meet **Real Patients** with our **Exclusive** Video Program

Enhance Your Understanding of Complex Abnormal Psychology Concepts!

Mark Durand's **Video Concept Reviews** are brief, high-interest video clips that review challenging topics that you may feel require more than one explanation. A list of these clips appears in every chapter and the actual videos can be found within **CengageNOW**. Over 200 key and difficult concepts are given further explanation to provide you with a deeper understanding of course topics.

Some of the key topics in the **Video Concept Reviews** include:

- **Integrative Approach**
- **Reciprocal Gene-Environment Model**
- **DSM-IV**
- **Independent/Dependent Variables**
- **Body Dysmorphic Disorder**
- **False and Recovered Memories, Malingering**
- **Bulimia Nervosa—Including Bingeing and Purging**
- **Normal Versus Abnormal Sexual Behavior**
- **Designer Drugs**
- **How Can Juries Decide Insanity?**

Basic Components of Research
- Research Design
  A method to test hypotheses
  - Independent variable - The variable that causes or influences behavior
  - Dependent variable - The behavior influenced by the independent variable

Body Dysmorphic Disorder
- Clinical Description
  - Preoccupation with imagined defect in appearance
  - Either fixation or avoidance of mirrors
  - Previously known as dysmorphophobia
  - Suicidal ideation and behavior are common
  - Often display ideas of reference for imagined defect

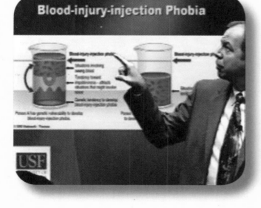

Blood-injury-injection Phobia

If your text did not come packaged with an access code for CengageNOW™ please visit **www.ichapters.com** where you can purchase immediate access to these study tools.

FIFTH EDITION

Abnormal Psychology
An Integrative Approach

David H. Barlow
Boston University

V. Mark Durand
University of South Florida–St. Petersburg

WADSWORTH
CENGAGE Learning

Australia • Brazil • Japan • Korea • Mexico • Singapore • Spain • United Kingdom • United States

WADSWORTH
CENGAGE Learning™

Abnormal Psychology:
An Integrative Approach, Fifth Edition
David H. Barlow / V. Mark Durand

Psychology Editor: Jaime Perkins

Development Editor: Kristin Makarewycz

Assistant Editor: Rachel Guzman

Editorial Assistant: Wilson Co

Technology Project Manager: Bessie Weiss

Marketing Manager: Kimberly Russell

Marketing Assistant: Melanie Cregger

Marketing Communications Manager: Linda Yip

Project Manager, Editorial Production:
    Jerilyn Emori

Creative Director: Rob Hugel

Art Director: Vernon Boes

Print Buyer: Rebecca Cross

Permissions Editor: Bob Kauser

Production Service: Anne Williams,
    Graphic World Inc.

Text and Cover Designer: Roy R. Neuhaus

Photo Researcher: Billie Porter

Cover Image: Lisa Spindler/Images.com/
    IPNstock

Compositor: Graphic World Inc.

For product information and technology assistance, contact us at
Cengage Learning Academic Resource Center, 1-800-423-0563

For permission to use material from this text or product,
submit all requests online at **www.cengage.com/permissions**
Further permissions questions can be emailed to
permissionrequest@cengage.com

Library of Congress Control Number: 2007937255

Student Edition:

ISBN-13: 978-0-495-09556-9

ISBN-10: 0-495-09556-7

Loose-leaf Edition:

ISBN-13: 978-0-495-50470-2

ISBN-10: 0-495-50470-X

Wadsworth Cengage Learning
10 Davis Drive
Belmont, CA 94002-3098
USA

Cengage Learning products are represented in Canada by Nelson Education, Ltd.

For your course and learning solutions, visit **academic.cengage.com.**

Purchase any of our products at your local college store or at our preferred online store **www.ichapters.com.**

Printed in Canada
2 3 4 5 6 7 12 11 10 09

I dedicate this book to my mother, Doris Elinor Barlow-Lanigan, for her multidimensional influence across my life span.
D. H. B.

To Wendy and Jonathan, whose patience, understanding, and love provided me the opportunity to complete such an ambitious project.
V. M. D.

About the Authors

David H. Barlow is an internationally recognized pioneer and leader in clinical psychology. A professor of psychology and psychiatry at Boston University, Dr. Barlow is Founder and Director Emeritus of the Center for Anxiety and Related Disorders, one of the largest research clinics of its kind in the world, and from 1996 to 2004 directed the clinical psychology programs. From 1979 to 1996, he was distinguished professor at the University at Albany–State University of New York. From 1975 to 1979, he was professor of psychiatry and psychology at Brown University, where he also founded the clinical psychology internship program. From 1969 to 1975, he was professor of psychiatry at the University of Mississippi, where he founded the Medical School psychology residency program. Dr. Barlow received his B.A. from the University of Notre Dame, his M.A. from Boston College, and his Ph.D. from the University of Vermont.

A fellow of every major psychological association, Dr. Barlow has received many awards in honor of his excellence in scholarship, including the National Institute of Mental Health Merit Award for long-term contributions to the clinical research effort; the 2000 Distinguished Scientist Award for applications of psychology from the American Psychological Association; the Distinguished Scientist Award from the Society of Clinical Psychology of the American Psychological Association; and a certificate of appreciation from the APA section on the clinical psychology of women, for "outstanding commitment to the advancement of women in psychology." In 2004, he received the C. Charles Burlingame Award from the Institute of Living and was awarded an Honorary Doctorate of Humane Letters degree from the Massachusetts School of Professional Psychology. He also received career contribution awards from the Massachusetts, Connecticut, and California Psychological Associations, and, in 2000, was named Honorary Visiting Professor at the Chinese People's Liberation Army General Hospital and Postgraduate Medical School.

In addition, the annual Grand Rounds in Clinical Psychology at Brown University was named in his honor, and he was awarded the first graduate alumni scholar award at the University of Vermont. During the 1997–1998 academic year he was Fritz Redlich Fellow at the Center for Advanced Study in the Behavioral Sciences in Menlo Park, California.

Dr. Barlow has edited 3 journals, served on the editorial boards of 19 different journals, and is currently Editor in Chief of the "Treatments that Work" series for Oxford University Press.

He has published more than 500 scholarly articles and written over 65 books and clinical manuals, including *Anxiety and Its Disorders,* 2nd edition, Guilford Press; *Clinical Handbook of Psychological Disorders: A Step-by-Step Treatment Manual,* 4th edition, Guilford Press; *Single-Case Experimental Designs: Strategies for Studying Behavior Change,* 3rd edition, Allyn & Bacon (with Matthew Nock and Michael Hersen); *The Scientist-Practitioner: Research and Accountability in the Age of Managed Care,* 2nd edition, Allyn & Bacon (with Steve Hayes and Rosemery Nelson); and *Mastery of Your Anxiety and Panic,* Oxford University Press (with Michelle Craske). The book and manuals have been translated in over 20 languages, including Arabic, Chinese, and Russian.

Dr. Barlow was one of three psychologists on the task force that was responsible for reviewing the work of more than 1,000 mental health professionals who participated in the creation of DSM-IV. He also chaired the APA Task Force on Psychological Intervention Guidelines, which created a template for clinical practice guidelines. His current research program focuses on the nature and treatment of anxiety and related emotional disorders.

At leisure he plays golf, skis, and retreats to his home in Nantucket, where he loves to write, walk on the beach, and visit with his island friends.

V. Mark Durand is known worldwide as an authority in the area of autism spectrum disorders. He is a professor of psychology at the University of South Florida–St. Petersburg, where he was the founding Dean of Arts & Sciences and Vice Chancellor for Academic Affairs. Dr. Durand is a fellow of the American Psychological Association. He has received over $4 million in continuous federal funding since the beginning of his career to study the nature, assessment, and treatment of behavior problems in children with disabilities. Before moving to Florida he served in a variety of leadership positions at the University at Albany, including associate director for clinical training for the doctoral psychology program from 1987 to 1990, chair of the psychology department from 1995 to 1998, and interim dean of Arts and Sciences from 2001 to 2002. There he established the Center for Autism and Related Disabilities at the University at Albany, SUNY. He received his B.A., M.A., and Ph.D.—all in psychology—at the State University of New York–Stony Brook.

Dr. Durand was awarded the University Award for Excellence in Teaching at SUNY–Albany in 1991 and in 1989 was named Distinguished Reviewer of the Year for the *Journal of the Association for Persons with Severe Handicaps.* Dr. Durand is currently a member of the Professional Advisory Board for the Autism Society of America and is on the board of directors of the International Association of Positive Behavioral Support. He serves on a number of editorial boards, reviews for dozens of journals, and has over 100 publications on functional communication, educational programming, and behavior therapy. His books include *Severe Behavior Problems: A Functional Communication Training Approach, Sleep Better! A Guide to Improving Sleep for Children with Special Needs,* and most recently, *When Children Don't Sleep Well: Interventions for Pediatric Sleep Disorders.*

Dr. Durand developed a unique treatment for severe behavior problems that is currently mandated by states across the country and is used worldwide. He also developed an assessment tool that is used internationally and has been translated into more than 15 languages. In 1993 he was the keynote speaker for the Australian National Conference on Behaviour Modification; he has also lectured throughout Norway. He has been consulted by the departments of education in numerous states and by the U.S. Departments of Justice and Education. His current research program includes the study of prevention models and treatments for such serious problems as self-injurious behavior.

In his leisure time, he enjoys long-distance running and has just completed his second marathon.

Brief Contents

CHAPTER 1

Abnormal Behavior in Historical Context 1

CHAPTER 2

An Integrative Approach to Psychopathology 30

CHAPTER 3

Clinical Assessment and Diagnosis 68

CHAPTER 4

Research Methods 98

CHAPTER 5

Anxiety Disorders 120

CHAPTER 6

Somatoform and Dissociative Disorders 170

CHAPTER 7

Mood Disorders and Suicide 206

CHAPTER 8

Eating and Sleep Disorders 260

CHAPTER 9

Physical Disorders and Health Psychology 308

CHAPTER 10

Sexual and Gender Identity Disorders 344

CHAPTER 11

Substance-Related and Impulse-Control Disorders 388

CHAPTER 12

Personality Disorders 430

CHAPTER 13

Schizophrenia and Other Psychotic Disorders 466

CHAPTER 14

Developmental Disorders 500

CHAPTER 15

Cognitive Disorders 532

CHAPTER 16

Mental Health Services: Legal and Ethical Issues 556

Contents

CHAPTER 1

Abnormal Behavior in Historical Context   1

Understanding Psychopathology   2
What Is a Psychological Disorder?   2
The Science of Psychopathology   5
Historical Conceptions of Abnormal Behavior   7

The Supernatural Tradition   8
Demons and Witches   8
Stress and Melancholy   8
Treatments for Possession   9
Mass Hysteria   10
Modern Mass Hysteria   10
The Moon and the Stars   10
Comments   11

The Biological Tradition   11
Hippocrates and Galen   11
The 19th Century   12
The Development of Biological Treatments   13
Consequences of the Biological Tradition   14

The Psychological Tradition   14
Moral Therapy   14
Asylum Reform and the Decline of Moral Therapy   15
Psychoanalytic Theory   16
Humanistic Theory   21
The Behavioral Model   22

The Present: The Scientific Method and an Integrative Approach   25

Summary   26

Key Terms   26

Answers to Concept Checks   27

CHAPTER 2

An Integrative Approach to Psychopathology   30

One-Dimensional or Multidimensional Models   31
What Caused Judy's Phobia?   31
Outcome and Comments   33

Genetic Contributions to Psychopathology   34
The Nature of Genes   34
New Developments in the Study of Genes and Behavior   35
The Interaction of Genetic and Environmental Effects   36
Nongenomic "Inheritance" of Behavior   39

Neuroscience and Its Contributions to Psychopathology   40
The Central Nervous System   40
The Structure of the Brain   42
The Peripheral Nervous System   44
Neurotransmitters   46
Implications for Psychopathology   50
Psychosocial Influences on Brain Structure and Function   51
Interactions of Psychosocial Factors with Brain Structure and Function   52
Comments   53

Behavioral and Cognitive Science   54
Conditioning and Cognitive Processes   54
Learned Helplessness   54
Social Learning   55
Prepared Learning   56
Cognitive Science and the Unconscious   56

Emotions   57
The Physiology and Purpose of Fear   57
Emotional Phenomena   58
The Components of Emotion   58
Anger and Your Heart   59
Emotions and Psychopathology   60

Cultural, Social, and Interpersonal Factors   60
Voodoo, the Evil Eye, and Other Fears   60
Gender   61
Social Effects on Health and Behavior   62
Global Incidence of Psychological Disorders   64

Life-Span Development   64

Conclusions   65

Summary   66

Key Terms   66

Answers to Concept Checks   67

CHAPTER 3

Clinical Assessment and Diagnosis   68

Assessing Psychological Disorders   69
Key Concepts in Assessment   71
The Clinical Interview   71
Physical Examination   74
Behavioral Assessment   74
Psychological Testing   77
Neuropsychological Testing   82
Neuroimaging: Pictures of the Brain   82
Psychophysiological Assessment   84

Diagnosing Psychological Disorders   85
Classification Issues   86
Diagnosis Before 1980   88
DSM-III   88
DSM-IV   89
Creating a Diagnosis   92
Conclusions   94

Summary   96

Key Terms   96

Answers to Concept Checks   96

CHAPTER 4

Research Methods   98

Examining Abnormal Behavior   99
Important Concepts   99
Basic Components of a Research Study   99
Statistical Versus Clinical Significance   101
The "Average" Client   102

Types of Research Methods   102
Studying Individual Cases   102
Research by Correlation   103
Research by Experiment   105
Single-Case Experimental Designs   107

Genetics and Research Across Time and Cultures   110
Studying Genetics   110
Studying Behavior Over Time   112
Studying Behavior Across Cultures   114
The Power of a Program of Research   115
Replication   116
Research Ethics   116

Summary   118

Key Terms   118

Answers to Concept Checks   119

CHAPTER 5

Anxiety Disorders   120

The Complexity of Anxiety Disorders   121
Anxiety, Fear, and Panic: Some Definitions   121
Causes of Anxiety Disorders   123
Comorbidity of Anxiety Disorders   126
Comorbidity With Physical Disorders   126
Suicide   127

Generalized Anxiety Disorder   127
Clinical Description   127
Statistics   129
Causes   129
Treatment   131

Panic Disorder With and Without Agoraphobia   132
Clinical Description   133
Statistics   134
Causes   136
Treatment   138

Specific Phobia   141
Clinical Description   141
Statistics   144
Causes   145
Treatment   147

Social Phobia   148
Clinical Description   148
Statistics   149
Causes   149
Treatment   151

Posttraumatic Stress Disorder 152
    Clinical Description 152
    Statistics 154
    Causes 156
    Treatment 157

Obsessive-Compulsive Disorder 159
    Clinical Description 159
    Statistics 161
    Causes 161
    Treatment 162

FUTURE DIRECTIONS

Drugs That Make Psychological Treatments Work Better 164

Summary 164

Key Terms 165

Answers to Concept Checks 165

CHAPTER 6

Somatoform and Dissociative Disorders 170

Somatoform Disorders 171
    Hypochondriasis 171
    Somatization Disorder 175
    Conversion Disorder 179
    Pain Disorder 184
    Body Dysmorphic Disorder 185

Dissociative Disorders 189
    Depersonalization Disorder 190
    Dissociative Amnesia 191
    Dissociative Fugue 192
    Dissociative Trance Disorder 193
    Dissociate Identity Disorder 193

FUTURE DIRECTIONS

Somatoform Disorders in DSM-V: Possible Changes 202

Summary 202

Key Terms 203

Answers to Concept Checks 203

CHAPTER 7

Mood Disorders and Suicide 206

Understanding and Defining Mood Disorders 207
    An Overview of Depression and Mania 208
    The Structure of Mood Disorders 209
    Depressive Disorders 210
    Bipolar Disorders 215
    Additional Defining Criteria 217

Prevalence of Mood Disorders 221
    In Children and Adolescents 222
    In the Elderly 224
    Across Cultures 225
    Among the Creative 225

The Overlap of Anxiety and Depression 226

Causes of Mood Disorders 228
    Biological Dimensions 228
    Brain Wave Activity 231
    Psychological Dimensions 231
    Social and Cultural Dimensions 235
    An Integrative Theory 237

Treatment of Mood Disorders 239
    Medications 239
    Electroconvulsive Therapy and Transcranial Magnetic Stimulation 242
    Psychological Treatments 243
    Combined Treatments 245
    Preventing Relapse 246
    Psychological Treatments for Bipolar Disorder 246

Suicide 248
    Statistics 249
    Causes 250
    Risk Factors 251
    Is Suicide Contagious? 252
    Treatment 252

FUTURE DIRECTIONS

Evidence for an Integrative Approach to Causes of Depression 254

Summary 255

Key Terms 256

Answers to Concept Checks 256

CHAPTER 8

Eating and Sleep Disorders 260

Major Types of Eating Disorders 261
Bulimia Nervosa 262
Anorexia Nervosa 265
Binge-Eating Disorder 268
Statistics 268

Causes of Eating Disorders 272
Social Dimensions 272
Biological Dimensions 276
Psychological Dimensions 276
An Integrative Model 277

Treatment of Eating Disorders 278
Drug Treatments 278
Psychological Treatments 279
Preventing Eating Disorders 282

Obesity 283
Statistics 283
Disordered Eating Patterns in Cases of Obesity 284
Causes 286
Treatment 286

Sleep Disorders: The Major Dyssomnias 288
An Overview of Sleep Disorders 288
Primary Insomnia 290
Primary Hypersomnia 293
Narcolepsy 294
Breathing-Related Sleep Disorders 295
Circadian Rhythm Sleep Disorders 295

Treatment of Sleep Disorders 298
Medical Treatments 298
Environmental Treatments 298
Psychological Treatments 299
Preventing Sleep Disorders 299
Parasomnias and Their Treatment 300

FUTURE DIRECTIONS
Should the Government Regulate What We Eat? 303

Summary 303

Key Terms 304

Answers to Concept Checks 304

CHAPTER 9

Physical Disorders and Health Psychology 308

Psychological and Social Factors That Influence Health 309
Health and Health-Related Behavior 311
The Nature of Stress 311
The Physiology of Stress 312
Contributions to the Stress Response 313
Stress, Anxiety, Depression, and Excitement 313
Stress and the Immune Response 315

Psychosocial Effects on Physical Disorders 318
AIDS 318
Cancer 319
Cardiovascular Problems 321
Hypertension 321
Coronary Heart Disease 323
Chronic Pain 325
Chronic Fatigue Syndrome 328

Psychosocial Treatment of Physical Disorders 330
Biofeedback 331
Relaxation and Meditation 332
A Comprehensive Stress- and Pain-Reduction Program 332
Drugs and Stress-Reduction Programs 333
Denial as a Means of Coping 334
Modifying Behaviors to Promote Health 334

FUTURE DIRECTIONS
Placebo Effects and the Brain 339

Summary 339

Key Terms 340

Answers to Concept Checks 340

CHAPTER 10

Sexual and Gender Identity Disorders 344

What Is Normal Sexuality? 345
Gender Differences 346
Cultural Differences 348
The Development of Sexual Orientation 348

Gender Identity Disorder 350
Defining Gender Identity Disorder 350
Causes 351
Treatment 352

An Overview of Sexual Dysfunctions 354
Sexual Desire Disorders 355
Sexual Arousal Disorders 357
Orgasm Disorders 358
Sexual Pain Disorders 360

Assessing Sexual Behavior 361
Interviews 362
Medical Examination 362
Psychophysiological Assessment 362

Causes and Treatment of Sexual Dysfunction 363
Causes of Sexual Dysfunction 363
Treatment of Sexual Dysfunction 367

Paraphilia: Clinical Descriptions 371
Fetishism 372
Voyeurism and Exhibitionism 373
Transvestic Fetishism 373
Sexual Sadism and Sexual Masochism 374
Pedophilia and Incest 376
Paraphilia in Women 377
Causes of Paraphilia 377

Assessing and Treating Paraphilia 379
Psychological Treatment 379
Drug Treatments 381
Summary 381

FUTURE DIRECTIONS
Gender Nonconformity in Children 382

Summary 382

Key Words 383

Answers to Concept Checks 384

Depressants 395
Alcohol Use Disorders 395
Sedative, Hypnotic, or Anxiolytic Substance Use Disorders 399

Stimulants 401
Amphetamine Use Disorders 401
Cocaine Use Disorders 402
Nicotine Use Disorders 403
Caffeine Use Disorders 405

Opioids 406

Hallucinogens 407
Marijuana 407
LSD and Other Hallucinogens 408

Other Drugs of Abuse 409

Causes of Substance-Related Disorders 411
Biological Dimensions 411
Psychological Dimensions 412
Cognitive Factors 413
Social Dimensions 414
Cultural Dimensions 415
An Integrative Model 415

Treatment of Substance-Related Disorders 417
Biological Treatments 417
Psychosocial Treatments 419
Prevention 421

Impulse-Control Disorders 422
Intermittent Explosive Disorder 422
Kleptomania 422
Pyromania 423
Pathological Gambling 423
Trichotillomania 424

FUTURE DIRECTIONS
Two New Approaches to Prevention 425

Summary 425

Key Terms 426

Answers to Concept Checks 426

CHAPTER 11

Substance-Related and Impulse-Control Disorders 388

Perspectives on Substance-Related Disorders 389
Levels of Involvement 390
Diagnostic Issues 394

CHAPTER 12

Personality Disorders 430

An Overview Of Personality Disorders 431
Aspects of Personality Disorders 431
Categorical and Dimensional Models 432
Personality Disorder Clusters 432

Statistics and Development   433
Gender Differences   435
Comorbidity   436
Personality Disorders Under Study   436

Cluster A Personality Disorders   438
Paranoid Personality Disorder   438
Schizoid Personality Disorder   439
Schizotypal Personality Disorder   441

Cluster B Personality Disorders   443
Antisocial Personality Disorder   443
Borderline Personality Disorder   450
Histrionic Personality Disorder   454
Narcissistic Personality Disorder   455

Cluster C Personality Disorders   457
Avoidant Personality Disorder   457
Dependent Personality Disorder   458
Obsessive-Compulsive Personality Disorder   459

FUTURE DIRECTIONS

DSM-V and the Personality Disorders   461

Summary   461

Key Terms   462

Answers to Concept Checks   462

CHAPTER 13

Schizophrenia and Other Psychotic Disorders   466

Perspectives on Schizophrenia   467
Early Figures in Diagnosing Schizophrenia   467
Identifying Symptoms   468

Clinical Description, Symptoms, and Subtypes   469
Positive Symptoms   470
Negative Symptoms   472
Disorganized Symptoms   473
Schizophrenia Subtypes   474
Other Psychotic Disorders   476

Prevalence and Causes of Schizophrenia   479
Statistics   479
Development   479
Cultural Factors   480
Genetic Influences   480
Neurobiological Influences   483
Psychological and Social Influences   487

Treatment of Schizophrenia   488
Biological Interventions   489
Psychosocial Interventions   491
Treatment Across Cultures   494
Prevention   494

FUTURE DIRECTIONS

Using Virtual Reality and Text Messaging in Assessment   495

Summary   495

Key Terms   496

Answers to Concept Checks   496

CHAPTER 14

Developmental Disorders   500

Common Developmental Disorders   501
What Is Normal? What Is Abnormal?   501
Attention Deficit/Hyperactivity Disorder   502
Learning Disorders   507

Pervasive Developmental Disorders   511
Autistic Disorder   511
Asperger's Disorder   515
Treatment of Pervasive Developmental Disorders   516

Mental Retardation   518
Clinical Description   519
Statistics   521
Causes   521
Treatment of Mental Retardation   524
Prevention of Developmental Disorders   525

FUTURE DIRECTIONS

Helpful "Designer Drugs"   526

Summary   527

Key Terms   527

Answers to Concept Checks   528

CHAPTER 15

Cognitive Disorders 532

Perspectives on Cognitive Disorders 533

Delirium 533
  Clinical Description and Statistics 534
  Treatment 535
  Prevention 535

Dementia 535
  Clinical Description and Statistics 536
  Dementia of the Alzheimer's Type 538
  Vascular Dementia 540
  Dementia Due to Other General Medical Conditions 541
  Substance-Induced Persisting Dementia 543
  Causes of Dementia 543
  Treatment 546
  Prevention 549

Amnestic Disorder 549

FUTURE DIRECTIONS

Are We Close to an Alzheimer's Vaccine? 551

Summary 551

Key Terms 551

Answers to Concept Checks 551

CHAPTER 16

Mental Health Services: Legal and Ethical Issues 556

Perspectives on Mental Health Law 557

Civil Commitment 557
  Criteria for Civil Commitment 558
  Changes Affecting Civil Commitment 560
  An Overview of Civil Commitment 562

Criminal Commitment 563
  The Insanity Defense 563
  Reactions to the Insanity Defense 564
  Therapeutic Jurisprudence 566
  Competence to Stand Trial 566
  Duty to Warn 567
  Mental Health Professionals as Expert Witnesses 567

Patients' Rights and Clinical Practice Guidelines 568
  The Right to Treatment 568
  The Right to Refuse Treatment 569
  Research Participants' Rights 569
  Evidence-Based Practice and Clinical Practice Guidelines 570

Conclusions 572

FUTURE DIRECTIONS

Brain Blame 572

Summary 573

Key Terms 573

Answers to Concept Checks 574

Glossary G-1

References G-16

Name Index I-1

Subject Index I-21

Preface

Science is a constantly evolving field, but every now and then something groundbreaking occurs that alters our way of thinking. For example, evolutionary biologists, who long assumed that the process of evolution was gradual, suddenly had to adjust to evidence that it happens in fits and starts in response to such cataclysmic, environmental events as meteor impacts. Similarly, geology has been revolutionized by the discovery of plate tectonics.

Until several years ago, the science of psychopathology had been compartmentalized, with psychopathologists examining the separate effects of psychological, biological, and social influences. This approach is still reflected in popular media accounts that describe, for example, a newly discovered gene, a biological dysfunction (chemical imbalance), or early childhood experiences as a "cause" of a psychological disorder. This way of thinking still dominates discussions of causality and treatment in some psychology textbooks: "The psychoanalytic views of this disorder are . . . ," "the biological views are . . . ," and, often in a separate chapter, "psychoanalytic treatment approaches for this disorder are . . . ," "cognitive behavioral treatment approaches are . . . ," or "biological treatment approaches are. . . ."

In the first edition of this text we tried to do something very different. We thought the field had advanced to the point that it was ready for an integrative approach in which the intricate interactions of biological, psychological, and social factors are explicated in as clear and convincing a manner as possible. Recent explosive advances in knowledge confirm this approach as the only viable way of understanding psychopathology. To take just one example, Chapter 2 now contains a description of a study demonstrating that stressful life events can lead to depression, but not everyone shows this response. Rather, stress is more likely to cause depression in individuals who already carry a particular gene that influences serotonin at the brain synapses. On the other hand, the entire section on genetics has been rewritten to highlight the new emphasis on gene-environment interaction, along with recent thinking from leading behavioral geneticists that the goal of basing the classification of psychological disorders on the firm foundation of genetics is fundamentally flawed. Also descriptions of the emerging field of epigenetics, or the influence of the environment on gene expression, is woven into the chapter, along with new studies on the seeming ability of extreme environments to largely override the effects of genetic contributions. Studies elucidating the mechanisms of epigenetics or specifically how environmental events influence gene expression are described.

These results confirm the integrative approach in this book: Psychological disorders cannot be explained by genetic or environmental factors alone but rather from their interaction. We now understand that psychological and social factors directly affect neurotransmitter function and even genetic expression. Similarly, we cannot study behavioral, cognitive, or emotional processes without appreciating the contribution of biological and social factors to psychological and psychopathological expression. Instead of compartmentalizing psychopathology, we use a more accessible approach that accurately reflects the current state of our clinical science.

As colleagues, you are aware that we understand some disorders better than others. But we hope you will share our excitement in conveying to students both what we currently know about the causes and treatment of psychopathology and how far we have yet to go in understanding these complex interactions.

INTEGRATIVE APPROACH

As noted earlier, the first edition of *Abnormal Psychology* pioneered a new generation of abnormal psychology textbooks, which offer an integrative and multidimensional perspective. (We acknowledge such one-dimensional approaches as biological, psychosocial, and supernatural as historic trends.) We include substantial current evidence of the reciprocal influences of biology and behavior, and of psychological and social influences on biology. Our examples hold students' attention; for example, we discuss genetic contributions to divorce, the effects of early social and behavioral experience on later brain function and structure, new information on the relation of social networks to the common cold, and new data on psychosocial treatments for cancer. We emphasize the fact that in the phenomenon of implicit memory and blind sight, which may have parallels in dissociative experiences, psychological science verifies the existence of the unconscious (although it does not much resemble the seething caldron of conflicts envisioned by Freud). We present new evidence confirming the effects of psychological treatments on neurotransmitter flow and brain function. We acknowledge the often neglected area of emotion theory for its rich contributions to psychopathology, for example, the effects of anger on cardiovascular disease. We weave scientific findings from the study of emotions together with behavioral, biological, cognitive, and social discoveries to create an integrated tapestry of psychopathology.

Life-Span Developmental Influences

No modern view of abnormal psychology can ignore the importance of life-span developmental factors to the manifestation and treatment of psychopathology. In this edition, for the first time, studies highlighting developmental windows for the influence of the environment on gene expression are highlighted. Accordingly, while we include a developmental disorders chapter (Chapter 14), we consider the importance of development throughout the text; we discuss childhood and geriatric anxiety, for example, in the context of the anxiety disorders chapter. This organization, which is for the most part consistent with DSM-IV, helps students appreciate the need to study each disorder from childhood through adulthood and old age. We note findings on developmental considerations in separate sections of each disorder chapter and, as appropriate, discuss how specific developmental factors affect causation and treatment.

Scientist-Practitioner Approach

We go to some length to explain why the scientist-practitioner approach to psychopathology is both practical and ideal. Like most of our colleagues, we view this as something more than simple awareness of how scientific findings apply to psychopathology. We show how every clinician contributes to general scientific knowledge through astute and systematic clinical observations, functional analyses of individual case studies, and systematic observations of series of cases in clinical settings. For example, we explain how

---

CULTURE INDEX

Throughout the book we consider the relationship of culture to many subjects, including:

African Americans, 135, 136, 186–187, 225, 249, 269, 397, 398, 448, 480, 508, 546
Alcohol use disorders, 251, 364, 393, 395–399, 418–420
Asian Americans, 173, 271, 291, 336–337, 397–398, 415, 546, 560
Body dysmorphic disorder, 185–189
Conversion disorder, 179–184
Coronary heart disease, 323–325, 337–338
Dementia, 396, 535–549, 555
Depression, 11, 92–93, 226–229, 231, 233–234, 265, 313–315
Diagnostic guidelines, 89–90, 90–93
Dissociative trance disorder, 193
Eating disorders, 261–262, 268–269, 271–283, 306
Fear, 60–61
Gender identity disorders, 351–352

Hispanic Americans, 135, 145, 249, 269, 291, 397–398
Native Americans, 222, 225, 397–398
Obesity, 284–286
Obsessive-compulsive disorder, 161–162
Panic disorder, 132–141
Personality disorders, 431
Phobias, 2, 141–152, 172
Posttraumatic stress disorder, 156–157, 199
Research, 114–115
Schizophrenia, 480
Sexual dysfunctions, 366–367
Sexuality, 348
Sleep disorders, 288–290
Smoking, 330–331
Somatization disorder, 177–179
Somatoform disorders, 176–179
Substance-related disorders, 411–417
Suicide, 250–251

GENDER INDEX

Gender issues are considered throughout the book in relation to numerous topics, including:

Agoraphobia, 132–134
Body dysmorphic disorder, 188–189
Conversion disorder, 183–184
Dementia, 543–546
Developmental disorders, 348–350
Eating disorders, 262, 271–276
Gender identity disorders:
    causes, 351–352
    treatment for, 352–354
Generalized anxiety disorder, 129–131
Hypochondriasis, 174–175

Insomnia, 291–292
Mood disorders, 225, 228–235
Obsessive-compulsive disorder, 161–162
Pain, 328
Paraphilias, 377–379
Personality disorders, 435–436
Phobias, 141–152
Premenstrual dysphoric disorder, 93–94
Sexual dysfunctions, 355, 366–367
Sexuality, 346–348
Social phobia, 149–151
Somatization disorder, 177–179
Substance-related disorders, 411–417
Suicide, 250–251

information on dissociative phenomena provided by early psychoanalytic theorists remains relevant today. We also describe the formal methods used by scientist-practitioners, showing how abstract research designs are actually implemented in research programs.

Clinical Cases of Real People

We have enriched the book with authentic clinical histories to illustrate scientific findings on the causes and treatment of psychopathology. We have both run active clinics for years, so 95 percent of the cases are from our own files, and they provide a fascinating frame of reference for the findings we describe. Most chapters begin with a case description, and most discussion of the latest theory and research is related to these very human cases.

Disorders in Detail

We cover the major psychological disorders in eleven chapters, focusing on three broad categories: clinical description, causal factors, and treatment and outcomes. We pay considerable attention to case studies and DSM-IV criteria, and we include statistical data, such as prevalence and incidence rates, sex ratio, age of onset, and the general course or pattern for the disorder as a whole. Throughout, we explore how biological, psychological, and social dimensions may interact to cause a particular disorder. Finally, by covering treatment and outcomes within the context of specific disorders, we provide a realistic sense of clinical practice.

Treatment

One of the best received innovations in the first four editions is that we discuss treatment in the same chapter as the disorders themselves instead of in a separate chapter, an approach that is supported by the development of specific psychosocial and pharmacological treatment procedures for specific disorders. We have retained this integrative format and have improved on it, and we include treatment procedures in the key terms and glossary.

Legal and Ethical Issues

In our closing chapter we integrate many of the approaches and themes that have been discussed throughout the text. We include case studies of people who have been involved directly with many legal and ethical issues and with the delivery of mental health services. We also provide a historical context for current perspectives so students will understand the effects of social and cultural influences on legal and ethical issues.

Diversity

Issues of culture and gender are integral to the study of psychopathology. Throughout the text we describe current thinking about which aspects of the disorders are culturally specific and which are universal, and about the strong and sometimes puzzling effects of gender roles. For instance, we discuss the current information on topics such as the gender imbalance in depression, how panic disorders are expressed differently in various Asian cultures, the ethnic

differences in eating disorders, treatment of schizophrenia across cultures, and the diagnostic differences of attention deficit hyperactivity disorder (ADHD) in boys and girls. Clearly, our field will grow in depth and detail as these subjects and others become standard research topics. For example, why do some disorders overwhelmingly affect females and others appear predominantly in males? And why does this apportionment sometimes change from one culture to another? In answering questions like these, we adhere closely to science, emphasizing that gender and culture are each one dimension among several that constitute psychopathology.

NEW TO THIS EDITION

A Thorough Update

This exciting field moves at a rapid pace, and we take particular pride in how our book reflects the most recent developments. Therefore, once again, every chapter has been carefully revised to reflect the latest research studies on psychological disorders. Hundreds of new references from 2005–2007 (and some still "in press") appear for the first time in this edition, and some of the information they contain stuns the imagination. Nonessential material has been eliminated, some new headings have been added, and DSM-IV criteria are included in their entirety as tables in the appropriate disorder chapters.

The chapters on Anxiety Disorders (Chapter 5), Mood Disorders and Suicide (Chapter 7), Eating and Sleep Disorders (Chapter 8), Substance-Related and Impulse-Control Disorders (Chapter 11), Schizophrenia and Other Psychotic Disorders (Chapter 13), and Developmental Disorders (Chapter 14) have been the most heavily revised to reflect new research, but all chapters have been significantly updated and freshened. Some highlights of the changes include:

- In Chapter 2, the entire section on genetics has been rewritten to highlight the new emphasis on gene-environment interaction. The emerging field of epigenetics is integrated throughout the chapter.
- In Chapter 4, a new concept that is now the focus of intense study—endophenotypes—is introduced.
- Chapter 5 now includes exciting new information on the discovery of the drug D-cycloserine, which facilitates the psychological treatment of anxiety disorders.
- Chapter 6 presents new information on the nature, prevalence, causes, and treatment of hypochondriasis, including cross-cultural variations.
- Chapter 7 discusses new and more precise presentations of the components of mood disorders, including major depressive episode, mania, hypomanic episode, and mixed episodes.
- Also in Chapter 7, new findings on depression are presented, including the growing evidence for the inextricable interaction of biological and psychological causes of depression, menopause as a trigger, new information on the sudden surge of depression in girls reaching puberty, the latest updates on new biological treatments, and a rewritten section on the latest efforts in preventing depression.
- In Chapter 8, new data from the National Comorbidity Survey on patterns of comorbidity of eating disorders is in-

cluded, along with new data on heritable risk factors, projections on changes for DSM-V criteria, and new information on the course, causes, cultural influences, drug and psychological treatments, and prevention of eating disorders.

- Chapter 8 also discusses very recent research that suggests that the effects of jet lag can be quite serious—at least among the elderly.
- In Chapter 9, new information is presented on the effects of psychological factors—including the role of both positive and negative emotions—on coronary heart disease.
- Chapter 10 includes new information on sexual dysfunction, including the prevalence, social and psychological determinants, treatments, and likely changes to DSM-V for sexual dysfunction.
- Chapter 11 describes an exciting new study on hallucinogen use, which compared volunteers' reactions to the hallucinogen psilocybin and a control drug, with interesting results.
- Chapter 12 includes broadened coverage of borderline personality disorder. A completely revised section on genetics in antisocial personality disorder reflects recent trends to investigate endophenotypes, such as serotonin and dopamine levels or the relative lack of anxiety or fear seen in these individuals.
- An entirely new "Development" section is presented in Chapter 13, which includes a new figure to illustrate the complex development of the phases of schizophrenia from early childhood through old age.
- In Chapter 14, a great deal of new information on ADHD is presented, including a new section on ADHD comorbidity, new information on ADHD prevalence globally, significantly expanded coverage of genetics including the only gene-environment interaction study, updated material on brain structural differences in children with ADHD, and a new discussion of the overlap among ADHD and opposition defiant disorder (ODD), conduct disorder, and bipolar disorder. In addition, treatments for adults with ADHD is covered, along with completely revised sections on genetics and neurobiological causes of learning disorders.
- Also in Chapter 14, a new theory of autism is introduced involving research on the amygdala and the role of the stress hormone cortisol. The controversy surrounding vaccinations and the causes of autism are also discussed.
- Chapter 15 includes a new discussion on the recent advances in neuron regeneration, which may offer new hope for cognitive disorders. For dementia, the prevention section is completely revised to highlight a large study in Sweden that concluded the best ways to prevent dementia are to control your blood pressure and lead an active physical and social life.

New Features

In addition to the changes highlighted earlier, we have added two new features to the fifth edition:

- Mark Durand's *Video Concept Reviews*—over 200—are newly created video clips that review challenging topics that typically need more than one explanation. A list of these clips appears in every chapter and the actual videos can be found within CengageNOW.

- At the end of every disorders chapter is a new feature called *Future Directions,* which discusses forward-thinking concepts such as new markers for depression, junk food taxes, drug prevention treatments on the horizon, using virtual reality and text messaging in assessment, an Alzheimer's vaccine, and previews of DSM-V.

DSM-IV, DSM-IV-TR, AND DSM-V

Much has been said about the mix of political and scientific considerations that resulted in DSM-IV, and naturally we have our own opinions. (David H. Barlow had the interesting experience of sitting on the task force.) Psychologists are often concerned about turf issues in what has become, for better or worse, the nosological standard in our field, and with good reason: In previous DSM editions, scientific findings sometimes gave way to personal opinions. However, for DSM-IV most professional biases were left at the door while the task force almost endlessly debated the data. This process produced enough new information to fill every psychopathology journal for a year with integrative reviews, reanalysis of existing databases, and new data from field trials. From a scholarly point of view, the process was both stimulating and exhausting. This book contains highlights of various debates that created the nomenclature, as well as recent updates. For example, we summarize and update the data and discussion of premenstrual dysphoric disorder and mixed anxiety depression, two disorders that did not make it into the final criteria. Students can thus see the process of making diagnoses, as well as the mix of data and inference that are part of it.

In 2000, the American Psychiatric Association published a revision of the text accompanying the DSM-IV diagnostic criteria, which updated the scientific literature and changed some of the criteria themselves, mostly in minor ways. Several senior clinical investigators from one of our research centers (DHB) participated in the text revision and this information is included. For example, the text revision (DSM-IV-TR) discusses the intense continuing debate on categorical and dimensional approaches to classification. We describe some of the compromises the Task Force made to accommodate data, such as why it does not yet seem possible to dimensionalize personality disorders, although almost everyone agrees that when we can we will prefer to do so.

Now the planning process is underway for DSM-V, and a senior scientist from one of our Centers is a member of the Planning Committee. The first phase of this massive project involved a joint effort by the National Institute of Mental Health and the American Psychiatric Association focused on delineating needed research efforts to provide crucial information for the DSM-V process. Research planning workgroups were formed in areas such as neuroscience, problems/gaps in the current system, cross-cultural issues, and developmental issues with the charge of producing "white papers" outlining the required research agenda. The white papers, along with an article summarizing important recommendations, were published in 2002. The Planning Committee then organized a series of conferences to further these efforts. Eleven conferences were held from 2004 through 2007, chaired by members of the American and international research communities on topics such as: externalizing disorders of childhood; personality disorders; and stress-induced and fear circuitry disorders. In 2007, the DSM-V task force and the major committees covering large classes of disorders (anxiety—mood—schizophrenia—and so on) were appointed with the goal of producing DSM-V by 2011–2012. It is already clear that DSM-V will incorporate a more dimensional approach to classification, and preliminary recommendations along these lines are presented in Chapter 4 and in many of the disorder chapters.

Prevention

Looking ahead into the future of abnormal psychology as a field, the prospect of helping the most people who display psychological disorders may lie in our ability to prevent these difficulties. Although this has long been a goal of many, we are now at the precipice of what appears to be the beginning of a new age in prevention research. Numerous scientists from all over the globe are developing the methodologies and techniques that may at long last provide us with the means to interrupt the debilitating toll of emotional distress caused by the disorders chronicled in this book. We therefore highlight these cutting-edge prevention efforts—such as preventing eating disorders, suicide, and health problems such as HIV and injuries—in appropriate chapters as a means of celebrating these important events, as well as to spur on the field to continue this important work.

RETAINED FEATURES

Visual Summaries

At the end of each disorder chapter is a colorful, two-page visual overview that succinctly summarizes the causes, development, symptoms, and treatment of each disorder covered in the chapter. Our integrative approach is instantly evident in these diagrams, which show the interaction of biological, psychological, and social factors in the etiology and treatment of disorders. The visual summaries will help instructors wrap up discussions and students will appreciate them as study aids.

Pedagogy

Each chapter contains several Concept Checks, which let students verify their comprehension at regular intervals. Answers are at the end of each chapter, along with a more detailed Summary; the Key Terms are listed in the order they appear in the text and thus form a sort of outline that students can study. Finally, each chapter concludes with two elements: connections to the *Abnormal Psychology Live CD-ROM,* which is packaged free with every new copy of the text purchased in the United States and Canada, and a link to the CengageNOW online study tool which includes Mark Durand's *Video Concept Reviews* on challenging topics.

LEARNING AIDS FOR THE STUDENT

Abnormal Psychology Live Student CD-ROM

Every new copy of the fifth edition is packaged with a free CD-ROM, *Abnormal Psychology Live,* which includes video clips of actual clients discussing their disorders. Each video clip has specific questions written around it, and students can write their responses on-screen, as well as print them out. By chapter, the videos include:

- **Chapter 2, An Integrative Approach to Psychopathology:** Integrative Approach
- **Chapter 3, Clinical Assessment and Diagnosis:** Arriving at a Diagnosis; Psychological Assessment
- **Chapter 4, Research Methods:** Research Methods
- **Chapter 5, Anxiety Disorders:** Panic Disorder: Steve; Obsessive-Compulsive Disorder: Chuck; Virtual Reality Therapy; Snake Phobia Treatment
- **Chapter 6, Somatoform and Dissociative Disorders:** Dissociative Identity Disorder: Rachel; Body Dysmorphic Disorder: Doug
- **Chapter 7, Mood Disorders and Suicide:** Major Depressive Disorder: Barbara; Major Depressive Disorder: Evelyn; Bipolar Disorder: Mary
- **Chapter 8, Eating and Sleep Disorders:** Anorexia Nervosa: Susan; Anorexia Nervosa/Bulimia: Twins; Weight Control: The Obesity Epidemic; Sleep Cycle
- **Chapter 9, Physical Disorders and Health Psychology:** Social Support/HIV: Orel; The Immune System: Effects of Stress and Emotion; Cancer: Education and Support Groups
- **Chapter 10, Sexual and Gender Identity Disorders:** Erectile Dysfunction: Clark; Changing Over: Jessica
- **Chapter 11, Substance-Related and Impulse-Control Disorders:** Substance-Use Disorder: Tim; Nicotine Dependence
- **Chapter 12, Personality Disorders:** Antisocial Personality Disorder: George; Borderline Personality Disorders; Dialectical Behavior Therapy
- **Chapter 13, Schizophrenia and Other Psychotic Disorders:** Schizophrenia: Etta; Positive Versus Negative Symptoms; Common Symptoms of Schizophrenia
- **Chapter 14, Developmental Disorders:** ADHD: Sean; ADHD: Edward; Life Skills Training; Bullying Prevention; Autism: The Nature of the Disorder; Autism: Christina; Autism: Rebecca; Down Syndrome: Lauren
- **Chapter 15, Cognitive Disorders:** Alzheimer's Disease: Tom; Amnestic Disorder: Mike; Amnestic Patient Interview: Endel Tulving; Neural Networks: Cognition and Dementia
- **Chapter 16, Mental Health Services:** Legal and Ethical Issues: False Memory Research

CengageNOW

CengageNOW is an easy-to-use online resource that helps students study in less time to get the grade they want—NOW. Featuring CengageNOW Personalized Study (a diagnostic study tool containing valuable text-specific resources) students focus on just what they don't know and learn more in less time to get a better grade. If the textbook does not include an access code card, students can go to academic.cengage.com/now to get CengageNOW.

Video Concept Reviews

For extra help with concepts that students have identified as the most difficult in the course, students can watch award-winning teacher Mark Durand provide additional information on challenging topics. In this age of "YouTube," students can instantly access hundreds of video clips covering important topics for each chapter, which can be found within CengageNOW.

Student Study Guide

The fifth edition *Study Guide* by David Santogrossi of Purdue University encourages collaborative learning and active reading, listening, and study skills. It contains chapter summaries, key words, sample questions, activities, and Internet resources for every chapter of the text. 0-495-50749-0

Barlow and Durand Book Companion Website

The book-specific website (at academic.cengage.com/psychology/barlow) offers students practice quizzes and links to related sites for each chapter of the text, as well as flashcards, glossaries, research activities, and more.

Audio Study Tools

Audio Study Tools provides audio reinforcement of key concepts that students can listen to from their personal computer or MP3 player. Created specifically for Barlow and Durand's *Abnormal Psychology*, Fifth Edition, Audio Study Tools provides approximately ten minutes of audio content for each chapter, giving students a quick and convenient way to master key concepts. Audio content allows students to test their knowledge with quiz questions, listen to a brief overview reflecting the major themes of each chapter, and review key terminology. Order Audio Study Tools directly at www.ichapters.com.

iChapters

Tell your students about www.iChapters.com and give them more choices for your course. At www.iChapters.com, students can select from over 10,000 print and digital study tools, including the option to buy individual e-chapters and e-books. The first e-chapter is FREE!

TEACHING AIDS FOR THE INSTRUCTOR

Videos

- *Abnormal Psychology: Inside/Out,* Volume I 0-534-20359-0
- *Abnormal Psychology: Inside/Out,* Volume II 0-534-36480-2
- *Abnormal Psychology: Inside/Out,* Volume III 0-534-50759-X
- *Abnormal Psychology: Inside/Out,* Volume IV 0-534-63369-2
- *ABC Video: Abnormal Child Psychology* 0-495-09531-1

Classroom Presentation Materials

- *PowerLecture CD-ROM*, the one-stop digital library and presentation tool. This CD-ROM includes preassembled Microsoft® PowerPoint® lecture slides by Kristoffer Rhoads of the University of Washington. Built around the Fifth Edition, these PowerPoint lecture slides feature most of the figures from the text, as well as relevant video clips. In addition to a full Instructor's Manual and Test Bank, PowerLecture also includes ExamView® testing software with all the test items from the printed Test Bank in electronic format that enables you to create customized tests in print or online, and JoinIn™ Student Response System, a book-specific system that allows you to transform your classroom and assess your students' progress with instant in-class quizzes and polls. 0-495-50904-3

Additional Resources

- *Test Bank* by Mary McNaughton-Cassill of The University of Texas at San Antonio contains 125 items per chapter in multiple-choice and essay formats. All test items are sorted into factual, conceptual, and applied questions, are tied to learning objectives, and are page-referenced to the main text. Each chapter contains at least 10 items that are located on the book companion website and 10 questions from the study guide. 0-495-50748-2
- *Instructor's Manual* by Bryan Cochran of the University of Montana contains chapter summaries, learning objectives, lecture outlines with discussion topics, key terms, classroom activities, demonstrations, and lecture topics, suggested supplemental reading material, video resources, and Internet resources. 0-495-50728-8
- *CengageNOW* provides your teaching and learning resources in one intuitive program organized around the essential activities you perform for class—lecturing, creating assignments, grading, quizzing, and tracking student progress and performance. CengageNOW's intuitive "tabbed" design allows you to navigate to all key functions with a single click and a unique homepage tell you just what needs to be done and when. CengageNOW provides students access to an integrated e-book, interactive tutorials, videos, animations, and other multimedia tools that help them get the most out of your course.
- *WebTutor Toolbox:* **WebTutor ToolBox for WebCT or Blackboard** provides access to all the content of this text's rich Book Companion website from within a professor's course management system. ToolBox offers a wide array of Web quizzes, activities, exercises, and Web links. Robust communication tools—such as a course calendar, asynchronous discussion, real-time chat, a whiteboard, and an integrated e-mail system—make it easy to stay connected to the course.

Titles of Interest

- *Looking into Abnormal Psychology: Contemporary Readings* by Scott O. Lilienfeld is a fascinating 234-page reader comprised of 40 articles from popular magazines and journals.

Each article explores ongoing controversies regarding mental illness and its treatment. 0-534-35416-5

• *Casebook in Abnormal Psychology* by Timothy A. Brown and David H. Barlow is a comprehensive casebook that reflects the integrative approach, which considers the multiple influences of genetics, biology, familial, and environment factors into a unified model of causality as well as maintenance and treatment of the disorder. The casebook reflects treatment methods that are the most effective interventions developed for a particular disorder. It also presents two undiagnosed cases in order to give students an appreciation for the complexity of disorders. The cases are strictly teaching/learning exercises similar to what many instructors use on their examinations. 0-534-36316-4

ACKNOWLEDGMENTS

Finally, this book in all of its editions would not have begun and certainly would not have been finished without the inspiration and coordination of Marianne Taflinger, our senior editor at Cengage Wadsworth as this edition began. And to our new editor, Jaime Perkins, thanks for the seamless transition, and we look forward to an equally long relationship. We also thank Michele Sordi, publisher at Cengage Wadsworth, for her hands-on leadership. Many thanks to developmental editor Kristin Makarewycz, who came up with fresh ideas and persuaded us that it would be worth the effort to implement them. It has been a pleasure to work with you. Bessie Weiss did an outstanding job on the media products. Kim Russell and Rachel Guzman were hardworking, enthusiastic, and organized from beginning to end.

In the production process, many individuals worked as hard as we did to complete this project. In Boston, Cherryl Blanding and Mara Fleischer assisted enormously in typing and integrating a vast amount of new information into each chapter. Their ability to find missing references and track down information was remarkable. It is an understatement to say we couldn't have done it without you. To project manager Anne Williams at Graphic World Inc. and copy editor Barbara Sidleck, let's just say your attention to detail puts the folks at CSI to shame. We thank Billie Porter for her commitment to finding the best photos possible. At Wadsworth, Vernon Boes guided the design down to the last detail. Jerilyn Emori coordinated all of the details with grace under pressure.

Numerous colleagues and students provided superb feedback on the previous editions, and to them we express our deepest gratitude. Although not all comments were favorable, all were important. Readers who take the time to communicate their thoughts offer the greatest reward to writers or scholars.

Finally, you share with us the task of communicating knowledge and discoveries in the exciting field of psychopathology, a challenge that none of us takes lightly. In the spirit of collegiality, we would greatly appreciate your comments on the content and style of this book and recommendations for improving it further.

REVIEWERS

Creating this book has been both stimulating and exhausting, and we could not have done it without the valuable assistance of colleagues who read one or more chapters and provided extraordinarily perceptive critical comments, corrected errors, pointed to relevant information, and, on occasion, offered new insights that helped us achieve a successful, integrative model of each disorder. We thank the following reviewers:

Kerm Almos, *Capital University*
Frank Andrasik, *University of West Florida*
Robin Apple, *Stanford University Medical Center*
Barbara Beaver, *University of Wisconsin*
James Becker, *Pulaski Technical College*
Dorothy Bianco, *Rhode Island College*
Sarah Bisconer, *College of William & Mary*
Susan Blumenson, *City University of New York, John Jay College of Criminal Justice*
Robert Bornstein, *Gettysburg College*
James Calhoun, *University of Georgia*
Montie Campbell, *Oklahoma Baptist University*
Robin Campbell, *Brevard Community College*
Shelley Carson, *Harvard University*
Richard Cavasina, *California University of Pennsylvania*
Antonio Cepeda-Benito, *Texas A & M University*
Kristin Christodulu, *State University of New York–Albany*
Bryan Cochran, *University of Montana*
Julie Cohen, *University of Arizona*
Dean Cruess, *University of Pennsylvania*
Robert Doan, *University of Central Oklahoma*
Juris Draguns, *Pennsylvania State University*
Melanie Duckworth, *University of Houston*
Mitchell Earlywine, *University of Southern California*
Chris Eckhardt, *Southern Methodist University*
Elizabeth Epstein, *Rutgers University*
Donald Evans, *Drake University*
Ronald G. Evans, *Washburn University*
Anthony Fazio, *University of Wisconsin–Milwaukee*
Diane Finley, *Prince George's Community College*
Allen Frances, *Duke University*
Louis Franzini, *San Diego State University*
Maximillian Fuhrmann, *California State University–Northridge*
Noni Gaylord, *Loyola University–Chicago*
Trevor Gilbert, *Athabasca University*
David Gleaves, *Texas A & M University*
Frank Goodkin, *Castleton State College*
Irving Gottesman, *University of Virginia*
Laurence Grimm, *University of Illinois–Chicago*
Mark Grudberg, *Purdue University*
Marjorie Hardy, *Muhlenberg College*
Keith Harris, *Canyon College*
Christian Hart, *Santa Monica College*
William Hathaway, *Regent University*
Brian Hayden, *Brown University*
Stephen Hinshaw, *University of California–Berkeley*
Alexandra Hye-Young Park, *Humboldt State University*
William Iacono, *University of Minnesota*
Heidi Inderbitzen-Nolan, *University of Nebraska–Lincoln*
Thomas Jackson, *University of Arkansas*
Kristine Jacquin, *Mississippi State University*
Boaz Kahana, *Cleveland State University*
Arthur Kaye, *Virginia Commonwealth University*
Christopher Kearney, *University of Nevada–Las Vegas*

Ernest Keen, *Bucknell University*

Elizabeth Klonoff, *San Diego State University*

Ann Kring, *Vanderbilt University*

Marvin Kumler, *Bowling Green State University*

Thomas Kwapil, *University of North Carolina–Greensboro*

George Ladd, *Rhode Island College*

Michael Lambert, *Brigham Young University*

Travis Langley, *Henderson State University*

Christine Larson, *Michigan State University*

Cynthia Ann Lease, *Virginia Polytechnic Institute and State University*

Richard Leavy, *Ohio Weslyan University*

Karen Ledbetter, *Portland State University*

Scott Lilienfeld, *Emory University*

Kristi Lockhart, *Yale University*

Michael Lyons, *Boston University*

Jerald Marshall, *Valencia Community College*

Janet Matthews, *Loyola University*

Dean McKay, *Fordham University*

Mary McNaughton-Cassill, *University of Texas at San Antonio*

Suzanne Meeks, *University of Louisville*

Michelle Merwin, *University of Tennessee–Martin*

Thomas Miller, *Murray State University*

Scott Monroe, *University of Oregon*

Greg Neimeyer, *University of Florida*

Sumie Okazaki, *University of Wisconsin–Madison*

John Otey, *South Arkansas University*

Christopher Patrick, *University of Minnesota*

P. B. Poorman, *University of Wisconsin–Whitewater*

Katherine Presnell, *Southern Methodist University*

Lynn Rehm, *University of Houston*

Kim Renk, *University of Central Florida*

Alan Roberts, *Indiana University*

Melanie Rodriguez, *Utah State University*

Carol Rothman, *City University of New York, Herbert H. Lehman College*

Steve Schuetz, *University of Central Oklahoma*

Stefan Schulenberg, *University of Mississippi*

Paula K. Shear, *University of Cincinnati*

Steve Siaz, *State University of New York–Plattsburgh*

Jerome Small, *Youngstown State University*

Ari Solomon, *Williams College*

Michael Southam-Gerow, *Virginia Commonwealth University*

John Spores, *Purdue University–North Central*

Brian Stagner, *Texas A & M University*

Irene Staik, *University of Montevallo*

Rebecca Stanard, *State University of West Georgia*

Chris Tate, *Middle Tennessee State University*

Lisa Terre, *University of Missouri–Kansas City*

Gerald Tolchin, *Southern Connecticut State University*

Michael Vasey, *Ohio State University*

Larry Ventis, *College of William and Mary*

Richard Viken, *Indiana University*

Lisa Vogelsang, *University of Minnesota–Duluth*

Philip Watkins, *Eastern Washington University*

Kim Weikel, *Shippensburg University of Pennsylvania*

Amy Wenzel, *University of North Dakota*

W. Beryl West, *Middle Tennessee State University*

Michael Wierzbicki, *Marquette University*

Richard Williams, *State University of New York, College at Potsdam*

John Wincze, *Brown University*

Bradley Woldt, *South Dakota State University*

Nancy Worsham, *Gonzaga University*

Ellen Zaleski, *Fordham University*

Raymond Zurawski, *St. Norbert College*

CHAPTER 1

Abnormal Behavior in Historical Context

©Jerry Cooke/Corbis

UNDERSTANDING PSYCHOPATHOLOGY
What Is a Psychological Disorder?
The Science of Psychopathology
Historical Conceptions of Abnormal Behavior

THE SUPERNATURAL TRADITION
Demons and Witches
Stress and Melancholy
Treatments for Possession
Mass Hysteria
Modern Mass Hysteria
The Moon and the Stars
Comments

THE BIOLOGICAL TRADITION
Hippocrates and Galen
The 19th Century
The Development of Biological Treatments
Consequences of the Biological Tradition

THE PSYCHOLOGICAL TRADITION
Moral Therapy
Asylum Reform and the Decline of Moral Therapy
Psychoanalytic Theory
Humanistic Theory
The Behavioral Model

**THE PRESENT: THE SCIENTIFIC METHOD
AND AN INTEGRATIVE APPROACH**

A clear and complete insight into the nature of madness, a correct and distinct concept of what constitutes the difference between the sane and the insane has, as far as I know, not been found.

Arthur Schopenhauer
The World as Will and Idea

UNDERSTANDING PSYCHOPATHOLOGY

Today you may have gotten out of bed, had breakfast, gone to class, studied, and, at the end of the day, enjoyed the company of your friends before dropping off to sleep. It probably did not occur to you that many physically healthy people are not able to do some or any of these things. What they have in common is a **psychological disorder,** a psychological dysfunction within an individual associated with distress or impairment in functioning and a response that is not typical or culturally expected. Before examining exactly what this means, let's look at one individual's situation.

JUDY: The Girl Who Fainted at the Sight of Blood

Judy, a 16-year-old, was referred to our anxiety disorders clinic after increasing episodes of fainting. About 2 years earlier, in her first biology class, the teacher showed a movie of a frog dissection to illustrate various points about anatomy.

This was a particularly graphic film, with vivid images of blood, tissue, and muscle. About halfway through, Judy felt a bit lightheaded and left the room. But the images did not leave her. She continued to be bothered by them and occasionally felt slightly queasy. She began to avoid situations in which she might see blood or injury. She stopped looking at magazines that might have gory pictures. She found it difficult to look at raw meat, or even Band-Aids, because they brought the feared images to mind. Eventually, anything her friends or parents said that evoked an image of blood or injury caused Judy to feel lightheaded. It got so bad that if one of her friends exclaimed, "Cut it out!" she felt faint. Beginning about 6 months before her visit to the clinic, Judy actually fainted when she unavoidably encountered something bloody. Her family physician could find nothing wrong with her, nor could several other physicians. By the time she was referred to our clinic she was fainting 5 to 10 times a week, often in class. Clearly, this was problematic for her and disruptive in school; each time she fainted, the other students flocked around her, trying to help, and class was interrupted. Because no one could find anything wrong with her, the principal finally concluded that she was being manipulative and suspended her from school, even though she was an honor student.

Judy was suffering from what we now call *blood–injury–injection phobia.* Her reaction was quite severe, thereby meeting the criteria for **phobia,** a psychological disorder characterized by marked and persistent fear of an object or situation. But many people have similar reactions that are not as severe when they receive an injection or see someone who is injured, whether blood is visible or not. For people who react as severely as Judy, this phobia can be disabling. They may avoid certain careers, such as medicine or nursing, and, if they are so afraid of needles and injections that they avoid them even when they need them, they put their health at risk.

What Is a Psychological Disorder?

Keeping in mind the real-life problems faced by Judy, let's look more closely at the definition of psychological disorder, or **abnormal behavior:** It is a psychological dysfunction within an individual that is associated with distress or impairment in functioning and a response that is not typical or culturally expected (see ■ Figure 1.1). On the surface, these three criteria may seem obvious, but they were not easily arrived at and it is worth a moment to explore what they mean. You will see, importantly, that no one criterion has yet been developed that fully defines abnormality.

■ Psychological Dysfunction

Psychological dysfunction refers to a breakdown in cognitive, emotional, or behavioral functioning. For example, if you are out on a date, it should be fun. But if you experience severe fear all evening and just want to go home, even though there is nothing to be afraid of, and the severe fear happens on every date, your emotions are not functioning properly. However, if all your friends agree that the person who asked you out is unpredictable and dangerous in some way, then it would not be dysfunctional for you to be fearful and avoid the date.

A dysfunction was present for Judy: She fainted at the sight of blood. But many people experience a mild version of this reaction (feeling queasy at the sight of blood) without meeting the criteria for the disorder, so knowing where to draw the line between normal and abnormal dysfunction is often difficult. For this reason, these problems are often considered to be on a continuum or a dimension rather than to be categories that are either present or absent. This, too, is a reason why just having a dysfunction is not enough to meet the criteria for a psychological disorder.

■ Personal Distress

That the disorder or behavior must be associated with distress adds an important component and seems clear: The criterion is satisfied if the individual is extremely upset. We can certainly say that Judy was distressed and even suffered with her phobia. But remember, by itself this criterion does not define abnormal behavior. It is often quite normal to be distressed—for example, if someone close to you dies. The human condition is such that suf-

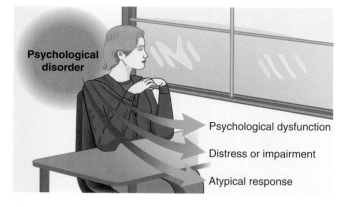

■ **FIGURE 1.1**   The criteria defining a psychological disorder.

Distress and suffering are a natural part of life and do not in themselves constitute a psychological disorder.

fering and distress are very much part of life. This is not likely to change. Furthermore, for some disorders, by definition, suffering and distress are absent. Consider the person who feels extremely elated and may act impulsively as part of a manic episode. As you will see in Chapter 7, one of the major difficulties with this problem is that some people enjoy the manic state so much they are reluctant to begin treatment or stay long in treatment. Thus, defining psychological disorder by distress alone doesn't work, although the concept of distress contributes to a good definition.

The concept of *impairment* is useful, although not entirely satisfactory. For example, many people consider themselves shy or lazy. This doesn't mean that they're abnormal. But if you are so shy that you find it impossible to date or even interact with people and you make every attempt to avoid interactions even though you would like to have friends, then your social functioning is impaired.

Judy was clearly impaired by her phobia, but many people with similar, less severe reactions are not impaired. This difference again illustrates the important point that most psychological disorders are simply extreme expressions of otherwise normal emotions, behaviors, and cognitive processes.

■ **Atypical or Not Culturally Expected**

Finally, the criterion that the response be *atypical* or *not culturally expected* is important but also insufficient to determine abnormality. At times, something is considered abnormal because it occurs infrequently; it deviates from the average. The greater the deviation, the more abnormal it is. You might say that someone is abnormally short or abnormally tall, meaning that the person's height deviates substantially from average, but this obviously isn't a definition of disorder. Many people are far from the average in their behavior, but few would be considered disordered. We might call them talented or eccentric. Many artists, movie stars, and athletes fall in this category. For example, it's not normal to masturbate in

public, but Madonna used to simulate it on stage. The novelist J. D. Salinger, who wrote *Catcher in the Rye,* retreated to a small town in New Hampshire and refused to see any outsiders for years, but he continued to write. Some male rock singers wear heavy makeup on stage. These people are well paid and seem to enjoy their careers. In most cases, the more productive you are in the eyes of

Some religious behaviors may seem unusual to us but are culturally or individually appropriate.

©Wenn Landov

We accept extreme behaviors by entertainers, such as Marilyn Manson, that would not be tolerated in other members of our society.

society, the more eccentricities society will tolerate. Therefore, "deviating from the average" doesn't work well as a definition.

Another view is that your behavior is abnormal if you are violating social norms, even if a number of people are sympathetic to your point of view. This definition is useful in considering important cultural differences in psychological disorders. For example, to enter a trance state and believe you are possessed reflects a psychological disorder in most Western cultures but not in many other societies, where the behavior is accepted and expected (see Chapter 6). (A cultural perspective is an important point of reference throughout this book.) An informative example of this view is provided by Robert Sapolsky (2002), the prominent neuroscientist who, during his studies, worked closely with the Masai tribe in East Africa. One day, Sapolsky's Masai friend Rhoda asked him to bring his jeep as quickly as possible to the Masai village where a woman had been acting aggressively and had been hearing voices. The woman had actually killed a goat with her own hands. Sapolsky and several Masai were able to subdue her and transport her to a local health center. Realizing that this was an opportunity to learn more of the Masai's view of psychological disorders, Sapolsky had the following discussion:

> "So, Rhoda," I began laconically, "what do you suppose was wrong with that woman?"
> She looked at me as if I was mad.
> "She is crazy."
> "But how can you tell?"
> "She's crazy. Can't you just see from how she acts?"
> "But how do you decide that she is crazy? What did she do?"
> "She killed that goat."

> "Oh," I said with anthropological detachment, "but Masai kill goats all the time."
> She looked at me as if I were an idiot. "Only the men kill goats," she said.
> "Well, how else do you know that she is crazy?"
> "She hears voices."
> Again, I made a pain of myself. "Oh, but the Masai hear voices sometimes." (At ceremonies before long cattle drives, the Masai trance-dance and claim to hear voices.) And in one sentence, Rhoda summed up half of what anyone needs to know about cross-cultural psychiatry.
> "But she hears voices at the wrong time." (p. 138)

However, a social standard of *normal* has been misused. Consider, for example, the practice of committing political dissidents to mental institutions because they protest the policies of their government, which was common in Iraq before the fall of Saddam Hussein. Although such dissident behavior clearly violated social norms, it should not alone be cause for commitment.

Jerome Wakefield (1992, 1999), in a thoughtful analysis of the matter, uses the shorthand definition of harmful dysfunction. A related concept that is also useful is to determine whether the behavior is out of the individual's control (something the person doesn't want to do) or not (Widiger & Sankis, 2000). Variants of these approaches are most often used in current diagnostic practice, as outlined in the text revision, fourth edition of the Diagnostic and Statistical Manual (DSM-IV-TR) (American Psychiatric Association, 2000), which contains the current listing of criteria for psychological disorders. These approaches guide our thinking in this book.

■ An Accepted Definition

In conclusion, it is difficult to define "normal" and "abnormal" (Lilienfeld & Marino, 1995, 1999)—and the debate continues (Houts, 2001; Clark, 1999; Klein, 1999; Spitzer, 1999; Wakefield, 2003). The most widely accepted definition used in DSM-IV-TR describes behavioral, psychological, or biological dysfunctions that are unexpected in their cultural context and associated with present distress and impairment in functioning, or increased risk of suffering, death, pain, or impairment. This definition can be useful across cultures and subcultures if we pay careful attention to what is functional or dysfunctional (or out of control) in a given society. But it is never easy to decide what represents dysfunction, and some scholars have argued persuasively that the health professions will never be able to satisfactorily define *disease* or *disorder* (see, for example, Lilienfeld & Marino, 1995, 1999). The best we may be able to do is to consider how the apparent disease or disorder matches a "typical" profile of a disorder—for example, major depression or schizophrenia—when most or all symptoms that experts would agree are part of the disorder are present. We call this typical profile a *prototype,* and, as described in Chapter 3, the diagnostic criteria from DSM-IV-TR found throughout this book are all prototypes. This means that the patient may have only some features or symptoms of the disorder (a minimum number) and still meet criteria for the disorder because his or her set of symptoms is close to the prototype. This concept is described more fully in Chapter 3, where the diagnosis of psychological disorder is discussed.

The process for creating the fifth edition of the *Diagnostic and Statistical Manual* (DSM-V) is in progress (Brown & Barlow, 2005; Krueger, Watson, & Barlow, 2005; Mitchell, Cook-Myers, & Wonderlich, 2005; Kupfer, First, & Regier, 2002) and the planning committees have already begun to wrestle with improvements they can make to definitions of disorder. To assist this process, the planning committees have conceptualized three research questions that form the basis for further investigation. First, they propose to do a careful analysis of the concepts that underlie disorders accepted in DSM-IV-TR, evaluating the degree to which they might conform (or not) to the numerous ways we have of understanding disorders at present. Second, they propose to conduct surveys of mental health professionals in the United States and around the world to attempt to get a better idea of the concepts of mental disorders used worldwide to see whether some striking commonalities emerge. Finally, using the same survey process, they would look to see what, in the eyes of mental health professionals around the world, separates those people who would truly meet criteria for a disorder from other individuals who might have a mild form of the same problem such that it would not interfere with their functioning (Rounsaville et al., 2002). It is hoped that these surveys would begin to shed light on the difficult problem of defining a psychological disorder.

To leave you with a final challenge, take the problem of defining abnormal behavior a step further and consider this: What if Judy passed out so often that after a while neither her classmates nor her teachers even noticed because she regained consciousness quickly? Furthermore, what if Judy continued to get good grades? Would fainting all the time at the mere thought of blood be a disorder? Would it be impairing? Dysfunctional? Distressing? What do you think?

The Science of Psychopathology

Psychopathology is the scientific study of psychological disorders. Within this field are specially trained professionals, including clinical and counseling psychologists, psychiatrists, psychiatric social workers, and psychiatric nurses, as well as marriage and family therapists and mental health counselors. *Clinical* and *counseling psychologists* receive the Ph.D. degree (or sometimes an Ed.D., doctor of education, or Psy.D., doctor of psychology) and follow a course of graduate-level study, lasting approximately 5 years, that prepares them to conduct research into the causes and treatment of psychological disorders and to diagnose, assess, and treat these disorders. Although there is a great deal of overlap, counseling psychologists tend to study and treat adjustment and vocational issues encountered by relatively healthy individuals, and clinical psychologists usually concentrate on more severe psychological disorders. Also, programs in professional schools of psychology, where the degree is often a Psy.D., focus on clinical training and de-emphasize or eliminate research training, compared to Ph.D. programs in universities, which integrate clinical and research training. Psychologists with other specialty training, such as experimental and social psychologists, concentrate on investigating the basic determinants of behavior but do not assess or treat psychological disorders.

Psychiatrists first earn an M.D. degree in medical school and then specialize in psychiatry during residency training that lasts 3 to 4 years. Psychiatrists also investigate the nature and causes of psychological disorders, often from a biological point of view; make diagnoses; and offer treatments. Many psychiatrists emphasize drugs or other biological treatments, although most use psychosocial treatments as well.

Psychiatric social workers typically earn a master's degree in social work as they develop expertise in collecting information relevant to the social and family situation of the individual with a psychological disorder. Social workers also treat disorders, often concentrating on family problems associated with them. *Psychiatric nurses* have advanced degrees such as a master's or even a Ph.D. and specialize in the care and treatment of patients with psychological disorders, usually in hospitals as part of a treatment team.

Finally, *marriage and family therapists* and *mental health counselors* typically spend 1–2 years earning a master's degree and are employed to provide clinical services by hospitals or clinics, usually under the supervision of a doctoral-level clinician.

■ The Scientist-Practitioner

The most important development in the recent history of psychopathology is the adoption of scientific methods to learn more about the nature of psychological disorders, their causes, and their treatment. Many mental health professionals take a scientific approach to their clinical work and therefore are called **scientist-practitioners** (Barlow, Hayes, & Nelson, 1984; Hayes, Barlow, & Nelson-Gray, 1999). Mental health practitioners may function as scientist-practitioners in one or more of three ways (see ■ Figure 1.2). First, they may keep up with the latest scientific developments in their field and therefore use the most current diagnostic and treatment procedures. In this sense, they are consumers of the science of psychopathology to the advantage of their patients. Second, scientist-practitioners evaluate their own assessments or treatment procedures to see whether they work. They are accountable not only to their patients but also to the government agencies and insurance companies that pay for the treatments, so they must demonstrate clearly that their treatments work. Third, scientist-practitioners might conduct research, often in clinics or hospitals, that produces new information about disorders or their treatment, thus becoming immune to the fads that plague our

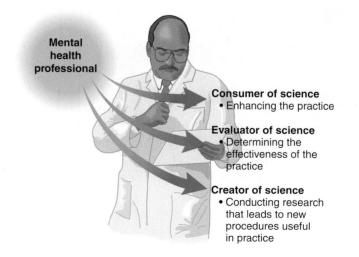

Mental health professional

Consumer of science
• Enhancing the practice

Evaluator of science
• Determining the effectiveness of the practice

Creator of science
• Conducting research that leads to new procedures useful in practice

■ **FIGURE 1.2** Functioning as a scientist-practitioner.

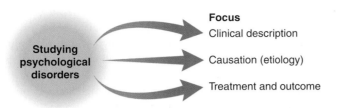

■ **FIGURE 1.3** Three major categories make up the study and discussion of psychological disorders.

field, often at the expense of patients and their families. For example, new "miracle cures" for psychological disorders that are reported several times a year in popular media would not be used by a scientist-practitioner if there were no sound scientific data showing that they work. Such data flow from research that attempts three basic things: to describe psychological disorders, to determine their causes, and to treat them (see ■ Figure 1.3). These three categories compose an organizational structure that recurs throughout this book and that is formally evident in the discussions of specific disorders beginning in Chapter 5. A general overview of them now will give you a clearer perspective on our efforts to understand abnormality.

■ Clinical Description

In hospitals and clinics, we often say that a patient "presents" with a specific problem or set of problems or we discuss the **presenting problem.** *Presents* is a traditional shorthand way of indicating why the person came to the clinic. Describing Judy's presenting prob-

lem is the first step in determining her **clinical description,** which represents the unique combination of behaviors, thoughts, and feelings that make up a specific disorder. The word *clinical* refers both to the types of problems or disorders that you would find in a clinic or hospital and to the activities connected with assessment and treatment. Throughout this text are excerpts from many more individual cases, most of them from our personal files.

Clearly, one important function of the clinical description is to specify what makes the disorder different from normal behavior or from other disorders. Statistical data may also be relevant.

For example, how many people in the population as a whole have the disorder? This figure is called the **prevalence** of the disorder. Statistics on how many new cases occur during a given period, such as a year, represent the **incidence** of the disorder. Other statistics include the *sex ratio*—that is, what percentage of males and females have the disorder—and the typical age of onset, which often differs from one disorder to another.

In addition to having different symptoms, age of onset, and possibly a different sex ratio and prevalence, most disorders follow a somewhat individual pattern, or **course.** For example, some disorders, such as schizophrenia (see Chapter 13), follow a *chronic course,* meaning that they tend to last a long time, sometimes a lifetime. Other disorders, like mood disorders (see Chapter 7), follow an *episodic course,* in that the individual is likely to recover within a few months only to suffer a recurrence of the disorder at a later time. This pattern may repeat throughout a person's life. Still other disorders may have a *time-limited course,* meaning the disorder will improve without treatment in a relatively short period.

Closely related to differences in course of disorders are differences in onset. Some disorders have an *acute onset,* meaning that they begin suddenly; others develop gradually over an extended period, which is sometimes called an *insidious onset.* It is important to know the typical course of a disorder so that we can know what to expect in the future and how best to deal with the problem. This is an important part of the clinical description. For example, if someone is suffering from a mild disorder with acute onset that we know is time limited, we might advise the individual not to bother with expensive treatment because the problem will be over soon enough, like a common cold. However, if the disorder is likely to last a long time (become chronic), the individual might want to seek treatment and take other appropriate steps. The anticipated course of a disorder is called the **prognosis.** So we might say, "the prognosis is good," meaning the individual will prob-ably recover, or "the prognosis is guarded," meaning the probable outcome doesn't look good.

The patient's age may be an important part of the clinical description. A specific psychological disorder occurring in childhood may present differently from the same disorder in adulthood or old age. Children experienc-

Children experience panic and anxiety differently from adults, so their reactions may be mistaken for symptoms of physical illness.

ing severe anxiety and panic often assume that they are physically ill because they have difficulty understanding that there is nothing physically wrong. Because their thoughts and feelings are different from those experienced by adults with anxiety and panic, children are often misdiagnosed and treated for a medical disorder.

We call the study of changes in behavior over time *developmental psychology,* and we refer to the study of changes in abnormal behavior as *developmental psychopathology.* When you think of developmental psychology, you probably picture researchers studying the behavior of children. However, because we change throughout our lives, researchers also study development in adolescents, adults, and older adults. Study across the entire age span is referred to as *life-span developmental psychopathology.* The field is relatively new but expanding rapidly.

■ Causation, Treatment, and Etiology Outcomes

Etiology, or the study of origins, has to do with why a disorder begins (what causes it) and includes biological, psychological, and social dimensions. Because the etiology of psychological disorders is so important to this field, we devote an entire chapter (Chapter 2) to it. Treatment is often important to the study of psychological disorders.

If a new drug or psychosocial treatment is successful in treating a disorder, it may give us some hints about the nature of the disorder and its causes. For example, if a drug with a specific known effect within the nervous system alleviates a certain psychological disorder, we know that something in that part of the nervous system might either be causing the disorder or helping maintain it. Similarly, if a psychosocial treatment designed to help clients regain a sense of control over their lives is effective with a certain disorder, a diminished sense of control may be an important psychological component of the disorder itself.

As you will see in the next chapter, psychology is never that simple. This is because the *effect* does not necessarily imply the *cause.* To use a common example, you might take an aspirin to relieve a tension headache you developed during a grueling day of taking exams. If you then feel better, that does not mean that the headache was caused by a lack of aspirin. Nevertheless, many people seek treatment for psychological disorders, and treatment can provide interesting hints about the nature of the disorder.

In the past, textbooks emphasized treatment approaches in a general sense, with little attention to the disorder being treated. For example, a mental health professional might be thoroughly trained in a single theoretical approach, such as psychoanalysis or behavior therapy (both described later in the chapter), and then use that approach on every disorder. More recently, as our science has advanced, we have developed specific effective treatments that do not always adhere neatly to one theoretical approach or another but that have grown out of a deeper understanding of the disorder in question. For this reason, there are no separate chapters in this book on such types of treatment approaches as psychodynamic, cognitive behavioral, or humanistic. Rather, the latest and most effective drug and psychosocial treatments are described in the context of specific disorders in keeping with our integrative multidimensional perspective.

We now survey many early attempts to describe and treat abnormal behavior and to comprehend its causes, which will give you a better perspective on current approaches. In Chapter 2, we exam-

ine exciting contemporary views of causation and treatment. In Chapter 3, we discuss efforts to describe, or classify, abnormal behavior. In Chapter 4, we review research methods—our systematic efforts to discover the truths underlying description, cause, and treatment that allow us to function as scientist-practitioners. In Chapters 5 through 15, we examine specific disorders; our discussion is organized in each case in the now familiar triad of description, cause, and treatment. Finally, in Chapter 16 we examine legal, professional, and ethical issues relevant to psychological disorders and their treatment today. With that overview in mind, let us turn to the past.

Historical Conceptions of Abnormal Behavior

For thousands of years, humans have tried to explain and control problematic behavior. But our efforts always derive from the theories or models of behavior popular at the time. The purpose of these models is to explain why someone is "acting like that." Three major models that have guided us date back to the beginnings of civilization.

Humans have always supposed that agents outside our bodies and environment influence our behavior, thinking, and emotions. These agents, which might be divinities, demons, spirits, or other phenomena such as magnetic fields or the moon or the stars, are the driving forces behind the *supernatural model.* In addition, since ancient Greece, the mind has often been called the *soul* or the *psyche* and considered separate from the body. Although many have thought that the mind can influence the body and, in turn, the body can influence the mind, most philosophers looked for causes of abnormal behavior in one or the other. This split gave rise to two traditions of thought about abnormal behavior, summarized as the *biological model* and the *psychological model.*

These three models—the supernatural, the biological, and the psychological—are very old but continue to be used today.

CONCEPT CHECK 1.1

Part A
Write the letter for any or all of the following definitions of abnormality in the blanks: (a) societal norm violation, (b) impairment in functioning, (c) dysfunction, and (d) distress.

1. Miguel recently began feeling sad and lonely. Although still able to function at work and fulfill other responsibilities, he finds himself feeling down much of the time and he worries about what is happening to him. Which of the definitions of abnormality apply to Miguel's situation?

_____

2. Three weeks ago, Jane, a 35-year-old business executive, stopped showering, refused to leave her apartment, and started watching television talk shows. Threats of being fired have failed to bring Jane back to reality, and she continues to spend her days staring blankly at the television screen. Which of the definitions seems to describe Jane's behavior? _____

(continued)

THE SUPERNATURAL TRADITION

For much of our recorded history, deviant behavior has been considered a reflection of the battle between good and evil. When confronted with unexplainable, irrational behavior and by suffering and upheaval, people perceived evil. In fact, in the Great Persian Empire from 900 to 600 B.C., all physical and mental disorders were considered the work of the devil (Millon, 2004). Barbara Tuchman, a noted historian, chronicled the second half of the 14th century, a particularly difficult time for humanity, in *A Distant Mirror* (1978). She ably captures the conflicting tides of opinion on the origins and treatment of insanity during that bleak and tumultuous period.

Demons and Witches

One strong current of opinion put the causes and treatment of psychological disorders squarely in the realm of the supernatural. During the last quarter of the 14th century, religious and lay authorities supported these popular superstitions and society as a whole began to believe more strongly in the reality and power of demons and witches. The Catholic Church had split, and a second center, complete with a pope, emerged in the south of France to compete with Rome. In reaction to this schism, the Roman Church fought back against the evil in the world that must have been behind this heresy.

People increasingly turned to magic and sorcery to solve their problems. During these turbulent times, the bizarre behavior of people afflicted with psychological disorders was seen as the work of the devil and witches. It followed that individuals possessed by evil spirits were probably responsible for any misfortune experienced by the townspeople, which inspired drastic action against the possessed. Treatments included **exorcism,** in which various religious rituals were performed to rid the victim of evil spirits. Other approaches included shaving the pattern of a cross in the hair of the victim's head and securing sufferers to a wall near the front of a church so that they might benefit from hearing Mass.

The conviction that sorcery and witches are causes of madness and other evils continued into the 15th century, and evil continued to be blamed for unexplainable behavior, even after the founding of our own country, as evidenced by the Salem, Massachusetts, witch trials.

Stress and Melancholy

An equally strong opinion, even during this period, reflected the enlightened view that insanity was a natural phenomenon, caused by mental or emotional stress, and that it was curable (Alexander & Selesnick, 1966; Maher & Maher, 1985a). Mental depression and anxiety were recognized as illnesses (Kemp, 1990; Schoeneman, 1977), although symptoms such as despair and lethargy were often identified by the church with the sin of *acedia,* or sloth (Tuchman, 1978). Common treatments were rest, sleep, and a

During the Middle Ages, individuals with psychological disorders were sometimes thought to be possessed by evil spirits that had to be exorcised through rituals.

©Mary Evans Picture Library/The Image Works

healthy and happy environment. Other treatments included baths, ointments, and various potions. Indeed, during the 14th and 15th centuries, the insane, along with the physically deformed or disabled, were often moved from house to house in medieval villages as neighbors took turns caring for them. We now know that this medieval practice of keeping people who have psychological disturbances in their own community is beneficial (see Chapter 13). (We return to this subject when we discuss biological and psychological models later in this chapter.)

One of the chief advisers to the king of France, a bishop and philosopher named Nicholas Oresme, also suggested that the disease of melancholy (depression) was the source of some bizarre behavior, rather than demons. Oresme pointed out that much of the evidence for the existence of sorcery and witchcraft, particularly among the insane, was obtained from people who were tortured and who, quite understandably, confessed to anything.

These conflicting crosscurrents of natural and supernatural explanations for mental disorders are represented more or less strongly in various historical works, depending on the sources consulted by historians. Some assumed that demonic influences were the predominant explanations of abnormal behavior during the Middle Ages (for example, Zilboorg & Henry, 1941); others believed that the supernatural had little or no influence. As we see in the handling of the severe psychological disorder experienced by late-14th-century King Charles VI of France, both influences were strong, sometimes alternating in the treatment of the same case.

CHARLES VI: The Mad King

©Mary Evans Picture Library/ The Image Works

In the summer of 1392, King Charles VI of France was under a great deal of stress, partly because of the division of the Catholic Church. As he rode with his army to the province of Brittany, a nearby aide dropped his lance with a loud clatter and the king, thinking he was under attack, turned on his own army, killing several prominent knights before being subdued from behind. The army immediately marched back to Paris. The king's lieutenants and advisers concluded that he was mad.

During the following years, at his worst the king hid in a corner of his castle believing he was made of glass or roamed the corridors howling like a wolf. At other times he couldn't remember who or what he was. He became fearful and enraged whenever he saw his own royal coat of arms and would try to destroy it if it was brought near him.

The people of Paris were devastated by their leader's apparent madness. Some thought it reflected God's anger, because the king failed to take up arms to end the schism in the Catholic Church; others thought it was God's warning against taking up arms; and still others thought it was divine punishment for heavy taxes (a conclusion some people might make today). But most thought the king's madness was caused by sorcery, a belief strengthened by a great drought that dried up the ponds and rivers, causing cattle to die of thirst. Merchants claimed their worst losses in 20 years.

Naturally, the king was given the best care available. The most famous healer in the land was a 92-year-old physician whose treatment program included moving the king to one of his residences in the country where the air was thought to be the cleanest in the land. The physician prescribed rest, relaxation, and recreation. After some time, the king seemed to recover. The physician recommended that the king not be burdened with the responsibilities of running the kingdom, claiming that if he had few worries or irritations, his mind would gradually strengthen and further improve.

Unfortunately, the physician died and the insanity of King Charles VI returned more seriously than before. This time, however, he came under the influence of the conflicting crosscurrent of supernatural causation. "An unkempt evil-eyed charlatan and pseudo-mystic named Arnaut Guilhem was allowed to treat Charles on his claim of possessing a book given by God to Adam by means of which man could overcome all affliction resulting from original sin" (Tuchman, 1978, p. 514). Guilhem insisted that the king's malady was caused by sorcery, but his treatments failed to bring about a cure.

A variety of remedies and rituals of all kinds were tried, but none worked. High-ranking officials and doctors of the university called for the "sorcerers" to be discovered and punished. "On one occasion, two Augustinian friars, after getting no results from magic incantations and a liquid made from powdered pearls, proposed to cut incisions in the king's head. When this was not allowed by the king's council, the friars accused those who opposed their recommendation of sorcery" (Tuchman, 1978, p. 514). Even the king himself, during his lucid moments, came to believe that the source of madness was evil and sorcery. "In the name of Jesus Christ," he cried, weeping in his agony, "if there is any one of you who is an accomplice to this evil I suffer, I beg him to torture me no longer but let me die!" (Tuchman, 1978, p. 515).

If Judy had lived during the late 14th century, it is quite possible that she would have been seen as possessed and subjected to exorcism. You may remember the movie *The Exorcist,* in which a young girl, behaving very strangely, was screened for every possible mental and physical disorder before authorities reluctantly resorted to an exorcism.

Treatments for Possession

With a perceived connection between evil deeds and sin on the one hand and psychological disorders on the other, it is logical to conclude that the sufferer is largely responsible for the disorder, which might well be a punishment for evil deeds. Does this sound familiar? The acquired immune deficiency syndrome (AIDS) epidemic was associated with a similar belief among some people, particularly in the 1990s. Because the human immunodeficiency

In hydrotherapy, patients were shocked back to their senses by being submerged in ice-cold water.

©Culver Pictures

virus (HIV) is, in Western societies, most prevalent among individuals with homosexual orientation, many people believe it is a divine punishment for what they consider disgusting behavior. This view has dissipated as the AIDS virus spreads to other, "less sinful" segments of the population, yet it persists.

Possession, however, is not always connected with sin but may be seen as involuntary and the possessed individual as blameless. Furthermore, exorcisms at least have the virtue of being relatively painless. Interestingly, they sometimes work, as do other forms of faith healing, for reasons we explore in subsequent chapters. But what if they did not? In the Middle Ages, if exorcism failed, some authorities thought that steps were necessary to make the body uninhabitable by evil spirits, and many people were subjected to confinement, beatings, and other forms of torture (Kemp, 1990).

Somewhere along the way, a creative "therapist" decided that hanging people over a pit full of poisonous snakes might scare the evil spirits right out of their bodies (to say nothing of terrifying the people themselves). Strangely, this approach sometimes worked; that is, the most disturbed, oddly behaving individuals would suddenly come to their senses and experience relief from their symptoms, if only temporarily. Naturally, this was reinforcing to the therapist, so snake pits were built in many institutions. Many other treatments based on the hypothesized therapeutic element of shock were developed, including dunkings in ice-cold water.

Mass Hysteria

Another fascinating phenomenon is characterized by large-scale outbreaks of bizarre behavior. To this day, these episodes puzzle historians and mental health practitioners. During the Middle Ages, they lent support to the notion of possession. In Europe, whole groups of people were simultaneously compelled to run out in the streets, dance, shout, rave, and jump around in patterns as if they were at a particularly wild party late at night (still called a *rave*), but without the music. This behavior was known by several names, including Saint Vitus's Dance and tarantism. It is most interesting that many people behaved in this strange way at once. In an attempt to explain the inexplicable, several reasons were offered in addition to possession. One reasonable guess was reaction to insect bites. Another possibility was what we now call *mass hysteria*. Consider the following example.

Modern Mass Hysteria

One Friday afternoon an alarm sounded over the public address system of a community hospital calling all physicians to the emergency room immediately. Arriving from a local school in a fleet of ambulances were 17 students and 4 teachers who reported dizziness, headache, nausea, and stomach pains. Some were vomiting; most were hyperventilating.

All the students and teachers had been in four classrooms, two on each side of the hallway. The incident began when a 14-year-old girl reported a funny smell that seemed to be coming from a vent. She fell to the floor, crying and complaining that her stomach hurt and her eyes stung. Soon, many of the students and most of the teachers in the four adjoining classrooms, who could see and hear what was happening, experienced similar symptoms. Of 86 susceptible people (82 students and 4 teachers in the four classrooms), 21 patients (17 students and 4 teachers) experienced symptoms severe enough to be evaluated at the hospital. Inspection of the school building by public health authorities revealed no apparent cause for the reactions, and physical examinations by teams of physicians revealed no physical abnormalities. All the patients were sent home and quickly recovered (Rockney & Lemke, 1992).

Mass hysteria may simply demonstrate the phenomenon of *emotion contagion,* in which the experience of an emotion seems to spread to those around us (Hatfield, Cacioppo, & Rapson, 1994; Wang, 2006). If someone nearby becomes frightened or sad, chances are that for the moment you also will feel fear or sadness. When this kind of experience escalates into full-blown panic, whole communities are affected (Barlow, 2002). People are also suggestible when they are in states of high emotion. Therefore, if one person identifies a "cause" of the problem, others will probably assume that their own reactions have the same source. In popular language, this shared response is sometimes referred to as *mob psychology.*

The Moon and the Stars

Paracelsus, a Swiss physician who lived from 1493 to 1541, rejected notions of possession by the devil, suggesting instead that the movements of the moon and stars had profound effects on

Emotions are contagious and can escalate into mass hysteria.

THE BIOLOGICAL TRADITION

Physical causes of mental disorders have been sought since early in history. Important to the biological tradition are a man, Hippocrates; a disease, syphilis; and the early consequences of believing that psychological disorders are biologically caused.

Hippocrates and Galen

The Greek physician Hippocrates (460–377 B.C.) is considered to be the father of modern Western medicine. He and his associates left a body of work called the *Hippocratic Corpus,* written between 450 and 350 B.C. (Maher & Maher, 1985a), in which they suggested that psychological disorders could be treated like any other disease. They did not limit their search for the causes of psychopathology to the general area of "disease," because they believed that psychological disorders might also be caused by brain pathology or head trauma and could be influenced by heredity (genetics). These are remarkably astute deductions for the time, and they have been supported in recent years. Hippocrates considered the brain to be the seat of wisdom, consciousness, intelligence, and emotion. Therefore, disorders involving these functions would logically be located in the brain. Hippocrates also recognized the importance of psychological and interpersonal contributions to psychopathology, such as the sometimes-negative effects of family stress; on some occasions, he removed patients from their families.

The Roman physician Galen (approximately 129–198 A.D.) later adopted the ideas of Hippocrates and his associates and developed them further, creating a powerful and influential school of thought within the biological tradition that extended well into the 19th century. One of the more interesting and influential legacies of the Hippocratic-Galenic approach is the *humoral theory* of disorders. Hippocrates assumed that normal brain functioning was related to four bodily fluids or *humors:* blood, black bile, yellow bile, and phlegm. Blood came from the heart, black bile from the spleen, phlegm from the brain, and choler or yellow bile from the liver. Physicians believed that disease resulted from too much or too little of one of the humors; for example, too much black bile was thought to cause melancholia (depression). In fact, the term *melancholer,* which means black bile, is still used today in its derivative form *melancholy* to refer to aspects of depression. The humoral theory was, perhaps, the first example of associating psychological disorders with chemical imbalance, an approach that is widespread today.

The four humors were related to the Greeks' conception of the four basic qualities: heat, dryness, moisture, and cold. Each humor was associated with one of these qualities. Terms derived from the four humors are still sometimes applied to personality traits. For example, *sanguine* (red, like blood) describes someone

people's psychological functioning. This influential theory inspired the word *lunatic,* which is derived from the Latin word for moon, *luna.* You might hear some of your friends explain something crazy they did last night by saying, "It must have been the full moon." The belief that heavenly bodies affect human behavior still exists, although there is no scientific evidence to support it. Despite much ridicule, millions of people around the world are convinced that their behavior is influenced by the stages of the moon or the position of the stars. This belief is most noticeable today in followers of astrology, who hold that their behavior and the major events in their lives can be predicted by their day-to-day relationship to the position of the planets. However, no serious evidence has ever confirmed such a connection.

Comments

The supernatural tradition in psychopathology is alive and well, although it is relegated, for the most part, to small religious sects in this country and to nontechnological cultures elsewhere. Members of organized religions in most parts of the world look to psychology and medical science for help with major psychological disorders; in fact, the Roman Catholic Church requires that all health-care resources be exhausted before spiritual solutions such as exorcism can be considered. Nonetheless, miraculous cures are sometimes achieved by exorcism, magic potions and rituals, and other methods that seem to have little connection with modern science. It is fascinating to explore them when they do occur, and we return to this topic in subsequent chapters. But such cases are relatively rare, and almost no one would advocate supernatural treatment for severe psychological disorders except, perhaps, as a last resort.

©Associated Press

who is ruddy in complexion, presumably from copious blood flowing through the body, and cheerful and optimistic, although insomnia and delirium were thought to be caused by excessive blood in the brain. *Melancholic* means depressive (depression was thought to be caused by black bile flooding the brain). A *phlegmatic* personality (from the humor phlegm) indicates apathy and sluggishness but can also mean being calm under stress. A *choleric* person (from yellow bile or choler) is hot tempered (Maher & Maher, 1985a).

Excesses of one or more humors were treated by regulating the environment to increase or decrease heat, dryness, moisture, or cold, depending on which humor was out of balance. One reason King Charles VI's physician moved him to the less stressful countryside was to restore the balance in his humors (Kemp, 1990). In addition to rest, good nutrition, and exercise, two treatments were developed. In one, *bleeding* or *bloodletting,* a carefully measured amount of blood was removed from the body, often with leeches. The other was to induce vomiting; indeed, in a well-known treatise on depression published in 1621, *Anatomy of Melancholy,* Robert Burton recommended eating tobacco and a half-boiled cabbage to induce vomiting (Burton, 1621/1977). In ancient China and throughout Asia, a similar idea existed. But rather than "humors," the Chinese focused on the movement of air or "wind" throughout the body. Unexplained mental disorders were caused by blockages of wind or the presence of cold, dark wind (yin) as opposed to warm, life-sustaining wind (yang). Treatment involved restoring proper flow of wind through various methods, including acupuncture. Three hundred years ago, Judy might have been diagnosed with an illness, a brain disorder, or some other physical problem and been given the proper medical treatments of the day: bed rest, a healthful diet, exercise, and other ministrations as indicated.

Bloodletting, the extraction of blood from patients, was intended to restore the balance of humors in the body.

Hippocrates also coined the word *hysteria* to describe a concept he learned about from the Egyptians, who had identified what we now call the *somatoform disorders.* In these disorders, the physical symptoms appear to be the result of an organic pathology for which no organic cause can be found, such as paralysis and some kinds of blindness. Because these disorders occurred primarily in women, the Egyptians (and Hippocrates) mistakenly assumed that they were restricted to women. They also presumed a cause: The empty uterus wandered to various parts of the body in search of conception (the Greek for uterus is *hysteron*). Numerous physical symptoms reflected the location of the wandering uterus. The prescribed cure might be marriage or, occasionally, fumigation of the vagina to lure the uterus back to its natural location (Alexander & Selesnick, 1966). Knowledge of physiology eventually disproved the wandering uterus theory; however, the tendency to stigmatize dramatic women as hysterical continued unabated well into the 1970s, when mental health professionals became sensitive to the prejudicial stereotype the term implied. As you will learn in Chapter 6, somatoform disorders (and the traits associated with them) are not limited to one sex or the other.

The 19th Century

The biological tradition waxed and waned during the centuries after Hippocrates and Galen but was reinvigorated in the 19th century because of two factors: the discovery of the nature and cause of syphilis and strong support from the well-respected American psychiatrist John P. Grey.

■ Syphilis

Behavioral and cognitive symptoms of what we now know as *advanced syphilis,* a sexually transmitted disease caused by a bacterial microorganism entering the brain, include believing that everyone is plotting against you (delusion of persecution) or that you are God (delusion of grandeur), as well as other bizarre behaviors. Although these symptoms are similar to those of *psychosis*—psychological disorders characterized in part by beliefs that are not based in reality (delusions), perceptions that are not based in reality (hallucinations), or both—researchers recognized that a subgroup of apparently psychotic patients deteriorated steadily, becoming paralyzed and dying within 5 years of onset. This course of events contrasted with that of most psychotic patients, who remained fairly stable. In 1825, the condition was designated a disease, *general paresis,* because it had consistent symptoms (presentation) and a consistent course that resulted in death. The relationship between general paresis and syphilis was only gradually established. Louis Pasteur's germ theory of disease, around 1870, facilitated the identification of the specific bacterial microorganism that caused syphilis. Pasteur stated that all symptoms of a disease were caused by a germ (bacterium) that had invaded the body.

Of equal importance was the discovery of a cure for general paresis. Physicians observed a surprising recovery in patients who had contracted malaria and deliberately injected others with blood from a soldier who was ill with malaria. Many recovered because the high fever "burned out" the syphilis bacteria. Obviously, this type of experiment would not be ethically possible today. Ultimately, clinical investigators discovered that penicillin cures syphilis, but with the malaria cure, "madness" and associated behavioral and cognitive symptoms for the first time were traced directly to a curable infection. Many mental health professionals then assumed that comparable causes and cures might be discovered for all psychological disorders.

■ John P. Grey

The champion of the biological tradition in the United States was the most influential American psychiatrist of the time, John P. Grey (Bockoven, 1963). In 1854, Grey was appointed superintendent of the Utica State Hospital in New York, the largest in the country. He also became editor of the *American Journal of Insanity,* the precursor of the current *American Journal of Psychiatry,* the flagship publication of the American Psychiatric Association (APA). Grey's position was that the causes of insanity were *always* physical. Therefore, the mentally ill patient should be treated as physically ill. The emphasis was again on rest, diet, and proper room temperature and ventilation, approaches used for centuries by previous therapists in the biological tradition. Grey even invented the rotary fan to ventilate his large hospital.

Under Grey's leadership, the conditions in hospitals greatly improved and they became more humane, livable institutions. But in subsequent years they also became so large and impersonal that individual attention was not possible.

In fact, leaders in psychiatry at the end of the 19th century were alarmed at the increasing size and impersonality of mental hospitals and recommended that they be downsized. It was almost 100 years before the community mental health movement was successful in reducing the population of mental hospitals with the controversial policy of deinstitutionalization, in which patients were released into their communities. Unfortunately, this practice has as many negative consequences as positive ones, including a large increase in the number of chronically disabled patients homeless on the streets of our cities.

The Development of Biological Treatments

On the positive side, renewed interest in the biological origin of psychological disorders led, ultimately, to greatly increased understanding of biological contributions to psychopathology and to the development of new treatments. In the 1930s, the physical interventions of electric shock and brain surgery were often used. Their effects, and the effects of new drugs, were discovered quite by accident. For example, insulin was occasionally given to stimulate appetite in psychotic patients who were not eating, but it also seemed to calm them down. In 1927, a Viennese physician, Manfred Sakel, began using increasingly higher dosages until, finally, patients convulsed and became temporarily comatose (Sakel, 1958). Some actually recovered their mental health, much to the surprise of everybody, and their recovery was attributed to the convulsions. The procedure became known as *insulin shock therapy,* but it was abandoned because it was too dangerous, often resulting in prolonged coma or even death. Other methods of producing convulsions had to be found.

Benjamin Franklin made numerous discoveries during his life with which we are familiar, but most people don't know that he discovered accidentally, and then confirmed experimentally in the 1750s, that a mild and modest electric shock to the head produced a brief convulsion and memory loss (amnesia) but otherwise did little harm. A Dutch physician who was a friend and colleague of Franklin's tried it on himself and discovered that the shock also made him "strangely elated" and wondered if it might be a useful treatment for depression (Finger & Zaromb, 2006, p. 245).

Independently in the 1920s, Joseph von Meduna observed that schizophrenia was rarely found in individuals with epilepsy (which ultimately did not prove to be true). Some of his followers concluded that induced brain seizures might cure schizophrenia. Following suggestions on the possible benefits of applying electric shock directly to the brain—notably, by two Italian physicians, Ugo Cerletti and Lucio Bini, in 1938—a surgeon in London treated a depressed patient by sending six small shocks directly through his brain, producing convulsions (Hunt, 1980). The patient recovered. Although greatly modified, shock treatment is still with us today. The controversial modern uses of *electroconvulsive therapy* are described in Chapter 7. It is interesting that even now we have little knowledge of how it works.

During the 1950s, the first effective drugs for severe psychotic disorders were developed in a systematic way. Before that time, a number of medicinal substances, including opium (derived from poppies), had been used as sedatives, along with countless herbs and folk remedies (Alexander & Selesnick, 1966). With the discovery of

In the 19th century, psychological disorders were attributed to mental or emotional stress, so patients were often treated sympathetically in a restful and hygienic environment.

Rauwolfia serpentine (later renamed *reserpine*) and another class of drugs called *neuroleptics* (major tranquilizers), for the first time hallucinatory and delusional thought processes could be diminished in some patients; these drugs also controlled agitation and aggressiveness. Other discoveries included *benzodiazepines* (minor tranquilizers), which seemed to reduce anxiety. By the 1970s, the benzodiazepines (known by such brand names as Valium and Librium) were among the most widely prescribed drugs in the world. As drawbacks and side effects of tranquilizers became apparent, along with their limited effectiveness, prescriptions decreased somewhat (we discuss the benzodiazepines in more detail in Chapters 5 and 11).

Throughout the centuries, as Alexander and Selesnick point out, "The general pattern of drug therapy for mental illness has been one of initial enthusiasm followed by disappointment" (1966, p. 287). For example, bromides, a class of sedating drugs, were used at the end of the 19th century and beginning of the 20th century to treat anxiety and other psychological disorders. By the 1920s, they were reported as being effective for many serious psychological and emotional symptoms. By 1928, one of every five prescriptions in the United States was for bromides. When their side effects, including various undesirable physical symptoms, became widely known, and experience began to show that their overall effectiveness was relatively modest, bromides largely disappeared from the scene.

Neuroleptics have also been used less as attention has focused on their many side effects, such as tremors and shaking. However, the positive side effects of these drugs on some patients' psychotic symptoms of hallucinations, delusions, and agitation revitalized both the search for biological contributions to psychological disorders and the search for new and more powerful drugs, a search that has paid many dividends, as documented in later chapters.

Consequences of the Biological Tradition

In the late 19th century, Grey and his colleagues ironically reduced or eliminated interest in treating mental patients because they thought that mental disorders were the result of some as-yet-undiscovered brain pathology and were therefore incurable. The only available course of action was to hospitalize these patients. Around the turn of the century, some nurses documented clinical success in treating mental patients but were prevented from treating others for fear of raising hopes of a cure among family members. In place of treatment, interest centered on diagnosis, legal questions concerning the responsibility of patients for their actions during periods of insanity, and the study of brain pathology itself.

Emil Kraepelin (1856–1926) was the dominant figure during this period and one of the founding fathers of modern psychiatry. He was extremely influential in advocating the major ideas of the biological tradition, but he was little involved in treatment. His lasting contribution was in the area of diagnosis and classification, which we discuss in detail in Chapter 3. Kraepelin (1913) was one of the first to distinguish among various psychological disorders, seeing that each may have a different age of onset and time course, with somewhat different clusters of presenting symptoms, and probably a different cause. Many of his descriptions of schizophrenic disorders are still useful today.

By the end of the 1800s, a scientific approach to psychological disorders and their classification had begun with the search for biological causes. Furthermore, treatment was based on humane principles. However, there were many drawbacks, the most unfortunate being that active intervention and treatment were all but eliminated in some settings, despite the availability of some effective approaches. It is to these that we now turn.

CONCEPT CHECK 1.2

For thousands of years, humans have tried to understand and control abnormal behavior. Check your understanding of these historical theories and match them to the treatments used to "cure" abnormal behavior: (a) bloodletting; induced vomiting; (b) patient placed in socially facilitative environments; and (c) exorcism; burning at the stake.

1. Supernatural causes; evil demons took over the victims' bodies and controlled their behaviors. _____
2. The humoral theory reflected the belief that normal functioning of the brain required a balance of four bodily fluids or humors. _____
3. Maladaptive behavior was caused by poor social and cultural influences within the environment. _____

THE PSYCHOLOGICAL TRADITION

It is a long leap from evil spirits to brain pathology as the cause of psychological disorders. In the intervening centuries, where was the body of thought that put psychological development, both normal and abnormal, in an interpersonal and social context? In fact, this approach has a long and distinguished tradition. Plato, for example, thought that the two causes of maladaptive behavior were the social and cultural influences in one's life and the learning that took place in that environment. If something was wrong in the environment, such as abusive parents, one's impulses and emotions would overcome reason. The best treatment was to reeducate the individual through rational discussion so that the power of reason would predominate (Maher & Maher, 1985a). This was very much a precursor to modern **psychosocial** approaches to the causation of pyschopathology, which focus not only on psychological factors but on social and cultural ones as well. Other well-known early philosophers, including Aristotle, also emphasized the influence of social environment and early learning on later psychopathology. These philosophers wrote about the importance of fantasies, dreams, and cognitions and thus anticipated, to some extent, later developments in psychoanalytic thought and cognitive science. They also advocated humane and responsible care for the psychologically disturbed.

Moral Therapy

During the first half of the 19th century, a strong psychosocial approach to mental disorders called **moral therapy** became influential. The term *moral* really meant emotional or psychological

Patients with psychological disorders were freed from chains and shackles as a result of the influence of Philippe Pinel (1745–1826), a pioneer in making mental institutions more humane.

early work at Pennsylvania Hospital. It then became the treatment of choice in the leading hospitals. *Asylums* had appeared in the 16th century, but they were more like prisons than hospitals. It was the rise of moral therapy in Europe and the United States that made asylums habitable and even therapeutic.

In 1833, Horace Mann, chairman of the board of trustees of the Worcester State Hospital, reported on 32 patients who had been given up as incurable. These patients were treated with moral therapy, cured, and released to their families. Of 100 patients who were viciously assaultive before treatment, no more than 12 continued to be violent a year after beginning treatment. Before treatment, 40 patients had routinely torn off any new clothes provided by attendants; only 8 continued this behavior after a period of treatment. These were remarkable statistics then and would be remarkable even today (Bockoven, 1963).

rather than a code of conduct. Its basic tenets included treating institutionalized patients as normally as possible in a setting that encouraged and reinforced normal social interaction (Bockoven, 1963), thus providing them with many opportunities for appropriate social and interpersonal contact. Relationships were carefully nurtured. Individual attention clearly emphasized positive consequences for appropriate interactions and behavior; the staff made a point of modeling this behavior. Lectures on various interesting subjects were provided, and restraint and seclusion were eliminated.

Once again, little is new under the sun. The principles of moral therapy date back to Plato and beyond. For example, the Greek Asclepiad Temples of the 6th century B.C. housed the chronically ill, including those with psychological disorders. Here, patients were well cared for, massaged, and provided with soothing music. Similar enlightened practices were evident in Muslim countries in the Middle East (Millon, 2004). But moral therapy as a system originated with the well-known French psychiatrist Philippe Pinel (1745–1826) (Zilboorg & Henry, 1941). A former patient, Pussin, long since recovered, was working in the Parisian hospital La Bicêtre when Pinel took over. Pussin had already instituted remarkable reforms, remembering, perhaps, being shackled as a patient himself. Pussin persuaded Pinel to go along with the changes. Much to Pinel's credit, he did, first at La Bicêtre and then at the women's hospital Salpêtrière (Maher & Maher, 1985b; Weiner, 1979), where a humane, socially facilitative atmosphere produced "miraculous" results.

After William Tuke (1732–1822) followed Pinel's lead in England, Benjamin Rush (1745–1813), often considered the founder of American psychiatry, introduced moral therapy in his

Asylum Reform and the Decline of Moral Therapy

Unfortunately, after the mid-19th century, humane treatment declined because of a convergence of factors. First, it was widely recognized that moral therapy worked best when the number of patients in an institution was 200 or fewer, allowing for a great deal of individual attention. After the Civil War, enormous waves of immigrants arrived in the United States, yielding their own populations of mentally ill. Patient loads in existing hospitals increased to 1,000, 2,000, and more. Because immigrant groups were thought not to deserve the same privileges as "native" Americans (whose ancestors had immigrated perhaps only 50 or 100 years earlier!), they were not given moral treatments even when there were sufficient hospital personnel.

A second reason for the decline of moral therapy has an unlikely source. The great crusader Dorothea Dix (1802–1887) campaigned endlessly for reform in the treatment of the insane. A schoolteacher who had worked in various institutions, she had firsthand knowledge of the deplorable conditions imposed on the insane, and she made it her

Dorothea Dix (1802–1887) began the mental hygiene movement and spent much of her life campaigning for reform in the treatment of the mentally ill.

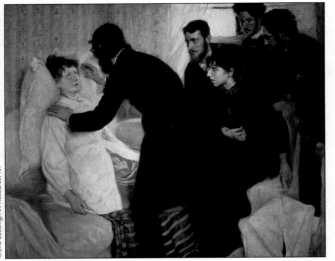

Anton Mesmer (1734–1815) and other early therapists used strong suggestions to cure their patients, who were often hypnotized.

life's work to inform the American public and their leaders of these abuses. Her work became known as the **mental hygiene movement.**

In addition to improving the standards of care, Dix worked hard to make sure that everyone who needed care received it, including the homeless. Through her efforts, humane treatment became more widely available in American institutions. As her career drew to a close, she was rightly acknowledged as a hero of the 19th century.

Unfortunately, an unforeseen consequence of Dix's heroic efforts was a substantial increase in the number of mental patients. This influx led to a rapid transition from moral therapy to custodial care because hospitals were inadequately staffed. Dix reformed our asylums and single-handedly inspired the construction of numerous new institutions here and abroad. But even her tireless efforts and advocacy could not ensure sufficient staffing to allow the individual attention necessary to moral therapy.

A final blow to the practice of moral therapy was the decision, in the middle of the 19th century, that mental illness was caused by brain pathology and, therefore, was incurable.

The psychological tradition lay dormant for a time, only to reemerge in several different schools of thought in the 20th century. The first major approach was **psychoanalysis,** based on Sigmund Freud's (1856–1939) elaborate theory of the structure of the mind and the role of unconscious processes in determining behavior. The second was **behaviorism,** associated with John B. Watson, Ivan Pavlov, and B. F. Skinner, which focuses on how learning and adaptation affect the development of psychopathology.

Psychoanalytic Theory

Have you ever felt as if someone cast a spell on you? Have you ever been mesmerized by a look across the classroom from a beautiful man or woman, or a stare from a rock musician as you sat down in front at a concert? If so, you have something in common with the patients of Anton Mesmer (1734–1815) and with millions of people since his time who have been hypnotized. Mesmer suggested to his patients that their problem was caused by an undetectable fluid found in all living organisms called "animal magnetism," which could become blocked.

Mesmer had his patients sit in a dark room around a large vat of chemicals with rods extending from it and touching them. Dressed in flowing robes, he might then identify and tap various areas of their bodies where their animal magnetism was blocked while suggesting strongly that they were being cured. Because of his rather unusual techniques, Mesmer was considered an oddity and maybe a charlatan, strongly opposed by the medical establishment (Winter, 1998). In fact, none less than Benjamin Franklin put animal magnetism to the test by conducting a brilliant experiment in which patients received either magnetized water or nonmagnetized water with strong suggestions that they would get better. Neither the patient nor the therapist knew which water was which, making it a double-blind experiment (see Chapter 4). When both groups got better, Franklin concluded that animal magnetism, or mesmerism, was nothing more than strong suggestion (Gould, 1991; McNally, 1999). Nevertheless, Mesmer is widely regarded as the father of hypnosis, a state in which extremely suggestible subjects sometimes appear to be in a trance.

Many distinguished scientists and physicians were interested in Mesmer's powerful methods of suggestion. One of the best known, Jean-Martin Charcot (1825–1893), was head of the Salpêtrière Hospital in Paris, where Philippe Pinel had introduced psychologi-

Jean Charcot (1825–1893) studied hypnosis and influenced Sigmund Freud to consider psychosocial approaches to psychological disorders.

Josef Breuer (1842–1925) worked on the celebrated case of Anna O. and, with Sigmund Freud, developed the theory of psychoanalysis.

cal treatments several generations earlier. A distinguished neurologist, Charcot demonstrated that some techniques of mesmerism were effective with a number of psychological disorders, and he did much to legitimize the fledgling practice of hypnosis. Significantly, in 1885 a young man named Sigmund Freud came from Vienna to study with Charcot.

After returning from France, Freud teamed up with Josef Breuer (1842–1925), who had experimented with a somewhat different hypnotic procedure. While his patients were in the highly suggestible state of hypnosis, Breuer asked them to describe their problems, conflicts, and fears in as much detail as they could. Breuer observed two extremely important phenomena during this process. First, patients often became extremely emotional as they talked and felt quite relieved and improved after emerging from the hypnotic state. Second, seldom would they have gained an understanding of the relationship between their emotional problems and their psychological disorder. In fact, it was difficult or impossible for them to recall some details they had described under hypnosis. In other words, the material seemed to be beyond the awareness of the patient. With this observation, Breuer and Freud had "discovered" the **unconscious** mind and its apparent influence on the production of psychological disorders. This is one of the most important developments in the history of psychopathology and, indeed, of psychology as a whole.

A close second was their discovery that it is therapeutic to recall and relive emotional trauma that has been made unconscious and to release the accompanying tension. This release of emotional material became known as **catharsis.** A fuller understanding of the relationship between current emotions and earlier events is referred to as *insight.* As you shall see throughout this book, particularly in Chapters 5 and 6 on anxiety and somatoform disorders, the existence of "unconscious" memories and feelings and the importance of processing emotion-filled information have been verified and reaffirmed.

Bertha Pappenheim (1859–1936), famous as Anna O., was described as "hysterical" by Breuer.

Sigmund Freud (1856–1939) is considered the founder of psychoanalysis.

Freud and Breuer's theories were based on case observations, some of which were made in a surprisingly systematic way for those times. An excellent example is Breuer's classic description of his treatment of "hysterical" symptoms in Anna O. in 1895 (Breuer & Freud, 1957). Anna O. was a bright, attractive young woman who was perfectly healthy until she reached 21 years of age. Shortly before her problems began, her father developed a serious chronic illness that led to his death. Throughout his illness, Anna O. had cared for him; she felt it necessary to spend endless hours at his bedside. Five months after her father became ill, Anna noticed that during the day her vision blurred and that from time to time she had difficulty moving her right arm and both legs. Soon, additional symptoms appeared. She began to experience some difficulty speaking, and her behavior became unpredictable. Shortly thereafter, she consulted Breuer.

In a series of treatment sessions, Breuer dealt with one symptom at a time through hypnosis and subsequent "talking through," tracing each symptom to its hypothetical causation in circumstances surrounding the death of Anna's father. One at a time her "hysterical" ailments disappeared, but only after treatment was administered for each respective behavior. This process of treating one behavior at a time fulfills a basic requirement for drawing scientific conclusions about the effects of treatment in an individual case study, as you will see in Chapter 4. We will return to the fascinating case of Anna O. in Chapter 6.

Freud took these basic observations and expanded them into the **psychoanalytic model,** the most comprehensive theory yet constructed on the development and structure of our personalities. He also speculated on where this development could go wrong and produce psychological disorders. Although many of Freud's views changed over time, the basic principles of mental functioning that he originally proposed remained constant through his writings and are still applied by psychoanalysts today.

Although most of it remains unproven, psychoanalytic theory has had a strong influence, and it is still important to be familiar with its basic ideas; what follows is a brief outline of the theory. We focus on its three major facets: (1) the structure of the mind and the distinct functions of personality that sometimes clash with one another; (2) the defense mechanisms with which the mind defends itself from these clashes, or conflicts; and (3) the stages of early psychosexual development that provide grist for the mill of our inner conflicts.

■ The Structure of the Mind

The mind, according to Freud, has three major parts or functions: the id, ego, and superego (see ■ Figure 1.4). These terms, like many from psychoanalysis, have found their way into our com-

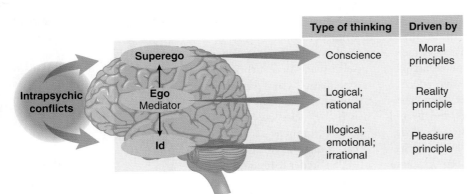

■ **FIGURE 1.4** Freud's structure of the mind.

mon vocabulary, but although you may have heard them, you may not be aware of their meaning. The **id** is the source of our strong sexual and aggressive feelings or energies. It is, basically, the animal within us; if totally unchecked, it would make us all rapists or killers. The energy or drive within the id is the *libido.* Even today, some people explain low sex drive as an absence of libido. A less important source of energy, not as well conceptualized by Freud, is the death instinct, or *thanatos.* Much like matter and antimatter, these two basic drives, toward life and fulfillment on the one hand and death and destruction on the other, are continually in opposition.

The id operates according to the *pleasure principle,* with an overriding goal of maximizing pleasure and eliminating any associated tension or conflicts. The goal of pleasure, which is particularly prominent in childhood, often conflicts with social rules and regulations, as you shall see later. The id has its own characteristic way of processing information; referred to as the *primary process,* this type of thinking is emotional, irrational, illogical, filled with fantasies, and preoccupied with sex, aggression, selfishness, and envy.

Fortunately for all of us, in Freud's view, the id's selfish and sometimes dangerous drives do not go unchecked. In fact, only a few months into life, we know we must adapt our basic demands to the real world. In other words, we must find ways to meet our basic needs without offending everyone around us. Put yet another way, we must act realistically. The part of our mind that ensures that we act realistically is called the **ego,** and it operates according to the *reality principle* instead of the pleasure principle. The cognitive operations or thinking styles of the ego are characterized by logic and reason and are referred to as the *secondary process,* as opposed to the illogical and irrational primary process of the id.

The third important structure within the mind, the **superego,** or what we might call conscience, represents the *moral principles* instilled in us by our parents and our culture. It is the voice within us that nags at us when we know we're doing something wrong. Because the purpose of the superego is to counteract the potentially dangerous aggressive and sexual drives of the id, the basis for conflict is readily apparent.

The role of the ego is to mediate conflict between the id and the superego, juggling their demands with the realities of the world. The ego is often referred to as the executive or manager of our minds. If it mediates successfully, we can go on to the higher

intellectual and creative pursuits of life. If it is unsuccessful, and the id or superego becomes too strong, conflict will overtake us and psychological disorders will develop. Because these conflicts are all within the mind, they are referred to as **intrapsychic conflicts.**

Now think back to the case of Anna O., in which Breuer observed that patients cannot always remember important but unpleasant emotional events. From these and other observations, Freud conceptualized the mental structures described in this section to explain unconscious processes. He believed that the id and the superego are almost entirely unconscious. We are fully aware only of the secondary processes of the ego, which is a relatively small part of the mind.

■ Defense Mechanisms

The ego fights a continual battle to stay on top of the warring id and superego. Occasionally, their conflicts produce anxiety that threatens to overwhelm the ego. The anxiety is a signal that alerts the ego to marshal **defense mechanisms,** unconscious protective processes that keep primitive emotions associated with conflicts in check so that the ego can continue its coordinating function.

Although Freud first conceptualized defense mechanisms, it was his daughter, Anna Freud, who developed the ideas more fully.

We all use defense mechanisms at times—they are sometimes adaptive and at other times maladaptive. For example, have you ever done poorly on a test because the professor was unfair in the grading? And then when you got home you yelled at your brother or perhaps even your dog? This is an example of the defense mechanism of *displacement.* The ego adaptively decides that expressing primitive anger at your professor might not be in your best interest. Because your brother and your dog don't have the authority to affect you in an adverse way, your anger is displaced to one of them. Some people may redirect energy from conflict or underlying anxiety into a more constructive outlet such as work, where they may be more efficient because of the redirection. This process is called *sublimation.*

More severe internal conflicts that produce a lot of anxiety or other emotions can trigger self-defeating defensive processes or symptoms. Phobic and obsessive symptoms are especially common self-defeating defensive reactions that, according to Freud, reflect an inadequate attempt to deal with an internally dangerous situation. Phobic symptoms typically incorporate elements of the danger. For example, a dog phobia may be connected to an infantile fear of castration; that is, a man's internal conflict involves a fear of being attacked and castrated, a fear that is consciously expressed as a fear of being attacked and bitten by a dog, even if he knows the dog is harmless.

Defense mechanisms have been subjected to scientific study, and there is some evidence that they may be of potential import in the study of psychopathology (Vaillant, Bond, & Vaillant, 1986). For example, different psychological disorders seem to be associated with different defense mechanisms (Pollack & Andrews, 1989), which might be important in planning treatment. Indeed, the DSM-IV-TR includes an axis of defense mechanisms in the appendix. Vaillant (1976) noted that healthy defense mechanisms, such as humor and sublimation, correlated with psychological health. Thus, the concept of defense mechanisms—*coping styles,* in contemporary terminology—continues to be important to the study of psychopathology.

Examples of defense mechanisms are listed below (based on DSM-IV-TR, APA, 2000):

Denial: Refuses to acknowledge some aspect of objective reality or subjective experience that is apparent to others

Displacement: Transfers a feeling about, or a response to, an object that causes discomfort onto another, usually less-threatening, object or person

Projection: Falsely attributes own unacceptable feelings, impulses, or thoughts to another individual or object

Rationalization: Conceals the true motivations for actions, thoughts, or feelings through elaborate reassuring or self-serving but incorrect explanations

Reaction formation: Substitutes behavior, thoughts, or feelings that are the direct opposite of unacceptable ones

Repression: Blocks disturbing wishes, thoughts, or experiences from conscious awareness

Sublimation: Directs potentially maladaptive feelings or impulses into socially acceptable behavior

■ Psychosexual Stages of Development

Freud also theorized that during infancy and early childhood we pass through a number of **psychosexual stages of development** that have a profound and lasting impact. This makes Freud one of the first to take a developmental perspective on the study of abnormal behavior, which we look at in detail throughout this book. The stages—oral, anal, phallic, latency, and genital—represent distinctive patterns of gratifying our basic needs and satisfying our drive for physical pleasure. For example, the oral stage, typically extending for approximately 2 years from birth, is characterized by a central focus on the need for food. In the act of sucking, necessary for feeding, the lips, tongue, and mouth become the focus of libidinal drives and, therefore, the principal source of pleasure. Freud hypothesized that if we did not receive appropriate gratification during a specific stage or if a specific stage left a particularly strong impression (which he termed fixation), an individual's personality would reflect the stage throughout adult life. For example, fixation at the oral stage might result in excessive thumb sucking and emphasis on oral stimulation through eating, chewing pencils, or biting fingernails. Adult personality characteristics theoretically associated with oral fixation include dependency and passivity or, in reaction to these tendencies, rebelliousness and cynicism.

One of the more controversial and frequently mentioned psychosexual conflicts occurs during the phallic stage (from age 3 to age 5 or 6), which is characterized by early genital self-stimulation.

This conflict is the subject of the Greek tragedy *Oedipus Rex,* in which Oedipus is fated to kill his father and, unknowingly, to marry his mother. Freud asserted that all young boys relive this fantasy when genital self-stimulation is accompanied by images of sexual interactions with their mothers. These fantasies, in turn, are accompanied by strong feelings of envy and perhaps anger toward their fathers, with whom they identify but whose place they wish to take. Furthermore, strong fears develop that the father may punish that lust by removing the son's penis—thus, the phenomenon of **castration anxiety.** This fear helps the boy keep his lustful impulses toward his mother in check. The battle of the lustful impulses on the one hand and castration anxiety on the other creates a conflict that is internal, or intrapsychic, called the *Oedipus complex.* The phallic stage passes uneventfully only if several things happen. First, the child must resolve his ambivalent relationship with his parents and reconcile the simultaneous anger and love he has for his father. If this happens, he may go on to channel his libidinal impulses into heterosexual relationships while retaining harmless affection for his mother.

The counterpart conflict in girls, called the *Electra complex,* is even more controversial. Freud viewed the young girl as wanting to replace her mother and possess her father. Central to this possession is the girl's desire for a penis, so as to be more like her father and brothers—hence the term *penis envy.* According to Freud, the conflict is successfully resolved when females develop healthy heterosexual relationships and look forward to having a baby, which he viewed as a healthy substitute for having a penis. Needless to say, this particular theory has provoked marked consternation over the years as being sexist and demeaning. It is important to remember that it is theory, not fact; no systematic research exists to support it.

In Freud's view, all nonpsychotic psychological disorders resulted from underlying unconscious conflicts, the anxiety that resulted from those conflicts, and the implementation of ego defense mechanisms. Freud called such disorders **neuroses,** or *neurotic disorders,* from an old term referring to disorders of the nervous system.

■ Later Developments in Psychoanalytic Thought

Freud's original psychoanalytic theories have been greatly modified and developed in a number of different directions, mostly by his students or followers. Some theorists simply took one component of psychoanalytic theory and developed it more fully. Others broke with Freud and went in entirely new directions.

Anna Freud (1895–1982), Freud's daughter, concentrated on the way in which the defensive reactions of the ego determine our behavior. In so doing, she was the first proponent of the modern field of **ego psychology** or self-psychology. Her book *Ego and the Mechanisms of Defense* (1946) is still influential. According to Anna Freud, the individual slowly accumulates adaptational capacities, skill in reality testing, and defenses. Abnormal behavior

©Hulton Archive/Getty Images

Anna Freud (1895–1982), here with her father, contributed the concept of defense mechanisms to the field of psychoanalysis.

develops when the ego is deficient in regulating such functions as delaying and controlling impulses or in marshaling appropriate normal defenses to strong internal conflicts.

A related area that is quite popular today is referred to as **object relations.** In this school of thought are theorists Melanie Klein and Otto Kernberg. Kernberg's work on *borderline personality disorder,* in which some behaviors "borderline" on being out of touch with reality and thus psychotic, has been widely applied (see Chapter 12). Object relations is the study of how children incorporate the images, the memories, and sometimes the values of a person who was important to them and to whom they were (or are) emotionally attached. *Object* in this sense refers to these important people, and the process of incorporation is called *introjection.* Introjected objects can become an integrated part of the ego or may assume conflicting roles in determining the identity, or self. For example, your parents may have conflicting views on relationships or careers, which, in turn, may be different from your own partly developed point of view. To the extent that these varying positions have been incorporated, the potential for conflict arises. One day you may feel one way about your career direction, and the next day you may feel quite differently. According to object relations theory, you tend to see the world through the eyes of the person incorporated into your self. Object relations theorists focus on how these disparate images come together to make up a person's identity and on the conflicts that may emerge.

Carl Jung (1875–1961) and Alfred Adler (1870–1937) were students of Freud who came to reject his ideas and form their own schools of thought. Jung, rejecting many of the sexual aspects of Freud's theory, introduced the concept of the collective unconscious, a wisdom accumulated by society and culture over the millennia that is stored deep in individual memories and passed down from generation to generation. Jung also suggested that spiritual and religious drives are as much a part of human nature

as are sexual drives; this emphasis and the idea of the **collective unconscious** continue to draw the attention of mystics. Jung emphasized the importance of enduring personality traits such as introversion (the tendency to be shy and withdrawn) and extroversion (the tendency to be friendly and outgoing).

Adler focused on feelings of inferiority and the striving for superiority; he created the term *inferiority complex.* Unlike Freud, both Jung and Adler also believed that the basic quality of human nature is positive and that there is a strong drive toward self-actualization. Jung and Adler believed that by removing barriers to both internal and external growth the individual would improve and flourish.

Others took psychoanalytical theorizing in different directions, emphasizing development over the life span and the influence of culture and society on personality. Karen Horney (1885–1952) and Erich Fromm (1900–1980) are associated with these ideas, but the best-known theorist is Erik Erikson (1902–1994). Erikson's greatest contribution was his theory of development across the life span, in which he described in some detail the crises and conflicts that accompany eight specific stages. For example, in the last of these stages, the *mature age,* beginning about age 65, individuals review their lives and attempt to make sense of them, experiencing both satisfaction at having completed some lifelong goals and despair at having failed at others. Scientific developments have borne out the wisdom of considering psychopathology from a developmental point of view.

■ Psychoanalytic Psychotherapy

Many techniques of psychoanalytic psychotherapy, or psychoanalysis, are designed to reveal the nature of unconscious mental processes and conflicts through catharsis and insight. Freud developed techniques of **free association,** in which patients are instructed to say whatever comes to mind without the usual socially required censoring. Free association is intended to reveal emotionally charged material that may be repressed because it is too painful or threatening to bring into consciousness. Freud's patients lay on a couch, and he sat behind them so that they would not be distracted. This is how the couch became the symbol of psychotherapy. Other techniques include **dream analysis** (still quite popular today), in which the content of dreams, supposedly reflecting the primary process thinking of the id, is systematically related to symbolic aspects of unconscious conflicts. The therapist interprets the patient's thoughts and feelings from free association and the content of dreams and relates them to various unconscious conflicts. This procedure is often difficult because the patient may resist the efforts of the therapist to uncover repressed and sensitive conflicts and may deny the interpretations. The goal of this stage of therapy is to help the patient gain insight into the nature of the conflicts.

The relationship between the therapist, called the **psychoanalyst,** and the patient is important. In the context of this relationship as it evolves, the therapist may discover the nature of the patient's intrapsychic conflict. This is because, in a phenomenon called **transference,** patients come to relate to the therapist much as they did to important figures in their childhood, particularly their parents. Patients who resent the therapist but can verbalize no good reason for it may be reenacting childhood resentment toward a parent. More often, the patient will fall deeply in love with the therapist, which reflects strong positive feelings that existed earlier for a parent. In the phenomenon of *countertransference,* therapists project some of their own personal issues and feelings, usually positive, onto the patient. Therapists are trained to deal with their own feelings as well as those of their patients, whatever the mode of therapy, and it is strictly against all ethical canons of the mental health professions to accept overtures from patients that might lead to relationships outside therapy.

Classical psychoanalysis requires therapy four to five times a week for 2 to 5 years to analyze unconscious conflicts, resolve them, and restructure the personality to put the ego back in charge. Reduction of symptoms (psychological disorders) is relatively inconsequential because they are only expressions of underlying intrapsychic conflicts that arise from psychosexual developmental stages. Thus, eliminating a phobia or depressive episode would be of little use unless the underlying conflict was dealt with adequately, because another set of symptoms would almost certainly emerge *(symptom substitution).* Because of the extraordinary expense of psychoanalysis, and the lack of evidence that it is effective in alleviating psychological disorders, this approach is seldom used today.

Classical psychoanalysis is still practiced, particularly in some large cities, but many psychotherapists employ a loosely related set of approaches referred to as **psychodynamic psychotherapy.** Although conflicts and unconscious processes are still emphasized, and efforts are made to identify trauma and active defense mechanisms, therapists use an eclectic mixture of tactics, with a social and interpersonal focus. Seven tactics that characterize psychodynamic psychotherapy include (1) a focus on affect and the expression of patients' emotions; (2) an exploration of patients' attempts to avoid topics or engage in activities that hinder the progress of therapy; (3) the identification of patterns in patients' actions, thoughts, feelings, experiences, and relationships; (4) an emphasis on past experiences; (5) a focus on patients' interpersonal experiences; (6) an emphasis on the therapeutic relationship; and (7) an exploration of patients' wishes, dreams, or fantasies (Blagys & Hilsenroth, 2000). Two additional features characterize psychodynamic psychotherapy. First, it is significantly briefer than classical psychoanalysis. Second, psychodynamic therapists deemphasize the goal of personality reconstruction, focusing instead on relieving the suffering associated with psychological disorders.

■ Comments

Pure psychoanalysis is of historical more than current interest, and classical psychoanalysis as a treatment has been diminishing in popularity for years. In 1980, the term *neurosis,* which specifically implied a psychoanalytic view of the causes of psychological disorders, was dropped from the DSM, the official diagnostic system of the APA.

A major criticism of psychoanalysis is that it is basically unscientific, relying on reports by the patient of events that happened years ago. These events have been filtered through the experience of the observer and then interpreted by the psychoanalyst in ways that certainly could be questioned and might differ from one analyst to the next. Finally, there has been no careful measurement of any of these psychological phenomena and no obvious way to prove or disprove the basic hypotheses of psychoanalysis. This is important because measurement and the ability to prove or disprove a theory are the foundations of the scientific approach.

Nevertheless, psychoanalytic concepts and observations have been valuable, not only to the study of psychopathology and psychodynamic psychotherapy but also to the history of ideas in Western civilization. Careful scientific studies of psychopathology have supported the observation of unconscious mental processes, the notion that basic emotional responses are often triggered by hidden or symbolic cues, and the understanding that memories of events in our lives can be repressed and otherwise avoided in a variety of ingenious ways. The relationship of the therapist and the patient, called the *therapeutic alliance,* is an important area of study across most therapeutic strategies. These concepts, along with the importance of various coping styles or defense mechanisms, will appear repeatedly throughout this book.

Freud's revolutionary ideas that pathological anxiety emerges in connection with some of our deepest and darkest instincts brought us a long way from witch trials and incurable brain pathology. Before Freud, the source of good and evil and of urges and prohibitions was conceived as external and spiritual, usually in the guise of demons confronting the forces of good. Since Freud, we ourselves have become the battleground for these forces, and we are inexorably caught up in the battle, sometimes for better and sometimes for worse.

Humanistic Theory

We have already seen that Jung and Adler broke sharply with Freud. Their fundamental disagreement concerned the very nature of humanity. Freud portrayed life as a battleground where we are continually in danger of being overwhelmed by our darkest forces. Jung and Adler, by contrast, emphasized the positive, optimistic side of human nature. Jung talked about setting goals, looking toward the future, and realizing one's fullest potential. Adler believed that human nature reaches its fullest potential when we contribute to other individuals and to society as a whole. He believed that we all strive to reach superior levels of intellectual and moral development. Nevertheless, both Jung and Adler retained many of the principles of psychodynamic thought. Their general philosophies were adopted in the middle of the century by personality theorists and became known as *humanistic psychology.*

Self-actualizing was the watchword for this movement. The underlying assumption is that all of us could reach our highest potential, in all areas of functioning, if only we had the freedom to grow. Inevitably, a variety of conditions may block our actualization. Because every person is basically good and whole, most blocks originate outside the individual. Difficult living conditions or stressful life or interpersonal experiences may move you away from your true self.

Abraham Maslow (1908–1970) was most systematic in describing the structure of personality. He postulated a *hierarchy of needs,* beginning with our most basic physical needs for food and sex and ranging upward to our needs for self-actualization, love, and self-esteem. Social needs such as friendship fall somewhere between. Maslow hypothesized that we cannot progress up the hierarchy until we have satisfied the needs at lower levels.

Carl Rogers (1902–1987) is, from the point of view of therapy, the most influential humanist. Rogers (1961) originated client-centered therapy, later known as **person-centered therapy.** In this approach, the therapist takes a passive role, making as few interpretations as possible. The point is to give the individual a chance to develop during the course of therapy, unfettered by threats to the self. Humanist theorists have great faith in the ability of human relations to foster this growth. **Unconditional positive regard,** the complete and almost unqualified acceptance of most of the client's feelings and actions, is critical to the humanistic approach. *Empathy* is the sympathetic understanding of the individual's particular view of the world. The hoped-for result of person-centered therapy is that clients will be more straightforward and honest with themselves and will access their innate tendencies toward growth.

Like psychoanalysis, the humanistic approach has had a substantial effect on theories of interpersonal relationships. For example, the human potential movements so popular in the 1960s and 1970s were a direct result of humanistic theorizing. This approach also emphasized the importance of the therapeutic relationship in a way quite different from Freud's approach. Rather than seeing the relationship as a means to an end (transference), humanistic therapists believed that relationships, including the therapeutic relationship, were the single most positive influence in facilitating human growth. In fact, Rogers made substantial contributions to the scientific study of therapist–client relationships.

Nevertheless, the humanistic model contributed relatively little new information to the field of psychopathology. One reason for this is that its proponents, with some exceptions, had little interest in doing research that would discover or create new knowledge. Rather, they stressed the unique, nonquantifiable experiences of the individual, emphasizing that people are more different than alike. As Maslow noted, the humanistic model found its greatest application among individuals without psychological disorders. The application of person-centered therapy to more severe psychological disorders has decreased substantially over the decades, although certain variations have periodically arisen in some areas of psychopathology.

The Behavioral Model

As psychoanalysis swept the world at the beginning of the 20th century, events in Russia and the United States would eventually provide an alternative psychological model that was every bit as powerful. The **behavioral model,** which is also known as the *cognitive-behavioral* or *social learning model,* brought the systematic development of a more scientific approach to psychological aspects of psychopathology.

■ Pavlov and Classical Conditioning

In his classic study examining why dogs salivate before the presentation of food, physiologist Ivan Petrovich Pavlov (1849–1936) of St. Petersburg, Russia, initiated the study of **classical conditioning,** a type of learning in which a neutral stimulus is paired with a response until it elicits that response. The word *conditioning* (or *conditioned response*) resulted from an accident in translation from the original Russian. Pavlov was really talking about a re-

sponse that occurred only on the condition of the presence of a particular event or situation (stimulus)—in this case, the footsteps of the laboratory assistant at feeding time. Thus, "conditional response" would have been more accurate. Conditioning is one way in which we acquire new information, particularly information that is somewhat emotional in nature. This process is not as simple as it first seems, and we continue to uncover many more facts about its complexity (Bouton, 2005; Craske, Hermans, & Vansteenwegen, 2006; Rescorla, 1988). But it can be quite automatic. Let's look at a powerful contemporary example.

Ivan Pavlov (1849–1936) identified the process of classical conditioning, which is important to many emotional disorders.

Psychologists working in oncology units have studied a phenomenon well known to many cancer patients, their nurses and physicians, and their families. Chemotherapy, a common treatment for some forms of cancer, has side effects including severe nausea and vomiting. But these patients often experience severe nausea and, occasionally, vomiting when they merely see the medical personnel who administered the chemotherapy or any equipment associated with the treatment, even on days when their treatment is not delivered (Morrow & Dobkin, 1988). For some patients, this reaction becomes associated with a variety of stimuli that evoke people or things present during chemotherapy—anybody in a nurse's uniform or even the sight of the hospital. The strength of the response to similar objects or people is usually a function of how similar these objects or people are. This phenomenon is called *stimulus generalization* because the response generalizes to similar stimuli. In any case, this particular reaction is distressing and uncomfortable, particularly if it is associated with a variety of objects or situations. Psychologists have had to develop specific treatments to overcome this response (Redd & Andrykowski, 1982); they are described more fully in Chapter 9.

Whether the stimulus is food, as in Pavlov's laboratory, or chemotherapy, the classical conditioning process begins with a stimulus that would elicit a response in almost anyone and requires no learning; no conditions must be present for the response to occur. For these reasons, the food or chemotherapy is called the *unconditioned stimulus (UCS).* The natural or unlearned response to this stimulus—in these cases, salivation or nausea—is called the *unconditioned response (UCR).* Now the learning comes in. As we have already seen, any person or object associated with the unconditioned stimulus (food or chemotherapy) acquires the power to elicit the same response, but now the response, because it was elicited by the conditional or *conditioned stimulus (CS),* is termed a *conditioned response (CR).* Thus, the nurse associated with the chemotherapy becomes a conditioned stimulus. The nauseous sensation, which is almost the same as that experienced during chemotherapy, becomes the conditioned response.

With unconditioned stimuli as powerful as chemotherapy, a conditioned response can be learned in one trial. However, most learning of this type requires repeated pairing of the unconditioned stimulus (for example, chemotherapy) and the conditioned stimulus (for instance, nurses' uniforms or hospital equipment). When Pavlov began to investigate this phenomenon, he substituted a metronome for the footsteps of his laboratory assistants so that he could quantify the stimulus more accurately and, therefore, study the approach more precisely. What he also learned is that presentation of the conditioned stimulus (for example, the metronome) *without* the food for a long enough period would eventually eliminate the conditioned response to the food. In other words, the dog learned that the metronome no longer meant that a meal might be on the way. This process was called **extinction.**

Because Pavlov was a physiologist, it was natural for him to study these processes in a laboratory and to be quite scientific about it. This required precision in measuring and observing relationships and in ruling out alternative explanations. Although this approach is common in biology, it was uncommon in psychology at that time. For example, it was impossible for psychoanalysts to measure unconscious conflicts precisely, or even observe them. Even early experimental psychologists such as Edward Titchener (1867–1927) emphasized the study of **introspection.** Subjects simply reported on their inner thoughts and feelings after experiencing certain stimuli, but the results of this "armchair" psychology were inconsistent and discouraging to many experimental psychologists.

■ Watson and the Rise of Behaviorism

An early American psychologist, John B. Watson (1878–1958), is considered the founder of behaviorism. Strongly influenced by the work of Pavlov, Watson decided that to base psychology on introspection was to head in the wrong direction; that psychology could be made as scientific as physiology; and that psychology no more needs introspection or other nonquantifiable methods than do chemistry and physics (Watson, 1913). This point of view is reflected in a famous quote from a seminal article published by Watson in 1913: "Psychology, as the behaviorist views it, is a purely objective experimental branch of natural science. Its theoretical goal is the prediction and control of behavior. Introspection forms no essential part of its methods" (p. 158). This, then, was the beginning of behaviorism and, like most revolutionaries, Watson took his cause to extremes. For example, he wrote that thinking, for purposes of science, could be equated with subvocal talking and that one need only measure movements around the larynx to study this process objectively.

Most of Watson's time was spent developing behavioral psychology as a radical empirical science, but he did dabble briefly in the study of psychopathology. In 1920, he and a student, Rosalie Rayner, presented an 11-month-old boy named Albert with a harmless fluffy white rat to play with. Albert was not afraid of the small animal and enjoyed playing with it. However, every time Albert reached for the rat, the experimenters made a loud noise behind him. After only five trials, Albert showed the first signs of fear if the white rat came near. The experimenters then determined that Albert displayed mild fear of any white furry object, even a Santa Claus mask with a white fuzzy beard. You may not think that this is surprising, but keep in mind that this was one of the first examples ever recorded in a laboratory of producing fear of an object not previously feared. Of course, this experiment would be considered unethical by today's standards.

Another student of Watson's, Mary Cover Jones (1896–1987), thought that if fear could be learned or classically conditioned in this way, perhaps it could also be unlearned or extinguished. She worked with a boy named Peter, who at 2 years, 10 months old was already quite afraid of furry objects. Jones decided to bring a white rabbit into the room where Peter was playing for a short time each day. She also arranged for other children, whom she knew did not fear rabbits, to be in the same room. She noted that Peter's fear gradually diminished. Each time it diminished, she brought the rabbit closer. Eventually Peter was touching and even playing with the rabbit (Jones, 1924a, 1924b), and years later the fear had not returned.

■ The Beginnings of Behavior Therapy

The implications of Jones's research were largely ignored for two decades, given the fervor associated with more psychoanalytic conceptions of the development of fear. But in the late 1940s and early 1950s, Joseph Wolpe (1915–1997), a pioneering psychiatrist from South Africa, became dissatisfied with prevailing psychoanalytic interpretations of psychopathology and began looking for something else. He turned to the work of Pavlov and became familiar with the wider field of behavioral psychology. He developed a variety of behavioral procedures for treating his patients, many of whom suffered from phobias. His best-known technique was termed **systematic desensitization.** In principle, it was similar to the treatment of little Peter: Individuals were gradually introduced to the objects or situations they feared so that their fear could extinguish; that is, they could test reality and see that nothing bad happened in the presence of the phobic object or scene. Wolpe added another element by having his patients do something that was incompatible with fear while they were in the presence of the dreaded object or situation. Because he could not always reproduce the phobic object in his office, Wolpe had his patients carefully and systematically *imagine* the phobic scene, and the response he chose was relaxation because it was convenient.

Mary Cover Jones (1896–1987) was one of the first psychologists to use behavioral techniques to free a patient from phobia.

©Bettmann/Corbis

B. F. Skinner (1904–1990) studied operant conditioning, a form of learning that is central to psychopathology.

For example, Wolpe treated a young man with a phobia of dogs by training him first to relax deeply and then imagine he was looking at a dog across the park. Gradually, he could imagine the dog across the park and remain relaxed, experiencing little or no fear. Wolpe then had him imagine that he was closer to the dog. Eventually, the young man imagined that he was touching the dog while maintaining a relaxed, almost trancelike state.

Wolpe reported great success with systematic desensitization, one of the first wide-scale applications of the new science of behaviorism to psychopathology. Wolpe, working with fellow pioneers Hans Eysenck and Stanley Rachman in London, called this approach **behavior therapy.** Although Wolpe's procedures are seldom used today, they paved the way for modern-day fear and anxiety reduction procedures in which severe phobias can be eliminated in as little as 1 day (see Chapter 5).

■ B. F. Skinner and Operant Conditioning

Sigmund Freud's influence extended far beyond psychopathology into many aspects of our cultural and intellectual history. Only one other behavioral scientist has made a similar impact: Burrhus Frederic (B. F.) Skinner (1904–1990). In 1938 he published *The Behavior of Organisms,* in which he laid out, in a comprehensive manner, the principles of *operant conditioning,* a type of learning in which behavior changes as a function of what follows the behavior. Skinner observed early on that a large part of our behavior is not automatically elicited by an unconditioned stimulus and that we must account for this. In the ensuing years, Skinner did not confine his ideas to the laboratories of experimental psychology. He ranged far and wide in his writings, describing, for example, the potential applications of a science of behavior to our culture. Some best-known examples of his ideas are in the novel *Walden Two* (Skinner, 1948), in which he depicts a fictional society run on the principles of operant conditioning. In another well-known work, *Beyond Freedom and Dignity* (1971), Skinner lays out a broader statement of problems facing our culture and suggests solutions based on his own view of a science of behavior.

Skinner was strongly influenced by Watson's conviction that a science of human behavior must be based on observable events and relationships among those events. The work of psychologist Edward L. Thorndike (1874–1949) also influenced Skinner. Thorndike is best known for the *law of effect,* which states that behavior is either strengthened (likely to be repeated more frequently) or weakened (likely to occur less frequently) depending on the consequences of that behavior. Skinner took the simple notions that Thorndike had tested in the animal laboratories, using food as a reinforcer, and developed them in a variety of complex ways to apply to much of our behavior. For example, if a 5-year-old boy starts shouting at the top of his lungs in McDonald's, much to the annoyance of the people around him, it is unlikely that his behavior was automatically elicited by an unconditioned stimulus. Also, he will be less likely to do it in the future if his parents scold him, take him out to the car to sit for a bit, or consistently reinforce more appropriate behavior. Then again, if the parents think his behavior is cute and laugh, chances are he will do it again.

Skinner coined the term *operant conditioning* because behavior operates on the environment and changes it in some way. For example, the boy's behavior affects his parents' behavior and probably the behavior of other customers. Therefore, he changes his environment. Most things that we do socially provide the context for other people to respond to us in one way or another, thereby providing consequences for our behavior. The same is true of our physical environment, although the consequences may be long term (polluting the air eventually will poison us). Skinner preferred the term **reinforcement** to "reward" because it connotes the effect on the behavior. Skinner once said that he found himself a bit embarrassed to be talking continually about reinforcement, much as Marxists used to see class struggle everywhere. But he pointed out that all of our behavior is governed to some degree by reinforcement, which can be arranged in an endless variety of ways, in *schedules of reinforcement.* Skinner wrote a whole book on different schedules of reinforcement (Ferster & Skinner, 1957). He also believed that using punishment as a consequence is relatively ineffective in the long run and that the primary way to develop new behavior is to positively reinforce desired behavior. Much like Watson, Skinner did not see the need to go beyond the observable and quantifiable to establish a satisfactory science of behavior. He did not deny the influence of biology or the existence of subjective states of emotion or cognition; he simply explained these phenomena as relatively inconsequential side effects of a particular history of reinforcement.

The subjects of Skinner's research were usually animals, mostly pigeons and rats. Using his new principles, Skinner and his disciples taught the animals a variety of tricks, including dancing, playing Ping-Pong, and playing a toy piano. To do this he used a procedure called **shaping,** a process of reinforcing successive approximations to a final behavior or set of behaviors. If you want a pigeon to play Ping-Pong, first you provide it with a pellet of food every time it moves its head slightly toward a Ping-Pong ball tossed in its direction. Gradually you require the pigeon to move its head ever closer to the Ping-Pong ball until it touches it. Finally, receiving the food pellet is contingent on the pigeon hitting the ball back with its head.

Pavlov, Watson, and Skinner contributed significantly to behavior therapy (see, for example, Wolpe, 1958), in which scientific principles of psychology are applied to clinical problems. Their ideas have substantially contributed to current psychosocial treatments and so are referred to repeatedly in this book.

■ Comments

The behavioral model has contributed greatly to the understanding and treatment of psychopathology, as is apparent in the chapters that follow. Nevertheless, this model is incomplete and inadequate to account for what we now know about psychopathology. In the past, there was little or no room for biology in behaviorism because disorders were considered, for the most part, environmentally determined reactions. The model also fails to account for development of psychopathology across the life span. Recent advances in our knowledge of how information is processed, both consciously and subconsciously, have added a layer of complexity. Integrating all these dimensions requires a new model of psychopathology.

THE PRESENT: THE SCIENTIFIC METHOD AND AN INTEGRATIVE APPROACH

As William Shakespeare wrote, "What's past is prologue." We have just reviewed three traditions or ways of thinking about causes of psychopathology: the supernatural, the biological, and the psychological (further subdivided into two major historical components: psychoanalytic and behavioral).

Supernatural explanations of psychopathology are still with us. Superstitions prevail, including beliefs in the effects of the moon and the stars on our behavior. However, this tradition has little influence on scientists and other professionals. Biological, psychoanalytic, and behavioral models, by contrast, continue to further our knowledge of psychopathology, as you will see in the next chapter.

Each tradition has failed in important ways. First, scientific methods were not often applied to the theories and treatments within a tradition, mostly because methods that would have produced the evidence necessary to confirm or disprove the theories and treatments had not been developed. Lacking such evidence, various fads and superstitions were widely accepted that ultimately proved to be untrue or useless. New fads often superseded truly useful theories and treatment procedures. This trend was at work in the "discovery" of the drug reserpine, which, in fact, had been around for thousands of years. King Charles VI was subjected to a variety of procedures, some of which have since been proved useful and others that were mere fads or even harmful. How we use scientific methods to confirm or disconfirm findings in psychopathology is described in Chapter 4. Second, health professionals tend to look at psychological disorders narrowly, from their own point of view alone. Grey assumed that psychological disorders were the result of brain disease and that other factors had no influence. Watson assumed that all behaviors, including disordered behavior, were the result of psychological and social influences and that the contribution of biological factors was inconsequential.

In the 1990s, two developments came together as never before to shed light on the nature of psychopathology: (1) the increasing sophistication of scientific tools and methodology and (2) the realization that no one influence—biological, behavioral, cognitive, emotional, or social—ever occurs in isolation. Literally, every time we think, feel, or do something, the brain and the rest of the body are hard at work. Perhaps not as obvious, however, is that our thoughts, feelings, and actions inevitably influence the function and even the structure of the brain, sometimes permanently. In other words, our behavior, both normal and abnormal, is the product of a continual interaction of psychological, biological, and social influences.

The view that psychopathology is multiply determined had its early adherents. Perhaps the most notable was Adolf Meyer (1866–1950), often considered the dean of American psychiatry. Whereas most professionals during the first half of the century held narrow views of the cause of psychopathology, Meyer steadfastly emphasized the equal contributions of biological, psychological, and sociocultural determinism. Although Meyer had some proponents, it was 100 years before the wisdom of his advice was fully recognized in the field.

By 2000, a veritable explosion of knowledge about psychopathology had occurred. The young fields of cognitive science and neuroscience began to grow exponentially as we learned more about the brain and about how we process, remember, and use information. At the same time, startling new findings from behavioral science revealed the importance of early experience in determining later development. It was clear that a new model was needed that would consider biological, psychological, and social influences on behavior. This approach to psychopathology would combine findings from all areas with our rapidly growing understanding of how we experience life during different developmental periods, from infancy to old age. In the remainder of this book, we explore some of these reciprocal influences and demonstrate that the only currently valid model of psychopathology is multidimensional and integrative.

CONCEPT CHECK 1.3

Match the treatment with the corresponding psychological theory of behavior: (a) behavioral model, (b) moral therapy, (c) psychoanalytic theory, and (d) humanistic theory.

1. Treating institutionalized patients as normally as possible and encouraging social interaction and relationship development. _____
2. Hypnosis, psychoanalysis like free association and dream analysis, and balance of the id, ego, and superego. _____
3. Person-centered therapy with unconditional positive regard. _____
4. Classical conditioning, systematic desensitization, and operant conditioning. _____

SUMMARY

Understanding Psychopathology

■ A psychological disorder is (1) a psychological dysfunction within an individual that is (2) associated with distress or impairment in functioning and (3) a response that is not typical or culturally expected. All three basic criteria must be met; no one criterion alone has yet been identified that defines the essence of abnormality.

■ The field of psychopathology is concerned with the scientific study of psychological disorders. Trained mental health professionals range from clinical and counseling psychologists to psychiatrists and psychiatric social workers and nurses. Each profession requires a specific type of training.

■ Using scientific methods, mental health professionals can function as scientist-practitioners. They not only keep up with the latest findings but also use scientific data to evaluate their own work, and they often conduct research within their clinics or hospitals.

■ Research about psychological disorders falls into three basic categories: description, causation, and treatment and outcomes.

The Supernatural, Biological, and Psychological Traditions

■ Historically, there have been three prominent approaches to abnormal behavior. In the supernatural tradition, abnormal behavior is attributed to agents outside our bodies or social environment, such as demons, spirits, or the influence of the moon and stars; although still alive, this tradition has been largely replaced by biological and psychological perspectives. In the biological tradition, disorders are attributed to disease or biochemical imbalances; in the psychological tradition, abnormal behavior is attributed to faulty psychological development and to social context.

■ Each tradition has its own way of treating individuals who suffer from psychological disorders. Supernatural treatments include exorcism to rid the body of the supernatural spirits. Biological treatments typically emphasize physical care and the search for medical cures, especially drugs. Psychological approaches use psychosocial treatments, beginning with moral therapy and including modern psychotherapy.

■ Sigmund Freud, the founder of psychoanalytic therapy, offered an elaborate conception of the unconscious mind, much of which is still conjecture. In therapy, Freud focused on tapping into the mysteries of the unconscious through such techniques as catharsis, free association, and dream analysis. Although Freud's followers steered from his path in many ways, Freud's influence can still be felt today.

■ One outgrowth of Freudian therapy is humanistic psychology, which focuses more on human potential and self-actualizing than on psychological disorders. Therapy that has evolved from this approach is known as person-centered therapy; the therapist shows almost unconditional positive regard for the client's feelings and thoughts.

■ The behavioral model moved psychology into the realm of science. Both research and therapy focus on things that are measurable, including such techniques as systematic desensitization, reinforcement, and shaping.

The Present: The Scientific Method and an Integrative Approach

■ With the increasing sophistication of our scientific tools, and new knowledge from cognitive science, behavioral science, and neuroscience, we now realize that no contribution to psychological disorders ever occurs in isolation. Our behavior, both normal and abnormal, is a product of a continual interaction of psychological, biological, and social influences.

Key Terms

psychological disorder, 2
abnormal behavior, 2
phobia, 2
psychopathology, 5
scientist-practitioner, 5
presenting problem, 6
clinical description, 6
prevalence, 6
incidence, 6
course, 6
prognosis, 6
etiology, 7
exorcism, 8

psychosocial, 14
moral therapy, 14
mental hygiene movement, 16
psychoanalysis, 16
behaviorism, 16
unconscious, 17
catharsis, 17
psychoanalytic model, 17
id, 18
ego, 18
superego, 18
intrapsychic conflicts, 18
defense mechanisms, 18

psychosexual stages of
    development, 19
castration anxiety, 19
neurosis, 19
ego psychology, 19
object relations, 20
collective unconscious, 20
free association, 20
dream analysis, 20
psychoanalyst, 20
transference, 20
psychodynamic
    psychotherapy, 21

self-actualizing, 21
person-centered therapy, 22
unconditional positive regard,
    22
behavioral model, 22
classical conditioning, 22
extinction, 23
introspection, 23
systematic desensitization, 23
behavior therapy, 24
reinforcement, 24
shaping, 24

Answers to Concept Checks

1.1

Part A

1. d; 2. b, c

Part B

3. d; 4. c; 5. a; 6. f; 7. e; 8. b

1.2

1. c; 2. a; 3. b

1.3

1. b; 2. c; 3. d; 4. a

The Abnormal Psychology Book Companion Website

See **academic.cengage.com/psychology/barlow** for practice quiz questions, interactive activities, Internet links, critical thinking exercises, discussion forums, and more. Also accessible from the Wadsworth Psychology Resource Center (**academic.cengage.com/login**).

 **CengageNOW**

Go to **academic.cengage.com/now** to link to CengageNOW, your online study tool. First take the Pre-Test for this chapter to get your personalized study plan, which will identify topics you need to review and direct you to online resources. Then take the Post-Test to determine what concepts you have mastered and what you still need work on.

Video Concept Reviews

CengageNOW also contains Mark Durand's *Video Concept Reviews* on these challenging topics.

- Concept Check—Abnormality
- Psychopathology
- Mental Health Professions
- The Scientist–Practitioner
- Presenting Problem
- Prevalence
- Incidence
- Course
- Prognosis
- Supernatural Views—Historical
- Supernatural Views—Current
- Emotion Contagion
- Hippocrates
- Bodily Humors
- Moral Therapy
- Concept Check—Integrative Approach

Timeline of Significant Events

400 B.C.–1825

400 B.C.: Hippocrates suggests that psychological disorders have both biological and psychological causes.

1300s: Superstition runs rampant and mental disorders are blamed on demons and witches; exorcisms are performed to rid victims of evil spirits.

1400–1800: Bloodletting and leeches are used to rid the body of unhealthy fluids and restore chemical balance.

1793: Philippe Pinel introduces moral therapy and makes French mental institutions more humane.

400 B.C.	1300s	1500s	1825–1875

200 B.C.: Galen suggests that normal and abnormal behavior are related to four bodily fluids, or humors.

1400s: Enlightened view that insanity is caused by mental or emotional stress gains momentum, and depression and anxiety are again regarded by some as disorders.

1500s: Paracelsus suggests that the moon and the stars affect people's psychological functioning, rather than possession by the devil.

1825–1875: Syphilis is differentiated from other types of psychosis in that it is caused by a specific bacterium; ultimately, penicillin is found to cure syphilis.

1930–1968

1930: Insulin shock therapy, electric shock treatments, and brain surgery begin to be used to treat psychopathology.

1943: The *Minnesota Multiphasic Personality Inventory* is published.

1950: The first effective drugs for severe psychotic disorders are developed. Humanistic psychology (based on ideas of Carl Jung, Alfred Adler, and Carl Rogers) gains some acceptance.

1958: Joseph Wolpe effectively treats patients with phobias using systematic desensitization based on principles of behavioral science.

1930	1943	1950	1968

1938: B. F. Skinner publishes *The Behavior of Organisms,* which describes the principles of operant conditioning.

1946: Anna Freud publishes *Ego and the Mechanisms of Defense.*

1952: The first edition of the *Diagnostic and Statistical Manual* (DSM-I) is published.

1968: DSM-II is published.

1848: Dorothea Dix successfully campaigns for more humane treatment in American mental institutions.

1870: Louis Pasteur develops his germ theory of disease, which helps identify the bacterium that causes syphilis.

1900: Sigmund Freud publishes *The Interpretation of Dreams.*

1913: Emil Kraepelin classifies various psychological disorders from a biological point of view and publishes work on diagnosis.

1848	**1870**	**1900**	**1920**

1854: John P. Grey, head of New York's Utica Hospital, believes that insanity is the result of physical causes, thus deemphasizing psychological treatments.

1895: Josef Breuer treats the "hysterical" Anna O., leading to Freud's development of psychoanalytic theory.

1904: Ivan Pavlov receives the Nobel Prize for his work on the physiology of digestion, which leads him to identify conditioned reflexes in dogs.

1920: John B. Watson experiments with conditioned fear in Little Albert using a white rat.

1990s: Increasingly sophisticated research methods are developed; no one influence—biological or environmental—is found to cause psychological disorders in isolation from the other.

1980: DSM-III is published.

2000: DSM-IV-TR is published.

1980	**1990s**	**2000**

1987: DSM-III-R is published.

1994: DSM-IV is published.

CHAPTER 2

An Integrative Approach to Psychopathology

©Royalty-Free/Getty Images

ONE-DIMENSIONAL OR MULTIDIMENSIONAL MODELS
What Caused Judy's Phobia?
Outcome and Comments

GENETIC CONTRIBUTIONS TO PSYCHOPATHOLOGY
The Nature of Genes
New Developments in the Study of Genes and Behavior
The Interaction of Genetic and Environmental Effects
Nongenomic "Inheritance" of Behavior

NEUROSCIENCE AND ITS CONTRIBUTIONS TO PSYCHOPATHOLOGY
The Central Nervous System
The Structure of the Brain
The Peripheral Nervous System
Neurotransmitters
Implications for Psychopathology
Psychosocial Influences on Brain Structure and Function
Interactions of Psychosocial Factors with Brain Structure and Function
Comments

BEHAVIORAL AND COGNITIVE SCIENCE
Conditioning and Cognitive Processes
Learned Helplessness
Social Learning
Prepared Learning
Cognitive Science and the Unconscious

EMOTIONS
The Physiology and Purpose of Fear
Emotional Phenomena
The Components of Emotion
Anger and Your Heart
Emotions and Psychopathology

CULTURAL, SOCIAL, AND INTERPERSONAL FACTORS
Voodoo, the Evil Eye, and Other Fears
Gender
Social Effects on Health and Behavior
Global Incidence of Psychological Disorders

LIFE-SPAN DEVELOPMENT

CONCLUSIONS

ABNORMAL PSYCHOLOGY LIVE CD-ROM
Integrative Approach
Web Link

The spirit within nourishes, and the mind, diffused through all the members, sways the mass and mingles with the whole frame.

Virgil
The Aeneid

Remember Judy from Chapter 1? We knew she suffered from blood–injury–injection phobia, but we did not know why. Here, we address the issue of causation. In this chapter, we examine the specific components of a **multidimensional integrative approach** to psychopathology (see Figure 2.1). Biological dimensions include causal factors from the fields of genetics and neuroscience. Psychological dimensions include causal factors from behavioral and cognitive processes, including learned helplessness, social learning, prepared learning, and even unconscious processes (in a different guise than in the days of Sigmund Freud). Emotional influences contribute in a variety of ways to psychopathology, as do social and interpersonal influences. Finally, developmental influences figure in any discussion of causes of psychological disorders. You will become familiar with these areas as they relate to psychopathology and learn about some of the latest developments relevant to psychological disorders. But keep in mind what we confirmed in the last chapter: No influence operates in isolation. Each dimension, biological or psychological, is strongly influenced by the others and by development, and they weave together in various complex and intricate ways to create a psychological disorder.

Here, we explain briefly why we have adopted a multidimensional integrative model of psychopathology. Then we preview various causal influences and interactions, using Judy's case as background. After that, we look more deeply at specific causal influences in psychopathology, examining both the latest research and integrative ways of viewing what we know.

ONE-DIMENSIONAL OR MULTIDIMENSIONAL MODELS

To say that psychopathology is caused by a physical abnormality or by conditioning is to accept a linear or one-dimensional model, which attempts to trace the origins of behavior to a single cause. A linear causal model might hold that schizophrenia or a phobia is caused by a chemical imbalance or by growing up surrounded by overwhelming conflicts among family members. In psychology and psychopathology, we still encounter this type of thinking occasionally, but most scientists and clinicians believe abnormal behavior results from multiple influences. A system, or feedback loop, may have independent inputs at many different points, but as each input becomes part of the whole it can no longer be considered independent. This perspective on causality is *systemic,* which derives from the word *system;* it implies that any particular influence contributing to psychopathology cannot be considered out of context. Context, in this case, is the biology and behavior of the individual, as well as the cognitive, emotional, social, and cultural environment, because any one component of the system inevitably affects the other components. This is a multidimensional model.

What Caused Judy's Phobia?

From a multidimensional perspective, let's look at what might have caused Judy's phobia (see ■ Figure 2.1).

■ Behavioral Influences
The cause of Judy's phobia might at first seem obvious. She saw a movie with graphic scenes of blood and injury and had a bad reaction to it. Her reaction, an unconditioned response, became associated with situations similar to the scenes in the movie, depending on how similar they were. But Judy's reaction reached such an extreme that even hearing someone say, "Cut it out!" evoked queasiness. Is Judy's phobia a straightforward case of classical conditioning? It might seem so, but one puzzling question arises: Why didn't the other kids in Judy's class develop the same phobia? As far as Judy knew, nobody else even felt queasy.

■ Biological Influences
We now know that more is involved in blood–injury–injection phobia than a simple conditioning experience, although, clearly, conditioning and stimulus generalization contribute. We have learned a lot about this phobia (Antony & Barlow, 2002a; Exeter-Kent & Page, 2006; Marks, 1988; Page, 1994, 1996). Physiologically, Judy experienced a *vasovagal syncope,* which is a common cause of fainting. When she saw the film, she became mildly distressed, as many people would, and her heart rate and blood pressure increased accordingly, which she probably did not notice. Then her body took over, immediately compensating by decreasing her vascular resistance, lowering her heart rate and, eventually, lowering her blood pressure. The amount of blood reaching her brain diminished until she lost consciousness. *Syncope* means "sinking feeling" or "swoon" caused by low blood pressure in the head. If Judy had quickly bent down and put her head between her knees, she might have avoided fainting, but it happened so quickly she had no time to use this strategy.

A possible cause of the vasovagal syncope is an overreaction of a mechanism called the *sinoaortic baroreflex arc,* which compensates for sudden increases in blood pressure by lowering it. Interestingly, the tendency to overcompensate seems to be inherited, a trait that may account for the high rate of blood–injury–injection phobia in families. Do you ever feel queasy at the sight of blood? If so, chances are your mother, your father, or someone else in your immediate family has the same reaction. In one study, 61% of the family members of individuals with this phobia had a similar condition, although somewhat milder in most cases (Öst, 1992). You might think, then, that we have discovered the cause of blood–injury–injection phobia and that all we need to do is develop a pill to regulate the baroreflex. But many people with rather severe syncope reaction tendencies do *not* develop phobias. They cope with their reaction in various ways, including tensing their muscles whenever they are confronted with blood. Tensing the muscles quickly raises blood pressure and prevents the fainting

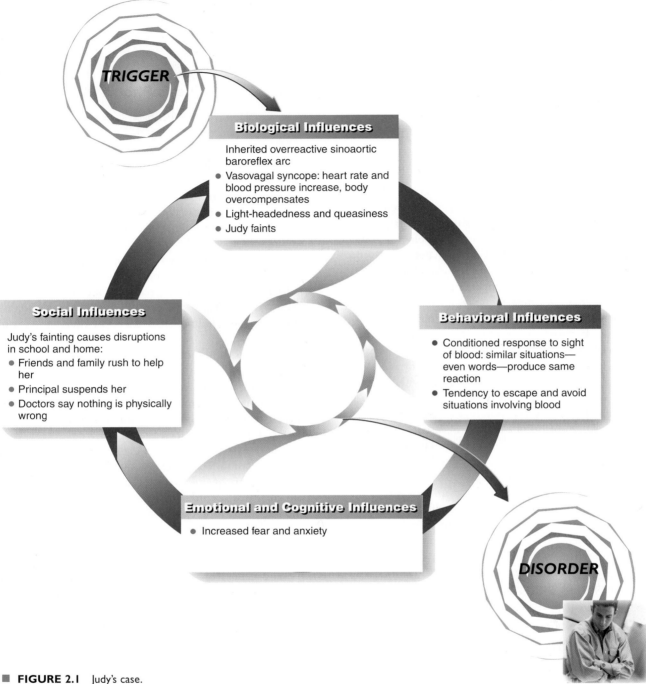

TRIGGER

Biological Influences

Inherited overreactive sinoaortic baroreflex arc
- Vasovagal syncope: heart rate and blood pressure increase, body overcompensates
- Light-headedness and queasiness
- Judy faints

Social Influences

Judy's fainting causes disruptions in school and home:
- Friends and family rush to help her
- Principal suspends her
- Doctors say nothing is physically wrong

Behavioral Influences

- Conditioned response to sight of blood: similar situations—even words—produce same reaction
- Tendency to escape and avoid situations involving blood

Emotional and Cognitive Influences

- Increased fear and anxiety

DISORDER

■ **FIGURE 2.1** Judy's case.

response. Furthermore, some people with little or no syncope reaction develop the phobia anyway (Öst, 1992). Therefore, the cause of blood–injury–injection phobia is more complicated than it seems. If we said that the phobia is caused by a biological dysfunction (an overactive vasovagal reaction probably because of a particularly sensitive baroreflex mechanism) or a traumatic experience (seeing a gruesome film) and subsequent conditioning, we would be partly right on both counts, but in adopting a one-dimensional causal model we would miss the most important point: To cause blood–injury–injection phobia, a complex *interaction* must occur between behavioral and biological factors. Inher-

iting a strong syncope reaction definitely puts a person at risk for developing this phobia, but other influences are at work as well.

■ Emotional Influences

Judy's case is a good example of biology influencing behavior. But behavior, thoughts, and feelings can also influence biology, sometimes dramatically. What role did Judy's fear and anxiety play in the development of her phobia, and where did they come from? Emotions can affect physiological responses such as blood pressure, heart rate, and respiration, particularly if we know rationally there is nothing to fear, as Judy did. In her case, rapid increases in

©Anton Vengo/SuperStock

People who experience the same traumatic event will have different long-term reactions.

heart rate, caused by her emotions, may have triggered a stronger and more intense baroreflex. Emotions also changed the way she thought about situations involving blood and injury and motivated her to behave in ways she didn't want to, avoiding all situations connected with blood and injury, even if it was important not to avoid them. As we see throughout this book, emotions play a substantial role in the development of many disorders.

■ Social Influences

We are all social animals; by our very nature we tend to live in groups such as families. Social and cultural factors make direct contributions to biology and behavior. Judy's friends and family rushed to her aid when she fainted. Did their support help or hurt? Her principal rejected her and dismissed her problem. What effect did this behavior have on her phobia? Rejection, particularly by authority figures, can make psychological disorders worse than they otherwise would be. Then again, being supportive only when somebody is experiencing symptoms is not always helpful because the strong effects of social attention may actually increase the frequency and intensity of the reaction.

■ Developmental Influences

One more influence affects us all—the passage of time. As time passes, many things about ourselves and our environments change in important ways, causing us to react differently at different ages. Thus, at certain times we may enter a *developmental critical period* when we are more or less reactive to a given situation or influence than at other times. To go back to Judy, it is possible she was previously exposed to other situations involving blood. Important questions to ask are these: Why did this problem develop when she was 16 years old and not before? Is it possible that her susceptibility to having a vasovagal reaction was highest in her teenage years? It may be that the timing of her physiological reaction, along with viewing the disturbing biology film, provided just the right (but unfortunate) combination to initiate her severe phobic response.

Outcome and Comments

Fortunately for Judy, she responded well to brief but intensive treatment at one of our clinics, and she was back in school within 7 days. Judy was gradually exposed, with her full cooperation, to words, images, and situations describing or depicting blood and injury while a sudden drop in blood pressure was prevented. We began with something mild, such as the phrase "cut it out!" By the end of the week Judy was witnessing surgical procedures at the local hospital. Judy required close therapeutic supervision during this program. At one point, while driving home with her parents from an evening session, she had the bad luck to pass a car crash, and she saw a bleeding accident victim. That night, she dreamed about bloody accident victims coming through the walls of her bedroom. This experience made her call the clinic and request emergency intervention to reduce her distress, but it did not slow her progress. (Programs for treating phobias and related anxiety disorders are described more fully in Chapter 5. It is the issue of etiology or causation that concerns us here.)

As you can see, finding the causes of abnormal behavior is a complex and fascinating process. Focusing on biological or behavioral factors would not have given us a full picture of the causes of Judy's disorder; we had to consider a variety of other influences and how they might interact. A discussion in more depth follows, examining the research underlying the many biological, psychological, and social influences that must be considered as causes of any psychological disorder.

CONCEPT CHECK 2.1

Theorists have abandoned the notion that any one factor can explain abnormal behavior; they favor an integrative model. Match each of the following scenarios to its most likely influence or influences: (a) behavioral, (b) biological, (c) emotional, (d) social, and (e) developmental.

1. The fact that some phobias are more common than others (such as fear of heights and snakes) and may have contributed to the survival of the species in the past

(continued)

GENETIC CONTRIBUTIONS TO PSYCHOPATHOLOGY

What causes you to look like one or both of your parents or, perhaps, your grandparents? Obviously, the genes you inherit are from your parents and from your ancestors before them. **Genes** are long molecules of deoxyribonucleic acid (DNA) at various locations on chromosomes, within the cell nucleus. Ever since Gregor Mendel's pioneering work in the 19th century, we have known that physical characteristics such as hair and eye color and, to a certain extent, height and weight are determined—or at least strongly influenced—by our genetic endowment. However, other factors in the environment influence our physical appearance. To some extent, our weight and even our height are affected by nutritional, social, and cultural factors. Consequently, our genes seldom determine our physical development in any absolute way. They do provide some boundaries to our development. Exactly where we go within these boundaries depends on environmental influences.

Although this is true for most of our characteristics, it is not true for all of them. Some of our characteristics are strongly determined by one or more genes, including natural hair and eye color. A few rare disorders are determined in this same kind of way, including Huntington's disease, a degenerative brain disease that appears in early to middle age, usually the early 40s. This disease has been traced to a genetic defect that causes deterioration in a specific area of the brain, the basal ganglia. It causes broad changes in personality, cognitive functioning, and, particularly, motor behavior, including involuntary shaking or jerkiness throughout the body. We have not yet discovered a way to environmentally influence the course of Huntington's disease. Another example of genetic influence is a disorder known as phenylketonuria (PKU), which can result in mental retardation. This disorder, present at birth, is caused

by the inability of the body to metabolize (break down) phenylalanine, a chemical compound found in many foods. Like Huntington's disease, PKU is caused by a defect in a single gene, with little contribution from other genes or the environmental background. PKU is inherited when both parents are carriers of the gene and pass it on to the child. Given the genetic determination of PKU, how do you think we could best intervene to prevent or correct this disorder? One possibility is genetic counseling. If the risk for a PKU baby is high, people might be advised not to have children. Fortunately, researchers have discovered a simpler way: We can change the way the environment interacts with and affects the genetic expression of this disorder. Specifically, by detecting PKU early enough (which is now routinely done), we can simply restrict the amount of phenylalanine in the baby's diet until the child develops to the point where a normal diet does not harm the brain, usually 6 or 7 years of age. Disorders such as Huntington's disease and PKU, in which cognitive impairment of various kinds is the prominent characteristic, are covered in more detail in Chapter 15.

Except for identical twins, every person has a unique set of genes unlike those of anyone else in the world. Because there is plenty of room for the environment to influence our development within the constraints set by our genes, there are many reasons for the development of individual differences.

What about our behavior and traits, our likes and dislikes? Do genes influence personality and, by extension, abnormal behavior? This question of nature (genes) versus nurture (upbringing and other environmental influences) is age old in psychology, and the answers beginning to emerge are fascinating. Before discussing them, let's review briefly what we know.

The Nature of Genes

We have known for a long time that each normal human cell has 46 chromosomes arranged in 23 pairs. One chromosome in each pair comes from the father and one from the mother. We can see these chromosomes through a microscope, and we can sometimes tell when one is faulty and predict what problems it will cause.

The first 22 pairs of chromosomes provide programs for the development of the body and brain, and the last pair, called the *sex chromosomes,* determines an individual's sex. In females, both chromosomes in the 23rd pair are called *X chromosomes.* In males, the mother contributes an X chromosome but the father contributes a *Y chromosome.* This one difference is responsible for the variance in biological sex. Abnormalities in the sex chromosomal pair can cause ambiguous sexual characteristics (see Chapter 10).

The DNA molecules that contain genes have a certain structure, a double helix that was discovered only a few decades ago. The shape of a helix is like a spiral staircase. A double helix is two spirals intertwined, turning in opposite directions. Located on this double spiral are simple pairs of molecules bound together and arranged in different orders. On the X chromosome there are approximately 160 million pairs. The ordering of these base pairs influences how the body develops and works.

A *dominant gene* is one of a pair of genes that strongly influences a particular trait, and we only need one of them to determine, for example, our eye or hair color. A *recessive gene,* by contrast, must be paired with another (recessive) gene to determine a

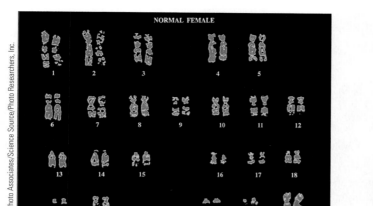

A normal female has 23 pairs of chromosomes.

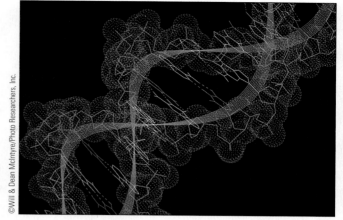

A DNA molecule, which contains genes, resembles a double spiral, or helix.

trait. Otherwise, it won't have any effect. Gene dominance occurs when one member of a gene pair is consistently expressed over the other (for example, a brown-eyed gene is dominant over a blue-eyed gene). When we have a dominant gene, using Mendelian laws of genetics we can predict fairly accurately how many offspring will develop a certain trait, characteristic, or disorder, depending on whether one or both of the parents carry that dominant gene.

Most of the time, predictions are not so simple. Much of our development and, interestingly, most of our behavior, personality, and even intelligence quotient (IQ) score are probably *polygenic*—that is, influenced by many genes, each contributing only a tiny effect, all of which, in turn, may be influenced by the environment. For this reason, most scientists have decided that we must look for patterns of influence across these genes, using procedures called quantitative genetics and multivariate analyses (Kendler, 2006; Plomin, 1990; Plomin, DeFries, McClearn, & Rutter, 1997; Rutter, Moffitt, & Caspi, 2006). *Quantitative genetics* basically sums up all the tiny effects across many genes without necessarily telling us which genes are responsible for which effects, although researchers are now using molecular genetic techniques (the study of the actual structure of genes) in an attempt to identify some specific genes that contribute to individual differences (for ex-

ample, Gershon, Kelsoe, Kendler, & Watson, 2001; Gottesman, 1997; Hariri et al., 2002; Plomin et al., 1995; Rutter et al., 2006). *Multivariate analysis* is a statistical method of analyzing more than one variable at a time. It is also important to understand how genes work. Genes exert their influences on our bodies and our behavior through a series of steps that produce proteins. Although all cells contain our entire genetic structure, only a small proportion of the genes in any one cell are "turned on" or expressed. In this way, cells become specialized, with some influencing liver function and others affecting personality. What is interesting is that many factors that determine whether genes are "turned on" are in the environment in the form of social and cultural influences. The study of gene expression and gene–environment interaction is the current frontier in the study of genetics (Kendler, 2006; Rutter, in press; Rutter, Moffitt, & Caspi, 2006). In Chapter 4, we look at the actual methods scientists use to study the influence of genes. Here, our interest is in what they are finding.

New Developments in the Study of Genes and Behavior

Scientists have now identified, in a preliminary way, the genetic contribution to psychological disorders and related behavioral patterns. The best estimates attribute about half of our enduring personality traits and cognitive abilities to genetic influence. For example, it seems that the heritability of general cognitive ability (as shown through IQ testing) is approximately 62%, and this figure is relatively stable throughout adult life (Gottesman, 1997). This estimate is based on an important study by McClearn et al. (1997), who compared 110 Swedish identical twin pairs, at least 80 years old, with 130 same-sex fraternal twin pairs of a similar age. This work built on earlier important twin studies, with different age groups showing similar results (for example, Bouchard, Lykken, McGue, Segal, & Tellegen, 1990). In the McClearn et al. (1997) study, heritability estimates for specific cognitive abilities, such as memory, or ability to perceive spatial relations ranged from 32% to 62%. More recent studies have shown, however, that adverse life events such as a "chaotic" childhood can overwhelm the influence of genes (Turkheimer, Haley, Waldron, D'Onofrio, & Gottesman, 2003). In other studies, the same calculation for per-

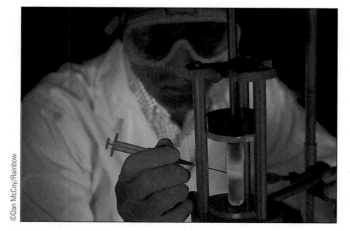

Scientists can now isolate DNA for study.

Genetic contributions to behavior are evident in twins who were raised apart. When these brothers were finally reunited, they were both firefighters, and they discovered many other shared characteristics and interests.

sonality traits such as shyness or activity levels ranges between 30% and 50% (Bouchard et al., 1990; Kendler, 2001; Loehlin, 1992; Saudino & Plomin, 1996; Saudino, Plomin, & DeFries, 1996). For psychological disorders, the evidence indicates that genetic factors make some contribution to all disorders but account for less than half of the explanation. If one of a pair of identical twins has schizophrenia, there is a less-than-50% likelihood that the other twin will also (Gottesman, 1991). Similar or lower rates exist for other psychological disorders (Plomin et al., 1997), with the possible exception of alcoholism (Kendler et al., 1995).

Behavioral geneticists have reached general conclusions in the past several years on the role of genes and psychological disorders relevant to our purposes. First, specific genes or small groups of genes may ultimately be found to be associated with certain psychological disorders, as suggested in several important studies described later. But much of the current evidence suggests that contributions to psychological disorders come from many genes, each having a relatively small effect (Rutter, in press). It is extremely important that we recognize this probability and continue to make every attempt to track

Eric Kandel won the Nobel Prize for establishing the effects of learning on biological functioning among other accomplishments.

the group of genes implicated in various disorders. Advances in gene mapping, molecular genetics, and linkage studies help with this difficult research (for example, Gershon et al., 2001; Hettema, Prescott, Myers, Neale, & Kendler, 2005; Plomin et al., 1997). In linkage studies, when individuals have the same disorder and share other features, such as eye color, where the location of the gene is known, this allows scientists to attempt to "link" known gene locations with the possible location of a gene contributing to the disorder (see Chapter 4).

Second, as noted earlier, it has become increasingly clear that genetic contributions cannot be studied in the absence of interactions with events in the environment that trigger genetic vulnerability or "turn on" specific genes. It is to this fascinating topic that we now turn.

The Interaction of Genetic and Environmental Effects

In 1983, the distinguished neuroscientist and Nobel Prize winner Eric Kandel speculated that the process of learning affects more than behavior. He suggested that the very genetic structure of cells may change as a result of learning if genes that were inactive or dormant interact with the environment in such a way that they become active. In other words, the environment may occasionally turn on certain genes. This type of mechanism may lead to changes in the number of receptors at the end of a neuron, which, in turn, would affect biochemical functioning in the brain.

Although Kandel was not the first to propose this idea, it had enormous effect. Most of us assume that the brain, like other parts of the body, may well be influenced by environmental changes during development. But we also assume that once maturity is reached, the structure and function of our internal organs and most of our physiology are set or, in the case of the brain, hardwired. The competing idea is that the brain and its functions are plastic, subject to continual change in response to the environment, even at the level of genetic structure. Now there is evidence supporting that view (Kolb, Gibb, & Robinson, 2003; Owens, Mulchahey, Stout, & Plotsky, 1997).

With these new findings in mind, we can now explore gene–environment interactions as they relate to psychopathology. Two models have received the most attention: the diathesis–stress model and reciprocal gene–environment model (or gene–environment correlations).

■ The Diathesis–Stress Model

For years, scientists have assumed a specific method of interaction between genes and environment. According to this **diathesis–stress model,** individuals inherit tendencies to express certain traits or behaviors, which may then be activated under conditions of stress (see ■ Figure 2.2). Each inherited tendency is a *diathesis,*

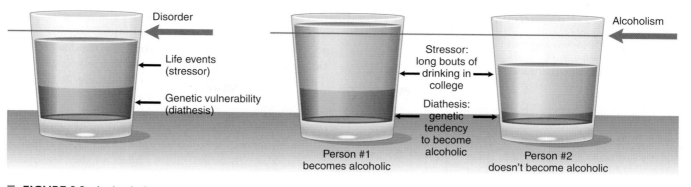

FIGURE 2.2 In the diathesis–stress model, the greater the underlying vulnerability, the less stress is needed to trigger a disorder.

which means, literally, a condition that makes someone susceptible to developing a disorder. When the right kind of life event, such as a certain type of stressor, comes along, the disorder develops. For example, according to the diathesis–stress model, Judy inherited a *tendency* to faint at the sight of blood. This tendency is the diathesis, or **vulnerability.** It would not become prominent until certain environmental events occurred. For Judy, this event was the sight of an animal being dissected when she was in a situation in which escape, or at least closing her eyes, was not acceptable. The stress of seeing the dissection under these conditions activated her genetic tendency to faint. Together, these factors led to her developing a disorder. If she had not taken biology, she might have gone through life without ever knowing she had the tendency, at least to such an extreme, although she might have felt queasy about minor cuts and bruises. You can see that the "diathesis" is genetically based and the "stress" is environmental but that they must interact to produce a disorder.

We might also take the case of someone who inherits a vulnerability to alcoholism, which would make that person substantially different from a close friend who does not have the same tendency.

During college, both engage in extended drinking bouts, but only the individual with the so-called addictive genes begins the long downward spiral into alcoholism. The friend doesn't. Having a particular vulnerability doesn't mean you will develop the associated disorder. The smaller the vulnerability, the greater the life stress required to produce the disorder; conversely, with greater vulnerability, less life stress is required. This model of gene–environment interactions has been popular, although, in view of the relationship of the environment to the structure and function of the brain, it is greatly oversimplified.

This relationship has been demonstrated in an elegant way in a landmark study by Caspi et al. (2003). These investigators are studying a group of 847 individuals who have undergone a variety of assessments for more than two decades, starting at the age of 3. They also noted whether the subjects, at age 26, had been depressed during the past year. Overall, 17% of the study participants reported that they had experienced a major depressive episode during the prior year, and 3% reported that they felt suicidal. But the crucial part of the study is that the investigators also identified the genetic makeup of the individuals and, in particular, a gene that produces a substance called a *chemical transporter* that affects the transmission of serotonin in the brain. Serotonin, one of

the four neurotransmitters we talk about later in the chapter, is particularly implicated in depression and related disorders. But the gene that Caspi et al. were studying comes in two common versions, or *alleles:* the long allele and the short allele. There was reason to believe, from prior work with animals, that individuals with at least two copies of the long allele (LL) were able to cope better with stress than individuals with two copies of the short allele (SS). Because the investigators have been recording stressful life events in these individuals most of their lives, they were able to test this relationship. In people with two S alleles, the risk for having a major depressive episode doubled if they had at least four stressful life events, compared with subjects experiencing four stressful events who had two L alleles. But the interesting finding occurs when we look at the childhood experience of these individuals. In people with the SS alleles, severe and stressful maltreatment during childhood more than doubled their risks of depression in adulthood compared to those individuals carrying the SS alleles who were not maltreated or abused (63% versus 30%). For individuals carrying the LL alleles, on the other hand, stressful childhood experiences did not affect the incidence of depression in adulthood; 30% of this group became depressed if they had experienced stressful childhoods, maltreatment or not. This relationship is shown in ■ Figure 2.3. Therefore, unlike this SS group, depression in the LL allele group seems related to stress in their recent past rather than childhood experiences. This study is by far the most important yet in demonstrating clearly that neither genes nor life experiences (environmental events) can explain the onset of a disorder such as depression. It takes a complex interaction of the two factors. Other groups of genes almost certainly play a role in the development of depression, perhaps differing, depending on the type of life circumstances with which they interact.

Other studies have replicated or supported to these findings (Rutter et al., 2006). For example, Hariri et al. (2002, 2005) found that individuals with SS alleles who were watching frightening pictures demonstrated greater activity in an area of the brain known as the amygdala than individuals with LL alleles as assessed by brain imaging (see Chapter 3).

Also, in a study of the same group of New Zealand individuals by the investigators who carried out the study described earlier, Caspi et al. (2002) found that a different set of genes from those associated with depression seems to contribute to violent and antisocial behavior in adults. But again, this genetic contribu-

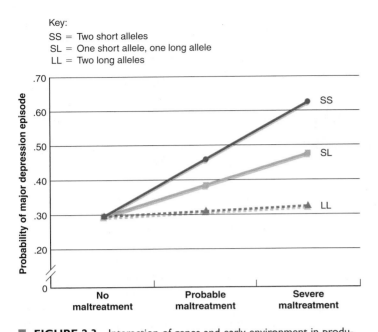

Key:
SS = Two short alleles
SL = One short allele, one long allele
LL = Two long alleles

■ **FIGURE 2.3** Interaction of genes and early environment in producing adult major depression. *(Reprinted, with permission, from Caspi, A., Sugden, K., Moffitt, T. E., Taylor, A., Craig, I. W., Harrington, H., et al., 2003. Influence of life stress on depression: Moderation by a polymorphism in the 5-HTT gene. Science, 301, 386–389, © 2003 AAAS.)*

tion occurs only if they were maltreated as children. That is, some children who were maltreated turned out to be violent and antisocial as adults, but they were four times more likely to do their share of rape, robbery, and assault if they had a certain genetic makeup than were those who didn't have the genetic makeup. These studies require replication, but they do provide powerful support for the gene–environment interaction model that has had only indirect support until this time.

■ The Reciprocal Gene–Environment Model

But it becomes more complex. Some evidence now indicates that genetic endowment may *increase the probability* that an individual will experience stressful life events (for example, Kendler, 2001, 2006; Rutter, in press; Saudino, Pedersen, Lichtenstein, McClearn, & Plomin, 1997). For example, people with a genetic vulnerability to develop a certain disorder, such as blood–injury–injection phobia, may also have a personality trait—let's say impulsiveness—that

makes them more likely to be involved in minor accidents that would result in their seeing blood. In other words, they may be accident prone because they are continually rushing to complete things or to get to places without regard for their physical safety. These people, then, might have a genetically determined tendency to create the very environmental risk factors that trigger a genetic vulnerability to blood–injury–injection phobia.

This is the **reciprocal gene–environment model** or gene–environment correlation model (Kendler, 2001) (see ■ Figure 2.4). Some evidence indicates that it applies to the development of depression, because some people may tend to seek out difficult relationships or other circumstances that lead to depression (Bebbington et al., 1988; Kendler et al., 1995; McGuffin, Katz, & Bebbington, 1988). However, this did not seem to be the case in the New Zealand study described earlier (Caspi et al., 2003), because stressful episodes during adulthood occurred with about the same frequency in the SS and the LL groups. McGue and Lykken (1992) have even applied the reciprocal gene–environment model to some fascinating data on the influence of genes on the divorce rate. Many of us think divorces occur because people simply marry the wrong partner. Some people may stick it out because their religion forbids divorce or for other reasons. But a successful marriage depends on finding the ideal partner, right? Not necessarily. For example, if you and your spouse each have an identical twin, and both identical twins have been divorced, the chance that you will also divorce increases greatly. Furthermore, if your identical twin and your parents and your spouse's parents have been divorced, the chance that you will divorce is 77.5%. Conversely, if none of your family members on either side has been divorced, the probability that you will divorce is only 5.3%.

This is the extreme example, but McGue and Lykken (1992) demonstrated that the probability of your divorcing doubles over the probability in the population at large if your fraternal twin is also divorced and increases sixfold if your identical twin is divorced. Obviously, no one gene causes divorce. To the extent it is genetically determined, the tendency to divorce is almost certainly related to various inherited traits, such as being high strung, impulsive, or short tempered (Jockin, McGue, & Lykken, 1996). Another possibility is that an inherited trait makes it more likely you will choose an incompatible spouse. To take a simple example, if you are passive and unassertive, you may well choose a strong,

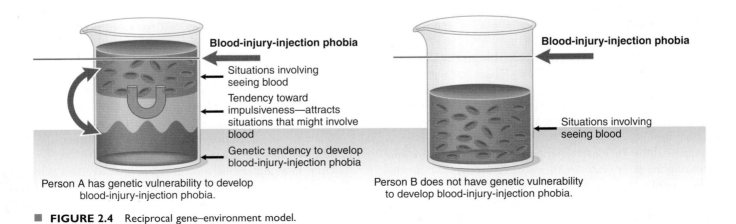

Person A has genetic vulnerability to develop blood-injury-injection phobia.

Blood-injury-injection phobia

Situations involving seeing blood

Tendency toward impulsiveness—attracts situations that might involve blood

Genetic tendency to develop blood-injury-injection phobia

Person B does not have genetic vulnerability to develop blood-injury-injection phobia.

Blood-injury-injection phobia

Situations involving seeing blood

■ **FIGURE 2.4** Reciprocal gene–environment model.

dominant mate who turns out to be impossible to live with. You get divorced but then find yourself attracted to another individual with the same personality traits, who is also impossible to live with. Some people write this kind of pattern off to poor judgment. Social, interpersonal, psychological, and environmental factors play major roles in whether we stay married, but, just possibly, our genes contribute to how we create our own environment.

Nongenomic "Inheritance" of Behavior

To make things a bit more interesting but also more complicated, a number of recent reports suggest that studies to date have overemphasized the extent of genetic influence on our personalities, our temperaments, and their contribution to the development of psychological disorders. This overemphasis may be partly the result of the manner in which these studies have been conducted (Moore, 2001; Turkheimer & Waldron, 2000). Several intriguing lines of evidence have come together in the recent years to buttress this conclusion.

For example, in their animal laboratories, Crabbe, Wahlsten, and Dudek (1999) conducted a clever experiment in which three types of mice with different genetic makeups were raised in virtually identical environments at three sites, the home universities of the behavioral geneticists just named. Each mouse of a given type (for example, type A) was genetically indistinguishable from all other mice of that type at each of the universities. The experimenters went out of their way to make sure the environments (for example, laboratory, cage, and lighting conditions) were the same at each university. For example, each site had the same kind of sawdust bedding that was changed on the same day of the week. If the animals had to be handled, all of them were handled at the same time by experimenters wearing the same kind of glove. When their tails were marked for identification, the same type of pen was used. If genes determine the behavior of the mice, then mice with virtually identical genetic makeup (type A) should have performed the same at all three sites on a series of tests, as should have type B and type C mice. But the results showed that this did not happen. Although a certain type of mouse might perform similarly on a specific test across all three sites, on other tests that type of mouse performed differently. Robert Sapolsky, a prominent neuroscientist, concluded, "genetic influences are often a lot less powerful than is commonly believed. The environment, even working subtly, can still mold and hold its own in the biological interactions that shape who we are" (Sapolsky, 2000a, p. 15).

In another fascinating program of research with rats (Cameron et al., 2005; Francis, Diorio, Liu, & Meaney, 1999; Weaver et al., 2004), the investigators studied stress reactivity and how it is passed through generations, using a powerful experimental procedure called cross-fostering. They first demonstrated, as had many other investigators, that maternal behavior affected how the young rats tolerated stress. If the mothers were calm and supportive, their rat pups were less fearful and better able to tolerate stress. We don't know if this effect results from genetic influences or from being raised by calm mothers. This is where cross-fostering comes in. Francis et al. (1999) took some newly born rat pups of fearful and easily stressed mothers and placed them for rearing

with calm mothers. Other young rats remained with their easily stressed mothers. With this interesting scientific twist, Francis et al. (1999) demonstrated that calm and supportive behavior by the mothers could be passed down through generations of rats *independent of genetic influences,* because rats born to easily stressed mothers but reared by calm mothers grew up more calm and supportive. The authors concluded, "these findings suggest that individual differences in the expression of genes in brain regions that regulate stress reactivity can be transmitted from one generation to the next through behavior. . . . The results . . . suggest that the mechanism for this pattern of inheritance involves differences in maternal care" (p. 1158). In subsequent studies from this group (Cameron et al., 2005), the investigators demonstrated that the maternal behavior had lastingly altered the endocrine response to stress by affecting gene expression. But this effect only occurred if the rat mother was calm and nurturing during the rat pups' first week of life. After that—it didn't matter. This highlights the importance of early experience on behavior.

Other scientists have reported similar results (Anisman, Zaharia, Meaney, & Merali, 1998; Harper, 2005). For example, Suomi (1999), working with rhesus monkeys and using the cross-fostering strategies just described, showed that if genetically reactive and emotional young monkeys are reared by calm mothers for the first 6 months of their lives, the animals behaved, in later life, as if they were nonemotional and not reactive to stress at birth. In other words, the environmental effects of early parenting seem to override any genetic contribution to be anxious, emotional, or reactive to stress. Suomi (1999) also demonstrated that these emotionally reactive monkeys raised by "calm, supportive" parents were also calm and supportive when raising their own children, thereby influencing and even reversing the genetic contribution to the expression of personality traits or temperaments.

Strong effects of the environment have also been observed in humans. For example, Tienari et al. (1994) found that children of parents with schizophrenia who were adopted away as babies demonstrated a tendency to develop psychiatric disorders (including schizophrenia) themselves only if they were adopted into dysfunctional families. Those children adopted into functional families with high-quality parenting did not develop the disorders. Collins and colleagues (Collins, Maccoby, Steinberg, Hetherington, & Bornstein, 2000), in reviewing the contributions of nature (genes) versus nurture (environment), concluded, with respect to the influence of parenting, that "this new generation of evidence on the role of parenting should add to the conviction, long held by many scholars, that broad general main effects for either heredity or environment are unlikely in research on behavior and personality" (p. 228). That is, a specific genetic predisposition, no matter how strong, may never express itself in behavior unless the individual is exposed to a certain kind of environment. On the other hand, a certain kind of (maladaptive) environment may have little effect on a child's development unless that child carries a particular genetic endowment. Thus, it is too simplistic to say the genetic contribution to a personality trait or to a psychological disorder is approximately 50%. We can talk of a heritable (genetic) contribution only in the context of the individual's past and present environment.

In support of this conclusion, Suomi (2000) demonstrated that for young monkeys with a specific genetic pattern associated with a highly reactive temperament (emotional or susceptible to the effects of stress), early maternal deprivation (disruptions in mothering) will have a powerful effect on their neuroendocrine functioning and their later behavioral and emotional reactions. However, for animals not carrying this genetic characteristic, maternal deprivation will have little effect, just as was found in the New Zealand study in humans by Caspi et al. (2003).

These new conceptualizations of the role of genetic contributions as constraining environmental influences have implications for preventing unwanted personality traits or temperaments and even psychological disorders. That is, it seems that environmental manipulations, particularly early in life, may do much to override the genetically influenced tendency to develop undesirable behavioral and emotional reactions. Although current research suggests the influence of everything in our environment in its totality, such as peer groups and schools, affects this genetic expression, the strongest evidence exists for the effects of early parenting influences and other early experiences (Cameron et al., 2005; Collins et al., 2000).

Nowhere is the complexity of the interaction of genetic and environmental influences more apparent than in the famous cases of Chang and Eng, a pair of conjoined identical twins born to parents living in Thailand in 1810 (known as Siam at the time) who were joined at the chest. These individuals, who traveled around the world performing at exhibitions, were the source of the name "Siamese twins." In fact, during their lives, these twins were entrepreneurial and successful with their entertaining and exhibitions, and they amassed a small fortune. In 1839, they became naturalized citizens of the United States and settled down with their wives, a pair of sisters. These two marital pairs produced 12 children each.

What is important for our purposes here is that these identical twins obviously shared identical genes, as well as nearly identical environments throughout their lives. Thus, we would certainly expect them to behave in similar ways when it comes to personality features, temperaments, and psychological disorders. But everybody who knew these twins noted that they had distinct personalities. Chang was prone to moodiness and depression, and he finally started drinking heavily. Eng, on the other hand, was more cheerful, quiet, and thoughtful (Moore, 2001).

In summary, a complex interaction between genes and the environment plays an important role in every psychological disorder (Kendler, 2001; Rutter, 2002, in press; Turkheimer, 1998). Our genetic endowment does contribute to our behavior, our emotions, and our cognitive processes and constrains the influence of environmental factors, such as upbringing, on our later behavior, as is evident in the New Zealand study (Caspi et al., 2003). Environmental events, in turn, seem to affect our very genetic structure by determining whether certain genes are activated or not (Gottlieb, 1998). Furthermore, strong environmental influences alone may be sufficient to override genetic diatheses. Thus, neither nature (genes) nor nurture (environmental events) alone, but a complex interaction of the two, influences the development of our behavior and personalities.

NEUROSCIENCE AND ITS CONTRIBUTIONS TO PSYCHOPATHOLOGY

Knowing how the nervous system and, especially, how the brain works is central to any understanding of our behavior, emotions, and cognitive processes. This is the focus of **neuroscience.** To comprehend the newest research in this field, we first need an overview of how the brain and the nervous system function. The human nervous system includes the *central nervous system,* consisting of the brain and the spinal cord, and the *peripheral nervous system,* consisting of the somatic nervous system and the autonomic nervous system (see ■ Figure 2.5).

The Central Nervous System

The central nervous system processes all information received from our sense organs and reacts as necessary. It sorts out what is relevant, such as a certain taste or a new sound, from what isn't, such as a familiar view or ticking clock; checks the memory banks to determine why the information is relevant; and implements the right reaction, whether it is to answer a question or to play a Chopin étude. This is a lot of exceedingly complex work. The spinal cord is part of the central nervous system, but its primary function is to facilitate the sending of messages to and from the brain, which is the other major component of the central nervous system and the most complex organ in the body. The brain uses an average of 140 billion nerve cells, called **neurons,** to control every thought and action. Neurons transmit information throughout the nervous system. Understanding how they work is important for our purposes because current research has confirmed that neurons contribute to psychopathology.

The typical neuron contains a central cell body with two kinds of branches. One kind of branch is called a *dendrite.* Dendrites have numerous *receptors* that receive messages in the form of

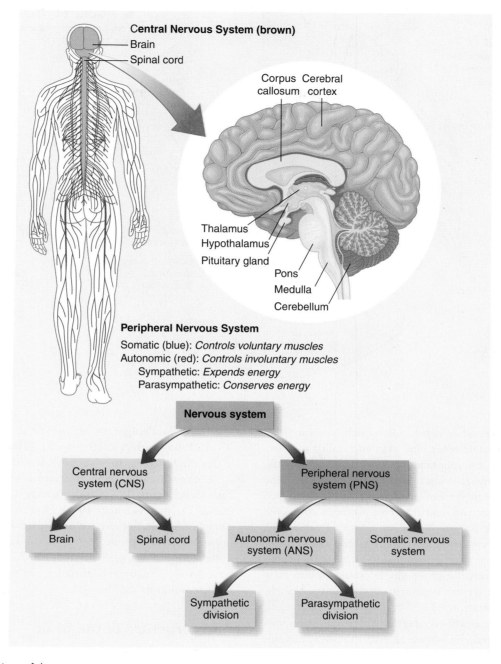

Central Nervous System (brown)
- Brain
- Spinal cord

Corpus Cerebral
callosum cortex

Thalamus
Hypothalamus
Pituitary gland
Pons
Medulla
Cerebellum

Peripheral Nervous System

Somatic (blue): *Controls voluntary muscles*
Autonomic (red): *Controls involuntary muscles*
  Sympathetic: *Expends energy*
  Parasympathetic: *Conserves energy*

Nervous system → Central nervous system (CNS) → Brain, Spinal cord
Nervous system → Peripheral nervous system (PNS) → Autonomic nervous system (ANS), Somatic nervous system
Autonomic nervous system (ANS) → Sympathetic division, Parasympathetic division

■ **FIGURE 2.5** Divisions of the nervous system. *(Reprinted from Kalat, J. W., 2007. Biological Psychology, 9th edition, © 2007 Wadsworth.)*

©David Young-Wolff/PhotoEdit

The central nervous system screens out information that is irrelevant to the current situation. From moment to moment we notice what moves or changes more than what remains the same.

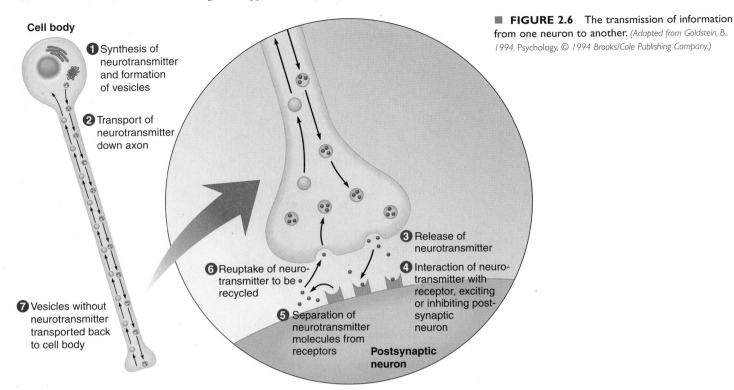

Cell body

❶ Synthesis of neurotransmitter and formation of vesicles

❷ Transport of neurotransmitter down axon

❼ Vesicles without neurotransmitter transported back to cell body

❻ Reuptake of neuro-transmitter to be recycled

❺ Separation of neurotransmitter molecules from receptors

❸ Release of neurotransmitter

❹ Interaction of neuro-transmitter with receptor, exciting or inhibiting post-synaptic neuron

Postsynaptic neuron

■ **FIGURE 2.6** The transmission of information from one neuron to another. *(Adapted from Goldstein, B., 1994. Psychology, © 1994 Brooks/Cole Publishing Company.)*

chemical impulses from other nerve cells, which are converted into electrical impulses. The other kind of branch, called an *axon,* transmits these impulses to other neurons. Any one nerve cell may have multiple connections to other neurons. The brain has billions of nerve cells, so you can see how complicated the system becomes, far more complicated than the most powerful computer that has ever been built (or will be for some time). In the 1997 victory of a powerful computer over the reigning world chess champion, the computer was programmed to estimate probabilities only of one move versus another among possible moves on a chessboard. The central nervous system, in contrast, must organize every facet of our existence.

Nerve cells are not actually connected. There is a small space through which the impulse must pass to get to the next neuron. The space between the axon of one neuron and the dendrite of another is called the **synaptic cleft** (see Figure 2.6). What happens in this space is of great interest to psychopathologists. The chemicals that are released from the axon of one nerve cell and transmit the impulse to the receptors of another nerve cell are called **neurotransmitters.** These were mentioned briefly when we described the genetic contribution to the depression in the New Zealand study (Caspi et al., 2003). Only in the past several decades have we begun to understand their complexity. Now, using increasingly sensitive equipment and techniques, scientists have identified many types of neurotransmitters.

Major neurotransmitters relevant to psychopathology include norepinephrine (also known as noradrenaline), serotonin, dopamine, gamma-aminobutyric acid (GABA), and glutamate. You will see these terms many times in this book. Excesses or insufficiencies in some neurotransmitters are associated with different groups of psychological disorders. For example, reduced levels of GABA

were initially thought to be associated with excessive anxiety (Costa, 1985). Early research (Snyder, 1976, 1981) linked increases in dopamine activity to schizophrenia. Other early research found correlations between depression and high levels of norepinephrine (Schildkraut, 1965) and, possibly, low levels of serotonin (Siever, Davis, & Gorman, 1991). However, more recent research, described later in this chapter, indicates that these early interpretations were too simplistic. Many types and subtypes of neurotransmitters are just being discovered, and they interact in complex ways. In view of their importance, we return to the subject of neurotransmitters shortly.

The Structure of the Brain

Having an overview of the brain is useful because many structures described here are later mentioned in the context of specific disorders. One way to view the brain (see ■ Figure 2.7) is to see it in two parts—the *brain stem* and the *forebrain.* The brain stem is the

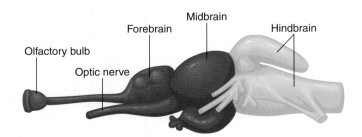

Olfactory bulb

Optic nerve

Forebrain

Midbrain

Hindbrain

■ **FIGURE 2.7a** Three divisions of the brain. *(Reprinted, with permission, from Kalat, J. W., 2007. Biological Psychology, 9th edition, © 2007 Wadsworth.)*

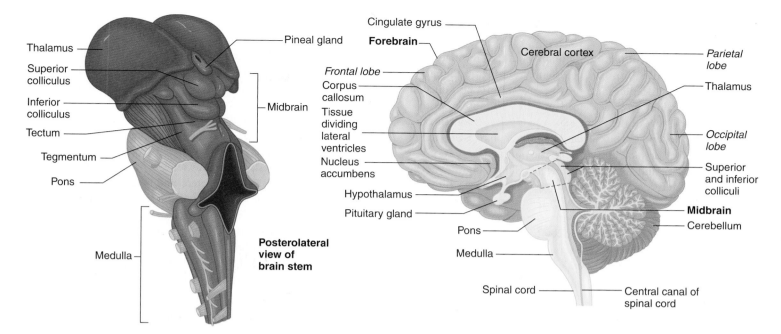

FIGURE 2.7b Major structures of the brain. *(Reprinted, with permission, from Kalat, J. W., 2007. Biological Psychology, 9th edition, © 2007 Wadsworth.)*

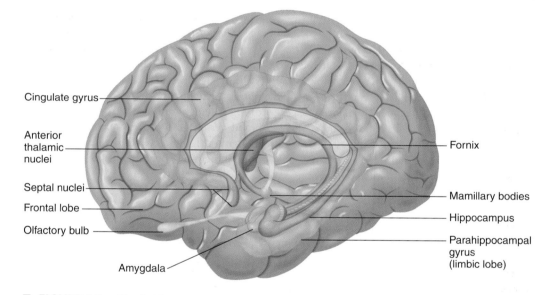

FIGURE 2.7c The limbic system. *(Reprinted, with permission, from Kalat, J. W., 2007. Biological Psychology, 9th edition, © 2007 Wadsworth.)*

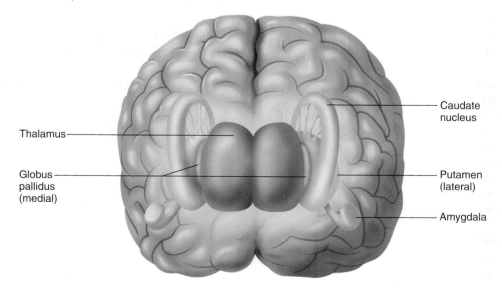

FIGURE 2.7d The basal ganglia. *(Reprinted, with permission, from Kalat, J. W., 2007. Biological Psychology, 9th edition, © 2007 Wadsworth.)*

lower and more ancient part of the brain. Found in most animals, this structure handles most of the essential automatic functions, such as breathing, sleeping, and moving around in a coordinated way. The forebrain is more advanced and evolved more recently.

The lowest part of the brain stem, the *hindbrain,* contains the *medulla,* the *pons,* and the *cerebellum.* The hindbrain regulates many automatic activities, such as breathing, the pumping action of the heart (heartbeat), and digestion. The cerebellum controls motor coordination, and recent research suggests that abnormalities in the cerebellum may be associated with the psychological disorder autism, although the connection with motor coordination is not clear (Courchesne, 1997; Lee et al., 2002) (see Chapter 14).

The *midbrain* coordinates movement with sensory input and contains parts of the *reticular activating system,* which contributes to processes of arousal and tension, such as whether we are awake or asleep.

At the top of the brain stem are the *thalamus* and *hypothalamus,* which are involved broadly with regulating behavior and emotion. These structures function primarily as a relay between the forebrain and the remaining lower areas of the brain stem. Some anatomists even consider the thalamus and hypothalamus to be parts of the forebrain.

At the base of the forebrain, just above the thalamus and hypothalamus, is the *limbic system. Limbic* means border, so named because it is located around the edge of the center of the brain. The limbic system, which figures prominently in much of psychopathology, includes such structures as the *hippocampus* (sea horse), *cingulated gyrus* (girdle), *septum* (partition), and *amygdala* (almond), all of which are named for their approximate shapes. This system helps regulate our emotional experiences and expressions and, to some extent, our ability to learn and to control our impulses. It is also involved with the basic drives of sex, aggression, hunger, and thirst.

The *basal ganglia,* also at the base of the forebrain, include the *caudate* (tailed) *nucleus.* Because damage to these structures may make us change our posture or twitch or shake, they are believed to control motor activity. Later in this chapter, we review some interesting findings on the relationship of this area to obsessive-compulsive disorder.

The largest part of the forebrain is the *cerebral cortex,* which contains more than 80% of all neurons in the central nervous system. This part of the brain provides us with our distinctly human qualities, allowing us to look to the future and plan, to reason, and to create. The cerebral cortex is divided into two hemispheres. Although the hemispheres look alike structurally and operate relatively independently (both are capable of perceiving, thinking, and remembering), recent research indicates that each has different specialties. The left hemisphere seems to be chiefly responsible for verbal and other cognitive processes. The right hemisphere seems to be better at perceiving the world around us and creating images. The hemispheres may play differential roles in specific psychological disorders. For example, current theories about dyslexia (a learning disability involving reading) suggest that it may be a result of specific problems in processing information in the left hemisphere and that the right hemisphere may attempt to compensate by involving visual cues from pictures while reading (Shaywitz, 2003). Each hemisphere consists of four separate areas,

or *lobes:* temporal, parietal, occipital, and frontal (see ■ Figure 2.8). Each is associated with different processes: the *temporal lobe* with recognizing various sights and sounds and with long-term memory storage; the *parietal* lobe with recognizing various sensations of touch; the *occipital lobe* with integrating and making sense of various visual inputs. These three lobes, located toward the back (posterior) of the brain, work together to process sight, touch, hearing, and other signals from our senses.

The *frontal lobe* is the most interesting from the point of view of psychopathology. It carries most of the weight of our thinking and reasoning abilities, as well as memory. It also enables us to relate to the world around us and the people in it, to behave as social animals. When studying areas of the brain for clues to psychopathology, most researchers focus on the frontal lobe of the cerebral cortex, as well as on the limbic system and the basal ganglia.

The Peripheral Nervous System

The peripheral nervous system coordinates with the brain stem to make sure the body is working properly. Its two major components are the *somatic nervous system* and the *autonomic nervous system.* The somatic nervous system controls the muscles, so damage in this area might make it difficult for us to engage in any voluntary movement, including talking. The autonomic nervous system includes the *sympathetic nervous system* and *parasympathetic nervous system.* The primary duties of the autonomic nervous system are to regulate the cardiovascular system (for example, the heart and blood vessels) and the endocrine system (for example, the pituitary, adrenal, thyroid, and gonadal glands) and to perform various other functions, including aiding digestion and regulating body temperature (see ■ Figure 2.9).

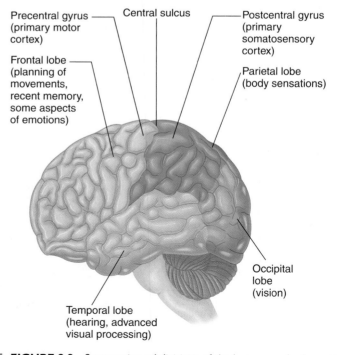

Precentral gyrus (primary motor cortex)

Central sulcus

Postcentral gyrus (primary somatosensory cortex)

Frontal lobe (planning of movements, recent memory, some aspects of emotions)

Parietal lobe (body sensations)

Occipital lobe (vision)

Temporal lobe (hearing, advanced visual processing)

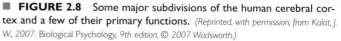

■ **FIGURE 2.8** Some major subdivisions of the human cerebral cortex and a few of their primary functions. *(Reprinted, with permission, from Kalat, J. W., 2007. Biological Psychology, 9th edition, © 2007 Wadsworth.)*

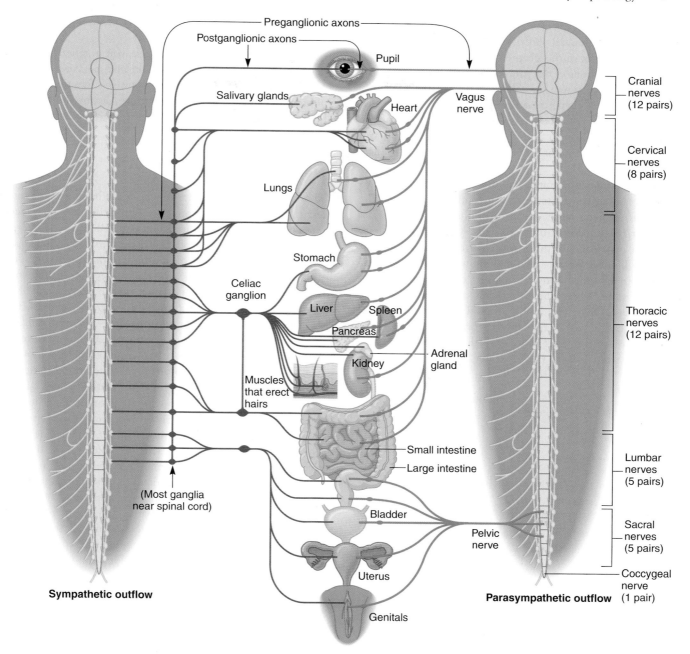

■ **FIGURE 2.9**   The sympathetic nervous system (red lines) and parasympathetic nervous system (blue lines).   *(Reprinted, with permission, from Kalat, J. W., 2007. Biological Psychology, 9th edition, © 2007 Wadsworth.)*

The *endocrine system* works a bit differently from other systems in the body. Each endocrine gland produces its own chemical messenger, called a **hormone,** and releases it directly into the bloodstream. The adrenal glands produce *epinephrine* (also called *adrenaline*) in response to stress, as well as salt-regulating hormones; the thyroid gland produces *thyroxine,* which facilitates energy metabolism and growth; the pituitary is a master gland that produces a variety of regulatory hormones; and the gonadal glands produce sex hormones such as estrogen and testosterone. The endocrine system is closely related to the immune system; it is also implicated in a variety of disorders, particularly the stress-related physical disorders discussed in Chapter 9. The sympathetic and parasympathetic divisions of the autonomic nervous system often

operate in a complementary fashion. The sympathetic nervous system is primarily responsible for mobilizing the body during times of stress or danger by rapidly activating the organs and glands under its control. When the sympathetic division goes on alert, the heart beats faster, thereby increasing the flow of blood to the muscles; respiration increases, allowing more oxygen to get into the blood and brain; and the adrenal glands are stimulated. All these changes help mobilize us for action. If we are threatened by some immediate danger, such as a mugger coming at us on the street, we are able to run faster or defend ourselves with greater strength than if the sympathetic nervous system had not innervated our internal organs. When you read in the newspaper that a woman lifted a heavy object to free a trapped child, you can be sure her sympathetic nervous system was working overtime. This system mediates a substantial part of our "emergency" or "alarm" reaction, discussed later in this chapter and in Chapter 5.

One of the functions of the parasympathetic system is to balance the sympathetic system. In other words, because we could not operate in a state of hyperarousal and preparedness forever, the parasympathetic nervous system takes over after the sympathetic nervous system has been active for a while, normalizing our arousal and facilitating the storage of energy by helping the digestive process.

One brain connection implicated in some psychological disorders involves the hypothalamus and the endocrine system. The hypothalamus connects to the adjacent pituitary gland, which is the master or coordinator of the endocrine system. The pituitary gland, in turn, may stimulate the cortical part of the adrenal glands on top of the kidneys. As we noted previously, surges of epinephrine tend to energize us, arouse us, and get our bodies ready for threat or challenge. When athletes say their adrenaline was really flowing, they mean they were highly aroused and up for the competition. The cortical part of the adrenal glands also produces the stress hormone cortisol. This system is called the *hypothalamic–pituitary–adrenocortical axis,* or *HPA axis* (see ■ Figure 2.10); it has

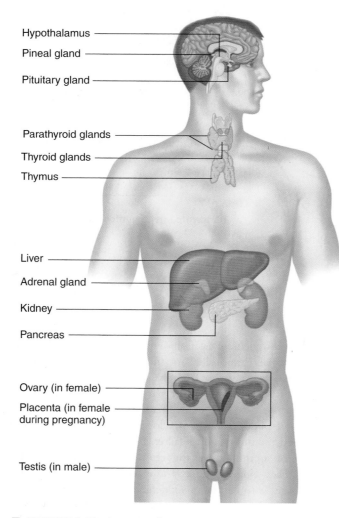

Hypothalamus
Pineal gland
Pituitary gland

Parathyroid glands
Thyroid glands
Thymus

Liver
Adrenal gland
Kidney
Pancreas

Ovary (in female)
Placenta (in female during pregnancy)

Testis (in male)

■ **FIGURE 2.10** Location of some major endocrine glands. *(Reprinted, with permission, from Kalat, J. W., 2007. Biological Psychology, 9th edition, © 2007 Wadsworth.)*

been implicated in several psychological disorders and is mentioned in Chapters 5, 7, and 9.

This brief overview should give you a general sense of the structure and function of the brain and nervous system. New procedures for studying brain structure and function that involve photographing the working brain are discussed in Chapter 3. Here, we focus on what these studies reveal about the nature of psychopathology.

Neurotransmitters

The biochemical neurotransmitters in the brain and nervous system that carry messages from one neuron to another are receiving intense attention by psychopathologists (Bloom & Kupfer, 1995; Bloom, Nelson, & Lazerson, 2001; LeDoux, 2002; Secko, 2005). These chemicals were discovered only in the past several decades, and only in the past few years have we developed the extraordinarily sophisticated procedures necessary to study them. One way to think of neurotransmitters is as narrow currents flowing through the ocean of the brain. Sometimes they run parallel with other currents, only to separate again. Often they seem to meander aimlessly, looping back on themselves before moving on. Neurons that are sensitive to one type of neurotransmitter cluster together and form paths from one part of the brain to the other.

Often these paths overlap with the paths of other neurotransmitters, but, as often as not, they end up going their separate ways (Bloom et al., 2001; Dean, Kelsey, Heller, & Ciaranello, 1993). There are thousands, perhaps tens of thousands, of these **brain circuits,** and we are just beginning to discover and map them. Recently, neuroscientists have identified several that seem to play roles in various psychological disorders (LeDoux, 2002).

Almost all drug therapies work by either increasing or decreasing the flow of specific neurotransmitters. Some drugs directly inhibit, or block, the production of a neurotransmitter. Other drugs increase the production of competing biochemical substances that may deactivate the neurotransmitter. Yet other drugs do not affect neurotransmitters directly but prevent the chemical from reaching the next neuron by closing down, or occupying, the receptors in that neuron. After a neurotransmitter is released, it is quickly drawn back from the synaptic cleft into the same neuron. This process is called **reuptake.** Some drugs work by blocking the reuptake process, thereby causing continued stimulation along the brain circuit.

New neurotransmitters are frequently discovered, and existing neurotransmitter systems must be subdivided into separate classifications. Current estimates suggest that more than 100 different neurotransmitters, each with multiple receptors, are functioning in various parts of the nervous system (Borodinsky et al., 2004). Because this dynamic field of research is in a state of considerable flux, the neuroscience of psychopathology is an exciting area of study; however, research findings that seem to apply to psychopathology today may no longer be relevant tomorrow. Many years of study will be required before it is all sorted out.

You may still read reports that certain psychological disorders are "caused" by biochemical imbalances, excesses, or deficiencies in certain neurotransmitter systems. For example, abnormal activity of the neurotransmitter serotonin is often described as causing depression, and abnormalities in the neurotransmitter dopamine have been implicated in schizophrenia. However, increasing evidence indicates that this is an enormous oversimplification. We are now learning that the effects of neurotransmitter activity are less specific. They often seem to be related to the way we process information (Bloom et al., 2001; Depue, Luciana, Arbisi, Collins, & Leon, 1994; Kandel, Schwartz, & Jessell, 2000; LeDoux, 2002; Sullivan & LeDoux, 2004). Changes in neurotransmitter activity may make people more or less likely to exhibit certain kinds of behavior in certain situations without causing the behavior directly. In addition, broad-based disturbances in our functioning are almost always associated with interactions of the various neurotransmitters rather than with alterations in the activity of any one system (Depue & Spoont, 1986; Depue & Zald, 1993; LeDoux, 2002; Owens et al., 1997; Secko, 2005; Xing, Zhang, Russell, & Post, 2006). In other words, the currents intersect so often that changes in one result in changes in the other, often in a way scientists have not yet been able to predict.

Research on neurotransmitter function focuses primarily on what happens when activity levels change. We can study this in several ways. We can introduce substances called **agonists** that effectively *increase* the activity of a neurotransmitter by mimicking its effects; substances called **antagonists** that *decrease,* or block, a neurotransmitter; or substances called **inverse agonists** that produce effects *opposite* to those produced by the neurotransmitter. By systematically manipulating the production of a neurotransmitter in different parts of the brain, scientists are able to learn more about its effects. In fact, most drugs could be classified as either agonistic or antagonistic, although they may achieve these results in a variety of ways. We now describe the five neurotransmitter systems most often mentioned in connection with psychological disorders.

■ Glutamate and GABA

Two major neurotransmitters affect much of what we do. Each of these substances is in the amino acid category of neurotransmitters. The first, **glutamate,** is an excitatory transmitter that "turns on" many different neurons, leading to action. A second type of amino acid transmitter is **gamma-aminobutyric acid,** or **GABA** for short, which is an inhibiting neurotransmitter. Thus, the job of GABA is to inhibit (or regulate) the transmission of information and action potentials. Because these two neurotransmitters work in concert to balance functioning in the brain, they have been referred to as the "chemical brothers" (LeDoux, 2002).

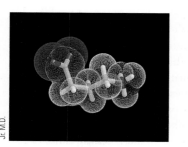

Computer-generated model of GABA.

Glutamate and GABA operate relatively independently at a molecular level, but the relative balance of each in a cell will determine whether the neuron is activated (fires) or not.

Another characteristic of these "chemical brothers" is that they are fast acting, as they would have to be for the brain to keep up with the welter of influences from the environment that require action or restraint. Overactivity of the glutamate system could literally burn out sections of nervous system in a worst-case scenario. Some people who like Chinese food and who are sensitive to glutamate may have experienced a few adverse reactions from a common additive in Chinese food referred to as MSG. MSG stands for monosodium glutamate and can increase the amount of glutamate in the body, causing headaches, ringing in the ears, or other physical symptoms in some people. We return to some exciting new findings involving glutamate-specific receptors when we discuss new treatments for anxiety disorders in Chapter 5.

As noted earlier, GABA reduces postsynaptic activity, which, in turn, inhibits a variety of behaviors and emotions; GABA was discovered before glutamate and has been studied for a longer period, but its best-known effect is to reduce anxiety (Charney & Drevets, 2002; Davis, 2002; Sullivan & LeDoux, 2004). Scientists have discovered that a particular class of drugs, the *benzodiazepines,* or minor tranquilizers, makes it easier for GABA molecules to attach themselves to the receptors of specialized neurons. Thus, the higher the level of benzodiazepine, the more GABA becomes attached to neuron receptors and the calmer we become (to a point). Neuroscientists thus assume that we must have within us substances much like the benzodiazepine class of drugs—in other words, natural benzodiazepines. However, we have yet to discover them (Bloom & Kupfer, 1995).

As with other neurotransmitter systems, we now know that GABA's effect is not specific to anxiety but has a broader influence. The GABA system rides on many circuits distributed widely throughout the brain. GABA seems to reduce overall arousal somewhat and to temper our emotional responses. For example, in addition to reducing anxiety, minor tranquilizers have an anticonvulsant effect, relaxing muscle groups that may be subject to spasms. Furthermore, this system seems to reduce levels of anger, hostility, aggression, and perhaps even positive emotional states such as eager anticipation and pleasure, making GABA a generalized inhibiting neurotransmitter, much as glutamate has a generalized excitatory function (Bond & Lader, 1979; Lader, 1975). We are also learning that the GABA system is not just one system working in only one manner but is composed of a number of subsystems. Different types of GABA receptors seem to act in different ways, with perhaps only one of the subtypes having an affinity for the benzodiazepine component (Gray, 1985; LeDoux, 2002; Pritchett, Lüddens, & Seeburg, 1989). Therefore, the conclusion that this system is responsible for anxiety seems just as out of date as concluding that the serotonin system is responsible for depression (see the next section).

■ Serotonin

The technical name for **serotonin** is 5-hydroxytryptamine (5HT). It is in the monoamine category of neurotransmitters, along with norepinephrine and dopamine, discussed next. Approximately six major circuits of serotonin spread from the midbrain, looping around its various parts (Azmitia, 1978) (see ■ Figure 2.11). Because of the widespread nature of these circuits, many of them ending up in the cortex, serotonin is believed to influence a great deal of our behavior, particularly the way we process information (Depue & Spoont, 1986; Spoont, 1992). It was genetically influ-

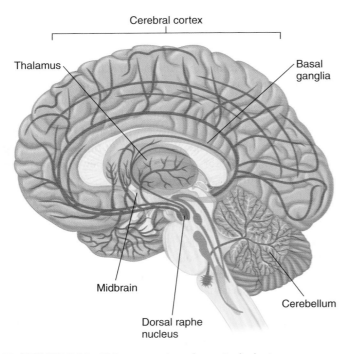

Cerebral cortex

Thalamus

Basal ganglia

Midbrain

Dorsal raphe nucleus

Cerebellum

■ **FIGURE 2.11** Major serotonin pathways in the brain.

enced dysregulation in this system that contributed to depression in the New Zealand study described earlier (Caspi et al., 2003).

The serotonin system regulates our behavior, moods, and thought processes. Extremely low activity levels of serotonin are associated with less inhibition and with instability, impulsivity, and the tendency to overreact to situations. Low serotonin activity has been associated with aggression, suicide, impulsive overeating, and excessive sexual behavior. However, these behaviors do not *necessarily* happen if serotonin activity is low. Other currents in the brain, or other psychological or social influences, may well compensate for low serotonin activity. Therefore, low serotonin activity may make us more vulnerable to certain problematic behavior without directly causing it (as mentioned earlier). On the other end, high levels of serotonin may interact with GABA to counteract glutamate (the same fact is emerging about other neurotransmitter systems).

To add to the complexity, serotonin has slightly different effects depending on the type or subtype of receptors involved, and

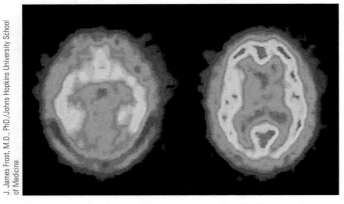

A positron emission tomography scan shows the distribution of serotonergic neurons.

we now know there are at least 15 different receptors in the serotonin system (Owens et al., 1997). Several classes of drugs primarily affect the serotonin system, including the tricyclic antidepressants such as imipramine (known by its brand name, Tofranil). However, the class of drugs called serotonin-specific reuptake inhibitors (SSRIs), including fluoxetine (Prozac) (see ■ Figure 2.12), affects serotonin more directly than other drugs, such as tricyclic antidepressants. These drugs are used to treat a number of psychological disorders, particularly anxiety, mood, and eating disorders. The herbal medication St. John's wort, available in health stores, also affects serotonin levels.

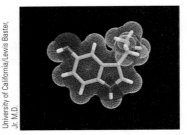

Computer-generated model of serotonin.

■ Norepinephrine

A third neurotransmitter system important to psychopathology is **norepinephrine** (also known as **noradrenaline**) (see ■ Figure 2.13). We have already seen that norepinephrine, like epinephrine (referred to as a catecholamine), is part of the endocrine system.

Norepinephrine seems to stimulate at least two groups (and probably several more) of receptors called *alpha-adrenergic* and *beta-adrenergic receptors*. Someone in your family may be taking a widely used class of drugs called *beta-blockers,* particularly if that person has hypertension or difficulties with regulating heart rate. As the name indicates, these drugs block the beta-receptors so that their response to a surge of norepinephrine is reduced, which keeps blood pressure and heart rate down. In the central nervous system, a number of norepinephrine circuits have been identified. One major circuit begins in the hindbrain, an area that controls basic bodily functions such as respiration. Another circuit appears to influence the emergency reactions or alarm responses (Charney & Drevets, 2002; Gray, 1987; Gray & McNaughton, 1996; Sullivan & LeDoux, 2004) that occur when we suddenly find ourselves in a dangerous situation, suggesting that norepinephrine may bear some relationship to states of panic (Charney et al., 1990; Gray & McNaughton, 1996). More likely, however, is that this system, with all its varying circuits coursing through the brain, acts in a more general way to regulate or modulate certain behavioral tendencies and is not directly involved in specific patterns of behavior or in psychological disorders.

■ Dopamine

Finally, **dopamine** is a major neurotransmitter also classified as a catecholamine because of the similarity of its chemical structure to epinephrine and norepinephrine. Dopamine has been implicated in psychological disorders such as schizophrenia (see ■ Figure 2.14). Remember the wonder drug reserpine mentioned in Chapter 1 that reduced psychotic behaviors associated with schizophrenia? This drug and more modern antipsychotic treatments affect a number of neurotransmitter systems, but their greatest impact may be that they block specific dopamine receptors, thus lowering dopamine activity (for example, Snyder, Burt,

How Neurotransmitters Work

Neurotransmitters are stored in tiny sacs at the end of the neuron **A**. An electric jolt makes the sacs merge with the outer membrane, and the neurotransmitter is released into the synapse **B**. The molecules diffuse across the gap and bind receptors, specialized proteins, on the adjacent neuron **C**. When sufficient neurotransmitter has been absorbed, the receptors release the molecules, which are then broken down or reabsorbed by the first neuron and stored for later use **D**.

How Serotonin Drugs Work

Prozac enhances serotonin's effects by preventing it from being absorbed **E**. Redux and fenfluramine (antiobesity drugs) cause the release of extra serotonin into the synapse **F**.

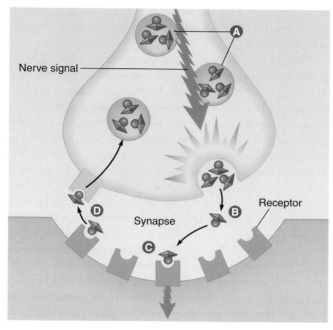

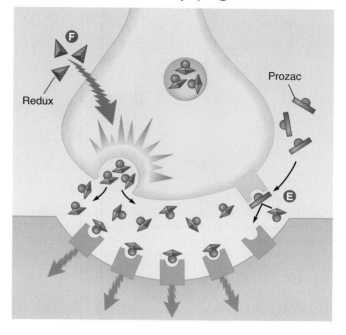

Receptor Variation

There are at least 15 different serotonin receptors, each associated with a different function.

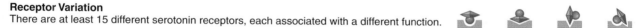

■ **FIGURE 2.12** Manipulating serotonin in the brain.

& Creese, 1976). Thus, it was long thought possible that in schizophrenia dopamine circuits may be too active. The recent development of new antipsychotic drugs such as clozapine, which has only weak effects on certain dopamine receptors, suggests this idea may need revising. We explore the dopamine hypothesis in some detail in Chapter 13.

In its various circuits throughout specific regions of the brain, dopamine also seems to have a more general effect, best described as a switch that turns on various brain circuits possibly associated with certain types of behavior. Once the switch is turned on, other neurotransmitters may then inhibit or facilitate emotions or behavior (Oades, 1985; Spoont, 1992). Dopamine circuits merge and cross with serotonin circuits at many points and therefore influence many of the same behaviors. For example, dopamine activity is associated with exploratory, outgoing, pleasure-seeking behaviors (Elovainio, Kivimaki, Viikari, Ekelund, & Keltikangas-

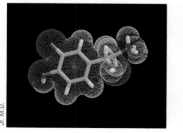

Computer-generated model of norepinephrine.

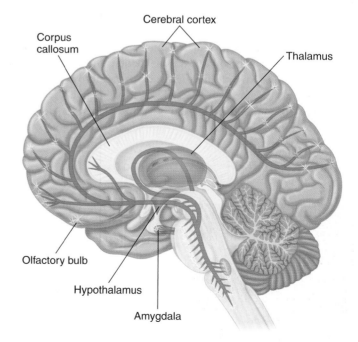

■ **FIGURE 2.13** Major norepinephrine pathways in the human brain.

(Adapted from Kalat, J. W., 2007. Biological Psychology, 9th edition, © 2007 Wadsworth.)

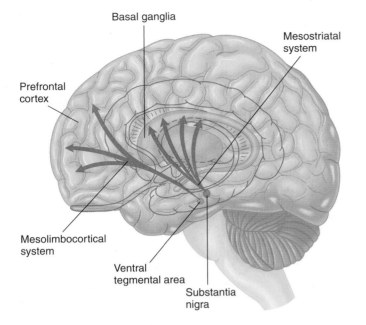

Basal ganglia

Mesostriatal system

Prefrontal cortex

Mesolimbocortical system

Ventral tegmental area

Substantia nigra

■ **FIGURE 2.14** Two major dopamine pathways. The mesolimbic system is apparently implicated in schizophrenia; the path to the basal ganglia contributes to problems in the locomotor system, such as tardive dyskinesia, which sometimes results from use of neuroleptic drugs. *(Adapted from Kalat, J. W., 2007. Biological Psychology, 9th edition, © 2007 Wadsworth.)*

Jarvinen, 2005), and serotonin is associated with inhibition and constraint; thus, in a sense they balance each other (Depue et al., 1994). Again, we see that the effects of a neurotransmitter—in this case, dopamine—are more complex than we originally thought. Researchers have thus far discovered at least five different receptor sites that are selectively sensitive to dopamine (Owens et al., 1997). One of a class of drugs that affects the dopamine circuits specifically is L-dopa, which is a dopamine agonist (increases levels of dopamine). One of the systems that dopamine switches on is the locomotor system, which regulates ability to move in a coordinated way and, once turned on, is influenced by serotonin activity. Because of these connections, deficiencies in dopamine have been associated with disorders such as Parkinson's disease, in which a marked deterioration in motor behavior includes tremors, rigidity of muscles, and difficulty with judgment. L-dopa has been successful in reducing some of these motor disabilities.

Implications for Psychopathology

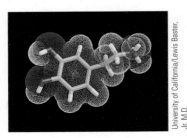

Computer-generated model of dopamine.

Psychological disorders typically mix emotional, behavioral, and cognitive symptoms, so identifiable lesions (or damage) localized in specific structures of the brain do not, for the most part, cause them. Even widespread damage most often results in motor or sensory deficits, which are usually the province of the medical specialty

of neurology; neurologists often work with neuropsychologists to identify specific lesions. But psychopathologists are also beginning to theorize about the more general role of brain function in the development of personality, considering how different types of biologically driven personalities might be more vulnerable to developing certain types of psychological disorders. For example, genetic contributions might lead to patterns of neurotransmitter activity that influence personality. Thus, some impulsive risk takers may have low serotonergic activity and high dopaminergic activity.

Procedures for studying images of the functioning brain have recently been applied to *obsessive-compulsive disorder (OCD)*. Individuals with this severe anxiety disorder suffer from intrusive, frightening thoughts—for example, that they might have become contaminated with poison and will poison their loved ones if they touch them. To prevent this drastic consequence, they engage in compulsive rituals such as frequent washing to try to scrub off the imagined poison. A number of investigators have found intriguing differences between the brains of patients with OCD and those of other people. Although the size and structure of the brain are the same, patients with OCD have increased activity in the part of the frontal lobe of the cerebral cortex called the *orbital surface*. Increased activity is also present in the cingulate gyrus and, to a lesser extent, in the caudate nucleus, a circuit that extends from the orbital section of the frontal area of the cortex to parts of the thalamus. Activity in these areas seems to be correlated; that is, if one area is active, the other areas are also. These areas contain several pathways of neurotransmitters, and one of the most concentrated is serotonin.

Remember that one of the roles of serotonin seems to be to moderate our reactions. Eating behavior, sexual behavior, and aggression are under better control with adequate levels of serotonin. Research, mostly on animals, demonstrates that lesions (damage) that interrupt serotonin circuits seem to impair the ability to ignore irrelevant external cues, making the organism overreactive. Thus, if we were to experience damage or interruption in this brain circuit, we might find ourselves acting on every thought or impulse that enters our heads.

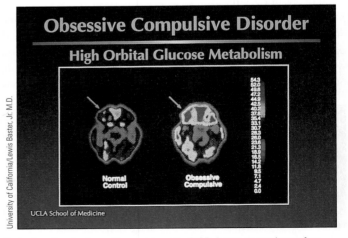

Brain function is altered in people with OCD, but it normalizes after effective psychosocial treatment.

Thomas Insel (1992) described a case originally reported by Eslinger and Damasio (1985) of a man who had been successful as an accountant, husband, and father of two before undergoing surgery for a brain tumor. He made a good recovery from surgery and seemed to be fine, but in the following year his business failed and he separated from his family. Although his scores on IQ tests were as high as ever and all his mental functions were intact, he was unable to keep a job or even be on time for an appointment. What was causing all these problems? He was engaging in lengthy and uncontrollable compulsive rituals. Most of his days were consumed with washing, dressing, and rearranging things in the single room where he lived. In other words, he had classic obsessive-compulsive symptoms. The area of his brain damaged by removal of the tumor was a small area of his orbital frontal cortex.

This information seems to support a biological cause for psychopathology—in this case, OCD. You might think there is no need to consider social or psychological influences here. Maybe there is some wisdom to the strategy of adopting a one-dimensional or linear causal model that traces all psychopathology to certain brain circuits. But Insel and other neuroscientists interpret these findings cautiously. First, this case involves only one individual. Other individuals with the *same* lesion might react differently. Also, brain-imaging studies are often inconsistent with one another on many important details. Sometimes pinpointing the increased or decreased activity is difficult because brains differ in their structure, just as bodies and faces do. Also, the orbital frontal cortex is implicated in other anxiety disorders and maybe other emotional disorders (Sullivan & LeDoux, 2004), so the damage in this area of the brain may just increase negative affect more generally rather than OCD specifically. Therefore, more work has to be done, and perhaps technology has to improve further, before we can be confident about the relation of the orbital frontal cortex to OCD. It is possible that activity in this area may simply be a result of the repetitive thinking and ritualistic behavior that characterizes OCD, rather than a cause. To take a simple analogy, if you were late for class and began running, massive changes would occur throughout your body and brain. If someone who did not know that you had just sprinted to class then examined you with brain scans, your brain functions would look different from those of the brain of a person who had walked to class. If you were doing well in the class, the scientist might conclude, wrongly, that your unusual brain function "caused" your intelligence.

Psychosocial Influences on Brain Structure and Function

At the same time that psychopathologists are exploring the causes of psychopathology, whether in the brain or in the environment, people are suffering and require the best treatments we have.

Sometimes the effects of treatment tell us something about the nature of psychopathology. For example, if a clinician thinks OCD is caused by a specific brain function or dysfunction or by learned anxiety to scary or repulsive thoughts, this view would determine choice of treatment, as we noted in Chapter 1. Directing a treatment at one or the other of these theoretical causes of the disorder and then observing whether the patient gets better will prove or disprove the accuracy of the theory. This common

strategy has one overriding weakness. Successfully treating a patient's particular feverish state or toothache with aspirin does not mean the fever or toothache was caused by an aspirin deficiency, because an effect does not imply a cause. Nevertheless, this line of evidence gives us some hints about causes of psychopathology, particularly when it is combined with other, more direct experimental evidence.

If you knew that someone with OCD might have a somewhat faulty brain circuit, what treatment would you choose? Maybe you would recommend brain surgery. Psychosurgery to correct severe psychopathology is an option still chosen today on occasion, particularly in the case of OCD when the suffering is severe (Jenike et al., 1991). For the accountant described previously, the removal of his brain tumor seems to have inadvertently eliminated an inhibitory part of the brain circuit implicated in OCD. Precise surgical lesions might dampen the runaway activity that seems to occur in or near this particular area of the brain. This result would probably be welcome if all other treatments have failed, although psychosurgery is used seldom and has not been studied systematically.

Nobody wants to do surgery if less intrusive treatments are available. To use the analogy of a television set that has developed the "disorder" of going fuzzy, if you had to rearrange and reconnect wires on the circuit board every time the disorder occurred, the correction would be a major undertaking. Alternatively, if you could simply push some buttons on the remote and eliminate the fuzziness, the correction would be simpler and less risky. The development of drugs affecting neurotransmitter activity has given us one of those buttons. We now have drugs that, although not a cure or even an effective treatment in all cases, do seem to be beneficial in treating OCD. As you might suspect, most of them act by increasing serotonin activity in one way or another.

But is it possible to get at this brain circuit without either surgery or drugs? Could psychological treatment be powerful enough to affect the circuit directly? The answer now seems to be yes. To take one of the first examples, Lewis R. Baxter and his colleagues used brain imaging on patients who had not been treated and then took an additional, important scientific step (Baxter et al., 1992). They treated the patients with a cognitive-behavioral therapy known to be effective in OCD called *exposure and response prevention* (described more fully in Chapter 5) and then repeated the brain imaging. In a remarkable finding, widely noted in the world of psychopathology, Baxter and his colleagues discovered that the brain circuit had been changed (normalized) by a psychological intervention. The same team of investigators then replicated the experiment with a different group of patients and found the same changes in brain function (Schwartz, Stoessel, Baxter, Martin, & Phelps, 1996). In other examples, two investigating teams noted changes in brain function after successful psychological treatment for depression (Brody et al., 2001; Martin et al., 2001), and another team observed normalization of brain circuits after successful treatment for a specific phobia, which they termed "re-wiring the brain" (Paquette et al., 2003). In yet another intriguing study, Leuchter, Cook, Witte, Morgan, and Abrams (2002) treated patients with major depressive disorder with either antidepressant medications or placebo medications. (Remember that it is common for inactive placebo medications, which are just sugar pills, to result in behavioral and emotional changes in patients, presumably as a result of psychological factors such as increasing hope and expectations). Measures of brain function showed that both antidepressant medications and placebos changed brain function but in somewhat different parts of the brain, suggesting different mechanisms of action for these two interventions. Placebos alone are not usually as effective as active medication, but every time clinicians prescribe pills, they are also treating the patient psychologically by inducing positive expectation for change, and this intervention changes brain function.

Petrovic, Kalso, Petersson, and Ingvar (2002), in an important study, looked more deeply into how "placebo" pills (in other words, psychological factors) can change brain function. Normal subjects were given (with their consent) a harmless but painful condition in which their left hand was subjected to intense heat. These subjects were informed that two potent analgesics (pain-reducing medications) would be used in the experiment. In fact, one of these drugs was an opioid, and the other was a placebo. Opioid-based drugs are used routinely in medical settings to relieve severe pain. Each subject experienced the painful stimulus under three conditions: (1) under the influence of an opioid drug, (2) under the influence of a placebo pill that the patient assumed was an opioid-based drug, and (3) with no drug (pain only). All subjects experienced each condition multiple times, while brain-imaging procedures monitored their brain functioning (see Chapter 3) during administration of the painful stimulus. Whereas both the placebo drug and the opiate drug reduced pain to less than the level with no drug, the surprising results indicated that both treatments activated overlapping although not identical regions in the brain, primarily within the anterior cingulate cortex and the brain stem. These areas were not activated during the pain-only condition. Thus, it appears that the anterior cingulate cortex is responsible for control of the pain response in the brain stem and that cognitive expectations of pain relief created by the placebo condition cause these brain circuits to be turned on. It would seem that psychological treatments are another button on the remote with which we can directly change brain circuits. Gorman, Kent, Sullivan, and Coplan (2000), a team of distinguished neuroscientists, have speculated further on more generalized changes in brain function caused by psychological interventions and on how these changes may differ from those that occur with medication.

Interactions of Psychosocial Factors with Brain Structure and Function

Several experiments illustrate the interaction of psychosocial factors and brain function on neurotransmitter activity, with implications for the development of disorders. Some even indicate that psychosocial factors directly affect levels of neurotransmitters. For example, Insel, Scanlan, Champoux, and Suomi (1988) raised two

Rhesus monkeys injected with a specific neurotransmitter react with anger or fear, depending on their early psychological experiences.

groups of rhesus monkeys identically except for their ability to control things in their cages. One group had free access to toys and food treats, but the second group got these toys and treats only when the first group did. In other words, members of the second group had the same number of toys and treats but could not choose when they got them. Therefore, they had less control over their environment. In psychological experiments, we say the second group was "yoked" with the first group because their treatment depended entirely on what happened to the first group. In any case, the monkeys in the first group grew up with a sense of control over things in their lives and those in the second group didn't.

Later in their lives, all these monkeys were administered a benzodiazepine inverse agonist, a neurochemical that has the *opposite* effect of the neurotransmitter GABA; the effect is an extreme burst of anxiety. (The few times this neurochemical has been administered to people, usually scientists administering it to one another, the recipients have reported the experience—which lasts only a short time—to be one of the most horrible sensations they had ever endured.) When this substance was injected into the monkeys, the results were interesting. The monkeys that had been raised with little control over their environment ran to a corner of their cage where they crouched and displayed signs of severe anxiety and panic. But the monkeys that had a sense of control behaved quite differently. They did not seem anxious. Rather, they seemed angry and aggressive, even attacking other

Thomas Insel, the leading investigator in the monkey study, conducts research on the interaction of neurotransmitters and psychosocial factors at the National Institute of Mental Health where he is now Director.

monkeys near them. Thus, the same level of a neurochemical substance, acting as a neurotransmitter, had different effects, depending on the psychological histories of the monkeys.

The Insel and colleagues (Insel, Scanlan, Champoux, & Suomi, 1988) experiment is an example of a significant interaction between neurotransmitters and psychosocial factors. Other experiments suggest that psychosocial influences directly affect the functioning and perhaps even the structure of the central nervous system. Scientists have observed that psychosocial factors routinely change the activity levels of many of our neurotransmitter systems, including norepinephrine and serotonin (Coplan et al., 1996, 1998; Heim & Nemeroff, 1999; Ladd et al., 2000; Roma, Champoux, & Suomi, 2006; Sullivan, Kent, & Coplan, 2000). It also seems that the structure of neurons themselves, including the number of receptors on a cell, can be changed by learning and experience (Gottlieb, 1998; Kandel, 1983; Kandel, Jessell, & Schacter, 1991; Ladd et al., 2000; Owens et al., 1997) and that these effects on the central nervous system continue throughout our lives (Cameron et al., 2005).

We are now beginning to learn how psychosocial factors affect brain function and structure (Kolb, Gibb, & Robinson, 2003; Kolb & Whishaw, 1998). For example, William Greenough and his associates, in a series of classic experiments (Greenough, Withers, & Wallace, 1990), studied the cerebellum, which coordinates and controls motor behavior. They discovered that the nervous systems of rats raised in a rich environment requiring a lot of learning and motor behavior develop differently from those in rats that were couch potatoes. The active rats had many more connections between nerve cells in the cerebellum and grew many more dendrites. The researchers also observed that certain kinds of learning decreased the connections between neurons in other areas. In a follow-up study, Wallace, Kilman, Withers, and Greenough (1992) reported that these structural changes in the brain began in as little as 4 days in rats, suggesting enormous plasticity in brain structure as a result of experience. Similarly, stress during early development can lead to substantial changes in the functioning of the HPA axis described here that, in turn, make primates more or less susceptible to stress later in life (Barlow, 2002; Coplan et al., 1998; Suomi, 1999). It may be something similar to this mechanism that was responsible for the effects of early stress on the later development of depression in genetically susceptible individuals in the New Zealand study described earlier (Caspi et al., 2003). So, we can conclude that early psychological experience affects the development of the nervous system and thus determines vulnerability to psychological disorders later in life. It seems that the very structure of the nervous system is constantly changing as a result of learning and experience, even into old age, and that some of these changes become permanent (Kolb, Gibb, & Gorny, 2003). This plasticity of the central nervous system helps us adapt more readily to our environment. These findings will be important when we discuss the causes of anxiety disorders and mood disorders in Chapters 5 and 7.

Scientists have begun to pin down the complex interaction among psychosocial factors, brain structure, and brain function as reflected in neurotransmitter activity. Yeh, Fricke, and Edwards (1996) studied two male crayfish battling to establish dominance in their social group. When one of the crayfish won the battle and

William Greenough and his associates raised rats in a complex environment that required significant learning and motor behavior, which affected the structure of the rats' brains. This supports the role of psychological factors on biological development.

established dominance, the scientists found that serotonin made a specific set of neurons more likely to fire; but in the animal that lost the battle, serotonin made the same neurons less likely to fire. Thus, unlike the Insel et al. experiment, where monkeys were injected with a neurotransmitter, Edwards et al. discovered that naturally occurring neurotransmitters have different effects depending on the previous psychosocial experience of the organism. Furthermore, this experience directly affects the structure of neurons at the synapse by altering the sensitivity of serotonin receptors. The researchers also discovered that the effects of serotonin are reversible if the losers again become dominant. Similarly, Suomi (2000) demonstrated in primates that early stressful experiences produced deficits in serotonin (as well as other neuroendocrine changes) in genetically susceptible individuals, deficits that did not occur in the absence of early stress.

Comments

More recently, Berton et al. (2006) discovered, much to their surprise, that putting into a cage big mice that then proceeded to "bully" a smaller mouse produced changes in the mesolimbic dopamine system of the smaller mouse. These changes were associated with smaller mice wanting no part of other mice under any circumstances. The small mouse chose to become a recluse. Interestingly, the mesolimbic system is ordinarily associated with reward and even addiction. But in this case, certain chemicals that produce new learning and other positive changes in other parts of the brain, specifically brain development neurotrophic factor (BDNF), were turned on in the mesolimbic dopamine system by a psychological experience—bullying—such that the mesolimbic dopamine system had different effects on the mouse than it usually does because of the mouse's unique experience. That is, the "bullying" experience produced BDNF, which changed the usual functioning of the mesolimbic dopamine system from facilitating reinforcement and even addiction to facilitating avoidance and isolation.

The specific brain circuits involved in psychological disorders are complex systems identified by pathways of neurotransmitters traversing the brain. The existence of these circuits suggests that the structure and function of the nervous system play major roles in psychopathology. But other research suggests the circuits are strongly influenced, perhaps even created, by psychological and social factors. Furthermore, both biological interventions, such as drugs, and psychological interventions or experience seem capable of altering the circuits. Therefore, we cannot consider the nature and cause of psychological disorders without examining both biological and psychological factors. We now turn to an examination of psychological factors.

CONCEPT CHECK 2.3

Check your understanding of the brain structures and neurotransmitters. Match each with its description below: (a) frontal lobe, (b) brain stem, (c) GABA, (d) midbrain, (e) serotonin, (f) dopamine, (g) norepinephrine, and (h) cerebral cortex.

1. Movement, breathing, and sleeping depend on the ancient part of the brain, which is present in most animals. _____

2. Which neurotransmitter binds to neuron receptor sites, inhibiting postsynaptic activity and reducing overall arousal? _____

3. Which neurotransmitter is a switch that turns on various brain circuits? _____

4. Which neurotransmitter seems to be involved in your emergency reactions or alarm responses? _____

5. This area contains part of the reticular activating system and coordinates movement with sensory output. _____

6. Which neurotransmitter is believed to influence the way we process information, as well as to moderate or inhibit our behavior? _____

7. More than 80% of the neurons in the human central nervous system are contained in this part of the brain, which gives us distinct qualities. _____

8. This area is responsible for most of our memory, thinking, and reasoning capabilities and makes us social animals. _____ .

BEHAVIORAL AND COGNITIVE SCIENCE

Enormous progress has been made in understanding behavioral and cognitive influences in psychopathology. Some new information has come from the rapidly growing field of **cognitive science,** which is concerned with how we acquire and process information and how we store and ultimately retrieve it (one of the processes involved in memory). Scientists have also discovered that a great deal goes on inside our heads of which we are not necessarily aware. Because, technically, these cognitive processes are unconscious, some findings recall the unconscious mental processes that are so much a part of Sigmund Freud's theory of psy-

choanalysis (although they do not look much like the ones he envisioned). A brief account of current thinking on what is happening during the process of classical conditioning will start us on our way.

Conditioning and Cognitive Processes

During the 1960s and 1970s, behavioral scientists in animal laboratories began to uncover the complexity of the basic processes of classical conditioning (Bouton, 2005; Bouton, Mineka, & Barlow, 2001; Eelen & Vervliet, 2006; Mineka & Zinbarg, 1996, 1998). Robert Rescorla (1988) concluded that simply pairing two events closely in time (such as the meat powder and the metronome in Ivan Pavlov's laboratories) is not what's important in this type of learning; at the least, it is a simple summary. Rather, a variety of judgments and cognitive processes combine to determine the final outcome of this learning, even in lower animals such as rats.

To take just one simple example, Pavlov would have predicted that if the meat powder and the metronome were paired, say, 50 times, then a certain amount of learning would take place. But Rescorla and others discovered that if one animal never saw the meat powder except for the 50 trials following the metronome sound, whereas the meat powder was brought to the other animal many times *between* the 50 times it was paired with the metronome, the two animals would learn different things; that is, even though the metronome and the meat powder were paired 50 times for each animal, the metronome was less meaningful to the second animal (see ■ Figure 2.15). Put another way, the first animal learned that the sound of the metronome meant meat powder came next; the second animal learned that the meat sometimes came after the sound and sometimes without the sound. That two different conditions produce two different learning outcomes is a commonsense notion, but it demonstrates, along with many far more complex scientific findings, that basic classical (and operant) conditioning paradigms facilitate the learning of the relationship among events in the environment.

This type of learning enables us to develop working ideas about the world that allow us to make appropriate judgments. We can then respond in a way that will benefit or at least not hurt us. In other words, complex cognitive, as well as emotional, processing of information is involved when conditioning occurs, even in animals.

Learned Helplessness

Along similar lines, Martin Seligman, also working with animals, described the phenomenon of **learned helplessness,** which occurs when rats or other animals encounter conditions over which they have no control. If rats are confronted with a situation in which they receive occasional foot shocks, they can function well if they learn they can cope with these shocks by doing something to avoid them (say, pressing a lever). But if the animals learn their behavior has no effect on their environment—sometimes they get shocked and sometimes they don't, no matter what they do—they become "helpless"; in other words, they give up attempting to cope and seem to develop the animal equivalent of depression.

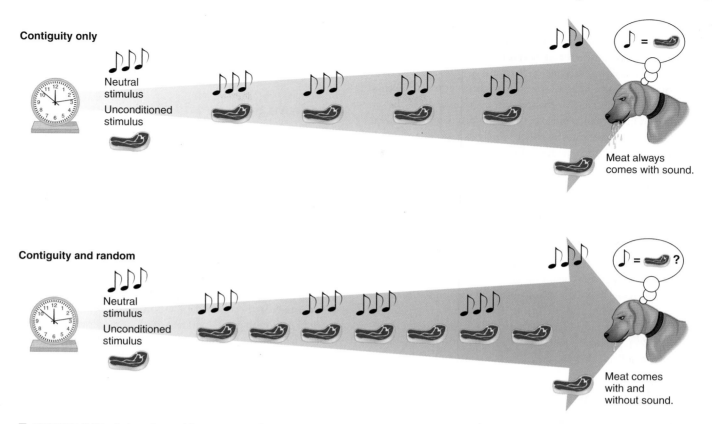

■ FIGURE 2.15 Robert Rescorla's experiment that showed contiguity—pairing a neutral stimulus and an unconditioned stimulus—does not result in the same kind of conditioning. The dog in the contiguity-only group (top panel) experiences the usual conditioning procedure: Pairing a tone and meat causes the tone to take on properties of the meat. For the dog in the contiguity-and-random group, the meat appeared away from the tones, as well as with it, making the tone less meaningful.

Seligman drew some important conclusions from these observations. He theorized that the same phenomenon may happen with people who are faced with uncontrollable stress in their lives. Subsequent work revealed this to be true under one important condition: People become depressed if they "decide" or "think" they can do little about the stress in their lives, even if it seems to others that there is something they could do. People make an *attribution* that they have no control, and they become depressed (Abramson, Seligman, & Teasdale, 1978; Miller & Norman, 1979). We revisit this important psychological theory of depression in Chapter 7. It illustrates, again, the necessity of recognizing that different people process information about events in the environment in different ways. These cognitive differences are an important component of psychopathology.

Lately, Seligman has turned his attention to a different set of attributions, which he terms "learned optimism" (Seligman, 1998,

Martin Seligman first described the concept of learned helplessness.

2002). In other words, if people faced with considerable stress and difficulty in their lives nevertheless display an optimistic, upbeat attitude, they are likely to function better psychologically and physically. We return to this theme repeatedly throughout this book but particularly in Chapter 9, when we talk about the effects of psychological factors on health. But consider this one example: In a study by Levy, Slade, Kunkel, & Kasl (2002), individuals between ages 50 and 94 who had positive views about themselves and positive attitudes toward aging lived 7.5 years longer than those without such positive, optimistic attitudes. This connection was still true after the investigators controlled for age, sex, income, loneliness, and physical capability to engage in household and social activities. This effect is extremely powerful, and it exceeds the 1–4 years of added life associated with other factors, such as low blood pressure, low cholesterol levels, and no history of obesity or cigarette smoking. Studies such as this have created interest in a new field of study called *positive psychology,* in which investigators explore factors that account for positive attitudes and happiness (Diener, 2000; Lyubomirsky, 2001). We return to these themes in the chapters describing specific disorders.

Social Learning

Another influential psychologist, Albert Bandura (1973, 1986), observed that organisms do not have to experience certain events in their environment to learn effectively. Rather, they can learn just as much by observing what happens to someone else in a given situation. This fairly obvious discovery came to be known as **modeling** or **observational learning.** What is important is that, even in animals, this type of learning requires a symbolic integration of the experiences of others with judgments of what might happen to oneself; in other words, even an animal that is not intelligent by human standards, such as a monkey, must make a decision about the conditions under which its own experiences would be similar to those of the animal it is observing. Bandura expanded his observations into a network of ideas in which behavior, cognitive factors, and environmental influences converged to produce the complexity of behavior that confronts us. He also specified in some detail the importance of the social context of our learning; that is, much of what we learn depends on our interactions with other people around us.

The basic idea in all Bandura's work is that a careful analysis of cognitive processes may well produce the most accurate scientific predictions of behavior. Concepts of probability learning, information processing, and attention have become increasingly important in psychopathology (Barlow, 2002; Craighead, Ilardi, Greenberg, & Craighead, 1997; Davey, 2006; Lovibond, 2006; Mathews & MacLeod, 1994).

Prepared Learning

It is clear that biology and, probably, our genetic endowment influence what we learn. This conclusion is based on the fact that we learn to fear some objects more easily than others. In other words, we learn fears and phobias selectively (Mineka & Sutton, 2006; Morris, Öhman, & Dolan, 1998; Öhman, Flykt, & Lundqvist, 2000; Öhman & Mineka, 2001). Why might this be? According to the concept of **prepared learning,** we have become highly prepared for learning about certain types of objects or situations over the course of evolution because this knowledge contributes to the survival of the species (Mineka, 1985b; Seligman, 1971). Even without any contact, we are more likely to learn to fear snakes or spiders than rocks or flowers, even if we know rationally that the snake or spider is harmless (for example, Fredrikson, Annas, & Wik, 1997; Pury & Mineka, 1997). In the absence of experience, however, we are less likely to fear guns or electrical outlets, even though they are potentially deadlier.

Why do we so readily learn to fear snakes or spiders? One possibility is that when our ancestors lived in caves, those who avoided snakes and spiders eluded deadly varieties and therefore survived in greater numbers to pass down their genes to us, thus contributing to the survival of the species. This is just a theory, but at present it seems a likely explanation. Something within us recognizes the connection between a certain signal and a threatening event. In other words, certain unconditioned stimuli and conditioned stimuli "belong" to one another. If you've ever gotten sick on cheap wine or bad food, chances are you won't make the same mistake again. This quick or "one-trial" learning also occurs in animals that eat something that tastes bad, causes nausea, or may contain poison. It is easy to see that survival is associated with quickly learning to avoid poisonous food. If animals are shocked instead of poisoned when eating certain foods, however, they do not learn this association nearly as quickly, probably because in nature shock is not a consequence of eating, whereas being poisoned may be. Perhaps these selective associations are also facilitated by our genes (Barlow, 2002; Cook, Hodes, & Lang, 1986; Garcia, McGowan, & Green, 1972).

Cognitive Science and the Unconscious

Advances in cognitive science have revolutionized our conceptions of the unconscious. We are not aware of much of what goes on inside our heads, but our unconscious is not necessarily the seething caldron of primitive emotional conflicts envisioned by Freud. Rather, we simply seem able to process and store information, and act on it, without having the slightest awareness of what the information is or why we are acting on it (Bargh & Chartrand, 1999). Is this surprising? Consider briefly these two examples.

Lawrence Weiskrantz (1992) describes a phenomenon called *blind sight* or *unconscious vision.* He relates the case of a young man who, for medical reasons, had a small section of his visual cortex (the center for the control of vision in the brain) surgically removed. Although the operation was considered a success, the young man became blind in both eyes. Later, during routine tests, a physician raised his hand to the left of the patient who, much to the shock of his doctors, reached out and touched it. Subsequently, scientists determined that he could not only reach accurately for objects but could also distinguish among objects and perform most of the functions usually associated with sight. Yet, when asked about his abilities, he would say, "I couldn't see anything, not a darn thing," and that all he was doing was guessing.

The phenomenon in this case is associated with real brain damage. More interesting, from the point of view of psychopathology, is that the same thing seems to occur in healthy individuals who have been hypnotized (Hilgard, 1992; Kihlstrom, 1992); that is, normal individuals, provided with hypnotic suggestions that they are blind, are able to function visually but have no awareness or memory of their visual abilities. This condition, which illustrates a process of *dissociation* between behavior and consciousness, is the basis of the dissociative disorders discussed in Chapter 6.

A second example, more relevant to psychopathology, is called **implicit memory** (Bowers & Marsolek, 2003; Craighead et al., 1997; Graf, Squire, & Mandler, 1984; Kihlstrom, Barnhardt, & Tataryn, 1992; McNally, 1999; Schacter, Chiu, & Ochsner, 1993). Implicit memory is apparent when someone clearly acts on

1. RED	6. GREEN	11. BLUE
2. PURPLE	7. PURPLE	12. PURPLE
3. GREEN	8. BROWN	13. BROWN
4. BLUE	9. BLUE	14. RED
5. BROWN	10. RED	15. GREEN

The Stroop paradigm. Have someone keep time as you name the colors of the words but not the words themselves and again while you name the words and colors together.

the basis of things that have happened in the past but can't remember the events. (A good memory for events is called *explicit memory.*) But implicit memory can be selective for only certain events or circumstances. Clinically, we have already seen in Chapter 1 an example of implicit memory at work in the story of Anna O., the classic case first described by Breuer and Freud (1895/1957) to demonstrate the existence of the unconscious. It was only after therapy that Anna O. remembered events surrounding her father's death and the connection of these events to her paralysis. Thus, Anna O.'s behavior (occasional paralysis) was evidently connected to implicit memories of her father's death. Many scientists have concluded that Freud's speculations on the nature and structure of the unconscious went beyond the evidence, but the existence of unconscious processes has since been demonstrated, and we must take them into account as we study psychopathology.

What methods do we have for studying the unconscious? The *black box* refers to unobservable feelings and cognitions inferred by an individual's self-report. In recent decades, psychologists, confident in an established science of behavior, have returned to the black box with new methods, attempting to reveal the unobservable. Several methods for studying the unobservable unconscious have been made possible by advances in technology. One of them is the Stroop color-naming paradigm.

In the Stroop paradigm, subjects are shown a variety of words, each printed in a different color. They are shown these words quickly and asked to name the colors in which they are printed while ignoring their meaning. Color naming is delayed when the meaning of the word attracts the subject's attention, despite efforts to concentrate on the color; that is, the meaning of the word interferes with the subject's ability to process color information. For example, experimenters have determined that people with certain psychological disorders, like Judy, are much slower at naming the colors of words associated with their problem (for example, *blood, injury,* and *dissect*) than the colors of words that have no relation to the disorder. Thus, psychologists can now uncover particular patterns of emotional significance, even if the subject cannot verbalize them or is not even aware of them. These developments in our understanding of the nature of psychopathology will come up repeatedly as we discuss specific disorders. Again, note that these findings support Freud's theories about the unconscious, up to a point. But no assumptions are made about an elaborate structure existing within the mind that is continually in conflict (Freud's id, ego, and superego). As cognitive science advances, it is less important to assume the existence of an unconscious with such a complex structure and array of functions.

EMOTIONS

Emotions play an enormous role in our day-to-day lives and can contribute in major ways to the development of psychopathology (Gross, 1999). Consider the emotion of fear. Have you ever found yourself in a really dangerous situation? Have you ever almost crashed your car and known for several seconds beforehand what was going to happen? Have you ever been swimming in the ocean and realized you were out too far or caught in a current? Have you ever almost fallen from a height, such as a cliff or a roof? In any of these instances, you would have felt an incredible surge of

Charles Darwin: Evolution of the Species, 1896

Charles Darwin (1809–1882) drew this cat frightened by a dog to show the flight or fight reaction.

arousal. As the first great emotion theorist, Charles Darwin (1872), pointed out more than 100 years ago, this kind of reaction seems to be programmed in all animals, including humans, which suggests that it serves a useful function. The alarm reaction that activates during potentially life-threatening emergencies is called the **flight or fight response.** If you are caught in ocean currents, your almost instinctual tendency is to struggle toward shore. You might realize rationally that you're best off just floating until the current runs its course and then, more calmly, swimming in later. Yet somewhere, deep within, ancient instincts for survival won't let you relax, even though struggling against the ocean will only wear you out and increase your chance of drowning. Still, this kind of reaction might momentarily give you the strength to lift a car off your trapped brother or fight off an attacker. The whole purpose of the physical rush of adrenaline that we feel in extreme danger is to mobilize us to escape the danger (flight) or to withstand it (fight).

The Physiology and Purpose of Fear

How do physical reactions prepare us to respond this way? The great physiologist Walter Cannon (1929) speculated on the reasons. Fear activates your cardiovascular system. Your blood vessels constrict, thereby raising arterial pressure and decreasing the blood flow to your extremities (fingers and toes). Excess blood is redirected to the skeletal muscles, where it is available to the vital organs that may be needed in an emergency. Often people seem "white with fear"; that is, they turn pale as a result of decreased blood flow to the skin. "Trembling with fear," with your hair standing on end, may be the result of shivering and piloerection (in which body hairs stand erect), reactions that conserve heat when your blood vessels are constricted.

These defensive adjustments can also produce the hot-and-cold spells that often occur during extreme fear. Breathing becomes faster and, usually, deeper to provide necessary oxygen to rapidly circulating blood. Increased blood circulation carries oxygen to the brain, stimulating cognitive processes and sensory functions, which make you more alert and able to think more quickly during emergencies. An increased amount of glucose (sugar) is released from the liver into the bloodstream, further energizing various crucial muscles and organs, including the brain. Pupils dilate, presumably to allow a better view of the situation. Hearing becomes more acute, and digestive activity is suspended, resulting in a reduced flow of saliva (the "dry mouth" of fear). In the short term, voiding the body of all waste material and eliminating digestive processes further prepare the organism for concentrated action and activity, so there is often pressure to urinate and defecate and, occasionally, to vomit. (This will also protect you if you have ingested poisonous substances during the emergency.)

It is easy to see why the flight or fight reaction is fundamentally important. Millennia ago, when our ancestors lived in unstable circumstances, those with strong emergency reactions were more likely to live through attacks and other dangers than those with weak emergency responses, and the survivors passed their genes down to us.

Emotional Phenomena

The **emotion** of fear is a subjective feeling of terror, a strong motivation for behavior (escaping or fighting), and a complex physiological or arousal response. To define "emotion" is difficult, but most theorists agree that it is an *action tendency* (Lang, 1985, 1995; Lang, Bradley, & Cuthbert, 1998); that is, a tendency to behave in a certain way (for example, escape), elicited by an external event (a threat) and a feeling state (terror) and accompanied by a (possibly) characteristic physiological response (Gross, 1999, in press; Gross & Muñoz, 1995; Izard, 1992; R. S. Lazarus, 1991, 1995). One purpose of a feeling state is to motivate us to carry out a behavior: If we escape, our terror, which is unpleasant, will be decreased, so decreasing unpleasant feelings motivates us to escape (Campbell-Sills & Barlow, in press; Gross, 1999, in press; Öhman, 1996). As Öhman (1996; Öhman, Flykt, & Lundquist, 2000) points out, the principal function of emotions can be understood as a clever means, guided by evolution, to get us to do what we have to do to pass on our genes successfully to coming generations. How do you think this works with anger or with love? What is the feeling state? What is the behavior?

Emotions are usually short-lived, temporary states lasting from several minutes to several hours, occurring in response to an external event. **Mood** is a more persistent period of affect or emotionality. Thus, in Chapter 7 we describe enduring or recurring states of depression or excitement (mania) as mood disorders. But anxiety disorders, described in Chapter 5, are characterized by enduring or chronic anxiety and, therefore, could also be called *mood disorders.* Alternatively, both anxiety disorders and mood disorders could be called *emotional disorders,* a term not formally used in psychopathology. This is only one example of the occasional inconsistencies in the terminology of abnormal psychology.

A related term you will see occasionally, particularly in Chapters 3 and 13, is **affect,** which usually refers to the momentary emotional tone that accompanies what we say or do. For example, if you just got an A+ on your test but you look sad, your friends might think your reaction strange because your affect is not ap-

propriate to the event. The term *affect* can also be used more generally to summarize commonalities among emotional states characteristic of an individual. Thus, someone who tends to be fearful, anxious, and depressed is experiencing negative affect. Positive affect would subsume tendencies to be pleasant, joyful, excited, and so on.

The Components of Emotion

Emotion theorists now agree that emotion is composed of three related components—*behavior, physiology,* and *cognition*—but most emotion theorists tend to concentrate on one component or another (see ■ Figure 2.16). Emotion theorists who concentrate on behavior think that basic patterns of emotion differ from one another in fundamental ways; for example, anger may differ from sadness not only in how it feels but also behaviorally and physiologically. These theorists also emphasize that emotion is a way of communicating between one member of the species and another. One function of fear is to motivate immediate and decisive action, such as running away. But if you look scared, your facial expression will quickly communicate the possibility of danger to your friends, who may not have been aware that a threat is imminent. Your facial communication increases their chance for survival because they can now respond more quickly to the threat when it occurs. This may be one reason emotions are contagious, as we observed in Chapter 1 when discussing mass hysteria (Hatfield, Cacioppo, & Rapson, 1994; Wang, 2006).

Other scientists have concentrated on the physiology of emotions, most notably Cannon (1929). In some pioneering work, he viewed emotion as primarily a brain function. Research in this tradition suggests that areas of the brain associated with emotional expression are generally more ancient and primitive than areas associated with higher cognitive processes, such as reasoning.

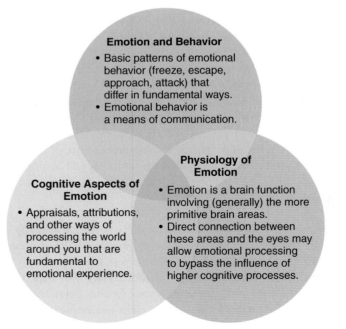

■ **FIGURE 2.16** Emotion has three important and overlapping components: behavior, cognition, and physiology.

Our emotional reaction depends on context. Fire, for example, can be threatening or comforting.

Other research demonstrates direct neurobiological connections between emotional centers of the brain and parts of the eye (the retina) or the ear that allow emotional activation without the influence of higher cognitive processes (LeDoux, 1996, 2002; Öhman, Flykt, & Lundqvist, 2000; Zajonc, 1984, 1998); in other words, you may experience various emotions quickly and directly without necessarily thinking about them or being aware of why you feel the way you do.

Finally, a number of prominent theorists concentrate on studying the cognitive aspects of emotion. Notable among these theorists was the late Richard S. Lazarus (for example, 1968, 1991, 1995), who proposed that changes in a person's environment are appraised in terms of their potential impact on that person. The type of appraisal you make determines the emotion you experience. For example, if you see somebody holding a gun in a dark alley, you will probably appraise the situation as dangerous and experience fear. You would make a different appraisal if you saw a tour guide displaying an antique gun in a museum. Lazarus would suggest that thinking and feeling cannot be separated, but other cognitive scientists are concluding otherwise by suggesting that, although cognitive and emotional systems interact and overlap, they are fundamentally separate (Teasdale, 1993). All components of emotion—behavior, physiology, and cognition—are important, and theorists are adopting more integrative approaches by studying their interaction (Gross, in press; Gross & John, 2003).

Anger and Your Heart

When we discussed Judy's blood phobia, we observed that behavior and emotion may strongly influence biology. Scientists have made important discoveries about the familiar emotion of anger. We have known for years that negative emotions such as hostility and anger increase a person's risk of developing heart disease (Chesney, 1986; MacDougall, Dembroski, Dimsdale, & Hackett, 1985). Sustained hostility with angry outbursts contributes more strongly to death from heart disease than other well-known risk factors, including smoking, high blood pressure, and high cholesterol levels (Finney, Stoney, & Engebretson, 2002; Suarez, Lewis, & Kuhn, 2002; Williams, Haney, Lee, Kong, & Blumenthal, 1980).

Why is this, exactly? Ironson and colleagues (1992) asked a number of people with heart disease to recall something that made them angry in the past. Sometimes these events had occurred many years earlier. In one case, an individual who had spent time in a Japanese prisoner-of-war camp during World War II became angry every time he thought about it, especially when he thought about reparations paid by the U.S. government to Japanese Americans who had been held in internment camps during the war. Ironson and associates compared the experience of anger to stressful events that increased heart rate but were not associated with anger. For example, some participants imagined making a speech to defend themselves against a charge of shoplifting. Others tried to figure out difficult problems in arithmetic within a time limit. Heart rates during these angry situations and stressful ones were then compared to heart rates that increased as a result of exercise (riding a stationary bicycle). The investigators found that the ability of the heart to pump blood efficiently through the body dropped significantly during anger but not during stress or exercise. In fact, remembering being angry was sufficient to cause the anger effect. If subjects were really angry, their heart-pumping efficiency dropped even more, putting them at risk for dangerous disturbances in heart rhythm (arrhythmias).

This study was the first to prove that anger affects the heart through decreased pumping efficiency, at least in people who already have heart disease. Other studies, such as one by Williams and colleagues (1980), demonstrated that anger also affects people without heart disease. Medical students who were often angry were seven times more likely to die by the age of 50 than students in the same class who had lower levels of hostility. Now, Suarez et al. (2002) have demonstrated how anger may cause this effect. Inflammation produced by an overactive immune system in particularly hostile individuals may contribute to clogged arteries (and decreased heart pumping efficiency). Shall we conclude that too much anger causes heart attacks? This would be another example of one-dimensional causal modeling. Increasing evidence, including the studies just mentioned, suggests that anger and hostility contribute to heart disease, but so do many other factors, including a genetically determined biological vulnerability. We discuss cardiovascular disease in Chapter 9.

Emotions and Psychopathology

We now know that suppressing almost any kind of emotional response, such as anger or fear, increases sympathetic nervous system activity, which may contribute to psychopathology (Barlow, Allen, & Choate, 2004; Campbell-Sills & Barlow, in press; Gross & Levenson, 1997). Other emotions seem to have a more direct effect. In Chapter 5, we study the phenomenon of *panic* and its relationship to anxiety disorders. One interesting possibility is that a panic attack is simply the normal emotion of fear occurring at the wrong time, when there is nothing to be afraid of. Some patients with mood disorders become overly excited and joyful. They think they have the world on a string and they can do anything they want and spend as much money as they want because everything will turn out all right. Every little event is the most wonderful and exciting experience they have ever had. These individuals are suffering from *mania,* which is part of the serious mood disorder discussed in Chapter 7. People who suffer from mania usually alternate periods of excitement with periods of extreme sadness and distress, when they feel that all is lost and the world is a gloomy and hopeless place. During extreme sadness or distress, people are unable to experience any pleasure in life and often find it difficult even to get out of bed and move around. If hopelessness becomes acute, they are at risk for suicide. This emotional state is *depression,* a defining feature of many mood disorders.

Thus, basic emotions of fear, anger, sadness or distress, and excitement may contribute to many psychological disorders and may even define them. Emotions and mood also affect our cognitive processes: If your mood is positive, then your associations, interpretations, and impressions also tend to be positive (Bower, 1981; Diener et al., 2003). Your impression of people you first meet and even your memories of past events are colored to a great extent by your current mood. If you are consistently negative or depressed, then your memories of past events are likely to be unpleasant. The pessimist or depressed person sees the bottle as half empty. In contrast, the cheerful optimist is said to see the world through rose-colored glasses and to see the bottle as half full. This is a rich area of investigation for cognitive scientists (Eysenck, 1992; Teasdale, 1993), particularly those interested in the close interconnection of cognitive and emotional processes. Leading psychopathologists are beginning to outline the nature of emotion disruption (or dysregulation) and to understand how these disruptions interfere with thinking and behavior in various psychological disorders (Barlow et al., 2004; Campbell-Sills & Barlow, in press; Gross, 1999, in press; Kring & Bachorowski, 1999).

> ### CONCEPT CHECK 2.4
>
> Check your understanding of behavioral and cognitive influences by identifying the descriptions. Choose your answers from (a) learned helplessness, (b) modeling, (c) prepared learning, and (d) implicit memory.
>
> *(continued)*

> ### CONCEPT CHECK 2.4
>
> *(continued)*
>
> 1. Karen noticed that every time Don behaved well at lunch, the teacher praised him. Karen decided to behave better to receive praise herself. _____
> 2. Josh stopped trying to please his father because he never knows whether his father will be proud or outraged. _____
> 3. Greg fell into a lake as a baby and almost drowned. Even though Greg has no recollection of the event, he hates to be around large bodies of water. _____
> 4. Christal was scared to death of the tarantula, even though she knew it wasn't likely to hurt her. _____

CULTURAL, SOCIAL, AND INTERPERSONAL FACTORS

Given the welter of neurobiological and psychological variables impinging on our lives, is there any room for the influence of social, interpersonal, and cultural factors? Studies are beginning to demonstrate the substantial power and depth of such influences. Researchers have now established that cultural and social influences can kill you. Consider the following example.

Voodoo, the Evil Eye, and Other Fears

In many cultures around the world, individuals may suffer from *fright disorders,* exaggerated startle responses, and other observable fear reactions. One example is the Latin American *susto,* characterized by various anxiety-based symptoms, including insomnia, irritability, phobias, and the marked somatic symptoms of sweating and increased heart rate (tachycardia). But *susto* has only one cause: The individual becomes the object of black magic, or witchcraft, and is suddenly badly frightened. In some cultures, the sinister influence is called the *evil eye* (Good & Kleinman, 1985; Tan, 1980), and the resulting fright disorder can be fatal. Cannon (1942), examining the Haitian phenomenon of voodoo death, suggested that the sentence of death by a medicine man may create an intolerable autonomic arousal in the subject, who has little ability to cope because there is no social support. That is, friends and family ignore the individual after a brief period of grieving because they assume death has already occurred. Ultimately, the condition leads to damage to internal organs and death. Thus, from all accounts, an individual who is from a physical and psychological point of view functioning in a perfectly healthy and adaptive way suddenly dies because of marked changes in the social environment.

Fear and phobias are universal, occurring across all cultures. But *what* we fear is strongly influenced by our social environment. Israeli and Bedouin researchers studied the fears of hundreds of Jewish and Bedouin children living in the same region of Israel (Elbedour, Shulman, & Kedem, 1997). Although they all feared potentially life-threatening events, Jewish children, whose society emphasizes individuality and autonomy, have fewer fears than

A "possessed" person receives treatment in a voodoo ritual.

Bedouin children, who grow up in a strongly paternalistic society in which the group and family are central and who are taught to be cautious about the rest of the world. Bedouin and Jewish children have different fears, and the Bedouin children have more of them, many centering on the possible disintegration of the family. Thus, cultural factors influence the form and content of psychopathology and may differ even among cultures side by side in the same country.

Gender

Gender roles have a strong and sometimes puzzling effect on psychopathology. Everyone experiences anxiety and fear, and phobias are found all over the world. But phobias have a peculiar characteristic: The likelihood of your having a particular phobia is powerfully influenced by your gender. For example, someone who complains of an insect or small-animal phobia severe enough to prohibit field trips or visits to friends in the country is almost certain to be female, as are 90% of the people with this phobia. But a social phobia strong enough to keep someone from attending parties or meetings affects men and women equally.

We think these substantial differences have to do with cultural expectations of men and women, or our *gender roles.* For example, an equal number of men and women may have an experience that could lead to an insect or small-animal phobia, such as being bitten by one, but in our society it isn't always acceptable for a man to show or even admit fear. So a man is more likely to hide or endure the fear until he gets over it. It is more acceptable for women to acknowledge fearfulness, so a phobia develops. It is also more acceptable for a man to be shy than to show fear, so he is more likely to admit social discomfort.

To avoid or survive a panic attack, an extreme experience of fear, some males drink alcohol instead of admitting they're afraid (see Chapter 5). In many cases, this attempt to cope may lead to alcoholism, a disorder that affects many more males than females (see Chapter 11). One reason for this gender imbalance is that males are more likely than females to self-medicate their fear and panic with alcohol and in so doing start down the slippery slope to addiction.

Jewish children, whose culture emphasizes individuality and autonomy, have been found to be less fearful of outsiders than Bedouin children in the same community, whose culture emphasizes the group and the family.

Bulimia nervosa, the severe eating disorder, occurs almost entirely in young females. Why? As you will see in Chapter 8, a cultural emphasis on female thinness plagues our society and, increasingly, societies around the world. The pressures for males to be thin are less apparent, and of the few males who develop bulimia, a substantial percentage are gay; for these individuals, cultural imperatives to be thin are present in many specific instances (Rothblum, 2002).

Finally, in an exciting new finding, Taylor (2002; Taylor et al., 2000) describes a unique way in which females in many species respond to stress in their lives. This unique response to stress is called "tend and befriend" and refers to protecting themselves and their young through nurturing behavior (tend) and forming alliances with larger social groups, particularly other females (befriend). Taylor et al. (2000) supposed that this response fits better with the way females respond to stress because it builds on the brain's attachment–caregiving system and leads to nurturing and affiliative behavior. Furthermore, the response is characterized by identifiable neurobiological processes in the brain.

Our gender doesn't cause psychopathology. But because gender role is a social and cultural factor that influences the form and content of a disorder, we attend closely to it in the chapters that follow.

Social Effects on Health and Behavior

A large number of studies have demonstrated that the greater the number and frequency of social relationships and contacts, the longer you are likely to live. Conversely, the lower you score on a social index that measures the richness of your social life, the shorter your life expectancy. Studies documenting this finding have been reported in the United States (Berkman & Syme, 1979; House, Robbins, & Metzner, 1982; Schoenbach, Kaplan, Fredman, & Kleinbaum, 1986), as well as in Sweden and Finland. They take into account existing physical health and other risk factors for dying young, such as high blood pressure, high cholesterol levels, and smoking habits, and they still produce the same result. Studies also show that social relationships seem to protect individuals against many physical and psychological disorders, such as high blood pressure, depression, alcoholism, arthritis, the progression to AIDS, and low birth weight in newborns (Cobb, 1976; House, Landis, & Umberson, 1988; Leserman et al., 2000).

Even whether or not we come down with a cold is strongly influenced by the quality and extent of our social network. Cohen, Doyle, Skoner, Rabin, and Gwaltney (1997) used nasal drops to expose 276 healthy volunteers to one of two different rhinoviruses (cold viruses), then they quarantined the subjects for a week. The authors measured the extent of participation in 12 types of social relationships (for example, spouse, parent, friend, and colleague), as well as other factors, such as smoking and poor sleep quality, that are likely to increase susceptibility to colds. The surprising results were that the greater the extent of social ties, the smaller the chance of catching a cold, even after all other factors were taken into consideration (controlled for). Those with the fewest social ties were more than four times more likely to catch a cold than those with the greatest number of ties. This effect also extends to pets! Compared to people without pets, those with pets evidenced lower resting heart rate and blood pressure and

responded with smaller increases in these variables during laboratory stressors (Allen, Bloscovitch, & Mendes, 2002). What could account for this? Again, social and interpersonal factors seem to influence psychological and neurobiological variables such as the immune system—sometimes to a substantial degree. Thus, we cannot study psychological and biological aspects of psychological disorders (or physical disorders, for that matter) without taking into account the social and cultural context of the disorder.

That a multidimensional point of view is necessary is shown time and again. Consider a classic experiment with primates that illustrates the dangers of ignoring social context. Many monkeys were injected with amphetamine, a central nervous system stimulant (Haber & Barchas, 1983). Surprisingly, the drug had no reliable effect on the average behavior of the monkeys as a group. When the investigators divided the monkeys according to social dominance and submissiveness, however, dramatic effects appeared. Amphetamine increased dominant behaviors in primates that were high in the social hierarchy and submissive behaviors in those that were low in the hierarchy. Thus, the effects of a biological factor (the drug) on psychological characteristics (the behavior) were uninterpretable unless the social context of the experiment was considered.

Returning to human studies, how do social relationships have such a profound impact on our physical and psychological characteristics? We don't know for sure, but there are some intriguing hints. Some people think interpersonal relationships give meaning to life and that people who have something to live for can overcome physical deficiencies and even delay death. You may have known an elderly person who far outlived his or her expected time to witness a significant family event, such as a grandchild's graduation from college. Once the event has passed, the person dies. Another common observation is that if one spouse in a long-standing marital relationship dies, particularly an elderly wife, the other often dies soon after, regardless of health status. It is also possible that social relationships facilitate health-promoting behaviors, such as restraint in the use of alcohol and drugs, getting proper sleep, and seeking appropriate health care (House, Landis, & Umberson, 1988; Leserman et al., 2000).

Sometimes social upheaval is an opportunity for studying the impact of social networks on individual functioning. When the Sinai Peninsula was dismantled and evacuated as part of peace negotiations with Egypt, Steinglass, Weisstub, and Kaplan De-Nour (1988) studied residents of an Israeli community threatened with dissolution. They found that believing oneself embedded firmly in a social context was just as important as having a social network. Poor long-term adjustment was best predicted in those who *perceived* that their social network was disintegrating, regardless of whether it actually did or not.

In another example, whether you live in a city or the country may be associated with your chances of developing schizophrenia, a severe disorder. Lewis, David, Andreasson, and Allsbeck (1992) found that the incidence of schizophrenia was 38% greater in men who had been raised in cities than in those raised in rural areas. We have known for a long time that more schizophrenia exists in the city than in the country, but researchers thought people with schizophrenia who drifted to cities *after* developing schizophrenia or other endemic urban factors, such as drug use or unstable fam-

A long and productive life usually includes strong social relationships and interpersonal relations.

physically ill. This finding raises the unfortunate possibility that it may be advantageous for elderly people to become physically ill, because illness allows them to reestablish the social support that makes life worth living. If further research indicates this is true, involving their families before they become ill might help maintain their physical health (and significantly reduce health-care costs).

The study of older adults is growing at a rapid pace. The U.S. Census Bureau has estimated that by 2080 the number of people age 85 and older will grow from the current 3.3 million to 18.7 million. With this growth will come a corresponding increase in the number of older adults with mental health problems, many of whom will not receive appropriate care (Gatz & Smyer, 1992). As you can see, understanding and treating the disorders experienced by older adults is necessary and important.

ily relationships, might be the real culprit. But Lewis and associates carefully controlled for such factors, and it now seems something about cities beyond those influences may contribute to the development of schizophrenia. We do not yet know what it is. This finding, if it is replicated and shown to be true, may be important in view of the mass migration of individuals to overcrowded urban areas, particularly in less developed countries.

In summary, we cannot study psychopathology independently of social and interpersonal influences, and we still have much to learn. Juris Draguns (1990, 1995) and Fanny Cheung (1998) have nicely summarized our knowledge in concluding that many major psychological disorders, such as schizophrenia and major depressive disorder, seem to occur in all cultures but they may look different from one culture to another because individual symptoms are strongly influenced by social and interpersonal context. For example, as you will see in Chapter 7, depression in Western culture is reflected in feelings of guilt and inadequacy and in developing countries with physical distress such as fatigue or illness.

■ Social and Interpersonal Influences on the Elderly

Finally, the effect of social and interpersonal factors on the expression of physical and psychological disorders may differ with age. Grant, Patterson, and Yager (1988) studied 118 men and women 65 years or older who lived independently. Those with fewer meaningful contacts and less social support from relatives had consistently higher levels of depression and more reports of unsatisfactory quality of life. However, if these individuals became physically ill, they had more substantial support from their families than those who were not

■ Social Stigma

Other factors make the consideration of social and cultural issues imperative to the study of psychopathology. Psychological disorders continue to carry a substantial stigma in our society. To be anxious or depressed is to be weak and cowardly. To be schizophrenic is to be unpredictable and crazy. For physical injuries in times of war, we award medals. For psychological injuries, the unfortunate soldiers earn scorn and derision, as anyone knows who has seen the movies *Patton* or *Born on the Fourth of July*. Often, a patient with psychological disorders does not seek health insurance reimbursement for fear a coworker might learn about the problem. With far less social support than for physical illness, there is less chance of full recovery. We discuss some consequences of social attitudes toward psychological disorders in Chapter 16.

In developing countries, personal upheaval because of political strife affects mental health.

Global Incidence of Psychological Disorders

Behavioral and mental health problems in developing countries are exacerbated by political strife, technological change, and massive movements from rural to urban areas. An important study from the World Health Organization (WHO), reveals that 10% to 20% of all primary medical services in poor countries are sought by patients with psychological disorders, principally anxiety and mood disorders (including suicide attempts), as well as alcoholism, drug abuse, and childhood developmental disorders (WHO 2001). Record numbers of young men are committing suicide in Micronesia. Alcoholism levels among adults in Latin America have risen to 20%. Treatments for disorders such as depression and addictive behaviors that are successful in the United States can't be administered in countries where mental health care is limited. In Cambodia, after the bloody reign of the Khmer Rouge, all mental health professionals either died or disappeared. As of 2006, only 26 psychiatrists were available to see 12 million people. In sub–Saharan Africa it's even worse, with only 1 psychiatrist per 1 million people (Miller, 2006). In the United States, 200,000 mental health professionals serve 250 million people, yet only 1 in 3 people with a psychological disorder in the United States has ever received treatment of any kind. And yet, the goals of the wonderful efforts of the Bill and Melinda Gates Foundation, "Grand Challenges in Global Health," don't even mention mental health. These shocking statistics suggest that in addition to their role in causation, social and cultural factors substantially maintain disorders because most societies have not yet developed the social context for alleviating and ultimately preventing them. Changing society's attitude is just one of the challenges facing us as the century unfolds.

LIFE-SPAN DEVELOPMENT

Life-span developmental psychopathologists point out that we tend to look at psychological disorders from a snapshot perspective: We focus on a particular point in a person's life and assume it represents the whole person. The inadequacy of this way of looking at people should be clear. Think back on your own life over the past few years. The person you were, say, 3 years ago, is different from the person you are now, and the person you will be 3 years from now will have changed in important ways. To understand psychopathology, we must appreciate how experiences during different periods of development may influence our vulnerability to other types of stress or to differing psychological disorders (Rutter, 2002).

Important developmental changes occur at all points in life. For example, adulthood, far from being a relatively stable period, is highly dynamic, with important changes occurring into old age. Erik Erikson (1982) suggested that we go through eight major crises during our lives, each determined by our biological maturation and the social demands made at particular times. Unlike Freud, who envisioned no developmental stages beyond adolescence, Erikson believed that we grow and change beyond the age of 65. During older adulthood, for example, we look back and view our lives either as rewarding or as disappointing.

Although aspects of Erikson's theory of psychosocial development have been criticized as being too vague and not supported by research (Shaffer, 1993), it demonstrates the comprehensive approach to human development advocated by life-span developmen-

talists. Basic research is beginning to confirm the importance of this approach. In one experiment Kolb, Gibb, and Gorny (2003) placed animals in complex environments as juveniles, as adults, or in old age when cognitive abilities were beginning to decline (senescence). They found that the environment had different effects on the brains of these animals depending on their developmental stage. Basically, the complex and challenging environments increased the size and complexity of neurons in the motor and sensory cortical regions in the adult and aged animals, but unlike the older groups, decreased the spine density of neurons in young animals. Nevertheless, this decrease was associated with enhanced motor and cognitive skills when the animals became adults. Even prenatal experience seems to affect brain structure, because the offspring of an animal housed in a rich and complex environment during the term of her pregnancy have the advantage of more complex cortical brain circuits after birth (Kolb, Gibb, & Robinson, 2003). You may remember the study by Cameron et al. (2005) discussed earlier in the chapter, in which mother rats' behavior in this first week of their pups' lives, but not thereafter, strongly influenced the ability of the pups to handle stress throughout their lives.

Thus, we can infer that the influence of developmental stage and prior experience has a substantial impact on the development and presentation of psychological disorders, an inference that is receiving confirmation from sophisticated life-span developmental psychologists such as Laura Carstensen (Carstensen, Charles, Isaacowitz, & Kenney, 2003; Isaacowitz, Smith, & Carstensen, 2003). For example, in depressive (mood) disorders, children and adolescents do not receive the same benefit from antidepressant drugs as do adults (Hazell, O'Connell, Heathcote, Robertson, & Henry, 1995). Also, the gender distribution in depression is approximately equal until puberty, when it becomes more common in girls (Compas et al., 1997; Hankin et al., 1998).

■ The Principle of Equifinality

Like a fever, a particular behavior or disorder may have a number of causes. The principle of **equifinality** is used in developmental psychopathology to indicate that we must consider a number of paths to a given outcome (Cicchetti, 1991). There are many examples of this principle. A delusional syndrome may be an aspect of schizophrenia, but it can also arise from amphetamine abuse. Delirium, which involves difficulty focusing attention, often occurs in older adults after surgery, but it can also result from thiamine deficiency or renal (kidney) disease. Autism can sometimes occur in children whose mothers are exposed to rubella during pregnancy, but it can also occur in children whose mothers experience difficulties during labor.

Different paths can also result from the interaction of psychological and biological factors during various stages of development. How someone copes with impairment resulting from organic causes may have a profound effect on that person's overall functioning. For example, people with documented brain damage may have different levels of disorder. Those with healthy systems of social support, consisting of family and friends, as well as highly adaptive personality characteristics, such as marked confidence in their abilities to overcome challenges, may experience only mild behavioral and cognitive disturbance despite an organic pathology. Those without comparable support and personality may be incapacitated. This may be clearer if you think of people you know with physical disabilities. Some, paralyzed from the waist down by accident or disease (paraplegics), have nevertheless become superb athletes or accomplished in business or the arts. Others with the same condition are depressed and hopeless; they have withdrawn from life or, even worse, ended their lives. Even the content of delusions and hallucinations that may accompany a disorder, and the degree to which they are frightening or difficult to cope with, is partly determined by psychological and social factors.

Researchers are exploring not only what makes people experience particular disorders but also what protects others from having the same difficulties. If you were interested in why someone would be depressed, for example, you would first look at people who display depression. But you could also study people in similar situations and from similar backgrounds who are not depressed. An excellent example of this approach is research on "resilient" children, which suggests that social factors may protect some children from being hurt by stressful experiences, such as one or both parents suffering a psychiatric disturbance (Garmezy & Rutter, 1983; Hetherington & Blechman, 1996; Weiner, 2000). The presence of a caring adult friend or relative can offset the negative stresses of this environment, as can the child's own ability to understand and cope with unpleasant situations. Those of us brought up in violent or otherwise dysfunctional families who have successfully gone on to college might want to look back for the factors that protected us. Perhaps if we better understand why some people do not encounter the same problems as others in similar circumstances, we can better understand particular disorders, assist those who suffer from them, and even prevent some cases from occurring.

CONCLUSIONS

We have examined modern approaches to psychopathology, and we have found the field to be complex indeed. In this brief overview (even though it may not seem brief), we have seen that contributions from (1) psychoanalytic theory, (2) behavioral and cognitive science, (3) emotional influences, (4) social and cultural influences, (5) genetics, (6) neuroscience, and (7) life-span developmental factors all must be considered when we think about psychopathology. Even though our knowledge is incomplete, you can see why we could never resume the one-dimensional thinking typical of the various historical traditions described in Chapter 1.

And yet, books about psychological disorders and news reports in the popular press often describe the causes of these disorders in one-dimensional terms without considering other influences. For example, how many times have you heard that a psychological disorder such as depression, or perhaps schizophrenia, is caused by a "chemical imbalance" without considering other possible causes? When you read that a disorder is *caused* by a chemical imbalance, it sounds like nothing else really matters and all you have to do is correct the imbalance in neurotransmitter activity to "cure" the problem.

Based on research we review when we talk about specific psychological disorders, there is no question that psychological disorders are associated with altered neurotransmitter activity and other aspects of brain function (a chemical imbalance). But you have learned in this chapter that a "chemical imbalance" could, in turn, be caused by psychological or social factors such as stress, strong emotional reactions, difficult family interactions, changes

caused by aging, or, most likely, some interaction of all of these factors. Therefore, it is inaccurate and misleading to say that a psychological disorder is "caused" by a chemical imbalance, even though chemical imbalances almost certainly exist.

Similarly, how many times have you heard that alcoholism or other addictive behaviors were caused by "lack of willpower," implying that if these individuals simply developed the right attitude they could overcome their addiction? There is no question that people with severe addictions may well have faulty cognitive processes as indicated by rationalizing their behavior, or other faulty appraisals, or by attributing their problems to stress in their lives or some other "bogus" excuse. They may also misperceive the effects that alcohol has on them, and all of these cognitions and attitudes contribute to developing addictions. But considering only cognitive processes without considering other factors as causes of addictions would be as incorrect as saying that depression is caused by a chemical imbalance. Our genes play a role in the development of addictive behaviors, as you will learn in Chapter 11. There is also evidence that brain function in people suffering from addictions may well be different from brain function in those individuals who may ingest similar amounts of alcohol but not develop addictive behavior. Interpersonal, social, and cultural factors also contribute strongly to the development of addictive behaviors. To say, then, that addictive behaviors such as alcoholism are caused by lack of willpower or certain faulty ways of thinking is also highly simplistic and just plain wrong.

If you learn one thing from this book, it should be that psychological disorders do not have just one cause. They have many causes—these causes all interact with one another—and we must understand this interaction to appreciate fully the origins of psychological disorders. To do this requires a multidimensional integrative approach. In chapters covering specific psychological disorders, we return to cases like Judy's and consider them from this multidimensional integrative perspective. But first we must explore the processes of assessment and diagnosis used to measure and classify psychopathology.

CONCEPT CHECK 2.5

Fill in the blanks to complete these statements relating to the cultural, social, and developmental factors influencing psychopathology.

1. What we _____ is strongly influenced by our social environments.
2. The likelihood of your having a particular phobia is powerfully influenced by your _____.
3. A large number of studies have demonstrated that the greater the number and frequency of _____ relationships and _____, the longer you are likely to live.
4. The effect of social and interpersonal factors on the expression of physical and psychological disorders may differ with _____.
5. The principle of _____ is used in developmental psychopathology to indicate that we must consider a number of paths to a given outcome.

SUMMARY

One-Dimensional or Multidimensional Models

- The causes of abnormal behavior are complex and fascinating. You can say that psychological disorders are caused by nature (biology) and by nurture (psychosocial factors), and you would be right on both counts—but also wrong on both counts.

- To identify the causes of various psychological disorders, we must consider the interaction of all relevant dimensions: genetic contributions, the role of the nervous system, behavioral and cognitive processes, emotional influences, social and interpersonal influences, and developmental factors. Thus, we have arrived at a multidimensional integrative approach to the causes of psychological disorders.

Genetic Contributions to Psychopathology

- The genetic influence on much of our development and most of our behavior, personality, and even IQ score is polygenic—that is, influenced by many genes. This is assumed to be the case in abnormal behavior as well, although research is beginning to identify specific small groups of genes that relate to some major psychological disorders.

- In studying causal relationships in psychopathology, researchers look at the interactions of genetic and environmental effects. In the diathesis–stress model, individuals are assumed to inherit certain vulnerabilities that make them susceptible to a disorder when the right kind of stressor comes along. In the reciprocal gene–environment, or gene–environment correlation model, the individual's genetic vulnerability toward a certain disorder may make it more likely that the person will experience the stressor that, in turn, triggers the genetic vulnerability and thus the disorder.

Neuroscience and Its Contributions to Psychopathology

- The field of neuroscience promises much as we try to unravel the mysteries of psychopathology. Within the nervous system, levels of neurotransmitter and neuroendocrine activity interact in complex ways to modulate and regulate emotions and behavior and contribute to psychological disorders.

- Critical to our understanding of psychopathology are the neurotransmitter currents called brain circuits. Of the neurotransmitters that may play a key role, we investigated five: serotonin, gamma-aminobutyric acid (GABA), glutamate, norepinephrine, and dopamine.

Behavioral and Cognitive Science

- The relatively new field of cognitive science provides a valuable perspective on how behavioral and cognitive influences affect the learning and adaptation each of us experience throughout life. Clearly, such influences not only contribute to psychological disorders but also may directly modify brain functioning, brain structure, and even genetic expression. We examined some research in this field by looking at learned helplessness, modeling, prepared learning, and implicit memory.

Emotions

- Emotions have a direct and dramatic impact on our functioning and play a central role in many disorders. Mood, a persistent period of emotionality, is often evident in psychological disorders.

Cultural, Social, and Interpersonal Factors

- Social and interpersonal influences profoundly affect both psychological disorders and biology.

Life-Span Development

- In considering a multidimensional integrative approach to psychopathology, it is important to remember the principle of equifinality, which reminds us that we must consider the various paths to a particular outcome, not just the result.

Key Terms

multidimensional integrative approach, 31
genes, 34
diathesis–stress model, 36
vulnerability, 37
reciprocal gene–environment model, 38
neuroscience, 40
neuron, 40
synaptic cleft, 42

neurotransmitters, 42
hormone, 45
brain circuits, 46
reuptake, 46
agonist, 47
antagonist, 47
inverse agonist, 47
glutamate, 47

gamma-aminobutyric acid (GABA), 47
serotonin, 47
norepinephrine (also nor-adrenaline), 48
dopamine, 48
cognitive science, 54
learned helplessness, 54

modeling (also observational learning), 56
prepared learning, 56
implicit memory, 56
flight or fight response, 57
emotion, 58
mood, 58
affect, 58
equifinality, 64

Answers to Concept Checks

2.1

1. b; 2. a (best answer) or c; 3. e; 4. a (initial), c (maintenance)

2.2

1. F (first 22 pairs); 2. T; 3. T; 4. F (reciprocal gene–environment model); 5. F (complex interaction of both nature and nurture)

2.3

1. b; 2. c; 3. f; 4. g; 5. d; 6. e; 7. h; 8. a

2.4

1. b; 2. a; 3. d; 4. c

2.5

1. fear; 2. gender; 3. social, contacts; 4. age; 5. equifinality

The Abnormal Psychology Book Companion Website

See **academic.cengage.com/psychology/barlow** for practice quiz questions, interactive activities, Internet links, critical thinking exercises, discussion forums, and more. Also accessible from the Wadsworth Psychology Resource Center **(academic.cengage .com/login).**

Abnormal Psychology Live CD-ROM

- *Integrative Approach:* This clip summarizes the integrative approach, showing how psychological factors affect our biology and our brain influences our behavior.

 **CengageNOW**

Go to **academic.cengage.com/now** to link to CengageNOW, your online study tool. First take the Pre-Test for this chapter to get your personalized study plan, which will identify topics you need to review and direct you to online resources. Then take the Post-Test to determine what concepts you have mastered and what you still need work on.

Video Concept Reviews

CengageNOW also contains Mark Durand's *Video Concept Reviews* on challenging topics.

- Multidimensional Models
- Genetics: Phenotype and Genotype
- Genetics: Nature of Genes
- Genetics: Dominant Versus Recessive Genes
- Genetics: Polygenic
- Diathesis-Stress Model
- Concept Check—Reciprocal Gene-Environment Model
- Neuroscience
- Neuroimaging
- Neurons
- Neurotransmitters/Reuptake
- Agonist/Antagonist
- Implicit Memory/Stroop Test
- Emotion

CHAPTER 3

Clinical Assessment and Diagnosis

©Zigy Kaluzny/Getty Images

ASSESSING PSYCHOLOGICAL DISORDERS
Key Concepts in Assessment
The Clinical Interview
Physical Examination
Behavioral Assessment
Psychological Testing
Neuropsychological Testing
Neuroimaging: Pictures of the Brain
Psychophysiological Assessment

DIAGNOSING PSYCHOLOGICAL DISORDERS
Classification Issues
Diagnosis Before 1980

DSM-III
DSM-IV
Creating a Diagnosis
Conclusions

 ABNORMAL PSYCHOLOGY LIVE CD-ROM

Arriving at a Diagnosis
Psychological Assessment
Web Link

> *It is not the illness but the human being that needs help. As a doctor I am not concerned with the illness but with the human being.*

Georg Goddeck
The Meaning of Illness

ASSESSING PSYCHOLOGICAL DISORDERS

The processes of clinical assessment and diagnosis are central to the study of psychopathology and, ultimately, to the treatment of psychological disorders. **Clinical assessment** is the systematic evaluation and measurement of psychological, biological, and social factors in an individual presenting with a possible psychological disorder. **Diagnosis** is the process of determining whether the particular problem afflicting the individual meets all criteria for a psychological disorder, as set forth in the fourth edition, text revision, of the *Diagnostic and Statistical Manual of Mental Disorders,* or *DSM-IV-TR* (American Psychiatric Association, 2000). In this chapter, after demonstrating assessment and diagnosis within the context of an actual case, we examine the development of the DSM into a widely used classification system for abnormal behavior. Then we review the many assessment techniques available to the clinician. Finally, we turn to diagnostic issues and the related challenges of classification.

FRANK: Young, Serious, and Anxious

Frank was referred to one of our clinics for evaluation and possible treatment of severe distress and anxiety centering on his marriage. He arrived neatly dressed in his work clothes (he was a mechanic). He reported that he was 24 years old and that this was the first time he had ever seen a mental health professional. He wasn't sure that he needed (or wanted) to be there, but he felt he was beginning to "come apart" because of his marital difficulties. He figured that it certainly wouldn't hurt to come once to see whether we could help. What follows is a transcript of parts of this first interview.

THERAPIST: What sorts of problems have been troubling you during the past month?
FRANK: I'm beginning to have a lot of marital problems. I was married about 9 months ago, but I've been really tense around the house and we've been having a lot of arguments.
THERAPIST: Is this something recent?
FRANK: Well, it wasn't too bad at first, but it's been worse lately. I've also been really uptight in my job, and I haven't been getting my work done.

Note that we always begin by asking the patient to describe for us, in a relatively open-ended way, the major difficul-

ties that brought him or her to the office. When dealing with adults, or children old enough (or verbal enough) to tell us their story, this strategy tends to break the ice. It also allows us to relate details of the patient's life revealed later in the interview to the central problems as seen through the patient's eyes.

After Frank described this major problem in some detail, we asked him about his marriage, his job, and other current life circumstances. Frank reported that he had worked steadily in an auto body repair shop for the past 4 years and that, 9 months previously, he had married a 17-year-old woman. After getting a better picture of his current situation, we returned to his feeling of distress and anxiety.

THERAPIST: When you feel uptight at work, is it the same kind of feeling you have at home?
FRANK: Pretty much; I just can't seem to concentrate, and lots of times I lose track of what my wife's saying to me, which makes her mad and then we'll have a big fight.
THERAPIST: Are you thinking about something when you lose your concentration, such as your work, or maybe other things?
FRANK: Oh, I don't know; I guess I just worry a lot.
THERAPIST: What do you find yourself worrying about most of the time?
FRANK: Well, I worry about getting fired and then not being able to support my family. A lot of the time I feel like I'm going to catch something—you know, get sick and not be able to work. Basically I guess I'm afraid of getting sick and then failing at my job and in my marriage, and having my parents and her parents both telling me what an ass I was for getting married in the first place.

During the first 10 minutes or so of the interview, Frank seemed to be quite tense and anxious and would often look down at the floor while he talked, glancing up only occasionally to make eye contact. Sometimes his right leg would twitch a bit. Although it was not easy to see at first because he was looking down, Frank was also closing his eyes tightly for a period of 2 to 3 seconds. It was during these periods when his eyes were closed that his right leg would twitch.

The interview proceeded for the next half hour, exploring marital and job issues. It became increasingly clear that Frank was feeling inadequate and anxious about handling situations in his life. By this time, he was talking freely and looking up a little more at the therapist, but he was continuing to close his eyes and twitch his right leg slightly.

THERAPIST: Are you aware that once in a while you're closing your eyes while you're telling me this?
FRANK: I'm not aware all the time, but I know I do it.
THERAPIST: Do you know how long you've been doing that?
FRANK: Oh, I don't know, maybe a year or two.
THERAPIST: Are you thinking about anything when you close your eyes?

FRANK: Well, actually I'm trying not to think about something.

THERAPIST: What do you mean?

FRANK: Well, I have these really frightening and stupid thoughts, and . . . it's hard to even talk about it.

THERAPIST: The thoughts are frightening?

FRANK: Yes, I keep thinking I'm going to take a fit, and I'm just trying to get that out of my mind.

THERAPIST: Could you tell me more about this fit?

FRANK: Well, you know, it's those terrible things where people fall down and they froth at the mouth, and their tongues come out, and they shake all over. You know, seizures. I think they call it epilepsy.

THERAPIST: And you're trying to get these thoughts out of your mind?

FRANK: Oh, I do everything possible to get those thoughts out of my mind as quickly as I can.

THERAPIST: I've noticed you moving your leg when you close your eyes. Is that part of it?

FRANK: Yes, I've noticed if I really jerk my leg and pray real hard for a little while the thought will go away.

(Excerpt from Nelson, R. O., & Barlow, D. H., 1981. Behavioral assessment: Basic strategies and initial procedures. In D. H. Barlow, Ed., *Behavioral assessment of adult disorders.* New York: Guilford Press.)

What's wrong with Frank? The first interview reveals an insecure young man experiencing substantial stress as he questions whether he is capable of handling marriage and a job. He reports that he loves his wife very much and wants the marriage to work and he is attempting to be as conscientious as possible on his job, a job from which he derives a lot of satisfaction and enjoyment. Also, for some reason, he is having troubling thoughts about seizures. Now let's consider one more case for purposes of illustration.

Brian was 20 years old and had recently been discharged from a tour of duty in the army. He was referred by a psychiatrist in another state for evaluation of sexual problems. What follows is a greatly abbreviated transcript.

THERAPIST: What seems to be the problem?

BRIAN: I'm a homosexual.

THERAPIST: You're a homosexual?

BRIAN: Yes, and I want to be straight. Who wants to be queer?

THERAPIST: Do you have any homosexual friends or lovers?

BRIAN: No, I wouldn't get near them.

THERAPIST: How often do you engage in homosexual behavior?

BRIAN: Well, I haven't as of yet, but it's no secret that I'm homosexual, and it's just a matter of time before it happens, I suppose.

THERAPIST: Do you have somebody specifically in mind? Are you attracted to somebody?

BRIAN: No, but others are attracted to me. I can tell by the way they look at me.

THERAPIST: The way they look at you?

BRIAN: Yes, the look in their eyes.

THERAPIST: Has anyone ever actually approached you or said anything to you about being homosexual?

BRIAN: No, not to me; they wouldn't dare. But I know they talk about me behind my back.

THERAPIST: How do you know that?

BRIAN: Well, sometimes the guys will be talking in the next room and the only thing they could be talking about is that I'm queer. (Nelson & Barlow, 1981, p. 20)

So where do we go from here? How do we determine whether Frank has a psychological disorder or if he is simply one of many young men suffering the normal stresses and strains of a new marriage who, perhaps, could benefit from some marital counseling? And what about Brian? Where do you think he got those ideas? The purpose of this chapter is to illustrate how mental health clinicians address these types of questions in a systematic way, assessing patients to study the basic nature of psychopathology, as well as to make diagnoses and plan treatment.

During their first meeting, the mental health professional focuses on the problem that brought the person to treatment.

Key Concepts in Assessment

The process of clinical assessment in psychopathology has been likened to a funnel (Hawkins, 1979; Peterson, 1968). The clinician begins by collecting a lot of information across a broad range of the individual's functioning to determine where the source of the problem may lie. After getting a preliminary sense of the overall functioning of the person, the clinician narrows the focus by ruling out problems in some areas and concentrating on areas that seem most relevant.

To understand the different ways clinicians assess psychological problems, we need to understand three basic concepts that help determine the value of our assessments: reliability, validity, and standardization (see ■ Figure 3.1). Assessment techniques are subject to a number of strict requirements, not the least of which is some evidence (research) that they actually do what they are designed to do. One of the more important requirements of these assessments is that they be reliable. **Reliability** is the degree to which a measurement is consistent. Imagine how irritated you would be if you had stomach pain and you went to four competent physicians and got four different diagnoses and four different treatments. The diagnoses would be said to be unreliable because two or more "raters" (the physicians) did not agree on the conclusion. We expect, in general, that presenting the same symptoms to different physicians will result in similar diagnoses. One way psychologists improve their reliability is by carefully designing their assessment devices and then conducting research on them to ensure that two or more raters will get the same answers (called *interrater reliability*). They also determine whether these techniques are stable across time. In other words, if you go to a clinician on Tuesday and are told you have an IQ of 110, you should expect a similar result if you take the same test again on Thursday. This is known as *test–retest reliability*. We return to the concept of reliability when we talk of diagnoses and classification.

Validity is whether something measures what it is designed to measure—in this case, whether a technique assesses what it is supposed to. Comparing the results of an assessment measure under consideration with the results of others that are better known allows you to begin to determine the validity of the first measure. This comparison is called *concurrent* or *descriptive validity*. For example, if the results from a standard, but long, IQ test were essentially the same as the results from a new, brief version, you could conclude that the brief version had concurrent validity. Predictive validity is how well your assessment tells you what will happen in the future. For example, does it predict who will succeed in school and who will not, which is one of the goals of an IQ test?

Standardization is the process by which a certain set of standards or norms is determined for a technique to make its use consistent across different measurements. The standards might apply to the procedures of testing, scoring, and evaluating data. For example, the assessment might be given to large numbers of people who differ on important factors such as age, race, gender, socioeconomic status, and diagnosis; their scores would then be used as a standard, or norm, with others like them, for comparison purposes. For example, if you are an African American male, 19 years old, and from a middle-class background, your score on a psychological test should be compared to the scores of others like you and not to the scores of different people, such as a group of women of Asian descent in their 60s from working-class backgrounds. Reliability, validity, and standardization are important to all forms of psychological assessment.

Clinical assessment consists of a number of strategies and procedures that help clinicians acquire the information they need to understand their patients and assist them. These procedures include a clinical interview and, within the context of the interview, a mental status exam that can be administered either formally or informally; often a thorough physical examination; a behavioral observation and assessment; and psychological tests (if needed).

The Clinical Interview

The clinical interview, the core of most clinical work, is used by psychologists, psychiatrists, and other mental health professionals. The interview gathers information on current and past behavior, attitudes, and emotions, as well as a detailed history of the individual's life in general and of the presenting problem. Clinicians determine when the specific problem started and identify other events (for example, life stress, trauma, or physical illness) that might have occurred about the same time. In addition, most clinicians gather at least some information on the patient's current and past interpersonal and social history, including family makeup (for example, marital status, number of children, or college student currently living with parents), and on the individual's upbringing. Information on sexual development, religious attitudes (current and past), relevant cultural concerns (such as stress induced by discrimination), and educational history are also routinely collected. To organize information obtained during an interview, many clinicians use a **mental status exam.**

■ The Mental Status Exam

In essence, the mental status exam involves the systematic observation of somebody's behavior. This type of observation occurs when any one person interacts with another. All of us, clinicians

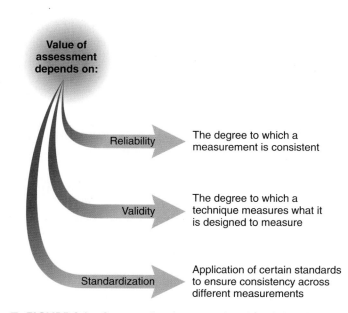

■ **FIGURE 3.1** Concepts that determine the value of clinical assessments.

and nonclinicians alike, perform daily pseudo-mental status exams. The trick for clinicians is to organize their observations of other people in a way that gives them sufficient information to determine whether a psychological disorder might be present (Nelson & Barlow, 1981). Mental status exams can be structured and detailed (Wing, Cooper, & Sartorius, 1974), but mostly they are performed relatively quickly by experienced clinicians in the course of interviewing or observing a patient. The exam covers five categories:

1. *Appearance and behavior.* The clinician notes any overt physical behaviors, such as Frank's leg twitch, as well as the individual's dress, general appearance, posture, and facial expression. For example, slow and effortful motor behavior, sometimes referred to as *psychomotor retardation,* may indicate severe depression.

2. *Thought processes.* When clinicians listen to a patient talk, they're getting a good idea of that person's thought processes. They might look for several things here. For example, what is the rate or flow of speech? Does the person talk quickly or slowly? What about continuity of speech? In other words, does the patient make sense when talking, or are ideas presented with no apparent connection? In some patients with schizophrenia, a disorganized speech pattern, referred to as *loose association* or *derailment,* is quite noticeable. Clinicians sometimes ask specific questions. If the patient shows difficulty with continuity or rate of speech, a clinician might ask, "Can you think clearly, or is there some problem putting your thoughts together? Do your thoughts tend to be mixed up or come slowly?"

   In addition to rate or flow and continuity of speech, what about the content? Is there any evidence of *delusions* (distorted views of reality)? Typical delusions would be *delusions of persecution,* in which someone thinks people are after him and out to get him all the time, or *delusions of grandeur,* in which one individual thinks she is all-powerful in some way. The individual might also have *ideas of reference,* in which everything everyone else does somehow relates back to the individual. The most common example would be thinking that a conversation between two strangers on the other side of the room must be about you. *Hallucinations* are things a person sees or hears when those things really aren't there. For example, the clinician might say, "Let me ask you a couple of routine questions that we ask everybody. Do you ever see things or maybe hear things when you know there is nothing there?"

   Now think back to the case of Brian. Extensive questioning of Brian revealed no evidence of homosexual arousal patterns, fantasies, or behavior. In fact, he had been quite active heterosexually over the past several years and had strong patterns of heterosexual fantasies. What would you say about Brian's thought processes during the interview? What kinds of ideas was he expressing? Notice the conclusion he drew when he happened to see other men looking at him. What did he think when a group of men happened to have a conversation he was not part of? This would be an example of ideas of reference. That is, Brian thought everything that anyone else did or said referred to him. However, his strongly held conviction about his homosexuality had no basis in reality. It was a delusion. On the other hand, his negative attitudes toward homosexuality, referred to as *homophobia,* were clearly evident.

3. *Mood and affect.* Determining mood and affect is an important part of the mental status exam. *Mood* is the predominant feeling state of the individual, as we noted in Chapter 2. Does the person appear to be down in the dumps or continually elated? Does the individual talk in a depressed or hopeless fashion? How pervasive is this mood? Are there times when the depression seems to go away? *Affect,* by contrast, refers to the feeling state that accompanies what we say at a given point. Usually our affect is "appropriate"; that is, we laugh when we say something funny or look sad when we talk about something sad. If a friend just told you his mother died and is laughing about it, or if your friend has just won the lottery and she is crying, you would think it strange, to say the least. A mental health clinician would note that your friend's affect is "inappropriate." Then again, you might observe your friend talking about a range of happy and sad things with no affect whatsoever. In this case, a mental health clinician would say the affect is "blunted" or "flat."

4. *Intellectual functioning.* Clinicians make a rough estimate of others' intellectual functioning just by talking to them. Do they seem to have a reasonable vocabulary? Can they talk in abstractions and metaphors (as most of us do much of the time)? How is the person's memory? Clinicians usually make some gross or rough estimate of intelligence that is noticeable only if it deviates from normal, such as concluding the person is above or below average intelligence.

5. *Sensorium.* *Sensorium* is our general awareness of our surroundings. Do the individuals know what the date is, what time it is, where they are, who they are, and who you are? Most of us are fully aware of these facts. People with permanent brain damage or dysfunction—or temporary brain damage or dysfunction, often because of drugs or other toxic states—may not know the answer to these questions. If the patient knows who he is and who the clinician is and has a good idea of the time and place, the clinician would say that the patient's sensorium is "clear" and is "oriented times three" (to person, place, and time).

What can we conclude from these informal behavioral observations? Basically, they allow the clinician to make a preliminary determination of which areas of the patient's behavior and condition should be assessed in more detail and perhaps more formally. If psychological disorders remain a possibility, the clinician may begin to hypothesize which disorders might be present. This process, in turn, provides more focus for the assessment and diagnostic activities to come.

Returning to our case, what have we learned from this mental status exam (see ■ Figure 3.2)? Observing Frank's persistent motor behavior in the form of a twitch led to the discovery of a connection (functional relationship) with some troublesome thoughts regarding seizures. Beyond this, his appearance was appropriate, and the flow and content of his speech was reasonable; his intelligence was well within normal limits, and he was oriented times three. He did display an anxious mood; however, his

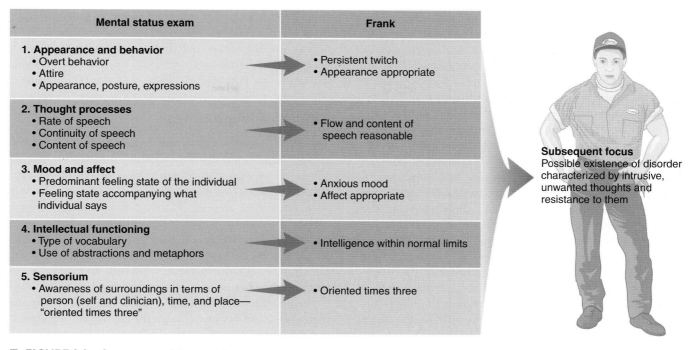

Mental status exam	Frank
1. Appearance and behavior • Overt behavior • Attire • Appearance, posture, expressions	• Persistent twitch • Appearance appropriate
2. Thought processes • Rate of speech • Continuity of speech • Content of speech	• Flow and content of speech reasonable
3. Mood and affect • Predominant feeling state of the individual • Feeling state accompanying what individual says	• Anxious mood • Affect appropriate
4. Intellectual functioning • Type of vocabulary • Use of abstractions and metaphors	• Intelligence within normal limits

5. Sensorium
• Awareness of surroundings in terms of
  person (self and clinician), time, and place—
  "oriented times three"
	• Oriented times three

Subsequent focus
Possible existence of disorder characterized by intrusive, unwanted thoughts and resistance to them

■ **FIGURE 3.2**   Components of the mental status exam.

affect was appropriate to what he was saying. These observations suggested that we direct the remainder of the clinical interview and additional assessment and diagnostic activities to identify the possible existence of a disorder characterized by intrusive, unwanted thoughts and the attempt to resist them—in other words, *obsessive-compulsive disorder (OCD)*. Later we describe some specific assessment strategies, from among many choices, that we would use with Frank.

Patients usually have a good idea of their major concerns in a general sense ("I'm depressed" or "I'm phobic"); occasionally, the problem reported by the patient may not, after assessment, be the major issue in the eyes of the mental health clinician. The case of Frank illustrates this point well: He complained of distress relating to marital problems, but the clinician decided, on the basis of the initial interview, that the principal difficulties lay elsewhere. Frank wasn't attempting to hide anything from the clinician. Frank just didn't think his intrusive thoughts were the major problem; in addition, talking about them was difficult for him because they were quite frightening.

This example illustrates the importance of conducting the clinical interview in a way that elicits the patient's trust and empathy. Psychologists and other mental health professionals are trained extensively in methods that put patients at ease and facilitate communication, including nonthreatening ways of seeking information and appropriate listening skills. Information provided by patients to psychologists and psychiatrists is protected by laws of "privileged communication" or confidentiality in most states; that is, even if authorities want the information the therapist has received from the patient, they cannot have access to it without the expressed consent of the patient. The only exception to this rule occurs when the clinician judges that, because of the patient's condition, some harm or danger to either the patient or someone else is imminent. At the outset of the initial interview, the therapist

should inform the patient of the confidential nature of their conversation and the (quite rare) conditions under which that confidence would not hold.

Despite these assurances of confidentiality and the clinician's interview skills, patients sometimes find it difficult to volunteer sensitive information. In our own files is the case of a man in his early 20s who came to therapy once a week for 5 months. He wanted help with what he viewed as deficient interpersonal skills and anxieties that were impeding his ability to relate to other people. Only after 5 months, and quite by chance during a particularly emotional session, did he reveal his secret. He was strongly sexually attracted to small boys and confessed that he found their feet and associated objects such as socks and shoes to be nearly irresistible. Although he had never actually approached any young boys, he had hidden in his home a large collection of small socks and shoes. Confidentiality had been assured, and the therapist was there to help. Nevertheless, the patient found it almost impossible to volunteer this information. There may well have been signs that something else was going on during the 5 months of treatment, but if there were, the therapist missed them.

■ Semistructured Clinical Interviews

Until relatively recently, most clinicians, after training, developed their own methods of collecting necessary information from patients. Different patients seeing different psychologists or other mental health professionals might encounter markedly different types and styles of interviews. Unstructured interviews follow no systematic format. *Semistructured interviews* are made up of questions that have been carefully phrased and tested to elicit useful information in a consistent manner so that clinicians can be sure they have inquired about the most important aspects of particular disorders. Clinicians may also depart from set questions to follow up on specific issues—thus the label "semistructured." Because the wording and sequencing of questions has been carefully worked out over a number of years, the clinician can feel confident that a semistructured interview will accomplish its purpose. The disadvantage is that it robs the interview of some of the spontaneous quality of two people talking about a problem. Also, if applied too rigidly, this type of interview may inhibit the patient from volunteering useful information that is not directly relevant to the questions being asked. Therefore, fully structured interviews administered wholly by a computer have not caught on, although they are used in some settings. An increasing number of mental health professionals routinely use semistructured interviews. Some are quite specialized. For example, Frank's clinician, in probing further into a possible obsessive-compulsive disorder, might use the *Anxiety Disorders Interview Schedule for DSM-IV (ADIS-IV)* (DiNardo, Brown, & Barlow, 1994). According to this interview schedule, shown in Table 3.1, the clinician first asks if the patient is bothered by thoughts, images, or impulses (obsessions) or feels driven to experience some behavior or thought repeatedly (compulsions). Based on an 8-point rating scale that ranges from "never" to "constantly," the clinician then asks the patient to rate each obsession on two measures: persistence–distress (how often it occurs and how much distress it causes) and resistance (types of attempts the patient makes to get rid of the obsession). For compulsions, the patient provides a rating of their frequency.

Physical Examination

Many patients with problems first go to a family physician and are given a physical. If the patient presenting with psychological problems has not had a physical exam in the past year, a clinician might recommend one, with particular attention to the medical conditions sometimes associated with the specific psychological problem. Many problems presenting as disorders of behavior, cognition, or mood may, on careful physical examination, have a clear relationship to a temporary toxic state. This toxic state could be caused by bad food, the wrong amount or type of medicine, or onset of a medical condition. For example, thyroid difficulties, particularly hyperthyroidism (overactive thyroid gland), may produce symptoms that mimic certain anxiety disorders, such as generalized anxiety disorder. Hypothyroidism (underactive thyroid gland) might produce symptoms consistent with depression. Certain psychotic symptoms, including delusions or hallucinations, might be associated with the development of a brain tumor. Withdrawal from cocaine often produces panic attacks, but many patients presenting with panic attacks are reluctant to volunteer information about their addiction, which may lead to an inappropriate diagnosis and improper treatment.

Usually, psychologists and other mental health professionals are well aware of the medical conditions and drug use and abuse that may contribute to the kinds of problems described by the patient. If a current medical condition or substance abuse situation exists, the clinician must ascertain whether it is merely coexisting or is causal, usually by looking at the onset of the problem. If a patient has suffered from severe bouts of depression for the past 5 years but within the past year has also developed hypothyroid problems or begun taking a sedative drug, then we would not conclude the depression was caused by the medical or drug condition. If the depression developed simultaneously with the initiation of sedative drugs and diminished considerably when the drugs were discontinued, we would be likely to conclude the depression was part of a substance-induced mood disorder.

Behavioral Assessment

The mental status exam is one way to begin to sample how people think, feel, and behave and how these actions might contribute to or explain their problems. **Behavioral assessment** takes this process one step further by using direct observation to assess formally an individual's thoughts, feelings, and behavior in specific situations or contexts. Indeed, behavioral assessment may be more appropriate than any interview in terms of assessing individuals who are not old enough or skilled enough to report their problems and experiences. Clinical interviews sometimes provide limited assessment information. For instance, young children or individuals who are not verbal because of the nature of their disorder or because of cognitive deficits or impairments are not good candidates for clinical interviews. As we already mentioned, sometimes people withhold information deliberately because it is embarrassing or unintentionally because they aren't aware it is important. In addition to talking with a patient in an office about a problem, some clinicians go to the person's home or workplace or even into the local community to observe the person and the reported problems directly. Others set up role-play simulations in a clinical setting to see how people might behave in similar situations in their daily lives. These techniques are all types of behavioral assessment.

In behavioral assessment, target behaviors are identified and observed with the goal of determining the factors that seem to influence them. It may seem easy to identify what is bothering a particular person (that is, the target behavior), but even this aspect of assessment can be challenging. For example, when the mother of a 7-year-old child with a severe conduct disorder came to one of our clinics for assistance, she told the clinician, after much prodding, that her son "didn't listen to her" and he sometimes had an "attitude." The boy's schoolteacher, however, painted a different picture. She spoke candidly of his verbal violence—of his threats toward other children and to herself, threats she took seriously. To get a clearer picture of the situation at home, the clinician visited one afternoon. Approximately 15 minutes after the visit began, the boy got up from the kitchen table without removing the drinking glass he was using. When his mother quite meekly asked him to put the glass in the sink, he picked it up and threw it across the room, sending broken glass throughout the kitchen. He giggled and went into his room to watch television. "See," she said. "He doesn't listen to me!"

Obviously, this mother's description of her son's behavior at home didn't portray what he was really like. It also didn't accurately describe her response to his violent outbursts. Without the home visit, the clinician's assessment of the problem and recommendations for treatment would have been different. Clearly this was more than simple disobedience. We developed strategies to teach the mother how to make requests of her son and how to follow up if he was violent.

TABLE 3.1   Sample Questions for Assessing Obsessive-Compulsive Disorder

I. Initial inquiry

   a. Currently, are you bothered by thoughts, images, or impulses that keep recurring to you and seem inappropriate or nonsensical but that you can't stop from coming into your mind?   yes _____ no _____

     If YES, specify:_____

   _____

   b. Currently, do you feel driven to repeat some behavior or to repeat something in your mind to try to feel less uncomfortable?

                                                                                             yes _____ no _____

     If YES, specify: _____

Obsessions:

For each obsession, make separate ratings of persistence–distress and resistance using the scales and suggested queries that follow.

Persistence–distress:

How often does the obsession enter your mind? How distressing is it to you when _____ enters your mind? (What is the time frame?)

0	1	2	3	4	5	6	7	8
Never/		Rarely/		Occasionally/		Frequently/		Constantly/
no distress		mild distress		moderate distress		marked distress		extreme distress

Resistance:

How often do you attempt to get rid of the obsession by ignoring, suppressing, or trying to neutralize it with some thought or action?

0	1	2	3	4	5	6	7	8
Never		Rarely		Occasionally		Frequently		Constantly

Current obsession	Persistence–distress	Resistance	Comments
a. Doubting (for example, locks, turning appliances off, and completion or accuracy of tasks)	_____	_____	_____
b. Contamination (for example, contracting germs from doorknobs, toilets, or money)	_____	_____	_____
c. Nonsensical impulses (for example, shouting or undressing in public)	_____	_____	_____
d. Aggressive impulses (for example, hurting self or others intentionally or destroying objects)	_____	_____	_____
e. Sexual (for example, obscene thoughts or images)	_____	_____	_____
f. Religious or satanic (for example, blasphemous thoughts or impulses)	_____	_____	_____
g. Accidental harm to others (for example, poisoning or hurting someone unknowingly)	_____	_____	_____
h. Horrific images (for example, mutilated bodies)	_____	_____	_____
i. Nonsensical thoughts or images (for example, numbers, letters, or songs)	_____	_____	_____
j. Other	_____	_____	_____
k. Other	_____	_____	_____

(continued)

TABLE 3.1   (continued)

For each compulsion, make ratings of frequency using the scale and suggested queries that follow.

Frequency:

How often are you driven to perform such an action? (What is the time frame?)

0	1	2	3	4	5	6	7	8
Never		Rarely		Occasionally		Frequently		Constantly

Current compulsion	Frequency	Comments
a. Counting (for example, certain letters or numbers or other objects in the environment)		
b. Checking (for example, locks, appliances, driving routes, important papers, or wastebaskets)		
c. Washing		
d. Hoarding (for example, newspapers, garbage, or trivial items)		
e. Internal repetition (for example, phrases, words, or prayers)		
f. Adhering to certain rules or sequences (for example, ensuring symmetry, performing ritualistic acts, or adhering to a specific routine for daily activities)		
g. Other		
h. Other		

Source: *Adapted and reprinted, with permission, from DiNardo, P.A., Brown, T.A., & Barlow, D. H., 1994.* Anxiety Disorders Interview Schedule for DSM-IV (ADIS-IV). *New York, NY: Oxford University Press.*

To go back to Frank and his anxiety about his marriage, how do we know he is telling the "truth" about his relationship with his wife? Is what he is not telling us important? What would we find if we observed Frank and his wife interacting in their home, or if they had a typical conversation in front of us in a clinical setting? Most clinicians assume that a complete picture of a person's problems requires direct observation in naturalistic environments. But going into a person's home, workplace, or school isn't always possible or practical, so clinicians sometimes arrange *analog,* or similar, settings (Roberts, 2001). For example, one of us studies children with autism (a disorder characterized by social withdrawal and communication problems; see Chapter 14). The reasons for self-hitting (called *self-injurious*) behavior are discovered by placing the children in simulated classroom situations, such as sitting alone at a desk, working in a group, or being asked to complete a difficult task (Durand, 2003). Observing how they behave in these different situations helps clinicians determine why they hit themselves so that they can design a successful treatment to eliminate the behavior.

Some areas of psychopathology are difficult to study without resorting to analog models. For instance, one study examined the tendency of some men to sexually harass women (Nagayama Hall, DeGarmo, Eap, Teten, & Sue, 2006). They showed the men two films—one with potentially offensive sexual content and one without—and then had them choose which film to watch with a woman who was (unbeknownst to them) part of the study. Choosing to show the potentially embarrassing film corresponded

with the men's self-reports of previous sexually coercive behavior. These types of observations are useful when developing screenings and treatments.

■ The ABCs of Observation

Observational assessment is usually focused on the here and now. Therefore, the clinician's attention is usually directed to the immediate behavior, its antecedents (what happened just before the behavior), and its consequences (what happened afterward) (Hersen, 2006). To use the example of the violent boy, an observer would note that the sequence of events was (1) his mother asking him to put his glass in the sink (antecedent), (2) the boy throwing the glass (behavior), and (3) his mother's lack of response (consequence). This antecedent–behavior–consequence sequence (the ABCs) might suggest that the boy was being reinforced for his violent outburst by not having to clean up his mess. And because there was no negative consequence for his behavior (his mother didn't scold or reprimand him), he will probably act violently the next time he doesn't want to do something (see ■ Figure 3.3).

This is an example of a relatively *informal observation*. A problem with this type of observation is that it relies on the observer's recollection, as well as interpretation, of the events. *Formal observation* involves identifying specific behaviors that are observable and measurable (called an *operational definition*). For example, it would be difficult for two people to agree on what "having an attitude" looks like. An operational definition, however, clarifies this behavior by specifying that this is "any time the boy does not comply

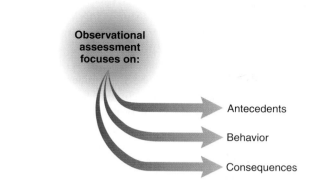

FIGURE 3.3 The ABCs of observation.

with his mother's reasonable requests." Once the target behavior is selected and defined, an observer writes down each time it occurs, along with what happened just before (antecedent) and just after (consequence). The goal of collecting this information is to see whether there are any obvious patterns of behavior and then to design a treatment based on these patterns.

People can also observe their own behavior to find patterns, a technique known as *self-monitoring* or *self-observation* (Haynes, 2000). People trying to quit smoking may write down the number of cigarettes they smoke and the times when and places where they smoke. This observation can tell them exactly how big their problem is (for example, they smoke two packs a day) and what situations lead them to smoke more (for example, talking on the phone). When behaviors occur only in private (such as purging by people with bulimia), self-monitoring is essential. Because the people with the problem are in the best position to observe their own behavior throughout the day, clinicians often ask patients to self-monitor their behavior to get more detailed information.

A more formal and structured way to observe behavior is through checklists and *behavior rating scales,* which are used as assessment tools before treatment and then periodically during treatment to assess changes in the person's behavior (Blacker, 2005; Myers & Collett, 2006). Of the many such instruments for assessing a variety of behaviors, the *Brief Psychiatric Rating Scale* (Lachar et al., 2001), which can be completed by staff, assesses 18 general areas of concern. Each symptom is rated on a 7-point scale from 0 (not present) to 6 (extremely severe). The rating scale screens for moderate to severe psychotic disorders and includes such items as somatic concern (preoccupation with physical health, fear of physical illness, hypochondriasis), guilt feelings (self-blame, shame, remorse for past behavior), and grandiosity (exaggerated self-opinion, arrogance, conviction of unusual power or abilities) (American Psychiatric Association, 2006).

A phenomenon known as *reactivity* can distort any observational data. Any time you observe how people behave, the mere fact of your presence may cause them to change their behavior (Hersen, 2006). To test reactivity, you can tell a friend you are going to record every time she says the word *like.* Just before you reveal your intent, however, count the times your friend uses this word in a 5-minute period. You will probably find that your friend uses the word less often when you are recording it. Your friend will react to the observation by changing the behavior. The

same phenomenon occurs if you observe your own behavior, or self-monitor. Behaviors people want to increase, such as talking more in class, tend to increase, and behaviors people want to decrease, such as smoking, tend to decrease when they are self-monitored (for example, Hufford, Shields, Shiffman, Paty, & Balabanis, 2002). Clinicians sometimes depend on the reactivity of self-monitoring to increase the effectiveness of their treatments.

Psychological Testing

We are confronted with so-called psychological tests in the popular press almost every week: "12 Questions to Test Your Relationship," "Every Guy's Private Marriage Checklist," "Are You a Type 'Z' Personality?" Although we may not want to admit it, many of us have probably purchased a magazine at some point to take one of these tests. Many are no more than entertainment, designed to make you think about the topic (and to make you buy the magazine). They are typically made up for the purposes of the article and include questions that, on the surface, seem to make sense. We are interested in these tests because we want to understand better why we and our friends behave the way we do. In reality, they usually tell us little.

In contrast, the tests used to assess psychological disorders must meet the strict standards we have noted. They must be reliable so that two or more people administering the same test to the same person will come to the same conclusion about the problem, and they must be valid so that they measure what they say they are measuring.

Psychological tests include specific tools to determine cognitive, emotional, or behavioral responses that might be associated with a specific disorder and more general ones that assess long-standing personality features, such as a tendency to be suspicious. Specialized areas include intelligence testing to determine the structure and patterns of cognition. Neuropsychological testing determines the possible contribution of brain damage or dysfunction to the patient's condition. Neuroimaging uses sophisticated technology to assess brain structure and function.

■ Projective Testing

We saw in Chapter 1 how Sigmund Freud brought to our attention the presence and influence of unconscious processes in psychological disorders. At this point we should ask, "If people aren't aware of these thoughts and feelings, how do we assess them?" To address this intriguing problem, psychoanalytic workers developed several assessment measures known as **projective tests.** They include a variety of methods in which ambiguous stimuli, such as pictures of people or things, are presented to people who are asked to describe what they see. The theory here is that people project their own personality and unconscious fears onto other people and things—in this case, the ambiguous stimuli—and, without realizing it, reveal their unconscious thoughts to the therapist.

Because these tests are based in psychoanalytic theory, they have been, and remain, controversial. Even so, the use of projective tests is quite common, with a majority of clinicians administering them at least occasionally and most doctoral programs providing training in their use (Durand, Blanchard, & Mindell, 1988). Three of the more widely used are the Rorschach inkblot test, the Thematic Apperception Test, and the sentence-completion method.

More than 80 years ago, a Swiss psychiatrist named Hermann Rorschach developed a series of inkblots, initially to study perceptual processes, then to diagnose psychological disorders. The *Rorschach inkblot test* is one of the early projective tests. In its current form, the test includes 10 inkblot pictures that serve as the ambiguous stimuli (see ■ Figure 3.4). The examiner presents the inkblots one by one to the person being assessed, who responds by telling what he sees.

Although Rorschach advocated a scientific approach to studying the answers to the test (Rorschach, 1951), he died at the age of 38, before he had fully developed his method of systematic interpretation. Unfortunately, much of the early use of the Rorschach is extremely controversial because of the lack of data on reliability or validity, among other things. Until relatively recently, therapists administered the test any way they saw fit, although one of the most important tenets of assessment is that the same test be given in the same way each time—that is, according to standardized procedures. If you encourage someone to give more detailed answers during one testing session but not during a second session, you may get different responses as the result of your administering the test differently on the two occasions—not because of problems with the test or administration by another person (interrater reliability).

To respond to the concerns about reliability and validity, John Exner developed a standardized version of the Rorschach inkblot test, called the *Comprehensive System* (Exner, 2003). Exner's system of administering and scoring the Rorschach specifies how the

cards should be presented, what the examiner should say, and how the responses should be recorded (Erdberg, 2000). Varying these steps can lead to varying responses by the patient. Unfortunately, despite the attempts to bring standardization to the use of the Rorschach test, its use remains controversial. Critics of the Rorschach question whether research on the Comprehensive System supports its use as a valid assessment technique for people with psychological disorders (Wood, Nezworski, Lilienfeld, & Garb, 2003).

The *Thematic Apperception Test (TAT)* is perhaps the best-known projective test after the Rorschach. It was developed in 1935 by Christiana Morgan and Henry Murray at the Harvard Psychological Clinic (Aronow, Weiss, & Reznikoff, 2001). The TAT consists of a series of 31 cards: 30 with pictures on them and 1 blank card, although only 20 cards are typically used during each administration. Unlike the Rorschach, which involves asking for a fairly straightforward description of what the test taker sees, the instructions for the TAT ask the person to tell a dramatic story about the picture. The tester presents the pictures and tells the patient, "This is a test of imagination, one form of intelligence." The person being assessed can "let your imagination have its way, as in a myth, fairy story, or allegory" (Stein, 1978, p. 186). Again like the Rorschach, the TAT is based on the notion that people will reveal their unconscious mental processes in their stories about the pictures (Dana, 1996).

Several variations of the TAT have been developed for different groups, including a Children's Apperception Test (CAT) and a Senior Apperception Technique (SAT). In addition, modifications of the test have evolved for use with a variety of racial and ethnic groups, including African Americans, Native Americans, and people from India, South Africa, and the South Pacific Micronesian culture (Bellak, 1975; Dana, 1996). These modifications have included changes not only in the appearance of people in the pictures but also in the situations depicted. Like the Comprehensive System used with the Rorschach, researchers have developed formal scoring systems for TAT stories, including the Social Cognition and Object Relations Scale (Westen, 1991).

Unfortunately, the TAT and its variants continue to be used inconsistently. How the stories people tell about these pictures are interpreted depends on the examiner's frame of reference, as well as what the patient may say. It is not surprising, therefore, that questions remain about its use in psychopathology (Garb, Wood, Nezworski, Grove, & Stejskal, 2001; Gieser & Stein, 1999; Karon, 2000).

Despite the popularity and increasing standardization of these tests, most clinicians who use projective tests have their own methods of administration and interpretation. When used as ice-breakers, for getting people to open up and talk about how they feel about things going on in their lives, the ambiguous stimuli in these tests can be valuable tools. However, their relative lack of reliability and validity makes them less useful as diagnostic tests (Wood, Garb, Lilienfeld, & Nezworski, 2002). Concern over the inappropriate use of projective tests should remind you of the importance of the scientist–practitioner approach. Clinicians not only are responsible for knowing how to administer tests but also need to be aware of research that suggests they have limited usefulness as a means of diagnosing psychopathology.

■ **FIGURE 3.4** This inkblot resembles the ambiguous figures presented in the Rorschach test.

■ Personality Inventories

The questions in psychological tests published in mainstream magazines typically make sense when you read them. This is called having *face validity:* The wording of the questions seems to fit the type of information desired. But is this necessary? A famous psychologist, the late Paul Meehl, presented his position on this issue more than 60 years ago and subsequently influenced a whole field of study on **personality inventories** (Meehl, 1945). Put simply, Meehl pointed out that what is necessary from these types of tests is not whether the questions necessarily make sense on the surface but, rather, what the answers to these questions predict. If we find that people who have schizophrenia tend to respond "true" to "I have never been in love with anyone," then it doesn't matter whether we have a theory of love and schizophrenia. If people with certain disorders tend, as a group, to answer a variety of questions in a certain way, this pattern may predict who else has this disorder. The content of the questions becomes irrelevant. The importance lies in what the answers predict.

Although many personality inventories are available, we look at the most widely used personality inventory in the United States, the *Minnesota Multiphasic Personality Inventory (MMPI),* which was developed in the late 1930s and early 1940s and first published in 1943 (Hathaway & McKinley, 1943). In stark contrast to projective tests, which rely heavily on theory for an interpretation, the MMPI and similar inventories are based on an *empirical* approach, that is, the collection and evaluation of data. The administration of the MMPI is straightforward. The individual being assessed reads statements and answers either "true" or "false." Following are some statements from the MMPI:

Cry readily

Often happy for no reason

Am being followed

Fearful of things or people that can't hurt me*

There is little room for interpretation of MMPI responses, unlike responses to projective tests such as the Rorschach and the TAT. A problem with administering the MMPI, however, is the time and tedium of responding to the 550 items on the original version and now the 567 items on the MMPI-2 (published in 1989). A version of the MMPI is also now available that is appropriate for adolescents—MMPI-A (published in 1992) (Nezami & Butcher, 2000). Individual responses on the MMPI are not examined; instead, the pattern of responses is reviewed to see whether it resembles patterns from groups of people who have specific disorders (for example, a pattern similar to a group with schizophrenia). Each group is represented on separate standard scales (Butcher, 2006) (see Table 3.2).

Fortunately, clinicians can have these responses scored by computer; the program also includes an interpretation of the results, thereby reducing problems of reliability. One concern that arose early in the development of the MMPI was the potential of some people to answer in ways that would downplay their problems; skilled individuals would ascertain the intent of statements such as "Worry about saying things that hurt peoples' feelings,"

TABLE 3.2 MMPI-2 Content Scales	
Scale	**Description of Content and Correlates**
ANX (anxiety)	General symptoms of anxiety and tension, sleep and concentration problems, somatic correlation of anxiety, excessive worrying, difficulty making decisions, and willingness to admit to these problems.
FRS (fears)	Many specific fears and phobias, including those related to animals, high places, insects, blood, fire, storms, water, the dark, being indoors, and dirt.
OBS (obsessiveness)	Excessive rumination, difficulty making decisions, compulsive behaviors, rigidity, and feelings of being overwhelmed.
DEP (depression)	Depressive thoughts, anhedonia, feelings of hopelessness and uncertainty, and possible suicidal thoughts.
HEA (health concerns)	Many physical symptoms across several body systems: gastrointestinal, neurological, sensory, cardiovascular, dermatological, and respiratory. Reports of pain and general worries about health.
BIZ (bizarre mentation)	Psychotic thought processes, auditory, visual, or olfactory hallucinations, paranoid ideation, and delusions.
ANG (anger)	Anger-control problems, irritability, impatience, loss of control, and past or potential abusiveness.
CYN (cynicism)	Misanthropic beliefs, negative expectations about the motives of others, generalized distrust.
ASP (antisocial practices)	Cynical attitudes, problem behaviors, trouble with the law, stealing, and belief in getting around rules and laws for personal gain.
TPA (Type A)	Hard-driving, work-oriented behavior; impatience and irritability; annoyance; feelings of time pressure; and interpersonally overbearing.
LSE (low self-esteem)	Low self-worth and overwhelming feelings of being unlikable, unimportant, unattractive, useless, and so on.
SOD (social discomfort)	Uneasiness around others, shyness, and a preference for being alone.
FAM (family problems)	Family discord, possible abuse in childhood, lack of love and affection or marriage, and feelings of hate for family members.
WRK (work interference)	Behaviors or attitudes likely to interfere with work performance, such as low self-esteem, obsessiveness, tension, poor decision making, lack of family support, and negative attitudes toward career or coworkers.
TRL (negative treatment indicators)	Negative attitudes toward doctors and mental health treatment, preference for giving up rather than attempting change, and discomfort discussing any personal concerns.

and fake the answers. To assess this possibility, the MMPI includes four additional scales that determine the validity of each administration. For example, on the Lie scale (L), a statement such as "Have hurt someone when angry," when answered "false" might be an indication that the person may be falsifying answers to look good. The other scales are the Infrequency scale (F), which measures false claims about psychological problems or determines whether the person is answering randomly; the Defensiveness scale (K), which assesses whether the person sees herself in unrealistically positive ways; and the Cannot-Say (?) scale, which simply measures the number of items the test taker did not answer.

■ Figure 3.5 is an MMPI *profile* or summary of scores from an individual being clinically assessed. Before we tell you why this 27-year-old man (we'll call him James S.) was being evaluated, let's see what his MMPI profile tells us about him (note that these scores were obtained on the original version of the MMPI). The first three data points represent scores on the L, F, and K scales; the high scores on these scales were interpreted to mean that James S. made a naive attempt to look good for the evaluator and may have been trying to fake an appearance of having no problems. Another

important part of his profile is the very high score on the psychopathic deviation (Pd) scale, which measures the tendency to behave in antisocial ways. The interpretation of this score from the assessing clinician is that James S. is "aggressive, unreliable, irresponsible; unable to learn from experience; may initially make a good impression but then psychopathic features will surface in longer interactions or under stress."

Why was James S. being evaluated? He was a young man with a criminal record that began in his childhood. He was evaluated as part of his trial for kidnapping, raping, and murdering a middle-aged woman. Throughout his trial, he made up a number of contradictory stories to make himself look innocent (remember his high scores on the L, F, and K scales), including blaming his brother. However, there was overwhelming evidence of his guilt, and he was sentenced to life in prison. His answers on the MMPI resembled those of others who act in violent and antisocial ways.

The MMPI is one of the most extensively researched assessment instruments in psychology (Butcher, 2006). The original standardization sample—the people who first responded to the statements and set the standard for answers—included many peo-

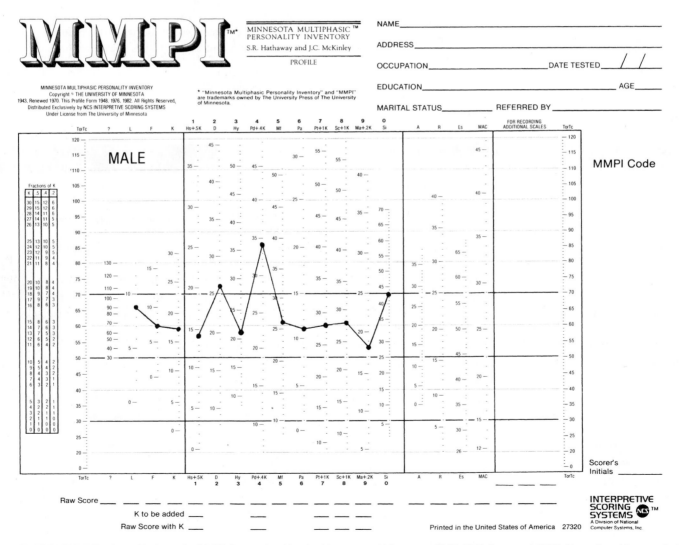

■ **FIGURE 3.5** A profile from the MMPI. Copyrighted by the University of Minnesota 1942, 1943 (renewed 1970). Reproduced by permission of the University of Minnesota Press).

ple from Minnesota who had no psychological disorders and several groups of people who had particular disorders. The more recent versions of this test, the MMPI-2 and the MMPA-A, eliminate problems with the original version, problems partly resulting from the original selective sample of people and partly resulting from the wording of questions (Graham, 2006). For example, some questions were sexist. One item on the original version asks the respondent to say whether she has ever been sorry she is a girl (Worell & Remer, 1992). Another item states, "Any man who is willing to work hard has a good chance of succeeding" (Hathaway & McKinley, 1943). Other items were criticized as insensitive to cultural diversity. Items dealing with religion, for example, referred almost exclusively to Christianity (Butcher, Graham, Williams, & Ben-Porath, 1990). The MMPI-2 has also been standardized with a sample that reflects the 1980 U.S. Census figures, including African Americans and Native Americans for the first time. In addition, new items have been added that deal with contemporary issues such as type A personality, low self-esteem, and family problems.

Reliability of the MMPI is excellent when it is interpreted according to standardized procedures, and thousands of studies on the original MMPI attest to its validity with a range of psychological problems (Butcher, 2006). But a word of caution is necessary here. As they might with any other form of assessment, some clinicians look at an MMPI profile and interpret the scales on the basis of their own clinical experience and judgment only. By not relying on the standard means of interpretation, this practice compromises the instrument's reliability and validity.

■ Intelligence Testing

"She must be very smart. I hear her IQ is 180!" What is "IQ?" What is "intelligence?" And how are they important in psychopathology? As many of you know from your introductory psychology course, intelligence tests were developed for one specific purpose: to predict who would do well in school. In 1904, a French psychologist, Alfred Binet, and his colleague, Théodore Simon, were commissioned by the French government to develop a test that would identify "slow learners" who would benefit from remedial help. The two psychologists identified a series of tasks that presumably measured the skills children need to succeed in school, including tasks of attention, perception, memory, reasoning, and verbal comprehension. Binet and Simon gave their original series of tasks to a large number of children; they then eliminated tasks that did not separate the slow learners from the children who did well in school. After several revisions and sample administrations, they had a test that was relatively easy to administer and that did what it was designed to do—predict academic success. In 1916, Lewis Terman of Stanford University translated a revised version of this test for use in the United States; it became known as the *Stanford-Binet test*.

The test provided a score known as an **intelligence quotient, or IQ.** Initially, IQ scores were calculated by using the child's *mental age*. For example, a child who passed all questions on the 7-year-old level and none of the questions on the 8-year-old-level received a mental age of 7. This mental age was then divided by the child's *chronological age* and multiplied by 100 to get the IQ score. However, there were problems with using this type of formula for calculating an IQ score. For example, a 4-year-old

This child is concentrating on a standard psychological assessment test.

needed to score only 1 year above his or her chronological age to be given an IQ score of 125, although an 8-year-old had to score 2 years above his or her chronological age to be given the same score (Bjorklund, 1989). Current tests use what is called a *deviation IQ*. A person's score is compared only to scores of others of the same age. The IQ score, then, is an estimate of how much a child's performance in school will deviate from the average performance of others of the same age.

In addition to the revised version of the Stanford-Binet (*Stanford-Binet V*; Roid & Pomplun, 2005), there is another widely used set of intelligence tests, developed by psychologist David Wechsler. The Wechsler tests include versions for adults (*Wechsler Adult Intelligence Scale,* third edition, or *WAIS-III*), children (*Wechsler Intelligence Scale for Children,* fourth edition, or *WISC-IV*), and young children (*Wechsler Preschool and Primary Scale of Intelligence,* third edition, or *WPPSI-III*). All these tests contain *verbal scales* (which measure vocabulary, knowledge of facts, short-term memory, and verbal reasoning skills) and *performance scales* (which assess psychomotor abilities, nonverbal reasoning, and ability to learn new relationships) (Zhu & Weiss, 2005).

One of the biggest mistakes nonpsychologists (and a distressing number of psychologists) make is to confuse IQ with intelligence. An IQ is a score on one of the intelligence tests we just described. An IQ score significantly higher than average means the person has a significantly greater than average chance of doing well in our educational system. By contrast, a score significantly lower than average suggests the person will probably not do well in school. Does a lower-than-average IQ score mean a person is not intelligent? Not necessarily. First, there are numerous reasons for a low score. For example, if the IQ test is administered in English and that is not the person's native language, the results will be affected.

Perhaps more important, however, is the continued development of models (Moses, 2006) that answer the question, "What constitutes intelligence?" Remember that the IQ tests measure abilities such as attention, perception, memory, reasoning, and verbal comprehension. But do these skills represent the totality of what we consider intelligence? Some recent theorists believe that what we think of as intelligence involves more, including the ability to adapt to the environment, the ability to generate new ideas, and the ability to process information efficiently (Flanagan & Harrison, 2005). Later, we discuss disorders that involve cognitive impairment, such as delirium and mental retardation, and IQ tests are typically used in assessing these disorders. Keep in mind, however, that we are discussing IQ and not necessarily intelligence. In general, however, IQ tests tend to be reliable, and to the extent that they predict academic success, they are valid assessment tools.

Neuropsychological Testing

Sophisticated tests now exist that can pinpoint the location of brain dysfunction (Swanda & Haaland, 2005). Fortunately, these techniques are generally available and relatively inexpensive. Technological advances in interactive teleconferencing have led to efforts to conduct such assessments for people in remote areas (Schopp, Johnstone, & Merrell, 2000). **Neuropsychological testing** measures abilities in areas such as receptive and expressive language, attention and concentration, memory, motor skills, perceptual abilities, and learning and abstraction in such a way that the clinician can make educated guesses about the person's performance and the possible existence of brain impairment. In other words, this method of testing assesses brain dysfunction by observing its effects on the person's ability to perform certain tasks. Although you do not see damage, you can see its effects.

A fairly simple neuropsychological test often used with children is the *Bender Visual–Motor Gestalt Test* (Canter, 1996). A child is given a series of cards on which are drawn various lines and shapes. The task is for the child to copy what is drawn on the card. The errors on the test are compared to test results of other children of the same age; if the number of errors exceeds a certain amount, then brain dysfunction is suspected. This test is less sophisticated than other neuropsychological tests because the nature or location of the problem cannot be determined with this test. The Bender Visual–Motor Gestalt Test can be useful for psychologists, however, because it provides a simple screening instrument that is easy to administer and can detect possible problems. Two of the most popular advanced tests of organic damage that allow more precise determinations of the location of the problem are the *Luria-Nebraska Neuropsychological Battery* (Golden, Hammeke, & Purisch, 1980) and the *Halstead-Reitan Neuropsychological Battery* (Reitan & Davison, 1974). These offer an elaborate battery of tests to assess a variety of skills in adolescents and adults. For example, the Halstead-Reitan Neuropsychological Battery includes the *Rhythm Test* (which asks the person to compare rhythmic beats, thus testing sound recognition, attention, and concentration), the *Strength of Grip Test* (which compares the grips of the right and left hands), and the *Tactile Performance Test* (which requires the test taker to place wooden blocks in a form board while blindfolded, thus testing learning and memory skills) (Swanda & Haaland, 2005).

Research on the validity of neuropsychological tests suggests they may be useful for detecting organic damage. One study found that the Halstead-Reitan and the Luria–Nebraska test batteries were equivalent in their abilities to detect damage and were about 80% correct (Goldstein & Shelly, 1984). However, these types of studies raise the issue of **false positives** and **false negatives.** For any assessment strategy, there will be times when the test shows a problem when none exists (false positives) and times when no problem is found even though some difficulty is present (false negatives). The possibility of false results is particularly troublesome for tests of brain dysfunction; a clinician who fails to find damage that exists might miss an important medical problem that needs to be treated. Fortunately, neuropsychological tests are used primarily as screening devices and are routinely paired with other assessments to improve the likelihood that real problems will be found. They do well with regard to measures of reliability and validity. On the downside, they can require hours to administer and are therefore not used unless brain damage is suspected.

Neuroimaging: Pictures of the Brain

For more than a century, we have known that many things we do, think, and remember are partially controlled by specific areas of the brain. In recent years we have developed the ability to look inside the brain and take increasingly accurate pictures of its structure and function using a technique called **neuroimaging** (Vythilingam, Shen, Drevets, & Innis, 2005). Neuroimaging can be divided into two categories. One category includes procedures that examine the structure of the brain, such as the size of various parts and whether there is any damage. In the second category are procedures that examine the actual functioning of the brain by mapping blood flow and other metabolic activity.

■ Images of Brain Structure

The first technique, developed in the early 1970s, uses multiple X-ray exposures of the brain from different angles; that is, X rays are passed directly through the head. As with any X ray, these are partially blocked or attenuated more by bone and less by brain tissue. The degree of blockage is picked up by detectors in the opposite side of the head. A computer then reconstructs pictures of various slices of the brain. This procedure, which takes about 15 minutes, is called a *computerized axial tomography (CAT) scan* or *CT scan*. It is relatively noninvasive and has proved useful in identifying and locating abnormalities in the structure or shape of the brain. It is particularly useful in locating brain tumors, injuries, and other structural and anatomical abnormalities. One difficulty, however, is that these scans, like all X rays, involve repeated X radiation, which poses some risk of cell damage (Vythilingam et al., 2005).

Several more recently developed procedures give greater resolution (specificity and accuracy) than a CT scan without the inherent risks of X rays. A now commonly used scanning technique is called nuclear *magnetic resonance imaging (MRI)*. The patient's head is placed in a high-strength magnetic field through which radio frequency signals are transmitted. These signals "excite" the brain tissue, altering the protons in the hydrogen atoms. The alteration is measured, along with the time it takes the protons to "relax" or return to normal. Where there are lesions or damage, the signal is lighter or darker (Vythilingam et al., 2005). Technology now exists that allows the computer to view the brain in layers, which enables precise examination of the structure. Al-

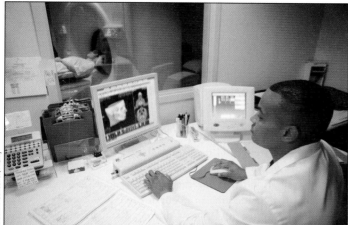

The patient is being positioned for an MRI scan.

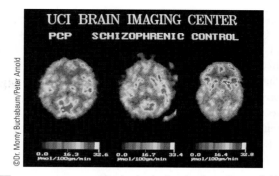

The PET scans compare activity in the brain of a drug abuser (left), a person with schizophrenia (center), and in a normal brain (right).

though an MRI is more expensive than a CT scan and originally took as long as 45 minutes, this is changing as technology improves. Newer versions of MRI procedures take as little as 10 minutes; the time and cost are decreasing yearly. Another disadvantage of MRI at present is that someone undergoing the procedure is totally enclosed inside a narrow tube with a magnetic coil surrounding the head. People who are somewhat claustrophobic often cannot tolerate an MRI.

Although neuroimaging procedures are useful for identifying damage to the brain, only recently have they been used to determine structural or anatomical abnormalities that might be associated with various psychological disorders. We review some tantalizing studies in subsequent chapters on specific disorders.

■ Images of Brain Functioning

Several widely used procedures are capable of measuring the actual functioning of the brain, as opposed to its structure. The first is called *positron emission tomography (PET) scan*. Subjects undergoing a PET scan are injected with a tracer substance attached to

radioactive isotopes, or groups of atoms that react distinctively. This substance interacts with blood, oxygen, or glucose. When parts of the brain become active, blood, oxygen, or glucose rushes to these areas of the brain, creating "hot spots" picked up by detectors that identify the location of the isotopes. Thus, we can learn what parts of the brain are working and what parts are not. To obtain clear images, the individual undergoing the procedure must remain motionless for 40 seconds or more. These images can be superimposed on MRI images to show the precise location of the active areas. The PET scans are also useful in supplementing MRI and CT scans when localizing the sites of trauma resulting from head injury or stroke, as well as when localizing brain tumors. More important, PET scans are used increasingly to look at varying patterns of metabolism that might be associated with different disorders. Recent PET scans have demonstrated that many patients with early Alzheimer's-type dementia show reduced glucose metabolism in the parietal lobes. Other intriguing findings have been reported for obsessive-compulsive disorder and bipolar disorder (see Chapters 5 and 7). PET scanning is expensive: The cost is about $6 million to set up a PET facility and $500,000 a year to run it. Therefore, these facilities are available only in large medical centers.

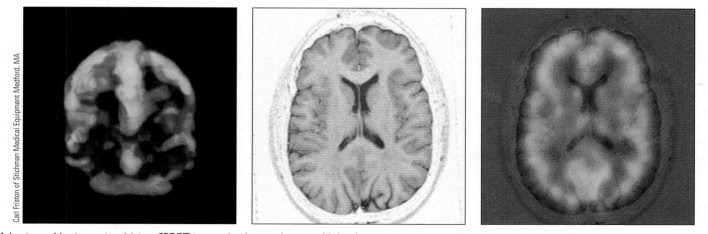

A horizontal brain section (a) in a SPECT image clearly reveals parietal lobe damage in a person with schizophrenia. Images (b) and (c) are MRI photographs. SPECT images show metabolic activity and thus indicate the relationship between the person's brain and the person's behavior. The higher-resolution MRI images show tissue variations.

A second procedure used to assess brain functioning is called *single photon emission computed tomography (SPECT)*. It works much like PET, although a different tracer substance is used and it is somewhat less accurate. It is also less expensive, however, and requires far less sophisticated equipment to pick up the signals. Therefore, it is used more often.

The most exciting advances involve MRI procedures that have been developed to work more quickly than the regular MRI (Fujita, Kugaya, & Innis, 2005). Using sophisticated computer technology, these procedures take only milliseconds and, therefore, can actually take pictures of the brain at work, recording its changes from one second to the next. Because these procedures measure the functioning of the brain, they are called *functional MRI, or fMRI*. fMRI procedures have largely replaced PET scans in the leading brain-imaging centers because they allow researchers to see the immediate response of the brain to a brief event, such as seeing a new face. This response is called an *event-related fMRI*. Even more powerful technology based on light sources is on the way (Gibson, Hebden, & Arridge, 2005). Shining near-infrared light through the head—called *diffuse optical imaging*—and picking up changes as the light is scattered by brain tissue at work may be a less expensive and more accurate way of learning how the brain works.

Brain imagery procedures hold enormous potential for illuminating the contribution of neurobiological factors to psychological disorders. For example, in Chapter 5 on anxiety disorders, you will learn what fMRI procedures reveal about brain functioning in individuals such as Frank, who has obsessive-compulsive disorder.

Psychophysiological Assessment

Yet another method for assessing brain structure and function specifically and nervous system activity generally is called **psychophysiological assessment.** As the term implies, *psychophysiology* refers to measurable changes in the nervous system that reflect emotional or psychological events. The measurements may be taken either directly from the brain or peripherally from other parts of the body.

Frank feared that he might have seizures. If we had any reason to suspect he might have periods of memory loss or exhibit bizarre, trancelike behavior, if only for a short period, it would be important for him to have an **electroencephalogram (EEG).** Measuring electrical activity in the head related to the firing of a specific group of neurons reveals brain wave activity, the low-voltage electrical current ongoing in the brain, usually from the cortex. A person's brain waves can be assessed in both waking and sleeping states. In an EEG, electrodes are placed directly on various places on the scalp to record the different low-voltage currents.

We have learned much about EEG patterns in the past decades (Ovsiew, 2005). Usually we measure ongoing electrical activity in the brain. When brief periods of EEG patterns are recorded in response to specific events, such as hearing a psychologically meaningful stimulus, the response is called an *event-related potential (ERP)* or *evoked potential*. We have learned that EEG patterns are often affected by psychological or emotional factors and can be an index of these reactions, or a psycho-

physiological measure. In a normal, healthy, relaxed adult, waking activities are characterized by a regular pattern of changes in voltage termed *alpha waves.*

Many types of stress-reduction treatments attempt to *increase* the frequency of the alpha waves, often by relaxing the patients in some way. The alpha wave pattern is associated with relaxation and calmness. During sleep, we pass through several stages of brain activity, at least partially identified by EEG patterns. During the deepest, most relaxed stage, typically occurring 1 to 2 hours after a person falls asleep, EEG recordings show a pattern of *delta waves.* These brain waves are slower and more irregular than the alpha waves, which is normal for this stage of sleep. You will see in Chapter 5 that panic attacks occurring while a person is sound asleep come almost exclusively during the delta wave stage. If frequent delta wave activity occurred during the waking state, it might indicate dysfunction of localized areas of the brain.

Psychophysiological assessment of other bodily responses may also play a role in assessment. These responses include heart rate, respiration, and *electrodermal responding,* formerly referred to as *galvanic skin response (GSR),* which is a measure of sweat gland activity controlled by the peripheral nervous system. Remember from Chapter 2 that the peripheral nervous system and, in particular, the sympathetic division of the autonomic nervous system are responsive to stress and emotional arousal.

Assessing psychophysiological response to emotional stimuli is important in many disorders, one being posttraumatic stress disorder. Stimuli such as sights and sounds associated with the trauma evoke strong psychophysiological responses, even if the patient is not fully aware that this is happening.

Psychophysiological assessment is also used with many sexual dysfunctions and disorders. For example, sexual arousal can be assessed through direct measurement of penile circumference in males or vaginal blood flow in females in response to erotic stimuli, usually movies or slides (see Chapter 10). Sometimes the individual might be unaware of specific patterns of sexual arousal.

Physiological measures are also important in the assessment and treatment of conditions such as headaches and hypertension (Nicassio, Meyerowitz, & Kerns, 2004); they form the basis for the treatment we call *biofeedback.* In biofeedback, as we explain in Chapter 9, levels of physiological responding, such as blood pressure readings, are fed back to the patient (provided on a continuous basis) by meters or gauges so that the patient can try to regulate these responses.

Nevertheless, physiological assessment is not without its limitations because it requires a great deal of skill and some technical expertise. Even when administered properly, the measures sometimes produce inconsistent results because of procedural or technical difficulties or the nature of the response itself. Therefore, only clinicians specializing in certain disorders in which these measures are particularly important are likely to make extensive use of psychophysiological recording equipment, although more straightforward applications, such as monitoring heart rate during relaxation exercises, are more common. More sophisticated psychophysiological assessment is most often used in theoretical investigations of the nature of certain psychological disorders, particularly emotional disorders (Barlow, 2002; Ovsiew, 2005).

DIAGNOSING PSYCHOLOGICAL DISORDERS

Thus far, we have looked at Frank's functioning on an individual basis; that is, we have closely observed his behavior, cognitive processes, and mood, and we have conducted semistructured interviewing, behavioral assessment, and psychological tests. These operations tell us what is unique about Frank, not what he may have in common with other individuals.

Learning how Frank may resemble other people in terms of the problems he presents is important for several reasons. If in the past people came in with similar problems or psychological profiles, we can go back and find a lot of information from their cases that might be applicable to Frank's case. We can see how the problems began for those other individuals, what factors seemed influential, and how long the problem or disorder lasted. Did the

problem in the other cases just go away on its own? If not, what kept it going? Did it need treatment? Most important, what treatments seemed to relieve the problem for those other individuals? These general questions are useful because they evoke a wealth of clinical and research information that enables the investigator to make certain inferences about what will happen next and what treatments may work. In other words, the clinician can establish a *prognosis,* a term we discussed in Chapter 1 that refers to the likely future course of a disorder under certain conditions. If you can make these general conclusions, you don't have to start at square one every time someone new comes into your office.

Both strategies are essential in the study and treatment of psychopathology. If we want to determine what is unique about an individual's personality, cultural background, or circumstances, we use what is known as an **idiographic strategy.** This information lets us tailor our treatment to the person. But to take advantage of the information already accumulated on a particular problem or disorder, we must be able to determine a general class of problems to which the presenting problem belongs. This is known as a **nomothetic strategy.** In other words, we are attempting to name or classify the problem. When we identify a specific psychological disorder, such as a mood disorder, in the clinical setting, we are making a diagnosis. We can also identify a general class or grouping of problems by determining a particular personality profile on a psychological test such as the MMPI. For example, when it was noted earlier in the section on the MMPI that James S. scored high on the Pd scale, we concluded that he shared personality features of aggressiveness and irresponsibility with others who have elevated scores on that scale. Before proceeding, let's define some additional terms more precisely.

Because classification is such an integral part of science and, indeed, of our human experience, we describe its various aspects individually (Millon, 1991). The term **classification** itself is broad, referring simply to any effort to construct groups or categories and to assign objects or people to these categories on the basis of their shared attributes or relations—a nomothetic strategy. If the classification is in a scientific context, it is most often called **taxonomy,** which is the classification of entities for scientific purposes, such as insects, rocks, or—if the subject is psychology—behaviors. If you apply a taxonomic system to psychological or medical phenomena or other clinical areas, you use the word **nosology.** All diagnostic systems used in health-care settings, such as those for infectious diseases, are nosological systems. The term **nomenclature** describes the names or labels of the disorders that make up the nosology (for example, anxiety or mood disorders). Most mental health professionals use the classification system contained in the DSM-IV-TR (American Psychiatric Association, 2000). This is the official system in the United States, and it is used widely throughout the world. A clinician refers to the DSM-IV to identify a specific psychological disorder in the process of making a diagnosis.

During the past several years, we have seen enormous changes in how we think about classifying psychopathology. Because these developments affect so much of what we do, we examine carefully the processes of classification and diagnosis as they are used in psychopathology. We look first at different approaches, examine the concepts of reliability and validity as they pertain to diagnosis, and then discuss our current system of classification, the DSM-IV.

Classification Issues

Classification is at the heart of any science, and much of what we have said about it is common sense. If we could not order and label objects or experiences, scientists could not communicate with one another and our knowledge would not advance. Everyone would have to develop a personal system that would mean nothing to anyone else. In your biology or geology courses, when you study insects or rocks, classification is fundamental. Knowing how one species of insects differs from another allows us to study its functioning and origins. When we are dealing with human behavior or human behavioral disorders, however, the subject of classification becomes controversial. Some people have questioned whether it is proper or ethical to classify human behavior. Even among those who recognize the necessity of classification, major controversies have arisen in several areas. Within psychopathology, for example, definitions of "normal" and "abnormal" are questioned, as is the assumption that a behavior or cognition is part of one disorder and not another. Some would prefer to talk about behavior and feelings on a continuum from happy to sad or fearful to nonfearful rather than to create such categories as mania, depression, and phobia. For better or worse, classifying behavior and people is something we all do. Few of us talk about our own emotions or those of our friends by using a number on a scale (where 0 is totally unhappy and 100 is totally happy), although this approach might be more accurate. ("How do you feel about that?" "About 65.") Rather, we talk about being happy, sad, angry, depressed, fearful, and so on.

■ Categorical and Dimensional Approaches

To avoid reinventing the wheel every time we see a new set of problem behaviors and to seek general principles of psychopathology, in what different ways can we classify human behavior? We have already alluded to two possibilities. We can have distinct categories of disorders that have little or nothing in common with one another; for example, you either hear voices talking to you from the refrigerator (auditory hallucination) and have other symptoms of schizophrenia or you don't. Alternatively, we can quantify the various attributes of a psychological disorder along several dimensions, coming up with a composite score. An MMPI profile is a good example; another is "dimensionalizing" depression on a continuum of severity, from feeling mildly depressed in the morning (something most of us experience once in a while) to feeling so deeply

Emil Kraepelin (1856–1926) was one of the first psychiatrists to classify psychological disorders from a biological point of view.

depressed and hopeless that suicide is the only solution. Which system is better? Each has its strengths and its faults (Brown & Barlow, 2005; Rounsaville et al., 2002; Widiger & Coker, 2003; Widiger & Samuel, 2005). Let's look at both.

The **classical** (or pure) **categorical approach** to classification originates in the work of Emil Kraepelin (1856–1926) and the biological tradition in the study of psychopathology. Here we assume that every diagnosis has a clear underlying pathophysiological cause, such as a bacterial infection or a malfunctioning endocrine system, and that each disorder is unique. When diagnoses are thought of in this way, the causes could be psychological or cultural instead of pathophysiological, but there is still only one set of causative factors per disorder, which does not overlap with those of other disorders. Because each disorder is fundamentally different from every other, we need only one set of defining criteria, which everybody in the category has to meet. If the criteria for a major depressive episode are (1) the presence of depressed mood, (2) significant weight loss or gain when not dieting, (3) diminished ability to think or concentrate, and 7 additional specific symptoms, then, to be diagnosed with depression, an individual would have to meet all of the criteria. In that case, according to the classical categorical approach, the clinician would know the cause of the disorder.

Classical categorical approaches are quite useful in medicine. It is extremely important for a physician to make accurate diagnoses. If a patient has a fever accompanied by stomach pain, the doctor must determine quickly whether the cause is a stomach flu or an infected appendix. This is not always easy, but physicians are trained to examine the signs and symptoms closely, and they usually reach the correct conclusion. To understand the cause of symptoms (infected appendix) is to know what treatment will be effective (surgery). But if someone is depressed or anxious, is there a similar type of underlying cause? As you saw in Chapter 2, probably not. Most psychopathologists believe psychological and social factors interact with biological factors to produce a disorder. Therefore, despite the beliefs of Kraepelin and other early biological investigators, the mental health field has not adopted a classical categorical model of psychopathology. As Frances and Widiger (1986) point out, the classical categorical approach is clearly inappropriate to the complexity of psychological disorders.

Despite their wide physical variation, all dogs belong to the same class of animals.

A second strategy is a **dimensional approach,** in which we note the variety of cognitions, moods, and behaviors with which the patient presents and quantify them on a scale. For example, on a scale of 1 to 10, a patient might be rated as severely anxious (10), moderately depressed (5), and mildly manic (2) to create a profile of emotional functioning (10, 5, 2). Although dimensional approaches have been applied to psychopathology—particularly to personality (Axis II) disorders (Widiger & Coker, 2003; Widiger & Samuel, 2005)—they have been relatively unsatisfactory until now (First & Pincus, 2002; Rounsaville et al., 2002). Most theorists have not been able to agree on how many dimensions are required: some say 1 dimension is enough; others have identified as many as 33 (Millon, 1991, 2004).

A third strategy for organizing and classifying behavioral disorders has found increasing support in recent years as an alternative to classical categorical or dimensional approaches. It is a categorical approach but with the twist that it basically combines some features of each of the former approaches. Called a **prototypical approach,** this alternative identifies certain essential characteristics of an entity so that you (and others) can classify it, but it also allows certain nonessential variations that do not necessarily change the classification. For example, if someone were to ask you to describe a dog, you could easily give a general description (the essential, categorical characteristics), but you might not exactly describe a specific dog. Dogs come in different colors, sizes, and even species (the nonessential, dimensional variations), but they all share certain doggish characteristics that allow you to classify them separately from cats. Thus, requiring a certain number of prototypical criteria and only some of an additional number of criteria is adequate. This system is not perfect because there is a greater blurring at the boundaries of categories, and some symptoms apply to more than one disorder. However, it has the advantage of fitting best with the current state of our knowledge of psychopathology, and it is relatively user friendly.

DSM-IV-TR

DSM TABLE 3.1   Criteria for a Major Depressive Episode

A. Five (or more) of the following symptoms have been present during the same 2-week period and represent a change from previous functioning; at least one of the symptoms is either (a) depressed mood or (b) loss of interest or pleasure.
Note: Symptoms that are clearly due to a general medical condition or mood-incongruent delusions or hallucinations should not be included.
1. Depressed mood most of the day
2. Markedly diminished interest or pleasure in all, or almost all, activities
3. Significant weight loss (when not dieting) or weight gain
4. Insomnia or hypersomnia nearly every day
5. Psychomotor agitation or retardation
6. Fatigue or loss of energy nearly every day
7. Feelings of worthlessness or excessive or inappropriate guilt
8. Diminished ability to think or concentrate or indecisiveness
9. Recurrent thoughts of death

Source: Reprinted, with permission, from American Psychiatric Association. (2000). *Diagnostic and statistical manual of mental disorders* (4th ed., text revision). Washington, DC: Author. Copyright © 2000 American Psychiatric Association.

When this approach is used in classifying a psychological disorder, many possible features or properties of the disorder are listed and any candidate must meet enough of them to fall into that category. Consider the DSM-IV criteria defining a major depressive episode.

As you can see, the criteria include many nonessential symptoms, but if you have either depressed mood or marked loss of interest or pleasure in most activities and at least four of the remaining eight symptoms, you come close enough to the prototype to meet the criteria for a major depressive episode. One person might have depressed mood, significant weight loss, insomnia, psychomotor agitation, and loss of energy, whereas another person who also meets the criteria for major depressive episode might have markedly diminished interest or pleasure in activities, fatigue, feelings of worthlessness, difficulty thinking or concentrating, and ideas of committing suicide. Although both have the requisite five symptoms that bring them close to the prototype, they look different because they share only one symptom. This is a good example of a prototypical category. The DSM-IV-TR is based on this approach.

■ Reliability

Any system of classification should describe specific subgroups of symptoms that are clearly evident and can be readily identified by experienced clinicians. If two clinicians interview the patient at separate times on the same day (and assuming the patient's condition does not change during the day), the two clinicians should see, and perhaps measure, the same set of behaviors and emotions. The psychological disorder can thus be identified reliably. If the disorder is not readily apparent to both clinicians, the resulting diagnoses might represent bias. For example, someone's clothes might provoke some comment. One of your friends might later say, "She looked kind of sloppy tonight." Another might comment, "No, that's just a real funky look; she's right in style." Perhaps a third friend would say, "Actually, I thought she was dressed kind of neatly." You might wonder if they had all seen the same person. In any case, there would be no reliability to their observations. Getting your friends to agree about someone's appearance would require a careful set of definitions that they all accept.

As we noted before, unreliable classification systems are subject to bias by clinicians making diagnoses. One of the most unreliable categories in current classification is the area of personality disorders—chronic, traitlike sets of inappropriate behaviors and emotional reactions that characterize a person's way of interacting with the world. Although great progress has been made, particularly with certain personality disorders, determining the presence or absence of this type of disorder during one interview is still difficult. Morey and Ochoa (1989) asked 291 mental health professionals to describe an individual with a personality disorder they had recently seen, along with their diagnoses. Morey and Ochoa also collected from these clinicians detailed information about the actual signs and symptoms present in these patients. In this way, they were able to determine whether the actual diagnosis made by the clinicians matched the objective criteria for the diagnosis as determined by the symptoms. In other words, was the clinician's diagnosis accurate, based on the presence of symptoms that define the diagnosis?

Morey and Ochoa found substantial bias in making diagnoses. For example, for some reason clinicians who were either less experienced or female diagnosed borderline personality disorder more often than the criteria indicated. More experienced clinicians and male clinicians diagnosed the condition less often than the criteria indicated.

Patients who were white, female, or poor were diagnosed with borderline personality disorder more often than the criteria indicated. Although bias among clinicians is always a potential problem, the more reliable the nosology, or system of classification, the less likely bias is to creep in during diagnosis.

■ Validity

In addition to being reliable, a system of nosology must be valid. Earlier we described *validity* as whether something measures what it is designed to measure. There are several types of diagnostic validity. For one, the system should have *construct validity*. This means the signs and symptoms chosen as criteria for the presence of the diagnostic category are consistently associated or hang together and what they identify differs from other categories. Someone meeting the criteria for depression should be discriminable from someone meeting the criteria for social phobia. This discriminability might be evident not only in presenting symptoms but also in the course of the disorder and possibly in the choice of treatment. It may also predict **familial aggregation,** the extent to which the disorder would be found among the patient's relatives (Blashfield & Livesley, 1991; Cloninger, 1989; Kupfer, First, & Regier, 2002).

In addition, a valid diagnosis tells the clinician what is likely to happen with the prototypical patient; it may predict the course of the disorder and the likely effect of one treatment or another. This type of validity is referred to often as *predictive validity* and sometimes as *criterion validity,* when the outcome is the criterion by which we judge the usefulness of the category. Finally, there is *content validity,* which simply means that if you create criteria for a diagnosis of, say, social phobia, it should reflect the way most experts in the field think of social phobia, as opposed to, say, depression. In other words, you need to get the label right.

Diagnosis Before 1980

The classification of psychopathology, as the old adage goes, has a long past but a recent history. Observations of depressed, phobic, or psychotic features stretch back to the earliest recorded observations of human behavior. Many of these observations were so detailed and complete that we could make a diagnosis today of the individuals they described. Nevertheless, only recently have we attempted the difficult task of creating a formal nosology that would be useful for scientists and clinicians around the world. As late as 1959 there were at least nine systems of varying usefulness for classifying psychological disorders worldwide, but only three of the nine systems listed "phobic disorder" as a separate category (Marks, 1969). One reason for this confusion is that creating a useful nosology is easier said than done.

Early efforts to classify psychopathology arose out of the biological tradition, particularly the work of Kraepelin as described in Chapter 1 and mentioned earlier. Kraepelin first identified what we now know as the disorder of schizophrenia. His term for the disorder at the time was *dementia praecox*. Dementia praecox refers to deterioration of the brain that sometimes occurs with advancing age (dementia) and develops earlier than it is supposed to, or "prematurely" (praecox). This label (later changed to *schizophrenia*) reflected Kraepelin's belief that brain pathology is the cause of this particular disorder. Kraepelin's landmark 1913 book *(Psychiatry: A Textbook for Students and Physicians)* described not only dementia praecox but also bipolar disorder, then called *manic depressive psychosis*. Kraepelin also described a variety of organic brain syndromes. Other well-known figures in their time, such as French psychiatrist Philippe Pinel, characterized psychological disorders, including depression (melancholia), as separate entities, but Kraepelin's theorizing that psychological disorders are basically biological disturbances had the greatest impact on the development of our nosology and led to an early emphasis on classical categorical strategies.

It was not until 1948 that the World Health Organization (WHO) added a section classifying mental disorders to the sixth edition of the *International Classification of Diseases and Related Health Problems* (ICD). However, this early system did not have much influence. Nor did the first *Diagnostic and Statistical Manual* (DSM-I), published in 1952 by the American Psychiatric Association. Only in the late 1960s did systems of nosology begin to have some real influence on mental health professionals. In 1968, the American Psychiatric Association published a second edition of its *Diagnostic and Statistical Manual* (DSM-II). In 1969, WHO published the eighth edition of the ICD. Nevertheless, these systems lacked precision, often differing substantially from one another and relying heavily on unproven theories of etiology not widely accepted by all mental health professionals. To make matters worse, the systems had little reliability. Two mental health practitioners looking at the same patient often came to different conclusions based on the nosology at that time. Even as late as the 1970s, many countries such as France and Russia had their own systems of nosology. In these countries, the same disorders would be labeled and interpreted differently.

DSM-III

The year 1980 brought a landmark in the history of nosology: the third edition of the *Diagnostic and Statistical Manual* (DSM-III) (American Psychiatric Association, 1980). Under the leadership of Robert Spitzer, DSM-III departed radically from its predecessors. Three changes stood out. First, DSM-III attempted to take an atheoretical approach to diagnosis, relying on precise descriptions of the disorders as they presented to clinicians rather than on psychoanalytic or biological theories of etiology. With this focus, DSM-III became a tool for clinicians with a variety of points of view. For example, rather than classifying phobia under the broad category "neurosis," defined by intrapsychic conflicts and defense mechanisms, it was assigned its own category within a new broader group, "anxiety disorders."

The second major change in DSM-III was that the specificity and detail with which the criteria for identifying a disorder were listed made it possible to study their reliability and validity. Although not all categories in DSM-III (and its 1987 revision, DSM-III-R) achieved perfect reliability and validity, this system was a vast improvement over what was available before. Third, DSM-III (and DSM-III-R) allowed individuals with possible psychological disorders to be rated on five dimensions, or axes. The disorder itself, such as schizophrenia or mood disorder, was represented only on the first axis. More enduring (chronic) disorders of personality were listed on Axis II. Axis III consisted of physical disorders and conditions. On Axis IV the clinician rated, in a dimensional fashion, the amount of psychosocial stress the person reported, and the current level of adaptive functioning was indicated on Axis V. This framework, called the *multiaxial system,* allowed the clinician to gather information about the individual's functioning in a number of areas rather than limiting information to the disorder itself.

■ Problems With DSM-III and DSM-III-R

Despite the conceptual advances of DSM-III and its revision, DSM-III-R (American Psychiatric Association, 1987), a number of problems remained. First, the reliability of some diagnostic categories was often unacceptably low. Researchers discovered that, even under optimal conditions, experienced interviewers watching videotapes could not always agree on whether a disorder was present. This lack of consensus occurred more for some disorders, such as somatoform and personality disorders, than for others (for example, see Hyler, Williams, & Spitzer, 1982; Spitzer, Forman, & Nee, 1979). Even when reliability was better, as with the anxiety disorders, it was difficult for clinicians to agree on the presence or absence of some specific disorders, such as generalized anxiety disorder or even simple phobia (DiNardo, Moras, Barlow, Rapee, & Brown, 1993; DiNardo, O'Brien, Barlow, Waddell, & Blanchard, 1983). Identifying a phobia seems to be a fairly straightforward task, but clinicians often could not agree whether the condition was severe enough to be a disorder. This lack of consensus is just one example of how complex a challenge it is to categorize psychopathology.

In addition, many criteria for DSM-III and DSM-III-R, although empirically based and potentially measurable, were established by committee consensus (Spitzer, 1991); that is, a group of experts attempted to decide what should be part of the diagnosis and what should not. Decisions by consensus sometimes produce strange results.

For example, one criterion for panic disorder in DSM-III-R was four panics in a 4-week period. Why four? Did this reflect some study indicating that three panics in a 4-week period are qualitatively different from four or five? Of course not—the criterion was simply the result of a committee offering a ballpark figure that sounded reasonable. Committee members knew the figure was nothing more than a convenient approximation, but tens of thousands of other clinicians subsequently operated under the assumption that the criteria were hard and fast and a person with three attacks didn't have a panic disorder, despite cautions published in the DSM itself. Such a mind-set reflects a tendency by some clinicians, often inexperienced ones, to *reify* a diagnostic category, which means to take it too literally. This is a mistake. Systems of nosology are simply our best working estimate of the optimal ways of classifying psychopathology and should not be taken as a permanent gold standard.

Despite these shortcomings, DSM-III and DSM-III-R had a substantial impact. Maser, Kaelber, and Weise (1991) surveyed the international usage of various diagnostic systems and found that DSM-III had become popular for a number of reasons. Primary among them were its precise descriptive format and its neutrality with regard to presuming a cause for diagnosis. The multiaxial format, which emphasizes a broad consideration of the whole individual rather than a narrow focus on the disorder alone, was also useful. Therefore, more clinicians around the world used DSM-III-R at the beginning of the 1990s than the ICD system designed to be applicable internationally.

David Kupfer is the chair of the task force for the 5th edition of the *Diagnostic and Statistical Manual of Mental Disorders (DSM),* which is due to appear in 2011 or later.

DSM-IV

By the late 1980s, clinicians and researchers realized the need for a consistent, worldwide system of nosology. The 10th edition of the *International Classification of Diseases* (ICD-10) would be published in 1993, and the United States is required by treaty obligations to use the ICD-10 codes in all matters related to health. To make the ICD-10 and DSM as compatible as possible, work proceeded more or less simultaneously on both the ICD-10 and the fourth edition of the DSM (DSM-IV). Concerted efforts were made to share research data and other information to create an empirically based worldwide system of nosology for psychological disorders. The DSM-IV task force decided to rely as little as possible on a consensus of experts. Any changes in the diagnostic system were to be based on sound scientific data. The revisers attempted to review the voluminous literature in all areas pertaining to the diagnostic system (Widiger et al., 1996, 1998) and to identify large sets of data that might have been collected for other reasons but that, with reanalysis, would be useful to DSM-IV. Finally, 12 independent studies or field trials examined the reliability and validity of alternative sets of definitions or criteria and, in some cases, the possibility of creating a new diagnosis. (See Widiger et al., 1998. A description of one of these field trials appears on p. 93.)

Perhaps the most substantial change in DSM-IV is that the distinction between organically based disorders and psychologically based disorders that was present in previous editions has been eliminated. As you saw in Chapter 2, we now know that even disorders associated with known brain pathology are substantially affected by psychological and social influences. Similarly, disorders previously described as psychological in origin certainly have biological components and, most likely, identifiable brain circuits.

■ The Multiaxial Format in DSM-IV

The multiaxial system remains in DSM-IV, with some changes in the five axes. Specifically, only personality disorders and mental retardation are now coded on Axis II. Pervasive developmental disorders, learning disorders, motor skills disorders, and communication disorders, previously coded on Axis II, are now all coded on Axis I. Axis IV, which rated the patient's amount of psychosocial stress, was not useful and has been replaced. The new Axis IV is used for reporting psychosocial and environmental problems that might have an impact on the disorder. Axis V is essentially unchanged. In addition, optional axes have been included for rating dimensions of behavior or functioning that may be important in some cases. There are axes for defense mechanisms or coping styles, social and occupational functioning, and relational functioning; clinicians might use them to describe the quality of relationships that provide the interpersonal context for the disorder. Finally, a number of new disorders were introduced in DSM-IV, and some disorders in DSM-III-R were either deleted or subsumed into other DSM-IV categories.

In 2000, a committee updated the text that describes the research literature accompanying the DSM-IV diagnostic category and made minor changes to some of the criteria themselves to improve consistency (First & Pincus, 2002; American Psychiatric Association, 2000). This text revision (DSM-IV-TR) helped clarify many issues related to the diagnosis of psychological disorders.

■ DSM-IV and Frank

In Frank's case, initial observations indicate an anxiety disorder on Axis I, specifically obsessive-compulsive disorder. However, he might also have long-standing personality traits that lead him systematically to avoid social contact. If so, there might be a diagnosis of schizoid personality disorder on Axis II. Unless Frank has an identifiable medical condition, there is nothing on Axis III. Job and marital difficulties would be coded on Axis IV, where clinicians note psychosocial or environmental problems that are not part of the disorder but might make it worse. Frank's difficulties with work would be noted by checking "occupational problems" and specifying "threat of job loss"; for "problems with primary support group," "marital difficulties" would be noted. On Axis V, the clinician would rate the highest overall level of Frank's current functioning on a 0-to-100 scale (100 indicates superior functioning in a variety of situations). At present, Frank's score is 55, which indicates moderate interference with functioning at home and at work.

It is important to emphasize that impairment is a crucial determination in making any diagnosis. For example, if someone, such as Frank, has all of the symptoms of obsessive-compulsive disorder but finds them only mildly annoying because the intrusive thoughts are not severe and don't occur that often, that person would not merit criteria for a psychological disorder. It is essential that the various behaviors and cognitions comprising the diagnosis interfere with functioning in some substantial manner. Thus, the criteria for disorders include the provision that the disorder must cause clinically significant distress or impairment in social, occupational, or other important areas of functioning. Individuals who have all the symptoms as noted earlier but do not cross this "threshold" of impairment could not be diagnosed with a disorder. In one of our own clinics, in addition to rating overall impairment on Axis V, impairment specifically associated with the Axis I disorder (if present) is also rated. A scale of 0 to 8 is used, where 0 is no impairment and 8 is severely disturbing or disabling (usually housebound and barely functional). The disorder must be rated at least a 4 in severity (definitely disturb-

ing or disabling) to meet criteria for a psychological disorder. Many times, disorders such as obsessive-compulsive disorder would be rated a 2 or 3, meaning that all of the symptoms are there but in too mild a form to impair functioning; in this case, the disorder would be termed *subthreshold*. Subthreshold examples of emotional symptoms are mentioned again when we consider the diagnosis of mixed anxiety-depression later in this chapter. In diagnostic reports produced every day at one of our clinics, a summary of Frank's profile based on the multiaxial formulation would look like this:

Axis I	Obsessive-compulsive disorder
Axis II	Schizoid personality disorder
Axis III	None
Axis IV	Occupational problems: threat of job loss; problems with primary support group: marital difficulties
Axis V	55 (current)

This multiaxial system organizes a range of important information that might be relevant to the likely course of the disorder and, perhaps, treatment. For example, two people might present with obsessive-compulsive disorder but look different on Axes II through V; such differences would greatly affect the clinician's recommendations for the two cases.

■ Social and Cultural Considerations in DSM-IV

By emphasizing levels of stress in the environment, DSM-III and DSM-IV facilitate a more complete picture of the individual. Furthermore, DSM-IV corrects a previous omission by including a plan for integrating important social and cultural influences on diagnosis. The plan, referred to as the "cultural formulation guidelines," allows the disorder to be described from the perspective of the patient's personal experience and in terms of the primary social and cultural group, such as Hispanic or Chinese. The following are suggestions for accomplishing these goals (Mezzich et al., 1993, 1999).

The DSM-IV-TR diagnostic guidelines take cultural considerations into account.

1. What is the primary cultural reference group of the patient? For recent immigrants to the country, as well as other ethnic minorities, how involved are they with their "new" culture versus their old culture? Have they mastered the language of their new country (for example, English in the United States), or is language a continuing problem?

2. Does the patient use terms and descriptions from his or her "old" country to describe the disorder? For example, *ataques de nervios* in the Hispanic subculture is a type of anxiety disorder close to panic disorder. Does the patient accept Western models of disease or disorder for which treatment is available in health-care systems, or does the patient also have an alternative health-care system in another culture (for example, traditional herbal doctors in Chinese subcultures)?

3. What does it mean to be "disabled?" Which kinds of "disabilities" are acceptable in a given culture and which are not? For example, is it acceptable to be physically ill but not to be anxious or depressed? What are the typical family, social, and religious supports in the culture? Are they available to the patient? Does the clinician understand the first language of the patient, as well as the cultural significance of the disorder?

These cultural considerations must not be overlooked in making diagnoses and planning treatment, and they are assumed throughout this book. But, as yet, there is no research supporting the use of these cultural formulation guidelines (Alarcon et al., 2002). The consensus is that we have a lot more work to do in this area to make our nosology truly culturally sensitive.

■ Criticisms of DSM-IV

Because the collaboration among groups creating the ICD-10 and DSM-IV was largely successful, it is clear that DSM-IV (and the closely related ICD-10 mental disorder section) is the most advanced, scientifically based system of nosology ever developed. Nevertheless, we cannot assume that the system is final or even completely correct. Any nosological system should be considered a work in progress (Brown & Barlow, 2005; Millon, 2004).

We still have "fuzzy" categories that blur at the edges, making diagnostic decisions difficult at times. As a consequence, individuals are often assigned more than one psychological disorder at the same time, sometimes as many as three or four. (Several disorders exist in a state of **comorbidity.**) How can we conclude anything definite about the course of a disorder, the response to treatment, or the likelihood of associated problems if we are dealing with combinations of disorders (Follette & Houts, 1996; Kupfer et al., 2002)? In the future, people who require an assignment of three or four disorders may have an entirely new class in our nosological system. Resolution of these tough problems simply awaits the long, slow process of science.

Criticisms center on two other aspects of DSM-IV and ICD-10. First, the systems strongly emphasize reliability, sometimes at the expense of validity. This is understandable, because reliability is so difficult to achieve unless you are willing to sacrifice validity. If the sole criterion for establishing depression were to hear the patient say at some point during an interview, "I feel depressed," the clinician could theoretically achieve perfect reliability (unless the clinician didn't hear the patient, which sometimes happens). But this achievement would be at the expense of validity because many people with differing psychological disorders, or none, occasionally say they are depressed. Thus, clinicians could agree that the statement occurred, but it would be of little use (Carson, 1991; Meehl, 1989). Second, as Carson (1996) points out, methods of constructing our nosology have a way of perpetuating definitions handed down to us from past decades, even if they might be fundamentally flawed. Carson (1991) makes a strong argument that it might be better to start fresh once in a while and create a new system of disorders based on emerging scientific knowledge rather than to simply fine-tune old definitions, but this is unlikely to happen because of the enormous effort and expense involved, and the necessity of discarding the accumulated wisdom of previous versions.

A thoughtful alternative was offered by Follette and Houts (1996), who argue that our system of nosology should become more theoretical. For example, depression can have a number of causes. One individual might be depressed because a loved one died, another because it results in attention from a girlfriend. Mild depression might lead to drug abuse, which deepens the depression. If we can't include *why* someone is depressed, we will never truly advance our system of classification, and without testing one theory (for example, biochemical changes resulting from stress) against another theory (for example, changes in social support), we won't understand causation. This theoretical approach emphasizes the function of behavior (why it occurs) rather than just the fact that it exists. It has been applied to alcoholism and pedophilia (Wulfert, Greenway, & Dougher, 1996) (see Chapters 10 and 11) and to anxiety disorder (Hayes, Wilson, Gifford, Follette, & Strosahl, 1996) (see Chapter 5). But the perspective still requires

The kinds of disabilities accepted in a given culture are socially determined.

considerable development and testing to determine whether it will be a useful addition to systems of classification.

In addition to the frightful complexity of categorizing psychopathology in particular and human behavior in general, systems are subject to misuse, some of which can be dangerous and harmful. Diagnostic categories are just a convenient format for organizing observations that help professionals communicate, study, and plan. But if we reify a category, we literally make it a "thing," assuming it has a meaning that, in reality, does not exist. Categories may change occasionally with new knowledge, so none can be written in stone. If a case falls on the fuzzy borders between diagnostic categories, we should not expend all our energy attempting to force it into one category or another. It is a mistaken assumption that everything has to fit neatly somewhere.

■ A Caution About Labeling

A related problem that occurs any time we categorize people is **labeling.** You may remember Kermit the Frog from *Sesame Street* sharing with us that "It's not easy being green." Something in human nature causes us to use a label, even one as superficial as skin color, to characterize the totality of an individual ("He's green . . . he's different from me"). We see the same phenomenon among psychological disorders ("He's a schizo"). Furthermore, if the disorder is associated with an impairment in cognitive or behavioral functioning, the label itself has negative connotations and becomes pejorative.

There have been many attempts over the years to categorize mental retardation. Most of the categories were based on the severity of the impairment or highest level of developmental ability that the individual could reach. But we have had to change the "labels" for these categories of cognitive impairment periodically as the stigma associated with them builds up. One early categorization described levels of severity as *moron, imbecile,* and *idiot.* When these terms were introduced they were rather neutral, simply describing the severity of a person's cognitive and developmental impairment. But as they began to be used in common language, they picked up negative connotations and were used as insults. As these terms gradually became pejorative, it was necessary to eliminate them from the categorical lexicon and come up with a new set of classifying labels that were less pejorative. One of the more recent developments is to categorize mental retardation functionally in terms of the levels of support needed by these individuals. In others words, a person's degree of mental retardation is determined by how much assistance he requires (that is, intermittent, limited, extensive, or pervasive) rather than by his IQ score (Lubinski, 2004; Luckasson et al., 1992).

Once labeled, individuals with a disorder may identify with the negative connotations associated with the label. This affects their self-esteem. Early attempts to document the detrimental effects of labeling produced mixed results (Segal, 1978), but a recent incisive analysis (Ruscio, 2004) indicates that the negative meanings associated with labeling are not a necessary consequence of making a diagnosis if it is relayed in a compassionate manner. Nevertheless, if you think of your own reactions to the mentally ill, you will probably recognize the tendency to generalize inappropriately from the label. We have to remember that terms in psychopathology do not describe people but identify patterns of

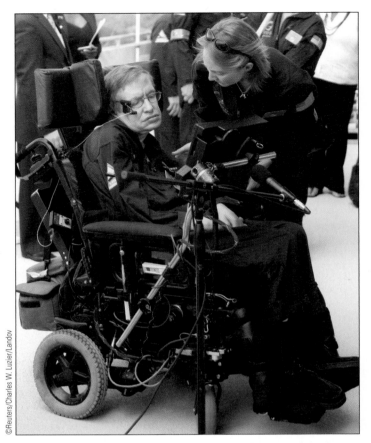

©Reuters/Charles W. Luzier/Landov

Would we label this man? Stephen Hawking, one of the world's leading physicists, is severely disabled by amyotrophic lateral sclerosis, a rare progressive degenerative disease of the spinal cord. Because he cannot activate his voice box or move his lips, Hawking types his words into an electronic voice synthesizer that "speaks" for him. He uses his thumbprint to autograph his books. "I have been lucky," he says. "I don't have anything to be angry about."

behavior that may or may not occur in certain circumstances. Thus, whether the disorder is medical or psychological, we must resist the temptation to identify the person with the disorder: Note the different implications of "John is a diabetic" and "John is a person who has diabetes."

Creating a Diagnosis

During the extensive deliberations by thousands of people that led to the publication of DSM-IV, a number of potentially new diagnostic categories were considered. Because one of us was a member of the task force, we can offer brief examples to illustrate how diagnostic categories are created.

■ Mixed Anxiety-Depression

Family physicians' offices, clinics, hospitals, and so on, are called *primary care settings* because they are where a person goes first with a problem. For years, people coming to these primary care clinics have complained of minor aches and pains that prove to have no physical basis. They also complain of feeling uptight, down in the dumps, and anxious. Health-care professionals examining these individuals report that their symptoms of both anxiety and depression are classic but not frequent or severe enough to meet criteria for an existing anxiety or mood disorder.

The DSM-IV task force was concerned about issues like this for several reasons. First, because many individuals present with some minor symptoms of a given disorder, it is important to set thresholds high enough that only people who clearly are suffering some impairment qualify for the category. (A *threshold* is the minimum number of criteria required to meet the definition of a disorder.) The primary reason for this concern is that substantial legal and policy implications are contingent on a diagnosis. That is, someone who presents with a psychological disorder that clearly qualifies for a diagnosis becomes part of the loosely organized medicolegal system and is eligible to ask (or sue) the government or private insurance companies for financial reimbursement or disability payments. This money actually comes from taxpayers, who are already burdened by skyrocketing health-care costs. Clearly, if the diagnostic system includes people who have only minor symptoms, who are not particularly impaired and just "feel down" from time to time, or who don't like their job and want disability (an all-too-common request in mental health clinics), the health-care system would be even more strained and would have fewer resources to treat the seriously impaired. But if people are experiencing considerable suffering and impairment in functioning, they should be covered in any health-care system. Therefore, minor complaints of dysphoric mood, characterized by vague complaints of anxiety and depression, were not considered sufficiently severe to constitute a formal diagnosis.

In 1989, Klerman and Weissman, reporting on a large study by Wells et al. (1989), found that patients who claimed to be anxious and mildly depressed were impaired in a number of areas when compared with normal controls and with patients with chronic medical conditions. It was *worse* than the impairment of many patients with chronic medical conditions. The evidence also suggested that these individuals were already imposing an enormous burden on the health-care system by appearing in large numbers at community clinics and the offices of family doctors. Barrett, Barrett, Oxman, and Gerber (1988), assessing patients from a rural primary care practice, found that as many as 14.4% of patients presented with principal complaints of anxiety and depression. Other studies supported this finding (Katon & Roy-Byrne, 1991; Roy-Byrne & Katon, 2000). Finally, evidence suggested that such people were at greatly increased risk of developing more severe mood or anxiety disorders (Moras et al., 1996; Roy-Byrne & Katon, 2000).

Therefore, we concluded that it might be valuable to identify these people and find out more about the etiology, course, and maintenance of the problem. The authors of the ICD-10, recognizing this phenomenon is prevalent throughout the world, had created a category of mixed anxiety-depression, but they had not defined it or created any criteria that would allow further examination of the potential disorder. Therefore, to explore the possibility of creating a new diagnostic category (Zinbarg & Barlow, 1996; Zinbarg et al., 1994, 1998), a study was undertaken that had three specific goals. First, if mental health professionals carefully administered semistructured interviews (the ADIS-IV), would they find patients who fit the new category? Or would careful examination find the criteria for existing disorders that had been

overlooked by health professionals not well trained in identifying psychological disorders? Second, if mixed anxiety-depression did exist, was it really more prevalent in medical primary care settings than in outpatient mental health settings? Third, what set of criteria (for example, types and number of symptoms) would best identify the disorder?

The study to answer these questions was conducted simultaneously in seven sites around the world (Zinbarg et al., 1994, 1998). Results indicated that people presenting with a number of anxious and depressed symptoms who *did not meet* criteria for an existing anxiety or mood disorder (because they did not have the right mix and/or severity of anxious or depressed symptoms) were common in primary care settings. Furthermore, they were substantially impaired in their occupational and social functioning and experienced a great deal of distress. Additional analysis revealed that such people could be distinguished from people with existing anxiety or mood disorders on the basis of their symptoms. Specifically, they presented with a set of emotional and behavioral symptoms that fall into the general category of *negative affect*, including behaviors such as difficulty sleeping and difficulty concentrating. These behaviors are often part of anxiety and mood disorders but are not specific to either. (Negative affect and its symptoms are described more fully in Chapter 7.) In any case, because these people appeared both anxious and depressed, the potential new category possessed content validity.

This study also established some criteria important in determining construct validity for the new category of mixed anxiety-depression. However, because the category is so new, we do not have information on additional criteria important in establishing construct validity, such as course, response to treatment, and the extent to which the disorder aggregates in families, and we cannot yet verify the reliability of the diagnosis or anything about predictive validity. Therefore, the decision of the DSM-IV task force was to place this mixed anxiety-depression diagnosis in the appendix, which is reserved for new diagnoses under study. It may become a full diagnostic category in future editions, but more research needs to be done first (First et al., 2002). Recently, Widiger and Samuel (2005) pointed out that this disorder fills a gap between anxiety and depression because it has symptoms of both. Therefore, they suggest that this might be a good reason to incorporate anxiety and depressive (mood) disorders into a larger, dimensionalized construct (discussed later).

■ Premenstrual Dysphoric Disorder

This disorder evokes a different issue that must be considered in the creation of any diagnostic category: bias and stigmatization. Evaluation of this extremely controversial category began well before the publication of DSM-III-R in 1987. Clinicians had identified a small group of women who presented with severe and sometimes incapacitating emotional reactions associated with the late luteal phase of their menstrual period (Rivera-Tovar, Pilkonis, & Frank, 1992). Subsequently, proposals were made to consider inclusion of this disorder in the DSM-III-R. In view of the suffering and impairment associated with the condition, the proponents argued, women deserved the attention, care, and financial support that inclusion in a diagnostic category would provide. In addition, as with mixed anxiety-depression, the creation of this category would promote a substantial increase in research into the nature and treatment of the problem.

Nevertheless, arguments against the category were marshaled along several fronts. First, opponents noted that relatively little scientific information existed in either the clinical or the research literature on this topic. The available information was insufficient to warrant the creation of a new diagnostic category. More important were substantial objections that what could be a normal endocrinological stage experienced by all or most women would be stigmatized as a psychiatric disorder. The seeming similarities with the once widely accepted category of "hysteria" described in Chapter 1 were also noted. (Remember that this so-called disorder, characterized by a variety of incapacitating physical complaints without a medical basis, was thought to be caused by the wandering of the uterus.) Questions were raised about whether the disorder would best be described as endocrinological or gynecological rather than mental. Because premenstrual dysphoric disorder occurs only in women, should we include a comparable disorder associated with, for example, aggressiveness related to excessive male hormones?

The DSM-III-R task force decided to place this disorder in the appendix in the hope of promoting further study. The task force also wanted to clearly differentiate this syndrome from premenstrual syndrome (PMS), which has less severe and specific premenstrual symptomatology. One way of accomplishing this was by naming the condition *late luteal phase dysphoric disorder (LLPDD)*.

After the publication of DSM-III-R, LLPDD attracted a great deal of research attention. By 1991, some observers estimated that one research article per month on LLPDD was published (Gold et al., 1996). A variety of scientific findings began to accrue that supported the inclusion of this disorder in DSM-IV. For example, although the rather vague and less severe symptoms of PMS occur in 20 to 40% of women (Severino & Moline, 1989), only a small proportion of them—about 4.6%—suffer from the more severe and incapacitating symptoms associated with LLPDD (Rivera-Tovar & Frank, 1990). In addition, a substantial number of women with no other psychological disorder meet the criteria for LLPDD. Among other findings supporting the inclusion of this disorder in DSM-IV were abnormalities in several biological systems associated with clinically significant premenstrual dysphoria (Gold et al., 1996) and the revelation that several types of treatment show some promise of being effective against LLPDD (for example, see Stone, Pearlstein, & Brown, 1991). Hurt and colleagues, in a reanalysis of data from 670 women, recommended a set of criteria for this disorder that were not very different from those proposed in DSM-III-R (Hurt et al., 1992).

Nevertheless, arguments continue against including this disorder in the diagnostic system. Most of them cite the issue of stigmatization, warning that recognition might confirm the cultural belief that menstruation and resulting disability make women unfit for positions of responsibility. (There have been several cases in which accusations of the less severe condition of PMS have been used against a mother in an attempt to win child custody for the father; see Gold et al., 1996.) Also, elevating the condition to the category of a disorder might sustain and strengthen religious and cultural taboos associated with the menstrual cycle that range from prohibition of sexual intercourse to actual banishment from regular living quarters. Those arguing against the disorder also point out that some symptoms are associated with anger, which would not be viewed as inappropriate in a male. Only in a female does society presume that anger signifies something is wrong.

What would you do? Would you call this condition a disorder to ensure that women suffering from it receive the attention and treatment they need? Or would you be more concerned with the potential for misuse of the diagnosis, particularly the social stigmatization? Interestingly, many women with this disorder are quite comfortable with the label. Some women presenting with other psychological disorders, such as depression, refuse to accept the suggestion that they have a "psychiatric problem," insisting it is really PMS (Rapkin, Chang, & Reading, 1989). Early in 1994, the DSM-IV task force decided to retain the disorder in the appendix as needing further study. Among other problems, the committee wanted to see more data on the prevalence of this condition using the new criteria and to examine more carefully the data on the relation of this problem to existing mood disorders.

Several additional research findings indicated that the name *late luteal phase dysphoric disorder* was not entirely accurate because the symptoms may not be exclusively related to the endocrine state of the late luteal phase. Therefore, the name has been changed to *premenstrual dysphoric disorder (PMDD)*.

Since 1994, research has continued, and even accelerated, on the nature of PMDD, with thousands of papers published on this general topic (Gold, 1999; Grady-Weliky, 2003; Perlstein, Yonkers, Fayyad, & Gillespie, 2005). Epidemiological studies from around the world now support the existence of disabling premenstrual symptoms in about 8% of women, with another 14% to 18% experiencing moderate symptoms (Angst, Sellaro, Stolar, Merikangas, & Endicott, 2001; J. H. Gold, 1997; Ko, Lee, Chang, & Huang, 1996; Wittchen, Becker, Lieb, & Krause, 2002). And the American College of Obstetricians and Gynecology has published systematic clinical practice guidelines recommending specific treatments (American College of Obstetricians and Gynecologists, 2002). One of the difficulties encountered has been distinguishing PMDD from premenstrual exacerbations of other disorders, such as binge eating disorder or mood disorders (Perlstein et al., 2005). Hartlage and Gehlert (2001) proposed a method that carefully considers the nature and timing of the symptoms to make a valid distinction between PMDD and premenstrual exacerbations of other disorders. For example, the symptoms of PMDD must be absent or present only mildly postmenstrually. Also, to distinguish from a mood disorder, at least some symptoms must be different from those associated with a mood disorder, such as certain physical symptoms or anxiety. The accumulating evidence thus far seems to suggest that PMDD is best considered a disorder of mood rather than, for example, an endocrine disorder and that it should continue to be considered a mental disorder (Gold, 1999). Whether further study will continue to support PMDD as a distinct psychological disorder for DSM-V remains to be seen.

Conclusions

The process of changing the criteria for existing diagnoses and creating new ones will continue as our science advances. New findings on brain circuits, cognitive processes, and cultural factors that affect our behavior could date diagnostic criteria relatively quickly.

Now the process to create the fifth edition of the *Diagnostic and Statistical Manual of Mental Disorders* (DSM-V) has begun. Initially, a series of research planning conferences resulted in a monograph detailing a research agenda for DSM-V (Kupfer et al., 2002). It is now clear to most professionals involved in this process that an exclusive reliance on discrete diagnostic categories has not achieved its objective in achieving a satisfactory system of nosology (Krueger, Watson, & Barlow, 2005). In addition to problems noted earlier with comorbidity and the fuzzy boundary between diagnostic categories, little evidence has emerged validating these categories, such as discovering specific underlying causes associated with each category. In addition, not one biological marker, such as a laboratory test, that would clearly distinguish one disorder from another has been discovered (Widiger & Samuel, 2005). It is also clear that the current categories lack treatment specificity. That is, certain treatments such as cognitive behavioral therapies or specific antidepressant drugs are effective for a large number of diagnostic categories that are not supposed to be all that similar. Therefore, the DSM-V planners are beginning to assume that the limitations of the current diagnostic system are substantial enough that continued research on these diagnostic categories may never be successful in uncovering their underlying causes or helping us develop new treatments. It may be time for a new approach. Most people agree that this approach will incorporate a dimensional strategy to a much greater extent than in DSM-IV (Krueger et al., 2005; Kupfer et al., 2002; Widiger & Coker, 2003; Widiger & Sankis, 2000).

For example, in the area of personality disorders, Livesley, Jang, and Vernon (1998), in studying both clinical samples of patients with personality disorders and community samples, concluded that personality disorders were not qualitatively distinct from the personalities of normal-functioning individuals in community samples. Instead, personality disorders simply represent maladaptive, and perhaps extreme, variants of common personality traits (Widiger & Samuel, 2005). Even the genetic structure of personality is not consistent with discrete categorical personality disorders. That is, personality dispositions more broadly defined, such as being shy and inhibited or outgoing, have a stronger genetic influence (higher genetic loading) than personality disorders as currently defined (First et al., 2002; Livesley et al., 1998; Rutter, Moffitt, & Caspi, 2006). For the anxiety and mood disorders, Brown, Chorpita, and Barlow (1998) have demonstrated that anxiety and depression have more in common than previously thought and may best be represented as points on a continuum of negative affect (see Barlow, 2002; Brown & Barlow, 2005; Clark, 2005; Mineka, Watson, & Clark, 1998; Watson, 2005). Even for severe disorders with seemingly stronger genetic influences, such as schizophrenia, it appears that dimensional classification strategies might prove superior (Charney et al., 2002; Lenzenweger &

Dworkin, 1996; Toomey, Faraone, Simpson, & Tsuang, 1998; Widiger, 1997; Widiger & Samuel, 2005; Widiger & Sankis, 2000).

At the same time, exciting new developments from the area of neuroscience relating to brain structure and function will provide enormously important information on the nature of psychological disorders. This information could then be integrated with more psychological, social, and cultural information into a diagnostic system. But even neuroscientists are abandoning the notion that groups of genes or brain circuits will be found that are specifically associated with DSM-IV diagnostic categories, as noted in Chapter 2. Rather, it is now assumed that neurobiological processes will be discovered that are associated with specific cognitive, emotional, and behavioral patterns or traits (for example, behavioral inhibition) that do not necessarily correspond closely with current diagnostic categories. The plan is that the work groups for DSM-V will be assembled in 2007, with the new criteria for DSM-V appearing around 2011 or later.

With this in mind, we can turn our attention to the current state of our knowledge about a variety of major psychological disorders. Beginning with Chapter 5, we attempt to predict the next major scientific breakthroughs affecting diagnostic criteria and definitions of disorders. But first we review the all-important area of research methods and strategies used to establish new knowledge of psychopathology.

CONCEPT CHECK 3.2

Identify each of the following statements related to diagnosing psychological disorders as either true (T) or false (F).

1. ____ The classical categorical approach to classification assumes there is only one set of causative factors per disorder with no overlap between disorders, and the prototypical approach uses essential, defining features, as well as a range of other characteristics.

2. ____ As in earlier versions, DSM-IV retains a distinction between organically and psychologically based disorders.

3. ____ The DSM-IV eradicated the problem of comorbidity, the identification of two or more disorders in an individual at one time, which was previously caused by imprecise categories.

4. ____ If two or more clinicians agree on a patient's classification, the assessments are said to be valid.

5. ____ A danger in psychological classification is that a diagnostic label might be used to characterize personally the total individual.

SUMMARY

Assessing Psychological Disorders

■ Clinical assessment is the systematic evaluation and measurement of psychological, biological, and social factors in an individual with a possible psychological disorder; diagnosis is the process of determining that those factors meet all criteria for a specific psychological disorder.

■ Reliability, validity, and standardization are important components in determining the value of a psychological assessment.

■ To assess various aspects of psychological disorders, clinicians may first interview and take an informal mental status exam of the patient. More systematic observations of behavior are called behavioral assessment.

■ A variety of psychological tests can be used during assessment, including projective tests, in which the patient responds to ambiguous stimuli by projecting unconscious thoughts; personality inventories, in which the patient takes a self-report questionnaire designed to assess personal traits; and intelligence testing, which provides a score known as an intelligence quotient (IQ).

■ Biological aspects of psychological disorders may be assessed through neuropsychological testing designed to identify possible areas of brain dysfunction. Neuroimaging can be used more directly to identify brain structure and function. Finally, psychophysiological assessment refers to measurable changes in the nervous system, reflecting emotional or psychological events that might be relevant to a psychological disorder.

Diagnosing Psychological Disorders

■ The term *classification* refers to any effort to construct groups or categories and to assign objects or people to the categories on the basis of their shared attributes or relations. Methods of classification include classical categorical, dimensional, and prototypical approaches. Our current system of classification, the *Diagnostic and Statistical Manual,* fourth edition, text revision (DSM-IV), is based on a prototypical approach in which certain essential characteristics are identified but certain "nonessential" variations do not necessarily change the classification. The DSM-IV-R categories are based on empirical findings to identify the criteria for each diagnosis. Although this system is the best to date in terms of scientific underpinnings, it is far from perfect, and research continues on the most useful way to classify psychological disorders as we begin to plan for DSM-V.

Key Terms

clinical assessment, 69	personality inventories, 79	electroencephalogram (EEG), 84	classical categorical approach, 86
diagnosis, 69	intelligence quotient (IQ), 81	idiographic strategy, 85	dimensional approach, 87
reliability, 71	neuropsychological testing, 82	nomothetic strategy, 85	prototypical approach, 87
validity, 71	false positive, 82	classification, 85	familial aggregation, 88
standardization, 71	false negative, 82	taxonomy, 85	comorbidity, 91
mental status exam, 71	neuroimaging, 82	nosology, 85	labeling, 92
behavioral assessment, 74	psychophysiological assessment, 84	nomenclature, 85	
projective tests, 77			

Answers to Concept Checks

3.1

Part A

1. thought processes; 2. appearance and behavior; 3. sensorium; 4. mood and affect; 5. intellectual functioning

Part B

6. R,V; 7. NR, NV; 8. R,V; 9. NR, NV

3.2

1. T; 2. F; 3. F (still a problem); 4. F (reliable); 5. T

The Abnormal Psychology Book Companion Website

See **academic.cengage.com/psychology/barlow** for practice quiz questions, interactive activities, Internet links, critical thinking exercises, discussion forums, and more. Also accessible from the Wadsworth Psychology Resource Center **(academic.cengage .com/login)**.

Abnormal Psychology Live CD-ROM

■ *Arriving at a Diagnosis:* A team discusses how it arrived at the conclusion that a patient has a panic disorder.

■ *Psychological Assessment:* The psychological team discusses factors in dysfunctional beliefs, family relationships, and behavior patterns that might be contributing to a woman's major depressive disorder.

CengageNOW

Go to **academic.cengage.com/now** to link to CengageNOW, your online study tool. First take the Pre-Test for this chapter to get your personalized study plan, which will identify topics you need to review and direct you to online resources. Then take the Post-Test to determine what concepts you have mastered and what you still need work on.

Video Concept Reviews

CengageNOW also contains Mark Durand's *Video Concept Reviews* on challenging topics.

- Clinical Assessment
- Reliability/Validity
- Standardization
- Mental Status Exam
- Behavioral Assessment
- Projective Tests
- Concept Check—Data-Based Approach
- Neuropsychological Testing
- False Positive/False Negative
- Psychophysiological Assessment
- Diagnosis/Classification
- Taxonomy/Nosology/Nomenclature
- Concept Check—Categorical Versus Dimensional
- Classification Systems
- DSM-IV

CHAPTER 4

Research Methods

©Design Pics Inc./Alamy

EXAMINING ABNORMAL BEHAVIOR
Important Concepts
Basic Components of a Research Study
Statistical Versus Clinical Significance
The "Average" Client

TYPES OF RESEARCH METHODS
Studying Individual Cases
Research by Correlation
Research by Experiment
Single-Case Experimental Designs

GENETICS AND RESEARCH ACROSS TIME AND CULTURES
Studying Genetics
Studying Behavior Over Time
Studying Behavior Across Cultures
The Power of a Program of Research
Replication
Research Ethics

ABNORMAL PSYCHOLOGY LIVE CD-ROM
Research Methods
Web Link

Traditional scientific method has always been at the very best 20–20 hindsight. It's good for seeing where you've been. It's good for testing the truth of what you think you know, but it can't tell you where you ought to go.

Robert M. Pirsig
Zen and the Art of Motorcycle Maintenance

EXAMINING ABNORMAL BEHAVIOR

Behavioral scientists explore human behavior the same way other scientists study the path of a comet or the AIDS virus: They use the scientific method. As you've already seen, abnormal behavior is a challenging subject because of the interaction of biological and psychological dimensions. Rarely are there any simple answers to such questions as "Why do some people have hallucinations?" or "How do you treat someone who is suicidal?"

In addition to the obvious complexity of human nature, another factor that makes an objective study of abnormal behavior difficult is the inaccessibility of many important aspects of this phenomenon. We can't get inside the minds of people except indirectly. Fortunately, some creative individuals have accepted this challenge and have developed many ingenious methods for studying scientifically what behaviors constitute problems, why people suffer from behavioral disorders, and how to treat these problems. Some of you will ultimately contribute to this important field by applying the methods described in this chapter. Many critical questions regarding abnormal behavior have yet to be answered, and we hope that some of you will be inspired to take them on. However, understanding research methods is extremely important for everyone. You or someone close to you may need the services of a psychologist, psychiatrist, or other mental health provider. You may have questions such as these:

- Should childhood aggression be cause for concern, or is it a phase my child will grow out of?
- The *Today* show just reported that increased exposure to sunlight alleviates depression. Instead of seeing a therapist, should I buy a ticket to Hawaii?
- I read a story about the horrors of shock therapy. Should I advise my neighbor not to let her daughter have this treatment?
- My brother has been in therapy for 3 years but doesn't seem to be any better. Should I tell him to look elsewhere for help?
- My mother is still in her 50s but seems to be forgetting things. Friends tell me this is natural as you grow older. Should I be concerned?

To answer such questions, you need to be a good consumer of research. When you understand the correct ways of obtaining information—that is, research methodology—you will know when you are dealing with fact and not fiction. Knowing the difference between a fad and an established approach to a problem can be the difference between months of suffering and a quick resolution to a disturbing problem.

Important Concepts

As we said from the start, we examine several aspects of abnormal behavior in this book. First, "What problems cause distress and impair functioning?" Second, "Why do people behave in unusual ways?" And third, "How do we help them behave in more adaptive ways?" The first question is about the nature of the problems people report; we explore research strategies that help us answer this question. The second question considers the causes, or *etiology,* of abnormal behavior; we explore strategies for discovering why a disorder occurred. Finally, because we want to help people who have disorders, we describe how researchers evaluate treatments. Before we discuss specific strategies, however, we must consider several general ways of evaluating research.

Basic Components of a Research Study

The basic research process is simple. You start with an educated guess, called a **hypothesis,** about what you expect to find. When you decide how you want to test this hypothesis, you have a **research design** that includes the aspects you want to measure in the people you are studying (the **dependent variable**) and the influences on their behaviors (the **independent variable**). Finally, two forms of validity are specific to research studies: internal validity and external validity. **Internal validity** is the extent to which you can be confident that the independent variable is causing the dependent variable to change. **External validity** refers to how well the results relate to things outside your study—in other words, how well your findings describe similar individuals who were not among the study subjects. Although we discuss a variety of research strategies, they all have these basic elements. Table 4.1 shows the essential components of a research study.

TABLE 4.1	The Basic Components of a Research Study
Component	**Description**
Hypothesis	An educated guess or statement to be supported by data.
Research design	The plan for testing the hypothesis. Affected by the question addressed, by the hypothesis, and by practical considerations.
Dependent variable	Some aspect of the phenomenon that is measured and is expected to be changed or influenced by the independent variable.
Independent variable	The aspect manipulated or thought to influence the change in the dependent variable.
Internal validity	The extent to which the results of the study can be attributed to the independent variable.
External validity	The extent to which the results of the study can be generalized or applied outside the immediate study.

Hypothesis

A close friend lost his younger brother in a motorcycle accident. The senseless loss of this fine young man created a tremendous amount of grief and bitterness. The family wanted to know *why*—what was the purpose, the reason for this tragedy?

Human beings look for order and purpose. We want to know why the world works as it does, why people behave the way they do. Robert Kegan (cited in Lefrancois, 1990) describes us as "meaning-making" organisms, constantly striving to make sense of what is going on around us. It is interesting to note that this orientation is reflected in such physiological processes as vision. We often see only parts of things—the side of a person's head, the way she walks down a hall. Yet the brain can take these parts and put them together to make a meaningful whole—your best friend.

The familiar search for meaning and order also characterizes the field of abnormal behavior. Almost by definition, abnormal behavior defies the regularity and predictability we desire. It is this departure from the norm that makes the study of abnormal behavior so intriguing. In an attempt to make sense of these phenomena, behavioral scientists construct hypotheses and then test them. Hypotheses are nothing more than educated guesses about the world. You may believe that watching violent television programs will cause children to be more aggressive. You may think that bulimia is influenced by media depictions of supposedly ideal female body types. You may suspect that someone abused as a child is likely to become a spouse abuser and child abuser. These concerns are all testable hypotheses.

Once a scientist decides what to study, the next step is to put it in words that are unambiguous and in a form that is testable. Consider a study of changes in marital satisfaction after the birth of a couple's first baby. Marc Schulz, Carolyn Pape Cowan, and Philip Cowan studied 66 couples who were expecting their first child (Schulz, Cowan, & Cowan, 2006). They knew from previous research that the transition to parenthood often strained these relationships. In their study, these researchers posed the following hypothesis: "A preventive intervention would help them maintain their satisfaction in the relationship after the birth of their baby." The way the hypothesis is stated suggests the researchers already know the answer to their question. This is an advantage because it doesn't assume anything until the experiment is completed. They won't know what they will find until the study is completed, but phrasing the hypothesis in this way makes it testable. If, for example, marital satisfaction declines even after the use of their treatment, then other efforts must be used. This concept of **testability** (the ability to support the hypothesis) is important for science because it allows us to say that in this case, either (1) the intervention prevents a decline in satisfaction, so maybe it should be used with other couples, or (2) the intervention is not effective, so let's try another approach.

When they develop an experimental hypothesis, researchers also specify dependent and independent variables. A dependent variable is what is expected to change or be influenced by the study. Psychologists studying abnormal behavior typically measure an aspect of the disorder, such as overt behaviors, thoughts, and feelings, or biological symptoms. In the study by Schulz and colleagues, the main dependent variable was the couples' responses on a questionnaire about their marital satisfaction (the Locke-Wallace Marital Adjustment Test). Independent variables are those factors thought to affect the dependent variables. The independent variable in the study by Schulz and colleagues was whether or not the couple received the prevention intervention. In other words, the treatment itself is expected to influence behavior and is therefore an independent variable.

Internal and External Validity

The researchers in the study on marital satisfaction solicited couples through a community newsletter and local medical practices. Suppose they found that, unknown to them, most couples who agree to participate in these types of studies are less dissatisfied with their marriages than typical couples. This would have affected the data in a way not related to the treatment, which would change the meaning of their results. This situation, which relates to internal validity, is called a **confound** (or **confounding variable**), defined as any factor occurring in a study that makes the results uninterpretable because a variable (in this instance, study participants who are more happily married than is typical) other than the independent variable (receiving or not receiving preventive intervention) may also affect the dependent variable (marital satisfaction). Interestingly for this study, another group of researchers found that how you locate couples does influence who participates. For example, recruiting at bridal shows leads to finding more satisfied couples, whereas radio and television ads attract more dissatisfied couples (Rogge et al., 2006). The degree to which confounds are present in a study is a measure of internal validity, the extent to which the results can be explained by the independent variable. If the study by Schulz found no differences in treatment because there was little dissatisfaction in any of the couples (because of how they were selected), then this would be a confound. Such a hypothetical confound in the Schulz study would have made this research internally invalid because it would have reduced the ability to explain the results in terms of the independent variable—the preventive intervention.

Scientists use many strategies to ensure internal validity in their studies, three of which we discuss here: control groups, randomization, and analog models. In a **control group,** people are similar to the experimental group in every way except that members of the experimental group are exposed to the independent variable and those in the control group are not. Because researchers can't prevent people from being exposed to many things around them that could affect the outcomes of the study, they try to compare people who receive the treatment with people who go through similar experiences except for the treatment (control group). Control groups help rule out alternative explanations for results, thereby strengthening internal validity.

Randomization is the process of assigning people to different research groups in such a way that each person has an equal chance of being place in any group. Researchers can, for example, randomly place people in groups but still end up with more of certain people (for example, people with more severe depression) in one group than another. Placing people in groups by flipping a coin or using a random number table helps improve internal

Studying people as part of a group sometimes masks individual differences.

validity by eliminating any systematic bias in assignment, but it does not necessarily eliminate bias in your group. You will see later that people sometimes "put themselves in groups," and this self-selection can affect study results. Perhaps a researcher treating people with depression offers them the choice of being either in the treatment group, which requires coming into the clinic twice a week for 2 months, or in a wait-list control group, which means waiting until some later time to be treated. The most severely depressed individuals may not be motivated to come to frequent treatment sessions and so will choose the wait-list group. If members of the treated group are less depressed after several months, it could be because of the treatment or because group members were less depressed to begin with. Groups assembled randomly avoid these problems.

Analog models create in the controlled conditions of the laboratory aspects that are comparable (analogous) to the phenomenon under study. Bulimia researchers could ask volunteers to binge eat in the laboratory, questioning them before they ate, while they were eating, and after they finished to learn whether eating in this way made them feel more or less anxious, guilty, and so on. If they used volunteers of any age, gender, race, or background, the researchers could rule out influences on the subjects' attitudes about eating that they might not be able to dismiss if the group contained only people with bulimia. In this way, such "artificial" studies help improve internal validity.

In a research study, internal and external validity often seem to be in opposition. On the one hand, we want to be able to control as many things as possible to conclude that the independent variable (the aspect of the study we manipulated) was responsible for the changes in the dependent variables (the aspects of the study we expected to change). On the other hand, we want the results to apply to people other than the subjects of the study and in other settings; this is **generalizability,** the extent to which results apply to everyone with a particular disorder. If we control all aspects of

a study so that only the independent variable changes, the result is not relevant to the real world. For example, if you reduce the influence of gender issues by only studying males, and if you reduce age variables by only selecting people from 25–30 years of age, and finally, if you limit your study to those with college degrees so that education level isn't an issue—then what you study (in this case, 25- to 30-year-old male college graduates) may not be relevant to many other populations. Internal and external validity are in this way often inversely related. Researchers constantly try to balance these two concerns and, as you will see later in this chapter, the best solution for achieving both internal and external validity may be to conduct several related studies.

Statistical Versus Clinical Significance

The introduction of statistics is part of psychology's evolution from a prescientific to a scientific discipline. Statisticians gather, analyze, and interpret data from research. In psychological research, statistical significance typically means the probability of obtaining the observed effect by chance is small. As an example, consider a study evaluating whether a drug (naltrexone)—when added to a psychological intervention—helps those with alcohol addiction stay sober longer (Anton et al., 2006). The study found that the combination of medication and psychotherapy helped people stay abstinent 77 days on average and those receiving a placebo stayed abstinent only 75 days on average. This difference was statistically significant. But is it an important difference? The difficulty is in the distinction between **statistical significance** and **clinical significance.**

Closer examination of the results leads to concern about the size of the effect. Because this research studied a large group of people dependent on alcohol (1,383 volunteers), even this small difference (75 versus 77 days) was statistically different. However, few of us would say staying sober for 2 extra days was worth taking medication and participating in extensive therapy.

Fortunately, concern for the clinical significance of results has led researchers to develop statistical methods that address not just that groups are different but also how large these differences are, or *effect size.* Calculating the actual statistical measures involves fairly sophisticated procedures that take into account how much each treated and untreated person in a research study improves or worsens (Reichardt, 2006). In other words, instead of just looking at the results of the group as a whole, individual differences are considered as well. Some researchers have used more subjective ways of determining whether truly important change has resulted from treatment. The late behavioral scientist Montrose Wolf (1978) advocated the assessment of what he called *social validity.* This technique involves obtaining input from the person being treated, as well as from significant others, about the importance of the changes that have occurred. In the example here, we might ask the volunteers and family members if they thought the treatment led to truly important improvements in alcohol abstinence. If the effect of the treatment is large enough to impress those who are directly involved, the treatment effect is clinically significant. Statistical techniques of measuring effect size and assessing subjective judgments of change will let us better evaluate the results of our treatments.

The "Average" Client

Too often we look at results from studies and make generalizations about the group, ignoring individual differences. Kiesler (1966) labeled the tendency to see all participants as one homogeneous group the **patient uniformity myth.** Comparing groups according to their mean scores ("Group A improved by 50% over Group B") hides important differences in individual reactions to our interventions.

The patient uniformity myth leads researchers to make inaccurate generalizations about disorders and their treatments. To continue with our previous example, what if the researchers studying the treatment of alcoholism concluded that the experimental treatment was a good approach? And suppose we found that, although some participants improved with treatment, others worsened. Such differences would be averaged out in the analysis of the group as a whole, but for the person whose drinking increased with the experimental treatment, it would make little difference that "on the average" people improved. Because people differ in such ways as age, cognitive abilities, gender, and history of treatment, a simple group comparison may be misleading. Practitioners who deal with all types of disorders understand the heterogeneity of their clients and therefore do not know whether treatments that are statistically significant will be effective for a given individual. In our discussions of various disorders, we return to this issue.

CONCEPT CHECK 4.1

In each of the statements provided, fill in the blanks with one of the following: hypothesis, dependent variable, independent variable, internal validity, external validity, or confound.

1. In a treatment study, the introduction of the treatment to the participants is referred to as the _____.
2. After the treatment study was completed, you found that many people in the control group received treatment outside of the study. This is called a _____.
3. A researcher's guess about what a study might find is labeled the _____.
4. Scores on a depression scale improved for a treatment group after therapy. The change in these scores would be referred to as a change in the _____.
5. A relative lack of confounds in a study would indicate good _____, whereas good generalizability of the results would be called good _____.

TYPES OF RESEARCH METHODS

Behavioral scientists use several forms of research when studying the causes of behavior. We now examine individual case studies, correlational research, experimental research, and single-case experimental studies.

Studying Individual Cases

Consider the following scenario: A psychologist thinks she has discovered a new disorder. She has observed several men who seem to have similar characteristics. All complain of a specific sleep disorder: falling asleep at work. Each man has obvious cognitive impairments that were evident during the initial interviews, and all are similar physically, each with significant hair loss and a pear-shaped physique. Finally, their personality styles are extremely egocentric, or self-centered. On the basis of these preliminary observations, the psychologist has come up with a tentative name, the Homer Simpson disorder, and she has decided to investigate this condition and possible treatments. But what is the best way to begin exploring a relatively unknown disorder? One method is to use the **case study method,** investigating intensively one or more individuals who display the behavioral and physical patterns (Yin, 2006).

One way to describe the case study method is by noting what it is not. It does not use the scientific method. Few efforts are made to ensure internal validity and, typically, many confounding variables are present that can interfere with conclusions. Instead, the case study method relies on a clinician's observations of differences among one person or one group with a disorder, people with other disorders, and people with no psychological disorders. The clinician usually collects as much information as possible to obtain a detailed description of the person. Historically, interviewing the person under study yields a great deal of information on personal and family background, education, health, and work history, as well as the person's opinions about the nature and causes of the problems being studied.

Case studies are important in the history of psychology. Sigmund Freud developed psychoanalytic theory and the methods of psychoanalysis on the basis of his observations of dozens of cases. Freud and Josef Breuer's description of Anna O. (see Chapter 1) led to development of the clinical technique known as free association. Sex researchers Virginia Johnson and William Masters based their work on many case studies and helped shed light on numerous myths regarding sexual behavior (Masters & Johnson, 1966). Joseph Wolpe, author of the landmark book *Psychotherapy by Reciprocal Inhibition* (1958), based his work with systematic desensitization on more than 200 cases. As our knowledge of psychological disorders has grown, psychological researchers have relied decreasingly on the case study method.

One difficulty with depending heavily on individual cases is that sometimes coincidences occur that are irrelevant to the condition under study. Unfortunately, coincidences in people's lives often lead to mistaken conclusions about what causes certain conditions and what treatment appears to be effective. Because a case study does not have the controls of an experimental study, the results may be unique to a particular person without the researcher realizing it or may derive from a special combination of factors that are not obvious. Complicating our efforts to understand abnormal behavior is the portrayal of sensational cases in the media. Just before mass murderer Ted Bundy was executed in Florida, he proclaimed that pornography was to blame for his abhorrent behavior. The case of Jeffrey Dahmer, who killed, mutilated, and cannibalized his victims, is known throughout the world. Attempts have been made to discover childhood experiences that could possibly explain his adult behavior. What conclusions should we draw? Did Bundy have valuable insight into his own behavior, or was he attempting to evade responsibility? Can acquaintances and friends of the Dahmer family shed accurate light on his development? We must be careful about concluding anything from such sensational portrayals.

Researchers in cognitive psychology point out that the public and researchers themselves are often, unfortunately, more highly influenced by dramatic accounts than by scientific evidence (Nisbett & Ross, 1980). Remembering our tendency to ignore this fact, we highlight research findings in this book. To advance our understanding of the nature, causes, and treatment of abnormal behavior, we must guard against premature and inaccurate conclusions.

Research by Correlation

One of the fundamental questions posed by scientists is whether two variables relate to each other. A statistical relationship between two variables is called a **correlation.** For example, is schizophrenia related to the size of ventricles (spaces) in the brain? Are people with depression more likely to have negative attributions? Is the frequency of hallucinations higher among older people? The answers depend on determining how one variable (for example, number of hallucinations) is related to another (for example, age). Unlike experimental designs, which involve manipulating or changing conditions, correlational designs are used to study phenomena just as they occur. The result of a correlational study—whether variables occur together—is important to the ongoing search for knowledge about abnormal behavior.

One of the clichés of science is that correlation does not imply causation. In other words, two things occurring together does not necessarily mean that one caused the other. For example, the occurrence of marital problems in families is correlated with behavior problems in children (Erath, Bierman, & Conduct Problems Prevention Research Group, 2006). If you conduct a correlational study in this area, you will find that in families with marital problems you tend to see children with behavior problems; in families with fewer marital problems, you are likely to find children with fewer behavior problems. The most obvious conclusion is that having marital problems will cause children to misbehave. If only it were as simple as that! The nature of the relationship between marital discord and childhood behavior problems can be explained in a number of ways. It may be that problems in a marriage cause disruptive behavior in the children. However, some evidence suggests the opposite may be true as well: The disruptive behavior of children may cause marital problems (Rutter & Giller, 1984). In addition, evidence suggests genetic influences may play a role in conduct disorders and in marital discord (D'Onofrio et al., 2006; Lynch et al., 2006).

This example points out the problems in interpreting the results of a correlational study. We know that variable A (marital problems) is correlated with variable B (child behavior problems). We do not know from these studies whether A causes B (marital problems cause child problems), whether B causes A (child problems cause marital problems), or whether some third variable, C, causes both (genes influence both marital problems and child problems).

The association between marital discord and child problems represents a **positive correlation.** This means that great strength or quantity in one variable (a great deal of marital distress) is associated with great strength or quantity in the other variable (more child disruptive behavior). At the same time, lower strength or quantity in one variable (marital distress) is associated with lower strength or quantity in the other (disruptive behavior). If you have trouble conceptualizing statistical concepts, you can think about this mathematical relationship in the same way you would a social relationship. Two people who are getting along well tend to go places together: "Where I go, you will go!" The correlation (or **correlation coefficient**) is represented as $+1.00$. The plus sign means there is a positive relationship, and the 1.00 means that it is a "perfect" relationship, in which the people are inseparable. Obviously, two people who like each other do not go everywhere together. The strength of their relationship ranges between 0.00 and $+1.00$ (0.00 means no relationship exists). The higher the number, the stronger the relationship, whether the number is positive or negative (for example, a correlation of $+0.80$ is "stronger" than a correlation of $+0.75$). You would expect two strangers, for example, to have a relationship of 0.00 because their behavior is not related; they sometimes end up in the same place together, but this occurs rarely and randomly. Two people who know each other but do not like each other would be represented by a negative sign, with the range of -1.00 to 0.00, and a strong negative relationship would be -1.00, which means, "Anywhere you go, I won't be there!"

Using this analogy, marital problems in families and behavior problems in children have a relatively strong positive correlation represented by a number around $+0.50$. They tend to go together. On the other hand, other variables are strangers to each other. Schizophrenia and height are not related, so they don't go together and probably would be represented by a number close to 0.00. If A and B have no correlation, their correlation coefficient would approximate 0.00. Other factors have negative relationships: As one increases, the other decreases. (See ■ Figure 4.1 for an illustration of positive and negative correlations.) We used an example of **negative correlation** in Chapter 2, when we discussed social supports and illness. The more social supports that are present, the less likely it is that a person will become ill. The negative relationship between social supports and illness could be represented by a number such as -0.40. The next time someone wants to break up with you, ask if the goal is to weaken the strength of your positive relationship to something like $+0.25$ (friends), to become complete strangers at 0.00, or to have an intense negative relationship approximating -1.00 (enemies).

A correlation allows us to see whether a relationship exists between two variables but not to draw conclusions about whether either variable causes the effects. This is a problem of **directional-**

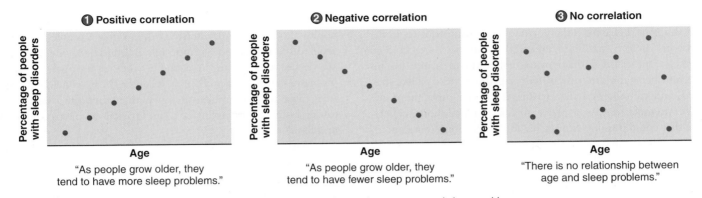

❶ Positive correlation

Percentage of people with sleep disorders

Age

"As people grow older, they tend to have more sleep problems."

❷ Negative correlation

Percentage of people with sleep disorders

Age

"As people grow older, they tend to have fewer sleep problems."

❸ No correlation

Percentage of people with sleep disorders

Age

"There is no relationship between age and sleep problems."

■ **FIGURE 4.1** These three graphs represent hypothetical correlations between age and sleep problems.

ity. In this case, it means that we do not know whether A causes B, B causes A, or a third variable, C, causes A and B. Therefore, even an extremely strong relationship between two variables (+0.90) shows nothing about the direction of causality.

■ Epidemiological Research

Scientists often think of themselves as detectives, searching for the truth by studying clues. One type of correlational research that is much like the efforts of detectives is called **epidemiology,** the study of the incidence, distribution, and consequences of a particular problem or set of problems in one or more populations. Epidemiologists expect that by tracking a disorder among many people they will find important clues as to why the disorder exists. One strategy involves determining *prevalence,* the number of people with a disorder at any one time. For example, the prevalence of binge drinking (having five or more drinks in a row) among U.S. college students is about 40% (Substance Abuse and Mental Health Services Administration, 2006; Windle & Windle, 2006). A related strategy is to determine the *incidence* of a disorder, the estimated number of new cases during a specific period. For example, incidence of binge drinking among college students is reduced only slightly from 1980 until the present (Substance Abuse and Mental Health Services Administration, 2006), suggesting that despite efforts to reduce such heavy drinking, it continues to be a problem. Epidemiologists study the incidence and prevalence of disorders among different groups of people. For instance, data from epidemiological research indicate that the prevalence of alcohol abuse among African Americans is lower than that among whites (Substance Abuse and Mental Health Services Administration, 2006).

Although the primary goal of epidemiology is to determine the extent of medical problems, it is also useful in the study of psychological disorders. In the early 1900s, a number of Americans displayed symptoms of a strange mental disorder. Its symptoms were similar to those of organic psychosis, which is often caused by mind-altering drugs or great quantities of alcohol. Many patients appeared to be catatonic (immobile for long periods) or exhibited symptoms similar to those of para-

noid schizophrenia. Victims were likely to be poor and African American, which led to speculation about racial and class inferiority. However, using the methods of epidemiological research, Joseph Goldberger found correlations between the disorder and diet, and he identified the cause of the disorder as a deficiency of the B vitamin niacin among people with poor diets. The symptoms were successfully eliminated by niacin therapy and improved diets among the poor. A long-term, widespread benefit of Goldberger's findings was the introduction of vitamin-enriched bread in the 1940s (Gottesman, 1991).

Researchers have used epidemiological techniques to study the effects of stress on psychological disorders. On the morning of September 11, 2001, approximately 3,000 people died from three separate terrorist attacks in lower Manhattan, at the Pentagon, and in Pennsylvania. DeLisi and colleagues (DeLisi et al., 2003) interviewed 1,009 men and women throughout Manhattan to assess their long-term emotional reactions to the attacks, especially given their proximity to the destroyed World Trade Center towers. These researchers found that individuals who had the most negative reactions to this traumatic event were those who had preexisting psychological disorders, those who had the greatest exposure to the attack (for example, being evacuated from the World Trade Center), and women. The most common negative reactions included anxiety and painful memories. This is a correlational

The more social supports people have, the less likely it is that they will become ill.

study because the investigators did not manipulate the independent variable. (The attack was not part of an experiment.)

If you have followed the work on the AIDS virus, you have seen how epidemiologists study a problem. By tracking the incidence of this disease among several populations (gay men, intravenous drug users, and spouses and children of infected individuals), researchers obtained important information about how the virus is passed from person to person. They inferred from the types of behaviors engaged in by members of these groups that the virus is probably spread by the transfer of bodily fluids through unprotected sex or by nonsterile hypodermic needles. Like other types of correlational research, epidemiological research can't tell us conclusively what causes a particular phenomenon. However, knowledge about the prevalence and course of psychological disorders is extremely valuable to our understanding because it points researchers in the right direction.

Research by Experiment

An **experiment** involves the manipulation of an independent variable and the observation of its effects. We manipulate the independent variable to answer the question of causality. If we observe a correlation between social supports and psychological disorders, we can't conclude which of these factors influenced the other. We can, however, change the extent of social supports and see whether there is an accompanying change in the prevalence of psychological disorders—in other words, do an experiment.

What will this experiment tell us about the relationship between these two variables? If we increase social supports and find no change in the frequency of psychological disorders, it may mean that lack of such supports does not cause psychological problems. On the other hand, if we find that psychological disorders diminish with increased social support, we can be more confident that nonsupport does contribute to them. However, because we are never 100% confident that our experiments are internally valid—that no other explanations are possible—we must be cautious about interpreting our results. In the following section, we describe different ways in which researchers conduct experiments and consider how each one brings us closer to understanding abnormal behavior.

■ Group Experimental Designs

With correlational designs, researchers observe groups to see how different variables are associated. In group experimental designs, researchers are more active. They actually change an independent variable to see how the behavior of the people in the group is affected. Suppose researchers design an intervention to help reduce insomnia in older adults, who are particularly affected by the condition (Irwin, Cole, & Nicassio, 2006). They treat a number of individuals and follow them for 10 years to learn whether their sleep patterns improve. The treatment is the independent variable; that is, it would not have occurred naturally. They then assess the treated group to learn whether their behavior changed as a function of what the researchers did. Introducing or withdrawing a variable in a way that would not have occurred naturally is also called *manipulating a variable.*

Unfortunately, a decade later the researchers find that the adults treated for sleep problems still, as a group, sleep less than 8 hours per night. Is the treatment a failure? Maybe not. The question that can't be answered in this study is what would have happened to group members if they hadn't been treated. Perhaps their sleep patterns would have been worse. Fortunately, researchers have devised ingenious methods to help sort out these complicated questions.

■ Control Groups

One answer to the what-if dilemma is to use a control group—people who are similar to the experimental group in every way except they are not exposed to the independent variable. The researchers also follow this group of people, assess them 10 years later, and look at their sleep patterns over this time. They probably observe that, without intervention, people tend to sleep fewer hours as they get older (Ancoli-Israel & Ayalon, 2006). Members of the control group, then, might sleep significantly less than people in the treated group, who might themselves sleep somewhat less than they did 10 years earlier. The control group allows the researchers to see that their treatment did help the treated subjects keep their sleep time from decreasing further.

Ideally, a control group is nearly identical to the treatment group in such factors as age, gender, socioeconomic backgrounds, and the problems they are reporting. Furthermore, a researcher would do the same assessments before and after the independent variable manipulation (for example, a treatment) to people in both groups. Any later differences between the groups after the change would, therefore, be attributable only to what was changed.

People in a treatment group often expect to get better. When behavior changes as a result of a person's expectation of change rather than as a result of any manipulation by an experimenter, the phenomenon is known as a **placebo effect** (from the Latin, which means "I shall please"). Conversely, people in the control group may be disappointed that they are not receiving treatment (analogously, we could label this a *frustro effect,* from the Latin "to disappoint"). Depending on the type of disorder they experience (for example, depression), disappointment may make them worse. This phenomenon would also make the treatment group look better by comparison.

One way researchers address the expectation concern is through **placebo control groups.** The word *placebo* typically refers to inactive medications such as sugar pills. The placebo is given to members of the control group to make them believe they are getting treatment (Stewart-Williams, 2004; Stewart-Williams & Podd, 2004). A placebo control in a medication study can be carried out with relative ease because people in the untreated group receive something that looks like the medication administered to the treatment group. In psychological treatments, however, it is not always easy to devise something that people believe may help them but does not include the component the researcher believes is effective. Clients in these types of control groups are often given part of the actual therapy—for example, the same homework as the treated group—but not the portions the researchers believe are responsible for improvements.

Note that you can look at the placebo effect as one portion of any treatment (Lambert, Shapiro, & Bergin, 1986). If someone

In comparative treatment research, different treatments are administered to comparable groups of people.

you provide with a treatment improves, you would have to attribute the improvement to a combination of your treatment and the client's expectation of improving (placebo effect). Therapists want their clients to expect improvement; this helps strengthen the treatment. However, when researchers conduct an experiment to determine what portion of a particular treatment is responsible for the observed changes, the placebo effect is a confound that can dilute the validity of the research. Thus, researchers use a placebo control group to help distinguish the results of positive expectations from the results of actual treatment.

The **double-blind control** is a variant of the placebo control group procedure. As the name suggests, not only are the participants in the study "blind," or unaware of what group they are in or what treatment they are given (single blind), but so are the researchers or therapists providing treatment (double blind). This type of control eliminates the possibility that an investigator might bias the outcome. For example, a researcher comparing two treatments who expected one to be more effective than the other might "try harder" if the "preferred" treatment wasn't working as well as expected. On the other hand, if the treatment that wasn't expected to work seemed to be failing, the researcher might not push as hard to see it succeed. This reaction might not be deliberate, but it does happen. This phenomenon is referred to as an *allegiance effect* (Westen, Novotny, & Thompson-Brenner, 2004). If, however, both the participants and the researchers or therapists are "blind," there is less chance that bias will affect the results.

A double-blind placebo control does not work perfectly in all cases. If medication is part of the treatment, participants and researchers may be able to tell whether or not they have received it by the presence or absence of physical reactions (side effects). Even with purely psychological interventions, participants often know whether or not they are receiving a powerful treatment, and they may alter their expectations for improvement accordingly.

■ Comparative Treatment Research

As an alternative to using no-treatment control groups to help evaluate results, some researchers compare different treatments. In this design, the researcher gives different treatments to two or more comparable groups of people with a particular disorder and can then assess how or whether each treatment helped the people who received it. This is called **comparative treatment research.** In the sleep study we discussed, two groups of older adults could be selected, with one group given medication for insomnia, the other given a cognitive–behavioral intervention, and the results compared.

The process and outcome of treatment are two important issues to be considered when different approaches are studied. Process research focuses on the mechanisms responsible for behavior change, or "why does it work?" In an old joke, someone goes to a physician for a new miracle cold cure. The physician prescribes the new drug and tells the patient the cold will be gone in 7 to 10 days. As most of us know, colds typically improve in 7 to 10 days without so-called miracle drugs. The new drug probably does nothing to further the improvement of the patient's cold. The process aspect of testing medical interventions involves evaluating biological mechanisms responsible for change. Does the medication cause lower serotonin levels, for example, and does this account for the changes we observe? Similarly, in looking at psychological interventions, we determine what is "causing" the observed changes. This is important for several reasons. First, if we understand what the "active ingredients" of our treatment are, we can often eliminate aspects that are not important, thereby saving clients time and money. For an example, one study of insomnia found that adding a relaxation training component to a treatment package provided no addition benefit—allowing clinicians to reduce the amount of training and focus on only those aspects that really improve sleep (for example, cognitive behavior therapy) (Harvey, Inglis, & Espie, 2002). In addition, knowing what is important about our interventions can help us create more powerful, newer versions that may be more effective.

Outcome research focuses on the positive, negative, or both results of the treatment. In other words, does it work? Remember, treatment process involves finding out why or how your treatment works. In contrast, treatment outcome involves finding out what changes occur after treatment.

Single-Case Experimental Designs

B. F. Skinner's innovations in scientific methodology were among his most important contributions to psychopathology. Skinner formalized the concept of **single-case experimental designs.** This method involves the systematic study of individuals under a variety of experimental conditions. Skinner thought it was much better to know a lot about the behavior of one individual than to make only a few observations of a large group for the sake of presenting the "average" response. Psychopathology is concerned with the suffering of specific people, and this methodology has greatly helped us understand the factors involved in individual psychopathology (Hayes, Barlow, & Nelson-Gray, 1999). Many applications throughout this book reflect Skinnerian methods.

Single-case experimental designs differ from case studies in their use of various strategies to improve internal validity, thereby reducing the number of confounding variables. As you will see, these strategies have strengths and weaknesses in comparison with traditional group designs. Although we use examples from treatment research to illustrate the single-case experimental designs, they, like other research strategies, can help explain why people engage in abnormal behavior, as well as how to treat them.

■ Repeated Measurements

One of the more important strategies used in single-case experimental design is **repeated measurement,** in which a behavior is measured several times instead of only once before you change the independent variable and once afterward. The researcher takes the same measurements repeatedly to learn how variable the behavior is (how much does it change from day to day?) and whether it shows any obvious trends (is it getting better or worse?). Suppose a young woman, Wendy, comes into the office complaining about feelings of anxiety. When asked to rate the level of her anxiety, she gives it a 9 (10 is the worst). After several weeks of treatment, Wendy rates her anxiety at 6. Can we say that the treatment reduced her anxiety? Not necessarily.

Suppose we had measured Wendy's anxiety each day during the weeks before her visit to the office (repeated measurement) and observed that it differed greatly. On particularly good days, she rated her anxiety from 5 to 7. On bad days, it was up between 8 and 10. Suppose further that, even after treatment, her daily ratings continued to range from 5 to 10. The rating of 9 before treatment and 6 after treatment may only have been part of the daily variations she experienced normally. Wendy could just as easily have had a good day and reported a 6 before treatment and then

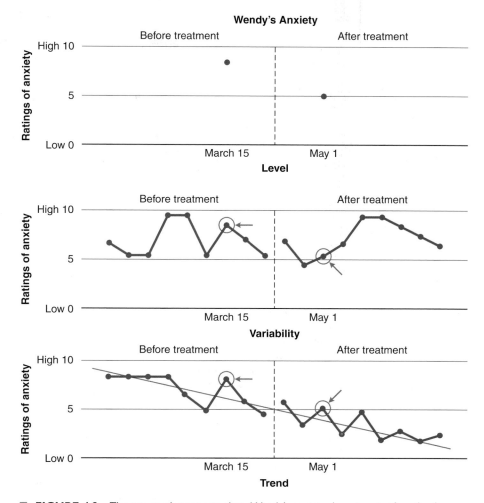

■ **FIGURE 4.2**   The top graph seems to show Wendy's anxiety dropping significantly after treatment (measuring level). However, when you look at repeated measures before and after treatment, the middle graph reveals little change because her anxiety fluctuated a great deal (measuring variability). A different scenario is illustrated in the bottom graph (measuring trend), where her anxiety also varied. In general, there was a downward movement (improved anxiety) even before treatment, suggesting that she might have improved without help. Examining variability and trend can provide more information about the true nature of the change.

had a bad day and reported a 9 after treatment, which would imply that the treatment made her worse!

Repeated measurement is part of each single-subject experimental design. It helps identify how a person is doing before and after intervention and whether the treatment accounted for any changes. ■ Figure 4.2 summarizes Wendy's anxiety and the added information obtained by repeated measurement. The top graph shows Wendy's original before-and-after ratings of her anxiety. The middle graph shows that with daily ratings her reports are variable and that just by chance the previous measurement was probably misleading. She had good and bad days both before and after treatment and doesn't seem to have changed much.

The bottom graph shows a different possibility: Wendy's anxiety was on its way down before the treatment, which would also have been obscured with just before-and-after measurements. Maybe she was getting better on her own and the treatment didn't have much effect. Although the middle graph shows how the **variability** from day to day could be important in an interpretation of the effect of treatment, the bottom graph shows how the

trend itself can also be important in determining the cause of any change. The three graphs illustrate important parts of repeated measurements: (1) the **level** or degree of behavior change with different interventions (top); (2) the variability or degree of change over time (middle); and (3) the trend or direction of change (bottom). Again, before-and-after scores alone do not necessarily show what is responsible for behavioral changes.

■ Withdrawal Designs

One of the more common strategies used in single-subject research is a **withdrawal design,** in which a researcher tries to determine whether the independent variable is responsible for changes in behavior. The effect of Wendy's treatment could be tested by stopping it for some time to see whether her anxiety increased. A simple withdrawal design has three parts. First, a person's condition is evaluated before treatment, to establish a **baseline.** Then comes the change in the independent variable—in Wendy's case, the beginning of treatment. Last, treatment is withdrawn ("return to baseline") and the researcher assesses whether Wendy's anxiety level changes again as a function of this last step. If with the treatment her anxiety lessens in comparison to baseline and then worsens after treatment is withdrawn, the researcher can conclude the treatment has reduced Wendy's anxiety.

How is this design different from a case study? An important difference is that the change in treatment is designed specifically to show whether treatment caused the changes in behavior. Although case studies often involve treatment, they don't include any effort to learn whether the person would have improved without the treatment. A withdrawal design gives researchers a better sense of whether or not the treatment itself caused behavior change.

Despite their advantages, withdrawal designs are not always appropriate. The researcher is required to remove what might be an effective treatment, a decision that is sometimes difficult to justify for ethical reasons. In Wendy's case, a researcher would have to decide there was a sufficient reason to risk making her anxious again. A withdrawal design is also unsuitable when the treatment can't be removed. Suppose Wendy's treatment involved visualizing herself on a beach on a tropical island. It would be difficult—if not impossible—to stop her from imagining something. Similarly, some treatments involve teaching people skills, which might be impossible to unlearn. If Wendy learned how to be less anxious in social situations, how could she revert to being socially apprehensive?

Several counterarguments support the use of withdrawal designs (Hayes et al., 1999). Treatment is routinely withdrawn when medications are involved. *Drug holidays* are periods when the medication is withdrawn so that clinicians can determine whether it is responsible for the treatment effects. Any medication can have negative side effects, and unnecessary medication should be avoided. Sometimes treatment withdrawal happens naturally. Withdrawal does not have to be prolonged; a brief withdrawal may still clarify the role of the treatment.

■ Multiple Baseline

Another single-case experimental design strategy used often that doesn't have some of the drawbacks of a withdrawal design is the **multiple baseline.** Rather than stopping the intervention to see whether it is effective, the researcher starts treatment at different times across settings (home versus school), behaviors (yelling at spouse or boss), or people. After waiting for a while and taking repeated measures of Wendy's anxiety both at home and at her office (the baseline), the clinician could treat her first at home. When the treatment begins to be effective, intervention could begin at work. If she improves only at home after beginning treatment but improves at work after treatment is used there also, we could conclude the treatment was effective. This is an example of using a multiple baseline across settings. Does internal validity improve with a multiple baseline? Yes. Any time other explanations for results can be ruled out, internal validity is improved. Wendy's anxiety improved only in the settings where it was treated, which rules out competing explanations. For example, if she had won the lottery at the same time treatment started and her anxiety decreased in all situations, we couldn't conclude her condition was affected by treatment.

Suppose a researcher wanted to assess the effectiveness of a treatment for a child's problem behaviors. Treatment could focus first on the child's crying then on a second problem, such as fighting with siblings. If the treatment was first effective only in reducing crying, and effective for fighting only after the second intervention, the researcher could conclude that the treatment, not something else, accounted for the improvements. This is a multiple baseline conducted across behaviors.

Single-case experimental designs are sometimes criticized because they tend to involve only a small number of cases, leaving their external validity in doubt. In other words, we can't say the results we saw with a few people would be the same for everyone. However, although they are called *single-case* designs, researchers can and often do use them with several people at once, in part to address the issue of external validity. One of us studied the effectiveness of a treatment for the severe behavior problems of children with autism (Durand, 1999) (see ■ Figure 4.3). We taught the children to communicate instead of misbehave, using a procedure known as *functional communication training* (we discuss this in more detail in Chapter 14). Using a multiple baseline, we introduced this treatment to a group of five children. Our dependent variables were the incidence of the children's behavior problems and their newly acquired communication skills. As Figure 4.3 shows, only when we began treatment did each child's behavior problems improve and communication begin. This design let us rule out coincidence or some other change in the children's lives as explanations for the improvements.

Among the advantages of the multiple baseline design in evaluating treatments is that it does not require withdrawal of treatment and, as you've seen, withdrawing treatment is sometimes difficult or impossible. Furthermore, the multiple baseline typically resembles the way treatment would naturally be implemented. A clinician can't help a client with numerous problems simultaneously but can take repeated measures of the relevant behaviors and observe when they change. A clinician who sees predictable and orderly changes related to where and when the treatment is used can conclude the treatment is causing the change.

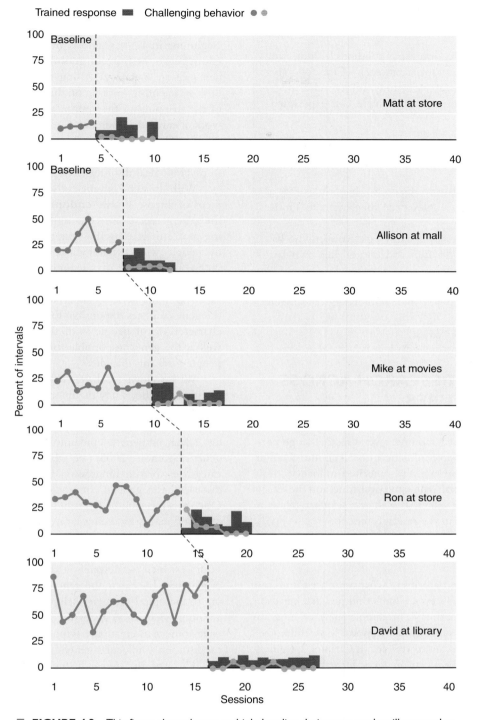

■ **FIGURE 4.3** This figure shows how a multiple baseline design was used to illustrate that the treatment—functional communication training—was responsible for improvements in the children's behaviors. The circles represent how often each child exhibited behavior problems (called challenging behavior), and the blue-shaded areas show how often they communicated without help from the teacher (referred to as unprompted communication). (From Durand, V. M., 1999. Functional communication training using assistive devices: recruiting natural communities of reinforcement, *Journal of Applied Behavior Analysis, 32(3),* 247–267. Reprinted by permission of the Society for the Experimental Analysis of Human Behavior.)

GENETICS AND RESEARCH ACROSS TIME AND CULTURES

Examining the origin and strategies for treating an individual's behavior problem or disorder requires several factors to be considered so that multiple possible influences are taken into account. The factors include determining any inherited influences, how behavior will change or remain the same over time, and the effects of culture. We discuss these issues, as well as research replication and ethics, as key elements in the research process.

Studying Genetics

We tend to think of genetics in terms of what we inherit from our parents: "He's got his mother's eyes." "She's thin just like her dad." "She's stubborn like her mother." This simple view of how we become the people we are suggests that how we look, think, feel, and behave is predetermined. Yet, as you saw in Chapter 2, we now know that the interaction between our genetic makeup and our experiences is what determines how we will develop. The goal of behavioral geneticists (people who study the genetics of behavior) is to tease out the role of genetics in these interactions.

Genetic researchers examine **phenotypes,** the observable characteristics or behavior of the individual, and **genotypes,** the unique genetic makeup of individual people. For example, a person with Down syndrome typically has some level of mental retardation and a variety of other physical characteristics, such as slanted eyes and a thick tongue. These characteristics are the phenotype. The genotype is the extra 21st chromosome that causes Down syndrome.

Our knowledge of the phenotypes of different psychological disorders exceeds our knowledge of the genotypes, but that may soon change. Ever since the discovery of the double helix in 1953 by James Watson and Francis Crick, scientists have known we have

to map the structure and location of every gene on all 46 chromosomes if we are to fully understand our genetic endowment. Beginning in 1990, scientists around the world, in a coordinated effort, began the **human genome project** (*genome* means all the genes of an organism). Using the latest advances in molecular biology, scientists working on this project completed a rough draft of the mapping of the approximately 25,000 human genes. This work identified hundreds of genes that contribute to inherited diseases. These exciting findings represent truly astounding progress in deciphering the nature of genetic endowment and its role in psychological disorders.

With the rapid advance of science, a third concept is now the focus of intense study—**endophenotypes.** Endophenotypes are the genetic mechanisms that ultimately contribute to the underlying problems causing the symptoms and difficulties experienced by people with psychological disorders (Gottesman & Gould, 2005). In the case of schizophrenia (a disorder we discuss in Chapter 13), for example, researchers are not looking for a "schizophrenia gene" (genotype); instead, they are searching for the gene or genes responsible for the working memory problems characteristic of people with this disorder (endophenotype), as well as the genes responsible for other problems experienced by people with this disorder.

What follows is a brief review of the research strategies scientists use as they study the interaction between environment and genetics in psychological disorders. These complex approaches can be summarized into four categories: basic genetic epidemiology, advanced genetic epidemiology, gene finding, and molecular genetics (Kendler, 2005) (see Table 4.2). The table shows that these categories form a progression that starts by finding whether a disorder has a genetic component (basic genetic epidemiology). Once this is established, researchers explore the nature of the genetic influences by seeing how genetics affect aspects of the disorder (advanced genetic epidemiology). Going deeper still, scientists use sophisticated statistical methods (linkage and association studies), which we describe next, to find out just where the gene or genes are located in the genome (gene finding). Finally, switching to biological strategies, scientists are just at the genesis of examining what these genes do and how they interact with the environment to create the symptoms associated with psychological disorders (molecular genetics).

The specific research techniques used in the study of genetics—family studies, adoption studies, twin studies, genetic linkage analysis, and association studies—are described next.

■ Family Studies

In **family studies,** scientists simply examine a behavioral pattern or emotional trait in the context of the family. The member with the trait singled out for study is called the **proband.** If there is a genetic influence, presumably the trait should occur more often in first-degree relatives (parents, siblings, or offspring) than in second-degree or more distant relatives. The presence of the trait in distant relatives, in turn, should be somewhat greater than in the population as a whole. In Chapter 1 you met Judy, the adolescent with blood–injury–injection phobia who fainted at the sight of blood. The tendency of a trait to run in families, or familial aggregation, is as high as 60% for this disorder; that is, 60% of the

TABLE 4.2 The Basic Approaches Used to Assess Gene-Environment Influences in Psychological Disorders

Approach	Method	Question
Basic genetic epidemiology	Statistical analysis of family, twin, and adoption studies	Is the disorder inherited (heritability), and if so, how much of the disorder is attributable to genetics?
Advanced genetic epidemiology	Statistical analysis of family, twin, and adoption studies	If the disorder is found to be inherited, what are the factors that influence the disorder (for example, is the change something that occurs early in development, is it different between males and females, and do the genetic influences affect environmental risk factors)?
Gene finding	Statistical analysis of specific families or individuals (linkage and/or association studies)	Where is the gene (or genes) that influences the disorder?
Molecular genetics	Biological analysis of individual DNA samples	What biological processes do the genes affect to produce the symptoms of the disorder?

Source: Adapted from Kendler, K. S. (2005). Psychiatric genetics: A methodological critique. In N. C. Andreasen (Ed.), *Research advances in genetics and genomics: Implications for psychiatry.* Washington, DC: American Psychiatric Publishing, Table 1, p. 6.

first-degree relatives of someone with blood–injury–injection phobia have the same reaction to at least some degree. This is one of the highest rates of familial aggregation for any psychological disorder we have studied.

The problem with family studies is that family members tend to live together and there might be something in their shared environment that causes the high familial aggregation. For example, Mom might have developed a bad reaction to blood as a young girl after witnessing a serious accident. Every time she sees blood she has a strong emotional response. Because emotions are contagious, the young children watching Mom probably react similarly. In adulthood, they pass it on, in turn, to their own children.

Adoption Studies

How do we separate environmental from genetic influences in families? One way is through **adoption studies.** Scientists identify adoptees who have a particular behavioral pattern or psychological disorder and attempt to locate first-degree relatives who were raised in different family settings. Suppose a young man has a disorder and scientists discover his brother was adopted as a baby and brought up in a different home. The researchers would then examine the brother to see whether he also displays signs of the disorder. If they can identify enough sibling pairs (and they usually do after a lot of hard work), they can assess whether siblings brought up in different families display the disorder to the same extent as the original subject. If the siblings raised with different families have the disorder more often than would be expected by chance, the researchers can infer that genetic endowment is a contributor.

Twin Studies

Nature presents an elegant experiment that gives behavioral geneticists their closest possible look at the role of genes in development: identical (monozygotic) twins. These twins not only look alike but also have identical genes. Fraternal (dizygotic) twins, on the other hand, come from different eggs and have only about 50% of their genes in common, as do all first-degree relatives. In **twin studies,** the obvious scientific question is whether identical twins share the same trait—say, fainting at the sight of blood—more often than fraternal twins. Determining whether a trait is shared is easy with some physical traits, such as height. As Plomin (1990) points out, correlations in height are 0.45 for both first-degree relatives and fraternal twins and 0.90 for identical twins. These findings show that heritability of height is about 90%, so approximately 10% of the variance is the result of environmental factors. But the case of conjoined identical twins with different personalities (who we mention in Chapter 2) reminds us that the 90% estimate is the *average* contribution. An identical twin who was severely physically abused or selectively deprived of proper foods might be substantially different in height from the other twin.

Michael Lyons and his colleagues (1995) conducted a study of antisocial behavior among members of the Vietnam Era Twin

Courtesy of Mary Anne Shahidi

Although family members often resemble one another, genetics has to do with far more than what we inherit from our parents.

Registry. The individuals in the study were about 8,000 twin men who served in the military from 1965 to 1975. The investigators found that among identical twins there was a greater degree of resemblance for antisocial traits than among fraternal twins. The difference was greater for adult antisocial behavior—that is, identical twins' behavior was more similar than fraternal twins' behavior in adulthood—than for juvenile antisocial behavior. The researchers concluded that the family environment is a stronger influence than genetic factors on juvenile antisocial traits and that antisocial behavior in adulthood is more strongly influenced by genetic factors. In other words, after the individual grew up and left the family of origin, early environmental influences mattered less and less. This way of studying genetics isn't perfect. You can assume identical twins have the same genetic makeup and fraternal twins do not. However, a complicating concern is whether identical twins have the same experiences or environment as fraternal twins. Some identical twins are dressed alike and are even given similar names. Yet the twins themselves influence each other's behavior, and in some cases, identical twins may affect each other more than fraternal twins (Carey, 1992).

One way to address this problem is by combining the adoption study and twin study methods. If you can find identical twins, one of whom was adopted as an infant, you can estimate the relative roles of genes and the environment (nature versus nurture) in the development of behavioral patterns.

■ Genetic Linkage Analysis and Association Studies

The results of a series of family, twin, and adoption studies may suggest that a particular disorder has a genetic component, but they can't provide the location of the implicated gene or genes. To locate a defective gene, there are two general strategies: genetic linkage analysis and association studies (Merikangas & Risch, 2005).

The basic principle of **genetic linkage analysis** is simple. When a family disorder is studied, other inherited characteristics are assessed at the same time. These other characteristics—called **genetic markers**—are selected because we know their exact location. If a match or link is discovered between the inheritance of the disorder and the inheritance of a genetic marker, the genes for the disorder and the genetic marker are probably close together on the same chromosome. For example, bipolar disorder (manic depression) was studied in a large Amish family (Egeland et al., 1987). Researchers found that two markers on chromosome 11, genes for insulin and a known cancer gene, were linked to the presence of mood disorder in this family, suggesting that a gene for bipolar disorder might be on chromosome 11. Unfortunately, although this is a genetic linkage study, it also illustrates the danger of drawing premature conclusions from research. This linkage study and a second study that purported to find a linkage between bipolar disorder and the X chromosome (Biron et al., 1987) have yet to be replicated; that is, different researchers have not been able to show similar linkages in other families (Craddock & Jones, 2001).

The inability to replicate findings in these studies is quite common (Kendler, 2005). This type of failure casts doubt on conclusions that only one gene is responsible for such complex disorders. Be mindful of such limitations the next time you read in a newspaper or hear on television that a gene has been identified as causing some disorder.

The second strategy for locating specific genes, **association studies,** also uses genetic markers. Whereas linkage studies compare markers in a large group of people with a particular disorder, association studies compare such people to people without the disorder. If certain markers occur significantly more often in the people with the disorder, it is assumed the markers are close to the genes involved with the disorder. This type of comparison makes association studies better able to identify genes that may only weakly be associated with a disorder. Both strategies for locating specific genes shed new light on the origins of specific disorders and may inspire new approaches to treatment (Merikangas & Risch, 2005).

Studying Behavior Over Time

Sometimes we want to ask, "How will a disorder or behavior pattern change (or remain the same) over time?" This question is important for several reasons. First, the answer helps us decide whether to treat a particular person. For example, should we begin an expensive and time-consuming program for a young adult who is depressed over the loss of a grandparent? You might not if you knew that with normal social supports the depression is likely to diminish over the next few months without treatment. On the other hand, if you have reason to believe a problem isn't likely to go away on its own, you might decide to begin treatment. For example, as you will see later, aggression among young children does not usually go away naturally and should be dealt with as early as possible.

It is also important to understand the developmental changes in abnormal behavior because sometimes these can provide insight into how problems are created and how they become more serious. For example, you will see that some researchers identify people who are at risk for schizophrenia through their family histories and follow them through the entire risk period (18–45 years of age) (see Tsuang, Stone, & Faraone, 2002). The goal is to discover the factors (for example, social status and family psychopathology) that predict who will manifest the disorder. (This complex and fascinating research is described in Chapter 13.)

■ Prevention Research

An additional reason for studying clinical problems over time is that we may be able to design interventions and services to prevent these problems. Clearly, preventing mental health difficulties would save countless families significant emotional distress, and the financial savings could be substantial. Prevention research has expanded over the years to include a broad range of approaches. These different methods can be viewed in four broad categories: health promotion or positive development strategies, universal prevention strategies, selective prevention strategies, and indicated prevention strategies (Weisz, Sandler, Durlak, & Anton, 2005). Health promotion or positive development strategies involve efforts to blanket entire populations of people—even those who may not be at risk—to prevent later problems and promote protective behaviors. The intervention is not designed to fix existing problems but, instead, focuses on skill building, for example, to keep problems from developing. For example, the Seattle Social Development Program targets young children in public elementary schools in the Seattle school system that are in high-crime areas, providing intervention with teachers and parents to engage the children in learning and positive behaviors. Although this approach does not target one particular problem (for example, drug use), long-term follow-up of these children suggests multiple positive effects in achievement and reductions in delinquency (Lonczak, Abbott, Hawkins, Kosterman, & Catalano, 2002). Universal prevention strategies focus on entire populations and target certain specific risk factors (for example, behavior problems in inner-city classrooms) without focusing on specific individuals. The third approach—selective prevention—specifically targets whole groups at risk (for example, children who have parents who have died) and designs specific interventions aimed at helping them avoid future problems. Finally, indicated prevention is a strategy for those individuals who are beginning to show signs of problems (for example, depressive symptoms) but do not yet have a psychological disorder.

To evaluate the effectiveness of each of these approaches, the research strategies used in prevention research for examining psychopathology across time combine individual and group research methods, including both correlational and experimental designs. We look next at two of the most often used: cross-sectional and longitudinal designs.

Cross-Sectional Designs   A variation of correlation research is to compare different people at different ages. For a **cross-sectional design,** researchers take a cross section of a population across the different age groups and compare them on some characteristic. For example, if they were trying to understand the development of alcohol abuse and dependence, they could take groups of adolescents at 12, 15, and 17 years of age and assess their beliefs about alcohol use. In an early comparison, Brown and Finn (1982) made some interesting discoveries. They found that 36% of the 12-year-olds thought the primary purpose of drinking was to get drunk. This percentage increased to 64% with 15-year-olds, but dropped again to 42% for the 17-year-old students. The researchers also found that 28% of the 12-year-olds reported drinking with their friends at least sometimes, a rate that increased to 80% for the 15-year-olds and to 88% for the 17-year-olds. Brown and Finn used this information to develop the hypothesis that the reason for excessive drinking among teens is a deliberate attempt to get drunk rather than a mistake in judgment once they are under the influence of alcohol. In other words, teenagers do not, as a group, appear to drink too much because once they've had a drink or two they show poor judgment and drink excessively. Instead, their attitudes before drinking seem to influence how much they drink later.

In cross-sectional designs, the participants in each age group are called **cohorts;** Brown and Finn studied three cohorts: 12-year-olds, 15-year-olds, and 17-year-olds. The members of each cohort are the same age at the same time and thus have all been exposed to similar experiences. Members of one cohort differ from members of other cohorts in age and in their exposure to cultural and historical experiences. You would expect a group of 12-year-olds in the early 1990s to have received a great deal of education about drug and alcohol use ("Just Say No"), whereas the 17-year-olds may not have. Differences among cohorts in their opinions about alcohol use may be related to their respective cognitive and emotional development at these different ages and to their dissimilar experiences. This **cohort effect,** the con-

founding of age and experience, is a limitation of the cross-sectional design.

Researchers prefer cross-sectional designs to study changes over time partly because they are easier to use than longitudinal designs (discussed next). In addition, some phenomena are less likely to be influenced by different cultural and historical experiences and therefore less susceptible to cohort effects. For example, the prevalence of Alzheimer's disease among people at ages 60 and 70—assumed to be strongly influenced by biology—is not likely to be greatly affected by different experiences among the study subjects.

One question not answered by cross-sectional designs is how problems develop in individuals. For example, do children who refuse to go to school grow up to have anxiety disorders? Researchers cannot answer this question simply by comparing adults with anxiety problems and children who refuse to go to school. They could ask the adults whether they were anxious about school when they were children, but this **retrospective information** (looking back) is usually less than accurate. To get a better picture of how individuals develop over the years, researchers use longitudinal designs.

Longitudinal Designs   Rather than looking at different groups of people of differing ages, researchers may follow one group over time and assess change in its members directly. The advantages of **longitudinal designs** are that they do not suffer from cohort effect problems and they allow the researchers to assess individual change. (■ Figure 4.4 illustrates both longitudinal and cross-sectional designs.) Researchers in Australia, for example, conducted a longitudinal study of adolescents who had some symptoms of depression (Sheffield et al., 2006). They compared different prevention strategies—including universal and indicated prevention strategies—to assess if they could prevent these mildly depressed youth from becoming more depressed by giving them problem-solving skills. They followed 2,479 depressed ninth graders in 34 schools over a 12-month period and found, surprisingly, that the interventions had no significant impact compared to no treatment. Although these results are disappointing, they show the value of longitudinal designs when assessing the durability of treatment.

Imagine conducting a major longitudinal study. Not only must the researcher persevere over months and years, but so must the people who participate in the study. They must remain willing to continue in the project, and the researcher must hope they will not move away, or worse, die. Longitudinal research is costly and time consuming; it is also subject to the distinct possibility that the research question will have become irrelevant by the time the study is complete. Finally, longitudinal designs can suffer from a phenomenon similar to the cohort effect on cross-sectional designs. The **cross-generational effect** involves trying to generalize the findings to groups whose experiences are different from those of the study participants. For example, the drug use histories of people who were young adults in the 1960s and early 1970s are vastly different from those of people born in the 1990s.

Sometimes psychopathologists combine longitudinal and cross-sectional designs in a strategy called the **sequential design,** which involves repeated study of different cohorts over time. Laurie Chassin and her colleagues study children's beliefs about

Longitudinal design

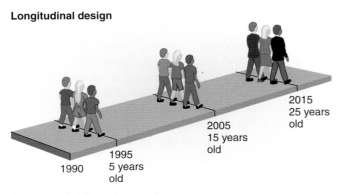

1990
1995
5 years
old
2005
15 years
old
2015
25 years
old

Same people followed across time

Cross-sectional design

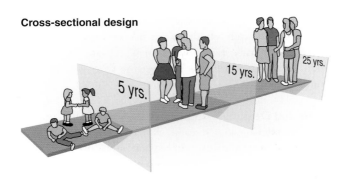

5 yrs.

15 yrs.

25 yrs.

People of different ages viewed at the same time

■ **FIGURE 4.4** Two research designs.

cigarette smoking (Chassin, Presson, Rose, & Sherman, 2001). These researchers have followed 10 cohorts of middle- and high-school-age children (cross-sectional design) since the early 1980s (longitudinal design). Through questionnaires, they have tracked how these children (and later, adults) viewed the health risks associated with smoking from their youth into their mid-30s. For example, the researchers would ask participants whether they believed in the following statement: "A person who eats right and

exercises regularly can smoke without harming his/her health." The results suggest that as middle schoolers (ages 11–14) the children viewed smoking as less risky to them personally and believed that there were positive psychological benefits (for example, making them appear more mature). These beliefs changed as the children went into high school and entered adulthood, but they point to the importance of targeting smoking prevention programs during the middle-school period (Chassin et al., 2001).

Studying Behavior Across Cultures

Just as we can become narrowly focused when we study people only at a certain age, we can also miss important aspects by studying people from only one culture. Studying the differences in behavior of people from different cultures can tell us a great deal about the origins and possible treatments of abnormal behaviors. Unfortunately, most research literature originates in Western cultures (Lambert et al., 1992), producing an ethnocentric view of psychopathology that can limit our understanding of disorders in general and can restrict the way we approach treatment (Draguns & Tanaka-Matsumi, 2003). Researchers in Malaysia—where psychological disorders are commonly believed to have supernatural origins—have described a disorder they call *sakit gila,* which has some features of schizophrenia but differs in important ways (Barrett et al., 2005). Could we learn more about schizophrenia (and *sakit gila*) by comparing the disorders themselves and the cultures in which they are found? Increasing awareness of the limited cultural scope of our research is creating a corresponding increase in cross-cultural research on psychopathology.

The designs we have described are adapted for studying abnormal behavior across cultures. Some researchers view the effects of different cultures as though they were different treatments (Hobfoll, Canetti-Nisim, & Johnson, 2006). In other words, the independent variable is the effect of different cultures on behavior, rather than, say, the effect of cognitive therapy versus simple exposure for the treatment of fears. The difference between looking at culture as a "treatment" and our typical design, however, is important. In cross-cultural research, we can't randomly assign infants to different cultures and observe how they develop. People

Longitudinal studies can be complicated by the cross-generational effect; for example, young people in the 1960s shared experiences that were different from those of young people today.

The same behavior—in this case a woman baring her legs and having her head uncovered in public—would be acceptable in some cultures but not in others.

from varying cultures can differ in any number of important ways—their genetic backgrounds, for one—that could explain variations in their behavior for reasons other than culture.

The characteristics of different cultures can also complicate research efforts. Symptoms or descriptions of them can be dissimilar in different societies. Nigerians who are depressed complain of heaviness or heat in the head, crawling sensations in the head or legs, burning sensations in the body, and a feeling that the belly is bloated with water (Ebigno, 1982). In contrast, people in the United States report feeling worthless, being unable to start or finish anything, losing interest in usual activities, and thinking of suicide. Natives of China, on the other hand, are less likely to report feeling depressed or losing interest in favorite things but may have thoughts of suicide or worthlessness (Phillips et al., 2007). These few examples illustrate that applying a standard definition of depression across different cultures will result in vastly different outcomes.

An additional complicating factor is varying tolerances, or thresholds, for abnormal behavior. If people in different cultures see the same behaviors differently, researchers will have trouble comparing incidence and prevalence rates. Lambert and colleagues (1992) found that Jamaican parents and teachers report fewer incidents of abnormal child behavior than do their American counterparts. Does this represent a biological or environmental difference in the children themselves, the effects of different thresholds of tolerance in the societies, or a combination of both? Understanding cultural attitudes and customs is essential to such research.

Finally, treatment research is also complicated by cross-cultural differences. Cultures develop treatment models that reflect their own values. In Japan, psychiatric hospitalization is organized in terms of a family model, with caregivers assuming parental roles. A family model was common in psychiatric institutions in 19th-century North America until it was replaced with the medical model common today (Blue & Gaines, 1992; Dwyer,

1992). In Saudi Arabia, women are veiled when outside the home, which prevents them from uncovering their faces in the presence of therapists; custom thus complicates efforts to establish a trusting and intimate therapeutic client–therapist relationship (Dubovsky, 1983). Because in the Islamic view medicine and religion are inseparable, medical and religious treatments are combined (Baasher, 2001). As you can see, something as basic as comparing treatment outcomes is highly complex in a cross-cultural context.

The Power of a Program of Research

When we examine different research strategies independently, as we have done here, we often have the impression that some approaches are better than others. It is important to understand that this is not true. Depending on the type of question you are asking and the practical limitations inherent in the inquiry, any of the research techniques would be appropriate. Significant issues often are resolved not by one perfectly designed study but rather by a series of studies that examine different aspects of the problem—in a program of research. In an outstanding example of this approach, Gerald Patterson and his colleagues at the University of Oregon studied the aggressive behavior of children.

Their earliest research focused on basic concerns, such as why children are aggressive. The researchers first did a series of correlational studies to determine what variables were associated with aggression in children. One study was conducted in a state institution for girls with various problem behaviors (Buehler, Patterson, & Furniss, 1966). Researchers found that the delinquent behaviors—including rule breaking, criticizing adults, and aggressiveness—were likely to be reinforced by the girls' peers, who encouraged them.

Using strategies from epidemiology, Patterson also looked at the prevalence of aggression in children. He found that the likelihood of inappropriate behavior among children who are identified as not having a disorder ranged from 41% to 11%, with a mean of approximately 25% (Patterson, Cobb, & Ray, 1972). In other words, some level of aggression appears to be normal. Children are seen as "deviant" not for displaying a behavior but when that behavior exceeds an acceptable level of frequency or intensity.

As you should remember, interpreting the results from correlation studies can be difficult, especially if the intent is to determine causation. To forestall this criticism, Patterson also conducted experimental studies. One strategy he used was a single-case experimental design (withdrawal design) in which he observed how a 5-year-old boy reacted to his mother's attempts to change his problem behavior (Patterson, 1982). Patterson asked the boy's mother to restrain the child if he was aggressive but not to talk to him during this time. Patterson observed that the boy whined and complained when he was restrained. In the experimental condition, Patterson asked the mother to talk with her son in a positive way when he complained. Later, Patterson had her again ignore her son's complaints (a withdrawal design). He found the boy was more likely to complain about being restrained when his mother talked with him. One conclusion was that reinforcement (verbal communication) from the mother encouraged the boy to try to escape her restraint by complaining. By observing both the boy's behavior (the dependent variable) and the mother's behavior (the independent variable), Patterson could make stronger conclusions about the role of the mother in influencing her son's behavior.

One of the questions about aggression in children concerns development. How does aggressiveness change over time? Patterson used cross-sectional research to observe children at different ages. In one study, he found that the rate of aggression decreases as children get older (Patterson, 1982). It seems that children are less often aggressive as they get older but their aggression may become more intense or destructive.

Using treatment outcome research, this group of researchers has also examined the effects of a combination of treatments on the aggressive behavior of children. Patterson and Fleischman (1979) introduced a behavioral treatment involving parent training (see Chapter 12) and described the results of the treatment on the behavior of both parents and their children. The researchers found they could reduce inappropriate child behavior and improve the parenting skills of the parents; these changes persisted a year after treatment.

As this example indicates, research is conducted in stages, and a complete picture of any behavior can be seen only after looking at it from many perspectives. An integrated program of research can help researchers explore various aspects of abnormal behavior.

Replication

The motto of the state of Missouri is "Show Me." The motto of science could be "Show Me Again." Scientists in general, and behavioral scientists in particular, are never really convinced something is "true." People are skeptical when it comes to claims about causes or treatment outcomes. Replicating findings is what makes researchers confident that what they are observing isn't a coincidence. We noted when we described the case study method that if we look at a disorder in only one person, no matter how carefully we describe and document what we observe, we cannot draw strong conclusions.

The strength of a research program is in its ability to replicate findings in different ways to build confidence in the results. If you look back at the research strategies we have described, you will find that replication is one of the most important aspects of each. The more times researchers repeat a process (and the behavior they are studying changes as expected), the surer they are about what caused the changes.

Research Ethics

An important final issue involves the ethics of doing research in abnormal psychology. For example, the appropriateness of a clinician's delaying treatment to people who need it, just to satisfy the requirements of an experimental design, is often questioned. One single-case experimental design, the withdrawal design, can in-

volve removing treatment for some time. Treatment is also withheld when placebo control groups are used in group experimental designs. Researchers across the world—in an evolving code of ethics referred to as the Declaration of Helsinki—are developing guidelines to determine just when it would be appropriate to use placebo-controlled trials (Carpenter, Appelbaum, & Levine, 2003). The fundamental question is this: When does a scientist's interest in preserving the internal validity of a study outweigh a client's right to treatment?

One answer to this question involves **informed consent**—a research participant's formal agreement to cooperate in a study following full disclosure of the nature of the research and the participant's role in it (Simon, 1999). The concept of informed consent is derived from the war trials after World War II. Revelations that the Nazis had forced prisoners into so-called medical experiments helped establish the informed consent guidelines that are still used today. In studies using some form of treatment delay or withdrawal, the participant is told why it will occur and the risks and benefits, and permission to proceed is then obtained. In placebo-control studies, participants are told they may not receive an active treatment (all participants are blind to or unaware of which group they are placed in), but they are usually given the option of receiving treatment after the study ends.

True informed consent is at times elusive. The basic components are competence, voluntarism, full information, and comprehension on the part of the subject (Bankert & Madur, 2006). In other words, research participants must be capable of consenting to participation in the research, they must volunteer or not be coerced into participating, they must have all the information they need to make the decision, and they must understand what their participation will involve. In some circumstances, all these conditions are difficult to attain. Children, for example, often do not fully appreciate what will occur during research. Similarly, individuals with cognitive impairments such as mental retardation or schizophrenia may not understand their role or their rights as participants. In institutional settings, participants should not feel coerced into taking part in research.

Certain general protections help ensure that these concerns are properly addressed. First, research in university and medical settings must be approved by an institutional review board (Bankert & Madur, 2006). These are committees made up of university faculty and nonacademic people from the community, and their purpose is to see that the rights of research participants are protected. The committee structure allows people other than the researcher to look at the research procedures to determine whether sufficient care is being taken to protect the welfare and dignity of the participants.

To safeguard those who participate in psychological research and to clarify the responsibilities of researchers, the American Psychological Association has published *Ethical Principles of Psychologists and Code of Conduct,* which includes general guidelines for conducting research (American Psychological Association, 2002b). People in research experiments must be protected from both physical and psychological harm. In addition to the issue of informed consent, these principles stress the investigators' responsibility for the research participants' welfare, because the researcher must ensure that the welfare of the research participants is given priority over any other consideration, including experimental design.

Psychological harm is difficult to define, but its definition remains the responsibility of the investigators. Researchers must hold in confidence all information obtained from participants, who have the right to concealment of their identity on all data, either written or informal. Whenever deception is considered essential to research, the investigator must satisfy a committee of peers that this judgment is correct. If deception or concealment is used, participants must be debriefed—that is, told in language they can understand the true purpose of the study and why it was necessary to deceive them.

The Society for Research in Child Development (1990) has endorsed ethical guidelines for research that address some issues unique to research on children. For example, these guidelines not only call for confidentiality, protection from harm, and debriefing but also require informed consent from children's caregivers and from the children themselves if they are age 7 or older. These guidelines specify that the research must be explained to children in language they can understand so that they can decide whether they wish to participate. Many other ethical issues extend beyond protection of the participants, including how researchers deal with errors in their research, fraud in science, and the proper way to give credit to others. Doing a study involves more than selecting the appropriate design. Researchers must be aware of numerous concerns that involve the rights of the people in the experiment, as well as their own conduct.

A final and important development in the field that will help to "keep the face" on psychological disorders is the involvement of consumers in important aspects of this research (Hanley, Truesdale, King, Elbourne, & Chalmers, 2001). The concern over not only how people are treated in research studies but also how the information is interpreted and used has resulted in many government agencies providing guidance on how the people who are the targets of the research (for example, those with schizophrenia, depression, or anxiety disorders) should be involved in the process. The hope is that if people who experience these disorders are partners in designing, running, and interpreting this research, the relevance of the research, as well as the treatment of the participants in these studies, will be markedly improved.

CONCEPT CHECK 4.3

Part A

The following are some advantages and limitations of methods used in research across time. Sort them out by marking CS for cross-sectional designs and L for longitudinal designs.

Benefits:

1. ____ Shows individual development
2. ____ Easier
3. ____ No cohort effects

Limitations:

4. ____ Cohort effects
5. ____ Cross-generational effect
6. ____ No individual development data

Part B

Indicate whether the following statements are true (T) or false (F).

7. ____ After the nature of the experiment and their role in it are disclosed to the participants, they must be allowed to refuse or agree to sign an informed consent form.
8. ____ If the participant is in the control group or taking a placebo, informed consent is not needed.
9. ____ Research in universities or medical settings must be approved by the institution's review board regarding whether or not the participants lack the cognitive skills to protect themselves from harm.
10. ____ Participants have a right to concealment of their identity on all data collected and reported.
11. ____ When deception is essential to the research, participants do not have to be debriefed regarding the true purpose of the study.

SUMMARY

Examining Abnormal Behavior

■ Research involves establishing a hypothesis that is then tested. In abnormal psychology, research focuses on hypotheses meant to explain the nature, the causes, or the treatment of a disorder.

Types of Research Methods

■ The individual case study is used to study one or more individuals in depth. Although case studies have an important role in the theoretical development of psychology, they are not subject to experimental control and must necessarily be suspect in terms of both internal and external validity.

■ Research by correlation can tell us whether a relationship exists between two variables, but it does not tell us if that relationship is a causal one. Epidemiological research is a type of correlational research that reveals the incidence, distribution, and consequences of a particular problem in one or more populations.

■ Research by experiment can follow one of two designs: group or single case. In both designs, a variable (or variables) is manipulated and the effects are observed to determine the nature of a causal relationship.

Genetics and Research Across Time and Cultures

■ Genetic research focuses on the role of genetics in behavior. These research strategies include family studies, adoption studies, twin studies, genetic linkage analyses, and association studies.

■ Research strategies that examine psychopathology across time include cross-sectional and longitudinal designs. Both focus on differences in behavior or attitudes at different ages, but the former does so by looking at different individuals at different ages and the latter looks at the same individuals at different ages.

■ Prevention research can be viewed in four broad categories: health promotion or positive development strategies, universal prevention strategies, selective prevention strategies, and indicated prevention strategies.

■ The clinical picture, causal factors, and treatment process and outcome can all be influenced by cultural factors.

■ The more the findings of a research program are replicated, the more they gain in credibility.

■ Ethics are important to the research process, and ethical guidelines are spelled out by many professional organizations in an effort to ensure the well-being of research participants.

■ Ethical concerns are being addressed through informed consent and through the inclusion of consumers in research design, implementation, and interpretation.

Key Terms

hypothesis, 99
research design, 99
dependent variable, 99
independent variable, 99
internal validity, 99
external validity, 99
testability, 100
confound, 100
confounding variable, control group, 100
randomization, 100
analog model, 101
generalizability, 101
statistical significance, 101
clinical significance, 101
effect size, 101

patient uniformity myth, 102
case study method, 102
correlation, 103
positive correlation, 103
correlation coefficient, 103
negative correlation, 103
directionality, 103
epidemiology, 104
experiment, 105
manipulating a variable, 105
placebo effect, 105
placebo control group, 105
double-blind control, 106
comparative treatment research, 106

single-case experimental design, 107
repeated measurement, 107
variability, 107
trend, 108
level, 108
withdrawal design, 108
baseline, 108
multiple baseline, 108
phenotype, 110
genotype, 110
human genome project, 110
endophenotypes, 110
family studies, 110

proband, 110
adoption studies, 111
twin studies, 111
genetic linkage analysis, 112
genetic marker, 112
association studies, 112
cross-sectional design, 113
cohort, 113
cohort effect, 113
retrospective information, 113
longitudinal design, 113
cross-generational effect, 113
sequential design, 113
informed consent, 116

Answers to Concept Checks

4.1

1. independent variable; 2. confound; 3. hypothesis; 4. dependent variable; 5. internal validity, external validity

4.2

1. d; 2. b; 3. a; 4. e

4.3

Part A

1. L; 2. CS; 3. L; 4. CS; 5. L; 6. CS

Part B

7. T; 8. F; 9. T; 10. T; 11. F

The Abnormal Psychology Book Companion Website

See **academic.cengage.com/psychology/barlow** for practice quiz questions, interactive activities, Internet links, critical thinking exercises, discussion forums, and more. Also accessible from the Wadsworth Psychology Resource Center **(academic.cengage .com/login).**

Abnormal Psychology Live CD-ROM

■ *Research Methods:* David Barlow discusses the protocols and procedures in doing ethical research on clients with psychological problems. He explains the safeguards and the changes in the practices over time.

CENGAGENOW™ CengageNOW

Go to **academic.cengage.com/now** to link to CengageNOW, your online study tool. First take the Pre-Test for this chapter to get your personalized study plan, which will identify topics you need to review and direct you to online resources. Then take the Post-Test to determine what concepts you have mastered and what you still need work on.

Video Concept Reviews

CengageNOW also contains Mark Durand's *Video Concept Reviews* on challenging topics.

■ Hypothesis/Testability
■ Independent/Dependent Variables
■ Internal/External Validity
■ Statistical Versus Clinical Significance
■ Case Study Method
■ Correlational Research
■ Correlation Coefficient
■ Experiment
■ Placebo Control Group
■ Double-Blind Control
■ Single-Case Experimental Design (Repeated Measures)
■ Genetic Research (Family and Adoptee Studies)
■ Genetic Research (Twin, Genetic Linkage, and Association Studies)
■ Longitudinal and Cross-Sectional Designs

CHAPTER 5

Anxiety Disorders

© Jupiterimages/Creatas/Alamy

THE COMPLEXITY OF ANXIETY DISORDERS
Anxiety, Fear, and Panic: Some Definitions
Causes of Anxiety Disorders
Comorbidity of Anxiety Disorders
Comorbidity With Physical Disorders
Suicide

GENERALIZED ANXIETY DISORDER
Clinical Description
Statistics
Causes
Treatment

PANIC DISORDER WITH AND WITHOUT AGORAPHOBIA
Clinical Description
Statistics
Causes
Treatment

SPECIFIC PHOBIA
Clinical Description
Statistics
Causes
Treatment

SOCIAL PHOBIA
Clinical Description
Statistics
Causes
Treatment

POSTTRAUMATIC STRESS DISORDER
Clinical Description
Statistics
Causes
Treatment

OBSESSIVE-COMPULSIVE DISORDER
Clinical Description
Statistics
Causes
Treatment

ABNORMAL PSYCHOLOGY LIVE CD-ROM
Panic Disorder: Steve
Obsessive-Compulsive Disorder: Chuck
Virtual Reality Therapy
Snake Phobia Treatment
Web Link

One thing is certain, that the problem of anxiety is a nodal point, linking up all kinds of the most important questions; a riddle of which the solution must cast a flood of light upon our whole mental life.

Sigmund Freud

Introductory Lectures on Psychoanalysis

THE COMPLEXITY OF ANXIETY DISORDERS

Anxiety is complex and mysterious, as Sigmund Freud realized many years ago. In some ways, the more we learn about it, the more baffling it seems. "Anxiety" is a specific type of disorder, but it is more than that. It is an emotion implicated so heavily across the full range of psychopathology that we begin by exploring its general nature, both biological and psychological. Next, we consider fear, a somewhat different but clearly related emotion. We suggest that panic is fear that occurs when there is nothing to be afraid of and, therefore, at an inappropriate time. With these important ideas clearly in mind, we focus on specific anxiety disorders.

Anxiety, Fear, and Panic: Some Definitions

Have you ever experienced anxiety? A silly question, you might say, because most of us feel some anxiety almost every day of our lives. Did you have a test in school today for which you weren't "perfectly" prepared? Did you have a date last weekend with somebody new? And how about that job interview coming up? Even thinking about that might make you nervous. But have you ever stopped to think about the nature of anxiety? What is it? What causes it?

Anxiety is a negative mood state characterized by bodily symptoms of physical tension and by apprehension about the future (American Psychiatric Association, 1994; Barlow, 2002). It is important to note that anxiety is hard to study. In humans it can be a subjective sense of unease, a set of behaviors (looking worried and anxious or fidgeting), or a physiological response originating in the brain and reflected in elevated heart rate and muscle tension. Because anxiety is difficult to study in humans, much of the research has been done with animals. For example, we might teach laboratory rats that a light signals an impending shock. The animals certainly look and act anxious when the light comes on. They may fidget, tremble, and perhaps cower in a corner. We might give them an anxiety-reducing drug and notice a reduction of anxiety in their reaction to the light. But is the rats' experience of anxiety the same as that of humans? It seems to be similar, but we don't know for sure; research with animals provides only general information about the nature of anxiety in humans. Thus, anxiety remains a mystery, and we are only beginning our journey of discovery. Anxiety is also closely related to depression (Barlow, 2000,

2002; Barlow, Chorpita, & Turovsky, 1996; Brown & Barlow, 2005; Clark, 2005), so much of what we say here is relevant to Chapter 7.

Anxiety is not pleasant, so why do we seem programmed to experience it almost every time we do something important? Surprisingly, anxiety is good for us, at least in moderate amounts. Psychologists have known for over a century that we perform better when we are a little anxious (Yerkes & Dodson, 1908). You would not have done so well on that test the other day if you had had no anxiety. You were a little more charming and lively on that date last weekend because you were anxious. And you will be better prepared for that job interview coming up if you are anxious. In short, physical and intellectual performances are driven and enhanced by anxiety. Without it, few of us would get much done. Howard Liddell (1949) first proposed this idea when he called anxiety the "shadow of intelligence." He thought the human ability to plan in some detail for the future was connected to that gnawing feeling that things could go wrong and we had better be prepared for them. This is why anxiety is a future-oriented mood state. If you were to put it into words, you might say, "Something might go wrong, and I'm not sure I can deal with it, but I've got to be ready to try. Maybe I'd better study a little harder (or check the mirror one more time before my date, or do a little more research on that company before the interview)."

But what happens when you have too much anxiety? You might actually fail the exam because you can't concentrate on the questions. All you can think about when you're too anxious is how terrible it will be if you fail. You might blow the interview for the same reason. On that date with a new person, you might spend the evening with perspiration running off your face, a sick feeling in your stomach, unable to think of even one reasonably interesting thing to say. Too much of a good thing can be harmful, and few sensations are more harmful than severe anxiety that is out of control.

What makes the situation worse is that severe anxiety usually doesn't go away—that is, even if we "know" there is nothing to be afraid of, we remain anxious. We constantly see examples of this kind of irrationality. John Madden, the well-known sports announcer and former professional football coach, suffers from claustrophobia. He has written about his anxiety and used it as a source of humor in several television commercials. Despite his imposing size (6 feet 4 inches, 260 pounds), Madden has had to overcome the stigma, embarrassment, and effect of anxiety on his

"First time it happened to me, I was driving down the highway, and I had a kind of a knot in my chest. I felt like I had swallowed something and it got stuck, and it lasted pretty much overnight. . . . I felt like I was having a heart attack. . . . I assumed that's what was happening. I felt very panicky. A flushed feeling came over my whole body. I felt as though I was going to pass out."

everyday life, but he hasn't overcome the claustrophobia itself. Madden, who may have to announce a game in New York one Sunday and in San Francisco the next, cannot travel by air. For a long time he took trains around the country; now he uses a well-equipped private bus. Madden and countless other individuals who suffer from anxiety-based disorders are well aware that there is little to fear in the situations they find so stressful. Madden must have long since realized that, because flying is the safest way to travel, it is in his best interest to fly to save time and help maintain his lucrative career. And yet he cannot abandon his self-defeating behavior. Nor can other celebrities who have talked openly about their experiences with severe anxiety, including Carly Simon, Oprah Winfrey, Nicolas Cage, Courtney Love, and the All-Pro NFL running back Ricky Williams.

All the disorders discussed in this chapter are characterized by excessive anxiety, which takes many forms. In Chapter 2 you saw that **fear** is an immediate alarm reaction to danger. Like anxiety, fear can be good for us. It protects us by activating a massive response from the autonomic nervous system (increased heart rate and blood pressure, for example), which, along with our subjective sense of terror, motivates us to escape (flee) or, possibly, to attack (fight). As such, this emergency reaction is often called the flight or fight response.

There is much evidence that fear and anxiety reactions differ psychologically and physiologically (Barlow, 2002; Bouton, 2005; Waddell, Morris, & Bouton, 2006). As noted earlier, anxiety is a future-oriented mood state, characterized by apprehension because we cannot predict or control upcoming events. Fear, on the other hand, is an immediate emotional reaction to current danger characterized by strong escapist action tendencies and, often, a surge in the sympathetic branch of the autonomic nervous system (Barlow, Brown, & Craske, 1994). Someone experiencing fear might say, "I've got to get out of here right now or I may not make it."

What happens if you experience the alarm response of fear when there is nothing to be afraid of—that is, if you have a false alarm? Consider the case of Gretchen, who appeared at one of our clinics.

GRETCHEN: Attacked by Panic

I was 25 when I had my first attack. It was a few weeks after I'd come home from the hospital. I had had my appendix out. The surgery had gone well, and I wasn't in any danger, which is why I don't understand what happened. But one night I went to sleep and I woke up a few hours later—I'm not sure how long—but I woke up with this vague feeling of apprehension. Mostly I remember how my heart started pounding. And my chest hurt; it felt like I was dying—that I was having a heart attack. And I felt kind of queer, as if I were detached from the experience. It seemed like my bedroom was covered with a haze. I ran to my sister's room, but I felt like I was a puppet or a robot who was under the control of somebody else while I was running. I think I scared her almost as much as I was frightened myself. She called an ambulance (Barlow, 2002).

The roots of the panic experience are deeply embedded in our cultural myths. Pan, the Greek god of nature, lived in the country, presiding over rivers, woods, streams, and grazing animals. But Pan did not look like the typical god. He was ugly and short, with legs resembling a goat's. Unfortunately for travelers, Pan habitually napped in a small cave or thicket near the road. When traveling Greeks disturbed him, he let out a bloodcurdling scream that was so intense many terrified travelers died of fright. This sudden overwhelming reaction came to be known as **panic,** after the irate god. In psychopathology, a **panic attack** is defined as an abrupt experience of intense fear or acute discomfort, accompanied by physical symptoms that usually include heart palpitations, chest pain, shortness of breath, and, possibly, dizziness.

Three basic types of panic attacks are described in DSM-IV: situationally bound, unexpected, and situationally predisposed. If you know you are afraid of high places or of driving over long bridges, you might have a panic attack in these situations but not anywhere else; this is a *situationally bound (cued) panic attack.* By contrast, you might experience *unexpected (uncued) panic attacks* if you don't have a clue when or where the next attack will occur. The third type of panic attack, the *situationally predisposed panic attack,* is between these two types. You are more likely to, but will not inevitably, have an attack where you have had one before; for example, in a large mall. If you don't know whether it will happen today and it does, the attack is situationally predisposed. We mention these types of attacks because they play a role in several anxiety disorders. Unexpected and situationally predisposed attacks are important in panic disorder. Situationally bound attacks are more common in specific phobias or social phobia (see ■ Figure 5.1).

Remember that fear is an intense emotional alarm accompanied by a surge of energy in the autonomic nervous system that motivates us to flee from danger. Does Gretchen's panic attack

DSM-IV-TR

DSM TABLE 5.1 Diagnostic Criteria for Panic Attack

The predominant complaint is a discrete period of intense fear or discomfort in which at least four (or more) of the following symptoms developed abruptly and reached a peak within 10 minutes:
1. Palpitations, pounding heart, or accelerated heart rate
2. Sweating
3. Trembling or shaking
4. Sensations of shortness of breath or smothering
5. Feeling of choking
6. Chest pain or discomfort
7. Nausea or abdominal distress
8. Feeling dizzy, unsteady, lightheaded, or faint
9. Derealization (feelings of unreality) or depersonalization (being detached from oneself)
10. Fear of losing control or going crazy
11. Fear of dying
12. Paresthesias (numbness or tingling sensations)
13. Chills or hot flushes

Source: Reprinted, with permission, from American Psychiatric Association. (2000). *Diagnostic and statistical manual of mental disorders* (4th ed., text revision). Washington, DC: Author, © 2000 American Psychiatric Association.

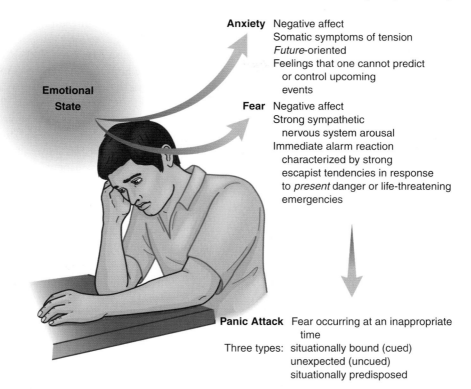

Anxiety Negative affect
Somatic symptoms of tension
Future-oriented
Feelings that one cannot predict
or control upcoming
events

Fear Negative affect
Strong sympathetic
nervous system arousal
Immediate alarm reaction
characterized by strong
escapist tendencies in response
to *present* danger or life-threatening
emergencies

Panic Attack Fear occurring at an inappropriate
time
Three types: situationally bound (cued)
unexpected (uncued)
situationally predisposed

■ **FIGURE 5.1** The relationships among anxiety, fear, and panic attack.

sound like it could be the emotion of fear? A variety of evidence suggests it is (Barlow, 2002; Barlow et al., 1996; Bouton, 2005), including similarities in reports of the experience of fear and panic, similar behavioral tendencies to escape, and similar underlying neurobiological processes.

Over the years we have recorded panic attacks during physiological assessments of patients (see, for example, Hofmann & Barlow, 1996). The physiological surge recorded in one patient is shown in ■ Figure 5.2. Notice the sudden dramatic increase in heart rate from minute 11 through minute 13, accompanied by increases in muscle tension (frontalis EMG) and finger temperature. This massive autonomic surge peaked and subsided within 3 minutes. The panic attack in the laboratory occurred quite unexpectedly from the patient's point of view and from ours. As the figure shows, fear and panic are experienced suddenly, which is necessary to mobilize us for instantaneous reaction to impending danger.

Causes of Anxiety Disorders

You learned in Chapters 1 and 2 that excessive emotional reactions have no simple one-dimensional cause but come from multiple sources. Next, we explore the biological, psychological, and social contributors and how they interact to produce anxiety disorders.

■ Biological Contributions

Increasing evidence shows that we inherit a tendency to be tense or uptight (Clark, 2005; Eysenck, 1967; Gray & McNaughton, 1996; Lader & Wing, 1964). As with almost all psychological disorders, no single gene seems to cause anxiety. Instead, contributions from collections of genes in several areas on chromosomes

make us vulnerable to anxiety (Kendler, 2006; Kendler et al., 1995; Plomin, DeFries, McClearn, & Rutter, 1997; Rutter et al., 2006) when the right psychological and social factors are in place. The tendency to panic also seems to run in families and may have a genetic component (Barlow, 2002). Some evidence indicates that genetic contributions to panic and anxiety differ (Craske, 1999; Craske & Barlow, in press; Kendler et al., 1995); still, in both situations, genetic vulnerability, particularly in a person who is under stress, may create the condition for panic but does not cause it directly. Scientists are beginning to discover groups of genes and relevant areas on a number of chromosomes that might contribute to anxiety and panic (Schumacher et al., 2005; Thorgeirsson et al., 2003). For example, activation of genes that promote corticotropin-releasing factor (CRF) seem to place children at risk for developing panic disorder and possibly phobia (Smoller, Rosenbaum, & Biederman, 2003; Smoller, Yamaki, & Fagerness, 2005). CRF is a neurohormone that is part of our sympathetic nervous system described in Chapter 2. We discuss the CRF system in more detail later in this chapter and in Chapter 9. Also, you saw in Chapter 2 that scientists are beginning to pinpoint small groups of genes that seem to play a particularly important role in making people vulnerable to developing not only depression but also anxiety (Caspi et al., 2003) because the genetic makeup underlying anxiety and that underlying depression seem to be the same (as discussed later). But overall, studies of genes associated with anxiety and panic have provided inconsistent results (Roy-Byrne, Craske, & Stein, in press).

Anxiety is also associated with specific brain circuits and neurotransmitter systems. For example, depleted levels of GABA, part of the GABA–benzodiazepine system, are associated with increased anxiety, although the relationship is not quite so direct.

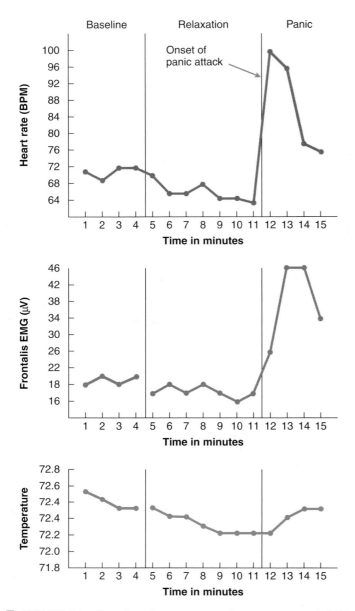

■ **FIGURE 5.2** Physiological measurements during a panic attack. BPM, beats per minute; EMG, electromyography. (Reprinted, with permission, from Cohen, A. S., Barlow, D. H., & Blanchard, E. B., 1985. Psychophysiology of relaxation-associated panic attacks. *Journal of Abnormal Psychology, 94, 98,* © 1985 by the American Psychological Association.)

The noradrenergic system has also been implicated in anxiety, and evidence from basic animal studies, as well as studies of normal anxiety in humans, suggest the serotonergic neurotransmitter system is also involved (Deakin & Graeff, 1991; Lesch et al., 1996; Maier, 1997). But increasing attention in the last several years is focusing on the role of CRF system as central to the expression of anxiety (and depression) (Heim & Nemeroff, 1999; Ladd et al., 2000; Smoller et al., 2005; Sullivan, Kent, & Coplan, 2000). This is because CRF activates the hypothalamic–pituitary–adrenocortical (HPA) axis, described in Chapter 2, which is part of the CRF system, and this CRF system has wide-ranging effects on areas of the brain implicated in anxiety, including the emotional brain (the limbic system), particularly the hippocampus and the amygdala;

the locus coeruleus in the brain stem; the prefrontal cortex; and the dopaminergic neurotransmitter system. The CRF system is also directly related to the GABA–benzodiazepine system and the serotonergic and noradrenergic neurotransmitter systems.

The area of the brain most often associated with anxiety is the limbic system (Charney & Drevets, 2002; Gray & McNaughton, 1996; LeDoux, 1996, 2002; see Figure 2.7c), which acts as a mediator between the brain stem and the cortex. The more primitive brain stem monitors and senses changes in bodily functions and relays these potential danger signals to higher cortical processes through the limbic system. The late Jeffrey Gray, a prominent British neuropsychologist, identified a brain circuit in the limbic system of animals that seems heavily involved in anxiety (Gray, 1982, 1985; McNaughton & Gray, 2000) and may be relevant to humans. This circuit leads from the septal and hippocampal area in the limbic system to the frontal cortex. (The septal–hippocampal system is activated by CRF and serotonergic- and noradrenergic-mediated pathways originating in the brain stem.) The system that Gray calls the **behavioral inhibition system (BIS)** is activated by signals from the brain stem of unexpected events, such as major changes in body functioning that might signal danger. Danger signals in response to something we see that might be threatening descend from the cortex to the septal–hippocampal system. The BIS also receives a big boost from the amygdala (Davis, 1992; LeDoux, 1996, 2002). When the BIS is activated by signals that arise from the brain stem or descend from the cortex, our tendency is to freeze, experience anxiety, and apprehensively evaluate the situation to confirm that danger is present.

The BIS circuit is distinct from the circuit involved in panic. Gray (1982; Gray & McNaughton, 1996) and Graeff (1987, 1993; Deakin & Graeff, 1991) identified what Gray calls the **fight/flight system (FFS).** This circuit originates in the brain stem and travels through several midbrain structures, including the amygdala, the ventromedial nucleus of the hypothalamus, and the central gray matter. When stimulated in animals, this circuit produces an immediate alarm-and-escape response that looks very much like panic in humans (Gray & McNaughton, 1996). Gray and McNaughton (1996) and Graeff (1993) think the FFS is activated partly by deficiencies in serotonin.

It is likely that factors in your environment can change the sensitivity of these brain circuits, making you more or less susceptible to developing anxiety and its disorders, a finding that has been demonstrated in several laboratories (Francis, Diorio, Plotsky, & Meaney, 2002). For example, one important study suggested that cigarette smoking as a teenager is associated with greatly increased risk for developing anxiety disorders as adults, particularly panic disorder and generalized anxiety disorder (J. G. Johnson et al., 2000). Nearly 700 adolescents were followed into adulthood. Teens who smoked 20 or more cigarettes daily were 15 times more likely to develop panic disorder and 5 times more likely to develop generalized anxiety disorder than teens who smoked less or didn't smoke. The complex interaction between smoking and panic disorder has been confirmed in more recent research (Zvolensky & Bernstein, 2005). One possible explanation is that chronic exposure to nicotine, an addictive drug that increases somatic symptoms, as well as respiratory problems, triggers additional anxiety and panic, thereby increasing biological vulnerability to develop severe anxiety disorders, even though many smokers may start smoking because they think it will calm them.

Research into the neurobiology of anxiety and panic is still new, but we have made exciting progress by implicating two seemingly different brain systems and confirming the crucial role of the CRF system and the amygdala. Brain-imaging procedures will undoubtedly yield more information in the years to come, and this has already begun to happen (Charney & Drevets, 2002).

■ Psychological Contributions

In Chapter 2, we reviewed some theories on the nature of psychological causes of anxiety. Remember that Freud thought anxiety was a psychic reaction to danger surrounding the reactivation of an infantile fearful situation. Behavioral theorists view anxiety as a product of early classical conditioning, modeling, or other forms of learning (Bandura, 1986). Evidence is accumulating (see, for example, Barlow, 2002; Suàrez, Bennett, Goldstein, & Barlow, in press) that supports an integrated model of anxiety involving a variety of factors. In childhood, we may acquire an awareness that events are not always in our control (Chorpita & Barlow, 1998). The continuum of this perception may range from total confidence in our control of all aspects of our lives to deep uncertainty about ourselves and our ability to deal with upcoming events. The perception that events may be out of our control is most evident as a set of danger-laden beliefs. If you are anxious about schoolwork, you may think you will do poorly on the next exam and that there is no way you can pass the course, even though all your grades have been A's and B's. A general "sense of uncontrollability" may develop early as a function of upbringing and other environmental factors.

Interestingly, the actions of parents in early childhood seem to do a lot to foster this sense of control or a sense of uncontrollability (Chorpita & Barlow, 1998). Generally, it seems that parents who interact in a positive and predictable way with their children by responding to their needs, particularly when the child communicates needs for attention, food, relief from pain, and so on, perform an important function. These parents teach their children that they have control over their environment and their responses have an effect on their parents and their environment. In addition, parents who allow their children to explore their world and develop the necessary skills to cope with unexpected occurrences enable their children to develop a healthy sense of control. What seems to be important is providing a "secure home base" for your children so you are there for them if they need you while they explore their world (Chorpita & Barlow, 1998). In contrast, parents who are overprotective and overintrusive and who "clear the way" for their children, never letting them experience any adversity, create a situation in which children never learn how to cope with adversity when it comes along. Therefore, these children don't learn that they can control their environment. A variety of evidence has accumulated supporting these ideas (Barlow, 2002; Chorpita & Barlow, 1998; Chorpita, Brown, & Barlow, 1998; Gunnar & Fisher, in press; Lieb et al., 2000; Nolen-Hoeksema, Wolfson, Mumme, & Guskin, 1995; White, Brown, Somers, & Barlow, 2006). A sense of control (or lack of it) that develops from these early experiences is the psychological factor that makes us more or less vulnerable to anxiety in later life.

Most psychological accounts of panic invoke conditioning and cognitive explanations that are difficult to separate (Bouton, Mineka, & Barlow, 2001). Thus, a strong fear response initially occurs during extreme stress or perhaps as a result of a dangerous situation in the environment (a true alarm). This emotional response then becomes associated with a variety of external and internal cues. In other words, these cues, or conditioned stimuli, provoke the fear response and an assumption of danger, whether or not danger is actually present (Bouton, 2005; Bouton et al., 2001; Martin, 1983; Mineka & Zinbarg, 2006; Razran, 1961). This is the conditioning process described in Chapter 2. External cues are places or situations similar to the one where the initial panic attack occurred. Internal cues are increases in heart rate or respiration that were associated with the initial panic attack, even if they are now the result of normal circumstances, such as exercise. Thus, when your heart is beating fast you are more likely to think of and, perhaps, experience a panic attack than when it is beating normally. Furthermore, you may not be aware of the cues or triggers of severe fear; that is, they are unconscious. This is most likely because experimental work with animals demonstrates that these cues or triggers may travel from the eyes directly to the amygdala in the emotional brain without going through the cortex, the source of awareness (Bouton et al., 2001; LeDoux, 2002).

■ Social Contributions

Stressful life events trigger our biological and psychological vulnerabilities to anxiety. Most are social and interpersonal in nature—marriage, divorce, difficulties at work, death of a loved one, pressures to excel in school, and so on. Some might be physical, such as an injury or illness.

The same stressors can trigger physical reactions such as headaches or hypertension and emotional reactions such as panic attacks (Barlow, 2002). The particular way we react to stress seems to run in families. If you get headaches when under stress, chances are other people in your family also get headaches. If you have panic attacks, other members of your family probably do also. This finding suggests a possible genetic contribution, at least to initial panic attacks.

■ An Integrated Model

Putting the factors together in an integrated way, we have described a theory of the development of anxiety and related disorders called the *triple vulnerability theory* (Barlow, 2000, 2002; Suàrez et al., in press). The first vulnerability (or diathesis) is a *generalized biological vulnerability*. We can see that a tendency to be uptight or high-strung might be inherited. But a generalized biological vulnerability to develop anxiety is not anxiety itself. The second vulnerability is a *generalized psychological vulnerability*. That is, you might also grow up believing the world is dangerous and out of control and you might not be able to cope when things go wrong based on your early experiences. If this perception is strong, you have a generalized psychological vulnerability to anxiety. The third vulnerability is a *specific psychological vulnerability* in which you learn from early experience, such as being taught by your parents, that some situations or objects are fraught with danger (even if they really aren't). Possible examples are dogs, if one of your parents is afraid of dogs, or being evaluated negatively by

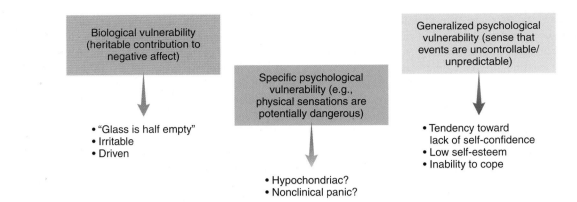

■ FIGURE 5.3 The three vulnerabilities that contribute to the development of anxiety disorders. If individuals possess all three, the odds are greatly increased that they will develop an anxiety disorder after experiencing a stressful situation. (From Barlow, D. H., 2002. *Anxiety and its disorders: The nature and treatment of anxiety and panic* (2nd ed.). New York: Guildford Press.)

others, if this is something your parents worry about. These triple vulnerabilities are presented in ■ Figure 5.3 and revisited when we describe each anxiety disorder. If you are under a lot of pressure, particularly from interpersonal stressors, a given stressor could activate your biological tendencies to be anxious and your psychological tendencies to feel you might not be able to deal with the situation and control the stress. Once this cycle starts, it tends to feed on itself, so it might not stop even when the particular life stressor has long since passed. Anxiety can be general, evoked by many aspects of your life. But it is usually focused on one area, such as social evaluations or grades (Barlow, 2002).

Panic is also a characteristic response to stress that runs in families and may have a genetic component that is separate from anxiety. Because an individual associates the panic attack with internal or external cues (conditioning is one form of learning), the attacks are called *learned alarms.* Even if you have a legitimate fear response to a dangerous situation (true alarm), your reaction can become associated with a variety of cues that may then trigger an attack *in the absence* of any danger, making it a learned alarm. Furthermore, anxiety and panic are closely related (Barlow, 2002; Suàrez et al., in press) in that anxiety increases the likelihood of panic. This relationship makes sense from an evolutionary point of view, because sensing a possible future threat or danger (anxiety) should prepare us to react instantaneously with an alarm response if the danger becomes imminent (Bouton, 2005). Anxiety and panic need not occur together, but it makes sense that they often do.

Comorbidity of Anxiety Disorders

Before describing the specific anxiety disorders, it is important to note that they often co-occur. As we described in Chapter 3, the co-occurrence of two or more disorders in a single individual is referred to as *comorbidity.* The high rates of comorbidity among anxiety disorders (and depression) emphasize how all of these disorders share the common features of anxiety and panic described here. They also share the same vulnerabilities, biological and psychological, to develop anxiety and panic. They differ only in the focus of anxiety (what are they anxious about?) and, perhaps, the patterning of panic attacks. Of course, if each patient

with an anxiety disorder also had every other anxiety disorder, there would be little sense in distinguishing among the specific disorders. It would be enough to say, simply, that the patient had an anxiety disorder. But this is not the case, and, although rates of comorbidity are high, they vary somewhat from disorder to disorder (Allen et al., in press; Bruce et al., 2005; Tsao, Mystkowski, Zucker, & Craske, 2002). A large-scale study recently completed at one of our centers examined the comorbidity of *Diagnostic and Statistical Manual of Mental Disorders,* fourth edition (DSM-IV) anxiety and mood disorders (Brown & Barlow, 2002; Brown, Campbell, Lehman, Grisham, & Mancill, 2001). Data were collected from 1,127 patients carefully diagnosed using a semistructured interview in our center. If we examine just rates of comorbidity at the time of assessment, the results indicate that 55% of the patients who received a principal diagnosis of an anxiety or depressive disorder had at least one additional anxiety or depressive disorder at the time of the assessment. If we consider whether the patient met criteria for an additional diagnosis at any time in his life, rather than just at the time of the assessment, the rate increases to 76%.

By far, the most common additional diagnosis for all anxiety disorders was major depression, which occurred in 50% of the cases over the course of the patient's life. This becomes important when we discuss the relationship of anxiety and depression later in this chapter. Also important is the finding that additional diagnoses of depression or alcohol or drug abuse makes it less likely that you will recover from an anxiety disorder and more likely that you will relapse if you do recover (Bruce et al., 2005).

Comorbidity With Physical Disorders

Anxiety disorders also co-occur with several physical conditions. A recent important study indicated that the presence of any anxiety disorder was uniquely and significantly associated with thyroid disease, respiratory disease, gastrointestinal disease, arthritis, migraine headaches, and allergic conditions (Sareen et al., 2006). Thus, people with these physical conditions are likely to have an anxiety disorder but are not any more likely to have another psychological disorder. Furthermore, the anxiety disorder most often begins before the physical disorder, suggesting (but not proving) that something about having an anxiety disorder might cause, or contribute to the cause of, the physical disorder. Finally, if someone has both an anxiety disorder and one of the physical disorders mentioned earlier, that person will suffer from greater disability and a poorer quality of life from both the physical and the emotional problem than if that individual had just the physical disorder alone. Some of these results are presented in ■ Figure 5.4. Other studies have also favored the same relationship between anxiety disorders, particularly panic disorders, and cardiovascular (heart) disease (see, for example, Gomez-Caminero, Blumentals, Russo, Brown, & Castilla-Puentes, 2005).

Suicide

Based on epidemiological data, Weissman and colleagues found in an earlier study that 20% of patients with panic disorder had attempted suicide. They concluded that such attempts were associated with panic disorder. They also concluded that the risk of someone with panic disorder attempting suicide is comparable to that for individuals with major depression (Johnson, Weissman, & Klerman, 1990; Weissman, Klerman, Markowitz, & Ouellette, 1989). This finding was frightening, because panic disorder is quite prevalent and clinicians had generally not been on the lookout for possible suicide attempts in such patients. The investigators also found that even patients with panic disorder who did not have accompanying depression were at risk for suicide.

A major study confirms that having any anxiety disorder, not just panic disorder, uniquely increases the chances of having thoughts about suicide (suicidal ideation) or making suicidal attempts (Sareen et al., 2006). Even if an individual has depression, which we know is a big risk for suicide attempts (see Chapter 7), anxiety disorders combined with depression will make the risk of suicide significantly greater than the risk for a person who has depression alone.

We now turn to descriptions of the individual anxiety disorders. But keep in mind that approximately 50% of individuals

---

with these disorders will present with one or more additional anxiety or depressive disorders and, perhaps, some other disorders, particularly substance abuse disorders, as described later.

GENERALIZED ANXIETY DISORDER

Specific anxiety disorders are complicated by panic attacks or other features that are the focus of the anxiety. In generalized anxiety disorder, the focus is generalized to the events of everyday life. Therefore, we consider generalized anxiety disorder first.

Clinical Description

Is somebody in your family a worrywart? Is somebody in your family a perfectionist? Perhaps it is you! Most of us worry to some extent. As we have said, worry can be useful. It helps us plan for the future, make sure that we're prepared for that test, or double-check that we've thought of everything before we head home for the holidays. The worry process itself is not pleasant, but without it nothing would go smoothly. But what if you worry indiscriminately about everything? Furthermore, what if worrying is unproductive: No matter how much you worry, you can't seem to decide what to do about an upcoming problem or situation. And what if you can't stop worrying, even if you know it is doing you no good and probably making everyone else around you miserable? These features characterize **generalized anxiety disorder (GAD).** Consider the case of Irene.

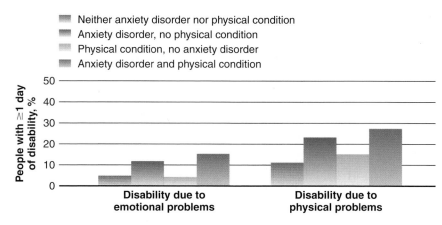

■ **FIGURE 5.4** The relationship of anxiety disorders and physical conditions with a disability within the past 30 days. The anxiety disorder and physical condition group had significantly increased associations with disability due to emotional problems and physical conditions compared with neither the anxiety disorder nor the physical condition group and the physical condition alone group. (From Sareen, J., Jacobi, F., Cox, B. J., Belik, S., Clara, I., & Stein, B. M., 2006. Disability and poor quality of life associated with comorbid anxiety disorders and physical conditions. *Archives of Internal Medicine, 166,* 2109–2116.)

IRENE: Ruled by Worry

Irene was a 20-year-old college student with an engaging personality but not many friends. She came to the clinic complaining of excessive anxiety and general difficulties in controlling her life. Everything was a catastrophe for Irene. Although she carried a 3.7 grade point average, she was convinced she would flunk every test she took. As a result, she repeatedly threatened to drop courses after only several weeks of classes because she feared that she would not understand the material.

Irene worried until she dropped out of the first college she attended after 1 month. She felt depressed for a while, then decided to take a couple of courses at a local junior college, believing she could handle the work there better. After achieving straight A's at the junior college for 2 years, she enrolled once again in a 4-year college as a junior. After a short time, she began calling the clinic in a state of extreme agitation, saying she had to drop this or that course because she couldn't handle it. With great difficulty, her therapist and parents persuaded her to stay in the courses and to seek further help. In any course Irene completed, her grade was between an A and a B-minus, but she still worried about every test and every paper, afraid she would fall apart and be unable to understand and complete the work.

Irene did not worry only about school. She was also concerned about relationships with her friends, and whenever she was with her new boyfriend she feared making a fool of herself and losing his interest. She reported that each date went extremely well but she knew the next one would probably be a disaster. As the relationship progressed and some sexual contact seemed natural, Irene was worried sick that her inexperience would make her boyfriend consider her naive and stupid. Nevertheless, she reported enjoying the early sexual contact and admitted that he seemed to enjoy it also, but she was convinced that the next time a catastrophe would happen.

Irene was also concerned about her health. She had minor hypertension, probably because she was somewhat overweight. She then approached every meal as if death itself might result if she ate the wrong types or amounts of food. She became reluctant to have her blood pressure checked for fear it would be high or to weigh herself for fear she was not losing weight. She severely restricted her eating and as a result had an occasional episode of binge eating, although not often enough to warrant concern.

In addition, Irene worried about her religious faith and about her relationships with her family, particularly her mother and sister. Although Irene had an occasional panic attack, this was not a major issue to her. As soon as the panic subsided, she focused on the next possible catastrophe. In addition to high blood pressure, Irene had tension headaches and a "nervous stomach," with a lot of gas, occasional diarrhea, and some abdominal pain. Irene's life was a series of impending catastrophes. Her mother reported that she dreaded a phone call from Irene, let alone a visit, because she knew she would have to see her daughter through a crisis. For the same reason, Irene had few friends. Even so, when she temporarily gave up her anxiety, she was fun to be with.

Irene suffered from GAD, which is, in many ways, the basic syndrome that characterizes every anxiety disorder considered in this chapter (Brown, Barlow, & Liebowitz, 1994). The DSM-IV-TR criteria specify that at least 6 months of excessive anxiety and worry (apprehensive expectation) must be ongoing more days than not. Furthermore, it must be difficult to turn off or control the worry process. This is what distinguishes pathological worrying from the normal kind we all experience occasionally as we prepare for an upcoming event or challenge. Most of us worry for a time but can set the problem aside and go on to another task. Even if the upcoming challenge is a big one, as soon as it is over the worrying stops. For Irene, it never stopped. She turned to the next crisis as soon as the current one was over.

DSM-IV-TR

DSM TABLE 5.2 Diagnostic Criteria for Generalized Anxiety Disorder

A. Excessive anxiety and worry (apprehensive expectation), occurring more days than not for at least 6 months about a number of events or activities (such as work or school performance).

B. The person finds it difficult to control the worry.

C. The anxiety and worry are associated with at least three (or more) of the following six symptoms (with at least some symptoms present for more days than not for the past 6 months) (Note: Only one item is required in children):
   1. Restlessness or feeling keyed up or on edge
   2. Being easily fatigued
   3. Difficulty concentrating or mind going blank
   4. Irritability
   5. Muscle tension
   6. Sleep disturbance (difficulty falling or staying asleep or restless, unsatisfying sleep)

D. The focus of the anxiety and worry is not confined to features of an Axis I disorder; that is, the anxiety or worry is not about having a panic attack (as in panic disorder), being embarrassed in public (as in social phobia), being contaminated (as in obsessive-compulsive disorder), being away from home or close relatives (as in separation anxiety disorder), gaining weight (as in anorexia nervosa), or having a serious illness (as in hypochondriasis), and is not part of posttraumatic stress disorder.

E. The anxiety, worry, or physical symptoms cause clinically significant distress or impairment in social, occupational, or other important areas of functioning.

F. The disturbance is not due to the direct physiological effects of a substance (e.g., drugs of abuse [or] medication) or a general medical condition (e.g., hyperthyroidism), and does not occur exclusively during a mood disorder, psychotic disorder, or a pervasive developmental disorder.

Source: Reprinted, with permission, from American Psychiatric Association. (2000). *Diagnostic and statistical manual of mental disorders* (4th ed., text revision). Washington, DC: Author, © 2000 American Psychiatric Association.

The physical symptoms associated with generalized anxiety and GAD differ somewhat from those associated with panic attacks and panic disorder (covered next). Whereas panic is associated with autonomic arousal, presumably as a result of a sympathetic nervous system surge (for instance, heart rate increases and palpitations, perspiration, and trembling), GAD is characterized by muscle tension, mental agitation (Brown, Marten, & Barlow, 1995), susceptibility to fatigue (probably the result of chronic excessive muscle tension), some irritability, and difficulty sleeping. Focusing attention is difficult as the mind quickly switches from crisis to crisis. For children, only one physical symptom is required, and research validates this strategy (Tracey, Chorpita, Douban, & Barlow, 1997). People with GAD mostly worry about minor, everyday life events, a characteristic that distinguishes GAD from other anxiety disorders. When asked, "Do you worry excessively about minor things?" 100% of individuals with GAD respond "yes" compared to approximately 50% of individuals with other anxiety disorder categories. Such a difference is statistically significant. Major events quickly become the focus of anxiety and worry, too. Adults typically focus on possible misfortune to their children, family health, job responsibilities, and more minor things such as household chores or being on time for appointments. Children with GAD most often worry about competence in academic, athletic, or social performance, as well as family issues (Albano & Hack, 2004; Silverman, La Greca, & Wasserstein, 1995; Weems, Silverman, & La Greca, 2000). The elderly tend to focus, understandably, on health (Beck & Averill, 2004; Person & Borkovec, 1995); they also have difficulty sleeping, which seems to make the anxiety worse (Beck & Stanley, 1997).

Statistics

Although worry and physical tension are common, the severe generalized anxiety experienced by Irene is quite rare. Approximately 3.1% of the population meets criteria for GAD during a given 1-year period (Kessler, Chiu, Demler, & Walters, 2005) and 5.7% at some point during their lifetime (Kessler, Berglund, Demler, Jin, & Walters, 2005). This is still quite a large number, making GAD one of the most common anxiety disorders. Similar rates are reported from around the world, for example, from rural South Africa (Bhagwanjee, Parekh, Paruk, Petersen, & Subedar, 1998). However, relatively few people with GAD come for treatment compared to patients with panic disorder. Anxiety clinics like ours report that only approximately 10% of their patients meet criteria for GAD compared to 30% to 50% for panic disorder. This may be because most patients with GAD seek help from their primary care doctors, where they are found in large numbers (Roy-Byrne & Katon, 2000).

About two-thirds of individuals with GAD are female in both clinical samples (Woodman, Noyes, Black, Schlosser, & Yagla, 1999; Yonkers, Warshaw, Massion, & Keller, 1996) and epidemiological studies, which include people who do not necessarily seek treatment (Blazer, George, & Hughes, 1991; Carter, Wittchen, Pfister, & Kessler, 2001; Wittchen, Zhao, Kessler, & Eaton, 1994). But this sex ratio may be specific to developed countries. In the South African study mentioned here, GAD was more common in males.

Some people with GAD report onset in early adulthood, usually in response to a life stressor. Nevertheless, most studies find that GAD is associated with an earlier and more gradual onset than most other anxiety disorders (Anderson, Noyes, & Crowe, 1984; Barlow, 2002; Brown et al., 1994; Sanderson & Barlow, 1990; Woodman et al., 1999). The median age of onset based on interviews is 31 (Kessler, Berglund, et al., 2005), but like Irene, many people have felt anxious and tense all their lives. Once it develops, GAD is chronic. One study found only an 8% probability of becoming symptom free after 2 years of follow-up (Yonkers et al., 1996). More recently, Bruce and colleagues (2005) reported that 12 years after the beginning of an episode of GAD there was only a 58% chance of recovering. But 45% of those individuals who recovered were likely to relapse later. This suggests that GAD, like most anxiety disorders, follows a chronic course, characterized by waxing and waning of symptoms.

GAD is prevalent among the elderly. In the large national comorbidity study, GAD was found to be most common in the group over 45 years of age and least common in the youngest group, age 15 to 24 (Wittchen et al., 1994). Flint (1994) reported prevalence rates of GAD in older adults to be as high as 7%. We also know that the use of minor tranquilizers in the elderly is high, ranging from 17% to 50% in one study (Salzman, 1991). It is not entirely clear why drugs are prescribed with such frequency for the elderly. One possibility is that the drugs may not be entirely intended for anxiety. Prescribed drugs may be primarily for sleeping problems or other secondary effects of medical illnesses. In any case, benzodiazepines (minor tranquilizers) interfere with cognitive function and put the elderly at greater risks for falling down and breaking bones, particularly their hips (Barlow, 2002). Major difficulties that hamper the investigation of anxiety in the elderly include the lack of good assessment instruments and treatment studies, largely because of a lack of sufficient research interest (Beck & Stanley, 1997; Sheikh, 1992).

In a classic study, Rodin and Langer (1977) demonstrated that the elderly may be particularly susceptible to anxiety about failing health or other life situations that begin to diminish whatever control they retain over events in their lives. This increasing lack of control, failing health, and gradual loss of meaningful functions may be a particularly unfortunate by-product of the way the elderly are treated in Western culture. The result is substantial impairment in quality of life in the elderly with GAD (Wetherell et al., 2004). If it were possible to change our attitudes and behavior, we might well reduce the frequency of anxiety, depression, and early death among our elderly citizens.

Causes

What causes GAD? We have learned a great deal in the past several years. As with most anxiety disorders, there seems to be a generalized biological vulnerability, as is reflected in studies examining a genetic contribution to GAD. This conclusion is based on studies showing that GAD tends to run in families (Noyes, Clarkson, Crowe, Yates, & McChesney, 1987; Noyes et al., 1992). Twin studies strengthen this suggestion (Kendler, Neale, Kessler, Heath, & Eaves, 1992a). Kendler and colleagues (1995; Hettema, Prescott, Myers, Neale, & Kendler, 2005) confirmed that what seems to be inherited is the tendency to become anxious rather than GAD itself. Genetic contributions to the personality trait "neuroticism" and GAD are very similar if not identical (Hettema, Prescott, & Kendler, 2004).

For a long time, GAD has posed a real puzzle to investigators. Although the definition of the disorder is relatively new, originating in 1980 with DSM-III, clinicians and psychopathologists were working with people with generalized anxiety long before diagnostic systems were developed. For years, clinicians thought that people who were generally anxious had simply not focused their anxiety on anything specific. Thus, such anxiety was described as "free floating." But now scientists have looked more closely and have discovered some interesting distinctions from other anxiety disorders.

The first hints of difference were found in the physiological responsivity of individuals with GAD. It is interesting that individuals with GAD do not respond as strongly as individuals with anxiety disorders in which panic is more prominent. Several studies have found that individuals with GAD show *less responsiveness* on most physiological measures, such as heart rate, blood pressure, skin conductance, and respiration rate (Borkovec & Hu, 1990; Hoehn-Saric, McLeod, & Zimmerli, 1989; Roemer, Orsillo, & Barlow, 2002), than do individuals with other anxiety disorders. Therefore, people with GAD have been called *autonomic restrictors* (Barlow, Chorpita, & Turovsky, 1996; Thayer, Friedman, & Borkovec, 1996).

When individuals with GAD are compared to nonanxious "normal" subjects, the one physiological measure that consistently distinguishes the anxious group is muscle tension (Marten et al., 1993). People with GAD are chronically tense. To understand this phenomenon, we may have to know what's going on in the minds of people with GAD. With new methods from cognitive science, we are beginning to uncover the sometimes-unconscious mental processes ongoing in GAD (McNally, 1996).

The evidence indicates that individuals with GAD are highly sensitive to threat in general, particularly to a threat that has personal relevance. That is, they allocate their attention more readily to sources of threat than do people who are not anxious (Aikins & Craske, 2001; Barlow, 2002; Bradley, Mogg, White, Groom, & de Bono, 1999; Butler & Mathews, 1983; MacLeod, Mathews, & Tata, 1986; Mathews, 1997; Mogg, Mathews, & Weinman, 1989). This high sensitivity may have arisen in early stressful experiences where they learned that the world is dangerous and out of control, and they might not be able to cope (generalized psychological vulnerability). Furthermore, this acute awareness of potential threat, particularly if it is personal, seems to be entirely automatic or unconscious. Using the Stroop color-naming task described in Chapter 2, MacLeod and Mathews (1991) presented threatening words on a screen for only 20 milliseconds and still found that individuals with GAD were slower to name the colors of the words than were nonanxious individuals. Remember that in this task words in colored letters are presented briefly and subjects are asked to name the *color* rather than the word. The fact that the colors of threatening words were named more slowly suggests the *words* were more relevant to people with GAD, which interfered with their naming the color—even though the words were not present long enough for the individuals to be conscious of them.

Mogg, Bradley, Millar, and White (1995) reported similar results. Investigators using other paradigms have come to similar conclusions (Eysenck, 1992; Mathews, 1997; McNally, 1996).

How do mental processes link up with the tendency of individuals with GAD to be autonomic restrictors? Tom Borkovec and his colleagues have suggested some possibilities. These researchers noticed that although the peripheral autonomic arousal of individuals with GAD is restricted, they showed marked increases in electroencephalogram (EEG)

Tom Borkovec and his colleagues theorized that people with GAD worry excessively to avoid images of deep-seated emotional threat. Borkovec has also developed effective psychosocial treatments for GAD.

beta activity, reflecting intense cognitive processing in the frontal lobes, particularly in the left hemisphere. This finding suggests to Borkovec and Inz (1990) that people with GAD engage in frantic, intense thought processes or worry without accompanying images (which would be reflected by activity in the right hemisphere of the brain) (Borkovec, Alcaine, & Behar, 2004). Borkovec suggests that this kind of worry may be what causes these individuals to be autonomic restrictors (Borkovec, Shadick, & Hopkins, 1991; Roemer & Borkovec, 1993). That is, they are thinking so hard about upcoming problems that they don't have the attentional capacity left for the all-important process of creating images of the potential threat, images that would elicit more substantial negative affect and autonomic activity. In other words, they *avoid* all negative affect associated with the threat (Borkovec et al., 2004; Craske, 1999). But from the point of view of therapy, it is important to "process" the images and negative affect associated with anxiety (Craske & Barlow, 2006; Zinbarg, Craske, & Barlow, 2006). Because people with GAD do not seem to engage in this process, they may avoid much of the unpleasantness and pain associated with the negative affect and imagery, but they are never able to work through their problems and arrive at solutions. Therefore, they become chronic worriers, with accompanying autonomic inflexibility and quite severe muscle tension. Thus, intense worrying for an individual with GAD may serve the same maladaptive purpose as avoidance does for people with phobias. It prevents the person from facing the feared situation, so adaptation never occurs.

In summary, some people inherit a tendency to be tense (generalized biological vulnerability), and they develop a sense early on that important events in their lives may be uncontrollable and potentially dangerous (generalized psychological vulnerability). Significant stress makes them apprehensive and vigilant. This sets off intense worry with resulting physiological changes, leading to GAD (Roemer et al., 2002; Turovsky & Barlow, 1996). This model is current, as it combines findings from cognitive science with biological data from both the central and the peripheral nervous systems. Time will tell if the model is correct, although supporting data continue to come in (Borkovec et al., 2004; Craske, 1999; DiBartolo, Brown, & Barlow, 1997; Mineka & Zinbarg, 2006). In any case, it is consistent with our view of anxiety as a future-oriented mood state focused on potential danger or threat, as opposed to an emergency or alarm reaction to actual present danger. A model of the development of GAD is presented in ■ Figure 5.5.

Treatment

GAD is quite common, and available treatments, both drug and psychological, are reasonably effective. Benzodiazepines are most often prescribed for generalized anxiety, and the evidence indicates that they give some relief, at least in the short term. Few studies have looked at the effects of these drugs for a period longer than 8 weeks. Those that have suggest benefits seem to continue for approximately 6 months (Schweizer & Rickels, 1996). But the therapeutic effect is relatively modest. Furthermore, benzodiazepines carry some risks. First, they seem to impair both cognitive and motor functioning (see, for example, Hindmarch, 1986, 1990; O'Hanlon, Haak, Blaauw, & Riemersma, 1982; van Laar, Volkerts, & Verbaten, 2001). Specifically, people don't seem to be as alert on the job or at school when they are taking benzodiazepines. The drugs may impair driving, and in the elderly they

seem to be associated with falls, resulting in hip fractures (Ray, Gurwitz, Decker, & Kennedy, 1992; Wang, Bohn, Glynn, Mogun, & Avorn, 2001). More important, benzodiazepines seem to produce both psychological and physical dependence, making it difficult for people to stop taking them (Noyes, Garvey, Cook, & Suelzer, 1991; Rickels, Schweizer, Case, & Greenblatt, 1990; Schweizer, Rickels, Case, & Greenblatt, 1990). There is reasonably wide agreement that the optimal use of benzodiazepines is for the short-term relief of anxiety associated with a temporary crisis or stressful event, such as a family problem (Craske & Barlow, 2006). Under these circumstances, a physician may prescribe a benzodiazepine until the crisis is resolved but for no more than a week or two. There is better evidence for the usefulness of antidepressants in the treatment of GAD, such as imipramine (Tofranil) (see, for example, Rickels, Downing, Schweizer, & Hassman, 1993), paroxetine (Paxil) (Rickels, Rynn, Ivengar, & Duff, 2006), and venlafaxine (Effexor) (Schatzberg, 2000). These drugs may prove to be a better choice (Brawman-Mintzer, 2001; Craske & Barlow, 2006).

In the short term, psychological treatments seem to confer about the same benefit as drugs in the treatment of GAD, but they are probably better in the long term (Barlow, Allen, & Basden, in press; Barlow & Lehman, 1996; Borkovec, Newman, Pincus, & Lytle, 2002; Gould, Otto, Pollack, & Yap, 1997; Roemer et al., 2002). Recent reports of innovations in brief psychological treatments are encouraging. As we learn more about generalized anxiety, we may find that helping people with this disorder focus on what is actually threatening is useful. Because we now know that individuals with GAD seem to avoid "feelings" of anxiety and the negative effect associated with images, clinicians have designed treatments to help them process the information on an emotional level, using images, so that they will feel anxious. These treatments have other components, such as teaching patients how to relax deeply to combat tension. Borkovec and his colleagues found such a treatment to be significantly better than a placebo psychological treatment, not only at posttreatment but also at a 1-year follow-up (Borkovec & Costello, 1993).

In the early 1990s, we developed a cognitive-behavioral treatment (CBT) for GAD in which patients evoke the worry process during therapy sessions and confront anxiety-provoking images and thoughts head-on. The patient learns to use cognitive therapy and other coping techniques to counteract and control the worry process (Craske & Barlow, 2006; Wetherell, Gatz, & Craske, 2003). A brief adaptation of this treatment has also been used successfully to improve quality of life in a primary care office (family doctors and nurses) where GAD is a frequent complaint (Rollman, Belnap, & Mazumdar, 2005). Borkovec and Ruscio (2001) reviewed 13 controlled studies evaluating CBTs for GAD and found substantial gains compared to no treatment or alternative treatment such as psychodynamic therapy. Studies indicate that brief psychological treatments such as these alter the sometimes-unconscious cognitive biases associated with GAD (Mathews, Mogg, Kentish, & Eysenck, 1995; Mogg, Bradley, Millar, & White, 1995). Despite this success, it is clear we need more powerful treatments, both drug and psychological, for this chronic, treatment-resistant condition. Recently, a new psychological treatment for GAD has been developed that incorporates procedures focusing on acceptance rather than avoidance of distressing thoughts

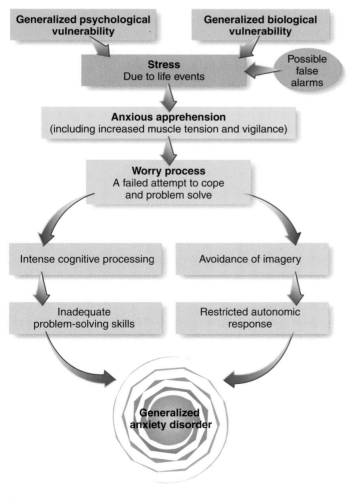

■ **FIGURE 5.5** An integrative model of GAD.

and feelings in addition to cognitive therapy. Meditational approaches help teach the patient to be more tolerant of these feelings (Orsillo, Roemer, & Barlow, 2003; Roemer & Orsillo, 2002; Roemer et al., 2002). Preliminary results are encouraging (Roemer & Orsillo, in press).

There is particularly encouraging evidence that psychological treatments are effective with children who suffer from generalized anxiety (Albano & Hack, 2004). Barrett, Dadds, and Rapee (1996) found significant benefit in children with severe GAD when cognitive-behavioral procedures were combined with family therapy. After treatment, 95% of the children receiving this combination of therapies no longer met criteria for the diagnosis. Even more encouraging was a 6-year follow-up showing that the gains were largely maintained, with 85.7% still not meeting criteria for diagnosis (Barrett, Duffy, Dadds, & Rapee, 2001); Kendall and colleagues (1997) randomly assigned 94 children from 9 to 13 years of age to CBT or a wait-list control group. The majority of the children were diagnosed with GAD, but some had social phobia or separation anxiety. Based on teacher ratings, 70% of the treated children were functioning normally after treatment, gains maintained for at least 1 year. Similarly, progress is also being made in adapting our treatments for the elderly, as important studies show (Beck & Stanley, 1997; Stanley, Beck, & Glassco, 1997; Stanley et al., 2003; Wetherell, Lenz, & Stanley, 2005).

After trying a number of different drugs, Irene was treated with the CBT approach developed at our clinic and found herself more able to cope with life. She completed college and graduate school, married, and is successful in her career as a counselor in a nursing home. But even now, Irene finds it difficult to relax and stop worrying. She continues to experience mild to moderate anxiety, particularly when under stress; she occasionally takes minor tranquilizers to support her psychological coping skills.

CONCEPT CHECK 5.2

True (T) or false (F)?

1. ____ GAD is characterized by muscle tension, mental agitation, irritability, sleeping difficulties, and susceptibility to fatigue.
2. ____ Most studies show that in the majority of cases of GAD, onset is early in adulthood as an immediate response to a life stressor.
3. ____ GAD is prevalent in the elderly and in females in our society.
4. ____ GAD has no genetic basis.
5. ____ Cognitive-behavioral treatment and other psychological treatments for GAD are probably better than drug therapies in the long run.

PANIC DISORDER WITH AND WITHOUT AGORAPHOBIA

Did you have a relative, an eccentric aunt, for example, who never seemed to leave the house? Family reunions or visits always had to be at her house. She never went anywhere else. Most people attributed their old aunt's behavior to her being a little odd or perhaps just not fond of travel. She was warm and friendly when people came to visit, so she retained contact with the family.

Your aunt may not have been just odd or eccentric. She may have suffered from a debilitating anxiety disorder called **panic disorder with agoraphobia (PDA),** in which individuals experience severe, unexpected panic attacks; they may think they're dying or otherwise losing control. Because they never know when an attack might occur, they develop **agoraphobia,** fear and avoidance of situations in which they would feel unsafe in the event of a panic attack or symptoms. These situations include those from which it would be hard or embarrassing to escape to get home or to a hospital. In severe cases, people with PDA are unable to leave the house, sometimes for years on end, as in the example of Mrs. M.

MRS. M.: Self-Imprisoned

Mrs. M. was 67 years old and lived in a second-floor walk-up apartment in a lower-middle-class section of the city. Her adult daughter, one of her few remaining contacts with the world, had requested an evaluation with Mrs. M.'s consent. I rang the bell and entered a narrow hallway; Mrs. M. was nowhere in sight. Knowing that she lived on the second floor, I walked up the stairs and knocked on the door at the top. When I heard Mrs. M. ask me to come in, I opened the door. She was sitting in her living room, and I could quickly see the layout of the rest of the apartment. The living room was in the front; the kitchen was in the back, adjoining a porch. To the right of the stairs was the one bedroom, with a bathroom opening from it.

Mrs. M. was glad to see me and friendly, offering me coffee and homemade cookies. I was the first person she had seen in 3 weeks. Mrs. M. had not left that apartment in 20 years, and she had suffered from PDA for more than 30 years.

As she told her story, Mrs. M. conveyed vivid images of a wasted life. And yet she continued to struggle in the face of adversity and to make the best she could of her limited existence. Even areas in her apartment signaled the potential for terrifying panic attacks. She had not answered the door herself for the past 15 years because she was afraid to look into the hallway. She could enter her kitchen and go into the areas containing the stove and refrigerator, but for the past 10 years she had not been to the part of the room that overlooked the backyard or out onto the back porch. Thus, her life for the past decade had been confined to her bedroom, her living room, and the front half of her kitchen. She relied on her adult daughter to bring groceries and visit once a week. Her only other visitor was the parish priest, who came to deliver communion every 2 to 3 weeks when he could. Her only other contact with the outside world was through the television and the radio. Her husband, who had abused both alcohol and Mrs. M., had died 10 years earlier of alcohol-related causes. Early in her stressful marriage she had her first terrifying panic attack and had gradually withdrawn from the world. As long as she stayed in her apartment, she was relatively free of panic. Therefore, and because in her mind there were few reasons left near the end of her life to venture out, she declined treatment.

Clinical Description

At the beginning of the chapter, we talked about the related phenomena of anxiety and panic. In PDA, anxiety and panic are combined with *phobic avoidance* in an intricate relationship that can become as devastating as it was for Mrs. M. Many people who have panic attacks do not necessarily develop panic disorder. Similarly, many people experience anxiety and panic without developing agoraphobia. In those cases, the disorder is called **panic disorder without agoraphobia (PD).**

To meet criteria for panic disorder (with or without agoraphobia), a person must experience an unexpected panic attack and develop substantial anxiety over the possibility of having another attack or about the implications of the attack or its consequences. In other words, the person must think that each attack is a sign of impending death or incapacitation. A few individuals do not report concern about another attack but still change their behavior in a way that indicates the distress the attacks cause them. They may avoid going to certain places or neglect their duties around the house for fear an attack might occur if they are too active.

■ The Development of Agoraphobia

Many people with panic disorder develop agoraphobia. The term *agoraphobia* was coined in 1871 by Karl Westphal, a German physician, and, in the original Greek, refers to fear of the marketplace. This is an appropriate term because the *agora,* the Greek marketplace, was a busy, bustling area. One of the most stressful places for individuals with agoraphobia today is the shopping mall, the modern-day agora.

All the evidence now points to the conclusion that agoraphobic avoidance behavior is simply one complication of severe, unexpected panic attacks (Barlow, 2002; Craske & Barlow, 1988, in press). Simply put, if you have had unexpected panic attacks and are afraid you may have another one, you want to be in a safe place or at least with a safe person who knows what you are experiencing if another attack occurs so that you can quickly get to a hospital or at least go into your bedroom and lie down (the home is usually a safe place). We know that anxiety is diminished for individuals with agoraphobia if they think a location or person is "safe," even if there is nothing effective the person could do if something bad did happen. If you are in a shopping mall or a crowded movie theater or church, not only is it difficult to leave but you are probably going to embarrass yourself if you try. You may think you will have to climb over everyone in church to get out or get up in the middle of the movie and run out—or worse, faint in the movie theater (in fact, individuals with agoraphobia

seldom do any of these things). For these reasons, when they do go to church or to the movies, people with agoraphobia always plan for rapid escape (for example, by sitting near the door). A list of typical situations commonly avoided by someone with agoraphobia is found in Table 5.1.

Although agoraphobic behavior initially is closely tied to the occasions of panic, it can become relatively independent of panic attacks (Craske & Barlow, 1988; Craske, Rapee, & Barlow, 1988; White & Barlow, 2002). In other words, an individual who has not had a panic attack for years may still have strong agoraphobic avoidance, like Mrs. M. Agoraphobic avoidance seems to be determined by the extent to which you think or expect you might have another attack rather than by how many attacks you actually have or how severe they are. Thus, agoraphobic avoidance is simply one way of coping with unexpected panic attacks.

Other methods of coping with panic attacks include using (and eventually abusing) drugs and/or alcohol. Some individuals do not avoid agoraphobic situations but endure them with "intense dread." For example, people who must go to work each day or, perhaps, travel as part of the job will suffer untold agonies of anxiety and panic simply to achieve their goals. Thus, DSM-IV notes that agoraphobia may be characterized either by avoiding the situations or by enduring them with marked distress.

Most patients with severe agoraphobic avoidance (and some with little) also display another cluster of avoidant behaviors that we call *interoceptive avoidance,* or avoidance of internal physical sensations (Barlow & Craske, 2007; Brown, White, & Barlow, 2005; Craske & Barlow, in press; Shear et al., 1997). These behaviors involve removing yourself from situations or activities that might produce the physiological arousal that somehow resembles the beginnings of a panic attack. Some patients might avoid exercise because it produces increased cardiovascular activity or faster respiration that reminds them of panic attacks and makes them think one might be beginning. Other patients might avoid sauna baths or any rooms in which they might perspire. Psychopathologists are beginning to recognize that this cluster of avoidance behaviors is every bit as important as more classical agoraphobic avoidance. A list of situations or activities typically avoided within the interoceptive cluster is found in Table 5.2.

TABLE 5.1	Typical Situations Avoided by People With Agoraphobia
Shopping malls	Being far from home
Cars (as driver or passenger)	Staying at home alone
Buses	Waiting in line
Trains	Supermarkets
Subways	Stores
Wide streets	Crowds
Tunnels	Planes
Restaurants	Elevators
Theaters	Escalators

Source: Adapted, with permission, from Barlow, D. H., & Craske, M. G. (2007). *Mastery of your anxiety and panic* (4th ed., p. 5). New York: Oxford University Press.

DSM-IV-TR

DSM TABLE 5.3 Diagnostic Criteria for Panic Disorder With Agoraphobia

A. Both 1 and 2:

1. Recurrent unexpected panic attacks are present.
2. At least one of the attacks has been followed by 1 month (or more) of one (or more) of the following: (a) persistent concern about having additional attacks, (b) worry about the implications of the attack or its consequences (e.g., losing control, having a heart attack, "going crazy"), or (c) a significant change in behavior related to the attacks.

B. The presence of agoraphobia in which the predominant complaint is anxiety about being in places or situations from which escape might be difficult or embarrassing, or in which help may not be available in the event of an unexpected or situationally predisposed panic attack or paniclike symptoms. Agoraphobic fears typically involve characteristic clusters of situations that include being outside the home alone; being in a crowd or standing in a line; being on a bridge; and traveling in a bus, train, or automobile.

C. The panic attacks are not due to the direct physiological effects of a substance (e.g., drug of abuse, medication) or a general medical condition (e.g., hyperthydroidism).

D. The panic attacks are not better accounted for by another mental disorder, such as social phobia (e.g., occurring on exposure to feared social situations), specific phobia (e.g., on exposure to a specific social situation), obsessive-compulsive disorder (e.g., on exposure to dirt, in someone with an obsession about contamination), posttraumatic stress disorder (e.g., in response to stimuli associated with a severe stressor), or separation anxiety disorder (e.g., in response to being away from home or close relatives).

Source: Reprinted, with permission, from American Psychiatric Association. (2000). *Diagnostic and statistical manual of mental disorders* (4th ed., text revision). Washington, DC: Author. © 2000 American Psychiatric Association.

TABLE 5.2 Interoceptive Daily Activities Typically Avoided by People With Agoraphobia

Running up flights of stairs	Getting involved in "heated" debates
Walking outside in intense heat	
Hot, stuffy rooms	Having showers with the doors and windows closed
Hot, stuffy cars	
Hot, stuffy stores or shopping malls	Having a sauna
	Hiking
Walking outside in very cold weather	Sports
Aerobics	Drinking coffee or any caffeinated beverages
Lifting heavy objects	
Dancing	Eating chocolate
Sexual relations	Standing quickly from a sitting position
Watching horror movies	
Eating heavy meals	Getting angry
Watching exciting movies or sports events	

Source: Adapted, with permission, from Barlow, D. H., & Craske, M. G. (2007). *Mastery of your anxiety and panic* (4th ed., p. 11). New York: Oxford University Press.

Statistics

PD or PDA is fairly common. Approximately 2.7% of the population meet criteria for PD or PDA during a given 1-year period (Kessler, Chiu, et al., 2005) and 4.7% met them at some point during their lives, two-thirds of them women (Eaton, Kessler, Wittchen, & Magee, 1994; Kessler, Berglund et. al., 2005). Another smaller group (1.4% at some point during their lives) develops agoraphobia without ever having a full-blown panic attack. Typically, these individuals will have only one or two severe symptoms, such as dizziness, rather than the minimum of four required to be called a panic attack. This condition is called *agoraphobia without a history of panic disorder,* but it looks much the same as PDA and is treated with the same treatments (Craske & Barlow, in press).

Michelle Craske demonstrated that agoraphobic avoidance is simply one way of coping with panic. She and Ron Rapee, working with David H. Barlow, also developed an effective psychological treatment for panic disorder.

Onset of panic disorder usually occurs in early adult life—from mid-teens through about 40 years of age. The median age of onset is between 20 and 24 (Kessler, Berglund, et al., 2005). Prepubescent children have been known to experience unexpected panic attacks and occasionally panic disorder, although this is quite rare (Albano, Chorpita, & Barlow, 1996; Kearney, Albano, Eisen, Allan, & Barlow, 1997; Moreau & Weissman, 1992). Most initial unexpected panic attacks begin at or after puberty. Puberty seems a better predictor of unexpected panic attacks than age because higher rates of panic attacks are found in girls after puberty compared to before puberty (Hayward et al., 1992). Furthermore, many prepubertal children who are seen by general medical practitioners have symptoms of hyperventilation that may well be panic attacks. However, these children do not report fear of dying or losing control—perhaps because they are not at a stage of their cognitive development where they can make these attributions (Nelles & Barlow, 1988).

Important work on anxiety in the elderly suggests that health and vitality are the primary focus of anxiety in the elderly population (Wisocki, 1988; Wisocki, Handen, & Morse, 1986). Lindesay (1991) studied 60 confirmed cases of phobic disorder in the elderly and found that they differed from younger adults in several ways, such as age of onset and prevalence. The primary phobia in this group was agoraphobia, which had a late onset (after age 50) and was often related to a stressful life event, usually an illness or injury. In general, the prevalence of PD or PDA decreases among the elderly, from 5.7% at ages 30–44 to 2.0% after age 60 (Kessler, Berglund, et al., 2005).

As we have said, 75% or more of those who suffer from agoraphobia are women (Barlow, 2002; Myers et al., 1984; Thorpe & Burns, 1983). For a long time, we didn't know why, but now it seems the most logical explanation is cultural (Arrindell et al.,

2003a). It is more accepted for women to report fear and to avoid numerous situations. Men, however, are expected to be stronger and braver, to "tough it out." The higher the severity of agoraphobic avoidance, the greater the proportion of women. For example, in our clinic, out of a group of patients suffering from panic disorder with mild agoraphobia, 72% were women; but if the agoraphobia was moderate, the percentage was 81%. Similarly, if agoraphobia was severe, the percentage was 89%.

What happens to men who have severe unexpected panic attacks? Is cultural disapproval of fear in men so strong that most of them simply endure panic? The answer seems to be "no." A large proportion of males with unexpected panic attacks cope in a culturally acceptable way: They consume large amounts of alcohol. The problem is that they become dependent on alcohol, and many begin the long downward spiral into serious addiction. Thus, males may end up with an even more severe problem than PDA. Because these men are so impaired by alcohol abuse, clinicians may not realize they also have PDA. Furthermore, even if they are successfully treated for their addiction, the anxiety disorder requires treatment (Chambless, Cherney, Caputo, & Rheinstein, 1987; Cox, Swinson, Schulman, Kuch, & Reikman, 1993; Kushner, Abrams, & Borchardt, 2000; Kushner, Sher, & Beitman, 1990).

■ Cultural Influences

Panic disorder exists worldwide, although its expression may vary from place to place. In Lesotho, Africa, the prevalence of panic disorder (and GAD) was found to be equal to or greater than in North America (Hollifield, Katon, Spain, & Pule, 1990). In a more comprehensive study, prevalence rates for panic disorder were remarkably similar in the United States, Canada, Puerto Rico, New Zealand, Italy, Korea, and Taiwan, with only Taiwan showing somewhat lower rates (Horwath & Weissman, 1997). The rate and types of symptoms of panic attacks among Iranian college students is similar to those among Western college students (Nazemi et al., 2003). Rates are also similar among different ethnic groups in the United States, including African Americans. Furthermore, black and white patients with panic disorder show no significant differences in symptoms (Friedman, Paradis, & Hatch, 1994). However, note that panic disorder often co-occurs with hypertension in African American patients (Neal, Nagle-Rich, & Smucker, 1994; Neal-Barnett & Smith, 1997).

Somatic symptoms of anxiety may be emphasized in Third World cultures. Subjective feelings of dread or angst may not be part of the cultural idiom; that is, individuals in these cultures do not attend to these feelings and do not report them, focusing only on bodily sensations. In Chapter 2, we described a fright disorder called *susto* in Latin America characterized by sweating, increased heart rate, and insomnia but not reports of anxiety or fear, even though a severe fright is the cause. An anxiety-related, culturally defined syndrome prominent among Hispanic Americans, particularly those from the Caribbean, is called *ataques de nervios* (Hinton, Chong, Pollack, Barlow, & McNally, in press; Liebowitz et al., 1994). The symptoms of an ataque seem quite similar to those of a panic attack, although such manifestations as shouting uncontrollably or bursting into tears may be associated more often with ataque than with panic.

Finally, Devon Hinton, a psychiatrist/anthropologist, and his colleagues have recently described a fascinating manifestation of panic disorder among Khmer (Cambodian) and Vietnamese refugees in the United States. Both of these groups seem to suffer from a high rate of panic disorder. But a substantial number of these panic attacks are associated with orthostatic dizziness (dizziness if one stands up quickly) and "sore neck." What Hinton's group discovered is that the Khmer concept of *kyol goeu* or "wind overload" becomes the focus of catastrophic thinking during panic attacks (Hinton, Pich, Chhean, Pollack, & Barlow, 2004; Hinton, Pollack, Pich, Fama, & Barlow, 2005; Hinton et al., in press).

■ Nocturnal Panic

Think back to the case of Gretchen, whose panic attack was described earlier. Is there anything unusual about her report? She was sound asleep when it happened. Approximately 60% of the people with panic disorder have experienced such nocturnal attacks (Craske & Rowe, 1997; Uhde, 1994). In fact, panic attacks occur more often between 1:30 A.M. and 3:30 A.M. than any other time (Taylor et al., 1986). In some cases, people are afraid to go to sleep at night. What's happening to them? Are they having nightmares? Research indicates they are not. Nocturnal attacks are studied in a sleep laboratory. Patients spend a few nights sleeping while attached to an electroencephalograph machine that monitors their brain waves (see Chapter 3). We all go through various stages of sleep that are reflected by different patterns on the electroencephalogram. (Stages of sleep are discussed fully in Chapter 8.) We have learned that nocturnal panics occur during delta wave or slow wave sleep, which typically occurs several hours after we fall asleep and is the deepest stage of sleep. People with panic disorder often begin to panic when they start sinking into delta sleep, then they awaken amid an attack. Because there is no obvious reason for them to be anxious or panicky when they are sound asleep, most of these individuals think they are dying (Craske & Barlow, 1988; Craske & Rowe, 1997).

What causes nocturnal panic? Currently, our best information is that the change in stages of sleep to slow wave sleep produces physical sensations of "letting go" that are frightening to an individual with panic disorder (Craske et al., 2002). This process is described more fully later when we discuss causes of panic disorder. Several other events also occur during sleep that resemble nocturnal panic and are mistakenly thought to be the cause of nocturnal panic by some. Initially, it was thought it might be nightmares, but nightmares and other dreamlike activity occur only during a stage of sleep characterized by rapid eye movement (REM sleep), which typically occurs much later in the sleep cycle. Therefore, people are not dreaming when they have nocturnal panics, a conclusion consistent with patient reports. Some therapists are not aware of the stage of sleep associated with nocturnal panic attacks and so assume that patients are "repressing" their dream material, perhaps because it might relate to an early trauma too painful to be admitted to consciousness. As we've seen, this is virtually impossible because nocturnal panic attacks do not occur during REM sleep, so there is no well-developed dream or nightmare activity going on when they happen. Thus, it is not possible for these patients to be dreaming anything.

Some therapists assume that patients with nocturnal panic might have a breathing disorder called *sleep apnea,* an interruption of breathing during sleep that may feel like suffocation. This condition is often found in people who are substantially overweight. But sleep apnea has a cycle of awakening and falling back to sleep that is not characteristic of nocturnal panics.

A related phenomenon occurring in children is called *sleep terrors,* which we describe in more detail in Chapter 8 (Durand, 2006). Often children awake imagining that something is chasing them around the room. It is common for them to scream and get out of bed as if something were after them. However, they do not wake up and have no memory of the event in the morning. In contrast, individuals experiencing nocturnal panic attacks do wake up and later remember the event clearly. Sleep terrors also tend to occur at a later stage of sleep (stage 4 sleep), a stage associated with sleepwalking.

Finally, there is a fascinating condition called *isolated sleep paralysis* that seems culturally determined. Have you ever heard the expression "the witch is riding you"? If you're white, you probably haven't, but if you're African American, chances are you at least know somebody who has had this frightening experience because it seems to be more common in this ethnic group in the United States (Bell, Dixie-Bell, & Thompson, 1986; Neal-Barnett & Smith, 1997; Ramsawh, Raffa, White, & Barlow, in press). Isolated sleep paralysis occurs during the transitional state between sleep and waking, when a person is either falling asleep or waking up, but mostly when waking up. During this period, the individual is unable to move and experiences a surge of terror that resembles a panic attack; occasionally, there are also vivid hallucinations. One possible explanation is that REM sleep is spilling over into the waking cycle. This seems likely because one feature of REM sleep is lack of bodily movement. Another is vivid dreams, which could account for the experience of hallucination. Paradis, Friedman, and Hatch (1997) confirmed that the occurrence of isolated sleep paralysis was significantly higher in African Americans with panic disorder (59.6%) as compared with other groups (see ■ Figure 5.6). More recently, Ramsawh and colleagues (in press) replicated this finding and discovered that African Americans with isolated sleep paralysis had a history of trauma and more frequent diagnoses of panic disorder and posttraumatic stress disorder than African Americans without isolated sleep paralysis. Even more interesting is that the disorder does not seem to occur in Nigerian blacks. The prevalence in Nigerian blacks is about the same as it is in American whites. The reasons for this distribution are not clear, although all factors point to a cultural explanation.

Causes

It is not possible to understand panic disorder (with or without agoraphobia) without referring to the triad of contributing factors mentioned throughout this book: biological, psychological, and social. Strong evidence indicates that agoraphobia develops after a person has unexpected panic attacks (or panic-like sensations); but whether agoraphobia develops and how severe it becomes seem to be socially and culturally determined, as we noted earlier. Panic attacks and panic disorder, however, seem to be related most strongly to biological and psychological factors and their interaction.

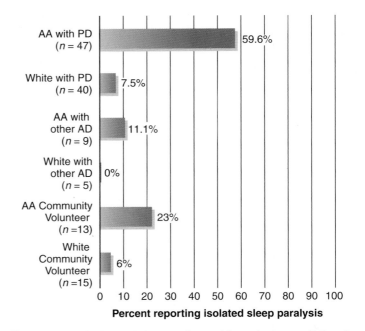

■ **FIGURE 5.6**   Isolated sleep paralysis in African Americans (AA) and Caucasian Americans with panic disorder (PD), other anxiety disorder (AD) but not panic disorder, and community volunteers with no disorder. (Adapted from Paradis, C. M., Friedman, S., & Hatch, M., 1997. Isolated sleep paralysis in African-Americans with panic disorder. *Cultural Diversity & Mental Health, 3,* 69–76.)

At the beginning of the chapter, we discussed the triple vulnerability model of how biological, psychological, and social factors may contribute to the development and maintenance of anxiety and to an initial unexpected panic attack (Bouton et al., 2001; Bouton, 2005; Suàrez et al., in press; White & Barlow, 2002) (see Figure 5.3).

As noted earlier, we all inherit—some more than others—a vulnerability to stress, which is a tendency to be generally neurobiologically overreactive to the events of daily life (generalized biological vulnerability). But some people are also more likely than others to have an emergency alarm reaction (unexpected panic attack) when confronted with stress-producing events. These may include stress on the job or at school, death of a loved one, divorce, and positive events that are nevertheless stressful, such as graduating from school and starting a new career, getting married, or changing jobs. (Remember that other people might be more likely to have headaches or high blood pressure in response to the same kinds of stress.) Particular situations quickly become associated in an individual's mind with external and internal cues that were present during the panic attack (Bouton et al., 2001). The next time the person's heart rate increases during exercise, she might assume she is having a panic attack (conditioning). Harmless exercise is an example of an internal cue or a conditioned stimulus for a panic attack. Being in a movie theater when panic first occurred would be an external cue that might become a conditioned stimulus for future panics. Because these cues become associated with a number of different internal and external stimuli through a learning process, we call them *learned alarms.*

But none of this would make much difference without the next step. The individuals must be susceptible to developing anxiety over the possibility of having another panic attack (a generalized psychological vulnerability). That is, they think the physical sensations associated with the panic attack mean something terrible is about to happen, perhaps death. This is what creates panic disorder. In other words, when people have a tendency to expect the worst as they experience strong physical sensations, some of them focus their anxiety on the possibility of *future* panic attacks—perhaps because they've been taught in childhood that unexpected bodily sensations may be dangerous—whereas other people experiencing these attacks do not. This tendency to believe that unexpected bodily sensations are dangerous reflects a specific psychological vulnerability to develop panic and related disorders. This causal sequence is depicted in ■ Figure 5.7.

Approximately 8% to 12% of the population has an occasional unexpected panic attack, often during a period of intense stress (Mattis & Ollendick, 2002; Norton, Harrison, Hauch, & Rhodes, 1985; Salge, Beck, & Logan, 1988; Suàrez et al., in press; Telch, Lucas, & Nelson, 1989). Most of these people do not develop anxiety (Telch et al., 1989). Only approximately 5% go on to develop anxiety over future panic attacks and thereby meet the criteria for panic disorder. What happens to those individuals who don't develop anxiety? They seem to attribute the attack to events of the moment, such as an argument with a friend, something

they ate, or a bad day, and go on with their lives, perhaps experiencing an occasional panic attack when they are under stress again. We can now measure one aspect of this psychological vulnerability, using an instrument known as the *anxiety sensitivity index* (Reiss, Peterson, Gursky, & McNally, 1986). One of the best tests of anxiety sensitivity as a vulnerability to experience panic attacks was demonstrated in an experiment conducted by Brad Schmidt and his colleagues (Schmidt, Lerew, & Jackson, 1997; Schmidt et al., 1999). Schmidt and colleagues (1997) administered the Anxiety Sensitivity Index to a large number of military recruits undergoing a stressful basic training regimen. High scores on the anxiety sensitivity index before basic training predicted the onset of unexpected panic attacks in the 5 weeks following basic training. It is likely that the anxiety these recruits experienced in response to their stress-related panic reactions made panic attacks more noticeable (Barlow, 2002). In a different study, high scores on this index also predicted future panic attacks and anxiety in adolescents (Hayward, Killen, Kraemer, & Taylor, 2000). The experience of panic, in turn, elevated scores on the Anxiety Sensitivity Index at a later date, underscoring the cycle of panic and anxiety in those who are vulnerable (Schmidt, Lerew, & Jackson, 1999; Weems, Hayward, Killen, & Taylor, 2002). The influential cognitive theories of David Clark (1986, 1996) explicate in more detail some cognitive processes that may be ongoing in panic disorder. Clark emphasizes the specific psychological vulnerability

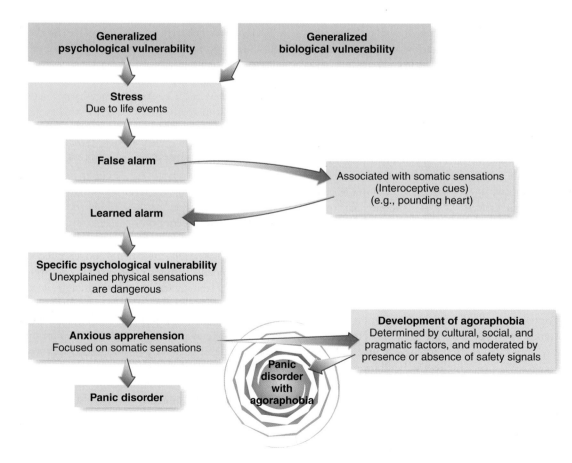

■ **FIGURE 5.7** A model of the causes of panic disorder with or without agoraphobia. (Reprinted, with permission, from White, K. S., & Barlow, D. H., 2002. Panic disorder and agoraphobia. In D. H. Barlow, *Anxiety and its disorders: The nature and treatment of anxiety and panic,* 2nd ed. New York: Guilford Press, © 2002 by Guilford Press.)

of people with this disorder to interpret normal physical sensations in a catastrophic way. In other words, although we all typically experience rapid heartbeat after exercise, if you have a psychological or cognitive vulnerability, you might interpret the response as dangerous and feel a surge of anxiety. This anxiety, in turn, produces more physical sensations because of the action of the sympathetic nervous system, you perceive these additional sensations as even more dangerous, and a vicious cycle begins that results in a panic attack. Thus, Clark emphasizes the cognitive process as most important in panic disorder.

Supporting this model, Ehlers and Breuer (1992, 1996) had panic disorder patients and several control groups try to estimate how fast their hearts were beating. The exercise demonstrated that patients with panic disorder paid much closer attention to their internal somatic sensations because they were more accurate at estimating how fast their hearts were beating than individuals without panic disorder. In other words, because they are anxious about bodily sensations to begin with, because these sensations might indicate an unexpected panic is about to occur, the patients are more vigilant for internal sensations, or more interoceptively aware. But this awareness helps maintain the vicious cycle because they quickly notice *any* somatic response and interpret it (Zoellner & Craske, 1999) as dangerous. Some studies however, could not replicate this finding (Antony et al., 1993), so we need to study the phenomenon more closely.

One hypothesis that panic disorder and agoraphobia evolve from psychodynamic causes suggested that early object loss and/or separation anxiety might predispose someone to develop the condition as an adult. Object loss, or separation anxiety, is what a child might feel at the threat of separation or upon actual separation from an important caregiver, such as the mother or father. Dependent personality tendencies often characterize a person with agoraphobia. These characteristics were hypothesized as a possible reaction to early separation. Nevertheless, despite some intriguing suggestions, little evidence indicates that patients who have PDA experienced separation anxiety during childhood more often than individuals with other psychological disorders or, for that matter, "normals" (Barlow, 2002; Thyer, 1993; van der Molen, van den Hout, van Dieren, & Griez, 1989). It is still possible, however, that the trauma of early separation might predispose someone to psychological disorders in general. (Separation anxiety disorder is discussed in the section on specific phobias.)

Treatment

As we noted in Chapter 1, research on the effectiveness of new treatments is important to psychopathology. Responses to certain specific treatments, whether drug or psychological, may indicate the causes of the disorder. We now discuss the benefits and some drawbacks of medication, psychological interventions, and a combination of these two treatments.

■ Medication

In some of his pioneering work, Donald Klein (1964) analyzed the effects of various drugs on panic and anxiety in an attempt to determine their causes. He noticed that drugs affecting primarily the serotonergic and noradrenergic neurotransmitter systems, spe-

cifically a tricyclic antidepressant drug called imipramine, blocked panic attacks but did not seem to affect generalized anxiety. Benzodiazepines, however, reduced anxiety but did not seem to block panic attacks. Thus, he developed his theory that panic was different from anxiety, which led to biological theories suggesting different locations in the brain for panic and anxiety responses.

Although subsequent studies strongly suggest that anxiety and panic may well be separate processes, the differential effects of the two classes of drugs have not been as strongly supported. It seems that some high-potency benzodiazepines are just as effective for panic disorder as are tricyclic antidepressants such as imipramine, which have been largely replaced by the newer serotonin specific reuptake inhibitors (SSRIs) such as Prozac and Paxil. These drugs are also antidepressants. A large number of drugs affecting the noradrenergic, serotonergic, or GABA–benzodiazepine neurotransmitter systems or some combination seem effective in treating panic disorder (Barlow, 2002; Barlow & Craske, 2007; Pollack, 2005; Spiegel, Wiegel, Baker, & Greene, 2000).

There are advantages and disadvantages to each class of drugs. SSRIs are currently the indicated drug for panic disorder based on all available evidence, although sexual dysfunction seems to occur in 75% or more of people taking these medications (Lecrubier, Bakker, et al., 1997; Lecrubier, Judge, et al., 1997). On the other hand, high-potency benzodiazepines such as alprazolam (Xanax), commonly used for panic disorder, work quickly but are hard to stop taking because of psychological and physical dependence and addiction. Therefore, they are not recommended as strongly as the SSRIs. Nevertheless, benzodiazepines remain the most widely used class of drugs in practice (Bruce et al., 2003). Also, all benzodiazepines adversely affect cognitive and motor functions to some degree. Therefore, people taking them in high doses often find their ability to drive a car or study somewhat reduced.

Approximately 60% of patients with panic disorder are free of panic as long as they stay on an effective drug (Lecrubier, Bakker, et al., 1997), but relapse rates are high (approximately 50%) once the medication is stopped (Hollon et al., 2005; Spiegel et al., 2000). The relapse rate is closer to 90% for those who stop taking benzodiazepines (see, for example, Fyer et al., 1987).

■ Psychological Intervention

Psychological treatments have proved quite effective for panic disorder. Originally, such treatments concentrated on reducing agoraphobic avoidance, using strategies based on exposure to feared situations. The strategy of exposure-based treatments is to arrange conditions in which the patient can gradually face the feared situations and learn there is nothing to fear. Most patients with phobias are well aware of this rationally, but they must be convinced on an emotional level as well by "reality testing" the situation. Sometimes the therapist accompanies the patients on their exposure exercises. At other times, the therapist simply helps patients structure their own exercises and provides them with a variety of psychological coping mechanisms to help them complete the exercises, which are typically arranged from least to most difficult. A sample of these is listed in Table 5.3. The therapist identifies situations relevant to the patient and then arranges them in order of difficulty.

Gradual exposure exercises, sometimes combined with anxiety-reducing coping mechanisms such as relaxation or breath-

TABLE 5.3 Situation-Exposure Tasks (From Least to Most Difficult)
Shopping in a crowded supermarket for 30 minutes alone
Walking five blocks away from home alone
Driving on a busy highway for 5 miles with spouse and alone
Eating in a restaurant, seated in the middle
Watching a movie while seated in the middle of the row

Source: Adapted, with permission, from Barlow, D. H., & Craske, M. G. (2007). *Mastery of your anxiety and panic* (4th ed., p. 133). New York: Oxford University Press.

ing retraining, have proved effective in helping patients overcome agoraphobic behavior. As many as 70% of patients undergoing these treatments substantially improve as their anxiety and panic are reduced and their agoraphobic avoidance is greatly diminished. Few, however, are cured, because many still experience some anxiety and panic attacks, although at a less severe level.

Effective psychological treatments have recently been developed that treat panic attacks directly (Barlow & Craske, 2007; Craske & Barlow, in press Clark et al., 1994; Klosko, Barlow, Tassinari, & Cerny, 1990). **Panic control treatment (PCT)** developed at one of our clinics concentrates on exposing patients with panic disorder to the cluster of interoceptive sensations that remind them of their panic attacks. The therapist attempts to create "mini" panic attacks in the office by having the patients exercise to elevate their heart rates or perhaps by spinning them in a chair to make them dizzy. A variety of exercises have been developed for this purpose (see Table 5.4). Patients also receive cognitive therapy. Basic attitudes and perceptions concerning the dangerousness of the feared but objectively harmless situations are identified and modified. As you learned earlier, many of these attitudes and perceptions are beyond the patient's awareness. Uncovering these unconscious cognitive processes requires a great deal of therapeutic skill. Sometimes, in addition to exposure to interoceptive sensations and cognitive therapy, patients are taught relaxation or breathing retraining to help them cope with increases in anxiety and to reduce excess arousal, but we are using these strategies less often because we find they are not necessary.

These psychological procedures are highly effective for panic disorder. Follow-up studies of patients who receive PCT indicate that most of them remain better after at least 2 years (Craske & Barlow, in press; Craske, Brown, & Barlow, 1991). Remaining agoraphobic behavior can then be treated with more standard exposure exercises. Although these treatments are quite effective, they are relatively new and not yet available to many individuals who suffer from panic disorder because administering them requires therapists to have advanced training (Barlow, Levitt, & Bufka, 1999).

■ Combined Psychological and Drug Treatments

Partly because primary care physicians are usually the first clinicians to treat these people and psychological treatments are not available

TABLE 5.4 Exercises to Create the Sensation of Panic
1. Shake your head loosely from side to side for 30 seconds (to produce dizziness or disorientation).
2. Place your head between your legs for 30 seconds and then lift it quickly (to produce lightheadedness or blood rushing).
3. Take one step up, using stairs, a box, or a footstool, and immediately step down. Do this repeatedly at a fast enough rate to notice your heart pumping quickly for 1 minute (to produce racing heart and shortness of breath).
4. Hold your breath for as long as you can or about 30 to 45 seconds (to produce chest tightness and smothering feelings).
5. Tense every part of your body for 1 minute without causing pain. Tense your arms, legs, stomach, back, shoulders, face—everything. Alternatively, try holding a push-up position for 1 minute or for as long as you can (to produce muscle tension, weakness, and trembling).
6. Spin in a chair for 1 minute. If you have a chair that spins, such as a desk chair, this is ideal. It's even better if someone is there to spin you around. Otherwise, stand up and turn around quickly to make yourself dizzy. Be near a soft chair or couch that you can sit in after 1 minute is up. This will produce dizziness and perhaps nausea.
7. Hyperventilate for 1 minute. Breathe deep and fast, using a lot of force. Sit down as you do this. This exercise might produce unreality, shortness of breath, tingling, cold or hot feelings, dizziness, or headache.
8. Breathe through a thin straw for 1 minute. Don't allow any air through your nose; hold your nostrils together (to produce feelings of restricted airflow or smothering).
9. Stare at a small spot on the wall or stare at yourself in the mirror for 2 minutes. Stare as hard as you can to produce feelings of unreality.

Source: Reprinted, with permission, from Barlow, D. H., & Craske, M. G. (2007). *Mastery of your anxiety and panic* (4th ed.) New York: Oxford University Press.

in those settings, when patients do get referred for psychological treatment, they are often already taking medications. So, important questions are as follows: How do these treatments compare to each other? And do they work together? One major study sponsored by the National Institute of Mental Health looked at the separate and combined effects of psychological and drug treatments (Barlow, Gorman, Shear, & Woods, 2000). In this double-blind study, 312 carefully screened patients with panic disorder were treated at four sites, two known for their expertise with medication treatments and two known for their expertise with psychological treatments. The purpose of this arrangement was to control for any bias that might affect the results because of the allegiance of investigators committed to one type of treatment or the other. Patients were randomized into five treatment condi-

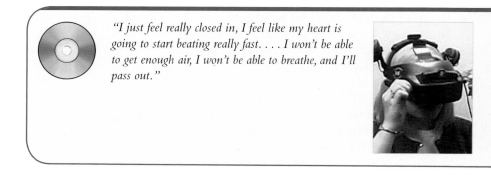

"I just feel really closed in, I feel like my heart is going to start beating really fast. . . . I won't be able to get enough air, I won't be able to breathe, and I'll pass out."

tions: psychological treatment alone (CBT); drug treatment alone (imipramine—IMI—a tricyclic antidepressant, was used); a combined treatment condition (IMI + CBT); and two "control" conditions, one using placebo alone (PBO), and one using PBO + CBT (to determine the extent to which any advantage for combined treatment was caused by placebo contribution).

■ Figure 5.8 shows the results in terms of the percentage of patients who had responded to treatment by the end of 3 months of active treatment (termed the acute response), during which patients were seen weekly. Data were based on the judgment of an independent evaluator using the panic disorder severity scale and include patients who dropped out along the way and were counted as failures. The data indicate that all treatment groups were significantly better than placebo, with some evidence that, among those who responded to treatment, people taking the drug alone did a little better than those receiving the CBT alone, but approximately the same number of patients responded to both treatments. Combined treatment was no better than individual treatments.

Figure 5.8 also presents the results after 6 additional months of maintenance treatment (9 months after treatment was initiated), during which patients were seen once per month. At this point, the results looked much as they did after initial treatment, except there was a slight advantage for combined treatment at this point and the number of people responding to placebo had diminished.

■ Figure 5.9 shows the last set of results, 6 months after treatment was discontinued (15 months after it was initiated). At this point, patients on medication, whether combined with CBT or not, had deteriorated somewhat, and those receiving CBT without the drug had retained most of their gains. For example, 14 of 29 patients, or 48% of those who began the 6-month follow-up phase, who were taking the drug IMI + CBT relapsed, with those who dropped out during this period counted as failures (intent to follow). Forty percent, or 10 of 25, of those patients who completed the follow-up phase relapsed. Notice the much lower relapse figure for the conditions containing CBT. Thus, treatments containing CBT without the drug tended to be superior at this point, because they had more enduring effects. Most studies show that drugs, particularly benzodiazepines, may interfere with the effects of psychological treatments (Craske & Barlow, in press). Because of this, our multisite collaborative team asked whether a sequential strategy where one treatment was delayed until later and only given to those patients who didn't do as well as hoped would work better than giving both treatments at the same time.

In this study, currently in preparation for publication, 256 patients with PD or PDA completed 3 months of initial treatment with CBT. Fifty-eight of those patients did not reach an optimal level of functioning (high end-state functioning) and entered a trial where they either received continued CBT or paroxetine. The paroxetine was administered for up to 1 year, whereas the CBT was delivered for 3 months. At the end of the 1-year period, there was a strong suggestion, represented as

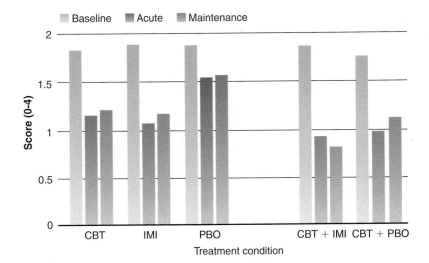

■ **FIGURE 5.8** Responders based on the panic disorder severity scale average item score after acute and after maintenance conditions. (Adapted from Barlow, D. H., Gorman, J. M., Shear, K. M., & Woods, S. W., 2000. Cognitive-behavioral therapy, imipramine, or their combination for panic disorder: A randomized controlled trial. *Journal of the American Medical Association, 283*(19), 2529–2536.)

a statistical trend, that more of the patients receiving paroxetine achieved responder status compared to those receiving continued CBT. Specifically, 60% of the nonresponders receiving paroxetine became responders compared to 35% receiving continued CBT. Although this finding represented only a "trend" toward statistical significance (p ≤ 0.083), further evaluation of effect sizes will help us evaluate the importance of this difference.

Looking at it the other way, another recent study (Craske et al., 2005) found that in the primary care setting, adding CBT to the treatment of patients already on medications resulted in significant further improvement compared to those by patients on medication who did not have CBT added. Thus, a "stepped care"

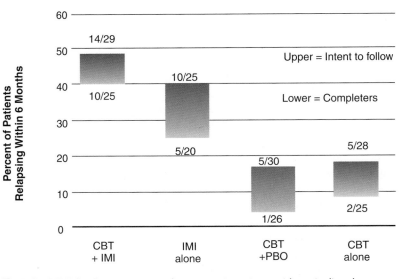

■ **FIGURE 5.9** Posttreatment relapse rates in patients with panic disorder. (Adapted from Barlow, D. H., Gorman, J. M., Shear, K. M., & Woods, S. W., 2000. Cognitive-behavioral therapy, imipramine, or their combination for panic disorder: A randomized controlled trial. *Journal of the American Medical Association, 283*(19), 2529–2536.)

approach may be superior to combining treatments from the beginning.

Conclusions from this large and important study suggest no advantage to combining drug and CBTs because any incremental effect of combined treatment seems to be a placebo effect, not a true drug effect. Furthermore, the psychological treatments seemed to perform better in the long run (6 months after treatment had stopped). The public health recommendation emanating from this study, based on the principle of using the least intrusive treatment first, suggests the psychological treatment should be offered initially, followed by drug treatment for those patients who do not respond adequately or for whom psychological treatment is not available. Because this was such a large study involving so many research centers, it has had a substantial impact on national health care policy.

CONCEPT CHECK 5.3

True (T) or false (F)?

1. ___ PD is a disorder in which an individual experiences anxiety and panic with phobic avoidance of what that person considers an "unsafe" situation.
2. ___ About 40% of the population meets the criteria for panic disorder at some point in their lives.
3. ___ Some individuals with panic disorder are suicidal, have nocturnal panic, and/or are agoraphobic.
4. ___ Psychological treatments like PCT or CBT are highly effective for treating panic disorder.

SPECIFIC PHOBIA

Remember Judy in Chapter 1? When she saw a film of the frog being dissected, Judy began feeling queasy. Eventually she reached the point of fainting if someone simply said, "Cut it out." Earlier in this chapter you read about John Madden's difficulties with flying. Judy and Madden have in common what we call a specific phobia.

Clinical Description

A **specific phobia** is an irrational fear of a specific object or situation that markedly interferes with an individual's ability to function. Before DSM-IV, this category was called "simple" phobia to distinguish it from the more complex agoraphobia condition, but we now recognize there is nothing simple about it. Many of you might be afraid of something that is not dangerous, such as going to the dentist, or have a greatly exaggerated fear of something that is only slightly dangerous, such as driving a car or flying. Therefore, most people can identify to some extent with a phobia. Recent surveys indicate that specific fears of a variety of objects or situations occur in a majority of the population (Myers et al., 1984). But the very commonness of fears, even severe fears, often causes people to trivialize the psychological disorder known as a specific phobia. These phobias, in their severe form, can be extremely disabling, as we saw with Judy. DSM Table 5.4 lists some

DSM-IV-TR

DSM TABLE 5.4 Diagnostic Criteria for Specific Phobia

A. Marked and persistent fear that is excessive or unreasonable, cued by the presence or anticipation of a specific object or situation (e.g., flying, heights, animals, receiving an injection, seeing blood).
B. Exposure to the phobic stimulus almost invariably provokes an immediate anxiety response, which may take the form of a situationally bound or situationally predisposed panic attack. Note: In children, the anxiety may be expressed by crying, tantrums, freezing, or clinging.
C. The person recognizes that the fear is excessive or unreasonable. Note: In children, this feature may be absent.
D. The phobic situation(s) is avoided or else is endured with intense anxiety or distress.
E. The avoidance, anxious anticipation, or distress in the feared situations interferes significantly with the person's normal routine, occupational (or academic) functioning, or social activities or relationships, or there is marked distress about having the phobia.
F. In individuals under age 18, the duration is at least 6 months.
G. The anxiety, panic attacks, or phobic avoidance associated with the specific object or situation are not better accounted for by another mental disorder, such as obsessive-compulsive disorder (e.g., fear of dirt, in someone with an obsession about contamination), posttraumatic stress disorder (e.g., avoidance of stimuli associated with a severe stressor), separation anxiety disorder (e.g., avoidance of school), social phobia (e.g., avoidance of social situations because of fear of embarrassment), panic disorder with agoraphobia, or agoraphobia without history of panic disorder.

Specify type:
1. Animal type
2. Natural environment type (e.g., heights, storms, and water)
3. Blood–injection–injury type
4. Situational type (e.g., planes, elevators, or enclosed places)
5. Other type (e.g., phobic avoidance of situations that may lead to choking, vomiting, or contracting an illness; or in children, avoidance of loud sounds or costumed characters)

Source: Reprinted, with permission, from American Psychiatric Association. (2000). *Diagnostic and statistical manual of mental disorders* (4th ed., text revision). Washington, DC: Author, © 2000 American Psychiatric Association.

other examples of particularly impairing phobias seen at our clinics (Antony & Barlow, 2002a).

For people such as Madden, on the other hand, phobias are a nuisance—sometimes an extremely inconvenient nuisance—but people can adapt to life with a phobia by simply working around it somehow. In upstate New York and New England, some people are afraid to drive in the snow. We have had people come to our clinics who have been so severely phobic that during the winter they were ready to uproot, change their jobs and their lives, and move south. That is one way of dealing with a phobia. We discuss some other ways at the end of this chapter.

The major characteristic held in common by Judy and Madden is the DSM-IV criterion of marked and persistent fear that is set off by a specific object or situation. Both also have recognized that their fear and anxiety are excessive or unreasonable. Finally, both went to considerable lengths to avoid situations in which their phobic response might occur.

There the similarities end. There are as many phobias as there are objects and situations. The variety of Greek and Latin names contrived to describe phobias stuns the imagination. Table 5.5 gives only the phobias beginning with the letter "a" from a long list compiled by Jack D. Maser from medical dictionaries and other diverse sources (Maser, 1985). This sort of list has little or no value for people studying psychopathology, but it does show the extent of the named phobias.

Before the publication of DSM-IV in 1994, no meaningful classification of specific phobias existed. However, we have now learned that the cases of Judy and Madden represent types of specific phobia that differ in major ways. Four major subtypes of specific phobia have been identified: blood–injury–injection type, situational type (such as planes, elevators, or enclosed places), natural environment type (for example, heights, storms, and water), and animal type. A fifth category, "other," includes phobias that do not fit any of the four major subtypes (for example, situations that may lead to choking, vomiting, or contracting an illness or, in children, avoidance of loud sounds or costumed characters). Although this subtyping strategy is useful, we also know that most people who suffer from phobia tend to have multiple phobias of several types (Hofmann, Lehman, & Barlow, 1997). This fact weakens the utility of subtyping.

TABLE 5.5 Phobias Beginning With "A"

Term	Fear of
Acarophobia	Insects, mites
Achluophobia	Darkness, night
Acousticophobia	Sounds
Acrophobia	Heights
Aerophobia	Air currents, drafts, wind
Agoraphobia	Open spaces
Agyiophobia	Crossing the street
Aichmophobia	Sharp, pointed objects; knives; being touched by a finger
Ailurophobia	Cats
Algophobia	Pain
Amathophobia	Dust
Amychophobia	Laceration; being clawed, scratched
Androphobia	Men (and sex with men)
Anemophobia	Air currents, wind, drafts
Anginophobia	Angina pectoris (brief attacks of chest pain)
Anthropophobia	Human society
Antlophobia	Floods
Apeirophobia	Infinity
Aphephobia	Physical contact, being touched
Apiphobia	Bees, bee stings
Astraphobia	Thunderstorms, lightning
Ataxiophobia	Disorder
Atephobia	Ruin
Auroraphobia	Northern lights
Autophobia	Being alone, solitude, oneself, being egotistical

Source: Reprinted, with permission, from Maser, J. D. (1985). List of phobias. In A. H. Tuma & J. D. Maser (Eds.), Anxiety and the anxiety disorders (p. 805). Mahwah, NJ: Erlbaum, © 1985 Lawrence Erlbaum Associates.

■ Blood–Injury–Injection Phobia

How do phobia subtypes differ from each other? We have already seen one major difference in the case of Judy. Rather than the usual surge of activity in the sympathetic nervous system and increased heart rate and blood pressure, Judy experienced a marked drop in heart rate and blood pressure and fainted as a consequence. Many people who suffer from phobias and experience panic attacks in their feared situations report that they feel like they are going to faint, but they never do because their heart rate and blood pressure are actually increasing. Therefore, those with **blood–injury–injection phobias** almost always differ in their physiological reaction from people with other types of phobia (Barlow & Liebowitz, 1995; Craske, Anthony, & Barlow, 2006; Öst, 1992). We also noted in Chapter 2 that blood–injury–injection phobia runs in families more strongly than any phobic disorder we know. This is probably because people with this phobia inherit a strong vasovagal response to blood, injury, or the possibility of an injection, all of which cause a drop in blood pressure and a tendency to faint. The phobia develops over the possibility of having this response. The average age of onset for this phobia is approximately 9 years (Antony, Brown, & Barlow, 1997a; Öst, 1989).

■ Situational Phobia

Phobias characterized by fear of public transportation or enclosed places are called **situational phobias.** Claustrophobia, a fear of small, enclosed places, is situational, as is a phobia of planes. Psychopathologists first thought that situational phobia was similar to PDA. One similarity in these two disorders is age of onset. Both situational phobia and PDA tend to emerge in an individual's early to mid-20s (Antony et al., 1997a; Craske et al., 2006). The extent to which PDA and situational phobias run in families is also similar (Curtis, Hill, & Lewis, 1990; Curtis, Himle, Lewis, & Lee, 1989; Fyer et al., 1990), with approximately 30% of first-degree relations having the same or a similar phobia. But more recent analyses, both descriptive (Antony et al., 1997a) and laboratory based (Antony, Brown, & Barlow, 1997b), do not support the similarity as anything more than superficial. The main difference between situational phobia and PDA is that people with situational phobia never experience panic attacks outside the context of their phobic object or situation. Therefore, they can relax when they don't have to confront their phobic situation. People with panic disorder, in contrast, might experience unexpected, uncued panic attacks at any time.

■ Natural Environment Phobia

Sometimes very young people develop fears of situations or events occurring in nature. These fears are called **natural environment phobias.** The major examples are heights, storms, and water. These fears also seem to cluster together (Antony & Barlow, 2002a; Hofmann et al., 1997): If you fear one situation or event, such as deep water, you are likely to fear another, such as storms. Many of these situations have some danger associated with them and, therefore, mild to moderate fear can be adaptive. For example, we should be careful in a high place or in deep water. It is entirely possible that we are somewhat prepared to be afraid of these situations; as we discussed in Chapter 2, something in our genes makes us sensitive to these situations if any sign of danger is pres-

People who develop a natural environment phobia intensely fear such places as heights and events such as lightning.

ent. In any case, these phobias have a peak age of onset of about 7 years. They are not phobias if they are only passing fears. They have to be persistent and to interfere substantially with the person's functioning, leading to avoidance of boat trips or summer vacations in the mountains where there might be a storm.

Animal Phobia

Fears of animals and insects are called **animal phobias.** Again, these fears are common but become phobic only if severe interference with functioning occurs. For example, we have seen cases in our clinic in which people with snake or mice phobias are unable to read magazines for fear of unexpectedly coming across a picture of one of these animals. There are many places that these people are unable to go, even if they want to very much, such as to the country to visit someone. The fear experienced by people with animal phobias is different from an ordinary mild revulsion. The age of onset for these phobias, like that of natural environment phobias, peaks around 7 years (Antony et al., 1997a; Öst, 1987).

Other Phobias

Several additional types of phobias from the "other" category are described briefly here because they appear in considerable numbers and can cause substantial problems. If you are afraid of contracting a disease and go to excessive and irrational lengths to avoid exposure to that disease, you may have an *illness phobia*. In these cases, the individuals do not believe they have the disease but are afraid they might acquire it in any number of ways (Barlow & Liebowitz, 1995; Craske et al., 1996). When this fear occurs in severe form, it can be incapacitating, because individuals with illness phobia may avoid all contact with people from which or places where they might catch something. Illness phobia has become more prevalent during the AIDS epidemic. People may have no reason to believe they have AIDS, and they will test negatively for HIV, but they may avoid public restrooms, some restaurants, and any contact with strangers for fear of contracting the disease. Illness phobia can also resemble other disorders, such as obsessive-compulsive disorder (discussed later in the chapter) or hypochondriasis (see Chapter 6), but is sufficiently different to be classified as a type of specific phobia. We return to this issue when we discuss these two disorders.

Choking phobia is characterized by fear and avoidance of swallowing pills, foods, or fluids and can produce significant weight loss. Other names for choking phobia include *hypersensitive gag reflex* or *globus hystericus* (McNally, 1994a). Phobias of choking and vomiting are relatively common and almost always originate in the traumatic experience of choking on a piece of food. In some people, the consequences are that they are unable to eat solid food and, in addition to weight loss, suffer severe nutritional and dental problems. If the phobia is prolonged, the person is likely to experience deterioration in gum tissue and tooth structure from lack of use and, ultimately, tooth loss. These people often maintain themselves on liquid diets. Fortunately, the condition responds to direct, structured treatment (Ball & Otto, 1994; Chorpita, Vitali, & Barlow, 1997).

Separation Anxiety Disorder

All anxiety disorders described in this chapter may occur during childhood, and there is one additional anxiety disorder unique to children. **Separation anxiety disorder** is characterized by children's unrealistic and persistent worry that something will happen to their parents or other important people in their life or that something will happen to the children themselves that will separate them from their parents (for example, they will be lost, kidnapped, killed, or hurt in an accident). Children often refuse to go to school or even to leave home, not because they are afraid of school but because they are afraid of separating from loved ones. These fears can result in refusing to sleep alone and may be characterized by nightmares involving possible separation and by physical symptoms, distress, and anxiety (Barlow, Pincus, Heinrichs, & Choate, 2003).

All young children experience separation anxiety to some extent; this fear usually decreases as they grow older. Therefore, a clinician must judge whether the separation anxiety is greater than would be expected at

Tom Ollendick is a leading investigator into the nature and treatment of anxiety disorders in children.

that particular age (Barlow et al., 2003; Ollendick & Huntzinger, 1990). It is also important to differentiate separation anxiety from school phobia. In school phobia, the fear is clearly focused on something specific to the school situation; the child can leave the parents or other attachment figures to go somewhere other than school. In separation anxiety, the act of separating from the parent or attachment figure provokes anxiety and fear.

Francis, Last, and Strauss (1987) found that the prevalence of certain symptoms varies as a function of age. For example, the prominent symptom among the youngest children (age 5–8) was worry that something would happen to their loved ones. Excessive distress on being separated was prominent in the middle age group of children (age 9–12), and physical complaints on school days characterized separation anxiety in adolescents (age 13–16).

Statistics

Specific fears occur in a majority of people. The ones most commonly found in the population at large, categorized by Agras, Sylvester, and Oliveau (1969), are presented in Table 5.6. Not surprisingly, fears of snakes and heights rank near the top. Notice also that the sex ratio among common fears is overwhelmingly female with a couple of exceptions. Among these exceptions is fear of heights, for which the sex ratio is approximately equal. Few people who report specific fears qualify as having a phobia, but for approximately 12.5% of the population, their fears are at some point in their lives severe enough to be classified as disorders and earn the label "phobia." These numbers seem to be increasing in younger generations (Magee, Eaton, Wittchen, McGonagle, & Kessler, 1996; Kessler, Berglund, et al., 2005). During a given 1-year period the prevalence is 8.7%. This is a high percentage, making specific phobia one of the most common psychological disorders in the United States and around the world (Arrindell et al., 2003b; Kessler, Berglund et al., 2005). As with common fears, the sex ratio for specific phobias is, at 4:1, overwhelmingly female; this is also consistent around the world (Arrindell et al., 2003b; Craske et al., 2006).

Even though phobias may interfere with an individual's functioning, only the most severe cases come for treatment because affected people tend to work around their phobias; for example, someone with a fear of heights arranges her life so she never has to be in a tall building or other high place. Table 5.7 presents the distribution of the 48 patients who recently came to our anxiety disorders clinic with a specific phobia as their primary problem; these are broken down by type. As you can see, people with situational phobias of such things as driving, flying, or small enclosed places most often come for treatment. However, there is reason to believe that people with blood–injury–injection phobias are quite prevalent in the population (Agras et al., 1969; Myers et al., 1984); they might seek help if they knew good treatments are available.

The median age of onset for specific phobia is 7 years of age, the youngest of any anxiety disorder except separation anxiety disorder (Kessler, Berglund et al., 2005). Once a phobia develops, it tends to last a lifetime (run a chronic course) (see, for example, Antony et al., 1997a; Barlow, 2002; Kessler, Berglund, et al., 2005); thus, the issue of treatment, described shortly, becomes important.

TABLE 5.6 Prevalence of Intense Fears and Phobias

Intense Fear	Prevalence per 1,000 Population	Sex Distribution	SE by Sex
Snakes	253	M: 118 F: 376	M: 34 F: 48
Heights	120	M: 109 F: 128	M: 33 F: 36
Flying	109	M: 70 F: 144	M: 26 F: 38
Enclosures	50	M: 32 F: 63	M: 18 F: 25
Illness	33	M: 31 F: 35	M: 18 F: 19
Death	33	M: 46 F: 21	M: 21 F: 15
Injury	23	M: 24 F: 22	M: 15 F: 15
Storms	31	M: 9 F: 48	M: 9 F: 22
Dentists	24	M: 22 F: 26	M: 15 F: 16
Journeys alone	16	M: 0 F: 31	M: 0 F: 18
Being alone	10	M: 5 F: 13	M: 7 F: 11

Phobia	Prevalence per 1,000 Population*	Sex Distribution	SE by Sex
Illness/injury	31 (42%)	M: 22 F: 39	M: 15 F: 20
Storms	13 (18%)	M: 0 F: 24	M: 0 F: 15
Animals	11 (14%)	M: 6 F: 18	M: 8 F: 13
Agoraphobia	6 (8%)	M: 7 F: 6	M: 8 F: 8
Death	5 (7%)	M: 4 F: 6	M: 6 F: 8
Crowds	4 (5%)	M: 2 F: 6	M: 5 F: 7
Heights	4 (5%)	M: 7 F: 0	M: 9 F: 0

SE, standard error.

*Percentages of the total of those with phobias are in parentheses.

Source: Adapted, with permission, from Agras, W. S., Sylvester, D., & Oliveau, D. (1969). The epidemiology of common fears and phobias. *Comprehensive Psychiatry, 10,* 151–156, © 1969 Elsevier.

Although most anxiety disorders look much the same in adults and in children, clinicians must be aware of the types of normal fears and anxieties experienced throughout childhood so that they can distinguish them from specific phobias (Albano et al., 1996; King, 1993; Silverman & Rabian, 1993). Infants, for example, show marked fear of loud noises and strangers. At 1 to 2 years of age, children quite normally are anxious about separating

TABLE 5.7	Frequency of Principal or Co-Principal Diagnoses of Specific Phobias	
Type of Phobia	**2005 Number**	**2006 Number**
Animal	1	4
Natural environment	4	2
Blood and injury	0	2
Situational	11	6
Other	5	5
Total	21	19

Note: Patients were seen at the authors' anxiety disorders clinic (Center for Anxiety and Related Disorders) from January 1, 2005, to October 31, 2006.

from parents, and fears of animals and the dark also develop and may persist into the fourth or fifth year of life. Fear of various monsters and other imaginary creatures may begin about age 3 and last for several years. At age 10, children may fear evaluation by others and feel anxiety over their physical appearance. Generally, reports of fear decline with age, although performance-related fears of such activities as taking a test or talking in front of a large group may increase with age. Specific phobias seem to decline with old age (Blazer et al., 1991; Sheikh, 1992).

The prevalence of specific phobias varies from one culture to another. Hispanics are two times more likely to report specific phobias than white Americans (Magee et al., 1996), for reasons not entirely clear. A variant of phobia in Chinese cultures is called *Pa-leng,* sometimes *frigo phobia* or "fear of the cold." *Pa-leng* can be understood only in the context of traditional ideas—in this case, the Chinese concepts of *yin* and *yang* (Tan, 1980). Chinese medicine holds that there must be a balance of yin and yang forces in the body for health to be maintained. Yin represents the cold, dark, windy, energy-sapping aspects of life; yang refers to the warm, bright, energy-producing aspects of life. Individuals with *Pa-leng* have a morbid fear of the cold. They ruminate over loss of body heat and may wear several layers of clothing even on a hot day. They may complain of belching and flatulence (passing gas), which indicate the presence of wind and therefore of too much yin in the body. As discussed earlier, these ideas also play a role in phobia and anxiety disorders in other Asian cultures (Hinton, Pich, Pollack, & Barlow, 2003).

Causes

For a long time, we thought that most specific phobias began with an unusual traumatic event. For example, if you were bitten by a dog, you would develop a phobia of dogs. We now know this is not always the case (Barlow, 2002; Craske et al., 2006; Öst, 1985; Rachman, 2002). This is not to say that traumatic conditioning experiences do not result in subsequent phobic behavior. Almost every person with a choking phobia has had some kind of a choking experience. An individual with claustrophobia who recently came to our clinic reported being trapped in an elevator for an extraordinarily long period. These are examples of phobias acquired by *direct experience,* where real danger or pain results in an

©Masterfile (Royalty Free Division)

A child with separation anxiety disorder persistently worries that parting with an important person drastically endangers either the loved one or the child.

alarm response (a true alarm). This is one way of developing a phobia, and there are at least three others: *experiencing* a false alarm (panic attack) in a specific situation, *observing* someone else experience severe fear (vicarious experience), or, under the right conditions, *being told* about danger.

Remember our earlier discussion of unexpected panic attacks? Studies show that many phobics do not necessarily experience a true alarm resulting from real danger at the onset of their phobia. Many initially have an unexpected panic attack in a specific situation, related, perhaps, to current life stress. A phobia of that situation may then develop. Munjack (1984; Mineka & Zinbarg, 2006) studied people with specific phobias of driving. He noted that about 50% of the people who could remember when their phobia started had experienced a true alarm because of a traumatic experience such as a car accident. The others had had nothing terrible happen to them while they were driving, but they had experienced an unexpected panic attack during which they felt they were going to lose control of the car and wipe out half the people on the highway. Their driving was not impaired, and their catastrophic thoughts were simply part of the panic attack.

Chinese medicine is based on the concept that *yin* (dark, cold, enervating forces) and *yang* (bright, warm, energizing forces) must harmonize in the body. In this traditional representation of the yin–yang balance, note that each aspect contains something of the other.

We also learn fears vicariously. Seeing someone else have a traumatic experience or endure intense fear may be enough to instill a phobia in the watcher. Remember, we noted earlier that emotions are contagious. If someone you are with is either happy or fearful, you will probably feel a tinge of happiness or fear also. Öst (1985) describes how a severe dental fear developed in this way. An adolescent boy sat in the waiting room at the school dentist's office partly observing, but fully hearing, his friend who was being treated. Evidently, the boy's reaction to pain caused him to move suddenly, and the drill punctured his cheek. The boy in the waiting room who overhead the accident bolted from the room and developed a severe and long-lasting fear of dental situations. Nothing actually happened to the second person, but you can certainly understand why he developed his phobia. Susan Mineka and her colleagues, in an elegant series of experiments, have shown that a monkey can develop a phobia simply by watching another monkey experience fear (Mineka, Davidson, Cook, & Keir, 1984).

Sometimes just being warned repeatedly about a potential danger is sufficient for someone to develop a phobia. Öst (1985) describes the case of a woman with an extremely severe snake phobia who had never encountered a snake. Rather, she had been told repeatedly while growing up about the dangers of snakes in the high grass. She was encouraged to wear high rubber boots to guard against this imminent threat—and she did so even when walking down the street. We call this mode of developing a phobia *information transmission*.

Terrifying experiences alone do not create phobias. As we have said, a true phobia also requires anxiety over the possibility of another extremely traumatic event or false alarm. Remember,

when we are anxious, we persistently anticipate something terrible and we are likely to avoid situations in which that terrible thing might occur. If we don't develop anxiety, our reaction would presumably be in the category of normal fears experienced by more than half the population. Normal fear can cause mild distress, but it is usually ignored and forgotten. This point is best illustrated by Peter DiNardo and his colleagues (1988), who studied a group of dog phobics, as well as a matched group who did not have the phobia. Like Munjack's (1984) driving phobics, about 50% of the dog phobics had had a frightening encounter with a dog, usually involving a bite. However, in another group of individuals who did not have dog phobia, about 50% had also had a frightening encounter with a dog. Why hadn't they become phobics as well? They had not developed anxiety about another encounter with a dog, unlike the people who did become phobic (reflecting a generalized psychological vulnerability). A diagram of the etiology of specific phobia is presented in ■ Figure 5.10.

In summary, several things have to occur for a person to develop a phobia. First, a traumatic conditioning experience often plays a role (even hearing about a frightening event is sufficient for some individuals). Second, fear is more likely to develop if we are "prepared"; that is, we seem to carry an inherited tendency to fear situations that have always been dangerous to the human race, such as being threatened by wild animals or trapped in small places (see Chapter 2).

We also have to be susceptible to developing anxiety focused on the possibility that the event will happen again. We have discussed the biological and psychological reasons for anxiety and have seen that at least one phobia, blood–injury–injection phobia, is highly heritable (Öst, 1989; Page & Martin, 1998). Öst found that 64% of 25 patients had at least one first-degree relative with blood phobia. Patients with blood phobia probably also inherit a strong vasovagal response that makes them susceptible to fainting. This alone would not be sufficient to ensure their becoming phobic, but it combines with anxiety to produce strong vulnerability.

Several years ago, Fyer and colleagues (1990) demonstrated that approximately 31% of the first-degree relatives of people with specific phobias also had a phobia, compared with 11% of the first-degree relatives of "normal" controls. More recently, in a collaborative study between Fyer's clinic and our center, we replicated these results, finding a 28% prevalence in the first-degree relatives of patients with phobia compared to 10% in relatives of controls. More interestingly, it seems that each subtype of phobia "bred true," in that relatives were likely to have identical types of phobia. Kendler, Karkowski, and Prescott (1999) and Page and Martin (1998) found relatively high estimates for heritability of individual specific

Peter DiNardo and his colleagues, who studied people with dog phobias, made important discoveries about the causes of phobias in general.

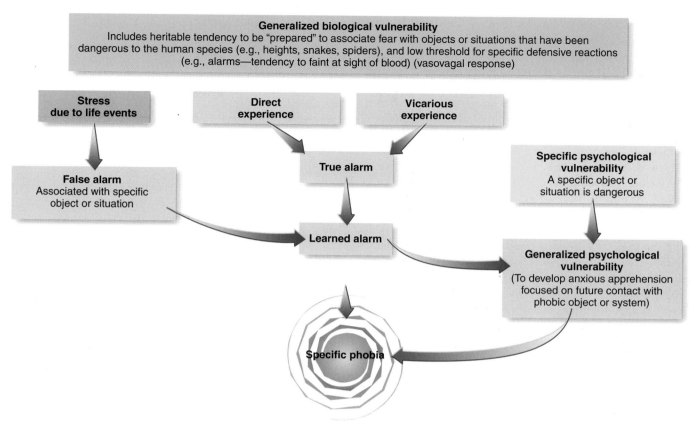

Generalized biological vulnerability
Includes heritable tendency to be "prepared" to associate fear with objects or situations that have been dangerous to the human species (e.g., heights, snakes, spiders), and low threshold for specific defensive reactions (e.g., alarms—tendency to faint at sight of blood) (vasovagal response)

Stress due to life events

Direct experience

Vicarious experience

True alarm

Specific psychological vulnerability
A specific object or situation is dangerous

False alarm
Associated with specific object or situation

Learned alarm

Generalized psychological vulnerability
(To develop anxious apprehension focused on future contact with phobic object or system)

Specific phobia

■ **FIGURE 5.10**   A model of the various ways a specific phobia may develop. (From Barlow, D. H., 2002. *Anxiety and its disorders: The nature and treatment of anxiety and panic* (2nd ed.). New York: Guildford Press.)

phobias. We do not know for sure whether the tendency for phobias to run in families is caused by genes or by modeling, but the findings are at least suggestive of a unique genetic contribution to specific phobia (Antony & Barlow, 2002a; Hettema et al., 2005; Smoller et al., 2005).

Finally, social and cultural factors are strong determinants of who develops and reports a specific phobia. In most societies, it is almost unacceptable for males to express fears and phobias. Thus, the overwhelming majority of reported specific phobias occur in women (Arrindell et al., 2003b). What happens to the males? Possibly they work hard to overcome their fears by repeatedly exposing themselves to their feared situations. A more likely possibility is that they simply endure their fears without telling anyone about them and without seeking treatment (Antony & Barlow, 2002a). Pierce and Kirkpatrick (1992) asked male and female college students to report their fears on two occasions before watching a videotape of something frightening. Before the second evaluation, subjects were told their heart rate would be monitored to assess the "truthfulness" of their report. Reports from women were the same on both occasions, but men reported substantially more fear when it was important to be truthful. More recently, Ginsburg and Silverman (2000) reported that level of reported fear in children with anxiety disorders was a function of gender role but not biological sex. That is, a more masculine "tom-boyish" girl would report less fear than a more feminine girl, illustrating the contribution of culture to the development of fear and phobia.

Treatment

Although the development of phobias is relatively complex, the treatment is fairly straightforward. Almost everyone agrees that specific phobias require structured and consistent exposure-based exercises (Craske et al., 2006). Nevertheless, most patients who expose themselves gradually to what they fear must be under therapeutic supervision. Individuals who attempt to carry out the exercises alone often attempt to do too much too soon and end up escaping the situation, which may strengthen the phobia. In addition, if they fear having another unexpected panic attack in this situation, it is helpful to direct therapy at panic attacks in the

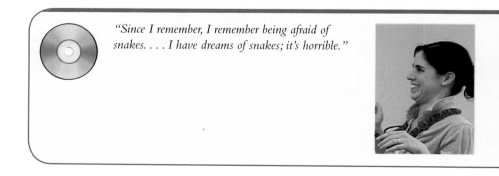

"Since I remember, I remember being afraid of snakes. . . . I have dreams of snakes; it's horrible."

manner described for panic disorder (Antony, Craske, & Barlow, 2006; Craske et al., 2006). For separation anxiety, parents are often included to help structure the exercises and work with parental reaction to childhood anxiety (Choate, Pincus, Eyberg, & Barlow, 2005). Finally, in cases of blood–injury–injection phobia, where fainting is a real possibility, graduated exposure-based exercises must be done in specific ways. Individuals must tense various muscle groups during exposure exercises to keep their blood pressure sufficiently high to complete the practice (Öst & Sterner, 1987). New developments make it possible to treat many specific phobias, including blood phobia, in a single, daylong session (see, for example, Antony & Barlow, 2002a; Antony et al., 2006; Craske et al., 2006; Öst, Ferebee, & Furmark, 1997; Öst, Svensson, Hellström, & Lindwall, 2001). Basically, the therapist spends most of the day with the individual, working through exposure exercises with the phobia object or situation. The patient then practices approaching the phobic situation at home, checking in occasionally with the therapist. It is interesting that in these cases not only does the phobia disappear but the tendency to experience the vasovagal response at the sight of blood also lessens considerably. It is also now clear based on brain-imaging work that these treatments change brain functioning by modifying neural circuitry. That is, these treatments "rewire" the brain (Paquette et al., 2003).

SOCIAL PHOBIA

Are you shy? If so, you have something in common with 20% to 50% of college students, depending on which survey you read. A much smaller number of people, who suffer severely around others, have **social phobia.** Consider the case of Billy, a 13-year-old boy.

BILLY: Too Shy

Billy was the model boy at home. He did his homework, stayed out of trouble, obeyed his parents, and was generally so quiet and reserved he didn't attract much attention. However, when he got to junior high school, something his parents had noticed earlier became painfully evident. Billy had no friends. He was unwilling to attend social or sporting activities connected with school, even though most of the other kids in his class went to these events. When his parents decided to check with the guidance counselor, they found that she had been about to call them. She reported that Billy did not socialize or speak up in class and was sick to his stomach all day if he knew he was going to be called on. His teachers had difficulty getting anything more than a yes-or-no answer from him. More troublesome was that he had been found hiding in a stall in the boy's restroom during lunch, which he said he had been doing for several months instead of eating. After Billy was referred to our clinic, we diagnosed a severe case of social phobia, an irrational and extreme fear of social situations. Billy's phobia took the form of extreme shyness. He was afraid of being embarrassed or humiliated in the presence of almost everyone except his parents.

Clinical Description

Social phobia is more than exaggerated shyness (Schneier et al., 1996). The cases described here are typical of many that appear occasionally in the press.

STEVE AND CHUCK: Star Players?

In the second inning of an All-Star game, Los Angeles Dodger second baseman Steve Sax fielded an easy grounder, straightened up for the lob to first, and bounced the ball past first baseman Al Oliver, who was less than 40 feet away. It was a startling error even in an All-Star game studded with bush-league mishaps. But hard-core baseball fans knew it was one more manifestation of a leading mystery of the 1983 season: Sax, 23, the National League Rookie of the Year, could not seem to make routine throws to first base. (Of his first 27 errors that season, 22 were bad throws.)

Chuck Knoblauch won the Golden Glove Award in 1997 but led the league in errors in 1999 with 26, most of them throwing errors. Announcers and reporters observed that his throws would be hard and on target to first base if he made a difficult play and had to quickly turn and throw the ball "without thinking about it." But if he fielded a routine ground ball and had time to think about the accuracy of his throw, he would throw awkwardly and slowly—and often off target. The announcers and reporters concluded that, because his arm seemed fine on the difficult plays, his problem must be "mental." For the 2001 season, he was moved to left field to avoid having to make that throw and by 2003 was out of baseball.

Whereas Knoblauch continued to struggle, Sax overcame his problem and went on to play for a number of major league teams. Many other athletes are not so fortunate. This problem is not limited to athletes but is also developed by well-known lecturers and performers. Singer Carly Simon gave up live shows for several years because of intolerable performance anxiety. NFL player Ricky Williams interrupted his career partly because of severe social anxiety. The inability of a skilled athlete to throw a baseball to first base or a seasoned performer to appear on stage certainly does not match the concept of "shyness" with which we are all familiar. Many of these performers may well be among our more gregarious citizens. What holds these two seemingly different conditions together? Billy, Knoblauch, Sax, Simon, and Williams all experienced marked and persistent fear of one or more social or performance situations. In Billy's case, these situations were any in which he might have to interact with people. For Knoblauch and Simon, they were specific to performing some special behavior in public. Individuals with performance anxiety usually have no difficulty with social interaction, but when they must do something specific in front of people, anxiety takes over and they focus on the possibility that they will embarrass themselves.

The most common type of performance anxiety, to which most people can relate, is public speaking. Other common situations are eating in a restaurant, signing a paper in front of a clerk, or, for males, urinating in a public restroom ("bashful bladder"). Males with this problem must wait until a stall is available, a difficult task at times. What these examples have in common is that the individual is required to *do* something while others are watching and, to some extent, evaluating their behavior. This is truly a social phobia because the people have no difficulty eating, writing, or urinating in private. Only when others are watching does the behavior deteriorate.

Individuals who are extremely and painfully shy in almost all social situations meet DSM-IV-TR criteria for the subtype *social phobia generalized type,* occasionally called *social anxiety disorder.* It is particularly prominent in children. In the child program in one of our clinics, 100% of children and adolescents with social phobia met criteria for the generalized type (Albano, DiBartolo, Heimberg, & Barlow, 1995). Billy also fits this subtype (Schneier et al., 1996).

DSM-IV-TR

DSM TABLE 5.5 Diagnostic Criteria for Social Phobia

A. A marked and persistent fear of one or more social or performance situations in which the person is exposed to unfamiliar people or to possible scrutiny by others. The individual fears that he or she will act in a way (or show anxiety symptoms) that will be humiliating or embarrassing. *Note:* In children, there must be evidence of the capacity for age-appropriate social relationships with familiar people and the anxiety must occur in peer settings, not just in interactions with adults.

B. Exposure to the feared social situation almost invariably provokes anxiety, which may take the form of a situationally bound or situationally predisposed panic attack. *Note:* In children, the anxiety may be expressed by crying, tantrums, freezing, or shrinking from social situations with unfamiliar people.

C. The person recognizes that the fear is excessive or unreasonable. *Note:* In children, this feature may be absent.

D. The feared social or performance situations are avoided or are endured with intense anxiety or distress.

E. The avoidance, anxious anticipation, or distress in the feared social or performance situation(s) interferes significantly with the person's normal routine, occupational (academic) functioning, or social activities or relationships, or there is marked distress about having the phobia.

F. In individuals under age 18, duration is at least 6 months.

G. The fear or avoidance is not due to the direct physiological effects of a substance (e.g., a drug of abuse, medication) or a general medical condition, and is not better accounted for by another mental disorder (e.g., panic disorder with or without agoraphobia, separation anxiety disorder, body dysmorphic disorder, a pervasive developmental disorder, or schizoid personality disorder).

H. If a general medical condition or another mental disorder is present, the fear in criterion A is unrelated to it: e.g., the fear is not of stuttering, trembling in Parkinson's disease, or exhibiting abnormal eating behavior in anorexia nervosa or bulimia nervosa.

Specify if:

Generalized: If the fears include most social situations (also consider the additional diagnosis of avoidant personality disorder)

Source: Reprinted, with permission, from American Psychiatric Association. (2000). *Diagnostic and statistical manual of mental disorders* (4th ed., text revision). Washington, DC: Author, © 2000 American Psychiatric Association.

Statistics

As many as 12.1% of the general population suffer from social phobia at some point in their lives (Kessler, Berglund, et al., 2005). In a given 1-year period, the prevalence is 6.8% (Kessler, Chiu, et al., 2005). This makes social phobia second only to specific phobia as the most prevalent anxiety disorder, afflicting more than 35 million people in the United States alone, based on current population estimates. Many more people are shy, but not severely enough to meet criteria for social phobia. The sex ratio favors females only somewhat (1.4 to 1.0), unlike other anxiety disorders for which females predominate (Magee et al., 1996). This distribution differs a bit from the sex ratio of social phobics appearing at clinics, which is nearly 50:50 (Hofmann & Barlow, 2002; Marks, 1985), suggesting that males may seek help more often, perhaps because of career-related issues. Overall, 45.6% of people suffering from social phobia sought professional help in a recent 12-month period (Wang et al., 2005). Social phobia usually begins during adolescence, with a peak age of onset around 13 years, later than specific phobias but earlier than panic disorder (Kessler, Berglund, et al., 2005). Social phobia also tends to be more prevalent in people who are young (18–29 years), undereducated, single, and of low socioeconomic class. Alarmingly, the number of young people with social phobia seems to be increasing somewhat (Magee et al., 1996). Prevalence declines among the elderly and is less than half as prevalent among individuals over 60 (6.6%) as it is among individuals 18–29 (13.6%) (Kessler, Berglund, et al., 2005).

Considering their difficulty meeting people, it is not surprising that a greater percentage of individuals with social phobia are single than in the population at large. Social phobias distribute relatively equally among different ethnic groups (Magee et al., 1996). In Japan, the clinical presentation of anxiety disorders is best summarized under the label *shinkeishitsu.* One of the most common subcategories is referred to as *taijin kyofusho* (Kirmayer, 1991; Kleinknecht, Dinnel, Kleinknecht, Hiruma, & Harada, 1997). Japanese people with this form of social phobia strongly fear looking people in the eye and are afraid that some aspect of their personal presentation (blushing, stuttering, body odor, and so on) will appear reprehensible. Thus, the focus of anxiety in this disorder is on offending or embarrassing others rather than embarrassing oneself as in social phobia, although these two disorders overlap considerably (Dinnel, Kleinknecht, & Tanaka-Matsumi, 2002). Japanese males with this disorder outnumber females by a 3:2 ratio (Takahasi, 1989).

Causes

We have noted that we seem to be prepared by evolution to fear certain wild animals and dangerous situations in the natural environment. Similarly, it seems we are also prepared to fear angry, critical, or rejecting people (Mineka & Zinbarg, 1996, 2006; Mogg, Philippot, & Bradley, 2004; Öhman, 1986). In a series of studies, Öhman and colleagues (see, for example, Dimberg & Öhman, 1983; Öhman & Dimberg, 1978) noted that we learn more quickly to fear angry expressions than other facial expressions, and this fear diminishes more slowly than other types of learning. Lundh and Öst (1996) demonstrated that people with social phobia who saw a number of pictures of faces were likely to remember critical expressions and Mogg and colleagues (2004) showed that socially anxious individuals were more vigilant for angry faces than "normals" and recognized these faces more quickly, whereas "normals" remembered the accepting expressions. More recently, one study demonstrated that even "normals" show more activation of their emotional brain to new and possibly threatening faces compared to familiar faces (Schwartz et al., 2003), and another study showed that individuals with generalized social phobia react to angry faces with greater activation of the amygdala than "normals" (Stein, Goldin, Sareen, Zorrilla, & Brown, 2002). More recently, Fox and Damjanovic (2006) demonstrated that the eye region specifically is the threatening area of the face. Why should we inherit a tendency to fear angry faces? Our ancestors probably avoided hostile, angry, domineering people who might attack or kill them. In all species, dominant, aggressive individuals, high in the social hierarchy, tend to be avoided. Possibly, individuals who avoided people with angry faces were more likely to survive and pass their genes down to us. Of course, this is just a theory.

Jerome Kagan and his colleagues (see, for example, Kagan, 1994, 1997; Kagan, Reznick, & Snidman, 1988; Kagan & Snidman, 1991, 1999) have demonstrated that some infants are born with a temperamental profile or trait of inhibition or shyness that is evident as early as 4 months of age. Four-month-old infants with this

trait become more agitated and cry more frequently when presented with toys or other age-appropriate stimuli than infants without the trait. There is now evidence that individuals with excessive behavioral inhibition are at increased risk for developing phobic behavior (Biederman et al., 1990; Hirschfeld et al., 1992). In any case, inhibition relates more to generalized social phobia than to discrete performance anxiety such as public speaking. A model of the etiology of social phobia would look somewhat like models of panic disorder and specific phobia. Three pathways to social phobia are possible, as depicted in ■ Figure 5.11. First, someone could inherit a generalized biological vulnerability to develop anxiety, a biological tendency to be socially inhibited, or both. The existence of a generalized psychological vulnerability—as reflected in a sense that events, particularly stressful events, are potentially uncontrollable—would increase an individual's vulnerability. When under stress, anxiety and self-focused attention could increase to the point of disrupting performance, even in the absence of a false alarm (panic attack). Second, when under stress, someone might have an unexpected panic attack in a social situation that would become associated (conditioned) to social cues. The individual would then become anxious about having additional (learned) alarms (panic attacks) in the same or similar social situations. Third, someone might experience a real social trauma resulting in a true alarm. Anxiety would then develop (be conditioned) in the same

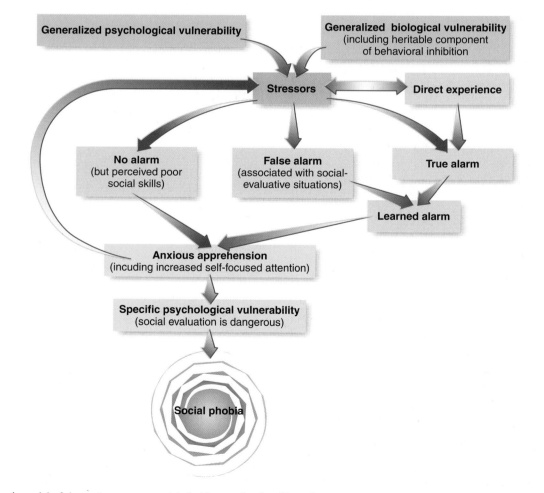

■ **FIGURE 5.11** A model of the various ways a social phobia may develop. (From Barlow, D. H., 2002. *Anxiety and its disorders: The nature and treatment of anxiety and panic.* (2nd ed.). New York: Guilford Press.)

Jerome Kagan discovered that shyness is evident as early as 4 months of age and is probably inherited.

or similar social situations. Traumatic social experiences may also extend back to difficult periods in childhood. Early adolescence—usually ages 12 through 15—is when children may be brutally taunted by peers who are attempting to assert their own dominance. This experience may produce anxiety and panic that are reproduced in future social situations. For example, McCabe, Anthony, Summerfeldt, Liss, and Swinson (2003) noted that 92% of adults with social phobia in their sample experienced severe teasing and bullying in childhood, compared to only 35% to 50% among other anxiety disorders.

But one more factor must fall into place to make it a social anxiety disorder. The individual with the vulnerabilities and experiences just described must also have learned growing up that social evaluation in particular can be dangerous, creating a specific psychological vulnerability to develop social anxiety. Evidence indicates that some social phobics are predisposed to focus their anxiety on events involving social evaluation. Some investigators (Bruch & Heimberg, 1994; Rapee & Melville, 1997) suggest that the parents of patients with social phobia are significantly more socially fearful and concerned with the opinions of others than are the parents of patients with panic disorder and that they pass this concern on to their children (Lieb et al., 2000). Fyer, Mannuzza, Chapman, Liebowitz, and Klein (1993) reported that the relatives of people with social phobia had a significantly greater risk of developing it than the relatives of individuals without social phobia (16% versus 5%)—thus, the specific psychological vulnerability depicted in Figure 5.11. As you can see, a combination of biological and psychological events seem to lead to the development of social phobia.

Treatment

Effective treatments have been developed for social phobia only in the past several years (Barlow & Lehman, 1996; Hofmann, 2004; Taylor, 1996; Turk, Heimberg, & Magee, in press). Rick Heimberg and colleagues developed a cognitive-behavioral group therapy (CBGT) program in which groups of patients rehearse or role-play their socially phobic situations in front of one another (Heimberg et al., 1990; Turk et al., in press). The group members participate in the role-playing, for example, acting as audience for someone who has extreme difficulty giving a speech. At the same time, the therapist conducts rather intensive cognitive therapy aimed at uncovering and changing the automatic or unconscious perceptions of danger that the socially phobic client assumes to exist. These treatments have been more effective than education about anxiety and social phobia and social support for stressful life events. More important, a follow-up after 5 years indicates that the therapeutic gains are maintained (Heimberg, Salzman, Holt, &

Blendell, 1993). More recently, Clark and colleagues (2006) evaluated a new and improved cognitive therapy program that emphasized more real-life experiences during therapy to disprove automatic perceptions of danger. This program substantially benefited 84% of individuals receiving treatment, and these results were maintained at a 1-year follow-up. This outcome is the best yet for this difficult condition and significantly better than previous approaches to which it has been compared.

Some studies have suggested that the exposure-based behavioral rehearsal of anxiety-provoking situations is a more important part of treatment than the cognitive therapy component (Feske & Chambless, 1995; Gould, Buckminster, Pollack, Otto, & Yap, 1997; Hofmann & Barlow, 2002), but that to be effective all treatments must change socially phobic cognitive processes (Hofmann, in press). We have adapted these protocols for use with adolescents, directly involving parents in the group treatment process. Preliminary results suggest that severely socially phobic adolescents can attain relatively normal functioning in school and other social settings (Albano & Barlow, 1996) and that including the parents in the treatment process produces better outcomes than treating the adolescents alone (Albano, Pincus, Tracey, & Barlow, 2007).

Effective drug treatments have been discovered as well. For a time, clinicians assumed that beta-blockers (drugs that lower heart rate and blood pressure, such as Inderal) worked well, particularly for performance anxiety, but the evidence does not seem to support that contention (Liebowitz et al., 1992; Turner, Beidel, & Jacob, 1994). Most recently, tricyclic antidepressants and, particularly, monoamine oxidase (MAO) inhibitors have been found to be more effective than placebo in the treatment of severe social anxiety (Liebowitz et al., 1992). Since 1999, the SSRIs, Paxil, Zoloft, and Effexor have received approval from the Food and Drug Administration for treatment of social anxiety disorder based on studies showing effectiveness compared to placebo (see, for example, Stein et al., 1998).

Several major studies have compared psychological and drug treatments. One large and important study compared MAO inhibitors, among the most powerful drugs for social anxiety disorder, to the psychological treatments described earlier. In this study (Heimberg et al., 1998; Liebowitz et al., 1999) 133 patients were randomly assigned to phenelzine (the MAO inhibitor), CBGT, drug placebo, or an educational-supportive group therapy that served as a placebo for the psychological treatment because it did not contain the cognitive-behavioral component. Results show that both active treatments are highly and equally effective compared to the two placebo conditions but that relapse tends to be more common after treatment stops among those taking medication. The combined effect of these treatments is being evaluated. Another impressive study compared Clark's cognitive therapy described earlier to the SSRI drug Prozac, along with instructions to the patients with generalized social phobia to attempt to engage in more social situations (self-exposure). A third group received placebo plus instructions to attempt to engage in more social activities. Assessments were conducted before the 16-week treatment, at the midpoint of treatment, posttreatment, and then after 3 months of booster sessions. Finally, researchers followed up with patients in the two treatment groups 12 months later (Clark et al., 2003). Results are presented in ■ Figure 5.12. Both treat-

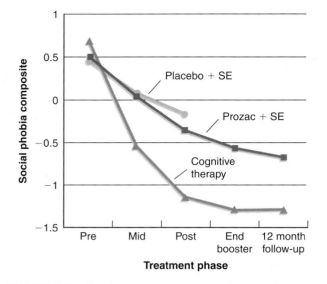

■ FIGURE 5.12 Results from a comparison of Prozac and instructions to attempt more social interactions or "self-exposure" (Prozac + SE), placebo and the same instruction (placebo + SE), and cognitive therapy (CT) in the treatment of patients with generalized social phobia. (Reprinted, with permission, from Clark, D. M., Ehlers, A., McManus, F., Hackmann, A., Fennell, M., Campbell, H., Flower, T., Davenport, C., & Louis, B., 2003. Cognitive therapy versus fluoxetine in generalized social phobia: A randomized placebo-controlled trial. *Journal of Consulting and Clinical Psychology, 71,* 1058–1067, © 2003 American Psychological Association.

ments did well, but the psychological treatment was substantially better at all times. This study is also notable because of the *extent* of change in treatment (most patients were cured or nearly cured with few remaining symptoms). Davidson, Foa, and Huppert (2004) found that a cognitive-behavioral treatment and an SSRI were comparable in efficacy but that the combination was no better than the two individual treatments. But now an exciting new study suggests that adding the drug D-cycloserine (DCS) to cognitive-behavioral treatments significantly enhances the effects of treatment (Hofmann et al., 2006). Unlike SSRIs, this drug is known to facilitate the extinction of anxiety, an important part of cognitive-behavioral treatments, by modifying neurotransmitter flow in the glutamate system as described in Chapter 2. Research is now under way to test the combination of DCS and cognitive-behavioral treatments for other anxiety disorders. Both drug and psychological treatments change brain function in similar areas of the emotional brain (Furmark et al., 2002).

CONCEPT CHECK 5.4

Identify the following specific phobias: (a) blood–injury–injection, (b) acrophobia, (c) animal, (d) social, (e) natural environment, and (f) other. The same phobia may apply to more than one statement.

1. Mark had no friends at school and hid in the boys' bathroom during both lunch and recess. _____

(continued)

CONCEPT CHECK 5.4

(continued)

2. Dennis fears and strenuously avoids storms. Not surprisingly, on his first oceangoing cruise, he found that deep water terrified him, too. _____
3. Rita was comfortable at the zoo until the old terror gripped her at the insect display. _____
4. Armando would love to eat fish with his fishing buddies, but he experiences an inordinate fear of choking on a bone. _____
5. John had to give up his dream of becoming a surgeon because he faints at the sight of blood. _____
6. Rachel turned down several lucrative job offers that involved public speaking for a low-paying desk job. _____ _____
7. Farrah can't visit her rural friends because of her fear of snakes. _____

POSTTRAUMATIC STRESS DISORDER

In recent years, we have heard a great deal about the severe and long-lasting emotional disorders that can occur after a variety of traumatic events. Perhaps the most impressive traumatic events have been war, the recent tragedy of the World Trade Center and the Pentagon on September 11, 2001, or Hurricane Katrina in 2005. Still, emotional disorders also occur after physical assault (particularly rape), car accidents, natural catastrophes, or the sudden death of a loved one. One emotional disorder that follows a trauma is known as **posttraumatic stress disorder (PTSD).**

Clinical Description

DSM-IV-TR describes the setting event for PTSD as exposure to a traumatic event during which someone feels fear, helplessness, or horror. Afterward, victims reexperience the event through memories and nightmares. When memories occur suddenly and the victims find themselves reliving the event, they are having a *flashback.* Victims avoid anything that reminds them of the trauma. They display a characteristic restriction or numbing of emotional responsiveness, which may be disruptive to interpersonal relationships. They are sometimes unable to remember certain aspects of the event. It is possible that victims unconsciously attempt to avoid the experience of emotion itself, like people with panic disorder, because intense emotions could bring back memories of the trauma. Finally, victims typically are chronically overaroused, easily startled, and quick to anger.

PTSD was first named in 1980 in DSM-III (American Psychiatric Association, 1980), but it has a long history. In 1666, the British diarist Samuel Pepys witnessed the Great Fire of London that caused substantial loss of life and property and threw the city into chaos for a time. He captured the events in an account that is still read today. But Pepys did not escape the effects of the horrific event. Six months later, he wrote, "It is strange to think how to this very day I cannot sleep a night without great terrors of fire;

Exposure to a traumatic event may create profound fear and helplessness. People who suffer from PTSD may reexperience such feelings in flashbacks, involuntarily reliving the horrifying event.

©The Christian Science Monitor/Getty Images

and this very night could not sleep to almost 2 in the morning through thoughts of fire" (Daly, 1983, p. 66). The DSM-IV criteria show that difficulty sleeping and recurring intrusive dreams of the event are prominent features of PTSD. Pepys described his guilt at saving himself and his property while others died. He also experienced a sense of detachment and a numbing of his emotions concerning the fire, common experiences in PTSD.

Consider the case of the Joneses from one of our clinics.

THE JONESES: One Victim, Many Traumas

Mrs. Betty Jones and her four children arrived at a farm to visit a friend. (Mr. Jones was at work.) Jeff, the oldest child, was 8 years old. Marcie, Cathy, and Susan were 6, 4, and 2 years of age. Mrs. Jones parked the car in the driveway, and they all started across the yard to the front door. Suddenly Jeff heard growling somewhere near the house. Before he could warn the others, a large German shepherd charged and leapt at Marcie, the 6-year-old, knocking her to the ground and tearing viciously at her face. The family, too stunned to move, watched the attack helplessly. After what seemed like an eternity, Jeff lunged at the dog and it moved away. The owner, in a state of panic, ran to a nearby house to get help. Mrs. Jones immediately put pressure on Marcie's facial wounds in an attempt to stop the bleeding. The owner had neglected to retrieve the dog, and it stood a short distance away, growling and barking at the frightened family. Eventually, the dog was restrained and Marcie was rushed to the hospital. Marcie, who was hysterical, had to be restrained on a padded board so that emergency room physicians could stitch her wounds.

This case is unusual because not only did Marcie develop PTSD but so did her 8-year-old brother. In addition, Cathy, 4, and Susan, 2, although quite young, showed symptoms of the disorder, as did their mother (see Table 5.8) (Albano, Miller, Zarate, Côté, & Barlow, 1997). Jeff evidenced classic survivor guilt symptoms, reporting that he should have saved Marcie or at least put himself between Marcie and the dog. Both Jeff and Marcie regressed developmentally, wetting the bed (nocturnal enuresis) and experiencing nightmares and separation fears. In addition, Marcie, having been strapped down and given local anesthetic and stitches, became frightened of any medical procedures and even of such routine daily events as having her nails trimmed or taking a bath. Furthermore, she refused to be tucked into bed, something she had enjoyed all her life, probably because it reminded her of the hospital board. Jeff started sucking his fingers, which he had not done for years. These behaviors, along with intense separation anxiety, are common, particularly in younger children (Eth, 1990; Silverman & La Greca, 2002). Cathy, the 4-year-old, evidenced considerable fear and avoidance when tested but denied having any problem when she was interviewed by a child psychologist. Susan, the 2-year-old, also had some symptoms, as shown in Table 5.8, but was too young to talk about them. However, for several months following the trauma she repeatedly said, without provocation, "Doggy bit sister."

| TABLE 5.8 | Symptoms of Posttraumatic Stress Disorder (PTSD) Evidenced by Marcie and Her Siblings |

Symptoms	Jeff	Marcie	Cathy	Susan
Repetitive play—trauma themes		X	X	X
Nightmares	X	X	X	X
Reexperiencing		X		
Distress at exposure to similar stimuli	X	X	X	X
Avoidance of talk of trauma		X	X	
Avoidance of trauma recollections		X		
Regressive behavior	X	X		
Detachment	X	X		
Restricted affect	X	X		
Sleep disturbance	X	X	X	X
Anger outbursts	X	X		
Hypervigilance		X	X	
Startle response	X	X		
DSM-III-R PTSD diagnosis met	X	X		

Source: From Albano, A. M., Miller, P. P., Zarate, R., Côté, G., & Barlow, D. H. (1997). Behavioral assessment and treatment of PTSD in prepubertal children: Attention to developmental factors and innovative strategies in the case study of a family. *Cognitive and Behavioral Practice, 4,* 245–262.

Children's memories of traumatic events can become embellished over the years. For example, some children incorporate a superhero coming to the rescue. These intense memories are malleable and subject to distortion.

As indicated in the criteria, PTSD is subdivided into acute and chronic. *Acute PTSD* can be diagnosed 1 month after the event occurs. When PTSD continues longer than 3 months, it is considered chronic. *Chronic PTSD* is usually associated with more prominent avoidance behaviors (Davidson, Hughes, Blazer, & George, 1991), as well as with the more frequent co-occurrence of additional diagnoses, such as social phobia. In *PTSD with delayed onset,* individuals show few or no symptoms immediately after a trauma, but later, perhaps years afterward, they develop full-blown PTSD. Why onset is delayed in some individuals is not yet clear.

As we noted, PTSD cannot be diagnosed until a month after the trauma. New to DSM-IV-TR is a disorder called **acute stress disorder.** This is really PTSD occurring within the first month after the trauma, but the different name emphasizes the severe reaction that some people have immediately. PTSD-like symptoms are accompanied by severe dissociative symptoms, such as amnesia for all or part of the trauma, emotional numbing, and derealization, or feelings of unreality. According to one study, 63% to 70% of individuals with acute stress disorder from motor vehicle accidents went on to develop PTSD up to 2 years after the trauma. In addition, 13% who did not meet criteria for acute stress disorder went on to develop PTSD. If the victim experienced strong arousal and emotional numbing as part of acute stress disorder, the likelihood of later developing PTSD was greater (Harvey & Bryant, 1998). Acute stress disorder was included in DSM-IV because many people with severe early reactions to trauma could not otherwise be diagnosed and, therefore, could not receive insurance coverage for immediate treatment.

Statistics

Determining the prevalence rates for PTSD seems relatively straightforward: Simply observe victims of a trauma and see how many are suffering from PTSD. But a number of studies have demonstrated the remarkably low prevalence of PTSD in popula-

---

DSM-IV-TR

DSM TABLE 5.6 Diagnostic Criteria for Posttraumatic Stress Disorder

A. The person has been exposed to a traumatic event in which both of the following were present:
 1. The person experienced, witnessed, or was confronted with an event or events that involve actual or threatened death or serious injury, or a threat to the physical integrity of self or others
 2. The person's response involved intense fear, helplessness, or horror. *Note:* in children, it may be expressed instead by disorganized or agitated behavior
B. The traumatic event is persistently reexperienced in one (or more) of the following ways:
 1. Recurrent and intrusive distressing recollections of the event, including images, thoughts, or perceptions. *note:* in young children, repetitive play may occur in which themes or aspects of the trauma are expressed
 2. Recurrent distressing dreams of the event. *note:* in children, there may be frightening dreams without recognizable content
 3. Acting or feeling as if the traumatic event were recurring (includes a sense of reliving the experience, illusions, hallucinations, and dissociative flashback episodes, including those that occur on awakening or when intoxicated). *note:* in young children, trauma-specific reenactment may occur
 4. Intense psychological distress at exposure to internal or external cues that symbolize or resemble an aspect of the traumatic event
 5. Physiologic reactivity on exposure to internal or external cues that symbolize or resemble an aspect of the traumatic event
C. Persistent avoidance of stimuli associated with the trauma and numbing of general responsiveness (not present before the trauma), as indicated by three (or more) of the following:
 1. Efforts to avoid thoughts, feelings, or conversations associated with the trauma
 2. Efforts to avoid activities, places, or people that arouse recollections of the trauma
 3. Inability to recall an important aspect of the trauma
 4. Markedly diminished interest or participation in significant activities
 5. Feeling of detachment or estrangement from others
 6. Restricted range of affect (e.g., unable to have loving feelings)
 7. Sense of a foreshortened future (e.g., does not expect to have a career, marriage, children, or a normal life span)
D. Persistent symptoms of increased arousal (not present before the trauma), as indicated by two (or more) of the following:
 1. Difficulty falling or staying asleep
 2. Irritability or outbursts of anger
 3. Difficulty concentrating
 4. Hypervigilance
 5. Exaggerated startle response
E. Duration of the disturbance (symptoms in B, C, and D) is more than one month.
F. The disturbance causes clinically significant distress or impairment in social, occupational, or other important areas of functioning.
Specify if:
 1. Acute: If duration of symptoms is less than 3 months
 2. Chronic: If duration of symptoms is 3 months or more
Specify if:
With delayed onset: If onset of symptoms at least 6 months after the stressor

Source: Reprinted, with permission, from American Psychiatric Association. (2000). *Diagnostic and statistical manual of mental disorders* (4th ed., text revision). Washington, DC: Author, © 2000 American Psychiatric Association.

tions of trauma victims. Rachman (1978) studied the British citizenry who endured numerous life-threatening air raids during Word War II. He concluded that "a great majority of people endured the air raids extraordinarily well, contrary to the universal expectation of mass panic. Exposure to repeated bombings did not produce a significant increase in psychiatric disorders. Although short-lived fear reactions were common, surprisingly few persistent phobic reactions emerged" (Rachman, 1991, p. 162). Similar results have been observed after disastrous fires, earthquakes, and floods (Green, Grace, Lindy, Titchener, & Lindy, 1983).

Phillip Saigh (1984) made some interesting observations when he was teaching at the American University in Beirut, Lebanon, just before and during the Israeli invasion in the early 1980s. Saigh had been collecting questionnaires measuring anxiety among university students just before the invasion. When the invasion began, half these students escaped to the surrounding mountains and were safe. The other half endured intense shelling and bombing for a period. Saigh continued administering the questionnaires and found a surprising result. There were no essential long-term differences between the group in the mountains and the group in the city, although a few students in the city who were closely exposed to danger and death did develop emotional reactions that progressed into PTSD. On the other hand, some studies have found a high incidence of PTSD after trauma. Kilpatrick and colleagues (1985) sampled more than 2,000 adult women who had personally experienced such trauma as rape, sexual molestation, robbery, and aggravated assault. Subjects were asked whether they had thought about suicide after the trauma, attempted suicide, or had a *nervous breakdown* (a lay term that has no meaning in psychopathology but is commonly used to refer to a severe psychological upset). The authors also analyzed the results based on whether the attack was completed or attempted, as shown in Table 5.9. Rape had the most significant emotional im-

TABLE 5.9 Proportion of Victimization Groups Experiencing Major Mental Health Problems

	Problem					
	Nervous Breakdown		Suicidal Ideation		Suicide Attempt	
Group	n	%	n	%	n	%
Attempted rape	7	9.0	23	29.5	7	8.9
Completed rape	16	16.3	44	44.0	19	19.2
Attempted molestation	2	5.4	12	32.4	3	8.1
Completed molestation	1	1.9	12	21.8	2	3.6
Attempted robbery	0	0.0	3	9.1	4	12.1
Completed robbery	5	7.8	7	10.8	2	3.1
Aggravated assault	1	2.1	7	14.9	2	4.3
Nonvictims	51	3.3	106	6.8	34	2.2

Source: Reprinted, with permission, from Kilpatrick, D. G., Best, C. L., Veronen, L. V., Amick, A. E., Villeponteaux, L. A., & Ruff, G. A. (1985). Mental health correlates of criminal victimization: A random community survey. *Journal of Consulting and Clinical Psychology, 53,* 866–873, © 1985 American Psychological Association.

pact. Compared to 2.2% of nonvictims, 19.2% of rape victims had attempted suicide, and 44% reported suicidal ideation at some time following the rape. Similarly, Resnick, Kilpatrick, Dansky, Saunders, and Best (1993) found that 32% of rape victims met criteria for PTSD at some point in their lives. Looking at all types of trauma (for example, physical assault and accidents) in a large sample of U.S. adult women, Resnick and colleagues (1993) found that 17.9% experienced PTSD. Taylor and Koch (1995) found that 15% to 20% of people experiencing severe auto accidents developed PTSD. Other surveys indicate that among the population as a whole, 6.8% have experienced PTSD at some point in their life (Kessler, Berglund, et al., 2005) and 3.5% during the past year (Kessler, Chiu, et al., 2005), and combat and sexual assault are the most common traumas (Kessler, Sonnega, Bromet, Hughes, & Nelson, 1995).

What accounts for the discrepancies between the low rate of PTSD in citizens who endured bombing and shelling in London and Beirut and the relatively high rate in victims of crime? Investigators have now concluded that during air raids many people may not have directly experienced the horrors of dying, death, and direct attack. Close exposure to the trauma seems to be necessary to developing this disorder (Keane & Barlow, 2002; King, King, Foy, & Gudanowski, 1996). But this is also evident among Vietnam veterans, where 18.7% developed PTSD, with prevalence rates directly related to amount of combat exposure (Dohrenwend et al., 2006). Preliminary surveys of 76 victims of Hurricane Katrina also report a doubling of severe mental illness (Kessler, Golea, Jones & Parker, 2006). Nowhere is this more starkly evident than in the tragedy of 9/11. Schlenger and colleagues (2002) interviewed a nationally representative sample of adults and found that the percentage of people who probably met criteria for PTSD was higher in New York City (11.2%) than in other major cities (between 2.3% and 3.6%). Galea and colleagues (2002) contacted a representative sample of adults living south of 110th Street in Manhattan and found that 7.5% reported symptoms consistent with a diagnosis of acute stress disorder or PTSD. But among respondents who lived close to the World Trade Center (south of Canal Street) the prevalence of the disorder was 20%. Again, those who experienced the disaster most personally and directly seemed to be the ones most affected.

In addition, tens of thousands of public school children in New York City who lived close to the disaster experienced chronic nightmares, fear of public places, and other symptoms of PTSD. After the attack, a large study conducted with the help of federal agencies estimates that 75,000 schoolchildren in New York City in grades 4 through 12, or 10.5% of children in those grades, suffered PTSD after September 11 (Goodnough, 2002). In addition, 155 suffered from agoraphobia, or a fear of leaving a safe place such as home. Many of these children feared riding public transportation. Two-thirds of the children sampled lived near the World Trade Center or in other neighborhoods directly affected by the tragedy, such as Staten Island, home to many who were killed, or Brooklyn, where smoke drifted over its neighborhoods for days. We also know that once it appears PTSD tends to last (runs a chronic course) (Perkonigg et al., 2005).

But is this the whole story? It seems not. Some people experience the most horrifying traumas imaginable and emerge psychologically healthy. For others, even relatively mild stressful events are sufficient to produce a full-blown disorder. To understand how this can happen, we must consider the etiology of PTSD.

Causes

PTSD is the one disorder for which we are sure of the etiology: Someone personally experiences a trauma and develops a disorder. However, whether a person develops PTSD or not is a surprisingly complex issue involving biological, psychological, and social factors. David Foy and his colleagues (Foy, Sipprelle, Rueger, & Carroll, 1984) concluded that the intensity of combat exposure contributed to the etiology of PTSD in a group of Vietnam War veterans, a finding recently confirmed, as noted earlier (Dohrenwend et al., 2006), but did not account for all of it. For example, approximately 67% of prisoners of war developed PTSD (Foy, Resnick, Sipprelle, & Carroll, 1987). This means that 33% of the prisoners who endured long-term deprivation and torture *did not* develop the disorder; perhaps the best known among the group is Senator John McCain. Similarly, Resnick, Kilpatrick, Dansky, Saunders, and Best (1993) demonstrated that the percentage of female crime victims who developed PTSD increased as a function of the severity of the trauma (see ■ Figure 5.13). Finally, children experiencing severe burns will develop PTSD in proportion to the severity of the burns and the pain associated with them (Saxe et al., 2005). At lower levels of trauma, some people develop PTSD but most do not. What accounts for these differences?

As with other disorders, we bring our own generalized biological and psychological vulnerabilities with us. The greater the vulnerability, the more likely we are to develop PTSD. If certain characteristics run in your family, you have a much greater chance

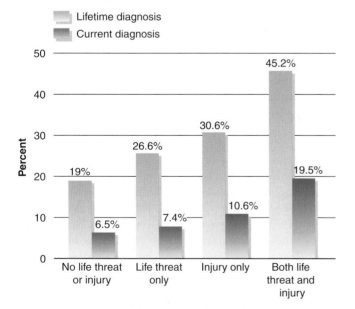

■ **FIGURE 5.13** Prevalence of lifetime and current PTSD associated with assault characteristics. (Reprinted, with permission, from Resnick, H. S., Kilpatrick, D. G., Dansky, B. S., Sanders, B. E., & Best, C. L., 1993. Prevalence of civilian trauma and posttraumatic stress disorder in a representative national sample of women. *Journal of Consulting and Clinical Psychology, 61,* 984–991, © 1993 American Psychological Association.)

of developing the disorder (Davidson, Swartz, Storck, Krishnan, & Hammett, 1985; Foy et al., 1987). A family history of anxiety suggests a generalized biological vulnerability for PTSD. True and colleagues (1993) reported that, given the same amount of combat exposure and one twin with PTSD, a monozygotic (identical) twin was more likely to develop PTSD than a dizygotic (fraternal) twin. The correlation of symptoms in identical twins was between 0.28 and 0.41, whereas for fraternal twins it was between 0.11 and 0.24, which suggests some genetic influence in the development of PTSD.

Breslau, Davis, and Andreski (1995) demonstrated among a random sample of 1,200 individuals that characteristics such as a tendency to be anxious, as well as factors such as minimal education, predict exposure to traumatic events in the first place and therefore an increased risk for PTSD. Breslau, Lucia, and Alvarado (2006) elaborated on this finding by showing that 6-year-old children with externalizing (acting out) problems were more likely to encounter trauma (such as assaults), probably because of their acting out, and later develop PTSD. Higher intelligence predicted decreased exposure to these types of traumatic events. That is, personality and other characteristics, some of them at least partially heritable, may predispose people to the experience of trauma by making it likely that they will be in (risky) situations where trauma is likely to occur. This is reminiscent of the studies on reciprocal gene–environment interactions we described in Chapter 2, in which existing vulnerabilities, some of them heritable, may help determine the kind of environment in which someone lives and, therefore, the type of psychological disorder that person may develop.

Also, there seems to be a generalized psychological vulnerability described in the context of other disorders based on early experiences with unpredictable or uncontrollable events. Foy and colleagues (1987) discovered that at high levels of trauma, these vulnerabilities did not matter as much, because the majority of prisoners (67%) developed PTSD. However, at low levels of stress or trauma, vulnerabilities matter a great deal in determining whether the disorder will develop. Family instability is one factor that may instill a sense that the world is an uncontrollable, potentially dangerous place (Chorpita & Barlow, 1998; Suàrez et al., in press), so it is not surprising that individuals from unstable families are at risk for developing PTSD if they experience trauma. This factor was relevant in a study of more than 1,600 male and female Vietnam veterans (King et al., 1996).

Basoglu and colleagues (1997) studied two groups of torture victims in Turkey. Thirty-four survivors had no history of political activity, commitment to a political cause or group, or expectations of arrest and torture. Compared with 55 tortured political activists, the nonactivists were subjected to less horrendous abuse but showed higher levels of psychopathology. It seemed that the political activists were more prepared psychologically for torture, which they generally experienced as predictable, thereby reducing later psychological symptoms. This study further demonstrates psychological factors that either protect against or increase the risk of developing PTSD.

Finally, social and cultural factors play a major role in the development of PTSD (see, for example, Carroll, Rueger, Foy, & Donahoe, 1985). The results from a number of studies are consistent in showing that, if you have a strong and supportive group of people around you, it is much less likely you will develop PTSD after a trauma. These factors seem to be true around the world because the reaction to trauma is similar across cultures, as a recent study comparing American and Russian adolescents demonstrated (Ruchkin et al., 2005). In a particularly interesting study, Vernberg, La Greca, Silverman, and Prinstein (1996) studied 568 elementary school children 3 months after Hurricane Andrew hit the coast of south Florida. More than 55% of these children reported moderate to severe levels of PTSD symptoms, a typical result for this type of disaster (La Greca & Prinstein, 2002). When the authors examined factors contributing to who developed PTSD symptoms and who didn't, social support from parents, close friends, classmates, and teachers was a important protective factor. Similarly, positive coping strategies involving active problem solving seemed to be protective, whereas becoming angry and placing blame on others were associated with higher levels of PTSD. The broader and deeper the network of social support, the less chance of developing PTSD. Schuster and colleagues (2001) reported that people who experienced PTSD symptoms following the attack of 9/11 coped with the stress mostly by looking to friends and family for support.

Why is this? As you saw in Chapter 2, we are all social animals, and something about having a loving, caring group of people around us directly affects our biological and psychological responses to stress. A number of studies show that support from loved ones reduces cortisol secretion and HPA axis activity in children during stress (see, for example, Nachmias, Gunnar, Mangelsdorf, Parritz, & Buss, 1996). It is likely that one reason for the high prevalence of PTSD in Vietnam veterans is the tragic absence of social support when they returned from the war.

It seems clear that PTSD involves a number of neurobiological systems (Amat et al., 2005; Charney, Deutch, Krystal, Southwick, & Davis, 1993; Gunnar & Fisher, in press; Heim & Nemeroff, 1999; Ladd et al., 2000; Shin et al., 2004; Sullivan et al., 2000). Dennis Charney and other investigators conducted research on animals, mostly rats who were exposed to strong uncontrollable stress such as repeated shock. Their findings revealed that stressful and threatening cues may activate input from several regions of the brain. These inputs then activate the CRF system, as noted earlier in the chapter. Note also that two critical brain structures related to anxiety and fear, the locus coeruleus and the central nucleus of the amygdala, are strongly stimulated by CRF nerve terminals. Of course, work with animals is only suggestive of what happens with humans. Some of these investigators have extended their work to patients with PTSD and confirmed the existence of elevated CRF, which indicates the heightened activity in the HPA axis described in Chapter 2 and here.

You may remember that primates studied in the wild under extreme stress also have elevated levels of CRF and cortisol, the stress hormones. Chronic activation of stress hormones in these primates seems to result in permanent damage to the hippocampus, which regulates the stress hormones. Thus, chronic arousal and some other symptoms of PTSD may be directly related to changes in brain function and structure (Bremner, 1999; Bremner et al., 1997; McEwen & Magarinos, 2004). Evidence of damage to the hippocampus has appeared in groups of patients with war-

related PTSD (Gurvits et al., 1996), adult survivors of childhood sexual abuse (Bremner et al., 1995), and firefighters exposed to extreme trauma (Shin et al., 2003). The hippocampus is a part of the brain that plays an important role in learning and memory. Thus, if there is damage to the hippocampus, we might expect some disruptions in learning and memory. Disruptions in memory functions, including short-term memory and recalling events, have been demonstrated in patients with PTSD (Sass et al., 1992). These memory deficits are also evident in veterans of the Gulf War (Vasterling, Brailey, Constans, & Sotker, 1998) and Holocaust survivors with PTSD, as compared to Holocaust survivors without PTSD or healthy Jewish adults (Golier et al., 2002). Bremner, Vermetten, Southwick, Krystal, and Charney (1998) suggest that the fragmentation of memory often seen in patients with PTSD may account for difficulties in recalling at least some aspects of their trauma.

Fortunately, as Bremner (1999) points out, some evidence indicates this damage to the hippocampus may be reversible. For example, Starkman and colleagues (1999) reported results from patients who had some damage to their hippocampus because of Cushing's disease, which causes chronic activation of the HPA axis and increased flow of cortisol. They found increases of up to 10% in hippocampal volume following successful treatment for this disease. Further studies will confirm if the changes as a result of trauma can be reversed by treatment. Earlier we described a panic attack as an adaptive fear response occurring at an inappropriate time. It is not surprising that Southwick, Krystal, Johnson, and Charney (1992) traced a brain circuit for PTSD that is similar to the brain circuit for panic attacks, originating in the locus coeruleus in the brain stem. We have speculated that the alarm reaction is similar in both panic disorder and PTSD but that in panic disorder the alarm is false. In PTSD, the initial alarm is true in that real danger is present (Jones & Barlow, 1990; Keane & Barlow, 2002). If the alarm is severe enough, we may develop a conditioned or learned alarm reaction to stimuli that remind us of the trauma (for example, being tucked into bed reminded Marcie of the emergency room board). We may also develop anxiety about the possibility of additional uncontrollable emotional experiences (such as flashbacks, which are common in PTSD). Whether or not we develop anxiety partly depends on our vulnerabilities. This model of the etiology of PTSD is presented in ■ Figure 5.14.

Treatment

From the psychological point of view, most clinicians agree that victims of PTSD should face the original trauma to develop effective coping procedures and thus overcome the debilitating effects of the disorder (Barlow & Lehman, 1996; Keane & Barlow, 2002; Najavits, 2007; Resick, Monson, & Rizvi, in press). In psychoanalytic therapy, reliving emotional trauma to relieve emotional suffering is called *catharsis*. The trick is in arranging the reexposure so that it will be therapeutic rather than traumatic again. Unlike the object of a specific phobia, a traumatic event is difficult to recreate, and few therapists want to try. Therefore, *imaginal exposure,* in which the content of the trauma and the emotions associated with it are worked through systematically, has been used for decades under a variety of names. At present, the most common strategy to

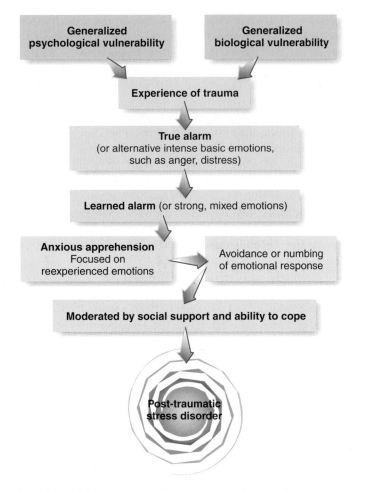

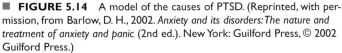

■ **FIGURE 5.14** A model of the causes of PTSD. (Reprinted, with permission, from Barlow, D. H., 2002. *Anxiety and its disorders: The nature and treatment of anxiety and panic* (2nd ed.). New York: Guilford Press, © 2002 Guilford Press.)

achieve this purpose with adolescents or adults is to work with the victim to develop a narrative of the traumatic experience that is then reviewed extensively in therapy. Cognitive therapy to correct negative assumptions about the trauma, such as blaming oneself in some way, feeling guilty, or both, is often part of treatment (Najavits, 2007; Resick et al., in press).

Another complication is that trauma victims often repress the emotional side of their memories of the event and sometimes, it seems, the memory itself. This happens automatically and unconsciously. Occasionally, with treatment, the memories flood back and the patient dramatically relives the episode. Although this may be frightening to both patient and therapist, it can be therapeutic if handled appropriately. Evidence is now accumulating that early, structured interventions delivered as soon after the trauma as possible to those who require help are useful in preventing the development of PTSD (Bryant, Moulds, & Nixon, 2003; Ehlers et al., 2003; Litz, Gray, Bryant, & Adler, 2002). For example, in the study by Ehlers and colleagues (2003) of patients who had experienced a scary car accident and were clearly at risk for developing PTSD, only 11% developed PTSD after 12 sessions of cognitive therapy, compared with 61% of those receiving a detailed self-help booklet or 55% of those who were just assessed repeatedly over time but had no intervention. All patients who needed it were then

treated with cognitive therapy. On the other hand, there is evidence that subjecting trauma victims to a single debriefing session, in which they are forced to express their feelings whether they are distressed or not, can be harmful (Ehlers & Clark, 2003).

Both Marcie, the young girl bitten by the dog, and her brother were treated simultaneously at our clinic. The primary difficulty was Marcie's reluctance to be seen by a doctor or to undergo any physical examinations, so a series of experiences was arranged from least to most intense (see Table 5.10). Mildly anxiety-provoking procedures for Marcie included having her pulse taken, lying on an examination table, and taking a bath after accidentally cutting herself. The most intense challenge was being strapped on a restraining board. First Marcie watched her brother go through these exercises. He was not afraid of these particular procedures, although he was anxious about being strapped to a board because of Marcie's terror at the thought. After she watched her brother experience these situations with little or no fear, Marcie tried each one in turn. The therapist took instant photographs of her that she kept after completing the procedures. Marcie was also asked to draw pictures of the situations. The therapist and her family warmly congratulated her as she completed each exercise. Because of Marcie's age, she was not adept at imaginatively recreating memories of the traumatic medical procedures. Therefore, her treatment offered experiences designed to alter her current perceptions of the situations. Marcie's PTSD was successfully treated, and her brother's guilt was greatly reduced as a function of helping in her treatment.

Drug can also be effective for symptoms of PTSD (Golier, Legge, & Yehuda, 2007). Some of the drugs, such as SSRIs (Prozac and Paxil), effective for anxiety disorders in general have been shown to be helpful for PTSD, perhaps because they relieve the severe anxiety and panic attacks so prominent in this disorder.

TABLE 5.10	Fear and Avoidance Hierarchy for Marcie	
	Pretreatment Fear Rating	**Posttreatment Fear Rating**
Being strapped on a board	4	0
Having an electrocardiogram	4	0
Having a chest X ray	4	0
Having doctor listen to heart with stethoscope	3	0
Lying on examination table	3	0
Taking a bath after sustaining an accidentally inflicted cut	3	0
Allowing therapist to put Band-Aid on a cut	2	0
Letting therapist listen to heart with stethoscope	1	0
Having pulse taken	1	0
Allowing therapist to examine throat with tongue depressor	1	0

Source: From Albano, A. M., Miller, P. P., Zarate, R., Côté, G., & Barlow, D. H. (1997). Behavioral assessment and treatment of PTSD in prepubertal children: Attention to developmental factors and innovative strategies in the case study of a family. *Cognitive and Behavioral Practice, 4,* 254, © 1997 Association for Advancement of Behavior Therapy.

Match the correct preliminary diagnosis with the following cases: (a) acute posttraumatic stress disorder, (b) acute stress disorder, and (c) delayed onset posttraumatic stress disorder.

1. Judy witnessed a horrific tornado level her farm 3 weeks ago. Since then, she's had many flashbacks of the incident, trouble sleeping, and a fear of going outside in storms. _____

2. Jack was involved in a car accident 6 weeks ago in which the driver of the other car was killed. Since then, Jack has been unable to get into a car because it brings back the horrible scene he witnessed. Nightmares of the incident haunt him and interfere with his sleep. He is irritable and has lost interest in his work and hobbies. _____

   _____

3. Patricia was raped at the age of 17, 30 years ago. Just recently, she has been having flashbacks of the event, difficulty sleeping, and fear of sexual contact with her husband. _____

OBSESSIVE-COMPULSIVE DISORDER

A client with an anxiety disorder who needs hospitalization is likely to have **obsessive-compulsive disorder (OCD).** A client referred for psychosurgery (neurosurgery for a psychological disorder) because every psychological and pharmacological treatment has failed and the suffering is unbearable probably has OCD. OCD is the devastating culmination of the anxiety disorders. It is not uncommon for someone with OCD to experience severe generalized anxiety, recurrent panic attacks, debilitating avoidance, and major depression, all occurring simultaneously with obsessive-compulsive symptoms. With OCD, establishing even a foothold of control and predictability over the dangerous events in life seems so utterly hopeless that victims resort to magic and rituals.

Clinical Description

In other anxiety disorders, the danger is usually in an external object or situation, or at least in the memory of one. In OCD, the dangerous event is a thought, image, or impulse that the client attempts to avoid as completely as someone with a snake phobia avoids snakes (Clark & O'Connor, 2005). For example, has anyone ever told you not to think of pink elephants? If you really concentrate on not thinking of pink elephants, using every mental means possible, you will realize how difficult it is to suppress a suggested thought or image. Individuals with OCD fight this battle all day, every day, sometimes for most of their lives, and they usually fail miserably. In Chapter 3, we discussed the case of Frank, who experienced involuntary thoughts of epilepsy or seizures and prayed or shook his leg to try to distract himself. **Obsessions** are intrusive and mostly nonsensical thoughts, images, or urges that the individual tries to resist or eliminate. **Compulsions** are the thoughts or actions used to suppress the obsessions and provide

relief. Frank had both obsessions and compulsions, but his disorder was mild compared to the case of Richard.

RICHARD: Enslaved by Ritual

Richard, a 19-year-old college freshman majoring in philosophy, withdrew from school because of incapacitating ritualistic behavior. He abandoned personal hygiene because the compulsive rituals that he had to carry out during washing or cleaning were so time consuming that he could do nothing else. Almost continual showering gave way to no showering. He stopped cutting and washing his hair and beard, brushing his teeth, and changing his clothes. He left his room infrequently and, to avoid rituals associated with the toilet, defecated on paper towels, urinated in paper cups, and stored the waste in the closet. He ate only late at night when his family was asleep. To be able to eat he had to exhale completely, making a lot of hissing noises, coughs, and hacks, and then fill his mouth with as much food as he could while no air was in his lungs. He would eat only a mixture of peanut butter, sugar, cocoa, milk, and mayonnaise. All other foods he considered contaminants. When he walked he took small steps on his toes while continually looking back, checking and rechecking. Occasionally, he ran quickly in place. He withdrew his left arm completely from his shirt sleeve as if he were crippled and his shirt was a sling.

Like everyone with OCD, Richard experienced intrusive and persistent thoughts and impulses; in his case they were about sex, aggression, and religion. His various behaviors were efforts to suppress sexual and aggressive thoughts or to ward off the disastrous consequences he thought would ensue if he did not perform his rituals. Richard performed most of the repetitive behaviors and mental acts mentioned in the DSM-IV criteria. Compulsions can be either behavioral (hand-washing or checking) or mental (thinking about certain words in a specific order, counting, praying, and so on) (Foa et al., 1996; Steketee & Barlow, 2002). The important thing is that they are believed to reduce stress or prevent a dreaded event. Compulsions are often "magical" in that they often bear no logical relation to the obsession.

■ Obsessions

Jenike, Baer, and Minichiello (1986) noted that the most common obsessions in a sample of 100 patients were contamination (55%), aggressive impulses (50%), sexual content (32%), somatic concerns (35%), and the need for symmetry (37%). Of those sampled, 60% displayed multiple obsessions. "Need for symmetry" refers to keeping things in perfect order or doing something in a specific way. As a child, were you careful not to step on cracks in the sidewalk? You and your friends might have kept this up for a few minutes before tiring of it. But what if you had to spend your whole life avoiding cracks, on foot or in a car? You wouldn't have much fun. People with obsessive impulses may feel they are about to yell out a swear word in church. One patient of ours, a young

"I'm a little bit obsessive-compulsive. . . . It's a little difficult to deal with. The obsessive part—I'll get a thought in my head, and I can't put it out. It's just there all the time. I think about it when I go to bed, I think about it when I get up. . . . I'm a 'checker'—I have to check things. . . . I don't cook, but I have to check the stove every morning . . . not always really rational."

and moral woman, was afraid to ride the bus for fear that if a man sat down beside her she would grab his crotch! In reality, this would be the last thing she would do, but the impulse was so horrifying that she made every attempt possible to suppress it and to avoid riding the bus or similar situations where the impulse might occur.

Compulsions

Leckman, Grice, and colleagues (1997) analyzed types of compulsions in several large groups of patients and found that checking, ordering, and arranging, along with washing and cleaning, were the major categories of rituals. Most patients with OCD present with cleaning and washing or checking rituals. For people who fear contact with objects or situations that may be contaminating, washing or cleaning restores a sense of safety and control (Rachman, 2006). Checking rituals serve to prevent an imagined disaster or catastrophe. Most are logical, such as repeatedly checking the stove to see whether you turned it off, but severe cases can be illogical. For example, Richard thought that if he did not eat in a certain way he might become possessed. If he didn't take small steps and look back, some disaster might happen to his family. A mental act, such as counting, can also be a compulsion. Like Richard, many patients have both kinds of rituals.

Certain kinds of obsessions are strongly associated with certain kinds of rituals (Calamari et al., 2004; Leckman, Grice, 1997). For example, aggression and sexual obsessions seem to lead to checking rituals. Obsessions with symmetry lead to ordering and arranging or repeating rituals; obsessions with contamination lead to washing rituals. It is also common for tic disorder, characterized by involuntary movement (sudden jerking of limbs, for example) or involuntary vocalizations to co-occur in patients with OCD or in their families (Grados et al., 2001). In some cases, these movements may be compulsions, as they were in the case of Frank. Observations among one small group of children presenting with OCD and tics suggest that these problems occurred after a bout of strep throat. This syndrome has been referred to as Pediatric Autoimmune Disorder associated with Streptococcal Infection, or "Pandas." Confirmation of this association awaits further research (Radomsky & Taylor, 2005; Swedo, 2002).

On rare occasions, patients, particularly children, will present with few or no identifiable obsessions. We saw an 8-year-old child who felt compelled to undress, put on his pajamas, and turn down the covers in a time-consuming fashion each night; he always repeated the ritual three times. He could give no particular reason for his behavior; he simply had to do it.

Hoarding

Recently, a group of patients have come to the attention of specialty clinics because they compulsively hoard things, fearing that if they throw something away, even a 10-year-old newspaper, they then might urgently need it (Frost, Steketee, & Williams, 2002; Grisham & Barlow, 2005; Samuels et al., 2002; Steketee & Frost, 2007a, 2007b). It is not uncommon for some patients' houses and yards to come to

DSM-IV-TR

DSM TABLE 5.7 Diagnostic Criteria for Obsessive-Compulsive Disorder

A. Either obsessions or compulsions.
  Obsessions are defined by 1, 2, 3, and 4:
  1. Recurrent and persistent thoughts, impulses, or images that are experienced, at some time during the disturbance, as intrusive and inappropriate and cause marked anxiety or distress
  2. The thoughts, impulses, or images are not simply excessive worries about reallife problems
  3. The person attempts to ignore or suppress such thoughts, impulses, or images, or to neutralize them with some other thought or action
  4. The person recognizes that the obsessional thoughts, impulses, or images are a product of his or her own mind (not imposed from without as in thought insertion)
  Compulsions as defined by 1 and 2:
  1. Repetitive behaviors (e.g., handwashing, ordering, checking) or mental acts (e.g., praying, counting, repeating words silently) that the person feels driven to perform in response to an obsession, or according to rules that must be applied rigidly
  2. The behaviors or mental acts are aimed at preventing or reducing distress or preventing some dreaded event or situation; however, these behaviors or mental acts either are not connected in a realistic way with what they are designed to neutralize or prevent or are clearly excessive
B. At some point during the course of the disorder, the person has recognized that the obsessions or compulsions are excessive or unreasonable. *Note:* This does not apply to children.
C. The obsessions or compulsions cause marked distress, are time-consuming (take more than 1 hour a day), or significantly interfere with the person's normal routine, occupational (or academic) functioning, or usual social activities or relationships.
D. If another Axis I disorder is present, the content of the obsessions or compulsions is not restricted to it (e.g., preoccupation with food in the presence of an eating disorder; hair pulling in the presence of trichotillomania; concern with appearance in the presence of body dysmorphic disorder; preoccupation with drugs in the presence of a substance use disorder; preoccupation with having a serious illness in the presence of hypochondriasis; preoccupation with sexual urges or fantasies in the presence of a paraphilia; or guilty ruminations in the presence of major depressive disorder).
E. The disturbance is not due to the direct effects of a substance (e.g., drugs of abuse, medication) or a general medical condition.
Specify if:
With poor insight: If, for most of the time during the current episode, the person does not recognize that the obsessions and compulsions are excessive or unreasonable

Source: Reprinted, with permission, from American Psychiatric Association. (2000). *Diagnostic and statistical manual of mental disorders* (4th ed., text revision). Washington, DC: Author, © 2000 American Psychiatric Association.

People with obsessive compulsive hoarding are so afraid they may throw something important away that clutter piles up in their homes.

the attention of public health authorities. One patient's house and yard was condemned because junk was piled so high it was both unsightly and a fire hazard. Among her hoard was a 20-year collection of used sanitary napkins.

Basically, these individuals usually begin acquiring things during their teenage years and often experience great pleasure, even euphoria from shopping or otherwise collecting various items. Shopping or collecting things may be a response to feeling down or depressed and is sometimes called, facetiously, "retail therapy." But unlike most people who like to shop or collect, these individuals then experience strong anxiety and distress about throwing anything away because everything has either some potential use or sentimental value in their minds, and their homes or apartments may become almost impossible to live in. Most of these individuals don't consider that they have a problem until family members or authorities insist that they receive help. The average age when these people come for treatment is approximately 50, after many years of hoarding (Grisham, Frost, Steketee, Kim, & Hood, 2006). Often they live alone. New treatments are in development at our clinic that teach people to assign different values to objects and to reduce anxiety about throwing away items that are somewhat less valued (Steketee & Frost, 2007a). Preliminary results are promising, but more information on long-term effects of these treatments is needed.

Statistics

The lifetime prevalence of OCD is approximately 1.6% (Kessler, Berglund, et al., 2005), and in a given 1-year period the prevalence is 1% (Kessler, Chiu, et al., 2005). Not all cases meeting criteria for OCD are as severe as Richard's. Obsessions and compulsions can be arranged along a continuum, like most clinical features of anxiety disorders. Intrusive and distressing thoughts are common in nonclinical ("normal") individuals (Clark & Rhyno,

2005). Randy Frost and his colleagues found that between 10% and 15% of "normal" college students engaged in checking behavior substantial enough to score within the range of patients with OCD (Frost, Sher, & Geen, 1986).

It would also be unusual *not* to have an occasional intrusive or strange thought. Many people have bizarre, sexual, or aggressive thoughts, particularly if they are bored—for example, when sitting in class. Gail Steketee and her colleagues collected examples of thoughts from ordinary people who do not have OCD. Some of these thoughts are listed in Table 5.11.

Have you had any of these thoughts? Most people do, but they let these thoughts go in one ear and out the other, so to speak. Certain individuals, however, are horrified by such thoughts, considering them signs of an alien, intrusive, evil force. The majority of individuals with OCD are female, but the ratio is not as large as for some other anxiety disorders. Rasmussen and Tsuang (1984, 1986) reported that 55% of 1,630 patients were female. An epidemiology study noted 60% females in their sample of people with OCD (Karno & Golding, 1991). Interestingly, in children the sex ratio is reversed, with more males than females (Hanna, 1995). This seems to be because boys tend to develop OCD earlier. By mid-adolescence, the sex ratio is approximately equal before becoming predominantly female in adulthood (Albano et al., 1996). Age of onset ranges from childhood through the 30s, with a median age of onset of 19 (Kessler, Berglund, et al., 2005). The age of onset peaks earlier in males (at 13 to 15) than in females (at 20 to 24) (Rasmussen & Eisen, 1990). Once OCD develops, it tends to become chronic (Eisen & Steketee, 1998; Steketee & Barlow, 2002).

In Arabic countries, OCD is easily recognizable, although as always cultural beliefs and concerns influence the content of the obsessions and the nature of the compulsions. In Saudi Arabia and Egypt, obsessions are primarily related to religious practices, specifically the Muslim emphasis on cleanliness. Contamination themes are also highly prevalent in India. Nevertheless, OCD looks remarkably similar across cultures. Insel (1984) reviewed studies from England, Hong Kong, India, Egypt, Japan, and Norway and found essentially similar types and proportions of obsessions and compulsions, as did Weissman and colleagues (1994) reviewing studies from Canada, Finland, Taiwan, Africa, Puerto Rico, Korea, and New Zealand.

Causes

Many of us sometimes have intrusive, even horrific thoughts and occasionally engage in ritualistic behavior, especially when we are under stress (Parkinson & Rachman, 1981a, 1981b). But few of us develop OCD. Again, as with panic disorder and PTSD, someone must develop anxiety focused on the possibility of having additional intrusive thoughts.

TABLE 5.11 Obsessions and Intrusive Thoughts Reported by Nonclinical Samples*

Harming

Impulse to jump out of high window

Idea of jumping in front of a car

Impulse to push someone in front of train

Wishing a person would die

While holding a baby, having a sudden urge to kick it

Thoughts of dropping a baby

The thought that if I forget to say goodbye to someone, they might die

Thought that thinking about horrible things happening to a child will cause it

Contamination or Disease

Thought of catching a disease from public pools or other public places

Thoughts I may have caught a disease from touching toilet seat

Idea that dirt is always on my hand

Inappropriate or Unacceptable Behavior

Idea of swearing or yelling at my boss

Thought of doing something embarrassing in public, like forgetting to wear a top

Hoping someone doesn't succeed

Thought of blurting out something in church

Thought of "unnatural" sexual acts

Doubts About Safety, Memory, and So On

Thought that I haven't locked the house up properly

Idea of leaving my curling iron on the carpet and forgetting to pull out the plug

Thought that I've left the heater and stove on

Idea that I've left the car unlocked when I know I've locked it

Idea that objects are not arranged perfectly

*Examples were obtained from Rachman and deSilva (1978) and from unpublished research by Dana Thordarson, Ph.D., and Michael Kyrios, Ph.D. (personal communications, 2000). Source: Reprinted, with permission, from Steketee, G., & Barlow, D. H. (2002). Obsessive-compulsive disorder. In D. H. Barlow, *Anxiety and its disorders: The nature and treatment of anxiety and panic* (2nd ed., p. 529), © 2002 Guilford Press.

The repetitive, intrusive, unacceptable thoughts of OCD may well be regulated by the hypothetical brain circuit described in Chapter 2. However, the tendency to develop anxiety over having additional compulsive thoughts may have the same generalized biological and psychological precursors as anxiety in general (Suàrez et al., in press).

Why would people with OCD focus their anxiety on the occasional intrusive thought rather than on the possibility of a panic attack or some other external situation? One hypothesis is that early experiences taught them that some thoughts are dangerous and unacceptable because the terrible things they are thinking might happen and they would be responsible. The experiences would result in a specific psychological vulnerability to

develop OCD. They learn this through the same process of misinformation that convinced the person with snake phobia that snakes were dangerous and could be everywhere. Clients with OCD equate thoughts with the specific actions or activity represented by the thoughts. This is called *thought–action fusion*. Thought–action fusion may, in turn, be caused by attitudes of excessive responsibility and resulting guilt developed during childhood when even a bad thought is associated with evil intent (Clark & O'Connor, 2005; Salkovskis, Shafran, Rachman, & Freeston, 1999; Steketee & Barlow, 2002). One patient believed thinking about abortion was the moral equivalent of having an abortion. Richard finally admitted to having strong homosexual impulses that were unacceptable to him and to his minister father, and he believed the impulses were as sinful as actual acts. Many people with OCD who believe in the tenets of fundamental religions, whether Christian, Jewish, or Islamic, present with similar attitudes of inflated responsibility and thought–action fusion. Several studies showed that the strength of religious belief, but not the type of belief, was associated with thought–action fusion and severity of OCD (Rassin & Koster, 2003; Steketee, Quay, & White, 1991). Of course, most people with fundamental beliefs do not develop OCD. But what if the most frightening thing in your life was not a snake, or speaking in public, but a terrible thought that happened to pop into your head? You can't avoid it as you would a snake, so you resist this thought by attempting to suppress it or "neutralize" it using mental or behavioral strategies, such as distraction, praying, or checking. These strategies become compulsions, but they are doomed to fail in the long term, because these strategies backfire and actually increase the frequency of the thought (Purdon, 1999; Wegner, 1989). Again, generalized biological and psychological vulnerabilities must be present for this disorder to develop. Believing some thoughts are unacceptable and therefore must be suppressed (a specific psychological vulnerability) may put people at greater risk of OCD (Amir, Cashman, & Foa, 1997; Parkinson & Rachman, 1981b; Salkovskis & Campbell, 1994). A model of the etiology of OCD that is somewhat similar to other models of anxiety disorders is presented in ■ Figure 5.15.

Treatment

Studies evaluating the effects of drugs on OCD are showing some promise (Steketee & Barlow, 2002; Zohar et al., 1996). The most effective seem to be those that specifically inhibit the reuptake of serotonin, such as clomipramine or the SSRIs, which benefit up to 60% of patients with OCD, with no particular advantage to one drug over another. However, the average treatment gain is moderate at best (Greist, 1990), and relapse often occurs when the drug is discontinued (Lydiard, Brawman-Mintzer, & Ballenger, 1996).

Highly structured psychological treatments work somewhat better than drugs, but they are not readily available. The most effective approach is called *exposure and ritual prevention (ERP),* a process whereby the rituals are actively prevented and the patient is systematically and gradually exposed to the feared thoughts or situations (Barlow & Lehman, 1996; Foa & Franklin, 2001; Steketee & Barlow, 2002). Richard would be systematically ex-

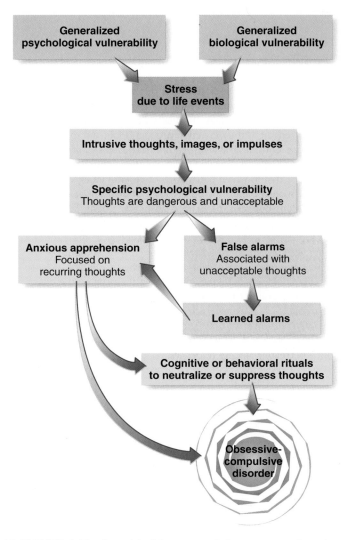

■ **FIGURE 5.15** A model of the causes of obsessive-compulsive disorder. (Reprinted, with permission, from Steketee, G., & Barlow, D. H., 2002. Obsessive-compulsive disorder. In *Anxiety and its disorders: The nature and treatment of anxiety and panic* (2nd ed., p. 536). New York: Guilford Press, © 2002 Guilford Press.)

posed to harmless objects or situations that he thought were contaminated, including certain foods and household chemicals, and his washing and checking rituals would be prevented. Usually this can be done by simply working closely with patients to see that they do not wash or check. In severe cases, patients may be hospitalized and the faucets removed from the bathroom sink for a period to discourage repeated washing. However the rituals are prevented, the procedures seem to facilitate "reality testing," because the client soon learns, at an emotional level, that no harm will result whether he carries out the rituals or not. Studies are now available examining the combined effects of medication and psychological treatments. In the largest study to date (Foa et al., 2005), ERP was compared to the drug clomipramine, as well as to a combined condition. ERP, with or without the drug, produced superior results to the drug alone, with 86% responding to ERP alone versus 48% to the drug alone. Combining the treatments did not produce any additional advantage. Also, relapse rates were high from the medication-only group when the drug was withdrawn.

Psychosurgery is one of the more radical treatments for OCD. "Psychosurgery" is a misnomer that refers to neurosurgery for a psychological disorder. Jenike and colleagues (1991) reviewed the records of 33 patients with OCD, most of them extremely severe cases who had failed to respond to either drug or psychological treatment. After a specific surgical lesion to the cingulate bundle (cingulotomy), approximately 30% benefited substantially. Considering that these patients seemed to have no hope from other treatments, surgery deserves consideration as a last resort. Each year, we understand more about the causes of OCD, and our treatments are improving. Before long, such radical treatments as psychosurgery will no longer be employed.

CONCEPT CHECK 5.6

Fill in the blanks to form facts about OCD.

1. _____ are intrusive and nonsensical thoughts, images, or urges an individual tries to eliminate or suppress.
2. The practices of washing, counting, and hoarding to suppress obsessions and provide relief are called _____ _____.
3. The lifetime prevalence of OCD is approximately _____, or even lower.
4. _____ is a radical treatment for OCD involving a surgical lesion to the cingulate bundle.

FUTURE DIRECTIONS

Drugs That Make Psychological Treatments Work Better

Until now, many clinicians combined the use of both drugs and psychological interventions to treat anxiety disorders. Surprisingly, recent research has shown that combining these treatments does not produce any added benefit for treating anxiety. That is, the combined treatments usually work only as well as each individual treatment in the anxiety disorders where this has been studied. Now research is beginning on a different drug that looks like it might enhance the effects of the best psychological interventions for anxiety disorders. This drug is called D-cycloserine (DCS), and it is an antibiotic that has been around a while but used mostly to treat bacterial infections or tuberculosis. But neuroscientists working in the laboratory, such as Michael Davis at Emory University, made some interesting discoveries about this drug. Davis found that when rats who had learned a fear response, by pairing a light with a brief electric shock, for example, were put into extinction trials in which the light that they had learned to fear was no longer paired with a frightening electric shock, an interesting thing happened. As always happens, the animals gradually learned not to fear the light (their fear extinguished), but providing them with the medication DCS during these extinction trials made extinction work faster and last longer (Walker, Ressler, Lu, & Davis,

2002). Further research indicated that this drug works in the amygdala, a structure in the brain very much implicated in the learning and unlearning of fear and anxiety. It affects neurotransmitter flow in a way that strengthens the extinction process (Hofmann, in press).

Most recently, several investigators have used this drug with humans. DCS is only given approximately an hour before the extinction or exposure trial in which patients practice interacting with people or giving a speech, depending on the form of their social anxiety. The individual does not take the drug in an ongoing basis. For example, Stefan Hofmann and his colleagues in our center (Hofmann et al., 2006) administered the most effective psychological intervention to patients with severe social anxiety either with or without the drug. (That is, one group got the drug and the other group got a placebo. The patients didn't know who was getting the drug or the placebo. Nor did the therapists know which group was getting the drug, making it a double-blind experiment.) The people who got the drug improved significantly more during treatment than those who didn't get the drug. If these results are replicated, we may have an important advance in treating anxiety disorders.

SUMMARY

The Complexity of Anxiety Disorders

- Anxiety is a future-oriented state characterized by negative affect in which a person focuses on the possibility of uncontrollable danger or misfortune; in contrast, fear is a present-oriented state characterized by strong escapist tendencies and a surge in the sympathetic branch of the autonomic nervous system in response to current danger.

- A panic attack represents the alarm response of real fear, but there is no actual danger.

- Panic attacks may be (1) unexpected (without warning), (2) situationally bound (always occurring in a specific situation), or (3) situationally predisposed (likely but unpredictable in a specific situation).

- Panic and anxiety combine to create different anxiety disorders.

Generalized Anxiety Disorder

- In generalized anxiety disorder (GAD), anxiety focuses on minor everyday events, not one major worry or concern.

- Both genetic and psychological vulnerabilities seem to contribute to the development of GAD.

- Although drug and psychological treatments may be effective in the short term, drug treatments are no more effective in the long term than placebo treatments. Successful treatment may help individuals with GAD focus on what is really threatening to them in their lives.

Panic Disorder With and Without Agoraphobia

- In panic disorder with or without agoraphobia (a fear and avoidance of situations considered to be "unsafe"), anxiety is focused on the next panic attack.

- We all have some genetic vulnerability to stress, and many of us have had a neurobiological overreaction to some stressful event—that is, a panic attack. Individuals who develop panic disorder then develop anxiety over the possibility of having another panic attack.

- Both drug and psychological treatments have proved successful in the treatment of panic disorder. One psychological method, panic control treatment, concentrates on exposing patients to clusters of sensations that remind them of their panic attacks.

Specific Phobia

- In phobic disorders, the individual avoids situations that produce severe anxiety, panic, or both. In specific phobia, the fear is focused on a particular object or situation.

- Phobias can be acquired by experiencing some traumatic event; they can also be learned vicariously or even be taught.

- Treatment of phobias is rather straightforward, with a focus on structured and consistent exposure-based exercises.

Social Phobia

- Social phobia is a fear of being around others, particularly in situations that call for some kind of "performance" in front of other people.
- Although the causes of social phobia are similar to those of specific phobias, treatment has a different focus that includes rehearsing or role-playing socially phobic situations. In addition, drug treatments have been effective.

Posttraumatic Stress Disorder

- Posttraumatic stress disorder (PTSD) focuses on avoiding thoughts or images of past traumatic experiences.
- The underlying cause of PTSD is obvious—a traumatic experience. But mere exposure is not enough. The intensity of the experience seems to be a factor in whether an individual develops PTSD; biological vulnerabilities, as well as social and cultural factors, appear to play a role as well.
- Treatment involves reexposing the victim to the trauma to overcome the debilitating effects of PTSD.

Obsessive-Compulsive Disorder

- Obsessive-compulsive disorder (OCD) focuses on avoiding frightening or repulsive intrusive thoughts (obsessions) or neutralizing these thoughts through the use of ritualistic behavior (compulsions).
- As with all anxiety disorders, biological and psychological vulnerabilities seem to be involved in the development of OCD.
- Drug treatment seems to be only modestly successful in treating OCD. The most effective treatment approach is exposure and response prevention.

Key Terms

anxiety, 121
fear, 122
panic, 122
panic attack, 122
behavioral inhibition system (BIS), 124
fight/flight system (FFS), 124
generalized anxiety disorder (GAD), 127

panic disorder with agoraphobia (PDA), 132
agoraphobia, 132
panic disorder without agoraphobia (PD), 133
panic control treatment (PCT), 139
specific phobia, 141

blood–injury–injection phobia, 142
situational phobia, 142
natural environment phobia, 142
animal phobia, 143
separation anxiety disorder, 143

social phobia, 148
posttraumatic stress disorder (PTSD), 152
acute stress disorder, 154
obsessive-compulsive disorder (OCD), 159
obsessions, 159
compulsions, 159

Answers to Concept Checks

5.1

1. b; 2. c; 3. e, d; 4. a; 5. f

5.2

1. T; 2. F (more gradual); 3. T; 4. F; 5. T

5.3

1. F (with agoraphobia); 2. F (3.5%); 3. T; 4. T

5.4

1. d; 2. e; 3. c; 4. f; 5. a; 6. d; 7. c

5.5

1. b; 2. a; 3. c

5.6

1. obsessions; 2. compulsions; 3. 1.6%; 4. psychosurgery

The Abnormal Psychology Book Companion Website

See **academic.cengage.com/psychology/barlow** for practice quiz questions, interactive activities, Internet links, critical thinking exercises, discussion forums, and more. Also accessible from the Wadsworth Psychology Resource Center **(academic.cengage .com/login).**

Abnormal Psychology Live CD-ROM

- *Steve, a Patient With Panic Disorder:* Steve discusses how panic attacks have disrupted his life.
- *Chuck, a Client With Obsessive-Compulsive Disorder:* Chuck discusses how his obsessions affect his everyday life, going to work, planning a vacation, and so on.
- *Virtual Reality Therapy:* A virtual reality program helps one woman overcome her fear of riding the subway.
- *Snake Phobia Treatment:* A demonstration of exposure therapy helps a snake phobic overcome her severe fear of snakes in just 3 hours.

CengageNOW

Go to **academic.cengage.com/now** to link to CengageNOW, your online study tool. First take the Pre-Test for this chapter to get your personalized study plan, which will identify topics you need to review and direct you to online resources. Then take the Post-Test to determine what concepts you have mastered and what you still need work on.

Video Concept Reviews

CengageNOW also contains Mark Durand's *Video Concept Reviews* on challenging topics.

- Anxiety
- Fear

- Characteristics of Anxiety Disorders
- Panic
- Panic Attacks
- Generalized Anxiety Disorder (GAD)—Description
- Panic Disorder
- Panic Control Treatment
- Concept Check: Medical Versus Psychological Treatment
- Specific Phobia
- Phobia Subtypes
- Social Phobia
- Posttraumatic Stress Disorder (PTSD)
- Obsessive-Compulsive Disorder (OCD)

Exploring Anxiety Disorders

People with anxiety disorders:
- *Feel overwhelming tension, apprehension, or fear when there is no actual danger*
- *May take extreme action to avoid the source of their anxiety*

Biological Influences
- Inherited vulnerability to experience anxiety and/or panic attacks
- Activation of specific brain circuits, neurotransmitters, and neurohormonal systems

TRIGGER

Social Influences
- Social support reduces intensity of physical and emotional reactions to triggers or stress
- Lack of social support intensifies symptoms

CAUSES

Behavioral Influences
- Marked avoidance of situations and/or people associated with fear, anxiety, or panic attack

Emotional and Cognitive Influences
- Heightened sensitivity to situations or people perceived as threats
- Unconscious feeling that physical symptoms of panic are catastrophic (intensifies physical reaction)

TREATMENT FOR ANXIETY DISORDERS

Cognitive-Behavioral Therapy
- Systematic exposure to anxiety-provoking situations or thoughts
- Learning to substitute positive behaviors and thoughts for negative ones
- Learning new coping skills: relaxation exercises, controlled breathing, etc.

Drug Treatment
- Reduces the symptoms of anxiety disorders by influencing brain chemistry
  —antidepressants (Tofranil, Paxil, Effexor)
  —benzodiazepines (Xanax, Klonopin)

Other Treatments
- Managing stress through a healthy lifestyle: rest, exercise, nutrition, social support, and moderate alcohol or other drug intake

TYPES OF ANXIETY DISORDERS

Panic Disorders

People with panic disorders have had one or more panic attacks and are anxious and fearful about having future attacks.

What is a panic attack?
A person having a panic attack feels:
- Apprehension leading to intense fear
- Sensation of "going crazy" or of losing control
- Physical signs of distress: racing heartbeat, rapid breathing, dizziness, nausea, or sensation of heart attack or imminent death

When/why do panic attacks occur?
Panic attacks can be:
- *Situationally bound:* Always occurring in the same situation, which may lead to extreme avoidance of triggering people, places, or events (see specific and social phobias)
- *Unexpected:* Can lead to extreme avoidance of any situation or place felt to be unsafe (agoraphobia)
- *Situationally predisposed:* Attacks may or may not occur in specific situations (between situationally bound and unexpected)

Phobias

People with phobias avoid situations that produce severe anxiety and/or panic. There are three main types:

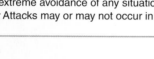

Agoraphobia
- Fear and avoidance of situations, people, or places where it would be unsafe to have a panic attack: malls, grocery stores, buses, planes, tunnels, etc.
- In the extreme, inability to leave the house or even a specific room
- Begins after a panic attack but can continue for years even if no other attacks occur

Specific Phobia
- Fear of specific object or situation that triggers attack: heights, closed spaces, insects, snakes, or flying
- Develops from personal or vicarious experience of traumatic event with the triggering object or situation or from misinformation

Social Phobia
Fear of being called for some kind of "performance" that may be judged: speaking in public, using a public restroom (for males), or generally interacting with people

Other Types of Anxiety Disorders

Generalized Anxiety Disorder
- Uncontrollable unproductive worrying about everyday events
- Feeling impending catastrophe even after successes
- Inability to stop the worry–anxiety cycle: e.g., Irene's fear of failure about school relationships and health even though everything seemed fine
- Physical symptoms of muscle tension

Posttraumatic Stress Disorder
- Fear of reexperiencing a traumatic event: rape, war, life-threatening situation, etc.
- Nightmares or flashbacks (of the traumatic event)
- Avoidance of the intense feelings of the event through emotional numbing

Obsessive-Compulsive Disorder
- Fear of unwanted and intrusive thoughts (obsessions)
- Repeated ritualistic actions or thoughts (compulsions) designed to neutralize the unwanted thoughts: e.g., Richard's attempts to suppress "dangerous" thoughts about sex, aggression, and religion with compulsive washing and cleaning rituals

Somatoform and Dissociative Disorders

© Dennis MacDonald/Alamy

SOMATOFORM DISORDERS
Hypochondriasis
Somatization Disorder
Conversion Disorder
Pain Disorder
Body Dysmorphic Disorder

DISSOCIATIVE DISORDERS
Depersonalization Disorder
Dissociative Amnesia

Dissociative Fugue
Dissociative Trance Disorder
Dissociative Identity Disorder

 ABNORMAL PSYCHOLOGY LIVE CD-ROM
Dissociative Identity Disorder: Rachel
Body Dysmorphic Disorder: Doug
Web Link

Why I became more afraid of living and of dying than others will forever remain an enigma.

Carla Cantor

Phantom Illness: Shattering the Myth of Hypochondria

Do you know somebody who's a hypochondriac? Most of us do. Maybe it's you! The popular image of hypochondria is of someone who exaggerates the slightest physical symptom. Many people continually run to the doctor even though there is nothing really wrong with them. This is usually a harmless tendency that may even be worth some good-natured jokes. But for a few individuals, the preoccupation with their health or appearance becomes so great that it dominates their lives. Their problems fall under the general heading of **somatoform disorders.** *Soma* means body, and the problems preoccupying these people seem, initially, to be physical disorders. What the disorders have in common is that there is usually no identifiable medical condition causing the physical complaints.

Have you ever felt "detached" from yourself or your surroundings? ("This isn't really me," or "That doesn't really look like my hand," or "There's something unreal about this place.") During these experiences, some people feel as if they are dreaming. These mild sensations that most people experience occasionally are slight alterations, or detachments, in consciousness or identity, and they are known as *dissociation* or *dissociative experiences.* For a few people, these experiences are so intense and extreme that they lose their identity entirely and assume a new one or they lose their memory or sense of reality and are unable to function. We discuss several types of **dissociative disorders** in the second half of this chapter.

Somatoform and dissociative disorders are strongly linked historically, and increasing evidence indicates they share common features (Kihlstrom, 1994; Prelior, Yutzy, Dean, & Wetzel, 1993). They used to be categorized under one general heading, "hysterical neurosis." You may remember (from Chapter 1) that the term *hysteria,* which dates back to the Greek, Hippocrates, and the Egyptians before him, suggests that the cause of these disorders, which were thought to occur primarily in women, can be traced to a "wandering uterus." But the term *hysterical* came to refer more generally to physical symptoms without known organic cause or to dramatic or "histrionic" behavior thought to be characteristic of women. Sigmund Freud (1894–1962) suggested that in a condition called *conversion hysteria* unexplained physical symptoms indicated the conversion of unconscious emotional conflicts into a more acceptable form. The historical term *conversion* remains with us (without the theoretical implications); however, the prejudicial and stigmatizing term *hysterical* is no longer used.

The term *neurosis,* as defined in psychoanalytic theory, suggested a specific cause for certain disorders. Specifically, neurotic disorders resulted from underlying unconscious conflicts, anxiety that resulted from those conflicts, and the implementation of ego defense mechanisms. *Neurosis* was eliminated from the diagnostic system in 1980 because it was too vague, applying to almost all nonpsychotic disorders, and because it implied a specific but unproven cause for these disorders.

Somatoform and dissociative disorders are not well understood, but they have intrigued psychopathologists and the public for centuries. A fuller understanding provides a rich perspective on the extent to which normal, everyday traits found in all of us can evolve into distorted, strange, and incapacitating disorders.

SOMATOFORM DISORDERS

The fourth edition, text revision, of the *Diagnostic and Statistical Manual of Mental Disorders* (DSM-IV-TR) lists five basic somatoform disorders: hypochondriasis, somatization disorder, conversion disorder, pain disorder, and body dysmorphic disorder. In each, individuals are pathologically concerned with the appearance or functioning of their bodies.

Hypochondriasis

Like many terms in psychopathology, **hypochondriasis** has ancient roots. To the Greeks, the *hypochondria* was the region below the ribs, and the organs in this region affected mental state. For example, ulcers and abdominal disorders were once considered part of the hypochondriac syndrome. As the actual causes of such disorders were discovered, physical complaints without a clear cause continued to be labeled *hypochondriasis* (Barsky, Wyshak, & Klerman, 1986). In hypochondriasis, severe anxiety is focused on the possibility of having a serious disease. The threat seems so real that reassurance from physicians does not seem to help. Consider the case of Gail.

GAIL: Invisibly Ill

Gail was married at 21 and looked forward to a new life. As one of many children in a lower-middle-class household, she felt weak and somewhat neglected and suffered from low self-esteem. An older stepbrother berated and belittled her when he was drunk. Her mother and stepfather refused to listen to her or believe her complaints. But she believed that marriage would solve everything; she was finally someone special. Unfortunately, it didn't work out that way. She soon discovered her husband was continuing an affair with an old girlfriend.

Three years after her wedding, Gail came to our clinic complaining of anxiety and stress. She was working part-time as a waitress and found her job extremely stressful. Although to the best of her knowledge her husband had stopped seeing his former girlfriend, she had trouble getting the affair out of her mind.

Although Gail complained initially of anxiety and stress, it soon became clear that her major concerns were about her health. Any time she experienced minor physical symptoms such as breathlessness or a headache, she was afraid she had a serious illness. A headache indicated a brain tumor. Breathlessness was an impending heart attack. Other sensations were quickly elaborated into the possibility of AIDS or cancer. Gail was afraid to go to sleep at night for fear that she would stop breathing. She avoided exercise, drinking, and even laughing because the resulting sensations upset her. Public restrooms and, on occasion, public telephones were feared as sources of infection.

The major trigger of uncontrollable anxiety and fear was the news in the newspaper and on television. Each time an article or show appeared on the "disease of the month," Gail found herself irresistibly drawn into it, intently noting symptoms that were part of the disease. For days afterward she was vigilant, looking for the symptoms in herself and others. She even watched her dog closely to see whether he was coming down with the dreaded disease. Only with great effort could she dismiss these thoughts after several days. Real illness in a friend or relative would incapacitate her for days at a time.

Gail's fears developed during the first year of her marriage, around the time she learned of her husband's affair. At first, she spent a great deal of time and more money than they could afford going to doctors. Over the years, she heard the same thing during each visit: "There's nothing wrong with you; you're perfectly healthy." Finally, she stopped going, as she became convinced her concerns were excessive, but her fears did not go away and she was chronically miserable.

■ Clinical Description

Gail's problems are fairly typical of hypochondriasis. Research indicates that hypochondriasis shares many features with the anxiety and mood disorders, particularly panic disorder (Craske et al., 1996; Creed & Barsky, 2004), including similar age of onset, personality characteristics, and patterns of familial aggregation (running in families). Indeed, anxiety and mood disorders are often comorbid with hypochondriasis; that is, if individuals with a hypochondriacal disorder have additional diagnoses, these most likely are anxiety or mood disorders (Côté et al., 1996; Creed & Barsky, 2004; Rief, Hiller, & Margraf, 1998; Simon, Gureje, & Fullerton, 2001).

Hypochondriasis is characterized by anxiety or fear that one has a serious disease. Therefore, the essential problem is anxiety, but its expression is different from that of the other anxiety disorders. In hypochondriasis, the individual is preoccupied with bodily symptoms, misinterpreting them as indicative of illness or disease. Almost any physical sensation may become the basis for concern for individuals with hypochondriasis. Some may focus on normal bodily functions such as heart rate or perspiration, others on minor physical abnormalities such as a cough. Some individuals complain of vague symptoms, such as aches or fatigue. Because a key feature of this disorder is preoccupation with physical symptoms, individuals with hypochondriasis almost always go initially to family physicians. They come to the attention of mental health professionals only after family physicians have ruled out realistic medical conditions as a cause.

Another important feature of hypochondriasis is that reassurances from numerous doctors that all is well and the individual is healthy have, at best, only a short-term effect. It isn't long before patients like Gail are back in the office of another doctor on the assumption that the previous doctors have missed something. In studying this feature for purposes of modifying the diagnostic criteria in DSM-IV-TR, researchers confirmed a subtle but interesting distinction (Côté et al., 1996; Craske et al., 1996; Kellner, Hernandez, & Pathak, 1992). Individuals who fear *developing* a disease, and therefore avoid situations they associate with contagion, are different from those who are anxious that they *have* the disease. Individuals who have marked fear of developing a disease are classified as having an *illness phobia* (see Chapter 5). Individuals who mistakenly believe they have a disease are diagnosed with hypochondriasis. These two groups differ further. Individuals with high disease conviction are more likely to misinterpret physical symptoms and display higher rates of checking behaviors and trait anxiety than individuals with illness phobia (Côté et al., 1996; Haenen, de Jong, Schmidt, Stevens, & Visser, 2000). Individuals with illness phobia have an earlier age of onset than those with disease conviction. Disease conviction has become the core feature of hypochondriasis. Some people may have both a disease conviction and a fear of developing additional diseases (Kellner, 1986). In one study, 60% of a group of patients with illness phobia went on to develop hypochondriasis, as well as panic disorder (Benedetti et al., 1997).

If you have just read Chapter 5, you may think that patients with panic disorder resemble patients with hypochondriasis. Patients with panic disorder also misinterpret physical symptoms as the beginning of the next panic attack, which they believe may kill them. Craske and colleagues (1996) and Hiller, Leibbrand, Rief, and Fichter (2005) suggested several differences. Although both disorders include characteristic concern with physical symptoms, patients with panic disorder typically fear immediate symptom-related catastrophes that may occur during the few minutes they are having a panic attack, and these concerns lessen between attacks. Individuals with hypochondriacal concerns, on the other hand, focus on a long-term process of illness and disease (for example, cancer or AIDS). Hypochondriacal patients also continue to seek the opinions of additional doctors in an attempt to rule out (or perhaps confirm) a disease process and are more likely to demand unnecessary medical treatments. Despite numerous assurances that they are healthy, they remain unconvinced and unreassured. In contrast, panic patients continue to believe their panic attacks might kill them, but most learn rather quickly to stop going to doctors and emergency rooms, where they are told repeatedly that nothing is wrong with them. Finally, the anxieties of individuals with panic disorder tend to focus on the specific set of 10 or 15 sympathetic nervous system symptoms associated with a panic attack. Hypochondriacal concerns range much wider. Nevertheless, there are probably more similarities than differences between these groups.

Minor, seemingly hypochondriacal concerns are common in young children, who often complain of abdominal aches and pains that do not seem to have a physical basis. In most cases, these complaints are passing responses to stress and do not develop into a full-blown chronic hypochondriacal syndrome.

DSM-IV-TR

DSM TABLE 6.1   Diagnostic Criteria for Hypochondriasis

A. Preoccupation with fears of having, or the idea that one has, a serious disease based on the person's misinterpretation of bodily symptoms.

B. The preoccupation persists despite appropriate medical evaluation and reassurance.

C. The belief in criterion A is not of delusional intensity (as in delusional disorder, somatic type) and is not restricted to a circumscribed concern about appearance (as in body dysmorphic disorder).

D. The preoccupation causes clinically significant distress or impairment in social, occupational, or other important areas of functioning.

E. The duration of the disturbance is at least 6 months.

F. The preoccupation is not better accounted for by generalized anxiety disorder, obsessive-compulsive disorder, panic disorder, a major depressive episode, separation anxiety, or another somatoform disorder.

Specify if:

With poor insight: If, for most of the time during the current episode, the person does not recognize that the concern about having a serious illness is excessive or unreasonable

Source: Reprinted, with permission, from American Psychiatric Association. (2000). *Diagnostic and statistical manual of mental disorders* (4th ed., text revision). Washington, DC: Author. © 2000 American Psychiatric Association.

■ Statistics

We know little about the prevalence of hypochondriasis in the general population. Early estimates indicate that anywhere between 1% and 14% of medical patients are diagnosed with hypochondriasis (Barsky, Wyshak, Klerman, & Latham, 1990). A recent review of five studies in primary care settings suggests that the median prevalence rate for hypochondriasis in these settings is 6.7% (Creed & Barsky, 2004). Although historically considered one of the "hysterical" disorders unique to women, the sex ratio is actually 50-50 (Creed & Barsky, 2004; Kellner, 1986; Kirmayer & Robbins, 1991; Kirmayer et al., 2003). It was thought for a long time that hypochondriasis was more prevalent in elderly populations, but this does not seem to be true (Barsky, Frank, Cleary, Wyshak, & Klerman, 1991). In fact, hypochondriasis is spread fairly evenly across various phases of adulthood. Naturally, more elderly people go to see physicians, making the *absolute number* of patients with hypochondriasis in this age group somewhat higher than in the younger population, but the proportion of all those seeing a doctor who have hypochondriasis is about the same. Hypochondriasis may emerge at any time of life, with the peak age periods found in adolescence, middle age (40s and 50s), and after age 60 (Kellner, 1986). As with most anxiety and mood disorders, hypochondriasis is chronic. In one study (Barsky, Fama, Bailey, & Ahern, 1998), a large group of more than 100 patients with hypochondriasis was followed for 4 to 5 years, as was a comparable nonhypochondriacal patient group from the same setting. Two-thirds of the patients still met criteria for the diagnosis of hypochondriasis, and these patients remained significantly more symptomatic than the comparison group. Other studies have found similar or somewhat lower percentages (Creed & Barsky, 2004).

As with anxiety disorders, culture-specific syndromes seem to fit comfortably with hypochondriasis. Among these is the disorder of *koro,* in which there is the belief, accompanied by severe anxiety and sometimes panic, that the genitals are retracting into the abdomen. Most victims of this disorder are Chinese males, although it is also reported in females; there are few reports of the problem in Western cultures. Why does *koro* occur in Chinese cultures? Rubin (1982) points to the central importance of sexual functioning among Chinese males. He notes that typical sufferers are guilty about excessive masturbation, unsatisfactory intercourse, or promiscuity. These kinds of events may predispose men to focus their attention on their sexual organs, which could exacerbate anxiety and emotional arousal, much as it does in the anxiety disorders, thereby setting off an "epidemic."

Another culture-specific disorder, prevalent in India, is an anxious concern about losing semen, something that obviously occurs during sexual activity. The disorder, called *dhat,* is associated with a vague mix of physical symptoms, including dizziness, weakness, and fatigue, that are not so specific as those in *koro.* These low-grade depressive or anxious symptoms are simply attributed to a physical factor, semen loss (Ranjith & Mohan, 2004). Other specific culture-bound somatic symptoms associated with emotional factors would include hot sensations in the head or a sensation of something crawling in the head, specific to African patients (Ebigno, 1986), and a sensation of burning in the hands and feet in Pakistani or Indian patients (Kirmayer & Weiss, 1993).

Somatic symptoms may be among the more challenging manifestations of psychopathology. First, a physician must rule out a physical cause for the somatic complaints before referring the patient to a mental health professional. Second, the mental health professional must determine the nature of the somatic complaints to know whether they are associated with a specific somatoform disorder or are part of some other psychopathological syndrome, such as a panic attack. Third, the clinician must be acutely aware of the specific culture or subculture of the patient, which often requires consultation with experts in cross-cultural presentations of psychopathology.

©Michael Newman/PhotoEdit

In hypochondriasis, normal experiences and sensations are often transformed into life-threatening illnesses.

■ Causes

Investigators with generally differing points of view agree on psychopathological processes ongoing in hypochondriasis. Faulty interpretation of physical signs and sensations as evidence of physical illness is central, so almost everyone agrees that hypochondriasis is basically a disorder of cognition or perception with strong emotional contributions (Adler, Côte, Barlow, & Hillhouse, 1994; Barsky & Wyshak, 1990; Kellner, 1985; Rief et al., 1998; Salkovskis & Clark, 1993; Taylor & Asmundson, 2004).

Individuals with hypochondriasis experience physical sensations common to all of us, but they quickly focus their attention on these sensations. Remember that the very act of focusing on yourself increases arousal and makes the physical sensations seem more intense than they are (see Chapter 5). If you also tend to misinterpret these as symptoms of illness, your anxiety will increase further. Increased anxiety produces additional physical symptoms, in a vicious cycle (see ■ Figure 6.1) (Salkovskis, Warwick, & Deale, 2003; Warwick & Salkovskis, 1990).

Using procedures from cognitive science such as the Stroop test (see Chapter 2), a number of investigators (Hitchcock & Mathews, 1992; Pauli & Alpers, 2002) have confirmed that subjects with hypochondriasis show enhanced perceptual sensitivity to illness cues. They also tend to interpret ambiguous stimuli as threatening (Haenen et al., 2000). Thus, they quickly become aware (and frightened) of any sign of possible illness or disease. A minor headache, for example, might be interpreted as a sure sign of a brain tumor. Smeets, de Jong, and Mayer (2000) demonstrated that individuals with hypochondriasis, compared to "normals," take a "better safe than sorry" approach to dealing with even minor physical symptoms by getting them checked out as soon as possible. More fundamentally, they have a restrictive concept of health as being symptom free (Rief et al., 1998).

What causes individuals to develop this pattern of somatic sensitivity and distorted beliefs? Although it is not certain, it is safe to say the solution is unlikely to be found in isolated biological or psychological factors. There is every reason to believe the fundamental causes of hypochondriasis are similar to those implicated in the anxiety disorders. For example, evidence shows that hypochondriasis runs in families (Kellner, 1985), suggesting (but not proving) a possible genetic contribution. But this contribution may be nonspecific, such as a tendency to overrespond to stress, and thus may be indistinguishable from the nonspecific genetic contribution to anxiety disorders. Hyperresponsivity might combine with a tendency to view negative life events as unpredictable and uncontrollable and, therefore, to be guarded against at all times (Noyes et al., 2004). As we noted in Chapter 5, these factors would constitute biological and psychological vulnerabilities to anxiety.

Why does this anxiety focus on physical sensations and illness? We know that children with hypochondriacal concerns often report the same kinds of symptoms that other family members may have reported at one time (Kellner, 1985; Kirmayer et al., 2003; Pilowsky, 1970). It is therefore quite possible, as in panic disorder, that individuals who develop hypochondriasis have *learned* from family members to focus their anxiety on specific physical conditions and illness.

Three other factors may contribute to this etiological process (Côte et al., 1996; Kellner, 1985). First, hypochondriasis seems to develop in the context of a stressful life event, as do many disorders, including anxiety disorders. Such events often involve death or illness (Noyes et al., 2004; Sandin, Chorot, Santed, & Valiente, 2004). (Gail's traumatic first year of marriage seemed to coincide with the beginning of her disorder.) Second, people who develop hypochondriasis tend to have had a disproportionate incidence of disease in their family when they were children. Thus, even if they did not develop hypochondriasis until adulthood, they carry strong memories of illness that could easily become the focus of anxiety. Third, an important social and interpersonal influence may be operating (Noyes et al., 2003). Some people who come from families where illness is a major issue seem to have learned

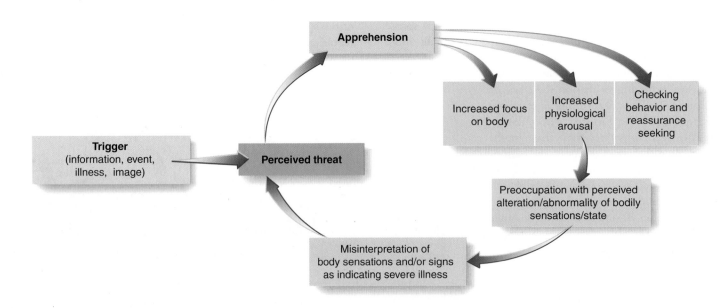

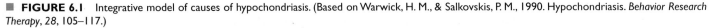

■ **FIGURE 6.1** Integrative model of causes of hypochondriasis. (Based on Warwick, H. M., & Salkovskis, P. M., 1990. Hypochondriasis. *Behavior Research Therapy, 28,* 105–117.)

that an ill person is often paid increased attention. The "benefits" of being sick might contribute to the development of the disorder. A "sick person" who thus receives more attention and less responsibility is described as adopting a "sick role." These issues may be even more significant in somatization disorder.

■ Treatment

Unfortunately, relatively little is known about treating hypochondriasis. Although it is common clinical practice to uncover unconscious conflicts through psychodynamic psychotherapy, results on the effectiveness of this kind of treatment have seldom been reported. In one study, Ladee (1966) noted that only 4 of 23 patients seemed to derive any benefit.

Scientifically controlled studies have appeared only recently (Taylor, Asmundson, & Coons, 2005). Surprisingly, clinical reports indicate that reassurance and education seems to be effective in some cases (Haenen et al., 2000; Kellner, 1992)—"surprisingly" because, by definition, patients with hypochondriasis are not supposed to benefit from reassurance about their health. However, reassurance is usually given only briefly by family doctors who have little time to provide the ongoing support and reassurance that might be necessary. Mental health professionals may well be able to offer reassurance in a more effective and sensitive manner, devote sufficient time to all concerns the patient may have, and attend to the "meaning" of the symptoms (for example, their relation to the patient's life stress). Fava, Grandi, Rafanelli, Fabbri, and Cazzaro (2000) tested this idea by assigning 20 patients who met diagnostic criteria for hypochondriasis to two groups. One received "explanatory therapy" in which the clinician went over the source and origins of their symptoms in some detail. These patients were assessed immediately after the therapy and again at a 6-month follow-up. The other group was a wait-list control group that did not receive the explanatory therapy until after their 6 months of waiting. All patients received usual medical care from their physicians. In both groups, taking the time to explain in some detail the nature of the patient's disorder in an educational framework was associated with a significant reduction in hypochondriacal fears and beliefs and a decrease in health-care usage, and these gains were maintained at the follow-up. For the wait-list group, treatment gains did not occur until they received explanatory therapy, suggesting this treatment is effective. Although this is a small study and follow-ups occurred only for 6 months, the results are promising, but, most likely, only benefit those with more mild forms of hypochondriasis (Taylor et al., 2005). Participation in support groups may also give these people the reassurance they need.

Evaluations of more robust treatments are beginning to appear. Warwick, Clark, Cobb, and Salkovskis (1996) randomly assigned 32 patients to either cognitive-behavioral treatment (CBT) or a no-treatment wait-list control group. Treatment focused on identifying and challenging illness-related misinterpretations of physical sensations and on showing patients how to create "symptoms" by focusing attention on certain body areas. Bringing on their own symptoms persuaded many patients that such events were under their control. Patients were also coached to seek less reassurance regarding their concerns. Patients in the treatment group improved an average of 76%, and those in the wait-list group

improved only 5%; benefits were maintained for 3 months. Clark and colleagues (1998) replicated this result in a larger study and also found that a general stress-management treatment (see Chapter 9) was substantially more effective than assignment to the wait-list group. Both the CBT and stress-management treatment retained their gain at 1 year follow-up. In the most ambitious and well-done study to date, Barsky and Ahern (2005) randomized 187 patients with hypochondriasis to receive either six sessions of CBT from trained therapists, similar to that tested by Warwick and colleagues (1996), described earlier, or treatment as usual from primary care physicians. Results can be seen in ■ Figure 6.2 as scores on the Whiteley index of hypochondriacal symptoms. CBT was more effective after treatment and at each follow-up point for both symptoms of hypochondriasis and overall changes in functioning and quality of life. But results were still "modest," and many eligible patients refused to enter treatment because they were convinced their problems were medical rather than psychological.

A few recent reports suggest that drugs may help some people (Fallon et al., 2003; Kjernisted, Enns, & Lander, 2002; Taylor et al., 2005). Not surprisingly, these same types of drugs (antidepressants) are useful for anxiety and depression. In one recent study, CBT and the drug paroxetine (Paxil), a serotonin-specific reuptake inhibitor (SSRI), were both effective, but only CBT was significantly different from a placebo condition. Specifically 45% in the CBT group, 30% in the Paxil group, and 14% in the placebo group responded to treatment among all patients who entered the study (Van Balkom et al. 2007). It is likely we will see more research on the treatment of hypochondriasis in the future.

Somatization Disorder

In 1859, Pierre Briquet, a French physician, described patients who came to see him with seemingly endless lists of somatic complaints for which he could find no medical basis (American

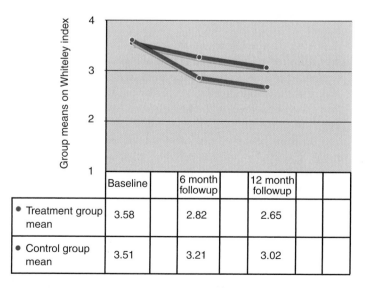

	Baseline	6 month followup	12 month followup	
● Treatment group mean	3.58	2.82	2.65	
● Control group mean	3.51	3.21	3.02	

■ **FIGURE 6.2**   Reduction in symptoms of hypochondriasis after six sessions of CBT or medical care as usual. (Adapted from Barsky, A. J., & Ahern, D. K., 2005. Cognitive behavior therapy for hypochondriasis: A randomized controlled trial. *JAMA, 291*, 1464-1470.)

Psychiatric Association, 1980). Despite his negative findings, patients returned shortly with either the same complaints or new lists containing slight variations. For more than 100 years, this disorder was called *Briquet's syndrome,* before being changed in 1980 to **somatization disorder.** Consider the case of Linda.

LINDA: Full-Time Patient

Linda, an intelligent woman in her 30s, came to our clinic looking distressed and pained. As she sat down she noted that coming into the office was difficult for her because she had trouble breathing and considerable swelling in the joints of her legs and arms. She was also in some pain from chronic urinary tract infections and might have to leave at any moment to go to the restroom, but she was extremely happy she had kept the appointment. At least she was seeing someone who could help alleviate her considerable suffering. She said she knew we would have to go through a detailed initial interview, but she had something that might save time. At this point, she pulled out several sheets of paper and handed them over. One section, some five pages long, described her contacts with the health-care system for *major difficulties only.* Times, dates, potential diagnoses, and days hospitalized were noted. The second section, one-and-a-half single-spaced pages, consisted of a list of all medications she had taken for various complaints.

Linda felt she had any one of a number of chronic infections that nobody could properly diagnose. She had begun to have these problems in her teenage years. She often discussed her symptoms and fears with doctors and clergy. Drawn to hospitals and medical clinics, she had entered nursing school after high school. However, during hospital training, she noticed her physical condition deteriorating rapidly: She seemed to pick up the diseases she was learning about. A series of stressful emotional events resulted in her leaving nursing school.

After developing unexplained paralysis in her legs, Linda was admitted to a psychiatric hospital, and after a year she regained her ability to walk. On discharge she obtained disability status, which freed her from having to work full time, and she volunteered at the local hospital. With her chronic but fluctuating incapacitation, on some days she could go in and on some days she could not. She was currently seeing a family practitioner and six specialists, who monitored various aspects of her physical condition. She was also seeing two ministers for pastoral counseling.

■ **Clinical Description**

Linda easily met and exceeded all DSM-IV diagnostic criteria for somatization disorder. Do you notice any differences between Linda, who presented with somatization disorder, and Gail, who presented with hypochondriacal disorder? Linda was more severely impaired and had suffered in the past from symptoms of paralysis (which we refer to as a conversion symptom; see p. 179).

But the more telling difference is that Linda was *not so afraid* as Gail that she had a disease. Linda was concerned with the symptoms themselves, not with what they might mean. Although there is some overlap between the conditions (Creed & Barsky, 2004; Leibbrand, Hiller, & Fichter, 2000), individuals with hypochondriasis most often take immediate action on noticing a symptom by calling the doctor or taking medication. People with somatization, on the other hand, do not feel the urgency to take action but continually feel weak and ill, and they avoid exercising, thinking it will make them worse (Rief et al., 1998). Furthermore, Linda's entire life revolved around her symptoms; she once told her therapist that her symptoms were her identity: Without them she would not know who she was. By this she meant that she would not know how to relate to people except in the context of discussing her symptoms much as other people might talk about their day at the office or their kids' accomplishments at school.

DSM-IV-TR

DSM TABLE 6.2 Diagnostic Criteria for Somatization Disorder

A. A history of many physical complaints beginning before age 30 that occur over several years and result in treatment being sought or significant impairment in social, occupational, or other important areas of functioning.

B. Each of the following criteria must have been met, with individual symptoms occurring at any time during the course of disturbance:

 1. Four pain symptoms: A history of pain related to at least four sites or functions (such as head, abdomen, back, joints, extremities, chest, rectum, during sexual intercourse, during menstruation, or during urination)

 2. Two gastrointestinal symptoms: A history of at least two gastrointestinal symptoms other than pain (such as nausea, diarrhea, bloating, vomiting other than during pregnancy, or intolerance of several foods)

 3. One sexual symptom: A history of at least one sexual or reproductive symptom other than pain (such as sexual indifference, erectile or ejaculatory dysfunction, irregular menses, excessive menstrual bleeding, or vomiting throughout pregnancy)

 4. One pseudo-neurological symptom: A history of at least one symptom or deficit suggesting a neurological disorder not limited to pain (conversion symptoms such as blindness, double vision, deafness, loss of touch or pain sensation, hallucinations, aphonia, impaired coordination or balance, paralysis or localized weakness, difficulty swallowing, difficulty breathing, urinary retention, or seizures; dissociative symptoms such as amnesia; or loss of consciousness other than fainting)

C. Either 1 or 2:

 1. After appropriate investigation, each of the symptoms in criterion B cannot be fully explained by a known general medical condition or the direct effects of a substance (for example, a drug of abuse or a medication)

 2. When there is a related general medical condition, the physical complaints or resulting social or occupational impairment are in excess of what would be expected from the history, physical examination, or laboratory findings

D. The symptoms are not intentionally produced or feigned (as in factitious disorder or malingering).

Source: Reprinted, with permission, from American Psychiatric Association. (2000). *Diagnostic and statistical manual of mental disorders* (4th ed., text revision). Washington, DC: Author. © 2000 American Psychiatric Association.

Her few friends who were not health-care professionals had the patience to relate to her sympathetically, through the veil of her symptoms, and she thought of them as friends because they "understood" her suffering.

Statistics

Somatization disorder is rare. DSM-III-R criteria required 13 or more symptoms from a list of 35, making diagnosis difficult. The criteria were greatly simplified for DSM-IV, with only 8 symptoms required (Cloninger, 1996). These criteria have been validated as easier to use and more accurate than alternative or past criteria (Yutzy et al., 1995). Katon and colleagues (1991) demonstrated that somatization disorder occurs on a continuum: People with only a few somatic symptoms of unexplained origin may experience sufficient distress and impairment of functioning to be considered to have a "disorder." Although it has its own name, *undifferentiated somatoform disorder,* it is just somatization disorder with fewer than eight symptoms. Using between four and six symptoms as criteria, Escobar and Canino (1989) found a prevalence of somatization disorder of 4.4% in one large city. The median prevalence in six samples of a large number of patients in a primary care setting meeting these criteria was 16.6% (Creed & Barsky, 2004).

Linda's disorder developed during adolescence, apparently the typical age of onset. A number of studies have demonstrated that individuals with somatization disorder tend to be women, unmarried, and from lower socioeconomic groups (see, for example, Creed & Barsky, 2004; Lieb et al., 2002; Swartz et al., 1986). For instance, 68% of the patients in a large sample studied by Kirmayer and Robbins (1991) were female. In addition to a variety of somatic complaints, individuals may have psychological complaints, usually anxiety or mood disorders (Adler et al., 1994; Kirmayer & Robbins, 1991; Lieb et al., 2002; Rief et al., 1998). Lenze, Miller, Munir, Pornoppadol, and North (1999) found that patients with somatization disorder who happened to be in psychiatric clinics reported seemingly endless psychological complaints, including psychotic symptoms, in addition to their physical complaints. Suicidal attempts that appear to be manipulative gestures rather than true death efforts are frequent (Chioqueta & Stiles, 2004). Although symptoms may come and go, somatization disorder and the accompanying sick role behavior are chronic, often continuing into old age.

For a long time, we thought that expressing psychological distress or somatic complaints was particularly common in non-Western or developing countries. But on closer inspection this does not seem to be the case, and the impression may have been because of the ways in which early studies were conducted (see, for example, Cheung, 1995). Thus, "somatizing" psychological distress is fairly common, and fairly uniform, throughout the world (Gureje, 2004). We must be particularly careful to rule out medical causes of somatic complaints in developing countries, where parasitic and other infectious diseases and physical conditions associated with poor nutrition are common and not always easy to diagnose. Table 6.1 presents data from a large World Health Organization study on individuals presenting to primary care settings either with somatic complaints that would not be sufficient to meet criteria for disorder or with somatization disorder. Notice that the rates are relatively uniform around the world for somatic complaints, as is the sex ratio (Gureje, Simon, Ustun, & Goldberg, 1997). When the problem is severe enough to meet criteria for disorder, the sex ratio is approximately 2:1 female.

Causes

Somatization disorder shares some features with hypochondriasis, including a history of family illness or injury during childhood. But this is a minor factor at best because countless families experience chronic illness or injuries without passing on the sick role to children. Something else contributes strongly to somatization disorder.

Given the past difficulty in making a diagnosis, few etiological studies of somatization disorder have been done. Early studies of possible genetic contributions had mixed results. For example, in a sophisticated twin study, Torgersen (1986) found no increased prevalence of somatization disorder in monozygotic pairs, but most studies find substantial evidence that the disorder runs in families and may have a heritable basis (Bell, 1994; Guze, Cloninger, Martin, & Clayton, 1986; Katon, 1993). A more startling finding emerged from these studies, however. Somatization disorder is strongly linked in family and genetic studies to *antisocial personality disorder (ASPD)* (see Chapter 12), which is characterized by vandalism, persistent lying, theft, irresponsibility with finances and at work, and outright physical aggression. Individuals with ASPD seem insensitive to signals of punishment and to the negative consequences of their often impulsive behavior, and they apparently experience little anxiety or guilt.

ASPD occurs primarily in males and somatization disorder in females, but they share a number of features. Both begin early in life, typically run a chronic course, predominate among lower socioeconomic classes, are difficult to treat, and are associated with marital discord, drug and alcohol abuse, and suicide attempts, among other complications (Cloninger, 1978; Goodwin & Guze, 1984; Lilienfeld, 1992; Mai, 2004). Both family and adoption studies suggest that ASPD and somatization disorder tend to run in

©Stockbyte Platinum/Alamy

In somatization disorder, primary relationships are often with medical caregivers; one's symptoms are one's identity.

TABLE 6.1	Frequency of Two Forms of Somatization in a Cross-Cultural Study ($N = 5,438$)*					
	ICD-10 Somatization Disorder (%)			**Somatic Symptom Index (%)**		
Center	**Men**	**Women**	**Overall Prevalence**	**Men**	**Women**	**Overall Prevalence**
Ankara, Turkey	1.3	2.2	1.9	22.3	26.7	25.2
Athens, Greece	0.4	1.8	1.3	7.7	13.5	11.5
Bangalore, India	1.3	2.4	1.8	19.1	20.0	19.6
Berlin, Germany	0.3	2.0	1.3	24.9	25.9	25.5
Groningen, the Netherlands	0.8	4.1	2.8	14.7	19.9	17.8
Ibadan, Nigeria	0.5	0.3	0.4	14.4	5.0	7.6
Mainz, Germany	1.0	4.4	3.0	24.9	17.3	20.6
Manchester, United Kingdom	0	0.5	0.4	21.4	20.0	20.5
Nagasaki, Japan	0	0.2	0.1	13.3	7.9	10.5
Paris, France	0.5	3.1	1.7	18.6	28.2	23.1
Rio de Janeiro, Brazil	1.5	11.2	8.5	35.6	30.6	32.0
Santiago, Chile	33.8	11.2	17.7	45.7	33.3	36.8
Seattle, Washington, United States	0.7	2.2	1.7	10.0	9.8	9.8
Shanghai, China	0.3	2.2	1.5	17.5	18.7	18.3
Verona, Italy	0	0.2	0.1	9.7	8.5	8.9
Total	1.9	3.3	2.8	19.8	19.7	19.7

Note: Criteria from *The International Classification of Diseases* (10th ed.) were used in this study.
*Weighted to the first-stage (intake) sample.

Source: Adapted from Gureje, O., Simon, G. E., Ustun, T. B., & Goldberg, D. P. (1997). Somatization in cross-cultural perspective: A World Health Organization study in primary care. *American Journal of Psychiatry, 154,* 989–995.

families and may well have a heritable component (see, for example, Bohman, Cloninger, von Knorring, & Sigvardsson, 1984; Cadoret, 1978), although it is also possible that the behavioral patterns could be learned in a maladaptive family setting.

Yet, the aggressiveness, impulsiveness, and lack of emotion characteristic of ASPD seem to be at the other end of the spectrum from somatization disorder. What could these two disorders possibly have in common? Although we don't yet have the answers, Scott Lilienfeld (1992; Lilienfeld & Hess, 2001) reviews a number of hypotheses; we look at some of them here because they are a fascinating example of integrative biopsychosocial thinking about psychopathology.

One model with some support suggests that somatization disorder and ASPD share a neurobiologically based disinhibition syndrome characterized by impulsive behavior (see, for example, Cloninger, 1987; Gorenstein & Newman, 1980). Evidence indicates that impulsiveness is common in ASPD (see, for example, Newman, Widom, & Nathan, 1985). How does this apply to people with somatization disorder? Many of the behaviors and traits associated with somatization disorder also seem to reflect the impulsive characteristic of short-term gain at the expense of long-term problems. The continual development of new somatic symptoms gains immediate sympathy and attention (for a while) but eventually leads to social isolation (Goodwin & Guze, 1984). Other behaviors that seem to indicate short-term gratification are the novelty-seeking and provocative sexual behavior often present

in people with somatization disorder (Kimble, Williams, & Agras, 1975). One study confirmed that these patients are more impulsive and pleasure seeking than anxiety patients (Battaglia, Bertella, Bajo, Politi, & Bellodi, 1998).

If individuals with ASPD and somatization disorder share the same underlying neurophysiological vulnerability, why do they behave so differently? The explanation is that social and cultural factors exert a strong effect. Both Cathy Spatz Widom (1984) and Robert Cloninger (1987) have pointed out that the major difference between the disorders is their degree of dependence. Aggression is strongly associated with males in most mammalian species, including rodents (Gray & Buffery, 1971). Dependence and lack of aggression are strongly associated with females. Thus, both aggression and ASPD are strongly associated with males, and dependence and somatization disorder are strongly associated with females. In support of this idea, Lilienfeld and Hess (2001), working with college students, found tendencies for females with antisocial and aggressive traits to report more somatic symptoms. Gender roles are among the strongest components of identity. It is possible that gender socialization accounts almost entirely for the profound differences in the expression of the same biological vulnerability among men and women.

These theoretical models are still preliminary and require a great deal more data before we can have confidence in their validity. But such ideas are at the forefront of our knowledge, and they reflect the kinds of integrative approaches to psychopathology (described in Chapter 2) that will inevitably emerge as our knowledge increases.

Might these assumptions apply to Linda or her family? Linda's sister had been married briefly and had two children. She had been in therapy for most of her adult life. Occasionally, Linda's sister visited doctors with various somatic complaints, but her primary difficulty was unexplained periods of recurring amnesia that might last several days; these spells alternated with blackout periods during which she was rushed to the hospital.

Were there signs of sexual impulsivity or ASPD in this family? The sister's older daughter, after a stormy adolescence characterized by truancy and delinquency, was sentenced to jail for violations involving drugs and assault. Amid one session with us, Linda noted that she had kept a list of people with whom she had had sexual intercourse. The list numbered well over 20, and most of the sexual episodes occurred in the offices of mental health professionals or clergy!

This development in Linda's relationship with caregivers was important because she saw it as the ultimate sign that the caregivers were concerned about her as a person and she was important to them. But the relationships almost always ended tragically. Several of the caregivers' marriages disintegrated, and at least one mental health professional committed suicide. Linda herself was never satisfied or fulfilled by the relationships but was greatly hurt when they inevitably ended. The American Psychological Association has decreed that it is *always* unethical to have *any* sexual contact with a patient at any time during treatment. Violations of this ethical canon have nearly always had tragic consequences.

■ Treatment

Somatization disorder is exceedingly difficult to treat. Although there are treatments with proven effectiveness, mostly cognitive-behavioral ones, none seem to "cure" the syndrome. In our clinic, we concentrate on initially providing reassurance, reducing stress, and, in particular, reducing the frequency of help-seeking behaviors. One of the most common patterns is the person's tendency to visit numerous medical specialists to address the symptom of the week. There is an extensive medical and physical workup with every visit to a new physician (or to one who has not been seen for a while). Several studies found that the costs of these patients to the health-care system was more than double that of the average patient (Barsky, Orav, & Bates, 2005; Hiller, Fichter, & Rief, 2003). In treatment, to limit these visits, a gatekeeper physician is assigned each patient to screen all physical complaints. Subsequent visits to specialists must be specifically authorized by this gatekeeper. In the context of a positive therapeutic relationship, most patients are amenable to this arrangement.

Additional therapeutic attention is directed at reducing the supportive consequences of relating to significant others on the basis of physical symptoms alone. More appropriate methods of interacting with others are encouraged, along with additional procedures to promote healthy social and personal adjustment without relying on being "sick." Based on existing studies, CBTs to accomplish these goals are most often considered the treatment of choice, particularly if simpler strategies are not working (Allen, Woolfolk, Lehrer, Gara, & Escobar, 2001; Kroenke & Swindle, 2000; Mai, 2004). Because Linda, like many patients with this

disorder, had become eligible for disability payments from the state, additional goals involved encouraging at least part-time employment, with the ultimate goal of discontinuing disability.

Other specialists in somatization disorder have enumerated similar therapeutic goals. For example, G. R. Smith, Monson, and Ray (1986) and R. J. Smith (1991) evaluated a similar procedure and found that, although it did not improve the patient's mental or physical health, it did substantially reduce the help-seeking behavior. This is an extremely important goal, because, as noted earlier, the cost in dollars—to the patient, to the medical system, and, ultimately, to society—is enormous. Now family doctors are being trained in how better to manage these patients using some of these principles (Garcia-Campayo, Claraco, Sanz-Carrillo, Arevalo, & Monton, 2002). Antidepressant drugs have shown some promise (Menza et al., 2001; Okugawa, Yagi, Kusaka, & Kinoshita, 2002) but are not the first choice for treatment because somatic or physical side effects such as nausea, agitation, or headaches are often frightening to these patients, making the drugs difficult to tolerate (Mai, 2004).

Conversion Disorder

The term *conversion* has been used off and on since the Middle Ages (Mace, 1992) but was popularized by Freud, who believed the anxiety resulting from unconscious conflicts somehow was "converted" into physical symptoms to find expression. This allowed the individual to discharge some anxiety without actually experiencing it. As in phobic disorders, the anxiety resulting from unconscious conflicts might be "displaced" onto another object.

■ Clinical Description

Conversion disorders generally have to do with physical malfunctioning, such as paralysis, blindness, or difficulty speaking (aphonia), without any physical or organic pathology to account for the malfunction. Most conversion symptoms suggest that some kind of neurological disease is affecting sensory–motor systems, although conversion symptoms can mimic the full range of physical malfunctioning.

Conversion disorders provide us with some of the most intriguing, sometimes astounding, examples of psychopathology. What could possibly account for somebody going blind when all visual processes are normal or experiencing paralysis of the arms or legs when there is no neurological damage? Consider the case of Eloise.

ELOISE: Unlearning Walking

Eloise sat on a chair with her legs under her, refusing to put her feet on the floor. Her mother sat close by, ready to assist her if she needed to move or get up. Her mother had made the appointment and, with the help of a friend, had all but carried Eloise into the office. Eloise was a 20-year-old of borderline intelligence who was friendly and personable during the initial interview and who readily answered all questions with a big smile. She obviously enjoyed the social interaction.

Eloise's difficulty walking developed over 5 years. Her right leg had given way and she began falling. Gradually, the condition worsened to the point that 6 months before her admission to the hospital Eloise could move around only by crawling on the floor.

Physical examinations revealed no physical problems. Eloise presented with a classic case of conversion disorder. Although she was not paralyzed, her specific symptoms included weakness in her legs and difficulty keeping her balance, with the result that she fell often. This particular type of conversion symptom is called *astasia-abasia.*

Eloise lived with her mother, who ran a gift shop in the front of her house in a small rural town. Eloise had been schooled through exceptional education programs until she was about 15; after this, no further programs were available. When Eloise began staying home, her walking began to deteriorate.

In addition to blindness, paralysis, and aphonia, conversion symptoms may include total mutism and the loss of the sense of touch. Some people have seizures, which may be psychological in origin, because no significant electroencephalogram (EEG) changes can be documented. Another relatively common symptom is *globus hystericus,* the sensation of a lump in the throat that makes it difficult to swallow, eat, or sometimes talk (Finkenbine & Miele, 2004).

DSM-IV-TR

DSM TABLE 6.3 Diagnostic Criteria for Conversion Disorder

A. One or more symptoms or deficits affecting voluntary motor or sensory function that suggest a neurological or general medical condition.

B. Psychological factors are judged to be associated with the symptom or deficit because the initiation or exacerbation of the symptom or deficit is preceded by conflicts or other stressors.

C. The symptom or deficit is not intentionally produced or feigned (as in factitious disorder or malingering).

D. The symptom or deficit cannot, after appropriate investigation, be fully explained by a general medical condition, by the direct effects of a substance, or as a culturally sanctioned behavior or experience.

E. The symptom or deficit causes clinically significant distress or impairment in social, occupational, or other important areas of functioning or warrants medical evaluation.

F. The symptom or deficit is not limited to pain or sexual dysfunction, does not occur exclusively during the course of somatization disorder, and is not better accounted for by another mental disorder.

Specify type of symptom or deficit:
  With motor symptom or deficit
  With sensory symptom or deficit
  With seizures or convulsions
  With mixed presentation

Closely Related Disorders Distinguishing among conversion reactions, real physical disorders, and outright **malingering** (faking) is sometimes difficult. Several factors can help, but one symptom, widely regarded as a diagnostic sign, has proved not to be useful.

It was long thought that patients with conversion reactions had the same quality of indifference to the symptoms thought to be present in somatization disorder. This attitude, referred to as *la belle indifférence,* was considered a hallmark of conversion reactions, but, unfortunately, this turns out not to be the case. Stone, Smyth, Carson, Warlow, and Sharpe (2006) found a blasé attitude toward illness is sometimes displayed by people with actual physical disorders, and some people with conversion symptoms do become quite distressed. Specifically, only 21% of 356 patients with conversion symptoms displayed *la belle indifférence* compared to 29% of 157 patients with organic disease.

Other factors may be more helpful in making this distinction., Conversion symptoms are often precipitated by marked stress. C.V. Ford (1985) noted that the incidence of marked stress preceding a conversion symptom occurred in 52% to 93% of the cases. Thus, if the clinician cannot identify a stressful event preceding the onset of the conversion symptom, the clinician might more carefully consider the presence of a true physical condition. In addition, although people with conversion symptoms can usually function normally, they seem truly unaware either of this ability or of sensory input. For example, individuals with the conversion symptom of blindness can usually avoid objects in their visual field, but they will tell you they can't see the objects. Similarly, individuals with conversion symptoms of paralysis of the legs might suddenly get up and run in an emergency and then be astounded they were able to do this. It is possible that at least some people who experience miraculous cures during religious ceremonies may have been suffering from conversion reactions. These factors may help in distinguishing between conversion and organically based physical disorders, but clinicians sometimes make mistakes, although it is not common with modern diagnostic techniques. For example, Moene and colleagues (2000) carefully reassessed 85 patients diagnosed with conversion disorder and found 10 (11.8%) had developed some evidence of a neurological disorder approximately 2.5 years after the first exam. Stone and colleagues (2005), summarizing a number of studies, estimate the rate of misdiagnosis of conversion disorders that are really physical problems is approximately 4%, having improved considerably from earlier decades.

It can also be difficult to distinguish between individuals who are truly experiencing conversion symptoms in a seemingly involuntary way and malingerers who are good at faking symptoms. Once malingerers are exposed, their motivation is clear: They are either trying to get out of something, such as work or legal difficulties, or they are attempting to gain something, such as a financial settlement. Malingerers are fully aware of what they are doing and are clearly attempting to manipulate others to gain a desired end.

More puzzling is a set of conditions called **factitious disorders,** which fall somewhere between malingering and conversion disorders. The symptoms are under voluntary control, as with malingering, but there is *no obvious reason* for voluntarily producing the symptoms except, possibly, to assume the sick role and receive increased attention. Tragically, this disorder may extend to

TABLE 6.2 Child Abuse Associated With Munchausen Syndrome by Proxy Versus Typical Child Abuse		
	Typical Child Abuse	**Atypical Child Abuse (Munchausen Syndrome by Proxy)**
Physical presentation of the child	Results from direct physical contact with the child; signs often detected on physical examination	Misrepresentation of an acute or accidental medical or surgical illness not usually obvious on physical examination
Obtaining the diagnosis	The perpetrator does not invite the discovery of the manifestation of the abuse	The perpetrator usually presents the manifestations of the abuse to the health-care system
Victims	Children are either the objects of frustration and anger or are receiving undue or inappropriate punishment	Children serve as the vector in gaining the attention the mother desires; anger is not the primary causal factor
Awareness of abuse	Usually present	Not usually present

Source: Reprinted, with permission, from Check, J. R. (2005). Munchausen syndrome by proxy: An atypical form of child abuse. *Journal of Practical Psychiatry and Behavioral Health,* 1998, p. 341, Table 6.2. © 1998 Lippincott, Williams & Wilkins.

other members of the family. An adult, almost always a mother, may purposely make her child sick, evidently for the attention and pity then given to the mother who is causing the symptoms. When an individual deliberately makes someone else sick, the condition is called *factitious disorder by proxy* or, sometimes, *Munchausen syndrome by proxy,* but it is really an atypical form of child abuse (Check, 1998). Table 6.2 presents differences between typical child abuse and Munchausen syndrome by proxy.

The offending parent may resort to extreme tactics to create the appearance of illness in the child. For example, one mother stirred a vaginal tampon obtained during menstruation in her child's urine specimen. Another mother mixed feces into her child's vomit (Check, 1998). Because the mother typically establishes a positive relationship with a medical staff, the true nature of the illness is most often unsuspected and the staff members perceive the parent as remarkably caring, cooperative, and involved in providing for her child's well-being. In fact, the mother typically becomes overly involved in the care of her child, often helping with the administration of drugs and the examination of laboratory results, as well as advising medical staff. Therefore, the mother is often successful at eluding suspicion. Helpful proce-

dures to assess the possibility of Munchausen syndrome by proxy include a trial separation of the mother and the child or video surveillance of the child while in the hospital. An important study has appeared validating the utility of surveillance in hospital rooms of children with suspected Munchausen syndrome by proxy. In this study, 41 patients presenting with chronic, difficult-to-diagnose physical problems were monitored by video during their hospital stay. In 23 of these cases, the diagnoses turned out to be Munchausen syndrome by proxy, where the parent was responsible for the child's symptoms, and in more than half of these 23 cases, video surveillance was the method used to establish the diagnosis. In the other patients, laboratory tests or "catching" the mother in the act of inducing illness in her child confirmed the diagnosis. In one case, a child was suffering from recurring *Escherichia coli,* or *E. coli,* infections, and cameras caught the mother injecting her own urine into the child's intravenous line. In another case, a mother gagged herself and vomited and told doctors the vomit was her child's (Hall, Eubanks, Meyyazhagan, Kenney, & Cochran Johnson, 2000).

Unconscious Mental Processes Unconscious cognitive processes seem to play a role in much of psychopathology (although not necessarily as Freud envisioned it), but nowhere is this phenomenon more readily and dramatically apparent than when we attempt to distinguish between conversion disorders and related conditions. To take a closer look at the "unconscious" mental process in these conditions, we review briefly the case of Anna O. (see Chapter 2).

As you may remember, when Anna O. was 21 years old she was nursing her dying father. This was a difficult time for her. She reported that after many days by the sick bed, her mind wandered. Suddenly she found herself imagining (dreaming?) that a black snake was moving across the bed, about to bite her father. She tried to grab the snake, but her right arm had gone to sleep and she could not move it. Looking at her arm and hand, she imagined that her fingers had turned into little poisonous snakes. Horrified, all she could do was pray, and the only prayer that came to mind was in English (Anna O.'s native language was German). After this, she experienced paralysis in her right arm whenever she remembered this hallucination. The paralysis gradually extended to the right side of her body and, on occasion, to other parts of her body. She also experienced a number of other conver-

---

DSM-IV-TR

DSM TABLE 6.4   Diagnostic Criteria for Factitious Disorders

A. Intentional production or feigning of physical or psychological signs or symptoms.

B. The motivation for the behavior is to assume the sick role.

C. External incentives for the behavior (such as economic gain, avoiding legal responsibility, or improving physical well-being, as in malingering) are absent.

Specify if:

With predominantly psychological signs and symptoms: If psychological signs and symptoms predominate in the clinical presentation

With predominantly physical signs and symptoms: If physical signs and symptoms predominate in the clinical presentation

With combined psychological and physical signs and symptoms: If neither psychological nor physical signs and symptoms predominate in the clinical presentation

Source: Reprinted, with permission, from American Psychiatric Association. (2000). *Diagnostic and statistical manual of mental disorders* (4th ed., text revision). Washington, DC: Author, © 2000 American Psychiatric Association.

sion symptoms such as deafness and, intriguingly, an inability to speak German, although she remained fluent in English. In Josef Breuer's treatment of Anna O., she relived her traumatic experiences in her imagination. Under hypnosis, she was able to recreate the memory of her horrific hallucination. As she recalled and processed the images, her paralysis left her and she regained her ability to speak German. Breuer called the therapeutic reexperiencing of emotionally traumatic events *catharsis* (purging, or releasing). Catharsis has proved to be an effective intervention with many emotional disorders, as we noted in Chapter 5.

Were Anna O.'s symptoms really "unconscious," or did she realize at some level that she could move her arm and the rest of her body if she wanted to and it simply served her purpose not to? This question has long bedeviled psychopathologists. Now new information (reviewed in Chapter 2) on unconscious cognitive processes becomes important. We are all capable of receiving and processing information in a number of sensory channels (such as vision and hearing) without being aware of it. Remember the phenomenon of blind sight or unconscious vision? Weiskrantz (1980) and others discovered that people with small, localized damage to certain parts of their brains could identify objects in their field of vision but that they had no awareness whatsoever that they could see. Could this happen to people without brain damage? Consider the case of Celia.

CELIA: Seeing Through Blindness

A 15-year-old girl named Celia suddenly was unable to see. Shortly thereafter, she regained some of her sight, but her vision was so severely blurred that she could not read. When she was brought to a clinic for testing, psychologists arranged a series of sophisticated vision tests that did not require her to report when she could or could not see. One of the tasks required her to examine three triangles displayed on three separate screens and to press a button under the screen containing an upright triangle. Celia performed perfectly on this test without being aware that she could see anything (Grosz & Zimmerman, 1970). Was Celia faking? Evidently not, or she would have purposely made a mistake.

Sackeim, Nordlie, and Gur (1979) evaluated the potential difference between real unconscious process and faking by hypnotizing two subjects and giving each a suggestion of total blindness. One subject was also told it was extremely important that she appear to everyone to be blind. The second subject was not given further instructions. The first subject, evidently following instructions to appear blind at all costs, performed far below chance on a visual discrimination task similar to the upright triangle task. On almost every trial, she chose the wrong answer. The second subject, with the hypnotic suggestion of blindness but no instructions to "appear" blind at all costs, performed perfectly on the visual discrimination tasks—although she reported she could not see anything. How is this relevant to identifying malingering? In an earlier case, Grosz and Zimmerman (1965) evaluated a male who

seemed to have conversion symptoms of blindness. They discovered that he performed much more poorly than chance on a visual discrimination task. Subsequent information from other sources confirmed that he was almost certainly malingering. To review these distinctions, someone who is truly blind would perform at a chance level on visual discrimination tasks. People with conversion symptoms, on the other hand, can see objects in their visual field and therefore would perform well on these tasks, but this experience is dissociated from their awareness of sight. Malingerers and, perhaps, individuals with factitious disorders simply do everything possible to pretend they can't see.

■ Statistics

We have already seen that conversion disorder may occur with other disorders, particularly somatization disorder, as in the case of Linda. Linda's paralysis passed after several months and did not return, although on occasion she would report "feeling as if" it were returning. Comorbid anxiety and mood disorders are also common (see, for example, Pehlivanturk & Unal, 2002). Conversion disorders are relatively rare in mental health settings, but remember that people who seek help for this condition are more likely to consult neurologists or other specialists. The prevalence estimates in neurological settings vary dramatically from 1% to 30% (Allin, Streeruwitz, & Curtis, 2005; Marsden, 1986; Trimbell, 1981), with one study estimating that 10% to 20% of all patients referred to epilepsy centers have psychogenic, nonepileptic seizures (Benbadis & Allen-Hauser, 2000).

Like somatization disorder, conversion disorders are found primarily in women (Folks, Ford, & Regan, 1984; Rosenbaum, 2000) and typically develop during adolescence or slightly thereafter. However, they occur relatively often in males at times of extreme stress (Chodoff, 1974). Conversion reactions are not uncommon in soldiers exposed to combat (Mucha & Reinhardt, 1970). The conversion symptoms often disappear after a time, only to return later in the same or similar form when a new stressor occurs. In one study, 56 patients with psychogenic nonepileptic seizures (16 males and 40 females), who had their disorder for an

The seizures and trances that may be symptomatic of conversion disorder are also common in some rural fundamentalist religious groups in the United States.

average of 8 years, were followed for 18 months after initial diagnosis (Ettinger, Devinsky, Weisbrot, Ramakrishna, & Goyal, 1999). Outcome was generally poor for these patients, with only about half of the patients recovering. Even among those patients whose seizures had gotten better, rehospitalizations were common. Approximately 20% of this group had attempted suicide, and this proportion did not differ between those whose seizures had gotten better during the period and those whose seizures had not gotten better. If the patients believed the diagnosis when it was given to them, and otherwise perceived themselves as being in good health and functioning well at work and at home, they had a better chance of recovering from their psychologically based seizures. Fortunately, children and adolescents seem to have a better long-term outlook than adults. In one study from Turkey, fully 85% of 40 children had recovered 4 years after initial diagnoses, with those diagnosed early having the best chance (Pehlivanturk et al., 2002). Whether this is also true in Europe or North America requires further study.

In the beginning of the chapter, we noted that conversion disorder and dissociative disorders share common features. Several studies provide evidence for this. In one recent study, 72 patients with conversion disorders were compared with a control group of 96 psychiatric patients suffering from various emotional disorders who were matched for gender and age. Dissociative symptoms such as feelings of unreality were significantly more common in the patients with conversion disorder than in the control group based on responses to a questionnaire (Spitzer, Spelsberg, Grabe, Mundt, & Freyberger, 1999). This finding was basically replicated in another report on 54 patients with conversion disorder compared to 50 matched patients with mood or anxiety disorders (Roelofs, Keijsers, Hoogduin, Naring, & Moene, 2002). In other cultures, some conversion symptoms are common aspects of religious or healing rituals. Seizures, paralysis, and trances are common in some rural fundamentalist religious groups in the United States (Griffith, English, & Mayfield, 1980), and they are often seen as evidence of contact with God. Individuals who exhibit such symptoms are thus held in high esteem by their peers. These symptoms do not meet criteria for a "disorder" unless they persist and interfere with an individual's functioning.

■ Causes

Freud described four basic processes in the development of conversion disorder. First, the individual experiences a traumatic event—in Freud's view, an unacceptable, unconscious conflict. Second, because the conflict and the resulting anxiety are unacceptable, the person represses the conflict, making it unconscious. Third, the anxiety continues to increase and threatens to emerge into consciousness, and the person "converts" it into physical symptoms, thereby relieving the pressure of having to deal directly with the conflict. This reduction of anxiety is considered to be the *primary gain* or reinforcing event that maintains the conversion symptom. Fourth, the individual receives greatly increased attention and sympathy from loved ones and may also be allowed to avoid a difficult situation or task. Freud considered such attention or avoidance to be the *secondary gain,* the secondarily reinforcing set of events.

We believe Freud was basically correct on at least three counts but probably not on the fourth, although firm evidence

supporting any of these ideas is sparse and Freud's views were far more complex than represented here. What seems to happen is that individuals with conversion disorder have experienced a traumatic event that must be escaped at all costs. This might be combat, where death is imminent, or an impossible interpersonal situation. Because simply running away is unacceptable in most cases, the socially acceptable alternative of getting sick is substituted; but getting sick on purpose is also unacceptable, so this motivation is detached from the person's consciousness. Finally, because the escape behavior (the conversion symptoms) is successful to an extent in obliterating the traumatic situation, the behavior continues until the underlying problem is resolved. One study confirms these hypotheses, at least partially (Wyllie, Glazer, Benbadis, Kotagal, & Wolgamuth, 1999). In this study, 34 child and adolescent patients, 25 of them girls, were evaluated after receiving a diagnosis of psychologically based pseudo-seizures (psychogenic nonepileptic seizures). Many of these children and adolescents presented with additional psychological disorders, including 32% with mood disorders and 24% with separation anxiety and school refusal. Other anxiety disorders were present in some additional patients.

When the extent of psychological stress in the lives of these children was examined, it was found that most of the patients had substantial stress, including a history of sexual abuse, recent parental divorce or death of a close family member, and physical abuse. The authors concluded that major mood disorders and severe environmental stress, especially sexual abuse, are common among children and adolescents with the conversion disorder of pseudo-seizures, as have other studies (Roelofs et al., 2002).

In another study, 15 adolescents who had exhibited visual problems in childhood that were of psychological origin were compared with a control group of adolescents who had experienced childhood visual problems because of known physical problems. Adolescents with the conversion disorder were more likely to have experienced some significant stress and adjustment difficulties, such as substantial school difficulties, or the loss of a significant figure in their lives, and they rated their mothers as overinvolved and overprotective on a rating scale. Rating mothers as "overinvolved" or "overprotective" suggests that these psychologically based visual symptoms may have been strongly attended to and reinforced (Wynick, Hobson, & Jones, 1997).

The one step in Freud's progression of events about which some questions remain is the issue of primary gain. The notion of primary gain accounts for the feature of *la belle indifférence* (cited previously), where individuals seem not the least bit distressed about their symptoms. In other words, Freud thought that because symptoms reflected an unconscious attempt to resolve a conflict, the patient would not be upset by them. But formal tests of this feature provide little support for Freud's claim. For example, Lader and Sartorius (1968) compared patients with conversion disorder with control groups of anxious patients without conversion symptoms. The patients with conversion disorder showed equal or greater anxiety and physiological arousal than the control group. Also Stone and colleagues (2006) in the study described earlier on "indifference" to conversion symptoms found no difference in distress over symptoms among patients with conversion disorder compared to patients with organic disease. The impression of indifference may be more in the mind of the therapist than true of the patient.

Social and cultural influences also contribute to conversion disorder, which, like somatization disorder, tends to occur in less educated, lower socioeconomic groups where knowledge about disease and medical illness is not well developed (Binzer, Andersen, & Kullgren, 1997; Kirmayer, Looper, & Taillefer, 2003; Swartz, Blazer, Woodbury, George, Landerman, 1986). For example, Binzer and colleagues (1997) noted that 13% of their group of 30 patients with motor disabilities resulting from conversion disorder had attended high school compared to 67% in a control group of motor symptoms because of a physical cause. Prior experience with real physical problems, usually among other family members, tends to influence the later choice of specific conversion symptoms; that is, patients tend to adopt symptoms with which they are familiar (see, for example, Brady & Lind, 1961). Furthermore, the incidence of these disorders has decreased over the decades (Kirmayer et al., 2003). The most likely explanation is that increased knowledge of the real causes of physical problems by both patients and loved ones eliminates much of the possibility of secondary gain so important in these disorders.

Finally, many conversion symptoms seem to be part of a larger constellation of psychopathology. Linda had broad-ranging somatization disorder, as well as the severe conversion symptoms, that resulted in her hospitalization. In similar cases, individuals may have a marked biological vulnerability to develop the disorder when under stress, with biological processes like those discussed in the context of somatization disorder. For countless other cases, however, biological contributory factors seem to be less important than the overriding influence of interpersonal factors, in this case the actions of Eloise's mother, as you will see. We talk about Eloise's treatment in the next section. There you will see that the extent of her suffering and its successful resolution point primarily to a psychological and social etiology.

■ Treatment

Although few systematic controlled studies have evaluated the effectiveness of treatment for conversion disorders, we often treat these conditions in our clinics, as do others (see, for example, Campo & Negrini, 2000; Moene, Spinhoven, Hoogduin, & van Dyck, 2002), and our methods closely follow our thinking on etiology. Because conversion disorder has much in common with somatization disorder, many of the treatment principles are similar.

A principal strategy is to identify and attend to the traumatic or stressful life event, if it is still present (either in real life or in memory). As in the case of Anna O., therapeutic assistance in reexperiencing or "reliving" the event (catharsis) is a reasonable first step.

The therapist must also work hard to reduce any reinforcing or supportive consequences of the conversion symptoms (secondary gain). For example, it was quite clear that Eloise's mother found it convenient if Eloise stayed in one place most of the day while her mother attended to the store in the front of the house. Eloise's immobility was thus strongly reinforced by motherly attention and concern. Any unnecessary mobility was punished. The therapist must collaborate with both the patient and the family to eliminate such self-defeating behaviors.

Many times, removing the secondary gain is easier said than done. Eloise was successfully treated in the clinic. Through intensive daily work with the staff, she was able to walk again. To accomplish this, she had to practice walking every day with considerable support, attention, and praise from the staff. When her mother visited, the staff noticed that she verbalized her pleasure with Eloise's progress but that her facial expressions or *affect* conveyed a different message. The mother lived a good distance from the clinic, so she could not attend sessions, but she promised to carry out the program at home after Eloise was discharged. But she didn't. A follow-up contact 6 months after Eloise was discharged revealed that she had relapsed and was again spending almost all her time in a room in the back of the house while her mother attended to business out front.

Following similar cognitive-behavioral programs, 65% of a group of 45 patients with mostly motor behavior conversions (for example, difficulty walking) responded well to treatment. Interestingly, hypnosis, which was administered to approximately half the patients, did not add any benefit to the CBT (Moene et al., 2002).

Pain Disorder

A related somatoform disorder about which little is known is **pain disorder.** Pain disorder refers to pain in one or more sites in the body that is associated with significant distress or impairment. In pain disorder, there may have been clear physical reasons for pain, at least initially, but psychological factors play a major role in maintaining it. In the placement of this disorder in DSM-IV, serious consideration was given to removing it from the somatoform disorders and putting it in a separate section, because a person rarely presents with localized pain without some physical basis, such as an accident or illness. Therefore, it was difficult to separate the cases in which the causes were judged to be primarily psychological from the ones in which the causes are primarily physical. Because pain disorder fits most closely within the somatoform cluster (an individual presents with physical symptoms judged to have strong psychological contributions), the decision was made to leave pain disorder in the somatoform section. However, the three subtypes of pain disorder run the gamut from pain judged to be due primarily to psychological factors to pain judged to be due primarily to a general medical condition. Several studies from Germany suggest that this is a fairly common condition, with 5% to 12% of the population meeting criteria for pain disorder (Frohlich, Jacobi, & Wittchen, 2006; Grabe et al., 2003).

An important feature of pain disorder is that the pain is real and it hurts, regardless of the causes (Aigner & Bach, 1999; King & Strain, 1991). Consider the two cases described here.

THE MEDICAL STUDENT:
Temporary Pain

During her first clinical rotation, a 25-year-old third-year medical student in excellent health was seen at her student health service for intermittent abdominal pain of several weeks' duration. The student claimed no past history of similar pain. Physical examination revealed no physical problems, but she told the physician that she had recently separated from her husband. The student was referred to the health service psychiatrist. No other psychiatric problems were found. She was taught relaxation techniques and given supportive therapy to help her cope with her current stressful situation. The student's pain subsequently disappeared, and she successfully completed medical school.

THE WOMAN WITH CANCER:
Managing Pain

A 56-year-old woman with metastatic breast cancer who appeared to be coping appropriately with her disease had severe pain in her right thigh for a month. She initially obtained relief from a combination of drugs and subsequently received hypnotherapy and group therapy. These treatment modalities provided additional pain relief and enabled the patient to decrease her narcotic intake with no increase in pain.

The medical student's pain was seen as purely psychological. In the case of the second woman, the pain was probably related to cancer. But we now know that whatever its cause, pain has a strong psychological component. If medical treatments for existing physical conditions are in place and pain remains, or if the pain seems clearly related to psychological factors, psychological interventions are appropriate. Because of the complexity of pain itself and the variety of narcotics and other medications prescribed for it, multidisciplinary pain clinics are part of most large hospitals. (In Chapter 9, we discuss health psychology and the contribution of psychological factors to physical disorders, and we delve more deeply into types of pain disorders, their causes, and treatment.)

Body Dysmorphic Disorder

Did you ever wish you could change part of your appearance? Maybe or the size of your nose or the way your ears stick out? Most people fantasize about improving something, but some relatively normal-looking people think they are so ugly they refuse to interact with others or otherwise function normally for fear that people will laugh at their ugliness. This curious affliction is called **body dysmorphic disorder (BDD),** and at its center is a preoccupation with some imagined defect in appearance by someone who actually looks reasonably normal. The disorder has been referred to as "imagined ugliness" (Phillips, 1991). Consider the case of Jim.

DSM-IV-TR

DSM TABLE 6.5 Diagnostic Criteria for Pain Disorder

A. Pain in one or more anatomical sites is the predominant focus of the clinical presentation and is of sufficient severity to warrant clinical attention.
B. The pain causes clinically significant distress or impairment in social, occupational, or other important areas of functioning.
C. Psychological factors are judged to have an important role in the onset, severity, exacerbation, or maintenance of the pain.
D. The symptom or deficit is not intentionally produced or feigned (as in factitious disorder or malingering).
E. The pain is not better accounted for by a mood, anxiety, or psychotic disorder and does not meet criteria for dyspareunia.
Specify if:
Acute (duration of less than 6 months)
Chronic (duration of 6 months or more)

Source: Reprinted, with permission, from American Psychiatric Association. (2000). *Diagnostic and statistical manual of mental disorders* (4th ed., text revision). Washington, DC: Author, © 2000 American Psychiatric Association.

JIM: Ashamed to Be Seen

In his mid-20s, Jim was diagnosed with suspected social phobia; he was referred to our clinic by another professional. Jim had just finished rabbinical school and had been offered a position at a synagogue in a nearby city. However, he found himself unable to accept because of marked social difficulties. Lately he had given up leaving his small apartment for fear of running into people he knew and being forced to stop and interact with them.

Jim was a good-looking young man of about average height, with dark hair and eyes. Although he was somewhat depressed, a mental status exam and a brief interview focusing on current functioning and past history did not reveal any remarkable problems. There was no sign of a psychotic process (he was not out of touch with reality). We then focused on Jim's social difficulties. We expected the usual kinds of anxiety about interacting with people or "doing something" (performing) in front of them. But this was not Jim's concern. Rather, he was convinced that everyone, even his good friends, were staring at a part of his body that he found grotesque. He reported that strangers would never mention his deformity and his friends felt too sorry for him to mention it. Jim thought his head was square! Like the Beast in *Beauty and the Beast* who could not imagine people reacting to him with anything less than revulsion, Jim could not imagine people getting past his square head. To hide his condition as well as he could, Jim wore soft floppy hats and was most comfortable in winter, when he could all but completely cover his head with a large stocking cap. To us, Jim looked normal.

Clinical Description

To give you a better idea of the types of concerns people with BDD present to health professionals, the locations of imagined defects in 200 patients are shown in Table 6.3. The average number of body areas of concern to these individuals was 5 to 7 (Phillips, Menard, Fay, & Weisberg, 2005). In another group of 23 adolescents with BDD, 61% focused on their skin and 55% on their hair (Albertini & Phillips, 1999). A variety of checking or compensating rituals are common in people with BDD in attempts to alleviate their concerns. For example, excessive tanning is common, with 25% of one group of 200 patients tanning themselves in an attempt to hide skin defects (Phillips, Menard, Fay, & Weisberg, 2005). Excessive grooming and skin picking are also common. Many people with this disorder become fixated on mirrors (Veale & Riley, 2001). They often check their presumed ugly feature to see whether any change has taken place. Others avoid mirrors to an almost phobic extent. Quite understandably, suicidal ideation, suicide attempts, and suicide itself are typical consequences of this disorder (Phillips, Menard, Fay, & Weisberg, 2005; Zimmerman & Mattia, 1998). People with BDD also have "ideas of reference," which means they think everything that goes on in their world somehow is related to them—in this case, to their imagined defect. This disorder can cause considerable disruption in the patient's life. Many patients with severe cases become housebound for fear of showing themselves to other people.

If this disorder seems strange to you, you are not alone. For decades, this condition, previously known as *dysmorphophobia* (literally, fear of ugliness), was thought to represent a psychotic delusional state because the affected individuals were unable to realize, even for a fleeting moment, that their ideas were irrational. Whether this is true is still debated.

In the context of obsessive-compulsive disorder (OCD) (see Chapter 5), a similar issue arose as to whether patients believe in their obsessions or realize they are irrational. A minority (10% or less) of people with OCD believe their fears about contaminating others or need to prevent catastrophes with their rituals are perfectly realistic and reasonable. This brings up the major issue of what is "delusional" and what isn't, which is even more important in BDD.

For example, in 200 cases examined by Phillips and colleagues (2005) and in 50 cases reported by Veale, Boocock, and colleagues (1996), between 33% and 50% subjects were convinced their imagined bodily defect was real and a reasonable source of concern. Is this delusional? The DSM-IV task force wrestled long and hard with this issue and decided that individuals with BDD whose beliefs are so firmly held that they could be called delusional should receive a second diagnosis in addition to BDD of delusional disorder, somatic type (see Chapter 14). Phillips, Menard, Pagano, Fay, and Stout (2006) looked closely at differences that may exist between delusional and nondelusional types and found nothing significant, beyond the fact that the delusional type was more severe and less educated. Thus, in DSM-V, it's likely that patients would receive just a BDD diagnosis, whether they are "delusional" or not.

Statistics

The prevalence of BDD is hard to estimate because by its very nature it tends to be kept secret. However, the best estimates are that it is far more common than we had previously thought. Without some sort of treatment, it tends to run a lifelong course (Phillips, 1991; Veale, Boocock, et al., 1996). One of the patients with BDD reported by Phillips and colleagues (1993) had suffered from her condition for 71 years, since the age of 9. If you think a college friend seems to have at least a mild version of BDD, you're probably correct. One study suggested that as many as 70% of college students report at least some dissatisfaction with their bodies; 28% of these appear to meet all the criteria for the disorder (Fitts, Gibson, Redding, & Deiter, 1989). However, this study was done by questionnaire and may well have reflected the large percentage of students who are concerned simply with weight. Another, study investigated the prevalence of BDD specifically in an ethnically diverse sample of 566 adolescents between the ages of 14 and 19. The overall prevalence of BDD in this group was 2.2%, with adolescent girls more dissatisfied with their bodies than boys and African Americans of both genders less dissatisfied with their bodies than Caucasians, Asians, and Hispanics (Mayville, Katz,

TABLE 6.3	Location of Imagined Defects in 200 Patients With Body Dysmorphic Disorder*		
Location	**%**	**Location**	**%**
Skin	80	Overall appearance of face	19
Hair	58	Small body build	18
Nose	39	Legs	18
Stomach	32	Face size or shape	16
Teeth	30	Chin	15
Weight	29	Lips	14.5
Breasts	26	Arms or wrists	14
Buttocks	22	Hips	13
Eyes	22	Cheeks	11
Thighs	20	Ears	11
Eyebrows	20		

Adapted from Phillips, K.A., Menard, B.A., Fay, C., & Weisberg, R., (2005). Demographic characteristics, phenomenology, comorbidity, and family history in 200 individuals with body dysmorphic disorder. *Psychosomatics*, 46:4, 317–325. © 2005 The Academy of Psychosomatic Medicine.

DSM-IV-TR

DSM TABLE 6.6 Diagnostic Criteria for Body Dysmorphic Disorder

A. Preoccupation with an imagined defect in appearance. If a slight physical anomaly is present, the person's concern is markedly excessive.

B. The preoccupation causes significant distress or impairment in social, occupational, or other important areas of functioning.

C. The preoccupation is not better accounted for by another mental disorder (for example, dissatisfaction with body shape and size in anorexia nervosa).

Source: Reprinted, with permission, from American Psychiatric Association. (2000). *Diagnostic and statistical manual of mental disorders* (4th ed., text revision). Washington, DC: Author, © 2000 American Psychiatric Association.

Gipson, & Cabral, 1999; Roberts, Cash, Feingold, & Johnson, 2006). Overall, about 1% of individuals in community samples meet criteria for BDD, and from 2% to 13% of student samples not in treatment (Phillips, Menard, Fay, & Weisberg, 2005). A somewhat higher proportion of individuals with BDD are interested in art or design compared to individuals without BDD, reflecting, perhaps, a strong interest in aesthetics or appearance (Veale, Ennis, & Lambrou, 2002).

"I didn't want to talk to anybody. . . . I was afraid because what I saw on my face . . . they saw. . . . If I could see it, they could see it. And I thought there was like an arrow pointing at it. And I was very self-conscious. And I felt like the only time I felt comfortable was at night, because it was dark time."

In mental health clinics, the disorder is also uncommon because most people with BDD seek other types of health professionals, such as plastic surgeons and dermatologists. BDD is equally seen in both men and women. In the larger series of 200 individuals reported by Phillips and colleagues (2005), 68.5% were female, but 62% of a large number of individuals with BDD in Japan were males. Generally, there are more similarities than differences between men and women, but some differences have been noted (Phillips, Menard, & Fay, 2006). Men tend to focus on body build, genitals, and thinning hair and tend to be more severe. A focus on muscle defects and body building is nearly unique to men (Pope et al., 2005).

Woman focus on more varied body areas and are more likely to also have an eating disorder. As you might suspect, few people with this disorder get married. Age of onset ranges from early adolescence through the 20s, peaking at the age of 16–17 (Phillips, Menard, Fay, & Weisberg, 2005; Veale, Boocock, et al., 1996; Zimmerman & Mattia, 1998). Individuals are somewhat reluctant to seek treatment. In many cases, a relative will force the issue, demanding the individual get help; this insistence may reflect the disruptiveness of the disorder for family members. Severity is also reflected in the high percentage (24%) of past suicide attempts among the 50 cases described by Veale, Boocock, and colleagues (1996); 27.5% of the 200 cases described by Phillips and colleagues (2005); and 21% of a group of 33 adolescents (Albertini & Phillips, 1999).

One study of 62 consecutive outpatients with BDD found that the degree of psychological stress, quality of life, and impairment were generally worse than comparable indices in patients with depression, diabetes, or a recent myocardial infarction (heart attack) on several questionnaire measures (Phillips, 2000). Similar results were recently reported on a larger sample of 176 patients (Phillips, Menard, Fay, & Pagano, 2005). Thus, BDD is among the more serious of psychological disorders, and depression and substance abuse are common consequences of BDD (Gustad & Phillips, 2003). Further reflecting the intense suffering that accompanies this disorder, Veale (2000) collected information on 25 patients with BDD who had sought cosmetic surgery in the past. Of these, 9 patients who could not afford surgery, or were turned down for other reasons, had attempted by their own hand to alter their appearance dramatically, often with tragic results. One example was a man preoccupied by his skin, who believed it was too "loose." He used a staple gun on both sides of his face to try to keep his skin taut. The staples fell out after 10 minutes and he narrowly missed damaging his facial nerve. In a second example, a woman was preoccupied by her skin and the shape of her face. She filed down her teeth to alter the appearance of her jawline.

Yet another woman who was preoccupied by the ugliness of multiple areas of her body and desired liposuction, but could not afford it, used a knife to cut her thighs and attempted to squeeze out the fat. BDD is also stubbornly chronic. In a recent prospective study of 183 patients, only 21% were somewhat improved over the course of a year, and 15% of that group relapsed during that year (Phillips, Pagano, Menard, & Stout, 2006).

Individuals with BDD react to what they think is a horrible or grotesque feature. Thus, the psychopathology lies in their reacting to a "deformity" that others cannot perceive. Social and cultural determinants of beauty and body image largely define what is "deformed." (Nowhere is this more evident than in the greatly varying cultural standards for body weight and shape, factors that play a major role in eating disorders, as you will see in Chapter 8.)

For example, in most cultures, it is desirable for a woman's skin to be lighter and smoother than a man's skin (Fallon, 1990; Liggett, 1974). Over the centuries freckles have not been popular, and in many cultures chemical solutions were used to remove them. Unfortunately, whole layers of skin disappeared and the underlying flesh was severely damaged (Liggett, 1974). Concerns with the width of the face, so common in BDD, can also be culturally determined. Until recently, in some areas of France, Africa, Greenland, and Peru, the head of a newborn infant was reshaped, either by hand or by tight caps secured by strings. Sometimes the face was elongated; other times it was widened. Similarly, attempts were made to flatten the noses of newborn infants, usually by hand (Fallon, 1990; Liggett, 1974).

©LIVERANI-UNEP/Peter Arnold, Inc.

In various cultures, a child's head or face is manipulated to produce desirable features, as in the addition of rings to lengthen the neck of this Burmese girl.

Other mutilations to enhance beauty are familiar to readers of the *National Geographic*. For example, in Uganda and Ethiopia, it is common practice to insert a large disk or plate into the lower lip, stretching the skin to fit. In Australia and Papua New Guinea, the two top front teeth are knocked out to celebrate adolescents' reaching adulthood. In some tribes, holes are drilled through the six front teeth and star-shaped plugs of brass are inserted; these teeth are also filed to sharp points. In Burma, women wear brass neck rings from an early age to lengthen the neck. One woman's neck was nearly 16 inches long (Morris, 1985).

Finally, many are aware of the old practice in China of binding girls' feet, often preventing the foot from growing to more than one-third of its normal size. Women's bound feet forced them to walk in a way that was thought seductive. As Brownmiller (1984) points out, the myth that an unnaturally small foot signifies extraordinary beauty and grace is still with us. Can you think of the fairy tale where a small foot becomes the identifying feature of the beautiful heroine?

What can we learn about BDD from such practices of mutilation around the world? The behavior of individuals with BDD seems remarkably strange, because they go *against* current cultural practices that put less emphasis on altering facial features. In other words, people who simply conform to the expectations of their culture do not have a disorder (as noted in Chapter 1). Nevertheless, aesthetic plastic surgery, particularly for the nose and lips, is still widely accepted and, because it is most often undertaken by the wealthy, carries an aura of elevated status. In this light, BDD may not be so strange. As with most psychopathology, its characteristic attitudes and behavior may simply be an exaggeration of normal culturally sanctioned behavior.

■ Causes and Treatment

We know little about either the etiology or the treatment of BDD. We have almost no information on whether it runs in families, so we can't investigate a specific genetic contribution. Similarly, we do not have any meaningful information on biological or psychological predisposing factors or vulnerabilities. Psychoanalytic speculations are numerous, but most center on the defensive mechanism of displacement—that is, an underlying unconscious conflict would be too anxiety provoking to admit into consciousness, so the person displaces it onto a body part.

What little evidence we do have on etiology comes from a weak source: the pattern of comorbidity of BDD with other disorders. BDD is a somatoform disorder because its central feature is a psychological preoccupation with somatic issues. For example, in hypochondriasis the focus is on physical sensations, and in BDD the focus is on physical appearance. We have already seen that many of the somatoform disorders tend to co-occur. Linda presented with somatization disorder but also had a history of conversion disorder. However, BDD does not tend to co-occur with the other somatoform disorders, nor does it occur in family members of patients with other somatoform disorders.

A disorder that does often co-occur with BDD and is found among other family members is OCD (Gustad & Phillips, 2003; Phillips & Stout, 2006; Tynes, White, & Steketee, 1990; Zimmerman & Mattia, 1998). Is BDD a variant of OCD? There are a lot of similarities. People with BDD complain of persistent,

intrusive, and horrible thoughts about their appearance, and they engage in such compulsive behaviors as repeatedly looking in mirrors to check their physical features. BDD and OCD also have approximately the same age of onset and run the same course. One recent brain-imaging study demonstrated similar abnormal brain functioning between patients with BDD and patients with OCD (Rauch et al., 2003). Perhaps most significantly, there are two, and only two, treatments for BDD with any evidence of effectiveness. First, drugs that block the reuptake of serotonin, such as clomipramine (Anafranil) and fluvoxamine (Luvox), provide relief to at least some people (Hadley, Kim, Priday, & Hollander, 2006). One controlled study of the effects of drugs on BDD demonstrated that clomipramine was significantly more effective than desipramine, a drug that does not specifically block reuptake of serotonin, for the treatment of BDD, even BDD of the delusional type (Hollander et al., 1999). A second controlled study reported similar findings for fluoxetine (Prozac), with 53% showing a good response compared to 18% on placebo after 3 months (Phillips, Albertini, & Rasmussen, 2002). Intriguingly, these are the same drugs that have the strongest effect in OCD. Second, exposure and response prevention, the type of cognitive behavior therapy effective with OCD, has also been successful with BDD (McKay et al., 1997; Rosen, Reiter, & Orosan, 1995; Veale, Gournay, et al., 1996; Wilhelm, Otto, Lohr, & Deckersbach, 1999). In the Rosen and colleagues (1995) study, 82% of patients treated with this approach responded, although these patients may have been somewhat less severe than other series (Wilhelm et al., 1999; Williams, Hadjistavropoulos, & Sharpe, 2006). Furthermore, patients with BDD and OCD have similar rates of response to these treatments (Saxena et al., 2001; Williams et al., 2006). If BDD does turn out to be a variant of OCD, we will know a lot more about some biological and psychological factors that may lead to its development (Veale, Boocock, et al., 1996).

Another interesting lead on causes of BDD comes from cross-cultural explorations of similar disorders. You may remember the Japanese variant of social phobia, *taijin kyofusho* (see Chapter 5), in which individuals may believe they have horrendous bad breath or body odor and thus avoid social interaction. But people with *taijin kyofusho* also have all the other characteristics of social phobia. Patients who would be diagnosed with BDD in our cul-

Jackson as a child and as an adult. Many people alter their features through surgery. However, people with BDD are seldom satisfied with the results.

ture might simply be considered to have severe social phobia in Japan and Korea. Possibly, then, social anxiety is fundamentally related to BDD, a connection that would give us further hints on the nature of the disorder. Studies of comorbidity indicate that social phobia, along with OCD, is also commonly found in cases of BDD (Phillips & Stout, 2006).

Plastic Surgery and Other Medical Treatments   Patients with BDD believe they are physically deformed in some way and go to medical doctors to attempt to correct their deficits. Phillips, Grant, Siniscalchi, and Albertini (2001) studied the treatments sought by 289 patients with BDD, including 39 children or adolescents, and found that fully 76.4% had sought this type of treatment and 66% were receiving it. Dermatology (skin) treatment was the most often received (45.2%), followed by plastic surgery (23.2%). Looking at it another way, in one recent study of 268 patients seeking care from a dermatologist, 11.9% met criteria for BDD (Phillips, Dufresne, Wilkel, & Vittorio, 2000).

Because the concerns of people with BDD involve mostly the face or head, it is not surprising that the disorder is big business for the plastic surgery profession—but it's bad business. These patients do not benefit from surgery and may return for additional surgery or, on occasion, file malpractice lawsuits. Even worse, a study found that the preoccupation with imagined ugliness increased in people who had plastic surgery, dental work, or special skin treatments for their perceived problems (Phillips et al., 1993). In one newspaper report, a former patient sued one of the past presidents of the American Society of Plastic Surgeons, her surgeon of the past 7 years, over severe scarring from multiple surgeries. The patient reported that a number of surgeons had performed liposuction on her chin, stomach, and knees and thighs; several eyelid lifts; eyebrow tattoos; injections of fat to remove wrinkles; a tummy tuck; a nose job, and other surgeries over 29 years. The patient claimed in court that her current surgeon should have known she had a psychological condition that gave her a distorted image of her own body and that she was, therefore, incapable of giving informed consent to surgery (Barnard, 2000). It is important that plastic surgeons screen out these patients; many do so by collaborating with medically trained psychologists (Pruzinsky, 1988).

Other investigators estimate that as many as 8–25% of all patients who request plastic surgery may have BDD (Barnard, 2000; Crerand et al., 2004). The most common procedures are rhinoplasties (nose jobs), face-lifts, eyebrow elevations, liposuction, breast augmentation, and surgery to alter the jawline. Surgery of this type is increasing rapidly. Between 1992 and 1999, according to the American Society of Plastic Surgeons, eyelid surgery increased 139% to 142,033 surgeries annually and breast enlargement increased 413% to 167,318 surgeries annually. The problem is that surgery on the proportion of these people with BDD seldom produces the desired results. These individuals return for additional surgery on the same defect or concentrate on some new defect. Hollander, Liebowitz, Winchel, Klumker, and Klein (1989) describe one patient who had four separate rhinoplasties and then became concerned about his thinning hair and sloped shoulders. Andreasen and Bardach (1977) noted that some patients become "synthetic creations of artificial noses, breasts, ears,

and hips." Phillips and colleagues (2005) report that of 81% of 50 individuals seeking surgery or similar medical consults were dissatisfied with the result. In 88% of a large group seeking medical rather than psychological treatment, the severity of the disorder and accompanying distress either did not change or *increased* after surgery. Similar discouraging or negative results are evident from other forms of medical treatment, such as skin treatments (Phillips et al., 2001).

CONCEPT CHECK 6.1

Diagnose the somatoform disorders described here by choosing one of the following: (a) pain disorder, (b) hypochondriasis, (c) somatization disorder, (d) conversion disorder, and (e) body dysmorphic disorder.

1. Emily constantly worries about her health. She has been to numerous doctors for her concerns about cancer and other serious diseases, only to be reassured of her well-being. Emily's anxiousness is exacerbated by each small ailment (for example, headaches or stomach pains) that she considers to be indications of a major illness. _____

   _____

2. D. J. arrived at Dr. Blake's office with a folder crammed full of medical records, symptom documentation, and lists of prescribed treatments and drugs. Several doctors are monitoring him for his complaints, ranging from chest pain to difficulty swallowing. D. J. recently lost his job for using too many sick days. _____

3. Sixteen-year-old Chad suddenly lost the use of his arms with no medical cause. The complete paralysis slowly improved to the point that he could slightly raise them. However, Chad cannot drive, pick up objects, or perform most tasks necessary for day-to-day life. _____

   _____

4. Loretta is 32 and has been preoccupied with the size and shape of her nose for 2 years. She has been saving money for plastic surgery, after which, she is sure, her career will improve. Trouble is, three honest plastic surgeons have told her that her nose is fine as it is. _____

5. Betty had considerable pain when she broke her arm. A year after it healed and all medical tests indicate her arm is fine, she still complains of the pain. It seems to intensify when she fights with her husband. _____

DISSOCIATIVE DISORDERS

At the beginning of the chapter, we said that when individuals feel detached from themselves or their surroundings, almost as if they are dreaming or living in slow motion, they are having dissociative experiences. Morton Prince, the founder of the *Journal of Abnormal Psychology*, noted more than 100 years ago that many people experience something like dissociation occasionally (Prince, 1906–1907). It is most likely to happen after an extremely stressful event, such as an accident. It might also happen when you're tired or under physical or mental pressure from, say, staying up all night cramming for an exam. Perhaps because you knew the cause, the dissociation may not have bothered you much (Dixon, 1963; Noyes, Hoenk, Kuperman, & Slymen, 1977). On the other hand, it may have been extremely frightening. Transient experiences of dissociation will occur in about half of the general population at some point in their lives, and studies show that if someone experiences a traumatic event, between 31% and 66% will have this feeling at that time (Hunter & Sierra, 2004).

Investigators at Stanford University surveyed the reactions of journalists who witnessed one of the first executions in California in many decades, a traumatic experience for many (Freinkel, Koopman, & Spiegel, 1994). The prisoner, Robert Alton Harriss, had been found guilty of the particularly brutal murder of two 16-year-old boys. As is customary, a number of journalists were invited to witness the execution. Because there were a number of stays of execution, they ended up spending all night at the prison as Harriss was repeatedly led into and back out of the gas chamber before he was finally executed near daybreak. Several weeks later, the journalists filled out acute stress reaction questionnaires. Between 40% and 60% of the journalists experienced several dissociative symptoms. For example, during the execution, things around them seemed unreal or dreamlike and they felt time had stopped. They also felt estranged from other people and distant from their own emotions; a number of them felt they were strangers to themselves.

These kinds of experiences can be divided into two types. During an episode of *depersonalization,* your perception alters so that you temporarily lose the sense of your own reality. During an episode of **derealization,** your sense of the reality of the external world is lost. Things may seem to change shape or size; people may seem dead or mechanical. These sensations of unreality are characteristic of the dissociative disorders because, in a sense, they are a psychological mechanism whereby one "dissociates" from reality. Depersonalization is often part of a serious set of conditions in which reality, experience, and even identity seem to disintegrate. As we go about our day-to-day lives, we ordinarily have an excellent sense of who we are and a general knowledge of the identity of other people. We are also aware of events around us, of where we are, and of why we are there. Finally, except for occasional small lapses, our memories remain intact so that events leading up to the current moment are clear in our minds.

But what happens if we can't remember why we are in a certain place or even who we are? What happens if we lose our sense that our surroundings are real? Finally, what happens if we not only forget who we are but also begin thinking we are somebody else—somebody who has a different personality, different memories, and even different physical reactions, such as allergies we never had? These are examples of disintegrated experience (Cardeña & Gleaves, 2003; Putnam, 1991; Spiegel & Cardeña, 1991). In each case, there are alterations in our relationship to the self, to the world, or to memory processes.

Although we have much to learn about these disorders, we briefly describe four of them—depersonalization disorder, dissociative amnesia, dissociative fugue, and dissociative trance disorder—before examining the fascinating condition of dissociative identity disorder. As you will see, the influence of social and cultural factors is strong in dissociative disorders. Even in severe cases, the expression of the pathology does not stray far from socially and culturally sanctioned forms (Kihlstrom, 2005).

Depersonalization Disorder

When feelings of unreality are so severe and frightening that they dominate an individual's life and prevent normal functioning, clinicians may diagnose the rare **depersonalization disorder.** Consider the case of Bonnie.

BONNIE: Dancing Away From Herself

Bonnie, a dance teacher in her late 20s, was accompanied by her husband when she first visited the clinic and complained of "flipping out." When asked what she meant, she said, "It's the most scary thing in the world. It often happens when I'm teaching my modern dance class. I'll be up in front and I will feel focused on. Then, as I'm demonstrating the steps, I just feel like it's not really me and that I don't really have control of my legs. Sometimes I feel like I'm standing in back of myself just watching. Also I get tunnel vision. It seems like I can only see in a narrow space right in front of me and I just get totally separated from what's going on around me. Then I begin to panic and perspire and shake." It turns out that Bonnie's problems began after she smoked marijuana for the first time about 10 years before. She had the same feeling then and found it scary, but with the help of friends she got through it. Lately the feeling recurred more often and more severely, particularly when she was teaching dance class.

You may remember from Chapter 5 that during an intense panic attack many people (approximately 50%) experience feelings of unreality. People undergoing intense stress or experiencing a traumatic event may also experience these symptoms, which characterize the newly defined *acute stress disorder.* Feelings of depersonalization and derealization are part of several disorders (Boon & Draijer, 1991). But when severe depersonalization and derealization are the primary problem, the individual meets criteria for depersonalization disorder (Steinberg, 1991). Recent small surveys suggest that this disorder exists in approximately 0.8% of the population (Johnson, Cohen, Kasen, & Brook, 2006). Simeon, Knutelska, Nelson, and Guralnik (2003) described 117 cases approximately equally split between men and women; Table 6.4 summarizes the 10 most commonly experienced symptoms in these patients. Mean age of onset was 16 years, and the course tended to be chronic. All patients were substantially impaired. Anxiety, mood, and personality disorders are also commonly found in these individuals (Simeon et al., 2003; Johnson et al., 2006). Among the 117 patients described, 73% suffered from additional mood disorders and 64% from anxiety disorders at some point in their lives.

Guralnik, Schmeidler, and Simeon (2000) compared 15 patients with depersonalization disorder to 15 matched normal-comparison subjects on a comprehensive neuropsychological test battery that assessed cognitive function. Although both groups were of equal intelligence, the subjects with depersonalization disorder showed a distinct cognitive profile, reflecting some specific cognitive deficits on measures of attention, short-term memory, and spatial reasoning. Basically, these patients were easily distracted and had some trouble perceiving three-dimensional objects because they tended to "flatten" these objects into two dimensions. It is not clear how these cognitive and perceptual deficits develop, but they seem to correspond with reports of "tunnel vision" (perceptual distortions) and "mind emptiness" (difficulty absorbing new information) that characterize these patients.

Specific aspects of brain functioning are also associated with depersonalization (see, for example, Sierra & Berrios, 1998; Simeon et al., 2000). Sierra and colleagues (2002) compared skin conductance responding, a psychophysiological measure of emotional responding (see Chapter 3), among 15 patients with depersonalization disorder, 11 patients with anxiety disorders, and 15 control subjects without any disorder. Patients with depersonalization disorder showed greatly reduced emotional responding compared to other groups, reflecting a tendency to selectively inhibit emotional expression. Brain-imaging studies now confirm deficits in perception (Simeon et al., 2000) and emotion regulation (Phillips et al., 2001). Other studies note dysregulation in the hypothalamic–pituitary–adrenocortical (HPA) axis among these patients, compared to normal controls (Simeon, Guralnik, Knutelska, Hollander, & Schmeidler, 2001), suggesting, again, deficits in emotional responding. Psychological treatments have not been systematically studied. A recent evaluation of the drug

DSM-IV-TR

DSM TABLE 6.7 Diagnostic Criteria for Depersonalization Disorder

A. Persistent or recurrent experiences of feeling detached from, and as if one is an outside observer of, one's mental processes or body (for example, feeling like one is in a dream).
B. During the depersonalization experience, reality testing remains intact.
C. The depersonalization causes clinically significant distress or impairment in social, occupational, or other important areas of functioning.
D. The depersonalization experience does not occur exclusively during the course of another mental disorder, such as schizophrenia, panic disorder, acute stress disorder, or another dissociative disorder, and is not due to the direct physiological effects of a substance (for example, a drug of abuse or a medication) or a general medical condition (for example, temporal lobe epilepsy).

Source: Reprinted, with permission, from American Psychiatric Association. (2000). *Diagnostic and statistical manual of mental disorders* (4th ed., text revision). Washington, DC: Author, © 2000 American Psychiatric Association.

Prozac did not show any treatment effect compared to placebo (Simeon, Guralnik, Schneider, & Knutelska, 2004).

Dissociative Amnesia

Perhaps the easiest to understand of the severe dissociative disorders is one called **dissociative amnesia,** which includes several patterns. People who are unable to remember anything, including who they are, are said to suffer from **generalized amnesia.** Generalized amnesia may be lifelong or may extend from a period in the more recent past, such as 6 months or a year previously.

THE WOMAN WHO LOST HER MEMORY

Several years ago, a woman in her early 50s brought her daughter to one of our clinics because of the girl's refusal to attend school and other severely disruptive behavior. The father, who refused to come to the session, was quarrelsome, a heavy drinker, and, on occasion, abusive. The girl's brother, now in his mid-20s, lived at home and was a burden on the family. Several times a week a major battle erupted, complete with shouting, pushing, and shoving, as each member of the family blamed the others for all their problems. The mother, a strong woman, was clearly the peacemaker responsible for holding the family together. Approximately every 6 months, usually after a family battle, the mother lost her memory and the family had her admitted to the hospital. After a few days away from the turmoil, the mother regained her memory and went home, only to repeat the cycle in the coming months. Although we did not treat this family (they lived too far away), the situation resolved itself when the children moved away and the stress decreased.

TABLE 6.4 Dissociative Experiences Scale Item Scores in 117 Subjects With Depersonalization Disorder (Arranged in Descending Frequency)

Item No.	Abbreviated Description	Mean	SD
12	Surroundings seem unreal	67.4	29.6
28	Looking at the world through a fog	60.0	37.3
13	Body does not belong to one	50.6	34.7
2	Did not hear part of conversation	43.6	29.3
16	Finding familiar place strange and unfamiliar	35.3	33.0
20	Staring off into space; unaware of time	32.7	31.8
23	Can't remember if just did something or thought it	31.6	28.8
22	Do usually difficult things with ease/spontaneity	31.2	31.2
21	Act so differently/feel like two different people	28.7	32.5
20	Talk out loud to oneself when alone	28.4	32.2

SD = standard deviation.
Adapted from Simeon, D., Knutelska, M., Nelson, D., & Guralnik, O., (2003). Feeling unreal: A depersonalization disorder update of 119 cases. *Journal of Clinical Psychiatry,* 185, 31–36. © Physicians Post Graduate Press, Inc.

DSM-IV-TR

DSM TABLE 6.8 Diagnostic Criteria for Dissociative Amnesia

A. The predominant disturbance is one or more episodes of inability to recall important personal information, usually of a traumatic or stressful nature, that is too extensive to be explained by ordinary forgetfulness.

B. The disturbance does not occur exclusively during the course of dissociative identity disorder, dissociative fugue, PTSD, acute stress disorder, or somatization disorder and is not due to the direct physiological effects of a substance (for example, a drug of abuse or a medication) or a neurological or other general medical condition (for example, amnestic disorder due to head trauma).

C. The symptoms cause clinically significant distress or impairment in social, occupational, or other important areas of functioning.

Source: Reprinted, with permission, from American Psychiatric Association. (2000). *Diagnostic and statistical manual of mental disorders* (4th ed., text revision). Washington, DC: Author, © 2000 American Psychiatric Association.

Far more common than general amnesia is **localized or selective amnesia,** a failure to recall specific events, usually traumatic, that occur during a specific period. Dissociative amnesia is common during war (Cardeña & Gleaves, 2003; Loewenstein, 1991; Spiegel & Cardeña, 1991). Sackeim and Devanand (1991) describe the interesting case of a woman whose father had deserted her when she was young. She had also been forced to have an abortion at the age of 14. Years later, she came for treatment for frequent headaches. In therapy she reported early events (for example, the abortion) rather matter-of-factly, but under hypnosis she would relive, with intense emotion, the early abortion and remember that subsequently she was raped by the abortionist. She also had images of her father attending a funeral for her aunt, one of the few times she ever saw him. Upon awakening from the hypnotic state, she had no memory of emotionally reexperiencing these events, and she wondered why she had been crying. In this case, the woman did not have amnesia for the *events themselves* but rather for her intense *emotional reactions to the events*. Absence of the subjective experience of emotion that is often present in depersonalization disorder and confirmed by brain-imaging studies (Phillips et al., 2001) becomes prominent here. In most cases of dissociative amnesia, the forgetting is selective for traumatic events or memories rather than generalized.

Dissociative Fugue

A related disorder is referred to as **dissociative fugue,** with *fugue* literally meaning "flight" (*fugitive* is from the same root). In these curious cases, memory loss revolves around a specific incident—an unexpected trip (or trips). Mostly, individuals just take off and later find themselves in a new place, unable to remember why or how they got there. Usually they have left behind an intolerable situation. During these trips, a person sometimes assumes a new identity or at least becomes confused about the old identity. Consider the case of Jeffrey Ingram, a 40-year-old male from Washington state, who found himself unexpectedly in Denver.

JEFFREY: A Troubled Trip

An amnesia sufferer who had been searching for his identity for more than a month was back in Washington state with his fiancée on Tuesday, but he still doesn't remember his past life or what happened, his mother said.

Jeffrey Alan Ingram, 40, was diagnosed in Denver with dissociative fugue, a type of amnesia.

He has had similar bouts of amnesia in the past, likely triggered by stress, once disappearing for 9 months. When he went missing this time, on September 6, he had been on his way to Canada to visit a friend who was dying of cancer, said his fiancée, Penny Hansen.

"I think that the stress, the sadness, the grief of facing a best friend dying was enough, and leaving me was enough to send him into an amnesia state," Hansen told KCNC-TV.

When Ingram found himself in Denver on September 10, he didn't know who he was. He said he walked around for about 6 hours asking people for help, then ended up at a hospital, where police spokeswoman Virginia Quinones said Ingram was diagnosed with a type of amnesia known as dissociative fugue.

Searched for his identity. Ingram's identity came to light last weekend after he appeared on several news shows asking the public for help: "If anybody recognizes me, knows who I am, please let somebody know."

"Penny's brother called her right away and told her 'Did you watch this newscast?' and 'I think that's Jeff that they're showing on television,'" said Marilyn Meehan, a spokeswoman for Hansen.

Hansen had filed a missing person report after Ingram failed to show up at her mother's home in Bellingham, Washington, on his way to Canada, but officials searching for him had turned up nothing.

On Monday night, two Denver police detectives accompanied Ingram on a flight to Seattle, where he was reunited with his fiancée.

His mother, Doreen Tompkins of Slave Lake, Alberta, was in tears as she talked about the struggle her son and the family still face.

"It's going to be very difficult again, but you know what, I can do it," she told CTV news of Edmonton, Alberta. "I did it before, I can do it again. I'll do it as many times as I have to just so I can have my son."

Memory never fully regained. Ingram had experienced an episode of amnesia in 1995 when he disappeared during a trip to a grocery store. Nine months later, he was found in a Seattle hospital, according to Thurston County, Washington, officials. His mother said he never fully regained his memory.

Meehan, who works with Hansen at the state Utilities and Transportation Commission, said the couple would not give interviews because they want to concentrate on Ingram's effort to regain his memory.

"They're taking it one step at a time," Meehan said.

"He said that while her face wasn't familiar to him, her heart was familiar to him," she said. "He can't remember his home, but he said their home felt like home to him."

Dissociative amnesia and fugue states seldom appear before adolescence and usually occur in adulthood. It is rare for these states to appear for the first time after an individual reaches the age of 50 (Sackeim & Devanand, 1991). However, once they do appear, they may continue well into old age.

Fugue states usually end rather abruptly, and the individual returns home, recalling most, if not all, of what happened. In this disorder, the disintegrated experience is more than memory loss, involving at least some disintegration of identity, if not the complete adoption of a new one.

An apparently distinct dissociative disorder not found in Western cultures is called *amok* (as in "running amok"). Most people with this disorder are males. Amok has attracted attention because individuals in this trancelike state often brutally assault and sometimes kill people or animals. If the person is not killed himself, he probably will not remember the episode. Running amok is only one of a number of "running" syndromes in which an individual enters a trancelike state and suddenly, imbued with a mysterious source of energy, runs or flees for a long time. Except for amok, the prevalence of running disorders is somewhat greater in women, as with most dissociative disorders. Among native peoples of the Arctic, running disorder is termed *pivloktoq*. Among the Navajo tribe, it is called *frenzy witchcraft*. Despite their different culturally determined expression, running disorders seem to meet criteria for dissociative fugue, with the possible exception of amok.

Dissociative Trance Disorder

Dissociative disorders differ in important ways across cultures. In many areas of the world, dissociative phenomena may occur as a trance or possession. The usual sorts of dissociative symptoms, such as sudden changes in personality, are attributed to possession by a spirit important in the particular culture. Often this spirit demands and receives presents or favors from the family and friends of the victim. Like other dissociative states, trance disorder seems to be most common in women and is often associated with stress or trauma, which, as in dissociative amnesia and fugue states, is current rather than in the past.

Trance and possession are a common part of some traditional religious and cultural practices and are not considered abnormal in that context. Dissociative trances commonly occur in India, Nigeria (where they are called *vinvusa*), Thailand *(phii pob),* and other Asian and African countries (Mezzich et al., 1992; Saxena & Prasad, 1989; van Duijil, Cardeña, & de Jong, 2005). In the United States, culturally accepted dissociation commonly occurs during African American prayer meetings (Griffith et al., 1980), Native American rituals (Jilek, 1982), and Puerto Rican spiritist sessions (Comas-Diaz, 1981). Among Bahamians and African Americans from the

Jeffrey Alan Ingram found himself in Denver not knowing who he was or why he was there after having gone missing a month earlier from Washington state.

South, trance syndromes are often referred to colloquially as "falling out." Currently this condition is not a diagnostic category in DSM-IV-TR, but when the state is *undesirable* and considered pathological by members of the culture, a proposal exists to diagnose it defined as a **dissociative trance disorder (DTD).** The personality profiles of 58 cases of dissociative trance disorder in Singapore, derived from objective testing, revealed that these individuals tended to be nervous, excitable, and emotionally unstable relative to "normals" in Singapore (Ng, Yap, Su, Lim, & Ong, 2002). Although trance and possession are almost never seen in Western cultures, they are among the most common forms of dissociative disorders elsewhere. A category to include these states has been proposed for DSM-V.

Dissociative Identity Disorder

People with **dissociative identity disorder (DID)** may adopt as many as 100 new identities, all simultaneously coexisting, although the average number is closer to 15. In some cases, the

DSM-IV-TR
DSM TABLE 6.9 Diagnostic Criteria for Dissociative Fugue
A. The predominant disturbance is sudden, unexpected travel away from home or one's customary place of work, with inability to recall one's past. B. Confusion about personal identity or assumption of new identity (partial or complete). C. The disturbance does not occur exclusively during the course of dissociative identity disorder and is not due to the direct physiological effects of a substance (for example, a drug of abuse or a medication) or a general medical condition (for example, temporal lobe epilepsy). D. The symptoms cause clinically significant distress or impairment in social, occupational, or other important areas of functioning.

Source: Reprinted, with permission, from American Psychiatric Association. (2000). *Diagnostic and statistical manual of mental disorders* (4th ed., text revision). Washington, DC: Author, © 2000 American Psychiatric Association.

DSM-IV-TR

DSM TABLE 6.10 Research Criteria for Dissociative Trance Disorder

A. Either 1 or 2:
  1. Trance, that is, temporary marked alteration in the state of consciousness or loss of customary sense of personal identity without replacement by an alternate identity, associated with at least one of the following:
     a. Narrowing of awareness of immediate surroundings, or unusually narrow and selective focusing on environmental stimuli
     b. Stereotyped behaviors or movements experienced as being beyond one's control
  2. Possession trance, a single or episodic alteration in the state of consciousness characterized by the replacement of customary sense of personal identity by a new identity. This is attributed to the influence of a spirit, power, deity, or other person, as evidenced by one (or more) of the following:
     a. Stereotyped and culturally determined behaviors or movements experienced as being controlled by the possessing agent
     b. Full or partial amnesia for the event
B. The trance or possession trance state is not accepted as a normal part of a collective cultural or religious practice.
C. The trance or possession trance state causes clinically significant distress or impairment in social, occupational, or other important areas of functioning.
D. The trance or possession trance state does not occur exclusively during the course of a psychotic disorder (including mood disorder with psychotic features and brief reactive psychosis) or dissociative identity disorder and is not due to the direct physiological effects of a substance or a general medical condition.

Source: Reprinted, with permission, from American Psychiatric Association. (2000). *Diagnostic and statistical manual of mental disorders* (4th ed., text revision). Washington, DC: Author, © 2000 American Psychiatric Association.

identities are complete, each with its own behavior, tone of voice, and physical gestures. But in many cases, only a few characteristics are distinct, because the identities are only partially independent. Therefore, the name of the disorder was changed in DSM-IV from multiple personality disorder to DID. Consider the case of Jonah, originally reported by Ludwig, Brandsma, Wilbur, Bendfeldt, and Jameson (1972).

JONAH: Bewildering Blackouts

Jonah, 27 years old and black, suffered from severe headaches that were unbearably painful and lasted for increasingly longer periods. Furthermore, he couldn't remember things that happened while he had a headache, except that sometimes a great deal of time passed. Finally, after a particularly bad night, when he could stand it no longer, he arranged for admission to the local hospital. What prompted Jonah to come to the hospital, however, was that other people told him what he did during his severe headaches. For example, he was told that the night before he had a violent fight with another man and attempted to stab him. He fled the scene and was shot at dur-

ing a high-speed chase by the police. His wife told him that during a previous headache he chased her and his 3-year-old daughter out of the house, threatening them with a butcher knife. During his headaches, and while he was violent, he called himself "Usoffa Abdulla, son of Omega." Once he attempted to drown a man in a river. The man survived, and Jonah escaped by swimming a quarter of a mile upstream. He woke up the next morning in his own bed, soaking wet, with no memory of the incident.

■ Clinical Description

During Jonah's hospitalization, the staff was able to observe his behavior directly, both when he had headaches and during other periods that he did not remember. He claimed other names at these times, acted differently, and generally seemed to be another person entirely. The staff distinguished three separate identities, or **alters,** in addition to Jonah. (*Alters* is the shorthand term for the different identities or personalities in DID.) The first alter was named Sammy. Sammy seemed rational, calm, and in control. The second alter, King Young, seemed to be in charge of all sexual activity and was particularly interested in having as many heterosexual interactions as possible. The third alter was the violent and dangerous Usoffa Abdulla. Characteristically, Jonah knew nothing of the three alters. Sammy was most aware of the other personalities. King Young and Usoffa Abdulla knew a little bit about the others but only indirectly.

In the hospital, psychologists determined that Sammy first appeared when Jonah was about 6, immediately after Jonah saw his mother stab his father. Jonah's mother sometimes dressed him as a girl in private. On one of these occasions, shortly after Sammy emerged, King Young appeared. When Jonah was 9 or 10, he was brutally attacked by a group of white youths. At this point, Usoffa Abdulla emerged, announcing that his sole reason for existence was to protect Jonah.

DSM-IV-TR criteria for DID include amnesia, as in dissociative amnesia and dissociative fugue. Here, however, identity has also fragmented. How many personalities live inside one body is relatively unimportant, whether there are 3, 4, or even 100 of them. Again, the defining feature of this disorder is that certain aspects of the person's identity are dissociated, accounting for the change in the name of this disorder in DSM-IV from multiple personality disorder to DID. This change also corrects the notion that multiple people somehow live inside one body.

Characteristics The person who becomes the patient and asks for treatment is usually a "host" identity. Host personalities usually attempt to hold various fragments of identity together but end up being overwhelmed. The first personality to seek treatment is seldom the original personality of the person. Usually, the host personality develops later (Putnam, 1992). Many patients have at least one impulsive alter who handles sexuality and generates income, sometimes by acting as a prostitute. In other cases, all alters may abstain from sex. Cross-gendered alters are not uncommon. For example, a small agile woman might have a strong powerful male alter who serves as a protector.

DSM-IV-TR

DSM TABLE 6.11 Diagnostic Criteria for Dissociative Identity Disorder (Multiple Personality Disorder)

A. The presence of two or more distinct identities or personality states (each with its own relatively enduring pattern of perceiving, relating to, and thinking about the environment and self).

B. At least two of these identities or personality states recurrently take control of the person's behavior.

C. Inability to recall important personal information that is too extensive to be explained by ordinary forgetfulness.

D. The disturbance is not due to the direct physiological effects of a substance (for example, blackouts or chaotic behavior during alcohol intoxication) or a general medical condition (for example, complex partial seizures). Note: In children, the symptoms are not attributable to imaginary playmates or other fantasy play.

Source: Reprinted, with permission, from American Psychiatric Association. (2000). *Diagnostic and statistical manual of mental disorders* (4th ed., text revision). Washington, DC: Author, © 2000 American Psychiatric Association.

The transition from one personality to another is called a *switch*. Usually, the switch is instantaneous (although in movies and on television it is often drawn out for dramatic effect). Physical transformations may occur during switches. Posture, facial expressions, patterns of facial wrinkling, and even physical disabilities may emerge. In one study, changes in handedness occurred in 37% of the cases (Putnam, Guroff, Silberman, Barban, & Post, 1986).

Can DID Be Faked? Are the fragmented identities "real," or is the person faking them to avoid responsibility or stress? As with conversion disorders, it is difficult to answer this question, for several reasons (Kluft, 1999). First, evidence indicates that individuals with DID are suggestible (Bliss, 1984; Kihlstrom, 2005). It is possible that alters are created in response to leading questions from therapists, either during psychotherapy or while the person is in a hypnotic state.

KENNETH: The Hillside Strangler

During the late 1970s, Kenneth Bianchi brutally raped and murdered 10 young women in the Los Angeles area and left their bodies naked and in full view on the sides of various hills. Despite overwhelming evidence that Bianchi was the "Hillside Strangler," he continued to assert his innocence, prompting some professionals to think he might have DID. His lawyer brought in a clinical psychologist, who hypnotized him and asked whether there were another part of Ken with whom he could speak. Guess what? Somebody called "Steve" answered and said he had done all the killing. Steve also said that Ken knew nothing about the murders. With this

evidence, the lawyer entered a plea of not guilty by reason of insanity.

The prosecution called on the late Martin Orne, a distinguished clinical psychologist and psychiatrist who was one of the world's leading experts on hypnosis and dissociative disorders (Orne, Dinges, & Orne, 1984). Orne used procedures similar to those we described in the context of conversion blindness to determine whether Bianchi was simulating DID or had a true psychological disorder. For example, Orne suggested during an in-depth interview with Bianchi that a true multiple personality disorder included at least three personalities. Bianchi soon produced a third personality. By interviewing Bianchi's friends and relatives, Orne established that there was no independent corroboration of different personalities before Bianchi's arrest. Psychological tests also failed to show significant differences among the personalities; true fragmented identities often score differently on personality tests. Several textbooks on psychopathology were found in Bianchi's room; therefore, he presumably had studied the subject. Orne concluded that Bianchi responded like someone simulating hypnosis, not someone deeply hypnotized. On the basis of Orne's testimony, Bianchi was found guilty and sentenced to life in prison.

Some investigators have studied the ability of individuals to fake dissociative experiences. Spanos, Weeks, and Bertrand (1985) demonstrated in an experiment that a college student could simulate an alter if it was suggested that faking was plausible, as in the interview with Bianchi. All the students in the group were told to play the role of an accused murderer claiming his innocence. The subjects received exactly the same interview as Orne administered to Bianchi, word for word. More than 80% simulated an alternate personality to avoid conviction. Groups given vaguer instructions, and no direct suggestion an alternate personality might exist, were much less likely to use one in their defense.

In an important experiment along the same lines, Spanos, James, and de Groot (1990) compared subjects with hypnotically induced amnesia (similar to the type in dissociative disorders) with subjects who were instructed to *simulate* amnesia. All the subjects were asked to memorize a list of words. They were then given a list that included the memorized words and many new ones. Subjects under hypnosis exhibited above-chance levels of recognition of the original words. Simulators, on the other hand, had below-chance recognition for the same words. Below-chance levels of recognition are more consistent with faked amnesia because faking subjects tend to overcompensate. Objective assessment of memory, particularly implicit (unconscious) memory, reveals that the memory processes in patients with DID do not differ from "normals" when the methodologies of cognitive science are used (Allen & Movius, 2000; Huntjens et al., 2002; Huntjens, Postma, Peters, Woertman, & van der Hart, 2003). Huntjens and colleagues (2006) showed that patients with DID acted more like simulators concerning other identities, about which they profess no memory (inter-identity amnesia), suggest-

The late Martin Orne was a leading expert worldwide on hypnosis and dissociative disorders.

ing the possibility of faking. This is in contrast to reports from interviews with patients with DID that suggest that memories are different from one alter to the next.

These findings on faking and the effect of hypnosis led Spanos (1996) to suggest that the symptoms of DID could mostly be accounted for by therapists who inadvertently suggested the existence of alters to suggestible individuals, a model known as the "sociocognitive model" because the possibility of identity fragments and early trauma is socially reinforced by a therapist (Kihlstrom, 2005; Lilienfeld et al., 1999). A recent survey of American psychiatrists showed little consensus on the scientific validity of DID, with only one-third in the sample believing that the diagnosis should have been included without reservation in DSM-IV (Pope, Oliva, Hudson, Bodkin, & Gruber, 1999). (We return to this point of view when we discuss false memories.)

On the other hand, some objective tests suggest that many people with fragmented identities are not consciously and voluntarily simulating (Kluft, 1991, 1999). Condon, Ogston, and Pacoe (1969) examined a film about Chris Sizemore, the real-life subject of the book and movie *The Three Faces of Eve.* They determined that one of the personalities (Eve Black) showed a transient microstrabismus (difference in joined lateral eye movements) that was not observed in the other personalities. These optical differences have been confirmed by S. D. Miller (1989), who demonstrated that DID subjects had 4.5 times the average number of changes in optical functioning in their alter identities than control subjects who simulated alter personalities. Miller concludes that optical changes, including measures of visual acuity, manifest refraction, and eye muscle balance, would be difficult to fake. Ludwig and colleagues (1972) found that Jonah's various identities had different physiological responses to emotionally laden words, including electrodermal activity, a measure of otherwise imperceptible sweat gland activity, and EEG brain waves. Using up-to-date functional magnetic resonance imaging procedures, changes in brain function were observed in one patient while switching from one personality to another. Specifically, this patient showed changes in hippocampal and medial temporal activity after the switch (Tsai, Condie, Wu, & Chang, 1999). A number of subsequent studies confirm that various alters have unique psychophysiological profiles (Cardeña & Gleaves, 2003; Putnam, 1997). Kluft (1999) suggests a number of additional clinical strategies to distinguish malingerers from patients with DID, including the observations that malingerers are usually eager to demonstrate their symptoms and do so in a fluid fashion. Patients with DID, on the other hand, are more likely to attempt to hide symptoms.

ANNA O.: Revealed

We return one more time to the famous case that prompted early insights into the unconscious and contributed to the development of psychoanalysis. Earlier we described Anna O.'s conversion symptoms of paralysis in her right arm, anesthesia of her right side, and the loss of the ability to speak her native German (although she retained perfect command of English). As Anna confronted her traumatic memories of watching her father die while she nursed him, she increasingly recovered her physical abilities.

Anna O.'s real name was Bertha Pappenheim, and she was an extraordinary woman. What many people don't realize is that she was never completely cured by Breuer, who finally gave up on her in 1882. During the next decade, she was institutionalized several times with severe recurrences of her conversion symptoms before beginning a slow recovery. She went on to become a pioneering social worker and staunch crusader against the sexual abuse of women (Putnam, 1992). She devoted her life to freeing women who were trapped in prostitution and slavery throughout Europe, Russia, and the Near East. Risking her own life, she entered brothels to liberate women from their captors. She wrote a play, *Women's Rights,* about sadistic men and the ongoing abuse of women. She founded a league of Jewish women in 1904 and a home for unwed mothers in 1907. In recognition of her extraordinary contributions as one of the first militant feminists, a commemorative stamp was later issued in her honor by the West German government (Sulloway, 1979).

Pappenheim's friends remarked that she seemed to lead a "double life." On the one hand, she was a radical feminist

Chris Sizemore's history of DID was dramatized in *The Three Faces of Eve.*

and reformer. On the other hand, she belonged to the cultural elite in Vienna at the end of the 19th century. It is clear from Breuer's notes that there were "two Anna O.'s" and that she suffered from DID. One personality was somewhat depressed and anxious but otherwise relatively normal. But in an instant she would turn dark and foreboding. Breuer was convinced that during these times "Anna" was someone else, someone who hallucinated and was verbally abusive. And it was the second Anna O. who experienced conversion symptoms. The second Anna O. spoke only English or garbled mixtures of four or five languages. The first Anna O. spoke fluent French and Italian, as well as her native German. Characteristically, one personality had no memory of what happened when the other was "out." Almost anything might cause an instant switch in personalities—for example, the sight of an orange, which was Anna O.'s primary source of nourishment when she nursed her dying father. Putnam (1992, p. 36) reports that when Pappenheim died of cancer in 1936, "It is said that she left two wills, each written in a different hand."

■ Statistics

Jonah had 4 identities, and Anna O. only 2, but the average number of alter personalities is reported by clinicians as closer to 15 (Ross, 1997; Sackeim & Devanand, 1991). Of people with DID, the ratio of females to males is as high as 9:1, although these data are based on accumulated case studies rather than survey research (Maldonado, Butler, & Spiegel, 1998). The onset is almost always in childhood, often as young as 4 years of age, although it is usually approximately 7 years after the appearance of symptoms before the disorder is identified (Maldonado et al., 1998; Putnam et al., 1986). Once established, the disorder tends to last a lifetime in the absence of treatment. The form it takes does not seem to vary substantially over the person's life span, although some evidence indicates the frequency of switching decreases with age (Sackeim & Devanand, 1991). Different personalities may emerge in response to new life situations, as was the case with Jonah.

There are not good epidemiological studies on the prevalence of the disorder in the population at large, although investigators now think it is more common than previously estimated (Kluft, 1991; Ross, 1997). For example, semistructured interviews of large numbers of severely disturbed inpatients found prevalence rates of DID of between 3% and 6% in North America (Ross, 1997; Ross, Anderson, Fleisher, & Norton, 1991; Saxe et al., 1993) and approximately 2% in Holland (Friedl & Draijer, 2000). In the best survey to date in a nonclinical (community) setting, a prevalence of 1.5% was found during the previous year (Johnson et al., 2006).

A large percentage of DID patients have simultaneous psychological disorders that may include anxiety, substance abuse, depression, and personality disorders (Johnson et al., 2006; Kluft, 1999; Ross et al., 1990). In one sample of more than 100 patients, more than seven additional diagnoses were noted on the average (Ellason & Ross, 1997). Another study of 42 patients documented a pattern of severe comorbid personality disorders, including se-

vere borderline pathology (Dell, 1998). It seems likely that different personalities will present with differing patterns of comorbidity, but the research has not yet been done. In some cases, this high rate of comorbidity may reflect that certain disorders, such as borderline personality disorder, share many features with DID—for example, self-destructive, sometimes suicidal behavior, and emotional instability. Mostly, however, the high frequency of additional disorders accompanying DID simply reflects an intensely severe reaction to what seems to be in almost all cases horrible child abuse. Because auditory hallucinations are common, DID is often misdiagnosed as a psychotic disorder. But the voices in DID are reported by patients as coming from inside their heads, not outside as in psychotic disorders. Because patients with DID are usually aware the voices are hallucinations, they don't report them and try to suppress them. These voices often encourage doing something against the person's will, so some individuals, particularly in other cultures, appear to be possessed by demons (Putnam, 1997). Although systematic studies are lacking, DID seems to occur in a variety of cultures throughout the world (Boon & Draijer, 1993; Coons, Bowman, Kluft, & Milstein, 1991; Ross, 1997). For example, Coons and colleagues (1991) found reports of DID in 21 different countries.

■ Causes

It is informative to examine current evidence on causes for all dissociative disorders, as we do later, but our emphasis here is on the etiology of DID. Life circumstances that encourage the development of DID seem quite clear in at least one respect. Almost every patient presenting with this disorder reports being horribly, often unspeakably, abused as a child.

SYBIL: Continual Abuse

You may have seen the movie that was based on Sybil's biography (Schreiber, 1973). Sybil's mother had schizophrenia, and her father refused or was unable to intervene in the mother's brutality. Day after day throughout her childhood, Sybil was sexually tortured and occasionally nearly murdered. Before she was 1 year old, her mother began tying her up in various ways and, on occasion, suspending her from the ceiling. Many mornings, her mother placed Sybil on the kitchen table and forcefully inserted various objects into her vagina. Sybil's mother reasoned, psychotically, that she was preparing her daughter for adult sex. In fact, she so brutally tore the child's vaginal canal that scars were evident during adult gynecological exams. Sybil was also given strong laxatives but prohibited from using the bathroom. Because of her father's detachment and the normal appearance of the family, the abuse continued without interruption throughout Sybil's childhood.

Imagine you are a child in a situation like this. What can you do? You're too young to run away. You're too young to call the authorities. Although the pain may be unbearable, you have no way of knowing it is unusual or wrong. But you can do one thing. You can escape into a fantasy world; you can be somebody else. If the escape blunts the physical and emotional pain just for a minute or makes the next hour bearable, chances are you'll escape again. Your mind learns there is no limit to the identities that can be created as needed. Fifteen? Twenty-five? A hundred? Such numbers have been recorded in some cases. You do whatever it takes to get through life. Most surveys report a high rate of childhood trauma in cases of DID (Gleaves, 1996; Ross, 1997). Putnam and colleagues (1986) examined 100 cases and found that 97% of the patients had experienced significant trauma, usually sexual or physical abuse. Sixty-eight percent reported incest. Ross and colleagues (1990) reported that, of 97 cases, 95% reported physical or sexual abuse. Unfortunately, the abuse seems often as bizarre and sadistic as what Sybil suffered. Some children were buried alive. Some were tortured with matches, steam irons, razor blades, or glass. Investigators have corroborated the existence of at least some early sexual abuse in 12 patients with DID, whose backgrounds were extensively investigated by examining early records, interviewing relatives and acquaintances, and so on (Lewis, Yeager, Swica, Pincus, & Lewis, 1997), although Kluft (1996, 1999) notes that some reports by patients are not true but have been confabulated (made up).

Not all the trauma is caused by abuse. Putnam (1992) describes a young girl in a war zone who saw both her parents blown to bits in a minefield. In a heart-wrenching response, she tried to piece the bodies back together, bit by bit.

Such observations have led to wide-ranging agreement that DID is rooted in a natural tendency to escape or "dissociate" from the unremitting negative affect associated with severe abuse (Kluft, 1984, 1991). A lack of social support during or after the abuse also seems implicated. A study of 428 adolescent twins demonstrated that a surprisingly major portion of the cause of dissociative experience could be attributed to a chaotic, nonsupportive family environment. Individual experience and personality factors also contributed to dissociative experiences (Waller & Ross, 1997).

The behavior and emotions that make up disorders seem related to otherwise normal tendencies present in all of us to some extent. It is quite common for otherwise normal individuals to escape in some way from emotional or physical pain (Butler, Duran, Jasiukaitis, Koopman, & Spiegel, 1996; Spiegel & Cardeña, 1991). Noyes and Kletti (1977) surveyed more than 100 survivors of various life-threatening situations and found that most had experienced some type of dissociation, such as feelings of unreality, a blunting of emotional and physical pain, and even separation from their bodies. Dissociative amnesia and fugue states are clearly reactions to severe life stress. But the life stress or trauma is in the present rather than the past, as in the case of the overwrought mother who suffered from dissociative amnesia. Many patients are escaping from legal difficulties or severe stress at home or on the job (Sackeim & Devanand, 1991). But sophisticated statistical analyses indicate that "normal" dissociative reactions differ substantially from the pathological experiences we've described (Waller, Putnam, & Carlson, 1996; Waller & Ross, 1997) and that at least some people do not develop severe pathological dissociative experiences, no matter how extreme the stress. These findings are consistent with our diathesis–stress model in that only with

the appropriate vulnerabilities (the diathesis) will someone react to stress with pathological dissociation.

You may have noticed that DID seems similar in its etiology to posttraumatic stress disorder (PTSD). Both conditions feature strong emotional reactions to experiencing a severe trauma (Butler et al., 1996). But remember that not everyone goes on to experience PTSD after severe trauma. Only people who are biologically and psychologically vulnerable to anxiety are at risk for developing PTSD in response to moderate levels of trauma. However, as the severity of the trauma increases, a greater percentage of people develop PTSD as a consequence. Still, some people do not become victims of the disorder even after the most severe traumas, suggesting that individual psychological and biological factors interact with the trauma to produce PTSD.

There is a growing body of opinion that DID is an extreme subtype of PTSD, with a much greater emphasis on the process of dissociation than on symptoms of anxiety, although both are present in each disorder (Butler et al., 1996). Some evidence also shows that the "developmental window" of vulnerability to the abuse that leads to DID closes at approximately 9 years of age (Putnam, 1997). After that, DID is unlikely to develop, although severe PTSD might. If true, this is a particularly good example of the role of development in the etiology of psychopathology.

We also must remember that we know relatively little about DID. Our conclusions are based on retrospective case studies or correlations rather than on the prospective examination of people who may have undergone the severe trauma that seems to lead to DID (Kihlstrom, 2005; Kihlstrom, Glisky, & Anguilo, 1994). Therefore, it is hard to say what psychological or biological factors might contribute, but there are hints concerning individual differences that might play a role.

Suggestibility Suggestibility is a personality trait distributed normally across the population, much like weight and height. Some people are more suggestible than others; some are relatively immune to suggestibility; and the majority fall in the midrange.

Did you ever have an imaginary childhood playmate? Many people did, and it is one sign of the ability to lead a rich fantasy life, which can be helpful and adaptive. But it also seems to cor-

A person in a hypnotic trance is suggestible and may become absorbed in a particular experience.

relate with being suggestible or easily hypnotized (some people equate the terms *suggestibility* and *hypnotizability*). A hypnotic trance is also similar to dissociation (Bliss, 1986; Butler et al., 1996; Carlson & Putnam, 1989). People in a trance tend to be focused on one aspect of their world, and they become vulnerable to suggestions by the hypnotist. There is also the phenomenon of self-hypnosis, in which individuals can dissociate from most of the world around them and "suggest" to themselves that, for example, they won't feel pain in one of their hands.

According to the *autohypnotic model,* people who are suggestible may be able to use dissociation as a defense against extreme trauma (Putnam, 1991). As many as 50% of DID patients clearly remember imaginary playmates in childhood (Ross et al., 1990); whether they were created before or after the trauma is not entirely clear. When the trauma becomes unbearable, the person's very identity splits into multiple dissociated identities. Children's ability to distinguish clearly between reality and fantasy as they grow older may be what closes the developmental window for developing DID at approximately age 9. People who are less suggestible may develop a severe posttraumatic stress reaction but not a dissociative reaction. Once again, these explanations are all speculative because there are no controlled studies of this phenomenon (Kihlstrom et al., 1994).

Biological Contributions   As in PTSD, where the evidence is more solid, there is almost certainly a biological vulnerability to DID, but it is difficult to pinpoint. For example, in the large twin study mentioned earlier (Waller & Ross, 1997), none of the variance or identifiable causal factors was attributable to heredity: All of it was environmental. As with anxiety disorders, more basic heritable traits, such as tension and responsiveness to stress, may increase vulnerability. On the other hand, much as in PTSD, there is evidence of smaller hippocampal and amygdala volume in patients with DID compared to "normals" (Vermetten, Schmahl, Lindner, Loewenstein, & Bremner, 2006).

Interesting observations may provide some hints about brain activity during dissociation. Individuals with certain neurological disorders, particularly seizure disorders, experience many dissociative symptoms (Bowman & Coons, 2000; Cardeña, Lewis-Fernandez, Bear, Pakianathan, & Spiegel, 1996). Devinsky, Feldman, Burrowes, and Bromfield (1989) reported that approximately 6% of patients with temporal lobe epilepsy reported "out of body" experiences. About 50% of another series of patients with temporal lobe epilepsy displayed some kinds of dissociative symptoms (Schenk & Bear, 1981), including alternate identities or identity fragments.

Patients with dissociative experiences who have seizure disorders are clearly different from those who do not (Ross, 1997). The seizure patients develop dissociative symptoms in adulthood that are not associated with trauma, in clear contrast to DID patients without seizure disorders. This is an area for future study (Putnam, 1991).

Head injury and resulting brain damage may induce amnesia or other types of dissociative experience. But these conditions are usually easily diagnosed because they are generalized and irreversible and are associated with an identifiable head trauma (Butler et al., 1996).

Real Memories and False   Again, retrospective case studies suggest that individuals presenting with dissociation, and particularly DID, may have experienced severe trauma such as sexual abuse early in their lives but that they have dissociated themselves from this experience and "repressed" the memory. One of the most controversial issues in the field of abnormal psychology today concerns the extent to which memories of early trauma, particularly sexual abuse, are accurate or not. Some suggest that many such memories are simply the result of strong suggestions by careless therapists who assume people with this condition have been abused. The stakes in this controversy are enormous, with considerable opportunity for harm to innocent people on each side of the controversy.

On the one hand, if early sexual abuse did occur but is not remembered because of dissociative amnesia, it is crucially important to reexperience aspects of the trauma under the direction of a skilled therapist to relieve current suffering. Without therapy, the patient is likely to suffer from PTSD or a dissociative disorder indefinitely. It is also important that perpetrators are held accountable for their actions, perhaps through the legal system, because abuse of this type is a crime and prevention is an important goal.

On the other hand, if memories of early trauma are inadvertently created in response to a careless therapist but seem real to the patient, false accusations against loved ones could lead to irreversible family breakup and, perhaps, unjust prison sentences for those falsely accused as perpetrators. In recent years, allegedly inaccurate accusations because of false memories have led to substantial lawsuits against therapists resulting in awards of millions of dollars in damages. As with most issues that reach this level of contention and disagreement, it is clear that the final answer will not involve an all-or-none resolution. There is incontrovertible evidence that false memories *can* be created by reasonably well-understood psychological processes (Ceci, 2003; Lilienfeld et al., 1999; Loftus, 2003; Loftus & Davis, 2006; McNally, 2001, 2003; Schacter, 1995). But there is also good evidence that early traumatic experiences can cause selective dissociative amnesia, with substantial implications for psychological functioning (Gleaves, 1996; Gleaves, Smith, Butler, & Spiegel, 2004; Kluft, 1999; Spiegel, 1995).

Victims of accusations deriving from allegedly false memories have formed a society called the False Memory Syndrome Foundation. One goal is to educate the legal profession and the public about false memories after psychotherapy so that, in the absence of other objective evidence, such "memories" cannot be used to convict innocent people.

Evidence supporting the existence of distorted or illusory memories comes from experiments like one by the distinguished cognitive psychologist Elizabeth Loftus and her colleagues (Loftus, 2003; Loftus & Davis, 2006). Loftus, Coan, and Pickrell (1996) successfully convinced a number of individuals that they had been lost for an extended period when they were approximately 5 years old, which was not true. A trusted companion was recruited to "plant" the memory. In one case, a 14-year-old boy was told by his older brother that he had been lost in a nearby shopping mall when he was 5 years old, rescued by an older man, and reunited with his mother and brother. Several days after receiving this suggestion, the boy reported remembering the event and even that he felt frightened when he was lost. As time went by, the boy remembered more and more details of the event, beyond those described in the "plant," including an exact description of the older man. When he was finally told the incident never happened, the boy was surprised, and he continued to describe details of the event as if they were true.

Young children are particularly unreliable in reporting accurate details of events (Bruck, Ceci, Francouer, & Renick, 1995). Thirty-five 3-year-old girls were given a genital exam as part of their routine medical checkup; another 35 girls were not (the control group). Shortly after the exam, with her mother present, each girl was asked to describe where the doctor had touched her. She was then presented with an anatomically correct doll and asked again to point out where the doctor had touched her. The findings indicated that the children were inaccurate in reporting what happened. Approximately 60% of those who were touched in the genital region refused to indicate this, whether the dolls were used or not. On the other hand, of the children in the control group, approximately 60% indicated genital insertions or other intrusive acts by the doctor, even though nothing of the sort had occurred.

In another set of studies, preschool children were asked to think about actual events that they had experienced, such as an accident, and about fictitious events, such as having to go to the hospital to get their fingers removed from a mousetrap. Each week for 10 consecutive weeks, an interviewer asked each child to choose one of the scenes and to "think very hard and tell me if this ever happened to you." The child thus experienced thinking hard and visualizing both real and fictitious scenes over an extended period. After 10 weeks, the children were examined by a new interviewer who had not participated in the experiment.

Ceci and his colleagues conducted several experiments using this paradigm (Ceci, 1995, 2003). In one study, 58% of the preschool children described the fictitious event as if it had happened. Another 25% of the children described the fictitious events as real a majority of the time. Furthermore, the children's narratives were detailed, coherent, and embellished in ways that were not suggested originally. More telling was that in one study 27% of the children, when told their memory was false, claimed that they did remember the event.

Clancy and colleagues, in a fascinating experiment, studied the process of false memory creation in a group who reported having recovered memories of traumatic events unlikely to have occurred: abduction by space aliens. Among three groups—those reporting recovered memories of alien abduction, those who believe they were abducted but have no memories of it (repressed memories), and people who have no such beliefs or memories—some interesting differences emerged (Clancy, McNally, Schacter, Lenzenweger, & Pitman, 2002). Those reporting recovered and repressed memories of abduction also evidenced more false recall and recognition on some cognitive tasks in the laboratory and scored higher on measures of suggestibility and depression than control subjects. These studies collectively indicate that memories

are malleable and easily distorted, particularly in some individuals with certain personality traits and characteristics.

But there is also plenty of evidence that therapists need to be sensitive to signs of trauma that may not be fully remembered in patients presenting with symptoms of dissociative disorder or PTSD. Even if patients are unable to report or remember early trauma, it can sometimes be confirmed through corroborating evidence (Coons, 1994). In one study, Williams (1994) interviewed 129 women with previously documented histories, such as hospital records, of having been sexually abused as children. Thirty-eight percent did not recall the incidents that had been reported to authorities at least 17 years earlier, even with extensive probing of their abuse histories. This lack of recall was more extensive if the victim had been young and knew the abuser. As noted earlier, Lewis and colleagues (1997) provided similar documentation of severe early abuse. But Goodman and colleagues (2003) interviewed 175 individuals with documented child sexual abuse histories and found that most subjects (81%) remembered and reported the abuse. Older age when the abuse ended and emotional support following initial disclosure of the abuses were associated with higher rates of disclosures. Although "forgetting" or other reasons for not disclosing are present, it is still possible that some subjects "repressed" their memories.

As Brewin, Andrews, and Gotlib (1993) also point out, the available data from cognitive science do not necessarily support an extreme reconstructive model of (false) memory induced by careless therapists, because most individuals can recall important details of their childhood, particularly if they are unique and unexpected.

How will this controversy be resolved? Because false memories can be created through strong repeated suggestions by an authority figure, therapists must be fully aware of the conditions under which this is likely to occur, particularly when dealing with young children. This requires extensive knowledge of the workings of memory and other aspects of psychological functioning and illustrates, again, the dangers of dealing with inexperienced or inadequately trained psychotherapists. Elaborate tales of satanic abuse of children under the care of elderly women in day care centers are most likely cases of memories implanted by aggressive and careless therapists or law enforcement officials (Lilienfeld et al., 1999; Loftus & Davis, 2006; McNally, 2003). In some cases, elderly caregivers have been sentenced to life in prison.

On the other hand, many people with dissociative disorder and PTSD have suffered documented extreme abuse and trauma, which could then become dissociated from awareness. It may be that future research will find that the severity of dissociative amnesia is directly related to the severity of the trauma in vulnerable individuals, and this type of severe dissociative reaction it is also likely to be proved as qualitatively different from "normal" dissociative experiences we all have occasionally, such as feeling unreal or not here for a moment or two. (See, for example, Kluft, 1999; Waller et al., 1996.) In other words, are there two kinds of memories: traumatic memories that can be dissociated and "normal" memories that cannot (although they could be just forgotten)? At present, this is the scientific crux of the issue.

Advocates on both sides of this issue agree that clinical science must proceed as quickly as possible to specify the processes under which the implantation of false memories is likely and to define the presenting features that indicate a real but dissociated traumatic experience (Gleaves et al., 2004; Kihlstrom, 1997, 2005; Lilienfeld et al., 1999; Pope, 1996, 1997). Until then, mental health professionals must be extremely careful not to prolong unnecessary suffering among both victims of actual abuse and victims falsely accused as abusers.

■ Treatment

Individuals who experience dissociative amnesia or a fugue state usually get better on their own and remember what they have forgotten. The episodes are so clearly related to current life stress that prevention of future episodes usually involves therapeutic resolution of the distressing situations and increasing the strength of personal coping mechanisms. When necessary, therapy focuses on recalling what happened during the amnesic or fugue states, often with the help of friends or family who know what happened, so that patients can confront the information and integrate it into their conscious experience. For more difficult cases, hypnosis or benzodiazepines (minor tranquilizers) have been used, with suggestions from the therapist that it is OK to remember the events (Maldonado et al., 1998).

For DID, however, the process is not so easy. With the person's very identity shattered into many elements, reintegrating the personality might seem hopeless. Fortunately, this is not always the case. Although no controlled research has been reported on the effects of treatment, there are many documented successes of attempts to reintegrate identities through long-term psychotherapy (Ellason & Ross, 1997; Putnam, 1989; Ross, 1997). Nevertheless, the prognosis for most people remains guarded. Coon (1986) found that only 5 of 20 patients achieved a full integration of their identities. Ellason and Ross (1997) reported that 12 of 54 (22.2%) patients had achieved integration 2 years after presenting for treatment, which in most cases had been continuous. These results could be attributed to other factors than therapy because no experimental comparison was present (Powell & Howell, 1998).

The strategies that therapists use today in treating DID are based on accumulated clinical wisdom, as well as on procedures that have been successful with PTSD (Maldonado et al., 1998; see Chapter 5). The fundamental goal is to identify cues or triggers that provoke memories of trauma, dissociation, or both and to neutralize them. More important, the patient must confront and relive the early trauma and gain control over the horrible events, at least as they recur in the patient's mind (Kluft, 1996, 1999; Ross, 1997). To instill this sense of control, the therapist must skillfully, and slowly, help the patient visualize and relive aspects of the trauma until it is simply a terrible memory instead of a current event. Because the memory is unconscious, aspects of the experience are often not known to either the patient or the therapist until they emerge during treatment. Hypnosis is often used to access unconscious memories and bring various alters into awareness. Because the process of dissociation may be similar to the process of hypnosis, the latter may be a particularly efficient way to access traumatic memories (Maldonado et al., 1998). (There is as yet no evidence that hypnosis is a *necessary* part of treatment.) DID seems to run a chronic course and seldom improves spontaneously, which confirms that current treatments, primitive as they are, have some effectiveness.

It is possible that reemerging memories of trauma may trigger further dissociation. The therapist must be on guard against this happening. Trust is important to any therapeutic relationship, but it is essential in the treatment of DID. Occasionally, medication is combined with therapy, but there is little indication that it helps much. What little clinical evidence there is indicates that antidepressant drugs might be appropriate in some cases (Coon, 1986; Kluft, 1996; Putnam & Loewenstein, 1993).

CONCEPT CHECK 6.2

Diagnose the dissociative disorders described here by choosing one of the following: (a) dissociative fugue, (b) depersonalization disorder, (c) generalized amnesia, (d) dissociative identity disorder, and (e) localized amnesia.

1. Ann was found wandering the streets, unable to recall any important personal information. After searching her purse and finding an address, doctors were able to contact her mother. They learned that Ann had just been in a terrible accident and was the only survivor. Ann could not remember her mother nor any details of the accident. She was distressed. _____

2. Karl was brought to a clinic by his mother. She was concerned because at times his behavior was strange. His speech and his way of relating to people and situations would change dramatically, almost as if he were a different person. What bothered her and Karl most was that he could not recall anything he did during these periods. _____

3. Terry complained about feeling out of control. She said she felt sometimes as if she were floating under the ceiling and just watching things happen to her. She also experienced tunnel vision and felt uninvolved in the things that went on in the room around her. This always caused her to panic and perspire. _____

4. Henry is 64 and recently arrived in town. He does not know where he is from or how he got here. His driver's license proves his name, but he is unconvinced it is his. He is in good health and not taking any medication. ___

5. Carol cannot remember what happened last weekend. On Monday she was admitted to a hospital, suffering from cuts, bruises, and contusions. It also appeared that she had been sexually assaulted. _____

FUTURE DIRECTIONS

Somatoform Disorders in DSM-V: Possible Changes

As noted in the beginning of this chapter, somatoform and dissociative disorders are among the oldest recognized mental disorders. And yet, recent evidence indicates that we have much to learn about the nature of these disorders and that neither grouping of disorders may comprise a uniform category that reflects some common underlying process for purposes of classification. For example, the grouping of somatoform disorders under the heading of "somatoform" is based largely on the assumption that "somatization" is a common process in which mental illness manifests itself in the form of physical symptoms. The associated disorders, then, simply reflect different ways that a mental disorder is manifested physically. Recently, major questions have arisen concerning the classification of somatoform disorders, and a proposal now exists that we do away with this broad category in upcoming revisions to our classification system in DSM-V.

Specifically, Richard Mayou and his colleagues (Mayou et. al., 2005) note that complaints of physical symptoms that could not be explained by a general medical condition and that were not clearly associated with other mood or anxiety diagnoses were combined in DSM-III to create a new category of somatoform disorders. But recent research has indicated several shortcomings in this grouping. The first is that this category separates symptoms that reflect a physical disease process from those that are psychological in origin. It is the latter that comprises the somatoform category. But we know that splitting symptoms in this way is overly simplistic (see Chapter 2). All complaints of physical symptoms have both psychological and physical origins, and no symptoms are purely psychological. Another objection is that making these diagnoses can be unacceptable to patients who assume they are being told that these symptoms are "all in their head." Nevertheless, it is clear that pain and other aspects of suffering produce substantial changes in brain function, whether the origin of the pain is a specific physical injury or some other source.

As an example of suggested changes, Mayou and colleagues (2005) proposed that hypochondriasis should be renamed "health anxiety disorder" and placed with the anxiety disorders. This is because patients with hypochondriasis present with anxiety about getting sick as the most notable complaint but the process of anxiety seems to be the major problem rather than what they are focusing on.

BDD, in which individuals are besieged by thoughts that they are ugly, seems to have more in common with OCD, also an anxiety disorder, and the treatments that have been successful with BDD are similar to those for OCD. The symptoms of conversion disorder are thought by some to be another example of dissociative symptoms, and discussion before DSM-IV centered on the possibility of grouping this disorder with the dissociative disorders. Finally, somatization disorder has much in common with some personality disorders on Axis II—specifically, ASPD and borderline personality disorder—and might be better grouped with these disorders.

This would leave a large group of patients who complain about various physical symptoms for which physicians can find no obvious physical (organic) cause. Physicians call these symptoms "dysfunctional" (rather than organic), simply reflecting that the symptom is not associated with an identifiable organic problem but is nevertheless distressing and real. An example is irritable bowel syndrome (IBS; see Chapter 9), in which the patient experiences very real physical symptoms of excessive gas, stomach pains, and maybe diarrhea but there is no known specific physical cause. Stress and anxiety are usually considered to be the cause. On the other hand, more severe abdominal disorders with a clearly identifiable physical cause resulting in similar symptoms to IBS may be made worse by stress and anxiety. The point is that the physical symptoms might be best considered "general medical syndromes" because the patient is distressed by physical symptoms in both cases. But psychological factors may play a larger contributing role in one case than in the other. Psychological factors in these cases could be handled under the existing heading in DSM-IV of "psychological factors affecting medical conditions," and the suggestion would be to continue this for DSM V.

Therefore, it may be that the somatoform disorders will no longer exist in DSM-V. Although the proposal by Mayou and colleagues (2005) will not necessarily be accepted as it stands, it seems clear that revisions of our conceptions of somatoform disorders will be an important future direction in the classification of mental disorders.

SUMMARY

Somatoform Disorders

- Individuals with somatoform disorders are pathologically concerned with the appearance or functioning of their bodies and bring these concerns to the attention of health professionals, who usually find no identifiable medical basis for the physical complaints.

- There are several types of somatoform disorders. Hypochondriasis is a condition in which individuals believe they are seriously ill and become anxious over this possibility. Somatization disorder is characterized by a seemingly unceasing and wide-ranging pattern of physical complaints that dominate the individual's life and interpersonal relationships. In conversion disorder, there is physical malfunctioning, such as paralysis, without any apparent physical problems. In pain disorder, psychological factors are judged to play a major role in maintaining physical suffering. In body dysmorphic disorder (BDD), a person who looks normal is obsessively preoccupied with some imagined defect in appearance (imagined ugliness).

- Distinguishing among conversion reactions, real physical disorders, and outright malingering, or faking, is sometimes difficult. Even more puzzling can be factitious disorder, in which the person's symptoms are feigned and under voluntary control, as with malingering, but for no apparent reason.

- The causes of somatoform disorders are not well understood, but some, including hypochondriasis and BDD, seem closely related to anxiety disorders.

- Treatment of somatoform disorders ranges from basic techniques of reassurance and social support to those meant to reduce stress and remove any secondary gain for the behavior. Recently, specifically tailored cognitive-behavioral therapy has proved successful with hypochondriasis. Patients suffering from BDD often turn to plastic surgery or other medical interventions, which more often than not increase their preoccupation and distress.

Dissociative Disorders

- Dissociative disorders are characterized by alterations in perceptions: a sense of detachment from one's own self, from the world, or from memories.
- Dissociative disorders include depersonalization disorder, in which the individual's sense of personal reality is temporarily lost (depersonalization), as is the reality of the external world (derealization). In dissociative amnesia, the individual may be unable to remember important personal information. In generalized amnesia, the individual is unable to remember anything; more commonly, the individual is unable to recall specific events that occur during a specific period (localized or selective amnesia). In dissociative fugue, memory loss is combined with an unexpected trip (or trips). In the extreme, new identities, or alters, may be formed, as in dissociative identity disorder (DID). Finally, the newly defined dissociative trance disorder is considered to cover dissociations that may be culturally determined.

- The causes of dissociative disorders are not well understood but often seem related to the tendency to escape psychologically from memories of traumatic events.
- Treatment of dissociative disorders involves helping the patient reexperience the traumatic events in a controlled therapeutic manner to develop better coping skills. In the case of DID, therapy is often long term and may include antidepressant drugs. Particularly essential with this disorder is a sense of trust between therapist and patient.

Key Terms

somatoform disorders, 171
dissociative disorder, 171
hypochondriasis, 171
somatization disorder, 176
conversion disorder, 179
malingering, 180

factitious disorder, 180
pain disorder, 184
body dysmorphic disorder (BDD), 185
derealization, 190

depersonalization disorder, 190
dissociative amnesia, 191
generalized amnesia, 191
localized or selective amnesia, 192

dissociative fugue, 192
dissociative trance disorder (DTD), 193
dissociative identity disorder (DID), 193
alters, 194

Answers to Concept Checks

6.1

1. b; 2. c; 3. d; 4. e; 5. a

6.2

1. c; 2. d; 3. b; 4. a; 5. e

The Abnormal Psychology Book Companion Website

See **academic.cengage.com/psychology/barlow** for practice quiz questions, interactive activities, Internet links, critical thinking exercises, discussion forums, and more. Also accessible from the Wadsworth Psychology Resource Center (**academic.cengage.com/login**).

Abnormal Psychology Live CD-ROM

- *Rachel, an Example of Dissociative Identity Disorder:* These three clips explore her multiple personalities, how she copes with them, and how they emerge in response to threats within the environment.
- *Doug, an Example of Body Dysmorphic Disorder:* This interview by Katharine Phillips, an authority on this disorder, shows how it cripples this man's life until he seeks treatment for it.

CENGAGENOW CengageNOW

Go to **academic.cengage.com/now** to link to CengageNOW, your online study tool. First take the Pre-Test for this chapter to get your personalized study plan, which will identify topics you need to review and direct you to online resources. Then take the Post-Test to determine what concepts you have mastered and what you still need work on.

Video Concept Reviews

CengageNOW also contains Mark Durand's *Video Concept Reviews* on challenging topics.

- Somatoform Disorders
- Hypochondriasis
- Concept Check: Hypochondriasis Versus Other Disorders
- Conversion Disorder
- Body Dysmorphic Disorder
- Dissociative Disorders
- Depersonalization Disorder
- Dissociative Amnesia
- Dissociative Fugue
- Dissociative Trance Disorder
- Dissociative Identity Disorder
- False and Recovered Memories, Malingering

Exploring Somatoform and Dissociative Disorders

These two sets of disorders share some common features and are strongly linked historically as "hysterical neuroses." Both are relatively rare and not yet well understood.

SOMATOFORM DISORDERS
Characterized by a pathological concern with physical functioning or appearance

HYPOCHONDRIASIS

Characteristics

- Severe anxiety over physical problems that are medically undetectable
- Affects women and men equally
- May emerge at any age
- Evident in diverse cultures

Faulty interpretation of physical sensations

Additional physical symptoms

CAUSES

Intensified focus on symptoms

Increased anxiety

Treatment

- Psychotherapy to challenge illness perceptions
- Counseling and/or support groups to provide reassurance

SOMATIZATION DISORDER

Characteristics

- Reports of multiple physical symptoms without a medical basis
- Runs in families; probably heritable basis
- Rare—most prevalent among unmarried women in low socioeconomic groups
- Onset usually in adolescence; often persists into old age

Continual development of new symptoms

Eventual social isolation

CAUSES

Immediate sympathy and attention

Treatment

- Hard to treat
- Cognitive-behavioral therapy (CBT) to provide reassurance, reduce stress, and minimize help-seeking behaviors
- Therapy to broaden basis for relating to others

CONVERSION DISORDER

Characteristics

- Severe physical dysfunctioning (e.g., paralysis and blindness) without corresponding physical pathology
- Affected people are genuinely unaware that they can function normally
- May coincide with other problems, especially somatization disorder
- Most prevalent in low socio-economic groups, women, and men under extreme stress (e.g., soldiers)

Life stresses or psychological conflict

Social influences (symptoms learned from observing real illness or injury)

CAUSES

Reduced by incapacitating symptoms

Treatment

- Same as for somatization disorder, with emphasis on resolving life stress or conflict and reducing help-seeking behaviors

BODY DYSMORPHIC DISORDER (BDD)

Characteristics

- Socially disabling preoccupation with a normal physical feature that is believed to be hideous ("imagined ugliness")
- Prevalence is not known; affects men and women equally
- Associated with obsessive-compulsive disorder

Intrusive, anxiety-provoking idea that individual has a physical defect apparent to everyone

Pathological attempts to "fix" the problem that prevents a more reality-based appraisal of the "defect"

CAUSES

Intensified focus on imagined defects accompanied by extreme self-consciousness

Increased anxiety

Treatment

- CBT treatments seem most effective
- Drug treatments can provide relief for some sufferers
- Without treatment, BDD lasts a lifetime

DISSOCIATIVE DISORDERS
Characterized by detachment from the self (depersonalization) and objective reality (derealization)

DISSOCIATIVE IDENTITY DISORDER (DID)

Characteristics

- Affected person adopts new identities, or alters, that coexist simultaneously; the alters may be complete and distinct personalities or only partly independent
- Average number of alters is 15
- Childhood onset; affects more women than men
- Patients often suffer from other psychological disorders simultaneously
- Rare outside of Western cultures

Treatment

- Long-term psychotherapy may reintegrate separate personalities in 25% of patients
- Treatment of associated trauma similar to posttraumatic stress disorder; lifelong condition without treatment

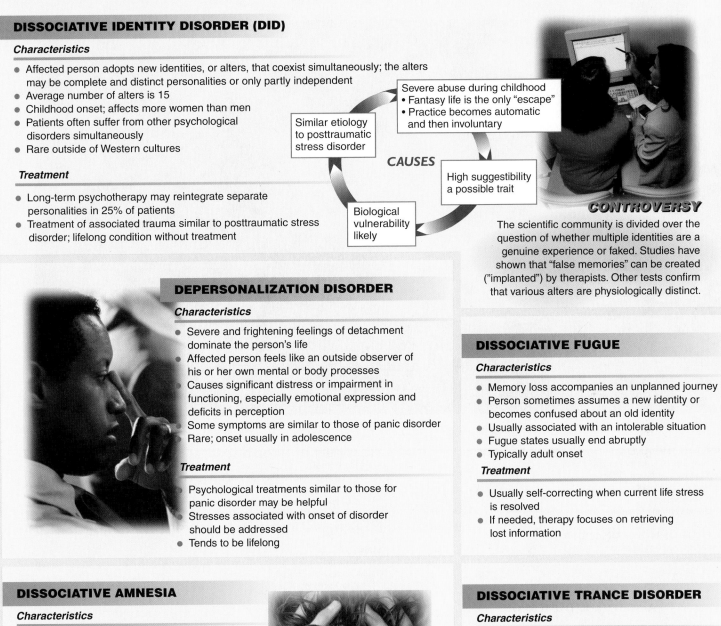

CAUSES

Similar etiology to posttraumatic stress disorder

Severe abuse during childhood
- Fantasy life is the only "escape"
- Practice becomes automatic and then involuntary

High suggestibility a possible trait

Biological vulnerability likely

CONTROVERSY

The scientific community is divided over the question of whether multiple identities are a genuine experience or faked. Studies have shown that "false memories" can be created ("implanted") by therapists. Other tests confirm that various alters are physiologically distinct.

DEPERSONALIZATION DISORDER

Characteristics

- Severe and frightening feelings of detachment dominate the person's life
- Affected person feels like an outside observer of his or her own mental or body processes
- Causes significant distress or impairment in functioning, especially emotional expression and deficits in perception
- Some symptoms are similar to those of panic disorder
- Rare; onset usually in adolescence

Treatment

- Psychological treatments similar to those for panic disorder may be helpful
- Stresses associated with onset of disorder should be addressed
- Tends to be lifelong

DISSOCIATIVE FUGUE

Characteristics

- Memory loss accompanies an unplanned journey
- Person sometimes assumes a new identity or becomes confused about an old identity
- Usually associated with an intolerable situation
- Fugue states usually end abruptly
- Typically adult onset

Treatment

- Usually self-correcting when current life stress is resolved
- If needed, therapy focuses on retrieving lost information

DISSOCIATIVE AMNESIA

Characteristics

- Generalized: Inability to remember anything, including identity; comparatively rare
- Localized: Inability to remember specific events (usually traumatic); frequently occurs in war
- More common than general amnesia
- Usually adult onset for both types

Treatment

- Usually self-correcting when current life stress is resolved
- If needed, therapy focuses on retrieving lost information

DISSOCIATIVE TRANCE DISORDER

Characteristics

- Sudden changes in personality accompany a trance or "possession"
- Causes significant distress and/or impairment in functioning
- Often associated with stress or trauma
- Prevalent worldwide, usually in a religious context; rarely seen in Western cultures
- More common in women than in men

Treatment

- Little is known

CHAPTER 7

Mood Disorders and Suicide

©Dion Ogust/The Image Works

UNDERSTANDING AND DEFINING MOOD DISORDERS
An Overview of Depression and Mania
The Structure of Mood Disorders
Depressive Disorders
Bipolar Disorders
Additional Defining Criteria

PREVALENCE OF MOOD DISORDERS
In Children and Adolescents
In the Elderly
Across Cultures
Among the Creative

THE OVERLAP OF ANXIETY AND DEPRESSION

CAUSES OF MOOD DISORDERS
Biological Dimensions
Brain Wave Activity
Psychological Dimensions
Social and Cultural Dimensions
An Integrative Theory

TREATMENT OF MOOD DISORDERS
Medications
Electroconvulsive Therapy and Transcranial Magnetic Stimulation
Psychological Treatments
Combined Treatments
Preventing Relapse
Psychological Treatments for Bipolar Disorder

SUICIDE
Statistics
Causes
Risk Factors
Is Suicide Contagious?
Treatment

ABNORMAL PSYCHOLOGY LIVE CD-ROM

Major Depressive Disorder: Barbara
Major Depressive Disorder: Evelyn
Bipolar Disorder: Mary
Web Link

My life is in ruins and . . . my body is uninhabitable. It is raging and weeping and full of destruction and wild energy gone amok. In the mirror I see a creature I don't know but must live and share my mind with.

Kay Redfield Jamison
An Unquiet Mind

UNDERSTANDING AND DEFINING MOOD DISORDERS

Think back over the last month of your life. It may seem normal in most respects; you studied during the week, socialized on the weekend, and thought about the future once in a while. Perhaps you were anticipating with some pleasure the next school break or seeing an old friend or a lover. But maybe sometime during the past month you also felt kind of down, because you broke up with your boyfriend or girlfriend or, worse yet, somebody close to you died. Think about your feelings during this period. Were you sad? Perhaps you remember crying. Maybe you felt listless, and you couldn't seem to get up the energy to go out with your friends. It may be that you feel this way once in a while for no good reason you can think of and your friends think you're moody.

If you are like most people, you know your mood will pass. You will be back to your old self in a day or two. If you never felt down and always saw only what was good in a situation, it might be more remarkable than if you were depressed once in a while. Feelings of depression (and joy) are universal, which makes it all the more difficult to understand disorders of mood, disorders that can be so incapacitating that violent suicide may seem by far a better option than living. Consider the case of Katie.

KATIE: Weathering Depression

Katie was an attractive but shy 16-year-old who came to our clinic with her parents. For several years, Katie had seldom interacted with anybody outside her family because of her considerable social anxiety. Going to school was difficult, and as her social contacts decreased her days became empty and dull. By the time she was 16, a deep, all-encompassing depression blocked the sun from her life. Here is how she described it later.

The experience of depression is like falling into a deep, dark hole that you cannot climb out of. You scream as you fall, but it seems like no one hears you. Some days you float upward without even trying; on other days, you wish that you would hit bottom so that you would never fall again. Depression affects the way you interpret events. It influences the way you see yourself and the way you see other people. I remember looking in the mirror and thinking that I was the ugliest creature in the world. Later in life, when some of these ideas would come back, I learned to remind myself that I did not have those thoughts yesterday and chances were that I would not have them tomorrow or the next day. It is a little like waiting for a change in the weather.

But at 16, in the depths of her despair, Katie had no such perspective. She often cried for hours at the end of the day. She had begun drinking alcohol the year before, with the blessing of her parents, strangely enough, because the pills prescribed by her family doctor did no good. A glass of wine at dinner had a temporary soothing effect on Katie, and both she and her parents, in their desperation, were willing to try anything that might make her a more functional person. But one glass was not enough. She drank increasingly more often. She began drinking herself to sleep. It was a means of escaping what she felt: "I had very little hope of positive change. I do not think that anyone close to me was hopeful, either. I was angry, cynical, and in a great deal of emotional pain." Katie's life continued to spiral downward.

For several years, Katie had thought about suicide as a solution to her unhappiness. At 13, in the presence of her parents, she reported these thoughts to a psychologist. Her parents wept, and the sight of their tears deeply affected Katie. From that point on, she never expressed her suicidal thoughts again, but they remained with her. By the time she was 16, her preoccupation with her own death had increased.

I think this was just exhaustion. I was tired of dealing with the anxiety and depression day in and day out. Soon I found myself trying to sever the few interpersonal connections that I did have, with my closest friends, with my mother, and my oldest brother. I was almost impossible to talk to. I was angry and frustrated all the time. One day I went over the edge. My mother and I had a disagreement about some unimportant little thing. I went to my bedroom where I kept a bottle of whiskey or vodka or whatever I was drinking at the time. I drank as much as I could until I could pinch myself as hard as I could and feel nothing. Then I got out a very sharp knife that I had been saving and slashed my wrist deeply. I did not feel anything but the warmth of the blood running from my wrist.

The blood poured out onto the floor next to the bed that I was lying on. The sudden thought hit me that I had failed, that this was not enough to cause my death. I got up from the bed and began to laugh. I tried to stop the bleeding with some tissues. I stayed calm and frighteningly pleasant. I walked to the kitchen and called my mother. I cannot imagine how she felt when she saw my shirt and pants covered in blood. She was amazingly calm. She asked to see the cut and said that it was not going to stop bleeding on its own and that I needed to go to the doctor immediately. I remember as the doctor shot novocaine into the cut he remarked that I must have used an anesthetic before cutting myself. I never felt the shot or the stitches.

After that, thoughts of suicide became more frequent and more real. My father asked me to promise that I would never do it again and I said I would not, but that promise meant nothing to me. I knew it was to ease his pains and fears and not mine, and my preoccupation with death continued.

Think for a moment about your own experience of depression. What are the major differentiating factors between your feelings and Katie's? Clearly, Katie's depression was outside the boundaries of normal experience because of its intensity and duration. In addition, her severe or "clinical" depression interfered substantially with her ability to function. Finally, a number of associated psychological and physical symptoms accompany clinical depression.

Because of their sometimes tragic consequences, we need to develop as full an understanding as possible of mood disorders. In the following sections, we describe how various emotional experiences and symptoms interrelate to produce specific mood disorders. We offer detailed descriptions of different mood disorders and examine the many criteria that define them. We discuss the relationship of anxiety and depression and the causes and treatment of mood disorders. We conclude with a discussion of suicide.

An Overview of Depression and Mania

The disorders described in this chapter used to be categorized under several general labels, such as "depressive disorders," "affective disorders," or even "depressive neuroses." Beginning with the third edition of the *Diagnostic and Statistical Manual* (DSM-III), these problems have been grouped under the heading **mood disorders** because they are characterized by gross deviations in mood.

The fundamental experiences of depression and mania contribute, either singly or together, to all the mood disorders. We describe each state and discuss its contributions to the various mood disorders. Then we briefly describe the additional defining criteria, features, or symptoms that define the specific disorders.

The most commonly diagnosed and most severe depression is called a **major depressive episode.** The DSM-IV-TR criteria indicate an extremely depressed mood state that lasts at least 2 weeks and includes cognitive symptoms (such as feelings of worthlessness and indecisiveness) and disturbed physical functions (such as altered sleeping patterns, significant changes in appetite and weight, or a notable loss of energy) to the point that even the slightest activity or movement requires an overwhelming effort. The episode is typically accompanied by a general loss of interest in things and an inability to experience any pleasure from life, including interactions with family or friends or accomplishments at work or at school. (The inability to experience pleasure is termed *anhedonia*.) Although all symptoms are important, evidence suggests that the most central indicators of a full major depressive episode (Buchwald & Rudick-Davis, 1993; Keller et al., 1995) are the physical changes (sometimes called *somatic* or *vegetative* symptoms), along with the behavioral and emotional "shutdown," as reflected by low scores on behavioral activation scales (Kasch, Rottenberg, Arnow, & Gotlib, 2002; Rottenberg, Gross, & Gotlib, 2005). Anhedonia (loss of energy and inability to engage in pleasurable activities or have any "fun") is more characteristic of these severe episodes of depression than are, for example, reports of sadness or distress (Kasch et al., 2002) or the tendency to cry, which occurs equally in depressed and nondepressed individuals (mostly women in both cases) (Rottenberg, Gross, Wilhelm, Najmi, & Gotlib, 2002). This anhedonia reflects that these episodes represent a state of low positive affect and not just

DSM-IV-TR

DSM TABLE 7.1 Criteria for Major Depressive Episode

A. Five (or more) of the following symptoms have been present during the same 2-week period and represent a change from previous functioning; at least one of the symptoms is either (1) depressed mood or (2) loss of interest or pleasure.

Note: Do not include symptoms that are clearly due to a general medical condition or mood-incongruent delusions or hallucinations.

 1. Depressed mood most of the day, nearly every day, as indicated by either subjective report (e.g., feels sad or empty) or observation made by others (e.g., appears tearful). *note:* in children and adolescents can be irritable mood.
 2. Markedly diminished interest or pleasure in all, or almost all, activities most of the day, nearly every day (as indicated by either subjective account or observation made by others)
 3. Significant weight loss when not dieting or weight gain (e.g., a change of more than 5% of body weight in a month), or decrease or increase in appetite nearly every day. *note:* in children, consider failure to make expected weight gains
 4. Insomnia or hypersomnia nearly every day
 5. Psychomotor agitation or retardation nearly every day (observable by others, not merely subjective feelings of restlessness or being slowed down)
 6. Fatigue or loss of energy nearly every day
 7. Feelings of worthlessness or excessive or inappropriate guilt (which may be delusional) nearly every day (not merely self-reproach or guilt about being sick)
 8. Diminished ability to think or concentrate, or indecisiveness, nearly every day (either by subjective account or as observed by others)
 9. Recurrent thoughts of death (not just fear of dying), recurrent suicidal ideation without a specific plan, or a suicide attempt or a specific plan for committing suicide

B. The symptoms do not meet criteria for a mixed episode.

C. The symptoms cause clinically significant distress or impairment in social, occupational, or other important areas of functioning.

D. The symptoms are not due to the direct physiological effects of a substance (e.g., a drug of abuse, a medication) or a general medical condition (e.g., hypothyroidism).

E. The symptoms are not better accounted for by bereavement, i.e., after the loss of a loved one, and persist for longer than 2 months or are characterized by marked functional impairment, morbid preoccupation with worthlessness, suicidal ideation, psychotic symptoms, or psychomotor retardation.

Source: Reprinted, with permission, from American Psychiatric Association. (2000). *Diagnostic and statistical manual of mental disorders* (4th ed., text revision). Washington, DC: Author. © 2000 American Psychiatric Association.

high negative affect (Kasch et al., 2002). The duration of a major depressive episode, if untreated, is approximately 4 to 9 months (Eaton et al., 1997; Hasin, Goodwin, Stinson, & Grant, 2005; Tollefson, 1993).

The second fundamental state in mood disorders is abnormally exaggerated elation, joy, or euphoria. In **mania,** individuals find extreme pleasure in every activity; some patients compare their daily experience of mania to a continuous sexual orgasm. They become extraordinarily active (hyperactive), require little sleep, and may develop grandiose plans, believing they can accomplish anything they desire. Speech is typically rapid and may become incoherent, because the individual is attempting to ex-

DSM-IV-TR

DSM TABLE 7.2   Criteria for Manic Episode

A. A distinct period of abnormally and persistently elevated, expansive, or irritable mood, lasting at least 1 week (or any duration if hospitalization is necessary).

B. During the period of mood disturbance, three (or more) of the following symptoms have persisted (four if the mood is only irritable) and have been present to a significant degree:
   1. Inflated self-esteem or grandiosity
   2. Decreased need for sleep (e.g., feels rested after only 3 hours of sleep)
   3. More talkative than usual or pressure to keep talking
   4. Flight of ideas or subjective experience that thoughts are racing
   5. Distractibility (i.e., attention too easily drawn to unimportant or irrelevant external stimuli)
   6. Increase in goal-directed activity (either socially, at work or school, or sexually) or psychomotor agitation
   7. Excessive involvement in pleasurable activities that have a high potential for painful consequences (e.g., engaging in unrestrained buying sprees, sexual indiscretions, or foolish business investments)

C. The symptoms do not meet criteria for a mixed episode.

D. The mood disturbance is sufficiently severe to cause marked impairment in occupational functioning or in usual social activities or relationships with others, or to necessitate hospitalization to prevent harm to self or others, or there are psychotic features.

E. The symptoms are not due to the direct physiological effects of a substance (e.g., a drug of abuse, a medication, or other treatment) or a general medical condition (e.g., hyperthyroidism).

Note: Manic-like episodes that are clearly caused by somatic antidepressant treatment (e.g., medication, electroconvulsive therapy, light therapy) should not count toward a diagnosis of bipolar I disorder.

Source: Reprinted, with permission, from American Psychiatric Association. (2000). *Diagnostic and statistical manual of mental disorders* (4th ed., text revision). Washington, DC: Author, © 2000 American Psychiatric Association.

press so many exciting ideas at once; this feature is typically referred to as *flight of ideas.*

DSM-IV-TR criteria for a manic episode require a duration of only 1 week, less if the episode is severe enough to require hospitalization. Hospitalization could occur, for example, if the individual was engaging in self-destructive buying sprees, charging thousands of dollars in the expectation of making a million dollars the next day. Irritability is often part of a manic episode, usually near the end. Paradoxically, being anxious or depressed is also commonly part of mania, as described later. The duration of an untreated manic episode is typically 3 to 6 months (Angst & Sellaro, 2000).

DSM-IV-TR also defines a **hypomanic episode,** a less severe version of a manic episode that does not cause marked impairment in social or occupational functioning. (*Hypo* means "below"; thus the episode is below the level of a manic episode.) A hypomanic episode is not in itself necessarily problematic, but it does contribute to the definition of several mood disorders.

The Structure of Mood Disorders

Individuals who experience either depression or mania are said to suffer from a *unipolar mood disorder,* because their mood remains at one "pole" of the usual depression-mania continuum. Mania by

itself (unipolar mania) does occur (Solomon et al., 2003) but is rare, because almost everyone with a unipolar mood disorder suffers from unipolar depression. Someone who alternates between depression and mania is said to have a bipolar mood disorder traveling from one "pole" of the depression–elation continuum to the other and back again. However, this label is somewhat misleading, because depression and elation may not exactly be at opposite ends of the same mood state; although related, they are often relatively independent. An individual can experience manic symptoms but feel somewhat depressed or anxious at the same time. This combination is called a **dysphoric manic episode** or a **mixed manic episode** (Angst & Sellaro, 2000; Cassidy, Forest, Murry, & Carroll, 1998; Freeman & McElroy, 1999; Hantouche, Akiskal, Azorin, Chatenet-Duchene, & Lancrenon, 2006). The patient usually experiences the symptoms of mania as being out of control or dangerous and becomes anxious or depressed about this uncontrollability. Research suggests that manic episodes are characterized by dysphoric (anxious or depressive) features more commonly than was thought, and dysphoria can be severe (Cassidy et al., 1998). In one recent study, 30% of 1,090 patients hospitalized for acute mania had mixed episodes (Hantouche et al., 2006). The rare individual who suffers from manic episodes alone also meets criteria for bipolar mood disorder because experience shows that most of these individuals can be expected to become depressed at a later time (Goodwin & Jamison, 2007; Miklowitz & Johnson, 2006).

Depression and mania may differ from one person to another in terms of their severity, their course (or the frequency with which they tend to recur), and, occasionally, the accompanying symptoms. Either losing or gaining weight and either losing sleep (insomnia) or sleeping too much (hypersomnia) might contribute to the diagnosis of a major depressive episode. Similarly, in a manic episode, one individual may present with clear and extreme euphoria and elation accompanied by inflated self-esteem or grandiosity, and another may appear irritable and exhibit flight of ideas. In reality, it is more common to see patients with a mix of such symptoms. As noted earlier, an important feature of major depressive episodes is that they don't go on forever, lasting from as little as 2 weeks to several months or more if untreated (Boland & Keller, 2002). Almost all major depressive episodes eventually abate on their own without treatment, although approximately 10% last 2 years or longer. Manic episodes abate on their own without treatment after approximately 3 to 4 months (Goodwin & Jamison, 2007). Therefore, it is important to determine the course or temporal patterning of the episodes. For example, do they tend to recur? If they do, does the patient recover fully between episodes? Do the depressive episodes alternate with manic or hypomanic episodes? All these different patterns come under the DSM-IV-TR general heading of "course modifiers for mood disorders."

Course modifiers characterize the mood state in the past, which helps us better predict the future of the disorder. Therefore, we determine the pattern of recurrence and whether the timing of the episode is related to other mood-related features (for example, it alternates with manic episodes) or a certain time of the year (usually winter).

The importance of course makes the goals of treating mood disorders somewhat different from those for other psychological disorders. Clinicians want to do everything possible to relieve people like Katie from their current depressive episode, but an equally important goal is to prevent future episodes—in other words, to help people like Katie stay well for a longer period. Studies have appeared that evaluate the effectiveness of treatment in terms of this second goal (Fava, Grandi, Zielezny, Rafanelli, & Canestrari, 1996; Hollon, Stewart, & Strunk, 2006; Teasdale et al., 2001).

"I've been sad, depressed most of my life. . . . I had a headache in high school for a year and a half. . . . There have been different periods in my life when I wanted to end it all. . . . I hate me, I really hate me. I hate the way I look, I hate the way I feel. I hate the way I talk to people. . . . I do everything wrong. . . . I feel really hopeless."

Depressive Disorders

DSM-IV-TR describes several types of depressive disorders. These disorders differ from one another in the frequency with which depressive symptoms occur and the severity of the symptoms.

■ Clinical Descriptions

The most easily recognized mood disorder is **major depressive disorder, single episode,** defined by the absence of manic or hypomanic episodes before or during the disorder. We now know that an occurrence of just one isolated depressive episode in a

lifetime is rare (Angst & Preizig, 1996; Judd, 1997, 2000; Mueller et al., 1999; Solomon et al., 2000).

If two or more major depressive episodes occurred and were separated by at least 2 months during which the individual was not depressed, **major depressive disorder, recurrent,** is diagnosed. Otherwise, the criteria are the same as for major depressive disorder, single episode. Recurrence is important in predicting the future course of the disorder, as well as in choosing appropriate treatments. As many as 85% of single-episode cases later experience a second episode and thus meet criteria for major depressive disorder, recurrent (Judd, 1997, 2000; Keller, Lavori, et al., 1992; Solomon et al., 2000), based on follow-ups as long as 15 years (Mueller et al., 1999). In the first year following an episode, the risk of recurrence is 20% (Boland & Keller, 2002). Because of this finding and others reviewed later, clinical scientists in just the last several years have concluded that unipolar depression is almost always a chronic condition that waxes and wanes over time but seldom disappears. The median lifetime number of major depressive episodes is four; in one large sample, 25% experienced six or more episodes (Angst, 1988; Angst & Preizig, 1996). The median duration of recurrent major depressive episodes is 4 to 5 months (Kessler et al., 2003; Solomon et al., 1997), somewhat shorter than the average length of the first episode (Eaton et al., 1997). On the basis of these criteria, how would you diagnose Katie? Katie suffered from severely depressed mood, feelings of worthlessness, difficulty concentrating, recurrent thoughts of death, sleep difficulties, and loss of energy. She clearly met the criteria for major depressive disorder, recurrent. Katie's depressive episodes were quite severe when they occurred, but she tended to cycle in and out of them.

Dysthymic disorder shares many of the symptoms of major depressive disorder but differs in its course. The symptoms are somewhat milder but remain relatively unchanged over long periods, sometimes 20 or 30 years or more (Akiskal & Cassano, 1997; Keller, Baker, & Russell, 1993; Klein, Schwartz, Rose, & Leader, 2000; Klein, Shankman, & Rose, 2006; Rush, 1993).

Dysthymic disorder is defined as a persistently depressed mood that continues at least 2 years, during which the patient cannot be symptom free for more than 2 months at a time. Dysthymic disorder differs from a major depressive episode only in the severity, chronicity, and number of its symptoms, which are milder and fewer but last longer. In a 10-year prospective follow-up study described later, 22% of people suffering from dysthymia eventually experienced a major depressive episode (Klein et al., 2006).

Double Depression Recently, individuals have been studied who suffer from both major depressive episodes and dysthymic

---

DSM-IV-TR

DSM TABLE 7.3 Diagnostic Criteria for Major Depressive Disorder, Single Episode

A. Presence of a single major depressive episode.

B. The major depressive episode is not better accounted for by schizoaffective disorder and is not superimposed on schizophrenia, schizophreniform disorder, delusional disorder, or psychotic disorder not otherwise specified.

C. There has never been a manic episode, a mixed episode, or a hypomanic episode. Note: This exclusion does not apply if all of the manic-like, mixed-like, or hypomanic-like episodes are substance or treatment induced or are due to the direct physiological effects of a general medical condition.

If the full criteria are currently met for a major depressive episode, specify its current clinical status and/or features:

  Mild, moderate, severe without psychotic features/severe with psychotic features

  Chronic

  With catatonic features

  With melancholic features

  With atypical features

  With postpartum onset

If the full criteria are not currently met for a MAJOR DEPRESSIVE EPISODE, specify the current clinical status of the major depressive disorder or features of the most recent episode:

  In partial remission, in full remission

  Chronic

  With catatonic features

  With melancholic features

  With atypical features

  With postpartum onset

Source: Reprinted, with permission, from American Psychiatric Association. (2000). Diagnostic and statistical manual of mental disorders (4th ed., text revision). Washington, DC: Author, © 2000 American Psychiatric Association.

DSM-IV-TR

DSM TABLE 7.4 Diagnostic Criteria for Dysthymic Disorder

A. Depressed mood for most of the day, for more days than not, as indicated either by subjective account or observation by others, for at least 2 years. *Note:* In children and adolescents, mood can be irritable and duration must be at least 1 year.

B. Presence, while depressed, of two (or more) of the following:
   1. Poor appetite or overeating
   2. Insomnia or hypersomnia
   3. Low energy or fatigue
   4. Low self-esteem
   5. Poor concentration or difficulty making decisions
   6. Feelings of hopelessness

C. During the 2-year period (1 year for children or adolescents) of the disturbance, the person has never been without the symptoms in criteria A and B for more than 2 months at a time.

D. No major depressive episode has been present during the first 2 years of the disturbance (1 year for children and adolescents); i.e., the disturbance is not better accounted for by chronic major depressive disorder, or major depressive disorder, in partial remission.

Note: There may have been a previous major depressive episode provided there was a full remission (no significant signs or symptoms for 2 months) before development of the dysthymic disorder. In addition, after the initial 2 years (1 year in children or adolescents) of dysthymic disorder, there may be superimposed episodes of major depressive disorder, in which case both diagnoses may be given when the criteria are met for a major depressive episode.

E. There has never been a manic episode, a mixed episode, or a hypomanic episode, and criteria have never been met for cyclothymic disorder.

F. The disturbance does not occur exclusively during the course of a chronic psychotic disorder, such as schizophrenia or delusional disorder.

G. The symptoms are not due to the direct physiological effects of a substance (e.g., a drug of abuse, a medication) or a general medical condition (e.g., hypothyroidism).

H. The symptoms cause clinically significant distress or impairment in social, occupational, or other important areas of functioning.

Specify if:
   Early onset: If onset is before age 21 years
   Late onset: If onset is age 21 years or older
   Specify (for most recent 2 years of dysthymic disorder):
   With atypical features

Source: Reprinted, with permission, from American Psychiatric Association. (2000). *Diagnostic and statistical manual of mental disorders* (4th ed., text revision). Washington, DC: Author, © 2000 American Psychiatric Association.

While his bride awaited him, Abraham Lincoln was suffering from a depressive episode that was so severe he was unable to proceed with the wedding until several days later.

JACK: A Life Kept Down

Jack was a 49-year-old divorced white man who lived at his mother's home with his 10-year-old son. He complained of chronic depression, saying he finally realized he needed help. Jack reported that he had been a pessimist and a worrier for much of his adult life. He consistently felt kind of down and depressed and did not have much fun. He had difficulty making decisions, was generally pessimistic about the future, and thought little of himself. During the past 20 years, the longest period he could remember in which his mood was "normal" or less depressed lasted only 4 or 5 days.

Despite his difficulties, Jack had finished college and obtained a master's degree in public administration. People told him his future was bright and he would be highly valued in state government. Jack did not think so. He took a job as a low-level clerk in a state agency, thinking he could always work his way up. He never did, remaining at the same desk for 20 years.

Jack's wife, fed up with his continued pessimism, lack of self-confidence, and relative inability to enjoy day-to-day events, became discouraged and divorced him. Jack moved in with his mother so that she could help care for his son and share expenses.

About 5 years before coming to the clinic, Jack had experienced a bout of depression worse than anything he had previously known. His self-esteem went from low to nonexistent. From indecisiveness, he became unable to decide anything. He was exhausted all the time and felt as if lead had filled his arms and legs, making it difficult even to move. He

disorder and who are therefore said to have **double depression.** Typically, dysthymic disorder develops first, perhaps at an early age, and then one or more major depressive episodes occur later (Eaton et al., 1997; Klein et al., 2006). Identifying this particular pattern is important because it is associated with severe psychopathology and a problematic future course (Akiskal & Cassano, 1997; Keller, Hirschfeld, & Hanks, 1997; Klein et al., 2006). For example, Keller, Lavori, Endicott, Coryell, and Klerman (1983) found that 61% of patients suffering from double depression had not recovered from the underlying dysthymic disorder 2 years after follow-up. The investigators also found that patients who had recovered from the superimposed major depressive episode experienced high rates of relapse and recurrence. Consider the case of Jack.

became unable to complete projects or to meet deadlines. Seeing no hope, he began to consider suicide. After tolerating a listless performance for years from someone they had expected to rise through the ranks, Jack's employers finally fired him.

After about 6 months, the major depressive episode resolved and Jack returned to his chronic but milder state of depression. He could get out of bed and accomplish some things, although he still doubted his own abilities. However, he was unable to obtain another job. After several years of waiting for something to turn up, he realized he was unable to solve his own problems and that without help his depression would continue. After a thorough assessment, we determined that Jack suffered from a classic case of double depression.

■ Onset and Duration

Generally the risk for developing major depression is fairly low until the early teens, when it begins to rise in a steady (linear) fashion. The mean age of onset for major depressive disorder is 30 years based on a large (43,000) and representative sample of the population of the United States (Hasin et al., 2005). A frightening finding is that the incidence of depression and consequent suicide seem to be steadily increasing (Cross-National Collaborative Group, 1992; Kessler et al., 2003; Lewinsohn, Rohde, Seeley, & Fischer, 1993). In 1989, Myrna Weissman and her colleagues published a survey of people in five U.S. cities (Klerman & Weissman, 1989; Wickramaratne, Weissman, Leaf, & Holford, 1989) that revealed a greatly increased risk of developing depression in younger Americans over the last several decades. Among Americans born before 1905, only 1% had developed depression by age 75; of those born since 1955, 6% had become depressed by age 24. Another study based on similar surveys conducted in Puerto Rico, Canada, Italy, Germany, France, Taiwan, Lebanon, and New Zealand (see ■ Figure 7.1) suggests that this trend toward developing

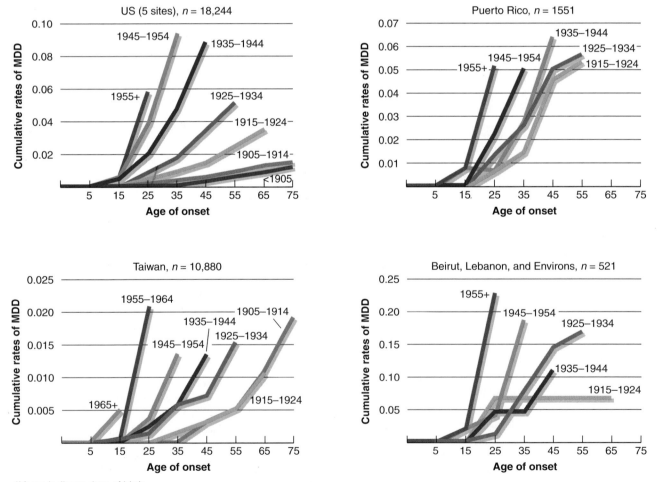

*Years indicate date of birth.

■ **FIGURE 7.1** Cross-cultural data on the onset of major depressive disorder (MDD). (Reprinted, with permission, from Cross-National Collaborative Group, 1992. The changing rate of major depression: Cross-national comparisons. *Journal of the American Medical Association, 268,* 3098-3105, © 1992 by the American Medical Association.)

depression at increasingly earlier ages is occurring worldwide (Cross-National Collaborative Group, 1992). A more recent sophisticated study surveying onset and prevalence of major depression in the United States confirmed this finding. Kessler and colleagues (2003) compared four age groups and found that fully 25% of people 18 to 29 years had already experienced major depression, a rate far higher than the rate for older groups when they were that age. There is some recent evidence that this trend is beginning to level off (Hasin et al., 2005).

As we noted previously, the length of depressive episodes is variable, with some lasting as little as 2 weeks; in more severe cases, an episode might last for several years, with the typical duration of the first episode being 4 to 9 months if untreated (Eaton et al., 1997; Hasin et al., 2005; Kessler et al., 2003; Tollefson, 1993). Although 9 months is a long time to suffer with a severe depressive episode, evidence indicates that even in the most severe cases, the probability of remission of the episode approaches 90% (Thase, 1990) within a 5-year period (Keller et al., 1992). Even in those severe cases in which the episode lasts 5 years or longer, 38% can be expected to recover (Mueller et al., 1996). Occasionally, however, episodes may not entirely clear up, leaving some residual symptoms. In this case, the likelihood of a subsequent episode is much higher (Judd et al., 1998b). It is also likely that subsequent episodes will be associated with incomplete inter-episode recovery. Knowing this is important to treatment planning, because treatment should be continued much longer in these cases.

Recent evidence also identifies important subtypes of dysthymic disorder. Although the typical age of onset has been estimated to be in the early 20s, Klein, Taylor, Dickstein, and Harding (1988) found that onset before 21 years of age, and often much earlier, is associated with three characteristics: (1) greater chronicity (it lasts longer), (2) relatively poor prognosis (response to treatment), and (3) stronger likelihood of the disorder running in the family of the affected individual. These findings have been replicated (Akiskal & Cassano, 1997). A greater prevalence of current personality disorders has been found in patients with early-onset dysthymia than in patients with major depressive disorder (Pepper et al., 1995). Adolescents who have recovered from dysthymic disorder still have a lower level of social support and higher levels of stress than adolescents with major depressive disorders or other nonmood disorders (Klein, Lewinsohn, & Seeley, 1997). These findings may account for the insidiousness of the psychopathology in early-onset dysthymia. Investigators have found a rather high prevalence of dysthymic disorder in children (Kovacs, Gatsonis, Paulauskas, & Richards, 1989), and Kovacs, Akiskal, Gatsonis, and Parrone (1994) found that 76% of a sample of dysthymic children later developed major depressive disorder.

Dysthymic disorder may last 20 to 30 years or more, although studies have reported a median duration of approximately 5 years in adults (Klein et al., 2006; Rounsaville, Sholomskas, & Prusoff, 1988) and 4 years in children (Kovacs et al., 1994). Klein and colleagues (2006), in the study mentioned earlier, conducted a 10-year follow-up of 97 adults with dysthymic disorder and found that 74% had recovered at some point but 71% of those had relapsed. The whole sample of 97 patients spent approximately 60% of the 10-year follow-up period meeting full criteria for a mood disorder. This compares to 21% of a group of patients with non-

chronic major depressive disorder also followed for 10 years. These findings demonstrate the chronicity of dysthymia. Even worse, patients with dysthymia were more likely to attempt suicide than a comparison group with episodes of major depressive disorder during a 5-year period. Kovacs and colleagues (1994), on the other hand, found that almost all children with dysthymia in their sample eventually recovered from it. It is relatively common for major depressive episodes and dysthymic disorder to co-occur (double depression) (McCullough et al., 2000). Among those who have had dysthymia, as many as 79% have also had a major depressive episode at some point in their lives. ■ Figure 7.2 presents data on the 10-year course of patients presenting with dysthymia alone, nonchronic major depressive disorder, or double depression. The dysthymic group, on the average, stays depressed. The double depression group starts off more severe, recovers from their major depressive episode as did Jack, but remains the most severely depressed after 10 years. The nonchronic major depressive disorder group evidences the most recovery (on average).

■ From Grief to Depression

At the beginning of the chapter, we asked whether you had ever felt down or depressed. Almost everyone has. But if someone you love has died—particularly if the death was unexpected and the

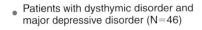

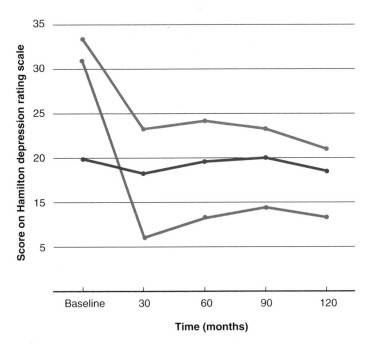

■ **FIGURE 7.2** Hamilton Depression Rating Scale scores of dysthymic disorder patients with and without concurrent major depressive disorder episode and patients with nonchronic major depressive disorder over a 10-year follow-up period. From Klein, D., Shankman, S., & Rose, S., (2006). Ten year prospective follow-up study of the naturalistic course of dysthymic disorder and double depression. *American Journal of Psychiatry, 163,* 872-880. © American Psychiatric Association.

person was a member of your immediate family—you may, after your initial reaction to the trauma, have experienced most of the symptoms of a major depressive episode: anxiety, emotional numbness, and denial. The frequency of severe depression following the death of a loved one is so high (approximately 62%) that mental health professionals do not consider it a disorder unless severe symptoms appear, such as psychotic features or suicidal ideation, or the less alarming symptoms last longer than 6 months (Maciejewski, Zhang, Block, & Prigerson, 2007). Some grieving individuals require immediate treatment because they are so incapacitated by their symptoms (for example, severe weight loss or no energy) that they cannot function.

We must confront death and process it emotionally. All religions and cultures have rituals, such as funerals and burial ceremonies, to help us work through our losses with the support and love of our relatives and friends (Bonanno & Kaltman, 1999; Shear, 2006). Usually the natural grieving process has peaked within the first 6 months, although some people grieve for a year or longer (Clayton & Darvish, 1979; Jacobs, Hansen, Berkman, Kasl, & Ostfeld, 1989; Maciejewski, Zhang, Block, & Prigerson, 2007). Grief often recurs at significant anniversaries, such as the birthday of the loved one, holidays, and other meaningful occasions, including the anniversary of the death. Mental health professionals are concerned when someone does not grieve after a death, because grieving is our natural way of confronting and handling loss.

When grief lasts beyond the normal time, mental health professionals again become concerned (C. G. Blanchard, Blanchard, & Becker, 1976). After a year or so, the chance of recovering from severe grief without treatment is considerably reduced, and for approximately 10% to 20% of bereaved individuals (Bonanno, 2006;

Jacobs, 1993; Middleton, Burnett, Raphael, & Martinek, 1996), a normal process becomes a disorder. At this stage, suicidal thoughts increase substantially (Stroebe, Stroebe, & Abakoumkin, 2005). Many of the psychological and social factors related to mood disorders in general, including a history of past depressive episodes (Horowitz et al., 1997; Jacobs et al., 1989), also predict the development of a normal grief response into a **pathological or impacted grief reaction,** although this reaction can develop without a preexisting depressed state (Bonanno, Wortman, & Nesse, 2004). Particularly prominent symptoms include intrusive memories and distressingly strong yearnings for the loved one and avoiding people or places that are reminders of the loved one (Horowitz et al., 1997; Lichtenthal, Cruess, & Prigerson, 2004; Shear, 2006). Indeed, some have proposed that this unique cluster of symptoms, combined with other differences, should be sufficient to make complicated grief a separate diagnostic category distinct from depression (Bonanno, 2006; Lichtenthal et al., 2004). Recent brain-imaging studies indicate that areas of the brain associated with close relationships and attachment are active in grieving people, in addition to areas of the brain associated with more general emotional responding (Gündel, O'Connor, Littrell, Fort, & Lane, 2003). In cases of long-lasting grief, the rituals intended to help us face and accept death were ineffective. As with victims suffering from posttraumatic stress, one therapeutic approach is to help grieving individuals reexperience the trauma under close supervision. Usually, the grieving person is encouraged to talk about the loved one, the death, and the meaning of the loss while experiencing all the associated emotions, until that person can come to terms with reality. This would include finding some meaning in the traumatic loss, incorporating positive emotions as-

Queen Victoria remained in such deep mourning for her husband, Prince Albert, that she was unable to perform as monarch for several years after his death. Actress Ashley Judd recently spoke of her struggles with depression and lifelong emotional problems.

sociated with memories of the relationship into the intense negative emotions connected with the loss, and arriving at the position that it is possible to cope with the pain and life will go on (Bonanno & Kaltman, 1999). An important study has demonstrated that this approach is successful compared to alternative psychological treatment that also focuses on grief and loss, interpersonal psychotherapy (Shear, Frank, Houck, & Reynolds, 2005).

Bipolar Disorders

The key identifying feature of bipolar disorders is the tendency of manic episodes to alternate with major depressive episodes in an unending roller-coaster ride from the peaks of elation to the depths of despair. Beyond that, bipolar disorders are parallel in many ways to depressive disorders. For example, a manic episode might occur only once or repeatedly. Consider the case of Jane.

JANE: Funny, Smart, and Desperate

Jane was the wife of a well-known surgeon and the loving mother of three children. They lived in an old country house on the edge of town with plenty of room for the family and pets. Jane was nearly 50; the older children had moved out; the youngest son, 16-year-old Mike, was having substantial academic difficulties in school and seemed anxious. Jane brought Mike to the clinic to find out why he was having problems.

As they entered the office, I observed that Jane was well dressed, neat, vivacious, and personable; she had a bounce to her step. She began talking about her wonderful and successful family before she and Mike even reached their seats. Mike, by contrast, was quiet and reserved. He seemed resigned and perhaps relieved that he would have to say little during the session. By the time Jane sat down, she had mentioned the personal virtues and material achievement of her husband, and the brilliance and beauty of one of her older children, and she was proceeding to describe the second child. But before she finished she noticed a book on anxiety disorders and, having read voraciously on the subject, began a litany of various anxiety-related problems that might be troubling Mike.

In the meantime, Mike sat in the corner with a small smile on his lips that seemed to be masking considerable distress and uncertainty over what his mother might do next. It became clear as the interview progressed that Mike suffered from obsessive-compulsive disorder, which disturbed his concentration both in and out of school. He was failing all his courses.

It also became clear that Jane herself was in the midst of a hypomanic episode, evident in her unbridled enthusiasm, grandiose perceptions, "uninterruptable" speech, and report that she needed little sleep these days. She was also easily distracted, as when she quickly switched from describing her children to the book on the table. When asked about her own psychological state, Jane readily admitted that she was a

"manic depressive" (the old name for bipolar disorder) and that she alternated rather rapidly between feeling on top of the world and feeling depressed; she was taking medication for her condition. I immediately wondered if Mike's obsessions had anything to do with his mother's condition.

Mike was treated intensively for his obsessions and compulsions but made little progress. He said that life at home was difficult when his mother was depressed. She sometimes went to bed and stayed there for 3 weeks. During this time, she seemed be in a depressive stupor, essentially unable to move for days. It was up to the children to care for themselves and their mother, whom they fed by hand. Because the older children had now left home, much of the burden had fallen on Mike. Jane's profound depressive episodes would remit after about 3 weeks, and she would immediately enter a hypomanic episode that might last several months or more. During hypomania, Jane was mostly funny, entertaining, and a delight to be with—if you could get a word in edgewise. Consultation with her therapist, an expert in the area, revealed that he had prescribed a number of medications but was so far unable to bring her mood swings under control.

Jane suffered from **bipolar II disorder,** in which major depressive episodes alternate with hypomanic episodes rather than full manic episodes. As we noted earlier, hypomanic episodes are less severe. Although she was noticeably "up," Jane functioned pretty well while in this mood state. The criteria for **bipolar I disorder** are the same, except the individual experiences a full manic episode. As in the criteria set for depressive disorder, for the manic episodes to be considered separate, there must be a symptom-free period of at least 2 months between them. Otherwise, one episode is seen as a continuation of the last.

The case of Billy illustrates a full manic episode. This individual was first encountered when he was admitted to a hospital.

BILLY: The World's Best at Everything

Before Billy reached the ward, you could hear him laughing and carrying on in a deep voice; it sounded like he was having a wonderful time. As the nurse brought Billy down the hall to introduce him to the staff, he spied the Ping-Pong table. Loudly, he exclaimed, "Ping-Pong! I love Ping-Pong! I have only played twice but that is what I am going to do while I am here; I am going to become the world's greatest Ping-Pong player! And that table is gorgeous! I am going to start work on that table immediately and make it the finest Ping-Pong table in the world. I am going to sand it down, take it apart, and rebuild it until it gleams and every angle is perfect!" Billy soon went on to something else that absorbed his attention.

DSM-IV-TR

DSM TABLE 7.5 Diagnostic Criteria for Bipolar II Disorder

A. Presence (or history) of one or more major depressive episodes.

B. Presence (or history) of at least one hypomanic episode.

C. There has never been a manic episode or a mixed episode.

D. The mood symptoms in criteria A and B are not better accounted for by schizoaffective disorder and are not superimposed on schizophrenia, schizophreniform disorder, delusional disorder, or psychotic disorder not otherwise specified.

E. The symptoms cause clinically significant distress or impairment in social, occupational, or other important areas of functioning.

Specify current or most recent episode:

   Hypomanic: If currently (or most recently) in a hypomanic episode

   Depressed: If currently (or most recently) in a major depressive episode

Specify (for current or most recent major depressive episode only if it is the most recent type of mood episode):

   Severity/psychotic/remission specifiers—Note: Fifth-digit codes specified cannot be used here because the code for bipolar II disorder already uses the fifth digit.

   Chronic

   With catatonic features

   With melancholic features

   With atypical features

   With postpartum onset

Specify:

   Longitudinal course specifiers (with and without interepisode recovery)

   With seasonal pattern (applies only to the pattern of major depressive episodes)

   With rapid cycling

Source: Reprinted, with permission, from American Psychiatric Association. (2000). *Diagnostic and statistical manual of mental disorders* (4th ed., text revision). Washington, DC: Author, © 2000 American Psychiatric Association.

The previous week, Billy had emptied his bank account, taken his credit cards and those of his elderly parents with whom he was living, and bought every piece of fancy stereo equipment he could find. He thought that he would set up the best sound studio in the city and make millions of dollars by renting it to people who would come from far and wide. This episode had precipitated his admission to the hospital.

During manic or hypomanic phases, patients often deny they have a problem, which was characteristic of Billy. Even after spending inordinate amounts of money or making foolish business decisions, these individuals, particularly if they are in the midst of a full manic episode, are so wrapped up in their enthusiasm and expansiveness that their behavior seems reasonable to them. The high during a manic state is so pleasurable that people may stop taking their medication during periods of distress or discouragement in an attempt to bring on a manic state again; this is a serious challenge to professionals.

Returning to the case of Jane, we continued to treat Jane's son Mike for several months. We made little progress before the school year ended. Because Mike was doing so poorly, the school administrators informed his parents that he would not be accepted back the next year. Mike and his parents wisely decided it might be a good idea if he got away from the house and did something different for a while, and he began working and living at a ski and tennis resort. Several months later, his father called to tell us that Mike's obsessions and compulsions had completely lifted since he'd been away from home. The father thought Mike should continue living at the resort, where he had entered school and was doing better academically. He now agreed with our previous assessment that Mike's condition might be related to his relationship with his mother. Several years later, we heard that Jane, in a depressive stupor, had killed herself, an all-too-tragic outcome in bipolar disorder.

A milder but more chronic version of bipolar disorder called **cyclothymic disorder** is similar in many ways to dysthymic disorder. Like dysthymic disorder, cyclothymic disorder is a chronic alternation of mood elevation and depression that does not reach the severity of manic or major depressive episodes. Individuals with cyclothymic disorder tend to be in one mood state or the other for years with relatively few periods of neutral (or euthymic) mood. This pattern must last for at least 2 years (1 year for children and adolescents) to meet criteria for the disorder. Individuals with cyclothymic disorder alternate between the kinds of mild depressive symptoms Jack experienced during his dysthymic states and the sorts of hypomanic episodes Jane experienced. In neither case was the behavior severe enough to require hospitalization or immediate intervention. Much of the time, such individuals are just considered moody. However, the chronically fluctuating mood states are, by definition, substantial enough to interfere with functioning. Furthermore, people with cyclothymia should be treated because of their increased risk to develop the more severe bipolar I or bipolar II disorder (Akiskal & Pinto, 1999; Akiskal, Khani, & Scott-Strauss, 1979; Alloy & Abramson, 2001; Depue et al., 1981; Goodwin & Jamison, 2007).

■ Onset and Duration

The average age of onset for bipolar I disorder is 18 and for bipolar II disorder is between 19 and 22, although cases of both can begin in childhood (Judd et al., 2003; Weissman, Bruce, Leaf, Florio, & Holzer, 1991). This is somewhat younger than the average age of onset for major depressive disorder, and bipolar disorders begin more acutely (Angst & Sellaro, 2000; Weissman et al., 1991; Winokur, Coryell, Endicott, & Akiskal, 1993). About one third of the cases of bipolar disorder begin in adolescence (Taylor & Abrams, 1981), and the onset is often preceded by minor oscillations in mood or mild cyclothymic mood swings (Goodwin & Ghaemi, 1998; Goodwin & Jamison, 2007). Only 10% to 13% of bipolar II disorder cases progress to full bipolar I syndrome (Coryell et al., 1995; Depression Guideline Panel, 1993). Prior evidence suggested that the distinction between unipolar and bipolar mood disorder also seemed well defined because few patients with unipolar depression experienced a manic episode during a 10-year follow-up period (Coryell, Endicott, et al., 1995). But Angst and Sellaro (2000), in reviewing some older studies, estimated the rate of depressed individuals later experiencing a full manic episode at closer to 25%. And Cassano and colleagues (2004), along with Akiskal (2006), found that as many as 67.5% of patients with unipolar depression experienced some manic symptoms. These studies raise questions about the true distinction between unipolar depression and bipolar disorder and suggest they may be on a continuum (called a spectrum in psychopathology).

It is relatively rare for someone to develop bipolar disorder after the age of 40. Once it does appear, the course is chronic; that is, mania and depression alternate indefinitely. Therapy usually involves managing the disorder with ongoing drug regimens that prevent recurrence of episodes. Suicide is an all-too-common consequence of bipolar disorder, almost always occurring during depressive episodes, as it did in the case of Jane (Valtonen et al., 2007). Estimates of suicide attempts in bipolar disorder range from an average of 17% for bipolar I to 24% for bipolar II, as compared to 12% in unipolar depression (Rihmer & Pestality, 1999). Rates of completed suicide are four times higher than for recurrent major depression (Brown, Beck, Steer, & Grisham, 2000; Miklowitz & Johnson, 2006). Even with treatment, patients with bipolar disorder tend to do poorly, with one study showing 60% of a large group experiencing poor adjustment during the first 5 years after treatment (Goldberg, Harrow, & Grossman, 1995; Goodwin et al., 2003). A more comprehensive and longer follow-up of 219 pa-

"Whoo, whoo, whoo—on top of the world! . . . It's going to be one great day! . . . I'm incognito for the Lord God Almighty. I'm working for him. I have been for years. I'm a spy. My mission is to fight for the American way . . . the Statue of Liberty. . . . I can bring up the wind, I can bring the rain, I can bring the sunshine, I can do lots of things. . . . I love the outdoors."

tients reported that only 16% recovered; 52% suffered from recurrent episodes, 16% had become chronically disabled, and 8% in one study had committed suicide (Angst & Sellaro, 2000) and 11% in another with a lengthy, 40-year follow-up (Angst, Angst, Gerber-Werder, & Gamma, 2005).

In typical cases, cyclothymia is chronic and lifelong. In about one third to one half of patients, cyclothymic mood swings develop into full-blown bipolar disorder (Kochman et. al., 2005; Waters, 1979). In one sample of cyclothymic patients, 60% were female, and the age of onset was quite young, often during the teenage years or before, with some data suggesting the most common age of onset to be 12 to 14 years (Depue et al., 1981). The disorder is often not recognized, and sufferers are thought to be high-strung, explosive, moody, or hyperactive (Biederman et al., 2000; Goodwin & Jamison, 2007). One subtype of cyclothymia is based on the predominance of mild depressive symptoms, one on the predominance of hypomanic symptoms, and another on an equal distribution of both.

Additional Defining Criteria

Other symptoms, or *specifiers,* may or may not accompany a mood disorder; when they do, they are often helpful in determining the most effective treatment. The specifiers are of two broad types: those that describe the most recent episode of the disorder and those that describe its course. We briefly review these here. As a guide through this maze of specifiers, refer to ■ Figure 7.3. What will be evident to you from the complexity of the figure is that diagnosing a mood disorder is not a straightforward task; great diversity of symptoms is possible within any of the diagnostic categories.

Six basic specifiers describe the most recent episode of a mood disorder: atypical, melancholic, chronic, catatonic, psychotic, and with postpartum onset.

1. *Atypical features specifier.* This specifier applies to depressive episodes and dysthymia but not manic episodes. Individuals with this specifier consistently oversleep and overeat during their depressive episodes and therefore gain weight (see, for example, Davidson, Miller, Turnbull, & Sullivan, 1982; Klein, 1989; Quitkin et al., 1988). Although they also have considerable anxiety, they can react with interest or pleasure to some things, unlike most depressed individuals. In addition, depression with atypical features, compared with more typical depression, is associated with a greater percentage of women and an earlier age of onset. The atypical group also had more symptoms, more severe symptoms, more suicide attempts, and

---

DSM-IV-TR

DSM TABLE 7.6 Diagnostic Criteria for Cyclothymic Disorder

A. For at least 2 years, the presence of numerous periods with hypomanic symptoms and numerous periods with depressive symptoms that do not meet criteria for a major depressive episode. *Note:* In children and adolescents, the duration must be at least 1 year.

B. During the above 2-year period (1 year in children and adolescents), the person has not been without the symptoms in criterion A for more than 2 months at a time.

C. No major depression episode, manic episode, or mixed episode has been present during the first 2 years of the disturbance.

Note: After the initial 2 years (1 year in children and adolescents) of cyclothymic disorder, there may be superimposed manic or mixed episodes (in which case both bipolar I disorder and cyclothymic disorder may be diagnosed) or major depressive episodes (in which case both bipolar II disorder and cyclothymic disorder may be diagnosed).

D. The symptoms in criterion A are not better accounted for by schizoaffective disorder and are not superimposed on schizophrenia, schizophreniform disorder, delusional disorder, or psychotic disorder not otherwise specified.

E. The symptoms are not due to the direct physiological effects of a substance (e.g., a drug of abuse, a medication) or a general medical condition (e.g., hyperthyroidism).

F. The symptoms cause clinically significant distress or impairment in social, occupational, or other important areas of functioning.

Source: Reprinted, with permission, from American Psychiatric Association. (2000). *Diagnostic and statistical manual of mental disorders* (4th ed., text revision). Washington, DC: Author. © 2000 American Psychiatric Association.

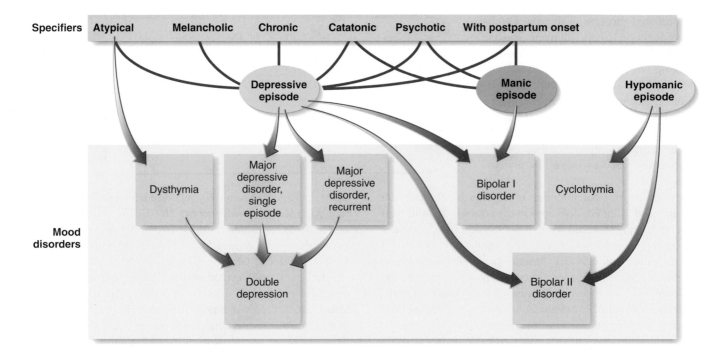

■ **FIGURE 7.3** Mood disorders and specifiers for the most recent episode of the disorder.

higher rate of comorbid disorders (Matza, Revicki, Davidson, & Stewart, 2003).

2. *Melancholic features specifier.* This specifier applies only if the full criteria for a major depressive episode have been met; it does not apply in the case of dysthymia. Melancholic specifiers include some of the more severe somatic symptoms, such as early-morning awakenings, weight loss, loss of libido (sex drive), excessive or inappropriate guilt, and anhedonia (diminished interest or pleasure in activities). The concept of "melancholic" does seem to signify, at the least, a severe type of depressive episode. Whether this type is anything more than a different point on a continuum of severity remains to be seen (Rush & Weissenburger, 1994).

3. *Chronic features specifier.* This specifier applies only if the full criteria for a major depressive episode have been met continuously for at least the past 2 years. Dysthymic disorder is not considered here because, for that disorder, a duration of at least 2 years is a primary diagnostic criterion. But with a requirement of a minimum of 2 years, both dysthymia and chronic major depression share the feature of chronicity (Mc-Cullough et al., 2000). Klein and colleagues (2006), in their 10-year prospective follow-up study, described earlier, suggest that chronicity (versus nonchronicity) may turn out to be the most important distinction in depression independent of whether the diagnosis is dysthymia or chronic major depression, because these two groups (chronic and nonchronic) seem different, not only in course over time but also in family history and cognitive style.

4. *Catatonic features specifier.* This specifier can be applied to major depressive episodes and even to manic episodes, although it is rare—and rarer still in mania. This serious condition involves an absence of movement (a stuporous state, as in the case of Jane) or **catalepsy,** in which the muscles are waxy and semi-

rigid, so a patient's arms or legs remain in any position in which they are placed. Catatonic symptoms may also involve excessive but random or purposeless movement. Catalepsy is more commonly associated with schizophrenia. In recent theorizing, this response maybe a common "end state" reaction to feelings of imminent doom and is found in many animals about to be attacked by a predator (Moskowitz, 2004).

5. *Psychotic features specifiers.* Some individuals in the midst of a major depressive or manic episode may experience psychotic symptoms, specifically **hallucinations** (seeing or hearing things that aren't there) and **delusions** (strongly held but inaccurate beliefs). Patients may also have somatic delusions, believing, for example, that their bodies are rotting internally and deteriorating into nothingness. Some may hear voices telling them how evil and sinful they are *(auditory hallucinations).* Such hallucinations and delusions are called *mood congruent* because they seem directly related to the depression. On rare occasions, depressed individuals might have other types of hallucinations or delusions such as *delusions of grandeur* (believing, for example, they are supernatural or supremely gifted) that do not seem consistent with the depressed mood. This is a *mood-incongruent* hallucination or delusion. Although quite rare, this condition signifies a serious type of depressive episode that may progress to schizophrenia (or may be a symptom of schizophrenia to begin with). Delusions of grandeur accompanying a manic episode are mood congruent (as in the photo on p. 217). Conditions in which psychotic symptoms accompany depressive episodes are relatively rare, occurring in 5% to 20% of identified cases of depression (Depression Guideline Panel, 1993; Flores & Schatzberg, 2006; Ohayon & Schatzberg, 2002; Thase, 1990). Ohayon and Schatzberg (2002), in a large community sample of almost 19,000 Europeans, found that 18.5% of individuals

meeting criteria for a major depressive episode had psychotic features. Symptoms of guilt and worthlessness were often associated with psychotic features. Psychotic features in general are associated with a poor response to treatment, greater impairment, and fewer weeks with minimal symptoms, compared to nonpsychotic depressed patients over a 10-year period (Chan, Janicak, Davis, & Altman, 1987; Coryell et al., 1996; Flint, Schaffer, Meyers, Rothschild, & Mulsant, 2006).

6. *Postpartum onset specifier.* This specifier can apply to both major depressive and manic episodes. Fully 13% of all women giving birth (one of eight) meet criteria for an episode of major depression. During the postpartum period (the 4-week period immediately following childbirth), early recognition of possible psychotic depressive or manic episodes is important because in a few tragic cases a mother in the midst of an episode has killed her newborn child (Purdy & Frank, 1993). Now a new study suggests that fathers don't entirely escape the emotional consequences of birth. Ramchandani and colleagues (2005) followed 11,833 mothers and 8,431 fathers for 8 weeks after the birth of their child. Of the mothers, 10% showed a marked increase in depressive symptoms on a rating scale, but so did 4% of the fathers. And depression in the fathers was associated with adverse emotional and behavioral outcomes in children 3.5 years later.

More minor reactions in adjustment to childbirth—called the "baby blues"—typically last a few days and occur in 50% to 80% of women between 1 and 5 days after delivery. During this period, new mothers may be tearful and have some temporary mood swings, but these are normal responses to the stresses of childbirth and disappear quickly (Kendell, 1985); the postpartum onset specifier does not apply to them (Wisner, Parry, & Piontek, 2002). However, in postpartum depression, most people, including the new mother herself, have difficulty understanding why she is depressed, because they assume this is a joyous time. Many new mothers forget that extreme stress can be brought on by physical exhaustion, new schedules, adjusting to nursing, and other changes that follow the birth. There is also some evidence that women with a history of postpartum depression meeting full criteria for an episode of major depression may be differentially susceptible to the rapid decline in reproductive hormones that occurs after delivery and that this may contribute to postpartum depression. This finding needs replication (Wisner et al., 2002). A close examination of women with postpartum depression revealed no essential differences between the characteristics of this mood disorder and others (Gotlib, Whiffen, Wallace, & Mount, 1991; Whiffen, 1992; Whiffen & Gotlib, 1993; Wisner et al., 2002). Therefore, postpartum depression did not seem to require a separate category in DSM-IV (Purdy & Frank, 1993), and approaches to treatment do not differ from those for nonpostpartum depression.

■ Differences in the Course of Mood Disorders

Three specifiers may accompany recurrent mania or depression: longitudinal course, rapid cycling, and seasonal pattern. Differences in course may require different treatment strategies.

1. *Longitudinal course specifiers.* Whether the individual suffering from an episode has had major episodes of depression or mania in the past is important, as is whether the individual fully

recovered between past episodes. Other important determinations are whether the patient with a major depressive episode suffered from dysthymia before the episode (double depression) and whether the patient with bipolar disorder experienced a previous cyclothymic disorder. Antecedent dysthymia or cyclothymia predicts a decreasing chance of full interepisode recovery (Judd et al., 1998b). Most likely, the patient will require a long and intense course of treatment to maintain a normal mood state for as long as possible after recovering from the current episode (Mueller et al., 1999; Rush, 1993; Solomon et al., 2000). Noting these longitudinal course specifiers—that is, whether there was full recovery between episodes and whether the patient had dysthymia or cyclothymia before the disorder—is important for recurrent major depressive disorder, bipolar I disorder, and bipolar II disorder.

2. *Rapid-cycling specifier.* This temporal specifier applies only to bipolar I and bipolar II disorders. Some people move quickly in and out of depressive or manic episodes. An individual with bipolar disorder who experiences at least four manic or depressive episodes within a year is considered to have a *rapid-cycling pattern,* which is apparently a severe variety of bipolar disorder that does not respond well to standard treatments (Bauer et al., 1994; Dunner & Fieve, 1974; Kilzieh & Akiskal, 1999; Kupka et al., 2005; Schneck et al., 2004). Coryell and colleagues (2003) demonstrated a higher probability of suicide attempts and more severe episodes of depression in 89 patients with a rapid-cycling pattern compared to a non-rapid-cycling group. Kupka and colleagues (2005) and Schneck and colleagues (2004) also found these patients' symptoms were more severe on a number of measures. Some evidence indicates that alternative drug treatment such as anticonvulsants and mood stabilizers rather than antidepressants may be more effective with this group of patients (Kilzieh & Akiskal, 1999; Post et al., 1989).

Approximately 20% to 40% of bipolar patients experience rapid cycling. From 60% to 90% are female, a higher rate than in other variations of bipolar disorder (see, for example, Coryell et al., 2003; Kupka et al., 2005; Schneck et al., 2004; Wehr, Sack, Rosenthal, & Cowdry, 1988), and this finding is consistent across 10 studies (Kilzieh & Akiskal, 1999). Unlike bipolar patients in general, most people with rapid cycling begin with a depressive episode rather than a manic episode (Kupka et al., 2005; McElroy & Keck, 1993). In most cases, rapid cycling tends to increase in frequency over time and can reach severe states in which patients cycle between mania and depression without any break. When this direct transition from one mood state to another happens, it is referred to as *rapid switching* or *rapid mood switching* and is a particularly treatment-resistant form of the disorder (MacKinnon, Zandi, Gershon, Nurnberger, & DePaulo, 2003; Maj, Pirozzi, Magliano, & Bartoli, 2002). Fortunately, rapid cycling does not seem to be permanent, because fewer than 3% of patients continue with rapid cycling across a 5-year period (Coryell, Endicott, & Keller, 1992), with 80% returning to a nonrapid-cycling pattern within 2 years (Coryell et al., 2003).

3. *Seasonal pattern specifier.* This temporal specifier applies both to bipolar disorders and to recurrent major depressive disor-

der. It accompanies episodes that occur during certain seasons (for example, winter depression). The most usual pattern is a depressive episode that begins in the late fall and ends with the beginning of spring. In bipolar disorder, individuals may become depressed during the winter and manic during the summer. This condition is called **seasonal affective disorder (SAD).**

Although some studies have reported seasonal cycling of manic episodes, the overwhelming majority of seasonal mood disorders involve winter depression, which has been estimated to affect as many as 2.7% of North Americans (Lam et al., 2006; Levitt & Boyle, 2002). But fully 15% to 25% of the population might have some vulnerability to seasonal cycling of mood that does not reach criteria for a disorder (Sohn & Lam, 2005). Unlike more severe melancholic types of depression, people with winter depressions tend toward excessive sleep (rather than decreased sleep) and increased appetite and weight gain (rather than decreased appetite and weight loss), symptoms shared with atypical depressive episodes. Although SAD seems a bit different from other major depressive episodes, family studies have not yet revealed any differential aggregation that would suggest winter depressions are a separate type (Allen, Lam, Remick, & Sadovnick, 1993).

Emerging evidence suggests that SAD may be related to daily and seasonal changes in the production of melatonin, a hormone secreted by the pineal gland. Because exposure to light suppresses melatonin production, it is produced only at night. Melatonin production also tends to increase in winter, when there is less sunlight. One theory is that increased production of melatonin might trigger depression in vulnerable people (Goodwin & Jamison, 2007; Lee et al., 1998). Wehr and colleagues (2001) have shown that melatonin secretion does increase in winter but only in patients with SAD and not healthy controls. (We return to this topic when we discuss biological contributions to depression.)

Another possibility is that circadian rhythms, which occur in approximately 24-hour periods, or cycles, and are thought to have some relationship to mood, are delayed in winter (Lewy & Sack, 1987; Wirz-Justice, 1998).

Cognitive and behavioral factors are also associated with SAD (Rohan, Sigmon, & Dorhofer, 2003). Women with SAD, compared to well-matched nondepressed women, reported more autonomous negative thoughts throughout the year and greater emotional reactivity to light in the laboratory, with low light associated with lower mood. Severity of worrying, or rumination, in the fall predicted symptom severity in the winter.

As you might expect, the prevalence of SAD is higher in extreme northern and southern latitudes because there is less winter sunlight. Studies have indicated less than 2% prevalence of SAD in Florida in contrast to nearly 10% prevalence in New Hampshire (Terman, 1988). A popular name for this type of reaction is *cabin fever.* SAD is quite prevalent in Fairbanks, Alaska, where 9% of the population appears to meet criteria for the disorder and another 19% have some seasonal symptoms of depression. The disorder also seems quite stable. In one group of 59 patients, 86% experienced a depressive episode each winter during a 9-year period of observation, with only 14% recovering during that time. For 26 (44%) of these patients, whose symptoms were more severe to begin with, depressive episodes began to occur during other seasons as well (Schwartz, Brown, Wehr, & Rosenthal, 1996). Rates in children and adolescents are between 1.7% and 5.5%, according to one study, with higher rates in postpubertal girls (Swedo et al., 1995), but the study needs replication.

Some clinicians reasoned that exposure to bright light might slow melatonin production in individuals with SAD (Blehar & Rosenthal, 1989; Lewy, Kern, Rosenthal, & Wehr, 1982). In phototherapy, a current treatment, most patients are exposed to 2 hours of bright light (2,500 lux) immediately on awakening. If the light exposure is effective, the patient begins to notice a lifting of mood within 3 to 4 days and a remission of winter depression in 1 to 2 weeks. Patients are also asked to avoid bright lights in the evening (from shopping malls and the like), so as not to interfere with the effects of the morning treatments. But this treatment is not without side effects. Approximately 19% of patients experience headaches, 17% have eyestrain, and 14% just feel "wired" (Levitt et al., 1993). Phototherapy is relatively new, but several studies strongly support its effectiveness (Eastman, Young, Fogg, Liu, & Meaden, 1998; Lewy et al., 1998; Terman, Terman, & Ross, 1998). In these studies, morning light was compared to evening light, which was predicted to be less effective. In two of these studies, a clever "negative ion generator" served as a placebo treatment in which patients sat in front of the box for the same amount of time as in the phototherapy and "expected" the treatment would work following instructions from the investigator but did not see the light. The results, presented in Table 7.1, showed a signifi-

Most SADs involve depression in winter, when the light is low and the days are short.

©2007 Jeff Schultz/AlaskaStock.com

TABLE 7.1	Summary of Remission Rates		
	Remission Rate % (Number of Patients)		
	Morning Light	**Evening Light**	**Placebo (Negative-Ion Generator)**
Terman et al., 1998			
First treatment	54 (25 of 46)	33 (13 of 39)	11 (2 of 19)
Crossover	60 (28 of 47)	30 (14 of 47)	Not done
Eastman et al., 1998			
First treatment	55 (18 of 33)	28 (9 of 32)	16 (5 of 31)
Lewy et al., 1998			
First treatment	22 (6 of 27)	4 (1 of 24)	Not done
Crossover	27 (14 of 51)	4 (2 of 51)	Not done

cantly better response for morning light compared to evening light or placebo. Evening light was better than placebo. The mechanism of action of this treatment has not been fully established, but one study indicated that morning light is superior to evening light because morning light produced phase advances of the melatonin rhythm, suggesting that changes in circadian rhythm are an important factor in treatment (Terman, Terman, Lo, & Cooper, 2001). In any case, it seems clear that light therapy is one important treatment for winter depression (Golden et al., 2005; Lam et al., 2006) and may even be effective for nonseasonal depression (Kripke, 1998).

Seemingly unique cognitive and behavioral factors are associated with SAD, as noted earlier, which suggests a role for cognitive-behavioral treatment (CBT). Now an important study by Rohan and colleagues (in press) indicates that CBT may be an effective treatment. Sixty-one adults received light therapy, CBT (twice a week in groups for 6 weeks), combination CBT and light therapy, or no treatment. All three treatment conditions were better than no treatment, with an advantage to the combined treatment in which 73% respond favorably. But when patients were followed for 1 year through the next winter (Rohan, Roecklein, Lacy, & Vacek, submitted for publication), only 5–6% of the groups receiving CBT alone, or in combination with light therapy, suffered a recurrence of depression compared to 39% of patients receiving light therapy alone. These results need to be replicated to confirm that CBT has more enduring effects with SAD.

CONCEPT CHECK 7.1

Match each description or case by choosing its corresponding disorder: (a) mania, (b) double depression, (c) dysthymic disorder, (d) major depressive episode, and (e) bipolar I disorder.

1. Last week, as he does about every 3 months, Ryan went out with his friends, buying rounds of drinks, socializing until early morning, and feeling on top of the world.

(continued)

CONCEPT CHECK 7.1

(continued)

Today Ryan will not even get out of bed to go to work, see his friends, or even turn on the lights. _____ _____

2. Feeling certain he would win the lottery, Charles went on an all-night shopping spree, maxing out all his credit cards without a worry. We know he's done this several times, feeling abnormally extreme elation, joy, and euphoria. _____

3. Heather has had some mood disorder problems in the past, although some days she's better than others. Many days it seems like she has fallen into a rut. Although she manages to get by, she has trouble making decisions because she doesn't trust herself. _____

4. For the past few weeks, Jennifer has been sleeping a lot. She feels worthless, can't get up the energy to leave the house, and has lost a lot of weight. Her problem is the most common and extreme mood disorder. _____ _____

5. Sanchez is always down and a bit blue, but occasionally he becomes so depressed that nothing pleases him. _____ _____

PREVALENCE OF MOOD DISORDERS

Several large epidemiological studies estimating the prevalence of mood disorder have been carried out in recent years (Kessler et al., 1994; Weissman et al., 1991). Wittchen, Knäuper, and Kessler (1994) compiled a summary of major studies, as shown in Table 7.2. Median prevalence rates during a period from 6 months to 1 year, as well as at some point during the respondents' lives, are shown for the principal disorders. At present, this table represents the best estimate of the worldwide prevalence of mood disorders. The figures for major depressive disorder of between 13% and 16.6% over a lifetime and 5.2% to 6.7% in the last year have recently been confirmed in two large and sophisticated studies (Hasin et al., 2005; Kessler et al., 2003, 2005). These studies agree that women are twice as likely to have mood disorders as men (Kessler, 2006).

Table 7.3 breaks down lifetime prevalence by four principal mood disorders. Notice here that the imbalance in prevalence between males and females is accounted for solely by major depressive disorder and dysthymia, because bipolar disorders are distributed approximately equally across gender. It is interesting that the prevalence of major depressive disorder and dysthymia is significantly lower among blacks than among whites (Hasin et al., 2005; Kessler et al., 1994; Weissman et al., 1991), although, again, no differences appear in bipolar disorders. One study of major depressive disorder in a community sample of African Americans found a prevalence of 3.1% during the previous year (Brown, Ahmed, Gary, & Milburn, 1995) and another found a prevalence of 4.52% during the previous year (Hasin et al., 2005). Fair or poor health status was the major predictor of depression in this popula-

TABLE 7.2 Prevalence of Affective Disorders Reported in Epidemiological Surveys Conducted Since 1980*

	Median % (Range)	
Disorder	**6 Months to 1 Year**	**Lifetime**
Major depression	6.5 (2.6 to 9.8)	16.1 (4.4 to 18.0)
Dysthymia	3.3 (2.3 to 4.6)	3.6 (3.1 to 3.9)
Bipolar	1.1 (1.0 to 1.7)	1.3 (0.6 to 3.3)

*Surveys used research diagnostic criteria (RDC); the third edition or third edition, text revision, of the *Diagnostic and Statistical Manual* (DSM-III or DSM-IIIR); or *International Classification of Diseases*, 10th edition (ICD-10), criteria.

Source: Adapted from Wittchen, H. U., Knäuper, B., & Kessler, R. C. (1994). Lifetime risk of depression. *British Journal of Psychiatry*, 165(Suppl. 26), 116–122.

TABLE 7.3 Lifetime Prevalence of Mood Disorder Subtypes by Age, Sex, and Ethnicity

	Lifetime Prevalence %			
	Bipolar I	**Bipolar II**	**Major Depression**	**Dysthymia**
Total	0.8	0.5	4.9	3.2
Age				
18–29	1.1	0.7	5.0	3.0
30–44	1.4	0.6	7.5	3.8
45–64	0.3	0.2	4.0	3.6
65+	0.1	0.1	1.4	1.7
Sex				
Men	0.7	0.4	2.6	2.2
Women	0.9	0.5	7.0	4.1
Ethnicity				
White	0.8	0.4	5.1	3.3
Black	1.0	0.6	3.1	2.5
Hispanic	0.7	0.5	4.4	4.0

Note: Significant variation within groups, adjusted for age, sex, or ethnicity.

Source: Adapted, with permission of The Free Press, a Division of Simon & Schuster Adult Publishing Group, from Robins, L. N., & Regier, D. A. (1991). *Psychiatric disorders in America: The epidemiologic catchment area study*. New York: Free Press, © 1991 Lee N. Robins and Darrel A. Regier.

tion. Few of these individuals received appropriate treatment, with only 11% coming in contact with a mental health professional (Brown et al., 1995). Native Americans, on the other hand, present with a significantly higher prevalence of depression (Hasin et al., 2005), although difficulties in translating the concept of depression to Native American cultures suggest this finding needs more study (Beals et al., 2005; Kleinman, 2004; see section later in this chapter on culture) Considering the chronicity and seriousness of mood

disorders (Klerman & Weissman, 1992), the prevalence is high indeed, demonstrating a substantial impact not only on the affected individuals and their families but also on society.

In Children and Adolescents

You might assume that depression requires some experience with life, that an accumulation of negative events or disappointments might create pessimism, which then leads to depression. Like many reasonable assumptions in psychopathology, this one is not uniformly correct. There is some evidence that 3-month-old babies can become depressed! Infants of depressed mothers display marked depressive behaviors (sad faces, slow movement, lack of responsiveness) even when interacting with a nondepressed adult (Field et al., 1988). Whether this behavior or temperament is caused by a genetic tendency inherited from the mother, the result of early interaction patterns with a depressed mother, or a combination is not yet clear.

Most investigators agree that mood disorders are fundamentally similar in children and in adults (Lewinsohn, Hops, Roberts, Seeley, & Andrews, 1993; Pataki & Carlson, 1990; Weiss & Garber, 2003). Therefore, no "childhood" mood disorders in DSM-IV-TR are specific to a developmental stage, unlike anxiety disorders. However, it also seems clear that the "look" of depression changes with age (see Table 7.4). For example, children under 3 years of age might manifest depression by their facial expressions, as well as by their eating, sleeping, and play behavior, quite differently from children between the ages of 9 and 12. Also, for preschool children (6 years old and under), Luby and colleagues (2003) report the necessity of setting aside the strict 2-week duration requirement because it is normal for mood to fluctuate at this young age. Furthermore, if these children clearly have the core symptoms of sadness or irritability and anhedonia (loss of pleasure), then a total of four symptoms rather than five seems sufficient. But even these core symptoms of anhedonia, hopelessness, and excessive sleep and social withdrawal seem to change with age, typically becoming more severe (Garber & Carter, 2005; Weiss & Garber, 2003). Adolescents forced to limit their activities because of illness or injury are at high risk for depression (Lewinsohn, Gotlib, & Seeley, 1997).

Estimates on the prevalence of mood disorders in children and adolescents vary widely, although more sophisticated studies are beginning to appear. The general conclusion is that depressive disorders occur less often in children than in adults but rise dramatically in adolescence (Garber & Carter, 2005; Kashani, Hoeper, Beck, & Corcoran, 1987; Lewinsohn, Hops, et al., 1993; Petersen, Compas, Brooks-Gunn, Stemmler, & Grant, 1993). Furthermore, some evidence indicates that, in young children, dysthymia is more prevalent than major depressive disorder, but this ratio reverses in adolescence. Like adults, adolescents experience major depressive disorder more often than dysthymia (Kashani et al., 1983, 1987). Major depressive disorder in adolescents is also a largely female disorder, as it is in adults, with puberty seemingly triggering this sex imbalance (Garber & Carter, 2005). Interestingly, this sex imbalance is not evident for more mild depression. Only among the adolescents referred to treatment does the sex imbalance exist (Compas et al., 1997). Some possible reasons more girls reach a more severe

TABLE 7.4 Speculative Manifestations of Depressive Symptoms Through Childhood

	Childhood Symptom				
Adult Symptom	**0–36 Months**	**3–5 Years**	**6–8 Years**	**9–12 Years**	**13–18 Years**
Dysphoric mood	Sad or expressionless face, gaze aversion, staring, irritability	Sad expression, somberness or labile mood, irritability	Prolonged unhappiness, somberness, irritability	Sad expression, apathy, irritability	Sad expression, apathy, irritability, increasing complaints of depression
Loss of interest or pleasure	No social play	Decreased socialization	Decreased socialization	Adult presentation	Adult presentation
Appetite or weight change	Feeding problems	Feeding problems	Adult presentation	Adult presentation	Adult presentation
Insomnia or hypersomnia	Sleep problems	Sleep problems	Sleep problems	Adult presentation	Adult presentation
Psychomotor agitation	Tantrums, irritability	Irritability, tantrums	Irritability, tantrums	Aggressive behavior	Aggressive behavior
Psychomotor retardation	Lethargy	Lethargy	Lethargy	Lethargy	Adult presentation
Loss of energy	Lethargy	Lethargy	Lethargy	Lethargy	Adult presentation
Feelings of worthlessness		Low self-esteem	Low self-esteem	Guilt, low self-esteem	Guilt
Diminished concentration		Accident proneness	Poor school performance	Poor school performance	Poor school performance
Recurrent thoughts of death or suicide		School phobia	Accident proneness, morbid outlook	Adult presentation	Adult presentation
Anxiety	Separation or attachment problems		Phobias, separation anxiety	Phobias, separation anxiety	Adult presentation
Somatic complaints		Present	Present	Present	Present

Source: Reprinted, with permission, from Carlson, G. A., & Kashani, J. H. (1988). Phenomenology of major depression from childhood through adulthood: Analysis of three studies. *American Journal of Psychiatry,* 145, 1222–1225, © 1988 American Psychiatric Association.

state requiring referral to treatment are suggested when we discuss sex differences in depression later in this chapter.

Looking at mania, children below the age of 9 seem to present with more irritability and emotional swings rather than classic manic states, and they are often mistaken as being hyperactive. In addition, their symptoms are more chronic in that they are always present rather than episodic, as in adults (Biederman et al., 2000), and this presentation seems to continue through adolescence (Faraone et al, 1997), although adolescents may appear more typically manic. Bipolar disorder seems to be rare in childhood, although case studies of children as young as 4 years of age displaying bipolar symptoms have been reported (Poznanski, Israel, & Grossman, 1984). However, the prevalence of bipolar disorder rises substantially in adolescence, which is not surprising in that many adults with bipolar disorder report a first onset during the teen years (Keller & Wunder, 1990).

©Royalty Free/Corbis

Among adolescents, severe major depressive disorder occurs mostly in girls.

One developmental difference between children and adolescents on the one hand and adults on the other is that children, especially boys, tend to become aggressive and even destructive during depressive episodes. Therefore, childhood depression (and mania) is sometimes misdiagnosed as attention deficit/hyperactivity disorder (ADHD) or, more often, conduct disorder in which aggression and even destructive behavior are common. Often conduct disorder and depression co-occur (Lewinsohn, Hops, et al., 1993; Petersen et al., 1993; Sanders, Dadds, Johnston, & Cash, 1992). Puig-Antich (1982) found that one third of prepubertal depressed boys met full criteria for a conduct disorder, which developed around the same time as the depressive disorder and ceased with the resolution of the depression. Biederman and colleagues (1987) found that 32% of children with ADHD also met criteria for major depression and between 60% to 90% of children and adolescents with mania also have ADHD (Biederman et al., 2000), a finding recently confirmed (Singh, DelBello, Kowatch, & Strakowski, 2006). In any case, successful treatment of the underlying depression (or spontaneous recovery) also resolves the associated problems in these specific cases. Adolescents with bipolar disorder may also become aggressive, impulsive, sexually provocative, and accident prone (Carlson, 1990; Keller & Wunder, 1990; Reiss, 1985).

Whatever the presentation, mood disorders in children and adolescents are serious because of their likely consequences. Fergusson and Woodward (2002), in a large prospective study, identified 13% of a group of 1,265 adolescents who developed major depressive disorder between 14 and 16 years of age. Later, between ages 16 and 21, this group was significantly at risk for occurrence of major depression, anxiety disorders, nicotine dependence, suicide attempts, and drug and alcohol abuse, as well as educational underachievement and early parenting, compared to adolescents who were not depressed. Lewinsohn, Rhode, Seeley, Klein, and Gotlib (2000) also followed 274 adolescents with major depressive

disorder into adulthood and identified several risk factors for additional depressive episodes as adults. Prominent among these were conflicts with parents, being female, and a higher proportion of family members experiencing depressive episodes. Jaffee and colleagues (2002) reported similar findings. Finally, Weissman and colleagues (1999) identified a group of 83 children with an onset of major depressive disorder before puberty and followed them for 10 to 15 years. Generally, there was also a poor adult outcome in this group, with high rates of suicide attempts and social impairment compared with children without major depressive disorder. Interestingly, these prepubertal children were more likely to develop substance abuse or other disorders as adults rather than continue with their depression, unlike adolescents with major depressive disorder. Even developing depressive symptoms that are not severe enough, or numerous enough to meet criteria for major depression (subthreshold symptoms), during adolescence poses a risk. Fergusson, Horwood, Ridder, and Beautrais (2005) found that extent and severity of depressive symptoms as an adolescent predicted extent of depression and suicidal behaviors as an adult. Clearly, becoming depressed as a child or adolescent is a dangerous, threatening event to be treated rapidly or prevented if possible.

In the Elderly

Only recently have we seriously considered the problem of depression in the elderly. Some studies estimate that 18% to 20% of nursing home residents may experience major depressive episodes (Katz, Leshen, Kleban, & Jethanandani, 1989; Rockwood, Stolee, & Brahim, 1991), which are likely to be chronic if they first appear after the age of 60 (Rapp, Parisi, & Wallace, 1991). In a large recent study, depressed elderly patients between 56 and 85 years of age were followed for 6 years; approximately 80% did not remit but continued to be depressed (or cycled in and out of depression) even if their depressive symptoms were not severe enough to meet diagnostic criteria for a disorder (Beekman et al., 2002). Late-onset depressions are associated with marked sleep difficulties, hypochondriasis (anxiety focused on possibly being sick or injured in some way), and agitation. It can be difficult to diagnose depression in the elderly because the presentation of mood disorders is often complicated by the presence of medical illnesses or symptoms of dementia (see, for example, Blazer, 1989; Delano-Wood & Abeles, 2005; Small, 1991). That is, elderly people who become physically ill or begin to show signs of dementia might become depressed about it, but the signs of depression would be attributed to the illness or dementia and thus missed. As many as 50% of patients with Alzheimer's disease suffer from comorbid depression, which makes life more difficult for their families (Lyketsos & Olin, 2002). Nevertheless, the overall prevalence of major depressive disorder for individuals over 65 is about half that of the general population (Hasin et al., 2005; Kessler et al., 2003), per-

Depression among the elderly is a serious problem that can be difficult to diagnose because the symptoms are often similar to those of physical illness or dementia.

©Matthew McVay/Stock, Boston

haps because stressful life events that trigger major depressive episodes decrease with age. But milder symptoms that do not meet criteria for major depressive disorder seem to be more common among the elderly (Beekman et al., 2002; Ernst & Angst, 1995; Gotlib & Nolan, 2001), perhaps because of illness and infirmity (Delano-Wood & Abeles, 2005; Roberts, Kaplan, Shema, & Strawbridge, 1997).

Anxiety disorders accompany depression in about one third of elderly patients, particularly generalized anxiety disorder and panic disorder (Lenze et al., 2000), and when they do, patients are more severely depressed. One third will also suffer from comorbid alcohol abuse (Devanand, 2002). Now, several studies have shown that entering menopause also increases rates of depression among women who have never previously been depressed (Cohen, Soares, Vitonis, Otto, & Harlow, 2006; Freeman, Sammel, Lin, & Nelson, 2006). This may be because of biological factors, such as hormonal changes, or the experience of distressing physical symptoms or other life events occurring during this period. Depression can also contribute to physical disease and death in the elderly (Grant, Patterson, & Yager, 1988; House, Landis, & Umberson, 1988). Being depressed doubles the risk of death in elderly patients who have suffered a heart attack or stroke (Schultz, Drayer, & Rollman, 2002). An even more tragic finding is that symptoms of depression are increasing substantially in our growing population of elderly people. Wallace and O'Hara (1992), in a longitudinal study, found that elderly citizens became increasingly depressed over a 3-year period. They suggest, with some evidence, that this trend is related to increasing illness and reduced social support; in other words, as we become frailer and more alone, the psychological result is depression, which increases the probability that we will become even frailer and have even less social support. Bruce (2002) confirmed that death of a spouse, caregiving burden for an ill spouse, and loss of independence because of medical illness are among the strongest risk factors for depression in this age group. This vicious cycle is deadly, because suicide rates are higher in the elderly than in any other age group (Conwell, Duberstein, & Caine, 2002).

The earlier gender imbalance in depression disappears after the age of 65. In early childhood, boys are more likely to be depressed than girls, but an overwhelming surge of depression in adolescent girls produces an imbalance in the sex ratio that is maintained until old age, when just as many women are depressed but increasing numbers of men are also affected (Wallace & O'Hara, 1992). From the perspective of the life span, this is the first time since early childhood that the sex ratio for depression is balanced.

Across Cultures

We noted the strong tendency of anxiety to take physical or somatic forms in some cultures; instead of talking about fear, panic, or general anxiety, many people describe stomach aches, chest pains or heart distress, and headaches. Much the same tendency exists across cultures for mood disorders, which is not surprising given the close relationship of anxiety and depression. Feelings of weakness or tiredness particularly characterize depression that is accompanied by mental or physical slowing or retardation

(Kleinman, 2004). Some cultures have their own idioms for depression; for instance, the Hopi, a Native American tribe, say they are "heartbroken" (Manson & Good, 1993).

Although somatic symptoms that characterize mood disorders seem roughly equivalent across cultures, it is difficult to compare subjective feelings. The way people think of depression may be influenced by the cultural view of the individual and the role of the individual in society (Jenkins, Kleinman, & Good, 1990; Kleinman, 2004). For example, in societies that focus on the *individual* instead of the *group,* it is common to hear statements such as "I feel blue" or "I am depressed." However, in cultures where the individual is tightly integrated into the larger group, someone might say, "Our life has lost its meaning," referring to the group in which the individual resides (Manson & Good, 1993). Despite these influences, it is generally agreed that the best way to study the nature and prevalence of mood disorders (or any other psychological disorder) in other cultures is first to determine their prevalence using standardized criteria (Neighbors, Jackson, Campbell, & Williams, 1989). The DSM criteria are increasingly used, along with semistructured interviews in which the same questions are asked, with some allowances for different words that might be specific to one subculture or another.

Weissman and colleagues (1991) looked at the lifetime prevalence of mood disorders in African American and Hispanic American ethnic groups (see Table 7.3). For each disorder, the figures are similar (although, as noted earlier, somewhat lower for African Americans in major depressive disorder and dysthymia), indicating no particular difference across subcultures. However, these figures were collected on a carefully constructed sample meant to represent the whole country.

In specific locations, results can differ dramatically. Kinzie, Leung, Boehnlein, and Matsunaga (1992) used a structured interview to determine the percentage of adult members of a Native American village who met criteria for mood disorders. The lifetime prevalence for any mood disorder was 19.4% in men, 36.7% in women, and 28% overall, approximately four times higher than in the general population. Examined by disorder, almost all the increase is accounted for by greatly elevated rates of major depression. Findings in the same village for substance abuse are similar to the results for major depressive disorder (see Chapter 11). Hasin and colleagues (2005) found a somewhat lower overall percentage of 19.17% in a different village, which was still 1.5 times higher than the percentage found in Caucasians, a significant difference. Beals and colleagues (2005), on the other hand, reported a considerably lower prevalence in two tribes they studied, perhaps because of differences in interviewing methods or because conditions and culture can differ greatly from tribe to tribe. Still, appalling social and economic conditions on many reservations fulfill all requirements for chronic major life stress, which is so strongly related to the onset of mood disorders, particularly major depressive disorder.

Among the Creative

Early in the history of the United States, Benjamin Rush, one of the signers of the U.S. Constitution and a founder of American psychiatry, observed something curious: "From a part of the brain

©Associated Press

As her diaries and letters demonstrate vividly, novelist Virginia Woolf suffered from both mania and depression. She committed suicide by drowning.

preternaturally elevated, but not diseased, the mind sometimes discovers not only unusual strengths and acuteness, but certain talents it never exhibited before. Talents for eloquence, poetry, music and painting, and uncommon ingenuity in several of the mechanical arts, are often evolved in this state of madness" (Rush, 1812, p. 153). This clinical observation has been made many times for thousands of years and applies not only to creativity but also to leadership. Aristotle pointed out that leading philosophers, poets, politicians, and artists all have tendencies toward "melancholia" (Ludwig, 1995).

Is there truth in the enduring belief that genius is allied to madness? Several researchers, including Kay Redfield Jamison and Nancy Andreasen, have attempted to find out. The results are surprising. Table 7.5 lists a group of famous American poets, many of whom won the coveted Pulitzer Prize. As you can see, all almost certainly had bipolar disorder. Many committed suicide. These 8 poets are among the 36 born in the 20th century who are represented in *The New Oxford Book of American Verse*, a collection reserved for the most distinguished poets in the country. It is certainly striking that about 20% of these 36 poets exhibited bipolar disorder, given the population prevalence of slightly less than 1%; but Goodwin and Jamison (2007) think that 20% is probably a conservative estimate, because the 28 remaining poets have not been studied in sufficient detail to determine whether they also suffered from bipolar disorder. Andreasen (1987) reported results similar to those shown in Table 7.5 in a study of 30 other creative writers, and Kaufman (2001, 2002) observed that

this effect was far more common in female poets even when compared to other artists or leaders. Why female poets in particular? Kaufman and Baer (2002) wonder whether the independent and sometimes rebellious qualities associated with creativity might be more stressful in a society that puts demands on women to be supportive and affiliative.

Many artists and writers, whether suspected of mood disorders or not, speak of periods of inspiration when thought processes quicken, moods lift, and new associations are generated (Jamison, 1989, 1993). Perhaps something inherent in manic states fosters creativity. On the other hand, it is possible that the genetic vulnerability to mood disorders is independently accompanied by a predisposition to creativity (Richards, Kinney, Lunde, Benet, & Merzel, 1988). In other words, the genetic patterns associated with bipolar disorder may also carry the spark of creativity. These ideas are little more than speculations at present, but the study of creativity and leadership, so highly valued in all cultures, may well be enhanced by a deeper understanding of "madness" (Goodwin & Jamison, 2007; Ludwig, 1995; Prien et al., 1984).

THE OVERLAP OF ANXIETY AND DEPRESSION

One of the mysteries faced by psychopathologists is the apparent overlap of anxiety and depression. Some of the latest theories on the causes of depression are based partly on this research. Several theorists have concluded that the two moods are more alike than different. This may seem strange, because you probably do not feel the same when you are anxious as when you are depressed. However, we now know that almost everyone who is depressed, particularly to the extent of having a disorder, is also anxious (Barlow, 2002; Brown, Campbell, Lehman, Grisham, & Mancill, 2001; DiNardo & Barlow, 1990), but not everyone who is anxious is depressed.

Let's examine this fact for a moment: *Almost all depressed patients are anxious, but not all anxious patients are depressed.* This means that certain core symptoms of depression are not found in anxiety and,

TABLE 7.5	Partial Listing of Major 20th-Century American Poets, Born Between 1895 and 1935, With Documented Histories of Manic-Depressive Illness (Bipolar Disorder)				
Poet	**Pulitzer Prize in Poetry**	**Treated for Major Depressive Illness**	**Treated for Mania**	**Committed Suicide**	
Hart Crane (1899–1932)		X	X	X	
Theodore Roethke (1908–1963)	X	X	X		
Delmore Schwartz (1913–1966)		X	X		
John Berryman (1914–1972)	X	X	X	X	
Randall Jarrell (1914–1965)		X	X	X	
Robert Lowell (1917–1977)	X	X	X		
Anne Sexton (1928–1974)	X	X	X	X	
Sylvia Plath* (1932–1963)	X	X		X	

*Plath, although not treated for mania, was probably bipolar II.

Source: Goodwin, F. K., & Jamison, K. R. (1990). *Manic depressive illness.* New York: Oxford University Press.

therefore, reflect what is "pure" about depression. These core symptoms include are the inability to experience pleasure (anhedonia) and a depressive "slowing" of both motor and cognitive functions until they are extremely labored and effortful (Brown, Chorpita, & Barlow, 1998; Clark & Watson, 1991; Moras et al., 1996; Rottenberg et al., 2002; Watson, 2005). Cognitive content (what one is thinking about) is also usually more negative in depressed individuals than in anxious ones (Greenberg & Beck, 1989).

Recently, our own ongoing research has identified symptoms that seem central to panic and anxiety even though they often are also found in depression. In panic, the symptoms (reflecting the flight or fight response, see Chapter 5), are primarily autonomic activation (excessive physiological symptoms such as heart palpitations and dizziness); muscle tension and apprehension (excessive worrying about the future) seem to reflect the essence of anxiety (Brown et al., 1998; Zinbarg & Barlow, 1996; Zinbarg et al., 1994). Many people with depression and even bipolar disorder (Frank et al., 2002; MacKinnon et al., 2003) also have the "central" symptoms of anxiety or panic just described. This is sometimes called *agitated depression* (Maj, Pirozzi, Magliano, & Bartoli, 2003). Earlier we discussed mixed manic episodes that seem to reflect mania and co-occurring anxiety. More important, a large number of symptoms are common in both anxiety and depressive disorders. Because these symptoms are not specific to either kind of disorder, they are called symptoms of *negative affect* (Brown et al., 1998; Clark, 2005). In Chapter 3, we talked about the process of creating a new diagnosis of mixed anxiety and depression. We noted that people who met criteria presented with symptoms of negative affect without any specific symptoms of anxiety or depression. Identifying pure anxious or depressive symptoms, as well as symptoms of negative affect that are common to both mood states, was an important step in creating this diagnosis (Brown et al., 1998; Moras et al., 1996; Zinbarg et al., 1994). Other researchers have reported finding similar shared and discrete symptoms (see, for example, Brown & Barlow, 2005; Clark & Watson, 1991).

Symptoms specific to anxiety, specific to depression, and common to both states are presented in Table 7.6. Research in this area may cause us to rethink our diagnostic criteria and combine anxiety and mood disorders into one larger category. Symptoms of negative affect alone are often less severe than full-blown anxiety or mood disorders, but their presence increases the risk of more severe disorders, suggesting that these symptoms are on a continuum with major depression and anxiety disorders (Clark, 2005; Nolen-Hoeksema, 2000a; Solomon & Haaga, 2003; Watson, 2005). In conclusion, most people who are depressed have both specific symptoms of anxiety and general symptoms of negative affect. But individuals with anxiety disorders may not have specific symptoms of depression.

Now think back for a minute to the case of Katie. You remember she was severely depressed and clearly had experienced a major depressive episode, along with serious suicidal ideation. A review of the list of depressive symptoms shows that Katie had all of them, thus meeting the criteria for major depressive disorder outlined in DSM-IV-TR. However, remember that Katie's difficulty began with her dread of interacting with her classmates or teachers for fear of making a fool of herself. Finally, she became

TABLE 7.6 Symptoms Specific to Anxiety and to Depression, as Well as Symptoms Shared by Both States

Pure Anxiety Symptoms

Apprehension

Tension

Edginess

Trembling

Excessive worry

Nightmares

Pure Depression Symptoms

Helplessness

Depressed mood

Loss of interest

Lack of pleasure

Suicidal ideation

Diminished libido

Mixed Anxiety and Depression Symptoms (Negative Affect)

Anticipating the worst

Worry

Poor concentration

Irritability

Hypervigilance

Unsatisfying sleep

Crying

Guilt

Fatigue

Poor memory

Middle or late insomnia

Sense of worthlessness

Hopelessness

Early insomnia

Source: Adapted from Zinbarg et al. (1994). The DSM-IV field trial for mixed anxiety depression. *American Journal of Psychiatry,* 151, 1153–1162.

so anxious that she stopped going to school. After seeing a doctor, who recommended she be "persuaded" to attend school, her parents became firmer. As Katie explained, however,

> I felt nauseated and sick each time that I went into the school building and so each day I was sent home. Uncomfortable physical experiences like sweaty palms, trembling, dizziness, and nausea accompanied my anxiety and fear. For me, being in a classroom, being in the school building, even the anticipation of being in school, triggered anxiety and illness. All of the sensations of anxiety draw your attention away from your surroundings and toward your own physical feelings. All of this would be bearable if it wasn't so extremely intense. I found myself battling the desire to escape and seek comfort. And, each escape brings with it a sense of failure and guilt. I understood that my physical sensations were inappropriate for the situation but I couldn't control them. I blamed myself for my lack of control.

CAUSES OF MOOD DISORDERS

In Chapter 2, we described *equifinality* as the same product resulting from possibly different causes. Just as there may be many reasons for a fever, there may also be a number of reasons for depression. For example, a depressive disorder that arises in winter has a different precipitant than a severe depression following a death, even though the episodes might look quite similar. Nevertheless, psychopathologists are identifying biological, psychological, and social factors that seem strongly implicated in the etiology of mood disorders, whatever the precipitating factor. An integrative theory of the etiology of mood disorders considers the interaction of biological, psychological, and social dimensions and notes the strong relationship of anxiety and depression. Before describing this, we review evidence pertaining to each contributing factor.

Biological Dimensions

Studies that would allow us to determine the genetic contribution to a particular disorder or class of disorders are complex and difficult to do. But several strategies—such as family studies and twin studies—can help us estimate this contribution.

Familial and Genetic Influences

In *family studies,* we look at the prevalence of a given disorder in the first-degree relatives of an individual known to have the disorder (the *proband*). We have found that, despite wide variability, the rate in relatives of probands with mood disorders is consistently about two to three times greater than in relatives of controls who don't have mood disorders (Gershon, 1990; Klein, Lewinsohn, Rohde, Seeley, & Durbin, 2002). Klein and colleagues (2002) also demonstrated that increasing severity and recurrence of major depression in the proband was associated with higher rates of depression in relatives.

The best evidence that genes have something to do with mood disorders comes from *twin studies,* in which we examine the frequency with which identical twins (with identical genes) have the disorder, compared to fraternal twins who share only 50% of their genes (as do all first-degree relatives). If a genetic contribution exists, the disorder should be present in identical twins to a much

greater extent than in fraternal twins. A number of twin studies suggest that mood disorders are heritable (see, for example, Kendler, Neale, Kessler, Heath, & Eaves, 1993; McGuffin & Katz, 1989; McGuffin et al., 2003). One of the strongest studies is presented in ■ Figure 7.4 (McGuffin et al., 2003). As you can see, an identical twin is two to three times more likely to present with a mood disorder than a fraternal twin if the first twin has a mood disorder (66.7% of identical twins compared to 18.9% of fraternal twins if the first twin has bipolar disorder; 45.6% versus 20.2% if the first twin has unipolar disorder). But notice that if one twin has unipolar disorder the chances of a co-twin having bipolar disorder are slim to none. Severity may also be related to amount of concordance (the degree to which something is shared). For example, Bertelsen, Harvald, and Hauge (1977) reported that if one twin had severe depression (defined as three or more major depressive episodes), then 59% of the identical twins and 30% of the fraternal twins also presented with a mood disorder. If the individual presented with fewer than three episodes, the concordance rate dropped to 33% in identical twins and 14% in fraternal twins. This means severe mood disorders may have a stronger genetic contribution than less severe disorders, a finding that was recently confirmed by Weissman and colleagues (2005) and holds true for most psychological disorders.

Kendler and colleagues (1993) also estimated heritability of major depressive disorders in a large number of female identical twins to be from 41% to 46%, well within the range reported in Figure 7.4. Even in older (nontwin) adults, estimates of heritability remain in the moderate range of approximately 35% (McGue & Christensen, 1997).

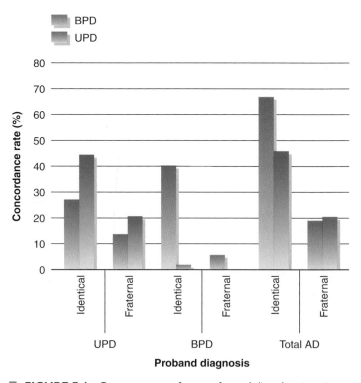

■ **FIGURE 7.4** Co-occurrence of types of mood disorders in twins for unipolar (UPD) and bipolar (BPD) affective disorder (AD). (Adapted, with permission, from McGuffin, P., Rijsdijk, F., Andrew, M., Sham, P., Katz, R., & Cardno, A., 2003. The heritability of bipolar affective disorder and the genetic relationship to unipolar depression. *Archives of General Psychiatry,* 60, 497–502, © 2003 American Medical Association.)

Two reports have appeared suggesting sex differences in genetic vulnerability to depression. Bierut and colleagues (1999) studied 2,662 twin pairs in the Australian twin registry and found the characteristically higher rate of depressive disorders in women. Estimates of heritability in women ranged from 36% to 44%, consistent with other studies. But estimates for men were lower and ranged from 18% to 24%. These results mostly agree with an important study of men in the United States by Lyons and colleagues (1998). The authors conclude that environmental events play a larger role in causing depression in men than in women.

Note from the studies just described that bipolar disorder confers an increased risk of developing some mood disorder in close relatives but not necessarily bipolar disorder. This conclusion supports an assumption noted previously that bipolar disorder may simply be a more severe variant of mood disorders rather than a fundamentally different disorder. Then again, of identical twins both having (concordant for) a mood disorder, 80% are also concordant for polarity. In other words, if one identical twin is unipolar, there is an 80% chance the other twin is unipolar. This finding suggests these disorders may be inherited separately and therefore be separate disorders after all (Nurnberger & Gershon, 1992).

McGuffin and colleagues (2003) conclude that both points are partially correct. Basically, they found that the genetic contributions to depression in both disorders are the same or similar but that the genetics of mania are distinct from depression. Thus, individuals with bipolar disorder are genetically susceptible to depression and independently genetically susceptible to mania.

Although these findings do raise continuing questions about the relative contributions of psychosocial and genetic factors to mood disorders, overwhelming evidence suggests that such disorders are familial and almost certainly reflect an underlying genetic vulnerability, particularly for women. As described in some detail in Chapter 2 (see p. 35), studies are now beginning to identify a small group of genes that confer this vulnerability, at least for some types of depression (Caspi et al., 2003; Garlow, Boone, Li, Owens, & Nemeroff, 2005). In this complex field, it is likely that many additional patterns of gene combinations will be found to contribute to varieties of depression.

In conclusion, the best estimates of genetic contributions to depression fall in the range of approximately 40% for women but seem to be significantly less for men (around 20%). Genetic contributions to bipolar disorder seem to be somewhat higher. This means that from 60% to 80% of the causes of depression can be attributed to environmental factors. As we noted in Chapter 4, behavioral geneticists break down environmental factors into events shared by twins (experiencing the same upbringing in the same house and, perhaps, experiencing the same stressful events) and events not shared. What part of our experience causes depression? There is wide agreement that it is the unique nonshared events rather than the shared ones that interact with biological vulnerability to cause depression (Bierut et al., 1999; Plomin, DeFries, McClearn, & Rutter, 1997).

■ Depression and Anxiety: Same Genes?

Although most studies have looked at specific disorders in isolation, a growing trend is to examine the heritability of related groups of disorders. Evidence supports the assumption of a close relationship among depression, anxiety, and panic (as well as other emotional disorders). For example, data from family studies indicate that the more signs and symptoms of anxiety and depression there are in a given patient, the greater the rate of anxiety, depression, or both in first-degree relatives and children (Hammen, Burge, Burney, & Adrian, 1990; Hudson et al., 2003; Kovacs et al., 1989; Leckman, Weissman, Merikangas, Pauls, & Prusoff, 1983; Puig-Antich & Rabinovich, 1986; Weissman, 1985). In several important reports from a major set of data on more than 2,000 female twins, Ken Kendler and his colleagues (Kendler, Heath, Martin, & Eaves, 1987; Kendler, Neale, Kessler, Heath, & Eaves, 1992b; Kendler et al., 1995) found that the same genetic factors contribute to both anxiety and depression. Social and psychological explanations seemed to account for the factors that differentiate anxiety from depression rather than genes. These findings again suggest that, with the possible exception of mania, the biological vulnerability for mood disorders may not be specific to that disorder but may reflect a more general predisposition to anxiety or mood disorders. The specific form of the disorder would be determined by unique psychological, social, or additional biological factors (Akiskal, 1997; Lyons et al., 1998; Weissman, 1985).

■ Neurotransmitter Systems

Mood disorders have been the subject of more intense neurobiological study than almost any other area of psychopathology, with the possible exception of schizophrenia. New and exciting findings describing the relationship of specific neurotransmitters and neurohormones to mood disorders appear almost monthly and are punctuated by occasional reports of so-called breakthroughs. In this difficult area, most breakthroughs prove to be illusory, but false starts provide us with an ever-deeper understanding of the enormous complexity of the neurobiological underpinnings of mood disorders (Garlow & Nemeroff, 2004; National Institute of Mental Health, 2003; Thase, 2005; Thase, Jindal, & Howland, 2002).

In Chapter 2, we observed that we now know that neurotransmitter systems have many subtypes and interact in many complex ways with one another and with neuromodulators (products of the endocrine system). Research implicates low levels of serotonin in the etiology of mood disorders, but only in relation to other neurotransmitters, including norepinephrine and dopamine (see, for example, Spoont, 1992; Thase, 2005; Thase et al., 2002). Remember that the apparent primary function of serotonin is to regulate our emotional reactions. For example, we are more impulsive, and our moods swing more widely, when our levels of serotonin are low. This may be because one of the functions of serotonin is to regulate systems involving norepinephrine and dopamine (Mandell & Knapp, 1979). According to the "permissive" hypothesis, when serotonin levels are low, other neurotransmitters are "permitted" to range more widely, become dysregulated, and contribute to mood irregularities, including depression. A drop in norepinephrine would be one of the consequences. Mann and colleagues (1996) used sophisticated brain-imaging procedures (PET scans) to confirm impaired serotonergic transmission in patients with depression. This theory is undoubtedly overly simplistic, but it does represent current strategies in the study of neurotransmitters and psychopathology. Current thinking is that the balance of the various neurotransmitters and their subtypes is more important than the absolute level of any one neurotransmitter.

In the context of this delicate balance, there is continued interest in the role of dopamine, particularly in relationship to manic episodes (Depue & Iacono, 1989) or psychotic features (Garlow & Nemeroff, 2003). For example, the dopamine agonist L-dopa seems to produce hypomania in bipolar patients (see, for instance, Van Praag & Korf, 1975), along with other dopamine agonists (Silverstone, 1985). But, as with other research in this area, it is quite difficult to pin down any relationships with certainty.

The Endocrine System

During the past several years, most attention has shifted to the endocrine system and the "stress hypothesis" of the etiology of depression (Nemeroff, 2004). This hypothesis focuses on overactivity in the hypothalamic–pituitary–adrenocortical (HPA) axis (discussed later), which produces stress hormones. Again, notice the similarity with the description of the neurobiology of anxiety in Chapter 5 (see, for example, Charney & Drevets, 2002). Investigators became interested in the endocrine system when they noticed that patients with diseases affecting this system sometimes became depressed. For example, hypothyroidism, or Cushing's disease, which affects the adrenal cortex, leads to excessive secretion of cortisol and, often, to depression (and anxiety).

In Chapter 2, and again in Chapter 5 on anxiety disorders, we discussed the brain circuit called the HPA axis, beginning in the hypothalamus and running through the pituitary gland, which coordinates the endocrine system (see Figure 2.10). Investigators have also discovered that neurotransmitter activity in the hypothalamus regulates the release of hormones that affect the HPA axis. These **neurohormones** are an increasingly important focus of study in psychopathology (see, for example, Garlow & Nemeroff, 2003; Ladd, Owens, & Nemeroff, 1996; Nemeroff, 2004). There are thousands of neurohormones. Sorting out their relationship to antecedent neurotransmitter systems (as well as determining their independent effects on the central nervous system) is likely to be a complex task indeed. One of the glands influenced by the pituitary is the cortical section of the adrenal gland, which produces the stress hormone cortisol that completes the HPA axis. Cortisol is called a *stress hormone* because it is elevated during stressful life events. (We discuss this system in more detail in Chapter 9.) For now, it is enough to know that cortisol levels are elevated in depressed patients, a finding that makes sense considering the relationship between depression and severe life stress (Gibbons, 1964; Gold, Goodwin, & Chrousos, 1988; Thase et al., 2002).

This connection led to the development of what was thought to be a biological test for depression, the *dexamethasone suppression test (DST)*. Dexamethasone is a glucocorticoid that suppresses cortisol secretion in normal subjects. However, when this substance was given to patients who were depressed, much *less* suppression was noticed than in normal subjects, and what did occur didn't last long (Carroll, Martin, & Davies, 1968; Carroll et al., 1980). Approximately 50% of depressed patients show this re-

duced suppression, particularly if their depression is severe (Rush et al., 1997). The thinking was that in depressed patients the adrenal cortex secreted enough cortisol to overwhelm the suppressive effects of dexamethasone. This theory was heralded as important, because it promised the first biological laboratory test for a psychological disorder. However, later research demonstrated that individuals with other disorders, particularly anxiety disorders, also demonstrate nonsuppression (Feinberg & Carroll, 1984; Goodwin & Jamison, 2007), which eliminated its usefulness as a test to diagnose depression.

Recent research has taken some exciting new turns. Recognizing that stressful hormones are elevated in patients with depression (and anxiety), researchers have begun to focus on the consequences of these elevations. Preliminary findings indicate that these hormones can be harmful to neurons in that they decrease a key ingredient that keeps neurons healthy and growing. You saw in Chapter 5 on anxiety disorders that individuals experiencing heightened levels of stress hormones over a long period undergo some shrinkage of a brain structure call the *hippocampus*. The hippocampus, among other things, is responsible for downregulating stress hormones and serves important functions in facilitating cognitive processes such as short-term memory. But the new finding, at least in animals, is that long-term overproduction of stress hormones makes the organism unable to develop new neurons (neurogenesis). Thus, some theorists suspect that the connection between high stress hormones and depression is the suppression of neurogenesis in the hippocampus (Heim, Plotsky, & Nemeroff, 2004; McEwen, 1999). Scientists have already observed that successful treatments for depression, including electroconvulsive therapy, seem to produce neurogenesis in the hippocampus, thereby reversing this process (Duman, 2004; Santarelli et al., 2003; Sapolsky, 2004). This is just a theory that must now undergo the slow process of scientific confirmation.

Sleep and Circadian Rhythms

Earlier we discussed the interesting new findings on SAD, noting that a characteristic symptom is an increase in sleeping. We have known for several years that sleep disturbances are a hallmark of most mood disorders. Most important, in people who are depressed, there is a significantly shorter period after falling asleep before *rapid eye movement (REM) sleep* begins. As you may remember from your introductory psychology or biology course, there are two major stages of sleep: REM sleep and non-REM sleep. When we first fall asleep, we go through several substages of progressively deeper sleep during which we achieve most of our rest. After about 90 minutes, we begin to experience REM sleep, when the brain arouses, and we begin to dream. Our eyes move rapidly back and forth under our eyelids, hence the name *rapid eye movement* sleep. As the night goes on, we have increasing amounts of REM sleep. (We discuss the process of sleep in more detail in Chapter 8.) In addition to entering REM sleep more quickly, depressed patients experience REM activity that is more intense, and the stages of deepest sleep, called *slow wave sleep,* don't occur until later if at all (Jindal et al., 2002; Kupfer, 1995). It seems that some sleep characteristics occur only while we are depressed and not at other times (Riemann, Berger, & Voderholzer, 2001; Rush et al., 1986), although more recent evidence suggests that disturbances in sleep continuity, as well as reduction of deep sleep, may be more traitlike in that they are present even when the individual is not depressed (Kupfer, 1995). Similar sleep pattern disturbances have been noted in depressed children (Garber & Carter, 2005). It is not yet clear whether sleep disturbances also characterize bipolar patients (Goodwin & Jamison, 2007), although preliminary evidence suggests patterns of *increased* rather than *decreased* sleep (Kupfer, 1995) and a longer rather than a shorter REM latency (Rao et al., 2002).

Another interesting finding is that depriving depressed patients of sleep, particularly during the second half of the night, causes temporary improvement in their condition (Giedke & Schwarzler, 2002; Wehr & Sack, 1988), although the depression returns when the patients start sleeping normally again. In any case, because sleep patterns reflect a biological rhythm, there may be a relationship among SAD, sleep disturbances in depressed patients, and a more general disturbance in biological rhythms. This would not be surprising if it were true, because most mammals are exquisitely sensitive to day length at the latitudes at which they live and this "biological clock" controls eating, sleeping, and weight changes. Thus, substantial disruption in circadian rhythm might be particularly problematic for some vulnerable individuals (Moore, 1999; Sohn & Lam, 2005).

Important research has examined the interaction of psychosocial factors and potentially important biological markers such as sleep characteristics. Monroe, Thase, and Simons (1992) reported that people with major depressive disorder who had experienced a major life stress just before their episode did not evidence reduced latency to REM sleep, but those without a precipitating life stress did have reduced REM latency values, indicating, perhaps, several pathways to depression. Thase, Simons, and Reynolds (1996) and Buysse and colleagues (1999) report that abnormal sleep profiles and, specifically, disturbances in REM sleep and poor sleep quality predict a somewhat poorer response to psychological treatment. This type of research prefaces more integrated strategies to come.

Brain Wave Activity

A new and promising area of investigation focuses on characteristics of brain waves in depressed and anxious individuals. Measuring electrical activity in the brain with electroencephalogram (EEG) was described in Chapter 3, where we also described a type of brain wave activity, alpha waves, that indicate calm, positive feelings. Davidson (1993) and Heller and Nitschke (1997) demonstrated that depressed individuals exhibit greater right-sided anterior activation of their brains (and less left-sided activation and, correspondingly, less alpha wave activity) than nondepressed individuals (Davidson, Pizzagalli, Nitschke, & Putnam, 2002). Furthermore, right-sided anterior activation is also found in patients who are no longer depressed (Gotlib, Ranganath, & Rosenfeld, 1998; Tomarken & Keener, 1998), suggesting this brain function might also exist *before* the individual becomes depressed and represent a vulnerability to depression. Similarly, adolescent offspring of depressed mothers tend to show this pattern, compared to offspring of nondepressed mothers (Tomarken, Dichter, Garber, & Simien, 2004). If these findings are confirmed (Gotlib & Abramson,

1999), this type of brain functioning could become an indicator of a biological vulnerability to depression.

Psychological Dimensions

In reviewing genetic contribution to the causes of depression, we noted that 60% to 80% of the causes of depression could be attributed to psychological experiences. Furthermore, most of those experiences are unique to the individual.

■ Stressful Life Events

Stress and trauma are among the most striking unique contributions to the etiology of all psychological disorders. This is reflected throughout psychopathology and is evident in the wide adoption of the diathesis–stress model of psychopathology presented in Chapter 2 (and referred to throughout this book), which describes possible genetic and psychological vulnerabilities. But in seeking what activates this vulnerability (diathesis), we usually look for a stressful or traumatic life event.

You would think it would be sufficient to ask people whether anything major had happened in their lives before they developed depression or some other psychological disorder. Most people who develop depression report losing a job, getting divorced, having a child, or graduating from school and starting a career. But, as with most issues in the study of psychopathology, the significance of a major event is not easily discovered (Kessler, 1997), so most investigators have stopped simply asking patients whether something bad (or good) happened and have begun to look at the context of the event, as well as the meaning it has for the individual.

For example, losing a job is stressful for most people, but it is far more difficult for some than others. A few people might even see it as a blessing. If you were laid off as a manager in a large corporation because of a restructuring but your wife is the president of another corporation and makes more than enough money to support the family, it might not be so bad. Furthermore, if you are an aspiring writer or artist who has not had time to pursue your art, becoming jobless might be the opportunity you have been waiting for, particularly if your wife has been telling you for years to devote yourself to your creative pursuits.

Now consider losing your job if you are a single mother of two young children living from day to day and, on account of a recent doctor's bill, you have to choose between paying the electric bill or buying food. The stressful life event is the same, but the context is different and transforms the significance of the event substantially. To complicate the scenario further, think for a minute about how such a woman might react to losing her job. One woman might well decide she is a total failure and thus becomes unable to carry on and provide for her children. Another woman might realize the job loss was not her fault and take advantage of a job training program while scraping by somehow. Thus, both the context of the life event and its meaning are important. This approach to studying life events, developed by George W. Brown (1989b) and associates in England, is represented in ■ Figure 7.5.

Brown's study of life events is difficult to carry out, and the methodology is still evolving. Psychologists such as Scott Monroe (Monroe & Roberts, 1990; Monroe, Rohde, Seeley, & Lewinsohn,

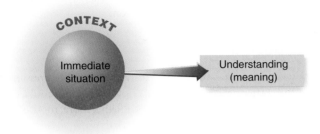

■ **FIGURE 7.5** Context and meaning in life stress situations. (Reprinted, with permission, from Brown, G. W., 1989b. Life events and measurement. In G. W. Brown & T. O. Harris, Eds., *Life events and illness.* New York: Guilford Press, © 1989 New York, NY: Guilford Press.)

1999; see also Dohrenwend & Dohrenwend, 1981; Hammen, 1991; Shrout et al., 1989) have developed new methods. One crucial issue is the bias inherent in remembering events. If you ask people who are currently depressed what happened when they first became depressed more than 5 years ago, you will probably get different answers from those they would give if they were not currently depressed. Because current moods distort memories, many investigators have concluded that the only useful way to study stressful life events is to follow people *prospectively,* to determine more accurately the precise nature of events and their relation to subsequent psychopathology.

In any case, in summarizing a large amount of research, it is clear that stressful life events are strongly related to the onset of mood disorders (Grant, Compas, Thurm, McMahon, & Gibson, 2004; Hammen, 2005; Kendler, Karkowski, & Prescott, 1999b; Kessler, 1997; Mazure, 1998; Monroe & Harkness, 2005; Monroe, Slavich, Torres, & Gotlib, 2007). Measuring the context of events and their impact in a random sample of the population, a number of studies have found a marked relationship between severe and, in some cases, traumatic life events and the onset of depression (Brown, 1989a; Brown, Harris, & Hepworth, 1994; Kendler et al., 1999b; Mazure, 1998). Severe events precede all types of depression except, perhaps, for a small group of patients with melancholic or psychotic features who are experiencing subsequent episodes (Brown et al., 1994). Major life stress is a somewhat stronger predictor for initial episodes of depression compared to recurrent episodes (Lewinsohn, Allen, Seeley, & Gotlib, 1999). In addition, for people with recurrent depression, the clear occurrence of a severe life stress before or early in the latest episode predicts a poorer response to treatment and a longer time before remission (Monroe, Kupfer, & Frank, 1992), as well as a greater likelihood of recurrence (Monroe, Roberts, Kupfer, & Frank, 1996). While the context and meaning are often more important than the exact nature of the event itself, there are some events that are particularly likely to lead to depression. One of them is the breakup of a relationship, which is difficult for both adolescents (Monroe, Rohde, Seeley, & Lewinsohn, 1999) and adults (Kendler, Hettema, Butera, Gardner, & Prescott, 2003). Kendler and colleagues (2003) demonstrated in an elegant twin study that if one twin experienced a loss, such as the death of a loved one, that twin was 10 times more likely to become depressed than the twin who didn't experience the loss. But if one twin is also humiliated by

the loss, as when, for example, a boyfriend or husband leaves the twin for a best friend and the twin still sees them all the time, then that twin would be 20 times more likely to get depressed than a twin with the same genes who didn't experience the event.

Despite this strong relationship between stress and depression, scientists are discovering that not all stressful events are independent of the depression. Remember in Chapter 2 where we noted that our genetic endowment might increase the probability that we will experience stressful life events? We referred to this as the *reciprocal gene–environment model* (Saudino, Pedersen, Lichenstein, McClearn, & Plomin, 1997). One example would be people who tend to seek difficult relationships because of genetically based personality characteristics that then lead to depression. Kendler and colleagues (1999a) report that about one third of the association between stressful life events and depression is not the usual arrangement where stress triggers depression but rather individuals vulnerable to depression who are placing themselves in high-risk stressful environments, such as difficult relationships or other risky situations where bad outcomes are common. What is important about the reciprocal model is that it can happen both ways in the same individual; stress triggers depression, and depressed individuals create or seek stressful events. Interestingly, if you ask mothers, they tend to say their adolescents created the problem, but adolescents blame the stressful event itself (Carter, Garber, Cielsa, & Cole, 2006). According to the reciprocal model, the truth lies somewhere between these two views.

The relationship of stressful events to the onset of episodes in bipolar disorder is also strong (Ellicott, 1988; Goodwin & Jamison, 2007; Johnson & Roberts, 1995; Johnson, Gruber, & Eisner, 2007; Reilly-Harrington, Alloy, Fresco, & Whitehouse, 1999). However, several issues may be particularly relevant to the etiology of bipolar disorders (Goodwin & Ghaemi, 1998). First, stressful life events seem to trigger early mania and depression, but as the disorder progresses, these episodes seem to develop a life of their own. In other words, once the cycle begins, a psychological or pathophysiological process takes over and ensures the disorder will continue (see, for example, Post, 1992; Post et al., 1989). Second, some precipitants of manic episodes seem related to loss of sleep, as in the postpartum period (Goodwin & Jamison, 2007) or as a result of jet lag—that is, disturbed circadian rhythms. In most cases of bipolar disorder, nevertheless, stressful life events are substantially indicated not only in provoking relapse but also in preventing recovery (Johnson & Miller, 1997).

Finally, although almost everyone who becomes depressed has experienced a significant stressful event, most people who experience such events do not become depressed. Although the data are not yet as precise as we would like, somewhere between 20% and 50% of individuals who experience severe events become depressed. Thus, between 50% and 80% of individuals do *not* develop depression or, presumably, any other psychological disorder. Again, data strongly support the interaction of stressful life events with some kind of vulnerability: genetic, psychological, or, more likely, a combination of the two influences (Barlow, 2002; Hankin & Abramson, 2001; Kendler, Kuhn, Vittum, Prescott, & Riley, 2005; Thase, 2005).

Given a genetic vulnerability (diathesis) and a severe life event (stress), what happens then? Research has isolated a number of psychological and biological processes. To illustrate one, let's return to Katie. Her life event was attending a new school. Katie's feeling of loss of control leads to another important psychological factor in depression: learned helplessness.

KATIE: No Easy Transitions

> I was a serious and sensitive 11-year-old at the edge of puberty and at the edge of an adventure that many teens and preteens embark on—the transition from elementary to junior high school. A new school, new people, new responsibilities, new pressures. Academically, I was a good student up to this point but I didn't feel good about myself and generally lacked self-confidence.

Katie began to experience severe anxiety reactions. Then she became quite ill with the flu. After recovering and attempting to return to school, Katie discovered that her anxieties were worse than ever. More important, she began to feel she was losing control.

> As I look back I can identify events that precipitated my anxieties and fears, but then everything seemed to happen suddenly and without cause. I was reacting emotionally and physically in a way that I didn't understand. I felt out of control of my emotions and body. Day after day I wished, as a child does, that whatever was happening to me would magically end. I wished that I would awake one day to find that I was the person I was several months before.

■ Learned Helplessness

To review our discussion in Chapter 2, Martin Seligman discovered that dogs and rats have an interesting emotional reaction to events over which they have no control. If rats receive occasional shocks, they can function reasonably well as long as they can cope with the shocks by doing something to avoid them, such as pressing a lever. But if they learn that nothing they do helps them avoid the shocks, they eventually become helpless, give up, and manifest an animal equivalent of depression (Seligman, 1975).

Do humans react the same way? Seligman suggests we seem to, but only under one important condition: People become anxious and depressed when they decide, or make an attribution, that they have no control over the stress in their lives (Abramson, Seligman, & Teasdale, 1978; Miller & Norman, 1979). These findings evolved into an important model called the **learned helplessness theory of depression.** Often overlooked is Seligman's point that anxiety is the first response to a stressful situation. Depression may follow marked hopelessness about coping with the difficult life events (Barlow, 1988, 2002). The depressive attributional style is (1) *internal,* in that the individual attributes negative events to personal failings ("it is all my fault"); (2) *stable,* in that, even after a particular negative event passes, the attribution that "additional bad things will always be my fault" remains; and (3) *global,* in that the attributions extend across a variety of issues. Research continues on this interesting concept, but you can see how it applies to Katie. Early in her difficulties with attending

school, she began to believe events were out of her control and that she was unable even to begin to cope. More important, in her eyes the bad situation was all her fault: "I blamed myself for my lack of control." A downward spiral into a major depressive episode followed.

But a major question remains: Is learned helplessness a cause of depression or a correlated side effect of becoming depressed? If it were a cause, learned helplessness would have to exist *before* the depressive episode. Results from a 5-year longitudinal study in children shed some light on this issue. Nolen-Hoeksema, Girgus, and Seligman (1992) reported that negative attributional style did not predict later symptoms of depression in young children; rather, stressful life events seemed to be the major precipitant of symptoms. However, as they grew older, they tended to develop more negative cognitive styles, which did tend to predict symptoms of depression in reaction to additional negative events. Nolen-Hoeksema and colleagues speculate that meaningful negative events early in childhood may give rise to negative attributional styles in a developmental fashion, making these children more vulnerable to future depressive episodes when stressful events occur. Indeed, most studies support the finding that negative cognitive styles precede and are a risk factor for depression (Alloy & Abramson, 2007; Garber & Carter, 2005).

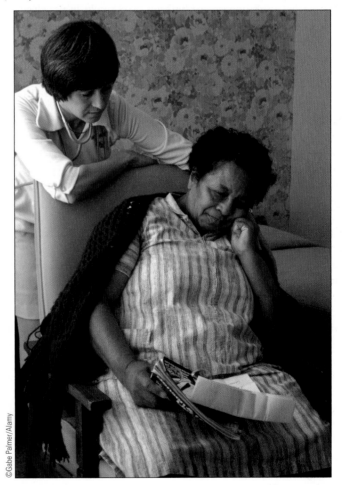

According to the learned helplessness theory of depression, people become depressed when they believe they have no control over the stress in their lives.

This thinking recalls the types of psychological vulnerabilities theorized to contribute to the development of anxiety disorders (Barlow, 1988, 2002). That is, in a person who has a nonspecific genetic vulnerability to either anxiety or depression, stressful life events activate a psychological sense that life events are uncontrollable (Barlow, 2002; Chorpita & Barlow, 1998). Evidence suggests that negative attributional styles are not specific to depression but characterize anxiety patients as well (Barlow, 2002; Hankin & Abramson, 2001; Heimberg, Klosko, Dodge, & Shadick, 1989). This may indicate that a psychological (cognitive) vulnerability is no more specific for mood disorders than a genetic vulnerability. Both types of vulnerabilities may underlie numerous disorders.

Abramson, Metalsky, and Alloy (1989) revised the learned helplessness theory to deemphasize specific attributions and highlight the development of a sense of hopelessness as a crucial cause of many forms of depression. Attributions are important only to the extent that they contribute to a sense of hopelessness. This fits well with recent thinking on crucial differences between anxiety and depression. Both anxious and depressed individuals feel helpless and believe they lack control, but only in depression do they give up and become hopeless about ever regaining control (Alloy & Abramson, 2007; Barlow, 1991, 2002; Chorpita & Barlow, 1998).

Some evidence indicates that a pessimistic style of attributing negative events to one's own character flaws results in hopelessness (Abramson, Alloy, & Metalsky, 1995; Gotlib & Abramson, 1999). This style may predate and therefore, in a sense, contribute to anxious or depressive episodes that follow negative or stressful events (Gotlib & Abramson, 1999).

Negative Cognitive Styles

In 1967, Aaron T. Beck (1967, 1976) suggested that depression may result from a tendency to interpret everyday events in a negative way, wearing gray- instead of rose-colored glasses. According to Beck, people with depression make the worst of everything; for them, the smallest setbacks are major catastrophes. In his extensive clinical work, Beck observed that all of his depressed patients thought this way, and he began classifying the types of "cognitive errors" that characterized this style. From the long list he compiled, two representative examples are *arbitrary inference* and *overgeneralization*. Arbitrary inference is evident when a depressed individual emphasizes the negative rather than the positive aspects of a situation. A high school teacher may assume he is a terrible instructor because two students in his class fell asleep. He fails to consider other reasons they might be sleeping (up all night partying) and "infers" that his teaching style is at fault. As an example of overgeneralization, when your professor makes one critical remark on your paper, you then assume you will fail the class despite a long string of positive comments and good grades on other papers. You are overgeneralizing from one small remark. According to Beck, people who are depressed think like this all the time. They make cognitive errors in thinking negatively about themselves, their immediate world, and their future, three areas that together are called the **depressive cognitive triad** (see ■ Figure 7.6).

In addition, Beck theorized, after a series of negative events in childhood, individuals may develop a deep-seated *negative schema,* an enduring negative cognitive belief system about some aspect of life (Beck, Epstein, & Harrison, 1983; Gotlib, Kurtzman,

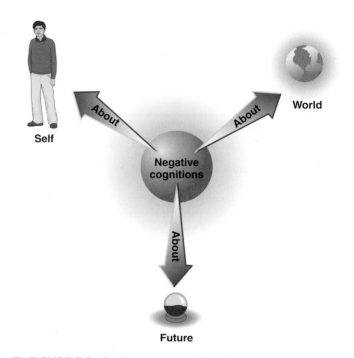

■ **FIGURE 7.6** Beck's cognitive triad for depression.

& Blehar, 1997; Gotlib & Krasnoperova, 1998; Gotlib & MacLeod, 1997; Young, Rygh, Weinberger, & Beck in press). In a self-blame schema, individuals feel personally responsible for every bad thing that happens. With a negative self-evaluation schema, they believe they can never do anything correctly. In Beck's view, these cognitive errors and schemas are automatic, that is, not necessarily conscious. Indeed, an individual might not even be aware of thinking negatively and illogically. Thus, minor negative events can lead to a major depressive episode.

A variety of evidence supports a cognitive theory of emotional disorders in general and depression in particular (Goodman & Gotlib, 1999; Mazure, Bruce, Maciejewski, & Jacobs, 2000; Reilly-Harrington et al., 1999; Segal et al., 2006). The thinking of depressed individuals is consistently more negative than that of nondepressed individuals (Gotlib & Abramson, 1999; Hollon, Kendall, & Lumry, 1986) in each dimension of the cognitive triad—the self, the world, and the future (see, for example, Bradley & Mathews, 1988; Garber & Carter, 2005; Segal, Hood, Shaw, & Higgins, 1988). Depressive cognitions seem to emerge from distorted and probably automatic methods of processing information. People are more likely to recall negative events when they are depressed than when they are not depressed or than are nondepressed individuals (Gotlib, Roberts, & Gilboa, 1996; Lewinsohn & Rosenbaum, 1987).

The implications of this theory are important. By recognizing cognitive errors and the underlying schemas, we can correct them and alleviate depression and related emotional disorders. In developing ways to do this, Beck became the father of cognitive therapy, one of the most important developments in psychotherapy in the last 50 years (see p. 243).

Cognitive Vulnerability for Depression: An Integration

Seligman and Beck developed their theories independently, and good evidence indicates their models are independent in that some people may have a negative outlook (dysfunctional attitudes) whereas others may explain things negatively (hopeless attributes) (Joiner & Rudd, 1996; Spangler, Simons, Monroe, & Thase, 1997). Nevertheless, the basic premises overlap a great deal and considerable evidence suggests depression is always associated with pessimistic explanatory style and negative cognitions. Evidence also exists that cognitive vulnerabilities predispose some people to view events in a negative way, putting them at risk for depression (see, for example, Mazure, Bruce, Maciejewski, & Jacobs, 2000; Reilly-Harrington et al., 1999; Segal et al., 2006).

Good evidence supporting this conclusion comes from the Temple-Wisconsin study of cognitive vulnerability to depression conducted by Lauren Alloy and Lyn Abramson (Alloy & Abramson, 2006; Alloy, Abramson, Safford, & Gibb, 2006). University freshmen who were not depressed at the time of the initial assessment were assessed every several months for up to 5 years to determine whether they experienced any stressful life events or diagnosable episodes of depression or other psychopathology. At the first assessment, the investigators determined whether the students were cognitively vulnerable to developing depression or not on the basis of their scores on questionnaires that measure dysfunctional attitudes and hopelessness attributions. Results indicated students at high risk because of dysfunctional attitudes reported higher rates of depression in the past compared to the low-risk group. But the really important results come from the prospective portion of the study. Negative cognitive styles do indicate a vulnerability to later depression. Even if participants had never suffered from depression before in their lives, high-risk participants (who scored high on the measures of cognitive vulnerability) were 6–12 times more likely than low-risk participants to experience a major depressive episode. In addition, 16% of the high-risk subjects versus only 2.7% of the low-risk subjects experienced major depressive episodes, and 46% versus 14% experienced minor depressive symptoms (Alloy & Abramson, 2006). The data are suggestive that cognitive vulnerabilities to developing depression do exist and, when combined with biological vulnerabilities, create a slippery path to depression.

Social and Cultural Dimensions

A number of social and cultural factors contribute to the onset or maintenance of depression. Among these, marital relationships, gender, and social support are most prominent.

■ Marital Relations

Marital dissatisfaction and depression are strongly related, as suggested earlier when it was noted that disruptions in relationships often lead to depression. Findings from a number of studies also indicate that marital disruption often precedes depression. Bruce and Kim (1992) collected data on 695 women and 530 men and then reinterviewed them up to 1 year later. During this period, a number of participants separated from or divorced their spouses, although the majority reported stable marriages. Approximately 21% of the women who reported a marital split during the study experienced severe depression, a rate three times higher than that for women who remained married. Nearly 17% of the men who reported a marital split developed severe depression, a rate *nine* times higher than that for men who remained married. However,

when the researchers considered only those participants with no history of severe depression, 14% of the men who separated or divorced during the period experienced severe depression, as did approximately 5% of the women. In other words, *only the men* faced a heightened risk of developing a mood disorder for the first time immediately following a marital split. Is remaining married more important to men than to women? It would seem so.

Monroe, Bromet, Connell, and Steiner (1986), as well as O'Hara (1986), also implicated factors in the marital relationship as predicting the later onset of depression. Important findings from the Monroe group's 1986 study emphasize the necessity of separating marital conflict from marital support. In other words, it is possible that high marital conflict and strong marital social support may both be present at the same time or may both be absent. High conflict, low support, or both are particularly important in generating depression (Barnett & Gotlib, 1988; Gotlib & Beach, 1995).

Another finding with considerable support is that depression, particularly if it continues, may lead to substantial deterioration in marital relationships (Beach, Sandeen, & O'Leary, 1990; Coyne, 1976; Gotlib & Beach, 1995; Paykel & Weissman, 1973; Uebelacker & Whisman, 2006; Whiffen & Gotlib, 1989). It is not hard to figure out why. Being around someone who is continually negative, ill tempered, and pessimistic becomes tiring after a while. Because emotions are contagious, the spouse probably begins to feel bad also. These kinds of interactions precipitate arguments or, worse, make the nondepressed spouse want to leave (Biglan et al., 1985; Whisman, Weinstock, & Tolejko, 2006).

But conflict within a marriage seems to have different effects on men and women. Depression seems to cause men to withdraw or otherwise disrupt the relationship. For women, on the other hand, problems in the relationship most often cause depression. Thus, for both men and women, depression and problems in marital relations are associated, but the causal direction is different (Fincham, Beach, Harold, & Osborne, 1997), a result also found by Spangler, Simons, Monroe, and Thase (1996). Given these factors, Beach and colleagues (1990) suggest that therapists treat disturbed marital relationships at the same time as the mood disorder to ensure the highest level of success for the patient and the best chance of preventing future relapses.

■ Mood Disorders in Women

Data on the prevalence of mood disorders indicate dramatic gender imbalances. Although bipolar disorder is evenly divided between men and women, almost 70% of the individuals with major depressive disorder and dysthymia are women (Bland, 1997; Hankin & Abramson, 2001; Kessler, 2006; Weissman et al., 1991). What is particularly striking is that this gender imbalance is constant around the world, even though overall rates of disorder may vary from country to country (Kessler, 2006; Weissman & Olfson, 1995; see ■ Figure 7.7). Often overlooked is the similar ratio for most anxiety disorders, particularly panic disorder and generalized anxiety disorder. Women represent an even greater proportion of specific phobias, as we noted in Chapter 2. What could account for this?

It may be that gender differences in the development of emotional disorders are strongly influenced by perceptions of

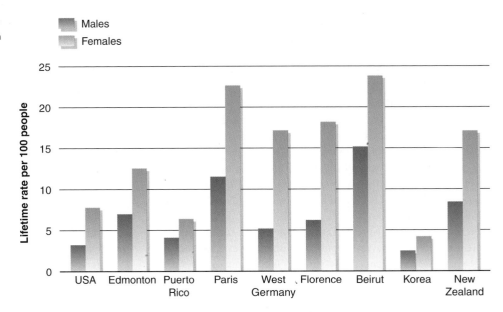

■ **FIGURE 7.7** Lifetime international rate per 100 people for major depression. (Reprinted, with permission, from Weissman, M. M., & Olfson, M., 1995. Depression in women: Implications for health care research. *Science, 269,* 799-801, © 1995 American Association for the Advancement of Science.)

uncontrollability (Barlow, 1988, 2002). If you feel a sense of mastery over your life and the difficult events we all encounter, you might experience occasional stress but you will not feel the helplessness central to anxiety and mood disorders. The source of these differences is cultural, in the sex roles assigned to men and women in our society. Males are strongly encouraged to be independent, masterful, and assertive; females, by contrast, are expected to be more passive, sensitive to other people, and, perhaps, to rely on others more than males do (needs for affiliation) (Cyranowski, Frank, Young, & Shear, 2000; Hankin & Abramson, 2001). Although these stereotypes are slowly changing, they still describe current sex roles to a large extent. But this culturally induced dependence and passivity may well put women at severe risk for emotional disorders by increasing their feelings of uncontrollability and helplessness. Evidence has accumulated that parenting styles encouraging stereotypic gender roles are implicated in the development of early psychological vulnerability to later depression or anxiety (Chorpita & Barlow, 1998), specifically, a smothering, overprotective style that prevents the child from developing initiative. Also interesting is the "sudden surge" in depression among girls mentioned earlier that occurs during puberty. Many thought this might be biologically based, but Kessler (2006) notes that low self-esteem emerges quickly in girls in seventh grade if the school system has a seventh- through ninth-grade middle school but not until ninth grade when the school has a kindergarten through eighth-grade primary school and a 4-year high school (Simmons & Blyth, 1987). These results suggest that the younger girls just entering a new school, whether it is seventh, ninth, or some other grade, find it stressful. Also girls who mature physically early have more distress and depression than girls who don't (Ge, Conger, & Elder, 1996).

Constance Hammen and her colleagues (Hammen, Marks, Mayol, & de Mayo, 1985) think that the value women place on intimate relationships may also put them at risk. Disruptions in such relationships, combined with an inability to cope with the disruptions, may be far more damaging to women than to men. Data from Fincham and colleagues (1997) and Spangler and colleagues (1996), described earlier, seem to support this view.

Cyranowski and associates (2000) note that the tendency for adolescent girls to express aggression by rejecting other girls, combined with a greater sensitivity to rejection, may precipitate more depressive episodes in these adolescent girls compared to boys. Kendler, Myers, and Prescott (2005) also observed that women tend to have larger and more intimate social networks than men and that emotionally supportive groups of friends protect against depression. However, data from Bruce and Kim (1992), reviewed earlier, suggest that if the disruption in a marital relationship reaches the stage of divorce, men who had previously been functioning well are at greater risk for depression.

Another potentially important gender difference has been suggested by Susan Nolen-Hoeksema (1987, 1990, 2000b; Nolen-Hoeksema, Larson, & Grayson, 1999). Women tend to ruminate more than men about their situation and blame themselves for being depressed. Men tend to ignore their feelings, perhaps engaging in activity to take their minds off them. This male behavior may be therapeutic because "activating" people (getting them busy doing something) is a common element of successful therapy for depression (Jacobson, Martell, & Dimidjian, 2001; Lewinsohn & Gotlib, 1995).

As Strickland (1992) pointed out, women are at a disadvantage in our society: They experience more discrimination, poverty, sexual harassment, and abuse than do men. They also earn less respect and accumulate less power. Three quarters of the people living in poverty in the United States are women and children. Women, particularly single mothers, have a difficult time entering the workplace. Interestingly, married women employed full time outside the home report levels of depression no greater than those of employed married men. Single, divorced, and widowed women experience significantly more depression than men in the same categories (Weissman & Klerman, 1977). This does not necessarily mean that anyone should get a job to avoid becoming depressed. Indeed, for a man or woman, feeling mastery, control, and value in the strongly socially supported role of homemaker and parent should be associated with low rates of depression.

Finally, other disorders may reflect gender role stereotypes, but in the opposite direction. Disorders associated with aggres-

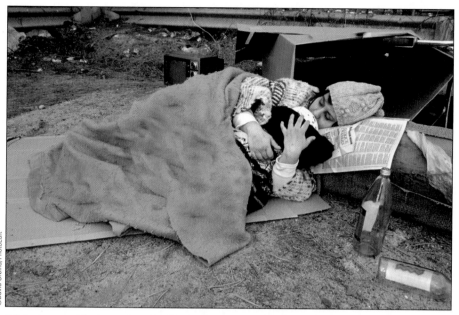

Of the impoverished people in the United States, three quarters are women and children.

siveness, overactivity, and substance abuse occur far more often in men than in women (Barlow, 1988, 2002). Identifying the reasons for gender imbalances across the full range of psychopathological disorders may prove important in discovering causes of disorders.

■ Social Support

In Chapter 2, we examined the powerful effect of social influences on our psychological and biological functioning. We cited several examples of how social influences seem to contribute to early death, such as the evil eye or lack of social support in old age. In general, the greater the number and frequency of your social relationships and contacts, the longer you are likely to live (see, for instance, House, Landis, & Umberson, 1988). It is not surprising, then, that social factors influence whether we become depressed.

In an early landmark study, G. W. Brown and Harris (1978) first suggested the important role of social support in the onset of depression. In a study of a large number of women who had experienced a serious life stress, they discovered that only 10% of the women who had a friend in whom they could confide became depressed, compared to 37% of the women who did not have a close supportive relationship. Later prospective studies have also confirmed the importance of social support (or lack of it) in predicting the onset of depressive symptoms at a later time (see, for instance, Cutrona, 1984; Joiner, 1997; Kendler, Kuhn et al., 2005; Lin & Ensel, 1984; Monroe, Imhoff, Wise, & Harris, 1983; Phifer & Murrell, 1986). The importance of social support in preventing depression holds true in China (Wang, Wang, & Shen, 2006) and every other country in which it has been studied. Other studies have established the importance of social support in speeding recovery from depressive episodes (Keitner et al., 1995; McLeod, Kessler, & Landis, 1992; Sherbourne, Hays, & Wells, 1995). Johnson, Winett, Meyer, Greenhouse, and Miller (1999) examined the effects of social support in speeding recovery from both manic and depressive episodes in patients with bipolar disorder, and they came

up with a surprising finding. A socially supportive network of friends and family helped speed recovery from depressive episodes but not from manic episodes. This finding highlights the uniquely different quality of manic episodes (McGuffin et al., 2003). In any case, these and related findings on the importance of social support have led to an exciting new psychological therapeutic approach for emotional disorders called interpersonal psychotherapy, which we discuss later in this chapter.

Let's return again to Katie. In reflecting on her turbulent times and the days when death seemed more rewarding than life, one thing sticks out clearly in her mind:

> My parents are the true heroes of these early years. I will always admire their strength, their love, and their commitment. My father is a high school graduate and my mother has an eighth-grade education. They dealt with complicated legal, medical, and psychological issues. They had little support from friends or professionals, yet they continued to do what they believed best. In my eyes there is no greater demonstration of courage and love.

Katie's parents did not have the social support that might have helped them through these difficult years, but they gave it to Katie. We return to her case later.

An Integrative Theory

How do we put all this together? Basically, depression and anxiety may often share a common, genetically determined biological vulnerability (Barlow, 2002; Barlow, Chorpita, & Turovsky, 1996) that can be described as an overactive neurobiological response to stressful life events. Again, this vulnerability is simply a general tendency to develop depression (or anxiety) rather than a specific vulnerability for depression or anxiety itself. But only between 20% and 40% of the causes of depression can be attributed to genes. For the remainder, we look at life experience.

People who develop mood disorders also possess a psychological vulnerability experienced as feelings of inadequacy for coping with the difficulties confronting them. As with anxiety, we may develop this sense of control in childhood (Barlow, 2002; Chorpita & Barlow, 1998). It may range on a continuum from total confidence to a complete inability to cope. When vulnerabilities are triggered, the "giving up" process seems crucial to the development of depression (Alloy, Kelly, Mineka, & Clements, 1990; Alloy et al., 2000; Alloy & Abramson, 2007).

A variety of evidence indicates that these attitudes and attributions correlate rather strongly with such biochemical markers of stress and depression as by-products of norepinephrine (see, for example, Nemeroff, 2004; Samson, Mirin, Hauser, Fenton, & Schildkraut, 1992) and with different levels of arousal in different hemispheres in the brain (hemispheric lateral asymmetry) (Davidson, 1993; Heller & Nitschke, 1997). It also shows that these vulnerabilities are associated with specific brain circuits

(Elliott, Rubinsztein, Sahakian, & Dolan, 2002; Liotti, Mayberg, McGinnis, Brannan, & Jerabek, 2002). The causes of this psychological vulnerability can be traced to early adverse experience in the form of childhood adversity, exposure to caregivers with psychopathology, or both—perhaps years before the onset of mood disorders. For example, a number of recent studies indicate that children of depressed parents are strongly at risk to develop depression and other disorders themselves (Rohde, Lewinsohn, Klein, & Seeley, 2005; Stoolmiller, Kim, & Capaldi, 2005; Weissman et al., 2006). Jaffee and colleagues (2002) demonstrated that more severe childhood anxiety was associated with an earlier onset of depression. This enduring psychological vulnerability intensifies the biochemical and cognitive response to stress later in life (Goodman & Gotlib, 1999; Nolen-Hoeksema, 2000a; Nolen-Hoeksema et al., 1992).

There is also good evidence that stressful life events trigger the onset of depression in most cases, particularly initial episodes. How do these factors interact? The best current thinking is that stressful life events activate stress hormones, which, in turn, have wide-ranging effects on neurotransmitter systems, particularly those involving serotonin, norepinephrine, and the corticotropin-releasing factor system. Evidence also indicates that activation of stress hormones over the long term may turn on certain genes, producing long-term structural and chemical changes in the brain (Kendler, Kuhn, et al., 2005). For example, processes triggered by long-term stress seem to lead to atrophy of neurons in the hippocampus that help regulate emotions, or, more important, an inability to generate new neurons (neurogenesis). Such structural change might permanently affect the regulation of neurotransmitter activity. The extended effects of stress may also disrupt the circadian rhythms in certain individuals, who then become susceptible to the recurrent episodic cycling that seems so uniquely characteristic of the mood disorders (Moore, 1999; Post, 1992). As noted earlier, triggering stressful life events also activates a dormant psychological vulnerability characterized by negative thinking and a sense of helplessness and hopelessness. What we have so far is a possible mechanism for the diathesis–stress model. Finally, it seems clear that factors such as interpersonal relationships or our gender may protect us from the effects of stress and therefore from developing mood disorders. Alternatively, these factors may at least determine whether we quickly recover from these disorders or not.

In summary, biological, psychological, and social factors all influence the development of mood disorders, as depicted in ■ Figure 7.8. This model does not account for the varied presentation of mood disorders—unipolar, bipolar, and so on—although mania in bipolar disorder may be associated with unique genetic contributions. But why would someone with an underlying genetic vulnerability who experiences a stressful life event develop a bipolar disorder rather than a unipolar disorder or, for that matter, an anxiety disorder? As with the anxiety disorders and other stress disorders, specific psychosocial circumstances, such as early learning experiences, may interact with specific genetic vulnerabilities and personality characteristics to produce the rich variety of emotional disorders. Only time will tell.

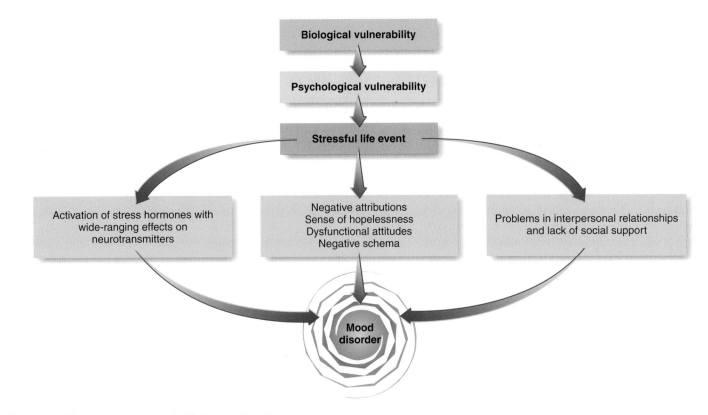

■ **FIGURE 7.8** An integrative model of mood disorders.

TREATMENT OF MOOD DISORDERS

We have learned a great deal about the neurobiology of mood disorders during the past several years. Findings on the complex interplay of neurochemicals are beginning to shed light on the nature of mood disorders. As we have noted, the principal effect of medications is to alter levels of these neurotransmitters and other related neurochemicals. Other biological treatments, such as electroconvulsive therapy, dramatically affect brain chemistry. A more interesting development, however, alluded to throughout this book, is that powerful psychological treatments also alter brain chemistry. Despite these advances, most cases of depression go untreated because neither health care professionals nor patients recognize and correctly identify or diagnose depression. Similarly, many professionals and patients are unaware of the existence of effective and successful treatments (Delano-Wood & Abeles, 2005; Hirschfeld et al., 1997). Therefore, it is important to learn about treatments for depression.

Medications

A number of medications are effective treatments for depression. New information often becomes available on new medications or the latest estimates of effectiveness of older medications.

■ Antidepressants

Three basic types of antidepressant medications are used to treat depressive disorders: tricyclic antidepressants, monoamine oxidase (MAO) inhibitors, and serotonin-specific reuptake inhibitors (SSRIs).

Tricyclic antidepressants were the most widely used treatments for depression before the introduction of SSRIs and are still in frequent use, particularly for severe depression. The best-known variants are probably imipramine (Tofranil) and amitriptyline (Elavil). It is not yet clear how these drugs work, but initially, at least, they block the reuptake of certain neurotransmitters, allowing them to pool in the synapse and, as the theory goes, desensitize or down-regulate the transmission of that particular neurotransmitter (so less of the neurochemical is transmitted). Tricyclic antidepressants seem to have their greatest effect by down-regulating norepinephrine, although other neurotransmitter systems, particularly serotonin, are also affected. This process then has a complex effect on both presynaptic and postsynaptic regulation of neurotransmitter activity, eventually restoring appropriate balance. Ultimately, as noted earlier, these drugs and other antidepressants may promote new nerve growth (neurogenesis) in the hippocampus (Santarelli et al., 2003). This process takes a while to work, often between 2 and 8 weeks. During this time, many patients feel a bit worse and develop a number of side effects, such as blurred vision, dry mouth, constipation, difficulty urinating, drowsiness, weight gain (at least 13 pounds on average), and, perhaps, sexual dysfunction. Therefore, as many as 40% of these patients may stop taking the drug, thinking the cure is worse than the disease. Nevertheless, with careful management, many side effects disappear. Tricyclics alleviate depression (but do not eliminate it) in approximately 50% of patients compared to approximately 25% to 30% of patients taking placebo pills, based on a summary analysis of more than 100 studies (American Psychiatric Association, 2000; Depression Guideline Panel, 1993; see Table 7.7). If dropouts are excluded and only those who complete treatment are counted, the percentage of patients receiving at least some benefit increases to between 65% and 70%. Another issue clinicians must consider is that tricyclics are *lethal* if taken in excessive doses; therefore, they must be prescribed with great caution to patients with suicidal tendencies.

MAO inhibitors work differently. As their name suggests, they block the enzyme MAO that breaks down such neurotransmitters

TABLE 7.7 Efficacy of Various Antidepressant Drugs for Major Depressive Disorder

Drug	Drug Efficacy		Drug–Placebo	
	Inpatient	Outpatient	Inpatient	Outpatient
Tricyclics	50.0%	51.5%	25.1%	21.3%
SD	(6.5)	(5.2)	(11.5)	(3.9)
N	[33]	[102]	[8]	[46]
Monoamine oxidase inhibitors	52.7%	57.4%	18.4%	30.9%
SD	(9.7)	(5.5)	(22.6)	(17.1)
N	[14]	[21]	[9]	[13]
Selective serotonin reuptake inhibitors	54.0%	47.4%	25.5%	20.1%
SD	(10.1)	(12.5)	(21.7)	(7.8)
N	[8]	[39]	[2]	[23]

Note: The percentage shown in the Drug Efficacy column is the anticipated percentage of patients provided the treatment shown who will respond. The Drug–Placebo column shows the expected percentage difference in patients given a drug versus a placebo based on direct drug–placebo comparisons in trials that included at least these two cells. The numbers in parentheses give the standard deviation (SD) of the estimated percentage of responders. The bracketed numbers give the number (N) of studies for which these estimates are calculated.

Source: Adapted from Depression Guideline Panel. (1993, April). *Depression in primary care: Vol. 1. Detection and diagnosis* (AHCPR Publication No. 93–0550). Clinical practice guideline, No. 5. Rockville, MD: U.S. Department of Health and Human Services, Public Health Service, Agency for Health Care Policy and Research.

as norepinephrine and serotonin. The result is roughly equivalent to the effect of the tricyclics. Because they are not broken down, the neurotransmitters pool in the synapse, leading to a down-regulation. The MAO inhibitors seem to be as effective as or slightly more effective than the tricyclics (American Psychiatric Association, 2000; Depression Guideline Panel, 1993), with some-what fewer side effects. Some evidence suggests they are relatively more effective for depression with atypical features (Thase & Kupfer, 1996). But MAO inhibitors are used far less often because of two potentially serious consequences: Eating and drinking foods and beverages containing tyramine, such as cheese, red wine, or beer, can lead to severe hypertensive episodes and, occasionally, death. In addition, many other drugs that people take daily, such as cold medications, are dangerous and even fatal in interaction with an MAO inhibitor. Therefore, MAO inhibitors are usually prescribed only when tricyclics are not effective.

Pharmaceutical companies have developed a new generation of more selective MAO inhibitors that are short acting and do not interact negatively with tyramine (Baldessarini, 1989; Nemeroff, 2006), but they are not available in the United States, although they are in other countries. In any case, use of these drugs has decreased considerably in recent years.

The class of drugs currently considered the first choice in drug treatment for depression seems to have a specific effect on the serotonin neurotransmitter system (although such drugs affect other systems to some extent). These *serotonin-specific reuptake inhibitors (SSRIs)* specifically block the presynaptic reuptake of sero-tonin. This temporarily increases levels of serotonin at the recep-tor site, but again the precise long-term mechanism of action is unknown, although levels of serotonin are eventually increased. Perhaps the best-known drug in this class is *fluoxetine* (Prozac). Like many other medications, Prozac was initially hailed as a breakthrough drug; it even made the cover of *Newsweek* (March 26, 1990). Then reports began to appear that it might lead to sui-cidal preoccupation, paranoid reactions, and, occasionally, violence (see, for example, Mandalos & Szarek, 1990; Teicher, Glod, & Cole, 1990). Prozac went from being a wonder drug in the eyes of the press to a potential menace to modern society. Neither conclusion was true. Findings indicated that the risks of suicide with this drug for the general population were no greater than with any other antidepressant (Fava & Rosenbaum, 1991), and the effectiveness is about the same as that of other antidepressants, including the tri-cycles.

Recently, concerns about suicidal risks (increased thoughts, and so on) have surfaced again, particularly among adolescents, and this time it looks like the concerns are justified, at least for adolescents (Baldessarini, Pompili, & Tondo, 2006; Fergusson, Doucette, et al., 2005; Hammad, Laughren, & Racoosin, 2006; Olfson, Marcus, & Schaffer, 2006). This had led to warnings from the Food and Drug Administration (FDA) and other regulatory agencies around the world about these drugs. On the other hand, Gibbons, Hur, Bhaumik, and Mann (2006) found that actual sui-cide rates were lower in sections of the United States where pre-scriptions for SSRIs were higher. In addition, the SSRIs were also associated with a small but statistically significant *decrease* in sui-cide among adolescents compared to depressed adolescents not taking these drugs, based on a large community survey (Olfson,

Shaffer, Marcus & Greenberg, 2003). These findings are *correla-tional,* meaning we can't conclude that increased prescriptions for SSRIs caused lower suicide rates. Research will continue on this important question. One possible conclusion is that SSRIs cause increased thoughts about suicide in the first few weeks in some adolescents but, once they start working after a month or more, may prevent the depression from leading to suicide (Simon, 2006). Prozac and other SSRIs have their own set of side effects, the most prominent of which are physical agitation, sexual dysfunc-tion, low sexual desire (which is prevalent, occurring in 50% to 75% of cases), insomnia, and gastrointestinal upset. But these side effects, on the whole, seem to bother most patients less than the side effects associated with tricyclic antidepressants, with the pos-sible exception of the sexual dysfunction. Studies suggest similar effectiveness of SSRIs and tricyclics with dysthymia (Lapierre, 1994).

Two newer antidepressants seem to have somewhat different mechanisms of neurobiological action. Venlafaxine is related to tricyclic antidepressants but acts in a slightly different manner, reducing some associated side effects, as well as the risk of damage to the cardiovascular system. Other typical side effects remain, including nausea and sexual dysfunction. Nefazodone is closely related to the SSRIs but seems to improve sleep efficiency instead of disrupting sleep. Both drugs are roughly comparable in effec-tiveness to older antidepressants (American Psychiatric Associa-tion, 2000; Nemeroff, 2006; Preskorn, 1995; Thase & Kupfer, 1996).

Finally, there was a great deal of interest several years ago in the antidepressant properties of the natural herb St. John's wort (hypericum). St. John's wort is popular in Europe, and a number of preliminary studies demonstrated it was better than placebo and worked about as well as low doses of other antidepressants (Amer-ican Psychiatric Association, 2000). St. John's wort produces few side effects and is relatively easy to produce. But it is now available only in health food stores and similar outlets, and there is no guar-antee that any given brand of St. John's wort contains the appropri-ate ingredients. Some preliminary evidence suggests the herb also somehow alters serotonin function. But the National Institutes of Health in the United States completed a major study examining its effectiveness (Hypericum Depression Trial Study Group, 2002), and surprisingly, this large study found no benefits from St. John's wort compared to placebo. Results from other studies in progress will be examined closely to confirm this finding.

Because the SSRI and other drugs relieve symptoms of de-pression to some extent in about 50% of all patients treated but eliminate depression or come close to it in only 25% to 30% of all patients treated (termed *remission*) (Trivedi et al., 2006), the question remains: What do clinicians do with those who need more treatment? A large study called the Sequenced Treatment Alternatives to Relieve Depression (STAR★D) examined whether offering those individuals who did not achieve remission the al-ternatives of either adding a second drug or switching to a second drug is useful. Among those who were willing, approximately 20% (for switching) to approximately 30% (for adding a second drug) achieved remission. When repeating this with a third drug among those who had failed to achieve remission with the first two drugs, the results weren't as good (between 10% and 20% achieved

Of the synthetic drugs for depression, fluoxetine (Prozac, left), is the most widely used; the common groundcover hypericum (St. John's wort, right) is being tested as an effective natural treatment.

remission) (Insel, 2006; Menza, 2006; Rush, 2007). The conclusion is that its worth being persistent, as long as individuals with depression are still willing to try new drugs, because some people who don't improve with the first drug could improve with a different drug. Later, we report on combining psychological treatments with drugs.

Current studies indicate that drug treatments effective with adults are not necessarily effective with children (American Psychiatric Association, 2000; Boulos et al., 1991; Geller et al., 1992; Ryan, 1992). Sudden deaths of children under 14 who were taking tricyclic antidepressants have been reported, particularly during exercise, as in routine school athletic competition (Tingelstad, 1991). The causes imply cardiac side effects. Traditional antidepressant drug treatments are usually effective with the elderly, but administering them takes considerable skill because older people may suffer from a variety of side effects not experienced by younger adults, including memory impairment and physical agitation (see, for example, Delano-Wood & Abeles, 2005; Deptula & Pomara, 1990; Marcopulos & Graves, 1990). Several studies evaluated a novel method for delivering better care to depressed elderly patients right in the office of their primary medical care doctor. Use of a depression care manager in these settings to encourage compliance with drug taking, monitor side effects unique to the elderly, and deliver a bit of psychotherapy was more effective than usual care (Alexopoulos et al., 2005; Unutzer et al., 2002).

Clinicians and researchers have concluded that recovery from depression, although important, may not be the most important therapeutic outcome (Frank et al., 1990; Prien & Kupfer, 1986). Most people eventually recover from a major depressive episode, some rather quickly. A more important goal is often to delay the next depressive episode or even prevent it entirely (National Institute of Mental Health, 2003; Prien & Potter, 1993; Thase, 1990; Thase & Kupfer, 1996). This is particularly important for patients who retain some symptoms of depression or have a past history of chronic depression or multiple depressive episodes. Because all these factors put people at risk for relapse, it is recommended that drug treatment go well beyond the termination of a depressive episode, continuing perhaps 6 to 12 months after the episode is over, or even longer (American Psychiatric Association, 2000; Insel, 2006). The drug is then gradually withdrawn over weeks or

months. (We return later to strategies for maintaining therapeutic benefits.) Long-term administration of antidepressants has not been studied extensively, and there is even some evidence that long-term treatment may worsen the course of depression (Fava, 2003).

Antidepressant medications have relieved severe depression and undoubtedly prevented suicide in tens of thousands of patients around the world. Although these medications are readily available, many people refuse or are not eligible to take them. Some are wary of long-term side effects. Women of childbearing age must protect themselves against the possibility of conceiving while taking antidepressants, because they can damage the fetus. In addition, approximately 30% of patients do not respond adequately to these drugs, and a substantial number of the remainder are left with residual symptoms.

■ Lithium

A fourth type of equally effective antidepressant drug, *lithium carbonate,* is a common salt widely available in the natural environment (Nemeroff, 2006). It is found in our drinking water in amounts too small to have any effect. However, the side effects of therapeutic doses of lithium are potentially more serious than those of other antidepressants. Dosage has to be carefully regulated to prevent toxicity (poisoning) and lowered thyroid functioning, which might intensify the lack of energy associated with depression. Substantial weight gain is also common. Lithium, however, has one major advantage that distinguishes it from other antidepressants: It is often effective in preventing and treating manic episodes. Therefore, it is most often referred to as a mood-stabilizing drug. Because antidepressants can induce manic episodes, even in individuals without preexisting bipolar disorder (Goodwin & Ghaemi, 1998; Goodwin & Jamison, 2007; Prien et al., 1984), lithium is the treatment of choice for bipolar disorder.

We are not sure how lithium works. It may limit the availability of dopamine and norepinephrine and may also have important effects on some neurohormones in the endocrine system, particularly those that influence the production and availability of sodium and potassium, electrolytes found in body fluids. But current thinking is that very basic biological activity in cells called signaling networks that actually influence neurotransmitters and neurohormones may be the most important target of lithium (Goodwin & Jamison, 2007). Results indicate that 50% of bipolar patients respond well to lithium initially, meaning at least a 50% reduction in manic symptoms.(Goodwin & Jamison, 2007). Thus, although effective, lithium provides many people with inadequate therapeutic benefit. Patients who don't respond can take other drugs with antimanic properties, including anticonvulsants such as carbamazepine and valproate (Divalproex), as well as calcium channel blockers such as verapamil (Keck & McElroy, 2002; Sachs & Rush, 2003; Thase & Kupfer, 1996). Valproate has recently overtaken lithium as the most commonly prescribed mood stabilizer (Goodwin et al., 2003; Keck & McElroy, 2002) and is equally effective, even for patients with a rapid-cycling feature (Calabrese et

Kay Redfield Jamison, an internationally respected authority on bipolar disorder, has suffered from the disease since adolescence.

al., 2005). But newer studies show that these drugs have one distinct disadvantage: They are less effective than lithium in preventing suicide (Thies-Flechtner, Muller-Oerlinghausen, Seibert, Walther, & Greil, 1996; Tondo, Jamison, & Baldessarini, 1997). Goodwin and colleagues (2003) reviewed records of more than 20,000 patients taking either lithium or valproate and found the rate of completed suicides was 2.7 times higher on valproate than on lithium. Thus, lithium remains the preferred drug for bipolar disorder (Goodwin & Ghaemi, 1998; Goodwin & Jamison, 2007).

For those patients who do respond to lithium, some studies suggest that maintaining adequate doses can prevent recurrence of manic episodes in approximately 66% of individuals (with 34% relapsing), based on 10 major double-blind studies comparing lithium to placebo. Relapse rates in the placebo group averaged a high 81% over several months to several years (Suppes, Baldessarini, Faedda, & Tohen, 1991). But newer studies following patients for up to 5 years report that approximately 70% relapse, even if they continue to take the lithium (Frank et al., 1999; Gitlin, Swendsen, Heller, & Hammen, 1995; Peselow, Fieve, Difiglia, & Sanfilipo, 1994). Nevertheless, for almost anyone with recurrent manic episodes, maintenance on lithium or a related drug is recommended to prevent relapse (Yatham et al., 2006). Another problem with drug treatment of bipolar disorder is that people usually like the euphoric or high feeling that mania produces and they often stop taking lithium to maintain or regain the state; that is, they do not comply with the medication regimen. Because the evidence now clearly indicates that individuals who stop their medication are at considerable risk for relapse, other methods, usually psychological in nature, are used to increase compliance.

Electroconvulsive Therapy and Transcranial Magnetic Stimulation

When someone does not respond to medication (or in an extremely severe case), clinicians may consider a more dramatic treatment, **electroconvulsive therapy (ECT),** the most controversial treatment for psychological disorders after psychosurgery. In Chapter 1, we described how ECT was used in the early 20th century. Despite many unfortunate abuses along the way, ECT is considerably changed today. It is now a safe and reasonably effective treatment for severe depression that has not improved with other treatments (American Psychiatric Association, 2000; Klerman, 1988; Nemeroff, 2006; National Institute of Mental Health, 2003).

In current administrations, patients are anesthetized to reduce discomfort and given muscle-relaxing drugs to prevent bone breakage from convulsions during seizures. Electric shock is administered directly through the brain for less than a second, producing a seizure and a series of brief convulsions that usually lasts for several minutes. In current practice, treatments are administered once every other day for a total of 6 to 10 treatments (fewer if the patient's mood returns to normal). Side effects are surprisingly few and generally limited to short-term memory loss and confusion that disappear after a week or two, although some patients may have long-term memory problems. For severely depressed inpatients with psychotic features, controlled studies (including some in which the control group undergoes a "sham" ECT procedure and doesn't actually receive shocks) indicate that approximately 50% of those *not responding* to medication will benefit. Continued treatment with medication or psychotherapy is then necessary because the relapse rate approaches 60% or higher (American Psychiatric Association, 2000; Depression Guideline Panel, 1993; Fernandez, Levy, Lachar, & Small, 1995; Prudic, Sackheim, & Devanand, 1990). For example, Sackeim and colleagues (2001) treated 84 patients with ECT and then randomly assigned them to follow-up placebo or one of several antidepressant drug treatments. All patients assigned to placebo relapsed within 6 months compared to 40% to 60% on medication. Thus, follow-up treatment with antidepressant drugs is necessary, but relapse is still high. Nevertheless, it may not be in the best interest of psychotically depressed and acutely suicidal inpatients to wait 3 to 6 weeks to determine whether a drug or psychological treatment is working; in these cases, immediate ECT may be appropriate.

We do not really know why ECT works. Repeated seizures induce massive functional and perhaps structural changes in the brain, which seems to be therapeutic. There is some evidence that ECT increases levels of serotonin, blocks stress hormones, and promotes neurogenesis in the hippocampus. Because of the controversial nature of this treatment, its use declined considerably during the 1970s and 1980s (American Psychiatric Association, 1990).

Recently, another method for altering electrical activity in the brain by setting up a strong magnetic field has been introduced. This procedure is called *transcranial magnetic stimulation (TMS),* and it works by placing a magnetic coil over the individual's head to generate a precisely localized electromagnetic pulse. Anesthesia is not required, and side effects are usually limited to headaches. Initial reports, as with most new procedures, showed promise in treating depression (Fitzgerald et al., 2003, 2006; George, Lisanby, & Sackheim, 1999). Now results from several important clinical trials have compared TMS to ECT in patients with severe or psychotic depression that is treatment resistant (has not responded to drugs or psychological treatments). Several studies found equal effectiveness (Grunhaus, Schreiber, Dolberg, Polak, & Dannon, 2003; Janicak et al., 2002), but Eranti and colleagues (2007) reported ECT to be clearly superior. More research is needed before concluding that TMS is a good alternative to ECT.

Several other nondrug approaches for treatment-resistant depression are in development. Vagus nerve stimulation involves implanting a pacemaker-like device that generates pulses to the vagus nerve, which, in turn, is thought to influence neurotransmitter production in the brain stem and limbic system (Marangell et al., 2002). Sufficient evidence has accumulated so that the FDA has approved this procedure. Deep brain stimulation has been used with a few severely depressed patients. In this procedure, electrodes are surgically implanted in the limbic system (the emotional brain). These electrodes are also connected to a pacemaker-like device (Mayberg et al., 2005). Time will tell if this is a useful treatment.

Psychological Treatments

Of the effective psychological treatments now available for depressive disorders, two major approaches have the most evidence supporting their efficacy. The first is a cognitive-behavioral approach; Aaron T. Beck, the founder of cognitive therapy, is most closely associated with this approach. The second approach, interpersonal psychotherapy, was developed by Myrna Weissman and Gerald Klerman.

■ Cognitive-Behavioral Therapy

Beck's **cognitive therapy** grew directly out of his observations of the role of deep-seated negative thinking in generating depression (Beck, 1967, 1976; Beck & Young, 1985; Young et al., in press). Clients are taught to examine carefully their thought processes while they are depressed and to recognize "depressive" errors in thinking. This task is not always easy, because many thoughts are automatic and beyond clients' awareness. Negative thinking seems natural to them. Clients are taught that errors in thinking can directly cause depression. Treatment involves correcting cognitive errors and substituting less depressing and (perhaps) more realistic thoughts and appraisals. Later in therapy, underlying negative cognitive schemas (characteristic ways of viewing the world) that trigger specific cognitive errors are targeted, not only in the office but also as part of the client's day-to-day life. The therapist purposefully takes a Socratic approach, making it clear that therapist and client are working as a team to uncover faulty thinking patterns and the underlying schemas from which they are generated. Therapists must be skillful and highly trained. Following is an example of an actual interaction between Beck and a client named Irene.

BECK AND IRENE: A Dialogue

Because an intake interview had already been completed by another therapist, Beck did not spend time reviewing Irene's symptoms in detail or taking a history. Irene began by describing her "sad states." Beck almost immediately started to elicit her automatic thoughts during these periods.

THERAPIST: What kind of thoughts go through your mind when you've had these sad feelings this past week?

PATIENT: Well . . . I guess I'm thinking what's the point of all this. My life is over. It's just not the same. . . . I have thoughts like, "What am I going to do?. . . Sometimes I feel mad at him, you know my husband. How could he leave me? Isn't that terrible of me? What's wrong with

me? How can I be mad at him? He didn't want to die a horrible death. . . . I should have done more. I should have made him go to the doctor when he first started getting headaches. . . . Oh, what's the use. . . ."

T: It sounds like you are feeling quite bad right now. Is that right?

P: Yes.

T: Keep telling me what's going through your mind right now.

P: I can't change anything. . . . It's over. . . . I don't know. . . . It all seems so bleak and hopeless. . . . What do I have to look forward to . . . sickness and then death. . . .

T: So one of the thoughts is that you can't change things and that it's not going to get any better?

P: Yes.

T: And sometimes you believe that completely?

P: Yeah, I believe it, sometimes.

T: Right now do you believe it?

P: I believe it—yes.

T: Right now you believe that you can't change things and it's not going to get better?

P: Well, there is a glimmer of hope but it's mostly. . . .

T: Is there anything in your life that you kind of look forward to in terms of your own life from here on?

P: Well, what I look forward to—I enjoy seeing my kids but they are so busy right now. My son is a lawyer and my daughter is in medical school. . . . So, they are very busy. . . . They don't have time to spend with me.

By inquiring about Irene's automatic thoughts, the therapist began to understand her perspective—that she would go on forever, mostly alone. This illustrates the hopelessness about the future that is characteristic of most depressed patients. A second advantage to this line of inquiry is that the therapist introduced Irene to the idea of looking at her own thoughts, which is central to cognitive therapy (J. E. Young et al., in press).

Between sessions, clients are instructed to *monitor and log* their thought processes carefully, particularly in situations where they might feel depressed. They also attempt to change their behavior by carrying out specific activities assigned as homework, such as tasks in which clients can test their faulty thinking. For example, a client who has to participate in an upcoming meeting might think, "If I go to that meeting, I'll just make a fool of myself and all my colleagues will think I'm stupid." The therapist might instruct the client to go to the meeting, predict ahead of time the reaction of the colleagues, and then see what really happens. This part of treatment is called *hypothesis testing* because the client makes a hypothesis about what's going to happen (usually a depressing outcome) and then, most often, discovers it is incorrect ("My colleagues congratulated me on my presentation"). The therapist typically schedules other activities to *reactivate* depressed patients who have given up most activities, helping them put some fun back into their lives. Cognitive therapy typically takes from 10 to 20 sessions, scheduled weekly.

Related cognitive-behavioral approaches to depression were developed by Peter Lewinsohn and colleagues (see, for example, Lewinsohn & Clarke, 1984; Lewinsohn & Gotlib, 1995) and Lynn Rehm and colleagues (see, for example, Rehm, Kaslow, & Rabin, 1987). Initially, Lewinsohn focused on behavioral change by reactivating depressed patients and countering their mood by bringing them in contact with various kinds of reinforcing events. For example, they might be assigned the task of going to the kind of social event they used to enjoy with their friends. During the past several years, however, this successful program has included cognitive procedures as well and is now more similar to the program developed by Beck. Similarly, Rehm emphasized behavioral change in developing self-control over moods and daily activities, with an approach that also includes cognitive components.

The late Neil Jacobson and colleagues have shown that increased activities alone can improve self-concept and lift depression (Dimidjian, Martell, Addis, & Herman-Dunn, in press; Jacobson et al., 1996). This more behavioral treatment has been reformulated because initial evaluation suggests it is as effective as or more effective than cognitive approaches (Jacobson et al., 2001). The new focus of this approach is on preventing avoidance of social and environmental cues that produce negative affect or depression and result in avoidance and inactivity. Rather, the individual is helped to face the cues or triggers and work through them and the depression they produce with the therapist by developing better coping skills. Similarly, programmed exercise over the course of weeks or months is surprisingly effective (Doyne et al., 1987; Ossip-Klein et al., 1989). Babyak and colleagues (2000) demonstrated that programmed aerobic exercise three times a week was as effective as treatment with antidepressive medication (Zoloft) or the combination of exercise and Zoloft after 4 months. More important, exercise was *better* at preventing relapse in the 6 months following treatment compared to the drug or combination treatment, particularly if the patients continued exercising. This general approach of focusing on activities is consistent with what we are learning about the most powerful methods to change dysregulated emotions (Barlow, Allen, & Choate, 2004; Campbell-Sills & Barlow, 2007), and we are likely to see more research on this approach in the near future.

Myrna Weissman and her husband, the late Gerald Klerman, developed IPT, which is effective with mood disorders and related conditions.

■ Interpersonal Psychotherapy

We have seen that major disruptions in our interpersonal relationships are an important category of stresses that can trigger mood disorders (Barnett & Gotlib, 1988; Coyne, 1976; Kendler et al., 2003). In addition, people with few, if any, important social relationships seem at risk for developing and sustaining mood disorders (Sherbourne et al., 1995). **Interpersonal psychotherapy (IPT)** (Bleiberg & Markowitz, in press; Klerman, Weissman, Rounsaville, & Chevron, 1984; Weissman, 1995) focuses on resolving problems in existing relationships and learning to form important new interpersonal relationships.

Like cognitive-behavioral approaches, IPT is highly structured and seldom takes longer than 15 to 20 sessions, usually scheduled once a week. After identifying life stressors that seem to precipitate the depression, the therapist and patient work collaboratively on the patient's current interpersonal problems. Typically, these include one or more of four interpersonal issues: *dealing with interpersonal role disputes,* such as marital conflict; *adjusting to the loss of a relationship,* such as grief over the death of a loved one; *acquiring new relationships,* such as getting married or establishing professional relationships; and *identifying and correcting deficits in social skills* that prevent the person from initiating or maintaining important relationships.

To take a common example, the therapist's first job is to identify and define an interpersonal dispute (Bleiberg & Markowitz, in press; Weissman, 1995), perhaps with a wife who expects her spouse to support her but has had to take an outside job to help pay bills. The husband might expect the wife to share equally in generating income. If this dispute seems to be associated with the onset of depressive symptoms and to result in a continuing series of arguments and disagreements without resolution, it would become the focus for IPT.

After helping identify the dispute, the next step is to bring it to a resolution. First, the therapist helps the patient determine the stage of the dispute.

1. *Negotiation stage.* Both partners are aware it is a dispute, and they are trying to renegotiate it.
2. *Impasse stage.* The dispute smolders beneath the surface and results in low-level resentment, but no attempts are made to resolve it.
3. *Resolution stage.* The partners are taking some action, such as divorce, separation, or recommitting to the marriage.

The therapist works with the patient to define the dispute clearly for both parties and develop specific strategies for resolving it. Along similar lines, Daniel O'Leary, Steve Beach, and their colleagues, as well as the late Neil Jacobson and his colleagues, have demonstrated that marital therapy is applicable to the large numbers of depressed patients they see, particularly women, who are in the midst of dysfunctional marriages (as is the case for as many as 50% of all depressed patients) (Beach et al., 1990; Jacobson, Dobson, Fruzzetti, Schmaling, & Salusky, 1991; Jacobson, Fruzzetti, Dobson, Whisman, & Hops, 1993; O'Leary & Beach, 1990).

Studies comparing the results of cognitive therapy and IPT to those of antidepressant drugs and other control conditions have found that psychological approaches and medication are equally effective, and all treatments are more effective than placebo conditions, brief psychodynamic treatments, or other appropriate control conditions for both major depressive disorder and dysthymia (Beck, Hollon, Young, Bedrosian, & Budenz, 1985; Blackburn & Moore, 1997; Hollon et al., 1992; Miller, Norman, & Keitner, 1989; Schulberg et al., 1996; Shapiro et al., 1995). Depending on how "success" is defined, approximately 50% or more of people benefit from treatment to a significant extent, compared to approximately 30% in placebo or control conditions (Craighead, Hart, Craighead, & Ilardi, 2002). One study, sponsored by the National Institute of Mental Health (NIMH) and carried out in three clinics in North America (Elkin et al., 1989), reported no essential differences in effectiveness among IPT, cognitive therapy, and tricyclic antidepressants when all patients who were treated were included in the results, whether they dropped out or not. At one clinic, medication was more effective than cognitive therapy if the patients were severely depressed (Elkin et al., 1995), a finding that may indicate less skillful cognitive therapists administering the treatment at that site (Hollon, 1993; Jacobson & Hollon, 1996a, 1996b).

Similar studies have not found a difference in treatment effectiveness based on severity of depression (Hollon et al., 1992; Hollon, Stewart, & Strunk, 2006; McLean & Taylor, 1992). DeRubeis, Gelfand, Tang, and Simons (1999) carefully evaluated the effects of cognitive therapy versus medication in severely depressed patients only, across four studies, and found no advantage for one treatment or the other. In any case, when patients in the NIMH study who *had* recovered were followed up for 18 months, the results of this study were disappointing (Shea et al., 1992). Of all patients entering treatment, only 30% of those who received cognitive therapy remained well compared to 26% of those who received IPT, 19% in the tricyclic drug group, and 20% in the placebo group. Shea and colleagues (1992) concluded that treatments were just not delivered long enough (or well enough) to effect meaningful change. More recently, O'Hara, Stuart, Gorman, and Wenzel (2000) demonstrated more positive effects for IPT in a group of women with postpartum depression, demonstrating that this approach is a worthwhile strategy in patients with postpartum depression who are reluctant to go on medication because, for example, they are breastfeeding. In one important related study, Spinelli and Endicott (2003) compared IPT to an alternative psychological approach in 50 depressed pregnant women unable to take drugs because of potential harm to the fetus. Fully 60% of these women recovered, leading the authors to recommend that IPT should be the first choice for pregnant depressed women. IPT has also been successfully administered to depressed adolescents by school-based clinicians trained to deliver IPT right in the school setting (Mufson et al., 2004). This practical approach shows good promise of reaching a larger number of depressed adolescents.

■ Prevention

In view of the seriousness of mood disorders in children and adolescents, work has begun on preventing these disorders in these age groups (Horowitz & Garber, 2006; Muñoz, 1993). Horowitz and Garber summarized results from three types of programs: *universal* programs, which are applied to everyone; *selected* interventions, which target individuals at risk for depression because of factors such as divorce, family alcoholism, and so on; and *indicated* interventions, where the individual is already showing mild symptoms of depression. As an example of selected interventions, some researchers focus on instilling social and problem-solving skills in children that are adequate to prevent the kinds of social stress so often associated with depression. Sanders and colleagues (1992) and Dadds, Sanders, Morrison, and Rebgetz (1992) determined that disordered communication and problem-solving skills, particularly within the family, are characteristic of depressed children and a natural target for preventive intervention.

Beardslee and colleagues (1997) have observed sustained effects from a preventive program directed at families with children between the ages of 8 and 15 in which one parent had experienced a recent episode of depression. Eighteen months after participating in 6 to 10 family sessions, these families were doing substantially better on most measures than the control families. In an even more intriguing preventive effort, Gilham, Reivich, Jaycox, and Seligman (1995) taught cognitive and social problem-solving techniques to 69 fifth- and sixth-grade children who were at risk for depression. Compared to children in a matched no-treatment control group, the prevention group reported fewer depressive symptoms during the 2 years they were followed. More important, moderate to severe symptoms were reduced by half, and the positive effects of this program increased during the period of follow-up. In an interesting replication, Seligman, Schulman, DeRubeis, and Hollon (1999) conducted a similar course for university students who were at risk for depression based on a pessimistic cognitive style. After 3 years, students taking the eight-session program experienced less anxiety and depression than a control group receiving the assessments only. This suggests that it might be possible to "psychologically immunize" at-risk children and adolescents against depression by teaching appropriate cognitive and social skills before they enter puberty.

Selected interventions have also been used effectively with pregnant women on public assistance at risk for postpartum depression (Zlotnick, Miller, Pearlstein, Howard, & Sweeney, 2006). These programs are clearly cost effective and, therefore, of great interest to public health authorities (Lynch et al., 2005). Preventive programs can also be effective in alleviating symptoms of depression when applied to all children, not just those at risk for depression (universal programs) (Gillham et al., 2007; Shochet et al., 2001; Spence, Sheffield, & Donovan, 2003), at least in the short term. After a year or more, the results are less certain, suggesting that prevention efforts should focus on those who are most at risk (Horowitz & Garber, 2006).

Combined Treatments

An increasing number of studies have tested the important question of whether combining psychosocial treatments with medication is effective in treating depression (see, for example, Beck et al., 1985; Blackburn & Moore, 1997; Hollon et al., 1992; Miller, Norman, Keitner, Bishop, & Down, 1989). These earlier studies, on the whole, did not strongly suggest any immediate advantage of combined treatment over separate drug or psychological treatment, but that perception is changing, mostly because of a large study reported by Keller and colleagues (2000) on the treatment of chronic major depression. In this, the largest study ever conducted on the treatment of depression, 681 patients at 12 clinics around the country were assigned to receive antidepressant medication (nefazodone), a CBT constructed specifically for chronically depressed patients, or the combination of two treatments. Researchers found that 48% of patients receiving each of the individual treatments were either remitted or responded in a clinically satisfactory way compared to 73% of the patients receiving combined treatment. Because this study was conducted with only a subset of depressed patients, those with chronic depression, the findings would need to be replicated before we could say combined treatment was useful for depression generally. In addition, because the study did not include a fifth condition in which the CBT was combined with placebo, we cannot rule out that the enhanced effectiveness of the combined treatment was the result of placebo factors. Nevertheless, a recent meta-analysis summarizing all studies conducted to date concludes that combined treatment does provide some advantage (Pampallona, Bollini, Tibaldi, Kupelnick, & Munizza, 2004). Notice how this conclusion differs from the conclusion in Chapter 5 on anxiety disorders, where no advantage of combining treatments was apparent. But, combining two treatments is also expensive, so many experts think that a sequential strategy makes more sense, where you start with one treatment first (maybe the one the patient prefers or the one that's available) and then switch to the other only if the first choice was not entirely satisfactory (see, for example, Schatzberg et al., 2005).

Preventing Relapse

In any case, drugs and CBTs clearly operate in different ways. Medication, when it works, does so more quickly than psychological treatments, which in turn have the advantage of increasing the patient's long-range social functioning (particularly in the case of IPT) and protecting against relapse or recurrence (particularly cognitive therapy). Combining treatments, therefore, might take advantage of the drugs' rapid action and the psychosocial protection against recurrence or relapse, thereby allowing eventual discontinuation of the medications. For example, Fava, Grandi, Zielezny, Rafanelli, and Canestrari (1996) assigned patients who had been successfully treated with antidepressant drugs to either CBT of residual symptoms or standard clinical management. Four years later, patients treated with cognitive-behavioral procedures had a substantially lower relapse rate (35%) than patients given the clinical management treatment (70%). In a second study, with patients with recurrent depressive episodes, the authors essentially replicated the results (Fava, Rafanelli, Grandi, Conti, & Belluardo, 1998), and at a 6-year follow-up 40% of the group receiving CBT experienced a recurrence compared to 90% of a comparison group receiving standard clinical management (Fava et al., 2004). Similarly, Paykel, Scott, and Teasdale (1999) found that adding cognitive therapy to medication was significantly more successful at preventing relapse than medication plus standard clinical management in patients who continued to have significant symptoms of depression after the initial course of drug treatment.

Given the high rate of recurrence in depression, it is not surprising that well more than 50% of patients on antidepressant medication relapse if their medication is stopped within 4 months after their last depressive episode (Hollon, Shelton, & Loosen, 1991; Thase, 1990). Therefore, one important question has to do with **maintenance treatment** to prevent relapse or recurrence over the long term. In a number of studies, cognitive therapy reduced rates of subsequent relapse in depressed patients by more than 50% over groups treated with antidepressant medication (see, for example, Evans et al., 1992; Hollon et al., 2005, 2006; Kovacs, Rush, Beck, & Hollon, 1981; Simons, Murphy, Levine, & Wetzel, 1986; Teasdale et al., 2000).

In one of the most impressive studies to date, patients were treated with either antidepressant medication or cognitive therapy compared to placebo (see DeRubeis et al., 2005), then the study began (Hollon et al., 2005; Hollon, Stewart, & Strunk, 2006). All patients who had responded well to treatment were followed for 2 years. During the first year, one group of patients who were originally treated with antidepressant medication continued on the medication but then stopped for the second year. Also included in this figure is a subgroup of patients from the antidepressant medication group who took their medication exactly as prescribed and, therefore, should have received maximum benefit from the drugs (perfect adherence). Patients originally receiving cognitive therapy were given up to three additional (booster) sessions during that first year but none after that. A third group was also originally treated with antidepressant medication but then switched to placebo. Patients who survived without relapse during the 2 years are presented in ■ Figure 7.9. During the first year, patients who were withdrawn from medication and placed onto pill placebo were considerably more likely to relapse over the ensuing 12-month interval than were patients continued on medication (23.8% survived without relapse on placebo versus 52.8% on medication). In comparison, 69.2% of patients with a history of cognitive therapy survived without relapse. At this point, there was no statistically significant difference in survival rates among patients who had received cognitive therapy versus those who continued on antidepressant medication. This suggests that prior cognitive therapy has an enduring effect that is at least as large in magnitude as keeping the patients on medications. In the second year, when all treatments had stopped, patients who had received medications were more likely to experience a recurrence than patients who had originally received cognitive therapy. Thus, the adjusted recurrence rates were 17.5% for prior cognitive therapy versus 56.3% for prior continuation antidepressant medication. These studies would seem to confirm that psychological treatments for depression are most notable for their enduring ability to prevent relapse or recurrence.

Psychological Treatments for Bipolar Disorder

Although medication, particularly lithium, seems a necessary treatment for bipolar disorder, most clinicians emphasize the need for psychological interventions to manage interpersonal and practical problems (for example, marital and job difficulties that result from the disorder) (Clarkin, Haas, & Glick, 1988). Until recently, the principal objective of psychological intervention was to increase compliance with medication regimens such as lithium

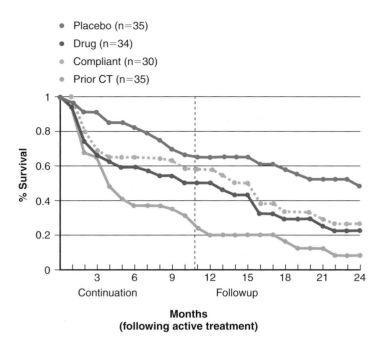

- Placebo (n=35)
- Drug (n=34)
- Compliant (n=30)
- Prior CT (n=35)

Months
(following active treatment)

■ FIGURE 7.9 Cumulative proportion of depressed treatment responders who survived without relapse during continuation (first 12 months), and cumulative proportion of recovered patients who survived without recurrence during the subsequent follow-up (months 13-24). Prior cognitive therapy (CT) allowed only three booster sessions following acute response (first 12 months) and no sessions following recovery (months 13-24). Continuation antidepressant medication patients (drug condition) continued on active medications following acute responses (first 12 months) then withdrew from all pills following recovery (months 13-24); compliant refers to a subset of drug condition who took the medication exactly as prescribed and should have received maximum benefit during the continuation phase. Placebo patients withdrew from active medications onto pill placebo following acute responses (first 12 months) then withdrew from all pills following recovery (months 13-24). (Adapted, with permission, from Hollon, S. D., Stewart, M. O., & Strunk, D., 2006. Cognitive behavior therapy has enduring effects in the treatment of depression and anxiety. *Annual Review of Psychology, 57,* 285-315, © 2005 American Medical Association.)

(Cochran, 1984). We noted before that the "pleasures" of a manic state make refusal to take lithium a major therapeutic obstacle. Giving up drugs between episodes or skipping dosages during an episode significantly undermines treatment. Therefore, increasing compliance with drug treatments is important (Goodwin & Jamison, 2007; Scott, 1995). For example, Clarkin, Carpenter, Hull, Wilner, and Glick (1998) evaluated the advantages of adding a psychological treatment to medication in inpatients and found it improved adherence to medication for all patients and resulted in better overall outcomes for the most severe patients compared to medication alone.

More recently, psychological treatments have also been directed at psychosocial aspects of bipolar disorder. In a new approach, Ellen Frank and her colleagues are testing a psychological treatment that regulates circadian rhythms by helping patients regulate their sleep cycles and other daily

schedules (Craighead, Miklowitz, Frank, & Vajk, 2002; Frank et al, 2005; Frank et al., 1997; Frank et al., 1999). In a major test of this approach, called interpersonal and social rhythm therapy (IPSRT) patients receiving IPSRT survived longer without a new manic or depressive episode compared to patients undergoing standard, intensive clinical management. Interestingly, this approach, which not only focuses on daily rhythms but also on interpersonal relationships, produced more regular social rhythms (sleeping and eating routines), and this seemed directly responsible for the success of IPSRT.

Ellen Frank and colleagues have developed important new treatments to prevent recurrences of mood disorders.

David Miklowitz and his colleagues found that family tension is associated with relapse in bipolar disorder. Preliminary studies indicate that treatments, directed at helping families understand symptoms and develop new coping skills and communication styles, change communication styles (Simoneau, Miklowitz, Richards, Saleem, & George, 1999) and prevent relapse (Miklowitz, 2001; Miklowitz & Goldstein, 1997; Miklowitz, Simoneau, Sachs-Ericsson, Warner, & Suddath, 1996). Miklowitz, George, Richards, Simoneau, and Suddath (2003) demonstrated that their family-focused treatment combined with medication results in significantly less relapse 1 year following initiation of treatment than patients receiving crisis management and medication over the same period (see ■ Figure 7.10). Specifically, only 35% of patients receiving family therapy plus medication relapsed compared to 54% in the comparison group. Similarly, family therapy

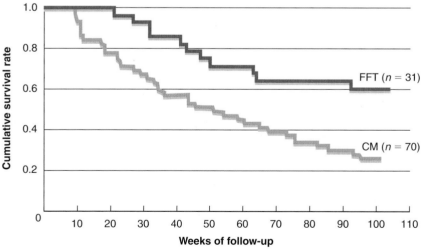

■ FIGURE 7.10 Survival curves for bipolar patients assigned to family-focused treatment (FFT) and medication or crisis management (CM) and medication (intent-to-treat analysis, N = 101). Comparison of the curves revealed that patients undergoing FFT had longer survival intervals without experiencing disease relapse than patients undergoing CM (Wilcoxon X^2_1 = 8.71, P = 0.003). (Adapted, with permission, from Miklowitz, D. J., George, E. L., Richards, J. A., Simoneau, T. L., & Suddath, R. L., 2003. A randomized study of family-focused psychoeducation and pharmacotherapy in the outpatient management of bipolar disorder. *Archives of General Psychiatry,* 60, 604-912, © 2003 American Medical Association.)

patients averaged over a year and a half (73.5 weeks) before relapsing, significantly longer than the comparison group. Rea, Tompson, and Miklowitz (2003) compared this approach to an individualized psychotherapy in which patients received the same number of sessions over the same period and continued to find an advantage for the family therapy after 2 years. In another important study, Lam et al. (2003) showed that patients with bipolar disorders treated with cognitive therapy plus medication relapsed significantly less over 1 year than a control group receiving just medication, replicating, in part, earlier results from Perry, Tarrier, Morriss, McCarthy, and Limb (1999). More recently, Lam, Hayward, Watkins, Wright, and Sham (2005) have reported similar results for 2 years following treatment.

Let us now return to Katie, who, you will remember, had made a serious suicide attempt amid a major depressive episode.

KATIE: The Triumph of the Self

Like the overwhelming majority of people with serious psychological disorders, Katie had never received an adequate course of treatment, although she was evaluated occasionally by various mental health professionals. She lived in a rural area where competent professional help was not readily available. Her life ebbed and flowed with her struggle to subdue anxiety and depression. When she could manage her emotions sufficiently, she took an occasional course in the high school independent study program. Katie discovered that she was fascinated by learning. She enrolled in a local community college at the age of 19 and did extremely well, even though she had not progressed beyond her freshman year in high school. At the college, she earned a high school equivalency degree. She went to work in a local factory. But she continued to drink heavily and to take Valium; occasionally, anxiety and depression would return and disrupt her life.

Finally, Katie left home, attended college full time, and fell in love. But the romance was one-sided, and she was rejected.

> One night after a phone conversation with him, I nearly drank myself to death. I lived in a single room alone in the dorm. I drank as much vodka as quickly as I could. I fell asleep. When I awoke, I was covered in vomit and couldn't recall falling asleep or being sick. I was drunk for much of the next day. When I awoke the following morning, I realized I could have killed myself by choking on my own vomit. More importantly, I wasn't sure if I fully wanted to die. That was the last of my drinking.

Katie decided to make some changes. Taking advantage of what she had learned in the little treatment she had received, she began looking at life and herself differently. Instead of dwelling on how inadequate and evil she was, she began to pay attention to her strengths. "But I now realized that I needed to accept myself as is, and work with any stumbling blocks that I faced. I needed to get myself through the world as happily and as comfortably as I could. I had a right to that."

Other lessons learned in treatment now became valuable, and Katie became more aware of her mood swings:

> I learned to objectify periods of depression as [simply] periods of "feeling." They are a part of who I am, but not the whole. I recognize when I feel that way, and I check my perceptions with someone that I trust when I feel uncertain of them. I try to hold on to the belief that these periods are only temporary.

Katie developed other strategies for coping successfully with life:

> I try to stay focused on my goals and what is important to me. I have learned that if one strategy to achieve some goal doesn't work there are other strategies that probably will. My endurance is one of my blessings. Patience, dedication, and discipline are also important. None of the changes that I have been through occurred instantly or automatically. Most of what I have achieved has required time, effort, and persistence.

Katie dreamed that if she worked hard enough she could help other people who had problems similar to her own. Katie pursued that dream and earned her Ph.D. in psychology.

CONCEPT CHECK 7.4

Indicate which type of treatment for mood disorders is being described in each statement.

1. The controversial but somewhat successful treatment involving the production of seizures through electrical current to the brain. _____

2. This teaches clients to carefully examine their thought process and recognize "depressive" styles in thinking. _____

3. These come in three main types (tricyclics, MAO inhibitors, and SSRIs) and are often prescribed but have numerous side effects. _____

4. This antidepressant must be carefully regulated to avoid illness but has the advantage of affecting manic episodes. _____

5. It is crucial to focus on resolving problems in existing relationships and learn to form new interpersonal relationships. _____

6. This is in an effort to prevent relapse or recurrence over the long run. _____

SUICIDE

Most days we are confronted with news about the war on cancer or the frantic race to find a cure for AIDS. We also hear never-ending admonitions to improve our diet and to exercise more to prevent heart disease. But another cause of death ranks right up there with the most frightening and dangerous medical conditions. This is the inexplicable decision to kill themselves made by approximately 30,000 people a year in the United States alone.

Statistics

According to the National Center for Health Statistics (Minino, Arias, Kochanek, Murphy, & Smith, 2002), suicide is officially the eighth leading cause of death in the United States for individuals age 25–34, and most epidemiologists agree that the actual number of suicides may be two to three times higher. Many of these unreported suicides occur when people deliberately drive into a bridge or off a cliff (Blumenthal, 1990). Around the world, suicide causes more deaths per year than homicide or war (World Health Organization, 2002).

Suicide is overwhelmingly a white phenomenon. Most minority groups, including African Americans and Hispanics, seldom resort to this violent alternative, as is evident in ■ Figure 7.11. When African Americans do commit suicide, they tend to do so at a young age and in a narrow, age-defined window of time (Garlow, Purselle, & Heninger, 2005). As you might expect from the incidence of depression in Native Americans, however, their suicide rate is extremely high (Beals et al., 2005; Hasin et al., 2005), although there is great variability across tribes (among the Apache, the rates are nearly four times the national average) (Berlin, 1987). Even more frightening is the dramatic increase in death by suicide in recent years, most evident among adolescents. ■ Figure 7.12 presents suicide rates for the population as a whole and rates for teenagers. As you can see, between 1960 and 1988 the suicide rate in adolescents rose from 3.6 to 11.3 per 100,000 population, an increase of 200% compared with a general population increase of 17%, before leveling off a bit. For teenagers, suicide is the *third* leading cause of death behind motor vehicle accidents and homicide (Minino et al., 2002; Ventura, Peters, Martin, & Maurer, 1997).

Note also the dramatic increase in suicide rates among the elderly in Figure 7.11. This rise has been connected to the growing incidence of medical illness in our oldest citizens and to their increasing loss of social support (Conwell, Duberstein, & Caine, 2002). As we have noted, a strong relationship exists between illness or infirmity and hopelessness or depression. In 2000, when approximately 12.5% of the population was 65 or older, this age group accounted for 18.1% of the suicide rate (Brown, Beck, Steer, & Grisham, 2000; Centers for Disease Control, 2003; Gallagher-Thompson & Osgood, 1997; National Center for Health Statistics, 1993). Suicide is not attempted only by adolescents and adults: Rosenthal and Rosenthal (1984) described 16 children 2 to 5 years of age who had attempted suicide at least

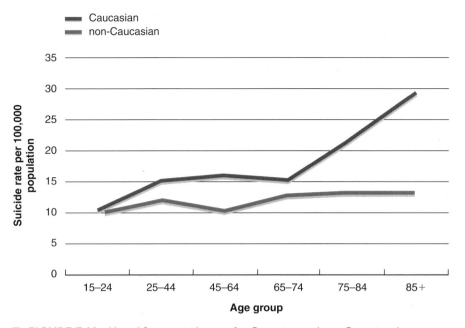

■ **FIGURE 7.11** United States suicide rates for Caucasians and non-Caucasians by age group, sexes combined (data from the National Center for Health Statistics, Vital Statistics of the United States, 2001). (From Centers for Disease Control and Prevention and Prevention, 2003a. Deaths: Final data for 2001. *National Vital Statistics Reports,* 52(3). Hyattsville, MD: National Center for Health Statistics.

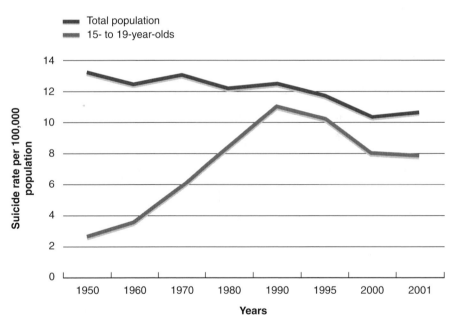

■ **FIGURE 7.12** Suicide rates per 100,000 in population for total population and for 15- to 19-year-olds (data from the National Center for Health Statistics, Vital Statistics of the United States, 2001). (From Centers for Disease Control and Prevention, 2003a. Deaths: Final data for 2001. *National Vital Statistics Reports,* 52(3). Hyattsville, MD: National Center for Health Statistics.

once, many injuring themselves severely, and suicide is the fifth leading cause of death from ages 5 to 14 (Minino et al., 2002).

Regardless of age, males are four to five times more likely to *commit* suicide than females (American Psychiatric Association, 2003). This startling fact seems to be related partly to gender differences in the types of suicide *attempts*. Males generally choose far more violent methods, such as guns and hanging; females tend

Men often choose violent methods of committing suicide. Nirvana's Kurt Cobain shot himself.

to rely on less violent options, such as drug overdose (Buda & Tsuang, 1990; Gallagher-Thompson & Osgood, 1997). More men commit suicide during old age and more women during middle age, partly because most attempts by older women are unsuccessful (Kuo, Gallo, & Tien, 2001). The suicide rate for young men in the United States is now the highest in the world, even surpassing rates in Japan and Sweden, countries long known for high rates of suicide (Blumenthal, 1990). But, as we noted, older men (over 65) in all countries are most at risk for completing suicide worldwide, with white men at highest risk (McIntosh, Santos, Hubbard, & Overholser, 1994).

Uniquely in China, more women commit suicide than men, particularly in rural settings (Murray, 1996; Murray & Lopez, 1996; Phillips, Li, & Zhang, 2002). What accounts for this culturally determined reversal? Chinese scientists agree that China's suicide rates, probably the highest in the world, are the result of an absence of stigma. Suicide, particularly among women, is often portrayed in classical Chinese literature as a reasonable solution to problems. A rural Chinese woman's family is her entire world, and suicide is an honorable solution if the family collapses. Furthermore, highly toxic farm pesticides are readily available and it is possible that many women who did not necessarily intend to kill themselves die after accidentally swallowing poison.

In addition to completed suicides, two other important indices of suicidal behavior are **suicidal attempts** (the person survives) and **suicidal ideation** (thinking seriously about suicide) (Kessler, Berglund, Borges, Nock, & Wang, 2005). Also, Nock and Kessler (2006) distinguish "attempters" (self-injurers with the intent to die), from "gesturers" (self-injurers who intend not to die but to influence or manipulate somebody or communicate a cry for help). Although males *commit* suicide more often than females in most of the world, females *attempt* suicide at least three times as often (Berman & Jobes, 1991; Kuo et al., 2001). This high incidence may reflect that more women than men are depressed and that depression is strongly related to suicide attempts (R. Frances, Franklin, & Flavin, 1986). Some estimates place the ratio of at-

tempted to completed suicides from 50:1 to 200:1 or higher (Garland & Zigler, 1993; Moscicki, 1997). In addition, results from another study (Kovacs, Goldston, & Gatsonis, 1993) suggested that among adolescents the ratio of *thoughts* about suicide to *attempts* is between 3:1 and 6:1. In other words, between 16% and 30% of adolescents in this study who had thought about killing themselves actually attempted it. "Thoughts" in this context does not refer to a fleeting philosophical type of consideration but rather to a serious contemplation of the act. The first step down the dangerous road to suicide is thinking about it.

In a study of college students (among whom suicide is the second leading cause of death), approximately 10% to 25% had thoughts about suicide during the past 12 months (Brener, Hassan, & Barrios, 1999; Meehan, Lamb, Saltzman, & O'Carroll, 1992; Schwartz & Whitaker, 1990). Only a minority of these college students with thoughts of suicide (perhaps around 15%) attempt to kill themselves, and only a few succeed (Kovacs et al., 1993). Nevertheless, given the enormity of the problem, suicidal thoughts are taken seriously by mental health professionals.

Causes

In the spring of 2003, Bernard Loiseau, one of the all-time great French chefs, learned that an important French restaurant guide, *GaultMillau,* was reducing the rating on one of his restaurants. This was the first time in his career that any of his restaurants had a rating reduced. Later that week, he killed himself. While police quickly ruled his death a suicide, most people in France did not consider it a suicide. Along with his fellow chefs, they accused the guidebook of murder! They claimed that he had been deeply affected by the ratings demotion, as well as speculation in the press that he might lose one of his three Michelin stars (Michelin publishes the most famous French restaurant guide). This series of events caused a sensation throughout France and, indeed, throughout the culinary world. But did *GaultMillau* kill Loiseau? Let's examine the causes of suicide.

■ Past Conceptions

The great sociologist Emile Durkheim (1951) defined a number of suicide types, based on the social or cultural conditions in which they occurred. One type is "formalized" suicides that were approved of, such as the ancient custom of *hara-kiri* in Japan, in which an individual who brought dishonor to himself or his family was expected to impale himself on a sword. Durkheim referred to this as *altruistic suicide.* Durkheim also recognized the loss of social supports as an important provocation for suicide; he called this *egoistic suicide.* (Elderly citizens who kill themselves after losing touch with their friends or family fit into this category.) Magne-Ingvar, Ojehagen, and Traskman-Bendz (1992) found that only 13% of 75 individuals who had seriously attempted suicide had an adequate social network of friends and relationships. *Anomic suicides* are the result of marked disruptions, such as the sudden loss of a high-prestige job. (*Anomie* is feeling lost and confused.) Finally, *fatalistic suicides* result from a loss of control over one's own destiny. The mass suicide of 39 Heaven's Gate cult members in 1997 is an example of this type because the lives of those people were largely in the hands of Marshall Applewhite, a supreme and charismatic leader. Durkheim's work was important in alerting us to the social contribution to suicide. Sigmund Freud (1917/1957) believed that suicide (and depression, to some extent) indicated unconscious hostility directed inward to the self rather than outward to the person or situation causing the anger. Indeed, suicide victims often seem to be psychologically "punishing" others who may have rejected them or caused some other personal hurt. Current thinking considers social and psychological factors but also highlights the potential importance of biological contributions.

Risk Factors

Edward Shneidman pioneered the study of risk factors for suicide (Shneidman, 1989; Shneidman, Farberow, & Litman, 1970). Among the methods he and others have used to study those conditions and events that make a person vulnerable is **psychological autopsy.** The psychological profile of the person who committed suicide is reconstructed through extensive interviews with friends and family members who are likely to know what the individual was thinking and doing in the period before death. This and other methods have allowed researchers to identify a number of risk factors for suicide.

■ Family History

If a family member committed suicide, there is an increased risk that someone else in the family will also (Kety, 1990; Mann, Waternaux, Haas, & Malone, 1999; Mann et al., 2005). Brent and colleagues (2002) noted a sixfold increased risk of suicide attempts in the offspring of family members who had attempted suicide compared to offspring of nonattempters. If a sibling was also a suicide attempter, the risk increased even more (Brent et al., 2003). This may not be surprising, because so many people who kill themselves are depressed, and depression runs in families. Nevertheless, the question remains: Are people who kill themselves simply adopting a familiar solution that they've witnessed in family members, or does an inherited trait, such as impulsivity, account for increased suicidal behavior in families? It seems both factors may contribute. If individuals have an early onset of their mood disorder, as well as aggressive or impulsive traits, then their families are at a greater risk for suicidal behavior (Mann et al., 2005). The possibility that something is inherited is also supported by several adoption studies. One found an increased rate of suicide in the biological relatives of adopted individuals who had committed suicide compared to a control group of adoptees who had not committed suicide (Schulsinger, Kety, & Rosenthal, 1979; Wender et al., 1986). In a small study of people whose twins had committed suicide, 10 out of 26 surviving monozygotic (identical) co-twins, and *none* of 9 surviving dizygotic (fraternal) co-twins, had themselves attempted suicide (Roy, Segal, & Sarchiapone, 1995). This suggests some biological (genetic) contribution to suicide, even if it is relatively small.

■ Neurobiology

A variety of evidence suggests that low levels of serotonin may be associated with suicide and with violent suicide attempts (Asberg, Nordstrom, & Traskman-Bendz, 1986; Cremniter et al., 1999; Winchel, Stanley, & Stanley, 1990). As we have noted, extremely low levels of serotonin are associated with impulsivity, instability, and the tendency to overreact to situations (Spoont, 1992). It is possible then that low levels of serotonin may contribute to creating a vulnerability to act impulsively. This may include killing oneself, which is sometimes an impulsive act, and the studies by Brent and colleagues (2002) and Mann and colleagues (2005) suggest that transmission of vulnerabilities for a mood disorder, including the trait of impulsivity, may mediate family transmission of suicide attempts.

■ Existing Psychological Disorders

More than 90% of people who kill themselves suffer from a psychological disorder (Black & Winokur, 1990; Brent & Kolko, 1990; Conwell et al., 1996; Garland & Zigler, 1993; Joe, Baser, Breeden, Neighbors, & Jackson, 2006; Orbach, 1997). Suicide is often associated with mood disorders, and for good reason. As many as 60% of suicides (75% of adolescent suicides) are associated with an existing mood disorder (Brent & Kolko, 1990; Frances et al., 1986; Oquendo et al., 2004). Lewinsohn, Rohde, and Seeley (1993) concluded that in adolescents suicidal behavior is largely an expression of severe depression, as did Oquendo and colleagues (2004) in adults. But many people with mood disorders do not attempt suicide, and, conversely, many people who attempt suicide do not have mood disorders. Therefore, depression and suicide, although strongly related, are still independent. Looking more closely at the relationship of mood disorder and suicide, some investigators have isolated hopelessness, a specific component of depression, as strongly predicting suicide (Beck, 1986; Beck, Steer, Kovacs, & Garrison, 1985; Goldston, Reboussin, & Daniel, 2006), a finding that also holds true in China (Cheung, Law, Chan, Liu, & Yip, 2006).

Alcohol use and abuse are associated with approximately 25% to 50% of suicides (see, for example, Frances et al., 1986) and are particularly evident in adolescent suicides (Brener et al., 1999; Conwell et al., 1996; Hawton, Houston, Haw, Townsend, & Harriss, 2003; Woods et al., 1997). Brent and colleagues (1988) found that about one third of adolescents who commit suicide were intoxicated when they died and that many more might have been under the influence of drugs. Combinations of disorders, such as substance abuse and mood disorders in adults or mood disorders and conduct disorder in children and adolescents, seem to create a stronger vulnerability than any one disorder alone (Conwell et al., 1996; Woods et al., 1997). For example, Hawton and colleagues (2003) noticed that the prevalence of previous attempts and repeated attempts doubled if a combination of disorders were present. For adolescents, Woods and colleagues (1997) found that substance abuse with other risk-taking behaviors, such as getting into fights, carrying a gun, or smoking, were predictive of teenage suicide, possibly reflecting impulsivity in these troubled adolescents. Esposito and Clum (2003) also noted that the presence of anxiety and mood (internalizing) disorders predicted suicide attempts in adolescents. Past suicide attempts are another strong risk factor and must be taken seriously. Cooper and colleagues (2005) followed almost 8,000 individuals who were treated in the emergency room for deliberate self-harm for up to 4 years. Sixty of these people had killed themselves, a 30-fold increase in risk compared to population statistics.

A disorder characterized more by impulsivity than depression is borderline personality disorder (see Chapter 12). Frances and Blumenthal (1989) suggest that these individuals, known for making manipulative and impulsive suicidal gestures without necessarily wanting to destroy themselves, sometimes kill themselves by mistake in as many as 10% of the cases. The combination of borderline personality disorder and depression is particularly deadly (Soloff, Lynch, Kelly, Malone, & Mann, 2000).

The association of suicide with severe psychological disorders, especially depression, belies the myth that it is a response to disappointment in people who are otherwise healthy.

■ Stressful Life Events

Perhaps the most important risk factor for suicide is a severe, stressful event experienced as shameful or humiliating, such as a failure (real or imagined) in school or at work, an unexpected arrest, or rejection by a loved one (Blumenthal, 1990; Brent et al., 1988; Conwell et al., 2002; Joiner & Rudd, 2000; Shaffer, Garland, Gould, Fisher, & Trautmen, 1988). Physical and sexual abuse are also important sources of stress (Wagner, 1997). Evidence confirms that the stress and disruption of natural disasters increase the likelihood of suicide (Krug et al., 1998). Based on data from 337 countries experiencing natural disasters in the 1980s, the authors concluded that the rates of suicide increased 13.8% in the 4 years after severe floods, 31% in the 2 years after hurricanes, and 62.9% in the first year after an earthquake. Given preexisting vulnerabilities—including psychological disorders, traits of impulsiveness, and lack of social support—a stressful event can often put a person over the edge. An integrated model of the causes of suicidal behavior is presented in ■ Figure 7.13.

Is Suicide Contagious?

We hear all too often of the suicide of a teenager or celebrity. Most people react with sadness and curiosity. Some people react by attempting suicide themselves, often by the same method they have just heard about. Gould (1990) reported an increase in sui-

cides during a 9-day period after widespread publicity about a suicide. Clusters of suicides (several people copying one person) seem to predominate among teenagers, with as many as 5% of all teenage suicides reflecting an imitation (Gould, 1990).

Why would anyone want to copy a suicide? First, suicides are often romanticized in the media: An attractive young person under unbearable pressure commits suicide and becomes a martyr to friends and peers by getting even with the (adult) world for creating such a difficult situation. Also, media accounts often describe in detail the methods used in the suicide, thereby providing a guide to potential victims. Little is reported about the paralysis, brain damage, and other tragic consequences of the incomplete or failed suicide or about how suicide is almost always associated with a severe psychological disorder. More important, even less is said about the futility of this method of solving problems (Gould, 1990; O'Carroll, 1990). To prevent these tragedies, the media should not inadvertently glorify suicides and mental health professionals must intervene immediately in schools and other locations with people who might be depressed or otherwise vulnerable to the contagion of suicide. But it isn't clear that suicide is "contagious" in the infectious disease sense. Rather, the stress of a friend's suicide or some other major stress may affect several individuals who are vulnerable because of existing psychological disorders (Joiner, 1999). Nevertheless, effective intervention is essential.

Treatment

Despite the identification of important risk factors, predicting suicide is still an uncertain art. Individuals with few precipitating factors unexpectedly kill themselves, and many who live with seemingly insurmountable stress and illness and have little social support or guidance somehow survive and overcome their difficulties.

Mental health professionals are thoroughly trained in assessing for possible suicidal ideation. Others might be reluctant to ask leading questions for fear of putting the idea in someone's head. However, we know it is far more important to check for these "secrets" than to do nothing, because the risk of inspiring suicidal

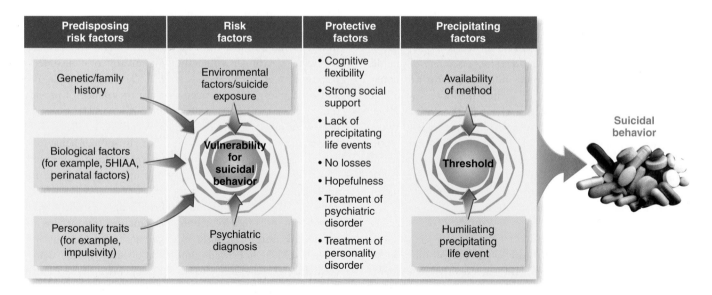

■ **FIGURE 7.13** Threshold model for suicidal behavior. 5HIAA = 5-hydroxyindoleacetic acid. (Reprinted, with permission, from Blumenthal, S. J., & Kupfer, D. J., 1988. Clinical assessment and treatment of youth suicide. *Journal of Youth and Adolescence, 17, 1-24,* © 1988 by Plenum Publishing.)

thoughts is small to nonexistent and the risk of leaving them undiscovered is enormous. Gould and colleagues (2005) found that more than 1,000 high school students who were asked about suicidal thoughts or behaviors during a screening program showed no risk of increased suicidal thoughts compared to a second group of 1,000 students who had the screening program without the questions about suicide. Therefore, if there is any indication that someone is suicidal, the mental health professional will inquire, "Has there been any time recently when you've thought that life wasn't worth living, or had some thoughts about hurting yourself or possibly killing yourself?"

The mental health professional will also check for possible recent humiliations and determine whether any of the factors are present that might indicate a high probability of suicide. For example, does a person who is thinking of suicide have a detailed plan or just a vague fantasy? If a plan is discovered that includes a specific time, place, and method, the risk is high. Does the detailed plan include putting all personal affairs in order, giving away possessions, and other final acts? If so, the risk is higher still. What specific method is the person considering? Generally, the more lethal and violent the method (guns, hanging, poison, and so on), the greater the risk it will be used. Does the person understand what might actually happen? Many people do not understand the effects of the pills on which they might overdose. Finally, has the person taken any precautions against being discovered? If so, the risk is extreme (American Psychiatric Association, 2003).

If a risk is present, clinicians attempt to get the individual to agree to or even sign a no-suicide contract. Usually this includes a promise not to do anything remotely connected with suicide without contacting the mental health professional first. If the person at risk refuses a contract (or the clinician has serious doubts about the patient's sincerity) and the suicidal risk is judged to be high, immediate hospitalization is indicated, even against the will of the patient. Whether the person is hospitalized or not, treatment aimed at resolving underlying life stressors and treating existing psychological disorders should be initiated immediately.

In view of the public health consequences of suicide, a number of programs have been implemented to reduce the rates of suicide. They include curriculum-based programs in which teams of professionals go into schools or other organizations to educate people about suicide and provide information on handling life stress. The Surgeon General of the United States has issued a comprehensive report on suicide prevention (U.S. Public Health Service, 2001), with a focus on older adults, a particularly high-risk group. Japan has developed programs for its elderly that focus on increasing social support (Ono, 2004). Unfortunately, most research indicates that such programs targeting the general population are not effective (Garfield & Zigler, 1993; Shaffer, Garland, Vieland, Underwood, & Busner, 1991).

More helpful are programs targeted to at-risk individuals, including adolescents in schools where a student has committed suicide. The Institute of Medicine (2002) recommends making services available immediately to friends and relatives of victims. An important step is limiting access to lethal weapons for anyone at risk for suicide. A recent analysis suggests that this may be the most powerful part of a suicide prevention program (Mann and colleagues, 2005). Telephone hotlines and other crisis intervention services also seem to be useful. Nevertheless, as Garfield and Zigler (1993) point out,

hotline volunteers must be backed up by competent mental health professionals who can identify potentially serious risks.

Specific treatments for people at risk have also been developed. For example, Salkovskis, Atha, and Storer (1990) treated 20 patients at high risk for repeated suicide attempts with a cognitive-behavioral problem-solving approach. Results indicated that they were significantly less likely to attempt suicide in the 6 months following treatment. Marshal Linehan and colleagues (see, for example, Linehan & Kehrer, 1993) developed a noteworthy treatment for the type of impulsive treatment suicidal behavior associated with borderline personality disorder (see Chapter 12). David Rudd and colleagues developed a brief psychological treatment targeting young adults who were at risk for suicide because of the presence of suicidal ideation accompanied by previous suicidal attempts, mood or substance use disorders, or both (Rudd et al., 1996). They randomly assigned 264 young people either to this new treatment or to treatment as usual in the community. Patients undergoing the new treatment spent approximately 9 hours each day for 2 weeks at a hospital treatment facility. Treatment consisted of problem solving, developing social competence, coping more adaptively with life's problems, and recognizing emotional and life experiences that may have precipitated the suicide attempt or ideation. Patients were assessed up to 2 years following treatment, and results indicated reductions in suicidal ideation and behavior, as well as marked improvement in problem-solving ability. Furthermore, the brief experimental treatment was significantly more effective at retaining the highest-risk young adults in the program. This program has been expanded into a psychological treatment for suicidal behavior with empirical support for its efficacy (Rudd, Joiner, & Rajab, 2001). Now, a landmark study has demonstrated that 10 sessions of cognitive therapy for recent suicide attempters cuts the risk of additional attempts by 50% over the next 18 months (Brown and colleagues, 2005). Specifically 24% of those in the cognitive therapy group made a repeat attempt compared to 42% in the care-as-usual group. The results are presented in ■ Figure 7.14. Because cognitive therapy is relatively widely available, this is an important development in suicide prevention.

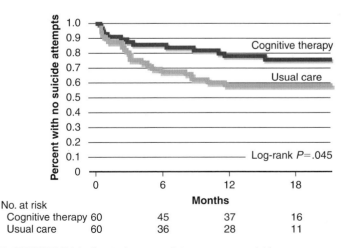

■ **FIGURE 7.14** Survival curves of time to repeat suicide attempt. From Brown, G., Have, T., and colleagues, (2005). Cognitive therapy for the prevention of suicide attempts: A randomized controlled trial. *JAMA, 294,* 563–570. © American Medical Association.

With the increased rate of suicide, particularly in adolescents, the tragic and paradoxical act is receiving increased scrutiny from public health authorities. The quest will go on to determine more effective and efficient ways of preventing the most serious consequences of any psychological disorder, the taking of one's own life.

CONCEPT CHECK 7.5

Match each of the following summaries with the correct suicide type, choosing from (a) altruistic, (b) egoistic, (c) anomic, and (d) fatalistic.

1. Ralph's wife left him and took the children. He is a well-known television personality, but, because of a conflict with the new station owners, he was recently fired. If Ralph kills himself, his suicide would be considered _____.

(continued)

CONCEPT CHECK 7.5

(continued)

2. Sam killed himself while a prisoner of war in Vietnam. _____

3. Sheiba lives in a remote village in Africa. She was recently caught in an adulterous affair with a man in a nearby village. Her husband wants to kill her but won't have to because of a tribal custom that requires her to kill herself. She leaps from the nearby "sinful woman's cliff." _____

4. Mabel lived in a nursing home for many years. At first, her family and friends visited her often; now they come only at Christmas. Her two closest friends in the nursing home died recently. She has no hobbies or other interests. Mabel's suicide would be identified as what type? _____

FUTURE DIRECTIONS

Evidence for an Integrative Approach to Causes of Depression

In our discussion of the causes of depression, the clear conclusion is that both biological and psychological processes are implicated. One biological process involves impaired neurotransmitter function, particularly concerning the serotonergic system. Remember that there is some evidence that low levels of serotonin in relation to other neurotransmitters may contribute to the onset of depressive episodes in certain individuals. We also reviewed evidence that negative cognitive styles are a core vulnerability marker for depression and that these pessimistic cognitive styles seem to predict the onset of future depressive episodes. But how do these two factors interact?

Booij and Van der Does (2007) have begun to investigate the relationship between these two vulnerability factors, or "markers" for depression. They collaborated with 39 patients who had suffered an episode of major depression but had recovered. These patients participated in two biological test or "challenge" procedures that had the effect of temporarily lowering levels of serotonin. This challenge procedure, called acute tryptophan depletion (ATD), temporarily lowers serotonin levels. This is accomplished fairly easily by altering diet for 1 day by restricting intake of tryptophan (a precursor to serotonergic functioning) and increasing a mixture of essential amino acids. It has previously been demonstrated that this challenge procedure temporarily exacerbates symptoms in about 50% of patients in remission from a previous depressive episode (Van der Does, 2001).

The subjects in the experiment are fully informed of these effects and collaborate willingly.

What Booij and Van der Does (2007) found was that this biological challenge was, as usual, effective in temporarily inducing a variety of depressive symptoms in some of these individuals but that these symptoms were more pronounced in those who also had evidence of the cognitive vulnerability marker. That is, cognitive vulnerability assessed before the biological challenge clearly predicted a depressive response. Interestingly, a challenge with ATD causes no significant changes in mood in healthy samples; rather, it is limited to those individuals who are vulnerable to depression. Two other risk factors for depression, neuroticism and behavioral inhibition, were not related to the biological challenge.

Depressive cognitive styles trigger a greater sensitivity to a reduction in serotonergic functioning, which moves researchers one step toward unifying cognitive and neurobiological theories of the cause of depression. More important, studies such as this one demonstrate conclusively that we cannot hold onto "single cause" models of the etiology of psychopathology (depression is caused by a chemical imbalance or depression is caused by disordered cognitive activity). It is clear that we have to continue to study the interaction of psychological and neurobiological factors.

SUMMARY

Understanding and Defining Mood Disorders

■ Mood disorders are among the most common psychological disorders, and the risk of developing them is increasing worldwide, particularly in younger people.

■ Two fundamental experiences can contribute either singly or in combination to all specific mood disorders: a major depressive episode and mania. A less severe episode of mania that does not cause impairment in social or occupational functioning is known as a hypomanic episode. An episode of mania coupled with anxiety or depression is known as a dysphoric manic or mixed episode.

■ An individual who suffers from episodes of depression only is said to have a unipolar disorder. An individual who alternates between depression and mania has a bipolar disorder.

■ Major depressive disorder may be a single episode or recurrent, but it is always time limited; in another form of depression, dysthymic disorder, the symptoms are somewhat milder but remain relatively unchanged over long periods. In cases of double depression, an individual experiences both depressive episodes and dysthymic disorder.

■ Approximately 20% of bereaved individuals may experience a pathological, complicated grief reaction in which the normal grief response develops into a full-blown mood disorder.

■ The key identifying feature of bipolar disorders is an alternation of manic episodes and major depressive episodes. Cyclothymic disorder is a milder but more chronic version of bipolar disorder.

■ Patterns of additional features that sometimes accompany mood disorders, called specifiers, may predict the course or patient response to treatment, as does the temporal patterning or course of mood disorders. One pattern, seasonal affective disorder, most often occurs in winter.

Prevalence of Mood Disorders

■ Mood disorders in children are fundamentally similar to mood disorders in adults.

■ Symptoms of depression are increasing dramatically in our elderly population.

■ The experience of anxiety across cultures varies, and it can be difficult to make comparisons, especially, for example, when we attempt to compare subjective feelings of depression.

The Overlap of Anxiety and Depression

■ Some of the latest theories on the causes of depression are based partly on research into the relationship between anxiety and depression. Anxiety almost always precedes depression, and everyone with depression is also anxious.

Causes of Mood Disorders

■ The causes of mood disorders lie in a complex interaction of biological, psychological, and social factors. From a biological perspective, researchers are particularly interested in the stress hypothesis and the role of neurohormones. Psychological theories of depression focus on learned helplessness and the depressive cognitive schemas, as well as interpersonal disruptions.

Treatment of Mood Disorders

■ A variety of treatments, both biological and psychological, have proved effective for the mood disorders, at least in the short term. For those individuals who do not respond to antidepressant drugs or psychosocial treatments, a more dramatic physical treatment, electroconvulsive therapy, is sometimes used. Two psychosocial treatments—cognitive therapy and interpersonal therapy—seem effective in treating depressive disorders.

■ Relapse and recurrence of mood disorders are common in the long term, and treatment efforts must focus on maintenance treatment, that is, on preventing relapse or recurrence.

Suicide

■ Suicide is often associated with mood disorders but can occur in their absence. In any case, the incidence of suicide has been increasing in recent years, particularly among adolescents, for whom it is the third leading cause of death.

■ In understanding suicidal behavior, two indices are important: suicidal attempts (that are not successful) and suicidal ideation (serious thoughts about committing suicide). Important, too, in learning about risk factors for suicides is the psychological autopsy, in which the psychological profile of an individual who has committed suicide is reconstructed and examined for clues.

Key Terms

mood disorders, 208

major depressive episode, 208

mania, 208

hypomanic episode, 209

mixed episode, 209

major depressive disorder, single or recurrent episode, 210

dysthymic disorder, 210

double depression, 211

pathological or impacted grief reaction, 214

bipolar II disorder, 215

bipolar I disorder, 215

cyclothymic disorder, 216

catalepsy, 218

hallucinations, 218

delusions, 218

seasonal affective disorder (SAD), 220

neurohormones, 230

learned helplessness theory of depression, 233

depressive cognitive triad, 234

electroconvulsive therapy (ECT), 242

cognitive therapy, 243

interpersonal psychotherapy (IPT), 244

maintenance treatment, 246

suicidal attempts, 250

suicidal ideation, 250

psychological autopsy, 251

Answers to Concept Checks

7.1

1. e; 2. a; 3. c; 4. d; 5. b

7.2

1. T; 2. F (it does not require life experience); 3. T; 4. T

7.3

1. genetics, neurotransmitter system abnormalities, endocrine system, circadian or sleep rhythms, neurohormones
2. stressful life events, learned helplessness, depressive cognitive triad, a sense of uncontrollability
3. marital dissatisfaction, gender, few social supports

7.4

1. electroconvulsive therapy; 2. cognitive therapy; 3. antidepressants; 4. lithium; 5. interpersonal psychotherapy; 6. maintenance treatment

7.5

1. c; 2. d; 3. a; 4. b

The Abnormal Psychology Book Companion Website

See **academic.cengage.com/psychology/barlow** for practice quiz questions, interactive activities, Internet links, critical thinking exercises, discussion forums, and more. Also accessible from the Wadsworth Psychology Resource Center (**academic.cengage .com/login**).

Abnormal Psychology Live CD-ROM

- *Barbara, a Client With Major Depressive Disorder:* Barbara suffers from a major depressive disorder that's rather severe and long-lasting.

- *Evelyn, a Patient With Major Depressive Disorder:* Evelyn has a major depressive disorder that gives a more positive view of long-term prospects for change.
- *Mary, a Client With Bipolar Disorder:* Mary is shown in both a manic and depressive phase of her illness. You may notice the similarity of the delusions in both phases of her illness.

CENGAGENOW CengageNOW

Go to **academic.cengage.com/now** to link to CengageNOW, your online study tool. First take the Pre-Test for this chapter to get your personalized study plan, which will identify topics you need to review and direct you to online resources. Then take the Post-Test to determine what concepts you have mastered and what you still need work on.

Video Concept Reviews

CengageNOW also contains Mark Durand's *Video Concept Reviews* on challenging topics:

- Overview of Moods
- Overview of Mood Disorders
- Major Depressive Disorder
- Major Depression: Single or Recurrent Episode
- Dysthymia
- Double Depression
- Bipolar I Disorder
- Bipolar II Disorder
- Cyclothymic Disorder
- Concept Check: Dysthymia Versus Major Depression
- Mood Disorders: Course Specifiers
- Learned Helplessness
- Electroconvulsive Therapy (ECT)
- Suicide

Exploring Mood Disorders

People with mood disorders experience one or both of the following:
*• **Mania:** A frantic "high" with extreme overconfidence and energy, often leading to reckless behavior*
*• **Depression:** A devastating "low" with extreme lack of energy, interest, confidence, and enjoyment of life*

TRIGGER

- Negative or positive life changes (death of a loved one, promotion, etc.)
- Physical illness

Biological Influences

- Inherited vulnerability
- Altered neurotransmitters and neurohormonal systems
- Sleep deprivation
- Circadian rhythm disturbances

Social Influences

- Women and minorities—social inequality and oppression and a diminished sense of control
- Social support can reduce symptoms
- Lack of social support can aggravate symptoms

CAUSES

Behavioral Influences

Depression
- General slowing down
- Neglect of responsibilities and appearance
- Irritability; complaints about matters that used to be taken in stride

Mania
- Hyperactivity
- Reckless or otherwise unusual behavior

Emotional and Cognitive Influences

Depression
- Emotional flatness or emptiness
- Inability to feel pleasure
- Poor memory
- Inability to concentrate
- Hopelessness and/or learned helplessness
- Loss of sexual desire
- Loss of warm feelings for family and friends
- Exaggerated self-blame or guilt
- Overgeneralization
- Loss of self-esteem
- Suicidal thoughts or actions

Mania
- Exaggerated feelings of euphoria and excitement

TYPES OF MOOD DISORDERS

DEPRESSIVE DISORDERS

Major Depressive Disorder
Symptoms of major depressive disorder:
- begin suddenly, often triggered by a crisis, change, or loss
- are extremely severe, interfering with normal functioning
- can be long term, lasting months or years if untreated

Some people have only one episode, but the pattern usually involves repeated episodes or lasting symptoms.

Dysthymia
Long-term unchanging symptoms of mild depression, sometimes lasting 20 to 30 years if untreated. Daily functioning not as severely affected, but over time impairment is cumulative.

Double Depression
Alternating periods of major depression and dysthymia

BIPOLAR DISORDERS

PEOPLE WHO HAVE A BIPOLAR DISORDER LIVE ON AN UNENDING EMOTIONAL ROLLER COASTER.

During the **Depressive Phase,** the person may:
- lose all interest in pleasurable activities and friends
- feel worthless, helpless, and hopeless
- have trouble concentrating
- lose or gain weight without trying
- have trouble sleeping or sleep more than usual
- feel tired all the time
- feel physical aches and pains that have no medical cause
- think about death or attempt suicide

During the **Manic Phase,** the person may:
- feel extreme pleasure and joy from every activity
- be extraordinarily active, planning excessive daily activities
- sleep little without getting tired
- develop grandiose plans leading to reckless behavior: unrestrained buying sprees, sexual indiscretions, foolish business investments, etc.
- have "racing thoughts" and talk on and on
- be easily irritated and distracted

Types of Bipolar Disorders

- **Bipolar I**: major depression and full mania
- **Bipolar II**: major depression and mild mania
- **Cyclothymia**: mild depression with mild mania, chronic and long term

TREATMENT OF MOOD DISORDERS

Treatment for mood disorders is most effective and easiest when it's started early. Most people are treated with a combination of these methods.

MEDICATION Antidepressants can help to control symptoms and restore neurotransmitter functioning.
Common types of antidepressants:
- Tricyclics (Tofranil, Elavil)
- Monamine oxidase inhibitors (MAOIs): (Nardil, Parnate); MAOIs can have severe side effects, especially when combined with certain foods or over-the-counter medications
- Selective serotonergic reuptake inhibitors or SSRIs (Prozac, Zoloft) are newer and cause fewer side effects than tricyclics or MAOIs
- Lithium is the preferred drug for bipolar disorder; side effects can be serious; and dosage must be carefully regulated

COGNITIVE-BEHAVIORAL THERAPY Helps depressed people:
- learn to replace negative depressive thoughts and attributions with more positive ones
- develop more effective coping behaviors and skills

INTERPERSONAL PSYCHOTHERAPY Helps depressed people:
- focus on the social and interpersonal triggers for their depression (such as the loss of a loved one)
- develop skills to resolve interpersonal conflicts and build new relationships

ELECTROCONVULSIVE THERAPY (ECT)
- For severe depression, ECT is used when other treatments have been ineffective. It usually has temporary side effects, such as memory loss and lethargy. In some patients, certain intellectual and/or memory functions may be permanently lost.

LIGHT THERAPY
- For seasonal affective disorder

Eating and Sleep Disorders

© Image Source/Corbis

MAJOR TYPES OF EATING DISORDERS
Bulimia Nervosa
Anorexia Nervosa
Binge-Eating Disorder
Statistics

CAUSES OF EATING DISORDERS
Social Dimensions
Biological Dimensions
Psychological Dimensions
An Integrative Model

TREATMENT OF EATING DISORDERS
Drug Treatments
Psychological Treatments
Preventing Eating Disorders

OBESITY
Statistics
Disordered Eating Patterns in Cases of Obesity
Causes
Treatment

SLEEP DISORDERS: THE MAJOR DYSSOMNIAS
An Overview of Sleep Disorders
Primary Insomnia
Primary Hypersomnia
Narcolepsy
Breathing-Related Sleep Disorders
Circadian Rhythm Sleep Disorders

TREATMENT OF SLEEP DISORDERS
Medical Treatments
Environmental Treatments
Psychological Treatments
Preventing Sleep Disorders
Parasomnias and Their Treatment

ABNORMAL PSYCHOLOGY LIVE CD-ROM
Anorexia Nervosa: Susan
Anorexia Nervosa/Bulimia: Twins
Weight Control: The Obesity Epidemic
Sleep Cycle
Web Link

I distinctly did not want to be seen as bulimic. I wanted to be an anorectic . . . a person whose passions were ascetic rather than hedonistic.

Marya Hornbacher

Wasted: A Memoir of Anorexia and Bulimia

We now begin a series of three chapters on the interaction of psychological and social factors and physical functioning. Most of us take our bodies for granted. We wake up in the morning assuming we will be alert enough to handle our required daily activities; we eat two or three meals a day and perhaps a number of snacks; we may engage in some vigorous exercise and, on some days, in sexual activity. We don't focus on our functioning to any great degree unless it is disrupted by illness or disease. Yet psychological and social factors can significantly disrupt these "activities of survival."

In this chapter we talk about psychological disruptions of two of our relatively automatic behaviors, eating and sleeping, which substantially affect the rest of our behavior. In Chapter 9, we discuss the psychological factors involved in physical malfunctioning: specifically, illness and disease. Finally, in Chapter 10, we discuss disordered sexual behavior.

MAJOR TYPES OF EATING DISORDERS

Although some disorders we discuss in this chapter can be deadly, many of us are not aware they are widespread among us. They began to increase during the 1950s or early 1960s and have spread insidiously over the ensuing decades. In **bulimia nervosa,** out-of-control eating episodes, or **binges,** are followed by self-induced vomiting, excessive use of laxatives, or other attempts to purge (get rid of) the food. In **anorexia nervosa,** the person eats nothing beyond minimal amounts of food, so body weight sometimes drops dangerously. The chief characteristic of these related disorders is an overwhelming, all-encompassing drive to be thin. Of the people with anorexia nervosa who are followed over a sufficient period, up to 20% die as a result of their disorder, with slightly more than 5% dying within 10 years (see, for example, Keel et al., 2003; Millar et al., 2005; Ratnasuriya, Eisler, Szmukler, & Russell, 1991; Sullivan, 1995; Theander, 1985; Zipfel, Lowe, Deter, & Herzog, 2000). In fact, anorexia nervosa has the highest mortality rate of any psychological disorder reviewed in this book, including depression (Park, 2007).

As many as half the deaths are suicides, which represents a fifty-fold increase in the relative risk of death from suicide in the general population (Agras, 2001; Chavez & Insel 2007; Keel et al., 2003; Thompson & Kinder, 2003). In binge-eating disorder, individuals may binge repeatedly and find it distressing but do not attempt to purge the food.

A growing number of studies in different countries indicate that eating disorders are widespread and increased dramatically in Western countries from about 1960 to 1995, according to the most recent data we have (Bulik et al., 2006; Hoek, 2002). In Switzerland, from 1956 to 1958, the number of new cases of anorexia nervosa under treatment among females between the ages of 12 and 25 was 3.98 per 100,000. There were 16.76 new cases per 100,000 during the 1973–1975 period, a fourfold increase (Willi & Grossman, 1983). Similar results were found in Scotland by Eagles, Johnston, Hunter, Lobban, and Millar (1995) between 1965 and 1991; by Lucas, Beard, O'Fallon, and Kurlan (1991) in Minnesota over a 50-year period; and by Moller-Madsen and Nystrup (1992) in Denmark between 1970 and 1989. Eagles and colleagues (1995) documented a steady increase of more than 5% per year in Scotland.

Even more dramatic are the data for bulimia nervosa. Garner and Fairburn (1988) reviewed rates of referral to a major eating disorder center in Canada. Between 1975 and 1986, the referral rates for anorexia rose slowly but the rates for bulimia rose dramatically—from virtually none to more than 140. Similar findings have been reported from other parts of the world (Hay & Hall, 1991; Lacey, 1992), although more recent surveys suggest that rates for bulimia are leveling off or even beginning to drop from highs reached in the 1990s (Keel, Heatherton, Dorer, Joiner, & Zalta, 2006). Nevertheless, a recent large-scale population survey (Hudson, Hiripi, Pope, & Kessler, 2007) continues to show a higher prevalence in younger age groups born between 1972 and 1985 than for older age groups, particularly for bulimia. So the "leveling off," if it's real, is recent.

Other studies estimate a sixfold increase in death rates from eating disorders compared to the normal population (Crisp, Callender, Halek, & Hsu, 1992; Patton, 1988). The mortality rate from eating disorders, particularly anorexia, is the highest for any psychological disorder, even depression (Harris & Barraclough, 1998; Keel et al., 2003; Millar et al., 2005; Vitiello & Lederhendler, 2000). Eating disorders were included for the first time as a separate group of disorders in the fourth edition of the *Diagnostic and Statistical Manual* (DSM-IV).

The increases in eating disorders during the last half of the twentieth century would be puzzling enough if they occurred across the population. What makes them even more intriguing is that they tend to be culturally specific. Until recently, eating disorders were not found in developing countries, where access to sufficient food is so often a daily struggle; only in the West, where food is generally plentiful, have they been rampant. Now this is changing; evidence suggests that eating disorders are going global. Unsystematic interviews with health professionals in Asia (Efon, 1997), as well as more formal studies (Lee, 1993), show estimates of prevalence in those countries, particularly Japan and Hong Kong, are approaching those in the United States and other Western countries. Not everyone in the world is at risk. Eating disorders tend to occur in a relatively small segment of the population. More than 90% of the severe cases are young females, mostly in families with upper-middle-class and upper-class socioeconomic status, who live in a socially competitive environment. Perhaps the most visible example is the late Diana, Princess of Wales, who recounted her 7-year battle with bulimia (Morton, 1992). She reported bingeing and vomiting four or more times a day during her honeymoon. Increasingly, this group of girls and young women with eating disorders seek one another out on the Internet at "pro-

The late Princess of Wales spoke candidly about her battle against bulimia.

ana" (anorexia) and "pro-mia" (bulimia) websites, where they find support and, in some cases, inspiration (pro-ana-nation, retrieved 2007).

The very specificity of these disorders in terms of sex, age, and social class is unparalleled and makes the search for causes all the more interesting. In these disorders, unlike most others, the strongest contributions to etiology seem to be sociocultural rather than psychological or biological factors.

Obesity is not considered an official disorder in the DSM, but we consider it here because it is thought to be one of the most dangerous epidemics confronting public health authorities around the world today. The latest surveys indicate that up to 65% of adults in the United States are overweight, more than 30% meet criteria for obesity, and these numbers have increased over the past 5 years (Ogden et el., 2006). Definitions of underweight, overweight, and obesity will be discussed further later, but they are based on body mass index (BMI), which is highly correlated with body fat. To determine your own BMI, refer to Table 8.1, which is applicable to both men and women. Keep in mind that the table may be off a bit for some people, such as a muscular football player who may look overweight on the charts or a person with normal weight who is out of shape and has a lot of fat. But this table is accurate for almost everyone and is in use around the world. In this chapter, we focus on serious undernourishment (BMI less than 18.5), as well as obesity (BMI greater than 29).

The more overweight someone is at a given height, the greater the risks to health. These risks are widespread and involve greatly increased prevalence of cardiovascular disease, diabetes, hypertension, stroke, gall bladder disease, respiratory disease, muscular skeletal problems, and hormone-related cancers (Flegal, Graubard, Williamson, & Gail, 2005; Henderson & Brownell, 2004; Must et al., 1999; Williams, Wake, Hesketh, Maher, & Waters, 2005). Obesity is included in this chapter because it is produced by the consumption of a greater number of calories than are expended in energy. The behavior that produces this distorted energy equation contradicts a common assumption—namely, that people with obesity do not necessarily eat more or exercise less than their lean counterparts. They do. Although the tendency to overeat and exercise too little unquestionably has a genetic component, as described later, the excessive eating at the core of the problem is the reason that obesity could be considered a disorder of eating.

We begin by examining bulimia nervosa and anorexia nervosa in some detail. We then briefly review obesity.

Bulimia Nervosa

You are probably familiar with bulimia nervosa from your own experience or a friend's. It is one of the most common psychological disorders on college campuses. Consider the case of Phoebe.

PHOEBE: Apparently Perfect

Phoebe was a classic all-American girl: popular, attractive, intelligent, and talented. By the time she was a senior in high school, she had accomplished a great deal. She was a class officer throughout high school, homecoming princess her sophomore year, and junior prom queen. She dated the captain of the football team. Phoebe had many talents, among them a beautiful singing voice and marked ability in ballet. Each year at Christmastime, her ballet company performed the *Nutcracker Suite,* and Phoebe attracted much attention with her poised performance in a lead role. She played on several of the school athletic teams. Phoebe maintained an A-minus average, was considered a model student, and was headed for a top-ranked university.

But Phoebe had a secret: She was haunted by her belief that she was fat and ugly. Every single bite of food that she put in her mouth was, in her mind, another step down the inexorable path that led to the end of her success and popularity. Phoebe had been concerned about her weight since she was 11. Ever the perfectionist, she began regulating her eating in junior high school. She would skip breakfast (over the protestations of her mother), eat a small bowl of pretzels at noon, and allow herself one half of whatever she was served for dinner.

This behavior continued into high school, as Phoebe struggled to restrict her eating to occasional binges on junk food. Sometimes she stuck her fingers down her throat after a binge (she even tried a toothbrush once), but this tactic was unsuccessful. During her sophomore year in high school, Phoebe reached her full adult height of 5 feet 2 inches and weighed 110 pounds; she continued to fluctuate between 105 and 110 pounds throughout high school. By the time she was a senior, Phoebe was obsessed with what she would eat and when. She used every bit of her willpower attempting to restrict her eating, but occasionally she failed. One day during the fall of her senior year, she came home after school and, alone in front of the television, she ate two big boxes of candy. Depressed, guilty, and desperate, she went to the bathroom and stuck her fingers further down her throat than she had ever before dared. She vomited. And she kept vomiting. Although so physically exhausted that she had to lie down for half an hour, Phoebe had never in her life felt such an overwhelming sense of relief from the anxiety, guilt, and tension that always accompanied her binges. She realized that she had gotten to eat all that candy and now her stomach was empty. It was the perfect solution to her problems.

TABLE 8.1   Body Mass Index (BMI) Table

Weight in Pounds

Height in Feet and Inches	120	130	140	150	160	170	180	190	200	210	220	230	240	250
4'6"	29	31	34	36	39	41	43	46	48	51	53	56	58	60
4'8"	27	29	31	34	36	38	40	43	45	47	49	52	54	56
4'10"	25	27	29	31	34	36	38	40	42	44	46	48	50	52
5'0"	23	25	27	29	31	33	35	37	39	41	43	45	47	49
5'2"	22	24	26	27	29	31	33	35	37	38	40	42	44	46
5'4"	21	22	24	26	28	29	31	33	34	36	38	40	41	43
5'6"	19	21	23	24	26	27	29	31	32	34	36	37	39	40
5'8"	18	20	21	23	24	26	27	29	30	32	34	35	37	38
5'10"	17	19	20	22	23	24	26	27	29	30	32	33	35	36
6'0"	16	18	19	20	22	23	24	26	27	28	30	31	33	34
6'2"	15	17	18	19	21	22	23	24	26	27	28	30	31	32
6'4"	15	16	17	18	20	21	22	23	24	26	27	28	29	30
6'6"	14	15	16	17	19	20	21	22	23	24	25	27	28	29
6'8"	13	14	15	17	18	19	20	21	22	23	24	25	26	28

Underweight Healthy weight Overweight Obese

Phoebe learned quickly what foods she could easily vomit. And she always drank lots of water. She began to restrict her eating even more. She ate almost nothing until after school, but then the results of her dreaming and scheming and planning all morning would be realized. Although the food sometimes varied, the routine did not. She might pick up a dozen doughnuts and a box of cookies. When she got home, she might make a bowl of popcorn.

And then she ate and ate, forcing down the doughnuts, cookies, and popcorn until her stomach hurt. Finally, with a mixture of revulsion and relief, she purged, forcing herself to vomit. When she was done, she stepped on the scale to make sure she had not gained any weight and then collapsed into bed and slept for about half an hour.

This routine went on for about 6 months, until April of her senior year in high school. By this time, Phoebe had lost much of her energy, and her schoolwork was deteriorating. Her teachers noticed this and saw that she looked bad. She was continually tired, her skin was broken out, and her face puffed up, particularly around her mouth. Her teachers and mother suspected that she might have an eating problem. When they confronted her, she was relieved her problem was finally out in the open.

In an effort to eliminate opportunities to binge and purge, her mother rearranged her schedule to be home in the afternoon when Phoebe got there; in general, her parents minimized the occasions when Phoebe was left alone, particularly after eating. This tactic worked for about a month. Mortally afraid of gaining weight and losing her popularity, Phoebe resumed her pattern, but she was now much better at hiding it. For 6 months, Phoebe binged and purged approximately 15 times a week.

When Phoebe went away to college that fall, things became more difficult. Now she had a roommate to contend with, and she was more determined than ever to keep her problem a secret. Although the student health service offered workshops and seminars on eating disorders for the freshman women, Phoebe knew that she could not break her cycle without the risk of gaining weight. To avoid the communal bathroom, she went to a deserted place behind a nearby building to vomit. Social life at college often involved drinking beer and eating fattening foods, so she vomited more often. Nevertheless, she gained 10 pounds and weighed 120 pounds. Gaining weight was common among freshmen, but her mother commented without thinking one day that Phoebe seemed to be putting on weight. This remark was devastating to Phoebe.

She kept her secret until the beginning of her sophomore year, when her world fell apart. One night, after drinking a lot of beer at a party, Phoebe and her friends went to Kentucky Fried Chicken. Although Phoebe did not truly binge because she was with friends, she did eat a lot of fried chicken, the most forbidden food on her list. Her guilt, anxiety, and tension increased to new heights. Her stomach throbbed with pain, but when she tried to vomit, her gag reflex seemed to be gone. Breaking into hysterics, she called her boyfriend and told him she was ready to kill herself. Her loud sobbing and crying attracted the attention of her friends in her dormitory, who attempted to comfort her. She confessed her problem to them. She also called her parents. At this point, Phoebe realized that her life was out of control and that she needed professional help.

Clinical Description

The hallmark of bulimia nervosa is eating a larger amount of food—typically, more junk food than fruits and vegetables—than most people would eat under similar circumstances (Fairburn & Cooper, 1993; Fairburn, Cooper, Shafran, & Wilson, in press). Patients with bulimia readily identify with this description, even though the actual caloric intake for binges varies significantly from person to person (Franko, Wonderlich, Little, & Herzog, 2004). Just as important as the *amount* of food eaten is that the eating is experienced as *out of control* (Fairburn, Cooper, & Cooper, 1986), a criterion that is an integral part of the definition of binge eating. Both criteria characterized Phoebe.

Another important criterion is that the individual attempts to *compensate* for the binge eating and potential weight gain, almost always by **purging techniques.** Techniques include self-induced vomiting immediately after eating, as in the case of Phoebe, and using laxatives (drugs that relieve constipation) and diuretics

---

DSM-IV-TR

DSM TABLE 8.1 Diagnostic Criteria for Bulimia Nervosa

A. Recurrent episodes of binge eating. An episode of binge eating is characterized by both of the following:
   1. Eating, in a discrete period of time (e.g., within any 2-hour period), an amount of food that is definitely larger than most people would eat during a similar period of time and under similar circumstances
   2. A sense of lack of control over eating during the episode (e.g., a feeling that one cannot stop eating or control what or how much one is eating)
B. Recurrent inappropriate compensatory behavior in order to prevent weight gain, such as self-induced vomiting; misuse of laxatives, diuretics or other medications; fasting; or excessive exercise.
C. The binge eating and inappropriate compensatory behaviors both occur, on average, at least twice a week for 3 months.
D. Self-evaluation is unduly influenced by body shape and weight.
E. The disturbance does not occur exclusively during episodes of anorexia nervosa.
Specify type:
   Purging type: During the current episode of bulimia nervosa, the person has regularly engaged in self-induced vomiting or the misuse of laxatives, diuretics, or enemas
   Nonpurging type: During the current episode of bulimia nervosa, the person has used other inappropriate compensatory behaviors, such as fasting or exercise, but has not regularly engaged in self-induced vomiting or the misuse of laxatives, diuretics, or enemas

Source: Reprinted, with permission, from American Psychiatric Association. (2000). *Diagnostic and statistical manual of mental disorders* (4th ed., text revision). Washington, DC: Author, © 2000 American Psychiatric Association

(drugs that result in loss of fluids through greatly increased frequency of urination). Some people use both methods; others attempt to compensate in other ways. Some exercise excessively (although rigorous exercising is more usually a characteristic of anorexia nervosa; Davis et al., 1997, found that 57% of a group of patients with bulimia nervosa exercised excessively but fully 81% of a group with anorexia did). Others fast for long periods between binges. Bulimia nervosa is subtyped in DSM-IV-TR into *purging type* (e.g., vomiting, laxatives, or diuretics) or *nonpurging type* (e.g., exercise and/or fasting). But the nonpurging type has turned out to be quite rare, accounting for only 6% to 8% of patients with bulimia (Hay & Fairburn, 1998; Striegel-Moore et al., 2001). Furthermore, these studies found little evidence of any differences between purging and nonpurging types of bulimia, nor were any differences evident in severity of psychopathology, frequency of binge episodes, or prevalence of major depression and panic disorder, raising questions about whether this is a useful subtype (Franko et al., 2004; Tobin, Griffing, & Griffing, 1997).

Purging is not a particularly efficient method of reducing caloric intake. Vomiting reduces approximately 50% of the calories just consumed, less if it is delayed (Kaye, Weltzin, Hsu, McConaha, & Bolton, 1993); laxatives and related procedures have little effect, acting, as they do, so long after the binge.

One of the more important additions to the DSM-IV criteria is the specification of a psychological characteristic clearly present in Phoebe. Despite her accomplishments and success, she felt her continuing popularity and self-esteem would largely be determined by the weight and shape of her body. Garfinkel (1992) noted that, of 107 women seeking treatment for bulimia nervosa, only 3% did not share this attitude. Recent investigations confirm the construct validity of the diagnostic category of bulimia nervosa, suggesting that the major features of the disorder (bingeing, purging, overconcern with body shape, and so on) "cluster together" in someone with this problem (Bulik, Sullivan, & Kendler, 2000; Fairburn, Stice, et al., 2003; Franko et al., 2004; Gleaves, Lowe, Snow, Green, & Murphy-Eberenz, 2000; Keel, Mitchell, Miller, Davis, & Crow, 2000).

■ Medical Consequences

Chronic bulimia with purging has a number of medical consequences (Pomeroy, 2004). One is salivary gland enlargement caused by repeated vomiting, which gives the face a chubby appearance. This was noticeable with Phoebe. Repeated vomiting also may erode the dental enamel on the inner surface of the front teeth. More important, continued vomiting may upset the chemical balance of bodily fluids, including sodium and potassium levels. This condition, called an *electrolyte imbalance,* can result in serious medical complications if unattended, including cardiac arrhythmia (disrupted heartbeat), seizures, and renal (kidney) failure, all of which can be fatal. Normalization of eating habits will quickly reverse the imbalance. Intestinal problems resulting from laxative abuse are also potentially serious; they can include severe constipation or permanent colon damage. Finally, some individuals with bulimia have marked calluses on their fingers or the backs of their hands caused by the friction of contact with the teeth and throat when repeatedly sticking their fingers down their throat to stimulate the gag reflex.

■ Associated Psychological Disorders

An individual with bulimia usually presents with additional psychological disorders, particularly anxiety and mood disorders. We compared 20 patients with bulimia nervosa to 20 individuals with panic disorder and another 20 with social phobia (Schwalberg, Barlow, Alger, & Howard, 1992). The most striking finding was that fully 75% of the patients with bulimia also presented with an anxiety disorder such as social phobia or generalized anxiety disorder. This finding was close to the results from the recent definitive national survey on the prevalence of eating disorders and associated psychological disorders, where 80.6 % of individuals with bulimia had an anxiety disorder at some point during their lives (Hudson et al., 2007). Patients with anxiety disorders in the study by Schwalberg and colleagues (1992), on the other hand, did not necessarily have an elevated rate of eating disorders. Mood disorders, particularly depression, also commonly co-occur with bulimia, with about 20% of bulimic patients meeting criteria for a mood disorder when interviewed and between 50% and 70% meeting criteria at some point during the course of their disorder (Agras, 2001; Hudson et al., 2007). For a number of years, one prominent theory suggested that eating disorders are simply a way of expressing depression. But most evidence indicates that depression *follows* bulimia and may be a reaction to it (Brownell & Fairburn, 1995; Hsu, 1990). Finally, substance abuse commonly accompanies bulimia nervosa. For example, Kendler and colleagues (1991) surveyed more than 2,000 twins who were not necessarily seeking treatment and found an elevated rate of alcoholism (15.5%) in subjects with bulimia. Keel and colleagues (2003) reported that 33% of their combined sample of individuals with bulimia, anorexia, or both also met criteria for substance abuse, including both alcohol and drugs. Hudson and colleagues (2007) reported similar figures: 36.8% of individuals with bulimia and 27% of individuals with anorexia. More recently, Wade, Bulik, Prescott, and Kendler (2004) in a twin study found that shared risk factors of novelty seeking and emotional instability accounted for the high rates of comorbidity between bulimia and anxiety and substance use disorder, although these factors differed somewhat as a function of biological sex. In summary, bulimia seems strongly related to anxiety disorders and somewhat less so to mood and substance use disorders. Underlying traits of emotional instability and novelty seeking in these individuals may account for these patterns of comorbidity.

Anorexia Nervosa

Like Phoebe, the overwhelming majority of individuals with bulimia are within 10% of their normal weight (Hsu, 1990). In contrast, individuals with anorexia nervosa (which literally means a "nervous loss of appetite," an incorrect definition because appetite often remains healthy) differ in one important way from individuals with bulimia. They are so successful at losing weight that they put their lives in considerable danger. Both anorexia and bulimia are characterized by a morbid fear of gaining weight and losing control over eating. The major difference seems to be whether the individual is successful at losing weight. People with anorexia are proud of both their diets and their extraordinary control. People with bulimia are ashamed of both the problem and their lack of control (Brownell & Fairburn, 1995). Consider the case of Julie.

JULIE: The Thinner, the Better

Julie was 17 years old when she first came for help. If you looked hard enough past her sunken eyes and pasty skin, you could see that she had once been attractive. But at present, she looked emaciated and unwell. Eighteen months earlier she had been overweight, weighing 140 pounds at 5 feet 1 inch. Her mother, a well-meaning but overbearing and demanding woman, nagged Julie incessantly about her appearance. Her friends were kinder but no less relentless. Julie, who had never had a date, was told by a friend she was cute and would have no trouble getting dates if she lost some weight. So she did! After many previous unsuccessful attempts, she was determined to succeed this time.

After several weeks on a strict diet, Julie noticed she was losing weight. She felt a control and mastery that she had never known before. It wasn't long before she received positive comments, not only from her friends but also from her mother. Julie began to feel good about herself. The difficulty was that she was losing weight too fast. She stopped menstruating. But now nothing could stop her from dieting. By the time she reached our clinic, she weighed 75 pounds but she thought she looked fine and, perhaps, could even stand to lose a bit more weight. Her parents had just begun to worry about her. Julie did not initially seek treatment for her eating behavior. Rather, she had developed a numbness in her left lower leg and a left foot drop that a neurologist determined was caused by peritoneal nerve paralysis believed to be related to inadequate nutrition. The neurologist referred her to our clinic.

Like most people with anorexia, Julie said she probably should put on a little weight, but she didn't mean it. She thought she looked fine, but she had "lost all taste for food," a report that may not have been true because most people with anorexia crave food at least some of the time but control their cravings. Nevertheless, she was participating in most of her usual activities and continued to do extremely well in school and in her extracurricular pursuits. Her parents were happy to buy her most of the workout videotapes available, and she began doing one every day, and then two. When her parents suggested she was exercising enough, perhaps too much, she worked out when no one was around. After every meal, she exercised with a workout tape until, in her mind, she burned up all the calories she had just taken in.

The tragic consequences of anorexia are well known in certain celebrities because their serious illnesses or deaths make headlines several times a year. In February 2007, 21-year-old Brazilian model Ana Carolina Reston died, weighing 88 pounds. At 5 feet 8 inches, she had a BMI of 13.4 (16 is considered starvation). In 2006, Spain caused a storm in the fashion world by banning models with a BMI less than 18 from its top fashion show (30% of models were turned away). Other countries are considering similar guidelines.

©Reuters/David Gray/Landov

In November 2006, Ana Carolina Reston, a 5-foot-8-inch Brazilian model suffering from anorexia, died weighing 88 pounds.

■ Clinical Description

Anorexia nervosa is less common than bulimia, but there is a great deal of overlap. For example, many individuals with bulimia have a history of anorexia; that is, they once used fasting to reduce their body weight below desirable levels (Fairburn et al., in press; Fairburn, Welch, Doll, Davies, & O'Connor, 1997).

Although decreased body weight is the most notable feature of anorexia nervosa, it is not the core of the disorder. Many people lose weight because of a medical condition, but people with an-

DSM-IV-TR

DSM TABLE 8.2 Diagnostic Criteria for Anorexia Nervosa

A. Refusal to maintain body weight at or above a minimally normal weight for age and height (e.g., weight loss leading to maintenance of body weight less than 85% of that expected or failure to make expected weight gain during period of growth, leading to body weight less than 85% of that expected).

B. Intense fear of gaining weight or becoming fat, even though underweight.

C. Disturbance in the way in which one's body weight or shape is experienced; undue influence of body weight or shape on self-evaluation, or denial of the seriousness of the current low body weight.

D. In post-menarcheal females, amenorrhea, that is, the absence of at least three consecutive menstrual cycles. (A woman is considered to have amenorrhea if her periods occur only following hormone, e.g., estrogen, administration.)

Specify type:

Restricting type: During the episode of anorexia nervosa, the person does not regularly engage in binge eating or purging behavior (i.e., self-induced vomiting or the misuse of laxatives or diuretics).

Binge-eating/purging type: During the episode of anorexia nervosa, the person has regularly engaged in binge eating or purging behavior (i.e., self-induced vomiting or the misuse of laxatives or diuretics).

Source: Reprinted, with permission, from American Psychiatric Association. (2000). *Diagnostic and statistical manual of mental disorders* (4th ed., text revision). Washington, DC: Author. © 2000 American Psychiatric Association

orexia have an intense fear of obesity and relentlessly pursue thinness (Fairburn et al., in press; Hsu, 1990; Schlundt & Johnson, 1990; Stice, Cameron, Killen, Hayward, & Taylor, 1999). As with Julie, the disorder most commonly begins in an adolescent who is overweight or who perceives herself to be. She then starts a diet that escalates into an obsessive preoccupation with being thin. As we noted, severe, almost punishing exercise is common, as with Julie (Davis et al., 1997). Dramatic weight loss is achieved through severe caloric restriction or by combining caloric restriction and purging.

DSM-IV specifies two subtypes of anorexia nervosa. In the *restricting type,* individuals diet to limit calorie intake; in the *binge-eating–purging type,* they rely on purging. Unlike individuals with bulimia, binge-eating–purging anorexics binge on relatively small amounts of food and purge more consistently, in some cases each time they eat. Approximately half the individuals who meet criteria for anorexia engage in binge eating and purging (Agras, 1987; Fairburn et al., in press; Garfinkel, Moldofsky, & Garner, 1979). Prospective data collected over 8 years on 136 individuals with anorexia reveal few differences between these two subtypes on severity of symptoms or personality (Eddy et al., 2002). At that time, fully 62% of the restricting subtype had begun bingeing or purging. Thus, subtyping may not be useful in predicting the future course of the disorder but rather may reflect a certain phase or stage of anorexia.

Individuals with anorexia are never satisfied with their weight loss. Staying the same weight from one day to the next or gaining any weight is likely to cause intense panic, anxiety, and depression. Only continued weight loss every day for weeks on end is satisfac-

tory. Although DSM-IV criteria specify body weight 15% below that expected, the average is approximately 25% to 30% below normal by the time treatment is sought (Hsu, 1990). Another key criterion of anorexia is a marked disturbance in body image. When Julie looked at herself in the mirror, she saw something different from what others saw. They saw an emaciated, sickly, frail girl in the throes of semistarvation. Julie saw a girl who needed to lose at least a few pounds from some parts of her body. For Julie, her face and buttocks were the problems. Other girls might focus on other parts, such as the arms or legs or stomach.

After seeing numerous doctors, people like Julie become good at mouthing what others expect to hear. They may agree they are underweight and need to gain a few pounds—but they don't believe it. Question further and they will tell you the girl in the mirror is fat. Therefore, individuals with anorexia seldom seek treatment on their own. Usually pressure from somebody in the family leads to the initial visit, as in Julie's case (Agras, 1987; Sibley & Blinder, 1988). Perhaps as a demonstration of absolute control over their eating, some anorexic individuals show increased interest in cooking and food. Some have become expert chefs, preparing all food for the family. Others hoard food in their rooms, looking at it occasionally.

■ Medical Consequences

One common medical complication of anorexia nervosa is cessation of menstruation (amenorrhea), which also occurs relatively often in bulimia (Crow, Thuras, Keel, & Mitchell, 2002). This feature can be an objective physical index of the degree of food restriction, but is inconsistent because it does not occur in all cases (Franko et al., 2004). Because of this inconsistency, amenorrhea is likely to be dropped as a diagnostic criteria in DSM-V (Fairburn et al., in press; Mitchell, Cook-Myers, & Wonderlich, 2005). Although some studies have demonstrated a strong correlation between ovulation and resulting menstruation and weight (Fairburn, Cooper, Doll, & Welch, 1999; Pirke, Schweiger, & Fichter, 1987), overwhelming evidence indicates that alterations in endocrine levels resulting in amenorrhea are a consequence of semistarvation rather than a cause. Other medical signs and symptoms of anorexia include dry skin, brittle hair or nails, and sensitivity to or intolerance of cold temperatures. Also, it is relatively common to see *lanugo,* downy hair on the limbs and cheeks. Cardiovascular problems, such as chronically low blood pressure and heart rate, can also result. If vomiting is part of the anorexia, electrolyte imbalance and resulting cardiac and kidney problems can result, as in bulimia.

■ Associated Psychological Disorders

As with bulimia nervosa, anxiety disorders and mood disorders are often present in individuals with anorexia (Agras, 2001; Kaye et al., 1993; Vitiello & Lederhendler, 2000), with Agras noting current depression in 33% of the cases and rates of depression occurring at some point during their lives in as many as 60% of cases. Interestingly, one anxiety disorder that seems to co-occur often with anorexia is obsessive-compulsive disorder (OCD) (see Chapter 5; Keel et al., 2004). In anorexia, unpleasant thoughts are focused on gaining weight, and individuals engage in a variety of behaviors, some of them ritualistic, to rid themselves of such

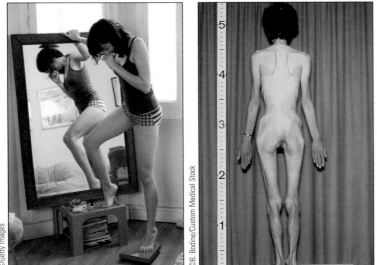

These women are at different stages of anorexia.

thoughts. Future research will determine whether anorexia and OCD are truly similar or simply resemble each other. Substance abuse is also common in individuals with anorexia nervosa (Keel et al., 2003; Wilson, 1993), and, in conjunction with anorexia, is a strong predictor of mortality, particularly by suicide.

Binge-Eating Disorder

Beginning in the 1990s, research focused on a group of individuals who experience marked distress because of binge eating but do *not* engage in extreme compensatory behaviors and therefore cannot be diagnosed with bulimia (Castonguay, Eldredge, & Agras, 1995; Fairburn et al., 1998; Spitzer et al., 1991). These individuals have **binge-eating disorder (BED).** Currently, BED is in the appendix of DSM-IV-TR as a potential new disorder requiring further study. Many investigators are beginning to conclude that it should be included as a full-fledged disorder in future editions of the DSM, or at least combined with existing disorders (Hudson et al., 2006). Bulik and colleagues (2000) studied anorectic and bulimic behavior in 2,163 female twins. They suggested there is enough evidence to support BED as a disorder in DSM-V. Castonguay and colleagues (1995), on the other hand, suggest that bulimia and BED could be combined because bingeing is a prominent feature of both disorders; individuals could then be subtyped as to whether they purge or not and whether they are obese or not. Further research will determine whether this designation would be useful (Fairburn, Hay, & Welch, 1993; Fairburn & Wilson, 1993). But this "transdiagnostic" approach to classifying eating disorders is gaining favor (Fairburn et al., in press). Individuals who meet preliminary criteria for BED are often found in weight-control programs. For example, Brody, Walsh, and Devlin (1994) studied mildly obese subjects in a weight-control program and identified 18.8% who met criteria for BED. In other programs, with the full range of obese subjects, close to 30% met criteria (see, for example, Spitzer et al., 1993). But Hudson and colleagues (2006) concluded that BED is a disorder caused by a separate set of factors from obesity without BED and is associated

with more severe obesity. Thus, this condition may require a different set of interventions than obesity without BED. The general consensus is that about 20% of obese individuals in weight-loss programs engage in binge eating, with the number rising to approximately 50% among candidates for bariatric surgery (surgery to correct severe or morbid obesity). Fairburn, Cooper, Doll, Norman, and O'Connor (2000), in a notable study, identified 48 individuals with BED and were able to prospectively follow 40 of them for 5 years. The prognosis was relatively good for this group, with only 18% retaining the full diagnostic criteria for BED at a 5-year follow-up. The percentage of this group who were obese, however, increased from 21% to 39%.

About half try dieting before bingeing, and half start with bingeing and then attempt to diet (Abbott et al., 1998); those who begin bingeing first become more severely affected and more likely to have additional disorders (Spurrell, Wilfley, Tanofsky, & Brownell, 1997). It's also increasingly clear that individuals with BED have some of the same concerns about shape and weight as people with anorexia and bulimia (Eldredge & Agras, 1996; Fairburn et al., in press; Hrabosky, Masheb, White, & Grilo, 2007; Wilfley, Schwartz, Spurrell, & Fairburn, 2000). It seems that approximately 33% binge to alleviate "bad moods" or negative affect (see, for example, Grilo, Masheb, & Wilson, 2001; Stice, Akutagawa, Gaggar, & Agras, 2000; Stice et al., 2001). These individuals are more psychologically disturbed than the 67% who represent a pure dieting subtype and do not use bingeing to regulate mood (Grilo et al., 2001).

Statistics

Clear cases of bulimia have been described for thousands of years (Parry-Jones & Parry-Jones, 2002), but bulimia nervosa was recognized as a distinct psychological disorder only in the 1970s (Boskind-Lodahl, 1976; Russell, 1979). Therefore, information on prevalence has been acquired relatively recently.

Among those who present for treatment, the overwhelming majority (90% to 95%) of individuals with bulimia are women; most are white and middle to upper-middle class. Males with bulimia have a slightly later age of onset, and a large minority are predominantly gay males or bisexual (Rothblum, 2002). For example, Carlat, Camargo, and Herzog (1997) accumulated information on 135 male patients with eating disorders who were seen over 13 years and found that 42% were either gay males or bisexual. Male athletes in sports that require weight regulation, such as wrestling, are another large group of males with eating disorders (Ricciardelli & McCabe, 2004). During 1998, stories were widely published about the deaths of three wrestlers from complications of eating disorders. Interestingly, the gender imbalance in bulimia was not always present. Historians of psychopathology note that for hundreds of years the vast majority of (unsystematically) recorded cases were male (Parry-Jones & Parry-Jones, 1994, 2002). Because women with bulimia are more common today, most of our examples are women.

Schlundt and Johnson (1990), summarizing a large number of surveys, suggest that between 6% and 8% of young women, especially on college campuses, meet criteria for bulimia nervosa.

Gross and Rosen (1988) reported that as many as 9% of high school girls would meet criteria, although only about 2% were purging at that age. Most people who seek treatment are in the purging subtype (Fairburn et al., in press).

A somewhat different view of the prevalence of bulimia comes from studies of the population rather than of specific groups of adolescents, with the most definitive study appearing in 2007 (Hudson et al., 2007). These results from the national comorbidity survey reflect lifetime and 12-month prevalence, not only for the three major eating disorders described here but also for "subthreshold" BED, where binge eating occurred at a high-enough frequency but some additional criteria, such as "marked distress" regarding the binge eating, was not required. Therefore, it did not meet the diagnostic "threshold" for BED. In addition, only 3-months duration was required for BED (or subthreshold BED), rather than the 6 months required in DSM-IV-TR. Thus, the results for BED may be slightly higher than if the DSM-IV 6-month criteria were used. Finally, if binge eating occurred at least twice a week for 3 months, even if it was just a symptom of the four other disorders in Table 8.2 rather than a separate condition, the case was listed under "Any binge eating." This latter category provides an overall picture of the prevalence of binge eating. These data are all presented in Table 8.2. As you can see, lifetime prevalence was consistently two to three times greater for females, with the exception of subthreshold BED. This sex ratio reflects a somewhat higher proportion of males than found in other samples, but because there are so few males in any study of

eating disorders, these results tend to be unstable. No 12-month cases of anorexia were found in this sample.

The median age of onset for all disorders occurred in a narrow range of 18–21 years. For anorexia, this age of onset was fairly consistent, with younger cases tending to begin at 15, but it was more common for cases of bulimia to begin as early as 10, as it did for Phoebe.

Once bulimia develops, it tends to be chronic if untreated (Fairburn et al., 2000; Fairburn, Stice, et al., 2003; Hudson et al., 2007; Keel & Mitchell, 1997); one study shows the "drive for thinness" and accompanying symptoms still present in a group of women 10 years after diagnosis (Joiner, Heatherton, & Keel, 1997). In an important study of the course of bulimia, referred to earlier, Fairburn and colleagues (2000) identified a group of 102 females with bulimia nervosa and followed 92 of them prospectively for 5 years. About a third improved to the point where they no longer met diagnostic criteria each year, but another third who had improved previously relapsed. Between 50% and 67% exhibited serious eating disorder symptoms at the end of each year of the 5-year study, indicating this disorder has a relatively poor prognosis. In a follow-up study, Fairburn and Stice (2003) reported that the strongest predictors of persistent bulimia were a history of childhood obesity and a continuing overemphasis on the importance of being thin. In addition, individuals tend to retain their bulimic symptoms, instead of shifting to symptoms of other eating disorders, which provides further validation for bulimia nervosa as a diagnostic category (Keel et al., 2000).

Once anorexia develops, its course seems chronic—although not so chronic as bulimia, based on data from Hudson and colleagues (2007), particularly if it is caught early and treated. But individuals with anorexia tend to maintain a low BMI over a long period, along with distorted perceptions of shape and weight, indicating that even if they no longer meet criteria for anorexia they continue to restrict their eating (Fairburn et al., in press). Perhaps for this reason, anorexia is thought to be more resistant to treatment than bulimia, based on clinical studies (Herzog et al., 1999; Vitiello & Lederhendler, 2000).

■ Cross-Cultural Considerations

We have already discussed the highly culturally specific nature of anorexia and bulimia. A particularly striking finding is that these disorders develop in immigrants who have recently moved to Western countries (Nasser, 1988). One of the more interesting studies is Nasser's 1986 survey of 50 Egyptian women in London universities and 60 Egyptian women in Cairo universities. There were no instances of eating disorders in Cairo, but 12% of the Egyptian women in England had developed eating disorders. Mumford, Whitehouse, and Platts (1991) found the same result with Asian women living in the United States.

Later, we discuss the increase in obesity among recent immigrant groups to the United States that might contribute to these findings (Goel, McCarthy, Phillips, & Wee, 2004). The prevalence of eating disorders varies among most North American minority populations, including African Americans, Hispanics, Native Americans, and Asians. Compared to Caucasians, the prevalence of eating disorders is lower among African American and Asian American females, equally common among Hispanic

TABLE 8.2 Lifetime and 12-Month Prevalence Estimates of DSM-IV-TR Eating Disorders and Related Problems			
	Male	**Female**	**Total**
	%	%	%
I. Lifetime prevalence			
Anorexia nervosa	0.3	0.9	0.6
Bulimia nervosa	0.5	1.5	1.0
Binge-eating disorder	2.0	3.5	2.8
Subthreshold binge-eating disorder	1.9	0.6	1.2
Any binge eating	4.0	4.9	4.5
II. 12-month prevalence*			
Bulimia nervosa	0.1	0.5	0.3
Binge-eating disorder	0.8	1.6	1.2
Subthreshold binge-eating disorder	0.8	0.4	0.6
Any binge eating	1.7	2.5	2.1
(n) Number of subjects	(1,220)	(1,760)	(2,980)

*None of the respondents met criteria for 12-month anorexia nervosa.

Source: From Hudson and colleagues, (2007). The prevalence and correlates of eating disorders in the national comorbidity survey replication. *Biological Psychiatry,* 61, 348–358. © Society for Biological Psychiatry.

females, and more common among Native Americans (Crago, Shisslak, & Estes, 1997). Generally, surveys reveal that African American adolescent girls have less body dissatisfaction, fewer weight concerns, a positive self-image, and perceive themselves to be thinner than they are compared to Caucasian adolescent girls (Celio, Zabinski, & Wilfley, 2002). Another good example is a recent study on the small relatively isolated Caribbean island of Curacao in the Netherlands Antilles, where the population is only approximately 150,000 (Hoek et al., 2005). Nevertheless, the incidence of anorexia from 1995 to 1998 was zero among the majority black population but approached levels observed in the Netherlands and United States for the minority white and mixed population. Striegel-Moore and colleagues (2003) surveyed 985 white women and 1,061 black women who had participated in a

10-year government study on growth and health and who were now 21 years old on average. The number in each group who developed anorexia, bulimia, or BED during that 10-year period is presented in ■ Figure 8.1. Major risk factors for eating disorders in all groups include overweight, higher social class, and acculturation to the majority (Crago et al., 1997; Grabe & Hyde, 2006; Raich et al., 1992; Smith & Krejci, 1991; Wilfley & Rodin, 2002). Greenberg and LaPorte (1996) observed in an experiment that young white males preferred somewhat thinner figures in women than African American males, which may contribute to the somewhat lower incidence of eating disorders in African American women.

There is a relatively high incidence of purging behavior in some minority groups. In most cases, the purging seems to be as-

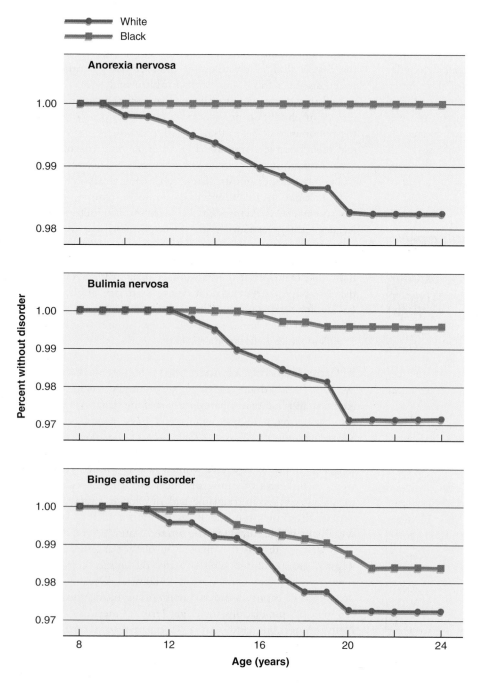

■ **FIGURE 8.1** Time to onset over 10 years of anorexia nervosa, bulimia nervosa, and BED for 2,046 white and black women, age 19–24 years, who ever met the DSM-IV criteria for each eating disorder. (Reprinted, with permission, from Striegel-Moore, R. H., Dohm, F. A., Kraemer, H. C., Taylor, C. B., Daniels, S., Crawford, P. B., & Schreiber, G. B., 2003. Eating disorders in white and black women. *American Journal of Psychiatry, 160*(7), 1,329, © 2003 American Psychiatric Press.)

©Getty Images

Anorexia seldom occurs among North American black women.

sociated with obesity. Rosen and colleagues (1988) found widespread purging and related behaviors in a group of American Indian Chippewa women. Among this group, 74% had dieted and 55% had used harmful weight-loss techniques such as fasting or purging; 12% had vomited and 6% reported use of laxatives or diuretics.

One culturally determined difference in criteria for eating disorders has been reported by Lee and colleagues (1991). In traditional Chinese cultures, it has been widely assumed that being slightly plump is highly valued, with ideals of beauty focused on the face rather than the body. Therefore, in this group, acne was more often reported as a precipitant for anorexia nervosa than a fear of being fat, and body image disturbance is rare (Lee, Hsu, & Wing, 1992). Patients said they refused to eat because of feelings of fullness or pain, although it is possible they related food intake to their skin conditions. Beyond that, they met all criteria for anorexia. More recent studies, however, call into question this ideal (Kawamura, 2002). Leung, Lam, and Sze (2001) analyzed data from the Miss Hong Kong beauty pageant from 1975 to 1999 and found that winners were taller and thinner than the average Chinese women, with a "curvaceous" narrow waist and full-hip body shape. They note that this ideal matches depictions of beauty in classical Chinese literature, and it challenges the notion that plumpness is valued, at least in Hong Kong.

In Japan, the prevalence of anorexia nervosa among teenage girls is still lower than the rate in North America, but, as mentioned previously, it seems to be increasing. The need to be thin or the fear of becoming overweight has not been as important in

Japanese culture as it is in North America, although this may be changing as cultures around the world become more westernized (Kawamura, 2002). Body image distortion and denial that a problem exists are clearly present in patients who have the disorder (Ritenbaugh, Shisslak, Teufel, Leonard-Green, & Prince, 1994).

In conclusion, anorexia and bulimia are relatively homogeneous and, until recently, were overwhelmingly associated with Western cultures. In addition, the frequency and pattern of occurrence among minority Western cultures differs somewhat but is associated with closer identification with Caucasian middle-class values.

■ Developmental Considerations

Because the overwhelming majority of cases begin in adolescence, it is clear that anorexia and bulimia are strongly related to development (Smith, Simmons, Flory, Annus, & Hill, 2007). As pointed out by Striegel-Moore, Silberstein, and Rodin (1986) and Attie and Brooks-Gunn (1995), differential patterns of physical development in girls and boys interact with cultural influences to create eating disorders. After puberty, girls gain weight primarily in fat tissue, whereas boys develop muscle and lean tissue. As the ideal look in Western countries is tall and muscular for men and thin and prepubertal for women, physical development brings boys closer to the ideal and takes girls further away.

Eating disorders, particularly anorexia nervosa, occasionally occur in children under the age of 11. In those rare cases of young children developing anorexia, they are likely to restrict fluid intake, as well as food intake, perhaps not understanding the difference (Gislason, 1988). This is particularly dangerous. Concerns about weight are somewhat less common in young children. Nevertheless, negative attitude toward being overweight emerges as early as 3 years of age, and more than half of girls age 6–8 would like to be thinner (Striegel-Moore & Franko, 2002). By 9 years of age, 20% of girls reported trying to lose weight, and by 14, 40% were trying to lose weight (Field et al., 1999).

Both bulimia and anorexia can occur in later years, particularly after the age of 55. Hsu and Zimmer (1988) reported that most of these individuals had had an eating disorder for decades with little change in their behavior. However, in a few cases onset did not occur until later years, and it is not yet clear what factors were involved. Generally, concerns with body image decrease with age (Tiggemann & Lynch, 2001; Whitbourne & Skultety, 2002).

CONCEPT CHECK 8.1

Check your understanding of eating disorders by identifying the proper disorder in the following scenarios: (a) bulimia nervosa, (b) anorexia nervosa, and (c) binge-eating disorder.

1. Jason has been having episodes lately when he eats prodigious amounts of food. He's been putting on a lot of weight because of it. _____
2. I noticed Elena eating a whole pie, a cake, and two bags of potato chips the other day when she didn't know I

(continued)

CONCEPT CHECK 8.1

(continued)

was there. She ran to the bathroom when she was finished and it sounded like she was vomiting. This disorder can lead to an electrolyte imbalance, resulting in serious medical problems. _____

3. Pam eats large quantities of food in a short time. She then takes laxatives and exercises for long periods to prevent weight gain. She has been doing this almost daily for several months and feels she will become worthless and ugly if she gains even an ounce. _____

4. Kirsten has lost several pounds and now weighs less than 90 pounds. She eats only a small portion of the food her mother serves her and fears that intake above her current 500 calories daily will make her fat. Since losing the weight, Kirsten has stopped having periods. She sees a fat person in the mirror. _____

CAUSES OF EATING DISORDERS

As with all disorders discussed in this book, biological, psychological, and social factors contribute to the development of these serious eating disorders, but the evidence is increasingly clear that the most dramatic factors are social and cultural.

Social Dimensions

Remember that anorexia and bulimia are the most culturally specific psychological disorders yet identified. What drives so many young people into a punishing and life-threatening routine of semistarvation or purging? For many young Western women, looking good is more important than being healthy. For young females in middle- to upper-class competitive environments, self-worth, happiness, and success are largely determined by body measurements and percentage of body fat, factors that have little or no correlation with personal happiness and success in the long run. The cultural imperative for thinness directly results in dieting, the first dangerous step down the slippery slope to anorexia and bulimia.

What makes the modern emphasis on thinness in women even more puzzling is that standards of desirable body sizes change much like fashion styles in clothes, if not as quickly (Cash & Pruzinsky, 2002). Several groups of investigators have documented this phenomenon in some interesting ways over the years. Garner, Garfinkel, Schwartz, and Thompson (1980) collected data from *Playboy* magazine centerfolds and from Miss America pageants from 1959 to 1978. During this period, both *Playboy* centerfolds and Miss America contestants became significantly thinner. Bust and hip measurements became smaller, although waists became somewhat larger, suggesting a change in what is considered desirable in the *shape* of the body in addition to weight. The preferred shape during the 1960s and 1970s was thinner and more tubular than before (Agras & Kirkley, 1986). Wiseman, Gray, Mosimann, and Ahrens (1992) updated the research, collecting

data from 1979 to 1988, and reported that 69% of the *Playboy* centerfolds and 60% of the Miss America contestants weighed 15% or more below normal for their age and height, meeting one of the criteria for anorexia. More recently, Rubinstein and Caballero (2000) compiled data on weight and height from winners of Miss America pageants from 1922 through 1999. Note that since the 1970s most Miss Americas would be considered undernourished. Just as important, when Wiseman and colleagues (1992) counted diet and exercise articles in six women's magazines from 1959 to 1988, they found a significant increase in both, with articles on exercise increasing dramatically during the 1980s, surpassing the number on diet.

Levine and Smolak (1996) refer to "the glorification of slenderness" in magazines and on television, where most females are thinner than average American women. Because overweight men are two to five times more common as television characters than overweight women, the message from the media to be thin is clearly aimed at women. Stice, Schupak-Neuberg, Shaw, and Stein (1994) established a strong relationship between amount of media exposure and symptoms of eating disorders in college women. In another study, girls who watched 8 or more hours of television per week reported significantly greater body dissatisfaction than girls who watched less television (Gonzalez-Lavin & Smolak, 1995; Levine & Smolak, 1996). An analysis of prime-time situation comedies revealed that 12% of female characters were dieting and many were making disparaging comments about their body image (Tiggemann, 2002). Finally, Thompson and Stice (2001) found that risk for developing eating disorders was directly related to the extent to which women internalize or "buy in" to the media messages and images glorifying thinness, a finding recently confirmed by Cafri, Yamamiya, Brannick, and Thompson (2005). Fortunately, women's investment in an unrealistically thin body image has begun to lessen in the last several years (Cash, Morrow, Hrabosky, & Perry, 2004).

The problem with today's standards is that they are increasingly difficult to achieve, because the size and weight of the average woman has increased over the years with improved nutrition; there is also a general increase in size throughout history (Brownell, 1991; Brownell & Rodin, 1994). Whatever the cause, the collision between our culture and our physiology (Brownell, 1991; Brownell & Fairburn, 1995) has had some negative effects, one of which is that women became dissatisfied with their bodies.

A second clear effect is the dramatic increase, especially among women, in dieting and exercise to achieve what may be an impossible goal. Look at the increase in dieting since the 1950s. Dwyer, Feldman, Seltzer, and Mayer reported in 1969 that more than 80% of female

Kelly Brownell documented the collision between culture and physiology that results in overwhelming pressure to be thinner.

Changing concepts of ideal weight are evident in a 17th-century painting by Peter Paul Rubens and in a photograph of a current fashion model.

high school seniors wished to lose weight and that 30% were diet-ing. Among their male counterparts, fewer than 20% wished to lose weight and only 6% were dieting. More recently, Hunnicutt and Newman (1993) surveyed a national sample of 3,632 eighth- and tenth-grade students and found that 60.6% of females and 28.4% of males were dieting. Although these studies are not di-rectly comparable, younger girls typically diet less than older girls, which suggests the increase is even more dramatic.

Fallon and Rozin (1985), studying male and female under-graduates, found that men rated their current size, their ideal size, and the size they figured would be most attractive to the opposite sex as approximately equal; indeed, they rated their ideal body weight as *heavier* than the weight females thought most attractive in men (see ■ Figure 8.2). Women, however, rated their current figures as much heavier than what they judged the most attractive, which in turn, was rated as heavier than what they thought was

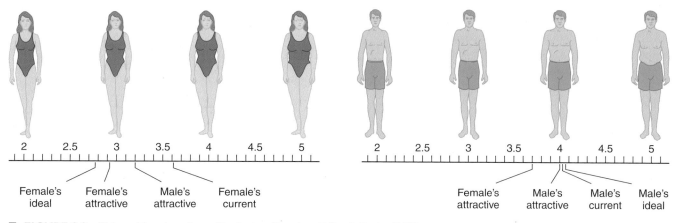

■ **FIGURE 8.2** Male and female ratings of body size. (Based on Fallon & Rozin, 1985.)

"Basically . . . I don't want to eat because it seems like, as soon as I eat, I just gain weight, get fat. . . . There are some times when I can't stop it, I just have to, and then, once I eat, there is a strong urge to either purge or take a laxative. . . . It never stops. . . . It becomes very obsessive, where you're getting on the scales ten times a day. . . . I weigh 96 pounds now."

ideal. This conflict between reality and fashion seems most closely related to the current epidemic of eating disorders. The efforts of some people to maintain thin, athletic shapes are almost superhuman. Miss America contestants work out an average of 14 hours per week, with some exercising 35 hours per week (Trebbe, 1979).

Interesting data are also available on body image perception among men. Pope and colleagues (2000) confirmed that men generally desire to be heavier and more muscular than they are. The authors measured the height, weight, and body fat of college-age men in three countries—Austria, France, and the United States. They asked the men to choose the body image that they felt represented (1) their own body, (2) the body they ideally would like to have, (3) the body of an average man of their age, and (4) the male body they believed was preferred by women. In all three countries, men chose an ideal body weight that was approximately 28 pounds more muscular than their current one. They also estimated that women would prefer a male body about 30 pounds more muscular than their current one. In contradiction to the impression, Pope and colleagues (2000) demonstrated, in a pilot study, that most women preferred an ordinary male body without the added muscle. Men who abuse anabolic–androgenic steroids to increase muscle mass and "bulk up" possess these distorted attitudes toward muscles, weight, and the "ideal man" to a greater degree than men who don't use steroids (Kanayama, Barry, & Pope, 2006).

We have some specific information on how these attitudes are socially transmitted in adolescent girls. Paxton, Schutz, Wertheim, and Muir (1999) explored the influence of close friendship groups on attitudes concerning body image, dietary restraint, and extreme weight-loss behaviors. In a clever experiment, the authors identified 79 different friendship cliques in a group of 523 adolescent girls. They found that these friendship cliques tended to share the same attitudes toward body image, dietary restraint, and the importance of attempts to lose weight. It was also clear from the study that these friendship cliques contributed significantly to the formation of individual body image concerns and eating behaviors. In other words, if your friends tend to use extreme dieting or other weight-loss techniques, there is a greater chance that you will, too (Field et al., 2001; Vander Wal & Thelen, 2000).

The abhorrence of fat can have tragic consequences. In one study, toddlers with affluent parents appeared at hospitals with "failure to thrive" syndrome, in which growth and development are severely retarded because of inadequate nutrition. In each case, the parents had put their young, healthy, but somewhat chubby

toddlers on diets in the hope of preventing obesity at a later date (Pugliese, Weyman-Daun, Moses, & Lifshitz, 1987).

Most people who diet don't develop eating disorders, but Patton, Johnson-Sabine, Wood, Mann, and Wakeling (1990) determined in a prospective study that adolescent girls who dieted were eight times more likely to develop an eating disorder 1 year later than those who weren't dieting. And Telch and Agras (1993) noted marked increases in bingeing during and after rigorous dieting in 201 obese women.

Stice and colleagues (1999) demonstrated that one of the reasons attempts to lose weight may lead to eating disorders is that weight reduction efforts in adolescent girls are more likely to result in weight *gain* than weight loss! To establish this finding, 692 girls, initially the same weight, were followed for 4 years. Girls who attempted dieting faced more than 300% greater risk of obesity than those who did not diet. Results are presented in ■ Figure 8.3.

It is not yet entirely clear why dieting leads to bingeing in only some people (Polivy & Herman, 1993), but the relationship is strong. In one study, Urbszat, Herman, and Polivy (2002) told 46 undergraduates that they would either be dieting for a week (Group 1) or not (Group 2) and then presented them with food under the pretext of giving them a taste test. But investigators were really looking at how much they ate during the test, not their ratings of taste. People who expected to go on a diet ate more than the group that didn't—but *only* if they were "restrained eaters" who were continually attempting to restrict their intake of food, particularly fattening food. Thus, attempts to restrict intake may put people at risk for bingeing. Fairburn, Cooper, Doll, and Davies (2005) examined a large group of 2,992 young women who were dieting and identified 104 who developed an eating disorder over the next 2 years. Among all of these dieters, several risk factors were identified. Those most at risk for developing an eating disor-

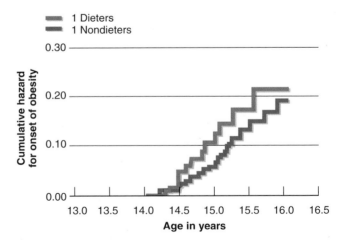

■ **FIGURE 8.3** The onset of obesity over 4 years for self-labeled dieters versus self-labeled nondieters. (From Stice, E., Cameron, R. P., Killen, J. D., Hayward, C., & Taylor, C. B., 1999. Naturalistic weight-reduction efforts prospectively predict growth in relative weight and onset of obesity among female adolescents. *Journal of Consulting and Clinical Psychology, 67,* 967–974.)

der were already binge eating and purging, were eating in secret, expressed a desire to have an empty stomach, were preoccupied with food, and were afraid of losing control over eating.

Distortions of body image in some males can also have tragic consequences. Olivardia, Pope, and Hudson (2000) have described a syndrome in men, particularly male weight lifters, that they initially termed "reverse anorexia nervosa." Men with this syndrome reported they were extremely concerned about looking small, even though they were muscular. Many of these men avoided beaches, locker rooms, and other places where their bodies might be seen. These men also were prone to using anabolic–androgenic steroids to bulk up, risking both the medical and the psychological consequences of taking steroids. Thus, although a marked gender difference in typical body image distortion is obvious, with many women thinking they're too big and some men thinking they're too small, both types of distortion can result in severe psychological and physical consequences (Corson & Andersen, 2002; Kanayama et al., 2006).

The conflict over body image would be bad enough if size were infinitely malleable, but it is not. Increasing evidence indicates a strong genetic contribution to body size; that is, some of us are born to be heavier than others, and we are all shaped differently. Although most of us can be physically fit, few can achieve the levels of fitness and shape so highly valued today. Biologically, it is nearly impossible (Brownell, 1991; Brownell & Fairburn, 2002). Nevertheless, many young people in our society fight biology to the point of starvation. In adolescence, cultural standards are often experienced as peer pressure and are more influential than reason and fact. The high number of males who are homosexual among the relatively small numbers of males with eating disorders has also been attributed to pressures among gay men to be physically trim (Carlat et al., 1997). Conversely, pressure to appear more fit and muscular is also apparent for a substantial proportion of men (Pope et al., 2000).

■ Dietary Restraint

During World War II, in what has become a classic study, Keys and colleagues (Keys, Brozek, Henschel, Michelson, & Taylor, 1950) conducted a semistarvation experiment involving 36 conscientious objectors who volunteered for the study as an alternative to military service. For 6 months, these healthy men were given about half their former full intake of food. This period was followed by a 3-month rehabilitation phase, during which food was gradually increased. During the diet, the subjects lost an average of 25% of their body weight. The results were carefully documented, particularly the psychological effects.

The investigators found that the subjects became preoccupied with food and eating. Conversations, reading, and daydreams revolved around food. Many began to collect recipes and to hoard food-related items. Some men never lost their obsession with food. The bizarre behavior of individuals with anorexia who become chefs for their families and hoard food could be an effect of dieting or starvation alone.

If cultural pressures to be thin are as important as they seem to be in triggering eating disorders, then such disorders would be expected to occur where these pressures are particularly severe, which is just what happens to ballet dancers, who are under extraordinary pressures to be thin. In an important study, Szmukler, Eisler, Gillis, and Haywood (1985) examined 100 adolescent female ballet students in London. Fully 7% were diagnosed with anorexia nervosa, and an additional 3% were borderline cases. Another 20% had lost a significant amount of weight, and 30% were clearly afraid of becoming fat even though they were below normal weight (Garner & Garfinkel, 1985). All these figures are much higher than in the population. In another study, Garner, Garfinkel, Rockert, and Olmsted (1987) followed a group of 11- to 14-year-old female students in ballet school. The conservative estimate was that at least 25% of these girls developed eating disorders during the 2 years of the study. Similar results are apparent among athletes, particularly females, such as gymnasts. What goes on in ballet classes that has such a devastating effect on girls? Consider the case of Phoebe again.

PHOEBE: Dancing to Destruction

Phoebe remembered clearly that during her early years in ballet the older girls talked incessantly about their weight. Phoebe performed well and looked forward to the rare compliment. The ballet mistress seemed to comment more on weight than on dance technique, often remarking, "You'd dance better if you lost weight." If one little girl lost a few pounds through heroic dieting, the instructor always pointed it out: "You've done well working on your weight; the rest of you had better follow this example." One day, without warning, the instructor said to Phoebe, "You need to lose 5 pounds before the next class." At that time, Phoebe was 5 feet 2 inches and weighed 98 pounds. The next class was in 2 days. After one of these admonitions and several days of restrictive eating, Phoebe experienced her first uncontrollable binge.

Early in high school, Phoebe gave up the rigors of ballet to pursue a variety of other interests. She did not forget the glory of her starring roles as a young dancer or how to perform the steps. She still danced occasionally by herself and retained the grace that serious dancers effortlessly display. But in college, as she stuck her head in the toilet bowl, vomiting her guts out for perhaps the third time that day, she realized there was one lesson she had learned in ballet class more deeply and thoroughly than any other—the life-or-death importance of being thin at all costs.

Thus, dieting is one factor that can contribute to eating disorders (Polivy & Herman, 2002).

■ Family Influences

Much has been made of the possible significance of family interaction patterns in cases of eating disorders. A number of investigators (see, for example, Attie & Brooks-Gunn, 1995; Bruch, 1985; Humphrey, 1986, 1988, 1989; Minuchin, Rosman, & Baker, 1978) have found that the "typical" family of someone with anorexia is successful, hard-driving, concerned about external appearances, and eager to maintain harmony. To accomplish these goals, family members often deny or ignore conflicts or negative feelings and tend to attribute their problems to other people at the expense of frank communication among themselves (Fairburn, Shafran, et al., 1999; Hsu, 1990).

Pike and Rodin (1991) confirmed the differences in interactions within the families of girls with disordered eating in comparison with control families. Basically, mothers of girls with disordered eating seemed to act as "society's messengers" in wanting their daughters to be thin (Steinberg & Phares, 2001). They were likely to be dieting themselves and, generally, were more perfectionistic than comparison mothers in that they were less satisfied with their families and family cohesion (Fairburn, Cooper, et al., 1997, 1999).

Whatever the preexisting relationships, after the onset of an eating disorder, particularly anorexia, family relationships can deteriorate quickly. Nothing is more frustrating than watching your daughter starve herself at a dinner table where food is plentiful. Educated and knowledgeable parents, including psychologists and psychiatrists with full understanding of the disorder, have reported resorting to physical violence (for example, hitting or slapping) in moments of extreme frustration, in a vain attempt to get their daughters to put some food, however little, in their mouths. The parents' guilt and anguish was considerable.

Biological Dimensions

Like most psychological disorders, eating disorders run in families and thus seem to have a genetic component (Strober, 2002). Although completed studies are only preliminary, they suggest that relatives of patients with eating disorders are four to five times more likely than the general population to develop eating disorders themselves, with the risks for female relatives of patients with anorexia a bit higher (see, for example, Hudson, Pope, Jonas, & Yurgelun-Todd, 1983; Strober, Freeman, Lampert, Diamond, & Kaye, 2000; Strober & Humphrey, 1987). In important twin studies of bulimia by Kendler and colleagues (1991) and of anorexia by Walters and Kendler (1995), researchers used structured interviews to ascertain the prevalence of the disorders among 2,163 female twins. In 23% of identical twin pairs, both twins had bulimia, as compared to 9% of fraternal twins. Because no adoption studies have yet been reported, strong sociocultural influences cannot be ruled out, and other studies have produced inconsistent results (Fairburn, Cowen, & Harrison, 1999). For anorexia, numbers were too small for precise estimates, but the disorder in one twin did seem to confer a significant risk for both anorexia and bulimia in the co-twin. In any case, an emerging consensus is that genetic makeup is about half of the equation among causes of anorexia and bulimia (Klump, Kaye, & Strober, 2001; Strober, 2002; Wade, Bulik, Neale, & Kendler, 2000). Again, there is no clear agreement on just *what* is inherited (Fairburn, Cowen, et al., 1999). Hsu (1990) speculates that nonspecific personality traits such as emotional instability and, perhaps, poor impulse control might be inherited. In other words, a person might inherit a tendency to be emotionally responsive to stressful life events and, as one consequence, might eat impulsively in an attempt to relieve stress and anxiety (Strober, 2002). Data from Kendler and colleagues (1995) would support this interpretation. Klump and col-

leagues (2001) mention perfectionist traits, along with negative affect. This biological vulnerability might then interact with social and psychological factors to produce an eating disorder.

Biological processes are quite active in the regulation of eating and thus of eating disorders, and substantial evidence points to the hypothalamus as playing an important role. Investigators have studied the hypothalamus and the major neurotransmitter systems—including norepinephrine, dopamine,

Courtesy of Judith Rodin

Judith Rodin and her colleagues have made important discoveries about the social influences on people with eating disorders.

and, particularly, serotonin—that pass through it to determine whether something is malfunctioning when eating disorders occur (Vitiello & Lederhendler, 2000). Low levels of serotonergic activity are associated with impulsivity generally and binge eating specifically (see Chapter 2). Thus, most drugs under study as treatments for bulimia target the serotonin system (see, for example, de Zwaan, Roerig, & Mitchell, 2004; Kaye et al., 1998; Walsh et al., 1997).

If investigators do find a strong association between neurobiological functions and eating disorders, the question of cause or effect remains. At present, the consensus is that some neurobiological abnormalities do exist in people with eating disorders but that they are a *result* of semistarvation or a binge–purge cycle rather than a cause, although they may well contribute to the *maintenance* of the disorder once it is established.

Psychological Dimensions

Clinical observations indicate that many young women with eating disorders have a diminished sense of personal control and confidence in their own abilities and talents (Bruch, 1973, 1985; Striegel-Moore, Silberstein, & Rodin, 1993; Walters & Kendler, 1995). This may manifest as strikingly low self-esteem (Fairburn, Cooper, & Shafran, 2003). They also display more perfectionistic attitudes, learned, perhaps, from their families, which may reflect attempts to exert control over important events in their lives (Fairburn, Shafran, et al., 1997, 1999; Joiner et al., 1997). Recently, Shafran, Lee, Payne, and Fairburn (2006) artificially raised perfectionistic standards in otherwise normal women by instructing them to pursue the highest possible standards in everything they do for the next 24 hours. These instructions caused them to eat fewer high-calorie foods, to restrict their eating, and to have more regret after eating than women told to just do the minimum for 24 hours. This occurred even though eating was not specifically mentioned as part of pursuing the "highest standards." Perfectionism alone, however, is only weakly associated with the development of an eating disorder, because individuals must consider themselves overweight and manifest low self-esteem before the trait of perfectionism makes a contribution (Vohs, Bardone, Joiner,

Abramson, & Heatherton, 1999). But when perfectionism is directed to distorted perception of body image, a powerful engine to drive eating disorder behavior is in place (Lilenfeld, Wonderlich, Riso, Crosby, & Mitchell, 2006; Shafran, Cooper, & Fairburn, 2002). Women with eating disorders are intensely preoccupied with how they appear to others (Fairburn, Stice, et al., 2003; Smith et al., 2007). They also perceive themselves as frauds, considering false any impressions they make of being adequate, self-sufficient, or worthwhile. In this sense, they feel like impostors in their social groups and experience heightened levels of social anxiety (Smolak & Levine, 1996). Striegel-Moore and colleagues (1993) suggest these social self-deficits are likely to increase as a consequence of the eating disorder, further isolating the woman from the social world.

Specific distortions in perception of body shape change often, depending on day-to-day experience. McKenzie, Williamson, and Cubic (1993) found that bulimic women judged their body size to be larger and their ideal weight to be less than same-size controls. Indeed, women with bulimia judged that their bodies were larger after they ate a candy bar and soft drink, whereas the judgments of women in control groups were unaffected by snacks. Thus, rather minor events related to eating may activate fear of gaining weight, further distortions in body image, and corrective schemes such as purging.

Rosen and Leitenberg (1985) observed substantial anxiety before and during snacks, which they theorized is *relieved* by purging. They suggested the state of relief strongly reinforces the purging, in that we tend to repeat behavior that gives us pleasure or relief from anxiety. This seemed to be true for Phoebe. However, other evidence suggests that in treating bulimia, reducing the anxiety associated with eating is less important than countering the tendency to overly restrict food intake and the associated negative attitudes about body image that lead to bingeing and purging (see, for example, Agras, Schneider, Arnow, Raeburn, & Telch, 1989; Fairburn, Agras, & Wilson, 1992; Fairburn et al., in press).

A more recent observation is that at least a subgroup of these patients has difficulty tolerating any negative emotion (mood intolerance) and may binge or engage in other behaviors, such as self-induced vomiting or intense exercise, in an attempt to regulate their mood (Paul, Schroeter, Dahme, & Nutzinger, 2002). This finding was recently confirmed. Mauler, Hamm, Weike, and Tuschen-Caffier (2006) investigated reaction to food cues in women with bulimia and a normal comparison group who had been food deprived. They discovered that women with bulimia, when hungry, had more intense negative emotional reactions (distress, anxiety, and depression) when viewing pictures of food and subsequently ate more at a buffet, presumably to decrease their anxiety and distress and make themselves feel better, even though this overeating would cause problems in the long run. These individuals, understandably, then evidenced even more intense negative affect after overeating and seemed threatened by food cues.

An Integrative Model

Although the three major eating disorders are identifiable by their unique characteristics, and the specific diagnoses have some validity, it is becoming increasingly clear that all eating disorders have much in common in terms of causal factors. It may be more useful to lump the eating disorders into one diagnostic category, simply noting which specific features occur, such as dietary restraint, bingeing, or purging. Recently Christopher Fairburn and colleagues have attempted to develop this approach (see, for example, Fairburn, Cooper, et al., 2003; Fairburn et al., 2007). Thus, we have integrated a discussion of the causes of eating disorders.

In putting together what we know about eating disorders, it is important to remember, again, that no one factor seems sufficient to cause them (see ■ Figure 8.4). Individuals with eating disorders may have some of the same biological vulnerabilities (such as being highly responsive to stressful life events) as individuals with anxiety disorders (Kendler et al., 1995; Rojo, Conesa, Bermudez, & Livianos, 2006). Anxiety and mood disorders are also common in the families of individuals with eating disorders (Schwalberg et al., 1992), and negative emotions, along with "mood intolerance," seem to trigger binge eating in many patients. In addition, as you will see, drug and psychological treatments with proven effectiveness for anxiety disorders are also the treatments of choice for eating disorders. Indeed, we could conceptualize eating disorders as anxiety disorders focused exclusively on a fear of becoming overweight.

In any case, it is clear that social and cultural pressures to be thin motivate significant restriction of eating, usually through severe dieting. Remember, however, that many people go on strict diets, including adolescent females, but only a small minority develop eating disorders, so dieting alone does not account for the disorders. It is also important to note that the interactions in high-income, high-achieving families may well be a factor. An emphasis on looks and achievement, and perfectionistic tendencies, may help establish strong attitudes about the overriding importance of physical appearance to popularity and success. These attitudes result in an exaggerated focus on body shape and weight. Finally, there is the question of why a small minority of individuals with eating disorders can successfully control their intake through dietary restraint, resulting in alarming weight loss (anorexia), whereas the majority are unsuccessful at losing weight and compensate in a cycle of bingeing and purging (bulimia), although most individuals with anorexia do go on to bingeing and purging at some point (Eddy et al., 2002). These differences, at least initially, may be determined by biology or physiology, such as a genetically determined disposition to be somewhat thinner initially. Then again, perhaps preexisting personality characteristics, such as a tendency to be overcontrolling, are important determinants of which disorder an individual develops.

Tim Walsh has made significant scientific contributions to our understanding of eating disorders.

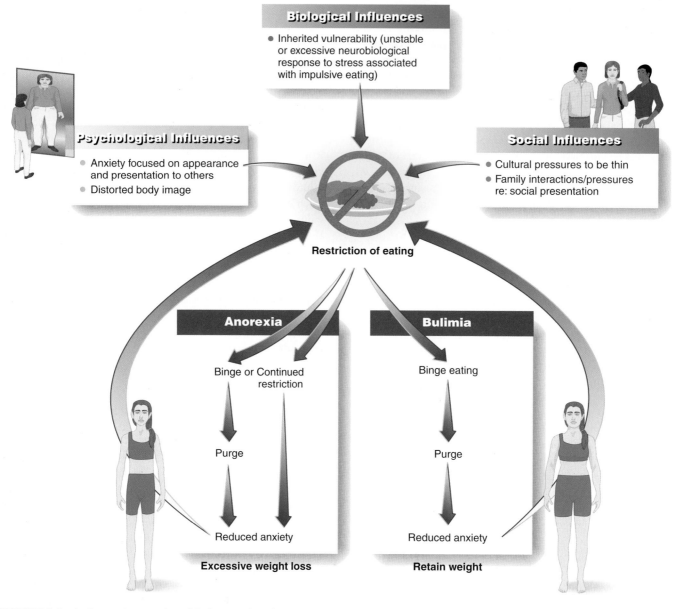

Biological Influences

- Inherited vulnerability (unstable or excessive neurobiological response to stress associated with impulsive eating)

Psychological Influences

- Anxiety focused on appearance and presentation to others
- Distorted body image

Social Influences

- Cultural pressures to be thin
- Family interactions/pressures re: social presentation

Restriction of eating

Anorexia

Binge or Continued restriction

Purge

Reduced anxiety

Excessive weight loss

Bulimia

Binge eating

Purge

Reduced anxiety

Retain weight

■ **FIGURE 8.4** An integrative causal model of eating disorders.

TREATMENT OF EATING DISORDERS

Only since the 1980s have there been treatments for bulimia; treatments for anorexia have been around much longer but were not well developed. Rapidly accumulating evidence indicates that at least one, and possibly two, psychological treatments are effective, particularly for bulimia nervosa. Certain drugs may also help, although the evidence is not so strong.

Drug Treatments

At present, drug treatments have not been found to be effective in the treatment of anorexia nervosa (see, for example, Attia, Haiman, Walsh, & Flater, 1998; de Zwaan et al., 2004; Garner & Needleman, 1996; Vitiello & Lederhendler, 2000; Wilson & Fairburn, 2002). For example, a recent definitive study reported that Prozac had no benefit in preventing relapse after weight has been restored (Walsh et al., 2006).

On the other hand, there is some evidence that drugs may be useful in some cases of bulimia. The drugs generally considered the most effective for bulimia are the same antidepressant medications that proved effective for mood disorders and anxiety disorders (Kaye, Strober, Stein, & Gendall, 1999; Walsh et al., 1997; Wilson et al., 1999; Wilson & Fairburn, 2002). The Food and Drug Administration (FDA) in 1996 approved Prozac as effective for eating disorders. Effectiveness is usually measured by reductions in the frequency of binge eating, as well as by the percentage of patients who stop binge eating and purging altogether, at least for a while. In two studies, one of tricyclic antidepressant drugs and the other of fluoxetine (Prozac), researchers found the average *reduction* in binge eating and purging was, respectively, 47% and 65% (Walsh, 1991; Walsh, Hadigan, Devlin, Gladis, & Roose, 1991). However, although antidepressants are more effective than placebo in the short term, and they may enhance the effects of psychological treatment somewhat (Whittal, Agras, & Gould,

Christopher Fairburn developed an effective psychosocial treatment for bulimia nervosa.

1999; Wilson et al., 1999), the available evidence suggests that antidepressant drugs alone do not have substantial long-lasting effects on bulimia nervosa (Walsh, 1995; Wilson & Fairburn, 2002).

Psychological Treatments

Until the 1980s, psychological treatments were directed at the patient's low self-esteem and difficulties in developing an individual identity. Disordered patterns of family interaction and communication were also targeted for treatment. However, these treatments alone did not have the effectiveness that clinicians hoped they might (see, for example, Minuchin et al., 1978; Russell, Szmukler, Dare, & Eisler, 1987). Short-term cognitive-behavioral treatments target problem eating behavior and associated attitudes about the overriding importance and significance of body weight and shape, and these strategies have become the treatment of choice for bulimia (Pike, Devlin, & Loeb, 2004; Wilson & Fairburn., 2002; Wilson, Grilo, & Vitousek, 2007).

■ Bulimia Nervosa

In the cognitive-behavioral treatment approach pioneered by Fairburn (1985), the first stage is teaching the patient the physical consequences of binge eating and purging, as well as the ineffectiveness of vomiting and laxative abuse for weight control. The adverse effects of dieting are also described, and patients are scheduled to eat small, manageable amounts of food five or six times per day with no more than a 3-hour interval between any planned meals and snacks, which eliminates the alternating periods of overeating and dietary restriction that are hallmarks of bulimia. In later stages of treatment, cognitive therapy focuses on altering dysfunctional thoughts and attitudes about body shape, weight, and eating. Coping strategies for resisting the impulse to binge and purge are also developed, including arranging activities so that the individual will not spend time alone after eating during the early stages of treatment (Fairburn, Marcus, & Wilson, 1993; Fairburn et al., in press). Evaluations of short-term (approximately 3 months) cognitive-behavioral treatments for bulimia have been good, showing superior efficacy to credible alternative treatments not only for bingeing and purging but also for distorted attitudes and accompanying depression. Furthermore, these results seem to last (Pike et al., 2003; Thompson-Brenner, Glass, & Westen, 2003; Whittal et al., 1999), although there are, of course, a number of patients who improve only modestly or do not benefit. Several studies are worth examining more closely.

In a thorough, carefully conducted study, Fairburn, Jones, Peveler, Hope, and O'Connor (1993) evaluated three treatments. *Cognitive-behavioral treatment* (CBT) focused on changing eating habits *and* changing attitudes about weight and shape; *behavior therapy* (BT) focused only on changing eating habits; and *interpersonal psychotherapy* (IPT) focused on improving interpersonal functioning. For patients receiving CBT, both binge eating and purging declined by more than 90% at a 1-year follow-up. In addition, 36% of the patients had ceased all binge eating and purging; the others had occasional episodes. Attitudes toward body shape and weight also improved. These results were significantly better than the results from BT. Even more interesting was the finding that IPT did as well as CBT at the 1-year follow-up, although CBT was more effective at the assessment immediately after treatment was completed. This result indicates that IPT caught up with CBT in terms of effectiveness by the end of the 1-year follow-up. This is particularly interesting because IPT does not concentrate directly on disordered eating patterns or dysfunctional attitudes about eating but rather on improving interpersonal functioning and reducing interpersonal conflict, a focus that may, in turn, promote changes in eating habits and attitudes. Both treatments were more effective than BT. Fairburn and colleagues (1995) combined patients from this study with those in another similar study and followed them up to 6 years. Some patients received a slightly different form of interpersonal therapy (that achieved almost identical results), which the authors called focal interpersonal therapy (FIT). Results from these two studies at a 6-year follow-up suggest that patients had retained their gains in the two effective treatments.

In a landmark study, Agras, Walsh, Fairburn, Wilson, and Kraemer (2000) randomly assigned 220 patients meeting diagnostic criteria for bulimia nervosa to 19 sessions of either CBT or IPT in an attempt to replicate and extend the intriguing results reported here. Again, the investigators found that, for those who completed treatment, CBT was significantly superior to IPT at the end of treatment, with 45% recovered in the CBT group versus 8% in the IPT group. The percentage who remitted (no longer met diagnostic criteria for an eating disorder but still had some problems) was 67% in the CBT group versus 40% in the IPT group. However, after 1 year, these differences again were no longer significant, as patients in the IPT group tended to "catch up" to patients in the CBT group. The results for both recovered and remitted patients, presented in ■ Figure 8.5, show that approximately the same percentage of patients (40%) remained recovered in the CBT group but 27% of those receiving IPT had now recovered. The results are similar for the less stringent criteria of remission. In a subsequent analysis, Agras and colleagues (2000) were able to demonstrate (see ■ Figure 8.6) that substantial improvement in the first six sessions was the best predictor of who would recover by the end of treatment.

The investigators conclude that CBT is the preferred psychological treatment for bulimia nervosa because it works significantly faster. Nevertheless, it is intriguing, again, that IPT was almost as effective after 1 year even though this treatment concentrates not directly on disordered eating patterns but rather on the interpersonal relationships of the patient. Clearly, we need to understand more about how to improve such treatments to deal more successfully with the growing number of patients with eating disorders.

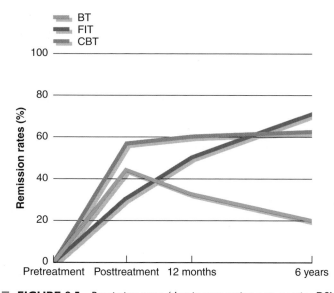

■ **FIGURE 8.5** Remission rates (that is, proportion not meeting DSM-IV criteria for eating disorder) in patients who received CBT ($n = 35$), BT ($n = 22$), or FIT ($n = 32$). Mean ((standard deviation) length of follow-up was 5.8 (2.0 years). (Reprinted, with permission, from Fairburn, C. G., Jones, R., Peveler, R. C., Hope, R. A., & O'Connor, M., 1993. Psychotherapy and bulimia nervosa: The longer-term effects of interpersonal psychotherapy, behaviour therapy and cognitive behaviour therapy. *Archives of General Psychiatry, 50,* 419–428, © 1993 American Medical Association.)

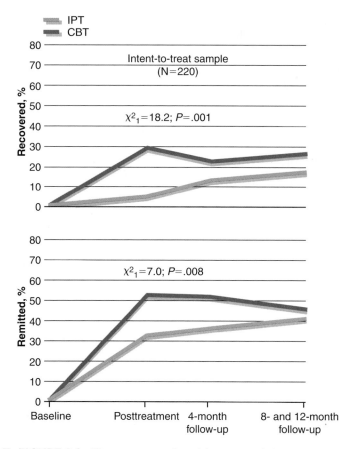

■ **FIGURE 8.6** The percentage of participants completing treatment who recovered in each treatment at each time point, and the percentage of participants remitted in each treatment. Significant differences between the treatment groups are indicated. (From Agras, W. S., Walsh, B. T., Fairburn, C. G., Wilson, G. T., & Kraemer, H. C., 2000. A multicenter comparison of cognitive-behavioral therapy and interpersonal psychotherapy for bulimia nervosa. *Archives of General Psychiatry, 57,* 459–466, © 2000 American Medical Association.)

PHOEBE: TAKING CONTROL

During her sophomore year in college, Phoebe entered the short-term CBT program outlined here. She made good progress during the first several months and worked carefully to eat regularly and gain control over her eating. She also made sure that she was with somebody during her high-risk times and planned alternative activities that would reduce her temptation to purge if she felt she had eaten too much at a restaurant or drunk too much beer at a party. During the first 2 months, Phoebe had three slips, and she and her therapist discussed what led to her temporary relapse. Much to Phoebe's surprise, she did not gain weight on this program, even though she did not have time to increase her exercise. Nevertheless, she still was preoccupied with food, was concerned about her weight and appearance, and had strong urges to vomit if she thought she had overeaten the slightest amount.

During the 9 months following treatment, Phoebe reported that her urges seemed to decrease somewhat, although she had one major slip after eating a big pizza and drinking a lot of beer. She reported that she was thoroughly disgusted with herself for purging and was quite careful to return to her program after this episode. Two years after finishing treatment, Phoebe reported that her urges to vomit had disappeared, a report confirmed by her parents. All that remained of her problem were some bad but increasingly vague and distant memories.

Short-term treatments for bulimia, although clearly effective for many, may not provide a lasting solution. Indeed, some people do not benefit from short-term CBT. Evidence now suggests that combining drugs with psychosocial treatments might boost the overall outcome, at least in the short term (Whittal et al., 1999; Wilson et al., 1999). In the largest study to date (Walsh et al., 1997), CBT was significantly superior to supportive psychotherapy (in which the therapist is understanding and sympathetic and encourages patients to achieve their goals) in the treatment of bulimia nervosa; adding two antidepressant medications to CBT, including a serotonin-specific reuptake inhibitor (SSRI), modestly increased the benefit of CBT. But CBT remains the preferred treatment for bulimia and is superior to medication alone (Wilson et al., 2002). There is also evidence that people who do not respond to CBT might benefit from interpersonal psychotherapeutic methods (Fairburn, Jones, et al., 1993; Klerman, Weissman, Rounsaville, & Chevron, 1984) or from antidepressant medication (Walsh et al., 2000).

■ Binge-Eating Disorder

Smith, Marcus, and Kaye (1992) adapted CBTs for bulimia to obese binge eaters, and the preliminary results looked promising. In their study, the frequency of binge eating was reduced by an average of 81%, with 50% of the subjects abstinent from bingeing by the end of treatment. Agras, Telch, Arnow, Eldredge, and Marnell (1997) followed 93 obese individuals with BED for 1 year and found that immediately after treatment, 41% of the participants abstained from bingeing and 72% binged less frequently. After 1 year, binge eating was reduced by 64%, and 33% of the group remained abstinent. Importantly, those who had stopped binge eating during CBT maintained a weight loss of approximately 9 pounds over this 1-year follow-up period; those who continued to binge gained approximately 8 pounds. Thus, stopping binge eating is critical to sustaining weight loss in obese patients, a finding consistent with other studies of weight-loss procedures (Marcus, Wing, & Hopkins, 1988; Marcus et al., 1990; Telch, Agras, & Rossiter, 1988).

In contrast to results with bulimia, it appears that IPT is every bit as effective as CBT for binge eating. Wilfley and colleagues (2002) treated 162 overweight or obese men and women with BED with either CBT or IPT and found comparable results from each treatment. Fully 60% were abstinent from bingeing at a 1-year follow-up. In an important comparative study of treatments for binge eating, Grilo, Masheb, and Wilson (2004) compared Prozac, placebo, CBT and Prozac, and CBT and placebo. Prozac showed no effect on BED compared to placebo, and both CBT treatments (with Prozac or placebo) were superior with no difference between them. Fully 73% of the CBT and placebo patients completing treatment did not binge for a month, which was the definition of remission. Thus, Prozac did not add anything to CBT, at least right after treatment terminated. If individuals began to respond rapidly to CBT treatment (by the fourth week), the response was particularly good, both short term and long term (Grilo, Masheb, & Wilson, 2006). Finally, one small study suggested that an antiobesity drug, sibutramine (Meridia), that reduces feelings of hunger, was more effective than placebo for BED (Appolinario et al., 2003).

Fortunately, it appears that self-help procedures may be useful in the treatment of BED. For example, both Peterson and colleagues (1998) and Loeb, Wilson, Gilbert, and Labouvie (2000) found that self-help manuals based on effective treatment procedures eliminated binge eating in 46% to 87% of patients. Furthermore, these results were as good as those in groups actively led by therapists. In one of the best studies of this approach, Carter and Fairburn (1998) randomly assigned 72 fe-

Stewart Agras has made many important contributions to our understanding of eating disorders.

males with BED to either a pure self-help group, in which participants were simply mailed their manual; guided self-help, in which therapists would meet with the patients periodically as they read the manual; or a wait-list control group. Fifty percent of the guided self-help group and 43% of the pure self-help group eliminated binge eating versus 8% of the wait-list control group. These improvements were maintained at a 6-month follow-up. If further studies confirm these findings, then a self-help approach should probably be the first treatment offered before engaging in more expensive and time-consuming therapist-led treatments.

■ Anorexia Nervosa

In anorexia, the most important initial goal is to restore the patient's weight to a point that is at least within the low-normal range (American Psychiatric Association, 1993). If body weight is below 70% of the average or if weight has been lost rapidly, inpatient treatment would be recommended (American Psychiatric Association, 1993; Casper, 1982) because severe medical complications, particularly acute cardiac failure, could occur if weight is not restored immediately. If the weight loss has been more gradual and seems to have stabilized, weight restoration can be accomplished on an outpatient basis.

Restoring weight is probably the easiest part of treatment. Clinicians who treat patients in different settings, as reported in a variety of studies, find that at least 85% will be able to gain weight. The gain is often as much as a half-pound to a pound a day until weight is within the normal range. Typical strategies used with inpatients are outlined in Table 8.3. Knowing they can leave the hospital when their weight gain is adequate is often sufficient to motivate young women (Agras, Barlow, Chapin, Abel, & Leitenberg, 1974). Julie gained about 18 pounds during her 5-week hospital stay.

Then the difficult stage begins. As Hsu (1988) and others have demonstrated, initial weight gain is a poor predictor of long-term outcome in anorexia. Without attention to the patient's underlying dysfunctional attitudes about body shape, as well as interpersonal disruptions in her life, she will almost always relapse. For restricting anorexics, the focus of treatment must shift to their marked anxiety over becoming obese and losing control of eating, as well as to their undue emphasis on thinness as a determinant of self-worth, happiness, and success. In this regard, effective treatments for restricting anorexics are similar to those for patients with bulimia nervosa (Fairburn, Shafran, & Cooper, 1999; Pike, Loeb, & Vitousek, 1996; Vitousek, Watson, & Wilson, 1998). In a recent study (Pike, Walsh, Vitousek, Wilson, & Bauer, 2003), extended (1-year) outpatient CBT was significantly better than continued nutritional counseling, with only 22% failing (relapsing or dropping out) with CBT versus 73% failing with nutritional counseling.

In addition, every effort is made to include the family to accomplish two goals. First, the negative and dysfunctional communication regarding food and eating must be eliminated and meals must be made more structured and reinforcing. Second, attitudes toward body shape and image distortion are discussed at some length in family sessions. Unless the therapist attends to these attitudes, individuals with anorexia are likely to face a lifetime preoccupation with weight and body shape, struggle to

TABLE 8.3 Strategies to Attain Weight Gain

1. Weight restoration occurs with other treatments, such as individual and family therapy, so that the patient does not feel that eating and weight gain are the only goals of treatment.

2. The patient trusts the treatment team and believes that she will not be allowed to become overweight.

3. The patient's fear of loss of control is contained; this may be accomplished by having her eat frequent, smaller meals (for example, four to six times per day, with 400 to 500 calories per meal) to produce a gradual but steady weight gain (for example, an average of 0.44 pounds per day).

4. A member of the nursing staff is present during mealtimes to encourage the patient to eat and to discuss her fears and anxiety about eating and weight gain.

5. Gradual weight gain rather than the amount of food eaten is regularly monitored, and the result is made known to the patient; thus, the patient should be weighed at regular intervals, and she should know whether she has gained or lost weight.

6. Some negative and positive reinforcements exist, such as the use of graduated level of activity and bed rest, whether or not these reinforcements are formally conceptualized as behavior modification techniques so that the patient may thereby learn that she can control not only her behavior but also the consequence of her behavior.

7. The patient's self-defeating behavior, such as surreptitious vomiting or purging, is confronted and controlled.

8. The dysfunctional conflict between the patient and the family about eating and food is not reenacted in the hospital or, if the pattern is to be reenacted in a therapeutic lunch session, the purpose is clearly defined.

Source: From Hsu, L. K. G., 1990. *Eating Disorders.* New York: Guilford Press, p. 136, © 1990 Guilford Press.

maintain marginal weight and social adjustment, and be subject to repeated hospitalization. Family therapy seems effective, particularly with young girls (less than 19 years of age) with a short history of the disorder. Under these circumstances, Eisler and colleagues (1997) found that 90% of a small group maintained substantial benefits for 5 years and family therapy was superior to individual therapy. In a second study, Eisler et al. (2000) found that seeing the parents separately from their daughter seemed more effective overall than seeing the family together, with about 76% responding well in the first group compared to 46% in the second group. Nevertheless, the long-term results of treatment for anorexia are more discouraging than for bulimia, with substantially lower rates of full recovery than for bulimia over a 7.5-year period (Herzog et al., 1999).

Preventing Eating Disorders

Attempts are being made to prevent the development of eating disorders. If successful methods are confirmed, they will be important, because many cases of eating disorders are resistant to treatment and most individuals who do not receive treatment suffer for years, in some cases all of their lives (Herzog et al., 1999; Keel et al., 1999; Killen, 1996). The development of eating disorders during adolescence is a risk factor for a variety of additional disorders during adulthood, including cardiovascular symptoms,

chronic fatigue and infectious diseases, and anxiety and mood disorders (Johnson, Cohen, Kasen, & Brook, 2002). Before implementing a prevention program, however, it is necessary to target specific behaviors to change. Killen and colleagues (1994) conducted a prospective analysis on a sample of 887 young adolescent girls. Over a 3-year interval, 32 girls, or 3.6% of the sample, developed symptoms of eating disorders.

Early concern about being overweight was the most powerful predictive factor of later symptoms. The instrument used to measure weight concerns is presented in Table 8.4. Girls who scored high on this scale (an average score of 58) were at substantial risk

TABLE 8.4 Weight Concerns*

1. How much *more* or *less* do you feel you worry about your weight and body shape than other girls your age?
   a. I worry a lot less than other girls (4)
   b. I worry a little less than other girls (8)
   c. I worry about the same as other girls (12)
   d. I worry a little more than other girls (16)
   e. I worry a lot more than other girls (20)

2. How afraid are you of gaining 3 pounds?
   a. Not afraid of gaining (4)
   b. Slightly afraid of gaining (8)
   c. Moderately afraid of gaining (12)
   d. Very afraid of gaining (16)
   e. Terrified of gaining (20)

3. When was the last time you went on a diet?
   a. I've never been on a diet (3)
   b. I was on a diet about 1 year ago (6)
   c. I was on a diet about 6 months ago (9)
   d. I was on a diet about 3 months ago (12)
   e. I was on a diet about 1 month ago (15)
   f. I was on a diet less than 1 month ago (18)
   g. I'm now on a diet (21)

4. How important is your weight to you?
   a. My weight is not important compared to other things in my life (5)
   b. My weight is a little more important than some other things (10)
   c. My weight is more important than most, but not all, things in my life (15)
   d. My weight is the most important thing in my life (20)

5. Do you ever feel fat?
   a. Never (4)
   b. Rarely (8)
   c. Sometimes (12)
   d. Often (16)
   e. Always (20)

*Value assigned to each answer is in parentheses. Thus, if you chose an answer worth 12 in questions 1, 2, 3, and 5 and an answer worth 10 in question 4, your score would be 58. (Remember that the prediction from this scale worked for girls age 11–13 but hasn't been evaluated in college students.)

Source: Killen, J. D. (1996). Development and evaluation of a school-based eating disorder symptoms prevention program. In L. Smolak, M. P. Levine, & R. Striegel-Moore (Eds.), *The developmental psychopathology of eating disorders: Implications for research, prevention, and treatment* (pp. 313–339). Mahwah, NJ: Erlbaum.

for developing serious symptoms compared to girls who scored lower (an average score of 33). Killen and colleagues (1996) then evaluated a prevention program on 967 sixth- and seventh-grade girls from 11 to 13 years of age. This is the universal approach described in Chapter 7, where the program is applied to everyone. Half the girls were put on the intervention program, and the other half were not. The program emphasized that female weight gain after puberty is normal and that excessive caloric restriction could cause increased gain. The interesting results were that the intervention had relatively little effect on the treatment group compared to the control group. But for those girls at high risk for developing eating disorders (as reflected by a high score on the scale in Table 8.4), the program significantly reduced weight concerns (Killen, 1996; Killen et al., 1994). The authors conclude from this preliminary study that the most cost-effective preventive approach would be to carefully screen 11- and 12-year-old girls who are at high risk for developing eating disorders and to apply the program selectively to them (Killen, 1996). This finding is similar to results from prevention efforts for depression, where a "selective" approach of targeting high-risk individuals was most successful (Stice & Shaw, 2004). Our best hope for dealing effectively with eating disorders may lie with preventive approaches such as this.

Could these preventive programs be delivered over the Internet? It seems they can! Winzelberg and colleagues (2000) studied a group of university women who did not have eating disorders at the time of the study but were concerned about their body image and the possibility of being overweight. College women in general are a high-risk group, and sorority women in particular are at higher risk than nonsorority women (Becker, Smith, & Ciao, 2005). The investigators developed the "student bodies program" (Winzelberg et al., 1998), a structured, interactive health education program designed to improve body image satisfaction and delivered through the Internet. The interactive software featured text, audio, and video components, as well as online self-monitoring journals and behavior change assignments. The program continued for 8 weeks with various assignments administered each week. In addition, participants were expected to post a message to a discussion group related to the themes under consideration that week. If participants missed their assignments, they were contacted by e-mail and encouraged to get back on track. The results indicated this program was markedly successful, because participants, compared to controls, reported a significant improvement in body image and a decrease in drive for thinness. Subsequently, these investigators developed innovations to improve compliance with this program to levels of 85% (Celio, Winzelberg, Dev, & Taylor, 2002). Stice and Shaw (2004) reviewed a large number of these prevention efforts and found that the best ones reduced risk factors and the development of eating disorders for up to 2 years. The best effects were observed in selected rather than universal programs, interactive rather than didactic programs, and programs offered just to females 15 years or older. Stice, Presnell, Gau, and Shaw (2007) confirmed that the key psychological variable that must change for these programs to be successful (the mediator of change) was strong belief (internalization) that being as thin as possible is an ideal. In view of the severity and chronicity of eating disorders, preventing these disorders through widespread educational and intervention efforts would be clearly preferable to waiting until the disorders develop.

CONCEPT CHECK 8.2

Mark the following statements about the causes and treatment of eating disorders as either true (T) of false (F).

1. ____ Many young women with eating disorders have a diminished sense of personal control and confidence in their own abilities and talents, are perfectionists, and/or are intensely preoccupied with how they appear to others.

2. ____ Biological factors, as well as the societal pressure to use diet and exercise to achieve nearly impossible weight goals, contribute to the high numbers of people with anorexia nervosa and bulimia nervosa.

3. ____ One study showed that males consider a smaller female body size to be more attractive than women do.

4. ____ Antidepressants help individuals overcome anorexia nervosa but have no effect on bulimia nervosa.

5. ____ Cognitive-behavioral treatment (CBT) and interpersonal psychotherapy (IPT) are both successful treatments for bulimia nervosa, although CBT is the preferred method.

6. ____ Attention must be focused on an anorexic's dysfunctional attitudes about body shape, or the individual will most likely relapse after treatment.

OBESITY

As noted at the beginning of the chapter, obesity is not formally considered an eating disorder in DSM. For example, rates of anxiety and mood disorders are only somewhat elevated over the normal population among obese people, and rates of substance abuse are actually somewhat lower (Phelan & Wadden, 2004; Simon et al., 2006). Indeed, the prevalence of obesity is so high that one might consider it statistically "normal" if it weren't for the serious implications for health, as well as for social and psychological functioning.

Statistics

The prevalence of obesity (BMI 30 or greater) among adults in the United States in 2000 was fully 30.5% of the population, and this increased to 30.6% in 2002 and 32.2% in 2004, a statistically significant increase (Ogden et al., 2006). What is particularly disturbing is that this prevalence of obesity represents close to a tripling from 12% of adults in 1991. This condition accounted for more than 164,000 deaths in the United States alone in 2000 (Flegal et al., 2005). The direct relationship between obesity and mortality (dying prematurely) is shown in ■ Figure 8.7. At a BMI of 30, risk of mortality increases by 30%, and at a BMI of 40 or more, risk of mortality is 100% or more (Manson et al., 1995; Wadden, Brownell, & Foster, 2002).

For children and adolescents, the numbers are even worse, with the rates of overweight people tripling in the past 25 years (Critser, 2003). In the last 5 years alone, rates of being overweight

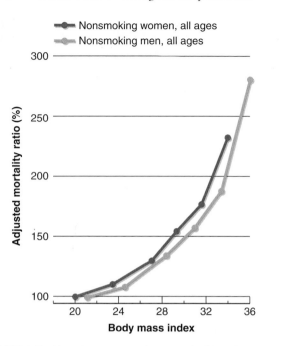

■ **FIGURE 8.7** Mortality rates in relation to the BMI of nonsmoking men and women (of all ages) who participated in the American Cancer Society study. (Reprinted, with permission, from Vanitallie, T. B., & Lew, E. A., 1992. Assessment of morbidity and mortality risk in the overweight patient. In T. A. Wadden and T. B. Vanitallie, Eds., *Treatment of the seriously obese patient* (p. 28). New York: Guilford Press, © 1992 Guilford Press.)

TABLE 8.5	Adult Obesity in 2002 and Estimated Level in 2010*			
Country	**2002**		**2010**	
	Males	**Females**	**Males**	**Females**
Bangladesh	0.1	0.1	0.2	0.2
Brazil	6.9	15.0	12.4	24.5
China	1.0	1.5	4.1	3.6
India	0.9	1.1	1.7	2.0
Indonesia	0.2	2.0	0.2	3.9
Japan	1.5	1.5	2.3	1.1
Malaysia	1.6	6.8	1.7	11.0
Mexico	20.3	31.6	30.1	41.0
Nigeria	1.6	4.9	3.0	8.1
Pakistan	0.8	2.9	1.6	5.0
United States	32.0	37.8	44.2	48.3
World	5.7	9.4	8.0	12.3
High income[†]	18.1	20.4	24.3	25.9
Upper-middle income	14.0	21.1	19.7	29.0
Lower-middle income	4.1	9.9	6.6	12.6
Low income	1.1	2.8	1.7	4.2

*Levels expressed as the percentage of people ≥ 15 years with BMI ≥ 30.
[†]World Bank Income Groups: high income, ≥ $9,206; upper-middle income, $2,976–$9,205; lower-middle income, $746–$2,975; low income, ≤ $745.

Source: World Development Indicators, World Bank, Washington, DC (2003). From Yach, D., Stuckler, D., & Brownell, K. D. (2006). Epidemiologic and economic consequences of the global epidemics of obesity and diabetes. *Nature Medicine, 12,* 62–66.

(defined as above the 95th percentile for sex-specific BMI for that age) have increased from 13.9% in 2000 to 17.1% in 2004 (Ogden et al., 2006). The stigma of obesity has a major impact on quality of life (Neumark-Stainer & Haines, 2004). For example, most overweight individuals are subjected to prejudice and discrimination in college, at work, and in housing (Henderson and Brownell, 2004). The high prevalence, along with the serious medical and social consequences, have resulted in obesity becoming the single most expensive health problem in the United States, with costs to the health-care system exceeding $117 billion per year. These costs surpass those for smoking and alcohol abuse. Ridicule and teasing in children may increase obesity through depression and binge eating (Schwartz & Brownell, 2007).

Obesity is not limited to North America. Rates of obesity in Eastern European nations are as high as 50% (Bjorntorp, 1997), and the rate is greatly increasing in developing nations. In Japan, obesity in men has doubled since 1992 and has nearly doubled in young women. Similar increases in obesity are occurring in China (Henderson & Brownell, 2004; World Health Organization, 1998) where the proportion of Chinese who are overweight increased from 6% to 8% in a 7-year period (Holden, 2005). Table 8.5 projects the prevalence of obesity in 2010 in selected countries compared to 2002, breaking it down by sex (Yach, Stuckler, & Brownell, 2006). Obesity is also the main driver of type 2 diabetes, which has reached epidemic status. Projected increases for diabetes in the same countries are presented in ■ Figure 8.8 (Yach et al., 2006). Additional facts documenting the global epidemic of obesity and its consequences are presented in ■ Figure 8.9 (Brownell & Yach, 2005). Ethnicity also is a factor in rates of obesity. In the United States, fully 50% of African American women

and 40% of Hispanic American women are obese compared to 30% of Caucasian women (Flegal, Carroll, Odgen, & Johnson, 2002). The percentage of overweight Latino and African American children doubled between 1986 and 1998 (Bellizzi, 2002).

Disordered Eating Patterns in Cases of Obesity

There are two forms of maladaptive eating patterns in people presenting with obesity. The first is binge eating, and the second is **night eating syndrome.** We discussed BED earlier in the chapter, but it is important to note that only a minority of patients with obesity, between 7% and 19%, present with patterns of binge eating. When they do, treatment for binge eating reviewed earlier should be integrated into weight-loss programs.

More interesting is the pattern of night eating syndrome that occurs in between 7% and 15% of obese individuals seeking weight-loss treatment but as much as 27% of those with extreme obesity seeking bariatric surgery (discussed later) (Lamberg, 2003; Sarwer et al., 2004). Individuals with night eating syndrome consume a third or more of their daily intake after their evening meal and get out of bed at least once during the night to have a high-calorie snack. In the morning, however, they are not hungry and do not usually eat breakfast. These individuals do not binge during their night eating and seldom purge. Occasionally, nonobese indi-

Countries (population >100 million)	Diabetes prevalence in 2000 (>20 years of age as a percentage)		Estimated prevalence in 2030 (>20 years of age as a percentage)	
Bangladesh	4.6		7.7	
Brazil	4.3		7.0	
China	2.4		3.7	
India	5.5		8.0	
Indonesia	6.7		10.6	
Japan	5.3		7.3	
Malaysia	7.6		10.8	
Mexico	3.9		6.4	
Nigeria	3.4		4.0	
Pakistan	7.7		8.7	
Russia	4.2		5.3	
United States	8.8		11.2	
World	4.6		6.4	
All developed	6.3		8.4	
All developing	4.1		6.0	

FIGURE 8.8 Diabetes prevalence in people over 20 years of age in 2000, and predicted prevalence in 2030 in countries with more than 100 million inhabitants. (From Yach, D., Stuckler, D., & Brownell, K. D. (2006). Epidemiologic and economic consequences of the global epidemics of obesity and diabetes. *Nature Medicine, 12,* 64.)

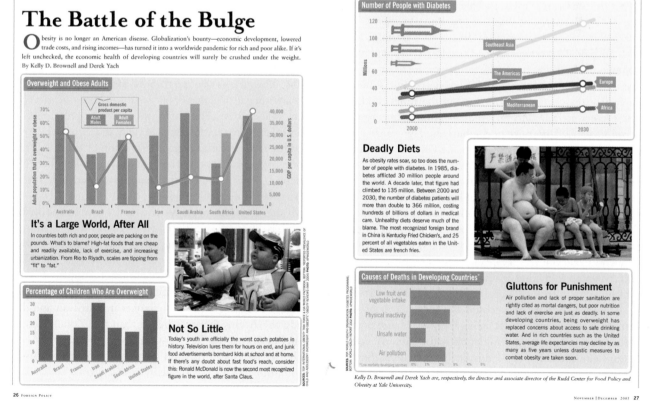

FIGURE 8.9 Worldwide prevalence and consequences of obesity. From Brownell, K.D., & Yach, D., (2005). The battle of the bulge. *Foreign Policy,* 26–27.

viduals will engage in night eating, but it is overwhelmingly associated with being overweight or obese (Lundgren et al., 2006). Notice that this condition is not the same as the nocturnal eating syndrome described later in the chapter in the section under sleep disorders. In that condition, individuals get up during the night and raid the refrigerator but never wake up. They also may eat uncooked or other dangerous foods while asleep. On the contrary, in night eating syndrome, the individuals are awake as they go about their nightly eating patterns. Night eating syndrome is an important target for treatment in any obesity program to reregulate patterns of eating so that individuals eat more during the day, when their energy expenditure is highest.

Causes

Henderson and Brownell (2004) make a point that this obesity epidemic is clearly related to the spread of modernization. In other words, as we advance technologically, we are getting fatter. That is, the promotion of an inactive, sedentary lifestyle and the consumption of a high-fat, energy-dense diet is the largest single contributor to the obesity epidemic (Levine, 2005). Kelly Brownell (2002, 2003) notes that in our modern society individuals are continually exposed to heavily advertised, inexpensive fatty foods that have low nutritional value. When consumption of these is combined with an increasingly inactive lifestyle, it is not surprising that the prevalence of obesity is increasing. Brownell has referred to this as the "toxic environment" (Schwartz & Brownell, 2007). He notes that the best example of this phenomenon comes from a study of the Pima Indians from Mexico. A portion of this tribe of Indians migrated to Arizona relatively recently. Examining the result of this migration, Ravussin, Valencia, Esparza, Bennett, and Schulz (1994) determined that Arizona Pima women consumed 41% of their total calories in fat on the average and weighed 44 pounds on average more than Pima women who stayed in Mexico, who consumed 23% of their calories from fat. Because this relatively small tribe retains a strong genetic similarity, it is likely that the "toxic environment" in the more modern United States has contributed to the epidemic. Immigrants to the United States in general more than doubled their prevalence of obesity from 8% to 19% after at least 15 years living in this country (Goel et al., 2004).

Not everyone exposed to this environment becomes obese, and this is where genetics, physiology, and personality come in. On average, genetic contributions may constitute a smaller portion of the cause of obesity than cultural factors, but it helps explain why some people become obese and some don't when exposed to the same environment. For example, genes influence the number of fat cells an individual has, the likelihood of fat storage, and, most likely, activity levels (Cope, Fernandez, & Allison, 2004). Generally, genes are thought to account for about 30% of the equation in causation of obesity (Bouchard, 2002). Physiological processes play a large role in the initiation and maintenance of eating and vary considerably from individual to individual (Smith & Gibbs, 2002), and psychological processes of affect regulation, impulse control, attitudes and motivation toward eating, and responsiveness to the consequences of eating are important (Blundell, 2002; Stice, Presnell, Shaw, & Rohde, 2005). Although the etiol-

ogy of obesity is extraordinarily complex, as with most disorders, an interaction of biological and psychological factors with a notably strong environmental and cultural contribution provides the most complete account.

Treatment

The treatment of obesity is only moderately successful at the individual level, with somewhat greater long-term evidence for effectiveness in children and adolescents compared to adults (Sarwer, Foster, & Wadden, 2004). Treatment is usually organized in a series of steps from least intrusive to most intrusive depending on the extent of obesity. One plan is presented in ■ Figure 8.10. As you can see, the first step is usually a self-directed weight-loss program in individuals who buy a popular diet book. The most usual result is that some individuals may lose some weight in the short term but almost always regain that weight. Furthermore, these books do little to change lifelong eating and exercise habits (Freedman, King, & Kennedy, 2001). Few individuals succeed on these diets, one of the reasons the latest one is always on the best-seller list. Similarly there is little evidence that physician counseling results in any changes. Nevertheless, physicians can play an important role by providing specific treatment recommendations, including referral to professionals (Sarwer et al., 2004).

The next step is commercial self-help programs such as Weight Watchers, Jenny Craig, and similar programs. Weight Watchers reports that more than 1 million people attend more than 44,000 meetings in 30 countries each week (Weight Watchers International, 2004). These programs stand a better chance of achieving some success, at least compared to self-directed programs (Heshka et al., 2003). Among members who successfully lost weight initially and kept their weight off for at least 6 weeks after completing the program, between 19% and 37% weighed within 5 pounds of their goal weight at least 5 years after treatment (Lowe, Miller-Kovach, Frie, & Phelan, 1999; Sarwer et al., 2004). This means that up to 80% of individuals, even if they are initially successful, are not successful in the long run. Several recent studies have compared the most popular diet programs. Dansinger, Gleason, Griffith, Secker, and Schaefer (2005) evaluated the Atkins (carbohydrate restriction), Ornish (fat restriction), Zone (macronutrients balance), and Weight Watchers (calorie restriction), diets among both men and women after 1 year. Weight loss averaged between 4 and 7 pounds, but only 50%–65% stuck with the diet. The most weight loss was observed in those who faithfully carried out their program. Gardiner and colleagues (2007) evaluated the same diets but substituted the popular LEARN program (Brownell, 2004) for Weight Watchers and restricted the sample to overweight, premenopausal women. The LEARN program emphasizes lifestyle changes in exercise and patterns of eating, as well as changes in nutrition and diet. In this study, the Atkins diet was better than the Zone program after 1 year, but Atkins was not significantly better than LEARN or Ornish. But the Atkins diet did seem safe, contrary to some previous assumptions about carbohydrate restrictions.

The most successful programs are professionally directed behavior modification programs, particularly if patients attend group maintenance sessions periodically in the year following initial

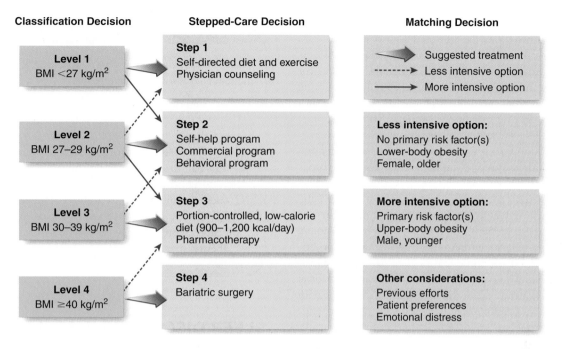

Classification Decision

Level 1
BMI <27 kg/m²

Level 2
BMI 27–29 kg/m²

Level 3
BMI 30–39 kg/m²

Level 4
BMI ≥40 kg/m²

Stepped-Care Decision

Step 1
Self-directed diet and exercise
Physician counseling

Step 2
Self-help program
Commercial program
Behavioral program

Step 3
Portion-controlled, low-calorie
diet (900–1,200 kcal/day)
Pharmacotherapy

Step 4
Bariatric surgery

Matching Decision

Suggested treatment
Less intensive option
More intensive option

Less intensive option:
No primary risk factor(s)
Lower-body obesity
Female, older

More intensive option:
Primary risk factor(s)
Upper-body obesity
Male, younger

Other considerations:
Previous efforts
Patient preferences
Emotional distress

■ **FIGURE 8.10** Treatment approaches for obesity in adults, shown as a conceptual scheme of a three-stage process for selecting treatment. Classification decision: Indicates which of four interventions is likely appropriate based on BMI. Stepped-care decision: Encourages all individuals to increase physical activity and consume an appropriate diet. Matching decision: Selects final treatment based on the individual's prior weight-loss efforts, treatment preferences, and need for weight reduction (as judged by overall health). Adjunct nutritional or psychological counseling is recommended for patients who report problems with meal planning, depression, body image, or similar difficulties. (Adapted from Wadden, T. A., Brownell, K. D., & Foster, G. D., 2002. Obesity: Responding to the global epidemic. *Journal of Consulting and Clinical Psychology, 70*, 510–525.)

weight reduction (Perri et al., 2001). Nevertheless, even these programs do not appear to be permanently effective (Sarwer et al., 2004).

For those individuals who have become more dangerously obese, very-low-calorie diets and possibly drugs, combined with behavior modification programs, are recommended. Patients lose as much as 20% of their weight on very-low-calorie diets, which typically consist of 4–6 liquid meal replacement products, or "shakes," a day. At the end of 3 or 4 months, they are then placed on a low-calorie balanced diet. As with all weight-loss programs, patients typically regain up to 50% of their lost weight in the year following treatment (Wadden & Osei, 2002). But more than half of them are able to maintain a weight loss of at least 5%, which is important in these very obese people (Sarwer et al., 2004). Similarly, drug treatments that reduce internal cues signaling hunger may be effective, particularly if combined with a behavioral approach targeting lifestyle change. Currently the FDA has approved two drugs for this purpose, sibutramine (Meridia) and orlistat (Xenical). For patients who remain on medication for more than 1 year, weight loss of 7% to 8% has been observed on average. Thus, there is promise for these combination treatments in maintaining some weight loss (Wadden, Berkowitz, Sarwer, Prus-Wisniewski, & Steinberg, 2001). On the other hand, medications produce a number of side effects and are not well tolerated by some.

Finally, the surgical approach to extreme obesity—called **bariatric surgery** and widely publicized by singer Carnie Wilson and television personality Al Roker—is an increasingly popular approach for individuals with a BMI of at least 40 (Wolfe

& Morton, 2005). Unfortunately, up to 5% of the population in the United States now falls into this category (Wolfe & Morton, 2005). Up to 172,000 individuals availed themselves of this treatment in 2005, compared to approximately 20,000 in 1998. Furthermore, it is more successful than diets, with patients losing approximately 30% to 50% of their body weight postoperatively and maintaining these results over a number of years (Buchwald et al., 2004; Kral, 2002). This surgery is reserved only for the most severely obese individuals for whom the obesity is an imminent health risk because the surgery is permanent. Typically, patients must have one or more obesity-related physical conditions, such as heart disease or diabetes. In the most common surgery, the stomach is stapled to create a small stomach pouch at the base of the esophagus, which severely limits food intake. Alternatively, a gastric bypass operation creates a bypass of the stomach, as the name implies, which limits not only food intake but also absorption of calories. Approximately 15% of patients who have bariatric surgery fail to lose significant weight or regain lost weight after surgery (Latfi, Kellum, DeMaria, & Sugarman, 2002). A small percentage of individuals, from 0.1% to 0.5%, do not survive the operation, and an additional 15% to 20% experience severe complications requiring rehospitalization and additional surgery within the first year after surgery and in each of the next 2 years after that (Zingmond, McGory, & Ko, 2005). The mortality rate may increase to as much as 2% in hospitals where the surgery is done less often, usually fewer than 100 operations for a given surgeon. Therefore, surgeons require patients to exhaust all other treatment options and to undergo a thorough psychological assessment to ascertain whether they can adapt to the radically changed eating patterns required postsurgery (Kral, 2002; Sarwer et al., 2004). New psychological programs have been designed specifically to prepare patients for this surgery (Apple, Lock, & Peebles, 2006). With these new programs, surgery is probably the best bet for the severely obese, but only 0.6% of those eligible are getting the surgery because clinicians still recommend relatively unsuccessful diets and drugs as a first-line treatment. (Santry, Gillen, & Lauderdale, 2005). This is likely to change in the coming years as the surgical procedures become more sophisticated and safer and the extreme health risks of severe obesity are more widely recognized.

In contrast to adults, the treatment of obesity in children and adolescents has achieved better outcome both short term and long term (Cooperberg & Faith, 2004; Epstein, Myers, Raynor, & Saelens, 1998). A number of studies report that behavior modification programs, particularly those that include parents, may produce a 20% reduction in overweight, a change maintained for at least several years after the end of the study. Again, these behavior modification programs include a number of strategies to change dietary habits, particularly decreasing high-calorie, high-fat snacks. These programs also target reduction of sedentary habits in children and adolescents, such as viewing television, playing video games, and sitting in front of a computer. These programs may be more successful than with adults because parents are typically fully engaged in the program and provide constant and continuing support. Also, dietary habits in children are less engrained than adults. In addition, children are generally more physically active if provided with appropriate activities (Cooperberg & Faith, 2004). For more seriously obese adolescents (BMI from 32 to 44), a recently completed and important study confirmed that combining medication with a comprehensive behavioral program was more effective than the behavioral program alone (Berkowitz, Wadden, Tershakovec, & Cronquist, 2003).

The greatest benefits may come from strategies that focus on prevention by altering factors in the "toxic environment" that strongly encourage the intake of unhealthy foods and a sedentary lifestyle (Brownell, 2002). Currently, policies in many countries in the Western world regarding diet are undergoing scrutiny. In the United States, many state and local governments are considering regulations on the type and amount of foods present in public schools, with the goal of eliminating unhealthy foods with low nutritional value and substituting healthier foods less likely to contribute to the epidemic of obesity in our culture (Brownell, 2003).

In addition, programs that directly involve children and their parents seem to have a better chance of working to some extent if they are brief, intensive, and focused on just eating and exercise, as opposed to focused on general health issues (Stice, Shaw, & Marti, 2006). These programs are in need of more development.

Most of us recognize that eating is essential to our survival. Equally important is sleep, a still relatively mysterious process crucial to everyday functioning and strongly implicated in many psychological disorders. We turn our attention to this additional survival activity in an effort to understand better how and why we can be harmed by sleep disturbances.

CONCEPT CHECK 8.3

Answer each of the following with either a T for true statements or an F for false statements.

1. ____ Obesity is the single most expensive health problem in the United States, surpassing both smoking and alcohol abuse.
2. ____ Individuals with night eating syndrome consume at least half their daily intake after their evening meal.
3. ____ Fatty foods and technology are not to blame for the obesity epidemic in the United States.
4. ____ Professionally directed behavior modification programs represent the most successful treatment for obesity.

SLEEP DISORDERS: THE MAJOR DYSSOMNIAS

We spend about one third of our lives asleep. That means most of us sleep nearly 3,000 hours per *year.* For many of us, sleep is energizing, both mentally and physically. Unfortunately, most people do not get enough sleep, and two out of every five Americans report getting less than 7 hours of sleep daily during the work week—which works out to about an hour and a half less than a century ago (National Sleep Foundation, 2005). Most of us know what it's like to have a bad night's sleep. The next day we're a little groggy, and as the day wears on we may become irritable. Research tells us that even minor sleep deprivation over only a few days impedes our ability to think clearly (Bliese, Wesensten, & Balkin, 2006). Now imagine, if you can, that it has been years since you've had a good night's sleep. Your relationships suffer, it is difficult to do your schoolwork, and your efficiency and productivity at work are diminished. Lack of sleep also affects you physically. People who do not get enough sleep report more health problems (Hale, 2005), perhaps because immune system functioning is reduced with the loss of even a few hours of sleep (Irwin et al., 1994; Jaffe, 2000).

Here you might ask yourself how sleep disorders fit into a textbook on abnormal psychology. Different variations of disturbed sleep clearly have physiological bases and therefore could be considered purely medical concerns. However, like other physical disorders, sleep problems interact in important ways with psychological factors.

An Overview of Sleep Disorders

The study of sleep has long influenced concepts of abnormal psychology. Moral treatment, used in the 19th century for people with severe mental illness, included encouraging patients to get adequate amounts of sleep as part of therapy (Armstrong, 1993). Sigmund Freud greatly emphasized dreams and discussed them with patients as a way of better understanding their emotional lives (Antrobus, 2000). Researchers who prevented people from sleeping for prolonged periods found that chronic sleep deprivation often had profound effects. An early study in this area looked at the effects of keeping 350 volunteers awake for 112 hours (Tyler, 1955). Seven volunteers engaged in bizarre behavior that seemed psychotic. Subsequent research suggested that interfering with the sleep of people with preexisting psychological problems can create these disturbing results (Brauchi & West, 1959). A number of the disorders covered in this book are often associated with sleep complaints, including schizophrenia, major depression, bipolar disorder, and anxiety-related disorders. Individuals with a range of developmental disorders (see Chapter 14) are also at greater risk for having sleep disorders (Durand, 1998). You may think at first that a sleep problem is the result of a psychological disorder. For example, how often have you been anxious about a future event (an upcoming exam, perhaps) and not

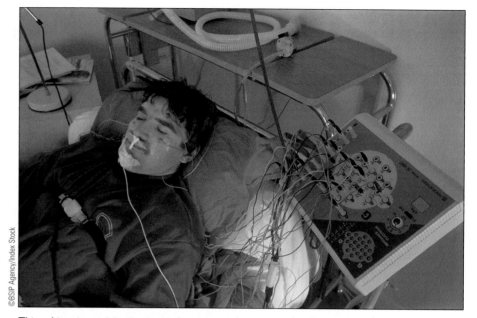

This subject is participating in a polysomnograph, an overnight electronic evaluation of sleep patterns.

been able to fall asleep? However, the relationship between sleep disturbances and mental health is more complex. Sleep problems may cause the difficulties people experience in everyday life (Mendelson, 2005), or they may result from some disturbance common to a psychological disorder.

In Chapter 5 we explained how a brain circuit in the limbic system may be involved with anxiety. We know that this region of the brain is also involved with our dream sleep, which is called **rapid eye movement (REM) sleep** (Benca, Chirelli, Rattenborg, & Tononi, 2005). This mutual neurobiological connection suggests that anxiety and sleep may be interrelated in important ways, although the exact nature of the relationship is still unknown. Similarly, REM sleep seems related to depression, as noted in Chapter 7 (Emslie, Rush, Weinberg, Rintelmann, & Roffwarg, 1994). Sleep abnormalities are preceding signs of serious clinical depression, which may suggest that sleep problems can help predict who is at risk for later mood disorders (Terman & Terman, 2006). In an intriguing study, researchers found that CBT improved symptoms among a group of depressed men and normalized REM sleep patterns (Nofzinger et al., 1994). Furthermore, sleep deprivation has temporary antidepressant effects on some people (Benedetti et al., 2003), although in people who are not already depressed sleep deprivation may bring on a depressed mood (Perlis et al., 2006). We do not fully understand how psychological disorders are related to sleep, yet accumulating research points to the importance of understanding sleep if we are to complete the broader picture of abnormal behavior.

Sleep disorders are divided into two major categories: **dyssomnias** and **parasomnias** (Table 8.6). Dyssomnias involve difficulties in getting enough sleep, problems with sleeping when you want to (not being able to fall asleep until 2 A.M. when you have a 9 A.M. class), and complaints about the quality of sleep, such as not feeling refreshed even though you have slept the whole night. Parasomnias are characterized by abnormal behavioral or

physiological events that occur during sleep, such as nightmares and sleepwalking.

The clearest and most comprehensive picture of your sleep habits can be determined only by a **polysomnographic (PSG) evaluation.** The patient spends one or more nights sleeping in a sleep laboratory being monitored on a number of measures, including respiration and oxygen desaturation (a measure of airflow); leg movements; brain wave activity, measured by an *electroencephalogram;* eye movements, measured by an *electrooculogram;* muscle movements, measured by an *electromyogram;* and heart activity, measured by an *electrocardiogram.* Daytime behavior and typical sleep patterns are also noted—for example, whether the person uses drugs or alcohol, is anxious about work or interpersonal problems, takes afternoon naps, or has a psychological disorder. Collecting all these data can be both time consuming and costly, but it is important to ensure an accurate diagnosis and treatment plan. One alternative to the comprehensive assessment of sleep is to use a wristwatch-size device called an **actigraph.** This instrument records the number of arm movements, and the data can be downloaded into a computer to determine the length and quality of sleep. Several studies have now tested the usefulness of this type of device in measuring the sleep of astronauts aboard the space shuttle, and they find it can reliably detect when they fall asleep, when they wake up, and how restful their in-space sleep is (Monk, Buysse, & Billy, 2006; Monk, Buysse, & Rose, 1999).

In addition, clinicians and researchers find it helpful to know the average number of hours the individual sleeps each day, taking into account **sleep efficiency (SE),** the percentage of time actually spent asleep, not just lying in bed trying to sleep. SE is calculated by dividing the amount of time sleeping by the amount of time in bed. An SE of 100% would mean you fall asleep as soon as your head hits the pillow and do not wake up during the night. In contrast, an SE of 50% would mean half your time in bed is spent trying to fall asleep; that is, you are awake half the time. Such

TABLE 8.6 Summary of DSM Sleep Disorders

	Sleep Disorder	Description
Dyssomnias	(Disturbances in the amount, timing, or quality of sleep)	
	Primary insomnia	Difficulty initiating or maintaining sleep, or sleep that is not restorative (person not feeling rested even after normal amounts of sleep)
	Primary hypersomnia	Complaint of excessive sleepiness that is displayed as either prolonged sleep episodes or daytime sleep episodes
	Narcolepsy	Irresistible attacks of refreshing sleep occurring daily, accompanied by episodes of brief loss of muscle tone (cataplexy)
	Breathing-related sleep disorder	Sleep disruption leading to excessive sleepiness or insomnia that is caused by sleep-related breathing difficulties
	Circadian rhythm sleep disorder (sleep–wake schedule disorder)	Persistent or recurrent sleep disruption leading to excessive sleepiness or insomnia that is due to a mismatch between the sleep–wake schedule required by a person's environment and his or her circadian sleep–wake pattern
Parasomnias	(Disturbances in arousal and sleep stage transition that intrude into the sleep process)	
	Nightmare disorder (dream anxiety disorder)	Repeated awakenings with detailed recall of extended and extremely frightening dreams, usually involving threats to survival, security, or self-esteem; the awakenings generally occur during the second half of the sleep period
	Sleep terror disorder	Recurrent episodes of abrupt awakening from sleep, usually occurring during the first third of the major sleep episode and beginning with a panicky scream
	Sleepwalking disorder	Repeated episodes of arising from bed during sleep and walking about, usually occurring during the first third of the major sleep episode

Source: Reprinted, with permission, from American Psychiatric Association. (2000). *Diagnostic and statistical manual of mental disorders* (4th ed., text revision). Washington, DC: Author, © 2000 American Psychiatric Association

measurements help the clinician determine objectively how well you sleep.

One way to determine whether a person has a problem with sleep is to observe his daytime sequelae, or behavior while awake. For example, if it takes you 90 minutes to fall asleep at night but this doesn't bother you and you feel rested during the day, then you do not have a problem. A friend who also takes 90 minutes to fall asleep but finds this delay anxiety provoking and is fatigued the next day might be considered to have a sleep problem. It is to some degree a subjective decision, partly depending on how the person perceives the situation and reacts to it.

Primary Insomnia

Insomnia is one of the most common sleep disorders. You may picture someone with insomnia as being awake all the time. However, it isn't possible to go completely without sleep. For example, after being awake for about 40 hours, a person begins having **microsleeps** that last several seconds or longer (Mendelson, 2005). In the rare occurrences of fatal familial insomnia (a degenerative brain disorder), total lack of sleep eventually leads to death (Polnitsky, 2006). Despite the common use of the term *insomnia* to mean "not sleeping," it actually applies to a number of complaints. People are considered to have insomnia if they have trouble falling asleep at night (difficulty initiating sleep), if they wake up frequently or too early and can't go back to sleep (difficulty maintaining sleep), or even if they sleep a reasonable number of hours but are still not rested the next day (nonrestorative sleep). Consider the case of Sonja.

SONJA: School on Her Mind

Sonja was a 23-year-old law student with a history of sleep problems. She reported that she never really slept well, both having trouble falling asleep at night and usually awakening again in the early morning. She had been using the nighttime cold medication Nyquil several times per week over the past few years to help her fall asleep. Unfortunately, since she started law school last year, her sleep problems had grown even worse. She would lie in bed awake until the early morning hours thinking about school, getting only 3–4 hours of sleep on a typical night. In the morning, she had a great deal of difficulty getting out of bed and was frequently late for her early morning class.

Sonja's sleep problems and their interference with her schoolwork were causing her to experience increasingly severe depression. In addition, she recently reported having a severe anxiety attack that woke her in the middle of the night. All of these difficulties caused her to be increasingly isolated from family and friends, who finally convinced her to seek help.

We return to Sonja later in this chapter.

■ Clinical Description

Sonja's symptoms meet the DSM-IV-TR criteria for **primary insomnia,** with *primary* indicating that the complaint is not related to other medical or psychiatric problems. Looking at sleep

DSM-IV-TR

DSM TABLE 8.3 Diagnostic Criteria for Primary Insomnia

A. The predominant complaint is difficulty initiating or maintaining sleep, or nonrestorative sleep, for at least 1 month.

B. The sleep disturbance (or associated daytime fatigue) causes clinically significant distress or impairment in social, occupational, or other important areas of functioning.

C. The sleep disturbance does not occur exclusively during the course of narcolepsy, breathing-related sleep disorder, circadian rhythm sleep disorder, or a parasomnia.

D. The disturbance does not occur exclusively during the course of another mental disorder (e.g., major depressive disorder, generalized anxiety disorder, a delirium).

E. The disturbance is not due to the direct physiological effects of a substance (e.g., a drug of abuse, a medication) or a general medical condition.

Source: Reprinted, with permission, from American Psychiatric Association. (2000). *Diagnostic and statistical manual of mental disorders* (4th ed., text revision). Washington, DC: Author, © 2000 American Psychiatric Association

disorders as primary recalls the overlap of sleep problems with psychological disorders such as anxiety and depression. Because not sleeping makes you anxious and anxiety further interrupts your sleep, which makes you more anxious, and so on, it is uncommon to find a person with a simple sleep disorder and no related problems.

Sonja's is a typical case of insomnia. She had trouble both initiating and maintaining sleep. Other people sleep all night but still feel as if they've been awake for hours. Although most people can carry out necessary day-to-day activities, their inability to concentrate can have serious consequences, such as debilitating accidents when they attempt to drive long distances (like bus drivers) or handle dangerous material (like electricians). Students with insomnia like Sonja's may do poorly in school because of difficulty concentrating.

■ Statistics

Almost a third of the population reports some symptoms of insomnia during any given year (National Sleep Foundation, 2005). For many of these individuals, sleep difficulties are a lifetime affliction (Mendelson, 2005). Approximately 35% of elderly people report excessive daytime sleepiness, with older black men reporting the most problems (Blazer, 1999; Whitney et al., 1998).

A number of psychological disorders are associated with insomnia. Total sleep time often decreases with depression, substance use disorders, anxiety disorders, and dementia of the Alzheimer's type. The interrelationship between alcohol use and sleep disorders can be particularly troubling. Alcohol is often used to initiate sleep (Neylan, Reynolds, & Kupfer, 2003). In small amounts, it helps make people drowsy, but it also interrupts ongoing sleep. Interrupted sleep causes anxiety, which often leads to repeated alcohol use and an obviously vicious cycle.

Women report insomnia twice as often as men. Does this mean that men sleep better than women? Not necessarily. Remember, a sleep problem is considered a disorder *only if you expe-*

rience discomfort about it. Women may be more often diagnosed as having insomnia because they more often report the problem, not necessarily because their sleep is disrupted more. Women may be more aware of their sleep patterns than men or may be more comfortable acknowledging and seeking help for problems.

Just as normal sleep needs change over time, complaints of insomnia differ in frequency among people of different ages. Children who have difficulty falling asleep usually throw a tantrum at bedtime or do not want to go to bed. Many children cry when they wake in the middle of the night. Estimates of insomnia among young children range from 25% to more than 40% (Owens, Rosen, & Mindell, 2003). Growing evidence points to both biological and cultural explanations for poor sleep among adolescents. As children move into adolescence, their biologically determined sleep schedules shift toward a later bedtime (Sadeh, Raviv, & Gruber, 2000). However, at least in the United States, children are still expected to rise early for school, causing chronic sleep deprivation. This problem is not observed among all adolescents, with ethnocultural differences reported among youth from different backgrounds. One study, for example, found that Chinese American youth reported the least problems with insomnia, and Mexican American adolescents reported the most difficulty sleeping (Roberts, Roberts, & Chen, 2000). The percentage of individuals who complain of sleep problems increases as they become older adults. A national sleep poll uncovered that among adults from 55 to 64 years of age 26% complain of sleep problems, but this decreases to about 21% for those from 65 to 84 years (National Sleep Foundation, 2005). This higher rate in reports of sleeping problems among older people makes sense when you remember that the number of hours we sleep decreases as we age. It is not uncommon for someone over 65 to sleep fewer than 6 hours and wake up several times each night.

■ Causes

Insomnia accompanies many medical and psychological disorders, including pain and physical discomfort, physical inactivity during the day, and respiratory problems.

Sometimes insomnia is related to problems with the biological clock and its control of temperature. People who can't fall asleep at night may have a delayed temperature rhythm: Their body temperature doesn't drop and they don't become drowsy until later at night (Morris, Lack, & Dawson, 1990). As a group, people with insomnia seem to have higher body temperatures than good sleepers, and their body temperatures seem to vary less; this lack of fluctuation may interfere with sleep (Monk & Moline, 1989).

Among the other factors that can interfere with sleeping are drug use and a variety of environmental influences such as changes in light, noise, or temperature. People admitted to hospitals often have difficulty sleeping because the noises and routines differ from those at home. Other sleep disorders, such as *sleep apnea* (a disorder that involves obstructed nighttime breathing) or *periodic limb movement disorder* (excessive jerky leg movements), can cause interrupted sleep and may seem similar to insomnia.

Finally, various psychological stresses can also disrupt your sleep. For example, one study looked at how medical and dental school students were affected by a particularly stressful event—in this case, participating in cadaver dissection (Snelling, Sahai, &

Ellis, 2003). Among the effects reported by the students was a decrease in their ability to sleep.

People with insomnia may have unrealistic expectations about how much sleep they need ("I need a full 8 hours") and about how disruptive disturbed sleep will be ("I won't be able to think or do my job if I sleep for only 5 hours") (Morin, Stone, Trinkle, Mercer, & Remsberg, 1993). It is important to recognize the role of cognition in insomnia; our thoughts alone may disrupt our sleep.

Is poor sleeping a learned behavior? It is generally accepted that people suffering from sleep problems associate the bedroom and bed with the frustration and anxiety that go with insomnia. Eventually, the arrival of bedtime itself may cause anxiety (Stepanski, 2006). Interactions associated with sleep may contribute to children's sleep problems. For example, one study found that when a parent was present when the child fell asleep, the child was more likely to wake during the night (Adair, Bauchner, Philipp, Levenson, & Zuckerman, 1991). Researchers think that some children learn to fall asleep only with a parent present; if they wake up at night, they are frightened at finding themselves alone and their sleep is disrupted. Despite widespread acceptance of the role of learning in insomnia, relatively little research has been done on this phenomenon, perhaps partly because this type of research would involve going into homes and bedrooms at an especially private time.

Cross-cultural sleep research has focused primarily on children. In the predominant culture in the United States, infants are expected to sleep on their own, in a separate bed, and, if possible, in a separate room. However, in many other cultures as diverse as rural Guatemala and Korea and urban Japan, the child spends the first few years of life in the same room and sometimes the same bed as the mother (Mosko, Richard, & McKenna, 1997). In many cultures, mothers report that they do not ignore the cries of their children (K. Lee, 1992; Morelli, Rogoff, Oppenheim, & Goldsmith, 1992), in stark contrast to the United States, where many pediatricians recommend that parents ignore the cries of their infants over a certain age at night (Ferber, 1985). One conclusion from this research is that sleep can be negatively affected by cultural norms, as in the United States. Unmet demands can

result in stress that negatively affects the ultimate sleep outcome for children (Durand, Mindell, Mapstone, & Gernert-Dott, 1998).

An integrative view of sleep disorders includes several assumptions. The first is that, at some level, both biological and psychological factors are present in most cases. A second assumption is that these multiple factors are reciprocally related. This can be seen in the study we just noted. Adair and colleagues (1991) observed that children who woke frequently at night often fell asleep in the presence of parents. However, they also noted that child temperament (or personality) may have played a role in this arrangement, because these children had comparatively difficult temperaments and their parents were presumably present to attend to sleep initiation difficulties. In other words, personality characteristics, sleep difficulties, and parental reaction interact in a reciprocal manner to produce and maintain sleep problems.

People may be biologically vulnerable to disturbed sleep. This vulnerability differs from person to person and can range from mild to more severe disturbances. For example, a person may be a light sleeper (easily aroused at night) or have a family history of insomnia, narcolepsy, or obstructed breathing. All these factors can lead to eventual sleeping problems. Such influences have been referred to as *predisposing conditions* (Spielman & Glovinsky, 1991); they may not, by themselves, always cause problems, but they may combine with other factors to interfere with sleep (see ■ Figure 8.11).

■ An Integrative Model

Biological vulnerability may, in turn, interact with *sleep stress* (Durand, in press, a), which includes a number of events that can negatively affect sleep. For example, poor bedtime habits (such as having too much alcohol or caffeine) can interfere with falling asleep (Stepanski, 2006). Note that biological vulnerability and sleep stress influence each other (see Figure 8.11). Although we may intuitively assume that biological factors come first, extrinsic influences such as poor sleep hygiene (the daily activities that affect how we sleep) can affect the physiological activity of sleep. One of the most striking examples of this phenomenon is jet lag, in which people's sleep patterns are disrupted, sometimes seri-

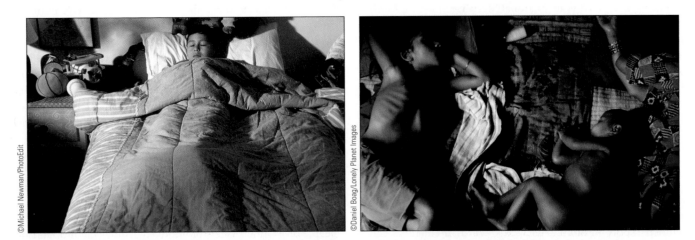

In the United States, children usually sleep alone (left). In many cultures, all family members share the same bed (right).

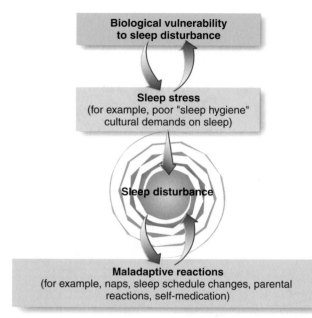

■ **FIGURE 8.11** An integrative, multidimensional model of sleep disturbance.

ously, when they fly across several time zones. Whether disturbances continue or become more severe may depend on how they are managed. For example, many people react to disrupted sleep by taking over-the-counter sleeping pills. Unfortunately, most people are not aware that **rebound insomnia**—where sleep problems reappear, sometimes worse—may occur when the medication is withdrawn. This rebound leads people to think they still have a sleep problem, readminister the medicine, and go through the cycle repeatedly. In other words, taking sleep aids can perpetuate sleep problems.

Other ways of reacting to poor sleep can also prolong problems. It seems reasonable that a person who hasn't had enough sleep can make up for this loss by napping during the day. Unfortunately, naps that alleviate fatigue during the day can also disrupt sleep the next night. Anxiety can also extend the problem. Lying in bed worrying about school, family problems, or even about not being able to sleep will interfere with sleep (Morin, 1993b). The behavior of parents can also help maintain these problems in children. Children who receive a great deal of positive attention at night when they wake up may wake up during the night more often (Durand, in press,a). Such maladaptive reactions, when combined with a biological predisposition to sleep problems and sleep stress, may account for continuing problems.

Primary Hypersomnia

Insomnia involves not getting enough sleep (the prefix *in* means "lacking" or "without"), and **hypersomnia** is a problem of sleeping too much (*hyper* means "in great amount" or "abnormal excess"). Many people who sleep all night find themselves falling asleep several times the next day. Consider the case of Ann.

ANN: Sleeping in Public

Ann, a college student, came to my office to discuss her progress in class. We talked about several questions that she got wrong on the last exam, and as she was about to leave she said that she never fell asleep during my class. This seemed like faint praise, but I thanked her for the feedback. "No," she said, "you don't understand. I usually fall asleep in *all* of my classes, but not in yours." Again, I didn't quite understand what she was trying to tell me and joked that she must pick her professors more carefully. She laughed. "That's probably true. But I also have this problem with sleeping too much."

As we talked more seriously, Ann told me that excessive sleeping had been a problem since her teenage years. In situations that were monotonous or boring, or when she couldn't be active, she fell asleep. This could happen several times a day, depending on what she was doing. Recently, large lecture classes had become a problem unless the lecturer was particularly interesting or animated. Watching television and driving long distances were also problematic.

Ann reported that her father had a similar problem. He had recently been diagnosed with narcolepsy (which we discuss next) and was now getting help at a clinic. Both she and her brother had been diagnosed with hypersomnia. Ann had been prescribed Ritalin (a stimulant medication) about 4 years ago and said that it was only somewhat effective in keeping her awake during the day. She said the drug helped reduce the sleep attacks but did not eliminate them altogether.

The DSM-IV-TR diagnostic criteria for hypersomnia include not only the excessive sleepiness that Ann described but also the subjective impression of this problem (American Psychiatric Association, 2000). Remember that whether insomnia is a problem depends on how it affects each person. Ann found her disorder disruptive because it interfered with driving and paying attention in class. Hypersomnia caused her to be less successful academically and upset her personally, both of which are defining features of this disorder. She slept approximately 8 hours each night, so her daytime sleepiness couldn't be attributed to insufficient sleep.

Several factors that can cause excessive sleepiness would not be considered hypersomnia. For example, people with insomnia (who get inadequate amounts of sleep) often report being tired during the day. In contrast, people with hypersomnia sleep through the night and appear rested upon awakening but still complain of being excessively tired throughout the day. Another sleep problem that can cause a similar excessive sleepiness is a breathing-related sleep disorder called **sleep apnea.** People with this problem have difficulty breathing at night. They often snore loudly, pause between breaths, and wake in the morning with a dry mouth and headache. In identifying hypersomnia, the clinician needs to rule out insomnia, sleep apnea, or other reasons for sleepiness during the day (American Psychiatric Association, 2000).

DSM TABLE 8.4 Diagnostic Criteria for Primary Hypersomnia

A. The predominant complaint is excessive sleepiness for at least 1 month (or less if recurrent) as evidenced by either prolonged sleep episodes or daytime sleep episodes that occur almost daily.
B. The excessive sleepiness causes clinically significant distress or impairment in social, occupational, or other important areas of functioning.
C. The excessive sleepiness is not better accounted for by insomnia, does not occur exclusively during the course of another sleep disorder (e.g., narcolepsy, breathing-related sleep disorder, circadian rhythm sleep disorder, or a parasomnia), and cannot be accounted for by an inadequate amount of sleep.
D. The disturbance does not occur exclusively during the course of another mental disorder.
E. The disturbance is not due to the direct physiological effects of a substance (e.g., a drug of abuse, a medication) or a general medical condition.

Specify if:
Recurrent: If there are periods of excessive sleepiness that last at least 3 days occurring several times a year for at least 2 years.

Source: Reprinted, with permission, from American Psychiatric Association. (2000). *Diagnostic and statistical manual of mental disorders* (4th ed., text revision). Washington, DC: Author. © 2000 American Psychiatric Association

Excessive sleepiness can be disruptive.

We are just beginning to understand the nature of hypersomnia, so relatively little research has been done on its causes. Genetic influences seem to be involved in a portion of cases, as 39% of people with hypersomnia have a family history of the disorder (Guilleminault & Pelayo, 2000; Parkes & Block, 1989). A significant subgroup of people diagnosed with hypersomnia previously were exposed to a viral infection such as mononucleosis, hepatitis, and viral pneumonia, which suggests there may be more than one cause (Guilleminault & Pelayo, 2000).

Narcolepsy

Ann described her father as having **narcolepsy,** a different form of the sleeping problem she and her brother shared (Pelayo & Lopes, 2006). In addition to daytime sleepiness, people with narcolepsy experience *cataplexy,* a sudden loss of muscle tone. Cataplexy occurs while the person is awake and can range from slight weakness in the facial muscles to complete physical collapse. Cataplexy lasts from several seconds to several minutes; it is usually preceded by strong emotion such as anger or happiness. Imagine that while cheering for your favorite team, you suddenly fall asleep; while arguing with a friend, you collapse to the floor in a sound sleep. You can imagine how disruptive this disorder can be!

Cataplexy appears to result from a sudden onset of REM sleep. Instead of falling asleep normally and going through the four non-rapid eye movement (NREM) stages that typically precede REM sleep, people with narcolepsy periodically progress right to this dream-sleep stage almost directly from the state of being awake. One outcome of REM sleep is the inhibition of input to the muscles, and this seems to be the process that leads to cataplexy.

Two other characteristics distinguish people who have narcolepsy (Pelayo & Lopes, 2006). They commonly report *sleep paraly-*

sis, a brief period after awakening when they can't move or speak that is often frightening to those who go through it. The last characteristic of narcolepsy is *hypnagogic hallucinations,* vivid and often terrifying experiences that begin at the start of sleep and are said to be unbelievably realistic because they include not only visual aspects but also touch, hearing, and even the sensation of body movement. Examples of hypnagogic hallucinations, which, like sleep paralysis, can be quite terrifying, include the vivid illusion of being caught in a fire or flying through the air. Narcolepsy is relatively rare, occurring in 0.03% to 0.16% of the population, with the numbers approximately equal among males and females. Although some cases have been reported in young children, the problems associated with narcolepsy usually are first seen during the teenage years. Excessive sleepiness usually occurs first, with cataplexy appearing either at the same time or with a delay of up to 30 years. Fortunately, the cataplexy, hypnagogic hallucinations, and sleep paralysis often decrease in frequency over time, although sleepiness during the day does not seem to diminish with age.

Sleep paralysis and hypnagogic hallucinations may serve a role in explaining a phenomenon—unidentified flying object (UFO) experiences. Each year, numerous people report sighting UFOs, and some even tell of visiting with inhabitants of other planets. A group of scientists examined people who had had such experiences, separating them into those who had nonintense experiences (seeing only lights and shapes in the sky) and those with intense experiences (seeing and communicating with aliens) (Spanos, Cross, Dickson, & DuBreuil, 1993). They found that a majority of the reported UFO incidents occurred at night and that 60% of the intense UFO stories were associated with sleep episodes. Specifically, the reports of these intense accounts were often described in ways that resembled accounts of people experiencing a frightening episode of sleep paralysis and hypnagogic hallucination, as illustrated by the following account (Spanos et al., 1993, p. 627):

> I was lying in bed facing the wall, and suddenly my heart started to race. I could feel the presence of three entities standing beside me. I was unable to move my body but could move my eyes. One of the entities, a male, was laughing at me, not verbally but with his mind. He made me feel stupid. He told me telepathically, "Don't you know by now that you can't do anything unless we let you?"

The realistic and frightening stories of people who have had UFO sightings may not be the products of an active imagination or the results of a hoax, but at least in some cases they may be a disturbance of sleep. Sleep paralysis and hypnagogic hallucinations do occur in a portion of people without narcolepsy, a phenomenon that may help explain why not everyone with these "otherworldly" experiences has narcolepsy. This condition commonly co-occurs with anxiety disorders in which it is termed isolated sleep paralysis (see p. 136).

Specific genetic models of narcolepsy are now being developed (Wieczorek et al., 2003). Previous research with Doberman pinschers and Labrador retrievers, who also inherit this disorder, suggests that narcolepsy is associated with a cluster of genes on chromosome 6, and it may be an autosomal recessive trait. Advances in understanding the etiology and treatment of such disorders can be credited to the help of "man's best friend."

Breathing-Related Sleep Disorders

For some people, sleepiness during the day or disrupted sleep at night has a physical origin, namely, problems with breathing while asleep. In DSM-IV-TR, these problems are diagnosed as **breathing-related sleep disorders.** People whose breathing is interrupted during their sleep experience numerous brief arousals throughout the night and do not feel rested even after 8 or 9 hours asleep (Sanders & Givelber, 2006). For all of us, the muscles in the upper airway relax during sleep, constricting the passageway somewhat and

making breathing a little more difficult. For some, unfortunately, breathing is constricted a great deal and may be labored *(hypoventilation)* or, in the extreme, there may be short periods (10 to 30 seconds) when they stop breathing altogether, called *sleep apnea.* Often the affected person is only minimally aware of breathing difficulties and doesn't attribute the sleep problems to the breathing. However, a bed partner usually notices loud snoring (which is one sign of this problem) or will have noticed frightening episodes of interrupted breathing. Other signs that a person has breathing difficulties are heavy sweating during the night, morning headaches, and episodes of falling asleep during the day *(sleep attacks)* with no resulting feeling of being rested (Sanders & Givelber, 2006).

There are three types of apnea, each with different causes, daytime complaints, and treatment: obstructive, central, and mixed sleep apnea. *Obstructive sleep apnea* occurs when airflow stops despite continued activity by the respiratory system (Sanders & Givelber, 2006). In some people, the airway is too narrow; in others, some abnormality or damage interferes with the ongoing effort to breathe. Everyone in a group of people with obstructive sleep apnea reported snoring at night (Guilleminault, 1989). Obesity is sometimes associated with this problem, as is increasing age. Sleep apnea is most common in males and is thought to occur in 10% to 20% of the population (Neylan, Reynolds, & Kupfer, 2003).

The second type, *central sleep apnea,* involves the complete cessation of respiratory activity for brief periods and is often associated with certain central nervous system disorders, such as cerebral vascular disease, head trauma, and degenerative disorders (Javaheri, 2006). Unlike people with obstructive sleep apnea, those with central sleep apnea wake up frequently during the night but they tend not to report excessive daytime sleepiness and often are not aware of having a serious breathing problem. Because of the lack of daytime symptoms, people tend not to seek treatment, so we know relatively little about its prevalence or course. The third breathing disorder, *mixed sleep apnea,* is a combination of both obstructive and central sleep apneas. All these breathing difficulties interrupt sleep and result in symptoms similar to those of insomnia.

Circadian Rhythm Sleep Disorders

"Spring ahead; fall back": People in most of the United States use this mnemonic device to remind themselves to turn the clocks ahead 1 hour in the spring and back again 1 hour in the fall. Most of us consider the shift to daylight saving time a minor inconvenience (although getting worse with so many watches and clocks to change) and are thus surprised to see how disruptive this time change can be. For at least a day or two, we may be sleepy during the day and have difficulty falling asleep at night, almost as if we had jet lag. The reason for this disruption is not just that we gain or lose 1 hour of sleep; our bodies adjust to this fairly easily. The difficulty has to do with how our biological clocks adjust to this change in time. Convention says to go to sleep at this new time while our brains are saying something different. If the struggle continues for any length of time, you may have what is called a **circadian rhythm sleep disorder.** This disorder is characterized by disturbed sleep (either insomnia or excessive sleepiness during the day) brought on by the brain's inability to synchronize its sleep patterns with the current patterns of day and night.

In the 1960s, German and French scientists identified several bodily rhythms that seem to persist without cues from the environment, rhythms that are self-regulated (Aschoff & Wever, 1962; Siffre, 1964). Because these rhythms don't exactly match our 24-hour day, they are called circadian (from *circa* meaning "about" and *dian* meaning "day"). If our circadian rhythms don't match the 24-hour day, why isn't our sleep completely disrupted over time?

Fortunately, our brains have a mechanism that keeps us in sync with the outside world. Our biological clock is in the *suprachiasmatic nucleus* in the hypothalamus. Connected to the suprachiasmatic nucleus is a pathway that comes from our eyes. The light we see in the morning and the decreasing light at night signal the brain to reset the biological clock each day. Unfortunately, some people have trouble sleeping when they want to because of problems with their circadian rhythms. The causes may be outside the person (for example, crossing several time zones in a short amount of time) or internal.

Not being synchronized with the normal wake and sleep cycles causes people's sleep to be interrupted when they do try to sleep and to be tired during the day. There are several types of circadian rhythm sleep disorders. *Jet lag type* is, as its name implies, caused by rapidly crossing multiple time zones (Monk, 2006). People with jet lag usually report difficulty going to sleep at the proper time and feeling fatigued during the day. Interestingly, older people, introverts (loners), and early risers (morning people) are most likely to be negatively affected by these time zone changes (Gillin, 1993). Research with mice suggests that the effects of jet lag can be quite serious—at least among the elderly. When older mice were exposed to repeated artificial jet lag, a significant number of them lived shorter lives (Davidson et al., 2006). *Shift work type* sleep problems are associated with work schedules (Richardson, 2006). Many people, such as hospital employees, police, or emergency personnel, work at night or must work irregular hours; as a result, they may have problems sleeping or experience excessive sleepiness during waking hours. Unfortunately, the problems of working (and thus staying awake) at unusual times can go beyond sleep and may contribute to cardiovascular disease, ulcers, and breast cancer in women (Richardson, 2006). Research suggests that people with circadian rhythm disorders are at greater risk of having one or more personality disorders (Dagan, Dela, Omer, Hallis, & Dar, 1996). Almost two thirds of all workers on rotating shifts complain of poor sleep (Neylan, Reynolds, & Kupfer, 2003).

In contrast with jet lag and shift work sleep-related problems, which have external causes such as long-distance travel and job selection, several circadian rhythm sleep disorders seem to arise from within the person experiencing the problems. Extreme night owls, people who stay up late and sleep late, may have a problem known as *delayed sleep phase type.* Sleep is delayed or later than normal bedtime. At the other extreme, people with an *advanced sleep phase type* of circadian rhythm disorder are "early to bed and early to rise." Here, sleep is advanced or earlier than normal bedtime. Partly because of our general lack of knowledge about them, DSM-IV-TR does not include these sleep phases as circadian rhythm sleep disorders.

Research on why our sleep rhythms are disrupted is advancing at a great pace, and we are beginning to understand the circadian rhythm process. Scientists believe the hormone *melatonin* contributes to the setting of our biological clocks that tell us when to sleep. This hormone is produced by the pineal gland, in the center of the brain. Melatonin (don't confuse with *melanin,* the chemical that determines skin color) has been nicknamed the "Dracula hormone" because its production is stimulated by darkness and ceases in daylight. When our eyes see that it is nighttime, this information is passed on to the pineal gland, which, in turn, begins producing melatonin. Researchers believe that both light and melatonin help set the biological clock (see ■ Figure 8.12).

DSM-IV-TR

DSM TABLE 8.7 Diagnostic Criteria for Circadian Rhythm Sleep Disorder (Formerly Sleep–Wake Schedule Disorder)

A. A persistent or recurrent pattern of sleep disruption leading to excessive sleepiness or insomnia that is due to a mismatch between the sleep–wake schedule required by a person's environment and his or her circadian sleep–wake pattern.

B. The sleep disturbance causes clinically significant distress or impairment in social, occupational, or other important areas of functioning.

C. The disturbance does not occur exclusively during the course of another sleep disorder or other mental disorder.

D. The disturbance is not due to the direct physiological effects of a substance (e.g., a drug of abuse, a medication) or a general medical condition.

Specify type:

Delayed sleep phase type: A persistent pattern of late sleep onset and late awakening times, with an inability to fall asleep and awaken at a desired earlier time

Jet lag type: Sleepiness and alertness that occur at an inappropriate time of day relative to local time, occurring after repeated travel across more than one time zone

Shift work type: Insomnia during major sleep period or excessive sleepiness during major awake period associated with night shift work or frequently changing shift work

Unspecified type

Source: Reprinted, with permission, from American Psychiatric Association. (2000). *Diagnostic and statistical manual of mental disorders* (4th ed., text revision). Washington, DC: Author, © 2000 American Psychiatric Association

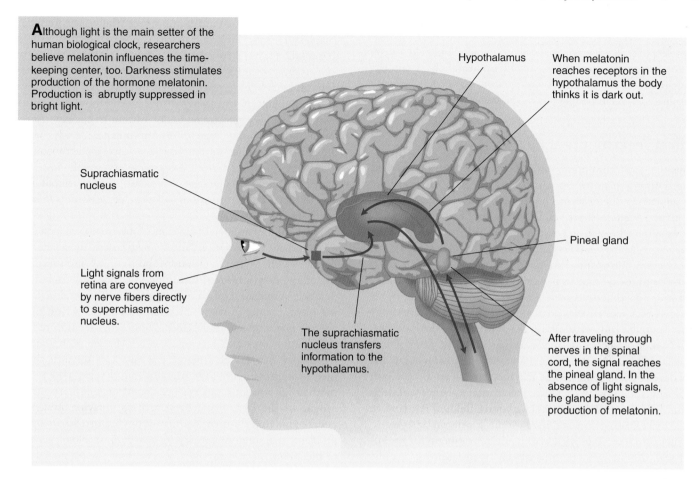

Although light is the main setter of the human biological clock, researchers believe melatonin influences the time-keeping center, too. Darkness stimulates production of the hormone melatonin. Production is abruptly suppressed in bright light.

Hypothalamus

When melatonin reaches receptors in the hypothalamus the body thinks it is dark out.

Suprachiasmatic nucleus

Pineal gland

Light signals from retina are conveyed by nerve fibers directly to superchiasmatic nucleus.

The suprachiasmatic nucleus transfers information to the hypothalamus.

After traveling through nerves in the spinal cord, the signal reaches the pineal gland. In the absence of light signals, the gland begins production of melatonin.

■ **FIGURE 8.12** Understanding the hormone of darkness. (Based on *New York Times,* 1992, November 3.)

CONCEPT CHECK 8.4

Match the following descriptions of sleeping problems with the correct term: (a) cataplexy, (b) primary hypersomnia, (c) primary insomnia, (d) sleep apnea, (e) sleep paralysis, (f) narcolepsy, (g) circadian rhythm sleep disorder, and (h) breathing-related sleep disorder.

1. Sometimes when Trudy awakens, she cannot move or speak. This is terrifying. _____
2. Susan's husband is extremely overweight. He snores every night and often wakes up exhausted as though he never slept. Susan suspects that he may be suffering from _____.
3. Suzy can hardly make it through a full day of work if she doesn't take a nap during her lunch hour. No matter how early she goes to bed in the evening, she still sleeps as late as possible in the morning. _____

(continued)

CONCEPT CHECK 8.4

(continued)
4. Jerod wakes up several times each night because he feels he is about to hyperventilate. He can't seem to get enough air, and often his wife will wake him to tell him to quit snoring. _____
5. Charlie has had considerable trouble sleeping since he started a new job that requires him to change shifts every 3 weeks. Sometime he works during the day and sleeps at night, and other times he works at night and sleeps during the day. _____
6. Jill has problems staying awake throughout the day. Even while talking on the phone or riding the bus across town, she often loses muscle tone and falls asleep for a while. _____

TREATMENT OF SLEEP DISORDERS

When we can't fall asleep or we awaken frequently, or when sleep does not restore our energy and vitality, we need help. A number of biological and psychological interventions have been designed and evaluated to help people regain the benefits of normal sleep.

Medical Treatments

Perhaps the most common treatments for insomnia are medical. People who complain of insomnia to a medical professional are likely prescribed one of several benzodiazepine or related medications, which include short-acting drugs such as *triazolam* (Halcion), zaleplon (Sonata), and zolpidem (Ambien) and long-acting drugs such as *flurazepam* (Dalmane). Short-acting drugs (those that cause only brief drowsiness) are preferred because the long-acting drugs sometimes do not stop working by morning and people report more daytime sleepiness. The long-acting medications are sometimes preferred when negative effects such as daytime anxiety are observed in people taking the short-acting drugs (Gillin, 1993). Newer medications, such as those that work directly with the melatonin system (ramelteon, Rozerem), for example, are also being developed to help people fall and stay asleep. People over the age of 65 are most likely to use medication to help them sleep, although people of all ages, including young children (Durand, in press, a), have been prescribed medications for insomnia.

There are several drawbacks to medical treatments for insomnia (Pagel, 2006). First, benzodiazepine medications can cause excessive sleepiness. Second, people can easily become dependent on them and rather easily misuse them, deliberately or not. Third, these medications are meant for short-term treatment and are not recommended for use longer than 4 weeks. Longer use can cause dependence and rebound insomnia. A newer concern for some medications (for example, Ambien) is that they may increase the likelihood of sleepwalking-related problems, such as sleep-related eating disorder (Morgenthaler & Silber, 2002). Therefore, although medications may be helpful for sleep problems that will correct themselves in a short period (for example, insomnia because of anxiety related to hospitalization), they are not intended for long-term chronic problems.

To help people with hypersomnia or narcolepsy, physicians usually prescribe a stimulant such as *methylphenidate* (Ritalin, the medication Ann was taking), *amphetamine,* or *modafinil* (Pelayo & Lopes, 2006). Cataplexy, or loss of muscle tone, can be treated with antidepressant medication, not because people with narcolepsy are depressed but because antidepressants suppress REM (or dream) sleep. Also, gamma-hydroxybutyr-ate (GHB) is the first medication specifically approved to treat cataplexy. (Some will recognize this as one of the "date rape" drugs that we discuss in Chapter 11.) Cataplexy seems to be related to the sudden onset of REM sleep; therefore, the antidepressant medication can be helpful in reducing these attacks.

Courtesy of Dr. William Dement

William C. Dement is a pioneering sleep researcher and director of the Sleep Disorders Center at Stanford University.

Treatment of breathing-related sleep disorders focuses on helping the person breathe better during sleep. For some, this means recommending weight loss. In some people who are obese, the neck's soft tissue compresses the airways. Unfortunately, as we have seen earlier in this chapter, voluntary weight loss is rarely successful in the long term; as a result, this treatment has not proved successful for breathing-related sleep disorders (Sanders & Givelber, 2006).

For mild or moderate cases of obstructive sleep apnea, treatment usually involves either a medication or a mechanical device—such as the continuous positive air pressure (CPAP) machine—that improves breathing. Medications include those that help stimulate respiration (for example, *medroxyprogesterone*) or the *tricyclic antidepressants,* which are thought to act on the locus coeruleus that affects REM sleep. These drugs seem to reduce the muscle tone loss usually seen during REM sleep, which means the respiratory muscles do not relax as much as usual at this time, thereby improving the person's breathing (Kryger, 2000). Certain mechanical devices have also been used to reposition either the tongue or the jaw during sleep to help improve breathing, but people tend to resist them because of discomfort. Severe breathing problems may require surgery to help remove blockages in parts of the airways.

An interesting treatment for people with mild apnea is being explored by researchers in collaboration with a Swiss didgeridoo instructor. A didgeridoo is a long instrument constructed from tree limbs hollowed out by termites. The instructor observed that people who practiced using this wind instrument had less daytime sleepiness. In one of a series of treatment studies, evidence points to the effectiveness of several months of daily practice using this instrument in improving the sleep of people with interrupted breathing (Puhan et al., 2006).

Environmental Treatments

Because medication as a primary treatment isn't usually recommended (Means & Edinger, 2006), other ways of getting people back in step with their sleep rhythms are usually tried. One general principle for treating circadian rhythm disorders is that *phase delays* (moving bedtime later) are easier than *phase advances* (moving bedtime earlier). In other words, it is easier to stay up several hours later than usual than to force yourself to go to sleep several hours earlier. Scheduling shift changes in a clockwise direction (going from day to evening schedule) seems to help workers adjust better. People can best readjust their sleep patterns by going to bed several hours later each night until bedtime is at the desired hour (Czeisler et al., 1981). A drawback of this approach is that it requires the person to sleep during the day for several days, which is difficult for people with regularly scheduled responsibilities.

Another strategy to help people with sleep problems involves using bright light to trick the brain into readjusting the biological clock. (In Chapter 7, we described light therapy for seasonal affective disorder.) Research indicates that bright light (also referred to as *phototherapy*) may help people with circadian rhythm problems readjust their sleep patterns (Dagan, Borodkin, & Ayalon, 2006). People typically sit in front of a bank of fluorescent lamps that generate light greater than 2,000 lux, an amount significantly different from normal indoor light (250 lux). Several hours of exposure to this bright light have successfully reset the circadian rhythms of many individuals (Czeisler & Allan, 1989). This type of treatment provides some hope for people with schedule-related sleep problems.

Psychological Treatments

As you can imagine, the limitations of using drugs to help people sleep better has led to the development of psychological treatments. Table 8.7 briefly describes some psychological approaches to insomnia. Different treatments help people with different kinds of sleep problems. For example, relaxation treatments reduce the physical tension that seems to prevent some people from falling asleep at night. Some people report that their anxiety about work, relationships, or other situations prevents them from sleeping or wakes them up in the middle of the night. To address this problem, cognitive treatments are used.

Research shows that some psychological treatments for insomnia may be more effective than others. For adult sleep problems, stimulus control may be recommended. People are instructed to use the bedroom only for sleeping and for sex and *not* for work or other anxiety-provoking activities (for example, watching the news on television). Progressive relaxation or sleep hygiene (changing daily habits that may interfere with sleep) alone may not be as effective as stimulus control alone for some people (Means & Edinger, 2006).

Sonja—the law student we profiled in the beginning of this section—was helped with her sleep problems using several techniques. She was instructed to limit her time in bed to about 4 hours of sleep time (sleep restriction), about the amount of time she slept each night. The period was lengthened when she began to sleep through the night. Sonja was also asked not to do any schoolwork while in bed and to get out of bed if she couldn't fall asleep within 15 minutes (stimulus control). Finally, therapy involved confronting her unrealistic expectations about how much sleep was enough for a person of her age (cognitive therapy). Within about 3 weeks of treatment, Sonja was sleeping longer (6 to 7 hours per night as opposed to 4 to 5 hours previously) and had fewer interruptions in her sleep. Also, she felt more refreshed in the morning and had more energy during the day. Sonja's results mirror those of studies that find combined treatments to be effective in older adults with insomnia (Petit, Azad, Byszewski, Sarazan, & Power, 2003). One such study, using a randomized placebo-control design, found that both medical and psychological approaches were effective in improving the sleep of older adults (Morin, Colecchi, Stone, Sood, & Brink, 1999). Over the long term, however, the psychological treatment was better able to maintain its effectiveness with this group.

For young children, some cognitive treatments may not be possible. Instead, treatment often includes setting up bedtime routines such as a bath, followed by a parent's reading a story, to help

TABLE 8.7 Psychological Treatments for Insomnia	
Sleep Treatment	**Description**
Cognitive	This approach focuses on changing the sleepers' unrealistic expectations and beliefs about sleep ("I must have 8 hours of sleep each night"; "If I get less than 8 hours of sleep, it will make me ill"). The therapist attempts to alter beliefs and attitudes about sleeping by providing information on topics such as normal amounts of sleep and a person's ability to compensate for lost sleep.
Guided imagery relaxation	Because some people become anxious when they have difficulty sleeping, this approach uses meditation or imagery to help with relaxation at bedtime or after a night waking.
Graduated extinction	Used for children who have tantrums at bedtime or wake up crying at night, this treatment instructs the parent to check on the child after progressively longer periods until the child falls asleep on his own.
Paradoxical intention	This technique involves instructing individuals in the opposite behavior from the desired outcome. Telling poor sleepers to lie in bed and try to stay awake as long as they can is used to try to relieve the performance anxiety surrounding efforts to try to fall asleep.
Progressive relaxation	This technique involves relaxing the muscles of the body in an effort to introduce drowsiness.

Source: World Development Indicators, World Bank, Washington, DC (2003). From Yach, D., Stuckler, D., & Brownell, K. D. (2006). Epidemiologic and economic consequences of the global epidemics of obesity and diabetes. *Nature Medicine, 12, 62–66.*

children go to sleep at night. Graduated extinction (described in Table 8.6) has been used with some success for bedtime problems, as well as for waking up at night (Durand, in press, b). Integrating both medical and behavioral treatments seems especially important for insomnia. Research suggests that short-term use of medication with other types of interventions may prove to be a quick and lasting treatment for insomnia (Petit et al., 2003).

Psychological treatment research for the other dyssomnias is virtually nonexistent. Mostly, counseling or support groups assist in managing the psychological and social effects of disturbed sleep, and they are especially helpful for people who suffer from feelings of low self-esteem and depression (Bootzin, Manber, Perlis, Salvio, & Wyatt, 1993).

Preventing Sleep Disorders

Sleep professionals generally agree that a significant portion of the sleep problems people experience daily can be prevented by following a few steps during the day. Referred to as *sleep hygiene,* these changes in lifestyle can be relatively simple to follow and can help avoid problems such as insomnia for some people (Means & Edinger, 2006). Some sleep hygiene recommendations rely on allowing the brain's normal drive for sleep to take over, replacing the restrictions we place on our activities that interfere with sleep. For example, setting a regular time to go to sleep and awaken each day can help make falling asleep at night easier. Avoiding the use of caffeine and nicotine—which are both stimulants—can also help prevent problems such as nighttime awakening. Table 8.8 illustrates a number of the sleep hygiene steps recommended for preventing sleep problems. Although there is little controlled prospective research on preventing sleep disorders, this approach appears to be among the most promising techniques available.

A few studies have investigated the value of educating parents about the sleep of their young children in an effort to prevent later difficulties (Kuhn & Elliott, 2003; Mindell, 1999). Kerr, Jowett, and Smith (1996), for example, provided information on proper sleep habits and developmental changes to the parents of 3-month-old children. They followed up on these children 6 months later and found that, compared to a randomly selected control group of children, the ones whose parents received education about sleep experienced fewer sleep problems at 9 months. Because so many children display disruptive sleep problems, this type of preventive effort could significantly improve the lives of many families.

Parasomnias and Their Treatment

Have you ever been told that you walk in your sleep? Talk in your sleep? Have you ever had troublesome nightmares? Do you grind your teeth in your sleep? If you answered yes to one or more of these questions (and it's likely you did), you have experienced sleep problems in the category of parasomnia. Parasomnias are not problems with sleep itself but abnormal events that occur either during sleep or during that twilight time between sleeping and waking. Some events associated with parasomnia are not unusual if they happen while you are awake (for example, walking to the kitchen to look into the refrigerator) but can be distressing if they take place while you are sleeping.

Parasomnias are of two types: those that occur during REM sleep, and those that occur during NREM sleep. As you might have guessed, **nightmares** occur during REM or dream sleep.

©PaloAlto/Alamy

A nightmare is distressing for both child and parent.

About 10% to 50% of children and 5% to 10% of adults experience them (Neylan, Reynolds, & Kupfer, 2003). To qualify as a nightmare disorder, according to DSM-IV-TR criteria, these experiences must be so distressful that they impair a person's ability to carry on normal activities. Some researchers distinguish nightmares from bad dreams by whether or not you wake up as a result. Nightmares are defined as disturbing dreams that awaken the sleeper; bad dreams are those that do not awaken the person experiencing them. Using this definition, college students report an average of 30 bad dreams and 10 nightmares per year (Zadra & Donderi, 2000). Because nightmares are so common, you would expect that a great deal of research would have focused on their causes and treatment. Unfortunately, this is not so, and we still know little about why people have nightmares and how to treat them. Fortunately, they tend to decrease with age.

Sleep terrors, which most commonly afflict children, usually begin with a piercing scream. The child is extremely upset, often sweating, and frequently has a rapid heartbeat. On the surface, sleep terrors appear to resemble nightmares—the child cries and appears frightened—but they occur during NREM sleep and therefore are not caused by frightening dreams. During sleep terrors, children cannot be easily awakened and comforted, as they can during a nightmare. Children do not remember sleep terrors, despite their often-dramatic effect on the observer (Durand, in press b). Approximately 5% of children (more boys than girls) may

TABLE 8.8 Good Sleep Habits

Establish a set bedtime routine.

Develop a regular bedtime and a regular time to awaken.

Eliminate all foods and drink that contain caffeine 6 hours before bedtime.

Limit any use of alcohol or tobacco.

Try drinking milk before bedtime.

Eat a balanced diet, limiting fat.

Go to bed only when sleepy and get out of bed if you are unable to fall asleep or back to sleep after 15 minutes.

Do not exercise or participate in vigorous activities in the hours before bedtime.

Do include a weekly program of exercise during the day.

Restrict activities in bed to those that help induce sleep.

Reduce noise and light in the bedroom.

Increase exposure to natural and bright light during the day.

Avoid extreme temperature changes in the bedroom (that is, too hot or too cold).

Source: Adapted, with permission, from Durand, V. M. (1998). Good sleep habits. In V. M. Durand, *Sleep better! A guide to improving sleep for children with special needs* (p. 60). Baltimore: Paul H. Brookes.)

DSM-IV-TR

DSM TABLE 8.8 Diagnostic Criteria for Nightmare Disorder

A. Repeated awakenings from the major sleep period or naps with detailed recall of extended and extremely frightening dreams, usually involving threats to survival, security, or self-esteem. The awakenings generally occur during the second half of the sleep period.

B. On awakening from the frightening dreams, the person rapidly becomes oriented and alert (in contrast to the confusion and disorientation seen in sleep terror disorder and some forms of epilepsy).

C. The dream experience, or the sleep disturbance resulting from the awakening, causes significant distress or impairment in social, occupational, or other important areas of functioning.

D. The nightmares do not occur exclusively during the course of another mental disorder (e.g., a delirium, posttraumatic stress disorder) and are not due to the direct physiological effects of a substance (e.g., a drug of abuse, a medication) or a general medical condition.

Source: Reprinted, with permission, from American Psychiatric Association. (2000). *Diagnostic and statistical manual of mental disorders* (4th ed., text revision). Washington, DC: Author, © 2000 American Psychiatric Association

experience sleep terrors; for adults, the prevalence rate is less than 1% (Buysse, Reynolds, & Kupfer, 1993). As with nightmares, we know relatively little about sleep terrors, although several theories have been proposed, including the possibility of a genetic component because the disorder tends to occur in families (Durand, in press b). Treatment for sleep terrors usually begins with a recommendation to wait and see if they disappear on their own. If the problem is frequent or continues a long time, sometimes antidepressants (imipramine) or benzodiazepines are recommended, although their effectiveness has not yet been clearly demonstrated (Mindell, 1993).

One approach to reducing chronic sleep terrors is the use of *scheduled awakenings.* In the first controlled study of its kind, Durand and Mindell (1999) instructed parents of children who were experiencing almost nightly sleep terrors to awaken their child briefly approximately 30 minutes before a typical episode. This simple technique, which was faded out over several weeks, was successful in almost eliminating these disturbing events.

It might surprise you to learn that **sleepwalking** (also called **somnambulism**) occurs during NREM sleep (Cartwright, 2006). This means that when people walk in their sleep, they are probably not acting out a dream. This parasomnia typically occurs during the first few hours while a person is in the deep stages of sleep. The DSM-IV-TR criteria for sleepwalking require that the person leave the bed, although less active episodes can involve small motor behaviors, such as sitting up in bed and picking at the blanket or gesturing. Because sleepwalking occurs during the deepest stages of sleep, waking someone during an episode is difficult; if the person is wakened, she typically will not remember what has happened. It is not true, however, that waking a sleepwalker is somehow dangerous.

Sleepwalking is primarily a problem during childhood, although a small proportion of adults are affected. A relatively large number of children—from 15% to 30%—have at least one episode of sleepwalking, with about 2% reported to have multiple incidents (Neylan, Reynolds, & Kupfer, 2003). Mostly, the course of sleepwalking is short, and few people over the age of 15 continue to exhibit this parasomnia.

We do not yet clearly understand why some people sleepwalk, although factors such as extreme fatigue, previous sleep deprivation, the use of sedative or hypnotic drugs, and stress have been implicated (Mendelson, 2005). On occasion, sleepwalking episodes have been associated with violent behavior, including homicide and suicide (Cartwright, 2006). In one case, a man drove to his in-laws' house, succeeded in killing his mother-in-law, and attempted to kill his father-in-law. He was acquitted of the charges of murder, using sleepwalking as his legal defense (Broughton, Billings, & Cartwright, 1994). These cases are still

DSM-IV-TR

DSM TABLE 8.9 Diagnostic Criteria for Sleep Terror Disorder

A. Recurrent episodes of abrupt awakening from sleep, usually occurring during the first third of the major sleep episode and beginning with a panicky scream.

B. Intense fear and signs of autonomic arousal, such as tachycardia, rapid breathing, and sweating, during each episode.

C. Relative unresponsiveness to efforts of others to comfort the person during the episode.

D. No detailed dream is recalled and there is amnesia for the episode.

E. The episodes cause clinically significant distress or impairment in social, occupational, or other important areas of functioning.

F. The disturbance is not due to the direct physiological effects of a substance (e.g., a drug of abuse, a medication) or a general medical condition.

Source: Reprinted, with permission, from American Psychiatric Association. (2000). *Diagnostic and statistical manual of mental disorders* (4th ed., text revision). Washington, DC: Author, © 2000 American Psychiatric Association

DSM-IV-TR

DSM TABLE 8.10 Diagnostic Criteria for Sleepwalking Disorder

A. Repeated episodes of rising from bed during sleep and walking about, usually occurring during the first third of the major sleep episode.

B. While sleepwalking, the person has a blank, staring face, is relatively unresponsive to the efforts of others to communicate with him or her, and can be awakened only with great difficulty.

C. On awakening (either from the sleepwalking episode or the next morning), the person has amnesia for the episode.

D. Within several minutes after awakening from the sleepwalking episode, there is no impairment of mental activity or behavior (although there may initially be a short period of confusion or disorientation).

E. The sleepwalking causes clinically significant distress or impairment in social, occupational, or other important areas of functioning.

F. The disturbance is not due to the direct physiological effects of a substance (e.g., a drug of abuse, a medication) or a general medical condition.

Source: Reprinted, with permission, from American Psychiatric Association. (2000). *Diagnostic and statistical manual of mental disorders* (4th ed., text revision). Washington, DC: Author, © 2000 American Psychiatric Association

controversial, although there is evidence for the legitimacy of some violent behavior coinciding with sleepwalking episodes. There also seems to be a genetic component to sleepwalking, with a higher incidence observed among identical twins and within families (Broughton, 2000). A related disorder, *nocturnal eating syndrome,* in which individuals rise from their beds and eat although they are still asleep, may be more frequent than previously thought, being found in almost 6% of individuals in one study who were referred because of insomnia complaints (Manni, Ratti, & Tartara, 1997; Winkelman, 2006).

There is an increasing awareness that sleep is important for both our mental and our physical well-being. Sleep problems are also comorbid with many other disorders and therefore can compound the difficulties of people with significant psychological difficulties. Researchers are coming closer to understanding the basic nature of sleep and its disorders, and we anticipate significant treatment advances in the years to come.

CONCEPT CHECK 8.5

Part A
Diagnose the sleep problems of the cases here using one of the following: (a) nocturnal eating syndrome, (b) sleep terrors, and (c) nightmares.

1. Ashley screams from her bed nearly every night. Her parents rush to comfort her, but she doesn't respond. Her heart rate is elevated during these episodes, and her pajamas are soaked in sweat. The next day, Ashley has no memory of the experience. _____

2. Rick has been dieting for more than a month but continues to gain weight. He has noticed that food is missing

(continued)

CONCEPT CHECK 8.5

(continued)

from the refrigerator but has no memory of eating. ____
_____

3. Eddie occasionally cries out from his bedroom at night. His parents take turns going into his room during these episodes and are eventually able to calm him down. He usually tells them that he was being chased by a big green monster and that he almost was caught. His parents noticed that these nighttime events may have started after he watched television at a friend's house. _____
_____

Part B
Fill in the blanks to make the following statements correct about the treatment of sleep disorders.

4. After Shirley's husband died at the age of 70, she could not sleep. For her insomnia, Shirley's family doctor prescribed enough _____ to get her through the hardest first week.

5. Dominic expressed concern to his doctor about developing a sleep disorder. His doctor suggested some relatively simple lifestyle changes otherwise known as good _____.

6. Ashley wakes up screaming every night, disregarding her parents' efforts to comfort her. Her heart rate is elevated in these episodes, and her pajamas are soaked in sweat. The next day, she has no memory of the experience. To help reduce these night terrors, Ashley's pediatrician used _____.

FUTURE DIRECTIONS

Should the Government Regulate What We Eat?

Several years ago, a professor of psychology at Yale University, Kelly Brownell, proposed in the *New York Times* that we should begin to discuss taxing high-calorie, high-fat, or high-sugar foods as a means of addressing the obesity epidemic. This proposal sparked a firestorm of controversy and came to be known as the "Twinkie tax." And yet, taxation is a powerful and commonly used tactic by governments around the world to set policy and shape the behavior of its citizens. A rapid increase in taxes on cigarettes has as one goal: reducing smoking in our citizens and improving health. Increasing taxes on fossil fuels, including gasoline, is conceived by many as one tool for promoting conservation and diminishing the release of harmful chemicals into our environment that contribute to global warming. Substantial tax breaks on alternative sources of energy such as wind power and solar energy are another government tool for promoting these sources.

Food taxes have also been discussed as a way to raise revenue that could be used in the fight against the obesity epidemic. In other words, could the government make it more attractive to eat healthy foods and less attractive to eat unhealthy foods by making the former less expensive and the latter more expensive? The Rudd Center for food policy and obesity at Yale is studying the issues intensely. Several states have put into place taxes on snack foods, although these efforts are just beginning. Also, well known are the states' initiatives to remove soft drink machines and other sources of unhealthy snack foods from public schools. The thinking is that taxes would have to be increased considerably to provide a substantial disincentive, perhaps 7% or more, depending on the food. There are many objections to large tax increases. Perhaps, the most persuasive argument is that the tax would be regressive in that it would disproportionately affect the poor, who tend to eat substantially more fast foods than well-to-do individuals. Also, any substantial tax, with its implications of government control of our behavior, would be controversial and roundly criticized by many.

Another approach suggested by the Rudd Center for discussion would be to institute a small tax that would not act as a disincentive but would produce revenue to fight obesity. For example, a tax of a penny a can on soft drinks in the United States would raise $1.5 billion annually but is likely to be well-tolerated by consumers. Expanding these small taxes across a number of unhealthy foods would increase revenue substantially.

These debates are now raging around the country and around the world. What would you do? Would you propose that governments intervene economically to change the nutrition of our citizens? Or would you rely solely on education and other means of persuasion? Governments will have to make these choices because it seems clear that the obesity epidemic is one of the greatest threats to health in recent history.

SUMMARY

- The prevalence of eating disorders has increased rapidly over the last half century. As a result, they were included for the first time as a separate group of disorders in DSM-IV.

Bulimia Nervosa and Anorexia Nervosa

- There are two prevalent eating disorders. In bulimia nervosa, dieting results in out-of-control binge-eating episodes that are often followed by purging the food through vomiting or other means. Anorexia nervosa, in which food intake is cut dramatically, results in substantial weight loss and sometimes dangerously low body weight.

Binge-Eating Disorder

- In binge-eating disorder, a pattern of binge eating is *not* followed by purging.

Statistics and Course for Eating Disorders

- Bulimia nervosa and anorexia nervosa are largely confined to young, middle- to upper-class women in Western cultures who are pursuing a thin body shape that is culturally mandated and biologically inappropriate, making it extremely difficult to achieve.

- Without treatment, eating disorders become chronic and can, on occasion, result in death.

Causes of Eating Disorders

- In addition to sociocultural pressures, causal factors include possible biological and genetic vulnerabilities (the disorders tend to run in families), psychological factors (low self-esteem), social anxiety (fears of rejection), and distorted body image (relatively normal-weight individuals view themselves as fat and ugly).

Treatment of Eating Disorders

- Several psychosocial treatments are effective, including cognitive-behavioral approaches combined with family therapy and interpersonal psychotherapy. Drug treatments are less effective at the current time.

Obesity

- Obesity is not a disorder in DSM but is one of the more dangerous epidemics confronting the world today. Cultures that encourage eating high-fat foods combine with genetic and other factors to cause obesity, which is difficulty to treat. Professionally directed behavior modification programs, possibly combined with drugs, are moderately successful.

Sleep Disorders

■ Sleep disorders are highly prevalent in the general population and are of two types: dyssomnias (disturbances of sleep) and parasomnias (abnormal events such as nightmares and sleepwalking that occur during sleep).

■ Of the dyssomnias, the most common disorder, primary insomnia, involves the inability to initiate sleep, problems maintaining sleep, or failure to feel refreshed after a full night's sleep. Other dyssomnias include primary hypersomnia (excessive sleep), narcolepsy (sudden and irresistible sleep attacks), circadian rhythm sleep disorders (sleepiness or insomnia caused by the body's inability to synchronize its sleep patterns with day and night), and breathing-related sleep disorders (disruptions that have a physical origin, such as sleep apnea, that leads to excessive sleepiness or insomnia).

■ The formal assessment of sleep disorders, a polysomnographic evaluation, is typically done by monitoring the heart, muscles, respiration, brain waves, and other functions of a sleeping client in the lab. In addition to such monitoring, it is helpful to determine the individual's sleep efficiency, a percentage based on the time the individual actually sleeps as opposed to time spent in bed trying to sleep.

■ Benzodiazepine medications have been helpful for short-term treatment of many of the dyssomnias, but they must be used carefully or they might cause rebound insomnia, a withdrawal experience that can cause worse sleep problems after the medication is stopped. Any long-term treatment of sleep problems should include psychological interventions such as stimulus control and sleep hygiene.

■ Parasomnias such as nightmares occur during rapid eye movement (or dream) sleep, and sleep terrors and sleepwalking occur during nonrapid eye movement sleep.

Key Terms

bulimia nervosa, 261
binge, 261
anorexia nervosa, 261
obesity, 262
purging techniques, 264
binge-eating disorder (BED), 268
night eating syndrome, 284

bariatric surgery, 287
rapid eye movement (REM) sleep, 289
dyssomnias, 290
parasomnias, 290
polysomnographic (PSG) evaluation, 290
actigraph, 290

sleep efficiency (SE), 290
microsleeps, 290
primary insomnia, 290
rebound insomnia, 293
hypersomnia, 293
sleep apnea, 293
narcolepsy, 294

breathing-related sleep disorders, 295
circadian rhythm sleep disorders, 296
nightmares, 300
sleep terrors, 300
sleepwalking, 301

Answers to Concept Checks

8.1

1. c; 2. a; 3. a; 4. b

8.2

1. T; 2. T; 3. F (females find a smaller size more attractive than do men); 4. F (they help with bulimia nervosa, not anorexia); 5. T; 6. T

8.3

1. T; 2. F (it's only one-third or more); 3. F; 4. T

8.4

1. e; 2. d; 3. b; 4. h; 5. g; 6. f

8.5

Part A

1. b; 2. a; 3. c

Part B

4. benzodiazepines 5. sleep hygiene 6. scheduled awakenings

The Abnormal Psychology Book Companion Website

See **academic.cengage.com/psychology/barlow** for practice quiz questions, interactive activities, Internet links, critical thinking exercises, discussion forums, and more. Also accessible from the Wadsworth Psychology Resource Center **(academic.cengage.com/login).**

Abnormal Psychology Live CD-ROM

■ *Susan, a Client With Anorexia Nervosa:* In this example of anorexia, Susan talks about her fears about not being "skinny enough" to be seen as a good enough example of the disorder.

■ *Twins With Anorexia Nervosa/Bulimia:* Two twins talk about their battle with food.

■ *Weight Control:* Consider how researchers are helping people deal with the obesity epidemic.

■ *Sleep Cycle:* This clip describes the normal cycle of REM and NREM sleep throughout the night—a cycle that may be altered in sleep disorders.

CengageNOW

Go to **academic.cengage.com/now** to link to CengageNOW, your online study tool. First take the Pre-Test for this chapter to get your personalized study plan, which will identify topics you need to review and direct you to online resources. Then take the Post-Test to determine what concepts you have mastered and what you still need work on.

Video Concept Reviews

CengageNOW also contains Mark Durand's *Video Concept Reviews* on challenging topics.

- Bulimia Nervosa—Including Bingeing and Purging
- Anorexia Nervosa
- Concept Check: Difference Between Anorexia and Bulimia
- Binge Eating Disorder
- Concept Check: Why Obesity Is Not in DSM-IV
- Dysomnias and Parasomnias
- Polysomnographic (PSG) Evaluation
- Primary Insomnia
- Hypersomnia
- Narcolepsy
- Alien Abduction and Sleep
- Circadian Rhythm Disorders

Exploring Eating Disorders

Individuals with eating disorders:
- *Feel a relentless, all-encompassing drive to be thin*
- *Are overwhelmingly young females from middle- to upper-class families, who live in socially competitive environments*
- *Lived only in Western countries until recently*

EATING DISORDERS

BULIMIA NERVOSA

Characteristics

- Out-of-control consumption of excessive amounts of mostly non-nutritious food within a short time
- Elimination of food through self-induced vomiting and/or abuse of laxatives or diuretics
- To compensate for binges, some bulimics exercise excessively or fast between binges
- Vomiting may enlarge salivary glands (causing a chubby face), erode dental enamel, and cause electrolyte imbalance resulting in cardiac failure or kidney problems
- Weight usually within 10% of normal
- Age of onset is typically 16 to 19 years of age

Treatment

- Drug treatment, such as antidepressants
- Short-term cognitive-behavioral therapy (CBT) to address behavior and attitudes on eating and body shape
- Interpersonal psychotherapy (IPT) to improve interpersonal functioning
- Tends to be chronic if left untreated

BINGE-EATING DISORDER

Characteristics

- Similar to bulimia with out-of-control food binges, but no attempt to purge the food (vomiting, laxatives, diuretics) or compensate for excessive intake
- Marked physical and emotional stress; some sufferers binge to alleviate bad moods
- Binge eaters share some concerns about weight and body shape as individuals with anorexia and bulimia
- Tends to affect more older people than either bulimia or anorexia

Treatment

- Short-term CBT to address behavior and attitudes on eating and body shape
- IPT to improve interpersonal functioning
- Drug treatments that reduce feelings of hunger
- Self-help approaches

ANOREXIA NERVOSA

Characteristics

- Intense fear of obesity and persistent pursuit of thinness; perpetual dissatisfaction with weight loss
- Severe caloric restriction, often with excessive exercise and sometimes with purging, to the point of semi-starvation
- Severely limiting caloric intake may cause cessation of menstruation, downy hair on limbs and cheeks, dry skin, brittle hair or nails, sensitivity to cold, and danger of acute cardiac or kidney failure
- Weight at least 15% below normal
- Average age of onset is about 13 years of age

Treatment

- Hospitalization (at 70% below normal weight)
- Outpatient treatment to restore weight and correct dysfunctional attitudes on eating and body shape
- Family therapy
- Tends to be chronic if left untreated; more resistant to treatment than bulimia

CAUSES

Social—Cultural and social emphasis on slender ideal, leading to body dissatisfaction and preoccupation with food and eating.

Psychological—Diminished sense of personal control and self-confidence, causing low self-esteem. Distorted body image.

Biological—Possible genetic tendency to poor impulse control, emotional instability, and perfectionistic traits

OBESITY

Characteristics

- Up to 65% of U.S. adults are overweight, and over 30% are obese
- Worldwide problem; increased risk in urban rather than rural settings
- Two forms of maladaptive eating patterns associated with obesity—binge eating and night eating syndrome
- Increases risk of cardiovascular disease, diabetes, hypertension, stroke, and other physical problems.

Treatment

- Self-directed weight loss programs
- Commercial self-help programs, such as Weight Watchers
- Professionally directed behavior modification programs, which are the most effective treatment
- Surgery, as a last resort

CAUSES

Social—Advancing technology promotes sedentary lifestyle and consumption of high fat foods.

Psychological—Affects impulse control, attitudes, and motivation towards eating, and responsiveness to the consequences of eating.

Biological—Genes influence an individual's number of fat cells, tendency toward fat storage, and activity levels.

Exploring Sleep Disorders

Characterized by extreme disruption in the everyday lives of affected individuals, and are an important factor in many psychological disorders.

SLEEP DISORDERS

DYSSOMNIAS

Disturbances in the timing, amount, or quality of sleep

Primary Insomnia

- Characteristics include difficulty initiating sleep, difficulty maintaining sleep, or nonrestorative sleep
- Causes include pain, insufficient exercise, drug use, environmental influences, anxiety, respiratory problems, and biological vulnerability.
- Treatment may be medical (benzodiazepines) or psychological (anxiety reduction, improved sleep hygiene); combined approach is usually most effective.

Narcolepsy

- Characteristics include sudden daytime onset of REM sleep combined with cataplexy, a rapid loss of muscle tone that can be quite mild or result in complete collapse. Often accompanied by sleep paralysis and/or hypnagogic hallucinations.
- Causes are likely to be genetic.
- Treatment is medical (stimulant drugs).

DIAGNOSING SLEEP DISORDERS

A polysomnographic (PSG) evaluation assesses an individual's sleep habits with various electronic tests to measure airflow, brain activity, eye movements, muscle movements, and heart activity. Results are weighed with a measure of sleep efficiency (SE), the percentage of time spent asleep.

Primary Hypersomnia

- Characteristics include abnormally excessive sleep and sleepiness, and involuntary daytime sleeping. Classified as a disorder only when it's subjectively perceived as disruptive.
- Causes may involve genetic link and/or excess serotonin.
- Treatment is usually medical (stimulant drugs).

Breathing-Related Sleep Disorder

- Characteristics include disturbed sleep and daytime fatigue resulting from hypoventilation (labored breathing) or sleep apnea (suspended breathing).
- Causes may include narrow or obstructed airway, obesity, and increasing age.
- Treatments to improve breathing are medical or mechanical.

Circadian Rhythm Sleep Disorder

- Characteristics include sleepiness or insomnia.
- Caused by inability to synchronize sleep patterns with current pattern of day and night due to jet lag, shift work, delayed sleep, or advanced sleep (going to bed earlier than normal bedtime).
- Treatment includes phase delays to adjust bedtime and bright light to readjust biological clock.

PARASOMNIAS

Abnormal behaviors that occur during sleep.

Nightmares

Frightening REM dreams that awaken the sleeper. Nightmares qualify as nightmare disorder when they are stressful enough to impair normal functioning. Causes are unknown, but they tend to decrease with age.

Sleep Terrors

Occur during non-REM (nondreaming) sleep and most commonly afflict children. Sleeping child screams, cries, sweats, sometimes walks, has rapid heartbeat, and cannot easily be awakened or comforted. More common in boys than girls, and possible genetic link since tend to run in families. May subside with time.

Sleepwalking

Occurs at least once during non-REM sleep in 15% to 30% of children under age 15. Causes may include extreme fatigue, sleep deprivation, sedative or hypnotic drugs, and stress. Adult sleepwalking is usually associated with other psychological disorders. May have a genetic link.

CHAPTER 9

Physical Disorders and Health Psychology

©Blend Images/SuperStock

PSYCHOLOGICAL AND SOCIAL FACTORS THAT INFLUENCE HEALTH
> Health and Health-Related Behavior
> The Nature of Stress
> The Physiology of Stress
> Contributions to the Stress Response
> Stress, Anxiety, Depression, and Excitement
> Stress and the Immune Response

PSYCHOSOCIAL EFFECTS ON PHYSICAL DISORDERS
> AIDS
> Cancer
> Cardiovascular Problems
> Hypertension
> Coronary Heart Disease
> Chronic Pain
> Chronic Fatigue Syndrome

PSYCHOSOCIAL TREATMENT OF PHYSICAL DISORDERS
> Biofeedback
> Relaxation and Meditation
> A Comprehensive Stress- and Pain-Reduction Program
> Drugs and Stress-Reduction Programs
> Denial as a Means of Coping
> Modifying Behaviors to Promote Health

ABNORMAL PSYCHOLOGY LIVE CD-ROM
Social Support/HIV: Orel
The Immune System: Effects of Stress and Emotion
Cancer: Education and Support Groups
Web Link

The story I want to tell is about heroism and sacrifice and love, but I will not be avoiding the anger.

Paul Monette

Borrowed Time: An AIDS Memoir

PSYCHOLOGICAL AND SOCIAL FACTORS THAT INFLUENCE HEALTH

The U.S. surgeon general and others have pointed out that at the beginning of the 20th century the leading causes of death were from infectious diseases such as influenza, pneumonia, diphtheria, tuberculosis, typhoid fever, measles, and gastrointestinal infections. Since then, the yearly death rate from these diseases has been reduced greatly, from 623 to 50 per 100,000 people (see Table 9.1). This reduction represents a revolution in public health that eliminated many infectious diseases and mastered many more. But the enormous success of our health-care system in reducing mortality from disease has revealed a more complex and challenging problem: At present, some major contributing factors to illness and death in this country are *psychological and behavioral.* Consider, for example, the relationship between genital herpes and stress.

There's a chance that someone you know has *genital herpes* and hasn't told you about it. It's not difficult to understand why: Genital herpes is an incurable sexually transmitted disease. Estimates indicate that more than 50 million Americans—about 20% of the entire population—have been infected by the herpes simplex virus I or II (Brentjens, Yeung-Yue, Lee, & Tyring, 2003). Because the disease is concentrated in young adults, the percentage in that group is much higher. The virus remains dormant until it is reactivated periodically. When it recurs, infected individuals usually experience any of a number of symptoms, including pain, itching, vaginal or urethral discharge, and, most commonly, ulcerative lesions (open sores) in the genital area. Lesions recur approximately four times each year but can appear more often. Cases of genital herpes have increased dramatically during the past 20 years, for reasons that are as much psychological and behavioral as biological. Although genital herpes is a biological disease, it spreads rapidly because people choose not to change their behavior by simply using a condom.

Increasing evidence suggests that stress plays a role in triggering recurrences (see, for example, Glaser, Kiecolt-Glaser, Speicher, & Holliday, 1985; Hoon et al., 1991; Pereira et al., 2003) by suppressing the immune system (Kemeny, Cohen, Zegans, & Conant, 1989). Stress-control procedures, particularly relaxation, may decrease recurrences of genital herpes, as well as the duration of each episode (Pereira et al., 2003). Burnette, Koehn, Kenyon-Jump, Hutton, and Stark (1991) treated seven women and one man using a single-case, multiple baseline, across-subjects design (see Chapter 4) in which treatment is introduced at a different time for each subject. If changes in the condition do not occur *until* treatment is introduced, we can be fairly confident the change is caused by the treatment and not some other factor, such as attention from the therapist. Data from five individuals who responded well to treatment are represented in ■ Figure 9.1. The data reflect the number of days per week that each person had a recurrence of genital herpes. On the horizontal line is the average number of recurrences before and after treatment. Note the response of subject 7. During some weeks she had outbreaks almost every day, but after stress-reduction treatment they were almost eliminated.

In addition to subject 7, four other patients responded reasonably well to treatment, but three others did not respond in a clinically significant way. At least one reported not practicing relaxation, which might account for the lack of progress; the other two, evidently, just did not benefit. Although these data are only

TABLE 9.1	The 10 Leading Causes of Death in the United States in 1900 and in 2001 (Rates per 100,000 Population)		
1900	**Rate**	**2001**	**Rate**
1. Cardiovascular diseases (heart disease, stroke)	345	1. Diseases of heart	258.2
2. Influenza and pneumonia	202	2. Cancer	200.9
3. Tuberculosis	194	3. Cerebrovascular diseases	60.9
4. Gastritis, duodenitis, enteritis, and colitis	143	4. Chronic lower respiratory diseases	44.3
5. Accidents	72	5. Accidents	35.6
6. Cancer	64	6. Diabetes	25.2
7. Diphtheria	40	7. Influenza and pneumonia	23.7
8. Typhoid fever	31	8. Alzheimer's disease	18.0
9. Measles	13	9. Nephritis, nephrotic syndrome, and nephrosis	13.5
10. Chronic liver diseases and cirrhosis	*	10. Septicemia	11.3
*Data unavailable.			

Source: Figures for 1900 from U.S. Bureau of the Census, 1975. *Historical Statistics of the United States: Colonial Times to 1970,* Pt. 1. Washington, DC: U.S. Government Printing Office. Figures for 2001 from U.S. Bureau of the Census, 2003. Deaths: Final data for 2001. *National Vital Statistics Reports,* 52, 8, © 2003 U.S. Government Printing Office.

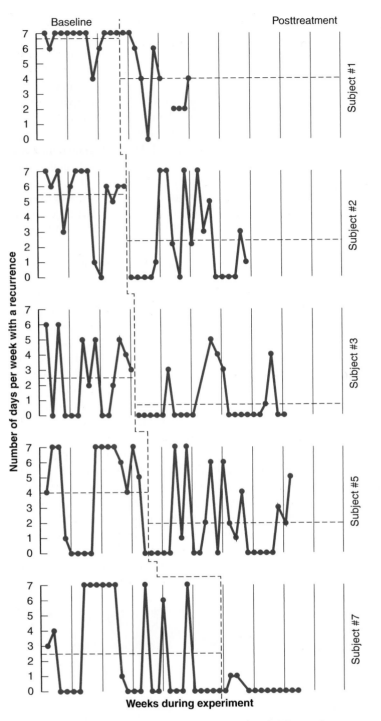

Number of days per week with a recurrence

Baseline   Posttreatment

Subject #1
Subject #2
Subject #3
Subject #5
Subject #7

Weeks during experiment

■ **FIGURE 9.1** Measures of genital herpes outbreaks. The graphs show before- and after-treatment measures of genital herpes outbreaks for five subjects who received stress-reduction treatment. The horizontal broken lines—representing the average number of outbreaks during baseline and posttreatment periods—show that these subjects experienced a significant decrease in outbreaks after treatment. (Adapted from Burnette, M. M., Koehn, K. A., Kenyon-Jump, R., & Stark, C., 1991. Control of genital herpes recurrences using progressive muscle relaxation. *Behavior Therapy, 22,* 237–247, © 1991 Association for Advancement of Behavior Therapy. Reprinted by permission of the author and publisher.)

preliminary, the findings strongly suggest a relationship between psychological factors and viral infections for some people.

In Chapter 2, we described the profound effects of psychological and social factors on brain structure and function. These factors seem to influence neurotransmitter activity, the secretion of neurohormones in the endocrine system, and, at a more fundamental level, gene expression. We have repeatedly looked at the complex interplay of biological, psychological, and social factors in the production and maintenance of psychological disorders. It will come as no surprise that psychological and social factors are important to a number of additional disorders, including endocrinological disorders such as diabetes and disorders of the immune system such as acquired immune deficiency syndrome (AIDS). The difference between these and the other disorders discussed in this chapter is that they are clearly *physical disorders.* They have known (or strongly inferred) physical causes and mostly observable physical pathology (for example, genital herpes, damaged heart muscle, malignant tumors, or measurable hypertension). Contrast this with the somatoform disorders discussed in Chapter 6: In conversion disorders, for example, clients complain of physical damage or disease but show no physical pathology. In the fourth edition, text revision, of the *Diagnostic and Statistical Manual* (DSM-IV-TR), physical disorders such as hypertension and diabetes are coded separately on Axis III. However, there is a provision for recognizing "psychological factors affecting medical condition."

The study of how psychological and social factors affect physical disorders used to be distinct and somewhat separate from the remainder of psychopathology. Early on, the field was called *psychosomatic medicine* (Alexander, 1950), which meant that *psychological* factors affected *somatic* (physical) function. *Psychophysiological disorders* was a label used to communicate a similar idea. Such terms are less often used today because they are misleading. Describing as psychosomatic a disorder with an obvious physical component gave the impression that psychological (mental) disorders of mood and anxiety did not have a strong biological component. As we now know, this assumption is not viable. Dividing the causes of mental disorders and physical disorders is not supported by current evidence. Biological, psychological, and social factors are implicated in the cause and maintenance of every disorder.

The contribution of psychosocial factors to the etiology and treatment of physical disorders is widely studied. Some of the discoveries are among the more exciting findings in all of psychology and biology. For example, in Chapter 2, we described briefly the specific harmful influences of anger on heart function. The tentative conclusion from that research was that the pumping efficiency of an angry person's heart is reduced, risking dangerous disturbances of heart rhythms (Ironson et al., 1992; Robins & Novaco, 2000). Remember, too, the tragic physical and mental deterioration among elderly people who are removed from social networks of family and friends (Broadhead, Kaplan, & James, 1983; Grant, Patterson, & Yager, 1988). Also, long-term unemployment among men who previously held steady jobs is associated with a doubling of the risk of death over the following 5 years compared to men who continued working (Morris, Cook, & Shaper, 1994). Researchers isolated stress resulting from economic uncertainty as the principal cause of plummeting ages of life expectancy in Eastern Europe after the fall of communism (Stone, 2000).

Health and Health-Related Behavior

The shift in focus from infectious disease to psychological factors has been called the second revolution in public health. Two closely related new fields of study have developed. In the first, **behavioral medicine** (Agras, 1982; Meyers, 1991), knowledge derived from behavioral science is applied to the prevention, diagnosis, and treatment of medical problems. This is an interdisciplinary field in which psychologists, physicians, and other health professionals work closely together to develop new treatments and preventive strategies (Schwartz & Weiss, 1978). A second field, **health psychology,** is not interdisciplinary, and it is usually considered a subfield of behavioral medicine. Practitioners study psychological factors that are important to the promotion and maintenance of health; they also analyze and recommend improvements in health-care systems and health policy formation within the discipline of psychology (Feuerstein, Labbe, & Kuczmierczyk, 1986; G. Stone, 1987; Taylor, 2006).

Psychological and social factors influence health and physical problems in *two* distinct ways (see ■ Figure 9.2). First, they can affect the basic biological processes that lead to illness and disease. Second, long-standing behavior patterns may put people at risk to develop certain physical disorders. Sometimes both these avenues contribute to the etiology or maintenance of disease (Kiecolt-Glaser & Newton, 2001; Miller & Blackwell, 2006; Schneiderman, 2004; Taylor, Repetti, & Seeman, 1997; Williams, Barefoot, & Schneiderman, 2003). Consider the tragic example of AIDS. AIDS is a disease of the immune system that is directly affected by stress (Cohen & Herbert, 1996; Kennedy, 2000), so stress may promote the deadly progression of AIDS (a conclusion pending confirmation from additional studies). This is an example of how psychological factors may directly influence biological processes. We also know that a variety of things we may choose to do put us at risk for AIDS—for example, having unprotected sex or sharing dirty needles. Because there is no medical cure for AIDS yet, our best weapon is large-scale behavior modification to *prevent acquisition* of the disease.

Other behavioral patterns contribute to disease. Fully 50% of deaths from the 10 leading causes of death in the United States can be traced to behaviors common to certain lifestyles (Centers for Disease Control, 2003). Smoking is the leading preventable cause of death in the United States and has been estimated to cause 19% of all deaths (Brannon & Feist, 1997; McGinnis & Foege, 1993). Other unhealthy behaviors include poor eating habits, lack of exercise, and insufficient injury control (not wearing seat belts, for example). These behaviors are grouped under the label *lifestyle* because they are mostly enduring habits that are an integral part of a person's daily living pattern (Faden, 1987; Oyama & Andrasik, 1992). We return to lifestyles in the closing pages of this chapter when we look at efforts to modify them and promote health.

We have much to learn about how psychological factors affect physical disorders and disease. Available evidence suggests that the same kinds of causal factors active in psychological disorders—social, psychological, and biological—play a role in some physical disorders (Mostofsky & Barlow, 2000; Taylor et al., 1997). But the factor attracting the most attention is *stress,* particularly the neurobiological components of the stress response.

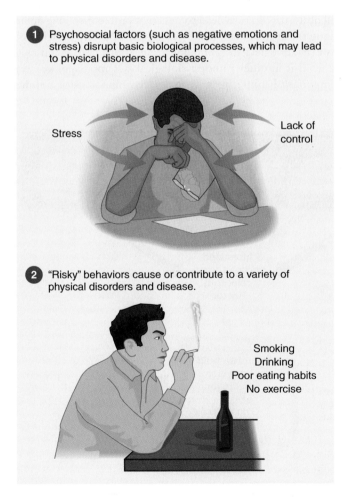

1 Psychosocial factors (such as negative emotions and stress) disrupt basic biological processes, which may lead to physical disorders and disease.

Stress

Lack of control

2 "Risky" behaviors cause or contribute to a variety of physical disorders and disease.

Smoking
Drinking
Poor eating habits
No exercise

■ **FIGURE 9.2** Psychosocial factors directly affect physical health in two ways.

The Nature of Stress

In 1936, a young scientist in Montreal, Canada, named Hans Selye noticed that one group of rats he injected with a certain chemical extract developed ulcers and other physiological problems, including atrophy of immune system tissues. But a control group of rats who received a daily saline (salty water) injection that should not have had any effect developed the *same* physical

Courtesy of Hans Selya

Hans Selye suggested in 1936 that stress contributes to certain physical problems.

problems. Selye pursued this unexpected finding and discovered that the daily injections themselves seemed to be the culprit rather than the injected substance. Furthermore, many types of environmental changes produced the same results. Borrowing a term from engineering, he decided the cause of this nonspecific reaction was *stress.* As so often happens in science, an accidental or serendipitous observation led to a new area of study, in this case, *stress physiology* (Selye, 1936).

Selye theorized that the body goes through several stages in response to *sustained stress.* The first phase is a type of *alarm* response to immediate danger or threat. With continuing stress, we seem to pass into a stage of *resistance,* in which we mobilize various coping mechanisms to respond to the stress. Finally, if the stress is too intense or lasts too long, we may enter a stage of *exhaustion,* in which our bodies suffer permanent damage or death (Selye, 1936, 1950). Selye called this sequence the **general adaptation syndrome (GAS).** Although Selye was not correct in all of the details of his theory, the idea that chronic stress may inflict permanent bodily damage or contribute to disease has been confirmed and elaborated on in recent years (Kemeny, 2003; McEwen & Stellar, 1993; Robles, Glaser, & Kiecolt-Glaser, 2005; Sapolsky, 1990, 2000).

The word *stress* means many things in modern life. In engineering, stress is the strain on a bridge when a heavy truck drives across it; stress is the *response* of the bridge to the truck's weight. But stress is also a *stimulus.* The truck is a "stressor" for the bridge, just as being fired from a job or facing a difficult final exam is a stimulus or stressor for a person. These varied meanings can create some confusion, but we concentrate on **stress** as the physiological response of the individual to a stressor.

The Physiology of Stress

In Chapter 2, we described the physiological effects of the early stages of stress, noting in particular its activating effect on the sympathetic nervous system, which mobilizes our resources during times of threat or danger by activating internal organs to prepare the body for immediate action, either fight or flight. These changes increase our strength and mental activity. We also noted in Chapter 2 that the activity of the endocrine system increases when we are stressed, primarily through activation of the hypothalamic–pituitary–adrenocortical (HPA) axis (see p. 46 in Chapter 2). Although a variety of neurotransmitters begin flowing in the nervous system, much attention has focused on the endocrine system's neuromodulators or neuropeptides, hormones affecting the nervous system that are secreted by the glands directly into the bloodstream (Krishnan, Doraiswamy, Venkataraman, Reed, & Richie, 1991; Owens et al., 1997). These neuromodulating hormones act much like neurotransmitters in carrying the brain's messages to various parts of the body. One of the

neurohormones, *corticotropin-releasing factor (CRF),* is secreted by the hypothalamus and stimulates the pituitary gland. Farther down the chain of the HPA axis, the pituitary gland (along with the autonomic nervous system) activates the adrenal gland, which secretes, among other things, the hormone *cortisol.* Because of their close relationship to the stress response, cortisol and other related hormones are known as the *stress hormones.*

Remember that the HPA axis is closely related to the limbic system. The hypothalamus, at the top of the brain stem, is right next to the limbic system, which contains the hippocampus and seems to control our emotional memories. The hippocampus is responsive to cortisol. When stimulated by this hormone during HPA axis activity, the hippocampus helps to *turn off* the stress response, completing a feedback loop between the limbic system and the various parts of the HPA axis (see ■ Figure 9.3).

This loop may be important for a number of reasons. Working with primates, Robert Sapolsky and his colleagues (see, for example, Sapolsky & Meaney, 1986; Sapolsky, 2000, 2007) showed that increased levels of cortisol in response to chronic stress may kill nerve cells in the hippocampus. If hippocampal activity is thus compromised, excessive cortisol is secreted and, over time, the ability to turn off the stress response decreases, which leads to further aging of the hippocampus. These findings indicate that chronic stress leading to chronic secretion of cortisol may have long-lasting effects on physical function, including brain damage. Cell death may, in turn, lead to deficient problem-solving abilities among the aged and, ultimately, dementia. This physiological process may also affect susceptibility to infectious disease and recovery from it in other pathophysiological systems. Sapolsky's work is important because we now know that hippocampal cell death

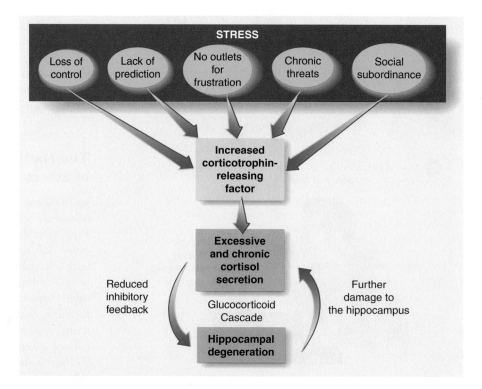

■ **FIGURE 9.3** Effects of psychological stress on the HPA axis and the hippocampus. Adapted from Sapolsky (1992, 2007) and Sapolsky and Ray (1989).

associated with chronic stress and anxiety occurs in humans with, for example, posttraumatic stress disorder (see Chapter 5) and depression (see Chapter 7). The long-term effects of this cell death are not yet known.

Contributions to the Stress Response

Stress physiology is profoundly influenced by psychological and social factors (Kemeny, 2003; Taylor et al., 1997). This link has been demonstrated by Sapolsky (1990, 2000, 2007). He is studying baboons living freely in a national reserve in Kenya because their primary sources of stress, like those of humans, are psychological rather than physical. As with many species, baboons arrange themselves in a social hierarchy with dominant members at the top and submissive members at the bottom. And life is tough at the bottom! The lives of subordinate animals are made difficult (Sapolsky calls it "stressful") by continual bullying from the dominant animals, and they have less access to food, preferred resting places, and sexual partners. Particularly interesting are Sapolsky's findings on levels of cortisol in the baboons as a function of their social rank in a dominance hierarchy. Remember from our description of the HPA axis that the secretion of cortisol from the adrenal glands is the final step in a cascade of hormone secretion that originates in the limbic system in the brain during periods of stress. The secretion of cortisol contributes to our arousal and mobilization in the short run but, if produced chronically, it can damage the hippocampus. In addition, muscles atro-

phy, fertility is affected by declining testosterone, hypertension develops in the cardiovascular system, and the immune response is impaired. Sapolsky discovered that dominant males in the baboon hierarchy ordinarily had *lower* resting levels of cortisol than subordinate males. When an emergency occurred, however, cortisol levels rose more quickly in the dominant males than in the subordinate males.

Sapolsky and his colleagues sought the causes of these differences by working backward up the HPA axis. They found an excess secretion of CRF by the hypothalamus in subordinate animals, combined with a diminished sensitivity of the pituitary gland (which is stimulated by CRF). Therefore, subordinate animals, unlike dominant animals, continually secrete cortisol, probably because their lives are so stressful. In addition, their HPA system is less sensitive to the effects of cortisol and therefore less efficient in turning off the stress response.

Sapolsky also discovered that subordinate males have fewer circulating lymphocytes (white blood cells) than dominant males, a sign of immune system suppression. In addition, subordinate males evidence less circulating high-density lipoprotein cholesterol, which puts them at higher risk for atherosclerosis and coronary heart disease, a subject we discuss later in this chapter.

What is it about being on top that produces positive effects? Sapolsky concluded that it is primarily the psychological benefits of having *predictability* and *controllability* concerning events in one's life. Parts of his data were gathered during years in which a number of male baboons were at the top of the hierarchy, with no clear "winner." Although these males dominated the rest of the animals in the group, they constantly attacked one another. Under these conditions, they displayed hormonal profiles more like those of subordinate males. Thus, dominance combined with stability produced optimal stress hormone profiles. But the most important factor in regulating stress physiology seems to be a sense of control (Sapolsky & Ray, 1989), a finding strongly confirmed in subsequent research (Kemeny, 2003; Sapolsky, 2007). Control of social situations and the ability to cope with any tension that arises go a long way toward blunting the long-term effects of stress. So-called personality characteristics in baboons that reflect a sense of control are shown in ■ Figure 9.4. Dominant males with these characteristics have basal levels of cortisol lower than those of dominant males without the characteristics.

©Thomas Dobner/Alamy

Baboons at the top of the social hierarchy have a sense of predictability and control that allows them to cope with problems and maintain physical health; baboons at the bottom of the hierarchy suffer the symptoms of stress because they have little control over access to food, resting places, and mates.

Stress, Anxiety, Depression, and Excitement

If you have read the chapters on anxiety, mood, and related psychological disorders, you might conclude, correctly, that stressful life events combined with psychological vulnerabilities such as an inadequate sense of

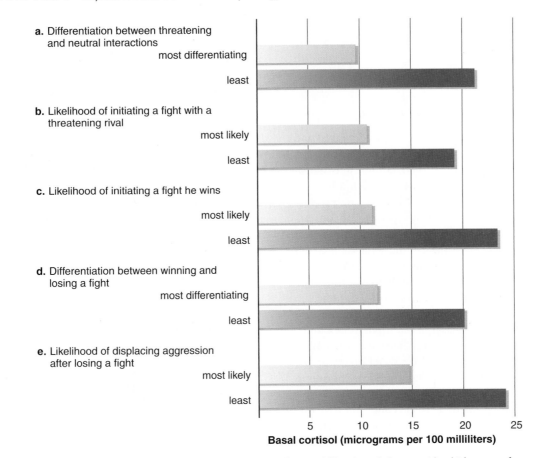

a. Differentiation between threatening and neutral interactions
most differentiating
least

b. Likelihood of initiating a fight with a threatening rival
most likely
least

c. Likelihood of initiating a fight he wins
most likely
least

d. Differentiation between winning and losing a fight
most differentiating
least

e. Likelihood of displacing aggression after losing a fight
most likely
least

5   10   15   20   25
Basal cortisol (micrograms per 100 milliliters)

■ **FIGURE 9.4** Personality characteristics in baboons that reflect a sense of control. Dominant baboons with a high sense of control (light bar) have lower base levels of cortisol than do other dominant males with a lower sense of control (dark bar), which suggests that attitude is a more important mediator of physiology than rank alone. Dominant males who can distinguish between the threatening and the neutral actions of a rival have cortisol levels about half as high as those of other dominant males (a). Similarly, low cortisol levels are found in males who start a fight with a threatening rival instead of waiting to be attacked (b); who know which fights to pick, and so are likely to win fights they initiate (c); who distinguish between having won and lost a fight (d); or who, when they do lose, take out their frustration on subordinates (e). (Reprinted, with permission, from Sapolsky, R., & Ray, J. C., 1989. Styles of dominance and their endocrine correlates among wild, live baboons. *American Journal of Primatology, 18*(1), 1–13, © 1989 by Wiley-Liss, a subsidiary of John Wiley & Sons.)

control are a factor in both psychological and physical disorders. Is there any relationship between psychological and physical disorders? There seems to be a strong one. George Vaillant (1979) studied more than 200 Harvard University sophomore men between 1942 and 1944 who were mentally and physically healthy. He followed these men closely for more than 30 years. Those who developed psychological disorders or who were highly stressed became chronically ill or died at a significantly higher rate than men who remained well adjusted and free from psychological disorders, a finding that has been repeatedly confirmed (see, for example, Katon, 2003; Robles et al., 2005). This suggests that the same types of stress-related psychological factors that contribute to psychological disorders may contribute to the later development of physical disorders and that stress, anxiety, and depression are closely related. Can you tell the difference among feelings of stress, anxiety, depression, and excitement? You might say, "No problem," but these four states have a lot in common. Which one you experience may depend on your *sense of control* at the moment or how well you think you can cope with the threat or challenge you are facing (Barlow, 2002; Barlow, Chorpita, & Turovsky, 1996; Barlow, Rapee, & Reisner, 2001). This continuum

of feelings from excitement to stress to anxiety to depression is shown in ■ Figure 9.5.

Consider how you feel when you are excited. You might experience a rapid heartbeat, a sudden burst of energy, or a jumpy stomach. But if you're well prepared for the challenge—for example, if you're an athlete, up for the game and confident in your abilities, or a musician, sure you are going to give an outstanding performance—these feelings of *excitement* can be pleasurable.

Sometimes when you face a challenging task, you feel you could handle it if you only had the time or help you need, but because you don't have these resources, you feel pressured. In response, you may work harder to do better and be perfect, even though you think you will be all right in the end. If you are under too much pressure, you may become tense and irritable or develop a headache or an upset stomach. This is what *stress* feels like. If something really is threatening and you believe there is little you can do about it, you may feel *anxiety*. The threatening situation could be anything from a physical attack to making a fool of yourself in front of someone. As your body prepares for the challenge, you worry about it incessantly. Your sense of control is considerably less than if you were stressed. In some cases, there

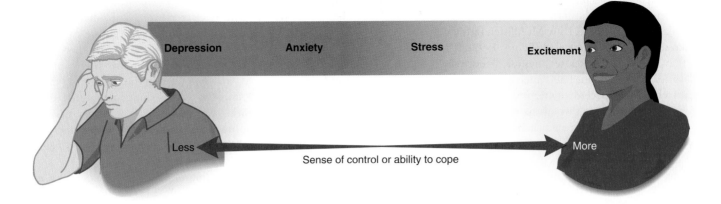

Depression   Anxiety   Stress   Excitement

Less ←   → More

Sense of control or ability to cope

■ **FIGURE 9.5**   Responses to threats and challenges. Our feelings range along a continuum from depression to anxiety to stress to excitement, depending partly on our sense of control and ability to cope. (Adapted, with permission, from Barlow, D. H., Rapee, R. M., & Reisner, L. C., 2001. *Mastering stress 2001: A lifestyle approach.* Dallas, TX: American Health, © 2001 American Health Publishing.)

may not be a difficult situation. Sometimes we are anxious for no reason except that we feel certain aspects of our lives are out of control. Finally, individuals who always perceive life as threatening may lose hope about ever having control and slip into a state of *depression,* no longer trying to cope.

To sum up, the underlying physiology of these particular emotional states seems relatively similar in some basic ways. This is why we refer to a similar pattern of sympathetic arousal and activation of specific neurotransmitters and neurohormones in discussing anxiety, depression, and stress-related physical disorders. On the other hand, there seem to be some differences. Blood pressure may increase when the challenges seem to overwhelm coping resources, resulting in a low sense of control (anxiety, depression), but blood pressure will be unchanged during excitement or marked stress (Blascovich & Tomaka, 1996). Nevertheless, it is psychological factors—specifically a sense of control and confidence that we can cope with stress or challenges, called **self-efficacy** by Bandura (1986)—that differ most markedly among these emotions, leading to different feelings (Taylor et al., 1997).

Stress and the Immune Response

Have you had a cold during the past several months? How did you pick it up? Did you spend the day with someone else who had a cold? Did someone sneeze nearby while you were sitting in class? Exposure to cold viruses is a necessary factor in developing a cold, but the level of stress you are experiencing at the time seems to play a major role in whether the exposure results in a cold. Sheldon Cohen and his associates (Cohen, 1996; Cohen, Doyle, & Skoner, 1999; Cohen, Tyrrell, & Smith, 1991, 1993) exposed volunteer subjects to a specific dosage of a cold virus and followed them closely. They found that the chance a subject would get sick was directly related to how much stress the person had experienced during the past year. In a later study, Cohen and colleagues (1995) linked the intensity of stress and negative affect at the time of exposure to the later *severity* of the

cold, as measured by mucus production. In an interesting twist, Cohen, Doyle, Turner, Alper, and Skoner (2003) have demonstrated that how sociable you are—that is, the quantity and quality of your social relationships—affects whether you come down with a cold when exposed to the virus, perhaps because socializing with friends relieves stress. These are among the first well-controlled studies to demonstrate that stress and related factors increase the risk of infection.

Think back to your last exam. Did you (or your roommate) have a cold? Exam periods are stressors that have been shown to produce increased infections, particularly of the upper respiratory tract (Glaser et al., 1987, 1990). Therefore, if you are susceptible to colds, maybe one way out is to skip final exams! A better solution is to learn how to control your stress before and during exams. Almost certainly, the effect of stress on susceptibility to infections is mediated through the **immune system,** which protects the body from any foreign materials that may enter it.

Research dating back to the original reports of Selye (1936) demonstrates the detrimental effects of stress on immune system functioning. Humans under stress show clearly increased rates of infectious diseases, including colds, herpes, and mononucleosis (see, for example, Cohen & Herbert, 1996; Vander, Plate, Aral, & Magder, 1988). Direct evidence links a number of stressful situations to lowered immune system functioning, including marital discord or relationship difficulties (Kiecolt-Glaser et al., 2005; Kiecolt-Glaser & Newton, 2001; Uchino et al., 1999), job loss, and the death of a loved one (Irwin, Daniels, Smith, Bloom, & Weiner, 1987; Morris et al., 1994; Pavalko, Elder, & Clipp, 1993). Furthermore, these stressful events affect the immune system rap-

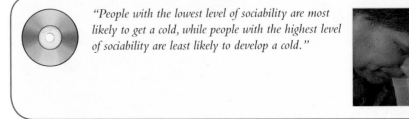

"People with the lowest level of sociability are most likely to get a cold, while people with the highest level of sociability are least likely to develop a cold."

idly. Studies in laboratories have demonstrated weakened immune system response within 2 hours of exposure to stress (Kiecolt-Glaser & Glaser, 1992; Weisse, Pato, McAllister, Littman, & Breier, 1990; Zakowski, McAllister, Deal, & Baum, 1992). It is therefore possible that stress contributes to physical illness, which Cohen and colleagues (1999) found. They infected 55 subjects with the influenza A virus. As expected, higher psychological stress was associated with a more severe case of the flu. But Cohen and colleagues (1999) also demonstrated that the stress hormones triggered cytokine interleukin 6, an immune system component that produces inflammation of tissues.

We have already noted that psychological disorders seem to make us more susceptible to developing physical disorders (Katon, 2003; Robles et al., 2005; Vaillant, 1979). We had assumed this was because of the effect of psychological disorders on the immune system. But direct evidence indicates that depression lowers immune system functioning (Herbert & Cohen, 1993; Miller & Blackwell, 2006; Stone, 2000; Weisse, 1992), particularly in the aged (Herbert & Cohen, 1993; Schleifer, Keller, Bond, Cohen, & Stein, 1989). It may be that the level of depression (and perhaps the underlying sense of uncontrollability that accompanies most depressions) is a more potent factor in lowering immune system functioning than are specific stressful life events, such as job loss (Miller & Blackwell, 2006; Robles et al., 2005; Weisse, 1992). Depression can also lead to poor self-care and a tendency to engage in riskier behaviors. For humans, like Sapolsky's baboons, the ability to retain a sense of control over events in our lives may be one of the most important psychological contributions to good health.

Most studies concerning stress and the immune system have examined a sudden or acute stressor. But *chronic stress* may be more problematic because the effects, by definition, last longer

(Schneiderman, 2004). In 1979, at Three Mile Island near Harrisburg, Pennsylvania, the nuclear power plant suffered a partial meltdown. Many residents feared that any exposure to radiation they might have sustained would lead to cancer or other illnesses, and they lived with this fear for years. More than 6 years after the event, some individuals who had been in the area during the crisis still had lowered immune system functioning (McKinnon, Weisse, Reynolds, Bowles, & Baum, 1989). A similar finding of lower immune system functioning has been reported for people who care for chronically ill family members, such as Alzheimer's disease patients (Kiecolt-Glaser & Glaser, 1987).

To understand how the immune system protects us, we must first understand how it works. We take a brief tour of the immune system next, using ■ Figure 9.6 as a visual guide, and then we examine psychological contributions to the biology of two diseases strongly related to immune system functioning: AIDS and cancer.

■ How the Immune System Works

The immune system identifies and eliminates foreign materials, called **antigens,** in the body. Antigens can be any of a number of substances, usually bacteria, viruses, or parasites. But the immune system also targets the body's own cells that have become aberrant or damaged in some way, perhaps as part of a malignant tumor. Donated organs are foreign, so the immune system attacks them after surgical transplant; consequently, it is necessary to suppress the immune system temporarily after surgery.

The immune system has two main parts: the humoral and the cellular. Specific types of cells function as agents of both. White blood cells, called *leukocytes,* do most of the work. There are several types of leukocytes. *Macrophages* might be considered one of the body's first lines of defense: They surround identifiable anti-

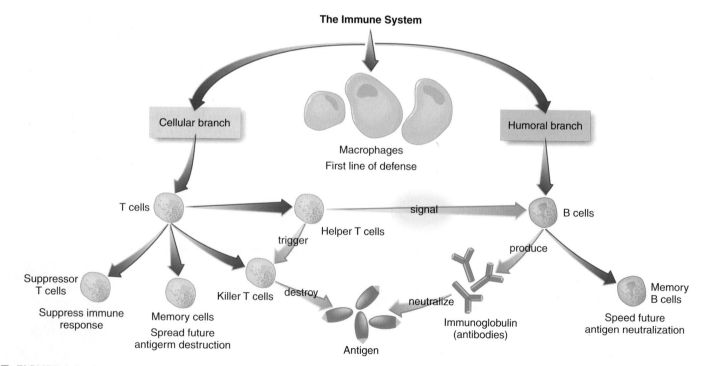

■ **FIGURE 9.6** An overview of the immune system.

gens and destroy them. They also signal *lymphocytes,* which consist of two groups, B cells and T cells.

The *B cells* operate within the humoral part of the immune system, releasing molecules that seek antigens in blood and other bodily fluids with the purpose of neutralizing them. The B cells produce highly specific molecules called *immunoglobulins* that act as *antibodies,* which combine with the antigens to neutralize them. After the antigens are neutralized, a subgroup called *memory B cells* are created so that the next time that antigen is encountered, the immune system response will be even faster. This action accounts for the success of inoculations you may have received for mumps or measles as a child. An inoculation contains small amounts of the targeted organism but not enough to make you sick. Your immune system then "remembers" this antigen and prevents you from coming down with the full disease when you are exposed to it.

Members of the second group of lymphocytes, called *T cells,* operate in the cellular branch of the immune system. These cells don't produce antibodies. Instead, one subgroup, *killer T cells,* directly destroys viral infections and cancerous processes (Borysenko, 1987; O'Leary, 1990; Roitt, 1988). When the process is complete, *memory T cells* are created to speed future responses to the same antigen. Other subgroups of T cells help regulate the immune system. For example, *T4 cells* are called *helper T cells* because they enhance the immune system response by signaling B cells to produce antibodies and telling other T cells to destroy the antigen. *Suppressor T cells* suppress the production of antibodies by B cells when they are no longer needed.

We should have twice as many T4 (helper) cells as suppressor T cells. With too many T4 cells, the immune system is overreactive and may attack the body's normal cells rather than antigens. When this happens, we have what is called an **autoimmune disease,** such as **rheumatoid arthritis.** With too many suppressor T cells, the body is subject to invasion by a number of antigens. The human immunodeficiency virus (HIV) directly attacks the helper T cells, lymphocytes that are crucial to both humoral and cellular immunity, thereby severely weakening the immune system and causing AIDS.

Until the mid-1970s, most scientists believed the brain and the immune system operate independently of each other. However, in 1974, Robert Ader and his colleagues (see, for example, Ader & Cohen, 1975, 1993) made a startling discovery. Working with a classical conditioning paradigm, they gave sugar-flavored water to rats, together with a drug that suppresses the immune system. Ader and Cohen then demonstrated that giving the same rats only the sweet-tasting water produced similar changes in the im-

Courtesy of Robert Ader

Robert Ader demonstrated that the immune system is responsive to environmental cues.

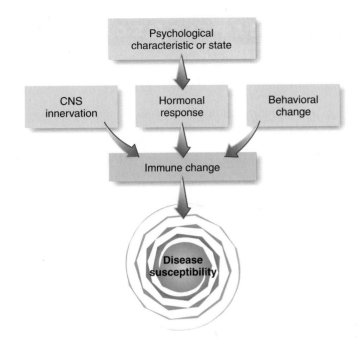

■ FIGURE 9.7   Pathways through which psychological factors might influence onset and progression of immune system–mediated disease. For simplicity, arrows are drawn in only one direction, from psychological characteristics to disease. No lack of alternative paths is implied. CNS = central nervous system. (From Cohen, S., & Herbert, T. B., 1996. Health psychology: Psychological factors and physical disease from the perspective of human psychoneuroimmunology. *Annual Review of Psychology, 47,* 113–142.)

mune system. In other words, the rats had "learned" (through classical conditioning) to respond to the water by suppressing their immune systems. We now know there are many connections between the nervous system and the immune system. These findings have generated a field of study known as **psychoneuroimmunology,** or **PNI** (Ader & Cohen, 1993), which simply means the object of study is *psych*ological influences on the *neuro*logical responding implicated in our *immune* response.

Cohen and Herbert (1996) illustrate pathways through which psychological and social factors may influence immune system functioning. Direct connections between the brain (central nervous system) and HPA axis (hormonal) and the immune system have already been described. Behavioral changes in response to stressful events, such as increased smoking or poor eating habits, may also suppress the immune system (■ Figure 9.7).

CONCEPT CHECK 9.1

Assess your knowledge of the immune system by matching components of the immune system with their function in the body: (a) macrophages, (b) B cells, (c) immunoglobins, (d) killer T cells, (e) suppressor T cells, and (f) memory B cells.

1. This subgroup targets viral infections within the cells by directly destroying the antigens. _____

(continued)

(continued)

2. A type of leukocyte that surrounds identifiable antigens and destroys them. _____

3. Highly specific molecules that act as antibodies. They combine with antigens to neutralize them. _____ _____

4. Lymphocytes that operate within the humoral part of the system and circulate in the blood and bodily fluids. _____

5. These are created so that when a specific antigen is encountered in the future, the immune response will be faster. _____

6. These T cells stop the production of antibodies by B cells when they are no longer needed. _____

PSYCHOSOCIAL EFFECTS ON PHYSICAL DISORDERS

With an enhanced understanding of the effects of emotional and behavioral factors on the immune system, we can now examine how these factors influence specific physical disorders. We begin with AIDS.

AIDS

The ravages of the AIDS epidemic have made this disease the highest priority of our public health system. In 2000, the total number of people around the world living with HIV was estimated at 34.3 million. By the end of 2003, the figure was 40 million, with 5 million new cases and 3 million deaths in 2003 alone (Stephenson, 2003). Only in 2006 had this trend begun to level off with aggressive treatment and prevention efforts in some parts of the world (Kuehn, 2006). Nevertheless, in the hardest hit regions in southern Africa, between 20% and 40% of the adult population are believed to be HIV positive. Furthermore, the United Nations estimates that at least two of every five girls and boys who are 15 years old today in these countries in southern Africa will die of AIDS. Indeed, of 11,000 new infections each day worldwide in 2005, nearly 14% were in children 15 years or younger (Kuehn, 2006). AIDS is spreading rapidly to the densely populated regions of India and China, where prevalence is expected to rise from a few thousand in 2000 to 10 million in 2010, far surpassing southern Africa (China U.N. Theme Group, 2001; Cohen, 2004; Stephenson, 2003). In Latin America, rates are projected to rise from 2 million in 2006 to 3.5 million by 2015 (Cohen, 2006).

Once a person is infected with HIV, the course of the disease is quite variable. After several months to several years with no symptoms, patients may develop minor health problems such as weight loss, fever, and night sweats, symptoms that make up the condition known as **AIDS-related complex (ARC).** A diagnosis of AIDS itself is not made until one of several serious diseases appears, such as pneumocystis pneumonia, cancer, dementia, or a

wasting syndrome in which the body literally withers away. The median time from initial infection to the development of full-blown AIDS has been estimated to range from 7.3 to 10 years or more (Moss & Bacchetti, 1989; Pantaleo, Graziosi, & Fauci, 1993). Although most people with AIDS die within 1 year of diagnosis, as many as 15% survive 5 years or longer (Kertzner & Gorman, 1992). Recently, clinical scientists have developed powerful new combinations of drugs referred to as highly active antiretroviral therapy (HAART) that seem to suppress the virus in those infected with HIV, even in advanced cases (Brechtl, Breitbart, Galietta, & Krivo-Rosenfeld, 2001; Hammer et al., 2006). Although this is a hopeful development, it does not seem to be a cure, because the most recent evidence suggests the virus is seldom eliminated but rather lies dormant in reduced numbers; thus, infected patients face a lifetime of taking multiple medications (Cohen, 2002; Hammer et al., 2006). Also, the percentage who drop out of HAART because of severe side effects is high—61% in one study (O'Brien, Clark, Besch, Myers, & Kissinger, 2003). Therefore, current recommendations are to deny treatment until those infected are in imminent danger of developing symptomatic disease (Cohen, 2002; Hammer et al., 2006). Even more discouraging is that drug-resistant strains of HIV are now being transmitted.

Because AIDS is a relatively new disease, with a long latency to development, we are still learning about the factors, including possible psychological factors, that extend survival (Kennedy, 2000). Investigators identified a group of people who have been exposed repeatedly to the AIDS virus but have not contracted the disease. A major distinction of these people is that their immune systems, particularly the cellular branch, are robust and strong (Ezzel, 1993), most likely because of genetic factors (Kaiser, 2006). Therefore, efforts to boost the immune system may contribute to the prevention of AIDS.

Can psychological factors affect the progression of AIDS? Learning we have an incurable terminal illness is extremely stressful for anyone. This happens every day to individuals stricken with HIV. The stress of learning you are carrying the AIDS virus can be devastating. Antoni and colleagues (1991) studied the effects of administering a psychosocial stress-reduction treatment to a group of individuals who believed they might have HIV during the weeks before they were tested for the virus. Half of the group received the stress-reduction program; the other half received the usual medical and psychological care. Unfortunately, many individuals in this group turned out to be HIV positive. However, those who had undergone the psychosocial stress-reduction procedures, unlike their counterparts, did not show substantial increases in anxiety and depression. Furthermore—and more important—they demonstrated *increases* in their immune system functioning as measured by such indices as helper T, inducer (CD4), and natural killer (NK) cells. In addition, participants in the stress-reduction program showed significant decreases in antibodies to two herpes viruses, suggesting improved functioning of the immune system (Esterling et al., 1992). This is important because herpes viruses are closely related to HIV and seem to promote further activation of HIV-infected cells, resulting in a faster and deadlier spread of HIV. What was most encouraging about this study, however, was that a follow-up showed less disease progression in the stress-reduction group 2 years later (Ironson et al.,

1994). A subsequent study has confirmed that high levels of stress and low levels of social support are associated with a faster progression to disease in a group of HIV-infected men without AIDS who were followed for 7.5 years (Leserman et al., 2000).

Remember, however, that the subjects in the study by Antoni and colleagues (1991) were in an early asymptomatic stage of the disease. Subsequent important studies suggest the same cognitive-behavioral stress-management (CBSM) program may have positive effects on the immune systems of individuals who are already symptomatic (Antoni et al., 2000; Lutgendorf et al., 1997). Specifically, Lutgendorf and colleagues (1997) used an intervention program that significantly decreased depression and anxiety compared to a control group that did not receive the treatment. More important, there was a significant reduction in antibodies to the herpes simplex virus II in the treatment group compared to the control group, which reflects the greater ability of the cellular component of the immune system to control the virus. In the study by Antoni and colleagues (2000), 73 gay or bisexual men already infected with HIV and symptomatic with the disease were assigned to a CBSM program or a control group receiving usual care without the program. As in previous studies, men receiving the stress-management treatment showed significantly lower post-treatment levels of anxiety, anger, and perceived stress than those in the control group, indicating the treatment was effective. More important, as long as a year after the intervention had ended, men who had received the treatment evidenced better immune system functioning as indicated by higher levels of T cells. These findings are presented in ■ Figure 9.8.

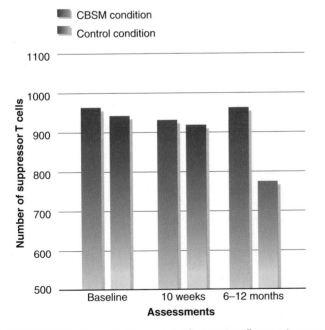

■ **FIGURE 9.8** Means for T suppressor/cytotoxic cells at preintervention (baseline), postintervention (10 weeks), and follow-up (6 to 12 months) in HIV-positive gay men assigned to CBSM (; n = 47) versus control (n = 26). (Adapted from Antoni, M. H., Cruess, D. G., Cruess, S., Lutgendorf, S., Kumar, M., Ironson, G., Klimas, N., Fletcher, M.A., & Schneiderman, N., 2000. Cognitive-behavioral stress management intervention effects on anxiety, 24-hr urinary norepinephrine output, and T-cytotoxic/suppressor cells over time among symptomatic HIV-infected gay men. *Journal of Consulting and Clinical Psychology, 68,* 31–45.)

Goodkin and colleagues (2001) reported that a 10-week psychological treatment significantly buffered against an increase in HIV viral load, which is a powerful and reliable predictor of progression to full-blown AIDS, when compared to a control group. Now, Antoni and colleagues (2006) have taken their important line of research a step further. HIV-positive men on HAART drug regimens received 10 weeks of training in how to take their medication properly by taking the exact amount prescribed as closely as possible to the assigned times. Half of this group also received the investigators' CBSM program. Men receiving CBSM actually showed a decrease in viral load 15 months later compared to those with medication training only, who showed no change. This reduction in viral load was primarily the result of decreases in depression, which, in turn, reduced the stress hormone cortisol. Thus, even in progressed, symptomatic HIV disease, psychological interventions may not only enhance psychological adjustment but also influence immune system functioning, and this effect may be long lasting.

It is too early to tell whether these results will be strong or persistent enough to translate into increased survival time for AIDS patients, although results from Antoni and colleagues (2000, 2006) suggest they might. If stress and related variables *are* clinically significant to immune response in HIV-infected patients, as suggested by Ironson and colleagues (1994) and Antoni and colleagues (2000, 2006), then psychosocial interventions to bolster the immune system might increase survival rates and, in the most optimistic scenario, prevent the slow deterioration of the immune system (Kennedy, 2000; Kiecolt-Glaser & Glaser, 1992). Few areas of study in behavioral medicine and health psychology are more urgent.

Cancer

Among the more mind-boggling developments in the study of illness and disease is the discovery that the development and course of different varieties of **cancer** are subject to psychosocial influences (Williams & Schneiderman, 2002). This has resulted in a new field of study called **psychoncology** (Andersen, 1992; Antoni & Goodkin, 1991; Antoni & Lutgendorf, 2007; Helgeson, 2005; Lutgendorf, Costanzo, & Siegel, 2007). *Oncology* means the study of cancer. David Spiegel, a psychiatrist at Stanford University, and his colleagues (1989) studied 86 women with advanced breast cancer that had metastasized to other areas of their bodies and was expected to kill them within 2 years. Clearly, the prognosis was poor indeed. Although Spiegel and his colleagues had little hope of affecting the disease itself, they thought that by treating these people in group psychotherapy at least they could relieve some of their anxiety, depression, and pain.

All patients had routine medical care for their cancer. In addition, 50 patients (of the 86) met with their therapist for psychotherapy once a week in small groups. Much to everyone's surprise, including Spiegel's, the therapy group's survival time was significantly longer than that of the control group who did not receive psychotherapy but otherwise benefited from the best care available. The group receiving therapy lived twice as long on average (approximately 3 years) as the controls (approximately 18 months). Four years after the study began, one third of the therapy patients

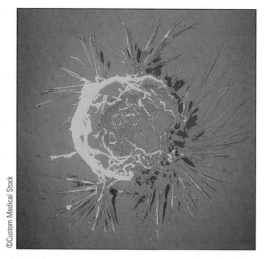

©Custom Medical Stock

Breast cancer cell.

were still alive and all the patients receiving the best medical care available *without* therapy had died. Subsequently, a careful reanalysis of medical treatment received by each group revealed no differences that could account for the effects of psychological treatment (Kogon, Biswas, Pearl, Carlson, & Spiegel, 1997). These findings do not mean that psychological interventions cured advanced cancer. At 10 years, only three patients in the therapy group still survived.

Supporting these findings, Fawzy and his colleagues studied 56 cancer patients with malignant melanoma (skin cancer) who, unlike the patients in the Spiegel study, had a reasonably good prognosis at the start of the study. Thirty-eight of these patients received six weekly, 1-hour treatment sessions delivered in small groups, where they were taught relaxation techniques, stress-management procedures, and generally how to cope with illness-related problems. Six months after treatment, immune functioning was higher in the group receiving psychotherapy than in a control group receiving only customary medical care (Fawzy, Cousins, et al., 1990; Fawzy, Kemeny, et al., 1990). More important, at a 5- to 6-year follow-up, control patients tended to have more recurrences of the cancer and were significantly more likely to die. Ten control patients and only three in the treatment group had died, replicating the findings of Spiegel and colleagues (1989) (Fawzy et al., 1993).

Spiegel and his colleagues (1996) later demonstrated that their treatment can be implemented relatively easily in oncology

clinics everywhere, which is necessary if the treatment is going to be truly useful. Clinical trials involving large numbers of patients with cancer are in progress to evaluate more thoroughly the life-prolonging and life-enhancing effects of psychosocial treatments for cancer.

The initial success of these psychological treatments in at least some studies has generated a great deal of interest in exactly how they might work, if they do work (Anderson & Baum, 2001; Antoni & Lutgendorf, 2007; Helgeson, 2005). Possibilities include better health habits, closer adherence to medical treatment, and improved endocrine functioning and response to stress, all of which may improve immune function (Classen, Diamond, & Spiegel, 1998). There is even preliminary evidence that psychological factors may contribute not only to the *course* but also to the *development* of cancer and other diseases (Antoni & Lutgendorf, 2007; Lutgendorf et al., 2007). Perceived lack of control, inadequate coping responses, overwhelmingly stressful life events, or the use of inappropriate coping responses (such as denial) may all contribute to the development of cancer, probably through changes in immune function but also through regulating the activity of cancer-causing viruses, deoxyribonucleic acid (DNA) repair processes, and the expression of genes that control the growth of tumors (Antoni & Lutgendorf, 2007; Lutgendorf et al., 2007; Williams & Schneiderman, 2002).

Not all studies find that psychological treatments prolong life. One such study confirmed that psychological treatments reduced depression and pain and increased well being, but it failed to replicate the survival-enhancing effects of treatment (Goodwin et al., 2001). Thus, it is safe to say that the jury is still out on a specific survival-enhancing effect of these treatments, but subsequent studies have clearly supported stress reduction effects, enhanced social adjustment and coping, and increases in quality of life (Anderson et al., 2006; Antoni et al., 2006; Nezu et al., 1999).

These studies have led to a renewed emphasis on an overlooked result of cancer: that is, some people discover some positive consequences. For example, many women with breast cancer experience an enhanced sense of purpose, deepening spirituality, closer ties to others, and changes in life priorities (Lechner & Antoni, 2004). These experiences have been called "benefit finding" and may reflect the types of traits, such as coping skills, a sense of control, and optimism, that underlie resiliency. It is these traits and skills that are among the most important goals of psychological treatment. Antoni and colleagues (2006) targeted these goals in 199 women with nonmetastatic breast cancer using a CBSM program, and they found substantially improved quality of life in the year following treatment.

Psychological factors are also prominent in treatment and recovery from cancer in children (Koocher, 1996). Many types of cancer require invasive and painful medical procedures; the suffering can be difficult to bear, not only for children but also for parents and health-care providers. Children usually struggle and cry hysterically, so to complete many of the procedures, they must be physically restrained. Not only does their behavior interfere with successful completion, but the stress

"Women who had low self-esteem, low body image, feelings of low control, low optimism, and a lack of support at home were even more likely to benefit from an education intervention."

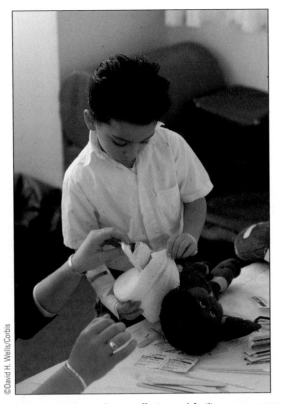

Psychological preparation reduces suffering and facilitates recovery in children who undergo surgery.

and anxiety associated with repeated painful procedures may have their own detrimental effect on the disease process. Psychological procedures designed to reduce pain and stress in these children include breathing exercises, watching films of exactly what happens to take the uncertainty out of the procedure, and rehearsal of the procedure with dolls, all of which make the interventions more tolerable and therefore more successful for young patients (Hubert, Jay, Saltoun, & Hayes, 1988; Jay, Elliott, Ozolins, Olson, & Pruitt, 1985; McGrath & DeVeber, 1986). Much of this work is based on the pioneering efforts of Barbara Melamed and her colleagues, who demonstrated the importance of incorporating psychological procedures into children's medical care, particularly children about to undergo surgery (see, for example, Melamed & Siegel, 1975). In any case, pediatric psychologists are making more routine use of these procedures. Reducing stress in parents who could then provide more supportive care is important. Sahler and colleagues (2005) treated mothers of children with newly diagnosed cancer with a cognitive-behavioral problem-solving intervention and compared the results to the usual care available to these mothers. Mothers in the problem-solving group became less negative, less stressed, and better problem solvers, certainly a positive outcome in parents who have to deal with the tragedy of cancer in their own children.

Cardiovascular Problems

The *cardiovascular system* comprises the heart, blood vessels, and complex control mechanisms for regulating their function. Many things can go wrong with this system and lead to **cardiovascular**

disease. For example, many individuals, particularly older individuals, suffer **strokes,** also called **cerebral vascular accidents (CVAs),** which are temporary blockages of blood vessels leading to the brain or a rupture of blood vessels in the brain that results in temporary or permanent brain damage and loss of functioning. People with Raynaud's disease lose circulation to peripheral parts of their bodies such as their fingers and toes, suffering some pain and continual sensations of cold in their hands and feet. The cardiovascular problems receiving the most attention these days are hypertension and coronary heart disease, and we look at both. First, let's consider the case of John.

JOHN: The Human Volcano

John is a 55-year-old business executive, married, with two teenage children. For most his adult life, John has smoked about a pack of cigarettes each day. Although he maintains a busy and active schedule, John is mildly obese, partly from regular meals with business partners and colleagues. He has been taking several medications for high blood pressure since age 42. John's doctor has warned him repeatedly to cut down on his smoking and to exercise more often, especially because John's father died of a heart attack. Although John has episodes of chest pain, he continues his busy and stressful lifestyle. It is difficult for John to slow down, as his business has been doing extremely well during the past 10 years.

Moreover, John believes that life is too short, that there is no time to slow down. He sees relatively little of his family and works late most evenings. Even when he's at home, John typically works into the night. It is difficult for him to relax; he feels a constant urgency to get as many things done as possible and prefers to work on several tasks simultaneously. For instance, John often proofreads a document, engages in a phone conversation, and eats lunch all at the same time. He attributes much of the success of his business to his working style. Despite his success, John is not well liked by his peers. His co-workers and employees often find him to be overbearing, easily frustrated, and, at times, even hostile. His subordinates in particular claim he is overly impatient and critical of their performance.

Do you think John has a problem? Most people would recognize that his behaviors and attitudes make his life unpleasant and possibly lethal. Some of these behaviors and attitudes appear to operate directly on the cardiovascular system and may result in hypertension and coronary heart disease.

Hypertension

Hypertension (high blood pressure) is a major risk factor not only for stroke and heart disease but also for kidney disease. This makes hypertension an extremely serious medical condition. Blood pressure increases when the blood vessels leading to organs and peripheral areas constrict (become narrower), forcing increasing amounts of blood to muscles in central parts of the body. Because so many blood vessels have constricted, the heart muscles must work much harder to force the blood to all parts of the body, which causes the increased pressure. These factors produce wear and tear on the ever-shrinking blood vessels and lead to cardio-vascular disease. A small percentage of cases of hypertension can be traced to specific physical abnormalities, such as kidney disease or tumors on the adrenal glands (Papillo & Shapiro, 1990), but the overwhelming majority have no specific verifiable physical cause and are considered **essential hypertension.** Blood pressure is defined as high by the World Health Organization if it exceeds 160 over 95 (Papillo & Shapiro, 1990), although measures of 140/90 or higher are cause for concern and more usually used to define hypertension (Wolf-Maier et al., 2003). The first value is called the *systolic blood pressure,* the pressure when the heart is pumping blood. The second value is the *diastolic blood pressure,* the pressure between beats when the heart is at rest. Elevations in diastolic pressure seem to be more worrisome in terms of risk of disease.

According to a recent comprehensive survey, 27.6% of individuals between the ages of 35 and 64 suffer from hypertension in North America, with a corresponding and shocking figure of 44.2% in six European countries (Wolf-Maier et al., 2003). These data, along with the percentage taking medication to control hypertension and body mass index (BMI) levels (see Chapter 8), are presented in Table 9.2. These are extraordinary numbers when you consider that hypertension, contributing to as many fatal diseases as it does, has been called the "silent killer." These num-

bers are much higher than for any single psychological disorder. The relationship of hypertension to risk of death from stroke in each country is presented in ■ Figure 9.9 and illustrates that hypertension is associated with premature mortality. Even more striking is that African Americans, both men and women, are approximately *twice* as likely to develop hypertension as whites (Anderson & Jackson, 1987; Brannon & Feist, 1997; Yan et al., 2003). More important, African Americans have hypertensive vascular diseases at a rate 5 to 10 times greater than whites. This makes hypertension a principal disorder of concern among the African American population. Saab and colleagues (1992) demonstrated that during laboratory stress tests African Americans without high blood pressure show greater vascular responsiveness, including heightened blood pressure. Thus, African Americans in general may be at greater risk to develop hypertension.

You will not be surprised to learn there are biological, psychological, and social contributions to the development of this potentially deadly condition. It has long been clear that hypertension runs in families and likely is subject to marked genetic influences (Papillo & Shapiro, 1990; Taylor, 2006; Williams et al., 2001). When stressed in the laboratory, even individuals with *normal* blood pressure show greater reactivity in their blood pressure if their parents have high blood pressure than do individuals with normal blood pressure whose parents also had normal blood pressure (Clark, 2003; Fredrikson & Matthews, 1990). In other words, it doesn't take much to activate an inherited vulnerability to hypertension. The offspring of parents with hypertension are at

TABLE 9.2	Hypertension Prevalence and Treatment and BMI Among People 35–64 Years Old in Six European Countries, Canada, and the United States*				
	Prevalence, %			Hypertensive Persons Taking	
Country	All	Men	Women	Medications, %	BMI
North America	27.6	30.4	24.8	44.4	27.1
United States	27.8	29.8	25.8	52.5	27.4
Canada	27.4	31.0	23.8	36.3	26.8
Europe	44.2	49.7	38.6	26.8	26.9
Italy	37.7	44.8	30.6	32.0	26.4
Sweden	38.4	44.8	32.0	26.2	26.5
England	41.7	46.9	36.5	24.8	27.1
Spain	46.8	49.0	44.6	26.8	27.4
Finland	48.7	55.7	41.6	25.0	27.1
Germany	55.3	60.2	50.3	26.0	27.3

*Age adjusted. BMI calculated as weight in kilograms divided by the height in meters squared.

Source: Reprinted, with permission, from Wolf-Maier, K., Cooper, R. S., Banegas, J. R., Giampaoli, S., Hense, H., Joffres, M., Kastarinen, M., Poulter, N., et al. (2003). Hypertension prevalence and blood pressure levels in six European countries, Canada, and the United States. *Journal of American Medical Association, 289,* 2363–2369, © 2003 American Medical Association.

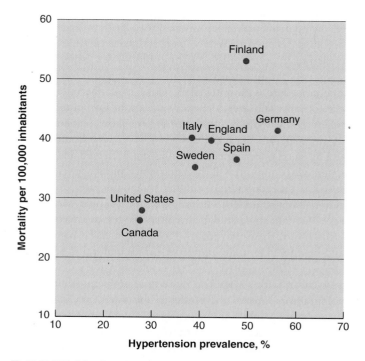

■ **FIGURE 9.9** Prevalence of hypertension versus stroke mortality in six European and two North American countries in men and women 35 to 64 years old, age adjusted. (Reprinted, with permission, from Wolf-Maier, K., Cooper, R. S., Banegas, J. R., Giampaoli, S., Hense, H., Joffres, M., Kastarinen, M., Poulter, N., et al., 2003. Hypertension prevalence and blood pressure levels in six European countries, Canada, and the United States. *Journal of the American Medical Association, 289,* 2367 (Figure 4), © 2003 American Medical Association.)

twice the risk of developing hypertension as children of parents with normal blood pressure (Brannon & Feist, 1997; Taylor, 2006).

Studies examining neurobiological causes of hypertension have centered on two factors central to the regulation of blood pressure: autonomic nervous system activity and mechanisms regulating sodium in the kidneys. When the sympathetic branch of the autonomic nervous system becomes active, one consequence is the constriction of blood vessels, which produces greater resistance against circulation; that is, blood pressure is elevated (Guyton, 1981). Because the sympathetic nervous system is responsive to stress, many investigators have long assumed that stress is a major contributor to essential hypertension. Sodium and water regulation, one of the functions of the kidneys, is also important in regulating blood pressure. Retaining too much salt increases blood volume and heightens blood pressure. This is one reason that people with hypertension are often told to restrict their intake of salt.

Psychological factors, such as personality, coping style, and, again, level of stress, have been used to explain individual differences in blood pressure (Winters & Schneiderman, 2000). For example, in a review of 28 studies, Uchino and colleagues (1996) found a strong relationship between levels of social support and blood pressure. Loneliness, depression, and feelings of uncontrollability are psychological mechanisms that may contribute to the association between hypertension and social support. But a more recently completed long-term study identifies two psychological factors, each of which almost doubles the risk of hypertension: hostility, particularly in interpersonal relations, and a sense of time urgency or impatience. To reach this conclusion, more than 5,000

African Americans suffer from hypertension in disproportionately high numbers.

black and white adults were followed for 15 years in the Coronary Artery Risk Development in Young Adults (CARDIA) study (Yan et al., 2003). It is likely that the combination of these two factors is an even more powerful risk factor. Also, both anger and hostility have been associated with increases in blood pressure in the laboratory setting (Jamner, Shapiro, Goldstein, & Hug, 1991; King, Taylor, Albright, & Haskell, 1990; Miller, Smith, Turner, Guijarro, & Hallet, 1996).

The notion that hostility or repressed hostility predicts hypertension (and other cardiovascular problems) can be traced back to Alexander (1939), who suggested that an inability to express anger could result in hypertension and other cardiovascular problems. What may be more important is not whether anger is suppressed but rather how often anger and hostility are experienced and expressed to others (Brondolo et al., 2003; Ironson et al., 1992; Miller et al., 1996; Winters & Schneiderman, 2000). Let's return to the case of John for a moment. John clearly suffered from hypertension. Do you detect any anger in John's case study? John's hypertension may well be related to his stressful lifestyle, frustration levels, and hostility. The ability to control anger by expressing these feelings constructively is associated with markedly lower blood pressure in the population (Davidson, MacGregor, Stuhr, Dixon, & MacLean, 2000), suggesting it might help patients, too.

Coronary Heart Disease

It may not surprise you that psychological and social factors contribute to high blood pressure, but can changes in behavior and attitudes prevent heart attacks? The answers are still not entirely clear, but increasing evidence indicates that psychological and social factors are implicated in coronary heart disease (Winters & Schneiderman, 2000). Why is this important? Heart disease is the number one cause of death in Western cultures.

Coronary heart disease (CHD), quite simply, is a blockage of the arteries supplying blood to the heart muscle (the *myocardium*). A number of terms describe heart disease. Chest pain resulting from partial obstruction of the arteries is called *angina pectoris* or, usually, just *angina*. *Atherosclerosis* occurs when a fatty substance or plaque builds up inside the arteries and causes an obstruction. *Ischemia* is the name for deficiency of blood to a body part caused by the narrowing of the arteries by too much plaque. And *myocardial infarction,* or *heart attack,* is the death of heart tissue when a specific artery becomes clogged with plaque. Arteries can constrict or become blocked for a variety of reasons other than plaque. For example, a blood clot might lodge in the artery.

It seems clear that we inherit a vulnerability to CHD (and to many other physical disorders), and other factors such as diet, exercise, and culture make important contributions to our cardiovascular status (Thoresen & Powell, 1992). But what sort of psychological factors contribute to CHD?

A variety of studies suggest strongly that stress, anxiety, and anger, combined with poor coping skills and low social support, are implicated in CHD (M. Friedman et al., 1984; Johnston, 1997; Lett et al., 2005; Matthews, 2005; Suls & Bunde, 2005; Winters & Schneiderman, 2000). Severe stress, as in learning that a family member suddenly died, can lead on rare occasions to a condition called *myocardial stunning,* which is basically heart failure (Wittstein et al., 2005). Some studies indicate that even healthy men who experience stress are later more likely to experience CHD than low-stress groups (Rosengren, Tibblin, & Wilhelmsen, 1991). For such individuals, stress-reduction procedures may prove to be an important preventive technique. There is a great deal of evidence on the value of stress-reduction procedures in preventing future heart attacks (Williams & Schneiderman, 2002). In one report summarizing results from 37 studies, and using analytic procedures that combine the results from these studies (meta-analysis), the effects of stress-reduction programs on CHD were quite apparent. Specifically, as a group, these studies yielded a 34% reduction in death from heart attacks, a 29% reduction in the recurrence of heart attacks; and a significant positive effect on blood pressure, cholesterol levels, body weight, and other risk factors for CHD (Dusseldorp, van Elderen, Maes, Meulman, & Kraaij, 1999). A more recent major clinical study confirmed the benefits of stress reduction and exercise in reducing emotional distress and improving heart function and risk for future attacks in a group of individuals with established heart disease (Blumenthal et al., 2005). This brings us to an important question: Can we identify, before an attack, people who are under a great deal of stress that might make them susceptible to a first heart attack? The answer seems to be yes, but the answer is more complex than we first thought.

Clinical investigators reported several decades ago that certain groups of people engage in a cluster of behaviors in stressful situations that seem to put them at considerable risk for CHD. These behaviors include excessive competitive drive, a sense of always being pressured for time, impatience, incredible amounts of energy that may show up in accelerated speech and motor activity, and angry outbursts. This set of behaviors, which came to be called the **type A behavior pattern,** was first identified by two cardiologists, Meyer Friedman and Ray Rosenman (1959, 1974). The **type B behavior pattern,** also described by these clinicians, applies to people who basically do not have type A attributes. In other words, the type B individual is more relaxed, less concerned about deadlines, and seldom feels the pressure or, perhaps, the excitement of challenges or overriding ambition.

Both type A behavior and CHD seem to be culturally determined.

The concept of the type A personality or behavior pattern is widely accepted in our hard-driving, goal-oriented culture. Indeed, some early studies supported the concept of type A behavior as putting people at risk for CHD (Friedman & Rosenman, 1974). But the most convincing evidence came from two large prospective studies that followed thousands of patients over a long period to determine the relationship of their behavior to heart disease. The first study was the Western Collaborative Group Study (WCGS). In this project, 3,154 healthy men, age 39 to 59, were interviewed at the beginning of the study to determine their typical behavioral patterns. They were then followed for 8 years. The basic finding was that the men who displayed a type A behavior pattern at the beginning of the study were at least twice as likely to develop CHD as the men with a type B behavior pattern. When the investigators analyzed the data for the younger men in the study (age 39 to 49), the results were even more striking, with CHD developing approximately six times more often in the type A group than in the type B group (Rosenman et al., 1975).

A second major study is the Framingham Heart Study that has been ongoing for more than 40 years (Haynes, Feinleib, & Kannel, 1980) and has taught us much of what we know about the development and course of CHD. In this study, 1,674 healthy men and women were categorized by a type A or type B behavior pattern and followed for 8 years. Again, both men and women with a type A pattern were more than twice as likely to develop CHD as their type B counterparts (in men, the risk was nearly three times as great). For women, the results were strongest for those with a low level of education (Eaker, Pinsky, & Castelli, 1992).

Population-based studies in Europe essentially replicated these results (De Backer, Kittel, Kornitzer, & Dramaix, 1983; French-Belgian Collaborative Group, 1982). It is interesting that a large study of Japanese men conducted in Hawaii did *not* replicate these findings (Cohen & Reed, 1985). The prevalence of type A behavior among Japanese men is much lower than among men in the United States (18.7% versus approximately 50%). Similarly, the prevalence of CHD is equally low in Japanese men (4%, compared to 13% in American men in the Framingham study) (Haynes & Matthews, 1988). In a study that illustrates the effects of culture more dramatically, 3,809 Japanese Americans were classified into groups according to how "traditionally Japanese" they were (in other words, they spoke Japanese at home, retained traditional Japanese values and behaviors, and so on). Japanese Americans who were the "most Japanese" had the lowest incidence of CHD, not significantly different from Japanese men in Japan. In contrast, the group that was the "least Japanese" had a three to five times greater incidence of CHD levels (Marmot & Syme, 1976; Matsumoto, 1996). Clearly, sociocultural differences are important.

Despite these straightforward results, at least in Western cultures, the type A concept has proved more complex and elusive than scientists had hoped. First, it is difficult to determine whether someone is type A from structured interviews, questionnaires, or other measures of this construct, because the measures often do not agree with one another. Many people have *some* characteristics of type A but not all of them, and others present with a mixture of types A and B. The notion that we can divide the world into two types of people—an assumption underlying the early work in this area—has long since been discarded. As a result, subsequent studies did not necessarily support the relationship of type A behavior to CHD (Dembroski & Costa, 1987; Hollis, Connett, Stevens, & Greenlick, 1990).

■ The Role of Chronic Negative Emotions

At this point, investigators decided that something might be wrong with the type A construct itself (Matthews, 1988; Rodin & Salovey, 1989). A consensus developed that some behaviors and emotions representative of the type A personality might be important in the development of CHD, but not all of them. The primary factor that seems to be responsible for much of the relationship is anger (Miller et al., 1996), which will come as no surprise if you read the Ironson study in Chapter 2 and the previous section on hypertension. As you may remember, Ironson and colleagues (1992) compared increased heart rate when they instructed individuals with heart disease to imagine situations or events in their own lives that made them angry with heart rates when they imagined other situations, such as exercise. They found that anger impaired the pumping efficiency of the heart, putting these individuals at risk for dangerous disturbances in heart rhythm (arrhythmias). This study confirms earlier findings relating the frequent experience of anger to later CHD (Dembroski, MacDougall, Costa, & Grandits, 1989; Houston, Chesney, Black, Cates, & Hecker, 1992; T. W. Smith, 1992). Results from an important study strengthen this conclusion. Iribarren and colleagues (2000) evaluated 374 young, healthy adults, both white and African American, over a period of 10 years. Those with high hostility and anger showed evidence of coronary artery calcification, an early sign of CHD.

Is type A irrelevant to the development of heart disease? Most investigators conclude that some components of the type A construct are important determinants of CHD, with a chronically high level of negative affect, such as anger, one of the prime candidates, and the time urgency or impatience factor another (Matthews, 2005; Thoresen & Powell, 1992; Williams, Barefoot, & Schneiderman, 2003; Winters & Schneiderman, 2000). Recall again the case of John, who had all the type A behaviors, including time urgency, but also had frequent angry outbursts. But what about people who experience closely related varieties of negative affect on a chronic basis? Look back to Figure 9.5 and notice the close relationship among stress, anxiety, and depression. Some evidence indicates that the physiological components of these emotions and their effects on the cardiovascular system may be identical, or at least similar (Suls & Bunde, 2005). We also know that the emotion of anger, so commonly associated with stress, is closely related to the emotion of fear, as evidenced in flight or fight response. Fight is the typical behavioral action tendency associated with anger, and flight or escape is associated with fear. But our bodily alarm response, activated by an immediate danger or threat, is associated with both emotions.

Some investigators, after reviewing the literature, have concluded that anxiety and depression are as important as anger in the development of CHD (Albert, Chae, Rexrode, Manson, & Kawachi, 2005; Barlow, 1988; Frasure-Smith & Lesperance, 2005; Suls & Bunde, 2005; Williams et al., 2003). In a study of 896 people who had suffered heart attacks, Frasure-Smith and colleagues (1999) found that patients who were depressed were three times more likely to die in the year following their heart attacks than those who were not depressed, regardless of how severe their initial heart disease was. Severe depression, as in major depressive episodes, is particularly implicated in cardiovascular damage (Agatisa et al., 2005). Thus, it may be that the chronic experience of the negative emotions of stress (anger), anxiety (fear), and depression (ongoing) and the neurobiological activation that accompanies these emotions provide the most important psychosocial contributions to CHD, and perhaps to other physical disorders. Indeed, Watkins and colleagues (2006) confirmed that both depression and anxiety predicted future arrhythmias in people with CHD.

Gallo and Matthews (2003; Matthews, 2005) provide a model of the contribution of psychosocial factors to CHD. Lower socioeconomic status and relatively few resources or low prestige is in the first box. Stressful life events are in the second. Coping skills and social support contribute to a reserve capacity that may buffer the effects of stress, as represented in the third box. Both negative emotions and negative cognitive styles then constitute a major risk factor. Positive emotions and an optimistic style, on the other hand, reduce the risk of CHD (Giltay, Geleijnse, Zitman, Hoekstra, & Schouten, 2004) and may turn out to be just as important as negative emotions in their effects of CHD. Both negative and positive emotions are in the fourth box. This model summarizes nicely what we know about the influence or psychosocial factors on CHD (see ■ Figure 9.10).

Chronic Pain

Pain is not in itself a disorder, yet for most of us it is the fundamental signal of injury, illness, or disease. The importance of pain in our lives cannot be underestimated. Without low levels of pain providing feedback on the functioning of the body and its various systems, we would incur substantially more injuries. For example, you might lie out in the hot sun a lot longer and be badly burned. You might not roll over while sleeping or shift your posture while sitting, thereby affecting your circulation in a way that might be harmful. Reactions to this kind of pain are mostly automatic; that is, we are not aware of the discomfort. When pain crosses the threshold of awareness, which varies a great deal from one person to another, we are forced to take action. If we can't relieve the pain ourselves or we are not sure of its cause, we usually seek medical help. The National Institutes of Health has identified chronic pain as the costliest medical problem in America, affecting nearly 100 million individuals (Byrne & Hochwarter, 2006; Otis & Pincus, in press). Overall the total cost of chronic pain, including treatments and indirect costs such as loss of productivity at work, have been estimated between $150 billion and $260 billion annually (Byrne & Hochwarter, 2006). Americans spend at least $125 billion annually on treatment for chronic pain, including over-the-counter medication to reduce temporary pain from headaches, colds, and other minor disorders (Turk & Gatchel, 1999; Gatchel, 2005). Pain is the cause of 80% of all visits to physicians (Gatchel, Peng, Peters, Fuchs, & Turk, 2007; Turk & Gatchel, 2002), making it by far the most common reason to see a primary care physician (Otis, MacDonald, & Dobscha, 2006). Yet most researchers now agree that the cause of chronic pain and the

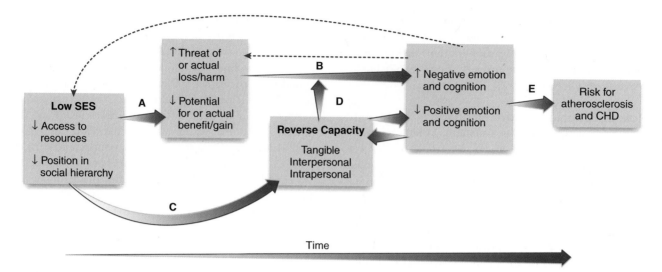

■ **FIGURE 9.10** The reserve capacity model for associations among environments of low socioeconomic status (SES), stressful experiences, psychosocial resources, and emotions and cognitions, which represent pathways to increased risk for CHD. *Note:* Arrow A depicts the direct influence of SES on exposure to stressful experiences. Arrow B indicates the direct impact of stress experiences on emotion and cognition. Arrow C shows that SES conditions and shapes the bank of resources (that is, the reserve capacity) available to manage stress. Arrow D shows that reserve capacity represents a potential moderator of the association between stress and emotional-cognitive factors. Arrow E indicates the direct effects of emotional-cognitive factors on intermediate pathways and risk for atherosclerosis and CHD. The dashed lines note the possible reverse influences. (Adapted from Gallo, L. C., & Matthews, K. A. (2003). Understanding the association between socioeconomic status and physical health: Do negative emotions play a role?" *Psychological Bulletin, 129,* 34 (Figure 1), © 2003 American Psychological Association. Reprinted, with permission, from Matthews, K. A. (2005). Psychological perspectives on the development of coronary heart disease. *American Psychologist, 60*(8), 791 (Figure 2), © 2005 American Psychological Association.)

resulting enormous drain on our health-care system *are substantially psychological and social* (Dersh, Polatin, & Gatchel, 2002; Gatchel and colleagues, 2007; Gatchel & Turk, 1999; Turk & Monarch, 2002).

There are two kinds of clinical pain: acute and chronic. **Acute pain** typically follows an injury and disappears once the injury heals or is effectively treated, often within a month (Philips & Grant, 1991). **Chronic pain,** by contrast, may begin with an acute episode but *does not decrease* over time, even when the injury has healed or effective treatments have been administered. Typically, chronic pain is in the muscles, joints, or tendons, particularly in the lower back. Vascular pain because of enlarged blood vessels may be chronic, as may headaches; pain caused by the slow degeneration of tissue, as in some terminal diseases; and pain caused by the growth of cancerous tumors that impinge on pain receptors (Melzack & Wall, 1982; Otis & Pincus, in press; Taylor, 2006). To better understand the experience of pain, clinicians and researchers generally make a clear distinction between the subjective experience termed *pain,* reported by the patient, and the overt manifestations of this experience, termed *pain behaviors.* Pain behaviors include changing the way one sits or walks, continually complaining about pain to others, grimacing, and, most important, avoiding various activities, particularly those involving work or leisure. Finally, an emotional component of pain called *suffering* sometimes accompanies pain and sometimes does not (Fordyce, 1988; Liebeskind, 1991). Because they are so important, we first review psychological and social contributions to pain.

■ Psychological and Social Aspects

In mild forms, chronic pain can be an annoyance that eventually wears you down and takes the pleasure out of your life. Severe chronic pain may cause you to lose your job, withdraw from your family, give up the fun in your life, and focus your entire awareness on seeking relief. What is interesting for our purposes is that the *severity* of the pain does not seem to predict the *reaction* to it. Some individuals experience intense pain frequently yet continue to work productively, rarely seek medical services, and lead reasonably normal lives; others become invalids. These differences appear to be primarily the result of psychological factors (Dersh et al., 2002; Gatchel, 2005; Gatchel & Turk, 1999; Keefe, Dunsmore, & Burnett, 1992; Turk & Monarch, 2002). It will come as no surprise that these factors are the same as those implicated in the stress response and other negative emotional states, such as anxiety and depression (Ohayon & Schatzberg, 2003) (see Chapters 5 and 7). The determining factor seems to be the individual's general sense of control over the situation: whether or not he can deal with the pain and its consequences in an effective and meaningful way. When a positive sense of control is combined with a generally optimistic outlook about the future, there is substantially less distress and disability (Bandura, O'Leary, Taylor, Gauthier, & Gossard, 1987; Gatchel & Turk, 1999; Keefe & France, 1999; Otis & Pincus, in press; Zautra, Johnson, & Davis, 2005). Positive psychological factors are also associated with active attempts to cope, such as exercise and other regimens, as opposed to suffering passively (Brown & Nicassio, 1987; Gatchel & Turk, 1999; Lazarus & Folkman, 1984; Strahl, Kleinknecht, & Dinnel, 2000; Turk & Gatchel, 2002; Zautra et al., 2005).

To take one example, Philips and Grant (1991) studied 117 patients who suffered from back and neck pain after an injury. Almost all were expected to recover quickly, but fully 40% of them still reported substantial pain at 6 months, thereby qualifying for "chronic pain" status. Of the 60% who reported no pain at the 6-month point, most had been pain free since approximately 1 month after the accident. Furthermore, Philips and Grant report that the relationship between the experience of pain and the subsequent disability was not as strongly related to the intensity of the pain as other factors, such as personality and socioeconomic differences and whether the person planned to initiate a lawsuit concerning the injury. Gatchel, Polatin, and Kinney (1995) found that preexisting anxiety and personality problems predicted who would suffer chronic pain. Generally, a profile of negative emotion such as anxiety and depression, poor coping skills, low social support, and the possibility of being compensated for pain through disability claims predict most types of chronic pain (Dersh et al., 2002; Gatchel and colleagues, 2007; Gatchel & Dersh, 2002; Gatchel & Epker, 1999). Yet another study of chronic pain patients undergoing a 4-week behavioral treatment program demonstrated that developing a greater sense of control and less anxiety focused on the pain resulted in less severe pain and less impairment after treatment (Burns, Glenn, Bruehl, Harden, & Lofland, 2003). Finally, Zautra and colleagues (2005) observed that positive affect in a group of 124 women with severe pain from arthritis or fibromyalgia predicted less pain in subsequent weeks than women with lower levels of positive affect.

That the experience of pain can be largely disconnected from disease or injury is perhaps best exemplified by *phantom limb pain*. In this not uncommon condition, people who have lost an arm or leg feel excruciating pain in the limb that is no longer there. Furthermore, they can describe in exquisite detail the exact location of the pain and its type, such as a dull ache or a sharp cutting pain. They are fully aware the limb is amputated, but this does

It is not uncommon for people to feel specific pain in limbs that are no longer part of them.

Some people with chronic pain or disability cope extremely well and become high achievers.

nothing to relieve the pain. Evidence suggests that changes in the sensory cortex of the brain may contribute to this phenomenon (Flor et al., 1995; Katz & Gagliese, 1999; Ramachandran, 1993). Generally, someone who thinks pain is disastrous, uncontrollable, or reflective of personal failure experiences more intense pain and greater psychological distress than someone who does not feel this way (Gatchel and colleagues 2007; Gil, Williams, Keefe, & Beckham, 1990; Turk & Gatchel, 2002). Thus, treatment programs for chronic pain concentrate on psychological factors.

Other examples of psychological influences on pain are encountered every day. Athletes with significant tissue damage often continue to perform and report relatively little pain. In an important study, 65% of war veterans wounded in combat reported feeling no pain when they were injured. Presumably, their attention was focused externally on what they had to do to survive rather than internally on the experience of pain (Melzack & Wall, 1982).

Social factors also influence how we experience pain (Fordyce, 1976, 1988). For example, family members who were formerly critical and demanding may become caring and sympathetic (Kearns et al., 2002; Otis & Pincus, in press; Romano, Jensen, Turner, Good, & Hops, 2000). This phenomenon is referred to as *operant* control of pain behavior because the behavior clearly seems under the control of social consequences. But these consequences have an uncertain relation to the amount of pain being experienced.

By contrast, a strong network of social support may reduce pain. Jamison and Virts (1990) studied 521 chronic pain patients (with back, abdominal, and chest conditions) and discovered that those who lacked social support from their families reported more pain sites and showed more pain behavior, such as staying in bed.

These patients also exhibited more emotional distress *without* rating their pain as any more intense than subjects with strong socially supportive families. The subjects with strong support returned to work earlier, showed less reliance on medications, and increased their activity levels more quickly than the others.

Although these results may seem to contradict studies on the operant control of pain, different mechanisms may be at work. General social support may reduce the stress associated with pain and injury and promote more adaptive coping procedures and control. However, specifically reinforcing pain behaviors, particularly in the absence of social supports, may powerfully increase such behavior. These complex issues have not yet been entirely sorted out.

■ Biological Aspects

No one thinks pain is entirely psychological, just as no one thinks it is entirely physical. As with other disorders, we must consider how they interact.

Gate Control Theory The *gate control theory of pain* (Melzack & Wall, 1965, 1982) accommodates both psychological and physical factors. According to this theory, nerve impulses from painful stimuli make their way to the spinal column and from there to the brain. An area called the *dorsal horns of the spinal column* acts as a "gate" and may open and transmit sensations of pain if the stimulation is sufficiently intense. Specific nerve fibers referred to as *small fibers* (A-delta and C fibers) and *large fibers* (A-beta fibers) determine the pattern, as well as the intensity, of the stimulation. Small fibers tend to open the gate, thereby increasing the transmission of painful stimuli, whereas large fibers tend to close the gate.

Most important for our purpose is that the brain sends signals back down the spinal cord that may affect the gating mechanism. For example, a person with negative emotions such as fear or anxiety may experience pain more intensely because the basic message from the brain is to be vigilant against possible danger or threat. Then again, in a person whose emotions are more positive or who is absorbed in an activity (such as a runner intent on finishing a long race), the brain sends down an inhibitory signal that closes the gate. Although many think that the gate control theory is overly simplistic (and it has recently been updated; see Melzack, 1999; 2005), research findings continue to support its basic elements, particularly as it describes the complex interaction of psychological and biological factors in the experience of pain (Gatchel and colleagues, 2007; Gatchel & Turk, 1999; Otis & Pincus, in press; Turk & Monarch, 2002).

Endogenous Opioids The neurochemical means by which the brain inhibits pain is an important discovery. Drugs such as heroin and morphine are manufactured from opioid substances. It now turns out that **endogenous** (natural) **opioids** exist within the body. Called *endorphins* or *enkephalins,* they act much like neurotransmitters. The brain uses them to shut down pain, even in the presence of marked tissue damage or injury. Because endogenous opioids are distributed widely throughout the body, they may be implicated in a variety of psychopathological conditions, including eating disorders and, more commonly, the "runners' high" that ac-

companies the release of endogenous opioids after intense (and sometimes painful) physical activity. Bandura and colleagues (1987) found that people with a greater sense of self-efficacy and control had a higher tolerance for pain than individuals with low self-efficacy and that they increased their production of endogenous opioids when they were confronted with a painful stimulus.

■ Gender Differences in Pain

Most animal and human studies have been conducted on males to avoid the complications of hormonal variation. But men and women seem to experience different types of pain. On the one hand, in addition to menstrual cramps and labor pains, women suffer more often than men from migraine headaches, arthritis, carpal tunnel syndrome, and temporomandibular joint (TMJ) pain in the jaw (Lipchik, Holroyd, & Nash, 2002; Miaskowski, 1999). Men, on the other hand, have more cardiac pain and backache. Both males and females have endogenous opioid systems, although in males it may be more powerful. But both sexes seem to have additional pain-regulating mechanisms that may be different. The female neurochemistry may be based on an estrogen-dependent neuronal system that may have evolved to cope with the pain associated with reproductive activity (Mogil, Sternberg, Kest, Marek, & Liebeskind, 1993). It is an "extra" pain-regulating pathway in females that, if taken away by removing hormones, has no implications for the remaining pathways, which continue to work. One implication of this finding is that males and females may benefit from different kinds of drugs, different kinds of psychological interventions, or unique combinations of these treatments to best manage and control pain.

Chronic Fatigue Syndrome

In the mid-19th century, a rapidly growing number of patients suffered from lack of energy, marked fatigue, a variety of aches and pains, and occasionally low-grade fever. No physical pathology could be discovered, and George Beard (1869) labeled the condition *neurasthenia,* literally "lack of nerve strength" (Abbey & Garfinkel, 1991; Costa e Silva & De Girolamo, 1990; Morey & Kurtz, 1989). The disease was attributed to the demands of the time, including a preoccupation with material success, a strong emphasis on hard work, and the changing role of women. Neurasthenia disappeared in the early 20th century in Western cultures but continues to remain one of the most common psychological diagnoses in China (Good & Kleinman, 1985; Kleinman, 1986). Now **chronic fatigue syndrome (CFS)** is spreading rapidly throughout the Western world (Jason, Fennell, & Taylor, 2006; Prins, van der Meer, & Bleijenberg, 2006). The symptoms of CFS, listed in Table 9.3, are almost identical to those of neurasthenia and have been attributed to viral infection, specifically the Epstein-Barr virus (Straus et al., 1985); immune system dysfunction (Straus, 1988); exposure to toxins; or clinical depression (Chalder, Cleare, & Wessely, 2000; Costa e Silva & De Girolamo, 1990). No evidence has yet to support any of these hypothetical physical causes (Chalder et al., 2000; Jason et al., 2003; Prins et al., 2006). Jason and colleagues (1999) conducted a sophisticated study of the prevalence of CFS in the community and reported that 0.4% of their sample was determined to have CFS, with

TABLE 9.3   Definition of Chronic Fatigue Syndrome

Inclusion Criteria

1. Clinically evaluated, medically unexplained fatigue of at least 6 months duration that is
   - of new onset (not lifelong)
   - not resulting from ongoing exertion
   - not substantially alleviated by rest
   - a substantial reduction in previous level of activities

2. The occurrence of four or more of the following symptoms:
   - Subjective memory impairment
   - Sore throat
   - Tender lymph nodes
   - Muscle pain
   - Joint pain
   - Headache
   - Unrefreshing sleep
   - Postexertional malaise lasting more than 24 hours

Source: Adapted from Fukuda, K., Straus, S. E., Hickie, I., Sharpe, M. B., Dobbins, J. G., & Komaroff, A. L. (1994). Chronic fatigue syndrome: A comprehensive approach to its diagnosis and management. *Annals of Internal Medicine,* 121, 953–959.

higher rates in Latino and African American respondents compared to whites. CFS can occur in up to 3% of patients in a primary care clinic, predominantly in women, and usually begins in early adulthood (Afari & Buchwald, 2003), but it can occur in children as young as 7 years (Sankey, Hill, Brown, Quinn, & Fletcher, 2006). A more recent study of 4,591 twins yielded a 2.7% prevalence rate (Furberg et al., 2005). To get a better idea of prevalence, large-scale population studies need to be done.

People with CFS suffer considerably and often must give up their careers, because the disorder runs a chronic course (Taylor et al., 2003). In a group of 100 patients followed for 18 months, chronic fatigue symptoms did not decrease significantly in fully 79% of cases. Better mental health to begin with, as well as less use of sedating medications and a more "psychological" as opposed to medical attribution for causes, led to better outcomes (Schmaling, Fiedelak, Katon, Bader, & Buchwald, 2003). Fortunately, CFS patients do not seem to be at risk for increased mortality (death) through disease or suicide compared to the general population (Smith, Noonan, & Buchwald, 2006). As Abbey and Garfinkel (1991) and Sharpe (1997) point out, both neurasthenia in the 19th century and CFS in the 20th century and the present have been attributed to an extremely stressful environment, the changing role of women, and the rapid dissemination of new technology and information. Both disorders are most common in women. It is possible that a virus or a specific immune system dysfunction will be found to account for CFS. Another possibility suggested by Abbey and Garfinkel (1991) is that the condition represents a rather nonspecific response to stress, and Heim and colleagues (2006) found a higher level of adverse early stressful events in people with CFS compared to nonfatigued controls, reminiscent of Sapolsky's monkeys (see p. 313). Furthermore, a recent large study looking at personality factors that may contribute to CFS

found preexisting stress and emotional instability to be important factors (Kato, Sullivan, Evengard, & Pederson, 2006). But it is not clear why certain individuals respond with chronic fatigue instead of some other psychological or physical disorder. Michael Sharpe (1997) has developed one of the first models of the causes of CFS that accounts for all of its features (see ■ Figure 9.11). Sharpe theorizes that individuals with particularly achievement-oriented lifestyles (driven, perhaps, by a basic sense of inadequacy) undergo a period of extreme stress or acute illness. They misinterpret the

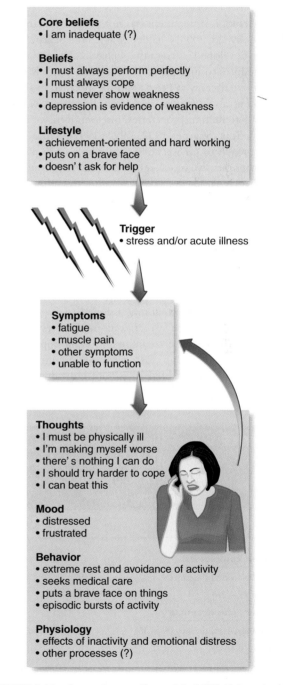

■ **FIGURE 9.11**   A complex-specific model of CFS. (Adapted, with permission, from Sharpe, M., 1997. Chronic fatigue syndrome. In D. M. Clark & C. G. Fairburn, Eds., *Science and Practice of Cognitive Behavior Therapy.* Oxford: Oxford University Press, pp. 381–414, © 1997 Oxford University Press.)

lingering symptoms of fatigue, pain, and inability to function at their usual high levels as a continuing disease that is worsened by activity and improved by rest. This results in behavioral avoidance, helplessness, depression, and frustration. They think they should be able to conquer the problem and cope with its symptoms. Chronic inactivity leads to lack of stamina, weakness, and increased feelings of depression and helplessness that in turn result in episodic bursts of long activity followed by further fatigue. Certainly genetic factors probably influence the impact of stress and psychological variables in causing CFS, as is the case with all disorders (Kaiser, 2006).

Pharmacological treatment has not proved effective for CFS (Afari & Buchwald, 2003; Chalder et al., 2000; Sharpe, 1992), but Sharpe has developed a cognitive-behavioral program that includes procedures to increase activity, regulate periods of rest, and direct cognitive therapy at the cognitions specified in Figure 9.11. This treatment also includes relaxation, breathing exercises, and general stress-reduction procedures, interventions we describe in the next section (Sharpe, 1992, 1993, 1997). Time will tell if Sharpe's approach to CFS is correct in whole or in part, but it is the first comprehensive model and it does have treatment implications. In an early controlled trial evaluating this approach, 60 patients were assigned to the cognitive-behavioral treatment or to treatment as usual. Seventy-three percent of the patients in the cognitive-behavioral treatment group improved on measures of fatigue, disability, and illness belief, a result far superior to that in the control group (Sharpe et al., 1996). In a second, more sophisticated, large-scale evaluation of a similar cognitive-behavioral approach to CFS (Deale, Chalder, Marks, & Wessely, 1997), 60 patients with CFS were randomly assigned to cognitive-behavioral therapy or relaxation exercises alone. The results indicated that fatigue diminished and overall functioning improved significantly more in the group that received cognitive-behavioral therapy. As is evident in Table 9.4, 70% of individuals who completed cognitive-behavioral therapy achieved substantial improve-

ment in physical functioning at a 6-month follow-up compared to only 19% of those in the relaxation-only group. A 5-year follow-up indicates the gains were largely maintained (Deale, Husain, Chalder, & Wessely, 2001). These results are encouraging and have been widely noted as one of the best treatment options to date (Bleijenberg, Prins, & Bazelmans, 2003; Whiting et al., 2001). A systematic program of exercise may also be helpful (Moss-Morris, Sharon, Tobin, & Baldi, 2005).

CONCEPT CHECK 9.2

Answer the following questions about the psychosocial effects on physical disorders.

1. Which of the following is not considered part of the experience of pain?
   a. The subjective impression of pain as reported by the patient
   b. Pain behaviors or overt manifestations of pain
   c. Cuts, bruises, and other injuries
   d. An emotional component called suffering
2. Some evidence shows that psychological factors may contribute to both the course and the _____ of cancer, AIDS, and other diseases, as well as treatment and recovery.
3. Psychosocial and biological factors contribute to the development of _____, a potentially deadly condition of high blood pressure, and to the development of _____, the blockage of arteries supplying blood to heart muscle.
4. Psychologists identified two types of behavior patterns that they alleged to contribute to the development of disease. What types were developed? _____ and _____
5. No evidence exists to show that there is a physical cause for the disease of _____ that often causes individuals to give up their careers and suffer considerably.

TABLE 9.4 Patients With Chronic Fatigue Syndrome Who Had Good Outcomes at 6-Month Follow-Up*

Study Group	N	%
Treatment completers		
Cognitive-behavioral therapy (N = 27)	19	70
Relaxation (N = 26)	5	19
Completers plus dropouts		
Cognitive-behavioral therapy (N = 30)	19	63
Relaxation (N = 30)	5	17

*An increase of 50 or more, from pretreatment to 6-month follow-up, or an end score of 83 or more on the physical functioning scale of the Medical Outcome Study Short-Form General Health Survey.

Source: Reprinted, with permission, from Deale, A., Chalder, T., Marks, I., & Wessely, S. (1997). Cognitive behavior therapy for chronic fatigue syndrome: A randomized controlled trial. *American Journal of Psychiatry,* 154, 408–414. © 1997 American Psychiatric Association.)

PSYCHOSOCIAL TREATMENT OF PHYSICAL DISORDERS

Certain experiments suggest that pain not only is bad for you but also may kill you. John Liebeskind and his colleagues (Page, Ben-Eliyahu, Yirmiya, & Liebeskind, 1993) demonstrated that postsurgical pain in rats doubles the rate at which a certain cancer metastasizes (spreads) to the lungs. Rats undergoing abdominal surgery *without* morphine developed twice the number of lung metastases as rats who were given morphine for the same surgery. The rats undergoing surgery with the pain-killing drug had even lower rates of metastases than rats that did not have surgery.

This effect may result from the interaction of pain with the immune system. Pain may reduce the number of natural killer cells in the immune system, perhaps because of the general stress reaction to the pain. Thus, if a rat is in *extreme* pain, the associated stress may further enhance the pain, completing a vicious circle. If this finding is found to apply to humans, it is important, because the consensus is that we are reluctant to use pain-killing medication in chronic diseases such as cancer. Some estimates suggest that fewer than half of all cancer patients in the United States receive sufficient pain relief. Direct evidence is available on the benefits of early pain relief in patients undergoing surgery (Coderre, Katz, Vaccarino, & Melzack, 1993; Keefe & France, 1999). Patients receiving pain medication before surgery reported less pain after surgery and requested less pain medication. Adequate pain-management procedures, either medical or psychological, are an essential part of the management of chronic disease.

A variety of psychological treatments have been developed for physical disorders and pain, including biofeedback, relaxation procedures, and hypnosis (Gatchel, 2005; Linden & Moseley, 2006; Otis & Pincus, in press; Turk & Gatchel, 2002). But because of the overriding role of stress in the etiology and maintenance of many physical disorders, comprehensive stress-management programs are increasingly incorporated into medical centers where such disorders are treated. We briefly review specific psychosocial approaches to physical disorders and describe a typical comprehensive stress-management program.

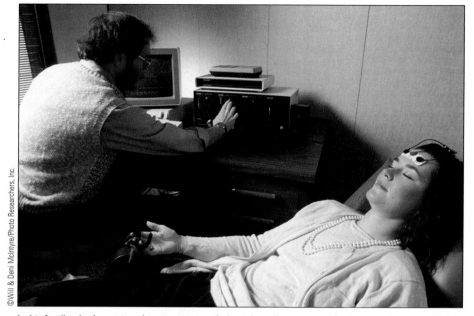

©Will & Deni McIntyre/Photo Researchers, Inc.

In biofeedback, the patient learns to control physiological responses that are visible on a screen.

Biofeedback

Biofeedback is a process of making patients aware of specific physiological functions that, ordinarily, they would not notice consciously, such as heart rate, blood pressure, muscle tension in specific areas of the body, electroencephalogram rhythms (brain waves), and patterns of blood flow (Andrasik, 2000; Schwartz & Andrasik, 2003). Conscious awareness is the first step, but the second step is more remarkable. In the 1960s, Neal Miller reported that rats could *learn to directly control* many of these responses. He used a variation of operant-conditioning procedures in which the animals were reinforced for increases or decreases in their physiological responses (N. E. Miller, 1969). Although it was subsequently difficult to replicate these findings with animals, clinicians applied the procedures with some success to humans who suffered from various physical disorders or stress-related conditions, such as hypertension and headache.

Clinicians use physiological monitoring equipment to make the response, such as heart rate, visible or audible to the patient. The patient then works with the therapist to learn to control the response. A successful response produces some type of signal. For example, if the patient is successful in lowering her blood pressure by a certain amount, the pressure reading will be visible on a gauge and a tone will sound. It wasn't long before researchers discovered that humans could discriminate changes in autonomic nervous system activity with a high degree of accuracy (Blanchard & Epstein, 1977). The question then became this: Why are people ordinarily so poor at discriminating their internal states? Zillmann

(1983) suggests that our abilities have always been highly developed in this regard but that we have simply lost our skills through lack of practice. Shapiro (1974) suggests that, in an evolutionary sense, it might have been adaptive to turn our attention from precise monitoring of our internal responses. He proposes that whether humans function as hunter-gatherers or in the home or office, they would be far less efficient if they were continually distracted by a turmoil of internal stimuli. In other words, to focus successfully on the task at hand, we may have found it necessary to ignore our internal functioning and leave it to the more automatic and less aware parts of the brain. Still, internal sensations often take control of our consciousness and make us fully aware of our needs. Consider, for example, the compelling sensations that signal the need to urinate or the insistence of hunger pangs. In any case, it does seem that through precise physiological feedback we can learn to control our responses, although the mechanisms by which we do so are not yet clearly known.

One goal of biofeedback has been to reduce tension in the muscles of the head and scalp, thereby relieving headaches. Pioneers in the area, such as Ed Blanchard, Ken Holroyd, and Frank Andrasik, found that biofeedback was successful in this area (Holroyd, Andrasik, & Noble, 1980), although no more successful than deep muscle relaxation procedures (Andrasik, 2000; Blanchard & Andrasik, 1982; Blanchard, Andrasik, Ahles, Teders, & O'Keefe, 1980; Holroyd & Penzien, 1986). Because of these results, some have thought that biofeedback might achieve its effects with tension headaches by simply teaching people to relax. However, Holroyd and colleagues (1984) concluded instead that the success of biofeedback, at least for headaches, may depend not on the reduction of tension but on the extent to which the procedures instill a sense of *control* over the pain. (How do you think this relates to the study of stress in baboons described in the beginning of the chapter?) Whatever the mechanism, biofeedback and relaxation are more effective treatments than, for example, placebo medication interventions, and the results of these two treatments are not altogether in-

Edward Blanchard was a pioneer in the development and testing of biofeedback.

terchangeable, in that some people benefit more from biofeedback and others benefit from relaxation procedures. Therefore, applying both treatments is a safe strategy (Andrasik, 2000; Schwartz & Andrasik, 2003). Several reviews have found that 38% to 63% of patients undergoing relaxation or biofeedback achieve significant reductions in headaches compared to approximately 35% who receive placebo medication (Blanchard, 1992; Blanchard et al., 1980; Holroyd & Penzien, 1986). Furthermore, the effects of biofeedback and relaxation seem to be long lasting (Andrasik, 2000; Blanchard, 1987; Lisspers & Öst, 1990).

Relaxation and Meditation

Various types of relaxation and meditation procedures have also been used, either alone or with other procedures, to treat physical disorder and pain patients. In *progressive muscle relaxation,* devised by Edmund Jacobson in 1938, people become acutely aware of any tension in their bodies and counteract it by relaxing specific muscle groups. A number of procedures focus attention either on a specific part of the body or on a single thought or image. This attentional focus is often accompanied by regular, slowed breathing. In *transcendental meditation,* attention is focused solely on a repeated syllable, or the *mantra.*

Herbert Benson stripped transcendental meditation of what he considered its nonessentials and developed a brief procedure he calls the **relaxation response,** in which a person silently repeats a mantra to minimize distraction by closing the mind to intruding thoughts. Although Benson suggested focusing on the word *one,* any neutral word or phrase would do. Individuals who meditate for 10 or 20 minutes a day report feeling calmer or more relaxed throughout the day. These brief, simple procedures can be powerful in reducing the flow of certain neurotransmitters and stress hormones, an effect that may be mediated by an increased sense of control and mastery (Benson, 1975, 1984). Benson's ideas are popular and are taught in 60% of U.S. medical schools and offered by many major hospitals (Roush, 1997). Relaxation has generally positive effects on headaches, hypertension, and acute and chronic pain, although the results are sometimes relatively modest (Taylor, 2006). Nonetheless, relaxation and meditation are almost always part of a comprehensive pain-management program.

A Comprehensive Stress- and Pain-Reduction Program

In our own stress-management program (Barlow, Rapee, & Reisner, 2001), individuals practice a variety of stress-management procedures presented to them in a workbook. First, they learn to monitor their stress closely and to identify the stressful events in their daily lives. (A sample of a daily stress record is in ■ Figure 9.12.) Note that clients are taught to be specific about recording the times they experience stress, the intensity of the stress, and what seems to trigger the stress. They also note the somatic symptoms and thoughts that occur when they are stressed. All this monitoring becomes important in carrying through with the program, but it can be helpful in itself because it reveals precise patterns and causes of stress and helps clients learn what changes to make to cope better.

After learning to monitor stress, clients are taught deep muscle relaxation, which involves, first, tensing various muscles to identify the location of different muscle groups. (Instructions for tensing specific muscle groups are included in Table 9.5.) Clients are then systematically taught to relax the muscle groups beyond the point of inactivity, that is, to actively let go of the muscle so that no tension remains in it.

Appraisals and attitudes are an important part of stress, and clients learn how they exaggerate the negative impact of events in their day-to-day lives. In the program, therapist and client use cognitive therapy to develop more realistic appraisals and attitudes, as exemplified in the case of Sally.

SALLY: Improving Her Perception

(Sally is a 45-year-old real estate agent.)

PATIENT: My mother is always calling just when I'm in the middle of doing something important and it makes me so angry, I find that I get short with her.

THERAPIST: Let's try and look at what you just said in another way. When you say that she *always* phones in the middle of something, it implies 100% of the time. Is that true? How likely is it really that she will call when you are doing something important?

P: Well, I suppose that when I think back over the last ten times she's called, most of the times I was just watching TV or reading. There was once when I was making dinner and it burned because she interrupted me. Another time, I was busy with some work I had brought home from the office, and she called. I guess that makes it 20% of the time.

T: OK, great; now let's go a bit further. So what if she calls at an inconvenient time?

P: Well, I know that one of my first thoughts is that she doesn't think anything I do is important. But before you say anything, I know that is a major overestimation since she obviously doesn't know what I'm doing when she calls. However, I suppose I also think that it's a major interruption and inconvenience to have to stop at that point.

T: Go on. What is the chance that it is a major inconvenience?

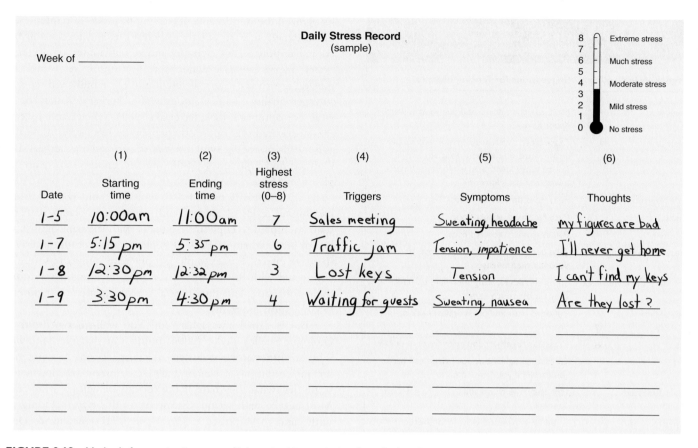

FIGURE 9.12 Methods for monitoring stress. (Adapted, with permission, from Barlow, D. H., Rapee, R. M., & Reisner, L. C., 2001. *Mastering stress 2001: A lifestyle approach* (p. 28). Dallas, TX: American Health, © 2001 American Health Publishing.)

P: When I was doing my work, I forgot what I was up to and it took me 10 minutes to work it out again. I guess that's not so bad; it's only 10 minutes. And when the dinner burned, it was really not too bad, just a little burned. Part of that was my fault anyway, because I could have turned the stove down before I went to the phone.

T: So, it sounds like quite a small chance that it would be a major inconvenience, even if your mother does interrupt you.

P: True. And I know what you are going to say next. Even if it is a major inconvenience, it's not the end of the world. I have handled plenty of bigger problems than this at work.

In this program, individuals work hard to identify unrealistic negative thoughts and to develop new appraisals and attitudes almost instantaneously when negative thoughts occur. Such assessment is often the most difficult part of the program. After the session just related, Sally began using what she had learned in cognitive therapy to reappraise stressful situations. Finally, clients in stress-reduction programs develop new coping strategies, such as time management and assertiveness training. During *time-management training,* patients are taught to prioritize their activities and pay less attention to nonessential demands. During *assertiveness training,* they learn to stand up for themselves in an appropri-

ate way. Clients also learn other procedures for managing everyday problems.

A number of studies have evaluated some version of this comprehensive program. The results suggest that it is generally more effective than individual components alone, such as relaxation or biofeedback, for chronic pain (Keefe et al., 1992; Otis & Pincus, in press; Turk, 2002), CFS (Deale et al., 1997), tension headaches (Blanchard et al., 1990; Lipchik et al., 2002), hypertension (Ward, Swan, & Chesney, 1987), temporomandibular joint (jaw) pain (Turner, Man, & Aaron, 2006) and cancer pain (Crichton & Morey, 2003; Fawzy, Cousins, et al., 1990). A summary "meta-analysis" of 22 studies of treatments for chronic lower back pain also found comprehensive psychological treatments effective (Hoffman, Papas, Chatkoff, & Kerns, 2007).

Drugs and Stress-Reduction Programs

We have already noted the enormous nationwide reliance on over-the-counter analgesic medication for pain, particularly headaches. Some evidence suggests that *chronic* reliance on these medications lessens the efficacy of comprehensive programs in the treatment of headache and may make headaches worse because patients experience *increased* headache pain every time the medication wears off or is stopped (rebound headaches) (Capobianco, Swanson, & Dodick, 2001). Michultka, Blanchard, Appelbaum, Jaccard, and Dentinger (1989) matched high analgesic users (people who took a lot of pain pills) to low analgesic users (people who took few or no pain pills)

TABLE 9.5	Suggestions for Tensing Muscles
Large Muscle Groups	**Suggestions for Tensing Muscles**
Lower arm	Make fist, palm down, and pull wrist toward upper arm.
Upper arm	Tense biceps; with arms by side, pull up per arm toward side without touching. (Try not to tense lower arm while doing this; let lower arm hang loosely.)
Lower leg and foot	Point toes upward to knees.
Thighs	Push feet hard against floor.
Abdomen	Pull in stomach toward back.
Chest and breathing	Take deep breath and hold it about 10 seconds, then release.
Shoulders and lower neck	Shrug shoulders, bring shoulders up until they almost touch ears.
Back of neck	Put head back and press against back of chair.
Lips	Press lips together; don't clench teeth or jaw.
Eyes	Close eyes tightly but don't close too hard (be careful if you have contacts).
Lower forehead	Pull eyebrows down and in (try to get them to meet).
Upper forehead	Raise eyebrows and wrinkle forehead.

Source: Adapted, with permission, from Barlow, D. H., Rapee, R. M., & Reisner, L. C. (2001). *Mastering Stress 2001: A Lifestyle Approach.* Dallas, TX: American Health, pp. 113–114, © 2001 American Health Publishing.

in terms of age, duration of headache activity, and response to comprehensive treatment. Only 29% of high users versus 55% of low users achieved at least a 50% reduction in headache activity.

In addition, Holroyd, Nash, Pingel, Cordingley, and Jerome (1991) compared a comprehensive cognitive-behavioral treatment to an antidepressant drug, amitriptyline, in the treatment of tension headache. The psychological treatment produced at least a 50% reduction in headache activity in 56% of the patients, whereas the drug produced a comparable reduction in only 27% of users. Grazzi and colleagues (2002) treated 61 patients with migraine headaches and analgesic overuse by withdrawing the patients from analgesics and then starting them on a more comprehensive but nonaddicting medication regimen, either with biofeedback and relaxation or without these (drugs only). After 3 years, significantly more individuals in the medication-only condition had relapsed by resuming analgesic use and were experiencing more headache pain. It is important that psychological treatment also seems to reduce drug consumption fairly consistently (Radnitz, Appelbaum, Blanchard, Elliott, & Andrasik, 1988), as it did in the study by Grazzi and colleagues (2002), not only for headaches but also for severe hypertension.

Denial as a Means of Coping

We have emphasized the importance of confronting and working through our feelings, particularly after stressful or traumatic events. Beginning with Sigmund Freud, mental health professionals have

recognized the importance of reliving or processing intense emotional experiences to put them behind us and to develop better coping responses. For example, individuals undergoing coronary artery bypass surgery who were optimistic recovered more quickly, returned to normal activities more rapidly, and reported a stronger quality of life 6 months after surgery than those who were not optimistic (Scheier et al., 1989). Scheier and colleagues also discovered that optimistic people are less likely to use denial as a means of coping with a severe stressor such as surgery. Bruce Compas and colleagues (2006) studied anxiety and pain complaints in 164 adolescents with recurrent abdominal pain. Adolescents who regularly used denial, avoidance, and wishful thinking had higher levels of anxiety and somatic complaints than those who attempted to cope more directly with the pain. Most mental health professionals work to eliminate denial because it has many negative effects. For example, people who deny the severe pain connected with disease may not notice meaningful variations in their symptoms, and they typically avoid treatment regimens or rehabilitation programs.

But is denial always harmful? The well-known health psychologist Shelley Taylor (2006) points out that most individuals who are functioning well deny the implications of a potentially serious condition, at least initially. A common reaction is to assume that what they have is not serious or will go away quickly. Most people with serious diseases react this way, including those with cancer (Meyerowitz, 1983) and CHD (Krantz & Deckel, 1983). Several groups of investigators (see, for example, Hackett & Cassem, 1973; Meyerowitz, 1983) have found that during that extremely stressful period when a person is first diagnosed, denial of the general implications and of anxiety and depression may help the patient endure the shock more easily. He is then better able to develop coping responses later. In one study, high initial denial resulted in less time in the intensive care section of the hospital (Levine et al., 1988), although, after discharge, the same patients were not as good at doing what they had to do to enhance their rehabilitation. Other studies show lower levels of corticosteroids and other stress-related responses among deniers during the most stressful phase of the illness (Katz, Weiner, Gallagher, & Hellman, 1970). Thus, the value of denial as a coping mechanism may depend more on timing than on anything else. In the long run, however, all evidence indicates that at some point we must face the situation, process our emotions, and come to terms with what is happening (Compas et al., 2006).

Modifying Behaviors to Promote Health

In the beginning of the chapter, we talked of psychological and social factors influencing health and physical problems in two distinct ways: by directly affecting biological processes and through unhealthy lifestyles. In this section, we consider the effects of an unhealthy lifestyle.

As early as 1991, the director of the National Institutes of Health said, "Our research is teaching us that many common diseases can be prevented and others can be postponed or controlled simply by making possible lifestyle changes" (U.S. Department of Health and Human Services, 1991). Unhealthy eating habits, lack of exercise, and smoking are three of the most common behaviors that put us at risk in the long term for a number of physical disorders. High-risk behaviors and conditions are listed in Table 9.6. Many of these behaviors contribute to diseases and physical disorders that are among the leading causes of death, including not only CHD and cancer but also accidents of various kinds (related to consumption of alcohol and the nonuse of safety restraints), cirrhosis of the liver (related to excessive consumption of alcohol), and a variety of respiratory diseases, including influenza and pneumonia (related to smoking and stress) (Sexton, 1979). Even now, fully 23.4% of adults in the United States are regular smokers, and smoking is the leading preventable cause of death, killing 440,000 people each year (Porter, Jackson, Trosclair, & Pederson, 2003).

Considerable work is ongoing to develop effective behavior modification procedures that improve diet, increase adherence to drug and medical treatment programs, and develop optimal exercise programs. Here we review briefly four areas of interest: injury control, the prevention of AIDS, efforts to reduce smoking in China, and a major community intervention known as the Stanford Three Community Study.

■ Injury Prevention

Accidents are the leading cause of death for people age 1 to 45 and the fifth leading cause of death among all causes in the United States (see Table 9.1). Furthermore, the loss of productivity to the

Courtesy of Lizette Peterson

Lizette Peterson developed important behavior-change procedures for preventing injuries in children.

individual and society, as well as years of life lost from injuries, is far greater than from the other four leading causes of death: heart disease, cancer, stroke, and respiratory disease (Institute of Medicine, 1999; Rice & MacKenzie, 1989). Therefore, the U. S. government has become interested in methods for reducing injury (Scheidt, Overpeck, Trifiletti, & Cheng, 2000). Spielberger and Frank (1992) point out that psychological variables are crucial in leading to virtually all factors that lead to injury. A good example is the work of the late Lizette Peterson and her colleagues (see, for example, Peterson & Roberts, 1992). Peterson was particularly interested in preventing accidents in children. Injuries kill more children than the next six causes of childhood death combined (Dershewitz & Williamson, 1977; Scheidt et al., 1995; Taylor, 2006), yet most people, including parents, don't think too much about prevention, even in their own children, because they usually consider injuries to be fated and, therefore, out of their hands (Peterson, Farmer, & Kashani, 1990; Peterson & Roberts, 1992).

However, a variety of programs focusing on behavior change have proved effective for preventing injuries in children (Sleet, Hammond, Jones, Thomas, & Whitt, 2003; Taylor, 2006). For example, children have been systematically and successfully taught to escape fires (Jones & Haney, 1984), identify and report emergencies (Jones & Ollendick, 2002; Jones & Kazdin, 1980), safely cross streets (Yeaton & Bailey, 1978), ride bicycles safely, and deal with injuries such as serious cuts (Peterson & Thiele, 1988). In many of these programs, the participating children maintained the safety skills they had learned for months after the intervention—as long as assessments were continued, in most cases. Because little evidence indicates that repeated warnings are effective in preventing injuries, programmatic efforts to change behavior are important. Such programs, however, are nonexistent in most communities.

■ AIDS Prevention

Earlier we documented the horrifying spread of AIDS, particularly in developing countries. Table 9.7 illustrates modes of transmission of AIDS in the United States as they existed through 2005. In developing countries, in Africa, for instance, AIDS is almost exclusively linked to heterosexual intercourse with an infected partner (Centers for Disease Control, 1994; Kuehn, 2006; World Health Organization, 2000). There is no vaccine for the disease. *Changing high-risk behavior is the only effective prevention strategy* (Catania et al., 2000).

Comprehensive programs are particularly important because testing alone to learn whether one is HIV positive or HIV negative does little to change behavior (see, for example, Landis, Earp, & Koch, 1992). Even educating at-risk individuals is generally

---

TABLE 9.6	Areas for Health-Risk Behavior Modifications

- Smoking
- Hyperlipidemia
- High blood pressure
- Dietary habits related to disease

  High sodium; low calcium, magnesium, and potassium—High blood pressure

  High fat—Cardiovascular disease and cancer of the prostate, breast, colon, and pancreas

  High simple carbohydrates—Diabetes mellitus

  Low fiber—Diabetes mellitus, digestive diseases, cardiovascular disease, and colon cancer

  Low intake of Vitamins A and C—Cancer
- Sedentary lifestyle
- Obesity
- Substance abuse (alcohol and drug)
- Nonuse of seat belts
- High-risk sexual behavior
- Nonadherence to recommended immunization and screening procedures
- High stress levels and type A personality
- High-risk situations for childhood accidents, neglect, and abuse
- Poor dental hygiene or infrequent care
- Sun exposure
- Poor quality relationships or supports
- Occupational risks

Source: Reprinted, with permission, from Johns, M. B., et al. (1987). Primary care and health promotion: A model for preventive medicine. *American Journal of Preventive Medicine,* 3(6), 351. © 1987 American Journal of Preventive Medicine.

TABLE 9.7 Estimated Number of AIDS Cases by Transmission Category Through (2005)*

Transmission Category	Adult and Adolescent Male	Adult and Adolescent Female	Total
Male-to-male sexual contact	454,106		454,106
Injection drug use	168,695	73,311	242,006
Male-to-male sexual contact and injection drug use	66,081		66,081
High-risk hetero-sexual contact[†]	61,914	102,936	164,850
Other[‡]	13,967	6,575	20,542

*Includes people with a diagnosis of AIDS from the beginning of the epidemic through 2005.
[†]Heterosexual contact with a person known to have, or to be at high risk for, HIV infection.
[‡]Includes hemophilia, blood transfusion, perinatal, and at risk not reported or not identified.

Source: From Centers for Disease Control (2007). Centers for Disease Control and Prevention. (2007, March). *Cases of HIV infection and AIDS in the United States and dependant areas.* Atlanta: U.S. Department of Health and Human Services, Public Health Services.

ineffective in changing high-risk behavior (Helweg-Larsen & Collins, 1997). One of the most successful behavior-change programs was carried out in San Francisco several years ago. Table 9.8 shows what behaviors were specifically targeted and what methods were used to achieve behavior change in various groups. Before this program was introduced, frequent unprotected sex was reported by 37.4% of one sample of gay men and 33.9% of another sample (Stall, McKusick, Wiley, Coates, & Ostrow, 1986). At a follow-up point in 1988, the incidence had dropped to 1.7% and 4.2%, respectively, in the same two samples (Ekstrand & Coates, 1990). These changes did not occur in comparable groups where a program of this type had not been instituted. In a similar, large, community-based program in eight small cities, Kelly and colleagues (1997) trained popular and well-liked members of the gay community to provide information and education. Risky sexual practices were substantially reduced in the four cities where the program occurred, compared to four cities where only educational pamphlets were distributed.

Careful evaluation of smaller at-risk groups or individuals demonstrates that high-risk sexual practices are reduced substantially by a comprehensive program of *cognitive-behavioral self-management training* and the development of an effective *social support network*. Kelly (1995) has developed an up-to-date program that is adjustable to the individual—young or old, woman or man, urban or rural—and emphasizes helping each one assess personal risk and change risky behavior. Analysis of factors that predict the adoption of safe-sex practices indicates that treatment programs should focus on instilling in participants a sense of self-efficacy and control over their own sexual practices (Aspinwall, Kemeny, Taylor, Schneider, & Dudley, 1991; Kelly, 1995; O'Leary, 1992).

It is crucial that these programs be extended to minorities and women, who often do not consider themselves at risk, probably because most media coverage has focused on gay white males (Mays & Cochran, 1988). Indeed, most research on the epidemiology and natural history of AIDS has largely ignored the disease in women (Cohn, 2003; Ickovics & Rodin, 1992). In 2003, women accounted for 50% of new AIDS cases (World Health Organization, 2003). Furthermore, the age of highest risk for women is between 15 and 25 years; the peak risk for men is during their late 20s and early 30s. In view of the different circumstances in which women put themselves at risk for HIV infection—for example, prostitution in response to economic deprivation—effective behavior-change programs for them must be different from those developed for men (World Health Organization, 2000). Recent reports from Uganda and Thailand, two countries hard hit by AIDS, are encouraging. In Uganda, under the president's strong leadership, intensive and explicit sex education and AIDS messages were introduced early in schools, while children were still forming attitudes about sex. The incidence of new cases declined markedly (Nantulya & Green, 2002). In Thailand, a 100% condom usage program was enforced among sex workers, along with required checkups. Just as important, strong peer support programs were set up to produce a greater sense of empowerment and control (UNAIDS, 2001). Both of these efforts involved strong, enforceable government actions that would be difficult in some Western countries.

■ Smoking in China

Despite efforts by the government to reduce smoking among its citizens, China has one of the most tobacco-addicted populations in the world. Approximately 250 million people in China are habitual smokers—90% of them male—a number that approximates the entire population of the United States. China consumes 33% of all cigarettes in the world, and smoking is projected to kill 100 million Chinese people in the next 50 years (Lam, Ho, Hedley, Mak, & Peto, 2001).

Unger and colleagues (2001) reported that 47% of Chinese boys in the seventh through ninth grades—but only 16% of girls—had already smoked cigarettes. In one early attempt to

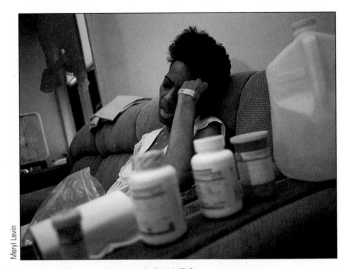

Women are increasingly at risk for AIDS.

TABLE 9.8 The San Francisco Model: Coordinated Community-Level Program to Reduce New HIV Infection

Information

Intervention: Media

Educate about how HIV is and is not transmitted.

Health-Care Establishments and Providers

Provide educational materials and classes about HIV transmission.

Schools

Distribute materials about HIV transmission and prevention.

Worksites

Distribute materials about HIV transmission and prevention.

STD, Family Planning, and Drug Abuse Treatment Centers

Distribute materials and video models about HIV transmission

Community Organizations (Churches, Clubs)

Make guest speakers, materials, and videos available.

Antibody Testing Centers

Distribute materials and instruction about HIV transmission.

Motivation

Provide examples of different kinds of individuals who have become HIV infected. Ask all patients about risk factors for HIV transmission.

Advise high-risk patients to be tested for HIV antibodies.

Provide models of teens who became infected with HIV.

Provide examples of co-workers who became infected with HIV.

Make detailed assessment of HIV risk.

Advise about testing for antibodies to HIV.

Provide examples that HIV-infected individuals are similar to club or organization membership.

STD = sexually transmitted disease.

Skills

Model how to clean needles and use condoms and spermicides.

Model skills for safe sex and needle negotiation.

Provide classes and videos to demonstrate safe-sex skills.

Provide classes and models for safe-sex and drug injection skills.

Instruct and rehearse safe-sex and drug injection skills during medical and counseling encounters.

Provide classes and videos for AIDS risk-reduction skills.

Norms

Publicize the low prevalence of high-risk behaviors.

Publicize public desirability of safe-sex classes and condom advertisements.

Advise patients about prevalent community norms.

Create a climate of acceptance for HIV-infected students and teachers.

Publicize student perceptions about desirability of safe sex.

Create a climate of acceptance for HIV-infected people.

Provide classes and videos for AIDS risk-reduction skills.

Policy and Legislation

Generate concern and action about policy.

Advocate policies and laws that will prevent spread of HIV.

Mobilize students and faculty to work to allow sex education to take place in the schools.

Install condom machines in public bathrooms.

Allow HIV-infected people to work.

Mobilize clients to request additional treatment slots and facilities.

Advocate beneficial laws and policies.

Advocate policy changes and laws suggesting AIDS risk reduction.

Advocate confidentiality and nondiscrimination.

Source: Reprinted, with permission, from Coates, T. J. (1990). Strategies for modifying sexual behavior for primary and secondary prevention of HIV disease. *Journal of Consulting and Clinical Psychology,* 58(1), 57–69, © 1990 American Psychological Association.

reach these individuals, health professionals took advantage of the strong family ties in China and decided to persuade the *children* of smokers to intervene with their fathers. In so doing, they conducted the largest study yet reported of attempted behavior modification to promote health. In 1989, they developed an antismoking campaign in 23 primary schools in Hangzhou, capital of Zhejiang province. Children took home antismoking literature and questionnaires to almost 10,000 fathers. They then wrote letters to their fathers asking them to quit smoking, and they submitted monthly reports on their fathers' smoking habits to the schools. Approximately 9 months later, the results were assessed. Indeed, the children's intervention had some effect. Almost 12% of the fathers in the intervention group had quit smoking for at least 6 months. By contrast, in a control group of another 10,000 males, the quit rate was only 0.2%.

Since then, the Chinese government has become more involved in smoking prevention efforts. One notable example is the Wuhan smoking prevention trial. In this public health effort, investigators from the United States and China are collaborating to prevent smoking by more than 5,000 adolescents in Wuhan and

southern California. In one initial investigation, Unger and colleagues (2002) found, somewhat surprisingly, that smoking by peers and availability of cigarettes were equally strong risk factors for smoking in adolescents in both China and the United States and would be one major target for prevention programs.

■ **Stanford Three Community Study**

One of the best-known and most successful efforts to reduce risk factors for disease in the community is the Stanford Three Community Study (Meyer, Nash, McAlister, Maccoby, & Farquhar, 1980). Although, it was conducted a number of years ago, it remains a model program. Rather than assemble three groups of people, these investigators studied three entire communities in central California that were reasonably alike in size and type of residents between 1972 and 1975. The target was reduction of risk factors for CHD. The positive behaviors that were introduced focused on smoking, high blood pressure, diet, and weight reduction. In Tracy, the first community, no interventions were conducted, but detailed information was collected from a random sample of adults to assess any increases in their knowledge of risk

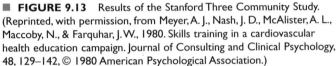

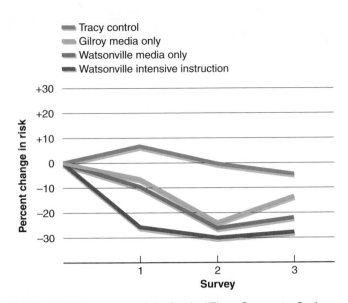

■ **FIGURE 9.13** Results of the Stanford Three Community Study. (Reprinted, with permission, from Meyer, A. J., Nash, J. D., McAlister, A. L., Maccoby, N., & Farquhar, J. W., 1980. Skills training in a cardiovascular health education campaign. Journal of Consulting and Clinical Psychology, 48, 129–142, © 1980 American Psychological Association.)

factors, as well as any changes in risk factors over time. In addition, participants in Tracy received a medical assessment of their cardiovascular factors. The residents of Gilroy and part of Watsonville were subjected to a media blitz on the dangers of behavioral risk factors for CHD, the importance of reducing these factors, and helpful hints for doing so. Most residents of Watsonville, the third community, also had a face-to-face intervention in which behavioral counselors worked with the townspeople judged to be at particularly high risk for CHD. Subjects in all three communities were surveyed once a year for a 3-year period following the intervention. Results indicate that the interventions were markedly successful at reducing risk factors for CHD in these communities (see ■ Figure 9.13). Furthermore, for the residents of Watsonville who also received individual counseling, risk factors were substantially lower than for people in Tracy or even for those in Gilroy and people in the part of Watsonville that received only the media blitz, and their knowledge of risk factors was substantially higher.

Interventions such as the Stanford study cost money, although in many communities the media are willing to donate time to such a worthy effort. Results show that mounting an effort like this is worthwhile to individuals, to the community, and to public health officials because many lives will be saved and disability leave will be decreased to an extent that will more than cover the original cost of the program. Unfortunately, implementation of this type of program is still not widespread.

CONCEPT CHECK 9.3

Check your understanding of psychosocial treatment by matching the treatments to the correct scenarios or statements: (a) biofeedback, (b) meditation and relaxation, (c) cognitive coping procedures, (d) denial, (e) modify behaviors to promote health, and (f) Stanford Three Community Study.

1. Mary is often upset by stupid things other people are always doing. Her doctor wants her to realize her exaggeration of these events and suggests _____.
2. Karl can't seem to focus on anything at work. He feels too stressed. He needs _____, a way of minimizing intruding thoughts that he can do at work in a short amount of time.
3. Harry's blood pressure soars when he feels stressed. His doctor showed him how to become aware of his body process to control them better by using _____.
4. At a world conference, leaders met to discuss how to reduce the risk of childhood injuries, AIDS risks, and the number of smoking-related diseases. Professionals suggested programs involving teaching individuals how to _____.
5. Initially, strong _____ can help a patient endure the shock of bad news; however, later it can inhibit or prevent the healing process.
6. The _____ is one of the best-known efforts to reduce community disease risk factors.

FUTURE DIRECTIONS

Placebo Effects and the Brain

Do "phony" placebo pills really decrease pain—or is just that individuals think or report that they are feeling less pain? This is one of the major controversies in the study of placebo responses, not only for pain but also for conditions such as depression. With the help of the latest brain-imaging technology, some new results are in. Several experiments have demonstrated that when pain is induced in some volunteers (for example, by injecting salt water in their jaws) after they are given a placebo, their brains operate in such a way that they actually feel less pain as opposed to simply thinking they feel less pain or reporting that they feel less pain (Wager, 2005; Zubieta et al., 2005). Specifically, broad areas of the brain are affected, but the most important system that is activated may be the endogenous opioid system (or endorphins), which, among other functions, suppresses pain. Increased endorphin activity across broad areas of the brain was associated with lower ratings of pain intensity, as well as reductions in the sensations of pain and emotional reactions to it. Thus, the studies show that the placebo effect is certainly not "all in your head."

"Phony" pills really do spur chemical changes in the brain that reduce pain. Because these placebo pills activate specific neurosystems, it is possible that placebo effects in pain may share a common brain circuitry with placebo effects in depression, Parkinson's disease, and other disorders (Wager, 2005).

There are several implications of these findings. First, it illustrates again the theme of this book. Specifically, you cannot easily separate brain function induced biochemically from brain function induced by psychological factors, including expectancies and appraisals. Second, there is the possibility of integrating placebo effects more efficiently with existing drugs, thus enhancing the therapeutic effect of drugs while possibly using less of the actual chemical ingredient. Finally, research on placebo effects can help us understand the mechanisms by which drugs and other treatments are effective. When we understand this process better, we will be closer to a full appreciation of how the mind regulates the body (Wager, 2005).

SUMMARY

Psychological and Social Factors That Influence Health

- Psychological and social factors play a major role in developing and maintaining a number of physical disorders.
- Two fields of study have emerged as a result of a growing interest in psychological factors contributing to illness. Behavioral medicine involves the application of behavioral science techniques to prevent, diagnose, and treat medical problems. Health psychology is a subfield that focuses on psychological factors involved in the promotion of health and well-being.
- Psychological and social factors may contribute directly to illness and disease through the psychological effects of stress on the immune system and other physical functioning. If the immune system is compromised, it may no longer be able to attack and eliminate antigens from the body effectively, or it may even begin to attack the body's normal tissue instead, a process known as autoimmune disease.
- Growing awareness of the many connections between the nervous system and the immune system has resulted in the new field of psychoneuroimmunology.
- Diseases that may be partly related to the effects of stress on the immune system include AIDS, rheumatoid arthritis, and cancer.

Psychosocial Effects on Physical Disorders

- Long-standing patterns of behavior or lifestyle may put people at risk for developing certain physical disorders. For example, unhealthy sexual practices can lead to AIDS and other sexually transmitted diseases, and unhealthy behavioral patterns, such as poor eating habits, lack of exercise, or type A behavior pattern, may contribute to cardiovascular diseases such as stroke, hypertension, and coronary heart disease.
- Of the 10 leading causes of death in the United States, fully 50% of deaths can be traced to lifestyle behaviors.
- Psychological and social factors also contribute to chronic pain. The brain inhibits pain through naturally occurring endogenous opioids, which may also be implicated in a variety of psychological disorders.
- Chronic fatigue syndrome is a relatively new disorder that is attributed at least partly to stress but may also have a viral or immune system dysfunction component.

Psychosocial Treatment of Physical Disorders

- A variety of psychosocial treatments have been developed with the goal of either treating or preventing physical disorders. Among these are biofeedback and relaxation response.
- Comprehensive stress- and pain-reduction programs include not only relaxation and related techniques but also new methods to encourage effective coping, including stress management, realistic appraisals, and improved attitudes through cognitive therapy.
- Comprehensive programs are generally more effective than individual components delivered singly.
- Other interventions aim to modify such behaviors as unsafe sexual practices, smoking, and unhealthy dietary habits. Such efforts have been made in a variety of areas, including injury control, AIDS prevention, smoking cessation campaigns in China, and the Stanford Three Community Study to reduce risk factors for disease.

Key Terms

behavioral medicine, 311
health psychology, 311
general adaptation syndrome (GAS), 312
stress, 312
self-efficacy, 315
immune system, 315
antigens, 316

autoimmune disease, 317
rheumatoid arthritis, 317
psychoneuroimmunology (PNI), 317
AIDS-related complex (ARC), 318
cancer, 319
psychoncology, 319

cardiovascular disease, 321
stroke/cerebral vascular accident (CVA), 321
hypertension, 321
essential hypertension, 322
coronary heart disease (CHD), 323
type A behavior pattern, 324

type B behavior pattern, 324
acute pain, 326
chronic pain, 326
endogenous opioids, 328
chronic fatigue syndrome (CFS), 328
biofeedback, 331
relaxation response, 332

Answers to Concept Checks

9.1

1. d; 2. a; 3. c; 4. b; 5. f; 6. e

9.2

1. c; 2. development; 3. hypertension, coronary heart disease; 4. type A (hard-driving, impatient), type B (relaxed, less concerned); 5. chronic fatigue syndrome

9.3

1. c; 2. b; 3. a; 4. e; 5. d; 6. f

The Abnormal Psychology Book Companion Website

See **academic.cengage.com/psychology/barlow** for practice quiz questions, interactive activities, Internet links, critical thinking exercises, discussion forums, and more. Also accessible from the Wadsworth Psychology Resource Center (**academic.cengage.com/login**).

Abnormal Psychology Live CD-ROM

■ *Orel, Social Support and HIV:* This African American client demonstrates the power of strong social support from family and friends, as well as pursuing personal interests such as art, to deal with the ongoing struggles of being an HIV/AIDS patient.

■ *The Immune System, Effects of Stress and Emotion:* This video illustrates recent findings on how emotional experiences—such as stress, loneliness, and sociability—affect physical health.

■ *Cancer, Education and Support Groups:* This clip investigates whether providing group support or group education is more helpful to women facing breast cancer.

CENGAGENOW™ CengageNOW

Go to **academic.cengage.com/now** to link to CengageNOW, your online study tool. First take the Pre-Test for this chapter to get your personalized study plan, which will identify topics you need to review and direct you to online resources. Then take the Post-Test to determine what concepts you have mastered and what you still need work on.

Video Concept Reviews

CengageNOW also contains Mark Durand's *Video Concept Reviews* on challenging topics.

■ Behavioral Medicine
■ Health Psychology
■ Stress
■ General Adaptation Syndrome (GAS)
■ HPA-Stress Response Cycle
■ AIDS-Related Complex (ARC)
■ Cancer and Psychoncology
■ Hypertension
■ Acute and Chronic Pain
■ Concept Check: Integrative Process With Physical Disorders
■ Chronic Fatigue Syndrome
■ Biofeedback and Relaxation Techniques

Exploring Physical Disorders and Health Psychology

Psychological and behavioral factors are major contributors to illness and death.
• Behavioral medicine applies behavioral science to medical problems.
• Health psychology focuses on psychological influences on health and improving health care.

PSYCHOLOGICAL AND SOCIAL FACTORS INFLUENCE BIOLOGY

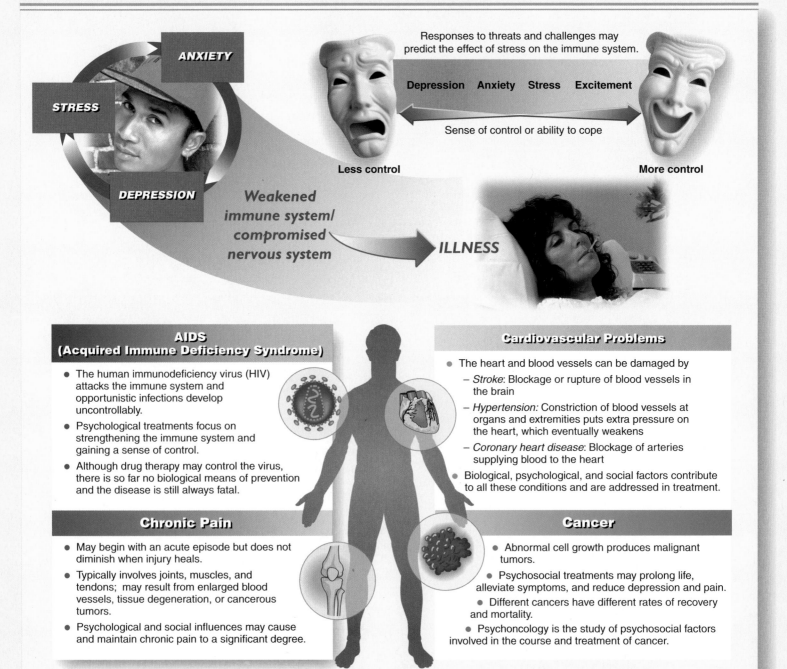

ANXIETY

STRESS

DEPRESSION

Weakened immune system/ compromised nervous system

ILLNESS

Responses to threats and challenges may predict the effect of stress on the immune system.

Depression   Anxiety   Stress   Excitement

Sense of control or ability to cope

Less control   **More control**

AIDS (Acquired Immune Deficiency Syndrome)

- The human immunodeficiency virus (HIV) attacks the immune system and opportunistic infections develop uncontrollably.
- Psychological treatments focus on strengthening the immune system and gaining a sense of control.
- Although drug therapy may control the virus, there is so far no biological means of prevention and the disease is still always fatal.

Cardiovascular Problems

- The heart and blood vessels can be damaged by
  - *Stroke*: Blockage or rupture of blood vessels in the brain
  - *Hypertension:* Constriction of blood vessels at organs and extremities puts extra pressure on the heart, which eventually weakens
  - *Coronary heart disease*: Blockage of arteries supplying blood to the heart
- Biological, psychological, and social factors contribute to all these conditions and are addressed in treatment.

Chronic Pain

- May begin with an acute episode but does not diminish when injury heals.
- Typically involves joints, muscles, and tendons; may result from enlarged blood vessels, tissue degeneration, or cancerous tumors.
- Psychological and social influences may cause and maintain chronic pain to a significant degree.

Cancer

- Abnormal cell growth produces malignant tumors.
- Psychosocial treatments may prolong life, alleviate symptoms, and reduce depression and pain.
- Different cancers have different rates of recovery and mortality.
- Psychoncology is the study of psychosocial factors involved in the course and treatment of cancer.

PSYCHOSOCIAL TREATMENTS FOR PHYSICAL DISORDERS

The stress reaction associated with pain may reduce the number of natural killer cells in the immune system:

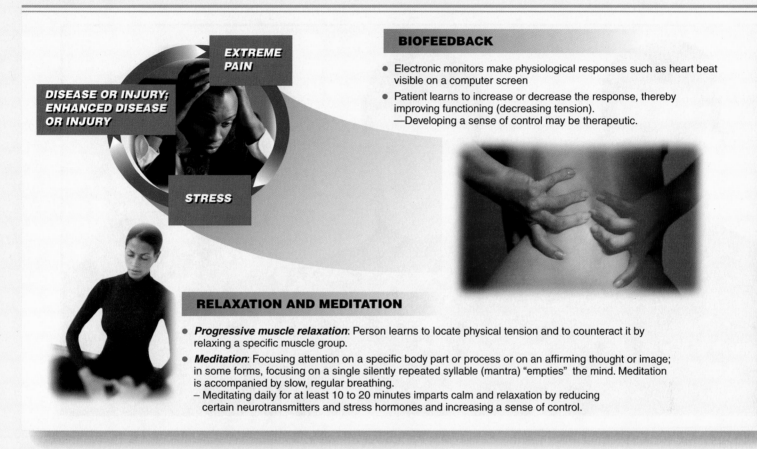

EXTREME PAIN

DISEASE OR INJURY; ENHANCED DISEASE OR INJURY

STRESS

BIOFEEDBACK

- Electronic monitors make physiological responses such as heart beat visible on a computer screen
- Patient learns to increase or decrease the response, thereby improving functioning (decreasing tension).
  —Developing a sense of control may be therapeutic.

RELAXATION AND MEDITATION

- **Progressive muscle relaxation**: Person learns to locate physical tension and to counteract it by relaxing a specific muscle group.
- **Meditation**: Focusing attention on a specific body part or process or on an affirming thought or image; in some forms, focusing on a single silently repeated syllable (mantra) "empties" the mind. Meditation is accompanied by slow, regular breathing.
  – Meditating daily for at least 10 to 20 minutes imparts calm and relaxation by reducing certain neurotransmitters and stress hormones and increasing a sense of control.

BEHAVIOR MODIFICATION TO PROMOTE HEALTH

Many injuries and diseases can be prevented or controlled through lifestyle changes involving diet, substance use, exercise, and safety precautions.

INJURY CONTROL

- Injuries are the leading cause of death for people age 1 to 45, especially children.
  - Most people consider injuries to be out of their control and therefore do not change high-risk behaviors.
  - In children, prevention focuses on
    – escaping fires
    – crossing streets
    – using car seats, seat belts, and bicycle helmets
    – first aid

AIDS PREVENTION

- Changing high-risk behavior through individual and community education is the only effective strategy.
  - Eliminate unsafe sexual practices through cognitive-behavioral self-management training and social support networks.
  - Show drug abusers how to clean needles and make safe injections.
- Target minorities and women, groups that do not perceive themselves to be at risk.
  - Media coverage focuses on gay white males.
  - More women are infected through heterosexual interactions than through intravenous drug use.

Sexual and Gender Identity Disorders

© Ron Chapple/Taxi/Getty Images

WHAT IS NORMAL SEXUALITY?
Gender Differences
Cultural Differences
The Development of Sexual Orientation

GENDER IDENTITY DISORDER
Defining Gender Identity Disorder
Causes
Treatment

AN OVERVIEW OF SEXUAL DYSFUNCTIONS
Sexual Desire Disorders
Sexual Arousal Disorders
Orgasm Disorders
Sexual Pain Disorders

ASSESSING SEXUAL BEHAVIOR
Interviews
Medical Examination
Psychophysiological Assessment

CAUSES AND TREATMENT OF SEXUAL DYSFUNCTION
Causes of Sexual Dysfunction
Treatment of Sexual Dysfunction

PARAPHILIA: CLINICAL DESCRIPTIONS
Fetishism
Voyeurism and Exhibitionism
Transvestic Fetishism
Sexual Sadism and Sexual Masochism
Pedophilia and Incest
Paraphilia in Women
Causes of Paraphilia

ASSESSING AND TREATING PARAPHILIA
Psychological Treatment
Drug Treatments
Summary

ABNORMAL PSYCHOLOGY LIVE CD-ROM
Erectile Dysfunction: Clark
Changing Over: Jessica
Web Link

> *When I first went through my gender change, I was working for an*
> *IBM subsidiary in Philadelphia. The biggest quandary there was*
> *"which bathroom is it going to use?"*

Kate Bornstein
Gender Outlaw: On Men, Women, and the Rest of Us

WHAT IS NORMAL SEXUALITY?

You have all read magazine surveys reporting sensational information on sexual practices. According to one, men can reach orgasm 15 or more times a day (in reality, such ability is rare) and women fantasize about being raped (this is even rarer). Surveys like this fail us on two counts: First, they claim to reveal sexual norms that are mostly distorted half-truths. Second, the facts they present typically are not based on any scientific methodology that would make them reliable, although they do sell magazines.

What is normal sexual behavior? As you will see, it depends. More to the point, when is sexual behavior that is somewhat different from the norm a disorder? Again, it depends. Current views tend to be quite tolerant of a variety of sexual expressions, even if they are unusual, unless the behavior is associated with a substantial impairment in functioning. Three kinds of sexual behavior meet this definition. In *gender identity disorder,* there is psychological dissatisfaction with one's biological sex. The disorder is not specifically sexual but rather a disturbance in the person's sense of identity as a male or a female. But these disorders are often grouped with sexual disorders, as in the fourth edition, text revision, of the *Diagnostic and Statistical Manual* (DSM-IV-TR). Individuals with *sexual dysfunction* find it difficult to function adequately while having sex; for example, they may not become aroused or achieve orgasm. And *paraphilia,* the relatively new term for sexual deviation, includes disorders in which sexual arousal occurs primarily in the context of inappropriate objects or individuals. *Philia* refers to a strong attraction or liking, and *para* indicates the attraction is abnormal. Paraphilic arousal patterns tend to be focused rather narrowly, often precluding mutually consenting adult patterns, even if desired. Before describing these three types of disorders, we return to our initial question, "What is normal sexual behavior?" to gain an important perspective.

Determining the prevalence of sexual practices accurately requires careful surveys that randomly sample the population. In a scientifically sound survey, Billy, Tanfer, Grady, and Klepinger (1993) reported data from 3,321 men in the United States age 20 to 39. The participants were interviewed, which is more reliable than having them fill out a questionnaire, and the responses were analyzed in detail. The purpose of this survey was to ascertain risk factors for sexually transmitted diseases, including AIDS. Some of the data are presented in ■ Figure 10.1. The most recent survey from the National Health and Nutrition Examination Survey sponsored by the Centers for Disease Control and Prevention (CDC) was just reported in June 2007 (Fryer et al., 2007). More than 6,000 men and women participated in this study, which provides some updated data, although the areas of sexual behavior sampled were more limited.

Virtually all men studied by Billy and colleagues and in the CDC study were sexually experienced, with vaginal intercourse a nearly universal experience, even for those who had never been married. Three fourths of the men in the study by Billy and colleagues also engaged in oral sex, but only one fifth had ever engaged in anal sex, a particularly high-risk behavior for AIDS transmission, and half of these had not had anal sex in the previous year and a half. Slightly more troublesome is the finding that 23.3% had had sex with 20 or more partners, another high-risk behavior. Then again, more than 70% had had only 1 sexual partner during the previous year, and fewer than 10% had had 4 or more partners during the same period. The CDC study reports similar figures, with 29% of men having sex with 15 or more partners during their lifetime (compared to 9% of women). Also, only 17% of men and 10% of women reported 2 or more partners during the past year. A surprising finding from Billy and colleagues is that the overwhelming majority of the men had engaged exclusively in **heterosexual behavior** (sex with the opposite sex). Only 2.3% had also en-

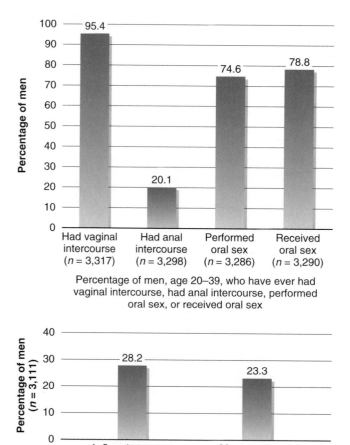

■ **FIGURE 10.1** Results of a survey of male sexual practices. (Data from Billy, J. O. G., Tanfer, K., Grady, W. R., & Klepinger, D. H., 1993. The sexual behavior of men in the United States. *Family Planning Perspectives, 25,* 52–60.)

gaged in **homosexual behavior** (sex with the same sex), and only 1.1% engaged exclusively in homosexual activity. These results require some rethinking of our assumptions, because for more than 40 years sex researchers and public health officials have relied on the comprehensive survey of sexual behaviors and attitudes by a pioneer investigator into sexual behavior, Alfred Kinsey. Kinsey and his colleagues (Kinsey, Pomeroy, & Martin, 1948; Kinsey, Pomeroy, Martin, & Gebhard, 1953) reported a figure of about 10% for any same-gender sexual activity. Because sampling procedures were not nearly so sophisticated in Kinsey's day as now, his data are presumed to be inaccurate, particularly in light of the additional surveys we report on in this chapter.

One study from Britain (Johnson, Wadsworth, Wellings, Bradshaw, & Field, 1992) and one from France (Spira et al., 1992) surveyed sexual behavior and practices among more than 20,000 men *and women* in each country. The results were surprisingly similar to those reported for American men. More than 70% of the respondents from all age groups in the British and French studies reported no more than one sexual partner during the past year. Women were somewhat more likely than men to have had fewer than two partners. Only 4.1% of French men and 3.6% of British men reported ever having had a male sexual partner, and this figure drops to 1.5% for British men if we consider only the last 5 years. Almost certainly, the percentage of males engaging exclusively in homosexual behavior would be considerably lower. The consistency of these data across three countries suggests strongly that the results represent something close to the norm, at least for Western countries. This has been confirmed in similar surveys (Seidman & Rieder, 1994). An update of the British survey (Johnson et al., 2001) indicates a small increase in number of partners over 5 years but also an increase in condom use. Still, more than 53% of males and 62% of females of all ages reported no more than one sexual partner over the last 5 years (contrasted to results for the past 1 year, reported previously). Also interesting is that sexual practices and the determinants of sexual satisfaction are now remarkably similar around the world, as recently demonstrated in a large survey of Chinese urban adults (Parish et al., 2007).

Another interesting set of data counters the many views we have of sexuality among elderly individuals. Sexual behavior can continue well into old age, even past 80 for some people. Table 10.1 presents the percentage by age group of married individuals in a community sample who were sexually active and continuing to have sexual intercourse (Diokno, Brown, & Herzog, 1990). Notably, 50% of men and 36% of women age 75 to 79 were sexually active. Reasons for the discrepancy between men and women are not clear, although given the earlier mortality of men, many older women lack a suitable partner; it is also possible that some women are married to men in an older age bracket. The sample of individuals over the age of 80 is too small to allow meaningful conclusions, although many remained sexually active. Decreases in sexual activity are mostly correlated with decreases in general mobility and various disease processes and consequent medication, which may reduce arousal; furthermore, the speed and intensity of various vasocongestive responses decrease with age. A large study of older individuals around the world, age 40–80, found men were generally more satisfied with their sexuality than women, particularly in non-Western countries, and that good physical and mental health, as well as a good relationship with a partner, were the best predictors of sexual well-being (Laumann et al., 2006).

Gender Differences

Although both men and women tend toward a monogamous (one partner) pattern of sexual relationships, gender differences in sexual behavior do exist, and some of them are quite dramatic. One common finding among sexual surveys is a much higher

Sexual behavior often continues well into old age.

TABLE 10.1 Sexual Activity of Elderly Married Respondents Classified by Age and Sex

Age	Males			Females		
	Yes	%	Total	Yes	%	Total
60–64	83	87.4	95	57	64.0	89
65–69	64	79.0	81	49	63.6	77
70–74	18	58.1	31	13	43.3	30
75–79	13	50.0	26	9	36.0	25
80+	4	28.6	14	1	25.0	4
Total	82	73.7	247	129	57.3	225

Source: Reprinted, with permission, from Diokno, A. C., Brown, M. B., & Herzog, A. R. (1990). Sexual function in the elderly. *Archives of Internal Medicine,* 150, 197–200, © 1990 American Medical Association.

percentage of men than women report that they masturbate (self-stimulate to orgasm) (Oliver & Hyde, 1993; Peplau, 2003). When Leitenberg, Detzer, and Srebnik (1993) surveyed 280 university students, they found this discrepancy remained (81% of men versus only 45% of women reported ever masturbating) even though for 25 years women had been encouraged to take more responsibility for their own sexual fulfillment and to engage in more sexual self-exploration.

Among those who did masturbate, the frequency was about three times greater for men than for women and had been throughout adolescence. Masturbation was not related to later sexual functioning; that is, whether individuals masturbated or not during adolescence had no influence on whether they had experienced intercourse, the frequency of intercourse, the number of partners, or other factors reflecting sexual adjustment.

Why women masturbate less frequently than men puzzles sex researchers, particularly when other long-standing gender differences in sexual behavior, such as the probability of engaging in premarital intercourse, have virtually disappeared (Clement, 1990). One traditional view accounting for differences in masturbatory behavior is that women have been taught to associate sex with romance and emotional intimacy, whereas men are more interested in physical gratification. But the discrepancy continues despite decreases in gender-specific attitudes toward sexuality. A more likely reason is anatomical. Because of the nature of the erectile response in men and their relative ease in providing sufficient stimulation to reach orgasm, masturbation may simply be more convenient for men than for women. This may explain why gender differences in masturbation are also evident in primates and other animals (Ford & Beach, 1951). In any case, incidence of masturbation continues to be the largest gender difference in sexuality.

Another continuing gender difference is reflected in attitudes toward casual premarital sex, with men expressing a far more permissive attitude than women, although this gap is becoming smaller. By contrast, results from a large number of studies suggest that *no* gender differences are currently apparent in attitudes about homosexuality (generally acceptable), the experience of sexual satisfaction (important for both), or attitudes toward masturbation (generally accepting). Small to moderate gender differences were evident in attitudes toward premarital intercourse when the couple was engaged or in a committed relationship (with men more approving than women) and in attitudes toward extramarital sex (sex outside of the marital relationship). As in the British and French studies, the number of sexual partners and the frequency of intercourse were slightly greater for men, and men were slightly younger at age of first sexual intercourse. Examining trends from 1943 to 1999, we find that almost all existing gender differences became smaller over time, especially in regard to attitudes toward premarital sex. Specifically, only 12% of young women approved of premarital sex in 1943 compared to 73% in 1999. The figures for men were 40% in 1943 and 79% in 1999 (Wells & Twenge, 2005).

Although they are decreasing, differences still exist between men and women in attitudes toward sexuality (Peplau, 2003). Hatfield, Sprecher, Pillemer, Greenberger, and Wexler (1988) assessed young, unmarried female undergraduates, as well as a sample of newly married couples (age 17 to 46 years), to determine what parts of the sexual relationship contributed most substantially to their satisfaction. Consistent with long-standing gender differences, women desired more demonstrations of love and intimacy during sex, and men were more interested in focusing on the arousal aspects. Although these attitudes may not correlate perfectly with actual behavior during sexual relations, they probably represent something basically different in the way men and women feel about sexual relations.

Differences also seem to exist in patterns of sexual arousal (Chivers, Rieger, Latty, & Bailey, 2004). Men are more specific and narrow in their patterns of arousal. That is, heterosexual men are aroused by female sexual stimuli but not male sexual stimuli. For gay men, it's the opposite. Men with gender identity disorder (discussed later) who had surgery to become female retained this specificity (attracted to males but not females). Females, on the other hand, whether heterosexual or lesbian, experience arousal to both male and female sexual stimuli, demonstrating a broader, more general pattern of arousal.

In an impressive series of studies, Barbara Andersen and her colleagues have assessed gender differences in basic or core beliefs about sexual aspects of one's self. These core beliefs about sexuality are referred to as "sexual self-schemas," and the findings echo those of Hatfield and colleagues (1988) a decade earlier. Specifically, in a series of studies (Andersen & Cyranowski, 1994; Andersen, Cyranowski, & Espindle, 1999; Cyranowski, Aarestad, & Andersen, 1999), Andersen and colleagues demonstrated that women tend to report the experience of passionate and romantic feelings as an integral part of their sexuality, as well as an openness to sexual experience. However, a substantial number of women also hold an embarrassed, conservative, or self-conscious schema that sometimes conflicts with more positive aspects of their sexual attitudes. Men, on the other hand, evidence a strong component of feeling powerful, independent, and aggressive as part of their sexuality, in addition to being passionate, loving, and open to experience. Also, men do not generally possess negative core beliefs reflecting self-consciousness, embarrassment, or feeling behaviorally inhibited. Peplau (2003) summarizes research to date on gender differences in human sexuality as highlighting four themes: (1) men show more sexual desire and arousal than women; (2) women emphasize committed relationships as a context for sex more than men; (3) men's sexual self-concept, unlike women's, is characterized partly by power, independence, and aggression; and (4) women's sexual beliefs are more "plastic" in that they are more easily shaped by cultural, social, and situational factors. For example, women are more likely to change sexual orientation over time or may be more variable in frequency of sex, alternating periods of high frequency with low frequency if a lover leaves.

What happened to the sexual revolution? Where are the effects of the "anything goes" attitude toward sexual expression and fulfillment that supposedly began in the 1960s and 1970s? Clearly there has been some change. The double standard has disappeared, in that most women no longer feel constrained by a stricter and more conservative social standard of sexual conduct. The sexes are definitely drawing together in their attitudes and behavior, although some differences in attitudes and core beliefs remain. Regardless, the overwhelming majority of individuals engage in heterosexual, vaginal intercourse in the context of a relationship with one partner. Based on these data, the sexual revolution may be largely a creation of the media, focusing as it does on extreme or sensational cases.

Cultural Differences

What is normal in this year in Western countries may not necessarily be normal in other parts of the world. The Sambia in Papua New Guinea believe semen is an essential substance for growth and development in young boys of the tribe. They also believe semen is *not* produced naturally; that is, the body is incapable of producing it spontaneously. Therefore, all young boys in the tribe, beginning at approximately age 7, become semen recipients by engaging exclusively in homosexual oral sex with teenage boys. Only oral sexual practices are permitted; masturbation is forbidden and absent. Early in adolescence, the boys switch roles and become semen providers to younger boys. Heterosexual relations and even contact with the opposite sex are prohibited until the boys become teenagers. Late in adolescence, the boys are expected to marry and begin exclusive heterosexual activity. And they do, with no exceptions (Herdt, 1987; Herdt & Stoller, 1989). By contrast, the Munda of northeast India require adolescents and children to live together. But in this group, both male and female children live in the same setting, and the sexual activity, consisting mostly of petting and mutual masturbation, is all heterosexual (Bancroft, 1989).

Even with Western cultures, there are some variations. Schwartz (1993) surveyed attitudes surrounding the first premarital experience of sexual intercourse in nearly 200 female undergraduates in the United States and compared them to a similar sample in Sweden, where attitudes toward sexuality are somewhat more permissive. The average age at the time of first intercourse for the woman and the age of her partner are presented in Table 10.2, as well as the age the women thought it would be socially acceptable in their culture for them to have sexual intercourse. Acceptable perceived ages for both men and women were significantly younger in Sweden, but few other differences existed, with one striking exception: 73.7% of Swedish women and only 56.7% of American women used some form of contraception during their first sexual intercourse, a significant difference. In about half of more than 100 societies surveyed worldwide, premarital sexual behavior is culturally accepted and encouraged; in the remaining half, premarital sex is unacceptable and discouraged (Bancroft, 1989; Broude & Greene, 1980). Thus, what is normal sexual behavior in one culture is not necessarily normal in another, and the

John Bancroft was one of the first researchers to describe the interaction of biology and psychology as determinants of sexual behavior.

Courtesy of John Bancroft

TABLE 10.2 Group Differences Between U.S. and Swedish Female Undergraduates Regarding Premarital Sex		
	United States	**Sweden**
Variable	**Mean (SD)**	**Mean (SD)**
Age at first coitus	16.97 (1.83)	16.80 (1.92)
Age of first coital partner	18.77 (2.88)	19.10 (2.96)
Perceived age of social acceptance for *females* to engage in premarital coitus	18.76 (2.57)	15.88 (1.43)
Perceived age of social acceptance for *males* to engage in premarital coitus	16.33 (2.13)	15.58 (1.20)

Source: Reprinted, with permission, from Schwartz, I. M. (1993). Affective reactions of American and Swedish women to their first premarital coitus: A cross comparison. *Journal of Sex Research,* 30(1), 18–26, © 1993 Society for the Scientific Study of Sex.

range of sexual expression must be considered in diagnosing the presence of a disorder.

The Development of Sexual Orientation

Reports suggest that homosexuality runs in families (Bailey & Benishay, 1993), and concordance for homosexuality is more common among identical twins than among fraternal twins or natural siblings. In two well-done twin studies, homosexual orientation was shared in approximately 50% of identical twins compared with 16% to 22% of fraternal twins. Approximately the same or a slightly lower percentage of nontwin brothers or sisters were gay (Bailey & Pillard, 1991; Bailey, Pillard, Neale, & Agyei, 1993; Whitnam, Diamond, & Martin, 1993). Other reports indicate that homosexuality is associated with differential exposure to hormones, particularly atypical androgen levels in utero (before birth) (Ehrhardt et al., 1985; Gladue, Green, & Hellman, 1984; Hershberger & Segal, 2004) and that the actual structure of the brain might be different in homosexuals and heterosexuals (Allen & Gorski, 1992; Byne et al., 2000; LeVay, 1991). Several findings lend some support to the theory of differential hormone exposure in utero. One is the observation that individuals with homosexual orientations have a 39% greater chance of being non–right handed (left handed or mixed handed) than those with heterosexual orientations (Lalumière, Blanchard, & Zucker, 2000), although this was not replicated in a later study (Mustanski, Bailey, & Kaspar, 2002). Another is the intriguing findings that males and masculine ("butch") lesbians tend to have a longer fourth ("ring") finger than index finger but that females and gay males show less of a difference or even have a longer second finger than fourth finger (Brown, Finn, Cooke, & Breedlove, 2002; Hall & Love, 2003), although this finding seems to be influenced by ethnic group membership (Loehlin, McFadden, Medland, & Martin, 2006; McFadden et al., 2005). Yet another report had suggested a possible gene (or genes) for homosexuality on the X chromosome (Hamer, Hu, Magnuson, Hu, & Pattatucci, 1993).

The principal conclusion drawn in the media is that sexual orientation has a biological cause. Gay rights activists are decidedly split on the significance of these findings. Some are pleased with the biological interpretation, because people can no longer assume gays have made a morally depraved choice of supposedly deviant arousal patterns. Others, however, note how quickly the public has pounced on the implication that something is biologically wrong with individuals with homosexual arousal patterns, assuming that someday the abnormality will be detected in the fetus and prevented, perhaps through genetic engineering.

Do such arguments over biological causes sound familiar? Think back to studies described in Chapter 2 that attempted to link complex behavior to particular genes. In almost every case, these studies could not be replicated, and investigators fell back on a model in which genetic contributions to behavioral traits and psychological disorders come from many genes, each making a relatively small contribution to a *vulnerability*. This generalized biological vulnerability then interacts in a complex way with various environmental conditions, personality traits, and other contributors to determine behavioral patterns. We also discussed reciprocal gene–environment interactions in which certain learning experiences and environmental events may affect brain structure and function and genetic expression.

The same thing is now happening with sexual orientation. For example, neither Bailey and colleagues (1999) nor Rice, Anderson, Risch, and Ebers (1999) in later studies could replicate the report suggesting a specific gene for homosexuality (Hamer et al., 1993). Most theoretical models outlining these complex interactions for sexual orientation imply that there may be many pathways to the development of heterosexuality or homosexuality and that no one factor—biological or psychological—can predict the outcome (Bancroft, 1994; Byne & Parsons, 1993). It is likely, too, that different types of homosexuality (and, perhaps, heterosexuality), with different patterns of etiology, may be discovered (Savin-Williams, 2006). Daryl Bem (1996) refers to his model of the development of sexual orientation as "exotic becomes erotic," a phrase that summarizes the principles of the theory nicely. Bem proposes that we inherit a temperament to behave in certain ways that later interacts with environmental factors to produce sexual orientation. For example, if a boy prefers active and aggressive or "boy typical" behaviors, he will feel similar to his same-sex peers. A young boy who feels less aggressive may avoid rough and tumble play in favor of "girl typical" activities. Their activities, whether typical or atypical, lead children to feel different from either their opposite or their same-sex peers. A young boy with boy-typical activities will feel more different from girls than he does from boys, making the opposite sex more "exotic." Sexual attraction in later years will be to the group of more exotic individuals. A young boy who engages in girl-typical activities is likely to feel more different from other boys than he does from girls. Therefore, what is exotic to this boy is other boys. Sexual attraction later follows. Bem has some evidence that gay men and women feel more different from their same-sex peers than heterosexual men and women, but little direct evidence indicates this feeling, in turn, determines sexual attraction. There is some evidence from other sources, however, regarding the attractiveness of novel or exotic stimuli. What is important for our purposes is that this theory combines biological and psychological or environmental variables and suggests how they interact to form sexual orientation (see ■ Figure 10.2). Almost certainly, in our view, scientists will pin down biological contributions to the formation of sexual orientation, both heterosexual and homosexual. And just as certainly, the environment and experience will be found to powerfully influence how these patterns of potential sexual arousal develop.

One of the more intriguing findings from the twin studies of Bailey and his colleagues is that approximately 50% of the identical twins with exactly the same genetic structure, as well as the same environment (growing up in the same house), *did not* have the same sexual orientation (Bailey & Pillard, 1991). There is even a case of identical male triplets in which two developed heterosexual and one developed homosexual orientation (Hershberger & Segal, 2004). Also intriguing is the finding in a study of 302 gay males that those growing up with older brothers are more likely to be gay, whereas having older sisters, or younger brothers or sisters, is not correlated with later sexual orientation. This study found that each additional older brother increased the odds of being gay by one third. This may suggest the importance of environmental influences, although the mechanism has not been identified (Blanchard & Bogaert, 1996, 1998; Cantor, Blanchard, Paterson, & Bogaert, 2002; Jones & Blanchard, 1998).

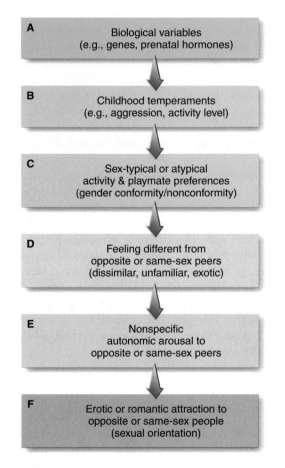

■ **FIGURE 10.2** The sequence of events leading to sexual orientation for most men and women in a gender-polarizing culture. (From Bem, D. J., 1996. Exotic becomes erotic: A developmental theory of sexual orientation. *Psychological Review, 103,* 320–335.)

In any case, the simple one-dimensional claims that homosexuality is caused by a gene or that heterosexuality is caused by healthy early developmental experiences will continue to appeal to the general population. Neither explanation is likely to be proved correct. Almost certainly, biology sets certain limits within which social and psychological factors affect development (Diamond, 1995).

GENDER IDENTITY DISORDER

What is it that makes you think you are a man? Or a woman? Clearly, it's more than your sexual arousal patterns or your anatomy. It's also more than the reactions and experiences of your family and society. The essence of your masculinity or femininity is a deep-seated personal sense called gender identity. **Gender identity disorder** is present if a person's physical gender is not consistent with the person's sense of identity. People with this disorder feel trapped in a body of the wrong sex. Consider the case of Joe.

JOE: Trapped in the Wrong Body

Joe was a 17-year-old male and the last of five children. Although his mother had wanted a girl, he became her favorite child. His father worked long hours and had little contact with the boy. For as long as Joe could remember, he had thought of himself as a girl. He began dressing in girls' clothes of his own accord before he was 5 years old and continued cross-dressing into junior high school. He developed interests in cooking, knitting, crocheting, and embroidering, skills he acquired by reading an encyclopedia. His older brother often scorned him for his distaste of such "masculine" activities as hunting.

Joe associated mostly with girls during this period, although he remembered being strongly attached to a boy in the first grade. In his sexual fantasies, which developed around 12 years of age, he pictured himself as a female having intercourse with a male. His extremely effeminate behavior made him the object of scorn and ridicule when he entered high school at age 15. Usually passive and unassertive, he ran away from home and attempted suicide. Unable to continue in high school, he attended secretarial school, where he was the only boy in his class. During his first interview with a therapist, he reported, "I am a woman trapped in a man's body and I would like to have surgery to become a woman."

Defining Gender Identity Disorder

Gender identity disorder (or *transsexualism,* as it used to be called) must be distinguished from transvestic fetishism, a paraphilic disorder (discussed later) in which individuals, usually males, are sexually aroused by wearing articles of clothing associated with the opposite sex. There is an occasional preference on the part of the male with transvestite patterns of sexual arousal for the female role, but the primary purpose of cross-dressing is sexual gratification. In the case of gender identity disorder, the primary goal is not sexual but rather the desire to live life openly in a manner consistent with that of the other gender.

Gender identity disorder must also be distinguished from *intersex individuals (hermaphrodites),* who are born with ambiguous genitalia associated with documented hormonal or other physical abnormalities. Depending on their particular mix of characteristics, they are usually "assigned" to a specific sex at birth, sometimes undergoing surgery, as well as hormonal treatments, to alter their sexual anatomy. Individuals with gender identity disorder, by contrast, have no demonstrated physical abnormalities. We return to the issue of intersex individuals later.

Finally, gender identity disorder must be distinguished from the homosexual arousal patterns of a male who sometimes behaves effeminately or a woman with homosexual arousal patterns and masculine mannerisms. Such an individual does not feel like a woman trapped in a man's body or have any desire to be a woman, or vice versa. Note also, as the DSM-IV-TR criteria do, that gender identity is independent of sexual arousal patterns (Savin-Williams, 2006). For example, a male-to-female transsexual (a biological male with a feminine gender identity) may be sexually attracted to females, which, technically, makes his arousal homosexual. Eli Coleman and his associates (Coleman, Bockting, & Gooren, 1993) reported on nine female-to-male cases in which the individuals were sexually attracted to men. Thus, heterosexual women before surgery were gay men after surgery. Chivers and Bailey (2000) compared a similar group of female-to-male individuals to a group of female-to-male individuals who were attracted to women both before and after surgery, and they found the groups did not differ in the strength of their gender identity (as males), although the latter group was more sexually assertive and, understandably, more interested in surgery to create an artificial penis. And Lawrence (2005) studied 232 male-to-female cases both before and after surgery and found that the majority (54%) were mostly heterosexual (attracted to women) before the surgery. This changed after surgery slightly for some and dramatically for a few such that 25% remained attracted to women after surgery, thus making them gay.

Gender identity disorder is relatively rare. The estimated incidence based on studies in Sweden, Australia, and the Netherlands is 1 in 37,000 in Sweden, 1 in 24,000 in Australia, and 1 in 11,000 in the Netherlands for biological males, compared to 1 in 103,000, 1 in 150,000, and 1 in 30,000 for biological females (Baker, van Kesteren, Gooren, & Bezemer, 1993; Ross, Walinder, Lundstrom, & Thuwe, 1981). Many countries now allow a series of legal steps to change gender identity. In Germany, between 2.1 and 2.4 per 100,000 in the population took at least the first legal steps of changing their first names in the 1990s. Here, the male–female ratio is 2.3:1 (Weitze & Osburg, 1996). In New York City as of 2006, people may choose to alter the sex listed on their birth certificates.

In some cultures, individuals with mistaken gender identity are often accorded the status of "shaman" or "seer" and treated as wisdom figures. A shaman is almost always a male adopting a female role (see, for example, Coleman, Colgan, & Gooren, 1992). Stoller (1976) reported on two contemporary feminized Native American men who were not only accepted but also esteemed by their tribes for their expertise in healing rituals. Contrary to the respect accorded these individuals in some cultures, social tolerance for them is relatively low in Western cultures, where they are the objects of curiosity at best and derision at worst.

Causes

Research has yet to uncover any specific biological contributions to gender identity disorder, although it seems likely that a biological predisposition will be discovered. Coolidge, Thede, and Young (2002) estimated that genetics contributed about 62% to creating a vulnerability to experience gender identity disorder in their twin sample. Thirty-eight percent of the vulnerability came from nonshared (unique) environmental events. A recent study from the

Netherlands twin registry suggested that 70% of the vulnerability for cross-gender behavior (behaving in a manner consistent with the opposite biological sex) was genetic as opposed to environmental, but this behavior is not the same as gender identity, which was not measured (as explained later) (van Beijsterveldt, Hudziak, & Boomsma, 2006). Segal (2006), on the other hand, found two monozygotic (identical) female twin pairs in which one twin had gender identity disorder and the other didn't. No unusual medical or life history factors were identified to account for this. Nevertheless, genetic contributions are clearly part of the picture.

Early research suggested that, as with sexual orientation, slightly higher levels of testosterone or estrogen at certain critical periods of development might masculinize a female fetus or feminize a male fetus (see, for example, Gladue et al., 1984; Imperato-McGinley, Peterson, Gautier, & Sturla, 1979). Variations in hormonal levels could occur naturally or because of medication that a pregnant mother is taking. More recently, scientists have studied girls age 5–12 with an intersex condition known as congenital adrenal hyperplasia (CAH). In CAH, the brains of these chromosomal females are flooded with male hormones (androgen), which, among other results, produces mostly masculine external genitalia, although internal organs (ovaries and so on) remain female. Meyer-Bahlburg and colleagues (2004) studied 15 girls with CAH, who had been correctly identified as female at birth and raised as girls, and looked at their development. Compared to groups of girls and boys without CAH, the CAH girls were masculine in their behavior, but there were no differences in gender identity. Thus, scientists have yet to establish a link between prenatal hormonal influence and later gender identity, although it is still possible that one exists. Structural differences in the area of the brain that controls male sex hormones have also been observed in individuals with male-to-female gender identity disorder (Zhou, Hofman, Gooren, & Swaab, 1995), with the result that the brains are comparatively more feminine. But it isn't clear whether this is a cause or an effect.

At least some evidence suggests that gender identity firms up between 18 months and 3 years of age (Ehrhardt & Meyer-Bahlburg, 1981; Money & Ehrhardt, 1972) and is relatively fixed after that. But newer studies suggest that possible preexisting biological factors have already had their impact. One interesting case illustrating this phenomenon was originally reported by Green and Money (1969), who described the sequence of events that occurred in the case of John/Joan. There do seem to be other case studies of children whose gender was reassigned at birth who adapted successfully (see, for example, Gearhart, 1989), but it certainly seems that biology expressed itself in John's case.

DSM-IV-TR

DSM TABLE 10.1   Criteria for Gender Identity Disorders

A. A strong and persistent cross-gender identification (not merely a desire for any perceived cultural advantages of being the other sex). In children, the disturbance is manifested by four (or more) of the following:

1. Repeatedly stated desire to be, or insistence that he or she is, the other sex
2. In boys, preference for cross-dressing of simulating female attire; in girls, insistence on wearing only stereotypical masculine clothing
3. Strong and persistent preferences for cross-sex roles in make-believe play or persistent fantasies of being the other sex
4. Intense desire to participate in the stereotypical games and pastimes of the other sex
5. Strong preference for playmates of the other sex
In adolescents and adults, the disturbance is manifested by symptoms such as a stated desire to be the other sex, frequent passing as the other sex, desire to live or be treated as the other sex, or the conviction that he or she has the typical feelings and reactions of the other sex.

B. Persistent discomfort with his or her sex or sense of inappropriateness in the gender role of that sex. In children, the disturbance is manifested by any of the following: in boys, assertion that his penis or testes are disgusting or will disappear or assertion that it would be better not to have a penis, or aversion toward rough-and-tumble play and rejection of male stereotypical toys, games, and activities; in girls, rejection of urinating in a sitting position, assertion that she has or will grow a penis, or assertion that she does not want to grow breasts or menstruate, or marked aversion toward normative feminine clothing. In adolescents and adults, the disturbance is manifested by symptoms such as preoccupation with getting rid of primary and secondary sex characteristics (e.g., request for hormones, surgery, or other procedures to physically alter sexual characteristics to simulate the other sex) or belief that he or she was born the wrong sex.

C. The disturbance is not concurrent with a physical intersex condition.

D. The disturbance causes clinically significant distress or impairment in social, occupational, or other important areas of functioning.
Specify if (for sexually mature individuals):
Sexually attracted to males
Sexually attracted to females
Sexually attracted to both
Sexually attracted to neither

Source: Reprinted, with permission, from American Psychiatric Association. (2000). *Diagnostic and statistical manual of mental disorders* (4th ed., text revision). Washington, DC: Author, © 2000 American Psychiatric Association.

JOHN/JOAN

A set of male identical twins was born into a well-adjusted family. Several months later, an unfortunate accident occurred. Although circumcision went routinely for one of the boys, the physician's hand slipped so that the electric current in the device burned off the penis of the second baby. After working through their hostility toward the physician, the parents consulted specialists in children with intersexual problems and were faced with a choice. The specialists pointed out that the easiest solution would be to reassign their son John as a girl, and the parents agreed. At the age of several months, John became "Joan." The parents purchased a new wardrobe and treated the child in every way possible as a girl. These twins were followed through childhood and, upon reaching puberty, the young girl was given hormonal replacement therapy. After 6 years, the doctors lost track of the case but assumed the child had adjusted well. However, Joan endured almost intolerable inner turmoil. We know this because two clinical scientists found this individual and reported a long-term follow-up (Diamond & Sigmundson, 1997). Joan never adjusted to her assigned gender. As a child, she preferred rough-and-tumble play and resisted wearing girls' clothes. In public bathrooms, she often insisted on urinating while standing up, which usually made a mess. By early adolescence, Joan was pretty sure she was a boy, but her doctors pressed her to act more feminine. When she was 14, she confronted her parents, telling them she was so miserable she was considering suicide. At that point, they told her the true story and the muddy waters of her mind began to clear. Shortly thereafter, Joan had additional surgery changing her back to John, who married and became the father of three adopted children. But the turmoil of his early life never fully resolved. Perhaps because of this, perhaps because his twin brother had recently died and he had lost his job and was divorcing, or perhaps because of a combination of these factors, David Reimer (his real name) committed suicide at age 38 in 2004.

interests. However, in following up these boys, Green discovered that few seem to develop the "wrong" gender identity. The most likely outcome is the development of homosexual preferences, but even this particular sexual arousal pattern seems to occur exclusively in only approximately 40% of the gender-nonconforming boys. Another 32% show some degree of *bisexuality*, sexual attraction to both their own and the opposite sex. Looking at it from the other side, 60% were functioning heterosexually.

This finding is not unique to American culture. For example, similar relationships between early gender-nonconforming behavior and later development exist among the Fa'afafine, a group of males in the pacific island country of Samoa with homosexual orientation (Bartlett & Vasey, 2006). And even in strict Muslim societies where any hint of gender-nonconforming behavior is severely discouraged, this disorder related to behavior, gender identity, or both may develop (Doğan & Doğan, 2006). We can safely say that the causes of mistaken gender identity are still something of a mystery.

Treatment

Treatment is available for gender identity disorder in a few specialty clinics around the world, although much controversy surrounds treatment (Carroll, 2000). At present, the most common decision is to alter the anatomy physically to be consistent with the identity through **sex reassignment surgery.** Recently, psychosocial treatments to directly alter mistaken gender identity itself have been attempted in a few cases.

Richard Green, a pioneering researcher in this area, has studied boys who behave in feminine ways and girls who behave in masculine ways, investigating what makes them that way and following what happens to them (Green, 1987). This set of behaviors and attitudes is referred to as **gender nonconformity** (see, for example, Skidmore, Linsenmeier, & Bailey, 2006). Green discovered that when most young boys spontaneously display "feminine" interests and behaviors, they are typically discouraged by most families and these behaviors usually cease. However, boys who consistently display these behaviors are not discouraged, and are sometimes encouraged.

Other factors, such as excessive attention and physical contact on the part of the mother, may also play some role, as may a lack of male playmates during the early years of socialization. These are just some factors identified by Green as characteristic of gender-nonconforming boys. Remember that as-yet-undiscovered biological factors may also contribute to the spontaneous display of cross-gender behaviors and

Alexis Arquette is a male to female transgender actress, musician, and cabaret drag performer who first came out as a gay male (left) and later chose sex reassignment surgery (right).

After gender reassignment as a baby and subsequently being raised as a girl, David Reimer reclaimed his male gender identity in his teens and lived his life as a man. He spoke out against infant gender reassignment until his death in 2004.

Sex Reassignment Surgery

To qualify for surgery at a reputable clinic, individuals must live in the opposite-sex role for 1 to 2 years so that they can be sure they want to change sex. They also must be stable psychologically, financially, and socially. In male-to-female candidates, hormones are administered to promote *gynecomastia* (the growth of breasts) and the development of other secondary sex characteristics. Facial hair is typically removed through electrolysis. If the individual is satisfied with the events of the trial period, the genitals are removed and a vagina is constructed.

For female-to-male transsexuals, an artificial penis is typically constructed through plastic surgery, using sections of skin and muscle from elsewhere in the body, such as the thigh. Breasts are surgically removed. Genital surgery is more difficult and complex in biological females. Estimates of transsexuals' satisfaction with surgery indicate predominantly successful adjustment (approximately 75% improved) among those who could be reached for follow-ups, with female-to-male conversions adjusting better than male-to-female ones (Bancroft, 1989; Blanchard & Steiner, 1992; Bodlund & Kullgren, 1996; Carroll, 2000; Green & Fleming, 1990; Kuiper & Cohen-Kettenis, 1988). However, many people were lost to follow-up. Approximately 7% of sex reassignment cases later regret surgery (Bancroft, 1989; Lundstrom, Pauly, & Walinder, 1984). This is unfortunate, because the surgery is irreversible. Also, as many as 2% attempt suicide after surgery, a rate much higher than the rate for the general population. One problem may be incorrect diagnosis and assessment. For example, one study of 186 Dutch psychiatrists reporting on 584 patients presenting with cross-gender identification revealed little consensus on diagnostic features of gender identity disorder or the minimum age at which sex reassignment surgery is safe. Rather, the decision seemed to rest on personal preferences of the psychiatrist (Campo, Nijman, Merckelbach, & Evers, 2003). These assessments are complex and

should always be done at highly specialized gender identity clinics. Nevertheless, surgery has made life worth living for some people who suffered the effects of existing in what they felt to be the wrong body.

Treatment of Intersexuality

As we noted, surgery and hormonal replacement therapy has been standard treatment for many intersex individuals (hermaphrodites) who may be born with physical characteristics of both sexes. Recently this group of individuals has been the subject of more careful evaluation, resulting in some new ideas and new approaches to treatment (Fausto-Sterling, 2000a, 2000b). Specifically, Anne Fausto-Sterling had suggested previously that there are actually five sexes: males; females; "herms," who are named after true hermaphrodites, or people born with both testes and ovaries; "merms," who are anatomically more male than female but possess some aspect of female genitalia; and "ferms," who have ovaries but possess some aspect of male genitalia. She estimates, based on the best evidence available, that for every 1,000 children born, 17, or 1.7%, may be intersexual in some form. What Fausto-Sterling (2000b) and others have noted is that individuals in this group are often dissatisfied with surgery, much as John was in the case we described. There have been instances in which doctors, upon observing anatomical sexual ambiguity after birth, treat it as an emergency and immediately perform surgery.

Fausto-Sterling suggests that an increasing number of pediatric endocrinologists, urologists, and psychologists are beginning to examine the wisdom of early genital surgery that results in an irreversible gender assignment. Instead, health professionals may

Physician Renee Richards played competitive tennis when she was a man, Richard Raskin, and after sex reassignment surgery

want to examine closely the precise nature of the intersex condition and consider surgery only as a last resort, and only when they are quite sure the particular condition will lead to a specific psychological gender identity. Otherwise, psychological treatments to help individuals adapt to their particular sexual anatomy, or their emerging gender identity, might be more appropriate.

CONCEPT CHECK 10.1

Answer the following questions about normal sexuality and gender identity disorder.

1. What gender differences exist in both sexual attitudes and sexual behavior? _____
2. Which sexual preference or preferences are normal, and how are they developed? _____
3. Charlie always felt out of place with the boys. At a young age, he preferred to play with girls and insisted that his parents call him "Charlene." He later claimed that he felt like a woman trapped in a man's body. What disorder could Charlie have? _____
4. What could be the cause of Charlie's disorder? _____
5. What treatments could be given to Charlie? _____

AN OVERVIEW OF SEXUAL DYSFUNCTIONS

Before describing **sexual dysfunction,** note that the problems that arise in the context of sexual interactions may occur in both heterosexual and homosexual relationships. Inability to become aroused or reach orgasm seems to be as common in homosexual as in heterosexual relationships, but we discuss them in the context of heterosexual relationships, which are the majority of cases we see in our clinic. The three stages of the sexual response cycle—desire, arousal, and orgasm (see ■ Figure 10.3)—are each associated with specific sexual dysfunctions. In addition, pain can become associated with sexual functioning, which leads to additional dysfunctions.

An overview of the DSM-IV-TR categories of the sexual dysfunctions we examine is in Table 10.3. As you can see, both males and females can experience parallel versions of most disorders, which take on specific forms determined by anatomy and other gender-specific characteristics. However, two disorders are sex specific: Premature ejaculation occurs only in males, and vaginismus—painful contractions or spasms of the vagina during attempted penetration—appears only in females. Sexual dysfunctions can be either lifelong or acquired. *Lifelong* refers to a chronic condition that is present during a person's entire sexual life; *acquired* refers to a disorder that begins after sexual activity has been relatively normal. In addition, disorders can either be *generalized,* occurring every time the individual attempts sex, or they can be

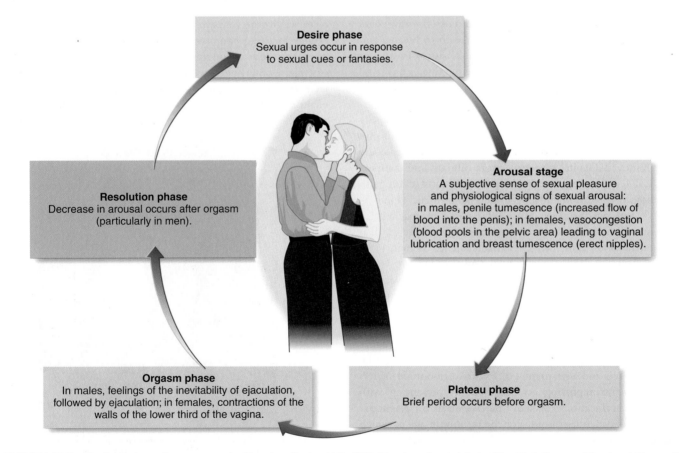

■ **FIGURE 10.3** The human sexual response cycle. (Based on Kaplan, H. S., 1979, *Disorders of sexual desire,* New York: Brunner/Mazel, and Masters, W. H., & Johnson, V. E., 1966, *Human sexual response,* Boston: Little, Brown.)

TABLE 10.3 Categories of Sexual Dysfunction Among Men and Women

Type of Disorder	Sexual Dysfunction Men	Sexual Dysfunction Women
Desire	Hypoactive sexual desire disorder (little or no desire to have sex)	Hypoactive sexual desire disorder (little or no desire to have sex)
	Sexual aversion disorder (aversion to and avoidance of sex)	Sexual aversion disorder (aversion to and avoidance of sex)
Arousal	Male erectile disorder (difficulty attaining or maintaining erections)	Female sexual arousal disorder (difficulty attaining or maintaining lubrication or swelling response)
Orgasm	Inhibited male orgasm; premature ejaculation	Inhibited female orgasm
Pain	Dyspareunia (pain associated with sexual activity)	Dyspareunia (pain associated with sexual activity); vaginismus (muscle spasms in the vagina that interfere with penetration)

Source: Reprinted, with permission, from Wincze, J. P., & Carey, M. P. (2001). *Sexual dysfunction: A guide for assessment and treatment.* New York: Guilford Press, © 1991 Guilford Press.

situational, occurring with some partners or at certain times but not with other partners or at other times. Finally, sexual dysfunctions are further specified as (1) due to psychological factors or (2) due to psychological factors combined with a general medical condition. The latter specification occurs when there is a demonstrable vascular, hormonal, or associated physical condition known to contribute to the sexual dysfunction. We learned much about the prevalence of the various sexual dysfunctions in the United States from a large and particularly well-done national probability sample of 1,749 women and 1,410 men age 18 to 59 years (Laumann, Paik, & Rosen, 1999). In the U.S. survey, the surprising estimates of prevalence are presented and discussed in the context of each disorder. But in the aggregate, fully 43% of all women and 31% of men suffer from sexual dysfunction, making this class of disorder the most prevalent of any psychological or physical disorder in the United States.

Before we describe the prevalence of specific sexual dysfunctions, we need to note an important study by Ellen Frank and her colleagues (1978), who carefully interviewed 100 well-educated, happily married couples who were not seeking treatment. More than 80% of these couples reported that their marital and sexual relations were happy and satisfying. Surprisingly, 40% of the men reported occasional erectile and ejaculatory difficulties and 63% of the women reported occasional dysfunctions of arousal or orgasm. But the crucial finding was that these dysfunctions did not detract from the respondents' overall sexual satisfaction. In another study, only 45% of women experiencing difficulties with orgasm reported the issue as problematic (Fugl-Meyer & Sjogren Fugl-Meyer, 1999). Bancroft, Loftus, and Long (2003) extended this analysis in a survey of close to 1,000 women in the United States involved in a heterosexual relationship for at least 6 months. The interesting results indicate that, although 44.3% met objective criteria for one of the disorders in Table 10.3, only 24.4% of these individuals were distressed about it. Many of these women just did not consider the issue to be a problem. Indeed, the best predictor of sexual distress among these women were deficits in general emotional well-being or emotional relationships with the partner during sexual relations, not lack of lubrication or orgasm. These studies indicate that sexual satisfaction and occasional sexual dysfunction are not mutually exclusive categories. In the context of a healthy relationship, occasional or partial sexual dysfunctions are easily accommodated. But this does raise problems for diagnosing sexual dysfunctions. Should a sexual problem be identified as a diagnosis when dysfunction is clearly present but the person is not distressed about it? This is one debate that will be taken up during discussions on DSM-V (Balon, Segraves, & Clayton, 2007).

Sexual Desire Disorders

Two disorders reflect problems with the desire phase of the sexual response cycle. Each of these disorders is characterized by little or no interest in sex that is causing problems in a relationship.

■ Hypoactive Sexual Desire Disorder

A person with **hypoactive sexual desire disorder** has little or no interest in any type of sexual activity. It is difficult to assess low sexual desire, and a great deal of clinical judgment is required (Pridal & LoPiccolo, 2000; Segraves & Woodard, 2006; Wincze, Bach, & Barlow, in press; Wincze & Barlow, 1997). You might gauge it by frequency of sexual activity—say, less than twice a month for a married couple. Or you might determine whether someone ever thinks about sex or has sexual fantasies. Then there is the person who has sex twice a week but really doesn't want to and thinks about it only because his wife is on his case to live up to his end of the marriage and have sex more often. This individual might have no desire, despite having frequent sex. Consider the cases of Judy and Ira and of Mr. and Mrs. C.

JUDY AND IRA: A Loving Marriage?

Judy, a married woman in her late 20s, reached a clinic staff member on the phone and reported that she thought her husband, Ira, was having an affair and that she was upset about it. The reason for her assumptions? He had demonstrated no interest in sex during the past 3 years, and they had not had sex for 9 months. However, Ira was willing to come into the clinic.

When he was interviewed, it became clear that Ira was not having an affair. In fact, he did not masturbate and hardly ever thought about sex. He noted that he loved his wife but that he had not been concerned about the issue until she raised it because he had too many other things to think about and he assumed they would eventually get back to having sex. He now realized that his wife was quite distressed about the situation, particularly because they were thinking about having children.

Although Ira did not have extensive sexual experience, he had engaged in several erotic relationships before his marriage, which Judy knew. During a separate interview, Ira confided that during his premarital affairs he would get a "hard on" just thinking about his lovers, each of whom was quite promiscuous. His wife, in contrast, was a pillar of the community and otherwise unlike these women, although attractive. Because he did not become aroused by thinking about his wife, he did not initiate sex.

MR. AND MRS. C.: Getting Started

Mrs. C., a 31-year-old successful businesswoman, was married to a 32-year-old lawyer. They had two children, ages 2 and 5, and had been married 8 years when they entered therapy. The presenting problem was Mrs. C.'s lack of sexual desire. Mr. and Mrs. C. were interviewed separately during the initial assessment, and both professed attraction to and love for their partner. Mrs. C. reported that she could enjoy sex once she got involved and almost always was orgasmic. The problem was her lack of desire to get involved. She avoided her husband's sexual advances and looked on his affection and romanticism with great skepticism and, usually, anger and tears. Mrs. C. was raised in an upper-middle-class family that was supportive and loving. However, from age 6 to age 12, she had been repeatedly pressured into sexual activity by a male cousin who was 5 years her senior. This sexual activity was always initiated by the cousin, always against her will. She did not tell her parents because she felt guilty, as the boy did not use physical force to make her comply. It appeared that romantic advances by Mr. C. triggered memories of abuse by her cousin.

The treatment of Mr. and Mrs. C. is discussed later in this chapter.

Problems of hypoactive sexual desire disorder used to be presented as marital rather than sexual difficulties. Since the recognition in the late 1980s of hypoactive sexual desire as a distinct disorder, however, increasing numbers of couples present to sex therapy clinics with one of the partners reporting this problem (Hawton, 1995; Pridal & LoPiccolo, 2000). Best estimates suggest that more than 50% of patients who come to sexuality clinics for help complain of hypoactive sexual desire (Kaplan, 1979; Pridal &

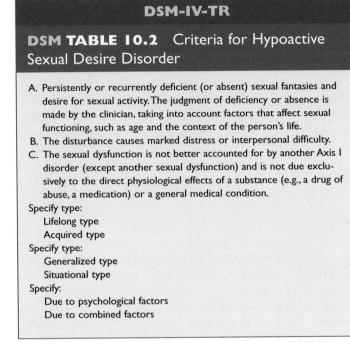

Source: Reprinted, with permission, from American Psychiatric Association. (2000). *Diagnostic and statistical manual of mental disorders* (4th ed., text revision). Washington, DC: Author. © 2000 American Psychiatric Association.

LoPiccolo, 2000). In many clinics, it is the most common presenting complaint of women; men present more often with erectile dysfunction (Hawton, 1995). Earlier studies (see, for example, Frank, Anderson, & Rubinstein, 1978) suggested that approximately 25% of individuals might have hypoactive sexual desire. The U.S. survey confirmed that 22% of women and 5% of men suffer from the disorder. For men, the prevalence increases with age; for women, it decreases with age (DeLamater & Sill, 2005; Laumann et al., 1999). Schreiner-Engel and Schiavi (1986) noted that patients with this disorder rarely have sexual fantasies, seldom masturbate (35% of the women and 52% of the men never masturbate, and most of the rest in their sample masturbate no more than once a month), and attempt intercourse once a month or less.

■ Sexual Aversion Disorder

On a continuum with hypoactive sexual desire disorder is **sexual aversion disorder,** in which even the thought of sex or a brief casual touch may evoke fear, panic, or disgust (Kaplan, 1987). In some cases, the principal problem might be panic disorder (see Chapter 5), in which the fear or alarm response is associated with the physical sensations of sex. In other cases, sexual acts and fantasies may trigger traumatic images or memories similar to but perhaps not as severe as those experienced by people with posttraumatic stress disorder (see Chapter 5). There are few data on prevalence, but the majority presenting to clinics seem to be women (Wincze et al., in press). Consider the case of Lisa from one of our clinics.

LISA: The Terror of Sex

Lisa was 36, had been married for 3 years, and was a full-time student working on an associate degree. She had been married once before. Lisa reported that sexual problems had begun 9 months earlier. She complained of poor lubrication during intercourse and of having "anxiety attacks" during sex. She had not attempted intercourse in 2 months and had tried only intermittently during the past 9 months. Despite their sexual difficulties, Lisa had a loving and close relationship with her husband. She could not remember precisely what happened 9 months ago except that she had been under a great deal of stress and experienced an anxiety attack during sex. Even her husband's touch was becoming increasingly intolerable because she was afraid it might bring on the scary feelings again. Her primary fear was of having a heart attack and dying during sex.

Among male patients presenting for sexual aversion disorder, 10% experienced panic attacks during attempted sexual activity. Kaplan (1987) reports that 25% of 106 patients presenting with sexual aversion disorder also met criteria for panic disorder. In such cases, treating the panic may be a necessary first step.

Sexual Arousal Disorders

Disorders of arousal are called **male erectile disorder** and **female sexual arousal disorder.** The problem here is not desire. Many individuals with arousal disorders have frequent sexual urges and fantasies and a strong desire to have sex. Their problem is in becoming physically aroused: A male has difficulty achieving or maintaining an erection, and a female cannot achieve or maintain adequate lubrication (Segraves & Althof, 1998; Wincze & Barlow, 1997; Wincze et al., in press). Consider the case of Bill.

BILL: Long Marriage, New Problem

Bill, a 58-year-old white man, was referred to our clinic by his urologist. He was a retired accountant who had been married for 29 years to his 57-year-old wife, a retired nutritionist. They had no children. For the past several years, Bill had had difficulties obtaining and maintaining an erection. He reported a rather rigid routine he and his wife had developed to deal with the problem. They scheduled sex for Sunday mornings. However, Bill had to do a number of chores first, including letting the dog out, washing the dishes, and shaving. The couple's current behavior consisted of mutual hand stimulation. Bill was "not allowed" to attempt insertion until after his wife had climaxed. Bill's wife was adamant that she was not going to change her sexual behavior and "become a whore," as she put it. This included refusing to try K-Y jelly as a lubricant appropriate to her postmenopausal decrease in lubrication. She described their behavior as "lesbian sex."

Bill and his wife agreed that despite marital problems over the years, they had always maintained a good sexual relationship until the onset of the current problem and that sex had kept them together during their earlier difficulties. Useful information was obtained in separate interviews. Bill masturbated on Saturday night in an attempt to control his erection the following morning; his wife was unaware of this. In addition, he quickly and easily achieved a full erection when viewing erotica in the privacy of the sexuality clinic laboratory (surprising the assessor). Bill's wife privately acknowledged being angry at her husband for an affair that he had had 20 years earlier.

At the final session, three specific recommendations were made: for Bill to cease masturbating the evening before sex, for the couple to use a lubricant, and for them to delay the morning routine until after they had had sexual relations. The couple called back 1 month later to report that their sexual activity was much improved.

The old and somewhat derogatory terms for male erectile disorder and female arousal disorder are *impotence* and *frigidity,* but these are imprecise labels that do not identify the specific phase of the sexual response in which the problems are localized. The man typically feels more impaired by his problem than the woman does by hers. Inability to achieve and maintain an erection makes intercourse difficult or impossible. Women who are unable to achieve vaginal lubrication, however, may be able to compensate by using a commercial lubricant (Schover & Jensen, 1988; Wincze & Barlow, 1997). In women, arousal and lubrication may decrease at any time but, as in men, such problems tend to accompany aging (Bartlik & Goldberg, 2000; DeLamater & Sill, 2005; Laumann

DSM-IV-TR

DSM TABLE 10.4 Diagnostic Criteria for Sexual Arousal Disorders

Female
A. Persistent or recurrent inability to attain, or to maintain until completion of the sexual activity, an adequate lubrication–swelling response of sexual excitement.
B. The disturbance causes marked distress or interpersonal difficulty.
C. The sexual dysfunction is not better accounted for by another Axis I disorder (except another sexual dysfunction) and is not due exclusively to the direct physiological effects of a substance (e.g., a drug of abuse, a medication) or a general medical condition.
Specify type:
    Lifelong type
    Acquired type
Specify type:
    Generalized type
    Situational type
Specify:
    Due to psychological factors
    Due to combined factors

Male
A. Persistent or recurrent inability to attain, or to maintain until completion of the sexual activity, an adequate erection.
B. The disturbance causes marked distress or interpersonal difficulty.
C. The erectile dysfunction is not better accounted for by another Axis I disorder (other than a sexual dysfunction) and is not due exclusively to the direct physiological effects of a substance (e.g., a drug of abuse, a medication) or a general medical condition.
Specify type:
    Lifelong type
    Acquired type
Specify type:
    Generalized type
    Situational type
Specify:
    Due to psychological factors
    Due to combined factors

Source: Reprinted, with permission, from American Psychiatric Association. (2000). *Diagnostic and statistical manual of mental disorders* (4th ed., text revision). Washington, DC: Author, © 2000 American Psychiatric Association.

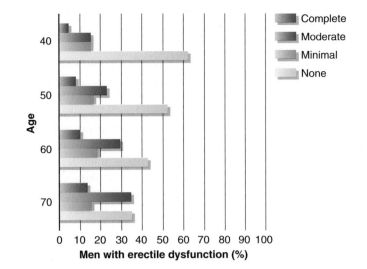

■ **FIGURE 10.4** Estimated prevalence and severity of erectile dysfunction in a sample of 1,290 men between 40 and 70 years of age. (Reprinted, with permission, from Feldman and colleagues (1994). Impotence and its medical and psychosocial correlates: Results of the Massachusetts male aging study. *Journal of Urology, 51,* 54–61.

et al., 1999; Morokoff, 1993; Rosen, 2000). In addition, until relatively recently, some women were not as concerned as men about experiencing intense pleasure during sex as long as they could consummate the act; this is generally no longer the case (Morokoff, 1993; Wincze & Carey, 2001). It is unusual for a man to be completely unable to achieve an erection. More typical is a situation like Bill's, where full erections are possible during masturbation and partial erections occur during attempted intercourse, but with insufficient rigidity to allow penetration.

The prevalence of erectile dysfunction is startlingly high and increases with age. Data from the U.S. survey indicate that 5% of men between 18 and 59 fully meet a stringent set of criteria for erectile dysfunction (Laumann et al., 1999). But this figure certainly underestimates the prevalence because erectile dysfunction increases rapidly in men after age 60. Rosen, Wing, Schneider, and Gendrano (2005) reviewed evidence from around the world and found that 60% of men 60 and over suffered from erectile dysfunction. Data from another study (shown in ■ Figure 10.4) suggest that at least some impairment is present in approximately 40% of men in their 40s and 70% of men in their 70s (Feldman, Goldstein, Hatzichristou, Krane, & McKunlay, 1994; Kim & Lipshultz, 1997); incidence (new cases) increases dramatically with age to 46 new cases each year per 1,000 men in their 60s (Johannes et al., 2000). Male erectile disorder is easily the most common problem for which men seek help, accounting for 50% or more of the men referred to specialists for sexual problems (Hawton, 1995).

The prevalence of female arousal disorders is somewhat more difficult to estimate because many women still do not consider absence of arousal to be a problem, let alone a disorder. The U.S. survey reports a prevalence of 14% of females experiencing an arousal disorder (Laumann et al., 1999). Because disorders of desire, arousal, and orgasm often overlap, it is difficult to estimate precisely how many women with specific arousal disorders present to sex clinics (Segraves & Althof, 1998; Wincze & Carey, 2001).

Orgasm Disorders

The orgasm phase of the sexual response cycle can also become disrupted in one of several ways. As a result, either the orgasm occurs at an inappropriate time or it does not occur.

■ Inhibited Orgasm

An inability to achieve an orgasm despite adequate sexual desire and arousal is commonly seen in women (Stock, 1993; Wincze & Barlow, 1997), but **inhibited orgasm** is relatively rare in men. Consider the case of Greta and Will.

GRETA AND WILL: Loving Disunion

Greta, a teacher, and Will, an engineer, were an attractive couple who came together to the first interview and entered the office clearly showing affection for each other. They had been married for 5 years and were in their late 20s. When asked about the problems that had brought them to the office, Greta quickly reported that she didn't think she had ever had an orgasm—"didn't think" because she wasn't really sure what an orgasm was. She loved Will and occasionally would initiate lovemaking, although with decreased frequency over the past several years.

Will certainly didn't think Greta was reaching orgasm. In any case, he reported, they were clearly going in "different directions" sexually, in that Greta's interest was decreasing. She had progressed from initiating sex occasionally early in their marriage to almost never doing so, except for an occasional spurt every 6 months or so, when she would initiate two or three times in a week. But Greta noted that it was the physical closeness she wanted most during these times rather than sexual pleasure. Further inquiry revealed that she did become sexually aroused occasionally but had never reached orgasm, even during several attempts at masturbation mostly before her marriage. Both Greta and Will reported that the sexual problem was a concern to them because everything else about their marriage was positive.

Greta had been brought up in a strict but loving and supportive Catholic family that more or less ignored sexuality. The parents were always careful not to display their affection in front of Greta, and when her mother caught Greta touching her genital area, she was cautioned rather severely to avoid that kind of activity.

We discuss Greta and Will's treatment later.

An inability to reach orgasm is the most common complaint among women who seek therapy for sexual problems. Although the U.S. survey did not estimate the prevalence of **female orgasmic disorder** specifically, approximately 25% of women report significant difficulty reaching orgasm (Heiman, 2000; Laumann et al., 1999). The problem is equally present in different age groups, and unmarried women were 1.5 times more likely than married women to experience orgasm disorder. In diagnosing this problem, it is necessary to determine that the women "never or almost never" reach orgasm (Wincze & Carey, 2001). This distinction is important because only approximately 20% of all women reliably experience regular orgasms during sexual intercourse (Lloyd, 2005). Therefore, approximately 80% do not achieve orgasm with every sexual encounter, unlike most men, who tend to experience orgasm more consistently. Thus, the "never or almost never" inquiry is important, along with establishing the extent of the couple's distress, in diagnosing orgasmic dysfunction.

In the U.S. survey, approximately 8% of men report having delayed orgasms or none during sexual interactions (Laumann et

DSM TABLE 10.5 Criteria for Orgasmic Disorder

Female

A. Persistent or recurrent delay in, or absence of, orgasm following a normal sexual excitement phase. Women exhibit wide variability in the type of intensity of stimulation that triggers orgasm. The diagnosis of female orgasmic disorder should be based on the clinician's judgment that the woman's orgasmic capacity is less than would be reasonable for her age, sexual experience, and the adequacy of sexual stimulation she receives.

B. The disturbance causes marked distress or interpersonal difficulty.

C. The orgasmic dysfunction is not better accounted for by another Axis I disorder (except another sexual dysfunction) and is not due exclusively to the direct physiological effects of a substance (e.g., a drug of abuse, a medication) or a general medical condition.

Specify type:
  Lifelong type
  Acquired type
Specify type:
  Generalized type
  Situational type
Specify:
  Due to psychological factors
  Due to combined factors

Male

A. Persistent or recurrent delay in, or absence of, orgasm following a normal sexual excitement phase during sexual activity that the clinician, taking into account the person's age, judges to be adequate in focus, intensity, and duration.

B. The disturbance causes marked distress or interpersonal difficulty.

C. The orgasmic dysfunction is not better accounted for by another Axis I disorder (except another sexual dysfunction) and is not due exclusively to the direct physiological effects of a substance (e.g., a drug of abuse, a medication) or a general medical condition.

Specify type:
  Lifelong type
  Acquired type
Specify type:
  Generalized type
  Situational type
Specify:
  Due to psychological factors
  Due to combined factors

Source: Reprinted, with permission, from American Psychiatric Association. (2000). *Diagnostic and statistical manual of mental disorders* (4th ed., text revision). Washington, DC: Author. © 2000 American Psychiatric Association.

al., 1999). Men seldom seek treatment for this condition. It is quite possible that in many cases some men reach climax through alternative forms of stimulation and that **male orgasmic disorder** is accommodated by the couple (Apfelbaum, 2000).

Some men who are unable to ejaculate with their partners can obtain an erection and ejaculate during masturbation. In the most usual pattern, ejaculation is delayed; this is called *retarded ejaculation.* Occasionally men suffer from *retrograde ejaculation,* in which ejaculatory fluids travel backward into the bladder rather than forward. This phenomenon is almost always caused by the effects of certain drugs or a coexisting medical condition and should not be confused with male orgasmic disorder.

■ Premature Ejaculation

A far more common male orgasmic disorder is **premature ejaculation,** ejaculation that occurs well before the man and his partner wish it to (Althof, 2006; Polonsky, 2000; Weiner, 1996). Consider the rather typical case of Gary.

GARY: Running Scared

Gary, a 31-year-old salesman, engaged in sexual activity with his wife three or four times a month. He noted that he would have liked to have had sex more often but his busy schedule kept him working about 80 hours a week. His primary difficulty was an inability to control the timing of his ejaculation. Approximately 70% to 80% of the time he ejaculated within seconds of penetration. This pattern had been constant since he met his wife approximately 13 years earlier. Previous experience with other women, although limited, was not characterized by premature ejaculation. In an attempt to delay his ejaculation, Gary distracted himself by thinking of nonsexual things (scores of ball games or work-related issues) and sometimes attempted sex soon after a previous attempt because he seemed not to climax as quickly under these circumstances. Gary reported masturbating seldom (three or four times a year at most). When he did masturbate, he usually attempted to reach orgasm quickly, a habit he acquired during his teens to avoid being caught by a family member.

One of his greatest concerns was that he was not pleasing his wife, and under no circumstances did he want her told that he was seeking treatment. Further inquiry revealed that he made many extravagant purchases at his wife's request, even though it strained their finances, because he wished to please her. He felt that if they had met recently, his wife probably would not even accept a date with him because he had lost much of his hair and she had lost weight and was more attractive than she used to be.

Treatment for Gary and his wife is described shortly.

The frequency of premature ejaculation seems to be quite high. In the U.S. survey, 21% of all men met criteria for premature ejaculation, making it the most common male sexual dysfunction (Laumann et al., 1999). This difficulty is also a presenting complaint in as many as 60% of men who seek treatment for sexual dysfunction (Malatesta & Adams, 1984; Polonsky, 2000). (But many of these men also present with erectile dysfunction as their major problem.) In one clinic, premature ejaculation was the principal complaint of 16% of men seeking treatment (Hawton, 1995).

It is difficult to define "premature." An adequate length of time before ejaculation varies from individual to individual. Some surveys indicate that men who complain of premature ejaculation typically climax no more than 1 or 2 minutes after penetration, compared with 7 to 10 minutes in individuals without this complaint (Strassberg, Kelly, Carroll, & Kircher, 1987). A perception of

---

DSM-IV-TR

DSM TABLE 10.6 Criteria for Premature Ejaculation

A. Persistent or recurrent ejaculation with minimal sexual stimulation before, on, or shortly after penetration and before the person wishes it. The clinician must take into account factors that affect duration of the excitement phase, such as age, novelty of the sexual partner or situation, and recent frequency of sexual activity.

B. The disturbance causes marked distress or interpersonal difficulty.

C. The premature ejaculation is not due exclusively to the direct effects of a substance (e.g., withdrawal from opioids).

Specify type:
  Lifelong type
  Acquired type
Specify type:
  Generalized type
  Situational type
Specify:
  Due to psychological factors
  Due to combined factors

Source: Reprinted, with permission, from American Psychiatric Association. (2000). *Diagnostic and statistical manual of mental disorders* (4th ed., text revision). Washington, DC: Author, © 2000 American Psychiatric Association.

---

lack of control over orgasm, however, may be the more important psychological determinant of premature ejaculation (Wincze et al., in press). Although occasional early ejaculation is normal, serious and consistent premature ejaculation appears to occur primarily in inexperienced men with less education about sex (Laumann et al., 1999).

Sexual Pain Disorders

In the **sexual pain disorders,** intercourse is associated with marked pain. For some men and women, sexual desire is present, and arousal and orgasm are easily attained, but the pain of intercourse is so severe that sexual behavior is disrupted. This subtype is named **dyspareunia,** which, in its original Greek, means "unhappily mated as bedfellows" (Wincze & Carey, 2001). This is not an accurate or descriptive name, but it has been used for decades and is accepted. Dyspareunia is diagnosed only if no medical reasons for pain can be found. It can be tricky to make this assessment (Binik, Bergeron, & Khalifé, 2000; Payne et al., 2005). Several years ago, a patient of ours described having sharp pains in his head, like a migraine headache, which began during ejaculation and lasted for several minutes. This man, in his 50s at the time, had had a healthy sexual relationship with his wife until a severe fall approximately 2 years earlier that left him partially disabled and with a severe limp. The pain during ejaculation developed shortly thereafter. Extensive medical examination from a number of specialists revealed no physical reason for the pain. Thus, he met the criteria for dyspareunia, and psychological interventions were administered—in this case, without benefit. He subsequently engaged in manual stimulation of his wife and, occasionally, intercourse, but he avoided ejaculation.

DSM-IV-TR

DSM TABLE 10.7 Criteria for Sexual Pain Disorders

Dyspareunia
A. Recurrent or persistent genital pain associated with sexual intercourse in either a male or a female.
B. The disturbance causes marked distress or interpersonal difficulty.
C. The disturbance is not caused exclusively by vaginismus or lack of lubrication, is not better accounted for by another Axis I disorder (except another sexual dysfunction), and is not due exclusively to the direct physiological effects of a substance (e.g., a drug of abuse, a medication) or a general medical condition.
Specify type:
   Lifelong type
   Acquired type
Specify type:
   Generalized type
   Situational type
Specify:
   Due to psychological factors
   Due to combined factors
Vaginismus
A. Recurrent or persistent involuntary spasm of the musculature of the outer third of the vagina that interferes with sexual intercourse.
B. The disturbance causes marked distress or interpersonal difficulty.
C. The disturbance is not better accounted for by another Axis I disorder (e.g., somatization disorder) and is not due exclusively to the direct physiological effects of a general medical condition.
Specify type:
   Lifelong type
   Acquired type
Specify type:
   Generalized type
   Situational type
Specify:
   Due to psychological factors
   Due to combined factors

Source: Reprinted, with permission, from American Psychiatric Association. (2000). *Diagnostic and statistical manual of mental disorders* (4th ed., text revision). Washington, DC: Author, © 2000 American Psychiatric Association.

Dyspareunia is rarely seen in clinics, with estimates ranging from 1% to 5% of men (Bancroft, 1989; Spector & Carey, 1990) and a more substantial 10% to 15% of women (Hawton, 1995; Rosen & Leiblum, 1995). Glatt, Zinner, and McCormack (1990) report that many women experience pain occasionally but it either resolves or is not sufficient to motivate them to seek treatment. Binik (2005) does not think that dyspareunia should be classified as a sexual disorder but rather as a "urogenital pain disorder." He believes that this would focus therapy on pain control.

A more common problem is **vaginismus,** in which the pelvic muscles in the outer third of the vagina undergo involuntary spasms when intercourse is attempted (Bancroft, 1997; Leiblum, 2000). The spasm reaction of vaginismus may occur during any attempted penetration, including a gynecological exam or insertion of a tampon (Beck, 1993). Women report sensations of "ripping, burning, or tearing during attempted intercourse" (Beck, 1993, p. 384). Consider the case of Jill.

JILL: Sex and Spasms

Jill was referred to our clinic by another therapist because she had not consummated her marriage of 1 year. At 23 years of age, she was an attractive and loving wife who managed a motel while her husband worked as an accountant. Despite numerous attempts in a variety of positions to engage in intercourse, Jill's severe vaginal spasms prevented penetration of any kind. Jill was also unable to use tampons. With great reluctance, she submitted to gynecological exams at infrequent intervals. Sexual behavior with her husband consisted of mutual masturbation or, occasionally, Jill had him rub his penis against her breasts to the point of ejaculation. She refused to engage in oral sex. Jill, an anxious young woman, came from a family in which sexual matters were seldom discussed and sexual contact between the parents had ceased some years before. Although she enjoyed petting, Jill's general attitude was that intercourse was disgusting. Furthermore, she expressed some fears of becoming pregnant despite taking adequate contraceptive measures. She also thought that she would perform poorly when she did engage in intercourse, therefore embarrassing herself with her new husband.

Although we have no data on the prevalence of vaginismus in community samples, best estimates are that it affects more than 5% of women who seek treatment in North America and 10% to 15% in Britain (Beck, 1993; Hawton, 1995). More recently Crowley, Richardson, and Goldmeir (2006) found that 25% of women who report suffering from some sexual dysfunction experience vaginismus. The prevalence of this condition in cultures with conservative views of sexuality, such as Ireland, may be higher—as high as 42% to 55% in at least two clinic samples (Barnes, Bowman, & Cullen, 1984; O'Sullivan, 1979). (Results from any one clinic may not be applicable even to other clinics, let alone to the population of Ireland.) Because vaginismus and dyspareunia both involve pain and overlap quite a bit in women, current proposals suggest combining these two problems in a single pain-related category (Binik, 2005; Payne et al., 2005). Results from the U.S. survey indicate that approximately 7% of women suffer from one or the other type of sexual pain disorder, with higher proportions of younger and less educated women reporting this problem (Laumann et al., 1999).

ASSESSING SEXUAL BEHAVIOR

There are three major aspects to the assessment of sexual behavior (Wiegel, Wincze, & Barlow, 2002):

1. *Interviews,* usually supported by numerous questionnaires because patients may provide more information on paper than in a verbal interview
2. A *thorough medical evaluation,* to rule out the variety of medical conditions that can contribute to sexual problems
3. A *psychophysiological assessment,* to directly measure the physiological aspects of sexual arousal

Interviews

All clinicians who conduct interviews for sexual problems should be aware of several useful assumptions (Wiegel et al., 2002; Wincze & Barlow, 1997). For example, they must demonstrate to the patient through their actions and interviewing style that they are comfortable talking about these issues. Because many patients do not know the various clinical terms professionals use to describe the sexual response cycle and various aspects of sexual behavior, clinicians must always be prepared to use the vernacular of the patient, realizing also that terms vary from person to person.

The following are examples of the questions asked in semistructured interviews in our sexuality clinic:

- How would you describe your current interest in sex?
- Do you avoid engaging in sexual behavior with a partner?
- Do you have sexual fantasies?
- How often do you currently masturbate?
- How often do you engage in sexual intercourse?
- How often do you engage in mutual caressing or cuddling without intercourse?
- Have you ever been sexually abused or raped or had a negative experience associated with sex?
- Do you have problems attaining an erection? [or] Do you have problems achieving or maintaining vaginal lubrication?
- Do you ever have problems reaching orgasm?
- Do you ever experience pain associated with sexual activity?

A clinician must be careful to ask these questions in a manner that puts the patient at ease. During an interview lasting approximately 2 hours, the clinician also covers nonsexual relationship issues and physical health and screens for the presence of additional psychological disorders. When possible, the partner is interviewed concurrently.

Patients may volunteer in writing some information they are not ready to talk about, so they are usually given a variety of questionnaires that help reveal sexual activity and attitudes toward sexuality.

Medical Examination

Any human sexuality clinician routinely inquires about medical conditions that affect sexual functioning. A variety of drugs, including some commonly prescribed for hypertension, anxiety, and depression, often disrupt sexual arousal and functioning. Recent surgery or concurrent medical conditions must be evaluated for their impact on sexual functioning; often the surgeon or treating physician will not have described possible side effects, or the patient may not have told the physician that a medical procedure or drug has affected sexual functioning. Most males with specific sexual dysfunctions such as erectile disorder have already visited a urologist—a physician specializing in disorders of the genitals, bladder, and associated structures—before coming to a sexuality clinic, and many females already have visited a gynecologist. These specialists may check levels of sexual hormones necessary for adequate sexual functioning and, in the case of males, evaluate vascular functioning necessary for an erectile response.

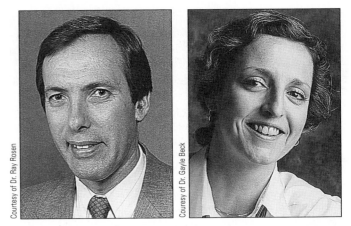

Ray Rosen (left) and Gayle Beck (right) pioneered research on the psychophysiological measurement of sexual arousal.

Psychophysiological Assessment

Many clinicians assess the ability of individuals to become sexually aroused under a variety of conditions by taking psychophysiological measurements while the patient is either awake or asleep. In men, penile erection is measured directly, using, for example, a *penile strain gauge* developed in our clinic (Barlow, Becker, Leitenberg, & Agras, 1970). As the penis expands, the strain gauge picks up the changes and records them on a polygraph. Note that subjects are often not aware of these more objective measures of their arousal; that is, their self-report of how aroused they are differs from the objective measure, and this discrepancy increases or decreases as a function of the type of sexual problem they have. Penile rigidity is also important to measure in cases of erectile dysfunction, because large erections with insufficient rigidity will not be adequate for intercourse (Wiegel et al., 2002).

The comparable device for women is a *vaginal photoplethysmograph,* developed by James Geer and his associates (Geer, Morokoff, & Greenwood, 1974; Prause & Janssen, 2006; Rosen & Beck, 1988). This device, which is smaller than a tampon, is inserted by the woman into her vagina. A light source at the tip of the instrument and two light-sensitive photoreceptors on the sides of the instrument measure the amount of light reflected back

John Wincze (left) and Michael Carey (right) developed new approaches for treating sexual dysfunction.

from the vaginal walls. Because blood flows to the vaginal walls during arousal, the amount of light passing through them decreases with increasing arousal.

Typically in our clinic, individuals undergoing physiological assessment view an erotic videotape for 2 to 5 minutes or, occasionally, listen to an erotic audiotape (see, for example, Bach, Brown, & Barlow, 1999; Weisburg, Brown, Wincze, & Barlow, 2001). The patient's sexual responsivity during this time is assessed psychophysiologically. Patients also report subjectively on the amount of sexual arousal they experience. This assessment allows the clinician to carefully observe the conditions under which arousal is possible for the patient. For example, many individuals with psychologically based sexual dysfunctions may achieve strong arousal in a laboratory but be unable to become aroused with a partner (Bancroft, 1997; Sakheim, Barlow, Abrahamson, & Beck, 1987).

Because erections most often occur during rapid eye movement (REM) sleep in physically healthy men, psychophysiological measurement of *nocturnal penile tumescence (NPT)* was often used in the past to determine a man's ability to obtain normal erectile response. If he could attain normal erections while he was asleep, the reasoning went, then the causes of his dysfunction were psychological. An inexpensive way to monitor nocturnal erections is for the clinician to provide a simple "snap gauge" that the patient fastens around his penis each night before he goes to sleep. If the snap gauge has come undone he has probably had a nocturnal erection. But this is a crude and often inaccurate screening device that should never supplant medical and psychological evaluation (Carey, Wincze, & Meisler, 1993; Mohr & Beutler, 1990; Wiegel et al., 2002). Finally, we now know that lack of NPT could also be the result of psychological problems, such as depression, or to a variety of medical difficulties that have nothing to do with physiological problems preventing erections (Rosen, 2000; Wiegel et al., 2002; Wincze et al., in press).

CONCEPT CHECK 10.2

Diagnose the following sexual dysfunctions.

1. Kay is in a serious sexual relationship and is quite content. Lately, however, the thought of her boyfriend's touch disgusts her. Kay has no idea what is causing this. She could be suffering from (a) panic disorder, (b) sexual arousal disorder, (c) sexual aversion disorder, or (d) both a and b.
2. After Bob was injured playing football, he started having pain in his arm during sex. All medical reasons for the pain have been ruled out. Bob is probably displaying (a) dyspareunia, (b) vaginismus, (c) penile strain gauge, or (d) male orgasmic disorder.
3. Kelly has no real desire for sex. She has sex only because she feels that otherwise her husband may leave her. Kelly suffers from (a) sexual aversion disorder, (b) hypoactive sexual disorder, (c) boredom, or (d) female sexual arousal disorder.

(continued)

CONCEPT CHECK 10.2

(continued)

4. Bill lacks the ability to control ejaculation. The majority of the time he ejaculates within seconds of penetration. He suffers from (a) male erectile disorder, (b) stress, (c) premature ejaculation, or (d) both a and b.
5. Samantha came into the office because she is unable to reach orgasm. She loves her husband but stopped initiating sex. She is most likely suffering from (a) female orgasmic disorder, (b) female sexual arousal disorder, (c) vaginismus, or (d) dislike for her husband.

CAUSES AND TREATMENT OF SEXUAL DYSFUNCTION

As with most disorders, biological, psychological, and social factors contribute to the development of sexual dysfunction. And these problems can be treated either psychologically or medically.

Causes of Sexual Dysfunction

Individual sexual dysfunctions seldom present in isolation. Usually, a patient referred to a sexuality clinic complains of a wide assortment of sexual problems, although one may be of most concern (Hawton, 1995; Wincze & Barlow, 1997). A 45-year-old man recently referred to our clinic had been free of problems until 10 years earlier, when he was under a great deal of pressure at work and was preparing to take a major career-related licensing examination. He began experiencing erectile dysfunction about 50% of the time, a condition that had progressed to approximately 80% of the time. In addition, he reported that he had no control over ejaculation, often ejaculating before penetration with only a semi-erect penis. Over the past 5 years, he had lost most interest in sex and was coming to treatment only at his wife's insistence. Thus, this man suffered simultaneously from erectile dysfunction, premature ejaculation, and low sexual desire.

Because of the frequency of such combinations, we discuss the causes of various sexual dysfunctions together, reviewing briefly the biological, psychological, and social contributions and specifying causal factors thought to be associated exclusively and specifically with one or another dysfunction.

■ Biological Contributions

A number of physical and medical conditions contribute to sexual dysfunction (Wiegel et al., 2002; Wincze et al., in press; Wincze & Carey, 2001). Although this is not surprising, most patients, and even many health professionals, are, unfortunately, unaware of the connection. Neurological diseases and other conditions that affect the nervous system, such as diabetes and kidney disease, may directly interfere with sexual functioning by reducing sensitivity in the genital area, and they are a common cause of erectile dysfunction in males (Schover & Jensen, 1988; Wincze & Barlow, 1997). Feldman and colleagues (1994) reported that 28% of men with diabetes experienced complete erectile failure. Vascular disease is a

"In the process of becoming aroused, all of a sudden it would be over. And I didn't understand that at all. So then everything is coupled with a bunch of depressing thoughts, like fear of failure. And so I begin to say, is this happening to me because I'm afraid I'm going to fail, and I don't want to be embarrassed by that? It's really very difficult to deal with emotionally. . . . The worse I feel about myself, the slower I am sexually, and sometimes I describe it as the fear of losing masculinity."

major cause of sexual dysfunction, because erections in men and vaginal engorgement in women depend on adequate blood flow. The two relevant vascular problems are arterial insufficiency (constricted arteries), which makes it difficult for blood to reach the penis, and venous leakage (blood flows out too quickly for an erection to be maintained) (Wincze & Carey, 2001).

Chronic illness can also indirectly affect sexual functioning. For example, it is not uncommon for individuals who have had heart attacks to be wary of the physical exercise involved in sexual activity to the point of preoccupation. They often become unable to achieve arousal despite being assured by their physicians that sexual activity is safe for them (Cooper, 1988). Also, coronary artery disease and sexual dysfunction commonly coexist, and it is now recommended that men presenting with erectile dysfunction should be screened for cardiovascular disease (Jackson, Rosen, Kloner, & Kostis, 2006).

A major physical cause of sexual dysfunction is prescription medication. Drug treatments for high blood pressure, called *antihypertensive medications,* in the class known as beta-blockers, including propranolol, may contribute to sexual dysfunction. Serotonin-specific reuptake inhibitor (SSRI) antidepressant medications and other antidepressant and antianxiety drugs may also interfere with sexual desire and arousal in both men and women (Balon, 2006; Segraves & Althof, 1998). A number of these drugs, particularly the psychoactive drugs, may dampen sexual desire and arousal by altering levels of certain subtypes of serotonin in the brain. Sexual dysfunction—specifically low sexual desire and arousal difficulties—is the most widespread side effect of the antidepressant SSRIs, such as Prozac (see Chapter 7), and as many as 80% of individuals who take these medications may experience some degree of sexual dysfunction, although estimates closer to 50% seem more reliable (Balon, 2006; Montejo-Gonzalez et al., 1997). Some people are aware that alcohol suppresses sexual arousal, but they may not know that most other drugs of abuse, such as cocaine and heroin, also produce widespread sexual dysfunction in frequent users and abusers, both male and female. Cocores, Miller, Pottash, and Gold (1988) and Macdonald, Waldorf, Reinarman, and Murphy (1988) reported that more than 60% of a large number of cocaine users had a sexual dysfunction. In the Cocores group's study, some patients also abused alcohol.

There is also the misconception that alcohol facilitates sexual arousal and behavior. What actually happens is that alcohol at low and moderate levels reduces social inhibitions so that people feel more like having sex (and perhaps are more willing to request it) (Crowe & George, 1989; Wiegel, Scepkowski, & Barlow, 2006). Physically, alcohol is a central nervous system suppressant, and for

men to achieve erection and women to achieve lubrication is more difficult when the central nervous system is suppressed (Schiavi, 1990). Chronic alcohol abuse may cause permanent neurological damage and may virtually eliminate the sexual response cycle. Such abuse may lead to liver and testicular damage, resulting in decreased testosterone levels and related decreases in sexual desire and arousal. This dual effect of alcohol (social disinhibition and physical suppression) has been recognized since the time of Shakespeare: "It provokes the desire, but it takes away the performance" (*Macbeth,* II, iii, 29).

Chronic alcoholism can also cause fertility problems in both men and women (Malatesta & Adams, 2001). Fahrner (1987) examined the prevalence of sexual dysfunction among male alcoholics and found that 75% had erectile dysfunction, low sexual desire, and premature or delayed ejaculation.

Many people report that cocaine or marijuana enhances sexual pleasure. Although little is known about the effects of marijuana across the range of use, it is unlikely that chemical effects increase pleasure. Rather, in those individuals who report some enhancement of sexual pleasure (and many don't), the effect may be psychological in that their attention is focused more completely and fully on sensory stimulation (Buffum, 1982), a factor that seems to be an important part of healthy sexual functioning. If so, imagery and attentional focus can be enhanced with non-drug procedures such as meditation, in which a person practices concentrating on something with as few distractions as possible. Finally, one report from Mannino, Klevens, and Flanders (1994), studying more than 4,000 male army veterans, found that cigarette smoking alone was associated with increased erectile dysfunction after controlling for other factors, such as alcohol and vascular disease (Wincze et al., in press).

■ Psychological Contributions

For years, most sex researchers and therapists thought the principal cause of sexual dysfunctions was anxiety (see, for example, Kaplan, 1979; Masters & Johnson, 1970). While evaluating the role of anxiety and sexual functioning in our own laboratory, we discovered it was not that simple. In certain circumstances, anxiety *increases* sexual arousal (Barlow, Sakheim, & Beck, 1983). We designed an experiment in which young, sexually functional men viewed erotic films under three conditions. In one condition, we attempted to replicate the kinds of performance anxiety that males might experience during a sexual interaction. Before viewing an erotic film, all subjects were exposed to a harmless but somewhat painful electric shock to the forearm. During one condition, subjects were told to relax and enjoy the film and that there was no chance of shock. This served as a control condition. In the second condition, subjects were told there was a 60% chance they would receive the shock at some time while they were watching the erotic film, no matter what they did (noncontingent shock threat). In the third condition, most closely paralleling the types of performance anxiety that some individuals might experience, subjects were told there was a 60% chance they would receive a shock if they did not achieve the average level of erection achieved by the previous subjects (contingent shock threat). No shocks were delivered during the viewing of the erotic films in any of the conditions, although subjects believed they might be administered.

The results, presented in ■ Figure 10.5, indicate that the noncontingent shock threat condition *increased* sexual arousal compared with the no-shock threat control condition. However, in an even more surprising development, the contingent shock threat condition (in which subjects were told there was a 60% chance they would be shocked if they did not achieve adequate arousal) increased sexual response even more significantly than the no-shock threat control condition. Similar results for women were reported by Hoon, Wincze, and Hoon (1977), Palace (1995), and Palace and Gorzalka (1990), who developed slightly different experimental paradigms, using the vaginal photoplethysmograph (Wiegel, Scepkowski, & Barlow, 2006).

These counterintuitive findings have some parallels outside the laboratory. In one unusual and startling report, Sarrel and Masters (1982) described the ability of men to perform sexually under threat of physical harm. These men, the victims of gang rape by women, reported later that they had been able to achieve erections and repeatedly engage in intercourse despite being constantly threatened with knives and other weapons if they failed. Certainly they experienced extreme levels of anxiety, yet they reported that their sexual performance was not impaired.

If anxiety does not necessarily decrease sexual arousal and performance, what does? A partial answer is distraction. In one experiment, subjects were asked to listen to a narrative through earphones while they watched an erotic film and were told that they would later have to report on the narrative to make sure they were listening. Sexually functional males demonstrated significantly less arousal based on penile strain gauge measurements when they were distracted by the narrative than when they were not distracted (Abrahamson, Barlow, Sakheim, Beck, & Athanasiou, 1985). To any male who has tried to concentrate on baseball scores or some other nonsexual event to reduce unwanted arousal, this result will come as no surprise. Males with erectile dysfunction in whom physical disease processes had been ruled out reacted somewhat differently from functional men to both shock threat and distraction conditions. Anxiety induced by shock threat ("You'll be shocked if you don't get aroused") did seem to reduce sexual arousal in males who were dysfunctional. Remember that the reverse was true for the normally functioning males. By contrast, the kind of neutral distracting conditions present in the experiment by Abrahamson and colleagues (1985) did not reduce arousal in those males who were dysfunctional. This discovery is puzzling.

Two other findings from different experiments are important. One revealed that patients with erectile dysfunction consistently underreport their actual levels of arousal; that is, at the same level of erectile responses (as measured by the penile strain gauge), men who are dysfunctional report far less sexual arousal than do sexually functional men (Sakheim et al., 1987). This result seems to be true for dysfunctional women as well (Meston & Gorzalka, 1995; Morokoff & Heiman, 1980; Wiegel et al., 2006). Another finding showed that inducing positive or negative mood by playing joyful or sad music directly affected sexual arousal, at least in normals, with sad music decreasing sexual arousal (Mitchell, DiBartolo, Brown, & Barlow, 1998).

How do we interpret this complex series of experiments to account for sexual dysfunction from a psychological perspective? Basically, we have to break the concept of performance anxiety into several components. One component is arousal, another is cognitive processes, and third is negative affect (Wiegel et al., 2006; Wincze et al., in press).

When confronted with the possibility of having sexual relations, individuals who are dysfunctional tend to expect the worst and find the situation to be relatively negative and unpleasant (Weisberg et al., 2001). As far as possible, they avoid becoming aware of any sexual cues (and therefore are not aware of how aroused they are physically, thus underreporting their arousal). They also may distract themselves with negative thoughts, such as, "I'm going to make a fool of myself; I'll never be able to get aroused; she [or he] will think I'm stupid." We know that as arousal increases, a person's attention focuses more intently and consistently. But the person who

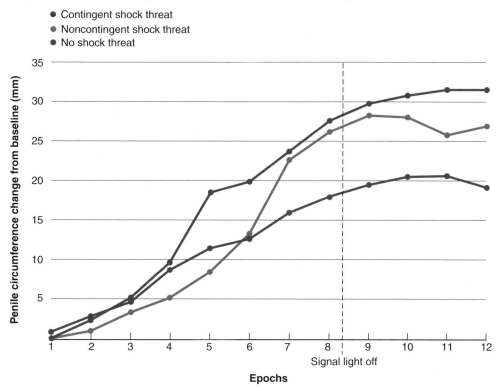

■ **FIGURE 10.5** Performance anxiety and sexual arousal in males. Shown here are the average changes in male sexual arousal (penile circumference change) during each of three conditions. An epoch is a period of 10 seconds. (From Barlow, D. H., Sakheim, D. K., & Beck, J. G., 1983. Anxiety increases sexual arousal. *Journal of Abnormal Psychology, 92,* 49–54.)

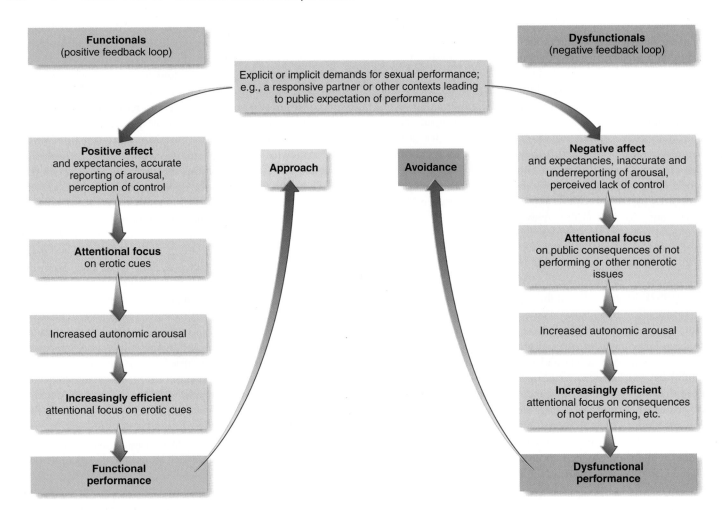

■ **FIGURE 10.6** A model of functional and dysfunctional sexual arousal. (Adapted from Barlow, D. H., 1986. Causes of sexual dysfunction: The role of anxiety and cognitive interference. *Journal of Consulting and Clinical Psychology, 54*, 140–148.)

is focusing on negative thoughts will find it impossible to become sexually aroused.

People with normal sexual functioning react to a sexual situation positively. They focus their attention on the erotic cues and do not become distracted. When they become aroused, they focus even more strongly on the sexual and erotic cues, allowing themselves to become increasingly sexually aroused. The model presented in ■ Figure 10.6 illustrates both functional and dysfunctional sexual arousal (Barlow, 1986, 2002). These experiments demonstrate that sexual arousal is strongly determined by psychological factors, particularly cognitive and emotional factors, that are powerful enough to determine whether blood flows to the appropriate areas of the body, such as the genitals, confirming again the strong interaction of psychological and biological factors in most of our functioning.

In summary, normally functioning individuals show increased sexual arousal during "performance demand" conditions, experience positive affect, are distracted by nonsexual stimuli, and have a good idea of how aroused they are. Individuals with sexual problems, such as erectile dysfunction in males, show decreased arousal during performance demand, experience negative affect, are not distracted by nonsexual stimuli, and do not have an accurate sense of how aroused they are. This process seems to apply to most sexual dysfunctions, which, you will remember, tend to

occur together, but it is particularly applicable to sexual arousal disorders (Wiegel et al., 2006).

We know little about the psychological (or biological) factors associated with premature ejaculation (Ertekin, Colakoglu, & Altay, 1995; Weiner, 1996). We do know that the condition is most prevalent in young men and that excessive physiological arousal in the sympathetic nervous system may lead to rapid ejaculation. These observations suggest some men may have a naturally lower threshold for ejaculation; that is, they require less stimulation and arousal to ejaculate. Unfortunately, the psychological factor of anxiety also increases sympathetic arousal. Thus, when a man becomes anxiously aroused about ejaculating too quickly, his concern only makes the problem worse. We return to the role of anxiety in sexual dysfunctions later.

■ Social and Cultural Contributions

The model of sexual dysfunction displayed in Figure 10.6 helps explain why some individuals may be dysfunctional *at the present time* but not how they *became* that way. Although we do not know for sure why some people develop problems, many people learn early that sexuality can be negative and somewhat threatening, and the responses they develop reflect this belief. Donn Byrne and his colleagues call this negative cognitive set *erotophobia*. They have demonstrated that erotophobia, presumably learned early in childhood from families, religious authorities, or others, seems to predict sexual difficulties later in life (Byrne & Schulte, 1990). Thus, for some individuals, sexual cues become associated early with negative affect. In other cases, both men and women may experience specific negative or traumatic events after a period of relatively well-adjusted sexuality. These negative events might include sudden failure to become aroused or actual sexual trauma such as rape, as well as early sexual abuse.

Laumann and colleagues (1999), in the U.S. sex survey, found a substantial impact of early traumatic sexual events on later sexual functioning, particularly in women. For example, if women were sexually victimized by an adult before puberty or were forced to have sexual contact of some kind, they were approximately twice as likely to have orgasmic dysfunction as women who had not been touched before puberty or forced to have sex at any time. For male victims of adult–child contact, the probability of experiencing erectile dysfunction is more than 3 times greater than if they had not had the contact. Interestingly, men who admitted sexually assaulting women are 3.5 times as likely to report erectile dysfunction as those who did not. Thus, traumatic sexual acts of all kinds have long-lasting effects on subsequent sexual functioning, in both men and women, sometimes lasting decades beyond the occurrence of the original event. Such stressful events may initiate negative affect, in which individuals experience a loss of control over their sexual response cycle, throwing them into the kind of dysfunctional pattern depicted in Figure 10.6. It is common for people who experience erectile failure during a particularly stressful time to continue sexual dysfunction long after the stressful situation has ended.

In addition to generally negative attitudes or experiences associated with sexual interactions, a number of other factors may contribute to sexual dysfunction. Among these, the most common is a marked deterioration in close interpersonal relationships (Wincze et al., in press). It is difficult to have a satisfactory sexual relationship in the context of growing dislike for a partner. Occasionally, the partner may no longer seem physically attractive. Finally it is also important to feel attractive yourself. Koch, Mansfield, Thurau, and Carey (2005) found that the more a woman perceived herself as less attractive than before, the more likely she was to have sexual problems. Kelly, Strassberg, and Kircher (1990) found that anorgasmic women, in addition to displaying more negative attitudes toward masturbation, greater sex guilt, and greater endorsement of sex myths, reported discomfort in telling their partners what sexual activities might increase their arousal or lead to orgasm, such as direct clitoral stimulation. Poor sexual skills might also lead to frequent sexual failure and, ultimately, lack of desire. For example, men with erectile dysfunction report a greatly restricted range of sexual behaviors, compared to men without these problems (Wincze, Bach, & Barlow, in press).

Thus, social and cultural factors seem to affect later sexual functioning. John Gagnon has studied this phenomenon and constructed an important concept called *script theory* of sexual functioning, according to which we all operate according to "scripts" that reflect social and cultural expectations and guide our behavior (Gagnon, 1990; Laumann, Gagnon, Michael, & Michaels, 1994). Discovering these scripts, both in individuals and across cultures, will tell us much about sexual functioning. For example, a person who learns that sexuality is potentially dangerous, dirty, or forbidden is more vulnerable to developing sexual dysfunction later in life. This pattern is most evident in cultures with restrictive attitudes toward sex. For example, vaginismus is relatively rare in North America but is the most common cause of unconsummated marriages in Ireland (Barnes, 1981; O'Sullivan, 1979). Cultural scripts may also contribute to the type of sexual dysfunction reported. In India, for example, Verma, Khaitan, and Singh (1998) reported that 77% of a large number of male patients in a sexuality clinic in India reported difficulties with premature ejaculation. In addition, 71% of male patients complained of being extremely concerned about nocturnal emissions associated with erotic dreams. The authors note that this focus on problems with ejaculation is most likely the result of a strong culturally held belief in India that loss of semen causes depletion of physical and mental energy. It is also interesting that out of 1,000 patients presenting to this clinic, only 36 were female, most likely reflecting the devaluation of sexual experiences for females for religious and social reasons in India.

Even in our own culture, certain socially communicated expectations and attitudes may stay with us despite our relatively enlightened and permissive attitude toward sex. Barbara Andersen and her colleagues (see, for example, Cyranowski et al., 1999) have demonstrated that a negative sexual self-schema, described earlier (being emotional and self-conscious about sex) and a concept similar to Byrne's erotophobia and Gagnon's scripts, may later lead to sexual difficulties under stressful situations. Zilbergeld (1999), one of the foremost authorities on male sexuality, has elaborated a number of myths about sex believed by many men, and Heiman and LoPiccolo (1988) have done the same for women. These myths are listed in Table 10.4. Baker and DeSilva (1988) converted an earlier version of Zilbergeld's male myths into a questionnaire and presented it to groups of sexually functional and dysfunctional men. They found that men with dysfunctions showed significantly greater belief in the myths than did men who were sexually functional. We explore such myths further in our discussion of treatment.

■ Interaction of Psychological and Physical Factors

Having reviewed the various causes, we must now say that seldom is any sexual dysfunction associated exclusively with either psychological or physical factors (Bancroft, 1997; Leiblum & Rosen, 2000; Wiegel et al., 2006). More often, there is a subtle combination of factors. To take a typical example, a young man, vulnerable to developing anxiety and holding to a certain number of sexual myths (the social contribution), may experience erectile failure unexpectedly after using drugs or alcohol, as many men do (the biological contribution). He will anticipate the next sexual encounter with anxiety, wondering if the failure might happen again. This combination of experience and apprehension activates the psychological sequence depicted in Figure 10.6, regardless of whether he's had a few drinks.

In summary, socially transmitted negative attitudes about sex may interact with a person's relationship difficulties and predispositions to develop performance anxiety and, ultimately, lead to sexual dysfunction. From a psychological point of view, it is not clear why some individuals develop one dysfunction and not another, although it is common for several dysfunctions to occur in

TABLE 10.4 Myths of Sexuality

Myths of Female Sexuality	Myths of Male Sexuality
1. Sex is only for women under 30.	1. We're liberated folks who are comfortable with sex.
2. Normal women have an orgasm every time they have sex.	2. A real man isn't into sissy stuff like feelings and communicating.
3. All women can have multiple orgasms.	3. All touching is sexual or should lead to sex.
4. Pregnancy and delivery reduce women's sexual responsiveness.	4. A man is always interested in and always ready for sex.
5. A woman's sex life ends with menopause.	5. Bigger is better.
6. There are different kinds of orgasm related to a woman's personality. Vaginal orgasms are more feminine and mature than clitoral orgasms.	6. Sex is centered on a hard penis and what's done with it.
7. A sexually responsive woman can always be turned on by her partner.	7. Sex equals intercourse.
8. Nice women aren't aroused by erotic books or films.	8. A man should be able to make the earth move for his partner, or at the least knock her socks off.
9. You are frigid if you don't like the more exotic forms of sex.	9. Good sex requires orgasm.
10. If you can't have an orgasm quickly and easily, there's something wrong with you.	10. Men don't have to listen to women in sex.
11. Feminine women don't initiate sex or become wild and unrestrained during sex.	11. Good sex is spontaneous, with no planning and no talking.
12. Double jeopardy: You're frigid if you don't want sex and wanton if you do.	12. Real men don't have sex problems.
13. Contraception is a woman's responsibility, and she's just making up excuses if she says contraceptive issues are inhibiting her sexuality.	13. Real men should be able to last all night.

Source: Left side of table reprinted, with permission of Simon & Schuster Adult Publishing Group, from Heiman, J. R., & LoPiccolo, J., 1988. *Becoming orgasmic: A sexual and personal growth program for women* (rev. ed.). New York: Prentice Hall, © 1976, 1988 Prentice Hall, a division of Simon & Schuster. Right side of table reprinted with permission of Bantamdell Publishing Group, a division of Random House Inc. From Zilbergeld, Z., (1999). The new male sexuality. New York: Bantam Books.

the same patient. Possibly, an individual's specific biological predispositions interact with psychological factors to produce a specific sexual dysfunction.

Treatment of Sexual Dysfunction

Unlike most other disorders discussed in this book, one surprisingly simple treatment is effective for a large number of individuals who experience sexual dysfunction: education. Ignorance of the most basic aspects of the sexual response cycle and intercourse often leads to long-lasting dysfunctions (Bach, Wincze, & Barlow, 2001; Wincze et al., in press; Wincze & Carey, 2001). Consider the case of Carl, who recently came to our sexuality clinic.

CARL: Never Too Late

Carl, a 55-year-old white man, was referred to our clinic by his urologist because he had difficulty maintaining an erection. Although he had never been married, he was involved in an intimate relationship with a 50-year-old woman. This was only his second sexual relationship. He was reluctant to ask his partner to come to the clinic because of his embarrassment in discussing sexual issues. A careful interview revealed that Carl engaged in sex twice a week, but requests by the clinician for a step-by-step description of his sexual activities revealed an unusual pattern: Carl skipped foreplay and immediately proceeded to intercourse. Unfortunately, because his partner was not aroused and lubricated, he was unable to penetrate her. His valiant efforts sometimes resulted in painful abrasions for both of them. Two sessions of extensive sex education, including specific step-by-step instructions for carrying out foreplay, provided Carl with a new outlook on sex. For the first time, he had successful, satisfying intercourse, much to his delight and his partner's.

In the case of hypoactive sexual desire disorder, a marked difference within a couple often leads to one partner being labeled as having low desire. For example, if one partner is quite happy with sexual relations once a week but the other partner desires sex every day, the latter partner may accuse the former of having low desire and, unfortunately, the former partner might agree. Facilitating better conditions often resolves these misunderstandings. Fortunately, for people with this and more complex sexual dysfunctions, treatments are now available, both psychosocial and biological (medical). Advances in medical treatments, particularly for erectile dysfunction, have been dramatic in just the last few years. We look first at psychosocial treatments; then we examine the latest medical procedures.

■ Psychosocial Treatments

Among the many advances in our knowledge of sexual behavior, none was more dramatic than the publication in 1970 by William Masters and Virginia Johnson of *Human Sexual Inadequacy*. The procedures outlined in this book literally revolutionized sex therapy by providing a brief, direct, and reasonably successful therapeutic program for sexual dysfunctions. Underscoring again the common basis of most sexual dysfunctions, a similar approach to therapy is taken with all patients, male and female, with slight variations depending on the specific sexual problem (for example, premature ejaculation or orgasmic disorder). This intensive program involves a male and a female therapist to facilitate communication between the dysfunctional partners. (Masters and Johnson were the original male and female therapists.) Therapy is conducted daily over a 2-week period.

The actual program is quite straightforward. In addition to providing basic education about sexual functioning, altering deep-seated myths, and increasing communication, the clinicians' primary goal is to eliminate psychologically based performance anxiety (refer back to Figure 10.6). To accomplish this, Masters and Johnson introduced *sensate focus* and *nondemand pleasuring*. In this exercise, couples are instructed to refrain from intercourse or genital caressing and simply to explore and enjoy each other's body through touching, kissing, hugging, massaging, or similar kinds of behavior. In the first phase, nongenital pleasuring, breasts and genitals are excluded from the exercises. After successfully accomplishing this phase, the couple moves to genital pleasuring but with a ban on orgasm and intercourse and clear instructions to the man that achieving an erection is not the goal.

At this point, arousal should be reestablished and the couple should be ready to attempt intercourse. So as not to proceed too quickly, this stage is also broken down into parts. For example, a couple might be instructed to attempt the beginnings of penetration; that is, the depth of penetration and the time it lasts are only gradually built up, and both genital and nongenital pleasuring continue. Eventually, full intercourse and thrusting are accomplished. After this 2-week intensive program, recovery was reported by Masters and Johnson for the vast majority of more than 790 sexually dysfunctional patients, with some differences in the rate of recovery depending on the disorder. Close to 100% of individuals with premature ejaculation recovered, whereas the rate for more difficult cases of lifelong generalized erectile dysfunction was closer to 60%.

Specialty sexuality clinics based on the pioneering work of Masters and Johnson were established around the country to administer these new treatment techniques. Subsequent research revealed that many of the structural aspects of the program did not seem necessary. For example, one therapist seems to be as effective as two (LoPiccolo, Heiman, Hogan, & Roberts, 1985), and seeing patients once a week seems to be as effective as seeing them every day (Heiman & LoPiccolo, 1983a). It has also become clear in the succeeding decades that the results achieved by Masters and Johnson were better than those achieved in clinics around the world using similar procedures. Reasons for this are not entirely clear. One possibility is that because patients had to take at least 2 weeks off and fly to St. Louis to meet with Masters and Johnson, they were highly motivated.

Sex therapists have expanded on and modified these procedures over the years to take advantage of recent advances in knowledge (see, for example, Bancroft, 1997; Leiblum & Rosen, 2000; Wincze & Barlow, 1997; Wincze et al., in press). Results with sex therapy for erectile dysfunction indicate that as many as 60% to 70% of the cases show a positive treatment outcome for at least several years, although there may be some slipping after that

(Sarwer & Durlak, 1997; Segraves & Althof, 1998). For better treatment of specific sexual dysfunctions, sex therapists integrate specific procedures into the context of general sex therapy. For example, to treat premature ejaculation, most sex therapists use a procedure developed by Semans (1956), sometimes called the *squeeze* technique, in which the penis is stimulated, usually by the partner, to nearly full erection. At this point, the partner firmly squeezes the penis near the top where the head of the penis joins the shaft, which quickly reduces arousal. These steps are repeated until (for heterosexual partners) eventually the penis is briefly inserted in the vagina without thrusting. If arousal occurs too quickly, the penis is withdrawn and the squeeze technique is employed again. In this way, the man develops a sense of control over arousal and ejaculation. Reports of success with this approach over the past 20 years suggest that 60% to 90% of men benefit, but the success rates drop to about 25% after 3 years or more of follow-up (Polonsky, 2000; Segraves & Althof, 1998). Gary, the 31-year-old salesman, was treated with this method, and his wife was cooperative during the procedures. Brief marital therapy also persuaded Gary that his insecurity over his perception that his wife no longer found him attractive was unfounded. After treatment, he reduced his work hours somewhat, and the couple's marital and sexual relations improved.

Lifelong female orgasmic disorder may be treated with explicit training in masturbatory procedures. For example, Greta was still unable to achieve orgasm with manual stimulation by her husband, even after proceeding through the basic steps of sex therapy. At this point, following certain standardized treatment programs for this problem (see, for example, Heiman, 2000; Heiman & LoPiccolo, 1988), Greta and Will purchased a vibrator and Greta was taught to let go of her inhibitions by talking out loud about how she felt during sexual arousal, even shouting or screaming if she wanted to. In the context of appropriate genital pleasuring and disinhibition exercises, the vibrator brought on Greta's first orgasm. With practice and good communication, the couple eventually learned how to bring on Greta's orgasm with-

A therapist usually treats a dysfunction in one partner by seeing the couple together.

©Romilly Lockyer/Brand X Pictures/Picture Quest

out the vibrator. Although Will and Greta were both delighted with her progress, Will was concerned that Greta's screams during orgasm would attract the attention of the neighbors. When they planned a vacation at a lake, they were concerned about whether the cabin had electricity to power the vibrator in case they needed it. Summaries of results from a number of studies suggest 70% to 90% of women will benefit from treatment, and these gains are stable and even improve further over time (Heiman, 2000; Heiman & Meston, 1997; Segraves & Althof, 1998).

To treat vaginismus, the woman and, eventually, the partner gradually insert increasingly larger dilators at the woman's pace. After the woman (and then the partner) can insert the largest dilator, in a heterosexual couple, the woman gradually inserts the man's penis. These exercises are carried out in the context of genital and nongenital pleasuring so as to retain arousal. Close attention must be accorded to any increased fear and anxiety that may be associated with the process, which may trigger memories of early sexual abuse that may have contributed to the onset of the condition. These procedures are highly successful, with a large majority of women (80% to 100%) overcoming vaginismus in a relatively short period (Beck, 1993; Leiblum, 2000; Segraves & Althof, 1998; ter Kuile et al., 2007).

A variety of treatment procedures have also been developed for low sexual desire (see, for example, Pridal & LoPiccolo, 2000; Wincze & Barlow, 1997; Wincze & Carey, 2001). At the heart of these treatments are the standard reeducation and communication phases of traditional sex therapy with, possibly, the addition of masturbatory training and exposure to erotic material. Each case may require individual strategies. Remember Mrs. C., who was sexually abused by her cousin? Therapy involved helping the couple understand the impact of the repeated, unwanted sexual experiences in Mrs. C.'s past and to approach sex so that Mrs. C. was more comfortable with foreplay. She gradually lost the idea that once sex was started she had no control. She and her husband worked on starting and stopping sexual encounters. Cognitive restructuring was used to help Mrs. C. interpret her husband's amorousness in a positive rather than a skeptical light. In general, approximately 50% to 70% of individuals with low sexual desire benefit from sex therapy, at least initially (Hawton, 1995; Segraves & Althof, 1998).

■ Medical Treatments

A variety of pharmacological and surgical techniques have been developed in recent years to treat sexual dysfunction, almost all focusing on male erectile disorder. The drug Viagra, introduced in 1998, and similar drugs such as Levitra and Cialis, introduced subsequently, are the best known. We look at the four most popular procedures: oral medication, injection of vasoactive substances directly into the penis, surgery, and vacuum device therapy. Before we begin, note that it is important to combine any medical treatment with a comprehensive educational and sex therapy program to ensure maximum benefit.

In 1998, the drug sildenafil (trade name Viagra) was introduced for erectile dysfunction. Approval from the Food and Drug Administration occurred early in 1998, and results from several clinical trials suggested that between 50% and 80% of a large number of men benefit from this treatment (Conti, Pepine, &

Sweeney, 1999; Goldstein et al., 1998) in that erections become sufficient for intercourse, compared to approximately 30% who benefit from placebo. Results are similar with Cialis and Levitra (Carrier et al., 2005). However, as many as 30% may suffer severe headaches as a side effect, particularly at higher doses (Rosen, 2000; Virag, 1999), and reports of sexual satisfaction are not optimal. For example, Virag (1999) evaluated a large number of men treated with Viagra and found that 32% of the men were successful if success was defined as an erection sufficient to engage in intercourse and satisfaction of at least 7 on the 0-to-10 scale. Results were categorized as fair for 29% who reported adequate erection but satisfaction from 4 to 6, and unsatisfactory for 39% with inadequate erection and satisfaction rated as 0 to 3. Thus, erections were sufficiently firm for intercourse in 61% of the men, consistent with other studies, but only 32% rated the results as at least good, suggesting the need for, perhaps, additional drug or psychological treatment. If men are particularly anxious about sex, results are not as good with the drug (Rosen et al., 2006). To address this issue Bach, Barlow, and Wincze (2004) evaluated the addition of cognitive-behavioral treatment (CBT) to treatment with Viagra. Results were encouraging because couples reported greater satisfaction and increased sexual activity after combined drug and CBT, compared to a period when only drug was used.

There was also some hope that Viagra would be useful for dysfunction in postmenopausal women, but results were disappointing (Kaplan et al., 1999). Berman and colleagues (2003) reported some improvement from Viagra in postmenopausal women with female sexual arousal disorder, but only in those women with no diminishment in sexual desire.

For some time, testosterone (Schiavi, White, Mandeli, & Levine, 1997) has been used to treat erectile dysfunction. But although it is safe and has relatively few side effects, only negligible effects on erectile dysfunction have been reported (Mann et al., 1996). Some urologists teach patients to inject vasodilating drugs such as *papaverine* or *prostaglandin* directly into the penis when they want to have sexual intercourse. These drugs dilate the blood vessels, allowing blood to flow to the penis and thereby producing an erection within 15 minutes that can last from 1 to 4 hours (Kim & Lipshultz, 1997; Rosen, 2000; Segraves & Althof, 1998). Because this procedure is a bit painful (although not as much as you might think), a substantial number of men, usually 50% to 60%, stop using it after a short time. In one study, 50 of 100 patients discontinued papaverine for various reasons (Lakin, Montague, Vanderbrug Medendorp, Tesar, & Schover, 1990; Segraves & Althof, 1998). Side effects include bruising and, with repeated injections, the development of fibrosis nodules in the penis (Gregoire, 1992; Rosen, 2000). Although some patients have found papaverine helpful, it is not widely used, and scientists are attempting to develop more palatable ways to deliver the drug. A soft capsule that contains the drug, called MUSE, can be inserted directly into the urethra, but this is somewhat painful, is less effective than injections, and remains awkward and artificial enough to preclude wide acceptance (Delizonna, Wincze, Litz, Brown, & Barlow, 2001). On the other hand, Heiman and colleagues (2006) recently demonstrated that topical application of this drug externally to women's genitalia produced vasocongestion and arousal in postmenopausal woman compared to placebo in the laboratory.

Studies must now determine whether this treatment is effective outside of the laboratory.

Insertion of *penile prostheses* or implants has been a surgical option for almost 100 years; only recently are they good enough to approximate normal sexual functioning. One procedure involves implanting a semirigid silicone rod that can be bent by the male into correct position for intercourse and maneuvered out of the way at other times. In a more popular procedure, the male squeezes a small pump that is surgically implanted into the scrotum, forcing fluid into an inflatable cylinder and thus producing an erection. The newest model of penile prosthetic device is an inflatable rod that contains the pumping device, which is more convenient than having the pump outside the rod. However, surgical implants fall short of restoring presurgical sexual functioning or assuring satisfaction in most patients (Gregoire, 1992; Kim & Lipshultz, 1997); they are now generally used only if other approaches don't work. On the other hand, this procedure has proved useful for men who must have a cancerous prostate removed, which most often causes erectile dysfunction, although newer "nerve-sparing" surgeries lessen the effect to some extent (Ramsawh, Morgentaler, Covino, Barlow, & DeWolf, 2005). Vascular surgery to correct arterial or venous malfunctions has also been attempted (see, for example, Bennett, 1988). Although the initial results are often successful, follow-up evaluations reveal a high failure rate.

Another approach is *vacuum device therapy,* which works by creating a vacuum in a cylinder placed over the penis. The vacuum draws blood into the penis, which is then trapped by a specially designed ring placed around the base of the penis. Although using the vacuum device is rather awkward, between 70% and 100% of users report satisfactory erections, particularly if psychological sex therapy is ineffective (Segraves & Althof, 1998; Witherington, 1988). The procedure is also less intrusive than surgery or injections, but it remains awkward and artificial enough to preclude wide acceptance (Delizonna et al., 2001).

■ Summary

Treatment programs, both psychosocial and medical, offer hope to most people who suffer from sexual dysfunctions. Unfortunately, such programs are not readily available in many locations because few health and mental health professionals are trained to apply them, although the availability of drugs for male erectile dysfunction is widespread. Psychological treatment of sexual arousal disorders requires further improvement, and treatments for low sexual desire are largely untested. New medical developments appear yearly, but most are still intrusive and clumsy, although drugs such as Viagra and Levitra exhibit some success for erectile dysfunction and many more such drugs are in development.

Unfortunately, most health professionals tend to ignore the issue of sexuality in the aging. Along with the usual emphasis on communication, education, and sensate focus, appropriate lubricants for women and a discussion of methods to maximize the erectile response in men should be a part of any sexual counseling for older couples. More important, even with reduced physical capabilities, continued sexual relations, not necessarily including intercourse, should be an enjoyable and important part of an aging couple's relationship. Further research and development in the treatment of sexual dysfunction must address all these issues. Nevertheless, the overwhelming consensus is that a combination of psychological and drug treatment, when indicated, will continue to be the treatment strategy of choice.

CONCEPT CHECK 10.3

Determine whether the following statements are true (T) or false (F) in regard to the causes and treatments of sexual dysfunctions.

1. ___ Many physical and medical conditions and their treatments (for example, prescription medications) contribute to sexual dysfunction; however, many doctors are unaware of the connection.
2. ___ Anxiety always decreases or even eradicates sexual arousal.
3. ___ Sexual dysfunctions can result from a growing dislike for a partner, traumatic sexual events, or childhood lessons about the negative consequences of sexual behavior.
4. ___ A simple, effective treatment for many disorders is education.
5. ___ All sexual dysfunctions are treated with the same psychosocial technique.
6. ___ Most surgical and pharmacological treatments of recent years have focused on male erectile disorder.

PARAPHILIA: CLINICAL DESCRIPTIONS

If you are like most people, your sexual interest is directed to other physically mature adults (or late adolescents), all of whom are capable of freely offering or withholding their consent. But what if you are sexually attracted to something or somebody other than another adult, such as animals (particularly horses and dogs) (Williams & Weinberg, 2003) or a vacuum cleaner? (Yes, it does happen!) Or what if your only means of obtaining sexual

An inflatable penile implant may be used for men with inadequate sexual functioning.

©Larry Mulvehill/The Image Works

©Robert Brenner/PhotoEdit

A crowded subway car is a typical setting for frotteuristic activity, in which a person takes advantage of forced physical contact with strangers to become aroused.

satisfaction is to commit a brutal murder? Such patterns of sexual arousal and countless others exist in a large number of individuals, causing untold human suffering both for them and, if their behavior involves other people, for their victims. As noted in the beginning of the chapter, these disorders of sexual arousal are called **paraphilias.**

Over the years, we have assessed and treated a large number of these individuals, ranging from the slightly eccentric and sometimes pitiful case to some of the most dangerous killer–rapists encountered anywhere. We begin by describing briefly the major types of paraphilia, using in all instances cases from our own files. As with sexual dysfunctions, it is unusual for an individual to have just one paraphilic pattern of sexual arousal. Many of our cases may present with two, three, or more patterns, although one is usually dominant (Abel et al., 1987; Abel, Becker, Cunningham-Rathner, Mittelman, & Rouleau, 1988; Brownell, Hayes, & Barlow, 1977). Furthermore, it is not uncommon for individuals with paraphilia to also suffer from comorbid mood, anxiety, and substance abuse disorders (Raymond, Coleman, Ohlerking, Christenson, & Miner, 1999). Although paraphilias are not widely prevalent and estimates of their frequency are hard to come by,

some disorders, such as transvestic fetishism, seem relatively common (Bancroft, 1989; Mason, 1997). You may have been the victim of **frotteurism** in a large city, typically on a crowded subway or bus. (We mean really crowded, with people packed in like sardines.) In this situation, women have been known to experience more than the usual jostling and pushing from behind. What they discover, much to their horror, is a male with a frotteuristic arousal pattern rubbing against them until he is stimulated to the point of ejaculation. Because the victims cannot escape easily, the frotteuristic act is usually successful.

Fetishism

In **fetishism,** a person is sexually attracted to nonliving objects. There are almost as many types of fetishes as there are objects, although women's undergarments and shoes are popular. Fetishistic arousal is associated with two classes of objects or activities: (1) an inanimate object or (2) a source of specific tactile stimulation, such as rubber, particularly clothing made out of rubber. Shiny black plastic is also used (Bancroft, 1989; Junginger, 1997). Most of the person's sexual fantasies, urges, and desires focus on this object. A third source of attraction (sometimes called *partialism*) is a part of the body, such as the foot, buttocks, or hair, but this attraction is no longer technically classified as a fetish because distinguishing it from more normal patterns of arousal is often difficult.

In one U.S. city for several months, bras hung out on a woman's backyard clothesline disappeared. The women in the neighborhood soon began talking to each other and discovered that bras were missing from every clothesline for blocks around. A police stakeout caught the perpetrator, who turned out to have a strong fetish for brassieres. It is relatively common for a urologist to be called to the emergency room to remove surgically a long thin object, like a pencil or the arm of an eyeglass frame, from the urethra. Men who insert such objects think that partially blocking the urethra in this way can increase the in-

DSM-IV-TR

DSM TABLE 10.8 Criteria for Frotteurism

A. Over a period of at least 6 months, recurrent, intense sexually arousing fantasies, sexual urges, or behaviors involving touching and rubbing against a nonconsenting person.
B. The person has acted on these sexual urges, or the sexual urges or fantasies cause marked distress or interpersonal difficulty.

Source: Reprinted, with permission, from American Psychiatric Association. (2000). *Diagnostic and statistical manual of mental disorders* (4th ed., text revision). Washington, DC: Author, © 2000 American Psychiatric Association.

DSM-IV-TR

DSM TABLE 10.9 Criteria for Fetishism

A. Over a period of at least 6 months, recurrent, intense sexually arousing fantasies, sexual urges, or behaviors involving the use of nonliving objects (e.g., female undergarments).
B. The fantasies, sexual urges, or behaviors cause clinically significant distress or impairment in social, occupational, or other important areas of functioning.
C. The fetish objects are not limited to articles of female clothing used in cross-dressing (as in transvestic fetishism) or devices designed for the purpose of tactile genital stimulation (e.g., a vibrator).

Source: Reprinted, with permission, from American Psychiatric Association. (2000). *Diagnostic and statistical manual of mental disorders* (4th ed., text revision). Washington, DC: Author, © 2000 American Psychiatric Association.

tensity of ejaculation during masturbation. However, if the entire object slips into the penis, major medical intervention is required.

Voyeurism and Exhibitionism

Voyeurism is the practice of observing, to become aroused, an unsuspecting individual undressing or naked. **Exhibitionism,** by contrast, is achieving sexual arousal and gratification by exposing genitals to unsuspecting strangers. Consider the case of Robert.

ROBERT: Outside the Curtains

Robert, a 31-year-old, married, blue-collar worker, reported that he first started "peeping" into windows when he was 14. He rode around the neighborhood on his bike at night, and when he spotted a female through a window he stopped and stared. During one of these episodes, he felt the first pangs of sexual arousal. Eventually he began masturbating while watching, thereby exposing his genitals, although out of sight. When he was older, he drove around until he spotted some prepubescent girls. He parked his car near them, unzipped his fly, called them over, and attempted to carry on a nonsexual conversation. Later he was sometimes able to talk a girl into mutual masturbation and *fellatio,* or oral stimulation of the penis. Although he was arrested several times, paradoxically, the threat of arrest increased his arousal (Barlow & Wincze, 1980).

Remember that anxiety actually increases arousal under some circumstances. Many voyeurs just don't get the same satisfaction from attending readily available strip shows at a local bar. Although paraphilias may occur separately, it is not unusual to find them co-occurring. Exhibitionism is often associated with lower

---

DSM-IV-TR

DSM TABLE 10.10 Criteria for Voyeurism and Exhibitionism

Voyeurism
A. Over a period of at least 6 months, recurrent, intense sexually arousing fantasies, sexual urges, or behaviors involving the act of observing an unsuspecting person who is naked, in the process of disrobing, or engaging in sexual activity.
B. The person has acted on these sexual urges, or the sexual urges or fantasies cause marked distress or interpersonal difficulty.
Exhibitionism
A. Over a period of at least 6 months, recurrent, intense sexually arousing fantasies, sexual urges, or behaviors involving the exposure of one's genitals to an unsuspecting stranger.
B. The person has acted on these sexual urges, or the sexual urges or fantasies cause marked distress or interpersonal difficulty.

levels of education, but not always. Note again that the thrilling element of risk is an important part of exhibitionism.

The Lawyer Who Needed the Bus

Several years ago, a distinguished lawyer reported that he needed help and that his career was on the line. An intelligent, good-looking single man, he noted, without bragging, that he could have sex with any number of beautiful women in the course of his law practice. However, the only way he could become aroused was to leave his office, go down to the bus stop, ride around the city until a reasonably attractive young woman got on, expose himself just before the next stop, and then run off the bus, often with people chasing after him. To achieve maximal arousal, the bus could not be full or empty; there had to be just a few people sitting on the bus, and the woman getting on had to be the right age. Sometimes hours would pass before these circumstances lined up correctly. The lawyer observed that if he was not fired for exhibitionism he would be fired for all the time he was missing from work. On several occasions he had requested a girlfriend to role-play sitting on a bus in his apartment. Although he exposed himself to her, he could not achieve sexual arousal and gratification because the activity just wasn't exciting.

In a recent random sample of 2,450 adults in Sweden, 31% reported at least one incident of being sexually aroused by exposing their genitals to a stranger and 7.7% reported at least one incident of being sexually aroused by spying on others having sex (Langstrom & Seto, 2006). To meet diagnosis for exhibitionism, the behavior must occur repeatedly and be compulsive or out of control.

Transvestic Fetishism

In **transvestic fetishism,** sexual arousal is strongly associated with the act of dressing in clothes of the opposite sex, or cross-dressing. Consider the case of Mr. M.

MR. M.: Strong Man in a Dress

Mr. M., a 31-year-old married police officer, came to our clinic seeking treatment for uncontrollable urges to dress in women's clothing and appear in public. He had been doing this for 16 years and had been discharged from the Marine Corps for cross-dressing. Since then, he had risked public disclosure on several occasions. Mr. M.'s wife had threatened to divorce him because of the cross-dressing, yet she often purchased women's clothing for him and was "compassionate" while he wore them.

DSM TABLE 10.11 Criteria for Transvestic Fetishism

A. Over a period of at least 6 months, in a heterosexual male, recurrent, intense sexually arousing fantasies, sexual urges, or behaviors involving cross-dressing.

B. The fantasies, sexual urges, or behaviors cause clinically significant distress or impairment in social, occupational, or other important areas of functioning.

Specify if:

With gender dysphoria: If the person has persistent discomfort with gender role or identity

Source: Reprinted, with permission, from American Psychiatric Association. (2000). *Diagnostic and statistical manual of mental disorders* (4th ed., text revision). Washington, DC: Author, © 2000 American Psychiatric Association.

DSM TABLE 10.12 Criteria for Sexual Sadism and Sexual Masochism

Sexual Sadism

A. Over a period of at least 6 months, recurrent, intense sexually arousing fantasies, sexual urges, or behaviors involving acts (real, not simulated) in which the psychological or physical suffering (including humiliation) of the victim is sexually exciting to the person.

B. The person has acted on these sexual urges with a nonconsenting person, or the sexual urges or fantasies cause marked distress or interpersonal difficulty.

Sexual Masochism

A. Over a period of at least 6 months, recurrent, intense sexually arousing fantasies, sexual urges, or behaviors involving the act (real, not simulated) of being humiliated, beaten, bound, or otherwise made to suffer.

B. The fantasies, sexual urges, or behaviors cause clinically significant distress or impairment in social, occupational, or other important areas of functioning.

Source: Reprinted, with permission, from American Psychiatric Association. (2000). *Diagnostic and statistical manual of mental disorders* (4th ed., text revision). Washington, DC: Author, © 2000 American Psychiatric Association.

Note that Mr. M. was in the Marine Corps before he joined the police force. It is not unusual for males who are strongly inclined to dress in female clothes to compensate by associating with so-called macho organizations. Some of our cross-dressing patients have been associated with various paramilitary organizations. Nevertheless, most individuals with this disorder do not seem to display any compensatory behaviors. The same survey in Sweden mentioned earlier found 2.8% of men and 0.4% of women reported at least one episode of transvestic fetishism (Langstrom & Zucker, 2005).

Interestingly, the wives of many men who cross-dress have accepted their husbands' behavior and can be quite supportive if it is a private matter between them. Docter and Prince (1997) reported that 60% of more than 1,000 cases of transvestic fetishism were married at the time of the survey. Some people, both married and single, join cross-dressing clubs that meet periodically or subscribe to newsletters devoted to the topic. Research suggests that transvestic fetishism is indistinguishable from other fetishes in most respects (Freund, Seto, & Kuban, 1996).

Sexual Sadism and Sexual Masochism

Both **sexual sadism** and **sexual masochism** are associated with either inflicting pain or humiliation (sadism) or suffering pain or humiliation (masochism). Although Mr. M. was extremely concerned about his cross-dressing, he was also disturbed by another problem. To maximize his sexual pleasure during intercourse with his wife, he had her wear a collar and leash, tied her to the bed, and handcuffed her. He sometimes tied himself with ropes, chains, handcuffs, and wires, all while he was cross-dressed. Mr. M. was concerned he might injure himself seriously. As a member of the police force, he had heard of cases and even investigated one himself in which an individual was found dead, tightly and completely bound in harnesses, handcuffs, and ropes. In many such cases, something goes wrong and the individual accidentally hangs himself, an event that should be distinguished from the closely related condition called *hypoxiphilia,* which involves self-strangulation to reduce the flow of oxygen to the brain and enhance the sensation of orgasm. It may seem paradoxical that someone has to either inflict or receive pain to become sexually aroused, but these types of cases are not uncommon. On many occasions, the behaviors themselves are quite mild and harmless, but they can become dangerous and costly. It was not unusual that Mr. M. presented with three patterns of deviant arousal—in his case, sexual masochism, sexual sadism, and transvestic fetishism.

▪ Sadistic Rape

After murder, rape is the most devastating assault one person can make on another. It is not classified as a paraphilia because most instances of rape are better characterized as an assault by a male (or, quite rarely, a female) whose patterns of sexual arousal are not paraphilic. Instead, many rapists meet criteria for antisocial personality disorder (see Chapter 12) and may engage in a variety of antisocial and aggressive acts (McCabe & Wauchope, 2005). Many rapes could be described as opportunistic, in that an aggressive or antisocial individual with a marked lack of empathy and disregard for inflicting pain on others (Bernat, Calhoun, & Adams, 1999) spontaneously took advantage of a vulnerable and unsuspecting woman. These unplanned assaults often occur during robberies or other criminal events. Rapes can also be motivated by anger and vindictiveness against specific women and may have been planned in advance (Hucker, 1997; Knight and Prentky, 1990; McCabe & Wauchope, 2005).

A number of years ago, we determined in our sexuality clinic that certain rapists do fit definitions of paraphilia closely and could probably better be described as sadists, a finding that has since been confirmed (McCabe & Wauchope, 2005). We constructed two audiotapes on which were described (1) mutually enjoyable sexual intercourse and (2) sexual intercourse involving force on the part of the male (rape). Each tape was played twice for selected listeners. Response differences between rapists and nonrapists are presented in ▪ Figure 10.7 (Abel, Barlow, Blanchard, & Guild, 1977). As you can see, the nonrapists became sexually

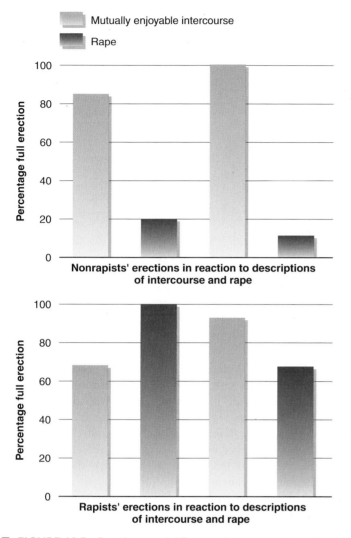

■ **FIGURE 10.7** Erectile arousal differences between rapists and non-rapists. Nonrapists became aroused to descriptions of mutually enjoyable intercourse but not to descriptions of rape; rapists experienced significant arousal to both types of descriptions. (Reprinted, with permission, from Abel, G. G., Barlow, D. H., Blanchard, E. B., & Guild, D., 1977. The components of rapists' sexual arousal. *Archives of General Psychiatry, 34,* 895–903, © 1977 American Medical Association.)

aroused to descriptions of mutually consenting intercourse but not to those involving force. Rapists, however, became aroused to both types of descriptions.

Among the rapists we were evaluating, a subgroup seemed to be particularly aroused when force and acts of cruelty were involved. To assess this reaction more completely, we put together a third audiotape consisting of aggression and assault without any sexual content. A number of individuals displayed strong sexual arousal to nonsexual aggressive themes, as well as to rape, and little or no arousal to mutually enjoyable intercourse, as depicted by the data from one individual in ■ Figure 10.8. This man was the most brutal rapist we have ever encountered. By his own report, he had raped more than 100 times. His last victim spent 2 weeks in the hospital recovering from various injuries. He would bite his victim's breasts, burn her with cigarettes, beat her with belts and switches, and pull out her pubic hair while shoving objects in her vagina. Although some evidence indicated he had

Murderer Jeffrey Dahmer obtained sexual gratification from acts of sadism and cannibalism. (In prison, he was killed by fellow inmates.)

killed at least three of his victims, it was not sufficient to convict him. Nevertheless, he was convicted of multiple assaults and rapes and was about to begin a life sentence in a closely guarded area of the maximum-security state prison. Realizing his behavior was hopelessly out of control, he was eager to get there. He reported that all his waking hours were spent ruminating uncontrollably on

In 2002, the Catholic Church in the United States was forced to acknowledge a series of cover-ups involving pedophilia by a number of clergy that went back several decades.

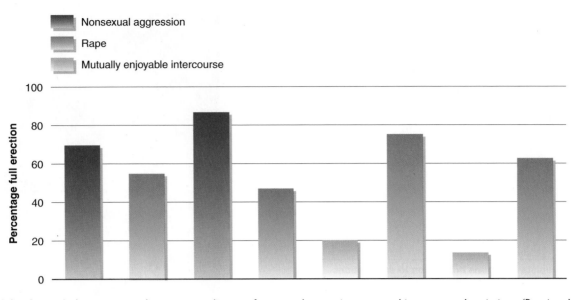

■ **FIGURE 10.8** One sadist's erections on listening to audiotape of nonsexual aggression, rape, and intercourse descriptions. (Reprinted, with permission, from Abel, G. G., Barlow, D. H., Blanchard, E. B., & Guild, D., 1977. The components of rapists' sexual arousal. *Archives of General Psychiatry, 34,* 895–903, © 1977 American Medical Association.)

sadistic fantasies. He knew he was going to spend the rest of his life in prison, probably in solitary confinement, but hoped there was something we could do to relieve him of his obsession. By any definition, this man met criteria for sexual sadism.

Pedophilia and Incest

Perhaps the most tragic sexual deviance is a sexual attraction to children (or young adolescents), called **pedophilia.** People around the world have become more aware of this problem following the well-publicized scandal in the Catholic Church, where priests,

many of whom undoubtedly met criteria for pedophilia, abused children repeatedly, only to be transferred to another church where they would do it again. Individuals with this pattern of arousal may be attracted to male children, female children, or both. In one survey, as many as 12% of men and 17% of women reported being touched inappropriately by adults when they were children, while another survey estimated that the number of sexually abused children rose 125% in the 1990s to more than 330,000 children in the United States (Fagan, Wise, Schmidt, & Berlin, 2002). Approximately 90% of abusers are male, and 10% are female (Fagan et al., 2002). Child pornography investigations have made much news lately, and individuals convicted of downloading child pornography often defend themselves by pointing out that they were "just looking" and are not pedophiles. But now an important study indicates that being charged with a child pornography offense is one of the best diagnostic indications of pedophilia (Seto, Cantor, & Blanchard, 2006).

If the children are the person's relatives, the pedophilia takes the form of **incest.** Although pedophilia and incest have much in common, victims of pedophilia tend to be young children and victims of incest tend to be girls beginning to mature physically

---

DSM-IV-TR

DSM TABLE 10.13 Criteria for Pedophilia

A. Over a period of at least 6 months, recurrent, intense sexually arousing fantasies, sexual urges, or behaviors involving sexual activity with a prepubescent child or children (generally age 13 years or younger).
B. The person has acted on these sexual urges, or the sexual urges or fantasies cause marked distress or interpersonal difficulty.
C. The person is at least age 16 years and at least 5 years older than the child or children in criterion A.
Note: Do not include an individual in late adolescence involved in an ongoing sexual relationship with a 12- or 13-year-old.
Specify if:
Sexually attracted to males
Sexually attracted to females
Sexually attracted to both
Specify if:
Limited to incest
Specify type:
Exclusive type (attracted only to children)
Nonexclusive type

Source: Reprinted, with permission, from American Psychiatric Association. (2000). *Diagnostic and statistical manual of mental disorders* (4th ed., text revision). Washington, DC: Author, © 2000 American Psychiatric Association.

DSM-IV-TR

DSM TABLE 10.14 Criteria for Paraphilia Not Otherwise Specified

This category is included for coding paraphilias that do not meet the criteria for any of the specific categories. Examples include, but are not limited to, telephone scatologia (obscene phone calls), necrophilia (corpses), partialism (exclusive focus on part of body), zoophilia (animals), coprophilia (feces), klismaphilia (enemas), and urophilia (urine).

Source: Reprinted, with permission, from American Psychiatric Association. (2000). *Diagnostic and statistical manual of mental disorders* (4th ed., text revision). Washington, DC: Author, © 2000 American Psychiatric Association.

(Rice & Harris, 2002). Marshall, Barbaree, and Christophe (1986) and Marshall (1997) demonstrated by using penile strain gauge measures that incestuous males are, in general, more aroused by adult women than are males with pedophilia, who tend to focus exclusively on children. Thus, incestuous relations may have more to do with availability and interpersonal issues ongoing in the family than pedophilia, as in the case of Tony.

TONY: More and Less a Father

Tony, a 52-year-old married television repairman, came in depressed. About 10 years earlier he had begun sexual activity with his 12-year-old daughter. Light kissing and some fondling gradually escalated to heavy petting and, finally, mutual masturbation. When his daughter was 16 years old, his wife discovered the ongoing incestuous relationship. She separated from her husband and eventually divorced him, taking her daughter with her. Soon, Tony remarried. Just before his initial visit to our clinic, Tony visited his daughter, then 22 years old, who was living alone in a different city. They had not seen each other for 5 years. A second visit, shortly after the first, led to a recurrence of the incestuous behavior. At this point, Tony became extremely depressed and told his new wife the whole story. She contacted our clinic with his full cooperation while his daughter sought treatment in her own city.

We return to the case of Tony later, but several features are worth noting. First, Tony loved his daughter and was bitterly disappointed and depressed over his behavior. Occasionally, a child molester is abusive and aggressive, sometimes killing the victims; in these cases, the disorder is often both sexual sadism and pedophilia. But most child molesters are *not* physically abusive. Rarely is a child physically forced or injured. From the molester's perspective, no harm is done because there is no physical force or threats. Child molesters often rationalize their behavior as "loving" the child or teaching the child useful lessons about sexuality. The child molester almost never considers the psychological damage the victim suffers, yet these interactions often destroy the child's trust and ability to share intimacy. Child molesters rarely gauge their power over the children, who may participate in the molestation without protest yet be frightened and unwilling. Often children feel responsible for the abuse because no outward force or threat was used by the adult, and only after the abused children grow up are they able to understand they were powerless to protect themselves and not responsible for what was done to them.

Paraphilia in Women

Paraphilia is seldom seen in women and was thought to be absent in women for many years, with the possible exception of sadomasochistic practices. But in recent years, several reports have appeared describing individual cases or small series of cases. Now estimates suggest that approximately 5% to 10% of all sexual offenders are women (Wiegel, 2007). For example, Federoff, Fishell, and Federoff (1999) have reported 12 cases of women with paraphilia seen in their clinic. Although some women had more than one paraphilia, 5 of the 12 presented with pedophilia, 4 presented with exhibitionism, and 3 presented with sadomasochistic tendencies.

To take several examples, one heterosexual woman had been convicted of sexually molesting an unrelated 9-year-old boy while she was babysitting. It seems she had touched the boy's penis and asked him to masturbate in front of her while she watched religious programs on television. It is not unusual for individuals with paraphilia to rationalize their behavior by engaging in some other practices that they consider to be morally correct or uplifting at the same time. Yet another woman came to treatment because of her "uncontrollable" rituals of undressing in front of her apartment window and masturbating approximately five times a month. In addition she would, occasionally, drive her truck through the neighborhood, where she would attempt to befriend cats and dogs by offering them food. She would then place honey or other food substances on her genital area so that the animals would lick her. As with most paraphilias, the woman herself was horrified by this activity and was seeking treatment to eliminate it, although she found it highly sexually arousing. Wiegel (2007) is in the process of analyzing information from more than 175 females who have admitted sexually abusing children or adolescents.

Causes of Paraphilia

Although no substitute for scientific inquiry, case histories often provide hypotheses that can then be tested by controlled scientific observations. Let's return to the cases of Robert and Tony to see if their histories contain any clues.

ROBERT: Revenge on Repression

Robert (who sought help for exhibitionism) was raised by a stern authoritarian father and a passive mother in a small Texas town. His father, who was a firm believer in old-time religion, often preached the evils of sexual intercourse to his family. Robert learned little about sex from his father except that it was bad, so he suppressed any emerging heterosexual urges and fantasies and as an adolescent felt uneasy around girls his own age. By accident, he discovered a private source of sexual gratification: staring at attractive and unsuspecting females through the window. This led to his first masturbatory experience.

Robert reported in retrospect that being arrested was not so bad because it disgraced his father, which was his only way of getting back at him. The courts treated him lightly (which is not unusual), and his father was publicly humiliated, forcing the family to move from their small Texas town (Barlow & Wincze, 1980).

TONY: Trained Too Young

Tony, who sought help because of an incestuous relationship with his daughter, reported an early sexual history that contained a number of interesting events. Although he was brought up in a reasonably loving and outwardly normal Catholic family, he had an uncle who did not fit the family pattern. When he was 9 or 10, Tony was encouraged by his uncle to observe a game of strip poker that the uncle was playing with a neighbor's wife. During this period, he also observed his uncle fondling a waitress at a drive-in restaurant and shortly thereafter was instructed by his uncle to fondle his young female cousin. Thus, he had an early model for mutual fondling and masturbation and obtained some pleasure from interacting in this way with young girls. Although the uncle never touched Tony, his behavior was clearly abusive. When Tony was about 13, he engaged in mutual manipulation with a sister and her girlfriend, which he remembers as pleasurable. Later, when Tony was 18, a brother-in-law took him to a prostitute and he first experienced sexual intercourse. He remembered this visit as unsatisfactory because, on that and subsequent visits to prostitutes, he ejaculated prematurely—a sharp contrast to his early experience with young girls. Other experiences with adult women were also unsatisfactory. When he joined the service and was sent overseas, he sought out prostitutes who were often as young as 12.

These cases remind us that deviant patterns of sexual arousal often occur in the context of other sexual and social problems. Undesired kinds of arousal may be associated with deficiencies in levels of "desired" arousal with consensual adults; this was certainly true for both Tony and Robert, whose sexual relationships with adults were incomplete. In many cases, an inability to develop adequate social relations with the appropriate people for sexual relationships seems to be associated with a developing of inappropriate sexual outlets (Barlow & Wincze, 1980; Marshall, 1997). However, many people with deficient sexual and social skills do not develop deviant patterns of arousal.

Early experience seems to have an effect that may be quite accidental. Tony's early sexual experiences just happened to be of the type he later found sexually arousing. Many pedophiles also report being abused themselves as children, which turns out to be a strong predictor of later sexual abuse by the victim (Fagan et al., 2002). Robert's first erotic experience occurred while he was "peeping." But many of us do not find our early experiences reflected in our sexual patterns.

Another factor may be the nature of the person's early sexual fantasies. For example, Rachman and Hodgson (1968; see also Bancroft, 1989) demonstrated that sexual arousal could become associated with a neutral object—a boot, for example—if the boot was repeatedly presented while the individual was sexually aroused. One of the most powerful engines for the development of unwanted arousal may be early sexual fantasies that are repeatedly reinforced through the strong sexual pleasure associated with

masturbation. Before a pedophile or sadist ever acts on his behavior, he may fantasize about it thousands of times while masturbating. Expressed as a clinical or operant-conditioning paradigm, this is another example of a learning process in which a behavior (sexual arousal to a specific object or activity) is repeatedly reinforced through association with a pleasurable consequence (orgasm). This mechanism may explain why paraphilias are almost exclusively male disorders. The basic differences in frequency of masturbation between men and women that exist across cultures may contribute to the differential development of paraphilias. As you have seen, on rare occasions, cases of women with paraphilia do turn up (Federoff et al., 1999; Hunter & Mathews, 1997; Stoller, 1982), and a comprehensive national study of 175 female child sexual abusers is under way (Wiegel, 2007).

However, if early experiences contribute strongly to later sexual arousal patterns, then what about the Sambia males who practice exclusive homosexual behavior during childhood and early adolescence and yet are exclusively heterosexual as adults? In such cohesive societies, the social demands or "scripts" for sexual interactions are stronger and more rigid than in our culture and thus may override the effects of early experiences (Baldwin & Baldwin, 1989).

In addition, therapists and sex researchers who work with paraphilics have observed what seems to be an incredibly strong sex drive. It is not uncommon for some paraphilics to masturbate three or four times a day. In one case seen in our clinic, a sadistic

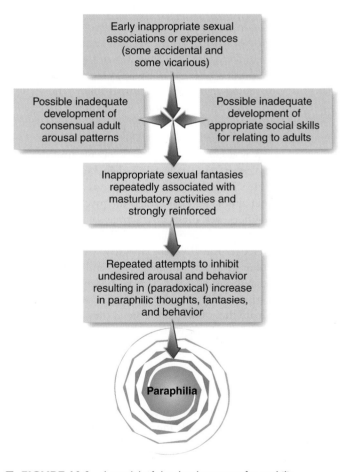

 **FIGURE 10.9** A model of the development of paraphilia.

rapist masturbated approximately every half hour all day long, just as often as it was physiologically possible. We have speculated elsewhere that activity this consuming may be related to the obsessional processes of obsessive-compulsive disorder (Barlow, 2002). In both instances, the very act of trying to suppress unwanted, emotionally charged thoughts and fantasies seems to have the paradoxical effect of *increasing* their frequency and intensity (see Chapter 5). This process is also ongoing in eating disorders and addictions, when attempts to restrict strong addictive cravings lead to uncontrollable increases in the undesired behaviors. Psychopathologists are becoming interested in the phenomenon of weak inhibitory control across these disorders, which may indicate a weak biologically based behavioral inhibition system (BIS) in the brain (Fowles, 1993; Kafka, 1997) that might repress serotonergic functioning. (You may remember from Chapter 5 that the BIS is a brain circuit associated with anxiety and inhibition.)

The model shown in ■ Figure 10.9 incorporates the factors thought to contribute to the development of paraphilia. Nevertheless, all speculations, including the hypotheses we have described, have little scientific support at this time. For example, this model does not include the biological dimension. Excess arousal in paraphilics could be biologically based. Before we can make any steadfast conclusions here, more research is needed.

ASSESSING AND TREATING PARAPHILIA

In recent years, we have developed sophisticated methods for assessing specific patterns of sexual arousal (Maletzky, 1998). This development is important in studying paraphilia because sometimes even the individual presenting with the problem is not fully aware of what caused arousal. An individual once came in complaining of uncontrollable arousal to open-toed white sandals worn by women. He noted that he was irresistibly drawn to any woman wearing such sandals and would follow her for miles. These urges occupied much of his summer. Subsequent assessment revealed that the sandal itself had no erotic value for this individual; rather, he had a strong sexual attraction to women's feet, particularly moving in a certain way.

Using the model of paraphilia described previously, we assess each patient not only for the presence of deviant arousal but also for levels of appropriate arousal to adults, for social skills, and for the ability to form relationships. Tony had no problems with social skills: He was 52 years old, reasonably happily married, and generally compatible with his second wife. His major difficulty was his continuing strong, incestuous attraction to his daughter. Nevertheless, he loved his daughter and wished strongly to interact in a normal fatherly way with her.

Psychological Treatment

A number of treatment procedures are available for decreasing unwanted arousal. Most are behavior therapy procedures directed at changing the associations and context from arousing and pleasurable to neutral. One procedure, carried out entirely in the imagination of the patient, called **covert sensitization,** was first described by Joseph Cautela (1967; see also Barlow, 1993). In this treatment, sexually arousing images are associated in the imagination with some reasons why the behavior is harmful or dangerous. The patient knows about these reasons, but the immediate pleasure and strong reinforcement the sexual activity provides is enough to overcome any thoughts of possible harm or danger that might arise in the future. This process is what happens in much unwanted addictive behavior, where the short-term pleasure outweighs the long-term harm, including bulimia.

In imagination, harmful or dangerous consequences can be associated quite directly with the unwanted behavior and arousal in a powerful and emotionally meaningful way. One of the most powerful negative aspects of Tony's behavior was his embarrassment over the thought of being discovered by his current wife, other family members, or, most important, the family priest. Therefore, he was guided through the fantasy described here.

TONY: Imagining the Worst

You are alone with your daughter in your trailer. You realize that you want to caress her breasts. So you put your arm around her, slip your hand inside her blouse, and begin to caress her breasts. Unexpectedly the door to the trailer opens and in walks your wife with Father X. Your daughter immediately jumps up and runs out the door. Your wife follows her. You are left alone with Father X. He is looking at you as if waiting for an explanation of what he has just seen. Seconds pass, but they seem like hours. You know what Father X must be thinking as he stands there staring at you. You are embarrassed and want to say something, but you can't seem to find the right words. You realize that Father X can no longer respect you as he once did. Father X finally says, "I don't understand this; this is not like you." You both begin to cry. You realize that you may have lost the love and respect of both Father X and your wife, who are important to you. Father X asks, "Do you realize what this has done to your daughter?" You think about this and you hear your daughter crying; she is hysterical. You want to run, but you can't. You are miserable and disgusted with yourself. You don't know if you will ever regain the love and respect of your wife and Father X.

(Reproduced, with permission of the authors and publisher, from Harbert, T. L., Barlow, D. H., Hersen, M., & Austin, J. B., 1974. Measurement and modification of incestuous behavior: A case study. *Psychological Reports, 34,* 79–86, © 1974 Psychological Reports.)

During six or eight sessions, the therapist narrates such scenes dramatically, and the patient is then instructed to imagine them daily until all arousal disappears. The results of Tony's treatment are presented in ■ Figure 10.10. "Card-sort scores" are a measure of how much Tony wanted sexual interactions with his daughter in comparison with his wish for nonsexual fatherly interactions. His incestuous arousal was largely eliminated after 3 to 4 weeks, but the treatment did not affect his desire to interact with his daugh-

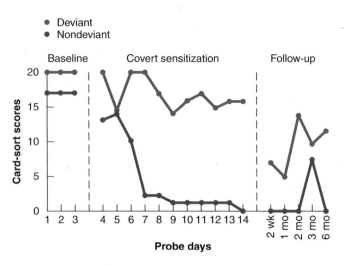

● Deviant
● Nondeviant

■ FIGURE 10.10 Ratings of Tony's incestuous urges (deviant) and desire for normal interactions with his daughter (nondeviant) during covert sensitization treatment. (Reproduced, with permission, from Harbert, T. L., Barlow, D. H., Hersen, M., & Austin, J. B., 1974. Measurement and modification of incestuous behavior: A case study. *Psychological Reports, 34,* 79–86, © 1974 Psychological Reports.)

ter in a healthier manner. These results were confirmed by psychophysiological measurement of his arousal response. A return of some arousal at a 3-month follow-up prompted us to ask Tony if anything unusual was happening in his life. He confessed that his marriage had taken a turn for the worse and sexual relations with his wife had all but ceased. A period of marital therapy restored the therapeutic gains (see Figure 10.10). Several years later, after his daughter's therapist decided she was ready, she and Tony resumed a nonsexual relationship, which they both wanted.

Two major areas in Tony's life needed treatment: deviant (incestuous) sexual arousal and marital problems. Most individuals with paraphilic arousal patterns need a great deal of attention to family functioning or other interpersonal systems in which they operate (Barbaree & Seto, 1997; Fagan et al., 2002; Rice & Harris, 2002). In addition, many require intervention to help strengthen appropriate patterns of arousal. In **orgasmic reconditioning,** patients are instructed to masturbate to their usual fantasies but to substitute more desirable ones just before ejaculation. With repeated practice, subjects should be able to begin the desired fantasy earlier in the masturbatory process and still retain their arousal. This technique, first described by Gerald Davison (1968), has been used with some success in a variety of settings (Brownell et al., 1977; Maletzky, 2002). Finally, as with most strongly pleasurable but undesirable behaviors (including addiction), care must be taken to provide the patient with coping skills to prevent slips or relapses. *Relapse prevention* treatment created for addictions (Laws, 1989; Laws & O'Donohue, 1997) does just that. Patients are taught to recognize the early signs of temptation and to institute a variety of self-control procedures before their urges become too strong.

The success of treatment with this rich array of procedures is surprisingly high when carried out by an experienced professional. Barry Maletzky, a psychiatrist at the University of Oregon Medical School, and his staff reported on the treatment of more than 8,000 sexual offenders of numerous types over 20 years. A

variety of procedures were used in a program of 3 to 4 months in a clinic devoted exclusively to this type of treatment. The numbers of people successfully treated are presented by category in Table 10.5 (Maletzky, 2002).

In this table, someone with pedophilia classified as "situational" would be living with the victim and well known to the victim, such as an uncle or stepfather. Usually there would be only one victim over a fairly long period. To be classified as "predatory," the offender would not be living with the victim nor even known to the victim, and there is typically a pattern of multiple offenses. The outcomes reported by Maletzky are truly impressive. What makes them even more impressive is that Maletzky collected objective physiological outcome measures on almost every case, in addition to patients' reports of progress. In many cases, he also obtained corroborating information from families and legal authorities.

In his follow-up of these patients, Maletzky defined a treatment as successful when someone had (1) completed all treatment sessions, (2) demonstrated no deviant sexual arousal on objective physiological testing at any annual follow-up testing session, (3) reported no deviant arousal or behavior at any time since treatment ended, and (4) had no legal record of any charges of deviant sexual activity, even if unsubstantiated. He defined as a treatment failure anyone who was not a success. Any offender who did not

TABLE 10.5   Treatment Outcome for Paraphilias (N = 7,156)

Category	N	Percentage (%) Meeting Criteria for Success*
Situational pedophilia, heterosexual	3,312	95.6
Predatory pedophilia, heterosexual	1,064	88.3
Situational pedophilia, homosexual	917	91.8
Predatory pedophilia, homosexual	796	80.1
Exhibitionism	1,230	95.4
Rape	643	75.5
Voyeurism	83	93.9
Public masturbation	77	94.8
Frotteurism	65	89.3
Fetishism	33	94.0
Transvestic fetishism	14	78.6
Telephone scatologia	29	93.1
Zoophilia	23	95.6

*A treatment success was defined as an offender who fulfilled the following:
1. Completed all treatment sessions. Any offender who dropped out of treatment, even if the offender met other criteria for success, was counted as a treatment failure.
2. Reported no covert or overt deviant sexual behavior at the end of treatment or at any follow-up session. Follow-up sessions occurred at 6, 12, 24, 36, 48, and 60 months after the end of active treatment.
3. Demonstrated no deviant sexual arousal, defined as greater than 20% on the penile plethysmograph, at the end of treatment or at any follow-up session.
4. Had no repeat legal charges for any sexual crime at the end of treatment or at any follow-up session.

Source: From Maletzky, B. (2002). The paraphilias: Research and treatment. In P. E. Nathan & J. M. Gorman (Eds.), *A guide to treatments that work* (2nd ed., pp. 525-557). New York: Oxford University Press.

complete treatment for any reason was counted as a failure, even though some may well have benefited from the partial treatment and gone on to recover.

Although these results are extremely good overall, Maletzky points out that men who rape have the lowest success rate among all offenders with a single diagnosis and that individuals with multiple paraphilias have the lowest success rate of any group. Maletzky also examined factors associated with failure. Among the strongest predictors were a history of unstable social relationships, an unstable employment history, strong denial the problem exists, a history of multiple victims, and a situation in which the offender continues to live with a victim (as might be typical in cases of incest).

Other groups using similar treatment procedures have achieved comparable success rates (Abel, 1989; Becker, 1990; Fagan et al., 2002; Pithers, Martin, & Cumming, 1989). In general, results are less satisfactory when general summaries of the outcomes from all studies are evaluated, including programs that do not always incorporate these approaches (see, for example, Nagayama Hall, 1995). Thus, therapist knowledge and expertise seem to be important. Judith Becker used the procedures described previously in a program for adolescent sexual offenders in an inner-city setting (see, for example, Becker, 1990; Morenz & Becker, 1995). Preliminary results indicate that a relatively low 10% of those who completed treatment had committed further sex crimes. These findings were important both because many adolescent offenders carry the AIDS virus and literally are putting their victims' lives in danger and because the recidivism rate of sexual offenders without treatment is high (see, for example, Hanson, Steffy, & Gauthier, 1993; Nagayama Hall, 1995), just as it is for all pleasurable but undesirable behavior, including substance abuse. More recently, an important study found that intervening with aggressive, victimizing, or highly inappropriate sexual behavior in children age 5–12 with a CBT was effective in preventing sexual offending once they reached adolescence and adulthood 10 years later compared to a group receiving play therapy (Carpentier, Silovsky, & Chaffin, 2006). Only 2% had future sexual offenses. Preventing adult sexual offending would be an important advance if these results are replicated.

Drug Treatments

The most popular drug used to treat paraphilics (Bradford, 1997) is an antiandrogen called *cyproterone acetate*. This drug eliminates sexual desire and fantasy by reducing testosterone levels dramatically, but fantasies and arousal return as soon as the drug is removed. This is the "chemical castration" treatment you may have read about in the news. A second drug is *medroxyprogesterone* (Depo-Provera is the injectable form), a hormonal agent that reduces testosterone (Fagan et al., 2002). These drugs may be useful for dangerous sexual offenders who do not respond to alternative treatments or to temporarily suppress sexual arousal in patients

who require it, but it is not always successful. In an earlier report of the Maletzky series (Maletzky, 1991), it was necessary to administer the drug to only 8 of approximately 5,000 patients. Rösler and Witztum (1998) report successful "chemical castration" of 30 men with severe long-standing paraphilia using triptorelin, which inhibits gonadotropin secretion in men. This drug appears to be somewhat more effective than the other drugs mentioned here with fewer side effects, based on this one study.

Summary

Based on evidence from a number of clinics, the psychosocial treatment of paraphilia is surprisingly effective. Success rates ranging from 70% to 100%, with follow-ups for longer than 10 years in some cases, seem to make this one of the more treatable psychological disorders. However, most results are uncontrolled observations from a small number of clinical research centers, and it seems they are not as good in other clinics and offices. In any case, like treatment for sexual dysfunctions, psychosocial approaches to paraphilia are not readily available outside of specialized treatment centers. In the meantime, the outlook for most individuals with this disorder is bleak because paraphilias run a chronic course and recurrence is common.

CONCEPT CHECK 10.4

Check your understanding of sexual paraphilias by matching the scenarios with the correct label: (a) exhibitionism, (b) voyeurism, (c) fetishism, or (d) sexual masochism.

1. Jane enjoys being slapped with leather whips during foreplay. Without such stimulation, she is unable to achieve orgasm during sex. _____
2. Michael has a collection of women's panties that arouse him. He loves to look at, collect, and wear them. _____
3. Sam finds arousal in walking up to strangers in the park and showing them his genitals. _____
4. Peeping Tom loves to look through Susie's bedroom window and watch her undress. He gets extremely excited as she disrobes. He is practicing _____.
5. What Peeping Tom does not realize is that Susie knows that he is watching. She is aroused by slowly undressing while others are watching, and she fantasizes about what they are thinking. Susie's behavior is called _____.
6. What Peeping Tom will be shocked to find out is that "Susie" is actually Scott, a man who can become aroused only if he wears feminine clothing. Scott's behavior is _____.

FUTURE DIRECTIONS

Gender Nonconformity in Children

Earlier in this chapter, we discussed the findings on what is now called gender nonconformity in children. Long-term prospective follow-up studies indicate a complex relationship between gender nonconformity as a child and the development of gender identity, sexual orientation, or both as an adult. Briefly, findings indicate that a higher proportion of gender-nonconforming children develop a homosexual orientation as adults compared to those who are gender conforming. But most individuals with homosexual orientations as adults conform to their biological sex as children (boys act like boys and so on). It is also clear that a small minority of gender-nonconforming children are expressing a gender identity disorder in which their gender is different from their biological sex. These individuals will consistently identify with the opposite sex, thereby meeting diagnostic criteria for gender identity disorder in adulthood.

©Jim Wilson/The New York Times/Redux

A question under debate is whether to refer gender-nonconforming children for interventions early on that would bring their behavior and interests more into line with their biological sex. On the one hand, some segments of society, particularly in more traditionally tolerant areas of the country such as San Francisco and New York, are becoming more open to gender variations in both children and adults. In 2006, New York City decided to let people alter the sex listed on their birth certificates. In some schools, children are being allowed and even encouraged to dress and appear in gender-nonconforming ways on the assumption that this gives freer rein to who they "really are" (Brown, 2006). On the other hand, Skidmore and colleagues (2006) examined whether gender nonconformity was related to psychological distress in a community-based sample of gay men and lesbians. Gender nonconformity was measured by self-reports of childhood gender nonconformity, as well as ratings of current behavior. They found that gender nonconformity was related to psychological distress (depression, anxiety), but only for gay men and not for lesbians. Nevertheless, both lesbian and gay male participants reported a more positive attitude in the community toward gender conformity than nonconformity.

Although only a minority of gay men report gender nonconformity as boys, research indicates that many of these gender-nonconforming boys defeminize as they reach adulthood, probably because of persistent social pressure from their family and peers. Also, interventions exist to alter gender-nonconforming behavior in young children to avoid the ostracism and scorn these children encounter in most school settings (Rekers, Kilgus, & Rosen, 1990).

Thus, society is faced with a dilemma that requires more research. Should the free expression of gender nonconformity be encouraged knowing that, in most parts of world, this will make for difficult social adaptation leading to substantial psychological distress for decades to come? Or will psychological adjustment be more positive if gender nonconformity is allowed and facilitated? If research confirms the latter finding, then large-scale campaigns to alter social norms may well occur along the lines of the successful campaigns of the last several decades for gay rights, after a consensus developed in the 1990s that homosexuality was not a disorder. Research will continue on this important and interesting topic.

SUMMARY

What Is Normal Sexuality?

■ Patterns of sexual behavior, both heterosexual and homosexual, vary around the world in terms of both behavior and risks. Approximately 20% of individuals who have been surveyed engage in sex with numerous partners, which puts them at risk for sexually transmitted diseases such as AIDS. Recent surveys also suggest that as many as 60% of American college females practice unsafe sex by not using appropriate condoms.

■ Three types of disorders are associated with sexual functioning and gender identity: gender identity disorder, sexual dysfunctions, and paraphilias.

Gender Identity Disorder

■ Gender identify disorder is a dissatisfaction with one's biological sex and the sense that one is really the opposite gender (for example, a woman trapped in a man's body). A person develops gender identity between 18 months and 3 years of age, and it seems that both appropriate gender identity and mistaken gender identity have biological roots influenced by learning.

■ Treatment for adults may include sex reassignment surgery integrated with psychological approaches.

Overview of Sexual Dysfunctions

■ Sexual dysfunction includes a variety of disorders in which people find it difficult to function adequately during sexual relations.

■ Specific sexual dysfunctions include disorders of sexual desire (hypoactive sexual desire disorder and sexual aversion disorder) in which interest in sexual relations is extremely low or nonexistent; disorders of sexual arousal (male erectile disorder and female sexual arousal disorder) in which achieving or maintaining adequate penile erection or vaginal lubrication is problematic; and orgasmic disorders (female orgasmic disorder and male orgasmic disorder) in which orgasm occurs too quickly or not at all. The most common disorder in this category is premature ejaculation, which occurs in males; inhibited orgasm is commonly seen in females.

■ Sexual pain disorders, in which unbearable pain is associated with sexual relations, include dyspareunia and vaginismus.

Assessing Sexual Behavior

■ The three components of assessment are interviews, a complete medical evaluation, and psychophysiological assessment.

Causes and Treatment of Sexual Dysfunction

■ Sexual dysfunction is associated with socially transmitted negative attitudes about sex, interacting with current relationship difficulties, and anxiety focused on sexual activity.

■ Psychosocial treatment of sexual dysfunctions is generally successful but not readily available. In recent years, various medical approaches have become available, including the drug Viagra. These treatments focus mostly on male erectile dysfunction and are promising.

Paraphilia: Clinical Descriptions

■ Paraphilia is sexual attraction to inappropriate people, such as children, or to inappropriate objects, such as articles of clothing.

■ The paraphilias include fetishism, in which sexual arousal occurs almost exclusively in the context of inappropriate objects or individuals; exhibitionism, in which sexual gratification is attained by exposing one's genitals to unsuspecting strangers; voyeurism, in which sexual arousal is derived from observing unsuspecting individuals undressing or naked; transvestic fetishism, in which individuals are sexually aroused by wearing clothing of the opposite sex; sexual sadism, in which sexual arousal is associated with inflicting pain or humiliation; sexual masochism, in which sexual arousal is associated with experiencing pain or humiliation; and pedophilia, in which there is a strong sexual attraction toward children. Incest is a type of pedophilia in which the victim is related, often a son or daughter.

■ The development of paraphilia is associated with deficiencies in consensual adult sexual arousal, deficiencies in consensual adult social skills, deviant sexual fantasies that may develop before or during puberty, and attempts by the individual to suppress thoughts associated with these arousal patterns.

Assessing and Treating Paraphilia

■ Psychosocial treatments of paraphilia, including covert sensitization, orgasmic reconditioning, and relapse prevention, seem highly successful but are available only in specialized clinics.

Key Terms

heterosexual behavior, 345
homosexual behavior, 346
gender nonconformity, 352
sex reassignment surgery, 352
sexual dysfunction, 354
hypoactive sexual desire
    disorder, 355
sexual aversion disorder, 356

male erectile disorder, 357
female sexual arousal disorder, 357
inhibited orgasm, 358
female orgasmic disorder, 359
male orgasmic disorder, 359
premature ejaculation, 360

sexual pain disorders
    (dyspareunia), 360
vaginismus, 361
paraphilias, 371
frotteurism, 372
fetishism, 372
voyeurism, 373
exhibitionism, 373

transvestic fetishism, 373
sexual sadism, 374
sexual masochism, 374
pedophilia, 376
incest, 376
covert sensitization, 379
orgasmic reconditioning, 380

Answers to Concept Checks

10.1

1. More men masturbate and do it more often; men are more permissive about casual sex; women want more intimacy from sex, and so on.
2. Both heterosexuality and homosexuality are normal; genetics appear to play some role in the development of sexual preference.
3. Gender identity disorder
4. Abnormal hormone levels during development, social or parental influences
5. Sex reassignment surgery, psychosocial treatment to adjust to either gender

10.2

1. c; 2. a; 3. b; 4. c; 5. a

10.3

1. T; 2. F (sometimes increases arousal); 3. T; 4. T; 5. F (nondemand pleasuring, squeeze technique, and so on); 6. T

10.4

1. d; 2. c; 3. a; 4. b; 5. a; 6. c

The Abnormal Psychology Book Companion Website

See **academic.cengage.com/psychology/barlow** for practice quiz questions, interactive activities, Internet links, critical thinking exercises, discussion forums, and more. Also accessible from the Wadsworth Psychology Resource Center **(academic.cengage .com/login).**

Abnormal Psychology Live CD-ROM

- *Clark, a Man With Erectile Dysfunction:* This illustrates a rather complicated case in which depression, physical symptoms, and cultural expectations all seem to play a role in Clark's problem.
- *Jessica, Changing Over:* Jessica discusses her life as a transsexual, both before and after her sex reassignment surgery.

CENGAGENOW CengageNOW

Go to **academic.cengage.com/now** to link to CengageNOW, your online study tool. First take the Pre-Test for this chapter to get your personalized study plan, which will identify topics you need to review and direct you to online resources. Then take the Post-Test to determine what concepts you have mastered and what you still need work on.

Video Concept Reviews

CengageNOW also contains Mark Durand's *Video Concept Reviews* on challenging topics.

- Normal Versus Abnormal Sexual Behavior
- Sexual Orientation
- Sexual and Gender Identity Disorders
- Gender Identity Disorders
- Concept Check: Gender Identity Disorder, Transvestic Fetishism, and Transgendered
- Sexual Reassignment Surgery
- Human Sexual Response Cycle
- Hypoactive Sexual Desire Disorder
- Sexual Aversion Disorder
- Male Erectile Disorder and Female Sexual Arousal Disorder
- Inhibited Orgasm
- Premature Ejaculation
- Sexual Pain Disorders (Dyspareunia)
- Vaginismus
- Paraphilias

Exploring Sexual and Gender Identity Disorders

- *Sexual behavior is considered normal in our culture unless it is associated with one of three kinds of impaired functioning—gender identity disorder, sexual dysfunction, or paraphilia.*
- *Sexual orientation probably has a strong biological basis that is influenced by environmental and social factors.*

GENDER IDENTITY DISORDERS

Present when a person feels trapped in a body that is the "wrong" sex, that does not match his or her innate sense of personal identity. (Gender identity is independent of sexual arousal patterns.) Relatively rare.

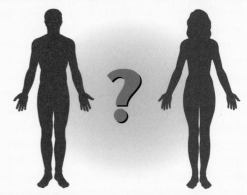

Biological Influences

- Not yet confirmed, although likely to involve prenatal exposure to hormones
- Hormonal variations may be natural or result from medication

Psychosocial Influences

- Gender identity develops between 1 1/2 and 3 years of age
- "Masculine" behaviors in girls and "feminine" behaviors in boys evoke different responses in different families

Treatment

- Sex reassignment surgery: removal of breasts or penis; genital reconstruction
- Requires rigorous psychological preparation and financial and social stability
- Psychosocial intervention to change gender identity
- Usually unsuccessful except as temporary relief until surgery

PARAPHILIAS

Sexual arousal occurs almost exclusively in the context of inappropriate objects or individuals.

Causes

- Preexisting deficiencies
  - In levels of arousal with consensual adults
  - In consensual adult social skills
- Treatment received from adults during childhood
- Early sexual fantasies reinforced by masturbation
- Extremely strong sex drive combined with uncontrollable thought processes

Treatment

- *Covert sensitization:* Repeated mental reviewing of aversive consequences to establish negative associations with behavior
- *Relapse prevention:* Therapeutic preparation for coping with future situations
- *Orgasmic reconditioning:* Pairing appropriate stimuli with masturbation to create positive arousal patterns
- *Medical:* Drugs that reduce testosterone to suppress sexual desire; fantasies and arousal return when drugs are stopped

Types of Paraphilias

Fetishism: Sexual attraction to nonliving objects

Voyeurism: Sexual arousal achieved by viewing unsuspecting person undressing or naked

Exhibitionism: Sexual gratification from exposing one's genitals to unsuspecting strangers

Transvestite fetishism: Sexual arousal from wearing opposite-sex clothing (cross-dressing)

Sexual sadism: Sexual arousal associated with inflicting pain or humiliation

Sexual masochism: Sexual arousal associated with experiencing pain or humiliation

Pedophilia: Strong sexual attraction to children

Incest: Sexual attraction to family member

SEXUAL DYSFUNCTIONS

Sexual dysfunctions can be
- **Lifelong:** Present during entire sexual history
- **Acquired:** Interrupts normal sexual pattern
- **Generalized:** Present in every encounter
- **Situational:** Present only with certain partners or at certain times

Types of Sexual Dysfunctions

Sexual Desire Disorders
Hypoactive sexual desire disorder: Apparent lack of interest in sexual activity or fantasy
Sexual aversion disorder: Extreme persistent dislike of sexual contact
Sexual Arousal Disorders
Male erectile disorder: Recurring inability to achieve or maintain adequate erection
Female sexual arousal disorder: Recurring inability to achieve or maintain adequate lubrication
Orgasm Disorders
Inhibited orgasm: Inability to achieve orgasm despite adequate desire and arousal
Premature ejaculation: Ejaculation before it is desired, with minimal stimulation
Sexual Pain Disorders
Dyspareunia: Marked pain associated with intercourse for which there is no medical cause; occurs in males and females
Vaginismus: Involuntary muscle spasms in the front of the vagina that prevent or interfere with intercourse

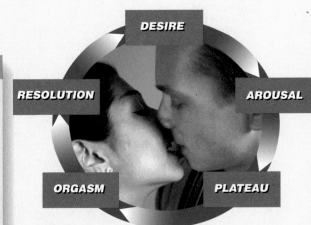

DESIRE

RESOLUTION

AROUSAL

ORGASM

PLATEAU

THE HUMAN SEXUAL RESPONSE CYCLE
A dysfunction is an impairment in one of the sexual response stages.

Psychological Contributions

- Distraction
- Underestimates of arousal
- Negative thought processes

Psychological and Physical Interactions

- A combination of influences is almost always present
- Specific biological predisposition *and* psychological factors may produce a particular disorder

CAUSES

Sociocultural Contributions

- Erotophobia, caused by formative experiences of sexual cues as alarming
- Negative experiences, such as rape
- Deterioration of relationship

Treatment

Psychosocial: Therapeutic program to facilitate communication, improve sexual education, and eliminate anxiety. Both partners participate fully.

Medical: Almost all interventions focus on male erectile disorder, including drugs, prostheses, and surgery. Medical treatment is combined with sexual education and therapy to achieve maximum benefit.

Biological Contributions

- Neurological or other nervous system problems
- Vascular disease
- Chronic illness
- Prescription medication
- Drugs of abuse, including alcohol

Substance-Related and Impulse-Control Disorders

©Palais Didier/SuperStock

PERSPECTIVES ON SUBSTANCE-RELATED DISORDERS
Levels of Involvement
Diagnostic Issues

DEPRESSANTS
Alcohol Use Disorders
Sedative, Hypnotic, or Anxiolytic Substance Use Disorders

STIMULANTS
Amphetamine Use Disorders
Cocaine Use Disorders
Nicotine Use Disorders
Caffeine Use Disorders

OPIOIDS

HALLUCINOGENS
Marijuana
LSD and Other Hallucinogens

OTHER DRUGS OF ABUSE

CAUSES OF SUBSTANCE-RELATED DISORDERS
Biological Dimensions
Psychological Dimensions

Cognitive Factors
Social Dimensions
Cultural Dimensions
An Integrative Model

TREATMENT OF SUBSTANCE-RELATED DISORDERS
Biological Treatments
Psychosocial Treatments
Prevention

IMPULSE-CONTROL DISORDERS
Intermittent Explosive Disorder
Kleptomania
Pyromania
Pathological Gambling
Trichotillomania

ABNORMAL PSYCHOLOGY LIVE CD-ROM
Substance Use Disorder: Tim
Nicotine Dependence
Web Link

For a long time, when it's working, the drink feels like a path to self-enlightenment, something that turns us into the person we wish to be, or the person we think we really are. In some ways the dynamic is this simple: alcohol makes everything better until it makes everything worse.

Caroline Knapp
Drinking: A Love Story

Would you be surprised if we told you that a group of psychological disorders costs U.S. citizens hundreds of billions of dollars each year, kills 500,000 Americans annually, and is implicated in street crime, homelessness, and gang violence? Would you be even more surprised to learn that most of us have behaved in ways characteristic of these disorders at some point in our lives? You shouldn't. Smoking cigarettes, drinking alcohol, and using illegal drugs are all related to these disorders, and they are responsible for astronomical financial costs and the tragic waste of hundreds of thousands of human lives each year. In this chapter, we explore **substance-related disorders,** which are associated with the abuse of drugs such as alcohol, cocaine, and heroin and with a variety of other substances people take to alter the way they think, feel, and behave. These disorders represent a problem that has cursed us for millennia and continues to affect how we live, work, and play.

Equally disruptive to the people affected, **impulse-control disorders** represent a number of related problems that involve the inability to resist acting on a drive or temptation. Included in this group are those who cannot resist aggressive impulses or the impulse to steal, to set fires, to gamble, or, for some, to pull out their own hair. Controversy surrounds both substance-related and impulse-control disorders because our society sometimes believes that both these problems are simply a lack of "will." If you wanted to stop drinking, using cocaine, or gambling, well, you would just stop. We first examine those individuals who are being harmed by their use of a variety of chemical substances (substance-related disorders) and then turn our attention to the puzzling array of disorders that are under the heading of impulse-control disorders.

PERSPECTIVES ON SUBSTANCE-RELATED DISORDERS

The cost in lives, money, and emotional turmoil has made the issue of drug abuse a major concern worldwide. Currently, more than 8% of the general population is believed to be made up of users of illegal drugs (Substance Abuse and Mental Health Services Administration, 2006). Many U.S. presidential administrations have declared various "wars on drugs," but the problem remains. The Roman Catholic Church issued a universal catechism in 1992 that officially declared drug abuse and drunk driving to be sins (Riding, 1992). Yet from the deaths of rock stars Jimi Hendrix and Janis Joplin in 1970 to the drug involvement of contemporary celebrities such as Rush Limbaugh, Nicole Richie, and Kate Moss, illicit drug use occupies the lives of many. And stories such as these not only are about the rich and famous but are retold in every corner of our society.

As we have just seen, a significant number of people continue to use illicit drugs regularly. Consider the case of Danny, who has the disturbing but common habit of **polysubstance use,** using multiple substances. (We cover this issue in more detail later in the chapter.)

DANNY: Multiple Dependencies

At the age of 35, Danny was in jail, awaiting trial on charges that he broke into a gas station and stole money. Danny's story illustrates the lifelong pattern that characterizes the behavior of many people who are affected by substance-related disorders.

Danny grew up in the suburban United States, the youngest of three children. He was well liked in school and an average student. Like many of his friends, he smoked cigarettes in his early teens and drank beer with his friends at night behind his high school. Unlike most of his friends, however, Danny almost always drank until he was obviously drunk; he also experimented with many other drugs, including cocaine, heroin, "speed" (amphetamines), and "downers" (barbiturates).

After high school, Danny attended a local community college for one semester, but he dropped out after failing most of his courses. His dismal performance in school seemed to be related to his missing most classes rather than to an inability to learn and understand the material. He had difficulty getting up for classes after partying most of the night, which he did with increasing frequency. His moods were highly variable, and he was often unpleasant. Danny's family knew he occasionally drank too much, but they didn't know (or didn't want to know) about his other drug use. He had for years forbidden anyone to go into his room after his mother found little packets of white powder (probably cocaine) in his sock drawer. He said he was keeping them for a friend and that he would return them immediately. He was furious that his family might suspect him of using drugs. Money was sometimes missing from the house, and once some stereo equipment "disappeared," but if his family members suspected Danny they never admitted it.

Danny held a series of low-paying jobs, and when he was working his family reassured themselves that he was back on track and things would be fine. Unfortunately, he rarely held a job for more than a few months. The money he earned had a magical way of turning into drugs, and he was usually fired for poor job attendance and performance. Because he con-

---

tinued to live at home, Danny could survive despite frequent periods of unemployment. When he was in his late 20s, Danny seemed to have a personal revelation. He announced that he needed help and planned to check into an alcohol rehabilitation center; he still would not admit to using other drugs. His family's joy and relief were overwhelming, and no one questioned his request for several thousand dollars to help pay for the private program he said he wanted to attend. Danny disappeared for several weeks, presumably because he was in the rehabilitation program. However, a call from the local police station put an end to this fantasy: Danny had been found quite high, living in an abandoned building. As with many of these incidents, we never learned all the details, but it appears that Danny spent his family's money on drugs and had a 3-week binge with some friends. Danny's deceptiveness and financial irresponsibility greatly strained his relationship with his family. He was allowed to continue living at home, but his parents and siblings excluded him from their emotional lives. Danny seemed to straighten out, and he held a job at a gas station for almost 2 years. He became friendly with the station owner and his son, and he often went hunting with them during the season. However, without any obvious warning, Danny resumed drinking and using drugs and was arrested for robbing the very place that had kept him employed for many months.

Why did Danny become dependent on drugs when many of his friends and siblings did not? Why did he steal from his family and friends? What ultimately became of him? We return to Danny's frustrating story later when we look at the causes and treatment of substance-related disorders.

Model Kate Moss was photographed in 2005 preparing and snorting cocaine. There is an increasing concern that celebrity use of illegal drugs glamorizes their use without showing their negative effects.

Levels of Involvement

Although each drug described in this chapter has unique effects, there are similarities in the ways they are used and how people who abuse them are treated. We first survey some concepts that apply to substance-related disorders in general, noting important terminology and addressing several diagnostic issues.

Can you use drugs and not abuse them? Can you abuse drugs and not become addicted to them? To answer these important questions, we first need to outline what we mean by *substance use, substance intoxication, substance abuse,* and *dependence.* The term *substance* refers to chemical compounds that are ingested to alter mood or behavior. Although you might first think of drugs such as cocaine and heroin, this definition also includes more commonplace legal drugs such as alcohol, the nicotine found in tobacco, and the caffeine in coffee, soft drinks, and chocolate. As you will see, these so-called safe drugs also affect mood and behavior, they can be addictive, and they account for more health problems and a greater mortality rate than all illegal drugs combined. You could make a good argument for directing the war on drugs to cigarette smoking (nicotine use) because of its addictive properties and negative health consequences.

To understand substance-related disorders, we must first know what it means to ingest **psychoactive substances**—which alter mood, behavior, or both—to become intoxicated or high, to abuse these substances, and to become dependent on or addicted to them.

■ Substance Use

Substance use is the ingestion of psychoactive substances in moderate amounts that does not significantly interfere with social, educational, or occupational functioning. Most of you reading this chapter probably use some sort of psychoactive substance occasionally. Drinking a cup of coffee in the morning to wake up or smoking a cigarette and having a drink with a friend to relax are examples of substance use, as is the occasional ingestion of illegal drugs such as marijuana, cocaine, amphetamines, or barbiturates.

■ Intoxication

Our physiological reaction to ingested substances—drunkenness or getting high—is referred to as **substance intoxication.** For a person to become intoxicated depends on which drug is taken, how much is ingested, and the person's individual biological reaction. For many of the substances we discuss here, intoxication is experienced as impaired judgment, mood changes, and lowered motor ability (for example, problems walking or talking).

DSM-IV-TR

DSM TABLE 11.1 Diagnostic Criteria for Substance Intoxication

A. The development of a reversible substance-specific syndrome due to recent ingestion of (or exposure to) a substance. *Note:* Different substances may produce similar or identical syndromes.
B. Clinically significant maladaptive behavioral or psychological changes that are due to the effect of the substance on the central nervous system (e.g., belligerence, mood lability, cognitive impairment, impaired judgment, impaired social or occupational functioning) and develop during or shortly after use of the substance.
C. The symptoms are not due to a general medical condition and are not better accounted for by another mental disorder.

Source: Reprinted, with permission, from American Psychiatric Association. (2000). Diagnostic and statistical manual of mental disorders (4th ed., text revision). Washington, DC: Author, © 2000 American Psychiatric Association.

■ Substance Abuse

Defining **substance abuse** by how much of a substance is ingested is problematic. For example, is drinking two glasses of wine in an hour abuse? Three glasses? Six? Is taking one injection of heroin considered abuse? The fourth edition, text revision, of the *Diagnostic and Statistical Manual* (DSM-IV-TR) (American Psychiatric Association, 2000c) defines substance abuse in terms of how significantly it interferes with the user's life. If substances disrupt your education, job, or relationships with others, and put you in physically dangerous situations (for example, while driving), and if you have related legal problems, you would be considered a drug abuser.

DSM-IV-TR

DSM TABLE 11.2 Diagnostic Criteria for Substance Abuse

A. A maladaptive pattern of substance use leading to clinically significant impairment or distress, as manifested by one (or more) of the following, during the same 12-month period:
1. Recurrent substance use resulting in a failure to fulfill major role obligations at work, school, or home (e.g., repeated absences or poor work performance related to substance use; substance-related absences, suspensions, or expulsions from school; neglect of children or household)
2. Recurrent substance use in situations in which it is physically hazardous (e.g., driving an automobile or operating a machine when impaired by substance use)
3. Recurrent substance-related legal problems (e.g., arrests for substance-related disorderly conduct)
4. Continued substance use despite having persistent or recurrent social or interpersonal problems caused or exacerbated by the effects of the substance (e.g., arguments with spouse about consequences of intoxication, physical fights)
B. The symptoms have never met the criteria for substance dependence for this class of substance.

Source: Reprinted, with permission, from American Psychiatric Association. (2000). Diagnostic and statistical manual of mental disorders (4th ed., text revision). Washington, DC: Author, © 2000 American Psychiatric Association.

Danny seems to fit this definition of abuse. His inability to complete a semester of community college was a direct result of drug use. Danny often drove while drunk or under the influence of other drugs, and he had already been arrested twice. Danny's use of multiple substances was so relentless and pervasive that he would probably be diagnosed as drug dependent, which indicates a severe form of the disorder.

■ Substance Dependence

Drug dependence is usually described as addiction. Although we use the term *addiction* routinely when we describe people who seem to be under the control of drugs, there is some disagreement about how to define addiction, or **substance dependence** (Jaffe & Anthony, 2005). In one definition, the person is physiologically dependent on the drug or drugs, requires increasingly greater amounts of the drug to experience the same effect **(tolerance),** and will respond physically in a negative way when the substance is no longer ingested **(withdrawal)** (American Psychiatric Association, 2007). Tolerance and withdrawal are physiological reactions

DSM-IV-TR

DSM TABLE 11.3 Diagnostic Criteria for Substance Dependence

A maladaptive pattern of substance use, leading to clinically significant impairment or distress, as manifested by three (or more) of the following, occurring at any time in the same 12-month period:
1. Tolerance, as defined by either of the following:
   a. A need for markedly increased amounts of the substance to achieve intoxication or desired effect
   b. Markedly diminished effect with continued use of the same amount of the substance
2. Withdrawal, as manifested by either of the following:
   a. The characteristic withdrawal syndrome for the substance (refer to criteria A and B of the criteria sets for withdrawal from the specific substances)
   b. The same (or a closely related) substance is taken to relieve or avoid withdrawal symptoms
3. The substance is often taken in larger amounts or over a longer period than was intended
4. There is a persistent desire or unsuccessful efforts to cut down or control substance use
5. A great deal of time is spent in activities necessary to obtain the substance (e.g., visiting multiple doctors or driving long distances), use the substance (e.g., chain-smoking), or recover from its effects
6. Important social, occupational, or recreational activities are given up or reduced because of substance use
7. The substance use is continued despite knowledge of having a persistent or recurrent physical or psychological problem that is likely to have been caused or exacerbated by the substance (e.g., current cocaine use despite recognition of cocaine-induced depression, or continued drinking despite recognition that an ulcer was made worse by alcohol consumption)
Specify if:
   With physiological dependence: Evidence of tolerance or withdrawal (i.e., either item 1 or 2 is present)
   Without physiological dependence: No evidence of tolerance or withdrawal (i.e., neither item 1 nor 2 is present)

*Source: Reprinted, with permission, from American Psychiatric Association. (2000). **Diagnostic and statistical manual of mental disorders** (4th ed., text revision). Washington, DC: Author, © 2000 American Psychiatric Association.*

Substance use.

cold to smoke), and the likelihood that use will resume after a period of abstinence are behaviors that define the extent of drug dependence. Such behavioral reactions are different from the physiological responses to drugs we described before and are sometimes referred to in terms of psychological dependence. The DSM-IV-TR definition of substance dependence combines the physiological aspects of tolerance and withdrawal with their behavioral and psychological aspects (American Psychiatric Association, 2000c).

This definition of dependence must be seen as a "work in progress." By these criteria, many people can be considered dependent on such activities as sex, work, or even eating chocolate. ■ Figure 11.1 shows the results of applying the DSM-IV-TR definition of dependence to a variety of daily activities, including substance use (Franklin, 1990). Is your behavior on this list? What most people consider serious addiction to drugs is qualitatively different from dependence on shopping or television. The physiological and behavioral patterns may need to be further refined before we can separate the truly serious phenomenon of substance dependence from less debilitating so-called addictions.

to the chemicals being ingested. How many of you have experienced headaches when you didn't get your morning coffee? You were probably going through caffeine withdrawal. In a more extreme example, withdrawal from alcohol can cause alcohol withdrawal delirium, in which a person can experience frightening hallucinations and body tremors (a condition described later in this chapter). Withdrawal from many substances can bring on chills, fever, diarrhea, nausea and vomiting, and aches and pains. However, not all substances are physiologically addicting. For example, you do not go through severe physical withdrawal when you stop taking LSD or marijuana. Cocaine withdrawal has a pattern that includes anxiety, lack of motivation, and boredom (Kosten & Sofuoglu, 2004). We return to the ways drugs act on our bodies when we examine the causes of abuse and dependence.

Another view of substance dependence uses the "drug-seeking behaviors" themselves as a measure of dependence. The repeated use of a drug, a desperate need to ingest more of the substance (stealing money to buy drugs, standing outside in the

Let's go back to the questions we started with: "Can you use drugs and not abuse them?" and "Can you abuse drugs and not become addicted to or dependent on them?" The answer to the first question is yes. Some people drink wine or beer regularly without drinking to excess. Although it is not commonly believed, some people use drugs such as heroin, cocaine, or crack (a form of cocaine) occasionally (for instance, several times a year) without abusing them (Goldman & Rather, 1993). What is disturbing is that we do not know ahead of time who might be likely to lose control and abuse these drugs and who is likely to become dependent with even a passing use of a substance.

It may seem counterintuitive, but dependence can be present without abuse. For example, cancer patients who take morphine for pain may become dependent on the drug—build up a tolerance and go through withdrawal if it is stopped—without abusing it (Portenoy & Payne, 1997). Later in this chapter, we discuss biological and psychosocial theories of the causes of substance-related disorders and of why we have individualized reactions to these substances.

Intoxication.

Substance abuse.

ACCORDING TO THE STANDARD psychiatric definition, any drug user who passes three of the nine tests below is hooked. Several researchers were asked to apply the tests not only to drugs but also to other substances and activities—chocolate, sex, shopping. Their responses show it's possible to become addicted to all sorts of things. For example, serious runners could pass three of the tests by spending more time running than originally intended, covering increasing distances, and experiencing withdrawal symptoms (a devoted runner forced to stop because of an injury, say, might become anxious and irritable). Of course, that sort of dependency isn't necessarily destructive. Conversely, a drug that fails the addictiveness test—LSD, for instance—may be harmful just the same. That so many things are potentially addictive suggests the addiction's cause is not confined to the substance or activity—our culture may play a large role too.

	Nicotine	Alcohol	Caffeine	Cocaine	Crack	Heroin	Ice*	LSD	Marijuana	PCP	Valium, Xanax, etc.†	Steroids	Chocolate	Running	Gambling	Shopping	Sex	Work	Driving	Television	Mountain climbing
TAKES substance or does activity more than originally intended	✓	✓	✓	✓	✓	✓	✓		✓	✓	✓	✓	✓	✓	✓	✓	✓	✓		✓	✓
WANTS to cut back or has tried to cut back but failed	✓	✓	✓	✓	✓	✓	✓		✓	✓	✓	✓	✓	✓	✓	✓	✓	✓		✓	✓
SPENDS lots of time trying to get substance or set up activity, taking substance or doing activity, or recovering	✓	✓		✓	✓	✓	✓	✓	✓		✓			✓	✓	✓	✓			✓	✓
IS OFTEN intoxicated or suffers withdrawal symptoms when expected to fulfill obligations at work, school, or home		✓		✓	✓	✓	✓		✓	✓	✓										
CURTAILS or gives up important social, occupational, or recreational activities because of substance or activity		✓		✓	✓	✓	✓		✓	✓	✓			✓	✓	✓	✓	✓		✓	✓
USES substance or does activity despite persistent social, psychological, or physical problems caused by substance or activity	✓	✓	✓	✓	✓	✓	✓	✓	✓	✓	✓	✓	✓	✓	✓	✓	✓	✓		✓	✓
NEEDS more and more of substance or activity to achieve the same effect (tolerance)	✓	✓	✓	✓	✓	✓	✓				✓										
SUFFERS characteristic withdrawal symptoms when activity or substance is discontinued (cravings, anxiety, depression, jitters)	✓	✓	✓	✓	✓	✓	✓				✓			✓	✓	✓	✓	✓		✓	✓
TAKES substance or does activity to relieve or avoid withdrawal symptoms	✓	✓	✓	✓	✓	✓	✓				✓										

* Methamphetamine
† Benzodiazepines

Research by Valerie Fahey

■ **FIGURE 11.1** Ice, LSD, chocolate, TV: Is everything addictive? (Reprinted from Fahey, V., 1990, January/February. Is everything addictive? *In Health* © 1990 In Health.)

Experts in the substance use field were asked about the relative "addictiveness" of various drugs (Franklin, 1990). The survey results are shown in ■ Figure 11.2. You may be surprised to see nicotine placed just ahead of methamphetamine and crack cocaine as the most addictive of drugs. Although this is only a subjective rating by these experts, it shows that our society sanctions or forbids drugs based on factors other than their addictiveness.

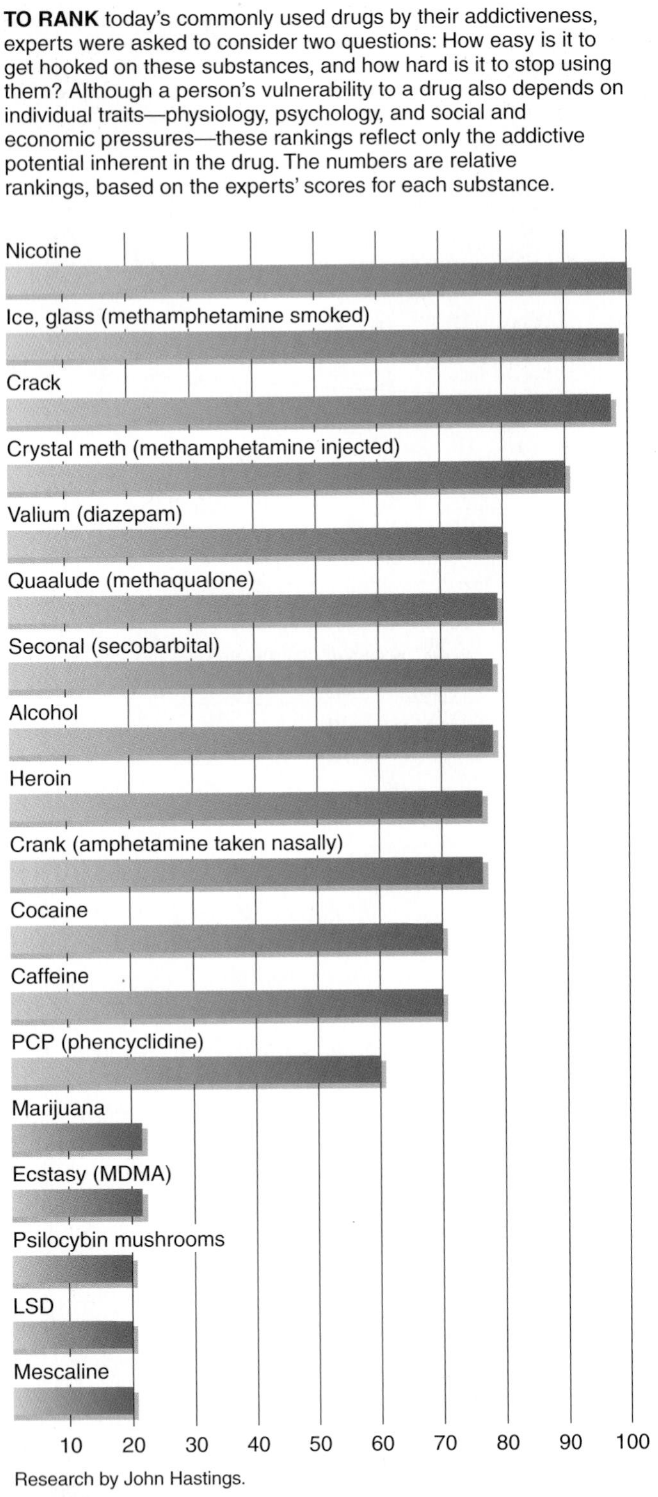

TO RANK today's commonly used drugs by their addictiveness, experts were asked to consider two questions: How easy is it to get hooked on these substances, and how hard is it to stop using them? Although a person's vulnerability to a drug also depends on individual traits—physiology, psychology, and social and economic pressures—these rankings reflect only the addictive potential inherent in the drug. The numbers are relative rankings, based on the experts' scores for each substance.

Research by John Hastings.

■ **FIGURE 11.2** Easy to get hooked on, hard to get off. (Reprinted, with permission, from Hastings, J., 1990, November/December. Easy to get hooked on, hard to get off. *In Health*, p. 37, © 1990 In Health.)

Diagnostic Issues

In early editions of the DSM, alcoholism and drug abuse weren't treated as separate disorders. Instead, they were categorized as "sociopathic personality disturbances" (a forerunner of the current *antisocial personality disorder,* which we discuss in Chapter 12),

because substance use was seen as a symptom of other problems. It was considered a sign of moral weakness, and the influence of genetics and biology was hardly acknowledged. A separate category was created in DSM-III, in 1980, and since then we have acknowledged the complex biological and psychological nature of the problem.

The DSM-IV-TR term *substance-related disorders* indicates several subtypes of diagnoses for each substance, including dependence, abuse, intoxication, withdrawal, or a combination of these. These distinctions help clarify the problem and focus treatment on the appropriate aspect of the disorder. Danny received the diagnosis "cocaine dependence" because of the tolerance he showed for the drug, his use of larger amounts than he intended, his unsuccessful attempts to stop using it, and the activities he gave up to buy it. His pattern of use was more pervasive than simple abuse, and the diagnosis of dependence provided a clear picture of his need for help.

Symptoms of other disorders can complicate the substance abuse picture significantly. For example, do some people take drugs to excess because they are depressed, or does drug use and its consequences (for example, loss of friends, job) create depression? Researchers estimate that almost three quarters of the people in addiction treatment centers have an additional psychiatric disorder, with mood disorders (such as major depression) observed in more than 40% and anxiety disorders and posttraumatic stress disorder seen in more than 25% of the cases (McGovern, Xie, Segal, Siembab, & Drake, 2006).

Substance use might occur concurrently with other disorders for several reasons (Jaffe & Anthony, 2005). Substance-related disorders and anxiety and mood disorders are highly prevalent in our society and may occur together so often just by chance. Drug intoxication and withdrawal can cause symptoms of anxiety, depression, and psychosis. Disorders such as schizophrenia and antisocial personality disorder are highly likely to include a secondary problem of substance use.

Because substance-related disorders can be so complicated, the DSM-IV-TR tries to define when a symptom is a result of substance use and when it is not. Basically, if symptoms seen in schizophrenia or in extreme states of anxiety appear during intoxication or within 6 weeks after withdrawal from drugs, they aren't considered signs of a separate psychiatric disorder. So, for example, individuals who show signs of severe depression just after they have stopped taking heavy doses of stimulants would not be diagnosed with a major mood disorder. However, individuals who were severely depressed before they used stimulants and those whose symptoms persist more than 6 weeks after they stop might have a separate disorder (Jaffe & Anthony, 2005).

We now turn to the individual substances themselves, their effects on our brains and bodies, and how they are used in our society. We have grouped the substances into five general categories.

- **Depressants:** These substances result in behavioral sedation and can induce relaxation. They include alcohol (ethyl alcohol) and the sedative, hypnotic, and anxiolytic drugs in the families of barbiturates (for example, Seconal) and benzodiazepines (for example, Valium, Halcion).

- **Stimulants:** These substances cause us to be more active and alert and can elevate mood. Included in this group are amphetamines, cocaine, nicotine, and caffeine.
- **Opiates:** The major effect of these substances is to produce analgesia temporarily (reduce pain) and euphoria. Heroin, opium, codeine, and morphine are included in this group.
- **Hallucinogens:** These substances alter sensory perception and can produce delusions, paranoia, and hallucinations. Marijuana and LSD are included in this category.
- **Other Drugs of Abuse:** Other substances that are abused but do not fit neatly into one of the categories here include inhalants (for example, airplane glue), anabolic steroids, and other over-the-counter and prescription medications (for example, nitrous oxide). These substances produce a variety of psychoactive effects that are characteristic of the substances described in the previous categories.

DEPRESSANTS

Depressants primarily *decrease* central nervous system activity. Their principal effect is to reduce our levels of physiological arousal and help us relax. Included in this group are alcohol and the sedative, hypnotic, and anxiolytic drugs, such as those prescribed for insomnia (see Chapter 8). These substances are among those most likely to produce symptoms of physical dependence, tolerance, and withdrawal. We first look at the most commonly used of these substances—alcohol—and the **alcohol use disorders** that can result.

Alcohol Use Disorders

Danny's substance abuse began when he drank beer with friends, a rite of passage for many teenagers. Alcohol has been widely used throughout history. Recently, for example, scientists found evidence of wine or beer in pottery jars at the site of a Sumerian trading post in western Iran that dates back 6,000 years (Goodwin & Gabrielli, 1997). For hundreds of years, Europeans drank large amounts of beer, wine, and hard liquor. When they came to North America in the early 1600s, they brought their considerable thirst for alcohol with them. In the United States during the early 1800s, consumption of alcohol (mostly whiskey) was more than 7 gallons per year for every person older than 15. This is more than three times the current rate of U.S. alcohol use (Goodwin & Gabrielli, 1997; Rorabaugh, 1991).

Alcohol is produced when certain yeasts react with sugar and water and *fermentation* takes place. Historically, we have been creative about fermenting alcohol from just about any fruit or vegetable, partly because many foods contain sugar. Alcoholic drinks have included mead from honey, sake from rice, wine from palm, mescal and pulque from agave and cactus, liquor from maple syrup, liquor from South American jungle fruits, wine from grapes, and beer from grains (Lazare, 1989).

■ Clinical Description
Although alcohol is a depressant, its initial effect is an apparent stimulation. We generally experience a feeling of well-being, our inhibitions are reduced, and we become more outgoing. This is

---

DSM-IV-TR

DSM TABLE 11.4 Diagnostic Criteria for Alcohol Intoxication

A. Recent ingestion of alcohol.
B. Clinically significant maladaptive behavioral or psychological changes (e.g., inappropriate sexual or aggressive behavior, mood lability, impaired judgment, impaired social or occupational functioning) that developed during, or shortly after, alcohol use.
C. One or more of the following signs, developing during, or shortly after, alcohol use:
   1. Slurred speech
   2. Incoordination
   3. Unsteady gait
   4. Nystagmus
   5. Impairment in attention or memory
   6. Stupor or coma
D. The symptoms are not due to a general medical condition and are not better accounted for by another mental disorder.

Source: Reprinted, with permission, from American Psychiatric Association. (2000). *Diagnostic and statistical manual of mental disorders* (4th ed., text revision). Washington, DC: Author. © 2000 American Psychiatric Association.

---

because what are initially depressed—or slowed—are the inhibitory centers in the brain. With continued drinking, however, alcohol depresses more areas of the brain, which impedes the ability to function properly. Motor coordination is impaired (staggering, slurred speech), reaction time is slowed, we become confused, our ability to make judgments is reduced, and even vision and hearing can be negatively affected, all of which help explain why driving while intoxicated is clearly dangerous.

■ Effects
Alcohol affects many parts of the body (see ■ Figure 11.3). After it is ingested, it passes through the esophagus (1 in Figure 11.3) and into the stomach (2), where small amounts are absorbed. From there, most of it travels to the small intestine (3), where it is easily absorbed into the bloodstream. The circulatory system distributes the alcohol throughout the body, where it contacts every major organ, including the heart (4). Some of the alcohol goes to the lungs, where it vaporizes and is exhaled, a phenomenon that is the basis for the *breathalyzer test* that measures levels of intoxication. As alcohol passes through the liver (5), it is broken down or metabolized into carbon dioxide and water by enzymes (Maher, 1997). ■ Figure 11.4 shows how much time it takes to metabolize one to four drinks, with the dotted line showing when driving becomes impaired (National Institute on Alcohol Abuse and Alcoholism, 1997).

Most substances we describe in this chapter, including marijuana, opiates, and tranquilizers, interact with specific receptors in the brain cells. The effects of alcohol, however, are more complex. Alcohol influences a number of neuroreceptor systems, which makes it difficult to study. For example, the *gamma-aminobutyric acid (GABA)* system, which we discussed in Chapters 2 and 5, seems to be particularly sensitive to alcohol. GABA, as you will recall, is an inhibitory neurotransmitter. Its major role is to interfere with the firing of the neuron it attaches to. When GABA

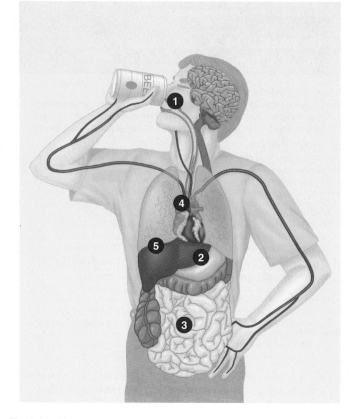

FIGURE 11.3 The path traveled by alcohol throughout the body (see text for complete description).

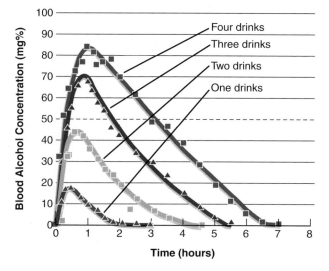

FIGURE 11.4 Blood alcohol concentration after the rapid consumption of different amounts of alcohol by eight adult, fasting, male subjects. 100 mg% is the legal level of intoxication in most states. 50 mg% is the level at which deterioration of driving skills begins. (From National Institute on Alcohol Abuse and Alcoholism, 1997. *Alcohol Alert: Alcohol-Metabolism.* No. 35, PH 371. Bethesda, MD: Author.)

attaches to its receptor, chloride ions enter the cell and make it less sensitive to the effects of other neurotransmitters. Alcohol seems to reinforce the movement of these chloride ions; as a result, the neurons have difficulty firing. In other words, although alcohol seems to loosen our tongues and makes us more sociable, it makes it difficult for neurons to communicate with one another (Jaffe & Anthony, 2005). Because the GABA system seems to act on our feelings of anxiety, alcohol's antianxiety properties may result from its interaction with the GABA system.

The *glutamate system* is under study for its role in the effects of alcohol. In contrast to the GABA system, the glutamate system is excitatory, helping neurons fire. It is suspected to involve learning and memory, and it may be the avenue through which alcohol affects our cognitive abilities. Blackouts, the loss of memory for what happens during intoxication, may result from the interaction of alcohol with the glutamate system. The serotonin system also appears to be sensitive to alcohol. This neurotransmitter system affects mood, sleep, and eating behavior and is thought to be responsible for alcohol cravings (Chastain, 2006). Because alcohol

affects so many neurotransmitter systems, we should not be surprised that it has such widespread and complex effects.

The long-term effects of heavy drinking are often severe. Withdrawal from chronic alcohol use typically includes hand tremors and, within several hours, nausea or vomiting, anxiety, transient hallucinations, agitation, insomnia, and, at its most extreme, **withdrawal delirium** (or **delirium tremens**—the **DTs**), a condition that can produce frightening hallucinations and body tremors. The devastating experience of delirium tremens can be reduced with adequate medical treatment (Schuckit & Tapert, 2004).

Whether alcohol will cause organic damage depends on genetic vulnerability, the frequency of use, the length of drinking binges, the blood alcohol levels attained during the drinking periods, and whether the body is given time to recover between binges (Mack, Franklin, & Frances, 2003). Consequences of long-term excessive drinking include liver disease, pancreatitis, cardiovascular disorders, and brain damage.

Part of the folklore concerning alcohol is that it permanently kills brain cells (neurons). As you will see later, this may not be true. Some evidence for brain damage comes from the experiences of people who are alcohol dependent and experience blackouts, seizures, and hallucinations. Memory and the ability to perform certain tasks may also be impaired. More seriously, two types of organic brain syndromes may result from long-term heavy alcohol use: dementia and Wernicke-Korsakoff syndrome. *Dementia,* which we discuss more fully in Chapter 15, involves the general loss of intellectual abilities and can be a direct result of neurotoxicity or "poisoning of the brain" by excessive amounts of alcohol (Jaffe & Anthony, 2005). *Wernicke-Korsakoff syndrome* results in confusion, loss of muscle coordination, and unintelligible speech (Gallant, 1999);

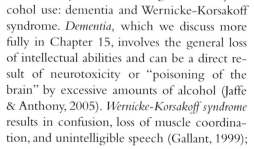

"When I drink, I don't care about anything, as long as I'm drinking. Nothing bothers me. The world doesn't bother me. So when I'm not drinking, the problems come back, so you drink again. The problems will always be there. You just don't realize it when you're drinking. That's why people tend to drink a lot."

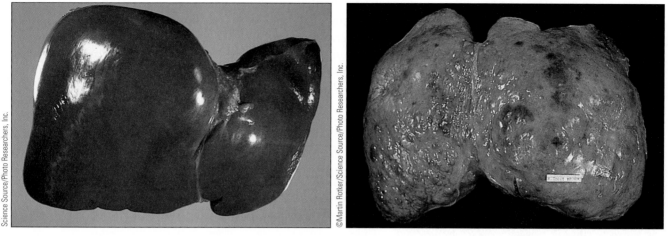

A healthy liver (left), and a cirrhotic liver scarred by years of alcohol abuse (right).

it is believed to be caused by a deficiency of thiamine, a vitamin metabolized poorly by heavy drinkers. The dementia caused by this disease does not go away once the brain is damaged.

The effects of alcohol abuse extend beyond the health and well-being of the drinker. **Fetal alcohol syndrome (FAS)** is now generally recognized as a combination of problems that can occur in a child whose mother drank while she was pregnant. These problems include fetal growth retardation, cognitive deficits, behavior problems, and learning difficulties (Simkin, 2005). In addition, children with FAS often have characteristic facial features.

It is interesting that not all women who drink during pregnancy are at equal risk for having children with FAS. African Americans and the Apache and Ute Indian tribes of the American Southwest appear to be at greater risk for having children with

FAS (May & Hymbaugh, 1983; Stoler, Ryan, & Holmes, 2002) than Caucasian women. We metabolize alcohol with the help of an enzyme called **alcohol dehydrogenase (ADH)** (Jaffe & Anthony, 2005). Three different forms of this enzyme have been identified (beta 1, beta 2, and beta 3 ADH); one form (beta 3 ADH) is found most often in African Americans. Initial work also shows that beta 3 ADH may be prevalent among children with FAS. What these two findings suggest is that, in addition to the drinking habits of the mother, the likelihood a child will have FAS may depend on whether there is a genetic tendency to have certain enzymes. Children from certain racial groups may thus be more susceptible to FAS than are others. If this research is confirmed, we may have a way of identifying parents who might put their children at increased risk for FAS.

■ Statistics on Use and Abuse

Because alcohol consumption is legal in the United States, we know more about it than about most other psychoactive substances we discuss in this chapter (with the possible exception of nicotine and caffeine, also legal here). Despite a national history of heavy alcohol use, most adults in the United States characterize themselves as light drinkers or abstainers. On the other hand, about half of all Americans over the age of 12 report being current drinkers of alcohol, and there are considerable differences among people from different racial and ethnic backgrounds (see ■ Figure 11.5; Substance Abuse and Mental Health Services Administration, 2006). Whites report the highest frequency of drinking (56.5%); drinking is lowest among Native Hawaiians (37.3%).

About 54 million (23%) Americans report binge drinking (five or more drinks on the same occasion) in the past month—an alarming statistic (Substance Abuse and Mental Health Services Administration, 2006).

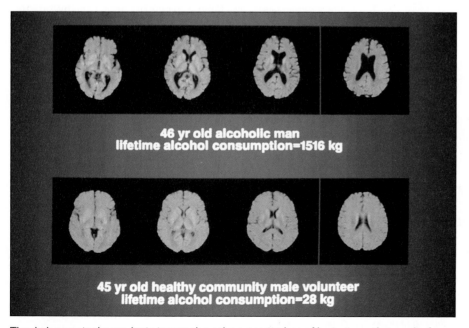

The dark areas in the top brain images show the extensive loss of brain tissue that results from heavy alcohol use.

Physical characteristics of FAS include skin folds at the corners of the eyes, low nasal bridge, short nose, groove between nose and upper lip, small head circumference, small eye opening, small midface, and thin upper lip.

Again, there are racial differences, with Asians reporting the lowest level of binge drinking (12.7%) and American Indians reporting the highest (32.8%). In a large survey among college-age men and women, about 42% of respondents said they had gone on a binge of heavy drinking once in the preceding 2 weeks (Presley & Meilman, 1992). Men, however, were more likely to report several binges in the 2-week period. The same survey found that students with a grade point average of A had no more than 3 drinks per week, whereas D and F students averaged 11 alcoholic drinks per week (Presley & Meilman, 1992). Overall, these data point to the popularity and pervasiveness of drinking in our society.

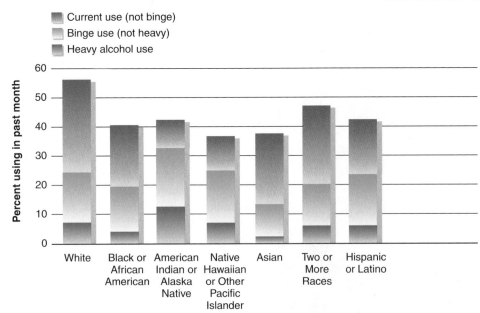

■ **FIGURE 11.5** Alcohol use across racial groups. Binge drinking is defined as drinking five or more drinks on one occasion at least once per month, and heavy alcohol use is defined as binge drinking for five or more days in a month. (From Substance Abuse and Mental Health Services Administration, Office of Applied Studies., 2006. *Results from the 2005 National Survey on Drug Use and Health: National Findings,* NSDUH Series H-30, DHHS Publication No. SMA 06-4194. Rockville, MD: Author.)

Statistics on Dependence

Our everyday experience tells us that not everyone who drinks becomes dependent on alcohol or abuses it. However, researchers estimate that more than 15 million adults are alcohol dependent (Substance Abuse and Mental Health Services Administration, 2006).

Outside the United States, rates of alcohol abuse and dependence vary widely. The prevalence of alcohol dependence in Peru is about 35%; in South Korea, it is approximately 22%; it is about 3.5% in Taipei and as low as 0.45% in Shanghai (Helzer & Canino, 1992; Yamamoto, Silva, Sasao, Wang, & Nguyen, 1993). Such cultural differences can be accounted for by different attitudes toward drinking, the availability of alcohol, physiological reactions, and family norms and patterns.

Progression

Remember that Danny went through periods of heavy alcohol and drug use but also had times when he was relatively "straight" and did not use drugs. Similarly, many people who abuse alcohol or are dependent on it fluctuate between drinking heavily, drinking "socially" without negative effects, and being abstinent (not drinking) (Schuckit & Tapert, 2004; Vaillant, 1983). It seems that about 20% of people with severe alcohol dependence have a spontaneous remission (they are able to stop drinking on their own) and do not reexperience problems with drinking (Ludwig, 1985; Vaillant, 1983).

It used to be thought that once problems arose with drinking they would become steadily worse, following a predictable downward pattern as long as the person kept drinking (Sobell & Sobell, 1993). In other words, like a disease that isn't treated properly, alcoholism will get progressively worse if left unchecked. First championed by Jellinek more than 50 years ago, this view continues to influence the way people view and treat the disorder (Jellinek, 1946, 1952, 1960). Unfortunately, Jellinek based his model of the progression of alcohol use on a now famous but faulty study (Jellinek, 1946), which we briefly review.

In 1945, the newly formed self-help organization Alcoholics Anonymous (AA) sent out some 1,600 surveys to its members asking them to describe symptoms related to drinking, such as feelings of guilt or remorse and rationalizations about their actions, and to note when these reactions first occurred. Only 98 of the almost 1,600 surveys were returned, however. As you know, such a small response could seriously affect data interpretation. A group of 98 may be different from the group as a whole, so they may not represent the typical person with alcohol problems. Also, because the responses were retrospective (participants were recalling past events), their reports may be inaccurate. Despite these and other problems, Jellinek agreed to analyze the data, and he developed a four-stage model for the pro-

Intoxication is often involved in cases of domestic violence.

gression of alcoholism based on this limited information (Jellinek, 1952). According to his model, individuals go through a *prealcoholic stage* (drinking occasionally with few serious consequences), a *prodromal stage* (drinking heavily but with few outward signs of a problem), a *crucial stage* (loss of control, with occasional binges), and a *chronic stage* (the primary daily activities involve getting and drinking alcohol). Attempts by other researchers to confirm this progression of stages have not been successful (Schuckit, Smith, Anthenelli, & Irwin, 1993).

It appears instead that the course of alcohol dependence may be progressive for most people, although the course of alcohol abuse may be more variable. For example, early use of alcohol may predict later abuse. A study of almost 6,000 lifetime drinkers found that drinking at an early age—from ages 11 to 14—was predictive of later alcohol use disorders (DeWitt, Adlaf, Offord, & Ogborne, 2000). A second study followed 636 male inpatients in an alcohol rehabilitation center (Schuckit et al., 1993). Among these chronically alcohol-dependent men, a general progression of alcohol-related life problems did emerge, although not in the specific pattern proposed by Jellinek. Three quarters of the men reported moderate consequences of their drinking, such as demotions at work, in their 20s. During their 30s, the men had more serious problems, such as regular blackouts and signs of alcohol withdrawal. By their late 30s and early 40s, these men demonstrated long-term serious consequences of their drinking, which included hallucinations, withdrawal convulsions, and hepatitis or pancreatitis. This study suggests a common pattern among people with chronic alcohol abuse and dependence, one with increasingly severe consequences. This progressive pattern is not inevitable for everyone who abuses alcohol, although we do not as yet understand what distinguishes those who are and those who

are not susceptible (Sobell & Sobell, 1993; Vaillant & Hiller-Sturmhöfel, 1997).

Finally, statistics often link alcohol with violent behavior (Bye, 2007). Numerous studies have found that many people who commit such violent acts as murder, rape, and assault are intoxicated at the time of the crime (Murdoch, Pihl, & Ross, 1990). We hope you are skeptical of this type of correlation. Just because drunkenness and violence overlap does not mean that alcohol will necessarily make you violent. Laboratory studies show that alcohol does make subjects more aggressive (Bushman, 1993). However, whether a person behaves aggressively outside the laboratory probably involves a number of interrelated factors, such as the quantity and timing of alcohol consumed, the person's history of violence, expectations about drinking, and what happens to the individual while intoxicated. Alcohol does not *cause* aggression, but it may increase a person's likelihood of engaging in impulsive acts and it may impair the ability to consider the consequences of acting impulsively (Bye, 2007). Given the right circumstances, such impaired rational thinking may increase a person's risk of behaving aggressively.

Sedative, Hypnotic, or Anxiolytic Substance Use Disorders

The general group of depressants also includes sedative (calming), hypnotic (sleep-inducing), and anxiolytic (anxiety-reducing) drugs (Jaffe & Anthony, 2005). These drugs include barbiturates and benzodiazepines. **Barbiturates** (which include Amytal, Seconal, and Nembutal) are a family of sedative drugs first synthesized in Germany in 1882 (Cozanitis, 2004). They were prescribed to help people sleep and replaced such drugs as alcohol and opium. Barbiturates were widely prescribed by physicians during the 1930s and 1940s, before their addictive properties were fully understood. By the 1950s, they were among the drugs most abused by adults in the United States (Franklin & Frances, 1999).

Benzodiazepines (which today include Valium, Xanax, Rohypnol, and Halcion) have been used since the 1960s, primarily to reduce anxiety. These drugs were originally touted as a miracle cure for the anxieties of living in our highly pressured technological society. Although in 1980 the Food and Drug Administration ruled that they are not appropriate for reducing the tension and anxiety resulting from everyday stresses and strains, an estimated 3.7 billion doses of benzodiazepines are consumed by Americans each year (Shabecoff, 1987). In general, benzodiazepines are considered much safer than barbiturates, with less risk of abuse and dependence (Jaffe & Anthony, 2005). Reports on the misuse of Rohypnol, however, show how dangerous these drugs can be. Rohypnol (otherwise known as "roofies" and the "date rape drug") gained a following among teenagers in the 1990s because it has the same effect as alcohol without the telltale odor. However, there are disturbing reports of men giving the drug to women without their knowledge, making it easier for them to engage in date rape (Smith & Wesson, 1999).

■ Clinical Description

At low doses, barbiturates relax the muscles and can produce a mild feeling of well-being. However, larger doses can have results similar to those of heavy drinking: slurred speech and problems walking, concentrating, and working. At extremely high doses, the diaphragm muscles can relax so much that they cause death by suffocation. Overdosing on barbiturates is a common means of suicide.

Like the barbiturates, benzodiazepines are used to calm an individual and induce sleep. In addition, drugs in this class are prescribed as muscle relaxants and anticonvulsants (antiseizure medications). (Jaffe & Anthony, 2005). People who use them for nonmedical reasons report first feeling a pleasant high and a reduction of inhibition, similar to the effects of drinking alcohol. However, with continued use, tolerance and dependence can develop. Users who try to stop taking the drug experience symptoms like those of alcohol withdrawal (anxiety, insomnia, tremors, and delirium).

The DSM-IV-TR criteria for sedative, hypnotic, and anxiolytic drug use disorders do not differ substantially from those for alcohol disorders. Both include maladaptive behavioral changes such as inappropriate sexual or aggressive behavior, variable moods, impaired judgment, impaired social or occupational functioning, slurred speech, motor coordination problems, and unsteady gait.

Like alcohol, sedative, hypnotic, and anxiolytic drugs affect the brain by influencing the GABA neurotransmitter system (Jaffe & Anthony, 2005), although by slightly different mechanisms; as a result, when people combine alcohol with any of these drugs, there can be synergistic effects. In other words, if you drink alcohol after taking a benzodiazepine or barbiturate, the total effects can reach dangerous levels. One theory about actress Marilyn Monroe's death in 1962 is that she combined alcohol with too many barbiturates and unintentionally killed herself.

■ Statistics

Barbiturate use has declined and benzodiazepine use has increased since 1960 (Substance Abuse and Mental Health Services Administration, 2006). Of those seeking treatment for substance-related

---

DSM-IV-TR

DSM TABLE 11.5 Diagnostic Criteria for Sedative, Hypnotic, or Anxiolytic Intoxication

A. Recent use of a sedative, hypnotic, or anxiolytic drug.
B. Clinically significant maladaptive behavioral or psychological changes (e.g., inappropriate sexual or aggressive behavior, mood lability, impaired judgment, impaired social or occupational functioning) that developed during, or shortly after, sedative, hypnotic, or anxiolytic use.
C. One or more of the following signs, developing during, or shortly after, sedative, hypnotic, or anxiolytic use:
 1. Slurred speech
 2. Incoordination
 3. Unsteady gait
 4. Nystagmus
 5. Impairment in attention or memory
 6. Stupor or coma
D. The symptoms are not due to a general medical condition and are not better accounted for by another mental disorder.

Source: Reprinted, with permission, from American Psychiatric Association. (2000). *Diagnostic and statistical manual of mental disorders* (4th ed., text revision). Washington, DC: Author, © 2000 American Psychiatric Association.

---

problems, less than 1% present problems with benzodiazepines compared to other drugs of abuse. Those who do seek help with these drugs tend to be female, Caucasian, and over the age of 35 (Substance Abuse and Mental Health Services Administration, 2006).

CONCEPT CHECK 11.1

Part A

Check your understanding of substance-related definitions by stating whether the following case summaries describe (a) use, (b) intoxication, (c) abuse, or (d) dependence.

1. Joe is a member of the high school football team and is out celebrating a big win. Joe doesn't believe in drinking alcohol, but he doesn't mind taking a hit of marijuana every now and then. Because Joe had such a good game, he decides to smoke marijuana to celebrate. Despite his great performance in the game, Joe is easily irritated, laughing one minute and yelling the next. The more Joe boasts about his stats, the more difficult it is to understand him. _____

2. Jill routinely drinks diet cola. Instead of having coffee in the morning, she heads for the fridge. Another habit of Jill's is having a cigarette immediately after dinner. If for some reason Jill is unable to have her diet cola in the morning or her cigarette in the evening, she is not dependent on them and can still function normally. _____

3. Steve is a 23-year-old college student who started drinking heavily when he was 16. Instead of getting drunk at weekend parties, Steve drinks a moderate amount every night. In high school, Steve would become drunk after about six beers; now his tolerance has more than doubled. Steve claims alcohol relieves the pressures of college life. He once attempted to quit drinking, but he had chills, fever, diarrhea, nausea and vomiting, and body aches and pains. _____

4. Jan is 32 and has just been fired from her third job in 1 year. She has been absent from work 2 days a week for the past 3 weeks. Not only did her boss telephone her and find her speech slurred, but she was also seen at a local pub in a drunken state during regular office hours. During her previous job, she came to work with alcohol on her breath and was unable to conduct herself in an orderly fashion. When confronted about her problems, Jan went home and tried to forget the situation by drinking more. _____

Part B

Match the following disorders with their corresponding effects: (a) substance-related disorder, (b) dementia, (c) impulse-control disorder, (d) alcohol use disorder, and (e) Wernicke-Korsakoff syndrome.

(continued)

CONCEPT CHECK 11.1

(continued)

5. Disorder in which the effects of the drug impede the ability to function properly by affecting vision, motor control, reaction time, memory, and hearing. _____ _____

6. Disorder that deprives a person of the ability to resist acting on a drive or temptation. _____

7. Disorder that affects the way people think, feel, and behave. _____

8. Disorder involving the decline of intellectual abilities through, for example, excess consumption of alcohol. __ _____

DSM TABLE 11.6 Diagnostic Criteria for Amphetamine (or Related Substance) Intoxication

A. Use of amphetamine or a related substance (e.g., methylphenidate).

B. Clinically significant maladaptive behavioral or psychological changes (e.g., euphoria or affective blunting; changes in sociability; hypervigilance; interpersonal sensitivity, anxiety, tension, or anger; stereotyped behaviors; impaired judgment or impaired social or occupational functioning) that developed during, or shortly after, use of amphetamine or a related substance.

C. Two (or more) of the following, developing during, or shortly after, use of amphetamine or a related substance:
  1. Tachycardia or bradycardia
  2. Pupillary dilation
  3. Elevated or lowered blood pressure
  4. Perspiration or chills
  5. Nausea or vomiting
  6. Evidence of weight loss
  7. Psychomotor agitation or retardation
  8. Muscular weakness, respiratory depression, chest pain, or cardiac arrhythmias
  9. Confusion, seizures, dyskinesias, dystonias, or coma

D. The symptoms are not due to a general medical condition and are not better accounted for by another mental disorder.

Specify if:
  With perceptual disturbances

Source: Reprinted, with permission, from American Psychiatric Association. (2000). *Diagnostic and statistical manual of mental disorders* (4th ed., text revision). Washington, DC: Author, © 2000 American Psychiatric Association.

STIMULANTS

Of all the psychoactive drugs used in the United States, the most commonly consumed are stimulants. Included in this group are caffeine (in coffee, chocolate, and many soft drinks), nicotine (in tobacco products such as cigarettes), amphetamines, and cocaine. You probably used caffeine when you got up this morning. In contrast to the depressant drugs, stimulants—as their name suggests—make you more alert and energetic. They have a long history of use. Chinese physicians, for example, have used an amphetamine compound called Ma-huang *(Ephedra sinica)* for more than 5,000 years (King & Ellinwood, 1997). We describe several stimulants and their effects on behavior, mood, and cognition.

Amphetamine Use Disorders

At low doses, amphetamines can induce feelings of elation and vigor and can reduce fatigue. You literally feel "up." However, after a period of elevation, you come back down and "crash," feeling depressed or tired. In sufficient quantities, stimulants can lead to **amphetamine use disorders.**

Amphetamines are manufactured in the laboratory; they were first synthesized in 1887 and later used as a treatment for asthma and as a nasal decongestant (King & Ellinwood, 1997). Because amphetamines also reduce appetite, some people take them to lose weight. Adolf Hitler, partly because of his other physical maladies, became addicted to amphetamines (Heston & Heston, 2000). Long-haul truck drivers, pilots, and some college students trying to "pull all-nighters" use amphetamines to get that extra energy boost and stay awake. Amphetamines are prescribed for people with *narcolepsy,* a sleep disorder characterized by excessive sleepiness. Some of these drugs (Ritalin) are even given to children with *attention deficit/hyperactivity disorder (ADHD)* (discussed in Chapter 14), although these too are being abused for their psychostimulant effects. One study found that as many as 1 in 10 students at one college reported using prescription stimulants illegally (Carroll, McLaughlin, & Blake, 2006).

DSM-IV-TR diagnostic criteria for amphetamine intoxication include significant behavioral symptoms, such as euphoria or affective blunting (a lack of emotional expression), changes in sociability, interpersonal sensitivity, anxiety, tension, anger, stereotyped behaviors, impaired judgment, and impaired social or occupational functioning. In addition, physiological symptoms occur during or shortly after amphetamine or related substances are ingested and can include heart rate or blood pressure changes, perspiration or chills, nausea or vomiting, weight loss, muscular weakness, respiratory depression, chest pain, seizures, or coma. The danger in using amphetamines and the other stimulants is their negative effects. Severe intoxication or overdose can cause hallucinations, panic, agitation, and paranoid delusions (Jaffe, Ling, & Rawson, 2005). Amphetamine tolerance builds quickly, making it doubly dangerous. Withdrawal often results in apathy, prolonged periods of sleep, irritability, and depression.

Periodically, certain "designer drugs" appear in local mini-epidemics. An amphetamine called methylene-dioxymethamphetamine (MDMA), first synthesized in 1912 in Germany, was used as an appetite suppressant (Grob & Poland, 1997). Recreational use of this drug, now commonly called Ecstasy, rose sharply in the late 1980s. After methamphetamine, MDMA is the club drug most often bringing people to emergency rooms, and it has passed LSD in frequency of use (Substance Abuse and Mental Health Services Administration, 2006). Its effects are best described by a user: "just like speed but without the comedown, and you feel warm and trippy like acid, but without the possibility of a major freak-out" (O'Hagan, 1992, p. 10). A purified, crystallized form of amphetamine, called crystal meth (or "ice"), is ingested through smoking. This drug causes marked aggressive tendencies and stays in the system longer than cocaine, making it particularly dangerous. This drug gained popularity in the gay community, although its use is now spreading to others (Parsons, Kelley, & Weiser, in press). However enjoyable these various amphetamines may be in the short term, the potential for users to become dependent on them is extremely high, with great risk for long-term difficulties.

Amphetamines stimulate the central nervous system by enhancing the activity of norepinephrine and dopamine. Specifically, amphetamines help the release of these neurotransmitters and block their reuptake, thereby making more of them available throughout the system (Jaffe & Anthony, 2005). Too much amphetamine—and therefore too much dopamine and norepinephrine—can lead to hallucinations and delusions. As we see in Chapter 13, this effect has stimulated theories on the causes of schizophrenia, which can also include hallucinations and delusions.

Cocaine Use Disorders

The use and misuse of drugs, such as those leading to **cocaine use disorders,** wax and wane according to societal fashion, moods, and sanctions. Cocaine replaced amphetamines as the stimulant of choice in the 1970s (Jaffe, Rawson, & Ling, 2005). Cocaine is derived from the leaves of the coca plant, a flowering bush indigenous to South America. In his essay "On Coca" (1885/1974, p. 60), a young Sigmund Freud wrote of cocaine's magical properties: "I have tested [the] effect of coca, which wards off hunger, sleep, and fatigue and steels one to intellectual effort, some dozen times on myself."

Latin Americans have chewed coca leaves for centuries to get relief from hunger and fatigue (Musto, 1992). Cocaine was intro-

duced into the United States in the late 19th century; it was widely used from then until the 1920s. In 1885, Parke, Davis & Co. manufactured coca and cocaine in 15 forms, including coca-leaf cigarettes and cigars, inhalants, and crystals. For people who couldn't afford these products, a cheaper way to get cocaine was in Coca-Cola, which up until 1903 contained a small amount (60 mg of cocaine per 8-ounce serving) (Jaffe, Rawson, et al., 2005).

■ Clinical Description

Like the amphetamines, in small amounts cocaine increases alertness, produces euphoria, increases blood pressure and pulse, and causes insomnia and loss of appetite. Remember that Danny snorted (inhaled) cocaine when he partied through the night with his friends. He later said the drug made him feel powerful and invincible—the only way he really felt self-confident. The effects of cocaine are short lived; for Danny they lasted less than an hour, and he had to snort repeatedly to keep himself up. During these binges, he often became paranoid, experiencing exaggerated fears that he would be caught or that someone would steal his cocaine. Such paranoia—referred to as *cocaine-induced paranoia*—is common among cocaine abusers, occurring in two thirds or more (Kalayasiri et al., 2006). Cocaine also makes the heart beat more rapidly and irregularly, and it can have fatal consequences, depending on a person's physical condition and the amount of the drug ingested. John Entwistle, bassist for the rock group the Who, died of a heart attack in 2002 as the result of cocaine ingestion—his heart already weakened by chronic cocaine use.

We saw that alcohol can damage the developing fetus. It has also been suspected that the use of cocaine (especially crack) by

For centuries, Latin Americans have chewed coca leaves for relief from hunger and fatigue.

DSM-IV-TR

DSM TABLE 11.7 Diagnostic Criteria for Cocaine Intoxication

A. Recent use of cocaine.
B. Clinically significant maladaptive behavioral or psychological changes (e.g., euphoria or affective blunting; changes in sociability; hypervigilance; interpersonal sensitivity; anxiety, tension, or anger; stereotyped behaviors; impaired judgment or impaired social or occupational functioning) that developed, during or shortly after, use of cocaine.
C. Two (or more) of the following, developing during, or shortly after, cocaine use:
  1. Tachycardia or bradycardia
  2. Pupillary dilation
  3. Elevated or lowered blood pressure
  4. Perspiration or chills
  5. Nausea or vomiting
  6. Evidence of weight loss
  7. Psychomotor agitation or retardation
  8. Muscular weakness, respiratory depression, chest pain, or cardiac arrhythmias
  9. Confusion, seizures, dyskinesias, dystonias, or coma
D. The symptoms are not due to a general medical condition and are not better accounted for by another mental disorder.
Specify if:
  With perceptual disturbances

pregnant women *may* adversely affect their babies. Crack babies appear at birth to be more irritable than normal babies and have long bouts of high-pitched crying. They were originally thought to have permanent brain damage, although recent research suggests that the effects are less dramatic than first feared (Schiller & Allen, 2005). Numerous negative effects were initially attributed to the mother's cocaine use. However, a closer look at these children suggests that we may have been too quick to blame cocaine exclusively. Some work suggests that many children born to mothers who have used cocaine during pregnancy may have decreased birth weight and decreased head circumference, but they show no evidence of problems with cognitive or motor skills at birth or 1 month later (Gold, 1997; Woods, Eyler, Behnke, & Conlon, 1992). The problem with evaluating most children born to mothers who used cocaine is that their mothers almost always used other substances as well, including alcohol and nicotine. Many of these children are raised in disrupted home environments, which further complicates the picture. It may be that damage once attributed only to cocaine results from a combination of drugs, inadequate parenting, or both. Continuing research should help us better understand the negative effects of cocaine on children. One study suggests that prenatal cocaine exposure may affect the fetus's "biological clock"—the suprachiasmatic nucleus (Weaver, Rivkees, & Reppert, 1992), which would cause a reaction similar to jet lag that might contribute to the irritability and other problems experienced by the newborn.

■ Statistics

In the United States, more than 1.5 million people 12 years and older report abusing or being dependent upon cocaine, more than any other drug besides marijuana (Substance Abuse and Mental Health Services Administration, 2006). White males account for about a third of all admissions to emergency rooms for cocaine-related problems (29%) followed by black males (23%), white females (18%), and black females (12%) (Substance Abuse and Mental Health Services Administration, 2002). Approximately 17% of cocaine users have also used crack cocaine (a crystallized form of cocaine that is smoked) (Closser, 1992). In 1991, one estimate was that about 0.2% of Americans had tried crack and that an increasing proportion of the abusers seeking treatment were young, unemployed adults living in urban areas (Closser, 1992).

Cocaine is in the same group of stimulants as amphetamines because it has similar effects on the brain. The "up" seems to come primarily from the effect of cocaine on the dopamine system. Look at ■ Figure 11.6 to see how this action occurs. Cocaine enters the bloodstream and is carried to the brain. There the cocaine molecules block the reuptake of dopamine. As you know, neurotransmitters released at the synapse stimulate the next neuron and then are recycled back to the original neuron. Cocaine seems to bind to places where dopamine neurotransmitters reenter their home neuron, blocking their reuptake. The dopamine that cannot be taken in by the neuron remains in the synapse, causing repeated stimulation of the next neuron. This stimulation of the dopamine neurons in the "pleasure pathway" (the site in the brain that seems to be involved in the experience of pleasure) causes the high associated with cocaine use.

As late as the 1980s, many felt cocaine was a wonder drug that produced feelings of euphoria without being addictive (Jaffe, Rawson et al., 2005). Such a conservative source as the *Comprehensive Textbook of Psychiatry* in 1980 indicated that, "taken no more than two or three times per week, cocaine creates no serious problems" (Grinspoon & Bakalar, 1980). Just imagine—a drug that gives you extra energy, helps you think clearly and more creatively, and lets you accomplish more throughout the day, all without any negative side effects! In our highly competitive and complex technological society, this would be a dream come true. But, as you probably realize, such temporary benefits have a high cost. Cocaine fooled us. Dependence does not resemble that of many other drugs early on; typically, people only find that they have a growing inability to resist taking more (Jaffe, Rawson, et al., 2005). Few negative effects are noted at first; however, with continued use, sleep is disrupted, increased tolerance causes a need for higher doses, paranoia and other negative symptoms set in, and the cocaine user gradually becomes socially isolated.

Again, Danny's case illustrates this pattern. He was a social user for a number of years, using cocaine only with friends and only occasionally. Eventually, he had more frequent episodes of excessive use or binges, and he found himself increasingly craving the drug between binges. After the binges, Danny would crash and sleep. Cocaine withdrawal isn't like that of alcohol. Instead of rapid heartbeat, tremors, or nausea, withdrawal from cocaine produces pronounced feelings of apathy and boredom. Think for a minute how dangerous this type of withdrawal is. First, you're bored with everything and find little pleasure from the everyday activities of work or relationships. The one that can "bring you back to life" is cocaine. As you can imagine, a particularly vicious cycle develops: Cocaine is abused, withdrawal causes apathy, cocaine abuse resumes. The atypical withdrawal pattern misled people into believing that cocaine was not addictive. We now know that cocaine abusers go through patterns of tolerance and withdrawal comparable to those experienced by abusers of other psychoactive drugs (Jaffe, Rawson, et al., 2005).

Nicotine Use Disorders

When you think of addicts, what image comes to mind? Do you see dirty and disheveled people huddled on an old mattress in an abandoned building, waiting for the next fix? Do you picture businesspeople huddled outside a city building on a rainy afternoon furtively smoking cigarettes? Both these images are accurate, because the nicotine in tobacco is a psychoactive substance that produces patterns of dependence, tolerance, and withdrawal—**nicotine use disorders**—comparable to those of the other drugs we have discussed so far (Hughes, 2005). In 1942, the Scottish physician Lennox Johnson "shot up" nicotine extract and found after 80 injections that he liked it more than cigarettes and felt deprived without it (Kanigel, 1988). This colorless, oily liquid—called nicotine after Jean Nicot, who introduced tobacco to the French court in the 16th century—is what gives smoking its pleasurable qualities.

The tobacco plant is indigenous to North America, and Native Americans cultivated and smoked the leaves centuries ago. Today, about 25% of all Americans smoke, which is down from the

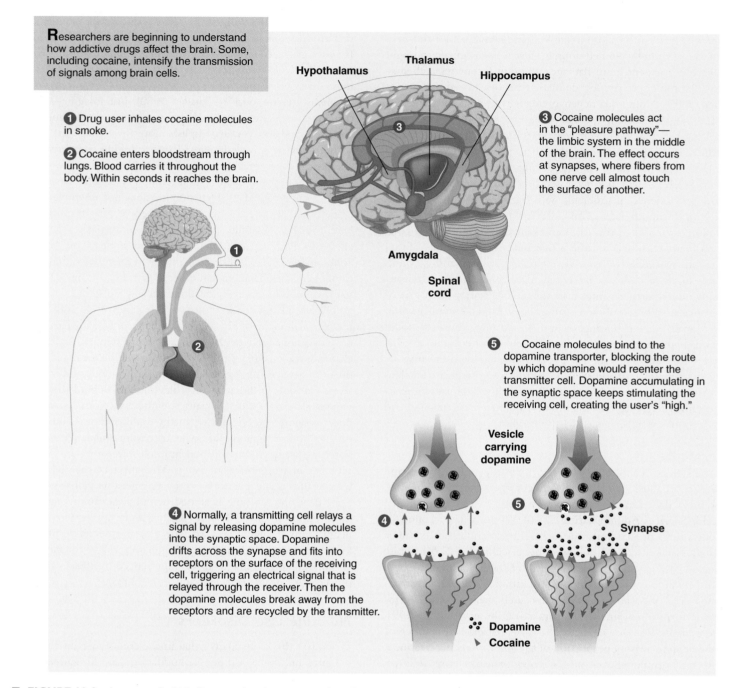

Researchers are beginning to understand how addictive drugs affect the brain. Some, including cocaine, intensify the transmission of signals among brain cells.

1 Drug user inhales cocaine molecules in smoke.

2 Cocaine enters bloodstream through lungs. Blood carries it throughout the body. Within seconds it reaches the brain.

Hypothalamus
Thalamus
Hippocampus
Amygdala
Spinal cord

3 Cocaine molecules act in the "pleasure pathway"—the limbic system in the middle of the brain. The effect occurs at synapses, where fibers from one nerve cell almost touch the surface of another.

5 Cocaine molecules bind to the dopamine transporter, blocking the route by which dopamine would reenter the transmitter cell. Dopamine accumulating in the synaptic space keeps stimulating the receiving cell, creating the user's "high."

Vesicle carrying dopamine

4 Normally, a transmitting cell relays a signal by releasing dopamine molecules into the synaptic space. Dopamine drifts across the synapse and fits into receptors on the surface of the receiving cell, triggering an electrical signal that is relayed through the receiver. Then the dopamine molecules break away from the receptors and are recycled by the transmitter.

Synapse

Dopamine
Cocaine

■ **FIGURE 11.6** Anatomy of a high. (Reprinted, with permission, from Booth, W., 1990. The anatomy of a high. *Washington Post National Weekly Edition*, March 26–April 1, p. 38, © 1990 The Washington Post.)

42.4% who were smokers in 1965 (National Institute on Drug Abuse, 2006).

DSM-IV-TR does not describe an intoxication pattern for nicotine. Rather, it lists withdrawal symptoms, which include depressed mood, insomnia, irritability, anxiety, difficulty concentrating, restlessness, and increased appetite and weight gain. Nicotine in small doses stimulates the central nervous system; it can relieve stress and improve mood. But it can also cause high blood pressure and increase the risk of heart disease and cancer (Hughes, 2005). High doses can blur your vision, cause confusion, lead to convulsions, and sometimes even cause death. Once smokers are dependent on nicotine, going without it causes these withdrawal symptoms. If you doubt the addictive power of nicotine, consider that the rate of relapse among people trying to give up drugs is equivalent among those using alcohol, heroin, and cigarettes (see ■ Figure 11.7).

Nicotine is inhaled into the lungs, where it enters the bloodstream. Only 7 to 19 seconds after a person inhales the smoke, the nicotine reaches the brain (Benowitz, 1996). Nicotine appears to stimulate specific receptors—nicotinic acetylcholine receptors (nAChRs)—in the midbrain reticular formation and the limbic system, the site of the pleasure pathway mentioned earlier (Hughes, 2005). Some evidence also points to how nicotine may affect the fetal brain, possibly increasing the likelihood that chil-

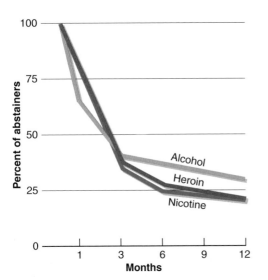

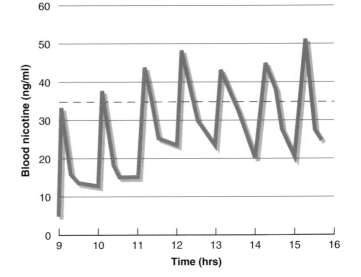

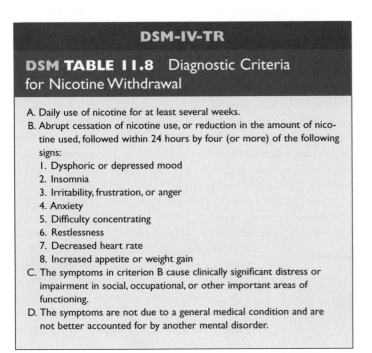

■ **FIGURE 11.7**   Relapse rates for nicotine compared to alcohol and heroin. Smokers trying to give up cigarettes backslide about as often as alcoholics and heroin addicts. (Adapted, with permission, from Kanigel, R., 1988, October/November. Nicotine becomes addictive. *Science Illustrated,* pp. 12–14, 19–21, © 1988 Science Illustrated.)

■ **FIGURE 11.8**   Smoking patterns and nicotine levels. This subject smoked one cigarette an hour, illustrating how smokers inhale more or less deeply or often, to get the desired blood levels of nicotine—on average 35 nanograms per milliliter. Adapted, with permission, from Kanigel, R., 1988, October/November. Nicotine becomes addictive. *Science Illustrated,* pp. 12–14, 19–21, ©1988 Science Illustrated.)

dren of mothers who smoke during pregnancy will smoke later in life (Kandel, Wu, & Davies, 1994). Smokers dose themselves throughout the day in an effort to keep nicotine at a steady level in the bloodstream (see ■ Figure 11.8; Dalack, Glassman, & Covey, 1993).

Smoking has been linked with signs of negative affect, such as depression, anxiety, and anger (Rasmusson, Anderson, Krishnan-Sarin, Wu, & Paliwal, 2006). For example, many people who quit smoking but later resume report that feelings of depression

DSM-IV-TR

DSM TABLE 11.8   Diagnostic Criteria for Nicotine Withdrawal

A. Daily use of nicotine for at least several weeks.

B. Abrupt cessation of nicotine use, or reduction in the amount of nicotine used, followed within 24 hours by four (or more) of the following signs:
1. Dysphoric or depressed mood
2. Insomnia
3. Irritability, frustration, or anger
4. Anxiety
5. Difficulty concentrating
6. Restlessness
7. Decreased heart rate
8. Increased appetite or weight gain

C. The symptoms in criterion B cause clinically significant distress or impairment in social, occupational, or other important areas of functioning.

D. The symptoms are not due to a general medical condition and are not better accounted for by another mental disorder.

Source: Reprinted, with permission, from American Psychiatric Association. (2000). *Diagnostic and statistical manual of mental disorders* (4th ed., text revision). Washington, DC: Author, © 2000 American Psychiatric Association.

or anxiety were responsible for the relapse (Hughes, 2005). This finding suggests that nicotine may help improve mood.

There is a complex relationship between cigarette smoking and negative affect. For example, severe depression is found to occur significantly more often among people with nicotine dependence (Breslau, Kilbey, & Andreski, 1993). Kenneth Kendler, conducted a large-scale twin study of depression among women, and found that among identical twins there was a relationship between smoking and depression only if both pairs of identical twins had a history of depression or smoking (Kendler, Neale, MacLean, et al., 1993). In other words, if only one of the pair had a history of depression, then no relationship existed between depression and smoking. What does this mean? It suggests that, in some women, a genetic vulnerability, combined with personal experiences, may lead to both depression and smoking, not that depression causes smoking or smoking causes depression. (We discuss evidence for the genetics of smoking when we cover the causes of substance abuse later in this chapter.)

Caffeine Use Disorders

Caffeine is the most common of the psychoactive substances, used regularly by 90% of all Americans (Goldstein, 1994). Called the "gentle stimulant" because it is thought to be the least harmful of all addictive drugs, caffeine can still lead to **caffeine use disorders.** This drug is found in tea, coffee, many cola drinks sold today, and cocoa products.

As most of you have experienced firsthand, caffeine in small doses can elevate your mood and decrease fatigue. In larger doses, it can make you feel jittery and can cause insomnia. Because caffeine takes a relatively long time to leave our bodies (it has a blood half-life of about 6 hours), sleep can be disturbed if the caffeine is ingested in the hours close to bedtime. This effect is especially

DSM-IV-TR

DSM TABLE 11.9 Diagnostic Criteria for Caffeine Intoxication

A. Recent consumption of caffeine, usually in excess of 250 mg (e.g., more than 2–3 cups of brewed coffee).

B. Five (or more) of the following signs, developing during, or shortly after, caffeine use:
  1. Restlessness
  2. Nervousness
  3. Excitement
  4. Insomnia
  5. Flushed face
  6. Diuresis
  7. Gastrointestinal disturbance
  8. Muscle twitching
  9. Rambling flow of thought and speech
  10. Tachycardia or cardiac arrhythmia
  11. Periods of inexhaustibility
  12. Psychomotor agitation

C. The symptoms in criterion B cause clinically significant distress or impairment in social, occupational, or other important areas of functioning.

D. The symptoms are not due to a general medical condition and are not better accounted for by another mental disorder (e.g., anxiety disorder).

Source: Reprinted, with permission, from American Psychiatric Association. (2000). *Diagnostic and statistical manual of mental disorders* (4th ed., text revision). Washington, DC: Author. © 2000 American Psychiatric Association.

pronounced among those already suffering from insomnia (Saln-Pascual, Castao, Shiromani, Valencia-Flores, & Campos, 2006). As with the other psychoactive drugs, people react variously to caffeine; some are sensitive to it, and others can consume relatively large amounts with little effect. Research suggests that moderate use of caffeine (a cup of coffee per day) by pregnant women does not harm the developing fetus (Mills et al., 1993).

As with other stimulants, regular caffeine use can result in tolerance and dependence on the drug. Those of you who have experienced headaches, drowsiness, and a generally unpleasant mood when denied your morning coffee have had the withdrawal symptoms characteristic of this drug (Strain & Griffiths, 2005). Caffeine's effect on the brain seems to involve the neurotransmitters adenosine and, to a lesser extent, *serotonin* (Greden & Walters, 1997). Caffeine seems to block adenosine reuptake. However, we do not yet know the role of adenosine in brain function or whether the interruption of the adenosine system is responsible for the elation and increased energy that come with caffeine use.

"You can't simply focus on nicotine itself. Many medications do that—they focus on replacing the nicotine, such as nicotine gum or the patch—and that's valuable, but you really have to focus on all the triggers, the cues, and the environment."

OPIOIDS

The word *opiate* refers to the natural chemicals in the opium poppy that have a narcotic effect (they relieve pain and induce sleep). In some circumstances, they can cause **opioid use disorders.** The broader term *opioids* refers to the family of substances that includes natural opiates, synthetic variations (methadone, pethidine), and the comparable substances that occur naturally in the brain (enkephalins, beta-endorphins, and dynorphins) (Jaffe & Strain, 2005). References to the use of opium as a medicine date back more than 3,500 years (Jaffe & Anthony, 2005). In *The Wizard of Oz,* the Wicked Witch of the West puts Dorothy, Toto, and their companions to sleep by making them walk through a field of poppies, a literary allusion to the opium poppies used to produce morphine, codeine, and heroin.

Just as the poppies lull the Tin Man, the Scarecrow, Dorothy, the Cowardly Lion, and Toto, opiates induce euphoria, drowsiness, and slowed breathing. High doses can lead to death if respiration is completely depressed. Opiates are also analgesics, substances that help relieve pain. People are sometimes given morphine before and after surgery to calm them and help block pain.

Withdrawal from opioids can be so unpleasant that people may continue to use these drugs despite a sincere desire to stop. However, barbiturate and alcohol withdrawal can be even more distressing. The perception among many people that opioid withdrawal can be life threatening stems from the experiences of heroin addicts in the 1920s and 1930s. These users had access to cheaper and purer forms of the drug than are available today, and withdrawal had more serious side effects than withdrawal from the weaker versions currently in use (McKim, 1991). Even so, people who cease or reduce their opioid intake begin to experience symptoms within 6 to 12 hours; these include excessive yawning, nausea and vomiting, chills, muscle aches, diarrhea, and insomnia—temporarily disrupting work, school, and social relationships. The symptoms can persist for 1 to 3 days, and the withdrawal process is completed in about a week.

Abuse of and dependence on heroin—the most commonly abused opiate—are reported in about one-quarter million people in the United States (Substance Abuse and Mental Health Services Administration, 2006). Emergency room admissions resulting from heroin abuse between 1995 and 2002 indicate a 34.5% increase during this period (Substance Abuse and Mental Health Services Administration, 2003a). People who use opiates face risks beyond addiction and the threat of overdose. Because these drugs are usually injected intravenously, users are at increased risk for HIV infection and therefore AIDS.

The life of an opiate addict can be bleak. Results from a 33-year follow-up study of more than 80 addicts in an English town highlight a pessimistic view of many of their lives (Rathod, Addenbrooke, & Rosenbach, 2005). At the follow-up, 22% of addicts had died, about twice the national rate of about 12%. More than half the deaths were the result of drug overdose, and several took their own lives. The good news from this study was that of those who survived, 80% were no longer using opioids and the remaining 20% were being treated with methadone.

Opium poppies.

The high or "rush" experienced by users comes from activation of the body's natural opioid system. In other words, the brain already has its own opioids—called enkephalins and endorphins—that provide narcotic effects (Jaffe & Strain, 2005). Heroin, opium, morphine, and other opiates activate this system. The discovery of the natural opioid system was a major breakthrough in the field of psychopharmacology: Not only does it allow us to study the effects of addictive drugs on the brain, but it also has led to important discoveries that may help us treat people dependent on these drugs.

HALLUCINOGENS

The substances we have examined so far affect people by making them feel "up," if they are stimulants such as cocaine, caffeine, and nicotine, or "down," if they are depressants such as alcohol and the

DSM-IV-TR

DSM TABLE 11.10 Diagnostic Criteria for Opioid Intoxication

A. Recent use of an opioid.
B. Clinically significant maladaptive behavioral or psychological changes (e.g., initial euphoria followed by apathy, dysphoria, psychomotor agitation or retardation, impaired judgment, or impaired social or occupational functioning) that developed during, or shortly after, opioid use.
C. Pupillary constriction (or pupillary dilation due to anoxia from severe overdose) and one (or more) of the following signs, developing during, or shortly after, opioid use:
  1. Drowsiness or coma
  2. Slurred speech
  3. Impairment in attention or memory
D. The symptoms are not due to a general medical condition and are not better accounted for by another mental disorder.
Specify if:
  With perceptual disturbances

Source: Reprinted, with permission, from American Psychiatric Association. (2000). *Diagnostic and statistical manual of mental disorders* (4th ed., text revision). Washington, DC: Author, © 2000 American Psychiatric Association.

barbiturates. Next, we explore the substances that can lead to **hallucinogen use disorder.** They essentially change the way the user perceives the world. Sight, sound, feelings, taste, and even smell are distorted, sometimes in dramatic ways, when a person is under the influence of drugs such as marijuana and LSD.

Marijuana

Marijuana (Cannabis sativa) was the drug of choice in the 1960s and early 1970s. Although it has decreased in popularity, it is still the most routinely used illegal substance, with 14.6 million Americans reporting they used the drug in the past month (Substance Abuse and Mental Health Services Administration, 2006). Marijuana is the name given to the dried parts of the cannabis or hemp plant (its full scientific name is *Cannabis sativa*) (Hall & Degenhardt, 2005). Cannabis grows wild throughout the tropical and temperate regions of the world, which accounts for one of its nicknames, "weed."

> Three men, so the story goes, arrived one night at the closed gates of a Persian city. One was intoxicated by alcohol, another was under the spell of opium, and the third was steeped in marihuana.
> The first blustered: "Let's break the gates down."
> "Nay," yawned the opium eater, "let us rest until morning, when we may enter through the wide-flung portals."
> "Do as you like," was the announcement of the marihuana addict. "But I shall stroll in through the keyhole!" (Rowell & Rowell, 1939)

As demonstrated by this parable, people who smoke marijuana often experience altered perceptions of the world.

Reactions to marijuana usually include mood swings. Otherwise-normal experiences seem extremely funny, or the person might enter a dreamlike state in which time seems to stand still. Users often report heightened sensory experiences, seeing vivid colors, or appreciating the subtleties of music. Perhaps more than any other drug, however, marijuana can produce different reactions in people. It is not uncommon for someone to report having no reaction to the first use of the drug; it also appears that people can "turn off" the high if they are sufficiently motivated (Hall & Degenhardt, 2005). The feelings of well-being produced by small doses can change to paranoia, hallucinations, and dizziness when larger doses are taken. High school–age marijuana smokers get lower grades and are less likely to graduate (Lynskey & Hall, 2000). Research on frequent marijuana users suggests that impairments of memory, concentration, relationships with others, and employment may be negative outcomes of long-term use, although some researchers suggest that that some psychological problems precede usage—increasing the likelihood that someone will use marijuana (Macleod et al., 2004).

The evidence for marijuana tolerance is contradictory. Chronic and heavy users report tolerance, especially to the euphoric high (Johnson, 1991); they are unable to reach the levels of pleasure they experienced earlier. However, evidence also indicates "reverse tolerance," when regular users experience more pleasure from the drug after repeated use. Major signs of withdrawal do not usually occur with marijuana. Chronic users who stop taking the drug report a period of irritability, restlessness, ap-

©Thomas R. Fletcher/Stock, Boston, Inc.

Marijuana.

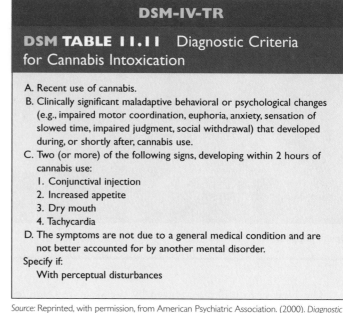

DSM TABLE 11.11 Diagnostic Criteria for Cannabis Intoxication

A. Recent use of cannabis.
B. Clinically significant maladaptive behavioral or psychological changes (e.g., impaired motor coordination, euphoria, anxiety, sensation of slowed time, impaired judgment, social withdrawal) that developed during, or shortly after, cannabis use.
C. Two (or more) of the following signs, developing within 2 hours of cannabis use:
　1. Conjunctival injection
　2. Increased appetite
　3. Dry mouth
　4. Tachycardia
D. The symptoms are not due to a general medical condition and are not better accounted for by another mental disorder.
Specify if:
　With perceptual disturbances

Source: Reprinted, with permission, from American Psychiatric Association. (2000). *Diagnostic and statistical manual of mental disorders* (4th ed., text revision). Washington, DC: Author, © 2000 American Psychiatric Association.

petite loss, nausea, and difficulty sleeping (National Institute on Drug Abuse, 2005), but no evidence suggests they go through the craving and psychological dependence characteristic of other substances (Grinspoon & Bakalar, 1997).

Controversy surrounds the use of marijuana for medicinal purposes. The popular media often describe individuals who illegally use marijuana to help ward off the nausea associated with chemotherapy or to ease the symptoms of other illnesses such as glaucoma, and the medical benefits of this drug may be promising (National Institute on Drug Abuse, 2005). Unfortunately, marijuana smoke may contain as many carcinogens as tobacco smoke, and long-term use may contribute to diseases such as lung cancer. This potential health risk should be weighed against the benefits of using marijuana under certain medical circumstances.

Most marijuana users inhale the drug by smoking the dried leaves in marijuana cigarettes; others use preparations such as hashish, which is the dried form of the resin in the leaves of the female plant. Marijuana contains more than 80 varieties of the chemicals called *cannabinoids,* which are believed to alter mood and behavior. The most common of these chemicals includes the *tetrahydrocannabinols,* otherwise known as *THC.* An exciting finding in the area of marijuana research is that the brain makes its own version of THC, a neurochemical called *anandamide* after the Sanskrit word *ananda,* which means "bliss" (Fackelmann, 1993). Scientists are only beginning to explore how this neurochemical affects the brain and behavior.

LSD and Other Hallucinogens

On a Monday afternoon in April 1943, Albert Hoffmann, a scientist at a large Swiss chemical company, prepared to test a newly synthesized compound. He had been studying derivatives of ergot, a fungus that grows on diseased kernels of grain, and sensed that he had missed something important in the 25th compound of the lysergic acid series. Ingesting what he thought was an infinitesimally small amount of this drug, which he referred to in his notes as LSD-25, he waited to see what subtle changes might come over him as a result. Thirty minutes later he reported no change, but some 40 minutes after taking the drug he began to feel dizzy and had a noticeable desire to laugh. Riding his bicycle home, he hallucinated that the buildings he passed were moving and melting. By the time he arrived home, he was terrified he was losing his mind. Hoffmann was experiencing the first recorded "trip" on LSD (Jones, 2005).

LSD (*d*-lysergic acid diethylamide) (sometimes referred to as "acid") is the most common hallucinogenic drug. It is produced synthetically in laboratories, although naturally occurring derivatives of this grain fungus (ergot) have been found historically. In Europe during the Middle Ages, an outbreak of illnesses occurred as a result of people's eating grain that was infected with the fungus. One version of this illness—later called *ergotism*—constricted the flow of blood to the arms or legs and eventually resulted in gangrene and the loss of limbs. Another type of illness resulted in convulsions, delirium, and hallucinations. Years later, scientists connected ergot with the illnesses and began studying versions of this fungus for possible benefits. This is the type of work Hoffmann was engaged in when he discovered LSD's hallucinogenic properties.

LSD remained in the laboratory until the 1960s, when it was first produced illegally for recreational use. The mind-altering effects of the drug suited the social effort to reject established culture and enhanced the search for enlightenment that characterized the mood and behavior of many people during the decade. The late Timothy Leary, at the time a Harvard University research professor, first used LSD in 1961 and immediately began a movement to have every child and adult try the drug and "turn on, tune in, and drop out."

There are a number of other hallucinogens, some occurring naturally in a variety of plants: *psilocybin* (found in certain species of mushrooms); *lysergic acid amide* (found in the seeds of the morning glory plant); *dimethyltryptamine (DMT)* (found in the bark of the Virola tree, which grows in South and Central America); and *mescaline* (found in the peyote cactus plant).

The DSM-IV-TR diagnostic criteria for hallucinogen intoxication are similar to those for marijuana: perceptual changes such as the subjective intensification of perceptions, depersonalization, and hallucinations. Physical symptoms include pupillary dilation, rapid heartbeat, sweating, and blurred vision (American Psychiatric Association, 2000c). Many users have written about hallucinogens, and they describe a variety of experiences. In one of the few well-designed placebo-controlled studies of hallucinogens, researchers at Johns Hopkins School of Medicine gave volunteers either the hallucinogen psilocybin or a control drug (the ADHD medication Ritalin) and assessed their reactions (Griffiths, Richards, McCann, & Jesse, 2006). Psilocybin ingestion resulted in

individualized reactions including perceptual changes (for example, mild visual hallucinations) and mood changes (for example, joy or happiness, anxiety, or fearfulness). Interestingly, the drug increased reports of mystical experiences (for example, deeply felt positive mood), and 2 months later many rated the experience as having a spiritual significance. More research is needed to explore how these types of drugs work, and this research may also tell us how our brains process experiences such as personal meaning and spirituality.

Tolerance develops quickly to a number of hallucinogens, including LSD, psilocybin, and mescaline (Jones, 2005). If taken repeatedly over a period of days, these drugs lose their effectiveness. However, sensitivity returns after about a week of abstinence. For most hallucinogens, no withdrawal symptoms are reported. Even so, a number of concerns have been expressed about their use. One is the possibility of psychotic reactions. Stories in the popular press about people who jumped out of windows because they believed they could fly or who stepped into moving traffic with the mistaken idea that they couldn't be hurt have provided for sensational reading, but little evidence suggests that using hallucinogens produces a greater risk than being drunk or under the influence of any other drug. People do report having "bad trips"; these are the sort of frightening episodes in which clouds turn into threatening monsters or deep feelings of paranoia take over. Usually someone on a bad trip can be "talked down" by supportive people who provide constant reassurance that the experience is the temporary effect of the drug and it will wear off in a few hours.

We still do not fully understand how LSD and the other hallucinogens affect the brain. Most of these drugs bear some resemblance to neurotransmitters; LSD, psilocybin, lysergic acid amide, and DMT are chemically similar to serotonin; mescaline resembles norepinephrine; and a number of other hallucinogens we have not discussed are similar to acetylcholine. However, the mechanisms responsible for the hallucinations and other perceptual changes that users experience remain unknown.

OTHER DRUGS OF ABUSE

A number of other substances are used by individuals to alter sensory experiences. These drugs do not fit neatly into the classes of substances we just described but are nonetheless of great concern because they can be physically damaging to those who ingest them. We briefly describe inhalants, steroids, and a group of drugs commonly referred to as designer drugs.

Inhalants include a variety of substances found in volatile solvents—making them available to breathe into the lungs directly. Among the more common inhalants used for abuse include spray paint, hair spray, paint thinner, gasoline, amyl nitrate, nitrous oxide ("laughing gas"), nail polish remover, felt-tipped markers, airplane glue, contact cement, dry-cleaning fluid, and spot remover (Crowley & Sakai, 2005). Inhalant use is most commonly observed among young males (age 13–15 years) who are economically disadvantaged (Franklin & Frances, 1999). These drugs are rapidly absorbed into the bloodstream through the lungs by inhaling them from containers or on a cloth held up to the mouth and nose. The high associated with the use of inhalants resembles that of alcohol

---

DSM-IV-TR

DSM TABLE 11.12 Diagnostic Criteria for Hallucinogen Intoxication

A. Recent use of a hallucinogen.

B. Clinically significant maladaptive behavioral or psychological changes (e.g., marked anxiety or depression, ideas of reference, fear of losing one's mind, paranoid ideation, impaired judgment, or impaired social or occupational functioning) that developed during, or shortly after, hallucinogen use.

C. Perceptual changes occurring in a state of full wakefulness and alertness (e.g., subjective intensification of perceptions, depersonalization, derealization, illusions, hallucinations, synesthesia) that developed during, or shortly after, hallucinogen use.

D. Two (or more) of the following signs developing during, or shortly after, hallucinogen use:

  1. Pupillary dilation

  2. Tachycardia

  3. Sweating

  4. Palpitations

  5. Blurring of vision

  6. Tremors

  7. Incoordination

E. The symptoms are not due to a general medical condition and are not better accounted for by another mental disorder.

Source: Reprinted, with permission, from American Psychiatric Association. (2000). *Diagnostic and statistical manual of mental disorders* (4th ed., text revision). Washington, DC: Author, © 2000 American Psychiatric Association.

intoxication and usually includes dizziness, slurred speech, incoordination, euphoria, and lethargy (American Psychiatric Association, 2000c). Users build up a tolerance to the drugs, and withdrawal—which involves sleep disturbance, tremors, irritability, and nausea—can last from 2 to 5 days. Unfortunately, use can also increase aggressive and antisocial behavior, and long-term use can damage bone marrow, kidneys, liver, and the brain (Crowley & Sakai, 2005).

Anabolic–androgenic steroids (more commonly referred to as steroids or "roids") are derived from or are a synthesized form of the hormone testosterone (Pope & Brower, 2005). The legitimate medical uses of these drugs focus on people with asthma, anemia, breast cancer, and males with inadequate sexual development. However, the anabolic action of these drugs (that can produce increased body mass) has resulted in their illicit use by those wishing to bulk up and improve their physical abilities. Steroids can be taken orally or through injection, and some estimates suggest that approximately 2% of males will use the drug illegally at some point in their lives (Pope & Brower, 2005). Users sometimes administer the drug on a schedule of several weeks or months followed by a break from its use—called "cycling"—or combine several types of steroids—called "stacking." Steroid use differs from other drug use because the substance does not produce a desirable high but instead is used to enhance performance and body size. Dependence on the substance therefore seems to involve the desire to maintain the performance gains obtained rather than a need to reexperience an altered emotional or physical state. Research on the long-term effects of steroid use seems to suggest that mood disturbances are common (for example, depression, anxiety, and panic attacks) (Pope & Brower, 2005), and there is a concern that more serious physical consequences may result from its regular use.

Another class of drugs—dissociative anesthetics—causes drowsiness, pain relief and the feeling of being out of one's body (Javitt & Zukin, 2005). Sometimes referred to as designer drugs, there are a growing group of drugs developed by pharmaceutical companies to target specific diseases and disorders. It was only a matter of time before some would use the developing technology to design "recreational drugs." We have already described one of the more common illicit designer drugs—MDMA, or Ecstasy—in the section on stimulants. This amphetamine is one of a small but feared growing list of related substances that includes 3,4-methelenedioxy-ethamphetamine (MDEA, or Eve), and 2-(4-bromo-2,5-dimethoxy-phenyl)-ethylamine (BDMPEA, or Nexus). Their ability to heighten a person's auditory and visual perception, as well as the senses of taste and touch, has been incorporated into the activities of those who attend nightclubs, all-night dance parties (raves), or large social gatherings of primarily gay men (called "circuit parties") (McDowell, 1999). Phencyclidine (or PCP) is snorted, smoked, or injected intravenously, and it causes impulsivity and aggressiveness. A drug related to phencyclidine and associated with the "drug club" scene is ketamine (street names include K, Special K, and Cat Valium), a dissociative anesthetic that produces a sense of detachment, along with a reduced awareness of pain (Jaffe, Ling, et al., 2005). Gamma-hydroxybutyrate (GHB, or liquid Ecstasy) is a central nervous system depressant that was marketed in health food stores in the 1980s as a means of stimulating muscle growth. Users report that, at low doses, it can produce a state of relaxation and increased tendency to verbalize but that at higher doses or with alcohol or other drugs it can result in seizures, severe respiratory depression, and coma. Use of all these drugs can result in tolerance and dependence, and their increasing popularity among adolescents and young adults raises significant public health concerns.

©Associated Press

The proliferation of new recreational drugs such as Ecstasy inspires ever more vigilance on the part of the legal system.

CONCEPT CHECK 11.2

Determine whether the following statements about stimulants are true (T) or false (F).

1. ___ Amphetamines have been used as appetite suppressants.
2. ___ Use of crack cocaine by pregnant mothers adversely affects all their babies.
3. ___ Stimulants have been used for more than 5,000 years.
4. ___ Regular use of stimulants can result in tolerance and dependence on the drugs.
5. ___ Amphetamines are naturally occurring drugs that induce feelings of elation and vigor and can reduce fatigue.
6. ___ Compared to all other drugs, caffeine can produce the most variable reactions in people.
7. ___ An ingredient of the beverage Coca-Cola in the 1800s was cocaine.

CAUSES OF SUBSTANCE-RELATED DISORDERS

People continue to use psychoactive drugs for their effects on mood, perception, and behavior despite the obvious negative consequences of abuse and dependence. We saw that despite his clear potential as an individual, Danny continued to use drugs to his detriment. Various factors help explain why people like Danny persist in using drugs. Drug abuse and dependence, once thought to be the result of moral weakness, are now believed to be influenced by a combination of biological and psychosocial factors.

Why do some people use psychoactive drugs without abusing or becoming dependent on them? Why do some people stop using these drugs or use them in moderate amounts after being dependent on them and others continue a lifelong pattern of dependence despite their efforts to stop? These questions continue to occupy the time and attention of numerous researchers throughout the world.

Biological Dimensions

In 2007, Anna Nicole Smith created a sensation when she died from an apparent accidental overdose of at least nine prescription medications, including methadone, valium, and the sedative chloral hydrate. Tragically, just months before, her only son Daniel died,

Anna Nicole Smith and her son Daniel both died from drug complications, raising questions about how environment and biology played roles in their drug use.

also from an apparent drug overdose. Did the son inherit a vulnerability to addiction from his mother? Did he pick up Anna Nicole's habits from living with her over the years? Is it just a coincidence that both mother and son were so involved with drugs?

■ Familial and Genetic Influences

As you already have seen throughout this book, many psychological disorders are influenced in important ways by genetics. Mounting evidence indicates that drug abuse generally, and alcohol abuse specifically, follows this pattern. A great deal of animal research confirms the importance of genetic influences on substance abuse (see, for example, Le et al., 2006). In work with humans, twin, family, and adoption studies indicate that certain people are genetically vulnerable to drug abuse (Rutter, Moffitt, & Caspi, 2006; Volkow, 2005). Twin studies of smoking, for example, find a moderate genetic influence (Lerman et al., 1999). However, most genetic data on substance abuse come from research on alcoholism, which is widely studied because alcohol use is legal and many people are dependent on it (Gordis, 2000d; Lerman et al., 1999). Research in general suggests that genetic risk factors cut across all illicit drugs (Compton, Thomas, Conway, & Colliver, 2005).

In a major twin study, the role of the environment, as well as the role of genetics, was examined in substance use, abuse, and dependence. Researchers studied more than 1,000 pairs of males and questioned them about their use of marijuana, cocaine, hallucinogens, sedatives, stimulants, and opiates (Kendler, Jacobson, Prescott, & Neale, 2003). The findings—which may have major implications for how we approach treatment and prevention—suggest that there are common genetic influences on the use of all of these drugs. However, the *use* of illegal drugs was primarily influenced by environmental factors, while *abuse and dependence* may be influenced primarily by as yet unspecified genetic factors. Therefore, whether or not you use drugs such as cocaine or heroin may be a factor of whom and what you are exposed to, but whether you will become addicted is largely a function of your biology. As the search for the genes influencing alcoholism continues, the next obvious question is how these genes work to affect addiction—a field of research called *functional genomics.*

Genetic research to date tells us that substance abuse in general is affected by our genes but no one gene causes substance abuse or dependence. Research suggests that genetic factors may affect how people experience certain drugs, which in turn may partly determine who will or will not become abusers.

■ Neurobiological Influences

In general, the pleasurable experiences reported by people who use psychoactive substances partly explain why people continue to use them (Volkow, 2005). In behavioral terms, people are positively reinforced for using drugs. But what mechanism is responsible for such experiences? Complex and fascinating studies indicate the brain appears to have a natural "pleasure pathway" that mediates our experience of reward. All abused substances seem to affect this internal reward center. In other words, what psychoactive drugs may have in common is their ability to activate this reward center and provide the user with a pleasurable experience, at least for a time.

The pleasure center was discovered more than 50 years ago by James Olds, who studied the effects of electrical stimulation of rat brains (Olds, 1956; Olds & Milner, 1954). If certain areas were stimulated with small amounts of electricity, the rats behaved as if they had received something pleasant, such as food. The exact location of the area in the human brain is still subject to debate, although it is believed to include the *dopaminergic system* and its *opioid-releasing neurons,* which begin in the midbrain *ventral tegmental area* and then work their way forward through the *nucleus accumbens* and on to the frontal cortex (Jaffe & Anthony, 2005).

How do different drugs that affect different neurotransmitter systems all converge to activate the pleasure pathway, which is primarily made up of dopamine-sensitive neurons? Researchers are only beginning to sort out the answers to this question, but some surprising findings have emerged in recent years. For example, we know that amphetamines and cocaine act directly on the dopamine system. Other drugs, however, appear to increase the availability of dopamine in more roundabout and intricate ways. For example, the neurons in the ventral tegmental area are kept from continuous firing by GABA neurons. (Remember that the GABA system is an inhibitory neurotransmitter system that blocks other neurons from sending information.) One thing that keeps us from being on an unending high is the presence of these GABA neurons, which act as the "brain police," or superegos of the reward neurotransmitter system. Opiates (opium, morphine, heroin) inhibit GABA, which in turn stops the GABA neurons from inhibiting dopamine, which makes more dopamine available in the reward center. Drugs that stimulate the reward center directly or indirectly include not only amphetamine, cocaine, and opiates but also nicotine and alcohol (Jaffe & Anthony, 2005).

This complicated picture is far from complete. Other pleasure pathways may exist in the brain (Wise, 1988). The coming years should yield interesting insights into the interaction of drugs and the brain. One aspect that awaits explanation is how drugs not only provide pleasurable experiences (positive reinforcement) but also help remove unpleasant experiences such as pain, feelings of illness, or anxiety (negative reinforcement). Aspirin is a negative reinforcer: We take it not because it makes us feel good but because it stops us from feeling bad. In much the same way, one property of the psychoactive drugs is that they stop people from feeling bad, an effect as powerful as making them feel good.

With several drugs, negative reinforcement is related to the anxiolytic effect, the ability to reduce anxiety (discussed briefly in the section on the sedative, hypnotic, and anxiolytic drugs). Alcohol has an anxiolytic effect. The neurobiology of how these drugs reduce anxiety seems to involve the septal–hippocampal system (Gray, 1987), which includes a large number of GABA-sensitive neurons. Certain drugs may reduce anxiety by enhancing the activity of GABA in this region, thereby inhibiting the brain's normal reaction (anxiety or fear) to anxiety-producing situations (Gordis, 2000a; Pihl, Peterson, & Lau, 1993).

Researchers have identified individual differences in the way people respond to alcohol. Understanding these response differences is important because they may help explain why some people continue to use drugs until they acquire a dependence on them, whereas others stop before this happens. A number of studies compare individuals with and without a family history of al-

coholism (Gordis, 2000a). They concluded that, compared to the sons of nonalcoholics, the sons of alcoholics may be more sensitive to alcohol when it is first ingested and then become less sensitive to its effects as the hours pass after drinking. This finding is significant because the euphoric effects of alcohol occur just after drinking but the experience after several hours is often sadness and depression. People who are at risk for developing alcoholism (in this case, the sons of alcoholics) may be better able to appreciate the initial highs of drinking and be less sensitive to the lows that come later, making them ideal candidates for continued drinking. In support of this observation, follow-up research over a 10-year period found that those men who tended to be less sensitive to alcohol also tended to drink more heavily and more often (Schuckit, 1994, 1998).

One line of research involves studying the brain-wave patterns of people who are at risk for developing alcoholism. The sons of people with alcohol problems are recruited to participate because of their own increased likelihood of having alcohol problems. Participants are asked to sit quietly and listen for a particular tone. When they hear the tone, they are to signal the researcher. During this time, their brain waves are monitored and a particular pattern emerges called the *P300 amplitude.* Approximately 300 milliseconds (the origin of the "P300" designation) after the tone is presented, a characteristic spike in brain waves occurs that indicates the brain is processing this information. In general, researchers find this spike is lower among males with a family history of alcoholism (Jaffe & Anthony, 2005).

Is this brain-wave difference somehow connected to the reasons people later develop a dependence on alcohol, or is it just a marker or sign that these individuals have in common but is not related to their drinking? One piece of evidence that argues against the P300 differences as a marker for alcoholism is that individuals with a variety of other psychological disorders (for example, schizophrenia and depression) also show lower P300 amplitude than control subjects (Polich, Pollock, & Bloom, 1994). Researchers are continuing to try to understand this interesting but puzzling phenomenon.

Psychological Dimensions

We have shown that the substances people use to alter mood and behavior have unique effects. The high from heroin differs substantially from the experience of smoking a cigarette, which in turn differs from the effects of amphetamines or LSD. Nevertheless, it is important to point out the similarities in the way people react to most of these substances.

■ Positive Reinforcement

The feelings that result from using psychoactive substances are pleasurable in some way, and people will continue to take the drugs to recapture the pleasure. Research shows quite clearly that many drugs used and abused by humans also seem to be pleasurable to animals (Young & Herling, 1986). Laboratory animals will work to have injected into their bodies drugs such as cocaine, amphetamines, opiates, sedatives, and alcohol, which demonstrates that even without social and cultural influences these drugs are pleasurable.

Human research also indicates that to some extent all psychoactive drugs provide a pleasurable experience (Jaffe & Anthony, 2005). In addition, the social contexts for drug taking may encourage its use, even when the use alone is not pleasurable. One study found that among volunteers who preferred not to take Valium, pairing money with pill taking caused participants to switch from a placebo to Valium (Alessi, Roll, Reilly, & Johanson, 2002). Positive reinforcement in the use and the situations surrounding the use of drugs contributes to whether or not people decide to try and continue using drugs.

■ Negative Reinforcement

Most researchers have looked at how drugs help reduce unpleasant feelings through negative reinforcement. Many people are likely to initiate and continue drug use to escape from unpleasantness in their lives. In addition to the initial euphoria, many drugs provide escape from physical pain (opiates), from stress (alcohol), or from panic and anxiety (benzodiazepines). This phenomenon has been explored under a number of different names, including *tension reduction, negative affect,* and *self-medication,* each of which has a somewhat different focus (Jaffe & Anthony, 2005; Measelle, Stice, & Springer, 2006).

Basic to many views of abuse and dependence is the premise that substance use becomes a way for users to cope with the unpleasant feelings that go along with life circumstances (Ahmed & Koob, 2005). Drug use by soldiers in Vietnam is one tragic example of this phenomenon. Almost 42% of these mostly young men experimented with heroin, half of whom became dependent, because the drug was readily available and because of the extreme stress of the war (Jaffe, Knapp, & Ciraulo, 1997). It is interesting that only 12% of these soldiers were still using heroin 3 years after their return to the United States (Robins, Helzer, & Davis, 1975), which suggests that once the stressors were removed they no longer needed the drug to relieve their pain. People who experience trauma such as sexual abuse are more likely to abuse alcohol (Stewart, 1996). This observation emphasizes the important role played by each aspect of abuse and dependence—biological, psychological, social, and cultural—in determining who will and who will not have difficulties with these substances.

In a study that examined substance use among adolescents as a way to reduce stress (Chassin, Pillow, Curran, Molina, & Barrera, 1993), researchers compared a group of adolescents with alcoholic parents with a group whose parents did not have drinking problems. The average age of the adolescents was 12.7 years. The researchers found that just having a parent with alcohol dependence was a major factor in predicting who would use alcohol and other drugs. However, they also found that adolescents who reported negative affect, such as feeling lonely, crying a lot, or being tense, were more likely than others to use drugs. The researchers further determined that the adolescents tended to use drugs as a way to cope with unpleasant feelings. This study and others (see, for example, Pardini, Lochman, & Wells, 2004) suggest that one contributing factor to adolescent drug use is the desire to escape from unpleasantness. It also suggests that to prevent people from using drugs we may need to address influences such as stress and anxiety, a strategy we discuss in our section on treatment.

Many people who use psychoactive substances experience a crash after being high. If people reliably crash, why don't they just stop taking drugs? One explanation is given by Solomon and Corbit in an interesting integration of both the positive and the negative reinforcement processes (Solomon, 1980; Solomon & Corbit, 1974). The *opponent-process theory* holds that an increase in positive feelings will be followed shortly by an increase in negative feelings. Similarly, an increase in negative feelings will be followed by a period of positive feelings. Athletes often report feeling depressed after finally attaining a long-sought goal. The opponent-process theory claims that this mechanism is strengthened with use and weakened by disuse. So a person who has been using a drug for some time will need more of it to achieve the same results (tolerance). At the same time, the negative feelings that follow drug use tend to intensify. For many people, this is the point at which the motivation for drug taking shifts from desiring the euphoric high to alleviating the increasingly unpleasant crash. Unfortunately, the best remedy is more of the same drug. People who are hung over after drinking too much alcohol are often advised to have "the hair of the dog that bit you." The sad irony here is that the very drug that can make you feel so bad is also the one thing that can take away your pain. You can see why people can become enslaved by this insidious cycle.

Researchers have also looked at substance abuse as a way of self-medicating for other problems. If people have difficulties with anxiety, for example, they may be attracted to barbiturates or alcohol because of their anxiety-reducing qualities. In one study, researchers were successful in treating a group of cocaine addicts who had ADHD with methylphenidate (Ritalin) (Levin, Evans, Brooks, & Garawi, 2007). They had hypothesized that these individuals used cocaine to help focus their attention. Once their ability to concentrate improved with the methylphenidate, the users reduced their use of cocaine. Research is just beginning to outline the complex interplay among stressors, negative feelings, other psychological disorders, and negative reactions to the drugs themselves as causative factors in psychoactive drug use.

Cognitive Factors

What people expect to experience when they use drugs influences how they react to them (Leventhal & Schmitz, 2006). A person who expects to be less inhibited when she drinks alcohol will act less inhibited whether she actually drinks alcohol or a placebo she thinks is alcohol (Cooper, Russell, Skinner, Frone, & Mudar, 1992; Wilson, 1987). This observation about the influence of how we think about drug use has been labeled an *expectancy effect* and has received considerable research attention.

Expectancies develop before people actually use drugs, perhaps as a result of parents' and peers' drug use, advertising, and media figures who model drug use (Miller, Smith, & Goldman, 1990). In one study, a large group of seventh and eighth graders were given questionnaires that focused on their expectations about drinking. The researchers reexamined the students 1 year later to see how their expectancies predicted their later drinking (Christiansen, Smith, Roehling, & Goldman, 1989). One surprising finding was the marked increase in drinking among the students only 1 year later. When researchers first questioned them, about 10% of the students reported getting drunk two to four times per year. This number had risen to 25% by the next year.

The students' expectations of drinking did predict who would later have drinking problems. Students who thought that drinking would improve their social behavior and their cognitive and motor abilities (despite all evidence to the contrary) were more likely to have drinking problems 1 year later. These results suggest that adolescents may begin drinking partly because they believe drinking will have positive effects.

Expectations appear to change as people have more experience with drugs, although their expectations are similar for alcohol, nicotine (Brandon & Baker, 1992; Wetter et al., 1994), marijuana, and cocaine (Schafer & Brown, 1991). Some evidence points to positive expectancies—believing you will feel good if you take a drug—as an indirect influence on drug problems. In other words, what these beliefs may do is increase the likelihood you will take certain drugs, which in turn will increase the likelihood that problems arise (Leventhal & Schmitz, 2006).

Once people stop taking drugs after prolonged or repeated use, powerful urges called "cravings" can interfere with efforts to remain off these drugs (Jaffe & Anthony, 2005). If you've ever tried to give up ice cream and then found yourself compelled to have some, you have a limited idea of what it might be like to crave a drug. These urges seem to be triggered by factors such as the availability of the drug, contact with things associated with drug taking (for example, sitting in a bar), specific moods (for example, being depressed), or having a small dose of the drug. For example, the sight and smell of beer will increase the likelihood of a drinker consuming even more beer (Perkins, Ciccocioppo, Jacobs, & Doyle, 2003). This suggests that, in the case of addiction, our brain's ability to learn and remember things works too well—causing these people to reuse drugs when exposed to certain situations (Hyman, 2004).

Research is under way to determine how cravings may work in the brain and if certain medications can be used to reduce these urges and help supplement treatment (Jaffe & Anthony, 2005). One interesting study simulated situations that caused cravings among recently abstinent smokers using "virtual reality" technology (Baumann & Sayette, 2006). These researchers created three-dimensional representations of environments such as packs of cigarettes in restaurants, people smoking, and a bar scene with alcohol, sports on television, and smoking. They found that the simulations caused reports of cravings similar to studies placing people in real-life situations, but they had the advantage of simulating more complex situations in a controlled setting. This type of technology may make it easier for clinicians to assess potential problem areas for clients, which can then be targeted to help keep them from relapsing.

Social Dimensions

Previously, we pointed out the importance of exposure to psychoactive substances as a necessary prerequisite to their use and possible abuse. You could probably list a number of ways people are exposed to these substances—through friends, through the media, and so on. For example, research on the consequences of cigarette advertising suggests the effects of media exposure may be more influential than peer pressure in determining whether teens smoke (Jackson, Brown, & L'Engle, 2007). One study looked at

how, besides advertising, young children might be introduced to drugs (Noll, Zucker, & Greenberg, 1990). Children between the ages of 3 and 6 were given a smelling task at school. They were told to close their eyes and try to tell just by smelling what was in a jar. Nine different substances were presented to them: apple juice, Play-Doh, popcorn, coffee, perfume, beer, whiskey, wine, and cigarettes. Of the older children in this group, more than half could already recognize either beer, wine, or whiskey, and 20% of the youngest children were able to identify alcohol. The importance of this study is in its suggestion that many children are exposed to alcohol as preschoolers; it seems that they learn about alcohol from relatives and acquaintances rather than from television alone.

Research suggests that drug-addicted parents spend less time monitoring their children than parents without drug problems (Dishion, Patterson, & Reid, 1988) and that this is an important contribution to early adolescent substance use (Barnes, Hoffman, Welte, Farrell, & Dintcheff, 2006). When parents did not provide appropriate supervision, their children tended to develop friendships with peers who supported drug use. Children influenced by drug use at home may be exposed to peers who use drugs as well. A self-perpetuating pattern seems to be associated with drug use that extends beyond the genetic influences we discussed previously.

How does our society view people who are dependent on drugs? This issue is of tremendous importance because it affects efforts to legislate the sale, manufacture, possession, and use of these substances. It also dictates how drug-dependent individuals are treated. Two views of substance abuse and dependence characterize contemporary thought: the moral weakness and the disease models of dependence. According to the *moral weakness model of chemical dependence,* drug use is seen as a failure of self-control in the face of temptation; this is a psychosocial perspective. Drug users lack the character or moral fiber to resist the lure of drugs. We saw earlier, for example, that the Catholic Church made drug

Many young children are exposed to drug use.

abuse an official sin—an indication of its disdain. The *disease model of dependence,* in contrast, assumes that drug dependence is caused by an underlying physiological disorder; this is a biological perspective. Just as diabetes or asthma can't be blamed on the afflicted individuals, neither should drug dependence. AA and similar organizations see drug dependence as an incurable disease over which the addict has no control (Marlatt, 1985).

Neither perspective does justice to the complex interrelationship between the psychosocial and the biological influences that affect substance disorders. Viewing drug use as moral weakness leads to punishing those afflicted with the disorder, whereas a disease model includes seeking treatment for a medical problem. On the other hand, people certainly help determine the outcome of treatment for drug abuse and dependence, and messages that the disorder is out of their control can at times be counterproductive. A comprehensive view of substance-related disorders that includes both psychosocial and biological influences is needed for this important societal concern to be addressed adequately.

In many cultures, alcohol is used ceremonially.

Cultural Dimensions

When we examine a behavior as it appears in different cultures, it is necessary to reexamine what is considered abnormal (Lopez & Guarnaccia, 2000). Each culture has its own preferences for psychoactive drugs, as well as its own prohibitions for substances it finds unacceptable. Keep in mind that in addition to defining what is or is not acceptable, cultural norms affect the rates of substance abuse and dependence in important ways. For example, poor economic conditions in certain parts of the world limit the availability of drugs, which appears partly to account for the relatively low prevalence of substance abuse in Mexico and Brazil (de Almeidia-Filho, Santana, Pinto, & de Carvalho-Neto, 1991; Ortiz & Medicna-Mora, 1988).

On the other hand, in certain cultures, including Korea, members are expected to drink alcohol heavily on certain social occasions (C. K. Lee, 1992). As we have seen before, exposure to these substances, in addition to social pressure for heavy and frequent use, may facilitate their abuse, and this may explain the high abuse rates in countries like Korea. This cultural influence provides an interesting natural experiment when exploring gene–environment interactions. People of Asian descent are more likely to have the ALDH2 gene, which produces a severe "flushing" effect (reddening and burning of the face) after drinking alcohol. This flushing effect was thought to be responsible for a relatively low rate of drinking in the population. However, between 1979 and 1992—when increased drinking became socially expected—there was an increase in alcohol abuse (Higuchi et al., 1994). The protective value of having the ALDH2 gene was diminished by the change in cultural norms (Rutter et al., 2006).

Cultural factors not only influence the rates of substance abuse but also determine how it is manifest. Research indicates that alcohol consumption in Poland and Finland is relatively low, yet conflicts related to drinking and arrests for drunkenness in those countries are high compared to those in the Netherlands, which has about the same rate of alcohol consumption (Osterberg, 1986). Our discussion of expectancies may provide some insight into how the same amount of drinking can have different behavioral outcomes. Expectancies about the effects of alcohol use differ across cultures (for example, "Drinking makes me more aggressive" versus "Drinking makes me more withdrawn"); these differing expectancies may partially account for the variations in the consequences of drinking in Poland, Finland, and the Netherlands. Whether substance use is considered a harmful dysfunction often depends on the assumptions of the cultural group.

An Integrative Model

Any explanation of substance use, abuse, and dependence must account for the basic issue raised earlier in this chapter: Why do some people use drugs but not abuse them or become dependent? ■ Figure 11.9 illustrates how the multiple influences we have discussed may interact to account for this process. Access to a drug is a necessary but not a sufficient condition for abuse or dependence. Exposure has many sources, including the media, parents, peers, and, indirectly, lack of supervision. Whether people use a drug depends also on social and cultural expectations, some encouraging and some discouraging, such as laws against possession or sale of the drug.

The path from drug use to abuse and dependence is more complicated (see Figure 11.9). As major stressors aggravate many disorders we have discussed, so do they increase the risk of abuse and dependence on psychoactive substances. Genetic influences may be of several types. Some individuals may inherit a greater

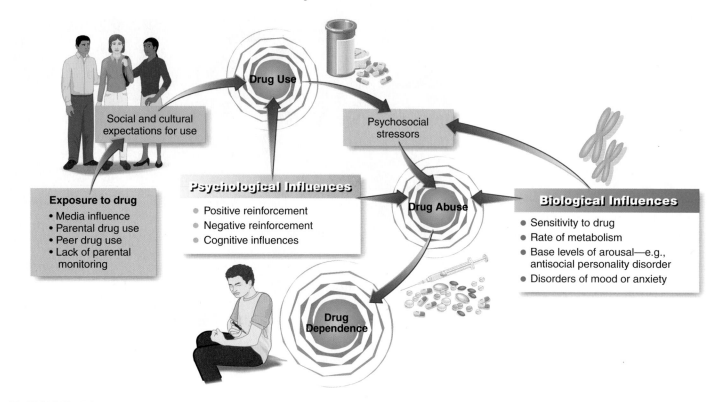

■ **FIGURE 11.9** An integrative model of substance-related disorders.

sensitivity to the effects of certain drugs; others may inherit an ability to metabolize substances more quickly and are thereby able to tolerate higher (and more dangerous) levels. Other psychiatric conditions may indirectly put someone at risk for substance abuse. Antisocial personality disorder, characterized by the frequent violation of social norms (see Chapter 12), is thought to include a lowered rate of arousal; this may account for the increased prevalence of substance abuse in this group. People with mood disorders or anxiety disorders may self-medicate by using drugs to relieve the negative symptoms of their disorder, and this may account for the high rates of substance abuse in this group.

We know also that continued use of certain substances changes the way our brains work through a process called neuroplasticity. We tend to think of neuroplasticity—the brain's tendency to reorganize itself by forming new neural connections—when we hear stories of people recovering abilities after some brain damage. This ability to adapt to change is something we hope for when injury occurs to the brain. The other side of this ability shows itself in drug addiction. With the continued use of substances such as alcohol, cocaine, or the other drugs we explore in this chapter, the brain reorganizes itself to adapt. Unfortunately, this change in the brain increases the drive to obtain the drug and decreases the desire for other nondrug experiences—both of which contribute to continued use and relapse (Kalivas, 2005).

It is clear that abuse and dependence cannot be predicted from one factor, be it genetic, neurobiological, psychological, or cultural. For example, *some* people with the genes common to many with substance abuse problems do not become abusers. Many people who experience the most crushing stressors, such as abject poverty or bigotry and violence, cope without resorting to

drug use. There are different pathways to abuse, and we are only now beginning to identify their basic outlines.

Once a drug has been used repeatedly, biology and cognition conspire to create dependence. Continual use of most drugs causes tolerance, which requires the user to ingest more of the drug to produce the same effect. Conditioning is also a factor. If pleasurable drug experiences are associated with certain settings, a return to such a setting will later cause urges to develop, even if the drugs themselves are not available.

This complex picture still does not convey the intricate lives of people who develop substance-related disorders. Each person has a story and path to abuse and dependence. We have only begun to discover the commonalities of substance disorders; we need to understand a great deal more about how all the factors interact to produce them.

CONCEPT CHECK 11.3

Part A

Match the following descriptions with their corresponding stimulants: (a) opioids, (b) amphetamines, (c) cocaine, (d) hallucinogens, (e) nicotine, and (f) caffeine.

1. These drugs, including LSD, influence perception, distorting feelings, sights, sounds, and smells. _____
_____

(continued)

(continued)

2. These create feelings of elation and vigor and reduce fatigue. They are prescribed to people with narcolepsy and ADHD. _____

3. These lead to euphoria, drowsiness, and slowed breathing. These substances are analgesics, relieving pain. Users tend to be secretive, preventing a great deal of research in this area. _____

4. This substance causes euphoria, appetite loss, and increased alertness. Dependence appears after years of use. Mothers addicted to this have the potential to give birth to irritable babies. _____

5. This is the most common psychoactive substance because it is legal, elevates mood, and decreases fatigue. It's readily available in many beverages. _____

6. This substance stimulates the nervous system and relieves stress. The DSM-IV-TR describes withdrawal symptoms instead of an intoxication pattern. _____

Part B

Indicate whether these statements about the causes of substance-related disorders are true (T) or false (F).

1. ____ Research with both animals and humans indicates that substance abuse in general is affected by our genes, although not one particular gene.

2. ____ To some extent, all psychoactive drugs provide a pleasurable experience, creating positive reinforcement.

3. ____ Negative reinforcement is involved in the continuance of drug use because drugs often provide escape from pain, stress, panic, and so on.

4. ____ The expectancy effect is illustrated when a person who expects to be less inhibited when drinking alcohol is given a placebo and acts or feels normally.

5. ____ The media and parental influences have no effect on adolescent drug use; it is solely a peer pressure factor.

TREATMENT OF SUBSTANCE-RELATED DISORDERS

When we left Danny, he was in jail, awaiting the legal outcome of being arrested for robbery. At this point in his life, Danny needs more than legal help; he needs to free himself from his addiction to alcohol and cocaine. And the first step in his recovery has to come from him. Danny must admit he needs help, that he does indeed have a problem with drugs, and that he needs others to help him overcome his chronic dependence. The personal motivation to work on a drug problem appears to be essential in the treatment of substance abuse (Miller, 1985). A therapist cannot help someone who doesn't want to change, and this can be a problem in treating substance abuse just as it is for people with disorders such as anorexia nervosa and antisocial personality disorder. Fortunately (and at last), Danny's arrest seemed to shock him into realizing how serious his problems had become, and he was ready to confront them head-on.

Treating people who have substance-related disorders is a difficult task. Perhaps because of the combination of influences that often work together to keep people hooked, the outlook for those who are dependent on drugs is often not positive. You will see in the case of heroin dependence, for example, that a best-case scenario is often just trading one addiction (heroin) for another (methadone). And even people who successfully cease taking drugs may feel the urge to resume drug use all their lives.

Treatment for substance-related disorders focuses on several areas. Sometimes the first step is to help someone through the withdrawal process; typically, the ultimate goal is abstinence. In other situations, the goal is to get a person to maintain a certain level of drug use without escalating its intake, and sometimes it is geared toward preventing exposure to drugs. Because substance abuse arises from so many influences, it should not be surprising that treating people with substance-related disorders is not a simple matter of finding just the right drug or the best way to change thoughts or behavior.

We discuss the treatment of substance-related disorders as a group because treatments have so much in common. For example, many programs that treat people for dependence on a variety of substances also teach skills for coping with life stressors. Some biological treatments focus on how to mask the effects of the ingested substances. We discuss the obvious differences among substances as they arise.

Biological Treatments

There have been a variety of biologically based approaches designed primarily to change the way substances are experienced. In other words, scientists are trying to find ways to prevent people from experiencing the pleasant highs associated with drug use or to find alternative substances that have some of the positive effects (for example, reducing anxiety) without their addictive properties. Table 11.1 lists the current recommended medical treatments for many of the more intractable substance dependence problems.

■ Agonist Substitution

Increased knowledge about how psychoactive drugs work on the brain has led researchers to explore ways of changing how they are experienced by people who are dependent on them. One method, **agonist substitution,** involves providing the person with a safe drug that has a chemical makeup similar to the addictive drug (therefore the name *agonist*). *Methadone* is an opiate agonist that is often given as a heroin substitute (O'Brien & Kampman, 2004). Methadone is a synthetic narcotic developed in Germany during World War II when morphine was not available for pain control; it was originally called *adolphine* after Adolph Hitler (Bellis, 1981). Although it does not give the quick high of heroin, methadone initially provides the same analgesic (pain reducing) and sedative effects. However, when users develop a tolerance for methadone it loses its analgesic and sedative qualities. Because heroin and methadone have *cross-tolerance,* meaning they act on the same neurotransmitter receptors, a heroin addict who takes methadone may become addicted to the methadone instead (O'Brien, 1996). Research suggests that when addicts combine methadone with counseling, many reduce their use of heroin and

TABLE 11.1 Medical Treatments		
Substance	**Treatment Goal**	**Treatment Approach**
Nicotine	Reduce withdrawal symptoms and cravings	Nicotine replacement therapy (patch, gum, spray, lozenge, and inhaler)
	Reduce withdrawal symptoms and cravings	Bupropion (Zyban)
Alcohol	Reduce reinforcing effects of alcohol	Naltrexone
	Reduce alcohol craving in abstinent individuals	Acamprosate (Campral)
	Maintenance of abstinence	Disulfiram (Antabuse)
Marijuana		No specific medical interventions recommended
Cocaine		No specific medical interventions recommended
Opioids	Maintenance of abstinence	Methadone
	Maintenance of abstinence	Buprenorphine (Subutex)

Source: From American Psychiatric Association. (2007). Practice guidelines for the treatment of patients with substance use disorders (2nd ed.). *American Journal of Psychiatry, 164*(Suppl.), 1–14.

engage in less criminal activity (Schwartz, Jaffe, Highfield, Callaman, & O'Grady, 2007). The news is not all good, however. A proportion of people under methadone treatment continue to abuse other substances, such as cocaine (Condelli, Fairbank, Dennis, & Rachal, 1991) and benzodiazepines (Iguchi et al., 1990). Research suggests that some people who use methadone as a substitute for heroin benefit significantly but they may be dependent on methadone for the rest of their lives (O'Brien & Kampman, 2004). A newer agonist—buprenorphine—blocks the effects of opiates and seems to encourage better compliance than would a nonopiate or opiate antagonist (Vocci, Acri, & Elkashef, 2005).

Addiction to cigarette smoking is also treated by a substitution process. The drug is provided to smokers in the form of nicotine gum, patch, inhaler, or nasal spray, which lack the carcinogens included in cigarette smoke; the dose is later tapered off to lessen withdrawal from the drug. In general, these replacement strategies successfully help people stop smoking, although it works best with supportive psychological therapy (Mitrouska, Bouloukaki, & Siafakas, 2007; Shiffman, Ferguson, & Hellebusch, 2007). People must be taught how to use the gum properly, and about 20% of people who successfully quit smoking become dependent on the gum itself (Hughes, Gust, Skoog, Keenan, & Fenwick, 1991). The nicotine patch, which requires less effort and provides a steadier nicotine replacement, may be somewhat more effective in helping people quit smoking (Hatsukami et al., 2000; Hughes, 1993; Tiffany, Cox, & Elash, 2000). However, if either treatment is used without a comprehensive psychological treatment program (see later), a substantial number of smokers relapse after they stop using the gum or patch (American Psychiatric Association, 2007). Another medical treatment for smoking—bupropion—is actually the antidepressant Wellbutrin. It is not thought that this helps people by making them less depressed, but instead it curbs the cravings without being an agonist for nicotine (American Psychiatric Association, 2007).

■ Antagonist Treatments

We described how many psychoactive drugs produce euphoric effects through their interaction with the neurotransmitter systems in the brain. What would happen if the effects of these drugs were blocked so that the drugs no longer produced the pleasant

results? Would people stop using the drugs? **Antagonist drugs** block or counteract the effects of psychoactive drugs, and a variety of drugs that seem to cancel out the effects of opiates have been used with people dependent on a variety of substances. The most often prescribed opiate-antagonist drug, *naltrexone,* has had only limited success with individuals who are not simultaneously participating in a structured treatment program (Jaffe & Strain, 2005). When it is given to a person who is dependent on opiates, it produces immediate withdrawal symptoms, an extremely unpleasant effect. A person must be withdrawn from the opiate completely before starting naltrexone, and because it removes the euphoric effects of opiates, the user must be highly motivated to continue treatment. Acamprosate also seems to decrease cravings in people dependent upon alcohol, and it works best with highly motivated people who are also participating in psychosocial interventions. The brain mechanisms for the effects of this drug are not well understood (Heilig & Egli, 2006).

Overall, naltrexone or the other drugs being explored are not the magic bullets that would shut off the addict's response to psychoactive drugs and put an end to dependence. They do appear to help some drug abusers handle withdrawal symptoms and the craving that accompanies attempts to abstain from drug use; antagonists may therefore be a useful addition to other therapeutic efforts.

■ Aversive Treatment

In addition to looking for ways to block the euphoric effects of psychoactive drugs, clinicians in this area may prescribe drugs that make ingesting the abused substances extremely unpleasant. The expectation is that a person who associates the drug with feelings of illness will avoid using the drug. The most commonly known aversive treatment uses *disulfiram (Antabuse)* with people who are alcohol dependent (Suh, Pettinati, Kampman, & O'Brien, 2006). Antabuse prevents the breakdown of acetaldehyde, a by-product of alcohol, and the resulting buildup of acetaldehyde causes feelings of illness. People who drink alcohol after taking Antabuse experience nausea, vomiting, and elevated heart rate and respiration. Ideally, Antabuse is taken each morning, before the desire to drink wins (Nathan, 1993). Unfortunately, noncompliance is a major concern, and a person who skips the Antabuse for a few days is able to resume drinking.

Efforts to make smoking aversive have included the use of *silver nitrate* in lozenges or gum. This chemical combines with the saliva of a smoker to produce a bad taste in the mouth. Research has not shown it to be particularly effective (Jensen, Schmidt, Pedersen, & Dahl, 1991). Both Antabuse for alcohol abuse and silver nitrate for cigarette smoking have generally been less than successful as treatment strategies on their own, primarily because they require that people be extremely motivated to continue taking them outside the supervision of a mental health professional (Leccese, 1991).

■ Other Biological Approaches

Medication is often prescribed to help people deal with the often-disturbing symptoms of withdrawal. *Clonidine,* developed to treat hypertension, has been given to people withdrawing from opiates. Because withdrawal from certain prescribed medications such as the sedatives can cause cardiac arrest or seizures, these drugs are gradually tapered off to minimize dangerous reactions. In addition, sedative drugs (benzodiazepines) are often prescribed to help minimize discomfort for people withdrawing from other drugs, such as alcohol (American Psychiatric Association, 2007).

Psychosocial Treatments

Most biological treatments for substance abuse show some promise with people who are trying to eliminate their drug habit. However, not one of these treatments alone is successful for most people (American Psychiatric Association, 2007). Most research indicates a need for social support or therapeutic intervention. Because so many people need help to overcome their substance disorder, a number of models and programs have been developed. Unfortunately, in no other area of psychology have unvalidated and untested methods of treatment been so widely accepted. A reminder: A program that has not been subject to the scrutiny of research *may* work, but the sheer number of people receiving services of unknown value is still cause for concern. We next review several therapeutic approaches that *have* been evaluated.

■ Inpatient Facilities

The first specialized facility for people with substance abuse problems was established in 1935, when the first federal narcotic "farm" was built in Lexington, Kentucky. Now mostly privately run, such facilities are designed to help people get through the initial withdrawal period and to provide supportive therapy so that they can go back to their communities (Morgan, 1981). Inpatient care can be extremely expensive (Bender, 2004). The question arises, then, as to how effective this type of care is compared to outpatient therapy that can cost 90% less. Research suggests there may be no difference between intensive residential setting programs and quality outpatient care in the outcomes for alcoholic patients (Miller & Hester, 1986) or for drug treatment in general (Guydish, Sorensen, Chan, Werdegar, & Acampora, 1999; Smith, Kraemer, Miller, DeBusk, & Taylor, 1999). Although some people do improve as inpatients, they may not need this expensive care.

■ Alcoholics Anonymous and Its Variations

Without question, the most popular model for the treatment of substance abuse is a variation of the Twelve Steps program first developed by AA. Established in 1935 by two alcoholic professionals, William "Bill W." Wilson and Robert "Dr. Bob" Holbrook Smith, the foundation of AA is the notion that alcoholism is a disease and alcoholics must acknowledge their addiction to alcohol and its destructive power over them. The addiction is seen as more powerful than any individual; therefore, they must look to a higher power to help them overcome their shortcomings. Central to the design of AA is its independence from the established medical community and the freedom it offers from the stigmatization of alcoholism (Denzin, 1987; Robertson, 1988). An important component is the social support it provides through group meetings.

Since 1935, AA has steadily expanded to include almost 97,000 groups in more than 100 countries (Emrick, 1999). In one survey, more than 3% of the adult population in the United States reported they had at one time attended an AA meeting (Room, 1993). The Twelve Steps of AA are the basis of its philosophy (see Table 11.2). In them, you can see the reliance on prayer and a belief in God.

Reaction is rarely neutral to AA and similar organizations, like Cocaine Anonymous and Narcotics Anonymous (Miller, Gold, & Pottash, 1989). Many people credit the approach with saving their lives, whereas others object that its reliance on spirituality and its adoption of a disease model foster dependence. Because participants attend meetings anonymously and only

TABLE 11.2   Twelve Suggested Steps of Alcoholics Anonymous

1. We admitted we were powerless over alcohol—that our lives had become unmanageable.
2. Came to believe that a power greater than ourselves could restore us to sanity.
3. Made a decision to turn our will and our lives over to the care of God as we understood Him.
4. Made a searching and fearless moral inventory of ourselves.
5. Admitted to God, to ourselves, and to another human being the exact nature of our wrongs.
6. Were entirely ready to have God remove all these defects of character.
7. Humbly asked Him to remove our shortcomings.
8. Made a list of all persons we had harmed, and became willing to make amends to them all.
9. Made direct amends to such people wherever possible, except when to do so would injure them or others.
10. Continued to take personal inventory and, when we were wrong, promptly admitted it.
11. Sought through prayer and meditation to improve our conscious contact with God as we understood Him, praying only for knowledge of His will for us and the power to carry that out.
12. Having had a spiritual awakening as the result of these steps, we tried to carry this message to alcoholics and to practice these principles in all our affairs.

Source: The Twelve Steps are reprinted with permission of Alcoholics Anonymous World Services (AAWS). Permission to reprint the Twelve Steps does not mean that AAWS has reviewed or approved the contents of this publication or that AAWS necessarily agrees with the views expressed herein. AA is a program of recovery from alcoholism only—use of the Twelve Steps in connection with programs and activities which are patterned after AA, but which address other problems, or in any other non-AA context, does not imply otherwise.

when they feel the need to, conducting systematic research on its effectiveness has been unusually difficult (Miller & McCrady, 1993). Nevertheless, there have been numerous attempts to evaluate AA's effect on alcoholism (Emrick, Tonigan, Montgomery, & Little, 1993). Although there are not enough data to show what percentage of people abstain from using alcohol as a result of participating in AA, research finds that those people who regularly participate in AA activities—or other similar supportive approaches—and follow its guidelines carefully are more likely to have a positive outcome (Moos & Moos, 2007). AA is clearly an effective treatment for highly motivated people with alcohol dependence. We do not yet know, however, who is likely to succeed and who is likely to fail in AA. Other treatments are needed for the large numbers of people who do not respond to AA's approach.

■ Controlled Use

One of the tenets of AA is total abstinence; recovering alcoholics who have just one sip of alcohol are believed to have "slipped" until they again achieve abstinence. However, some researchers question this assumption and believe at least a portion of abusers of several substances (notably alcohol and nicotine) may be capable of becoming social users without resuming their abuse of these drugs. Some people who smoke only occasionally are thought to react differently to nicotine than heavy users (Goldstein, 1994).

In the alcoholism treatment field, the notion of teaching people **controlled drinking** is extremely controversial, partly because of a classic study showing partial success in teaching severe abusers to drink in a limited way (Sobell & Sobell, 1978). The subjects were 40 male alcoholics in an alcoholism treatment program at a state hospital who were thought to have a good prognosis. The men were assigned either to a program that taught them how to drink in moderation (experimental group) or to a group that was abstinence oriented (control group). The researchers, Mark and Linda Sobell, followed the men for more than 2 years, maintaining contact with 98% of them. During the second year after treatment, those who participated in the controlled drinking group were functioning well 85% of the time, whereas the men in the abstinence group were reported to be doing well only 42% of the time. Although results in the two groups differed significantly, some men in both groups suffered serious relapses and required rehospitalization and some were incarcerated. The results of this study suggest that controlled drinking may be a viable alternative to abstinence for some alcohol abusers, although it clearly isn't a cure.

The controversy over this study began with a paper published in the prestigious journal *Science* (Pendery, Maltzman, & West, 1982). The authors reported they had contacted the men in the Sobell study after 10 years and found that only 1 of the 20 men in the experimental group maintained a pattern of controlled drinking. Although this reevaluation made headlines and was the subject of a segment on the *60 Minutes* television show, it had a number of flaws (Marlatt, Larimer, Baer, & Quigley, 1993). Most serious was the lack of data on the abstinence group over the same 10-year follow-up period. Because no treatment study on substance abuse pretends to help everyone who participates, control groups are added to compare progress. In this case, we need to know how well the controlled drinking group fared compared to the abstinence group.

The controversy over the Sobell study still had a chilling effect on controlled drinking as a treatment of alcohol abuse in the United States. In contrast, controlled drinking is widely accepted as a treatment for alcoholism in the United Kingdom (Rosenberg, 1993). Despite opposition, research on this approach has been conducted in the ensuing years (Marlatt et al., 1993), and the results seem to show that controlled drinking is at least as effective as abstinence but that neither treatment is successful for 70% to 80% of patients over the long term—a rather bleak outlook for people with alcohol dependence problems.

■ Component Treatment

Most comprehensive treatment programs aimed at helping people with substance abuse and dependence problems have a number of components thought to boost the effectiveness of the "treatment package." We saw in our review of biological treatments that their effectiveness is increased when psychologically based therapy is added. In aversion therapy, which uses a conditioning model, substance use is paired with something extremely unpleasant, such as a brief electric shock or feelings of nausea. For example, a person might be offered a drink of alcohol and receive a painful shock when the glass reaches his lips. The goal is to counteract the positive associations with substance use with negative associations. The negative associations can also be made by imagining unpleasant scenes in a technique called *covert sensitization* (Cautela, 1966); the person might picture herself beginning to snort cocaine and be interrupted with visions of herself becoming violently ill.

One component that seems to be a valuable part of therapy for substance use is *contingency management* (Higgins et al., 2006). Here, the clinician and the client together select the behaviors that the client needs to change and decide on the reinforcers that will reward reaching certain goals, perhaps money or small retail items like CDs. In a study of cocaine abusers, clients received cash vouchers (up to almost $2,000) for having cocaine-negative urine specimens (Higgins et al., 2006). This study found greater abstinence rates among cocaine-dependent users with the contingency management approach and other skills training than among users in a more traditional counseling program that included a 12-step approach to treatment.

Another package of treatments is the community reinforcement approach (American Psychiatric Association, 2007). In keeping with the multiple influences that affect substance use, several facets of the drug problem are addressed to help identify and correct aspects of the person's life that might contribute to substance use or interfere with efforts to abstain. First, a spouse, friend, or relative who is not a substance user is recruited to participate in relationship therapy to help the abuser improve relationships with other important people. Second, clients are taught how to identify the antecedents and consequences that influence their drug taking. For example, if they are likely to use cocaine with certain friends, clients are taught to recognize the relationship and encouraged to avoid the associations. Third, clients are given assistance with employment, education, finances, or other social service areas that may help reduce their stress. Fourth, new recreational options help the person replace substance use with new activities. Preliminary studies of the community reinforcement approach with alcohol and cocaine abusers appear encouraging, although more research is needed to assess its long-term effectiveness.

Because people present such different challenges to substance abuse treatment, a "shotgun-like" effort, using a variety of approaches, is often required to cover the range of problems influencing substance use. This type of treatment matching has received increased attention from workers in the area of substance abuse. For example, the National Institute on Alcohol Abuse and Alcoholism initiated Project MATCH (Matching Alcoholism Treatment to Client Heterogeneity) to assess whether people with differing characteristics (for example, some have little hope for improvement, and others are searching for spiritual meaning) would respond better or worse to different treatments (Project MATCH Research Group, 1993). Initial reports suggest that well-run programs of various types can be effective with a range of people with substance use problems (Project MATCH Research Group, 1997). Although no exact matches are yet recommended, research is ongoing to help clinicians tailor their treatments to the particular needs of their clients (Jaffe et al., 1996; Project MATCH Research Group, 1998). By identifying the factors that support a person's substance abuse and treating them in an integrated fashion, clinicians may improve the success rates of the various approaches we have discussed.

■ Relapse Prevention

Another kind of treatment directly addresses the problem of relapse. Marlatt and Gordon's (1985) **relapse prevention** treatment model looks at the learned aspects of dependence and sees relapse as a failure of cognitive and behavioral coping skills (Witkiewitz & Marlatt, 2004). Therapy involves helping people remove any ambivalence about stopping their drug use by examining their beliefs about the positive aspects of the drug ("There's nothing like a cocaine high") and confronting the negative consequences of its use ("I fight with my wife when I'm high"). High-risk situations are identified ("having extra money in my pocket"), and strategies are developed to deal with potentially problematic situations, as well as with the craving that arises from abstinence. Incidents of relapse are dealt with as occurrences from which the person can recover; instead of looking on these episodes as inevitably leading to more drug use, people in treatment are encouraged to see them as episodes brought on by temporary stress or a situation that can be changed. Research on this technique suggests that it may be particularly effective for alcohol problems (Irvin, Bowers, Dunn, & Wang, 1999), as well as in treating a variety of other substance use disorders (see, for example, Burleson & Kaminer, 2005).

Prevention

Over the past few years, the strategies for preventing substance abuse and dependence have shifted from education-based approaches (for example, teaching schoolchildren that drugs can be harmful) to more wide-ranging approaches, including changes in the laws regarding drug possession and use and community-based interventions (Holder, 2004). Many states, for example, have implemented education-based programs in schools to try to deter students from using drugs. The widely used Drug Abuse Resistance Education (DARE) program encourages a "no drug use" message through fear of consequences, rewards for commitments not to use drugs, and strategies for refusing offers of drugs. Unfortunately, several extensive evaluations suggest that this type of program may not have its intended effects (Pentz, 1999). Fortunately, more comprehensive programs that involve skills training to avoid or resist social pressures (such as peers) and environmental pressures (such as media portrayals of drug use) can be effective in preventing drug abuse among some. For example, one large-scale longitudinal study used a community-based intervention strategy to reduce binge drinking and alcohol-related injuries (for example, car crashes and assaults) (Holder et al., 2000). Three communities were mobilized to encourage responsible beverage service (that is, not serving too much alcohol to bar patrons), limit alcohol access to underage drinkers, and increase local enforcement of drinking and driving laws to limit access to alcohol. Self-reports by community members of drinking too much and drinking and driving were fewer after the intervention, as were alcohol-related car accidents and assaults. These types of comprehensive programs may need to be replicated across communities and extended to more pervasive influences (for example, how drug use is portrayed in the media) to affect significant prevention results.

It may be that our most powerful preventive strategy involves cultural change. Over the past 25 years or so, we have gone from a "turn on, tune in, drop out," "if it feels good, do it," and "I get by with a little help from my friends" society to one that champions statements like "Just say no to drugs." The social unacceptability of excessive drinking, smoking, and other drug use is probably responsible for this change. The sociocultural disapproval of cigarette smoking, for example, is readily apparent in the following description by a former smoker (Cook, 1993, p. 1750):

> I began smoking (in Boy Scouts!) at age 11. By the time I was a college freshman, freed from the restrictions of school and home, my smoking had increased to a pack a day. The seminal Surgeon General's Report *Smoking and Health* was issued that year (1964), but I didn't notice. The warnings that began appearing on cigarette packs a couple of years later were also easy to ignore, since I had grown up knowing that smoking was unhealthy. As a graduate student and young professor I often smoked while leading class discussions, as had some of my favorite teachers. That ended in 1980, when an undergraduate student, no doubt empowered by the antismoking movement, asked me to stop because smoke bothered him. A few years later there were hardly any social situations left in which it was acceptable to smoke. Even my home was no longer a refuge, since my children were pestering me to quit. And so I did. Now my status as former smoker puts me in company with fully half of all those who have ever smoked regularly and are alive today. For many of us the deteriorating social environment for smoking made it easier to quit.

Implementing this sort of intervention is beyond the scope of one research investigator or even a consortium of researchers collaborating across many sites. It requires the cooperation of governmental, educational, and even religious institutions. We may need to rethink our approach to preventing drug use and abuse.

CONCEPT CHECK 11.4

Determine whether you understand how treatments for substance-related disorders work by matching the examples with the following terms: (a) dependent, (b) cross-tolerant, (c) agonist substitution, (d) antagonist, (e) relapse prevention, (f) controlled drinking, (g) aversion therapy, (h) covert sensitization, (i) contingency management, and (j) anonymous.

1. Methadone is used to help heroin addicts kick their habit in a method called _____.
2. Heroin and methadone are _____, which means they affect the same neurotransmitter receptors.
3. Unfortunately, the heroin addict may become permanently _____ on methadone.
4. _____ drugs block or counteract the effects of psychoactive drugs and are sometimes effective in treating addicts.
5. In _____, substance use is paired with something extremely unpleasant (like alcohol and vomiting with Antabuse).
6. The _____ model involves therapy that helps individuals remove ambivalence about stopping their drug use by examining their beliefs about the positive and negative aspects of drug use.
7. By imagining unpleasant scenes, the _____ technique helps the person associate the negative effects of the drug with drug use.
8. It has been difficult to evaluate rigorously the effectiveness of Alcoholics Anonymous because the participants are _____.
9. _____ is a controversial treatment for alcohol abuse because of a negative but flawed experimental finding, but also because it conflicts with the belief in total abstinence.
10. In _____, the clinician and the client work together to decide which behaviors the client needs to change and which reinforcers will be used as rewards for reaching set goals.

IMPULSE-CONTROL DISORDERS

A number of the disorders we describe in this book start with an irresistible impulse—usually one that will ultimately be harmful to the person affected. Typically, the person experiences increasing tension leading up to the act and, sometimes, pleasurable anticipation of acting on the impulse. For example, paraphilias such as pedophilia (sexual attraction to children), eating disorders, and the substance-related disorders in this chapter often commence with temptations or desires that are destructive but difficult to resist. DSM-IV-TR includes five additional impulse-control disorders (labeled "impulse-control disorders not elsewhere classified") that are not included under other categories—intermittent explosive disorder, kleptomania, pyromania, pathological gambling, and trichotillomania (Greenberg, 2005).

Intermittent Explosive Disorder

People with **intermittent explosive disorder** have episodes in which they act on aggressive impulses that result in serious assaults or destruction of property (American Psychiatric Association, 2000). Although it is unfortunately common among the general population to observe aggressive outbursts, when you rule out the influence of other disorders (for example, antisocial personality disorder, borderline personality disorder, a psychotic disorder, and Alzheimer's disease) or substance use, this disorder is only rarely diagnosed. One small study found that from 3.4% to 10.4% of those in a psychiatric facility had the characteristics of intermittent explosive disorder at some point in their lives (Grant, Levine, Kim, & Potenza, 2005).

This diagnosis is controversial and has been debated throughout the development of the DSM. One concern, among others, is that by validating a general category that covers aggressive behavior it may be used as a legal defense—insanity—for all violent crimes (Greenberg, 2005).

Research is at the beginning stages for this disorder and focuses on the influence of neurotransmitters such as serotonin and norepinephrine and testosterone levels, along with their interaction with psychosocial influences (stress, disrupted family life, and parenting styles). These and other influences are being examined to explain the origins of this disorder (Scott, Hilty, & Brook, 2003). Cognitive-behavioral interventions (for example, helping the person identify and avoid "triggers" for aggressive outbursts) and approaches modeled after drug treatments appear the most effective for these individuals, although few controlled studies yet exist (Greenberg, 2005).

Kleptomania

The story of wealthy actress Winona Ryder stealing $5,500 worth of merchandise from Saks Fifth Avenue in Beverly Hills, California, was as puzzling as it was titillating. Why risk a multimillion-dollar career over some clothes that she could easily afford? Was hers a case of **kleptomania**—a recurrent failure to resist urges to steal things that are not needed for personal use or their monetary value? This disorder appears to be rare, but it is not well studied, partly because of the stigma associated with identifying oneself as acting out this illegal behavior. The patterns described by those with this disorder are strikingly similar—the person begins to feel a sense of tension just before stealing, which is followed by feelings of pleasure or relief while the theft is committed (Greenberg, 2005). People with kleptomania score high on assessments of impulsivity, reflecting their inability to judge the immediate gratification of stealing compared to the long-term negative consequences (for example, arrest, embarrassment) (Grant & Kim, 2002). Brain-imaging research supports this observation, with one study finding damage in areas of the brain associated with poor decision making (inferior frontal regions) (Grant, Correia, & Brennan-Krohn, 2006).

There appears to be high comorbidity between kleptomania and mood disorders, and to a lesser extent with substance abuse and dependence (Baylé, Caci, Millet, Richa, & Olié, 2003). Some refer to kleptomania as an "antidepressant" behavior, or a reaction

In 2002, actress Winona Ryder was found guilty of shoplifting items worth several thousand dollars from a Beverly Hills department store.

Pathological Gambling

Gambling has a long history—for example, dice have been found in Egyptian tombs (Greenberg, 2005). It is growing in popularity in this country, and in many places it is a legal and acceptable form of entertainment. Perhaps as a result, and unlike the other impulse-control disorders, which are relatively rare, **pathological gambling** affects an increasing number of people, estimated between 3% and 5% of adult Americans (Greenberg, 2005). It is estimated that among pathological gamblers, 14% have lost at least one job, 19% have declared bankruptcy, 32% have been arrested, and 21% have been incarcerated (Gerstein et al., 1999). The DSM-IV-TR criteria for pathological gambling set forth the associated behaviors that characterize people who are problem gamblers. These include the same pattern of urges we observe in the other impulse-control disorders. Note too the parallels with substance dependence, with the need to gamble increasing amounts of money over time and the "withdrawal symptoms" such as restlessness and irritability when attempting to stop.

There is a growing body of research on the nature and treatment of pathological gambling. For example, work is under way to explore the biological origins of the urge to gamble among pathological gamblers. In one study, brain-imaging technology (echoplanar functional magnetic resonance imaging) was used to observe brain function while gamblers observed videotapes of other people gambling (Potenza et al., 2003). A decreased level of

on the part of some to relieve unpleasant feelings through stealing (Fishbain, 1987). To date, only case study reports of treatment exist, and these involve either behavioral interventions or use of antidepressant medication.

Pyromania

Just as we know that someone who steals does not necessarily have kleptomania, it is also true that not everyone who sets fires is considered to have **pyromania**—an impulse-control disorder that involves having an irresistible urge to set fires. Again, the pattern parallels that of kleptomania, where the person feels a tension or arousal before setting a fire and a sense of gratification or relief while the fire burns. These individuals will also be preoccupied with fires and the associated equipment involved in setting and putting out these fires (American Psychiatric Association, 2000). Also rare, pyromania is diagnosed in less than 4% of arsonists (Scott et al., 2003), because arsonists can include people who set fires for monetary gain or revenge rather than to satisfy a physical or psychological urge. Because so few people are diagnosed with this disorder, research on etiology and treatment is almost nonexistent. Research that has been conducted follows the general group of arsonists (of which only a small percentage have pyromania) and examines the role of a family history of fire setting along with comorbid impulse disorders (antisocial personality disorder and alcoholism). Treatment is generally cognitive-behavioral and involves helping the person identify the signals that initiate the urges and teaching coping strategies to resist the temptation to start fires.

DSM-IV-TR

DSM TABLE 11.13 Diagnostic Criteria for Pathological Gambling

A. Persistent and recurrent maladaptive gambling behavior as indicated by five (or more) of the following:
  1. Is preoccupied with gambling (e.g., preoccupied with reliving past gambling experiences, handicapping or planning the next venture, or thinking of ways to get money with which to gamble)
  2. Needs to gamble with increasing amounts of money in order to achieve the desired excitement
  3. Has repeated unsuccessful efforts to control, cut back, or stop gambling
  4. Is restless or irritable when attempting to cut down or stop gambling
  5. Gambles as a way of escaping from problems or of relieving dysphoric mood (e.g., feelings of helplessness, guilt, anxiety, depression)
  6. After losing money gambling, often returns another day to get even ("chasing" one's losses)
  7. Lies to family members, therapist, or others to conceal the extent of involvement with gambling
  8. Has committed illegal acts such as forgery, fraud, theft, or embezzlement to finance gambling
  9. Has jeopardized or lost a significant relationship, job, or educational or career opportunity because of gambling
  10. Relies on others to provide money to relieve a desperate financial situation caused by gambling
B. The gambling behavior is not better accounted for by a manic episode.

activity was observed in those regions of the brain that are involved in impulse regulation when compared to controls, suggesting an interaction between the environmental cues to gamble and the brain's response (which may be to decrease the ability to resist these cues). Abnormalities in the dopamine system (which may account for the pleasurable consequences of gambling) and the serotonin system (involved in impulsive behavior) have been found in some studies of pathological gamblers (Scott et al., 2003).

Treatment of gambling problems is difficult. Those with pathological gambling exhibit a combination of characteristics—including denial of the problem, impulsivity, and continuing optimism ("One big win will cover my losses!")—that interfere with effective treatment. Treatment is often similar to substance dependence treatment, and there is a parallel Gambler's Anonymous that incorporates the same 12-step program we discussed previously. However, the evidence of effectiveness for Gambler's Anonymous suggests that 70% to 90% drop out of these programs and that the desire to quit must be present before intervention (McElroy & Arnold, 2001). Cognitive-behavioral interventions are also being studied, with one study including a variety of components—setting financial limits, planning alternative activities, preventing relapse, and imaginal desensitization. This preliminary research provides a more optimistic view of potential outcomes (Dowling, Smith, & Thomas, in press).

Trichotillomania

The urge to pull out one's own hair from anywhere on the body, including the scalp, eyebrows, and arms, is referred to as **trichotillomania.** This behavior results in noticeable hair loss, distress, and significant social impairments. This disorder can often have severe social consequences, and, as a result, those affected can go to great lengths to conceal their behavior. Compulsive hair pulling is more common than once believed and is observed in between 1% and 5% of college students, with females reporting the problem more than males (Scott et al., 2003). There may be some genetic influence on trichotillomania, with one study finding a unique genetic mutation in a small number of people (Zuchner et al., 2006). Stress also seems to be involved, and there is an increased over-

lap with posttraumatic stress disorder (Chamberlain, Menzies, Sahakian, & Fineberg, 2007).

Research using serotonin-specific reuptake inhibitors holds some promise for treatment, as do cognitive behavioral interventions, although rigorous research trials have yet to be conducted (Chamberlain et al., 2007).

In addition to these five impulse-control disorders, other impulsive behaviors may occasionally rise to the level of these difficulties. Some individuals show the same irresistible urges to engage in compulsive buying or shopping (oniomania), self-mutilation, skin picking (psychogenic excoriation), severe nail biting (onychophagia), and excessive computer use ("Internet addiction") (McElroy & Arnold, 2001). There is a limited but growing literature that will help us understand and ultimately treat these impulse-control problems.

CONCEPT CHECK 11.5

Match the following disorders with their corresponding symptoms: (a) pathological gambling, (b) trichotillomania, (c) intermittent explosive disorder, (d) kleptomania, and (e) pyromania.

1. This disorder refers to compulsive hair pulling and is more common in females than males. _____
2. Individuals with this disorder are preoccupied with fires and the equipment involved in setting and putting out fires. _____
3. This disorder begins with the person feeling a sense of tension that is released and followed with pleasure after they have committed a robbery. _____
4. This disorder affects somewhere between 3% and 5% of the adult American population and is characterized by the need to gamble. _____
5. This rarely diagnosed disorder is characterized by episodes of aggressive impulses and can sometimes be treated with cognitive-behavioral interventions, drug treatments, or both. _____

FUTURE DIRECTIONS

Two New Approaches to Prevention

We see that the problem with drug abuse is not just its use. A complicating factor in drug abuse includes the brain's desire to continue to use the drug, especially when in the presence of stimuli and situations usually associated with the drug. This "drug seeking" and relapse continue to interfere with successful treatment. Groundbreaking research is now exploring where in the brain these processes occur, which in turn may lead to new approaches to help people remain drug free (Kalivas, 2005).

Taking this one step further, new research with animals suggests the possibility of creating "vaccines" that would use the immune system to fight drugs such as heroin, just as your body attacks infectious bacteria (Anton & Leff, 2006). A vaccine that would take away the pleasurable aspects of smoking is now being tested with humans (Dorey, 2006). What this means is that—theoretically—children could be vaccinated early in their lives and that if they tried a drug it would not have the pleasurable effects that would encourage repeated use. These "vice vaccines" could hold the answer to one of our most pressing social issues.

On the other end of the intervention spectrum, new and more comprehensive prevention approaches may help many individuals avoid initially trying dangerous drugs. One such approach is being used in Montana—called the Montana Meth Project (Generations United, 2006). Initially funded by software billionaire Timothy Siegel, this initiative supports advertising and community action programs to inform youth across the state about the devastating effects of methamphetamine use. Using dramatic and sometimes shocking pictures and video ads, the project's surveys suggest that attitudes about meth use changed in many 12–17-year-olds. Although no controlled research yet exists, this may be an additional powerful tool for reducing drug dependence.

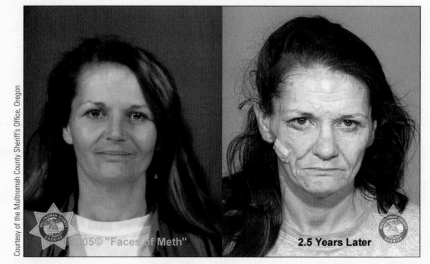

The Montana Meth Project used photos like these from Faces of Meth, a project of the Multnomah County Sheriff's Office in Portland, Oregon.

SUMMARY

Perspectives on Substance-Related Disorders

- In DSM-IV-TR, substance-related disorders are divided into depressants (alcohol, barbiturates, and benzodiazepines), stimulants (amphetamine, cocaine, nicotine, and caffeine), opiates (heroin, codeine, and morphine), and hallucinogens (marijuana and LSD).
- Specific diagnoses are further categorized as substance dependence, substance abuse, substance intoxication, and substance withdrawal.
- Nonmedical drug use in the United States has declined in recent times, although it continues to cost billions of dollars and seriously impairs the lives of millions of people each year.

Depressants, Stimulants, Opioids, and Hallucinogens

- Depressants are a group of drugs that decrease central nervous system activity. The primary effect is to reduce our levels of physiological arousal and help us relax. Included in this group are alcohol and sedative, hypnotic, and anxiolytic drugs, such as those prescribed for insomnia.
- Stimulants, the most commonly consumed psychoactive drugs, include caffeine (in coffee, chocolate, and many soft drinks), nicotine (in tobacco products such as cigarettes), amphetamines, and cocaine. In contrast to the depressant drugs, stimulants make us more alert and energetic.

- Opiates include opium, morphine, codeine, and heroin; they have a narcotic effect—relieving pain and inducing sleep. The broader term *opioids* is used to refer to the family of substances that includes these opiates and synthetic variations created by chemists (methadone and pethidine) and the similarly acting substances that occur naturally in our brains (enkephalins, beta-endorphins, and dynorphins).

- Hallucinogens essentially change the way the user perceives the world. Sight, sound, feelings, and even smell are distorted, sometimes in dramatic ways, in a person under the influence of drugs such as marijuana and LSD.

Causes and Treatment of Substance-Related Disorders

- Most psychotropic drugs seem to produce positive effects by acting directly or indirectly on the dopaminergic mesolimbic system (the pleasure pathway). In addition, psychosocial factors such as expectations, stress, and cultural practices interact with the biological factors to influence drug use.

- Substance dependence is treated successfully only in a minority of those affected, and the best results reflect the motivation of the drug user and a combination of biological and psychosocial treatments.

- Programs aimed at preventing drug use may have the greatest chance of significantly affecting the drug problem.

Impulse-Control Disorders

- In DSM-IV-TR, impulse-control disorders include five separate disorders: intermittent explosive disorder, kleptomania, pyromania, pathological gambling, and trichotillomania.

Key Terms

substance-related disorders, 389
impulse-control disorders, 389
polysubstance use, 389
psychoactive substances, 390
substance intoxication, 390
substance abuse, 391
substance dependence, 391
tolerance, 391
withdrawal, 391
depressants, 394
stimulants, 395

opiates, 395
hallucinogen, 395
alcohol use disorders, 395
withdrawal delirium (delirium tremens/DTs), 396
fetal alcohol syndrome (FAS), 397
alcohol dehydrogenase (ADH), 397
barbiturates, 399
benzodiazepines, 399

amphetamine use disorders, 401
cocaine use disorders, 402
nicotine use disorders, 403
caffeine use disorders, 405
opioid use disorders, 406
hallucinogen use disorders, 407
marijuana (*Cannabis sativa*), 407
LSD (*d*-lysergic acid diethylamide), 408

agonist substitution, 417
antagonist drugs, 418
controlled drinking, 420
relapse prevention, 421
intermittent explosive disorder, 422
kleptomania, 422
pyromania, 423
pathological gambling, 423
trichotillomania, 424

Answers to Concept Checks

11.1

Part A

1. b; 2. a; 3. d; 4. c

Part B

5. d; 6. c; 7. a; 8. b

11.2

1. True; 2. False (the use of crack by pregnant mothers adversely affects only some babies); 3. True; 4. True; 5. False (amphetamines are produced in the lab); 6. False (marijuana produces the most variable reactions in people); 7. True

11.3

Part A

1. d; 2. b; 3. a; 4. c; 5. f; 6. e

Part B

1. T; 2. T; 3. T; 4. F (they would still act uninhibited); 5. F (all have an effect)

11.4

1. c; 2. b; 3. a; 4. d; 5. g; 6. e; 7. h; 8. j; 9. f; 10. i;

11.5

1. b; 2. e; 3. d; 4. a; 5. c

The Abnormal Psychology Book Companion Website

See **academic.cengage.com/psychology/barlow** for practice quiz questions, interactive activities, Internet links, critical thinking exercises, discussion forums, and more. Also accessible from the Wadsworth Psychology Resource Center (**academic.cengage .com/login**).

Abnormal Psychology Live CD-ROM

- *Tim, an Example of Substance Use Disorder:* Tim describes the key criteria and shows how the disorder has had an impact on his life.
- *Nicotine Dependence:* Learn how nicotine increases the power of cues associated with smoking and how this research might help in the design of more effective programs to help people quit tobacco.

CENGAGENOW™ CengageNOW

Go to **academic.cengage.com/now** to link to CengageNOW, your online study tool. First take the Pre-Test for this chapter to get your personalized study plan, which will identify topics you need to review and direct you to online resources. Then take the Post-Test to determine what concepts you have mastered and what you still need work on.

Video Concept Reviews

CengageNOW also contains Mark Durand's *Video Concept Reviews* on challenging topics.

- Substance Intoxication, Abuse and Dependence
- Tolerance and Withdrawal
- Alcohol Use Disorders
- Sedative, Hypnotic, and Anxiolytic Substances
- Stimulants
- Amphetamine Use Disorders
- Cocaine Use Disorders
- Nicotine Use Disorders
- Caffeine Use Disorders
- Opioid Use Disorders
- Hallucinogen Use Disorders
- Marijuana
- LSD and Other Hallucinogens
- Inhalants
- Anabolic Steroids
- Designer Drugs
- Drug Use: Psychological Perspective
- Concept Check: Impulse Control Disorders Versus Substance Use

Exploring Substance-Related Disorders

- *Many kinds of problems can develop when people use and abuse substances that alter the way they think, feel, and behave.*
- *Once seen as due to personal weakness, drug abuse and dependence are now thought influenced by both biological and psychosocial factors.*

Social Influences

- Exposure to drug—through media, peers, parents, or lack of parental monitoring—versus no exposure to drug
- Social expectations and cultural norms for use
- Family/culture/society, and peers (all or some) supportive versus unsupportive of drug use

Psychological Influences

Not to use
- Fear of effects of drug use
- Decision not to use drugs
- Feeling of confidence and self-esteem without drug use

To use
- Drug use for pleasure; association with "feeling good" (positive reinforcement)
- Drug use to avoid pain and escape unpleasantness by "numbing out" (negative reinforcement)
- Feeling of being in control
- Positive expectations/urges about what drug use will be like
- Avoidance of withdrawal symptoms
- Present of other psychological disorders: mood anxiety, etc.

CAUSES OF DRUG USE AND DRUG ABUSE

Biological Influences

- Inherited genetic vulnerability affects
—Body's sensitivity to drug (ADH gene)
—Body's ability to metabolize drug (presence of specific enzymes in liver)
- Drugs activate natural reward center ("pleasure pathway") in brain
- Neuroplasticity increases drug-seeking and relapse

TREATMENT
Best to use multiple approaches

Psychosocial Treatments

- Aversion therapy—to create negative associations with drug use (shocks with drinking, imagining nausea with cocaine use)
- Contingency management to change behaviors by rewarding chosen behaviors
- Alcoholics Anonymous and its variations
- Inpatient hospital treatment (can be expensive)
- Controlled use
- Community reinforcement
- Relapse prevention

Biological Treatments

- Agonist substitution
—Replacing one drug with a similar one (methadone for heroin, nicotine gum and patches for cigarettes)
- Antagonist substitution
—Blocking one drug's effect with another drug (naltrexone for opiates and alcohol)
- Aversive treatments
—Making taking drug very unpleasant (using Antabuse, which causes nausea and vomiting when mixed with alcohol, to treat alcoholism)
- Drugs to help recovering person deal with withdrawal symptoms (clonidine for opiate withdrawal, sedatives for alcohol, etc.)

Types of Drugs

Depressants

Examples:
Alcohol, barbiturates (sedatives: Amytal, Seconal, Nembutal), benzodiazepines (antianxiety: Valium, Xanax, Halcion)

Effects:
- Decreased central nervous system activity
- Reduced levels of body arousal
- Relaxation

Stimulants

Examples:
Amphetamines, cocaine, nicotine, caffeine

Effects:
- Increased physical arousal
- User feels more alert and energetic

Opiates

Examples:
Heroin, morphine, codeine

Effects:
- Narcotic—reduce pain and induce sleep and euphoria by mirroring opiates in the brain (endorphins, etc.)

Hallucinogens

Examples:
Marijuana, LSD, Ecstasy

Effects:
- Altered mental and emotional perception
- Distortion (sometimes dramatic) of sensory perceptions

Exploring Impulse-Control Disorders

Characterized by inability to resist acting on a drive or temptation. Sufferers often perceived by society as having a problem simply due to a lack of "will."

TYPES OF IMPULSE-CONTROL DISORDERS

INTERMITTENT EXPLOSIVE DISORDER

Characteristics

- Acting on aggressive impulses that result in assaults or destruction of property
- Current research is focused on how neurotransmitters and testosterone levels interact with psychosocial influences (stress, parenting styles)

Treatment

- Cognitive-behavioral interventions (helping person identify and avoid triggers for aggressive outbursts) and approaches modeled after drug treatments appear most effective

KLEPTOMANIA

Characteristics

- Recurring failure to resist urges to steal unneeded items
- Feeling tense just before stealing, followed by feelings of pleasure or relief when committing the theft
- High comorbity with mood disorders, and to a lesser degree with substance abuse/dependence

Treatment

- Behavioral interventions or antidepressant medication

PATHOLOGICAL GAMBLING

Characteristics

- Preoccupation with gambling/with need to gamble increasing amounts of money to feel the same excitement
- "Withdrawal symptoms" of restlessness and irritability when attempting to stop
- May have a biological component, involving brain activity (decreased activity in brain region controlling impulse regulation, abnormalities in dopamine and serotonin systems)

Treatment

- Gamblers Anonymous; similar to substance-dependence treatment

TRICHOTILLOMANIA

Characteristics

- Urge to pull out one's own hair from anywhere on the body
- Sufferers go to great lengths to conceal behavior
- Relatively common (seen 1%–5% of college students)

Treatment

- SSRIs may help; cognitive-behavior interventions hold promise

PYROMANIA

Characteristics

- Irresistible urge to set fires
- Feeling aroused prior to setting fire then a sense of gratification or relief while the fire burns
- Rare; diagnosed in less than 4% of arsonists

Treatment

- Cognitive-behavioral interventions (helping person identify signals triggering urges, and teaching coping strategies to resist setting fires)

CHAPTER 12

Personality Disorders

©Janine Wiedel Photolibrary/Alamy

AN OVERVIEW OF PERSONALITY DISORDERS
Aspects of Personality Disorders
Categorical and Dimensional Models
Personality Disorder Clusters
Statistics and Development
Gender Differences
Comorbidity
Personality Disorders Under Study

CLUSTER A PERSONALITY DISORDERS
Paranoid Personality Disorder
Schizoid Personality Disorder
Schizotypal Personality Disorder

CLUSTER B PERSONALITY DISORDERS
Antisocial Personality Disorder
Borderline Personality Disorder
Histrionic Personality Disorder
Narcissistic Personality Disorder

CLUSTER C PERSONALITY DISORDERS
Avoidant Personality Disorder
Dependent Personality Disorder
Obsessive-Compulsive Personality Disorder

 ABNORMAL PSYCHOLOGY LIVE CD-ROM
Antisocial Personality Disorder: George
Borderline Personality Disorders
Dialectical Behavior Therapy
Web Link

When I was supposed to be awake, I was asleep; when I was supposed to speak, I was silent; when a pleasure offered itself to me, I avoided it.

Susanna Kaysen
Girl, Interrupted

AN OVERVIEW OF PERSONALITY DISORDERS

According to the fourth edition, text revision, of the *Diagnostic and Statistical Manual* (DSM-IV-TR), **personality disorders** are "enduring patterns of perceiving, relating to, and thinking about the environment and oneself that are exhibited in a wide range of social and personal contexts," and "are inflexible and maladaptive, and cause significant functional impairment or subjective distress" (American Psychiatric Association, 2000, p. 686). Now that you have taken out your yellow marker and highlighted this definition of personality disorders, what do you think it means?

We all think we know what a personality is. It's all the characteristic ways a person behaves and thinks: "Michael tends to be shy"; "Mindy likes to be dramatic"; "Juan is always suspicious of others"; "Annette is outgoing"; "Bruce seems to be sensitive and gets upset easily over minor things"; "Sean has the personality of an eggplant!" We tend to type people as behaving in one way in many situations. For example, like Michael, many of us are shy with people we don't know, but we won't be shy around our friends. A truly shy person is shy even among people he has known for some time. The shyness is part of the way the person behaves in most situations. We also have all probably behaved in all the other ways noted here (dramatic, suspicious, outgoing, easily upset). However, we usually consider a way of behaving part of a person's personality only if it occurs in many times and places. In this chapter, we look at characteristic ways of behaving in relation to personality disorders. First we examine how we conceptualize personality disorders and the issues related to them; then we describe the disorders themselves.

Aspects of Personality Disorders

What if a person's characteristic ways of thinking and behaving cause significant distress to the self or others? What if the person can't change this way of relating to the world and is unhappy? We might consider this person to have a personality disorder. The DSM-IV-TR definition notes that these personality characteristics are "inflexible and maladaptive and cause significant functional impairment or subjective distress." Unlike many of the disorders we have already discussed, personality disorders are chronic; they do not come and go but originate in childhood and continue throughout adulthood. Because they affect personality, these chronic problems pervade every aspect of a person's life. If a woman is overly suspicious, for example (a sign of a possible paranoid personality disorder), this trait will affect almost everything she does, including her employment (she may have to change jobs often if she believes coworkers conspire against her), her relationships (she may not be able to sustain a lasting relationship if she can't trust anyone), and even where she lives (she may have to move often if she suspects her landlord is out to get her).

DSM-IV-TR notes that having a personality disorder may distress the affected person. However, individuals with personality disorders may not feel any subjective distress; indeed, it may be acutely felt by others because of the actions of the person with the disorder. This is particularly common with antisocial personality disorder, because the individual may show a blatant disregard for the rights of others yet exhibit no remorse (Patrick, 2006). In certain cases, someone other than the person with the personality disorder must decide whether the disorder is causing significant functional impairment, because the affected person often cannot make such a judgment.

DSM-IV-TR lists 10 specific personality disorders and several others that are being studied for future consideration; we review them all. Although the prospects for treatment success for people who have personality disorders may be more optimistic than previously thought (see, for example, Svartberg, Stiles, & Seltzer, 2004), unfortunately, as you will see later, many people who have personality disorders in addition to other psychological problems (for example, major depression) tend to do poorly in treatment. One factor important to the success (or lack of success) of treatment is how the therapist feels about the client. The emotions of therapists brought out by clients (called "countertransference" by Sigmund Freud) tend to be negative for those diagnosed with personality disorders, especially those (as you will see next) in Cluster A (the odd or eccentric cluster) and Cluster B (the dramatic, emotional, or erratic cluster) (Rossberg, Karterud, Pedersen, & Friis, 2007). Therapists especially need to guard against letting their personal feelings interfere with treatment when working with people who have personality disorders.

Most disorders we discuss in this book are in Axis I of the DSM-IV-TR, which includes the standard traditional disorders. The personality disorders are included in a separate axis, Axis II, because as a group they are distinct. The characteristic traits are more ingrained and inflexible in people who have personality disorders, and the disorders themselves are less likely to be successfully modified.

Having personality disorders on a separate axis requires the clinician to consider in each symptom whether the person has a personality disorder. In the axis system, a patient can receive a diagnosis on only Axis I, only Axis II, or on both axes. A diagnosis on both Axis I and Axis II indicates that a person has both a current disorder (Axis I) and a more chronic problem (for example, personality disorder). As you will see, it is not unusual for one person to be diagnosed on both axes.

You may be surprised to learn that the category of personality disorders is controversial, because it involves a number of unresolved issues. Examining these issues can help you understand all the disorders described in this book.

Categorical and Dimensional Models

Most of us are sometimes suspicious of others and a little paranoid, overly dramatic, too self-involved, or reclusive. Fortunately, these characteristics have not lasted long or been overly intense, and they haven't significantly impaired how we live and work. People with personality disorders, however, display problem characteristics over extended periods and in many situations, which can cause great emotional pain for themselves, others, or both. Their difficulty, then, can be seen as one of *degree* rather than *kind;* in other words, the problems of people with personality disorders may just be extreme versions of the problems many of us experience temporarily, such as being shy or suspicious.

The distinction between problems of degree and problems of kind is usually described in terms of *dimensions* instead of *categories.* The issue that continues to be debated in the field is whether personality disorders are extreme versions of otherwise normal personality variations (dimensions) or ways of relating that are different from psychologically healthy behavior (categories) (Widiger & Trull, 2007). You can see the difference between dimensions and categories in everyday life. For example, we tend to look at gender categorically. Our society views us as being in one category—"female"—or the other—"male." Yet we could also look at gender in terms of dimensions. For example, we know that "maleness" and "femaleness" are partly determined by hormones. We could identify people along testosterone, estrogen, or both dimensions and rate them on a continuum of maleness and femaleness rather than in the absolute categories of male or female. We also often label people's size categorically, as tall, average, or short. But height, too, can be viewed dimensionally, in inches or centimeters.

Many researchers and clinicians in this field see personality disorders as extremes on one or more personality dimensions. Yet because of the way people are diagnosed with the DSM, the personality disorders—like most other disorders—end up being viewed in categories. You have two choices—either you do ("yes") or you do not ("no") have a disorder. For example, either you have antisocial personality disorder or you don't. The DSM doesn't rate how dependent you are; if you meet the criteria, you are labeled as having dependent personality disorder. There is no "somewhat" when it comes to personality disorders.

There are advantages to using categorical models of behavior, the most important being their convenience. With simplification, however, come problems. One is that the mere act of using categories leads clinicians to reify them; that is, to view disorders as real "things," comparable to the realness of an infection or a broken arm. Some argue that personality disorders are not things that exist but points at which society decides a particular way of relating to the world has become a problem. There is the important unresolved issue again: Are personality disorders just an extreme variant of normal personality, or are they distinctly different disorders?

Some have proposed that the DSM-IV-TR personality disorders section be replaced or at least supplemented by a dimensional model (Widiger & Trull, 2007) in which individuals would not only be given categorical diagnoses but also would be rated on a series of personality dimensions. Widiger (1991) believes such a system would have at least three advantages over a purely categorical system: (1) It would retain more information about each individual, (2) it would be more flexible because it would permit both categorical and dimensional differentiations among individuals, and (3) it would avoid the often arbitrary decisions involved in assigning a person to a diagnostic category.

Although no general consensus exists about what the basic personality dimensions might be, there are several contenders (Eysenck & Eysenck, 1975; Tellegen, 1978; Watson, Clark, & Harkness, 1994). One of the more widely accepted is called the *five-factor model,* or the "Big Five," and is taken from work on normal personality (Costa & McCrae, 1990; Costa & Widiger, 1994; Goldberg, 1993; Tupes & Christal, 1992). In this model, people can be rated on a series of personality dimensions, and the combination of five components describes why people are so different. The five factors or dimensions are *extroversion* (talkative, assertive, and active versus silent, passive, and reserved); *agreeableness* (kind, trusting, and warm versus hostile, selfish, and mistrustful); *conscientiousness* (organized, thorough, and reliable versus careless, negligent, and unreliable); *neuroticism* (even-tempered versus nervous, moody, and temperamental); and *openness to experience* (imaginative, curious, and creative versus shallow and imperceptive) (Goldberg, 1993). On each dimension, people are rated high, low, or somewhere between.

Cross-cultural research establishes the universal nature of the five dimensions—although there are individual differences across cultures (Hofstede & McCrae, 2004). For example, one study found that in general Austrian, Swiss, and Dutch samples scored the highest on openness to experience, whereas the Danes, Malaysians, and Telugu Indians (India) scored the lowest on this factor (McCrae, 2002). A number of researchers are trying to determine whether people with personality disorders can also be rated in a meaningful way along these dimensions and whether the system will help us better understand these disorders (Skodol et al., 2005).

An alternative model that derives from clinical work with people who have personality disorders is proposed by Westen and Shedler (1999). Their model identifies 12 personality dimensions (as opposed to the five in the five-factor model) that not only overlap with DSM criteria but also introduce new aspects of personality not previously tapped in the DSM (see Table 12.1). This system has yet to receive the extensive research support required for wide acceptance, but it may bring us a step closer to better understanding these complex problems.

Again, an obstacle to the adoption of a dimensional approach to personality disorders is the lack of consensus regarding the most appropriate framework. However, there is a growing consensus that the next version of the *Diagnostic and Statistical Manual—DSM-V*—should incorporative aspects of a dimensional approach to personality disorders (Widiger & Trull, 2007).

Personality Disorder Clusters

DSM-IV-TR divides the personality disorders into three groups, or clusters; this will probably continue until a strong scientific basis is established for viewing them differently (American Psychiatric Association, 2000). The cluster division is based on resemblance. Cluster A is called the odd or eccentric cluster; it includes paranoid, schizoid, and schizotypal personality disorders. Cluster B

TABLE 12.1 Two Dimensional Models of Personality

Dimension	Description
Five-Factor Model	
Neuroticism	Proneness to psychological distress and impulsive behavior
Extroversion	Tendency to join in social situations and feel joy and optimism
Openness to experience	Curiosity, receptivity to new ideas, and emotional expressiveness
Agreeableness	Extent to which someone shows both compassion and hostility toward others
Conscientiousness	Degree of organization and commitment to personal goals
Westen and Shedler Model	
Psychological health	Ability to love others, find meaning in life, and gain personal insights
Psychopathy	Lack of remorse, presence of impulsiveness, and tendency to abuse drugs
Hostility	Deep-seated ill will
Narcissism	Self-importance, grandiose assumptions about oneself, and tendency to treat others as an audience to provide admiration
Emotional dysregulation	Intense and uncontrolled emotional reactions
Dysphoria	Depression, shame, humiliation, and lack of any pleasurable experiences
Schizoid orientation	Constricted emotions, inability to understand abstract concepts such as metaphors, and few or no friends
Obsessionality	Absorption in details, stinginess, and fear of dirt and contamination
Thought disorder	Such as believing one has magical powers over others or can directly read their minds
Oedipal conflict	Adult pursuit of romantic partners who are already involved with others, inappropriate seductiveness, and intense sexual jealousy
Dissociated consciousness	Fragmenting of thought and perception often related to past sexual abuse
Sexual conflict	Anxieties and fears regarding sexual intimacy

Source: Bower, B. (1999). Personality conflicts: A clinical upstart elbows its way into the personality-assessment fray. *Science News,* 156, 88–90.

DSM-IV-TR

DSM TABLE 12.1 Personality Disorders

Personality Disorder	Description
Cluster A—Odd or Eccentric Disorders	
Paranoid personality disorder	A pervasive distrust and suspiciousness of others such that their motives are interpreted as malevolent.
Schizoid personality disorder	A pervasive pattern of detachment from social relationships and a restricted range of expression of emotions in interpersonal settings.
Schizotypal personality disorder	A pervasive pattern of social and interpersonal deficits marked by acute discomfort with reduced capacity for close relationships, as well as by cognitive or perceptual distortions and eccentricities of behavior.
Cluster B—Dramatic, Emotional, or Erratic Disorders	
Antisocial personality disorder	A pervasive pattern of disregard for and violation of the rights of others.
Borderline personality disorder	A pervasive pattern of instability of interpersonal relationships, self-image, affects, and control over impulses.
Histrionic personality disorder	A pervasive pattern of excessive emotion and attention seeking.
Narcissistic personality disorder	A pervasive pattern of grandiosity (in fantasy or behavior), need for admiration, and lack of empathy.
Cluster C—Anxious or Fearful Disorders	
Avoidant personality disorder	A pervasive pattern of social inhibition, feelings of inadequacy, and hypersensitivity to negative evaluation.
Dependent personality disorder	A pervasive and excessive need to be taken care of, which leads to submissive and clinging behavior and fears of separation.
Obsessive-compulsive personality disorder	A pervasive pattern of preoccupation with orderliness, perfectionism, and mental and interpersonal control, at the expense of flexibility, openness, and efficiency.

Source: Reprinted, with permission, from American Psychiatric Association. (2000). *Diagnostic and statistical manual of mental disorders* (4th ed., text revision). Washington, DC: Author, © 2000 American Psychiatric Association.

is the dramatic, emotional, or erratic cluster; it consists of antisocial, borderline, histrionic, and narcissistic personality disorders. Cluster C is the anxious or fearful cluster; it includes avoidant, dependent, and obsessive-compulsive personality disorders. We follow this order in our review.

Statistics and Development

Because many people with these problems do not seek help on their own like those with the Axis I disorders, gathering information about the prevalence of personality disorders is difficult and therefore varies a great deal. For example, DSM-IV-TR indicates that personality disorders are found in 0.5% to 2.5% of the general population, 10% to 30% of all individuals served in inpatient settings, and 2% to 10% of those individuals in outpatient settings (American Psychiatric Association, 2000). However, an important population survey suggests that as many as 1 in 10 adults in the United States may have a diagnosable personality disorder (Lenzenweger, Lane, Loranger, & Kessler, in press) which makes them relatively common (see Table 12.2). This difference in prevalence estimates may be the result of surveying people in clinical settings versus surveying the general population—even those not seeking assistance. Similarly, gender differences in the disorders—for example, more women diagnosed with borderline personality disorder and more men identified with antisocial personality disorder—are not apparent when surveying the general population. There may be several reasons for this discrepancy, including bias in diagnoses and differences in help-seeking behavior and tolerance of behavior in a culture. We discuss several of these concerns later in the chapter.

Personality disorders are thought to originate in childhood and continue into the adult years (Svrakic & Cloninger, 2005); they are also thought to be so ingrained that an onset is difficult to pinpoint. Maladaptive personality characteristics develop over time into the maladaptive behavior patterns that create distress for the affected person and draw the attention of others. Our relative lack of information about such important features of personality disorders as their developmental course is a repeating theme. The gaps in our knowledge of the course of about half these disorders are visible in Table 12.2. One reason for this dearth of research is that many individuals do not seek treatment in the early developmental phases of their disorder but only after years of distress. This makes it difficult to study people with personality disorders from the beginning, although a few research studies have helped us understand the development of several disorders.

People with borderline personality disorder are characterized by their volatile and unstable relationships; they tend to have persistent problems in early adulthood, with frequent hospitalizations, unstable personal relationships, severe depression, and suicidal gestures. Almost 10% attempt suicide, and approximately 6% succeed in their attempts (Perry, 1993; Stone, 1989; Yen et al., 2004). On the bright side, their symptoms gradually improve if they survive into their 30s (Zanarini, Frankenburg, Hennen, Reich, & Silk, 2006), although elderly individuals may have difficulty making plans and

---

TABLE 12.2 Statistics and Development of Personality Disorders

Disorder	Prevalence*	Gender Differences†	Course
Paranoid personality disorder	In the clinical population: 4.2%	In the clinical population: More common in males	Insufficient information
	In the general population: 2.3%–2.4%	In the general population: No difference	
Schizoid personality disorder	In the clinical population: 1.4%	In the clinical population: More common in males	Insufficient information
	In the general population: 1.7%–4.9%	In the general population: No difference	
Schizotypal personality disorder	In the clinical population: 0.6%	In the clinical population: More common in males	Chronic; some go on to develop schizophrenia
	In the general population: 0.6%–3.3%	In the general population: No difference	
Antisocial personality disorder	In the clinical population: 3.6%	In the clinical population: More common in males	Dissipates after age 40 (Hare, McPherson, & Forth, 1988)
	In the general population: 0.7%–1%	In the general population: No difference	
Borderline personality disorder	In the clinical population: 9.3%	In the clinical population: More common in females	Symptoms gradually improve if individuals survive into their 30s (Zanarini et al., 2006); approximately 6% die by suicide (Perry, 1993)
	In the general population: 0.7%–1.6%	In the general population: No difference	
Histrionic personality disorder	In the clinical population: 1.0%	In the clinical population: No difference	Chronic
	In the general population: >1%–2.0%	In the general population: No difference	
Narcissistic personality disorder	In the clinical population: 2.3%	In the clinical population: More common in males	May improve over time (Cooper & Ronningstam, 1992; Gunderson, Ronningstam, & Smith, 1991)
	In the general population: >1%	In the general population: No difference	
Avoidant personality disorder	In the clinical population: 14.7%	In the clinical population: No difference	Insufficient information
	In the general population: 5.0%–5.2%	In the general population: No difference	
Dependent personality disorder	In the clinical population: 1.4%	In the clinical population: No difference	Insufficient information
	In the general population: .6%–1.5%	In the general population: No difference	
Obsessive-compulsive personality disorder	In the clinical population: 8.7%	In the clinical population: More common in males	Insufficient information
	In the general population: 2.0%–2.4%	In the general population: No difference	

*Clinical population data reported in Zimmerman, Rothschild, and Chelminski, 2005. General population data reported from two community samples, Lenzenweger et al. (in press) and Torgersen, Kringlen, and Cramer (2001).

†Clinical population data reported in DSM-IV-TR (American Psychiatric Association, 2000) and general population data from Lenzenweger et al. (in press).

may be disruptive in nursing homes (Rosowsky & Gurian, 1992). People with antisocial personality disorder display a characteristic disregard for the rights and feelings of others; they tend to continue their destructive behaviors of lying and manipulation through adulthood. Fortunately, some tend to "burn out" after the age of about 40 and engage in fewer criminal activities (Douglas, Vincent, & Edens, 2006). As a group, however, the problems of people with personality disorders continue, as shown when researchers follow their progress over the years (Phillips & Gunderson, 2000).

Gender Differences

Borderline personality disorder is diagnosed more often in females (although as you will see next, this may be the result of diagnostic bias), who make up about 75% of the identified cases (Svrakic & Cloninger, 2005) (see Table 12.2). Historically, histrionic and dependent personality disorders were identified by clinicians more often in women (Dulit, Marin, & Frances, 1993; Stone, 1993), but according to more recent studies of their prevalence in the general population, equal numbers of males and females may have histrionic and dependent personality disorders (see Table 12.2). If this observation holds up in future studies, why have these disorders been predominantly diagnosed among females in general clinical practice and in other studies?

Do the disparities indicate differences between men and women in certain basic experiences that are genetic, sociocultural, or both, or do they represent biases on the part of the clinicians who make the diagnoses? Take, for example, a classic study by Maureen Ford and Thomas Widiger (1989), who sent fictitious case histories to clinical psychologists for diagnosis. One case described a person with *antisocial personality disorder*, which is characterized by irresponsible and reckless behavior and usually diagnosed in males; the other case described a person with *histrionic personality disorder*, which is characterized by excessive emotionality and attention seeking and more often diagnosed in females. The subject was identified as male in some versions of each case and as female in others, although everything else was identical. As the graph in ■ Figure 12.1 shows, when the antisocial personality disorder case was labeled male, most psychologists gave the correct diagnosis. However, when the same case of antisocial personality disorder was labeled female, most psychologists diagnosed it as histrionic personality disorder rather than antisocial personality disorder. In the case of histrionic personality disorder, being labeled a woman increased the likelihood of that diagnosis. Ford and Widiger (1989) concluded that the psychologists incorrectly diagnosed more women as having histrionic personality disorder.

This gender difference in diagnosis has also been criticized by other authors (see, for example, Kaplan, 1983) on the grounds that histrionic personality disorder, like several of the other personality disorders, is biased against females. As Kaplan (1983) points out,

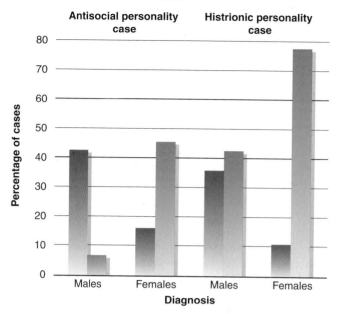

■ **FIGURE 12.1** Gender bias in diagnosing personality disorders (P.D.). Data are shown for the percentage of cases clinicians rated as antisocial personality disorder or histrionic personality disorder, depending on whether the case was described as a male or a female. (From Ford, M. R., & Widiger, T. A., 1989. Sex bias in the diagnosis of histrionic and antisocial personality disorders. *Journal of Consulting and Clinical Psychology, 57*, 301–305.)

many of the features of histrionic personality disorder, such as overdramatization, vanity, seductiveness, and overconcern with physical appearance, are characteristic of the Western "stereotypical female." This disorder may simply be the embodiment of extremely "feminine" traits (Chodoff, 1982); branding such an individual mentally ill, according to Kaplan, reflects society's inherent bias against females. (See Table 12.3 for a humorous take on a male

©Bonnie Kamin/PhotoEdit

Personality disorders tend to begin in childhood.

TABLE 12.3 Diagnostic Criteria for "Independent" Personality Disorders

A. Puts work (career) above relationships with loved ones (for example, travels a lot on business, works late at night and on weekends).

B. Is reluctant to take into account others' needs when making decisions, especially concerning the individual's career or use of leisure time, for example, expects spouse and children to relocate to another city because of individual's career plans.

C. Passively allows others to assume responsibility for major areas of social life because of inability to express necessary emotion (for example, lets spouse assume most child-care responsibilities).

Source: From Kaplan, M., 1983. A woman's view of DSM-III. *American Psychologist, 38,* 786–792.

version of a personality disorder). Interestingly, the "macho" personality (Mosher & Sirkin, 1984), in which the individual possesses stereotypically masculine traits, is nowhere to be found in the DSM.

The issue of gender bias in diagnosing personality disorder remains highly controversial. Remember, however, that just because certain disorders are observed more in men or women doesn't necessarily indicate bias (Lilienfeld, Van Valkenburg, Larntz, & Akiskal, 1986). When it is present, bias can occur at different stages of the diagnostic process. Widiger and Spitzer (1991) point out that the criteria for the disorder may themselves be biased *(criterion gender bias),* or the assessment measures and the way they are used may be biased *(assessment gender bias).* In general, the criteria themselves do not appear to have strong gender bias (Jane, Oltmanns, South, & Turkheimer, 2007), although there may be some tendency for clinicians to use their own bias when using the criteria and therefore diagnose males and females differently (Morey, Alexander, & Boggs, 2005). As research efforts continue, we will try to make the diagnosis of personality disorders more accurate with respect to gender and more useful to clinicians.

Comorbidity

Looking at Table 12.2 and adding up the prevalence rates across the personality disorders, you might conclude that up to 25% of all people are affected. In fact, the percentage of people in the population with a personality disorder is likely closer to 10% (Lenzenweger et al., in press). What accounts for this discrepancy? A major concern with the personality disorders is that people tend to be diagnosed with more than one. The term *comorbidity* historically describes the condition in which a person has multiple diseases (Caron & Rutter, 1991). A fair amount of disagreement is ongoing about whether the term should be used with psychological disorders because of the frequent overlap of different disorders (Skodol, 2005). In just one example, Zimmerman, Rothschild, and Chelminski (2005) conducted a study of 859 psychiatric outpatients and assessed how many had one or more personality disorders. Table 12.4 shows the odds that a person with a particular personality disorder would also meet the criteria for other disorders. For example, a person identified with borderline personality disorder is also likely to receive diagnoses of paranoid, schizotypal, antisocial, narcissistic, avoidant, and dependent personality disorders.

Do people really tend to have more than one personality disorder? Are the ways we define these disorders inaccurate, and do we need to improve our definitions so that they do not overlap? Or did we divide the disorders in the wrong way, and do we need to rethink the categories? Such questions about comorbidity are just a few of the important issues faced by researchers who study personality disorders.

Personality Disorders Under Study

We started this chapter by noting difficulties in categorizing personality disorders; for example, there is much overlap of the categories, which suggests there may be other ways to arrange these pervasive difficulties of character. It shouldn't surprise you to learn that other personality disorders have been proposed for inclusion in the DSM—for example, sadistic personality disorder, which includes people who receive pleasure by inflicting pain on others (Morey, Hopwood, & Klein, in press), and self-defeating personality disorder, which includes people who are overly passive and accept the pain and suffering imposed by others (Skodol, 2005). However, few studies support the existence of these disorders, so they were not included in the DSM-IV-TR (Svrakic & Cloninger, 2005).

Two new categories of personality disorder are under study. *Depressive personality disorder* includes self-criticism, dejection, a judgmental stance toward others, and a tendency to feel guilt. Some evidence indicates this may indeed be a personality disorder

©Blend Images/Alamy

Gender bias may affect the diagnosis of clinicians who associate certain behavioral characteristics with one sex or the other.

TABLE 12.4 Diagnostic Overlap of Personality Disorders

Odds Ratio[†] of People Qualifying for Other Personality Disorder Diagnoses

Diagnosis	Paranoid	Schizoid	Schizotypal	Antisocial	Borderline	Histrionic	Narcissistic	Avoidant	Dependent	Obsessive-Compulsive
Paranoid		2.1	37.3*	2.6	12.3*	0.9	8.7*	4.0*	0.9	5.2*
Schizoid	2.1		19.2	1.1	2.0	3.9	1.7	12.3*	2.9	5.5*
Schizotypal	37.3*	19.2		2.7	15.2*	9.4	11.0	3.9*	7.0	7.1
Antisocial	2.6	1.1	2.7		9.5*	8.1*	14.0*	0.9	5.6	0.2
Borderline	12.3*	2.0	15.2*	9.5*		2.8	7.1*	2.5*	7.3*	2.0
Histrionic	0.9	3.9	9.4	8.1*	2.8		13.2*	0.3	9.5	1.3
Narcissistic	8.7*	1.7	11.0	14.0*	7.1*	13.2*		0.3	4.0	3.7*
Avoidant	4.0*	12.3*	3.9*	0.9	2.5*	0.3	0.3		2.0	2.7
Dependent	0.9	2.9	7.0	5.6	7.3*	9.5	4.0	2.0		0.9
Obsessive-compulsive	5.2*	5.5*	7.1	0.2	2.0	1.3	2.0	2.7	0.9	

†The "odds ratio" indicates how likely it is that a person would have both disorders. The odds ratios with an asterisk (*) indicate that, statistically, people are likely to be diagnosed with both disorders—with a higher number meaning people are more likely to have both. Some higher odds ratios are not statistically significant because the number of people with the disorder in this study was relatively small.

Source: Reprinted, with permission, from Zimmerman, M., Rothschild, L., & Chelminski, I., 2005. The prevalence of DSM-IV personality disorders in psychiatric outpatients. *American Journal of Psychiatry,* 162, 1911–1918, © 2005 American Psychiatric Association.

distinct from dysthymic disorder (the mood disorder described in Chapter 7 that involves a persistently depressed mood lasting at least 2 years); research is continuing in this area (Laptook, Klein, & Dougherty, 2006). *Negativistic personality disorder* is characterized by passive aggression in which people adopt a negativistic attitude to resist routine demands and expectations. This category is an expansion of a previous DSM-III-R category, *passive-aggressive personality disorder,* and may be a subtype of a narcissistic personality disorder (Fossati et al., 2000). Neither depressive personality disorder nor negativistic personality disorder has yet had enough research attention to warrant inclusion as additional personality disorders in the DSM.

We now review the personality disorders currently in DSM-IV-TR, 10 in all. Then we look briefly at a few categories being considered for inclusion.

CONCEPT CHECK 12.1

Fill in the blanks to complete the following statements about personality disorders.

1. Unlike many disorders, personality disorders are _____; they originate in childhood and continue throughout adulthood.

(continued)

CONCEPT CHECK 12.1

(continued)

2. Personality disorders as a group are distinct and therefore placed on a separate axis, _____.
3. It's debated whether personality disorders are extreme versions of otherwise normal personality variations (therefore classified as dimensions) or ways of relating that are different from psychologically healthy behavior (classified as _____).
4. The personality disorders are divided into three clusters or groups: _____ contains the odd or eccentric disorders; _____ the dramatic, emotional, and erratic disorders; and _____ the anxious and fearful disorders.
5. Gender differences are evident in the research of personality disorders, although some differences in the findings may be the result of _____.
6. People with personality disorders are often diagnosed with other disorders, a phenomenon called _____

CLUSTER A PERSONALITY DISORDERS

Three personality disorders—paranoid, schizoid, and schizotypal—share common features that resemble some of the psychotic symptoms seen in schizophrenia. These odd or eccentric personality disorders are described next.

Paranoid Personality Disorder

Although it is probably adaptive to be a little wary of other people and their motives, being too distrustful can interfere with making friends, working with others, and, in general, getting through daily interactions in a functional way. People with **paranoid personality disorder** are excessively mistrustful and suspicious of others, without any justification. They assume other people are out to harm or trick them; therefore, they tend not to confide in others. Consider the case of Jake.

JAKE: Research Victim

Jake grew up in a middle-class neighborhood, and although he never got in serious trouble, he had a reputation in high school for arguing with teachers and classmates. After high school he enrolled in the local community college, but he flunked out after the first year. Jake's lack of success in school was partly attributable to his failure to take responsibility for his poor grades. He began to develop conspiracy theories about fellow students and professors, believing they worked together to see him fail. Jake bounced from job to job, each time complaining that his employer was spying on him while at work and at home.

At age 25—and against his parents' wishes—he moved out of his parents' home to a small town out of state. Unfortunately, the letters Jake wrote home daily confirmed his parents' worst fears. He was becoming increasingly preoccupied with theories about people who were out to harm him. Jake spent enormous amounts of time on his computer exploring websites, and he developed an elaborate theory about how research had been performed on him in childhood. His letters home described his belief that researchers working with the CIA drugged him as a child and implanted something in his ear that emitted microwaves. These microwaves, he believed, were being used to cause him to develop cancer. Over 2 years, he became increasingly preoccupied with this theory, writing letters to various authorities trying to convince them he was being slowly killed. After he threatened harm to some local college administrators, his parents were contacted and they brought him to a psychologist, who diagnosed him with paranoid personality disorder and major depression.

■ Clinical Description

The defining characteristic of people with paranoid personality disorder is a pervasive unjustified distrust (American Psychiatric Association, 2000). Certainly, there may be times when someone is deceitful and "out to get you"; however, people with paranoid personality disorder are suspicious in situations in which most other people would agree their suspicions are unfounded. Even events that have nothing to do with them are interpreted as personal attacks (Skodol, 2005). These people would view a neighbor's barking dog or a delayed airline flight as a deliberate attempt to annoy them. Unfortunately, such mistrust often extends to people close to them and makes meaningful relationships difficult. Imagine what a lonely existence this must be. Suspiciousness and mistrust can show themselves in a number of ways. People with paranoid personality disorder may be argumentative, may complain, or may be quiet. This style of interaction is communicated, sometimes nonverbally, to others, often resulting in discomfort among those who come in contact with them because of the volatility. They often appear tense and are "ready to pounce" when they think they've been slighted by someone. These individuals are sensitive to criticism and have an excessive need for autonomy (Bernstein, Useda, & Siever, 1993).

■ Causes

Evidence for biological contributions to paranoid personality disorder is limited. Some research suggests the disorder may be slightly more common among the relatives of people who have schizophrenia, although the association does not seem to be strong (Tienari et al., 2003). In other words, relatives of individuals with schizophrenia may be more likely to have paranoid per-

---

DSM-IV-TR

DSM TABLE 12.2 Diagnostic Criteria for Paranoid Personality Disorder

A. A pervasive distrust and suspiciousness of others such that their motives are interpreted as malevolent, beginning by early adulthood and present in a variety of contexts, as indicated by four (or more) of the following:
 1. Suspects, without sufficient basis, that others are exploiting, harming, or deceiving him or her
 2. Is preoccupied with unjustified doubts about the loyalty or trustworthiness of friends or associates
 3. Is reluctant to confide in others because of unwarranted fear that the information will be used maliciously against him or her
 4. Reads hidden demeaning or threatening meanings into benign remarks or events
 5. Persistently bears grudges, i.e., is unforgiving of insults, injuries, or slights
 6. Perceives attacks on his or her character or reputation that are not apparent to others and is quick to react angrily or to counterattack
 7. Has recurrent suspicions, without justification, regarding fidelity of spouse or sexual partner
B. Does not occur exclusively during the course of schizophrenia, a mood disorder with psychotic features, or another psychotic disorder and is not due to the direct physiological effects of a general medical condition.
Note: If criteria are met prior to the onset of schizophrenia, add "premorbid," e.g., "paranoid personality disorder (premorbid)."

Source: Reprinted, with permission, from American Psychiatric Association. (2000). *Diagnostic and statistical manual of mental disorders* (4th ed., text revision). Washington, DC: Author, © 2000 American Psychiatric Association.

sonality disorder than people who do not have a relative with schizophrenia. As you will see later with the other odd or eccentric personality disorders in Cluster A, there seems to be some relationship with schizophrenia, although its exact nature is not yet clear. In general, however, there appears to be a strong role for genetics in paranoid personality disorder (Kendler et al., 2006).

Psychological contributions to this disorder are even less certain, although some interesting speculations have been made. Retrospective research—asking people with this disorder to recall events from their childhood—suggests that early mistreatment or traumatic childhood experiences may play a role in the development of paranoid personality disorder (Johnson, Bromley, & McGeoch, 2005). Caution is warranted when interpreting these results because, clearly, there may be strong bias in the recall of these individuals, who are already prone to viewing the world as a threat.

Some psychologists point directly to the thoughts of people with paranoid personality disorder as a way of explaining their behavior. One view is that people with this disorder have the following basic mistaken assumptions about others: "People are malevolent and deceptive," "They'll attack you if they get the chance," and "You can be OK only if you stay on your toes" (Freeman, Pretzer, Fleming, & Simon, 1990). This is a maladaptive way to view the world, yet it seems to pervade every aspect of the lives of these individuals. Although we don't know why they develop these perceptions, some speculation is that the roots are in their early upbringing. Their parents may teach them to be careful about making mistakes and to impress on them that they are different from other people (Turkat & Maisto, 1985). This vigilance causes them to see signs that other people are deceptive and malicious (Beck & Freeman, 1990). It is certainly true that people are not always benevolent and sincere, and our interactions are sometimes ambiguous enough to make other people's intentions unclear. Looking too closely at what other people say and do can sometimes lead you to misinterpret them.

Cultural factors have also been implicated in paranoid personality disorder. Certain groups of people such as prisoners, refugees, people with hearing impairments, and the elderly are thought to be particularly susceptible because of their unique experiences (Christenson & Blazer, 1984; O'Brien, Trestman, & Siever, 1993). Imagine how you might view other people if you were an immigrant who had difficulty with the language and the customs of your new culture. Such innocuous things as other people laughing or talking quietly might be interpreted as somehow directed at you. The late musician Jim Morrison of The Doors described this phenomenon in his song "People Are Strange" (words and music by The Doors, © 1967 Doors Music Co., used by permission):

> People are strange,
> When you're a stranger,
> Faces look ugly,
> When you're alone.

You have seen how someone could misinterpret ambiguous situations as malevolent. Therefore, cognitive and cultural factors may interact to produce the suspiciousness observed in some people with paranoid personality disorder.

People with paranoid personality disorder often believe that impersonal situations exist specifically to annoy or otherwise disturb them.

■ Treatment

Because people with paranoid personality disorder are mistrustful of everyone, they are unlikely to seek professional help when they need it and they have difficulty developing the trusting relationships necessary for successful therapy (Schlesinger & Silk, 2005). Establishing a meaningful therapeutic alliance between the client and the therapist therefore becomes an important first step (Bender, 2005). When these individuals finally do seek therapy, the trigger is usually a crisis in their lives—such as Jake's threats to harm strangers—or other problems such as anxiety or depression, not necessarily their personality disorder (Kelly, Casey, Dunn, Ayuso-Mateos, & Dowrick, 2007).

Therapists try to provide an atmosphere conducive to developing a sense of trust (Bender, 2005). They often use cognitive therapy to counter the person's mistaken assumptions about others, focusing on changing the person's beliefs that all people are malevolent and most people cannot be trusted (Tyrer & Davidson, 2000). Be forewarned, however, that to date there are no confirmed demonstrations that any form of treatment can significantly improve the lives of people with paranoid personality disorder. A survey of mental health professionals indicated that only 11% of therapists who treat paranoid personality disorder thought these individuals would continue in therapy long enough to be helped (Quality Assurance Project, 1990).

Schizoid Personality Disorder

Do you know someone who is a "loner"? Someone who would choose a solitary walk over an invitation to a party? A person who comes to class alone, sits alone, and leaves alone? Now, magnify this preference for isolation many times over and you can begin to grasp the impact of **schizoid personality disorder** (Svrakic

& Cloninger, 2005). People with this personality disorder show a pattern of detachment from social relationships and a limited range of emotions in interpersonal situations (Skodol, 2005). They seem aloof, cold, and indifferent to other people. The term *schizoid* is relatively old, having been used by Bleuler (1924) to describe people who have a tendency to turn inward and away from the outside world. These people were said to lack emotional expressiveness and pursued vague interests. Consider the case of Mr. Z.

MR. Z.: All on His Own

A 39-year-old scientist was referred after his return from a tour of duty in Antarctica where he had stopped cooperating with others, had withdrawn to his room, and begun drinking on his own. Mr. Z. was orphaned at 4 years, raised by an aunt until 9, and subsequently looked after by an aloof housekeeper. At university he excelled at physics, but chess was his only contact with others. Throughout his subsequent life he made no close friends and engaged primarily in solitary activities. Until the tour of duty in Antarctica, he had been quite successful in his research work in physics. He was now, some months after his return, drinking at least a bottle of Schnapps each day, and his work had continued to deteriorate. He presented as self-contained and unobtrusive and was difficult to engage effectively. He was at a loss to explain his colleagues' anger at his aloofness in Antarctica and appeared indifferent to their opinion of him. He did not appear to require any interpersonal relations, although he did complain of some tedium in his life and at one point during the interview became sad, expressing longing to see his uncle in Germany, his only living relation.

(Cases and excerpts reprinted, with permission of the Royal Australian and New Zealand College of Psychiatrists, from Quality Assurance Project, 1990. Treatment outlines for paranoid, schizotypal and schizoid personality disorders. *Australian and New Zealand Journal of Psychiatry, 24,* 339–350.)

■ Clinical Description

Individuals with schizoid personality disorder seem neither to desire nor to enjoy closeness with others, including romantic or sexual relationships. As a result they appear cold and detached and do not seem affected by praise or criticism. One of the changes in DSM-IV-TR from previous versions is the recognition that at least some people with schizoid personality disorder are sensitive to the opinions of others but are unwilling or unable to express this emotion. For them, social isolation may be extremely painful. Unfortunately, homelessness appears to be prevalent among people with this personality disorder, perhaps as a result of their lack of close friendships and lack of dissatisfaction about not having a sexual relationship with another person (Rouff, 2000).

The social deficiencies of people with schizoid personality disorder are similar to those of people with paranoid personality disorder, although they are more extreme. As Beck and Freeman (1990, p. 125) put it, they "consider themselves to be observers rather than participants in the world around them." They do not seem to have the unusual thought processes that characterize the other disorders in Cluster A (Skodol, 2005) (see Table 12.5). For example, people with paranoid and schizotypal personality disorders often have ideas of reference, mistaken beliefs that meaningless events relate just to them. In contrast, those with schizoid personality disorder share the social isolation, poor rapport, and constricted affect (showing neither positive nor negative emotion) seen in people with paranoid personality disorder. You will see in Chapter 13 that this distinction among psychotic-like symptoms is important to understanding people with schizophrenia, some of whom show the "positive" symptoms (actively unusual behaviors such as ideas of reference) and others only the "negative" symp-

TABLE 12.5 Grouping Schema for Cluster A Disorders

	Psychotic-Like Symptoms	
Cluster A Personality Disorder	**Positive** (for example, Ideas of Reference, Magical Thinking, and Perceptual Distortions)	**Negative** (for example, Social Isolation, Poor Rapport, and Constricted Affect)
Paranoid	Yes	Yes
Schizoid	No	Yes
Schizotypal	Yes	No

Source: Adapted from Siever, L. J. 1992. Schizophrenia spectrum personality disorders. In A. Tasman & M. B. Riba (Eds.), *Review of psychiatry* (Vol. 11, pp. 25–42). Washington, DC: American Psychiatric Press.

DSM-IV-TR

DSM TABLE 12.3 Diagnostic Criteria for Schizoid Personality Disorder

A. A pervasive pattern of detachment from social relationships and a restricted range of expression of emotions in interpersonal settings, beginning by early adulthood and present in a variety of contexts, as indicated by four (or more) of the following:
  1. Neither desires nor enjoys close relationships, including being part of a family
  2. Almost always chooses solitary activities
  3. Has little, if any, interest in having sexual experiences with another person
  4. Takes pleasure in few, if any, activities
  5. Lacks close friends or confidants other than first-degree relatives
  6. Appears indifferent to the praise or criticism of others
  7. Shows emotional coldness, detachment, or flattened affectivity
B. Does not occur exclusively during the course of schizophrenia, a mood disorder with psychotic features, another psychotic disorder, or a pervasive developmental disorder and is not due to the direct physiological effects of a general medical condition.
Note: If criteria are met prior to the onset of schizophrenia, add "premorbid," e.g., "schizoid personality disorder (premorbid)."

Source: Reprinted, with permission, from American Psychiatric Association. (2000). *Diagnostic and statistical manual of mental disorders* (4th ed., text revision). Washington, DC: Author. © 2000 American Psychiatric Association.

toms (the more passive manifestations of social isolation or poor rapport with others).

■ Causes and Treatment

Extensive research on the genetic, neurobiological, and psychosocial contributions to schizoid personality disorder remains to be conducted (Phillips, Yen, & Gunderson, 2003). Childhood shyness is reported as a precursor to later adult schizoid personality disorder. It may be that this personality trait is inherited and serves as an important determinant in the development of this disorder. Abuse and neglect in childhood are also reported among individuals with this disorder (Johnson et al., 2005). Research over the past several decades point to biological causes of autism (a disorder we discuss in more detail in Chapter 14), and parents of children with autism are more likely to have schizoid personality disorder (Wolff, Narayan, & Moyes, 1988). It is possible that a biological dysfunction found in both autism and schizoid personality disorder combines with early learning or early problems with interpersonal relationships to produce the social deficits that define schizoid personality disorder (Wolff, 2000). For example, research on the neurochemical dopamine suggests that people with a lower density of dopamine receptors scored higher on a measure of "detachment" (Farde, Gustavsson, & Jonsson, 1997). It may be that dopamine (which seems to be involved with schizophrenia as well) may contribute to the social aloofness of people with schizoid personality disorder.

It is rare for a person with this disorder to request treatment except in response to a crisis such as extreme depression or losing a job (Kelly et al., 2007). Therapists often begin treatment by pointing out the value in social relationships. The person with the disorder may even need to be taught the emotions felt by others to learn empathy (Beck & Freeman, 1990). Because their social skills were never established or have atrophied through lack of use, people with schizoid personality disorder often receive social skills training. The therapist takes the part of a friend or significant other in a technique known as role-playing and helps the patient practice establishing and maintaining social relationships (Beck & Freeman, 1990). This type of social skills training is helped by identifying a social network—a person or people who will be supportive (Bender, 2005). Outcome research on this type of approach is unfortunately quite limited, so we must be cautious in evaluating the effectiveness of treatment for people with schizoid personality disorder.

Schizotypal Personality Disorder

People with **schizotypal personality disorder** are typically socially isolated, like those with schizoid personality disorder. In addition, they also behave in ways that would seem unusual to many of us, and they tend to be suspicious and to have odd beliefs (Svrakic & Cloninger, 2005). Schizotypal personality disorder is considered by some to be on a continuum of disorders with schizophrenia—the severe disorder we discuss in the next chapter. (Siever & Davis, 2004)—but without some of the more debilitating symptoms, such as hallucinations and delusions. Consider the case of Mr. S.

MR. S.: Man With a Mission

Mr. S. was a 35-year-old chronically unemployed man who had been referred by a physician because of a vitamin deficiency. This was thought to have developed because Mr. S. avoided any foods that "could have been contaminated by machine." He had begun to develop alternative ideas about diet in his 20s and soon left his family and began to study an eastern religion. "It opened my third eye, corruption is all about," he said.

He now lived by himself on a small farm, attempting to grow his own food, bartering for items he could not grow himself. He spent his days and evenings researching the origins and mechanisms of food contamination and, because of this knowledge, had developed a small band who followed his ideas. He had never married and maintained little contact with his family: "I've never been close to my father. I'm a vegetarian."

He said he intended to do a herbalism course to improve his diet before returning to his life on the farm. He had refused medication from the physician and became uneasy when the facts of his deficiency were discussed with him.

(Cases and excerpts reprinted, with permission of the Royal Australian and New Zealand College of Psychiatrists, from Quality Assurance Project, 1990. Treatment outlines for paranoid, schizotypal and schizoid personality disorders. *Australian and New Zealand Journal of Psychiatry, 24,* 339–350.)

■ Clinical Description

People given a diagnosis of schizotypal personality disorder have psychotic-like (but not psychotic) symptoms (such as believing everything relates to them personally), social deficits, and sometimes cognitive impairments or paranoia (Siever & Davis, 2004). These individuals are often considered odd or bizarre because of how they relate to other people, how they think and behave, and even how they dress. They have *ideas of reference,* which means they think insignificant events relate directly to them. For example, they may believe that somehow everyone on a passing city bus is talking about them, yet they may be able to acknowledge this is unlikely. Again, as you will see in Chapter 13, some people with schizophrenia also have ideas of reference, but they are usually not able to "test reality" or see the illogic of their ideas.

Individuals with schizotypal personality disorder also have odd beliefs or engage in "magical thinking," believing, for example, that they are clairvoyant or telepathic. In addition, they report unusual perceptual experiences, including such illusions as feeling the presence of another person when they are alone. Notice the subtle but important difference between *feeling* as if someone else is in the room and the more extreme perceptual distortion in people with schizophrenia who might report there *is* someone else in the room when there isn't. Unlike people who simply have unusual interests or beliefs, those with schizotypal personality disorder tend to be suspicious and have paranoid thoughts, express little emotion, and may dress or behave in unusual ways (for example, wear many layers of clothing in the summertime or mumble to themselves) (Siever & Davis, 2004). Prospective research on children who later develop schizotypal personality disorder found that they tend to be passive and unengaged and are hypersensitive to criticism (Olin et al., 1997).

Clinicians have to be warned that different cultural beliefs or practices may lead to a mistaken diagnosis of schizotypal personality disorder. For example, some people who practice certain religious rituals—such as speaking in tongues, practicing voodoo, or mind reading—may do so with such obsessiveness as to make them seem extremely unusual, thus leading to a misdiagnosis (American Psychiatric Association, 2000). Mental health workers have to be particularly sensitive to cultural practices that may differ from their own and can distort their view of certain seemingly unusual behaviors.

■ Causes

Historically, the word *schizotype* was used to describe people who were predisposed to develop schizophrenia (Meehl, 1962; Rado, 1962). Schizotypal personality disorder is viewed by some to be one phenotype of a schizophrenia genotype. Recall that a *phenotype* is one way a person's genetics is expressed. Your *genotype* is the gene or genes that make up a particular disorder. However, depending on a variety of other influences, the way you turn out,

your phenotype, may vary from other people with a similar genetic makeup. Some people are thought to have "schizophrenia genes" (the genotype) yet, because of the relative lack of biological influences (for example, prenatal illnesses) or environmental stresses (for example, poverty), some will have the less severe schizotypal personality disorder (the phenotype).

The idea of a relationship between schizotypal personality disorder and schizophrenia arises partly from the way people with the disorders behave. Many characteristics of schizotypal personality disorder, including ideas of reference, illusions, and paranoid thinking, are similar but milder forms of behaviors observed among people with schizophrenia. Genetic research also seems to support a relationship. Family, twin, and adoption studies have shown an increased prevalence of schizotypal personality disorder among relatives of people with schizophrenia who do not also have schizophrenia themselves (Siever & Davis, 2004). However, these studies also tell us that the environment can strongly influence schizotypal personality disorder. For example, some research suggests a woman's exposure to influenza in pregnancy may increase the chance of schizotypal personality disorder in her children (Venables, 1996). Accumulating evidence points to genetic and environmental influences that may protect some frontal lobe abilities of people with schizotypal personality disorder that in turn protects them from developing schizophrenia (Siever & Davis, 2004).

Cognitive assessment of people with this disorder point to mild to moderate decrements in their ability to perform on tests involving memory and learning, suggesting some damage in the left hemisphere (Siever & Davis, 2004). Other research using magnetic resonance imaging points to generalized brain abnormalities in this group (Dickey et al., 2000).

DSM-IV-TR

DSM TABLE 12.4 Diagnostic Criteria for Schizotypal Personality Disorder

A. A pervasive pattern of social and interpersonal deficits marked by acute discomfort with, and reduced capacity for, close relationships, as well as by cognitive or perceptual distortions and eccentricities of behavior, beginning by early adulthood and present in a variety of contexts, as indicated by five (or more) of the following:
  1. Ideas of reference (excluding delusions of reference)
  2. Odd beliefs or magical thinking that influences behavior and is inconsistent with subcultural norms (e.g., superstitiousness, belief in clairvoyance, telepathy, or "sixth sense"; in children and adolescents, bizarre fantasies or preoccupations)
  3. Unusual perceptual experiences, including bodily illusions
  4. Odd thinking and speech (e.g., vague, circumstantial, metaphorical, overelaborate, or stereotyped)
  5. Suspiciousness or paranoid ideation
  6. Inappropriate or constricted affect
  7. Behavior or appearance that is odd, eccentric, or peculiar
  8. Lack of close friends or confidants other than first-degree relatives
  9. Excessive social anxiety that does not diminish with familiarity and tends to be associated with paranoid fears rather than negative judgments about self
B. Does not occur exclusively during the course of schizophrenia, a mood disorder with psychotic features, another psychotic disorder, or a pervasive developmental disorder.

Note: If criteria are met prior to the onset of schizophrenia, add "premorbid," e.g., "schizotypal personality disorder (premorbid)."

Source: Reprinted, with permission, from American Psychiatric Association. (2000). *Diagnostic and statistical manual of mental disorders* (4th ed., text revision). Washington, DC: Author, © 2000 American Psychiatric Association.

■ Treatment

Some estimate that between 30% and 50% of the people with this disorder who request clinical help also meet the criteria for major depressive disorder. Treatment will include some of the medical and psychological treatments for depression (Goldberg, Schultz, Resnick, Hamer, & Schultz, 1987; M. H. Stone, 2001).

Controlled studies of attempts to treat groups of people with schizotypal personality disorder are few. However, there is now growing interest in treating this disorder because it is being viewed as a precursor to schizophrenia. One study used a combination of approaches, including antipsychotic medication, community treatment (a team of support professionals providing therapeutic services), and social skills training, to treat the symptoms experienced by individuals with this disorder. Researchers found that this combination of approaches either reduced their symptoms or postponed the onset of later schizophrenia (Nordentoft et al., 2006).

Further research on the treatment of people with this disorder is important for a variety of reasons. They tend not to improve over time, and, as you have seen, some evidence indicates that some will go on to develop the more severe characteristics of schizophrenia.

CONCEPT CHECK 12.2

Which personality disorders are described here?

1. Carlos, who seems eccentric, never shows much emotion. He has always sought solitary activities in school and at home. He has no close friends. At birthday parties during his adolescence, he would take his gifts to a corner to play. Carlos appears indifferent to what others say, has never had a girlfriend, and expresses no desire to have sex. He is meeting with a therapist only because his family tricked him into going. _____

2. Paul trusts no one and incorrectly believes other people want to harm him or cheat him out of his life earnings. He is sure his wife is having an affair, although he has no proof. He no longer confides in friends or divulges any information to coworkers for fear that it will be used against him. He dwells for hours on harmless comments by family members. _____

3. Alison lives alone out in the country and has little contact with relatives or any other individuals in a nearby town. She is extremely concerned with pollution, fearing that harmful chemicals are in the air and water around her. If it is necessary for her to go outside, she covers her body with excessive clothing and wears a face mask to avoid the contaminated air. She has developed her own water purification system and makes her own clothes. _____

CLUSTER B PERSONALITY DISORDERS

People diagnosed with the Cluster B personality disorders—antisocial, borderline, histrionic, and narcissistic—all have behaviors that have been described as dramatic, emotional, or erratic. These personality disorders with exaggerated presentations are described next.

Antisocial Personality Disorder

People with **antisocial personality disorder** are among the most puzzling of the individuals a clinician will see in a practice and are characterized as having a history of failing to comply with social norms. They perform actions most of us would find unacceptable, such as stealing from friends and family. They also tend to be irresponsible, impulsive, and deceitful (Lykken, 2006). Robert Hare, a pioneer in the study of people with this disorder, describes them as "social predators who charm, manipulate, and ruthlessly plow their way through life, leaving a broad trail of broken hearts, shattered expectations, and empty wallets. Completely lacking in conscience and empathy, they selfishly take what they want and do as they please, violating social norms and expectations without the slightest sense of guilt or regret" (Hare, 1993, p. xi). Just who are these people with antisocial personality disorder? Consider the case of Ryan.

RYAN: The Thrill Seeker

I first met Ryan on his 17th birthday. Unfortunately, he was celebrating the event in a psychiatric hospital. He had been truant from school for several months and had gotten into some trouble; the local judge who heard his case had recommended psychiatric evaluation one more time, even though Ryan had been hospitalized six previous times, all for problems related to drug use and truancy. He was a veteran of the system and already knew most of the staff. I interviewed him to assess why he was admitted this time and to recommend treatment.

My first impression was that Ryan was cooperative and pleasant. He pointed out a tattoo on his arm that he had made himself, saying that it was a "stupid" thing to have done and that he now regretted it. He regretted many things and was looking forward to moving on with his life. I later found out that he was never truly remorseful for anything.

Our second interview was quite different. During those 48 hours, Ryan had done a number of things that showed why he needed a great deal of help. The most serious incident involved a 15-year-old girl named Ann who attended class with Ryan in the hospital school. Ryan had told her that he was going to get himself discharged, get in trouble, and be sent to the same prison Ann's father was in, where he would rape her father. Ryan's threat so upset Ann that she hit her teacher and several of the staff. When I spoke to Ryan about this, he smiled slightly and said he was bored and that it was fun to upset Ann. When I asked whether it bothered him that his behavior might extend her stay in the hospital, he looked puzzled and said, "Why should it bother me? She's the one who'll have to stay in this hell hole!"

Just before Ryan's admittance, a teenager in his town was murdered. A group of teens went to the local cemetery at night to perform satanic rituals, and a young man was stabbed to death, apparently over a drug purchase. Ryan was in the group, although he did not stab the boy. He told me that they occasionally dug up graves to get skulls for their parties—not because they really believed in the devil but because it was fun and it scared the younger kids. I asked, "What if this was the grave of someone you knew, a relative or a friend? Would it bother you that strangers were digging up the remains?" He shook his head. "They're dead, man; they don't care. Why should I?"

Ryan told me he loved PCP, or "angel dust," and that he would rather be dusted than anything else. He routinely made the 2-hour trip to New York City to buy drugs in a particularly dangerous neighborhood. He denied that he was ever nervous. This wasn't machismo; he really seemed unconcerned.

Ryan made little progress. I discussed his future in family therapy sessions and we talked about his pattern of showing supposed regret and remorse and then stealing money from his parents and going back onto the street. Most of our discussions centered on trying to give his parents the courage to say no to him and not to believe his lies.

One evening, after many sessions, Ryan said he had seen the "error of his ways" and that he felt bad he had hurt his parents. If they would only take him home this one last time, he would be the son he should have been all these years. His speech moved his parents to tears, and they looked at me gratefully as if to thank me for curing their son. When Ryan finished talking, I smiled, applauded, told him it was the best performance I had ever seen. His parents turned on me in anger. Ryan paused for a second, then he, too, smiled and said, "It was worth a shot!" Ryan's parents were astounded that he had again tricked them into believing him; he hadn't meant a word of what he had just said. Ryan was eventually discharged to a drug rehabilitation program. Within 4 weeks, he had convinced his parents to take him home, and within 2 days he had stolen all their cash and disappeared; he apparently went back to his friends and to drugs.

When he was in his 20s, after one of his many arrests for theft, he was diagnosed as having antisocial personality disorder. His parents never summoned the courage to turn him out or refuse him money, and he continues to con them into providing him with a means of buying more drugs.

DSM-IV-TR

DSM TABLE 12.5 Diagnostic Criteria for Antisocial Personality Disorder

A. There is a pervasive pattern of disregard for and violation of the rights of others occurring since age 15 years, as indicated by three (or more) of the following:
 1. Failure to conform to social norms with respect to lawful behaviors as indicated by repeatedly performing acts that are grounds for arrest
 2. Deceitfulness, as indicated by repeated lying, use of aliases, or conning others for personal profit or pleasure
 3. Impulsivity or failure to plan ahead
 4. Irritability and aggressiveness, as indicated by repeated physical fights or assaults
 5. Reckless disregard for safety of self or others
 6. Consistent irresponsibility, as indicated by repeated failure to sustain consistent work behavior or honor financial obligations
 7. Lack of remorse, as indicated by being indifferent to or rationalizing having hurt, mistreated, or stolen from another
B. The individual is at least age 18 years.
C. There is evidence of conduct disorder with onset before age 15 years.
D. The occurrence of antisocial behavior is not exclusively during the course of schizophrenia or a manic episode.

Source: Reprinted, with permission, from American Psychiatric Association. (2000). *Diagnostic and statistical manual of mental disorders* (4th ed., text revision). Washington, DC: Author, © 2000 American Psychiatric Association.

■ Clinical Description

Individuals with antisocial personality disorder tend to have long histories of violating the rights of others (Lykken, 2006). They are often described as being aggressive because they take what they want, indifferent to the concerns of other people. Lying and cheating seem to be second nature to them, and often they appear unable to tell the difference between the truth and the lies they make up to further their own goals. They show no remorse or concern over the sometimes-devastating effects of their actions. Substance abuse is common, occurring in 60% of people with antisocial personality disorder, and appears to be a lifelong pattern among these individuals (Taylor & Lang, 2006). The long-term outcome for people with antisocial personality disorder is usually poor, regardless of gender (Douglas et al., 2006). One study, for example, followed 1,000 delinquent and nondelinquent boys over a 50-year period (Laub & Vaillant, 2000). Many of the delinquent boys would today receive a diagnosis of conduct disorder, which you will see later may be a precursor to antisocial personality disorder in adults. The delinquent boys were more than twice as likely to die an unnatural death (for example, accident, suicide, or homicide) as their nondelinquent peers, which may be attributed to factors such as alcohol abuse and poor self-care (for example, infections and reckless behavior).

Antisocial personality disorder has had a number of names over the years. Philippe Pinel (1809; 1962) identified what he called *manie sans délire* (mania without delirium) to describe people with unusual emotional responses and impulsive rages but no deficits in reasoning ability (Sutker, Bugg, & West, 1993). Other labels have included moral insanity, egopathy, sociopathy, and psychopathy. A great deal has been written about these labels; we focus on the two that have figured most prominently in psy-

chological research: **psychopathy** and DSM-IV-TR's antisocial personality disorder. As you will see, there are important differences between the two.

Defining Criteria Hervey Cleckley (1941; 1982), a psychiatrist who spent much of his career working with the "psychopathic personality," identified a constellation of 16 major characteristics, most of which are personality traits and are sometimes referred to as the "Cleckley criteria." Hare and his colleagues, building on the descriptive work of Cleckley, researched the nature of psychopathy (see, for example, Hare, 1970; Harpur, Hare, & Hakstian, 1989) and developed a 20-item checklist that serves as an assessment tool. Six of the criteria that Hare includes in his Revised Psychopathy Checklist (PCL-R) are as follows (Hare & Neumann, 2006):

1. Glibness/superficial charm
2. Grandiose sense of self-worth
3. Proneness to boredom/need for stimulation
4. Pathological lying
5. Conning/manipulative
6. Lack of remorse

With some training, clinicians are able to gather information from interviews with a person, along with material from significant others or institutional files (for example, prison records), and assign the person scores on the checklist, with high scores indicating psychopathy (Hare & Neumann, 2006).

The DSM-IV-TR criteria for antisocial personality focus almost entirely on observable *behaviors* (for example, "repeated lying, use of aliases, or conning others for personal profit"). In contrast,

Courtesy of Dr. Robert Hare

Robert Hare has made extensive studies of people with psychopathic personalities.

the Cleckley/Hare criteria focus primarily on underlying *personality traits* (for example, being self-centered or manipulative). DSM-IV-TR and previous versions chose to use only observable behaviors so that clinicians could reliably agree on a diagnosis. The framers of the criteria felt that trying to assess a personality trait—for example, whether someone was manipulative—would be more difficult than determining whether the person engaged in certain behaviors, such as repeated fighting.

Antisocial Personality, Psychopathy, and Criminality

Although Cleckley did not deny that many psychopaths are at greatly elevated risk for criminal and antisocial behaviors, he did emphasize that some have few or no legal or interpersonal difficulties. In other words, some psychopaths are not criminals and some do not display the aggressiveness that is a DSM-IV-TR criterion for antisocial personality disorder. Although the relationship between psychopathic personality and antisocial personality disorder is uncertain, the two syndromes clearly do not overlap perfectly (Lykken, 2006). ■ Figure 12.2 illustrates the relative overlap among the characteristics of psychopathy as described by Cleckley and Hare, antisocial personality disorder as outlined in DSM-IV-TR, and criminality, which includes all people who get into trouble with the law.

As you can see in the diagram, not everyone who has psychopathy or antisocial personality disorder becomes involved with the legal system. What separates many in this group from those who get into trouble with the law may be their intelligence quotient (IQ). In a classic prospective, longitudinal study, White, Moffitt, and Silva (1989) followed almost 1,000 children, begin-

ning at age 5, to see what predicted antisocial behavior at age 15. They found that, of the 5-year-olds determined to be at high risk for later delinquent behavior, 16% did indeed have run-ins with the law by the age of 15 and 84% did not. What distinguished these two groups? In general, the at-risk children with lower IQs were the ones who got in trouble. This suggests that having a higher IQ may help protect some people from developing more serious problems, or may at least prevent them from getting caught.

Some psychopaths function quite successfully in certain segments of society (for example, politics, business, and entertainment). Because of the difficulty in identifying these people, such "successful" or "subclinical" psychopaths (who meet some the criteria for psychopathy) have not been the focus of much research. In a clever exception, Widom (1977) recruited a sample of subclinical psychopaths through advertisements in underground newspapers that invited many of the major personality characteristics of psychopathy. For example, one of the advertisements read as follows:

> Wanted: charming, aggressive, carefree people who are impulsively irresponsible but are good at handling people and at looking after number one.

Widom found that her sample appeared to possess many of the same characteristics as imprisoned psychopaths; for example, a large percentage of them received low scores on questionnaire measures of empathy and socialization and their parents tended to have higher rates of psychopathology, including alcoholism. But many of these individuals had stable occupations and had managed to stay out of prison. Widom's study, although lacking a control group, shows that at least some individuals with psychopathic personality traits avoid repeated contact with the legal system and may even function successfully in society.

Identifying psychopaths among the criminal population seems to have important implications for predicting their future criminal behavior. As you can imagine, having personality characteristics such as a lack of remorse and impulsivity can lead to difficulty staying out of trouble with the legal system. In general, people who score high on measures of psychopathy commit crimes at a higher rate than those with lower scores and are at greater risk for more violent crimes and recidivism (repeating offenses) (Widiger, 2006).

As we review the literature on antisocial personality disorder, note that the people included in the research may be members of only one of the three groups (those with antisocial personality disorder, psychopathy, and criminals) we have described. For example, genetic research is usually conducted with criminals because they and their families are easier to identify than members of the other groups. As you now know, the criminal group may include people other than those with antisocial personality disorder or psychopathy. Keep this in mind as you read on.

Conduct Disorder Before we discuss causal factors, it is important to note the developmental nature of antisocial behavior. DSM-IV-TR provides a separate diagnosis for children who engage in behaviors that violate society's norms: *conduct disorder*. Many children with conduct disorder—most often diagnosed in boys (Eme, 2007)—become juvenile offenders (Eppright, Kashani,

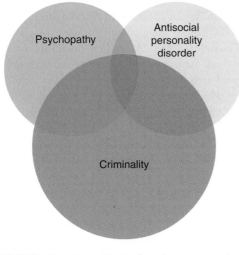

■ **FIGURE 12.2** Overlap and lack of overlap among antisocial personality disorder, psychopathy, and criminality.

"I have hatred inside me. I don't care how much I be somebody.... The more I hear somebody, the more anger I get inside me.... I used drugs when I was ... probably 9 or 10 years old ... smoked marijuana.... First time I drank some alcohol I think I was probably about 3 years old.... I assaulted a woman.... I had so much anger.... I was just like a bomb ... it's just ticking ... and the way I'm going, that bomb was going to blow up in me. I wouldn't be able to get away from it ... going to be a lot of people hurt.... I'm not going out without taking somebody with me."

Robison, & Reid, 1993) and tend to become involved with drugs (VanKammen, Loeber, & Stouthamer-Loeber, 1991). Ryan fit into this category. More important, the lifelong pattern of antisocial behavior is evident because young children who display antisocial behavior are likely to continue these behaviors as they grow older (Soderstrom, Sjodin, Carlstedt, & Forsman, 2004). Data from long-term follow-up research indicate that many adults with antisocial personality disorder or psychopathy had conduct disorder as children (Robins, 1978; Salekin, 2006); the likelihood increases if the child has both conduct disorder and attention deficit/hyperactivity disorder (Lynam, 1996). In many cases, the types of norm violations that an adult would engage in—irresponsibility regarding work or family—appear as younger versions in conduct disorder: truant from school, running away from home. A major difference is that lack of remorse is included under antisocial personality disorder but not in the conduct disorder criteria.

There is a tremendous amount of interest in studying a group that causes a great deal of harm to society. Research has been conducted for a number of years, and so we know a great deal more about antisocial personality disorder than about the other personality disorders.

■ Genetic Influences

Family, twin, and adoption studies all suggest a genetic influence on both antisocial personality disorder and criminality (Waldman & Rhee, 2006). For example, Crowe (1974) examined children whose mothers were felons and who were later adopted by other families and compared them with adopted children of normal mothers. All were separated from their mothers as newborns, minimizing the possibility that environmental factors from their biological families were responsible for the results. Crowe found that the adopted offspring of felons had significantly higher rates of arrests, conviction, and antisocial personality than did the adopted offspring of normal mothers, which suggests at least some genetic influence on criminality and antisocial behavior.

However, Crowe found something else quite interesting: The adopted children of felons who themselves later became criminals had spent more time in interim orphanages than either the adopted children of felons who did not become criminals or the adopted children of normal mothers. As Crowe points out, this suggests a gene–environment interaction; in other words, genetic factors may be important only in the presence of certain environmental influences (alternatively, certain environmental influences are important only in the presence of certain genetic predisposi-

tions). Genetic factors may present a vulnerability, but actual development of criminality may require environmental factors, such as a deficit in early, high-quality contact with parents or parent surrogates.

This gene–environment interaction was demonstrated most clearly by Cadoret, Yates, Troughton, Woodworth, and Stewart (1995), who studied adopted children and their likelihood of developing conduct problems. If the children's biological parents had a history of antisocial personality disorder and their adoptive families exposed them to chronic stress through marital, legal, or psychiatric problems, the children were at greater risk for conduct problems. Again, research shows that genetic influence does not necessarily mean certain disorders are inevitable. Large-scale research on twins with conduct disorder supports the role of genetic and environmental influences on this disorder as well (Slutske et al., 1997, 1998).

If you remember back to Chapter 4, we introduced the concept of an *endophenotype*—underlying aspects of a disorder that might be more directly influenced by genes. In the case of antisocial personality disorder, gene researchers are looking for genetic differences that may influence factors such as serotonin and dopamine levels or the relative lack of anxiety or fear seen in these individuals (which we discuss next) (van Goozen, Fairchild, Snoek, & Harold, 2007; Waldman & Rhee, 2006). Although at its early stages, this research is refining the search for genes—not for ones that "cause antisocial personality disorder" but for genes that create the unusual aspects of an antisocial personality, such as aggressiveness, impulsivity, and lack of remorse.

■ Neurobiological Influences

A great deal of research has focused on neurobiological influences that may be specific to antisocial personality disorder. One thing seems clear: General brain damage does not explain why some people become psychopaths or criminals; these individuals appear to score as well on neuropsychological tests as the rest of us (Hart, Forth, & Hare, 1990). However, such tests are designed to detect significant damage in the brain and will not pick up subtle changes in chemistry or structure that could affect behavior.

Arousal Theories The fearlessness, seeming insensitivity to punishment, and thrill-seeking behaviors characteristic of those with antisocial personality disorder (especially those with psychopathy) sparked interest in what neurobiological processes might contribute to these unusual reactions. Early theoretical work on people with antisocial personality disorder emphasized two hypotheses: the underarousal hypothesis and the fearlessness hypothesis. According to the *underarousal hypothesis,* psychopaths have abnormally low levels of cortical arousal (Quay, 1965). There appears to be an inverted U-shaped relation between arousal and performance. The *Yerkes-Dodson curve* suggests that people with either high or low levels of arousal tend to experience negative affect and perform poorly in many situations, whereas individuals with intermediate levels of arousal tend to be relatively content and perform satisfactorily in most situations.

DSM-IV-TR

DSM TABLE 12.6 Diagnostic Criteria for Conduct Disorder

A. A repetitive and persistent pattern of behavior in which the basic rights of others or major age-appropriate societal norms or rules are violated, as manifested by the presence of three (or more) of the following criteria in the past 12 months with at least one criterion present in the past 6 months:

Aggression to people and animals

1. Often bullies, threatens, or intimidates others
2. Often initiates physical fights
3. Has used a weapon that can cause serious physical harm to others (e.g., a bat, brick, broken bottle, knife, gun)
4. Has been physically cruel to people
5. Has been physically cruel to animals
6. Has stolen while confronting a victim (e.g., mugging, purse snatching, extortion, armed robbery)
7. Has forced someone into sexual activity

Destruction of property

8. Has deliberately engaged in fire setting with the intention of causing serious damage
9. Has deliberately destroyed others' property (other than by fire setting)

Deceitfulness or theft

10. Has broken into someone else's house, building, or car
11. Often lies to obtain goods or favors or to avoid obligations (i.e., "cons" others)
12. Has stolen items of nontrivial value without confronting a victim (e.g., shoplifting, but without breaking and entering; forgery)

Serious violations of rules

13. Often stays out at night despite parental prohibitions, beginning before age 13 years
14. Has run away from home overnight at least twice while living in parental or parental surrogate home (or once without returning for a lengthy period)
15. Is often truant from school, beginning before age 13 years

B. The disturbance in behavior causes clinically significant impairment in social, academic, or occupational functioning.

C. If the individual is age 18 years or older, criteria are not met for antisocial personality disorder.

Specify type based on age at onset:

Childhood-onset type: Onset of at least one criterion characteristic of conduct disorder prior to age 10 years

Adolescent-onset type: Absence of any criteria characteristic of conduct disorder prior to age 10 years

Specify severity:

Mild: Few if any conduct problems in excess of those required to make the diagnosis and conduct problems cause only minor harm to others

Moderate: Number of conduct problems and effect on others intermediate between "mild" and "severe"

Severe: Many conduct problems in excess of those required to make the diagnosis or conduct problems cause considerable harm to others

Source: Reprinted, with permission, from American Psychiatric Association. (2000). *Diagnostic and statistical manual of mental disorders* (4th ed., text revision). Washington, DC: Author, © 2000 American Psychiatric Association.

©Joel Gordon

Many prisons allow visits between inmates and their children, partly to help reduce later problems in those children.

According to the underarousal hypothesis, the abnormally low levels of cortical arousal characteristic of psychopaths are the primary cause of their antisocial and risk-taking behaviors; they seek stimulation to boost their chronically low levels of arousal. This means that Ryan lied, took drugs, and dug up graves to achieve the same level of arousal we might get from talking on the phone with a good friend or watching television. Several researchers have examined childhood and adolescent psychophysiological predictors of adult antisocial behavior and criminality. Raine, Venables, and Williams (1990), for example, assessed a sample of 15-year-olds on a variety of autonomic and central nervous system variables. They found that future criminals had lower skin conductance activity, lower heart rate during rest periods, and more slow-frequency brain wave activity, all indicative of low arousal.

According to the fearlessness hypothesis, psychopaths possess a higher threshold for experiencing fear than most other individuals (Lykken, 1957, 1982). In other words, things that greatly frighten the rest of us have little effect on the psychopath. Remember that Ryan was unafraid of going alone to dangerous neighborhoods to buy drugs. According to proponents of this hypothesis, the fearlessness of the psychopath gives rise to all the other major features of the syndrome.

Theorists have tried to connect what we know about the workings of the brain with clinical observations of people with antisocial personality disorder, especially those with psychopathy. Several theorists have applied Jeffrey Gray's (1987) model of brain functioning to this population (Fowles, 1988; Quay, 1993). According to Gray, three major brain systems influence learning and emotional behavior: the behavioral inhibition system (BIS), the reward system, and the fight/flight system. The BIS is responsible for our ability to stop or slow down when we are faced with impending punishment, nonreward, or novel situations, which leads to anxiety and frustration. The BIS is thought to be located in the septohippocampal system and involves the noradrenergic and serotonergic neurotransmitter systems. The reward system is responsible for our approach behavior—in particular, our approach to positive rewards—and is associated with hope and relief. This system probably involves the dopaminergic system in the mesolimbic area of the brain, which we previously noted as the "pleasure pathway" for its role in substance use and abuse (see Chapter 11).

If you think about the behavior of psychopaths, the possible malfunctioning of these systems is clear. An imbalance between the BIS and the reward system may make the fear and anxiety produced by the BIS less apparent and the positive feelings associated with the reward system more prominent (Levenston, Patrick, Bradley, & Lang, 2000; Quay, 1993). Theorists have proposed that this type of neurobiological dysfunction may explain why psychopaths aren't anxious about committing the antisocial acts that characterize their disorder.

Researchers continue to explore how differences in neurotransmitter function (for example, serotonin) and neurohormone function (for example, androgens such as testosterone and the stress neurohormone cortisol) in the brains of these individuals can explain the callousness, superficial charm, lack of remorse, and impulsivity that characterize people with psychopathy. Integrative theories that link these differences to both genetic and environmental influences are just now beginning to be outlined (van Goozen et al., 2007) and may lead to better understanding and treatments for this debilitating disorder.

■ Psychological and Social Dimensions

What goes on in the mind of a psychopath? In one of several studies of how psychopaths process reward and punishment, Newman, Patterson, and Kosson (1987) set up a card-playing task on a computer; they provided five-cent rewards and fines for correct and incorrect answers to psychopathic and nonpsychopathic criminal offenders. The game was constructed so that at first players were rewarded about 90% of the time and fined only about 10% of the time. Gradually, the odds changed until the probability of getting a reward was 0%. Despite feedback that reward was no longer forthcoming, the psychopaths continued to play and lose. As a result of this and other studies, the researchers hypothesized that once psychopaths set their sights on a reward goal, they are less likely than nonpsychopaths to be deterred despite signs the goal is no longer achievable (Hiatt & Newman, 2006). Again, considering the reckless and daring behavior of some psychopaths (robbing banks without a mask and getting caught immediately), failure to abandon an unattainable goal fits the overall picture.

Interesting research suggests that this pattern of persisting in the face of failure may not be true for psychopaths from different racial groups. In replicating the type of research just described across samples of Caucasian and African American offenders, Newman and Schmitt (1998) found that the African American offenders did not make the same types of errors as their Caucasian counterparts. One explanation for this difference may be that because African American males are incarcerated at a higher rate than people from other groups, the population in prison may have a lower rate of psychopathy and therefore may be less likely to commit such errors (Newman & Schmitt, 1998).

Remember our discussion in Chapter 4 of Gerald Patterson's studies of aggressive children, who may develop antisocial personality disorder or psychopathy (Robins, 1978)? Patterson's influential work suggests that aggression in such children may escalate, partly as a result of their interactions with their parents (Granic & Patterson, 2006; Patterson, 1982). He found that the parents often give in to the problem behaviors displayed by their children. For example, parents ask their son to make his bed and he refuses. One parent yells at the boy. He yells back and becomes abusive. At some point, his interchange becomes so aversive that the parent stops fighting and walks away, thereby ending the fight but also letting the son not make his bed. Giving in to these problems results in short-term gains for both the parent (calm is restored in the house) and the child (he gets what he wants), but it results in continuing problems. The child has learned to continue fighting and not give up, and the parent learns that the only way to "win" is to withdraw all demands. This "coercive family process" combines with other factors, such as parental depression, poor monitoring of their child's activities, and less parental involvement, to help maintain the aggressive behaviors (Chronis et al., 2007; Patterson, DeBaryshe, & Ramsey, 1989).

Although little is known about which environmental factors play a direct role in causing antisocial personality disorder and psychopathy (as opposed to childhood conduct disorders), evidence from adoption studies strongly suggests that shared environmental factors—that tend to make family members similar—are important to the etiology of criminality and perhaps antisocial personality disorder. For example, in the adoption study by Sigvardsson, Cloninger, Bohman, and von-Knorring (1982), low social status of the adoptive parents increased the risk of nonviolent criminality among females. Like children with conduct disorders, individuals with antisocial personality disorder come from homes with inconsistent parental discipline (see, for example, Robins, 1966). It is not known for certain, however, whether inconsistent discipline directly causes antisocial personality disorder; it is conceivable, for example, that parents have a genetic vulnerability to antisocial personality disorder that they pass on to their children but that also causes them to be inadequate parents.

A final factor that has been implicated in antisocial personality disorder is the role of stress. One study found that trauma associated with combat may increase the likelihood of antisocial behavior. Barrett, Resnick, and colleagues (1996) studied more than 2,000 army veterans of the Vietnam War. Even after adjusting for histories of childhood problems, the researchers found that those who had been exposed to the most traumatic events were most likely to engage in violence, illegal activities, lying, and using aliases.

■ Developmental Influences

The forms that antisocial behaviors take change as children move into adulthood, from truancy and stealing from friends to extortion, assaults, armed robbery, or other crimes. Fortunately, clinical lore, as well as scattered empirical reports (Robins, 1966), suggest that rates of antisocial behavior begin to decline rather markedly around the age of 40. Hare and colleagues (1988) provided empirical support for this phenomenon. They examined the conviction rates of male psychopaths and male nonpsychopaths who had been incarcerated for a variety of crimes. The researchers found that between the ages of 16 and 45 the conviction rates of nonpsychopaths remained relatively constant. In contrast, the conviction rates of psychopaths remained relatively constant up until about 40, at which time they decreased markedly (see ■ Figure 12.3). Why antisocial behavior often declines around middle age remains unanswered.

■ An Integrative Model

How can we put all this information together to get a better understanding of people with antisocial personality disorder? Remember that the research just discussed sometimes involved people labeled as having antisocial personality disorder but at other times included people labeled as psychopathic or even criminals. Whatever the label, it appears these people have a genetic vulnerability to antisocial behaviors and personality traits. As you have seen, genetics may lead to differences in neurotransmitter and neurohormone function that influences aggressiveness (serotonin and testosterone) and neurohormone function

Children with conduct disorder may become adults with antisocial personality disorder.

that affect the way people deal with stress (cortisol) in the brains of these individuals may lead to personality traits such as callousness, impulsivity, and aggressiveness that characterize people with psychopathy (van Goozen et al., 2007).

These biological influences further interact with environmental experiences such as early childhood adversity. In a family that may already be under stress because of divorce or substance abuse (Hetherington, Stanley-Hagan, & Anderson, 1989; Patterson et al., 1989), there may be an interaction style that encourages antisocial behavior on the part of the child (Wootton, Frick, Shelton, & Silverthorn, 1997). The child's antisocial and impulsive behavior—partly caused by the child's difficult temperament and impulsivity (Chronis et al., 2007; Kochanska, Aksan, & Joy, 2007)—alienates other children who might be good role models and attracts others who encourage antisocial behavior (Vuchinich, Bank, & Patterson, 1992). These behaviors may also result in the child dropping out of school and a poor occupational history in adulthood, which help create increasingly frustrating life circumstances that further incite acts against society (Caspi, Elder, & Bem, 1987).

This is, admittedly, an abbreviated version of a complex scenario. The important element is that in this integrative model of antisocial behavior, biological, psychological, and cultural factors combine in intricate ways to create someone like Ryan.

■ Treatment

One of the major problems with treating people in this group is typical of numerous personality disorders: They rarely identify themselves as needing treatment. Because of this, and because they can be manipulative even with their therapists, most clinicians are pessimistic about the outcome of treatment for adults who have antisocial personality disorder, and there are few documented success stories (Meloy, 2001). An interesting test of "therapeutic communities"—essentially intensive group therapy (usually in a prison setting) for up to 80 hours per week—provides some revealing results. This study followed up groups of psychopathic and nonpsychopathic offenders more than 10 years after treatment using this approach and found that although the nonpsychopathic offenders were less likely to reoffend, the psychopathic inmates were more likely to reoffend violently (Rice, Harris, & Cormier, 1992). One theory is that both groups improved their interpersonal skills through the program but that the psychopathic offend-

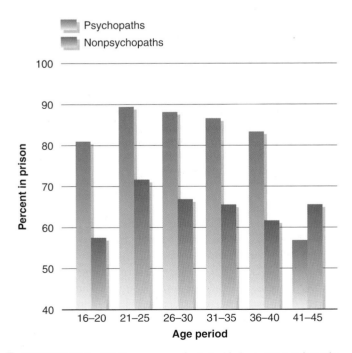

■ **FIGURE 12.3** Lifetime course of criminal behavior in psychopaths and nonpsychopaths. (Based on Hare, R. D., McPherson, L. M., & Forth, A. E., 1988. Male psychopaths and their criminal careers. *Journal of Consulting and Clinical Psychology, 56,* 710–714.)

ers used these new skills to better manipulate and exploit others when they were released (Harris & Rice, 2006). In general, therapists agree with incarcerating these people to deter future antisocial acts. Clinicians encourage identification of high-risk children so that treatment can be attempted before they become adults (Patterson, 1982).

The most common treatment strategy for children involves parent training (Patterson, 1986; Sanders, 1992). Parents are taught to recognize behavior problems early and how to use praise and privileges to reduce problem behavior and encourage prosocial behaviors. Treatment studies typically show that these types of programs can significantly improve the behaviors of many children who display antisocial behaviors (Harris & Rice, 2006). A number of factors, however, put families at risk either for not succeeding in treatment or for dropping out early; these include cases with a high degree of family dysfunction, socioeconomic disadvantage, high family stress, a parent's history of antisocial behavior, and severe conduct disorder on the part of the child (Dumas & Wahler, 1983; Kazdin, Mazurick, & Bass, 1993).

■ Prevention

We have seen a dramatic increase in the amount of research on prevention strategies focused on children at risk for later antisocial personality disorder. The aggressive behavior of young children is remarkably stable, meaning that children who hit, insult, and threaten others are likely to continue as they grow older. Unfortunately, these behaviors become more serious over time and are the early signs of the homicides and assaults seen among some adults (Eron & Huesmann, 1990; Singer & Flannery, 2000).

Approaches to change this aggressive course are being implemented mainly in school and preschool settings and emphasize behavioral supports for good behavior and skills training to improve social competence (Flannery et al., 2003). A number of types of these programs are under evaluation, and the results look promising. For example, research using parent training for young children (toddlers from 1½ to 2½ years) suggests that early intervention may be particularly helpful (Shaw, Dishion, Supplee, Gardner, & Arnds, 2006). Aggression can be reduced and social competence (for example, making friends and sharing) can be improved among young children, and these results generally maintain over a few years (Flannery et al., 2003). It is too soon to assess the success of such programs in preventing adult antisocial behaviors typically observed among people with this personality disorder. However, given the ineffectiveness of treatment for adults, prevention may be the best approach to this problem.

Borderline Personality Disorder

People with **borderline personality disorder** lead tumultuous lives. Their moods and relationships are unstable, and usually they have a poor self-image. These people often feel empty and are at great risk of dying by their own hands. Consider the case of Claire.

CLAIRE: A Stranger Among Us

I have known Claire for more than 30 years and have watched her through the good but mostly bad times of her often shaky and erratic life as a person with borderline personality disorder. Claire and I went to school together from the eighth grade through high school, and we've kept in touch periodically. My earliest memory of her is of her hair, which was cut short rather unevenly. She told me that when things were not going well she cut her own hair severely, which helped to "fill the void." I later found out that the long sleeves she usually wore hid scars and cuts that she had made herself.

Claire was the first of our friends to smoke. What was unusual about this and her later drug use was not that they occurred (this was in the 1960s when "If it feels good, do it" hadn't been replaced by "Just say no") or that they began early; it was that she didn't seem to use them to get attention, like everyone else. Claire was also one of the first whose parents divorced, and both of them seemed to abandon her emotionally. She later told me that her father was an alcoholic who had regularly beaten her and her mother. She did poorly in school and had a low opinion of herself. She often said she was stupid and ugly, yet she was neither.

Throughout our school years, Claire left town periodically, without any explanation. I learned many years later that she was in psychiatric facilities to get help with her suicidal depression. She often threatened to kill herself, although we didn't guess that she was serious.

In our later teens, we all drifted away from Claire. She had become increasingly unpredictable, sometimes berating us for a perceived slight ("You're walking too fast. You don't want to be seen with me!"), and at other times desperate to be around us. We were confused by her behavior. With some people, emotional outbursts can bring you closer together. Unfortunately for Claire, these incidents and her overall demeanor made us feel that we didn't know her. As we all grew older, the "void" she described in herself became overwhelming and eventually shut us all out.

Claire married twice, and both times had passionate but stormy relationships interrupted by hospitalizations. She tried to stab her first husband during a particularly violent rage. She tried a number of drugs but mainly used alcohol to "deaden the pain."

Now, in her mid-50s, things have calmed down some, although she says she is rarely happy. Claire does feel a little better about herself and is doing well as a travel agent. Although she is seeing someone, she is reluctant to become involved because of her personal history. Claire was ultimately diagnosed with major depression and borderline personality disorder.

■ Clinical Description

Borderline personality disorder is one of the most common personality disorders observed in clinical settings; it is observed in every culture and is seen in about 1% to 2% of the general population (Lenzenweger et al., in press; Torgersen, Kringlen, & Cramer, 2001). Claire's life illustrates the instability characteristic of people with borderline personality disorder. They tend to have turbulent relationships, fearing abandonment but lacking control over their emotions (Phillips et al., 2003). They often engage in behaviors that are suicidal, self-mutilative, or both, cutting, burning, or punching themselves. Claire sometimes used her cigarette to burn her palm or forearm, and she carved her initials in her arm. A significant proportion—about 6%—succeed at suicide (Stone, 1989; Widiger & Trull, 1993). On the positive side, the long-term outcomes for people with borderline personality disorder is encouraging, with up to 88% achieving remission more than 10 years after initial treatment (Zanarini et al., 2006).

People with this personality disorder are often intense, going from anger to deep depression in a short time. Dysfunction in the area of emotion is sometimes considered one of the core features of borderline personality disorder (Gunderson, 2001; Linehan, 1993) and is one of the best predictors of suicide in this group (Yen et al., 2004).

These individuals also are characterized by impulsivity, which can be seen in their drug abuse and self-mutilation. Although not so obvious as to why, the self-injurious behaviors such as cutting sometimes are described as tension reducing by people who engage in these behaviors (Bohus et al., 2000). Claire's empty feeling is also common; these people are sometimes described as chronically bored and have difficulties with their own identities (Wilkinson-Ryan & Westen, 2000). The mood disorders we discussed in Chapter 7 are common among people with borderline personality disorder, with 24% to 74% having major depression and 4% to 20% having bipolar disorder (Widiger & Rogers, 1989). Eating disorders are also common, particularly bulimia (see Chapter 8): Almost 25% of bulimics also have borderline personality disorder (Levin & Hyler, 1986). Up to 67% of the people with this disorder are also diagnosed with at least one substance use disor-

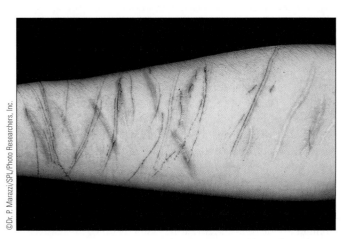

Borderline personality disorder is often accompanied by self-mutilation.

©Dr. P. Marazzi/SPL/Photo Researchers, Inc.

DSM-IV-TR

DSM TABLE 12.7 Diagnostic Criteria for Borderline Personality Disorder

A pervasive pattern of instability of interpersonal relationships, self-image, and affects, and marked impulsivity beginning by early adulthood and present in a variety of contexts, as indicated by five (or more) of the following:

1. Frantic efforts to avoid real or imagined abandonment; *note:* do not include suicidal or self-mutilating behavior covered in criterion 5
2. A pattern of unstable and intense interpersonal relationships characterized by alternating between extremes of idealization and devaluation
3. Identity disturbance: Markedly and persistently unstable self-image or sense of self
4. Impulsivity in at least two areas that are potentially self-damaging (e.g., spending, sex, substance abuse, reckless driving, binge eating); *note:* do not include suicidal or self-mutilating behavior covered in criterion 5
5. Recurrent suicidal behavior, gestures, or threats, or self-mutilating behavior
6. Affective instability due to a marked reactivity of mood (e.g., intense episodic dysphoria, irritability, or anxiety usually lasting a few hours and only rarely more than a few days)
7. Chronic feelings of emptiness
8. Inappropriate, intense anger or difficulty controlling anger (e.g., frequent displays of temper, constant anger, recurrent physical fights)
9. Transient, stress-related paranoid ideation or severe dissociative symptoms

Source: Reprinted, with permission, from American Psychiatric Association. (2000). *Diagnostic and statistical manual of mental disorders* (4th ed., text revision). Washington, DC: Author, © 2000 American Psychiatric Association.

der (Dulit et al., 1993; Skodol, Oldham, & Gallaher, 1999). As with antisocial personality disorder, people with borderline personality disorder tend to improve during their 30s and 40s, although they may continue to have difficulties into old age (Rosowsky & Gurian, 1992).

■ Causes

The results from almost 20 family studies suggest that borderline personality disorder is more prevalent in families with the disorder and somehow linked with mood disorders (see, for example, Baron, Gruen, Asnis, & Lord, 1985; Links, Steiner, & Huxley, 1988; Zanarini, Gunderson, Marino, Schwartz, & Frankenburg, 1988). A study of monozygotic and dizygotic twins indicated a higher concordance rate among monozygotic twins, further supporting the role of genetics in the expression of borderline personality disorder (Torgersen et al., 2000).

The emotional reactivity that is a central aspect of borderline personality disorder has led researchers to look at this aspect of their personality for clues about inherited influences (endophenotypes). Important genetic studies are investigating genes associated with the neurochemical serotonin because dysfunction in this system has been linked to the emotional instability, suicidal behaviors, and impulsivity seen in people with this disorder (Ni et al., 2006). One study found that a mutation of a serotonin transporter gene (the protein in brain cells that recycles the chemical messenger after it has been secreted into the synapse) was present among people with this disorder when compared to healthy control subjects (Ni et al., 2006). Importantly, serotonin dysfunction is also implicated in the mood disorders (see Chapter 7) and may help explain the overlap between borderline personality disorder and depression.

Neuroimaging studies, designed to locate areas in the brain contributing to the disorder, point to the frontolimbic network (Schmahl & Bremner, 2006). Significantly, this area in the brain is involved in emotion regulation and dysfunctional serotonin neurotransmission, linking these findings with genetic research.

To further "zero in" on the nature of this disorder, it is necessary to refine the concept of emotional reactivity in borderline personality disorder. When asked about their experiences, people with this disorder will report greater emotional fluctuations and greater emotional intensity, primarily in negative emotions such as anger and anxiety (Rosenthal et al., in press). Some research—using "morphing" technology—is looking at how sensitive these individuals are to the emotions of others. One study tested how people with and without borderline personality disorder could correctly identify the emotion of a face that was morphing on screen (changing slowly from a neutral expression to an emotional expression such as anger) (Lynch et al., 2006) and found those with borderline personality disorder were more accurate than controls.

In one study, the emotion "shame" was explored in people with this disorder (Rusch et al., 2007). For example, people were given the following scenario:

> You attend your coworker's housewarming party and you spill red wine on a new cream-colored carpet, but you think no one notices.

Participants are then asked to say which of the following four reactions they would have:

- "You would wish you were anywhere but at the party" (indicating shame proneness)
- "You would stay late to help clean up the stain after the party" (guilt proneness)
- "You think your coworker should have expected some accidents at such a big party" (detachment)
- "You would wonder why your coworker chose to serve red wine with the new light carpet" (externalization)

This study found that women with borderline personality disorder (no men were included in this study) were more likely to report shame than healthy women and women with social phobia. Importantly, the researchers also found that this elevated tendency to experience shame was associated with low self-esteem, low quality of life, and high levels of anger and hostility (Rusch et al., 2007).

Cognitive factors in borderline personality disorder are just beginning to be explored. Here, the questions are, just how do people with this disorder process information, and does this contribute to their difficulties? One study that takes a look at the thought processes of these individuals asked people with and without borderline personality disorder to look at words projected on a computer screen and try to remember some of the

words and try to forget others (Korfine & Hooley, 2000). When the words were not related to the symptoms of borderline personality disorder—for example, "celebrate," "charming," and "collect"—both groups performed equally well. However, when they were presented with words that might be relevant to the disorder—for example, "abandon," "suicidal," and "emptiness"—individuals with borderline personality disorder remembered more of these words despite being instructed to forget them. This preliminary evidence for a memory bias may hold clues to the nature of this disorder and may someday be helpful in designing more effective treatment.

An important environmental risk factor in a gene–environment interaction explanation for borderline personality disorder is the possible contribution of early trauma, especially sexual and physical abuse. Numerous studies show that people with this disorder are more likely to report abuse than are healthy individuals or those with other psychiatric conditions (see, for example, Bandelow et al., 2005; Goldman, D'Angelo, DeMaso, & Mezzacappa, 1992; Ogata et al., 1990). Although we do not know whether abuse and neglect cause later borderline personality disorder (these studies are all based on recollection and a correlation between the two phenomena), they may be predisposing factors in at least some cases. If childhood abuse or neglect does lead to most cases of borderline personality disorder, the connection may well explain why women are affected more often than men. Girls are two or three times more likely to be sexually abused than boys (Herman, Perry, & van der Kolk, 1989).

The extremely high rates of reported abuse among people diagnosed with borderline personality disorder begs the question, does everyone with this disorder have a history of abuse? Although not everyone with this diagnosis recalls some form of early trauma, this could be the result of their being unwilling to report it or because they lack a memory of the events (as with *implicit memory,* which we discussed in Chapter 2). This is an extremely controversial topic in the area of personality disorders.

On the one hand, if we assume that every person who displays the characteristics associated with borderline personality has been the subject of abuse, then it clearly removes any fault or blame for the actions of these people—actions that can be excessively disruptive and can seriously interfere with therapeutic efforts. Treatment for all individuals with borderline personality disorder can then progress as though trauma has occurred. Yet, should we assume that people who do not remember abuse have faulty memories (Graybar & Boutilier, 2002)? You could make a counterargument that some individuals are inaccurately recalling early abuse because of the inherent problems associated with retrospective reporting of information.

It is clear that a majority of people who receive the diagnosis of borderline personality disorder have suffered terrible abuse or neglect from both parents, sexual abuse, physical abuse by others, or a combination of these. For those who have not reported such histories, some workers are now examining just how they could develop borderline personality disorder. For example, factors such as temperament (emotional nature, such as being impulsive, irritable, or hypersensitive) or neurological impairments (being exposed prenatally to alcohol or drugs) and how they interact with parental styles may account for some cases of borderline personality disorder (Graybar & Boutilier, 2002). A scientific perspective to these types of issues focuses on attempting to remain objective—it is possible that some individuals with borderline personality disorder do not have histories of abuse—in the face of social and political pressures to adopt a particular view.

Building on the possible link to abuse, Gunderson and Sabo (1993) argued that borderline personality disorder is similar to posttraumatic stress disorder (PTSD); they see many resemblances in the two behavior patterns. Herman and colleagues (1989) have drawn similar parallels; for example, difficulties in the regulation of mood, impulse control, and interpersonal relationships. This discussion about borderline personality disorder and PTSD can be viewed from a political perspective. Some writers argue that what the mental health profession calls borderline personality disorder is simply a case of PTSD among women and that a diagnosis of PTSD puts the emphasis on the victimization of women rather than on their mental illness. This distinction in assigning a diagnosis is an important one and represents a debate that will continue for some time (Becker, 2000). These observations all seem to support the hypothesis that borderline personality disorder may be caused by early trauma. It is important to remember, however, that not all cases of borderline personality disorder resemble PTSD (Zanarini et al., 1998).

Borderline personality disorder has been observed among people who have gone through rapid cultural changes. The problems of identity, emptiness, fears of abandonment, and low anxiety threshold have been found in child and adult immigrants (Laxenaire, Ganne-Vevonec, & Streiff, 1982; Skhiri, Annabi, Bi, & Allani, 1982). These observations further support the possibility that early trauma may, in some individuals, lead to borderline personality disorder.

Remember, however, that a history of childhood trauma, including sexual and physical abuse, occurs in a number of other disorders such as somatoform disorder (see Chapter 6), panic disorder (see Chapter 5), and dissociative identity disorder (see Chapter 6). In addition, a portion of individuals with borderline personality disorder have no apparent history of such abuse (Gunderson & Sabo, 1993). Although childhood sexual and physical abuse seems to play some role in the etiology of borderline personality disorder, neither appears to be necessary or sufficient to produce the syndrome.

■ An Integrative Model

Although there is no currently accepted integrative model for this disorder, it is tempting to borrow from the work on anxiety disorders to outline a possible view. If you recall from Chapter 5, we describe the "triple vulnerability" theory (Barlow, 2000, 2002; Suàrez et al., in press). The first vulnerability (or diathesis) is a generalized biological vulnerability. We can see the genetic vulnerability to emotional reactivity in people with borderline personality disorder and how this affects specific brain function. The second vulnerability is a generalized psychological vulnerability. In the case of people with this personality disorder, they tend to view the world as threatening and to react strongly to real and perceived threats. The third vulnerability is a specific psychological vulnerability in which people learn from early environmental experiences, and this is where early trauma, abuse, or both may

advance this sensitivity to threats. When stressed, a person's biological tendency to be overly reactive interacts with the psychological tendency to feel threatened. This may result in the outbursts and suicidal behaviors commonly observed in this group. This preliminary model awaits validation and further research.

■ Treatment

In stark contrast to individuals with antisocial personality disorder who rarely acknowledge requiring help, those with borderline personality disorder appear quite distressed and are more likely to seek treatment even than people with anxiety and mood disorders (Ansell, Sanislow, McGlashan, & Grilo, in press). Many people appear to respond positively to a variety of medications, including serotonin-specific reuptake inhibitors and related antidepressant medications and lithium (Svrakic & Cloninger, 2005). However, efforts to provide successful treatment are complicated by problems with drug abuse, compliance with treatment, and suicide attempts. As a result, many clinicians are reluctant to work with people who have borderline personality disorder.

One of the most thoroughly researched psychosocial treatments was developed by Linehan (1987, 1993). This approach—which she calls *dialectical behavior therapy (DBT)*—involves helping people cope with the stressors that seem to trigger suicidal behaviors. Priority in treatment is first given to those behaviors that may result in harm (suicidal behaviors), then those behaviors that interfere with therapy, and, finally, those that interfere with the patient's quality of life. Weekly individual sessions provide support, and patients are taught how to identify and regulate their emotions. Problem solving is emphasized so that they can handle difficulties more effectively. In addition, they receive treatment similar to that used for people with PTSD, in which prior traumatic events are reexperienced to help extinguish the fear associated with them (see Chapter 5). In the final stage of therapy, clients learn to trust their own responses rather than depend on the validation of others, sometimes by visualizing themselves not reacting to criticism.

Results from a number of studies suggest that DBT may help reduce suicide attempts, dropouts from treatment, and hospitalizations (Linehan, Armstrong, Suarez, Allmon, & Heard, 1991; Linehan, Heard, & Armstrong, 1992). A follow-up of 39 women who received either dialectic behavior therapy or general therapeutic support (called "treatment as usual") for 1 year showed that, during the first 6 months of follow-up, the women in the DBT group were less suicidal, less angry, and better adjusted socially (Linehan & Kehrer, 1993). Another study examined how treating these individuals with DBT in an inpatient setting—psychiatric hospital—for approximately 3 months before discharge to home would improve their outcomes (Bohus et al., 2000). The participants improved in a number of areas, such as with a reduction in self-injury (for example, cutting themselves), depression, and anxiety. A growing body of evidence is now available to document the effectiveness of this approach to aid many individuals with this debilitating disorder (Stanley & Brodsky, 2005).

Probably some of the most intriguing research we describe in this book involves using the techniques in brain imaging to see how our psychological treatment influences brain function. One pilot study examined emotional reactions to upsetting photos (for example, pictures of women being attacked) in controls and in women with borderline personality disorder (Schnell & Herpertz, 2007). This study found that among the women who benefited from treatment, arousal (in the amygdala and hippocampus) to the upsetting photos moderated over time as a function of treatment. No changes occurred in controls or in women who did not have positive treatment experiences. This type of integrative research holds enormous promise for our understanding of borderline personality disorder and the mechanisms underlying successful treatment.

Histrionic Personality Disorder

Individuals with **histrionic personality disorder** tend to be overly dramatic and often seem almost to be acting, which is why the term *histrionic,* which means theatrical in manner, is used. Consider the case of Pat.

PAT: Always Onstage

When we first met, Pat seemed to radiate enjoyment of life. She was single, in her mid-30s, and was going to night school for her master's degree. She often dressed flamboyantly. During the day she taught children with disabilities, and when she didn't have class she was often out late on a date. When I first spoke with her, she enthusiastically told me how impressed she was with my work in the field of developmental disabilities and that she had been extremely successful in using some of my techniques with her students. She was clearly overdoing the praise, but who wouldn't appreciate such flattering comments?

Because some of our research included children in her classroom, I saw Pat often. Over a period of weeks, however, our interactions grew strained. She often complained of various illnesses and injuries (falling in the parking lot, twisting her neck looking out a window) that interfered with her work. She was disorganized, often leaving to the last minute tasks that required considerable planning. Pat made promises to other people that were impossible to keep but seemed to be aimed at winning their approval; when she broke the promise, she usually made up a story designed to elicit sympathy and compassion. For example, she promised the mother of one of her students that she would put on a "massive and unique" birthday party for her daughter but forgot about it until the mother showed up with cake and juice. Upon seeing her, Pat flew into a rage and blamed the principal for keeping her late after school, although there was no truth to this accusation.

Pat often interrupted meetings about research to talk about her latest boyfriend. The boyfriends changed almost weekly, but her enthusiasm ("Like no other man I have ever met!") and optimism about the future ("He's the guy I want to spend the rest of my life with!") remained high for each

of them. Wedding plans were seriously discussed with almost every one, despite their brief acquaintance. Pat was ingratiating, especially to the male teachers, who often helped her out of trouble she got into because of her disorganization.

When it became clear that she would probably lose her teaching job because of her poor performance, Pat managed to manipulate several of the male teachers and the assistant principal into recommending her for a new job in a nearby school district. A year later, she was still at the new school but had been moved twice to different classrooms. According to teachers she worked with, Pat still lacked close interpersonal relationships, although she described her current relationship as "deeply involved." After a rather long period of depression, Pat sought help from a psychologist, who diagnosed her as also having histrionic personality disorder.

■ Clinical Description

People with histrionic personality disorder are inclined to express their emotions in an exaggerated fashion, for example, hugging someone they have just met or crying uncontrollably during a sad movie (Svrakic & Cloninger, 2005). They also tend to be vain, self-centered, and uncomfortable when they are not in the limelight. They are often seductive in appearance and behavior, and they are typically concerned about their looks. (Pat, for example, spent a great deal of money on unusual jewelry and was sure to point it out to anyone who would listen.) In addition, they seek reassurance and approval constantly and may become upset or angry when others do not attend to them or praise them. People with histrionic personality disorder also tend to be impulsive and have great difficulty delaying gratification.

The cognitive style associated with histrionic personality disorder is impressionistic (Beck, Freeman, & Davis, 2007), characterized by a tendency to view situations in global, black-and-white terms. Speech is often vague, lacking in detail, and characterized by exaggeration (Pfohl, 1991). For example, when Pat was

People with histrionic personality disorder tend to be vain, extravagant, and seductive.

©Mark Segal/Index Stock Imagery/Picture Quest

DSM-IV-TR

DSM TABLE 12.8 Diagnostic Criteria for Histrionic Personality Disorder

A pervasive pattern of excessive emotionality and attention seeking, beginning by early adulthood and present in a variety of contexts, as indicated by five (or more) of the following:

1. Is uncomfortable in situations in which he or she is not the center of attention
2. Interaction with others is often characterized by inappropriate sexually seductive or provocative behavior
3. Displays rapidly shifting and shallow expression of emotions
4. Consistently uses physical appearance to draw attention to self
5. Has a style of speech that is excessively impressionistic and lacking in detail
6. Shows self-dramatization, theatricality, and exaggerated expression of emotion
7. Is suggestible, i.e., easily influenced by others or circumstances
8. Considers relationships to be more intimate than they actually are

Source: Reprinted, with permission, from American Psychiatric Association. (2000). *Diagnostic and statistical manual of mental disorders* (4th ed., text revision). Washington, DC: Author, © 2000 American Psychiatric Association.

asked about a date she had had the night before, she might say it was "way cool" but fail to provide more detailed information.

The high rate of this diagnosis among women versus men raises questions about the nature of the disorder and its diagnostic criteria. As we first discussed in the beginning of this chapter, there is some thought that the features of histrionic personality disorder, such as overdramatization, vanity, seductiveness, and overconcern with physical appearance, are characteristic of the Western "stereotypical female" and may lead to an overdiagnosis among women. Sprock (2000) examined this important question and found some evidence for a bias among psychologists and psychiatrists to associate the diagnosis with women rather than men.

■ Causes

Despite its long history, little research has been done on the causes or treatment of histrionic personality disorder. The ancient Greek philosophers believed that many unexplainable problems of women were caused by the uterus (hysteria) migrating within the body (Abse, 1987). As you have seen, however, histrionic personality disorder also occurs among men.

One hypothesis involves a possible relationship with antisocial personality disorder. Evidence suggests that histrionic personality and antisocial personality co-occur more often than chance would account for. Lilienfeld and colleagues (1986), for example, found that roughly two-thirds of people with a histrionic personality also met criteria for antisocial personality disorder. The evidence for this association has led to the suggestion (see, for example, Cloninger, 1978; Lilienfeld, 1992) that histrionic personality and antisocial personality may be sex-typed alternative expressions of the same unidentified underlying condition. Females with the underlying condition may be predisposed to exhibit a predominantly histrionic pattern, whereas males with the underlying condition may be predisposed to exhibit a predominantly antisocial pattern.

■ Treatment

Although a great deal has been written about ways of helping people with this disorder, little research demonstrates success (Dulit et al., 1993; Horowitz, 2001). Some therapists have tried to modify the attention-getting behavior. Kass, Silvers, and Abrams (1972) worked with five women, four of whom had been hospitalized for suicide attempts and all of whom were later diagnosed with histrionic personality disorder. The women were rewarded for appropriate interactions and fined for attention-getting behavior. The therapists noted improvement after an 18-month follow-up, but they did not collect scientific data to confirm their observation.

A large part of therapy for these individuals usually focuses on the problematic interpersonal relationships. They often manipulate others through emotional crises, using charm, sex, seductiveness, or complaining (Beck et al., 2007). People with histrionic personality disorder often need to be shown how the short-term gains derived from this interactional style result in long-term costs, and they need to be taught more appropriate ways of negotiating their wants and needs.

Narcissistic Personality Disorder

We all know people who think highly of themselves—perhaps exaggerating their real abilities. They consider themselves somehow different from others and deserving of special treatment. In **narcissistic personality disorder,** this tendency is taken to its extreme. In Greek mythology, Narcissus was a youth who spurned the love of Echo, so enamored was he of his own beauty. He spent his days admiring his own image reflected in a pool of water. Psychoanalysts, including Freud, used the term *narcissistic* to describe people who show an exaggerated sense of self-importance and are preoccupied with receiving attention (Beck et al., 2007). Consider the case of Willie.

WILLIE: It's All About Me

Willie was an office assistant in a small attorney's office. Now in his early 30s, Willie had an extremely poor job history. He never stayed employed at the same place for more than 2 years, and he spent considerable time working through temporary employment agencies. Your first encounter, however, would make you believe that he was extremely competent and that he ran the office. If you entered the waiting room you were greeted by Willie, even though he wasn't the receptionist. He would be extremely solicitous, asking how he could be of assistance, offer you coffee, and ask you to make yourself comfortable in "his" reception area. Willie liked to talk, and any conversation was quickly redirected in a way that kept him the center of attention.

This type of ingratiating manner was welcomed at first but soon annoyed other staff. This was especially true when he referred to the other workers in the office as his staff, even though he was not responsible for supervising any of them. The conversations with visitors and staff often consumed a great deal of his time and the time of other staff, and this was becoming a problem.

He quickly became controlling in his job—a pattern revealed in his other positions as well—eagerly taking charge of duties assigned to others. Unfortunately, he did not complete these tasks well, and this created a great deal of friction.

When confronted with any of these difficulties, Willie would first blame others. Ultimately, however, it would become clear that Willie's self-centeredness and controlling nature were at the root of many of the office inefficiencies. During a disciplinary meeting with all of the law firm's partners, an unusual step, Willie became explosively abusive and blamed them for being out to get him. He insisted that his performance was exceptional at all of his previous positions—something contradicted by his previous employers—and that they were at fault. After calming down, he revealed a previous drinking problem, a history of depression, and multiple family problems, all of which he believed contributed to any difficulties he experienced.

The firm recommended he be seen at a university clinic as a condition of his continued employment, where he was diagnosed with major depression, as well as narcissistic personality disorder. Ultimately, his behavior—including lateness and incomplete work—resulted in his termination. In a revealing turn of events, Willie reapplied for another position at the same firm 2 years later. A mix-up in records failed to reveal his previous termination, but he lasted only 3 days—showing up late to work on his second and third days. He was convinced he could be successful, yet he could not change his behavior to conform to even the minimal standards needed to be successful at work.

■ Clinical Description

People with narcissistic personality disorder have an unreasonable sense of self-importance and are so preoccupied with themselves that they lack sensitivity and compassion for other people (Miller, Campbell, & Pilkonis, 2007). They aren't comfortable unless someone is admiring them. Their exaggerated feelings and their fantasies of greatness, called *grandiosity,* create a number of negative attributes. They require and expect a great deal of special attention—the best table in the restaurant, the illegal parking space in front of the movie theater. They also tend to use or exploit others for their own interests and show little empathy. When confronted with other successful people, they can be extremely envious and arrogant. And because they often fail to live up to their own expectations, they are often depressed.

■ Causes and Treatment

We start out as infants being self-centered and demanding, which is part of our struggle for survival. However, part of the socialization process involves teaching children empathy and altruism. Some writers, including Kohut (1971, 1977), believe that narcis-

DSM-IV-TR

DSM TABLE 12.9 Diagnostic Criteria for Narcissistic Personality Disorder

A pervasive pattern of grandiosity (in fantasy or behavior), need for admiration and lack of empathy, beginning by early adulthood and present in a variety of contexts, as indicated by five (or more) of the following:

1. Has a grandiose sense of self-importance (e.g., exaggerates achievements and talents, expects to be recognized as superior without commensurate achievements)
2. Is preoccupied with fantasies of unlimited success, power, brilliance, beauty, or ideal love
3. Believes that he or she is "special" and unique and can only be understood by, or should associate with, other special or high-status people (or institutions)
4. Requests excessive admiration
5. Has a sense of entitlement, i.e., unreasonable expectations of especially favorable treatment or automatic compliance with his or her expectations
6. Is interpersonally exploitative, i.e., takes advantage of others to achieve his or her own ends
7. Lacks empathy: Is unwilling to recognize or identify with the feelings and needs of others
8. Is often envious of others or believes that others are envious of him or her
9. Shows arrogant, haughty behaviors or attitudes

Source: Reprinted, with permission, from American Psychiatric Association. (2000). *Diagnostic and statistical manual of mental disorders* (4th ed., text revision). Washington, DC: Author, © 2000 American Psychiatric Association.

sistic personality disorder arises largely from a profound failure of modeling empathy by the parents early in a child's development. As a consequence, the child remains fixated at a self-centered, grandiose stage of development. In addition, the child (and later the adult) becomes involved in an essentially endless and fruitless search for the ideal person who will meet her unfulfilled empathic needs.

In a sociological view, Christopher Lasch (1978) wrote in his popular book *The Culture of Narcissism* that this personality disorder is increasing in prevalence in most Western societies, primarily as a consequence of large-scale social changes, including greater emphasis on short-term hedonism, individualism, competitiveness, and success. According to Lasch, the "me generation" has produced more than its share of individuals with narcissistic personality disorder. Indeed, reports confirm that narcissistic personality disorder is increasing in prevalence (Cooper & Ronningstam, 1992). However, this apparent rise may be a consequence of increased interest in and research on the disorder.

Treatment research is extremely limited in both number of studies and reports of success (Groopman & Cooper, 2001). When therapy is attempted with these individuals, it often focuses on their grandiosity, their hypersensitivity to evaluation, and their lack of empathy toward others (Beck et al., 2007). Cognitive therapy aims at replacing their fantasies with a focus on the day-to-day pleasurable experiences that are truly attainable. Coping strategies such as relaxation training are used to help them face and accept criticism. Helping them focus on the feelings of others is also a goal. Because individuals with this disorder are vulnerable to severe depressive episodes, particularly in middle age, treatment is often initiated for the depression. However, it is impossible to draw any conclusions about the impact of such treatment on the actual narcissistic personality disorder.

CONCEPT CHECK 12.3

Correctly identify the type of personality disorder described here.

1. Matt is 19 and has been in trouble with the law since he was 14. He lies to his parents, vandalizes buildings in the community, and, when caught, shows no remorse. He often fights with others and doesn't care whom he injures. _____

2. Alan is involved in drugs and has casual sexual encounters. He feels empty unless he does dangerous and exciting things. He threatens to commit suicide if his girlfriend suggests getting help or if she talks about leaving him. He alternates between loving her and hating her. He has low self-esteem and has recently experienced high levels of stress. _____

3. The therapist immediately notices that Joan displays extreme emotional behavior a great deal when she speaks, so much so that she seems to be acting. _____ _____

4. Katherine thinks she is the best candidate for any job, thinks her performance is always excellent, and looks for admiration from others. _____

CLUSTER C PERSONALITY DISORDERS

People diagnosed with the next three personality disorders we highlight—avoidant, dependent, and obsessive-compulsive—share common features with people who have anxiety disorders. These anxious or fearful personality disorders are described next.

Avoidant Personality Disorder

As the name suggests, people with **avoidant personality disorder** are extremely sensitive to the opinions of others and therefore avoid most relationships. Their extremely low self-esteem, coupled with a fear of rejection, causes them to be limited in their friendships and dependent on those they feel comfortable with. Consider the case of Jane.

JANE: Not Worth Noticing

Jane was raised by an alcoholic mother who had borderline personality disorder and who abused her verbally and physically. As a child, she made sense of her mother's abusive treat-

ment by believing that she (Jane) must be an intrinsically unworthy person to be treated so badly. As an adult in her late 20s, Jane still expected to be rejected when others found out that she was inherently unworthy and bad.

Jane was highly self-critical and predicted that she would not be accepted. She thought that people would not like her, that they would see she was a loser, and that she would not have anything to say. She became upset if she perceived that someone in even the most fleeting encounter was reacting negatively or neutrally. If a newspaper vendor failed to smile at her, or a sales clerk was slightly curt, Jane automatically thought it must be because she (Jane) was somehow unworthy or unlikable. She then felt quite sad. Even when she was receiving positive feedback from a friend, she discounted it. As a result, Jane had few friends and certainly no close ones.

(Case and excerpt reprinted, with permission, from Beck, A. T., & Freeman, A., 1990. *Cognitive therapy of personality disorders.* New York: Guilford Press, © 1990 Guilford Press.)

■ Clinical Description

Theodore Millon (1981), who initially proposed this diagnosis, notes that it is important to distinguish between individuals who are asocial because they are apathetic, affectively flat, and relatively uninterested in interpersonal relationships (comparable to what DSM-IV-TR terms *schizoid personality disorder*) and individuals who are asocial because they are interpersonally anxious and fearful of rejection. It is the latter who fit the criteria of avoidant personality disorder (Millon & Martinez, 1995). These individuals feel chronically rejected by others and are pessimistic about their future.

DSM-IV-TR

DSM TABLE 12.10 Diagnostic Criteria for Avoidant Personality Disorder

A pervasive pattern of social inhibition, feelings of inadequacy, and hypersensitivity to negative evaluation, beginning by early adulthood and present in a variety of contexts, as indicated by four (or more) of the following:

1. Avoids occupational activities that involve significant interpersonal contact, because of fears of criticism, disapproval, or rejection
2. Is unwilling to get involved with people unless certain of being liked
3. Shows restraint within intimate relationships because of the fear of being shamed or ridiculed
4. Is preoccupied with being criticized or rejected in social situations
5. Is inhibited in new interpersonal situations because of feelings of inadequacy
6. Views self as socially inept, personally unappealing, or inferior to others
7. Is unusually reluctant to take personal risks or to engage in any new activities because they may prove embarrassing

Source: Reprinted, with permission, from American Psychiatric Association. (2000). *Diagnostic and statistical manual of mental disorders* (4th ed., text revision). Washington, DC: Author, © 2000 American Psychiatric Association.

Causes

Some evidence exists pointing to this personality disorder as related to other sub-schizophrenia-related disorders—occurring more often in relatives of people who have schizophrenia (Fogelson et al., 2007). A number of theories have been proposed that integrate biological and psychosocial influences as the cause of avoidant personality disorder. Millon (1981), for example, suggests that these individuals may be born with a difficult temperament or personality characteristics. As a result, their parents may reject them, or at least not provide them with enough early, uncritical love. This rejection, in turn, may result in low self-esteem and social alienation, conditions that persist into adulthood. Limited support does exist for psychosocial influences in the cause of avoidant personality disorder. For example, Stravynski, Elie, and Franche (1989) questioned a group of people with avoidant personality disorder and a group of control subjects about their early treatment by their parents. Those with the disorder remembered their parents as more rejecting, more guilt engendering, and less affectionate than the control group, suggesting parenting may contribute to the development of this disorder. Similarly, Meyer and Carver (2000) found that these individuals were more likely to report childhood experiences of isolation, rejection, and conflict with others.

Treatment

In contrast to the scarcity of research into most other personality disorders, there are a number of well-controlled studies on approaches to therapy for people with avoidant personality disorder (Beck et al., 2007). Behavioral intervention techniques for anxiety and social skills problems have had some success (Alden, 1989; Alden & Capreol, 1993; Renneberg, Goldstein, Phillips, & Chambless, 1990; Stravynski, Lesage, Marcouiller, & Elie, 1989). Because the problems experienced by people with avoidant personality disorder resemble those of people with social phobia, many of the same treatments are used for both groups (see Chapter 5). Therapeutic alliance—the collaborative connection between therapist and client—appears to be an important predictor for treatment success in this group (Strauss et al., 2006).

Dependent Personality Disorder

We all know what it means to be dependent on another person. People with **dependent personality disorder,** however, rely on others to make ordinary decisions as well as important ones, which results in an unreasonable fear of abandonment. Consider the case of Karen.

KAREN: Whatever You Say

Karen was a 45-year-old married woman who was referred for treatment by her physician for problems with panic attacks. During the evaluation, she appeared to be worried, sensitive, and naive. She was easily overcome with emotion

and cried on and off throughout the session. She was self-critical at every opportunity throughout the evaluation. For example, when asked how she got along with other people, she reported that "others think I'm dumb and inadequate," although she could give no evidence as to what made her think that. She reported that she didn't like school because "I was dumb" and that she always felt that she was not good enough.

Karen described staying in her first marriage for 10 years, even though "it was hell." Her husband had affairs with many other women and was verbally abusive. She tried to leave him many times but gave in to his repeated requests to return. She was finally able to divorce him, and shortly afterward she met and married her current husband, whom she described as kind, sensitive, and supportive. Karen stated that she preferred to have others make important decisions and agreed with other people to avoid conflict. She worried about being left alone without anyone to take care of her and reported feeling lost without other people's reassurance. She also reported that her feelings were easily hurt, so she worked hard not to do anything that might lead to criticism.

(Case and excerpt reprinted, with permission, from Beck, A. T., & Freeman, A., 1990. *Cognitive therapy of personality disorders.* New York: Guilford Press, © 1990 by Guilford Press.)

Clinical Description

Individuals with dependent personality disorder sometimes agree with other people when their own opinion differs so as not to be rejected (Hirschfeld, Shea, & Weise, 1995). Their desire to obtain and maintain supportive and nurturant relationships may lead to their other behavioral characteristics (Bornstein, 1997), including submissiveness, timidity, and passivity. People with this disorder are similar to those with avoidant personality disorder in their feelings of inadequacy, sensitivity to criticism, and need for reassurance. However, people with avoidant personality disorder respond to these feelings by avoiding relationships, whereas those with dependent personality disorder respond by clinging to relationships (Svrakic & Cloninger, 2005).

Causes and Treatment

We are all born dependent on other people for food, physical protection, and nurturance. Part of the socialization process involves helping us live independently (Bornstein, 1992). It is thought that such disruptions as the early death of a parent or neglect or rejection by caregivers may cause people to grow up fearing abandonment (Stone, 1993). This view comes from work in child development on "attachment," or how children learn to bond with their parents and other people who are important in their lives (Bowlby, 1977). If early bonding is interrupted, individuals may be constantly anxious that they will lose people close to them.

The treatment literature for this disorder is mostly descriptive; little research exists to show whether a particular treatment is effective (Svartberg et al., 2004). On the surface, because of their

DSM-IV-TR

DSM TABLE 12.11 Diagnostic Criteria for Dependent Personality Disorder

A pervasive and excessive need to be taken care of that leads to submissive and clinging behavior and fears of separation, beginning by early adulthood and present in a variety of contexts, as indicated by five (or more) of the following:

1. Has difficulty making everyday decisions without an excessive amount of advice and reassurance from others
2. Needs others to assume responsibility for most major areas of his or her life
3. Has difficulty expressing disagreement with others because of fear of loss of support or approval; *note:* do not include realistic fears of retribution
4. Has difficulty initiating projects or doing things on his or her own (because of a lack of self-confidence in judgment or abilities rather than a lack of motivation or energy)
5. Goes to excessive lengths to obtain nurturance and support from others, to the point of volunteering to do things that are unpleasant
6. Feels uncomfortable or helpless when alone because of exaggerated fears of being unable to care for himself or herself
7. Urgently seeks another relationship as a source of care and support when a close relationship ends
8. Is unrealistically preoccupied with fears of being left to take care of himself or herself

Source: Reprinted, with permission, from American Psychiatric Association. (2000). *Diagnostic and statistical manual of mental disorders* (4th ed., text revision). Washington, DC: Author, © 2000 American Psychiatric Association.

attentiveness and eagerness to give responsibility for their problems to the therapist, people with dependent personality disorder can appear to be ideal patients. However, their submissiveness negates one of the major goals of therapy, which is to make the person more independent and personally responsible. Therapy therefore progresses gradually as the patient develops confidence in his ability to make decisions independently (Beck et al., 2007). There is a particular need for care that the patient does not become overly dependent on the therapist.

Obsessive-Compulsive Personality Disorder

People who have **obsessive-compulsive personality disorder** are characterized by a fixation on things being done "the right way." Although many might envy their persistence and dedication, this preoccupation with details prevents them from completing much of anything. Consider the case of Daniel.

DANIEL: Getting It Exactly Right

Each day at exactly 8 A.M., Daniel arrived at his office at the university where he was a graduate student in psychology. On his way, he always stopped at the 7-Eleven for coffee and the *New York Times*. From 8 to 9:15 A.M., he drank his coffee and read the paper. At 9:15 A.M., he reorganized the files that held the hundreds of papers related to his doctoral dissertation, now several years overdue. From 10 A.M. until noon, he read one of these papers, highlighting relevant passages. Then he took the paper bag that held his lunch (always a peanut butter and jelly sandwich and an apple) and went to the cafeteria to purchase a soda and eat by himself. From 1 P.M. until 5 P.M. he held meetings, organized his desk, made lists of things to do, and entered his references into a new database program on his computer. At home, Daniel had dinner with his wife, then worked on his dissertation until after 11 P.M., although much of the time was spent trying out new features of his home computer.

Daniel was no closer to completing his dissertation than he had been 4 years ago. His wife was threatening to leave him because he was equally rigid about everything at home and she didn't want to remain in this limbo of graduate school forever. When Daniel eventually sought help from a therapist for his anxiety over his deteriorating marriage, he was diagnosed as having obsessive-compulsive personality disorder.

■ Clinical Description

Like many with this personality disorder, Daniel is work oriented, spending little time going to movies or parties or doing anything that isn't related to his graduate studies. Because of their general rigidity, these people tend to have poor interpersonal relationships (Svrakic & Cloninger, 2005).

This personality disorder seems to be only distantly related to obsessive-compulsive disorder, one of the anxiety disorders we described in Chapter 5. People like Daniel tend not to have the obsessive thoughts and the compulsive behaviors seen in the like-named obsessive-compulsive disorder. Although people with the anxiety disorder sometimes show characteristics of the personality disorder, they show the characteristics of other personality disorders as well (for example, avoidant, histrionic, or dependent) (Stone, 1993).

An intriguing theory suggests that the psychological profiles of many serial killers point to the role of obsessive-compulsive personality disorder. Ferreira (2000) notes that these individuals do not often fit the definition of someone with a severe mental illness—such as schizophrenia—but are "masters of control" in manipulating their victims. Their need to control all aspects of the crime fits the pattern of people with obsessive-compulsive personality disorder, and some combination of this disorder and unfortunate childhood experiences may lead to this disturbing behavior pattern. Obsessive-compulsive personality disorder may also play a role among some sex offenders—in particular, pedophiles. Brain-imaging research on pedophiles suggests that brain functioning in these individuals is similar to those with obsessive-compulsive personality disorder (Schiffer et al., 2007). At the other end of the behavioral spectrum, it is also common to find obsessive-compulsive personality disorder among gifted children, whose quest for perfectionism can be quite debilitating (Nugent, 2000).

DSM-IV-TR

DSM TABLE 12.12 Diagnostic Criteria for Obsessive-Compulsive Personality Disorder

A pervasive pattern of preoccupation with orderliness, perfectionism, and mental and interpersonal control, at the expense of flexibility, openness, and efficiency, beginning by early adulthood and present in a variety of contexts, as indicated by four (or more) of the following:

1. Is preoccupied with details, rules, lists, order, organization, or schedules to the extent that the major point of the activity is lost
2. Shows perfectionism that interferes with task completion (e.g., is unable to complete a project because his or her own overly strict standards are not met)
3. Is excessively devoted to work and productivity to the exclusion of leisure activities and friendships (not accounted for by obvious economic necessity)
4. Is overconscientious, scrupulous, and inflexible about matters of morality, ethics, or values (not accounted for by cultural or religious identification)
5. Is unable to discard worn-out or worthless objects even when they have no sentimental value
6. Is reluctant to delegate tasks or to work with others unless they submit to exactly his or her way of doing things
7. Adopts a miserly spending style toward both self and others; money is viewed as something to be hoarded for future catastrophes
8. Shows rigidity and stubbornness

Source: Reprinted, with permission, from American Psychiatric Association. (2000). *Diagnostic and statistical manual of mental disorders* (4th ed., text revision). Washington, DC: Author, © 2000 American Psychiatric Association.

People with obsessive-compulsive personality disorder are preoccupied with doing things "the right way."

■ Causes and Treatment

There seems to be a weak genetic contribution to this disorder (McKeon & Murray, 1987; Stone, 1993). Some people may be predisposed to favor structure in their lives, but to reach the level it did in Daniel may require parental reinforcement of conformity and neatness.

Therapy often attacks the fears that seem to underlie the need for orderliness. These individuals are often afraid that what they do will be inadequate, so they procrastinate and excessively ruminate about important issues and minor details alike. Therapists help the individual relax or use distraction techniques to redirect the compulsive thoughts. This form of cognitive behavior therapy—following along the lines of treatment on obsessive-compulsive disorder (see Chapter 5)—appears to be effective for people with this personality disorder (Svartberg et al., 2004).

CONCEPT CHECK 12.4

Match the following scenarios with the correct personality disorder.

1. Lynn is afraid to be alone and seeks constant reassurance from her family and friends. Only 1 month after her first abusive marriage ended, she jumped into another marriage with a man she hardly knew. She thinks that if she shows any resolve or initiative she will be abandoned and will have to take care of herself. Lynn is self-critical and claims she is unintelligent and has no skills. _____ _____

2. The therapist discovers that Tim has yet to fill out the information form, although he was given at least 15 minutes. Tim says he first had to resharpen the pencil, clean it of debris, and then he noticed the pencil sharpener wasn't clean. The paper also wasn't properly placed on the clipboard. _____

3. Jeffery is especially anxious at even the thought of social interaction. He disregards compliments and reacts excessively to criticism, which only feeds his pervasive feelings of inadequacy. Jeffery takes everything personally, assuming that neighbors don't say hello because he is a nuisance to live by. _____

FUTURE DIRECTIONS

DSM-V and the Personality Disorders

We opened the chapter discussing the controversies surrounding the classification of the personality disorders. The great degree of overlap (comorbidity) of the disorders—for example, some people are diagnosed with three or more personality disorders—and the use of categories as opposed to dimensions continue to concern the researchers who study these disorders and the clinicians who care for these individuals (Sheets & Craighead, 2007). For example, the organization that we use in the chapter (the three clusters of A,

B and C) is also used by DSM-IV but is nothing more than a convenient way for clinicians to remember the disorders and is not based on any scientific evidence (Widiger, 2007). Perhaps the most anticipated change in this field is a radical redefinition of the disorders using dimensions, and we expect that the next version of DSM—DSM-V—will introduce this new approach and perhaps make us rethink how we view many of the other disorders we cover in this book (Widiger & Trull, 2007).

SUMMARY

An Overview of Personality Disorders

- The personality disorders represent long-standing and ingrained ways of thinking, feeling, and behaving that can cause significant distress. Because people may display two or more of these maladaptive ways of interacting with the world, considerable disagreement remains over how to categorize the personality disorders.

- DSM-IV-TR includes 10 personality disorders that are divided into three clusters: Cluster A (odd or eccentric) includes paranoid, schizoid, and schizotypal personality disorders; Cluster B (dramatic, emotional, or erratic) includes antisocial, borderline, histrionic, and narcissistic personality disorders; and Cluster C (anxious or fearful) includes avoidant, dependent, and obsessive-compulsive personality disorders.

Cluster A Personality Disorders

- People with paranoid personality disorder are excessively mistrustful and suspicious of other people, without any justification. They tend not to confide in others and expect other people to do them harm.

- People with schizoid personality disorder show a pattern of detachment from social relationships and a limited range of emotions in interpersonal situations. They seem aloof, cold, and indifferent to other people.

- People with schizotypal personality disorder are typically socially isolated and behave in ways that would seem unusual to most of us. In addition, they tend to be suspicious and have odd beliefs about the world.

Cluster B Personality Disorders

- People with antisocial personality disorder have a history of failing to comply with social norms. They perform actions most of us would find unacceptable, such as stealing from friends and family. They also tend to be irresponsible, impulsive, and deceitful.

- In contrast to the DSM-IV-TR criteria for antisocial personality, which focuses almost entirely on observable behaviors (for

example, impulsively and repeatedly changing employment, residence, or sexual partners), the related concept of psychopathy primarily reflects underlying personality traits (for example, self-centeredness or manipulativeness).

- People with borderline personality disorder lack stability in their moods and in their relationships with other people, and they usually have poor self-esteem. These individuals often feel empty and are at great risk of suicide.

- Individuals with histrionic personality disorder tend to be overly dramatic and often appear almost to be acting.

- People with narcissistic personality disorder think highly of themselves—beyond their real abilities. They consider themselves somehow different from others and deserving of special treatment.

Cluster C Personality Disorders

- People with avoidant personality disorder are extremely sensitive to the opinions of others and therefore avoid social relationships. Their extremely low self-esteem, coupled with a fear of rejection, causes them to reject the attention others desire.

- Individuals with dependent personality disorder rely on others to the extent of letting them make everyday decisions, as well as major ones; this results in an unreasonable fear of being abandoned.

- People who have obsessive-compulsive personality disorder are characterized by a fixation on things being done "the right way." This preoccupation with details prevents them from completing much of anything.

- Treating people with personality disorders is often difficult because they usually do not see that their difficulties are a result of the way they relate to others.

- Personality disorders are important for the clinician to consider because they may interfere with efforts to treat more specific problems such as anxiety, depression, or substance abuse. Unfortunately, the presence of one or more personality disorders is associated with a poor treatment outcome and a generally negative prognosis.

Key Terms

personality disorders, 431
paranoid personality disorder, 438
schizoid personality disorder, 439
schizotypal personality disorder, 441

antisocial personality disorder, 443
psychopathy, 444
borderline personality disorder, 450

histrionic personality disorder, 454
narcissistic personality disorder, 455
avoidant personality disorder, 457

dependent personality disorder, 458
obsessive-compulsive personality disorder, 459

Answers to Concept Checks

12.1

1. chronic; 2. Axis II; 3. categories; 4. Cluster A, Cluster B, Cluster C; 5. bias; 6. comorbidity

12.2

1. schizoid; 2. paranoid; 3. schizotypal

12.3

1. antisocial; 2. borderline; 3. histrionic; 4. narcissistic

12.4

1. dependent; 2. obsessive-compulsive; 3. avoidant

The Abnormal Psychology Book Companion Website

See **academic.cengage.com/psychology/barlow** for practice quiz questions, interactive activities, Internet links, critical thinking exercises, discussion forums, and more. Also accessible from the Wadsworth Psychology Resource Center (**academic.cengage.com/login**).

Abnormal Psychology Live CD-ROM

- *George, an Example of Antisocial Personality Disorder:* George describes his long history of violating people's rights.
- *Borderline Personality Disorders:* These women discuss the most troubling symptoms of their disorder.
- *Dialectical Behavior Therapy:* Marsha Linehan discusses the effects of borderline personality disorders with a few clients.

CENGAGENOW™ CengageNOW

Go to **academic.cengage.com/now** to link to CengageNOW, your online study tool. First take the Pre-Test for this chapter to get your personalized study plan, which will identify topics you need to review and direct you to online resources. Then take the Post-Test to determine what concepts you have mastered and what you still need work on.

Video Concept Reviews

CengageNOW also contains Mark Durand's *Video Concept Reviews* on challenging topics.

- Personality Disorders
- Paranoid Personality Disorder
- Schizoid Personality Disorder
- Schizotypal Personality Disorder
- Antisocial Personality Disorder
- Borderline Personality Disorder
- Histrionic Personality Disorder
- Narcissistic Personality Disorder
- Concept Check: Histrionic Versus Narcissistic Personality Disorder
- Avoidant Personality Disorder
- Dependent Personality Disorder
- Obsessive-Compulsive Personality Disorder

Exploring Personality Disorders

- People with personality disorders think and behave in ways that cause distress to themselves and/or the people who care about them.
- There are three main groups, or clusters, of personality disorders, which usually begin in childhood.

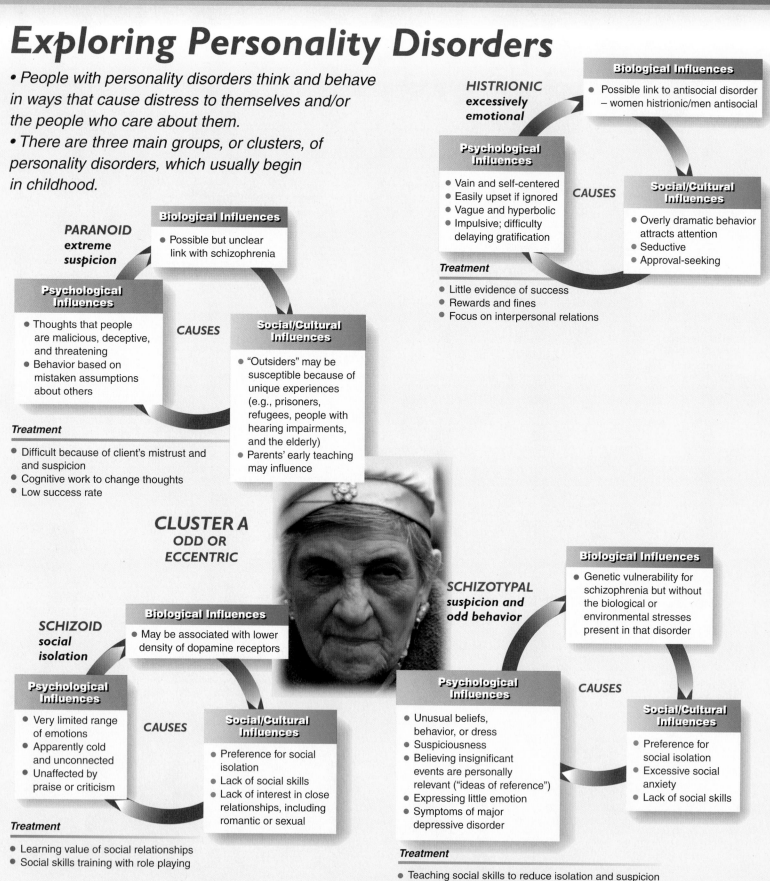

PARANOID
extreme suspicion

Biological Influences
- Possible but unclear link with schizophrenia

Psychological Influences
- Thoughts that people are malicious, deceptive, and threatening
- Behavior based on mistaken assumptions about others

CAUSES

Social/Cultural Influences
- "Outsiders" may be susceptible because of unique experiences (e.g., prisoners, refugees, people with hearing impairments, and the elderly)
- Parents' early teaching may influence

Treatment
- Difficult because of client's mistrust and and suspicion
- Cognitive work to change thoughts
- Low success rate

HISTRIONIC
excessively emotional

Biological Influences
- Possible link to antisocial disorder – women histrionic/men antisocial

Psychological Influences
- Vain and self-centered
- Easily upset if ignored
- Vague and hyperbolic
- Impulsive; difficulty delaying gratification

CAUSES

Social/Cultural Influences
- Overly dramatic behavior attracts attention
- Seductive
- Approval-seeking

Treatment
- Little evidence of success
- Rewards and fines
- Focus on interpersonal relations

CLUSTER A
ODD OR ECCENTRIC

SCHIZOID
social isolation

Biological Influences
- May be associated with lower density of dopamine receptors

Psychological Influences
- Very limited range of emotions
- Apparently cold and unconnected
- Unaffected by praise or criticism

CAUSES

Social/Cultural Influences
- Preference for social isolation
- Lack of social skills
- Lack of interest in close relationships, including romantic or sexual

Treatment
- Learning value of social relationships
- Social skills training with role playing

SCHIZOTYPAL
suspicion and odd behavior

Biological Influences
- Genetic vulnerability for schizophrenia but without the biological or environmental stresses present in that disorder

Psychological Influences
- Unusual beliefs, behavior, or dress
- Suspiciousness
- Believing insignificant events are personally relevant ("ideas of reference")
- Expressing little emotion
- Symptoms of major depressive disorder

CAUSES

Social/Cultural Influences
- Preference for social isolation
- Excessive social anxiety
- Lack of social skills

Treatment
- Teaching social skills to reduce isolation and suspicion
- Medication (haloperidol) to reduce ideas of reference, odd communication, and isolation
- Low success rate

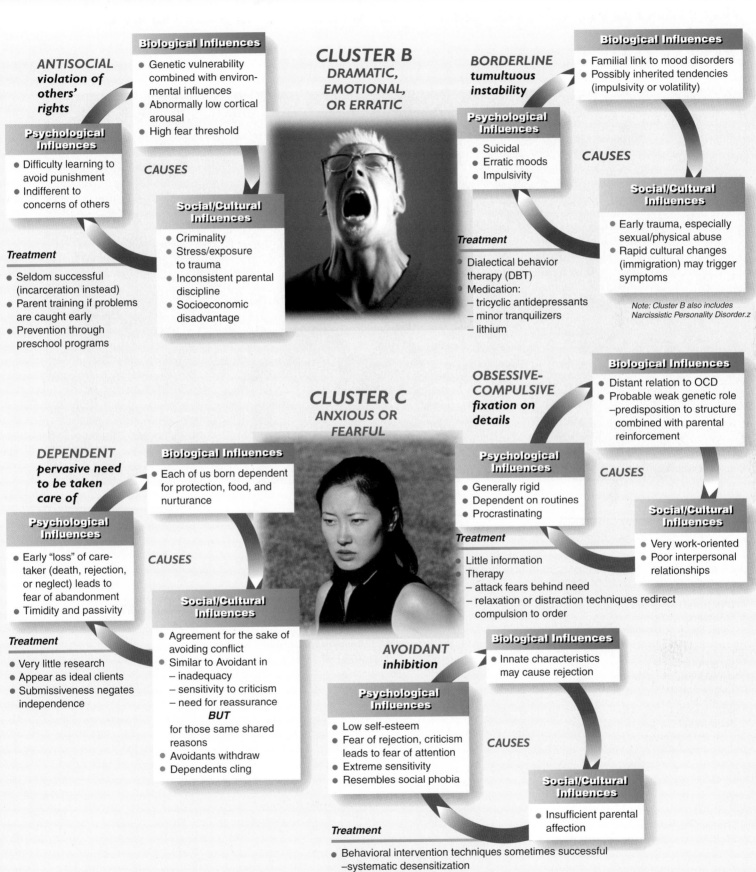

ANTISOCIAL
violation of others' rights

Biological Influences
- Genetic vulnerability combined with environmental influences
- Abnormally low cortical arousal
- High fear threshold

Psychological Influences
- Difficulty learning to avoid punishment
- Indifferent to concerns of others

CAUSES

Social/Cultural Influences
- Criminality
- Stress/exposure to trauma
- Inconsistent parental discipline
- Socioeconomic disadvantage

Treatment
- Seldom successful (incarceration instead)
- Parent training if problems are caught early
- Prevention through preschool programs

CLUSTER B
DRAMATIC, EMOTIONAL, OR ERRATIC

BORDERLINE
tumultuous instability

Biological Influences
- Familial link to mood disorders
- Possibly inherited tendencies (impulsivity or volatility)

Psychological Influences
- Suicidal
- Erratic moods
- Impulsivity

CAUSES

Social/Cultural Influences
- Early trauma, especially sexual/physical abuse
- Rapid cultural changes (immigration) may trigger symptoms

Treatment
- Dialectical behavior therapy (DBT)
- Medication:
  – tricyclic antidepressants
  – minor tranquilizers
  – lithium

Note: Cluster B also includes Narcissistic Personality Disorder.z

CLUSTER C
ANXIOUS OR FEARFUL

DEPENDENT
pervasive need to be taken care of

Biological Influences
- Each of us born dependent for protection, food, and nurturance

Psychological Influences
- Early "loss" of caretaker (death, rejection, or neglect) leads to fear of abandonment
- Timidity and passivity

CAUSES

Treatment
- Very little research
- Appear as ideal clients
- Submissiveness negates independence

Social/Cultural Influences
- Agreement for the sake of avoiding conflict
- Similar to Avoidant in
  – inadequacy
  – sensitivity to criticism
  – need for reassurance
  BUT
  for those same shared reasons
- Avoidants withdraw
- Dependents cling

OBSESSIVE-COMPULSIVE
fixation on details

Biological Influences
- Distant relation to OCD
- Probable weak genetic role –predisposition to structure combined with parental reinforcement

Psychological Influences
- Generally rigid
- Dependent on routines
- Procrastinating

CAUSES

Social/Cultural Influences
- Very work-oriented
- Poor interpersonal relationships

Treatment
- Little information
- Therapy
  – attack fears behind need
  – relaxation or distraction techniques redirect compulsion to order

AVOIDANT
inhibition

Biological Influences
- Innate characteristics may cause rejection

Psychological Influences
- Low self-esteem
- Fear of rejection, criticism leads to fear of attention
- Extreme sensitivity
- Resembles social phobia

CAUSES

Social/Cultural Influences
- Insufficient parental affection

Treatment
- Behavioral intervention techniques sometimes successful
  –systematic desensitization
  –behavioral rehearsal
- Improvements usually modest

Schizophrenia and Other Psychotic Disorders

© Roberty Daly/Getty Images

PERSPECTIVES ON SCHIZOPHRENIA
    Early Figures in Diagnosing Schizophrenia
    Identifying Symptoms

CLINICAL DESCRIPTION, SYMPTOMS, AND SUBTYPES
    Positive Symptoms
    Negative Symptoms
    Disorganized Symptoms
    Schizophrenia Subtypes
    Other Psychotic Disorders

PREVALENCE AND CAUSES OF SCHIZOPHRENIA
    Statistics
    Development
    Cultural Factors
    Genetic Influences
    Neurobiological Influences
    Psychological and Social Influences

TREATMENT OF SCHIZOPHRENIA
    Biological Interventions
    Psychosocial Interventions
    Treatment Across Cultures
    Prevention

ABNORMAL PSYCHOLOGY LIVE CD-ROM
    Schizophrenia: Etta
    Positive Versus Negative Symptoms
    Common Symptoms of Schizophrenia
    Web Link

I was out of control, lost in my world of confusion. I realized that something was going wrong with my reasoning.

Ross David Burke

When the Music's Over: My Journey into Schizophrenia

PERSPECTIVES ON SCHIZOPHRENIA

A middle-aged man walks the streets of New York City with aluminum foil on the inside of his hat so Martians can't read his mind. A young woman sits in her college classroom and hears the voice of God telling her she is a vile and disgusting person. You try to strike up a conversation with the supermarket bagger, but he stares at you vacantly and will say only one or two words in a flat, toneless voice. Each of these people may have **schizophrenia,** the startling disorder characterized by a broad spectrum of cognitive and emotional dysfunctions including delusions and hallucinations, disorganized speech and behavior, and inappropriate emotions.

Schizophrenia is a complex syndrome that inevitably has a devastating effect on the lives of the person affected and on family members. This disorder can disrupt a person's perception, thought, speech, and movement: almost every aspect of daily functioning. Society often devalues these individuals. For example, people with these severe mental health problems are twice as likely to be harassed in public as are people without schizophrenia (Berzins, Petch, & Atkinson, 2003). And despite important advances in treatment, complete recovery from schizophrenia is rare. This catastrophic disorder takes a tremendous emotional toll on everyone involved. In addition to the emotional costs, the financial drain is considerable. The annual cost of schizophrenia in the United States is estimated to exceed $65 billion when factors such as family caregiving, lost wages, and treatment are considered (American Psychiatric Association, 2004). Because schizophrenia is so widespread, affecting approximately 1 of every 100 people at some point in their lives, and because its consequences are so severe, research on its causes and treatment has spread rapidly. Given the attention it has received, you would think the question, "What is schizophrenia?" would by now be answered easily. It is not.

In this chapter, we explore this intriguing disorder and review efforts to determine whether schizophrenia is distinct or a combination of disorders. The search is complicated by the presence of subtypes: different presentations and combinations of symptoms such as hallucinations, delusions, and disorders of speech, emotion, and socialization. After discussing the characteristics of people with schizophrenia, we describe research into its causes and treatment.

Early Figures in Diagnosing Schizophrenia

The history of schizophrenia as it has evolved over the years is unparalleled by any other disorder covered in this book. Knowing something about it will help you understand that the nature of the disorder is multifaceted and treatment is correspondingly complex.

In *Observations on Madness and Melancholy,* published in 1809, John Haslam eloquently portrayed what he called "a form of insanity." In the following passage, Haslam mentions some symptoms that inform our current conception of schizophrenia:

The attack is almost imperceptible; some months usually elapse before it becomes the subject of particular notice; and fond relatives are frequently deceived by the hope that it is only an abatement of excessive vivacity, conducting to a prudent reserve, and steadiness of character. A degree of apparent thoughtfulness and inactivity precede, together with a diminution of the ordinary curiosity, concerning that which is passing before them; and they therefore neglect those objects and pursuits which formerly proved courses of delight and instruction. The sensibility appears to be considerably blunted: they do not bear the same affection towards their parents and relations: they become unfeeling to kindness, and careless of reproof. . . . I have painfully witnessed this hopeless and degrading change, which in a short time has transformed the most promising and vigorous intellect into a slavering and bloated idiot. (Haslam, 1809/1976, pp. 64–67)

About the same time Haslam was writing his description in England, the French physician Philippe Pinel was writing about people we would describe as having schizophrenia (Pinel, 1809, 1962). Some 50 years later, another physician, Benedict Morel, used the French term *démence* (loss of mind) *précoce* (early, premature), because the onset of the disorder is often during adolescence.

Toward the end of the 19th century, the German psychiatrist Emil Kraepelin (1899) built on the writings of Haslam, Pinel, and Morel (among others) to give us what stands today as the most enduring description and categorization of schizophrenia. Two of Kraepelin's accomplishments are especially important. First, he combined several symptoms of insanity that had usually been viewed as reflecting separate and distinct disorders: **catatonia** (alternating immobility and excited agitation), **hebephrenia** (silly and immature emotionality), and **paranoia** (delusions of grandeur or persecution). Kraepelin thought these symptoms shared similar underlying features and included them under the Latin term **dementia praecox.** Although the clinical manifestation might differ from person to person, Kraepelin believed an early onset at the heart of each disorder develops into "mental weakness."

In a second important contribution, Kraepelin (1898) distinguished dementia praecox from manic-depressive illness (bipolar disorder). For people with dementia praecox, an early age of onset and a poor outcome were characteristic; in contrast, these patterns were not essential to manic depression (Peters, 1991). Kraepelin also noted the numerous symptoms in people with dementia praecox, including hallucinations, delusions, negativism, and stereotyped behavior.

A second major figure in the history of schizophrenia was Kraeplin's contemporary, Eugen Bleuler (1908), a Swiss psychiatrist who introduced the term *schizophrenia.* The label was significant because it signaled Bleuler's departure from Kraepelin on what he thought was the core problem. *Schizophrenia,* which

Eugen Bleuler (1857–1939), a Swiss psychiatrist, introduced the term *schizophrenia* and was a pioneer in the field.

©Bettmann/Corbis

comes from the combination of the Greek words for "split" *(skhizein)* and "mind" *(phren)*, reflected Bleuler's belief that underlying all the unusual behaviors shown by people with this disorder was an **associative splitting** of the basic functions of personality. This concept emphasized the "breaking of associative threads," or the destruction of the forces that connect one function to the next. Furthermore, Bleuler believed that a difficulty keeping a consistent train of thought characteristic of all people with this disorder led to the many and diverse symptoms they displayed. Whereas Kraepelin focused on early onset and poor outcomes, Bleuler highlighted what he believed to be the universal underlying problem. Unfortunately, the concept of "split mind" inspired the common but incorrect use of the term *schizophrenia* to mean split or multiple personality. For a summary of the early contributors to the concept of schizophrenia, see Table 13.1.

Identifying Symptoms

It is not easy to point to one thing that makes a person "schizophrenic." As you read about different disorders in this book, you have learned that a particular behavior, way of thinking, or emotion usually defines or is characteristic of each disorder. For example, depression always includes feelings of sadness, and panic disorder is always accompanied by intense feelings of anxiety. Surprisingly, this isn't the case for schizophrenia. Schizophrenia is a number of behaviors or symptoms that aren't necessarily shared by all people who are given this diagnosis. Kraepelin described the situation when he outlined his view of dementia praecox in the late 1800s:

The complexity of the conditions which we observe in the domain of dementia praecox is very great, so that their inner connection is at first recognizable only by their occurring one after the other in the course of the same disease. In any case certain fundamental disturbances, even though they cannot for the most part be regarded as characteristic, yet return frequently in the same form, but in the most diverse combinations. (Kraepelin, 1919, p. 5)

This heterogeneity was also highlighted by Bleuler in the title of his 1911 book, *Dementia Praecox or the Group of Schizophrenias,* which emphasizes the complexity of the disorder. The varied nature of schizophrenia is something we come back to throughout this chapter. Individuals who have schizophrenia have varying symptoms, and we find that the causes vary as well.

Despite these complexities, researchers have identified clusters of symptoms that make up the disorder of schizophrenia. Later we describe these dramatic symptoms, such as seeing or hearing things that others do not (hallucinations) or having beliefs that are unrealistic, bizarre, and not shared by others in the same culture (delusions). But first, consider the following case of an individual who had an intense but relatively rare short-term episode of psychotic behavior.

ARTHUR: Saving the Children

We first met 22-year-old Arthur at an outpatient clinic in a psychiatric hospital. Arthur's family was extremely concerned and upset by his unusual behavior and was desperately seeking help for him. They said that he was "sick" and "talking like a crazy man," and they were afraid he might harm himself.

Arthur had a normal childhood in a middle-class suburban neighborhood. His parents had been happily married until his father's death several years earlier. Arthur was an average student throughout school and had completed an associate's degree in junior college. His family seemed to think he regretted not continuing on to receive a bachelor's degree. Arthur had worked in a series of temporary jobs, and his mother reported that he seemed satisfied with what he was doing. He lived and worked in a major city, some 15 minutes from his mother and his married brother and sister.

Arthur's family said that about 3 weeks before he came to the clinic he had started speaking strangely. He had been laid off from his job a few days before because of cutbacks

TABLE 13.1	Early Figures in the History of Schizophrenia	
Date	**Historical Figure**	**Contribution**
1809	John Haslam (1764–1844)	Superintendent of a British hospital. In *Observations on Madness and Melancholy,* he outlined a description of the symptoms of schizophrenia.
1801/1809	Philippe Pinel (1745–1826)	A French physician who described cases of schizophrenia.
1852	Benedict Morel (1809–1873)	Physician at a French institution who used the term *démence précoce* (in Latin, *dementia praecox*), meaning early or premature *(précoce)* loss of mind *(démence)* to describe schizophrenia.
1898/1899	Emil Kraepelin (1856–1926)	A German psychiatrist who unified the distinct categories of schizophrenia (hebephrenic, catatonic, and paranoid) under the name *dementia praecox.*
1908	Eugen Bleuler (1857–1939)	A Swiss psychiatrist who introduced the term *schizophrenia,* meaning splitting of the mind.

and hadn't communicated with any of his family members for several days. When they next spoke with him, his behavior startled them. Although he had always been idealistic and anxious to help other people, he now talked about saving all the starving children in the world with his "secret plan." At first, his family assumed this was just an example of Arthur's sarcastic wit, but his demeanor changed to one of extreme concern and he spoke nonstop about his plans. He began carrying several spiral notebooks that he claimed contained his scheme for helping starving children; he said he would reveal it only at the right time to the right person. Suspecting that Arthur might be taking drugs, which could explain the sudden and dramatic change in his behavior, his family searched his apartment. Although they didn't find any evidence of drug use, they did find his checkbook and noticed a number of strange entries. Over the past several weeks, Arthur's handwriting had deteriorated, and he had written notes instead of the usual check information ("Start to begin now"; "This is important!"; "They must be saved"). He had also made unusual notes in several of his most prized books, a particularly alarming development given his reverence for these books.

As the days went on, Arthur showed dramatic changes in emotion, often crying and acting apprehensive. He stopped wearing socks and underwear and, despite the extremely cold weather, wouldn't wear a jacket when he went outdoors. At the family's insistence, he moved into his mother's apartment. He slept little, and kept the family up until the early morning. His mother said it was like being in a living nightmare. Each morning she would wake up with a knot in her stomach, not wanting to get out of bed because she felt so helpless to do anything to rescue Arthur from his obvious distress.

The family's sense of alarm grew as Arthur revealed more details of his plan. He said that he was going to the German embassy because that was the only place people would listen to him. He would climb the fence at night when everyone was asleep and present his plan to the German ambassador. Fearing that Arthur would be hurt trying to enter the embassy grounds, his family contacted a local psychiatric hospital, described Arthur's condition, and asked that he be admitted. Much to their surprise and disappointment, they were told that Arthur could commit himself but that they couldn't bring him in involuntarily unless he was in danger of doing harm to himself or others. The fear that Arthur might be harmed wasn't sufficient reason to admit him involuntarily.

His family finally talked Arthur into meeting the staff at the outpatient clinic. In our interview, it was clear he was delusional, firmly believing in his ability to help all starving children. After some cajoling, I finally convinced him to let me see his books. He had written random thoughts (for example, "The poor, starving souls"; "The moon is the only place") and made drawings of rocket ships. Parts of his plan involved building a rocket ship that would go to the moon, where he would create a community for all malnourished children, a place where they could live and be helped. After a few brief comments on his plan, I began to ask him about his health.

"You look tired; are you getting enough sleep?"

"Sleep isn't really needed," he noted. "My plans will take me through, and then they can all rest."

"Your family is worried about you," I said. "Do you understand their concern?"

"It's important for all concerned to get together, to join together," he replied.

With that, he got up and walked out of the room and out of the building, after telling his family that he would be right back. After 5 minutes they went to look for him, but he had disappeared. He was missing for 2 days, which caused his family a great deal of concern about his health and safety. In an almost miraculous sequence of events, they found him walking the streets of the city. He acted as if nothing had happened. Gone were his notebooks and the talk of his secret plan.

What caused Arthur to act so strangely? Was it being fired from his job? Was it the death of his father? Was it a genetic predisposition to have schizophrenia or another disorder that kicked in during a period of stress? Unfortunately, we will never know exactly what happened to Arthur to make him behave so bizarrely and then recover so quickly and completely. However, research that we discuss next may shed some light on schizophrenia and potentially help other Arthurs and their families.

CLINICAL DESCRIPTION, SYMPTOMS, AND SUBTYPES

The case of Arthur shows the range of problems experienced by people with schizophrenia or other psychotic disorders. The term **psychotic behavior** has been used to characterize many unusual behaviors, although in its strictest sense it usually involves delusions (irrational beliefs) and/or hallucinations (sensory experiences in the absence of external events). Schizophrenia is one of the disorders that involve psychotic behavior; we describe others in more detail later.

Schizophrenia can affect all the functions we rely on each day. Before we describe the symptoms, it is important to look carefully at the specific characteristics of people who exhibit these behaviors, partly because we constantly see distorted images of people with schizophrenia. Headlines such as "Ex-Mental Patient Kills Family" falsely imply that everyone with schizophrenia is dangerous and violent. Popular accounts also contribute to this misinformation. Evidence for violence among people with schizophrenia suggests although they may be slightly more likely to commit violent acts than the general population, you are more likely to see violence from people with substance abuse problems and personality disorders (Kirkpatrick & Tek, 2005). Despite this information, more than 70% of characters in prime-time television dramas with schizophrenia are portrayed as violent, with more than one fifth depicted as murderers (Wahl, 1995). As in mistakenly assuming that *schizophrenia* means "split personality," the popular press misrepresents abnormal psychology to the detriment of people who experience these debilitating disorders.

The fourth edition, text revision, of the *Diagnostic and Statistical Manual* (DSM-IV-TR) has a multiple-part process for determining whether or not someone has schizophrenia. Later we discuss the symptoms the person experiences during the disorder (active phase symptoms), the course of the disorder, and the subtypes of schizophrenia currently in use.

Mental health workers typically distinguish between *positive* and *negative* symptoms of schizophrenia. A third dimension, *disorganized* symptoms, also appears to be an important aspect of the disorder (Kirkpatrick & Tek, 2005). There is not yet universal agreement about which symptoms should be included in these categories. Positive symptoms generally include the more active manifestations of abnormal behavior or an excess or distortion of normal behavior; these include delusions and hallucinations. Negative symptoms involve deficits in normal behavior in such areas as speech and motivation. Disorganized symptoms include rambling speech, erratic behavior, and inappropriate affect (Lindenmayer & Khan, 2006). A diagnosis of schizophrenia requires that two or more positive, negative, and/or disorganized symptoms be present for at least 1 month.

A great deal of research has focused on the different symptoms of schizophrenia, each of which is described here in some detail.

Positive Symptoms

We next describe the **positive symptoms** of schizophrenia, which are the more obvious signs of psychosis. These include the disturbing experiences of delusions and hallucinations. Between 50% and 70% of people with schizophrenia experience hallucinations, delusions, or both (Lindenmayer & Khan, 2006).

Delusions

A belief that would be seen by most members of a society as a misrepresentation of reality is called a *disorder of thought content,* or a *delusion*. Because of its importance in schizophrenia, delusion has been called "the basic characteristic of madness" (Jaspers, 1963, p. 93). If, for example, you believe that squirrels are aliens sent to Earth on a reconnaissance mission, you would be considered delusional. The media often portray people with schizophrenia as believing they are famous or important people (such as Napoleon or Jesus Christ). Arthur's belief that he could end starvation for all the world's children is also a *delusion of grandeur.*

DSM-IV-TR
DSM TABLE 13.1 Diagnostic Criteria for Schizophrenia

A. *Characteristic symptoms:* Two (or more) of the following, each present for a significant portion of time during a 1-month period (or less if successfully treated):
  1. Delusions
  2. Hallucinations
  3. Disorganized speech (e.g., frequent derailment or incoherence)
  4. Grossly disorganized or catatonic behavior
  5. Negative symptoms (i.e., affective flattening, alogia, or avolition)
Note: Only one criterion A symptom is required if delusions are bizarre, or hallucinations consist of a voice keeping up a running commentary on the person's behavior or thoughts or two or more voices conversing with each other.
B. *Social/occupational dysfunction:* For a significant portion of the time since the onset of the disturbance, one or more major areas of functioning such as work, interpersonal relations, or self-care are markedly below the level achieved prior to the onset (or when the onset is in childhood or adolescence, failure to achieve expected level of interpersonal, academic, or occupational achievement).
C. *Duration:* Continuous signs of the disturbance persist for at least 6 months. This 6-month period must include at least 1 month of symptoms (or less if successfully treated) that meet criterion A (i.e., active-phase symptoms) and may include periods of prodromal or residual symptoms. During these prodromal or residual periods, the signs of the disturbance may be manifested by only negative symptoms or two or more symptoms listed in criterion A present in an attenuated form (e.g., odd beliefs, unusual perceptual experiences).
D. *Schizoaffective and mood disorder exclusion:* Schizoaffective disorder and mood disorder with psychotic features have been ruled out because either (1) no major depressive, manic, or mixed episodes have occurred concurrently with the active-phase symptoms; or (2) if mood episodes have occurred during active-phase symptoms, their total duration has been brief relative to the duration of the active and residual periods.
E. *Substance/general medical condition exclusion:* The disturbance is not due to the direct physiological effects of a substance (e.g., a drug of abuse, a medication) or a general medical condition.
F. *Relationship to a pervasive developmental disorder:* If there is a history of autistic disorder or another pervasive developmental disorder, the additional diagnosis of schizophrenia is made only if prominent delusions or hallucinations are also present for at least a month (or less if successfully treated).
Classification of longitudinal course (can be applied only after at least 1 year has elapsed since the initial onset of active-phase symptoms):
Episodic with interepisode residual symptoms (episodes are defined by the reemergence of prominent psychotic symptoms); *also specify if:* with prominent negative symptoms
Episodic with no interepisode residual symptoms
Continuous (prominent psychotic symptoms are present throughout the period of observation); *also specify if:* with prominent negative symptoms
Single episode in partial remission; *also specify if:* with prominent negative symptoms
Single episode in full remission
Other or unspecified pattern

Source: Reprinted, with permission, from American Psychiatric Association. (2000). *Diagnostic and statistical manual of mental disorders* (4th ed., text revision). Washington, DC: Author, © 2000 American Psychiatric Association.

A common delusion in people with schizophrenia is that others are "out to get them." Called *delusions of persecution,* these beliefs can be most disturbing. One of us worked with a world-class cyclist who was on her way to making the Olympic team. Tragically, however, she developed a belief that other competitors were determined to sabotage her efforts, which forced her to stop riding for years. She believed opponents would spray her bicycle with chemicals that would take her strength away, and they would slow her down by putting small pebbles in the road that only she would ride over. These thoughts created a great deal of anxiety, and she refused even to go near her bicycle for some time.

Other more unusual delusions include Capgras syndrome, in which the person believes someone they know has been replaced by a double, and Cotard's syndrome, in which the person believes he is dead (McKay, Langdon, & Coltheart, in press).

A man recovering from schizophrenia frankly described his delusional experiences (Fleshner, 1995):

> When I went to the polls, voting was not by machine but rather by ballot. After receiving instructions on how to fill out the ballot I thought I heard the registrar say to initial it in the lower right-hand corner. I wondered why I would have to initial a ballot. It was supposed to be a secret ballot. Immediately I suspected that my vote and my vote alone would determine the destiny of the presidency. . . . I thought Clinton was the power boss who controlled everything including his "evil empire." So later, while watching TV, I saw what I perceived to be a rather sheepish, maybe slightly devilish glance from Clinton and a thumbs up (presumably at me) for having cast my vote the way I did. You see I had an additional delusion that while watching TV the subject being televised can peer right into your living room. . . . In my deluded mind, the thumbs up was for me personally for voting as I did. (pp. 704–705)

Why would someone come to believe such obviously improbable things (for example, a friend is replaced by a double or your vote will determine the outcome of a national election)? A number of theories exist and can be summarized into two themes—motivational or deficit theories (McKay et al., in press). A motivational view of delusions would look at these beliefs as attempts to deal with and relieve anxiety and stress. A person develops "stories" around some issue—for example, a famous person is in love with them (erotomania)—that in a way helps the person make sense out of uncontrollable anxieties in a tumultuous world. Preoccupation with the delusion distracts the individual from the upsetting aspects of the world, such as hallucinations. In contrast, a deficit view of delusion sees these beliefs as resulting from brain dysfunction that creates these disordered cognitions or perceptions. Much work remains to develop an integrative account for these intriguing but debilitating symptoms of schizophrenia.

■ Hallucinations

Did you ever think someone called your name, only to discover that no one was there? Did you ever think you saw something move by you, yet nothing did? We all have fleeting moments when we think we see or hear something that isn't there. However, for many people with schizophrenia, these perceptions are real and occur regularly. The experience of sensory events without any input from the surrounding environment is called a *hallucination.* The case of David illustrates the phenomena of hallucina-

tions, as well as other disorders of thought that are common among people with schizophrenia.

DAVID: Missing Uncle Bill

David was 25 years old when I met him; he had been living in a psychiatric hospital for about 3 years. He was a little overweight and of average height; he typically dressed in a T-shirt and jeans and tended to be active. I first encountered him while I was talking to another man who lived on the same floor. David interrupted us by pulling on my shoulder. "My Uncle Bill is a good man. He treats me well." Not wanting to be impolite, I said, "I'm sure he is. Maybe after I've finished talking to Michael here, we can talk about your uncle." David persisted, "He can kill fish with a knife. Things can get awfully sharp in your mind, when you go down the river. I could kill you with my bare hands—taking things into my own hands. . . . I know you know!" He was now speaking quickly and had gained emotionality, along with speed, as he spoke. I talked to him quietly until he calmed down for the moment; later, I looked into David's file for some information about his background.

David was brought up on a farm by his Aunt Katie and Uncle Bill. His father's identity is unknown and his mother, who had mental retardation, couldn't care for him. David, too, was diagnosed as having mental retardation, although his functioning was only mildly impaired, and he attended school. The year David's Uncle Bill died, his high school teachers first reported unusual behavior. David occasionally talked to his deceased Uncle Bill in class. Later, he became increasingly agitated and verbally aggressive toward others and was diagnosed as having schizophrenia. He managed to graduate from high school but never obtained a job after that; he lived at home with his aunt for several years. Although his aunt sincerely wanted him to stay with her, his threatening behavior escalated to the point that she requested he be seen at the local psychiatric hospital.

I spoke with David again and had a chance to ask him a few questions. "Why are you here in the hospital, David?" "I really don't want to be here," he told me. "I've got other things to do. The time is right, and you know, when opportunity knocks." He continued for a few minutes until I interrupted him. "I was sorry to hear that your Uncle Bill died a few years ago. How are you feeling about him these days?" "Yes, he died. He was sick and now he's gone. He likes to fish with me, down at the river. He's going to take me hunting. I have guns. I can shoot you and you'd be dead in a minute."

David's conversational speech resembled a ball rolling down a rocky hill. Like an accelerating object, his speech gained momentum the longer he went on and, as if bouncing off obstacles, the topics almost always went in unpredictable directions. If he continued for too long, he often became agitated and spoke of harming others. David also told me that his uncle's voice spoke to him repeatedly. He heard other voices also, but he couldn't identify them or tell me what they said. We return to David's case later in this chapter when we discuss causes and treatments.

Hallucinations can involve any of the senses, although hearing things that aren't there, or *auditory hallucination*, is the most common form experienced by people with schizophrenia. David had frequent auditory hallucinations, usually of his uncle's voice. When David heard a voice that belonged to his Uncle Bill, he often couldn't understand what his uncle was saying; on other occasions, the voice was clearer. "He told me to turn off the TV. He said, 'It's too damn loud, turn it down, turn it down.'" This is consistent with recent views of hallucinations as being related to metacognition or "thinking about thinking." Most of us have had an occasional intrusive thought that we try not to focus on (for example, thinking "I wish she were dead!" when you know that's not appropriate). People who experience hallucinations appear to have intrusive thoughts, but they believe they are coming from somewhere or someone else (David thinking he is hearing his uncle's voice when it is probably his own thoughts he is "hearing"). They then worry about having these thoughts and engage in metaworry—or worrying about worrying (Morrison & Wells, 2007; Stirling, Barkus, & Lewis, 2007).

Exciting research on hallucinations uses sophisticated brain-imaging techniques to try to localize these phenomena in the brain. Using single photon emission computed tomography (SPECT) to study the cerebral blood flow of men with schizophrenia who also had auditory hallucinations, researchers in London made a surprising discovery (McGuire, Shah, & Murray, 1993). The researchers used the brain-imaging technique while the men were experiencing hallucinations and while they were not, and they found that the part of the brain most active during hallucinations was Broca's area (see ■ Figure 13.1). This is surprising because Broca's area is known to be involved in speech production. Because auditory hallucinations usually involve understanding the "speech" of others, you might expect more activity in Wernicke's area, which involves language comprehension. However, this study supports an earlier finding by a different group of researchers who also found that Broca's area was more active than Wernicke's area during hallucinations (Cleghorn et al., 1992). These observations support the metacognition theory that people who are hallucinating are *not* hearing the voices of others but are listening to their own thoughts or their own voices and cannot recognize the difference (Fitzgerald et al., 2007; Hoffman, Rapaport, Mazure, & Quinlan, 1999).

Negative Symptoms

In contrast to the active presentations that characterize the positive symptoms of schizophrenia, the **negative symptoms** usually indicate the absence or insufficiency of normal behavior. They include emotional and social withdrawal, apathy, and poverty of thought or speech, and approximately 25% of people with schizophrenia display these symptoms (Kirkpatrick & Tek, 2005).

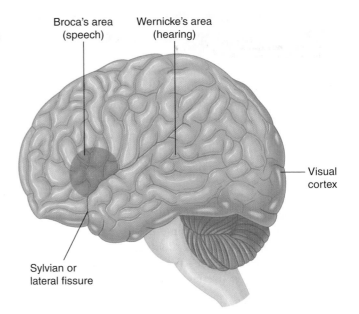

■ **FIGURE 13.1** Major areas of functioning of the cerebral cortex. In most people, only the left hemisphere is specialized for language.

Avolition

Combining the prefix *a,* meaning "without," and *volition,* which means "an act of willing, choosing, or deciding," **avolition** is the inability to initiate and persist in activities. People with this symptom (also referred to as *apathy*) show little interest in performing even the most basic day-to-day functions, including those associated with personal hygiene.

Alogia

Derived from the combination of *a* ("without") and *logos* ("words"), **alogia** refers to the relative absence of speech. A person with alogia may respond to questions with brief replies that have little content and may appear uninterested in the conversation. For example, to the question, "Do you have any children?" most parents might reply, "Oh yes, I have two beautiful children, a boy and a girl. My son is 6 and my daughter is 12." In the following exchange, someone with alogia responds to the same question:

INTERVIEWER: Do you have any children?
CLIENT: Yes.
I: How many children do you have?
C: Two.
I: How old are they?
C: Six and twelve.

Such deficiency in communication is believed to reflect a negative thought disorder rather than inadequate communication skills. Some researchers, for example, suggest that people with alogia may have trouble finding the right words to formulate their thoughts (Sumiyoshi et al., 2005). Sometimes alogia takes the form of delayed comments or slow responses to questions. Talking with individuals who manifest this symptom can be extremely frustrating, making you feel as if you are "pulling teeth" to get them to respond.

■ Anhedonia

A related symptom is called **anhedonia,** which derives from the combination of *a* ("without") and *hedonic,* pertaining to pleasure. Anhedonia is the presumed lack of pleasure experienced by some people with schizophrenia. Like some mood disorders, anhedonia signals an indifference to activities that would typically be considered pleasurable, including eating, social interactions, and sexual relations.

■ Affective Flattening

Imagine that people wore masks at all times: You could communicate with them verbally, but you wouldn't be able to see their emotional reactions. Approximately one quarter of the people with schizophrenia exhibit what is called **flat affect** (Kirkpatrick & Tek, 2005). They are similar to people wearing masks because they do not show emotions when you would normally expect them to. They

Negative symptoms of schizophrenia include social withdrawal and apathy.

may stare at you vacantly, speak in a flat and toneless manner, and seem unaffected by things going on around them. However, although they do not react openly to emotional situations, they may be responding on the inside.

Howard Berenbaum and Thomas Oltmanns (1992) compared people with schizophrenia who had flat (or "blunted") affect with those who did not. The two groups were shown clips from comedies and dramas selected to create emotional reactions in the viewer. Berenbaum and Oltmanns found that the people with flat affect showed little change in facial expression, although they reported experiencing the appropriate emotions. The authors concluded that the flat affect in schizophrenia may represent difficulty expressing emotion, not a lack of feeling. Researchers can now use computer analyses of facial expressions to more objectively assess the emotional expressiveness of people with disorders such as schizophrenia. One such study confirmed the difficulty of people with this disorder to express themselves properly with facial expressions (Alvino et al., in press).

The expression of affect—or the lack of this expression—may be an important symptom of the development of schizophrenia. In a particularly innovative study, researchers videotaped high-risk children (those with one or more parents who had schizophrenia) eating lunch in 1972 and followed them up almost 20 years later (Schiffman et al., 2004). The researchers were able to show that children who later went on to develop schizophrenia typically displayed less positive and more negative affect than those children who did not develop the disorder. This suggests that emotional expression may be one way to identify potential schizophrenia in children.

Disorganized Symptoms

Perhaps the least studied and therefore the least understood symptoms of schizophrenia are referred to as the "disorganized symptoms." These include a variety of erratic behaviors that affect speech, motor behavior, and emotional reactions. The prevalence of these behaviors among those with schizophrenia is unclear.

■ Disorganized Speech

A conversation with someone who has schizophrenia can be particularly frustrating. If you want to understand what is bothering or upsetting this person, eliciting relevant information is especially difficult. For one thing, people with schizophrenia often lack *insight,* an awareness that they have a problem. In addition, they experience what Bleuler called "associative splitting" and what Paul Meehl called "cognitive slippage" (Bleuler, 1908; Meehl, 1962). These phrases help describe the speech problems of people with schizophrenia: Sometimes they jump from topic to topic, and at other times they talk illogically. DSM-IV-TR uses the term **disorganized speech** to describe such communication problems. Let's go back to our conversation with David to demonstrate the symptom.

"If anyone gets into the house, they say I'd get shot. . . . [Who said?] That's the eagle. . . . The eagle works through General Motors. They have something to do with my General Motors check I get every month . . . when you do the 25 of the clock, it means that you leave the house 25 after 1 to mail letters so that they can check on you . . . and they know where you're at. That's the eagle. . . . If you don't do something they tell you to do, Jesus makes the shotgun sound, and then . . . not to answer the phone or the doorbell . . . because you'd get shot [by the] eagle."

LWA–Dan Tardiff/Corbis

VMD: Why are you here in the hospital, David?

DAVID: I really don't want to be here. I've got other things to do. The time is right, and you know, when opportunity knocks . . .

David didn't really answer the question he was asked. This type of response is called *tangentiality*—that is, going off on a tangent instead of answering a specific question (Andreasen, 1979). David also abruptly changed the topic of conversation to unrelated areas, a behavior that has variously been called *loose association* or *derailment* (Cutting, 1985).

VMD: I was sorry to hear that your Uncle Bill died a few years ago. How are you feeling about him these days?

DAVID: Yes, he died. He was sick, and now he's gone. He likes to fish with me, down at the river. He's going to take me hunting. I have guns. I can shoot you and you'd be dead in a minute.

Again, David didn't answer the question. It was unclear whether he didn't understand the question, couldn't focus his attention, or found it too difficult to talk about his uncle. You can see why people spend a great deal of time trying to interpret all the hidden meanings behind this type of conversation. Unfortunately, however, such analyses have yet to provide us with useful information about the nature of schizophrenia or its treatment.

■ Inappropriate Affect and Disorganized Behavior

Occasionally, people with schizophrenia display **inappropriate affect,** laughing or crying at improper times. Sometimes they exhibit bizarre behaviors such as hoarding objects or acting in unusual ways in public. People with schizophrenia engage in a number of other "active" behaviors that are usually viewed as unusual. For example, catatonia is one of the most curious symptoms in some individuals with schizophrenia; it involves motor dysfunctions that range from wild agitation to immobility. On the active side of the continuum, some people pace excitedly or move their fingers or arms in stereotyped ways. At the other end of the extreme, people hold unusual postures, as if they were fearful of something terrible happening if they move **(catatonic immobility).** This manifestation can also involve *waxy flexibility,* or the tendency to keep their bodies and limbs in the position they are put in by someone else.

Again, to receive a diagnosis of schizophrenia, a person must display two or more positive, negative, and/or disorganized symptoms for a major portion of at least 1 month. Depending on the combination of symptoms displayed, two people could receive the same diagnosis but behave differently, for example, one having marked hallucinations and delusions and the other displaying disorganized speech and some negative symptoms. Proper treatment depends on differentiating individuals in terms of their varying symptoms.

Schizophrenia Subtypes

As we noted earlier, the search for subtypes of schizophrenia began before Kraepelin described his concept of schizophrenia. Three divisions have persisted: paranoid (delusions of grandeur or persecution), disorganized (or hebephrenic; silly and immature emotionality), and catatonic (alternate immobility and excited agitation). Although these categories continue to be used in DSM-IV-TR, their usefulness is in question. As research advances on the underlying biological influences (endophenotypes) of this disorder, it is not clear that they will match these subtypes. In addition, people can sometimes change diagnosis over the course of their illness, moving from one category to another (Kirkpatrick & Tek, 2005). However, we describe them next for their historic value and because the current diagnostic system relies on these distinctions.

■ Paranoid Type

People with the **paranoid type of schizophrenia** stand out because of their delusions or hallucinations; at the same time, their cognitive skills and affect are relatively intact. They generally do not have disorganized speech or flat affect, and they typically have a better prognosis than people with other forms of schizophrenia. The delusions and hallucinations usually have a theme, such as grandeur or persecution. The DSM-IV-TR criteria for inclusion in this subtype specify preoccupation with one or more delusions or frequent auditory hallucinations but without a marked display of disorganized speech, disorganized or catatonic behavior, or flat or inappropriate affect (American Psychiatric Association, 2000c).

■ Disorganized Type

In contrast to the paranoid type of schizophrenia, people with the **disorganized type of schizophrenia** show marked disruption in their speech and behavior; they also show flat or inappropriate affect, such as laughing in a silly way at the wrong times (American Psychiatric Association, 2000c). They also seem unusually self-absorbed and may spend considerable amounts of time looking at themselves in the mirror (Kirkpatrick & Tek, 2005). If delusions or hallucinations are present, they tend not to be organized around a central theme, as in the paranoid type, but are more fragmented. This subtype was previously called *hebephrenic.* Individuals with this diagnosis tend to show signs of difficulty early, and their problems are often chronic, lacking the remissions (improvement of symptoms) that characterize other forms of the disorder (Lindenmayer & Khan, 2006).

DSM-IV-TR

DSM TABLE 13.2 Diagnostic Criteria for Paranoid Type

A type of schizophrenia in which the following criteria are met:

A. Preoccupation with one or more delusions or frequent auditory hallucinations.

B. None of the following is prominent: disorganized speech, disorganized or catatonic behavior, or flat or inappropriate affect.

Source: Reprinted, with permission, from American Psychiatric Association. (2000). *Diagnostic and statistical manual of mental disorders* (4th ed., text revision). Washington, DC: Author. © 2000 American Psychiatric Association.

DSM-IV-TR

DSM TABLE 13.4 Diagnostic Criteria for Catatonic Type

A type of schizophrenia in which the clinical picture is dominated by at least two of the following:
1. Motoric immobility as evidenced by catalepsy (including waxy flexibility) or stupor
2. Excessive motor activity (that is apparently purposeless and not influenced by external stimuli)
3. Extreme negativism (an apparently motiveless resistance to all instructions or maintenance of a rigid posture against attempts to be moved) or mutism
4. Peculiarities of voluntary movement as evidenced by posturing (voluntary assumption of inappropriate or bizarre postures), stereotyped movements, prominent mannerisms, or prominent grimacing
5. Echolalia or echopraxia

Source: Reprinted, with permission, from American Psychiatric Association. (2000). *Diagnostic and statistical manual of mental disorders* (4th ed., text revision). Washington, DC: Author, © 2000 American Psychiatric Association.

©Michael Newman/PhotoEdit

Homeless people who suffer from paranoid schizophrenia often bear the additional burden of persecutory delusions, which interfere with outside efforts to help.

Catatonic Type

In addition to the unusual motor responses of remaining in fixed positions (called "waxy flexibility" because their limbs and body position can be moved by others) and engaging in excessive activity, individuals with the **catatonic type of schizophrenia** sometimes display odd mannerisms with their bodies and faces, including grimacing (American Psychiatric Association, 2000c). They sometimes repeat or mimic the words of others *(echolalia)* or the movements of others *(echopraxia)*. There may be subtypes of catatonic schizophrenia, with some individuals showing primarily symptoms of labeled "negative withdrawal" (immobility, posturing, mutism), "automatic" (routine obedience, waxy flexibility), "repetitive/echo" (grimacing, perseveration, echolalia) and "agitated/resistive" excitement, impulsivity, combativeness) (Ungvari, Goggins, Leung, & Gerevich, 2007).

Undifferentiated Type

People who do not fit neatly into these subtypes are classified as having an **undifferentiated type of schizophrenia;** they include people who have the major symptoms of schizophrenia but who do not meet the criteria for paranoid, disorganized, or catatonic types.

Residual Type

People who have had at least one episode of schizophrenia but who no longer manifest major symptoms are diagnosed as having the **residual type of schizophrenia.** Although they may not suffer from bizarre delusions or hallucinations, they may display residual or "leftover" symptoms, such as negative beliefs, or they may still have unusual ideas that are not fully delusional. Residual symptoms can include social withdrawal, bizarre thoughts, inactivity, and flat affect. All versions of the DSM (from DSM-I through DSM-IV-TR) have included a residual type to describe the condition of individuals who have less severe problems associated with an episode of schizophrenia.

Research suggests that the paranoid subtype may have a stronger familial link than the others and that these people may function better before and after episodes of schizophrenia than people diagnosed with other subtypes (Kirkpatrick & Tek, 2005). More work will determine whether dividing schizophrenia into five subtypes helps us understand and treat people. Several other disorders also characterized by psychotic behaviors such as hallu-

DSM-IV-TR

DSM TABLE 13.3 Diagnostic Criteria for Disorganized Type

A type of schizophrenia in which the following criteria are met:
A. All the following are prominent:
1. Disorganized speech
2. Disorganized behavior
3. Flat or inappropriate affect
B. The criteria are not met for catatonic type.

Source: Reprinted, with permission, from American Psychiatric Association. (2000). *Diagnostic and statistical manual of mental disorders* (4th ed., text revision). Washington, DC: Author, © 2000 American Psychiatric Association.

DSM-IV-TR

DSM TABLE 13.5 Diagnostic Criteria for Residual Type

A type of schizophrenia in which the following criteria are met:
A. Absence of prominent delusions, hallucinations, disorganized speech, and grossly disorganized or catatonic behavior.
B. There is continuing evidence of the disturbance, as indicated by the presence of negative symptoms or two or more symptoms listed in criterion A for schizophrenia, present in an attenuated form (e.g., odd beliefs, unusual perceptual experiences).

Source: Reprinted, with permission, from American Psychiatric Association. (2000). *Diagnostic and statistical manual of mental disorders* (4th ed., text revision). Washington, DC: Author, © 2000 American Psychiatric Association.

cinations and delusions do not manifest in the same way as schizophrenia. In the next section, we first distinguish them from schizophrenia and then describe them in greater detail.

Other Psychotic Disorders

The psychotic behaviors of some individuals do not fit neatly under the heading of schizophrenia as we have just described. Several other categories of disorders depict these significant variations.

Schizophreniform Disorder

Some people experience the symptoms of schizophrenia for a few months only; they can usually resume normal lives. The symptoms sometimes disappear as the result of successful treatment, but they often do so for reasons unknown. The label **schizophreniform disorder** classifies these symptoms, but because relatively few studies are available on this disorder, data on important aspects of it are sparse. It appears, however, that the lifetime prevalence is approximately 0.2% (American Psychiatric Association, 2000c). The DSM-IV-TR diagnostic criteria for schizophreniform disorder include onset of psychotic symptoms within 4 weeks of the first noticeable change in usual behavior, confusion at the height of the psychotic episode, *good premorbid* (before the psychotic episode) social and occupational functioning (functioning before the psychotic episode), and the absence of blunted or flat affect (Naz, Fochtmann & Bromet, 2005).

Schizoaffective Disorder

Historically, people who had symptoms of schizophrenia and who exhibited the characteristics of mood disorders (for example, depression or bipolar affective disorder) were lumped in the category of schizophrenia. Now, however, this mixed bag of problems is diagnosed as **schizoaffective disorder** (Fennig, Fochtmann, & Carlson, 2005). The prognosis is similar to the prognosis for people with schizophrenia—that is, individuals tend not to get better on their own and are likely to continue experiencing major life difficulties for many years. DSM-IV-TR criteria for schizoaffective disorder require, in addition to the presence of a mood disorder, delusions or hallucinations for at least 2 weeks in the absence

DSM-IV-TR

DSM TABLE 13.6 Diagnostic Criteria for Schizophreniform Disorder

A. criteria A, D, and E of schizophrenia are met.
B. An episode of the disorder (including prodromal, active, and residual phases) lasts at least 1 month but less than 6 months. (When the diagnosis must be made without waiting for recovery, it should be qualified as "provisional.")
Specify if:
Without good prognostic features
With good prognostic features: As evidenced by two (or more) of the following:
  1. Onset of prominent psychotic symptoms within 4 weeks of the first noticeable change in usual behavior or functioning
  2. Confusion or perplexity at the height of the psychotic episode
  3. Good premorbid social and occupational functioning
  4. Absence of blunted or flat affect

Source: Reprinted, with permission, from American Psychiatric Association. (2000). *Diagnostic and statistical manual of mental disorders* (4th ed., text revision). Washington, DC: Author, © 2000 American Psychiatric Association.

of prominent mood symptoms (American Psychiatric Association, 2000c).

Delusional Disorder

Delusions are beliefs that are not generally held by other members of a society. The major feature of **delusional disorder** is a persistent belief that is contrary to reality, in the absence of other characteristics of schizophrenia. For example, a woman who believes without any evidence that coworkers are tormenting her by put-

DSM-IV-TR

DSM TABLE 13.7 Diagnostic Criteria for Schizoaffective Disorder

A. An uninterrupted period of illness during which, at some time, there is either a major depressive episode, a manic episode, or a mixed episode concurrent with symptoms that meet criterion A for schizophrenia.
Note: The major depressive episode must include criterion A1: depressed mood.
B. During the same period of illness, there have been delusions or hallucinations for at least 2 weeks in the absence of prominent mood symptoms.
C. Symptoms that meet criteria for a mood episode are present for a substantial portion of the total duration of the active and residual periods of the illness.
D. The disturbance is not due to the direct physiological effects of a substance (e.g., a drug of abuse, a medication) or a general medical condition.
Specify type:
Bipolar type: If the disturbance includes a manic or a mixed episode (or a manic or a mixed episode and major depressive episodes)
Depressive type: If the disturbance only includes major depressive episodes

Source: Reprinted, with permission, from American Psychiatric Association. (2000). *Diagnostic and statistical manual of mental disorders* (4th ed., text revision). Washington, DC: Author, © 2000 American Psychiatric Association.

DSM-IV-TR

DSM TABLE 13.8 Diagnostic Criteria for Delusional Disorder

A. Nonbizarre delusions (i.e., involving situations that occur in real life, such as being followed, poisoned, infected, loved at a distance, or deceived by spouse or lover, or having a disease) of at least 1 month's duration.

B. Criterion A for schizophrenia has never been met. *Note:* Tactile and olfactory hallucinations may be present in delusional disorder if they are related to the delusional theme.

C. Apart from the impact of the delusion(s) or its ramifications, functioning is not markedly impaired and behavior is not obviously odd or bizarre.

D. If mood episodes have occurred concurrently with delusions, their total duration has been brief relative to the duration of the delusional periods.

E. The disturbance is not due to the direct physiological effects of a substance (e.g., a drug of abuse, a medication) or a general medical condition.

Specify type (the following types are assigned based on the predominant delusional theme):

Erotomanic type: Delusions that another person, usually of higher status, is in love with the individual

Grandiose type: Delusions of inflated worth, power, knowledge, identity, or special relationship to a deity or famous person

Jealous type: Delusions that the individual's sexual partner is unfaithful

Persecutory type: Delusions that the person (or someone to whom the person is close) is being malevolently treated in some way

Somatic type: Delusions that the person has some physical defect or general medical condition

Mixed type: Delusions characteristic of more than one of the above types but no one theme predominates

Unspecified type

Source: Reprinted, with permission, from American Psychiatric Association. (2000). *Diagnostic and statistical manual of mental disorders* (4th ed., text revision). Washington, DC: Author, © 2000 American Psychiatric Association.

ting poison in her food and spraying her apartment with harmful gases has a delusional disorder. This disorder is characterized by a persistent delusion that is not the result of an organic factor such as brain seizures or of any severe psychosis. Individuals tend not to have flat affect, anhedonia, or other negative symptoms of schizophrenia; importantly, however, they may become socially isolated because they are suspicious of others. The delusions are often long standing, sometimes persisting over several years (Fennig, Fochtmann, & Bromet, 2005).

DSM-IV-TR recognizes the following delusional subtypes: erotomanic, grandiose, jealous, persecutory, and somatic. An *erotomanic type* of delusion is the irrational belief that one is loved by another person, usually of higher status. Some individuals who stalk celebrities appear to have erotomanic delusional disorder. The *grandiose type* of delusion involves believing in one's inflated worth, power, knowledge, identity, or special relationship to a deity or famous person. A person with the *jealous type* of delusion believes the sexual partner is unfaithful. The *persecutory type* of delusion involves believing oneself (or someone close) is being malevolently treated in some way. Finally, with the *somatic delusions* the person feels afflicted by a physical defect or general medical condition. These delusions differ from the more bizarre types of-

ten found in people with schizophrenia because in delusional disorder *the imagined events could be happening but aren't* (for example, mistakenly believing you are being followed); in schizophrenia, however, *the imagined events aren't possible* (for example, believing your brain waves broadcast your thoughts to other people around the world).

Delusional disorder seems to be relatively rare, affecting 24 to 30 people out of every 100,000 in the general population. Among those people with psychotic disorders in general, between 2% and 8% are thought to have delusional disorder (Fennig, Fochtmann, & Bromet, 2005). Researchers can't be confident about the percentages because they know that many of these individuals have no contact with the mental health system.

The onset of delusional disorder is relatively late: The average age of first admission to a psychiatric facility is between 40 and 49 (Munro, 1999). However, because many people with this disorder can lead relatively normal lives, they may not seek treatment until their symptoms become most disruptive. Delusional disorder seems to afflict more females than males (55% and 45%, respectively, of the affected population).

In a longitudinal study, Opjordsmoen (1989) followed 53 people with delusional disorder for an average of 30 years and found they tended to fare better in life than people with schizophrenia but not as well as those with some other psychotic disorders, such as schizoaffective disorder. About 80% of the 53 individuals had been married at some time, and half were employed, which demonstrates an ability to function relatively well despite delusions.

We know relatively little about either the biological or the psychosocial influences on delusional disorder (Fennig, Fochtmann, & Bromet, 2005). Research on families suggests that the characteristics of suspiciousness, jealousy, and secretiveness may occur more often among the relatives of people with delusional disorder than among the population at large, suggesting some aspect of this disorder may be inherited (Winokur, 1985).

A number of other disorders can cause delusions, and their presence should be ruled out before diagnosing delusional disorder. For example, abuse of amphetamines, alcohol, and cocaine can cause delusions, as can brain tumors, Huntington's disease, and Alzheimer's disease (Fennig, Fochtmann, & Bromet, 2005).

■ Brief Psychotic Disorder

Recall the puzzling case of Arthur, who suddenly experienced the delusion that he could save the world and whose intense emotional swings lasted for only a few days. He would receive the DSM-IV-TR diagnosis of **brief psychotic disorder,** which is characterized by the presence of one or more positive symptoms such as delusions, hallucinations, or disorganized speech or behavior lasting 1 month or less. Individuals like Arthur regain their previous ability to function well in day-to-day activities. Brief psychotic disorder is often precipitated by extremely stressful situations.

■ Shared Psychotic Disorder (Folie à Deux)

Relatively little is known about **shared psychotic disorder (folie à deux),** the condition in which an individual develops delusions simply as a result of a close relationship with a delusional

DSM-IV-TR

DSM TABLE 13.9 Diagnostic Criteria for Brief Psychotic Disorder

A. Presence of one (or more) of the following symptoms:
   1. Delusions
   2. Hallucinations
   3. Disorganized speech (e.g., frequent derailment or incoherence)
   4. Grossly disorganized or catatonic behavior
Note: Do not include a symptom if it is a culturally sanctioned response pattern.

B. Duration of an episode of the disturbance is at least 1 day but less than 1 month, with eventual full return to premorbid level of functioning.

C. The disturbance is not better accounted for by a mood disorder with psychotic features, schizoaffective disorder, or schizophrenia and is not due to the direct physiological effects of a substance (e.g., a drug of abuse, a medication) or a general medical condition.

Specify if:

With marked stressor(s) (brief reactive psychosis): If symptoms occur shortly after and apparently in response to events that, singly or together, would be markedly stressful to almost anyone in similar circumstances in the person's culture

Without marked stressor(s): If psychotic symptoms do *not* occur shortly after, or are not apparently in response to events that, singly or together, would be markedly stressful to almost anyone in similar circumstances in the person's culture

With postpartum onset: If onset within 4 weeks postpartum

Source: Reprinted, with permission, from American Psychiatric Association. (2000). *Diagnostic and statistical manual of mental disorders* (4th ed., text revision). Washington, DC: Author, © 2000 American Psychiatric Association.

individual. The content and nature of the delusion originate with the partner and can range from the relatively bizarre, such as believing enemies are sending harmful gamma rays through your house, to the fairly ordinary, such as believing you are about to receive a major promotion despite evidence to the contrary. About 50% of the dyads involve mother–daughter or sister–sister pairs, and some level of cognitive impairment in the secondary member is common (Reif & Pfuhlmann, 2004).

Schizotypal personality disorder, discussed in Chapter 12, is a related psychotic disorder. As you may recall, the charac-

DSM-IV-TR

DSM TABLE 13.10 Diagnostic Criteria for Shared Psychotic Disorder

A. A delusion develops in an individual in the context of a close relationship with another person(s), who has an already-established delusion.

B. The delusion is similar in content to that of the person who already has the established delusion.

C. The disturbance is not better accounted for by another psychotic disorder (e.g., schizophrenia) or a mood disorder with psychotic features and is not due to the direct physiological effects of a substance (e.g., a drug of abuse, a medication) or a general medical condition.

Source: Reprinted, with permission, from American Psychiatric Association. (2000). *Diagnostic and statistical manual of mental disorders* (4th ed., text revision). Washington, DC: Author, © 2000 American Psychiatric Association.

teristics are similar to those experienced by people with schizophrenia but are less severe. Some evidence also suggests that schizophrenia and schizotypal personality disorder may be genetically related as part of a "schizophrenia spectrum."

Remember that although people with related psychotic disorders display many of the characteristics of schizophrenia, these disorders differ significantly.

CONCEPT CHECK 13.1

Part A

Determine which subtype of schizophrenia is described in each scenario.

1. Gary often has delusions and hallucinations that convince him enemies are out to persecute him. _____

2. Sally displays motor immobility, and she often repeats words said by others around her. _____

3. Carrie had an episode of schizophrenia in the past, but she no longer displays the major symptoms of the disorder. She does, however, still have some negative, unusual ideas and displays flat affect on occasion. _____

4. Tim suffers from a type of schizophrenia that is identified by disruption and incoherence in his speech and behavior. He also shows inappropriate affect, often laughing in sad or upsetting situations. _____

5. You sit down next to a gentleman who suddenly giggles. When you ask what he's laughing at, he answers, but you can't make sense of what he says. _____

Part B

Diagnose the type of psychotic disorders described in each of the following. Choose from (a) schizophreniform disorder, (b) schizoaffective disorder, (c) delusional disorder, and (d) shared psychotic disorder.

6. Carol reveals to her therapist that she hears numerous voices talking to her and giving her orders. For the past month or so, these voices have been commenting on her everyday behavior. Her doctor has just sent her to this therapist for what he believes to be a major depressive episode. She had begun to sleep all the time and contemplated suicide often. _____

7. Scott believes his wife is unfaithful and has been this way for years. He has absolutely no proof. A private investigator was hired, and he claimed Scott's wife is loving and devoted. Scott disregarded this and considered the possibility that the investigator was one of his wife's lovers. _____

8. Sarah believes the government is out to get her. She thinks agents follow her daily, monitor her calls, and read her mail. Her roommate Courtney tried to convince her otherwise. However, after a year of this, Courtney began

(continued)

(continued)

to believe Sarah was correct and the government was out to get her, too. _____

9. If Brooke's schizophrenic symptoms disappeared after about 4 months and she returned to her normal life, what diagnosis might she have received? _____

PREVALENCE AND CAUSES OF SCHIZOPHRENIA

Studying schizophrenia reveals the many levels on which we must decipher what makes us behave the way we do. To uncover the causes of this disorder, researchers look in several areas: (1) the possible genes involved in schizophrenia, (2) the chemical action of the drugs that help many people with this disorder, and (3) abnormalities in the working of the brains of people with schizophrenia (Sawa & Snyder, 2002). As we survey the work of many specialists, we examine many state-of-the-art techniques for studying both biological and psychosocial influences, a process that may be slow going at times but will bring new insight to your understanding of psychopathology. We now examine the nature of schizophrenia and learn how researchers have attempted to understand and treat people who have it.

Statistics

Schizophrenia sometimes defies our desire for simplicity. We have seen how different symptoms can be displayed by individuals who would all be considered to have the disorder; in some people they develop slowly, and in others they occur suddenly. Schizophrenia is generally chronic, and most people with the disorder have a difficult time functioning in society. This is especially true of their ability to relate to others; they tend not to establish or maintain significant relationships, so many people with schizophrenia never marry or have children. Unlike the delusions of people with other psychotic disorders, the delusions of people with schizophrenia are likely to be outside the realm of possibility. Finally, even when individuals with schizophrenia improve with treatment, they are likely to experience difficulties throughout their lives.

Worldwide, the lifetime prevalence rate of schizophrenia is roughly equivalent for men and women, and it is estimated to be 0.2% to 1.5% in the general population (Buchanan & Carpenter, 2005), which means the disorder will affect around 1% of the population at some point. Life expectancy is slightly less than average, partly because of the higher rate of suicide and accidents among people with schizophrenia. Although there is some disagreement about the distribution of schizophrenia between men and women, the difference between the sexes in age of onset is clear. For men, the likelihood of onset diminishes with age, but it can still first occur after the age of 75. The onset for women is lower than for men until age 36, when the relative risk for onset switches, with more women than men being affected later in life (Murray & Bramon, 2005). Women appear to have more favorable outcomes than do men.

Development

The more severe symptoms of schizophrenia first occur in late adolescence or early adulthood, although we saw that there may be signs of the development of the disorder in early childhood (Murray & Bramon, 2005). Children who go on to develop schizophrenia show early clinical features such as mild physical abnormalities, poor motor coordination, and mild cognitive and social problems (Lieberman et al., 2001; Schiffman et al., 2004). Unfortunately, these types of early problems are not specific enough to schizophrenia—meaning they could also be signs of other problems, such as the pervasive developmental disorders we review in Chapter 14—to be able to say for sure that a particular child will later develop schizophrenia.

Up to 85% of people who later develop schizophrenia go through a *prodromal stage*—a 1- to 2-year period before the serious symptoms occur but when less severe yet unusual behaviors start to show themselves (Murray & Bramon, 2005; Yung, Phillips, Yuen, & McGorry, 2004). These behaviors (which you should recognize from Chapter 12 as symptoms seen in schizotypal personality disorders) include ideas of reference (thinking insignificant events relate directly to them), magical thinking (believing they have special abilities such as being clairvoyant or telepathic), and illusions (such as feeling the presence of another person when they are alone). In addition, other symptoms are common, such as increased anxiety or irritability, attentional problems, social withdrawal, and obsessive behaviors (Lieberman et al., 2001).

Once the symptoms of schizophrenia develop, it typically takes 1–2 years before the person is diagnosed and receives treatment (Woods et al., 2001). Part of this delay may be the result of hiding symptoms from others (sometimes because of increasing paranoia). Once treated, patients with this disorder will often improve. Unfortunately, most will also go through a pattern of relapse and recovery (Murray & Bramon, 2005). This relapse rate is important when discussing the course of schizophrenia. For example, the data from one study show the course of schizophrenia among four prototypical groups (Zubin, Steinhauer, & Condray, 1992). About 22% of the group had one episode of schizophrenia and improved without lasting impairment. However, the remaining 78% experienced several episodes, with differing degrees of impairment between them. People with schizophrenia have a poorer prognosis than those with most of the other disorders we describe in this book—including a high risk of successful suicide—although a significant number of individuals can experience long periods of recovery (Jobe & Harrow, 2005). Relapses are an important subject in the field of schizophrenia; we return to this phenomenon when we discuss causes and treatment. To illustrate this complex developmental picture, ■ Figure 13.2 graphically depicts the developmental course of schizophrenia. Life stages (from before birth to the end of life) are listed across the top of the graph, with the colored regions showing periods of decline and recovery.

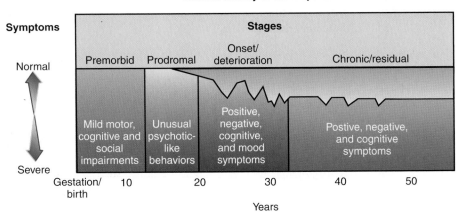

FIGURE 13.2 The longitudinal course of schizophrenia is depicted starting at birth through old age. The severity of the symptoms is shown on the left axis, and the changes in symptoms across each phase (premorbid, prodromal, onset, and chronic) are labeled. (Adapted from Lieberman, J. A., Perkins, D., Belger, A., Chakos, M., Jarskog, F., Boteva, K., & Gilmore, J., 2001. The early stages of schizophrenia: Speculations on pathogenesis, pathophysiology, and therapeutic approaches. *Biological Psychiatry, 50,* p. 885).

Cultural Factors

Because schizophrenia is so complex, the diagnosis itself can be controversial. Some have argued that "schizophrenia" does not really exist but is a derogatory label for people who behave in ways outside the cultural norm (see, for example, Laing, 1967; Sarbin & Mancuso, 1980; Szasz, 1961). This concern takes us back to our discussions in the first chapter about the difficulty of defining what is abnormal. Although the idea that schizophrenia exists only in the minds of mental health professionals is certainly provocative, this extreme view is contradicted by experience. We have both had a great deal of contact with people who have this disorder and with their families and friends, and the tremendous amount of emotional pain resulting from schizophrenia gives definite credence to its existence. In an interesting historical note, Kraepelin, who we described as developing the modern-day view of schizophrenia, traveled to Asia at the turn of the last century to confirm that this unusual set of behaviors was experienced by cultures other than those of Western Europe (Lauriello, Bustillo, & Keith, 2005). We now know that people in extremely diverse cultures have the symptoms of schizophrenia, which supports the notion that it is a reality for many people worldwide. Schizophrenia is thus universal, affecting all racial and cultural groups studied so far.

However, the course and outcome of schizophrenia vary from culture to culture. For example, in Colombia, India, and Nigeria, more people improve significantly or recover than in other countries (Draguns & Tanaka-Matsumi, 2003). These differences may be the result of cultural variations or prevalent biological influences such as immunization, but we cannot yet explain these differences in outcomes.

In the United States, proportionately more African Americans receive the diagnosis of schizophrenia than Caucasians (Lindsey & Paul, 1989). Research from both England and the United States suggests that people from devalued ethnic minority groups (Afro-Caribbean in England and African Americans and Puerto Ricans in the United States) may be victims of bias and stereotyping (Jones & Gray, 1986; Lewis, Croft-Jeffreys, & Anthony, 1990); in other words, they may be more likely to receive a diagnosis of schizophrenia than members of a dominant group. One prospective study of schizophrenia among different ethnic groups in London found that although the outcomes of schizophrenia appear similar across these groups, blacks were more likely to be detained against their will, brought to the hospital by police, and given emergency injections (Goater et al., 1999). The differing rates of schizophrenia, therefore, may be the result of *misdiagnosis* rather than any real cultural distinctions. However, an additional factor contributing to this imbalance is being revealed in our advancing knowledge of genetics. There may be genetic variants unique to certain racial groups that contribute to the development of schizophrenia (Glatt, Tampilic, Christie, DeYoung, & Freimer, 2004), a factor we explore in detail next.

Genetic Influences

We could argue that no other area of abnormal psychology so clearly illustrates the enormous complexity and intriguing mystery of genetic influences on behavior as does the phenomenon of schizophrenia (Braff, Schork, & Gottesman, 2007). Despite the possibility that schizophrenia may be several different disorders, we can safely make one generalization: *Genes are responsible for making some individuals vulnerable to schizophrenia.* We look at a range of research findings from family, twin, adoptee, offspring of twins, and linkage and association studies. We conclude by discussing the compelling reasons that no one gene is responsible for schizophrenia; rather, multiple genes combine to produce vulnerability. For a more detailed but highly readable discussion of this research, refer to *Schizophrenia Genesis: The Origins of Madness* by Irving Gottesman (1991).

Family Studies

In 1938, Franz Kallmann published a major study of the families of people with schizophrenia (Kallmann, 1938). Kallmann examined family members of more than 1,000 people diagnosed with schizophrenia in a Berlin psychiatric hospital. Several of his observations continue to guide research on schizophrenia. Kallmann

Irving Gottesman, a psychologist at the University of Virginia, has contributed significantly to our understanding of schizophrenia.

showed that the severity of the parent's disorder influenced the likelihood of the child's having schizophrenia: The more severe the parent's schizophrenia, the more likely the children were to develop it. Another observation was important: All forms of schizophrenia (for example, catatonic and paranoid) were seen within the families. In other words, it does not appear that you inherit a predisposition for, say, paranoid schizophrenia. Instead, you may inherit a general predisposition for schizophrenia that manifests in the same form or differently from that of your parent. More recent research confirms this observation and suggests that families that have a member with schizophrenia are at risk not just for schizophrenia alone or for all psychological disorders; instead, there appears to be some familial risk for a spectrum of psychotic disorders related to schizophrenia.

Gottesman (1991) summarized the data from about 40 studies of schizophrenia, as shown in ■ Figure 13.3. The most striking feature of this graph is its orderly demonstration that the risk of having schizophrenia varies according to how many genes an individual shares with someone who has the disorder. For example, you have the greatest

The Genain quadruplets all had schizophrenia but exhibited different symptoms over the years.

Dr. Allan F. Mirsky/National Institute of Mental Health

chance (approximately 48%) of having schizophrenia if it has affected your identical (monozygotic) twin, a person who shares 100% of your genetic information. Your risk drops to about 17% with a fraternal (dizygotic) twin, who shares about 50% of your genetic information. And having any relative with schizophrenia makes you more likely to have the disorder than someone without such a relative (about 1%). Because family studies can't separate genetic influence from the impact of the environment, we use twin and adoption studies to help us evaluate the role of shared experiences in the cause of schizophrenia.

■ **Twin Studies**

If they are raised together, identical twins share 100% of their genes and 100% of their environment, whereas fraternal twins share only about 50% of their genes and 100% of their environment. If the environment is solely responsible for schizophrenia, we would expect little difference between identical and fraternal twins with regard to this disorder. If only genetic factors are relevant, both identical twins would always have schizophrenia (be concordant) and the fraternal twins would both have it about 50% of the time. Research from twin studies indicates that the truth is somewhere in the middle (Braff et al., 2007).

In one of the most fascinating of "nature's experiments," identical quadruplets, all of whom have schizophrenia, have been studied extensively. Nicknamed the "Genain" quadruplets (from the Greek, meaning "dreadful gene"), these women have been followed by David Rosenthal and his colleagues at the National Institute of Mental Health for a number of years (Rosenthal, 1963). The fictitious names of the girls reported in studies of their lives—Nora, Iris, Myra, and Hester—represent the letters NIMH for the National Institute of Mental Health. In a sense, the women represent the complex interaction between genetics and environment. All four shared the same genetic predisposition, and all were brought up in the same particularly dysfunctional household; yet the time of onset for schizophrenia, the symptoms and diagnoses,

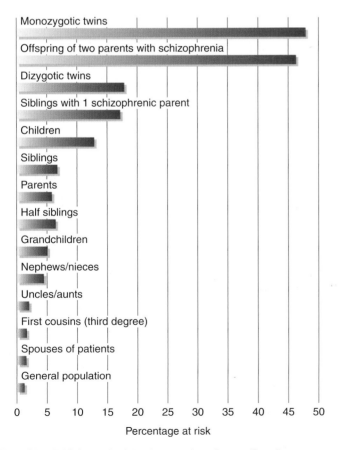

Monozygotic twins

Offspring of two parents with schizophrenia

Dizygotic twins

Siblings with 1 schizophrenic parent

Children

Siblings

Parents

Half siblings

Grandchildren

Nephews/nieces

Uncles/aunts

First cousins (third degree)

Spouses of patients

General population

0 5 10 15 20 25 30 35 40 45 50

Percentage at risk

■ **FIGURE 13.3** Risk of developing schizophrenia. (Based on Gottesman, I. I., 1991, *Schizophrenia genesis: The origins of madness.* New York: W. H. Freeman.)

the course of the disorder, and, ultimately, their outcomes, differed significantly from sister to sister.

The case of the Genain quadruplets reveals an important consideration in studying genetic influences on behavior—*unshared environments* (Plomin, 1990). We tend to think that siblings, and especially identical multiples, are brought up the same way. The impression is that "good" parents expose their children to favorable environments and "bad" parents give them unstable experiences. However, even identical siblings can have different prenatal and family experiences and therefore be exposed to varying degrees of biological and environmental stress. For example, Hester, one of the Genain sisters, was described by her disturbed parents as a habitual masturbator, and she had more social problems than her sisters as she grew up. Hester was the first to experience severe symptoms of schizophrenia, at age 18, but her sister Myra was not hospitalized until 6 years later. This unusual case demonstrates that even siblings who are close in every aspect of their lives can still have considerably different experiences physically and socially as they grow up, which may result in vastly different outcomes. A follow-up on the lives of these women showed the progression of their disorder stabilized and in some cases improved when they were assessed at age 66 (Mirsky et al., 2000).

Adoption Studies

Several adoption studies have distinguished the roles of the environment and genetics as they affect schizophrenia. These studies often span many years; because people often do not show the first signs of schizophrenia until middle age, researchers need to be sure all the offspring reach that point before drawing conclusions. Many schizophrenia studies are conducted in Europe, primarily because of the extensive and comprehensive records kept in countries where socialized medicine is practiced.

The largest adoption study is currently being conducted in Finland (Tienari, 1991). From a sample of almost 20,000 women with schizophrenia, the researchers found 190 children who had been given up for adoption. The data from this study support the idea that schizophrenia represents a spectrum of related disorders, all of which overlap genetically. If an adopted child had a biological mother with schizophrenia, that child had about a 5% chance of having the disorder (compared to about only 1% in the general population). However, if the biological mother had schizophrenia or one of the related psychotic disorders (for example, delusional disorder or schizophreniform disorder), the risk that the adopted child would have one of these disorders rose to about 22% (Tienari et al., 2003; Tienari, Wahlberg, & Wynne, 2006). Even when raised away from their biological parents, children of parents with schizophrenia have a much higher chance of having the disorder themselves. Something other than living in the home of a person with schizophrenia must account for this disorder.

The Offspring of Twins

Twin and adoption studies strongly suggest a genetic component for schizophrenia, but what about children who develop schizophrenia even though their parents do not? For example, the study by Tienari and colleagues (2003, 2006) we just discussed found that 1.7% of the children with nonschizophrenic parents developed schizophrenia. Does this mean you can develop schizophrenia without "schizophrenic genes"? Or are some people carriers, having the genes for schizophrenia but for some reason not showing the disorder themselves? An important clue to this question comes from research on the children of twins with schizophrenia.

In a study begun in 1971 by Margit Fischer and later continued by Irving Gottesman and Aksel Bertelsen, 21 identical twin pairs and 41 fraternal twin pairs with a history of schizophrenia were identified, along with their children (Fischer, 1971; Gottesman & Bertelsen, 1989). The researchers wanted to determine the relative likelihood that a child would have schizophrenia if her parent did and if the parent's twin had schizophrenia but the parent did not. ■ Figure 13.4 illustrates the findings from this study. For example, if your parent is an identical (monozygotic) twin with schizophrenia, you have about a 17% chance of having the disorder yourself, a figure that holds if you are the child of an unaffected identical twin whose co-twin has the disorder.

On the other hand, look at the risks for the child of a fraternal (dizygotic) twin. If your parent is the twin with schizophrenia, you have about a 17% chance of having schizophrenia yourself. However, if your parent does not have schizophrenia but your parent's fraternal twin does, your risk is only about 2%. The only way to explain this finding is through genetics. The data clearly indicate that you can have genes that predispose you to schizophrenia, not show the disorder yourself, but still pass on the genes to your children. In other words, you can be a "carrier" for schizophrenia. This is some of the strongest evidence yet that people are genetically vulnerable to schizophrenia. Remember, however, there is only a 17% chance of inheritance, meaning that other factors help determine who will have this disorder.

Linkage and Association Studies

Recall from Chapter 4 that genetic linkage and association studies rely on traits such as blood types (whose exact location on the chromosome is already known) inherited in families with the disorder you are looking for—in this case, schizophrenia. Because we know the location of the genes for these traits (called *marker*

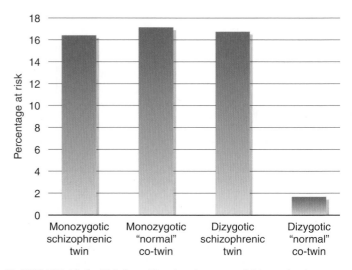

■ **FIGURE 13.4** Risk for schizophrenia among children of twins.

genes), we can make a rough guess about the location of the disorder genes inherited with them. To date, researchers have looked at several sites for genes that may be responsible for schizophrenia. For example, regions of chromosomes 1, 2, 3, 5, 6, 8, 11, 14, 20, and 22 are implicated in this disorder (Sullivan, Owen, O'Donovan, & Freedman, 2006).

Endophenotypes Genetic research on schizophrenia is evolving, and the information on the findings from these sophisticated studies is now being combined with advances in understanding the specific deficits found in people with this disorder. Remember, in complex disorders such as this, we are not looking for a "schizophrenia gene" or genes. Instead, we try to find basic processes that contribute to the behaviors or symptoms of the disorder and then find the gene or genes that cause these difficulties—a strategy called *endophenotyping* (Braff et al., 2007).

Several potential candidates for endophenotypes for schizophrenia have been studied over the years. One of the more highly researched is called *smooth-pursuit eye movement*, or eye-tracking. Keeping your head still, you must be able to track a moving pendulum, back and forth, with your eyes. The ability to track objects smoothly across the visual field is deficient in many people who also have schizophrenia (Clementz & Sweeney, 1990; Holzman & Levy, 1977; Iacono, Bassett, & Jones, 1988); it does not appear to be the result of drug treatment or institutionalization (Lieberman et al., 1993). It also seems to be a problem for relatives of these people (Lenzenweger, McLachlan, & Rubin, 2007). ■ Figure 13.5 shows the decreasing likelihood of observing this abnormal eye-tracking ability the further a person is genetically from someone with schizophrenia. When all these observations are combined, they suggest an eye-tracking deficit may be an endophenotype for schizophrenia that could be used in further study.

Other such research is looking at the social, cognitive, and emotional deficits characteristic of schizophrenia. One study, for example, looked at multiple generations of families who had someone with schizophrenia (Gur et al., 2007). They tested them on a variety of skills for identified cognitive deficits in areas we described previously—such as emotion identification—and showed that specific problems were inherited in the same manner as schizophrenia. Combining genetic research—in this case, a large family study—with neurocognitive assessment may bring us closer to understanding just what is inherited in this disorder (Braff et al., 2007).

Neurobiological Influences

A parent of someone with schizophrenia wrote the following statement:

> Many of us who have a son, daughter, or other relative with schizophrenia have observed so great a change in the person's behavior with the onset of the psychosis that we know intuitively that the cause had to be something basic, such as an alteration of the brain's functioning. (Johnson, 1989, p. 553)

The belief that schizophrenia involves a malfunctioning brain goes back as far as the writings of Kraepelin (1856–1926). It is therefore not surprising that a great deal of research has focused on the brain.

■ Dopamine

One of the most enduring yet controversial theories of the cause of schizophrenia involves the neurotransmitter *dopamine* (Javitt & Laruelle, 2006). Before we consider the research, however, let's review briefly how neurotransmitters operate in the brain and how they are affected by neuroleptic medications, which reduce hallucinations and delusions. In Chapter 2, we discussed the sensitivity of specific neurons to specific neurotransmitters and described how they cluster throughout the brain. The top of ■ Figure 13.6 shows two neurons and the important synaptic gap that separates them. Neurotransmitters are released from the storage vessels (synaptic vesicles) at the end of the axon, cross the gap, and are taken up by receptors in the dendrite of the next axon. Chemical "messages" are transported in this way from neuron to neuron throughout the brain.

This process can be influenced in a number of ways, and the rest of Figure 13.6 illustrates some of them. The chemical messages can be increased by agonistic agents or decreased by antagonistic agents. (Remember the word *antagonistic* means hostile or unfriendly; in some way, this is the effect of antagonistic agents on the chemical messenger service.) Antagonistic effects slow or stop messages from being transmitted by preventing the release of the neurotransmitter, blocking uptake at the level of the dendrite, or causing leaks that reduce the amount of neurotransmitter released. On the other hand, agonistic effects assist with the transference of chemical messages and, if extreme, can produce too much neurotransmitter activity by increasing production or release of the

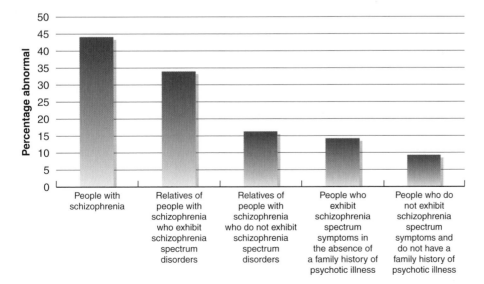

■ **FIGURE 13.5** Abnormal smooth-pursuit eye movements and schizophrenia. (Adapted, with permission, from Thaker, G. K., & Avila, M., 2003. Schizophrenia, V: Risk markers. *American Journal of Psychiatry, 160,* 1578, © 2003 American Psychiatric Association.)

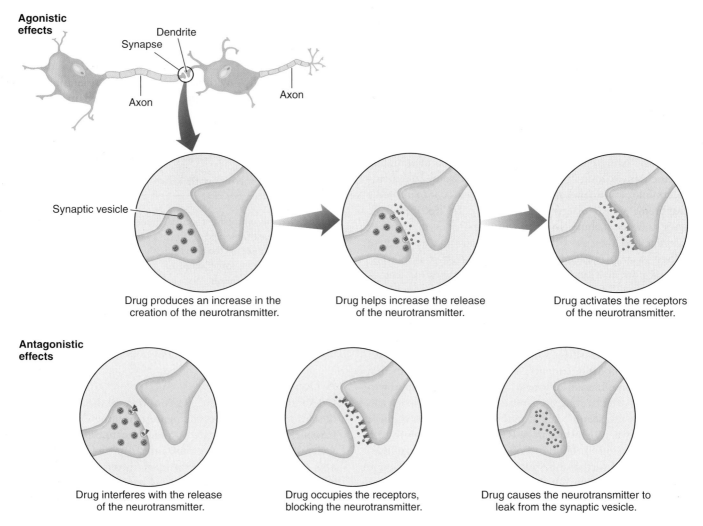

Agonistic effects

Dendrite
Synapse
Axon
Axon

Synaptic vesicle

Drug produces an increase in the creation of the neurotransmitter.

Drug helps increase the release of the neurotransmitter.

Drug activates the receptors of the neurotransmitter.

Antagonistic effects

Drug interferes with the release of the neurotransmitter.

Drug occupies the receptors, blocking the neurotransmitter.

Drug causes the neurotransmitter to leak from the synaptic vesicle.

■ **FIGURE 13.6** Some ways drugs affect neurotransmission.

neurotransmitter and by affecting more receptors at the dendrites.

What we've learned about antipsychotic medications points to the possibility that the dopamine system is too active in people with schizophrenia. The simplified picture in Figure 13.6 does not show that there are different receptor sites and that a chemical such as dopamine produces different results depending on which of those sites it affects. In schizophrenia, attention has focused on several dopamine sites, in particular those referred to simply as D_1 and D_2.

In a story that resembles a mystery plot, several pieces of "circumstantial evidence" are clues to the role of dopamine in schizophrenia:

1. Antipsychotic drugs (neuroleptics) often effective in treating people with schizophrenia are dopamine antagonists, partially blocking the brain's use of dopamine (Creese, Burt, & Snyder, 1976; Seeman, Lee, Chau Wong, & Wong, 1976).
2. These drugs can produce negative side effects similar to those in Parkinson's disease, a disorder known to be caused by insufficient dopamine.
3. The drug L-dopa, a dopamine agonist used to treat people with Parkinson's disease, produces schizophrenia-like symptoms in some people (Davidson et al., 1987).

4. Amphetamines, which also activate dopamine, can make psychotic symptoms worse in some people with schizophrenia (van Kammen, Docherty, & Bunney, 1982).

In other words, when drugs are administered that are known to increase dopamine (agonists), there is an increase in schizophrenic behavior; when drugs that are known to decrease dopamine activity (antagonists) are used, schizophrenic symptoms tend to diminish. Taking these observations together, researchers theorized that schizophrenia in some people was attributable to excessive dopamine activity.

Despite these observations, some evidence contradicts the dopamine theory (Javitt & Laruelle, 2006):

1. A significant number of people with schizophrenia are not helped by the use of dopamine antagonists.
2. Although the neuroleptics block the reception of dopamine quite quickly, the relevant symptoms subside only after several days or weeks, more slowly than we would expect.
3. These drugs are only partly helpful in reducing the negative symptoms (for example, flat affect or anhedonia) of schizophrenia.

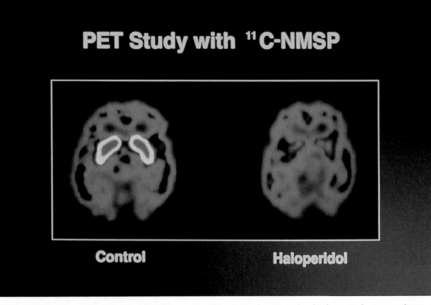

These PET images show the brain of a man with schizophrenia who had never been medicated (left) and after he received haloperidol (right). The red and yellow areas indicate activity in the D_2 receptors; haloperidol evidently reduced dopamine activity.

In addition to these concerns, there is evidence of a "double-edged sword" with respect to schizophrenia. A medication called *olanzapine*—along with a family of similar drugs—is effective with many people who were not helped with traditional neuroleptic medications (Wahlbeck, Cheine, Essali, & Adams, 1999). That's the good news. The bad news for the dopamine theory is that olanzapine and these other new medications are weak dopamine antagonists, much less able to block the sites than other drugs (Javitt & Laruelle, 2006). Why would a medication inefficient at blocking dopamine be as effective as a treatment for schizophrenia if schizophrenia is caused by excessive dopamine activity?

The answer may be that although dopamine is involved in the symptoms of schizophrenia, the relationship is more complicated than we once thought (Javitt & Laruelle, 2006). Current thinking—based on growing evidence from highly sophisticated research techniques—points to *at least three specific neurochemical abnormalities* simultaneously at play in the brains of people with schizophrenia.

Strong evidence now leads us to believe that schizophrenia is partially the result of excessive stimulation of striatal dopamine D_2 receptors (Javitt & Laruelle, 2006). Recall that the striatum is part of the basal ganglia found deep within the brain. These cells control movement, balance, and walking, and they rely on dopamine to function. Current work on Huntington's disease (which involves a deterioration of motor function) is pointing to deterioration in this area of the brain. How do we know that excessive stimulation of D_2 receptors is involved in schizophrenia? One clue is that the most effective antipsychotic drugs all share dopamine D_2 receptor antagonism—meaning they help block the stimulation of the D_2 receptors. Using brain-imaging techniques such as SPECT, scientists can view the living brain of a person with schizophrenia and can observe how the newer, "second-generation" antipsychotic medications work on these specific dopamine sites.

A second area of interest to scientists investigating the cause of schizophrenia is the observation of a deficiency in the stimulation of prefrontal dopamine D_1 receptors (Javitt & Laruelle, 2006). Therefore, while some dopamine sites may be overactive (for example, striatal D_2), a second type of dopamine site in the part of the brain that we use for thinking and reasoning (prefrontal D_1 receptors) appears to be less active and may account for other symptoms common in schizophrenia. As you will see later in this chapter, people with schizophrenia display a range of deficits in the prefrontal section of the brain, and this area may be less active in people with schizophrenia (a condition known as *hypofrontality*, discussed later).

Finally, a third and more recent area of neurochemical interest involves research on alterations in prefrontal activity involving glutamate transmission (Javitt & Laruelle, 2006). Glutamate is an excitatory neurotransmitter that is found in all areas of the brain and is only now being studied in earnest. Just as we saw with dopamine (for example, D_1 and D_2 receptors), glutamate has different types of receptors, and the ones being studied for their role in schizophrenia are the N-methyl-d-aspartate (NMDA) receptors. And, just as researchers were led to the study of dopamine by observations from the effects of dopamine-specific drugs on behavior, the effects of certain drugs that affect NMDA receptors point to clues to schizophrenia. Two recreational drugs described in Chapter 11—phencyclidine (PCP) and ketamine—can result in psychotic-like behavior in people without schizophrenia and can exacerbate psychotic symptoms in those with schizophrenia. Both PCP and ketamine are also NMDA antagonists, suggesting that a deficit in glutamate or blocking of NMDA sites may be involved in some symptoms of schizophrenia (Goff & Coyle, 2001).

You can see that research on these two neurotransmitters and their relationship to each other is complex and awaits further clarification. However, advances in technology are leading us closer to the clues behind this enigmatic disorder and closer still to better treatments.

■ Brain Structure

Evidence for neurological damage in people with schizophrenia comes from a number of observations. A child with a parent who has the disorder, and who is thus at risk, tends to show subtle but observable neurological problems, such as abnormal reflexes and inattentiveness (Fish, 1977; Hans & Marcus, 1991). These difficulties are persistent: Adults who have schizophrenia show deficits in their ability to perform certain tasks and to attend during reaction time exercises (Cleghorn & Albert, 1990). Such findings suggest that brain damage or dysfunction may cause or accompany schizophrenia, although no one site is probably responsible for the whole range of symptoms (Belger & Dichter, 2006).

One of the most reliable observations about the brain in people with schizophrenia involves the size of the ventricles (see

Figure 13.7). As early as 1927, these liquid-filled cavities showed enlargement in some brains examined in people with schizophrenia (Jacobi & Winkler, 1927). Since then, more sophisticated techniques have been developed for observing the brain, and in the dozens of studies conducted on ventricle size, the great majority show abnormally large lateral ventricles in people with schizophrenia (Belger & Dichter, 2006). Ventricle size may not be a problem, but the dilation (enlargement) of the ventricles indicates that adjacent parts of the brain either have not developed fully or have atrophied, thus allowing the ventricles to become larger.

Ventricle enlargement is not seen in everyone who has schizophrenia. Several factors seem to be associated with this finding. For example, enlarged ventricles are observed more often in men than in women (Goldstein & Lewine, 2000). Also, ventricles seem to enlarge in proportion to age and to the duration of the schizophrenia. One study found that individuals with schizophrenia who were exposed to influenza prenatally may be more likely to have enlarged ventricles (Takei, Lewis, Jones, Harvey, & Murray, 1996). (We describe the possible role of prenatal exposure to influenza and schizophrenia in the next section.)

In a study of ventricle size, researchers investigated the possible role of genetics (Staal et al., 2000). Using a brain-imaging technique, magnetic resonance imaging, investigators compared brain structure among people with schizophrenia, their same-sex siblings who did not have schizophrenia, and healthy volunteers. Both the people with schizophrenia and their otherwise unaffected siblings had enlargement of the third ventricle compared to the volunteers. This suggests that the enlargement of ventricles may be related to susceptibility to schizophrenia.

We touched on the concept of unshared environments in the section on genetics (Jang, 2005; Plomin, 1990). Although twins are identical genetically, they can experience a number of environmental differences, even before they are born. For instance, in the

intrauterine environment, twins must compete for nutrients, and they may not be equally successful. In addition, birth complications, such as the loss of oxygen (anoxia), could affect only one of the twins (Jang, 2005). Obstetrical complications appear often among twins with schizophrenia in discordant identical pairs and among the more severely affected if both twins have schizophrenia (McNeil, 1987). Different experiences among twins already predisposed to the disorder could damage the brain and cause the types of symptoms we associate with schizophrenia.

The frontal lobes of the brain have also interested people looking for structural problems associated with schizophrenia (Belger & Dichter, 2006). As we described in the section on neurotransmitters, this area may be less active in people with schizophrenia than in people without the disorder, a phenomenon sometimes known as *hypofrontality* (*hypo* means "less active," or "deficient"). Research by Weinberger and other scientists at the National Institute of Mental Health further refined this observation, suggesting that deficient activity in a particular area of the frontal lobes, the dorsolateral prefrontal cortex (DLPFC), may be implicated in schizophrenia (Berman & Weinberger, 1990; Weinberger, Berman, & Chase, 1988). When people with and without schizophrenia are given tasks that involve the DLPFC, less activity (measured by cerebral blood flow) is recorded in the brains of those with schizophrenia. Follow-up studies show that some individuals with schizophrenia show *hyperfrontality* (that is, too much activity), indicating that the dysfunction is reliable, but hyperfrontality displays itself differently in different people (Callicott et al., 2003; Garrity et al., 2007).

It appears that several brain sites are implicated in the cognitive dysfunction observed among people with schizophrenia, especially the prefrontal cortex, various related cortical regions, and subcortical circuits, including the thalamus and the stratum (Belger & Dichter, 2006). Remember that this dysfunction seems to occur *before the onset* of schizophrenia. In other words, brain damage may develop progressively, beginning before the symptoms of the disorder are apparent, perhaps prenatally.

■ Prenatal and Perinatal Influences

There is a great deal of evidence that the prenatal (before birth) and perinatal (around the time of birth) environment are correlated with the development of schizophrenia (Gilmore & Murray, 2006). Fetal exposure to viral infection, pregnancy complications, and delivery complications are among the environmental influences that seem to affect whether or not someone develops schizophrenia.

Several studies have shown that schizophrenia may be associated with prenatal exposure to influenza. For example, Sarnoff Mednick and colleagues followed a large number of people after a severe Type A2 influenza epidemic in Helsinki, Finland, and found that those whose mothers were exposed to influenza during the second trimester of pregnancy were more likely to have schizophrenia than others (Cannon, Barr, & Mednick, 1991). This observation has been confirmed by some researchers (see, for example, O'Callaghan, Sham, Takei, Glover, & Murray, 1991; Venables, 1996) but not by others (Buchanan & Carpenter, 2005). The indications that virus-like diseases may cause damage to the fetal brain, which later may cause the symptoms of schizophrenia,

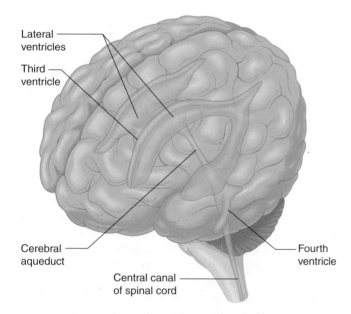

Lateral ventricles

Third ventricle

Cerebral aqueduct

Central canal of spinal cord

Fourth ventricle

■ FIGURE 13.7 Location of the cerebrospinal fluid in the human brain. This extracellular fluid surrounds and cushions the brain and spinal cord. It also fills the four interconnected cavities (cerebral ventricles) within the brain and the central canal of the spinal cord.

are suggestive and may help explain why some people with schizophrenia behave the way they do (Gilmore & Murray, 2006).

The evidence of pregnancy complications (for example, bleeding) and delivery complications (for example, asphyxia or lack of oxygen) and their relationship to later schizophrenia on the surface suggest that this type of environmental stress may trigger the expression of the disorder (Gilmore & Murray, 2006). However, it is possible that the genes carried by the fetus that make it vulnerable to schizophrenia may themselves contribute to the birth complications (Buchanan & Carpenter, 2005).

Psychological and Social Influences

That one identical twin may develop schizophrenia and the other may not suggests that schizophrenia involves something in addition to genes. We know that early brain trauma, perhaps resulting from a second-trimester virus-like attack or obstetrical complications, may generate physical stress that contributes to schizophrenia. All these observations show clearly that schizophrenia does not fall neatly into a few simple causal packages. For instance, not all people with schizophrenia have enlarged ventricles, nor do they all have a hypofrontality or disrupted activity in their dopamine systems. The causal picture may be further complicated by psychological and social factors. We next look at research into psychosocial factors. Do emotional stressors or family interaction patterns *initiate* the symptoms of schizophrenia? If so, how might those factors cause people to relapse after a period of improvement?

■ Stress

It is important to learn how much and what kind of stress makes a person with a predisposition for schizophrenia develop the disorder. Think back to the two cases we presented at the beginning of this chapter. Did you notice any precipitating events? Arthur's father had died several years earlier, and Arthur was laid off from his job around the time his symptoms first appeared. David's uncle had died the same year he began acting strangely. Were these stressful events just coincidences, or did they contribute to the men's later problems?

Researchers have studied the effects of a variety of stressors on schizophrenia. Dohrenwend and Egri (1981), for instance, observed that otherwise healthy people who engage in combat during a war often display temporary symptoms that resemble those of schizophrenia. In a classic study, Brown and Birley (1968; Birley & Brown, 1970) examined people whose onset of schizophrenia could be dated within a week. These individuals had experienced a high number of stressful life events in the 3 weeks before they started showing signs of the disorder. In a large-scale study sponsored by the World Health Organization, researchers also looked at the role of life events in the onset of schizophrenia (Day et al., 1987). This cross-national study confirmed the findings of Brown and Birley across eight research centers.

The *retrospective* nature of such research creates problems. Each study relies on after-the-fact reports, collected after the person showed signs of schizophrenia. One always wonders whether such reports are biased in some way and therefore misleading. At the same time, there are strong individual differences in how people experience the same life events, and people with schizophrenia may experience events differently from the experiences of those without the disorder (Phillips, Francey, Edwards, & McMurray, 2007).

Do the symptoms of schizophrenia become worse as a result of stressful life experiences? This vulnerability–stress model of schizophrenia suggests that this is the case, and it may be helpful in predicting problems. One research study used a natural disaster—the 1994 Northridge, California, earthquake—to assess how people with schizophrenia would react to this stress when compared to those with bipolar disorder and healthy controls (Horan et al., 2007). Both patient groups reported more stress-related symptoms compared to the controls, however, the people with schizophrenia reported lower levels of self-esteem after the disaster and were more likely to engage in avoidance coping (not thinking about the problem or becoming resigned to difficulties) than the other two groups. Research on sociocultural stress, such as poverty, homelessness, and the stress of being in a new country (Cantor-Graae & Selten, 2005) extend the types of psychosocial stressors influential in schizophrenia beyond stressful life events. These types of studies point to the particular vulnerability of people with schizophrenia to stress and may help suggest useful treatments (such as cognitive-behavior therapy to cope more appropriately) (Phillips et al., 2007).

■ Families and Relapse

A great deal of research has studied how interactions within the family affect people who have schizophrenia. For example, the term **schizophrenogenic mother** was used for a time to describe a mother whose cold, dominant, and rejecting nature was thought to cause schizophrenia in her children (Fromm-Reichmann, 1948). In addition, the term **double bind communication** was used to portray a communication style that produced conflicting messages, which, in turn, caused schizophrenia to develop (Bateson, 1959). Here, the parent presumably communicates messages that have two conflicting meanings; for example, a mother responds coolly to her child's embrace but says, "Don't you love me anymore?" when the child withdraws. Although these theories are no longer supported, they have been—and in some cases continue to be—destructive, producing guilt in parents who are persuaded that their early mistakes caused devastating consequences.

Recent work has focused more on how family interactions contribute not to the onset of schizophrenia but to relapse after initial symptoms are observed. You will see that this research is similar to the work on vulnerability to stress in general that we just discussed. Research has focused on a particular emotional communication style known as **expressed emotion (EE).** This concept was formulated by George W. Brown and his colleagues in London. Following a sample of people who had been discharged from the hospital after an episode of schizophrenic symptoms, the researchers found that former patients who had limited contact with their relatives did better than the patients who spent longer periods with their families (Brown, 1959). Additional research results indicated that if the levels of criticism (disapproval), hostility (animosity), and emotional overinvolvement (intrusiveness) expressed by the families were high, patients tended to relapse (Brown, Monck, Carstairs, & Wing, 1962).

Other researchers have since found that ratings of high expressed emotion in a family are a good predictor of relapse among

Courtesy of Jill Hooley

Jill Hooley of Harvard University is a noted researcher of expressed emotion in families with schizophrenia.

people with chronic schizophrenia (Butzlaff & Hooley, 1998). If you have schizophrenia and live in a family with high expressed emotion, you are 3.7 times more likely to relapse than if you lived in a family with low expressed emotion (Kavanagh, 1992; Parker & Hadzi-Pavlovic, 1990). Here are examples of interviews that show how families of people with schizophrenia might communicate expressed emotion (Hooley, 1985, p. 134).

High Expressed Emotion

- I always say, "Why don't you pick up a book, do a crossword or something like that to keep your mind off it." That's even too much trouble.
- I've tried to jolly him out of it and pestered him into doing things. Maybe I've overdone it, I don't know.

Low Expressed Emotion

- I know it's better for her to be on her own, to get away from me and try to do things on her own.
- Whatever she does suits me.
- I just tend to let it go because I know that when she wants to speak she will speak.

This style suggests that families with high expressed emotion view the symptoms of schizophrenia as controllable and that the hostility arises when family members think that patients just do not want to help themselves (Hooley & Campbell, 2002; McNab, Haslam, & Burnett, 2007). The literature on expressed emotion is valuable to our understanding of why symptoms of schizophrenia recur and may show us how to treat people with this disorder and their families so that they do not experience further psychotic episodes.

An interesting issue that arises when studying family influences is whether what we see is unique to our culture or universal. Looking at expressed emotion across different cultures may help us learn whether it is a *cause* of schizophrenia. Remember that schizophrenia is observed to be about the same rate worldwide, with a prevalence of about 1% in the global population. If a factor like high expressed emotion in families is a causal agent, we should see the same rates in families across cultures; however, they differ, as you can see in ■ Figure 13.8. These data come from an analysis of the concept of expressed emotion in several studies from India, Mexico, United Kingdom, and the United States (Jenkins & Karno, 1992). The differences suggest there are cultural variations in how families react to someone with schizophrenia and their reactions do not cause the disorder (Weisman de Mamani, Kymalainen, Rosales, & Armesto, 2007). However, critical and hostile environments clearly provide additional stressors that can, in turn, lead to more relapses.

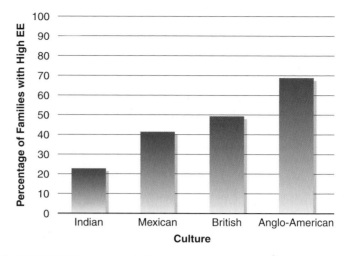

■ **FIGURE 13.8** Cultural differences in expressed emotion.

CONCEPT CHECK 13.2

Check your understanding of genetic vulnerability by filling in the blanks of the statements associated with family, twin, and adoption studies. Choose from (a) higher, (b) lower, (c) equal, (d) severity, (e) type, (f) identical twin, (g) specific, (h) fraternal twin, and (i) general.

1. The likelihood of a child's having schizophrenia is influenced by the _____ of the parent's disorder. One may inherit a predisposition for _____ schizophrenia that is the same or different from that of the parent.
2. The greatest risk of having schizophrenia is in those who have a(n) _____ or _____ with schizophrenia. Any relative with schizophrenia will make your chances of developing the disorder _____ than those of the general population.
3. Raised in a home other than that of their biological parents, adopted children of parents with schizophrenia have a(n) _____ chance of having the disorder themselves. Children of people with schizophrenia adopted into families without schizophrenia have a _____-than-average chance of having schizophrenia.

TREATMENT OF SCHIZOPHRENIA

If you remember our descriptions of Arthur and David, you will recall their families' concern for them. Arthur's mother spoke of the "living nightmare," and David's aunt expressed concern for both her safety and David's. In each case, the family was desperate to help, but what do you do for someone who has delusions, hears his dead uncle's voice, or can't communicate complete thoughts? The search for help has taken many paths, sometimes down some disturbing roads; for example, in the 1500s primitive surgery was conducted to remove the "stone of madness," which was thought to cause disturbed behavior. As barbaric as this practice may seem today, it is not different from the prefrontal lobotomies performed on people with schizophrenia as late as the 1950s. This procedure severed the frontal lobes from the lower portion of the brain, which sometimes calmed the patient but also caused cognitive and emotional deficits. Even today, some societies use crude surgical procedures to eliminate the symptoms of schizophrenia. In Kenya, for instance, Kisii tribal doctors listen to their patients to find the location of the noises in their heads (hallucinations), then get them drunk, cut out a piece of scalp, and scrape the skull in the area of the voices (Mustafa, 1990).

In the Western world today, treatment usually begins with one of the neuroleptic drugs invaluable in reducing the symptoms of schizophrenia for many people. They are typically used with a variety of psychosocial treatments to reduce relapse, compensate for skills deficits, and improve cooperation for taking the medications (American Psychiatric Association, 2004).

Biological Interventions

Researchers have assumed for more than 100 years that schizophrenia requires some form of biological intervention. Kraepelin, who so eloquently described dementia praecox in the late 19th century, saw the disorder as a brain disease. Lacking a biological treatment, he routinely recommended that the physician use "good patience, kindly disposition, and self-control" to calm excited patients (Nagel, 1991). This approach was seen as only a temporary way of helping the person through disturbing times and was not thought to be an actual treatment.

During the 1930s, several novel biological treatments were tried. One approach was to inject massive doses of insulin—the drug that given in smaller doses is used to treat diabetes—to induce comas in people suffering from schizophrenia. Insulin coma therapy was thought for a time to be helpful, but closer examination showed it carried great risk of serious illness and death. Dur-

ing this time, *psychosurgery,* including prefrontal lobotomies, was introduced, and in the late 1930s, electroconvulsive therapy (ECT) was advanced as a treatment for schizophrenia. As with earlier drastic treatments, initial enthusiasm for ECT faded because it was found not to be beneficial for most people with schizophrenia—although it is still used with a limited number of people today (Shimizu et al., 2007). As we explained in Chapter 7, ECT is sometimes recommended for people who experience severe episodes of depression.

■ Antipsychotic Medications

A breakthrough in the treatment of schizophrenia came during the 1950s with the introduction of several drugs that relieved symptoms in many people (Kane & Marder, 2005). Called *neuroleptics* (meaning "taking hold of the nerves"), these medications provided the first real hope that help was available for people with schizophrenia. When they are effective, neuroleptics help people think more clearly and reduce hallucinations and delusions. They work by affecting the positive symptoms (delusions, hallucinations, and agitation) and to a lesser extent the negative and disorganized ones, such as social deficits. Table 13.2 shows the classes of these drugs (based on their chemical structure) and their trade names.

Recall from our discussion of the dopamine theory of schizophrenia that the neuroleptics are dopamine antagonists. One of their major actions in the brain is to interfere with the

An early 16th-century painting of psychosurgery, in which part of the brain is removed to treat mental illness.

TABLE 13.2   Commonly Used Antipsychotic Medications

Class	Example*	Degree of Extrapyramidal Side Effects
Conventional Antipsychotics		
Phenothiazines	Chlorpromazine/*Thorazine*	Moderate
	Fluphenazine/*Prolixin*	High
	Mesoridazine/*Serentil*	Low
	Perphenazine/*Trilafon*	High
	Thioridazine/*Mellaril*	Low
	Trifluoperazine/*Stelazine*	High
Butyrophenone	Haloperidol/*Haldol*	High
Others	Loxapine/*Loxitane*	High
	Molindone/*Moban*	Low
	Thiothixene/*Navane*	High
Second-Generation Agents		
	Aripiprazole/*Abilify*	Low
	Clozapine/*Clozaril*	Low
	Olanzapine/*Zyprexa*	Low
	Quetiapine/*Seroquel*	Low
	Risperidone/*Risperdal*	Low
	Ziprasidone/*Geodon*	Low

Source: Adapted from American Psychiatric Association. (2004). Practice guideline for the treatment of patients with schizophrenia, 2nd edition. *American Journal of Psychiatry,* 161(Suppl.), 1–56.
*The trade name is in italics.

dopamine neurotransmitter system. However, they can also affect other systems, such as the serotonergic and glutamate system. We are just beginning to understand the mechanisms by which these drugs work.

In general, each drug is effective with some people and not with others. Clinicians and patients often must go through a trial-and-error process to find the medication that works best, and some individuals do not benefit significantly from any of them. The earliest neuroleptic drugs, called conventional or first-generation antipsychotics, are effective for approximately 60% of people who try them (American Psychiatric Association, 2004). However, many people are not helped by antipsychotics or experience unpleasant side effects. Fortunately, some people respond well to newer medications—sometimes called atypical or second-generation antipsychotics; the most common are risperidone and olanzapine. These newer drugs hold promise for helping patients who were previously unresponsive to medications (American Psychiatric Association, 2004; Stroup, Kraus, & Marder, 2006); the drugs were thought to have fewer serious side effects than the conventional antipsychotics. However, a large-scale study of 1,493 people the drugs with schizophrenia demonstrated that the majority discontinued their use of medication—whether it was the traditional or the atypical antipsychotic—and both classes of these drugs had comparable negative side effects (Lieberman et al., 2005).

■ Noncompliance With Medication: Why?

Despite the optimism generated by the effectiveness of antipsychotics, they work only when they are taken properly, and many people with schizophrenia do not routinely take their medication. David frequently "cheeked" the Haldol pills that were helpful in reducing his hallucinations, holding them in his mouth until he was alone and then spitting them out. In the large-scale study we just mentioned, 74% had stopped taking their medications 18 months after initial use (Lieberman et al., 2005).

A number of factors seem to be related to patients' noncompliance with a medication regimen, including negative doctor–patient relationships, cost of the medication, and poor social support (Miller, McEvoy, Jest, & Marder, 2006). Not surprisingly, negative side effects are a major factor in patient refusal. Antipsychotics can produce a number of unwanted physical symptoms, such as grogginess, blurred vision, and dryness of the mouth. Because the drugs affect neurotransmitter systems, more serious side effects, called *extrapyramidal symptoms,* can also result (Kane & Marder, 2005). These symptoms include the motor difficulties similar to those experienced by people with Parkinson's disease, sometimes called parkinsonian symptoms. *Akinesia* is one of the most common; it includes an expressionless face, slow motor activity, and monotonous speech. Another extrapyramidal symptom is *tardive dyskinesia,* which involves involuntary movements of the tongue, face, mouth, or jaw and can include protrusions of the tongue, puffing of the cheeks, puckering of the mouth, and chewing movements. Tardive dyskinesia seems to result from long-term use of high doses of antipsychotic medication and is often irreversible. The risk increases with time, with 3%–5% of people displaying tardive dyskinesia each year it is used over the first 5 years (Kane, 2006). These serious negative side effects have justifiably concerned people who otherwise benefit from the drugs.

One of the major obstacles to drug treatment for schizophrenia is compliance. Patients discontinue their medication for a variety of reasons, including the negative side effects.

©Ian O'Leary/Getty Images

To learn what patients themselves say, Windgassen (1992) questioned 61 people who had had recent onsets of schizophrenia. About half reported the feeling of sedation or grogginess as an unpleasant side effect: "I always have to fight to keep my eyes open," "I felt as though I was on drugs . . . drowsy, and yet really wound up" (p. 407). Other complaints included deterioration in the ability to think or concentrate (18%), problems with salivation (16%), and blurred vision (16%). Although a third of the patients felt the medications were beneficial, about 25% had a negative attitude toward them. A significant proportion of people who could benefit from antipsychotic medications find them unacceptable as a treatment, which may explain the relatively high rates of refusal and noncompliance.

Researchers have made this a major treatment issue in schizophrenia, realizing that medications can't be successful if they aren't taken regularly. Researchers hoped compliance rates would improve with the introduction of injectable medications. Instead of taking an oral antipsychotic every day, patients can have their medications injected every few weeks. Unfortunately, noncompliance remains an issue, primarily because patients do not return to the hospital or clinic for repeated doses (Weiden et al., 1991). Psychosocial interventions are now used not only to treat schizophrenia but also to increase medication-taking compliance by helping patients communicate better with professionals about their concerns.

An interesting but as yet not-well-validated treatment for the hallucinations experienced by many people with schizophrenia involves exposing the individual to magnetic fields. Called *transcranial magnetic stimulation,* this technique uses wire coils to repeatedly generate magnetic fields—up to 50 times per second—that pass through the skull to the brain. This input seems to interrupt temporarily the normal communication to that part of the brain. Hoffman and colleagues (2000, 2003) used this technique to stimulate the area of the brain involved in hallucinations for individuals with schizophrenia who experienced auditory hallucinations. They found that many of the individuals experienced improvement following transcranial magnetic stimulation. Again, more research is required to assess the true value of this technique for people with hallucinations (Haraldsson, Ferrarelli, Kalin, & Tononi, 2004).

Psychosocial Interventions

Historically, a number of psychosocial treatments have been tried for schizophrenia, reflecting the belief that the disorder results from problems in adapting to the world because of early experiences (Swartz, Lauriello, & Drake, 2006). Many therapists have thought that individuals who could achieve insight into the presumed role of their personal histories could be safely led to deal with their current situations. Although clinicians who take a psychodynamic or psychoanalytic approach to therapy continue to use this type of treatment, research suggests that their efforts at best may not be beneficial and at worst may be harmful (Mueser & Berenbaum, 1990; Scott & Dixon, 1995b).

Today, few believe that psychological factors cause people to have schizophrenia or that traditional psychotherapeutic approaches will cure them. Nevertheless, you will see that psychological methods have an important role. Despite the great promise of drug treatment, the problems with ineffectiveness, inconsistent use, and relapse suggest that by themselves drugs may not be effective with many people. As with a number of the disorders discussed in this text, recent work in the area of psychosocial intervention has suggested the value of an approach that uses both kinds of treatment (Fenton, 2005).

Until relatively recently, most people with severe and chronic cases of schizophrenia were treated in hospital settings. During the 19th century, inpatient care involved "moral treatment," which emphasized improving patients' socialization, helping them establish routines for self-control, and showing them the value of work and religion (Armstrong, 1993). Various types of such "milieu" treatments (changing the physical and social environment—usually to normalize institutional settings) have been popular, but, with one important exception, none seems to have helped people with schizophrenia (Tucker, Ferrell, & Price, 1984).

Gordon Paul and Robert Lentz conducted pioneering work in the 1970s at a mental health center in Illinois (Paul & Lentz, 1977). Borrowing from the behavioral approaches used by Ted Ayllon and Nate Azrin (1968), Paul and Lentz designed an environment for inpatients that encouraged appropriate socialization, participation in group sessions, and self-care such as bed making while discouraging violent outbursts. They set up an elaborate **token economy,** in which residents could earn access to meals and small luxuries by behaving appropriately. A patient could, for example, buy cigarettes with the tokens he earned for keeping his room neat. On the other hand, a patient would be fined (lose tokens) for being disruptive or otherwise acting inappropriately. This incentive system was combined with a full schedule of daily activities. Paul and Lentz compared the effectiveness of applied behavioral (or social learning) principles to traditional inpatient environments. In general, they found that patients who went through their program did better than others on social, self-care, and vocational skills, and more of them could be discharged from the hospital. This study was one of the first to show that people suffering from the debilitating effects of schizophrenia can learn to perform some skills they need to live more independently.

During the years since 1955, many efforts have combined to halt the routine institutionalization of people with schizophrenia in the United States (Talbott, 1990). This trend has occurred partly because of court rulings that limit involuntary hospitalization (as we saw in Arthur's case) and partly because of the relative success of antipsychotic medication. The bad news is that policies of deinstitutionalization have often been ill conceived, with the result that many people who have schizophrenia or other serious psychological disorders are homeless—the number is estimated at more than 200,000 people in the United States alone (National Resource Center on Homelessness and Mental Illness, 2003). The good news is that more attention is being focused on supporting these people in their communities, among their friends and families. The trend is away from creating better hospital environments and toward the perhaps more difficult task of addressing complex problems in the less predictable and insecure world outside. So far, only a small fraction of the growing number of homeless individuals with mental disorders is being helped.

One of the more insidious effects of schizophrenia is its negative impact on a person's ability to relate to other people.

©Ghislain & Marie David de Lossy/Getty Images

A mother is glad to have her daughter home from a psychiatric hospital, but acknowledges that "Now the real struggle begins."

Although not as dramatic as hallucinations and delusions, this problem can be the most visible impairment displayed by people with schizophrenia and can prevent them from getting and keeping jobs and making friends. Clinicians attempt to reteach social skills such as basic conversation, assertiveness, and relationship building to people with schizophrenia (Bellack, Mueser, Gingerich, & Agresta, 2004; Bustillo, Lauriello, Horan, & Keith, 2001).

Therapists divide complex social skills into their component parts, which they model. Then the clients do role-playing and ultimately practice their new skills in the "real world," all the while receiving feedback and encouragement at signs of progress. This isn't as easy as it may sound. For example, how would you teach someone to make a friend? Many skills are involved, such as maintaining eye contact when you talk to someone and providing the prospective friend with some (but not too much) positive feedback on her own behavior ("I really enjoy talking to you"). Such individual skills are practiced and then combined until they can be used naturally (Swartz et al., 2006). Basic skills can be taught to people with schizophrenia, but there is some disagreement about how successful the treatment is (Bellack & Mueser, 1992; Hogarty et al., 1992). The challenge of teaching social skills, as with all therapies, is to maintain the effects over a long period.

In addition to social skills, programs often teach a range of ways people can adapt to their disorder yet live in the community. At the Independent Living Skills Program at the University of California, Los Angeles, for example, the focus is on helping people take charge of their own care by such methods as identifying signs that warn of a relapse and learning how to manage their medication (see Table 13.3) (Corrigan, Wallace, Schade, & Green,

1994; Eckman et al., 1992). Preliminary evidence indicates that this type of training may help prevent relapses by people with schizophrenia, although longer-term outcome research is needed to see how long the effects last. To address some obstacles to this much-desired maintenance, such programs combine skills training with the support of a multidisciplinary team that provides services directly in the community, which seems to reduce hospitalization (Swartz et al., 2006). The more time and effort given to these services, the more likely the improvement.

In our discussion of the psychosocial influences on schizophrenia, we reviewed some work linking the person's social and emotional environments to the recurrence of schizophrenic episodes (McNab et al., 2007). It is logical to ask whether families could be helped by learning to reduce their level of expressed emotion and whether this would result in fewer relapses and better overall functioning for people with schizophrenia. Several studies have addressed these issues in a variety of ways (Falloon et al., 1985; Hogarty et al., 1986, 1991), and behavioral family therapy has been used to teach the families of people with schizophrenia to be more supportive (Dixon & Lehman, 1995; Mueser, Liberman, & Glynn, 1990). Research on professionals who provide care for people who have schizophrenia, and who may display high levels of expressed emotion, is also an active area of study.

In contrast to traditional therapy, behavioral family therapy resembles classroom education (Falloon et al., 1985). Family members are informed about schizophrenia and its treatment, relieved of the myth that they caused the disorder, and taught practical facts about antipsychotic medications and their side ef-

TABLE 13.3 Independent Living Skills program at UCLA		
Module	**Skill Areas**	**Learning Objectives**
Symptom management	Identifying warning signs of relapse	To identify personal warning signs
		To monitor personal warning signs with assistance from others
	Managing warning signs	To obtain assistance from health-care providers in differentiating personal warning signs from persistent symptoms, medication side effects, and variations in mood; to develop an emergency plan for responding to warning signs
	Coping with persistent symptoms	To recognize and monitor persistent personal symptoms; to obtain assistance from health-care providers in differentiating persistent symptoms from warning signs, medication side effects, and variations in mood; to use specific techniques for coping with persistent symptoms
		To monitor persistent symptoms daily
	Avoiding alcohol and street drugs	To identify adverse effects of alcohol and illicit drugs and benefits of avoiding them; to refuse offers of alcohol and street drugs; to know how to resist using these substances in coping with anxiety, low self-esteem, or depression; to discuss openly use of alcohol and drugs with health-care providers
Medication management	Obtaining information about antipsychotic medication	To understand how these drugs work, why maintenance drug therapy is used, and the benefits of taking medication
	Knowing correct self-administration and evaluation	To follow the appropriate procedures for taking medication; to evaluate responses to medication daily
	Identifying side effects of medication	To know the specific side effects that sometimes result from taking medication and what to do when these problems occur
	Negotiating medication issues with health-care providers	To practice ways of obtaining assistance when problems occur with medication

Source: Reprinted, with permission, from Eckman, T. A., Wirshing, W. C., Marder, S. R., Liberman, R. P., Johnston-Cronk, K., Zimmermann, K., & Mintz, J. (1992). Techniques for training schizophrenic patients in illness self-management: A controlled trial. *American Journal of Psychiatry,* 149, 1549–1555, © 1992 American Psychiatric Association.

fects. They are also helped with communication skills so that they can become more empathic listeners, and they learn constructive ways of expressing negative feelings to replace the harsh criticism that characterizes some family interactions. In addition, they learn problem-solving skills to help them resolve conflicts that arise. Like the research on social skills training, outcome research suggests that the effects of behavioral family therapy are significant during the first year but less robust 2 years after intervention (Montero, Masanet, Bellver, & Lacruz, 2006; Montero et al., 2005). This type of therapy, therefore, must be ongoing if patients and their families are to benefit from it.

Adults with schizophrenia face great obstacles to maintaining gainful employment. Their social skills deficits make reliable job performance and adequate employee relationships a struggle. To address these difficulties, some programs focus on vocational rehabilitation, such as supportive employment. Supportive employment involves providing coaches who give on-the-job training, and these efforts can help some people with schizophrenia maintain meaningful jobs (Mueser et al., 2004).

Research suggests that individual social skills training, family intervention, and vocational rehabilitation may be helpful additions to biological treatment for schizophrenia. Significant relapses may be avoided or delayed by such psychosocial interventions. ■ Figure 13.9 illustrates the studies reviewed by one group (Falloon, Brooker, & Graham-Hole, 1992), which show that multilevel treatments reduce the number of relapses among people receiving drug therapy in comparison with simple social support or educational efforts.

Where treatment occurs, it has expanded over the years from locked wards in large mental hospitals, to family homes, to local communities. In addition, the services have expanded to include self-advocacy and self-help groups. Former patients have organized programs such as Fountain House in New York City to provide mutual support. Psychosocial clubs have differing models, but all are "person centered" and focus on obtaining positive experiences through employment opportunities, friendship, and empowerment. Many see this consumer-run self-help model as an added component to more specific interventions such as social

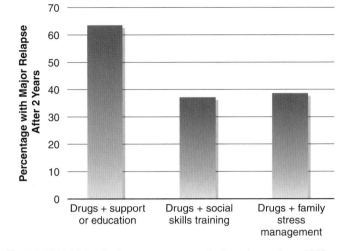

■ **FIGURE 13.9** Studies on treatment of schizophrenia from 1980 to 1992. (From Falloon, I. R. H., Brooker, C., & Graham-Hole, V., 1992. Psychosocial interventions for schizophrenia. *Behaviour Change, 9,* 238–245.)

skills training, family intervention, and medical management of symptoms. Some research indicates that participation may help reduce relapses, but as it is also possible that those who participate may be a special group of individuals, it is difficult to interpret improvements (Goering et al., 2006).

Because schizophrenia is a complex disorder that affects multiple areas of functioning, effective treatment is carried out at several levels. Table 13.4 lists six approaches to treatment that have proved effective in assisting these individuals to achieve higher-quality lives. Probably the most extensively studied program is the assertive community treatment (ACT) program that grew out of work by researchers in Madison, Wisconsin (Swartz et al., 2006). ACT involves using a multidisciplinary team of professionals to provide broad-ranging treatment across all domains, including medication management, psychosocial treatment, and vocational training and support. As you can see, one approach alone is not sufficient to address the many needs of people with schizophrenia and their families.

TABLE 13.4	An Integrative Treatment Approach
Treatment	**Description**
Collaborative psychopharmacology	Using antipsychotic medications to treat the main symptoms of the disorder (hallucinations, delusions), as well as using other medications for secondary symptoms (for example, antidepressant medication for people with secondary depression)
Assertive community treatment	Providing support in the community, with emphasis on small caseloads for care providers, services in the community setting rather than a clinic, and 24-hour coverage
Family psychoeducation	Assisting family members, including educating them about the disorder and its management, helping them reduce stress and tension in the home, and providing social support
Supportive employment	Providing sufficient support before and during employment so that the person can find and keep a meaningful job
Illness management and recovery	Helping the individual become an active participant in treatment, including providing education about the disorder, teaching effective use of medication strategies for collaborating with clinicians, and coping with symptoms when they reoccur
Integrated dual-disorders treatment	Treating coexisting substance use

Treatment Across Cultures

Treatment of schizophrenia and its delivery differ from one country to another and across cultures within countries. Hispanics, for example, may be less likely than other groups to seek help in institutional settings, relying instead on family support (Dassori, Miller, & Saldana, 1995). Adapting treatments to make them culturally relevant—in this case, adding important relatives to the social skills training of Latinos with schizophrenia—is essential for effectiveness (Kopelowicz, Mintz, Liberman, Zarate, & Gonzalez-Smith, 2004). In one interesting study, beliefs about symptoms and treatments were compared between British and Chinese populations (Furnham & Wong, 2007). Native Chinese hold more religious beliefs about both the causes and the treatments of schizophrenia than those living in England—for example, endorsing statements such as, "Schizophrenia is due to evil done in a previous life" and "Ancestor worship (burning candles and joss sticks) will help treat schizophrenia." These different beliefs translate into practice—with the British using more biological, psychological, and community treatments and the Chinese relying more on alternative medicine (Furnham & Wong, 2007). Supernatural beliefs about the cause of schizophrenia among family members in Bali leads to limited use of antipsychotic medication in treatment (Kurihara, Kato, Reverger, & Gusti Rai Tirta, 2006). In many countries in Africa, people with schizophrenia are kept in prisons, primarily because of the lack of adequate alternatives (Mustafa, 1990). In general, the movement from housing people in large institutional settings to community care is ongoing in most Western countries.

Prevention

One strategy for preventing a disorder such as schizophrenia—which typically first shows itself in early adulthood—is to identify and treat children who may be at risk for getting the disorder later in life. In our discussion of genetics, we noted that approximately 17% of the children born to parents who have schizophrenia are likely themselves to develop the disorder. These high-risk children have been the focus of several studies, both prospective (before and during an expected situation) and longitudinal (over long periods).

In China, acupuncture and herbal medicine are often used with antipsychotic medications for schizophrenia.

A classic at-risk study was initiated in the 1960s by Sarnoff Mednick and Fini Schulsinger (1965, 1968). They identified 207 Danish children of mothers who had severe cases of schizophrenia and 104 control children born to mothers who had no history of the disorder. The average age of these children was about 15 when they were first identified, and the researchers followed them for 10 more years to determine whether any factors had predicted who would and would not develop schizophrenia. We have already discussed pregnancy and delivery-related complications. Mednick and Schulsinger also identified *instability of early family rearing environment,* which suggests that environmental influences may trigger the onset of schizophrenia (Cannon et al., 1991). Poor parenting may place additional strain on a vulnerable person who is already at risk. When the at-risk children in the Danish study enter middle age, we will know the eventual outcomes for all of them; until then, we cannot draw strong conclusions from the study (Mirsky, 1995).

As we await the outcomes of these long-term studies, other approaches may prove valuable for reducing the rates of this disorder. For example, we have seen that factors such as birth complications and certain early illnesses (for example, viruses) may trigger the onset of schizophrenia, especially among those individuals who are genetically predisposed. Therefore, interventions such as vaccinations against viruses for women of childbearing age and interventions related to improving prenatal nutrition and care may be effective preventive measures (McGrath, 2000).

CONCEPT CHECK 13.3

Read the descriptions and then match them to the following words: (a) olanzapine, (b) extrapyramidal symptoms, (c) serotonin, (d) dopamine, (e) metabolites, (f) token economy, (g) vocational rehabilitation, (h) social skills training, (i) family intervention.

1. Recent studies sometimes indicate that the relationship of the neurotransmitters _____ and _____ may explain some positive symptoms of schizophrenia.
2. Setting up an elaborate _____ in which patients are fined for disruptive or inappropriate behavior and rewarded for appropriate behavior is beneficial in hospitals.
3. Difficult cases of schizophrenia seem to improve with a serotonin and dopamine antagonist called _____.
4. In _____ clinicians attempt to reteach such behaviors as basic conversation, assertiveness, and relationship building to people with schizophrenia.
5. Because antipsychotic medications may cause serious side effects, some patients stop taking them. One serious side effect is called _____, which may include parkinsonian symptoms.
6. Aside from social skills training, two psychosocial treatments for schizophrenia, _____ (teaching family members to be supportive) and _____ (teaching meaningful jobs), may be helpful.

FUTURE DIRECTIONS

Using Virtual Reality and Text Messaging in Assessment

Is there a role for new technologies in the diagnosis and treatment of schizophrenia? Creative researchers are answering this question in a number of exciting developments for the field. One study looked to improve the diagnosis of schizophrenia by using virtual reality technology to simulate multiple cognitive tasks (Sorkin, Weinshall, Modai, & Peled, 2006). Researchers created a gamelike task to test aspects of working memory and perseveration (focusing on the same things repeatedly) and found not only could this approach create real-life simulations that revealed deficits but also that the tasks could be fun!

Other researchers are using text messaging to alert medical professionals that their patients might be prone to relapse. In the Czech Republic, one center has patients and their family members complete a 10-item early warning signs questionnaire and the scores are sent to their psychiatrist's cell phones through short message service (text messaging) (Spaniel & Motlova, 2007). The scores provide a warning for signs of relapse, and the clinician knows immediately when to intervene early. These types of innovative uses of current technology could lead to improved services for people with schizophrenia.

SUMMARY

Clinical Description, Symptoms, and Subtypes

- Schizophrenia is characterized by a broad spectrum of cognitive and emotional dysfunctions that include delusions and hallucinations, disorganized speech and behavior, and inappropriate emotions.

- The symptoms of schizophrenia can be divided into positive, negative, and disorganized. Positive symptoms are active manifestations of abnormal behavior, or an excess or distortion of normal behavior, and include delusions and hallucinations. Negative symptoms involve deficits in normal behavior on such dimensions as affect, speech, and motivation. Disorganized symptoms include rambling speech, erratic behavior, and inappropriate affect.

- DSM-IV-TR divides schizophrenia into five subtypes. People with the paranoid type of schizophrenia have prominent delusions or hallucinations while their cognitive skills and affect remain relatively intact. People with the disorganized type of schizophrenia tend to show marked disruption in their speech and behavior; they also show flat or inappropriate affect. People with the catatonic type of schizophrenia have unusual motor responses, such as remaining in fixed positions (waxy flexibility), excessive activity, and being oppositional by remaining rigid. In addition, they display odd mannerisms with their bodies and faces, including grimacing. People who do not fit neatly into these subtypes are classified as having an undifferentiated type of schizophrenia. Some people who have had at least one episode of schizophrenia but who no longer have major symptoms are diagnosed as having the residual type of schizophrenia.

- Several other disorders are characterized by psychotic behaviors, such as hallucinations and delusions; these include schizophreniform disorder (which includes people who experience the symptoms of schizophrenia for less than 6 months); schizoaffective disorder (which includes people who have symptoms of schizophrenia and who exhibit the characteristics of mood disorders, such as depression and bipolar affective disorder); delusional disorder (which includes people with a persistent belief that is contrary to reality, in the absence of the other characteristics of schizophrenia); brief psychotic disorder (which includes people with one or more positive symptoms, such as delusions, hallucinations, or disorganized speech or behavior over the course of less than a month); and shared psychotic disorder (which includes individuals who develop delusions simply as a result of a close relationship with a delusional individual).

Prevalence and Causes of Schizophrenia

- A number of causative factors have been implicated for schizophrenia, including genetic influences, neurotransmitter imbalances, structural damage to the brain caused by a prenatal viral infection or birth injury, and psychological stressors.

- Relapse appears to be triggered by hostile and critical family environments characterized by high expressed emotion.

Treatment of Schizophrenia

- Successful treatment for people with schizophrenia rarely includes complete recovery. However, the quality of life for these individuals can be meaningfully affected by combining antipsychotic medications with psychosocial approaches, employment support, and community-based and family interventions.

- Treatment typically involves antipsychotic drugs that are usually administered with a variety of psychosocial treatments, with the goal of reducing relapse and improving skills in deficits and compliance in taking the medications. The effectiveness of treatment is limited, because schizophrenia is typically a chronic disorder.

Key Terms

schizophrenia, 467
catatonia, 467
hebephrenia, 467
paranoia, 467
dementia praecox, 467
associative splitting, 468
psychotic behavior, 469
positive symptoms, 470
negative symptoms, 470
avolition, 472
alogia, 472

anhedonia, 473
flat affect, 473
disorganized speech, 473
inappropriate affect, 474
catatonic immobility, 474
paranoid type of
    schizophrenia, 474
disorganized type of
    schizophrenia, 474
catatonic type of
    schizophrenia, 475

undifferentiated type of
    schizophrenia, 475
residual type of schizophrenia,
    475
schizophreniform disorder,
    476
schizoaffective disorder, 476
delusional disorder, 476
brief psychotic disorder, 477
shared psychotic disorder
    (folie à deux), 477

schizotypal personality
    disorder, 478
schizophrenogenic mother,
    487
double bind communication,
    487
expressed emotion (EE), 487
token economy, 491

Answers to Concept Checks

13.1

Part A

1. paranoid; 2. catatonic; 3. residual; 4. disorganized; 5. disorganized

Part B

6. b; 7. c; 8. d; 9. a

13.2

1. d, i; 2. f, h, a; 3. a, a

13.3

1. d, c; 2. f; 3. a; 4. h; 5. b; 6. i, g

The Abnormal Psychology Book Companion Website

See **academic.cengage.com/psychology/barlow** for practice quiz questions, interactive activities, Internet links, critical thinking exercises, discussion forums, and more. Also accessible from the Wadsworth Psychology Resource Center (**academic.cengage.com/login**).

Abnormal Psychology Live CD-ROM

■ *Etta, a Patient With Schizophrenia:* An example of a lower-functioning patient with schizophrenia.

■ *Positive Versus Negative Symptoms:* A team of clinicians describe the differences between positive and negative symptoms.

■ *Common Symptoms of Schizophrenia:* A clinician reviews the most common psychotic symptoms in schizophrenia, and his discussion is interspersed with patients who exemplify these symptoms.

 **CengageNOW**

Go to **academic.cengage.com/now** to link to CengageNOW, your online study tool. First take the Pre-Test for this chapter to get your personalized study plan, which will identify topics you need to review and direct you to online resources. Then take the Post-Test to determine what concepts you have mastered and what you still need work on.

Video Concept Reviews

CengageNOW also contains Mark Durand's *Video Concept Reviews* on challenging topics.

■ Schizophrenia
■ Positive Symptoms
■ Delusions
■ Hallucinations
■ Negative Symptoms
■ Avolition, Alogia, Anhedonia, and Flat Affect
■ Disorganized Symptoms
■ Paranoid Type of Schizophrenia
■ Catatonic Type of Schizophrenia
■ Delusional Disorder
■ Brief Psychotic Disorder and Shared Psychotic Disorder
■ Expressed Emotion and Stress
■ Concept Check: The Relevance of Psychologists to the Treatment of Schizophrenia

Exploring Schizophrenia

• Schizophrenia disrupts perception of the world, thought, speech, movement, and almost every other aspect of daily functioning.
• Usually chronic with a high relapse rate, complete recovery from schizophrenia is rare.

TRIGGER

- Stressful, traumatic life event
- High expressed emotion (family criticism, hostility, and/or intrusion)
- Sometimes no obvious trigger

Biological Influences

- Inherited tendency (multiple genes) to develop disease
- Prenatal/birth complications— viral infection during pregnancy/ birth injury affect child's brain cells
- Brain chemistry (abnormalities in the dopamine and glutamate systems)
- Brain structure (enlarged ventricles)

Social Influences

- Environment (early family experiences) can trigger onset
- Culture influences interpretation of disease/symptoms (hallucinations, delusions)

CAUSES

Behavioral Influences

- **Positive symptoms:**
  —Active manifestations of abnormal behavior (delusions, hallucinations, disorganized speech, odd body movements, or catatonia)
- **Negative symptoms:**
  —Flat affect (lack of emotional expression)
  —Avolition (lack of initiative, apathy)
  —Alogia (relative absence in amount or content of speech)

Emotional and Cognitive Influences

- Interaction styles that are high in criticism, hostility, and emotional overinvolvement can trigger a relapse

TREATMENT OF SCHIZOPHRENIA

Individual, Group, and Family Therapy

- Can help patient and family understand the disease and symptom triggers.
- Teaches families communication skills.
- Provides resources for dealing with emotional and practical challenges.

Social Skills Training

- Can occur in hospital or community settings.
- Teaches the person with schizophrenia social, self-care, and vocational skills.

Medications

- Taking neuroleptic medications may help people with schizophrenia to:
  —Clarify thinking and perceptions of reality
  —Reduce hallucinations and delusions
- Drug treatment must be consistent to be effective. Inconsistent dosage may aggravate existing symptoms or create new ones.

SYMPTOMS OF SCHIZOPHRENIA

People with schizophrenia do not all show the same kinds of symptoms. Symptoms vary from person to person and may be cyclical. Common symptoms include:

DELUSIONS

- Unrealistic and bizarre beliefs not shared by others in the culture
- May be delusions of grandeur (that you are really Mother Teresa or Napoleon) or delusions of persecution (the cyclist who believed her competitors were sabotaging her by putting pebbles in the road)

HALLUCINATIONS

- Sensory events that aren't based on any external event (hearing voices, seeing people who have died)
- Many have auditory hallucinations (David hears his dead uncle talking to him)

DISORGANIZED SPEECH

- Jumping from topic to topic
- Talking illogically (not answering direct questions, going off on tangents)
- Speaking in unintelligible words and sentences

BEHAVIORAL PROBLEMS

- Pacing excitably, wild agitation
- Catatonic immobility
- Waxy flexibility (keeping body parts in the same position when they are moved by someone else)
- Inappropriate dress (coats in the summer, shorts in the winter)
- Inappropriate affect
- Ignoring personal hygiene

WITHDRAWAL

- Lack of emotional response (flat speech, little change in facial expressions)
- Apathy (little interest in day-to-day activities)
- Delayed and brief responses in conversation
- Loss of enjoyment in pleasurable activities (eating, socializing, sex)

Types of Schizophrenia

Paranoid
- Delusions of grandeur or persecution
- Hallucinations (especially auditory)
- Higher level of functioning between episodes
- May have stronger familial link than other types

Disorganized
- Disorganized speech and/or behavior
- Immature emotionality (inappropriate affect)
- Chronic and lacking in remissions

Catatonic
- Alternating immobility and excited agitation
- Unusual motor responses (waxy flexibility, rigidity)
- Odd facial or body mannerisms (often mimicking others)
- Rare

Residual
- Has had at least one schizophrenic episode but no longer shows major symptoms
- Still shows "leftover" symptoms (social withdrawal, bizarre thoughts, inactivity, flat affect)

Undifferentiated
- Symptoms of several types that taken together do not neatly fall into one specific category

CHAPTER 14

Developmental Disorders

© Harry Sieplinga/HMS Images/Getty Images

COMMON DEVELOPMENTAL DISORDERS
What Is Normal? What Is Abnormal?
Attention Deficit/Hyperactivity Disorder
Learning Disorders

PERVASIVE DEVELOPMENTAL DISORDERS
Autistic Disorder
Asperger's Disorder
Treatment of Pervasive Developmental Disorders

MENTAL RETARDATION
Clinical Description
Statistics
Causes
Treatment of Mental Retardation
Prevention of Developmental Disorders

ABNORMAL PSYCHOLOGY LIVE CD-ROM
ADHD: Sean
ADHD: Edward
Life Skills Training
Bullying Prevention
Autism: The Nature of the Disorder
Autism: Christina
Autism: Rebecca
Down Syndrome: Lauren
Web Link

Anything I tried to learn, unless it was something I sought and taught myself, closed me out and became hard to comprehend, just like any other intrusion from "the world."

Donna Williams

Nobody Nowhere: The Extraordinary Autobiography of an Autistic

COMMON DEVELOPMENTAL DISORDERS

Almost all disorders described in this book are developmental disorders in the sense that they change over time. Most disorders originate in childhood, although the full presentation of the problem may not manifest itself until much later. Disorders that show themselves early in life often persist as the person grows older, so the term *childhood disorder* may be misleading. In this chapter, we cover those disorders that are revealed in a clinically significant way during a child's developing years and are of concern to families and educators. Remember, however, that these difficulties often persist through adulthood and are typically lifelong problems, not problems unique to children.

Again, a number of difficulties and, indeed, distinct disorders begin in childhood. In certain disorders, some children are fine except for difficulties with talking. Others have problems relating to their peers. Still other children have a combination of conditions that significantly hinder their development, as illustrated by the case of Timmy.

TIMMY: The Boy Who Looked Right Through You

Timmy, a beautiful blond baby, was born with the umbilical cord wrapped around his neck, so he had been without oxygen for an unknown period. Nonetheless, he appeared to be a healthy little boy. His mother later related that he was a good baby who rarely cried, although she was concerned he didn't like to be picked up and cuddled. His family became worried about his development when he was 2 years old and didn't talk (his older sister had at that age). They also noticed that he didn't play with other children; he spent most of his time alone, spinning plates on the floor, waving his hands in front of his face, and lining up blocks in a certain order.

The family's pediatrician assured them that Timmy was just developing at a different rate and would grow out of it. When, at age 3, Timmy's behavior persisted, his parents consulted a second pediatrician. Neurological examinations revealed nothing unusual but suggested, on the basis of Timmy's delay in learning such basic skills as talking and feeding himself, that he had mild mental retardation.

Timmy's mother did not accept this diagnosis, and over the next few years she consulted numerous other professionals and received numerous diagnoses (including childhood schizophrenia, childhood psychosis, and developmental delay). By age 7, Timmy still didn't speak or play with other children, and he was developing aggressive and self-injurious behaviors. His parents brought him to a clinic for children with severe disabilities. Here, Timmy was diagnosed as having autism.

The clinic specialists recommended a comprehensive educational program of intensive behavioral intervention to help Timmy with language and socialization and to counter his increasing tendency to engage in tantrums. The work continued daily for approximately 10 years, both at the clinic and at home. During this time, Timmy learned to say only three words: "soda," "cookie," and "Mama." Socially, he appeared to like other people (especially adults), but his interest seemed to center on their ability to get him something he wanted, such as a favorite food or drink. If his surroundings were changed in even a minor way, Timmy became disruptive and violent to the point of hurting himself; to minimize his self-injurious behavior, the family took care to ensure that his surroundings stayed the same as much as possible. However, no real progress was made toward eliminating his violent behavior, and as he grew bigger and stronger, he became increasingly difficult to work with; he hurt his mother physically on several occasions. With great reluctance, she institutionalized Timmy when he was 17.

As clinicians have grown to appreciate the far-reaching effects of childhood problems and the importance of early intervention in treating most disorders, they have become more interested in understanding the diversity of severe problems experienced in early life. Timmy was diagnosed with autism in the early 1970s. Almost four decades later, we know more—although still not enough—about how to help children who have autism. Who can say what the prognosis for Timmy might be today, especially if he were diagnosed correctly at age 2 instead of at age 7?

What Is Normal? What Is Abnormal?

Before we discuss specific disorders, we need to address the broad topic of development in relation to disorders usually first diagnosed in infancy, childhood, or adolescence. What can we learn from children like Timmy, and what effect do the early disruptions in their skills have on their later lives? Does it matter when in the developmental period certain problems arise? Are disruptions in development permanent, thus making any hope for treatment doubtful?

Recall that in Chapter 2 we described developmental psychopathology as the study of how disorders arise and how they change with time. Childhood is considered particularly important because the brain changes significantly for several years after birth; this is also when critical developments occur in social, emotional, cognitive, and other important competency areas. These changes mostly follow a pattern: The child develops one skill before acquiring the next. Although this pattern of change is only one aspect of development, it is an important concept at this point because it implies that any disruption in the development of early skills will, by the very nature of this sequential process, disrupt the development of later skills. For example, some researchers believe that people with autism suffer from a disruption in early social development, which prevents them from developing important social relationships, even with their parents. From a developmental perspective, the absence of early and meaningful social relationships has serious consequences. Children whose motivation to interact with others is disrupted may have a more difficult time learning to communicate; that is, they may not want to learn to speak if other people are not important to them. We don't know whether a disruption in communication skills is a direct outcome of the disorder or a by-product of disrupted early social development.

Understanding this type of developmental relationship is important for several reasons. Knowing what processes are disrupted will help us understand the disorder better and may lead to more appropriate intervention strategies. It may be important to identify children with attention deficit/hyperactivity disorder, for example, because their problems with impulsivity may interfere with their ability to create and maintain friendships, an important developmental consideration. Similarly, identifying a disorder such as autism at an early age is important for these children so that their social deficits can be addressed before they affect other skill domains, such as language and communication. Too often, people see early and pervasive disruptions in developmental skills (such as you saw with Timmy) and expect a negative prognosis, with the problems predetermined and permanent. However, remember that biological and psychosocial influences continuously interact with each other. Therefore, even for disorders such as attention deficit/hyperactivity disorder and autism that have clear biological bases, the presentation of the disorder is different for each individual. Changes at the biological or the psychosocial level may reduce the impact of the disorder.

One note of caution is appropriate here. There is real concern in the profession, especially among developmental psychologists, that some workers in the field may view aspects of normal development as symptoms of abnormality. For example, echolalia, which involves repeating the speech of others, was once thought to be a sign of autism. However, when we study the development of speech in children without disorders, we find that repeating what someone else says is an intermediate step in language development. In children with autism, therefore, echolalia is just a sign of relatively delayed language skills and not a symptom of their disorder (Durand, 2004). Knowledge of development is important for understanding the nature of psychological disorders.

With that caveat in mind, we now examine several disorders usually diagnosed first in infancy, childhood, or adolescence, including *attention deficit/hyperactivity disorder,* which involves characteristics of inattention or hyperactivity and impulsivity, and *learning disorders,* which are characterized by one or more difficulties in areas such as reading and writing. We then focus on *autistic disorder,* a more severe disability, in which the child shows significant impairment in social interactions and communication and has restricted patterns of behavior, interest, and activities, and we

discuss the less severe *Asperger's disorder.* Finally, we examine *mental retardation,* which involves significant deficits in cognitive abilities.

Attention Deficit/Hyperactivity Disorder

Do you know people who flit from activity to activity, who start many tasks but seldom finish one, who have trouble concentrating, and who don't seem to pay attention when others speak? These people may have **attention deficit/hyperactivity disorder (ADHD),** one of the most common reasons children are referred for mental health services in the United States (Hechtman, 2005). The primary characteristics of such people include a pattern of inattention, such as not paying attention to school- or work-related tasks, or of hyperactivity and impulsivity. These deficits can significantly disrupt academic efforts, as well as social relationships. Consider the case of Danny.

DANNY: The Boy Who Couldn't Sit Still

Danny, a handsome 9-year-old boy, was referred to us because of his difficulties at school and at home. Danny had a great deal of energy and loved playing most sports, especially baseball. Academically, his work was adequate, although his teacher reported that his performance was diminishing and she believed he would do better if he paid more attention in class. Danny rarely spent more than a few minutes on a task without some interruption: He would get up out of his seat, rifle through his desk, or constantly ask questions. His peers were frustrated with him because he was equally impulsive during their interactions: He never finished a game, and in sports he tried to play all positions simultaneously.

At home, Danny was considered a handful. His room was a constant mess because he became engaged in a game or activity only to drop it and initiate something else. Danny's parents reported that they often scolded him for not carrying out some task, although the reason seemed to be that he forgot what he was doing rather than that he deliberately tried to defy them. They also said that, out of their own frustration, they sometimes grabbed him by the shoulders and yelled, "Slow down!" because his hyperactivity drove them crazy.

Clinical Description

Danny has many characteristics of ADHD. Like Danny, people with this disorder have a great deal of difficulty sustaining their attention on a task or activity (Barkley, 2006e). As a result, their tasks are often unfinished and they often seem not to be listening when someone else is speaking. In addition to this serious disruption in attention, some people with ADHD display motor hyperactivity. Children with this disorder are often described as fidgety in school, unable to sit still for more than a few minutes. Danny's restlessness in his classroom was a considerable source of concern for his teacher and peers, who were frustrated by his impatience.

In addition to hyperactivity and problems sustaining attention, impulsivity—acting apparently without thinking—is a common complaint made about people with ADHD. For instance, during meetings of his baseball team, Danny often shouted responses to the coach's questions even before the coach had a chance to finish his sentence.

For ADHD, the fourth edition, text revision, of the *Diagnostic and Statistical Manual* (DSM-IV-TR) differentiates three types of symptoms. The first includes problems of *inattention*. People may appear not to listen to others; they may lose necessary school assignments, books, or tools; and they may not pay enough attention to details, making careless mistakes. The second type of symptom includes *hyperactivity,* which includes fidgeting, having trouble sitting for any length of time, always being on the go. The third general symptom is *impulsivity,* which includes blurting out answers before questions have been completed and having trouble waiting turns. Either the first (inattention) or the second and third (hyperactivity and impulsivity) domains of symptoms must be present for someone to be diagnosed with ADHD.

Inattention, hyperactivity, and impulsivity often cause other problems that appear secondary to ADHD. Academic performance tends to suffer, especially as the child progresses in school. The cause of this poor performance is not known. It could be a result of the problems with attention and impulsivity characteristic of ADHD, and in some children this can be made worse by factors such as concurrent learning disabilities, which are common in boys with ADHD (Barkley, 2006b). Children with ADHD are likely to be unpopular and rejected by their peers (Hoza et al., 2005). Here, the difficulty appears to be directly related to the behaviors symptomatic of ADHD. For example, one study found that young girls with ADHD in general were likely to be rejected by peers but that this likelihood was more pronounced in those with hyperactivity, impulsivity, and inattention when compared to girls who had only the inattentive type (Hinshaw, 2002). You would think that problems with peers, combined with frequent negative feedback from parents and teachers, would cause these children to view themselves negatively. However, evidence suggests that some children with ADHD (who are not also depressed) actually have an inflated sense of their own competence in areas such as social acceptance, physical appearance, and self-worth (Hoza et al., 2004).

■ Statistics

ADHD is estimated to occur in 3–7% of school-age children in the United States, and an important analysis of prevalence suggests that the disorder is found in about 5.2% of the child populations across all regions of the world (Polanczyk, de Lima, Horta, Biederman, & Rohde, 2007). This finding of comparable rates of ADHD across the world is important because debates continue to rage about the validity of ADHD as a real disorder. Some people believe that children who are just normally "active" are being misdiagnosed with ADHD. Previously, there were historic differences in the number of people diagnosed with this disorder. Children were more likely to receive the label of ADHD in the

"He's very, very intelligent; his grades don't reflect that because he will just neglect to do a 240-point assignment if somebody doesn't stay behind it. . . . What I try to do with him is come in and cut it down to 'this is what I want by tomorrow, this is what I want day after tomorrow.'"

United States than anywhere else. Based on this difference, some argue that ADHD in children is simply a cultural construct—meaning that the behavior of these children is typical from a developmental perspective and it is Western society's intolerance (due to the loss of extended family support, pressure to succeed academically, and busy family life) that causes labeling ADHD as a disorder (Timimi & Taylor, 2004). However, with improvements in diagnosis worldwide, countries that previously reported lower rates of ADHD are now finding similar numbers of these children being brought to the attention of helping professionals (Barkley, 2006e). This change suggests that the disorder may not simply be a reflection of a lack of tolerance on the part of teachers or parents in the United States for active or impulsive children but rather is an indication that ADHD is a valid disorder that affects a significant number of children all over the world (Moffitt & Melchior, 2007).

Boys are three times more likely to be diagnosed with ADHD than girls, and this discrepancy increases when you look at those children being seen in clinics. The reason for this gender difference is largely unknown. It may be that adults are more tolerant of hyperactivity among girls, who tend to be less active than boys with ADHD. Boys tend to be more aggressive, which will more likely result in attention by mental health professionals (Barkley, 2006e). Girls with ADHD, on the other hand, tend to display more behaviors referred to as "internalizing"—specifically, anxiety and depression (Barkley, 2006e).

The higher prevalence of boys identified as having ADHD has led some to question whether the DSM-IV-TR diagnostic criteria for this disorder are applicable to girls. Here is the quandary. Most research over the last several decades has used young boys as subjects. This focus on boys may have been the result of their active and disruptive behaviors, which caused concern among families and school personnel and therefore prompted research into the nature, causes, and treatment of these problems. More boys displayed these behaviors, which made it easier to find subjects to study. But did this almost-singular focus on boys result in ignoring how young girls experience this disorder?

This concern is being raised by some psychologists, including Kathleen Nadeau (a clinical psychologist who specializes in girls with ADHD), who argues the need for more research on ADHD in girls: "Girls experience significant struggles that are often overlooked because their ADHD symptoms bear little resemblance to those of boys" (Crawford, 2003, p. 28). It appears that girls with ADHD were neglected because their symptoms differ so dramatically from boys' symptoms.

It seems that ADHD as a disorder may not be gender specific but that girls and boys may be likely to display the disorder differently (Barkley, 2006e). Just as we are now exploring ADHD

DSM-IV-TR

DSM TABLE 14.1 Diagnostic Criteria for Attention Deficit/Hyperactivity Disorder

A. Either (1) or (2):
1. Six (or more) of the following symptoms of inattention have persisted for at least 6 months to a degree that is maladaptive and inconsistent with developmental level:

Inattention
   a. often fails to give close attention to details or makes careless mistakes in schoolwork, work, or other activities
   b. Often has difficulty sustaining attention in tasks or play activities
   c. Often does not seem to listen when spoken to directly
   d. Often does not follow through on instructions and fails to finish schoolwork, chores, or duties in the workplace (not due to oppositional behavior or failure to understand instructions)
   e. Often has difficulty organizing tasks and activities
   f. Often avoids, dislikes, or is reluctant to engage in tasks that require sustained mental effort (such as schoolwork or homework)
   g. Often loses things necessary for tasks or activities (e.g., toys, school assignments, pencils, books, or tools)
   h. Is often easily distracted by extraneous stimuli
   i. Is often forgetful in daily activities
2. Six (or more) of the following symptoms of hyperactivity/impulsivity have persisted for at least 6 months to a degree that is maladaptive and inconsistent with developmental level:

Hyperactivity
   a. Often fidgets with hands or feet or squirms in seat
   b. Often leaves seat in classroom or in other situations in which remaining seated is expected
   c. Often runs about or climbs excessively in situations in which it is inappropriate (in adolescents or adults, may be limited to subjective feelings of restlessness)
   d. Often has difficulty playing or engaging in leisure activities quietly
   e. Is often "on the go" or often acts as if "driven by a motor"
   f. Often talks excessively

Impulsivity
   g. Often blurts out answers before questions have been completed
   h. Often has difficulty awaiting turn
   i. Often interrupts or intrudes on others (e.g., butts into conversations or games)

B. Some hyperactive/impulsive or inattentive symptoms that caused impairment were present before age 7 years.
C. Some impairment from the symptoms is present in two or more settings (e.g., at school [or work] and at home).
D. There must be clear evidence of clinically significant impairment in social, academic, or occupational functioning.
E. The symptoms do not occur exclusively during the course of a pervasive developmental disorder, schizophrenia, or other psychotic disorder and are not better accounted for by another mental disorder (e.g., mood disorder, anxiety disorder, dissociative disorder, or a personality disorder).

Source: Reprinted, with permission, from American Psychiatric Association. (2000). *Diagnostic and statistical manual of mental disorders* (4th ed., text revision). Washington, DC: Author, © 2000 American Psychiatric Association.

among adults, in addition to children, more research is now addressing the relative lack of research on girls and women. This expansion of research across age and gender bodes well for a fuller understanding of the disorder.

Children with ADHD are first identified as different from their peers around age 3 or 4; their parents describe them as active, mischievous, slow to toilet train, and oppositional (Conners, March, Frances, Wells, & Ross, 2001). The symptoms of inattention, impulsivity, and hyperactivity become increasingly obvious during the school years. Despite the perception that children grow out of ADHD, their problems usually continue: it is estimated that about half of the children with ADHD have ongoing difficulties through adulthood (McGough, 2005). Over time, children with ADHD seem to be less impulsive, although inattention persists. During adolescence, the impulsivity manifests itself in different areas; for example, they are at greater risk for teen pregnancy and contracting sexually transmitted diseases. They are also more likely to have driving difficulties, such as crashes; to be cited for speeding; and to have their licenses suspended (Barkley, 2006a). In short, although the manifestations of ADHD change as people grow older, many of their problems persist.

Up to 80% of children with ADHD are diagnosed with one or more other disorders as well (Wilens et al., 2002). This information is important for several reasons. First, it speaks to the causes of the disorder, which may overlap with others. Second, it tells clinicians to look for other problems in these children that may complicate efforts to treat them. Common comorbid disorders in children include anxiety, depression, and disruptive behavior (Barkley, 2006c). Similarly, almost 90% of adults with ADHD are likely to have at least one other disorder, including disruptive behavior, depression, anxiety, and substance use disorders (McGough et al., 2005).

As you can see, diagnosing children with ADHD is complicated. Several other DSM-IV disorders, also found in children, appear to overlap significantly with this disorder. Specifically, oppositional defiant disorder (ODD), conduct disorder, and bipolar disorder all have characteristics seen in children with ADHD. ODD is a DSM-IV disorder that includes symptoms such as "often loses temper," "argues with adults," "often deliberately annoys people," "touchy and easily annoyed by others," and "often spiteful and vindictive." The impulsivity and hyperactivity observed in children with ADHD can manifest themselves in some of these symptoms. It's been estimated that at least half of those with ADHD could also be diagnosed with ODD (Barkley, 2006c). Similarly, conduct disorder—which, as you saw in Chapter 12, can be a precursor to antisocial personality disorder—is also observed in many children with ADHD. Bipolar disorder—which you will recall is one of the mood disorders—also overlaps significantly with ADHD. This overlap can complicate diagnosis in these children.

■ Causes

As with many other disorders, we are at a period when important information about the genetics of ADHD is beginning to be uncovered (Waldman & Gizer, 2006). We have known for some time that ADHD is more common in families in which one person has the disorder. For example, the relatives of children with ADHD have been found to be more likely to have ADHD themselves than would be expected in the general population (Biederman et al., 1992). Importantly, these families display an increase in psy-

"[He] would never think before he did stuff. And actually, the thing that really made me go, 'Something is desperately wrong here'—we had a little puppy. Real tiny little dog. And Sean was upstairs playing with it. And my daughter had gone upstairs, and went, 'Mom, something's wrong with the dog's paw.' And I looked and this poor little dog had a broken paw. Sean had dropped her. But—didn't say anything to anyone. Just left the poor little dog sitting there. And I thought, 'Wow. This is just not normal.'"

chopathology in general, including conduct disorder, mood disorders, anxiety disorders, and substance abuse (Faraone et al., 2000). This research and the comorbidity in the children themselves suggest that some shared genetic deficits may contribute to the problems experienced by individuals with these disorders (Faraone, 2003).

ADHD is considered to be highly influenced by genetics, with a relatively small role played by environmental influences in the cause of the disorder when compared to many other disorders we discuss in this book. As with other disorders, researchers are finding that more than one gene is probably responsible for ADHD (Bobb, Castellanos, Addington, & Rapoport, 2006). Research in this area is following the same progression as for other disorders and involves large collaborative studies across many laboratories worldwide. Most attention to date focuses on genes associated with the neurochemical dopamine, although norepinephrine, serotonin, and gamma-aminobutyric acid are also implicated in the cause of ADHD. More specifically, there is strong evidence that ADHD is associated with the dopamine D_4 receptor gene, the dopamine transporter gene (DAT1), and the dopamine D_5 receptor gene. DAT1 is of particular interest because methylphenidate (Ritalin)—one of the most common medical treatments for ADHD—inhibits this gene and increases the amount of dopamine available. Such research helps us understand at a microlevel what might be going wrong and how to design new interventions.

As with several other disorders we've discussed, researchers are looking for endophenotypes, those basic deficits—such as specific attentional problems—characteristic of ADHD. The goal is to link these deficits to specific brain dysfunctions. Not surprisingly, specific areas of current interest for ADHD are the brain's executive attention system, working memory functions, inattentiveness, and impulsivity. Researchers are now trying to tie specific genetic defects to these cognitive processes to make the link between genes and behavior (Kim, Kim, & Cho, 2006).

The strong genetic influence in ADHD does not rule out any role for the environment (Sharp et al., 2003; Waldman & Gizer, 2006). In one of the few gene–environment interaction studies of ADHD, researchers found that children with a specific mutation involving the dopamine system (called the DAT1 genotype) were more likely to exhibit the symptoms of ADHD if their mothers smoked during pregnancy (Kahn, Khoury, Nichols, & Lanphear, 2003). Prenatal smoking seemed to interact with this

genetic predisposition to increase the risk for hyperactive and impulsive behavior.

For several decades, ADHD has been thought to involve brain damage, and this notion is reflected in the previous use of labels such as "minimal brain damage" or "minimal brain dysfunction" (Ross & Pelham, 1981). The rapid advances in scanning technology now permit us to see just how the brain may be involved in this disorder. A great deal of research on the structure and the function of the brain for children with this disorder has been conducted just over the past few years. In general, we now know that the overall volume of the brain in those with this disorder is slightly smaller (3% to 4%) than in children without this disorder. A number of areas in the brains of those with ADHD appear affected (Valera, Faraone, Murray, & Seidman, 2007). In addition, more research is starting to focus on the structure and function of the brain in adults with ADHD.

A variety of such toxins as allergens and food additives have been considered as possible causes of ADHD over the years, although little evidence supports the association. The theory that food additives such as artificial colors, flavorings, and preservatives are responsible for the symptoms of ADHD has had a substantial impact. Feingold (1975) presented this view, along with recommendations for eliminating these substances as a treatment for ADHD. Hundreds of thousands of families have put their children on the Feingold diet, despite evidence that it has little or no effect on the symptoms of ADHD (Barkley, 1990; Kavale & Forness, 1983).

A child with ADHD is likely to behave inappropriately regardless of the setting.

As you saw in the discussion of genetics, one of the more consistent findings among children with ADHD involves its association with maternal smoking. In addition, a variety of other pregnancy complications (for example, maternal alcohol consumption and low birth weight) seem to play a role in increasing the chance that a child with a genetic predisposition for ADHD will display the symptoms characteristic of this disorder (Barkley, 2006d).

Psychological and social dimensions of ADHD may further influence the disorder itself—especially how the child fares over time. Negative responses by parents, teachers, and peers to the affected child's impulsivity and hyperactivity may contribute to feelings of low self-esteem, especially in children who are also depressed (Barkley, 1989). Years of constant reminders by teachers and parents to behave, sit quietly, and pay attention may create a negative self-image in these children, which, in turn, can negatively affect their ability to make friends. Thus, the possible biological influences on impulsivity, hyperactivity, and attention, combined with attempts to control these children, may lead to rejection and consequent poor self-image. An integration of the biological and psychological influences on ADHD suggests that both need to be addressed when designing effective treatments (Rapport, 2001).

■ Treatment of ADHD

Treatment for ADHD has proceeded on two fronts: biological and psychosocial interventions. Typically, the goal of biological treatments is to reduce the children's impulsivity and hyperactivity and to improve their attentional skills. Psychosocial treatments generally focus on broader issues such as improving academic performance, decreasing disruptive behavior, and improving social skills. Although these two kinds of approaches have typically developed independently, recent efforts combine them to have a broader impact on people with ADHD.

The first class of medication used for children with ADHD is the stimulants. Since the use of stimulant medication with children with ADHD was first described (Bradley, 1937), hundreds of studies have documented the effectiveness of this kind of medication in reducing the core symptoms of the disorder. It is estimated that more than 2.5 million children in the United States are being treated with these medications (Centers for Disease Control and Prevention, 2005). Drugs such as methylphenidate (Ritalin, Metadate, Concerta) and D-amphetamine (Dexedrine, Dextrostat) have proved helpful for more than 70% of cases in at least temporarily reducing hyperactivity and impulsivity and improving concentration on tasks (Connor, 2006). Adderall, which is a longer-acting version of these psychostimulants, reduces the need for multiple doses for children during the day but has similar positive effects (Connor, 2006).

Originally, it seemed paradoxical or contrary to expect that children would calm down after taking a stimulant. However, on the same low doses, children and adults with and without ADHD react in the same way. It appears that stimulant medications reinforce the brain's ability to focus attention during problem-solving tasks (Connor, 2006). Although the use of stimulant medications remains controversial, especially for children, most clinicians recommend them temporarily, in combination with psychosocial interventions, to help improve children's social and academic skills.

The concerns over the use of stimulant medications now include their potential for abuse. You saw in Chapter 11 that drugs such as Ritalin are sometimes abused for their ability to create elation and reduce fatigue. This is particularly worrisome for children with ADHD because they are at increased risk for later substance abuse (Spencer, 2006). A newer drug—Strattera (or atomoxetine)—also appears effective for some children with ADHD, but it is a selective norepinephrine-reuptake inhibitor and therefore does not produce the same "highs" when used in larger doses. Research suggests that other drugs, such as one of the antidepressants (bupropion, imipramine) and a drug used for treating high blood pressure (clonidine), may have similar effects on people with ADHD (Spencer, 2006). Not all children with ADHD have depression or high blood pressure (although depression can be a problem in a portion of these children), but these drugs work on the same neurotransmitter systems (norepinephrine and dopamine) involved in ADHD. All these drugs seem to improve compliance and decrease negative behaviors in many children, and their effects do not usually last when the drugs are discontinued.

Some portion of children with ADHD do not respond to medications, and most children who do respond show improvement in ability to focus their attention but do not show gains in the important areas of academics and social skills (Smith, Barkley, & Shapiro, 2006). In addition, the medications often result in unpleasant side effects, such as insomnia, drowsiness, or irritability (Connor, 2006). Because of these findings, researchers have applied various behavioral interventions to help these children at home and in school. In general, the programs set such goals as increasing the amount of time the child remains seated, the number of math papers completed, or appropriate play with peers. Reinforcement programs reward the child for improvements and, at times, punish misbehavior with loss of rewards. Other programs incorporate parent training to teach families how to respond constructively to their child's behaviors and how to structure the child's day to help prevent difficulties (Sonuga-Barke, Daley, Thompson, Laver-Bradbury, & Weeks, 2001). Social skills training for these children, which includes teaching them how to interact appropriately with their peers, also seems to be an important treatment component (de Boo & Prins, 2007). For adults with ADHD, cognitive-behavioral intervention for the distractibility and organizational skills problems appears quite helpful. Most clinicians typically recommend a combination of approaches designed to individualize treatments for those with ADHD, targeting both short-term management issues (decreasing hyperactivity and impulsivity) and long-term concerns (preventing and reversing academic decline and improving social skills).

To determine whether or not a combined approach to treatment is the most effective, a large-scale study initiated by the National Institute of Mental Health was conducted by six teams of researchers (Jensen et al., 2001). Labeled the Multimodal Treatment of Attention Deficit/Hyperactivity Disorder (MTA) study, this project included 579 children who were randomly assigned to one of four groups. One group of the children received routine care without medication or specific behavioral interventions (community care). The three treatment groups consisted of medication management (usually methylphenidate), intensive behavioral treatment, and a combination of the two treatments, and the study lasted 14 months. Initial reports from the study suggested that the combination of behavioral treatments and medication and that medication alone were superior to behavioral treatment alone and *community intervention* for ADHD symptoms. For problems that went beyond the specific symptoms of ADHD, such as social skills, academics, parent–child relations, oppositional behavior, and anxiety or depression, results suggested slight advantages of combination over single treatments (medication management, behavioral treatment) and community care.

Some controversy surrounds the interpretation of these findings—specifically, whether or not the combination of behavioral and medical treatments is superior to medication alone (Biederman, Spencer, Wilens, & Greene, 2001; Pelham, 1999). One of the concerns surrounding the study was that although medication continued to be dispensed, the behavioral treatment was faded over time, which may account for the observed differences.

Practically, if there is no difference between these two treatments, most parents and therapists would opt for simply providing medication for these children. As we mentioned previously, behavioral interventions have the added benefit of improving aspects of the child and family that are not directly affected by medication. Reinterpretations of the data from this large-scale study continue, and more research likely will be needed to clarify the combined and separate effects of these two approaches to treatment (Smith et al., 2006). Despite these advances, however, children with ADHD continue to pose a considerable challenge to their families and to the educational system.

Learning Disorders

Academic achievement is highly valued in our society. We often compare the performance of our schoolchildren with that of children in other cultures to estimate whether we are succeeding or failing as a world leader and economic force. On a personal level, because parents often invest a great deal of time and emotional energy into ensuring their children's academic success, it can be extremely upsetting when a child with no obvious intellectual deficits does not achieve as expected. In this section, we describe **learning disorders** in reading, mathematics, and written expression—all characterized by performance that is substantially below what would be expected given the person's age, intelligence quotient (IQ) score, and education. We also look briefly at disorders that involve how we communicate. Consider the case of Alice.

ALICE: Taking a Reading Disorder to College

Alice, a 20-year-old college student, sought help because of her difficulty in several of her classes. She reported that she had enjoyed school and had been a good student until about the sixth grade, when her grades suffered significantly. Her teacher informed her parents that she wasn't working up to

her potential and she needed to be better motivated. Alice had always worked hard in school but promised to try harder. However, with each report card her mediocre grades made her feel worse about herself. She managed to graduate from high school, but by that time she felt she was not as bright as her friends.

Alice enrolled in the local community college and again found herself struggling with the work. Over the years, she had learned several tricks that seemed to help her study and at least get passing grades. She read the material in her textbooks aloud to herself; she had earlier discovered that she could recall the material much better this way than if she just read silently to herself. In fact, reading silently, she could barely remember any of the details just minutes later.

After her sophomore year, Alice transferred to the university, which she found even more demanding and where she failed most of her classes. After our first meeting, I suggested that she be formally assessed to identify the source of her difficulty. As suspected, Alice had a learning disability.

Scores from an IQ test placed her slightly above average, but she was assessed to have significant difficulties with reading. Her comprehension was poor, and she could not remember most of the content of what she read. We recommended that she continue with her trick of reading aloud, because her comprehension for what she heard was adequate. In addition, Alice was taught how to analyze her reading—that is, how to outline and take notes. She was even encouraged to audiotape her lectures and play them back to herself as she drove around in her car. Although Alice did not become an A student, she was able to graduate from the university, and she now works with young children who themselves have learning disabilities.

■ Clinical Description

According to DSM-IV-TR criteria, Alice would be diagnosed as having a **reading disorder,** which is defined as a significant discrepancy between a person's reading achievement and what would be expected for someone of the same age—referred to by some as "unexpected underachievement" (Fletcher, Lyon, Fuchs, & Barnes, 2007). More specifically, the criteria require that the person read at a level significantly below that of a typical person of the same age, cognitive ability (as measured on an IQ test), and educational background. In addition, this disability cannot be caused by a sensory difficulty, such as trouble with sight or hearing, and should not be the result of poor or absent instruction. Similarly, DSM-IV-TR defines a **mathematics disorder** as achievement below expected performance in mathematics and a **disorder of written expression** as achievement below expected performance in writing. In each of these disorders, the difficulties are sufficient to interfere with the students' academic achievement and to disrupt their daily activities.

There is some controversy over using the discrepancy between IQ and achievement as part of the process of identifying children with learning disorders. Part of the criticism involves the delay between when learning problems occur and when they fi-

DSM-IV-TR

DSM TABLE 14.2 Diagnostic Criteria for Learning Disorders* for Reading Disorder (Developmental Reading Disorder), Mathematics Disorder (Developmental Arithmetic Disorder), and Disorder of Written Expression (Developmental Expressive Writing Disorder)

A. (Reading achievement) (Mathematical ability) (Writing skill), as measured by individually administered standardized tests, is substantially below that expected given the person's chronological age, measured intelligence, and age-appropriate education.

B. The disturbance in criterion A significantly interferes with academic achievement or activities of daily living that require (reading skills) (mathematical ability) (composition of written texts).

C. If a sensory deficit is present, the learning difficulties are in excess of those usually associated with it.

*The three separate learning disorders are combined here because the basic criteria are identical, with the exception of the specific ability that is affected.

Source: Reprinted, with permission, from American Psychiatric Association. (2000). *Diagnostic and statistical manual of mental disorders* (4th ed., text revision). Washington, DC: Author, © 2000 American Psychiatric Association.

nally result in a large enough difference between IQ scores and achievement scores—which may not be measurable until later in a child's academic life. An alternative approach—called "response to intervention"—is now being used by many clinicians. It involves identifying a child as having a learning disorder when the response to a known effective intervention (for example, an early reading program) is significantly inferior to the performance by peers (Compton, Fuchs, Fuchs, & Bryant, 2006). This provides an early warning system and focuses on providing effective instruction.

■ Statistics

Estimates of how prevalent learning disorders are range from 5% to 10% (Altarac & Saroha, 2007), although the frequency of this diagnosis appears to increase in wealthier regions of the country—suggesting that with better access to diagnostic services, more children are identified (see ■ Figure 14.1). It is currently believed that nearly 6 million children in the United States are diagnosed as having a specific learning disorder (Altarac & Saroha, 2007). There do appear to be racial differences in the diagnosis of learning disorders. Approximately 1% of white children and 2.6% of black children were receiving services for problems with learning in 2001 (Bradley, Danielson, & Hallahan, 2002). However, this research also suggests that the differences were related to the economic status of the child, not ethnic background.

Difficulties with reading are the most common of the learning disorders and occur in some form in 4% to 10% of the general population (Tannock, 2005b). Mathematics disorder appears in approximately 1% of the population (Tannock, 2005a), but we have limited information about the prevalence of disorder of written expression among children and adults. Early studies suggested that boys were more likely to have a reading disorder than girls, although more contemporary research indicates that boys and girls may be equally affected by this disorder (Feinstein & Phillips, 2006). Students with learning disorders are more likely to drop out of school (Vogel & Reder, 1998), more likely to be unemployed (Shapiro & Lentz, 1991), and more likely to have suicidal thoughts and attempt suicide (Daniel et al., 2006).

Interviews with adults who have learning disabilities reveal that their school experiences were generally negative and the effects often lasted beyond graduation. One man who did not have special assistance during school reports the following:

> I faked my way through school because I was very bright. I resent most that no one picked up my weaknesses. Essentially I judge myself on my failures. . . . [I] have always had low self-esteem. In hindsight I feel that I had low self-esteem in college. . . . I was afraid to know myself. A blow to my self-esteem when I was in school was that I could not write a poem or a story. . . . I could not write with a pen or pencil. The computer has changed my life. I do everything on my computer. It acts as my memory. I use it to structure my life and for all of my writing since my handwriting and written expression has always been so poor. (Polloway, Schewel, & Patton, 1992, p. 521)

A group of disorders loosely identified as verbal or *communication disorders* seems closely related to learning disorders. These dis-

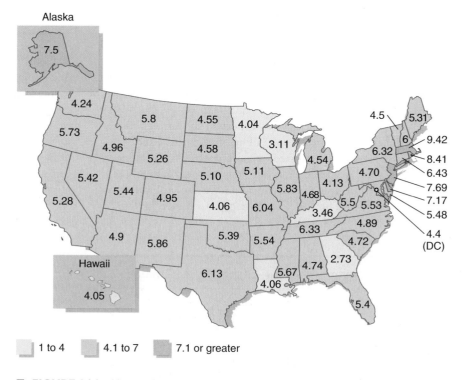

■ **FIGURE 14.1** Uneven distribution. The highest percentages of schoolchildren diagnosed with learning disabilities are in the wealthiest states.

orders can appear deceptively benign, yet their presence early in life can cause wide-ranging problems later. For a brief overview of these disorders, which include **stuttering, expressive language disorder, selective mutism,** and **tic disorder,** see Box 14.1.

■ Causes

Theories about the causes of learning disorders include genetic, neurobiological, and environmental factors. The genetic research in this area is particularly complex. It is clear that learning disorders run in families, and sophisticated family and twin studies bear this out (Fletcher et al., 2007). Yet, analyses of the genes involved suggest that many effects are not specific—meaning that there are not different genes responsible for reading disorders and mathematics disorders. Instead, there are genes that affect learning and they may contribute to problems across domains (reading, mathematics, writing) (Plomin & Kovas, 2005).

It should be obvious that the different problems associated with learning themselves have different origins. For example, children (and adults) often have very different problems associated with reading. Reading disorders are sometimes broken into problems with word recognition (difficulty decoding single words—sometimes called *dyslexia*), fluency (problems being able to read words and sentences smoothly and automatically), and comprehension (difficulty getting meaning from what is read) (Fletcher et al., 2007). Most research to date focuses on problems with word recognition, and there is evidence that some develop these problems primarily through their genes while others develop problems as a result of environmental factors (Shaywitz, Mody, & Shaywitz, 2006). Genes located on chromosomes 2, 6, 15, and 18 have all been repeatedly linked to these difficulties. At the same time, environmental influences such as the home reading habits of families can significantly affect outcomes—especially with skills such as

---

BOX 14.1 Communication and Related Disorders

STUTTERING

Clinical Description
A disturbance in speech fluency that includes a number of problems with speech, such as repeating syllables or words, prolonging certain sounds, making obvious pauses, or substituting words to replace ones that are difficult to articulate.

Statistics
Occurs twice as often among boys as among girls. Begins most often in children under the age of 3, and 98% of cases occur before the age of 10. Approximately 80% of children who stutter before they enter school will no longer stutter after they have been in school a year or so (Kroll & Beitchman, 2005).

Causes
Rather than anxiety causing stuttering, stuttering makes people socially anxious (Craig, Hancock, Tran, & Craig, 2003). Multiple brain pathways appear to be involved, and genetic influences may be a factor (Kroll & Beitchman, 2005).

Treatment
Parents are counseled about how to talk to their children. *Regulated-breathing method* is a promising behavioral treatment in which the person is instructed to stop speaking when a stuttering episode occurs and then to take a deep breath (exhale, then inhale) before proceeding (Woods, Twohig, Fuqua, & Hanley, 2000). Some works shows that altered auditory feedback (electronically changing speech feedback to people who stutter) can improve speech (Lincoln, Packman, & Onslow, 2006), as can using forms of self-monitoring, in which

people modify their own speech for the words they stutter (Venkatagiri, 2005).

EXPRESSIVE LANGUAGE DISORDERS

Clinical Description
Limited speech in *all* situations. *Expressive language* (what is said) is significantly below *receptive language* (what is understood); the latter is usually average.

Statistics
Occurs in 10% to 15% of children younger than 3 years of age (Johnson & Beitchman, 2005) and is almost five times as likely to affect boys as girls (Whitehurst et al., 1988).

Causes
An unfounded psychological explanation is that the children's parents may not speak to them enough. A biological theory is that middle ear infection is a contributory cause.

Treatment
May be self-correcting and may not require special intervention.

SELECTIVE MUTISM

Clinical Description
Persistent failure to speak in specific situations—such as school—despite the ability to do so.

Statistics
Occurs in less than 1% of children and most often between the ages of 5 and 7. More prevalent among girls than boys.

Causes
Not much is known. Anxiety is one possible cause (Bergman & Piacentini, 2005).

Treatment
Contingency management: Giving children praise and reinforcers for speaking while ignoring their attempts to communicate in other ways.

TIC DISORDERS

Clinical Description
Involuntary motor movements *(tics),* such as head twitching, or vocalizations, such as grunts, that often occur in rapid succession, come on suddenly, and happen in idiosyncratic or stereotyped ways. In one type, *Tourette's disorder,* vocal tics often include the involuntary repetition of obscenities.

Statistics
Of all children, 12% to 18% show some tics during their growing years, and 10 to 80 children out of every 10,000 have Tourette's disorder (Scahill & Leckman, 2005). Usually develops before the age of 14. High comorbidity between tics and ADHD, as well as obsessive-compulsive disorder (Scahill & Leckman, 2005).

Causes
Strong genetic component, but the nature of the genes is as yet unknown (Scahill & Leckman, 2005).

Treatment
Psychological: Self-monitoring, relaxation training, and habit reversal.
Pharmacological: Haloperidol; more recently, risperidone and ziprasidone.

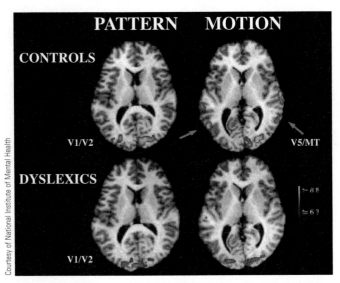

These functional MRI scans of composite data from six dyslexic adults and eight controls show a horizontal slice through the brain, with the face at the top. Imaging shows atypical brain activity associated with dyslexia. The scans were performed while subjects tracked a pattern of moving dots on a computer screen. A brain area (V5/MT) normally active during such motion tasks did not switch on in dyslexic subjects (right). Their brain activity was more similar to that of controls during a pattern recognition task (left).

Specially designed computer games may help children with learning disorders improve their language skills.

word recognition—suggesting that reading to children at risk for reading disorders can lessen the impact of the genetic influence (Petrill, Deater-Deckard, Thompson, DeThorne, & Schatschneider, 2006).

Various forms of subtle brain damage have also been thought responsible for learning disabilities; some of the earliest theories involve a neurological explanation (Hinshelwood, 1896). Research suggests structural, as well as functional, differences in the brains of people with learning disabilities. Specifically, three areas of the left hemisphere appear to be involved in problems with dyslexia (word recognition)—Broca's area (which affects articulation and word analysis), an area in the left parietotemporal area (which affects word analysis), and an area in the left occipitotemporal area (which affects recognizing word form) (Shaywitz et al., 2006). A different area in the left hemisphere—the intraparietal sulcus—seems to be critical for the development of a sense of numbers and is implicated in mathematics disorder (Fletcher et al., 2007). In contrast, there is no current evidence for specific deficits responsible for disorders of written expression.

Disorders of reading have been diagnosed more often in English-speaking countries. Although some have thought that this may simply be a difference in diagnostic practices, biological research now suggests it may involve the relative complexity of the written word in English. Researchers tested individuals who displayed reading disorders and who spoke English, French, or Italian (Paulesu et al., 2001). Although those who spoke Italian did better on tests of reading, brain imaging (positron emission tomography) while all subjects were reading indicated each experienced the same reduced activity in the left temporal lobe. It was hypothesized that the complexity of reading English may account for these cultural differences.

You saw that Alice persisted despite the obstacles caused by her learning disorder, as well as by the reactions of teachers and others. What helped her continue toward her goal when others choose, instead, to drop out of school? Psychological and motivational factors that have been reinforced by others seem to play an important role in the eventual outcome of people with learning disorders. Factors such as socioeconomic status, cultural expectations, parental interactions and expectations, and child management practices, together with existing neurological deficits and the types of support provided in the school, seem to determine outcome (Fletcher et al., 2007).

■ Treatment of Learning Disorders

As you will see in the case of mental retardation, learning disorders primarily require educational intervention. Biological treatment is typically restricted to those individuals who may also have ADHD, which you have seen involves impulsivity and an inability to sustain attention and can be helped with certain stimulant medications, such as methylphenidate (Ritalin). Educational efforts can be broadly categorized into (1) specific skills instruction, including instruction on vocabulary, finding the main idea, and finding facts in readings, and (2) strategy instruction, which includes efforts to improve cognitive skills through decision making and critical thinking (Fletcher et al., 2007).

Many programs are used to assist children with their problems related to learning. One of the approaches that has received considerable research support is called Direct Instruction (Carnine, Silbert, Kame'enui, & Tarver, 2004). Among the components that make up this program are systematic instruction, using highly scripted lesson plans, placing students together in small groups based on their progress, and teaching for mastery (teaching students until they understand all concepts). In addition, children are constantly assessed and plans are modified based on progress or lack of progress. Direct Instruction and a number of related training programs appear to significantly improve academic skills in children with learning disorders (Gajria, Jitendra, Sood, & Sacks, 2007).

How do these behavioral and educational approaches help children with reading difficulties? Are they just tricks or adaptations to learning, or do these treatments have a more profound effect on the way these children process information? Exciting research using brain-imaging technology is allowing us to answer these important questions. One study used functional magnetic resonance imaging scanning to compare how children with and without reading disorders processed simple tasks (Temple et al., 2003). The children with reading difficulties were then exposed to 8 weeks of intensive training on a computer program that helped them work on their auditory and language processing skills. Not only did the children improve their reading skills, but their brains started functioning in a way similar to the brains of their peers who were good readers. This and similar studies (Simos et al., 2007) mirror results seen with other disorders—namely, that behavioral interventions can change the way the brain works and that we can use such interventions to help individuals with significant problems.

CONCEPT CHECK 14.1

Assign a label to each of the following cases: (a) ADHD, (b) attention deficit disorder without hyperactivity, (c) selective mutism, (d) Tourette's disorder, or (e) reading disorder.

1. Ten-year-old Michael is frequently off-task at school. He often forgets to bring his homework to school and typically comes home without an important book. He works quickly and makes careless mistakes. _____
2. Jan was a good student until the fifth grade. She studied a great deal, but her grades continued to drop. Now, as a high school senior concerned about graduation, Jan has sought help. She places above average on an IQ test but shows significant problems with reading and comprehension. _____

(continued)

CONCEPT CHECK 14.1

(continued)

3. Mike's developmental disorder is characterized by uncontrollable yelps, sniffs, and grunting noises. _____
4. Nine-year-old Evan can be frustrating to his parents, teachers, and friends. He often calls out answers in school, sometimes before the complete question is asked. He has trouble waiting his turn during games and does things seemingly without thinking. _____
5. Nine-year-old Cathy is described by everyone as a "handful." She fidgets constantly in class, drumming her fingers on the desk, squirming in her chair, and getting up and down. She has trouble waiting her turn at work or at play, and she sometimes has violent outbursts. _____
6. At home, 8-year-old Hanna has been excitedly telling her cousins about a recent trip to a theme park. This would surprise her teachers, who have never heard her speak. _____

PERVASIVE DEVELOPMENTAL DISORDERS

People with **pervasive developmental disorders** all experience problems with language, socialization, and cognition (Durand, 2005). The word *pervasive* means that these problems are not relatively minor but significantly affect individuals throughout their lives. Included under the heading of pervasive developmental disorders are autistic disorder (or autism), Asperger's disorder, **Rett's disorder, childhood disintegrative disorder,** and **pervasive developmental disorder, not otherwise specified.** We focus on two of the more prevalent pervasive developmental disorders—autistic disorder and Asperger's disorder; the other disorders are highlighted in Box 14.2.

Autistic Disorder

Autistic disorder (autism) is a childhood disorder characterized by significant impairment in social interactions and communication and by restricted patterns of behavior, interest, and activities (Durand, 2004). Individuals have a puzzling array of symptoms. Consider the case of Amy.

AMY: In Her Own World

Amy, 3 years old, spends much of her day picking up pieces of lint. She drops the lint in the air and then watches intently as it falls to the floor. She also licks the back of her hands and stares at the saliva. She hasn't spoken yet and can't feed or dress herself. Several times a day she screams so loudly that the neighbors at first thought she was being abused. She doesn't seem to be interested in her mother's love and affection but will take her mother's hand to lead her to the refrigerator. Amy likes to eat butter—whole pats of it, several at a time. Her mother uses the pats of butter that you get at some restaurants to help Amy learn and to keep her well behaved. If Amy helps with dressing herself, or if she sits quietly for several minutes, her mother gives her some butter. Amy's mother knows that the butter isn't good for her, but it is the only thing that seems to get through to the child. The family's pediatrician has been concerned about Amy's developmental delays for some time and has recently suggested that she be evaluated by specialists. The pediatrician thinks Amy may have autism and the child and her family will probably need extensive support.

■ Clinical Description

Three major characteristics of autism are expressed in DSM-IV-TR: impairment in social interactions, impairment in communication, and restricted behavior, interests, and activities (American Psychiatric Association, 2000).

Impairment in Social Interactions   One of the defining characteristics of people with autistic disorder is that they do not develop the types of social relationships expected for their age (Durand, 2004). Amy never made friends among her peers and

often limited her contact with adults to using them as tools—for example, taking the adult's hand to reach for something she wanted. For young children, the signs of social problems usually include a failure to engage in skills such as joint attention (Dawson et al., 2004; MacDonald et al., 2006). When sitting with a parent in front of a favorite toy, young children will typically look back and forth between the parent and the toy, smiling, in an attempt to engage the parent with the toy. However, this skill in joint attention is noticeably absent in children with autism.

Research using sophisticated eye-tracking technology shows how this social awareness problem evolves as the children grow older. In one study, scientists showed an adult man with autism scenes from some movies and compared how he looked at social scenes with how a man without autism did so (Klin, Jones, Schultz, Volkmar, & Cohen, 2002). You can see from the photo (on the next page) that the man with autism (indicated by the red lines) scanned nonsocial aspects of the scene (the actors' mouth and jacket), while the man without autism looked at the socially meaningful sections (looking from eye to eye of the people conversing). This research suggests that people with autism—for reasons we do not yet fully understand—may not be interested in social situations and therefore may not enjoy meaningful relationships with others or have the ability to develop them.

Impairment in Communication   People with autism nearly always have severe problems with communicating. About one-third never acquire speech (Wetherby & Prizant, 2005). In those with some speech, much of their communication is unusual. Some

---

BOX 14.2   Additional Pervasive Developmental Disorders

RETT'S DISORDER

Clinical Description
A progressive neurological disorder that primarily affects girls. It is characterized by constant hand-wringing, increasingly severe mental retardation, and impaired motor skills, all of which appear *after* an apparently normal start in development (Van Acker, Loncola, & Van Acker, 2005). Motor skills seem to deteriorate progressively over time; social skills, however, develop normally at first, decline between the ages of 1 and 3, and then partially improve.

Statistics
Rett's disorder is relatively rare, occurring in approximately 1 per 12,000 to 15,000 live female births.

Causes
A mutation of a gene on the X chromosome (MECP2) appears responsible for the majority of cases.

Treatment
Focuses on teaching self-help and communication skills and on efforts to reduce problem behaviors.

CHILDHOOD DISINTEGRATIVE DISORDER

Clinical Description
Involves severe regression in language, adaptive behavior, and motor skills after a 2- to 4-year period of normal development (Volkmar, Koenig, & State, 2005).

Statistics
Rare, occurring in 1 of approximately every 100,000 births.

Causes
Although no specific cause has been identified, several factors suggest an accumulation of a number of rare genetic mutations (Volkmar, Koenig, & State, 2005).

Treatment
Typically involves behavioral interventions to regain lost skills and behavioral and pharmacological treatments to help reduce behavioral problems.

PERVASIVE DEVELOPMENTAL DISORDER, NOT OTHERWISE SPECIFIED

Clinical Description
Severe and pervasive impairments in social interactions but without all criteria for autistic disorder. These individuals may not display the early avoidance of social interaction but still may exhibit significant social problems. Their problems may become more obvious after 3 years of age.

Statistics
Little good evidence for prevalence at this time, although appears more common than autistic disorder.

Causes
Some of the same genetic influences and neurobiological impairments common in autism are likely involved in these individuals as well (Towbin, 2005).

Treatment
Focuses on teaching socialization and communication skills and on efforts to reduce problem behaviors.

Researchers are exploring how people with autism view social interactions among other people. (From Klin, A., Jones, W., Schultz, R., Volkmar, F., & Cohen, D., 2002. Defining and quantifying the social phenotype in autism. *American Journal of Psychiatry, 159*, 895–908.)

repeat the speech of others, a pattern called echolalia we referred to before as a sign of delayed speech development. If you say, "My name is Eileen, what's yours?" they will repeat all or part of what you said: "Eileen, what's yours?" And often, not only are your words repeated, but so is your intonation. Some who can speak are unable or unwilling to carry on conversations with others.

Restricted Behavior, Interests, and Activities The more striking characteristics of autism include *restricted patterns of behavior, interests,* and *activities.* Amy appeared to like things to stay the same: She became extremely upset if even a small change was introduced (such as moving her toys in her room). This intense preference for the status quo has been called *maintenance of sameness.* Often, people with autism spend countless hours in *stereotyped and ritualistic behaviors,* making such stereotyped movements as spinning around in circles, waving their hands in front of their eyes with their heads cocked to one side, or biting their hands.

▪ Statistics

Autism was once thought to be a rare disorder, although more recent estimates of its occurrence seem to show an increase in its prevalence. Previous estimates found a rate of 2 to 20 per 10,000 people, although it is now believed to be as high as 1 in every 500 births (Shattuck, 2006). The prevalence of autism spectrum disorders (which include autistic disorder; pervasive developmental disorder, not otherwise specified; and Asperger's disorder) is estimated as high as 1 in every 150 births (Centers for Disease Control and Prevention, 2007). This rise in the rates may be the result of increased awareness on the part of professionals to distinguish the pervasive developmental disorders from mental retardation. Gender differences for autism vary depending on the IQ level of the person affected. For people with IQs under 35, autism is more prevalent among females; in the higher IQ range, it is more prevalent among males. We do not know the reason for these differences (Volkmar, Szatmari, & Sparrow, 1993). Autistic disorder appears to be a universal phenomenon, identified in every part of

---

DSM-IV-TR

DSM TABLE 14.3 Diagnostic Criteria for Autistic Disorder

A. A total of six (or more) items from (1), (2), and (3), with at least two from (1) and one each from (2) and (3):
  1. Qualitative impairment in social interaction, as manifested by at least two of the following:
     a. Marked impairment in the use of multiple nonverbal behaviors such as eye-to-eye gaze, facial expression, body postures, and gestures to regulate social interaction
     b. Failure to develop peer relationships appropriate to developmental level
     c. A lack of spontaneous seeking to share enjoyment, interests, or achievements with other people (e.g., by a lack of showing, bringing, or pointing out objects of interest)
     d. Lack of social or emotional reciprocity
  2. Qualitative impairments in communication as manifested by at least one of the following:
     a. Delay in, or total lack of, the development of spoken language (not accompanied by an attempt to compensate through alternative modes of communication such as gesture or mime)
     b. In individuals with adequate speech, marked impairment in the ability to initiate or sustain a conversation with others
     c. Stereotyped and repetitive use of language or idiosyncratic language
     d. Lack of varied, spontaneous make-believe play or social imitative play appropriate to developmental level
  3. Restricted repetitive and stereotyped patterns of behavior, interests, and activities, as manifested by at least one of the following:
     a. Encompassing preoccupation with one or more stereotyped and restricted patterns of interest that is abnormal in either intensity or focus
     b. Apparently inflexible adherence to specific, nonfunctional routines or rituals
     c. Stereotyped and repetitive motor mannerisms (e.g., hand or finger flapping or twisting, or complex whole-body movements)
     d. Persistent preoccupation with parts of objects
B. Delays or abnormal functioning in at least one of the following areas, with onset prior to age 3 years: (1) social interaction, (2) language as used in social communication, or (3) symbolic or imaginative play.
C. The disturbance is not better accounted for by Rett's disorder or childhood disintegrative disorder.

Source: Reprinted, with permission, from American Psychiatric Association. (2000). *Diagnostic and statistical manual of mental disorders* (4th ed., text revision). Washington, DC: Author. © 2000 American Psychiatric Association.

the world, including Sweden (Gillberg, 1984), Japan (Sugiyama & Abe, 1989), Russia (Lebedinskaya & Nikolskaya, 1993), and China (Chung, Luk, & Lee, 1990). Most people with autism develop the associated symptoms before the age of 36 months (American Psychiatric Association, 2000).

There are people with autism along the continuum of IQ scores. Earlier estimates placed the rate of mental retardation among children with autism as high as 75%, although more recent work—using more appropriate tests for these children—indicates the range between 40% and 55% (Chakrabarti & Fombonne, 2001; Edelson, 2006).

IQ measures are used to determine prognosis: The higher children score on IQ tests, the less likely they are to need extensive support by family members or people in the helping professions. Conversely, young children with autistic disorder who score

"Last year she used (the communication book) a lot more in communicating with us. We have different pictures in the book. They're called picture symbols to represent what she might want, what she might need, what she's asking of us."

poorly on IQ tests are more likely to be severely delayed in acquiring communication skills and to need a great deal of educational and social support as they grow older. Usually, language abilities and IQ scores are reliable predictors of how children with autistic disorder will fare later in life: The better the language skills and IQ test performance, the better the prognosis.

■ Causes: Psychological and Social Dimensions

Autism is a puzzling condition, so you should not be surprised to find numerous theories of why it develops. One generalization is that autistic disorder probably does not have a single cause (Tsai, 2005). Instead, a number of biological contributions may combine with psychosocial influences to result in the unusual behaviors of people with autism. Because historical context is important to research, it is helpful to examine past, as well as more recent, theories of autism. (In doing this, we are departing from our usual format of providing biological dimensions first.)

Historically, autistic disorder was seen as the result of failed parenting (Bettelheim, 1967; Ferster, 1961; Tinbergen & Tinbergen, 1972). Mothers and fathers of children with autism were characterized as perfectionistic, cold, and aloof (Kanner, 1949), with relatively high socioeconomic status (Allen, DeMyer, Norton, Pontius, & Yang, 1971; Cox, Rutter, Newman, & Bartak, 1975) and higher IQs than the general population (Kanner, 1943). Descriptions such as these inspired theories holding parents responsible for their children's unusual behaviors. These views were devastating to a generation of parents, who felt guilty and responsible for their children's problems. Imagine being accused of such coldness toward your own child as to cause serious and permanent disabilities. More sophisticated research using larger samples of children and families suggests that the parents of individuals with autism may not differ substantially from parents of children without disabilities (Bhasin & Schendel, 2007).

Other theories about the origins of autism were based on the unusual speech patterns of some individuals—namely, their tendency to avoid first-person pronouns such as *I* and *me* and to use *he* and *she* instead. For example, if you ask a child with autism, "Do you want something to drink?" he might say, "He wants something to drink" (meaning "I want something to drink"). This observation led some theorists to wonder whether autism involves a lack of self-awareness (Goldfarb, 1963; Mahler, 1952). Imagine, if you can, not understanding that your existence is distinct. There is no "you," only "them." Such a debilitating view of the world was used to explain the unusual ways people with autism behaved. Theorists suggested that the withdrawal seen among people with autistic disorder reflected a lack of awareness of their own existence.

However, later research has shown that some people with autistic disorder do seem to have self-awareness (Dawson & McKissick, 1984; Spiker & Ricks, 1984) and that it follows a developmental progression. Just like children without a disability, those with cognitive abilities below the level expected for a child of 18 to 24 months show little or no self-recognition, but people with more advanced abilities do demonstrate self-awareness. Self-concept may be lacking when people with autism also have cognitive disabilities or delays, not because of autism itself.

Myths about people with autism are perpetuated when the idiosyncrasies of the disorder are highlighted. These perceptions are furthered by portrayals such as Dustin Hoffman's in *Rain Man*—his character could, for instance, instantaneously and accurately count hundreds of toothpicks falling to the floor. This type of ability—referred to as savant skills—is rare among people with autism. It is important always to separate myth from reality and to be aware that such portrayals do not accurately represent the full range of manifestations of this complex disorder.

The phenomenon of echolalia, repeating a word or phrase spoken by another person, was once believed to be an unusual characteristic of this disorder. Subsequent work in developmental psychopathology, however, demonstrated that repeating the speech of others is part of the normally developing language skills observed in most young children (Wetherby & Prizant, 2005). Even a behavior as disturbing as the self-injurious behavior sometimes seen in people with autism is observed in milder forms, such as head banging, among typically developing infants (de Lissovoy, 1961). This type of research has helped clinicians isolate the facts from the myths about autism and clarify the role of development in the disorder. Primarily, it appears that what clearly distinguish people with autism from others are social deficiencies.

■ Causes: Biological Dimensions

At present, few workers in the field of autism believe that psychological or social influences play a major role in the development of this disorder. To the relief of many families, it is now clear that poor parenting is not responsible for autism. Deficits in such skills as socialization and communication appear to be biological in origin. Biological theories about the origins of autism, examined next, have received much empirical support.

Genetic Influences It is now clear that autism has a genetic component (Volkmar, Klin, & Schultz, 2005). We know that families

"Getting her out of her routine is something that sets her off. . . . Routine is extremely, extremely important with her."

Temple Grandin has a Ph.D. in animal science and a successful career designing humane equipment for handling livestock. She also has autism.

that have one child with autism have a 5% to 10% risk of having another child with the disorder. This rate is 50 to 200 times the risk in the general population, providing strong evidence of a genetic component in the disorder. The exact genes involved in the development of autism remain elusive. There is evidence for some involvement with numerous chromosomes, and work is ongoing in this complex field (Autism Genome Project Consortium, 2007). One area that is receiving attention involves the genes responsible for the neuropeptide oxytocin. Because oxytocin is shown to have a role in how we bond with others and in our social memory, researchers are looking for whether genes responsible for this neurochemical are involved with the disorder. Preliminary work identifies an association between autism and an

Timothy plays violin and piano, as well as baseball. Autistic disorder occurs in all cultures and races.

oxytocin receptor gene (Jacob et al., 2007), and researchers expect more connections will be identified in the coming years.

Neurobiological Influences As in the area of genetics, many neurobiological influences are being studied to help explain the social and communication problems observed in autism (Volkmar, Klin, & Schultz, 2005). One intriguing theory involves research on the amygdala—the area of the brain that, as you saw in Chapter 5, is involved in emotions such as anxiety and fear. Researchers studying the brains of people with autism after they died note that adults with and without the disorder have amygdalae of about the same size but that those with autism have fewer neurons in this structure (Schumann & Amaral, 2006). Earlier research showed that young children with autism actually have a larger amygdala. The theory being proposed is that the amygdala in children with autism is enlarged early in life—causing excessive anxiety and fear (perhaps contributing to their social withdrawal). With continued stress, the release of the stress hormone cortisol damages the amygdala, causing the relative absence of these neurons in adulthood. The damaged amygdala may account for the different way people with autism respond to social situations.

An additional neurobiological influence we mentioned in the section on genetics involves the neuropeptide oxytocin. Remember that this is an important social neurochemical that influences bonding and is found to increase trust and reduce fear. Some research on children with autism found lower levels of oxytocin in their blood (Modahl et al., 1998), and giving people with autism oxytocin improved their ability to remember and process information with emotion content (such as remembering happy faces), a problem that is symptomatic of autism (Hollander et al., 2007). This is one of a number of theories being explored as possible contributors to this puzzling disorder.

One highly controversial theory is that mercury—specifically, the mercury previously used as a preservative in childhood vaccines (thimerosol)—is responsible for the increases seen in autism over the last decade. Large epidemiological studies conducted in Denmark show that there is no increased risk of autism in children who are vaccinated (Madsen et al., 2002). Despite this and other convincing evidence, the correlation between when a child is vaccinated for measles, mumps, and rubella (12–15 months) and when the symptoms of autism first become evident (before 3 years), continues to fuel the belief by many families that there must be some connection.

The study of autism is a relatively young field and still awaits an integrative theory. It is likely, however, that further research will identify the biological mechanisms that may explain the social aversion experienced by many people with the disorder. Also to be outlined are the psychological and social factors that interact early with the biological influences, producing deficits in socialization and communication, as well as the characteristic unusual behaviors.

Asperger's Disorder

Asperger's disorder involves a significant impairment in the ability to engage in meaningful social interaction, along with restricted and repetitive stereotyped behaviors but without the severe delays in language or other cognitive skills characteristic of people with autism (American Psychiatric Association, 2000). First described by Hans Asperger in 1944, it was Lorna Wing in the early 1980s who recommended that Asperger's disorder be reconsidered as a separate disorder from autism, with an emphasis on the unusual and limited interests (such a train schedules) displayed by these individuals (Volkmar, Klin, & Schultz, 2005).

■ Clinical Description

People with this disorder display impaired social relationships and restricted or unusual behaviors or activities (such as following airline schedules or memorizing ZIP codes), but unlike individuals with autism they can often be quite verbal. This tendency to be obsessed with esoteric facts over people, along with their often formal and academic style of speech, has led some to refer to the disorder as the "little professor syndrome." Individuals show few severe cognitive impairments and usually have IQ scores within the average range (Volkmar, Klin, & Schultz, 2005). They often exhibit clumsiness and poor coordination. Some researchers think Asperger's disorder may be a milder form of autism rather than a separate disorder.

What must it be like to have this disorder? Is it an exquisite solitude, divorced from the stressors of modern life? Or is it an oppressive state of anxiety, filled with the need to try constantly to maintain sameness in a chaotic world? Such fundamental questions have led some researchers to interview these individuals, hoping to gain a better understanding of the disorder so as to aid those who have it. This is just one of these statements that reflects the highly logical and factual nature of their thinking:

> My name is Robert Edwards. I am an intelligent, unsociable but adaptable person. I would like to dispel any untrue rumors about me. I am not edible. I cannot fly. I cannot use telekinesis. My brain is not large enough to destroy the entire world when unfolded. I did not teach my long-haired guinea pig, Chronos, to eat everything in sight (that is the nature of the long-haired guinea pig). (Volkmar, Klin, & Schultz, 2005, p. 3179)

As we gain access to more of these accounts, our understanding of Asperger's disorder should grow, allowing us to offer greater assistance to those with this disorder.

■ Statistics

Until recently, most diagnosticians were relatively unfamiliar with this disorder, and it is generally believed that many individuals went undiagnosed. Current estimates of the prevalence are between 1 and 2 per 10,000, and it is believed to occur more often in boys than in girls (Volkmar, Klin, & Schultz, 2005).

■ Causes

Little causal research exists, although a possible genetic contribution is suspected. Asperger's disorder does seem to run in families, and there appears to be a higher prevalence of both autism and Asperger's disorder in some families. Because of the social–emotional disturbances observed in people with this disorder, as you just saw with autism, researchers are looking at the amygdala for its possible role in the cause (Schultz, Romanski, & Tsatsanis, 2000), although to date there is no conclusive evidence for a specific biological or psychological model.

DSM-IV-TR

DSM TABLE 14.4 Diagnostic Criteria for Asperger's Disorder

A. Qualitative impairment in social interaction, as manifested by at least two of the following:
 1. Marked impairment in the use of multiple nonverbal behaviors such as eye-to-eye gaze, facial expression, body postures, and gestures to regulate social interaction
 2. Failure to develop peer relationships appropriate to developmental level
 3. A lack of spontaneous seeking to share enjoyment, interests, or achievements with other people (e.g., by a lack of showing, bringing, or pointing out objects of interest to other people)
 4. Lack of social or emotional reciprocity
B. Restricted repetitive and stereotyped patterns of behavior, interests, and activities, as manifested by at least one of the following:
 1. Encompassing preoccupation with one or more stereotyped and restricted patterns of interest that is abnormal either in intensity or focus
 2. Apparently inflexible adherence to specific, nonfunctional routines or rituals
 3. Stereotyped and repetitive motor mannerisms (e.g., hand or finger flapping or twisting, or complex whole-body movements)
 4. Persistent preoccupation with parts of objects
C. The disturbance causes clinically significant impairment in social, occupational, or other important areas of functioning.
D. There is no clinically significant delay in cognitive development or in the development of age-appropriate self-help skills, adaptive behavior (other than in social interaction), and curiosity about the environment in childhood.
F. Criteria are not met for another specific pervasive developmental disorder or schizophrenia.

Source: Reprinted, with permission, from American Psychiatric Association. (2000). *Diagnostic and statistical manual of mental disorders* (4th ed., text revision). Washington, DC: Author, © 2000 American Psychiatric Association.

Treatment of Pervasive Developmental Disorders

Most treatment research has focused on children with autism, so we primarily discuss treatment research for these individuals. However, because treatment for all the pervasive developmental disorders relies on a similar approach, this research should be relevant across disorders. One generalization that can be made about autism, as well as the other pervasive developmental disorders, is that no completely effective treatment exists. We have not been successful in eliminating the social problems experienced by these individuals. Rather, like the approach to individuals with mental retardation, most efforts at treating people with pervasive developmental disorders focus on enhancing their communication and daily living skills and on reducing problem behaviors, such as tantrums and self-injury (Durand, 2005). We describe some of these approaches next, including work on early intervention for young children with autism.

■ Psychosocial Treatments

Early psychodynamic treatments were based on the belief that autism is the result of improper parenting, and they encouraged ego development (the creation of a self-image) (Bettelheim,

1967). Given our current understanding about the nature of the disorder, we should not be surprised to learn that treatments based solely on ego development have not had a positive impact on the lives of people with autism (Kanner & Eisenberg, 1955). Greater success has been achieved with behavioral approaches that focus on skill building and behavioral treatment of problem behaviors. This approach is based on the early work of Charles Ferster and Ivar Lovaas. Although the work of Ferster and Lovaas has been greatly refined over the past 40 years, the basic premise—that people with autism can learn and that they can be taught some skills they lack—remains central. There is a great deal of overlap between the treatment of autism and the treatment of mental retardation. With that in mind, we highlight several treatment areas that are particularly important for people with autism, including communication and socialization.

Problems with communication and language are among the defining characteristics of this disorder. People with autism often do not acquire meaningful speech; they tend either to have limited speech or to use unusual speech, such as echolalia. Teaching people to speak in a useful way is difficult. Think about how we teach languages: It mostly involves imitation. Imagine how you would teach a young girl to say the word *spaghetti*. You could wait for several days until she said a word that sounded something like *spaghetti* (maybe *confetti*) and then reinforce her. You could then spend several weeks trying to shape *confetti* into something closer to *spaghetti*. Or you could just prompt, "Say 'spaghetti.'" Fortunately, most children can imitate and learn to communicate efficiently. But a child who has autism can't or won't imitate.

In the mid-1960s, Lovaas and his colleagues took a monumental first step toward addressing the difficulty of getting children with autism to respond. They used the basic behavioral procedures of shaping and discrimination training to teach these nonspeaking children to imitate others verbally (Lovaas, Berberich, Perloff, & Schaeffer, 1966). The first skill the researchers taught them was to imitate other people's speech. They began by reinforcing a child with food and praise for making any sound while watching the teacher. After the child mastered that step, they reinforced the child only if she made a sound after the teacher made a request—such as the phrase, "Say 'ball'" (a procedure known as *discrimination training*). Once the child reliably made some sound after the teacher's request, the teacher used *shaping* to reinforce only approximations of the requested sound, such as the sound of the letter "b." Sometimes the teacher helped the child with physical prompting—in this case, by gently holding the lips together to help the child make the sound of "b." Once the child responded successfully, a second word was introduced—such as "mama"—and the procedure was repeated. This continued until the child could correctly respond to multiple requests, demonstrating imitation by copying the words or phrases made by the teacher. Once the children could imitate, speech was easier, and progress was made in teaching some of them to use labels, plurals, sentences, and other more complex forms of language (Lovaas, 1977). Despite the success of some children in learning speech, other children do not respond to this training, and workers sometimes use alternatives to vocal speech, such as sign language and devices that have vocal output and can literally "speak" for the child (Wetherby & Prizant, 2005).

One of the most striking features of people with autism is their unusual reactions to other people. Although social deficits are among the more obvious problems experienced by people with autism, they can also be the most difficult to teach. A number of approaches are now used to teach social skills (for example, how to carry on a conversation and ask questions of other people), including the use of peers who do not have autism as trainers, and there is evidence that those with autism can improve their socialization skills (Zager & Shamow, 2005).

Timing and Settings for Treatment   Lovaas and his colleagues at University of California, Los Angeles, reported on their early intervention efforts with young children (Lovaas, 1987). They used intensive behavioral treatment for communication and social skills problems for 40 hours or more per week, which seemed to improve intellectual and educational functioning. Follow-up suggests that these improvements are long lasting (McEachin, Smith, & Lovaas, 1993). These studies created considerable interest, as well as controversy. Some critics question the research on practical, as well as experimental, grounds, claiming that one-on-one therapy for 40 hours per week was too expensive and time consuming; they also criticized the studies for having no proper control group. Nevertheless, the results from this important study and a number of replications around the world suggest that early intervention is promising for children with autism (Lord et al., 2005).

Biological Treatment   No one medical treatment has been found to cure autism. In fact, medical intervention has had little success on the core symptoms of social and language difficulties. A variety of pharmacological treatments are used to decrease agitation, and the major tranquilizers and serotonin-specific reuptake inhibitors seem helpful here (Volkmar, Klin, & Schultz, 2005).

Because autism may result from a variety of deficits, it is unlikely that one drug will work for everyone with this disorder. Much current work is focused on finding pharmacological treatments for specific behaviors or symptoms.

Integrating Treatments   The treatment of choice for people with pervasive developmental disorder combines various approaches to the many facets of this disorder. For children, most therapy consists of school education with special psychological supports for problems with communication and socialization. Behavioral approaches have been most clearly documented as benefiting children in this area. Pharmacological treatments can help some of them temporarily. Parents also need support because of the great demands and stressors involved in living with and caring for such children. As children with autism grow older, intervention focuses on efforts to integrate them into the community, often with supported living arrangements and work settings. Because the range of abilities of people with autism is so great, however, these efforts differ dramatically. Some people are able to live in their own apartments with only minimal support from family members. Others, with more severe forms of cognitive impairment, require more extensive efforts to support them in their communities.

CONCEPT CHECK 14.2

Determine how well you are able to diagnose the disorder in each of the following situations by labeling them (a) autistic disorder, (b) Asperger's disorder, (c) Rett's disorder, (d) childhood disintegrative disorder, or (e) pervasive developmental disorder, not otherwise specified.

1. Once Kevin turned 4, his parents noticed that his motor skills and language abilities were beginning to regress dramatically. _____

2. Six-year-old Megan doesn't entirely avoid social interactions, but she experiences many problems in communicating and dealing with people. _____

3. Five-year-old Sally has a low IQ and enjoys sitting in the corner by herself, where she arranges her blocks in little lines or watches the pump bubble in the fish tank. She cannot communicate verbally, but she throws temper tantrums when her parents try to get her to do something she doesn't want to do. _____

4. Three-year-old Abby has severe mental retardation and trouble walking on her own. One of the characteristics of her disorder is constant hand-wringing. _____

5. Brad's parents first noticed when he was an infant that he did not like to play with other children or to be touched or held. At an early age, he became preoccupied with geography and could name all of the state capitals. His speech development, however, was not delayed. ___

_____

Actor Chris Burke, who has Down syndrome, played an angel with Down syndrome on the television show *Touched by an Angel.*

starred in the television series *Life Goes On* and appeared on *Touched by an Angel,* in which he played an angel with Down syndrome. Others with mental retardation have significant cognitive and physical impairments and require considerable assistance to carry on day-to-day activities. Consider the case of James.

MENTAL RETARDATION

Mental retardation is a disorder evident in childhood as significantly below-average intellectual and adaptive functioning (King, Hodapp, & Dykens, 2005). People with mental retardation experience difficulties with day-to-day activities to an extent that reflects both the severity of their cognitive deficits and the type and amount of assistance they receive. Perhaps more than any other group you have studied in this text, people with mental retardation have throughout history received treatment that can best be described as shameful (Scheerenberger, 1983). With notable exceptions, societies throughout the ages have devalued individuals whose intellectual abilities are deemed less than adequate.

The field of mental retardation has undergone dramatic and fundamental changes during the past two decades. What it means to have mental retardation, how to define it, and how people with this disorder are treated have been scrutinized, debated, and fought over by a variety of concerned groups. We describe the disorder in the context of these important changes, explaining both the status of people who have mental retardation and our current understanding of its causes and treatment.

The manifestations of mental retardation are varied. Some individuals function quite well, even independently, in our complex society, one example being the actor Chris Burke, who

JAMES: Up to the Challenge

James's mother contacted us because he was disruptive at school and at work. James was 17 and attended the local high school. He had Down syndrome and was described as likable and, at times, mischievous. He enjoyed skiing, bike riding, and many other activities common among teenage boys. His desire to participate was a source of some conflict between him and his mother: He wanted to take the driver's education course at school, which his mother felt would set him up for failure, and he had a girlfriend he wanted to date, a prospect that also caused his mother concern.

School administrators complained because James didn't participate in activities such as physical education, and at the work site that was part of his school program he was often sullen, sometimes lashing out at the supervisors. They were considering moving him to a program with more supervision and less independence.

James's family had moved often during his youth, and they experienced striking differences in the way each community responded to James and his mental retardation. In some school districts, he was immediately placed in classes with other children his age and his teachers were provided with additional assistance and consultation. In others, it was just as quickly recommended that he be taught separately. Sometimes the school district had a special classroom in the local school for children with mental retardation. Other districts had programs in other towns, and James would have to travel an hour to and from school each day. Every time he was assessed in a new school, the evaluation was similar to earlier ones. He received scores on his IQ tests in the range of 40 to 50, which placed him in the moderate range of mental retardation. Each school gave him the same diagnosis: Down syndrome with moderate mental retardation. At each school, the teachers and other professionals were competent and caring individuals who wanted the best for James and his mother. Yet some believed that to learn skills James needed a separate program with specialized staff. Others felt they could provide a program with specialized staff. Still others felt they could provide a comparable education in a regular classroom and that to have peers without disabilities would be an added benefit.

In high school, James had several academic classes in a separate classroom for children with learning problems, but he participated in some classes, such as gym, with students who did not have mental retardation. His current difficulties in gym (not participating) and at work (being oppositional) were jeopardizing his placement in both programs. When I spoke with James's mother, she expressed frustration that the work program was beneath him because he was asked to do boring, repetitious work such as folding paper. James expressed a similar frustration, saying that he was treated like a baby. He could communicate fairly well when he wanted to, although he sometimes would become confused about what he wanted to say and it was difficult to understand everything he tried to articulate. On observing him at school and at work, and after speaking with his teachers, we realized that a common paradox had developed. James resisted work he thought was too easy. His teachers interpreted his resistance to mean that the work was too hard for him, and they gave him even simpler tasks. He resisted or protested more vigorously, and they responded with even more supervision and structure.

Clinical Description

People with mental retardation display a broad range of abilities and personalities. Individuals like James, who have mild or moderate impairments, can, with proper preparation, carry out most of the day-to-day activities expected of any of us. Many can learn to use mass transportation, purchase groceries, and hold a variety of jobs. Those with more severe impairments may need help to eat, bathe, and dress themselves, although with proper training and support they can achieve a degree of independence. These individuals experience impairments that affect most areas of functioning. Language and communication skills are often the most obvious. James was only mildly impaired in this area, needing help with articulation. In contrast, people with more severe forms of mental retardation may never learn to use speech as a form of

DSM-IV-TR

DSM TABLE 14.5 Diagnostic Criteria for Mental Retardation

A. Significantly subaverage intellectual functioning: an IQ of approximately 70 or below on an individually administered IQ test (for infants, a clinical judgment of significantly subaverage intellectual functioning).

B. Concurrent deficits or impairments in present adaptive functioning (i.e., the person's effectiveness in meeting the standards expected for his or her age by his or her cultural group) in at least two of the following areas: communication, self-care, home living, social/interpersonal skills, use of community resources, self-direction, functional academic skills, work, leisure, health, and safety.

C. The onset is before age 18 years.

Code based on degree of severity reflecting level of intellectual impairment:

Mild mental retardation: IQ level 50–55 to approximately 70

Moderate mental retardation: IQ level 35–40 to 50–55

Severe mental retardation: IQ level 20–25 to 35–40

Profound mental retardation: IQ level below 20 or 25

Mental retardation, severity unspecified: When there is strong presumption of mental retardation but the person's intelligence is untestable by standard tests

Source: Reprinted, with permission, from American Psychiatric Association. (2000). *Diagnostic and statistical manual of mental disorders* (4th ed., text revision). Washington, DC: Author. © 2000 American Psychiatric Association.

communication, requiring alternatives such as sign language or special communication devices to express even their most basic needs. Because many cognitive processes are adversely affected, individuals with mental retardation have difficulty learning, the level of challenge depending on how extensive the cognitive disability is.

Before examining the specific criteria for mental retardation, note that, like the personality disorders we described in Chapter 12, mental retardation is included on Axis II of DSM-IV-TR. Remember that separating disorders by axes serves two purposes: first, indicating that disorders on Axis II tend to be more chronic and less amenable to treatment, and second, reminding clinicians to consider whether these disorders, if present, are affecting an Axis I disorder. People can be diagnosed on both Axis I (for example, generalized anxiety disorder) and Axis II (for example, mild mental retardation).

The DSM-IV-TR criteria for mental retardation are in three groups. First, a person must have *significantly subaverage intellectual functioning,* a determination made with one of several IQ tests with a cutoff score set by DSM-IV-TR of approximately 70. Roughly 2% to 3% of the population score at 70 or below on these tests. The American Association on Mental Retardation (AAMR), which has its own, similar definition of mental retardation, has a cutoff score of approximately 70 to 75 (King et al., 2005).

The second criterion of both the DSM-IV-TR and the AAMR definitions for mental retardation calls for *concurrent deficits or impairments in adaptive functioning.* In other words, scoring "approximately 70 or below" on an IQ test is not sufficient for a diagnosis of mental retardation; a person must also have significant difficulty in at least two of the following areas: communication, self-care, home living, social and interpersonal skills, use of community resources, self-direction, functional academic skills, work, leisure, health, and safety. To illustrate, although James had many strengths, such as his ability to communicate and his social and interpersonal skills (he had several good friends), he was not as proficient as other teenagers at caring for himself in areas such as home living, health, and safety or in academic areas. This aspect of the definition is important because it excludes people who can function quite well in society but for various reasons do poorly on IQ tests. For instance, someone whose primary language is not English may do poorly on an IQ test but may still function at a level comparable to peers. This person would not be considered to have mental retardation even with a score of below 70 on the IQ test.

The final criterion for mental retardation is the *age of onset*. The characteristic below-average intellectual and adaptive abilities must be evident before the person is 18. This cutoff is designed to identify affected individuals when the brain is developing and therefore when any problems should become evident. The age criterion rules out the diagnosis of mental retardation for adults who suffer from brain trauma or forms of dementia that impair their abilities. The age of 18 is somewhat arbitrary, but it is the age at which most children leave school, when our society considers a person an adult.

The imprecise definition of mental retardation brings up an important issue: Mental retardation, perhaps more than any of the other disorders, is defined by society. The cutoff score of 70 or 75 is based on a statistical concept (two or more standard deviations from the mean), not on qualities inherent in people who supposedly have mental retardation. There is little disagreement about the diagnosis for people with the most severe disabilities; however, the majority of people diagnosed with mental retardation are in the mild range of cognitive impairment. They need some support and assistance, but remember that the criteria for using the label of mental retardation are based partly on a somewhat arbitrary cutoff score for IQ that can (and does) change with changing social expectations.

People with mental retardation differ significantly in their degree of disability. Almost all classification systems have differentiated these individuals in terms of their ability or on the cause of the mental retardation (King et al., 2005). Traditionally (and still evident in the DSM-IV-TR), classification systems have identified four levels of mental retardation: *mild,* which is identified by an IQ score between 50–55 and 70; *moderate,* with a range of 35–40 to 50–55; *severe,* ranging from 20–25 to 35–40; and *profound,* which includes people with IQ scores below 20–25. It is difficult to categorize each level of mental retardation according to "average" individual achievements by people at each level. A person with severe or profound mental retarda-

tion tends to have extremely limited formal communication skills (no spoken speech or only one or two words) and may require great or even total assistance in dressing, bathing, and eating. Yet people with these diagnoses have a range of skills that depend on training and the availability of other supports. Similarly, people like James, who have mild or moderate mental retardation, should be able to live independently or with minimal supervision; again, however, their achievement depends partly on their education and the community support available to them.

Perhaps the most controversial change in the AAMR definition of mental retardation is its description of different levels of this disorder, which are based on the level of support or assistance people need: *intermittent, limited, extensive,* or *pervasive* (Luckasson et al., 1992). The important difference is that the AAMR system identifies the role of "needed supports" in determining level of functioning, whereas DSM-IV-TR implies that the ability of the person is the sole determining factor. The AAMR system focuses on specific areas of assistance a person needs that can then be translated into training goals. Whereas his DSM-IV-TR diagnosis might be "moderate mental retardation," James might receive the following AAMR diagnosis: "a person with mental retardation who needs limited supports in home living, health and safety, and in academic skills." The AAMR definition emphasizes the types of support James and others require, and it highlights the need to identify what assistance is available when considering a person's abilities and potential. However, at this writing, the AAMR system has not been assessed empirically to determine whether it has greater value than traditional systems.

An additional method of classification has been used in the educational system to identify the abilities of students with mental retardation. It relies on three categories: *educable mental retardation* (based on an IQ of 50 to approximately 70–75), *trainable mental retardation* (IQ of 30 to 50), and *severe mental retardation* (IQ

Although he cannot speak, this man is learning to communicate with an eye-gaze board, pointing to or simply looking at the image that conveys his message.

©Photodisc/Getty Images

Mental retardation can be defined in terms of the level of support people need.

severe impairments require more assistance to participate in work and community life.

Over the last century, a curious thing has occurred—IQ scores have risen. This phenomenon is known as the Flynn effect (Flynn, 1984). As these scores rise, those who make up IQ tests adjust the assessments every decade or two to keep the average score around 100. For most people, these changes have no practical effect. However, for people hovering at the cutoff point for mental retardation, this may mean the difference between receiving the diagnosis or not (Durand & Christodulu, 2006). In one study, the number of people scoring just below 70 (the cutoff for mild mental retardation) tripled when they were administered one of the revised IQ tests (Kanaya, Scullin, & Ceci, 2003). These results emphasize the caution we need to take when interpreting who does or does not have mental retardation.

below 30) (Cipani, 1991). The assumption is that students with educable mental retardation (comparable to mild mental retardation) could learn basic academic skills; students with trainable mental retardation (comparable to moderate mental retardation) could not master academic skills but could learn rudimentary vocational skills; and students with severe mental retardation (comparable to severe and profound mental retardation) would not benefit from academic or vocational instruction. Built into this categorization system is the automatic negative assumption that certain individuals cannot benefit from certain types of training. This system and the potentially stigmatizing and limiting DSM-IV-TR categories (mild, moderate, severe, and profound mental retardation) inspired the AAMR categorization of needed supports. Current trends are away from the educational system of classification, because it inappropriately creates negative expectations in teachers. Clinicians continue to use the DSM-IV-TR system; we have yet to see whether the AAMR categories will be widely adopted.

Statistics

Approximately 90% of people with mental retardation fall under the label of mild mental retardation (IQ of 50 to 70), and when you add individuals with moderate, severe, and profound mental retardation (IQ below 50), the total population of people with this disorder represents 1% to 3% of the general population (King et al., 2005).

The course of mental retardation is chronic, meaning that people do not go through periods of remission, such as with substance use disorders or anxiety disorders. However, the prognosis for people with this disorder varies considerably. Given appropriate training and support, individuals with less severe forms can live relatively independent and productive lives. People with more

Causes

There are literally hundreds of known causes of mental retardation, including the following:

Environmental: For example, deprivation, abuse, and neglect
Prenatal: For instance, exposure to disease or drugs while still in the womb
Perinatal: Such as difficulties during labor and delivery
Postnatal: For example, infections and head injury

As we mentioned in Chapter 11, heavy use of alcohol among pregnant women can produce a disorder in their children called *fetal alcohol syndrome,* a condition that can lead to severe learning disabilities. Other prenatal factors that can produce mental retardation include the pregnant woman's exposure to disease and chemicals and the child's poor nutrition. In addition, lack of oxygen (anoxia) during birth, and malnutrition and head injuries during the developmental period can lead to severe cognitive impairments. Despite the rather large number of known causes of mental retardation, keep one fact in mind: Nearly 75% of cases either cannot be attributed to any known cause or are thought to be the result of social and environmental influences (King et al., 2005). Most affected individuals have mild mental retardation and are sometimes referred to as having cultural–familial mental retardation.

■ Biological Dimensions

Most research on the causes of mental retardation focuses on biological influences. We next look at biological dimensions that appear to be responsible for the more common forms of mental retardation.

Genetic Influences Almost 300 genes have been identified as having the potential to contribute to mental retardation, and it is expected that there are many more (Inlow & Restifo, 2004). A portion of the people with more severe mental retardation have identifiable single-gene disorders, involving a *dominant gene* (expresses itself when paired with a normal gene), a *recessive gene* (expresses itself only when paired with another copy of itself), or an *X-linked gene* (present on the X or sex chromosome).

Only a few dominant genes result in mental retardation, probably because of natural selection: Someone who carries a dominant gene that results in mental retardation is less likely to have children and thus less likely to pass the gene to offspring. Therefore, this gene becomes less likely to continue in the population. However, some people, especially those with mild mental retardation, do marry and have children, thus passing on their genes. One example of a dominant gene disorder, *tuberous sclerosis,* is relatively rare, occurring in 1 of approximately every 30,000 births. About 60% of the people with this disorder have mental retardation, and most have seizures (uncontrolled electrical discharges in the brain) and characteristic bumps on the skin that during their adolescence resemble acne (Pulsifer, Winterkorn, & Thiele, 2007).

The next time you drink a diet soda, notice the warning, "Phenylketonurics: Contains Phenylalanine." This is a caution for people with the recessive disorder called *phenylketonuria (PKU),* which affects 1 of every 14,000 newborns and is characterized by an inability to break down a chemical in our diets called phenylalanine. Until the mid-1960s, the majority of people with this disorder had mental retardation, seizures, and behavior problems, resulting from high levels of this chemical. However, researchers developed a screening technique that identifies the existence of PKU; infants are now routinely tested at birth, and any individuals identified with PKU can be successfully treated with a special diet that avoids the chemical phenylalanine. This is a rare example of the successful prevention of one form of mental retardation.

Ironically, successful early identification and treatment of people with PKU has some worried that an outbreak of PKU-related mental retardation will recur. The special diet to prevent symptoms is necessary only until the person reaches age 6 or 7. At this point, people tend to become lax and eat a regular diet—fortunately, with no harmful consequences for themselves. Because untreated maternal PKU can harm the developing fetus, there is concern now that women with PKU who are of childbearing age may not stick to their diets and inadvertently cause PKU-related mental retardation in their children before birth. Many physicians now recommend dietary restriction through the childbearing period—thus the warnings on products with phenylalanine (Hendriksz & Walter, 2004).

Lesch-Nyhan syndrome, an X-linked disorder, is characterized by mental retardation, signs of cerebral palsy (spasticity or tightening of the muscles), and self-injurious behavior, including finger and lip biting (Nyhan, 1978). Only males are affected, because a recessive gene is responsible; when it is on the X chromosome in males, it does not have a normal gene to balance it because males do not have a second X chromosome. Women with this gene are carriers and do not show any of the symptoms.

As our ability to detect genetic defects improves, more disorders will be identified genetically. The hope is that our increased knowledge will be accompanied by improvements in our ability to treat or, as in the case of PKU, prevent mental retardation and other negative outcomes.

Chromosomal Influences   It was only about 50 years ago that the number of chromosomes—46—was correctly identified in human cells (Tjio & Levan, 1956). Three years later, researchers found that people with Down syndrome (the disorder James displayed) had an additional small chromosome (Lejeune, Gauthier, & Turpin, 1959). Since that time, a number of other chromosomal aberrations that result in mental retardation have been identified. We describe Down syndrome and fragile X syndrome in some detail, but there are hundreds of other ways in which abnormalities among the chromosomes can lead to mental retardation.

Down syndrome, the most common chromosomal form of mental retardation, was first identified by the British physician Langdon Down in 1866. Down had tried to develop a classification system for people with mental retardation based on their resemblance to people of other races; he described individuals with this particular disorder as "mongoloid" because they resembled people from Mongolia (Scheerenberger, 1983). The term *mongoloidism* was used for some time but has been replaced with the term *Down syndrome.* The disorder is caused by the presence of an extra 21st chromosome and is therefore sometimes referred to as *trisomy 21.* For reasons we don't completely understand, during cell division two of the 21st chromosomes stick together (a condition called nondisjunction), creating one cell with one copy that dies and one cell with three copies that divide to create a person with Down syndrome.

People with Down syndrome have characteristic facial features, including folds in the corners of their upwardly slanting eyes, a flat nose, and a small mouth with a flat roof that makes the tongue protrude somewhat. Like James, they tend to have congenital heart malformations. Tragically, nearly *all* adults with Down syndrome past the age of 40 show signs of dementia of the Alzheimer's type, a degenerative brain disorder that causes impairments in memory and other cognitive disorders (Visser et al., 1997). This disorder among people with Down syndrome occurs earlier than usual (sometimes in their early 20s) and has led to the finding that at least one form of Alzheimer's disease is attributable to a gene on the 21st chromosome.

The incidence of children born with Down syndrome has been tied to maternal age: As the age of the mother increases, so does her chance of having a child with this disorder (see ■ Figure 14.2). A woman at age 20 has a 1 in 2,000 chance of having a child with Down syndrome, at the age of 35 this risk increases to 1 in 500, and at the age of 45 it increases again to 1 in 18 births

"The speech has been the most difficult . . . and communication naturally just causes tremendous behavior difficulties. . . . If there is not a way for her to communicate to us what her needs are and how she's feeling . . . it really causes a lot of actual shutdowns with Lauren. . . . She knows exactly what she wants and she is going to let you know even though she can't verbalize it."

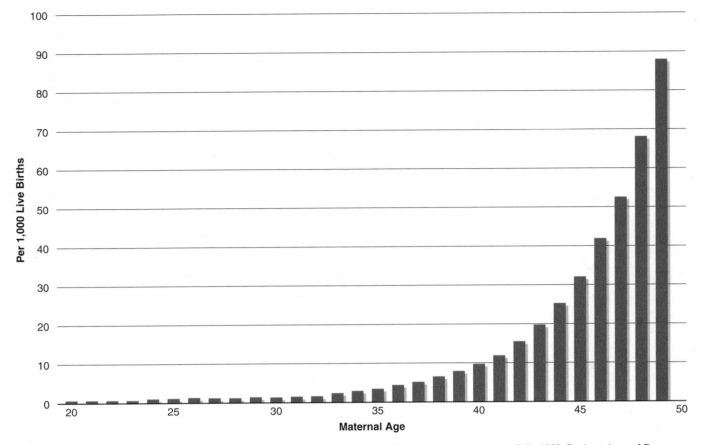

Rates of Down Syndrome Births

y-axis: Per 1,000 Live Births (0 to 100)
x-axis: Maternal Age (20 to 50)

■ **FIGURE 14.2** The increasing likelihood of Down syndrome with maternal age. (Based on data from Hook, E. B., 1982. Epidemiology of Down syndrome. In S. M. Pueschel & J. E. Rynders, Eds., *Down syndrome: Advances in biomedicine and the behavioral sciences* (pp. 11–88). Cambridge, MA: Ware Press, © 1982 Ware University Press.)

(Evans & Hammerton, 1985; Hook, 1982). Despite these numbers, many more children with Down syndrome are born to younger mothers because, as women get older, they tend to have fewer children. The reason for the rise in incidence with maternal age is not clear. Some suggest that because a woman's ova (eggs) are all produced in youth, the older ones have been exposed to toxins, radiation, and other harmful substances over longer periods. This exposure may interfere with the normal meiosis (division) of the chromosomes, creating an extra 21st chromosome (Pueschel & Goldstein, 1991). Others believe the hormonal changes that occur as women age are responsible for this error in cell division (Crowley, Hayden, & Gulati, 1982).

For some time, it has been possible to detect the presence of Down syndrome—but not the degree of mental retardation—through **amniocentesis,** a procedure that involves removing and testing a sample of the fluid that surrounds the fetus in the amniotic sac. This type of test is not always desirable because it is an invasive procedure (inserting a needle that could cause unwanted damage to the developing fetus). Fortunately, there are now more sophisticated tests of a mother's blood that can be used to detect Down syndrome as early as the first trimester of pregnancy (Wax, 2007).

Fragile X syndrome is a second common chromosomally related cause of mental retardation (King et al., 2005). As its name suggests, this disorder is caused by an abnormality on the X chromosome, a mutation that makes the tip of the chromosome look

as though it were hanging from a thread, giving it the appearance of fragility. As with Lesch-Nyhan syndrome, which also involves the X chromosome, fragile X primarily affects males because they do not have a second X chromosome with a normal gene to balance out the mutation. Unlike Lesch-Nyhan carriers, however,

©Photofusion Picture Library/Alamy

An adult with Down syndrome.

women who carry fragile X syndrome commonly display mild to severe learning disabilities (Koukoui & Chaudhuri, 2007). Men with the disorder display moderate to severe levels of mental retardation and have higher rates of hyperactivity, short attention spans, gaze avoidance, and perseverative speech. In addition, such physical characteristics as large ears, testicles, and head circumference are common. Estimates are that 1 of every 1,000 males and 1 of every 3,000 females are born with fragile X syndrome (King et al., 2005).

■ Psychological and Social Dimensions

Up to 75% of the cases of mental retardation fall in the mild range and are not associated with any obvious genetic or physical disorders. Sometimes referred to as **cultural–familial retardation,** people with these characteristics are thought to have cognitive impairments that result from a combination of psychosocial and biological influences, although the specific mechanisms that lead to this type of mental retardation are not yet understood. The cultural influences that may contribute to this condition include abuse, neglect, and social deprivation.

It is sometimes useful to consider people with mental retardation in two distinct groups: those with cultural–familial and those with biological (or "organic") forms of mental retardation. People in the latter group have more severe forms of mental retardation that are usually traceable to known causes such as fragile X syndrome. ■ Figure 14.3 shows that the cultural–familial group is composed primarily of individuals at the lower end of the IQ continuum, whereas in the organic group, genetic, chromosomal, and other factors affect intellectual performance. The organic group increases the number of people at the lower end of the IQ continuum so that it exceeds the expected rate for a normal distribution (King et al., 2005).

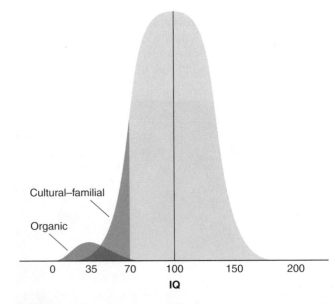

■ **FIGURE 14.3** The actual distribution of IQ scores for individuals with cultural–familial retardation and organic retardation. Note that the cultural–familial group represents the normal expected lower end of the continuum but the organic group is a separate and overlapping group. (Adapted, with permission, from Zigler, E., & Hodapp, R. M., 1986. *Understanding mental retardation.* Cambridge: Cambridge University Press, © 1986 Cambridge University Press.)

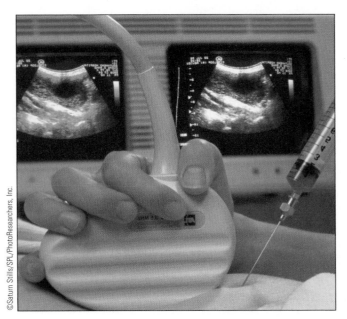

Amniocentesis can detect the presence of Down syndrome in a fetus. Guided by an ultrasound image, the doctor withdraws amniotic fluid for analysis.

Treatment of Mental Retardation

Direct biological treatment of mental retardation is currently not a viable option. Generally, the treatment of individuals with mental retardation parallels that of people with pervasive developmental disorders, attempting to teach them the skills they need to become more productive and independent. For individuals with mild mental retardation, intervention is similar to that for people with learning disorders. Specific learning deficits are identified and addressed to help the student improve such skills as reading and writing. At the same time, these individuals often need additional support to live in the community. For people with more severe disabilities, the general goals are the same; however, the level of assistance they need is often more extensive. Remember that the expectation for all people with mental retardation is that they will in some way participate in community life, attend school and later hold a job, and have the opportunity for meaningful social relationships. Advances in electronic and educational technologies have made this goal realistic even for people with profound mental retardation.

People with mental retardation can acquire skills through the many behavioral innovations first introduced in the early 1960s to teach such basic self-care as dressing, bathing, feeding, and toileting to people with even the most severe disabilities (Durand & Christodulu, 2006). The skill is broken into its component parts (a procedure called a *task analysis*), and people are taught each part in succession until they can perform the whole skill. Performance on each step is encouraged by praise and by access to objects or activities the people desire (reinforcers). Success in teaching these skills is usually measured by the level of independence people can attain by using them. Typically, most individuals, regardless of their disability, can be taught to perform some skills.

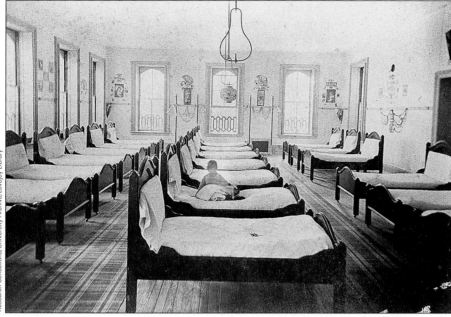

The Illinois Asylum for Feeble-Minded Children, about 1880. Today, great efforts are made to keep children with mental retardation in their homes and communities.

Communication training is important for people with mental retardation. Making their needs and wants known is essential for personal satisfaction and for participation in most social activities. The goals of communication training differ, depending on the existing skills. For people with mild levels of mental retardation, the goals may be relatively minor (for example, improving articulation) or more extensive (for example, organizing a conversation) (Sigafoos, Arthur-Kelly, & Butterfield, 2006). Some, like James, have communication skills that are already adequate for day-to-day needs.

For individuals with the most severe disabilities, this type of training can be particularly challenging, because they may have multiple physical or cognitive deficits that make spoken communication difficult or impossible. Creative researchers, however, use alternative systems that may be easier for these individuals, including the sign language, used primarily by people with hearing disabilities, and *augmentative communication strategies*. Augmentative strategies may use picture books, teaching the person to make a request by pointing to a picture—for instance, pointing to a picture of a cup to request a drink (Beukelman & Mirenda, 2005). A variety of computer-assisted devices can be programmed so that the individual presses a button to produce complete spoken sentences (for example, "Would you come here? I need your help."). People with limited communication skills can be taught to use these devices, which helps them reduce the frustration of not being able to relate their feelings and experiences to other people (Durand, 2001).

Concern is often expressed by parents, teachers, and employers that some people with mental retardation can be physically or verbally aggressive or may hurt themselves. Considerable debate has ensued over the proper way to reduce these behavior problems; the most heated discussions involve whether to use painful punishers (Repp & Singh, 1990). Alternatives to punishment that

may be equally effective in reducing behavior problems such as aggression and self-injury (Durand, 1999a) include teaching people how to communicate their need or desire for such things as attention that they seem to be getting with their problem behaviors. Important advances are being made in significantly reducing even severe behavior problems for some people.

In addition to ensuring that people with mental retardation are taught specific skills, caretakers focus on the important task of supporting them in their communities. "Supported employment" involves helping an individual find and participate satisfactorily in a competitive job (Hall, Butterworth, Winsor, Gilmore, & Metzel, 2007). Research has shown not only that people with mental retardation can be placed in meaningful jobs but also that, despite the costs associated with supported employment, it can be cost-effective (Sandys, 2007). The benefits to people who achieve the satisfaction of being a productive part of society are incalculable.

There is general agreement about *what* should be taught to people with mental retardation. The controversy in recent years has been over *where* this teaching should take place. Should people with mental retardation, especially the severe forms, be taught in specially designed separate classrooms or workshops, or should they attend their neighborhood public schools and work at local businesses? Increasingly, teaching strategies to help these students learn are being used in regular classrooms and in preparing them to work at jobs in the community (Frankel & Gold, 2007). There is at present no cure for mental retardation, but the current prevention and treatment efforts suggest that meaningful changes can be achieved in the lives of these people.

Prevention of Developmental Disorders

Prevention efforts for the developmental disorders outlined in this chapter are in their early stages of development. One such effort—early intervention—has been described for the pervasive developmental disorders and appears to hold considerable promise for some children. In addition, early intervention can target and assist children who, because of inadequate environments, are at risk for developing cultural–familial mental retardation (Fewell & Glick, 1996; Ramey & Ramey, 1992). The national Head Start program is one such effort at early intervention; it combines educational, medical, and social supports for these children and their families. One project identified a group of children shortly after birth and provided them with an intensive preschool program, along with medical and nutritional supports. This intervention continued until the children began formal education in kindergarten (Martin, Ramey, & Ramey, 1990). The authors of this study found that for all but one of the children in a control group who received medical and nutritional support but not the intensive educational experiences, each had IQ scores below 85 at age 3 but that 3-year-olds in the experimental group all tested above 85. Such findings are important because they show the potential for creating a lasting impact on the lives of these children and their families.

Although it appears that many children can make significant progress if interventions are initiated early in life (Henry, Gordon, & Rickman, 2006), a number of important questions remain regarding early intervention efforts. Not all children, for example, benefit significantly from such efforts, and future research will need to resolve a number of lingering concerns. For example, we need to determine how best to identify children and families who will benefit from such programs, how early in the child's development it is important to begin programs, and how long to continue them to produce desirable outcomes.

Given recent advances in genetic screening and technology, it may someday be possible to detect and correct genetic and chromosomal abnormalities—research that could fundamentally change our approach to children with developmental disorders. For example, one study used mice with a disease similar to an inherited enzyme deficiency (Sly disease) that is found in some individuals with mental retardation. Researchers found that they could transplant healthy brain cells into the diseased young mice to correct the disease (Snyder, Taylor, & Wolfe, 1995). Someday, it may be possible for similar research to be performed prenatally on children identified as having syndromes associated with mental retardation. For example, it may soon be possible to conduct prenatal gene therapy, where a developing fetus that has been screened for a genetic disorder may be the target of intervention before birth (Ye, Mitchell, Newman, & Batshaw, 2001). This prospect is not without its difficulties, however (Durand, 2001).

One cause of concern is the reliability of gene therapy. This technology is not sufficiently advanced to produce intended results consistently. Currently, any such intervention may cause unwanted mutations or other complications, which in turn could be fatal to the fetus. Gene therapy will probably not be practical for those disorders that involve numerous genes, but rather may be limited to single gene disorders such as PKU.

Advances in biomedical technology will need support from psychological researchers to make sure that any needed treatments are carried out properly. For example, biological risk factors for several developmental disorders include malnutrition and exposure to toxins such as lead and alcohol. Although medical researchers can identify the role of these biological events in cognitive development, psychologists will need to support these efforts. Behavioral intervention for safety training (for example, involving lead-based paints in older homes), substance-use treatment and prevention, and behavioral medicine (for example, "wellness" efforts) are examples of crucial roles played by psychologists that may contribute to preventing certain forms of developmental disorders.

CONCEPT CHECK 14.3

In the following situations, label each level of mental retardation as mild, moderate, severe, or profound. Also label the corresponding levels of necessary support: intermittent, limited, extensive, or pervasive.

1. Bobby received an IQ score of 45. He lives in a fully staffed group home and needs a great deal of help with many tasks. He is beginning to receive training for a job in the community. _____, _____
2. James received an IQ score of 20. He needs help with all his basic needs, including dressing, bathing, and eating. _____, _____
3. Robin received an IQ score of 65. He lives at home, goes to school, and is preparing to work when he is through with school. _____, _____
4. Katie received an IQ score of 30. She lives in a fully staffed group home where she is trained in basic adaptive skills and communication. She is improving over time and can communicate by pointing or using her eye-gaze board. _____, _____

FUTURE DIRECTIONS

Helpful "Designer Drugs"

Get ready to learn a new word—*psychopharmacogenetics*. Psychopharmacogenetics is the study of how your genetic makeup influences your response to certain drugs. The hope for this field is that medications can be matched or even "designed" for individuals to better complement their specific needs (Weinshilboum, 2003). For example, one study looked at the use of methylphenidate (Ritalin) for children and adolescents with ADHD (Polanczyk, Zeni, et al., 2007). For those who had a specific gene defect—the adrenergic alpha-2A receptor gene (ADRA2A)—methylphenidate had a strong positive effect, especially on their problems with inattention. This was not the case for those with ADHD who did not have the ADRA2A gene defect. Currently, the use of drug treatments tends to be by trial and error. A medication is attempted at a particular dose. If it is not effective, the dose is changed. If that does not work, a different medication

is tried. This new study holds the promise of potentially eliminating this guesswork and tailoring the treatment to the person.

This exciting new approach to medical treatment for mental illness brings with it some weighty concerns. Central to these concerns are issues of privacy and confidentiality. Genetic screening to identify defects is likely to identify any number of potential genetic problems in each of us. How will schools, employment sites, and insurance companies view this information if they have access? The concern is that people will be discriminated against based on this information (for example, having the genes that may or may not lead to having ADHD or another disorder). Will the desire to better target drug treatments outweigh these types of ethical concerns? Most new technical advances, like those promised with psychopharmacogenetics, also uncover new problems, and it is essential that ethical issues be part of the discussion as we move forward in this area.

SUMMARY

Common Developmental Disorders

- Developmental psychopathology is the study of how disorders arise and change with time. These changes usually follow a pattern, with the child mastering one skill before acquiring the next. This aspect of development is important because it implies that any disruption in the acquisition of early skills will, by the very nature of the developmental process, also disrupt the development of later skills.

- The primary characteristics of people with attention deficit/hyperactivity disorder are a pattern of inattention (such as not paying attention to school- or work-related tasks), hyperactivity/impulsivity, or both. These deficits can significantly disrupt academic efforts and social relationships.

- DSM-IV-TR groups the learning disorders as reading disorder, mathematics disorder, and disorder of written expression. All are defined by performance that falls far short of expectations based on intelligence and school preparation.

- Verbal or communication disorders seem closely related to learning disorders. They include stuttering, a disturbance in speech fluency; expressive language disorder, limited speech in all situations but without the types of cognitive deficits that lead to language problems in people with mental retardation or one of the pervasive developmental disorders; selective mutism, refusal to speak despite having the ability to do so; and tic disorders, which include involuntary motor movements such as head twitching and vocalizations such as grunts that occur suddenly, in rapid succession, and in idiosyncratic or stereotyped ways.

Pervasive Developmental Disorders

- People with pervasive developmental disorders all experience trouble progressing in language, socialization, and cognition. The use of the word *pervasive* means these are not relatively minor problems (like learning disabilities) but are conditions that significantly affect how individuals live. Included in this group are autistic disorder, Rett's disorder, Asperger's disorder, and childhood disintegrative disorder.

- Autistic disorder, or autism, is a childhood disorder characterized by significant impairment in social interactions, gross and significant impairment in communication, and restricted patterns of behavior, interest, and activities. It probably does not have a single cause; instead, a number of biological conditions may contribute, and these, in combination with psychosocial influences, result in the unusual behaviors displayed by people with autism.

- Asperger's disorder is characterized by impairments in social relationships and restricted or unusual behaviors or activities, but it does not present the language delays observed in people with autism.

- Rett's disorder, almost exclusively observed in females, is a progressive neurological disorder characterized by constant hand-wringing, mental retardation, and impaired motor skills.

- Childhood disintegrative disorder involves severe regression in language, adaptive behavior, and motor skills after a period of normal development for 2 to 4 years.

- Pervasive developmental disorder, not otherwise specified, is a childhood disorder characterized by significant impairment in social interactions, gross and significant impairment in communication, and restricted patterns of behavior, interest, and activities. Children who have this disorder are similar to those with autism but may not meet the age criterion or may not meet the criteria for the other symptoms.

Mental Retardation

- The definition of mental retardation has three parts: significantly subaverage intellectual functioning, concurrent deficits or impairments in present adaptive functioning, and an onset before the age of 18.

- Down syndrome is a type of mental retardation caused by the presence of an extra 21st chromosome. It is possible to detect the presence of Down syndrome in a fetus through a process known as amniocentesis.

- Two other types of mental retardation are common: fragile X syndrome, which is caused by a chromosomal abnormality of the tip of the X chromosome, and cultural–familial mental retardation, the presumed cause, possibly by a combination of psychosocial and biological factors, of up to 75% of mental retardation.

Key Terms

attention deficit/hyperactivity disorder (ADHD), 502
learning disorders, 507
reading disorder, 507
mathematics disorder, 507
disorder of written expression, 507

stuttering, 509
expressive language disorder, 509
selective mutism, 509
tic disorder, 509
pervasive developmental disorders, 511

Rett's disorder, 511
childhood disintegrative disorder, 511
autistic disorder (autism), 511
Asperger's disorder, 515
mental retardation, 518

Down syndrome, 522
amniocentesis, 523
fragile X syndrome, 523
cultural–familial retardation, 524

Answers to Concept Checks

14.1

1. b; 2. e; 3. d; 4. b; 5. a; 6. c

14.2

1. d; 2. e; 3. a; 4. c; 5. b

14.3

1. moderate, limited support; 2. profound, pervasive support; 3. mild, intermittent support; 4. severe, extensive support

The Abnormal Psychology Book Companion Website

See **academic.cengage.com/psychology/barlow** for practice quiz questions, interactive activities, Internet links, critical thinking exercises, discussion forums, and more. Also accessible from the Wadsworth Psychology Resource Center **(academic.cengage .com/login).**

Abnormal Psychology Live CD-ROM

■ *Sean and Modifying Behavior:* This child's mother and psychologists describe and discuss Sean's behavior before his treatment with a behavior modification program at school and at home. The eminent clinician, Jim Swanson, also discusses what we believe is involved in ADHD.

■ *Edward, a Student With ADHD:* This segment shows interviews with Edward, who suffers from ADHD, and his teacher, who describes Edward's struggles in school and the various strategies to help his grades reflect his high level of intelligence.

■ *Life Skills:* This segment shows an empirically validated program that teaches anger management to reduce violence in school-age and adolescent students.

■ *Bullying Prevention:* This segment features an empirically validated program that shows how to teach students specific strategies for dealing with bullying behaviors in school.

■ *Nature of the Disorder—Autism:* Mark Durand's research program deals with the motivation behind problem behaviors and how communication training can be used to lessen such behaviors.

■ *Christina, a Student With Autism:* This clip shows Christina's school, where you see how she spends a typical day in a mainstreamed classroom. There are interviews with her teacher's aide and a background interview with Mark Durand to describe functional communication issues and other cutting-edge research trends in autism.

■ *Rebecca, an Autistic Child:* This segment shows an autistic child in a mainstreamed first-grade classroom and interviews her teachers about what strategies work best in helping Rebecca learn and control her behavior.

■ *Lauren, a Child With Down Syndrome:* The teacher and mother of a kindergartner with Down syndrome are interviewed to discuss strategies for teaching her new skills and managing her behavior difficulties.

CENGAGENOW™ CengageNOW

Go to **academic.cengage.com/now** to link to CengageNOW, your online study tool. First take the Pre-Test for this chapter to get your personalized study plan, which will identify topics you need to review and direct you to online resources. Then take the Post-Test to determine what concepts you have mastered and what you still need work on.

Video Concept Reviews

CengageNOW also contains Mark Durand's *Video Concept Reviews* on challenging topics.

■ Attention-Deficit/Hyperactivity Disorder (ADHD)
■ Reading Disorder
■ Mathematics Disorder
■ Pervasive Developmental Disorders
■ Autistic Disorder (Autism)
■ Asperger's Disorder
■ Mental Retardation

Exploring Developmental Disorders

Disorders that appear early in life disrupt the normal course of development.
• Interrupting or preventing the development of one skill impedes mastery of the skill that is normally acquired next.
• Knowing what skills are disrupted by a particular disorder is essential to developing appropriate intervention strategies.

COGNITION
LANGUAGE
SOCIALIZATION

TYPES OF DEVELOPMENTAL DISORDERS

ATTENTION DEFICIT/HYPERACTIVITY DISORDER (ADHD)

Description:
- Inattentive, overactive, and impulsive behavior
- Disrupted schooling and relationships
- Symptoms may change with maturity, but problems persist.
- More prevalent in boys than girls

Causes
- Research suggests hereditary factor
- Abnormal neurology
- Possible link with maternal smoking
- Negative responses by others create low self-esteem.

Treatment
- Biological (medication)
  – improves compliance
  – decreases negative behaviors
  – effects not long term
- Psychological (behavioral)
  – goal setting and reinforcement

LEARNING DISORDERS

Description:
- Reading, math, and written expression fall behind IQ, age, and education
- May also be accompanied by ADHD

Causes
- Theories assume genetic, neurobiological, and environmental factors.

Treatment
- Education intervention
  —basic processing
  —cognitive and behavioral skills

COMMUNICATION DISORDERS

Closely related to learning disorders, but comparatively benign. Early appearance, wide range of problems later in life.

Types of Communication Disorders

STUTTERING
Description:
Disturbance in speech fluency (repeating words, prolonging sounds, extended pauses)
Treatment:
- Psychological
- Pharmacological

EXPRESSIVE LANGUAGE DISORDERS
Description:
Limited speech in all situations
Treatment:
- May be self-correcting

SELECTIVE MUTISM
Description:
Failure to speak in specific situations (e.g., school)
Treatment:
- Contingency management

TIC DISORDERS
Description:
Involuntary motor movements (tics), such as physical twitches or vocalizations
Treatment:
- Psychological
- Pharmacological

Infancy　　　　**Childhood**　　　　**Adolescence**

PERVASIVE DEVELOPMENTAL DISORDERS

AUTISTIC DISORDER

Description:
- Severely impaired socialization and communication
- Restricted behavior, interests, and activities
  - echolalia
  - maintenance of sameness
  - stereotyped, ritualistic behaviors
- Symptoms almost always develop before 36 months of age.

Causes

- Little conclusive data
- Numerous biological factors
  - clear genetic component
  - evidence of brain damage (cognitive deficits) combined with psychosocial influences

Treatment

- Behavioral focus
  - communication
  - socialization
  - living skills
- Inclusive schooling
- Temporary benefits from medication

ASPERGER'S DISORDER

Description:
Impaired socialization and restricted/unusual behaviors, but without language delays
- Few cognitive impairments (average IQ)
- May be mild autism, not separate disorder

RETT'S DISORDER

Description:
Progressive neurological disorder after apparently normal early development
- Primarily affects girls
- Mental retardation
- Deteriorating motor skills
- Constant hand-wringing

CHILDHOOD DISINTEGRATIVE DISORDER

Description:
Severe regression after 2–4 years normal development
- Affects language, adaptive behavior, and motor skills
- Evidence of neurological origin

MENTAL RETARDATION

Description:
- Adaptive and intellectual functioning significantly below average
  - language and communication impairments
- Wide range of impairment—from mild to profound— in daily activities (90% of affected individuals have mild impairments.)

Causes

- Hundreds of identified factors
  - genetic
  - prenatal
  - perinatal
  - postnatal
  - environmental
- Nearly 75% of cases cannot be attributed to any known cause.

Treatment

- No biological intervention
- Behavioral focus similar to that for autism
- Prevention
  - genetic counseling
  - biological screening
  - maternal care

CHAPTER 15

Cognitive Disorders

© Eduardo Jose Bernardino 2007/Shutterstock.com

PERSPECTIVES ON COGNITIVE DISORDERS

DELIRIUM
    Clinical Description and Statistics
    Treatment
    Prevention

DEMENTIA
    Clinical Description and Statistics
    Dementia of the Alzheimer's Type
    Vascular Dementia
    Dementia Due to Other General Medical Conditions
    Substance-Induced Persisting Dementia
    Causes of Dementia
    Treatment
    Prevention

AMNESTIC DISORDER

ABNORMAL PSYCHOLOGY LIVE CD-ROM

Alzheimer's Disease: Tom
Amnestic Disorder: Mike
Amnestic Patient Interview: Endel Tulving
Neural Networks: Cognition and Dementia
Web Link

As my grip upon the present slips, more and more comfort is found within my memories of the past. Childhood nostalgia is so keen I can actually smell the aroma of the small town library where I spent so many childhood hours.

Diana Friel McGowin
Living in the Labyrinth: A Personal Journey Through the Maze of Alzheimer's

PERSPECTIVES ON COGNITIVE DISORDERS

Research on the brain and its role in psychopathology has increased at a rapid pace, and we have described many of the latest advances throughout this book. All the disorders we have reviewed are in some way influenced by the brain. You have seen, for example, that relatively subtle changes in neurotransmitter systems can significantly affect mood, cognition, and behavior. Unfortunately, the brain is sometimes affected profoundly, and, when this happens, drastic changes occur. In previous editions of this book, the tone of this chapter was quite dark given the lack of information on these cognitive disorders that impair all aspects of mental functioning. The typically poor prognosis of the people afflicted led to pessimistic conclusions. However, a great deal of new research is leading us to be more optimistic about the future for this area. For example, we used to think that once neurons died there was no hope of any replacement, yet we now know brain cells can regenerate even in the aging brain (Khachaturian, 2007). In this chapter, we examine this exciting new work for the brain disorders that affect cognitive processes, such as learning, memory, and consciousness.

Whereas mental retardation and other learning disorders are believed to be present from birth (see Chapter 14), most cognitive disorders develop much later in life. In this section, we review three classes of cognitive disorders: *delirium,* an often temporary condition displayed as confusion and disorientation; *dementia,* a progressive condition marked by gradual deterioration of a range of cognitive abilities; and *amnestic disorders,* dysfunctions of memory resulting from a medical condition or a drug or toxin.

The label "cognitive disorders" in the fourth edition, text revision, of the *Diagnostic and Statistical Manual* (DSM-IV-TR) reflects a shift in the way these disorders are viewed (Davis, 2005). In previous editions of the DSM, they were labeled "organic mental disorders," along with mood, anxiety, personality, hallucinosis, and delusional disorders. The word *organic* indicated that brain damage or dysfunction was believed to be involved. Although brain dysfunction is still thought to be the primary cause, we now know that some dysfunction in the brain is involved in most disorders described in DSM-IV-TR (American Psychiatric Association Practice Guideline, 2000a).

We have repeatedly emphasized the complex relationship between neurological and psychosocial influences in many psychological disorders. Few people would disagree, for example, that schizophrenia involves some damage to the brain. In one sense, then, most disorders are "organic." This fundamental shift in perspective immediately affected the categorizing of disorders. The term *organic mental disorders* covered so many as to make any distinction meaningless. Consequently, the traditional organic disorders—delirium, dementia, and amnestic disorders—were kept together, and the others—organic mood, anxiety, personality, hallucinosis, and delusional disorders—were categorized with disorders that shared their symptoms (such as anxiety and mood disorders).

Once the term *organic* was dropped, attention moved to developing a better label for delirium, dementia, and the amnestic disorders. The label "cognitive disorders" signifies that their predominant feature is the impairment of such cognitive abilities as memory, attention, perception, and thinking. Although disorders such as schizophrenia and depression also involve cognitive problems, they are not believed to be primary characteristics (Weiner, 2003). Problems still exist with this term, however, because although the cognitive disorders usually first appear in older adults, mental retardation and learning disorders, which are apparent early, also have cognitive impairment as a predominant characteristic. Forthcoming research may provide a more useful way of distinguishing among disorders.

As with certain other disorders, it may be useful to clarify why cognitive disorders are discussed in a textbook on abnormal psychology. Because they so clearly have organic causes, you could argue that they are purely medical concerns. You will see, however, that the consequences of a cognitive disorder often include profound changes in a person's behavior and personality. Intense anxiety, depression, or both are common, especially among people with dementia. In addition, paranoia is often reported, as are extreme agitation and aggression. Families and friends are also profoundly affected by such changes. Imagine your emotional distress as a loved one is transformed into a different person, often one who no longer remembers who you are or your history together. The deterioration of cognitive ability, behavior, and personality and the effects on others are major concerns for mental health professionals.

DELIRIUM

The disorder known as **delirium** is characterized by impaired consciousness and cognition during the course of several hours or days. Delirium is one of the earliest-recognized mental disorders: Descriptions of people with these symptoms were written more than 2,500 years ago (Samuels & Neugroschl, 2005). Consider the case of Mr. J.

MR. J.: Sudden Distress

Mr. J., an older gentleman, was brought to the hospital emergency room. He didn't know his own name, and at times he didn't seem to recognize his daughter, who was with him. Mr. J. appeared confused, disoriented, and a little agitated. He had difficulty speaking clearly and could not focus his attention to answer even the most basic questions. Mr. J.'s daughter reported that he had begun acting this way the night before, had been awake most of the time since then, was frightened, and seemed even more confused today. She told the nurse that this behavior was not normal for him and she was worried that he was becoming senile. She mentioned that his doctor had just changed his hypertension medication and wondered whether the new medication could be causing her father's distress. Mr. J. was ultimately diagnosed as having substance-induced delirium (a reaction to his new medication); once the medication was stopped, he improved significantly over the course of the next 2 days.

The preceding scenario is played out daily in most major metropolitan hospital emergency rooms.

Clinical Description and Statistics

People with delirium appear confused, disoriented, and out of touch with their surroundings. They cannot focus and sustain their attention on even the simplest tasks. There are marked impairments in memory and language. Mr. J. had trouble speaking; he was not only confused but also couldn't remember basic facts, such as his own name. As you saw, the symptoms of delirium do not come on gradually but develop over hours or a few days, and they can vary over the course of a day.

Delirium is estimated to be present in as many as 10% to 30% of the people who come into acute care facilities such as emergency rooms (American Psychiatric Association Practice Guideline, 2000b). It is most prevalent among older adults, people undergoing medical procedures, cancer patients, and people with acquired immune deficiency syndrome (AIDS) (Bourgeois, Seaman, & Servis, 2003). Delirium subsides relatively quickly, with full recovery expected in most cases within several weeks. Some individuals continue to have problems on and off; some even lapse into a coma and may die. Concern by medical professionals is increasing—perhaps because of the increased number of adults living longer—leading some to recommend that delirium be included as one of the "vital signs" (along with heart beat, breathing rate, temperature, and blood pressure) that physicians routinely check when seeing older adults (Flaherty et al., 2007).

Many medical conditions that impair brain function have been linked to delirium, including intoxication by drugs and poisons; withdrawal from drugs such as alcohol and sedative, hypnotic, and anxiolytic drugs; infections; head injury; and various other types of brain trauma (Samuels & Neugroschl, 2005). DSM-IV-TR recognizes several causes of delirium among its subtypes. The criteria for delirium due to a general medical condition include a disturbance of consciousness (reduced awareness of the environment) and a change in cognitive abilities such as memory and language skills, occurring over a short period and brought about by a general medical condition. Other subtypes include the diagnosis received by Mr. J.—substance-induced delirium—as well as delirium due to multiple etiologies and delirium not oth-

erwise specified. The rise in the use of drugs such as Ecstasy (methylene-dioxymethamphetamine) is of particular concern because of such drugs' potential to produce delirium (Samuels & Neugroschl, 2005). The last two categories indicate the often-complex nature of delirium.

That delirium can be brought on by the improper use of medication is a particular problem for older adults, because they tend to use prescription medications more than any other age group. The risk of problems among the elderly is increased further because they tend to eliminate drugs from their systems less efficiently than younger individuals. It is not surprising, then, that adverse drug reactions resulting in hospitalization are almost six times higher among elderly people than in other age groups (Col, Fanale, & Kronholm, 1990). And it is believed that delirium is responsible for many of the falls that cause debilitating hip fractures in the elderly (Stenvall et al., 2006), and the 16,000 serious car accidents that occur each year in the United States among elderly drivers (Ray, Fought, & Decker, 1992). Although there has been some improvement in the use of medication among older adults, improper use continues to produce serious side effects, including symptoms of delirium (Cole, 2004). Because possible combinations of illnesses and medications are so numerous, determining the cause of delirium is extremely difficult (Samuels & Neugroschl, 2005).

Delirium may be experienced by children who have high fevers or who are taking certain medications and is often mistaken for noncompliance (Onoe & Nishigaki, 2004). It often occurs during the course of dementia; as many as 50% of people with dementia suffer at least one episode of delirium (Kwok, Lee, Lam, & Woo, in press). Because many of the primary medical conditions can be treated, delirium is often reversed within a relatively short time. Yet, in about a quarter of cases, delirium can be a sign of the end of life (Wise, Hilty, & Cerda, 2001).

Factors other than medical conditions can trigger delirium. Age itself is an important factor; older adults are more susceptible to developing delirium as a result of mild infections or medication changes (American Psychiatric Association Practice Guidelines,

---

DSM-IV-TR

DSM TABLE 15.1 Diagnostic Criteria for Delirium Due to . . . [Indicate the General Medical Condition]

A. Disturbance of consciousness (i.e., reduced clarity of awareness of the environment) with reduced ability to focus, sustain, or shift attention.

B. A change in cognition (such as memory deficit, disorientation, language disturbance) or the development of a perceptual disturbance that is not better accounted for by a preexisting, established, or evolving dementia.

C. The disturbance develops over a short period of time (usually hours to days) and tends to fluctuate during the course of the day.

D. There is evidence from the history, physical examination, or laboratory findings that the disturbance is caused by the direct physiological consequences of a general medical condition.

Source: Reprinted, with permission, from American Psychiatric Association. (2000). *Diagnostic and statistical manual of mental disorders* (4th ed., text revision). Washington, DC: Author, © 2000 American Psychiatric Association.

2000b). Sleep deprivation, immobility, and excessive stress can also cause delirium (Samuels & Neugroschl, 2005).

Treatment

Delirium brought on by withdrawal from alcohol or other drugs is usually treated with haloperidol or other antipsychotic medications, which help calm the individual. Infections, brain injury, and tumors are given the necessary and appropriate medical intervention. The antipsychotic drug haloperidol is also prescribed for individuals in acute delirium when the cause is unknown (Samuels & Neugroschl, 2005).

Psychosocial interventions may also be beneficial (American Psychiatric Association Practice Guidelines, 2000b). The goal of nonmedical treatment is to reassure the person to help her deal with the agitation, anxiety, and hallucinations of delirium. A person in the hospital may be comforted by familiar personal belongings such as family photographs (Gleason, 2003). Also, a patient who is included in all treatment decisions retains a sense of control (Katz, 1993). This type of psychosocial treatment can help the person manage during this disruptive period until the medical causes are identified and addressed. Some evidence suggests that this type of support can also delay institutionalization for elderly patients (Rahkonen et al., 2001).

Prevention

Preventive efforts may be most successful in assisting people who are susceptible to delirium. Proper medical care for illnesses and therapeutic drug monitoring can play significant roles in prevent-

Patients in care facilities are often comforted by having their personal belongings nearby.

ing delirium (Inouye et al., 1999). For example, the increased number of older adults involved in managed care and patient counseling on drug use appear to have led to more appropriate use of prescription drugs among the elderly (U.S. General Accounting Office, 1995).

CONCEPT CHECK 15.1

Match the terms with the following descriptions of delirium: (a) elderly, (b) counseling, (c) trauma, (d) memory, (e) confused, and (f) cause.

1. Various types of brain _____, such as head injury or infection, have been linked to delirium.
2. Delirium severely affects people's _____, making tasks such as recalling one's own name difficult.
3. Treatment of delirium depends upon the _____ of the episode and can include medications, psychosocial intervention, or both.
4. People who suffer from delirium appear to be _____ or out of touch with their surroundings.
5. Managed care and patient _____ have been successful in preventing delirium in older adults.
6. The _____ population is at the greatest risk of experiencing delirium resulting from improper use of medications.

DEMENTIA

Few things are more frightening than the possibility that you will one day not recognize those you love, that you will not be able to perform the most basic of tasks, and, worse yet, that you will be acutely aware of this failure of your mind. When family members show these signs, initially adult children often deny any difficulty, coming up with excuses ("I forget things, too") for their parents' failing abilities. **Dementia** is the cognitive disorder that makes these fears real: a gradual deterioration of brain functioning that affects judgment, memory, language, and other advanced cognitive processes. Dementia is caused by several medical conditions and by the abuse of drugs or alcohol that cause negative changes in cognitive functioning. Some of these conditions—for instance, infection or depression—can cause dementia, although it is often reversible through treatment of the primary condition. Some forms of the disorder, such as Alzheimer's disease, are at present irreversible. Although delirium and dementia can occur together, dementia has a gradual progression as opposed to delirium's acute onset; people with dementia are not disoriented or confused in the early stages, unlike people with delirium. Like delirium, however, dementia has many causes, including a variety of traumas to the brain such as stroke (which destroys blood vessels), the infectious diseases of syphilis and HIV, severe head injury, the introduction of certain toxic or poisonous substances, and diseases such as Parkinson's, Huntington's, and, the most common cause of dementia, Alzheimer's. Consider the now-classic personal account by Diana, a woman who poignantly writes of her experiences with this disorder (McGowin, 1993).

DIANA: Humiliation and Fear

At the age of 45, Diana Friel McGowin was a successful legal assistant, wife, and mother, but she was beginning to experience "lapses." She writes about developing these problems just before a party she was planning for her family.

> Nervously, I checked off the table appointments on a list retrieved from my jumpsuit pocket. Such a list had never been necessary before, but lately I noticed frequent little episodes of confusion and memory lapses.
>
> I had decided to "cheat" on this family buffet and have the meal prepared on a carry-out basis. Cooking was also becoming increasingly difficult, due to what my children and my husband Jack teasingly referred to as my "absentmindedness." (pp. 1–2)

In addition to memory difficulties, other problems began at this time, including brief dizzy spells. Diana wrote of her family's growing awareness of the additional symptoms.

> Shaun walked past me on his way to the kitchen, and paused. "Mom, what's up? You look ragged," he commented sleepily. "Late night last night, plenty of excitement, and then up early to get your father off to work," I answered. Shaun laughed disconcertingly. I glanced up at him ruefully. "What is so funny?" I demanded. "You, Mom! You are talking as though you are drunk or something! You must really be tired!" (pp. 4–5)

In the early stages of her dementia, Diana tended to explain these changes in herself as temporary, with such causes as tension at work. However, the extent of her dysfunction continued to increase, and she had more frightening experiences. In one episode, she describes an attempt to drive home from a brief errand.

> Suddenly, I was aware of car horns blowing. Glancing around, nothing was familiar. I was stopped at an intersection and the traffic light was green. Cars honked impatiently, so I pulled straight ahead, trying to get my bearings. I could not read the street sign, but there was another sign ahead; perhaps it would shed some light on my location. A few yards ahead, there was a park ranger building. Trembling, I wiped my eyes, and breathing deeply, tried to calm myself. Finally, feeling ready to speak, I started the car again and approached the ranger station. The guard smiled and inquired how he could assist me. "I appear to be lost," I began, making a great effort to keep my voice level, despite my emotional state. "Where do you need to go?" the guard asked politely. A cold chill enveloped me as I realized I could not remember the name of my street. Tears began to flow down my cheeks. I did not know where I wanted to go. (pp. 7–8)

Diana's difficulties continued. She sometimes forgot the names of her children, and once she astounded her nephew when she didn't recognize him. If she left home, she almost invariably got lost. She learned to introduce herself as a tour-ist from out of town, because people would give her better directions. She felt as if there "was less of me every day than there was the day before" (p. 33).

During initial medical examinations, Diana didn't recall this type of problem in her family history. However, a look through some of her late mother's belongings revealed that she was not the first to experience symptoms of dementia.

> Then I noticed the maps. After mother's death I had found mysterious hand drawn maps and bits of directions scribbled on note papers all over her home. They were in her purses, in bureau drawers, in the desks, seemingly everywhere. Too distraught at the time to figure out their purpose, I simply packed them all away with other articles in the box. Now I smoothed out each map and scrawled note, and placed them side by side. They covered the bedroom floor. There were maps to every place my mother went about town, even to my home and my brother's home. As I deciphered each note and map, I began recollecting my mother's other eccentric habits. She would not drive out of her neighborhood. She would not drive at night. She was teased by both myself and my brother about "memory goofs" and would become irate with both of her children over their loving teasing.
>
> Then with a chill, I recalled one day when I approached my mother to tell her something, and she did not recognize me. (p. 52)

After several evaluations, which included magnetic resonance imaging (MRI) showing some damage in several parts of her brain, Diana's neurologist concluded that she had dementia. The cause could be a stroke she had had years before that damaged several small areas of her brain by breaking or blocking several blood vessels. The dementia could also indicate Alzheimer's disease. People at the same stage of decline as Diana will continue to deteriorate and eventually may die from complications of their disorder.

Clinical Description and Statistics

Depending on the individual and the cause of the disorder, the gradual progression of dementia may have somewhat different symptoms, although all aspects of cognitive functioning are eventually affected. In the initial stages, memory impairment is typically seen as an inability to register ongoing events. In other words, a person can remember how to talk and may remember events from many years ago but will have trouble remembering what happened in the past hour. For example, Diana still knew how to use the stove but couldn't remember whether she had turned it on or off.

Diana couldn't find her way home because visuospatial skills are impaired among people with dementia. **Agnosia,** the inability to recognize and name objects, is one of the most familiar symptoms. **Facial agnosia,** the inability to recognize even familiar faces, can be extremely distressing to family members. Diana failed to recognize not only her nephew but also coworkers whom she had seen daily for years. A general deterioration of intellectual function results from impairment in memory, planning, and abstract reasoning.

Perhaps partly because victims of dementia are aware that they are deteriorating mentally, emotional changes often occur as well. Common side effects are delusions (irrational beliefs), depression, agitation, aggression, and apathy (Neugroschi, Kolevzon, Samuels, & Marin, 2005). Again, it is difficult to establish the cause-and-effect relationship. We don't know how much behavioral change is caused by progressive brain deterioration directly and how much is a result of the frustration and discouragement that inevitably accompany the loss of function and the isolation of "losing" loved ones. Cognitive functioning continues to deteriorate until the person requires almost total support to carry out day-to-day activities. Ultimately, death occurs as the result of inactivity, combined with the onset of other illnesses, such as pneumonia.

Globally, it is estimated that one new case of dementia is identified every 7 seconds (Ferri et al., 2005). Dementia can occur at almost any age, although this disorder is more frequent in older adults. Current estimates in the United States suggest a prevalence of a little more than 5% in people older than 65; this rate increases to 20%–40% in those older than 85 (Neugroschi et al., 2005). Estimates of the increasing number of people with just one form of dementia—dementia of the Alzheimer's type—are alarming. Table 15.1 illustrates how the prevalence of dementia of the Alzheimer's type is projected to dramatically increase in older adults, partly as a result of the increase of baby boomers who will enter the ranks of the elderly (Hebert, Scherr, Bienias, Bennett, & Evans, 2003). Among the eldest of adults, research on centenarians (people 100 years and older) indicates that up to 100% showed signs of dementia (Imhof et al., 2007). Dementia of the Alzheimer's type rarely occurs in people under 45 years of age.

A problem with confirming prevalence figures for dementia is that survival rates alter the outcomes. Because adults are generally living longer and therefore more are at greater risk of devel-

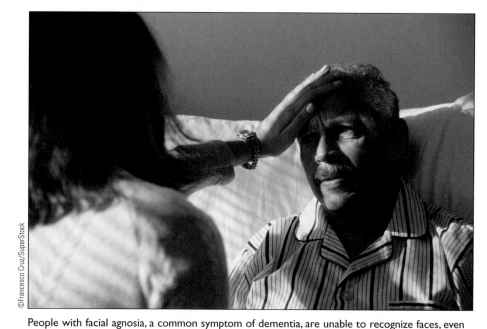

People with facial agnosia, a common symptom of dementia, are unable to recognize faces, even of their closest friends and relatives.

oping dementia, it is not surprising that dementia is more prevalent. Incidence studies, which count the number of new cases in a year, may thus be the most reliable method for assessing the frequency of dementia, especially among the elderly. Research shows that the rate for new cases doubles with every 5 years of age after age 75. Many studies find greater increases of dementia among women (Neugroschi et al., 2005), although this may be because of the tendency of women to live longer. Dementia of the Alzheimer's type may, as we discuss later, be more prevalent among women. Together, results suggest that dementia is a relatively common disorder among older adults and the chances of developing it increase rapidly after the age of 75.

In addition to the human costs of dementia, the financial costs are staggering. Estimates of the costs of caring for people with dementia of the Alzheimer's type are often quoted to be about $100 billion per year in the United States. One estimate indicates that the total worldwide societal cost of dementia is more than $315 billion (Wimo, Winblad, & Jonsson, 2007). However, these numbers do not factor in the costs to businesses for health care in the form of insurance and for those who care for these individuals—estimated to be more than $60 billion in 2002 alone (Koppel, 2002). Many times, family members care for an afflicted person around the clock, which is an inestimable personal and financial commitment (Neugroschi et al., 2005).

The statistics on prevalence and incidence cover dementias that arise from a variety of causes. DSM-IV-TR groups are based on presumed cause, but determining the cause of dementia is an inexact process. Sometimes, as with dementia of the Alzheimer's type, clinicians rely on ruling out alternative explanations—identifying all the things that are not the cause—instead of determining the precise origin.

Five classes of dementia based on etiology have been identified: (1) dementia of the Alzheimer's type; (2) vascular dementia; (3) dementia due to other general medical conditions; (4) substance-

TABLE 15.1	Estimates of Prevalence of Alzheimer's Disease in the United States Through 2050 (in millions)		
Year	Age 65–74	Age 75–84	Age 85 and older
2000	0.3	2.4	1.8
2010	0.3	2.4	2.4
2020	0.3	2.6	2.8
2030	0.5	3.8	3.5
2040	0.4	5.0	5.6
2050	0.4	4.8	8.0

Source: Adapted from Hebert, L. E., Scherr, P. A., Bienias, J. L., Bennett, D. A., & Evans, D. A. (2003). Alzheimer disease in the U.S. population: Prevalence estimates using the 2000 Census. Archives of Neurology. 60, 1119–1122.

induced persisting dementia; and (5) dementia due to multiple etiologies. A sixth, dementia not otherwise specified, is included when cause cannot be determined. We emphasize dementia of the Alzheimer's type because of its prevalence (almost half of those with dementia exhibit this type) and the relatively large amount of research conducted on its etiology and treatment.

Dementia of the Alzheimer's Type

The German psychiatrist Alois Alzheimer first described the disorder that bears his name in 1907. He wrote of a 51-year-old woman who had a "strange disease of the cerebral cortex" that manifested as a progressive memory impairment and other behavioral and cognitive problems, including suspiciousness (Neugroschi et al., 2005). He called the disorder an "atypical form of senile dementia"; thereafter, it was referred to as **Alzheimer's disease.**

■ Description and Statistics

The DSM-IV-TR diagnostic criteria for **dementia of the Alzheimer's type** include multiple cognitive deficits that develop gradually and steadily. Predominant are impairment of memory, orientation, judgment, and reasoning. The inability to integrate new information results in failure to learn new associations. Individuals with Alzheimer's disease forget important events and lose objects. Their interest in nonroutine activities narrows. They tend to lose interest in others and, as a result, become more socially isolated. As the disorder progresses, they can become agitated, confused, depressed, anxious, or even combative. Many of these difficulties become more pronounced late in the day—in a phenomenon referred to as "sundowner syndrome"—perhaps as a result of fatigue or a disturbance in the brain's biological clock (Weiner, 2003).

People with dementia of the Alzheimer's type also display one or more other cognitive disturbances, including aphasia (difficulty with language), apraxia (impaired motor functioning), agnosia (failure to recognize objects), or difficulty with activities such as planning, organizing, sequencing, or abstracting information. These cognitive impairments have a serious negative impact on social and occupational functioning, and they represent a significant decline from previous abilities.

Research using brain scans is being conducted on people with mild cognitive impairment to see whether changes in brain structure early in the development of Alzheimer's disease can be detected, which can lead to early diagnosis (Rabins, 2006). Currently, a definitive diagnosis of Alzheimer's disease can be made only after an autopsy determines that certain characteristic types of damage are present in the brain, although clinicians are accurate in identifying this condition in living patients 70% to 90% of the time (Bourgeois et al., 2003). To make a diagnosis without direct examination of the brain, a simplified version of a mental status exam is used to assess language and memory problems (see Table 15.2).

In an interesting, somewhat controversial study—referred to as the "Nun Study"—the writings of a group of Catholic nuns collected over several decades appeared to indicate early in life which women were most likely to develop Alzheimer's disease later (Snowdon et al., 1996). Researchers observed that samples from the nuns' journals over the years differed in the number of ideas each contained, which the scientists called "idea density." In other words, some sisters described events in their lives simply: "I was born in Eau Claire, Wis, on May 24, 1913 and was baptized in St. James Church." Others were more elaborate in their prose: "The happiest day of my life so far was my First Communion Day

TABLE 15.2 Testing for Dementia of the Alzheimer's Type

Type*	Maximum Score†	Question
Orientation	5	Ask the patient, "What is the (year) (season) (date) (day) (month)?"
	5	Ask the patient, "Where are we—(state) (country) (town) (hospital) (floor)?"
Registration	3	Name three objects, using 1 second to say each. Then ask the patient all three after you have said them. (Give one point for each correct answer.) Then repeat them until the patient learns all three. (Count and record the number of trials.)
Attention and Calculation	5	Count backward from given number (like 100) by subtracting 7s. (Give one point for each correct answer; stop after five answers.) Alternatively, spell "world" backward.
Recall	3	Have the patient name the three objects learned previously. (Give one point for each correct answer.)
Language	9	Have the patient name a pencil and a watch. (1 point) Have the patient repeat the following: "No ifs, ands, or buts." (1 point) Have the patient follow a three-stage command: "Take a piece of paper in your right hand, fold it in half, and put it on the floor." (3 points) Have the patient read and obey the following: "Close your eyes." (1 point) Have the patient write a sentence. (1 point) Have the patient copy a design. (1 point)

Note: One part of the diagnosis of the dementia of Alzheimer's disease uses a relatively simple test of the patient's mental state and abilities, like this one, called the Mini Mental State Inpatient Consultation Form. A low score on such a test does not necessarily indicate a medical diagnosis of dementia.
*The examination also includes an assessment of the patient's level of consciousness: alert, drowsy, stupor, or coma.
†Total maximum score is 30.

Adapted from the Mini Mental State Inpatient Consultation Form, Folstein M.F., Folstein, S.E., & McHugh, P.R. (1975). "Mini-mental state." A practical method for grading the cognitive state of patients for the clinician. *Journal of Psychiatric Research, 12*, 189–198.

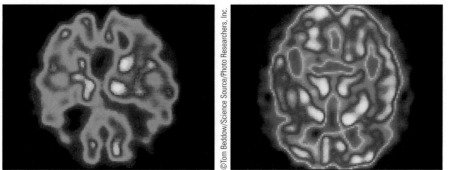

The PET scan of a brain afflicted with Alzheimer's disease (left) shows significant tissue deterioration in comparison with a normal brain (right).

which was in June nineteen hundred and twenty when I was but eight years of age, and four years later in the same month I was confirmed by Bishop D. D. McGavich" (Snowdon et al., 1996, p.530). When findings of autopsies on 14 of the nuns were correlated with idea density, the simple writing (low idea density) occurred among all 5 nuns with Alzheimer's disease (Snowdon et al., 1996). This is an elegant research study, because the daily lives of the nuns were similar, which ruled out many other possible causes. However, we must be cautious in depending on this study, because only a small number of people were examined. It is not yet clear that dementia of the Alzheimer's type has such early signs, but research continues in the hope of early detection so that early intervention can be developed.

Cognitive deterioration of the Alzheimer's type is slow during the early and later stages but more rapid during the middle stages (Neugroschi et al., 2005). The average survival time is estimated to be about 8 years, although many individuals live dependently for more than 10 years. In some forms, the disease can occur relatively early, during the 40s or 50s (sometimes referred to as *presenile dementia*), but it usually appears during the 60s or 70s. Approximately 50% of the cases of dementia are found to be the result of Alzheimer's disease, which is believed to afflict more than 5 million Americans and millions more worldwide (Alzheimer's Association, 2007).

Some early research on prevalence suggested that Alzheimer's disease may occur more often in people who are poorly educated (Fratiglioni et al., 1991; Korczyn, Kahana, & Galper, 1991). Greater impairment among uneducated people might indicate a much earlier onset, suggesting that Alzheimer's disease causes intellectual dysfunction that in turn hampers educational efforts. Or there could be something about intellectual achievement that prevents or delays the onset or symptoms of the disorder. Later research seems to confirm the latter explanation. It appears that educational level may predict a delay in the observation of symptoms. Unfortunately, people who attain a higher level of education also decline more rapidly once the symptoms start to occur (Scarmeas, Albert, Manly, & Stern, 2006), suggesting the education does not prevent Alzheimer's disease but just provides a buffer period of better functioning. Educational attainment may somehow create a mental "reserve," a learned set of skills that help someone cope longer with the cognitive deterioration that marks the beginning of dementia. Like Diana's mother, who made copi-

ous notes and maps to help her function despite her cognitive deterioration, some people may adapt more successfully than others and thus escape detection longer. Brain deterioration may thus be comparable for both groups, but better-educated individuals may be able to function successfully on a day-to-day basis for a longer period. This tentative hypothesis may prove useful in designing treatment strategies, especially during the early stages of the disorder.

A biological version of this theory—the cognitive reserve hypothesis—suggests that the more synapses a person develops throughout life, the more neuronal death must take place before the signs of dementia are obvious (Bourgeois et al., 2003; Scarmeas & Stern, 2003). Mental activity that occurs with education presumably builds up this reserve of synapses and serves as a protective factor in the development of the disorder. It is likely that both skill development and the changes in the brain with education may contribute to how quickly the disorder progresses.

DSM-IV-TR

DSM TABLE 15.2 Diagnostic Criteria for Dementia of the Alzheimer's Type

A. The development of multiple cognitive deficits manifested by both
  1. Memory impairment (impaired ability to learn new information or to recall previously learned information)
  2. One (or more) of the following cognitive disturbances:
    a. Aphasia (language disturbance)
    b. Apraxia (impaired ability to carry out motor activities despite intact motor function)
    c. Agnosia (failure to recognize or identify objects despite intact sensory function)
    d. Disturbance in executive functioning (i.e., planning, organizing, sequencing, abstracting)
B. The cognitive deficits in criteria A1 and A2 each cause significant impairment in social or occupational functioning and represent a significant decline from a previous level of functioning.
C. The course is characterized by gradual onset and continuing cognitive decline.
D. The cognitive deficits in criteria A1 and A2 are not due to any of the following:
  1. Other central nervous system conditions that cause progressive deficits in memory and cognition (e.g., cerebrovascular disease, Parkinson's disease, Huntington's disease, subdural hematoma, normal-pressure hydrocephalus, brain tumor)
  2. Systemic conditions that are known to cause dementia (e.g., hypothyroidism, vitamin B12 or folic acid deficiency, niacin deficiency, hypercalcemia, neurosyphillis, HIV infection)
  3. Substance-induced conditions
E. The deficits do not occur exclusively during the course of a delirium.
F. The disturbance is not better accounted for by another Axis I disorder (e.g., major depressive disorder, schizophrenia).
Specify if:
  With behavioral disturbance

Research suggests that Alzheimer's disease may be more prevalent among women (Garre-Olmo et al., 2004), even when women's higher survival rate is factored into the statistics. In other words, because women live longer than men on average, they are more likely to experience Alzheimer's and other diseases, but longevity alone does not account for the higher prevalence of the disorder among women. A tentative explanation involves the hormone estrogen. Women lose estrogen as they grow older, so perhaps it is protective against the disease. A large and important study—the Women's Health Initiative Memory Study—looked at hormone use among women and its effect on Alzheimer's disease (Shumaker et al., 2004). In its initial findings, the study followed women over age 65 using a type of combined estrogen plus progestin known as Prempro and observed an increased risk for Alzheimer's disease. More research is ongoing into the individual effects of these two types of hormones on dementia.

Finally, there appear to be questions about the prevalence of Alzheimer's disease according to racial identity. Early research seemed to suggest that certain populations (such as those with Japanese, Nigerian, certain Native American, and Amish backgrounds) were less likely to be affected (for example, see Pericak-Vance et al., 1996; Rosenberg et al., 1996). However, more recent work indicates that some of these differences may have been the result of differences in who seeks assistance (which is seen as unacceptable in some cultural groups), as well as differences in education (which we saw may delay the onset of obvious symptoms) (Fitzpatrick et al., 2004). Alzheimer's disease is found in roughly the same numbers across all ethnic groups, with one study finding a slightly lower rate among American Indians (Weiner, Hynan, Beekly, Koepsell, & Kukull, 2007). As you will see, findings like these help bring us closer to understanding the causes of this devastating disease.

Vascular Dementia

Each year, 500,000 people die from strokes (any diseases or traumas to the brain that result in restriction or cessation of blood flow). Although stroke is the third leading cause of death in the

©Associated Press

Former first lady Nancy Reagan was widely respected for her unwavering support of her husband Ronald Reagan, who died in 2004 of complications of Alzheimer's disease.

United States, many people survive, but one potential long-term consequence can be severely debilitating. **Vascular dementia** is a progressive brain disorder that is second only to Alzheimer's disease as a cause of dementia (Neugroschi et al., 2005).

■ Description and Statistics

The word *vascular* refers to blood vessels. When the blood vessels in the brain are blocked or damaged and no longer carry oxygen and other nutrients to certain areas of brain tissue, damage results. MRI scans of Diana's brain showed a number of damaged areas, or multiple infarctions, left by a stroke several years earlier; this was one probable cause of her dementia. Because multiple sites in the brain can be damaged, the profile of degeneration—the particular skills that are impaired—differs from person to person. DSM-IV-TR lists as criteria for vascular dementia the memory and other cognitive disturbances that are identical to those for dementia of the Alzheimer's type. However, certain neurological signs of brain tissue damage, such as abnormalities in walking and weakness in the limbs, are observed in many people with vascular dementia but not in people in the early stages of dementia of the Alzheimer's type.

In comparison with research on dementia of the Alzheimer's type, there are fewer studies on vascular dementia, perhaps because of its lower incidence rates. The prevalence of vascular dementia is approximately 1.5% in people 70 to 75 years of age and increases to 15% for those over the age of 80 (Neugroschi et al., 2005). The risk for men is higher than among women, in contrast with the higher risk among women for Alzheimer's type dementia (Report of the Advisory Panel on Alzheimer's Disease, 1995). The relatively high rate of cardiovascular disease among men in general may account for their increased risk of vascular dementia. The onset of vascular dementia is typically more sudden than the onset for the Alzheimer's type, probably because the disorder is the result of stroke, which inflicts brain damage immediately. The outcome, however, is similar for people with both types: Ultimately, they will require formal nursing care until they succumb to an infectious disease such as pneumonia—because of weakening of the immune system.

Dementia Due to Other General Medical Conditions

In addition to Alzheimer's disease and vascular damage, a number of other neurological and biochemical processes can lead to de-

---

DSM-IV-TR

DSM TABLE 15.4 Diagnostic Criteria for Dementia Due to Other General Medical Conditions

A. The development of multiple cognitive deficits manifested by both
  1. Memory impairment (impaired ability to learn new information or to recall previously learned information)
  2. One (or more) of the following cognitive disturbances:
     a. Aphasia (language disturbance)
     b. Apraxia (impaired ability to carry out motor activities despite intact motor function)
     c. Agnosia (failure to recognize or identify objects despite intact sensory function)
     d. Disturbance in executive functioning (i.e., planning, organizing, sequencing, abstracting)
B. The cognitive deficits in criteria A1 and A2 each cause significant impairment in social or occupational functioning and represent a significant decline from a previous level of functioning.
C. There is evidence from the history, physical examination, or laboratory findings that the disturbance is the direct physiological consequence of one of the general medical conditions listed below.
D. The deficits do not occur exclusively during the course of a delirium.
Dementia due to HIV disease
Dementia due to head trauma
Dementia due to Parkinson's disease
Dementia due to Huntington's disease
Dementia due to Pick's disease
Dementia due to Creutzfeldt-Jakob disease
Dementia due to (indicate the general medical condition not listed above)
For example, normal-pressure hydrocephalus, hypothyroidism, brain tumor, vitamin B12 deficiency, intracranial radiation

Source: Reprinted, with permission, from American Psychiatric Association. (2000). *Diagnostic and statistical manual of mental disorders* (4th ed., text revision). Washington, DC: Author. © 2000 American Psychiatric Association.

---

mentia. As you will see next, a variety of diseases can cause the loss of previous levels of cognitive abilities.

■ Descriptions and Statistics

DSM-IV-TR lists several other types with specific causes, including dementia due to HIV disease, dementia due to head trauma, dementia due to Parkinson's disease, dementia due to Huntington's disease, dementia due to Pick's disease, and dementia due to Creutzfeldt-Jakob disease. Each of these is discussed here. Other medical conditions that can lead to dementia include normal pressure hydrocephalus (excessive water in the cranium, resulting from brain shrinkage), hypothyroidism (an underactive thyroid gland), brain tumor, and vitamin B12 deficiency. In their effect on cognitive ability, these disorders are comparable to the other forms of dementia we have discussed so far.

The **human immunodeficiency virus type 1 (HIV-1)**, which causes AIDS, can also cause dementia (Bottiggi et al., in press). This impairment seems to be independent of the other infections that accompany HIV; in other words, the HIV infection itself seems to be responsible for the neurological impairment (Neugroschi et al., 2005). The early symptoms of dementia resulting from HIV are cognitive slowness, impaired attention, and forgetfulness. Affected individuals also tend to be clumsy, to show repetitive movements such as tremors and leg weakness, and to become apathetic and socially withdrawn.

People with HIV seem particularly susceptible to impaired thinking in the later stages of HIV infection, although significant declines in cognitive abilities may occur earlier. Cognitive impairments were highly common among those infected with AIDS, but with the introduction of new medications (highly active antiretroviral therapies, or HAARTs) less than 10% of patients now experience dementia (Neugroschi et al., 2005). HIV-1 accounts for a relatively small percentage of people with dementia compared to Alzheimer's disease and vascular causes, but its presence can complicate an already-devastating set of medical conditions.

Like dementia from Parkinson's disease, Huntington's disease, and several other causes, dementia resulting from HIV is sometimes referred to as *subcortical dementia,* because it affects primarily the inner areas of the brain, below the outer layer called the cortex (Bourgeois et al., 2003). The distinction between cortical (including dementia of the Alzheimer's type) and subcortical is important because of the different expressions of dementia in these two categories (see Table 15.3). **Aphasia,** which involves impaired language skills, occurs among people with dementia of the Alzheimer's type but not among people with subcortical dementia. In contrast, people with subcortical dementia are more likely to experience severe depression and anxiety than those with dementia of the Alzheimer's type. In general, motor skills including speed and coordination are impaired early on among those with subcortical dementia. The differing patterns of impairment can be attributed to the different areas of the brain affected by the disorders.

Head trauma, injury to the head and therefore to the brain, is typically caused by accidents and can lead to cognitive impairments in both children and adults. Memory loss is the most common symptom (Lipton & Weiner, 2003).

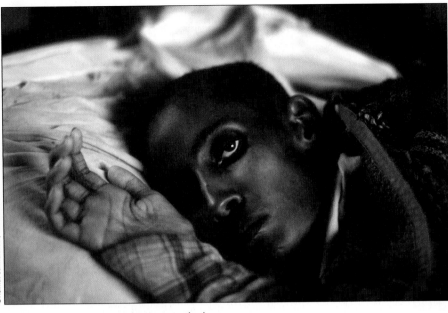

The AIDS virus may cause dementia in the later stages.

Parkinson's disease is a degenerative brain disorder that affects about 1 in every 1,000 people worldwide (Mehta et al., in press). Movie and television star Michael J. Fox and former Attorney General Janet Reno both suffer from this progressive disorder. Motor problems are characteristic among people with Parkinson's disease, who tend to have stooped posture, slow body movements (called *bradykinesia*), tremors, and jerkiness in walking. The voice is also affected; afflicted individuals speak in a soft monotone. The changes in motor movements are the result of damage to dopamine pathways. Because dopamine is involved in complex movement, a reduction in this neurotransmitter makes affected individuals increasingly unable to control their muscle movements, which leads to tremors and muscle weakness. The course of the disease varies widely, with some individuals functioning well with treatment.

Some people with Parkinson's disease develop dementia; conservative estimates place the rate at twice that found in the general population (Neugroschi et al., 2005). The pattern of impairments for these individuals fits the general pattern of subcortical dementia (see Table 15.3).

Huntington's disease is a genetic disorder that initially affects motor movements, typically in the form of *chorea*, involun-

tary limb movements (Ward et al., 2006). People with Huntington's disease can live for 20 years after the first signs of the disease appear, although skilled nursing care is often required during the last stages. Just as with Parkinson's disease, only a portion of people with Huntington's disease go on to display dementia—somewhere between 20% and 80%—although some researchers believe that all patients with Huntington's disease would eventually display dementia if they lived long enough (Neugroschi et al., 2005). Dementia resulting from Huntington's disease also follows the subcortical pattern.

The search for the gene responsible for Huntington's disease is like a detective story. For some time, researchers have known that the disease is inherited as an autosomal dominant disorder, meaning that approximately 50% of the offspring of an adult with Huntington's disease will develop the disease. Since 1979, behavioral scientist Nancy Wexler and a team of researchers have been studying the largest known extended family in the world afflicted by Huntington's disease, in small villages in Venezuela. The villagers have cooperated with the research, partly because Wexler herself lost her mother, three uncles, and her maternal grandfather to Huntington's disease, and she, too, may develop the disorder (Wexler & Rawlins, 2005). Using genetic linkage analysis techniques (see Chapter 4), these researchers first mapped the deficit to an area on chromosome 4 (Gusella et al., 1983) and then identified the elusive gene (Huntington's Disease Collaborative Research Group, 1993). Finding that one gene causes a disease is exceptional; research on other inherited mental disorders typically points to multiple gene (polygenic) influences.

Pick's disease is a rare neurological condition—occurring in about 5% of those people with dementia—that produces a cortical dementia similar to that of Alzheimer's disease. The course of this disease is believed to last from 5 to 10 years, although its cause is as yet unknown (Hardin, Hardin, & Schooley, 2002). Like Huntington's disease, Pick's disease usually occurs relatively early in life—during a person's 40s or 50s—and is therefore considered an example of presenile dementia. An even rarer condition, **Creutzfeldt-Jakob disease,** is believed to affect only one in

TABLE 15.3	Characteristics of Dementias	
Characteristic	**Dementia of the Alzheimer's Type**	**Subcortical Dementias**
Language	Aphasia (difficulties with articulating speech)	No aphasia
Memory	Both recall and recognition are impaired	Impaired recall; normal or less impaired recognition
Visuospatial skills	Impaired	Impaired
Mood	Less severe depression and anxiety	More severe depression and anxiety
Motor speed	Normal	Slowed
Coordination	Normal until late in the progression	Impaired

Source: Adapted, with permission of Oxford University Press, from Cummings, J. L. (Ed.) (1990). *Subcortical dementia.* New York: Oxford University Press, © 1990 Jeffrey L. Cummings.

Michael J. Fox provides his time and celebrity status to efforts to cure Parkinson's disease, a degenerative disease that is severely affecting his life.

Nancy Wexler headed the team of scientists who found the gene for Huntington's disease.

every million individuals (Edwards, 1994). An alarming development in the study of Creutzfeldt-Jacob disease is the finding of 10 cases of a new variant that may be linked to bovine spongiform encephalopathy, more commonly referred to as "mad cow disease" (Neugroschi et al., 2005). This discovery led to a ban on exporting beef from the United Kingdom because the disease might be transmitted from infected cattle to humans. We do not yet have definitive information about the link between mad cow disease and the new form of Creutzfeldt-Jacob disease.

Substance-Induced Persisting Dementia

Prolonged drug use, especially combined with poor diet, can damage the brain and, in some circumstances, can lead to dementia. This impairment unfortunately lasts beyond the period involved in intoxication or withdrawal from these substances.

■ Description and Statistics

As many as 7% of individuals dependent on alcohol meet the criteria for dementia (Neugroschi et al., 2005). DSM-IV-TR identifies several drugs that can lead to symptoms of dementia, including alcohol, inhalants such as glue or gasoline (which some people inhale for the euphoric feeling they produce), and sedative, hypnotic, and anxiolytic drugs (see Chapter 11). These drugs pose a threat because they create dependence, making it difficult for a user to stop ingesting them. The resulting brain damage can be permanent and can cause the same symptoms as seen in dementia of the Alzheimer's type. The DSM-IV-TR criteria for substance-induced persisting dementia are essentially the same as those for the other forms of dementia; they include memory impairment

and at least one of the following cognitive disturbances: aphasia (language disturbance), apraxia (inability to carry out motor activities despite intact motor function), agnosia (failure to recognize or identify objects despite intact sensory function), or a disturbance in executive functioning (such as planning, organizing, sequencing, and abstracting).

Causes of Dementia

As our technology for studying the brain advances, so does our understanding of the many and varied causes of dementia. A complete description of what we know about the origins of this type of brain impairment is beyond the scope of this book, but we highlight some insights available for more common forms of dementia.

■ Biological Influences

Cognitive abilities can be adversely compromised in many ways. As you have seen, dementia can be caused by a number of processes: Alzheimer's disease, Huntington's disease, Parkinson's disease, head trauma, substance abuse, and others. The most common cause of dementia, Alzheimer's disease, is also the most mysterious. Because of its prevalence and our relative ignorance about the factors responsible for it, Alzheimer's disease has held the attention of many researchers, who are trying to find the cause and ultimately a treatment or cure for this devastating condition.

Findings from Alzheimer's research seem to appear almost daily. We should be cautious when interpreting the output of this fast-paced and competitive field; too often, as you have seen in other areas, findings are heralded prematurely as conclusive and important. Remember that "discoveries" of a single gene for bipolar disorder, schizophrenia, and alcoholism were later shown to be based on overly simplistic accounts. Similarly, findings from Alzheimer's research are sometimes too quickly sanctioned as accepted truths before they have been replicated, an essential validation process.

One lesson in scientific caution comes from research that demonstrates a negative correlation between cigarette smoking and Alzheimer's disease (Brenner et al., 1993). In other words, the study found that smokers are less likely than nonsmokers to develop Alzheimer's disease. Does this mean smoking has a protective effect, shielding a person against the development of this disease? On close examination, the finding may instead be the result of the differential survival rates of those who smoke and those who do not. In general, nonsmokers tend to live longer and are thereby more likely to develop Alzheimer's disease, which appears later in life. Some even believe the relative inability of cells to repair themselves, a factor that may be more pronounced among people with Alzheimer's disease, may interact with cigarette smoking to shorten the lives of smokers who are at risk for Alzheimer's disease (Riggs, 1993). Put another way, smoking may exacerbate the degenerative process of Alzheimer's disease, causing people with the disease who also smoke to die earlier than nonsmokers who have Alzheimer's disease. These types of studies and the conclusions drawn from them should make us sensitive to the complicated nature of the disorders we study.

What do we know about Alzheimer's disease, the most common cause of dementia? After the death of the patient he described as having a "strange disease of the cerebral cortex," Alois Alzheimer performed an autopsy. He found that the brain contained large numbers of tangled, strandlike filaments (referred to as *neurofibril-*

lary tangles). This type of damage occurs in everyone with Alzheimer's disease. A second type of degeneration results from gummy protein deposits—called *amyloid plaques* (also referred to as *neuritic* or *senile plaques*)—that accumulate in the brains of people with this disorder. Amyloid plaques are also found in older adults who do not have symptoms of dementia, but they have far fewer of them than do individuals with Alzheimer's disease (Bourgeois et al., 2003). Both forms of damage—neurofibrillary tangles and amyloid plaques—accumulate over the years and are believed to produce the characteristic cognitive disorders we have been describing.

These two types of degeneration affect extremely small areas and can be detected only by a microscopic examination of the brain. Even sophisticated brain-scan techniques are not yet powerful enough to observe these changes in the living brain, which is why a definitive diagnosis of Alzheimer's disease requires an autopsy. In addition to having neurofibrillary tangles and amyloid plaques, over time the brains of many people with Alzheimer's disease atrophy (shrink) to a greater extent than would be expected through normal aging (Neugroschi et al., 2005). Because brain shrinkage has many causes, however, only by observing the tangles and plaques can a diagnosis of Alzheimer's disease be properly made.

Rapid advances are being made toward uncovering the genetic bases of Alzheimer's disease (Becker, Mestre, Ziolko, & Lopez, 2007). Because important discoveries happen almost daily, we cannot speak conclusively; however, certain overall themes have arisen from genetic research. As with most other behavioral disorders we have examined, multiple genes seem to be involved in the development of Alzheimer's disease. Table 15.4 illustrates what we know so far. Genes on chromosomes 21, 19, 14, 12, and 1 have all been linked to certain forms of Alzheimer's disease (Neugroschi et al., 2005). The link to chromosome 21 was discovered first, and it resulted from the unfortunate observation that individuals with Down syndrome, who have three copies of chromosome 21 instead of the usual two, developed the disease at an unusually high rate (Report of the Advisory Panel on Alzheimer's Disease, 1995). More recent work has located relevant genes on other chromosomes. These discoveries indicate that there is more than one genetic cause of Alzheimer's disease. Some forms, including the one associated with chromosome 14, have an early onset. Diana may have an early-onset form, because she started noting symptoms at the age of 45. In contrast, Alzheimer's disease

TABLE 15.4 Genetic Factors in Alzheimer's Disease

Gene	Chromosome	Age of Onset (years)
APP	21	43 to 59
Presenilin 1	14	33 to 60
Presenilin 2	1	50 to 90
apo E4	19	60
A2M	12	70

A2M = alpha-2-macroglobulin; AAP = amyloid precursor protein; apo E4 = apolipoprotein E4.

associated with chromosome 19 seems to be a late-onset form of the disease that has an effect only after the age of about 60.

Some genes that are now identified are **deterministic,** meaning that if you have one of these genes you have a nearly 100% chance of developing Alzheimer's disease (Gatz, 2007). Deterministic genes such as the precursor gene for small proteins called amyloid beta peptides (also referred to as beta-amyloid or A(β) and the Presenilin 1 and Presenilin 2 genes will inevitably lead to Alzheimer's disease, but, fortunately, these genes are also rare in the general population. For treatment purposes, this means that even if we can find a way to prevent these genes from leading to Alzheimer's disease, it will only help a relatively small number of people. On the other hand, some genes—including the *apolipoprotein E4 (apo E4)* gene—are known as **susceptibility** genes. These genes only slightly increase the risk of developing Alzheimer's disease, but in contrast to the deterministic genes, these are more common in the general population (Gatz, 2007). If future research can find ways to interfere with the apo E4 gene, many people will be helped.

Although closing in on the genetic origins of Alzheimer's disease has not brought immediate treatment implications, researchers are nearer to understanding how the disease develops, which may result in medical interventions. Genetic research has advanced our knowledge of how the amyloid plaques develop in the brains of people with Alzheimer's disease and may hold a clue to its origins. In the core of the plaques is a solid waxy substance made up of Aβ. Just as cholesterol buildup on the walls of blood vessels chokes the blood supply, deposits of Aβ are believed by some researchers to cause the cell death associated with Alzheimer's disease (Gatz, 2007). An important question then is, Why does this protein accumulate in the brain cells of some people but not of others?

Two mechanisms that may account for amyloid protein buildup are being studied. The first involves *amyloid precursor protein* (APP), a large protein that is eventually broken down into the *amyloid protein* found in the amyloid plaques. Important work resulted in identifying the gene responsible for producing APP, on chromosome 21 (Neugroschi et al., 2005). This finding may help integrate two observations about Alzheimer's disease: (1) APP produces the amyloid protein found in the amyloid plaques, and (2) Down syndrome, associated with an extra 21st chromosome, results in a higher incidence of the disease. The gene responsible for producing APP and, ultimately, amyloid protein, may be responsible for the relatively infrequent early-onset form of the disease, and its location could explain why people with Down syndrome—who have an extra 21st chromosome and therefore an extra APP gene—are more likely than the general population to develop Alzheimer's disease.

A second, more indirect way that amyloid protein may build up in brain cells is through apolipoprotein E (apo E), which normally helps transport cholesterols, including amyloid protein, through the bloodstream. There are at least three forms of this transporter protein: apo E2, apo E3, and apo E4. Individuals who have late-onset Alzheimer's disease, the most common form, are likely to carry the gene associated with apo E4, located on chromosome 19. Researchers have found that the majority of people with Alzheimer's disease who also have a family history of the disease will have at least one gene for apo E4 (Gatz, 2007). In contrast, approximately 64% of individuals with Alzheimer's disease who have no family history of the disease have at least one gene for apo E4, and only 31% of nonaffected individuals have the gene. Having two genes for apo E4 (one on each member of the chromosome 19 pair) increases the risk for Alzheimer's disease: As many as 90% of people with two genes developed Alzheimer's disease (Reiman et al., 2007). In addition, having two apo E4 genes seemed to decrease the mean age of onset from 84 years to 68 years. These results suggest that apo E4 may be responsible for late-onset Alzheimer's disease and that a gene on chromosome 19 is responsible. What is still not completely understood is how apo E4 causes amyloid proteins to build up in the neurons of people who ultimately exhibit Alzheimer's disease and whether this process is responsible for the disease.

Researchers are just beginning to try to examine potential gene–environment interactions in Alzheimer's disease. Several isolated studies suggest a few areas of promise. For example, one study found that among African Americans having low levels of cholesterol seemed to reduce risk of Alzheimer's disease—but only among those who did not carry the apo E4 gene (Evans et al., 2000). In another study, physical exercise reduced the likelihood of developing the disease but, like the previous study, only among those without the apo E4 gene (Podewils et al., 2005). This type of research holds the potential for better understanding the complex nature of Alzheimer's disease and may lead to important prevention strategies (such as lowering cholesterol levels and exercising regularly).

For all disorders described in this book, we have identified the role of biological, psychological, or both types of stressors as partially responsible for the onset of the disorder. Does dementia of the Alzheimer's type—which appears to be a strictly biological event—follow the same pattern? One of the leading candidates for an external contributor to this disorder is head trauma. It appears that repeated blows to the head can bring on dementia pugilistica, named after the boxers who suffer from this type of dementia. Fighters who carry the apo E4 gene may be at greater risk for developing dementia attributed to head trauma (Jordan et al., 1997). News accounts suggest links to the trauma experienced by NFL players and the development of dementia in these former athletes (Schwarz, 2007). Head trauma may be one of the stressors that initiates the onset of dementias of varying types. Other such stressors including having diabetes, high blood pressure, or herpes simplex virus-1 (Merikangas & Risch, 2003). As with each of the disorders discussed, psychological and biological stressors may interact with physiological processes to produce Alzheimer's disease.

We opened the section with a word of caution, which it is appropriate at this point to repeat. Some of the findings just reviewed are considered controversial. We are clearly learning, but many questions remain to be answered about this destructive condition.

■ Psychological and Social Influences

Research has mostly focused on the biological conditions that produce dementia. Although few would claim that psychosocial influences directly cause the type of brain deterioration seen in people with dementia, they may help determine onset and course. For example, a person's lifestyle may involve contact with factors that can cause dementia. You saw, for instance, that substance abuse can lead to dementia and, as we discussed previously (see Chapter 11), whether a person abuses drugs is determined by a combination of biological and psychosocial factors. In the case of vascular dementia, a person's biological vulnerability to vascular disease will influence the chances of strokes that can lead to this form of dementia. Lifestyle issues such as diet, exercise, and stress influence cardiovascular disease and therefore help determine who experiences vascular dementia.

Cultural factors may also affect this process. For example, hypertension and strokes are prevalent among African Americans and certain Asian Americans (King, Mainous, & Geesey, in press), which may explain why vascular dementia is more often observed in members of these groups. In an extreme example, exposure to a viral infection can lead to dementia similar in form to Creutzfeldt-Jakob disease through a condition known as kuru. This virus is passed on through a ritual form of cannibalism practiced in Papua New Guinea as a part of mourning (Collinge et al., 2006). Dementia caused by head trauma and malnutrition are relatively prevalent in preindustrial rural societies (Del Parigi, Panza, Capurso, & Solfrizzi, 2006). Not getting enough of vitamins B9 and B12 in particular seems to lead to dementia, although the process is as yet unknown. These findings suggest that occupational safety and economic conditions influencing diet also affect the prevalence of certain forms of dementia. It is apparent that psychosocial factors help influence who does and who does not develop certain forms of dementia. Brain deterioration is a biological process but, as you have seen throughout this text, even biological processes are influenced by psychosocial factors.

Psychosocial factors themselves influence the course of dementia. Recall that educational attainment may affect the onset of dementia (Scarmeas et al., 2006). Having certain skills may help some people cope better than others with the early stages of dementia. As you saw earlier, Diana's mother was able to carry on her day-to-day activities by making maps and using other tricks to help compensate for her failing abilities. The early stages of confusion and memory loss may be better tolerated in cultures with lowered expectations of older adults. In certain cultures, including the Chinese, younger people are expected to take the demands of work and care from older adults after a certain age, and symptoms of dementia are viewed as a sign of normal aging (Elliot, Di Minno, Lam, & Mei Tu, 1996). Dementia may go undetected for years in these societies.

Much remains to be learned about the cause and course of most types of dementia. As you saw with Alzheimer's disease and Huntington's disease, certain genetic factors make some individuals vulnerable to progressive cognitive deterioration. In addition, brain trauma, some diseases, and exposure to certain drugs, such as alcohol, inhalants, and sedative, hypnotic, and anxiolytic drugs, can cause the characteristic decline in cognitive abilities. We also noted that psychosocial factors can help determine who is subject to these causes and how they cope with the condition. Looking at dementia from this integrative perspective should help you view treatment approaches in a more optimistic light. It may be possible to protect people from conditions that lead to dementia and to support them in dealing with the devastating consequences of having it. We next review attempts to help from both biological and psychosocial perspectives.

Treatment

For many of the disorders we have considered, treatment prospects are fairly good. Clinicians can combine various strategies to reduce suffering significantly. Even when treatment does not bring expected improvements, mental health professionals have usually been able to stop problems from progressing. This is not the case in the treatment of dementia.

One factor preventing major advances in the treatment of dementia is the nature of the damage caused by this disorder. The brain contains billions of neurons, many more than are used. Damage to some can be compensated for by others because of plasticity. However, there is a limit to where and how many neurons can be destroyed before vital functioning is disrupted. Researchers are closing in on how to use the brain's natural process of regeneration to potentially reverse the damage caused in dementia (Khachaturian, 2007). Currently, however, with extensive brain damage, no known treatment can restore lost abilities. The goals of treatment therefore become (1) trying to prevent certain conditions, such as substance abuse, that may bring on dementia; (2) trying to delay the onset of symptoms to provide better quality of life; and (3) attempting to help these individuals and their caregivers cope with the advancing deterioration. Most efforts in treating dementia have focused on the second and third goals, with biological treatments aimed at stopping the cerebral deterioration and psychosocial treatments directed at helping patients and caregivers cope.

A troubling statistic further clouds the tragic circumstances of dementia: About 25% of caregivers of people with dementia—usually relatives—eventually become clinically depressed (Cuijpers, 2005). Compared with the public, these caregivers use more psychotropic medications and report stress symptoms at three times the normal rate. Caring for people with dementia, especially in its later stages, is clearly a trying experience. As a result, clinicians are becoming increasingly sensitive to the needs of these caregivers, and research is now exploring interventions to assist them to care for people with dementia (Majerovitz, 2007).

■ Biological Treatments

Dementia resulting from known infectious diseases, nutritional deficiencies, and depression can be treated if it is caught early. Unfortunately, however, no known treatment exists for most types of dementia that are responsible for the vast majority of cases. Dementia caused by stroke, HIV, Parkinson's disease, or Huntington's disease is not currently treatable because there is no effective treatment for the primary disorder. However, exciting research in several related areas has brought us closer to helping individuals with these forms of dementia. Substances that may help preserve and perhaps restore neurons—called glial cell–derived neurotrophic factor—may someday be used to help reduce or reverse the progression of degenerative brain diseases (Heese, Low, & Inoue, 2006). Researchers are also looking into the possible benefits of transplanting stem cells (fetal brain tissue) into the brains of people with such diseases. Preliminary results from these studies appear promising (Heese et al., 2006). Dementia brought on by strokes may now be more preventable by new drugs that help prevent much of the damage inflicted by the blood clots characteristic of stroke (Bourgeois et al., 2003). Most current attention is on a treatment for dementia of the Alzheimer's type, because it affects so many people. Here, too, however, success has been modest at best.

Much work has been directed at developing drugs that will enhance the cognitive abilities of people with dementia of the Alzheimer's type. Many seem to be effective initially, but long-term improvements have not been observed in placebo-controlled studies (Bourgeois et al., 2003). Several drugs that have had a modest impact on cognitive abilities in some patients include donepezil (Aricept), rivastigmine (Exelon), and galantamine (Reminyl). *Tacrine hydrochloride* (Cognex), another in this family of drugs, is rarely used today because of the potential for liver damage (Rabins, 2006). These drugs prevent the breakdown of the neurotransmitter acetylcholine, which is deficient in people with Alzheimer's disease, thus making more acetylcholine available to the brain. Research suggests that people's cognitive abilities improve to the point where they were 6 months earlier (Knapp et al., 1994; Rogers & Friedhoff, 1996; Samuels & Davis, 1997). But the gain is not permanent. Even people who respond positively do not stabilize but continue to experience the cognitive decline associated with Alzheimer's disease. In addition, if they stop taking the drug—as almost three-quarters of the patients do because of negative side effects such as liver damage and nausea—they lose even that 6-month gain (Neugroschi et al., 2005). The drugs and required testing can cost more than $250 per month, so the affected person and the family must decide whether the cost is worth the temporary benefit.

Several other medical approaches are being explored to slow the course of Alzheimer's disease, but initial excitement generated by these approaches has waned with the findings from researchers. For example, most of you have heard of using *Ginkgo biloba* (maidenhair) to improve memory. Initial research suggested that this herbal remedy may produce modest improvements in the memory of people with Alzheimer's disease, but other studies have not replicated this benefit (Rabins, 2006). Similarly, the effects of vitamin E have been evaluated. One large study found that among individuals with moderately severe impairment, high doses of the vitamin (2,000 international units per day) delayed progression compared to a placebo (Sano et al., 1997), but it did not prevent the development of the disease. Modest slowing of the progression of the disease also may be obtained by introducing exercise to patients (Rockwood & Middleton, 2007; Teri et al., 2003). To date, however, no medical interventions are available that directly treat and therefore stop the progression of the conditions that cause the cerebral damage in Alzheimer's disease.

Medical interventions for dementia also include the use of drugs to help with some associated symptoms. A variety of antidepressants—such as serotonin-specific reuptake inhibitors—are commonly recommended to alleviate the depression and anxiety that too often accompany the cognitive decline. Antipsychotic medication is sometimes used for those who become unusually agitated (Neugroschi et al., 2005). In addition to medical interventions, we next describe psychosocial approaches that are used with medication to address the variety of problems that accompany memory difficulties.

> *"Our cognitive activity arises from the neural networks in the brain. Whenever you lose an individual neuron, you're not losing an idea, you're just losing a tiny bit of the resolution, or the crispness, of that idea."*

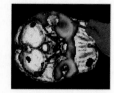

■ Psychosocial Treatments

Psychosocial treatments are now receiving a great deal of attention for their ability to delay the onset of severe cognitive decline. These efforts focus on enhancing the lives of people with dementia, as well as those of their families.

People with dementia can be taught skills to compensate for their lost abilities. Recall that Diana's mother learned on her own to make maps to help her get from place to place. Diana herself began making lists so that she would not forget important things. Some researchers have evaluated more formal adaptations to help people in the early stages of dementia. Michelle Bourgeois (1992, 1993) created "memory wallets" to help people with dementia carry on conversations. On white index cards inserted into a plastic wallet are printed declarative statements such as, "My husband John and I have 3 children," or "I was born on January 6, 1921, in Pittsburgh." In one of her studies, Bourgeois (1992) found that adults with dementia could, with minimal training, use this memory aid to improve their conversations with others. Adaptations such as these help people communicate with others, help them remain aware of their surroundings, and can reduce the frustration that comes with the awareness of their own decline.

Cognitive stimulation—encouraging people with dementia to practice learning and memory skills—seems to be an effective method for delaying the onset of the more severe cognitive effects of this disorder (Livingston et al., 2005). These activities include word games, tests of memory of famous and familiar faces, and practice with numbers (for example, how much change back you would receive from a purchase). They can maintain cognitive activity and improve the quality of life in those patients when compared to controls.

What impact do the medical and nonmedical treatments have on those with Alzheimer's disease? ■ Figure 15.1 illustrates how

A resident of an assistive living facility practices cognitive stimulation using one of several computer-based systems (the Dakim [m]Power Brain Fitness System).

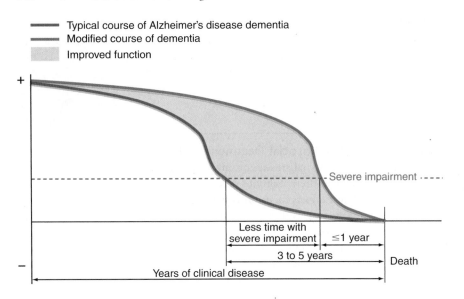

■ FIGURE 15.1 Improving the course of Alzheimer's disease with medical and nonmedical interventions. (From Becker, J. T., Mestre, L. T., Ziolko, S., & Lopez, O. L., 2007. Gene–environment interactions with cognition in late life and compression of morbidity. *American Journal of Psychiatry, 164,* 849–852.)

these interventions may delay the worst of the symptoms—essentially compressing the time when the person is most impaired (Becker et al., 2007). The red line illustrates the typical course of the disease, which results in 3 to 5 years of severe impairment before death. However, with the interventions we highlighted (illustrated by the blue line), people are able to live more fully for a longer period, despite the still-inevitable impairment and death. Families find this extra time with their loved ones to be invaluable, and hopefully with more advancements we will see progress on improving mortality rates of this progressive disease.

Individuals with advanced dementia are not able to feed, bathe, or dress themselves. They cannot communicate with or recognize even familiar family members. They may wander away from home and become lost. Because they are no longer aware of social stigma, they may engage in public displays of sexual behavior, such as masturbation. They may be frequently agitated or even physically violent. To help both the person with dementia and the

caregiver, researchers have explored interventions for dealing with these consequences of the disorder (Neugroschi et al., 2005). For example, some research indicates that a combination of exercise for patients and instruction for caregivers on how to handle behavior problems can improve the overall health and the depression in people with Alzheimer's disease (Teri et al., 2003).

Of great concern is the tendency of people with dementia to wander. Sometimes they wind up in places or situations that may be dangerous (for example, stairwells or the street). Often, the person is tied to a chair or bed, or sedated, to prevent roaming. Unfortunately, physical and medical restraint has its own risks, including additional medical complications; it also adds greatly to the loss of control and independence that already plague the person with dementia. Psychological treatment as an alternative to restraint sometimes involves providing cues for people to help them safely navigate around their home or other areas. New innovations in surveillance technology—creating a "smart home" that can monitor the location of the patient and warn caregivers—may provide more piece of mind for those who care for these patients. At the same time, ethical concerns are being raised about the use of this technology because of its ability to invade privacy (Mahoney et al., 2007).

Someone with dementia can become agitated and sometimes verbally and physically aggressive. This behavior is understandably stressful for people trying to provide care. In these situations, medical intervention is often used, although many times with only modest results (Franco & Messinger-Rapport, 2006). Caregivers are often given assertiveness training to help them deal with hostile behaviors (see Table 15.5). Otherwise, caregivers may either passively accept all criticism inflicted by the person with dementia, which increases stress, or become angry and aggressive in return. This last response is of particular concern because of the potential for elder abuse. Withholding food or medication or inflicting physical abuse is most common among caregivers of elderly people

TABLE 15.5 Sample Assertive Responses	
Patient Behavior	**Assertive Response**
	Calmly but firmly say:
1. The patient refuses to eat, bathe, or change clothes.	"We agreed to do this at this time so that we will be able to (give specific activity or reward)."
2. The patient wants to go home.	"I know you miss some of the places we used to be. This is our home now, and together we are safe and happy here."
3. The patient demands immediate gratification.	"It's not possible to have everything we want. As soon as I've finished (describe specific task or action), we can discuss other things we want to do."
4. The patient accuses the caregiver of taking the patient's possessions.	"We both enjoy our own things. I'll help you look for (specific item missing) so that you can enjoy it just as soon as I have finished (describe specific task or action)."
5. The patient is angry, rebellious, or both.	"I like to be treated fairly just as you do. Let's discuss what's bothering you so that we can go back to our usual good relationship."

Source: Adapted, with permission, from Edwards, A. J., 1994. *When memory fails: Helping the Alzheimer's and dementia patient.* New York: Plenum Press, p. 174, © 1994 Plenum Press.

who have cognitive deficits (Hansberry, Chen, & Gorbien, 2005). It is important to teach caregivers how to handle stressful circumstances so that they do not escalate into abusive situations. Not a great deal of objective evidence supports the usefulness of assertiveness training for reducing caregiver stress, and we await research to guide future efforts.

In general, families of people with dementia can benefit from supportive counseling to help them cope with the frustration, depression, guilt, and loss that take a heavy emotional toll. However, clinicians must first recognize that the ability to adapt to stressors differs among people. One study, for example, found cultural differences in the coping styles of caregivers. In one area of rural Alabama, white caregivers used acceptance and humor as coping strategies, while black caregivers used religion and denial (Kosberg, Kaufman, Burgio, Leeper, & Sun, 2007). One group, which conducted a large-scale study of 555 principal caregivers over a 3-year period, identified a number of steps that can be taken to support caregivers through this difficult time (Aneshensel, Pearlin, Mullan, Zarit, & Whitlatch, 1995). Early on, caregivers need basic information on the causes and treatment of dementia, financial and legal issues, and locating help for the patient and the family. As the dementia progresses, and the affected person requires increasing amounts of assistance, caregivers will need help managing behavioral difficulties (wandering away or violent outbursts) and developing effective ways to communicate with the patient. Clinicians also assist the family with decisions about hospitalizations and, finally, help them adjust during bereavement (Martin-Cook, Svetlik, & Weiner, 2003).

Overall, the outlook for slowing (but not stopping) the cognitive decline characteristic of dementia is optimistic. The best available medications provide some recovery of function, but they do not stop the progressive deterioration. Psychological interventions may help people cope more effectively with the loss of cognitive abilities, especially in the earlier stages of this disorder. In addition, emphasis is placed on helping caregivers—the other victims of dementia—as the person they care for continues to decline.

Prevention

Without treatment, we need to rely even more heavily on prevention strategies for dementia. You can imagine that it is difficult to study prevention efforts for dementia because of the need to follow individuals for long periods to see whether the efforts are effective. One major study conducted in Sweden—where socialized medicine provides complete medical histories of all residents—looked at many of the risk factors (those factors that increase the chance of having dementia) and protective factors (those that decrease the risk) under study today (Fratiglioni, Winblad, & von Strauss, in press). They looked at the medical records of 1,810 participants who were older than 75 at the time and followed them for about 13 years. Through interviews and medical histories, they came to two major conclusions: control your blood pressure, and lead an active physical and social life! These two recommendations came out as the major factors that individuals can change—because you cannot change your genetics, for example—that will decrease the chances of developing dementia. Additional prevention research is ongoing, and there may be other potentially fruitful research areas that can lead to the successful prevention of this devastating disorder.

CONCEPT CHECK 15.2

Part A

Identify following symptoms of dementia from the descriptions: (a) facial agnosia, (b) agnosia, and (c) aphasia.

1. Your elderly Aunt Bessie can no longer form complete, coherent sentences. _____

2. She does not recognize her own home any longer. _____

3. Aunt Bessie no longer recognizes you when you visit, even though you are her favorite niece. _____

Part B

Identify the cognitive disorders described.

4. A decline in cognitive functioning that is gradual and continuous and has been associated with neurofibrillary tangles and amyloid plaques. _____

5. José is a recovering alcoholic. Ask him about his wild partying days, and his stories usually end quickly because he can't remember the whole tale. He even has to write down things he has to do in a notebook; otherwise, he's likely to forget. _____

6. Grandpa has suffered from a number of strokes but can still care for himself. However, his ability to remember important things has been declining steadily for the past few years. _____

"I still have a pretty major memory problem, which has since brought about a divorce and which I now have a new girlfriend, which helps very much. I even call her . . . my new brain or my new memory. . . . If I want to know something, besides on relying on this so-called memory notebook, which I jot notes down in constantly and have it every day dated, so I know what's coming up or what's for that day. She also helps me very much with the memory. My mother types up the pages for this notebook, which has each half hour down and the date, the day and the date, which anything coming within an hour or two or the next day or the next week, I can make a note of it so that when that morning comes, and I wake up, I right away, one of the first things, is look at the notebook. What have I got to do today?"

AMNESTIC DISORDER

Say these three words to yourself: *apple, bird, roof.* Try to remember them, and then count backward from 100 by 3s. After about 15 seconds of counting, can you still recall the three words? Probably so. However, people with **amnestic disorder** will not remember them, even after such a short period (Grossman, 2005). The loss of this type of memory, which we described as a primary characteristic of dementia, can occur without the loss of other high-level cognitive functions. The main deficit of amnestic disorder appears to be the inability to transfer information like the list we just described into long-term memory, which can cover minutes, hours, or years. This disturbance in memory is caused by either the physiological effects of a medical condition, such as head trauma, or the long-term effects of a drug. Consider the case of S. T.

S. T.: Remembering Fragments

S. T., a 67-year-old white woman, suddenly fell, without loss of consciousness. She appeared bewildered and anxious but oriented to person and place. Language functioning was normal. Yet she was not oriented to time. She was unable to recall her birthplace, the ages of her children, or any recent presidents of the United States. She could not remember three objects for 1 minute, nor recall what she had eaten for her last meal. She could not name the color of any object shown to her but could correctly name the color related to certain words—for example, *grass* and *sky*. Object naming was normal. Examined 1 year later, she could repeat five digits forward and backward but could not recall her wedding day, the cause of her husband's death, or her children's ages. She did not know her current address or phone number and remembered none of three objects after 5 minutes. While she was described by her family as extremely hard-working before her illness, after hospitalization she spent most of her time sitting and watching television. She was fully oriented, displayed normal language function, and performed simple calculations without error (Cole, Winkelman, Morris, Simon, & Boyd, 1992, pp. 63–64).

The DSM-IV-TR criteria for amnestic disorder describe the inability to learn new information or to recall previously learned information. As with all cognitive disorders, memory disturbance causes significant impairment in social and occupational functioning. The woman just described was diagnosed with a type of amnestic disorder called *Wernicke-Korsakoff syndrome,* which is caused by damage to the thalamus, a small region deep inside the brain that acts as a relay station for information from many other parts of the brain. In her case, the damage to the thalamus was believed to be the result of a stroke that caused vascular damage. Another common cause of the Wernicke-Korsakoff syndrome is chronic heavy alcohol use. As you saw, S. T. had pronounced difficulty recalling information presented just minutes before. Although she could repeat a series of numbers, she couldn't remember three objects presented to her a few minutes earlier. As with other people with amnestic disorder, despite these obvious deficits with her memory, her language command was fine and she could perform simple chores. Yet these individuals are often significantly

DSM-IV-TR

DSM TABLE 15.6 Diagnostic Criteria for Amnestic Disorder Due to . . . [Indicate the General Medical Condition]

A. The development of memory impairment as manifested by impairment in the ability to learn new information or the inability to recall previously learned information.
B. The memory disturbance causes significant impairment in social or occupational functioning and represents a significant decline from a previous level of functioning.
C. The memory disturbance does not occur exclusively during the course of a delirium or a dementia.
D. There is evidence from the history, physical examination, or laboratory findings that the disturbance is the direct physiological consequence of a general medical condition (including physical trauma).

Specify if:
  Transient: If memory impairment lasts for 1 month or less
  Chronic: If memory impairment lasts for more than 1 month

Source: Reprinted, with permission, from American Psychiatric Association. (2000). *Diagnostic and statistical manual of mental disorders* (4th ed., text revision). Washington, DC: Author. © 2000 American Psychiatric Association.

impaired in social or vocational functioning because of the importance of memory to such activities.

As you saw with the other cognitive impairments, a range of traumas to the brain can cause permanent amnestic disorders. Research has focused on attempting to prevent the damage associated with Wernicke-Korsakoff syndrome. Specifically, a deficiency in thiamine (vitamin B1) resulting from alcohol abuse in people developing Wernicke-Korsakoff syndrome is leading researchers to try supplementing this vitamin, especially for heavy drinkers (Sechi & Serra, 2007). To date, however, there is little research pointing to successful long-term assistance in treating people with amnestic disorders (Grossman, 2005).

CONCEPT CHECK 15.3

Insert either a T for true or an F for false for statements pertaining to amnestic disorder.

1. ____ The abuse of alcohol and trauma to the brain can cause amnestic disorders.
2. ____ Amnestic disorders can be either transient, lasting 1 month or less, or chronic, lasting more than 1 month.
3. ____ *Ginkgo biloba* has been found to be effective in treating amnestic disorders.
4. ____ Amnestic disorder refers to the inability to learn new information or to recall previously learned information.

FUTURE DIRECTIONS

Are We Close to an Alzheimer's Vaccine?

We described in Chapter 11 how researchers are striving to create a vaccine that would use the immune system to fight drugs such as heroin, just as your body attacks infectious bacteria. Other researchers are targeting vaccines that would potentially treat and prevent—rather than just delay—the symptoms of Alzheimer's disease. Much of the research is attempting to get the immune system to attack the process that overproduces the small proteins (Aβ) that lead to cell death. Prior efforts early in this decade had to be abandoned because of the severe negative side effects of the vaccine, which included serious brain inflammation. More recent research with humans and animals indicates that there may be several vaccines that could be effective in preventing the damage caused by Aβ formation and therefore represent the first glimmer of hope for patients and their families (Melnikova, 2007). Researchers are optimistic that there may finally be intervention approaches that would reverse the current trend of increasing numbers of people with dementia.

SUMMARY

Delirium

- Delirium is a temporary state of confusion and disorientation that can be caused by brain trauma, intoxication by drugs or poisons, surgery, and a variety of other stressful conditions, especially among older adults.

Dementia

- Dementia is a progressive and degenerative condition marked by gradual deterioration of a range of cognitive abilities including memory, language, and planning, organizing, sequencing, and abstracting information.
- Alzheimer's disease is the leading cause of dementia, affecting approximately 4 million Americans; there is currently no known cause or cure.

- To date, there is no effective treatment for the irreversible dementias caused by Alzheimer's disease, Parkinson's disease, Huntington's disease, and various less common conditions that produce this progressive cognitive impairment. Treatment often focuses on helping patients cope with the continuing loss of cognitive skills and helping caregivers deal with the stress of caring for affected individuals.

Amnestic Disorder

- Amnestic disorders involve a dysfunction in the ability to recall recent and past events. The most common is Wernicke-Korsakoff syndrome, a memory disorder usually associated with chronic alcohol abuse.

Key Terms

delirium, 533
dementia, 535
agnosia, 536
facial agnosia, 536
Alzheimer's disease, 538

dementia of the Alzheimer's type, 538
vascular dementia, 540
human immunodeficiency virus type 1 (HIV-1), 541

aphasia, 541
head trauma, 541
Parkinson's disease, 542
Huntington's disease, 542
Pick's disease, 542

Creutzfeldt-Jakob disease, 542
deterministic, 545
susceptibility, 545
amnestic disorder, 549

Answers to Concept Checks

15.1

1. c; 2. d; 3. f; 4. e; 5. b; 6. a

15.2

Part A

1. c; 2. b; 3. a

Part B

4. dementia of Alzheimer's type; 5. substance-induced persisting dementia; 6. vascular dementia

15.3

1. T; 2. T; 3. F; 4. T

 The Abnormal Psychology Book Companion Website

See **academic.cengage.com/psychology/barlow** for practice quiz questions, interactive activities, Internet links, critical thinking exercises, discussion forums, and more. Also accessible from the Wadsworth Psychology Resource Center **(academic.cengage.com/login).**

Abnormal Psychology Live CD-ROM

- *Tom, a Patient With Alzheimer's Disease:* This is a rather moving clip in which Tom's family talks about him and you see a surprising example of memory that still works.
- *Mike, an Amnestic Patient:* Following an accident, Mike struggles with memory problems that affect his employment, his relationship, and his sense of self. You'll notice how he expresses himself both in his language and in the flatness of his emotion.
- *Amnestic Patient Interview:* This clip shows Endel Tulving interviewing a patient who demonstrates intact procedural memory, gross deficits of episodic memory, and a good example of a screening for cognitive impairment.
- *Neural Networks: Cognition and Dementia:* In this clip, James McClelland proposes that computer simulations of the brain's neural networks can reveal how human cognition works—and even how cognition fails in dementia.

CENGAGENOW™ **CengageNOW**

Go to **academic.cengage.com/now** to link to CengageNOW, your online study tool. First take the Pre-Test for this chapter to get your personalized study plan, which will identify topics you need to review and direct you to online resources. Then take the Post-Test to determine what concepts you have mastered and what you still need work on.

Video Concept Reviews

CengageNOW also contains Mark Durand's *Video Concept Reviews* on challenging topics.

- Dementia
- Agnosia
- Facial Agnosia
- Dementia of the Alzheimer's Type
- Vascular Dementia
- Human Immunodeficiency Virus Type 1 (HIV-1)
- Head Trauma
- Amnestic Disorder

Exploring Cognitive Disorders

• When the brain is damaged, the effects are irreversible, accumulating until learning, memory, or consciousness are obviously impaired.

• Cognitive disorders develop much later than mental retardation and other learning disorders, which are believed to be present at birth.

TYPES OF COGNITIVE DISORDERS

DELIRIUM

Description
- Impaired consciousness and cognition for several hours or days
  – confusion, disorientation, inability to focus
- Most prevalent among older adults, people with AIDS, and patients on medication

Causes (subtypes)
- Delirium due to a general medical condition
- Substance-induced delirium
- Delirium due to multiple etiologies
- Delirium not otherwise specified

Treatment
- Pharmacological
  – benzodiazepines
  – antipsychotics
- Psychosocial
  – reassurance
  – presence of personal objects
  – inclusion in treatment decisions

AMNESTIC DISORDER

Description
- Permanent short-term memory loss without impairment of other cognitive functions
  – inability to learn new information or recall previously learned information
  – significant impairment in social and occupational functioning

Causes
- Medical condition such as head trauma
- Lasting effects of a drug, even after the substance is no longer ingested

Treatment
- Prevention: proper medical care and drug monitoring
- No long-term success at combating damage

Subtype: Wernicke/Korsakoff Syndrome

Caused by damage to the thalamus from injury (stroke) or chronic heavy alcohol use (thiamine depletion)

Dementia

• *Gradual deterioration of brain functioning that affects judgment, memory, language, and other advanced cognitive processes*
• *Caused by medical condition or drug abuse*
• *Some forms are irreversible, some are resolved by treatment of primary condition.*

TYPES OF DEMENTIA

DEMENTIA OF THE ALZHEIMER'S TYPE

Description
- Increasing memory impairment and other multiple behavioral and cognitive deficits, affecting language, motor functioning, ability to recognize people or things, and/or planning.
- Most prevalent dementia
- Subject of most research

Causes
- Progressive brain damage, evident in neurofibrillary tangles and neuritic plaque, confirmed by autopsy but assessed by simplified mental status exam
- Involves multiple genes

Treatment
- No cure so far, but hope lies in genetic research and amyloid protein in neurine plaques
- Management may include lists, maps, and notes to help maintain orientation.
- New medications that prevent acetylcholine breakdown and vitamin therapy show promise.

SUBSTANCE-INDUCED PERSISTING DEMENTIA

- Caused by brain damage due to prolonged drug use, especially in combination with poor diet, as in alcohol dependency; other substances may include inhalants, and the sedative, hypnotic, and anxiolytic drugs.
- Treatment focuses on prevention.

VASCULAR DEMENTIA

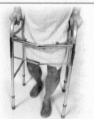

- Permanent deterioration due to blocked or damaged blood vessels in the brain (stroke)
- Symptoms identical to Alzheimer's and may also include problems with walking and weakness of limbs
- Treatment focuses on coping.

DEMENTIA DUE TO OTHER GENERAL MEDICAL CONDITIONS

- Similar in effect to other cognitive disorders, but caused by:
  – head trauma
  – HIV, Parkinson's, Huntington's, Pick's, or Creutzfeldt-Jakob disease
  – hydrocephalus, hypothyroidism, brain tumor, and vitamin B12 deficiency
- Treatment of primary condition is sometimes possible

CHAPTER 16

Mental Health Services:
Legal and Ethical Issues

©Richard Laird/Getty Images

PERSPECTIVES ON MENTAL HEALTH LAW

CIVIL COMMITMENT
    Criteria for Civil Commitment
    Changes Affecting Civil Commitment
    An Overview of Civil Commitment

CRIMINAL COMMITMENT
    The Insanity Defense
    Reactions to the Insanity Defense
    Therapeutic Jurisprudence
    Competence to Stand Trial
    Duty to Warn
    Mental Health Professionals as Expert Witnesses

PATIENTS' RIGHTS AND CLINICAL PRACTICE GUIDELINES
    The Right to Treatment
    The Right to Refuse Treatment
    Research Participants' Rights
    Evidence-Based Practice and Clinical Practice Guidelines

CONCLUSIONS

ABNORMAL PSYCHOLOGY LIVE CD-ROM

    False Memory Research
    Web Link

Mind is the great lever of all things: human thought is the process by which human ends are ultimately answered.

Daniel Webster

PERSPECTIVES ON MENTAL HEALTH LAW

We begin this chapter with a return to Arthur, whom we described in Chapter 13 as having psychotic symptoms. Revisiting the case from his family's perspective reveals the complexities of mental health law and the ethical aspects of working with people who have psychological disorders.

ARTHUR: A Family's Dilemma

As you remember, Arthur was brought to our clinic by family members because he was speaking and acting strangely. He talked incessantly about his "secret plan" to save all the starving children in the world. His family's concern intensified when Arthur said he was planning to break into the German embassy and present his plan to the German ambassador. Alarmed by his increasingly inappropriate behavior and fearing he would be hurt, the family was astounded to learn they could not force him into a psychiatric hospital. Arthur could admit himself—which was not likely, given his belief that nothing was wrong with him—but they had no power to admit him involuntarily unless he was in danger of doing harm to himself or others. Even if they sincerely believed some harm might be forthcoming, this wasn't sufficient reason to admit him involuntarily. The family coped with this emergency as best they could for several weeks until the worst of Arthur's behaviors began to diminish.

Arthur suffered from what is known as brief psychotic disorder (see Chapter 13). Fortunately for him, this is one of the few psychotic disorders that is not chronic. What is important here is to see how the mental health system responded. Because Arthur had not hurt himself or someone else, he had to seek help on his own before the hospital would assist him, even though everyone involved realized that such action on his part was unlikely. This response by the mental health system added one more layer of helplessness to the family's already desperate emotional state. Why wouldn't the mental health facility admit Arthur, who was clearly out of touch with reality and in need of help? Why couldn't his own family authorize the mental health facility to act? What would have happened if Arthur had entered the German embassy and hurt or, worse, killed someone? Would he have gone to jail, or would he have finally received help from the mental health community? Would Arthur have been held responsible if he hurt other people while he was delusional? These are just a few of the many issues that surface when we try to balance the rights of people who have psychological disorders with the responsibilities of society to provide care.

Mental health professionals face such questions daily. They must both diagnose and treat people and consider individual and societal rights and responsibilities. As we describe how systems of ethics and legal concepts have developed, remember they change with time and with shifting societal and political perspectives on mental illness. How we treat people with psychological disorders is partly a function of how society views them. For example, do people with mental illness need help and protection, or does society need protection from them? As public opinion about people with mental illness changes, so do the laws affecting them, and legal and ethical issues affect both research and practice. As you will see, the issues affecting research and practice are often complementary. For example, confidentiality is required to protect the identity of a participant in a research study and of a patient seeking help for a psychological disorder. Because people who receive mental health services often simultaneously participate in research studies, we must consider the concerns of both constituencies.

CIVIL COMMITMENT

The legal system exercises significant influence over the mental health system, for better or for worse. Laws have been designed to protect people who display abnormal behavior and to protect society. Often, achieving this protection is a delicate balancing act, with the scales sometimes thought to be tipped in favor of the rights of individuals and at other times in favor of society. For example, each state has **civil commitment laws** that detail when a person can be legally declared to have a mental illness and be placed in a hospital for treatment (Meyer & Weaver, 2006). When Arthur's family tried to have him involuntarily committed to a mental health facility, hospital officials decided that because he was not in imminent danger of hurting himself or others he could not be committed against his will. In this case, the laws protected Arthur from involuntary commitment, but they also put him and others at potential risk by not compelling him to get help. In a now-classic book, La Fond and Durham (1992) argue that two clear trends in mental health law are evident in the recent history of the United States. According to these authors, a "liberal era" from 1960 to 1980 was characterized by a commitment to individual rights and fairness. In contrast, 1980 to the present has been a "neoconservative era," partly in reaction to the liberal reforms of the 1960s and 1970s, that has focused on majority concerns, including law and order. In the liberal era, the rights of people with mental illness dominated; in the neoconservative era, the rights of people with mental illness have been limited to provide greater protection to society.

Civil commitment laws in the United States date back to the late 19th century. Before this time, almost all people with severe mental illness were cared for by family members or the commu-

People with mental illness are treated differently in different cultures.

nity or were left to care for themselves. With the development of a large public hospital system devoted to treating such individuals came an alarming trend: involuntary commitment of people for reasons unrelated to mental illness (Meyer & Weaver, 2006). There were even instances in which women were committed to psychiatric hospitals by their husbands simply for holding differing personal or political views. In the 1800s, Mrs. E. P. W. Packard crusaded for better civil commitment laws after being involuntarily confined to a psychiatric hospital for 3 years (Weiner & Wettstein, 1993).

Criteria for Civil Commitment

Historically, states have permitted commitment when several conditions have been met: (1) The person has a "mental illness" and is in need of treatment, (2) the person is dangerous to himself or herself or others, or (3) the person is unable to care for himself, a situation considered a "grave disability." How these conditions are interpreted has varied over the years and has always been controversial. It is important to see that the government justifies its right to act against the wishes of an individual—in this case, to commit someone to a mental health facility—under two types of authority: police power and *parens patriae* ("state or country as the parent") power. Under police power, the government takes responsibility for protecting the public health, safety, and welfare and can create laws and regulations to ensure this protection. Criminal offenders are held in custody if they are a threat to society. The state applies *parens patriae* power when citizens are not likely to act in their own best interest, for example, to assume custody of chil-

dren who have no living parents. Similarly, it is used to commit individuals with severe mental illness to mental health facilities when it is believed that they might be harmed because they are unable to secure the basic necessities of life, such as food and shelter (grave disability), or because they do not recognize their need for treatment (Meyer & Weaver, 2006). Under *parens patriae* power, the state acts as a surrogate parent, presumably in the best interests of a person who needs help.

A person in need of help can always voluntarily request admission to a mental health facility; after an evaluation by a mental health professional, a patient may be accepted for treatment. However, when an individual does not voluntarily seek help but others feel that treatment or protection is necessary, the formal process of civil commitment can be initiated. The specifics of this process differ from state to state, but it usually begins with a petition by a relative or mental health professional to a judge. The court may then request an examination to assess psychological status, ability for self-care, need for treatment, and potential for harm. The judge considers this information and decides whether commitment is appropriate. This process is similar to other legal proceedings, and the person under question has all the rights and protections provided by the law. In most states, the person can even request that a jury hear the evidence and make a determination. In all cases, the person must be notified that the civil commitment proceedings are taking place, must be present during the trial, must have representation by an attorney, and can examine the witnesses and request an independent evaluation. These safeguards are built into the civil commitment process to guarantee the rights of the person being examined and to ensure that no one is involuntarily

©Bruce Ayres/Getty Images

The government can exert *parens patriae* to protect people from hurting themselves.

committed to a psychiatric facility for other than legitimate reasons.

In emergency situations, when there is clearly immediate danger, a short-term commitment can be made without the formal proceedings required of a civil commitment. Family members or sometimes police officers certify that the person presents a "clear and present danger" to herself or to others (Meyer & Weaver, 2006). Arthur's family was unsuccessful in having him admitted on an emergency basis because it was not clear that anyone was in immediate danger, only that someone might be hurt. Again, deciding what is a clear and present danger sometimes requires a great deal of subjective judgment from the court and from mental health professionals.

■ Defining Mental Illness

The concept of mental illness figures prominently in civil commitment, and it is important to understand how it is defined. **Mental illness** is a legal concept, typically meaning severe emotional or thought disturbances that negatively affect an individual's health and safety. Each state has its own definition. For example, in New York, "'Mental illness' means an affliction with a mental disease or mental condition which is manifested by a disorder or disturbance in behavior, feeling, thinking, or judgment to such an extent that the person afflicted requires care, treatment and rehabilitation" (*New York Mental Hygiene Law,* 1992). In contrast, in Connecticut, "'Mentally ill person' means a person who has a mental or emotional condition that has substantial adverse effects on his or her ability to function and who requires care and treatment, and specifically excludes a person who is an alcohol-

dependent person or a drug-dependent person" (Conn. Gen. Stat. Ann., 1992). Many states exclude mental retardation or substance-related disorders from the definition of mental illness.

Mental illness is *not* synonymous with psychological disorder; in other words, receiving a diagnosis according to the fourth edition, text revision, of the *Diagnostic and Statistical Manual* (DSM-IV-TR) does not necessarily mean that a person's condition fits the legal definition of mental illness. Although the DSM is quite specific about criteria that must be met for diagnosis, there is considerable ambiguity about what constitutes a "mental condition" or what are "adverse effects on his or her ability to function." This allows flexibility in making decisions individually, but it also maintains the possibility of subjective impression and bias as influences on these decisions.

■ Dangerousness

Assessing whether someone is a danger to self or others is a critical determinant of the civil commitment process. **Dangerousness** is a particularly controversial concept for the mentally ill: Popular opinion tends to be that people who are mentally ill are more dangerous than those who are not. Although this conclusion is questionable, it is still widespread, partly because of sensational media reports. Such views are important to the process of civil commitment if they bias a determination of dangerousness and unfairly link it with severe mental illness.

There is a widespread popular belief that mental illness causes a person to be violent (Van Dorn, Swanson, Elbogen, & Swartz, 2005). The results of research on dangerousness and mental illness are often mixed, but evidence points to a moderately increased rate of violence among people with mental illness (Fazel & Grann, 2006). Closer examination of this kind of research reveals that although having a mental illness generally does increase the likelihood of future violence, specific symptoms (such as hallucinations, delusions, or having a comorbid personality disorder) appear to be associated with people at increased risk of violence (Elbogen, Tomkins, Pothuloori, & Scalora, 2003; Harris & Lurigio, in press). Even previously violent individuals with mental illness are not necessarily going to commit violent crimes after they are released, although the presence of certain symptoms may increase the risk.

Unfortunately, the widely held misperception that people with mental illness are more dangerous may differentially affect ethnic minorities and women (Spector, 2001). Women, for example, are likely to be viewed as more dangerous than men when they engage in similar aggressive behaviors (Coughlin, 1994). Homeless women are more likely to be involuntarily committed even in warm climates because they are perceived as less capable than men of caring for themselves, and thus at greater risk of harming themselves (Stefan, 1996). Black males are often perceived as dangerous, even when they don't exhibit any violent behavior (Bond, DeCandia, & MacKinnon, 1988), which may partly explain why blacks are overrepresented among those who are involuntarily committed to state psychiatric institutions (Lawson, Hepler, Holladay, & Cuffel, 1994; Spector, 2001).

To return to the general issue, how do you determine whether a person is dangerous to others? How accurate are mental health professionals at predicting who will and who will not later be violent? The answers bear directly on the process of civil commitment, as well as on protection for society. If we can't accurately predict dangerousness, how can we justify involuntary commitment?

Clinicians are better at assessing the relative risk required of the legal system than determining dangerousness case by case (Scott & Resnick, 2006). Stated in another way, mental health professionals can identify groups of people who are at greater risk than the general population for being violent—such as having a previous history of both violence and drug or alcohol dependence—and can so advise the court. What clinicians cannot yet do is predict with certainty whether a particular person will or will not become violent.

Changes Affecting Civil Commitment

Clearly, there are significant problems with the process of civil commitment. In particular, deciding whether a person has a mental illness or is dangerous requires considerable subjective judgment and, because of varying legal language, this determination can differ from state to state. These problems have resulted in a number of significant legal developments. We look next at how changes in civil commitment procedures have resulted in significant economic and social consequences, including an impact on one of our more important social problems: homelessness.

■ The Supreme Court and Civil Commitment

In 1957, the parents of Kenneth Donaldson had him committed to the Florida State Hospital for treatment of paranoid schizophrenia. Donaldson was not considered dangerous, yet, despite repeated offers of placement in a halfway house or with a friend, Dr. O'Connor, the superintendent of the hospital, refused to release him for almost 15 years, during which Donaldson received virtually no treatment (Donaldson, 1976). Donaldson successfully sued Dr. O'Connor for damages, winning $48,500. In deciding the case, the Supreme Court found that "a State cannot constitutionally confine . . . a non-dangerous individual who is capable of surviving safely in freedom by himself or with the help of willing and responsible family and friends" (*O'Connor v. Donaldson,* 1975).

Here, and in a subsequent decision known as *Addington v. Texas* (1979), the Supreme Court said that more than just a promise of improving quality of life is required to commit someone

involuntarily. If nondangerous people can survive in the community with the help of others, they should not be detained against their will. Needing treatment or having a grave disability was not sufficient to commit someone involuntarily with a mental illness. The effect of this decision was to limit substantially the government's ability to commit individuals unless they were dangerous (Meyer & Weaver, 2006).

■ Criminalization

Because of the tightened restrictions on involuntary commitment that prevailed in the 1970s and 1980s, many people who would normally have been committed to mental health facilities for treatment were instead being handled by the criminal justice system. In other words, people with severe mental illness were now living in the community, but many were not receiving the mental health services they needed and would eventually run afoul of the legal system because of their behavior. This "criminalization" of the mentally ill was of great concern because the criminal justice system was not prepared to care for these individuals (Meyer & Weaver, 2006). Family members were increasingly frustrated that they couldn't obtain treatment for their loved ones, who were instead languishing in jail without help.

■ Deinstitutionalization and Homelessness

In addition to criminalization, two other trends emerged at this time: an increase in the number of people who were homeless and **deinstitutionalization,** the movement of people with severe mental illness out of institutions. Remember that homelessness is not exclusively a problem of the mentally ill. Approximately 2 million to 3 million people will experience a night of homelessness in the United States each year, and estimates place the numbers of homeless people at 800,000 on any given night (U.S. Department of Health and Human Services, 2007). About 25% have a previous history of hospitalization for mental health problems, and about a third of the people with a history of hospitalization are considered seriously mentally ill (Folsom et al., 2005). One study found that as many as 15% of people experiencing severe psychiatric disturbances for the first time had been homeless before their psychological difficulties (Herman, Susser, Jandorf, Lavelle, & Bromet, 1998). For reasons not yet fully understood, ethnicity may also play a part in who among people with mental illness become homeless. In a large study in San Diego County, Latinos and Asian Americans with mental illness were less likely to become homeless, but African Americans were more likely to be homeless (Folsom et al., 2005).

Information on the characteristics of people who are homeless is important because it provides us with clues about why people become homeless, and it dispels the notion that all homeless people have mental health problems. For a time, homelessness was blamed on strict civil commitment criteria and deinstitutionalization (Meyer & Weaver, 2006); that is, policies to severely limit who can be involuntarily committed, the limits placed on the stays of people with severe

Larry Hogue was involuntarily committed to a psychiatric hospital because, homeless and under the influence of drugs (left), he terrorized residents of a New York City neighborhood for years. Once off drugs (right), Hogue was able to control himself.

© Associated Press
© Associated Press

People become homeless because of many factors, including economic conditions, mental health status, and drug use.

mental illness, and the concurrent closing of large psychiatric hospitals were held responsible for the substantial increase in homelessness during the 1980s. Although a sizable percentage of homeless people have mental illness, the rise in homelessness is also the result of such economic factors as increased unemployment and a shortage of low-income housing (U.S. Conference of Mayors-Sodexho, 2005). Yet the perception that civil commitment restrictions and deinstitutionalization caused homelessness resulted in movements to change commitment procedures.

Reforms in civil commitment that made it more difficult to commit someone involuntarily occurred at the same time the policy of deinstitutionalization was closing large psychiatric hospitals (Turkheimer & Parry, 1992). Deinstitutionalization had two goals: (1) to close the large state mental hospitals and (2) to create a network of community mental health centers where the released individuals could be treated. Although the first goal appears to have been substantially accomplished, with about a 75% decrease in the number of hospitalized patients (Kiesler & Sibulkin, 1987), the essential goal of providing alternative community care appears not be have been attained. Instead, there was **transinstitutionalization,** or the movement of people with severe mental illness from large psychiatric hospitals to nursing homes or other group residences, including jails and prisons, many of which provide only marginal services (Perez, Leifman, & Estrada, 2003). Because of the deterioration in care for many people who had previously been served by the mental hospital system, deinstitutionalization is largely considered a failure. Although many praise the ideal of providing community care for people with severe mental illness, the support needed to provide this type of care has been severely deficient.

■ Reactions to Strict Commitment Procedures

Arthur's psychotic reaction and his family's travails in trying to get help occurred during the mid-1970s, a time characterized by greater concern for individual freedom than for society's rights and by the belief that people with mental illness were not properly served by being forced into treatment. Others, however, especially relatives of afflicted people, felt that by not coercing some individuals into treatment, the system was sanctioning their men-

tal decline and placing them at grave risk of harm. The culmination of a number of factors—such as the lack of success with deinstitutionalization, the rise in homelessness, and the criminalization of people with severe mental illness—gave rise to a backlash against their perceived causes, including the strict civil commitment laws. The case of Joyce Brown captures this clash of concerns between individual freedoms for people with mental illness and society's responsibility to treat them.

JOYCE BROWN: Homeless but Not Helpless

During a 1988 winter emergency in New York City, Mayor Ed Koch ordered that all homeless people who appeared to be mentally ill should be involuntarily committed to a mental health facility for their protection. He used the legal principle of *parens patriae* to justify this action, citing the need to protect these individuals from the cold and from themselves. One of the people who was taken off the streets, 40-year-old Joyce Brown, was picked up against her will and admitted to Bellevue Hospital, where she received a diagnosis of paranoid schizophrenia. She had been homeless for some time, swearing at people as they walked by; at one point, she adopted the name Billie Boggs after a New York television personality with whom she fantasized a relationship. Supported by the New York Civil Liberties Union, Brown contested her commitment and was released after 3 months (Kasindorf, 1988).

This case is important because it illustrates the conflicting interests over civil commitment. Brown's family had for some time been concerned about her well-being and had tried unsuccessfully to have her involuntarily committed. Although she had never hurt anyone or tried to commit suicide, they felt that living on the streets of New York City was too hazardous, and they feared for her welfare. City officials expressed concern for Brown and others like her, especially during the dangerously cold winter, although some suspected that this was an excuse to remove people with disturbing behavior from the streets of affluent sections (Kasindorf, 1988). Brown chose not to seek treatment and resisted efforts to place her in alternative settings. At times, she could be quite articulate in making a case for her freedom of choice. Only weeks after she was released from the hospital, she was again living on the streets. Brown was involuntarily committed to a mental health facility again in early 1994 and was released at her insistence a short time later. This continued a pattern that lasted for years (Failer, 2002).

Rulings such as *O'Connor v. Donaldson* and *Addington v. Texas* had argued that mental illness and dangerousness should be criteria for involuntary commitment. However, because of cases like Brown's and concerns about homelessness and criminalization, a movement has emerged calling for a return to broader civil procedures that would permit commitment not only of those who showed dangerousness to self or others but also of individuals who were not dangerous but were in need of treatment and of those with grave disability. Groups including the National Alliance for the Mentally Ill, a coalition of family members of people with mental illness, argued for legal reform to make involuntary commitment easier—an emotional response to the failure to protect and treat people with mental illness. Several states in the late 1970s and early 1980s changed their civil commitment laws in an attempt to address these concerns. For example, the state of Washington revised its laws in 1979 to allow commitment of people who were judged to be in need of treatment, which produced a 91% increase in the number of involuntary commitments in the first year it was in effect (Durham & La Fond, 1985). There was essentially no change in the size of the hospital population at this time, only in the status under which patients were committed (La Fond & Durham, 1992). Whereas people were previously detained because of violence, they were now admitted under *parens patriae* powers; also, whereas most admissions had been voluntary, they were now involuntary. Hospitals began to fill up because of longer stays and repeated admissions and they accepted only involuntary admissions; therefore, the result of easing the procedure for involuntarily committing people with mental illness was only to change the authority under which they were admitted.

The special case of sex offenders has attracted public attention in recent years, and the issue of how to treat repeat offenders is at the heart of the concerns over civil commitment. In the years between 1930 and 1960, some states passed "sexual psychopath laws" that provided hospitalization instead of incarceration, but for an indefinite period (La Fond, 2005). Sex offenders (rapists and pedophiles) could be civilly committed until they demonstrated that treatment was effective. However, because treatment is often unsuccessful when attempted with uncooperative clients (see Chapter 10) and because public opinion moved from a priority to treat to a priority to punish, these laws were repealed or went unused. Recent efforts have focused on incarcerating sex offenders for their crimes and, if they are judged still dangerous at the end of their sentences, civilly committing them. Such "sexual predator" laws were first enacted in 1990, and the Kansas version was upheld as constitutional by the U.S. Supreme Court (*Kansas v. Hendricks,* 1997). Confinement of this type was viewed by the court as acceptable because it was seen as treatment, even though the justices conceded that such treatment is often ineffective (Zonana, 1997). Some are greatly concerned that these types of laws give the government too much latitude in using civil commitment just to keep certain individuals away from others in society (La Fond, 2005).

An Overview of Civil Commitment

What should the criteria be for involuntarily committing someone with severe mental illness to a mental health facility? Should imminent danger to self or others be the only justification, or should society act as a parent and coerce people who appear to be in distress and in need of asylum or safety? How do we address the concerns of families like Arthur's who see their loved ones overcome by psychological problems? And what of our need not to be harassed by people like Brown? When do these rights take precedence over the rights of an individual to be free from un-

A significant number of the homeless are individuals with mental disorders, many of whom live with their children in shelters or on the streets.

wanted incarceration? It is tempting to conclude that the legal system has failed to address these issues and reacts only to the political whims of the times.

However, from another point of view, the periodic change in laws is a sign of a healthy system that responds to the limitations of previous decisions. The reactions by the Supreme Court in the 1970s to the coercive and arbitrary nature of civil commitment were as understandable as more recent attempts to make it easier to commit people in obvious need of help. As the consequences of these changes become apparent, the system responds to correct injustices. Although improvements may seem excruciatingly slow and may not always correctly address the issues in need of reform, the fact that laws can be changed should make us optimistic that the needs of individuals and of society can ultimately be addressed through the courts.

CONCEPT CHECK 16.1

Check your understanding of civil commitment by filling in the blanks.

Several conditions must be met before the state is permitted to commit a person involuntarily: The person has a(n) (1) _____ and is in need of treatment, the person is considered (2) _____ to herself or others, and the person is unable to care for himself or herself, also known as (3) _____.

Mental illness is a(n) (4) _____ concept, typically meaning severe emotional or thought disturbances that negatively affect an individual's health and safety, although this definition differs from state to state. When the laws about civil commitment emerged, (5) _____ (movement of disabled individuals out of mental institutions) and (6) _____ (movement of disabled individuals to a lesser facility) also occurred.

CRIMINAL COMMITMENT

What would have happened if Arthur had been arrested for trespassing on embassy grounds or, worse yet, if he had hurt or killed someone in his effort to present his plan for saving the world? Would he have been held responsible for his actions, given his obvious disturbed mental state? How would a jury have responded to him when he seemed fine just several days later? If he was not responsible for his behavior then, why does he seem so normal now?

These questions are of enormous importance as we debate whether people should be held responsible for their criminal behavior despite the possible presence of mental illness. Cases such as that of Andrea Yates, who was first convicted and sentenced to life in prison for drowning her five children in a bathtub in 2001 but later found not guilty by reason of insanity (NGRI), causes some to wonder whether the laws have gone too far. **Criminal commitment** is the process by which people are held because (1) they have been accused of committing a crime and are detained in a mental health facility until they can be assessed as fit or unfit to participate in legal proceedings against them or (2) they have been found not guilty of a crime by reason of insanity.

The Insanity Defense

The purpose of our criminal justice system is to protect our lives, our liberty, and our pursuit of happiness, but not all people are punished for criminal behavior. The law recognizes that, under certain circumstances, people are not responsible for their behavior and it would be unfair and perhaps ineffective to punish them. Current views originate from a case recorded more than 150 years ago in England. Daniel M'Naghten today might receive the diagnosis of paranoid schizophrenia. He held the delusion that the English Tory party was persecuting him, and he set out to kill the British prime minister. He mistook the man's secretary for the prime minister and killed the secretary instead. In what has become known as the M'Naghten rule, the English court decreed that people are not responsible for their criminal behavior if they do not know what they are doing or if they don't know that what they are doing is wrong. This ruling was, in essence, the beginning of the *insanity defense* (see summary in Table 16.1). For more than 100 years, this rule was used to determine culpability when a person's mental state was in question.

In the intervening years, other standards have been introduced to modify the M'Naghten rule because many critics felt that simply relying on an accused person's knowledge of right or wrong was too limiting and a broader definition was needed (Guttmacher & Weihofen, 1952). Mental illness alters not only a person's cognitive abilities but also that person's emotional functioning, and mental health professionals believed the entire range of functioning should be taken into account when a person's responsibility was determined. One influential decision, known as the Durham rule, was initiated in 1954 by Judge David Bazelon of the Federal Circuit Court of Appeals for the District of Columbia and based on the case *Durham v. United States* (1954). The Durham rule broadened the criteria for responsibility from knowledge of right or wrong to include the presence of a "mental disease or defect" (see Table 16.1). This decision was initially hailed by mental health professionals because it allowed them to present to a judge or jury a complete picture of the person with mental illness. Unfortunately, it was soon apparent that mental health professionals did not have the expertise to assess reliably whether a person's mental illness caused the criminal behavior in question and therefore that decisions were being based on unscientific opinions (Arens, 1974). Although the Durham rule is no longer used, it caused a reexamination of the criteria used in the insanity defense.

TABLE 16.1 Important Factors in the Evolution of the Insanity Defense

Factor	Date	Quotation
M'Naghten rule	1843	[I]t must be clearly proved that at the time of committing the act, the party accused was labouring under such a defect of reason, from disease of the mind, as not to know the nature and quality of the act he was doing; or if he did know it, that he did not know he was doing what was wrong. (101 Cl. & F. 200, 8 Eng. Rep. 718, H.L. 1843)
Durham rule	1954	An accused is not criminally responsible if his unlawful act was the product of mental disease or mental defect. (*Durham v. United States*, 1954)
American Law Institute (ALI) rule	1962	1. A person is not responsible for criminal conduct if at the time of such conduct as a result of mental disease or defect he lacks substantial capacity either to appreciate the criminality (wrongfulness) of his conduct or to conform his conduct to the requirements of law. 2. As used in the Article, the terms "mental disease or defect" do not include an abnormality manifested only by repeated criminal or otherwise antisocial conduct. (American Law Institute, 1962)
Diminished capacity	1978	Evidence of abnormal mental condition would be admissible to affect the degree of crime for which an accused could be convicted. Specifically, those offenses requiring intent or knowledge could be reduced to lesser included offenses requiring only reckless or criminal neglect. (New York State Department of Mental Hygiene, 1978)
Insanity Defense Reform Act	1984	A person charged with a criminal offense should be found not guilty by reason of insanity if it is shown that, as a result of mental disease or mental retardation, he was unable to appreciate the wrongfulness of his conduct at the time of his offense. (American Psychiatric Association, 1983, p. 685)

Source: Reprinted, with permission, from Silver, E., Cirincione, C., & Steadman, H. J., 1994. Demythologizing inaccurate perceptions of the insanity defense. *Law and Human Behavior,* 18, 63–70, © 1994 Plenum Press.

An influential study of this question was conducted around the same time as the Durham decision by a group of attorneys, judges, and law scholars who belonged to the American Law Institute (ALI). Their challenge was to develop criteria for determining whether a person's mental competence makes him answerable for criminal behavior. The ALI first reaffirmed the importance of distinguishing the behavior of people with mental illness from that of people without mental disorders. Its members pointed out that the threat of punishment was unlikely to deter someone who had severe mental illness; the group's position was that these individuals should instead be treated until they improve and should then be released. (This recommendation is discussed further when we examine recent developments and criticisms of the insanity defense.) The ALI concluded that people are not responsible for their criminal behavior if, because of their mental illness, they cannot recognize the inappropriateness of their behavior or control it (ALI, 1962). The criteria shown in Table 16.1, known as the ALI test, stipulate that a person must either be unable to distinguish right from wrong—as set forth in the M'Naghten rule—or be incapable of self-control to be shielded from legal consequences.

The ALI also included provisions for the concept of **diminished capacity** (see Table 16.1), which holds that people's ability to understand the nature of their behavior and therefore their criminal intent can be diminished by their mental illness. The theory of criminal intent—otherwise called *mens rea,* or having a "guilty mind"—is important legally because to convict someone of a crime, there must be proof of the physical act *(actus rea)* and the mental state *(mens rea)* of the person committing the act (Meyer & Weaver, 2006). For example, if a woman accidentally hits someone who steps in front of her car and the person subsequently dies, the woman would not be held criminally responsible; although a person was killed, there was no criminal intent—the driver didn't deliberately hit the person and attempt murder. The diminished capacity concept proposes that a person with mental illness who commits a criminal offense may not, because of the illness, have criminal intent and therefore cannot be held responsible.

Reactions to the Insanity Defense

Judicial rulings through the 1960s and 1970s regarding criminal responsibility parallel the course of civil commitment. An effort was made to focus on the needs of people with mental illness who also broke the law, providing mental health treatment instead of punishment. However, the successful use of concepts such as *insanity* or *diminished capacity* in criminal cases alarmed large segments of the population. For instance, in 1979 a man successfully pleaded NGRI after being arrested for writing bad checks. His case was based on the testimony of an expert witness who said he suffered from pathological gambling disorder and he therefore could not distinguish right from wrong (*State v. Campanaro,* 1980). Other successful defenses were based on disorders in the DSM, such as posttraumatic stress disorder, and on disorders not in this system, including battered wife syndrome.

Without question, the case that prompted the strongest outrage against the insanity defense and the most calls for its abolition

James Brady, President Ronald Reagan's press secretary, was wounded in 1981 by a gunman attempting to assassinate the president. In 1994, Brady and his wife Sarah celebrated the passage of the Brady law, which imposed stricter controls on the possession of handguns.

©Dirk Halstead/Getty Images

is that of John W. Hinckley, Jr. (Simon, 2005). On March 31, 1981, as President Ronald Reagan walked out of the Washington Hilton Hotel, Hinckley fired several shots, hitting and seriously wounding the president, a Secret Service agent, and James Brady, the president's press secretary. In an instant, Secret Service agents tackled and disarmed Hinckley. Hinckley was obsessed with actress Jodie Foster; he claimed he tried to kill the president to impress her. Hinckley was judged by a jury to be NGRI, using the ALI standard. The verdict sent shock waves throughout the country and legal community (Simon, 2005). One of the many consequences of this event was that James Brady and his wife Sarah became advocates for stricter gun control laws and saw the ultimate passage of the Brady law in 1994.

Although there was already criticism of the insanity defense, one study found that after Hinckley's verdict more than half the states considered abolishing it (Keilitz & Fulton, 1984). As you have seen before, such impulses often are based more on emotion than on fact. Highly publicized cases such as those of Hinckley, Charles Manson, Jeffrey Dahmer, and Ted Kaczynski, with the media characterization of people with mental illness as excessively violent, have created an unfavorable public perception of the insanity defense. One telephone survey study found that 91% of people who responded agreed with the statement, "judges and juries have a hard time telling whether the defendants are really sane or insane" (Hans, 1986). Almost 90% agreed the "insanity plea is a loophole that allows too many guilty people to go free." In a similar study, 90% of people agreed "the insanity plea is used too much. Too many people escape responsibilities for crimes by pleading insanity" (Pasewark & Seidenzahl, 1979). Is there hard evidence that the insanity defense is used too often?

A study of the public's impression of the insanity defense compared it to the actual use of the defense and its outcomes (Silver, Cirincione, & Steadman, 1994). As Table 16.2 shows, the public's perception that this defense is used in 37% of all felony cases is a gross overestimate; the actual figure is less than 1%. The public also overestimates how often the defense is successful, as well as how often people judged NGRI are set free. People tend to underestimate the length of hospitalization of those who are acquitted. This last issue is important: In contrast to public perceptions, the length of time a person is confined to a hospital after being judged NGRI may exceed the time the person would have spent in jail had that person been convicted of the crime (Gracheck, 2006). Hinckley, for example, has been a patient in St. Elizabeth's Hospital for more than 25 years. Other research shows that individuals with mental illness who are found guilty of *nonviolent* crimes can be committed more than eight times as long as those people without mental illness placed in prison (Perlin, 2000). People with mental illness apparently do not often "beat the rap" as a result of being judged NGRI.

Theodore Kaczynski, once a promising mathematician (left), became a notorious terrorist who killed 3 people and injured 23 more with handmade bombs sent through the mail. Awaiting trial as the Unabomber (right), Kaczynski refused to cooperate with his lawyers, who fought to have him declared mentally ill to save his life. Ironically, the prosecution, in pressing for the death penalty, supported his claim of sanity. (In the end, Kaczynski pleaded guilty and accepted a life sentence.)

TABLE 16.2	Comparison of Public Perceptions With the Actual Occurrence of the Insanity Defense	
	Public Perception (%)	**Actual Occurrence (%)**
Use of Insanity Defense		
Felony indictments resulting in an insanity plea	37.0	0.9
Insanity pleas resulting in acquittal	44.0	26.0
Disposition of Insanity Acquittees		
Insanity acquittees sent to a mental hospital	50.6	84.7
Insanity acquittees set free	25.6	15.3
Conditional release		11.6
Outpatient		2.6
Release		1.1
Length of Confinement of Insanity Acquittees (in months)		
All crimes	21.8	32.5
Murder		76.4

Source: Reprinted, with permission, from Silver, E., Cirincione, C., & Steadman, H. J., 1994. Demythologizing inaccurate perceptions of the insanity defense. *Law and Human Behavior,* 18, 63–70, © 1994 Plenum Press.

Despite sound evidence that it is not used excessively and does not result in widespread early release of dangerous individuals, major changes were made in the criteria for the insanity defense after the Hinckley verdict. Both the American Psychiatric Association (1983) and the American Bar Association (1984) recommended modifications, moving back toward M'Naghten-like definitions. Shortly afterward, Congress passed the Insanity Defense Reform Act of 1984, which incorporated these suggestions and made successful use of the insanity defense more difficult.

Another attempt at reforming the insanity plea has been to replace the NGRI verdict with a verdict of guilty but mentally ill (GBMI) (Simon, 2005). Although there are several versions of the GBMI verdict, the shared premise is that the consequences for a person ruled GBMI are different from those for a person who is NGRI. People found to be NGRI are not sent to prison but are evaluated at a psychiatric facility until such time as they are judged ready for release. A person determined to be no longer mentally ill must be released. If Arthur had committed a crime and was found NGRI, because his brief psychotic disorder was quickly resolved, he would probably have been released immediately. In contrast, one version of the GBMI verdict in theory allows the system both to treat and to punish the individual. The person found guilty is given a prison term just as if there were no question of mental illness. Whether the person is incarcerated in prison or in a mental health facility is decided by legal authorities. If the person recovers from mental illness before the sentence has passed, that person can be confined in prison for the maximum length of the term. If Arthur were found GBMI under this system, he could serve a full prison sentence, even though his mental illness was resolved. This version of GBMI has been adopted by a number of states (The evolving insanity defense, 2006).

The second version of GBMI is even harsher for the mentally ill offender. Convicted individuals are imprisoned, and prison authorities may provide mental health services if they are available. The verdict itself is simply a declaration by the jury that the person was mentally ill at the time the crime was committed and does not result in differential treatment for the perpetrator. Idaho, Montana, and Utah have abandoned the insanity defense altogether and have adopted this version of GBMI (The evolving insanity defense, 2006).

As noted, the GBMI verdict was a reaction to the perceived loophole provided by the insanity defense. It has been used in several states for more than 15 years, and its effects have been investigated by researchers. Two studies have shown that people who receive the GBMI verdict are more likely to be imprisoned and to receive longer sentences than people pleading NGRI (Callahan, McGreevy, Cirincione, & Steadman, 1992; Keilitz, 1987). Research also indicates that individuals receiving GBMI verdicts are no more likely to receive treatment than other prisoners who have mental illness (Keilitz, 1987; Smith & Hall, 1982). Currently, the type of verdicts available (NGRI versus GBMI) depends on the laws of the particular state where the crimes were committed.

Therapeutic Jurisprudence

There is a built-in tension between the judicial system and the mental health system. The legal system is, by design, adversarial. In other words, it was created with prosecutors and defendants, winners and losers. In contrast, the mental health system is set up to find solutions to important psychological problems without placing blame on any parties. The goal is for both sides to "win." Fortunately, there is an increasing recognition in the legal system that a strict adversarial approach to dealing with people with mental health problems may be harmful to everyone. As a result of this change in thinking, when individuals with psychological disorders break the law, they may now find themselves in one of a variety of "problem-solving courts" (Winick & Wexler, 2006). These new courts are designed to address the unique needs of people with specific problems. For example, today in many states you can find drug treatment courts, domestic violence courts, and mental health courts, among others. Interestingly, models of problem-solving courts have their roots in the legal systems of tribal societies in the United States, Canada, Australia, and New Zealand (Winick & Wexler, 2003).

These problem-solving courts are based on the concept of therapeutic jurisprudence—in essence, using what we know about behavior change to help people in trouble with the law. In drug treatment court, for example, a judge might be assigned to all criminal cases involving drug-addicted defendants. The judge would have the leeway to delay sentencing under the condition that the accused obtained and held a job for 6 months, received drug treatment during that time, and remained drug free. Similarly, a defendant in a mental health court might be helped by referrals to existing programs in the community and involvement of family members. Rather than simply trying to decide between prison and freedom, the court can serve as an instrument of social change. This evolving concept may provide effective alternatives in the criminal justice system for people with severe mental illness.

Society has long recognized the need to identify criminals who may not be in control of their behavior and who may not benefit from simple incarceration. The challenge is in trying to do what may be impossible: determining whether the person knew what she was doing, knew right from wrong, and could control her behavior. Mental health professionals cannot assess mental health retrospectively. An additional dilemma is the desire, on the one hand, to provide care to people with mental illness and, on the other, to treat them as responsible individuals. Finally, we must resolve the simultaneous and conflicting interests of wanting to assist people with mental illness and wanting to be protected from them. The recent trend of using problem-solving courts may be one way to address these concerns. We must reach a national consensus about the basic value of people with mental illness to decide how they should be dealt with legally. We hope the recent trend of favoring law and order over the rights of people with mental illness can be moderated to provide attention to both concerns.

Competence to Stand Trial

Before people can be tried for a criminal offense, they must be able to understand the charges against them and to assist with their own defense, criteria outlined by the Supreme Court in *Dusky v. United States* (1960). Thus, in addition to interpreting a person's state of mind during the criminal act, experts must also anticipate his state of mind during the subsequent legal proceedings. A person could be ruled NGRI because of his mental illness at the time of the criminal act yet still be competent to stand trial, a situation that would have occurred in Arthur's case had he committed a crime.

A person determined to be incompetent to stand trial typically loses the authority to make decisions and faces commitment. Because a trial requires a determination of **competence,** most people with obvious and severe impairments who commit crimes are never tried. Some observers estimate that for every person who receives a verdict of NGRI, 45 others are committed to a mental health facility with a diagnosis of severe mental illness (Butler, 2006). The length of stay is the time it takes the committed person to regain competence. Because this period can be drawn out, the courts have ruled it cannot be indefinite and that, after a reasonable amount of time, the person must be found competent, set free, or committed under civil law (*Jackson v. Indiana,* 1972). Laws are often not precise in their language, and the phrase "reasonable amount of time" is open to a great deal of interpretation.

A final issue relates to the legal concept of burden of proof, the weight of evidence needed to win a case. In decisions of competence to stand trial, an important ruling placed responsibility on the defendant to provide the burden of proof—in this case, that she is incompetent to stand trial (*Medina v. California,* 1992). Again, public concern that dangerous individuals with mental illness are routinely acquitted and let loose on society after committing multiple violent offenses flies in the face of the facts. More realistically, a person with mental illness commits a nonviolent crime and receives treatment through legal actions, such as the competence proceedings.

Duty to Warn

Do mental health professionals have any responsibility for the actions of the people they serve? This is especially important when we consider the dangerous behavior exhibited by a minority of people with severe mental illness. What are the responsibilities of professionals who suspect that someone with whom they are working may hurt or even kill another person? Must they contact the appropriate authority or the person who may be harmed, or are they forbidden to discuss information disclosed during therapy sessions?

These issues were the subject of a tragic case known as *Tarasoff v. Regents of the University of California* (1974, 1976). In 1969, Prosenjit Poddar, a graduate student at the University of California, killed a fellow student, Tatiana Tarasoff, who had previously rejected his romantic advances. At the time of the murder, he was being seen by two therapists at the University Health Center and had received a diagnosis of paranoid schizophrenia. At his last session, Poddar hinted that he was going to kill Tarasoff. His therapist believed this threat was serious and contacted the campus police, who investigated the allegation and received assurances from Poddar that he would leave Tarasoff alone. Weeks later, after repeated attempts to contact her, Poddar shot and stabbed Tarasoff until she died.

After learning of the therapists' role in the case, Tarasoff's family sued the university, the therapists, and the university police, saying they should have warned Tarasoff that she was in danger. The court agreed, and the Tarasoff case has been used ever since as a standard for therapists concerning their **duty to warn** a client's potential victims. Related cases have further defined the role of the therapist in warning others (Simone & Fulero, 2005). Courts have generally ruled that the threats must be specific. In *Thompson v. County of Alameda* (1980), the California Supreme Court ruled that a therapist does not have a duty to warn when a person makes nonspecific threats against nonspecific people. It is difficult for therapists to know their exact responsibilities for protecting third parties from their clients. Good clinical practice dictates that any time they are in doubt they should consult with colleagues. A second opinion can be just as helpful to a therapist as to a client.

Mental Health Professionals as Expert Witnesses

Judges and juries often have to rely on **expert witnesses,** individuals who have specialized knowledge, to assist them in making decisions (Simon, 2003). We have alluded to several instances in which mental health professionals serve in such a capacity, providing information about a person's dangerousness or ability to understand and participate in the defense. The public's perception of expert witnesses is characterized by ambivalence. On one hand, they see the value of persuasive expert testi-

mony in educating a jury; on the other, they see expert witnesses as "hired guns" whose opinions suit the side that pays their bills (Hollien, 1990). How reliable are the judgments of mental health professionals who act as expert witnesses?

To take one example, in deciding whether someone should be civilly committed, the assessor must determine the person's potential for future violence. Research suggests that mental health professionals can make reliable predictions of dangerousness over the short term, for 2 to 20 days after the evaluation (Lidz, Mulvey, Appelbaum, & Cleveland, 1989; McNiel & Binder, 1991). However, they have not been able to make reliable predictions of violence after longer periods (Tardiff, 2003). A second area in which mental health professionals are often asked to provide consultation is in assigning a diagnosis. In Chapter 3, we discussed the development of systems to ensure the reliability of diagnoses. Recent revisions of diagnostic criteria, most notably DSM-III-R and the current DSM-IV-TR, have addressed this issue directly, thus helping clinicians make diagnoses that are generally reliable. Remember, however, that the legal definition of mental illness is not matched by a comparable disorder in DSM-IV-TR. Therefore, statements about whether someone has a "mental illness" reflect determinations made by the court, not by mental health professionals.

Mental health professionals appear to have expertise in identifying *malingering* and in assessing competence. Remember that to malinger is to fake or grossly exaggerate symptoms, usually to be absolved from blame. For example, a person might claim to have been actively hallucinating at the time of the crime and therefore not responsible. Research indicates that the Minnesota Multiphasic Personality Inventory test is extremely accurate in revealing malingering in people claiming to have serious mental illness. The examiners look for true symptoms, but ones people

Elizabeth Loftus, a psychologist at the University of California, Irvine, and an expert in human memory, testifies during the pretrial hearing of former White House official Lewis "Scooter" Libby.

©Associated Press

with mental illness rarely report. Malingerers, in their rush to fake their illness, will often overreport these problems, perhaps to convince others they are mentally ill (Gassen, Pietz, Spray, & Denney, 2007). Mental health professionals also appear capable of providing reliable information about a person's competence, or ability to understand and assist with a defense (Shulman, Cohen, Kirsh, Hull, & Champine, 2007). Overall, mental health professionals can provide judges and juries with reliable and useful information in certain areas (Meyer & Weaver, 2006).

The research described here does not indicate how accurate expert testimony is under everyday conditions. In other words, under the right circumstances, experts can make accurate determinations of the short-term risks that a person will commit an act of violence, is faking certain symptoms, or is competent to stand trial and of what diagnosis should be made. Still, other factors conspire to influence expert testimony. Personal and professional opinions that exceed the competence of the expert witness can influence what information is or is not presented, as well as how it is relayed to the court (Simon, 2003). For instance, if the expert witness believes generally that people should not be involuntarily committed to mental health facilities, this opinion will likely influence how the witness presents clinical information in civil commitment court proceedings.

CONCEPT CHECK 16.2

Check your understanding of criminal commitment by identifying the following concepts: (a) competence to stand trial, (b) diminished capacity, (c) American Law Institute rule, (d) Durham rule, (e) M'Naghten rule, (f) malingering, (g) expert witness, and (h) duty to warn.

1. The person could not distinguish between right and wrong at the time of the crime. _____
2. The person is not criminally responsible if the crime was the result of "mental disease or mental defect." _____

   _____
3. The person is not responsible for the crime if he is not able to appreciate the wrongfulness of behavior caused by mental disease or defect. _____
4. A mental disorder could lessen a person's ability to understand criminal behavior and to form criminal intent.

   _____
5. The defendant does not go to trial because she is unable to understand the proceedings and assist in the defense.

   _____
6. One of my clients threatened his mother's life during his session today. Now I must decide whether I have a(n) _

   _____.
7. Dr. X testified in court that the defendant was faking and exaggerating symptoms to evade responsibility. Dr. X is acting as a(n) _____, and the defendant is ___

   _____.

PATIENTS' RIGHTS AND CLINICAL PRACTICE GUIDELINES

Until about 30 years ago, people in mental health facilities were accorded few rights. What treatment they received and whether they could make phone calls, send and receive mail, or have visitors were typically decided by hospital personnel who rarely consulted with the patient. However, abuses of this authority led to legal action and subsequent rulings by the courts concerning the rights of people in these facilities.

The Right to Treatment

One of the most fundamental rights of people in mental health facilities is the right to treatment. For too many and for too long, conditions were poor and treatment was lacking in numerous large mental health facilities. Starting in the early 1970s, a series of class-action lawsuits (filed on behalf of many individuals) helped establish the rights of people with mental illness and mental retardation. A landmark case, *Wyatt v. Stickney* (1972), grew out of a lawsuit filed by the employees of large institutions in Alabama who were fired because of funding difficulties and established for the first time the minimum standards that facilities had to meet in relation to the people who were hospitalized. Among the standards set by *Wyatt v. Stickney* were minimum staff–patient ratios and physical requirements, such as a certain number of showers and toilets for a given number of residents. The case also mandated that facilities make positive efforts to attain treatment goals for their patients.

Wyatt v. Stickney went further and expanded on a concept called the "least restrictive alternative," indicating that, wherever possible, people should be provided with care and treatment in the least confining and limiting environment. For example, the court noted the following for those with mental retardation:

> Residents shall have a right to the least restrictive conditions necessary to achieve the purpose of habilitation. To this end the institution shall make every attempt to move residents from (1) more to less structured living; (2) large to smaller facilities; (3) large to smaller living units; (4) group to individual residences; (5) segregated from the community to integrated into the community; (6) dependent living to independent living.

Despite this movement to secure treatment for people in mental health facilities, a gap was left as to what constituted proper treatment. The case of *Youngberg v. Romeo* (1982) reaffirmed the need to treat people in nonrestrictive settings but essentially left to professionals the decision about the type of treatment to be provided. This concerned patient advocates because, historically, leaving treatment to professional judgment has not always resulted in the intended end for the people in need of help. In 1986, Congress provided a number of safeguards by passage of the Protection and Advocacy for Mentally Ill Individuals Act (Woodside & Legg, 1990), which established a series of protection and advocacy agencies in each state to investigate allegations of abuse and neglect and to act as legal advocates. This layer of protection has resulted in a balance between professional concerns and needs and rights of patients in mental health facilities.

The Right to Refuse Treatment

One of the most controversial issues in mental health today is the right of people, especially those with severe mental illness, to refuse treatment (Meyer & Weaver, 2006). In recent times, the argument has centered on the use of antipsychotic medications. On one side of the issue is the mental health professional who believes that, under certain circumstances, people with severe mental illness are not capable of making a decision in their own best interest and that the clinician is therefore responsible for providing treatment, despite the protestations of the affected people. On the other side, patients and their advocates argue that all people have a fundamental right to make decisions about their own treatment, even if doing so is not in their own best medical interests.

Although this controversy is not yet resolved, one court case has responded to a related question: Can people be "forced" to become competent to stand trial? This is an interesting dilemma: If people facing criminal charges are delusional or have such frequent severe hallucinations that they cannot fully participate in the legal proceedings, can they be forced against their will to take medication to reduce these symptoms, thereby making them competent to stand trial? A Supreme Court ruling, *Riggins v. Nevada* (1992), stated that, because of the potential for negative side effects (such as tardive dyskinesia), people cannot be forced to take antipsychotic medication. Although this decision does not settle the issue of refusing treatment, it does indicate the high court's wish to honor individual choice (Watters, 2005).

Research Participants' Rights

Throughout this text we have described research conducted worldwide with people who have psychological disorders. We also touched briefly in Chapter 4 on the issue of the rights of these individuals. In general, people who participate in psychological research have the following rights (American Psychological Association, 2002b):

1. The right to be informed about the purpose of the research study
2. The right to privacy
3. The right to be treated with respect and dignity
4. The right to be protected from physical and mental harm
5. The right to choose to participate or to refuse to participate without prejudice or reprisals
6. The right to anonymity in the reporting of results
7. The right to the safeguarding of their records

These rights are particularly important for people with psychological disorders who may not be able to understand them fully. One of the most important concepts in research is that those who participate must be fully informed about the risks and benefits of the study. Simple consent is not sufficient; it must be *informed consent,* or formal agreement by the subject to participate after being fully apprised of all important aspects of the study, including any possibility of harm. An important case underlines the significance of informed consent and the sometimes-gray areas that exist in applied research.

GREG ALLER: Concerned About Rights

In 1988, 23-year-old Greg Aller signed a consent form agreeing to participate in a treatment study at the University of California at Los Angeles (UCLA) Neuropsychiatric Institute (Willwerth, 1993). Since the previous year, Greg had experienced vivid and frightening hallucinations and delusions about space aliens. His parents had contacted UCLA for assistance. They learned that the university was initiating a new study to evaluate people in the early stages of schizophrenia and to assess the effects of the withdrawal of medication. If Greg participated, he could receive extremely expensive drug therapy and counseling free. After taking the drug Prolixin for 3 months as part of the study, he improved dramatically; the hallucinations and delusions were gone. He was now able to enroll in college, and he made the dean's list.

Although overjoyed with the results, Greg's parents were concerned about the second phase of the study, which involved taking him off the medication. They were reassured by the researchers that this was an important and normal part of treatment for people with schizophrenia and that the potential for negative side effects of taking the drug for too long was great. They were also told the researchers would put Greg back on the medication if he grew considerably worse without it.

Greg Aller (right, with his parents) participated in a drug study at UCLA and suffered a severe relapse of psychotic symptoms when medication was withdrawn. He and his family subsequently raised the issue of informed consent for such research.

Toward the end of 1989, Greg was slowly taken off the drug, and he soon started having delusions about then-President Ronald Reagan and space aliens. Although his deterioration was obvious to his parents, Greg did not indicate to the researchers that he needed the medication or tell them of his now-continuous hallucinations and delusions. Greg continued to deteriorate, at one point threatening to kill his parents. After several more months, Greg's parents persuaded him to ask for more medication. Although better than he was earlier, Greg has still not returned to the much-improved state he achieved following his first round of medication.

This case highlights the conflicts that can arise when researchers attempt to study important questions in psychopathology. Administrators at the National Institutes of Health reported that the UCLA researchers did not give Greg and his family all the information about the risks of treatment and the possibility of other approaches (Hilts, 1994). Critics claim that informed consent in this and similar situations is too often not fully met and that information is often colored to ensure participation. However, the UCLA researchers note that what they did was no different from what would have happened outside the research study: They attempted to remove Greg from potentially dangerous antipsychotic medication. The controversy emerging from this case should be an added warning to researchers about their responsibilities to people who participate in their studies and their obligation to design added safeguards to protect the welfare of their study subjects. Some are now exploring methods to assess formally whether participants with mental illness fully understand the risks and benefits associated with these studies (Moser et al., 2005; Wirshing, Sergi, & Mintz, 2005).

Evidence-Based Practice and Clinical Practice Guidelines

Health-care delivery systems around the world have become extremely interested in determining whether treatments commonly used for both physical and psychological disorders are effective. This concern stems partly from the greatly increased expense of health care and from the fact that much of the cost is picked up by governments around the world. As a result, governments and health-care policy makers are increasingly promoting evidence-based practice (EBP)—health-care practices supported by research findings demonstrating that they are effective. EBP is one of those ideas that comes along occasionally and takes the world by storm. Although some tenets of EBP have been around for decades, it is only in the past 10 years that EBP has been formally identified as a systematic method of delivering clinical care (Institute of Medicine, 2001; Sackett, Strauss, Richardson, Rosenberg, & Haynes, 2000). In the United States, the President's New Freedom Commission on Mental Health (2003, p. 21) made the principle recommendation of its final report to advance EBPs and "expand the workforce providing evidence-based mental health services and supports." The American Psychological Association Presidential Task Force in 2006 adopted as policy a report describing EBP in psychology and encouraging wide adoption of the notion of basing principles of psychological practice on evidence.

As described throughout this book, evidence has accumulated on the effectiveness of psychological treatments for specific disorders both in research clinics and in clinics that serve the public directly. When this evidence is put in the form of recommen-

dations on how to treat a particular problem, these recommendations are called clinical practice guidelines. In 1989, legislation established a new branch of the federal government called the Agency for Health Care Policy and Research. In 1999, this agency was reauthorized by Congress and renamed the Agency for Healthcare Research and Quality. The purpose of this agency is to establish uniformity in the delivery of effective health and mental health care and to communicate to practitioners, policy makers, and patients alike throughout the country the latest developments in treating certain disorders effectively. The agency is also responsible for research into improving systems for the delivery of health and mental health services.

The government hopes not only to reduce costs by eliminating unnecessary or ineffective treatments but also to facilitate the dissemination of effective interventions based on the latest research evidence. Treating people effectively—alleviating their pain and distress—is the most important way to reduce health-care costs because these individuals will no longer request one treatment after another in an unending search for relief.

Recognizing the importance of this trend and the necessity that clinical practice guidelines be sound and valid, a task force of the American Psychological Association composed a template, or set, of principles for constructing and evaluating guidelines for clinical interventions for both psychological disorders and psychosocial aspects of physical disorders. These principles were published in 1995 and revised in 2002 with relatively few changes (American Psychological Association, 2002). As envisioned by the task force creating the template, the guidelines developed from it should help both the practitioner and the patient make decisions about appropriate treatment interventions for cognitive, emotional, and behavioral disorders and dysfunctions, as well as psychosocial aspects of physical disorders. Ideally, the guidelines will also restrain administrators of health-care plans from sacrificing or not providing sufficient resources for effective treatment, or limiting the amount of clinician time necessary to deliver treatment, to cut costs. The task force also felt that guidelines for psychosocial interventions could never be inflexible, because they must allow for the individual issues that arise in treating people with psychological disorders.

The task force decided that clinical practice guidelines for specific disorders should be constructed on the basis of two simultaneous considerations, or axes: the clinical efficacy axis and the clinical utility axis. The **clinical efficacy axis** is a thorough consideration of the scientific evidence to determine whether the intervention in question is effective. This evidence would answer the question, Is the treatment effective when compared to an alternative treatment or to no treatment in a controlled clinical research context? In Chapter 4, we reviewed the various research strategies used to determine whether an intervention is effective.

As you will remember, for many reasons, a treatment might seem effective when it is not. For instance, if patients improve on their own while being treated simply because of the passage of time or the natural healing process, the treatment had little to do with the improvement. It is possible that nonspecific effects of the treatment—perhaps just meeting with a caring health professional—are enough to make someone feel better without any contribution from the particular treatment technique. To determine clinical efficacy, experiments must establish whether the intervention in question is better than no therapy, better than a nonspecific therapy, or better than an alternative therapy. (The latter finding provides the highest level of evidence for a treatment's effectiveness.) Clinicians might also rely on information collected from various clinics where a large number of practitioners are treating the disorder in question. If these clinicians collect systematic data on the outcomes of their patients, they can ascertain how many are "cured," how many improve somewhat without recovering, and how many fail to respond to the intervention. Such data are referred to as quantified clinical observations or clinical replication series. Finally, a clinical consensus of leading experts is also a valuable source of information, although not as valuable as data from quantified clinical observations or randomized control trials.

The **clinical utility axis** is concerned with the effectiveness of the intervention in the practice setting in which it is to be applied, regardless of research evidence on its efficacy; in other words, will an intervention with proven efficacy in a research setting also be effective in the various clinical settings where the interventions are most often applied? Also, is application of the intervention in the settings where it is needed feasible and cost-effective? This axis is concerned with external validity, the extent to which an internally valid intervention is effective in different settings or under different circumstances from those where it was tested.

The first major issue to consider on the clinical utility axis is feasibility. Will patients accept the intervention and comply with its requirements, and is it relatively easy to administer? As noted in Chapter 7, electroconvulsive therapy is an effective treatment for severe depression in many cases, but it is extremely frightening to patients, many of whom refuse it. The treatment also requires sophisticated procedures and close supervision by medical personnel, usually in a hospital setting. Therefore, it is not particularly feasible.

A second issue on the clinical utility axis is generalizability, which refers to the extent to which an intervention is effective with patients of differing backgrounds (ethnicity, age, or sex), as well as in different settings (inpatient, outpatient, or community) or with different therapists. Again, an intervention could be effective in a research setting with one group of patients but generalize poorly across different ethnic groups. For a summary of these two axes, see Table 16.3.

In reading the disorder chapters (Chapters 5–15 of this book), you will have noted a number of effective treatments, both psychosocial and medical. In the future, we will see a great deal of additional research to establish both the clinical efficacy and the clinical utility of various interventions for psychological disorders.

TABLE 16.3 Overview of Template for Constructing Psychological Intervention Guidelines

Clinical Efficacy (Internal Validity)	Clinical Utility (External Validity)
A. Better than alternative therapy (randomized controlled trials, or RCTs)	A. Feasibility
B. Better than nonspecific therapy (RCTs)	1. Patient acceptability (cost, pain, duration, side effects, and so on)
C. Better than no therapy (RCTs)	2. Patient choice in face of relatively equal efficacy
D. Quantified clinical observations	3. Probability of compliance
E. Clinical consensus	4. Ease of dissemination (number of practitioners with competence, requirements for training, opportunities for training, need for costly technologies or additional support personnel, and so on)
1. Strongly positive	B. Generalizability
2. Mixed	1. Patient characteristics
3. Strongly negative	a. Cultural background issues
F. Contradictory evidence	b. Gender issues
	c. Developmental level issues
	d. Other relevant patient characteristics
	2. Therapist characteristics
	3. Issues of robustness when applied in practice settings with different time frames, and so on
	4. Contextual factors regarding setting in which treatment is delivered
	C. Costs and benefits
	1. Costs of delivering intervention to individual and society
	2. Costs to individual and society of withholding intervention

Note: Confidence in treatment efficacy is based on both (a) absolute and relative efficacy of treatment and (b) quality and replicability of studies in which this judgment is made.

Note: Confidence in clinical utility as reflected on these three dimensions should be based on systematic and objective methods and strategies for assessing these characteristics of treatment as they are applied in actual practice. In some cases, randomized controlled trials will exist. More often, data will be in the form of quantified clinical observations (clinical replication series) or other strategies, such as health economic calculations.

Source: Reprinted, with permission, from American Psychological Association Board of Professional Affairs Task Force on Psychological Intervention Guidelines, 1995. *Template for developing guidelines: Interventions for mental disorders and psychosocial aspects of physical disorders.* Approved by APA Council of Representatives, February 1995. Washington, D.C.: American Psychological Association, © 1995 American Psychological Association.

In Chapter 1, we reviewed various activities that make up the role of scientist-practitioners in the mental health professions, who take a scientific approach to their clinical work to provide the most effective assessment procedures and interventions. Changes in the delivery of mental health services are likely to be accompanied by considerable disruption, because this is a major system that affects millions of people. But the change will also bring opportunities. Scientist-practitioners will contribute to the process of guidelines development in several ways. For example, as attempts are made to assess the clinical utility or external validity of interventions, the collected experience of thousands of mental health professionals will be immensely valuable. Most information relevant to clinical utility or external validity will be collected by these clinicians in the course of their practice. Thus, they will truly fulfill the scientist-practitioner role to the benefit of patients in our field.

CONCLUSIONS

Therapy and scientific progress do not occur in a vacuum. People who study and treat abnormal behavior are responsible not only for mastering the wealth of information we have only touched on in this book but also for understanding and appreciating their role in society and in the world. Every facet of life—from the biological to the social, political, and legal—interacts with every other facet; if we are to help people, we must appreciate this complexity.

We hope we have given you a good sense of the challenges faced by workers in the field of mental health and have spurred some of you to join us in this rewarding work.

CONCEPT CHECK 16.3

Identify the following situation using one of these terms: (a) informed consent, (b) refuse treatment, (c) clinical utility, (d) clinical efficacy, and (e) reduce costs.

1. The clinical researcher knows the potential for harm of the participants is slight but is nevertheless careful to tell them about it and asks them whether they agree to give their _____.
2. Recently, clinical practice guidelines were established on two axes. The _____ axis is a consideration of the scientific evidence to determine whether the intervention in question is effective.
3. The Supreme Court ruling in *Riggins v. Nevada* helped support a patient's right to _____.
4. The _____ axis is concerned with an intervention's effectiveness in the clinical setting where it will be applied, not in the research setting.
5. Clinical practice guidelines are designed to safeguard clients and _____.

FUTURE DIRECTIONS

Brain Blame

Throughout this book, we were privileged to chronicle advances in the variety of sciences that contribute to our understanding of abnormal behavior. The integration of these sciences is just now revealing mysteries that only a few years ago were assumed to be out of the reach of our ability to explore why people behave the way they do. As has been true throughout history, however, advancing technology often outpaces society's ability to incorporate this new knowledge in its social and ethical structure. Take, for example, new research on moral decision making. Research using functional imaging technologies reveals that our ability to "feel the pain" of other people—feeling empathetic to others in distress—involves activation of the prefron-

tal cortex (Robertson et al., 2007) and damage to this area prevents people from using empathy to make moral decisions (Damasio, 2007). How long will it take before this important research finds its way to the courtroom? Will it be argued that defendants who have psychopathy (see Chapter 12), for example, be judged not responsible for their behavior because their inability to empathize with others has its origin in the brain? This "brain blame" will become more prominent in coming years because our definitions of insanity have not kept up with our understanding of the combined contributions of the environment and biology to mental illness and criminal behavior.

SUMMARY

Perspectives on Mental Health Law

- Societal views of people with mental illness change with time, often as responses to perceived problems with and as intended improvements of relevant laws. According to researchers, a "liberal era" between 1960 and 1980 in the United States was characterized by a commitment to individual rights and fairness; the "neoconservative era" that followed focuses on majority concerns and on law and order.

Civil Commitment

- Civil commitment laws determine the conditions under which a person may be certified legally to have a mental illness and therefore to be placed in a hospital, sometimes in conflict with the person's own wishes.

- Historically, states have permitted commitment when several conditions have been met: (1) the person has a mental illness and is in need of treatment, (2) the person is dangerous to himself or to others, or (3) the person is unable to care for himself.

- *Mental illness* as used in legal system language is not synonymous with *psychological disorder;* each state has its own definition of mental illness, usually meant to include people with severe disturbances that negatively affect their health and safety.

- Having a mental illness does not seem to increase the likelihood of dangerousness, that is, that a person will commit violent acts in the future, although having symptoms of hallucinations and delusions does seem to indicate more risk for behaving violently.

- The combination of the lack of success with deinstitutionalization, which has resulted instead in transinstitutionalization; the rise in homelessness; and the criminalization of people with severe mental illness led to a backlash against the perceived causes of these factors, including the strict civil commitment laws.

Criminal Commitment

- Criminal commitment is the process by which people are held for one of two reasons: (1) They have been accused of committing a crime and are detained in a mental health facility until they can be determined fit or unfit to participate in legal proceedings against them, or (2) they have been found not guilty of a crime by reason of insanity.

- The insanity defense is defined by a number of legal rulings: The M'Naghten rule states that people are not responsible for criminal behavior if they do not know what they are doing, or if they do know and they don't know it is wrong. The Durham rule broadened the criteria for responsibility from knowledge of right or wrong to the presence of a "mental disease or defect." The American Law Institute criteria concluded that people were not responsible for their criminal behavior if, because of their mental illness, they lacked either the cognitive ability to recognize the inappropriateness of their behavior or the ability to control their behavior.

- The concept of diminished capacity holds that people's ability to understand the nature of their behavior and therefore their criminal intent could be lessened by their mental illness.

- A determination of competence must be made before an individual can be tried for a criminal offense: To stand trial, people must be competent—able to understand the charges against them and to assist with their own defense.

- Duty to warn is a standard that sets forth the responsibility of the therapist to warn potential victims that a client may attempt to hurt or kill them.

- Individuals who have specialized knowledge and who assist judges and juries in making decisions, especially about such issues as competence and malingering, are called expert witnesses.

Patients' Rights and Clinical Practice Guidelines

- One of the more fundamental rights of patients in mental facilities is their right to treatment; that is, they have a legal right to some sort of ongoing effort to both define and strive toward treatment goals. By contrast, a great deal of controversy exists over whether all patients are capable of making a decision to refuse treatment. This is an especially difficult dilemma in the case of antipsychotic medications that may improve patients' symptoms but bring with them severe negative side effects.

- Subjects who participate in any research study must be fully informed of the risks and benefits and formally give their informed consent to indicate they have been fully informed.

- Clinical practice guidelines can play a major role in providing information about types of interventions that are likely to be effective for a specific disorder. Critical to such a determination are measures of clinical efficacy (internal validity) and clinical utility (external validity); in other words, the former is a measure of whether a treatment works, and the latter is a measure of whether the treatment is effective in a variety of settings.

Key Terms

civil commitment laws, 557
mental illness, 559
dangerousness, 559

deinstitutionalization, 560
transinstitutionalization, 561
criminal commitment, 563

diminished capacity, 564
competence, 566
duty to warn, 567

expert witness, 567
clinical efficacy axis, 570
clinical utility axis, 571

Answers to Concept Checks

16.1

1. mental disorder; 2. dangerous; 3. grave disability; 4. legal; 5. deinstitutionalization; 6. transinstitutionalization

16.2

1. e; 2. d; 3. c; 4. b; 5. a; 6. h; 7. g, f

16.3

1. a; 2. d; 3. b; 4. c; 5. e

 The Abnormal Psychology Book Companion Website

See **academic.cengage.com/psychology/barlow** for practice quiz questions, interactive activities, Internet links, critical thinking exercises, discussion forums, and more. Also accessible from the Wadsworth Psychology Resource Center **(academic.cengage.com/login).**

Abnormal Psychology Live CD-ROM

- *False Memory Research:* This clip of Elizabeth Loftus raises a host of questions about the use of testimony in trials related to child abuse that arise in therapy.

 **CengageNOW**

Go to **academic.cengage.com/now** to link to CengageNOW, your online study tool. First take the Pre-Test for this chapter to get your personalized study plan, which will identify topics you need to review and direct you to online resources. Then take the Post-Test to determine what concepts you have mastered and what you still need work on.

Video Concept Reviews

CengageNOW also contains Mark Durand's *Video Concept Reviews* on challenging topics.

- Civil Commitment Laws
- Parens Patriae and Police Power
- Mental Illness
- Dangerousness
- Criminal Commitment
- Concept Check: How Can Juries Decide Insanity?
- The Insanity Defense
- Competence
- Expert Witness

Glossary

Note: Many familiar words have specialized meanings and usage in psychology. A number of these, used in the text, are defined here.

abnormal behavior   Actions that are unexpected and often evaluated negatively because they differ from typical or usual behavior.

acetylcholine   Neurotransmitter, pervasive throughout the nervous system, that contributes to movement, attention, arousal, and memory. A deficiency of acetylcholine is found in people with **Alzheimer's disease.**

actigraph   Small electronic device that is worn on the wrist like a watch and records body movements. This device can be used to record sleep–wake cycles.

acute onset   Sudden beginning of a disease or disorder (contrast with **insidious onset**).

acute pain   Pain that typically follows an injury and disappears once the injury heals or is effectively treated.

acute PTSD   Posttraumatic stress disorder diagnosed 1 to 3 months following the traumatic event.

acute stress disorder   Severe reaction immediately following a terrifying event, often including amnesia about the event, emotional numbing, and **derealization.** Many victims later develop **posttraumatic stress disorder.**

addiction   Informal term for **substance dependence.**

adoption studies   In genetics research, the study of first-degree relatives reared in different families and environments. If they share common characteristics, such as a disorder, this finding suggests that those characteristics have a genetic component.

advanced sleep phase type   Type of circadian rhythm problem, not a DSM-IV-TR disorder, involving a persistent pattern of early sleep onset and awakening times.

affect   Conscious, subjective aspect of an **emotion** that accompanies an action at a given time.

age of onset   Person's age when developing or exhibiting symptoms of a disease or condition.

agnosia   Inability to recognize and name objects; may be a symptom of **dementia** or other brain disorders.

agonist   Chemical substance that effectively increases the activity of a **neurotransmitter** by imitating its effects.

agonist substitution   Replacement of a drug on which a person is dependent with one that has a similar chemical makeup, an **agonist.** Used as a treatment for **substance dependence.**

agoraphobia   Anxiety about being in places or situations from which escape might be difficult.

agreeableness   One of the dimensions of the five-factor model of personality and individual differences, involving being warm, kind, and trusting as opposed to hostile, selfish, and mistrustful.

AIDS-related complex (ARC)   Group of minor health problems such as weight loss, fever, and night sweats that appears after HIV infection but before development of full-blown AIDS.

akinesia   Extrapyramidal symptom involving slow motor activity, an expressionless face, and emotionless speech.

alcohol   By-product of the **fermentation** of yeasts, sugar, and water; the most commonly used and abused **depressant** substance.

alcohol dehydrogenase (ADH)   Enzyme that helps humans metabolize **alcohol.** Different levels of its subtypes may account for different susceptibilities to disorders such as **fetal alcohol syndrome.**

alcohol use disorders   Cognitive, biological, behavioral, and social problems associated with **alcohol** use and abuse.

alogia   Deficiency in the amount or content of speech, a disturbance often seen in people with **schizophrenia.**

alpha adrenergic receptors   Group of nervous system **receptors** stimulated by the **neurotransmitter norepinephrine.**

alpha waves   Regular pattern of brain-wave voltage changes typical of calm relaxation.

alters   Shorthand term for alter egos, the different personalities or identities in **dissociative identity disorder.**

altruistic suicide   Formalized suicide approved of and even expected by some cultures.

Alzheimer's disease   "Strange disease of the cerebral cortex" that causes an "atypical form of senile dementia," discovered in 1906 by German **psychiatrist** Alois Alzheimer.

amnestic disorder   Deterioration in the ability to transfer information from short- to long-term memory, in the absence of other **dementia** symptoms, as a result of **head trauma** or drug abuse.

amniocentesis   Prenatal medical procedure that allows the detection of abnormalities (for example, **Down syndrome**) in the developing fetus. It involves removal and analysis of amniotic fluid from the mother.

amok   One of several running disorders seen in non-Western cultures—as in "running amok"—in which individuals enter a trancelike state and may commit violent acts. Later, they will have amnesia about the episode.

amphetamine   Stimulant medication used to treat hypersomnia by keeping the person awake during the day, and to treat **narcolepsy,** including sudden onset episodes, by suppressing **rapid eye movement sleep.**

amphetamine use disorders   Psychological, biological, behavioral, and social problems associated with **amphetamine** use and abuse.

amygdala   Part of the brain's limbic system that regulates **emotions** and the ability to learn and control impulses; figures prominently in some **psychopathology.**

amyloid plaque   Clusters of dead **neurons** found during autopsy in the brains of people with **Alzheimer's disease.** Also known as *neuritic* or *senile plaque.*

amyloid precursor protein   Large protein, controlled by a **gene** on chromosome 21, that breaks down to contribute to the **amyloid plaque** characteristic of people with **Alzheimer's disease.**

amyloid protein   Solid, waxy substance forming the core of the **amyloid plaque** characteristic of people with **Alzheimer's disease.**

analgesic rebound headache   Headache, more severe than the original one, that occurs after the medication used to treat headache pain has "worn off."

analog model   Approach to research that employs subjects who are similar to clinical clients, allowing **replication** of a clinical problem under controlled conditions.

anandamide   Neurochemical that seems to be a naturally occurring version of the active chemical in **marijuana.**

angina pectoris   Chest pain caused by partial blockage of the arteries that supply blood to the heart.

anhedonia   Inability to experience pleasure, associated with some **mood** and schizophrenic disorders.

animal phobia   Unreasonable, enduring **fear** of animals or insects that usually develops early in life.

anomic suicide   Suicide motivated by loss and confusion caused by a major life disruption.

anorexia nervosa   Eating disorder characterized by recurrent food refusal, leading to dangerously low body weight.

Antabuse   See **disulfiram.**

antagonist   In **neuroscience,** a chemical substance that decreases or blocks the effects of a **neurotransmitter.**

antagonist drugs   Medications that block or counteract the effects of psychoactive drugs.

antibodies   Highly specific molecules called immunoglobulins produced by **B cells** to combine with and neutralize **antigens.**

antigens   Foreign materials that enter the body, including bacteria and parasites.

antisocial personality disorder (ASPD)   Cluster B (dramatic, emotional, or erratic) **personality disorder** involving a pervasive pattern of disregard for and violation of the rights of others. Similar to the non-DSM-IV-TR label **psychopathy** but with greater emphasis on overt behavior rather than **personality traits.**

anxiety   Mood state characterized by marked **negative affect** and bodily symptoms of tension in which a person apprehensively anticipates future danger or misfortune. Anxiety may involve feelings, behaviors, and physiological responses.

Anxiety Disorders Interview Schedule-IV (ADIS-IV)   Specialized, structured interview protocol to assess **anxiety** and related disorders.

apathy   See **avolition.**

aphasia   Impairment or loss of language skills resulting from brain damage caused by **stroke, Alzheimer's disease,** or other illness or trauma.

apnea   See **sleep apnea.**

apolipoprotein E (apo E)   Protein involved in the transport of cholesterol. High concentration of one subtype, controlled by a **gene** on chromosome 19, is associated with **Alzheimer's disease.**

arrhythmia Irregular heartbeat.

Asperger's disorder **Pervasive developmental disorder** characterized by impairments in social relationships and restricted or unusual behaviors, but without the language delays seen in **autism.**

assertiveness training Instruction in which individuals learn to cope with **stress** by rehearsing ways to protect their time and personal rights in appropriate ways to avoid being exploited and feeling used. For example, caregivers of people with **Alzheimer's disease** learn assertiveness to prevent them from resorting to abuse in frustration.

assessment gender bias Possibility that gender differences in the reported prevalence or **diagnosis** of certain diagnostic categories may be the result of prejudice in the assessment measures or the ways they are used.

association studies Research strategies for comparing **genetic markers** in groups of people with and without a particular disorder.

associative splitting Separation among basic functions of human personality (for example, cognition, **emotion,** and perception) seen by some as the defining characteristic of **schizophrenia.**

asylum Safe refuge; specifically, an institution to house mentally disordered people.

atherosclerosis Process by which a fatty substance or plaque builds up inside arteries to form obstructions.

attention deficit/hyperactivity disorder (ADHD) Developmental disorder featuring maladaptive levels of inattention, excessive activity, and impulsiveness.

atypical depressive episode Depressive episode characterized by some ability to experience interest and pleasure, increased **anxiety,** overeating, and oversleeping.

auditory hallucinations Psychotic disturbance in perception in which a person hears sounds or voices although these are not real or actually present. The voices are often critical, accusatory, or demanding.

augmentative communication strategies Pictures or computer aids to assist people with communication deficits so that they can communicate.

autistic disorder (autism) **Pervasive developmental disorder** characterized by significant impairment in social interactions and communication and restricted patterns of behavior, interest, and activity.

autoimmune disease Condition in which the body's **immune system** attacks healthy tissue rather than **antigens.**

autonomic nervous system Part of the **peripheral nervous system** that regulates cardiovascular (heart and blood vessel), endocrine (**hormone**), and digestive functions. Includes the **sympathetic** and **parasympathetic nervous systems.**

autonomic restrictors Term for people with **generalized anxiety disorder** because they show lower heart rate, blood pressure, skin conductance, and respiration rate activity than do people with other anxiety disorders.

avoidant personality disorder Cluster C (anxious or fearful) **personality disorder** featuring a pervasive pattern of social inhibition, feelings of inadequacy, and hypersensitivity to criticism.

avolition *Apathy,* or the inability to initiate or persist in important activities.

axes Several dimensions for which information is provided in DSM-IV-TR **diagnosis** protocols—for example, clinical disorders and medical conditions.

axon Nerve cell branches that transmit outgoing electrochemical impulses to other **neurons.**

B cells Special type of white blood cells produced in bone marrow. They release into the **humoral branch** of the **immune system** molecules that circulate in the blood to seek, identify, and neutralize **antigens.**

barbiturates Sedative (and addictive) drugs including Amytal, Seconal, and Nembutal that are used as sleep aids.

bariatric surgery Surgical approach to extreme **obesity,** usually accomplished by stapling the stomach to create a small stomach pouch or bypassing the stomach through gastric bypass surgery.

basal ganglia Brain area at the base of the **forebrain** that seems to control motor behavior and to be involved in **obsessive-compulsive disorder.**

baseline Measured rate of a behavior before introduction of an intervention that allows comparison and assessment of the effects of the intervention.

behavioral assessment Measuring, observing, and systematically evaluating (rather than inferring) the client's thoughts, feelings, and behavior in the actual problem situation or context.

behavioral inhibition system (BIS) Brain circuit in the **limbic system** that responds to threat signals by inhibiting activity and causing **anxiety.**

behavioral medicine Interdisciplinary approach applying behavioral science to the prevention, **diagnosis,** and treatment of medical problems.

behavioral model Explanation of human behavior, including dysfunction, based on principles of learning and adaptation derived from experimental psychology.

behavioral rehearsal **Behavior therapy** technique in which the client practices coping with troublesome or anxiety-arousing situations in a safe and supervised situation.

behaviorism Explanation of human behavior, including dysfunction, based on principles of learning and adaptation derived from experimental psychology.

behavior rating scales Structured assessment instruments used before and during treatment to evaluate the frequency and severity of specific behaviors.

behavior therapy Array of therapy methods based on the principles of behavioral and **cognitive science,** as well as principles of learning as applied to clinical problems. It considers specific behaviors rather than inferred conflicts as legitimate targets for change.

Bender Visual-Motor Gestalt Test Neuropsychological test for children in which they copy a variety of lines and shapes.

benzodiazepines Antianxiety drugs including Valium, Xanax, Dalmane, and Halcion also used to treat insomnia. Effective against **anxiety** (and, at high potency, panic disorder), they show some side effects, such as some cognitive and motor impairment, and may result in **substance dependence.** **Relapse** rates are extremely high when the drug is discontinued.

beta adrenergic receptors Group of nervous system **receptors** stimulated by the **neurotransmitter norepinephrine** to increase blood pressure and heart rate. Drugs called beta-blockers act at this level to control high blood pressure.

binge Relatively brief episode of uncontrolled, excessive consumption, usually of food or **alcohol.**

binge-eating disorder (BED) Pattern of eating involving distress-inducing **binges** not followed by purging behaviors; being considered as a new DSM diagnostic category.

biofeedback Use of physiological monitoring equipment to make individuals aware of their own bodily functions, such as blood pressure or brain waves, that they cannot normally access, with the purpose of controlling these functions.

biological model Explanation of psychological dysfunction that primarily emphasizes brain disorder or illness as the cause.

bipolar I disorder Alternation of **major depressive episodes** with full **manic episodes.**

bipolar II disorder Alternation of **major depressive episodes** with **hypomanic episodes** (not full manic episodes).

bisexuality Attraction to both same- and opposite-sex sexual partners.

black box Concept of the inner workings of the organism, such as thoughts and feelings that cannot be observed directly.

blind sight Phenomenon in which a person is able to perform visual functions while having no awareness or memory of these abilities. Also called *unconscious vision.*

blood–injury–injection phobia Unreasonable **fear** and avoidance of exposure to blood, injury, or the possibility of an injection. Victims experience fainting and a drop in blood pressure.

body dysmorphic disorder (BDD) **Somatoform disorder** featuring a disruptive preoccupation with some imagined defect in appearance ("imagined ugliness").

borderline personality disorder Cluster B (dramatic, emotional, or erratic) **personality disorder** involving a pervasive pattern of instability of interpersonal relationships, self-image, affects, and control over impulses.

bradykinesia Slowed body movements, as occur in **Parkinson's disease.**

brain circuits Neurotransmitter currents or neural pathways in the brain.

brain stem Ancient lower part of the brain responsible for many life-sustaining automatic functions, such as breathing and coordinated movement.

breathalyzer test Measure of **alcohol** intoxication that uses a breath sample because some consumed alcohol is vaporized in the lungs and exhaled.

breathing-related sleep disorders Sleep disruption leading to excessive sleepiness or insomnia, caused by a breathing problem such as interrupted (**sleep apnea**) or labored (**hypoventilation**) breathing.

Brief Psychiatric Rating Scale Behavior rating scale used to assess the severity of patient problem areas, such as guilt feelings and preoccupation with health.

brief psychotic disorder Psychotic disturbance involving **delusions, hallucinations,** or **disorganized speech** or behavior but lasting less than 1 month; often occurs in reaction to a stressor.

Briquet's syndrome Obsolete term for **somatization disorder.**

bulimia nervosa Eating disorder involving recurrent episodes of uncontrolled excessive (**binge**) eating followed by compensatory actions to remove the food (for example, deliberate vomiting, laxative abuse, and excessive exercise).

caffeine use disorders Cognitive, biological, behavioral, and social problems associated with the use and abuse of caffeine.

cancer Category of often-fatal medical conditions involving abnormal cell growth and malignancy.

cannabinoids Family of chemicals in **marijuana** believed to be responsible for its mood- and behavior-altering ability.

cardiovascular disease Afflictions in the mechanisms, including the heart, blood vessels, and their controllers, responsible for transporting blood to the body's tissues and organs. Psychological factors may play important roles in such diseases and their treatments.

cardiovascular system Heart, blood vessels, and their controlling mechanisms, all of which transport blood and nutrients to the tissues of the body.

case study method Research procedure in which a single person or small group is studied in detail. The method does not allow conclusions about cause-and-effect relationships, and findings can be generalized only with great caution (contrast with **single-case experimental design**).

castration anxiety In **psychoanalysis,** the **fear** in young boys that they will be mutilated genitally because of their lust for their mothers.

catalepsy Motor movement disturbance seen in people with some psychoses and **mood disorders** in which body postures are waxy and can be "sculpted" to remain fixed for long periods.

cataplexy Sudden loss of muscle tone that accompanies **narcolepsy.**

catatonia Disorder of movement involving immobility or excited agitation.

catatonic immobility Disturbance of motor behavior in which the person remains motionless, sometimes in an awkward posture, for extended periods.

catatonic type of schizophrenia Type of **schizophrenia** in which motor disturbances (rigidity, agitation, and odd mannerisms) predominate.

catecholamine Outdated, simplistic theory of the **etiology** of **mood disorders** stating that **norepinephrine** (a catecholamine) excess causes **mania,** and that low levels of it cause some forms of depression.

catharsis Rapid or sudden release of emotional tension thought to be an important factor in psychoanalytic therapy.

caudate nucleus Brain structure; part of the **basal ganglia** that controls motor behavior and is implicated in **obsessive-compulsive disorder.**

cellular branch Branch of the **immune system** using specialized cells to protect the body cells against viral and parasite infections.

central nervous system Brain and spinal cord.

central sleep apnea Brief periods of cessation in respiratory activity during sleep that may be associated with **central nervous system** disorders. Most clients awaken often as a result but do not report sleepiness and may be unaware of any problem.

cerebellum Part of the **hindbrain** in the **brain stem** that controls motor coordination and may be involved in **autism.**

cerebral cortex Largest part of the **forebrain,** divided into two hemispheres; responsible for human functions such as perceiving, reasoning, planning, creating, and remembering.

chemical imbalance Relative excess or deficit in brain chemicals, such as **neurotransmitters,** that may be implicated in some **psychological disorders.**

childhood disintegrative disorder Pervasive **developmental disorder** involving severe regression in language, adaptive behavior, and motor skills after a 2- to 4-year period of normal development.

choking phobia Fear and avoidance of swallowing pills, foods, and fluids, which may lead to significant weight loss. Also known as *hypersensitive gag reflex* or *globus hystericus.*

chorea Motor problems characterized by involuntary limb movements.

chronic fatigue syndrome (CFS) Incapacitating exhaustion following only minimal exertion, accompanied by fever, headaches, muscle and joint pain, depression, and **anxiety.**

chronic pain Enduring pain that does not decrease over time; may occur in muscles, joints, and the lower back, and may be caused by enlarged blood vessels or degenerating or cancerous tissue. Other significant factors are social and psychological.

chronic PTSD **Posttraumatic stress disorder** that endures longer than 3 months and is associated with greater avoidance and a higher likelihood of **comorbidity** with additional disorders.

chronic stage Final of E. Morton Jellinek's four stages identified in the progression of alcoholism, where the individual's primary daily activities revolve around obtaining and drinking **alcohol.**

chronological age Person's age in calendar years.

circadian rhythm sleep disorders Sleep disturbances resulting in sleepiness or insomnia, caused by the body's inability to synchronize its sleep patterns with the current pattern of day and night.

civil commitment laws Legal proceedings that determine a person is mentally disordered and may be hospitalized, even involuntarily.

classical categorical approach **Classification** method founded on the assumption of clear-cut differences among disorders, each with a different known cause.

classical conditioning Fundamental learning process first described by Ivan Pavlov. An event that automatically elicits a response is paired with another stimulus event that does not (a neutral stimulus). After repeated pairings, the neutral stimulus becomes a **conditioned stimulus** that by itself can elicit the desired response.

classification Assignment of objects or people to categories on the basis of shared characteristics.

clinical assessment Systematic evaluation and measurement of psychological, biological, and social factors in a person presenting with a possible **psychological disorder.**

clinical description Details of the combination of behaviors, thoughts, and feelings of an individual that make up a particular disorder.

clinical efficacy axis One of a proposed set of guidelines for evaluating clinical interventions on the evidence of their effectiveness (compare with **clinical utility axis**).

clinical psychologist Person who has earned a Ph.D. or related degree (for example, Psy.D.) in psychology and is trained to conduct research into the causes and treatment of severe **psychological disorders,** as well as to diagnose, assess, and treat them.

clinical significance Degree to which research findings have useful and meaningful applications to real problems.

clinical utility axis One of a proposed set of guidelines for evaluating clinical interventions by whether they can be applied effectively and cost effectively in real clinical settings (compare with **clinical efficacy axis**).

clonidine Medical treatment for **hypertension** that is often used to reduce the negative symptoms of **withdrawal** from **opiates.**

clozapine One of the newer medications for **schizophrenia** (trade name Clozaril), a weak **dopamine antagonist** that seems effective in some previously untreatable cases and with fewer serious side effects.

cocaine Derivative of coca leaves used medically as a local anesthetic and narcotic; often a substance of abuse.

cocaine use disorders Cognitive, biological, behavioral, and social problems associated with the use and abuse of **cocaine.**

codeine Opiate; a mild, medical narcotic derived from **morphine.**

cognitive-behavioral treatment (CBT) Group of treatment procedures aimed at identifying and modifying faulty thought processes, attitudes and attributions, and problem behaviors; often used synonymously with **cognitive therapy.**

cognitive relaxation Use of meditation or imagery to combat **anxiety** that may result from sleeplessness.

cognitive restructuring **Cognitive therapy** procedure used to change negative or unrealistic thoughts or attributions.

cognitive science Field of study that examines how humans and other animals acquire, process, store, and retrieve information.

cognitive therapy Treatment approach that involves identifying and altering negative thinking styles related to **psychological disorders** such as depression and **anxiety** and replacing them with

more positive beliefs and attitudes—and, ultimately, more adaptive behavior and coping styles.

cohort Participants in each age group of a study with a **cross-sectional design.**

cohort effect Observation that people of different age groups differ in their values and experiences.

collective unconscious Accumulated wisdom of a culture collected and remembered across generations, a psychodynamic concept introduced by Carl Jung.

communication disorders Problems in transmitting or conveying information, including stuttering, **selective mutism,** and **expressive language disorder.**

community intervention Approach to treating and preventing disorders by directing action at the organizational, agency, and community levels rather than at individuals.

comorbidity Presence of two or more disorders in an individual at the same time.

comparative treatment research Outcome research that contrasts two or more treatment methods to determine which is most effective.

competence Ability of legal defendants to participate in their own defense and understand the charges and the roles of the trial participants.

Comprehensive System Standardized system of administering and scoring the **Rorschach inkblot test** that seeks to improve its **reliability** and **validity.**

compulsions Repetitive, ritualistic, time-consuming behaviors or mental acts a person feels driven to perform.

computerized axial tomography (CAT) scan (CT scan) Noninvasive imaging procedure useful in identifying abnormalities in the structure or shape of the brain.

concurrent (descriptive) validity Condition of testing in which the results from one test correspond to the results of other measures of the same phenomenon.

conditioned response (CR) Learned reaction, similar to the **unconditioned response,** elicited by a **conditioned stimulus** following **classical conditioning.**

conditioned stimulus (CS) Environmental event that acquires the ability to elicit a learned response as a result of **classical conditioning** associated with an **unconditioned stimulus.**

conditioning Process by which behaviors can be learned or modified through interaction with the environment. See **classical conditioning** and **operant conditioning.**

confound Any factor occurring in a study that makes the results uninterpretable because its effects cannot be separated from those of the variables being studied.

confounding variable Variable in a research study that was not part of the intended design and that may contribute to changes in the **dependent variable.**

conscientiousness One of the dimensions of the five-factor model of personality and individual differences involving being organized, thorough, and reliable as opposed to careless, negligent, and unreliable.

construct validity Degree to which signs and symbols used to categorize a disorder relate to one another while differing from those for other disorders.

content validity Degree to which the characteristics of a disorder are a true sample of the phenomenon in question.

contingency management Encouragement of reinforcers to promote and maintain desired behaviors and removal of those reinforcers that maintain undesired behaviors.

control group Group of individuals in a study who are similar to the experimental subjects in every way but are not exposed to the treatment received by the experimental group. Their presence allows for a comparison of the differential effects of the treatment.

controlled drinking An extremely controversial treatment approach to **alcohol** dependence, in which severe abusers are taught to drink in moderation.

conversion disorder Physical malfunctioning, such as blindness or paralysis, suggesting neurological impairment but with no organic pathology to account for it.

conversion hysteria Obsolete term for **conversion disorder** derived from the Freudian notion that physical symptoms represented a conversion of **unconscious** conflicts into a more acceptable form.

coping styles See **defense mechanisms.**

coronary heart disease (CHD) Blockage of the arteries supplying blood to the heart muscle; a major cause of death in Western culture, with social and psychological factors involved.

correlation Degree to which two variables are associated. In a **positive correlation,** the two variables increase or decrease together. In a **negative correlation,** one variable decreases as the other increases.

correlation coefficient Computed statistic reflecting the strength and direction of any association between two variables. It can range from +1.00 through 0.00 (indicating no association) to (1.00, with the absolute value indicating the strength and the sign reflecting the direction.

correlational study Research procedure in which variables are measured and compared to detect any association but are not manipulated. Conclusions about cause-and-effect relationships are not permissible.

corticosteroids Hormones, including **cortisol,** released by the adrenal gland in response to stressors to activate and, later, to turn off the body's **stress** response. Also called **stress hormones.**

corticotropin-releasing factor (CRF) Neuromodulator hormone secreted into the blood by the **hypothalamus.** It stimulates the pituitary gland as part of a reaction chain called the **stress** response. It may be implicated in **mood disorders,** as well as physical problems.

cortisol Stress hormone (corticosteroid) secreted by the cortex of the adrenal glands as part of the **stress** response.

counseling psychologist Person who has earned a Ph.D. or related degree in psychology and is trained to study and treat adjustment and vocational issues in relatively healthy people.

countertransference Psychoanalytic concept involving personal issues the therapist brings to professional relationships with clients.

course Pattern of development and change of a disorder over time.

course modifiers Patterns of development in a disorder that help predict its future course. These include recurrence, time sequences, and **seasonal pattern.**

covert sensitization Cognitive-behavioral intervention to reduce unwanted behaviors by having clients imagine the extremely aversive consequences of the behaviors and establish negative rather than positive associations with them.

crack Cocaine in a highly potent, solid, rocklike form.

crack babies Infants who were exposed to **cocaine** prenatally because of their mothers' use. Their characteristic irritability and high-pitched crying may be caused by abuse or neglect, in addition to the cocaine itself.

Creutzfeldt-Jakob disease Extremely rare condition that causes **dementia.**

criminal commitment Legal procedure by which a person found not guilty of a crime by reason of **insanity** must be confined in a psychiatric hospital.

criterion gender bias Possibility that gender differences in the reported prevalence or **diagnosis** of certain diagnostic categories may be the result of prejudice in the defining criteria for the disorder.

criterion validity Extent to which categorization accurately predicts the future **course** of a disorder, whether treated or untreated. See also **predictive validity.**

cross-generational effect Limit on the **generalizability** of longitudinal research because the group under study may differ from others in culture and experience.

cross-sectional design Methodology to examine a characteristic by comparing individuals of different ages (contrast with **longitudinal design**).

cross-tolerance Condition in which a person may replace **addiction** to one drug with addiction to another when the two drugs have similar chemical makeup and act on the same **neurotransmitter receptors.**

crucial stage Third of four of E. Morton Jellinek's stages identified in the progression of alcoholism, involving a loss of control of drinking and occasional **binges** of heavy drinking.

cultural–familial mental retardation Mild **mental retardation** that may be caused largely by environmental influences.

cyclothymic disorder Chronic (at least 2 years) **mood disorder** characterized by alternating **mood** elevation and depression levels that are not as severe as **manic** or **major depressive episodes.**

dangerousness Tendency to violence that, contrary to popular opinion, is not more likely among mental patients.

deep sleep Sleep stage characterized by slow brainwave (**delta wave**) patterns. A person in deep sleep is difficult to rouse and slow to become alert.

defense mechanisms Common patterns of behavior, often adaptive coping styles when they occur in moderation, observed in response to particular situations. In **psychoanalysis,** these are thought to be **unconscious** processes originating in the **ego.**

deinstitutionalization Systematic removal of people with severe mental illness or **mental retardation** from institutions like psychiatric hospitals.

delayed-onset PTSD Posttraumatic stress disorder with onset more than 6 months after the traumatic event.

delayed sleep phase type of circadian rhythm sleep disorder Persistent pattern of late sleep onset and awakening time.

delirium Rapid-onset reduced clarity of consciousness and cognition, with confusion, disorientation, and deficits in memory and language.

delta waves Relatively slow and irregular pattern of brain waves typical of the deepest, most relaxed stage of sleep. This is the time when sleeping **panic attacks** may occur. Delta activity during wakefulness may indicate brain dysfunction. Also known as *slow wave sleep.*

delusion Psychotic symptom involving disorder of thought content and presence of strong beliefs that are misrepresentations of reality.

delusional disorder Psychotic disorder featuring a persistent belief contrary to reality (**delusion**) but no other symptoms of **schizophrenia.**

delusion of grandeur Psychotic symptom; people's unfounded belief that they are more famous or important than is true.

delusion of persecution People's unfounded belief that others seek to harm them.

démence précoce French-language form of **dementia praecox.**

dementia Gradual-onset deterioration of brain functioning, involving memory loss, inability to recognize objects or faces, and problems in planning and abstract reasoning. These are associated with frustration and discouragement.

dementia of the Alzheimer's type Gradual onset of cognitive deficits caused by **Alzheimer's disease,** principally identified by a person's inability to recall newly or previously learned material. The most common form of **dementia.**

dementia praecox Latin term meaning "premature loss of mind," an early label for what is now called **schizophrenia,** emphasizing the disorder's frequent appearance during adolescence. Called *démence précoce* in France.

dendrite Nerve cell branches that receive incoming electrochemical information for transmission along the **neuron.**

dependent personality disorder Cluster C (anxious or fearful) **personality disorder** characterized by a person's pervasive and excessive need to be taken care of, a condition that leads to submissive and clinging behavior and fears of separation.

dependent variable In an experimental study, the phenomenon that is measured and expected to be influenced (compare with **independent variable**).

depersonalization Altering of perception that causes people to temporarily lose a sense of their own reality; most prevalent in people with the **dissociative disorders.** There is often a feeling of being outside observers of their own behavior.

depersonalization disorder Dissociative disorder in which feelings of **depersonalization** are so severe they dominate the client's life and prevent normal functioning.

depressants Psychoactive substances that result in behavioral sedation, including **alcohol** and the sedative, hypnotic, and anxiolytic drugs.

depressive cognitive triad Thinking errors in depressed people negatively focused in three areas: themselves, their immediate world, and their future.

depressive personality disorder Pervasive pattern dominated by dejection, self-criticism, and a judgmental stance toward other people; under consideration as a future DSM category.

depressive stupor (catatonic depressive episode) Rare but severe depressive episode experienced by someone with a **mood disorder,** featuring, usually, substantial reduction in spontaneous motor movement or, occasionally, agitation or odd mannerisms.

derailment See **loose associations.**

derealization Situation in which the individual loses a sense of the reality of the external world.

desire phase First stage of sexual activity, when sexual urges, thoughts, or fantasies occur, either in reaction to or even in the absence of a stimulating cue.

deterministic In genetics, **genes** that lead to nearly a 100% chance of developing the associated disorder. These are rare in the population.

developmental psychology Study of changes in behavior that occur over time.

developmental psychopathology Study of changes in **abnormal behavior** that occur over time.

deviation IQ Intelligence test score that estimates how much a child's school performance will deviate from the average performance of others of the same age.

dexamethasone suppression test (DST) Proposed biological test for depression. The test failed to discriminate depression from other disorders.

diagnosis Process of determining whether a **presenting problem** meets the established criteria for a specific **psychological disorder.**

Diagnostic and Statistical Manual, Fourth Edition, Text Revision (DSM-IV-TR) Current version of the official **classification** system for **psychological disorders,** published by the American Psychiatric Association.

dialectical behavioral therapy (DBT) Promising treatment for **borderline personality disorder** that involves exposing the client to stressors in a controlled situation, as well as helping the client regulate **emotions** and cope with stressors that might trigger suicidal behavior.

diastolic blood pressure   Blood pressure level when the heart is at rest or between heartbeats.

diathesis–stress model   Hypothesis that both an inherited tendency (a **vulnerability**) and specific stressful conditions are required to produce a disorder.

dimensional approach   Method of categorizing characteristics on a continuum rather than on a binary, either-or, or all-or-none basis.

dimethyltryptamine (DMT)   Natural **hallucinogen** from the bark of trees that grow in Central and South America.

diminished capacity   Evidence of an abnormal mental condition in people that causes criminal charges against them requiring intent or knowledge to be reduced to lesser offenses requiring only reckless or criminal neglect.

directionality   Possibility that when two variables, A and B, are correlated variable A causes variable B or variable B causes variable A.

discrimination training   Arrangement of experiences in which the person or animal learns to respond under certain conditions and not to respond under other conditions.

disease conviction   Core feature of **hypochondriasis;** people's firm belief that they currently have a disease, based on the misinterpretation of their own symptoms and sensations.

disease model of dependence   View that drug dependence is caused by a physiological disorder. This implies the user is a blameless victim of an illness.

disorder of written expression   Condition in which writing performance is significantly below the standard for that age level.

disorganized speech   Style of talking often seen in people with **schizophrenia,** involving incoherence and a lack of typical logic patterns.

disorganized type of schizophrenia   Type of **schizophrenia** featuring disrupted speech and behavior, disjointed **delusions** and **hallucinations,** and silly or **flat affect.**

displacement   **Defense mechanism** in which a person directs a problem impulse toward a safe substitute.

dissociation   Detachment or loss of integration between identity or reality and consciousness.

dissociative amnesia   **Dissociative disorder** featuring the inability to recall personal information, usually of a stressful or traumatic nature.

dissociative disorder   Disorder in which individuals feel detached from themselves or their surroundings and reality, experience, and identity may disintegrate.

dissociative fugue   **Dissociative disorder** featuring sudden, unexpected travel away from home, along with an inability to recall the past, sometimes with assumption of a new identity.

dissociative identity disorder (DID)   Formerly known as multiple personality disorder; a disorder in which as many as 100 personalities or fragments of personalities coexist within one body and mind.

dissociative trance disorder (DTD)   Altered state of consciousness in which people firmly believe they are possessed by spirits; considered a disorder only where there is distress and dysfunction.

disulfiram   Chemical used as an aversion treatment for heavy drinking because it causes a buildup in the body of an **alcohol** by-product, making the person vomit after drinking. Clients must continue taking it for the chemical to remain effective. Also known as *Antabuse.*

dominant gene   One **gene** of any pair of genes that determines a particular trait.

dopamine   Neurotransmitter whose generalized function is to activate other **neurotransmitters**

and to aid in exploratory and pleasure-seeking behaviors (thus balancing **serotonin**). A relative excess of **dopamine** is implicated in **schizophrenia** (although contradictory evidence suggests the connection is not simple), and its deficit is involved in **Parkinson's disease.**

dopaminergic system   Parts of the nervous system activated by the **neurotransmitter dopamine;** involved in many functions, including the experience of reward.

dorsal horns of the spinal cord   Sections of the spinal cord responsible for transmitting sensory input to the brain. They function as a "gate" that allows transmission of pain sensations if the stimulation is sufficiently intense.

double bind communication   According to an obsolete, unsupported theory, the practice of transmitting conflicting messages that was thought to cause **schizophrenia.**

double-blind control   Procedure in outcome studies that prevents bias by ensuring that neither the subjects nor the providers of the experimental treatment know who is receiving treatment and who is receiving placebo.

double depression   Severe **mood disorder** typified by **major depressive episodes** superimposed over a background of **dysthymic disorder.**

Down syndrome   Type of **mental retardation** caused by a chromosomal aberration (chromosome 21) and involving characteristic physical appearance. Sometimes known as trisomy 21.

dream analysis   Psychoanalytic therapy method in which dream contents are examined as symbolic of **id** impulses and **intrapsychic conflicts.**

duty to warn   Mental health professional's responsibility to break confidentiality and notify the potential victim whom a client has specifically threatened.

dysfunctional attitudes   Cognitive errors seen in depressed individuals, who may automatically assume the worst, draw negative conclusions arbitrarily, and treat minor problems as major ones.

dyslexia   Learning disability involving problems in reading.

dysmorphophobia   Literally, "fear of ugliness," an obsolete term for **body dysmorphic disorder.**

dysphoric manic episode   See **mixed manic episode.**

dyssomnias   Problems in getting to sleep or in obtaining sufficient quality sleep.

dysthymic disorder   **Mood disorder** involving persistently depressed **mood,** with low self-esteem, **withdrawal,** pessimism, or despair, present for at least 2 years, with no absence of symptoms for more than 2 months.

echolalia   Repetition or echoing of the speech of others, a normal intermediate step in the development of speech skills. Originally thought to be a unique symptom of **autism,** it is now seen as evidence of developmental delay involved in that disorder.

echoplanar magnetic resonance imaging   Experimental version of **magnetic resonance imaging** that can make rapid multiple sequential images of the brain as it functions.

echopraxia   The involuntary imitation of the movement of another person.

educable mental retardation   Obsolete term referring to level of retardation comparable to the DSM-IV-TR "mild" designation that assumes the individual can learn basic academic skills.

ego   In **psychoanalysis,** the psychical entity responsible for finding realistic and practical ways to satisfy **id** drives.

egoistic suicide   Suicide that occurs in the context of diminished social supports, as in the case of some elderly people who have lost friends and family contacts.

ego psychology   Derived from **psychoanalysis,** this theory emphasizes the role of the **ego** in development and attributes **psychological disorders** to failure of the ego to manage impulses and internal conflicts. Also known as *self-psychology.*

Electra complex   In **psychoanalysis,** a young girl's intrapsychic desire to replace her mother, possess her father, and acquire a penis. The resolution of this complex results in development of the **superego.**

electrocardiogram   Measure of electrical activity generated by heart muscle exertion used to detect and evaluate heart diseases.

electroconvulsive therapy (ECT)   Biological treatment for severe, chronic depression involving the application of electrical impulses through the brain to produce seizures. The reasons for its effectiveness are unknown.

electroencephalogram (EEG)   Measure of electrical activity patterns in the brain, taken through electrodes placed on the scalp.

electromyogram (EMG)   Measure of muscle movement.

electrooculogram (EOG)   Measure of eye muscle movement particularly relevant to detecting dream stages during sleep.

emotion   Pattern of action elicited by an external event and a feeling state, accompanied by a characteristic physiological response.

emotional stability   One of the dimensions of the five-factor model of personality and individual differences, involving being even-tempered as opposed to nervous, moody, and temperamental.

emotion contagion   Situation in which an emotional reaction spreads from one individual to others nearby.

empathy   Condition of sharing and understanding the **emotions** of another person.

endocrine system   Network of glands that affect bodily functions by releasing **hormones** into the bloodstream. Some endocrine activity is implicated in **psychological disorders.**

endogenous opioids   Substances occurring naturally throughout the body that function like **neurotransmitters** to shut down pain sensation even in the presence of marked tissue damage. These may contribute to psychological problems such as eating disorders. Also known as *endorphins* or *enkephalins.*

endophenotypes   Genetic mechanisms that contribute to the underlying problems causing the symptoms and difficulties experienced by people with **psychological disorders.**

endorphins   See **endogenous opioids.**

enkephalins   See **endogenous opioids.**

epidemiology   **Psychopathology** research method examining the prevalence, distribution, and consequences of disorders in populations.

episodic course   Pattern of a disorder alternating between recovery and recurrence.

equifinality   **Developmental psychopathology** principle that a behavior or disorder may have several causes.

erotomanic type   Type of **delusional disorder** featuring belief that another person, usually of higher status, is in love with the individual.

erotophobia   Learned negative reaction to or attitude about sexual activity, perhaps developed as a result of a negative or even traumatic event, such as rape.

essential hypertension   High blood pressure with no verifiable physical cause, which makes up the overwhelming majority of high blood pressure cases.

etiology   Cause or source of a disorder.

event-related potential (ERP)   Brain's electrical reaction to a psychologically meaningful environment event, as measured by the **electroencephalogram.** Also known as evoked potential.

exhibitionism Sexual gratification attained by exposing genitals to unsuspecting strangers.

exorcism Religious ritual that attributes disordered behavior to possession by demons and seeks to treat the individual by driving the demons from the body.

expectancy effect People's response to a substance on the basis of their beliefs about it, even if it contains no active ingredient. This phenomenon demonstrates that cognitive, as well as physiological, factors are involved in drug reaction and dependence.

experiment Research method that can establish causation by manipulating the variables in question and controlling for alternative explanations of any observed effects.

expert witness Person who because of special training and experience is allowed to offer opinion testimony in legal trials.

explicit memory Good recollection of actual events (contrast with **implicit memory**).

expressed emotion (EE) Hostility, criticism, and overinvolvement demonstrated by some families toward a family member with a **psychological disorder.** This can often contribute to the person's **relapse.**

expressive language Communication with words.

expressive language disorder An individual's problems in spoken communication, as measured by significantly low scores on standardized tests of **expressive language** relative to nonverbal intelligence test scores. Symptoms may include a markedly limited vocabulary or errors in verb tense.

extensive support retardation Retardation level characterized by the long-term and regular care required for individuals with this degree of disability.

external validity Extent to which research findings generalize, or apply, to people and settings not involved in the study.

extinction Learning process in which a response maintained by **reinforcement** in **operant conditioning** or pairing in **classical conditioning** decreases when that reinforcement or pairing is removed; also the procedure of removing that reinforcement or pairing.

extrapyramidal symptoms Serious side effects of **neuroleptic** medications resembling the motor difficulties of **Parkinson's disease.** They include **akinesia** and **tardive dyskinesia.** Also called *parkinsonian symptoms.*

extroversion One of the dimensions of the five-factor model of personality and individual differences, involving being talkative, assertive, and active as opposed to silent, passive, and reserved.

eye-tracking See **smooth-pursuit eye movement.**

face validity Condition of testing in which test items appear plausible for their intended purposes, even if they are not truly valid discriminators.

facial agnosia Type of **agnosia** characterized by a person's inability to recognize even familiar faces.

factitious disorder Nonexistent physical or **psychological disorder** deliberately faked for no apparent gain except possibly sympathy and attention.

failure to thrive Stunted physical growth and maturation in children, often associated with psychosocial factors such as lack of love and nurturing.

false negative Assessment error in which no pathology is noted (that is, test results are negative) when one is actually present.

false positive Assessment error in which pathology is reported (that is, test results are positive) when none is actually present.

family studies Genetic studies that examine patterns of traits and behaviors among relatives.

fatalistic suicide Suicide in the context of a person's hopelessness and loss of the feeling of control over personal destiny.

fear Emotion of an immediate alarm reaction to present danger or life-threatening emergencies.

fearlessness hypothesis One of the major theories of the **etiology** of **antisocial personality disorder,** stating that psychopaths are less prone to **fear** and thus less inhibited from dangerous or illicit activities.

female orgasmic disorder Recurring delay or absence of orgasm in some women following a normal sexual excitement phase, relative to their prior experience and current stimulation. Also known as **inhibited orgasm** (female).

female sexual arousal disorder Recurrent inability in some women to attain or maintain adequate lubrication and sexual excitement swelling responses until completion of sexual activity.

fermentation Decomposition process by which yeasts, water, and sugar form **alcohol.**

fetal alcohol syndrome (FAS) Pattern of problems including learning difficulties, behavior deficits, and characteristic physical flaws, resulting from heavy drinking by the victim's mother when she was pregnant with the victim.

fetishism Long-term, recurring, intense sexually arousing urges, fantasies, or behavior involving the use of nonliving, unusual objects, which cause distress or impairment in life functioning.

fight/flight system (FFS) Brain circuit in animals that when stimulated causes an immediate alarm and escape response resembling human **panic.**

fixation In **psychoanalysis,** stopping or concentrating at a psychosexual stage because of a lack of appropriate gratification at that stage.

flashback Sudden, intense reexperiencing of a previous, usually traumatic, event.

flat affect Apparently emotionless demeanor (including toneless speech and vacant gaze) when a reaction would be expected.

flight or fight response Biological reaction to alarming stressors that musters the body's resources (for example, blood flow and respiration) to resist or flee a threat.

fluoxetine Serotonin-specific reuptake inhibitor (trade name Prozac) that acts on the serotonergic system as a treatment for depression, **obsessive-compulsive disorder,** and **bulimia nervosa.**

flurazepam Long-acting medication for insomnia (trade name Dalmane) that may cause daytime sleepiness.

forebrain Top section of the brain that includes the limbic system, **basal ganglia, caudate nucleus,** and **cerebral cortex.** Also called *telencephalon.*

formal observation Structured recording of behaviors that are measurable and well defined.

fragile X syndrome Pattern of **abnormality** caused by a defect in the **X chromosome** resulting in **mental retardation,** learning problems, and unusual physical characteristics.

free association Psychoanalytic therapy technique intended to explore threatening material repressed into the **unconscious.** The patient is instructed to say whatever comes to mind without censoring.

frenzy witchcraft Running frenzy disorder among the Navajo tribe that seems equivalent to **dissociative fugue.**

frontal lobe Forward section of each cerebral hemisphere, most responsible for thinking, reasoning, memory, the experience of reward, and social behavior and thus most likely to be involved in a range of **psychopathology.**

frotteurism **Paraphilia** in which the person gains sexual gratification by rubbing against unwilling victims in crowds from which they cannot escape.

functional communication training Teaching of speech or nonspeech communication skills to replace undesired behavior. The new skills are useful to the person and will be maintained because of the effects they have on others.

functional genomics The study of how genes function to create changes in the organism.

GABA–benzodiazepine system Chemical benzodiazepines (minor tranquilizers) that facilitate the effects of the **neurotransmitter gamma-aminobutyric acid** in reducing **anxiety.** Such a system suggests the existence of natural benzodiazepines in the nervous system that have not yet been discovered.

gamma-aminobutyric acid (GABA) **Neurotransmitter** that reduces activity across the synapse and thus inhibits a range of behaviors and **emotions,** especially generalized **anxiety.**

gate control theory of pain View that psychological factors can enhance or diminish the sensation and perception of pain by influencing the transmission of pain impulses through the section of the spinal cord that acts as a "gate."

gender identity disorder Psychological dissatisfaction with biological gender, a disturbance in the sense of identity as a male or female. The primary goal is not sexual arousal but rather to live the life of the opposite gender.

general adaptation syndrome (GAS) Sequence of reactions to sustained **stress** described by Hans Selye. These stages are alarm, resistance, and exhaustion, which may lead to death.

generalizability Extent to which research results apply to a range of individuals not included in the study.

generalized amnesia Loss of memory of all personal information, including identity.

generalized anxiety disorder (GAD) Anxiety disorder characterized by intense, uncontrollable, unfocused, chronic, and continuous worry that is distressing and unproductive, accompanied by physical symptoms of tenseness, irritability, and restlessness.

genes Long deoxyribonucleic acid (DNA) molecules, the basic physical units of heredity that appear as locations on chromosomes.

genetic linkage analysis Study that seeks to match the inheritance pattern of a disorder to that of a **genetic marker.** This helps researchers establish the location of the **gene** responsible for the disorder.

genetic marker Inherited characteristic for which the chromosomal location of the responsible **gene** is known.

genital herpes Incurable sexually transmitted viral disease with alternating periods of dormancy and activity. The active periods involve pain, liquid discharge, itching, and ulcerative lesions, and their recurrence may be influenced by **stress.**

genome All of the hereditary information of an organism that is encoded in DNA.

genotype Specific genetic makeup of an individual.

globus hystericus Sensation of a lump in the throat causing the person difficulty in swallowing, eating, and talking. A conversion symptom or part of **choking phobia.**

glutamate Amino acid **neurotransmitter** that excites many different **neurons,** leading to action.

glutamate system Excitatory **neurotransmitter** system that may be the avenue by which **alcohol** affects cognitive abilities.

good premorbid Outdated **classification** for **schizophrenia,** referring to the quality of social functioning of the individual just before the emergence of the disorder.

graduated extinction Monitoring of a desired behavior, such as sleeping or compliance by children, with decreasing frequency to encourage independence.

grandiose type Type of **delusional disorder** featuring beliefs of inflated worth, power, knowledge, identity, or a special relationship to a deity or famous person.

hallucinations Psychotic symptoms of perceptual disturbance in which things are seen, heard, or otherwise sensed although they are not actually present.

hallucinogen Any **psychoactive substance** such as **LSD** or **marijuana** that can produce **delusions, hallucinations, paranoia,** and altered sensory perception.

hallucinogen use disorders Cognitive, biological, behavioral, and social problems associated with the use and abuse of hallucinogenic substances.

Halstead-Reitan Neuropsychological Battery Relatively precise instrument that helps identify and locate organic damage by testing various skills, including rhythm, grip, and tactile performance.

head trauma Injury to the head and, therefore, to the brain, typically caused by accidents; can lead to cognitive impairments, including memory loss.

health psychology Subfield of **behavioral medicine** that studies psychological factors important in health promotion and maintenance.

hebephrenia Silly and immature emotionality, a characteristic of some types of **schizophrenia.**

helper T cells T-type lymphocyte that enhances the **immune system** response by signaling **B cells** to produce **antibodies** and other **T cells** to destroy **antigens.**

hermaphrodites See **intersex individuals.**

heterosexual behavior Sexual activity with members of the opposite gender.

hierarchy of needs Ranking of human necessities from basic food to self-actualization, proposed by Abraham Maslow.

high blood pressure See **hypertension.**

hindbrain Lowest part of the **brain stem;** regulates many automatic bodily functions, such as breathing and digestion, and includes the **medulla, pons,** and **cerebellum.**

hippocampus Part of the brain's **limbic system** that regulates **emotions** and the ability to learn and control impulses; figures prominently in some **psychopathology.**

histrionic personality disorder Cluster B (dramatic, emotional, or erratic) **personality disorder** involving a pervasive pattern of excessive emotionality and attention seeking.

homosexual behavior Sexual activity with members of the same gender.

hormone Chemical messenger produced by the endocrine glands.

human genome project Ongoing scientific attempt to develop a comprehensive map of all human **genes.**

human immunodeficiency virus type 1 (HIV-l) Disease that causes AIDS.

humoral branch One of two main branches of the **immune system;** operates in the blood and other bodily fluids to develop **antibodies** and neutralize **antigens.**

humoral theory Ancient belief that **psychological disorders** were caused by imbalances in bodily **humors** or fluids.

humors Bodily fluids (blood, black and yellow bile, and phlegm) that early theorists believed controlled normal and abnormal functioning.

Huntington's disease Genetic disorder marked by involuntary limb movements and progressing to **dementia.**

hypersensitive gag reflex See **choking phobia.**

hypersomnia Abnormally excessive sleep. A person with this condition will fall asleep several times a day.

hypertension Major risk factor for **stroke** and heart and kidney disease that is intimately related to psychological factors. Also known as *high blood pressure.*

hypnagogic hallucinations Characteristic of **narcolepsy** involving frightening and vivid experiences during sleep that are visual, tactile, aural, and mobile.

hypoactive sexual desire disorder Apparent lack of interest in sexual activity or fantasy that would

not be expected considering the person's age and life situation.

hypochondriasis **Somatoform disorder** involving severe **anxiety** over belief in having a disease process without any evident physical cause.

hypofrontality Relative deficiency in activity in the **frontal lobes** of the brains of people with **schizophrenia;** associated with the negative symptoms of the disorder.

hypomanic episode Less severe and less disruptive version of a **manic episode** that is one of the criteria for several **mood disorders.**

hypothalamic–pituitary–adrenocortical (HPA) axis Brain–endocrine system connection implicated in some **psychological disorders.**

hypothalamus Part of the brain that lies beneath the **thalamus** and is broadly involved in the regulation of behavior and **emotion.**

hypothesis Educated guess or statement to be tested by research.

hypoventilation Reduced or labored breathing—for example, during sleep.

id In **psychoanalysis,** the **unconscious** psychical entity present at birth representing basic drives.

ideas of reference Person's **delusion** that the actions, thoughts, laughter, and meaningless activities of others are directed toward or refer to that person.

idiographic strategy Close and detailed investigation of an individual emphasizing what makes that person unique (compare with **nomothetic strategy**).

illness phobia Extreme **fear** of the possibility of contracting a disease (as opposed to the belief in already having it), combined with irrational behaviors to avoid contracting it.

imaginal exposure Presentation or **systematic exposure** of **emotions** or fearful or traumatic experiences in the imagination.

imipramine One of the **tricyclic antidepressant** drugs affecting the serotonergic and noradrenergic **neurotransmitter** systems. It blocks **panic attacks** but not more generalized **anxiety** and causes side effects such as dry mouth, dizziness, and, occasionally, **sexual dysfunction;** effective in some **mood** and **anxiety** disorders, as well as other disorders.

immune system Body's means of identifying and eliminating any foreign materials (for example, bacteria, parasites, and even transplanted organs) that enter.

implicit memory Condition of memory in which a person cannot recall past events despite acting in response to them (contrast with **explicit memory**).

impulse-control disorders Disorders in which a person acts on an irresistible, but potentially harmful, impulse.

inappropriate affect Emotional displays that are improper for the situation.

incest Deviant sexual attraction (**pedophilia**) directed toward a family member; often the attraction of a father toward a daughter who is maturing physically.

incidence Number of new cases of a disorder appearing during a specific period (compare with **prevalence**).

independent variable Phenomenon manipulated by the experimenter in a study and expected to influence the **dependent variable.**

inferiority complex Feeling of being inferior to others while striving for superiority.

informal observation Attention paid to behavior but without defining or recording it in any systematic fashion.

information transmission Warnings about the feared object repeated so often that the person develops a **phobia** solely on the basis of hearing them.

informed consent Ethical requirement whereby research subjects agree to participate in a study only after they receive full disclosure about the nature of the study and their own role in it.

inhibited orgasm Inability to achieve orgasm despite adequate sexual desire and arousal; commonly seen in women but relatively rare in men.

insanity Legal rather than psychological or medical concept involving both a **psychological disorder** and an inability to know or appreciate the wrongfulness of criminal acts.

insanity defense Legal plea that a defendant should not be held responsible for a crime because that person was mentally ill at the time of the offense.

insidious onset Development of a disorder that occurs gradually over an extended period (contrast with **acute onset**).

insight In **psychoanalysis,** recognition of the causes of emotional distress.

insulin shock therapy Dangerous biological treatment involving the administration of large doses of insulin to induce seizures.

intelligence quotient (IQ) Score on an intelligence test estimating a person's deviation from average test performance.

intermittent explosive disorder Episodes during which a person acts on aggressive impulses that result in serious assaults or destruction of property.

intermittent support retardation Retardation level characterized by the need for only episodic special care—for example, during crises and difficult life changes.

internal validity Extent to which the results of a study can be attributed to the **independent variable** after confounding alternative explanations have been ruled out.

interoceptive avoidance Avoidance of situations or activities, such as exercise, that produce internal physical arousal similar to the beginnings of a **panic attack.**

interpersonal psychotherapy (IPT) Brief treatment approach that emphasizes resolution of interpersonal problems and stressors, such as role disputes, in marital conflict or forming relationships in marriage or a new job. It has demonstrated effectiveness for such problems as depression.

interpersonal therapy Brief, structured treatment that focuses on teaching a person skills to improve existing relationships or develop new ones.

interrater reliability Degree to which two or more observers make the same ratings or measurements.

intersex individuals People born with ambiguous genitalia and hormonal abnormalities. They are assigned a gender at birth and then often provided **hormones** and surgery to complete the correspondence. Also known as *hermaphrodites.*

intrapsychic conflicts In **psychoanalysis,** the struggles among the **id, ego,** and **superego.**

introjection In **object relations** theory, the process of incorporating memories and values of individuals who are important and close to the person.

introspection Early, nonscientific approach to the study of psychology involving systematic attempts to report thoughts and feelings that specific stimuli evoked.

introversion Tendency to be shy and withdrawn.

inverse agonist Chemical substance that produces effects opposite those of a particular **neurotransmitter.**

isolated sleep paralysis A period of time upon going to sleep or upon awakening in which a person cannot perform voluntary movements.

ischemia Narrowing of arteries caused by plaque buildup within the arteries.

jealous type Type of **delusional disorder** featuring **delusions** that the individual's sexual partner is unfaithful.

jet lag type of circadian rhythm sleep disorder Disorder in which sleepiness and alertness patterns conflict with local time and occur after recent or repeated travel across time zones.

kleptomania Recurrent failure to resist urges to steal things not needed for personal use or their monetary value.

koro In Singapore, a condition of **mass hysteria** or group **delusion** in which people believe their genitals are retracting into their bodies.

labeling Applying a name to a phenomenon or a pattern of behavior. The label may acquire negative connotations or be applied erroneously to the person rather than that person's behaviors.

la belle indifférence Lack of distress shown by some individuals presenting conversion, somatization, or **amnestic disorders.**

large fibers Nerve fibers in the **dorsal horns of the spinal cord** that regulate the pattern and intensity of pain sensations. They close the gate, decreasing the transmission of painful stimuli.

lateral ventricles Naturally occurring cavities in the brain filled with cerebrospinal fluid. Some individuals with **schizophrenia** have enlarged ventricles, probably resulting from insufficient development or atrophy of surrounding tissue.

law of effect Edward L. Thorndike's principle that behaviors are strengthened or weakened by the environmental events that follow them.

learned helplessness Martin Seligman's theory that people become anxious and depressed when they make an attribution that they have no control over the **stress** in their lives (whether or not they do in reality).

learning disorders Reading, mathematics, or written expression performance substantially below levels expected relative to the person's age, IQ score, and education.

Lesch-Nyhan syndrome X-linked disorder characterized by **mental retardation,** signs of cerebral palsy, and **self-injurious** behavior.

leukocytes White blood cells of varying types that play specialized roles in the **immune system** to fight viral and parasitic infections.

level Degree of behavior change with different interventions (for example, high or low).

libido In **psychoanalysis,** the energy within the **id** that drives people toward life and fulfillment.

life-span developmental psychopathology Study of **psychological disorders** over the entire age range.

limbic system Part of the **forebrain** involved in **emotion,** the ability to learn and to control impulses, and the regulation of sex, hunger, thirst, and aggression drives. This system figures prominently in much of **psychopathology.**

limited support retardation Retardation level characterized by the special care needed on a consistent although time-limited basis—for example, during employment training.

lithium carbonate Common salt used in substantial doses to treat bipolar disorder. Clients often discontinue its use because they enjoy the manic periods, and **relapse** rates are high. The mechanism for its effects is unknown.

lobotomy Neurosurgery procedure intended to eliminate undesirable behaviors by severing the connections between the **thalamus** or **hypothalamus** and the **frontal lobes** of the brain.

localized or selective amnesia Memory loss limited to specific times and events, particularly traumatic events.

locus coeruleus Area in the **hindbrain** that is part of a noradrenergic (norepinephrine-sensitive) circuit. It is involved in emergency and alarm reactions and may be related to **panic** states.

longitudinal course Time patterns among **mood disorders** (for example, prior dysthymia or cyclothymia **rapid cycling** and **seasonal pattern**) that

may suggest their **course,** treatment, and **prognosis.**

longitudinal design Systematic study of changes in the same individual or group examined over time (contrast with **cross-sectional design**).

loose associations Deficits in logical continuity of speech, with abrupt movement between ideas. A characteristic of **schizophrenia** also called *derailment.*

LSD (*d*-lysergic acid diethylamide) Most common hallucinogenic drug; a synthetic version of the grain fungus ergot.

Luria-Nebraska Neuropsychological Battery Relatively precise instrument that helps identify and locate organic damage by testing various skills.

lysergic acid amide Naturally occurring **hallucinogen** found in the seeds of the morning glory plant.

magnetic resonance imaging (MRI) Procedure using radio signals generated in a strong magnetic field and passed through body tissue to produce detailed, even layered, images of its structure.

maintenance of sameness Necessity among people with **autism** that their familiar environments remain unchanged. They become upset when changes are introduced.

maintenance treatment Combination of continued **psychosocial treatment,** medication, or both designed to prevent **relapse** following therapy.

major depressive disorder, single or recurrent episode Mood disorder involving one *(single episode)* or more (separated by at least 2 months without depression—*recurrent*) **major depressive episodes.**

major depressive episode Most common and severe experience of depression, including feelings of worthlessness, disturbances in bodily activities such as sleep, loss of interest, and inability to experience pleasure, persisting at least 2 weeks.

male erectile disorder Recurring inability in some men to attain or maintain adequate penile erection until completion of sexual activity.

male orgasmic disorder Recurring delay in or absence of orgasm in some men following a normal sexual excitement phase, relative to age and current stimulation. Also known as **inhibited orgasm** (male).

malingering Deliberate faking of a physical or **psychological disorder** motivated by gain.

mania Period of abnormally excessive elation or euphoria, associated with some **mood disorders.**

manic episode Period of abnormally elevated or irritable **mood** that may include inflated self-esteem, decreased need for sleep, pressured speech, flight of ideas, agitation, or self-destructive behavior.

marijuana (*Cannabis sativa*) Dried part of the hemp plant; a **hallucinogen** that is the most widely used illegal substance.

marital therapy Interventions for the relationship problems of couples, whether married or not.

mass hysteria Phenomenon in which people in groups share the same **fear, delusion, abnormal behavior,** or even physical symptoms as a result of psychological processes and suggestion.

mathematics disorder Mathematics performance significantly below the standard for that age level.

medroxyprogesterone Medication that helps stimulate respiration and is used in treatment of **obstructive sleep apnea.**

medulla Part of the **hindbrain,** which regulates such automatic bodily functions as breathing and digestion.

melatonin Hormone produced by the pineal gland that is activated by darkness to control the body's biological clock and to induce sleep. It is implicated in **seasonal affective disorder** and

may be used in treatments for **circadian rhythm sleep disorder.**

memory B cells Specialized lymphocytes created after **antigens** are neutralized to help the **immune system** fight off new invasions by those antigens more rapidly. These account for the effectiveness of inoculations.

mental age Score a person achieves on an intelligence test representing the highest age-equivalent items passed.

mental disorder See psychological disorder.

mental hygiene movement Mid-19th-century effort to improve care of the mentally disordered by informing the public of their mistreatment.

mental illness Term formerly used to mean **psychological disorder** but less preferred because it implies that the causes of the disorder can be found in a medical disease process.

mental retardation Significantly subaverage intellectual functioning paired with deficits in adaptive functioning such as self-care or occupational activities, appearing before age 18.

mental status exam Relatively coarse preliminary test of a client's judgment, orientation to time and place, and emotional and mental state; typically conducted during an initial interview.

mescaline Naturally occurring **hallucinogen** found in the peyote cactus plant.

methadone **Opiate agonist** used as a treatment for heroin **addiction.** It initially provides the analgesic and sedative effects of heroin. After extended use, these effects diminish and **tolerance** develops. An effective treatment for some when combined with counseling.

methylphenidate **Stimulant** medicine (trade name Ritalin) used to treat **hypersomnia** (by keeping the person awake during the day); **narcolepsy,** including that with sudden onset (by suppressing **rapid eye movement sleep**); and **attention deficit/hyperactivity disorder.**

microsleeps Short, seconds-long periods of sleep that occur in people who have been deprived of sleep.

midbrain Section of the brain that coordinates movement with sensory input and contributes to the processes of arousal and tension.

migraine headache Debilitating, throbbing, or pulsing head pain with rapid onset, usually occurring on one side of the head.

mild mental retardation Level of retardation defined by IQ scores between 55 and 70.

Minnesota Multiphasic Personality Inventory (MMPI) Empirically derived standardized personality test that provides scales for assessing such abnormal functioning as depression and **paranoia.** One of the most widely used and heavily researched assessment instruments.

mixed manic episode Condition in which the individual experiences both elation and depression or **anxiety** at the same time. Also known as *dysphoric manic episode.*

mixed sleep apnea Combination of **obstructive** and **central sleep apnea,** such as brief interruptions in breathing during sleep caused by a blocked air passage and by cessation in respiratory activity.

modeling Learning through observation and imitation of the behavior of other individuals and consequences of that behavior.

moderate mental retardation Level of retardation defined by IQ scores between 40 and 55.

monoamine oxidase (MAO) inhibitors Medications that treat depression and severe social **anxiety** by blocking an enzyme that breaks down the **neurotransmitters norepinephrine** and **serotonin.**

mood Enduring period of emotionality.

mood congruent Consistent with the person's emotional level. **Hallucinations** and **delusions** may be congruent or incongruent with a depressed person's **mood** (contrast with **mood incongruent**).

mood disorders Group of disorders involving severe and enduring disturbances in emotionality ranging from elation to severe depression.

mood incongruent Not consistent with the person's emotional level. **Psychotic symptoms** associated with **mood disorders** may not be congruent with the person's **mood** (contrast with **mood congruent**).

moral therapy Psychosocial approach in the 19th century that involved treating patients as normally as possible in normal environments.

moral weakness model of chemical dependence View that substance abusers should be blamed because their behavior results from lack of self-control, character, or moral fiber.

morphine **Opiate** medication used as an analgesic (pain reliever) and narcotic that is sometimes a substance of abuse.

multiaxial system Categorization system, such as in DSM-IV-TR, employing several dimensions or **axes,** each used for differentiating among the categories.

multidimensional integrative approach Approach to the study of **psychopathology** that holds **psychological disorders** as always being the products of multiple interacting causal factors.

multiple baseline **Single-case experimental design** in which measures are taken on two or more behaviors or on a single behavior in two or more situations. A particular intervention is introduced for each at different times. If behavior change is coincident with each introduction, this is strong evidence the intervention caused the change.

multiple infarctions More than one area or incident of death to tissue (for example, in the brain or heart) because of blockage of blood flow.

myocardial infarction Death of heart tissue when its blood supply artery is blocked by plaque or a blood clot.

myocardium Heart muscle.

naltrexone Most widely used **opiate antagonist** drug. It produces immediate **withdrawal** and, thus, a great deal of discomfort. It may also contribute to the treatment of **alcohol** abuse but is not as successful for either substance as was originally hoped.

narcissistic personality disorder Cluster B (dramatic, emotional, or erratic) **personality disorder** involving a pervasive pattern of grandiosity in fantasy or behavior, need for admiration, and lack of **empathy.**

narcolepsy Sleep disorder involving sudden and irresistible **sleep attacks.**

natural environment phobia Fear of situations or events in nature, especially heights, storms, and water.

negative affect Emotional symptoms that are part of the definition of both **anxiety** and depression but are not specific to either of these. Also, **substance abuse** must be maintained because the substance causes an escape from unpleasant circumstances, responsibilities, or, especially, feelings.

negative correlation Association between two variables in which one increases as the other decreases.

negative schema Automatic, enduring, and stable negative cognitive bias or belief system about some aspect of life.

negative symptoms Less outgoing symptoms, such as **flat affect** and poverty of speech, displayed by some people with **schizophrenia.**

negativistic personality disorder Pervasive pattern of resisting routine requests and expectations and adopting a contrary attitude; considered for, but not included in, DSM-IV. Corresponds to former category known as **passive-aggressive personality disorder.**

nervous breakdown Lay term for a severe psychological upset that has no meaning in scientific or professional **psychopathology.**

neurasthenia Disorder common in the United States in the mid-1800s; the label is no longer used here (although it is still prevalent in China). Its symptoms include a lack of energy, a variety of aches and pains, and sometimes fever. This disorder is similar to present-day **chronic fatigue syndrome.**

neuritic plaque See **amyloid plaque.**

neurofibrillary tangles Brain damage in the form of large numbers of strandlike filaments found during autopsy in people with **Alzheimer's disease.**

neurohormones **Hormones** that affect the brain and are increasingly the focus of study in **psychopathology.**

neuroimaging Sophisticated computer-aided procedures that allow nonintrusive examination of nervous system structure and function.

neuroleptics Major antipsychotic medications, **dopamine antagonists,** that diminish **delusions, hallucinations,** and aggressive behavior in psychotic patients but may also cause serious side effects.

neuromodulators **Hormones** secreted into the blood to transmit brain messages throughout the body. Also known as *neuropeptides.*

neuron Individual nerve cell; responsible for transmitting information.

neuropeptides See **neuromodulators.**

neuropsychological testing Assessment of brain and nervous system functioning by testing an individual's performance on behavioral tasks.

neuroscience Study of the nervous system and its role in behavior, thoughts, and **emotions.**

neurosis Obsolete psychodynamic term for **psychological disorder** thought to result from **unconscious** conflicts and the **anxiety** they cause. Plural is *neuroses.*

neurotransmitters Chemicals that cross the **synaptic cleft** between nerve cells to transmit impulses from one **neuron** to the next. Their relative excess or deficiency is involved in several **psychological disorders.**

nicotine Toxic and addictive substance found in tobacco leaves.

nicotine gum Chewing gum that delivers **nicotine** to smokers without the carcinogens in cigarette smoke. This substitute may help people stop smoking, especially when combined with counseling.

nicotine patch Patch placed on the skin that delivers **nicotine** to smokers without the carcinogens in cigarette smoke. Somewhat more successful than nicotine gum because it requires less effort by the wearer and delivers the drug more consistently; should be coupled with counseling to stop smoking and avoid **relapse.**

nicotine use disorders Cognitive, biological, behavioral, and social problems associated with the use and abuse of **nicotine.**

night eating syndrome Consuming a third or more of daily food intake after the evening meal and getting out of bed at least once during the night to have a high-calorie snack. In the morning, however, individuals with night eating syndrome are not hungry and do not usually eat breakfast. These individuals do not **binge** during their night eating and seldom purge.

nightmares Frightening and anxiety-provoking dreams occurring during **rapid eye movement sleep.** The individual recalls the bad dreams and recovers alertness and orientation quickly.

nocturnal enuresis Urination while sleeping.

nocturnal penile tumescence (NPT) Erection of the penis during sleep, usually **rapid eye movement sleep.** If this normal reaction occurs in a man with erectile problems in the waking state, his problems may be assumed to have psychological origins.

nomenclature In a naming system or **nosology,** the actual labels or names that are applied. In **psychopathology,** these include **mood disorders** and eating disorders.

nomothetic strategy Identification and examination of large groups of people with the same disorder to note similarities and develop general laws (compare with **idiographic strategy**).

nondemand pleasuring Procedure to reestablish sexual arousal involving fondling and caressing while intercourse is forbidden. This method avoids the **anxiety** provoked by the need to perform sexually.

nondisjunction In **Down syndrome,** the failure of two of the 21st chromosomes to divide to create one cell with one copy that dies and one cell with three copies that continue to divide.

nonrapid eye movement (NREM) sleep Periods in the sleep cycle, divided into four substages, when the body may be active while the brain is relatively less active and dreaming does not occur.

norepinephrine (also noradrenaline) Neurotransmitter active in the **central** and **peripheral nervous systems,** controlling heart rate, blood pressure, and respiration, among other functions. Because of its role in the body's alarm reaction, it may also contribute generally and indirectly to **panic attacks** and other disorders.

nosology **Classification** and naming system for medical and psychological phenomena.

nucleus accumbens Complex of **neurons** that is part of the brain's "pleasure pathway" responsible for the experience of reward.

obesity Excess of body fat resulting in a body mass index (BMI, a ratio of weight to height) of 30 or more.

object relations Modern development in psychodynamic theory involving the study of how children incorporate the memories and values of people who are close and important to them.

obsessions Recurrent intrusive thoughts or impulses the client seeks to suppress or neutralize while recognizing they are not imposed by outside forces.

obsessive-compulsive disorder (OCD) Anxiety disorder involving unwanted, persistent, intrusive thoughts and impulses, as well as repetitive actions intended to suppress them.

obsessive-compulsive personality disorder Cluster C (anxious or fearful) **personality disorder** featuring a pervasive pattern of preoccupation with orderliness, perfectionism, and mental and interpersonal control at the expense of flexibility, openness, and efficiency.

obstructive sleep apnea Snoring and brief interruptions in breathing during sleep caused by blockage of the airway.

occipital lobe Section of each cerebral hemisphere that integrates and makes sense of visual inputs.

Oedipus complex In **psychoanalysis,** the intrapsychic struggle within a young boy between his lust for his mother and his **fear** of castration because of it. The resolution of this complex results in development of the **superego.**

operant conditioning Fundamental behavioral learning process in which responses are modified by their consequences (reinforcers, punishers, **extinction,** and so on).

operational definition Delineation of a concept on the basis of the operation used to measure it.

opiates Addictive **psychoactive substances** such as heroin, **opium,** and **morphine** that cause temporary euphoria and analgesia (pain reduction).

opioid-releasing neurons Nerve cells that release **endogenous opioids** and play a role in the brain's pleasure pathway controlling the experience of reward.

opioid use disorders Cognitive, biological, behavioral, and social problems associated with the use and abuse of **opiates** and their synthetic variants.

opioids Family of substances including **opiates** and **endorphins,** as well as synthetic variants such as **methadone,** that have a narcotic effect.

opium Naturally occurring compound from the poppy plant that is a strong narcotic, having pain-relieving and sleep- and euphoria-inducing effects. Its derivatives include **morphine** and heroin.

opponent-process theory Explanation of drug **tolerance** and dependence suggesting that when a person experiences positive feelings these will be followed shortly by negative feelings, and vice versa. Eventually, the motivation for drug taking shifts from a desire for the euphoric high to a need to relieve the increasingly unpleasant feelings that follow drug use. A vicious cycle develops: The drug that makes a person feel terrible is the one thing that can eliminate the pain.

orgasmic reconditioning Learning procedure to help clients strengthen appropriate patterns of sexual arousal by pairing appropriate stimuli with the pleasurable sensations of masturbation.

orgasm phase Stage of sexual activity involving ejaculation in men and vaginal wall contractions in women. Women are able to experience orgasm again immediately. Men are unable to form an erection for a time interval called a refractory period.

oriented times three Patients are aware of, or oriented to, their identity, location, and time (person, place, and time).

outcome research Studies examining the effectiveness and results, positive or negative, of treatment procedures.

pain behaviors Observable manifestations of the private experience of pain. These may include wincing or other facial expressions, verbal complaints of distress, and avoidance of activities that increase pain sensations.

pain disorder **Somatoform disorder** featuring true pain but for which psychological factors play an important role in onset, severity, or maintenance.

panic Sudden, overwhelming fright or terror.

panic attack Abrupt experience of intense **fear** or discomfort accompanied by a number of physical symptoms, such as dizziness or heart palpitations.

panic control treatment (PCT) Cognitive-behavioral treatment for **panic attacks,** involving gradual exposure to feared somatic sensations and modification of perceptions and attitudes about them.

panic disorder with agoraphobia (PDA) Fear and avoidance of situations the person believes might induce a dreaded **panic attack.**

panic disorder without agoraphobia (PD) **Panic attacks** experienced without development of **agoraphobia.**

papaverine Vasodilating medication used to treat male erectile disorder by dilating blood vessels, increasing blood flow to the penis to form an erection. The medication must be injected, and the procedure can be painful. It is so intrusive that it is often declined or discontinued by patients.

paradoxical intention Instructing clients to do the opposite of the desired behavior. Telling an impotent man not to have sex or an insomniac not to sleep reduces **anxiety** to perform.

paranoia People's irrational beliefs that they are especially important **(delusions of grandeur)** or that other people are seeking to do them harm.

paranoid personality disorder Cluster A (odd or eccentric) **personality disorder** involving pervasive distrust and suspiciousness of others such that their motives are interpreted as malevolent.

paranoid type of schizophrenia Type of **schizophrenia** in which symptoms primarily involve **de-**lusions and **hallucinations;** speech and motor and emotional behavior are relatively intact.

paraphilias Sexual disorders and deviations in which sexual arousal occurs almost exclusively in the context of inappropriate objects or individuals.

parasomnias Abnormal behaviors such as **nightmares** or **sleepwalking** that occur during sleep.

parasympathetic nervous system Part of the **autonomic nervous system** that regulates bodily systems (for example, digestion) while activity level is low and that balances **sympathetic nervous system** activity.

parens patriae Latin term (parent of his country) used to describe when the government takes on the role of guardian for a minor or person incapacitated.

parietal lobe Section of each cerebral hemisphere responsible for recognizing touch sensations.

parkinsonian symptoms See **extrapyramidal symptoms.**

Parkinson's disease Degenerative brain disorder principally affecting motor performance (for example, tremors and stooped posture) associated with reduction in **dopamine. Dementia** may be a result as well.

passive-aggressive personality disorder Former diagnostic category not included in DSM-IV-TR for lack of sufficient research. See a similar category: **negativistic personality disorder.**

pathological gambling Persistent and recurrent maladaptive gambling behavior.

pathological or impacted grief reaction Extreme reaction to the death of a loved one that involves psychotic features, **suicidal ideation,** or severe loss of weight or energy or that persists more than 2 months.

patient uniformity myth Tendency to consider all members of a category as more similar than they are, ignoring their individual differences.

pedophilia **Paraphilia** involving strong sexual attraction toward children.

penile prosthesis Surgical treatment for **male erectile disorder** involving the insertion of a prosthesis that may be a semirigid silicone rod or an inflatable tube.

penile strain gauge Psychophysiological monitoring device that measures male sexual arousal by changes in penis circumference.

performance scales In the Wechsler group of intelligence tests, subtests that assess psychomotor and nonverbal reasoning skills and the ability to learn new relationships.

peripheral nervous system Neural networks outside the brain and spinal cord, including the **somatic nervous system,** which controls muscle movement, and the **autonomic nervous system,** which regulates cardiovascular, endocrine, digestion, and regulation functions.

permissive hypothesis Theory that **neurotransmitter systems** contribute to **mood** irregularities when low **serotonin** levels permit them to range widely and become unregulated.

persecutory type A form of delusion that involves believing oneself (or someone close) is being malevolently treated in some way.

personality disorders Enduring maladaptive patterns for relating to the environment and self, exhibited in a range of contexts that cause significant functional impairment or subjective distress.

personality inventories Self-report questionnaires that assess personal traits by asking respondents to identify descriptions that apply to them.

personality trait Enduring tendency to behave in particular predisposed ways across situations.

person-centered therapy Therapy method in which the client, rather than the counselor, primarily directs the course of discussion, seeking self-discovery and self-responsibility.

pervasive developmental disorders Wide-ranging, significant, and long-lasting dysfunctions that appear before the age of 18.

pervasive support retardation Retardation level characterized by the constant, intensive care needed by the individual in all environments.

phantom limb pain Perception of pain in a limb that is absent because of amputation. This phenomenon suggests pain is not entirely a physical experience.

phencyclidine (PCP) Dangerous synthetic **hallucinogen,** also called angel dust, that may cause agitated or violent behavior, disorientation, convulsions, coma, and even death.

phenotype Observable characteristics or behaviors of an individual.

phenylketonuria (PKU) Recessive disorder involving the inability to break down a food chemical whose buildup causes retardation, seizures, and behavior problems. PKU can be detected by infant screening and prevented by a specialized diet.

phii pob Thailand's version of **dissociative trance** states.

phobia **Psychological disorder** characterized by marked and persistent **fear** of an object or situation.

phobic avoidance Extreme shunning of feared objects or situations displayed by people with **phobias.**

phototherapy Treatment of **seasonal affective disorder** with large doses of exposure to bright light.

Pick's disease Rare neurological disorder that results in **presenile dementia.**

pivloktoq Running frenzy disorder among native peoples of the Arctic that seems equivalent to **dissociative fugue.**

placebo A nonactive treatment that is successful due to suggestion.

placebo control group In an outcome **experiment,** a **control group** that does not receive the experimental manipulation but is given a similar procedure with an identical expectation of change, allowing the researcher to assess any **placebo effect.**

placebo effect Behavior change resulting from the person's expectation of change rather than from the experimental manipulation itself.

plasticity Phenomenon by which damage to **neurons** sometimes can be compensated for by the action of other **neurons.**

pleasure principle Tendency to seek pleasure and minimize discomfort.

polysomnographic (PSG) evaluation Assessment of sleep disorders in which a client sleeping in the lab is monitored for heart, muscle, respiration, brain wave, and other functions.

polysubstance use Use of multiple mind- and behavior-altering substances, such as drugs.

pons Part of the hindbrain that controls such automatic bodily functions as breathing and digestion.

positive correlation Association between two variables in which one increases as the other increases.

positive symptoms More overt symptoms, such as **delusions** and **hallucinations,** displayed by some people with **schizophrenia.**

positron emission tomography (PET) scan Imaging procedure in which a radioactive tracer that binds to blood glucose is detected as the glucose is metabolized during brain activity. This allows nonintrusive localization and observation of brain activity.

postpartum onset Disorder that first appears in mothers during the time immediately following childbirth.

posttraumatic stress disorder (PTSD) Enduring, distressing emotional disorder that follows exposure to a severe helplessness- or fear-inducing threat. The victim reexperiences the trauma, avoids stimuli associated with it, and develops a numbing of responsiveness and an increased vigilance and arousal.

prealcoholic stage First of E. Morton Jellinek's four stages identified in the progression of alcoholism, involving occasional drinking with few serious consequences.

predictive validity Degree to which an assessment instrument accurately predicts a person's future behavior. See also **criterion validity.**

premature ejaculation Recurring ejaculation before the person wishes it, with minimal sexual stimulation.

prepared learning An ability has been adaptive for evolution, allowing certain associations can be learned more readily than others.

presenile dementia Dementia that appears before old age, between 40 and 60 years.

presenting problem Original complaint reported by the client to the therapist. The actual treated problem may sometimes be a modification derived from the presenting problem.

prevalence Number of people displaying a disorder in the total population at any given time (compare with **incidence**).

primary gain Freudian notion that **anxiety** reduction is the principal reinforcement obtained for the display of psychological symptoms.

primary insomnia Difficulty in initiating, maintaining, or gaining from sleep; not related to other medical or psychological problems.

primary process In psychodynamic theory, the **id's** characteristic mode of thinking, which is emotional, irrational, and preoccupied with sex, aggression, and envy.

proband In genetics research, the individual displaying the trait or characteristic being studied.

prodromal stage Second of E. Morton Jellinek's four stages identified in the progression of alcoholism, featuring heavy drinking but with few outward signs of a problem.

profound mental retardation Level of retardation defined by IQ scores below 20 and extremely limited communication and self-help skills.

prognosis Predicted future development of a disorder over time.

progressive muscle relaxation Set of exercises to teach people to become aware of and actively counteract muscle tension to induce relaxation or drowsiness.

projective tests Psychoanalytically based measures that present ambiguous stimuli to clients on the assumption that their responses will reveal their **unconscious** conflicts. Such tests are inferential and lack high **reliability** and **validity.**

prototypical approach System for categorizing disorders using both essential, defining characteristics and a range of variation on other characteristics.

psilocybin Naturally occurring **hallucinogen** found in certain species of mushrooms.

psychiatric nurse Person with nursing training who specializes in care and treatment of psychiatric patients, usually in a hospital setting.

psychiatric social worker Person who has earned a master of social work (M.S.W.) degree or, occasionally, a doctor of social work (D.S.W.) degree and is trained to work with social agencies to help psychologically disordered clients and their families.

psychiatrist Person who has earned an M.D. degree and then has specialized in psychiatry during residency training. Such a person is trained to investigate primarily the biological nature and causes of psychiatric disorders and to diagnose and treat them.

psychoactive substances Substances, such as drugs, that alter **mood** or behavior.

psychoanalysis Psychoanalytic assessment and therapy, which emphasizes exploration of, and in-

sight into, **unconscious** processes and conflicts, pioneered by Sigmund Freud.

psychoanalyst Therapist who practices **psychoanalysis** after earning either an M.D. or a Ph.D. degree and receiving additional specialized postdoctoral training.

psychoanalytic model Complex and comprehensive theory originally advanced by Sigmund Freud that seeks to account for the development and structure of personality, as well as the origin of **abnormal behavior,** based primarily on inferred inner entities and forces.

psychodynamic psychotherapy Contemporary version of **psychoanalysis** that still emphasizes **unconscious** processes and conflicts but is briefer and more focused on specific problems.

psychological autopsy Postmortem psychological profile of a suicide victim constructed from interviews with people who knew the person before death.

psychological disorder Psychological dysfunction associated with distress or impairment in functioning that is not a typical or culturally expected response.

psychological model Explanation of human behavior and its dysfunction that emphasizes the influence of the social environment and early experience.

psychomotor retardation Deficits in motor activity and coordination development.

psychoncology Study of psychological factors involved in the **course** and treatment of **cancer.**

psychoneuroimmunology (PNI) Study of psychological influences on the neurological responding involved in the body's immune response.

psychopathology Scientific study of **psychological disorders.**

psychopathy Non–DSM-IV-TR category similar to **antisocial personality disorder** but with less emphasis on overt behavior. Indicators include superficial charm, lack of remorse, and other personality characteristics.

psychopharmacogenetics The study of how genetic makeup can affect individual reactions to drugs.

psychophysiological assessment Measurement of changes in the nervous system reflecting psychological or emotional events such as **anxiety, stress,** and sexual arousal.

psychophysiological disorders Outdated term, similar to **psychosomatic medicine,** for the study of psychological and social factors influencing physical disorders. The term is misleading because it falsely implies that other psychological problems, such as **mood disorders,** do not have significant biological components.

psychosexual stages of development In **psychoanalysis,** the sequence of phases a person passes through during development. Each stage is named for the location on the body where **id** gratification is maximal at that time.

psychosis Group of severe **psychological disorders,** including **schizophrenia,** featuring **delusions** and **hallucinations.**

psychosocial treatment Treatment practices that focus on social and cultural factors (such as family experience), as well as psychological influences. These approaches include cognitive, behavioral, and interpersonal methods.

psychosomatic medicine See **behavioral medicine.**

psychosurgery Biological treatment involving neurosurgery, such as **lobotomy,** for a **psychological disorder.** For example, a specific surgical lesion to the cingulate bundle may be an effective last-resort treatment for **obsessive-compulsive disorder.**

psychotic behavior Severe **psychological disorder** category characterized by **hallucinations** and loss of contact with reality.

psychotic symptoms **Delusions** and **hallucinations** that may appear during depressive or **manic episodes.**

purging techniques In the eating disorder **bulimia nervosa,** the self-induced vomiting or laxative abuse used to compensate for excessive food ingestion.

pyromania An **impulse-control disorder** that involves having an irresistible urge to set fires.

quantitative genetics Method of genetics research that examines patterns of genetic control over a range of **genes,** each of which may contribute only a small effect.

randomization Method for placing individuals into research groups that assures each an equal chance of being assigned to any group, thus eliminating any systematic differences across groups.

rapid cycling Temporal **course** of a bipolar disorder when transitions between **mania** and depression are quick, occurring four or more times in 1 year.

rapid eye movement (REM) sleep Periodic intervals of sleep during which the eyes move rapidly from side to side, and dreams occur, but the body is inactive.

rauwolfia serpentina More commonly known as *reserpine,* an early medication derived from the snakeroot plant that helps control the agitation and aggressiveness of some psychotic patients.

Raynaud's disease **Cardiovascular disease** involving blockage of blood circulation to the extremities, with resultant pain and cold sensations in the hands and feet.

reactivity Changes in one person's behavior as a result of observing the behavior in another.

reading disorder Reading performance significantly below the standard for that age level.

reality principle In psychodynamic theory, the logical reasoning style of the **ego** that ensures actions are practical and realistic.

rebound insomnia In a person with insomnia, the worsened sleep problems that can occur when medications are used to treat insomnia and then withdrawn.

receptive language Communicated material that is understood.

receptors Locations on nerve cell **dendrites** that receive chemical impulses for transmission through the **neuron.**

recessive gene **Gene** that must be paired with another recessive gene to determine a trait.

reciprocal gene–environment model **Hypothesis** that people with a genetic predisposition for a disorder may also have a genetic tendency to create environmental risk factors that promote the disorder.

reexperiencing Careful and systematic visualizing and reliving of traumatic life events to diminish their power and emotional effects as a means of treating **dissociative identity disorder** or **posttraumatic stress disorder.**

regulated-breathing method Intervention for **stuttering** in which the person is instructed to stop and take a deep breath whenever a stuttering episode begins.

reinforcement In **operant conditioning,** consequences for behavior that strengthen it or increase its frequency. Positive reinforcement involves the contingent delivery of a desired consequence. Negative reinforcement is the contingent escape from an aversive consequence. Unwanted behaviors may result from their reinforcement or the failure to reinforce desired behaviors.

relapse Reappearance of or return to problem behaviors after treatment or recovery.

relapse prevention Extending therapeutic progress by teaching the client how to cope with future troubling situations.

relaxation response Active components of meditation methods, including repetitive thoughts of a sound to reduce distracting thoughts and closing the mind to other intruding thoughts, that decrease the flow of **stress hormones** and **neurotransmitters** and cause a feeling of calm.

reliability Degree to which a measurement is consistent—for example, over time or among different raters.

repeated measurement When responses are measured on more than two occasions (not just before and after intervention) to assess trends.

replication Confirming the results of a study by repeating it, often by a separate, independent researcher.

repressed memories Concept involving recollections of traumatic events actively eliminated from memory. Controversy surrounds whether recall that seems to occur years later is real or accurate.

repression In psychoanalytic theory, a process that forces unwanted material from the conscious to the **unconscious.**

research design Plan of experimentation used to test a **hypothesis.**

reserpine See **rauwolfia serpentina.**

residual type of schizophrenia Diagnostic category for people who have experienced at least one episode of **schizophrenia** and who at no longer display its major symptoms but still show some bizarre thoughts or social **withdrawal.**

retarded ejaculation Male orgasmic disorder in which ejaculation is delayed; thus, the patient is unable to reach orgasm with his partner, although he is able to ejaculate during masturbation.

reticular activating system (RAS) Section of the **midbrain** responsible for tension and arousal processes, including sleep and wakefulness.

retrograde ejaculation Condition in which ejaculatory fluids travel backward into the bladder, usually as a result of certain drugs or a medical condition. This is not considered a DSM-IV-TR **male orgasmic disorder.**

retrospective information Literally "the view back"; data collected by examining records or recollections of the past. It is limited by the accuracy, **validity,** and thoroughness of the sources.

retrospective study Research that uses **retrospective information** and shares its limitations.

Rett's disorder Progressive neurological developmental disorder featuring constant hand-wringing, **mental retardation,** and impaired motor skills.

reuptake Action by which a **neurotransmitter** is quickly drawn back into the discharging **neuron** after being released into a **synaptic cleft.**

reversal design See **withdrawal design.**

rheumatoid arthritis Painful, degenerative disease in which the **immune system** essentially attacks itself, resulting in stiffness, swelling, and even destruction of the joints. **Cognitive-behavioral treatments** can help relieve pain and stiffness.

Rhythm Test Subtest of the **Halstead-Reitan Neuropsychological Battery** that asks respondents to compare rhythmic beats to assess sound recognition, attention, and concentration.

Rorschach inkblot test **Projective test** that uses irregular patterns of ink as its ambiguous stimuli.

sadistic personality disorder Pervasive pattern of deriving pleasure by inflicting pain on others; proposed as a category for DSM-III-R but not included in DSM-IV-TR.

Saint Vitus's Dance Instance of **mass hysteria** in which groups of people experienced a simultaneous **compulsion** to dance and shout in the streets. Also known as *tarantism.*

sakit gila Disorder reported in Malaysia, similar to **schizophrenia** but different in important ways that may illuminate details of both disorders.

scheduled awakening For children who wake frequently at night, awakening them about an hour before their usual times and from a deeper sleep than usual to help them learn to fall asleep on their own.

schedules of reinforcement In **operant conditioning**, the pattern of consequences following a behavior based on the number of responses emitted or the time intervals between them.

schizoaffective disorder Psychotic disorder featuring symptoms of both **schizophrenia** and major **mood disorder.**

schizoid personality disorder Cluster A (odd or eccentric) **personality disorder** featuring a pervasive pattern of detachment from social relationships and a restricted range of expression of **emotions.**

schizophrenia Devastating psychotic disorder that may involve characteristic disturbances in thinking **(delusions),** perception **(hallucinations),** speech, **emotions,** and behavior.

schizophreniform disorder Psychotic disorder involving the symptoms of **schizophrenia** but lasting less than 6 months.

schizophrenogenic mother According to an obsolete, unsupported theory, a cold, dominating, and rejecting parent who was thought to cause **schizophrenia** in her offspring.

schizotypal personality disorder Cluster A (odd or eccentric) **personality disorder** involving a pervasive pattern of interpersonal deficits featuring acute discomfort with, and reduced capacity for, close relationships, as well as cognitive or perceptual distortions and eccentricities of behavior.

scientist-practitioners Mental health professionals who are expected to apply scientific methods to their work. They must keep current in the latest research on **diagnosis** and treatment, they must evaluate their own methods for effectiveness, and they may generate their own research to discover new knowledge of disorders and their treatment.

script theory Theory of sexual functioning that suggests people's sexual behavior and attitudes are guided by scripts reflecting social and cultural expectations. Negative scripts may increase **vulnerability** to the development of **sexual dysfunction.**

seasonal affective disorder (SAD) Mood disorder involving a cycling of episodes corresponding to the seasons of the year, typically with depression occurring during the winter.

seasonal pattern Temporal **course** of bipolar or recurrent **major depressive disorders** in which episodes occur during particular seasons of the year.

secondary gain Additional reinforcers beyond **primary gain** that a person may obtain by the display of symptoms. These may include attention, sympathy, and avoidance of unwanted responsibilities.

selective mutism Developmental disorder characterized by the individual's consistent failure to speak in specific social situations despite speaking in other situations.

self-actualizing Process emphasized in humanistic psychology in which people strive to achieve their highest potential against difficult life experiences.

self-defeating personality disorder Pervasive pattern of being overly passive and accepting the pain and suffering imposed by others. A category proposed for DSM-III-R but not included in DSM-IV-TR for lack of research.

self-efficacy Perception of having the ability to cope with **stress** or challenges.

self-injurious Dangerous actions, including headbanging and hitting and biting oneself, seen in many children with **autism.**

self-medication Process by which some individuals may abuse substances in attempting to use them to relieve other problems such as **anxiety,** pain, or sleeplessness.

self-monitoring Action by which clients observe and record their own behaviors as either an assessment of a problem and its change or a treatment procedure that makes them more aware of their responses. Also called self-observation.

self-psychology See **ego psychology.**

semistructured interviews Interviews that employ preplanned, standardized questions to elicit information in a consistent way.

sensate focus Sex therapy in which couples concentrate on pleasurable sensations from caressing and fondling. Intercourse is forbidden to prevent focus on sexual performance and the **anxiety** it may provoke.

sensorium Person's general awareness of the surroundings, including time and place.

sentence-completion method **Projective test** in which the person is asked to finish a series of incomplete sentences.

separation anxiety disorder Excessive, enduring **fear** in some children that harm will come to them or their parents while they are apart.

septum Part of the **limbic system** that regulates **emotions** and the ability to learn and control impulses, as well as such drives as sex, hunger, thirst, and aggression.

sequential design Combination of the **cross-sectional** and **longitudinal designs** involving repeated study of different **cohorts** over time.

serotonin **Neurotransmitter** involved in processing of information and coordination of movement, as well as inhibition and restraint. It also assists in the regulation of eating, sexual, and aggressive behaviors, all of which may be involved in different **psychological disorders.** Its interaction with **dopamine** is implicated in **schizophrenia.**

serotonin reuptake blockers See **serotonin-specific reuptake inhibitors.**

serotonin-specific reuptake inhibitors (SSRIs) Class of medications for depression (including Prozac) that act on the serotonergic system by inhibiting the **reuptake** of the **neurotransmitter serotonin.**

severe mental retardation Level of retardation defined by IQ scores between 20 and 40 and with somewhat limited communication, self-help, social, and vocational skills.

sex ratio Percentage of men and women with a disorder.

sex reassignment surgery Surgical procedures to alter a person's physical anatomy to conform to that person's psychological gender identity.

sexual aversion disorder Extreme and persistent dislike of sexual contact or similar activities.

sexual dysfunction Sexual disorder in which the client finds it difficult to function adequately while having sex.

sexual masochism **Paraphilia** in which sexual arousal is associated with experiencing pain or humiliation.

sexual pain disorders (dyspareunia) Recurring genital pain in either males or females before, during, or after sexual intercourse.

sexual sadism **Paraphilia** in which sexual arousal is associated with inflicting pain or humiliation.

shaping In **operant conditioning,** the development of a new response by reinforcing successively more similar versions of that response. Both desirable and undesirable behaviors may be learned in this manner.

shared psychotic disorder (folie à deux) Psychotic disturbance in which individuals develop a **delusion** similar to that of a person with whom they share a close relationship.

shift work type Circadian rhythm sleep disorder characterized by insomnia during sleep time and sleepiness during wake time because of late-shift work or frequent work shift changes.

silver nitrate Chemical that can be used in gum or lozenges to make subsequent smoking aversive by producing a bad taste in the mouth. Research indicates this treatment approach is not particularly effective.

single-case experimental design Research tactic in which an **independent variable** is manipulated for a single individual, allowing cause-and-effect conclusions but with limited **generalizability** (contrast with **case study method**).

single photon emission computed tomography (SPECT) **Neuroimaging** procedure similar to a **positron emission tomography scan,** although less accurate, less complex, and less costly.

sinoaortic baroreflex arc Body mechanism to compensate for sudden blood pressure increases by decreasing pressure. This reaction causes some people to faint and may lead them to develop **phobias.**

situationally bound, or cued, panic attack **Panic attack** for which the triggering circumstances are known to the client.

situationally predisposed panic attack Circumstance that increases the likelihood a **panic attack** may be triggered.

situational phobia **Anxiety** involving enclosed places (for example, claustrophobia) or public transportation (for example, **fear** of flying).

sleep apnea Disorder involving brief periods when breathing ceases during sleep.

sleep attacks Unexpected episodes of falling asleep during the day.

sleep efficiency (SE) Percentage of time actually spent sleeping of the total time spent in bed.

sleep hygiene Psychological treatment for insomnia that teaches clients to recognize and eliminate environmental obstacles to sleep. These include the use of **nicotine,** caffeine, certain medications, and **alcohol,** as well as ill-timed exercise.

sleep paralysis Brief and frightening period at the beginning or end of sleep when the individual cannot move or speak; sometimes mistaken for nocturnal **panic attack.**

sleep restriction Treatment for insomnia that involves limiting time in bed to the actual amount spent sleeping so that the bed is associated with sleep and no other competing activities.

sleep stress Environmental events, such as ingesting excess caffeine, that can affect sleep negatively.

sleep terrors Episodes of apparent awakening from sleep, accompanied by signs of **panic,** followed by disorientation and amnesia for the incident. These occur during **nonrapid eye movement sleep** and so do not involve frightening dreams.

sleepwalking **Parasomnia** that involves leaving the bed during **nonrapid eye movement sleep.** See also **somnambulism.**

slow wave sleep See **delta waves.**

small fibers Nerve fibers in the **dorsal horns of the spinal cord** that regulate the pattern and intensity of pain sensations. They open the gate, increasing the transmission of painful stimuli.

smooth-pursuit eye movement Ability to follow moving targets visually. Deficits in this skill can be caused by a single **gene** whose location is known. This problem is associated with **schizophrenia** and, thus, may serve as a **genetic marker** for this disorder. Also called *eye-tracking.*

social phobia Extreme, enduring, irrational **fear** and avoidance of social or performance situations.

sociopathic personality disturbances Obsolete term corresponding to the current category **antisocial personality disorder.** It included **alcohol** and drug abuse because these were considered merely symptoms of other problems.

somatic delusions False and unfounded beliefs about the body—for example, that parts are rotting or turning to stone.

somatic nervous system Part of the **peripheral nervous system** that controls muscle movement.

somatic treatments Biological interventions that include medication, **electroconvulsive therapy,** and **psychosurgery.**

somatization disorder **Somatoform disorder** involving extreme and long-lasting focus on multi-

ple physical symptoms for which no medical cause is evident.

somatoform disorders Pathological concern of individuals with the appearance or functioning of their bodies, usually in the absence of any identifiable medical condition.

somnambulism Repeated **sleepwalking** that occurs during **nonrapid eye movement sleep** and so is not the acting out of a dream. The person is difficult to waken and does not recall the experience.

specific phobia Unreasonable **fear** of a specific object or situation that markedly interferes with daily life functioning.

specifiers In **mood disorders,** patterns of characteristics that sometimes accompany **major depressive** or **manic episodes** and may help predict their **course** and **prognosis.** These include psychotic, melancholic, atypical, catatonic, chronic, and with **postpartum onset.**

standardization Process of establishing specific norms and requirements for a measurement technique to ensure it is used consistently across measurement occasions. This includes instructions for administering the measure, evaluating its findings, and comparing these to data for large numbers of people.

Stanford-Binet test Early standardized intelligence test designed to identify children who will experience academic difficulties by assessing their attention, perception, reasoning, and comprehension.

statistical significance Probability that obtaining the observed research findings merely by chance is small.

statistics Branch of mathematics concerned with gathering, analyzing, and interpreting data from research.

stimulants **Psychoactive substances** that elevate **mood,** activity, and alertness, including **amphetamines,** caffeine, **cocaine,** and **nicotine.**

stimulus control Deliberate arrangement of the environment so that it encourages desired behaviors and discourages problem behaviors. For example, insomnia may be combated by limiting time in, and associations with, the bed.

Strength of Grip Test Subtest of the **Halstead-Reitan Neuropsychological Battery** that compares the grip strength of the client's right and left hands.

stress Body's physiological response to a stressor, which is any event or change that requires adaptation.

stress hormones Group of **hormones,** including **corticosteroids,** involved in the body's physiological **stress** response.

stress physiology Study of the body's response to stressful events.

stroke/cerebral vascular accident (CVA) Temporary blockage of blood vessels supplying the brain, or a rupture of blood vessels in the brain, resulting in temporary or permanent loss of brain functioning.

stuttering Disturbance in the fluency and time patterning of speech (for example, sound and syllable repetitions or prolongations).

subcortical dementia Disease affecting the inner areas of the brain below the cortex. It differs from **dementia of the Alzheimer's type** in that it involves impaired recall but normal recognition, more severe depression and **anxiety,** slowed motions, and impaired coordination but no **aphasia.**

sublimation Psychodynamic **defense mechanism** in which the person redirects energy from conflict and **anxiety** into more constructive outlets, such as work.

substance abuse Pattern of **psychoactive substance** use leading to significant distress or impairment in social and occupational roles and in hazardous situations.

substance dependence Maladaptive pattern of substance use characterized by the need for increased amounts to achieve the desired effect, negative physical effects when the substance is withdrawn, unsuccessful efforts to control its use, and substantial effort expended to seek it or recover from its effects. Also known as *addiction.*

substance intoxication Physiological reactions, such as impaired judgment and motor ability, as well as **mood** changes, resulting from the ingestion of **psychoactive substances.**

substance-related disorders Range of problems associated with the use and abuse of drugs such as **alcohol, cocaine,** heroin, and other substances people use to alter the way they think, feel, and behave. These are extremely costly in human and financial terms.

sufficient condition Circumstance that, by itself, is enough to cause or allow a particular phenomenon to occur.

suicidal attempts Efforts made to kill oneself.

suicidal ideation Serious thoughts about committing suicide.

superego In **psychoanalysis,** the psychical entity representing the internalized moral standards of parents and society.

supernatural model Explanation of human behavior and its dysfunction that posits important roles for spirits, demons, grace, sin, and so on.

susceptibility In genetics, **genes** that only slightly increase the risk of developing the disorder, but in contrast to the **deterministic** genes, these are more common in the general population.

sympathetic nervous system Part of the **autonomic nervous system** that prepares the body for activity or to respond to stressors—by increasing heart rate and blood flow to muscles, for instance.

symptom substitution Psychodynamic assertion that if overt problem behavior (the symptom) is treated without eliminating the underlying conflict thought to be causing it, that conflict will reemerge in the form of new, perhaps worse, symptoms.

synaptic cleft Space between nerve cells where chemical transmitters act to move impulses from one **neuron** to the next.

systematic desensitization Behavioral therapy technique to diminish excessive **fears,** involving gradual exposure to the feared stimulus paired with a positive coping experience, usually relaxation.

systemic perspective View that the many contributing causes of **abnormal behavior** form a system involving biology, behavior, cognition, **emotion,** culture, and society. Each component of the system affects all the others.

systolic blood pressure Blood pressure generated when the heart is at work pumping blood.

T cells Lymphocytes produced in bone marrow, developed in the thymus gland, and operating in the **cellular branch** of the **immune system.** Some attack **antigens** directly; others help regulate the system.

tacrine hydrochloride Medication for patients with **Alzheimer's disease** that prevents the breakdown of **acetylcholine,** keeping it available for use by the brain. Improvements are small, and the drug is expensive and causes serious side effects.

Tactile Performance Test Subtest of the **Halstead-Reitan Neuropsychological Battery** that asks the respondent to insert wooden shapes into a hidden form board, allowing the examiner to assess the subject's learning and memory skills.

taijin kyofusho Japanese variant of **social phobia.** In many cases, individuals avoid social interaction because they believe they have terrible body or breath odor.

tangentiality Characteristic of the loose cognitive and verbal associations seen in **schizophrenia** in which the person fails to answer questions and quickly moves the conversation to unrelated topics.

tarantism See **Saint Vitus's Dance.**

tardive dyskinesia Extrapyramidal symptom and sometimes irreversible side effect of long-term **neuroleptic** medication, involving involuntary motor movements, especially in the face and tongue.

task analysis Method for evaluating a skill to be learned, breaking it down into its component parts.

taxonomy System of naming and **classification** (for example, of specimens) in science.

telencephalon See **forebrain.**

telephone scatologia **Paraphilia** in which the person gains sexual gratification by making obscene phone calls, usually while masturbating.

temporal lobe Section of each cerebral hemisphere associated primarily with sight and sound recognition and with long-term memory storage.

temporal patterning **Course** modifier for **mood disorders** describing their time sequences, including recurrence, recovery, and alternation.

tension headaches Bilateral head pain characterized by a dull ache, usually starting at the front or back of the head.

tension reduction Negative reinforcement motivation account for **substance abuse,** suggesting it is maintained because it allows people to escape **anxiety.**

testability Ability of a **hypothesis,** for example, to be subjected to scientific scrutiny and to be accepted or rejected, a necessary condition for the **hypothesis** to be useful.

test–retest reliability Degree to which results of two administrations of a test to the same person are similar.

tetrahydrocannabinols (THC) Most common active chemicals in **marijuana** responsible for its ability to alter **mood** and behavior.

thalamus Small region deep inside the brain broadly associated with regulation of behavior and **emotion.**

thanatos Freudian concept of a human drive toward death and destruction.

Thematic Apperception Test (TAT) Projective test in which the respondent is asked to tell stories about a series of ambiguous drawings.

tic disorder Disruption in early development involving involuntary motor movements or vocalizations.

tics Sudden, rapid, and recurrent involuntary motor movements or vocalizations.

time–limited course Condition in which a disorder improves on its own in a relatively brief period.

time–management training Instruction that teaches patients to deal with **stress** by establishing priorities among activities and demands and paying less attention to the less important ones.

token economy Social learning behavior modification system in which individuals earn items they can exchange for desired rewards by displaying appropriate behaviors.

tolerance Need for increased amounts of a substance to achieve the desired effect, and a diminished effect with continued use of the same amount.

total sleep time Actual combined time a person spends sleeping each day.

Tourette's disorder Developmental disorder featuring multiple dysfunctional motor and vocal **tics.**

trainable mental retardation Obsolete term referring to level of retardation comparable to the DSM-IV-TR "moderate" designation that suggests the individual can learn rudimentary vocational but not academic skills.

transcendental meditation Technique for focusing attention by softly repeating a single syllable (mantra); often accompanied by slow and regular breathing.

transference Psychoanalytic concept suggesting that clients may seek to relate to the therapist as they do to important authority figures, particularly their parents.

transinstitutionalization Movement of people with severe mental illness from large psychiatric hospitals to smaller group residences.

transsexualism Obsolete term for **gender identity disorder.**

transvestic fetishism **Paraphilia** in which individuals, usually males, are sexually aroused or receive gratification by wearing clothing of the opposite sex.

treatment outcome research Studies of the effectiveness of clinical interventions, including the comparison of competing treatments.

trend Direction of change of a behavior or behaviors (for example, increasing or decreasing).

triazolam Short-acting benzodiazepine medication (trade name Halcion) used to treat insomnia. Possible negative side effects include drowsiness, dependence, short-term memory loss, or rebound.

trichotillomania People's urge to pull out their own hair from anywhere on the body, including the scalp, eyebrows, and arm.

tricyclic antidepressants Most common treatment for depression, a group of medications including **imipramine** and amitriptyline that block the **reuptake** of **neurotransmitters,** principally **serotonin** and **norepinephrine,** at the synapse. The drugs are effective for some **anxiety** disorders and **mood disorders.** They are also used to treat **obstructive sleep apnea** because they help maintain respiratory muscle tone to assist breathing during **rapid eye movement sleep.** Positive effects are delayed, and negative side effects may include dizziness and even death, so close monitoring is required. **Relapse** rates range from 20% to 50% when the drug is stopped.

tuberous sclerosis Rare **dominant gene** disorder characterized by bumps on the skin and sometimes **mental retardation** and seizures.

twin studies In genetics research, the comparison of twins with unrelated or less closely related individuals. If twins, particularly monozygotic twins who share identical **genotypes,** share common characteristics such as a disorder, even if they were reared in different environments, this is strong evidence of genetic involvement in those characteristics.

type A behavior pattern Cluster of behaviors including excessive competitiveness, time-pressured impatience, accelerated speech, and anger, originally thought to promote high risk for heart disease.

type B behavior pattern Cluster of behaviors including a relaxed attitude, indifference to time pressure, and less forceful ambition; originally thought to promote low risk for heart disease.

unconditional positive regard Acceptance by the counselor of the client's feelings and actions without judgment or condemnation.

unconditioned response (UCR) In **classical conditioning,** the natural or unlearned reaction to the **unconditioned stimulus.**

unconditioned stimulus (UCS) Environmental event that would elicit a response in almost anyone and requires no learning. In **classical conditioning,** it is paired with a neutral stimulus that, after training, may become a **conditioned stimulus.**

unconscious Part of the psychic makeup that is outside the awareness of the person.

unconscious vision See **blind sight.**

underarousal hypothesis Theory of the **etiology** of **antisocial personality disorder** suggesting psychopaths engage in dangerous or illicit behavior to stimulate the underaroused **cerebral cortex** in their brains.

undifferentiated somatoform disorder Somatization disorder with fewer than eight symptoms but still causing distress and impaired functioning.

undifferentiated type of schizophrenia Category for individuals who meet the criteria for **schizophrenia** but not for one of the defined subtypes.

unexpected, or uncued, panic attack **Panic attack** that has no identified triggering circumstance.

unipolar mood disorder **Mood disorder** characterized by depression or **mania** but not both. Most cases involve unipolar depression.

unshared environments Term indicating that even identical twins living in the same home may have different prenatal and family experiences.

vacuum device therapy Mechanical treatment for male erectile disorder that employs a vacuum cylinder to draw blood into the penis, where it is held by a ring placed at the base of the penis.

vaginal photoplethysmograph Light-sensitive psychophysiological monitoring device that measures female sexual arousal reflected by blood flow to the vagina.

vaginismus Recurring involuntary muscle spasms in the outer third of the vagina that interfere with sexual intercourse.

validity Degree to which a technique measures what it purports to measure.

variability Degree of change in a phenomenon over time.

vascular Pertaining to the vessels that transport blood and other fluids in the body.

vascular dementia Progressive brain disorder involving loss of cognitive functioning, caused by blockage of blood flow to the brain, that appears concurrently with other neurological signs and symptoms.

vasovagal syncope Fainting because of low blood pressure in the head and brain.

ventral tegmental area **Midbrain** region that includes part of the "pleasure pathway" responsible for the experience of reward.

verbal scales Sections of the Wechsler series of intelligence tests that assess vocabulary, memory, reasoning skills, and information facts.

vinvusa Nigerian variant of **dissociative trance** states.

visuospatial skills Ability to see, recognize, orient within, and negotiate between objects in space.

voyeurism **Paraphilia** in which sexual arousal is derived from observing unsuspecting individuals undressing or naked.

vulnerability **Susceptibility** or tendency to develop a disorder.

waxy flexibility Characteristic of **catatonia** in which the person remains in bodily postures positioned by another person.

Wechsler Adult Intelligence Scale—Revised (WAIS-R) Intelligence test for adults, assessing a range of verbal and performance abilities.

Wechsler Intelligence Scale for Children—3rd Edition (WISC-III) Intelligence test for children assessing a range of verbal and performance abilities.

Wechsler Preschool and Primary Scale of Intelligence—Revised (WPPSI-R) Intelligence test for young children that measures a range of performance, verbal, and preverbal abilities.

Wernicke-Korsakoff syndrome Organic brain syndrome resulting from prolonged heavy **alcohol** use, involving confusion, unintelligible speech, and loss of motor coordination. It may be caused by a deficiency of thiamine, a vitamin metabolized poorly by heavy drinkers.

withdrawal Severely negative physiological reaction to removal of a **psychoactive substance,** which can be alleviated by the same or a similar substance.

withdrawal delirium (delirium tremens/ DTs) Frightening hallucinations and body tremors that result when a heavy drinker withdraws from **alcohol.**

withdrawal design Removing a treatment to note whether it has been effective. In **single-case experimental designs,** a behavior is measured **(baseline),** an **independent variable** is introduced (intervention), and then the intervention is withdrawn. Because the behavior continues to be measured throughout (repeated measurement), any effects of the intervention can be noted. Also called *reversal design.*

X chromosome One of the two sex chromosomes that determine gender; females have two and males have one, contributed by the mother. X chromosome abnormalities are implicated in some physical and cognitive problems.

x-linked gene A gene on the X chromosome.

Y chromosome One of the two sex chromosomes that determine gender; its presence, contributed by the father, determines the offspring will be male.

Yerkes–Dodson curve Inverted U-shaped graphical relationship between arousal and performance. Optimal performance occurs at intermediate levels of arousal. Psychopaths may engage in stimulus-seeking behavior to increase their low arousal to more useful levels.

References

Abbey, S. E., & Garfinkel, P. E. (1991). Neurasthenia and chronic fatigue syndrome: The role of culture in the making of a diagnosis. *American Journal of Psychiatry, 148,* 1638–1646.

Abbott, D. W., de Zwaan, M., Mussell, M. P., Raymond, N. C., Seim, H. C., Crow, S. J., et al. (1998). Onset of binge eating and dieting in overweight women: Implications for etiology, associated features and treatment. *Journal of Psychosomatic Research, 44,* 367–374.

Abel, G. G. (1989). Behavioral treatment of child molesters. In A. J. Stunkard & A. Baum (Eds.), *Perspectives in behavioral medicine: Eating, sleeping and sex.* Hillsdale, NJ: Erlbaum.

Abel, G. G., Barlow, D. H., Blanchard, E. B., & Guild, D. (1977). The components of rapists' sexual arousal. *Archives of General Psychiatry, 34,* 895–903.

Abel, G. G., Becker, J. V., Cunningham-Rathner, J., Mittelman, M., & Rouleau, J. L. (1988). Multiple paraphilic diagnoses among sex offenders. *Bulletin of the American Academy of Psychiatry and Law, 16,* 153–168.

Abel, G. G., Becker, J. V., Mittelman, M., Cunningham-Rathner, J., Rouleau, J. L., & Murphy, W. E. (1987). Self-reported sex crimes of nonincarcerated paraphiliacs. *Journal of Interpersonal Violence, 2,* 3–25.

Abrahamson, D. J., Barlow, D. H., Sakheim, D. K., Beck, J. G., & Athanasiou, R. (1985). Effects of distraction on sexual responding in functional and dysfunctional men. *Behavior Therapy, 16,* 503–515.

Abramson, L. Y., Alloy, L. B., & Metalsky, J. I. (1995). Hopelessness depression. In J. N. Buchanan & M. E. P. Seligman (Eds.), *Explanatory style* (pp. 113–134). Hillsdale, NJ: Erlbaum.

Abramson, L. Y., Metalsky, G. I., & Alloy, L. B. (1989). Hopelessness depression: A theory-based subtype of depression. *Psychological Review, 96*(2), 358–372.

Abramson, L. Y., Seligman, M. E. P., & Teasdale, J. D. (1978). Learned helplessness in humans: Critique and reformulation. *Journal of Abnormal Psychology, 87,* 49–74.

Abse, D. W. (1987). *Hysteria and related mental disorders: An approach to psychological medicine.* Bristol: Wright.

Adair, R., Bauchner, H., Philipp, B., Levenson, S., & Zuckerman, B. (1991). Night waking during infancy: Role of parent presence at bedtime. *Pediatrics, 87,* 500–504.

Addington v. Texas, 99 S. Ct. 1804 (1979).

Ader, R., & Cohen, N. (1975). Behaviorally conditioned immunosuppression. *Psychosomatic Medicine, 37,* 333–340.

Ader, R., & Cohen, N. (1993). Psychoneuroimmunology: Conditioning and stress. *Annual Review of Psychology, 44,* 53–85.

Adler, C. M., Côte, G., Barlow, D. H., & Hillhouse, J. J. (1994). *Phenomenological relationships between somatoform, anxiety, and psychophysiological disorders.* Unpublished manuscript.

Afari, N., & Buchwald, D. (2003). Chronic fatigue syndrome: A review. *American Journal of Psychiatry, 160,* 221–236.

Agatisa, P., Matthews, K., Bromberger, J., Edmundowicz, D., Chang, Y., & Sutton-Tyrell, K. (2005). Coronary and aortic calcification in women with major depression history. *Archives of Internal Medicine, 165,* 1229–1236.

Agras, W. S. (1982). Behavioral medicine in the 1980s: Nonrandom connections. *Journal of Consulting and Clinical Psychology, 50,* 797–803.

Agras, W. S. (1987). *Eating disorders: Management of obesity, bulimia, and anorexia nervosa.* Elmsford, NY: Pergamon Press.

Agras, W. S. (2001). The consequences and costs of eating disorders. *Psychiatric Clinics of North America, 24,* 371–379.

Agras, W. S., & Kirkley, B. G. (1986). Bulimia: Theories of etiology. In K. D. Brownell & J. P. Foreyt (Eds.), *Handbook of eating disorders: Physiology, psychology, and treatment of obesity, anorexia, and bulimia* (pp. 367–378). New York: Basic Books.

Agras, W. S., Barlow, D. H., Chapin, H. N., Abel, G. G., & Leitenberg, H. (1974). Behavior modification of anorexia nervosa. *Archives of General Psychiatry, 30,* 279–286.

Agras, W. S., Schneider, J. A., Arnow, B., Raeburn, S. D., & Telch, C. F. (1989). Cognitive-behavioral and response-prevention treatments for bulimia nervosa. *Journal of Consulting and Clinical Psychology, 57,* 215–221.

Agras, W. S., Sylvester, D., & Oliveau, D. (1969). The epidemiology of common fears and phobia. *Comprehensive Psychiatry, 10,* 151–156.

Agras, W. S., Telch, C. F., Arnow, B., Eldredge, K., & Marnell, M. (1997). One year follow-up of cognitive-behavioral therapy of obese individuals with binge eating disorder. *Journal of Consulting and Clinical Psychology, 65,* 343–347.

Agras, W. S., Walsh, B. T., Fairburn, C. G., Wilson, G. T., & Kraemer, H. C. (2000). A multicenter comparison of cognitive-behavioral therapy and interpersonal psychotherapy for bulimia nervosa. *Archives of General Psychiatry, 57,* 459–466.

Ahmed, S. H., & Koob, G. F. (2005). Transition to drug addiction: A negative reinforcement model based on an allostatic decrease in reward function. *Psychopharmacology, 180,* 473–490.

Aigner, M., & Bach, M. (1999). Clinical utility of DSM-IV pain disorder. *Comprehensive Psychiatry, 40*(5), 353–357.

Aikins, D. E., & Craske, M. G. (2001). Cognitive theories of generalized anxiety disorder. *Psychiatric Clinics of North America, 24,* 57–74.

Akiskal, H. S. (1997). Overview of chronic depressions and their clinical management. In H. S. Akiskal & G. B. Cassano (Eds.), *Dysthymia and the spectrum of chronic depressions* (pp. 1–34). New York: Guilford Press.

Akiskal, H. (2006). Special issue on circular insanity and beyond: Historic contributions of French psychiatry to contemporary concepts and research on bipolar disorder. *Journal of Affective Disorders, 96,* 141–143.

Akiskal, H. S., & Cassano, G. B. (Eds.) (1997). *Dysthymia and the spectrum of chronic depressions.* New York: Guilford Press.

Akiskal, H. S., & Pinto, O. (1999). The evolving spectrum: Prototypes I, II, III, and IV. *The Psychiatric Clinics of North America, 22*(3), 517–534.

Akiskal, H. S., Khani, M. K., & Scott-Strauss, A. (1979). Cyclothymic temperamental disorders. *Psychiatric Clinics of North America, 2,* 527–554.

Alarcon, R. D., Bell, C. C., Kirmayer, L. J., Ling, K., Bedirhan, U., & Wisner, K. L. (2002). Beyond the funhouse mirrors: Research agenda on culture and psychiatric diagnosis. In D. Kupfer, M. First, & D. Regier (Eds.), *A research agenda for DSM-V* (pp. 219–281). Washington, DC: American Psychiatric Association.

Albano, A. M., & Barlow, D. H. (1996). Breaking the vicious cycle: Cognitive-behavioral group treatment for socially anxious youth. In E. D. Hibbs & P. S. Jensen (Eds.), *Psychosocial treatment research and adolescent disorders* (pp. 43–62). Washington, DC: APA Press.

Albano, A. M., & Hack, S. (2004). Children and adolescents. In R. G. Heimberg, C. L. Turk, & D. S. Mennin (Eds.), *Generalized anxiety disorder: Advances in research and practice* (pp. 383–408). New York: Guilford Press.

Albano, A. M., Chorpita, B. F., & Barlow, D. H. (1996). Childhood anxiety disorders. In E. J. Mash & R. A. Barkley (Eds.), *Child psychopathology* (pp. 196–241). New York: Guilford Press.

Albano, A. M., DiBartolo, P. M., Heimberg, R. G., & Barlow, D. H. (1995). Children and adolescents: Assessment and treatment. In R. G. Heimberg, M. R. Liebowitz, D. A. Hope, & F. Schneier (Eds.), *Social phobia: Diagnosis, assessment and treatment.* New York: Guilford Press.

Albano, A. M., Miller, P. P., Zarate, R., Côté, G., & Barlow, D. H. (1997). Behavioral assessment and treatment of PTSD in prepubertal children: Attention to development factors and innovative strategies in the case study of a family. *Cognitive and Behavioral Practice, 4,* 245–262.

Albano, A., Pincus, D. B., Tracey, S., & Barlow, D. H. (2003). Cognitive behavioral group treatment of social phobia in adolescents: Importance of parent inclusion in treatment. Manuscript in preparation.

Albert, C., Chae, C., Rexrode, K., Manson, J., & Kawachi, I. (2005). Phobic anxiety and risk of coronary heart disease and sudden cardiac among women. *Circulation, 111,* 480–487.

Albertini, R. S., & Phillips, K. A. (1999). Thirty-three cases of body dysmorphic disorder in children and adolescents. *Journal of the American Academy of Child and Adolescent Psychiatry, 38*(4), 453–459.

Alden, L. (1989). Short-term structured treatment for avoidant personality disorder. *Journal of Consulting and Clinical Psychology, 57,* 756–764.

Alden, L. E., & Capreol, M. J. (1993). Avoidant personality disorder: Interpersonal problems as predictors of treatment response. *Behavior Therapy, 24,* 357–376.

Alessi, S. M., Roll, J. M., Reilly, M. P., & Johanson, C. E. (2002). Establishment of a diazepam preference in human volunteers following a differential-conditioning history of placebo versus diazepam choice. *Experimental and Clinical Psychopharmacology, 10,* 77–83.

Alexander, F. G. (1939). Emotional factors in essential hypertension: Presentation of a tentative hypothesis. *Psychosomatic Medicine, 1,* 175–179.

Alexander, F. G. (1950). *Psychosomatic medicine.* New York: Norton.

Alexander, F. G., & Selesnick, S. T. (1966). *The history of psychiatry: An evaluation of psychiatric thought and practice from prehistoric times to the present.* New York: Harper & Row.

Alexopoulos, G., Katz, I., Bruce, M., Heo, M., Have, T., Raue, P., et al. (2005). Remission in depressed geriatric primary care patients: A report from the PROSPECT study. *American Journal of Psychiatry, 162,* 718–724.

Allen, J., DeMyer, M., Norton, J., Pontius, W., & Yang, G. (1971). Intellectuality in parents of psychotic, subnormal, and normal children. *Journal of Autism and Childhood Schizophrenia, 1,* 311–326.

Allen, J. J., & Movius, H. L. (2000). The objective assessment of amnesia in dissociative identity disorder using event-related potentials. *International Journal of Psychophysiology, 38,* 21–41.

Allen, J. M., Lam, R. W., Remick, R. A., & Sadovnick, A. D. (1993). Depressive symptoms and family history in seasonal and nonseasonal mood disorders. *American Journal of Psychiatry, 150*(3), 443–448.

Allen, K., Bloscovitch, J., & Mendes, W. B. (2002). Cardiovascular reactivity in the presence of pets, friends, and spouses: The truth about cats and dogs. *Psychosomatic Medicine, 64,* 727–739.

Allen, L. A., Woolfolk, R. L., Lehrer, P. M., Gara, M. A., & Escobar, J. I. (2001). Cognitive behavior therapy for somatization disorder: A preliminary investigation. *Journal of Behavior Therapy and Experimental Psychiatry, 32,* 53–62.

Allen, L. B., White, K. S., Barlow, D. H., Gorman, J. M., Shear, K. M., & Woods, S. W. (in press). Effects of cognitive-behavioral therapy (CBT) for panic disorder on comorbid depression and anxiety. *Journal of Consulting and Clinical Psychology.*

Allen, L. S., & Gorski, R. A. (1992). Sexual orientation and the size of the anterior commissure in the human brain. *Proceedings of the National Academy of Science, 89,* 7199–7202.

Allin, M., Streeruwitz, A., & Curtis, V. (2005). Progress in understanding conversation disorder. *Neuropsychiatric Disease and Treatment, 3,* 1–5.

Alloy, L., & Abramson, L. (2001). Cyclothymic personality. In W. E. Craighead & C. B. Nemeroff (Eds.), *The Corsini encyclopedia of psychology and behavioral science* (3rd ed., pp. 417–418). New York: Wiley & Sons.

Alloy, L., & Abramson, L. (2006). Prospective incidence of first onsets and recurrences of depression individuals at high and low cognitive risk for depression. *Journal of Abnormal Psychology, 115,* 145–156.

Alloy, L., & Abramson, L. (2007). The adolescent surge in depression and emergence of gender differences: A biocognitive vulnerability sress model in developmental context. In E. Walker & D. Romer (Eds.), *Adolescents psychopathology and the developing brain* (pp. 284–312). New York: Oxford University Press.

Alloy, L., Abramson, L. Y., Hogan, M. E., Whitehouse, W. G., Rose, D. T., Robinson, M. S., et al. (2000). The Temple-Wisconsin cognitive vulnerability to depression project: Lifetime history of axis I psychopathology in individuals at high and low cognitive risk for depression. *Journal of Abnormal Psychology, 109,* 403–418.

Alloy, L., Abramson, L., Safford, S., & Gibb, B. (2006). The cognitive vulnerability to depression (CVD) project: Current findings and future directions. In L. B. Alloy & J. H. Riskind (Eds.), *Cognitive vulnerability to emotional disorders* (pp. 33–61). Hillsdale, NJ: Erlbaum.

Alloy, L., Kelly, K. A., Mineka, S., & Clements, C. M. (1990). Comorbidity of anxiety and depressive disorders: A helplessness–hopelessness perspective. In J. D. Maser & C. R. Cloninger (Eds.), *Comorbidity of mood and anxiety disorders* (pp. 499–543). Washington, DC: American Psychiatric Press.

Altarac, M., & Saroha, E. (2007). Lifetime prevalence of learning disability among U.S. children. *Pediatrics, 119*(Suppl. 1), S77–S83.

Althof, S. (2006). The psychology of premature ejaculation: Therapies and consequences. *Journal of Sexual Medicine, 3,* 324–331.

Alvino, C., Kohler, C., Barrett, F., Gur, R. E., Gur, R. C., & Verma, R. (in press). Computerized measurement of facial expression of emotions in schizophrenia. *Journal of Neuroscience Methods.*

Alzheimer's Association. (2007). *Alzheimer's disease facts and figures: 2007.* Chicago: Alzheimer's Association.

Amat, J., Baratta, B. V., Paul, E., Bland, S. T., Watkins, L. R., & Maier, S. F. (2005). Medial prefrontal cortex determines how stressor controllability affects behavior and dorsal raphe nucleus. *Nature Neuroscience, 8,* 365–371.

American Bar Association Standing Committee on Association Standards for Criminal Justice. (1984). *Criminal justice and mental health standards.* Chicago: Author.

American College of Obstetricians and Gynecologists. (2002). Clinical management guidelines for obstetricians–gynecologists: Premenstrual syndrome. *ACOG Practice Bulletin.* No. 15. Washington, DC: American College of Obstetricians and Gynecologists.

American Law Institute. (1962). *Model penal code: Proposed official draft.* Philadelphia: Author.

American Psychiatric Association. (1980). *Diagnostic and statistical manual of mental disorders* (3rd ed.). Washington, DC: Author.

American Psychiatric Association. (1983). American Psychiatric Association statement on the insanity defense. *American Journal of Psychiatry, 140,* 681–688.

American Psychiatric Association. (1987). *Diagnostic and statistical manual of mental disorders* (3rd ed. rev.). Washington, DC: Author.

American Psychiatric Association. (1990). *Benzodiazepine dependence, toxicity, and abuse: A task force report of the American Psychiatric Association.* Washington, DC: Author.

American Psychiatric Association. (1993). Practice guideline for eating disorders. *American Journal of Psychiatry, 150*(2), 212–228.

American Psychiatric Association. (1994). *Diagnostic and statistical manual of mental disorders* (4th ed.). Washington, DC: Author.

American Psychiatric Association. (2000). *Diagnostic and statistical manual of mental disorders* (4th ed., text revision). Washington, DC: Author.

American Psychiatric Association. (2003). Practice guideline for the assessment and treatment of patients with suicidal behaviors. *American Journal of Psychiatry, 160*(Suppl.), 1–44.

American Psychiatric Association. (2004). Practice guideline for the treatment of patients with schizophrenia (2nd ed.). *American Journal of Psychiatry, 161*(Suppl.), 1–56.

American Psychiatric Association. (2006). Practice guideline for the psychiatric evaluation of adults (2nd ed.). *American Journal of Psychiatry, 163*(Suppl.), 1–36.

American Psychiatric Association. (2007). Practice guidelines for the treatment of patients with substance use disorders (2nd ed.). *American Journal of Psychiatry, 164*(Suppl.), 1–14.

American Psychiatric Association Practice Guideline. (2000a): *Practice guideline for the treatment of patients with Alzheimer's disease and other dementias of late life: Compendium 2000* (pp. 69–137). Washington, DC: Author.

American Psychiatric Association Practice Guideline. (2000b): *Practice guideline for the treatment of patients with delirium: Compendium 2000* (pp. 31–68). Washington, DC: Author.

American Psychiatric Association Practice Guideline. (2000c). Substance use disorders: Alcohol, cocaine, opioids. In *Practice guideline for the treatment of psychi-*

atric disorders: Compendium 2000 (pp. 139–238). Washington, DC: Author.

American Psychiatric Association Practice Guideline. (2000d). Schizophrenia. In *Practice guideline for the treatment of psychiatric disorders: Compendium 2000* (pp. 200–412). Washington, DC: Author.

American Psychiatric Association Practice Guideline. (2000e). Practice guideline for the treatment of patients with major depressive disorder (revision). *American Journal of Psychiatry, 157*(4 Suppl.).

American Psychological Association. (2002a). Criteria for practice guideline development and evaluation. *American Psychologist, 57,* 1048–1059.

American Psychological Association. (2002b). Ethical principles of psychologists and code of conduct. *American Psychologist, 57,* 1060–1073.

American Psychological Association Board of Professional Affairs Task Force on Psychological Intervention Guidelines (1995). *Template for developing guidelines: Interventions for mental disorders and psychosocial aspects of physical disorders.* Approved by APA Council of Representatives, February 1995. Washington, DC: American Psychological Association

American Psychological Association Presidential Task Force. (2006). Evidence-based practice in psychology. *American Psychologist, 61,* 271–285.

Amir, N., Cashman, L., & Foa, E. B. (1997). Strategies of thought control and obsessive-compulsive disorder. *BRAT, 35,* 775–777.

Ancoli-Israel, S., & Ayalon, L. (2006). Diagnosis and treatment of sleep disorders in older adults. *American Journal of Geriatric Psychiatry, 14,* 95–103.

Andersen, B. L. (1992). Psychological interventions for cancer patients to enhance the quality of life. Special issue: Behavioral medicine: An update for the 1990s. *Journal of Consulting and Clinical Psychology, 60*(4), 552–568.

Andersen, B. L., & Cyranowski, J. M. (1994). Women's sexual self-schema. *Journal of Personality and Social Psychology, 67*(6), 1079–1100.

Andersen, B. L., Cyranowski, J. M., & Espindle, D. (1999). Men's sexual self-schema. *Journal of Personality and Social Psychology, 76*(4), 645–661.

Anderson, B., & Baum, A. (2001). *Psychosocial interventions for cancer.* Washington, DC: American Psychological Association.

Anderson, D. J., Noyes, R., & Crowe, R. R. (1984). A comparison of panic disorder and generalized anxiety disorder. *American Journal of Psychiatry, 141,* 572–575.

Anderson, N. B., & Jackson, J. S. (1987). Race, ethnicity and health psychology: The example of essential hypertension. In C. M. Stone, S. M. Weiss, J. D. Matarazzo, N. E. Miller, J. Rodin, C. D. Belar, M. J. Follick, & J. E. Singer (Eds.), *Health psychology: A discipline and a profession.* Chicago: University of Chicago Press.

Andrasik, F. (2000). Biofeedback. In D. I. Mostofsky & D. H. Barlow (Eds.), *The management of stress and anxiety in medical disorders* (pp. 66–83). Needham Heights, MA: Allyn & Bacon.

Andreasen, N. C. (1979). Thought, language, and communication disorders: I. Clinical assessment, definition of terms, and evaluation of their reliability. *Archives of General Psychiatry, 36,* 1315–1321.

Andreasen, N. C. (1987). Creativity and mental illness: Prevalence rates in writers and their first-degree relatives. *American Journal of Psychiatry, 144*(10), 1288–1292.

Andreasen, N. C. (1997). Linking mind and brain in the study of mental illnesses: A project for a scientific psychopathology. *Science, 275,* 1586–1593.

Andreasen, N. C., & Bardach, J. (1977). Dysmorphophobia: Symptom or disease? *American Journal of Psychiatry, 134,* 673–676.

Aneshensel, C. S., Pearlin, L. I., Mullan, J. T., Zarit, S. H., & Whitlatch, C. J. (1995). *Profiles in caregiving:*

The unexpected career. San Diego, CA: Academic Press.

Angst, A., Angst, F., Gerber-Werder, R., & Gamma, A. (2005). Suicide in 406 mood disordered patients with and without long-term medication: A 40 to 44 years' follow-up. *Archives Suicide Research, 9,* 279–300.

Angst, J. (1988). Clinical course of affective disorders. In T. Helgason & R. J. Daly (Eds.), *Depressive illness: Prediction of course and outcome* (pp. 1–44). Berlin: Springer-Verlag.

Angst, J., & Preizig, M. (1996). Course of a clinical cohort of unipolar, bipolar and schizoaffective patients: Results of a prospective study from 1959 to 1985. *Schweizer Archiv fur Neurologie und Psychiatrie, 146,* 1–16.

Angst, J., & Sellaro, R. (2000). Historical perspectives and natural history of bipolar disorder. *Biological Psychiatry, 48*(6), 445–457.

Angst, J., Sellaro, R., Stolar, M., Merikangas, K. R., & Endicott, J. (2001). The epidemiology of premenstrual psychological symptoms. *Acta Psychiatrica Scandinavica, 104,* 110–116.

Anisman, H., Zaharia, M. D., Meaney, M. J., & Merali, Z. (1998). Do early life events permanently alter behavioral and hormonal responses to stressors? *International Journal of Developmental Neuroscience, 16*(3–4), 149–164.

Ansell, E. B., Sanislow, C. A., McGlashan, T. H., & Grilo, C. M. (in press). Psychosocial impairment and treatment utilization by patients with borderline personality disorder, other personality disorders, mood and anxiety disorders, and a healthy comparison group. *Comprehensive Psychiatry.*

Anton, B., & Leff, P. (2006). A novel bivalent morphine/heroin vaccine that prevents relapse to heroin addiction in rodents. *Vaccine, 24,* 3232–3240.

Anton, R. F., O'Malley, S. S., Ciraulo, D. A., Cisler, R. A., Couper, D., Donovan, D. M., et al., for the COMBINE Study Research Group. (2006). Combined pharmacotherapies and behavioral interventions for alcohol dependence: The COMBINE Study: A randomized controlled trial. *JAMA, 295,* 2003–2017.

Antoni, M. H., & Goodkin, K. (1991). The interaction of viral and psychological factors in the promotion of cervical neoplasia. In H. Balner & J. Have (Eds.), *Coping with cancer and beyond: Cancer treatment and mental health.* Amsterdam: Swets and Zeitlinger.

Antoni, M. H., & Lutgendorf, S. (2007). Psychosocial factors and disease progression in cancer. *Current Directions in Psychological Science, 16,* 42–46.

Antoni, M. H., Baggett, L., Ironson, G., LaPerriere, A., August, S., Klimas, N., et al. (1991). Cognitive-behavioral stress management intervention buffers distress responses and immunologic changes following notification of HIV-1 seropositivity. *Journal of Consulting and Clinical Psychology, 59*(6), 906–915.

Antoni, M. H., Cruess, D. G., Cruess, S., Lutgendorf, S., Kumar, M., Ironson, G., et al. (2000). Cognitive-behavioral stress management intervention effects on anxiety, 24-hr urinary norepinephrine output, and T-cytotoxic/suppressor cells over time among symptomatic HIV-infected gay men. *Journal of Consulting and Clinical Psychology, 68,* 31–45.

Antoni, M. H., Lechner, S., Kazi, A., Wimberly, S., Sifre, T., Urcuyo, K., et al. (2006). How stress management improves quality of life after treatment for breast cancer. *Journal of Consulting and Clinical Psychology, 74,* 1143–1152.

Antony, M. M., & Barlow, D. H. (2002a). Specific phobias. In D. H. Barlow, *Anxiety and its disorders: The nature and treatment of anxiety and panic* (2nd ed.). New York: Guilford Press.

Antony, M. M., & Barlow, D. H. (Eds.) (2002b). *Handbook of assessment and treatment planning for psychological disorders.* New York: Guilford Press.

Antony, M. M., Brown, T. A., & Barlow, D. H. (1997a). Heterogeneity among specific phobia types in DSM-IV. *Behavior Research and Therapy, 35,* 1089–1100.

Antony, M. M., Brown, T. A., & Barlow, D. H. (1997b). Response to hyperventilation and 5.5% CO_2 inhalation of subjects with types of specific phobia, panic disorder, or no mental disorder. *American Journal of Psychiatry, 154,* 1089–1095.

Antony, M. M., Brown, T. A., Craske, M. G., Barlow, D. H., Mitchell, W. B., & Meadows, E. A. (1993). *Accuracy of heart beat estimation in panic disorder, social phobic and non-anxious controls.* Manuscript submitted for publication.

Antony, M. M., Craske, M. G., & Barlow, D. H. (2006). *Mastering your fears and phobias: Workbook.* New York: Oxford University Press.

Antrobus, J. (2000). Theories of dreaming. In M. H. Kryger, T. Roth, & W. C. Dement (Eds.), *Principles and practice of sleep medicine* (3rd ed., pp. 472–481). Philadelphia: W. B. Saunders.

Apfelbaum, B. (2000). Retarded ejaculation: A much misunderstood syndrome. In S. R. Leiblum & R. C. Rosen (Eds.), *Principles and practice of sex therapy* (3rd ed., pp. 205–241). New York: Guilford Press.

Apple, R. F., Lock, J., & Peebles, R. (2006). *Preparing for weight loss surgery.* New York: Oxford University Press.

Appolinario, J. C., Bacaltchuk, J., Sichieri, R., Claudino, A. M., Godoy-Matos, A., Morgan, S., et al. (2003). A randomized, double-blind, placebo-controlled study of Sibutramine in the treatment of binge-eating disorder. *Archives of General Psychiatry, 60,* 1109–1116.

Arens, R. (1974). *Insanity defense.* New York: Philosophical Library.

Armstrong, H. E. (1993). Review of psychosocial treatments for schizophrenia. In D. L. Dunner (Ed.), *Current psychiatric therapy* (pp. 183–188). Philadelphia: W. B. Saunders.

Aronow, E., Weiss, K. A., & Reznikoff, M. (2001). *A practical guide to the Thematic Apperception Test: The TAT in clinical practice.* Philadelphia: Taylor & Francis.

Arrindell, W. A., Eisemann, M., Richter, J., Oei, T. P. S., Caballo, V. E., van der Ende, J., Sanavio, E., Bagés, N., Feldman, L., Torres, B., Sica, C., Iwawaki, S., Edelmann, R. J., et al. (2003a). Phobic anxiety in 11 nations Part I: Dimensional constancy of the five-factor model. *Behaviour Research and Therapy, 41,* 461–479.

Arrindell, W. A., Eisemann, M., Richter, J., Oei, T. P. S., Caballo, V. E., van der Ende, J., Sanavio, E., Bagés, N., Feldman, L., Torres, B., Sica, C., Iwawaki, S., Hatzichristou, C., et al. (2003b). Masculinity–feminity as a national characteristic and its relationship with national agoraphobic fear levels: Fodor's sex role hypothesis revitalized. *Behaviour Research and Therapy, 41,* 795–807.

Asberg, M., Nordstrom, P., & Traskman-Bendz, L. (1986). Cerebrospinal fluid studies in suicide: An overview. *Annals of the American Academy of Science, 487,* 243–255.

Aschoff, J., & Wever, R. (1962). Spontanperiodik des Menschen die Ausschlus aller Zeitgeber. *Die Naturwissenschaften, 49,* 337–342.

Aspinwall, L. G., Kemeny, M. E., Taylor, S. E., Schneider, S. G., & Dudley, J. P. (1991). Psychosocial predictors of gay men's AIDS risk-reduction behavior. *Health Psychology, 10*(6), 432–444.

Attia, E., Haiman, C., Walsh, B. T., & Flater, S. R. (1998). Does fluoxetine augment the inpatient treatment of anorexia nervosa? *American Journal of Psychiatry, 155*(4), 548–551.

Attie, I., & Brooks-Gunn, J. (1995). The development of eating regulation across the life span. In D. Cicchetti & D. J. Cohen (Eds.), *Developmental psychopathology* (Vol. 2). New York: Wiley.

Autism Genome Project Consortium. (2007). Mapping autism risk loci using genetic linkage and chromosomal rearrangements. *Nature Genetics, 39,* 319–328.

Ayllon, T., & Azrin, N. H. (1968). *The token economy: A motivational system for therapy and rehabilitation.* New York: Appleton-Century-Crofts.

Azmitia, E. C. (1978). The serotonin-producing neurons of the midbrain median and dorsal raphe nuclei. In L. Iverson, S. Iverson, & S. Snyder (Eds.), *Handbook of psychopharmacology: Vol. 9. Chemical pathways in the brain* (pp. 233–314). New York: Plenum Press.

Baasher, T. A. (2001). Islam and mental health. *Eastern Mediterranean Health Journal, 7,* 372–376.

Babyak, M., Blumenthal, J. A., Herman, S., Khatri, P., Doraiswamy, M., Moore, K., et al. (2000). Exercise treatment for major depression: Maintenance of therapeutic benefit at 10 months. *Psychosomatic Medicine, 62,* 633–638.

Bach, A. K., Barlow, D., & Wincze, J. (2004). The enhancing effects of manualized treatment for erectile dysfunction among men using slidenafil: A preliminary investigation. *Behaviour Therapy, 35,* 55–73.

Bach, A. K., Brown, T. A., & Barlow, D. H. (1999). The effects of false negative feedback on efficacy expectancies and sexual arousal in sexually functional males. *Behavior Therapy, 30,* 79–95.

Bach, A. K., Wincze, J. P., & Barlow, D. H. (2001). Sexual dysfunction. In D. H. Barlow (Ed.), *Clinical handbook of psychological disorders: A step-by-step treatment manual* (3rd ed.). New York: Guilford Press.

Bailey, J. M., & Benishay, D. S. (1993). Familial aggregation of female sexual orientation. *American Journal of Psychiatry, 150*(2), 272–277.

Bailey, J. M., & Pillard, R. C. (1991). A genetic study of male sexual orientation. *Archives of General Psychiatry, 48,* 1089–1096.

Bailey, J. M., Pillard, R. C., Dawood, K., Miller, M. B., Farrer, L. A., Trivedi, S., & Murphy, R. L. (1999). A family history study of male sexual orientation using three independent samples. *Behavior Genetics, 29,* 79–86.

Bailey, J. M., Pillard, R. C., Neale, M. C., & Agyei, Y. (1993). Heritable factors influence sexual orientation in women. *Archives of General Psychiatry, 50,* 217–223.

Baker, A., van Kesteren, P. J., Gooren, L. J. G., & Bezemer, P. D. (1993). The prevalence of transsexualism in The Netherlands. *Acta Psychiatrica Scandinavica, 87,* 237–238.

Baker, C. D., & DeSilva, P. (1988). The relationship between male sexual dysfunction and belief in Zilbergeld's myths: An empirical investigation. *Sexual and Marital Therapy, 3*(2), 229–238.

Baldessarini, R. J. (1989). Current status of antidepressants: Clinical pharmacology and therapy. *Journal of Clinical Psychiatry, 50*(4), 117–126.

Baldessarini, R., Pompili, M., & Tondo, L. (2006). Suicidal risk in antidepressant drug trials. *Archives General Psychiatry, 63.*

Baldwin, J. D., & Baldwin, J. I. (1989). The socialization of homosexuality and heterosexuality in a non-Western society. *Archives of Sexual Behavior, 18,* 13–29.

Ball, S. G., & Otto, M. W. (1994). Cognitive behavioral treatment of choking phobia: Three case studies. *Psychotherapy and Psychosomatics, 62,* 207–211.

Balon, R. (2006). SSRI-associated sexual dysfunction. *American Journal of Psychiatry, 163,* 1504–1512.

Balon, R., Segraves, R., & Clayton, A. (2007). Issues for DSM-V: Sexual dysfunction, disorder, or variation along normal distribution—Toward rethinking DSM criteria of sexual dysfunctions. *American Journal of Psychiatry, 164,* 198–200.

Bancroft, J. (1989). *Human sexuality and its problems* (2nd ed.). EdSchwartz Schwartzinburgh: Churchill Livingstone.

Bancroft, J. (1994). Homosexual orientation: The search for a biological basis. *British Journal of Psychiatry, 164,* 437–440.

Bancroft, J. (1997). Sexual problems. In D. M. Clark & C. G. Fairburn (Eds.), *Science and practice of cognitive behavior therapy* (pp. 243–257). New York: Oxford University Press.

Bancroft, J., Loftus, J., & Long, J. S. (2003). Distress about sex: A national survey of women in heterosexual relationships. *Archives of Sexual Behavior, 32,* 193–208.

Bandelow, B., Krause, J., Wedekind, D., Broocks, A., Hajak, G., & Ruther, E. (2005). Early traumatic life events, parental attitudes, family history, and birth risk factors in patients with borderline personality disorder and healthy controls. *Psychiatry Research, 134,* 169–179.

Bandura, A. (1973). *Aggression: A social learning analysis.* Englewood Cliffs, NJ: Prentice Hall.

Bandura, A. (1986). *Social foundations of thought and action: A social cognitive theory.* Englewood Cliffs, NJ: Prentice Hall.

Bandura, A., O'Leary, A., Taylor, C. B., Gauthier, J., & Gossard, D. (1987). Perceived self-efficacy and pain control: Opioid and nonopioid mechanisms. *Journal of Personality and Social Psychology, 53,* 563–571.

Bankert, E. A., & Madur, R. J. (2006). *Institutional Review Board: Management and Function.* Jones and Bartlett Publishers.

Barbaree, H. E., & Seto, M. C. (1997). Pedophilia: Assessment and treatment. In D. R. Laws & W. O. O'Donohue (Eds.), *Sexual deviance: Theory, assessment, and treatment* (pp. 175–193). New York: Guilford Press.

Bargh, J. A., & Chartrand, T. L. (1999). The unbearable automaticity of being. *American Psychologist, 54,* 462–479.

Barkley, R. A. (1989). Attention deficit-hyperactivity disorder. In E. J. Mash & R. A. Barkley (Eds.), *Treatment of childhood disorders* (pp. 39–72). New York: Guilford Press.

Barkley, R. A. (1990). *Attention deficit hyperactivity disorder: A handbook for diagnosis and treatment.* New York: Guilford Press.

Barkley, R. A. (2006a). ADHD in adults: Developmental course and outcome of children with ADHD, and ADHD in clinic-referred adults. In R. A. Barkley (Ed.), *Attention-deficit hyperactivity disorder: A handbook for diagnosis and treatment* (3rd ed., pp. 248–296). New York: Guilford Press.

Barkley, R. A. (2006b). Associated cognitive, developmental, and health problems. In R. A. Barkley (Ed.), *Attention-deficit hyperactivity disorder: A handbook for diagnosis and treatment* (3rd ed., pp. 122–183). New York: Guilford Press.

Barkley, R. A. (2006c). Comorbid disorders, social and family adjustment, and subtyping. In R. A. Barkley (Ed.), *Attention-deficit hyperactivity disorder: A handbook for diagnosis and treatment* (3rd ed., pp. 184–218). New York: Guilford Press.

Barkley, R. A. (2006d). Etiologies. In R. A. Barkley (Ed.), *Attention-deficit hyperactivity disorder: A handbook for diagnosis and treatment* (3rd ed., pp. 219–247). New York: Guilford Press.

Barkley, R. A. (2006e). Primary symptoms, diagnostic criteria, prevalence, and gender differences. In R. A. Barkley (Ed.), *Attention-deficit hyperactivity disorder: A handbook for diagnosis and treatment* (3rd ed., pp. 76–121). New York: Guilford Press.

Barlow, D. H. (1986). Causes of sexual dysfunction: The role of anxiety and cognitive interference. *Journal of Consulting and Clinical Psychology, 54,* 140–148.

Barlow, D. H. (1988). *Anxiety and its disorders: The nature and treatment of anxiety and panic.* New York: Guilford Press.

Barlow, D. H. (1991). Disorders of emotion. *Psychological Inquiry, 2*(1), 58–71.

Barlow, D. H. (1993). Covert sensitization for paraphilia. In J. R. Cautela & A. J. Kearney (Eds.), *Covert conditioning casebook* (pp. 187–198). Pacific Grove, CA: Brooks/Cole.

Barlow, D. H. (2000). Unraveling the mysteries of anxiety and its disorders from the perspective of emotion theory. *American Psychologist, 55,* 1245–1263.

Barlow, D. H. (2002). *Anxiety and its disorders: The nature and treatment of anxiety and panic* (2nd ed.). New York: Guilford Press.

Barlow, D. H., & Craske, M. G. (2007). *Mastery of your anxiety and panic* (4th ed.). New York, NY: Oxford University Press.

Barlow, D. H., & Lehman, C. L. (1996). Advances in the psychosocial treatment of anxiety disorders: Implications for national health care. *Archives of General Psychiatry, 53,* 727–735.

Barlow, D. H., & Liebowitz, M. R. (1995). Specific and social phobias. In H. I. Kaplan & B. J. Sadock (Eds.), *Comprehensive textbook of psychiatry: VI* (pp. 1204–1217). Baltimore: Williams & Wilkins.

Barlow, D. H., & Wincze, J. P. (1980). Treatment of sexual deviations. In S. R. Leiblun & L. A. Pervin (Eds.), *Principles and practice of sex therapy* (pp. 347–375). New York: Guilford Press.

Barlow, D. H., Allen, L. B., & Basden, S. (in press). Psychological treatments for panic disorders, phobias, and generalized anxiety disorder. In P. E. Nathan & J. M. Gorman (Eds.), *A guide to treatments that work* (3rd ed.). New York: Oxford University Press.

Barlow, D. H., Allen, L. B., & Choate, M. L. (2004). Toward a unified treatment for emotional disorders. *Behavior Therapy, 35,* 205–230.

Barlow, D. H., Becker, R., Leitenberg, H., & Agras, W. S. (1970). A mechanical strain gauge for recording penile circumference change. *Journal of Applied Behavior Analysis, 3,* 73–76.

Barlow, D. H., Brown, T. A., & Craske, M. G. (1994). Definitions of panic attacks and panic disorder in DSM-IV: Implications for research. *Journal of Abnormal Psychology, 103,* 553–554.

Barlow, D. H., Chorpita, B. F., & Turovsky, J. (1996). Fear, panic, anxiety, and disorders of emotion. In D. A. Hope (Ed.), *Perspectives on anxiety, panic and fear* (The 43rd Annual Nebraska Symposium on Motivation) (pp. 251–328). Lincoln: Nebraska University Press.

Barlow, D. H., Gorman, J. M., Shear, K. M., & Woods, S. W. (2000). Cognitive-behavioral therapy, imipramine, or their combination for panic disorder: A randomized controlled trial. *JAMA, 283*(19), 2529–2536.

Barlow, D. H., Hayes, S. C., & Nelson, R. O. (1984). *The scientist practitioner: Research and accountability in clinical and educational settings.* Boston: Allyn & Bacon.

Barlow, D. H., Levitt, J. T., & Bufka, L. F. (1999). The dissemination of empirically supported treatments: A view to the future. *Behaviour Research and Therapy, 37*(Suppl. 1), S147–162.

Barlow, D. H., Pincus, D. B., Heinrichs, N., & Choate, M. (2003). Anxiety disorders: A Lifespan developmental perspective. In I. Weiner (Ed.), *Comprehensive Handbook of Psychology* (Vol. 8). New York: John Wiley.

Barlow, D. H., Rapee, R. M., & Reisner, L. C. (2001). *Mastering stress 2001: A lifestyle approach.* Dallas, TX: American Health.

Barlow, D. H., Sakheim, D. K., & Beck, J. G. (1983). Anxiety increases sexual arousal. *Journal of Abnormal Psychology, 92,* 49–54.

Barnard, A. (2000, September 12). When plastic surgeons should just say "no." *Boston Globe,* pp. E1, E3.

Barnes, J. (1981). Non-consummation of marriage. *Irish Medical Journal, 74,* 19–21.

Barnes, J., Bowman, E. P., & Cullen, J. (1984). Biofeedback as an adjunct to psychotherapy in the treatment of vaginismus. *Biofeedback and Self-Regulation, 9,* 281–289.

Barnes, G. M., Hoffman, J. H., Welte, J. W., Farrell, M. P., & Dintcheff, B. A. (2006). Effects of parental monitoring and peer deviance on substance use and delinquency. *Journal of Marriage and the Family, 68,* 1084–1104.

Barnett, P. A., & Gotlib, I. H. (1988). Psychosocial functioning and depression: Distinguishing among antecedents, concomitants and consequences. *Psychological Bulletin, 104*(1), 97–126.

Baron, M., Gruen, R., Asnis, L., & Lord, S. (1985). Familial transmission of schizotypal and borderline personality disorders. *American Journal of Psychiatry, 142,* 927–934.

Barrett, D. H., Resnick, H. S., Foy, D. W., Dansky, B. S., Flanders, W. D., & Stroup, N. E. (1996). Combat exposure and adult psychosocial adjustment among U.S. Army veterans serving in Vietnam, 1965–1971. *Journal of Abnormal Psychology, 105,* 575–581.

Barrett, J. E., Barrett, J. A., Oxman, T. E., & Gerber, P. D. (1988). The prevalence of psychiatric disorders in a primary care practice. *Archives of General Psychiatry, 45,* 1100–1106.

Barrett, P. M., Dadds, M. R., & Rapee, R. M. (1996). Family treatment of childhood anxiety: A controlled trial. *Journal of Consulting and Clinical Psychology, 64,* 333–342.

Barrett, P. M., Duffy, A. L., Dadds, M. R., & Rapee, R. M. (2001). Cognitive-behavioral treatment of anxiety disorders in children: Long-term (6-year) follow-up. *Journal of Consulting and Clinical Psychology, 69,* 135–141.

Barrett, R., Loa, P., Jerah, E., Nancarrow, D., Chant, D., & Mowry, B. (2005). Rates of treated schizophrenia and its clinical and cultural features in the population isolate of the Iban of Sarawak: A tri-diagnostic approach. *Psychological Medicine, 35,* 281–293.

Barsky, A. J., & Ahern, D. K. (2005). Cognitive behavior therapy for hypochondriasis: A randomized controlled trial. *JAMA, 291,* 1464–1470.

Barsky, A. J., & Wyshak, G. (1990). Hypochondriasis and somatosensory amplification. *British Journal of Psychiatry, 157,* 404–409.

Barsky, A. J., Fama, J. M., Bailey, E. D., & Ahern, D. K. (1998). A prospective 4 to 5 year study of DSM-III-R hypochondriasis. *Archives of General Psychiatry, 55*(8), 737–744.

Barsky, A. J., Frank, C. B., Cleary, P. D., Wyshak, G., & Klerman, G. L. (1991). The relation between hypochondriasis and age. *American Journal of Psychiatry, 148,* 923–928.

Barsky, A. J., Orav, E., & Bates, D. (2005). Somatization increases medical utilization and costs independent of psychiatric and medical comorbidity. *Archives of General Psychiatry, 62,* 903–910.

Barsky, A. J., Wyshak, G., & Klerman, G. L. (1986). Hypochondriasis: An evaluation of the DSM-III criteria in medical outpatients. *Archives of General Psychiatry, 43,* 493–500.

Barsky, A. J., Wyshak, G., Klerman, G. L., & Latham, K. S. (1990). The prevalence of hypochondriasis in medical outpatients. *Social Psychiatry & Psychiatry Epidemiology, 25,* 89–94.

Bartlett, N., & Vasey, P. (2006). A retrospective study of childhood gender-atypical behavior in Samoan Fa'afafine. *Archives of Sexual Behavior, 35,* 695–666.

Bartlik, B., & Goldberg, J. (2000). Female sexual arousal disorder. In S. R. Leiblum & R. C. Rosen (Eds.), *Principles and practice of sex therapy* (3rd ed., pp. 85–117). New York: Guilford Press.

Basoglu, M., Mineka, S., Paker, M., Aker, T., Gok, S., & Livanou, M. (1997). Psychological preparedness for trauma as a protective factor in survivors of torture. *Psychological Medicine, 27,* 1421–1433.

Bateson, G. (1959). Cultural problems posed by a study of schizophrenic process. In A. Auerback (Ed.), *Schizophrenia: An integrated approach.* New York: Ronald Press.

Battaglia, M., Bertella, S., Bajo, S., Politi, E., & Bellodi, L. (1998). An investigation of the co-occurrence of panic and somatization disorders through temperamental variables. *Psychosomatic Medicine, 60*(6), 726–729.

Bauer, M. S., Calabrese, J., Dunner, D. L., Post, R., Whybrow, P. C., Gyulai, L., et al. (1994). Multisite data reanalysis of the validity of rapid cycling as a course modifier for bipolar disorder in DSM-IV. *American Journal of Psychiatry, 151,* 506–515.

Baumann, S. B., & Sayette, M. A. (2006). Smoking cues in a virtual world provoke cravings in cigarette smokers. *Psychology of Addictive Behaviors, 20,* 484–489.

Baxter, L. R., Jr., Schwartz, J. M., Bergman, K. S., Szuba, M. P., Guze, B. H., Mazziotta, J. C., et al. (1992). Caudate glucose metabolic rate changes with both drug and behavior therapy for obsessive-compulsive disorder. *Archives of General Psychiatry, 49,* 681–689.

Baylé, F. J., Caci, H., Millet, B., Richa, S., & Olié, J.-P. (2003). Psychopathology and comorbidity of psychiatric disorders in patients with kleptomania. *American Journal of Psychiatry, 160,* 1509–1513.

Beach, S. R. H., Sandeen, E. E., & O'Leary, K. D. (1990). Depression in marriage: A model for etiology and treatment. In D. H. Barlow (Ed.), *Treatment manuals for practitioners.* New York: Guilford Press.

Beals, J., Manson, S., Whitesell, N., Mitchell, C., Novins, D., Simpson, S., et al. (2005). Prevalence of major depressive episode in two American Indian reservation populations: Unexpected findings with a structured interview. *American Journal Psychiatry, 162,* 1713–1722.

Beard, G. M. (1869). Neurasthenia or nervous exhaustion. *Boston Medical Surgical Journal, 3,* 217–221.

Beardslee, W. R., Salt, P., Versage, E. M., Gladstone, T. R. G., Wright, E. J., & Rothberg, P. C. (1997). Sustained change in parents receiving preventive interventions for families with depression. *American Journal of Psychiatry, 154*(4), 510–515.

Bebbington, P. E., Brugha, T., MacCarthy, B., Potter, J., Sturt, E., Wykes, T., et al. (1988). The Camberwell Collaborative Depression Study: I. Depressed probands: Adversity and the form of depression. *British Journal of Psychiatry, 152,* 754–765.

Beck, A. T. (1967). *Depression: Clinical, experimental and theoretical aspects.* New York: Harper & Row.

Beck, A. T. (1976). *Cognitive therapy and the emotional disorders.* New York: International Universities Press.

Beck, A. T. (1986). Hopelessness as a predictor of eventual suicide. *Annals of the New York Academy of Science, 487,* 90–96.

Beck, A. T., & Freeman, A. (1990). *Cognitive therapy of personality disorders.* New York: Guilford Press.

Beck, A. T., & Young, J. E. (1985). Depression. In D. H. Barlow (Ed.), *Clinical handbook of psychological disorders.* New York: Guilford Press.

Beck, A. T., Epstein, N., & Harrison, R. (1983). Cognitions, attitudes and personality dimensions in depression. *British Journal of Cognitive Psychotherapy, 1*(1), 1–16.

Beck, A. T., Freeman, A., & Davis, D. D. (2007). *Cognitive therapy of personality disorders* (2nd ed.). New York: Guilford Press.

Beck, A. T., Hollon, S. D., Young, J. E., Bedrosian, R. C., & Budenz, D. (1985). Treatment of depression with cognitive therapy and amitriptyline. *Archives of General Psychiatry, 42,* 142–148.

Beck, A. T., Steer, R., Kovacs, M., & Garrison, B. (1985). Hopelessness and eventual suicide: A 10-year prospective study of patients hospitalized with suicidal ideation. *American Journal of Psychiatry, 142,* 559–563.

Beck, J. G. (1993). Vaginismus. In W. O'Donohue & J. H. Geer (Eds.), *Handbook of sexual dysfunctions: Assessment and treatment* (pp. 381–397). Boston: Allyn & Bacon.

Beck, J. G., & Averill, P. M. (2004). Older adults. In R. G. Heimberg, C. L. Turk, & D. S. Mennin (Eds.), *Generalized anxiety disorder: Advances in research and practice* (pp. 409–433). New York: Guilford Press.

Beck, J. G., & Stanley, M. A. (1997). Anxiety disorders in the elderly: The emerging role of behavior therapy. *Behavior Therapy, 28,* 83–100.

Becker, C. B., Smith, L. M., & Ciao, A. C. (2005). Reducing eating disorder risk factors in sorority members: A randomized trial. *Behavior Therapy, 36,* 245–253.

Becker, D. (2000). When she was bad: Borderline personality disorder in a posttraumatic age. *American Journal of Orthopsychiatry, 70,* 422–432.

Becker, J. T., Mestre, L. T., Ziolko, S., & Lopez, O. L. (2007). Gene–environment interactions with cognition in late life and compression of morbidity. *American Journal of Psychiatry, 164,* 849–852.

Becker, J. V. (1990). Treating adolescent sexual offenders. *Professional Psychology: Research and Practice, 21,* 362–365.

Beekman, A. T., Geerlings, S. W., Deeg, D. J., Smit, J. H., Schoevers, R. S., de Beurs, E., et al. (2002). The natural history of late-life depression: A 6-year prospective study in the community. *Archives of General Psychiatry, 59,* 605–611.

Belger, A., & Dichter, G. (2006). Structural and functional neuroanatomy. In J. A. Lieberman, T. S. Stroup, & D. O. Perkins (Eds.), *The American Psychiatric Publishing textbook of schizophrenia* (pp. 167–185). Washington, DC: American Psychiatric Publishing.

Bell, C. C., Dixie-Bell, D. D., & Thompson, B. (1986). Further studies on the prevalence of isolated sleep paralysis in black subjects. *Journal of the National Medical Association, 75,* 649–659.

Bell, I. R. (1994). Somatization disorder: Health care costs in the decade of the brain. *Biological Psychiatry, 35,* 81–83.

Bellack, A. S., & Mueser, K. T. (1992). Social skills training for schizophrenia? *Archives of General Psychiatry, 49,* 76.

Bellack, A. S., Mueser, K. T., Gingerich, S., & Agresta, J. (2004). *Social skills training for schizophrenia: A step-by-step guide* (2nd ed.). New York: Guilford Press.

Bellak, L. (1975). *The thematic apperception test, the children's apperception test, and the senior apperception technique in clinical use* (3rd ed.). New York: Grune & Stratton.

Bellis, D. J. (1981). *Heroin and politicians: The failure of public policy to control addiction in America.* Westport, CT: Greenwood Press.

Bellizzi, M. (2002). Childhood obesity: The emerging global epidemic. Paper presented at the 2002 convention of the World Health Assembly, Geneva, Switzerland.

Bem, D. J. (1996). Exotic becomes erotic: A developmental theory of sexual orientation. *Psychological Review, 103,* 320–335.

Benbadis, R. R., & Allen-Hauser, W. (2000). An estimate of the prevalence of psychogenic non-epileptic seizures. *Seizure, 9*(4), 280–281.

Benca, R. M., Chirelli, C., Rattenborg, N. C., & Tononi, G. (2005). Sleep disorders. In B. J. Sadock & V. A. Sadock (Eds.), *Kaplan & Sadock's comprehensive textbook of psychiatry* (pp. 280–295). Philadelphia: Lippincott, Williams & Wilkins.

Bender, D. S. (2005). Therapeutic alliance. In J. M. Oldham, A. E. Skodol, & D. S. Bender (Eds.), *Textbook of personality disorders* (pp. 405–420). Washington, DC: American Psychiatric Publishing.

Bender, E. (2004). Data show wide variation in addiction treatment costs. *Psychiatric News, 39,* 11.

Benedetti, A., Perugi, G., Toni, C., Simonetti, B., Mata, B., & Cassano, G. B. (1997). Hypochondriasis and illness phobia in panic-agoraphobic patients. *Comprehensive Psychiatry, 38*(2), 124–131.

Benedetti, F., Colombo, C., Serretti, A., Lorenzi, C., Pontiggia, A., Barbini, B., & Smeraldi, E. (2003). Antidepressant effects of light therapy combined with sleep deprivation are influenced by a functional polymorphism within the promoter of the serotonin transporter gene. *Biological Psychiatry, 54,* 687–692.

Bennett, A. H. (1988). Venous arterialization for erectile impotence. *Urologic Clinics of North America, 15,* 111–113.

Benowitz, N. L. (1996). Pharmacology of nicotine: Addiction and therapeutics. *Annual Review of Pharmacology and Toxicology, 36,* 597–613.

Benson, H. (1975). *The relaxation response.* New York: William Morrow.

Benson, H. (1984). *Beyond the relaxation response.* New York: Times Books.

Berenbaum, H., & Oltmanns, T. F. (1992). Emotional experience and expression in schizophrenia and depression. *Journal of Abnormal Psychology, 101,* 37–44.

Bergman, R. L., & Piacentini, J. (2005). Selective mutism. In B. J. Sadock & V. A. Sadock (Eds.), *Kaplan & Sadock's comprehensive textbook of psychiatry* (pp. 3302–3306). Philadelphia: Lippincott, Williams & Wilkins.

Berkman, L. F., & Syme, S. L. (1979). Social networks, host resistance, and mortality: A nine-year follow-up study of Alameda county residents. *American Journal of Epidemiology, 109,* 186.

Berkowitz, R. I., Wadden, T. A., Tershakovec, A. M., & Cronquist, J. L. (2003). Behavior therapy and Sibutramine for the treatment of adolescent obesity: A randomized controlled trial. *JAMA, 289,* 1805–1812.

Berlin, I. N. (1987). Suicide among American Indian adolescents: An overview. *Suicide and Life Threatening Behavior, 17*(3), 218–232.

Berman, A. L., & Jobes, D. A. (1991). *Adolescent suicide: Assessment and intervention.* Washington, DC: American Psychological Association.

Berman, J. R., Berman, L. A., Toler, S. M., Gill, J., Haughie, S., for the Sildenafil Study Group. (2003). Safety and efficacy of sildenafil citrate for the treatment of female sexual arousal disorder: A double-blind, placebo controlled study. *The Journal of Urology, 170,* 2333–2338.

Berman, K. F., & Weinberger, D. R. (1990). Lateralization of cortical function during cognitive tasks: Regional cerebral blood flow studies of normal individuals and patients with schizophrenia. *Journal of Neurology, Neurosurgery and Psychiatry, 53,* 150–160.

Bernat, J. A., Calhoun, K. S., & Adams, H. E. (1999). Sexually aggressive and nonaggressive men: Sexual arousal and judgments in response to acquaintance rape and consensual analogues. *Journal of Abnormal Psychology, 108,* 662–673.

Bernstein, D. P., Useda, D., & Siever, L. J. (1993). Paranoid personality disorder: Review of the literature and recommendations for DSM-IV. *Journal of Personality Disorders, 7,* 53–62.

Bertelsen, B., Harvald, B., & Hauge, M. (1977). A Danish twin study of manic-depressive disorders. *British Journal of Psychiatry, 130,* 330–351.

Berton, O., McClung, C. A., DiLeone, R. J., Krishnan, V., Renthal, W., Russo, S. J., et al. (2006). Essential role of BDNF in the mesolimbic dopamine pathway in social defeat stress. *Science, 311,* 864–868.

Berzins, K. M., Petch, A., & Atkinson, J. M. (2003). Prevalence and experience of harassment of people with mental health problems living in the community. *British Journal of Psychiatry, 183,* 526–533.

Bettelheim, B. (1967). *The empty fortress.* New York: Free Press.

Beukelman, D. R., & Mirenda, P. (Eds.) (2005). *Augmentative and alternative communication supporting children and adults with complex communication needs* (3rd ed.). Baltimore: Paul H. Brookes.

Bhagwanjee, A., Parekh, A., Paruk, Z., Petersen, I., & Subedar, H. (1998). Prevalence of minor psychiatric disorders in an adult African rural community in South Africa. *Psychological Medicine, 28,* 1137–1147.

Bhasin, T., & Schendel, D. (2007). Sociodemographic risk factors for autism in a U.S. metropolitan area. *Journal of Autism and Developmental Disorders, 37,* 667–677.

Biederman, J., Faraone, S. V., Keenan, K., Benjamin, J., Krifcher, B., Moore, C., et al. (1992). Further evidence for family–genetic risk factors in attention deficit hyperactivity disorder: Patterns of comorbidity in probands and relatives in psychiatrically and pediatrically referred samples. *Archives of General Psychiatry, 49,* 728–738.

Biederman, J., Mick, E., Faraone, S. V., Spencer, T., Wilens, T. E., & Wozniak, J. (2000). Pediatric mania: A developmental subtype of bipolar disorder? *Biological Psychiatry, 48*(6), 458–466.

Biederman, J., Munir, K., Knee, D., Armentano, M., Autor, S., Waternaux, C., & Tsuang, M. (1987). High rate of affective disorders in probands with attention deficit disorder and in their relatives: A controlled family study. *American Journal of Psychiatry, 144*(3), 330–333.

Biederman, J., Rosenbaum, J. F., Hirschfeld, D. R., Farone, S. V., Bolduc, E. A., Gersten, M., et al. (1990). Psychiatric correlates of behavioral inhibition in young children of parents with and without psychiatric disorders. *Archives of General Psychiatry, 47,* 21–26.

Biederman, J., Spencer, T., Wilens, T., & Greene, R. (2001). Attention-deficit/hyperactivity disorder. In G. O. Gabbard (Ed.), *Treatment of psychiatric disorders* (Vol. 1, 3rd ed., pp. 145–176). Washington, DC: American Psychiatric Publishing.

Bierut, L. J., Heath, A. C., Bucholz, K. K., Dinwiddie, S. H., Madden, P. A., Statham, D. J., et al. (1999). Major depressive disorder in a community-based twin sample: Are there different genetic and environmental contributions for men and women? *Archives of General Psychiatry, 56*(6), 557–563.

Biglan, A., Hops, H., Sherman, L., Friedman, L. S., Arthur, J., & Osteen, V. (1985). Problem solving interactions of depressed women and their husbands. *Behavior Therapy, 16,* 431–451.

Billy, J. O. G., Tanfer, K., Grady, W. R., & Klepinger, D. H. (1993). The sexual behavior of men in the United States. *Family Planning Perspectives, 25,* 52–60.

Binik, Y. (2005). Should dyspareunia be retained as a sexual dysfunction in DSM-V? A painful classification decision. *Archives of Sexual Behavior, 34,* 11–21.

Binik, Y. M., Bergeron, S., & Khalifé, S. (2000). Dyspareunia. In S. R. Leiblum & R. C. Rosen (Eds.), *Principles and practice of sex therapy* (3rd ed., pp. 154–180). New York: Guilford Press.

Binzer, M., Andersen, P. M., & Kullgren, G. (1997). Clinical characteristics of patients with motor disability due to conversion disorder: A prospective control group study. *Journal of Neurology, Neurosurgery, and Psychiatry, 63*(1), 83–88.

Birley, J., & Brown, G. W. (1970). Crisis and life changes preceding the onset or relapse of acute schizophrenia: Clinical aspects. *British Journal of Psychiatry, 16,* 327–333.

Biron, M., Risch, N., Hamburger, R., Mandel, B., Kushner, S., Newman, M., et al. (1987). Genetic linkage between X-chromosome markers and bipolar affective illness. *Nature, 326,* 289–292.

Bjorklund, D. F. (1989). *Children's thinking: Developmental function and individual differences.* Pacific Grove, CA: Brooks/Cole.

Bjorntorp, P. (1997). Obesity. *Lancet, 350,* 423–426.

Black, D. W., & Winokur, G. (1990). Suicide and psychiatric diagnosis. In S. J. Blumenthal & D. J. Kupfer (Eds.), *Suicide over the life cycle: Risk factors, assessment and treatment of suicidal patients.* Washington, DC: American Psychiatric Press.

Blackburn, I.-M., & Moore, R. G. (1997). Controlled acute and follow-up trial of cognitive therapy and pharmacotherapy in out-patients with recurrent depression. *British Journal of Psychiatry, 171,* 328–334.

Blacker, D. (2005). Psychiatric rating scales. In B. J. Sadock & V. A. Sadock (Eds.), *Kaplan & Sadock's comprehensive textbook of psychiatry* (pp. 929–955). Philadelphia: Lippincott Williams & Wilkins.

Blagys, M. D., & Hilsenroth, M. J. (2000). Distinctive features of short-term psychodynamic–interpersonal psychotherapy: A review of the comparative psychotherapy process literature. *Clinical Psychology: Science and Practice, 7,* 167–188.

Blanchard, C. G., Blanchard, E. B., & Becker, J. V. (1976). The young widow: Depressive symptomatology throughout the grief process. *Psychiatry, 39,* 394–399.

Blanchard, E. B. (1987). Long-term effects of behavioral treatment of chronic headache. *Behavior Therapy, 18,* 375–385.

Blanchard, E. B. (1992). Psychological treatment of benign headache disorders. Special issue: Behavioral medicine: An update for the 1990s. *Journal of Consulting and Clinical Psychology, 60*(4), 537–551.

Blanchard, E. B., & Andrasik, F. (1982). Psychological assessment and treatment of headache: Recent developments and emerging issues. *Journal of Consulting and Clinical Psychology, 50*(6), 859–879.

Blanchard, E. B., & Epstein, L. H. (1977). *A biofeedback primer.* Reading, MA: Addison-Wesley.

Blanchard, E. B., Andrasik, F., Ahles, T. A., Teders, S. J., & O'Keefe, D. (1980). Migraine and tension headache: A meta-analytic review. *Behavior Therapy, 11,* 613–631.

Blanchard, E. B., Appelbaum, K. A., Radnitz, C. L., Michultka, D., Morrill, B., Kirsh, C., et al. (1990). Placebo-controlled evaluation of abbreviated progressive muscle relaxation combined with cognitive therapy in the treatment of tension headache. *Journal of Consulting and Clinical Psychology, 58*(2), 210–215.

Blanchard, R., & Bogaert, A. (1996). Homosexuality in men and number of older brothers. *American Journal of Psychiatry, 153,* 27–31.

Blanchard, R., & Bogaert, A. (1998). Birth order in homosexual versus heterosexual sex offenders against children, pubescents, and adults. *Archives of Sexual Behavior, 27*(6), 595–603.

Blanchard, R., & Steiner, B. W. (1992). *Clinical management of gender identity disorders in children and adults.* Washington, DC: American Psychiatric Press.

Bland, R. C. (1997). Epidemiology of affective disorders: A review. *Canadian Journal of Psychiatry, 42,* 367–377.

Blascovich, J., & Tomaka, J. (1996). The biopsychosocial model of arousal regulation. *Advances in Experimental Social Psychology, 28,* 1–51.

Blashfield, R. K., & Livesley, W. J. (1991). Metaphorical analysis of psychiatric classification as a psychological test. *Journal of Abnormal Psychology, 100*(3), 262–270.

Blazer, D. (1999). Geriatric psychiatry. In R. E. Hales, S. C. Yudofsky, & J. A. Talbot (Eds.), *Textbook of psychiatry* (3rd ed., pp. 1447–1462). Washington, DC: American Psychiatric Press.

Blazer, D. G. (1989). Current concepts: Depression in the elderly. *New England Journal of Medicine, 320,* 164–166.

Blazer, D. G., George, L., & Hughes, D. (1991). The epidemiology of anxiety disorders: An age comparison. In C. Salzman & B. Liebowitz (Eds.), *Anxiety disorders in the elderly* (pp. 17–30). New York: Springer.

Blehar, M. C., & Rosenthal, N. E. (1989). Seasonal affective disorder and phototherapy. *Archives of General Psychiatry, 46,* 469–474.

Bleiberg, K. L., & Markowitz, J. C. (in press). Interpersonal psychotherapy for major depressive disorder. In D. H. Barlow (Ed.), *Clinical handbook of psychological disorders* (4th ed.). New York: Guilford Press.

Bleijenberg, G., Prins, J., & Bazelmans, E. (2003). Cognitive-behavioral therapies. In L. A. Jason, P. A. Fennell, & R. R. Taylor (Eds.), *Handbook of chronic fatigue syndrome.* Hoboken, NJ: John Wiley.

Bleuler, E. (1908). Die Prognose der Dementia praecox (Schizophreniegruppe). *Allgemeine Zeitschrift für Psychiatrie, 65,* 436–464.

Bleuler, E. (1911). *Dementia praecox or the group of schizophrenias* (Joseph Zinkin, Trans.) New York: International Universities Press.

Bleuler, E. (1924). *Textbook of psychiatry.* (A. A. Brill, Trans.) New York: Macmillan.

Bliese, P. D., Wesensten, N. J., & Balkin, T. J. (2006). Age and individual variability in performance during sleep restriction. *Journal of Sleep Research, 15*(4), 376–385.

Bliss, E. L. (1984). A symptom profile of patients with multiple personalities including MMPI results. *Journal of Nervous and Mental Diseases, 172,* 197–211.

Bliss, E. L. (1986). *Multiple personality allied disorders and hypnosis.* New York: Oxford University Press.

Bloom, F. E., & Kupfer, D. J. (1995). *Psychopharmacology: The fourth generation of progress.* New York: Raven Press.

Bloom, F. E., Nelson, C. A., & Lazerson, A. (2001). *Brain, mind, & behavior* (3rd ed.). New York: Worth Publishers.

Blue, A. V., & Gaines, A. D. (1992). The ethnopsychiatric répertoire: A review and overview of ethnopsychiatric studies. In A. D. Gaines (Ed.), *Ethnopsychiatry: The cultural construction of professional and folk psychiatries* (pp. 397–484). Albany: State University of New York Press.

Blumenthal, J. A., Sherwood, A., Babyak, M., Watkins, L., Waugh, R., Georgiades, A., et al. (2005). Effects of exercise and stress management training on markers of cardiovascular risk in patients with ischemic heart disease. *JAMA, 293,* 1626–1634.

Blumenthal, S. J. (1990). An overview and synopsis of risk factors, assessment, and treatment of suicidal patients over the life cycle. In S. J. Blumenthal & D. J. Kupfer (Eds.), *Suicide over the life cycle: Risk factors, assessment and treatment of suicidal patients.* Washington, DC: American Psychiatric Press.

Blumenthal, S. J., & Kupfer, D. J. (1988). Clinical assessment and treatment of youth suicide. *Journal of Youth and Adolescence, 17,* 1–24.

Bobb, A. J., Castellanos, F. X., Addington, A. M., & Rapoport, J. L. (2006). Molecular genetic studies of ADHD: 1991 to 2004. *American Journal of Medical Genetics Part B (Neuropsychiatric Genetics), 141,* 551–565.

Blundell, J. E. (2002). The psychobiological approach to appetite and weight control. In K. D. Brownell & C. G. Fairburn (Eds.), *Eating disorders and obesity: A comprehensive handbook* (2nd ed., pp. 13–20). New York: Guilford Press.

Bockoven, J. S. (1963). *Moral treatment in American psychiatry.* New York: Springer.

Bodlund, O., & Kullgren, G. (1996). Transsexualism—General outcome and prognostic factors: A five-year follow-up study of nineteen transsexuals in the process of changing sex. *Archives of Sexual Behavior, 25,* 303–316.

Bohman, M., Cloninger, C. R., von Knorring, A. L., & Sigvardsson, S. (1984). An adoption study of somatoform disorders: III. Cross-fostering analysis and genetic relationship to alcoholism and criminality. *Archives of General Psychiatry, 41,* 872–878.

Bohus, M., Haaf, B., Stiglmayr, C., Pohl, U., Bohme, R., & Linehan, M. (2000). Evaluation of inpatient dialectical–behavioral therapy for borderline personality disorder—A prospective study. *Behavior Research and Therapy, 38*(9), 875–887.

Boland, R., & Keller, M. (2002). Course and outcome of depression. In I. H. Gotlib & C. L. Hammen (Eds.), *Handbook of depression* (pp. 43–60). New York: Guilford Press.

Bonanno, G. (2006). Is complicated grief a valid construct? *Clinical Psychology Science Practice, 13,* 129–134.

Bonanno, G., & Kaltman, S. (1999). Toward an integrative perspective on bereavement. *Psychological Bulletin, 125*(6), 1004–1008.

Bonanno, G., Wortman, C., & Nesse, R. (2004). Prospective patterns of resilience and maladjustment during widowhood. *Psychology and Aging, 19,* 260–271.

Bond, A., & Lader, M. L. (1979). Benzodiazepines and aggression. In M. Sandler (Ed.), *Psychopharmacology of aggression.* New York: Raven Press.

Bond, C. F., DeCandia, C. G., & MacKinnon, J. (1988). Responses to race in a psychiatric setting: The role of patient's race. *Personality and Social Psychology Bulletin, 14,* 448–458.

Booij, L., & Van der Does, W. (2007). Cognitive and serotonergic vulnerability to depression: Convergent findings. *Journal of Abnormal Psychology, 116,* 86–94.

Boon, S., & Draijer, N. (1991). Diagnosing dissociative disorders in the Netherlands: A pilot study with the Structured Clinical Interview for DSM-III-R dissociative disorders. *American Journal of Psychiatry, 148,* 458–462.

Boon, S., & Draijer, N. (1993). Multiple personality disorder in the Netherlands: A clinical investigation of 71 cases. *American Journal of Psychiatry, 150,* 489–494.

Booth, W. (1990). The anatomy of a high. *Washington Post National Weekly Edition,* March 26–April 1, p. 38.

Bootzin, R. R., Manber, R., Perlis, M. L., Salvio, M., & Wyatt, J. K. (1993). Sleep disorders. In P. B. Sutker & H. E. Adams (Eds.), *Comprehensive handbook of psychopathology* (2nd ed., pp. 531–561). New York: Plenum Press.

Borkovec, T. D., & Costello, E. (1993). Efficacy of applied relaxation and cognitive-behavioral therapy in the treatment of generalized anxiety disorder. *Journal of Consulting and Clinical Psychology, 61*(4), 611–619.

Borkovec, T. D., & Hu, S. (1990). The effect of worry on cardiovascular response to phobic imagery. *Behaviour Research and Therapy, 28,* 69–73.

Borkovec, T. D., & Inz, J. (1990). The nature of worry in generalized anxiety disorder: A predominance of thought activity. *Behaviour Research and Therapy, 28,* 153–158.

Borkovec, T. D., & Ruscio, A. (2001). Psychotherapy for generalized anxiety disorder. *Journal of Clinical Psychiatry, 62,* 37–45.

Borkovec, T. D., Alcaine, O. M., & Behar, E. (2004). Avoidance theory of worry and generalized anxiety disorder. In R. G. Heimberg, C. L. Turk, & D. S. Mennin (Eds.), *Generalized anxiety disorder: Advances in research and practice* (pp. 77–108). New York: Guilford Press.

Borkovec, T. D., Newman, M. G., Pincus, A. L., & Lytle, R. (2002). A component analysis of cognitive-behavioral therapy for generalized anxiety disorder and the role of interpersonal problems. *Journal of Consulting and Clinical Psychology, 70,* 288–298.

Borkovec, T. D., Shadick, R., & Hopkins, M. (1991). The nature of normal and pathological worry. In R. M. Rapee & D. H. Barlow (Eds.), *Chronic anxiety, generalized anxiety disorder, and mixed anxiety depression.* New York: Guilford Press.

Bornstein, R. F. (1992). The dependent personality: Developmental, social, and clinical perspectives. *Psychological Bulletin, 112,* 3–23.

Bornstein, R. F. (1997). Dependent personality disorder in the DSM-IV and beyond. *Clinical Psychology: Science and Practice, 4,* 175–187.

Borodinsky, L. N., Root, C. M., Cronin, J. A., Sann, S. B., Gu, X., & Spitzer, N. C. (2004). Activity-dependent homeostatic specification of transmitter expression in embryonic neurons. *Nature, 429,* 523–530.

Borysenko, M. (1987). Area review: Psychoneuroimmunology. *Annals of Behavioral Medicine, 9,* 3–10.

Boskind-Lodahl, M. (1976). Cinderella's stepsisters: A feminist perspective on anorexia nervosa and bulimia. *Signs, 2,* 342–356.

Bottiggi, K. A., Chang, J. J., Schmitt, F. A., Avison, M. J., Mootoor, Y., Nath, A., & Berger, J. R. (in press). The HIV dementia scale: Predictive power in mild dementia and HAART. *Journal of the Neurological Sciences.*

Bouchard, C. (2002). Genetic influences on body weight and shape. In K. D. Brownell & C. G. Fairburn (Eds.), *Eating disorders and obesity: A comprehensive handbook* (2nd ed., pp. 21–26). New York: Guilford Press.

Bouchard, T. J., Jr., Lykken, D. T., McGue, M., Segal, N. L., & Tellegen, A. (1990). Sources of human psychological differences: The Minnesota study of twins reared apart. *Science, 250,* 223–228.

Boulos, C., Kutcher, S., Marton, P., Simeon, J., Ferguson, B., & Roberts, N. (1991). Response to desipramine treatment in adolescent major depression. *Psychopharmacology Bulletin, 27*(1), 59–65.

Bourgeois, J. A., Seaman, J. S., & Servis, M. E. (2003). Delirium, dementia, and amnestic disorders. In R. E. Hales & S. C. Yudofsky (Eds.), *Textbook of clinical psychiatry* (4th ed., pp. 259–308). Washington, DC: American Psychiatric Publishing.

Bourgeois, M. S. (1992). Evaluating memory wallets in conversations with persons with dementia. *Journal of Speech and Hearing Research, 35,* 1344–1357.

Bourgeois, M. S. (1993). Effects of memory aids on the dyadic conversations of individuals with dementia. *Journal of Applied Behavior Analysis, 26,* 77–87.

Bouton, M. E. (2005). Behavior systems and the contextual control of anxiety, fear, and panic. In L. Feldman Barrett, P. Niedenthal, & P. Winkielman (Eds.), *Emotion: Conscious and unconscious* (pp. 205–227). New York: Guilford Press.

Bouton, M. E., Mineka, S., & Barlow, D. H. (2001). A modern learning-theory perspective on the etiology of panic disorder. *Psychological Review, 108,* 4–32.

Bower, B. (1999). Personality conflicts: A clinical upstart elbows its way into the personality-assessment fray. *Science News, 156,* 88–90.

Bower, G. H. (1981). Mood and memory. *American Psychologist, 36,* 129–148.

Bowers, J. S., & Marsolek, C. J. (2003). *Rethinking implicit memory.* New York: Oxford University Press.

Bowlby, J. (1977). The making and breaking of affectionate bonds. *British Journal of Psychiatry, 130,* 201–210.

Bowman, E. S., & Coons, P. M. (2000). The differential diagnosis of epilepsy, pseudoseizures, dissociative identity disorder, and dissociative disorder not otherwise specified. *Bulletin of the Menninger Clinic, 64,* 164–180.

Bradford, J. (1997). Medical interventions in sexual deviance. In D. R. Laws & W. O'Donohue (Eds.), *Sexual deviance: Theory, assessment and treatment* (pp. 449–464). New York: Guilford Press.

Bradley, B. P., & Mathews, A. (1988). Memory bias in recovered clinical depressives. Special issue: Information processing and the emotional disorders. *Cognition and Emotion, 2*(3), 235–245.

Bradley, B. P., Mogg, K., White, J., Groom, C., & de Bono, J. (1999). Attentional bias for emotional faces in generalized anxiety disorder. *British Journal of Clinical Psychology, 38,* 267–278.

Bradley, R., Danielson, L., & Hallahan, D. P. (Eds.) (2002). *Identification of learning disabilities: Research to practice.* Mahwah, NJ: Erlbaum.

Bradley, W. (1937). The behavior of children receiving Benzedrine. *American Journal of Psychiatry, 94,* 577–585.

Brady, J. P., & Lind, D. L. (1961). Experimental analysis of hysterical blindness. *Archives of General Psychiatry, 4,* 331–339.

Braff, D., Schork, N. J., & Gottesman, I. I. (2007). Endophenotyping schizophrenia. *American Journal of Psychiatry, 164,* 705–707.

Brandon, T. H., & Baker, T. B. (1992). The smoking consequences questionnaire: The subjective utility of smoking in college students. *Psychological Assessment: A Journal of Consulting and Clinical Psychology, 3,* 484–491.

Brannon, L., & Feist, J. (1997). *Health psychology: An introduction to behavior and health.* Pacific Grove, CA: Brooks/Cole.

Brauchi, J. T., & West, L. J. (1959). Sleep deprivation. *JAMA, 171,* 11–14.

Brawman-Mintzer, O. (2001). Pharmacologic treatment of generalized anxiety disorder. *Psychiatric Clinics of North America, 24,* 119–137.

Brechtl, J. R., Breitbart, W., Galietta, M., Krivo, S., & Rosenfeld, B. (2001). The use of highly active antiretroviral therapy (HAART) in patients with advanced HIV infection: impact on medical, palliative care, and quality of life outcomes. *Journal of Pain Symptom Manage, 21,* 41–51.

Bremner, J. D. (1999). Does stress damage the brain? *Biological Psychiatry, 45,* 797–805.

Bremner, J. D., Licinio, J., Darnell, A., Krystal, A. H., Owens, M. J., Southwick, S. M., et al. (1997). Elevated CSF corticotropin-releasing factor concentrations in posttraumatic stress disorder. *American Journal of Psychiatry, 154,* 624–629.

Bremner, J. D., Randall, P. R., Scott, T. M., Bronen, R. A., Seibyl, J. P., Southwick, S. M., et al. (1995). MRI-based measurement of hippocampal volume in patients with combat-related posttraumatic stress disorder. *American Journal of Psychiatry, 152,* 973–981.

Bremner, J. D., Vermetten, E., Southwick, S. M., Krystal, J. H., & Charney, D. S. (1998). Trauma, memory, and dissociation: An integrative formulation. In J. D. Bremner & C. Marmar (Eds.), *Trauma, memory, and dissociation.* Washington, DC: American Psychiatric Press.

Brener, N. D., Hassan, S. S., & Barrios, L. C. (1999). Suicidal ideation among college students in the United States. *Journal of Consulting & Clinical Psychology, 67,* 1004–1008.

Brenner, D. E., Kukull, W. A., van Belle, G., Bowen, J. D., McCormick, W. C., Teri, L., & Larson, E. B. (1993). Relationship between cigarette smoking and Alzheimer's disease in a population-based case-control study. *Neurology, 43,* 293–300.

Brent, D. A., & Kolko, D. J. (1990). The assessment and treatment of children and adolescents at risk for suicide. In S. J. Blumenthal & D. J. Kupfer (Eds.), *Suicide over the life cycle: Risk factors, assessment and treatment of suicidal patients.* Washington, DC: American Psychiatric Press.

Brent, D. A., Oquendo, M., Birmaher, B., Greenhill, L., Kolko, D., Stanley, B., et al. (2002). Familial pathways to early-onset suicide attempt risk for suicidal behavior in offspring of mood-disordered suicide attempters. *Archives of General Psychiatry, 59,* 801–807.

Brent, D. A., Oquendo, M., Birmaher, B., Greenhill, L., Kolko, D., Stanley, B., et al. (2003). Peripubertal suicide attempts in offspring of suicide attempters with siblings concordant for suicidal behavior. *American Journal of Psychiatry, 160,* 1486–1493.

Brent, D. A., Perper, J. A., Goldstein, C. E., Kolko, D. J., Allan, M. J., Allman, C. J., & Zellenak, J. P. (1988). Risk factors for adolescent suicide: A comparison of adolescent suicide victims with suicidal inpatients. *Archives of General Psychiatry, 45,* 581–588.

Brentjens, M. H., Yeung-Yue, K. A., Lee, P. C., & Tyring, S. K. (2003). Recurrent genital herpes treatments and their impact on quality of life. *Pharmacoeconomics, 21*(12), 853–863.

Breslau, N., Davis, G. C., & Andreski, M. A. (1995). Risk factors for PTSD-related traumatic events: A prospective analysis. *American Journal of Psychiatry, 152,* 529–535.

Breslau, N., Kilbey, M. M., & Andreski, P. (1993). Nicotine dependence and major depression: New evidence from a prospective investigation. *Archives of General Psychiatry, 50,* 31–35.

Breslau, N., Lucia, V. C., & Alvarado, G. F. (2006). Intelligence and other predisposing factors in exposure to trauma and posttraumatic stress disorder. *Archives of General Psychiatry, 63,* 1238–1245.

Breuer, J., & Freud, S. (1957). *Studies on hysteria.* New York: Basic Books. (Original work published 1895.)

Brewin, C. R., Andrews, B., & Gotlib, I. H. (1993). Psychopathology in early experience: A reappraisal of retrospective reports. *Psychological Bulletin, 113,* 82–98.

Broadhead, W. E., Kaplan, B. H., & James, S. A. (1983). The epidemiologic evidence for a relationship between social support and health. *American Journal of Epidemiology, 117,* 521–537.

Brody, A. L., Saxena, S., Stoessel, P., Gillies, L. A., Fairbanks, L. A., Alborzian, S., et al. (2001). Regional brain metabolic changes in patients with major depression treated with either paroxetine or interpersonal therapy. *Archives of General Psychiatry, 48,* 631–640.

Brody, M. J., Walsh, B. T., & Devlin, M. J. (1994). Binge eating disorder: Reliability and validity of a new diagnostic category. *Journal of Consulting and Clinical Psychology, 62,* 381–386.

Brondolo, E., Rieppi, R., Erickson, S. A., Bagiella, E., Shapiro, P. A., McKinley, P., & Sloan, R. P. (2003). Hostility, interpersonal interactions, and ambulatory blood pressure. *Psychosomatic Medicine, 65,* 1003–1011.

Broude, G. J., & Greene, S. J. (1980). Cross-cultural codes on 20 sexual attitudes and practices. In H. Barry, III, & A. Schlegel (Eds.), *Cross-cultural samples and codes* (pp. 313–333). Pittsburgh: University of Pittsburgh Press.

Broughton, R. J. (2000). NREM arousal parasomnias. In M. H. Kryger, T. Roth, & W. C. Dement (Eds.), *Principles and practice of sleep medicine* (3rd ed., pp. 693–706). Philadelphia: W. B. Saunders.

Broughton, R., Billings, R., & Cartwright, R. (1994). Homicidal somnambulism: A case report. *Sleep, 17,* 253–264.

Brown, D. R., Ahmed, F., Gary, L. E., & Milburn, N. G. (1995). Major depression in a community sample of African Americans. *American Journal of Psychiatry, 152,* 373–378.

Brown, G. K., & Nicassio, P. M. (1987). The development of a questionnaire for the assessment of active and passive coping strategies in chronic pain patients. *Pain, 31,* 53–65.

Brown, G. K., Beck, A. T., Steer, R. A., & Grisham, J. R. (2000). Risk factor for psychiatric outpatients: A 20-year perspective study. *Journal of Consulting and Clinical Psychology, 63*(3), 371–377.

Brown, G. K., Have, T., Henriques, G., Xie, S., Hollander, J., & Beck, A. (2005). Cognitive therapy for the prevention of suicide attempts: A randomized controlled trial. *JAMA, 294,* 563–570.

Brown, G. W. (1959). Experiences of discharged chronic schizophrenic mental hospital patients in various types of living group. *Millbank Memorial Fund Quarterly, 37,* 105–131.

Brown, G. W. (1989a). Depression. In G. W. Brown & T. O. Harris (Eds.), *Life events and illness* (pp. 49–93). New York: Guilford Press.

Brown, G. W. (1989b). Life events and measurement. In G. W. Brown & T. O. Harris (Eds.), *Life events and illness.* New York: Guilford Press.

Brown, G. W., & Birley, J. L. T. (1968). Crisis and life change and the onset of schizophrenia. *Journal of Health and Social Behavior, 9,* 203–214.

Brown, G. W., & Harris, T. O. (1978). *Social origins of depression: A study of psychiatric disorder in women.* London: Tavistock.

Brown, G. W., Harris, T. O., & Hepworth, C. (1994). Life events and endogenous depression. *Archives of General Psychiatry, 51,* 525–534.

Brown, G. W., Monck, E. M., Carstairs, G. M., & Wing, J. K. (1962). Influence of family life on the course of schizophrenic illness. *British Journal of Preventive and Social Medicine, 16,* 55–68.

Brown, J., & Finn, P. (1982). Drinking to get drunk: Findings of a survey of junior and senior high school students. *Journal of Alcohol and Drug Education, 27,* 13–25.

Brown, P. L. (2006). Supporting boys or girls when the line isn't clear. *New York Times,* December 2, 2006.

Brown, T. A., & Barlow, D. H. (2002). Classification of anxiety and mood disorders. In D. H. Barlow, *Anxiety and its disorders: The nature and treatment of anxiety and panic.* (2nd ed.). New York: Guilford Press.

Brown, T. A., & Barlow, D. H. (2005). Dimensional versus categorical classification of mental disorders in the fifth edition of the diagnostic and statistical manual of mental disorders and beyond: Comment on the special section. Special issue: Toward a dimensionally based taxonomy of psychopathology. *Journal of Abnormal Psychology, 114*(4), 551–556.

Brown, T. A., Barlow, D. H., & Liebowitz, M. R. (1994). The empirical basis of generalized anxiety disorder. *American Journal of Psychiatry, 15*(9), 1272–1280.

Brown, T. A., Campbell, L. A., Lehman, C. L., Grisham, J. R., & Mancill, R. B. (2001). Current and lifetime comorbidity of the DSM-IV anxiety and mood disorders in a large clinical sample. *Journal of Abnormal Psychology.*

Brown, T. A., Chorpita, B. F., & Barlow, D. H. (1998). Structural relationships among dimensions of the DSM-IV anxiety and mood disorders and dimensions of negative affect, positive affect, and autonomic arousal. *Journal of Abnormal Psychology, 107*(2), 179–192.

Brown, T. A., Marten, P. A., & Barlow, D. H. (1995). Discriminant validity of the symptoms comprising the DSM-III-R and DSM-IV associated symptom criterion of generalized anxiety disorder. *Journal of Anxiety Disorders, 9,* 317–328.

Brown, T. A., White, K. S., & Barlow, D. H. (2005). A psychometric reanalysis of the Albany panic and phobia questionnaire. *Behaviour Research and Therapy, 43,* 337–355.

Brown, W. M., Finn, C. J., Cooke, B. M., & Breedlove, S. M. (2002). Differences in finger length ratios between self-identified "butch" and "femme" lesbians. *Archives of Sexual Behavior, 31,* 123–127.

Brownell, K. D. (1991). Dieting and the search for the perfect body: Where physiology and culture collide. *Behavior Therapy, 22,* 1–12.

Brownell, K. D. (2002). Eating disorders in athletes. In K. D. Brownell & C. G. Fairburn (Eds.), *Eating disorders and obesity: A comprehensive handbook* (2nd ed., pp. 191–196). New York: Guilford Press.

Brownell, K. D. (2003). *Food fight: The inside story of the food industry, America's obesity crisis and what we can do about it.* New York: McGraw-Hill.

Brownell, K. D., & Fairburn, C. G. (2002). Eating disorders and obesity: A comprehensive handbook (2nd ed.). New York: Guilford Press.

Brownell, K. D., & Fairburn, C. G. (Eds.) (1995). *Eating disorders and obesity: A comprehensive handbook.* New York: Guilford Press.

Brownell, K. D., & Rodin, J. (1994). The dieting maelstrom: Is it possible and advisable to lose weight? *American Psychologist, 49*(9), 781–791.

Brownell, K. D., & Yach, D. (2005). The battle of the bulge. *Foreign Policy,* 26–27.

Brownell, K. D., Hayes, S. C., & Barlow, D. H. (1977). Patterns of appropriate and deviant sexual arousal: The behavioral treatment of multiple sexual deviations. *Journal of Consulting and Clinical Psychology, 45*(6), 1144–1155.

Brownmiller, S. (1984). *Femininity.* New York: Ballantine Books.

Bruce, M. L. (2002). Psychosocial risk factors for depressive disorders in late life. *Biological Psychiatry, 52,* 175–184.

Bruce, M. L., & Kim, K. M. (1992). Differences in the effects of divorce on major depression in men and women. *American Journal of Psychiatry, 149*(7), 914–917.

Bruce, S. E., Vasile, R. G., Goisman, R. M., Salzman, C., Spencer, M., Machan, J. T., & Keller, M. B. (2003). Are benzodiazepines still the medication of choice for patients with panic disorder with or without agoraphobia? *American Journal of Psychiatry, 160,* 1432–1438.

Bruce, S. E., Yonkers, K. A., Otto, M. W., Eisen, J. L., Weisberg, R. B., Pagano, M., et al. (2005). Influence of psychiatric comorbidity on recovery and recurrence in generalized anxiety disorder, social phobia, and panic disorder: A 12-year prospective study. *American Journal of Psychiatry, 162,* 1179–1187.

Bruch, H. (1973). *Eating disorders: Obesity, anorexia nervosa, and the person within.* New York: Basic Books.

Bruch, H. (1985). Four decades of eating disorders. In D. M. Garner & P. E. Garfinkel (Eds.), *Handbook of psychotherapy for anorexia nervosa and bulimia* (pp. 7–18). New York: Guilford Press.

Bruch, M. A., & Heimberg, R. G. (1994). Differences in perceptions of parental and personal characteristics between generalized and non-generalized social phobics. *Journal of Anxiety Disorders, 8,* 155–168.

Bruck, M., Ceci, S., Francouer, E., & Renick, A. (1995). Anatomically detailed dolls do not facilitate preschoolers' reports of a pediatric examination involving genital touching. *Journal of Experimental Psychology: Applied, 1,* 95–109.

Bryant, R. A., Moulds, M. L., & Nixon, R. V. D. (2003). Cognitive behavior therapy of acute stress disorder: A four-year follow-up. *Behaviour Research and Therapy, 41,* 489–494.

Buchanan, R. W., & Carpenter, W. T. (2005). Schizophrenia and other psychotic disorders. In B. J. Sadock & V. A. Sadock (Eds.), *Kaplan & Sadock's comprehensive textbook of psychiatry* (pp. 1329–1345). Philadelphia: Lippincott, Williams & Wilkins.

Buchwald, A. M., & Rudick-Davis, D. (1993). The symptoms of major depression. *Journal of Abnormal Psychology, 102*(2), 197–205.

Buchwald, H., Avidor, Y., Braunwald, E., Jensen, M. D., Pories, W., Fahrbach, K., & Schoelles, K. (2004). Bariatric surgery: A systematic review and meta-analysis. *JAMA, 292,* 1724–1737.

Buda, M., & Tsuang, M. T. (1990). The epidemiology of suicide: Implications for clinical practice. In S. J. Blumenthal & D. J. Kupfer (Eds.), *Suicide over the life cycle: Risk factors, assessment and treatment of suicidal patients.* Washington, DC: American Psychiatric Press.

Buehler, R. E., Patterson, G. R., & Furniss, J. M. (1966). The reinforcement of behavior in institutional settings. *Behavior, Research, and Therapy, 4,* 157–167.

Buffum, J. (1982). Pharmacosexology: The effects of drugs on sexual function—A review. *Journal of Psychoactive Drugs, 14,* 5–44.

Bulik, C. M., Sullivan, P. F., & Kendler, K. S. (2000). An empirical study of the classification of eating disorders. *American Journal of Psychiatry, 157*(6), 886–895.

Bulik, C. M., Sullivan, P. F., Tozzi, F., Furberg, H., Lichtenstin, P., & Pederson, N. L. (2006). Prevalence, heritability, and prospective risk factors, for anorexia nervosa. *Archives of General Psychiatry, 63,* 305–312.

Burleson, J. A., & Kaminer, Y. (2005). Self-efficacy as a predictor of treatment outcome in adolescent substance use disorders. *Addictive Behaviors, 30,* 1751–1764.

Burnette, M. M., Koehn, K. A., Kenyon-Jump, R., Hutton, K., & Stark, C. (1991). Control of genital herpes recurrences using progressive muscle relaxation. *Behavior Therapy, 22,* 237–247.

Burns, J. W., Glenn, B., Bruehl, S., Harden, R. N., & Lofland, K. (2003). Cognitive factors influence outcome following multidisciplinary chronic pain treatment: A replication and extension of a cross-lagged panel analysis. *Behaviour Research and Therapy, 41,* 1163–1182.

Burton, R. (1977). *Anatomy of melancholy.* (Reprint edition). New York: Random House. (Original work published 1621.)

Bushman, B. J. (1993). Human aggression while under the influence of alcohol and other drugs: An integrative research review. *Psychological Science, 2,* 148–152.

Bustillo, J. R., Lauriello, J., Horan, W. P., & Keith, S. J. (2001). The psychosocial treatment of schizophrenia: An update. *American Journal of Psychiatry, 158*(2), 163–175.

Butcher, J. N. (2006). *MMPI-2: A practitioners guide.* Washington, DC: American Psychological Association.

Butcher, J. N., Graham, J. R., Williams, C. L., & Ben-Porath, Y. S. (1990). *Development and use of the MMPI-2 content scales.* Minneapolis: University of Minnesota Press.

Butler, B. (2006). NGRI revisited: Venirepersons' attitudes toward the insanity defense. *Journal of Applied Social Psychology, 36,* 1833–1847.

Butler, G., & Mathews, A. (1983). Cognitive processes in anxiety. *Advances in Behaviour Research and Therapy, 5,* 51–62.

Butler, L. D., Duran, R. E. F., Jasiukaitis, P., Koopman, C., & Spiegel, D. (1996). Hypnotizability and traumatic experience: A diathesis stress model of dissociative symptomatology. *American Journal of Psychiatry, 153,* 42–63.

Butzlaff, R. L., & Hooley, J. M. (1998). Expressed emotion and psychiatric relapse. *Archives of General Psychiatry, 55,* 547–552.

Buysse, D. J., Reynolds, C. F., & Kupfer, D. J. (1993). Classification of sleep disorders: A preview of the DSM-IV. In D. L. Dunner (Ed.), *Current psychiatric therapy* (pp. 360–361). Philadelphia: W. B. Saunders.

Buysse, D. J., Tu, X. M., Cherry, C. R., Begley, A. E., Kowalski, J., Kupfer, D. J., & Frank, E. (1999). Pretreatment REM sleep and subjective sleep quality distinguish depressed psychotherapy remitters and nonremitters. *Biological Psychiatry, 45*(2), 205–213.

Bye, E. K. (2007). Alcohol and violence: Use of possible confounders in a time-series analysis. *Addiction, 102,* 369–376.

Byne, W., & Parsons, B. (1993). Human sexual orientation: The biologic theories reappraised. *Archives of General Psychiatry, 50,* 228–239.

Byne, W., Lasco, M. S., Kemether, E., Edgar, M. A., Morgello, S., Jones, L. B., & Tobet, S. (2000). The interstitial nuclei of the human anterior hypothalamus: An investigation of sexual variation in volume and cell size, number and density. *Brain Research, 856,* 254–258.

Byrne, D., & Schulte, L. (1990). Personality dispositions as mediators of sexual responses. *Annual Review of Sex Research, 1,* 93–117.

Byrne, Z., & Hochwarter, W. (2006). I get by with a little help from my friends: The interaction of chronic pain and organizational support and performance. *Journal of Occupational Health Psychology, 11,* 215–227.

Cadoret, R. J. (1978). Psychopathology in the adopted-away offspring of biologic parents with antisocial behavior. *Archives of General Psychiatry, 35,* 176–184.

Cadoret, R. J., Yates, W. R., Troughton, E., Woodworth, G., & Stewart, M. A. (1995). Genetic–environment interaction in the genesis of aggressivity and conduct disorders. *Archives of General Psychiatry, 52,* 916–924.

Cafri, G., Yamamiya, Y., Brannick, M., & Thompson, J. K. (2005). The influence of sociocultural factors on body image: A meta-analysis. *Clinical Psychology: Science and Practice, 12,* 421–433.

Calabrese, J., Shelton, M, Rapport, D., Youngstrom, E., Jackson, K., Bilali, S., et al. (2005). A 20-month, double-blind, maintenance trial of lithium versus divalproex, in rapid-cycling bipolar disorder. *American Journal of Psychiatry, 162,* 2152–2161.

Calamari, J. E., Wiegartz, P. S., Riemann, B. C., Cohen, R. J., Greer, A., Jacobi, D. M., et al. (2004). Obsessive-compulsive disorder subtypes: An attempted replication and extension of symptom-based taxonomy. *Behavior Research and Therapy, 42,* 647–670.

Callahan, L. A., McGreevy, M. A., Cirincione, C., & Steadman, H. J. (1992). Measuring the effects of the guilty but mentally ill (GBMI) verdict: Georgia's 1982 GBMI reform. *Law and Human Behavior, 16,* 447–462.

Callicott, J. H., Mattay, V. S., Verchinski, B. A., Marenco, S., Egan, M. F., & Weinberger, D. R. (2003). Complexity of prefrontal cortical dysfunction in schizophrenia: More than up or down. *American Journal of Psychiatry, 160,* 2209–2215.

Cameron, N. M., Champagne, F. A., Parent, C., Fish, E. W., Ozaki-Kuroda, K., & Meaney, M. J. (2005). The programming of individual differences in defensive responses and reproductive strategies in the rat through variations in maternal care. *Neuroscience and Biobehavioral Reviews, 29,* 843–865.

Campbell-Sills, L., & Barlow, D. H. (2007). Incorporating emotion regulation into conceptualization and treatment of anxiety and mood disorders. In J. J. Gross (Ed.), *Handbook of emotion regulation* (pp. 542–560). New York: Guilford Press.

Campo, J. A., Nijman, H., Merckelbach, H., & Evers, C. (2003). Psychiatric comorbidity of gender identity disorders: A survey among Dutch psychiatrists. *American Journal of Psychiatry, 160,* 1332–1336.

Campo, J. V., & Negrini, B. J. (2000). Case study: Negative reinforcement and behavioral management of conversion disorder. *Journal of the American Academy of Child and Adolescent Psychiatry, 39*(6), 787–790.

Cannon, T. D., Barr, C. E., & Mednick, S. A. (1991). Genetic and perinatal factors in the etiology of schizophrenia. In E. F. Walker (Ed.), *Schizophrenia: A life-course developmental perspective* (pp. 9–31). New York: Academic Press.

Cannon, W. B. (1929). *Bodily changes in pain, hunger, fear and rage* (2nd ed.). New York: Appleton-Century-Crofts.

Cannon, W. B. (1942). Voodoo death. *American Anthropologist, 44,* 169–181.

Canter, A. (1996). The Bender-Gesalt Test (BGT). In C. S. Newmark (Ed.), *Major psychological assessment instruments* (pp. 400–430). Boston: Allyn & Bacon.

Cantor, J. M., Blanchard, R., Paterson, A. D., & Bogaert, A. F. (2002). How many gay men owe their sexual orientation to fraternal birth order? *Archives of Sexual Behavior, 31,* 63–71.

Capobianco, D. J., Swanson, J. W., & Dodick, D. W. (2001). Medication-induced (analgesic rebound) headache: Historical aspects and initial descriptions of the North American experience. *Headache, 41,* 500–502.

Cardeña, E. A., & Gleaves, D. H. (2003). Dissociative disorders: Phantoms of the self. Kirmayer, L. J., Looper, K. J., & Taillefer, S. (2003). Somatoform disorders. In M. Hersen & S. M. Turner (Eds.), *Adult psychopathology and diagnosis* (4th ed., pp. 476–505). New York: John Wiley.

Cardeña, E., Lewis-Fernandez, R., Bear, D., Pakianathan, I., & Spiegel, D. (1996). Dissociative disorders. In T. A. Widiger, A. J. Frances, H. A. Pincus, R. Ross, M. B. First, & W. W. Davis (Eds.), *DSM-IV sourcebook* (Vol. 2, pp. 973–1005). Washington, DC: American Psychiatric Press.

Carey, G. (1992). Twin imitation for antisocial behavior: Implications for genetic and family environment research. *Journal of Abnormal Psychology, 101,* 18–25.

Carey, M. P., Wincze, J. P., & Meisler, A. W. (1993). Sexual dysfunction: Male erectile disorder. In D. H. Barlow (Ed.), *Clinical handbook of psychological disorders* (2nd ed., pp. 442–480). New York Guilford Press.

Carlat, D. J., & Camargo, C. A., Jr., & Herzog, D. B. (1997). Eating disorders in males: A report on 135 patients. *American Journal of Psychiatry, 154,* 1127–1132.

Carlson, C. L., Lahey, B. B., & Neeper, R. (1984). Peer assessment of the social behavior of accepted, rejected, and neglected children. *Journal of Abnormal Child Psychology, 12,* 189–198.

Carlson, E. B., & Putnam, F. W. (1989). Integrating research on dissociation and hypnotizability: Are there two pathways to hypnotizability? *Dissociation, 2,* 32–38.

Carlson, G. A. (1990). Annotation: Child and adolescent mania—Diagnostic considerations. *Journal of Child Psychology and Psychiatry, 31*(3), 331–341.

Carlson, G. A., & Kashani, J. H. (1988). Phenomenology of major depression from childhood through adulthood: Analysis of three studies. *American Journal of Psychiatry, 145,* 1222–1225.

Carnine, D., Silbert, J., Kame'enui, E., & Tarver, S. (2004). *Direct instruction reading* (4th ed.). Upper Saddle River, NJ: Pearson.

Caron, C., & Rutter, M. (1991). Comorbidity in childhood psychopathology: Concepts, issues, and research strategies. *Journal of Child Psychology and Psychiatry, 32,* 1063–1080.

Carpenter, W. T., Appelbaum, P. S., & Levine, R. J. (2003). The Declaration of Helsinki and clinical trials: A focus on placebo-controlled trials in schizophrenia. *American Journal of Psychiatry, 160,* 356–362.

Carpentier, M., Silovsky, J., & Chaffin, M. (2006). Randomized trial of treatment for children with sexual behavior problems: Ten-year follow-up. *Journal of Consulting and Clinical Psychology, 74,* 482–488.

Carroll, B. C., McLaughlin, T. J., & Blake, D. R. (2006). Patterns and knowledge of nonmedical use of stimulants among college students. *Archives of Pediatrics and Adolescent Medicine, 160,* 481–485.

Carroll, B. J., Feinberg, M., Greden, J. F., Haskett, R. F., James, N. M., Steiner, M., & Tarika, J. (1980). Diagnosis of endogenous depression: Comparison of clinical, research, and neuroendocrine criteria. *Journal of Affective Disorders, 2,* 177–194.

Carroll, B. J., Martin, F. I., & Davies, B. (1968). Resistance to suppression by dexamethasone of plasma 11-O.H.C.S. levels in severe depressive illness. *British Medical Journal, 3,* 285–287.

Carroll, E. M., Rueger, D. B., Foy, D. W., & Donahoe, C. P. (1985). Vietnam combat veterans with post-traumatic stress disorder: Analysis of marital and cohabitating adjustment. *Journal of Abnormal Psychology, 94,* 329–337.

Carroll, R. A. (2000). Assessment and treatment of gender dysphoria. In S. R. Leiblum & R. C. Rosen (Eds.), *Principles and practice of sex therapy* (3rd ed., pp. 368–397). New York: Guilford Press.

Carson, R. C. (1991). Discussion: Dilemmas in the pathway of DSM-IV. *Journal of Abnormal Psychology, 100,* 302–307.

Carson, R. C. (1996). Aristotle, Galileo, and the *DSM* taxonomy: The case of schizophrenia. *Journal of Consulting and Clinical Psychology, 64*(6), 1133–1139.

Cartensen, L. L., Charles, S. T., Isaacowitz, D., & Kennedy, Q. (2003). Life-span personality development and emotion. In R. J. Davidson, K. Scherer, & H. H. Goldsmith (Eds.), *Handbook of affective sciences* (pp. 931–951). Oxford: Oxford University Press.

Carter, J. C., & Fairburn, C. G. (1998). Cognitive-behavioral self-help for binge eating disorder: A controlled effectiveness study. *Journal of Consulting and Clinical Psychology, 66,* 616–623.

Carter, J. S., Garber, J., Cielsa, J., & Cole, D. (2006). Modeling relations between hassles and internalizing and externalizing symptoms in adolescents: A four-year prospective study. *Journal of Abnormal Psychology, 115,* 428–442.

Carter, R. M., Wittchen, H. U., Pfister, H., & Kessler, R. C. (2001). One-year prevalence of subthreshold and threshold DSM-IV generalized anxiety disorder in a nationally representative sample. *Depression & Anxiety, 13,* 78–88.

Cartwright, R. D. (2006). Sleepwalking. In T. Lee-Chiong (Ed.), *Sleep: A comprehensive handbook* (pp. 429–433). Hoboken, NJ: John Wiley & Sons.

Cash, T. F., & Pruzinsky, T. (2002). Understanding body images. In T. F. Cash & T. Pruzinsky (Eds.), *Body image: A handbook of theory, research and clinical practice* (pp. 3–12). New York: Guilford Press.

Cash, T. F., Morrow, J. A., Hrabosky, J. I., & Perry, A. A. (2004). How has body image changed? A cross sectional investigation of college women and men from 1983 to 2001. *Journal of Consulting and Clinical Psychology, 72,* 1081–1089.

Casper, R. C. (1982). Treatment principles in anorexia nervosa. *Adolescent Psychiatry, 10,* 431–454.

Caspi, A., Elder, G. H., Jr., & Bem, D. L. (1987). Moving against the world: Life-course patterns of explosive children. *Developmental Psychology, 23,* 308–313.

Caspi, A., McClay, J., Moffitt, T. E., Mill, J., Martin, J., Craig, I. W., et al. (2002). Role of genotype in the cycle of violence in maltreated children. *Science, 297,* 851–853.

Caspi, A., Sugden, K., Moffitt, T. E., Taylor, A., Craig, I. W., Harrington, H., et al. (2003). Influence of life stress on depression: Moderation by a polymorphism in the 5-HTT gene. *Science, 301,* 386–389.

Cassano, G., Rucci, P., Frank, E., Fagiolini, A., Dell'Osso, L., Shear, K., et al. (2004). The mood spectrum in unipolar and bipolar disorder: Arguments for a unitary approach. *American Journal Psychiatry, 161,* 1264–1269.

Cassidy, F., Forest, K., Murry, E., & Carroll, B. J. (1998). A factor analysis of the signs and symptoms of mania. *Archives of General Psychiatry, 55,* 27–32.

Castonguay, L. G., Eldredge, K. L., & Agras, W. S. (1995). Binge eating disorder: Current state and directions. *Clinical Psychology Review, 15,* 815–890.

Catania, J. A., Morin, S. F., Canchola, J., Pollack, L., Chang, J., & Coates, T. J. (2000). U.S. priorities—HIV prevention. *Science, 290,* 717.

Cautela, J. R. (1966). Treatment of compulsive behavior by covert sensitization. *Psychological Record, 16,* 33–41.

Cautela, J. R. (1967). Covert sensitization. *Psychological Reports, 20,* 459–468.

Ceci, S. J. (1995). False beliefs: Some developmental and clinical considerations. In D. L. Schacter (Ed.), *Memory distortion: How minds, brains, and societies reconstruct the past* (pp. 91–125). Cambridge, MA: Harvard University Press.

Ceci, S. J. (2003). Cast in six ponds and you'll reel in something: Looking back on 25 years of research. *American Psychologist, 58,* 855–867.

Celio, A. A., Winzelberg, A. J., Dev, P., & Taylor, C. B. (2002). Improving compliance in on-line, structured self-help programs: Evaluation of an eating disorder prevention program. *Journal of Psychiatric Practice, 8,* 14–20.

Celio, A. A., Zabinski, M. F., & Wilfley, D. E. (2002). African American body images. In T. F. Cash & T. Pruzinsky (Eds.), *Body image: A handbook of theory, research and clinical practice* (pp. 234–242). New York: Guilford Press.

Centers for Disease Control and Prevention. (1994, September). *HIV/AIDS surveillance.* Atlanta: U.S. Department of Health and Human Services, Public Health Service.

Centers for Disease Control and Prevention. (2003a). Deaths: Final data for 2001. *National Vital Statistics Reports, 52*(3). Hyattsville, MD: National Center for Health Statistics.

Centers for Disease Control and Prevention. (2003b). Deaths, percent of total deaths, and death rates for the 15 leading causes of death in 5-year age groups, by race and sex: United States, 2000. Centers for Disease Control and National Center for Health Statistics, National Vital Statistics System.

Centers for Disease Control and Prevention. (2005). Prevalence of diagnosis and medication treatment for attention-deficit/hyperactivity disorder: United States, 2003. *MMWR, 54,* 842–847.

Centers for Disease Control and Prevention. (2007). Prevalence of autism spectrum disorders: Autism and developmental disabilities monitoring network, six sites, United States, 2000. Surveillance summaries, 2002. *MMWR, 56,* 1–11.

Centers for Disease Control and Prevention. (2007, March). *Cases of HIV infection and AIDS in the United States and dependant areas.* Atlanta: U.S. Department of Health and Human Services, Public Health Services.

Chakrabarti, S., & Fombonne, E. (2001). Pervasive developmental disorders in preschool children. *JAMA, 285,* 3093–3099.

Chalder, T., Cleare, A., & Wessely, S. (2000). The management of stress and anxiety in chronic fatigue syndrome. In D. I. Mostofsky & D. H. Barlow (Eds.), *The management of stress and anxiety in medical disorders* (pp. 160–179). Needham Heights, MA: Allyn & Bacon.

Chamberlain, S. R., Menzies, L., Sahakian, B. J., & Fineberg, N. A. (2007). Lifting the veil on trichotillomania. *American Journal of Psychiatry, 164,* 568–574.

Chambless, D. L., Cherney, J., Caputo, G. C., & Rheinstein, B. J. G. (1987). Anxiety disorders and alcoholism: A study with inpatient alcoholics. *Journal of Anxiety Disorders, 1,* 29–40.

Chan, C. H., Janicak, P. G., Davis, J. M., & Altman, E. (1987). Response of psychotic and nonpsychotic depressed patients to tricyclic antidepressants. *Journal of Clinical Psychiatry, 48,* 197–200.

Charney, D. S., Barlow, D. H., Botteron, K., Cohen, J. D., Goldman, D., Raquel, E. G., et al. (2002). Neuroscience research agenda to guide development of a pathophysiologically based classification system. In D. J. Kupfer, M. B. First & D. A. Regier (Eds.), *A research agenda for DSM-V* (pp. 31–83). Washington, DC: American Psychiatric Association.

Charney, D. S., & Drevets, W. C. (2002). Neurobiological basis of anxiety disorders. In K. L. Davis, D. Charney, J. T. Coyle & C. Nemeroff (Eds.), *Neuropsychopharmacology: The fifth generation of progress* (pp. 901–951). Philadelphia: Lippincott Williams & Wilkins.

Charney, D. S., Deutch, A. Y., Krystal, J. H., Southwick, S. M., & Davis, M. (1993). Psychobiological mechanisms of posttraumatic stress disorder. *Archives of General Psychiatry, 50,* 294–305.

Charney, D. S., Woods, S. W., Price, L. H., Goodman, W. K., Glazer, W. M., & Heninger, G. R. (1990). Noradrenergic dysregulation in panic disorder. In J. C. Ballenger (Ed.), *Neurobiology of panic disorder* (pp. 91–105). New York: Wiley-Liss.

Chassin, L., Pillow, D. R., Curran, P. J., Molina, B. S. G., & Barrera, M. (1993). Relation of parental alcoholism to early adolescent substance use: A test of three mediating mechanisms. *Journal of Abnormal Psychology, 102,* 3–19.

Chassin, L., Presson, C. C., Rose, J. S., & Sherman, S. J. (2001). From adolescence to adulthood: Age-related changes in beliefs about cigarette smoking in a midwestern community sample. *Health Psychology, 20,* 377–386.

Chastain, G. (2006). Alcohol, neurotransmitter systems, and behavior. *Journal of General Psychology, 133,* 329–335.

Chavez, M., & Insel, T. R. (2007). Eating disorders: National Institute of Mental Health perspective. *American Psychologist, 62,* 159–166.

Check, J. R. (1998). Munchausen syndrome by proxy: An atypical form of child abuse. *Journal of Practical Behavioral Health, 4,* 340–345.

Check, J. R. (2005). Munchausen syndrome by proxy: An atypical form of child abuse. *Journal of Practical Behavioral Health, 4,* 340–345.

Chesney, M. A. (1986, November). *Type A behavior: The biobehavioral interface.* Keynote address presented at the annual meeting of the Association for Advancement of Behavior Therapy, Chicago.

Cheung, F. M. (1995). Facts and myths about somatization among the Chinese. In T. Y. Lin, W. S. Tseng, & E. K. Yeh (Eds.), *Chinese societies and mental health* (pp. 156–166). Hong Kong: Oxford University Press.

Cheung, F. M. (1998). Cross-cultural psychopathology. *Comprehensive Clinical Psychology, 10,* 35–51.

Cheung, Y., Law, C., Chan, B, Liu, K., & Yip, P. (2006). Suicidal ideation and suicidal attempts in a population based study of Chinese people: Risk attributable to hopelessness, depression, and social factors. *Journal of Affective Disorders, 90,* 193–199.

China U.N. Theme Group on HIV/AIDS for the U.N. Country Team in China. (2001). HIV/AIDS: China's titanic peril. In *2001 update of the AIDS situation and needs assessment report.* Beijing: UNAIDS.

Chioqueta, A., & Stiles, T. (2004). Suicide risk in patients with somatization disorder. *Crisis: The Journal of Crisis Intervention and Suicide Prevention, 25*(1), 3–7.

Chivers, M. L., & Bailey, J. M. (2000). Sexual orientation of female-to-male transsexuals: A comparison of homosexual and nonhomosexual types. *Archives of Sexual Behavior, 29*(3), 259–279.

Chivers, M. L., Rieger, G., Latty, E., & Bailey, M. (2004). A sex difference in the specificity of sexual arousal. *Psychological Science, 15,* 736–744.

Choate, M. L., Pincus, D. B., Eyberg, S. M., & Barlow, D. B. (2005). Parent–child interaction therapy for treatment of separation anxiety disorder: A pilot study. *Cognitive and Behavioral Practice, 12*(1), 126–135.

Chodoff, P. (1974). The diagnosis of hysteria: An overview. *American Journal of Psychiatry, 131,* 1073–1078.

Chodoff, P. (1982). Hysteria in women. *American Journal of Psychiatry, 139,* 545–551.

Chorpita, B. F., & Barlow, D. H. (1998). The development of anxiety: The role of control in the early environment. *Psychological Bulletin, 124*(1), 3–21.

Chorpita, B. F., Brown, T. A., & Barlow, D. H. (1998). Perceived control as a mediator of family environment in etiological models of childhood anxiety. *Behavior Therapy, 29,* 457–476.

Chorpita, B. F., Vitali, A. E., & Barlow, D. H. (1997). Behavioral treatment of choking phobia in an adolescent: An experimental analysis. *Journal of Behavior Therapy & Experimental Psychiatry, 28*(4), 307–315.

Christenson, R., & Blazer, D. (1984). Epidemiology of persecutory ideation in an elderly population in the community. *American Journal of Psychiatry, 141,* 1088–1091.

Christiansen, B. A., Smith, G. T., Roehling, P.V., & Goldman, M. S. (1989). Using alcohol expectancies to predict adolescent drinking behavior after one year. *Journal of Consulting and Clinical Psychology, 57,* 93–99.

Chronis, A. M., Lahey, B. B., Pelham, W. E., Jr., Williams, S. H., Baumann, B. L., Kipp, H., et al. (2007). Maternal depression and early positive parenting predict future conduct problems in young children with attention-deficit/hyperactivity disorder. *Developmental Psychology, 43,* 70–82.

Chung, S.Y., Luk, S. L., & Lee, P. W. H. (1990). A follow-up study of infantile autism in Hong Kong. *Journal of Autism and Developmental Disorders, 20,* 221–232.

Cicchetti, D. (1991). A historical perspective on the discipline of developmental psychopathology. In J. Rolf, A. S. Masten, D. Cicchetti, K. H. Nuechterlein, & S. Weintraub (Eds.), *Risk and protective factors in the development of psychopathology* (pp. 2–28). New York: Cambridge University Press.

Cipani, E. (1991). Educational classification and placement. In J. L. Matson & J. A. Mulick (Eds.), *Handbook of mental retardation* (2nd ed., pp. 181–191). Elmsford, NY: Pergamon Press.

Clancy, S. A., McNally, R. J., Schacter, D. L., Lenzenweger, M. F., & Pitman, R. K. (2002). Memory distortion in people reporting abduction by aliens. *Journal of Abnormal Psychology, 111,* 455–461.

Clark, D. A., & O'Connor, K. (2005). Thinking is believing: Ego-dystonic intrusive thoughts in obsessive-compulsive disorder. In D. A. Clark (Ed.), *Intrusive Thoughts in Clinical Disorders* (pp. 145–174). New York: Guilford Press.

Clark, D. A., & Rhyno, S. (2005). Unwanted intrusive thoughts in nonclinical individuals: Implications for clinical disorders. In D. A. Clark (Ed.), *Intrusive thoughts in clinical disorders* (pp. 1–29). New York: Guilford Press.

Clark, D. M. (1986). A cognitive approach to panic. *Behaviour Research and Therapy, 24,* 461–470.

Clark, D. M. (1996). Panic disorder: From theory to therapy. In P. Salkovskis (Ed.), *Frontiers of cognitive therapy* (pp. 318–344). New York: Guilford Press.

Clark, D. M., Ehlers, A., Hackman, A., McManus, F., Fennell, M., Grey, N., et al. (2006). Cognitive therapy versus exposure and applied relaxation in social phobia: A randomized controlled trial. *Journal of Consulting and Clinical Psychology, 74,* 568–578.

Clark, D. M., Ehlers, A., McManus, F., Hackman, A., Fennell, M. J. V., Campbell, H., et al. (2003). Cognitive therapy versus fluoxetine in generalized social phobia: A randomized placebo-controlled trial. *Journal of Consulting and Clinical Psychology, 71,* 1058–1067.

Clark, D. M., Salkovskis, P. M. N., Hackmann, A., Wells, A., Fennell, M., Ludgate, S., et al. (1998). Two psychological treatments for hypochondriasis. *British Journal of Psychiatry, 173,* 218–225.

Clark, D. M., Salkovskis, P. M., Hackmann, A., Middleton, H., Anastasiades, P., & Gelder, M. (1994). A comparison of cognitive therapy, applied relaxation and imipramine in the treatment of panic disorder. *British Journal of Psychiatry.*

Clark, L. A. (1999). Introduction to the special section on the concept of disorder. *Journal of Abnormal Psychology, 108,* 371–373.

Clark, L. A. (2005). Temperament as a unifying basis for personality and psychopathology [Special issue]. *Journal of Abnormal Psychology, 114,* 505–521.

Clark, L. A., & Watson, D. (1991). Tripartite model of anxiety and depression: Psychometric evidence and taxonomic implications. Special issue: Diagnoses, dimensions, and DSM-IV: The science of classification. *Journal of Abnormal Psychology, 100*(3), 316–336.

Clark, R. (2003). Parental history of hypertension and coping responses predict blood pressure changes in black college volunteers undergoing a speaking task about perceptions of racism. *Psychosomatic Medicine, 65,* 1012–1019.

Clarkin, J. F., Carpenter, D., Hull, J., Wilner, P., & Glick, I. (1998). Effects of psychoeducational intervention for married patients with bipolar disorder and their spouses. *Psychiatric Services, 49*(4), 531–533.

Clarkin, J. F., Haas, G. L., & Glick, I. D. (1988). *Affective disorders in the family.* New York: Guilford Press.

Classen, C., Diamond, S., & Spiegel, D. (1998). Studies of life-extending psychosocial interventions. In J. Holland (Ed.), *Psycho-oncology.* Oxford: Oxford University Press.

Clayton, P. J., & Darvish, H. S. (1979). Course of depressive symptoms following the stress of bereavement. In J. E. Barrett (Ed.), *Stress and mental disorder.* New York: Raven.

Cleckley, H. M. (1982). *The mask of sanity* (6th ed.). St. Louis: Mosby. (Original work published 1941.)

Cleghorn, J. M., & Albert, M. L. (1990). Modular disjunction in schizophrenia: A framework for a pathological psychophysiology. In A. Kales, C. N. Stefanis, & J. A. Talbot (Eds.), *Recent advances in schizophrenia* (pp. 59–80). New York: Springer-Verlag.

Cleghorn, J. M., Franco, S., Szechtman, B., Kaplan, R. D., Szechtman, H., Brown, G. M., et al. (1992). To-

ward a brain map of auditory hallucinations. *American Journal of Psychiatry, 149,* 1062–1069.

Clement, U. (1990). Surveys of heterosexual behavior. *Annual Review of Sex Research, 1,* 45–74.

Clementz, B. A., & Sweeney, J. A. (1990). Is eye movement dysfunction a biological marker for schizophrenia? A methodological review. *Psychological Bulletin, 108,* 77–92.

Cloninger, C. R. (1978). The link between hysteria and sociopathy: An integrative model of pathogenesis based on clinical, genetic, and neurophysiological observations. In H. S. Akiskal & W. L. Webb (Eds.), *Psychiatric diagnosis: Exploration of biological predictors* (pp. 189–218). New York: Spectrum.

Cloninger, C. R. (1987). A systematic method for clinical description and classification of personality variants: A proposal. *Archives of General Psychiatry, 44,* 573–588.

Cloninger, C. R. (1989). Establishment of diagnostic validity in psychiatric illness: Robins and Guze's method revisited. In L. N. Robins & J. E. Barrett (Eds.), *The validity of psychiatric diagnosis* (pp. 9–16). New York: Raven Press.

Cloninger, C. R. (1996). Somatization disorder. Literature review for DSM-IV sourcebook. Washington, DC: American Psychiatric Press.

Closser, M. H. (1992). Cocaine epidemiology. In T. R. Kosten & H. D. Kleber (Eds.), *Clinician's guide to cocaine addiction: Theory, research, and treatment* (pp. 225–240). New York: Guilford Press.

Coates, T. J. (1990). Strategies for modifying sexual behavior for primary and secondary prevention of HIV disease. *Journal of Consulting and Clinical Psychology, 58*(1), 57–69.

Cobb, S. (1976). Social support as a moderator of life stress. *Psychosomatic Medicine, 38,* 300.

Cochran, S. D. (1984). Preventing medical noncompliance in the outpatient treatment of bipolar affective disorders. *Journal of Consulting and Clinical Psychology, 52*(5), 873–878.

Cocores, J. A., Miller, N. S., Pottash, A. C., & Gold, M. S. (1988). Sexual dysfunction in abusers of cocaine and alcohol. *American Journal of Drug and Alcohol Abuse, 14,* 169–173.

Coderre, T. J., Katz, J., Vaccarino, A. L., & Melzack, R. (1993). Contribution of central neuroplasticity to pathological pain: Review of clinical and experimental evidence. *Pain, 52,* 259–285.

Cohen, A. S., Barlow, D. H., & Blanchard, E. B., 1985. Psychophysiology of relaxation-associated panic attacks. *Journal of Abnormal Psychology, 94,* 98.

Cohen, J. (2002). Confronting the limits of success. *Science, 296,* 2320–2324.

Cohen, J. (2004). Asia and Africa: On different trajectories? *Science Magazine, 304,* 1932–1938.

Cohen, J. (2006, July 28th). The overlooked epidemic. *Science Magazine, 313,* 468–469.

Cohen, J. B., & Reed, D. (1985). Type A behavior and coronary heart disease among Japanese men in Hawaii. *Journal of Behavioral Medicine, 8,* 343–352.

Cohen, L., Soares, C., Vitonis, A., Otto, M., & Harlow, B. (2006). Risk for new onset of depression during the menopausal transition. *Archive General Psychiatry, 63,* 385–390.

Cohen, S. (1996). Psychological stress, immunity, and upper respiratory infections. *Current Directions in Psychological Science, 5,* 86–90.

Cohen, S., & Herbert, T. B. (1996). Health psychology: Psychological factors and physical disease from the perspective of human psychoneuroimmunology. *Annual Review of Psychology, 47,* 113–142.

Cohen, S., Doyle, W. J., & Skoner, D. P. (1999). Psychological stress, cytokine production, and severity of upper respiratory illness. *Psychosomatic Medicine, 61,* 175–180.

Cohen, S., Doyle, W. J., Skoner, D. P., Fireman, P., Gwaltney, J. M., Jr., & Newsome, J. T. (1995). State and trait negative affect as predictors of objective and subjective symptoms of respiratory viral infec-

tions. *Journal of Personality and Social Psychology, 68,* 159–169.

Cohen, S., Doyle, W. J., Turner, R., Alper, C. M., & Skoner, D. P. (2003). Sociability and susceptibility to the common cold. *Psychological Science, 14*(5), 389–395.

Cohen, S., Doyle, W., Skoner, D. P., Rabin, B. S., & Gwaltney, J. M. (1997). Social ties and susceptibility to the common cold. *JAMA, 277,* 1940–1944.

Cohen, S., Tyrrell, D. A., & Smith, A. P. (1991). Psychological stress and susceptibility to the common cold. *New England Journal of Medicine, 325,* 606–612.

Cohen, S., Tyrrell, D. A., & Smith, A. P. (1993). Negative life events, perceived stress, negative affect, and susceptibility to the common cold. *Journal of Personality and Social Psychology, 64*(1), 131–140.

Cohn, S. E. (2003). Women with HIV/AIDS: Treating the fastest-growing population. *The AIDS Reader, 13*(5): 241–242, 244.

Col, N., Fanale, J. E., & Kronholm, P. (1990). The role of medical noncompliance and adverse drug reactions in hospitalizations of the elderly. *Archives of Internal Medicine, 150,* 841–845.

Cole, M. G. (2004). Delirium in elderly patients. *American Journal of Geriatric Psychiatry, 12,* 7–21.

Cole, M., Winkelman, M. D., Morris, J. C., Simon, J. E., & Boyd, T. A. (1992). Thalamic amnesia: Korsakoff syndrome due to left thalamic infarction. *Journal of the Neurological Sciences, 110,* 62–67.

Coleman, E., Bockting, W. O., & Gooren, L. (1993). Homosexual and bisexual identity in sex-reassigned female-to-male transsexuals. *Archives of Sexual Behavior, 22,* 37–50.

Coleman, E., Colgan, P., & Gooren, L. (1992). Male cross-gender behavior in Myanmar (Burma): A description of the acault. *Archives of Sexual Behavior, 21*(3), 313–321.

Collinge, J., Whitfield, J., McKintosh, E., Beck, J., Mead, S., Thomas, D. J., & Alpers, M. P. (2006). Kuru in the 21st century: An acquired human prion disease with very long incubation periods. *Lancet, 367,* 2068–2074.

Collins, W. A., Maccoby, E. E., Steinberg, L., Hetherington, E. M., & Bornstein, M. H. (2000). Contemporary research on parenting: The case for nature and nurture. *American Psychologist, 55,* 218–232.

Comas-Diaz, L. (1981). Puerto Rican *espiritismo* and psychotherapy. *American Journal of Orthopsychiatry, 51*(4), 636–645.

Compas, B. E., Boyer, M., Stanger, C., Colletti, R., & Thomsen, A. (2006). Latent variable analysis of coping, anxiety/depression, and somatic symptoms in adolescents with chronic pain. *Journal of Consulting and Clinical Psychology, 74,* 1132–1142.

Compas, B. E., Oppedisano, G., Connor, J. K., Gerhardt, C. A., Hinden, B. R., Achenbach, T. M., & Hammen, C. (1997). Gender differences in depressive symptoms in adolescence: Comparison of national samples of clinically referred and nonreferred youths. *Journal of Consulting and Clinical Psychology, 65,* 617–626.

Compton, D. L., Fuchs, D., Fuchs, L. S., & Bryant, J. D. (2006). Selecting at-risk readers in first grade for early intervention: A two-year longitudinal study of decision rules and procedures. *Journal of Educational Psychology, 98,* 394–409.

Compton, W. M., Thomas, Y. F., Conway, K. P., & Colliver, J. D. (2005). Developments in the epidemiology of drug use and drug use disorders. *American Journal of Psychiatry, 162,* 1494–1502.

Condelli, W. S., Fairbank, J. A., Dennis, M. L., & Rachal, J. V. (1991). Cocaine use by clients in methadone programs: Significance, scope, and behavioral interventions. *Journal of Substance Abuse Treatment, 8,* 203–212.

Condon, W., Ogston, W., & Pacoe, L. (1969). Three faces of Eve revisited: A study of transient microstrabismus. *Journal of Abnormal Psychology, 74,* 618–620.

Conn. Gen. Stat. Ann. (1992). 319: Part II, 17a–495.

Conners, C. K., March, J. S., Frances, A., Wells, K. C., & Ross, R. (2001). *Treatment of attention-deficit/hyperactivity disorder: Expert consensus guidelines. Journal of Attention Disorders, 4*(Suppl. 1), 7–128.

Connor, D. F. (2006). Stimulants. In R. A. Barkley (Ed.), *Attention-deficit hyperactivity disorder: A handbook for diagnosis and treatment* (3rd ed., pp. 608–647). New York: Guilford Press.

Conti, C. R., Pepine, C. J., & Sweeney, M. (1999). Efficacy and safety of sildenafil citrate in the treatment of erectile dysfunction in patients with ischemic heart disease. *American Journal of Cardiology, 83,* 29C–34C.

Conwell, Y., Duberstein, P. R., & Caine, E. D. (2002). Risk factors for suicide in later life. *Biological Psychiatry, 52,* 193–204.

Conwell, Y., Duberstein, P. R., Cox, C., Hermmann, J. H., Forbes, N. T., & Caine, E. D. (1996). Relationships of age and axis I diagnoses in victims of completed suicide: A psychological autopsy study. *American Journal of Psychiatry, 153,* 1001–1008.

Cook, E. W., III, Hodes, R. L., & Lang, P. J. (1986). Preparedness and phobia: Effects of stimulus content on human visceral conditioning. *Journal of Abnormal Psychology, 95,* 195–207.

Cook, P. J. (1993). The matter of tobacco use. *Science, 262,* 1750–1751.

Coolidge, F., Thede, L., & Young, S. (2002). The heritability of gender identity disorder in a child and adolescent twin sample. *Behavior Genetics, 32,* 251–257.

Coon, P. M. (1986). Treatment progress in 20 patients with multiple personality disorder. *Journal of Nervous and Mental Disease, 174,* 715–721.

Coons, P. M. (1994). Confirmation of childhood abuse in child and adolescent cases of multiple personality disorder not otherwise specified. *Journal of Nervous & Mental Disease, 182,* 461–464.

Coons, P. M., Bowman, E. S., Kluft, R. P., & Milstein, V. (1991). The cross cultural occurrence of NPD: Additional cases from a recent survey. *Dissociation, 4,* 124–128.

Cooper, A. J. (1988). Sexual dysfunction and cardiovascular disease. *Stress Medicine, 4,* 273–281.

Cooper, A. M., & Ronningstam, E. (1992). Narcissistic personality disorder. In A. Tasman & M. B. Riba (Eds.), *Review of psychiatry* (Vol. 11, pp. 80–97). Washington, DC: Psychiatric Press.

Cooper, J., Kapur, N., Webb, R., Lawlor, M., Guthrie, E., Mackway-Jones, K., et al. (2005). Suicide after deliberate self-harm: A 4-year cohort study. *American Journal of Psychiatry, 162,* 297–303.

Cooper, M. L., Russell, M., Skinner, J. B., Frone, M. R., & Mudar, P. (1992). Stress and alcohol use: Moderating effects of gender, coping, and alcohol expectancies. *Journal of Abnormal Psychology, 101,* 139–152.

Cooperberg, J., & Faith, M. S. (2004). Treatment of obesity II: Childhood and adolescent obesity. In J. K. Thompson (Ed.), *Handbook of eating disorders and obesity* (pp. 443–450). New York: John Wiley.

Cope, M. B., Fernandez, J. R., & Allison, D. (2004). Genetic and biological risk factors. In J. K. Thompson (Ed.), *Handbook of eating disorders and obesity* (pp. 323–338). New York: John Wiley.

Coplan, J. D., Andrews, M. W., Rosenblum, L. A., Owens, M. J., Friedman, S., Gorman, J. M., & Nemeroff, C. B. (1996). Persistent elevations of cerebrospinal fluid concentrations of corticotropin-releasing factor in adult nonhuman primates exposed to early life stressors: Implications for the pathophysiology of mood and anxiety disorders. *Proceedings of the National Academy of Sciences, 93,* 1619–1623.

Coplan, J. D., Trost, R. C., Owens, M. J., Cooper, T. B., Gorman, J. M., Nemeroff, C. B., & Rosenblum, L. A. (1998). Cerebrospinal fluid concentrations of somatostatin and biogenic amines in grown primates reared by mothers exposed to manipulated forag-

ing conditions. *Archives of General Psychiatry, 55,* 473–477.

Corrigan, P. W., Wallace, C. J., Schade, M. L., & Green, M. F. (1994). Learning medication self-management skills in schizophrenia: Relationships with cognitive deficits and psychiatric symptoms. *Behavior Therapy, 25,* 5–15.

Corson, P. W., & Andersen, A. E. (2002). Body image issues among boys and men. In T. F. Cash & T. Pruzinsky (Eds.), *Body image: A handbook of theory, research and clinical practice* (pp. 192–199). New York: Guilford Press.

Coryell, W., Endicott, J., & Keller, M. (1992). Rapid cycling affective disorder: Demographics, diagnosis, family history, and course. *Archives of General Psychiatry, 49,* 126–131.

Coryell, W., Endicott, J., Maser, J. D., Keller, M. B., Leon, A. C., & Akiskal, H. S. (1995). Long-term stability of polarity distinctions in the affective disorders. *American Journal of Psychiatry, 152,* 385–390.

Coryell, W., Leon, A., Winokur, G., Endicott, J., Keller, M., Akiskal, H., & Solomon, D. (1996). Importance of psychotic features to long-term course in major depressive disorder. *American Journal of Psychiatry, 153,* 483–489.

Coryell, W., Solomon, D., Turvey, C., Keller, M., Leon, A. C., Endicott, J., et al. (2003). The long-term course of rapid-cycling bipolar disorder. *Archives of General Psychiatry, 60,* 914–920.

Costa e Silva, J. A., & De Girolamo, G. (1990). Neurasthenia: History of a concept. In N. Sartorius, D. Goldberg, G. De Girolamo, J. A. Costa e Silva, Y. Lecrubier, & U. Wittchen (Eds.), *Psychological disorders in general medical settings* (pp. 699–81). Toronto: Hogrefe and Huber.

Costa, E. (1985). Benzodiazepine-GABA interactions: A model to investigate the neurobiology of anxiety. In A. H. Tuma & J. D. Maser (Eds.), *Anxiety and the anxiety disorders.* Hillsdale, NJ: Erlbaum.

Costa, P. T., Jr., & McCrae, R. R. (1990). Personality disorders and the five-factor model of personality. *Journal of Personality Disorders, 4,* 362–371.

Costa, P. T., Jr., & Widiger, T. A. (Eds.) (1994). *Personality disorders and the five-factor model of personality.* Washington, DC: American Psychological Association.

Côté, G., O'Leary, T., Barlow, D. H., Strain, J. J., Salkovskis, P. M., Warwick, H. M. C., et al. (1996). Hypochondriasis. In T. A. Widiger, A. J. Frances, H. A. Pincus, R. Ross, M. B. First, & W. W. Davis (Eds.), *DSM-IV sourcebook* (Vol. 2, pp. 933–947). Washington, DC: American Psychiatric Association.

Coughlin, A. M. (1994). Excusing women. *California Law Review, 82,* 1–93.

Courchesne, E. (1997). Brainstem, cerebellar and limbic neuroanatomical abnormalities in autism. *Current Opinion in Neurobiology, 7,* 269–278.

Cox, A., Rutter, M., Newman, S., & Bartak, L. (1975). A comparative study of infantile autism and specific developmental receptive language disorder: II. Parental characteristics. *British Journal of Psychiatry, 126,* 146–159.

Cox, B. C., Swinson, R. P., Schulman, I. D., Kuch, K., & Reikman, J. T. (1993). Gender effects in alcohol use in panic disorder with agoraphobia. *BRAT, 31*(4), 413–416.

Coyne, J. C. (1976). Toward an interactional description of depression. *Psychiatry, 39*(1), 28–40.

Cozanitis, D. A. (2004). One hundred years of barbiturates and their saint. *Journal of the Royal Society of Medicine, 97,* 594–598.

Crabbe, J. C., Wahlsten, D., & Dudek, B. C. (1999). Genetics of mouse behavior: Interactions with laboratory environment. *Science, 284,* 1670–1672.

Craddock, N., & Jones, I. (2001). Molecular genetics of bipolar disorder. *British Journal of Psychiatry, 41,* 128–133.

Crago, M., Shisslak, C. M., & Estes, L. S. (1997). Eating disturbances among American minority groups:

A review. *The International Journal of Eating Disorders, 19,* 239–248.

Craig, A., Hancock, K., Tran, Y., & Craig, M. (2003). Anxiety levels in people who stutter: A randomised population study. *Journal of Speech, Language, and Hearing Research, 46,* 1197–1206.

Craighead, W. E., Hart, A. B., Craighead, L. W., & Ilardi, S. S. (2002). Psychosocial treatments for major depressive disorder. In P. E. Nathan & J. M. Gorman (Eds.), *A guide to treatments that work* (2nd ed., pp. 245–261). New York: Oxford University Press.

Craighead, W. E., Ilardi, S. S., Greenberg, M. P., & Craighead, L. W. (1997). Cognitive psychology: Basic theory and clinical implications. In A. Tasman, J. Key, & J. A. Lieberman (Eds.), *Psychiatry* (Vol. 1, pp. 350–368). Philadelphia: W. B. Saunders.

Craighead, W. E., Miklowitz, D. J., Frank, E., & Vajk, F. C. (2002). Psychosocial treatments for bipolar disorder. In P. E. Nathan & J. M. Gorman (Eds.), *A guide to treatments that work* (2nd ed., pp. 263–275). New York: Oxford University Press.

Craske, M. G. (1999). *Anxiety disorders: Psychological approaches to theory and treatment.* Boulder, CO: Westview Press.

Craske, M. G., & Barlow, D. H. (1988). A review of the relationship between panic and avoidance. *Clinical Psychology Review, 8,* 667–685.

Craske, M. G., & Barlow, D. H. (in press). Panic disorder and agoraphobia. In D. H. Barlow (Ed.), *Clinical handbook of psychological disorders: A step-by-step treatment manual* (4th ed.). New York: Guilford Press.

Craske, M. G., & Rowe, M. K. (1997). Nocturnal panic. *Clinical Psychology: Science & Practice, 4,* 153–174.

Craske, M. G., Antony, M. M., & Barlow, D. H. (2006). *Mastering your fears and phobias: Therapist guide.* New York: Oxford University Press.

Craske, M. G., Barlow, D. H., Clark, D. M., Curtis, G. C., Hill, E. M., Himle, J. A., et al. (1996). Specific (simple) phobia. In T. A. Widiger, A. J. Frances, H. A. Pincus, R. Ross, M. B. First, & W. W. Davis (Eds.), *DSM-IV sourcebook* (Vol. 2, pp. 473–506). Washington, DC: American Psychiatric Association.

Craske, M. G., Brown, T. A., & Barlow, D. H. (1991). Behavioral treatment of panic disorder: A two-year follow-up. *Behavior Therapy, 22,* 289–304.

Craske, M. G., Golinelli, D., Stein, M. B., Roy-Byrne, P., Bystritsky, A., Sherbourne, C. (2005). Does the addition of cognitive behavioral therapy improve panic disorder treatment outcome relative to medication alone in the primary-care setting? *Psychological Medicine, 35*(11), 1645–1654.

Craske, M. G., Hermans, D., & Vansteenwegen, D. (2006). *Fear and learning.* Washington, DC: American Psychological Association.

Craske, M. G., Lang, A. J., Rowe, M., DeCola, J. P., Simmons, J., Mann, C., et al. (2002). Presleep attributions about arousal during sleep: Nocturnal panic. *Journal of Abnormal Psychology, 111,* 52–62.

Craske, M. G., Rapee, R. M., & Barlow, D. H. (1988). The significance of panic expectancy for individual patterns of avoidance. *Behavior Therapy, 19,* 577–592.

Crawford, N. (2003). ADHD: A women's issue. *Monitor on Psychology, 35,* 28–30.

Creed, F., & Barsky, A. (2004). A systematic review of the epidemiology of somatisation disorder and hypochondriasis. *Journal of Psychosomatic Research, 56,* 391–408.

Creese, I., Burt, D. R., & Snyder, S. H. (1976). Dopamine receptor binding predicts clinical and pharmacological potencies of antischizophrenic drugs. *Science, 192,* 481–483.

Cremniter, D., Jamin, S., Kollenbach, K., Alvarez, J. C., Lecrubier, Y., Gilton, A., et al. (1999). CSF 5-HIAA levels are lower in impulsive as compared to nonimpulsive violent suicide attempts and control subjects. *Biological Psychiatry, 45*(12), 1572–1579.

Crerand, C., Sarwer, D., Magee, L., Gibbons, L., Lowe, M., Bartlett, S., et al. (2004). Rate of body dysmorphic disorder among patients seeking facial plastic surgery. *Psychiatric Annals, 34, 958–965.*

Crichton, P., & Morey, S. (2003). Treating pain in cancer patients. In D. C. Turk & R. J. Gatchel (Eds.), *Psychological approaches to pain management: A practitioner's handbook* (2nd ed.). New York: Guilford Press.

Crisp, A. H., Callender, J. S., Halek, C., & Hsu, L. K. G. (1992). Long-term mortality in anorexia nervosa: A 20-year follow-up of the St. George's and Aberdeen cohorts. *British Journal of Psychiatry, 161,* 104–107.

Critser, G. (2003). *Fat Land: How Americans Became the Fattest People in the World.* Boston: Houghton Mifflin.

Cross-National Collaborative Group. (1992). The changing rate of major depression: Cross-national comparisons. *JAMA, 268,* 3098–3105.

Crow, S. J., Thuras, P., Keel, P. K., & Mitchell, J. E. (2002). Long-term menstrual and reproductive function in patients with bulimia nervosa. *American Journal of Psychiatry, 159,* 1048–1050.

Crowe, L. C., & George, W. H. (1989). Alcohol and human sexuality: Review and integration. *Psychological Bulletin, 105*(3), 374–386.

Crowe, R. R. (1974). An adoption study of antisocial personality. *Archives of General Psychiatry, 31,* 785–791.

Crowley, P. H., Hayden, T. L., & Gulati, D. K. (1982). Etiology of Down syndrome. In S. M. Pueschel & J. E. Rynders (Eds.), *Down syndrome: Advances in biomedicine and behavioral sciences* (pp. 89–131). Cambridge, MA: Ware Press.

Crowley, T., & Sakai, J. (2005). Inhalant-related disorders. In B. J. Sadock & V. A. Sadock (Eds.), *Kaplan & Sadock's comprehensive textbook of psychiatry* (pp. 1247–1257). Philadelphia: Lippincott, Williams & Wilkins.

Crowley, T., Richardson, D., & Goldmeir, D. (2006). Recommendation for the management of vaginismus: BASHH special interest group for sexual dysfunction. *International Journal of STD and AIDS, 17,* 14–18.

Cuijpers, P. (2005). Depressive disorders in caregivers of dementia patients: A systematic review. *Aging & Mental Health, 9,* 325–330.

Cummings, J. L. (1990). *Subcortical dementia.* New York: Oxford University Press.

Curtis, G. C., Hill, E. M., & Lewis, J. A. (1990). *Heterogeneity of DSM-III-R simple phobia and the simple phobia/agoraphobia boundary: Evidence from the ECA study.* Preliminary report to the Simple Phobia subcommittee of the DSM-IV Anxiety Disorders Work Group.

Curtis, G. C., Himle, J. A., Lewis, J. A., & Lee, Y-J. (1989). *Specific situational phobias: Variant of agoraphobia?* Paper requested by the Simple Phobia subcommittee of the DSM-IV Anxiety Disorders Work Group.

Cutrona, C. E. (1984). Social support and stress in the transition to parenthood. *Journal of Abnormal Psychology, 93*(4), 378–390.

Cutting, J. (1985). *The psychology of schizophrenia.* New York: Churchill Livingstone.

Cyranowski, J. M., Aarestad, S. L., & Andersen, B. L. (1999). The role of sexual self-schema in a diathesis-stress model of sexual dysfunction. *Applied & Preventative Psychology, 8,* 217–228.

Cyranowski, J. M., Frank, E., Young, E. & Shear, M. K. (2000). Adolescent onset of the gender difference in lifetime rates of major depression. *Archives of General Psychiatry, 57,* 21–27.

Czeisler, C. A., & Allan, J. S. (1989). Pathologies of the sleep–wake schedule. In R. L. Williams, I. Karacan, & C. A. Morre (Eds.), *Sleep disorders: Diagnosis and treatment* (pp. 109–129). New York: John Wiley.

Czeisler, C. A., Richardson, G. S., Coleman, R. M., Zimmerman, J. C., Moore-Ede, M. C., Dement, W.

C., & Weitzman, E. D. (1981). Chronotherapy: Resetting the circadian clocks of patients with delayed sleep phase insomnia. *Sleep, 4,* 1–21.

D'Onofrio, B. M., Turkheimer, E., Emery, R. E., Slutske, W. S., Heath, A. C., Madden, P. A., & Martin, N. G. (2006). A genetically informed study of the processes underlying the association between parental marital instability and offspring adjustment. *Developmental Psychology, 42,* 486–499.

Dadds, M. R., Sanders, M. R., Morrison, M., & Rebgetz, M. (1992). Childhood depression and conduct disorder: II. An analysis of family interaction patterns in the home. *Journal of Abnormal Psychology, 101*(3), 505–513.

Dagan, Y., Borodkin, K., & Ayalon, L. (2006). Advanced, delayed, irregular, and free-running sleep–wake disorders. In T. Lee-Chiong (Ed.), *Sleep: A comprehensive handbook* (pp. 383–388). Hoboken, NJ: John Wiley & Sons.

Dagan, Y., Dela, H., Omer, H., Hallis, D., & Dar, R. (1996). High prevalence of personality disorders among circadian rhythm sleep disorders (CRSD) patients. *Journal of Psychosomatic Research, 41,* 357–363.

Dalack, G. W., Glassman, A. H., & Covey, L. S. (1993). Nicotine use. In D. L. Dunner (Ed.), *Current psychiatric therapy* (pp. 114–118). Philadelphia: W. B. Saunders.

Daly, R. J. (1983). Samuel Pepys and post traumatic stress disorder. *British Journal of Psychiatry, 143,* 64–68.

Damasio, A. (2007). Neuroscience and ethics: Intersections. *American Journal of Bioethics, 7*(1), 3–7.

Dana, R. H. (1996). The Thematic Apperception Test (TAT). In C. S. Newmark (Ed.), *Major psychological assessment instruments* (pp. 166–205). Boston: Allyn & Bacon.

Daniel, S. S., Walsh, A. K., Goldston, D. B., Arnold, E. M., Reboussin, B. A., & Wood, F. B. (2006). Suicidality, school dropout, and reading problems among adolescents. *Journal of Learning Disabilities, 39,* 507–514.

Dansinger, M. L., Gleason, J. A., Griffith, J. L., Selker, H. P., & Schaefer, E. J. (2005). Comparison of the Atkins, Ornish, Weight Watchers, and Zone diets for weight loss and heart disease risk reduction: A randomized trial. *JAMA, 293,* 43–53.

Darwin, C. R. (1872). *The expression of emotions in man and animals.* London: John Murray.

Dassori, A. M., Miller, A. L., & Saldana, D. (1995). Schizophrenia among Hispanics: Epidemiology, phenomenology, course, and outcome. *Schizophrenia Bulletin, 21,* 303–312.

Davey, G. (2006). Cognitive mechanisims in fear acquisition and maintenance. In M. G. Craske, D. Hermans, & D. Vansteenwegen (Eds.), *Fear and learning from basic processes to clinical implications.* Washington, DC: American Psychological Association.

Davidson, A. J., Sellix, M. T., Daniel, J., Yamazaki, S., Menaker, M., & Block, G. D. (2006). Chronic jet-lag increases mortality in aged mice. *Current Biology, 16,* R914–R916.

Davidson, J. R. T., Foa, E. B., & Huppert, J. D. (2004). Fluoxetine, comprehensive Cognitive behavioral therapy, and placebo in generalized social phobia. *Archives of General Psychiatry, 61,* 1005–1013.

Davidson, J. R. T., Hughes, D. L., Blazer, D. G., & George, L. K. (1991). Posttraumatic stress in the community: An epidemiological study. *Psychological Medicine, 21,* 713–721.

Davidson, J., Miller, R. D., Turnbull, C. D., & Sullivan, J. L. (1982). Atypical depression. *Archives of General Psychiatry, 39,* 527–534.

Davidson, J., Swartz, M., Storck, M., Krishnan, R. R., & Hammett, E. (1985). A diagnostic and family study of posttraumatic stress disorder. *American Journal of Psychiatry, 142,* 90–93.

Davidson, K., MacGregor, M. W., Stuhr, J., Dixon, K., & MacLean, D. (2000). Constructive anger verbal

behavior predicts blood pressure in a population-based sample. *Health Psychology, 19,* 55–64.

Davidson, M., Keefe, R. S. E., Mohs, R. C., Siever, L. J., Losonczy, M. F., Horvath, T. B., & Davis, K. L. (1987). L-Dopa challenge and relapse in schizophrenia. *American Journal of Psychiatry, 144,* 934–938.

Davidson, R., Pizzagalli, D., Nitschke, J., & Putnam, K. (2002). Depression: Perspectives from affective neuroscience. *Annual Review of Psychology, 53,* 545–574.

Davidson, R. J. (1993). Cerebral asymmetry and emotion: Methodological conundrums. *Cognition and Emotion, 7,* 115–138.

Davis, K. L. (2005). Cognitive disorders: Introduction and overview. In B. J. Sadock & V. A. Sadock (Eds.), *Kaplan & Sadock's comprehensive textbook of psychiatry* (pp. 1053–1054). Philadelphia: Lippincott, Williams & Wilkins.

Davis, K. L., Kahn, R. S., Ko, G., & Davidson, M. (1991). Dopamine in schizophrenia: A review and reconceptualization. *American Journal of Psychiatry, 148,* 1474–1486.

Davis, M. (1992). The role of the amygdala in fear and anxiety. *Annual Review of Neuroscience, 15,* 353–375.

Davis, M. (2002). Neural circuitry of anxiety and stress disorders. In K. L. Davis, D. Charney, J. T. Coyle, & C. Nemeroff (Eds.), *Neuropsychopharmacology: The fifth generation of progress* (pp. 901–930). Philadelphia: Lippincott Williams & Wilkins.

Davison, G. C. (1968). Elimination of a sadistic fantasy by a client-controlled counter-conditioning technique: A case study. *Journal of Abnormal Psychology, 73,* 91–99.

Dawson, G., & McKissick, F. C. (1984). Self-recognition in autistic children. *Journal of Autism and Developmental Disorders, 14,* 383–394.

Dawson, G., Toth, K., Abbott, R., Osterling, J., Munson, J., Estes, A., & Liaw, J. (2004). Early social attention impairments in autism: Social orienting, joint attention, and attention to distress. *Developmental Psychology, 40,* 271–283.

Day, R., Nielsen, J. A., Korten, A., Ernberg, G., Dube, K. C., Gebhart, J., et al. (1987). Stressful life events preceding the acute onset of schizophrenia: A cross-national study from the World Health Organization. *Cultural Medicine and Psychiatry, 11,* 123–205.

de Almeidia-Filho, N., Santana, V. S., Pinto, I. M., & de Carvalho-Neto, J. A. (1991). Is there an epidemic of drug misuse in Brazil? A review of the epidemiological evidence (1977–1988). *International Journal of the Addictions, 26,* 355–369.

De Backer, G., Kittel, F., Kornitzer, M., & Dramaix, M. (1983). Behavior, stress, and psychosocial traits as risk factors. *Preventative Medicine, 12,* 32–36.

de Boo, G. M., & Prins, P. J. M. (2007). Social incompetence in children with ADHD: Possible moderators and mediators in social-skills training. *Clinical Psychology Review, 27,* 78–97.

de Lissovoy, V. (1961). Head banging in early childhood. *Child Development, 33,* 43–56.

de Zwaan, M., Roerig, J. L., & Mitchell, J. E. (2004). Pharmacological treatment of anorexia nervosa, bulimia nervosa and binge eating disorder. In J. K. Thompson (Ed.), *Handbook of eating disorders and obesity* (pp. 186–217). New York: John Wiley.

Deakin, J. F. W., & Graeff, F. G. (1991). Critique: 5-HT and mechanisms of defence. *Journal of Psychopharmacology, 5*(4), 305–315.

Deale, A., Chalder, T., Marks, I., & Wessely, S. (1997). Cognitive behavior therapy for chronic fatigue syndrome: A randomized controlled trial. *American Journal of Psychiatry, 154,* 408–414.

Deale, A., Husain, K., Chalder, T., & Wessely, S. (2001). Long-term outcome of cognitive behavioral therapy versus relaxation therapy for chronic fatigue syndrome: A 5-year follow-up study. *American Journal of Psychiatry, 158,* 2038–2042.

Dean, R. R., Kelsey, J. E., Heller, M. R., & Ciaranello, R. D. (1993). Structural foundations of illness and treatment: Receptors. In D. L. Dunner (Ed.), *Current psychiatric therapy.* Philadelphia: W. B. Saunders.

Del Parigi, A., Panza, F., Capurso, C., & Solfrizzi, V. (2006). Nutritional factors, cognitive decline, and dementia. *Brain Research Bulletin, 69,* 1–19.

DeLamater, J., & Sill, M. (2005). Sexual desire in latter life. *Journal of Sex Research, 42,* 138–149.

Delano-Wood, L., & Abeles, N. (2005). Late-life depression: Detection, risk, reduction, and somatic intervention. *Clinical Psychology Science Practice, 12,* 207–217.

DeLisi, L. E., Maurizio, A., Yost, M., Papparozzi, C. F., Fulchino, C., Katz, C. L., et al. (2003). A survey of New Yorkers after the Sept. 11, 2001, terrorist attacks. *American Journal of Psychiatry, 160,* 780–783.

Delizonna, L. L., Wincze, J. P., Litz, B. T., Brown, T. A., & Barlow, D. H. (2001). A comparison of subjective and physiological measures of mechanically produced and erotically produced erections. (Or, is an erection an erection?) *Journal of Sex and Marital Therapy, 27,* 21–31.

Dell, P. F. (1998). Axis II pathology in outpatients with dissociative identity disorder. *Journal of Nervous and Mental Disease, 186*(6), 352–356.

Dembroski, T. M., & Costa, P. T., Jr. (1987). Coronary prone behavior: Components of the Type A pattern and hostility. *Journal of Personality, 55*(2), 211–235.

Dembroski, T. M., MacDougall, J. M., Costa, P. T., & Grandits, G. A. (1989). Components of hostility as predictors of sudden death and myocardial infarction in the multiple risk factor intervention trial. *Psychosomatic Medicine, 51*(5), 514–522.

Denzin, N. K. (1987). *The recovering alcoholic.* Newbury Park, CA: Sage.

Depression Guideline Panel. (1993, April). *Depression in primary care: Vol. 1. Detection and diagnosis* (AHCPR Publication No. 93–0550). Clinical practice guideline, No. 5. Rockville, MD: U.S. Department of Health and Human Services, Public Health Service, Agency for Health Care Policy and Research.

Deptula, D., & Pomara, N. (1990). Effects of antidepressants on human performance: A review. *Journal of Clinical Psychopharmacology, 10,* 105–111.

Depue, R. A., & Iacono, W. G. (1989). Neurobehavioral aspects of affective disorders. *Annual Review of Psychology, 40,* 457–492.

Depue, R. A., & Spoont, M. R. (1986). Conceptualizing a serotonin trait: A behavioral dimension of constraint. *Annals of the New York Academy of Sciences, 487,* 47–62.

Depue, R. A., & Zald, D. (1993). Biological and environmental processes in nonpsychotic psychopathology: A neurobehavioral system perspective. In C. Costello (Ed.), *Basic issues in psychopathology.* New York: Guilford Press.

Depue, R. A., Luciana, M., Arbisi, P., Collins, P., & Leon, A. (1994). Dopamine and the structure of personality: Relation of agonist-induced dopamine activity to positive emotionality. *Journal of Personality and Social Psychology, 67,* 485–498.

Depue, R. A., Slater, J. F., Wolfstetter-Kausch, H., Klein, D., Goplerud, E., & Farr, D. (1981). A behavioral paradigm for identifying persons at risk for bipolar depressive disorder: A conceptual framework and five validation studies. *Journal of Abnormal Psychological Monographs, 90,* 381–437.

Dersh, J., Polatin, P. B., & Gatchel, R. J. (2002). Chronic pain and psychopathology: Research findings and theoretical considerations. *Psychosomatic Medicine, 64,* 773–786.

Dershewitz, R. A., & Williamson, J. W. (1977). Prevention of childhood household injuries: A controlled clinical trial. *American Journal of Public Health, 67,* 1148–1153.

DeRubeis, R., Gelfand, L. A., Tang, T. Z., & Simons, A. D. (1999). Medications versus cognitive behavior therapy for severely depressed outpatients: Mega-analysis of four randomized comparisons. *American Journal of Psychiatry, 156,* 1007–1013.

DeRubeis, R., Hollon, S., Amsterdam, J., Shelton, R., Young, P., et al. (2005). Cognitive therapy vs. medications in the treatment of moderate to severe depression. *Archives of General Psychiatry, 62,* 409–416.

Devanand, D. P. (2002). Comorbid psychiatric disorders in late life depression. *Biological Psychiatry, 52,* 236–242.

Devinsky, O., Feldman, E., Burrowes, K., & Bromfield, E. (1989). Autoscopic phenomena with seizures. *Archives of Neurology, 46*(10), 1080–1088.

DeWitt, D. J., Adlaf, E. M., Offord, D. R., & Ogborne, A. C. (2000). Age at first alcohol use: A risk factor for the development of alcohol disorders. *American Journal of Psychiatry, 157,* 745–750.

Diamond, M. (1995). Biological aspects of sexual orientation and identity. In L. Diamant & R. D. McAnulty (Eds.), *The psychology of sexual orientation, behavior, and identity.* Westport, CT: Greenwood Press.

Diamond, M., & Sigmundson, K. (1997). Sex reassignment at birth: Long-term review and clinical implications. *Archives of Pediatric and Adolescent Medicine, 151,* 298–304.

DiBartolo, P. M., Brown, T. A., & Barlow, D. H. (1997). Effects of anxiety on attentional allocation and task performance: An information processing analysis. *BRAT, 35,* 1101–1111.

Dickey, C. C., Shenton, M. E., Hirayasu, Y., Fischer, I., Voglmaier, M. M., Niznikiewicz, M. A., et al. (2000). Large CSF volume is not attributable to ventricular volume in schizotypal personality disorder. *American Journal of Psychiatry, 157,* 48–54.

Diener, E. (2000). Subjective well-being: The science of happiness, and a proposal for a national index. *American Psychologist, 55,* 34–43.

Diener, E., Oishi, S., & Lucas, R. E. (2003). Personality, culture, and subjective well-being: Emotional and cognitive evaluations of life. *Annual Review of Psychology, 54,* 403–425.

Dimberg, U., & Öhman, A. (1983). The effects of directional facial cues on electrodermal conditioning to facial stimuli. *Psychophysiology, 20,* 160–167.

Dimidjian, S., Martell, C. R., Addis, M. E., & Herman-Dunn, R. (in press). *Behavioral activation for depression.* In D. H. Barlow (Ed.), *Clinical handbook of psychological disorders* (4th ed.) New York: Guilford Press.

DiNardo, P. A., & Barlow, D. H. (1990). Syndrome and symptom comorbidity in the anxiety disorders. In J. D. Maser & C. R. Cloninger (Eds.), *Comorbidity of mood and anxiety disorders* (pp. 205–230). Washington, DC: American Psychiatric Press.

DiNardo, P. A., Brown, T. A., & Barlow, D. H. (1994). *Anxiety disorders interview schedule for DSM-IV (ADIS-IV).* Albany, NY: Oxford University Press.

DiNardo, P. A., Guzy, L. T., Jenkins, J. A., Bak, R. M., Tomasi, S. F., & Copeland, M. (1988). Etiology and maintenance of dog fears. *Behaviour Research and Therapy, 26,* 241–244.

DiNardo, P. A., Moras, K., Barlow, D. H., Rapee, R. M., & Brown, T. A. (1993). Reliability of DSM-III-R anxiety disorder categories: Using the Anxiety Disorders Interview Schedule—Revised (ADIS-R). *Archives of General Psychiatry, 50,* 251–256.

DiNardo, P. A., O'Brien, G. T., Barlow, D. H., Waddell, M. T., & Blanchard, E. B. (1983). Reliability of DSM-III anxiety disorder categories using a new structured interview. *Archives of General Psychiatry, 40,* 1070–1074.

Dinnel, D. L., Kleinknecht, R. A., & Tanaka-Matsumi, J. (2002). A cross-cultural comparison of social phobia symptoms. *Journal of Psychopathology and Behavioral Assessment, 24,* 75–82.

Diokno, A. C., Brown, M. B., & Herzog, A. R. (1990). Sexual function in the elderly. *Archives of Internal Medicine, 150,* 197–200.

Dishion, T. J., Patterson, G. R., & Reid, J. R. (1988). Parent and peer factors associated with drug sampling in early adolescence: Implications for treatment. In E. R. Rahdert & J. Gabowski (Eds.), *Adolescent drug abuse: Analyses of treatment research* (NIDA Research Monograph No. 77, DHHS Publication No. ADM88–1523, pp. 69–93). Rockville, MD: National Institute on Drug Abuse.

Dixon, J. C. (1963). Depersonalization phenomena in a sample population of college students. *British Journal of Psychiatry, 109,* 371–375.

Dixon, L. B., & Lehman, A. F. (1995). Family interventions for schizophrenia. *Schizophrenia Bulletin, 21,* 631–643.

Docter, R. F., & Prince, V. (1997). Transvestism: A survey of 1032 cross-dressers. *Archives of Sexual Behavior, 26,* 589–605.

Do_an, S., & Do_an, M. (2006). Possible gender identity disorder in an extremely religious Muslim family. *Archives of Sexual Behavior, 35,* 645–646.

Dohrenwend, B. P., & Dohrenwend, B. S. (1981). Socioenvironmental factors, stress and psychopathology. *American Journal of Community Psychology, 9*(2), 128–164.

Dohrenwend, B. P., & Egri, G. (1981). Recent stressful life events and episodes of schizophrenia. *Schizophrenia Bulletin, 7,* 12–23.

Dohrenwend, B. P., Turner, J. B., & Turse, N. A. (2006). The psychological risks of Vietnam for U.S. veterans: A revisit with new data and methods. *Science, 313,* 979–982.

Donaldson, K. (1976). *Insanity inside out.* New York: Crown.

Donnellan, M. B., Ge, X., & Wenk, E. (2000). Cognitive abilities in adolescent-limited and life-course-persistent criminal offenders. *Journal of Abnormal Psychology, 109,* 396–402.

Dorey, E. (2006). The power of addiction: With increasing understanding of the causes of addiction comes growing commercial interest in its treatment. *Chemistry and Industry, 12,* 12.

Douglas, K. S., Vincent, G. M., & Edens, J. F. (2006). Psychopathy and substance use disorders. In C. J. Patrick (Ed.), *Handbook of psychopathy* (pp. 533–554). New York: Guilford Press.

Dowling, N., Smith, D., & Thomas, T. (in press). A comparison of individual and group cognitive-behavioural treatment for female pathological gambling. *Behaviour Research and Therapy.*

Doyne, E. J., Ossip-Klein, D. J., Bowman, E. D., Osborn, K. M., McDougall-Wilson, I. B., & Neimeyer, R. A. (1987). Running versus weight lifting in the treatment of depression. Special issue: Eating disorders. *Journal of Consulting and Clinical Psychology, 55*(5), 748–754.

Draguns, J. G. (1990). Normal and abnormal behavior in cross-cultural perspective: Specifying the nature of their relationship. In J. Berman (Ed.), *Cross-Cultural Perspectives: Nebraska Symposium on Motivation 1989* (pp. 235–277). Lincoln: University of Nebraska Press.

Draguns, J. G. (1995). Cultural influences upon psychopathology: Clinical and practical implications. *Journal of Social Distress and the Homeless, 4,* 79–103.

Draguns, J. G., & Tanaka-Matsumi, J. (2003). Assessment of psychopathology across and within cultures: Issues and findings. *Behavior Research and Therapy, 41,* 755–776.

Dubovsky, S. L. (1983). Psychiatry in Saudi Arabia. *American Journal of Psychiatry, 140,* 1455–1459.

Dulit, R. A., Marin, D. B., & Frances, A. J. (1993). Cluster B personality disorders. In D. L. Dunner (Ed.), *Current psychiatric therapy* (pp. 405–411). Philadelphia: W. B. Saunders.

Duman, R. (2004). Depression: A case of neuronal life and death? *Biological Psychiatry, 56,* 140–145.

Dumas, J., & Wahler, R. G. (1983). Predictors of treatment outcome in parent training: Mother insularity and socioeconomic disadvantage. *Behavioral Assessment, 5,* 301–313.

Dunner, D. D., & Fieve, R. (1974). Clinical factors in lithium carbonate prophylaxis failure. *Archives of General Psychiatry, 30,* 229–233.

Durand, V. M. (1998). *Sleep better: A guide to improving the sleep of children with special needs.* Baltimore: Paul H. Brookes.

Durand, V. M. (1999). Functional communication training using assistive devices: Recruiting natural communities of reinforcement. *Journal of Applied Behavior Analysis, 32(3),* 247–267.

Durand, V. M. (2001). Future directions for children and adolescents with mental retardation. *Behavior Therapy, 32,* 633–650.

Durand, V. M. (2003). Functional communication training to treat challenging behavior. In W. O'Donohue, J. E. Fisher, & S. C. Hayes (Eds.), *Empirically supported techniques of cognitive behavior therapy: A step-by-step guide for clinicians.* New York: John Wiley.

Durand, V. M. (2004). Past, present and emerging directions in education. In D. Zager (Ed.), *Autism: Identification, Education, and Treatment* (3rd ed.). Hillsdale, NJ: Erlbaum.

Durand, V. M. (2005). Past, present, and emerging directions in education. In D. Zager (Ed.), *Autism spectrum disorders: Identification, education, and treatment* (3rd ed., pp. 89–109). Hillsdale, NJ: Lawrence Erlbaum Associates.

Durand, V. M. (2006). Sleep terrors. In J. E. Fisher & W. T. O'Donohue (Eds.), *Evidence-based psychotherapy* (pp. 654–659). Reno, NV: Springer.

Durand, V. M. (in press a). *Pediatric sleep disorders.* New York: Oxford University Press.

Durand, V. M. (in press b). Sleep terrors. In J. E. Fisher & W. O'Donohue (Eds.), *Practice guidelines for evidence-based psychotherapy.* New York: Kluwer Academic Publications.

Durand, V. M., & Christodulu, K. V. (2006). Mental retardation. In M. Hersen (Ed.), *Clinician's handbook of child behavioral assessment* (pp. 459–475). Burlington, MA: Elsevier Academic Press.

Durand, V. M., & Mindell, J. A. (1999). Behavioral intervention for childhood sleep terrors. *Behavior Therapy, 30,* 705–715.

Durand, V. M., Blanchard, E. B., & Mindell, J. A. (1988). Training in projective testing: A survey of clinical training directors and internship directors. *Professional Psychology: Research and Practice, 19,* 236–238.

Durand, V. M., Mindell, J., Mapstone, E., & Gernert-Dott, P. (1998). Sleep problems. In T. S. Watson & F. M. Gresham (Eds.), *Handbook of child behavior therapy* (pp. 203–219). New York: Plenum Press.

Durham v. United States, 214 F.2d, 862, 874–875 (D.C. Cir., 1954).

Durham, M. L., & La Fond, J. Q. (1985). The empirical consequences and policy implications of broadening the statutory criteria for civil commitment. *Yale Law and Policy Review, 3,* 395–446.

Durkheim, E. (1951). *Suicide: A study in sociology.* (J. A. Spaulding & G. Simpson, Trans.). New York: Free Press.

Dusky v. United States, 362 U.S. 402 (1960).

Dusseldorp, E., van Elderen, T., Maes, S., Meulman, J., & Kraaij, V. (1999). A meta-analysis of psychoeducational programs for coronary heart disease patients. *Health Psychology, 18,* 506–519.

Dwyer, E. (1992). Attendants and their world of work. In A. D. Gaines (Ed.), *Ethnopsychiatry: The cultural construction of professional and folk psychiatries* (pp. 291–305). Albany: State University of New York Press.

Dwyer, J. T., Feldman, J. J., Seltzer, C. C., & Mayer, J. (1969). Body image in adolescents: Attitudes toward weight and perception of appearance. *American Journal of Clinical Nutrition, 20,* 1045–1056.

Eagles, J. M., Johnston, M. I., Hunter, D., Lobban, M., & Millar, H. R. (1995). Increasing incidence of anorexia nervosa in the female population of north-

east Scotland. *American Journal of Psychiatry, 152,* 1266–1271.

Eaker, E. D., Pinsky, J., & Castelli, W. P. (1992). Myocardial infarction and coronary death among women: Psychosocial predictors from a 20-year follow-up of women in the Framingham study. *American Journal of Epidemiology, 135,* 854–864.

Eastman, C. I., Young, M. A., Fogg, L. F., Liu, L., & Meaden, P. M. (1998). Bright light treatment of winter depression: A placebo-controlled trial. *Archives of General Psychiatry, 55*(10), 883–889.

Eaton, W. W., Anthony, J. C., Gallo, J., Cai, G., Tien, A., Romanoski, A., et al. (1997). Natural history of diagnostic interview schedule/DSM-IV major depression: The Baltimore Epidemiologic Catchment Area follow-up. *Archives of General Psychiatry, 54,* 993–999.

Eaton, W. W., Kessler, R. C., Wittchen, H. U., & McGee, W. J. (1994). Panic and panic disorder in the United States. *American Journal of Psychiatry, 151,* 413–420.

Ebigno, P. (1982). Development of a culture-specific screening scale of somatic complaints indicating psychiatric disturbance. *Culture, Medicine, and Psychiatry, 6,* 29–43.

Ebigno, P. O. (1986). A cross sectional study of somatic complaints of Nigerian females using the Enugu Somatization Scale. *Culture, Medicine, and Psychiatry, 10,* 167–186.

Eckman, T. A., Wirshing, W. C., Marder, S. R., Liberman, R. P., Johnston-Cronk, K., Zimmermann, K., & Mintz, J. (1992). Techniques for training schizophrenic patients in illness self-management: A controlled trial. *American Journal of Psychiatry, 149,* 1549–1555.

Eddy, K. T., Keel, P. K., Dorer, D. J., Delinsky, S. S., Franko, D. L., & Herzog, D. B. (2002). A longitudinal comparison of anorexia nervosa subtypes. *International Journal of Eating Disorders, 31,* 191–201.

Edelson, M. G. (2006). Are the majority of children with autism mentally retarded? *Focus on Autism and other Developmental Disabilities, 21,* 66–83.

Edwards, A. J. (1994). *When memory fails: Helping the Alzheimer's and dementia patient.* New York: Plenum Press.

Eelen, P., & Vervliet, B. (2006). Fear conditioning and clinical implications: What can we learn from the past? In M. G. Craske, D. Hermans, & D. Vansteenwegen, *Fear and learning: From basic processes to clinical implications* (pp. 17–35). Washington, DC: American Psychological Association.

Efon, S. (1997, October 19). Tsunami of eating disorders sweeps across Asia. *San Francisco Examiner,* p. A27.

Egeland, J. A., Gerhard, D. S., Pauls, D. L., Sussex, J. N., Kidd, K. K., Allen, C. R., et al. (1987). Bipolar affective disorders linked to DNA markers on chromosome 11. *Nature, 325*(6107), 783–787.

Ehlers, A., & Breuer, P. (1992). Increased cardiac awareness in panic disorder. *Journal of Abnormal Psychology, 101*(3), 371–382.

Ehlers, A., & Breuer, P. (1996). How good are patients with panic disorder at perceiving their heartbeats? [Special issue]. *Biological Psychology, 42,* 165–182.

Ehlers, A., & Clark, D. M. (2003). Early psychological interventions for adult survivors of trauma: A review. *Biological Psychiatry, 53,* 817–826.

Ehlers, A., Clark, D. M., Hackmann, A., McManus, F., Fennell, M., Herbert, C., et al. (2003). A randomized controlled trial of cognitive therapy, a self-help booklet, and repeated assessments as early interventions for posttraumatic stress disorder. *Archives of General Psychiatry, 60,* 1024–1032.

Ehrhardt, A. A., & Meyer-Bahlburg, H. F. L. (1981). Effects of prenatal sex hormones on gender-related behavior. *Science, 211,* 1312–1318.

Ehrhardt, A. A., Meyer-Bahlburg, H. F. L., Rosen, L. R., Feldman, J. F., Veridiano, N. P., Zimmerman, I., & McEwen, B. (1985). Sexual orientation after pre-

natal exposure to exogenous estrogen. *Archives of Sexual Behavior, 14*(1), 57–77.

Eisen, J., & Steketee, G. (1998). Course of illness in obsessive–compulsive disorder. In L. J. Dickstein, M. B. Riba, & J. M. Oldham (Eds.), *Review of psychiatry* (Vol. 16). Washington, DC: American Psychiatric Press.

Eisler, I., Dare, C., Hodes, M., Russell, G. F. M., Dodge, E., & Le Grange, D. (2000). Family therapy for adolescent anorexia nervosa: The results of a controlled comparison of two family interventions. *Journal of Child Psychology and Psychiatry, 41,* 727–736.

Eisler, I., Dare, C., Russell, G. F. M., Szmukler, G., le Grange, D., & Dodge, E. (1997). Family and individual therapy in anorexia nervosa: A five-year follow-up. *Archives of General Psychiatry, 54,* 1025–1030.

Ekstrand, M. L., & Coates, T. J. (1990). Maintenance of safer sexual behaviors and predictors of risky sex: The San Francisco men's health study. *American Journal of Public Health, 80,* 973–977.

Elbedour, S., Shulman, S., & Kedem, P. (1997). Children's fears: Cultural and developmental perspectives. *Behavior Research and Therapy, 35,* 491–496.

Elbogen, E. B., Tomkins, A. J., Pothuloori, A. P., & Scalora, M. J. (2003). Documentation of violence risk information in psychiatric hospital patient charts: An empirical examination. *Journal of the American Academy of Psychiatry and the Law, 31,* 58–64.

Eldredge, K. L., & Agras, W. S. (1996). Weight and shape overconcern and emotional eating in binge eating disorder. *International Journal of Eating Disorders, 19,* 73–82.

Elkin, I., Gibbons, R. D., Shea, M. T., Sotsky, S. M., Watkins, J. T., Pilkonis, P. A., & Hedeker, D. (1995). Initial severity and differential treatment outcome in the National Institute of Mental Health Treatment of Depression Collaborative Research Program. *Journal of Consulting and Clinical Psychology, 63,* 841–847.

Elkin, I., Shea, M. T., Watkins, J. T., Imber, S. D., Sotsky, S. M., Collins, J. F., et al. (1989). National Institute of Mental Health Treatment of Depression Collaborative Research Program: General effectiveness of treatments. *Archives of General Psychiatry, 46*(11), 971–982.

Ellason, J. W., & Ross, C. A. (1997). Two-year follow up of inpatients with dissociative identity disorder. *American Journal of Psychiatry, 154,* 832–839.

Ellicott, A. G. (1988). *A prospective study of stressful life events and bipolar illness.* Unpublished doctoral dissertation, University of California, Los Angeles.

Elliot, K. S., Di Minno, M., Lam, D., & Mei Tu, A. (1996). Working with Chinese families in the context of dementia. In G. Yeo & D. Gallagher-Thompson (Eds.), *Ethnicity and the dementias* (pp. 89–108). Washington, DC: Taylor & Francis.

Elliott, R., Rubinsztein, J. S., Sahakian, B. J., & Dolan, R. J. (2002). The neural basis of mood-congruent processing biases in depression. *Archives of General Psychiatry, 59,* 597–604.

Elovainio, M., Kivimaki, M., Viikari, J., Ekelund, J., & Keltikangas-Jarvinen, L. (2005). The mediating role of novelty seeking in the association between the type 4 dopamine receptor gene polymorphism and cigarette-smoking behavior. *Personality and Individual Differences, 38,* 639–645.

Eme, R. F. (2007). Sex differences in child-onset, life-course-persistent conduct disorder: A review of biological influence. *Clinical Psychology Review, 27,* 607–627.

Emrick, C. D. (1999). Alcoholics Anonymous and other 12-step groups. In M. Galanter & H. D. Kleber (Eds.), *Textbook of substance abuse treatment* (2nd ed., pp. 403–411). Washington, DC: American Psychiatric Press.

Emrick, C. D., Tonigan, J. S., Montgomery, H., & Little, L. (1993). Alcoholics Anonymous: What is currently known? In B. S. McCrady & W. R. Miler (Eds.), *Research on Alcoholics Anonymous: Opportunities and alternatives* (pp. 41–76). New Brunswick, NJ: Rutgers Center of Alcohol Studies.

Emslie, G. J., Rush, A. J., Weinberg, W. A., Rintelmann, J. W., & Roffwarg, H. P. (1994). Sleep EEG features of adolescents with major depression. *Biological Psychiatry, 36,* 573–581.

Eppright, T. D., Kashani, J. H., Robison, B. D., & Reid, J. C. (1993). Comorbidity of conduct disorder and personality disorders in an incarcerated juvenile population. *American Journal of Psychiatry, 150,* 1233–1236.

Epstein, L. H., Myers, M. D., Raynor, H., & Saelens, B. E. (1998). Treatment of pediatric obesity. *Pediatrics, 101,* 554–570.

Eranti, S., Mogg, A., Pluck, G., Landau, S., Purvis, R., Brown, R., et al. (2007). A randomized controlled trial with 6-month follow-up of repetitive transcranial magnetic stimulation and electroconvulsive therapy for severe depression. *American Journal of Psychiatry, 164,* 73–81.

Erath, S. A., Bierman, K. L., & Conduct Problems Prevention Research Group. (2006). Aggressive marital conflict, maternal harsh punishment, and child aggressive–disruptive behavior: Evidence for direct and mediated relations. *Journal of Family Psychology, 20,* 217–226.

Erdberg, P. (2000). Rorschach assessment. In G. Goldstein & M. Hersen (Eds.), *Handbook of psychological assessment* (pp. 437–449). New York: Pergamon Press.

Erikson, E. (1982). *The life cycle completed.* New York: Norton.

Ernst, C., & Angst, J. (1995). Depression in old age: Is there a real decrease in prevalence? A review. *European Archives of Psychiatry and Clinical Neuroscience, 245*(6), 272–287.

Eron, L., & Huesmann, R. (1990). The stability of aggressive behavior—Even unto the third generation. In M. Lewis & S. Miller (eds.), *Handbook of developmental psychopathology* (pp. 147–156). New York: Plenum.

Ertekin, C., Colakoglu, Z., & Altay, B. (1995). Hand and genital sympathetic skin potentials in flaccid and erectile penile states in normal potent men and patients with premature ejaculation. *The Journal of Urology, 153,* 76–79.

Escobar, J. I., & Canino, G. (1989). Unexplained physical complaints: Psychopathology and epidemiological correlates. *British Journal of Psychiatry, 154,* 24–27.

Escobar, J. I., Gara, M., Waitzkin, H., Silver, R. C., Holman, A., & Compton, W. (1998). DSM-IV hypochondriasis in primary care. *General Hospital Psychiatry, 20*(3), 155–159.

Eslinger, P. J., & Damasio, A. R. (1985). Severe disturbance of higher cognition after bilateral frontal lobe ablation: Patient EVR. *Neurology, 35,* 1731–1741.

Esposito, C. L., & Clum, G. A. (2003). The relative contribution of diagnostic and psychosocial factors in the prediction of adolescent suicidal ideation. *Journal of Clinical Child and Adolescent Psychology, 32,* 386–395.

Esterling, B., Antoni, M., Schneiderman, N., LaPerriere, A., Ironson, G., Klimas, N., & Fletcher, M. A. (1992). Psychosocial modulation of antibody to Epstein-Barr viral capsid antigen and human herpes virus-Type 6 in HIV-1 infected and at-risk gay men. *Psychosomatic Medicine, 54,* 354–371.

Eth, S. (1990). Posttraumatic stress disorder in childhood. In M. Hersen & C. G. Last (Ed.), *Handbook of child and adult psychopathology: A longitudinal perspective.* Elmsford, NY: Pergamon Press.

Ettinger, A. B., Devinsky, O., Weisbrot, D. M., Ramakrishna, R. K., & Goyal, A. (1999). A comprehensive profile of clinical, psychiatric, and psychosocial characteristics of patients with psychogenic nonepileptic seizures. *Epilepsia, 40*(9), 1292–1298.

Evans, J. A., & Hammerton, J. L. (1985). Chromosomal anomalies. In A. M. Clarke, A. D. B. Clarke, & J. M. Berg (Eds.), *Mental deficiency: The changing outlook* (4th ed., pp. 213–266). New York: Free Press.

Evans, M. D., Hollon, S. D., DeRubeis, R. J., Pinsecki, J. M., Grove, W. M., Garvey, J. J., & Tuason, V. B. (1992). Differential relapse following cognitive therapy and pharmacotherapy for depression. *Archives of General Psychiatry, 49*(10), 802–808.

Evans, R. M., Emsley, C. L., Gao, S., Sahota, A., Hall, K. S., Farlow, M. R., & Hendrie, H. (2000). Serum cholesterol, APOE genotype, and the risk of Alzheimer's disease: A population-based study of African Americans. *Neurology, 54,* 240–242.

Exeter-Kent, H. A., & Page, A. C. (2006). The role of cognitions, trait anxiety and disgust sensitivity in generating faintness around blood–injury phobic stimuli [Special issue]. *Journal of Behavior Therapy and Experimental Psychiatry, 37,* 41–52.

Exner, J. E. (2003). *The Rorschach: A comprehensive system. Basic foundations and principles of interpretation* (4th ed.). New York: Wiley.

Eysenck, H. J. (Ed.) (1967). *The biological basis of personality.* Springfield, IL: Charles C. Thomas.

Eysenck, H. J., & Eysenck, S. B. G. (1975). *Manual for the Eysenck Personality Questionnaire.* London: Hodder & Stoughton.

Eysenck, M. W. (1992). *Anxiety: The cognitive perspective.* Hove, England: Erlbaum.

Ezzel, C. (1993). On borrowed time: Long-term survivors of HIV-l infection. *Journal of NIH Research, 5,* 77–82.

Fackelmann, K. A. (1993). Marijuana and the brain: Scientists discover the brain's own THC. *Science, 143,* 88–94.

Faden, R. R. (1987). Health psychology and public health. In G. L. Stone, S. M. Weiss, J. D. Matarazzo, N. E. Miller, J. Rodin, C. D. Belar, M. J. Follick, & J. E. Singer (Eds.), *Health psychology: A discipline and a profession.* Chicago: University of Chicago Press.

Fagan, P. J., Wise, T. N., Schmidt, C. W., & Berlin, M. D. (2002). Pedophilia. *JAMA, 288,* 2458–2465.

Fahey, V. (1990, January/February). Is everything addictive? *In Health,* p. 27.

Fahrner, E. M. (1987). Sexual dysfunction in male alcohol addicts: Prevalence and treatment. *Archives of Sexual Behavior, 16*(3), 247–257.

Failer, J. L. (2002). *Who qualifies for rights? Homelessness, mental illness, and civil commitment.* Ithaca, NY: Cornell University Press.

Fairburn, C. G. (1985). Cognitive-behavioral treatment for bulimia. In D. M. Garner & P. E. Garfinkel (Eds.), *Handbook of psychotherapy for anorexia nervosa and bulimia* (pp. 160–192). New York: Guilford Press.

Fairburn, C. G., & Cooper, Z. (1993). The eating disorder examination. In C. G. Fairburn & G. T. Wilson (Eds.), *Binge eating: Nature, assessment, and treatment.* (pp. 317–360). New York: Guilford Press.

Fairburn, C. G., & Wilson, G. T. (1993). Binge eating: Definition and classification. In C. G. Fairburn & G. T. Wilson (Eds.), *Binge eating: Nature, assessment, and treatment.* New York: Guilford Press.

Fairburn, C. G., Agras, W. S., & Wilson, G. T. (1992). The research on the treatment of bulimia nervosa: Practical and theoretical implications. In G. H. Anderson & S. H. Kennedy (Eds.), *The biology of feast and famine: Relevance to eating disorders* (pp. 317–340). New York: Academic Press.

Fairburn, C. G., Cooper, Z., & Cooper, P. J. (1986). The clinical features and maintenance of bulimia nervosa. In K. D. Brownell & J. P. Foreyt (Eds.), *Handbook of eating disorders: Physiology, psychology, and treatment of obesity, anorexia, and bulimia* (pp. 389–404). New York: Basic Books.

Fairburn, C. G., Cooper, Z., Doll, H. A., & Davies, B. A. (2005). Identifying dieters who will develop an eating disorder: A prospective, population-based study. *American Journal of Psychiatry, 162,* 2249–2255.

Fairburn, C. G., Cooper, Z., Doll, H. A., & Welch, S. L. (1999). Risk factors for anorexia nervosa. Three integrated case-control comparisons. *Archives of General Psychiatry, 56,* 468–476.

Fairburn, C. G., Cooper, Z., Doll, H. A., Norman, P., & O'Connor, M. (2000). The natural course of bulimia nervosa and binge eating disorder in young women. *Archives of General Psychiatry, 57,* 659–665.

Fairburn, C. G., Cooper, Z., & Shafran, R. (2003). Cognitive behavior therapy for eating disorders: A "transdiagnostic" theory and treatment. *Behaviour Research and Therapy, 41,* 509–528.

Fairburn, C. G., Cooper, Z., Shafran, R., & Wilson, T. (in press). Eating disorders: A transdiagnostic protocol. In D H. Barlow (Ed.), *Clinical handbook of psychological disorders: A step-by-step treatment manual* (4th ed.). New York: Guilford Press.

Fairburn, C. G., Cowen, P. J., & Harrison, P. J. (1999). Twin studies and the etiology of eating disorders. *International Journal of Eating Disorders, 26*(4), 349–358.

Fairburn, C. G., Doll, H. A., Welch, S. L., Hay, P. J., Davies, B. A., & O'Connor, M. E. (1998). Risk factors for binge eating disorder. *Archives of General Psychiatry, 55,* 425–432.

Fairburn, C. G., Hay, P. J., & Welch, S. L. (1993). Binge eating and bulimia nervosa: Distribution and determinants. In C. G. Fairburn & G. T. Wilson (Eds.), *Binge eating: Nature, assessment, and treatment.* New York: Guilford Press.

Fairburn, C. G., Jones, R., Peveler, R. C., Hope, R. A., & O'Connor, M. (1993). Psychotherapy and bulimia nervosa: The longer-term effects of interpersonal psychotherapy, behaviour therapy and cognitive behaviour therapy. *Archives of General Psychiatry, 50,* 419–428.

Fairburn, C. G., Marcus, M. D., & Wilson, G. T. (1993). Cognitive behaviour therapy for binge eating and bulimia nervosa: A comprehensive treatment manual. In C. G. Fairburn & G. T. Wilson (Eds.), *Binge eating: Nature, assessment, and treatment.* New York: Guilford Press.

Fairburn, C. G., Norman, P. A., Welch, S. L., O'Connor, M. E., Doll, H., & Peveler, R. C. (1995). A prospective study of outcome in bulimia nervosa and the long-term effects of three psychological treatments. *Archives of General Psychiatry, 52,* 304–312.

Fairburn, C. G., Shafran, R., & Cooper, Z. (1999). A cognitive behavioural theory of anorexia nervosa. *Behaviour Research and Therapy, 37,* 1–13.

Fairburn, C. G., Stice, E., Cooper, Z., Doll, H. A., Norman, P. A., & O'Connor, M. E. (2003). Understanding persistence in bulimia nervosa: A 5-year naturalistic study. *Journal of Consulting and Clinical Psychology, 71,* 103–109.

Fairburn, C. G., Welch, S. L., Doll, S. A., Davies, B. A., & O'Connor, M. E. (1997). Risk factors for bulimia nervosa: A community-based case-control study. *Archives of General Psychiatry, 54,* 509–517.

Fallon, A. (1990). Culture in the mirror: Sociocultural determinants of body image. In T. F. Cash & T. Pruzinsky (Eds.), *Body images: Development, deviance, and change* (pp. 80–109). New York: Guilford Press.

Fallon, A. E., & Rozin, P. (1985). Sex differences in perceptions of desirable body shape. *Journal of Abnormal Psychology, 94,* 102–105.

Fallon, B. A., Altamari, I., Qureshi, A. I., Schneier, F. R., Sanchez-Lacay, A., Vermes, D., et al. (2003). An open trial of fluvoxamine for hypochondriasis. *Psychosomatics, 44,* 298–303.

Fallon, I. R. H., Boyd, J. L., McGill, C. W., Williamson, M., Razani, J., Moss, H. B., et al. (1985). Family management in the prevention of morbidity of schizophrenia. *Archives of General Psychiatry, 42,* 887–896.

Fallon, I. R. H., Brooker, C., & Graham-Hole, V. (1992). Psychosocial interventions for schizophrenia. *Behaviour Change, 9,* 238–245.

Faraone, S.V. (2003). Report from the 4th international meeting of the attention deficit hyperactivity disorder molecular genetics network. *American Journal of Medical Genetics, 121,* 55–59.

Faraone, S.V., Biederman, J., Mick, E., Williamson, S., Wilens, T., Spencer, T., et al. (2000). Family study of girls with attention deficit hyperactivity disorder. *American Journal of Psychiatry, 157*(7), 1077–1083.

Faraone, S.V., Biederman, J., Woznaik, J., Mundy, E., Mennin, D., & O'Donnell, D. (1997). Comorbidity w/ ADHD a marker for juvenile onset mania? *Journal of the American Academy of Child and Adolescent Psychiatry, 36*(8), 1046–1055.

Farde, L., Gustavsson, J. P., & Jonsson, E. (1997). D2 dopamine receptors and personality traits. *Nature, 385,* 590.

Fausto-Sterling, A. (2000a). The five sexes, revisited. *The Sciences, 40*(4), 19–23.

Fausto-Sterling, A. (2000b). *Sexing the body.* New York: Basic.

Fava, G. A., Grandi, S., Rafanelli, C., Fabbri, S., & Cazzaro, M. (2000). Explanatory therapy in hypochondriasis. *Journal of Clinical Psychiatry, 61*(4), 317–322.

Fava, G. A., Grandi, S., Zielezny, M., Rafanelli, C., & Canestrari, R. (1996). Four-year outcome for cognitive behavioral treatment of residual symptoms in major depression. *American Journal of Psychiatry, 153,* 945–947.

Fava, G. A., Rafanelli, C., Grandi, S., Conti, S., & Belluardo, P. (1998). Prevention of recurrent depression with cognitive behavioral therapy: Preliminary finding. *Archives of General Psychiatry, 55*(9), 816–820.

Fava, G. A., Ruini, C., Rafanelli, C., Finos, L., Conti, S., & Grandi, S. (2004). Six-year outcome of cognitive behavior therapy for prevention of recurrent depression. *American Journal of Psychiatry, 161,* 1872–1876.

Fava, M. (2003). Can long-term treatment with antidepressant drugs worsen the course of depression? *The Journal of Clinical Psychiatry, 64,* 26–29.

Fava, M., & Rosenbaum, J. F. (1991). Suicidality and fluoxetine: Is there a relationship? *Journal of Clinical Psychiatry, 52*(3), 108–111.

Fawzy, F. I., Cousins, N., Fawzy, N. W., Kemeny, M. E., Elashoff, R., & Morton, D. (1990). A structured psychiatric intervention for cancer patients: I. Changes over time in methods of coping and affective disturbance. *Archives of General Psychiatry, 47,* 720–728.

Fawzy, F. I., Fawzy, N. W., Hyun, C. S., Elashoff, R., Guthrie, D., Fahey, J. L., & Morton, D. L. (1993). Malignant melanoma: Effects of an early structured psychiatric intervention, coping, and affective state on recurrence and survival 6 years later. *Archives of General Psychiatry, 50,* 681–689.

Fawzy, F. I., Kemeny, M. E., Fawzy, N. W., Elashoff, R., Morton, D., Cousins, N., & Fahey, J. L. (1990). A structured psychiatric intervention for cancer patients: II. Changes over time in immunological measures. *Archives of General Psychiatry, 47,* 729–735.

Fazel, S., & Grann, M. (2006). The population impact of severe mental illness on violent crime. *American Journal of Psychiatry, 163,* 1397–1403.

Federoff, J. P., Fishell, A., & Federoff, B. (1999). A case series of women evaluated for paraphilic sexual disorders. *Canadian Journal of Human Sexuality, 8*(2), 127–140.

Feinberg, M., & Carroll, B. J. (1984). Biological "markers" for endogenous depression: Effect of age, severity of illness, weight loss and polarity. *Archives of General Psychiatry, 41,* 1080–1085.

Feingold, B. F. (1975). *Why your child is hyperactive.* New York: Random House.

Feinstein, C., & Phillips, J. M. (2006). Developmental disorders of communication, motor skills, and learning. In M. K. Dulcan & J. M. Wiener (Eds.), *Essentials of child and adolescent psychiatry* (pp. 203–231). Washington, DC: American Psychiatric Publishing.

Feldman, H. A., Goldstein, I., Hatzichristou, D. G., Krane, R. J., & McKunlay, J. B. (1994). Impotence and its medical and psychosocial correlates: Results of the Massachusetts Male Aging Study. *Journal of Urology, 151,* 54–61.

Fennig, S., Fochtmann, L. J., & Bromet, E. J. (2005). Delusional disorder and shared psychotic disorder. In B. J. Sadock & V. A. Sadock (Eds.), *Kaplan & Sadock's comprehensive textbook of psychiatry* (pp. 1525–1533). Philadelphia: Lippincott, Williams & Wilkins.

Fennig, S., Fochtmann, L. J., & Carlson, G. A. (2005). Schizoaffective disorder. In B. J. Sadock & V. A. Sadock (Eds.), *Kaplan & Sadock's comprehensive textbook of psychiatry* (pp. 1533–1536). Philadelphia: Lippincott, Williams & Wilkins.

Fenton, W. S. (2005). Schizophrenia: Integrative treatment and functional outcomes. In B. J. Sadock & V. A. Sadock (Eds.), *Kaplan & Sadock's comprehensive textbook of psychiatry* (pp. 1487–1501). Philadelphia: Lippincott, Williams & Wilkins.

Ferber, R. (1985). *Solve your child's sleep problems.* New York: Simon & Schuster.

Fergusson, D., & Woodward, L. J. (2002). Mental health, educational, and social role outcomes of adolescents with depression. *Archives of General Psychiatry, 59,* 225–231.

Fergusson, D., Doucette, D., Glass, K., Shapiro, S., Healy, D., Herber, P., & Hutton, B. (2005). Association between suicide attempts and selective serotonin reuptake inhibitors: Systematic review of randomized controlled trials. *BMJ, 330,* 396–402.

Fergusson, D., Horwood, J., Ridder, E., & Beutrais, A. (2005). Subthreshold depression in adolescence and mental health outcomes in adulthood. *Archives General of Psychiatry, 62,* 66–72.

Fernandez, F., Levy, J. K., Lachar, B. L., & Small, G. W. (1995). The management of depression and anxiety in the elderly. *Journal of Clinical Psychiatry, 56*(Suppl. 2), 20–29.

Ferreira, C. (2000). Serial killers: Victims of compulsion or masters of control? In D. H. Fishbein (Ed.), *The science, treatment, and prevention of antisocial behaviors: Application to the criminal justice system* (pp. 15-1–15-18). Kingston, NJ: Civic Research Institute.

Ferri, C. P., Prince, M., Brayne, C., Brodaty, H., Fratiglioni, L., Ganguli, M., et al. (2005). Global prevalence of dementia: A Delphi consensus study. *Lancet, 366,* 2112–2117.

Ferster, C. B. (1961). Positive reinforcement and behavioral deficits of autistic children. *Child Development, 32,* 437–456.

Ferster, C. B., & Skinner, B. F. (1957). *Schedules of reinforcement.* New York: Appleton-Century-Crofts.

Feske, U., & Chambless, D. L. (1995). Cognitive behavioral versus exposure only treatment for social phobia: A meta-analysis. *Behavior Therapy, 26,* 695–720.

Feuerstein, M., Labbe, E. E., & Kuczmierczyk, A. R. (1986). *Health psychology: A psychobiological perspective.* New York: Plenum Press.

Fewell, R. R., & Glick, M. P. (1996). Program evaluation findings of an intensive early intervention program. *American Journal on Mental Retardation, 101,* 233–243.

Field, A. E., Camargo, C. A., Taylor, C. B., Bekey, C. S., Roberts, S. B., & Colditz, G. A. (2001). Peer, parent and media influences on the development of weight concerns and frequent dieting among preadolescent and adolescent girls and boys. *Pediatrics, 107,* 54–60.

Field, A. E., Cheung, L., Wolf, A. M., Herzog, D. B., Gortmaker, S. L., & Colditz, G. A. (1999). Exposure to the mass media and weight concerns among girls. *Pediatrics, 103,* e36.

Field, T., Healy, B., Goldstein, S., Perry, S., Bendell, D., Schanberg, S., Zimmerman, E. A., & Kuhn, C. (1988). Infants of depressed mothers show "depressed" behavior even with nondepressed adults. *Child Development, 59*(6), 1569–1579.

Fincham, F. D., Beach, S. R. H., Harold, G. T., & Osborne, L. N. (1997). Marital satisfaction and depression: Different causal relationships for men and women? *Psychological Science, 8*(5), 351–357.

Finger, S., & Zaromb, F. (2006). Benjamin Franklin and shock-induced amnesia. *American Psychologist, 61,* 240–248.

Finkenbine, R., & Miele, V. J. (2004). Globus hystericus: A brief review. *General Hospital Psychiatry, 26,* 78–82.

Finney, M. L., Stoney, C. M., & Engebretson, T. O. (2002). Hostility and anger expression in African-American and European American men is associated with cardiovascular and lipid reactivity. *Psychophysiology, 39,* 340–349.

First, M. B., & Pincus, H. A. (2002). The DSM-IV text revision: Rationale and potential impact on clinical practice. *Psychiatric Services, 53,* 288–292.

First, M. B., Bell, C. C., Cuthbert, B., Krystal, J. H., Malison, R., Offord, D. R., et al. (2002). Personality disorders and relational disorders: A research agenda for addressing crucial gaps in DSM. In D. J. Kupfer, M. B. First & D. A. Regier (Eds.), *A research agenda for DSM-V* (pp. 123–199). Washington, DC: American Psychiatric Association. Grady-Weliky, T. (2003). Premenstrual dysphoric disorder. *New England Journal of Medicine, 345,* 433–438.

Fischer, M. (1971). Psychoses in the offspring of schizophrenic monozygotic twins and their normal co-twins. *British Journal of Psychiatry, 118,* 43–52.

Fish, B. (1977). Neurobiological antecedents of schizophrenia in children: Evidence for an inherited, congenital, neurointegrative defect. *Archives of General Psychiatry, 34,* 1297–1313.

Fishbain, D. A. (1987). Kleptomania as risk-taking behavior in response to depression. *American Journal of Psychotherapy, 41,* 598–603.

Fitts, S. N., Gibson, P., Redding, C. A., & Deiter, P. J. (1989). Body dysmorphic disorder: Implications for its validity as a DSM-III-R clinical syndrome. *Psychological Reports, 64,* 655–658.

Fitzgerald, P., Benitez, J., de Castella, A., Daskalakis, Z., Brown, T., & Kulkarni, J. (2006). A randomized controlled trial of sequential bilateral repetitive transcranial magnetic stimulation for treatment-resistant depression. *American Journal of Psychiatry, 163,* 88–94.

Fitzgerald, P. B., Brown, T. L., Marston, N. A., Daskalakis, J., De Castella, A., & Kulkarni, J. (2003). Transcranial magnetic stimulation in the treatment of depression: A double-blind, placebo-controlled trial. *Archives of General Psychiatry, 60,* 1002–1008.

Fitzgerald, P. B., Sritharan, A., Benitez, J., Daskalakis, Z. J., Jackson, G., Kulkarni, J., & Egan, G. F. (2007). A preliminary fMRI study of the effects on cortical activation of the treatment of refractory auditory hallucinations with rTMS. *Psychiatry Research: Neuroimaging, 155,* 83–88.

Fitzpatrick, A. L., Kuller, L. H., Ives, D. G., Lopez, O. L., Jagust, W., Breitner, J. C., et al. (2004). Incidence and prevalence of dementia in the cardiovascular health study. *Journal of the American Geriatric Society, 52,* 195–204.

Flaherty, J. H., Rudolph, J., Shay, K., Kamholz, B., Boockvar, K. S., Shaughnessy, M., et al. (2007). Delirium is a serious and under-recognized problem: Why assessment of mental status should be the sixth vital sign. *Journal of the American Medical Directors Association, 8,* 273–275.

Flanagan, D. P., & Harrison, P. L. (Eds.) (2005). *Contemporary intellectual assessment: Theories, tests, and issues* (2nd ed.). New York: Guilford Press.

Flannery, D. J., Liau, A. K., Powell, K. E., Vesterdal, W., Vazsonyi, A. T., Guo, S., et al. (2003). Initial behavior outcomes for the PeaceBuilders universal school-based violence prevention program. *Developmental Psychology, 39,* 292–308.

Flegal, K. M., Carroll, M. D., Odgen, C. L., & Johnson, C. L. (2002). Prevalence and trends in obesity among U.S. adults, 1999–2000. *JAMA, 288,* 1723–1727.

Flegal, K. M., Graubard, B. I., Williamson, D. F., & Gail, M. H. (2005). Excess deaths associated with underweight, overweight, and obesity. *JAMA, 293,* 1861–1867.

Fleshner, C. L. (1995). First person account: Insight from a schizophrenia patient with depression. *Schizophrenia Bulletin, 21,* 703–707.

Fletcher, J. M., Lyon, G. R., Fuchs, L. S., & Barnes, M. A. (2007). *Learning disabilities: From identification to intervention.* New York: Guilford Press.

Flint, A. (1994). Epidemiology and co-morbidity of anxiety disorders in the elderly. *American Journal of Psychiatry, 151,* 640–649.

Flint, A., Schaffer, A., Meyers, B., Rothschild, A., & Mulsant, B. (2006). Research assessment of patients with psychotic depression: The STOP-PD approach. *Psychiatric Annals, 36,* 48–56.

Flor, H., Elbert, T., Kenecht, S., Weinbruch, C., Pantev, C., Birbaumer, N., et al. (1995). Phantom limb pain as a perceptual correlate of cortical reorganization following arm amputation. *Nature, 375,* 482–484.

Flynn, J. R. (1984). The mean IQ of Americans: Massive gains 1932 to 1978. *Psychological Bulletin, 95,* 29–51.

Foa, E. B., & Franklin, M. E. (2001). Obsessive compulsive disorder. In D. H. Barlow (Ed.), *Clinical Handbook of Psychological Disorders.* (3rd ed.). New York: Guilford Press.

Foa, E. B., Jenike, M., Kozak, M. J., Joffe, R., Baer, L., Pauls, D., et al. (1996). Obsessive-compulsive disorder. In T. A. Widiger, A. J. Frances, H. A. Pincus, M. R. Ross, M. B. First, & W. W. Davis (Eds.), *DSM-IV sourcebook* (Vol. 2, pp. 549– 576). Washington, DC: American Psychiatric Association.

Foa, E. B., Liebowitz, M. R., Kozak, M. J., Davies, S., Campeas, R., Franklin, M. E., et al. (2005). Randomized, placebo-controlled trial of exposure and ritual prevention, clomipramine, and their combination in the treatment of obsessive-compulsive disorder. *American Journal of Psychiatry, 162,* 151–161.

Fogelson, D. L., Nuechterlein, K. H., Asarnow, R. A., Payne, D. L., Subotnik, K. L., Jacobson, K. C., et al. (2007). Avoidant personality disorder is a separable schizophrenia-spectrum personality disorder even when controlling for the presence of paranoid and schizotypal personality disorders: The UCLA family study. *Schizophrenia Research, 91,* 192–199.

Folks, D. G., Ford, C. U., & Regan, W. M. (1984). Conversion symptoms in a general hospital. *Psychosomatics, 25*(4), 285–295.

Follette, W. C., & Houts, A. C. (1996). Models of scientific progress and the role of theory in taxonomy development: A case study of the DSM. *Journal of Consulting and Clinical Psychology, 64*(6), 1120–1132.

Folsom, D. P., Hawthorne, W., Lindamer, L., Gilmer, T., Bailey, A., Golshan, S., et al. (2005). Prevalence and risk factors for homelessness and utilization of mental health services among 10,340 patients with serious mental illness in a large public mental health system. *American Journal of Psychiatry, 162,* 370–376.

Folstein M. F., Folstein, S. E., & McHugh, P. R. (1975). "Mini-mental state." A practical method for grading the cognitive state of patients for the clinician. *Journal of Psychiatric Research*, 12, 189–198.

Ford, C.V. (1985). Conversion disorders: An overview. *Psychosomatics, 26,* 371–383.

Ford, C., & Beach, F. (1951). *Patterns of sexual behavior.* New York: Harper & Row.

Ford, M. R., & Widiger, T. A. (1989). Sex bias in the diagnosis of histrionic and antisocial personality disorders. *Journal of Consulting and Clinical Psychology, 57,* 301–305.

Fordyce, W. E. (1976). *Behavioral methods in chronic pain and illness.* St. Louis, MO: Mosby.

Fordyce, W. E. (1988). Pain and suffering: A reappraisal. *American Psychologist, 43*(4), 276–283.

Fossati, A., Maffei, C., Bagnato, M., Donati, D., Donini, M., Fiorilli, M., & Novella, L. (2000). A psychometric study of DSM-IV passive-aggressive (negativistic) personality disorder criteria. *Journal of Personality Disorders, 14,* 72–83.

Fowles, D. C. (1988). Psychophysiology and psychopathy: A motivational approach. *Psychophysiology, 25,* 373–391.

Fowles, D. C. (1993). A motivational theory of psychopathology. In W. Spaulding (Ed.), *Nebraska symposium on motivation: Integrated views of motivation, cognition, and emotion* (Vol. 41, pp. 181–238). Lincoln: University of Nebraska Press.

Fox, E., & Damjanovic, L. (2006) The eyes are sufficient to produce a threat superiority effect. *Emotion, 6,* 534–539.

Foy, D. W., Resnick, H. S., Sipprelle, R. C., & Carroll, E. M. (1987). Premilitary, military and postmilitary factors in the development of combat related posttraumatic stress disorder. *The Behavior Therapist, 10,* 3–9.

Foy, D. W., Sipprelle, R. C., Rueger, D. B., & Carroll, E. M. (1984). Etiology of posttraumatic stress disorder in Vietnam veterans: Analysis of premilitary, military, and combat exposure influences. *Journal of Consulting and Clinical Psychology, 52,* 79–87.

Frances, A., & Blumenthal, S. J. (1989). Personality disorders and characteristics in youth suicide. In *Alcohol, drug abuse and mental health administration. Report of the secretary's task force on youth suicide: Vol. 12, risk factors for youth suicide* (DHHS Publication No. ADM89-1622, pp. 172–185). Washington, DC: U.S. Government Printing Office.

Frances, A., & Widiger, T. A. (1986). Methodological issues in personality disorder diagnosis. In T. Millon & G. Klerman (Ed.), *Contemporary directions in psychopathology.* New York: Guilford Press.

Frances, R., Franklin, J., & Flavin, D. (1986). Suicide and alcoholism. *Annals of the New York Academy of Science, 287,* 316–326.

Francis, D. D., Diorio, J., Plotsky, P. M., & Meaney, M. J. (2002). Environmental enrichment reverses the effects of maternal separation on stress reactivity. *Journal of Neuroscience, 22,* 7840–7843.

Francis, D., Diorio, J., Liu, D., & Meaney, M. J. (1999). Nongenomic transmission across generations of maternal behavior and stress responses in the rat. *Science, 286,* 1155–1158.

Francis, G., Last, C. G., & Strauss, C. C. (1987). Expression of separation anxiety disorder: The roles of age and gender. *Child Psychiatry and Human Development, 18,* 82–89.

Franco, K. N., & Messinger-Rapport, B. (2006). Pharmacological treatment of neuropsychiatric symptoms of dementia: A review of the evidence. *Journal of the American Medical Directors Association, 7,* 201–202.

Frank, E., Anderson, C., & Rubinstein, D. (1978). Frequency of sexual dysfunction in "normal" couples. *New England Journal of Medicine, 299,* 111–115.

Frank, E., Cyranowski, J. M., Rucci, P., Shear, M. K., Fagiolini, A., Thase, M. E., et al. (2002). Clinical significance of lifetime panic spectrum symptoms in the treatment of patients with bipolar I disorder. *Archives of General Psychiatry. 59,* 905–911.

Frank, E., Hlastala, S., Ritenour, A., Houck, P., Tu, X. M., Monk, T. H., et al. (1997). Inducing lifestyle regularity in recovering bipolar disorder patients: Results from the Maintenance Therapies in Bipolar Disorder Protocol. *Biological Psychiatry, 41,* 1165–1173.

Frank, E., Kupfer, D. J., Perel, J. M., Cornes, C., Jarrett, D. B., Mallinger, A. G., et al. (1990). Three-year outcomes for maintenance therapies in recurrent depression. *Archives of General Psychiatry, 47*(12), 1093–1099.

Frank, E., Kupfer, D., Thase, M., Mallinger, A., Swartz, H., Eagiolini, A., et al. (2005). Two-year outcomes for interpersonal and social rhythm therapy in individuals with bipolar I disorder. *Archives of General Psychiatry, 62,* 996–1004.

Frank, E., Swartz, H. A., Mallinger, A. G., Thase, M. E., Weaver, E. V., & Kupfer, D. J. (1999). Adjunctive psychotherapy for bipolar disorder: Effects of changing treatment modality. *Journal of Abnormal Psychology, 108*(4), 579–587.

Frankel, E. B., & Gold, S. (2007). Principles and practices of early intervention. In I. Brown & M. Percy (Eds.), *A comprehensive guide to intellectual & developmental disabilities* (pp. 451–466). Baltimore: Paul H. Brookes.

Franklin, D. (1990, November/December). Hooked–Not hooked: Why isn't everyone an addict? *Health,* pp. 39–52.

Franklin, J. E., & Frances, R. J. (1999). Alcohol and other psychoactive substance use disorders. In R. E. Hales, S. C. Yudofsky, & J. A. Talbott (Eds.), *Textbook of psychiatry* (3rd ed., pp. 363–423). Washington, DC: American Psychiatric Press.

Franko, D. L., Wonderlich, S. A., Little, D., & Herzog, D. B. (2004). Diagnosis and classification of eating disorders. In J. K. Thompson (Ed.), *Handbook of eating disorders and obesity* (pp. 58–80). New York: John Wiley.

Frasure-Smith, N., & Lesperance, F. (2005). Depression and coronary heart disease: Complex synergism of mind, body, and environment. *Current Directions in Psychological Science, 14,* 39–43.

Frasure-Smith, N., Lesperance, F., Juneau, M., Talajic, M., & Bourassa, M. G. (1999). Gender, depression, and one-year prognosis after myocardial infarction. *Psychosomatic Medicine, 61,* 26–37.

Fratiglioni, L., Grut, M., Forsell, Y., Viitanen, M., Grafstrom, M., Holmen, K., et al. (1991). Prevalence of Alzheimer's disease and other dementias in an elderly urban population: Relationship with age, sex and education. *Neurology, 41,* 1886–1892.

Fratiglioni, L., Winblad, B., & von Strauss, E. (in press). Prevention of Alzheimer's disease and dementia: Major findings from the Kungsholmen project. *Physiology & Behavior.*

Fredrikson, M., & Matthews, K. A. (1990). Cardiovascular responses to behavioral stress and hypertension: A meta-analytic review. *Annals of Behavioral Medicine, 12*(1), 30–39.

Fredrikson, M., Annas, P., & Wik, G. (1997). Parental history, aversive exposure and the development of snake and spider phobia in women. *Behavior Research and Therapy, 35,* 23–28.

Freedman, M., King, J., & Kennedy, E. (2001). Popular diets: A scientific review. *Obesity Research, 9*(Suppl.), 1S–38.

Freeman, A., Pretzer, J., Fleming, B., & Simon, K. M. (1990). *Clinical applications of cognitive therapy.* New York: Plenum Press.

Freeman, E., Sammel, M., Lin, H., & Nelson, D. (2006). Associations of hormones and menopausal status with depressed mood in women with no history of depression. *Archive General Psychiatry, 63,* 375–382.

Freeman, M. P., & McElroy, S. L. (1999). Clinical picture and etiological models of mixed states. *Psychiatric Clinics of North America, 22*(3), 535–546.

Freinkel, A., Koopman, C., & Spiegel, D. (1994). Dissociative symptoms in media eyewitnesses of an execution. *American Journal of Psychiatry, 151,* 1335–1339.

French-Belgian Collaborative Group. (1982). Ischemic heart disease and psychological patterns: Prevalence and incidence studies in Belgium and France. *Advances in Cardiology, 29,* 25–31.

Freud, A. (1946). *Ego and the mechanisms of defense.* New York: International Universities Press.

Freud, S. (1957). Mourning and melancholia. In J. Strachey (Ed. and Trans.), *The standard edition of the complete psychological works of Sigmund Freud* (Vol. 14). London: Hogarth Press. (Original work published 1917.)

Freud, S. (1962). The neuro-psychoses of defence. In J. Strachey (Ed.), *The complete psychological works* (Vol. 3, pp. 45–62). London: Hogarth Press. (Original work published 1894.)

Freud, S. (1974). On coca. In R. Byck (Ed.), *Cocaine papers by Sigmund Freud* (pp. 49–73). New York: Stonehill. (Original work published 1885.)

Freund, K., Seto, M. C., & Kuban, M. (1996). Two types of fetishism. *Behaviour Research and Therapy, 34,* 687–694.

Friedl, M. C., & Draijer, N. (2000). Dissociative disorders in Dutch psychiatric inpatients. *American Journal of Psychiatry, 157*(6), 1012–1013.

Friedman, M., & Rosenman, R. H. (1959). Association of specific overt behavior pattern with blood and cardiovascular findings. *JAMA, 169,* 1286.

Friedman, M., & Rosenman, R. H. (1974). *Type A behavior and your heart.* New York: Knopf.

Friedman, M., Thoresen, C. E., Gill, J., Powell, L. H., Ulmer, D., Thompson, L., et al. (1984). Alteration of type A behavior and reduction in cardiac recurrences in post-myocardial infarction patients. *American Heart Journal, 108,* 237–248.

Friedman, S., Paradis, C. M., & Hatch, M. (1994). Characteristics of African-American and white patients with panic disorder and agoraphobia. *Hospital & Community Psychiatry, 45,* 798–803.

Frohlich, C., Jacobi, F., & Wittchen, H. (2006). DSM-IV pain disorder in the general population: An exploration of the structure and threshold of medically unexplained pain symptoms. *European Archives of Psychiatry and Clinical Neuroscience, 256,* 187–196.

Fromm-Reichmann, F. (1948). Notes on the development of treatment of schizophrenics by psychoanalytic psychotherapy. *Psychiatry, 11,* 263–273.

Frost, R. O., Sher, K. J., & Geen, T. (1986). Psychotherapy and personality characteristics of non-clinical compulsive checkers. *Behaviour Research and Therapy, 24,* 133–143.

Frost, R. O., Steketee, G., & Williams, L. (2002). Compulsive buying, compulsive hoarding, and obsessive-compulsive disorder. *Behavior Therapy, 33,* 201–214.

Fryar, C., Hirsch, R., Porter, K., Kottiri, B., Brody, D., & Louis, T. (2007). *Drug use and sexual behaviors reported by adults: United States, 1999–2002* (Advance data from Vital and Health Statistics, No. 384). Hyattsville, MD: National Center for Health Statistics.

Fugl-Meyer, A. R., & Sjogren Fugl-Meyer, K. (1999). Sexual disabilities, problems, and satisfaction in 18–74 year old Swedes. *Scandinavian Journal of Sexology, 3,* 79–105.

Fujita, M., Kugaya, A., & Innis, R. B. (2005). Radiotracer imaging: Basic principles and exemplary findings in neuropsychiatric disorders. In B. J. Sadock & V. A. Sadock (Eds.), *Kaplan & Sadock's comprehensive textbook of psychiatry* (pp. 222–235). Philadelphia: Lippincott Williams & Wilkins.

Fukuda, K., Straus, S. E., Hickie, I., Sharpe, M. B., Dobbins, J. G., & Komaroff, A. L. (1994). Chronic fatigue syndrome: A comprehensive approach to its diagnosis and management. *Annals of Internal Medicine, 121,* 953–959.

Furberg, H., Olarte, M., Afari, N., Goldberg, J., Buchwald, D., & Sullivan, P. (2005). The prevalence of self-reported chronic fatigue in a U.S. twin registry. *Journal of Psychosomatic Research, 59,* 283–290.

Furmark, T., Tillfors, M., Marteinsdottir, I., Fischer, H., Pissiota, A., Långström, B., et al. (2002). Common changes in cerebral blood flow in patients with social phobia treated with citalopram or cognitive-behavioral therapy. *Archives of General Psychiatry, 59,* 425–433.

Furnham, A., & Wong, L. (2007). A cross-cultural comparison of British and Chinese beliefs about the causes, behaviour manifestations and treatment of schizophrenia. *Psychiatry Research, 151,* 123–138.

Fyer, A. J., Mannuzza, S., Chapman, T. F., Liebowitz, M. R., & Klein, D. F. (1993). A direct interview family study of social phobia. *Archives of General Psychiatry, 50,* 286–293.

Fyer, A. J., Mannuzza, S., Gallops, M. S., Martin, L. Y., Aaronson, C., Gorman, J. M., et al. (1990). Familial transmission of simple phobias and fears: A preliminary report. *Archives of General Psychiatry, 47,* 252–256.

Fyer, A., Liebowitz, M., Gorman, J., Compeas, R., Levin, A., Davies, S., et al. (1987). Discontinuation of alprazolam treatment in panic patients. *American Journal of Psychiatry, 144,* 303–308.

Gagnon, J. H. (1990). The explicit and implicit use of the scripting perspective in sex research. *Annual Review of Sex Research, 1,* 1–43.

Gajria, M., Jitendra, A. K., Sood, S., & Sacks, G. (2007). Improving comprehension of expository text in students with LD: A research synthesis. *Journal of Learning Disabilities, 40,* 210–225.

Galea, S., Ahern, J., Resnick, H., Kilpatrick, D., Bucuvalas, M., Gold, J., et al. (2002). Psychological sequelae of the September 11 terrorist attacks in New York City. *New England Journal of Medicine, 346,* 982–987.

Gallagher-Thompson, D., & Osgood, N. J. (1997). Suicide later in life. *Behavior Therapy, 28,* 23–41.

Gallant, D. (1999). Alcohol. In M. Galanter & H. D. Kleber (Eds.), *Textbook of substance abuse treatment* (2nd ed., pp. 151–164). Washington, DC: American Psychiatric Press.

Gallo, L., & Matthews, K. (2003). Understanding the association between socioeconomic status and physical health: Do negative emotions play a role? *Psychological Bulletin, 129,* 10–51.

Garb, H. N., Wood, J. M., Nezworski, M. T., Grove, W. M., & Stejskal, W. J. (2001). Toward a resolution of the Rorschach controversy. *Psychological Assessment, 13,* 433–448.

Garber, J., & Carter, J. S. (2006). Major depression. In R. T. Ammerman (Ed.), *Comprehensive handbook of personality and psychopathology. Volume III: Child Psychopathology* (pp. 165–216). Hoboken, NJ: John Wiley & Sons.

Garcia, J., McGowan, B. K., & Green, K. F. (1972). Biological constraints on conditioning. In A. H. Black & W. F. Prokasy (Eds.), *Classical conditioning II: Current research and theory.* New York: Appleton-Century-Crofts.

Garcia-Campayo, J., Claraco, L. M., Sanz-Carrillo, C., Arevalo, E., & Monton, C. (2002). Assessment of a pilot course on the management of somatization disorder for family doctors. *General Hospital Psychiatry, 24,* 101–105.

Gardner, C., Kiazand, A., Alhassan, S., Soowon, K., Stafford, R., Balise, R., et al. (2007). Comparison of the Atkins, Zone, Ornish, and LEARN diets for change in weight and related risk factors among overweight premenopausal women. *JAMA, 297,* 969–977.

Garfield, A. F., & Zigler, E. (1993). Adolescent suicide prevention: Current research and social policy implications. *American Psychologist, 48*(2), 169–182.

Garfinkel, P. E. (1992). Evidence in support of attitudes to shape and weight as a diagnostic criterion of bulimia nervosa. *International Journal of Eating Disorders, 11*(4), 321–325.

Garfinkel, P. E., Moldofsky, H., & Garner, D. M. (1979). The heterogeneity of anorexia nervosa: Bulimia as a distinct subgroup. *Archives of General Psychiatry, 37,* 1036–1040.

Garland, A. F., & Zigler, E. (1993). Adolescent suicide prevention: Current research and social policy implications. *American Psychologist, 48,* 169–182.

Garlow, S., & Nemeroff, C. B. (2004). Neurochemistry of mood disorders: Clinical studies. In D. S. Charney & E. J. Nestler (Eds.), *The neurobiology of mental illness* (2nd ed.). New York: Oxford University Press.

Garlow, S., Boone, E., Li, W., Owens, M., & Nemeroff, C. (2005). Genetic analysis of the hypothalamic corticotrophin releasing factor system. *Endocrinology, 146,* 2362–2368.

Garlow, S., Purselle, D., & Heninger, M. (2005). Ethnic differences in patterns of suicide across the life cycle. *American Journal of Psychiatry, 162,* 319–323.

Garmezy, N., & Rutter, M. (Eds.) (1983). *Stress, coping and development in children.* New York: McGraw-Hill.

Garner, D. M., & Fairburn, C. G. (1988). Relationship between anorexia nervosa and bulimia nervosa: Diagnostic implications. In D. M. Garner & P. E. Garfinkel (Eds.), *Diagnostic issues in anorexia nervosa and bulimia nervosa.* New York: Brunner/Mazel.

Garner, D. M., & Garfinkel, P. E. (Eds.) (1985). *Handbook of psychotherapy for anorexia nervosa and bulimia.* New York: Guilford Press.

Garner, D. M., & Needleman, L. D. (1996). Step care and the decision-tree models for treating eating disorders. In J. K. Thompson (Ed.), *Body image, eating disorders and obesity* (pp. 225–252). Washington, DC: American Psychological Association.

Garner, D. M., Garfinkel, P. E., Rockert, W., & Olmsted, M. P. (1987). A prospective study of eating disturbances in the ballet. Ninth World Congress of the International College of Psychosomatic Medicine, Sydney, Australia. *Psychotherapy and Psychosomatics, 48,* 170–175.

Garner, D. M., Garfinkel, P. E., Schwartz, D., & Thompson, M. (1980). Cultural expectation of thinness in women. *Psychological Reports, 47,* 483–491.

Garre-Olmo, J., López-Pousa, S., Vilata-Franch, J., Turon-Estrada, A., Lozano-Gallego, M., Hernández-Ferràndiz, M., et al. (2004). Neuropsychological profile of Alzheimer's disease in women: Moderate and moderately severe cognitive decline. *Archives of Women's Mental Health, 7,* 27–36.

Garrity, A. G., Pearlson, G. D., McKiernan, K., Lloyd, D., Kiehl, K. A., & Calhoun, V. D. (2007). Aberrant "default mode" functional connectivity in schizophrenia. *American Journal of Psychiatry, 164,* 450–457.

Gassen, M. D., Pietz, C. A., Spray, B. J., & Denney, R. L. (2007). Accuracy of Megargee's Criminal Offender Infrequency (FC) Scale in detecting malingering among forensic examinees. *Criminal Justice and Behavior, 34,* 493–504.

Gatchel, R. (2005). *Clinical essentials of pain management.* Washington, DC: American Psychological Association.

Gatchel, R. J., & Dersh, J. (2002). Psychological disorders and chronic pain: Are there cause-and-effect relationships? In D. C. Turk & R. J. Gatchel (Eds.), *Psychological approaches to pain management: A practitioner's handbook* (2nd ed.). New York: Guilford Press.

Gatchel, R. J., & Epker, J. (1999). Psychosocial predictors of chronic pain and response to treatment. In R. J. Gatchel & D. C. Turk (Eds.), *Psychosocial factors in pain: Critical perspectives* (pp. 412–434). New York: Guilford Press.

Gatchel, R. J., & Turk, D. C. (Eds.) (1999). Psychosocial factors in pain: Critical perspectives. New York: Guilford Press.

Gatchel, R. J., Peng, Y. B., Peters, M. L., Fuchs, P. N., & Turk, D. C. (2007). The biopsychosocial approach to chronic pain: Scientific advances and future directions. *Psychological Bulletin, 133,* 581–624.

Gatchel, R. J., Polatin, P. B., & Kinney, R. K. (1995). Predicting outcome of chronic back pain using clinical predictors of psychopathology: A prospective analysis. *Health Psychology, 14,* 415–420.

Gatz, M. (2007). Genetics, dementia, and the elderly. *Current Directions in Psychological Science, 16,* 123–127.

Gatz, M., & Smyer, M. A. (1992). The mental health system and older adults in the 1990s. *American Psychologist, 47*(6), 741–751.

Ge, X., Conger, R., & Elder, G. (1996). Coming of age too early: Pubertal influences on girls vulnerability to psychological distress. *Child Development, 67,* 3386–3400.

Gearhart, J. P. (1989). Total ablation of the penis after circumcision electrocautery: A method of management and long term follow-up. *Journal of Urology, 42,* 789–801.

Geer, J. H., Morokoff, P., & Greenwood, P. (1974). Sexual arousal in women: The development of a measurement device for vaginal blood volume. *Archives of Sexual Behavior, 3,* 559–564.

Geller, B., Cooper, T. B., Graham, D. L., Fetaer, H. M., Marsteller, F. A., & Wells, J. M. (1992). Pharmacokinetically designed double blind placebo controlled study of nortriptyline in 6–12 year olds with major depressive disorder: Outcome: Nortriptyline and hydroxy-nortriptyline plasma levels; EKG, BP and side effect measurements. *Journal of the American Academy of Child and Adolescent Psychiatry, 31,* 33–44.

Generations United. (2006). *Meth and child welfare: Promising solutions for children, their parents and grandparents.* Washington, DC: Author.

George, M. S., Lisanby, S. H., & Sakheim, H. A. (1999). Transcranial magnetic stimulation. *Archives of General Psychiatry, 56,* 300–311.

Gershon, E. S. (1990). Genetics. In F. K. Goodwin & K. R. Jamison (Eds.), *Manic-depressive illness* (pp. 373–401). New York: Oxford University Press.

Gershon, E. S., Kelsoe, J. R., Kendler, K. S., & Watson, J. D. (2001). It's time to search for susceptibility genes for major mental illnesses. *Science, 294,* 5.

Gerstein, D. R., Volberg, R. A., Toce, M. T., Harwood, H., Johnson, R. A., Bule, T., et al. (1999). *Gambling impact and behavior study: Report to the national gambling impact study commission.* Chicago: National Opinion Research Center at the University of Chicago.

Gibbons, J. L. (1964). Cortisol secretion rates in depressive illness. *Archives of General Psychiatry, 10,* 572–575.

Gibbons, R., Hur, K., Bhaumik, D., & Mann, J. (2006). The relationship between antidepressant prescription rates and rate of early adolescent suicide. *American Journal of Psychiatry, 163,* 1898–1904.

Gibson, A. P., Hebden, J. C., & Arridge, S. R. (2005). Recent advances in diffuse optical imaging. *Physics in Medicine and Biology, 50,* R1–R43.

Giedke, H., & Schwarzler, F. (2002). Therapeutic use of sleep deprivation in depression. *Sleep Medicine Reviews, 6,* 361–377.

Gieser, L., & Stein, M. I. (Eds.) (1999). *Evocative images: The Thematic Apperception Test and the art of projection.* Washington, DC: American Psychological Association.

Gil, K., Williams, D., Keefe, F., & Beckham, J. (1990). The relationship of negative thoughts to pain and psychological distress. *Behavior Therapy, 21,* 349–362.

Gillham, J. E., Reivich, K. J., Freres, D., Chaplin, T., Shatte, A., Samuels, B., et al. (2007). School-based prevention of depressive symptoms: A randomized controlled study of the effectiveness and specificity of the Penn Resiliency program. *Journal of Consulting and Clinical Psychology, 75,* 9–19.

Gillham, J. E., Reivich, K. J., Jaycox, L. H., & Seligman, M. E. P. (1995). Prevention of depressive symptoms in schoolchildren: Two-year follow-up. *Psychological Science, 6*(6), 343–351.

Gillberg, C. (1984). Infantile autism and other childhood psychoses in a Swedish urban region: Epidemiological aspects. *Journal of Child Psychology and Psychiatry, 25,* 35–43.

Gillin, J. C. (1993). Clinical sleep–wake disorders in psychiatric practice: Dyssomnias. In D. L. Dunner (Ed.), *Current psychiatric therapy* (pp. 373–380). Philadelphia: W. B. Saunders.

Gilmore, J. H., & Murray, R. M. (2006). Prenatal and perinatal factors. In J. A. Lieberman, T. S. Stroup, & D. O. Perkins (Eds.), *The American Psychiatric Pub-*

lishing textbook of schizophrenia (pp. 55–67). Washington, DC: American Psychiatric Publishing.

Giltay, E., Geleijnse, J., Zitman, F., Hoekstra, T., & Schouten, E. (2004). Dispositional optimism and all-cause and cardiovascular mortality in a prospective cohort of elderly Dutch men and women. *Archives of the General Psychiatry, 61,* 1126–1135.

Ginsburg, G. S., & Silverman, W. K. (2000). Gender role orientation and fearfulness in children with anxiety disorders. *Journal of Anxiety Disorders, 14*(1), 57–67.

Gislason, I. L. (1988). Eating disorders in childhood (ages 4 through 11 years). In B. J. Blinder, B. F. Chaitin, & R. S. Goldstein (Eds.), *The eating disorders: Medical and psychological bases of diagnosis and treatment* (pp. 285–293). New York: PMA.

Gitlin, M. J., Swendsen, J., Heller, T. L., & Hammen, C. (1995). Relapse and impairment in bipolar disorder. *American Journal of Psychiatry, 152,* 1635–1640.

Gladue, B. A., Green, R., & Hellman, R. E. (1984). Neuroendocrine response to estrogen and sexual orientation. *Science, 225,* 1496–1499.

Glaser, R., Kennedy, S., Lafuse, W. P., Bonneau, R. H., Speicher, C. E., Hillhouse, J., & Kiecolt-Glaser, J. K. (1990). Psychological stress-induced modulation of IL-2 receptor gene expression and IL-2 production in peripheral blood leukocytes. *Archives of General Psychiatry, 47,* 707–712.

Glaser, R., Kiecolt-Glaser, J. K., Speicher, C. E., & Holliday, J. E. (1985). Stress, loneliness, and changes in herpes virus latency. *Journal of Behavioral Medicine, 8,* 249–260.

Glaser, R., Rice, J., Sheridan, J., Fertel, R., Stout, J., Speicher, C., et al. (1987). Stress-related immune suppression: Health implications. *Brain, Behavior, and Immunity, 1,* 7–20.

Glatt, A. E., Zinner, S. H., & McCormack, W. M. (1990). The prevalence of dyspareunia. *Obstetrics and Gynecology, 75,* 433–436.

Glatt, C. E., Tampilic, M., Christie, C., DeYoung, J., & Freimer, N. B. (2004). Re-screening serotonin receptors for genetic variants identifies population and molecular genetic complexity. *American Journal of Medical Genetics, 124,* 92–100.

Gleason, O. C. (2003). Delirium. *American Family Physician, 67,* 1027–1034.

Gleaves, D. H. (1996). The sociocognitive model of dissociative identity disorder: A reexamination of the evidence. *Psychological Bulletin, 120,* 42–59.

Gleaves, D. H., Lowe, M. R., Snow, A. C., Green, B. A., & Murphy-Eberenz, K. P. (2000). Continuity and discontinuity models of bulimia nervosa: A taxometric investigation. *Journal of Abnormal Psychology, 109*(1), 56–68.

Gleaves, D. H., Smith, S. M., Butler, L. D., & Spiegel, D. (2004). False and recovered memories in the laboratory and clinic: A review of experimental and clinical evidence. *Clinical Psychology: Science and Practice.*

Gloster, A. T. (2006). State of the field in late-life anxiety research: Brief history and promising future. *Anxiety disorders: A quarterly report* (Special Interest Group, ABCT), 1–3.

Goater, N., King, M., Cole, E., Leavey, G., Johnson-Sabine, E., Blizard, R., & Hoar, A. (1999). Ethnicity and outcomes of psychosis. *British Journal of Psychiatry, 175,* 34–42.

Goel, M. S., McCarthy, E. P., Phillips, R. S., & Wee, C. C. (2004). Obesity among U.S. immigrant subgroups by duration of residence. *JAMA, 292,* 2860–2867.

Goering, P., Durbin, J., Sheldon, C. T., Ochocka, J., Nelson, G., & Krupa, T. (2006). Who uses consumer-run self-help organizations? *American Journal of Orthopsychiatry, 76,* 367–373.

Goff, D. C., & Coyle, J. T. (2001). The emerging role of glutamate in the pathophysiology and treatment of schizophrenia. *American Journal of Psychiatry, 158,* 1367–1377.

Gold, J. H. (1997). Premenstrual dysphoric disorder: What's that? *JAMA, 278,* 1024–1025.

Gold, J. H. (1999). Premenstrual dysphoric disorder: An update. *Journal of Practical Psychiatry and Behavioral Health, 5,* 209–215.

Gold, J. H., Endicott, J., Parry, B. L., Severino, S. K., Stotland, N., & Frank, E. (1996). Late luteal phase dysphoric disorder. In T. A. Widiger, A. J. Frances, H. A. Pincus, Ross, R., First, M. B., & Davis, W. W. (Eds.), *DSM-IV sourcebook* (Vol. 2, pp. 317–394). Washington, DC: American Psychiatric Association.

Gold, M. S. (1997). Cocaine (and crack): Clinical aspects. In J. H. Lowinson, P. Ruiz, R. B. Millman, & J. G. Langrod (Eds.), *Substance abuse: A comprehensive textbook* (pp. 181–199). Baltimore: Williams & Wilkins.

Gold, P. W., Goodwin, F. K., & Chrousos, G. P. (1988). Clinical and biochemical manifestations of depression: Relation to the neurobiology of stress. *New England Journal of Medicine, 319,* 348–353.

Goldberg, J. F., Harrow, M., & Grossman, L. S. (1995). Course and outcome in bipolar affective disorder: A longitudinal follow-up study. *American Journal of Psychiatry, 152,* 379–384.

Goldberg, L. (1993). The structure of phenotypic personality traits. *American Psychologist, 48,* 26–34.

Goldberg, S. C., Schultz, C., Resnick, R. J., Hamer, R. M., & Schultz, P. M. (1987). Differential prediction of response to thiothixene and placebo in borderline and schizotypal personality disorders. *Psychopharmacology Bulletin, 23,* 342–346.

Golden, C. J., Hammeke, T. A., & Purisch, A. D. (1980). *The Luria-Nebraska Battery manual.* Palo Alto, CA: Western Psychological Services.

Golden, R., Gaynes, B., Ekstrom, R., Hmaer, R., Jacobsen, F., et al. (2005). The efficacy of light therapy in the treatment of mood disorders: A review and meta-analysis of the evidence. *American Journal Psychiatry, 162,* 656–662.

Goldfarb, W. (1963). Self-awareness in schizophrenic children. *Archives of General Psychiatry, 8,* 63–76.

Goldman, M. S., & Rather, B. C. (1993). Substance use disorders: Cognitive models and architecture. In K. S. Dobson & P. C. Kendall (Eds.), *Psychopathology and cognition* (pp. 245–292). New York: Academic Press.

Goldman, S. J., D'Angelo, E. J., DeMaso, D. R., & Mezzacappa, E. (1992). Physical and sexual abuse histories among children with borderline personality disorder. *American Journal of Psychiatry, 149,* 1723–1726.

Goldstein, A. (1994). *Addiction: From biology to drug policy.* New York: W. H. Freeman.

Goldstein, G., & Shelly, C. (1984). Discriminative validity of various intelligence and neuropsychological tests. *Journal of Consulting and Clinical Psychology, 52,* 383–389.

Goldstein, I., Lue, T. F., Padma-Nathan, H., Rosen, R. C., Steers, W. D., & Wicker, P. A., for the Sildenafil Study Group. (1998). Oral sildenafil in the treatment of erectile dysfunction. *New England Journal of Medicine, 338,* 1397–1404.

Goldstein, J. M., & Lewine, R. R. J. (2000). Overview of sex differences in schizophrenia: Where have we been and where do we go from here? In D. J. Castle, J. McGrath, & J. Kulkarni (Eds.), *Women and schizophrenia* (pp. 111–143). Cambridge University Press: Cambridge.

Goldston, D., Reboussin, B., & Daniel, S. (2006). Predictors of suicide attempts: State and trait components. *Journal of Abnormal Psychology, 115,* 842–849.

Golier, J., Yehuda, R., Lupien, S., Harvey, P., Grossman, R., & Elkin, A. (2002). Memory performance in Holocaust survivors with posttraumatic stress disorder. *American Journal of Psychiatry, 159,* 1682–1688.

Gomez-Caminero, A., Blumentals, W. A., Russo, L., Brown, R. R., & Castilla-Puentes, R. (2005). Does panic disorder increase the risk of coronary heart disease? A cohort study of a national managed care database. *Psychosomatic Medicine, 67,* 688–691.

Gonzalez-Lavin, A., & Smolak, L. (1995, March). *Relationships between television and eating problems in middle school girls.* Paper presented at the meeting of the Society for Research in Child Development, Indianapolis, IN.

Good, B. J., & Kleinman, A. M. (1985). Culture and anxiety: Cross-cultural evidence for the patterning of anxiety disorders. In A. H. Tuma & J. D. Maser (Eds.), *Anxiety and the anxiety disorders.* Hillsdale, NJ: Erlbaum.

Goodkin, K., Baldewicz, T. T., Asthana, D., Khamis, I., Blaney, N. T., Kumar, M., et al. (2001). A bereavement support group intervention affects plasma burden of human immunodeficiency virus type 1. Report of a randomized controlled trial. *Journal of Human Virology, 4,* 44–54.

Goodman, G. S., Ghetti, S., Quas, J. A., Edelstein, R. S., Alexander, K. W., Redlich, A. D., Cordon, I. M., & Jones, D. P. H. (2003). A prospective study of memory for child sexual abuse: New findings relevant to the repressed/lost memory controversy. *Psychological Science, 14*(2), 113–118.

Goodman, S. H., & Gotlib, I. H. (1999). Risk for psychopathology in the children of depressed mothers: A developmental model for understanding mechanisms of transmission. *Psychological Review, 106*(3), 458–490.

Goodnough, A. (2002). Post-9/11 pain found to linger in young minds. Available at http://www.nytimes.com/2002/05/02/health/02SCHO.html?todaysheadlines.

Goodwin, D. W., & Gabrielli, W. F. (1997). Alcohol: Clinical aspects. In J. H. Lowinson, P. Ruiz, R. B. Millman, & J. G. Langrod (Eds.), *Substance abuse: A comprehensive textbook* (pp. 142–148). Baltimore: Williams & Wilkins.

Goodwin, D. W., & Guze, S. B. (1984). *Psychiatric diagnosis* (3rd ed.). New York: Oxford University Press.

Goodwin, F. K., & Ghaemi, S. N. (1998). Understanding manic-depressive illness. *Archives of General Psychiatry, 55*(1), 23–25.

Goodwin, F. K., & Jamison, K. R. (1990). *Manic depressive illness.* New York: Oxford University Press.

Goodwin, F. K., & Jamison, K. R. (Eds.) (2007). *Manic depressive illness: Bipolar disorders and recurrent depression* (2nd ed.). New York: Oxford University Press.

Goodwin, F. K., Fireman, B., Simon, G. E., Hunkeler, E. M., Lee, J., & Revicki, D. (2003). Suicide risk in bipolar disorder during treatment with lithium and divalproex. *JAMA, 290,* 1467–1473.

Goodwin, P. J., Leszcz, M., Ennis, M., Koopmans, J., Vincent, L., Guther, H., et al. (2001). The effect of group psychosocial support on survival in metastatic breast cancer. *New England Journal of Medicine, 345,* 1719–1726.

Gordis, E. (2000a). Alcohol, the brain, and behavior: Mechanisms of addiction. *Alcohol Research & Health, 24*(1), 12–15.

Gordis, E. (2000d). Why do some people drink too much? The role of genetic and psychosocial influences. *Alcohol Research & Health, 24*(1), 17–26.

Gorenstein, E. E., & Newman, J. P. (1980). Disinhibitory psychopathology: A new perspective and a model for research. *Psychological Review, 87,* 301–315.

Gorman, J. M., Kent, J. M., Sullivan, G. M., & Coplan, J. D. (2000). Neuroanatomical hypothesis of panic disorder, revised. *American Journal of Psychiatry, 157,* 493–505.

Gotlib, I. H., & Abramson, L. Y. (1999). Attributional theories of emotion. In T. Dagleish & M. J. Power (Eds.), *Handbook of cognition and emotion.* Chichester, England: John Wiley.

Gotlib, I. H., & Beach, S. R. H. (1995). A marital/family discord model of depression: Implications for therapeutic intervention. In N. S. Jacobson & A. S. Gurman (Eds.), *Clinical handbook of couple therapy* (pp. 411–436). New York: Guilford Press.

Gotlib, I. H., & Krasnoperova, E. (1998). Biased information processing as a vulnerability factor for depression. *Behavior Therapy, 29,* 603–617.

Gotlib, I. H., & MacLeod, C. (1997). Information processing in anxiety and depression: A cognitive-developmental perspective. In J. Burack & J. Enns (Eds.), *Attention, development, and psychopathology* (pp. 350–378). New York: Guilford Press.

Gotlib, I. H., & Nolan, S. A. (2001). Depression. In A. S. Bellack & M. Hersen (Eds.), *Psychopathology in adulthood* (2nd ed.). Boston: Allyn & Bacon.

Gotlib, I. H., Kurtzman, H. S., & Blehar, M. C. (1997). Cognition and depression: Issues and future directions. *Cognition and Emotion, 11*(5/6), 663–673.

Gotlib, I. H., Ranganath, C., & Rosenfeld, J. P. (1998). Frontal EEG alpha asymmetry, depression, and cognitive functioning. *Cognition and Emotion, 12,* 449–478.

Gotlib, I. H., Roberts, J. E., & Gilboa, E. (1996). Cognitive interference in depression. In I. G. Sarason, G. R. Pierce, & B. R. Sarason (Eds.), *Cognitive interference: Theories, methods, and findings* (pp. 347–377). Mahwah, NJ: Erlbaum.

Gotlib, I. H., Whiffen, V. E., Wallace, P. M., & Mount, J. H. (1991). Prospective investigation of postpartum depression: Factors involved in onset and recovery. *Journal of Abnormal Psychology, 100*(2), 122–132.

Gottesman, I. I. (1991). *Schizophrenia genesis: The origins of madness.* New York: W. H. Freeman.

Gottesman, I. I. (1997, June 6). Twins: En route to QTLs for cognition. *Science, 276,* 1522–1523.

Gottesman, I. I., & Bertelsen, A. (1989). Dual mating studies in psychiatry—Offspring of inpatients with examples from reactive (psychogenic) psychoses. *International Review of Psychiatry, 1,* 287–296.

Gottesman, I. I., & Gould, T. D. (2005). The endophenotype concept in psychiatry: Etymology and strategic intentions. In N. C. Andreasen (Ed.), *Research advances in genetics and genomics: Implications for psychiatry* (pp. 63–84). Washington, DC: American Psychiatric Publishing.

Gottlieb, G. (1998). Normally occurring environmental and behavioral influences on gene activity: From central dogma to probabilistic epigenesis. *Psychological Review, 105,* 492–802.

Gould, M. (1990). Suicide clusters and media exposure. In S. J. Blumenthal & D. J. Kupfer (Eds.), *Suicide over the life cycle: Risk factors, assessment and treatment of suicidal patients.* Washington, DC: American Psychiatric Press.

Gould, M., Marrocco, F., Kleinman, M., Thomas, J., Mostkoff, K., et al. (2005). Evaluating iatrogenic risk of youth suicide screening programs. *JAMA, 293,* 1635–1643.

Gould, R. A., Buckminster, S., Pollack, M. H., Otto, M. W., & Yap, L. (1997). Cognitive-behavioral and pharmacological treatment for social phobia: A meta-analysis. *Clinical Psychology: Science and Practice, 4,* 291–306.

Gould, R. A., Otto, M. W., Pollack, M. H., & Yap, L. (1997). Cognitive behavioral and pharmacological treatment of generalized anxiety disorder: A preliminary meta-analysis. *Behavior Therapy, 28,* 285–305.

Gould, S. J. (1991). The chain of reason versus the chain of thumbs. In *Bully for brontosaurus: Reflections in natural history* (pp. 182–197). New York: Norton.

Grabe, H. J., Meyer, C., Hapke, U., Rumpf, H. J., Freyberger, H. J., Dilling, H., et al. (2003). Somatoform pain disorder in the general population. *Psychotherapy and Psychosomatics, 72,* 88–94.

Grabe, S., & Hyde, J. S. (2006). Ethnicity and body dissatisfaction among women in the United States: A meta-analysis. *Psychological Bulletin, 132,* 622–640.

Gracheck, J. E. (2006). The insanity defense in the twenty-first century: How recent United States Supreme Court case law can improve the system. *Indiana Law Journal, 81,* 1479–1501.

Grados, M. A., Riddle, M. A., Samuels, J. F., Liang, K-Y., Hoehn-Saric, R., Bienvenu, O. J., et al. (2001). The familial phenotype of obsessive-compulsive disorder in relation to tic disorders: The Hopkins OCD family study. *Biological Psychiatry, 50,* 559–565.

Grady-Weliky, T. (2003). Premenstrual dysphoric disorder. *New England Journal of Medicine, 345,* 433–438.

Graeff, F. G. (1987). The anti-aversive action of drugs. In T. Thompson, P. B. Dews, & J. Barrett (Eds.), *Advances in behavioral pharmacology* (Vol. 6). Hillside, NJ: Erlbaum.

Graeff, F. G. (1993). Role of 5-ht in defensive behavior and anxiety. *Review in the Neurosciences, 4,* 181–211.

Graf, P., Squire, L. R., & Mandler, G. (1984). The information that amnesic patients do not forget. *Journal of Experimental Psychology: Learning, Memory, and Cognition, 10,* 164–178.

Graham, J. R. (2006). *MMPI-2: Assessing personality and psychopathology* (4th ed.). New York: Oxford University Press.

Granic, I., & Patterson, G. R. (2006). Toward a comprehensive model of antisocial development: A dynamic systems approach. *Psychological Review, 113,* 101–131.

Grant, I., Patterson, T. L., & Yager, J. (1988). Social supports in relation to physical health and symptoms of depression in the elderly. *American Journal of Psychiatry, 145*(10), 1254–1258.

Grant, J. E., & Kim, S. W. (2002). Temperament and early environmental influences in kleptomania. *Comprehensive Psychiatry, 43,* 223–229.

Grant, J. E., Correia, S., & Brennan-Krohn, T. (2006). White matter integrity in kleptomania: A pilot study. *Psychiatry Research: Neuroimaging, 147,* 233–237.

Grant, J. E., Levine, L., Kim, D., & Potenza, M. N. (2005). Impulse control disorders in adult psychiatric inpatients. *American Journal of Psychiatry, 162,* 2184–2188.

Grant, K. E., Compas, B. E., Thurm, A. E., McMahon, S. D., & Gipson, P. Y. (2004). Stressors and child and adolescent psychopathology: Measurement issues and prospective effects. *Journal of Clinical Child and Adolescent Psychology, 33*(2), 412–425.

Gray, J. A. (1982). *The neuropsychology of anxiety.* New York: Oxford University Press.

Gray, J. A. (1985). Issues in the neuropsychology of anxiety. In A. H. Tuma & J. D. Maser (Eds.), *Anxiety and the anxiety disorders* (pp. 5–25). Hillside, NJ: Erlbaum.

Gray, J. A. (1987). *The psychology of fear and stress* (2nd ed.). New York: Cambridge University Press.

Gray, J. A., & Buffery, A. W. H. (1971). Sex differences in emotional and cognitive behavior in mammals including man: Adaptive and neural bases. *Acta Psychologica, 35,* 89–111.

Gray, J. A., & McNaughton, N. (1996). The neuropsychology of anxiety: Reprise. In D. A. Hope (Ed.), *Perspectives on anxiety, panic and fear* (The 43rd Annual Nebraska Symposium on Motivation) (pp. 61–134). Lincoln: Nebraska University Press.

Graybar, S. R., & Boutilier, L. R. (2002). Nontraumatic pathways to borderline personality disorder. *Psychotherapy: Theory/Research/Practice/Training, 39,* 152–162.

Grazzi, L., Andrasik, F., D'Amico, D., Leone, M., Usai, S., Kass, S. J., & Bussone, G. (2002). Behavioral and pharmacologic treatment of transformed migraine with analgesic overuse: Outcome at 3 years. *Headache, 42,* 483–490.

Greden, J. F., & Walters, A. (1997). Caffeine. In J. H. Lowinson, P. Ruiz, R. B. Millman, & J. G. Langrod (Eds.), *Substance abuse: A comprehensive textbook* (pp. 294–307). Baltimore: Williams & Wilkins.

Green, B. L., Grace, M. C., Lindy, J. D., Titchener, J. L., & Lindy, J. G. (1983). Levels of functional impairment following a civilian disaster: The Beverly Hills Supper Club fire. *Journal of Consulting and Clinical Psychology, 51,* 573–580.

Green, R. (1987). *The "sissy boy syndrome" and the development of homosexuality.* New Haven: Yale University Press.

Green, R., & Fleming, D. T. (1990). Transsexual surgery follow-up: Status in the 1990s. *Annual Review of Sex Research, 1,* 163–174.

Green, R., & Money, J. (1969). *Transsexualism and sex reassignment.* Baltimore: Johns Hopkins Press.

Greenberg, D. R., & LaPorte, D. L. (1996). Racial differences in body type preferences of men for women. *International Journal of Eating Disorders, 19,* 275–278.

Greenberg, H. R. (2005). Impulse-control disorders not elsewhere classified. In B. J. Sadock & V. A. Sadock (Eds.), *Kaplan & Sadock's comprehensive textbook of psychiatry* (pp. 2035–2054). Philadelphia: Lippincott, Williams & Wilkins.

Greenberg, M. S., & Beck, A. T. (1989). Depression versus anxiety: A test of the content specificity. *Journal of Abnormal Psychology, 98*(1), 9–13.

Greenough, W. T., Withers, G. S., & Wallace, C. S. (1990). Morphological changes in the nervous system arising from behavioral experience: What is the evidence that they are involved in learning and memory? In L. R. Squire & E. Lindenlaub (Eds.), *The biology of memory, Symposia Medica Hoescht 23* (pp. 159–183). Stuttgart/New York: Schattauer Verlag.

Gregoire, A. (1992). New treatments for erectile impotence. *British Journal of Psychiatry, 160,* 315–326.

Greist, J. H. (1990). Treatment of obsessive compulsive disorder: Psychotherapies, drugs, and other somatic treatments. *Journal of Clinical Psychiatry, 51,* 44–50.

Griffith, E. E. H., English, T., & Mayfield, U. (1980). Possession, prayer and testimony: Therapeutic aspects of the Wednesday night meeting in a black church. *Psychiatry, 43*(5), 120–128.

Griffiths, R. R., Richards, W. A., McCann, U., & Jesse, R. (2006). Psilocybin can occasion mystic-type experiences having substantial and sustained personal meaning and spiritual significance. *Psychopharmacology, 187,* 268–283.

Grilo, C. M., Masheb, R. M., & Wilson, G. T. (2001). Subtyping binge eating disorder. *Journal of Consulting and Clinical Psychology, 69,* 1066–1072.

Grilo, C. M., Masheb, R. M., & Wilson, G. T. (2004). Efficacy of cognitive behavioral therapy and fluoxetine for the treatment of binge eating disorder: A randomized double-blind placebo-controlled comparison. *Biological Psychiatry, 57,* 301–309.

Grilo, C. M., Masheb, R. M., & Wilson, G. T. (2006). Rapid response to treatment for binge eating disorder. *Journal of Consulting and Clinical Psychology, 74,* 602–613.

Grinspoon, L., & Bakalar, J. B. (1980). Drug dependence: Non-narcotic agents. In H. I. Kaplan, A. M. Freedman, & B. J. Sadock (Eds.), *Comprehensive textbook of psychiatry* (3rd ed., pp. 1614–1629). Baltimore: Williams & Wilkins.

Grinspoon, L., & Bakalar, J. B. (1997). Marihuana. In J. H. Lowinson, P. Ruiz, R. B. Millman, & J. G. Langrod (Eds.), *Substance abuse: A comprehensive textbook* (pp. 199–206). Baltimore: Williams & Wilkins.

Grisham, J. R., & Barlow, D. H. (2005). Compulsive hoarding: Current research and theory. *Journal of Psychopathology and Behavioral Assessment, 27,* 45–52.

Grisham, J., Frost, R. O., Steketee, G., Kim, H. J., & Hood, S. (2006). Age of onset of compulsive hoarding. *Journal of Anxiety Disorders, 20,* 675–686.

Grob, C. S., & Poland, R. E. (1997). In J. H. Lowinson, P. Ruiz, R. B. Millman, & J. G. Langrod (Eds.), *Substance abuse: A comprehensive textbook* (pp. 269–275). Baltimore: Williams & Wilkins.

Groopman, L. C., & Cooper, A. M. (2001). Narcissistic personality disorder. In G. O. Gabbard (Ed.), *Treatment of psychiatric disorders* (Vol. 2, 3rd ed., pp.

2309–2326). Washington, DC: American Psychiatric Publishing.

Gross, J. J. (in press). *Handbook of emotion regulation.* New York: Guilford Press.

Gross, J. J. (1999). Emotion and emotion regulation. In L. A. Pervin & O. P. John (Eds.), *Handbook of personality: Theory and research* (2nd ed., pp. 525–552). New York: Guilford Press.

Gross, J. J., & John, O. P. (2003). Individual differences in two emotion regulation processes: Implications for affect, relationships, and well-being. *Journal of Personality and Social Psychology, 85,* 348–362.

Gross, J. J., & Levenson, R. W. (1997). Hiding feelings: The acute effects of inhibiting negative and positive emotion. *Journal of Abnormal Psychology, 108,* 95–103.

Gross, J. J., & Muñoz, R. F. (1995). Emotion regulation and mental health. *Clinical Psychology: Science and Practice, 2,* 151–164.

Gross, J., & Rosen, J. C. (1988). Bulimia in adolescents: Prevalence and psychosocial correlates. *International Journal of Eating Disorders, 7,* 51–61.

Grossman, H. (2005). Amnestic disorders. In B. J. Sadock & V. A. Sadock (Eds.), *Kaplan & Sadock's comprehensive textbook of psychiatry* (pp. 1093–1106). Philadelphia: Lippincott, Williams & Wilkins.

Grosz, H. J., & Zimmerman, J. (1965). Experimental analysis of hysterical blindness: A follow-up report and new experimental data. *Archives of General Psychiatry, 13,* 255–260.

Grosz, H. J., & Zimmerman, J. (1970). A second detailed case study of functional blindness: Further demonstration of the contribution of objective psychological laboratory data. *Behavior Therapy, 1,* 115–123.

Grunhaus, L., Schreiber, S., Dolberg, O. T., Polak, D., & Dannon, P. N. (2003). A randomized controlled comparison of electroconvulsive therapy and repetitive transcranial magnetic stimulation in severe and resistant nonpsychotic major depression. *Biological Psychiatry, 53,* 324–331.

Guilleminault, C. (1989). Clinical features and evaluation of obstructive sleep apnea. In M. H. Kryger, T. Roth, & W. C. Dement (Eds.), *Principles and practice of sleep medicine* (pp. 552–558). Philadelphia: W. B. Saunders.

Guilleminault, C., & Pelayo, R. (2000). Idiopathic central nervous system hypersomnia. In M. H. Kryger, T. Roth, & W. C. Dement (Eds.), *Principles and practice of sleep medicine* (3rd ed., pp. 687–692). Philadelphia: W. B. Saunders.

Gündel, H., O'Connor, M. F., Littrell, L., Fort, C., & Lane, R. D. (2003). Functional neuroanatomy of grief: An FMRI study. *American Journal of Psychiatry, 160,* 1946–1953.

Gunderson, J. G. (2001). *Borderline personality disorder: A clinical guide.* Washington, DC: American Psychiatric Publishing.

Gunderson, J. G., & Sabo, A. N. (1993). The phenomenological and conceptual interface between borderline personality disorder and PTSD. *American Journal of Psychiatry, 150,* 19–27.

Gunderson, J. G., Ronningstam, E., & Smith, L. E. (1991). Narcissistic personality disorder: A review of data on DSM-III-R descriptions. *Journal of Personality Disorders, 5,* 167–177.

Gunnar, M. R., & Fisher, P. A. (in press). Bringing basic research on early experience and stress neurobiology to bear on preventive interventions for neglected and maltreated children. *Development and Psychopathology.*

Gur, R. E., Nimgaonkar, V. L., Almasy, L., Calkins, M. E., Ragland, J. D., Pogue-Geile, M. F., et al. (2007). Neurocognitive endophenotypes in a multiplex multigenerational family study of schizophrenia. *American Journal of Psychiatry, 164,* 813–819.

Guralnik, O., Schmeidler, J., & Simeon, D. (2000). Feeling unreal: Cognitive processes in depersonalization. *American Journal of Psychiatry, 157*(1), 103–109.

Gureje, O. (2004). What can we learn from a cross-national study of somatic distress? *Journal of Psychosomatic Research, 56,* 409–412.

Gureje, O., Simon, G. E., Ustun, T. B., & Goldberg, D. P. (1997). Somatization in cross-cultural perspective: A World Health Organization study in primary care. *American Journal of Psychiatry, 154,* 989–995.

Gurvits, T. V., Shenton, M. E., Hokama, H., Ohta, H., Lasko, N. B., Gilbertson, M. W., et al. (1996). Magnetic resonance imaging study of hippocampal volume in chronic, combat-related posttraumatic stress disorder. *Biological Psychiatry, 40,* 1091–1099.

Gusella, J. F., Wexler, N. S., Conneally, P. M., Naylor, S. L., Anderson, M. A., Tanzi, R. E., et al. (1983). A polymorphic DNA marker genetically linked to Huntington's disease. *Nature, 306,* 234–239.

Guttmacher, M. S., & Weihofen, H. (1952). *Psychiatry and the law.* New York: Norton.

Guydish, J., Sorensen, J. L., Chan, M., Werdegar, D., & Acampora, A. (1999). A randomized trial comparing day and residential drug abuse treatment: 18-month outcomes. *Journal of Consulting and Clinical Psychology, 67*(3), 428–434.

Guyton, A. (1981). *Textbook of medical physiology.* Philadelphia: W. B. Saunders.

Guze, S. B., Cloninger, C. R., Martin, R. L., & Clayton, P. J. (1986). A follow-up and family study of Briquet's syndrome. *British Journal of Psychiatry, 149,* 17–23.

Haber, S. N., & Barchas, P. R. (1983). The regulatory effect of social rank on behavior after amphetamine administration. In P. R. Barchas (Ed.), *Social hierarchies: Essays toward a sociophysiological perspective* (pp. 119–132). Westport, CT: Greenwood Press.

Hackett, T. P., & Cassem, N. H. (1973). Psychological adaptation to convalescence in myocardial infarction patients. In J. P. Naughton, H. K. Hellerstein, & I. C. Mohler (Eds.), *Exercise testing and exercise training in coronary heart disease.* New York: Academic Press.

Hadley, S., Kim, S., Priday, L., & Hollander, E. (2006). Pharmacologic treatment of body dysmorphic disorder. *Primary Psychiatry, 13,* 61–69.

Haenen, M. A., de Jong, P. J., Schmidt, A. J. M., Stevens, S., & Visser, L. (2000). Hypochondriacs' estimation of negative outcomes: Domain-specificity and responsiveness to reassuring and alarming information. *Behaviour Research and Therapy, 38,* 819–833.

Hale, L. (2005). Who has time to sleep? *Journal of Public Health, 27,* 205–211.

Hall, A. C., Butterworth, J., Winsor, J., Gilmore, D., & Metzel, D. (2007). Pushing the employment agenda: Case study research of high performing States in integrated employment. *Intellectual and Developmental Disabilities, 45,* 182–198.

Hall, D. E., Eubanks, L., Meyyazhagan, S., Kenney, R. D., & Cochran Johnson, S. (2000). Evaluation of covert video surveillance in the diagnosis of Munchausen syndrome by proxy: Lessons from 41 cases. *Pediatrics, 6,* 1305–1312.

Hall, L. S., & Love, C. T. (2003). Finger-length ratios in female monozygotic twins discordant for sexual orientation. *Archives of Sexual Behavior, 32,* 23–28.

Hall, W., & Degenhardt, L. (2005). Cannabis-related disorders. In B. J. Sadock & V. A. Sadock (Eds.), *Kaplan & Sadock's comprehensive textbook of psychiatry* (pp. 1211–1220). Philadelphia: Lippincott, Williams & Wilkins.

Hamer, D. H., Hu, S., Magnuson, V. L., Hu, N., & Pattatucci, A. M. (1993). A linkage between DNA markers on the X chromosome and male sexual orientation. *Science, 261,* 321–327.

Hammad, T., Laughren, T., & Racoosin, J. (2006). Suicidality in pediatric patients treated with antidepressant drugs. *Archives of General Psychiatry, 63,* 332–339.

Hammen, C. (1991). The generation of stress in the course of unipolar depression. *Journal of Abnormal Psychology, 100,* 555–561.

Hammen, C. (2005). Stress and depression. *Annual Review of Clinical Psychology, 1,* 293–319.

Hammen, C., Burge, D., Burney, E., & Adrian, C. (1990). Longitudinal study of diagnoses in children of women with unipolar and bipolar affective disorder. *Archives of General Psychiatry, 47*(12), 1112–1117.

Hammen, C., Marks, T., Mayol, A., & de Mayo, R. (1985). Depressive self-schemas, life stress, and vulnerability to depression. *Journal of Abnormal Psychology, 94,* 308–319.

Hammer, S., Saag, M., Scheechter, M., Montaner, J., Schooley, R., Jacobsen, D., et al. (2006). Treatment for adult HIV infection. *JAMA, 296,* 827–843.

Hankin, B. L., & Abramson, L. Y. (2001). Development of gender differences in depression: An elaborated cognitive vulnerability–transactional stress theory. *Psychological Bulletin, 127,* 773–796.

Hankin, B. L., Abramson, L. Y., Moffitt, T. E., Silva, P. A., McGee, R., & Angell, K. E. (1998). Development of depression from preadolescence to young adulthood: Emerging gender differences in a 10-year longitudinal study. *Journal Abnormal Psychology, 107,* 128–140.

Hanley, B., Truesdale, A., King, A., Elbourne, D., & Chalmers, I. (2001). Involving consumers in designing, conducting, and interpreting randomized controlled trials: Questionnaire survey. *British Medical Journal, 322,* 519–523.

Hanna, G. L. (1995). Demographic and clinical features of obsessive-compulsive disorder in children and adolescents. *Journal of the American Academy of Child and Adolescent Psychiatry, 34,* 19–27.

Hans, S. L., & Marcus, J. (1991). Neurobehavioral development of infants at risk for schizophrenia: A review. In E. F. Walker (Ed.), *Schizophrenia: A life-course developmental perspective* (pp. 33–57). New York: Academic Press.

Hans, V. P. (1986). An analysis of public attitudes toward the insanity defense. *Criminology, 4,* 393–415.

Hansberry, M. R., Chen, E., & Gorbien, M. J. (2005). Dementia and elder abuse. *Clinics in Geriatric Medicine, 21,* 315–332.

Hanson, R. K., Steffy, R. A., & Gauthier, R. (1993). Long-term recidivism of child molesters. *Journal of Consulting and Clinical Psychology, 61,* 646–652.

Hantouche, E., Akiskal, H., Azorin, J., Chatenet-Duchene, L., & Lancrenon, S. (2006). Clinical and psychometric characterization of depression in mixed mania: A report from the French National Cohort of 1090 manic patients. *Journal of Affective Disorders, 96,* 225–232.

Haraldsson, H. M., Ferrarelli, F., Kalin, N. H., & Tononi, G. (2004). Transcranial magnetic stimulation in the investigation and treatment of schizophrenia: A review. *Schizophrenia Research, 71,* 1–16.

Harbert, T. L., Barlow, D. H., Hersen, M., & Austin, J. B. (1974). Measurement and modification of incestuous behavior: A case study. *Psychological Reports, 34,* 79–86.

Hardin, S., Hardin, S., & Schooley, B. (2002). A story of Pick's disease: A rare form of dementia. *Journal of Neuroscience Nursing, 34,* 117–122.

Hare, R. D. (1970). *Psychopathy: Theory and research.* New York: John Wiley.

Hare, R. D. (1993). *Without conscience: The disturbing world of the psychopaths among us.* New York: Pocket Books.

Hare, R. D., & Neumann, C. S. (2006). The PCL-R assessment of psychopathology: Development, structural properties, and new directions. In C. J. Patrick (Ed.), *Handbook of psychopathy* (pp. 58–88). New York: Guilford Press.

Hare, R. D., McPherson, L. M., & Forth, A. E. (1988). Male psychopaths and their criminal careers. *Journal of Consulting and Clinical Psychology, 56,* 710–714.

Hariri, A., Drabunt, E., Munoz, K., Kolachana, B., Venkata, S., Egan, M., & Weinberger, D. (2005). A susceptibility gene for affective disorders and the

response of the human amygdala. *Archives of General Psychiatry, 62,* 146–152.

Hariri, A. R., Mattay, V. S., Tessitore, A., Kolachana, B., Fera, F., Goldman, D., et al. (2002). Serotonin transporter genetic variation and the response of the human amygdala. *Science, 297,* 400–402.

Harper, L. V. (2005). Epigenic inheritance and the intergenerational transfer of experience. *Psychological Bulletin, 131,* 340–360.

Harpur, T. J., Hare, R. D., & Hakstian, A. R. (1989). Two-factor conceptualization of psychopathy: Construct validity and assessment implications. *Psychological Assessment: A Journal of Consulting and Clinical Psychology, 1,* 6–17.

Harris, A., & Lurigio, A. J. (in press). Mental illness and violence: A brief review of research and assessment strategies. *Aggression and Violent Behavior.*

Harris, E. C., & Barraclough, B. (1998). Excess mortality of mental disorder. *British Journal of Psychiatry, 173,* 11–53.

Harris, G. T., & Rice, M. E. (2006). Treatment of psychopathy: A review of empirical findings. In C. J. Patrick (Ed.), *Handbook of psychopathy* (pp. 555–572). New York: Guilford Press.

Hart, S. D., Forth, A. E., & Hare, R. D. (1990). Performance of criminal psychopaths on selected neuropsychological tests. *Journal of Abnormal Psychology, 99,* 374–379.

Hartlage, S., & Gehlert, S. (2001). Differentiating premenstrual dysphoric disorder from premenstrual exacerbations of other disorders: A methods dilemma. *Clinical Psychology: Science and Practice, 8*(2), 242–253.

Harvey, A. G., & Bryant, R. A. (1998). The relationship between acute stress disorder and posttraumatic stress disorder: A prospective evaluation of motor vehicle accident survivors. *Journal of Consulting and Clinical Psychology, 66,* 507–512.

Harvey, L., Inglis, S. J., & Espie, C. (2002). Insomniacs' reported use of CBT components and relationship to long-term clinical outcome. *Behaviour Research and Therapy, 40,* 75–83.

Hasin, D., Goodwin, R., Stinson, F., & Grant, B. (2005). Epidemiology of major depressive disorder. *Archives General Psychiatry, 62,* 1097–1106.

Haslam, J. (1976). *Observations on madness and melancholy.* New York: Arno Press. (Original work published in 1809.)

Hastings, J. (1990, November/December). Easy to get hooked on, hard to get off. *In Health,* p. 37.

Hatfield, E., Cacioppo, J. T., & Rapson, R. L. (1994). *Emotional contagion.* Cambridge: Cambridge University Press.

Hatfield, E., Sprecher, S., Pillemer, J. T., Greenberger, D., & Wexler, P. (1988). Gender differences in what is desired in the sexual relationship. *Journal of Psychology and Human Sexuality, 1*(2), 39–52.

Hathaway, S. R., & McKinley, J. C. (1943). *Manual for the Minnesota Multiphasic Personality Inventory.* New York: Psychological Corporation.

Hatsukami, D. K., Grillo, M., Boyle, R., Allen, S., Jensen, J., Bliss, R., & Brown, S. (2000). Treatment of spit tobacco users with transdermal nicotine system and mint snuff. *Journal of Consulting and Clinical Psychology, 68*(2), 241–249.

Hawkins, R. P. (1979). The functions of assessment: Implications for selection and development of devices for assessing repertoires in clinical, educational, and other settings. *Journal of Applied Behavior Analysis, 12,* 501–516.

Hawton, K. (1995). Treatment of sexual dysfunctions by sex therapy and other approaches. *British Journal of Psychiatry, 167,* 307–314.

Hawton, K., Houston, K., Haw, C., Townsend, E., & Harriss, L. (2003). Comorbidity of axis I and axis II disorders in patients who attempted suicide. *American Journal of Psychiatry, 160,* 1494–1500.

Hay, P. J., & Fairburn, C. (1998). The validity of the DSM-IV scheme for classifying bulimic eating dis-

orders. *International Journal of Eating Disorders, 23,* 7–15.

Hay, P. J., & Hall, A. (1991). The prevalence of eating disorders in recently admitted psychiatric in-patients. *British Journal of Psychiatry, 159,* 562–565.

Hayes, S. C., Barlow, D. H., & Nelson-Gray, R. O. (1999). *The scientist-practitioner: Research and accountability in the age of managed care* (2nd ed.). Boston: Allyn & Bacon.

Hayes, S. C., Wilson, K. G., Gifford, E. V., Follette, V. M., & Strosahl, K. (1996). Experiential avoidance and behavior disorders: A functional dimensional approach. *Journal of Consulting and Clinical Psychology, 64*(6), 1152–1168.

Haynes, S. G., & Matthews, K. A. (1988). Area review: Coronary-prone behavior: Continuing evolution of the concept: Review and methodologic critique of recent studies on type A behavior and cardiovascular disease. *Annals of Behavioral Medicine, 10*(2), 47–59.

Haynes, S. G., Feinleib, M., & Kannel, W. B. (1980). The relationship of psychosocial factors to coronary heart disease in the Framingham study: III. Eight-year incidence of coronary heart disease. *American Journal of Epidemiology, 111,* 37–58.

Haynes, S. N. (2000). Behavioral assessment of adults. In G. Goldstein & M. Hersen (Eds.), *Handbook of psychological assessment* (pp. 471–502). New York: Pergamon Press.

Hayward, G., Killen, J. D., Hammer, L. D., Litt, I. F., Wilson, D. M., Simmonds, B., & Taylor, C. B. (1992). Pubertal stage and panic attack history in sixth- and seventh-grade girls. *American Journal of Psychiatry, 149,* 1239–1243.

Hayward, C., Killen, J. D., Kraemer, H. C., & Taylor, C. B. (2000). Predictors of panic attacks in adolescents. *Journal of the American Academy of Child and Adolescent Psychiatry, 39*(2), 1–8.

Hazell, P., O'Connell, D., Heathcote, D., Robertson, J., & Henry, D. (1995). Efficacy of tricyclic drugs in treating child and adolescent depression: A meta-analysis. *British Medical Journal, 8,* 897–901.

Hebert, L. E., Scherr, P. A., Bienias, J. L., Bennett, D. A., & Evans, D. A. (2003). Alzheimer disease in the U.S. population: Prevalence estimates using the 2000 Census. *Archives of Neurology. 60,* 1119–1122.

Hechtman, L. (2005). Attention-deficit disorders. In B. J. Sadock & V. A. Sadock (Eds.), *Kaplan & Sadock's comprehensive textbook of psychiatry* (pp. 3183–3198). Philadelphia: Lippincott, Williams & Wilkins.

Heese, K., Low, J. W., & Inoue, N. (2006). Nerve growth factor, neural stem cells and Alzheimer's disease. *Neurosignals, 15,* 1–12.

Heilig, M., & Egli, M. (2006). Pharmacological treatment of alcohol dependence: Target symptoms and target mechanisms. *Pharmacology & Therapeutics, 111,* 855–876.

Heim, C., & Nemeroff, C. B. (1999). The impact on early adverse experiences on brain systems involved in the pathophysiology of anxiety and affective disorders. *Biological Psychiatry, 46*(11), 1509–1522.

Heim, C., Plotsky, P., & Nemeroff, C. (2004). Importance of studying the contributions of early adverse experience to neurobiological findings in depression. *Neuropsychopharmacology, 29,* 641–648.

Heim, C., Wagner, D., Maloney, E., Papanicolaou, D., Dimitris, A., Solomon, L., et al. (2006). Early adverse experience and risk for chronic fatigue syndrome. *Archives of General Psychiatry, 63,* 1258–1266.

Heiman, J. R. (2000). Orgasmic disorders in women. In S. R. Leiblum & R. C. Rosen (Eds.), *Principles and practice of sex therapy* (3rd ed., pp. 118–153). New York: Guilford Press.

Heiman, J. R., & LoPiccolo, J. (1983). Clinical outcome of sex therapy: Effects of daily versus weekly treatment. *Archives of General Psychiatry, 40,* 443–449.

Heiman, J. R., & LoPiccolo, J. (1988). *Becoming orgasmic: A sexual and personal growth program for women* (rev. ed.). New York: Prentice Hall.

Heiman, J. R., & Meston, C. M. (1997). Empirically validated treatment for sexual dysfunction. *Annual Review of Sex Research, 8,* 148–195.

Heiman, J. R., Gittelman, M., Costabile, R., Guay, A., Friedman, A., & Heard-Davison, A., et al. (2006). Topical alprostadil (PGE-sub-1) for the treatment of female sexual arousal disorder: In clinic evaluation of safety and efficacy. *Journal of Psychosomatic Obstetrics & Gynecology, 27,* 31–41.

Heimberg, R. G., Dodge, C. S., Hope, D. A., Kennedy, C. R., Zollo, L., & Becker, R. E. (1990). Cognitive behavioral group treatment for social phobia: Comparison to a credible placebo control. *Cognitive Therapy and Research, 14,* 1–23.

Heimberg, R. G., Klosko, J. S., Dodge, C. S., & Shadick, R. (1989). Anxiety disorders, depression and attributional style: A further test of the specificity of depressive attributions. *Cognitive Therapy and Research, 13*(1), 21–36.

Heimberg, R. G., Liebowitz, M. R., Hope, D. A., Schneier, F. R., Holt, C. S., Welkowitz, L. A., et al. (1998). Cognitive behavioral group therapy vs. phenelzine therapy for social phobia. *Archives of General Psychiatry, 55,* 1133–1141.

Heimberg, R. G., Salzman, D. G., Holt, C. S., & Blendell, K. A. (1993). Cognitive-behavioral group treatment for social phobia: Effectiveness at five-year follow-up. *Cognitive Therapy and Research, 17,* 325–339.

Helgeson, V. (2005). Recent advances in psychosocial oncology. *Journal of Consulting and Clinical Psychology, 73,* 268–271.

Heller, W., & Nitschke, J. B. (1997). Regional brain activity in emotion: A framework for understanding cognition in depression. *Cognition and Emotion, 11*(5–6), 737–661.

Helweg-Larsen, M., & Collins, B. E. (1997). A social psychological perspective on the role of knowledge about AIDS in AIDS prevention. *Current Directions in Psychological Science, 6,* 23–26.

Helzer, J. E., & Canino, G. (1992). Comparative analyses of alcoholism in 10 cultural regions. In J. Helzer & G. Canino (Eds.), *Alcoholism—North America, Europe and Asia: A coordinated analysis of population data from ten regions* (pp. 131–155). London: Oxford University Press.

Henderson, K. E., & Brownell, K. D. (2004). The toxic environment and obesity: Contribution and cure. In J. K. Thompson (Ed.), *Handbook of eating disorders and obesity* (pp. 339–348). New York: John Wiley.

Hendriksz, C. J., & Walter, J. H. (2004). Update on phenylketonuria. *Current Paediatrics, 14,* 400–406.

Henry, G. T., Gordon, C. S., & Rickman, D. K. (2006). Early education policy alternatives: Comparing quality and outcomes of head start and state prekindergarten. *Educational Evaluation and Policy Analysis, 28,* 77–99.

Herbert, T. B., & Cohen, S. (1993). Depression and immunity: A meta-analytic review. *Psychological Bulletin, 113*(3), 472–486.

Herdt, G. H. (1987). *The Sambia: Ritual and gender in New Guinea.* New York: Holt, Rinehart and Winston.

Herdt, G. H., & Stoller, R. J. (1989). Commentary to "The socialization of homosexuality and heterosexuality in a non-Western society." *Archives of Sexual Behavior, 18,* 31–34.

Herman, D. B., Susser, E. S., Jandorf, L., Lavelle, J., & Bromet, E. J. (1998). Homelessness among individuals with psychotic disorders hospitalized for the first time: Findings from the Suffolk County Mental Health Project. *American Journal of Psychiatry, 155,* 109–113.

Herman, J. L., Perry, C., & van der Kolk, B. A. (1989). Childhood trauma in borderline personality disorder. *American Journal of Psychiatry, 146,* 490–495.

Hersen, M. (Ed.) (2006). *Clinician's handbook of adult behavioral assessment.* Burlington, MA: Elsevier.

Hershberger, S., & Segal, N. (2004). The cognitive, behavioral, and personality profiles of a male monozygotic triplet set discordant for sexual orientation. *Archives of Sexual Behavior, 33,* 497–514.

Herzog, D. B., Dorer, D. J., Keel, P. K., Selwyn, S. E., Ekeblad, E. R., Flores, A. T., et al. (1999). Recovery and relapse in anorexia and bulimia nervosa: A 7.5-year follow-up study. *Journal of the American Academy of Child and Adolescent Psychiatry, 38*(7), 829–837.

Heshka, S., Anderson, J. W., Atkinson, R. L., Greenway, F. L., Hill, J. O., Phinney, S. D., et al. (2003). Weight loss with self-help compared with a structured commercial program: A randomized trial. *JAMA, 289,* 1792–1798.

Heston, L. L., & Heston, R. (2000). *The medical casebook of Adolph Hitler.* New York: Cooper Square Press.

Hetherington, E. M., & Blechman, E. A. (Eds.) (1996). *Stress, coping and resiliency in children and families.* Mahwah, NJ: Erlbaum.

Hetherington, E. M., Stanley-Hagan, M., & Anderson, E. R. (1989). Marital transitions: A child's perspective. *American Psychologist, 44,* 303–312.

Hettema, J. M., Prescott, C. A., & Kendler, K. S. (2004). Genetic and environmental sources of covariation between generalized anxiety disorder and neuroticism. *American Journal of Psychiatry, 161,* 1581–1587.

Hettema, J. M., Prescott, C. A., Myers, J. M., Neale, M. C., & Kendler, K. S. (2005). The structure of genetic and environmental risk factors for anxiety disorders in men and women. *Archives of General Psychiatry, 62,* 182–189.

Hiatt, K. D., & Newman, J. P. (2006). Understanding psychopathy: The cognitive side. In C. J. Patrick (Ed.), *Handbook of psychopathy* (pp. 334–352). New York: Guilford Press.

Higgins, S. T., Heil, S. H., Dantona, R., Donham, R., Matthews, M., & Badger, G. J. (2006). Effects of varying the monetary value of voucher-based incentives on abstinence achieved during and following treatment among cocaine-dependent outpatients. *Addiction, 102,* 271–281.

Higuchi, S., Matsushita, S., Imazeki, H., Kinoshita, T., Takagi, S., & Kono, H. (1994). Aldehyde dehydrogenase genotypes in Japanese alcoholics. *Lancet, 343,* 741–742.

Hilgard, E. R. (1992). Divided consciousness and dissociation. *Consciousness & Cognition, 1,* 16–31.

Hiller, W., Fichter, M. M., & Rief, W. (2003). A controlled treatment study of somatoform disorders including analysis of healthcare utilization and cost-effectiveness. *Journal of Psychosomatic Research, 54,* 369–380.

Hiller, W., Leibbrand, R., Rief, W., & Fichter, M. (2005). Differentiating hypochondriasis from panic disorder. *Journal of Anxiety Disorders, 19,* 29–49.

Hilts, P. J. (1994, March 10). Agency faults a UCLA study for suffering of mental patients. *New York Times,* p. A1.

Hindmarch, I. (1986). The effects of psychoactive drugs on car handling and related psychomotor ability: A review. In J. F. O'Hanlon & J. J. Gier (Eds.), *Drugs and driving* (pp. 71–79). London: Taylor & Francis.

Hindmarch, I. (1990). Cognitive impairment with anti-anxiety agents: A solvable problem? In D. Wheatley (Ed.), *The anxiolytic jungle: Where, next?* (pp. 49–61). Chichester, England: John Wiley.

Hinshaw, S. P. (2002). Preadolescent girls with attention-deficit/hyperactivity disorder: I. Background characteristics, comorbidity, cognitive and social functioning, and parenting practices. *Journal of Consulting and Clinical Psychology, 70,* 1086–1098.

Hinshelwood, J. A. (1896). A case of dyslexia: A peculiar form of word-blindness. *Lancet, 2,* 1451–1454.

Hinton, D., Chong, R., Pollack, M. H., Barlow D. H., & McNally, R. J. (in press). *Ataque de nervios:* Relationship to anxiety sensitivity and dissociation predisposition. D*epression and Anxiety.*

Hinton, D., Pich, V., Chhean, D., Pollack, M. H., & Barlow, D. H. (2004). Olfactory-triggered panic attacks among Cambodian refugees attending a psychiatric clinic. *General Hospital Psychiatry, 26*(5), 390–397.

Hinton, D., Pich, K., Pollack, M. H., & Barlow, D. H. (2004). Olfactory-triggered panic attacks among Khmer refugees attending a psychiatric clinic.

Hinton, D., Pollack, M. H., Pich, V., Fama, J. M., & Barlow, D. H. (2005). Orthosatically induced panic attacks among Cambodian refugees: Flashbacks, catastrophic cognitions, and associated psychopathology. *Cognitive Behavioral Practice, 12,* 301–311.

Hirschfeld, D. R., Rosenbaum, J. F., Biederman, J., Bolduc, E. A., Farone, S. V., Snidman, N., et al. (1992). Stable behavioral inhibition and its association with anxiety disorder. *Journal of the American Academy of Child and Adolescent Psychiatry, 31,* 103–111.

Hirschfeld, R. M. A., Keller, M. M., Panico, S., Arons, B. S., Barlow, D., Davidoff, F., et al. (1997). The National Depressive and Manic-Depressive Association consensus statement on the undertreatment of depression. *JAMA, 277*(4), 333–340.

Hirschfeld, R. M. A., Shea, M. T., & Weise, R. (1995). Dependent personality disorder. In W. J. Livesley (Ed.), *The DSM-IV personality disorders* (pp. 239–256). New York: Guilford Press.

Hitchcock, P. B., & Mathews, A. (1992). Interpretation of bodily symptoms in hypochondriasis. *Behaviour Research and Therapy, 30*(3), 223–234.

Hobfoll, S. E., Canetti-Nisim, D., & Johnson, R. J. (2006). Exposure to terrorism, stress-related mental health symptoms, and defensive coping among Jews and Arabs in Israel. *Journal of Consulting and Clinical Psychology, 74,* 207–218.

Hoehn-Saric, R., McLeod, D. R., & Zimmerli, W. D. (1989). Somatic manifestations in women with generalized anxiety disorder: Psychophysiological responses to psychological stress. *Archives of General Psychiatry, 46,* 1113–1119.

Hoek, H. W. (2002). The distribution of eating disorders. In K. D. Brownell & C. G. Fairburn (Eds.), *Eating disorders and obesity: A comprehensive handbook* (2nd ed., pp. 207–211). New York: Guilford Press.

Hoek, H. W., van Harten, P. N., Hermans, K., M. E., Katzman, M. A., Matroos, G. E., & Susser, E. S. (2005). The incidence of anorexia nervosa on Curacao. *American Journal of Psychiatry, 162,* 748–752.

Hoffman, B., Papas, R., Chatkoff, D., & Kerns, R. (2007). Meta-analysis of psychological interventions for chronic low back pain. *Health Psychology, 26,* 1–9.

Hoffman, R. E., Boutros, N. N., Hu, S., Berman, R. M., Krystal, J. H., & Charney, D. S. (2000). Transcranial magnetic stimulation and auditory hallucinations in schizophrenia. *Lancet, 355,* 1073–1075.

Hoffman, R. E., Hawkins, K. A., Gueorguieva, R., Boutros, N. N., Rachid, F., Carroll, K., & Krystal, J. H. (2003). Transcranial magnetic stimulation of left temporoparietal cortex and medication-resistant auditory hallucinations. *Archives of General Psychiatry, 60,* 49–56.

Hoffman, R. E., Rapaport, J., Mazure, C. M., & Quinlan, D. M. (1999). Selective speech perception alterations in schizophrenic patients reporting hallucinated "voices." *American Journal of Psychiatry, 156,* 393–399.

Hofmann, S. G. (2004). Cognitive mediation of treatment change in social phobia. *Journal of Consulting and Clinical Psychology, 72,* 393–399.

Hofmann, S. G. (in press). Enhancing exposure-based therapy from a translational research perspective. *Behavior Research and Therapy.*

Hofmann, S. G., & Barlow, D. H. (1996). Ambulatory psychophysiological monitoring: A potentially useful tool when treating panic relapse. *Cognitive and Behavioral Practice, 3,* 53–61.

Hofmann, S. G., & Barlow, D. H. (2002). Social phobia (social anxiety disorder). In D. H. Barlow, *Anxiety and its disorders: The nature and treatment of anxiety and panic* (2nd ed.). New York: Guilford Press.

Hofmann, S. G., Lehman, C. L., & Barlow, D. H. (1997). How specific are specific phobias? *Journal of Behavior Therapy and Experimental Psychiatry, 28,* 233–240.

Hofmann, S. G., Meuret, A. E., Smitts, J. A. J., Simon, N. M., Pollack, M. H., Eisenmenger, K., et al. (2006). Augmentation of exposure therapy with D-cycloserine for social anxiety disorder. *Archives of General Psychiatry, 63,* 298–304.

Hofstede, G., & McCrae, R. R. (2004). Personality and culture revisited: Linking traits and dimensions of culture. *Cross-Cultural Research, 38,* 52–88.

Hogarty, G. E., Anderson, C. M., Reiss, D. J., Kornblith, S. J., Greenwald, D. P., Javna, C. D., & Madonia, M. J. (1986). Family psychoeducation, social skills training, and maintenance chemotherapy in the aftercare treatment of schizophrenia: I. One year effects of a controlled study on relapse and expressed emotion. *Archives of General Psychiatry, 43,* 633–642.

Hogarty, G. E., Anderson, C. M., Reiss, D. J., Kornblith, S. J., Greenwald, D. P., Ulrich, R. F., Carter, M., & The Environmental–Personal Indicators in the Course of Schizophrenia (EPICS) Research Group. (1991). Family psychoeducation, social skills training, and maintenance chemotherapy in the aftercare treatment of schizophrenia. *Archives of General Psychiatry, 48,* 340–347.

Hogarty, G. E., Reis, D., Kornblith, S. J., Greenwald, D., Ulrich, R., & Carter, M. (1992). In reply. *Archives of General Psychiatry, 49,* 76–77.

Holden, C. (2005). Obesity in the east. *Science, 307,* 38.

Holder, H. D. (2004). Prevention of alcohol-related problems. In M. Galanter & H. D. Kleber (Eds.), *The American Psychiatry Publishing textbook of substance abuse treatment* (3rd ed., pp. 611–623). Washington, DC: American Psychiatric Publishing.

Holder, H. D., Gruenewald, P. J., Ponicki, W. R., Treno, A. J., Grube, J. W., Saltz, R. F., et al. (2000). Effect of community-based interventions on high-risk drinking and alcohol-related injuries. *JAMA, 284,* 2341–2347.

Hollander, E., Allen, A., Kwon, J., Aronwoitz, B., Schmeidler, J., Wong, C., & Simeon, D. (1999). Clomipramine vs. desipramine crossover trial in body dysmorphic disorder: Selective efficacy of a serotonin reuptake inhibitor in imagined ugliness. *Archives of General Psychiatry, 56*(11), 1033–1039.

Hollander, E., Bartz, J., Chaplin, W., Phillips, A., Sumner, J., Soorya, L., Anagnostou, E., & Wasserman, S. (2007). Oxytocin increases retention of social cognition in autism. *Biological Psychiatry, 61,* 498–503.

Hollander, E., Liebowitz, M. R., Winchel, R., Klumker, A., & Klein, D. F. (1989). Treatment of body-dysmorphic disorder with serotonin reuptake blockers. *American Journal of Psychiatry, 1989, 146,* 768–770.

Hollien, H. (1990). The expert witness: Ethics and responsibilities. *Journal of Forensic Sciences, 35,* 1414–1423.

Hollifield, M., Katon, W., Spain, D., & Pule, L. (1990). Anxiety and depression in a village in Lesotho, Africa: A comparison with the United States. *British Journal of Psychiatry, 156,* 343–350.

Hollis, J. F., Connett, J. E., Stevens, V. J., & Greenlick, M. R. (1990). Stressful life events, Type A behavior, and the prediction of cardiovascular and total mortality over six years. *Journal of Behavioral Medicine, 13*(3), 263–280.

Hollon, S. D. (1993). Review of psychosocial treatments for mood disorders. In D. L. Dunner (Ed.), *Current psychiatric therapy.* Philadelphia: W. B. Saunders.

Hollon, S. D., DeRubeis, R. J., Evans, M. D., Wiener, M. J., Garvey, M. J., Grose, W. M., & Tuason, V. B. (1992). Cognitive therapy and pharmacotherapy for depression: Singly and in combination. *Archives of General Psychiatry, 49*(10), 772–781.

Hollon, S. D., DeRubeis, R. J., Shelton, R. C., Amsterdam, J. D., Salomon, R. M., O'Reardon, J. P., et al. (2005). Prevention of relapse following cognitive therapy vs. medications in moderate to severe depression. *Archives of General Psychiatry, 62,* 417–422.

Hollon, S. D., Kendall, P. C., & Lumry, A. (1986). Specificity of depressotypic cognitions in clinical depression. *Journal of Abnormal Psychology, 95,* 52–59.

Hollon, S. D., Shelton, R. C., & Loosen, P. T. (1991). Cognitive therapy and pharmacotherapy for depression. *Journal of Consulting and Clinical Psychology, 59*(1), 88–99.

Hollon, S. D., Stewart, M. O., & Strunk, D. (2006). Cognitive behavior therapy has enduring effects in the treatment of depression and anxiety. *Annual Review of Psychology, 57,* 285–315.

Holroyd, K. A., & Penzien, D. B. (1986). Client variables in the behavioral treatment of current tension headache: A meta-analytic review. *Journal of Behavioral Medicine, 9,* 515–536.

Holroyd, K. A., Andrasik, F., & Noble, J. (1980). A comparison of EMG biofeedback and a credible pseudotherapy in treating tension headache. *Journal of Behavioral Medicine, 3,* 29–39.

Holroyd, K. A., Nash, J. M., Pingel, J. D., Cordingley, G. E., & Jerome, A. (1991). A comparison of pharmacological (amitriptyline HCL) and nonpharmacological (cognitive-behavioral) therapies for chronic tension headaches. *Journal of Consulting and Clinical Psychology, 59*(3), 387–393.

Holroyd, K. A., Penzien, D. B., Hursey, K. G., Tobin, D. L., Rogers, L., Holm, J. E., et al. (1984). Change mechanisms in EMG biofeedback training. Cognitive changes underlying improvements in tension headache. *Journal of Consulting and Clinical Psychology, 52,* 1039–1053.

Holzman, P. S., & Levy, D. L. (1977). Smooth pursuit eye movements and functional psychoses: A review. *Schizophrenia Bulletin, 3,* 15–27.

Homeless suit victor must stay in hospital, *New York Times.* (1994, February 2).

Hook, E. B. (1982). Epidemiology of Down syndrome. In S. M. Pueschel & J. E. Rynders (Eds.), *Down syndrome: Advances in biomedicine and the behavioral sciences* (pp. 11–88). Cambridge, MA: Ware Press.

Hooley, J. M. (1985). Expressed emotion: A review of the critical literature. *Clinical Psychology Review, 5,* 119–139.

Hooley, J. M., & Campbell, C. (2002). Control and controllability: Beliefs and behaviour in high and low expressed emotion relatives. *Psychological Medicine, 32,* 1091–1099.

Hoon, E. F., Hoon, P. W., Rand, K. H., Johnson, J., Hall, N. R., & Edwards, N. B. (1991). A psycho-behavioral model of genital herpes recurrence. *Journal of Psychosomatic Research, 35,* 25–36.

Hoon, P. W., Wincze, J. P., & Hoon, E. F. (1977). A test of reciprocal inhibition: Are anxiety and sexual arousal in women mutually inhibitory? *Journal of Abnormal Psychology, 86,* 65–74.

Horan, W. P., Ventura, J., Mintz, J., Kopelowicz, A., Wirshing, D., Christian-Herman, J., Foy, D., & Liberman, R. P. (2007). Stress and coping responses to a natural disaster in people with schizophrenia. *Psychiatry Research, 151,* 77–86.

Horowitz, J., & Garber, J. (2006). The prevention of depressive symptoms in children and adolescents: A meta-analytic review. *Journal of Consulting and Clinical Psychology, 74,* 401–415.

Horowitz, M. J. (2001). Histrionic personality disorder. In G. O. Gabbard (Ed.), *Treatment of psychiatric disorders* (Vol. 2, 3rd ed., pp. 2293–2307). Washington, DC: American Psychiatric Publishing.

Horowitz, M. J., Siegel, B., Holen, A., Bonanno, G. A., Milbrath, C., & Stinson, C. H. (1997). Diagnostic criteria for complicated grief disorder. *American Journal of Psychiatry, 154,* 904–910.

Horwath, E., & Weissman, M. (1997). Epidemiology of anxiety disorders across cultural groups. In S. Friedman (Ed.), *Cultural issues in the treatment of anxiety* (pp. 21–39.) New York: Guilford Press.

House, J. S., Landis, K. R., & Umberson, D. (1988). Social relationships and health. *Science, 241,* 540–545.

House, J. S., Robbins, C., & Metzner, H. M. (1982). The association of social relationships and activities with mortality: Prospective evidence from the Tecumseh community health study. *American Journal of Epidemiology, 116,* 123.

Houston, B. K., Chesney, M. A., Black, G. W., Cates, D. S., & Hecker, M. H. L. (1992). Behavioral clusters and coronary heart disease risk. *Psychosomatic Medicine, 54*(4), 447–461.

Houts, A. C. (2001). The diagnostic and statistical manual's new white coat and circularity of plausible dysfunctions: Response to Wakefield, Part I. *Behavior research and therapy, 39,* 315–345.

Hoza, B., Gerdes, A. C., Hinshaw, S. P., Arnold, L. E., Pelham, W. E., Molina, B. S. G., et al. (2004). Self-perceptions of competence in children with ADHD and comparison children. *Journal of Consulting and Clinical Psychology, 72,* 382–391.

Hoza, B., Mrug, S., Gerdes, A. C., Hinshaw, S. P., Bukowski, W. M., Gold, J. A., et al. (2005). What aspects of peer relationships are impaired in children with attention-deficit/hyperactivity disorder? *Journal of Consulting and Clinical Psychology, 73,* 411–423.

Hrabosky, J. I., Masheb, R. M., White, M. A., & Grilo, C. M. (2007). Overvaluation of shape and weight in binge eating disorder. *Journal of Consulting and Clinical Psychology, 75,* 175–180.

Hsu, L. K. G. (1988). The outcome of anorexia nervosa: A reappraisal. *Psychological Medicine, 18,* 807–812.

Hsu, L. K. G. (1990). *Eating disorders.* New York: Guilford Press.

Hsu, L. K. G., & Zimmer, B. (1988). Eating disorders in old age. *International Journal of Eating Disorders, 7,* 133–138.

Hubert, N. C., Jay, S. M., Saltoun, M., & Hayes, M. (1988). Approach-avoidance and distress in children undergoing preparation for painful medical procedures. *Journal of Clinical Child Psychology, 17,* 194–202.

Hucker, S. J. (1997). Sexual sadism: Psychopathology and theory. In D. R. Laws & W. T. O'Donohue (Eds.), *Sexual deviance: Theory, assessment, and treatment* (pp. 194–209). New York: Guilford Press.

Hudson, J. I., Hiripi, E., Pope, H. G., Jr., & Kessler, R. C. (2007). The prevalence and correlates of eating disorders in the national comorbidity survey replication. *Biological Psychiatry, 61,* 348–358.

Hudson, J. I., Lalonde, J. K., Berry, J. M., Pindych, L. J., Bulik, C. M., Crow, S. J., et al. (2006). Binge-eating disorder as a distinct familial phenotype in obese individuals. *Archives of General Psychiatry, 63,* 313–319.

Hudson, J. I., Mangweth, B., Pope, H. G., Jr., De Col, C., Hausmann, A., Gutweniger, S., et al. (2003). Family study of affective spectrum disorder. *Archives of General Psychiatry, 60,* 170–177.

Hudson, J., Pope, H., Jonas, J. M., & Yurgelun-Todd, D. (1983). Family history study of anorexia nervosa and bulimia. *British Journal of Psychiatry, 142,* 133–138.

Hufford, M. R., Shields, A. L., Shiffman, S., Paty, J., & Balabanis, M. (2002). Reactivity to ecological momentary assessment: An example using undergraduate problem drinkers. *Psychology of Addictive Behaviors, 16,* 205–211.

Hughes, J. R. (1993). Pharmacotherapy for smoking cessation: Unvalidated assumptions, anomalies, and suggestions for future research. *Journal of Consulting and Clinical Psychology, 61,* 751–760.

Hughes, J. R. (2005). Nicotine-related disorders. In B. J. Sadock & V. A. Sadock (Eds.), *Kaplan & Sadock's comprehensive textbook of psychiatry* (pp. 1257–1264). Philadelphia: Lippincott, Williams & Wilkins.

Hughes, J. R., Gust, S. W., Skoog, K., Keenan, R. M., & Fenwick, J. W. (1991). Symptoms of tobacco withdrawal: A replication and extension. *Archives of General Psychiatry, 48,* 52–61.

Humphrey, L. L. (1986). Structural analysis of parent–child relationships in eating disorders. *Journal of Abnormal Psychology, 95,* 395–402.

Humphrey, L. L. (1988). Relationships within subtypes of anorexic, bulimic, and normal families. *Journal of the American Academy of Child and Adolescent Psychiatry, 27,* 544–551.

Humphrey, L. L. (1989). Observed family interactions among subtypes of eating disorders using structural analysis of social behavior. *Journal of Consulting and Clinical Psychology, 57,* 206–214.

Hunicutt, C. P., & Newman, I. A. (1993). Adolescent dieting practices and nutrition knowledge. *Health Values: The Journal of Health Behavior, Education and Promotion, 17*(4), 35–40.

Hunt, W. A. (1980). History and classification. In A. E. Kazdin, A. S. Bellack, & M. Hersen (Eds.), *New perspectives in abnormal psychology.* New York: Oxford University Press.

Hunter, E., Sierra, M., & David, A. (2004). The epidemiology of depersonalisation and derealisation: A systematic review. *Social Psychiatry and Psychiatric Epidemiology, 39,* 9–18.

Hunter, J. A., Jr., & Mathews, R. (1997). Sexual deviance in females. In D. R. Laws & W. T. O'Donohue (Eds.), *Sexual deviance: Theory, assessment, and treatment* (pp. 465–490). New York: Guilford Press.

Huntington's Disease Collaborative Research Group. (1993). A novel gene containing a trinucleotide repeat that is expanded and unstable on Huntington's disease chromosomes. *Cell, 72,* 971–983.

Huntjens, R. J., Peters, M., Woertman, L., Bovenschen, L., Loes, M., Martin, R., et al. (2006). Inter-identity amnesia in dissociative identity disorder: A simulated memory impairment? *Psychological Medicine, 36,* 857–863.

Huntjens, R. J., Postma, A., Hamaker, E. L., Woertman, L., van der Hart, O., & Peters, M. (2002). Perceptual and conceptual priming in patients with dissociative identity disorder. *Memory & cognition, 30,* 1033–1043.

Huntjens, R. J., Postma, A., Peters, M., Woertman, L., & van der Hart, O. (2003). Interidentity amnesia for neutral, episodic information in dissociative identity disorder. *Abnormal Psychology, 112,* 290–7.

Hurt, S. W., Schnurr, P. P., Severino, S. K., Freeman, E. W., Gise, L. H., Rivera-Tovar, A., & Steege, J. F. (1992). Late luteal phase dysphoric disorder in 670 women evaluated for premenstrual complaints. *American Journal of Psychiatry, 149,* 525–530.

Hyler, S. E., Williams, J. B. W., & Spitzer, R. L. (1982). Reliability in the DSM-III field trials: Interview v. case summary. *Archives of General Psychiatry, 39,* 1275–1278.

Hyman, S. E. (2004). Addiction: A disease of learning and memory. *American Journal of Psychiatry, 162,* 1414–1422.

Hypericum Depression Trial Study Group. (2002). Effect of *Hypericum perforatum* (St John's wort) in major depressive disorder: A randomized controlled trial. *The JAMA, 287,* 1853–1854.

Iacono, W. G., Bassett, A. S., & Jones, B. D. (1988). Eye tracking dysfunction is associated with partial trisomy of chromosome 5 and schizophrenia. *Archives of General Psychiatry, 45*(12), 1140–1141.

Ickovics, J. R., & Rodin, J. (1992). Women and AIDS in the United States: Epidemiology, natural history, and mediating mechanisms. *Health Psychology, 11*(1), 1–16.

Iguchi, M. Y., Griffiths, R. R., Bickel, W. K., Handelsman, L., Childress, A. R., & McLellan, A. T. (1990). Relative abuse liability of benzodiazepines in methadone maintenance populations in three cities. *Problems of drug dependence* (pp. 364–365). NIDA

Publication No. ADM 90–1663. Washington, DC: U.S. Government Printing Office.

Imhof, A., Kovari, E., von Gunten, A., Gold, G., Rivara, C.-B., Herrmann, F. R., et al. (2007). Morphological substrates of cognitive decline in nonagenarians and centenarians: A new paradigm? *Journal of the Neurological Sciences, 257,* 72–79.

Imperato-McGinley, J., Peterson, R. E., Gautier, T., & Sturla, E. (1979). Androgens and the evolution of male-gender identity among male pseudohermaphrodites with 5-alpha-reductase deficiency. *New England Journal of Medicine, 300,* 1233–1237.

Inlow, J. K., & Restifo, L. L. (2004). Molecular and comparative genetics of mental retardation. *Genetics, 166,* 835–881.

Inouye, S. K., Bogardus, S. T., Charpentier, P. A., Leo-Summers, L., Acampora, D., Holford, T. R., & Cooney, L. M. (1999). A multicomponent intervention to prevent delirium in hospitalized older patients. *New England Journal of Medicine, 340,* 669–676.

Insel, T. R. (1992). Toward a neuroanatomy of obsessive-compulsive disorder. *Archives of General Psychiatry, 49,* 739–744.

Insel, T. R. (Ed.) (1984). *New findings in obsessive-compulsive disorder.* Washington, DC: American Psychiatric Press.

Insel, T. R. (2006). Beyond efficacy: The STAR★D trial. *American Journal of Psychiatry, 163,* 5–7.

Insel, T. R., Scanlan, J., Champoux, M., & Suomi, S. J. (1988). Rearing paradigm in a nonhuman primate affects response to B-CCE challenge. *Psychopharmacology, 96,* 81–86.

Institute of Medicine. (1999). *Reducing the burden of injury: Advancing prevention and treatment.* Washington, DC: National Academy of Sciences.

Institute of Medicine. (2001). *Crossing the quality chasm: A new health system for the 21st century.* Washington, DC: National Academies Press.

Institute of Medicine. (2002). Reducing suicide: A national imperative. Washington, DC: National Academic Press.

Iribarren, C., Sidney, S., Bild, D. E., Liu, K., Markovitz, J. H., Roseman, J. M., & Matthews, K. (2000). Association of hostility with coronary artery calcification in young adults. *JAMA, 283*(19), 2546–2551.

Ironson, G., Friedman, A., Klimas, N., Antoni, M., Fletcher, M. A., LaPerriere, A., et al. (1994). Distress, denial, and low adherence to behavioral interventions predict faster disease progression in gay men infected with human immunodeficiency virus. *International Journal of Behavioral Medicine, 1,* 90–105.

Ironson, G., Taylor, C. B., Boltwood, M., Bartzokis, T., Dennis, C., Chesney, M., et al. (1992). Effects of anger on left ventricular ejection fraction in coronary artery disease. *American Journal of Cardiology, 70,* 281–285.

Irvin, J. E., Bowers, C. A., Dunn, M. E., & Wang, M. C. (1999). Efficacy of relapse prevention: A meta-analytic review. *Journal of Consulting and Clinical Psychology, 67*(4), 563–570.

Irwin, M., Daniels, M., Smith, T. L., Bloom, E., & Weiner, H. (1987). Impaired natural killer cell activity during bereavement. *Brain, Behavior, and Immunity, 1,* 98–104.

Irwin, M., Mascovich, A., Gillin, J. C., Willoughby, R., Pike, J., & Smith, T. L. (1994). Partial sleep deprivation reduces natural killer cell activity in humans. *Psychosomatic Medicine, 56,* 493–498.

Isaacowitz, D., Smith, T. T., & Carstensen, L. L. (2003). Socioemotional selectivity, positive bias, and mental health among trauma survivors in old age. *Ageing International, 28,* 181–199.

Izard, C. E. (1992). Basic emotions, relations among emotions, and emotion–cognition relations. *Psychological Review, 99*(3), 561–565.

Jackson v. Indiana, 406 U.S. 715 (1972).

Jackson, C., Brown, J. D., & L'Engle, K. L. (2007). R-rated movies, bedroom televisions, and initiation of

smoking by white and black adolescents. *Archives of Pediatrics & Adolescent Medicine, 161,* 260–268.

Jackson, G., Rosen, R., Kloner, R., & Kostis, J. (2006). The second Princeton consensus on sexual dysfunction and cardiac risk: New guidelines for sexual medicine. *Journal of Sexual Medicine, 3,* 28–36.

Jacob, S., Brune, C. W., Carter, C. S., Leventhal, B. L., Lord, C., & Cook, J. E. H. (2007). Association of the oxytocin receptor gene (OXTR) in Caucasian children and adolescents with autism. *Neuroscience Letters, 417,* 6–9.

Jacobi, W., & Winkler, H. (1927). Encephalographische Studien an chronischen Schizophrenen. *Arch. Psychiatr. Nervenk.r, 81,* 299–332.

Jacobs, S. (1993). *Pathologic grief: Maladaptation to loss.* Washington, DC: American Psychiatric Press.

Jacobs, S., Hansen, F., Berkman, L., Kasl, S., & Ostfeld, A. (1989). Depressions of bereavement. *Comprehensive Psychiatry, 30*(3), 218–224.

Jacobson, E. (1938). *Progressive relaxation.* Chicago: University of Chicago Press.

Jacobson, N. S., & Hollon, S. D. (1996a). Cognitive behavior therapy vs. pharmacotherapy: Now that the jury's returned its verdict, it's time to present the rest of the evidence. *Journal of Consulting and Clinical Psychology, 64,* 74–80.

Jacobson, N. S., & Hollon, S. D. (1996b). Prospects for future comparisons between drugs and psychotherapy: Lessons from the CBT vs. pharmacotherapy exchange. *Journal of Consulting and Clinical Psychology, 64,* 104–108.

Jacobson, N. S., Dobson, K. S., Truax, P. A., Addis, M. E., Koerner, K., Gollan, J. K., et al. (1996). A component analysis of cognitive-behavioral treatment for depression. *Journal of Consulting and Clinical Psychology, 64,* 295–304.

Jacobson, N. S., Dobson, K., Fruzzetti, A. E., Schmaling, K. B., & Salusky, S. (1991). Marital therapy as a treatment for depression. *Journal of Consulting and Clinical Psychology, 59*(4), 547–557.

Jacobson, N. S., Fruzzetti, A. E., Dobson, K., Whisman, M., & Hops, H. (1993). Couple therapy as a treatment for depression: II. The effects of relationship quality and therapy on depressive relapse. *Journal of Consulting and Clinical Psychology, 61*(3), 516–519.

Jacobson, N. S., Martell, C. R., & Dimidjian, S. (2001). Behavioral activation treatment for depression: Returning to contextual roots. *Clinical Psychology: Science and Practice, 8*(3), 255–270.

Jaffe, A. J., Rounsaville, B., Chang, G., Schottenfeld, R. S., Meyer, R. E., & O'Malley, S. O. (1996). Naltrexone, relapse prevention, and supportive therapy with alcoholics: An analysis of patient treatment matching. *Journal of Consulting and Clinical Psychology, 64,* 1044–1053.

Jaffe, J. H., & Anthony, J. C. (2005). Substance-related disorders. In B. J. Sadock & V. A. Sadock (Eds.), *Kaplan & Sadock's comprehensive textbook of psychiatry* (pp. 1137–1168). Philadelphia: Lippincott, Williams & Wilkins.

Jaffe, J. H., & Strain, E. C. (2005). Opioid-related disorders. In B. J. Sadock & V. A. Sadock (Eds.), *Kaplan & Sadock's comprehensive textbook of psychiatry* (pp. 1265–1290). Philadelphia: Lippincott, Williams & Wilkins.

Jaffe, J. H., Knapp, C. M., & Ciraulo, D. A. (1997). Opiates: Clinical aspects. In J. H. Lowinson, P. Ruiz, R. B. Millman, & J. G. Langrod (Eds.), *Substance abuse: A comprehensive textbook* (pp. 158–166). Baltimore: Williams & Wilkins.

Jaffe, J. H., Ling, W., & Rawson, R. A. (2005). Amphetamine (or amphetamine-like)-related disorders. In B. J. Sadock & V. A. Sadock (Eds.), *Kaplan & Sadock's comprehensive textbook of psychiatry* (pp. 1188–1200). Philadelphia: Lippincott, Williams & Wilkins.

Jaffe, J. H., Rawson, R. A., & Ling, W. (2005). Cocaine-related disorders. In B. J. Sadock & V. A. Sadock (Eds.), *Kaplan & Sadock's comprehensive textbook* of psychiatry (pp. 1220–1238). Philadelphia: Lippincott, Williams & Wilkins.

Jaffe, S. E. (2000). Sleep and infectious disease. In M. H. Kryger, T. Roth, & W. C. Dement (Eds.), *Principles and practice of sleep medicine* (3rd ed., pp. 1093–1102). Philadelphia: W. B. Saunders.

Jaffee, S. R., Moffitt, T. E., Caspi, A., Fombonne, E., Poulton, R., & Martin, J. (2002). Differences in early childhood risk factors for juvenile-onset and adult-onset depression. *Archives of General Psychiatry, 59*, 215–222.

Jamison, K. R. (1989). Mood disorders and patterns of creativity in British writers and artists. *Psychiatry, 52*, 125–134.

Jamison, K. R. (1993). Touched with fire: Manic depressive illness and the artistic temperament. New York: Macmillan.

Jamison, R. N., & Virts, K. L. (1990). The influence of family support on chronic pain. *Behaviour Research and Therapy, 28*(4), 283–287.

Jamner, L. D., Shapiro, D., Goldstein, I. B., & Hug, R. (1991). Ambulatory blood pressure and heart rate in paramedics: Effects of cynical hostility and defensiveness. *Psychosomatic Medicine, 53*, 393–406.

Jane, J. S., Oltmanns, T. F., South, S. C., & Turkheimer, E. (2007). Gender bias in diagnostic criteria for personality disorders: An item response theory analysis. *Journal of Abnormal Psychology, 116*, 166–175.

Jang, K. L. (2005). *The behavioral genetics of psychopathology: A clinical guide.* Mahwah, NJ: Lawrence Erlbaum Associates.

Janicak, P. G., Dowd, S. M., Martis, B., Alam, D., Beedle, D., Krasuski, J., et al. (2002). Repetitive transcranial magnetic stimulation versus electroconvulsive therapy for major depression: Preliminary results of a randomized trial. *Biological Psychiatry*, 659–667.

Jason, L. A., Fennell, P. A., & Taylor, R. R. (2003). *Handbook of chronic fatigue syndrome.* Hoboken, NJ: John Wiley.

Jason, L. A., Richman, J. A., Rademaker, A. W., Jordan, K. M., Plioplys, A. V., Taylor, R. R., et al. (1999). A community-based study of chronic fatigue syndrome. *Archives of Internal Medicine, 159*, 2129–2137.

Jaspers, K. (1963). *General psychopathology* (J. Hoenig & M. W. Hamilton, Trans.). Manchester, England: Manchester University Press.

Javaheri, S. (2006). Central sleep apnea. In T. Lee-Chiong (Ed.), *Sleep: A comprehensive handbook* (pp. 249–262). Hoboken, NJ: John Wiley & Sons.

Javitt, D. C., & Laruelle, M. (2006). Neurochemical theories. In J. A. Lieberman, T. S. Stroup, & D. O. Perkins (Eds.), *The American Psychiatric Publishing textbook of schizophrenia* (pp. 85–116). Washington, DC: American Psychiatric Publishing.

Javitt, D., & Zukin, S. R. (2005). Phencyclidine (phencyclidine–like)-related disorders. In B. J. Sadock & V. A. Sadock (Eds.), *Kaplan & Sadock's comprehensive textbook of psychiatry* (pp. 1291–1300). Philadelphia: Lippincott, Williams & Wilkins.

Jay, S. M., Elliott, C. H., Ozolins, M., Olson, R. A., & Pruitt, S. D. (1985). Behavioral management of children's distress during painful medical procedures. *Behaviour Research and Therapy, 23*(5), 513–520.

Jellinek, E. M. (1946). Phases in the drinking histories of alcoholics. *Quarterly Journal of Studies on Alcohol, 7*, 1–88.

Jellinek, E. M. (1952). Phases of alcohol addiction. *Quarterly Journal of Studies on Alcohol, 13*, 673–684.

Jellinek, E. M. (1960). *The disease concept of alcohol.* New Brunswick, NJ: Hillhouse Press.

Jenike, M. A., Baer, L., & Minichiello, W. E. (Eds.) (1986). *Obsessive-compulsive disorders: Theory and management.* Littleton, MA: PSG Publishing.

Jenike, M. A., Baer, L., Ballantine, H. T., Martuza, R. L., Tynes, S., Giriunas, I., et al. (1991). Cingulotomy

for refractory obsessive-compulsive disorder: A long-term follow-up of 33 patients. *Archives of General Psychiatry, 48*, 548–555.

Jenkins, J. H., & Karno, M. (1992). The meaning of expressed emotion: Theoretical issues raised by cross-cultural research. *American Journal of Psychiatry, 149*, 9–21.

Jenkins, J. H., Kleinman, A., & Good, B. J. (1990). Cross-cultural studies of depression. In J. Becker & A. Kleinman (Eds.), *Psychosocial aspects of depression.* Hillsdale, NJ: Erlbaum.

Jensen, E. J., Schmidt, E., Pedersen, B., & Dahl, R. (1991). Effect on smoking cessation of silver acetate, nicotine and ordinary chewing gum. *Psychopharmacology, 104*, 470–474.

Jensen, P. S., Hinshaw, S. P., Swanson, J. M., Greenhill, L. L., Conners, C. K., Arnold, L. E., et al. (2001). Findings from the NIMH Multimodal Treatment Study of ADHD (MTA): Implications and applications for primary care providers. *Journal of Developmental and Behavioral Pediatrics, 22*(1), 60–73.

Jilek, W. G. (1982). Altered states of consciousness in North American Indian ceremonials. *Ethos, 10*(4), 326–343.

Jindal, R. D., Thase, M. E., Fasiczka, A. L., Friedman, E. S., Buysse, D. J., Frank, E., & Kupfer, D.J. (2002). Electroencephalographic sleep profiles in single-episode and recurrent unipolar forms of major depression: II. Comparison during remission. *Biological Psychiatry, 1*, 230–236.

Jobe, T. H., & Harrow, M. (2005). Long-term outcome of patients with schizophrenia: A review. *Canadian Journal of Psychiatry, 50*, 892–900.

Jockin, V., McGue, M., & Lykken, D. T. (1996). Personality and divorce: A genetic analysis. *Journal of Personality and Social Psychology, 71*, 288–299.

Joe, S., Baser, R., Breeden, G., Neighbors, H., & Jackson, J. (2006). Prevalence of and risk factors for lifetime suicide attempts among blacks in the United States. *JAMA, 296*, 2112–2123.

Johannes, C. B., Araujo, A. B., Feldman, H. A., Derby, C. A., Kleinman, K. P., & McKinlay, J. B. (2000). Incidence of erectile dysfunction in men 40 to 69 years old: Longitudinal results from the Massachusetts male aging study. *Journal of Urology, 163*, 460–463.

Johns, M. B., Hovell, M. F., Ganiats, T., Peddecord, M., & Agras, W. S. (1987). Primary care and health promotion: A model for preventive medicine. *American Journal of Preventive Medicine, 3*(6), 351.

Johnson, A. M., Mercer, C. H., Erens, B., Copas, A. J., McManus, S., Wellings, K., et al. (2001). Sexual behaviour in Britain: Partnerships, practices, and HIV risk behaviours. *The Lancet, 358*, 1835–1842.

Johnson, A. M., Wadsworth, J., Wellings, K., Bradshaw, S., & Field, J. (1992). Sexual lifestyles and HIV risk. *Nature, 360*, 410–412.

Johnson, B. A. (1991). Cannabis. In I. B. Glass (Ed.), *International handbook of addiction behaviour* (pp. 69–76). London: Tavistock/Routledge.

Johnson, C. J., & Beitchman, J. H. (2005). Expressive language disorder. In B. J. Sadock & V. A. Sadock (Eds.), *Kaplan & Sadock's comprehensive textbook of psychiatry* (pp. 3136–3142). Philadelphia: Lippincott, Williams & Wilkins.

Johnson, D. L. (1989). Schizophrenia as a brain disease: Implications for psychologists and families. *American Psychologist, 44*, 553–555.

Johnson, J. G., Bromley, E., & McGeoch, P. G. (2005). Role of childhood experiences in the development of maladaptive and adaptive traits. In J. M. Oldham, A. E. Skodol, & D. S. Bender (Eds.), *Textbook of personality disorders* (pp. 209–221). Washington, DC: American Psychiatric Publishing.

Johnson, J. G., Cohen, P., Kasen, S., & Brook, J. S. (2002). Eating disorders during adolescence and the risk for physical and mental disorders during early adulthood. *Archives of General Psychiatry, 59*, 545–552.

Johnson, J. G., Cohen, P., Kasen, S., & Brook, J. S. (2006). Dissociative disorders among adults in the community, impaired functioning, and Axis I and Axis II comorbidity. *Journal of Psychiatric Research, 40*, 131–140.

Johnson, J. G., Cohen, P., Pine, D. S., Klein, D. F., Kasen, S., & Brook, J. S. (2000). Association between cigarette smoking and anxiety disorders during adolescence and early adulthood. *JAMA, 284*, 2348–2351.

Johnson, J. G., Weissman, M. M., & Klerman, G. L. (1990). Panic disorder, comorbidity and suicide attempts. *Archives of General Psychiatry, 47*, 805–808.

Johnson, S. L., & Miller, I. (1997). Negative life events and time to recovery from episodes of bipolar disorder. *Journal of Abnormal Psychology, 106*(3), 449–457.

Johnson, S. L., & Roberts, J. E. (1995). Life events and bipolar disorder: Implications from biological theories. *Psychological Bulletin, 117*(3), 434–449.

Johnson, S. L., Gruber, J. L., & Eisner, L. R. (2007). Emotion and bipolar disorder. In J. Rottenberg & S. L. Johnson (Eds.), *Emotion and psychopathology* (pp. 123–150). Washington, DC: American Psychological Association.

Johnson, S. L., Winett, C. A., Meyer, B., Greenhouse, W. J., & Miller, I. (1999). Social support and the course of bipolar disorder. *American Psychological Association, 180*(4), 558–566.

Johnston, D. W. (1997). Cardiovascular disease. In D. M. Clark & C. G. Fairburn (Eds.), *Science and practice of cognitive behaviour therapy* (pp. 341–358). Oxford: Oxford University Press.

Joiner, T. E., Jr. (1997). Shyness and low social support as interactive diatheses, with loneliness as mediator: Testing an interpersonal–personality view of vulnerability to depressive symptoms. *Journal of Abnormal Psychology, 106*(3), 386–394.

Joiner, T. E., Jr. (1999). A test of interpersonal theory of depression in youth psychiatric inpatients. *Journal of Abnormal Child Psychology, 27*(1), 77–85.

Joiner, T. E., Jr., & Rudd, D. M. (1996). Toward a categorization of depression-related psychological constructs. *Cognitive Therapy and Research, 20*, 51–68.

Joiner, T. E., Jr., & Rudd, M. D. (2000). Intensity and duration of suicidal crises vary as a function of previous suicide attempts and negative life events. *Journal of Consulting and Clinical Psychology, 68*(5), 909–916.

Joiner, T. E., Jr., Heatherton, T. F., & Keel, P. K. (1997). Ten year stability and predictive validity of five bulimia-related indicators. *American Journal of Psychiatry, 154*, 1133–1138.

Jones, B. E., & Gray, B. A. (1986). Problems in diagnosing schizophrenia and affective disorders in blacks. *Hospital and Community Psychiatry, 37*, 61–65.

Jones, J. C., & Barlow, D. H. (1990). The etiology of posttraumatic stress disorder. *Clinical Psychology Review, 10*, 299–328.

Jones, M. B., & Blanchard, R. (1998). Birth order and male homosexuality: An extension of Slater's index. *Human Biology, 70*, 775–787.

Jones, M. C. (1924a). The elimination of children's fears. *Journal of Experimental Psychology, 7*, 383–390.

Jones, M. C. (1924b). A laboratory study of fear. The case of Peter. *Pedagogical Seminary, 31*, 308–315.

Jones, R. T. (2005). Hallucinogen-related disorders. In B. J. Sadock & V. A. Sadock (Eds.), *Kaplan & Sadock's comprehensive textbook of psychiatry* (pp. 1238–1247). Philadelphia: Lippincott, Williams & Wilkins.

Jones, R. T., & Haney, J. I. (1984). A primary preventive approach to the acquisition and maintenance of fire emergency responding: Comparison of external and self-instruction strategies. *Journal of Community Psychology, 12*(2), 180–191.

Jones, R. T., & Kazdin, A. E. (1980). Teaching children how and when to make emergency telephone calls. *Behavior Therapy, 11*(4), 509–521.

Jones, R. T., & Ollendick, T. H. (2002). Residential fires. In A. M. La Greca, W. K. Silverman, E. Vernberg, & M. C. Roberts (Eds.), *Helping Children in Disasters: Integrating Research and Practice.* Washington, DC: American Psychological Association.

Jordan, B. D., Relkin, N. R., Ravdin, L. D., Jacobs, A. R., Bennett, A., & Gandy, S. (1997). Apolipoprotein E Epsilon 4 associated with chronic traumatic brain injury in boxing. *JAMA, 278,* 136–140.

Judd, L. L. (1997). The clinical course of unipolar major depressive disorders. *Archives of General Psychiatry, 54,* 989–991.

Judd, L. L. (2000). Course and chronicity of unipolar major depressive disorder: Commentary on joiner. *Child Psychology Science and Practice, 7*(2), 219–223.

Judd, L. L., Akiskal, H. S., Maser, J. D., Zeller, P. J., Endicott, J., Coryell, W., et al. (1998). Major depressive disorder: A prospective study of residual subthreshold depressive symptoms as predictor of rapid release. *Journal of Affective Disorders, 50,* 97–108.

Judd, L. L., Akiskal, H., Schettler, P., Coryell, W., Endicott, J., Maser, J., et al. (2003). A prospective investigation of the natural history of the long-term weekly symptomatic status of the long-term weekly symptomatic status of bipolar II disorder. *Archives of General Psychiatry, 60,* 261–269.

Junginger, J. (1997). Fetishism: Assessment and treatment. In D. R. Laws & W. O'Donohue (Eds.), *Sexual deviance: Theory, assessment and treatment* (pp. 92–110). New York: Guilford Press.

Kafka, M. P. (1997). A monoamine hypothesis for the pathophysiology of paraphilic disorders. *Archives of Sexual Behavior, 26,* 343–358.

Kagan, J. (1994). *Galen's prophesy.* New York: Basic Books.

Kagan, J. (1997). Temperament and the reactions to unfamiliarity. *Child Development, 68,* 139–143.

Kagan, J., & Snidman, N. (1991). Infant predictors of inhibited and uninhibited profiles. *Psychological Science, 2,* 40–44.

Kagan, J., & Snidman, N. (1999). Early childhood predictors of adult anxiety disorders. *Biological Psychiatry, 46,* 1536–1541.

Kagan, J., Reznick, J. S., & Snidman, N. (1988). Biological bases of childhood shyness. *Science, 240,* 167–171.

Kaiser, J. (2006, May 5). Differences in immune cell "brakes" may explain chimp–human split on AIDS. *Science Magazine, 312,* 672–673.

Kahn, R. S., Khoury, J., Nichols, W. C., & Lanphear, B. P. (2003). Role of dopamine transporter genotype and maternal prenatal smoking in childhood hyperactive-impulsive, inattentive, and oppositional behaviors. *The Journal of Pediatrics, 143*(1), 104–110.

Kalat, J. W. (Ed.) (2007). *Biological Psychology* (9th ed.). Pacific Grove, CA: Brooks/Cole.

Kalayasiri, R., Kranzler, H. R., Weiss, R., Brady, K., Gueorguieva, R., Panhuysen, C., et al. (2006). Risk factors for cocaine-induced paranoia in cocaine-dependent sibling pairs. *Drug and Alcohol Dependence, 84,* 77–84.

Kalivas, P. W. (2005). New directions pharmacotherapy for addiction or can we forget to be addicted? *Clinical Neuroscience Research, 5,* 147–150.

Kallmann, F. J. (1938). *The genetics of schizophrenia.* New York: Augustin.

Kanaya, T., Scullin, M. H., & Ceci, S. J. (2003). The Flynn effect and U.S. policies: The impact of rising IQ scores on American society via mental retardation diagnoses. *American Psychologist, 58,* 778–790.

Kanayama, G., Barry, S., & Pope, H. G. (2006). Body image and attitudes toward male roles in anabolic–androgenic steroid users. *American Journal of Psychiatry, 163,* 697–703.

Kandel, D. B., Wu, P., & Davies, M. (1994). Maternal smoking during pregnancy and smoking by adolescent daughters. *American Journal of Public Health, 84,* 1407–1413.

Kandel, E. R. (1983). From metapsychology to molecular biology: Explorations into the nature of anxiety. *American Journal of Psychiatry, 140,* 1277–1293.

Kandel, E. R., Jessell, T. M., & Schacter, S. (1991). Early experience and the fine tuning of synaptic connections. In E. R. Kandel, J. H. Schwartz, & T. M. Jessell (Eds.), *Principles of neural science* (3rd ed., pp. 945–958). New York: Elsevier.

Kandel, E. R., Schwartz, J., & Jessell, T. M. (2000). *Principles of neural science* (4th ed.). New York: McGraw-Hill.

Kane, J. M. (2006). Tardive dyskinesia circa 2006. *American Journal of Psychiatry, 163,* 1316–1318.

Kane, J. M., & Marder, S. R. (2005). Schizophrenia: Somatic treatment. In B. J. Sadock & V. A. Sadock (Eds.), *Kaplan & Sadock's comprehensive textbook of psychiatry* (pp. 1467–1476). Philadelphia: Lippincott, Williams & Wilkins.

Kanigel, R. (1988, October/November). Nicotine becomes addictive. *Science Illustrated,* pp. 12–14, 19–21.

Kanner, L. (1943). Autistic disturbances of affective contact. *Nervous Child, 2,* 217–250.

Kanner, L. (1949). Problems of nosology and psychodynamics of early infantile autism. *American Journal of Orthopsychiatry, 19,* 416–426.

Kanner, L., & Eisenberg, L. (1955). Notes on the follow-up studies of autistic children. In P. Hoch & J. Zubin (Eds.), *Psychopathology of childhood* (pp. 227–239). New York: Grune & Stratton.

Kansas v. Hendricks, 117 S. Ct. 2072 (1997).

Kaplan, H. S. (1979). *Disorders of sexual desire.* New York: Brunner/Mazel.

Kaplan, H. S. (1987). *Sexual aversion, sexual phobias, and panic disorder.* New York: Brunner/Mazel.

Kaplan, M. (1983). A woman's view of DSM-III. *American Psychologist, 38,* 786–792.

Kaplan, S. A., Reis, R. B., Kohn, I. J., Ikeguchi, E. F., Laor, E., Te, A. E., & Martins, A. C. (1999). Safety and efficacy of sildenafil in postmenopausal women with sexual dysfunction. *Urology, 53,* 481–486.

Karno, M., & Golding, J. M. (1991). Obsessive-compulsive disorder. In L. N. Robins & D. A. Regier (Eds.), *Psychiatric disorders in America: The epidemiologic catchment area study* (pp. 204–219). New York: Free Press.

Karon, B. P. (2000). The clinical interpretation of the Thematic Apperception Test, Rorschach, and other clinical data: A reexamination of statistical versus clinical prediction. *Professional Psychology: Research and Practice, 31,* 230–233.

Kasch, K. L., Rottenberg, J., Arnow, B. A., & Gotlib, I. H. (2002). Behavioral activation and inhibition systems and the severity and course of depression. *Journal of Abnormal Psychology, 111,* 589–597.

Kashani, J. H., Hoeper, E. W., Beck, N. C., & Corcoran, C. M. (1987). Personality, psychiatric disorders, and parental attitude among a community sample of adolescents. *Journal of the American Academy of Child and Adolescent Psychiatry, 26*(6), 879–885.

Kashani, J. H., McGee, R. O., Clarkson, S. E. A., Walton, L. A., Williams, S., Silva, P. A., et al. (1983). Depression in a sample of 9-year-old children: Prevalence and associated characteristics. *Archives of General Psychiatry, 40,* 1217–1223.

Kasindorf, J. (1988, May 2). The real story of Billie Boggs: Was Koch right—Or the civil libertarians? *New York,* pp. 36–44.

Kass, D. J., Silvers, F. M., & Abrams, G. M. (1972). Behavioral group treatment of hysteria. *Archives of General Psychiatry, 26,* 42–50.

Kato, K., Sullivan, P., Evengard, B., & Pederson, N. (2006). Premorbid predictors of chronic fatigue. *Archives of General Psychiatry, 63,* 1267–1272.

Katon, W. (1993). Somatization disorder, hypochondriasis, and conversion disorder. In D. L. Dunner (Ed.), *Current psychiatric therapy* (pp. 314–320). Philadelphia: W. B. Saunders.

Katon, W. J. (2003). Clinical and health services relationships between major depression, depressive symptoms, and general medical illness. *Biological Psychiatry, 54,* 216–226.

Katon, W., & Roy-Byrne, P. P. (1991). Mixed anxiety and depression. *Journal of Abnormal Psychology, 100*(3), 337–345.

Katon, W., Lin, E., Von Korff, M., Russo, J., Lipscomb, P., & Bush, T. (1991). Somatization: A spectrum of severity. *American Journal of Psychiatry, 148,* 34–40.

Katz, I. R. (1993). Delirium. In D. L. Dunner (Ed.), *Current psychiatric therapy* (pp. 65–73). Philadelphia: W. B Saunders.

Katz, I. R., Leshen, E., Kleban, M., & Jethanandani, V. (1989). Clinical features of depression in the nursing home. *International Psychogeriatrics, 1,* 5–15.

Katz, J. L., Weiner, H., Gallagher, T. F., & Hellman, I. (1970). Stress, distress, and ego defenses: Psychoendocrine response to impending breast tumor biopsy. *Archives of General Psychiatry, 23,* 131–142.

Katz, J., & Gagliese, L. (1999). Phantom limb pain: A continuing puzzle. In R. J. Gatchel & D. C. Turk (Eds.), *Psychosocial factors in pain: Critical perspectives* (pp. 284–300). New York: Guilford Press.

Kaufman, J. C. (2001). The Sylvia Plath effect: Mental illness in eminent creative writers. *The Journal of Creative Behavior, 35,* 37–50.

Kaufman, J. C. (2002). Creativity and confidence: Price of achievement. *American Psychologist, 57,* 375–376.

Kaufman, J. C., & Baer, J. (2002). I bask in dreams of suicide: Mental illness, poetry, and women. *Review of General Psychology, 6,* 271–286.

Kavale, K. A., & Forness, S. R. (1983). Hyperactivity and diet treatment: A meta-analysis of the Feingold hypothesis. *Journal of Learning Disabilities, 16,* 324–330.

Kavanagh, D. J. (1992). Recent developments in expressed emotion and schizophrenia. *British Journal of Psychiatry, 160,* 601–620.

Kawamura, K. Y. (2002). Asian American body images. In T. F. Cash & T. Pruzinsky (Eds.), *Body image: A handbook of theory, research and clinical practice* (pp. 243–249). New York: Guilford Press.

Kaye, W. H., Greeno, C. G., Moss, H., Fernstrom, J., Fernstrom, M., Lilenfeld, L. R., et al. (1998). Alterations in serotonin activity and psychiatric symptoms after recovery from bulimia nervosa. *Archives of General Psychiatry, 55,* 927–935.

Kaye, W. H., Strober, M., Stein, D., & Gendall, K. (1999). New directions in treatment research of anorexia and bulimia nervosa. *Biological Psychiatry, 45,* 1285–1292.

Kaye, W. H., Weltzin, T. E., Hsu, L. K. G., McConaha, C. W., & Bolton, B. (1993). Amount of calories retained after binge eating and vomiting. *American Journal of Psychiatry, 150*(6), 969–971.

Kaysen, S. (1993). *Girl, interrupted.* New York: Turtle Bay Books.

Kazdin, A. E., Mazurick, J. L., & Bass, D. (1993). Risk for attrition in treatment of antisocial children and families. *Journal of Child Clinical Psychology, 22,* 2–16.

Keane, T. M., & Barlow, D. H. (2002). Posttraumatic stress disorder. In D. H. Barlow, *Anxiety and its disorders: The nature and treatment of anxiety and panic.* (2nd ed., pp. 418–453). New York: Guilford Press.

Kearney, C. A., Albano, A. M., Eisen, A. R., Allan, W. D., & Barlow, D. H. (1997). The phenomenology of panic disorder in youngsters: An empirical study of a clinical sample. *Journal of Anxiety Disorders, 11*(10), 49–62.

Keck, P. E., & McElroy, S. L. (2002). Pharmacological treatments for bipolar disorder. In P. E. Nathan & J. M. Gorman (Eds.), *A guide to treatments that work* (2nd ed., pp. 277–299). New York: Oxford University Press.

Keefe, F. J., & France, C. R. (1999). Pain: Biopsychosocial mechanisms and management. *Current Directions in Psychological Science, 8,* 137–141.

Keefe, F. J., Dunsmore, J., & Burnett, R. (1992). Behavioral and cognitive-behavioral approaches to chronic pain: Recent advances and future directions. Special issue: Behavioral medicine: An update for the 1990s. *Journal of Consulting and Clinical Psychology, 60*(4), 528–536.

Keel, P. K., & Mitchell, J. E. (1997). Outcome in bulimia nervosa. *American Journal of Psychiatry, 154,* 313–321.

Keel, P. K., Dorer, D. J., Eddy, K. T., Franko, D., Charatan, D. L., & Herzog, D. B. (2003). Predictors of mortality in eating disorders. *Archives of General Psychiatry, 60,* 179–183.

Keel, P. K., Fichter, M., Quadfleig, N., Bulik, C. M., Baxter, M. G., Thornton, L., et al. (2004). Application of a latent class analysis to empirically define eating disorder phenotypes. *Archives of General Psychiatry, 61,* 192–200.

Keel, P. K., Heatherton, T. F., Dorer, D. J., Joiner, T, E., & Zalta, A. K. (2006). Point prevalence of bulimia nervosa in 1982, 1992, and 2002. *Psychological Medicine, 36,* 119–127.

Keel, P. K., Mitchell, J. E., Miller, K., B. Davis, T. L., & Crow, S. J. (1999). Long-term outcome of bulimia nervosa. *Archives of General Psychiatry, 56,* 63–69.

Keel, P. K., Mitchell, J. E., Miller, K. B., Davis, T. L., & Crow, S. J. (2000). Predictive validity of bulimia nervosa as a diagnostic strategy. *American Journal of Psychiatry 157*(1), 136–138.

Keilitz, I. (1987). Researching and reforming the insanity defense. *Rutgers Law Review, 39,* 289–322.

Keilitz, I., & Fulton, J. P. (1984). *The insanity defense and its alternatives: A guide for policymakers.* Williamsburg, VA: National Center for State Courts.

Keitner, G. I., Ryan, C. E., Miller, I. W., Kohn, R., Bishop, D. S., & Epstein, N. B. (1995). Role of the family in recovery and major depression. *American Journal of Psychiatry, 152,* 1002–1008.

Keller, M. B., & Wunder, J. (1990). Bipolar disorder in childhood. In M. Hersen & C. G. Last (Eds.), *Handbook of child and adult psychopathology: A longitudinal perspective.* Elmsford, NY: Pergamon Press.

Keller, M. B., Baker, L. A., & Russell, C. W. (1993). Classification and treatment of dysthymia. In D. L. Dunner (Ed.), *Current psychiatric therapy.* Philadelphia: W. B. Saunders.

Keller, M. B., Hirschfeld, R. M. A., & Hanks, D. L. (1997). Double depression: A distinctive subtype of unipolar depression. *Journal of Affective Disorders, 45,* 65–73.

Keller, M. B., Klein, D. N., Hirschfeld, R. M. A., Kocsis, J. H., McCullough, J. P., Miller, I., et al. (1995). Results of the DSM-IV mood disorders field trial. *American Journal of Psychiatry, 152,* 843–849.

Keller, M. B., Lavori, P. W., Endicott, J., Coryell, W., & Klerman, G. L. (1983). "Double depression": Two year follow-up. *American Journal of Psychiatry, 140*(6), 689–694.

Keller, M. B., Lavori, P. W., Mueller, T. I., Endicott, J., Coryell, W., Hirschfeld, R. M. A., & Shea, T. (1992). Time to recovery, chronicity, and levels of psychopathology in major depression. *Archives of General Psychiatry, 49,* 809–816.

Keller, M. B., McCollough, J. P., Klein, D. N., Arnow, B., Dunner, D. L., Gelenberg, A. J., et al. (2000). A comparison of nefazodone, the cognitive behavioral-analysis system of psychotherapy, and their combination for the treatment of chronic depression. *New England Journal of Medicine, 342*(20), 1462–1470.

Kellner, R. (1985). Functional somatic symptoms and hypochondriasis: A survey of empirical studies. *Archives of General Psychiatry, 42,* 821–833.

Kellner, R. (1986). *Somatization and hypochondriasis.* New York: Praeger-Greenwood.

Kellner, R. (1992). Diagnosis and treatments of hypochondriacal syndromes. *Psychosomatics, 33*(3), 278–279.

Kellner, R., Hernandez, J., & Pathak, D. (1992). Hypochondriacal fears and beliefs, anxiety, and somatization. *British Journal of Psychiatry, 160,* 525–532.

Kelly, B. D., Casey, P., Dunn, G., Ayuso-Mateos, J. L., & Dowrick, C. (2007). The role of personality disorder in "difficult to reach" patients with depression: Findings from the ODIN study. *European Psychiatry, 22,* 153–159.

Kelly, J. A. (1995). *Changing HIV risk behavior: Practical strategies.* New York: Guilford Press.

Kelly, J. A., Murphy, D. A., Sikkema, K. J., McAuliffe, T. L., Roffman, R. A., Solomon, L. J., Winett, R. A., Kalichman, S. C., & the Community HIV Prevention Research Collaborative. (1997). Randomised, controlled community-level HIV-prevention intervention for sexual-risk behaviour among homosexual men in U.S. cities. *The Lancet, 350,* 1500–1505.

Kelly, M. P., Strassberg, D. S., & Kircher, J. R. (1990). Attitudinal and experiential correlates of anorgasmia. *Archives of Sexual Behavior, 19*(2), 165–177.

Kemeny, M. E. (2003). The psychobiology of stress. *Current Directions in Psychological Science, 12*(4), 124–129.

Kemeny, M. E., Cohen, F., Zegans, L. S., & Conant, M. A. (1989). Psychological and immunological predictors of genital herpes recurrence. *Psychosomatic Medicine, 51,* 195–208.

Kemp, S. (1990). *Medieval psychology.* New York: Greenwood Press.

Kendall, P. C., Flannery-Schroeder, E., Panichelli-Mindell, M., Southam-Gerow, M., Henin, A., & Warman, M. (1997). Therapy for youths with anxiety disorder: A second randomized clinical trial. *Journal of Consulting and Clinical Psychology, 65,* 366–380.

Kendell, R. (1985). Emotional and physical factors in the genesis of puerperal mental disorders. *Journal of Psychosomatic Research, 29,* 3–11.

Kendler, K. S. (2001). Twin studies of psychiatric illness. *Achieves of General Psychiatry, 58,* 1005–1013.

Kendler, K. S. (2005). Psychiatric genetics: A methodological critique. In N. C. Andreasen (Ed.), *Research advances in genetics and genomics: Implications for psychiatry* (pp. 5–25). Washington, DC: American Psychiatric Publishing.

Kendler, K. S. (2006). Reflections on the relationship between psychiatric genetics and psychiatric nosology. *American Journal of Psychiatry, 163,* 1138–1146.

Kendler, K. S., Czajkowski, N., Tambs, K., Torgersen, S., Aggen, S. H., Neale, M. C., & Reichborn-Kjennerud, T. (2006). Dimensional representations of DSM-IV cluster A personality disorders in a population-based sample of Norwegian twins: A multivariate study. *Psychological Medicine, 36,* 1583–1591.

Kendler, K. S., Heath, A. C., Martin, N. G., & Eaves, L. J. (1987). Symptoms of anxiety and symptoms of depression: Same genes, different environments? *Archives of General Psychiatry, 44*(5), 451–457.

Kendler, K. S., Hettema, J. M., Butera, F., Gardner, C. O., & Prescott, C. A. (2003). Life event dimensions of loss, humiliation, entrapment, and danger in the prediction of onsets of major depression and generalized anxiety. *Archives of General Psychiatry, 60,* 789–796.

Kendler, K. S., Jacobson, K. C., Prescott, C. A., & Neale, M. C. (2003). Specificity of genetic and environmental risk factors for use and abuse/dependence of cannabis, cocaine, hallucinogens, sedatives, stimulants, and opiates in male twins. *American Journal of Psychiatry, 160,* 687–695.

Kendler, K. S., Karkowski, L. M., & Prescott, C. A. (1999a). The assessment of dependence in the study of stressful life events: Validation using a twin design. *Psychological Medicine, 29*(6), 1455–1460.

Kendler, K. S., Karkowski, L. M., & Prescott, C. A. (1999b). Causal relationship between stressful life events and the onset of major depression. *American Journal of Psychiatry, 156*(6), 837–841.

Kendler, K. S., Karkowski, L. M., & Prescott, C. A. (1999c). Fear and phobias: Reliability and heritability. *Psychological Medicine, 29,* 539–553.

Kendler, K. S., Kessler, R. C., Walters, E. E., MacLean, C., Neale, M. C., Heath, A. C., & Eaves, L. J. (1995). Stressful life events, genetic liability, and onset of an episode of major depression in women. *American Journal of Psychiatry, 152,* 833–842.

Kendler, K. S., Kuhn, J., Vittum, J., Prescott, C. A., & Riley, B. (2005). The interaction of stressful life events and a serotonin transporter polymorphism in the prediction of episodes of major depression. *Archives of General Psychiatry, 62,* 529–535.

Kendler, K. S., MacLean, C., Neale, M., Kessler, R., Heath, A., & Eaves, L. (1991). The genetic epidemiology of bulimia nervosa. *American Journal of Psychiatry, 148*(12), 1627–1637.

Kendler, K. S., Myers, J., & Prescott, C. A. (2005). Sex differences in the relationship between social support and risk for major depression: A longitudinal study of opposite-sex twin pairs. *American Journal of Psychiatry, 162,* 250–256.

Kendler, K. S., Neale, M. C., Heath, A. C., Kessler, R. C., & Eaves, L. J. (1994). A twin-family study of alcoholism in women. *American Journal of Psychiatry, 151,* 707–715.

Kendler, K. S., Neale, M. C., Kessler, R. C., Heath, A. C., & Eaves, L. J. (1992a). Generalized anxiety disorder in women: A population-based twin study. *Archives of General Psychiatry, 49,* 267–272.

Kendler, K. S., Neale, M. C., Kessler, R. C., Heath, A. C., & Eaves, L. J. (1992b). Major depression and generalized anxiety disorder: Same genes, (partly) different environments? *Archives of General Psychiatry, 49,* 716–722.

Kendler, K. S., Neale, M. C., Kessler, R. C., Heath, A. C., & Eaves, L. J. (1993). A longitudinal twin study of 1-year prevalence of major depression in women. *Archives of General Psychiatry, 50,* 843–852.

Kendler, K. S., Neale, M. C., MacLean, C. J., Heath, A. C., Eaves, L. J., & Kessler, R. C. (1993). Smoking and major depression: A causal analysis. *Archives of General Psychiatry, 50,* 36–43.

Kennedy, S. (2000). Psychological factors and immunity in HIV infection: Stress, coping, social support, and intervention outcomes. In D. I. Mostofsky & D. H. Barlow (Eds.), *The management of stress and anxiety in medical disorders* (pp. 194–205). Needham Heights, MA: Allyn & Bacon.

Kerr, S. M., Jowett, S. A., & Smith, L. N. (1996). Preventing sleep problems in infants: A randomized controlled trial. *Journal of Advanced Nursing, 24,* 938–942.

Kertzner, R. M., & Gorman, J. M. (1992). Psychoneuroimmunology and HIV infection. In A. Tashan & M. B. Riba (Eds.), *Review of psychiatry* (Vol. 11). Washington, DC: American Psychiatric Press.

Kessler, R. C. (1997). The effects of stressful life events on depression. *Annual Review of Psychology, 48,* 191–214.

Kessler, R. C. (2006). The epidemiology of depression among women. In C. Keyes, S. Goodman (Eds.), *A handbook for the social, behavioral, and biomedical sciences: Women and depression* (pp. 22–37). New York: Cambridge University Press.

Kessler, R. C., Berglund, P., Demler, O., Jin, R., Koretz, D., Merikangas, K. R., et al. (2003). The epidemiology of major depressive disorder: Results from the National Comorbidity Survey Replication (NCS-R). *JAMA, 289,* 3095–3105.

Kessler, R. C., Berglund, P., Borges, G., Nock, M., & Wang, P. (2005). Trends in suicide ideation, plans, gestures, and attempts in the United States, 1990–1992 to 2001–2003. *JAMA, 293,* 2487–2495.

Kessler, R. C., Berglund, P., Demler, O., Jin, R., & Walters, E. E. (2005). Lifetime prevalence and age-of-onset distributions of DSM-IV disorders in the National Comorbidity Survey replication. *Archives of General Psychiatry, 62,* 593–602.

Kessler, R. C., Chiu, W. T., Demler, O., & Walters, E. E. (2005). Prevalence, severity, and comorbidity of 12-month DSM-IV disorders in the National Comorbidity Survey replication. *Archives of General Psychiatry, 62,* 617–627.

Kessler, R. C., Galea, S., Jones, R. T., & Parker, H. A. (2006). *Mental illness and suicidality after Hurricane Katrina.* Bulletin of the World Health Organization (WHO Publication No. 06-033019).

Kessler, R. C., McGonagle, K. A., Zhao, S., Nelson, C. B., Hughes, M., Eshleman, S., et al. (1994). Lifetime and 12-month prevalence of DSM-III-R psychiatric disorders among persons aged 15–54 in the United States: Results from the national comorbidity survey. *Archives of General Psychiatry.*

Kessler, R. C., Sonnega, A., Bromet, E., Hughes, M., & Nelson, C. B. (1995). Posttraumatic stress disorder in the national comorbidity survey. *Archives of General Psychiatry, 52,* 1048–1060.

Kety, S. S. (1990). Genetic factors in suicide: Family, twin, and adoption studies. In S. J. Blumenthal & D. J. Kupfer (Eds.), *Suicide over the life cycle: Risk factors, assessment and treatment of suicidal patients* (pp. 127–133). Washington, DC: American Psychiatric Press.

Keys, A., Brozek, J., Henschel, A., Michelson, O., & Taylor, H. L. (1950). *The biology of human starvation* (Vol. 1). Minneapolis: University of Minnesota Press.

Khachaturian, Z. S. (2007). Alzheimer's 101. *Alzheimer's and Dementia, 3,* 1–2.

Kiecolt-Glaser, J. K., & Glaser, R. (1987). Chronic stress and immunity in family caregivers of Alzheimer's disease victims. *Psychosomatic Medicine, 49*(5), 523–535.

Kiecolt-Glaser, J. K., & Glaser, R. (1992). Psychoneuroimmunology: Can psychological interventions modulate immunity? Special issue: Behavioral medicine: An update for the 1990s. *Journal of Consulting and Clinical Psychology, 60*(4), 569–575.

Kiecolt-Glaser, J. K., & Newton, T. L. (2001). Marriage and health: His and hers. *Psychological Bulletin, 127,* 475–503.

Kiecolt-Glaser, J. K., Loving, T., Stowell, J., Malarkey, W., Lemeshow, S., & Dickinson, S., et al. (2005). Hostile marital interactions, proinflammatory cytokine production, and wound healing. *Archives of General Psychiatry, 62,* 1377–1384.

Kiesler, C. A., & Sibulkin, A. E. (1987). *Mental hospitalization: Myths and facts about a national crisis.* Beverly Hills, CA: Sage.

Kiesler, D. J. (1966). Some myths of psychotherapy research and the search for a paradigm. *Psychological Bulletin, 65,* 110–136.

Kihlstrom, J. F. (1992). Dissociation and dissociations: A commentary on consciousness and cognition. *Consciousness & Cognition, 1,* 47–53.

Kihlstrom, J. F. (1994). One hundred years of hysteria. In S. J. Lynn & J. W. Rhue (Eds.), *Dissociation: Clinical and theoretical perspectives.* New York: Guilford Press.

Kihlstrom, J. F. (1997). Memory, abuse, and science. *American Psychologist, 52,* 994–995.

Kihlstrom, J. F. (2005). Dissociative disorders. In S. Nolen-Hoeksema, T. D. Cannon, & T. Widiger (Eds.), *Annual review of clinical psychology* (Vol. 1). Palo Alto, CA: Annual Reviews.

Kihlstrom, J. F., Barnhardt, T. M., & Tataryn, D. J. (1992). The psychological unconscious: Found, lost, and regained. *American Psychologist, 47*(6), 788–791.

Kihlstrom, J. F., Glisky, M. L., & Anguilo, M. J. (1994). Dissociative tendencies and dissociative disorders. *Journal of Abnormal Psychology, 103,* 117–124.

Killen, J. D. (1996). Development and evaluation of a school-based eating disorder symptoms prevention program. In L. Smolak, M. P. Levine, & R. Striegel-Moore (Eds.), *The developmental psychopathology of eating disorders: Implications for research, prevention, and treatment* (pp. 313–339). Mahwah, NJ: Erlbaum.

Killen, J. D., Taylor, C. B., Hayward, C., Haydel, F., Wilson, D. M., Hammer, L. D., et al. (1996). Weight concerns influence the development of eating disorders: A four-year prospective study. *Journal of Consulting and Clinical Psychology, 64,* 936–940.

Killen, J. D., Taylor, C. B., Hayward, C., Wilson, D. M., Hammer, L. D., Robinson, T. N., et al. (1994). The pursuit of thinness and onset of eating disorder symptoms in a community sample of adolescent girls: A three-year prospective analysis. *International Journal of Eating Disorders, 16,* 227–238.

Kilpatrick, D. G., Best, C. L., Veronen, L. J., Amick, A. E., Villeponteaux, L. A., & Ruff, G. A. (1985). Mental health correlates of criminal victimization: A random community survey. *Journal of Consulting and Clinical Psychology, 53,* 866–873.

Kilzieh, N., & Akiskal, H. S. (1999). Rapid-cycling bipolar disorder: An overview of research and clinical experience. *Psychiatric Clinics of North America, 22*(3), 585–607.

Kim, E. D., & Lipshultz, L. I. (1997, April 15). Advances in the treatment of organic erectile dysfunction. *Hospital Practice,* 101–120.

Kim, J.-W., Kim, B.-N., & Cho, S.-C. (2006). The dopamine transporter gene and the impulsivity phenotype in attention deficit hyperactivity disorder: A case-control association study in a Korean sample. *Journal of Psychiatric Research, 40,* 730–737.

Kimble, R., Williams, J. G., & Agras, W. S. (1975). A comparison of two methods of diagnosing hysteria. *American Journal of Psychiatry, 132*(11), 1197–1199.

King, A. C., Taylor, C. B., Albright, C. A., & Haskell, W. L. (1990). The relationship between repressive and defensive coping styles and blood pressure responses in healthy, middle-aged men and women. *Journal of Psychosomatic Research, 34,* 461–471.

King, B. H., Hodapp, R. M., & Dykens, E. M. (2005). Mental retardation. In B. J. Sadock & V. A. Sadock (Eds.), *Kaplan & Sadock's comprehensive textbook of psychiatry* (pp. 3076–3106). Philadelphia: Lippincott, Williams & Wilkins.

King, D. E., Mainous III, A. G., & Geesey, M. E. (in press). Turning back the clock: Adopting a healthy lifestyle in middle age. *American Journal of Medicine.*

King, D. W., King, L. A., Foy, D. W., & Gudanowski, D. M. (1996). Prewar factors in combat related posttraumatic stress disorder: Structural equation modeling with a national sample of female and male Vietnam veterans. *Journal of Consulting and Clinical Psychology, 64,* 520–531.

King, G. R., & Ellinwood, E. H. (1997). Amphetamines and other stimulants. In J. H. Lowinson, P. Ruiz, R. B. Millman, & J. G. Langrod (Eds.), *Substance abuse: A comprehensive textbook* (pp. 207–223). Baltimore: Williams & Wilkins.

King, N. J. (1993). Simple and social phobias. In T. H. Ollendick & R. J. Prinz (Eds.), *Advances in clinical child psychology* (Vol. 15, pp. 305–341). New York: Plenum Press.

King, S. A., & Strain, J. J. (1991). *Pain disorders: A proposed classification for DSM-IV.* Paper presented at the 144th annual meeting of the American Psychiatric Association, New Orleans.

Kinsey, A. C., Pomeroy, W. B., & Martin, C. E. (1948). *Sexual behavior in the human male.* Philadelphia: W. B. Saunders.

Kinsey, A. C., Pomeroy, W. B., Martin, C. E., & Gebhard, P. H. (1953). *Sexual behavior in the human female.* Philadelphia: W. B. Saunders.

Kinzie, J. D., Leung, P. K., Boehnlein, J., & Matsunaga, D. (1992). Psychiatric epidemiology of an Indian village: A 19-year replication study. *Journal of Nervous and Mental Disease, 180*(1), 33–39.

Kirkpatrick, B., & Tek, C. (2005). Schizophrenia: Clinical features and psychopathology concepts. In B. J. Sadock & V. A. Sadock (Eds.), *Kaplan & Sadock's comprehensive textbook of psychiatry* (pp. 1416–1436). Philadelphia: Lippincott, Williams & Wilkins.

Kirmayer, L. J. (1991). The place of culture in psychiatric nosology: Taijin kyofusho and DSM-III-R. *Journal of Nervous and Mental Disease, 179,* 19–28.

Kirmayer, L. J., & Robbins, J. M. (1991). Three forms of somatization in primary care: Prevalence, co-occurrence, and sociodemographic characteristics. *Journal of Nervous and Mental Disease, 179,* 647–655.

Kirmayer, L. J., & Weiss, M. (1993). *On cultural considerations for somatoform disorders in the DSM-IV.* In cultural proposals and supporting papers for DSM-IV. Submitted to the DSM-IV Task Force by the Steering Committee, NIMH-Sponsored Group on Culture and Diagnosis.

Kirmayer, L. J., Looper, K. J., & Taillefer, S. (2003). Somatoform disorders. In M. Hersen & S. M. Turner (Eds.), *Adult psychopathology and diagnosis* (4th ed. pp. 420–475). New York: John Wiley.

Kjernisted, K. D., Enns, M. W., & Lander, M. (2002). An open-label clinical trial of nefazodone in hypochondriasis. *Psychosomatics, 43,* 290–294.

Klein, D. F. (1964). Delineation of two drug responsive anxiety syndromes. *Psychopharmacologia, 5,* 397–408.

Klein, D. F. (1989). The pharmacological validation of psychiatric diagnosis. In L. Robins & J. Barrett (Eds.), *Validity of psychiatric diagnosis.* New York: Raven Press.

Klein, D. F. (1999). Harmful dysfunction, disorder, disease, illness, and evolution. *Journal of Abnormal Psychology, 108,* 421–429.

Klein, D. N., Lewinsohn, P. M., Rohde, P., Seeley, J. R., & Durbin, C. E. (2002). Clinical features of major depressive disorder in adolescents and their relatives: Impact on familial aggregation, implications for phenotype definition, and specificity of transmission. *Journal of Abnormal Psychology. 111,* 98–106.

Klein, D. N., Lewinsohn, P. M., & Seeley, J. R. (1997). Psychosocial characteristics of adolescents with a past history of dysthymic disorder: Comparison with adolescents with past histories of major depressive and non-affective disorders, and never mentally ill controls. *Journal of Affective Disorders, 42,* 127–135.

Klein, D. N., Schwartz, J. E., Rose, S., & Leader, J. B. (2000). Five-year course and outcome of dysthymic disorder: A prospective, naturalistic follow-up study. *American Journal of Psychiatry, 157*(6), 931–939.

Klein, D. N., Shankman, S., & Rose, S. (2006). Ten-year prospective follow-up study of the naturalistic course of dysthymic disorder and double depression. *American Journal of Psychiatry, 163,* 872–880.

Klein, D. N., Taylor, E. B., Dickstein, S., & Harding, K. (1988). The early–late onset distinction in DSM-III-R dysthymia. *Journal of Affective Disorders, 14*(1), 25–33.

Kleinknecht, R. A., Dinnel, D. L., Kleinknecht, E. E., Hiruma, N., & Harada, N. (1997). Cultural factors in social anxiety: A comparison of social phobia symptoms and *taijin kyofusho. Journal of Anxiety Disorders, 11,* 157–177.

Kleinman, A. (1986). *Social origins of distress and disease: Depression, neurasthenia, and pain in modern China.* New Haven, CT: Yale University Press.

Kleinman, A. (2004). Culture and depression. *New England Journal of Medicine, 351,* 951–953.

Klerman, G. L. (1988). Depression and related disorders of mood (affective disorders). In A. M. Nicholi Jr. (Ed.), *The new Harvard guide to psychiatry.* Cambridge, MA: Harvard University Press.

Klerman, G. L., & Weissman, M. M. (1989). Increasing rates of depression. *JAMA, 261,* 2229–2235.

Klerman, G. L., & Weissman, M. M. (1992). The course, morbidity, and costs of depression. *Archives of General Psychiatry, 49*(10), 831–834.

Klerman, G. L., Weissman, M. M., Rounsaville, B. J., & Chevron, E. S. (1984). *Interpersonal psychotherapy of depression.* New York: Basic Books.

Klin, A., Jones, W., Schultz, R., Volkmar, F., & Cohen, D. (2002). Defining and quantifying the social phenotype in autism. *American Journal of Psychiatry, 159,* 895–908.

Klosko, J. S., Barlow, D. H., Tassinari, R., & Cerny, J. A. (1990). A comparison of alprazolam and behavior therapy in treatment of panic disorder. *Journal of Consulting and Clinical Psychology, 58,* 77–84.

Kluft, R. P. (1984). Treatment of multiple personality disorder. *Psychiatric Clinics of North America, 7,* 9–29.

Kluft, R. P. (1991). Multiple personality disorder. In A. Tasman & S. W. Goldinger (Eds.), *Review of psychiatry* (Vol. 10). Washington, DC: American Psychiatric Press.

Kluft, R. P. (1996). Treating the traumatic memories of patients with dissociative identity disorder. *American Journal of Psychiatry, 153,* 103–110.

Kluft, R. P. (1999). Current issues in dissociative identity disorder. *Journal of Practical Psychology and Behavioral Health, 5,* 3–19.

Klump, K. L., Kaye, W. H., & Strober, M. (2001). The evolving genetic foundations of eating disorders. *The Psychiatric Clinics of North America, 24,* 215–225.

Knapp, C. (1997). *Drinking: A love story.* New York: Delta.

Knapp, M. J., Knopman, D. S., Solomon, P. R., Pendlebury, W. W., Davis, C. S., & Graxon, S. I. (1994). A 30-week randomized controlled trial of high-dose tacrine in patients with Alzheimer's disease. *JAMA, 271,* 985–991.

Knight, R. A., & Prentky, R. A. (1990). Classifying sexual offenders: The development and corroboration of taxonomic models. In W. L. Marshall, D. R. Laws, & H. E. Barbaree (Eds.), *Handbook of sexual assault: Issues, theories and treatment of the offender* (pp. 23–52). New York: Plenum Press.

Ko, H-C., Lee, L-R., Chang, R-B., & Huang, K-E. (1996). Comorbidity of premenstrual depression and postpartum blues among Chinese women. *Biological Psychiatry, 39,* 648.

Koch, P., Mansfield, P., Thurau, D., & Carey, M. (2005). "Feeling frumpy": The relationship between body image and sexual response changes in midlife women. *Journal of Sex Research, 42,* 215–223.

Kochanska, G., Aksan, N., & Joy, M. E. (2007). Children's fearfulness as a moderator of parenting in early socialization: Two longitudinal studies. *Developmental Psychology, 43,* 222–237.

Kochman, F. J., Hantouche, E. G., Ferrari, P., Lancrenon, S., Bayart, D., & Akiskal, H. S. (2005). Cyclothymic temperament as a prospective predictor of bipolarity and suicidality in children and adolescents with major depressive disorder. *Journal of Affective Disorders, 85,* 181–189.

Kogon, M. M., Biswas, A., Pearl, D., Carlson, R. W. L., & Spiegel, D. (1997). Effects of medical and psychotherapeutic treatment on the survival of women with metastatic breast carcinoma. *Cancer, 80,* 225–230.

Kohut, H. (1971). *The analysis of self.* New York: International Universities Press.

Kohut, H. (1977). *The restoration of the self.* New York: International Universities Press.

Kolb, B., & Whishaw, I. Q. (1998). Possible regeneration of rat medial front cortex following neonatal frontal lesions. *Behavioral Brain Research, 91,* 127–141.

Kolb, B., Gibb, R., & Gorny, G. (2003). Experience-dependent changes in dendritic arbor and spine density in neocortex vary qualitatively with age and sex. *Neurobiology of Learning & Memory, 79,* 1–10.

Kolb, B., Gibb, R., & Robinson, T. E. (2003). Brain plasticity and behavior. *Current Directions in Psychological Science, 12,* 1–5.

Koocher, G. P. (1996). Pediatric oncology: Medical crisis intervention. In R. J. Resnick & R. H. Rozensky (Eds.), *Health psychology through the life span: Practice and research opportunities* (pp. 213–225). Washington, DC: American Psychological Association.

Kopelowicz, A., Mintz, J., Liberman, R. P., Zarate, R., & Gonzalez-Smith, V. (2004). Disease management in Latinos with schizophrenia: A family-assisted, skills training approach. *Schizophrenia Bulletin, 29,* 211–227.

Koppel, R. (2002). *Alzheimer's disease: The costs to U.S. businesses in 2002.* Washington, DC: Alzheimer's Association.

Korczyn, A. D., Kahana, E., & Galper, Y. (1991). Epidemiology of dementia in Ashkelon, Israel. *Neuroepidemiology, 10,* 100.

Korfine, L., & Hooley, J. M. (2000). Directed forgetting of emotional stimuli in borderline personality disorder. *Journal of Abnormal Psychology, 109,* 214–221.

Kosberg, J. I., Kaufman, A. V., Burgio, L. D., Leeper, J. D., & Sun, F. (2007). Family caregiving to those with dementia in rural Alabama: Racial similarities and differences. *Journal of Aging and Health, 19,* 3–21.

Kosten, T. R., & Sofuoglu, M. (2004). Stimulants. In M. Galanter & H. D. Kleber (Eds.), *The American Psychiatry Publishing textbook of substance abuse treatment* (3rd ed., pp. 189–197). Washington, DC: American Psychiatric Publishing.

Koukoui, S. D., & Chaudhuri, A. (2007). Neuroanatomical, molecular genetic, and behavioral correlates of fragile X syndrome. *Brain Research Reviews, 53,* 27–38.

Kovacs, M., Akiskal, H. S., Gatsonis, C., & Parrone, P. L. (1994). Childhood-onset dysthymic disorder. *Archives of General Psychiatry, 51,* 365–374.

Kovacs, M., Gatsonis, C., Paulaukas, S. L., & Richards, C. (1989). Depressive disorders in childhood: IV. A longitudinal study of comorbidity with and risk for anxiety disorders. *Archives of General Psychiatry, 46*(9), 776–782.

Kovacs, M., Goldston, D., & Gatsonis, C. (1993). Suicidal behaviors and childhood-onset depressive disorders: A longitudinal investigation. *Journal of the American Academy of Child and Adolescent Psychiatry, 32,* 8–20.

Kovacs, M., Rush, A. J., Beck, A. T., & Hollon, S. D. (1981). Depressed outpatients treated with cognitive therapy or pharmacotherapy: A one-year follow-up. *Archives of General Psychiatry, 38*(1), 33–39.

Kraepelin, E. (1898). *The diagnosis and prognosis of dementia praecox.* Paper presented at the 29th Congress of Southwestern German Psychiatry, Heidelberg.

Kraepelin, E. (1899). *Kompendium der Psychiatrie* (6th ed.). Leipzig: Abel.

Kraepelin, E. (1913). *Psychiatry: A textbook for students and physicians.* Leipzig: Barth.

Kraepelin, E. (1919). *Dementia praecox and paraphrenia* (R. M. Barclay & G. M. Robertson, Trans.). New York: R. E. Krieger.

Kral, J. G. (2002). Surgical interventions for obesity. In K. D. Brownell & C. G. Fairburn (Eds.), *Eating disorders and obesity: A comprehensive handbook* (2nd ed., pp. 510–515). New York: Guilford Press.

Krantz, D. S., & Deckel, A. W. (1983). Coping with coronary heart disease and stroke. In T. G. Burish & L. A. Bradley (Eds.), *Coping with chronic disease: Research and applications.* New York: Academic Press.

Kring, A. M., & Bachorowski, J. (1999). Emotions and psychopathology. *Cognition and Emotion, 13*(5), 575–599.

Kripke, D. F. (1998). Light treatment for nonseasonal depression: Speed, efficiency, and combined treatment. *Journal of Affective Disorder, 49,* 109–117.

Krishnan, K. R., Doraiswamy, P. M., Venkataraman, S., Reed, D., & Richie, J. C. (1991). Current concepts in hypothalamo–pituitary–adrenal axis regulation. In J. A. McCubbin, P. G. Kaufmann, & C. B. Nemeroff (Eds.), *Stress, neuropeptides, and systemic disease* (pp. 19–35). San Diego: Academic Press.

Kroenke, K., & Swindle, R. (2000). Cognitive-behavioral therapy for somatization syndromes: A critical review of controlled trials. *Psychotherapy Psychosomatics, 9,* 205–215.

Kroll, R., & Beitchman, J. H. (2005). Stuttering. In B. J. Sadock & V. A. Sadock (Eds.), *Kaplan & Sadock's comprehensive textbook of psychiatry* (pp. 3154–3159). Philadelphia: Lippincott, Williams & Wilkins.

Krueger, R. F., Watson, D., & Barlow, D. H. (2005). Introduction to the special section: Toward a dimensionally based taxonomy of psychopathology [Special issue]. *Journal of Abnormal Psychology, 114,* 491–493.

Krug, E. G., Kresnow, M.-J., Peddicord, J. P., Dahlberg, L. L., Powell, K. E., Crosby, A. E., & Annest, J. L. (1998). Suicide after natural disasters. *New England Journal of Medicine, 338*(6), 373–378.

Kryger, M. H. (2000). Management of obstructive sleep apnea–hypoapnea syndrome: Overview. In M. H. Kryger, T. Roth, & W. C. Dement (Eds.), *Principles and practice of sleep medicine* (3rd ed., pp. 940–954). Philadelphia: W. B. Saunders.

Kuehn, B. (2006). UN–AIDS report: AIDS epidemic slowing, but huge challenges remain. *JAMA, 296,* 29–30.

Kuhn, B. R., & Elliott, A. J. (2003). Treatment efficacy in behavioral pediatric sleep medicine. *Journal of Psychosomatic Research, 54,* 587–597.

Kuiper, B., & Cohen-Kettenis, P. (1988). Sex reassignment surgery: A study of 141 Dutch transsexuals. *Archives of Sexual Behaviour, 17,* 439–457.

Kuo, W. H., Gallo, J. J., & Tien, A. Y. (2001). Incidence of suicide ideation and attempts in adults: The 13-year follow-up of a community sample in Baltimore, Maryland. *Psychological Medicine, 31,* 1181–91.

Kupfer, D. J. (1995). Sleep research in depressive illness: Clinical implications—A tasting menu. *Biological Psychiatry, 38,* 391–403.

Kupfer, D. J., First, M. B., & Regier, D. A. (2002). *A research agenda for DSM-V.* Washington, DC: American Psychiatric Association.

Kupka, R., Luckenbaugh, D., Post, R., Suppes, T., Altshuler, L., Keck, P., et al. (2005). Comparison of rapid-cycling and non-rapid-cycling bipolar disorder based on prospective mood ratings in 539 outpatients. *American Journal Psychiatry, 162,* 1273–1280.

Kurihara, T., Kato, M., Reverger, R., & Gusti Rai Tirta, I. (2006). Beliefs about causes of schizophrenia among family members: A community-based survey in Bali. *Psychiatric Services, 57,* 1795–1799.

Kushner, M. G., Abrams, K., & Borchardt, C. (2000). The relationship between anxiety disorders and alcohol use disorders: A review of major perspectives and findings. *Clinical Psychology Review, 20,* 149–171.

Kushner, M. G., Sher, K. J., & Beitman, B. D. (1990). The relation between alcohol problems and the anxiety disorders. *American Journal of Psychiatry, 147,* 685–695.

Kwok, T., Lee, J., Lam, L., & Woo, J. (in press). Vitamin B12 supplementation did not improve cognition but reduced delirium in demented patients with vitamin B12 deficiency. *Archives of Gerontology and Geriatrics.*

La Fond, J. Q. (2005). *Preventing sexual violence: How society should cope with sex offenders.* Washington, DC: American Psychological Association.

La Fond, J. Q., & Durham, M. L. (1992). *Back to the asylum: The future of mental health law and policy in the United States.* New York: Oxford University Press.

La Greca, A. M., & Prinstein, M. J. (2002). Hurricanes and earthquakes. In A. N. La Greca, W. K. Silverman & M. C. Roberts (Eds.), *Helping Children Cope with Disasters and Terrorism* (Vol. 1, pp. 107–138). Washington, DC: American Psychological Association.

Lacey, J. H. (1992). The treatment demand for bulimia: A catchment area report of referral rates and demography. *Psychiatric Bulletin, 16,* 203–205.

Lachar, D., Bailley, S. E., Rhoades, H. M., Espadas, A., Aponte, M., Cowan, K. A., Gummattira, P., Kopecky, C. R., & Wassef, A. (2001). New subscales for an anchored version of the Brief Psychiatric Rating Scale: Construction, reliability, and validity in acute psychiatric admissions. *Psychological Assessment, 13,* 384–395.

Ladd, C. O., Huot, R. L., Thrivikraman, K. V., Nemeroff, C. B., Meaney, M. J., & Plotsky, P. M. (2000). Long-term behavioral and neuroendocrine adaptations to adverse early experience. In E. A. Mayer & C. B. Saper (Eds.), *Progress in brain research: The biological basis for mind body interactions.* (Vol. 122, pp. 81–103). Amsterdam: Elsevier.

Ladd, C. O., Owens, M. J., & Nemeroff, C. B. (1996). Persistent changes in corticotropin-releasing factor neuronal systems induced by maternal deprivation. *Endocrinology, 137*(4), 1212–1218.

Ladee, G. A. (1966). *Hypochondriacal syndromes.* New York: Elsevier.

Lader, M. H. (1975). *The psychophysiology of mental illness.* London: Routledge & Kegan Paul.

Lader, M. H., & Wing, L. (1964). Habituation of the psycho-galvanic reflex in patients with anxiety states and in normal subjects. *Journal of Neurology, Neurosurgery, and Psychiatry, 27,* 210–218.

Lader, M., & Sartorius, N. (1968). Anxiety in patients with hysterical conversion symptoms. *Journal of Neurology, Neurosurgery, and Psychiatry, 31,* 490–495.

Laing, R. D. (1967). *The politics of experience.* New York: Pantheon.

Lakin, M. M., Montague, D. K., Vanderbrug Medendorp, S., Tesar, L., & Schover, L. R. (1990). Intracavernous injection therapy: Analysis of results and complications. *Journal of Urology, 143,* 1138–1141.

Lalumière, M. L., Blanchard, R., & Zucker, K. J. (2000). Sexual orientation and handedness in men and women: A meta-analysis. *Psychological Bulletin, 126,* 575–592.

Lam, D. H., Hayward, P., Watkins, E., Wright, K., & Sham, P. (2005). Relapse prevention in patients with bipolar disorder: Cognitive therapy outcome after 2 years. *American Journal of Psychiatry, 162,* 324–329.

Lam, D. H., Watkins, E. R., Hayward, P., Bright, J., Wright, K., Kerr, N., et al. (2003). A randomized controlled study of cognitive therapy for relapse prevention for bipolar affective disorder: Outcome of the first year. *Archives of General Psychiatry, 60,* 145–152.

Lam, R., Levitt, A., Levitan, R., Enns, M., Morehouse, R., Michalak, E., et al. (2006). The Can-Sad study: A randomized controlled trial of the effectiveness of light therapy and fluoxetine in patients with winter seasonal affective disorder. *American Journal of Psychiatry, 163,* 805–812.

Lam, T. H., Ho, S. Y., Hedley, A. J., Mak, K. H., & Peto, R. (2001). Mortality and smoking in Hong Kong: Case-control study of all adult deaths in 1998. *British Medical Journal, 323,* 361–362.

Lamberg, L. (2003). All night diners: Researchers take a new look at night eating syndrome. *JAMA, 290,* 1442.

Lambert, M. C., Weisz, J. R., Knight, F., Desrosiers, M., Overly, K., & Thesiger, C. (1992). Jamaican and American adult perspectives on child psychopathology: Further explorations of the threshold model. *Journal of Consulting and Clinical Psychology, 60,* 146–149.

Lambert, M. J., Shapiro, D. A., & Bergin, A. E. (1986). The effectiveness of psychotherapy. In S. L. Garfield & A. E. Bergin (Eds.), *Handbook of psychotherapy and behavior change* (3rd ed.). New York: John Wiley.

Landis, S. E., Earp, J. L., & Koch, G. G. (1992). Impact of HIV testing and counseling on subsequent sexual behavior. *AIDS Education and Prevention, 4*(1), 61–70.

Lang, P. J. (1985). The cognitive psychophysiology of emotion: Fear and anxiety. In A. H. Tuma & J. D. Maser (Eds.), *Anxiety and the anxiety disorders.* Hillsdale, NJ: Erlbaum.

Lang, P. J. (1995). The emotion probe: Studies of motivation and attention. *American Psychologist, 50,* 372–385.

Lang, P. J., Bradley, M. M., & Cuthbert, B. N. (1998). Emotion, motivation, and anxiety: Brain mechanisms and psychophysiology. *Biological Psychiatry, 44,* 1248–1263.

Langstrom, N., & Seto, M. (2006). Exhibitionistic and voyeuristic in a Swedish national population survey. *Archives of Sexual Behavior, 35,* 427–435.

Langstrom, N., & Zucker, K. (2005). Transvestic fetishism in the general population: Prevalence and correlates. *Journal of Sex & Marital Therapy, 31,* 87–95.

Lapierre, Y. D. (1994). Pharmacological therapy of dysthymia. *Acta Psychiatrica Scandinavica Supplemental, 89*(383), 42–48.

Laptook, R. S., Klein, D. N., & Dougherty, L. R. (2006). Ten-year stability of depressive personality disorder in depressed outpatients. *American Journal of Psychiatry, 163,* 865–871.

Lasch, C. (1978). *The culture of narcissism: American life in an age of diminishing expectations.* New York: W. W. Norton.

Latfi, R., Kellum, J. M., DeMaria, E. J., & Sugarman, H. J. (2002). Surgical treatment of obesity. In T. A. Wadden & A. J. Stunkard (Eds.), *Handbook of obesity treatment* (pp. 339–356). New York: Guilford Press.

Laub, J. H., & Vaillant, G. E. (2000). Delinquency and mortality: A 50-year follow-up study of 1,000 delinquent and nondelinquent boys. *American Journal of Psychiatry, 157,* 96–102.

Laumann, E., Gagnon, J., Michael, R., & Michaels, S. (1994). *The social organization of sexuality: Sexual practices in the United States.* Chicago: University of Chicago Press.

Laumann, E., Paik, A., Glasser, D., Kang, J., Wang, T., Levinson, B., et al. (2006). A cross-national study of subjective sexual well-being among older women and men: Findings from the global study of sexual attitudes and behaviors. *Archives of Sexual Behavior, 35,* 145–161.

Laumann, E., Paik, A., & Rosen, R. C. (1999). Sexual dysfunction in the United States. Prevalence and predictors. *JAMA, 281,* 537–544.

Lauriello, J., Bustillo, J. R., & Keith, S. J. (2005). Schizophrenia: Scope of the problem. In B. J. Sadock & V. A. Sadock (Eds.), *Kaplan & Sadock's comprehensive textbook of psychiatry* (pp. 1345–1354). Philadelphia: Lippincott, Williams & Wilkins.

Lawrence, A. (2005). Sexuality before and after male-to-female sex reassignment surgery. *Archives of Sexual Behavior, 34,* 147–166.

Laws, D. R. (Ed.) (1989). *Relapse prevention with sex offenders.* New York: Guilford Press.

Laws, D. R., & O'Donohue, W. (Eds.) (1997). *Sexual deviance: Theory, assessment and treatment.* New York: Guilford Press.

Lawson, W. B., Hepler, N., Holladay, J., & Cuffel, B. (1994). Race as a factor in inpatient and outpatient admissions and diagnosis. *Hospital and Community Psychiatry, 45,* 72–74.

Laxenaire, M., Ganne-Vevonec, M. O., & Streiff, O. (1982). Les problèmes d'identité chez les enfants des migrants. *Annales Medico-Psychologiques, 140,* 602–605.

Lazare, D. (1989, October 18–24). Drugs 'R' Us. *In These Times,* pp. 12–13.

Lazarus, R. A., & Folkman, S. (1984). *Stress, appraisal, and coping.* New York: Springer.

Lazarus, R. S. (1968). Emotions and adaptation: Conceptual and empirical relations. In W. J. Arnold (Ed.), *Nebraska Symposium on Motivation* (Vol. 16). Lincoln: University of Nebraska Press.

Lazarus, R. S. (1991). Progress on a cognitive-motivational relational theory of emotion. *American Psychologist, 46*(8), 819–834.

Lazarus, R. S. (1995). Psychological stress in the workplace. In R. Crandall, P. L. Perrewe (Eds.), *Occupational stress: A handbook* (pp. 3–14). Philadelphia: Taylor & Francis.

Le, A. D., Li, Z., Funk, D., Shram, M., Li, T. K., & Shaham, Y. (2006). Increased vulnerability to nicotine self-administration and relapse in alcohol-naive offspring of rats selectively bred for high alcohol intake. *Journal of Neuroscience, 26,* 1872–1879.

Lebedinskaya, K. S., & Nikolskaya, O. S. (1993). Brief report: Analysis of autism and its treatment in modern Russian defectology. *Journal of Autism and Developmental Disorders, 23,* 675–697.

Leccese, A. P. (1991). *Drugs and society: Behavioral medicines and abusable drugs.* Englewood Cliffs, NJ: Prentice Hall.

Lechner, S., Antoni, M. (2004). Posttraumatic growth and group based intervention for persons dealing with cancer: What have we learned so far? *Psychological Inquiry, 15,* 35–41.

Leckman, J. F., Grice, D. E., Boardman, J., Zhang, H., Vitali, A., Bondi, C., et al. (1997). Symptoms of obsessive-compulsive disorder. *American Journal of Psychiatry, 154,* 911–917.

Leckman, J. F., Weissman, M. M., Merikangas, K. R., Pauls, D. L., & Prusoff, B. A. (1983). Panic disorder and major depression. *Archives of General Psychiatry, 40,* 1055–1060.

Lecrubier, Y., Bakker, A., Dunbar, G., & the collaborative paroxetine panic study investigators. (1997). A comparison of paroxetine, clomipramine and placebo in the treatment of panic disorder. *Acta Psychiatrica Scandinavica, 95,* 145–152.

Lecrubier, Y., Judge, R., & and the collaborative paroxetine panic study investigators. (1997). Long term evaluation of paroxetine, clomipramine and placebo in panic disorder. *Acta Psychiatrica Scandinavica, 95,* 153–160.

LeDoux, J. E. (1996). *The emotional brain: The mysterious underpinnings of emotional life.* New York: Simon & Schuster.

LeDoux, J. E. (2002). *Synaptic self: How our brains become who we are.* New York: Penguin Books.

Lee, C. K. (1992). Alcoholism in Korea. In J. Helzer & G. Canino (Eds.), *Alcoholism—North America, Europe and Asia: A coordinated analysis of population data from ten regions* (pp. 247–262). London: Oxford University Press.

Lee, K. (1992). Pattern of night waking and crying of Korean infants from 3 months to 2 years old and its relation with various factors. *Journal of Developmental & Behavioral Pediatrics, 13,* 326–330.

Lee, M., Martin-Ruiz, C., Graham, A., Court, J., Jaros, E., Perry, R., et al. (2002). Nicotinic receptor abnormalities in the cerebellar cortex in autism. *Brain, 125,* 1483–1495.

Lee, S. (1993). How abnormal is the desire for slimness? A survey of eating attitudes and behavior among Chinese undergraduates in Hong Kong. *Psychological Medicines, 23,* 437–451.

Lee, S., Hsu, L. K. G., & Wing, Y. K. (1992). Bulimia nervosa in Hong Kong Chinese patients. *British Journal of Psychiatry, 161,* 545–551.

Lee, S., Leung, C. M., Wing, Y. K., Chiu, H. F., & Chen, C. N. (1991). Acne as a risk factor for anorexia nervosa in Chinese. *Australian and New Zealand Journal of Psychiatry, 25*(1), 134–137.

Lee, T. M., Chen, E. Y., Chan, C. C., Paterson, J. G., Janzen, H. L., & Blashko, C. A. (1998). Seasonal affective disorder. *Clinical Psychology: Science and Practice, 5,* 275–290.

Lefrancois, G. R. (1990). *The lifespan* (3rd ed.). Belmont, CA: Wadsworth.

Leibbrand, R., Hiller, W., & Fichter, M. M. (2000). Hypochondriasis and somatization: Two distinct aspects of somatoform disorders? *Journal of Clinical Psychology, 56,* 63–72.

Leiblum, S. R. (2000). Vaginismus: A most perplexing problem. In S. R. Leiblum & R. C. Rosen (Eds.), *Principles and practice of sex therapy* (3rd ed., pp. 181–202). New York: Guilford Press.

Leiblum, S. R., & Rosen, R. C. (Eds.) (2000). *Principles and practice of sex therapy* (3rd ed.). New York: Guilford Press.

Leitenberg, H., Detzer, M. J., & Srebnik, D. (1993). Gender differences in masturbation and the relation of masturbation experience in preadolescence and/or early adolescence to sexual behavior and sexual adjustment in young adulthood. *Archives of Sexual Behavior, 22*(2), 87–98.

Lejeune, J., Gauthier, M., & Turpin, R. (1959). Étude des chromosomes somatiques de neuf enfants mongoliens. *Comptes Rendus Hebdomadaires des Séances de l' Académie des Sciences. D: Sciences Naturelles (Paris), 248,* 1721–1722.

Lenze, E. J., Miller, A. R., Munir, Z. B., Pornoppadol, C., & North, C. S. (1999). Psychiatric symptoms endorsed by somatization disorder patients in a psychiatric clinic. *Annals of Clinical Psychiatry, 11*(2), 73–79.

Lenze, E. J., Mulsant, B. H., Shear, K. M., Schulberg, H. C., Dew, M. A., Begley, A. E., et al. (2000). Comorbid anxiety disorders in depressed elderly patients. *American Journal of Psychiatry, 157*(5), 722–728.

Lenzenweger, M. F., & Dworkin, R. H. (1996). The dimensions of schizophrenia phenomenology. Note one or two, at least three, perhaps four. *British Journal of Psychiatry, 168,* 432–440.

Lenzenweger, M. F., Lane, M. C., Loranger, A. W., & Kessler, R. C. (in press). DSV-IV personality disorders in the National Comorbidity Survey Replication. *Biological Psychiatry.*

Lenzenweger, M. F., McLachlan, G., & Rubin, D. B. (2007). Resolving the latent structure of schizophrenia endophenotypes using expectation-maximization-based finite mixture modeling. *Journal of Abnormal Psychology, 116,* 16–29.

Lerman, C., Caporaso, N. E., Audrain, J., Main, D., Bowman, E. D., Lockshin, B., et al. (1999). Evidence suggesting the role of specific genetic factors in cigarette smoking. *Health Psychology, 18*(1), 14–20.

Lesch, K.-P., Bengel, D., Heils, A., Sabol, S. Z., Greenberg, B. D., Petri, S., et al. (1996, November 29). Association of anxiety-related traits with a polymorphism in the serotonin transporter gene regulatory region. *Science, 274,* 1527–1531.

Leserman, J., Petitto, J. M., Golden, R. N., Gaynes, B. N., Gu, H., Perkins, D. O., et al. (2000). Impact of stressful life events, depression, social support, coping, and cortisol on progression to AIDS. *American Journal of Psychiatry, 157,* 1221–1228.

Lett, H., Blumenthal, J., Babyak, M., Strauman, T., Robins, C., & Sherwood, A. (2005). Social support and coronary heart disease: Epidemiologic evidence and implications for treatment. *Psychosomatic Medicine, 67,* 869–878.

Leuchter, A. F., Cook, I. A., Witte, E. A., Morgan, M., & Abrams, M. (2002). Changes in brain function of depressed subjects during treatment with placebo. *American Journal of Psychiatry, 159,* 122–129.

Leung, F., Lam, S., & Sze, S. (2001). Cultural expectations of thinness in Chinese women. *Eating Disorders: The Journal of Treatment and Prevention, 9,* 339–350.

LeVay, S. (1991). A difference in hypothalamic structure between heterosexual and homosexual men. *Science, 253,* 1034–1037.

Levenston, G. K., Patrick, C. J., Bradley, M. M., & Lang, P. J. (2000). The psychopath as observer: Emotion and attention in picture processing. *Journal of Abnormal Psychology, 109,* 373–385.

Leventhal, A. M., & Schmitz, J. M. (2006). The role of drug use outcome expectancies in substance abuse risk: An interactional–transformational model. *Addictive Behaviors, 31,* 2038–2062.

Levin, A., & Hyler, S. (1986). DSM-III personality diagnosis in bulimia. *Comprehensive Psychiatry, 27,* 47.

Levin, F. R., Evans, S. M., Brooks, D. J., & Garawi, F. (2007). Treatment of cocaine dependent treatment seekers with adult ADHD: Double-blind comparison of methylphenidate and placebo. *Drug and Alcohol Dependence, 87,* 20–29.

Levine, J. A., Lanningham-Foster, L. M., McCrady, S. K., Krizan, A. C., Olson, L. R., Kane, P. H., Jensen, M. D., & Clark, M. M. (2005). Interindividual variation in posture allocation: Possible role in human obesity. *Science, 307,* 584–586.

Levine, M. N., Guyatt, G. H., Gent, M., DePauw, S., Goodyear, M. D., Hryniuk, W. M., et al. (1988). Quality of life in stage II breast cancer: An instrument for clinical trials. *Journal of Clinical Oncology, 6,* 1798–1810.

Levine, M. P., & Smolak, L. (1996). Media as a context for the development of disordered eating. In L. Smolak, M. P. Levine, & R. Striegel-Moore (Eds.), *The developmental psychopathology of eating disorders: Implications for research, prevention, and treatment* (pp. 235–257). Mahwah, NJ: Erlbaum.

Levitt, A., & Boyle, M. (2002). The impact of latitude on the prevalence of seasonal depression. *Canadian Journal of Psychiatry, 46,* 650–654.

Levitt, A. J., Joffe, R. T., Moul, D. F., Lam, R. W., Teicher, M. H., Lebegue, B., et al. (1993). Side effects of light therapy in seasonal affective disorder. *American Journal of Psychiatry, 150,* 650–652.

Levy, B. R., Slade, M. D., Kunkel, S. R., & Kasl, S. V. (2002). Longevity increased by positive self-perceptions of aging. *Journal of Personality and Social Psychology, 83,* 261–270.

Lewinsohn, P. M., & Clarke, G. N. (1984). Group treatment of depressed individuals: The "coping with depression" course. *Advances in Behaviour Research and Therapy, 6*(2), 99–114.

Lewinsohn, P. M., & Gotlib, I. H. (1995). Behavioral therapy and treatment of depression. In E. E. Beckham & W. R. Leber (Eds.), *Handbook of depression* (pp. 352–375). New York: Guilford Press.

Lewinsohn, P. M., & Rosenbaum, M. (1987). Recall of parental behavior by acute depressives, remitted depressives and nondepressives. *Journal of Personality and Social Psychology, 52*(3), 611–619.

Lewinsohn, P. M., Allen, N. B., Seeley, J. R., & Gotlib, I. H. (1999). First onset versus recurrence of depression: Differential processes of psychosocial risk. *Journal of Abnormal Psychology, 108*(3), 483–489.

Lewinsohn, P. M., Gotlib, I. H., & Seeley, J. R. (1997). Depression-related psychosocial variables: Are they specific to depression in adolescents? *Journal of Abnormal Psychology, 106*(3), 365–375.

Lewinsohn, P. M., Hops, H., Roberts, R. E., Seeley, J. R., & Andrews, J. A. (1993). Adolescent psychopathology: I. Prevalence and incidence of depression and other DSM-III-R disorders in high school students. *Journal of Abnormal Psychology, 102*(1), 133–144.

Lewinsohn, P. M., Rohde, P., & Seeley, J. R. (1993). Psychosocial characteristics of adolescents with a history of suicide attempt. *Journal of the American Academy of Child and Adolescent Psychiatry, 32*(1), 60–68.

Lewinsohn, P. M., Rohde, P., Seeley, J. R., & Fischer, S. A. (1993). Age-cohort changes in the lifetime occurrence of depression and other mental disorders. *Journal of Abnormal Psychology, 102*(1), 110–120.

Lewinsohn, P. M., Rohde, P., Seeley, J. R., Klein, D. N., & Gotlib, I. H. (2000). Natural course of adolescent major depressive disorder on community sample: Predictors of recurrence in young adults. *American Journal of Psychiatry, 157*(10), 1584–1591.

Lewis, D. O., Yeager, C. A., Swica, Y., Pincus, J. H., & Lewis, M. (1997). Objective documentation of child abuse and dissociation in 12 murderers with dissociative identity disorder. *American Journal of Psychiatry, 154,* 1703–1710.

Lewis, G., Croft-Jeffreys, C., & Anthony, D. (1990). Are British psychiatrists racist? *British Journal of Psychiatry, 157,* 410–415.

Lewis, G., David, A., Andreasson, S., & Allsbeck, P. (1992). Schizophrenia and city life. *Lancet, 340,* 137–140.

Lewy, A. J., & Sack, R. L. (1987). Light therapy of chronobiological disorders. In A. Halaris (Ed.), *Chronobiology and psychiatric disorders* (pp. 181–206). New York: Elsevier.

Lewy, A. J., Bauer, V. K., Cutler, N. L., Ahmed, S., Thomas, K. H., Blood, M. L., & Letham Jackson, J. M. (1998). Morning vs. evening light treatment of patients with winter depression. *Archives of General Psychiatry, 55,* 890–896.

Lewy, A. J., Kern, H. E., Rosenthal, N. E., & Wehr, T. A. (1982). Bright artificial light treatment of a manic-depressive patient with a seasonal mood cycle. *American Journal of Psychiatry, 139,* 1496–1498.

Lichtenthal, W., Cruess, D., & Prigerson, H. (2004). A case for establishing complicated grief as a distinct mental disorder in DSM-V. *Clinical Psychology Review, 24,* 637–662.

Liddell, H. S. (1949). The role of vigilance in the development of animal neurosis. In P. Hoch & J. Zubin (Eds.), *Anxiety.* New York: Grune & Stratton.

Lidz, C. W., Mulvey, E. P., Appelbaum, P. S., & Cleveland, S. (1989). Commitment: The consistency of clinicians and the use of legal standards. *American Journal of Psychiatry, 146,* 176–186.

Lieb, R., Wittchen, H-U., Hofler, M., Fuetsch, M., Stein, M. B., & Merikangas, K. R. (2000). Parental psychopathology, parenting styles, and the risk of social phobia in offspring. *Archives of General Psychiatry, 57,* 859–866.

Lieb, R., Zimmermann, P., Friis, R. H., Hofler, M., Tholen, S., & Wittchen, H. U. (2002). The natural course of DSM-IV somatoform disorders and syndromes among adolescents and young adults: A prospective-longitudinal community study. *European Psychiatry, 17,* 321–331.

Lieberman, J. A., Jody, D., Alvir, J. M. J., Ashtari, M., Levy, D. L., Bogerts, B., et al. (1993). Brain morphology, dopamine, and eye-tracking abnormalities in first-episode schizophrenia. *Archives of General Psychiatry, 50,* 357–368.

Lieberman, J. A., Perkins, D., Belger, A., Chakos, M., Jarskog, F., Boteva, K., & Gilmore, J. (2001). The early stages of schizophrenia: Speculations on pathogenesis, pathophysiology, and therapeutic approaches. *Biological Psychiatry, 50,* 884–897.

Lieberman, J. A., Stroup, T. S., McEvoy, J. P., Swartz, M. S., Rosenheck, R. A., Perkins, D. O., et al.; Clinical Antipsychotic Trials of Intervention Effectiveness (CATIE) Investigators. (2005). Effectiveness of antipsychotic drugs in patients with chronic schizophrenia. *New England Journal of Medicine, 353,* 1209–1223.

Liebeskind, J. (1991). Pain can kill. *Pain, 44,* 3–4.

Liebowitz, M. R., Heimberg, R. G., Schneier, F. R., Hope, D. A., Davies, S., Holt, C. S., et al. (1999). Cognitive-behavioral group therapy versus phenelzine in social phobia: Long-term outcome. *Depression and Anxiety, 10,* 89–98.

Liebowitz, M. R., Salman, E., Jusino, C. M., Garfinkel, R., Street, L., Cardenas, D. L., et al. (1994). Ataque de nervios and panic disorder. *American Journal of Psychiatry, 151,* 871–875.

Liebowitz, M. R., Schneier, F., Campeas, R., Hollander, E., Hatterer, J., Fyer, A., et al. (1992). Phenelzine vs. atenolol in social phobia: A placebo controlled comparison. *Archives of General Psychiatry, 49,* 290–300.

Liggett, J. (1974). *The human face.* New York: Stein and Day.

Lilenfeld, L. R. R., Wonderlich, S., Riso, L. P., Crosby, R., & Mitchell, J. (2006). Eating disorders and personality: A methodological and empirical review. *Clinical Psychology Review, 26,* 299–320.

Lilienfeld, S. O. (1992). The association between antisocial personality and somatization disorders: A review and integration of theoretical models. *Clinical Psychology Review, 12,* 641–662.

Lilienfeld, S. O., & Hess, T. H. (2001). Psychopathic personality traits and somatization: Sex differences and the mediating role of negative emotionality.

Journal of Psychopathology and Behavioral Assessment, 23, 11–24.

Lilienfeld, S. O., Kirsch, I., Sarbin, T. R., Lynn, S. J., Chaves, J. F., & Ganaway, G. K. (1999). Dissociative identity disorder and the sociocognitive model: Recalling the lessons of the past. *Psychological Bulletin, 125*(5), 507–523.

Lilienfeld, S. O., VanValkenburg, C., Larntz, K., & Akiskal, H. S. (1986). The relationship of histrionic personality to antisocial personality and somatization disorders. *American Journal of Psychiatry, 143,* 718–722.

Lilienfeld, S. O., & Marino, L. (1999). Essentialism revisited: Evolutionary theory and the concept of mental disorder. *Journal of Abnormal Psychology, 108,* 400–411.

Lin, N., & Ensel, W. M. (1984). Depression-mobility and its social etiology: The role of life events and social support. *Journal of Health and Social Behavior, 25*(2), 176–188.

Lincoln, M., Packman, A., & Onslow, M. (2006). Altered auditory feedback and the treatment of stuttering: A review. *Journal of Fluency Disorders, 31,* 71–89.

Linden, W., & Moseley, J. (2006). The efficacy of behavioral treatments for hypertension. *Applied Psychophysiology and Biofeedback, 31,* 51–63.

Lindenmayer, J. P., & Khan, A. (2006). Psychopathology. In J. A. Lieberman, T. S. Stroup, & D. O. Perkins (Eds.), *The American Psychiatric Publishing textbook of schizophrenia* (pp. 187–221). Washington, DC: American Psychiatric Publishing.

Lindesay, J. (1991). Phobic disorders in the elderly. *British Journal of Psychiatry, 159,* 531–541.

Lindsey, K. P., & Paul, G. L. (1989). Involuntary commitments to public mental institutions: Issues involving the overrepresentation of blacks and assessment of relevant functioning. *Psychological Bulletin, 106,* 171–183.

Linehan, M. M. (1987). Dialectical behavior therapy for borderline personality disorder: Theory and method. *Bulletin of the Menninger Clinic, 51,* 261–276.

Linehan, M. M. (1993). *Cognitive behavioral treatment of borderline personality disorder.* New York: Guilford Press.

Linehan, M. M., & Kehrer, C. A. (1993). Borderline personality disorder. In D. H. Barlow (Ed.), *Clinical handbook of psychological disorders: A step by step treatment manual.* New York: Guilford Press.

Linehan, M. M., Armstrong, H. E., Suarez, A., Allmon, D., & Heard, H. L. (1991). Cognitive-behavioral treatment of chronically parasuicidal borderline patients. *Archives of General Psychiatry, 48,* 1060–1064.

Linehan, M. M., Heard, H. L., & Armstrong, H. E. (1992). *Naturalistic follow-up of a behavioral treatment for chronically parasuicidal borderline patients.* Unpublished manuscript, University of Washington, Seattle.

Links, P., Steiner, M., & Huxley, G. (1988). The occurrence of borderline personality disorder in families of borderline patients. *Journal of Personality Disorders, 2,* 14–20.

Liotti, M., Mayberg, H. S., McGinnis, S., Brannan, S. L., & Jerabek, P. (2002). Unmasking disease-specific cerebral blood flow abnormalities: Mood challenge in patients with remitted unipolar depression. *American Journal of Psychiatry, 159,* 1807–1808.

Lipchik, G. L., Holroyd, K. A., & Nash, J. M. (2002). Cognitive-behavioral management of recurrent headache disorders: A minimal-therapist-contact approach. In D. C. Turk & R. J. Gatchel (Eds.), *Psychological approaches to pain management: A practitioner's handbook* (2nd ed.). New York: Guilford Press.

Lipton, A. M., & Weiner, M. F. (2003). Differential diagnosis. In M. F. Weiner & A. M. Lipton (Eds.), *The dementias: Diagnosis, treatment and research* (3rd ed., pp. 137–180). Washington, DC: American Psychiatric Publishing.

Lisspers, J., & Öst, L. (1990). Long-term followup of migraine treatment: Do the effects remain up to six years? *Behaviour Research and Therapy, 28,* 313–322.

Litz, B. T., Gray, M. J., Bryant, R. A., & Adler, A. B. (2002). Early intervention for trauma: Current status and future directions. *Clinical Psychology: Science & Practice, 9,* 112–134.

Livesley, W. J., Jang, K. L., & Vernon, P. A. (1998). Phenotypic and genotypic structure of traits delineating personality disorder. *Archives of General Psychiatry, 55,* 941–948.

Livingston, G., Johnston, K., Katona, C., Paton, J., Lyketsos, C. G., & Old Age Task Force of the World Federation of Societies of Biological Psychiatry (2005). Systematic review of psychological approaches to the management of neuropsychiatric symptoms of dementia. *American Journal of Psychiatry, 162,* 1996–2021.

Lloyd, E. A. (2005). The case of the female orgasm: Bias in the science of evolution. Cambridge, MA: Harvard University Press.

Loeb, K. L., Wilson, G. T., Gilbert, J. S., & Labouvie, E. (2000). Guided and unguided self-help for binge eating. *Behaviour Research and Therapy, 38*(3), 259–272.

Loehlin, J., McFadden, D., Medland, S., & Martin, N. (2006). Population differences in finger-length ratios: Ethnicity or latitude? *Archives of Sexual Behavior, 35,* 739–742.

Loehlin, J. C. (1992). *Genes and environment in personality development.* Newbury Park, CA: Sage.

Loewenstein, R. J. (1991). An office mental status examination for complex chronic dissociative symptoms and multiple personality disorder. *The Psychiatric Clinics of North America, 14,* 567–604.

Loftus, E., & Davis, D. (2006). Recovered memories. *Annual Review of Clinical Psychology, 2,* 469–498.

Loftus, E. F. (2003). Make-believe memories. *American Psychologist, 58,* 867–873.

Loftus, E. F., Coan, J. A., & Pickrell, J. E. (1996). Manufacturing false memories using bits of reality. In L. Reder (Ed.), *Implicit memory and metacognition* (pp. 195–220). Mahwah, NJ: Erlbaum.

Lonczak, H. S., Abbott, R., Hawkins, J. D., Kosterman, R., & Catalano, R. F. (2002). Effects of the Seattle Social Development Project on sexual behavior, pregnancy, birth, and sexually transmitted disease outcomes by age 21 years. *Archives of Pediatric & Adolescent Medicine, 156,* 438–447.

Lopez, S. R., & Guarnaccia, P. J. (2000). Cultural psychopathology: Uncovering the social world of mental illness. *Annual Review of Psychology, 51,* Page 571–598.

LoPiccolo, J., Heiman, J. R., Hogan, D. R., & Roberts, C. W. (1985). Effectiveness of single therapists versus cotherapy teams in sex therapy. *Journal of Consulting and Clinical Psychology, 53*(3), 287–294.

Lord, C., Wagner, A., Rogers, S., Szatmari, P., Aman, M., Charman, T., et al. (2005). Challenges in evaluating psychosocial interventions for autistic spectrum disorders. *Journal of Autism and Developmental Disorders, 35,* 695–708.

Lovaas, O. I. (1977). *The autistic child: Language development through behavior modification.* New York: Irvington.

Lovaas, O. I. (1987). Behavioral treatment and normal educational and intellectual functioning in young autistic children. *Journal of Consulting and Clinical Psychology, 55,* 3–9.

Lovaas, O. I., Berberich, J. P., Perloff, B. F., & Schaeffer, B. (1966). Acquisition of imitative speech by schizophrenic children. *Science, 151,* 705–707.

Lovibond, P. (2006). Fear and avoidance: An integrated expectancy model. In M. G. Craske, D. Hermans, & D. Vansteenwegen, *Fear and learning: From basic processes to clinical implications* (pp. 117–132). Washington, DC: American Psychological Association.

Lowe, M. R., Miller-Kovach, K., Frie, N., & Phelan, S. P. (1999). An initial evaluation of a commercial weight loss program: Short-term effects on weight, eating behavior, and mood. *Obesity Research, 7,* 51–59.

Lubinski, D. (2004). Introduction to the special section of cognitive abilities: 100 years after Spearman's (1904) General intelligence, objectively determined and measured. *Journal of Personality and Social Psychology, 86,* 96–111.

Luby, J. L., Mrakotsky, C., Heffelfinger, A., Brown, K., Hessler, M., & Spitznagel, E. (2003). Modification of DSM-IV criteria for depressed preschool children. *American Journal of Psychiatry, 160,* 1169–1172.

Lucas, A. R., Beard, C. M., O'Fallon, W. M., & Kurlan, L. T. (1991). 50-year trends in the incidence of anorexia nervosa in Rochester, Minn.: A population-based study. *American Journal of Psychiatry, 148,* 917–922.

Luckasson, R., Coulter, D. L., Polloway, E. A., Reiss, S., Schalock, R. L., Snell, M. E., et al. (1992). *Mental retardation: Definition, classification, and systems of supports* (9th ed.). Washington, DC: American Association on Mental Retardation.

Ludwig, A. M. (1985). Cognitive processes associated with "spontaneous" recovery from alcoholism. *Journal of Studies on Alcohol, 46,* 53–58.

Ludwig, A. M. (1995). *The price of greatness: Resolving the creativity and madness controversy.* New York: Guilford Publications.

Ludwig, A., Brandsma, J., Wilbur, C., Bendfeldt, F., & Jameson, D. (1972). The objective study of a multiple personality. *Archives of General Psychiatry, 26,* 298–310.

Lundgren, J. D., Allison, K. C., Crow, S., O'Reardon, J. P., Berg, K. C., Galbraith, J., et al. (2006). Prevalence of the night eating syndrome in psychiatric population. *American Journal of Psychiatry, 163,* 156–158.

Lundh, L.-G., & Öst, L.-G. (1996). Recognition bias for critical faces in social phobics. *BRAT, 34,* 787–794.

Lundstrom, B., Pauly, I., & Walinder, J. (1984). Outcome of sex reassignment surgery. *Acta Psychiatrica Scandinavica, 70,* 289–294.

Lutgendorf, S., Costanzo, E., & Siegel, S. (2007). Psychosocial influences in oncology: An expanded model of biobehavioral mechanisms. In R. Ader, R. Glaser, N. Cohen, & M. Irwin (Eds.), *Psychoneuroimmunology* (4th ed., pp. 869–895). New York: Academic Press.

Lutgendorf, S. K., Antoni, M. H., Ironson, G., Klimas, N., Kumar, M., Starr, K., et al. (1997). Cognitive-behavioral stress management decreases dysphoric mood and herpes simplex virus-type 2 antibody titers in symptomatic HIV-seropositive gay men. *Journal of Consulting and Clinical Psychology, 65,* 31–43.

Lydiard, R. B., Brawman-Mintzer, O., & Ballenger, J. C. (1996). Recent developments in the psychopharmacology of anxiety disorders. *Journal of Consulting & Clinical Psychology, 64,* 660–668.

Lyketsos, C. G., & Olin, J. (2002). Depression in Alzheimer's disease: Overview and treatment. *Biological Psychiatry, 52,* 243–252.

Lykken, D. T. (1957). A study of anxiety in the sociopathic personality. *Journal of Abnormal and Social Psychology, 55,* 6–10.

Lykken, D. T. (1982). Fearfulness: Its carefree charms and deadly risks. *Psychology Today, 16,* 20–28.

Lykken, D. T. (2006). Psychopathic personality: The scope of the problem. In C. J. Patrick (Ed.), *Handbook of psychopathy* (pp. 3–13). New York: Guilford Press.

Lynam, D. R. (1996). Early identification of chronic offenders: Who is a fledgling psychopath? *Psychological Bulletin, 120,* 209–234.

Lynch, F., Hornbrook, M., Clarke, G., Perrin, N., Polen, M., O'Connor, E., & Dickerson, J. (2005). Cost-effectiveness of an intervention to prevent depression in at-risk teens. *Archives General Psychiatry, 62,* 1241–1248.

Lynch, S. K., Turkheimer, E., D'Onofrio, B. M., Mendle, J., Emery, R. E., Slutske, W. S., & Martin, N. G. (2006). A genetically informed study of the association between harsh punishment and offspring behavioral problems. *Journal of Family Psychology, 20,* 190–198.

Lynch, T. R., Rosenthal, M. Z., Kosson, D. S., Cheavens, J. S., Lejuez, C. W., & Blair, R. J. R. (2006). Heightened sensitivity to facial expressions of emotion in borderline personality disorder. *Emotion, 6,* 647–655.

Lynskey, M., & Hall, W. (2000). The effects of adolescent cannabis use on educational attainment: A review. *Addiction, 95,* 1621–1630.

Lyons, M. J., Eisen, S. A., Goldberg, J., True, W., Lin, N., Meyer, J. M., et al. (1998). A registry-based twin study of depression in men. *Archives of General Psychiatry, 55,* 468–472.

Lyons, M. J., True, W. R., Eisen, S. A., Goldberg, J., Meyer, J. M., Faraone, S. V., et al. (1995). Differential heritability of adult and juvenile antisocial traits. *Archives of General Psychiatry, 52,* 906–915.

Lyubomirsky, S. (2001). Why are some people happier than others? The role of cognitive and motivational processes in well-being. *American Psychologist, 56,* 239–249.

Macdonald, P. T., Waldorf, D., Reinarman, C., & Murphy, S. (1988). Heavy cocaine use and sexual behavior. *Journal of Drug Issues, 18,* 437–455.

MacDonald, R., Anderson, J., Dube, W. V., Geckeler, A., Green, G., Holcomb, W., et al. (2006). Behavioral assessment of joint attention: A methodological report. *Research in Developmental Disabilities, 27,* 138–150.

MacDougall, J. M., Dembroski, T. M., Dimsdale, J. E., & Hackett, T. P. (1985). Components of Type A, hostility, and anger-in: Further relationships to angiographic findings. *Health Psychology, 4*(2), 137–152.

Mace, C. J. (1992). Hysterical conversion II: A critique. *British Journal of Psychiatry, 161,* 378–389.

Maciejewski, P., Zhang, B., Block, S., & Prigerson, H. (2007). An empirical examination of the stage theory of grief. *JAMA, 297,* 716–723.

Mack, A. H., Franklin, J. E., & Frances, R. J. (2003). Substance use disorders. In R. E. Hales & S. C. Yudofsky (Eds.), *Textbook of clinical psychiatry* (4th ed., pp. 309–377). Washington, DC: American Psychiatric Publishing.

MacKinnon, D. F., Zandi, P. P., Gershon, E. S., Nurnberger, J. I., & DePaulo, J. R. (2003). Association of rapid mood switching with panic disorder and familial panic risk in familial bipolar disorder. *American Journal of Psychiatry, 160,* 1696–1698.

MacLeod, C., & Mathews, A. M. (1991). Cognitive-experimental approaches to the emotional disorders. In P. R. Martin (Ed.), *Handbook of behavior therapy and psychological science: An integrative approach* (pp. 116–150). Elmsford, NY: Pergamon Press.

MacLeod, C., Mathews, A., & Tata, P. (1986). Attentional bias in emotional disorders. *Journal of Abnormal Psychology, 95,* 15–20.

Macleod, J., Oakes, R., Copello, A., Crome, I., Egger, M., Hickman, M., et al. (2004). Psychological and social sequelae of cannabis and other illicit drug use by young people: A systematic review of longitudinal, general population studies. *Lancet, 363,* 1579–1588.

Madsen, K. M., Hviid, A., Vestergaard, M., Schendel, D., Wohlfahrt, J., Thorsen, P., et al. (2002). A population-based study of measles, mumps, and rubella vaccination and autism. *New England Journal of Medicine, 347,* 1477–1482.

Magee, W. J., Eaton, W. W., Wittchen, H.-U., McGonagle, K. A., & Kessler, R. C. (1996). Agoraphobia, simple phobia, and social phobia in the National Comorbidity Survey. *Archives of General Psychiatry, 53,* 159–168.

Magne-Ingvar, U., Ojehagen, A., & Traskman-Bendz, L. (1992). The social network of people who attempt suicide. *Acta Psychiatrica Scandinavica, 86,* 153–158.

Maher, B. A., & Maher, W. B. (1985a). Psychopathology: I. From ancient times to the eighteenth century. In G. A. Kimble & K. Schlesinger (Eds.), *Topics in the history of psychology* (pp. 251–294). Hillsdale, NJ: Erlbaum.

Maher, B. A., & Maher, W. B. (1985b). Psychopathology: II. From the eighteenth century to modern times. In G. A. Kimble & K. Schlesinger (Eds.), *Topics in the history of psychology* (pp. 295–329). Hillsdale, NJ: Erlbaum.

Maher, J. J. (1997). Exploring alcohol's effects on liver function. *Alcohol Health & Research World, 21,* 5–12.

Mahler, M. (1952). On childhood psychosis and schizophrenia: Autistic and symbiotic infantile psychosis. *Psychoanalytic Study of the Child, 7,* 286–305.

Mahoney, D. F., Purtilo, R. B., Webbe, F. M., Alwan, M., Bharucha, A. J., Adlam, T. D., et al. (2007). In-home monitoring of persons with dementia: Ethical guidelines for technology research and development. *Alzheimer's & Dementia, 3,* 217–226.

Mai, F. (2004). Somatization disorder: A practical review. *Canadian Journal of Psychiatry, 49,* 652–662.

Maier, S. F. (1997, September). *Stressor controllability, anxiety, and serotonin.* Paper presented at the National Institute of Mental Health Workshop on Cognition and Anxiety, Rockville, MD.

Maj, M., Pirozzi, R., Magliano, L., & Bartoli, L. (2002). The prognostic significance of "switching" in patients with bipolar disorder: A 10-year prospective follow-up study. *American Journal of Psychiatry, 159,* 1711–1717.

Maj, M., Pirozzi, R., Magliano, L., & Bartoli, L. (2003). Agitated depression in bipolar I disorder: Prevalence, phenomenology, and outcome. *American Journal of Psychiatry, 160,* 2134–2140.

Majerovitz, S. D. (2007). Predictors of burden and depression among nursing home family caregivers. *Aging & Mental Health, 11,* 323–329.

Malatesta, V. J., & Adams, H. E. (1984). The sexual dysfunctions. In H. E. Adams & P. B. Sutker (Eds.), *Comprehensive handbook of psychopathology* (pp. 725–775). New York: Plenum Press.

Malatesta, V. J., & Adams, H. E. (2001). Sexual dysfunctions. In H. E. Adams & P. B. Sutker (Eds.), *Comprehensive handbook of psychopathology* (3rd ed.). New York: Kluwer Academic/Plenum.

Maldonado, J. R., Butler, L. D., & Spiegel, D. (1998). Treatments for dissociative disorders. In P. E. Nathan & J. M. Gorman (Eds.), *A guide to treatments that work.* New York: Oxford University Press.

Maletzky, B. (2002). The paraphilias: Research and treatment. In P. E. Nathan & J. M. Gorman (Eds.), *A guide to treatments that work* (2nd ed., pp. 525–557). New York: Oxford University Press.

Maletzky, B. M. (1991). *Treating the sexual offender.* Newbury Park, CA: Sage.

Maletzky, B. M. (1998). The paraphilias: Research and treatment. In P. E. Nathan & J. M. Gorman (Eds.), *A guide to treatments that work* (pp. 472–500). New York: Oxford University Press.

Mandalos, G. E., & Szarek, B. L. (1990). Dose-related paranoid reaction associated with fluoxetine. *Journal of Nervous and Mental Disease, 178*(1), 57–58.

Mandell, A. J., & Knapp, S. (1979). Asymmetry and mood, emergent properties of serotonin regulation: A proposed mechanism of action of lithium. *Archives of General Psychiatry, 36*(8), 909–916.

Mann, J., Bertolote, J., Beautrais, A., Currier, D., et al. (2005). Suicide prevention strategies: A systematic review. *JAMA, 294,* 2064–2074.

Mann, J., Nortinger, J., Oquendo, M., Currier, D., Li, S., & Brent, D. (2005). Family history of suicidal behavior and mood disorders in probands with mood disorders. *American Journal of Psychiatry, 162,* 1672–1679.

Mann, J. J., Malone, K. M., Diehl, D. J., Perel, J., Cooper, T. B., & Mintun, M. A. (1996). Demonstration in vivo of reduced serotonin responsivity in the brain of untreated depressed patients. *American Journal of Psychiatry, 153,* 174–182.

Mann, J. J., Waternaux, C., Haas, G. L., & Malone, K. M. (1999). Toward a clinical model of suicidal behavior in psychiatric patients. *American Journal of Psychiatry, 156*(2), 181–189.

Mann, K., Klingler, T., Noe, S., Röschke, J., Müller, S., & Benkert, O. (1996). Effects of yohimbine on sexual experiences and nocturnal penile tumescence and rigidity in erectile dysfunction. *Archives of Sexual Behavior, 25,* 1–16.

Manni, R., Ratti, M. T., & Tartara, A. (1997). Nocturnal eating: Prevalence and features in 120 insomniac referrals. *Sleep, 20,* 734–738.

Mannino, D. M., Klevens, R. M., & Flanders, W. D. (1994). Cigarette smoking: An independent risk factor for impotence? *American Journal of Epidemiology, 140,* 1003–1008.

Manson, J. E., Willett, W. C., Stampfer, M. J., Colditz, G. A., Hunter, D. J., Hankinson, S. E., et al. (1995). Body weight and mortality among women. *New England Journal of Medicine, 333,* 677–685.

Manson, S. M., & Good, B. J. (1993, January). *Cultural considerations in the diagnosis of DSM-IV mood disorders.* Cultural proposals and supporting papers for DSM-IV. Submitted to the DSM-IV Task Force by the Steering Committee, NIMH-Sponsored Group on Culture and Diagnosis.

Marangell, L., Rush, A., George, M., Sackheim, H., Johnson, C, Husain, M., et al. (2002). Vagus nerve stimulation (VNS) for major depressive episodes: One year outcomes. *Biological Psychiatry, 51,* 280–287.

Marcopulos, B. A., & Graves, R. E. (1990). Antidepressant effect on memory in depressed older persons. *Journal of Clinical and Experimental Neuropsychology, 12*(5), 655–663.

Marcus, M. D., Wing, R. R., & Hopkins, J. (1988). Obese binge eaters: Affect, cognitions, and response to behavioral weight control. *Journal of Consulting and Clinical Psychology, 3,* 433–439.

Marcus, M. D., Wing, R. R., Ewing, L., Keern, E., Gooding, W., & McDermott, M. (1990). Psychiatric disorders among obese binge eaters. *International Journal of Eating Disorders, 9,* 69–77.

Marks, I. M. (1969). *Fears and phobias.* New York: Academic.

Marks, I. M. (1985). Behavioural treatment of social phobia. *Psychopharmacology Bulletin, 21,* 615–618.

Marks, I. M. (1988). Blood–injury phobia: A review. *American Journal of Psychiatry, 145,* 1207–1213.

Marlatt, G. A. (1985). Relapse prevention: Theoretical rationale and overview of the model. In G. A. Marlatt & J. R. Gordon (Eds.), *Relapse prevention: Maintenance strategies in the treatment of addictive behaviors* (pp. 3–70). New York: Guilford Press.

Marlatt, G. A., & Gordon, J. R. (1985). *Relapse prevention: Maintenance strategies in the treatment of addictive behaviors.* New York: Guilford Press.

Marlatt, G. A., Larimer, M. E., Baer, J. S., & Quigley, L. A. (1993). Harm reduction for alcohol problems: Moving beyond the controlled drinking controversy. *Behavior Therapy, 24,* 461–504.

Marmot, M. G., & Syme, S. L. (1976). Acculturation and coronary heart disease in Japanese Americans. *American Journal of Epidemiology, 104,* 225–247.

Marsden, C. D. (1986). Hysteria—A neurologist's view. *Psychological Medicine, 16,* 277–288.

Marshall, W. L. (1997). Pedophilia: Psychopathology and theory. In D. R. Laws & W. O'Donohue (Eds.), *Sexual deviance: Theory, assessment and treatment* (pp. 152–174). New York: Guilford Press.

Marshall, W. L., Barbaree, H. E., & Christophe, D. (1986). Sexual offenders against female children: Sexual preferences for age of victims and type of behavior. *Canadian Journal of Behavioral Science, 18,* 424–439.

Marten, P. A., Brown, T. A., Barlow, D. H., Borkovec, T. D., Shear, M. K., & Lydiard, M. B. (1993). Evaluation of the ratings comprising the associated symptom criterion of DSM-III-R generalized anxiety disorder. *Journal of Nervous and Mental Disease, 181,* 676–682.

Martin, I. (1983). Human classical conditioning. In A. Gale & J. A. Edward (Eds.), *Physiological correlates of human behavior: Vol. 2. Attention and performance.* London: Academic Press.

Martin, S. D., Martin, E., Rai, S. S., Richardson, M. A., & Royall, R. (2001). Brain blood flow changes in depressed patients treated with interpersonal psychotherapy or venlafaxine hydrochloride. *Archives of General Psychiatry, 58,* 641–648.

Martin, S. L., Ramey, C. T., & Ramey, S. L. (1990). The prevention of intellectual impairment in children of impoverished families: Findings of a randomized trial of educational daycare. *American Journal of Public Health, 80,* 844–847.

Martin-Cook, K., Svetlik, D., & Weiner, M. F. (2003). Supporting family caregivers. In M. F. Weiner & A. M. Lipton (Eds.), *The dementias: Diagnosis, treatment and research* (3rd ed., pp. 321–340). Washington, DC: American Psychiatric Publishing.

Maser, J. D. (1985). List of phobias. In A. H. Tuma & J. D. Maser (Eds.), *Anxiety and the anxiety disorders.* Hillsdale, NJ: Erlbaum.

Maser, J. D., Kaelber, C., & Weise, R. E. (1991). International use and attitudes toward DSM-III and DSM-III-R: Growing consensus in psychiatric classification. *Journal of Abnormal Psychology, 100*(3), 271–279.

Mason, F. L. (1997). Fetishism: Psychopathology and theory. In D. R. Laws & W. O'Donohue (Eds.), *Sexual deviance: Theory, assessment and treatment* (pp. 75–91). New York: Guilford Press.

Massie, H. N., Miranda, G., Snowdon, D. A., Greiner, L. H., Wekstein, D. R., Danner, D., et al. (1996). Linguistic ability in early life and Alzheimer disease in late life. *JAMA, 275,* 1879.

Masters, W. H., & Johnson, V. E. (1966). *Human sexual response.* Boston: Little, Brown.

Masters, W. H., & Johnson, V. E. (1970). *Human sexual inadequacy.* Boston: Little, Brown.

Mathews, A. (1997). Information processing biases in emotional disorders. In D. M. Clark & C. G. Fairburn (Eds.), *Science and practice of cognitive-behavior therapy* (pp. 47–66). Oxford: Oxford University Press.

Mathews, A., & MacLeod, C. (1994). Cognitive approaches to emotion and emotional disorders. *Annual Review of Psychology, 45,* 25–50.

Mathews, A., Mogg, K., Kentish, J., & Eysenck, M. (1995). Effective psychological treatment on cognitive bias and generalized anxiety disorder. *Behavior Research and Therapy, 33,* 293–303.

Matsumoto, D. (1996). *Culture and psychology.* Pacific Grove, CA: Brooks/Cole.

Matthews, K. (2005). Psychological perspectives on the development of coronary heart disease. *American Psychological Association, 60,* 780–796.

Matthews, K. A. (1988). Coronary heart disease and Type A behaviors: Update on and alternative to the Booth-Kewley and Friedman (1987) quantitative review. *Psychological Bulletin, 104*(3), 373–380.

Mattis, S. G., & Ollendick, T. H. (2002). Nonclinical panic attacks in late adolescence prevalence and associated psychopathology. *Journal of Anxiety Disorders, 16,* 351–367.

Matza, L. S., Revicki, D. A., Davidson, J. R., & Stewart, J. W. (2003). Depression with atypical features in the National Comorbidity Survey: Classification, description, and consequences. *Archives of General Psychiatry, 60,* 817–826.

Mauler, B. I., Hamm, A. O., Weike, A. I., & Tuschen-Caffier, B. (2006). Affect regulation and food intake in bulimia nervosa: Emotional responding to food cues after deprivation and subsequent eating. *Journal of Abnormal Psychology, 115,* 567–579.

Max, M. (2003). How to move pain research from the margin to the mainstream. *Journal of Pain, 4*(7), 2003.

May, P. A., & Hymbaugh, K. J. (1983). A pilot project of fetal alcohol syndrome among American Indians. *Alcohol Health and Research World, 7,* 3–9.

Mayberg, H., Lozano, A., Voon, V., McNeely, H., Seminowicz, D., Hanani, C., et al. (2005). Deep brain stimulation for treatment resistant depression. *Neuron, 45,* 651–660.

Mayou, R., Phil, M., Kirmayer, L., Simon, G., Kroenke, G., & Sharpe, M. (2005). Somatoform disorders: Time for a new approach in DSM-V. *American Journal of Psychiatry, 162,* 847–855.

Mays, V. M., & Cochran, S. D. (1988). Issues in the perception of AIDS risk and risk reduction activities by black and Hispanic/Latino women. *American Psychologist, 43*(11), 949–957.

Mayville, S., Katz, R. C., Gipson, M. T., & Cabral, K. (1999). Assessing the prevalence of body dysmorphic disorder in an ethnically diverse group of adolescents. *Journal of Child and Family Studies, 8*(3), 357–362.

Mazure, C. M. (1998). Life stressors as risk factors in depression. *Clinical Psychology: Science and Practice, 5*(3), 291–313.

Mazure, C. M., Bruce, M. L., Maciejewski, P. K., & Jacobs, S. C. (2000). Adverse life events and cognitive-personality characteristics in the prediction of major depression and antidepressant response. *American Journal of Psychiatry, 157*(6), 896–903.

McCabe, R., Antony, M. M., Summerfeldt, L. J., Liss, A., & Swinson, R. P. (2003). Preliminary examination of the relationship between anxiety disorders in adults and self-reported history of teasing or bullying experiences. *Cognitive Behaviour Therapy, 32,* 187–193.

McCabe, M., & Wauchope, M. (2005). Behavioral characteristics of men accused of rape: Evidence for different types of rapists. *Archives of Sexual Behavior, 34,* 241–253.

McClearn, G. E., Johansson, B., Berg, S., Pedersen, N. L., Ahern, F., Petrill, S. A., & Plomin, R. (1997). Substantial genetic influence on cognitive abilities in twins 80 or more years old. *Science, 276,* 1560–1563.

McCrae, R. R. (2002). NEO PI-R data from 36 cultures: Further intercultural comparisons. In R. McCrae & J. Allik (Eds.), *The five-factor model of personality across cultures* (pp. 105–126). New York: Kluwer Academic/Plenum Publishers.

McCullough, J. P., Jr., Klein, D. N., Keller, M. B., Holzer, C. E., III, Davis, S. M., Kornstein, S. G., et al. (2000). Comparison of DSM-III-R chronic major depression and major depression superimposed on dysthymia (double depression): Validity of the distinction. *Journal of Abnormal Psychology, 109,* 419–427.

McDowell, D. M. (1999). MDMA, ketamine, GHB, and the "club drug" scene. In M. Galanter & H. D. Kleber (Eds.), *Textbook of substance abuse treatment* (2nd ed., pp. 295–305). Washington, DC: American Psychiatric Press.

McEachin, J. J., Smith, T., & Lovaas, O. I. (1993). Long-term outcome for children with autism who received early intensive behavioral treatment. *American Journal on Mental Retardation, 97,* 359–372.

McElroy, S. L., & Arnold, L. M. (2001). Impulse-control disorders. In G. O. Gabbard (Ed.), *Treatment of psychiatric disorders* (Vol. 1, 3rd ed., pp. 2435–2471). Washington, DC: American Psychiatric Publishing.

McElroy, S. L., & Keck, P. E. (1993). Rapid cycling. In D. L. Dunner (Ed.), *Current psychiatric therapy* (pp. 226–231). Philadelphia: W. B. Saunders.

McEwen, B. S. (1999). Stress and hippocampal plasticity. *Annual Review of Neuroscience, 22,* 105–122.

McEwen, B. S., & Magarinos, A. M. (2004). Does Stress Damage the Brain? In J. M. Gorman, *Fear and anxiety: The benefits of translational research* (pp. 23–45). Washington, DC: American Psychiatric Publishing.

McEwen, B. S., & Stellar, E. (1993). Stress and the individual: Mechanisms leading to disease. *Archives of Internal Medicine, 153,* 2093–2101.

McFadden, D., Loehlin, J., Breedlove, S., Lippa, R., Manning, J., & Rahman, Q. (2005). A reanalysis of five studies on sexual orientation and the relative length of the 2nd and 4th fingers (the 2D: 4D ratio). *Archives of Sexual Behavior, 34,* 341–356.

McGinnis, J. M., & Foege, W. H. (1993). Actual causes of death in the United States. *JAMA, 270*(18), 2207–2212.

McGough, J. J. (2005). Adult manifestations of attention-deficit/hyperactivity disorder. In B. J. Sadock & V. A. Sadock (Eds.), *Kaplan & Sadock's comprehensive textbook of psychiatry* (pp. 3198–3204). Philadelphia: Lippincott, Williams & Wilkins.

McGough, J. J., Smalley, S. L., McCracken, J. T., Yang, M., Del'Homme, M., Lynn, D. E., & Loo, S. (2005). Psychiatric comorbidity in adult attention deficit hyperactivity disorder: Findings from multiplex families. *American Journal of Psychiatry, 162,* 1621–1627.

McGovern, M. P., Xie, H., Segal, S. R., Siembab, L., & Drake, R. E. (2006). Addiction treatment services and co-occurring disorders: Prevalence estimates, treatment practices, and barriers. *Journal of Substance Abuse Treatment, 31,* 267–275.

McGowin, D. F. (1993). *Living in the labyrinth: A personal journey through the maze of Alzheimer's.* New York: Delacorte Press.

McGrath, J. (2000). Universal interventions for the primary prevention of schizophrenia. *Australian and New Zealand Journal of Psychiatry, 34*(Suppl.), S58.

McGrath, P. A., & DeVeber, L. L. (1986). The management of acute pain evoked by medical procedures in children with cancer. *Journal of Pain and Symptom Management, 1,* 145–150.

McGue, M., & Christensen, K. (1997). Genetic and environmental contributions to depression symptomatology: Evidence from Danish twins 75 years of age and older. *Journal of Abnormal Psychology, 106*(3), 439–448.

McGue, M., & Lykken, D. T. (1992). Genetic influence on risk of divorce. *Psychological Science, 3*(6), 368–373.

McGuffin, P., & Katz, R. (1989). The genetics of depression and manic-depressive disorder. *British Journal of Psychiatry, 155,* 294–304.

McGuffin, P., Katz, R., & Bebbington, P. (1988). The Camberwell Collaborative Depression Study: III. Depression and adversity in the relatives of depressed probands. *British Journal of Psychiatry, 152,* 775–782.

McGuffin, P., Rijsdijk, F., Andrew, M., Sham, P., Katz, R., & Cardno, A. (2003). The heritability of bipolar affective disorder and the genetic relationship to unipolar depression. *Archives of General Psychiatry, 60,* 497–502.

McGuire, P. K., Shah, G. M. S., & Murray, R. M. (1993). Increased blood flow in Broca's area during auditory hallucinations in schizophrenia. *Lancet, 342,* 703–706.

McIntosh, J. L., Santos, J. F., Hubbard, R. W., & Overholser, J. C. (1994). *Elder suicide: Research, theory and treatment.* Washington, DC: American Psychological Association.

McKay, D., Todaro, J., Neziroglu, F., Campisi, T., Moritz, E. K., & Yaryura-Tobias, J. A. (1997). Body dysmorphic disorder: A preliminary evaluation of treatment and maintenance using exposure with response prevention. *Behaviour Research and Therapy, 35,* 67–70.

McKay, R., Langdon, R., & Coltheart, M. (in press). Models of misbelief: Integrating motivational and deficit theories of delusions. *Consciousness and Cognition.*

McKenzie, S. J., Williamson, D. A., & Cubic, B. A. (1993). Stable and reactive body image disturbances in bulimia nervosa. *Behavior Therapy, 24,* 195–207.

McKeon, P., & Murray, R. (1987). Familial aspects of obsessive-compulsive neuroses. *British Journal of Psychiatry, 151,* 528–534.

McKim, W. A. (1991). *Drugs and behavior: An introduction to behavioral pharmacology* (2nd ed.). Englewood Cliffs, NJ: Prentice Hall.

McKinnon, W., Weisse, C. S., Reynolds, C. P., Bowles, C. A., & Baum, A. (1989). Chronic stress, leukocyte subpopulations, and hormonal response to latent viruses. *Health Psychology, 8,* 399–402.

McLean, P., & Taylor, S. (1992). Severity of unipolar depression and choice of treatment. *Behaviour Research and Therapy, 30*(5), 443–451.

McLeod, J. D., Kessler, R. C., & Landis, K. R. (1992). Speed of recovery from major depressive episodes in a community sample of married men and women. *Journal of Abnormal Psychology, 101*(2), 277–286.

McNab, C., Haslam, N., & Burnett, P. (2007). Expressed emotion, attributions, utility beliefs, and distress in parents of young people with first episode psychosis. *Psychiatry Research, 151,* 97–106.

McNally, R. (2003). *Remembering trauma.* Cambridge, MA: Belknap Press.

McNally, R. J. (1994). Choking phobia: A review of the literature. *Comprehensive Psychiatry, 35,* 83–89.

McNally, R. J. (1996). Cognitive bias in the anxiety disorders. In D. A. Hope (Ed.), *Perspectives on anxiety, panic and fear* (The 43rd Annual Nebraska Symposium on Motivation) (pp. 211–250). Lincoln: Nebraska University Press.

McNally, R. J. (1999). EMDR and mesmerism: A comparative historical analysis. *Journal of Anxiety Disorders, 13,* 225–236.

McNally, R. J. (2001). The cognitive psychology of repressed and recovered memories of childhood sexual abuse: Clinical implications. *Psychiatric Annals, 31,* 509–514.

McNaughton, N., & Gray, J. H. (2000). Anxiolytic action on the behavioral inhibition system implies multiple types of arousal contribute to anxiety. *Journal of Affective Disorders, 61*(3), 161–176.

McNeil, T. F. (1987). Perinatal influences in the development of schizophrenia. In H. Helmchen & F. A. Henn (Eds.), *Biological perspectives of schizophrenia* (pp. 125–138). New York: John Wiley.

McNiel, D. E., & Binder, R. L. (1991). Clinical assessment of the risk of violence among psychiatric inpatients. *American Journal of Psychiatry, 148,* 1317–1321.

Means, M. K., & Edinger, J. D. (2006). Nonpharmacologic therapy of insomnia. In T. Lee-Chiong (Ed.), *Sleep: A comprehensive handbook* (pp. 133–136). Hoboken, NJ: John Wiley & Sons.

Measelle, J. R., Stice, E., & Springer, D. W. (2006). A prospective test of the negative affect model of substance abuse: Moderating effects of social support. *Psychology of Addictive Behaviors, 20,* 225–233.

Medina v. California, 112 S. Ct. 2575 (1992).

Mednick, S. A., & Schulsinger, F. (1965). A longitudinal study of children with a high risk for schizophrenia: A preliminary report. In S. Vandenberg (Ed.), *Methods and goals in human behavior genetics* (pp. 255–296). New York: Academic Press.

Mednick, S. A., & Schulsinger, F. (1968). Some premorbid characteristics related to breakdown in children with schizophrenic mothers. *Journal of Psychiatric Research, 6,* 267–291.

Meehan, P. J., Lamb, J. A., Saltzman, L. E., & O'Carroll, P. W. (1992). Attempted suicide among young adults: Progress toward a meaningful estimate of prevalence. *American Journal of Psychiatry, 149*(1), 41–44.

Meehl, P. E. (1945). The dynamics of "structured" personality tests. *Journal of Clinical Psychology, 1,* 296–303.

Meehl, P. E. (1962). Schizotaxia, schizotypy, schizophrenia. *American Psychologist, 17,* 827–838.

Meehl, P. E. (1989). Schizotaxia revisited. *Archives of General Psychiatry, 46,* 935–944.

Mehta, P., Kifley, A., Wang, J. J., Rochtchina, E., Mitchell, P., & Sue, C. M. (in press). Population prevalence and incidence of Parkinson's disease in an Australian community. *Internal Medicine Journal.*

Melamed, B. G., & Siegel, L. J. (1975). Reduction of anxiety in children facing hospitalization and surgery by use of filmed modeling. *Journal of Consulting and Clinical Psychology, 43*(4), 511–521.

Melnikova, I. (2007). Therapies for Alzheimer's disease. *Nature Reviews Drug Discovery, 6,* 341–342.

Meloy, J. R. (2001). Antisocial personality disorder. In G. O. Gabbard (Ed.), *Treatment of psychiatric disorders* (Vol. 2, 3rd ed., pp. 2251–2271). Washington, DC: American Psychiatric Publishing.

Melzack, R. (1999). From the gate to the neuromatrix. *Pain* (Suppl. 6), S121–S126.

Melzack, R. (2005). Evolution of the neuromatrix theory of pain. *Pain Practice, 5,* 85–94.

Melzack, R., & Wall, P. D. (1965). Pain mechanisms: A new theory. *Science, 150,* 971–979.

Melzack, R., & Wall, P. D. (1982). *The challenge of pain.* New York: Basic Books.

Mendelson, W. (2005). Sleep disorders. In B. J. Sadock & V. A. Sadock (Eds.), *Kaplan & Sadock's comprehensive textbook of psychiatry* (pp. 2022–2034). Philadelphia: Lippincott, Williams & Wilkins.

Menza, M. (2006). STAR★D: The results begin to roll in. *American Journal of Psychiatry, 163,* 1123–1125.

Menza, M., Lauritano, M., Allen, L., Warman, M., Ostella, F., Hamer, R. M., et al. (2001). Treatment of somatization disorder with nefazodone: a prospective, open-label study. *Annals of Clinical Psychiatry, 13,* 153–158.

Merikangas, K. R., & Risch, N. (2003). Will the genomics revolution revolutionize psychiatry? *American Journal of Psychiatry, 160,* 625–635.

Merikangas, K. R., & Risch, N. (2005). Will the genomics revolution revolutionize psychiatry? In N. C. Andreasen (Ed.), *Research advances in genetics and genomics: Implications for psychiatry* (pp. 37–61). Washington, DC: American Psychiatric Publishing.

Meston, C. M., & Gorzalka, B. B. (1995). The effects of sympathetic activation on physiological and subjective sexual arousal in women. *Behaviour Research and Therapy, 33,* 651–664.

Meyer, A. J., Nash, J. D., McAlister, A. L., Maccoby, M., & Farquhar, J. W. (1980). Skills training in a cardiovascular health education campaign. *Journal of Consulting and Clinical Psychology, 2,* 129–142.

Meyer, B., & Carver, C. S. (2000). Negative childhood accounts, sensitivity and pessimism: A study of avoidant personality disorder features in college students. *Journal of Personality Disorders, 14,* 233–248.

Meyer, R. G., & Weaver, C. M. (2006). *Law and mental health: A case-based approach.* New York: Guilford Press.

Meyer-Bahlburg, H., Dolezal, C., Baker, S., Carlson, A., Obeid, J., & New, M. (2004). Prenatal androgenization affects gender-related behavior but not gender identity in 5–12 year old girls with congenital adrenal hyperplasia. *Archives of Sexual Behavior, 33,* 97–104.

Meyerowitz, B. E. (1983). Postmastectomy coping strategies and quality of life. *Health Psychology, 2,* 117–132.

Meyers, A. (1991). Biobehavioral interactions in behavioral medicine. *Behavior Therapy, 22,* 129–131.

Mezzich, J. E., Good, B. J., Lewis-Fernandez, R., Guarnaccia, P., Lin, K. M., Parron, D., et al. (1993, September). *Cultural formulation guidelines.* Revised cultural proposals for DSM-IV. Submitted to the DSM-IV Task Force by the Steering Committee, NIMH-Sponsored Group on Culture and Diagnosis.

Mezzich, J. E., Kirmayer, L. J., Kleinman, A., Fabrega, H., Jr., Parron, D. L., Good, B. J., et al. (1999). The place of culture in DSM-IV. *Journal of Nervous and Mental Disease, 187,* 457–464.

Mezzich, J. E., Kleinman, A., Fabrega, H., Jr., Good, B., Johnson-Powell, G., Lin, K. M., et al. (1992). *Cultural proposals for DSM-IV.* Submitted to the DSM-IV Task Force by the Steering Committee, NIMH-Sponsored Group on Culture and Diagnosis.

Miaskowski, C. (1999). The role of sex and gender in pain perception and responses to treatment. In R. J. Gatchel & D. C. Turk (Eds.), *Psychosocial factors in pain: Critical perspectives* (pp. 401–411). New York: Guilford Press.

Michultka, D. M., Blanchard, E. B., Appelbaum, K. A., Jaccard, J., & Dentinger, M. P. (1989). The refractory headache patient: II. High medication consumption (analgesic rebound) headache. *Behaviour Research and Therapy, 27,* 411–420.

Middleton, W., Burnett, P., Raphael, B., & Martinek, N. (1996). The bereavement response: A cluster analysis. *British Journal of Psychiatry, 169,* 167–171.

Miklowitz, D. J. (2001). Bipolar disorder. In D. H. Barlow (Ed.), *Clinical handbook of psychological disorders* (3rd ed., pp. 523–561). New York: Guilford Publications.

Miklowitz, D. J., & Goldstein, M. J. (1997). *Bipolar disorder: A family focused treatment approach.* New York: Guilford Press.

Miklowitz, D. J., & Johnson, S. (2006). The psychopathology and treatment of bipolar disorder. In S. Nolen-Hoeksema, T. D. Cannon, & T. Widiger (Eds.), *Annual Review of Clinical Psychology* (pp. 199–235). Palo Alto, California: Annual Reviews.

Miklowitz, D. J., George, E. L., Richards, J. A., Simoneau, T. L., & Suddath, R. L. (2003). A randomized study of family-focused psychoeducation and pharmacotherapy in the outpatient management of bipolar disorder. *Archives of General Psychiatry, 60,* 904–912.

Miklowitz, D. J., Simoneau, T. L., Sachs-Ericsson, N., Warner, R., & Suddath, R. (1996). Family risk indicators in the course of bipolar affective disorder. In C. Mundt, M. J. Goldstein, K. Hahlweg, & P. Fiedler. (Eds.), *Interpersonal factors in the origin and course of affective disorders* (pp. 204–217). London: Gaskell Press.

Millar, H. R., Qrdell, F., Vyvyan, J. P., Naji, S. A., Prescott, G. J., & Eagles, J. M. (2005). Anorexia nervosa mortality in northeast Scotland 1965–1999. *American Journal of Psychiatry, 162,* 753–757.

Miller, A. L., McEvoy, J. P., Jeste, D. V., & Marder, S. R. (2006). Treatment of chronic schizophrenia. In J. A. Lieberman, T. S. Stroup, & D. O. Perkins (Eds.), *The American Psychiatric Publishing textbook of schizophrenia* (pp. 365–381). Washington, DC: American Psychiatric Publishing.

Miller, G. (2006). The unseen: Mental illness's global toll. *Science, 311,* 458–461.

Miller, G., & Blackwell, E. (2006). Turning up the heat: Inflammation as a mechanism linking chronic stress, depression, and heart disease. *Current Directions in Psychological Science, 15,* 269–277.

Miller, I. W., & Norman, W. H. (1979). Learned helplessness in humans: A review and attribution-theory model. *Psychological Bulletin, 86*(1), 93–118.

Miller, I. W., Norman, W. H., & Keitner, G. I. (1989). Cognitive-behavioral treatment of depressed inpatients: Six- and twelve-month follow-up. *American Journal of Psychiatry, 146,* 1274–1279.

Miller, I. W., Norman, W. H., Keitner, G. I., Bishop, S. B., & Down, M. G. (1989). Cognitive-behavioral treatment of depressed inpatients. *Behavior Therapy, 20*(1), 25–47.

Miller, J. D., Campbell, W. K., & Pilkonis, P. A. (2007). Narcissistic personality disorder: Relations with distress and functional impairment. *Comprehensive Psychiatry, 48,* 170–177.

Miller, N. E. (1969). Learning of visceral and glandular responses. *Science, 163,* 434–445.

Miller, N. S., Gold, M. S., & Pottash, A. C. (1989). A 12-step treatment approach for marijuana (cannabis) dependence. *Journal of Substance Abuse Treatment, 6,* 241–250.

Miller, P. M., Smith, G. T., & Goldman, M. S. (1990). Emergence of alcohol expectancies in childhood: A possible critical period. *Journal of Studies on Alcohol, 51,* 343–349.

Miller, S. D. (1989). Optical differences in cases of multiple personality disorder. *Journal of Nervous and Mental Disease, 177*(8), 480–486.

Miller, T. Q., Smith, T. W., Turner, C. W., Guijarro, M. L., & Hallet, A. J. (1996). A meta-analytic review of research on hostility and physical health. *Psychological Bulletin, 119*(2), 322–348.

Miller, W. R. (1985). Motivation for treatment: A review with special emphasis on alcoholism. *Psychological Bulletin, 98,* 84–107.

Miller, W. R., & Hester, R. K. (1986). Inpatient alcoholism treatment: Who benefits? *American Psychologist, 41,* 794–805.

Miller, W. R., & McCrady, B. S. (1993). The importance of research on Alcoholics Anonymous. In B. S. McCrady & W. R. Miller (Eds.), *Research on Alcoholics Anonymous: Opportunities and alternatives* (pp. 3–11). New Brunswick, NJ: Rutgers Center of Alcohol Studies.

Millon, T. (1981). *Disorders of personality: DSM-III, Axis II.* New York: John Wiley.

Millon, T. (1991). Classification in psychopathology: Rationale, alternatives, and standards. *Journal of Abnormal Psychology, 100*(3), 245–261.

Millon, T. (2004). *Masters of the mind.* Hoboken, NJ: Wiley & Sons.

Millon, T., & Martinez, A. (1995). Avoidant personality disorder. In W. J. Livesley (Ed.), *The DSM-IV personality disorders* (pp. 218–233). New York: Guilford Press.

Mills, J. L., Holmes, L. B., Aarons, J. H., Simpson, J. L., Brown, Z. A., Jovanovic-Peterson, L. G., et al. (1993). Moderate caffeine use and the risk of spontaneous abortion and intrauterine growth retardation. *JAMA, 269,* 593–597.

Mindell, J. A. (1993). Sleep disorders in children. *Health Psychology, 12,* 152–163.

Mindell, J. A. (1999). Empirically supported treatments in pediatric psychology: Bedtime refusal and night wakings in young children. *Journal of Pediatric Psychology, 24,* 465–481.

Mineka, S. (1985). The frightful complexity of the origins of fears. In F. R. Bruch & J. B. Overmier (Eds.), *Affect, conditioning, and cognition: Essays on the determinants of behavior.* Hillsdale, NJ: Erlbaum.

Mineka, S., & Sutton, J. (2006). In M. G. Craske, D. Hermans, & D. Vansteenwegen, *Fear and learning: From basic processes to clinical implications* (pp. 75–97), Washington, DC: American Psychological Association.

Mineka, S., & Watson, D., & Clark, L. A. (1998). Comorbidity of anxiety and unipolar mood disorders. *Annual Review of Psychology, 49,* 377–412.

Mineka, S., & Zinbarg, R. (1996). Conditioning and ethological models of anxiety disorders: Stress-in-dynamic-context anxiety models. In D. A. Hope (Ed.), *Perspectives on anxiety, panic and fear* (The 43rd Annual Nebraska Symposium on Motivation) (pp. 135–210). Lincoln: Nebraska University Press.

Mineka, S., & Zinbarg, R. (1998). Experimental approaches to understanding the mood and anxiety disorders. In J. Adair (Ed.), *Advances in psychological research, Vol. 2: Social, personal, and cultural aspects* (pp. 429–454). Hove, England: Psychology Press/Erlbaum.

Mineka, S., & Zinbarg, R. (2006). A contemporary learning theory perspective on the etiology of anxiety disorders. *American Psychologist, 61,* 10–26.

Mineka, S., Davidson, M., Cook, M., & Keir, R. (1984). Observational conditioning of snake fear in rhesus monkeys. *Journal of Abnormal Psychology, 93,* 355–372.

Minino, A. M., Arias, E., Kochanek, K. D., Murphy, S. L., & Smith, B. L. (2002). Deaths: Final data for 2000. *National Vital Statistics Reports, 50,* 1–119.

Minino, A. M., Heron, M., & Smith, B. (2006). Deaths: Preliminary data for 2004. *National Vital Statistics Report, 54,* 1–49.

Minuchin, S., Rosman, B. L., & Baker, L. (1978). *Psychosomatic families.* Cambridge, MA: Harvard University Press.

Mirsky, A. F. (1995). Israeli High-Risk Study: Editor's introduction. *Schizophrenia Bulletin, 21,* 179–182.

Mirsky, A. F., Bieliauskas, L. A., French, L. M., van Kammen, D. P., Jonsson, E., & Sedvall, G. (2000). A 39-year follow-up of the Genain quadruplets. *Schizophrenia Bulletin, 26,* 699–708.

Mitchell, J. E., Cook-Myers, T., & Wonderlich, S. A. (2005). Diagnostic criteria for anorexia nervosa: Looking ahead to DSM-V [Special issue]. *International Journal of Eating Disorders, 37,* S95–S97.

Mitchell, W. B., DiBartolo, P. M., Brown, T. A., & Barlow, D. H. (1998). Effects of positive and negative mood on sexual arousal in sexually functional males. *Archives of Sexual Behavior, 27*(2), 197–207.

Mitrouska, I., Bouloukaki, I., & Siafakas, N. M. (2007). Pharmacological approaches to smoking cessation. *Pulmonary Pharmacology & Therapeutics, 20,* 220–232.

Modahl, C., Green, L., Fein, D., Morris, M., Waterhouse, L., Feinstein, C., & Levin, H. (1998). Plasma oxytocin levels in autistic children. *Biological Psychiatry, 43,* 270–277.

Moene, F. C., Landberg, E. H., Hoogduin, K. A., Spinhoven, P., Hertzberger, L. I., Kleyweg, R. P., et al. (2000). Organic syndromes diagnosed as conversion disorder: Identification and frequency in a study of 85 patients. *Journal of Psychosomatic Research, 49,* 7–12.

Moene, F. C., Spinhoven, P., Hoogduin, K. A., & van Dyck, R. (2002). A randomised controlled clinical trial on the additional effect of hypnosis in a comprehensive treatment programme for in-patients with conversion disorder of the motor type. *Psychotherapy and psychosomatics, 71,* 66–76.

Moffitt, T. E., & Melchior, M. (2007). Why does the worldwide prevalence of childhood attention deficit hyperactivity disorder matter? *American Journal of Psychiatry, 164,* 856–858.

Mogg, K., Bradley, B. P., Millar, N., & White, J. (1995). A follow-up study of cognitive bias in generalized anxiety disorder. *BRAT, 33,* 927–935.

Mogg, K., Mathews, A., & Weinman, J. (1989). Selective processing of threat cues in anxiety states: A replication. *Behaviour Research and Therapy, 27,* 317–323.

Mogg, K., Philippot, P., & Bradley, B. P. (2004). Selective attention to angry faces in clinical social phobia. *Journal of Abnormal Psychology, 113,* 160–165.

Mogil, J. S., Sternberg, W. F., Kest, B., Marek, P., & Liebeskind, J. C. (1993). Sex differences in the antagonism of swim stress-induced analgesia: Effects of gonadectomy and estrogen replacement. *Pain, 53,* 17–25.

Mohr, D. C., & Beutler, L. E. (1990). Erectile dysfunction: A review of diagnostic and treatment procedures. *Clinical Psychology Review, 10*(1), 123–150.

Moller-Madsen, S., & Nystrup, J. (1992). Incidence of anorexia nervosa in Denmark. *Acta Psychiatrica Scandinavica, 86,* 197–200.

Money, J., & Ehrhardt, A. (1972). *Man and woman, boy and girl.* Baltimore: Johns Hopkins University Press.

Monk, T. H. (2006). Jet lag. In T. Lee-Chiong (Ed.), *Sleep: A comprehensive handbook* (pp. 389–393). Hoboken, NJ: John Wiley & Sons.

Monk, T. H., & Moline, M. L. (1989). The timing of bedtime and waketime decisions in free-running subjects. *Psychophysiology, 26,* 304–310.

Monk, T. H., Buysse, D. J., & Billy, B. J. (2006). Using daily 30-min phase advances to achieve a 6-hour advance: Circadian rhythm, sleep, and alertness. *Aviation Space and Environmental Medicine, 77,* 677–686.

Monk, T. H., Buysse, D. J., & Rose, L. R. (1999). Wrist actigraphic measures of sleep in space. *Sleep, 22,* 948–954.

Monroe, S., & Harkness, K. (2005). Life, stress, the "kindling" stress perspective. *Psychological Review, 112,* 417–445.

Monroe, S., Slavich, G., Torres, L., & Gotlib, I. (2007). Major life events and major chronic difficulties are differentially associated with history of major depressive disorders. *Journal of Abnormal Psychology, 116,* 116–124.

Monroe, S. M., & Roberts, J. E. (1990). Conceptualizing and measuring life stress: Problems, principles, procedures, progress. Special issue: II–IV. Advances in measuring life stress. *Stress Medicine, 6*(3), 209–216.

Monroe, S. M., Bromet, E. J., Connell, M. M., & Steiner, S. C. (1986). Social support, life events, and depressive symptoms: A 1 year prospective study. *Journal of Consulting and Clinical Psychology, 54*(4), 424–431.

Monroe, S. M., Imhoff, D. F., Wise, B. D., & Harris, J. E. (1983). Prediction of psychological symptoms under high-risk psychosocial circumstances: Life events, social support, and symptom specificity. *Journal of Abnormal Psychology, 92*(2), 338–350.

Monroe, S. M., Kupfer, D. J., & Frank, E. (1992). Life stress and treatment course of recurrent depression: I. Response during index episode. *Journal of Consulting and Clinical Psychology, 60*(5), 718–724.

Monroe, S. M., Roberts, J. E., Kupfer, D. J., & Frank, E. (1996). Life stress and treatment course of recurrent depression: II. Postrecovery associations with attrition, symptom course, and recurrence over 3 years. *Journal of Abnormal Psychology, 105*(3), 313–328.

Monroe, S. M., Rohde, P., Seeley, J. R., & Lewinsohn, P. M. (1999). Life events and depression in adolescence: For first onset of major depressive disorder. *Journal of Abnormal Psychology, 108*(4), 606–614.

Monroe, S. M., Thase, M. E., & Simons, A. D. (1992). Social factors and the psychobiology of depression: Relations between life stress and rapid eye movement sleep latency. *Journal of Abnormal Psychology, 101*(3), 528–537.

Montejo-Gonzalez, A. L., Liorca, G., Izquierdo, J. A., Ledesma, A., Bousono, M., Calcedo, A., et al. (1997). SSRI-induced sexual dysfunction: Fluoxetine, paroxetine, sertraline, and fluvoxamine in a prospective, multicenter, and descriptive clinical study of 344 patients. *Journal of Sex and Marital Therapy, 23,* 176–194.

Montero, I., Hernandez, I., Asencio, A., Bellver, F., La-Cruz, M., & Masanet, M. J. (2005). Do all people with schizophrenia receive the same benefit from different family intervention programs? *Psychiatry Research, 133*(2–3), 187–195.

Montero, I., Masanet, M. J., Bellver, F., & Lacruz, M. (2006). The long-term outcome of two family intervention strategies in schizophrenia. *Comprehensive Psychiatry, 47*(5), 362–367.

Moore, D. S. (2001). *The dependent gene: The fallacy of "nature vs. nurture."* New York: Henry Holt and Company.

Moore, R. Y. (1999). Circadian rhythms: A clock for the ages. *Science, 284,* 2102–2103.

Moos, R. H., & Moos, B. S. (2007). Protective resources and long-term recovery from alcohol use disorders. *Drug and Alcohol Dependence, 86,* 46–54.

Moras, K., Clark, L. A., Katon, W., Roy-Byrne, P., Watson, D., & Barlow, D. H. (1996). Mixed anxiety-depression. In T. A. Widiger, A. J. Frances, H. A. Pincus, R. Ross, M. B. First, & W. W. Davis (Eds.), *DSM-IV sourcebook* (Vol. 2, pp. 623–643). Washington, DC: American Psychiatric Association.

Moreau, D., & Weissman, M. M. (1992). Panic disorder in children and adolescents: A review. *American Journal of Psychiatry, 149,* 1306–1314.

Morelli, G. A., Rogoff, B., Oppenheim, D., & Goldsmith, D. (1992). Cultural variation in infants' sleeping arrangements: Questions of independence. *Developmental Psychology, 28,* 604–613.

Morenz, B., & Becker, J. (1995). The treatment of youthful sexual offenders. *Applied & Preventive Psychology, 4,* 247–256.

Morey, L. C., & Kurtz, J. E. (1989). *The place of neurasthenia in the DSM-IV.* Unpublished report to the DSM-IV subgroup on generalized anxiety disorder and mixed anxiety depression.

Morey, L. C,, & Ochoa, E. S. (1989). An investigation of adherence to diagnostic criteria: Clinical diagnosis of the DSM-III personality disorders. *Journal of Personality Disorders, 3*(3), 180–192.

Morey, L. C., Alexander, G. M., & Boggs, C. (2005). Gender. In J. M. Oldham, A. E. Skodol, & D. S. Bender (Eds.), *Textbook of personality disorders* (pp. 541–559). Washington, DC: American Psychiatric Publishing.

Morey, L. C., Hopwood, C. J., & Klein, D. N. (in press). Passive-aggressive, depressive, and sadistic personality disorders. In W. O'Donohue, K. Fowler, & S. O. Lilienfeld (Eds.), *Sage handbook of personality disorders.* Thousand Oaks, CA: Sage Publishing.

Morgan, H. W. (1981). *Drugs in America: A social history, 1800–1980.* Syracuse, NY: Syracuse University Press.

Morgenthaler, T. I., & Silber, M. H. (2002). Amnestic sleep-related eating disorder associated with zolpidem. *Sleep Medicine, 3,* 323–327.

Morin, C. M. (1993a). *Insomnia: Psychological assessment and management.* New York: Guilford Press.

Morin, C. M. (1993b). *Psychological management of insomnia.* New York: Guilford Press.

Morin, C. M., Colecchi, C., Stone, J., Sood, R., & Brink, D. (1999). Behavioral and pharmacological therapies for late-life insomnia: A randomized controlled trial. *JAMA, 281,* 991–999.

Morin, C. M., Stone, J., Trinkle, D., Mercer, J., & Remsberg, S. (1993). Dysfunctional beliefs and attitudes about sleep among older adults with and without insomnia complaints. *Psychology and Aging, 8,* 463–467.

Morokoff, P. J. (1993). Female sexual arousal disorder. In W. O'Donohue & J. H. Geer (Eds.), *Handbook of sexual dysfunctions: Assessment and treatment* (pp. 157–199). Boston: Allyn & Bacon.

Morokoff, P. J., & Heiman, J. R. (1980). Effects of erotic stimuli on sexually functional and dysfunctional women: Multiple measures before and after sex therapy. *Behaviour Research and Therapy, 18,* 127–137.

Morris, D. (1985). *Body watching: A field guide to the human species.* New York: Crown.

Morris, J. K., Cook, D. G., & Shaper, A. G. (1994). Loss of employment and mortality. *British Medical Journal, 308,* 1135–1139.

Morris, J. S., Öhman, A., & Dolan, R. J. (1998). Conscious and unconscious emotion learning in the human amygdala. *Nature, 393,* 467–470.

Morris, M., Lack, L., & Dawson, D. (1990). Sleep-onset insomniacs have delayed temperature rhythms. *Sleep, 13,* 1–14.

Morrison, A. P., & Wells, A. (2007). Relationships between worry, psychotic experiences and emotional distress in patients with schizophrenia spectrum diagnoses and comparisons with anxious and nonpatient groups. *Behaviour Research and Therapy, 45,* 1593–1600.

Morrow, G. R., & Dobkin, P. L. (1988). Anticipatory nausea and vomiting in cancer patients undergoing chemotherapy treatment: Prevalence, etiology, and behavioral interventions. *Clinical Psychology Review, 8,* 517–556.

Morton, A. (1992). *Diana: Her true story.* New York: Pocket Books.

Moscicki, E. (1997). Identification of suicide risk factors using epidemiological studies. *Psychiatric Clinics of North America, 20,* 499–517.

Moser, D. J., Reese, R. L., Schultz, S. K., Benjamin, M. L., Arndt, S., Fleming, F. W., & Andreasen, N. C. (2005). Informed consent in medication-free schizophrenia research. *American Journal of Psychiatry, 162*(6), 1209–1211.

Moses, J. A. (2006). Recent advances in intelligence assessment theory and practice. [Review of the book *Contemporary intellectual assessment: Theories, tests, and issues* (2nd ed.)]. *PsycCRITIQUES, 51*(5), Article 11.

Mosher, D. L., & Sirkin, M. (1984). Measuring a macho personality constellation. *Journal of Research in Personality, 18,* 150–163.

Mosko, S., Richard, C., & McKenna, J. C. (1997). Maternal sleep and arousals during bedsharing with infants. *Sleep, 20,* 142–150.

Moskowitz, A. (2004). "Scared stiff": Catatonia as an evolutionary based fear response. *Psychological Review, 111,* 984–1002.

Moss, A. R., & Bacchetti, P. (1989). Natural history of HIV infection. *AIDS, 3,* 55–61.

Moss-Morris, R., Sharon, C., Tobin, R., & Baldi, J. (2005). A randomized controlled graded exercise trial for chronic fatigue syndrome: Outcomes and mechanisms of change. *Journal of Health Psychology, 10,* 245–259.

Mostofsky, D. I., & Barlow, D. H. (Eds.) (2000). *The management of stress and anxiety in medical disorders.* Needham Heights, MA: Allyn & Bacon.

Mucha, T. F., & Reinhardt, R. F. (1970). Conversion reactions in student aviators. *American Journal of Psychiatry, 127,* 493–497.

Mueller, T. I., Leon, A. C., Keller, M. B., Solomon, D. A., Endicott, J., Coryell, W., et al. (1999). Recurrence after recovery from major depressive disorder during 15 years of observational follow-up. *American Journal of Psychiatry, 156*(7), 1000–1006.

Mueller, T., Keller, M. B., Leon, A. C., Solomon, D. A., Shea, M. T., Coryell, W., & Endicott, J. (1996). Recovery after 5 years of unremitting major depressive disorder. *Archives of General Psychiatry, 53,* 794–799.

Mueser, K. T., & Berenbaum, H. (1990). Psychodynamic treatment of schizophrenia: Is there a future? *Psychological Medicine, 20,* 253–262.

Mueser, K. T., Clark, R. E., Haines, M., Drake, R. E., McHugo, G. J., Bond, G. R., et al. (2004). The Hartford study of supported employment for persons with severe mental illness. *Journal of Consulting and Clinical Psychology, 72,* 479–490.

Mueser, K. T., Liberman, R. P., & Glynn, S. M. (1990). Psychosocial interventions in schizophrenia. In A. Kales, C. N. Stefanis, & J. A. Talbott (Eds.), *Recent advances in schizophrenia* (pp. 213–235). New York: Springer-Verlag.

Mufson, L., Pollack-Dorta, K., Wickramaratne, P., Nomura, Y., Olfson, M., & Weismann, M. (2004). A randomized effectiveness trial of interpersonal psychotherapy for depressed adolescents. *Archives General Psychiatry, 61,* 577–584.

Mumford, D. B., Whitehouse, A. M., & Platts, M. (1991). Sociocultural correlates of eating disorders among Asian schoolgirls in Bradford. *British Journal of Psychiatry, 158,* 222–228.

Munjack, D. J. (1984). The onset of driving phobias. *Journal of Behavior Therapy and Experimental Psychiatry, 15,* 305–308.

Muñoz, R. F. (1993). The prevention of depression: Current research and practice. *Applied and Preventative Psychology, 2,* 21–33.

Munro, A. (1999). *Delusional disorder: Paranoia and related illnesses.* New York: Cambridge University Press.

Murdoch, D., Pihl, R. O., & Ross, D. (1990). Alcohol and crimes of violence: Present issues. *International Journal of the Addictions, 25,* 1065–1081.

Murray, C. J. L. (1996). *Global health statistics.* Cambridge, MA: Harvard University Press.

Murray, C. J. L., & Lopez, A. (Eds.) (1996). *The global burden of disease.* Cambridge, MA: Harvard University Press.

Murray, R. M., & Bramon, E. (2005). Developmental model of schizophrenia. In B. J. Sadock & V. A. Sadock (Eds.), *Kaplan & Sadock's comprehensive textbook of psychiatry* (pp. 1381–1396). Philadelphia: Lippincott, Williams & Wilkins.

Must, A., Spadano, J., Coakley, E. H., Field, A. E., Colditz, G., & Dietz, W. H. (1999). The disease burden associated with overweight and obesity. *JAMA, 282,* 1523–1529.

Mustafa, G. (1990). Delivery systems for the care of schizophrenic patients in Africa—Sub-Sahara. In A. Kales, C. N. Stefanis, & J. A. Talbot (Eds.), *Recent advances in schizophrenia* (pp. 353–371). New York: Springer-Verlag.

Mustanski, B. S., Bailey, J. M., & Kaspar, S. (2002). Dermatoglyphics, handedness, sex, and sexual orientation. *Archives of Sexual Behavior, 31,* 113–122.

Musto, D. F. (1992). America's first cocaine epidemic: What did we learn? In T. R. Kosten & H. D. Kleber (Eds.), *Clinician's guide to cocaine addiction: Theory, research, and treatment* (pp. 3–15). New York: Guilford Press.

Myers, J. K., Weissman, M. M., Tischler, C. E., Holzer, C. E., III, Orvaschel, H., Anthony, J. C., et al. (1984). Six-month prevalence of psychiatric disorders in three communities. *Archives of General Psychiatry, 41,* 959–967.

Myers, K., & Collett, B. (2006). Rating scales. In M. K. Dulcan & J. M. Wiener (Eds.), *Essentials of child and adolescent psychiatry* (pp. 81–97). Washington, DC: American Psychiatric Publishing.

Nachmias, M., Gunnar, M., Mangelsdorf, S., Parritz, R. H., & Buss, K. (1996). Behavioral inhibition and stress reactivity: The moderating role of attachment security. *Child Development, 67*(2), 508–522.

Nagayama Hall, G. C. (1995). The preliminary development of theory-based community treatment for sexual offenders. *Professional Psychology: Research and Practice, 26*(5), 478–483.

Nagayama Hall, G. C., DeGarmo, D. S., Eap, S., Teten, A. L., & Sue, S. (2006). Initiation, desistance, and persistence of men's sexual coercion. *Journal of Consulting and Clinical Psychology, 74*(4), 732–742.

Nagel, D. B. (1991). Psychotherapy of schizophrenia: 1900–1920. In J. G. Howells (Ed.), *The concept of schizophrenia: Historical perspectives* (pp. 191–201). Washington, DC: American Psychiatric Press.

Najavits, L. M. (2007). Psychosocial treatments for posttraumatic stress disorder. In P. E. Nathan & J. M. Gorman (Eds.), *A guide to treatments that work* (3rd ed.). New York: Oxford University Press.

Nantulya, V., & Green, E. (2002, May 9). What accounts for Uganda's remarkable HIV prevalence and incidence decline? Seminar at Harvard University Center for Population and Development Studies, Cambridge, MA.

Nasser, M. (1986). Comparative study of the prevalence of abnormal eating attitudes among Arab female students of both London and Cairo universities. *Psychological Medicine, 16,* 621–625.

Nasser, M. (1988). Eating disorders: The cultural dimension. *Social Psychiatry and Psychiatric Epidemiology, 23,* 184–187.

Nathan, P. E. (1993). Alcoholism: Psychopathology, etiology, and treatment. In P. B. Sutker & H. E. Adams (Eds.), *Comprehensive handbook of psychopathology* (pp. 451–476). New York: Plenum Press.

National Center for Health Statistics. (1993). Advance report of final mortality statistics, 1990 (Monthly Vital Statistics Report, Vol. 41, No. 7, Suppl.). Hyattsville, MD: Public Health Service.

National Institute of Mental Health. (2003). *Breaking ground, breaking through: The strategic plan for mood disorders research.* (NIH Publication No. 03-5121). Washington, DC: U.S. Government Printing Office.

National Institute on Alcohol Abuse and Alcoholism. (1997). *Alcohol Alert: Alcohol-Metabolism.* No. 35, PH 371. Bethesda, MD: Author.

National Institute on Drug Abuse. (1993). NIDA Capsules, CAP 16. U.S. Department of Health and Human Services. Washington, DC: U.S. Government Printing Office.

National Institute on Drug Abuse. (2005). *NIDA research report: Marijuana abuse.* NIH Publication No. 05-3859.

National Institute on Drug Abuse. (2006). *NIDA research report: Tobacco addiction.* NIH Publication No. 06-4342, revised.

National Institutes of Health. (1998). *Clinical guidelines on the identification, evaluation, and treatment of overweight and obesity in adults: The evidence report* (NIH Publication No. 98-4083, pp. 139–140). Washington, DC: U.S. Government Printing Office.

National Resource Center on Homelessness and Mental Illness. (2003). *Fact Sheet: Who is Homeless?* Delmar, NY: National Resource Center on Homelessness and Mental Illness.

National Sleep Foundation. (2005). *2005 Sleep in America Poll.* Washington, DC: Author.

Naz, B., Fochtmann, L. J., & Bromet, E. J. (2005). Schizophreniform disorder. In B. J. Sadock & V. A. Sadock (Eds.), *Kaplan & Sadock's comprehensive textbook of psychiatry* (pp. 1522–1525). Philadelphia: Lippincott, Williams & Wilkins.

Nazemi, H., Kleinknecht, R. A., Dinnel, D. L., Lonner, W. J., Nazemi, S., Shamlo, S., & Sobhan, A. (2003). A study of panic attacks among university students in the Islamic Republic of Iran. *Journal of Psychopathology and Behavioral Assessment, 25,* 191– 201.

Neal, A. M., Nagle-Rich, L., & Smucker, W. D. (1994). The presence of panic disorder among African American hypertensives: A pilot study. *Journal of Black Psychology, 20,* 29–35.

Neal-Barnett, A. M., & Smith, J., Sr. (1997). African Americans. In S. Friedman (Ed.), *Cultural issues in the treatment of anxiety* (pp. 154–174). New York: Guilford Press.

Neighbors, H. W., Jackson, J. S., Campbell, L., & Williams, D. (1989). The influence of racial factors on psychiatric diagnosis: A review and suggestions for research. *Community Mental Health Journal, 25*(4), 301–311.

Nelles, W. B. N., & Barlow, D. H. (1988). Do children panic? *Clinical Psychology Review, 8*(4), 359–372.

Nelson, R. O., & Barlow, D. H. (1981). Behavioral assessment: Basic strategies and initial procedures. In D. H. Barlow (Ed.), *Behavioral assessment of adult disorders.* New York: Guilford Press.

Nemeroff, C. (2004). Early-life adversity, CRF dysregulation, and vulnerability to mood and anxiety disorders. *Psychopharmacology Bulletin, 38,* 14–20.

Nemeroff, C. (2006). The burden of severe depression: A review of diagnostic challenges and treatment alternatives. *Journal of Psychiatric Research, 1–18.*

Neugroschi, J. A., Kolevzon, A., Samuels, S. C., & Marin, D. B. (2005). Dementia. In B. J. Sadock & V. A. Sadock (Eds.), *Kaplan & Sadock's comprehensive textbook of psychiatry* (pp. 1068–1093). Philadelphia: Lippincott, Williams & Wilkins.

Neumark-Sztainer, D., & Haines, J. (2004). Psychosocial and behavioral consequences of obesity. In J. K. Thompson (Ed.), *Handbook of eating disorders and obesity* (pp. 349–371). New York: John Wiley.

New York Mental Hygiene Law. (1992). 1.03 (20).

New York State Department of Mental Hygiene (1978). *The insanity defense in New York.* New York: Author.

Newman, J. P., & Schmitt, W. A. (1998). Passive avoidance in psychopathic offenders: A replication and extension. *Journal of Abnormal Psychology, 107,* 527–532.

Newman, J. P., Patterson, C. M., & Kosson, D. S. (1987). Response perseveration in psychopaths. *Journal of Abnormal Psychology, 96,* 145–148.

Newman, J. P., Widom, C. S., & Nathan, S. (1985). Passive-avoidance in syndromes of disinhibition: Psychopathy and extraversion. *Journal of Personality and Social Psychology, 50,* 624–630.

Neylan, T. C., Reynolds, C. F., III, & Kupfer, D. J. (2003). Sleep disorders. In R. E. Hales & S. C. Yu-

dofsky (Eds.), *Textbook of clinical psychiatry* (4th ed., pp. 975–1000). Washington, DC: American Psychiatric Publishing.

Nezami, E., & Butcher, J. N. (2000). Objective personality assessment. In G. Goldstein & M. Hersen (Eds.), *Handbook of psychological assessment* (pp. 413–435). New York: Pergamon Press.

Nezu, C. M., Nezu, A. M., Friedman, S. H., Houts, P. S., DelliCarpini, L., Bildner, C., & Faddis, S. (1999). Cancer and psychological distress: Two investigations regarding the role of social problem-solving. *Journal of Psychosocial Oncology, 16*(3–4), 27–40.

Ng, B. Y., Yap, A. K., Su, A., Lim, D., & Ong, S. H. (2002). Personality profiles of patients with dissociative trance disorder in Singapore. *Comprehensive psychiatry, 43,* 121–126.

Ni, X., Bismil, R., Chan, K., Sicard, T., Bulgin, N., McMain, S., & Kennedy, J. L. (2006). Serotonin 2a receptor gene is associated with personality traits, but not to disorder, in patients with borderline personality disorder. *Neuroscience Letters, 408,* 214–219.

Ni, X., Chan, K., Bulgin, N., Sicard, T., Bismil, R., McMain, S., & Kennedy, J. L. (2006). Association between serotonin transporter gene and borderline personality disorder. *Journal of Psychiatric Research, 40,* 448–453.

Nicassio, P. M., Meyerowitz, B. E., & Kerns, R. D. (2004). The future of health psychology interventions. *Health Psychology, 23,* 132–137.

Nisbett, R. E., & Ross, L. (1980). *Human inference: Strategies and shortcomings in social judgment.* New York: Century.

Nock, M., & Kessler, R. (2006). Prevalence of and risk factors for suicide attempts versus suicide gestures: Analysis of the national comorbidity survey. *Journal of Abnormal Psychology, 115,* 616–623.

Nofzinger, E. A., Schwartz, C. F., Reynolds, C. F., Thase, M. E., Jennings, J. R., Frank, E., Fasiczka, A. L., Garamoni, G. L., & Kupfer, D. J. (1994). Affect intensity and phasic REM sleep in depressed men before and after treatment with cognitive-behavior therapy. *Journal of Consulting and Clinical Psychology, 62,* 83–91.

Nolen-Hoeksema, S. (1987). Sex differences in unipolar depression: Evidence and theory. *Psychological Bulletin, 101*(2), 259–282.

Nolen-Hoeksema, S. (1990). *Sex differences in depression.* Stanford, CA: Stanford University Press.

Nolen-Hoeksema, S. (2000a). Further evidence for the role of psychosocial factors in depression chronicity. *Clinical Psychology: Science and Practice, 7*(2), 224–227.

Nolen-Hoeksema, S. (2000b). The role of rumination in depressive disorders and mixed anxiety/depressive symptoms. *Journal of Abnormal Psychology, 109,* 504–511.

Nolen-Hoeksema, S., Girgus, J. S., & Seligman, M. E. P. (1992). Predictors and consequences of childhood depressive symptoms: A 5-year longitudinal study. *Journal of Abnormal Psychology, 101*(3), 405–422.

Nolen-Hoeksema, S., Larson, J., & Grayson, C. (1999). Explaining the gender differences in depressive symptoms. *Journal of Personality and Social Psychology, 77*(5), 1061–1072.

Nolen-Hoeksema, S., Wolfson, A., Mumme, D., & Guskin, K. (1995). Helplessness in children of depressed and nondepressed mothers. *Developmental Psychology, 31,* 377–387.

Noll, R. B., Zucker, R. A., & Greenberg, G. S. (1990). Identification of alcohol by smell among preschoolers: Evidence for early socialization about drugs occurring in the home. *Child Development, 61,* 1520–1527.

Nordentoft, M., Thorup, A., Petersen, L., Ohlenschlaeger, J., Melau, M., Christensen, T. O., et al. (2006). Transition rates from schizotypal disorder to psychotic disorder for first-contact patients in-

cluded in the opus trial: A randomized clinical trial of integrated treatment and standard treatment. *Schizophrenia Research, 83,* 29–40.

Norton, G. R., Harrison, B., Hauch, J., & Rhodes, L. (1985). Characteristics of people with infrequent panic attacks. *Journal of Abnormal Psychology, 94,* 216–221.

Noyes, R., & Kletti, R. (1977). Depersonalization in response to life-threatening danger. *Comprehensive Psychiatry, 18,* 375–384.

Noyes, R., Clarkson, C., Crowe, R. R., Yates, W. R., & McChesney, C. M. (1987). A family study of generalized anxiety disorder. *American Journal of Psychiatry, 144,* 1019–1024.

Noyes, R., Garvey, M. J., Cook, B., & Suelzer, M. (1991). Controlled discontinuation of benzodiazepine treatment for patients with panic disorder. *American Journal of Psychiatry, 148,* 517–523.

Noyes, R., Hoenk, P., Kuperman, S., & Slymen, D. (1977). Depersonalization in accident victims and psychiatric patients. *Journal of Nervous and Mental Disease, 164,* 401–407.

Noyes, R., Stuart, S. P., Langbehn, D. R., Happel, R. L., Longley, S. L., Muller, B. A., et al. (2003). Test of an interpersonal model of hypochondriasis. *Psychomatic Medicine, 65,* 292–300.

Noyes, R., Watson, D., Carney, C., Letuchy, E., Peloso, P., Black, D., et al. (2004). Risk factors for hypochondriacal concerns in a sample of military veterans. *Journal of Psychosomatic Research, 57,* 529–539.

Noyes, R., Woodman, C., Garvey, M. J., Cook, B. L., Suelzer, M., Clancy, J., & Anderson, D. J. (1992). Generalized anxiety disorder vs. panic disorder: Distinguishing characteristics and patterns of comorbidity. *Journal of Nervous and Mental Disease, 180,* 369–379.

Nugent, S. A. (2000). Perfectionism: Its manifestations and classroom-based interventions. *Journal of Secondary Gifted Education, 11,* 215–221.

Nurnberger, J. I., & Gershon, E. S. (1992). Genetics. In E. S. Paykel (Ed.), *Handbook of affective disorders* (pp. 126–145). New York: Guilford Press.

Nyhan, W. L. (1978). The Lesch-Nyhan syndrome. *Developmental Medicine and Child Neurology, 20,* 376–387.

O'Brien, C. P. (1996). Recent developments in the pharmacotherapy of substance abuse. *Journal of Consulting and Clinical Psychology, 64,* 677–686.

O'Brien, C. P., & Kampman, K. M. (2004). Opioids: Antagonists and partial agonists. In M. Galanter & H. D. Kleber (Eds.), *The American Psychiatry Publishing textbook of substance abuse treatment* (3rd ed., pp. 305–319). Washington, DC: American Psychiatric Publishing.

O'Brien, M. E., Clark, R. A., Besch, C. L., Myers, L., & Kissinger, P. (2003). Patterns and correlates of discontinuation of the initial HAART regimen in an urban outpatient cohort. *Journal of Acquired Immune Deficiency Syndrome, 34*(4), 407–414.

O'Brien, M. M., Trestman, R. L., & Siever, L. J. (1993). Cluster A personality disorders. In D. L. Dunner (Ed.), *Current psychiatric therapy* (pp. 399–404). Philadelphia: W. B. Saunders.

O'Callaghan, E., Sham, P., Takei, N., Glover, G., & Murray, R. M. (1991). Schizophrenia after prenatal exposure to 1957 A2 influenza epidemic. *Lancet, 337,* 1248–1250.

O'Carroll, P. W. (1990). Community strategies for suicide prevention and intervention. In S. J. Blumenthal & D. J. Kupfer (Eds.), *Suicide over the life cycle: Risk factors, assessment and treatment of suicidal patients.* Washington, DC: American Psychiatric Press.

O'Connor v. Donaldson, 95 S. Ct. 2486 (1975).

O'Hagan, S. (1992, February 22). Raving madness. *The Times Saturday Review,* pp. 10–12.

O'Hanlon, J. F., Haak, J. W., Blaauw, G. J., & Riemersma, J. B. J. (1982). Diazepam impairs lateral position control in highway driving. *Science, 27,* 79–81.

O'Hara, M. W. (1986). Social support, life events and depression during pregnancy and the puerperium. *Archives of General Psychiatry, 43*(6), 569–575.

O'Hara, M. W., Stuart, S., Gorman, L. L., & Wenzel, A. (2000). Efficacy of interpersonal psychotherapy for postpartum depression. *Archives of General Psychiatry, 57,* 1039–1045.

O'Leary, A. (1990). Stress, emotion, and human immune function. *Psychological Bulletin, 108*(3), 363–382.

O'Leary, A. (1992). Self-efficacy and health: Behavioral and stress-physiological mediation. *Cognitive Therapy and Research, 16*(2), 229–245.

O'Leary, K. D., & Beach, S. R. (1990). Marital therapy: A viable treatment for depression and marital discord. *American Journal of Psychiatry, 147*(2), 183–186.

O'Sullivan, K. (1979). Observations on vaginismus in Irish women. *Archives of General Psychiatry, 36,* 824–826.

Oades, R. D. (1985). The role of noradrenaline in tuning and dopamine in switching between signals in the CNS. *Neuroscience and Biobehavioral Reviews, 9,* 261–282.

Ogata, S. N., Silk, K. R., Goodrich, S., Lohr, N. E., Westen, D., & Hill, E. M. (1990). Childhood sexual and physical abuse in adult patients with borderline personality disorder. *American Journal of Psychiatry, 147,* 1008–1013.

Ogden, C. L., Carroll, M. D., Curtin, L. R., McDowell, M. A., Tabak, C. J., & Flegal, K. M. (2006). Prevalence of overweight and obesity in the United States, 1999–2004. *JAMA, 295,* 1549–1555.

Ohayon, M. M., & Schatzberg, A. F. (2002). Prevalence of depressive episodes with psychotic features in the general population. *American Journal of Psychiatry. 159,* 1855–1861.

Ohayon, M. M., & Schatzberg, A. F. (2003). Using chronic pain to predict depressive morbidity in the general population. *Archives of General Psychiatry, 60,* 39–47.

Öhman, A. (1986). Face the beast and fear the face: Animal and social fears as prototypes for evolutionary analyses of emotion. *Psychophysiology, 23,* 123–145.

Öhman, A. (1996). Preferential pre-attentive processing of threat in anxiety: Preparedness and attentional biases. In R. Rapee (Ed.), *Current controversies in the anxiety disorders* (pp. 253–290). New York: Guilford Press.

Öhman, A., & Dimberg, U. (1978). Facial expressions as conditioned stimuli for electrodermal responses: A case of preparedness? *Journal of Personality and Social Psychology, 36*(11), 1251–1258.

Öhman, A., & Mineka, S. (2001). Fears, phobias, and preparedness: Toward an evolved model of fear and fear learning. *Psychological Review.*

Öhman, A., Flykt, A., & Lundqvist, D. (2000). Unconscious emotion: Evolutionary perspective, psychophysiological data, and neuropsychological mechanisms. In R. Lane & L. Nadel (Eds.), *The cognitive neuroscience of emotion* (pp. 296–327). New York: Oxford University Press.

Okugawa, G., Yagi, A., Kusaka, H., & Kinoshita, T. (2002). Paroxetine for treatment of somatization disorder. *Journal of Neuropsychiatry Clinical Neuroscience, 14,* 464–465.

Olds, J. (1956). Pleasure centers in the brain. *Scientific American, 195,* 105–116.

Olds, J., & Milner, P. M. (1954). Positive reinforcement produced by electrical stimulation of septal area and other regions of rat brain. *Journal of Comparative and Physiological Psychology, 47,* 419–427.

Olfson, M., Marcus, S., & Schaffer, D. (2006). Antidepressant drug therapy and suicide in severely depressed children and adolescents. *Archives General Psychiatry, 63,* 865–872.

Olfson, M., Shaffer, D., Marcus, S. C., & Greenberg, T. (2003). Relationship between antidepressant medication treatment and suicide in adolescents. *Archives of General Psychiatry, 60,* 978–82.

Olin, S. S., Raine, A., Cannon, T. D., Parnas, J., Schulsinger, F., & Mednick, S. A. (1997). Childhood behavior precursors of schizotypal personality disorder. *Schizophrenia Bulletin, 23,* 93–103.

Olivardia, R., Pope, H. G., & Hudson, J. I. (2000). Muscle dysmorphia in male weightlifters: A case-control study. *American Journal of Psychiatry, 157,* 1291–1296.

Oliver, M. B., & Hyde, J. S. (1993). Gender differences in sexuality: A meta-analysis. *Psychological Bulletin, 114*(1), 29–51.

Ollendick, T. H., & Huntzinger, R. M. (1990). Separation anxiety disorder in childhood. In M. Hersen & C. G. Last (Eds.), *Handbook of child and adult psychopathology: A longitudinal perspective.* Elmsford, NY: Pergamon Press.

Ono, Y. (2004). Suicide prevention program for the elderly: The experience in Japan.

Onoe, S., & Nishigaki, T. (2004). EEG spectral analysis in children with febrile delirium. *Brain and Development, 26,* 513–518.

Opjordsmoen, S. (1989). Delusional disorders: I. Comparative long-term outcome. *Acta Psychiatrica Scandinavica, 80,* 603–612.

Oquendo, M., Galfalvy, H., Russo, S., Ellis, S., Grunebaum, M., Burke, A., et al. (2004). Prospective study of clinical predictors of suicidal acts after a major depressive episode in patients with major depressive disorder or bipolar disorder. *American Journal of Psychiatry, 161,* 1433–1441.

Orbach, I. (1997). A taxonomy of factors related to suicidal behavior. *Clinical Psychology: Science and Practice, 4,* 205–224.

Orne, M. T., Dinges, D. F., & Orne, E. C. (1984). On the differential diagnosis of multiple personality in the forensic context. *International Journal of Clinical and Experimental Hypnosis, 32,* 118–169.

Orsillo, S. M., Roemer, L., & Barlow, D. H. (2003). Integrating acceptance and mindfulness into existing cognitive-behavioral treatment for GAD: A case study. *Cognitive & Behavioral Practice, 10,* 222–230.

Ortiz, A., & Medicna-Mora, M. E. (1988). Research on drugs in Mexico: Epidemiology of drug abuse and issues among Native American populations. In Community Epidemiology Work Group Proceedings, December 1987. Contract No. 271–87–8321. Washington, DC: U.S. Government Printing Office.

Ossip-Klein, D. J., Doyne, E. J., Bowman, E. D., Osborn, K. M., McDougall-Wilson, I. B., & Neimeyer, R. A. (1989). Effects of running or weight lifting on self-concept in clinically depressed women. *Journal of Consulting and Clinical Psychology, 57*(1), 158–161.

Öst, L. G. (1985). Mode of acquisition of phobias. *Acta Universitatis Uppsaliensis* (Abstracts of Uppsala Dissertations from the Faculty of Medicine), *529,* 1–45.

Öst, L. G. (1987). Age at onset in different phobias. *Journal of Abnormal Psychology, 96,* 223–229.

Öst, L. G. (1989). *Blood phobia: A specific phobia subtype in DSM-IV.* Paper requested by the Simple Phobia subcommittee of the DSM-IV Anxiety Disorders Work Group.

Öst, L. G. (1992). Blood and injection phobia: Background and cognitive, physiological, and behavioral variables. *Journal of Abnormal Psychology, 101*(1), 68–74.

Öst, L. G., & Sterner, U. (1987). Applied tension: A specific behavioural method for treatment of blood phobia. *Behaviour Research and Therapy, 25,* 25–30.

Öst, L. G., Ferebee, I., & Furmark, T. (1997). One session group therapy of spiderphobia: Direct vs. indirect treatments. *BRAT, 35,* 721–732.

Öst, L. G., Svensson, L., Hellström, K., & Lindwall, R. (2001). One-session treatment of specific phobia in youths: A randomized clinical trial. *Journal of Consulting and Clinical Psychology, 69,* 814–824.

Osterberg, E. (1986). Alcohol-related problems in cross-national perspectives: Results of the ISACE study. Special issue: Alcohol and culture: Comparative perspectives from Europe and America (T. Babot, Ed.). *Annals of the New York Academy of Sciences, 472,* 10–20.

Otis, J., & Pincus, D. (in press). Chronic pain. In B. A. Boyer & I. Paharia, (Eds.), *Comprehensive handbook of clinical health psychology.* John Wiley & Son.

Otis, J., Macdonald, A., & Dobscha, A. (2006). Integration and coordination of pain management in primary care. *Journal of Clinical Psychology, 62,* 1333–1343.

Ovsiew, F. (2005). Neuropsychiatry and behavioral neurology. In B. J. Sadock & V. A. Sadock (Eds.), *Kaplan & Sadock's comprehensive textbook of psychiatry* (pp. 323–349). Philadelphia: Lippincott Williams & Wilkins.

Owens, J. A., Rosen, C. L., & Mindell, J. A. (2003). Medication use in the treatment of pediatric insomnia: Results of a survey of community-based pediatricians. *Pediatrics, 111,* 628–635.

Owens, M. J., Mulchahey, J. J., Stout, S. C., & Plotsky, P. M. (1997). Molecular and neurobiological mechanisms in the treatment of psychiatric disorders. In A. Tasman, J. Kay, & J. A. Lieberman (Eds.), *Psychiatry* (Vol. 1, pp. 210–257). Philadelphia: W. B. Saunders.

Oyama, O., & Andrasik, F. (1992). Behavioral strategies in the prevention of disease. In S. M. Turner, K. S. Calhoun, & H. E. Adams (Eds.), *Handbook of clinical behavior therapy* (2nd ed., pp. 397–413). New York: John Wiley.

Page, A. C. (1994). Blood–injury phobia. *Clinical Psychology Review, 14,* 443–461.

Page, A. C. (1996). Blood–injury–injection fears in medical practice. *Medical Journal of Australia, 164,* 189.

Page, A. C., & Martin, N. G. (1998). Testing a genetic structure of blood–injury–injection fears. *American Journal of Medical Genetics (Neuropsychiatric Genetics) 81:* 377–384.

Page, G. G., Ben-Eliyahu, S., Yirmiya, R., & Liebeskind, J. C. (1993). Morphine attenuates surgery-induced enhancement of metastatic colonization in rats. *Pain, 54*(1), 21–28.

Pagel, J. F. (2006). Medications that induce sleepiness. In T. Lee-Chiong (Ed.), *Sleep: A comprehensive handbook* (pp. 175–182). Hoboken, NJ: John Wiley & Sons.

Palace, E. M. (1995). Modification of dysfunctional patterns of sexual response through autonomic arousal and false physiological feedback. *Journal of Consulting and Clinical Psychology, 63,* 604–615.

Palace, E. M., & Gorzalka, B. B. (1990). The enhancing effects of anxiety on arousal in sexually dysfunctional and functional women. *Journal of Abnormal Psychology, 99*(4), 403–411.

Pampallona, S., Bollini, P., Tibaldi, G., Kupelnick, B., & Munizza, C. (2004). Combined pharmacotherapy and psychological treatment for depression. *Archives of General Psychiatry, 61,* 714–719.

Pantaleo, G., Graziosi, C., & Fauci, A. S. (1993). The immunopathogenesis of human immunodeficiency virus infection. *New England Journal of Medicine, 328,* 327–335.

Papillo, J. F., & Shapiro, D. (1990). The cardiovascular system. In J. T. Cacioppo & L. G. Tassinaryo (Eds.), *Principles of psychophysiology: Physical, social, and inferential elements.* New York: Cambridge University Press.

Paquette, V., Lévesque, J., Mensour, B., Leroux, J-M., Beudoin, G., Bourgouin, P., et al. (2003). "Change the mind and you change the brain": Effects of cognitive-behavioral therapy on the neural correlates of spider phobia. *Neuroimage, 18,* 401–409.

Paradis, C. M., Friedman, S., & Hatch, M. (1997). Isolated sleep paralysis in African-Americans with panic disorder. *Cultural Diversity & Mental Health, 3,* 69–76.

Pardini, D., Lochman, J., & Wells, K. (2004). Negative emotions and alcohol use initiation in high-risk boys: The moderating effect of good inhibitory control. *Journal of Abnormal Child Psychology, 32,* 505–518.

Parish, W., Luo, Y., Stolzenberg, R., Laumann, E., Farrer, G., & Pan, S. (2007). Sexual practices and sexual satisfaction: A population based study of Chinese urban adults. *Archives of Sexual Behavior, 36,* 5–20.

Park, D. C. (2007). Eating disorders: A call to arms. *American Psychologist, 62,* 158.

Parker, G., & Hadzi-Pavlovic, D. (1990). Expressed emotion as a predictor of schizophrenic relapse: An analysis of aggregated data. *Psychological Medicine, 20,* 961–965.

Parkes, J. D., & Block, C. (1989). Genetic factors in sleep disorders. *Journal of Neurology, Neurosurgery, and Psychiatry, 52,* 101–108.

Parkinson, L., & Rachman, S. (1981a). Intrusive thoughts: The effects of an uncontrived stress. *Advances in Behaviour Research and Therapy, 3,* 111–118.

Parkinson, L., & Rachman, S. (1981b). Speed of recovery from an uncontrived stress. *Advances in Behaviour Research and Therapy, 3,* 119–123.

Parloff, M. B. (1986). Placebo controls in psychotherapy research: A sine qua non or a placebo for research problems? *Journal of Consulting and Clinical Psychology, 54,* 79–87.

Parry-Jones, B., & Parry-Jones, W. L. (2002). History of bulimia and bulimia nervosa. In K. D. Brownell & C. G. Fairburn (Eds.), *Eating disorders and obesity: A comprehensive handbook* (2nd ed., pp. 145–150). New York: Guilford Press.

Parry-Jones, W. Li., & Parry-Jones, B. (1994). Implications of historical evidence for the classification of eating disorders. *British Journal of Psychiatry, 165,* 287–292.

Parsons, J. T., Kelly, B. C., & Weiser, J. D. (in press). Initiation into methamphetamine use for young gay and bisexual men. *Drug and Alcohol Dependence.*

Pasewark, R. A., & Seidenzahl, D. (1979). Opinions concerning the insanity plea and criminality among mental patients. *Bulletin of the American Academy of Psychiatry and Law, 7,* 199–202.

Pataki, C. S., & Carlson, G. A. (1990). Major depression in childhood. In M. Hersen & C. Last (Eds.), *Handbook of child and adult psychopathology: A longitudinal perspective.* Elmsford, NY: Pergamon Press.

Patrick, C. J. (Ed.) (2006). *Handbook of psychopathy.* New York: Guilford Press.

Patterson, G. R. (1982). *Coercive family process.* Eugene, OR: Castalia.

Patterson, G. R. (1986). Performance models for antisocial boys. *American Psychologist, 41,* 432–444.

Patterson, G. R., & Fleischman, M. J. (1979). Maintenance of treatment effects: Some considerations concerning family systems and follow-up data. *Behavior Therapy, 10,* 168–185.

Patterson, G. R., Cobb, J. A., & Ray, R. S. (1972). Direct intervention in the classroom: A set of procedures for the aggressive child. In F. Clark, D. Evans, & L. Hamerlynck (Eds.), *Implementing behavioral programs for schools and clinics.* Champaign, IL: Research Press.

Patterson, G. R., DeBaryshe, B. D., & Ramsey, E. (1989). A developmental perspective on antisocial behavior. *American Psychologist, 44,* 329–335.

Patton, G. C. (1988). Mortality in eating disorders. *Psychological Medicine, 18*(4), 947–951.

Patton, G. C., Johnson-Sabine, E., Wood, K., Mann, A. H., & Wakeling, A. (1990). Abnormal eating attitudes in London school girls—A prospective epidemiological study: Outcome at twelve month followup. *Psychological Medicine, 20,* 383–394.

Paul, G. L., & Lentz, R. J. (1977). *Psychosocial treatment of chronic mental patients: Milieu versus social learning programs.* Cambridge, MA: Harvard University Press.

Paul, T., Schroeter, K., Dahme, B., & Nutzinger, D. O. (2002). Self-injurious behavior in women with eating disorders. *American Journal of Psychiatry, 159,* 408–411.

Paulesu, E., Demonet, J. F., Fazio, F., McCrory, E., Chanoine, V., Brunswick, N., Cappa, S. F., Cossu, G., Habib, M., Frith, C. D., & Frith, U. (2001). Dyslexia: Cultural diversity and biological unity. *Science, 291*(5511), 2165–2167.

Pauli, P., & Alpers, G. W. (2002). Memory bias in patients with hypochondriasis and somatoform pain disorder. *Journal of Psychosomatic Research, 52,* 45–53.

Pavalko, E. K., Elder, G. H., Jr., & Clipp, E. C. (1993). Worklives and longevity: Insights from a life course perspective. *Journal of Health and Social Behavior, 34,* 363–380.

Paxton, S. J., Schutz, H. K., Wertheim, E. H., & Muir, S. L. (1999). Friendship clique and peer influences on body image concerns, dietary restraint, extreme weight-loss behaviors, and binge eating in adolescent girls. *Journal of Abnormal Psychology, 108,*(2), 255–266.

Paykel, E. S., & Weissman, M. M. (1973). Social adjustment and depression: A longitudinal study. *Archives of General Psychiatry, 28,* 659–663.

Paykel, E. S., Scott, J., & Teasdale, J. D. (1999). Prevention of relapse in residual depression by cognitive therapy: A controlled trial. *Archives of General Psychiatry, 56,* 829–835.

Payne, K., Reissing, E., Lahaie, M., Binik, Y., Amsel, R., & Khalife, S. (2005). What is sexual pain? A critique of DSM's classification of dyspareunia and vaginismus. In Karasic, D., & Drescher, J. (Eds.), *Sexual and gender diagnoses of the Diagnostic and Statistical Manual (DSM): A reevaluation.* New York: Haworth Press.

Pehlivanturk, B., & Unal, F. (2002). Conversion disorder in children and adolescents: A 4-year follow-up study. *Journal of Psychosomatic Research, 52,* 187–191.

Pelayo, R., & Lopes, M. C. (2006). Narcolepsy. In T. Lee-Chiong (Ed.), *Sleep: A comprehensive handbook* (pp. 145–150). Hoboken, NJ: John Wiley & Sons.

Pelham, W. E., Jr. (1999). The NIMH Multimodal Treatment Study for attention-deficit hyperactivity disorder: Just say yes to drugs alone? *Canadian Journal of Psychiatry, 44,* 981–990.

Pendery, M. L., Maltzman, I. M., & West, L. J. (1982). Controlled drinking by alcoholics? New findings and a reevaluation of a major affirmative study. *Science, 217,* 169–175.

Pentz, M. A. (1999). Prevention. In M. Galanter & H. D. Kleber (Eds.), *Textbook of substance abuse treatment* (2nd ed., pp. 535–544). Washington, DC: American Psychiatric Press.

Peplau, L. A. (2003). Human sexuality: How do men and women differ? *Current Directions in Psychological Science, 12,* 37–40.

Pepper, C. M., Klein, D. N., Anderson, R. L., Riso, L. P., Ouimette, P. C., & Lizardi, H. (1995). DSM-III-R Axis II comorbidity in dysthymia and major depression. *American Journal of Psychiatry, 152,* 239–247.

Pereira, D. B., Antoni, M. H., Danielson, A., Simon, T., Efantis-Potter, J., Carver, C. S., et al. (2003). Stress as a predictor of symptomatic genital herpes virus recurrence in women with human immunodeficiency virus. *Journal of Psychosomatic Research, 54*(3), 237–244.

Perez, A., Leifman, S., & Estrada, A. (2003). Reversing the criminalization of mental illness. *Crime & Delinquency, 49,* 62–78.

Pericak-Vance, M. A., Johnson, C. C., Rimmler, J. B., Saunders, A. M., Robinson, L. C., D'Hondt, E. G., et al. (1996). Alzheimer's disease and apolipoprotein E-4 allele in an Amish population. *Annals of Neurology, 39,* 700–704.

Perkins, K. A., Ciccocioppo, M., Jacobs, L., & Doyle, T. (2003). The subjective and reinforcing effects of visual and olfactory stimuli in alcohol drinking.

Experimental and Clinical Psychopharmacology, 11, 269–275.

Perkonigg, A., Pfister, H., Stein, M. B., Hofler, M., Lieb, R., Maercker, A., & Wittchen, H. (2005). Longitudinal course of posttraumatic stress disorder and posttraumatic stress disorder symptoms in a community sample of adolescents and young adults. *American Journal of Psychiatry, 162,* 1320–1327.

Perlin, M. L. (2000). *The hidden prejudice: Mental disability on trial.* Washington, DC: American Psychological Association.

Perlis, M. L., Smith, L. J., Lyness, J. M., Matteson, S. R., Pigeon, W. R., Jungquist, C. R., & Tu, X. (2006). Insomnia as a risk factor for onset of depression in the elderly. *Behavioral Sleep Medicine, 4,* 104–113.

Perlstein, T., Yonkers, K. A., Fayyad, R., & Gillespie, J. A. (2005). Pretreatment pattern of symptom expression in premenstrual dysphoric disorder. *Journal of Affective Disorder, 85,* 275–282.

Perri, M. G., Nezu, A. M., McKelvey, W. F., Shermer, R. L., Renjilian, D. A., & Viegener, B. J. (2001). Relapse prevention training and problem-solving therapy in the long-term management of obesity. *Journal of Consulting and Clinical Psychology, 69,* 722–726.

Perry, A., Tarrier, N., Morriss, R., McCarthy, E., & Limb, K. (1999). Randomised controlled trial of efficacy of teaching patients with bipolar disorder to identify early symptoms of relapse and obtain treatment. *British Medical Journal, 318,* 149–153.

Perry, J. C. (1993). Longitudinal studies of personality disorders. *Journal of Personality Disorders, 7,* 63–85.

Person, D. C., & Borkovec, T. D. (1995, August). *Anxiety disorders among the elderly: Patterns and issues.* Paper presented at the 103rd annual meeting of the American Psychological Association. New York.

Peselow, E. D., Fieve, R. R., Difiglia, C., & Sanfilipo, M. P. (1994). Lithium prophylaxis of bipolar illness: The value of combination treatment. *British Journal of Psychiatry, 164,* 208–214.

Peters, C. P. (1991). Concepts of schizophrenia after Kraepelin and Bleuler. In J. G. Howells (Ed.), *The concept of schizophrenia: Historical perspectives* (pp. 93–107). Washington, DC: American Psychiatric Press.

Petersen, A. C., Compas, B. E., Brooks-Gunn, J., Stemmler, M., Ey, S., & Grant, K. E. (1993). Depression in adolescence. *American Psychologist, 48*(2), 155–168.

Peterson, C. B., Mitchell, J. E., Engbloom, S., Nugent, S., Mussell, M. P., & Miller, J. P. (1998). Group cognitive-behavioral treatment of binge eating disorders: A comparison of therapist-led versus self-help formats. *International Journal of Eating Disorders, 24,* 125–136.

Peterson, D. R. (1968). *The clinical study of social behavior.* New York: Appleton-Century-Crofts.

Peterson, L., & Roberts, M. C. (1992). Complacency, misdirection, and effective prevention of children's injuries. *American Psychologist, 47*(8), 1040–1044.

Peterson, L., & Thiele, C. (1988). Home safety at school. *Child and Family Behavior Therapy, 10*(1), 1–8.

Peterson, L., Farmer, J., & Kashani, J. H. (1990). Parental injury prevention endeavors: A function of health beliefs? *Health Psychology, 9*(2), 177–191.

Petit, L., Azad, N., Byszewski, A., Sarazan, F. F. A., & Power, B. (2003). Non-pharmacological management of primary and secondary insomnia among older people: Review of assessment tools and treatments. *Age and Ageing, 32,* 19–25.

Petrill, S. A., Deater-Deckard, K., Thompson, L. A., DeThorne, L. S., & Schatschneider, C. (2006). Reading skills in early readers: Genetic and shared environmental influences. *Journal of Learning Disabilities, 39,* 48–55.

Pfohl, B. (1991). Histrionic personality disorder: A review of available data and recommendations for DSM-IV. *Journal of Personality Disorders, 5,* 150–166.

Phelan, S., & Wadden, T. A. (2004). Behavioral assessment of obesity. In J. K. Thompson (Ed.), Handbook of eating disorders and obesity (pp. 393–420). New York: John Wiley.

Phifer, J. F., & Murrell, S. A. (1986). Etiologic factors in the onset of depressive symptoms in older adults. Journal of Abnormal Psychology, 95, 282–291.

Philips, H. C., & Grant, L. (1991). Acute back pain: A psychological analysis. Behaviour Research and Therapy, 29, 429–434.

Phillips, K. A. (1991). Body dysmorphic disorder: The distress of imagined ugliness. American Journal of Psychiatry, 148, 1138–1149.

Phillips, K. A. (2000). Quality of life for patients with body dysmorphic disorder. Journal of Nervous and Mental Disease, 188(3), 170–175.

Phillips, K. A., & Gunderson, J. G. (2000). Personality disorders. In M. H. Kryger, T. Roth, & W. C. Dement (Eds.), Principles and practice of sleep medicine (3rd ed., pp. 795–823). Philadelphia: W. B. Saunders.

Phillips, K. A., & Stout, R. (2006). Association in the longitudinal course of body dysmorphic disorder with major depression, obsessive compulsive disorder, and social phobia. Journal of Psychiatric Research, 40, 360–369.

Phillips, K. A., Albertini, R. S., & Rasmussen, S. A. (2002). A randomized placebo-controlled trial of fluoxetine in body dysmorphic disorder. Evidence-based mental health, 5, 119.

Phillips, K. A., Dufresne, R. G., Wilkel, C. S., & Vittorio, C. C. (2000). Rate of body dysmorphic disorder in dermatology patients. Journal of the American Academy of Dermatology, 42, 436–441.

Phillips, K. A., Grant, J., Sinicalchi, J., & Albertini, R. S. (2001). Surgical and nonpsychiatric medical treatment of patients with body dysmorphic disorder. Psychosomatics, 42, 504–510.

Phillips, K. A., McElroy, S. L., Keck, P. E., Jr., Pope, H. G., Jr., & Hudson, J. I. (1993). Body dysmorphic disorder: 30 cases of imagined ugliness. American Journal of Psychiatry, 150, 302–308.

Phillips, K. A., Menard, W., Fay, C., & Pagano, M. E. (2005). Psychosocial functioning and quality of life in body dysmorphic disorder. Comprehensive Psychiatry, 46(4), 254–260.

Phillips, K. A., Menard, W., Fay, C., & Weisberg, R. (2005). Demographic characteristics, phenomenology, comorbidity, and family history in 200 individuals with body dysmorphic disorder. Psychosomatics, 46, 317–325.

Phillips, K. A., Menard, W., Pagano, M., Fay, C., & Stout, R. (2006). Delusional versus nondelusional body dysmorphic disorder: Clinical features and course of illness. Journal of Psychiatric Research, 40, 95–104.

Phillips, K. A., Pagano, M., Menard, W., & Stout, R. (2006). A 12-month follow-up study of the course of body dysmorphic disorder. American Journal of Psychiatry, 163, 907–912.

Phillips, K. A., Yen, S., & Gunderson, J. G. (2003). Personality disorders. In R. E. Hales & S. C. Yudofsky (Eds.), Textbook of clinical psychiatry (4th ed., pp. 804–832). Washington, DC: American Psychiatric Publishing.

Phillips, L. J., Francey, S. M., Edwards, J., & McMurray, N. (2007). Stress and psychosis: Towards the development of new models of investigation. Clinical Psychology Review, 27, 307–317.

Phillips, M. R., Li, X., & Zhang, Y. (2002). Suicide rates in China, 1995–99. Lancet, 359, 835–840.

Phillips, M. R., Shen, Q., Liu, X., Pritker, S., Streiner, D., Conner, K., & Yang, G. (2007). Assessing depressive symptoms in persons who die of suicide in mainland China. Journal of Affective Disorders, 98, 73–82.

Pierce, K. A., & Kirkpatrick, D. R. (1992). Do men lie on fear surveys? Behaviour Research and Therapy, 30, 415–418.

Pihl, R. O., Peterson, J. B., & Lau, M. A. (1993). A biosocial model of the alcohol-aggression relationship. Journal of Studies on Alcohol (Suppl. 11), 128–139.

Pike, K. M., & Rodin, J. (1991). Mothers, daughters, and disordered eating. Journal of Abnormal Psychology, 100(2), 198–204.

Pike, K. M., Devlin, M. J., & Loeb, C. (2004). Cognitive-behavioral therapy in the treatment of anorexia nervosa, and binge eating disorder. In J. K. Thompson (Ed.), Handbook of eating disorders and obesity (pp. 130–162). New York: John Wiley.

Pike, K. M., Loeb, K., & Vitousek, K. (1996). Cognitive-behavioral therapy for anorexia nervosa and bulimia nervosa. In J. K. Thompson (Ed.), Body image, eating disorders and obesity (pp. 253–302). Washington, DC: American Psychological Association.

Pike, K. M., Walsh, B. T., Vitousek, K., Wilson, G. T., & Bauer, J. (2003). Cognitive behavior therapy in the posthospitalization treatment of anorexia nervosa. American Journal of Psychiatry, 160, 2046–2048.

Pilowsky, I. (1970). Primary and secondary hypochondriasis. Acta Psychiatrica Scandinavica, 46, 273–285.

Pinel, P. (1962). A treatise on insanity. New York: Hafner. (Original work published in 1801.)

Pinel, P. H. (1809). Traité medico-philosophique sur l'aliénation mentale. Paris: Chez J. Ant Brosson.

Pirke, K. M., Schweiger, U., & Fichter, M. M. (1987). Hypothalamic–pituitary–ovarian axis in bulimia. In J. I. Hudson & H. G. Pope (Eds.), The psychobiology of bulimia (pp. 15–28). Washington, DC: American Psychiatric Press.

Pithers, W. D., Martin, G. R., & Cumming, G. F. (1989). Vermont treatment program for sexual aggressors. In D. R. Laws (Ed.), Relapse prevention with sex offenders (pp. 292–310). New York: Guilford Press.

Plomin, R. (1990). The role of inheritance in behavior. Science, 248, 183–188.

Plomin, R., & Kovas, Y. (2005). Generalist genes and learning disabilities. Psychological Bulletin, 131, 592–617.

Plomin, R., DeFries, J. C., McClearn, G. E., & Rutter, M. (1997). Behavioral Genetics: A primer (3rd ed.). New York: Freeman.

Plomin, R., McClearn, G. E., Smith, D. L., Skuder, P., Vignetti, S., Chorney, M. J., et al. (1995). Allelic association between 100 DNA markers and high versus low IQ. Intelligence, 21, 31–48.

Podewils, L. J., Guallar, E., Kuller, L. H., Fried, L. P., Lopez, O. L., Carlson, M., & Lyketsos, C. G. (2005). Physical activity, APOE genotype, and dementia risk: Findings from the Cardiovascular Health Cognition Study. American Journal of Epidemiology, 161, 639–651.

Polanczyk, G., de Lima, M. S., Horta, B. L., Biederman, J., & Rohde, L. A. (2007). The worldwide prevalence of ADHD: A systematic review and metaregression analysis. American Journal of Psychiatry, 164, 942–948.

Polanczyk, G., Zeni, C., Genro, J. P., Guimaraes, A. P., Roman, T., Hutz, M. H., & Rohde, L. A. (2007). Association of the adrenergic {alpha}2A receptor gene with methylphenidate improvement of inattentive symptoms in children and adolescents with attention-deficit/hyperactivity disorder. Archives of General Psychiatry, 64, 218–224.

Polich, J., Pollock, V. E., & Bloom, F. E. (1994). Meta-analysis of P300 amplitude from males at risk for alcoholism. Psychological Bulletin, 115, 55–73.

Polivy, J. M., & Herman, C. P. (1993). Etiology of binge eating: Psychological mechanisms. In C. G. Fairburn & G. T. Wilson (Eds.), Binge eating: Nature, assessment, and treatment. New York: Guilford Press.

Polivy, J., & Herman, C. P. (2002). Dieting and its relation to eating disorder. In K. D. Brownell & C. G. Fairburn (Eds.), Eating disorders and obesity: A comprehensive handbook (2nd ed., pp. 83–86). New York: Guilford Press.

Pollack, C., & Andrews, G. (1989). Defense styles associated with specific anxiety disorders. American Journal of Psychiatry, 146, 1500–1502.

Pollack, M. H. (2005). The pharmacotherapy of panic disorder. Journal of Clinical Psychiatry, 66, 23–27.

Polloway, E. A., Schewel, R., & Patton, J. R. (1992). Learning disabilities in adulthood: Personal perspectives. Journal of Learning Disabilities, 25, 520–522.

Polnitsky, C. A. (2006). Fatal familial insomnia. In T. Lee-Chiong (Ed.), Sleep: A comprehensive handbook (pp. 111–115). Hoboken, NJ: John Wiley & Sons.

Polonsky, D. C. (2000). Premature ejaculation. In S. R. Leiblum & R. C. Rosen (Eds.), Principles and practice of sex therapy (3rd ed., pp. 305–332). New York: Guilford Press.

Pomeroy, C. (2004). Assessment of medical status and physical factors. In J. K. Thompson (Ed.), Handbook of eating disorders and obesity (pp. 81–111). New York: John Wiley.

Pope, C., Pope, H., Menard, W., Fay, C., Olivardia, R., & Phillips, K. (2005). Clinical features of muscle dysmorphia among males with body dysmorphic disorder. Body Image, 4, 395–400.

Pope, H. D., Jr., Oliva, P. S., Hudson, J. I., Bodkin, J. A., & Gruber, A. J. (1999). Attitudes toward DSM-IV dissociative disorders diagnoses among board-certified American psychiatrists. American Journal of Psychiatry, 156(2), 321–323.

Pope, H. G., & Brower, K. J. (2005). Anabolic–androgenic steroid abuse. In B. J. Sadock & V. A. Sadock (Eds.), Kaplan & Sadock's comprehensive textbook of psychiatry (pp. 1318–1328). Philadelphia: Lippincott, Williams & Wilkins.

Pope, H. G., Jr., Gruber, A. J., Mangweth, B., Bureau, B., deCol, C., Jouvent, R., & Hudson, J. I. (2000). Body image perception among men in three countries. American Journal of Psychiatry, 157, 1297–1301.

Pope, K. S. (1996). Memory, abuse and science: Questioning claims about the false memory syndrome epidemic. American Psychologist, 51, 957–974.

Pope, K. S. (1997). Science as careful questioning: Are claims of a false memory syndrome epidemic based on empirical evidence? American Psychologist, 52, 997–1006.

Portenoy, R. K., & Payne, R. (1997). Acute and chronic pain. In J. H. Lowinson, P. Ruiz, R. B. Millman, & J. G. Langrod (Eds.), Substance abuse: A comprehensive textbook (pp. 563–589). Baltimore: Williams & Wilkins.

Porter, S., Jackson, K., Trosclair, A., & Pederson, L. L. (2003). Prevalence of current cigarette smoking among adults and changes in prevalence of current and some day smoking—United States, 1996–2001. The JAMA, 289(18), 2355–2356.

Post, R. M. (1992). Transduction of psychosocial stress into the neurobiology of recurrent affective disorder. American Journal of Psychiatry, 149(8), 999–1010.

Post, R. M., Rubinow, D. R., Uhde, T. W., Roy-Byrne, P. P., Linnoila, M., Rosoff, A., & Cowdry, R. (1989). Dysphoric mania: Clinical and biological correlates. Archives of General Psychiatry, 46, 353–358.

Potenza, M. N., Steinberg, M. A., Skudlarski, P., Fulbright, R. K., Lacadie, C. M., Wilber, M. K., Rounsaville, B. J., Gore, J. C., & Wexler, B. E. (2003). Gambling urges in pathological gambling: A functional magnetic resonance imaging study. Archives of General Psychiatry, 60, 828–836.

Powell, R. A., & Howell, A. J. (1998). Effectiveness of treatment for dissociative identity disorder. Psychological Reports, 83, 483–490.

Poznanski, E. O., Israel, M. C., & Grossman, J. A. (1984). Hypomania in a four year old. Journal of the American Academy of Child Psychiatry, 23(1), 105–110.

Prause, N., & Janssen, E. (2006). Blood flow: Vaginal photoplethysmography. In Goldstein, I., Meston, C. M., Davis, S. R., & Traish, A. M. (Eds.), Women's sexual function and dysfunction: Study, diagnostic and treatment (pp. 359–367). New York: Taylor and Francis.

Prelior, E. F., Yutzy, S. H., Dean, J. T., & Wetzel, R. D. (1993). Briquet's syndrome, dissociation and abuse. *American Journal of Psychiatry, 150,* 1507–1511.

President's New Freedom Commission on Mental Health. (2003). *Achieving the promise: Transforming mental health care in America—Final report* (DHHS Pub. No. SMA-03–3832). Rockville, MD: Substance Abuse and Mental Health Services Administration.

Preskorn, S. H. (1995). Comparison of the tolerability of bupropion, fluoxetine, imipramine, nefazodone, paroxetine, sertraline, and venlafaxine. *Journal of Clinical Psychiatry, 56*(Suppl. 6), 12–21.

Presley, C. A., & Meilman, P. W. (1992). *Alcohol and drugs on American college campuses: A report to college presidents.* Carbondale: Southern Illinois University Press.

Pridal, C. G., & LoPiccolo, J. (2000). Multielement treatment of desire disorders: Integration of cognitive, behavioral and systemic therapy. In S. R. Leiblum & R. C. Rosen (Eds.), *Principles and practice of sex therapy* (3rd ed., pp. 57–81). New York: Guilford Press.

Prien, R. F., & Kupfer, D. J. (1986). Continuation drug therapy for major depressive episodes: How long should it be maintained? *American Journal of Psychiatry, 143*(1), 18–23.

Prien, R. F., & Potter, W. Z. (1993). Maintenance treatment for mood disorders. In D. L. Dunner (Ed.), *Current psychiatric therapy* (pp. 255–260). Philadelphia: W. B. Saunders.

Prien, R. F., Kupfer, D. J., Mansky, P. A., Small, J. G., Tuason, V. B., Voss, C. B., & Johnson, W. E. (1984). Drug therapy in the prevention of recurrences in unipolar and bipolar affective disorders: Report of the NIMH collaborative study group comparing lithium carbonate, imipramine and a lithium carbonate–imipramine combination. *Archives of General Psychiatry, 41,* 1096–1104.

Prince, M. (1906–1907). Hysteria from the point of view of dissociated personality. *Journal of Abnormal Psychology, 1,* 170–187.

Prins, J., van der Meer, J., & Bleijenberg, G. (2006). Chronic fatigue syndrome. *Lancet, 367,* 346–355.

Pritchett, D. B., Lüddens, H., & Seeburg, P. H. (1989). Importance of a novel GABA receptor subunit for benzodiazepine pharmacology. *Nature, 338,* 582–585.

Pro-Ana-Nation. (n.d.). Available at http://www.pro-ana-nation.com//.

Project MATCH Research Group. (1993). Project MATCH: Rationale and methods for a multisite clinical trial matching patients to alcoholism treatment. *Alcoholism: Clinical and Experimental Research, 17,* 1130–1145.

Project MATCH Research Group. (1997). Matching alcoholism treatments to client heterogeneity: Project MATCH: Posttreatment drinking outcomes. *Journal of Studies on Alcohol, 58,* 7–29.

Project MATCH Research Group. (1998). Matching alcoholism treatments to client heterogeneity: Treatment main effects and matching effects on drinking during treatment. *Journal of Studies on Alcohol, 59*(6), 631–639.

Prudic, J., Sackeim, H. A., & Devanand, D. P. (1990). Medication resistance and clinical response to electroconvulsive therapy. *Psychiatry Research, 31,* 287–296.

Pruzinsky, T. (1988). Collaboration of plastic surgeon and medical psychotherapist: Elective cosmetic surgery. *Medical Psychotherapy, 1,* 1–13.

Pueschel, S. M., & Goldstein, A. (1991). Genetic counseling. In J. L. Matson & J. A. Mulick (Eds.), *Handbook of mental retardation* (2nd ed., pp. 279–291). Elmsford, NY: Pergamon Press.

Pugliese, M. T., Weyman-Daun, M., Moses, N., & Lifshitz, F. (1987). Parental health beliefs as a cause of nonorganic failure to thrive. *Pediatrics, 80,* 175–182.

Puhan, M. A, Suarez, A., Lo Cascio, C., Zahn, A., Heitz, M., & Braendli, O. (2006). Didgeridoo playing as alternative treatment for obstructive sleep apnoea syndrome: Randomised controlled trial. *British Medical Journal, 332,* 266–270.

Puig-Antich, J. (1982). Major depression and conduct disorder in prepuberty. *Journal of the American Academy of Child Psychiatry, 21,* 118–128.

Puig-Antich, J., & Rabinovich, H. (1986). Relationship between affective and anxiety disorders in childhood. In R. G. Helman (Ed.), *Anxiety disorders of childhood* (pp. 136–156). New York: John Wiley.

Pulsifer, M. B., Winterkorn, E. B., & Thiele, E. A. (2007). Psychological profile of adults with tuberous sclerosis complex. *Epilepsy & Behavior, 10,* 402–406.

Purdon, C. (1999). Thought suppression and psychopathology. *Behaviour Research and Therapy, 37,* 1029–1054.

Purdy, D., & Frank, E. (1993). Should postpartum mood disorders be given a more prominent or distinct place in DSM-IV? *Depression, 1,* 59–70.

Pury, C. L. S., & Mineka, S. (1997). Covariation bias for blood–injury stimuli and aversion outcomes. *Behavior Research and Therapy, 35,* 35–47.

Putnam, F. W. (1989). *Diagnosis and treatment of multiple personality disorder.* New York: Guilford Press.

Putnam, F. W. (1991). Dissociative phenomena. In A. Tasman & S. M. Goldinger (Eds.), *American Psychiatric Press review of psychiatry* (Vol. 10). Washington, DC: American Psychiatric Press.

Putnam, F. W. (1992). Altered states: Peeling away the layers of a multiple personality. *Sciences, 32*(6), 30–36.

Putnam, F. W. (1997). *Dissociation in children and adolescents: A developmental perspective.* New York: Guilford Press.

Putnam, F. W., & Loewenstein, R. J. (1993). Treatment of multiple personality disorder: A survey of current practices. *American Journal of Psychiatry, 150,* 1048–1052.

Putnam, F. W., Guroff, J. J., Silberman, E. K., Barban, L., & Post, R. M. (1986). The clinical phenomenology of multiple personality disorder: Review of 100 recent cases. *Journal of Clinical Psychiatry, 47,* 285–293.

Quality Assurance Project. (1990). Treatment outlines for paranoid, schizotypal and schizoid personality disorders. *Australian and New Zealand Journal of Psychiatry, 24,* 339–350.

Quay, H. C. (1965). Psychopathic personality as pathological stimulation seeking. *American Journal of Psychiatry, 122,* 180–183.

Quay, H. C. (1993). The psychobiology of undersocialized aggressive conduct disorder: A theoretical perspective. *Development and Psychopathology, 5,* 165–180.

Quitkin, F. M., Stewart, J. W., McGrath, P. J., Liebowitz, M. R., Harrison, W. M., Tricamo, E., et al. (1988). Phenelzine versus imipramine in the treatment of probable atypical depression: Defining syndrome boundaries of selective MAOI responders. *American Journal of Psychiatry, 145,* 306–311.

Rabins, P. V. (2006). *Guideline watch: Practice guidelines for the treatment of patients with Alzheimer's disease and other dementias of late life.* Washington, DC: American Psychiatric Association.

Rachman, S. (1978). *Fear and courage.* San Francisco: W. H. Freeman.

Rachman, S. (1991). Neo-conditioning and the classical theory of fear acquisition. *Clinical Psychology Review, 11,* 155–173.

Rachman, S. (2002). Fears born and bred: Non-associative fear acquisition? *Behaviour Research and Therapy, 40,* 121–126.

Rachman, S. (2006). *Fear of Contamination.* New York: Oxford University Press.

Rachman, S., & de Silva, P. (1978). Abnormal and normal obsessions. *Behaviour Research and Therapy, 16,* 233–248.

Rachman, S., & Hodgson, R. (1968). Experimentally induced "sexual fetishism": Replication and development. *Psychological Record, 18*(1), 25–27.

Radnitz, C. L., Appelbaum, K. A., Blanchard, E. B., Elliott, L., & Andrasik, F. (1988). The effect of self-regulatory treatment on pain behavior in chronic headache. *Behaviour Research and Therapy, 26,* 253–260.

Rado, S. (1962). Theory and therapy: The theory of schizotypal organization and its application to the treatment of decompensated schizotypal behavior. In S. Rado (Ed.), *Psychoanalysis of behavior* (Vol. 2, pp. 127–140). New York: Grune & Stratton.

Radomsky, A. S., & Taylor, S. (2005). Subtyping OCD: Prospects and problems. *Behavior Therapy, 36,* 371–379.

Rahkonen, T., Eloniemi-Sulkava, U., Paanila, S., Halonen, P., Sivenius, J., & Sulkava, R. (2001). Systematic intervention for supporting community care of elderly people after a delirium episode. *International Psychogeriatrics, 13*(1), 37–49.

Raich, R. M., Rosen, J. C., Deus, J., Perez, O., Requiena, A., & Gross, J. (1992). Eating disorder symptoms among adolescents in the United States and Spain: A comparative study. *International Journal of Eating Disorders, 11,* 63–72.

Raine, A., Venables, P. H., & Williams, M. (1990). Relationships between central and autonomic measures of arousal at age 15 years and criminality at age 24 years. *Archives of General Psychiatry, 47,* 1003–1007.

Ramachandran, V. S. (1993). Filling in the gaps in perception II: Scotomas and phantom limbs. *Current Directions in Psychological Science, 2,* 56–65.

Ramchandani, P., Stein, A., Evans, J., O'Connor, T., & the ALSPAC Study Team. (2005). Paternal depression in the postnatal period and child development: A prospective population study. *Lancet, 365,* 2201–2205.

Ramey, C. T., & Ramey, S. L. (1992). Effective early intervention. *Mental Retardation, 30,* 337–345.

Ramsawh, H., Raffa, S. D., White, K. S., & Barlow, D. H. (in press). *Isolated sleep paralysis: Anxiety sensitivity and other risk factors in an African American sample.*

Ramsawh, H. J., Morgentaler, A., Covino, N., Barlow, D. H., & DeWolf, W. C. (2005). Quality of life following simultaneous placement of penile prosthesis with radical prostatectomy. *Journal of Urology, 174* (4, Part 1 of 2), 1395–1398.

Ranjith, G., & Mohan, R. (2004). Dhat syndrome: A functional somatic syndrome? {Letter to the editor}. *British Journal of Psychiatry,* pp. 200–209.

Rao, U., Dahl, R. E., Ryan, N. D., Birmaher, B., Williamson, D. E., Rao, R., et al. (2002). Heterogeneity in EEG sleep findings in adolescent depression: Unipolar versus bipolar clinical course. *Journal of Affective Disorders, 70,* 273–280.

Rapee, R. M., & Melville, L. F. (1997). Recall of family factors in social phobia and panic disorder: Comparison of mother and offspring reports. *Depression and Anxiety, 5,* 7–11.

Rapkin, A. J., Chang, L. C., & Reading, A. E. (1989). Mood and cognitive style in premenstrual syndrome. *Obstetrics and Gynecology, 74,* 644–649.

Rapp, S. R., Parisi, S. A., & Wallace, C. E. (1991). Comorbid psychiatric disorders in elderly medical patients: A 1-year prospective study. *Journal of the American Geriatrics Society, 39*(2), 124–131.

Rapport, M. D. (2001). Bridging theory and practice: Conceptual understanding of treatments for children with attention deficit hyperactivity disorder (ADHD), obsessive-compulsive disorder (OCD), autism, and depression. *Journal of Clinical Child Psychology, 30*(1), 3–7.

Rasmussen, S. A., & Eisen, J. L. (1990). Epidemiology of obsessive-compulsive disorder. *Journal of Clinical Psychiatry, 51,* 10–14.

Rasmussen, S. A., & Tsuang, M. T. (1984). The epidemiology of obsessive-compulsive disorder. *Journal of Clinical Psychiatry, 45,* 450–457.

Rasmussen, S. A., & Tsuang, M. T. (1986). Clinical characteristics and family history in DSM-III obsessive-compulsive disorder. *American Journal of Psychiatry, 143,* 317–322.

Rasmusson, A. M., Anderson, G. M., Krishnan-Sarin, S., Wu, R., & Paliwal, P. (2006). A decrease in plasma DHEA to cortisol ratio during smoking abstinence may predict relapse: A preliminary study. *Psychopharmacology, 186,* 473–480.

Rassin, E., & Koster, E. (2003). The correlation between thought–action fusion and religiosity in a normal sample. *Behaviour Research and Therapy, 41,* 361–368.

Rathod, N. H., Addenbrooke, W. M., & Rosenbach, A. F. (2005). Heroin dependence in an English town: 33-year follow-up. *British Journal of Psychiatry, 187,* 421–425.

Ratnasuriya, R. H., Eisler, I., Szmukler, G. I., & Russell, G. F. (1991). Anorexia nervosa: Outcome and prognostic factors after 20 years. *British Journal of Psychiatry, 158,* 495–502.

Rauch, S. L., Phillips, K. A., Segal, E., Markis, N., Shin, L. M., Whalen, P. J., et al. (2003). A preliminary morphometric magnetic resonance imaging study of regional brain volumes in body dysmorphic disorder. *Psychiatry Research, 122,* 13–19.

Ravussin, E., Valencia, M. E., Esparza, J., Bennett, P. H., & Schulz, L. O. (1994). Effects of a traditional lifestyle on obesity in Pima Indians. *Diabetes Care, 17,* 1067–1074.

Ray, W. A., Fought, R. L., & Decker, M. D. (1992). Psychoactive drugs and the risk of injurious motor vehicle crashes in elderly drivers. *American Journal of Epidemiology, 136,* 873–883.

Ray, W. A., Gurwitz, J., Decker, M. D., & Kennedy, D. L. (1992). Medications and the safety of the older driver: Is there a basis for concern? Special issue: Safety and mobility of elderly drivers: II. *Human Factors, 34*(1), 33–47.

Raymond, N. C., Coleman, E., Ohlerking, F., Christenson, G. A., & Miner, M. (1999). Psychiatric comorbidity in pedophilic sex offenders. *American Journal of Psychiatry, 156,* 786–788.

Razran, G. (1961). The observable unconscious and the inferable conscious in current Soviet psychophysiology: Interoceptive conditioning, semantic conditioning, and the orienting reflex. *Psychological Review, 68,* 81–150.

Rea, M., Tompson, M. C., & Miklowitz, D. J. (2003). Family-focused treatment versus individual treatment for bipolar disorder: Results of a randomized clinical trial. *Journal of Consulting and Clinical Psychology, 71,* 482–492.

Redd, W. H., & Andrykowski, M. A. (1982). Behavioral intervention in cancer treatment: Controlling aversion reactions to chemotherapy. *Journal of Consulting and Clinical Psychology, 50,* 1018–1029.

Rehm, L. P., Kaslow, N. J., & Rabin, A. S. (1987). Cognitive and behavioral targets in a self-control therapy program for depression. *Journal of Consulting and Clinical Psychology, 55*(1), 60–67.

Reichardt, C. S. (2006). The principle of parallelism in the design of studies to estimate treatment effects. *Psychological Methods, 11,* 1–18.

Reif, A., & Pfuhlmann, B. (2004). Folie à deux versus genetically driven delusional disorder: Case reports and nosological considerations. *Comprehensive Psychiatry, 45,* 155–160.

Reilly-Harrington, N. A., Alloy, L. B., Fresco, D. M., & Whitehouse, W. G. (1999). Cognitive styles and life events interact to predict bipolar and unipolar symptomatology. *Journal of Abnormal Psychology, 108*(4), 567–578.

Reiman, E. M., Webster, J. A., Myers, A. J., Hardy, J., Dunckley, T., Zismann, V. L., et al. (2007). GAB2 alleles modify Alzheimer's risk in APOE E4 carriers. *Neuron, 54,* 713–720.

Reiss, A. L. (1985). Developmental manifestations in a boy with prepubertal bipolar disorder. *Journal of Clinical Psychiatry, 46*(10), 441–443.

Reiss, S., Peterson, R. A., Gursky, D. M., & McNally, R. J. (1986). Anxiety sensitivity, anxiety frequency, and the prediction of fearfulness. *Behaviour Research and Therapy, 24,* 1–8.

Reitan, R. M., & Davison, I. A. (1974). *Clinical neuropsychology: Current status and applications.* Washington, DC: V. H. Winston.

Rekers, G. A., Kilgus, M., & Rosen, A. C. (1990). Long-term effects of treatment for gender identity disorder of childhood. *Journal of Psychology & Human Sexuality, 3*(2), 121–153.

Renneberg, B., Goldstein, A. J., Phillips, D., & Chambless, D. L. (1990). Intensive behavioral group treatment of avoidant personality disorder. *Behavior Therapy, 21,* 363–377.

Report of the Advisory Panel on Alzheimer's Disease. (1995). *Alzheimer's disease and related dementias: Biomedical update.* U.S. Department of Health and Human Services. Washington, DC: U.S. Government Printing Office.

Repp, A. C., & Singh, N. N. (1990). *Perspectives on the use of nonaversive and aversive interventions for persons with developmental disabilities.* Sycamore, IL: Sycamore Publishing.

Rescorla, R. A. (1988). Pavlovian conditioning: It's not what you think it is. *American Psychologist, 43*(3), 151–160.

Resnick, H. S., Kilpatrick, D. G., Dansky, B. S., Saunders, B. E., & Best, C. L. (1993). Prevalence of civilian trauma in posttraumatic stress disorder in a representative national sample of women. *Journal of Consulting and Clinical Psychology, 61,* 984–991.

Resick, P. A., Monson, C. M., & Rizvi, S. L. (in press). Posttraumatic stress disorder. In D. H. Barlow (Ed.), *Clinical handbook of psychological disorders* (4th ed.). New York: Guilford Press.

Ricciardelli, L. A., & McCabe, M. P. (2004). A biopsychosocial model of disordered eating and the pursuit of muscularity in adolescent boys. *Psychological Bulletin, 130,* 170–205.

Rice, D. P., & MacKenzie, E. J. (1989). *Cost of injury in the United States: A report to Congress.* San Francisco: University of California and Injury Prevention Center, Institute for Health and Aging, and the Johns Hopkins University.

Rice, G., Anderson, C., Risch, N., & Ebers, G. (1999). Male homosexuality: Absence of linkage to microsatellite markers at Xq28. *Science, 284,* 665–667.

Rice, M. E., & Harris, G. T. (2002). Men who molest their sexually immature daughters: Is a special explanation required? *Journal of Abnormal Psychology, 111,* 329–339.

Rice, M. E., Harris, G. T., & Cormier, C. (1992). A follow-up of rapists assessed in a maximum security psychiatric facility. *Journal of Interpersonal Violence, 5,* 435–448.

Richards, R., Kinney, D. K., Lunde, I., Benet, M., & Merzel, A. P. C. (1988). Creativity in manic depressives, cyclothymes, their normal relatives, and control subjects. *Journal of Abnormal Psychology, 97*(3), 281–288.

Richardson, G. S. (2006). Shift work sleep disorder. In T. Lee-Chiong (Ed.), *Sleep: A comprehensive handbook* (pp. 395–399). Hoboken, NJ: John Wiley & Sons.

Rickels, K., Downing, R., Schweizer, E., & Hassman, H. (1993). Antidepressants for the treatment of generalized anxiety disorder. *Archives of General Psychiatry, 50,* 884–895.

Rickels, K., Rynn, M., Ivengar, M., & Duff, D. (2006). Remission of generalized anxiety disorder: A review of the paroxetine clinical trials database. *Journal of Clinical Psychiatry, 67,* 41–47.

Rickels, K., Schweizer, E., Case, W. G., & Greenblatt, D. J. (1990). Long-term therapeutic use of benzodiazepines: I. Effects of abrupt discontinuation. *Archives of General Psychiatry, 47,* 899–907.

Riding, A. (1992, November 17). New catechism for Catholics defines sins of modern world. *New York Times,* p. A14.

Rief, W., Hiller, W., & Margraf, J. (1998). Cognitive aspects of hypochondriasis and the somatization syndrome. *Journal of Abnormal Psychology, 107,* 587–595.

Riemann, D., Berger, M., & Voderholzer, U. (2001). Sleep and depression—Results from psychobiological studies: An overview. *Biological Psychology, 57,* 67–103.

Riggins v. Nevada, 112 S. Ct. 1810 (1992).

Riggs, J. E. (1993). Smoking and Alzheimer's disease: Protective effect or differential survival bias? *Lancet, 342,* 793–794.

Rihmer, Z., & Pestality, P. (1999). Bipolar II disorder and suicidal behavior. *The Psychiatric Clinics of North America, 22*(3), 667–674.

Ritenbaugh, C., Shisslak, C., Teufel, N., Leonard-Green, T. K., & Prince, R. (1994). Eating disorders: A cross-cultural review in regard to DSM-IV. In J. E. Mezzich, A. Kleinman, H. Fabrega, B. Good, G. Johnson-Powell, K. M. Lin, S. Manson, & D. Parron (Eds.), *Cultural proposals and supporting papers for DSM-IV.*

Rivera-Tovar, A. D., & Frank, E. (1990). Late luteal phase dysphoric disorder in young women. *American Journal of Psychiatry, 147,* 1634–1636.

Rivera-Tovar, A. D., Pilkonis, P., & Frank, E. (1992). Symptom patterns in late luteal-phase dysphoric disorder. *Journal of Psychopathology and Behavioral Assessment, 14,* 189–199.

Roberts, A., Cash, T., Feingold, A., & Johnson, B. (2006). Are black–white differences in females' body dissatisfaction decreasing? A meta-analytic review. *Journal of Consulting and Clinical Psychology, 74,* 1121–1131.

Roberts, M. W. (2001). Clinic observations of structured parent–child interaction designed to evaluate externalizing disorders. *Psychological Assessment, 13,* 46–58.

Roberts, R. E., Kaplan, G. A., Shema, S. J., & Strawbridge, W. J. (1997). Does growing old increase the risk for depression? *American Journal of Psychiatry, 154,* 1384–1390.

Roberts, R. E., Roberts, C. R., & Chen, I. G. (2000). Ethnocultural differences in sleep complaints among adolescents. *The Journal of Nervous and Mental Disease, 188,* 222–229.

Robertson, D., Snarey, J., Ousley, O., Harenski, K., Bowman, F. D., Gilkey, R., & Kilts, C. (2007). The neural processing of moral sensitivity to issues of justice and care. *Neuropsychologia, 45*(4), 755–766.

Robertson, N. (1988). *Getting better: Inside Alcoholics Anonymous.* New York: William Morrow.

Robins, L. N. (1966). *Deviant children grown up: A sociological and psychiatric study of sociopathic personality.* Baltimore: Williams & Wilkins.

Robins, L. N. (1978). Sturdy childhood predictors of adult antisocial behavior: Replications from longitudinal studies. *Psychological Medicine, 8,* 611–622.

Robins, L. N., Helzer, J. E., & Davis, D. H. (1975). Narcotic use in Southeast Asia and afterwards. *Archives of General Psychiatry, 32,* 955–961.

Robins, L. N., & Regier, D. A. (1991). *Psychiatric disorders in America: The epidemiologic catchment area study.* New York: Free Press.

Robins, S., & Novaco, R. W. (2000). Anger control as a health promotion mechanism. In D. I. Mostofsky & D. H. Barlow (Eds.), *The management of stress and anxiety in medical disorders* (pp. 361–377). Needham Heights, MA: Allyn & Bacon.

Robles, T., Glaser, R., & Kiecolt-Glaser, J. (2005). Out of balance: A new look at chronic stress, depression, and immunity. *Current Directions in Psychological Science, 14,* 111–115.

Rockney, R. M., & Lemke, T. (1992). Casualties from a junior–senior high school during the Persian Gulf war: Toxic poisoning or mass hysteria? *Developmental and Behavioral Pediatrics, 13*(5), 339–342.

Rockwood, K., & Middleton, L. (2007). Physical activity and the maintenance of cognitive function. *Alzheimer's & Dementia, 3,* S38–S44.

Rockwood, K., Stolee, P., & Brahim, A. (1991). Outcomes of admission to a psychogeriatric service. *Canadian Journal of Psychiatry, 36*(4), 275–279.

Rodin, J., & Langer, E. J. (1977). Long-term effects of a controlled relevant intervention with the institutionalized aged. *Journal of Personality and Social Psychology, 35*(12), 897–902.

Rodin, J., & Salovey, P. (1989). Health psychology. *Annual Review of Psychology, 40,* 533–579.

Roelofs, K., Keijsers, G. P., Hoogduin, K. A., Naring, G. W., & Moene, F. C. (2002). Childhood abuse in patients with conversion disorder. *American Journal of Psychiatry, 159,* 1908–1913.

Roemer, L., & Borkovec, T. D. (1993). Worry: Unwanted cognitive activity that controls unwanted somatic experience. In D. M. Wegner & J. W. Pennebaker (Eds.), *Handbook of mental control.* Englewood Cliffs, NJ: Prentice Hall.

Roemer, L., & Orsillo, S. M. (2002). Expanding our conceptualization of and treatment for generalized anxiety disorder: Integrating mindfulness/acceptance-based approaches with existing cognitive-behavioral models. *Clinical Psychology: Science and Practice, 9,* 54–68.

Roemer, L., & Orsillo, S. M. (in press). An open-trial investigation of an acceptance- based behavior therapy for generalized anxiety disorder. *Behavior Therapy.*

Roemer, L., Orsillo, S. M., & Barlow, D. H. (2002). Generalized anxiety disorder. In D. H. Barlow, *Anxiety and its disorders: The nature and treatment of anxiety and panic* (2nd ed.). New York: Guilford Press.

Rogers, C. R. (1961). *On becoming a person.* Boston: Houghton Mifflin.

Rogers, S. L., & Friedhoff, L. T. (1996). The efficacy and safety of donepezil in patients with Alzheimer's disease: Results of a U.S. multicentre, randomized, double-blind, placebo-controlled trial. The Donepezil Study Group. *Dementia, 7,* 293–303.

Rogge, R. D., Cobb, R. J., Story, L. B., Johnson, M. D., Lawrence, E. E., Rothman, A. D., & Bradbury, T. N. (2006). Recruitment and selection of couples for intervention research: Achieving developmental homogeneity at the cost of demographic diversity. *Journal of Consulting and Clinical Psychology, 74,* 777–784.

Rohan, K. J., Roecklein, K. A., Lacy, T. M., & Vacek, P. M. (submitted). Prevention of winter depression recurrence one year after cognitive-behavioral therapy, light therapy, or combination treatment.

Rohan, K. J., Roecklein, K. A., Tierney Lindsey, K., Johnson, L. G., Lippy, R. D., Lacy, T. M., & Barton, F. B. (in press). A randomized controlled trial of cognitive-behavioral therapy, light therapy, and their combination for seasonal affective disorder. *Journal of Consulting and Clinical Psychology.*

Rohan, K. J., Sigmon, S. T., & Dorhofer, D. M. (2003). Cognitive-behavioral factors in seasonal affective disorder. *Journal of Consulting and Clinical Psychology, 71,* 22–30.

Rohde, P., Lewisohn, P., Klein, D., & Seeley, J. (2005). Association of parental depression with psychiatric course from adolescence to young adulthood among formerly depressed individuals. *Journal of Abnormal Psychology, 114,* 409–420.

Roid, G. H., & Pomplun, M. (2005). Interpreting the Stanford–Binet intelligence scales (5th ed.). In D. P. Flanagan & P. L. Harrison, (Eds.), *Contemporary intellectual assessment: Theories, tests, and issues* (2nd ed., pp. 325–343). New York: Guilford Press.

Roitt, I. (1988). *Essential immunology* (6th ed.). Oxford: Blackwell.

Rojo, L., Conesa, L., Bermudez, O., & Livianos, L. (2006). Influence of stress in the onset of eating disorders: Data from a two stage epidemiologic controlled study. (2006). *Psychosomatic Medicine, 68,* 628–635.

Rollman, B. L., Belnap, B. H., & Mazumdar, S. (2005). A randomized trial to improve the quality of treatment for panic and generalized anxiety disorders in primary care. *Archives of General Psychiatry, 62,* 1332–1341.

Roma, P. G., Champoux, M., & Suomi, S. J. (2006). Environmental control, social context, and individual differences in behavioral and cortisol responses to novelty in infant rhesus monkeys. *Child Development, 77,* 118–131.

Romano, J. M., Jensen, M. P., Turner, J. A., Good, A. B., & Hops, H. (2000). Chronic pain patient–partner interactions: Further support for a behavioral model of chronic pain. *Behavior Therapy, 31,* 415–440.

Room, R. (1993). Alcoholics Anonymous as a social movement. In B. S. McCrady & W. R. Miller (Eds.), *Research on Alcoholics Anonymous: Opportunities and alternatives* (pp. 167–187). New Brunswick, NJ: Rutgers Center of Alcohol Studies.

Rorabaugh, W. J. (1991, Fall). Alcohol in America. *OAH Magazine of History,* pp. 17–19.

Rorschach, H. (1951). *Psychodiagnostics.* New York: Grune & Stratton. (Original work published 1921.)

Rosen, J. C., & Leitenberg, H. (1985). Exposure plus response prevention treatment of bulimia. In D. M. Garner & P. E. Garfinkel (Eds.), *Handbook of psychotherapy for anorexia nervosa and bulimia* (pp. 193–209). New York: Guilford Press.

Rosen, J. C., Reiter, J., & Orosan, P. (1995). Cognitive-behavioral body image therapy for body dysmorphic disorder. *Journal of Consulting Clinical Psychology, 63,* 263–269.

Rosen, L. W., Shafer, C. L., Dummer, G. M., Cross, L. K., Deuman, G. W., & Malmberg, S. R. (1988). Prevalence of pathogenic weight-control behaviors among Native American women and girls. *International Journal of Eating Disorders, 7*(6), 807–811.

Rosen, R., Janssen, E., Wiegel, M., Bancroft, J., Althof, S., Wincze, J., et al. (2006). Psychological and interpersonal correlates in men with erectile dysfunction and their partners: A pilot study of treatment outcome with sildenafil. *Journal of Sex & Marital Therapy, 32,* 215–234.

Rosen, R., Wing, R., Schneider, S., & Gendrano, N. (2005). Epidemiology of erectile dysfunction: The role of medical comorbidities and lifestyle factors. *Urological Clinics of North America, 32,* 403–417.

Rosen, R. C. (2000). Medical and psychological interventions for erectile dysfunction: Toward a combined treatment approach. In S. R. Leiblum & R. C. Rosen (Eds.), *Principles and practice of sex therapy* (3rd ed., pp. 276–304). New York: Guilford Press.

Rosen, R. C., & Beck, J. G. (1988). *Patterns of sexual arousal: Psychophysiological processes and clinical applications.* New York: Guilford Press.

Rosen, R. C., & Leiblum, S. R. (1995). Treatment of sexual disorders in the 1990s: An integrated approach. *Journal of Consulting and Clinical Psychology, 63,* 877–890.

Rosenbaum, M. (2000). Psychogenic seizures—Why women? *Psychosomatics, 41*(2), 147–149.

Rosenberg, H. (1993). Prediction of controlled drinking by alcoholics and problem drinkers. *Psychological Bulletin, 113,* 129–139.

Rosenberg, R. N., Richter, R. W., Risser, R. C., Taubman, K., Prado-Farmer, I., Ebalo, E., et al. (1996). Genetic factors for the development of Alzheimer's disease in the Cherokee Indian. *Archives of Neurology, 53,* 997–1000.

Rosengren, A., Tibblin, G., & Wilhelmsen, L. (1991). Self-perceived psychological stress and incidence of coronary artery disease in middle-aged men. *American Journal of Cardiology, 68,* 1171–1175.

Rosenman, R. H., Brand, R. J., Jenkins, C. D., Friedman, M., Straus, R., & Wurm, M. (1975). Coronary heart disease in the Western Collaborative Group Study: Final follow-up experience of 8 years. *JAMA, 233,* 872–877.

Rosenthal, D. (Ed.) (1963). *The Genain quadruplets: A case study and theoretical analysis of heredity and environment in schizophrenia.* New York: Basic Books.

Rosenthal, M. Z., Gratz, K. L., Kosson, D. S., Cheavens, J. S., Lejuez, C. W., & Lynch, T. R. (in press). Borderline personality disorder and emotional responding: A review of the research literature. *Clinical Psychology Review.*

Rosenthal, P. A., & Rosenthal, S. (1984). Suicidal behavior by preschool children. *American Journal of Psychiatry, 141,* 520–525.

Rösler, A., & Witztum, M. D. (1998). Treatment of men with paraphilia with a long-acting analogue of gonadotropin-releasing hormone. *New England Journal of Medicine, 338,* 416–422.

Rosowsky, E., & Gurian, B. (1992). Impact of borderline personality disorder in late life on systems of care. *Hospital and Community Psychiatry, 43,* 386–389.

Ross, A. O., & Pelham, W. E. (1981). Child psychopathology. *Annual Review of Psychology, 32,* 243–278.

Ross, C. A. (1997). *Dissociative identity disorder.* New York: John Wiley.

Ross, C. A., Anderson, G., Fleisher, W. P., & Norton, G. R. (1991). The frequency of multiple personality disorder among psychiatric inpatients. *American Journal of Psychiatry, 148,* 1717–1720.

Ross, C. A., Miller, S. D., Reagor, P., Bjornson, L., Fraser, G. A., & Anderson, G. (1990). Structured interview data on 102 cases of multiple personality disorder from four centers. *American Journal of Psychiatry, 147,* 596–601.

Ross, M. W., Walinder, J., Lundstrom, B., & Thuwe, I. (1981). Cross-cultural approaches to transsexualism: A comparison between Sweden and Australia. *Acta Psychiatrica Scandinavica, 63,* 75–82.

Rossberg, J. I., Karterud, S., Pedersen, G., & Friis, S. (2007). An empirical study of countertransference reactions toward patients with personality disorders. *Comprehensive Psychiatry, 48,* 225–230.

Rothblum, E. D. (2002). Gay and lesbian body images. In T. F. Cash & T. Pruzinsky (Eds.), *Body image: A handbook of theory, research and clinical practice* (pp. 257–265). New York: Guilford Press.

Rottenberg, J., Gross, J., & Gotlib, I. (2005). Emotion content insensitivity in major depressive disorder. *Journal of Abnormal Psychology, 114,* 627–639.

Rottenberg, J., Gross, J. J., Wilhelm, F. H., Najmi, S., & Gotlib, I. H. (2002). Crying threshold and intensity in major depressive disorder. *Journal of Abnormal Psychology, 111,* 302–312.

Rouff, L. (2000). Schizoid personality traits among the homeless mentally ill: A quantitative and qualitative report. *Journal of Social Distress and the Homeless, 9,* 127–141.

Rounsaville, B. J., Alarcon, R. D., Andrews, G., Jackson, J. S., Kendell, R. E., & Kendler, K. (2002). Basic nomenclature issues for DSM-V. In D. J. Kupfer, M. B. First, & D. A. Regier (Eds.), *A research agenda for DSM-V* (pp. 1–29). Washington, DC: American Psychiatric Association.

Rounsaville, B. J., Sholomskas, D., & Prusoff, B. A. (1988). Chronic mood disorders in depressed outpatients: Diagnosis and response to pharmacotherapy. *Journal of Affective Disorders, 2,* 72–88.

Roush, W. (1997). Herbert Benson: Mind–body maverick pushes the envelope. *Science, 276,* 357–359.

Rowell, E. A., & Rowell, R. (1939). *On the trail of marihuana: The weed of madness.* Mountain View, CA: Pacific Press.

Roy, A., Segal, N. L., & Sarchiapone, M. (1995). Attempted suicide among living co-twins of twin suicide victims. *American Journal of Psychiatry, 152,* 1075–1076.

Roy-Byrne, P. P., & Katon, W. (2000). Anxiety management in the medical setting: Rationale, barriers to diagnosis and treatment, and proposed solutions. In D. I. Mostofsky & D. H. Barlow (Eds.), *The management of stress and anxiety in medical disorders* (pp. 1–14). Needham Heights, MA: Allyn & Bacon.

Roy-Byrne, P. P., Craske, M. G., & Stein, M. B. (in press). Panic disorder. *Lancet.*

Rubin, R. T. (1982). Koro (Shook Yang): A culture-bound psychogenic syndrome. In C. T. H. Friedmann & R. A. Fauger (Eds.), *Extraordinary disorders of human behavior* (pp. 155–172). New York: Plenum Press.

Rubinstein, S., & Caballero, B. (2000). Is Miss America an undernourished role model? *JAMA, 283,* 1569.

Ruchkin, V., Schwab-Stone, M., Jones, S., Cicchetti, D. V., Koposov, R., & Vermeiren, R. (2005). Is post-traumatic stress in youth a culture-bound phenomenon? A comparison of symptom trends in selected U.S. and Russian communities. *American Journal of Psychiatry, 162,* 538–544.

Rudd, M. D., Joiner, Y., & Rajab, M. H. (2001). *Treating suicidal behavior.* New York: Guilford Press.

Rudd, M. D., Rajab, M. H., Orman, D. T., Stulman, D. A., Joiner, T., & Dixon, W. (1996). Effectiveness of an outpatient intervention targeting suicidal young adults: Preliminary results. *Journal of Consulting and Clinical Psychology, 64,* 179–190.

Rusch, N., Lieb, K., Gottler, I., Hermann, C., Schramm, E., Richter, H., et al. (2007). Shame and implicit self-concept in women with borderline personality disorder. *American Journal of Psychiatry, 164,* 500–508.

Ruscio, J. (2004). Diagnoses and the behaviors they denote: A critical evaluation of the labeling theory of mental illness. *Scientific Review of Mental Health Practice, 3,* 5–22.

Rush, A. (2007). STAR ★D: What have we learned? *American Journal of Psychiatry, 164,* 201–204.

Rush, A. J., & Weissenburger, J. E. (1994). Melancholic symptom features and DSM-IV. *American Journal of Psychiatry, 151,* 489–498.

Rush, A. J., Erman, M. K., Giles, D. E., Schlesser, M. A., Carpenter, G., Vasavada, N., & Roffwarg, H. P. (1986). Polysomnographic findings in recently drug-free and clinically remitted depressed patients. *Archives of General Psychiatry, 43,* 878–884.

Rush, A. J., Giles, D. E., Schlesser, M. A., Orsulak, P. J., Weissenburger, J. E., Fulton, C. L., et al. (1997). Dexamethasone response, thyrotropin-releasing hormone stimulation, rapid eye movement latency, and subtypes of depression. *Biological Psychiatry, 41,* 915–928.

Rush, B. (1812). *Medical inquiries and observations upon the diseases of the mind.* Philadelphia: Kimber and Richardson.

Rush, J. A. (1993). Mood disorders in DSM-IV. In D. L. Dunner (Ed.), *Current psychiatric therapy* (pp. 189–195). Philadelphia: W. B. Saunders.

Russell, G. F. M. (1979). Bulimia nervosa: An ominous variant of anorexia nervosa. *Psychological Medicine, 9,* 429–448.

Russell, G. F. M., Szmukler, G. I., Dare, C., & Eisler, I. (1987). An evaluation of family therapy in anorexia nervosa and bulimia nervosa. *Archives of General Psychiatry, 44,* 1047–1056.

Rutter, M. (2002). The interplay of nature, nurture, and developmental influences: The challenge ahead for mental health. *Archives of General Psychiatry, 59,* 996–1000.

Rutter, M. (in press). *Genes and behavior: Nature–nurture interplay.* Oxford: Blackwell.

Rutter, M., & Giller, H. (1984). *Juvenile delinquency: Trends and perspectives.* New York: Guilford Press.

Rutter, M., Moffitt, T. E., & Caspi, A. (2006). Gene–environment interplay and psychopathology: Multiple varieties but real effects. *Journal of Child Psychology and Psychiatry, 47,* 226–261.

Ryan, W. D. (1992). The pharmacologic treatment of child and adolescent depression. *Psychiatric Clinics of North America, 15,* 29–40.

Saab, P. G., Llabre, M. M., Hurwitz, B. E., Frame, C. A., Reineke, I., Fins, A. I., et al. (1992). Myocardial and peripheral vascular responses to behavioral challenges and their stability in black and white Americans. *Psychophysiology, 29*(4), 384–397.

Sachs, G. S., & Rush, A. J. (2003). Response, remission, and recovery in bipolar disorders: What are the realistic treatment goals? *Journal of Clinical Psychiatry, 64,* 18–22.

Sackeim, H. A., & Devanand, D. P. (1991). Dissociative disorders. In M. Hersen & S. M. Turner (Eds.), *Adult psychopathology & diagnosis* (2nd ed., pp. 279–322). New York: John Wiley.

Sackeim, H. A., Nordlie, J. W., & Gur, R. C. (1979). A model of hysterical and hypnotic blindness: Cognition, motivation and awareness. *Journal of Abnormal Psychology, 88,* 474–489.

Sackett, D. L., Strauss, S. E., Richardson, W. S., Rosenberg, W., & Haynes, R. B. (2000). *Evidence-based medicine: How to practice and teach EBM* (2nd ed.). London: Churchill Livingstone.

Sackheim, H., Haskett, R., Mulsant, B., Thase, M., Mann, J., Pettinati, H., et al. (2001). Continuation pharmacotherapy in the prevention of relapse following electroconvulsive therapy: A randomized controlled trial. *JAMA, 285,* 1299–1307.

Sadeh, A., Raviv, A., & Gruber, R. (2000). Sleep patterns and sleep disruptions in school-age children. *Developmental Psychology, 36,* 291–301.

Sahler, O., Fairclough, D., Phipps, S., Mukhern, R., Dolgin, M., & Noll, R. (2005). Using problem solving skills training to reduce negative affectivity in mothers of children with newly diagnosed cancer: Report of a multisite randomized trial. *Journal of Consulting and Clinical Psychology, 73,* 272–283.

Saigh, P. A. (1984). Pre- and postinvasion anxiety in Lebanon. *Behavior Therapy, 15,* 185–190.

Sakel, M. (1958). *Schizophrenia.* New York: Philosophical Library.

Sakheim, D. K., Barlow, D. H., Abrahamson, D. J., & Beck, J. G. (1987). Distinguishing between organogenic and psychogenic erectile dysfunction. *Behaviour Research and Therapy, 25,* 379–390.

Salekin, R. T. (2006). Psychopathy in children and adolescents: Key issues in conceptualization and assessment. In C. J. Patrick (Ed.), *Handbook of psychopathy* (pp. 389–414). New York: Guilford Press.

Salge, R. A., Beck, J. G., & Logan, A. (1988). A community survey of panic. *Journal of Anxiety Disorder, 2,* 157–167.

Salkovskis, P. M., & Campbell, P. (1994). Thought suppression induces intrusion in naturally occurring negative intrusive thoughts. *Behaviour Research and Therapy, 32*(1), 1–8.

Salkovskis, P. M., & Clark, D. M. (1993). Panic disorders and hypochondriasis. Special issue: Panic, cognitions and sensations. *Advances in Behavioral Research and Therapy, 5,* 23–48.

Salkovskis, P. M., Atha, C., & Storer, D. (1990). Cognitive-behavioural problem solving in the treatment of patients who repeatedly attempt suicide: A controlled trial. *British Journal of Psychiatry, 157,* 871–876.

Salkovskis, P., Shafran, R., Rachman, S., & Freeston, M. H. (1999). Multiple pathways to inflated responsibility beliefs in obsessional problems: Possible origins and implications for therapy and research. *Behaviour Therapy and Research, 37,* 1055–1072.

Salkovskis, P., Warwick, H., & Deale, A. (2003). Cognitive-behavioral treatment for severe and persistent health anxiety. *Brief Treatment and Crisis Intervention, 3,* 353–367.

Saln-Pascual, R. J., Castao, A., Shiromani, P. J., Valencia-Flores, M., & Campos, R. M. (2006). Caffeine challenge in insomniac patients after total sleep deprivation. *Sleep Medicine, 7,* 141–145.

Salzman, C. (1991). Pharmacologic treatment of the anxious elderly patient. In C. Salzman & B. D. Lebowitz (Eds.), *Anxiety in the elderly: Treatment and research* (pp. 149–173). New York: Springer.

Samson, J. A., Mirin, S. M., Hauser, S. T., Fenton, B. T., & Schildkraut, J. J. (1992). Learned helplessness and urinary MHPG levels in unipolar depression. *American Journal of Psychiatry, 149*(6), 806–809.

Samuels, J., Bienvenu III, O. J., Riddle, M. A., Cullen, B. A. M., Grados, M. A., Liang, K.-Y., et al. (2002). Hoarding in obsessive compulsive disorder: Results from a case-control study. *Behaviour Research Therapy, 40,* 517–528.

Samuels, S. C., & Davis, K. L. (1997). A risk–benefit assessment of tacrine in the treatment of Alzheimer's disease. *Drug Safety, 16,* 66–77.

Samuels, S. C., & Neugroschl, J. A. (2005). Delirium. In B. J. Sadock & V. A. Sadock (Eds.), *Kaplan & Sadock's comprehensive textbook of psychiatry* (pp. 1054–1068). Philadelphia: Lippincott, Williams & Wilkins.

Sanders, M. H., & Givelber, R. J. (2006). Overview of obstructive sleep apnea in adults. In T. Lee-Chiong (Ed.), *Sleep: A comprehensive handbook* (pp. 231–240). Hoboken, NJ: John Wiley & Sons.

Sanders, M. R. (1992). Enhancing the impact of behavioural family intervention with children: Emerging perspectives. *Behaviour Change, 9,* 115–119.

Sanders, M. R., Dadds, M. R., Johnston, B. M., & Cash, R. (1992). Childhood depression and conduct disorder: I. Behavioral, affective and cognitive aspects of family problem solving interactions. *Journal of Abnormal Psychology, 101*(3), 495–504.

Sanderson, W. C., & Barlow, D. H. (1990). A description of patients diagnosed with DSM-III-R generalized anxiety disorder. *Journal of Nervous and Mental Disease, 178,* 588–591.

Sandin, B., Chorot, P., Santed, M., & Valiente, R. (2004). Differences in negative life events between patients with anxiety disorders, depression and hypochondriasis. *Anxiety, Stress & Coping: An International Journal, 17,* 37–47.

Sano, M., Ernesto, C., Thomas, R. G., Klauber, M. R., Schafer, K., Grundman, M., et al. (1997). A controlled trial of selegiline, alpha-tocopherol, or both as treatment for Alzheimer's disease. *New England Journal of Medicine, 336,* 1216–1222.

Santarelli, L., Saxe, M., Gross, C., Surget, A., Battaglia, F., Dulawa, S., et al. (2003). Requirement of hippocampal neurogenesis for the behavioral effects of antidepressants. *Science, 301,* 805–809.

Sandys, J. (2007). Work and employment for people with intellectual and developmental disabilities. In I. Brown & M. Percy (Eds.), *A comprehensive guide to intellectual & developmental disabilities* (pp. 527–543). Baltimore: Paul H. Brookes.

Sankey, A., Hill, C., Brown, J., Quinn, L., & Fletcher, A. (2006). A follow-up study of chronic fatigue syndrome in children and adolescents: Symptoms persistence and school absenteeism. *Clinical Child Psychology and Psychiatry, 11,* 126–138.

Santry, H. P., Gillen, D. L., & Lauderdale, D. S. (2005). Trends in bariatric surgical procedures. *JAMA, 294,* 1909–1917.

Sapolsky, J. (2007). Stress, stress-related disease, and emotional regulation. In J. J. Gross (Ed.), *Handbook of Emotion Regulation* (pp. 606–615). New York: Guilford Press.

Sapolsky, R. (1992). *Stress, the aging brain, and the mechanisms of neuron death.* Cambridge, MA: MIT Press.

Sapolsky, R. (2004). Is impaired neurogenesis relevant to the affective symptoms of depression? *Biological Psychiatry, 56,* 137–139.

Sapolsky, R. M. (1990, January). Stress in the wild. *Scientific American,* pp. 116–123.

Sapolsky, R. M. (2000a). Genetic hyping. *The Sciences, 40*(2), 12–15.

Sapolsky, R. M. (2000b). Glucocorticoids and hippocampal atrophy in neuropsychiatric disorders. *Archives of General Psychiatry, 57,* 925–935.

Sapolsky, R. M. (2002). *A primate's memoir.* New York: Simon & Schuster.

Sapolsky, R. M., & Meaney, M. J. (1986). Maturation of the adrenal stress response: Neuroendocrine control mechanisms and the stress hyporesponsive period. *Brain Research Review, 11,* 65–76.

Sapolsky, R. M., & Ray, J. C. (1989). Styles of dominance and their endocrine correlates among wild, live baboons. *American Journal of Primatology, 18*(1), 1–13.

Sarbin, T., & Mancuso, J. (1980). *Schizophrenia: Medical diagnosis or moral verdict?* Elmsford, NY: Pergamon Press.

Sareen, J., Jacobi, F., Cox, B. J., Belik, S., Clara, I., & Stein, B. M. (2006). Disability and poor quality of life associated with comorbid anxiety disorders and physical conditions. *Archives of Internal Medicine, 166*, 2109–2116.

Sarrel, P. M., & Masters, W. H. (1982). Sexual molestation of men by women. *Archives of Sexual Behavior, 11*, 117–131.

Sarwer, D. B., & Durlak, J. A. (1997). A field trial of the effectiveness of behavioral treatment for sexual dysfunctions. *Journal of Sex and Marital Therapy, 23*, 87–97.

Sarwer, D. B., Foster, G. D., & Wadden, T. A. (2004). Treatment of obesity I: Adult obesity. In J. K. Thompson (ed.). *Handbook of eating disorders and obesity* (pp. 421–442). New York: John Wiley.

Sass, K. J., Sass, A., Westerveld, M., Lencz, T., Novelly, R. A., Kim, J. H., & Spender, D. D. (1992). Specificity in the correlation of verbal memory and hippocampal neuron loss: Dissociation of memory, language, and verbal intellectual ability. *Journal of Clinical and Experimental Neuropsychology, 14*(5), 662–672.

Saudino, J. J., Pedersen, N. L., Lichenstein, P., Mc-Clearn, G. E., & Plomin, R. (1997). Can personality explain genetic influence on life events? *Journal of Personality & Social Psychology, 72*(1), 196–206.

Saudino, K. J., & Plomin, R. (1996). Personality and behavioral genetics: Where have we been and where are we going? *Journal of Research in Personality, 30*, 335–347.

Saudino, K. J., Plomin, R., & DeFries, J. C. (1996). Tester-rated temperament at 14, 20, and 24 months: Environmental change and genetic continuity. *British Journal of Developmental Psychology, 14*, 129–144.

Savin-Williams, R. (2006). Who's gay? Does it matter? *Current Directions in Psychological Science, 15*, 40–44.

Sawa, A., & Snyder, S. H. (2002). Schizophrenia: Diverse approaches to a complex disease. *Science, 296*, 692–695.

Saxe, G. N., Stoddard, F., Hall, E., Chawla, N., Lopez, C., Sheridan, R., et al. (2005). Pathways to PTSD: Part I. Children with burns. *American Journal of Psychiatry, 162*, 1299–1304.

Saxe, G. N., van der Kolk, B. A., Berkowitz, R., Chinman, G., Hall, K., Leiberg, G., & Schwartz, J. (1993). Dissociative disorders in psychiatric inpatients. *American Journal of Psychiatry, 150*, 1037–1042.

Saxena, S., & Prasad, K. (1989). DSM-III subclassifications of dissociative disorders applied to psychiatric outpatients in India. *American Journal of Psychiatry, 146*, 261–262.

Saxena, S., Winograd, A., Dunkin, J. J., Maidment, K., Rosen, R., Vapnik, T., et al. (2001). A retrospective review of clinical characteristics and treatment response in body dysmorphic disorder versus obsessive-compulsive disorder. *Journal of Clinical Psychiatry, 62*, 67–72.

Scahill, L., & Leckman, J. F. (2005). Tic disorders. In B. J. Sadock & V. A. Sadock (Eds.), *Kaplan & Sadock's comprehensive textbook of psychiatry* (pp. 3228–3236). Philadelphia: Lippincott, Williams & Wilkins.

Scarmeas, N, & Stern, Y. (2003). Cognitive reserve and lifestyle. *Journal of Clinical and Experimental Neuropsychology, 25*, 625–633.

Scarmeas, N., Albert, S. M., Manly, J. J., & Stern, Y. (2006). Education and rates of cognitive decline in incident Alzheimer's disease. *Journal of Neurology, Neurosurgery, and Psychiatry, 77*, 308–316.

Schacter, D. L. (Ed.) (1995). *Memory distortion: How minds, brains, and societies reconstruct the past.* Cambridge, MA: Harvard University Press.

Schacter, D. L., Chiu, P., & Ochsner, K. N. (1993). Implicit memory: A selective review. *Annual Review of Neuroscience, 16*, 159–182.

Schafer, J., & Brown, S. A. (1991). Marijuana and cocaine effect expectancies and drug use patterns. *Journal of Consulting and Clinical Psychology, 59*, 558–565.

Schatzberg, A. (2000). New indications for antidepressants. *Journal of Clinical Psychiatry, 61*(Suppl. 11), 9–17.

Schatzberg, A., Rush, J., Arnow, B., Banks, P., Blalock, J., Borian, F., Howland, R., et al. (2005). Chronic depression: Medication (Nefazodone) or psychotherapy (CBASP) is effective when the other is not. *Archives of General Psychiatry, 62*, 513–520.

Scheerenberger, R. C. (1983). *A history of mental retardation.* Baltimore: Paul H. Brookes.

Scheidt, P. C., Harel, Y., Trumble, A. C., Jones, D. H., Overpeck, M. D., & Bijur, P. E. (1995). The epidemiology of nonfatal injuries among U.S. children and youth. *American Journal of Public Health, 85*, 932–938.

Scheidt, P. C., Overpeck, M. D., Trifiletti, L. B., & Cheng, T. (2000). Child and adolescent injury research in 1998: A summary of abstracts submitted to the Ambulatory Pediatrics Association and the American Public Health Association. *Archives of Pediatrics and Adolescent Medicine, 154*, 442–445.

Scheier, M. F., Matthews, K. A., Owens, J. F., Magovern, G. J., Sr., Lefebvre, R. C., Abbott, R. A., & Carver, C. S. (1989). Dispositional optimism and recovery from coronary artery bypass surgery: The beneficial effects on physical and psychological well-being. *Journal of Personality and Social Psychology, 57*(6), 1024–1040.

Schenk, L., & Bear, D. (1981). Multiple personality and related dissociative phenomena in patients with temporal lobe epilepsy. *American Journal of Psychiatry, 138*, 1311–1316.

Schiavi, R. C. (1990). Chronic alcoholism and male sexual dysfunction. *Journal of Sex and Marital Therapy, 16*, 23–33.

Schiavi, R. C., White, D., Mandeli, J., & Levine, A. C. (1997). Effect of testosterone administration on sexual behavior and mood in men with erectile dysfunction. *Archives of Sexual Behavior, 26*, 231–241.

Schiffer, B., Peschel, T., Paul, T., Gizewski, E., Forsting, M., Leygraf, N., Schedlowski, M., & Krueger, T. H. C. (2007). Structural brain abnormalities in the frontostriatal system and cerebellum in pedophilia. *Journal of Psychiatric Research, 41*, 753–762.

Schiffman, J., Walker, E., Ekstrom, M., Schulsinger, F., Sorensen, H., & Mednick, S. (2004). Childhood videotaped social and neuromotor precursors of schizophrenia: A prospective investigation. *American Journal of Psychiatry, 161*, 2021–2027.

Schildkraut, J. J. (1965). The catecholamine hypothesis of affective disorders: A review of supporting evidence. *American Journal of Psychiatry, 122*, 509–522.

Schiller, C., & Allen, P. J. (2005). Follow-up of infants prenatally exposed to cocaine. *Pediatric Nursing, 31*, 427–436.

Schleifer, S. J., Keller, S. E., Bond, R. N., Cohen, J., & Stein, M. (1989). Major depressive disorder and immunity: Role of age, sex, severity, and hospitalization. *Archives of General Psychiatry, 46*, 81–87.

Schlenger, W. E., Caddell, J. M., Ebert, L., Jordan, B. K., Rourke, K. M., Wilson, D., et al. (2002). Psychological reactions to terrorist attacks. *JAMA, 288*, 581–588.

Schlesinger, A., & Silk, K. R. (2005). Collaborative treatment. In J. M. Oldham, A. E. Skodol, & D. S. Bender (Eds.), *Textbook of personality disorders* (pp. 431–446). Washington, DC: American Psychiatric Publishing.

Schlundt, O. G., & Johnson, W. G. (1990). *Eating disorders: Assessment and treatment.* Boston: Allyn & Bacon.

Schmahl, C., & Bremner, J. D. (2006). Neuroimaging in borderline personality disorder. *Journal of Psychiatric Research, 40*, 419–427.

Schmaling, K. B., Fiedelak, J. I., Katon, W. J., Bader, J. O., & Buchwald, D. S. (2003). Prospective study of the prognosis of unexplained chronic fatigue in a clinic-based cohort. *Psychosomatic Medicine, 65*, 1047–1054.

Schmidt, N. B., Lerew, D. R., & Jackson, R. J. (1997). The role of anxiety sensitivity in the pathogenesis of panic: Projective evaluation of spontaneous panic attacks during acute stress. *Journal of Abnormal Psychology, 106*, 355–364.

Schmidt, N. B., Lerew, D. R., & Jackson, R. J. (1999). Prospective evaluation of anxiety sensitivity in the pathogenesis of panic: Replication and extension. *Journal of Abnormal Psychology, 108*, 532–537.

Schneck, C., Miklowitz, D., Calabrese, J., Allen, M., Thomas, M., Wisniewski, S., et al. (2004). Phenomenology of rapid-cycling bipolar disorder: Data from the first 500 participants in the systematic treatment enhancement program. *American Journal Psychiatry, 161*, 1902–1908.

Schneiderman, N. (2004). Psychosocial, behavioral, and biological aspects of chronic diseases. *Current Directions in Psychological Science, 13*, 247–251.

Schneier, F. R., Liebowitz, M. R., Beidel, D. C., Fyer, A. J., George, M. S., Heimberg, R. G., et al. (1996). Social phobia. In T. A. Widiger, A. J. Frances, H. A. Pincus, R. Ross, M. B. First, & W. W. Davis (Eds.), *DSM-IV sourcebook* (Vol. 2, pp. 507–548). Washington, DC: American Psychiatric Association.

Schnell, K., & Herpertz, S. C. (2007). Effects of dialectic-behavioral-therapy on the neural correlates of affective hyperarousal in borderline personality disorder. *Journal of Psychiatric Research, 41*, 837–847.

Schoenbach, V. J., Kaplan, B. H., Fredman, L., & Kleinbaum, D. G. (1986). Social ties and mortality in Evans County, Georgia. *American Journal of Epidemiology, 123*, 577.

Schoeneman, T. J. (1977). The role of mental illness in the European witchhunts of the sixteenth and seventeenth centuries: An assessment. *Journal of the History of the Behavioral Sciences, 13*, 337–351.

Schopp, L., Johnstone, B., & Merrell, D. (2000). Telehealth and neuropsychological assessment: New opportunities for psychologists. *Professional Psychology: Research and Practice, 31*, 179–183.

Schover, L. R., & Jensen, S. B. (1988). *Sexuality and chronic illness: A comprehensive approach.* New York: Guilford Press.

Schreiber, F. R. (1973). *Sybil.* Chicago: Regnery.

Schreiner-Engel, P., & Schiavi, R. C. (1986). Lifetime psychopathology in individuals with low sexual desire. *Journal of Nervous and Mental Disease, 174*, 646–651.

Schuckit, M. A. (1994). Low level of response to alcohol as a predictor of future alcoholism. *American Journal of Psychiatry, 151*, 184–189.

Schuckit, M. A. (1998). Biological, psychological and environmental predictors of alcoholism risk: A longitudinal study. *Journal of Studies on Alcohol, 59*, 485–494.

Schuckit, M. A., & Tapert, S. (2004). Alcohol. In M. Galanter & H. D. Kleber (Eds.), *The American Psychiatry Publishing textbook of substance abuse treatment* (3rd ed., pp. 151–166). Washington, DC: American Psychiatric Publishing.

Schuckit, M. A., Smith, T. L., Anthenelli, R., & Irwin, M. (1993). Clinical course of alcoholism in 636 male inpatients. *American Journal of Psychiatry, 150*, 786–792.

Schulberg, H. C., Block, M. R., Madonia, M. J., Scott, C. P., Rodriguez, E., Imber, S. D., et al. (1996). Treating major depression in primary care practice: Eight-month clinical outcomes. *Archives of General Psychiatry, 53*, 913–919.

Schulsinger, F., Kety, S. S., & Rosenthal, D. (1979). A family study of suicide. In M. Schou & E. Stromgren (Eds.), *Origin, prevention, and treatment of affective disorders.* New York: Academic Press.

Schultz, R. T., Romanski, L. M., & Tsatsanis, K. D. (2000). Neurofunctional models of autistic disorder and Asperger syndrome: Clues from neuroimaging. In A. Klin, F. R. Volkmar, & S. S. Sparrow (Eds.), *Asperger syndrome* (pp. 172–209). New York: Guilford Press.

Schulz, M. S., Cowan, C. P., & Cowan, P. A. (2006). Promoting healthy beginnings: A randomized controlled trial of a preventive intervention to preserve marital quality during transition to parenthood. *Journal of Consulting and Clinical Psychology, 74,* 20–31.

Schulz, R., Drayer, R. A., & Rollman, B. L. (2002). Depression as a risk factor for non-suicide mortality in the elderly. *Biological Psychiatry, 52,* 205–225.

Schumacher, J., Jamra, R. A., Becker, T., Klopp, N., Franke, P., Jacob, C., et al. (2005). Investigation of the DAOA/G30 locus in panic disorder. *Molecular Psychiatry, 10,* 428–429.

Schumann, C. M., & Amaral, D. G. (2006). Stereological analysis of amygdala neuron number in autism. *Journal of Neuroscience, 26,* 7674–7679.

Schuster, M., Stein, B., Jaycox, L., Collins, R., Marshall, G., Elliott, M., et al. (2001). A national survey of stress reactions after the September 11, 2001, terrorist attacks. *New England Journal of Medicine, 345,* 1507–1512.

Schwalberg, M. D., Barlow, D. H., Alger, S. A., & Howard, L. J. (1992). Comparison of bulimics, obese binge eaters, social phobics, and individuals with panic disorder or comorbidity across DSM-III-R anxiety. *Journal of Abnormal Psychology, 101,* 675–681.

Schwartz, A. J., & Whitaker, L. C. (1990). Suicide among college students: Assessment, treatment, and intervention. In S. J. Blumenthal & D. J. Kupfer (Eds.), *Suicide over the life cycle: Risk factors, assessment and treatment of suicidal patients.* Washington, DC: American Psychiatric Press.

Schwartz, C. E., Wright, C. L., Shin, L. M., Kagan, J., Whalen, P. J., McMullin, K. G., et al. (2003). Differential amygdalar response to novel versus newly familiar neutral faces: A functional MRI probe developed for studying inhibited temperament. *Biological Psychiatry, 53,* 854–862.

Schwartz, G. E., & Weiss, S. M. (1978). Behavioral medicine revisited: An amended definition. *Journal of Behavioral Medicine, 1,* 249–252.

Schwartz, I. M. (1993). Affective reactions of American and Swedish women to the first premarital coitus: A cross-cultural comparison. *Journal of Sex Research, 30*(1), 18–26.

Schwartz, J. M., Stoessel, P. W., Baxter, L. R., Martin, K. M., & Phelps, M. E. (1996). Systematic changes in cerebral glucose metabolic rate after successful behavior modification treatment of obsessive compulsive disorder. *Archives of General Psychiatry, 53,* 109–113.

Schwartz, M. B., & Brownell, K. D. (2007). Actions necessary to prevent childhood obesity: Creating the climate for change. *Journal of Law, Medicine, & Ethics.*

Schwartz, M. S., & Andrasik, F. (Eds.) (2003). *Biofeedback: A practitioner's guide* (3rd ed.). New York: Guilford Press.

Schwartz, P. J., Brown, C., Wehr, T. A., & Rosenthal, N. E. (1996). Winter seasonal affective disorder: A follow-up study of the first 59 patients of the National Institute of Mental Health seasonal studies program. *American Journal of Psychiatry, 153,* 1028–1036.

Schwartz, R. P., Jaffe, J. H., Highfield, D. A., Callaman, J. M., & O'Grady, K. E. (2007). A randomized controlled trial of interim methadone maintenance: 10-month follow-up. *Drug and Alcohol Dependence, 86,* 30–36.

Schwarz, A. (2007, March 14). Wives united by husband's post-NFL trauma. *New York Times.* Available at http://www.nytimes.com.

Schweizer, E., & Rickels, K. (1996). Pharmacological treatment for generalized anxiety disorder. In M. R. Mavissakalian & R. F. Prien (Eds.), *Long-term treatments of anxiety disorders.* Washington, DC: American Psychiatric Press.

Schweizer, E., Rickels, K., Case, W. G., & Greenblatt, D. J. (1990). Long-term use of benzodiazepines: II. Effects of gradual taper. *Archives of General Psychiatry, 47,* 908–915.

Scott, C. L., & Resnick, P. J. (2006). Violence risk assessment in persons with mental illness. *Aggression and Violent Behavior, 11,* 598–611.

Scott, C. L., Hilty, D. M., & Brook, M. (2003). Impulse-control disorders not elsewhere classified. In R. E. Hales & S. C. Yudofsky (Eds.), *Textbook of clinical psychiatry* (4th ed., pp. 781–802). Washington, DC: American Psychiatric Publishing.

Scott, J. (1995). Psychotherapy for bipolar disorder. *British Journal of Psychiatry, 167,* 581–588.

Scott, J. E., & Dixon, L. B. (1995). Psychological interventions for schizophrenia. *Schizophrenia Bulletin, 21,* 621–630.

Sechi, G., & Serra, A. (2007). Wernicke's encephalopathy: New clinical settings and recent advances in diagnosis and management. *Lancet Neurology, 6,* 442–455.

Secko, D. (2005). Depression: More than just serotonin. *Canadian Medical Association Journal, 172,* 1551.

Seeman, P., Lee, T., Chau Wong, M., & Wong, K. (1976). Antipsychotic drug doses and neuroleptic/dopamine receptors. *Nature, 261,* 717–719.

Segal, N. (2006). Two monozygotic twin pairs discordant for female to male transsexualism. *Archives of Sexual Behavior, 35,* 347–358.

Segal, S. (1978). Attitudes toward the mentally ill: A review. *Social Work, 23,* 211–217.

Segal, Z. V., Hood, J. E., Shaw, B. F., & Higgins, E. (1988). A structural analysis of the self-schema construct in major depression. *Cognitive Therapy and Research, 12*(5), 471–485.

Segraves, R., & Althof, S. (1998). Psychotherapy and pharmacotherapy of sexual dysfunctions. In P. E. Nathan & J. M. Gorman (Eds.), *A guide to treatments that work* (pp. 447–471). New York: Oxford University Press.

Segraves, R., & Woodard, T. (2006). Female hypoactive sexual desire disorder: History and current status. *Journal of Sexual Medicine, 3,* 408–418.

Seidman, S. N., & Rieder, R. O. (1994). A review of sexual behavior in the United States. *American Journal of Psychiatry, 151,* 330–341.

Seligman, M. E. P. (1971). Phobias and preparedness. *Behavior Therapy, 2,* 307–320.

Seligman, M. E. P. (1975). *Helplessness: On depression, development and death.* San Francisco: W. H. Freeman.

Seligman, M. E. P. (1998). *Learned Optimism.* (2nd ed.). New York: Simon & Schuster.

Seligman, M. E. P. (2002). *Authentic Happiness: Using the new positive psychology to realize your potential for lasting fulfillment.* New York: Free Press/Simon & Schuster.

Seligman, M. E. P., Schulman, P., DeRubeis, R. J., & Hollon, S. D. (1999). The prevention of depression and anxiety. *Prevention and Treatment, 2,* 8.

Selye, H. (1936). A syndrome produced by diverse noxious agents. *Nature, 138,* 32.

Selye, H. (1950). *The physiology and pathology of exposure to stress.* Montreal: Acta.

Semans, J. H. (1956). Premature ejaculation: A new approach. *Southern Medical Journal, 49,* 353–358.

Seto, M., Cantor, J., & Blanchard, R. (2006). Child pornography offenses are a valid diagnostic indicator of pedophilia. *Journal of Abnormal Psychology, 115,* 610–615.

Severino, S. K., & Moline, M. L. (1989). *Premenstrual syndrome: A clinician's guide.* New York: Guilford Press.

Sexton, M. M. (1979). Behavioral epidemiology. In O. F. Pomerleau & J. P. Brady (Eds.), *Behavioral medicine: Theory and practice* (pp. 3–21). Baltimore: Williams & Wilkins.

Shabecoff, P. (1987, October 14). Stress and the lure of harmless remedies. *New York Times,* p. 12.

Shaffer, D. R. (1993). *Developmental psychology: Childhood and adolescence* (3rd ed.). Pacific Grove, CA: Brooks/Cole.

Shaffer, D., Garland, A., Vieland, V., Underwood, M., & Busner, C. (1991). The impact of curriculum based suicide prevention programs for teenagers. *Journal of the American Academy of Child and Adolescent Psychiatry, 30*(4), 588–596.

Shafran, R., Cooper, Z., & Fairburn, C. G. (2002). Clinical perfectionism: A cognitive-behavioural analysis. *Behaviour Research Therapy, 40,* 773–791.

Shafran, R., Lee, M., Payne, E., & Fairburn, C. G. (2006). The impact of manipulating personal standards on eating attitudes and behaviour. *Behaviour Research and Therapy, 44,* 897–906.

Shapiro, D. (1974). Operant-feedback control of human blood pressure: Some clinical issues. In P. A. Obrist, A. H. Black, J. Brener, & L. V. DiCara (Eds.), *Cardiovascular psychophysiology: Current issues in response mechanisms, biofeedback, and methodology.* Chicago: Aldine.

Shapiro, D. A., Rees, A., Barkham, M., Hardy, G., Reynolds, S., & Startup, M. (1995). Effects of treatment duration and severity of depression on the maintenance of gains after cognitive-behavioral and psychodynamic-interpersonal psychotherapy. *Journal of Consulting and Clinical Psychology, 63,* 378–387.

Shapiro, E. S., & Lentz, F. E. (1991). Vocational–technical programs: Follow-up of students with learning disabilities. *Exceptional Children, 58,* 47–59.

Sharp, W. S., Gottesman, R. F., Greenstein, D. K., Ebens, C. L., Rapoport, J. L., & Castellanos, F. X. (2003). Monozygotic twins discordant for attention-deficit/hyperactivity disorder: Ascertainment and clinical characteristics. *Journal of the American Academy of Child and Adolescent Psychiatry, 42,* 93–97.

Sharpe, M. (1992). Fatigue and chronic fatigue syndrome. *Current Opinion in Psychiatry, 5,* 207–212.

Sharpe, M. (1993). *Chronic fatigue syndrome* (pp. 298–317). Chichester, England: John Wiley.

Sharpe, M. (1997). Chronic fatigue. In D. M. Clark & C. G. Fairburn (Eds.), *Science and practice of cognitive behavior therapy* (pp. 381–414). Oxford: Oxford University Press.

Sharpe, M., Clements, A., Hawton, K., Young, A., Sargent, P., & Cowen, P. (1996). Increased prolactin response to buspirone in chronic fatigue syndrome. *Journal of Affective Disorders, 41,* 71–76.

Shattuck, P. T. (2006). The contribution of diagnostic substitution to the growing administrative prevalence of autism in U.S. special education. *Pediatrics, 117,* 1028–1037.

Shaw, D. S., Dishion, T. J., Supplee, L., Gardner, F., & Arnds, K. (2006). Randomized trial of a family-centered approach to the prevention of early conduct problems: 2-year effects of the family checkup in early childhood. *Journal of Consulting and Clinical Psychology, 74,* 1–9.

Shaywitz, S. (2003). *Overcoming Dyslexia: A new and complete science-based program for overcoming reading problems at any level.* New York: Knopf.

Shaywitz, S. E., Mody, M., & Shaywitz, B. A. (2006). Neural mechanisms in dyslexia. *Current Directions in Psychological Science, 15,* 278–281.

Shea, M. T., Elkin, I., Imber, S. D., Sotsky, S. M., Watkins, J. T., Collins, J. F., et al. (1992). Course of depressive symptoms over follow-up: Findings from the National Institute of Mental Health Treatment of Depression Collaborative Research Program. *Archives of General Psychiatry, 49*(10), 782–787.

Shear, K. (2006). Adapting imaginal exposure to the treatment of complicated grief. In Rothbaum, B.

(Ed.), *Pathological anxiety: Emotional processing in etiology and treatment* (pp. 215–226). New York: Guilford Press.

Shear, K., Frank, E., Houck, P., & Reynolds, C. (2005). Treatment of complicated grief: A randomized controlled trial. *JAMA, 293,* 2601–2608.

Shear, M. K., Brown, T. A., Barlow, D. H., Money, R., Sholomskas, D. E., Woods, S. W., et al. (1997). Multicenter collaborative panic disorder severity scale. *American Journal of Psychiatry, 154,* 1571–1575.

Sheets, E., & Craighead, W. E. (2007). Toward an empirically based classification of personality pathology. *Clinical Psychology: Science and Practice, 14,* 77–93.

Sheffield, J. K., Spence, S. H., Rapee, R. M., Kowalenko, N., Wignall, A., Davis, A., & McLoone, J. (2006). Evaluation of universal, indicated, and combined cognitive-behavioral approaches to the prevention of depression among adolescents. *Journal of Consulting and Clinical Psychology, 74,* 66–79.

Sheikh, J. I. (1992). Anxiety and its disorders in old age. In J. E. Birren, K. Sloan, & G. D. Cohen (Eds.), *Handbook of mental health and aging* (pp. 410–432). New York: Academic Press.

Sherbourne, C. D., Hays, R. D., & Wells, K. B. (1995). Personal and psychosocial risk factors for physical and mental health outcomes and course of depression among depressed patients. *Journal of Consulting and Clinical Psychology, 63,* 345–355.

Shiffman, S., Ferguson, S. G., & Hellebusch, S. J. (2007). Physicians' counseling of patients when prescribing nicotine replacement therapy. *Addictive Behaviors, 32,* 729–739.

Shimizu, E., Imai, M., Fujisaki, M., Shinoda, N., Handa, S., Watanabe, H., et al. (2007). Maintenance electroconvulsive therapy (ECT) for treatment-resistant disorganized schizophrenia. *Progress in Neuro-Psychopharmacology and Biological Psychiatry, 31,* 571–573.

Shin, L. M., Shin, P. S., Heckers, S., Krangel, T. S., Macklin, M. L., Orr, S. P., et al. (2004). Hippocampal function in posttraumatic stress disorder. *Hippocampus, 14,* 292–300.

Shneidman, E. S. (1989). Approaches and commonalities of suicide. In R. F. W. Diekstra, R. Mariss, S. Platt, A. Schmidtke, & G. Sonneck (Eds.), *Suicide and its prevention: The role of attitude and imitation. Advances in Suicidology* (Vol. 1). Leiden, Netherlands: E. J. Brill.

Shneidman, E. S., Farberow, N. L., & Litman, R. E. (Eds.) (1970). *The psychology of suicide.* New York: Science House.

Shochet, I. M., Dadds, M. R., Holland, D., Whitefield, K., Harnett, P. H., & Osgarby, S. (2001). The efficacy of a universal school-based program to prevent adolescent depression. *Journal of Clinical Child Psychology, 30,* 303–315.

Show, M. (1985). Practical problems of lithium maintenance treatment. *Advances in Biochemical Psychopharmacology, 40,* 131–138.

Shrout, P. E., Link, B. G., Dohrenwend, B. P., Skodol, A. E., Stueve, A., & Mirotznik, J. (1989). Characterizing life events as risk factors for depression: The role of fateful loss events. *Journal of Abnormal Psychology, 98,* 460–467.

Shulman, K. I., Cohen, C. A., Kirsh, F. C., Hull, I. M., & Champine, P. R. (2007). Assessment of testamentary capacity and vulnerability to undue influence. *American Journal of Psychiatry, 164*(5), 722–727.

Shumaker, S. A., Legault, C., Kuller, L., Rapp, S. R., Thal, L., Lane, D. S., et al., & Women's Health Initiative Memory Study. (2004). Conjugated equine estrogens and incidence of probable dementia and mild cognitive impairment in postmenopausal women: Women's Health Initiative Memory Study. *JAMA, 291,* 3005–3007.

Sibley, D. C., & Blinder, B. J. (1988). Anorexia nervosa. In B. J. Blinder, B. F. Chaitin, & R. S. Goldstein (Eds.), *The eating disorders: Medical and psychological bases of diagnosis and treatment* (pp. 247–258). New York: PMA.

Sierra, M., & Berrios, G. E. (1998). Depersonalization: Neurobiological Perspectives. *Society of Biological Psychiatry, 44,* 898–908.

Sierra, M., Senior, C., Dalton, J., McDonough, M., Bond, A., Phillips, M. L., et al. (2002). Autonomic response in depersonalization disorder. *Archives of General Psychiatry, 59,* 833–838.

Siever, L. J. (1992). Schizophrenia spectrum personality disorders. In A. Tasman & M. B. Riba (Eds.), *Review of Psychiatry* (Vol. 11, pp. 25–42). Washington, DC: American Psychiatric Press.

Siever, L. J., & Davis, K. L. (2004). The pathophysiology of schizophrenia disorders: Perspectives from the spectrum. *American Journal of Psychiatry, 161,* 398–413.

Siever, L. J., Davis, K. L., & Gorman, L. K. (1991). Pathogenesis of mood disorders. In K. Davis, H. Klar, & J. T. Coyle (Eds.), *Foundations of psychiatry.* Philadelphia: W. B. Saunders.

Siffre, M. (1964). *Beyond time* (H. Briffault, Ed. and Trans.). New York: McGraw-Hill.

Sigafoos, J., Arthur-Kelly, M., & Butterfield, N. (2006). *Enhancing everyday communication for children with disabilities.* Baltimore: Paul H. Brookes.

Sigvardsson, S., Cloninger, C. R., Bohman, M., & von-Knorring, A. L. (1982). Predisposition to petty criminality in Swedish adoptees. *Archives of General Psychiatry, 39,* 1248–1253.

Silver, E., Cirincione, C., & Steadman, H. J. (1994). Demythologizing inaccurate perceptions of the insanity defense. *Law and Human Behavior, 18,* 63–70.

Silverman, W. K., & La Greca, A. M. (2002). Children experiencing disasters: Definitions, reactions and predictors of outcomes. In A. N. La Greca, W. K. Silverman & M. C. Roberts (Eds.), *Helping Children Cope with Disasters and Terrorism* (Vol. 1, pp. 11–33). Washington, DC: American Psychological Association.

Silverman, W. K., & Rabian, B. (1993). Simple phobias. *Child and Adolescent Psychiatric Clinics of North America, 2,* 603–622.

Silverman, W. K., La Greca, A. M., & Wasserstein, S. (1995). What do children worry about? Worries & their relation to anxiety. *Child Development, 66,* 671–686.

Silverstone, T. (1985). Dopamine in manic depressive illness: A pharmacological synthesis. *Journal of Affective Disorders, 8*(3), 225–231.

Simeon, D., Guralnik, O., Hazlett, E. A., Spiegel-Cohen, J., Hollander, E., & Buchsbaum, M. S. (2000). Feeling unreal: A PET study of depersonalization disorder. *American Journal of Psychiatry, 157,* 1782–1788.

Simeon, D., Guralnik, O., Knutelska, M., Hollander, E., & Schmeidler, J. (2001). Hypothalamic–pituitary–adrenal axis dysregulation in depersonalization disorder. *Neuropsychopharmacology, 25,* 793–795.

Simeon, D., Guralnik, O., Schmeidler, J., & Knutelska, M. (2004). Fluoxetine therapy in depersonalization disorder: Randomised controlled trial. *British Journal of Psychiatry, 185,* 31–36.

Simeon, D., Knutelska, M., Nelson, D., & Guralnik, O. (2003). Feeling unreal: A depersonalization disorder update of 117 cases. *Journal of Clinical Psychiatry, 64,* 990–997.

Simkin, D. R. (2005). Adolescent substance abuse. In B. J. Sadock & V. A. Sadock (Eds.), *Kaplan & Sadock's comprehensive textbook of psychiatry* (pp. 3470–3490). Philadelphia: Lippincott, Williams & Wilkins.

Simmons, R., & Blyth, D. (1987). *Moving into adolescence: The impact of pubertal change and school context.* New York: Aldine de Gruyter.

Simon, G. (2006). How can we know whether antidepressants increase suicide risk? *American Journal of Psychiatry, 163,* 1861–1863.

Simon, G. E., Gureje, O., & Fullerton, C. (2001). Course of hypochondriasis in an international primary care study. *General Hospital Psychiatry, 23,* 51–55.

Simon, G. E., von Koff, M., Saunders, K., Miglioretti, D. L., Crane, P. K., van Belle, G., & Kessler, R. C. (2006). Association between obesity and psychiatric disorders in the U.S. adult population. *Archives of General Psychiatry, 63,* 824–830.

Simon, R. I. (1999). The law and psychiatry. In R. E. Hales, S. C. Yudofsky, & J. A. Talbott (Eds.), *The American Psychiatric Press Textbook of Psychiatry* (3rd ed., pp. 1493–1534). Washington, DC: American Psychiatric Press.

Simon, R. I. (2003). The law and psychiatry. In R. E. Hales & S. C. Yudofsky (Eds.), *Textbook of clinical psychiatry* (4th ed., pp. 1585–1626). Washington, DC: American Psychiatric Publishing.

Simon, R. I. (2005). Clinical–legal issues in psychiatry. In B. J. Sadock & V. A. Sadock (Eds.), *Kaplan & Sadock's comprehensive textbook of psychiatry* (pp. 3969–3988). Philadelphia: Lippincott, Williams & Wilkins.

Simone, S., & Fulero, S. M. (2005). Tarasoff and the duty to protect. *Journal of Aggression, Maltreatment & Trauma, 11,* 145–168.

Simoneau, T. L., Miklowitz, D. J., Richards, J. A., Saleem R., & George, E. L. (1999). Bipolar disorder and family communication: Effects of a psychoeducational treatment program. *Journal of Abnormal Psychology, 108,* 588–597.

Simons, A. D., Murphy, G. E., Levine, J. L., & Wetzel, R. D. (1986). Cognitive therapy and pharmacotherapy for depression: Sustained improvement over one year. *Archives of General Psychiatry, 43*(1), 43–48.

Simos, P. G., Fletcher, J. M., Sarkari, S., Billingsley-Marshall, R., Denton, C. A., & Papanicolaou, A. C. (2007). Intensive instruction affects brain magnetic activity associated with oral word reading in children with persistent reading disabilities. *Journal of Learning Disabilities, 40,* 37–48.

Singer, M., & Flannery, D. J. (2000). The relationship between children's threats of violence and violent behaviors. *Archives of Pediatrics and Adolescent Medicine, 154,* 785–790.

Singh, M., DelBello, M., Kowatch, R., & Strakowski, S. (2006). Co-occurrence of bipolar and attention-deficit hyperactivity disorders in children. *Bipolar Disorders, 8,* 710–720.

Skhiri, D., Annabi, S., Bi, S., & Allani, D. (1982). Enfants d'immigrés: Facteurs de liens ou de rupture? *Annales Medico-Psychologiques, 140,* 597–602.

Skidmore, W., Linsenmeier, J., & Bailey, J. (2006). Gender nonconformity and psychological distress in lesbians and gay men. *Archives of Sexual Behavior, 35,* 685–697.

Skinner, B. F. (1938). *The behavior of organisms.* New York: Appleton-Century-Crofts.

Skinner, B. F. (1948). *Walden two.* New York: Macmillan.

Skinner, B. F. (1971). *Beyond freedom and dignity.* New York: Knopf.

Skodol, A. E. (2005). Manifestations, clinical diagnosis, and comorbidity. In J. M. Oldham, A. E. Skodol, & D. S. Bender (Eds.), *Textbook of personality disorders* (pp. 57–87). Washington, DC: American Psychiatric Publishing.

Skodol, A. E., Oldham, J. M., Bender, D. S., Dyck, I. R., Stout, R. L., Morey, L. C., et al. (2005). Dimensional representations of DSM-IV personality disorders: Relationships to functional impairment. *American Journal of Psychiatry, 162,* 1919–1925.

Skodol, A. E., Oldham, J. M., & Gallaher, P. E. (1999). Axis II comorbidity of substance use disorders among patients referred for treatment of personality disorders. *American Journal of Psychiatry, 156,* 733–738.

Sleet, D. A., Hammond, R., Jones, R., Thomas, N., & Whitt, B. (2003). Using psychology for injury and violence prevention in the community. In R. H. Rozensky, N. G. Johson, C. D. Goodheart, & R. Hammond (Eds.), *Psychology Builds a Healthy World.* Washington, DC: American Psychological Association.

Slutske, W. S., Heath, A. C., Dinwiddie, S. H., Madden, P. A. F., Bucholz, K. K., Dunne, M. P., et al. (1997). Modeling genetic and environmental influences in the etiology of conduct disorder: A study of 2,682 adult twin pairs. *Journal of Abnormal Psychology, 106,* 266–279.

Slutske, W. S., Heath, A. C., Dinwiddie, S. H., Madden, P. A. F., Bucholz, K. K., Dunne, M. P., et al. (1998). Common genetic risk factors for conduct disorder and alcohol dependence. *Journal of Abnormal Psychology, 107,* 363–374.

Small, G. W. (1991). Recognition and treatment of depression in the elderly. The clinician's challenge: Strategies for treatment of depression in the 1990s. *Journal of Clinical Psychiatry, 52,* 11–22.

Smeets, G., de Jong, P. J., & Mayer, B. (2000). If you suffer from a headache, then you have a brain tumour: Domain-specific reasoning "bias" and hypochondriasis. *Behaviour Research and Therapy, 38,* 763–776.

Smith, B. H., Barkley, R. A., & Shapiro, C. J. (2006). Combined child therapies. In R. A. Barkley (Ed.), *Attention-deficit hyperactivity disorder: A handbook for diagnosis and treatment* (3rd ed., pp. 678–691). New York: Guilford Press.

Smith, D. E., & Wesson, D. R. (1999). Benzodiazepines and other sedative-hypnotics. In M. Galanter & H. D. Kleber (Eds.), *Textbook of substance abuse treatment* (2nd ed., pp. 239–250). Washington, DC: American Psychiatric Press.

Smith, D. E., Marcus, M. D., & Kaye, W. (1992). Cognitive-behavioral treatment of obese binge eaters. *International Journal of Eating Disorders, 12,* 257–262.

Smith, G. A., & Hall, J. A. (1982). Evaluating Michigan's guilty but mentally ill verdict: An empirical study. *Journal of Law Reform, 16,* 75–112.

Smith, G. P., & Gibbs, J. (2002). Peripheral physiological determinants for eating and body weight. In K. D. Brownell & C. G. Fairburn (Eds.), *Eating disorders and obesity: A comprehensive handbook* (2nd ed., pp. 8–12). New York: Guilford Press.

Smith, G. R., Monson, R. A., & Ray, D. B. (1986). Psychiatric consultation in somatization disorder. *New England Journal of Medicine, 314,* 1407–1413.

Smith, G. T., Simmons, J. R., Flory, K., Annus, A. M., & Hill, K. K. (2007). Thinness and eating expectancies predict subsequent binge-eating and purging behavior among adolescent girls. *Journal of Abnormal Psychology, 116,* 188–197.

Smith, J. E., & Krejci, J. (1991). Minorities join the majority: Eating disturbances among Hispanic and Native American youth. *International Journal of Eating Disorders, 10,* 179–186.

Smith, P. M., Kraemer, H. C., Miller, N. H., DeBusk, R. F., & Taylor, C. B. (1999). In-hospital smoking cessation programs: Who responds, who doesn't? *Journal of Consulting and Clinical Psychology, 67*(1), 19–27.

Smith, R. J. (1991). Somatization disorder: Defining its role in clinical medicine. *Journal of General Internal Medicine, 6,* 168–175.

Smith, T. W. (1992). Hostility and health: Current status of a psychosomatic hypothesis. *Health Psychology, 11*(3), 139–150.

Smith, W., Noonan, C., & Buchwald, D. (2006). Mortality in a cohort of chronically fatigued patients. *Psychological Medicine, 36,* 1301–1306.

Smolak, L., & Levine, M. P. (1996). Adolescent transitions and the development of eating problems. In L. Smolak, M. P. Levine, & R. Striegel-Moore (Eds.), *The developmental psychopathology of eating disorders: Implications for research, prevention, and treatment* (pp. 207–233). Mahwah, NJ: Erlbaum.

Smoller, J. W., Rosenbaum, J. F., & Biederman, J. (2003). Association of a genetic marker at the corticotropin-releasing hormone locus with behavioral inhibition. *Psychiatry, 54,* 1376–1381.

Smoller, J. W., Yamaki, L. H., & Fagerness, J. A. (2005). The corticotropin-releasing hormone gene and be-

havioral inhibition in children at risk for panic disorder. *Biological Psychiatry, 57,* 1485–1492.

Snelling, J., Sahai, A., & Ellis, H. (2003). Attitudes of medical and dental students to dissection. *Clinical Anatomy, 16,* 165–172.

Snowdon, D. A., Kemper, S. J., Mortimer, J. A., Greiner, L. H., Wekstein, D. R., & Markesbery, W. R. (1996). Linguistic ability in early life and cognitive function and Alzheimer's disease in late life: Findings from the nun study. *Journal of the American Medical Association, 275*(7), 528–532.

Snyder, E. Y., Taylor, R. M., & Wolfe, J. H. (1995). Neural progenitor cell engraftment corrects lysosomal storage throughout the MPS VII mouse brain. *Nature, 374,* 367–370.

Snyder, S. H. (1976). The dopamine hypothesis of schizophrenia: Focus on the dopamine receptor. *American Journal of Psychiatry, 133,* 197–202.

Snyder, S. H. (1981). Opiate and benzodiazepine receptors. *Psychosomatics, 22*(11), 986–989.

Snyder, S. H., Burt, D. R., & Creese, I. (1976). Dopamine receptor of mammalian brain: Direct demonstration of binding to agonist and antagonist states. *Neuroscience Symposia, 1,* 28–49.

Sobell, M. B., & Sobell, L. C. (1978). *Behavioral treatment of alcohol problems.* New York: Plenum Press.

Sobell, M. B., & Sobell, L. C. (1993). *Problem drinkers: Guided self-change treatment.* New York: Guilford Press.

Society for Research in Child Development, Committee for Ethical Conduct in Child Development Research. (1990, Winter). SRCD ethical standards for research with children. *SRCD Newsletter,* Chicago.

Soderstrom, H., Sjodin, A.-K., Carlstedt, A., & Forsman, A. (2004). Adult psychopathic personality with childhood-onset hyperactivity and conduct disorder: A central problem constellation in forensic psychiatry. *Psychiatry Research, 121,* 271–280.

Sohn, C., & Lam, R. (2005, August). Update on the biology of seasonal affective disorder. *CNS Spectrums, 10,* 635–646.

Soloff, P. H., Lynch, K. G., Kelley, T. M., Malone, K. M., & Mann, J. J. (2000). Characteristics of suicide attempts of patients with major depressive episode and borderline personality disorder: A comparative study. *American Journal of Psychiatry, 157*(4), 601–608.

Solomon, A., & Haaga, D. A. F. (2003). Reconsideration of self-complexity as a buffer against depression. *Cognitive Therapy & Research, 27,* 579–591.

Solomon, D. A., Keller, M. B., Leon, A. C., Mueller, T. I., Lavori, P. W., Shea, T., et al. (2000). Multiple recurrences of major depressive disorder. *American Journal of Psychiatry, 157*(2), 229–233.

Solomon, D. A., Keller, M. B., Leon, A. C., Mueller, T. I., Shea, M. T., Warshaw, M., et al. (1997). Recovery from major depression: A 10-year prospective follow-up across multiple episodes. *Archives of General Psychiatry, 54,* 1001–1006.

Solomon, D. A., Leon, A. C., Endicott, J., Coryell, W. H., Mueller, T. I., Posternak, M. A., et al. (2003). Unipolar mania over the course of a 20-year follow-up study. *American Journal of Psychiatry, 160,* 2049–2051.

Solomon, R. L. (1980). The opponent-process theory of acquired motivation: The costs of pleasure and the benefits of pain. *American Psychologist, 35,* 691–712.

Solomon, R. L., & Corbit, J. D. (1974). An opponent process theory of motivation: I. Temporal dynamics of affect. *Psychological Review, 81,* 119–145.

Sonuga-Barke, E. J., Daley, D., Thompson, M., Laver-Bradbury, C., & Weeks, A. (2001). Parent-based therapies for preschool attention-deficit/hyperactivity disorder: A randomized, controlled trial with a community sample. *Journal of the American Academy of Child & Adolescent Psychiatry, 40*(4), 402–408.

Southwick, S. M., Krystal, J. H., Johnson, D. R., & Charney, D. S. (1992). Neurobiology of posttrau-

matic stress disorder. In A. Tasman & M. B. Riba (Eds.), *Review of psychiatry* (Vol. 11, pp. 347–367). Washington, DC: American Psychiatric Press.

Sorkin, A., Weinshall, D., Modai, I., & Peled, A. (2006). Improving the accuracy of the diagnosis of schizophrenia by means of virtual reality. *American Journal of Psychiatry, 163,* 512–520.

Spangler, D. L., Simons, A. D., Monroe, S. M., & Thase, M. E. (1996). Gender differences in cognitive diathesis-stress domain match: Implications for differential pathways to depression. *Journal of Abnormal Psychology, 105,* 653–657.

Spangler, D. L., Simons, A. D., Monroe, S. M., & Thase, M. E. (1997). Comparison of cognitive models of depression: Relationships between cognitive constructs and cognitive diathesis-stress match. *Journal of Abnormal Psychology, 106,* 395–403.

Spaniel, F., & Motlova, L. (2007). Information technology aided relapse prevention in schizophrenia: ITAREPS. *European Psychiatry, 22*(Suppl. 1), S140.

Spanos, N. P. (1996). *Multiple identities and false memories: A sociocognitive prospective.* Washington, DC: American Psychological Association.

Spanos, N. P., Cross, P. A., Dickson, K., & DuBreuil, S. C. (1993). Close encounters: An examination of UFO experiences. *Journal of Abnormal Psychology, 102,* 624–632.

Spanos, N. P., James, B., & de Groot, H. P. (1990). Detection of simulated hypnotic amnesia. *Journal of Abnormal Psychology, 99*(2), 179–182.

Spanos, N. P., Weeks, J. R., & Bertrand, L. D. (1985). Multiple personality: A social psychological perspective. *Journal of Abnormal Psychology, 92,* 362–376.

Spector, I. P., & Carey, M. P. (1990). Incidence and prevalence of the sexual dysfunctions: A critical review of the empirical literature. *Archives of Sexual Behavior, 19*(4), 389–408.

Spector, R. (2001). Is there racial bias in clinicians' perceptions of the dangerousness of psychiatric patients? A review of the literature. *Journal of Mental Health, 10,* 5–15.

Spence, S. H., Sheffield, J. K., & Donovan, C. L. (2003). Preventing adolescent depression: An evaluation of the problem solving for life program. *Journal of Consulting and Clinical Psychology, 71,* 3–13.

Spencer, T. J. (2006). ADHD and comorbidity in childhood. *Journal of Clinical Psychiatry, 67*(Suppl 8), 27–31

Spiegel, D. (1995). Hypnosis and suggestion. In D. L. Schacter (Ed.), *Memory distortion: How minds, brains, and societies reconstruct the past.* Cambridge, MA: Harvard University Press.

Spiegel, D. (1996). Cancer and depression. *British Journal of Psychiatry, 168*(Suppl. 30), 109–116.

Spiegel, D., & Cardeña, E. (1991). Disintegrated experience: The dissociative disorders revisited. *Journal of Abnormal Psychology, 100*(3), 366–378.

Spiegel, D., Bloom, J. R., Kramer, H. C., & Gotheil, E. (1989). Effect of psychosocial treatment on survival of patients with metastatic breast cancer. *Lancet, 14,* 888–891.

Spiegel, D., Morrow, G. R., Classen, C., Riggs, G., Stott, P. B., Mudaliar, N., Pierce, H. I., Flynn, P. J., & Heard, L. (1996). Effects of group therapy on women with primary breast cancer. *The Breast Journal, 2*(1), 104–106.

Spiegel, D., Wiegel, M., Baker, S. L., & Greene, K. A. I. (2000). Pharmacological management of anxiety disorders. In D. I. Mostofsky & D. H. Barlow (Eds.), *The management of stress and anxiety in medical disorders* (pp. 36–65). Needham Heights, MA: Allyn & Bacon.

Spielberger, C. D., & Frank, R. G. (1992). Injury control: A promising field for psychologists. *American Psychologist, 47*(8), 1029–1030.

Spielman, A. J., & Glovinsky, P. (1991). The varied nature of insomnia. In P. J. Hauri (Ed.), *Case studies in insomnia* (pp. 1–15). New York: Plenum Press.

Spiker, D., & Ricks, M. (1984). Visual self-recognition in autistic children: Developmental relationships. *Child Development, 55,* 214–225.

Spinelli, M. G., & Endicott, J. (2003). Controlled clinical trial of interpersonal psychotherapy versus parenting education program for depressed pregnant women. *American Journal of Psychiatry, 160,* 555–562.

Spira, A., Bajos, N., Bejin, A., Beltzer, N., Bozon, M., Ducot, M., et al. (1992). AIDS and sexual behavior in France. *Nature, 360,* 407–409.

Spitzer, C., Spelsberg, B., Grabe, H. J., Mundt, B., & Freyberger, H. J. (1999). Dissociative experiences and psychopathology in conversion disorders. *Journal of Psychosomatic Research, 46*(3), 291–294.

Spitzer, R. L. (1991). An outsider–insider's views about revising the DSMs. *Journal of Abnormal Psychology, 100*(3), 294–296.

Spitzer, R. L. (1999). Harmful dysfunction and the DSM definition of mental disorder. *Journal of Abnormal Psychology, 108,* 430–432.

Spitzer, R. L., Devlin, M. J., Walsh, B. T., Hasin, D., Wing, R., Marcus, M. D., et al. (1991). Binge eating disorder: To be or not to be in DSM-IV. *International Journal of Eating Disorders, 10,* 627–629.

Spitzer, R. L., Forman, J. B. W., & Nee, J. (1979). DSM-III field trials: I. Initial interrater diagnostic reliability. *American Journal of Psychiatry, 136,* 815–817.

Spitzer, R. L., Yanovski, S. Z., Wadden, T., Wing, R., Marcus, M., Stunkard, A., et al. (1993). Binge eating disorder: Its further validation in a multi-site study. *International Journal of Eating Disorders, 13,* 137–153.

Spoont, M. R. (1992). Modulatory role of serotonin in neural information processing: Implications for human psychopathology. *Psychological Bulletin, 112*(2), 330–350.

Sprock, J. (2000). Gender-typed behavioral examples of histrionic personality disorder. *Journal of Psychopathology and Behavioral Assessment, 22,* 107–122.

Spurrell, E. B., Wilfley, D. E., Tanofsky, M. B., & Brownell, K. D. (1997). Age of onset for binge eating: Are there different pathways to binge eating? *International Journal of Eating Disorders, 21,* 55–65.

Staal, W. G., Pol, H. E. H., Schnack, H. G., Hoogendoorn, M. L. C., Jellema, K., & Kahn, R. S. (2000). Structural brain abnormalities in patients with schizophrenia and their healthy siblings. *American Journal of Psychiatry, 157,* 416–421.

Stall, R., McKusick, L., Wiley, J., Coates, T. J., & Ostrow, D. G. (1986). Alcohol and drug use during sexual activity and compliance with safe sex guidelines for AIDS. *Health Education Quarterly, 13,* 359–371.

Stanley, B., & Brodsky, B. S. (2005). Dialectical behavior therapy. In J. M. Oldham, A. E. Skodol, & D. S. Bender (Eds.), *Textbook of personality disorders* (pp. 307–320). Washington, DC: American Psychiatric Publishing.

Stanley, M. A., Beck, J. G., & Glassco, J. D. (1997). Generalized anxiety in older adults: Treatment with cognitive-behavioral and supportive approaches. *Behavior Therapy, 27,* 565–581.

Stanley, M. A., Beck, J. G., Novy, D. M., Averill, P. M., Swann, A. C., Diefenbach, G. J., & Hopko, D. R. (2003). Cognitive-behavioral treatment of late-life generalized anxiety disorder. *Journal of Consulting and Clinical Psychology, 71*(2), 309–319.

Starkman, M. N., Giordani, B., Gebarski, S. S., Berent, S., Schork, M. A., & Schteingart, D. E. (1999). Decrease in cortisol reverses human hippocampal atrophy following treatment of Cushing's disease. *Biological Psychiatry, 46,* 1595–1602.

State v. Campanaro, Nos. 632–79, 1309–79, 1317–79, 514–80, & 707–80 (S. Ct. N.J. Criminal Division, Union County, 1980).

Stefan, S. (1996). Issues relating to women and ethnic minorities in mental health treatment and law. In B. D. Sales & D. W. Shuman (Eds.), *Law, mental health, and mental disorder* (pp. 240–278). Pacific Grove, CA: Brooks/Cole.

Stein, M. B., Goldin, P. R., Sareen, J., Zorrilla, L. T., & Brown, G. G. (2002). Increased amygdala activation to angry and contemptuous faces in generalized social phobia. *Archives of General Psychiatry, 59,* 1027–1034.

Stein, M. B., Liebowitz, M. R., Lydiard, R. B., Pitts, C. D., Bushnell, W., & Gergel, I. (1998). Paroxetine treatment of generalized social phobia (social anxiety disorder). A randomized clinical trial. *JAMA, 280,* 708–713.

Stein, M. I. (1978). Thematic apperception test and related methods. In B. B. Wolman (Ed.), *Clinical diagnosis of mental disorders: A handbook* (pp. 179–235). New York: Plenum Press.

Steinberg, A. B., & Phares, V. (2001). Family functioning, body image, and eating disturbances. In J. K. Thompson & L. Smolak (Eds.), *Body image, eating disorders, and obesity in youth: Assessment, prevention and treatment* (127–147). Washington, DC: American Psychological Association.

Steinberg, M. (1991). The spectrum of depersonalization: Assessment and treatment. *Annual Review of Psychiatry, 10,* 223–247.

Steinglass, P., Weisstub, E., & Kaplan De-Nour, A. K. (1988). Perceived personal networks as mediators of stress reactions. *American Journal of Psychiatry, 145,* 1259–1264.

Steketee, G., & Frost, R. O. (2007a). *Compulsive hoarding and acquiring: Client workbook.* New York: Oxford University Press.

Steketee, G., & Frost, R. O. (2007b). *Compulsive hoarding and acquiring: Therapist guide.* New York: Oxford University Press.

Steketee, G., & Barlow, D. H. (2002). Obsessive-compulsive disorder. In D. H. Barlow, *Anxiety and its disorders: The nature and treatment of anxiety and panic* (2nd ed.). New York: Guilford Press.

Steketee, G., Quay, S., & White, K. (1991). Religion and guilt in OCD patients. *Journal of Anxiety Disorders, 5,* 359–367.

Stenvall, M., Olofsson, B., Lundstrom, M., Svensson, O., Nyberg, L., & Gustafson, Y. (2006). Inpatient falls and injuries in older patients treated for femoral neck fracture. *Archives of Gerontology and Geriatrics, 43,* 389–399.

Stepanski, E. J. (2006). Causes of insomnia. In T. Lee-Chiong (Ed.), *Sleep: A comprehensive handbook* (pp. 99–102). Hoboken, NJ: John Wiley & Sons.

Stephenson, J. (2003). Global AIDS epidemic worsens. *JAMA, 291,* 31–32.

Stewart, S. H. (1996). Alcohol abuse in individuals exposed to trauma: A critical review. *Psychological Bulletin, 120,* 85–112.

Stewart-Williams, S. (2004). The placebo puzzle: Putting together the pieces. *Health Psychology, 23,* 198–206.

Stewart-Williams, S., & Podd, J. (2004). The placebo effect: Dissolving the expectancy versus conditioning debate. *Psychological Bulletin, 130,* 324–340.

Stice, E., & Shaw, H. (2004). Eating disorder prevention programs: A meta-analytic review. *Psychological Bulletin, 130,* 206–227.

Stice, E., Agras, W. S., Telch, C. F., Halmi, K. A., Mitchell, J. E., & Wilson, G. T. (2001). Subtyping binge eating disordered women along dieting and negative affect dimension. *International Journal of Eating Disorders, 30,* 11–27.

Stice, E., Akutagawa, D., Gaggar, A., & Agras, W. S. (2000). Negative affect moderates the relation between dieting and binge eating. *International Journal of Eating Disorders, 27,* 218–229.

Stice, E., Cameron, R. P., Killen, J. D., Hayward, C., & Taylor, C. B. (1999). Naturalistic weight-reduction efforts prospectively predict growth in relative weight and onset of obesity among female adolescents. *Journal of Consulting and Clinical Psychology, 67,* 967–974.

Stice, E., Presnell, K., Gau, J., & Shaw, H. (2007). Testing mediators of intervention effects in randomized controlled trials: An evaluation of two eating disorder prevention programs. *Journal of Consulting and Clinical Psychology, 75,* 20–32.

Stice, E., Presnell, K., Shaw, H., & Rohde, P. (2005). Psychological and behavioral risk factors for obesity onset in adolescent girls: A prospective study. *Journal of Consulting and Clinical Psychology, 73,* 195–202.

Stice, E., Schupak-Neuberg, E., Shaw, H. E., & Stein, R. I. (1994). Relation of media exposure to eating disorder symptomatology: An examination of mediating mechanisms. *Journal of Abnormal Psychology, 103,* 836–840.

Stice, E., Shaw, H., & Marti, C. N. (2006). A meta-analytic review of obesity prevention programs for children and adolescents: The skinny on interventions that work. (2006). *Psychological Bulletin, 132,* 667–691.

Stirling, J., Barkus, E., & Lewis, S. (2007). Hallucination proneness, schizotypy and meta-cognition. *Behaviour Research and Therapy, 45,* 1401–1408.

Stock, W. (1993). Inhibited female orgasm. In W. O'Donohue & J. H. Geer (Eds.), *Handbook of sexual dysfunctions: Assessment and treatment* (pp. 253–277). Boston: Allyn & Bacon.

Stoler, J. M., Ryan, L. M., & Holmes, L. B. (2002). Alcohol dehydrogenase 2 genotypes, maternal alcohol use, and infant outcome. *The Journal of Pediatrics, 141,* 780–785.

Stoller, R. J. (1976). Two feminized male American Indians. *Archives of Sexual Behavior, 5,* 529–538.

Stoller, R. J. (1982). Transvestism in women. *Archives of Sexual Behavior, 11,* 99–115.

Stone, A. B., Pearlstein, T. B., & Brown, W. A. (1991). Fluoxetine in the treatment of late luteal phase dysphoric disorder. *Journal of Clinical Psychiatry, 52*(7), 290–293.

Stone, G. C. (1987). The scope of health psychology. In G. C. Stone, S. M. Weiss, J. D. Matarazzo, N. E. Miller, J. Rodin, D. D. Belar, M. J. Follick, & J. E. Singer (Eds.), *Health psychology: A discipline and a profession.* Chicago: University of Chicago Press.

Stone, J., Smyth, R., Carson, A., Lewis, S., Prescott, R., Warlow, C., et al. (2005). Systematic review of misdiagnosis of conversion symptoms and hysteria. *British Medical Journal, 331,* no pagination specified.

Stone, J., Smyth, R., Carson, A., Warlow, C., & Sharpe, M. (2006). La belle indifference in conversion symptoms and hysteria: Systematic review. *British Journal of Psychiatry, 188,* 204–209.

Stone, M. H. (1989). The course of borderline personality disorder. In A. Tasman, R. E. Hales, & A. J. Frances (Eds.), *Annual review of psychiatry* (Vol. 8, pp. 103–122). Washington, DC: American Psychiatric Press.

Stone, M. H. (1993). Cluster C personality disorders. In D. L. Dunner (Ed.), *Current psychiatric therapy* (pp. 411–417). Philadelphia: W. B. Saunders.

Stone, M. H. (2001). Schizoid and schizotypal personality disorders. In G. O. Gabbard (Ed.), *Treatment of psychiatric disorders* (Vol. 2, 3rd ed., pp. 2237–2250). Washington, DC: American Psychiatric Publishing.

Stone, R. (2000). Stress: The invisible hand in eastern Europe's death rates. *Science, 288,* 1732–1733.

Stoolmiller, M., Hyoun, K., & Capaldi, D. (2005). The course of depressive symptoms in men from early adolescence to young adulthood: Identifying latent trajectories and early predictors. *Journal of Abnormal Psychology, 114,* 331–345.

Strahl, C., Kleinknecht, R. A., & Dinnel, D. L. (2000). The role of pain anxiety, coping, and pain self-efficacy in rheumatoid arthritis patient functioning. *Behaviour Research and Therapy, 38,* 863–873.

Strain, E. C., & Griffiths, R. R. (2005). Caffeine-related disorders. In B. J. Sadock & V. A. Sadock (Eds.), *Kaplan & Sadock's comprehensive textbook of psychiatry* (pp. 1201–1210). Philadelphia: Lippincott, Williams & Wilkins.

Strassberg, D. S., Kelly, M. P., Carroll, C., & Kircher, J. C. (1987). The psychophysiological nature of premature ejaculation. *Archives of Sexual Behavior, 16,* 327–336.

Straus, S. E., Tosato, G., Armstrong, G., Lawley, T., Preble, O. T., Henle, W., et al. (1985). Persisting illness and fatigue in adults with evidence of Epstein Barr virus infection. *Annals of Internal Medicine, 102,* 7–16.

Strauss, J. L., Hayes, A. M., Johnson, S. L., Newman, C. F., Brown, G. K., Barber, J. P., et al. (2006). Early alliance, alliance ruptures, and symptom change in a nonrandomized trial of cognitive therapy for avoidant and obsessive-compulsive personality disorders. *Journal of Consulting and Clinical Psychology, 74,* 337–345.

Strauss, S. E. (1988). The chronic mononucleosis syndrome. *Journal of Infectious Disease, 157,* 405–412.

Stravynski, A., Elie, R., & Franche, R. L. (1989). Perception of early parenting by patients diagnosed with avoidant personality disorder: A test of the overprotection hypothesis. *Acta Psychiatrica Scandinavica, 80,* 415–420.

Stravynski, A., Lesage, A., Marcouiller, M., & Elie, R. (1989). A test of the therapeutic mechanism in social skills training with avoidant personality disorder. *Journal of Nervous and Mental Disease, 177,* 739–744.

Strickland, B. R. (1992). Women and depression. *Current Directions in Psychological Science, 1*(4), 132–135.

Striegel-Moore, R. H., & Franko, D. L. (2002). Body image issues among girls and women. In T. F. Cash & T. Pruzinsky (Eds.), *Body image: A handbook of theory, research and clinical practice* (pp. 183–191). New York: Guilford Press.

Striegel-Moore, R. H., Cachelin, F. M., Dohm, F. A., Pike, M., Wilfley, D. E., & Fairburn, C. G. (2001). Comparison of binge eating disorder and bulimia nervosa in a community sample. *International Journal of Eating Disorders, 29,* 157–165.

Striegel-Moore, R. H., Dohm, F. A., Kaemer, H. C., Taylor, C. B., Daniels, S., Crawford, P. B., et al. (2003). Eating disorders in white and black women. *American Journal of Psychiatry, 160,* 1326–1331.

Striegel-Moore, R. H., Silberstein, L. R., & Rodin, J. (1986). Toward an understanding of risk factors for bulimia. *American Psychologist, 3,* 246–263.

Striegel-Moore, R. H., Silberstein, L. R., & Rodin, J. (1993). The social self in bulimia nervosa: Public self-consciousness, social anxiety, and perceived fraudulence. *Journal of Abnormal Psychology, 102*(2), 297–303.

Strober, M. (2002). Family–genetic perspectives on anorexia nervosa and bulimia nervosa. In K. D. Brownell & C. G. Fairburn (Eds.), *Eating disorders and obesity: A comprehensive handbook* (2nd ed., pp. 212–218). New York: Guilford Press.

Strober, M., & Humphrey, L. L. (1987). Familial contributions to the etiology and course of anorexia nervosa and bulimia. Special issue: Eating disorders. *Journal of Consulting and Clinical Psychology, 55*(5), 654–659.

Strober, M., Freeman, R., Lampert, C., Diamond, J., & Kaye, W. (2000). Controlled family study of anorexia nervosa and bulimia nervosa: Evidence of shared liability and transmission of partial syndromes. *American Journal of Psychiatry, 157,* 393–401.

Stroebe, M., Stroebe, W., & Abakoumkin, G. (2005). The broken heart: Suicidal ideation in bereavement. *American Journal of Psychiatry, 162,* 2178–2180.

Stroup, T. S., Kraus, J. E., & Marder, S. R. (2006). Pharmacotherapies. In J. A. Lieberman, T. S. Stroup, & D. O. Perkins (Eds.), *The American Psychiatric Publishing textbook of schizophrenia* (pp. 303–325). Washington, DC: American Psychiatric Publishing.

Suarez, E. C., Lewis, J. G., & Kuhn, C. (2002). The relation of aggression, hostility, and anger to lipopolysaccharidestimulated tumor necrosis factor (TNF)-(by blood monocytes from normal men. *Behavior and Immunity, 16,* 675–684.

Suárez, L., Bennett, S., Goldstein, C., & Barlow, D. H. (in press). Understanding anxiety disorders from a "triple vulnerabilities" framework. In M. M. Antony & M. B. Stein (Eds.), *Oxford handbook of anxiety and related disorders.* New York: Oxford University Press.

Substance Abuse and Mental Health Services Administration, Office of Applied Studies. (2002). *Emergency department trends from the Drug Abuse Warning Network, final estimates 1994–2001,* DAWN Series D-21, DHHS Publication No. (SMA) 02-3635, Rockville, MD: Author.

Substance Abuse and Mental Health Services Administration, Office of Applied Studies. (2003). *Emergency department trends from the Drug Abuse Warning Network, final estimates 1995–2002,* DAWN Series D-24, DHHS Publication No. (SMA) 02-3780, Rockville, MD: Author.

Substance Abuse and Mental Health Services Administration, Office of Applied Studies. (2006). *Results from the 2005 national survey on drug use and health: National findings,* NSDUH Series H-30, DHHS Publication No. SMA 06-4194, Rockville, MD: Author.

Sugiyama, T., & Abe, T. (1989). The prevalence of autism in Nagoya, Japan: A total population study. *Journal of Autism and Developmental Disorders, 19,* 87–96.

Suh, J. J., Pettinati, H. M., Kampman, K. M., & O'Brien, C. P. (2006). The status of disulfiram: A half of a century later. *Journal of Clinical Psychopharmacology, 26,* 290–302.

Sullivan, G. M., Kent, J. M., & Coplan, J. D. (2000). The neurobiology of stress and anxiety. In D. I. Mostofsky & D. H. Barlow (Eds.), *The management of stress and anxiety in medical disorders* (pp. 15–35). Needham Heights, MA: Allyn & Bacon.

Sullivan, G. M., & LeDoux, J. E. (2004). Synaptic self: Conditioned fear, developed adversity, and the anxious individual. In J. M. Gorman (Ed.), *Fear and anxiety: The benefits of translational research* (pp. 1–22). Washington, DC: American Psychiatric Publishing.

Sullivan, P. F. (1995). Mortality in anorexia nervosa. *American Journal of Psychiatry, 152,* 1073–1074.

Sullivan, P. F., Owen, M. J., O'Donovan, M. C., & Freedman, R. (2006). Genetics. In J. A. Lieberman, T. S. Stroup, & D. O. Perkins (Eds.), *The American Psychiatric Publishing textbook of schizophrenia* (pp. 39–53). Washington, DC: American Psychiatric Publishing.

Sulloway, F. (1979). *Freud, biologist of the mind.* London: Burnett.

Suls, J., & Bunde, J. (2005). Anger, anxiety, and depression as risk factors for cardiovascular disease: The problems and implications of overlapping affective dispositions. *Psychological Bulletin, 131,* 260–300.

Sumiyoshi, C., Sumiyoshi, T., Nohara, S., Yamashita, I., Matsui, M., Kurachi, M., & Niwa, S. (2005). Disorganization of semantic memory underlies alogia in schizophrenia: An analysis of verbal fluency performance in Japanese subjects. *Schizophrenia Research, 74,* 91–100.

Suomi, S. J. (1999). Attachment in rhesus monkeys. In J. Cassidy & P. Shaver (Eds.), *Handbook of attachment: Theory, research, and clinical applications* (pp. 181–197). New York: Guilford Press.

Suomi, S. J. (2000). A biobehavioral perspective on developmental psychopathology. In A. J. Sameroff, J. Lewis, & S. M. Miller (Eds.), *Handbook of developmental psychopathology* (pp. 237–256). New York: Kluwer Academic/Plenum.

Suppes, T., Baldessarini, R. J., Faedda, G. L., & Tohen, M. (1991). Risk of recurrence following discontinuation of lithium treatment in bipolar disorder. *Archives of General Psychiatry, 48*(12), 1082–1088.

Sutker, P. B., Bugg, F., & West, J. A. (1993). Antisocial personality disorder. In P. B. Sutker & H. E. Adams (Eds.), *Comprehensive handbook of psychopathology* (2nd ed., pp. 337–369). New York: Plenum Press.

Svartberg, M., Stiles, T. C., & Seltzer, M. H. (2004). Randomized, controlled trial of the effectiveness of short-term dynamic psychotherapy and cognitive therapy for cluster C personality disorders. *American Journal of Psychiatry, 161,* 810–817.

Svrakic, D. M., & Cloninger, C. R. (2005). Personality disorders. In B. J. Sadock & V. A. Sadock (Eds.), *Kaplan & Sadock's comprehensive textbook of psychiatry* (pp. 2063–2104). Philadelphia: Lippincott, Williams & Wilkins.

Swanda, R. M., & Haaland, K. Y. (2005). In B. J. Sadock & V. A. Sadock (Eds.), *Kaplan & Sadock's comprehensive textbook of psychiatry* (pp. 860–874). Philadelphia: Lippincott Williams & Wilkins.

Swartz, M., Blazer, D., George, L., & Landerman, R. (1986). Somatization disorder in a community population. *American Journal of Psychiatry, 143,* 1403–1408.

Swartz, M., Blazer, D., Woodbury, M., George, L., & Landerman, R. (1986). Somatization disorder in a U.S. southern community: Use of a new procedure for analysis of medical classification. *Psychological Medicine, 16,* 595–609.

Swartz, M. S., Lauriello, J., & Drake, R. E. (2006). Psychosocial therapies. In J. A. Lieberman, T. S. Stroup, & D. O. Perkins (Eds.), *The American Psychiatric Publishing textbook of schizophrenia* (pp. 327–340). Washington, DC: American Psychiatric Publishing.

Swedo, S. E., (2002). Pediatric autoimmune neuropsychiatric disorders associated with streptococcal infections (PANDAS). *Molecular Psychiatry, 7,* S24–S35.

Swedo, S. E., Pleeter, J. D., Richter, D. M., Hoffman, C. L., Allen, A. J., Hamburger, S. D., et al. (1995). Rates of seasonal affective disorder in children and adolescents. *American Journal of Psychiatry, 152,* 1016–1019.

Szasz, T. (1961). *The myth of mental illness: Foundations of a theory of personal conduct.* New York: Hoeber-Harper.

Szmukler, G. I., Eisler, I., Gillis, C., & Haywood, M. E. (1985). The implications of anorexia nervosa in a ballet school. *Journal of Psychiatric Research, 19,* 177–181.

Takahasi, T. (1989). Social phobia syndrome in Japan. *Comprehensive Psychiatry, 30,* 45–52.

Takei, N., Lewis, S., Jones, P., Harvey, I., & Murray, R. M. (1996). Prenatal exposure to influenza and increased cerebrospinal fluid spaces in schizophrenia. *Schizophrenia Bulletin, 22,* 521–534.

Talbott, J. A. (1990). Current perspectives in the United States on the chronically mentally ill. In A. Kales, C. N. Stefanis, & J. A. Talbott (Eds.), *Recent advances in schizophrenia* (pp. 279–295). New York: Springer-Verlag.

Tan, E. S. (1980). Transcultural aspects of anxiety. In G. D. Burrows & B. Davies (Eds.), *Handbook of studies on anxiety.* Amsterdam: Elsevier/North-Holland.

Tannock, R. (2005a). Mathematics disorder. In B. J. Sadock & V. A. Sadock (Eds.), *Kaplan & Sadock's comprehensive textbook of psychiatry* (pp. 3116–3123). Philadelphia: Lippincott, Williams & Wilkins.

Tannock, R. (2005b). Reading disorder. In B. J. Sadock & V. A. Sadock (Eds.), *Kaplan & Sadock's comprehensive textbook of psychiatry* (pp. 3107–3116). Philadelphia: Lippincott, Williams & Wilkins.

Tarasoff v. Regents of University of California ("Tarasoff I"), 529 P.2d 553 (Cal. S. Ct. 1974).

Tarasoff v. Regents of University of California ("Tarasoff II"), 551 P.2d 334 (Cal. S. Ct. 1976).

Tardiff, K. J. (2003). Violence. In R. E. Hales & S. C. Yudofsky (Eds.), *Textbook of clinical psychiatry* (4th ed., pp. 1485–1509). Washington, DC: American Psychiatric Publishing.

Taylor, C. B., Sheikh, J., Agras, W. S., Roth, W. T., Margraf, J., Ehlers, A., et al. (1986). Self-report of panic attacks: Agreement with heart rate changes. *American Journal of Psychiatry, 143,* 478–482.

Taylor, J., & Lang, A. R. (2006). Psychopathy and substance use disorders. In C. J. Patrick (Ed.), *Handbook of psychopathy* (pp. 495–511). New York: Guilford Press.

Taylor, M. A., & Abrams, R. (1981). Early- and late-onset bipolar illness. *Archives of General Psychiatry, 38*(1), 58–61.

Taylor, R. R., Jason, L. A., Richman, J. A., Torres-Harding, S. R., King, C., & Song, S. (2003). Epidemiology. In L. A. Jason, P. A. Fennell, & R. R. Taylor (Eds.), *Handbook of chronic fatigue syndrome.* Hoboken, NJ: John Wiley.

Taylor, S. (1996). Meta-analysis of cognitive behavioral treatment for social phobia. *Journal of Behavior Therapy and Experimental Psychiatry, 27,* 1–9.

Taylor, S. (2003). *Health psychology* (5th ed.). San Francisco: McGraw-Hill.

Taylor, S., & Asmundson, J. G. (2004). *Treating health anxiety: A cognitive behavioral approach.* New York: Guilford Press.

Taylor, S., Asmundson, G., & Coons, M. (2005). Current directions in the treatment of hypochondriasis. *Journal of Cognitive Psychotherapy: An International Quarterly, 19,* 285–304.

Taylor, S. E. (1999). *Health psychology* (4th ed.). Boston: McGraw-Hill.

Taylor, S. E. (2002). *The tending instinct: How nurturing is essential to who we are and how we live.* New York: Henry Holt and Company.

Taylor, S. E., Klein, L. C., Lewis, B. P., Gruenewald, T. L., Gurung, R. A. R., & Updegraff, J. A. (2000). Biobehavioral responses to stress in females: Tend-and-befriend, not fight-or-flight. *Psychological Review, 107,* 411–429.

Taylor, S. E., Repetti, R. L., & Seeman, T. (1997). Health psychology: What is an unhealthy environment and how does it get under the skin? *Annual Review of Psychology, 48,* 411–447.

Taylor, S., & Koch, W. J. (1995). Anxiety disorders due to motor vehicle accidents: Nature and treatment. *Clinical Psychology Review, 15,* 721–738.

Teasdale, J. D. (1993). Emotion and two kinds of meaning: Cognitive therapy and applied cognitive science. *Behaviour Research and Therapy, 31*(4), 339–354.

Teasdale, J. D., Scott, J., Moore, R. G., Hayhurst, H., Scott, J., Pope, M., et al. (2001). How does cognitive therapy prevent relapse in residual depression? Evidence from a controlled trial. *Journal of Consulting and Clinical Psychology, 69,* 347–357.

Teasdale, J. D., Segal, Z. V., Williams, J. M., Ridgeway, V. A., Soulsby, J. M., & Lau, M. A. (2000). Prevention of relapse/recurrence in major depression by mindfulness-based cognitive therapy. *Journal of Consulting and Clinical Psychology, 4,* 615–623.

Teicher, M. H., Glod, C., & Cole, J. O. (1990). Emergence of intense suicidal preoccupation during fluoxetine treatment. *American Journal of Psychiatry, 147*(1), 207–210.

Telch, C. F., & Agras, W. S. (1993). The effects of a very low calorie diet on binge eating. *Behavior Therapy, 24,* 177–193.

Telch, C. F., Agras, W. S., & Rossiter, E. M. (1988). Binge eating increases with increasing adiposity. *International Journal of Eating Disorders, 7,* 115–119.

Telch, M. J., Lucas, J. A., & Nelson, P. (1989). Nonclinical panic in college students: An investigation of prevalence and symptomatology. *Journal of Abnormal Psychology, 98,* 300–306.

Tellegen, A. (1978). *Manual for the Multidimensional Personality Questionnaire.* Unpublished manuscript, University of Minnesota, Minneapolis.

Temple, E., Deutisch, G. K., Poldrack, R. A., Miller, S. L., Tallal, P., Merzenich, M. M., & Gabrieli, J. D. E. (2003). Neural deficits in children with dyslexia ameliorated by behavioral remediation: Evidence from functional MRI. *Proceedings of the National Academy of Sciences, 100,* 2860–2865.

ter Kuile, M., van Lankveld, J., Jacques, J., de Groot, E., Melles, R., Neffs, J., & Zanbergen, M. (2007). Cognitive-behavioral therapy for women with lifelong vaginismus: Process and prognostic factors. *Behaviour Research and Therapy, 45,* 359–373.

Teri, L., Gibbons, L. E., McCurry, S. M., Logsdon, R. G., Buchner, D. M., Barlow, W. E., et al. (2003). Exercise plus behavioral management in patients with Alzheimer's disease: A randomized controlled trial. *JAMA, 290,* 2015–2022.

Terman, J. S., Terman, M., Lo, E., & Cooper, T. B. (2001). Circadian time of morning light administration and therapeutic response in winter depression. *Archives of General Psychiatry, 58,* 69–75.

Terman, M. (1988). On the question of mechanism in phototherapy for seasonal affective disorder: Considerations of clinical efficacy and epidemiology. *Journal of Biological Rhythms, 3*(2), 155–172.

Terman, M., & Terman, J. S. (2006). Controlled trial of naturalistic dawn simulation and negative air ionization for seasonal affective disorder. *American Journal of Psychiatry, 163*(12), 2126–2133.

Terman, M., Terman, J. S., & Ross, D. C. (1998). A controlled trial of timed bright light and negative air ionization of treatment of winter depression. *Archives of General Psychiatry, 55,* 875–882.

Thaker, G. K., & Avila, M. (2003). Schizophrenia, V: Risk markers. *American Journal of Psychiatry, 160,* 1578.

Thase, M. (2005). Major depressive disorder. In Frank Adrasik (Ed.), *Comprehensive handbook of personality and psychopathology. Volume 2: Adult psychopathology* (pp. 207–230). New York: Wiley.

Thase, M., Jindal, R., & Howland, R. (2002). Biological aspects of depression. In I. H. Gotlib & C. L. Hammen (Eds.), *Handbook of depression* (pp. 192–218). New York: Guilford Press.

Thase, M. E. (1990). Relapse and recurrence in unipolar major depression: Short-term and long-term approaches. *Journal of Clinical Psychiatry, 51*(Suppl. 6), 51–57.

Thase, M. E., & Kupfer, D. J. (1996). Recent developments in the pharmacotherapy of mood disorders. *Journal of Consulting and Clinical Psychology, 64,* 646–659.

Thase, M. E., Simons, A. D., & Reynolds, C. F., III. (1996). Abnormal electroencephalographic sleep profiles in major depression. *Archives of General Psychiatry, 53,* 99–108.

Thayer, J. F., Friedman, B. H., & Borkovec, T. D. (1996). Autonomic characteristics of generalized anxiety disorder and worry. *Biological Psychiatry, 39,* 255–266.

The evolving insanity defense. (2006). *ABA Journal, 92,* 37–37.

Theander, S. (1985). Outcome and prognosis in anorexia nervosa and bulimia: Some results of previous investigations, compared with those of the Swedish long-term study. *Journal of Psychiatric Research, 19,* 493–508.

Thies-Flechtner, K., Muller-Oerlinghausen, B., Seibert, W., Walther, A., & Greil, W. (1996). Effect of prophylactic treatment on suicide risk in patients with major affective disorders: Data from a randomized prospective trial. *Pharmacopsychiatry, 29,* 103–107.

Thompson v. County of Alameda, 614 P.2d 728 (Cal. S. Ct. 1980).

Thompson, J. K., & Kinder, B. (2003). Eating disorders. In M. Hersen & S. Turner (Eds.), *Handbook of adult psychopathology* (4th ed., pp. 555–582). New York: Plenum.

Thompson, J. K., & Stice, E. (2001). Thin-idea internalization: Mounting evidence for a new risk factor for body-image disturbance and eating pathology. *Current Directions in Psychological Science, 11,* 181–183.

Thompson-Brenner, H., Glass, S., & Westen, D. (2003). A multidimensional meta-analysis of psychotherapy for bulimia nervosa. *Clinical Psychology: Science and Practice, 10,* 269–287.

Thoresen, C. E., & Powell, L. H. (1992). Type A behavior pattern: New perspectives on theory, assessment and intervention. Special issue: Behavioral medicine: An update for the 1990s. *Journal of Consulting and Clinical Psychology, 60*(4), 595–604.

Thorgeirsson, T. E., Oskarsson, H., Desnica, N., Kostic, J. P., Stefansson, J. G., Kolbeinsson, H., et al. (2003). Anxiety with panic disorder linked to chromosome 9q in Iceland. *American Journal of Human Genetics, 72,* 1221–1230.

Thorpe, G. L., & Burns, L. E. (1983). *The agoraphobic syndrome.* New York: John Wiley.

Thyer, B. A. (1993). Childhood separation anxiety disorder and adult-onset agoraphobia: Review of evidence. In C. Last (Ed.), *Anxiety across the lifespan: A developmental perspective* (pp. 128–145). New York: Springer.

Tienari, P. (1991). Interaction between genetic vulnerability and family environment: The Finnish adoptive family study of schizophrenia. *Acta Psychiatrica Scandinavica, 84,* 460–465.

Tienari, P., Wahlberg, K.-E., & Wynne, L. C. (2006). Finnish adoption study of schizophrenia: Implications for family interventions. *Families, Systems & Health, 24,* 442–451.

Tienari, P., Wynne, L. C., Laksy, K., Moring, J., Nieminen, P., Sorri, A., et al. (2003). Genetic boundaries of the schizophrenia spectrum: Evidence from the Finnish Adoptive Family Study of Schizophrenia. *American Journal of Psychiatry, 160,* 1567–1594.

Tienari, P., Wynne, L. C., Moring, J., Lahti, I., Naarala, M., Sorri, A., et al. (1994). The Finnish adoptive family study of schizophrenia: Implications for family research. *British Journal of Psychiatry, 23*(Suppl. 164), 20–26.

Tiffany, S. T., Cox, L. S., & Elash, C. A. (2000). Effects of transdermal nicotine patches on abstinence-induced and cue-elicited craving in cigarette smokers. *Journal of Consulting and Clinical Psychology, 68*(2), 233–240.

Tiggemann, M. (2002). Media influences on body image development. In T. F. Cash & T. Pruzinsky (Eds.), *Body image: A handbook of theory, research and clinical practice* (pp. 91–98). New York: Guilford Press.

Tiggemann, M., & Lynch, J. E. (2001). Body image across the life span in adult women: The role of self-objectification. *Developmental Psychology, 37,* 243–253.

Timimi, S., & Taylor, E. (2004). ADHD is best understood as a cultural construct. *British Journal of Psychiatry, 184,* 8–9.

Tinbergen, E. A., & Tinbergen, N. (1972). *Early childhood autism: An ethological approach.* Berlin: Paul Parey.

Tingelstad, J. B. (1991). The cardiotoxicity of the tricyclics. *Journal of the American Academy of Child and Adolescent Psychiatry, 30,* 845–846.

Tjio, J. H., & Levan, A. (1956). The chromosome number of man. *Hereditas, 42,* 1–6.

Tobin, D. L., Griffing, A., & Griffing, S. (1997). An examination of subtype criteria for bulimia nervosa. *International Journal of Eating Disorders, 22,* 179–186.

Tollefson, G. D. (1993). Major depression. In D. L. Dunner (Ed.), *Current psychiatric therapy.* Philadelphia: W. B. Saunders.

Tomarken, A., & Keener, A. (1998). Frontal brain asymmetry and depression: A self-regulatory perspective. *Cognition and Emotion, 12,* 387–420.

Tomarken, A., Dichter, G., Garber, J., & Simien, C. (2004). Relative left frontal hypo-activation in adolescents at risk for depression. *Biological Psychology, 67,* 77–102.

Tondo, L., Jamison, K. R., & Baldessarini, R. J. (1997). Effect of lithium maintenance on suicidal behavior in major mood disorders. In D. M. Stoff & J. J. Mann (Eds.), *The neurobiology of suicide: From the bench to the clinic* (Vol. 836, pp. 339–351). New York: Academy of Sciences.

Toomey, R., Faraone, S. V., Simpson, J. C., & Tsuang, M. T. (1998). Negative, positive, and disorganized symptom dimensions in schizophrenia, major depression, and bipolar disorder. *Journal of Nervous and Mental Disorders, 186,* 470–476.

Torgersen, S. (1986). Genetics of somatoform disorder. *Archives of General Psychiatry, 43,* 502–505.

Torgensen, S., Kringlen, E., & Cramer, V. (2001). The prevalence of personality disorders in a community sample. *Archives of General Psychiatry, 58,* 590–596.

Torgersen, S., Lygren, S., Oien, P. A., Skre, I., Onstad, S., Edvardsen, J., et al. (2000). A twin study of personality disorders. *Comprehensive Psychiatry, 41,* 416–425.

Towbin, K. E. (2005). Pervasive developmental disorder not otherwise specified. In F. R. Volkmar, R. Paul, A. Klin, & D. Cohen (Eds.), *Handbook of autism and pervasive developmental disorders. Volume 1: Diagnosis, development, neurobiology, and behavior* (pp. 165–200). Hoboken, NJ: John Wiley & Sons.

Tracey, S. A., Chorpita, B. F., Douban, J., & Barlow, D. H. (1997). Empirical evaluation of DSM-IV generalized anxiety disorder criteria in children and adolescents. *Journal of Clinical Child Psychology, 26,* 404–414.

Trebbe, A. (1979, September 15). Ideal is body beautiful and clean cut. *USA Today,* pp. 1–2.

Trimbell, M. R. (1981). *Neuropsychiatry.* Chichester, England: John Wiley.

Trivedi, M., Rush, A., Wisniewski, S., Nierenberg, A., Warden, D., Ritz, L., et al. (2006). Evaluation of outcomes with citalopram for depression using measurement-based care in STAR *D: Implications for clinical practice. *American Journal of Psychiatry, 163,* 28–40.

True, W. R., Rice, J., Eisen, S. A., Heath, A. C., Goldberg, J., Lyons, M. J., & Nowak, J. (1993). A twin study of genetic and environmental contributions to liability for posttraumatic stress symptoms. *Archives of General Psychiatry, 50,* 257–264.

Tsai, G. E., Condie, D., Wu, M. T., & Chang, I. W. (1999). Functional magnetic resonance imaging of personality switches in a woman with dissociative identity disorder. *Harvard Review of Psychiatry, 7*(2), 119–122.

Tsai, L. Y. (2005). Recent neurobiological research in autism. In D. Zager (Ed.), *Autism spectrum disorders: Identification, education, and treatment* (3rd ed., pp. 47–87). Hillsdale, NJ: Lawrence Erlbaum Associates.

Tsao, J. C. I., Mystkowski, J. L., Zucker, B. G., & Craske, M. G. (2002). Effects of cognitive-behavioral therapy for panic disorder on comorbid conditions: Replication and extension. *Behavior Therapy, 33,* 493–509.

Tsuang, M. T., Stone, W. S., & Faraone, S. V. (2002). Understanding predisposition to schizophrenia: Toward intervention and prevention. *Canadian Journal of Psychiatry, 47,* 518–526.

Tuchman, B. (1978). *A distant mirror.* New York: Ballantine Books.

Tucker, G. J., Ferrell, R. B., & Price, T. R. P. (1984). The hospital treatment of schizophrenia. In A. S. Bellack (Ed.), *Schizophrenia: Treatment, management, and rehabilitation* (pp. 175–191). New York: Grune & Stratton.

Tupes, E. C., & Christal, R. E. (1992). Recurrent personality factors based on trait ratings. *Journal of Personality, 60,* 225–251.

Turk, C. L., Heimberg, R. G., & Magee, L. (in press). Social anxiety. In D. H. Barlow (Ed.), *Clinical handbook of psychological disorders: A step-by-step treatment manual.* New York: Guilford Press.

Turk, D. C., & Gatchel, R. J. (Eds.) (1999). Psychosocial factors and pain: Revolution and evolution. In R. J. Gatchel & D. C. Turk (Eds.), *Psychosocial factors in pain: Critical perspectives* (pp. 481–493). New York: Guilford Press.

Turk, D. C. (2002). A cognitive-behavioral perspective on treatment of chronic pain patients. In D. C. Turk & R. J. Gatchel (Eds.), *Psychological approaches to pain management: A practitioner's handbook* (2nd ed.). New York: Guilford Press.

Turk, D. C., & Gatchel, R. J. (2002). *Psychological approaches to pain management: A practitioner's handbook* (2nd ed.). New York: Guilford Press.

Turk, D. C., & Monarch, E. S. (2002). Biopsychosocial perspective on chronic pain. In D. C. Turk & R. J. Gatchel (Eds.), *Psychological approaches to pain management: A practitioner's handbook* (2nd ed.). New York: Guilford Press.

Turkat, I. D., & Maisto, S. A. (1985). Personality disorders: Applications of the experimental method to the formulation and modification of personality disorders. In D. H. Barlow (Ed.), *Clinical handbook of psychological disorders.* New York: Guilford Press.

Turkheimer, E. (1998). Heritability and biological explanation. *Psychological Review, 105,* 782–791.

Turkheimer, E., Haley, A., Waldron, M., D'Onofrio, B., & Gottesman, I. I. (2003). Socioeconomic status modifies heritability of IQ in young children. *Psychological Science, 14,* 623–628.

Turkheimer, E., & Parry, C. D. H. (1992). Why the gap? Practice and policy in civil commitment hearings. *American Psychologist, 47,* 646–655.

Turkheimer, E., & Waldron, M. C. (2000). Nonshared environment: A theoretical, methodological, and quantitative review. *Psychological Bulletin, 126,* 78–108.

Turner, J., Mancl, L., & Aaron, L. (2006). Short- and long-term efficacy of brief cognitive behavioral therapy for patients with chronic temporomandibular disorder pain: A randomized, controlled trial. *Pain, 121,* 181–194.

Turner, S. M., Beidel, D. C., & Jacob, R. G. (1994). Social phobia: A comparison of behavior therapy and atenolol. *Journal of Consulting Psychology, 62,* 350–358.

Turovsky, J., & Barlow, D. H. (1996). Generalized anxiety disorder. In J. Margraf (Ed.), *Textbook of behavior therapy* (pp. 87–106). Berlin: Springer-Verlag.

Tyler, D. B. (1955). Psychological changes during experimental sleep deprivation. *Diseases of the Nervous System, 16,* 293–299.

Tynes, L. L., White, K., & Steketee, G. S. (1990). Toward a new nosology of obsessive-compulsive disorder. *Comprehensive Psychiatry, 31,* 465–480.

Tyrer, P., & Davidson, K. (2000). Cognitive therapy for personality disorders. In J. G. Gunderson & G. O. Gabbard (Eds.), *Psychotherapy for personality disorders* (pp. 131–149). Washington, DC: American Psychiatric Press.

U.S. Conference of Mayors-Sodexho. (2005). Hunger and homelessness survey. Available at http://www.mayors.org/uscm/hungersurvey/2005/HH-2005FINAL.pdf.

U.S. Congress, Office of Technology Assessment. (1992, September). *The biology of mental disorders,* OTA-BA-538. Washington, DC: U.S. Government Printing Office.

U.S. Department of Health and Human Services. (1991). *Health and behavior research.* National Institutes of Health: Report to Congress.

U.S. Department of Health and Human Services. (2007). *Strategic action plan on homelessness: Report from the Secretary's work group on ending chronic homelessness.* Washington, DC: U.S. Department of Health and Human Services.

U.S. General Accounting Office. (1995). *Prescription drugs and the elderly: Many still receive potentially harmful drugs despite recent improvements.* (GOA/HEHS-95-152). United States General Accounting Office: Report to Congress.

U.S. Public Health Service. (2001). National strategy for suicide prevention: Goals and objectives for action. U.S. Department of Health and Human Services (Ed.). Rockville, MD: Public Health Service, pp. 1–204.

Uchino, B. N., Cacioppo, J. T., & Kiecolt-Glaser, J. K. (1996). The relationship between social support and physiological processes: A review with emphasis on underlying mechanisms and implications for health. *Psychological Bulletin, 119*(3), 488–531.

Uchino, B. N., Uno, D., & Holt-Lunstad, J. (1999). Social support, physiological processes, and health. *Current Directions in Psychological Science, 8,* 145–148.

Uebelacker, L., & Whisman, M. (2006). Moderators of the association between relationship discord and major depression in a national population-based sample. *Journal of Family Psychology, 20,* 40–46.

Uhde, T. (1994). The anxiety disorder: Phenomenology and treatment of core symptoms and associated sleep disturbance. In M. Kryger, T. Roth, & W. Dement (Eds.), *Principles and practice of sleep medicine* (pp. 871–898). Philadelphia: Saunders.

UNAIDS. (2001, April). HIV prevention needs and successes: A tale of three countries: An update on the HIV prevention success in Senegal, Thailand, and Uganda. In UNAIDS, Best Practice Collection. Geneva: UNAIDS. Available at http://www.unaids.org/whatsnew/speeches/eng/wearsit280499.html.

Unger, J. B., Yan, L., Chen, X., Jiang, X., Azen, S., Qian, G., et al. (2001). Adolescent smoking in Wuhan, China: Baseline data from the Wuhan Smoking Prevention Trial. *American Journal of Preventive Medicine, 21*(3): 162–169.

Unger, J. B., Yan, L., Shakib, S., Rohrbach, L. A., Chen, X., Qian, G., et al. (2002). Peer influences and access to cigarettes as correlates of adolescent smoking: A cross-cultural comparison of Wuhan, China, and California. *Preventive Medicine, 34*(4), 476–484.

Ungvari, G. S., Goggins, W., Leung, S.-K., & Gerevich, J. (2007). Schizophrenia with prominent catatonic features (`catatonic schizophrenia'). II. Factor analysis of the catatonic syndrome. *Progress in Neuro-Psychopharmacology and Biological Psychiatry, 31,* 462–468.

Unutzer, J., Katon, W., Callahan, C. M., Williams, J. W., Hunkeler, E., Harpole, L., et al. (2002). Collaborative care management of late-life depression in the primary care setting: A randomized controlled trial. *JAMA, 288,* 2836–2845.

Urbszat, C., Herman, C. P., & Polivy, J. (2002). Eat, drink, and be merry, for tomorrow we diet: Effects of anticipated deprivation on food intake in restrained and unrestrained eaters. *Journal of Abnormal Psychology, 11,* 396–401.

Vaillant, G. E. (1976). Natural history of male psychological health V: The relation of choice of ego mechanisms of defense to adult adjustment. *Archives of General Psychiatry, 33,* 535–545.

Vaillant, G. E. (1979). Natural history of male psychological health. *New England Journal of Medicine, 301,* 1249–1254.

Vaillant, G. E. (1983). *The natural history of alcoholism.* Cambridge, MA: Harvard University Press.

Vaillant, G. E., & Hiller-Sturmhöfel, S. (1997). The natural history of alcoholism. *Alcohol Health & Research, 20,* 152–161.

Vaillant, G. E., Bond, M., & Vaillant, C. D. (1986). An empirically validated hierarchy of defense mechanisms. *Archives of General Psychiatry, 43,* 786–794.

Valera, E. M., Faraone, S. V., Murray, K. E., & Seidman, L. J. (2007). Meta-analysis of structural imaging findings in attention-deficit/hyperactivity disorder. *Biological Psychiatry, 61,* 1361–1369.

Valtonen, H. M., Suominen, K., Mantere, O., Leppämäki, S., Arvilommi, P., & Isometsä, E. (2007). Suicidal behaviour during different phases of bipolar disorder. *Journal of Affective Disorders, 97,* 101–107.

Van Acker, R., Loncola, J. A., & Van Acker, E. Y. (2005). Rett syndrome: A pervasive developmental disorder. In F. R. Volkmar, R. Paul, A. Klin, & D. Cohen (Eds.), *Handbook of autism and pervasive developmental disorders. Volume 1: Diagnosis, development, neurobiology, and behavior* (pp. 126–164). Hoboken, NJ: John Wiley & Sons.

Van Balkom, A., Visser, S., Merkelbach, J., Van Rood, Y., Van Dyck, R., Willem der Does, W., et al. (2007). Cognitive behavior therapy and paroxetine in the treatment of hypochondriasis: A randomized controlled trial. *American Journal of Psychiatry, 164,* 91–99.

van Beijsterveldt, C., Hudziak, J., & Boomsma, D. (2006). Genetic and environmental influences on cross-gender behavior and relation to behavior problems: A study of Dutch twins at ages 7 and 10 years. *Archives of Sexual Behavior, 35,* 647–658.

van der Molen, G. M., van den Hout, M. A., van Dieren, A. C., & Griez, E. (1989). Childhood separation anxiety and adult-onset panic disorders. *Journal of Anxiety Disorders, 3,* 97–106.

Van Dorn, R. A., Swanson, J. W., Elbogen, E. B., & Swartz, M. S. (2005). A comparison of stigmatizing attitudes toward persons with schizophrenia in four stakeholder groups: Perceived likelihood of violence and desire for social distance. *Psychiatry, 68,* 152–163.

van Duijil, M., Cardena, E., & de Jong, J. (2005). The validity of DSM-IV dissociative disorders in southwest Uganda. *Transcultural Psychiatry, 42, 219–241.*

van Goozen, S. H. M., Fairchild, G., Snoek, H., & Harold, G. T. (2007). The evidence for a neurobiological model of childhood antisocial behavior. *Psychological Bulletin, 133,* 149–182.

van Kammen, D. P., Docherty, J. P., & Bunney, W. E. (1982). Prediction of early relapse after pimozide discontinuation by response to d-amphetamine during pimozide treatment. *Biological Psychiatry, 17,* 223–242.

van Laar, M., Volkerts, E., & Verbaten, M. (2001). Subchronic effects of the GABA-agonist lorazepam and the 5-HT2A/2C antagonist ritanserin on driving performance, slow wave sleep and daytime sleepiness in healthy volunteers. *Psychopharmacology (Berlin), 154,* 189–197.

Van Praag, H. M., & Korf, J. (1975). Central monamine deficiency in depressions: Causative of secondary phenomenon? *Pharmakopsychiatr Neuropsychopharmakol, 8,* 322–326.

Vandenberg, S. G., Singer, S. M., & Pauls, D. L. (1986). *The heredity of behavior disorders in adults and children.* New York: Plenum Press.

Vander Plate, C., Aral, S. O., & Magder, L. (1988). The relationship among genital herpes simplex virus, stress, and social support. *Health Psychology, 7,* 159–168.

Vander Wal, J. S., & Thelen, M. H. (2000). Predictors of body image dissatisfaction in elementary-age school girls. *Eating Behaviors, 1,* 105–122.

Vanitallie, T. B., & Lew, E. A., 1992. Assessment of morbidity and mortality risk in the overweight patient. In T. A. Wadden and T. B. Vanitallie, Eds., *Treatment of the seriously obese patient* (p. 28). New York: Guilford Press.

VanKammen, W. B., Loeber, R., & Stouthamer-Loeber, M. (1991). Substance use and its relationship to conduct problems and delinquency in young boys. *Journal of Youth and Adolescence, 20,* 399–413.

Vasterling, J. J., Brailey, K., Constans, J. I., & Sotker, P. B. (1998). Attention and memory dysfunction in posttraumatic stress disorders. *Neuropsychology, 12*(1), 125–133.

Veale, D. (2000). Outcome of cosmetic surgery and "DIY" surgery inpatients with body dysmorphic disorder. *Psychiatric Bulletin, 24*(6), 218–221.

Veale, D., & Riley, S. (2001). Mirror, mirror on the wall, who is the ugliest of them all? The psychopathology of mirror gazing in body dysmorphic disorder. *Behaviour Research and Therapy, 39,* 1381–1393.

Veale, D., Boocock, A., Gournay, K., Dryden, W., Shah, F., Willson, R., & Walburn, J. (1996). Body dysmorphic disorder: A survey of 50 cases. *British Journal of Psychiatry, 169,* 196–201.

Veale, D., Ennis, M., & Lambrou, C. (2002). Possible association of body dysmorphic disorder with an occupation or education in art and design. *American Journal of Psychiatry, 159,* 1788–1790.

Veale, D., Gournay, K., Dryden, W., Boocock, A., Shah, F., Willson, R., & Walburn, J. (1996). Body dysmorphic disorder: A cognitive behavioral model and pilot randomized control trial. *Behaviour Research and Therapy, 34,* 717–729.

Venables, P. H. (1996). Schizotypy and maternal exposure to influenza and to cold temperature: The Mauritius study. *Journal of Abnormal Psychology, 105,* 53–60.

Venkatagiri, H. S. (2005). Recent advances in the treatment of stuttering: A theoretical perspective. *Journal of Communication Disorders, 38,* 375–393.

Ventura, S. L., Peters, K. D., Martin, J. A., & Mauer, J. D. (1997). Births and deaths: United States, 1996. *Monthly Vital Statistics Report, 46*(Suppl. 2) 1–41.

Verma, K. K., Khaitan, B. K., & Singh, O. P. (1998). The frequency of sexual dysfunction in patients attending a sex therapy clinic in North India. *Archives of Sexual Behavior, 27,* 309–314.

Vermetten, E., Schmahl, C., Lindner, S., Loewenstein, R., & Bremner, J. (2006). Hippocampal and amygdalar volumes in dissociative identity disorder. *American Journal of Psychiatry, 163,* 630–636.

Vernberg, E. M., LaGreca, A. M., Silverman, W. K., & Prinstein, M. J. (1996). Prediction of posttraumatic stress symptoms in children after Hurricane Andrew. *Journal of Abnormal Psychology, 105,* 237–248.

Virag, R. (1999). Indications and early results of sildenafil (Viagra) in erectile dysfunction. *Urology, 54,* 1073–1077.

Visser, F. E., Aldenkamp, A. P., van Huffelen, A. C., Kuilman, M., Overweg, J., & van Wijk, J. (1997). Prospective study of the prevalence of Alzheimer-type dementia in institutionalized individuals with Down syndrome. *American Journal on Mental Retardation, 101,* 400–412.

Vitiello, B., & Lederhendler, I. (2000). Research on eating disorders: Current status and future prospects. *Biological Psychiatry, 47,* 777–786.

Vitousek, K., Watson, S., & Wilson, G. T. (1998). Enhancing motivation for change in treatment-resistant eating disorders. *Clinical Psychological Review, 18,* 391–420.

Vocci, F., Acri, J., & Elkashef, A. (2005). Medications development for addictive disorders: The state of the science. *American Journal of Psychiatry, 162,* 1432–1440.

Vogel, S. A., & Reder, S. (1998). Educational attainment of adults with learning disabilities. In S. A. Vogel, S. A., & S. Reder, (Eds.), *Learning disabilities, literacy, and adult education* (pp. 5–28). Baltimore: Paul H. Brookes.

Vohs, K. D., Bardone, A. M., Joiner, T. E., Jr., Abramson, L. Y., & Heatherton, T. F. (1999). Perfectionism, perceived weight status, and self-esteem interact to predict bulimic symptoms: A model of bulimic symptom development. *Journal of Abnormal Psychology, 108,* 695–700.

Volkmar, F. R., Klin, A., & Schultz, R. T. (2005). Pervasive developmental disorders. In B. J. Sadock & V. A. Sadock (Eds.), *Kaplan & Sadock's comprehensive textbook of psychiatry* (pp. 3164–3182). Philadelphia: Lippincott, Williams & Wilkins.

Volkmar, F. R., Koenig, K., & State, M. (2005). Childhood disintegrative disorder. In F. R. Volkmar, R. Paul, A. Klin, & D. Cohen (Eds.), *Handbook of autism and pervasive developmental disorders. Volume 1: Diagnosis, development, neurobiology, and behavior* (pp. 70–87). Hoboken, NJ: John Wiley & Sons.

Volkmar, F. R., Szatmari, P., & Sparrow, S. S. (1993). Sex differences in pervasive developmental disorders. *Journal of Autism and Developmental Disorders, 23,* 579–591.

Volkow, N. D. (2005). What do we know about drug addiction? *American Journal of Psychiatry, 162,* 1401–1402.

Vuchinich, S., Bank, L., & Patterson, G. R. (1992). Parenting, peers, and the stability of antisocial behavior in preadolescent boys. *Developmental Psychology, 28,* 510–521.

Vythilingam, M., Shen, J., Drevets, W. C., & Innis, R. B. (2005). Nuclear magnetic resonance imaging: Basic principles and recent findings in neuropsychiatric disorders. In B. J. Sadock & V. A. Sadock (Eds.), *Kaplan & Sadock's comprehensive textbook of psychiatry* (pp. 201–222). Philadelphia: Lippincott Williams & Wilkins.

Waddell, J., Morris, R. W., & Bouton, M. E. (2006). Effects of bed nucleus of the stria terminalis lesions on conditioned anxiety: Aversive conditioning with long-duration conditional stimuli and reinstatement of extinguished fear. *Behavioral Neuroscience, 120,* 324–336.

Wadden, T. A., & Osei, S. (2002). The treatment of obesity: An overview. In T. A. Wadden & A. J. Stunkard (Eds.), *Handbook of obesity treatment* (pp. 229–248). New York: Guilford Press.

Wadden, T. A., Berkowitz, R. I., Sarwer, D. B., Prus-Wisniewski, R., & Steinberg, D. M. (2001). Benefits of lifestyle modification in the pharmacologic treatment of obesity: A randomized trial. *Archives of Internal Medicine, 161,* 218–227.

Wadden, T. A., Brownell, K. D., & Foster, G. D. (2002). Obesity: Responding to the global epidemic. *Journal of Consulting and Clinical Psychology, 70,* 510–525.

Wade, T. D., Bulik, C. M., Neale, M., & Kendler, K. S. (2000). Anorexia nervosa and major depression: Shared genetic and environmental risk factors. *American Journal of Psychiatry. 157,* 469–471.

Wade, T. D., Bulik, C. M., Prescott, C. A., & Kendler, K. S. (2004). Sex influences on shared risk factors for bulimia nervosa and other psychiatric disorders. *Archives of General Psychiatry, 61,* 251–256.

Wager, T. (2005). The neural bases of placebo effects in pain. *Current Directions in Psychological Science, 14,* 175–179.

Wagner, B. M. (1997). Family risk factors for child and adolescent suicidal behavior. *Psychological Bulletin, 121,* 246–298.

Wahl, O. (1995). *Media madness: Public images of mental illness.* New Brunswick, NJ: Rutgers University Press.

Wahlbeck, K., Cheine, M., Essali, A., & Adams, C. (1999). Evidence of clozapine's effectiveness in schizophrenia: A systematic review and meta-analysis of randomized trials. *American Journal of Psychiatry, 156,* 990–999.

Wakefield, J. C. (1992). The concept of mental disorder: On the boundary between biological facts and social values. *American Psychologist, 47,* 373–388.

Wakefield, J. C. (1999). Evolutionary versus prototype analyses of the concept of disorder. *Journal of Abnormal Psychology, 108, 3,* 374–399.

Wakefield, J. C. (2003). Dysfunction as a factual component of disorder. *Behavior Research and Therapy, 41,* 969–990.

Waldman, I. D., & Gizer, I. R. (2006). The genetics of attention deficit hyperactivity disorder. *Clinical Psychology Review, 26,* 396–432.

Waldman, I. D., & Rhee, S. H. (2006). Genetic and environmental influences on psychopathy and antisocial behavior. In C. J. Patrick (Ed.), *Handbook of psychopathy* (pp. 205–228). New York: Guilford Press.

Walker, D. L., Ressler, K. J., Lu, K.-T., & Davis, M. (2002). Facilitation of conditioned fear extinction by systemic administration or intra-amygdala infusions of D-cycloserine assessed with fear-potentiated startle. *Journal of Neuroscience, 22,* 2343–2351.

Wallace, C. S., Kilman, V. L., Withers, G. S., & Greenough, W. T. (1992). Increases in dendritic length in occipital cortex after 4 days of differential housing in weanling rats. *Behavioral and Neural Biology, 58,* 64–68.

Wallace, J., & O'Hara, M. W. (1992). Increases in depressive symptomatology in the rural elderly: Results from a cross-sectional and longitudinal study. *Journal of Abnormal Psychology, 101*(3), 398–404.

Waller, N. G., & Ross, C. A. (1997). The prevalence and biometric structure of pathological dissociation in the general population: Taxometric and behavior genetic findings. *Journal of Abnormal Psychology, 106,* 499–510.

Waller, N. G., Putnam, F. W., & Carlson, E. B. (1996). Types of dissociation and dissociative types: A taxometric analysis of dissociative experiences. *Psychological Methods, 1,* 300–321.

Walsh, B. T. (1991). Fluoxetine treatment of bulimia nervosa. *Journal of Psychosomatic Research, 35,* 471–475.

Walsh, B. T. (1995). Pharmacotherapy of eating disorders. In K. D. Brownell & C. G. Fairburn (Eds.), *Eating disorders and obesity: A comprehensive handbook* (pp. 313–317). New York: Guilford Press.

Walsh, B. T., Agras, W. S., Devlin, M. J., Fairburn, C. G., Wilson, G. T., Kahn, C., & Chally, M. K. (2000). Fluoxetine for bulimia nervosa following poor response to psychotherapy. *American Journal of Psychiatry, 157,* 1332–1334.

Walsh, B. T., Hadigan, C. M., Devlin, M. J., Gladis, M., & Roose, S. P. (1991). Long-term outcome of antidepressant treatment of bulimia nervosa. *Archives of General Psychiatry, 148,* 1206–1212.

Walsh, B. T., Kaplan, A. S., Attia, E., Olmsted, M., Parides, M., Carter, J. C., Pike, K. M., Devlin, M. J., Woodside, B., Roberto, C. A., & Rockert, W. (2006). Fluoxetine after weight restoration in anorexia nervosa. *JAMA, 295,* 2605–2612.

Walsh, B. T., Wilson, G. T., Loeb, K. L., Devlin, M. J., Pike, K. M., Roose, S. P., Fleiss, J., & Waternaux, C. (1997). Medication and psychotherapy in the treatment of bulimia nervosa. *American Journal of Psychiatry, 154,* 523–531.

Walters, E. E., & Kendler, K. S. (1995). Anorexia nervosa and anorexia-like syndromes in a population based female twin sample. *American Journal of Psychiatry, 152,* 64–71.

Wang, P. S., Berglund, P., Olfson, M., Pincus, H. A., Wells, K. B., & Kessler, R. C. (2005). Failure and delay in initial treatment contact after first onset of mental disorders in the national comorbidity survey replication. *Archives of General Psychiatry, 62,* 603– 613.

Wang, P. S., Bohn, R. L., Glynn, R. J., Mogun, H., & Avorn, J. (2001). Hazardous benzodiazepine regimens in the elderly: Effects of half-life, dosage, and duration on risk of hip fracture. *American Journal of Psychiatry, 158,* 892–898.

Wang, S. (2006). Contagious behavior. *Psychological Science, 19,* 22–26.

Wang, X., Wang, D., & Shen, J. (2006). The effects of social support on depression in the aged. *Chinese Journal of Clinical Psychology, 14,* 73.

Ward, J., Sheppard, J. M., Shpritz, B., Margolis, R. L., Rosenblatt, A., & Brandt, J. (2006). A four-year prospective study of cognitive functioning in Huntington's disease. *Journal of the International Neuropsychological Society, 12,* 445–454.

Ward, M. M., Swan, G. E., & Chesney, M. A. (1987). Arousal-reduction treatments for mild hypertension: A meta-analysis of recent studies. *Handbook of Hypertension, 9,* 285–302.

Warner, P., Bancroft, J., & members of the Edinburgh Human Sexuality Group (1987). A regional service for sexual problems: A three year study. *Sexual and Marital Therapy, 2,* 115–126.

Warwick, H. M. C., Clark, D. M., Cobb, A. M., & Salkovskis, P. M. (1996). A controlled trial of cognitive-behavioural treatment of hypochondriasis. *British Journal of Psychiatry, 169,* 189–195.

Warwick, H. M., & Salkovskis, P. M. (1990). Hypochondriasis. *Behavior Research Therapy, 28,* 105–117.

Waters, B. G. H. (1979). Early symptoms of bipolar affective psychosis: Research and clinical implications. *Canadian Psychiatric Association Journal, 2,* 55–60.

Watson, D. (2005). Rethinking the mood and anxiety disorders: A quantitative hierarchical model for DSM-V [Special issue]. *Journal of Abnormal Psychology, 114,* 522–536.

Watson, D., Clark, L. A., & Harkness, A. R. (1994). Structures of personality and their relevance to psychopathology. *Journal of Abnormal Psychology, 103,* 18–31.

Watson, J. B. (1913). Psychology as a behaviorist views it. *Psychology Review, 20,* 158–177.

Watters, T. (2005). Competence to stand trial with force medication: Placing defendants in harm's way? *Journal of Forensic Psychology Practice, 5,* 79–88.

Wax, J. R. (2007). Trends in state/population-based Down syndrome screening and invasive prenatal testing with introduction of first trimester combined Down syndrome screening, South Australia 1995–2005. *American Journal of Obstetrics and Gynecology, 196,* 285–286.

Weaver, D. R., Rivkees, S. A., & Reppert, S. M. (1992). D1-dopamine receptors activate c-fos expression in the fetal suprachiasmatic nuclei. *Proceedings of the National Academy of Science, 89,* 9201–9204.

Weaver, J. C. G., Cervoni, N., Champagne, F. A., D'Alessio, A. C., Charma, S., Seckl, J., et al. (2004). Epigenetic programming by maternal behavior. *Nature Neuroscience, 7,* 847–854.

Weems, C. F., Hayward, C., Killen, J., & Taylor, C. B. (2002). A longitudinal investigation of anxiety sensitivity in adolescence. *Journal of Abnormal Psychology, 111*(3), 471–477.

Weems, C. F., Silverman, W. K., & La Greca, A. M. (2000). What do youths referred for anxiety problems worry about?: Worry and its relation to anxiety and anxiety disorders in children and adolescents. *Journal of Abnormal Child Psychology, 28,* 63–72.

Wegner, D. (1989). *White bears and other unwanted thoughts.* New York: Viking.

Wehr, T. A., & Sack, D. A. (1988). The relevance of sleep research to affective illness. In W. P. Koella, F. Obal, H. Schulz, & P. Visser (Eds.), *Sleep '86* (pp. 207–211). New York: Gustav Fischer Verlag.

Wehr, T. A., Duncan, W. C., Jr., Sher, L., Aeschbach, D., Schwartz, P. J., Turner, E. H., et al. (2001). A circadian signal of change of season in patients with seasonal affective disorder. *Archives of General Psychiatry, 58,* 1108–1114.

Wehr, T., Sack, D., Rosenthal, N. E., & Cowdry, R. W. (1988). Rapid cycling affective disorder: Contributing factors and treatment response on 51 patients. *American Journal of Psychiatry, 145,* 179–184.

Weiden, P. J., Dixon, L., Frances, A., Appelbaum, P., Haas, G., & Rapkin, B. (1991). In C. A. Tamminga & S. C. Schulz (Eds.), *Advances in neuropsychiatry and psychopharmacology. 1: Schizophrenia research* (pp. 285–296). New York: Raven Press.

Weight Watchers International. (2004, January 15). Available at http://www.weightwatchers.com.

Weinberger, D. R., Berman, K. F., & Chase, T. N. (1988). Mesocortical dopaminergic function and human cognition. *Annals of the New York Academy of Sciences, 537,* 330–338.

Weiner, B. A., & Wettstein, R. M. (1993). *Legal issues in mental health care.* New York: Plenum Press.

Weiner, D. N. (1996). *Premature ejaculation: An evaluation of sensitivity to erotica.* Unpublished doctoral dissertation, State University of New York, Albany.

Weiner, J. M. (2000). Integration of nature and nurture: A new paradigm for psychiatry. *American Journal of Psychiatry, 157,* 1193–1194.

Weiner, M. F. (2003). Clinical diagnosis of cognitive dysfunction and dementing illness. In M. F. Weiner & A. M. Lipton (Eds.), *The dementias: Diagnosis, treatment and research* (3rd ed., pp. 1–48). Washington, DC: American Psychiatric Publishing.

Weiner, M. F., Hynan, L. S., Beekly, D., Koepsell, T. D., & Kukull, W. A. (2007). Comparison of Alzheimer's disease in American Indians, whites, and African Americans. *Alzheimer's & Dementia, 3,* 211–216.

Weinshilboum, R. (2003). Inheritance and drug response. *New England Journal of Medicine, 348,* 5 29–537.

Weisburg, R. B., Brown, T. A., Wincze, J. P., & Barlow, D. H. (2001). Causal attributions and male sexual arousal: The impact of attributions for a bogus erectile difficulty on sexual arousal, cognitions, and affect. *Journal of Abnormal Psychology, 110*(2), 324–334.

Weiskrantz, L. (1980). Varieties of residual experience. *Quarterly Journal of Experimental Psychology, 32,* 365–386.

Weiskrantz, L. (1992, September/October). Unconscious vision: The strange phenomenon of blindsight. *The Sciences,* pp. 23–28.

Weisman de Mamani, A. G., Kymalainen, J. A., Rosales, G. A., & Armesto, J. C. (2007). Expressed emotion and interdependence in white and Latino/Hispanic family members of patients with schizophrenia. *Psychiatry Research, 151,* 107–113.

Weiss, B., & Garber, J. (2003). Developmental differences in the phenomenology of depression. *Development and Psychopathology, 15,* 403–430.

Weisse, C. S. (1992). Depression and immunocompetence: A review of the literature. *Psychological Bulletin, 111*(3), 475–489.

Weisse, C. S., Pato, C. W., McAllister, C. G., Littman, R., & Breier, A. (1990). Differential effects of controllable and uncontrollable acute stress on lymphocyte proliferation and leukocyte percentages in humans. *Brain, Behavior, and Immunity, 4,* 339–351.

Weissman, M. (1985). The epidemiology of anxiety disorders: Rates, risks, and familial patterns. In A. H. Tuma & J. D. Maser (Eds.), *Anxiety and the anxiety disorders.* Hillsdale, NJ: Erlbaum.

Weissman, M. (1995). *Mastering depression: A patient's guide to interpersonal psychotherapy.* New York, NY: Oxford University Press .

Weissman, M., Pilowsky, D., Wickramaratne, P., Talati, A., Wisniewski, S., Fava, M., et al. (2006). Remissions in maternal depression and child psychopathology: A STAR★D-child report. *JAMA, 295,* 1389–1398.

Weissman, M., Wickramaratne, P., Nomura, Y., Verdeli, H., Pilowsky, D., Grillon, C., & Bruder, G. (2005). Families at high and low risk for depression: A 3-generation study. *Archives of General Psychiatry, 62,* 29–36.

Weissman, M. M., & Klerman, G. L. (1977). Sex differences and the epidemiology of depression. *Archives of General Psychiatry, 34,* 98–111.

Weissman, M. M., & Olfson, M. (1995). Depression in women: Implications for health care research. *Science, 269,* 799–801.

Weissman, M. M., Bruce, M. L., Leaf, P. J., Florio, L. P., & Holzer, C. (1991). Affective disorders. In L. N. Robins & D. A. Regier (Eds.), *Psychiatric disorders of America: The epidemiologic catchment area study* (pp. 53–80). New York: Free Press.

Weissman, M. M., Klerman, G. L., Markowitz, J. S., & Ouellette, R. (1989). Suicidal ideation and suicide attempts in panic disorder and attacks. *New England Journal of Medicine, 321,* 1209–1214.

Weissman, M. M., Wolk, S., Wickramaratne, P., Goldstein, R. B., Adams, P., Greenwald, S., et al. (1999). *Archives of General Psychiatry, 56,* 794–801.

Weissman, M., Bland, R., Canino, G., Greenwald, S., Hwo, H., Lee, C., et al. (1994). The cross national epidemiology of obsessive compulsive disorder. *Journal of Clinical Psychiatry, 55,* 5–10.

Weisz, J. R., Sandler, I. N., Durlak, J. A., & Anton, B. S. (2005). Promoting and protecting youth mental health through evidence-based prevention and treatment. *American Psychologist, 60,* 628–648.

Weitze, C., & Osburg, S. (1996). Transsexualism in Germany: Empirical data on epidemiology and application of the German transsexuals' act during its first ten years. *Archives of Sexual Behavior, 25,* 409–465.

Wells, B., & Twenge, J. (2005). Changes in young people's sexual behavior and attitudes, 1943–1999: A cross-temporal meta-analysis. *Review of General Psychology, 9,* 249–261.

Wells, K. B., Stewart, A., Hays, R. D., Burnam, M. A., Rogers, W., Daniels, M., et al. (1989). The functioning and well-being of depressed patients: Results from the medical outcomes study. *JAMA, 262*(7), 914–919.

Wender, P. H., Kety, S. S., Rosenthal, D., Schlusinger, F., Ortmann, J., & Lunde, I. (1986). Psychiatric disorders in the biological and adoptive families of adopted individuals with affective disorders. *Archives of General Psychiatry, 43,* 923–929.

Westen, D. (1991). Social cognition and object relations. *Psychological Bulletin, 109,* 429–455.

Westen, D., Novotny, C. M., & Thompson-Brenner, H. (2004). The empirical status of empirically supported psychotherapies: Assumptions, findings, and reporting in controlled clinical trials. *Psychological Bulletin, 130,* 631–663.

Westen, D., & Shedler, J. (1999). Revising and assessing axis II, part II: Toward an empirically based and clinically useful classification of personality disorders. *American Journal of Psychiatry, 156,* 273–285.

Westphal, C. (1871). Die Agoraphobia: Eine neuropathische Eischeinung. *Archives für Psychiatrie und Nervenkrankheiten, 3,* 384–412.

Wetherby, A. M., & Prizant, B. M. (2005). Enhancing language and communication development in autism spectrum disorders: Assessment and intervention guidelines. In D. Zager (Ed.), *Autism spectrum disorders: Identification, education, and treatment* (3rd ed., pp. 327–365). Hillsdale, NJ: Lawrence Erlbaum Associates.

Wetherell, J. L., Gatz, M., & Craske, M. G. (2003). Treatment of generalized anxiety disorder in older adults. *Journal of Consulting and Clinical Psychology, 71,* 31–40.

Wetherell, J. L., Lenze, E. J., & Stanley, M. (2005). Evidence-based treatment of geriatric anxiety disorders. *Psychiatric Clinics of North America, 28,* 871–896.

Wetherell, J. L., Thorp, S. R., Patterson, T. L., Golshan, S., Jeste, D. V., & Gatz, M. (2004). Quality of life in geriatric generalized anxiety disorder: A preliminary investigation. *Journal of Psychiatric Research, 38,* 305–312.

Wetter, D. W., Smith, S. S., Kenford, S. L., Jorenby, D. E., Fiore, M. C., Hurt, R. D., et al. (1994). Smoking outcome expectancies: Factor structure, predictive validity, and discriminant validity. *Journal of Abnormal Psychology, 103,* 801–811.

Wexler, N. S., & Rawlins, M. D. (2005). Prejudice in a portrayal of Huntington's disease. *Lancet, 366,* 1069–1070.

Whiffen, V. E. (1992). Is postpartum depression a distinct diagnosis? *Clinical Psychology Review, 12*(5), 485–508.

Whiffen, V. E., & Gotlib, I. H. (1989). Stress and coping in maritally distressed and nondistressed couples. *Journal of Social and Personal Relationships, 6*(3), 327–344.

Whiffen, V. E., & Gotlib, I. H. (1993). Comparison of postpartum and nonpostpartum depression: Clinical presentation, psychiatric history, and psychosocial functioning. *Journal of Consulting and Clinical Psychology, 61*(3), 485–494.

Whisman, M., Weinstock, L., & Tolejko, N. (2006). Marriage and depression. In L. M. Corey & S.

Goodman (Eds.), *A handbook for the social, behavioral, and biomedical sciences* (pp. 219–240). Boulder, CO: Cambridge University Press.

Whitbourne, S. K., & Skultety, K. M. (2002). Body image development: Adulthood and aging. In T. M. Cash & T. Pruzinsky (Eds.), *Body image: A handbook of theory, research, and clinical practice* (pp. 83–90). New York: Guilford Press.

White, J. L., Moffitt, T. E., & Silva, P. A. (1989). A prospective replication of the protective effects of IQ in subjects at high risk for juvenile delinquency. *Journal of Consulting and Clinical Psychology, 57,* 719–724.

White, K. S., Brown, T. A., Somers, T. J., & Barlow, D. H. (2006). Avoidance behavior in panic disorder: The moderating influence of perceived control. *Behaviour Research and Therapy, 44,* 147–157.

Whitehurst, G. J., Fischel, J. E., Lonigan, C. J., Valdez-Menchaca, M. C., DeBaryshe, B. D., & Caulfield, M. B. (1988). Verbal interaction in families of normal and expressive-language-delayed children. *Developmental Psychology, 24,* 690–699.

Whiting, P., Bagnall, A., Sowden, A. J., Cornell, J. E., Mulrow, C. D., & Ramirez, G. (2001). Interventions for the treatment and management of chronic fatigue syndrome. *JAMA, 286,* 1360–1366.

Whitnam, F. L., Diamond, M., & Martin, J. (1993). Homosexual orientation in twins: A report on 61 pairs and three triplet sets. *Archives of Sexual Behavior, 22*(3), 187–206.

Whitney, C. W., Enright, P. L., Newman, A. B., Bonekat, W., Foley, D., & Quan, S. F. (1998). Correlates of daytime sleepiness in 4578 elderly persons: The cardiovascular health study. *Sleep, 21,* 27–36.

Whittal, M. L., Agras, W. S., & Gould, R. A. (1999). *Behavior Therapy, 30,* 117–135.

Wickramaratne, P. J., Weissman, M. M., Leaf, D. J., & Holford, T. R. (1989). Age, period and cohort effects on the risk of major depression: Results from five United States communities. *Journal of Clinical Epidemiology, 42,* 333–343.

Widiger, T. A. (1991). Personality disorder dimensional models proposed for the DSM-IV. *Journal of Personality Disorders, 5,* 386–398.

Widiger, T. A. (1997). Mental disorders as discrete clinical conditions: Dimensional versus categorical classification. In S. M. Turner & M. Hersen (Eds.), *Adult psychopathology and diagnosis* (3rd ed., pp. 3–23). New York: John Wiley.

Widiger, T. A. (2006). Psychopathy and DSM-IV psychopathology. In C. J. Patrick (Ed.), *Handbook of psychopathy* (pp. 156–171). New York: Guilford Press.

Widiger, T. A. (2007). An empirically based classification of personality pathology: Where we are now and where do we go. *Clinical Psychology: Science and Practice, 14,* 94–98.

Widiger, T. A., & Coker, L. A. (2003). Mental disorders as discrete clinical conditions: Dimensional versus categorical classification. In M. Hersen & S. M. Turner (Eds.), *Adult psychopathology and diagnosis* (4th ed., pp. 3–35). New York: John Wiley.

Widiger, T. A., & Rogers, J. H. (1989). Prevalence and comorbidity of personality disorders. *Psychiatry Annual, 19,* 132.

Widiger, T. A., & Samuel, D. B. (2005). Diagnostic categories or dimensions? A question for the diagnostic and statistical manual of mental disorders (5th ed.). *Journal of Abnormal Psychology, 114,* 494–504.

Widiger, T. A., & Sankis, L. M. (2000). Adult psychopathology: Issues and controversies. *Annual Review of Psychology, 51,* 377–404.

Widiger, T. A., & Spitzer, R. L. (1991). Sex bias in the diagnosis of personality disorders: Conceptual and methodological issues. *Clinical Psychology Review, 11,* 1–22.

Widiger, T. A., & Trull, T. J. (1993). Borderline and narcissistic personality disorders. In P. B. Sutker &

H. E. Adams (Eds.), *Comprehensive handbook of psychopathology* (2nd ed., pp. 371–394). New York: Plenum Press.

Widiger, T. A., & Trull, T. J. (2007). Plate tectonics in the classification of personality disorder: Shifting to a dimensional model. *American Psychologist, 62,* 71–83.

Widiger, T. A., Frances, A. J., Pincus, H. A., Ross, R., First, M. B., & Davis, W. W. (Eds.) (1996). *DSM-IV sourcebook* (Vol. 2). Washington, DC: American Psychiatric Association.

Widiger, T. A., Frances, A. J., Pincus, H. A., Ross, R., First, M. B., Davis, W., & Kline, M. (Eds.) (1998). *DSM-IV sourcebook* (Vol. 4). Washington, DC: American Psychiatric Association.

Widom, C. S. (1977). A methodology for studying noninstitutionalized psychopaths. *Journal of Consulting and Clinical Psychology, 45,* 674–683.

Widom, C. S. (1984). Sex roles, criminality, and psychopathology. In C. S. Widom (Ed.), *Sex roles and psychopathology* (pp. 183–217). New York: Plenum Press.

Wieczorek, S., Gencik, M., Rujescu, D., Tonn, P., Giegling, I., Epplen, J. T., & Dahmen, N. (2003). TNFA promoter polymorphisms and narcolepsy. *Tissue Antigens, 61,* 437–442.

Wiegel, M. (2007). Manuscript in preparation.

Wiegel, M., Scepkowski, L. A., & Barlow, D. H. (2001). Cognitive-affective processes in sexual arousal and sexual dysfunction. In E. Janssen (Ed.), *The psychophysiology of sex.* Indiana: Indiana University Press.

Wiegel, M., Scepkowski, L., & Barlow, D. (2006). Cognitive and affective processes in female sexual dysfunctions. In I. Goldstein, C. Meston, S. Davis, & A. Traish (Eds.), *Women's sexual function and dysfunction: Study, diagnosis and treatment* (pp. 85–92). London: Taylor & Francis.

Wiegel, M., Wincze, J. P., & Barlow, D. H. (2002). Sexual dysfunction. In M. M. Antony & D. H. Barlow (Eds.), *Handbook of assessment and treatment planning for psychological disorders* (pp. 481–522). New York: Guilford Press.

Wilens, T. E., Biederman, J., Brown, S., Tanguay, S., Monuteaux, M. C., Blake, C., & Spencer, T. J. (2002). Psychiatric comorbidity and functioning in clinically referred preschool children and school-age youths with ADHD. *Journal of the American Academy of Child and Adolescent Psychiatry, 41,* 262–268.

Wilfley, D. E., & Rodin, J. (1995). Cultural influences on eating disorders. In K. D. Brownell & C. G. Fairburn (Eds.), *Eating disorders and obesity: A comprehensive handbook.* New York: Guilford Press, pp. 78–82.

Wilfley, D. E., Schwartz, J. N. B., Spurrell, B., & Fairburn, C. G. (2000). Using the Eating Disorder Examination to identify the specific psychopathology of binge eating disorder. *International Journal of Eating Disorders, 27,* 259–269.

Wilfley, D. E., Welch, R., Stein, R. I., Spurrell, E. B., Cohen, L. R., Saelens, B. E., et al. (2002). A randomized comparison of group cognitive-behavioral and group interpersonal psychotherapy for treatment of overweight individuals with binge-eating disorder. *Archives of General Psychiatry, 59,* 713–721.

Wilhelm, S., Otto, M. W., Lohr, B., & Deckersbach, T. (1999). Cognitive behavior group therapy for body dysmorphic disorder: A case series. *Behaviour Research and Therapy, 37,* 71–75.

Wilkinson-Ryan, T., & Westen, D. (2000). Identity disturbance in borderline personality disorder: An empirical investigation. *American Journal of Psychiatry, 157,* 528–541.

Willi, J., & Grossman, S. (1983). Epidemiology of anorexia nervosa in a defined region of Switzerland. *American Journal of Psychiatry, 140,* 564–567.

Williams, C. J., & Weinberg, M. S. (2003). Zoophilia in men: A study of sexual interest in animals. *Archives of Sexual Behavior, 32,* 523–535.

Williams, D. (1992). *Nobody nowhere: The extraordinary autobiography of an autistic.* New York: Times Books.

Williams, J., Hadjistavropoulos, T., & Sharpe, D. (2006). A meta-analysis of psychological and pharmacological treatments for body dysmorphic disorder. *Behaviour Research and Therapy, 44,* 99–111.

Williams, J., Wake, M., Hesketh, K., Maher, E., & Waters, E. (2005). Health-related quality of life of overweight and obese children, *JAMA, 293,* 70–76.

Williams, L. (1994). Recall of childhood trauma: A prospective study of women's memories of child sexual abuse. *Journal of Consulting and Clinical Psychology, 62,* 1167–1176.

Williams, R. B., & Schneiderman, N. (2002). Resolved: Psychosocial interventions can improve clinical outcomes in organic disease (Pro). *Psychosomatic Medicine, 64,* 552–557.

Williams, R. B., Barefoot, J. C., & Schneiderman, N. (2003). Psychosocial risk factors for cardiovascular disease; More than one culprit at work. *JAMA, 290,* 2190–2192.

Williams, R. B., Jr., Haney, T. L., Lee, K. L., Kong, V., & Blumenthal, J. A. (1980). Type A behavior, hostility, and coronary atherosclerosis. *Psychosomatic Medicine, 42,* 529–538.

Williams, R. B., Marchuk, D. A., Gadde, K. M., Barefoot, J. C., Grichnik, K., Helms, M. J., et al. (2001). Central nervous system serotonin function and cardiovascular responses to stress. *Psychosomatic Medicine, 63,* 300–305.

Willwerth, J. (1993, August 30). Tinkering with madness. *Time,* pp. 40–42.

Wilson, G. T. (1987). Cognitive studies in alcoholism. *Journal of Consulting and Clinical Psychology, 55,* 325–331.

Wilson, G. T. (1993). Psychological and pharmacological treatments of bulimia nervosa: A research update. *Applied and Preventive Psychology, 2,* 35–42.

Wilson, G. T., & Fairburn, C. G. (2002). Treatments for eating disorders. In P. E. Nathan, & J. M. Gorman (Eds.), *A guide to treatments that work* (2nd ed., pp. 559–592). New York: Oxford University Press.

Wilson, G. T., Grilo, C. M., & Vitousek, K. M. (2007). Psychological treatment of eating disorders. *American Psychologist, 62,* 199–216.

Wilson, G. T., Loeb, K. L., Walsh, B. T., Labouvie, E., Petkova, E., Liu, S., & Waternaux, C. (1999). Psychological versus pharmacological treatments of bulimia nervosa: Predictors and processes of change. *Journal of Consulting and Clinical Psychology, 67,* 451–459.

Wimo, A., Winblad, B., & Jonsson, L. (2007). An estimate of the total worldwide societal costs of dementia in 2005. *Alzheimer's and Dementia, 3,* 81–91.

Winchel, R. M., Stanley, B., & Stanley, M. (1990). Biochemical aspects of suicide. In S. J. Blumenthal & D. J. Kupfer (Eds.), *Suicide over the life cycle: Risk factors, assessment and treatment of suicidal patterns* (pp. 97–126). Washington, DC: American Psychiatric Press.

Wincze, J. P., & Barlow, D. H. (1997). *Enhancing sexuality: A problem-solving approach client workbook.* San Antonio, TX: Graywind Publications/The Psychological Corporation.

Wincze, J. P., & Carey, M. P. (2001). *Sexual dysfunction: A guide for assessment and treatment.* New York: Guilford Press.

Wincze, J. P., Bach, A., & Barlow, D. H. (in press). Sexual dysfunction. In D. H. Barlow (Ed.), *Clinical handbook of psychological disorders: A step-by-step treatment manual* (4th ed.). New York: Guilford Press.

Windgassen, K. (1992). Treatment with neuroleptics: The patient's perspective. *Acta Psychiatrica Scandinavica, 86,* 405–410.

Windle, M., & Windle, R. C. (2006). Alcohol consumption and its consequences among adolescents and young adults. In M. Galanter (Ed.), *Alcohol problems in adolescents and young adults: Epidemiology, neurobiology, prevention, and treatment* (pp. 67–83). New York: Springer Science + Business Media.

Wing, J. K., Cooper, J. E., & Sartorius, N. (1974). *The measurement and classification of psychiatric symptoms.* Cambridge, England: Cambridge University Press.

Winick, B. J., & Wexler, D. B. (Eds.) (2003). *Judging in a therapeutic key: Therapeutic jurisprudence and the courts.* Durham, NC: Carolina Academic Press.

Winick, B. J., & Wexler, D. B. (2006). The use of therapeutic jurisprudence in law school clinical education: Transforming the criminal law clinic. *Clinical Law Review, 13,* 605–632.

Winkelman, J. W. (2006). Efficacy and tolerability of open-label topiramate in the treatment of sleep-related eating disorder: A retrospective case series. *Journal of Clinical Psychiatry, 67,* 1729–1734.

Winokur, G. (1985). Familial psychopathology in delusional disorder. *Comprehensive Psychiatry, 26,* 241–248.

Winokur, G., Coryell, W., Endicott, J., & Akiskal, H. (1993). Further distinctions between manic-depressive illness (bipolar disorder) and primary depressive disorder (unipolar depression). *American Journal of Psychiatry, 150,* 1176–1181.

Winter, A. (1998). *Mesmerized powers of mind in Victorian Britain.* University of Chicago Press: Chicago.

Winters, R. W., & Schneiderman, N. (2000). Anxiety and coronary heart disease. In D. I. Mostofsky & D. H. Barlow (Eds.), *The management of stress and anxiety in medical disorders* (pp. 206–219). Needham Heights, MA: Allyn & Bacon.

Winzelberg, A. J., Eppstein, D., Eldredge, K. L., Wilfley, D., Dasmahapatra, R., Dev, P., & Taylor, C. B. (2000). Effectiveness of an internet-based program for reducing risk factors for eating disorders. *Journal of Consulting and Clinical Psychology, 68,* 346–350.

Winzelberg, A. J., Taylor, C. B., Sharpe, T., Eldredge, K. L., Dev, P., & Constantinou, P. S. (1998). Evaluation of a computer-mediated eating disorder intervention program. *International Journal of Eating Disorders, 24,* 339–349.

Wirshing, D. A., Sergi, M. J., & Mintz, J. (2005). A videotape intervention to enhance the informed consent process for medical and psychiatric treatment research. *American Journal of Psychiatry, 162*(1), 186–188.

Wirz-Justice, A. (1998). Beginning to see the light. *Archives of General Psychiatry, 55,* 861–862.

Wise, M. G., Hilty, D. M., & Cerda, G. M. (2001). Delirium due to a general medical condition, delirium due to multiple etiologies, and delirium not otherwise specified. In G. O. Gabbard (Ed.), *Treatment of psychiatric disorders* (Vol. 1, 3rd ed., pp. 387–412). Washington, DC: American Psychiatric Publishing.

Wise, R. A. (1988). The neurobiology of craving: Implications for the understanding and treatment of addiction. *Journal of Abnormal Psychology, 97,* 118–132.

Wiseman, C. V., Gray, J. J., Mosimann, J. E., & Ahrens, A. H. (1992). Cultural expectations of thinness in women: An update. *International Journal of Eating Disorders, 11,* 85–89.

Wisner, K. L., Parry, B. L., & Piontek, C. M. (2002). Postpartum depression. *New England Journal of Medicine, 347,* 194–199.

Wisocki, P. A. (1988). Worry as a phenomenon relevant to the elderly. *Behavior Therapy, 19,* 369–379.

Wisocki, P. A., Handen, B., & Morse, C. K. (1986). The Worry Scale as a measure of anxiety among homebound and community active elderly. *The Behavior Therapist, 5,* 91–95.

Witherington, R. (1988). Suction device therapy in the management of erectile impotence. *Urologic Clinics of North America, 15,* 123–128.

Witkiewitz, K., & Marlatt, G. A. (2004). Relapse prevention for alcohol and drug problems: That was Zen, this is Tao. *American Psychologist, 59,* 224–235.

Wittchen, H. U., Becker, E., Lieb, R., & Krause, P. (2002). Prevalence, incidence and stability of premenstrual dysphoric disorder in the community. *Psychological Medicine, 32,* 119–132.

Wittchen, H. U., Knäuper, B., & Kessler, R. C. (1994). Lifetime risk of depression. *British Journal of Psychiatry, 165*(Suppl. 26), 116–122.

Wittchen, H. U., Zhao, S., Kessler, R. C., & Eaton, W. W. (1994). DSM-III-R generalized anxiety disorder in the national comorbidity survey. *Archives of General Psychiatry, 51,* 355–364.

Wittstein, I., Thiemann, D., Lima, J., Baughman, K., Sculman, S., Gerstenblith, G., et al. (2005). Neurohumoral features of myocardial stunning due to sudden emotional stress. *New England Journal of Medicine, 352,* 539–548.

Wolf, M. M. (1978). Social validity: The case for subjective measurement or how applied behavior analysis is finding its heart. *Journal of Applied Behavior Analysis, 11,* 203–214.

Wolfe, B. M., & Morton, J. M. (2005). Weighing in on bariatric surgery. *JAMA, 294,* 1960–1963.

Wolff, S. (2000). Schizoid personality in childhood and Asperger syndrome. In A. Klin, F. R. Volkmar, & S. S. Sparrow (Eds.), *Asperger syndrome* (pp. 278–305). New York: Guilford Press.

Wolff, S., Narayan, S., & Moyes, B. (1988). Personality characteristics of parents of autistic children: A controlled study. *Journal of Child Psychology and Psychiatry, 29,* 143–153.

Wolf-Maier, K., Cooper, R. S., Banegas, J. R., Giampaoli, S., Hense, H., Joffres, M., et al. (2003). Hypertension prevalence and blood pressure levels in 6 European countries, Canada, and the United States. *JAMA, 289,* 2362–2369.

Wolpe, J. (1958). *Psychotherapy by reciprocal inhibition.* Stanford, CA: Stanford University Press.

Wood, J. M., Garb, H. N., Lilienfeld, S. O., & Nezworski, M. T. (2002). Clinical assessment. *Annual Review of Psychology, 53,* 519–542.

Wood, J. M., Nezworski, M. T., Lilienfeld, S. O., & Garb, H. N. (2003). *What's wrong with the Rorschach? Science confronts the controversial inkblot test.* New York: Wiley.

Woodman, C. L., Noyes, R., Black, D. W., Schlosser, S., & Yagla, S. J. (1999). A 5-year follow-up study of generalized anxiety disorder and panic disorder. *Journal of Nervous and Mental Disease, 187,* 3–9.

Woods, D. W., Twohig, M. P., Fuqua, R. W., & Hanley, J. M. (2000). Treatment of stuttering with regulated breathing: Strengths, limitations, and future directions. *Behavior Therapy, 31,* 547–568.

Woods, E. R., Lin, Y. G., Middleman, A., Beckford, P., Chase, L., & DuRant, R. H. (1997). The associations of suicide attempts in adolescents. *Pediatrics, 99,* 791–796.

Woods, N. S., Eyler, F. D., Behnke, M., & Conlon, M. (1992). Cocaine use during pregnancy: Maternal depressive symptoms and infant neurobehavior over first month. *Infant Behavior and Development, 16,* 83–98.

Woods, S. W., Miller, T. J., Davidson, L., Hawkins, K. A., Sernyak, M. J., & McGlashan, T. H. (2001). Estimated yield of early detection of prodromal or first episode patients by screening first-degree relatives of schizophrenic patients. *Schizophrenia Research, 52,* 21–27.

Woodside, M. R., & Legg, B. H. (1990). Patient advocacy: A mental health perspective. *Journal of Mental Health Counseling, 12,* 38–50.

Wootton, J. M., Frick, P. J., Shelton, K. K., & Silverthorn, P. (1997). Ineffective parenting and childhood conduct problems: The moderating role of callous-unemotional traits. *Journal of Consulting and Clinical Psychology, 65,* 301–308.

Worell, J., & Remer, P. (1992). *Feminist perspectives in therapy: An empowerment model for women.* New York: John Wiley.

World Health Organization. (1998). *Obesity: Preventing and managing the global epidemic.* Geneva, Switzerland: World Health Organizations.

World Health Organization. (2000). Women and HIV/AIDS: Fact sheet no. 242. Available at http://www.who.int/inf-fs/en/fact242.html.

World Health Organization. (2002). World report on violence and health. Geneva: World Health Organization.

World Health Organization. (2003). Global summary of the HIV/AIDS epidemic, December 2003. Available at http://www.who.int/hiv/pub/epidemiology/imagefile/en.html.

Wulfert, E., Greenway, D. E., & Dougher, M. J. (1996). A logical functional analysis of reinforcement-based disorders: Alcoholism and pedophilia. *Journal of Consulting and Clinical Psychology, 64*(6), 1140–1151.

Wyatt v. Stickney, 344 F. Supp. 373 (Ala. 1972).

Wyllie, E., Glazer, J. P., Benbadis, S., Kotagal, P., & Wolgamuth, B. (1999). Psychiatric features of children and adolescents with pseudoseizures. *Archives of Pediatrics and Adolescent Medicine, 153,* 244–248.

Wynick, S., Hobson, R. P., & Jones, R. B. (1997). Psychogenic disorders of vision in childhood ("visual conversion reaction"): Perspectives from adolescence: A research note. *Journal of Child Psychology and Psychiatry, 38*(3), 375–379.

Xing, G., Zhang, L., Russell, S., & Post, R. (2006). *Schizophrenia Research, 84,* 36–56.

Yach, D., Stuckler, D., & Brownell, K. D. (2006). Epidemiologic and economic consequences of the global epidemics of obesity and diabetes. *Nature Medicine, 12,* 62–66.

Yamamoto, J., Silva, A., Sasao, T., Wang, C., & Nguyen, L. (1993). Alcoholism in Peru. *American Journal of Psychiatry, 150,* 1059–1062.

Yan, L. L., Liu, K., Matthews, K. A., Daviglus, M. L., Ferguson, T. F., & Kiefe, C. I. (2003). Psychosocial risk factors and risk of hypertension: The coronary artery risk development in young adults (CARDIA) study. *JAMA, 290,* 2138–2148.

Yatham, L., Kennedy, S., O'Donovan, C., Parikh, Sagar, V., MacQueen, G., et al. (2006). Canadian Network for Mood and Anxiety Treatments (CANMAT) guidelines for the management of patients with bipolar disorder: Update 2007. *Bipolar Disorders, 8,* 721–739.

Ye, X., Mitchell, M., Newman, K., & Batshaw, M. L. (2001). Prospects for prenatal gene therapy in disorders causing mental retardation. *Mental Retardation and Developmental Disabilities Research Review, 7,* 65–72.

Yeaton, W. H., & Bailey, J. S. (1978). Teaching pedestrian safety skills to young children: An analysis and one-year follow-up. *Journal of Applied Behavior Analysis, 11,* 315–329.

Yeh, S.-R., Fricke, R. A., & Edwards, D. H. (1996, January 19). The effect of social experience on serotonergic modulation of escape circuit of crayfish. *Science, 271,* 355–369.

Yen, S., Shea, M. T., Sanislow, C. A., Grilo, C. M., Skodol, A. E., Gunderson, J. G., et al. (2004). Borderline personality disorder criteria associated with prospectively observed suicidal behavior. *American Journal of Psychiatry, 161,* 1296–1298.

Yerkes, R. M., & Dodson, J. D. (1908). The relation of strength of stimulus to rapidity of habit-formation. *Journal of Comprehensive Neurologic and Psychology, 18,* 459–482.

Yin, R. K. (2006). Case study methods. In J. L. Green, G. Camilli, & P. B. Elmore (Eds.), *Handbook of complementary methods in education research* (pp. 111–122). Mahwah, NJ: Erlbaum.

Yonkers, K. A., Warshaw, M., Massion, A. O., & Keller, M. B. (1996). Phenomenology and course of generalized anxiety disorder. *British Journal of Psychiatry, 168,* 308–313.

Yoon, C. K. (1996). New light on seasonal disorder (SAD) therapy. *Journal of NIH Research, 8,* 29–31.

Yoshida, A., Huang, I-Y., & Ikawa, M. (1984). Molecular abnormality of an inactive aldehyde dehydrogenase variant commonly found in Orientals. *Proceedings of the National Academy of Sciences, 81,* 258–261.

Young, A. M., & Herling, S. (1986). Drugs as reinforcers: Studies in laboratory animals. In S. R. Goldberg & I. P. Stolerman (Eds.), *Behavioral analysis of drug dependence* (pp. 9–67). Orlando, FL: Academic Press.

Young, J., Rygh, J., Weinberger, A., & Beck, A. T. (in press). Cognitive therapy for depression. In Barlow, D. H. (Ed.), *Clinical handbook of psychological disorders* (4th ed.). New York: Guilford Press.

Youngberg v. Romeo, 457 U.S. 307 (1982).

Yung, A. R., Phillips, L. J., Yuen, H. P., & McGorry, P. D. (2004). Risk factors for psychosis in an ultra high-risk group: Psychopathology and clinical features. *Schizophrenia Research, 67,* 131–142.

Yutzy, S. H., Cloninger, C. R., Guze, S. B., Pribor, E. F., Martin, R. L., Kathol, R. G., et al. (1995). DSM-IV field trial: Testing a new proposal for somatization disorder. *American Journal of Psychiatry, 152,* 97–101.

Zadra, A., & Donderi, D. C. (2000). Nightmares and bad dreams: Their prevalence and relationship to well-being. *Journal of Abnormal Psychology, 109,* 273–281.

Zager, D., & Shamow. (2005). Teaching students with autism spectrum disorders. In D. Zager (Ed.), *Autism spectrum disorders: Identification, education, and treatment* (3rd ed.) 295–326. Hillsdale, NJ: Lawrence, Erlbaum Associates, Inc.

Zajonc, R. B. (1984). On the primacy of affect. *American Psychologist, 39*(2), 117–123.

Zajonc, R. B. (1998). Emotions. In D. Gilbert, S. T. Fiske, & G. Lindzey (Eds.), *Handbook of social psychology* (Vol. 1, 4th ed., pp. 591–632). New York: McGraw-Hill.

Zakowski, S. G., McAllister, C. G., Deal, M., & Baum, A. (1992). Stress, reactivity, and immune function in healthy men. *Health Psychology, 11,* 223–32.

Zanarini, M. C., Frankenburg, F. R., Hennen, J., Reich, D. B., & Silk, K. R. (2006). Prediction of the 10-year course of borderline personality disorder. *American Journal of Psychiatry, 163,* 827–832.

Zanarini, M. C., Gunderson, J., Marino, M., Schwartz, E., & Frankenburg, F. (1988). DSM-III disorders in the families of borderline outpatients. *Journal of Personality Disorders, 2,* 292–302.

Zautra, A., Johnson, L., & Davis, M. (2005). Positive affect as a source of resilience for women in chronic pain. *Journal of Consulting and Clinical Psychology, 73,* 212–220.

Zhou, J. N., Hofman, M. A., Gooren, L. J., & Swaab, D. F. (1995). A sex difference in the human brain and its relation to transsexuality. *Nature, 378,* 68–70.

Zhu, J., & Weiss, L. (2005). The Wechsler Scales. In D. P. Flanagan, & P. L. Harrison, (Eds.). *Contemporary intellectual assessment: Theories, tests, and issues* (2nd ed., pp. 297–324). New York: Guilford Press.

Zigler, E., & Hodapp, R. M. (1986). *Understanding mental retardation.* Cambridge: Cambridge University Press.

Zilbergeld, B. (1999). *The new male sexuality.* New York: Bantam Books.

Zilboorg, G., & Henry, G. (1941). *A history of medical psychology.* New York: W. W. Norton.

Zillmann, D. (1983). Arousal and aggression. In R. G. Geen & E. Donnerstein (Eds.), *Aggression: Theoretical and empirical reviews* (Vol. 1). New York: Academic Press.

Zimmerman, M., & Mattia, J. I. (1998). Body dysmorphic disorder in psychiatric outpatients: Recognition, prevalence, comorbidity, demographic, and clinical correlates. *Comprehensive Psychiatry, 39*(5), 265–270.

Zimmerman, M., Rothschild, L., & Chelminski, I. (2005). The prevalence of DSM-IV personality disorders in psychiatric outpatients. *American Journal of Psychiatry, 162,* 1911–1918.

Zinbarg, R. E., & Barlow, D. H. (1996). Structure of anxiety and the anxiety disorders: A hierarchical model. *Journal of Abnormal Psychology, 105,* 181–193.

Zinbarg, R. E., Barlow, D. H., Liebowitz, M. R., Street, L., Broadhead, E., Katon, W., et al. (1998). The DSM-IV field trial for mixed anxiety-depression. In T. A. Widiger, A. J. Frances, H. A. Pincus, R. Ross, M. B. First, W. Davis, & M. Kline (Eds.), *DSM-IV sourcebook* (Vol. 4, pp. 735–799). Washington, DC: American Psychiatric Association.

Zinbarg, R. E., Barlow, D. H., Liebowitz, M., Street, L., Broadhead, E., Katon, W., et al. (1994). The DSM-IV field trial for mixed anxiety depression. *American Journal of Psychiatry, 151,* 1153–1162.

Zinbarg, R. E., Craske, M. G., & Barlow, D. H. (2006). *Mastery of your anxiety and worry: Therapist guide.* New York: Oxford University Press.

Zingmond, D. S., McGory, M. L., & Ko, C. Y. (2005). Hospitalization before and after gastric bypass surgery. *JAMA, 294,* 1918–1924.

Zipfel, S., Lowe, B., Deter, H. C., & Herzog, W. (2000). Long-term prognosis in anorexia nervosa: Lessons from a 21-year follow-up study. *Lancet, 355,* 721–722.

Zlotnick, C., Miller, I., Pearlstein, T., Howard, M., & Sweeney, P. (2006). A preventive intervention for pregnant women on public assistance at risk for postpartum depression. *American Journal of Psychiatry, 163,* 1443–1445.

Zoellner, L. A., & Craske, M. G. (1999). Interoceptive accuracy and panic. *Behaviour Research and Therapy, 37,* 1141–1158.

Zohar, J., Judge, R., & the OCD paroxetine study investigators. (1996). Paroxetine vs. clomipramine in the treatment of obsessive-compulsive disorder. *British Journal of Psychiatry, 169,* 468–474.

Zonana, H. (1997). The civil commitment of sex offenders. *Science, 278,* 1248–1249.

Zvolensky, M. J., & Bernstein, A. (2005). Cigarette smoking and panic psychopathology. *Current Directions in Psychological Science, 14,* 301–305.

Zubieta, J., Bueller, J., Jackson, L., Scott, D., Xu, Y., & Koeppe, R., et al. (2005). Placebo effects mediated by endogenous opioid activity on u-opioid receptors. *Journal of Neuroscience, 25,* 7754–7762.

Zubin, J., Steinhauer, S. R., & Condray, R. (1992). Vulnerability to relapse in schizophrenia. *British Journal of Psychiatry, 161,* 13–18.

Zuchner, S., Cuccaro, M. L., Tran-Viet, K. N., Cope, H., Krishnan, R. R., Pericak-Vance, M. A., Wright, H. H., Ashley-Koch, A. (2006). SLITRK1 mutations in trichotillomania. *Molecular Psychiatry, 11,* 887–889.

Photo Credits

Name Index

Aarestad, S. L., 347
Aaron, L., 333
Aarons, J. H., 406
Aaronson, C., 146
Abakoumkin, G., 214
Abbey, S. E., 328–329
Abbott, D. W., 268
Abbott, R., 113, 512
Abbott, R. A., 334
Abe, T., 513
Abel, G. G., 281, 372, 374–376, 381
Abeles, N., 224–225, 239, 241
Abrahamson, D. J., 363, 365
Abrams, G. M., 455
Abrams, K., 135
Abrams, M., 51
Abrams, R., 216
Abramson, L. Y., 55, 216, 231–237, 276
Abse, D. W., 455
Acampora, A., 419
Acampora, D., 535
Achenbach, T. M., 223
Acri, J., 418
Adair, R., 292, 317
Adams, C., 485
Adams, H. E., 360, 364, 374
Adams, P., 224
Addenbrooke, W. M., 406
Addington, A. M., 505
Addis, M. E., 244
Adlaf, E. M., 399
Adlam, T. D., 548
Adler, A., 20–21
Adler, C. M., 174
Adrian, C., 229
Aeschbach, D., 220
Afari, N., 329–330
Agatisa, P., 325
Aggen, S. H., 439
Agras, W. S., 135, 144, 172, 178, 261, 265, 267–268, 274, 277, 279–281, 311, 362
Agyei, Y., 348
Ahern, D. K., 173, 175
Ahern, F., 35
Ahern, J., 155
Ahles, T. A., 331–332
Ahmed, E., 221–222
Ahmed, S. H., 413
Ahrens, A. H., 272
Aigner, M., 184
Aikins, D. E., 130
Akiskal, H. S., 209–211, 213, 216–217, 219, 229, 436, 455
Aksan, N., 449
Akutagawa, D., 268
Alam, D., 242
Alarcon, R. D., 5, 91
Albano, A. M., 129, 132, 134, 144, 149, 151, 153, 158, 161
Albert, C., 325
Albert, M. L., 485
Albert, S. M., 539, 546
Albertini, R. S., 186–189, 191
Albright, C. A., 323

Alcaine, O. M., 130–131
Alden, L. E., 458
Aldenkamp, A. P., 522
Alessi, S. M., 413
Alexander, F. G., 8, 13–14, 310, 323
Alexander, G. M., 436
Alexander, K. W., 200
Alexopoulos, G., 241
Alger, S. A., 265, 277
Alhassan, S., 286
Allan, J. S., 299
Allan, M. J., 252
Allan, W. D., 134
Allani, D., 453
Allen, A., 188
Allen, C. R., 112
Allen, J., 514
Allen, J. J., 195
Allen, J. M., 220
Allen, K., 62
Allen, L., 179
Allen, L. B., 60, 126, 131, 244
Allen, L. S., 348
Allen, M., 219
Allen, P. J., 403
Allen, S., 418
Allen-Hauser, W., 182
Allin, M., 182
Allison, D., 286
Allman, C. J., 252
Allmon, D., 453
Alloy, L. B., 216, 232–235, 237
Allsbeck, P., 62
Almasy, L., 483
Almeida, G. F., 156
Alper, C. M., 315
Alpers, G. W., 174
Alpers, M. P., 546
ALSPAC Study Team, 219
Altamash, I., 175
Altay, B., 366
Althof, S., 355, 360, 364, 369–370
Altman, E., 219
Altshuler, L., 219
Alvarado, G. F., 156
Alvarez, J. C., 251
Alvir, J. M. J., 483
Alwan, M., 548
Alzheimer's Association, 539
Aman, M., 517
Amaral, D. G., 515
Amat, J., 157
American Bar Association, 565
American College of Obstetricians and Gynecologists, 94
American Law Institute, 564
American Medical Association, 212, 247
American Psychiatric Association, 4, 13, 21, 69, 77, 85, 87, 89–90, 121, 133, 141, 152, 154, 160, 173, 175–176, 180, 181, 185, 192–193, 194, 208–211, 216–217, 223, 239–240, 240–241, 241, 242, 253, 264, 267, 281, 289, 291, 293–296, 301, 351, 356–359, 361, 372–374, 376, 391–392, 395, 400,

402, 405–410, 418, 419, 420, 422–423, 431–434, 436, 438, 440, 442, 444, 447, 451, 455–457, 459–460, 467, 470, 474–478, 489–490, 492, 504, 508, 512, 513, 516, 519, 539, 540–541, 544, 550, 565
American Psychiatric Association Practice Guideline, 534–535
American Psychological Association, 116, 569–571
Amir, N., 162
Amsel, R., 360–361
Amsterdam, J. D., 138, 246
Anagnostou, E., 515
Anastasiades, P., 139, 175
Andersen, A. E., 275
Andersen, B. L., 319–320, 347
Andersen, P. M., 184
Anderson, C., 349, 355–356
Anderson, D. J., 129
Anderson, E. R., 449
Anderson, G. M., 197–199, 405
Anderson, J. W., 286, 512
Anderson, M. A., 542
Anderson, N. B., 322
Andrasik, F., 150, 311, 331–332, 334
Andreasen, N. C., 189, 226, 570
Andreasson, S., 62
Andreski, M. A., 156
Andreski, P., 405
Andrew, M., 228–229, 237
Andrews, B., 200
Andrews, G., 5
Andrews, J. A., 222, 224
Andrykowski, M. A., 22
Aneshensel, C. S., 548
Angst, A., 94
Angst, F., 217
Angst, J., 209, 210, 216–217, 225
Anguilo, M. J., 198–199
Anisman, H., 39
Annabi, S., 453
Annas, P., 56
Annest, J. L., 252
Annus, A. M., 271, 277
Ansell, E. B., 453
Anthenelli, R., 399
Anthony, D., 480
Anthony, J. C., 134, 138, 141, 142–144, 147–148, 208, 211, 213, 394, 396–397, 399–400, 402, 406, 412–414
Anthony, M. M., 151
Anton, B., 424
Anton, R. F., 101
Antoni, M. H., 309, 318–320
Antony, M. M., 31
Antrobus, J., 288
Apfelbaum, B., 359
Appelbaum, K. A., 333–334
Appelbaum, P. S., 116, 490, 567
Apple, R. F., 288
Appolinario, J. C., 281
Aral, S. O., 315
Araujo, A. B., 358

Arbisi, P., 47
Arens, R., 563
Arias, E., 249
Armentano, M., 224
Armesto, J. C., 488
Armstrong, G., 328
Armstrong, H. E., 288, 453, 491
Arnds, K., 450
Arndt, S., 570
Arnold, E. M., 508
Arnold, L. E., 506
Arnold, L. M., 424
Arnonow, E., 78
Arnow, B. A., 208, 246, 277, 281
Arons, B. S., 239
Aronwoitz, B., 188
Arridge, S. R., 84
Arrindell, W. A., 134, 144, 147
Arthur, J., 235
Arthur-Kelly, M., 525
Arvilommi, P., 217
Asarnow, R. A., 457–458
Asberger, H., 516
Aschoff, J., 296
Asencio, A., 493
Ashley-Koch, A., 424
Ashtari, M., 483
Asmundson, J. G., 174–175
Asnis, L., 451
Aspinwall, L. G., 336
Asthana, D., 319
Atha, C., 253
Athanasiou, R., 365
Atkinson, J. M., 467
Atkinson, R. L., 286
Attia, E., 278
Attie, I., 275
Audrain, J., 411
August, S., 318–319
Austin, J. B., 369–380
Autism Genome Project Consortium, 515
Autor, S., 224
Averill, P. M., 129, 132
Avidor, Y., 287
Avila, M., 483
Avison, M. J., 541
Avorn, J., 131
Ayalon, L., 299
Ayllon, T., 491
Ayuso-Mateos, J. L., 439, 441
Azad, N., 299
Azen, S., 336–337
Azorin, J., 209
Azrin, N., 491

Baasher, T. A., 115
Babyak, M., 324
Bacaltchuk, J., 281
Bacchetti, P., 318
Bach, A. T., 355–357, 363–364, 367, 369
Bach, M., 184
Bachorowski, J., 60
Bader, J. O., 329
Badger, G. J., 420

Baer, J. S., 226, 420
Baer, L., 51, 159, 163
Bagés, N., 134, 144, 147
Baggett, L., 318–319
Bagiella, E., 323
Bagnall, A., 330
Bagnato, M., 437
Bailey, A., 560
Bailey, E. D., 173
Bailey, J., 282
Bailey, J. M., 348–350, 352
Bailey, J. S., 335
Bailey, M., 347
Bajo, S., 178
Bajos, N., 346
Bak, R. M., 146
Bakalar, J. B., 403, 408
Baker, A., 350
Baker, L., 275, 279
Baker, S. L., 138, 210, 351
Baker, T. B., 414
Bakker, A., 138
Balabanis, M., 77
Baldessarini, R. J., 240, 242
Baldewicz, T. T., 319
Baldi, J., 330
Baldwin, J. D., 378
Baldwin, J. I., 378
Balise, R., 286
Balkin, T. J., 288
Ball, S. G., 143
Ballantine, H. T., 51, 163
Ballenger, J. C., 131, 162
Balon, R., 355, 364
Bancroft, J., 348–349, 353, 355, 358,
    361, 363, 368, 369, 372
Bandelow, B., 452
Bandura, A., 55–56, 125, 315,
    326–327
Banegas, J. R., 322
Bank, L., 449
Bankert, E. A., 116
Banks, P., 246
Baratta, B. V., 157
Barban, K., 195
Barbaree, H. E., 376, 380
Barber, J. P., 458
Barbini, B., 290
Barchas, P. R., 62
Bardach, J., 189
Bardone, A. M., 276
Barefoot, J. C., 322
Bargh, J. A., 56
Barkham, M., 245
Barkley, R. A., 502–505, 507
Barkus, E., 472
Barlow, D. H., 5, 10, 31, 53–54,
    56, 58, 60, 70, 72, 84, 86, 89,
    91, 93, 95, 107–108, 121–123,
    125–126, 128–145, 147–149, 151,
    153, 156–163, 172, 174, 226–227,
    232–234, 236–237, 239, 244, 253,
    265, 277, 311, 314–315, 325,
    332–334, 355–358, 361–366, 367,
    369–380, 453, 548
Barnard, A., 189
Barnes, G. M., 414
Barnes, J., 361, 367
Barnes, M. A., 507, 509–511
Barnhardt, T. M., 56
Baron, M., 451
Barr, C. E., 486, 494
Barraclough, B., 261
Barrera, M., 413
Barrett, D. H., 448
Barrett, J. A., 93
Barrett, J. E., 93
Barrett, P. A., 235, 244
Barrett, P. M., 132
Barrios, L. C., 250, 251
Barry, S., 274–275
Barsky, A. J., 171–175, 177, 179
Bartak, L., 514

Bartlett, N., 352
Bartlett, S., 189
Bartlik, B., 357
Bartoli, L., 219, 227
Bartz, J., 515
Bartzokis, T., 310, 323, 325
Basden, S., 131
Baser, R., 251
Bass, D., 450
Bassett, A. S., 483
Bates, D., 179
Bateson, G., 487
Battaglia, F., 230, 239
Battaglia, M., 178
Bauchner, H., 292
Bauer, J., 279, 281
Bauer, M. S., 219
Baughman, K., 324
Baum, A., 316, 320
Baumann, B. L., 448–449
Baumann, S. B., 414
Baxter, L. R., Jr., 51
Bayart, D., 217
Baylé, F.J., 422
Bazelman, E., 330
Beach, F., 347
Beach, S. R. H., 235–236, 244
Beals, J., 222, 225, 249
Bear, D., 199
Beard, C. M., 261
Beard, G., 328
Beardslee, W. R., 245
Bebbington, P. E., 38
Beck, A. T., 217, 227, 234, 243,
    245–246, 249, 251, 440–441,
    454–456, 458–459
Beck, J. G., 129, 132, 137, 361–365,
    370, 546
Beck, N. C., 222
Becker, D., 453
Becker, E., 94
Becker, J. T., 544, 548
Becker, J. V., 214, 372, 381
Becker, R., 362
Becker, T., 123
Beckford, P., 251
Beckham, J., 327
Bedrosian, R. C., 245
Beedle, D., 242
Beekly, D., 540
Beekman, A. T., 225
Begley, A. E., 225
Behar, E., 130–131
Behnke, M., 403
Beidel, D. C., 149, 151
Beitman, B. D., 135
Bejin, A., 346
Bekey, C. S., 274
Belger, A., 479–480, 485–486
Belik, S., 126–127
Bell, C. C., 95, 136
Bell, I. R., 177
Bellack, A. S., 492
Bellak, L., 78
Bellis, D. J., 417
Bellizzi, M., 284
Bellodi, L., 178
Belluardo, P., 246
Bellver, F., 493
Belnap, B. H., 131
Beltzer, N., 346
Bem, D. J., 349, 449
Benbadis, R. R., 182
Benbadis, S., 183
Benca, R. M., 289
Bendell, D., 222
Bender, D. S., 439
Bender, E., 419
Bendfeldt, F., 194
Benedetti, A., 172
Benedetti, F., 290
Ben-Eliyahu, S., 330

Benet, M., 226
Bengel, D., 124
Benishay, D. S., 348
Benitez, J., 472
Benjamin, M. L., 570
Benkert, O., 370
Bennett, A., 545
Bennett A H., 371
Bennett, D. A., 537
Bennett, P. H., 286
Bennett, S., 125, 136–137, 156, 453
Benowitz, N. L., 404
Ben-Porath, Y. S., 81
Benson, H., 332
Berenbaum, H., 473, 491
Berent, S., 157
Berg, K. C., 286
Berg, S., 35
Berger, J. R., 541
Berger, M., 230
Bergeron, S., 360
Bergin, A. E., 105
Berglund, P., 129, 134, 144, 149,
    155, 161, 212–213, 221, 224,
    250
Bergman, K. S., 51
Berkman, L. F., 62, 214
Berkowitz, R. I., 287, 288
Berlin, I. N., 249
Berlin, M. D., 376, 378, 380–381
Berman, A. L., 250
Berman, J. R., 370
Berman, K. F., 486
Berman, L. A., 370
Berman, R. M., 491
Bermudez, O., 276–277
Bernat, J. A., 374
Bernstein, D. P., 124, 438
Berrios, G. E., 190–191
Berry, J. M., 268
Bertella, S., 178
Bertelsen, A., 482
Bertelsen, B., 228
Berton, O., 53
Bertrand, L. D., 195
Berzins, K. M., 467
Besch, C. L., 318
Best, C. L., 155–156
Bettelheim, B., 514, 516
Beudoin, G., 51, 148
Beukelman, D. R., 525
Beutler, L. E., 363
Beutrais, A., 224
Bezemer, P. D., 350
Bhagwanjee, A., 129
Bharucha, A. J., 548
Bhasin, T., 514
Bhaumik, D., 240
Bi, S., 453
Biederman, J., 123, 147, 150, 217,
    223–224, 503–504, 506
Bieliauskas, L. A., 482
Bienias, J. L., 533–537, 537
Bienveunu, O. J., 160
Bierman, K. L., 103
Bierut, L. J., 229
Biglan, A., 235
Bilali, S., 241
Bildner, C., 320
Billingsley-Marshall, R., 511
Billy, B. J., 290
Binder, R. L., 298, 567
Binet, A., 81
Bini, L., 13
Binik, Y. M., 360–361
Binzer, M., 184
Birbaumer, N., 327
Birley, J. L. T., 487
Birmaher, B., 231, 251
Biron, M., 112
Bishop, D. S., 237
Bishop, S. B., 245
Bismil, R., 451–452

Biswas, A., 320
Bjorklund, D. F., 81
Bjornson, L., 197–199
Bjorntorp, P., 284
Blaauw, G. J., 131
Black, D. W., 129, 174, 251
Black, G. W., 325
Blackburn, I. M., 245
Blacker, D., 77
Blackwell, E., 311, 316
Blagys, M. D., 21
Blake, C., 504
Blake, D. R., 401
Blalock, J., 246
Blanchard, C. G., 214
Blanchard, E. B., 77, 89, 214,
    331–334, 374–376
Blanchard, R., 348–349, 353
Bland, R. C., 161, 174
Bland, S. T., 157
Blaney, N. T., 319
Blascovich, J., 315
Blashfield, R. K., 88
Blashko, C. A., 220
Blazer, D. G., 129, 145, 154, 177,
    184, 224, 291, 439
Blechman, E. A., 65
Blehar, E., 220
Blehar, M. C., 234
Bleiberg, K. L., 244
Blendell, K. A., 151
Bleuler, E., 440, 467–468, 473
Bliejenberg, G., 328, 330
Bliese, P. D., 288
Blinder, B. J., 267
Bliss, E. L., 195, 199
Bliss, R., 418
Blizard, R., 480
Block, C., 294
Block, M. R., 245
Block, S., 214
Bloom, E., 315
Bloom, F. E., 46–47, 412
Bloscovitch, J., 62
Blue, A. V., 115
Blumenthal, J. A., 59, 127, 249,
    252, 324
Blyth, D., 236
Boardman, J., 160
Bobb, A. J., 505
Bockoven, J. S., 15
Bockting, W. O., 350
Bodkin, J. A., 196
Bodlund, O., 353
Boehnlein, J., 225
Bogaert, A. F., 349
Bogardus, S. T., 535
Bogarts, B., 483
Boggs, C., 436
Bohman, 178, 448
Bohme, R., 451, 453
Bohn, R. L., 131
Bohus, M., 451, 453
Boland, R., 209–210
Bolduc, E. A., 150
Bollini, P., 246
Bolton, B., 265, 267
Boltwood, M., 310, 323, 325
Bonanno, G., 214–215
Bond, A., 47
Bond, G. R., 493
Bond, R. N., 316
Bondi, C., 160
Bonekat, W., 291
Boob, G. F., 413
Boockvar, K. S., 534
Boocock, A., 186–188
Booij, L., 254
Boomsma, D., 351
Boon, S., 190, 197
Boone, E., 229
Booth, W., 404
Bootzin, R. R., 299

Borchardt, C., 135
Borges, G., 155, 161, 221, 250
Borian, F., 246
Borkovec, T. D., 129–131
Bornstein, K., 345
Bornstein, M. H., 39–49
Bornstein, R. F., 458
Borodinsky, L. N., 46
Borodkin, K., 299
Borysenko, M., 317
Boskind-Lodahl, M., 267–268
Boteva, K., 479–480
Botteron, K., 95
Bottiggi, K. A., 541
Bouchard, C., 286
Bouchard, T. J., Jr., 35–36
Boulos, C., 241
Bouloukaki, I., 418
Bourassa, M. G., 325
Bourgeois, J. A., 534, 539, 541, 544, 546–547
Bourgouin, P., 51, 148
Boursono, M., 364
Boutilier, L. R., 452–453
Bouton, M. E., 22, 54, 122–123, 125, 136
Boutros, N. N., 491
Bowen, J. D., 544
Bower, G. H., 60
Bowers, C. A., 421
Bowers, J. S., 56
Bowlby, J., 458
Bowles, C. A., 316
Bowman, E. D., 244, 411
Bowman, E. P., 361
Bowman, E. S., 197, 199
Bowman, F. D., 572
Boyd, J. L., 492
Boyd, T. A., 550
Boyer, M., 334
Boyle, M., 220
Boyle, R., 418
Bozon, M., 346
Bradbury, T. N., 100
Bradford, J., 381
Bradhead, E., 227
Bradley, B. P., 130–131, 149–150, 234
Bradley, M. M., 58, 448
Bradley, R., 508
Bradshaw, S., 346
Brady, J. P., 184
Braendli, O., 298
Braff, D., 480–481, 483
Brahim, A., 224, 547
Brailey, K., 157
Bramon, E., 479
Brand, R. J., 324
Brandon, T. H., 414
Brandsma, J., 194
Brannan, S. L., 238
Brannick, M., 272
Brannon, L., 311, 322–323
Brauchi, J. T., 289
Braunwald, E., 287
Brawman-Mintzer, O., 131, 162
Brayne, C., 537
Brechtl, J. R., 318
Breeden, G., 251
Breedlove, S. M., 348
Breier, A., 316
Breitnern, J. C., 540
Bremmer, J. D., 157, 199
Bremner, J. D., 452
Brener, N. D., 251
Brennan-Krohn, T., 422
Brenner, D. E., 250, 544
Brent, D. A., 251–252, 253
Brentjens, M. H., 309
Breslau, N., 156, 405
Breuer, J., 17, 57, 102, 138, 197
Brewin, C. R., 200
Brietbart, W., 318

Bright, J., 248
Briquet, P., 175
Broadhead, W. E., 310
Brodaty, H., 537
Brodsky, B. S., 453
Brody, M. J., 51, 268
Bromberger, J., 325
Bromet, E. J., 155, 235, 476–477, 560
Bromfield, E., 199
Bromley, E., 439, 441
Brondolo, E., 323
Bronen, R. A., 157
Broocks, A., 452
Brook, J. S., 124, 190, 197, 282
Brook, M., 422–424
Brooker, C., 492–493
Brooks, D. J., 413
Brooks-Gunn, J., 222, 224, 275
Broude, G. J., 348
Broughton, R. J., 301–302
Brower, K. J., 410
Brown, C., 220
Brown, D. R., 221–222
Brown, G. G., 150
Brown, G. K., 217, 249, 326, 458
Brown, G. M., 472
Brown, G. W., 231, 237, 487
Brown, J., 113, 329
Brown, J. D., 414
Brown, K., 222
Brown, M. B., 346
Brown, P. L., 282
Brown, R. R., 127
Brown, S. A., 414, 418, 504
Brown, T. A., 5, 72, 86, 89, 91, 95, 121–122, 125, 128–131, 134, 139, 142–143, 226–227, 253, 363, 365, 370–371
Brown, T. L., 242
Brown, W. M., 348
Brown, Z. A., 406
Brownell, K. D., 262, 265, 268, 272, 275, 283–386, 288, 299, 303, 372, 380
Brownmiller, S., 188
Brozek, J., 275
Bruce, M. L., 234–236, 241
Bruce, S. E., 126, 129, 138, 216, 221, 225, 236
Bruch, H., 276
Bruch, M. A., 151, 275
Bruck, M., 200
Bruehl, S., 327
Brugha, T., 38
Brunswick, N., 510
Bryant, J. D., 508
Bryant, R. A., 154, 158
Buchanan, R. W., 479, 486–487
Buchner, D. M., 548
Bucholz, K. K., 229, 446
Buchwald, A. M., 208
Buchwald, D., 329–330
Buchwald, H., 287
Buckminster, S., 151
Bucuvalas, M., 147
Buda, M., 250
Budenz, D., 245
Buehler, R. E., 115
Bueller, J., 339
Buffery, A. W. H., 178
Buffman, J., 364
Bufka, L. F., 139
Bugg, F., 444
Bukowski, W. M., 503
Bule, T., 423
Bulgin, N., 451–52
Bulik, C. M., 261, 265, 268, 276
Bunde, J., 325
Bunney, W. E., 484
Bureau, B., 274–275
Burge, D., 229
Burgio, L. D., 548

Burleson, J. A., 421
Burman, M. A., 93
Burnett, P., 214, 488, 492
Burnett, R., 326, 333
Burnette, M. M., 309, 310
Burney, E., 229
Burns, J. W., 327
Burns, L. E., 134
Burrowes, K., 199
Burt, D. R., 48–49, 484
Burton, R., 12
Bush, T., 177
Bushman, B. J., 399
Busner, C., 253
Buss, K., 157
Bussone, G., 334
Bustillo, J. R., 480, 492
Butcher, J. N., 79–81
Butera, F., 232, 244
Butler, G., 130
Butler, L. D., 197–199, 201
Butterfield, N., 525
Butterworth, J., 525
Butzlaff, R. L., 488
Buysse, D. J., 229–231, 290, 301
Bye, E. K., 399
Byne, W., 348–349
Byrne, D., 325, 366
Bystritsky, A., 140
Byszewski, A., 299

Caballero, B., 272
Caballo, V. E., 134, 144, 147
Cabral, K., 186–187
Cachelin, F. M., 265
Caci, H., 422
Cacioppo, J. T., 10, 58, 323
Caddell, J. M., 155
Cadoret, R. J., 446
Cafri, G., 272
Cai, G., 208, 211, 213
Caine, E. D., 225, 249, 251–252
Calabrese, J., 219, 241
Calamri, J. W., 160
Calcedo, A., 364
Calhoun, K. S., 374
Calhoun, V. D., 486
Calkins, M. E., 483
Callahan, C. M., 241
Callahan, L. A., 566
Callaman, J. M., 418
Callender, J. S., 261
Callicott, J. H., 486
Calstedt, A., 446
Camargo, C. A., Jr., 268, 274–275
Cameron, N. M., 39–40, 53, 64
Cameron, R. P., 267, 274
Campbell, C., 488
Campbell, L. A., 225–226
Campbell, P., 162
Campbell, W. K., 456
Campbell-Sills, L., 58, 60, 244
Campeas, R., 163
Campo, J. A., 353
Campo, J. V., 184
Campos, R. M., 406
Campisi, T., 188
Canchola, J., 335
Canestrari, R., 210, 246
Canetti-Nisim, D., 114
Canino, G., 161, 177, 398
Cannon, T. D., 442, 486, 494
Cannon, W. B., 57–58
Canter, A., 82
Cantor, C., 171
Cantor, J. M., 340, 376
Cantor-Graae, E., 487
Capaldi, D., 238
Capobainco, D. J., 333
Caporaso, N. E., 411
Cappa, S. F., 510
Capreol, M. J., 458

Capurso, C., 546
Caputo, G. C., 135
Cardeña, E. A., 190, 192–193, 196, 199
Cardno, A., 228–229, 237
Carey, G., 112
Carey, M. P., 355, 358–359, 363, 367, 370
Carlat, D. J., 268, 274–275
Carlson, A., 351
Carlson, E. B., 198
Carlson, G. A., 222–224, 476
Carlson, M., 545
Carlson, R. W. L., 320
Carney, C., 174
Carnine, D., 511
Caron, C., 436
Carpenter, D., 246–247
Carpenter, G., 230
Carpenter, W. T., 116, 479, 486–487
Carpentier, M., 381
Carroll, B. C., 401
Carroll, B. J., 209, 230
Carroll, C., 360
Carroll, E. M., 156
Carroll, K., 491
Carroll, M. D., 262, 282, 284
Carroll, R. A., 352–353
Carson, A., 91, 180, 183
Carstairs, G. M., 487
Cartensen, L. L., 64
Carter, J. C., 276, 278, 281
Carter, J. S., 222, 231, 233–234
Carter, M., 492
Carter, R. M., 129
Cartwright, R. D., 301
Carver, C. S., 309, 334, 458
Case, W. G., 131
Casey, P., 439, 441
Cash, R., 224, 245
Cash, T. F., 272
Cashman, L., 162
Casper, R. C., 281
Caspi, A., 35, 37–38, 40, 42, 48, 53, 123, 224, 229, 411, 415, 449
Cassano, G. B., 172, 209–211, 213, 217
Cassem, N. H., 334
Cassidy, F., 209
Castao, A., 406
Castellanos, F. X., 505
Castelli, W. P., 324
Castilla-Puentes, R., 127
Castonguay, L. G., 268
Catalano, R. F., 113
Catania, J. A., 335
Cates, D. S., 325
Cautela, J., 379, 420
Cazzaro, M., 175
Ceci, S. J., 199, 521
Celio, A. A., 270, 283
Centers for Disease Control, 249, 311, 335–336, 345, 506, 513
Cerda, G. M., 534
Cerletti, U., 13
Cerny, J. A., 139
Cervoni, N., 39
Chae, C., 325
Chaffin, M., 381
Chakos, M., 479–480
Chakrabarti, S., 513
Chalder, T., 328, 330, 333
Chalmers, I., 117
Chamberlain, S. R., 424
Chambless, D. L., 135, 151, 458
Champagne, F. A., 39–40, 64
Champine, P. R., 568
Champoux, M., 52–53
Chan, B., 251
Chan, C. H., 219
Chan, K., 451–452

Chan, M., 419
Chang, G., 421
Chang, I. W., 196
Chang, J., 335
Chang, J. J., 541
Chang, L. C., 94
Chang, R. -B., 94
Chang, Y., 325
Chanoine, V., 510
Chapin, H. N., 281
Chaplin, T., 245
Chaplin, W., 515
Chapman, T. F., 151
Charatan, D. L., 261, 267
Charcot, J. -M., 16–17
Charles, S. T., 64
Charma, S., 39
Charman, T., 517
Charney, D. S., 47–48, 95, 124–125,
    157, 330, 491
Charpentier, P. A., 535
Chartrand, T. L., 56
Chase, L., 251
Chase, T. N., 486
Chassin, L., 113–114, 413
Chastain, G., 396
Chatener-Duchene, L., 209
Chatkoff, D., 333
Chau Wong, M., 484
Chaudhuri, A., 524
Chaves, J. F., 196, 199, 201
Chavez, M., 261
Chawla, N., 156
Chean, D., 135
Cheavens, J. S., 452
Check, J. R., 181
Cheine, M., 485
Chelminski, I., 436–437
Chen, C. C., 220
Chen, C. N., 271
Chen, E. Y., 220, 548
Chen, I. G., 291
Chen, X., 336–337
Cheng, T., 335
Cherney, J., 135
Chesney, M. A., 59, 310, 323, 325,
    333, 542
Cheung, F. M., 63, 177
Cheung, L., 271
Cheung, Y., 251
Chevron, E. S., 244, 280
China U. N. Theme Group, 318
Chioqueta, A., 177
Chirelli, C., 289
Chiu, H. F., 271
Chiu, P., 56
Chiu, R. C., 129
Chiu, W. T., 134, 149, 161
Chivers, M. L., 347, 350
Cho, S. -C., 505
Choate, M. L., 60, 143–144, 148,
    244
Chodoff, P., 182, 435
Chong, R., 135
Chorot, P., 174
Chorpita, B. F., 95, 121, 125, 128–
    130, 134, 143–144, 156, 161, 227,
    234, 236–237, 314
Christal, R. E., 431
Christensen, K., 228
Christensen, T. O., 442
Christenson, G. A., 372
Christenson, R., 439
Christian-Herman, J., 487
Christiansen, B. A., 413
Christie, C., 480
Christophe, D., 376
Chronis, A. M., 448–449
Chrousos, G. P., 230
Chung, S. Y., 513
Ciaranello, R. D., 46
Cicchetti, D. V., 64, 157
Ciccocioppo, M., 414

Cielsa, J., 232
Ciraulo, D. A., 101, 413
Cirincione, C., 563, 565–566
Cisler, R. A., 101
Clancy, S. A., 200
Clara, I., 126–127
Claraco, L. M., 179
Clark, D. A., 158–159, 162, 227
Clark, D. M., 137, 139, 151–152,
    172, 174, 175, 329
Clark, L. A., 4, 95, 123, 227, 431
Clark, R., 322
Clark, R. A., 318
Clark, R. E., 493
Clarke, G. N., 244
Clarkin, J. F., 246–247
Clarkson, C., 129
Classen, C., 320
Claudino, A. M., 281
Clayton, A., 177, 355
Cleare, A., 328, 330
Cleary, P. D., 173
Cleckley, H. M., 444, 445
Cleghorn, J. M., 472, 485
Clement, U., 347
Clements, C. M., 237
Clementz, B. A., 483
Cleveland, S., 567
Clipp, E. C., 315
Cloninger, C. R., 88, 177–178,
    434–436, 439, 441, 448, 453–454,
    455, 458–459
Closser, M. H., 403
Clum, G. A., 251
Coakley, E. H., 262
Coan, J. A., 199
Coates, T. J., 335, 336–337
Cobb, A. M., 175
Cobb, J. A., 115
Cobb, R. J., 100
Cobb, S., 62
Cochran Johnson, S., 181
Cochran, S. D., 247, 336
Cocores, J. A., 364
Coderre, T. J., 331
Cohen, C. A., 568
Cohen, D., 512
Cohen, F., 309
Cohen, J., 316, 318
Cohen, J. B., 324
Cohen, J. D., 95
Cohen, L., 225
Cohen, N., 317
Cohen, P., 124, 190, 197, 282
Cohen, R. J., 160
Cohen, S., 62, 311, 315–317
Cohn, S. E., 336
Coker, L. A., 86–87, 95
Col, N., 534
Colakoglu, Z., 366
Colditz, G., 262
Colditz, G. A., 271, 274, 283
Cole, D., 105, 232
Cole, J. O., 240
Cole, M. G., 534, 550
Coleman, E., 350, 372
Coleman, R. M., 298
Colgan, P., 350
Collett, B., 77
Colletti, R., 334
Collier, J. D., 411
Collinge, J., 546
Collins, B. E., 336
Collins, J. F., 245
Collins, P., 47
Collins, R., 157
Collins, W. A., 39–49
Colombo, C., 290
Coltheart, M., 471
Comas-Diaz, L., 193
Community HIV Prevention
    Research Collaborative, 336
Compas, B. E., 222–224, 232, 334

Compeas, R., 138
Compton, D. L., 508
Compton, W. M., 411
Conant, M. A., 309
Condelli, W. S., 418
Condie, D., 196
Condon, W., 196
Condray, R., 479
Conduct Problems Prevention
    Research Group, 103
Conesa, L., 276–277
Conger, R., 236
Conlon, M., 403
Conn. Gen. Stat. Ann., 559
Conneally, P. M., 542
Connell, M. M., 235
Conners, C. K., 504, 506
Connor, D. F., 506
Connor, J. K., 223
Constans, J. L., 157
Conti, S., 246, 370
Conway, K. P., 411
Conwell, Y., 225, 251–252
Cook, B., 131
Cook, D. G., 310, 315
Cook, E. W., III, 56
Cook, I. A., 51
Cook, M., 146
Cook, P. J., 421
Cook-Meyer, T., 5
Cooke, B. M., 348
Cooldge, F., 351
Cooney, L. M., 535
Coons, P. M., 175, 197, 199–200,
    201
Cooper, A. J., 363
Cooper, A. M., 456
Cooper, J. E., 72, 251
Cooper, M. L., 413
Cooper, P. J., 264
Cooper, R. S., 322
Cooper, T. B., 53, 229, 241
Cooper, T. M., 221
Cooper, Z., 264–265, 267, 269, 274,
    276–277, 279, 281
Cooperberg, J., 288
Copas, A. J., 346
Cope, H., 424
Cope, M. B., 286
Copeland, M., 146
Copello, A., 407
Coplan, J. D., 52–53, 124, 157
Corbit, J. D., 413
Corcoran, C. M., 222
Cordingley, G. E., 334
Cordon, I. M., 200
Cormir, C., 449
Cornell, J. E., 330
Cornes, C., 241
Correia, S., 422
Corrigan, P. W., 492
Corson, P. W., 275
Coryell, W. H., 209, 210–211, 213,
    216, 219
Costa, E., 42
Costa, P. T, Jr., 325
Costa, P. T., Jr., 431
Costa e Silva, J. A., 328
Costanzo, E., 319–320
Costello, E., 131
Côté, G., 153, 158, 172, 174
Coughlin, A. M., 559
Coulter, D. L., 92
Couper, D., 101
Courchesne, E., 44
Court, J., 44
Cousins, N., 320, 333
Covey, L. S., 405
Covino, N., 371
Cowan, C. P., 100
Cowan, P. A., 100
Cowdry, R. W., 219, 232
Cowen, P. J., 276

Cox, A., 514
Cox, B. C., 135
Cox, B. J., 126–127
Cox, C., 251
Cox, L. S., 418
Coyle, J. T., 485
Coyne, J. C., 235, 244
Cozanitis, D. A., 399
Crabbe, J. C., 39
Craddock, N., 112
Crago, M., 270
Craig, I. W., 37, 40, 42, 48, 53,
    123, 229
Craighead, L. W., 56, 245
Craighead, W. E., 56, 245, 247, 461
Cramer. V., 451
Crane, P. K., 283
Craske, M. G., 22, 93, 121–123,
    126, 130–131, 133–135, 138–141,
    143–145, 147–148, 172
Crawford, N., 503
Crawford, P. B., 270
Creed, F., 172–173, 176–177
Creese, I., 49, 484
Cremniter, D., 251
Crerand, C., 189
Crichton, P., 333
Crick, F., 110
Crisp, A. H., 261
Crister, G., 283
Croft-Jeffreys, C., 480
Crome, I., 407
Cronin, J. A., 46
Cronquist, J. L., 288
Crosby, A. E., 252
Crosby, R., 277
Cross, L. K., 271
Cross, P. A., 294–295
Cross-National Collaborative Group,
    212–213
Crow, S., 286
Crow, S. J., 265, 267–269, 282
Crowe, L. C., 364
Crowe, R. R., 129, 446
Crowley, P. H, 523
Crowley, T., 361, 409
Cruess, D. G., 214, 319
Cruess, S., 319
Cubic, B. A., 277
Cuccaro, M. L., 424
Cuffel, B., 559
Cuijpers, P., 546
Cullen, J., 361
Cumming, G. F., 381
Cunningham-Rathner, J., 372
Curran, P. J., 413
Currier, D., 253
Curtin, L. R., 262, 282
Curtis, G. C., 142, 172
Curtis, V., 182
Cuthbert, B. N., 58, 95
Cutrona, C. E., 237
Cutting, J., 474
Cyranowski, J. M., 227, 236, 347, 439
Czeisler, C. A., 298–299

Dadds, M. R., 132, 224, 245
Dagan, Y., 296, 299
Dahl, R. E., 231, 419
Dahlberg, L. L., 252
Dahme, B., 277
Dalack, G. W., 405
D'Alessio, A. C., 39
Daley, D., 506
Daly, R. J., 153
Damasio, A., 572
D'Amico, D., 334
Dana, R. H., 78
D'Angelo, E. J., 452
Daniel, S. S., 251, 508
Daniels, M., 93, 315
Daniels, S., 270
Danielson, A., 309

Danielson, L., 508
Dannon, P. N., 242
Dansinger, M. L., 286
Dansky, B. S., 155–156, 448
Dantona, R., 420
Dar, R., 296
Dare, C., 279, 282
Darwin, C., 57
Daskalakis, Z. J., 242, 472
Dasmahapatra, R., 283
Dassori, A. M., 494
Davey, G., 56
David, A., 62, 190
Davidoff, F., 239
Davidson, J., 156, 217–218
Davidson, J. R. T., 152, 154
Davidson, K., 323, 439
Davidson, L., 479
Davidson, M., 146, 484
Davidson, R. J., 231, 237
Davies, B., 230
Davies, B. A., 266, 268, 274, 276
Davies, M., 405
Davies, S., 138, 163
Daviglus, M. L., 322–323
Davis, A., 113
Davis, C. S., 547
Davis, D. D., 199–200, 454–456, 458–459
Davis, D. H., 413
Davis, G. C., 156
Davis, J. M., 219
Davis, K. L., 441–442, 484, 533, 547
Davis, M., 47, 124, 157, 164, 326–327
Davis, S. M., 213, 218
Davis, T. L., 265, 269, 282
Davis, K. L., 42
Davis, W. W., 89
Davison, G., 380
Davison, I. A., 82
Dawood, R. C., 349
Dawson, D., 291
Dawson, G., 512, 514
Day, R., 487
de Almeidia-Filho, N., 415
de Backer, G., 324
de Bono, J., 130
de Boo, G. M., 506
de Carvalho-Neto, J. A., 415
de Castella, A., 242
de Girolamo, G., 328
de Groot, H. P., 195
de Jong, P. J., 172, 174–175, 193
de Lima, M. S., 503
de Lissovoy, V., 514
de Mayo, R., 236
de Zwaan, M., 268, 276–277
Deakin, J. F. W., 124
Deal, M., 316
Deale, A., 174, 330, 333
Dean, J. T., 171
Dean, R. R., 46
Deater-Deckard, K., 510
DeBaryshe, B. D., 448–449
Debusk, R. F., 419
DeCarlson, G. A., 223
Deckel, A. W., 334
Decker, M. D., 131, 534
Deckersbach, T., 188
deCol, C., 274–275
DeFries, J. C., 35–36, 123, 229
DeGarmo, D. S., 76
Degenhardt, L., 407
Deiter, P. J., 186
Del Parigi, A., 546
Del'Homme, M., 504
Dela, H., 296
DeLamater, J., 356–357
Delano-Wood, L., 224–225, 239, 241
DelBello, M., 224
Delcol, C., 229
Delinsky, S. S., 267, 277

DeLisi, L. E., 104
Delizonna, L. L., 370–371
Dell, P. F., 197
DelliCarpini, L., 320
DeMaria, E. J., 287
DeMaso, D. R., 452
Dembroski, T. M., 59, 325
Dement, W. C., 298
Demler, O., 129, 155, 161, 212–213, 221, 224
Demonet, J. F., 510
DeMyer, M., 514
Denney, R. L., 568
Dennis, C., 310, 323, 325
Dennis, M. L., 418
Dentinger, M. P., 333
Denton, C. A., 511
Denzin, N. K., 419
DePaulo, J. R., 219, 227
DePauw, S., 334
Depression Guideline Panel, 216, 218, 239–240, 242
Deptula, D., 241
Depue, R. A., 47, 50, 216–217, 230
Derby, C. A., 358
Dersh, J., 326–327
Dershewitz, R. A., 335
DeRubeis, R. J., 138, 245–246
Desnica, N., 123
Desrosiers, M., 114–115
Deter, H. C., 261
DeThorne, L. S., 510
Detzer, M. J., 347
Deuman, G. W., 271
Deus, J., 270
Dev, P., 283
Devanand, D. P., 192–193, 197–198, 225, 242
DeVeber, L. L., 321
Devinsky, O., 183, 199
Devlin, M. J., 51, 268, 276, 278–279
Dew, M. A., 225
DeWitt, D. J., 399
DeWolf, W. C., 371
DeYoung, J., 480
Di Minno, M., 546
Diamond, J., 276
Diamond, M., 348, 352
Diamond, S., 320
DiBartolo, P. M., 131, 149, 365
Dichter, G., 231, 485–486
Dickerson, J., 245
Dickey, C. C., 442
Dickinson, S., 315
Dickson, K., 294–295
Dickstein, S., 213
Diefenbach, G. J., 132
Diehl, D. J., 229
Diener, E., 55, 60
Dietz ,W. H., 262
Difiglia, C., 242
DiLeone, R. J., 53
Dilling, H., 184
Dimberg, U., 149
Dimidjian, S., 236, 244
Dimitris, A., 329
Dimsdale, J. E., 59
DiNardo, P. A., 72, 89, 146, 226
Dinges, D. F., 195
Dinnel, D. L., 135, 149, 326
Dintcheff, B. A., 414
Dinwiddie, S. H., 229, 446
Diokno, A. C., 346
Diorio, J., 39, 124
Dishion, T. J., 414, 450
Dixie-Bell, D. D., 136
Dixon, J. C., 190
Dixon, K., 323, 490
Dixon, L. B., 491–492
Dixon, W., 237
Dobbins, J. G., 329

Dobkin, P. L., 22
Dobscha, A., 325
Dobson, K., 244
Docherty, J. P., 484
Docter, R. F., 374
Dodge, C. S., 234
Dodge, E., 282
Dodick, D. W., 333
Dodson, J. D., 121
Dohm, F. A., 265, 270
Dohrenwend, B. P., 155–156, 232, 487
Dohrenwend, B. S., 232
Dolan, R. J., 56, 238
Dolberg, O. T., 242
Dolezal, C., 351
Dolgin, M., 321
Doll, H. A., 265, 267–269, 274, 276–277, 279
Doll, S. A., 266
Donahoe, C. P., 156
Donaldson, K., 560
Donati, D., 437
Donderi, D. C., 300
Donham, R., 420
Donini, M., 437
Donovan, C. L., 245
Donovan, D. M., 101
Doraiswamy, P. M., 312
Dorer, D. J., 261, 267–269, 277
Dorey, E., 424
Dorhofer, D. M., 220
Doubin, J., 129
Doucette, D., 240
Dougher, M. J., 91
Dougherty, L. R., 437
Douglas, K. S., 435, 444
Dowd, S. M., 242
Dowling, N., 424
Down, M. G., 245
Downing, R., 131
Dowrick, C., 439, 441
Doyle, T., 414
Doyle, W. J., 62, 315–316
Doyne, E. J., 244
Drabunt, E., 35
Draguns, J. G., 63, 114, 480
Draijer, N., 190, 197
Drake, R. E., 394, 491, 492, 493
Dramaix, M., 324
Drayer, R. A., 225
Drevets, W. C., 47–48, 82, 124–125, 330
Dryden, W., 186, 188
Dube, K. C., 487
Dube, W. V., 512
Duberstein, P. R., 225, 249, 251–252
Dubovsky, S. L., 115
DuBreuil, S. C., 294–295
Ducot, M., 346
Dudek, B. C., 39
Dudley, J. P., 336
Duff, D., 131
Duffy, A. L., 132
Dufresne, R. G., 189
Dulawa, S., 230, 239
Dulit, R. A., 435, 451, 455
Duman, R., 230
Dumas, J., 450
Dummer, G. M., 271
Dunbar, G., 138
Duncan, W. C., Jr., 220
Dunckley, T., 545
Dunn, G., 439, 441
Dunn, M. E., 421
Dunne, M. P., 446
Dunner, D. L., 219, 246
Dunsmore, J., 326, 333
Duran, R. E. F., 198–199
Durand, V. M., 76–77, 108–109, 136, 292–293, 298–300, 502, 511–512, 516, 524–525

DuRant, R. H., 251
Durbin, C. E., 228
Durbin, J., 493
Durham, M. L., 557, 562
Durkheim, E., 250–251
Durlak, J. A., 369
Dusseldorp, E., 324
Dworkin, R. H., 95
Dwyer, E., 115
Dwyer, J. T., 272
Dykens, E. M., 518–521, 523, 524

Eagiolini, A., 247
Eagles, J. M., 261
Eaker, E. D., 324
Eap, S., 76
Earp, J. L., 335
Eastman, C. I., 220
Eaton, W. W., 129, 134, 144–145, 149, 208, 210–211, 213
Eaves, L. J., 129, 228–229, 265, 276–277
Ebens, C. L., 505
Ebers, G., 349
Ebert, L., 155
Ebigno, P. O., 115, 173
Eckman, T. A., 492
Eddy, K. T., 261, 267–268, 277
Edelson, M. G., 513
Edelstein, R. S., 200
Edens, J. F., 435, 444
Edgar, M. A., 348
Edinburgh Human Sexuality Group, 358
Edinger, J. D., 298–299
Edlemann, R. J., 134
Edmundowicz, D., 325
Edvardsen, J., 451
Edwards, A. J., 53, 537–543, 549
Edwards, D. H., 53
Edwards, J., 115, 487
Edwards, N. B., 309
Eelen, P., 54
Efantis-Potter, J., 309
Efron, S., 261
Egan, G. F., 472
Egan, M. F., 35, 486
Egeland, J. A., 112
Egger, M., 407
Egli, M., 418
Egri, G., 487
Ehlers, A., 135, 138, 151–152, 158
Ehrhardt, A. A., 348, 351
Eisemann, M., 134, 144, 147
Eisen, J. L., 126, 129, 134, 161, 229
Eisen, S. A., 111
Eisenberg, L., 517
Eisenmenger, K., 152, 164
Eisler, I., 261, 275, 279, 282
Eisner, L. R., 232
Ekeblad, E. R., 269, 282
Ekelund, J., 49–50
Ekstand, M. L., 336
Ekstrom, M., 473, 479
Ekstrom, R., 221
Elash, C. A., 418
Elbedour, S., 60
Elbert, T., 327
Elbogen, E. B., 559
Elbourne, D., 117
Elder, G. H., Jr., 236, 315, 449
Eldredge, K. L., 268, 281, 283
Elie, R., 458
Elkashef, A., 418
Elkin, I., 245
Ellason, J. W., 197, 201
Ellicott, A. G., 232
Ellinwood, E. H., 401
Elliot, K. S., 546
Elliott, A. J., 300
Elliott, C. H., 321
Elliott, L., 334

Elliott, M., 157
Elliott, R., 238
Ellis, H., 291
Eloniemi-Sulkava, U., 535
Elovainio, M., 49–50
Emery, R. E., 103, 452
Emrick, C. D., 419–420
Emsley, C. L., 545
Emslie, G. J., 289
Endicott, J., 94, 209–211, 213, 216, 219, 245
Engebretson, T. O., 59
English, T., 183, 193
Ennis, M. W., 320
Enns, M. W., 187, 220–221
Enright, P. L., 291
Ensel, W. M., 237
Epker, J., 327
Epplen, J. T., 295
Eppright, T. D., 445
Eppstein, D., 283
Epstein, L. H., 288, 331
Epstein, N. B., 234, 237
Erath, S. A., 103
Erdberg, P., 78
Erens, B., 346
Erickson, S. A., 323
Erikson, E., 20, 64
Erman, M. K., 230
Ernberg, G., 487
Ernesto, C., 547
Ernst, C., 225
Eron, L., 450
Ertekin, C., 366
Escobar, J. I., 177, 179
Espie, C., 106
Espindle, D., 347
Espostio, C. L., 251
Essali, A., 485
Esterling, B., 318
Estes, A., 512
Estes, L. S., 270
Estrada, A., 561
Eth, S., 153
Ettinger, A. B., 183
Eubanks, L., 181
Evan, D. A., 537
Evans, J., 219
Evans, J. A., 522
Evans, M. D., 245–246
Evengard B., 329
Evens, R. M., 545
Evens, S. M., 413
Evers, C., 353
Ewing, L., 281
Exeter-Kent, H. A., 31
Exner, J., 78
Ey, S., 222, 224
Eyberg, S. M., 148
Eyler, F. D., 403
Eysenck, H. J., 24, 60, 123, 431
Eysenck, M., 131
Eysenck, S. B. G., 431
Ezzel, C., 318

Fabbri, S., 175
Fabrega, H., Jr., 193
Faddis, S., 320
Faden, R. R., 311
Faedda, G. L., 241–242
Fagan, P. J., 376, 378, 380–381
Fagerness, J. A., 123
Fagiolini, A., 227
Fahey, J. L., 320
Fahey, V., 393
Fahrbach, K., 287
Fahrner, E. M., 364
Failer, J. L., 561
Fairbank, J. A., 418
Fairburn, C. G., 261, 264–269, 272, 274–280, 329
Fairchild, G., 446–447
Fairclough, D., 321

Faith, M. S., 288
Fallon, A. E., 273
Fallon, B. A., 175, 187
Falloon, I. R. H., 492–493
Fama, J. M., 135, 173
Fanale, J. E., 534
Faraone, S. V., 95, 111–112, 217, 223, 505
Farberow, N. L., 251
Farde, L., 441
Farlow, M. R., 545
Farmer, J., 335
Farone, S. V., 150
Farquhar, J. W., 337–338
Farr, D., 217
Farrell, M. P., 414
Farrer, G., 346
Farrer, L. A., 349
Fasiczka, A. L., 229–230, 290
Fauci, A. S., 318
Fausto-Sterling, A., 353
Fava, G. A., 175, 210, 246
Fava, M., 240–241
Fawzy, F. I., 320, 333
Fawzy, N. W., 320
Fay, C., 186–187
Fayyad, R., 94
Fazel, S., 559
Fazio, F., 510
Federoff, B., 377–378
Federoff, J. P., 377–378
Fein, D., 515
Feinberg, M., 230
Feingold, B. F., 505
Feinlieb, M., 324
Feinstein, C., 508, 515
Feist, J., 311, 322–323
Feldman, H. A., 358, 363
Feldman, J., 272, 348
Feldman, L., 134, 144, 147, 199
Fennell, M., 151–152
Fennell, P. A., 328
Fenning, S., 476–477
Fenton, B. T., 237
Fenton, W. S., 491
Fenwick, J. W., 418
Fera, F., 37
Ferber, R., 292
Ferebee, I., 148
Ferguson, D., 224, 240–241
Ferguson, S. G., 418
Ferguson, T. F., 322–323
Fernandez, F., 242
Fernandez, J. R., 286
Fernstrom, J., 276
Fernstrom, M., 276
Ferrarelli, F., 491
Ferrari, P., 217
Ferrell, R. B., 491
Ferrera, C., 459
Ferri, C. P., 537
Ferster, C. B., 24, 514, 517
Fertel, R., 315
Feske, U., 151
Fetaer, H. M., 241
Feuerstein, M., 311
Fewell, R. R., 525
Fichter, M., 172, 176, 179
Fiedelak, J. I., 329
Field, A. E., 262, 271, 274
Field, J., 346
Field, T., 222
Fieve, R. R., 219, 242
Fincham, F. D., 235–236
Fineberg, N. A., 424
Fineberg, N. A., 424
Fineman, S., 13
Finger, S., 13
Finkenbine, R., 180
Finn, C. J., 348
Finn, P., 113
Finney, M. L., 59
Fins, A. I., 322
Fiore, M. C., 414
Fiorilli, M., 437

Fireman, P., 315
First, M. B., 5, 88–91, 93, 95
Fischer, H., 152
Fischer, I., 442
Fischer, M., 482
Fischer, S. A., 212
Fish, B., 485
Fish, E. W., 39–40, 64
Fishell, A., 377
Fisher, P. A., 125, 157, 252
Fitts, S. N., 186
Fitzgerald, P. B., 242, 472
Fitzpatrick, A., 540
Flaherty, J. H., 534
Flanagan, D. P., 82
Flanders, W. D., 364, 448
Flannery, D. J., 450
Flater, S. R., 278
Flavin, D., 250
Flegal, K., 262, 282, 284
Flegal, K. M., 262
Fleischman, M. J., 115–116
Fleisher, W. P., 197
Fleming, B., 439
Fleming, D. T., 353
Fleming, F. W., 570
Fleshner, C. L., 471
Fletcher, A., 329
Fletcher, J. M., 507, 509–511
Fletcher, M. A., 318–319
Flint, A., 129, 219
Flor, H., 327
Flores, A. T., 218, 269, 282
Florio, L. P., 216, 221, 225
Flory, K., 271, 277
Flykt, A., 56, 58–59
Flynn, J. R., 521
Flynn, P. J., 320
Foa, E. B., 152, 159, 162–163
Fochtmann, L. J., 476–477
Foege, W. H., 311
Fogelson, D. L., 457–458
Fogg, L. F., 220
Foley, D., 291
Folkman, S., 326
Folks, D. G., 182
Follette, W. C., 91
Folsom, D. P., 560
Folstein, M. F., 538
Fombonne, E., 224, 513
Food and Drug Administration, 277
Forbes, N. T., 251
Ford, C., 346
Ford, C. U., 182
Ford, C. V., 180
Ford, M. R., 435
Fordyce, W. E., 326–327
Forest, K., 209
Forman, J. B. W., 89
Forness, S. R., 505
Forsell, Y., 539, 549
Forsman, A., 446
Forsting, M., 459
Fort, C., 214
Forth, A. E., 446, 448–449
Fossati, A., 437
Foster, G. D., 283, 284, 286
Fought, R. L., 534
Fowles, D. C., 379, 447
Foy, D. W., 155–156, 448, 487
Frame, C. A., 322
France, C. R., 326, 331
Frances, A., 490, 504
Frances, A. J., 86, 89, 251–252, 435, 451, 455
Frances, R. J., 250, 396, 399, 409
Frances, S. M., 115, 487
Franche, R. L., 458
Francis, D., 39, 124
Francis, G., 144
Franco, D. L., 267, 277
Franco, K. N., 264–265, 548

Franco, S., 472
Francouer, E., 200
Frank, C. B., 173
Frank, E., 93–94, 215, 219, 227, 230, 232, 236, 241–242, 247, 290, 355–356
Frank, R. G., 335
Franke, P., 123
Frankel, E. B., 525
Frankenburg, F. R., 434, 451, 453
Franklin, B., 13, 16, 162
Franklin, D., 391, 393
Franklin, J. E., 250, 396, 399, 409
Franklin, M. E., 163
Franko, D., 261, 267
Fraser, G. A., 197–199
Frasure-Smith, N., 325
Fratiglioni, L., 537, 539, 549
Fredman, L., 62
Fredrikson, M., 56, 322
Freedman, M., 286
Freedman, R., 483
Freeman, A., 439–441, 454–456, 458–459
Freeman, E. W., 94, 225
Freeman, M. P., 209
Freeman, R., 276
Freeston, M. H., 162
Freimer, N. B., 480
Freinkel, A., 190
French, L. M., 482
French-Belgian Collaborative Group, 324
Freres, D., 245
Fresco, D. M., 232, 234–235
Freud, A., 19–20
Freud, S., 16–17, 20–21, 54, 56–57, 77, 102, 125, 171, 181, 183, 334, 402
Freund, K., 374
Freyberger, H. J., 183, 184
Frick, P. J., 449
Fricke, R. A., 53
Frie, N., 286
Fried, L. P., 545
Friedhoff, L. T., 547
Friedl, M. C., 197
Friedman, A., 318–319
Friedman, B. H., 130
Friedman, E. S., 229–230
Friedman, L. S., 235
Friedman, M., 324
Friedman, S., 135–136
Friedman, S. H., 320
Friis, R., 177
Friis, S., 431
Frohlich, C., 184
Fromm, E., 20
Fromm-Reichmann, F., 487
Frone, M. R., 413
Frost, R. O., 160–161
Fruzzetti, A. E., 244
Fryer, A., 138
Fryer, A. J., 345
Fuchs, D., 508
Fuchs, L. S., 507–511
Fuchs, P. N., 325–328
Fuetsch, M., 125
Fugl-Meyer, A. R., 355
Fujisaki, M., 489
Fujita, M., 84
Fukuda, K., 329
Fulbright, R. K., 423
Fulchino, C., 104
Fulero, S. M., 567
Fullerton, G., 172
Fulton, C. L., 230
Fulton, J. P., 564
Furberg, H., 261, 329
Furmark, T., 148, 152
Furnham, A., 494
Furniss, J. M., 115
Fyer, A. J., 146, 149, 151

Gabrieli, J. D. E., 511
Gabrielli, W. F., 395
Gadde, K. M., 322
Gaggar, S. A., 268
Gagliese, L., 327
Gagnon, J., 367
Gail, M. H., 262, 283
Gaines, A. D., 115
Gajria, M., 511
Galbraith, J., 286
Galietta, M., 318
Gallagher, T. F., 334
Gallagher-Thompson, D., 249–250
Gallaher, P. E., 451
Gallant, D., 396
Gallo, J. J., 208, 211, 213, 250
Gallo, L. C., 325–326
Gallops, M. S., 146
Galper, Y., 539
Gamma, A., 217
Ganaway, G. K., 196, 199, 201
Gandy, S., 545
Ganguli, M., 537
Ganne-Vevonec, M. O., 453
Gao, S., 545
Gara, M. A., 179
Garamoni, G. L., 290
Garawi, F., 413
Garb, H. N., 78
Garber, J., 222, 231, 233–234, 245
Garcia, J., 56
Garcia-Campayo, J., 179
Gardner, C. O., 232, 244, 286
Gardner, F., 450
Garfield, A. F., 253
Garfinkel, P. E., 265, 267, 272, 275, 328–329
Garland, A. F., 250–252
Garlow, S., 229–330, 249
Garmezy, N., 65
Garner, D. M., 261, 267, 272, 275, 278
Garre-Olmo, J., 540
Garrison, B., 251
Garrity, A. G., 486
Garvey, M. J., 131, 245–246
Gary, J. J., 272
Gary, L. E., 221–222
Gassen, M. D., 568
Gatchel, R. J., 325–328, 331
Gatsonis, C., 213, 229, 250
Gatz, M., 63, 131, 545
Gau, J., 283, 286
Gauthier, J., 326–327
Gauthier, M., 522
Gauthier, R., 381
Gautier, T., 351
Gaynes, B. N., 62, 221, 319
Ge, X., 236
Gebarski, S. S., 157
Gebhard, P. H., 346
Gebhart, J., 487
Geckeler, A., 512
Geer, J. H., 362
Geesey, M. E., 546
Gelder, M., 139, 175
Gelea, S., 155
Gelenberg, A. J., 246
Gelfand, L. A., 245
Gelijnse, J., 325
Geller, B., 241
Gencik, M., 295
Gendrano, N., 358
Generations United, 425
Genro, J. P., 526
Gent, M., 334
George, E. L., 247
George, L. K., 129, 146, 154, 177, 184
George, M. S., 149, 242
George, W. H., 364
Georgiades, A., 324
Gerber, P. D., 93

Gerber-Werder, R., 217
Gerdes, A. C., 503
Gerevich, J., 475
Gerhard, D. S., 112
Gerhardt, C. A., 223
Gernert-Dott, P., 292
Gershon, E. S., 35–36, 219, 227–228
Gerstein, D. R., 423
Gersten, M., 150
Gerstenblith, G., 324
Ghaemi, S. N., 216, 232, 241–242
Ghetti, S., 200
Giampaoli, S., 322
Gibb, B., 235
Gibb, R., 36, 53, 64
Gibbons, J. L., 330
Gibbons, L. E., 189, 548
Gibbons, R., 240
Gibbons, R. D., 245
Gibbs, J., 286
Gibson, A. P., 84
Gibson, P., 186
Giedke, H., 231
Gieser, L., 78
Gifford, E. V., 91
Gil, K., 327
Gilbert, J. S., 281
Gilbertson, M. W., 157
Gilboa, E., 234
Giles, D. E., 230
Gilkey, R., 572
Gill, J., 370
Gillberg, C., 513
Giller, H., 103
Gillespie, J. A., 94
Gillham, J. E., 245
Gillin, J. C., 288, 296, 298
Gillis, C., 275
Gilmer, T., 560
Gilmore, D., 525
Gilmore, J. H., 479–480, 486–487
Giltay, E., 325
Gilton, A., 251
Ginsburg, G. S., 147
Giordani, B., 157
Gipson, M. T., 186–187
Gipson, P. Y., 232
Girgus, J. S., 233, 238
Giriunas, I., 51, 163
Gise, L. H., 94
Gitlin, M. J., 242
Givelber, R. J., 295, 298
Gizer, I. R., 504, 505
Gizewski, E., 459
Gladis, M., 277
Gladstone, T. R. G., 245
Gladue, B. A., 348, 351
Glaser, R., 309, 312, 314–316, 319
Glass, K., 240
Glass, S., 279
Glassco, J. D., 132
Glassman, A. H., 405
Glatt, A. E., 361
Glatt, C. E., 480
Glazer, J. P., 183
Gleason, J. A., 286
Gleason, O. C., 535
Gleaves, D. H., 190, 192, 196, 198–199, 201, 265
Glenn, B., 327
Glick, I., 246–247
Glick, M. P., 525
Glisky, M. L., 198–199
Glod, C., 240
Glover, M., 486
Glovinsky, P., 292
Glynn, R. J., 131
Glynn, S. M., 492
Goater, N., 480
Goddeck, G., 69
Godoy-Matos, A., 281
Goel, M. S., 269, 286

Goering, P., 493
Goff, D. C., 485
Goggins, W., 475
Gold, G., 537
Gold, J. A., 503
Gold, J. H., 94, 147
Gold, M. S., 364, 403, 419
Gold, P. W., 230
Gold, S., 525
Goldberg, D. P., 177–178
Goldberg, J. F., 111, 217, 229, 329, 357
Goldberg, L., 431
Goldberg, S. C., 442
Goldberger, J., 104
Golden, C. J., 82
Golden, R. N., 62, 221, 319
Goldfarb, W., 514
Goldin, P. R., 150
Golding, J. M., 161
Goldman, D., 37, 95
Goldman, M. S., 392, 413
Goldman, S. J., 452
Goldmeir, D., 361
Goldsmith, D., 292
Goldstein, A., 405, 420, 523
Goldstein, A. J., 458
Goldstein, C. E., 125, 136–137, 156, 252, 453
Goldstein, G., 82
Goldstein, I. B., 323, 358, 363, 370
Goldstein, J. M., 486
Goldstein, M. J., 247
Goldstein, R. B., 224
Goldstein, S., 222
Goldston, D. B., 250–251, 508
Golier, J., 158
Golinelli, D., 140
Golshan, S., 560
Gomez-Caminro, A., 127
Gonzales-Lavin, A., 272
Gonzalez-Smith, V., 494
Good, A. B., 327
Good, B. J., 60, 90, 193, 225, 328
Gooding, W., 281
Goodkin, K., 319
Goodman, G. S., 200
Goodman, S. H., 234, 238
Goodnough, A., 155
Goodrich, S., 452
Goodwin, D. W., 177–178, 395
Goodwin, F. K., 209, 216–217, 220, 226, 230–232, 241–242, 247
Goodwin, P. J., 320
Goodwin, R., 208, 212–213, 221–222, 224–225, 249
Goodyear, M. D., 334
Gooren, L. J. G., 350, 351
Goplerud, E., 217
Gorbien, M. J., 548
Gordis, E., 411, 412
Gordon, C. S., 526
Gore, J. C., 423
Gorenstein, E. E., 178
Gorman, J. M., 52, 126, 138, 139–140, 146, 318, 380
Gorman, L. K., 42
Gorman, L. L., 245
Gorny, G., 53, 64
Gorski, R. A., 348
Gortmaker, S. L., 271
Gorzalka, B. B., 364–365
Gossard, D., 326–327
Gotlib, I. H., 200, 208, 219, 222, 224, 225, 227, 231, 235, 238, 244
Gottesman, I. I., 35–36, 104, 480–483
Gottesman, R. F., 505
Gottler, I., 452
Gottlieb, G., 40, 53
Gould, M., 252–253
Gould, R. A., 131, 151, 277, 279–280

Gould, S. J., 16
Gournay, K., 186, 188
Goyal, A., 183
Grabe, H. J., 183, 184
Grabe, S., 270
Grace, M. C., 155
Gracheck, J. E., 565
Grados, M. A., 160
Grady, W. R., 345
Grady-Weliky, T., 94
Graeff, F. G., 124
Graf, P., 56
Grafstrom, M., 539, 549
Graham, A., 44, 79–81
Graham, D. L., 241
Graham-Hole, V., 492–493
Grandi, S., 175, 210, 246
Grandits, G. A., 325
Granic, I., 448
Grann, M., 559
Grant, B., 208, 212–213, 221–222, 224–225, 249
Grant, I., 63, 225, 310
Grant, J. E., 186–189, 191, 422
Grant, K. E., 222, 224, 232
Grant, L., 185
Gratz, K. L., 452
Graubard, B. I., 262, 283
Graves, R. E., 241
Graxon, S. I., 547
Gray, B. A., 480
Gray, J. A., 178, 412, 447
Graybar, S. R., 452–453
Grayson, C., 236
Graziosi, C., 318
Grazzi, L., 334
Greden, J. F., 230, 406
Green, B. A., 265
Green, B. L., 155
Green, E., 336
Green, G., 512
Green, K. F., 56
Green, L., 515
Green, M. F., 492
Green, R., 348, 351–353
Greenberg, B. D., 124
Greenberg, D., 347
Greenberg, G. S., 414
Greenberg, H. R., 270, 422–423
Greenberg, M. P., 56
Greenberg, M. S., 227
Greenberg, T., 240
Greenblatt, D. J., 131
Greene, K. A. I., 138
Greene, R., 507
Greene, S. J., 348
Greenhill, L. L., 251, 506
Greenhouse, W. J., 237
Greeno, C. G., 276
Greenough, W. T., 53
Greenstein, D. K., 505
Greenwald, D., 492
Greenwald, S., 161
Greenway, D. E., 91
Greenway, F. L., 286
Greenwood, P., 362
Greer, A., 160
Gregoire, A., 370
Greil, W., 242
Greiner, L. H., 538–539
Greist, 162
Grey, J. A., 47–48, 123–124
Grey, J. P., 12, 14
Grey, N., 151–152
Grice, D. E., 160
Grichnik, K., 322
Griez, E., 138
Griffing, A., 265
Griffing, S., 265
Griffith, E. E. H., 193
Griffith, J. L., 286
Griffiths, R. R., 406, 409
Griffth, E. E. H., 183

Grillo, M., 418
Grilo, C. M., 268, 279, 281, 434, 451, 453
Grinspoon, L., 403, 408
Grisham, J. R., 160–161, 217, 226, 249
Grob, C. S., 401
Groom, C., 130
Groopman, L. C., 456
Gross, C., 230, 239
Gross, H., 549–550
Gross, J. J., 57–60, 208, 227, 269, 270
Gross, W. M., 245
Grossman, J. A., 223
Grossman, L. S., 217
Grossman, S., 261
Grosz, H. J., 182
Grove, W. M., 78, 246
Grube, J. W., 421
Gruber, A. J., 196, 274–275
Gruber, J. L., 232
Gruber, R., 291
Gruenewald, P. J., 421
Gruenewald, T. L., 62
Grundman, M., 547
Grunhaus, L., 242
Grut, M., 539, 549
Gu, H., 62, 319
Gu, X., 46
Guallar, E., 545
Guarnaccia, P., 90
Guarnaccia, P. J., 415
Gudanowski, D. M., 155–156
Gueorguieva, R., 491
Guijarro, M. L., 323, 325
Guild, D., 374–376
Guilleminault, C., 294–295
Guimaraes, A. P., 526
Gulati, D. K., 523
Gündel, H., 214
Gunderson, J. G., 434–435, 441, 451, 453
Gunnar, M. R., 125, 157
Guo, S., 450
Gur, R. C., 182
Gur, R. E., 483
Guralnik, O., 190–191
Gureje, O., 172, 177–178
Gurian, B., 435, 451
Guroff, J. J., 195
Gursky, D. M., 137
Gurung, R. A. R., 62
Gurvits, T. V., 157
Gurwitz, J., 131
Gusella, J. F., 542
Guskin, L., 125
Gust, S. W., 418
Gustad, J., 187–188
Gustafson, Y., 534
Gustavsson, J. P., 441
Gusti Rai Tirta, I., 494
Guther, H., 320
Guthrie, D., 320
Guthrie, E., 251
Guttmacher, M. S., 563
Gutweniger, S., 229
Guyatt, G. H., 334
Guydish, J., 419
Guyton, R., 323
Guze, B. H., 51
Guze, S. B., 177–178
Guzy, L. T., 146
Gwaltnye, J. M., Jr., 62, 315
Gyulai, L., 219

Haaf, B., 451, 453
Haaga, D. A. F., 227
Haak, J. W., 131
Haaland, K. Y., 82
Haas, G. L., 251, 490
Haber, S. N., 62
Hack, S., 129, 132
Hackett, T. P., 59, 334

Hackmann, A., 139, 151–152, 175
Hadigan, C. M., 277
Hadjistavropoulos, T., 188
Hadley, S., 188
Hadzi-Pavlovic, D., 488
Haenen, M. A., 172, 174, 175
Haiman, C., 278
Haines, J., 384
Haines, M., 493
Hajak, G., 452
Hakstian, A. R., 444
Hale, L., 288
Halek, C., 261
Haley, A., 35
Hall, A. C., 261, 525
Hall, D. E., 181
Hall, E., 156
Hall, J. A., 566
Hall, K. S., 545
Hall, L. S., 348
Hall, N. R., 309
Hall, W., 407
Hallahan, D. P., 508
Hallet, A. J., 323, 325
Hallis, D., 296
Halonen, P., 535
Hamaker, E. L., 195
Hamburger, R., 112
Hamer, D. H., 348–349
Hamer, R. M., 179, 442
Hamm, A. O., 277
Hammad, T., 240
Hammeke, T. A., 82
Hammen, C., 223, 229, 232, 236, 242
Hammer, L. D., 134, 282–283
Hammer, S., 318
Hammerton, J. L., 522
Hammett, E., 156
Hammond, R., 335
Hanani, C., 243
Handa, S., 489
Handen, B., 134
Haney, J. I., 335
Haney, T. L., 59
Hankin, B. L., 232, 234–236
Hankinson, S. E., 283
Hanks, D. L., 211
Hanley, B., 117
Hanna, G. L., 161
Hans, S. L., 485
Hans, V. P., 564
Hansen, F., 214
Hanson, R. K., 381
Hantouche, E. G., 209, 217
Hapke, U., 184
Happel, R. L., 174
Har, A. B., 245
Harada, N., 149
Haraldsson, H. M., 491
Harbert, T. L., 379–380
Harden, R. N., 327
Hardin, S., 542
Harding, K., 213
Hardy, G., 245
Hardy, J., 545
Hare, R. D., 443–446, 448–449
Harenski, K., 572
Hariri, A., 35, 37
Harkness, A. R., 431
Harlow, B., 225
Harnett, P. H., 245
Harold, G. T., 235–236, 446–447
Harper, L. V., 39
Harpole, I., 241
Harpur, T. J., 444
Harrington, H., 37, 40, 42, 48, 53, 123, 229
Harris, E. C., 261
Harris, G. T., 376, 380, 449–550
Harris, J. E., 237
Harris, T. O., 237
Harrison, B., 137
Harrison, P. J., 276

Harrison, P. L., 82
Harrison, R., 234
Harrison, W. M., 217
Harriss, L., 251
Harrow, M., 217, 479
Hart, S. D., 446
Harvald, B., 228
Harvey, A. G., 154
Harvey, I., 486
Harvey, L., 106
Harwood, H., 423
Hasin, D., 208, 212–213, 221–222, 224–225, 249, 268
Haskell, W. L., 323
Haskett, R. F., 230
Haslam, J., 467
Haslam, N., 488, 492
Hassan, S. S., 250–251
Hassman, H., 131
Hastings, J., 394
Hatch, M., 135–136
Hatfield, E., 10, 58, 347
Hathaway, S. R., 79, 81
Hatsukami, D. K., 418
Hatzichrisou, C., 134, 144, 147
Hatzichristou, D. G., 358, 363
Hauch, J., 137
Hauge, M., 228
Haughie, S., 370
Hauser, S. T., 237
Hausmann, A., 229
Have, T., 241
Haw, C., 251
Hawkins, J. D., 113
Hawkins, K. A., 479, 491
Hawthorne, W., 560
Hawton, K., 251, 356, 358, 361, 370
Hay, P. J., 261, 265, 268
Haydel, F., 282–283
Hayden, T. L., 523
Hayes, A. M., 458
Hayes, M., 321
Hayes, S. C., 5, 91, 107–108, 372, 380
Hayhurt, 210
Haynes, R. B., 570
Haynes, S. G., 324
Haynes, S. N., 77
Hays, R. D., 93, 237, 244
Hayward, C., 267, 274, 282
Hayward, G., 134, 137
Hayward, R., 248
Haywood, M. E., 275
Hazell, P., 64
Healy, B, 222
Healy, D., 240
Heard, H. L., 453
Heath, A. C., 103, 123, 129, 228–229, 265, 276–277, 446
Heathcote, D., 64
Heatheron, T. F., 261, 276
Hebden, J. C., 84
Hebert, L. E., 537
Hechtman, L., 502
Hecker, M. H. L., 325
Hecker, S., 157
Hedeker, D., 245
Hedley, A. J., 336
Heese, K., 546
Heffelfinger, A., 222
Heil, S. H., 420
Heilig, M., 418
Heils, A., 124
Heim, C., 53, 124, 157, 230, 329
Heiman, J. R., 359, 365, 368–369
Heimberg, R. G., 149, 151, 234
Heinrichs, N., 143–144
Heitz, M., 298
Helgeson, V., 319–320
Hellebusch, S. J., 418
Heller, M. N., 46, 237
Hellman, I., 334
Hellman, R. E., 348, 351
Hellman, T. L., 242

Hellström, K., 148
Helms, E., 322
Helweg-Larsen, M., 336
Helzer, J. E., 398, 413
Henderson, K. E., 262, 284, 286
Hendrie, H., 545
Hendriksz, C. J., 522
Heninger, M., 249
Henle, W., 328
Hennen, J., 434, 451
Henry, D., 64
Henry, G. T., 9, 15, 526
Henschel, A., 275
Hense, H., 322
Heo, M., 241
Hepler, N., 559
Herber, P., 240
Herbert, L. E., 537
Herbert, T. B., 311, 315–317
Herdt, G. H., 348
Herling, S., 412
Herman, C. P., 274, 275
Herman, D. B., 560
Herman, J. L., 452–453
Herman-Dunn, R., 244
Hermann, C., 452
Hermans, D., 22, 144–145, 147
Hermmann, J. H., 251
Hernandez, I., 493
Hernandez, J., 172
Hernández-Ferràdiz, M., 540
Herpertz, S. C., 454
Herrmann, F. R., 537
Hersen, M., 76–77, 369–380
Hershberger, S., 348–349
Herzog, A. R., 346
Herzog, D. B., 264–265, 267–269, 271, 275, 277, 282
Herzog, W., 261
Heshka, S., 286
Hesketh, K., 262
Hess, T. H., 178
Hessler, M., 222
Hester, R. K., 419
Hethrington, E. M., 39–49, 65, 449
Hettema, J. M., 36, 129–130, 147, 232, 244
Hiatt, K. D., 448
Hickman, M., 407
Higgins, E., 234
Higgins, S. T., 420
Highfield, D. A., 418
Higuchi, S., 415
Hikama, H., 157
Hilgard, E. R., 56
Hill, C., 329
Hill, E. M., 142, 172, 452
Hill, J. O., 286
Hill, K. K., 271, 277
Hiller, W., 172, 174, 176, 179
Hiller-Sturmhöfel, S., 399
Hillhouse, J. J., 174
Hilsenroth, M. J., 21
Hilts, P. J., 570
Hilty, D. M., 534
Himle, J. A., 142, 172
Hinden, B. R., 223
Hindmarch, I., 131
Hinshaw, S. P., 503, 506
Hinshelwood, J. A., 510
Hinton, D., 135, 145
Hirayasu, Y., 442
Hiripi, E., 261, 265, 269
Hirschfeld, D. R., 150
Hirschfeld, R. M. A., 208, 211, 239, 458
Hiruma, N., 149
Hitchcock, P. B., 174
Hitty, D. M., 422–424
Hlastala, S., 247
Hmaer, R., 221
Hnasberry, M. R., 548
Ho, S. Y., 336

Hoar, A., 480
Hobfoll, S. E., 114
Hobson, R. P., 183
Hodapp, R. M., 518–521, 523, 524
Hodes, M., 282
Hodes, R. L., 56
Hodgson, R., 368
Hoehn-Saric, R., 130, 160
Hoek, H. W., 261
Hoekstra, T., 325
Hoenk, P., 190
Hoeper, E. W., 222
Hoffman, B., 333
Hoffman, J. H., 414
Hoffman, R. E., 472, 491
Hoffman, S. G., 152
Hofler, M., 125, 155, 177
Hofman, M. A., 351
Hofmann, S. G., 123, 142, 149, 151, 164
Hofstede, G., 431
Hogan, D. R., 369
Hogarty, G. E., 492
Holcomb, W., 512
Holden, C., 284
Holder, H. D., 421
Holen, A., 214
Holford, T. R., 212, 535
Holladay, J., 559
Holland, D., 245
Hollander, E., 188–189, 191, 515
Holliday, J. E., 309
Hollifield, M., 135
Hollon, S. D., 138, 210, 234, 245–247, 567
Holm, J. E., 331–332
Holmen, K., 539, 549
Holmes, L. B., 397, 406
Holroyd, K. A., 328, 331–334
Holt, C. S., 151
Holt-Lunstad, J., 315
Holzer, C. E., III, 134, 141, 144, 213, 216, 218, 221, 225
Holzman, P. S., 483
Hood, J. E., 234
Hood, S., 161
Hoogduin, K. A., 180, 183, 184
Hoogendoorn, M. L. C., 486
Hook, E. B., 522
Hooley, J. M., 452, 488
Hoon, E. F., 309, 364
Hoon, P. W., 309, 364
Hope, R. A., 279–280
Hopkins, J., 281
Hopkins, M., 130
Hopko, D. R., 132
Hops, H., 222, 224, 235, 327
Hopwood, C. J., 436
Horan, W. P., 487, 492
Hornbacher, M., 261
Hornbrook, M., 245
Horney, K., 20
Horowitz, M. J., 214, 245, 455
Horta, B. L., 503
Horvath, T. B., 484
Horwath, E., 135
Houck, P., 215, 247
House, J. S., 62, 237
Houston, B. K., 325
Houston, K., 251
Houts, A. C., 91
Houts, P. D., 320
Howard, L. J., 265, 277
Howard, M., 245
Howell, A. J., 201
Howland, R., 229–230, 246
Hoza, B., 503
Hrabosky, J. I., 268, 272
Hsu, L. K. G., 261, 265–267, 271, 276, 281–282
Hu, N., 348–349
Hu, S., 130, 348–349, 491

Huang, K. -E., 94
Hubbard, R. W., 250
Hubert, N. C., 321
Hucker, S. J., 374
Hudson, J. I., 196, 261, 265, 268–269, 274–275, 276
Hudziak, J., 351
Huesmann, R., 450
Hufford, M. R., 77
Hug, R., 323
Hughes, D., 129, 146
Hughes, D. L., 154
Hughes, J. R., 403, 405, 418
Hughes, M., 155, 221
Hull, I. M., 568
Hull, J., 246–247
Humphrey, L. L., 275–276
Hunkeler, E., 241
Hunnicutt, C. P., 273
Hunt, 13
Hunter, D. J., 261, 283
Hunter, E., 190
Hunter, J. A., Jr., 378
Huntington's Disease Collaborative Research Group, 542
Huntjens, R. J., 195
Huntzinger, R. M., 144
Huot, R. L., 53, 157
Huppert, J. D., 152
Hur, K., 240
Hursey, K. G., 331–332
Hurt, R. I., 414
Hurt, S. W., 94
Hurwitz, B. E., 322
Husain, K., 330
Husain, M., 241–242
Hutton, B, 240
Hutton, K., 309
Hutz, M. H., 526
Huxley, G., 451
Hviid, A., 515
Hwo, H., 161
Hyde, J. S., 270, 347
Hyler, S. E., 89, 451
Hymbaugh, K. J., 397
Hynan, L. S., 540
Hyoun, K., 238
Hypericum Depression Trial Study Group, 240
Hyrniuk, W. M., 334
Hyun, C. S., 320

Iacono, W. G., 230, 483
Ickovics, J. R., 336
Ikeguchi, E. F., 370
Ilardi, S. S., 56, 245
Imai, M., 489
Imazeki, M., 415
Imber, S. D., 245
Imhof, A., 537
Imhoff, D. F., 237
Imperato-McGinely, J., 351
Inglis, S. J., 106
Ingvar, M., 52
Inlow, J. K., 521
Innis, R. B., 82, 84
Inouye, N, 546
Inouye, S. K., 535
Insel, T. R., 52–53, 161, 241, 261
Institute of Medicine, 253, 335, 570
Inz, J., 130
Ironson, G., 310, 318–319, 323, 325
Irvin, J. E., 421
Irwin, D., 105
Irwin, M., 288, 315, 399
Isaacowitz, D., 64
Israel, M. C., 223
Ivengar, M., 131
Ives, D. G., 540
Iwawaki, S., 134, 144, 147
Izard, C. E., 58
Izquierdo, J. A., 364

Jaccard, J., 333
Jackson, C., 414
Jackson, G., 363, 472
Jackson, J. S., 5, 225, 251, 322
Jackson, K., 241, 335
Jackson, L., 339
Jackson, R. J., 137
Jacob, C., 123
Jacob, R. G., 151
Jacobi, D. M., 160
Jacobi, F., 126–127, 184
Jacobi, W., 485
Jacobs, A. R., 545
Jacobs, L., 414
Jacobs, S. C., 214, 234–235
Jacobsen, D., 318
Jacobsen, F., 221
Jacobsen, N. S., 236, 244–245
Jacobson, K. C., 411, 457–458
Jaffe, A. J., 421
Jaffe, J. H., 394, 396–397, 399–403, 406–407, 412–414, 418
Jaffe, S. E., 288
Jaffee, S. R., 224
Jagust, W., 540
James, B., 195
James, N. M., 230
James, S. A., 310
Jameson, D., 194
Jamin, S., 251
Jamison, K. R., 207, 209, 216–217, 220, 226, 231–232, 241, 242, 247
Jamison, R. N., 327
Jamner, L. D., 323
Jamra, R. A., 123
Jandorf, L., 560
Jane, J. S., 436
Jang, K. L., 95, 486
Janicak, P. G., 219, 242
Janssen, E., 362, 370
Janzen, H. L., 220
Jaros, E., 44
Jarrett, D. B., 241
Jarskog, F., 479–480
Jasiukaitis, P., 198–199
Jason, L. A., 328, 329
Jaspers, K., 470
Javahri, S., 295
Javitt, D., 410
Javitt, D. C., 484–485
Jay, S. M., 321
Jaycox, L., 157
Jellema, K., 486
Jellinek, E. M., 398–399
Jenike, M. A., 51, 159, 163
Jenkins, C. D., 324
Jenkins, J. A., 146
Jenkins, J. H., 488
Jennings, J. R., 290
Jensen, E. J., 419
Jensen, J., 418
Jensen, M. P., 287, 327
Jensen, P. S., 506
Jensen, S. B., 357, 363
Jerabek, P., 238
Jerome, A., 334
Jesse, R., 409
Jessell, T. M., 47, 53
Jest, D. V., 490
Jethanandani, V., 224
Jiang, X., 336–337
Jilek, W. G., 193
Jin, R., 129, 212–213, 221, 224, 229–230
Jindal, R. D., 229–230
Jitendra, A. K., 511
Jobe, T. H., 479
Jobes, D. A., 250
Jockin, V., 38
Jody, D., 483
Joe, S., 251
Joffe, R., 159
Joffres, M., 322

Johannes, C. B., 358
Johansson, B., 35
John, O. P., 59
Johns, M. B., 335
Johnson, A. M., 346
Johnson, B. A., 407
Johnson, B. M., 245
Johnson, C., 241–242
Johnson, C. E., 413
Johnson, C. L., 282
Johnson, D. L., 480–483
Johnson, D. R., 157
Johnson, J., 309
Johnson, J. G., 124, 127, 190, 197, 282, 439, 441
Johnson, K., 547
Johnson, L., 326–327
Johnson, M. D., 100
Johnson, M. I., 261
Johnson, R. A., 423
Johnson, R. J., 114
Johnson, S., 209, 217
Johnson, S. L., 232, 237, 458
Johnson, V. E., 102, 353, 364, 368–369
Johnson, W. E., 241
Johnson, W. G., 267–268
Johnson-Powell, G., 193
Johnson-Sabine, E., 274, 480
Johnston, B. M., 224
Johnston-Cronk, K., 492
Johnstone, B., 82
Joiner, T. E., Jr., 235, 237, 252, 261, 276
Jonas, J. M., 276
Jones, B. D., 483
Jones, B. E., 480
Jones, D. P H., 200
Jones, I., 112
Jones, J. C., 157
Jones, L. B., 348
Jones, M. C., 23
Jones, P., 486
Jones, R., 279–280
Jones, R. B., 183
Jones, R. T., 155, 335, 408
Jones, S., 157
Jones, W, 512–513
Jonsson, E., 441
Jonsson, L., 537
Jordan, B. D., 545
Jordan, B. K., 155
Jordan, K. M., 328
Jorenby, D. E., 414
Jourvent, R., 274–275
Jovanovic-Peterson, L. G., 406
Jowett, S. A., 300
Joy, M. E., 449
Judd, L. L., 210, 213, 216, 219
Judge, R., 138, 162
Juneau, M., 325
Jung, C., 20–21
Junginger, J., 372
Jungquist, C. R., 290

Kaelber, C., 89
Kafka, M. P., 379
Kagan, J., 150
Kahana, E., 539
Kahn, C., 280
Kahn, R. S., 486
Kaiser, J., 318, 330
Kalat, J. W., 42–43
Kalichman, S. C., 336
Kalin, N. H., 491
Kalivas, P. W., 424
Kalso, E., 52
Kaltman, S., 214–215
Kame'enui, E., 511
Kamholz, B., 534
Kaminer, Y., 421
Kampman, K. M., 417–418, 418
Kanaya, T., 521

Kanayama, G., 274–275
Kandel, D. B., 405
Kandel, E. R., 47, 53
Kane, J. M., 489, 490
Kanigel, R., 403, 405
Kannel, W. B., 324
Kanner, L., 514, 517
Kaplan, A. S., 278
Kaplan, B. H., 62, 310
Kaplan, G. A., 225
Kaplan, H. S., 356, 364
Kaplan, M., 435
Kaplan, R. D., 472
Kaplan, S. A., 370
Kaplan DeNour, A. K., 62
Kapur, N., 251
Karkowski, L. M., 146, 232
Karno, M., 161, 488
Karon, B. P., 78
Karterud, S., 431
Kasch, K. L., 208
Kasen, S., 124, 190, 197, 282
Kashani, J. H., 222, 223, 445
Kashani, K. H., 335
Kasindorf, J., 561
Kasl, S. V., 55, 214
Kaslow, N. J., 244
Kaspar, S., 348
Kass, D. J., 455
Kass, S. J., 334
Kastarinen, M., 322
Kathol, R., 177
Kato, K., 329
Kato, M., 494
Katon, E., 227
Katon, W., 93, 129, 135, 177, 227,
    241
Katon, W. J., 314, 316, 329
Katona, C., 547
Katz, C. L., 104
Katz, I. R., 224, 241, 535
Katz, J. L., 327, 331, 334
Katz, R. C., 38, 186–187, 228–229,
    237
Kaufman, A. V., 548
Kaufman, J. C., 226
Kavanagh, D. J., 488
Kavle, K. A., 505
Kawachi, I., 325
Kawamura, K. Y., 271
Kaye, W. H., 265, 267, 276, 281
Kazdin, A. E., 450
Kazi, A., 319–320
Keane, T. B., 155, 157
Kearney, C. A., 134
Keck, P., 219
Keck, P. E., 219, 241
Kedem, P., 60
Keefe, F. J., 326–327, 331, 333
Keefe, R. S. E., 484
Keel, P. K., 261, 265, 267–269,
    276–277, 282
Keenan, R. M., 418
Keener, A., 231
Keern, E., 281
Kegan, R., 100
Kehrer, C. A., 253, 453
Keijers, G. P., 183
Keilitz, I., 564, 565–566
Keir, R., 146
Keith, S. J., 480, 492
Keitner, G. I., 237, 245
Kelerman, G. L., 173, 280
Keller, M. B., 129, 208–211, 213,
    218–219, 223–224, 246
Keller, M. M., 239
Keller, S. E., 316
Kelley, T. M., 252
Kellner, R., 172–175
Kellum, J. M., 287
Kelly, B. D., 439, 441
Kelly, J. A., 336
Kelly, K. A., 237

Kelly, M. P., 360, 367
Kelpiner, D. H., 345
Kelsey, J. E., 46
Kelsoe, J. R., 35–36
Keltikangas-Jarvinen, L., 49–50
Kemeny, M. E., 309, 312–313, 320,
    333, 336
Kemether, E., 348
Kemp, S., 8, 10, 12
Kemper, S. J., 538–539
Kendall, P. C., 234
Kendell, R. E., 5, 132, 219
Kendler, K. S., 5, 35–36, 38, 40,
    112, 123, 129–130, 146–147,
    228–229, 232, 236–238, 244, 265,
    268, 276, 277, 411, 439
Kenecht, S., 327
Kenford, S. L., 414
Kennedy, D. L., 131
Kennedy, E., 286
Kennedy, J. L., 451–52
Kennedy, S., 242, 311, 318–319
Kenney, Q., 64
Kenney, R. D., 181
Kent, J. M., 53, 124, 157
Kentish, J., 131
Kenyon-Jump, R., 309, 310
Kern, H. E., 220
Kernberg, O., 20
Kerns, R., 333
Kerns, R. D., 84
Kerr, N., 248
Kerr, S. M., 300
Kertzner, R. M., 318
Kessler, R. C., 123, 129, 134,
    144–145, 149, 155, 161, 212–213,
    221, 224, 228–229, 231, 235,
    236–237, 250, 261, 265, 269, 276,
    277, 283, 434, 451
Kest, B., 328
Kety, S. S., 251
Keys, A., 275
Khachaturian, Z. S., 533, 546
Khaitan, B. K., 367
Khalifé, S., 360–361
Khamis, I., 319
Khan, A., 470, 474
Khani, M. K., 216
Kiazand, A., 286
Kidd, K. K., 112
Kiebeskind, J. C., 328
Kiecolt-Glaser, J. K., 309, 311–312,
    314–316, 319, 323
Kiefe, C. I., 322–323
Kiehl, K. A., 486
Kiesler, D. J., 102
Kiehl, K. A., 542
Kihlstrom, J. F., 56, 171, 190,
    195–196, 198–199, 201
Kilbey, M. M., 405
Kilgus, M., 282
Killen, J. D., 134, 137, 267, 274,
    282–283
Kilman, V. L., 53
Kils, C., 572
Kilsieh, N., 219
Kim, B. -N., 505
Kim, D., 422
Kim, D. R., 358, 370
Kim, H. L., 161
Kim, J. H., 157
Kim, K. M., 235–236
Kim, S. W., 188, 422
Kim, W. -W., 505
Kimble, R., 178
Kinder, B., 261
King, A., 117
King, A. C., 323
King, B. H., 518–521, 523, 524
King, C., 329
King, D. E., 546
King, D. W., 155–156
King, G. R., 401

King, J., 286
King, L. A., 155–156
King, M., 480
King, N. J., 144
King, S. A., 184
Kinney, D. K., 226
Kinney, R. K., 327
Kinoshita, T., 179, 415
Kinsey, A. C., 346
Kinzie, J. D., 225
Kipp, H., 448–449
Kircher, J. C., 360
Kircher, J. R., 367
Kirkley, B. G., 172
Kirkpatrick, B., 469–470, 472–475
Kirkpatrick, D. G., 147, 155–156
Kirmayer, L. J., 149, 173–174, 177,
    184, 202
Kirsch, I., 196, 199, 201
Kirsh, C., 333
Kirsh, F. C., 568
Kirshnan, P. R., 424
Kissinger, P., 318
Kittel, F., 324
Kivimaki, M., 49–50
Kjernisted, K. D., 175
Klauber, M. R., 547
Kleban, M., 224
Klein, D., 238
Klein, D. F., 4, 124, 151, 189
Klein, D. N., 207, 210–211, 213,
    217–218, 224, 228, 246, 436–437
Klein, L. C., 62
Klein, M., 20
Kleinbaum, D. G., 62
Kleinknecht, E. E., 149
Kleinknecht, R. A., 135, 149
Kleinman, A. M., 60, 193, 225, 328
Kleinman, K. P., 358
Kleinman, M., 253
Klerman, G. L., 93, 127, 171, 211,
    212, 222, 236, 242, 243
Kletti, R., 198
Klevens, R. M., 364
Klienknecht, R. A., 326
Klimas, N., 318–319
Klin, A., 512–517
Klingler, T., 370
Kloner, R., 363
Klosko, J. S., 139, 234
Kluft, R. P., 195–198, 201
Klumker, A., 189
Klump, K. L., 276
Knapp, C. M., 413
Knapp, M. J., 547
Knapp, S., 229
Knäuper, B., 221
Knee, D., 224
Knight, F., 114–115
Knight, R. A., 374
Knutelska, M., 190–191
Ko, C. Y., 287
Ko, H. -C., 94
Koch, G. G., 335
Koch, P., 367
Koch, W. J., 155
Kochanek, K. D., 249
Kochanska, G., 449
Kochman, F. J., 217
Kocsis, J. H., 208
Koehn, K. A., 309, 310
Koeppe, R., 339
Koepsell, T. D., 540
Kogon, M. M., 320
Kohn, I. J., 370
Kohn, R., 237
Kohut, H., 456
Kolachana, B., 35, 37
Kolb, B., 36, 53, 64
Kolevzon, A., 537–538, 539–544,
    547–548
Kolko, D. J., 251, 252
Kollenbach, K., 251

Kong, V., 59
Kono, H., 415
Koopman, C., 190, 198–199
Koopman, J., 320
Koplowicz, A., 487, 494
Koposov, R., 157
Koppel, R., 537
Korczyn, A. D., 539
Koretz, D., 212–213, 221, 224
Korf, J., 330
Korfine, L., 452
Kornblith, S. J., 492
Kornitzer, M., 324
Kornstein, S. G., 213, 218
Korten, A., 487
Kosberg, J. L., 548
Kositc, J. P., 123
Kosson, D. S., 448, 452
Kosten, T. R., 391
Koster, E., 162
Kosterman, R., 113
Kostis, J., 363
Kotegal, P., 183
Koukoui, S. D., 524
Kovacs, M., 213, 229, 246, 250–251
Kovari, E., 537
Kovas, Y., 509
Kowalenko, N., 113
Kowatch, R., 224
Kowk, T., 534
Kown, J., 188
Kozak, M. J., 159, 163
Kraaij, V., 324
Kraemer, H. C., 270, 279–280, 419,
    467–468
Kraemer, L. D., 137
Kraepelin, E., 14, 86, 480, 483, 489
Kral, J. G., 287–288
Krane, R. J., 358, 363
Krangel, T. S., 157
Krantz, D. S., 334
Krasnoperova, E., 234
Krasu, J. E., 490
Krasuski, J., 242
Krause, J., 452
Krause, P., 94
Krejci, J., 270
Kresnow, M. -J., 252
Kring, A. M., 60
Kringlen, E., 451
Krishnan, K. R., 312
Krishnan, R. R., 156
Krishnan, V., 53
Krishnan-Sarin, S., 405
Krivo, S., 318
Kroenke, G., 202
Kroenke, K., 179
Kronholm, P., 534
Krueger, R. F., 5, 95
Krueger, T. H. C., 459
Krug, E. G., 252
Krupa, T., 493
Kryger, M. H., 298
Krystal, J. H., 95, 157, 491
Kuban, M., 374
Kuch, K., 135
Kuczmierczyk, A. R., 311
Kuehn, B., 318, 335
Kugaya, A., 84
Kuhn, B. R., 300
Kuhn, C., 59, 222
Kuhn, J., 231–232, 237–238
Kuilman, M., 522
Kukull, W. A., 540, 544
Kulkarni, J., 242, 472
Kuller, L. H., 540, 545
Kullgren, G., 184, 353
Kumar, M., 319
Kunkel, S. R., 55
Kuo, W. H., 250
Kupelnick, B., 246
Kuperman, S., 190
Kupfer, D. J., 5, 46–47, 88, 91, 95,

230–231, 240–241, 247, 290–291, 295–296, 300–301
Kupka, R., 219
Kurachim, M., 472
Kurihara, T., 494
Kurlan, L. T., 261
Kurtz, J. E., 328
Kurtzman, H. S., 234
Kusaka, H., 179
Kushner, M. G., 135
Kushner, S., 112
Kutcher, S., 241
Kymalainen, J. A., 488

La Fond, J. Q., 557, 562
La Greca, A. M., 129, 153, 157
Labbe, E. E., 311
Labouvie, E., 279, 281
Lacadie, C. M., 423
Lacey, J. H., 261
Lachar, B. L., 242
Lack, L., 291
LaCruz, M., 493
Lacy, T. M., 221
Ladd, C. O., 53, 124, 157, 330
Ladee, G. A., 175
Lader, M. L., 47, 123, 183
Lahaie, M., 360–361
Lahey, B. B., 448–449
Lahti, I., 39
Lakin, M. M., 370
Laksy, K., 438, 482
Lalonde, J. K., 268
Lalumière, M. L., 348
Lam, D., 546
Lam, D. H., 248
Lam, L., 534
Lam, R., 220–221, 231
Lam, S., 271
Lam, T. H., 336
Lamb, J. A., 250
Lamberg, L., 284
Lambert, M. J., 105, 114–115
Lambrou, C., 187
Lampert, C., 276
Lancenon, S., 209
Lancrenon, S., 217
Lander, M., 175
Landerman, R., 177, 184
Landis, K. R., 62, 225, 237
Landis, S. E., 335
Lane, D. S., 540
Lane, M. C., 434, 451
Lane, R. D., 214
Lang, A. R., 444
Lang, P. J., 56, 58, 448
Langbehn, D. R., 174
Langdon, R., 471
Langer, P., 129
Långström, B., 152
Langstrom, N., 373–374
Laor, E., 370
LaPerriere, A., 318–319
LaPorte, D. L., 270
Laptook, R. S., 437
Larimer, M. E., 420
Larntz, K., 436, 455
Larson, E. B., 544
Larson, J., 236
Laruelle, M., 484–485
Lasch, C., 456
Lasko, N. B., 157
Lasoc, M. S., 348
Last, C. G., 144
Latfi, R., 287
Latham, K. S., 173
Latty, E., 347
Lau, M. A., 412
Laub, J. H., 444
Laughren, T., 240
Laumann, E., 346, 355–361, 367
Lauriello, J., 480, 491, 492
Lauritano, M., 179

Lavelle, J., 560
Laver-Bradbury, C., 506
Lavori, P. W., 210–211, 219
Law, C., 251
Lawley, T., 328
Lawlor, M., 251
Lawrence, A., 350
Lawrence, E. E., 100
Laws, D. R., 380
Lawson, W. B., 559
Laxenaire, M., 453
Lazare, D., 395
Lazarus, R. S., 58–59, 326
Lazerson, A., 46–47
Le, A. D., 411
Le Grange, D., 282
Leader, J. B., 210
Leaf, D. J., 212, 216, 221, 225
Leavey, G., 480
Lebedinskaya, K. S., 513
Leccese, A. P., 419
Lechner, S., 319–320
Leckman, J. F., 160, 229
Lecrubier, Y., 138, 251
Lederhendler, I., 267, 269, 276–277
Ledesma, A., 364
LeDoux, L. E., 46–48, 51, 59, 124–125
Lee, C. K., 161, 415
Lee, J., 534
Lee, K. L., 59, 292
Lee, L. -R., 94
Lee, M., 44
Lee, P. C., 309
Lee, P. W. H., 513
Lee, S., 261, 271
Lee, T. M., 220, 484
Lee, Y. J., 142
Leeper, J. D., 548
Lefebvre, R. C, 334
Leff, P., 424
Legault, C., 540
Legg, B. H., 158, 568
Lehman, A. F., 492
Lehman, C. L., 131, 142, 157, 162, 225–226
Lehrer, P. M., 179
Leibbrand, R., 172, 176
Leiblum, S. R., 361, 369–370
Leifman, S., 561
Leitenberg, H., 277, 281, 347, 362
Lejeune, J., 522
Lejuez, C. W., 452
Lemeshow, S., 315
Lemke, T., 10
Lencz, T., 157
L'Engle, K. L., 414
Lentz, F. E., 508
Lentz, P., 491
Lenze, E. J., 132, 177, 225
Lenzenweger, M. F., 95, 200, 434, 436, 451, 483
Leon, A. C., 47, 209–210, 213, 219
Leonard-Green, T. K., 271
Leone, M., 334
Leo-Summers, L., 535
Leppämäki, S., 217
Lerew, D. R., 137
Lerman, C., 411
Leroux, J. -M., 51, 148
Lesage, A., 458
Lesch, K. -P., 124
Leserman, J., 62, 319
Leshen, E., 224
Lesperance, F., 325
Leszcz, M., 320
Leuchter, A. F., 51
Leung, C. M., 271
Leung, F., 271
Leung, P. K., 225
Leung, S. -K., 475
Levan, A., 522
LeVay, S., 348

Levenson, R. W., 60
Levenson, S., 292
Levenston, G. K., 448
Leventhal, A. M., 413–414
Lévesque, J., 51, 148
Levin, A. C., 138, 370, 451
Levin, F. R., 413
Levin, H., 515
Levine, J. A., 286
Levine, J. L., 246
Levine, L., 422
Levine, M. P., 272, 277, 282, 334
Levine, R. J., 116
Levitan, R., 220–221
Levitt, A., 220–221
Levitt, J. T., 139
Levy, B. R., 55
Levy, D. L., 483
Levy, J. K., 242
Lew, E. A., 284
Lewin, R. R. J., 486
Lewinsohn, P. M., 212–213, 222, 224, 228, 231, 234, 236, 238, 244, 251
Lewis, B. P., 62
Lewis, D. O., 198, 200
Lewis, G., 62, 480
Lewis, J. A., 142
Lewis, J. G., 59
Lewis, M., 198, 200
Lewis, S., 472, 486
Lewis-Fernandez, R., 90, 199
Lewy, A. J., 220
Leygraf, N., 459
Li, S., 253
Li, T. K., 411
Li, W., 229
Li, X., 250
Li, Z., 411
Liang, K. -Y., 160
Liau, A. K., 450
Liaw, J., 512
Liberman, R. P., 487
Lichtenstein, P., 38, 232, 261
Lichtenthal, W., 214
Liddell, H., 121
Lidz, C. W., 567
Lieb, K., 452
Lieb, R., 94, 125, 151, 155, 177
Lieberman, J. A., 479–480, 483, 490, 492, 494
Liebeskind, J. C., 326, 330
Liebowitz, M. R., 128, 135, 138, 142–143, 149, 151, 163, 189, 217, 227
Lifshitz, F., 274
Liggett, J., 187
Lilienfeld, L. R., 276–277
Lilienfeld, S. O., 4, 78, 177–178, 196, 199, 201, 436, 455
Lim, D., 193
Lima, J., 324
Limb, K., 248
Lin, E., 177
Lin, H., 225
Lin, K. M., 90, 193
Lin, N, 111, 229, 237
Lin, Y. G., 251
Lind, D. L., 184
Lindamer, L., 560
Linden, W., 331
Lindenmayer, J. P., 470, 474
Lindesay, J., 134
Lindner, S., 199
Lindsey, K. P., 480
Lindwall, R., 148
Lindy, J. D., 155
Lindy, J. G., 155a
Linehan, M. M., 253, 451, 453
Ling, W., 401–403
Link, B. G., 232
Links, P., 451
Linnolia, M., 232

Linsenmeier, J., 282, 352
Liorca, G., 364
Liotti, M., 238
Lipchik, G. L., 328, 333
Lippa, R., 348
Lipscomb, P., 177
Lipshultz, L. I., 358, 370
Lipton, A. M., 540–541
Lisanby, S. H., 242
Liss, A., 151
Lisspers, J., 332
Litman, R. E., 251
Litt, I. F., 134
Little, D., 264–265, 267
Little, I., 420
Littman, R., 316
Littrell, L., 214
Litz, B. T., 370–371
Liu, D., 39
Liu, K., 251, 322–323
Liu, L., 220
Liu, S., 279
Livesley, W. J., 88, 95
Livianos, L., 276–277
Livingston, G., 547
Llabre, M. M., 322
Lloyd, D., 486
Lloyd, E. A., 359
Lo Cascio, C., 298
Lo, E., 221
Lobban, M., 261
Lochman, J., 413
Lock, J., 288
Lockshin, B., 411
Loeb, K. L., 276, 278–279, 281
Loeber, R., 446
Loehlin, J., 348
Loewenstein, R. J., 192, 199, 201
Lofland, K., 327
Loftus, E. F., 199–200
Loftus, J., 355
Logan, A., 137
Logsdon, R. G., 548
Lohr, B., 188
Lohr, N. E., 452
Lonczak, H. S., 113
Long, J. S., 355
Longley, S. L., 174
Lonner, W. J., 135
Loo, S., 504
Looper, K. J., 184
Loosen, P. T., 246
Lopes, M. C., 294, 298
Lopez, A., 250
Lopez, C., 156
Lopez, O. L., 540, 544–545, 548
Lopez, S. R., 415
López-Pousa, S., 540
LoPiccolo, J., 355–356, 368–370
Loranger, A. W., 434, 451
Lord, C., 517
Lord, S., 451
Lorenzi, C., 290
Losonczy, M. F., 484
Lovaas, O. I., 517
Love, C. T., 348
Lovibond, P., 56
Loving, T., 315
Lowe, B., 261
Lowe, L. W., 546
Lowe, M. R., 189, 265, 286
Lozano, A., 243
Lozano-Gallego, M., 540
Lu, K. -T., 164
Lubinski, D., 92
Luby, J. L., 222
Lucas, A. R., 261
Lucas, J. A., 137
Lucas, R. E., 60
Lucia, V. C., 156
Luciana, M., 47
Luckasson, R., 92
Luckenbaugh, D., 219

Lüddens, H., 47
Ludwig, A. M., 194, 196, 226, 398
Lue, T. F., 370
Luk, S. L., 513
Lumry, A., 234
Lunde, I., 226
Lundgren, J. D., 286
Lundh, L. G., 150
Lundqvist, A., 56, 58–59
Lundstrom, B., 350, 353
Lundstrum, M., 534
Luo, Y., 346
Lutchy, E., 174
Lutgendorf, S., 319–320
Lydiard, M. B., 130, 162
Lygren, S., 451
Lyketsos, C. G., 224, 545, 547
Lykken, D. T., 35–36, 38, 443–446
Lynam, D. R., 446
Lynch, F., 245
Lynch, K. G., 252
Lynch, S. K., 103, 452
Lynche, J. E., 271
Lyness, J. M., 290
Lynn, D. E., 504
Lynn, S. J., 196, 199, 201
Lynskey, M., 407
Lyon, G. R., 507, 509–511
Lyons, M. J., 111, 229
Lytle, R., 131
Lyubomirksy, S., 55

MacCarthy, B., 38
Maccoby, E. E., 39–40, 337–338
Macdonald, A., 325
Macdonald, P. T., 364
MacDonald, R., 512
MacDougall, J. M., 59, 325
Mace, C. J., 179
MacGregor, M. W., 323
Maciejewski, P., 214, 234–235
Mack, A. H., 396
MacKenzie, E. J., 335
MacKinnon, D. F., 219, 227
Macklin, M. L., 157
Mackway-Jones, K., 251
MacLean, C. J., 123, 229, 276–277, 405
MacLean, D., 323
MacLeod, C., 56, 130, 234
Macleod, J., 407
MacQueen, G., 242
Madden, P. A. F., 103, 229, 446
Madonia, M. J., 245
Madsen, K. M., 515
Madu, R. J., 116
Maercker, A., 155
Maes, S., 324
Magarinos, A. M., 157
Magder, L., 315
Magee, L., 151, 189
Magee, W. J., 134, 144–145, 149
Magliano, L., 219, 227
Magne-Ingvar, U., 250
Magnuson, V. L., 348–349
Magovern, G. J., Sr., 334
Maher, B. A., 8, 11–12, 14–15
Maher, E., 262
Maher, W. B., 8, 11–12, 14–15
Mahler, M., 514
Mahoney, D. F., 548
Mai, F., 177, 179
Maier, S. F., 124, 157
Main, D., 411
Mainous, A. G., III, 546
Maisto, S. A., 439
Maj, M., 219, 227
Majuerovitz, S. D., 546
Mak, K. H., 336
Malarkey, W., 315
Malatesta, V. J., 360, 364
Maldonado, J. R., 197, 201
Maletzky, B. M., 379–381

Mallinger, A. G., 241–242, 247
Malmberg, S. R., 271
Malone, K. M., 229, 251–252
Maloney, E., 329
Malsion, R., 95
Maltzman, I. M., 420
Man, L., 333
Manber, R., 299
Mancill, R. B., 226
Mancuso, J., 480
Mandalos, G. E., 240
Mandel, A. J., 229
Mandeli, J., 370
Mandler, G., 56
Mangelsdorf, S., 157
Mangweth, B., 274–275
Manly, J. J., 539, 546
Mann, A. H., 274
Mann, H., 15
Mann, J. J., 229, 240, 251–253
Mann, K., 370
Manni, R., 302
Manning, J., 348
Mannino, D. M., 364
Mannuzza, S., 146, 151
Mansfield, P., 367
Mansky, P. A., 241
Manson, J., 325
Manson, J. E., 283
Manson, S., 222, 225, 249
Mantere, O., 217
Mapstone, J. A., 292
Marangell, L., 242
March, J. S., 504
Marchuk, D. A., 322
Marcopulos, B. A., 241
Marcouiller, 458
Marcus, J., 485
Marcus, M. D., 268, 279, 281
Marcus, S., 240
Marder, S. R., 489, 490, 492
Marek, P., 328
Marenco, S., 486
Margraf, J., 135, 172, 174, 176
Marin, D. B., 435, 451, 455, 537–544, 547–548
Marino, L., 4
Marino, M., 453
Markesbery, W. R., 538–539
Markis, N., 188
Markowitz, J. C., 244
Markowitz, J. S., 127
Marks, I. M., 31, 88, 149, 330, 333
Marks, T., 236
Marlatt, G. A., 415, 420–421
Marmot, M. G., 324
Marnell, M., 281
Marrocco, F., 253
Marsden, C. D., 182
Marshall, S., 157
Marshall, W. L., 376, 378
Marsolek, C. J., 56
Marsteller, F. A., 241
Marston, N. A., 242
Marteinsdottir, I., 152
Martell, C. R., 236, 244
Marten, P. A., 130
Marti, C. N., 288
Martin, C. E., 346
Martin, E., 51
Martin, F. I., 230
Martin, G. R., 381
Martin, I., 125
Martin, J., 224, 348
Martin, J. A., 249
Martin, K. M., 51
Martin, L. Y., 146
Martin, N. G., 103, 146, 348
Martin, P. A., 129
Martin, R. L., 177
Martin, S. D., 51
Martin, S. L., 525
Martin-Cook, K., 548

Martin-Ruiz, C., 44
Martinek, N., 214
Martinez, A., 457
Martins, A. C., 370
Martis, B., 242
Marton, P., 241
Martuza, R. L., 51, 163
Masanet, M. J., 493
Mascovich, A., 288
Maser, J. D., 89, 142, 213, 216, 219
Masheb, R. M., 268, 281
Maslow, A., 21–22
Mason, F. L., 372
Massion, A. O., 129
Masters, W. H., 102, 353, 364–365, 368–369
Mata, B., 172
Mathews, A., 56, 130–131, 174, 234
Mathews, K. A., 322–323, 325–326
Mathews, R., 378
Matsui, M., 472
Matsumoto, D., 324
Matsunaga, D., 225
Matsushita, S., 415
Mattay, V. S., 37, 486
Matteson, S. R., 290
Matthews, K. A., 322, 325, 334
Matthews, J., 420
Mattia, J. I., 186–188
Mattis, S. G., 137
Matza, L. S., 218
Mauer, J. D., 249
Mauler, B. I., 277
Maurizio, A., 104
May, P. A., 397
Mayberg, H. S., 238, 243
Mayer, B., 174
Mayer, J., 272
Mayfield, U., 183, 193
Mayol, A., 236
Mayou, R., 202
Mays, V. M., 336
Mayville, S., 186–187
Mazumdar, S., 131
Mazure, C. M., 232, 234–235, 472
Mazurick, J. L., 450
Mazziotta, J. C., 51
McAlister, A. L., 337–338
McAllister, C. G., 316
McAuliffe, T. L., 336
McCabe, M. P., 268, 374
McCabe, R., 151
McCann, U., 409
McCarthy, E., 248
McCarthy, E. P., 269, 286
McChesney, C. M., 129
McClearn, G. E., 35–37, 38, 123, 229, 232
McClung, C. A., 53
McConaha, C. W., 265, 267
McCormack, W. M., 361
McCormick, W. C., 544
McCracken, J. T., 504
McCrady, B. S., 420
McCrae, R. R., 431
McCrory, E., 510
McCullough, J. P., Jr., 208, 213, 218, 246
McCurry, S. M., 548
McDermott, M., 281
McDougall-Wilson, I. B., 244
McDowell, D. M., 410
McDowell, M. A., 262, 282
McElroy, S. L., 209, 219, 241, 424
McEvoy, J. P., 490
McEwen, B., 348
McEwen, B. S., 157, 230, 312
McFadden, D., 348
McGeoch, P. G., 439, 441
McGill, C. W., 492
McGinnis, J. M., 311
McGinnis, S., 238

McGlashan, T. H., 453, 479
McGonagle, K. A., 134, 144–146, 149, 221
McGorry, P. D., 479
McGory, M. L., 287
McGough, J. J., 504
McGovern, M. P., 394
McGowan, B. K., 56
McGowin, D. F., 536
McGrath, J., 494
McGrath, P. A., 321
McGrath, P. J., 217
McGreevy, M. A., 566
McGue, M., 35–36, 38, 228
McGuffin, P., 38, 228–229, 237
McGuire, P. K., 472
McHugh, P. R., 538
McHugo, G. J., 493
McIntosh, J. L., 250
McKay, D., 188
McKay, R., 471
McKelvey, W. F., 287
McKenna, J. C., 292
McKenzie, S. J., 277
McKeon, P., 460
McKiernan, K., 486
McKim, W. A., 406
McKinlay, J. B., 358
McKinley, J. C., 79, 81
McKinley, P., 323
McKinnon, W., 316
McKintosh, E., 546
McKissick, F. C., 514
McKunlay, J. B., 358, 363
McKusick, L., 336
McLachlan, G., 483
McLaughlin, T. J., 401
McLean, C., 265
McLean, P., 245
McLeod, D. R., 130
McLeod, J. D., 237
McLoone, J., 113
McMahon, S. D., 232
McMain, S., 451–52
McManus, F., 151–152
McManus, S., 346
McMurray, N., 115, 487
McNab, C., 488, 492
McNally, R. J., 16, 56, 130, 135, 137, 143, 199–200
McNaughton, N., 48, 123–124
McNeely, H., 243
McNeil, D. E, 567
McNeil, T. F., 486
McPherson, L. M., 448–449
Mead, S., 546
Meaden, P. M., 220
Meaney, M. J., 39–49, 53, 64, 124, 157, 312
Means, M. K., 298–299
Measelle, J. R., 413
Medicna-Mora, M. E., 415
Medland, S., 348
Mednick, S. A., 442, 473, 479, 486, 494
Meehan, P. J., 250
Meehl, P. E., 79, 91, 442, 473
Mehta, P., 542
Mei Tu, A., 546
Meilman, P. W., 398
Meisler, A. W., 363
Melamed, B. G., 321
Melau, M., 442
Melchior, M., 503
Melnikova, I., 551
Meloy, J. R., 449
Melville, L. F., 151
Melzack, R., 326–327, 328, 331
Menard, W., 186–187
Mendelson, W., 289–291, 301
Mendes, W. B., 62
Mendle, J., 103, 452
Mennin, D., 223, 505

Mensour, B., 51, 148
Menza, M., 179
Menzies, L., 424
Merali, Z., 39
Mercer, C. H., 346
Mercer, J., 292, 299
Merckelbach, H., 353
Merikangas, K. R., 94, 112, 125, 212–213, 221, 224, 229, 545
Merkelbach, J., 175
Merrell, D., 82
Merzel, A. P. C., 226
Merzenich, M., 511
Mesmer, A., 16
Messinger-Rapport, B., 548
Meston, C. M., 365, 369
Mestre, L. T., 544, 548
Metalsky, G. I., 234
Metzel, D., 525
Metzner, H. M., 62
Meulman, J., 324
Meuret, A. E., 152, 164
Meyer, A. J., 25, 337–338
Meyer, B., 237, 458
Meyer, C., 184
Meyer, J. M., 111, 229
Meyer, R. E., 421
Meyer, R. G., 557–560, 564, 568–569
Meyer-Bahlburg, H. F. L., 348, 351
Meyerowitz, B. E., 84, 334
Meyers, B., 219
Meyyazhagan, S., 181
Mezzacappa, E., 452
Mezzich, J. E., 90, 193
Miaskowski, C., 328
Michael, R., 367
Michaels, S., 367
Michalak, E., 220–221
Michelson, O., 275
Michultka, D., 333
Mick, E., 217, 223, 505
Middleman, A., 251
Middleton, H., 139, 175
Middleton, W., 214
Miele, V. J., 180
Miglioretti, D. L., 283
Miklowitz, D. J., 209, 217, 247–248
Milbrath, C., 214
Milburn, N. G., 221–222
Milkowitz, D., 219
Millar, H. R., 261
Miller, A. L., 490, 494
Miller, A. R., 177
Miller, G., 64, 311, 316
Miller, I. W., 55, 208, 232, 233, 237, 245
Miller, J. D., 456
Miller, K. B., 265, 269, 282
Miller, M. B., 349
Miller, N., 130–131
Miller, N. H., 419
Miller, N. S., 364, 419
Miller, P. M., 413
Miller, P. P., 158
Miller, R. D., 217
Miller, S. D., 196–199
Miller, S. L., 511
Miller, T. J., 479
Miller, T. Q., 323, 325
Miller, W. R., 417, 419, 420
Miller-Kovach, K., 286
Millet, B., 422
Millon, P. P., 153
Millon, T., 8, 15, 85, 87, 91, 457–458
Mills, J. L., 406
Milner, P. M., 412
Milstein, V., 197
Mindell, J. A., 77, 291–292, 300–301
Mineka, S., 54, 56, 95, 131, 145–146, 149, 237
Miner, M., 372
Minino, A. M., 249

Mintun, M. A., 229
Mintz, J., 487, 492, 494, 570
Minuchin, S., 275, 279
Mirenda, P., 525
Mirin, S. M., 237
Mirotznik, J., 232
Mirsky, A. F., 348, 482
Mitchell, C., 222, 225, 249
Mitchell, J. E., 5, 265, 267–269, 276–277, 277, 282
Mitchell, M., 526
Mitchell, P., 542
Mitchell, W. B., 365
Mitrouska, I., 418
Mittelman, C., 372
Mnagweth, B., 229
Modahl, C., 515
Modai, I., 495
Mody, M., 509–510
Moene, F, C., 180, 183–184
Moffitt, T. E., 35, 40, 48, 53, 123, 224, 229, 411, 415, 445, 503
Mogg, K., 130–131, 149–150
Mogil, J. S., 328
Mogun, H., 131
Mohan, R., 173
Mohr, D. C., 363
Mohs, R. C., 484
Moldofsky, H., 267
Molina, B. S. G., 413
Moline, M. L., 94, 291
Moller-Madsen, S., 261
Monarch, E. S., 326, 328
Monck, E. M., 487
Monette, P., 309
Money, J., 351
Monk, T. H., 247, 290–291, 296
Monroe, S. M., 231, 235–236, 237
Monson, C. M., 156–158, 179
Montague, D. K., 370
Montaner, J., 318
Montejo-Gonzalez, A. L., 364
Montero, I., 493
Montgomery, H., 420
Monton, C., 179
Monuteaux, M. C., 504
Moor-Ede, M. C., 298
Moore, R. G., 39–40, 210, 245
Moore, R. Y., 231, 238
Moos, B. S., 420
Moos, R. H., 420
Mootoor, Y., 541
Moras, K., 89, 93, 227
Morel, B., 467
Morelli, G. A., 292
Morenz, B., 381
Morey, L. C., 87, 328, 436
Morey, S., 333
Morgan, C., 78
Morgan, H. W., 419
Morgan, M., 51
Morgan, S., 281
Morgello, S., 348
Morgentaler, A., 371
Morgenthaler, T. I., 298
Morin, C. M., 292–293, 299
Morin, S. F., 335
Moring, J., 39, 438, 482
Moritz, E. K., 188
Morokoff, P. J., 358, 362, 365
Morrill, B., 333
Morris, D., 188
Morris, J. C., 550
Morris, J. K., 310, 315
Morris, J. S., 56, 122
Morris, M., 291, 515
Morrison, A. P., 472
Morrison, M., 245
Morriss, R., 248
Morrow, G. R., 22, 320
Morrow, J. A., 272
Morse, C. K., 134

Mortimer, J. A., 538–539
Morton, A., 261
Morton, D., 320, 333
Morton, J. M., 287
Moscicki, E., 250
Moseley, J., 331
Moser, D. J., 570
Moses, J. A., 81
Moses, N., 274
Mosimann, J. E., 272
Mosko, S., 292
Moskowitz, A., 218
Moss, A. R., 318
Moss, H., 276
Moss, H. B., 492
Moss-Morris, R., 330
Mostkoff, K., 253
Mostofsky, D. I., 311
Moulds, M. L., 158
Mount, J. H., 219
Movius, H. L., 195
Moyes, B., 441
Mrakotsky, C., 222
Mrug, S., 503
Mucha, T. F., 182
Mudaliar, N., 320
Mudar, P., 413
Mueller, T. I., 209, 210, 213, 219
Mueser, K. T., 491, 493
Mufson, L., 245
Muir, S. L., 274
Mukhern, R., 321
Mulchahey, J. J., 36, 47–48, 50, 312
Mullan, J. T., 548
Muller, B. A., 174
Müller, B., 370
Muller-Oerlinghausen, B., 242
Mulrow, C. D., 330
Mulsant, B. H., 219, 225
Mulvey, E. P., 567
Mumford, D. B., 269
Mumme, D., 125
Mundt, B., 183
Mundy, E., 223, 505
Munir, K., 224
Munir, Z. B., 177
Munizza, C., 246
Munjack, D. J., 145–146
Munoz, K., 35
Muñoz, R. F., 58, 245
Munro, A., 477
Munson, J., 512
Murdoch, D., 399
Murphy, D. A., 336
Murphy, G. E., 246
Murphy, R. L., 349
Murphy, S. L., 249, 364
Murphy, W. E., 372
Murphy-Eberenz, K. P., 265
Murray, C. J. L., 250
Murray, H., 78
Murray, K. E., 505
Murray, R. M., 460, 472, 479, 486–487
Murry, E., 209
Mussell, M. P., 268
Must, A., 262
Mustafa, G., 489
Mustanski, B. S., 348
Musto, D. F., 402, 494
Myers, A. J., 545
Myers, J. K., 134, 141, 144, 146–147, 232, 236
Myers, J. M., 36, 129
Myers, K., 77
Myers, L., 318
Myers, M. D., 288
Mystkowski, J. L., 126

Naarala, M., 39
Nachmias, M., 157
Nadeau, K., 503
Nagayama Hall, G. C., 76, 381

Nagel, D. B., 489
Najavits, L. M., 156–158
Naji, A., 261
Najmi, S., 208, 227
Nantulya, V., 336
Narayan, S., 441
Naring, G. W., 183
Nash, J. D., 337–338
Nash, J. M., 328, 333–334
Nasser, M., 269
Nath, A., 541
Nathan, P. E., 380, 418
Nathan, S., 178, 242
National Center for Health Statistics, 249
National Institute on Alcohol and Alcoholism, 395–396
National Institute on Drug Abuse, 404, 408
National Institutes of Health, 263
National Institutes of Mental Health, 241, 245
National Resources Center on Homelessness and Mental Illness, 491
National Sleep Foundation, 288, 291
Naylor, S. L., 542
Naz, B., 476
Nazemi, H., 135
Nazemi, S., 135
Neal, A. M., 135
Neal-Barnett, A. M., 135–136
Neale, C., 276
Neale, M. C., 36, 123, 129, 147, 228–229, 265, 277, 348, 405, 411, 439
Neddleman, L. D., 278
Nee, J., 89
Negle-Rich, L., 135
Negrini, B. J., 184
Neighbors, H. W., 225, 251
Neimeyer, R. A., 244
Nells, W. B. N., 134
Nelson, C. A., 46–47
Nelson, C. B., 155, 221
Nelson, D., 190, 225
Nelson, G., 493
Nelson, P., 137
Nelson, R. O., 5, 70, 72
Nelson-Gray, R. O., 5, 107–108
Nemeroff, C. B., 53, 124, 157, 229–330, 237, 240–241
Nesse, R., 214
Neugroschl, J. A., 533–535, 537–538, 539–544, 547–548
Neumann, C. S., 444
Neumark-Stainer, D., 384
New York Mental Hygine Law, 559
New, M., 351
Newman, A. B., 291
Newman, C. F., 458
Newman, I. A., 273
Newman, M. G., 112, 131
Newman, S., 514
Newmann, J. P., 178, 448
Newmann, K., 526
Newsome, J. T., 315
Newton, T. L., 311, 315
Neylan, T. C., 291, 295–296, 300–301
Nezami, E., 79
Neziroglu, F., 188
Nezu, A. M., 287, 320
Nezu, C. M., 320
Nezworski, M. T., 78
Ng, B. Y., 193
Nguyan, L., 398
Ni, X., 451–452
Nicassio, P. M., 84, 105, 326
Nielsen, J. A., 487
Nieminen, P., 438, 482
Nijman, H., 353
Nikolskaya, O. S., 513

Nimgaonkar, V. L., 483
Nisbett, R. E., 103
Nishigaki, T., 534
Nitschke, J., 231, 237
Nixon, R. V. D., 158
Niznikiewicz, M., 442
Noble, J., 331
Nock, M., 155, 161, 221, 250
Noe, S., 370
Nofzinger, E. A., 290
Nohara, S., 472
Nolan, S. A., 225
Nolen-Hoeksema, S., 125, 227, 233, 236, 238
Noll, R. B., 321, 414
Nomura, Y., 161, 228
Noonan, C., 329
Nordentoft, M., 442
Nordile, J. W., 182
Nordstrom, P., 251
Norman, P. A., 265, 267–269, 277, 279
Norman, W. H., 55, 233, 245
North, C. S., 177
Nortinger, J., 253
Norton, G. R., 137, 197
Norton, J., 514
Novaco, R. W., 310
Novella, L., 437
Novelly, R. A., 157
Novins, D., 222, 225, 249
Novotny, C. M., 106
Novy, D. M., 132
Noyes, R., 129, 131, 174, 190, 198
Nuechterlein, K. H., 457–458
Nugent, S. A., 459
Nurnberger, J. I., 219, 227, 229
Nutzinger, D. O., 277
Nyberg, L., 534
Nyhan, W. L., 522
Nystrup, J., 261

O'Brien, C. P., 417–418
O'Brien, G. T., 89
O'Brien, M. E., 318
O'Brien, M. M., 439
O'Callaghan, E., 486
O'Carroll, P. W., 250, 252
O'Connell, D., 64
O'Connor, E., 245
O'Connor, K., 159, 162
O'Connor, M. E., 265–266, 269, 276–277, 279–280
O'Connor, M. F., 214
O'Connor, T., 219
O'Donnell, D., 223, 505
O'Donohue, W., 380
O'Donovan, C., 242
O'Donovan, M. C., 483
O'Fallon, W. M., 261
O'Grady, K. E., 418
O'Hagan, S., 401
O'Hanlon, J. F., 131
O'Hara, M. W., 225, 245
O'Keefe, S., 331–332
O'Leary, A., 317, 326–327, 336
O'Leary, K. D., 235, 244
O'Leary, T., 172
O'Malley, S. O., 421
O'Malley, S. S., 101
O'Reardon, J. P., 138, 246, 286
O'Sullivan, K., 361, 367
Oades, R. D., 49
Oakes, R., 407
Obeid, J., 351
Ochoa, E. S., 87
Ochocka, J., 493
Ochsner, K. N., 56
Oei, T. P. S., 134, 144, 147
Offord, D. R., 95, 399
Ogata, S. N., 452
Ogborne, A. C., 399
Ogden, C. L., 262, 283–284

Ogston, W., 196
Ohayon, A. F., 218, 326
Ohlenschlaeger, J., 442
Ohlerking, F., 372
Öhman, A., 56, 58–59, 149
Ohta, H., 157
Oien, P. A., 451
Oishi, S., 60
Ojehagen, A., 250
Okugawa, G., 179
Olarte, M., 329
Oldham, J. M., 451
Olds, J., 412
Olfson, M., 149, 235, 240
Olié, J. -P., 422
Olin, J., 224
Olin, S. S., 442
Oliva, P. S., 196
Olivardia, R., 187, 274
Oliveau, D., 144
Oliver, M. B., 347
Ollendick, T. H., 137, 144, 335
Olmsted, M. P., 275, 278
Olofsson, B., 534
Olson, R. A., 321
Oltmanns, T. F., 436, 473
Omer, H., 296
Ong, S. H., 193
Onoe, S., 534
Onstad, S., 451
Opjordsmoen, S., 477
Oppediasano, G., 223
Oppenheim, D., 292
Oquendo, M., 251, 253
Orav, E., 179
Orbach, I., 251
Oresme, N., 9
Orman, D. T., 253
Orne, E. C., 195
Orne, M. T., 195
Orr, S. P., 157
Orsan, P., 188
Orsillo, S. M., 130, 132
Orsulak, P. J., 230
Ortiz, A., 415
Ortmann, J., 251
Orvaschell, H., 134, 141, 144
Osborn, K. M., 244
Osborne, L. N., 235–236
Osburg, S., 350
Osei, S., 287
Osgarby, S., 245
Osgood, N. J., 249–250
Oskarsson, H., 123
Ossip-Klein, D. J., 244
Öst, L. -G., 31–32, 142–143, 145–146, 148, 150, 332
Osteen, V., 235
Ostella, F., 179
Osterberg, E., 415
Osterling, J., 512
Ostfeld, A., 214
Ostrow, D. G., 336
Otis, J., 325–328, 331, 333
Otto, M. W., 126, 129, 131, 143, 151, 188, 225
Ouellette, R., 127
Ousley, O., 572
Overholser, J. C., 250
Overly, K., 114–115
Overpeck, M. D., 335
Overweg, J., 522
Ovsiew, F., 84
Owen, M. J., 483
Owens, J. A., 291
Owens, J. F., 334
Owens, M., 229
Owens, M. J., 36, 47–48, 50, 53, 230, 312
Oxman, T. E., 93
Oyama, O., 311
Ozaki-Kuroda, K., 39–49, 64
Ozolins, M., 321

Paanila, S., 535
Pacoe, L., 196
Padma-Nathan, H., 370
Pagano, M., 126, 129, 187
Page, A. C., 31, 146, 330
Pagel, J. F., 298
Paik, A., 355–361, 366
Pakianathan, L., 199
Palace, E. M., 364
Paliwal, P., 405
Pampallona, S., 246
Pan, S., 346
Panico, S., 239
Pantaleo, G., 318
Pantev, C., 327
Panza, F., 546
Papanicolaou, A. C., 511
Papanicolaou, D., 329
Papas, R., 333
Papillo, J. F., 322
Papparozzi, C. F., 104
Paquette, V., 51, 148
Pardini, D., 413
Pardis, C. M., 135–136
Parekh, A., 129
Parent, C., 39–40, 64
Parides, M., 278
Parikh Sagar, V., 242
Parish, W., 346
Parisi, S. A., 224
Park, D. C., 261
Parker, G., 488
Parker, H. A., 155
Parkes, J. D., 294
Parkinson, L., 161–162
Parnas, J., 442
Parritz, R. H., 157
Parron, D., 90, 213
Parry, B. L., 94, 219
Parry, C. D. H., 561
Parry-Jones, B., 268
Parry-Jones, W. L., 268
Parsons, B., 249
Paruk, Z., 129
Pasewark, R. A., 565
Pataki, C. S., 222
Paterson, A. D., 349
Paterson, J. G., 220
Pathak, D., 172
Pato, C. W., 316
Paton, J., 547
Patrick, C. J., 448
Patrick, C. L., 431
Pattatucci, A. M., 348–349
Patterson, C. M., 448
Patterson, G. R., 115–116, 414, 448–450
Patterson, T. L., 63, 225, 310
Patton, G. C., 274
Patton, J. R., 508
Paty, J., 77
Paul, E., 157
Paul, G. L., 480, 491
Paul, T., 277, 459
Paulauskas, S. L., 213, 229
Paulesu, E., 510
Pauli, P., 174
Pauls, D. L., 112, 159, 229
Pauly, I., 353
Pavalko, E. K., 315
Pavlov, I. P., 22, 25, 54
Paxton, S. J., 274
Paykel, E. S., 235, 246
Payne, D. L., 457–458
Payne, K., 360–361
Payne, R., 392
Pearl, D., 320
Pearlin, L. I., 548
Pearlson, G. D., 486
Pearlstein, T., 245
Peddicord, J. P., 252
Pedersen, B., 419
Pedersen, G., 431

Pedersen, N. L., 35, 38, 232, 329
Pederson, L. L., 335
Pederson, N. L., 261
Peebles, R., 288
Pehlivanturk, B., 182–183
Pelayo, R., 294, 298
Peled, A., 495
Pelham, W. E., Jr., 448–449, 505, 507
Peloso, P., 174
Pendery, M. L., 420
Pendlebury, W. W., 547
Peng, Y. B., 325–328
Pentz, M. A., 421
Penzien, D. B., 331–332
Pepine, C. J., 370
Peplau, L. A., 347
Pereira, D. B., 309
Perel, J., 229, 241
Perez, A., 561
Perez, O., 270
Pericak-Vance, M. A., 424
Perkins, D. O., 62, 319, 479–480, 490
Perkins, K. A., 414
Perkonigg, A., 155
Perlin, M. L., 565
Perlis, M. L., 290, 299
Perlstein, T., 94
Perper, J. A., 252
Perri, M. G., 287
Perrin, N., 245
Perry, A. A., 248, 272
Perry, C., 452–453
Perry, J. C., 434
Perry, R., 44
Perry, S., 222
Perschel, T., 459
Person, D. C., 129
Perugi, G., 172
Peselow, E. D., 242
Pestality, P., 217
Petch, A., 467
Peters, C. P., 467
Peters, K. D., 249
Peters, M., 195
Peters, M. L., 325–328
Petersen, A. C., 222, 224
Petersen, I., 129
Petersen, L., 442
Petersson, K. M., 52
Peterson, J. B., 412
Peterson, L., 335
Peterson, R. A., 137
Peterson, R. E., 351
Petit, L., 299
Petitto, J. M., 62, 319
Petkova, E., 279
Peto, R., 336
Petri, S., 124
Petrill, S. A., 36, 510
Petrovic, P., 52
Pettinati, H. M., 418
Peveler, R. C., 279
Pfiser, H., 155
Pfister, H., 129
Pfohl, B., 454
Pfuhlmann, B., 478
Phares, V., 276
Phelan, S. P., 283, 286
Phelps, M. E., 51
Phil, M., 202
Philippot, P., 149–150
Philips, H. C., 326
Philips, K. A., 434–435
Phillips, A., 515
Phillips, B., 292
Phillips, D., 458
Phillips, J. M., 508
Phillips, K. A., 185–189, 191, 441, 451
Phillips, L. J., 115, 479, 487
Phillips, M. R., 250

Phillips, R. S., 269, 286
Phinney, S. D., 286
Pich, V., 135, 145
Pickrell, J. E., 199
Pierce, K. A., 147
Pierce, H. I., 320
Pietz, C. A., 568
Pigeon, W. R., 290
Pihl, R. O., 399, 412
Pike, J., 288
Pike, K. M., 265, 276–277, 279, 281
Pilkonis, P., 93
Pilkonis, P. A., 245, 456
Pillard, R. C., 348–349
Pillemer, J. T., 347
Pillow, D. R., 413
Pilowsky, I., 174, 228
Pincus, D. B., 143–144, 148,
    325–328, 331
Pincus, H. A., 89–90, 131, 149, 151
Pincus, J. H., 198, 200
Pindych, L. J., 268
Pine, D. S., 124
Pinel, P., 15, 16–17, 88, 444, 467
Pingel, J. D., 334
Pinseckie, J. M., 246
Pinsky, J., 324
Pinto, I. M., 415
Pinto, O., 216
Piontek, C. M., 219
Pirozzi, R., 219, 227
Pirsig, R. M., 99
Pissiota, A., 152
Pithers, W. D., 381
Pitman, P. K., 200
Pizzagalli, D., 231
Platts, M., 245, 269
Plioplys, A. V., 328
Plomin, R., 35–36, 38, 123, 229,
    232, 482, 486, 509
Plotsky, P. M., 36, 47–48, 50, 53,
    124, 157, 230, 312
Podd, J., 105
Podwils, L. J., 545
Pogue-Geile, M. F., 483
Pohl, U., 451, 453
Pol, H. E. H., 486
Polak, D., 242
Polanczyk, G., 503, 526
Poland, R. E., 401
Polatin, P. B., 326–327
Poldrack, R. A., 511
Polen, M., 245
Polich, J., 412
Politi, E., 178
Polivy, J., 275
Polivy, J. M., 274
Pollack, L., 335
Pollack, M. H., 131, 135, 138, 145,
    151, 152, 164
Pollack-Dorta, K., 245
Pollock, V. E., 412
Polloway, E. A., 92, 508
Polnitsky, C. A., 290
Polonsky, D. C., 360, 369
Pomara, N., 241
Pomeroy, C., 265
Pomeroy, W. B., 346
Pompili, M., 240
Pontiggia, A., 290
Pontius, W., 514
Pope, C., 187
Pope, H., 276
Pope, H. D., Jr., 187, 196, 229
Pope, H. G., Jr., 261, 265, 269,
    274–275, 410
Pope, K. S., 201
Pope, M., 210
Pories, W., 287
Pornoppadol, C., 177
Portenoy, R. K., 392
Porter, S., 335

Post, P., 47
Post, R. M., 195, 219, 232, 238
Posternak, M. A., 209
Postma, A., 195
Potenza, M. N., 422–423
Pothuloori, A. P., 559
Pottash, A. C., 364, 419
Potter, J., 38
Potter, W. Z., 241
Poulter, N., 322
Poulton, R., 224
Powell, K. E., 252, 450
Powell, L. H., 323, 325
Powell, R. A., 201
Power, B., 299
Poznanski, E. O., 223
Prasad, K., 193
Prause, N., 362
Preble, O. T., 328
Preizig, M., 210
Prelor, E. F., 171
Prentky, R. A., 374
Prescott, C. A., 36, 129, 146–147,
    232, 236–238, 244, 265, 411
Prescott, G. J., 261
President's New Freedom Commission
    on Mental Health, 570
Preskorn, S. H., 240
Presley, C. A., 398
Presnell, K., 283, 286
Presson, C. C., 113–114
Pretzer, J., 439
Pribor, E. F., 177
Price, T. R. P., 491
Pridal, C. G., 355–356, 370
Priday, L., 188
Prien, R. F., 241
Prigerson, H., 214
Prince, M., 189, 537
Prince, R., 271
Prince, V., 374
Prins, J., 328, 330
Prins, P. J. M., 506
Prinstein, M. J., 157
Priott, S. D., 321
Pritchett, D. B., 47
Prizant, B. M., 512, 514, 517
Pro-Ana-Nation, 262
Project MATCH Research Group,
    421
Prudic, J., 242
Prus-Wisniewski, R., 287
Pruzinsky, T., 189, 272
Prusoff, B. A., 86–87, 213, 229
Pueschel, S. M., 523
Pugliese, M. T., 274
Puhan, M. A., 298
Puig-Antich, J., 224
Pule, L., 135
Pulsifer, M. B., 522
Purdon, C., 162
Purdy, D., 219
Purisch, A. D., 82
Purselle, D., 249
Purtilo, R. B., 548
Pury, C. L. S., 56
Putnam, F. W., 190, 194–199, 201
Putnam, K., 231

Qian, G., 336–337
Qrdell, F., 261
Quality Assurance Project, 439
Quan, S. F., 291
Quas, J. A., 200
Quay, S., 162, 446–448
Quigley, L. A., 420
Quinlan, D. M., 472
Quinn, L., 329
Quitkin, F. M., 217
Qureshi, A. I., 175

Rabian, B., 62
Rabin, A. S., 244

Rabin, B. S., 62
Rabins, P. V., 538, 547
Rachal, J. V., 418
Rachid, F., 491
Rachman, S., 24, 146, 155, 160–
    162, 368
Racoosin, J., 240
Rademaker, A. W., 328
Radnitz, C. L., 333–334
Rado, S., 442
Radomsky, A. S., 160
Raebrun, S. D., 277
Rafanelli, C., 175, 210, 246
Raffa, S. D., 136
Ragland, J. D., 483
Rahkonen, T., 535
Rahman, Q., 348
Rai, S. S., 51
Raich, R. M., 270
Raine, A., 442, 447
Rajab, M. H., 253
Ramachandran, V. S., 327
Ramakrishna, R. K., 182
Ramchandani, P., 219
Ramey, C. T., 525
Ramey, S. L., 525
Ramirez, G., 330
Ramsawh, H., 136
Ramsawh, H. J., 371
Ramsey, E., 448–449
Rand, J. H., 309
Randall, P. R., 157
Ranganath, C., 231
Ranjith, G., 173
Rao, R., 231
Rao, U., 231
Rapaport, J., 472, 506
Rapee, R. M., 89, 113, 132, 134,
    151, 314–315, 332–334
Raphael, B., 214
Rapkin, A. J., 94
Rapkin, B., 490
Rapoport, J. L., 505
Rapp, S. R., 224, 540
Rapport, D., 241
Rapson, R. L., 10, 58
Raquel, E. G., 95
Rasmussen, S. A., 161, 188
Rasmusson, A. M., 405
Rassin, E., 162
Rather, B. C., 392
Rathod, N. H., 406
Ratnasuriya, R. H., 261
Rattenborg, N. C., 289
Ratti, M. T., 302
Rauch, S. L., 188
Raue, P., 241
Ravdin, L. D., 545
Raviv, A., 291
Ravyssin, E., 286
Rawlins, M. D., 542
Rawson, R. A., 401–402, 403
Ray, D. B., 179
Ray, J. C., 313–314
Ray, R. S., 115
Ray, W. A., 131, 534
Raymond, N. C., 268, 372
Rayner, R., 23
Raynor, H., 288
Razani, J., 492
Razran, G., 125
Reading, A. E., 94
Reagor, P., 197–199
Rebgetz, M., 245
Reboussin, B. A., 251, 508
Redd, W. H., 22
Redding, C. A., 186
Reder, S., 508
Redlich, A. D., 200
Reed, D., 312, 324
Rees, A., 245
Reese, R. L., 570
Regan, W. M., 182

Regier, D. A., 5, 88, 91
Rehm, L. P., 244
Reich, D. B., 434, 451
Reichardt, C. S., 101
Reichborn-Kjennerud, T., 439
Reid, J. C., 445
Reid, J. R., 414
Reif, A., 478
Reikman, J. T., 135
Reilly, M . P., 413
Reilly-Harrington, N. A., 232,
    234–235
Reiman, E. M., 545
Reinarman, C., 364
Reineke, I., 322
Reinhardt, R. F., 182
Reis, D., 492
Reisner, L. C., 314–315, 332–334
Reiss, A. L., 137
Reiss, R. B., 370
Reiss, S., 92
Reissing, E., 360–361
Reitan, R. M., 82
Reiter, J., 188
Reivich, K. J., 245
Rekers, G. A., 282
Relkin, N. R., 545
Remick, R. A., 220
Remsberg, S., 292, 299
Renick, A., 200
Renjilian, D. A., 287
Renneberg, B., 458
Renthal, W., 53
Repetti, R. L., 311, 315
Report of the Advisory Panel on
    Alzheimer's Disease, 541, 544
Repp, A. C., 525
Reppert, S. M., 403
Requiena, A., 270
Rescorla, R. A., 22, 54–55
Resick, P. A., 157–158
Resler, K. J., 164
Resnick, H. S., 155–156, 448
Resnick, R. J., 442
Restifo, L. L., 521
Reverger, R., 494
Revicki, D. A., 218
Rexrode, K., 325
Reynolds, C., 215
Reynolds, C. F., III, 231, 290, 291,
    295–296, 300–301
Reynolds, C. P., 316
Reynolds, S., 245
Reznick, J. S., 150
Reznickoff, M., 78
Rhee, S. H., 446
Rheinstein, B. J. G., 135
Rhodes, L., 137
Ricciardelli, L. A., 268
Rice, D. P., 335
Rice, G., 349
Rice, J., 315
Rice, M. E., 376, 380, 449–550
Richa, S., 422
Richard, C., 292
Richards, C., 213, 229
Richards, J. A., 247
Richards, R., 226
Richards, W. A., 409
Richardson, D., 361
Richardson, G. S., 296, 298
Richardson, M. A., 51
Richardson, W. S., 570
Richie, J. C., 312
Richman, J. A., 328, 329
Richter, H., 452
Richter, J., 134, 144, 147
Rick, M., 514
Rickels, K., 131
Rickman, D. K., 526
Ridder, E., 224
Riddle, M. A., 160
Ridgeway, V. A., 246

Riding, A., 389
Rieder, R. O., 346
Rief, W., 172, 174, 176, 179
Rieger, G., 347
Riemann, B. C., 160, 230
Riemersma, J. B. J., 131
Rieppi, R., 323
Riggs, G., 320
Riggs, J. E., 544
Rihmer, Z., 217
Rijsdijk, F., 228–229, 237
Riley, B., 237
Riley, S., 186
Rintelmann, J. W., 289
Risch, N., 112, 545
Riso, L. P., 277
Ritenbaugh, C., 271
Ritenour, A., 247
Rivara, C. -B., 537
Rivera-Tovar, A. D., 93–94
Rivkees, S. A., 403
Rizvi, S. L., 156–158
Robbins, C., 62, 173, 177
Robbins, D., 251, 481
Roberto, C. A., 278
Roberts, C. R., 291
Roberts, C. W., 369
Roberts, J. E., 231
Roberts, M. C., 335
Roberts, M. W., 76
Roberts, N., 241
Roberts, R. E., 222, 224, 225, 291
Roberts, S. B., 274
Robertson, D., 572
Robertson, J. E., 64, 232, 234
Robertson, N., 419
Robins, L. N., 413, 446
Robins, S., 310, 448
Robinson, T. E., 36, 53, 64
Robinson, T. N., 282–283
Robison, B. D., 445
Robles, T., 312, 314, 316
Rochtchina, E., 542
Rockert, W., 275
Rocket, W., 278
Rockney, R. M., 10
Rockwood, K., 224, 547
Rodin, J., 129, 270–272, 276–277, 325, 336
Rodriguez, E., 245
Roecklein, K. A., 221
Roehling, P. V., 413
Roelofs, K., 183
Roemer, L., 130–132
Roerig, J. L., 276–277
Roffmann, R. A., 336
Roffwarg, H. P., 230, 289
Rogers, C., 22
Rogers, J. H., 451
Rogers, L., 331–332
Rogers, S., 517
Rogers, S. L., 547
Rogers, W., 93
Rogge, R. D., 100
Rogoff, B., 292
Rohan, K. J., 220–221
Rohde, L. A., 526
Rohde, P., 212, 224, 228, 231, 238, 251, 503
Roitt, I., 317
Rojo, L., 276–277
Roll, J. M., 413
Rollman, B. L., 131, 225
Roma, P. G., 53
Roman, T., 526
Romano, J. M., 327
Romanoski, A., 208, 211, 213
Romanski, L. M., 516
Ronningstam, E., 456
Room, R., 419
Roose, S. P., 277
Root, C. M., 46
Rorschach, H., 78
Rosales, G. A., 488

Röschke, J., 370
Rose, J. S., 113–114
Rose, L. R., 290
Rose, S., 210–211, 213
Rosen, A. C., 282
Rosen, C. L., 291
Rosen, J. C., 188, 269, 270, 277
Rosen, L. R., 355–361, 363
Rosen, L. W., 271
Rosen, R. C., 355–357, 361–363, 366, 369–370
Rosenbach, A. F., 406
Rosenbaum, J. F., 123, 147, 150, 240
Rosenbaum, M., 182, 234
Rosenberg, H., 420
Rosenberg, W., 570
Rosenfeld, B., 318
Rosenfeld, J. P., 231
Rosengren, A., 324
Rosenheck, R. A., 490
Rosenman, R. H., 324
Rosenthal, D., 251, 481
Rosenthal, M. Z., 452
Rosenthal, N. E., 219, 220
Rosenthal, P. A., 249
Rosenthal, S., 249
Rösler, A., 381
Rosman, B. L., 275, 279
Rosoff, A., 232
Rosowsky, E., 435, 451
Ross, A. O., 505
Ross, C. A., 197–199, 201
Ross, D., 399
Ross, D. C., 220
Ross, L., 103
Ross, M. W., 350
Ross, R., 89, 504
Rossberg, J. I., 431
Rossiter, E. M., 281
Roth, W. T., 135
Rothberg, P. C., 245
Rothblum, E. D., 62, 268
Rothman, A. D., 100
Rothschild, A., 219
Rothschild, L., 436–437
Rottenberg, J., 208, 227
Rouff, L., 440
Rouleau, J. L., 372
Rounsaville, B., 421
Rounsaville, B. J., 5, 86–87, 213, 244, 280, 423
Rourke, K. M., 155
Roush, W., 332
Rowe, M. K., 135
Rowell, E. A., 407
Rowell, R., 407
Roy, A., 251
Royall, R., 51
Roy-Byrne, P. P., 93, 123, 129, 140, 227, 232
Rozin, P., 273
Rubin, D. B., 483
Rubin, R. T., 173
Rubinow, D. R., 232
Rubinstein, D., 355–356
Rubinstein, S., 272
Rubinsztein, J. S., 238
Rucci, P., 227
Ruchkin, V., 157
Rudd, D. M., 235, 252–253
Rudick-Davis, D., 208
Rudolph, J., 534
Rueger, D. B., 156
Rujescu, D., 295
Rumpf, H. J., 184
Rusch, N., 452
Ruscio, J., 92, 131
Rush, A. J., 230, 241–242, 246, 289
Rush, B., 15, 226
Rush, J. A., 210, 218–219, 246
Russell, G. F., 261
Russell, G. F. M., 279, 282

Russell, M., 413
Russell, S., 47, 210
Russo, J., 177
Russo, L., 127
Russo, S. J., 53
Ruther, E., 452
Rutter, M., 35–38, 40, 64–65, 95, 103, 123, 229, 411, 415, 436, 514
Ryan, C. E., 237
Ryan, L. M., 397
Ryan, N. D., 231
Rygh, J., 234, 243
Rynders, J. R., 523
Rynn, M., 131

Saab, P. G., 322
Saag, M., 318
Sabo, A. N., 453
Sabol, S. Z., 124
Sachs, G. S., 241
Sachs-Ericsson, N., 247
Sack, D., 219
Sack, D. A., 220
Sack, S. L., 220
Sackeim, H. A., 182, 192–193, 197–198, 242
Sackett, D. L., 570
Sacks, G., 511
Sadeh, A., 291
Sadovnick, A. D., 220
Saelens, B. E., 288
Safford, S., 235
Sahai, A., 291
Sahakian, B. J., 238, 424
Sahler, O., 321
Sahota, A., 545
Sakai, J., 409
Sakel, M., 13
Sakheim, D. K., 363–365
Sakheim, H. A., 242
Saldana, D., 494
Saleem, R., 247
Salekin, R. T., 446
Salge, R. A., 137
Salkovskis, P. M. N., 139, 162, 172, 174, 175, 253
Saln-Pascual, R. J., 406
Salomon, R. M., 138, 246
Salovey, P., 325
Salt, P., 245
Saltoun, M., 321
Saltz, R. F., 421
Saltzman, L. E., 250
Salusky, S., 244
Salvio, M., 299
Salzman, C., 129
Salzman, D. G., 151
Sammel, M., 225
Samson, J. A., 237
Samuel, D. B., 86–87, 93, 95
Samuels, B., 245
Samuels, J. F., 160
Samuels, S. C., 533–544, 547–548
Sanavio, E., 134, 144, 147
Sanchez-Lacay, A., 175
Sandeen, E. E., 235, 244
Sanders, B. E., 155–156, 224
Sanders, M. H., 295, 298
Sanders, M. R., 245, 450
Sanderson, W. C., 129
Sandin, B., 174
Sandys, J., 525
Sanfilipo, M. P., 242
Sankey, A., 329
Sankis, R. L., 4, 95
Sann, S. B., 46
Sano, M., 547
Santana, V. S., 415
Santarelli, L., 230, 239
Santed, M., 174
Santos, J. F., 250
Sanz-Carrillo, C., 179

Sapolsky, R., 4, 39, 312–314
Sarazan, F. F. A., 299
Sarbin, T. R., 196, 199, 201, 480
Sarchiapone, M., 251
Sareen, J., 126–127, 150
Sarkai, S., 511
Sarrel, P. M., 365
Sartorius, N., 72, 183
Sarwer, D. B., 189, 284, 286–287, 369
Sasao, T., 398
Sass, A., 157
Sass, K. J., 157
Saudino, J. J., 38, 232
Saudino, K. J., 36
Saunders, K., 283
Savin-Williams, R., 349–350
Sawa, A., 479
Saxe, G. N., 156
Saxe, M., 230, 239
Saxena, S., 193
Sayette, M. A., 414
Scalora, M. J., 559
Scanlan, J., 52–53
Scarmeas, N., 539, 546
Scepkowski, L. A., 364, 366
Schacter, D. L., 56, 199
Schacter, G., 53
Schade, M. L., 492
Schaefer, E. J., 286
Schafer, J., 414
Schafer, K., 547
Schaffer, A., 219
Schaffer, D., 240
Schalock, R. L., 92
Schanberg, S., 222
Schatcer, D. L., 200
Schatschneider, C., 510
Schatzberg, A., 246
Schatzberg, M. M., 218, 326
Schedlowski, M., 459
Scheechter, M., 318
Scheerenberger, R. C., 518, 522
Scheidt, P. C., 335
Scheier, M. F., 334
Schendel, D., 514, 515
Schenk, L., 199
Scherr, P. A., 533–537
Schettler, P., 213, 216
Schewel, R., 508
Schiavi, R. C., 356, 364, 370
Schiffer, B., 459
Schiffman, J., 473, 479
Schildkraut, J. J., 42, 237
Schiller, C., 403
Schleifer, S. J., 316
Schlenger, W. E., 155
Schlesinger, A., 439
Schlesser, M. A., 230
Schlosser, S., 129
Schlundt, O. G., 267–268
Schmahl, C., 199, 452
Schmaling, K. B., 244, 329
Schmeidler, J., 188, 190–191
Schmidt, A. J. M., 172, 174–175
Schmidt, C. W., 376, 378, 380–381
Schmidt, E., 419
Schmidt, N. B., 137
Schmitt, F. A., 541
Schmitt, W. A., 448
Schmitz, J. M., 413–414
Schnack, H. G., 486
Schneck, C., 219
Schneider, J. A., 277
Schneider, S. G., 336
Schneiderman, N., 311, 316, 318–320, 323–325
Schneier, F. R., 149, 175
Schnell, K., 454
Schnurr, P. P., 94
Schoellers, K., 287
Schoenbach, V. J., 62
Schoeneman, T. J., 8

Schok, M. A., 157
Schooley, B., 542
Schooley, R., 318
Schopp, L., 82
Schork, N. J., 480, 481, 483
Schottenfeld, R. S., 421
Schouten, E., 325
Schover, L. R., 357, 363, 370
Schramm, E., 452
Schreiber, F. R., 197
Schreiber, S., 242
Schreinger-Engel, P., 356
Schrieber, G. B., 270
Schroeter, K., 277
Schteingart, D. E., 157
Schuckit, M. A., 396, 398–399
Schulberg, H. C., 225, 245
Schulman, I. D., 135, 245
Schulsinger, F., 251, 442, 473, 479, 494
Schulte, L., 325, 366
Schultz, R. T., 512–517
Schultz, S. K., 570
Schulz, C., 442
Schulz, L. O., 286
Schulz, M. S., 100
Schulz, P. M., 442
Schulz, R., 225
Schumacher, J., 123
Schumann, C. M., 515
Schupak-Neuberg, E., 272
Schuster, M., 157
Schutz, H. K., 274
Schwab-Stone, M., 157
Schwalberg, M. D., 265, 277
Schwartz, C. F., 290
Schwartz, D., 272
Schwartz, E., 453
Schwartz, G. E., 311
Schwartz, I. M., 348
Schwartz, J., 47
Schwartz, J. E., 210
Schwartz, J. M., 51
Schwartz, M. B., 284
Schwartz, M. S., 150, 331–332
Schwartz, P. J., 220
Schwartz, R. P., 418
Schwarz, A., 545
Schwarz, M. B., 286
Schwarzler, F., 231
Schweizer, E., 131
Scneider, S., 358
Scott, C. L., 422–424
Scott, C. P., 245
Scott, D., 339
Scott, J. E., 210, 246–247, 491
Scott, T. M., 157
Scott-Strauss, A., 216
Scullin, M. H., 521
Sculman, S., 324
Seaman, J. S., 534, 539, 541, 544, 546–547
Secko, D., 46–47
Seeburg, P. H., 47
Seeley, J. R., 212–213, 222, 224, 228, 231, 238, 251
Seeman, P., 484
Seeman, T., 311, 315
Segal, E., 188
Segal, N. L., 35–36, 235, 251, 348–349, 351
Segal, S., 92
Segal, S. R., 394
Segal, Z. V., 234, 246
Segraves, R., 355, 357–358, 360, 364, 369–370
Seibert, W., 242
Seibyl, J. P., 157
Seidenzahl, D., 565
Seidman, L. J., 505
Seidman, S. N., 346
Seim, H. C., 268
Selesnick, S. T., 8, 13–14

Seligman, M. E. P., 54, 56, 233, 238, 245
Selker, H. P., 286
Sellaro, R., 94, 209, 216–217
Selten, J. P., 487
Seltzer, C. C., 272
Seltzer, M. H., 431, 458, 4608
Selwyn, S. E., 269, 282
Selye, H., 311–312, 315
Semans, J. H., 369
Seminowicz, D., 243
Sergi, M. J., 570
Sernyak, M. J., 479
Serretti, A., 290
Servis, M. E., 534, 539, 541, 544, 546–547
Seto, M., 373–374, 376, 380
Severino, S. K., 94
Sexton, M. M., 335
Shabecoff, P., 399
Shadick, R., 130, 234
Shafer, C. L., 271
Shaffer, D. R., 64, 252
Shafran, R., 162, 264, 267, 269, 276–277, 279, 281
Shah, F., 186, 188
Shah, G. M. S., 472
Shaham, Y., 411
Sham, P., 228–229, 237, 486
Shamlo, S., 135
Shamow, N., 517
Shankman, S., 210–211, 213
Shaper, A. G., 310, 315
Shapiro, C. J., 507
Shapiro, D. A., 105, 245, 322, 323, 331
Shapiro, E. S., 508
Shapiro, P. A., 323
Shapiro, S., 240
Sharom, D., 188
Sharon, C., 330
Sharp, W. S., 505
Sharpe, M. B., 180, 183, 202, 229–330, 329
Shatte, A., 245
Shattuck, P. T., 513
Shaughnessy, M., 534
Shaw, B. F., 234, 283, 286
Shaw, D. S., 450
Shaw, H. E., 272, 288
Shay, K., 534
Shaywitz, B. A., 509–510
Shaywitz, S. E., 44, 509–510
Shea, M. T., 245, 434, 451, 458
Shea, T., 210, 213, 219
Shear, K. M., 126, 130, 134, 139–140, 214–215, 225, 227
Shear, M. K., 236
Sheets, E., 461
Sheffield, J. K., 113, 245
Sheikh, J. I., 129, 135, 145
Sheldon, C. T., 493
Shelly, C., 82
Shelton, K. K., 449
Shelton, M., 241
Shelton, R. C., 138, 246
Shema, S. J., 225
Shen, J., 82, 237
Shenton, M. E., 157, 442
Sher, K. J., 135
Sher, L., 220
Sherboune, C. D., 140, 237, 244
Sheridan, J., 315
Sheridan, R., 156
Sherman, L., 235
Sherman, S. J., 113–114
Shermer, R. L., 287
Sherwood, A., 324
Shields, A. L., 77
Shiffman, S., 77, 418
Shimizu, E., 489
Shin, L. M., 157, 188
Shin, P. S., 157

Shinoda, N., 489
Shiromani, P. J., 406
Shisslak, C., 271
Shisslak, C. M., 270
Shneidman, E. S., 251
Shochet, I. M., 245
Sholomskas, D., 86–87, 213
Shram, M., 411
Shrout, P. E., 232
Shulman, K. I., 568
Shulman, S., 60
Shumaker, S. A., 540
Siafakas, N. M., 418
Sibley, D. C., 267
Sica, C., 134, 144, 147
Sicard, T., 451–452
Sichieri, R., 281
Siegel, B., 214, 319
Siegel, L. J., 321
Siegel, S., 319–320
Siembab, L., 394
Sierra, M., 190–191
Siever, L. J., 42, 438–439, 441–442, 484
Siffre, M., 296
Sifre, I., 319
Sifre, T., 320
Sigafoos, J., 525
Sigmon, S. T., 220
Sigmundson, K., 352
Sigvardsson, S., 178, 448
Sikkema, K. J., 336
Silber, M. H., 298
Silberman, E. K., 195
Silberstein, L. R., 270–271, 276–277
Silbert, J., 511
Sildenafil Study Group, 370
Silk, K. R., 434, 439, 451, 452
Sill, M., 356–357
Silovsky, J., 381
Silva, A., 398
Silva, P. A., 445
Silver, E., 563, 565
Silverman, W. K., 129, 144, 147, 153, 157
Silvers, R. M., 455
Silverstone, T., 330
Silverthorn, P., 449
Simeon, D., 188, 190
Simeon, J., 241
Simien, C., 231
Simkin, D. R., 397
Simmons, J. R., 271, 277
Simmons, R., 236
Simon, G. E., 172, 177–178, 202, 283
Simon, J. E., 550
Simon, K. M., 439
Simon, N. M., 152, 164
Simon, R. I., 116, 564–565, 567, 568
Simon, T., 309
Simone, S., 567
Simoneau, T. L., 247
Simonetti, B., 172
Simons, A. D., 231, 235–236, 245–246
Simos, P. J., 511
Simpson, J. C., 95
Simpson, J. L., 406
Simpson, S., 222, 225, 249
Singh, M., 224
Singh, N. N., 525
Singh, O. P., 367
Siniscalchi, J., 186–189, 191
Sipprelle, R. C., 156
Sivenius, J., 535
Sjodin, A. -K., 446
Sjogren Fugl-Meyer, K., 355
Skhiri, D., 453
Skidmore, W., 282, 352
Skinner, B. F., 16, 24–25, 107
Skinner, J. B., 413
Skodol, A. E., 232, 434, 436, 438, 440, 451

Skoner, D. P., 62, 315–316
Skoog, K., 418
Skre, I., 451
Skudlarski, P., 423
Skultety, K. M., 271
Slade, M. D., 55
Slater, J. F., 217
Sleet, D. A., 335
Sloan, R. P., 323
Slutske, W. S., 103, 446, 452
Slymen, D., 190
Small, G. W., 224, 242
Small, J. G., 241
Smalley, S. L., 504
Smeets, B., 174
Smeraldi, E., 290
Smith, A. P., 315
Smith, B. H., 507
Smith, B. L., 249
Smith, D., 424
Smith, D. E., 281, 399
Smith, G. A., 566
Smith, G. P., 286
Smith, G. R., 179
Smith, G. T., 271, 277, 413
Smith, J. E., 270
Smith, J., Sr., 135–136
Smith, L J., 290
Smith, L. N., 300
Smith, P. M., 419
Smith, S. M., 198–199, 201
Smith, S. S., 414
Smith, T. L., 288, 315, 399
Smith, T. T., 64
Smith, T. W., 323, 325
Smith, W., 329
Smitts, J. A. J., 152, 164
Smolak, L., 272, 277, 282
Smoller, J. W., 123, 147
Smucker, W. D., 135
Smyer, M. A., 63
Smyth, R., 180, 183
Snarey, J., 572
Snell, M. E., 92
Snelling, J., 291
Snidman, N., 150
Snoek, H., 446–447
Snow, A. C., 265
Snowdon, D. A., 538–539
Snyder, S. H., 42, 48–49, 479, 484
Soares, C., 225
Sobell, L. C., 398–399, 420
Sobell, M. B., 398–399, 420
Sobhan, A., 135
Society for Research in Child Development, 117
Soderstrom, H., 446
Sofuoglu, M., 391
Sohn, C., 220, 231
Solfrizzi, V., 546
Soloff, P. H., 252
Solomon, A., 227
Solomon, D. A., 209–210, 213, 218–219
Solomon, L. J., 329, 336
Solomon, P. R., 547
Solomon, R. L., 413
Somers, T.J., 125
Song, S., 329
Sonnega, A., 155
Sonuga-Barke, E. J., 506
Sood, S., 511
Soorya, L., 515
Soowon, K., 286
Sorensen, H., 473, 479
Sorensen, J. L., 419
Sorkin, A., 495
Sorri, A., 39, 438, 482
Sotker, P. B., 157
Sotsky, S. M., 245
Soulsby, J. M., 246
South, S. C., 436
Southwick, S. M., 157

Sowden, A. J., 330
Spadano, J., 262
Spain, D., 135
Spangler, D. L., 235–236
Spanos, N. P., 195–196, 294–295
Sparrow, S. S., 513
Spector, R., 559
Speicher, C. E., 309, 315
Spelsberg, B., 183
Spence, S. H., 113, 245
Spencer, T., 217, 223, 505–507
Spencer, T. J., 504
Spender, D. D., 157
Spiegel, D., 138, 190, 192, 197–199, 201, 320
Spielberger, C. D., 335
Spielman, A. J., 292
Spiker, D., 514
Spinelli, M. G., 245
Spinhoven, P., 180, 184
Spira, A., 346
Spitzer, C., 183
Spitzer, N. C., 46
Spitzer, R. L., 4, 88–89, 268, 435–436
Spitznagel, E., 222
Spoont, M. R., 47, 49, 229, 251
Spray, B. J., 568
Sprecher, S., 347
Springer, D. W., 413
Sprock, J., 455
Spurrell, E. B., 268
Squire, L. R., 56
Srebnik, D., 347
Sritharan, A., 472
Staal, W. G., 486
Stafford, R., 286
Stall, R., 336
Stampfer, M. J., 283
Stanely, B., 251
Stanger, C., 334
Stanley, B., 251, 453
Stanley, M., 251
Stanley, M. A., 129, 132
Stanley-Hagan, M., 449
Stark, C., 309, 310
Starkman, M. N., 157
Starr, K., 319
Startup, M., 245
Statham, D. J., 229
Steadman, H. J., 563, 565–566
Steer, R. A., 217, 249, 251
Steers, W. D., 370
Steeruwitz, A., 182
Stefan, S., 559
Steffy, R. A., 381
Stein, A., 219
Stein, B. M., 126–127, 157
Stein, M. B., 125, 140, 150–151, 155, 316
Stein, M. I., 78, 123
Stein, R. L., 272
Steinberg, A. B., 276
Steinberg, D. M., 287
Steinberg, L., 39–49
Steinberg, M. A., 190, 423
Steiner, B. W., 353
Steiner, M., 230, 451
Steiner, S. C., 235
Steinglass, P., 62
Steinhauer, S. R., 479
Stejskal, W. J., 78
Steketee, G., 159–163, 188
Stellar, E., 312
Stemmler, M., 222, 224
Stenvall, M., 534
Stepanski, E. J., 292
Stephenson, J., 318
Stern, Y., 539, 546
Sternberg, W. F., 328
Sterner, U., 148
Stevens, S., 172, 174–175
Stewart, A., 93

Stewart, J. W., 217–218
Stewart, M. A., 446
Stewart, M. O., 210, 245–247
Stewart, S. H., 413
Stewart-Williams, S., 105
Stice, E., 265, 267–269, 272, 274, 277, 283, 286, 288, 413
Stiglmayr, C., 451, 453
Stiles, T. C., 431, 458, 4608
Stinson, C. H., 214
Stinson, F., 208, 212–213, 221, 224–225, 249
Stirling, J., 472
Stock, W., 358
Stoddard, F., 156
Stoessell, P. W., 51
Stolar, M., 94
Stolee, P., 224, 547
Stoler, J. M., 397
Stoller, R. J., 348, 350, 378
Stolzenberg, R., 346
Stone, G., 311
Stone, J., 180, 183, 292, 299
Stone, M. H., 434, 442, 451, 458–460
Stone, R., 311
Stone, W. S., 112
Stoney, C. M., 59
Stoolmiller, M., 238
Storck, M., 156
Storer, D., 253
Storshal, K., 91
Story, L. B., 100
Stotland, N., 94
Stott, P. B., 320
Stout, R., 186–189
Stout, S. C., 36, 47–48, 50, 312, 315
Stouthamer-Loeber, M., 446
Stowell, J., 315
Strahl, C., 326
Strain, E. C., 406–407
Strain, J. J., 172, 184
Strakowski, S., 224
Strassberg, D. S., 360, 367
Straus, R., 324
Strauss, C. C., 144
Strauss, J. L., 458
Strauss, S. E., 328–329, 570
Stravynski, A., 458
Strawbridge, W. J., 225
Street, L., 227
Streiff, O., 453
Strickland, B. R., 236
Striegel-Moore, R. H., 265, 270–271, 276–277, 282
Strober, M., 276
Stroebe, M., 214
Stroebe, W., 214
Stroup, N. E., 448
Stroup, T. S., 490
Strunk, D., 210, 245–247
Stuart, S., 245
Stuart, S. P., 174
Stuckler, D., 284–285, 299
Stueve, A., 232
Stuhr, J., 323
Stuikes, T., 177
Stulman, D. A., 253
Sturia, E., 351
Sturt, E., 38
Su, A., 193
Suarez, A., 298, 453
Suàrez, E. C., 59
Suàrez, L., 136–137, 156, 453
Subedar, H., 129
Subotnik, K. L., 457–458
Substance Abuse and Mental Health Services Administration, 104, 389, 397–398, 400, 403, 406–407
Suddath, R., 247
Sue, C. M., 542
Sue, S., 76

Suelzer, M., 131
Sugarman, H. J., 287
Sugden, K., 37, 40, 42, 48, 53, 123, 229
Sugiyama, T., 513
Suh, J. J., 418
Sulkava, R., 535
Sullivan, G. M., 47–48, 51, 53, 124, 157
Sullivan, J. L., 217
Sullivan, P. F., 261, 265, 268, 329, 483
Sulloway, F., 196
Suls, J., 325
Sumiyoshi, C., 472
Sumiyoshi, T., 472
Summerfeldt, L. J., 151
Sumner, J., 515
Sun, F., 548
Suomi, S. J., 39, 52–53
Suominen, K., 217
Suppes, T., 219, 242
Supplee, L., 450
Surget, A., 230, 239
Susser, E. S., 560
Sussex, J. N., 112
Sutker, P. B., 444
Sutton-Tyrell, K., 325
Svartberg, M., 431, 458, 460
Svensson, L., 148
Svensson, O., 534
Svetlik, D., 548
Svrakic, D. M., 434–436, 439, 441, 453–454, 458–459
Swan, G. E., 333, 542
Swanda, R. M., 82
Swann, A. C., 132
Swanson, J. M., 506
Swanson, J. W., 333, 559
Swartz, H. A., 242, 247
Swartz, M., 156, 177, 184
Swartz, M. S., 490, 491, 492, 559
Swedo, S. E., 160, 220
Sweeney, J. A., 483
Sweeney, M., 370
Sweeney, P, 245
Swendsen, J., 242
Swica, Y., 198, 200
Swindle, R., 179
Swinson, R. P., 135, 151
Sylvester, A., 144
Syme, S. L., 62, 324
Szarek, B. L., 240
Szatmari, P., 513, 517
Sze, S., 271
Szechtman, B., 472
Szechtman, H., 472
Szmukler, G., 282
Szmukler, G. I., 261, 275, 279
Szuba, M. P., 51

Tabak, C. J., 262
Taillefer, S., 184
Takagi, S., 415
Takahasi, T., 149
Takei, N., 486
Talajic, M., 325
Talbott, J. A., 491
Tallal, P., 511
Tambs, K., 439
Tampilic, M., 480
Tan, E. S., 60, 145
Tanaka-Matsumi, J., 114, 149, 480
Tanfer, K., 345
Tang, T. Z., 245
Tanguay, S., 504
Tannock, R., 508
Tanofsky, M. B., 268
Tanzi, R. E., 542
Tapert, S., 396, 398
Tardiff, K. J., 567
Tarkika, J., 230
Tarrier, N., 248

Tartara, A., 302
Tarver, S., 511
Tassinari, R., 139
Tata, P., 130
Tataryn, D. J., 56
Taylor, A., 37, 40, 42, 48, 53, 123, 229
Taylor, C. B., 135, 137, 267, 270, 274, 282–283, 310, 323, 325, 326–327, 419
Taylor, E. B., 213, 503
Taylor, H. L., 275
Taylor, J., 444
Taylor, M. A., 216
Taylor, R. R., 328, 329
Taylor, S. E., 62, 151, 155, 160, 174, 175, 245, 311, 315, 322–323, 326, 332, 334, 336
Te, A. E., 370
Teasdale, J. D., 55, 59–60, 210, 233, 246
Teders, S. J., 331–332
Teicher, M. H., 240
Tek, C. F., 155, 469–470, 472–475
Telch, C. F., 268, 274, 277, 281
Telch, M. J., 137
Tellegen, A., 35–36, 431
Temple, E., 511
Teri, L., 544, 548
Terman, J. S., 220–221
Terman, L., 81
Terman, M., 220–221
Tershakovec, A. M., 288
Tesar, L., 370
Tessitore, A., 37
Teten, A. L., 76
Teufel, N., 271
Thaker, G. K., 483
Thal, L., 540
Thase, M. E., 218, 227, 229–231, 235–236, 240–241, 246–247, 290
Thayer, J. F., 130, 138
Theander, S., 261
Thede, L., 351
Thelen, M. H., 274
Thesiger, C., 114–115
Thiele, C., 335
Thiele, E. A., 522
Thiemann, D., 324
Thies-Flechtner, K., 242
Tholen, S., 177
Thomas, D. J., 546
Thomas, J., 253
Thomas, M., 219
Thomas, N., 335
Thomas, R. G., 547
Thomas, T., 424
Thomas, Y. F., 411
Thompson, B., 136
Thompson, J. K., 261, 272
Thompson, L. A., 510
Thompson, M., 272, 506
Thompson-Brenner, H., 106, 279
Thomsen, A., 334
Thoresen, C. E., 323, 325
Thorgeirsson, T. E., 123
Thorndike, E. L., 24
Thorpe, G. L., 134
Thorsen, P., 515
Thorup, A., 442
Thrivikraman, K. V., 53, 157
Thum, A. E., 232
Thuras, P., 267
Thurau, D., 367
Thuwe, I., 350
Tibaldi, G., 246
Tibblin, G., 324
Tichler, C. E., 141
Tien, A. Y., 208, 211, 213, 250
Tienari, P., 39, 438, 482
Tiffany, S. T., 418
Tiggemann, M., 271, 272
Tillfors, M., 152

Timimi, S., 503
Tingelstad, J. B., 241
Tischler, C. E., 134, 144
Titchener, E., 23
Titchener, J. L., 155
Tjio, J. H., 522
Tobet, S., 348
Tobin, D. L., 265, 331–332
Tobin, R., 330
Toce, M. T., 423
Todaro, J., 188
Tohen, M., 241–242
Tokejko, N., 235
Toler, S. M., 370
Tollefson, G. D., 213
Tomaka, J., 315
Tomarken, A., 231
Tomasi, S. F., 146
Tomkins, A. J., 559
Tondo, L., 240, 242
Toni, C., 172
Tonigan, J. S., 420
Tonn, P., 295
Tononi, G., 289, 491
Toomey, R., 95
Torgersen, S., 177, 439, 451
Torres, B., 134, 144, 147
Torres-Harding, S. R., 329
Tosato, G., 328
Toth, K., 512
Townsend, E., 251
Tozzi, F., 261
Tracy, S. A., 129, 151
Tran-Viet, K. N., 424
Traskman-Bendz, L., 250, 251
Trautmen, P., 252
Trebbe, A., 274
Treno, A. J., 421
Trestman, R. L., 439
Tricamo, E., 217
Trifiletti, L. B., 335
Trimbell, M. R., 182
Trinkle, D., 292, 299
Trivedi, L., 349
Trosclair, A., 335
Trost, R. C., 53
Troughton, E., 446
True, W. R., 111, 229
Truesdale, A., 117
Trull, T, J., 431, 451
Tsai, G. E., 196
Tsai, L. Y., 514
Tsao, J. C. I., 126
Tsatsanis, K. D., 516
Tsuang, M., 224
Tsuang, M. T., 95, 112, 161, 250
Tu, X. M., 247, 290
Tuason, V. B., 241, 245–246
Tuchman, B., 8–9
Tucker, G. J., 491
Tuke, W., 15
Tupes, E. C., 431
Turk, C. L., 151
Turk, D. C., 325–328, 331, 333
Turkat, I. D., 439
Turkheimer, E., 35, 39–40, 103, 436, 452, 561
Turnbull, C. D., 217
Turner, C. W., 323, 325
Turner, E., 220
Turner, J. A., 327, 333
Turner, J. B., 155
Turner, R., 315
Turner, S. M., 151
Turon-Estrada, A., 540
Turovsky, J., 121, 130, 237, 314
Turpin, R., 522
Turse, N. A., 155
Tuschen-Caffier, B., 277
Twenge, J., 347
Tyler, D. B., 289
Tynes, L. L., 188
Tynes, S., 51, 163

Tyrer, P., 439
Tyring, S. K., 309
Tyrrell, D. A., 315

U. S. Bureau of the Census, 309
U. S. Conference of Maryors-Sodexho, 561
U. S. Department of Health and Human Services, 334, 560
U. S. General Accounting Office, 535
U. S. Public Health Service, 253
Uchino, B. N., 315, 323
Uebelacker, L., 235
Uhde, T., 135
Uhde, T. W., 232
Ulrich, R., 492
Umberson, D., 62, 225, 237
UNAIDS, 336
Unal, F., 182–183
Underwood, M., 253
Unger, J. B., 336–337
Ungvari, G. S., 475
Uno, D., 315
Unutzer, J., 241
Urbszat, C., 274
Urcuyo, K., 319, 320
Usai, S., 334
Useda, D., 438
Ustun, T. B., 177–178

Vaccarino, A. L., 331
Vacek, P. M., 221
Vaillant, G. E., 314, 316, 398–399, 444
Vajk, F. C., 247
Valencia, M. E., 286
Valencia-Flores, M., 406
Valera, E. M., 505
Valiente, R., 174
Valtonen, H, M., 217
Van Balkom, A., 175
van Beijsterveldt, C., 351
van Belle, G., 544
Van der Does, W., 254
van der Ende, J., 134, 144, 147
van der Hart, O., 195
van der Hout, M. A., 138
van der Kolk, B. A., 452–453
van der Meer, J., 328
van der Molen, G. M., 138
van Dieren, A. C., 138
Van Dorn, R. A., 559
van Duijil, M., 193
van Dyck, R., 175, 180, 184
van Elderen, T., 324
van Goozen, S. H. M., 446–447
van Huffelen, A. C., 522
van Kammen, D. P., 482, 484
van Kesteren, P. J., 350
van Laar, M., 131
Van Praag, H. M., 330
Van Rood, Y., 175
van Wijk, J., 522
Vander Wal, J. S., 274
Vander, Plate, C., 315
Vanderbrug Medendorp, S., 370
Vanitallie, T. B., 284
VanKammen, D. P., 446
Vansteenwegen, D., 22, 144–145, 147
VanValkenburg, C., 436, 455
Vasavada, N., 230
Vassey, P., 352
Vasterling, J. J., 157
Vazsonyi, A. T., 450
Veale, D., 186–188
Venables, P. H., 447
Venkata, S., 35
Venkataraman, S., 312
Ventura, J., 487
Ventura, S. L., 249
Verbaten, M., 131

Verchinski, B. A., 486
Verdeli, H., 161, 228
Veridiano, N. P., 348
Verman, K. K., 367
Vermeiren, R., 157
Vermes, D., 175
Vermetten, E., 157
Vernberg, M., 157
Vernetten, E., 199
Vernon, P. A., 95
Versage, E. M., 245
Vervliet, B., 54
Vesterdal, W., 450
Vestergaard, M., 515
Viegener, B. J., 287
Vieland, V., 253
Vielenti, R., 174
Viikarik, J., 49–50
Viitanen, M., 539, 549
Vilata-Franch, J., 540
Vincent, G. M., 435, 444
Vincent, L., 320
Virag, R., 370
Virts, K. L., 327
Visser, F. E., 522
Visser, L., 172, 174–175
Visser, S., 175
Vitali, A. E., 143, 160
Vitiello, B., 267, 269, 276–277
Vitonis, A., 225
Vitousek, K. M., 279, 281
Vittorio, C. C., 189
Vittum, J., 231–232, 237–238
Vocci, F., 418
Voderholzer, U., 230
Vogel, S. A., 508
Voglmaier, M. M., 442
Vohs, K. D., 276
Volberg, R. A., 423
Volkers, E., 131
Volkmar, F., 512–517
Volkow, N. D., 411
von Gunten, A., 537
von Knorring, A. L., 178, 448
Von Korff, M., 177, 283
von Meduna, J., 13
Voon, V., 243
Voss, C. B., 241
Vuchinich, S., 449
Vythilingam, M., 82
Vyvyan, J. P., 261

Waddell, M.T., 89, 122
Wadden, T. A., 268, 283, 284, 286, 287–288
Wade, T. D., 276
Wadsworth, J., 346
Wager, T., 339
Wagner, A., 517
Wagner, B. M., 252
Wagner, D., 329
Wahl, O., 469
Wahlbeck, K., 485
Wahlberg, K. -E., 482
Wahler, R. G., 450
Wahlsten, D., 39
Wake, M., 262
Wakefield, J., 4
Wakeling, A., 274
Walburn, J., 186, 188
Waldman, I. D., 446, 504, 505
Waldorf, D., 364
Waldron, M., 35, 39
Walinder, J., 350, 353
Walker, D. L., 164
Walker, E., 473, 479
Wall, P. D., 326–328
Wallace, C. E., 224
Wallace, C. J., 492
Wallace, C. S., 53
Wallace, J., 225
Wallace, P. M., 219
Waller, N. G., 198–200
Walsh, A. K., 508

Walsh, B. T., 51, 268, 276, 278–281
Walter, J. H., 522
Walters, A., 406
Walters, E. E., 123, 129, 155, 161, 229, 275–276, 277
Walther, A., 242
Wang, C., 398
Wang, D., 237
Wang, J. J., 542
Wang, M. C., 421
Wang, P. S., 131, 149, 155, 161, 221, 250
Wang, S., 10, 58
Wang, X., 237
Ward, M. M., 333
Ward, S. M., 542
Warlow, C., 180, 183
Warman, M., 179
Warner, P., 358
Warner, R., 247
Warshaw, M., 129
Warwick, H. M. C., 172, 174–175
Wasserman, S., 515
Wasserstein, S., 129
Watanabe, H., 489
Waterhous, L., 515
Waternaux, C., 224, 251
Waters, E., 217, 262
Watkins, E. R., 248
Watkins, J. T., 245
Watkins, L. R., 157, 324
Watson, D., 5, 95, 174, 227, 431
Watson, J. B., 16, 23, 25, 110
Watson, J. D., 35–36
Watson, S., 281
Wauchope, M., 374
Waugh, R., 324
Wax, J. R., 523
Weaver, C. M., 557–560, 564, 568–569
Weaver, D. R., 403
Weaver, E. V., 241–242, 247
Weaver, J. C. G., 39
Webb, F. M., 548
Webb, R., 251
Webser, J. A., 545
Wechsler, D., 81
Wedekind, D., 452
Wee, C. C., 269, 286
Weeks, A., 506
Weeks, J. R., 195
Weems, C. F., 129, 137
Wegner, D., 162
Wehr, T. A., 219–220, 231
Weiden, P. J., 490
Weight Watchers International, 286
Weihbruch, C., 327
Weihofen, H., 563
Weinberg, M. S., 371
Weinberg, W. A., 289
Weinberger, A., 234, 243
Weinberger, D. R., 35, 486
Weiner, D. B., , 15
Weiner, B. A., 558
Weiner, D. N., 366
Weiner, H., 315, 334
Weiner, J. M., 65
Weiner, M. F., 533, 538, 540–541, 548
Weinman, J., 130
Weinshall, D., 495
Weinshilboum, R., 526
Weinstock, L., 235
Weisberg, R. B., 126, 129, 186–187, 363, 365
Weisbrot, D. M., 183
Weise, R. E., 89, 458
Weiskrantz, L., 56, 182
Weisman de Mamani, A. G., 488
Weiss, B., 222
Weiss, C. S., 316
Weiss, K. A., 78

Weiss, L., 81
Weiss, M., 173
Weiss, S. M., 311
Weissenburger, J. E., 218, 230
Weissman, M. M., 93, 127, 134,
  135, 141, 144, 161, 212, 216,
  221–222, 224–225, 228–229,
  235–236, 243–244, 280
Weisstub, E., 62
Weisz, J. R., 114–115
Weitze, C., 350
Weitzman, E. D., 298
Weke, A. I., 277
Wekstein, D. R., 538–539
Welch, S. L., 266–268, 276, 279
Wellings, K., 346
Wells, A., 472
Wells, B., 347
Wells, J. M., 241
Wells, K., 413
Wells, K. B., 93, 149, 237, 244
Wells, K. C., 504
Welte, J. W., 414
Weltzin, T. E., 265, 267
Wender, P. H., 251
Wenzel, A., 245
Werdegar, D., 419
Wertheim, E. H., 274
Wesensten, N. J., 288
Wessely, S., 328, 330, 333
Wesson, D. R., 399
West, J. A., 444
West, L. J., 289, 420
Westen, D., 78, 106, 279, 451, 452
Westerveld, M., 157
Westphal, K., 133
Wetherby, A. M., 512, 514, 517
Wetherell, J. L., 131–132
Wetter, D. W., 414
Wettstein, R. M., 558
Wetzel, R. D., 171, 246
Wever, R., 296
Wexler, B. E., 423
Wexler, D. B., 566
Wexler, N. S., 542
Wexler, P., 347
Weyman-Daun, M., 274
Whalen, P. J., 188
Whiffen, V. E., 219
Whishaw, I. Q., 53
Whisman, M., 235
Whitbourne, S. K., 271
White, D., 370
White, J., 130–131
White, J. L., 445
White, K., 188
White, K. S., 125–126, 134, 136,
  162, 253
White, M. A., 268
Whitefield, K., 245
Whitehouse, A. M., 269
Whitehouse, W. G., 232, 234–235
Whitesell, N., 222, 225, 249
Whitfield, J., 546
Whiting, P., 330
Whitlatch, C. J., 548
Whitnam, F. L., 348
Whitney, C. W., 291
Whitt, B., 335
Whittal, M. L., 277, 279–280
Whybow, P. C., 219
Wickramaratne, P. J., 212, 224, 228,
  245
Widiger, T. A., 4, 86–87, 89, 93, 95,
  251, 431, 435–436, 445, 451, 461
Widom, C. S., 178, 445
Wieczorek, S., 295
Wiegartz, P. S., 160
Wiegel, M., 138, 361–364, 366,
  377–378
Wiener, M. J., 245
Wignall, A., 113

Wik, G., 56
Wikel, C. S., 189
Wilber, C., 194
Wilber, M. K., 423
Wilens, T. E., 217, 223, 269, 504,
  505, 507
Wiley, J., 336
Wilfley, D. E., 265, 268, 270, 283
Wilhelm, F. H., 208, 227
Wilhelm, S., 188
Wilhelmen, L., 324
Wilkinson-Ryan, T., 451
Willem de Dos, W., 175
Willett, W. C., 283
Willi, J., 261
Williams, C. J., 371
Williams, C. L., 81
Williams, D., 225, 327
Williams, J., 188, 262
Williams, J. B. W., 89
Williams, J. G., 178
Williams, J. M., 246
Williams, J. W., 241
Williams, L., 160, 200
Williams, M., 447
Williams, R. B., Jr., 59, 319–320,
  322, 324
Williams, S. H., 448–449
Williamson, D. A., 277
Williamson, D. E., 231
Williamson, D. F., 262, 283
Williamson, J. W., 335
Williamson, M., 492
Williamson, S., 505
Willoughby, R., 288
Wilner, P., 246–247
Wilson, D., 155
Wilson, D. M., 134, 282–283
Wilson, G. T., 268, 276–281, 413
Wilson, K. G., 91
Wilson, R., 186, 188
Wilson, T., 264, 267, 277, 279
Wimberly, S., 319–320
Wimo, A., 537
Winblad, B., 537
Winchel, R., 189
Winchel, R. M., 251
Wincze, J. P., 355–359, 361–363,
  367, 369–370, 370–371, 373,
  377–378
Windgasen, K., 490
Windle, M., 104
Windle, R. C., 104
Windom, C. S., 295
Winett, C. A., 237
Winett, R. A., 336
Wing, J. K., 72, 123, 487
Wing, L., 516
Wing, R. R., 268, 281, 358
Wing, Y. K., 271
Winick, B. J., 566
Winkelman, M. D., 550
Winkler, H., 485
Winokur, G., 216, 219, 251, 477
Winsor, J., 525
Winter, A., 16
Winterkorn, E. B., 522
Winters, R. W., 323, 325
Winzelberg, A. J., 283
Wirshing, D., 487
Wirshing, D. A., 570
Wirshing, W. C., 492
Wirz-Justice, A., 220
Wiscocki, P. A., 134
Wise, B. D., 237
Wise, M. G., 534
Wise, R. A., 412–413
Wise, T. N., 376, 378, 380–381
Wiseman, C. V., 272
Wisner, K. L., 219
Wisniewski, S., 219
Witherington, R., 371

Withers, G. S., 53
Witkiewitz, K., 421
Wittchen, H. U., 94, 125, 129, 134,
  144–145, 149, 155, 177, 184, 221
Witte, E. A., 51
Wittstein, I., 324
Witztum, M. D., 381
Woertman, L., 195
Wohlfahrt, J., 515
Wolf, A. M., 271
Wolf, M. M., 101
Wolf-Maier, K., 322
Wolfe, B. M., 287
Wolff, S., 441
Wolfson, A., 125
Wolfstetter-Kausch, H., 217
Wolgamuth, B., 183
Wolk, S., 224
Wolpe, J., 23, 25, 102
Women's Health Initiative Memory
  Study, 540
Wonderlich, S. A., 5, 264–265, 267,
  277
Wong, C., 188
Wong, K., 484
Wong, L., 494
Woo, J., 534
Wood, F. B., 508
Wood, J. M., 78
Wood, K., 274
Woodard, T., 355
Woodbury, M., 177, 184
Woodman, C. L., 129
Woods, E. R., 251
Woods, N. S., 403
Woods, S. W., 126, 139–140, 479
Woodside, B., 278
Woodside, M. R., 568
Woodward, L. J., 224
Woodworth, G., 446
Woolfolk, R. L., 179
Wooton, J. M., 449
World Health Organization, 64, 249,
  284, 322, 335–336
Wortman, C., 214
Wozniak, J., 217, 223, 505
Wright, E. J, 245
Wright, H. H., 424
Wu, M. T., 196
Wu, P., 405
Wu, R., 405
Wulfert, E., 91
Wunder, J., 223–224
Wurm, M., 324
Wyatt, J. K., 299
Wykes, T., 38
Wyllie, E., 183
Wynick, S., 183
Wynne, L. C., 39, 438, 482
Wyshak, G., 171, 173–174

Xie, H., 394
Xing, G., 47
Xu, Y., 339

Yach, D., 284–285, 299
Yager, J., 63, 225, 310
Yagi, A., 179
Yagla, S. J., 129
Yamaki, L. H., 123
Yamamiya, Y., 272
Yamamoto, J., 398
Yamashita, I., 472
Yan, L. L., 322–323, 336–337
Yang, G., 514
Yang, M., 504
Yanovski, S. Z., 268
Yap, A. K., 193
Yap, L., 131, 151
Yaryura-Tobis, J. A., 188
Yates, W. R., 446
Ye, X., 526

Yeager, C. A., 198, 200
Yeaton, W. H., 335
Yeh, S. -R., 53
Yehuda, R., 158
Yen, S., 434, 441, 451
Yerkes, R. M., 121
Yeung-Yue, K. A., 309
Yin, R. K., 102
Yip, P., 251
Yirmiya, R., 330
Yonkers, K. A., 94, 126, 129
Yost, M., 104
Young, A. M., 412
Young, E., 236
Young, J. E., 234, 243–245
Young, M. A., 220
Young, P., 246
Young, S., 351
Youngstrom, E., 241
Yuen, H. P., 479
Yung, A. R., 479
Yurgelun-Todd, D., 276
Yutzy, S. H., 171, 177

Zabinski, M. F., 270
Zadra, A., 300
Zager, D., 517
Zaharia, M. D., 39
Zahn, A., 298
Zakowski, S. G., 316
Zald, D, 47
Zalta, A. K., 261
Zanarini, M. C., 434, 451, 453
Zandi, P. P., 219, 227
Zarate, R., 153, 158, 494
Zarit, S. H., 548
Zaromb, F., 13
Zautra, A., 326–327
Zegans, L. S., 309
Zellenak, J. P., 252
Zeller, P. J., 219
Zeni, C., 526
Zhang, B., 214
Zhang, H., 160
Zhang, L., 47
Zhang, Y., 250
Zhao, S., 129, 221
Zhou, J. N., 351
Zhu, J., 81
Zielezny, M., 210, 246
Zigler, E., 250–251, 253, 524
Zilboorg, G., 9, 15
Zillman, D., 331
Zimmer, B., 271
Zimmerli, W. D., 130
Zimmerman, E. A., 222
Zimmerman, I., 348
Zimmerman, J. C., 182, 298
Zimmerman, M., 186–188, 436–437
Zimmermann, K., 492
Zimmermann, P., 177
Zinbarg, R. E., 54, 93, 125,
  130–131, 146, 149, 227
Zingmond, D. S., 287
Zinner, S. H., 361
Ziolko, S., 544, 548
Zipfel, S., 261
Zismann, V. L., 545
Zitman, F., 325
Zlotnick, C., 245
Zoellner, L. A., 138
Zohar, J., 162
Zonana, H., 562
Zorrilla, L. T., 150
Zubeita, J., 339
Zubin, J., 479
Zuchner, S., 424
Zucker, B. G., 126
Zucker, K. J., 348, 373–374, 414
Zuckerman, B., 292
Zukin, S. R., 410
Zvolensky, M. J., 124

Subject Index

AAMR. *See* American Association of
  Mental Retardation
Abnormal behavior. *See*
  Psychological disorders
Acamprosate, 418
Acetaldehyde, 418
Acetylcholine receptors, 404
ACT (assertive community treat-
  ment), 493
Acute pain, 326
Acute PTSD, 154
Acute stress disorder, 154, 190
Addiction. *See* Dependence
Addington v. Texas, 560–561
ADH (alcohol dehydrogenase), 397
ADHD. *See* Attention deficit/
  hyperactivity disorder
Adler, Alfred, 20
Adolescents
  BDD in, 186–187
  conversion disorder in, 183
  eating disorders in, 269, 271
  insomnia in, 291
  MMPI for, 79
  mood disorders in, 222–224
  normal/abnormal behavior in,
    501–502
  obesity in, 283–284
  psychopaths, 448–449
  substance use, 413
  suicide in, 250, 251
Adoption studies, 111, 446, 482
ADRA2A (adrenergic alpha-2A
  receptor) gene, 526
Adrenaline. *See* Epinephrine
Advance sleep phase type, 296
Affect
  assessing, 72
  define, 58
  inappropriate, 474
Affective flattening, 473
African Americans
  alcohol use, 398
  antisocial personality disorder, 448
  BDD in, 186–187
  dementia in, 546
  FAS in, 397
  learning disorders in, 508
  mood disorders in, 225
  obesity in, 269
  panic disorder in, 135
  psychopaths, 448
  schizophrenia in, 480
  sleep paralysis in, 136
  suicide in, 249
Age, 18, 520
Aggression. *See also* Violence
  in children, 448, 450
  intermittent explosive disorder
    and, 422
Agnosia, 536
Agonist substitution, 417–418
Agonists, 47
Agoraphobia

development, 133
DSM-IV-TR criteria, 134
panic disorder with, 132
Agreeableness, 432
AIDS. *See* HIV/AIDS
Akinesia, 490
Alarm response, 312
Alcohol use disorder
  binge drinking, 397–398
  clinical description, 395
  dependency criteria, 393
  DSM-IV-TR criteria, 395
  effects, 395–397
  progression, 398–399
  sexual dysfunction and, 364
  statistics, 397–398
  suicide and, 251
  treatment approaches, 418–420
Alcoholics Anonymous
  critics of, 419–420
  establishment, 419
  survey, 398
  twelve steps, 419
ALDH2 gene, 415
Alleles, 37
Alogia, 472
Alpha waves, 84
Alpha-adrenergic receptors, 48
Altruistic suicides, 250
Alzheimer, Alois, 544
Alzheimer's disease
  biological factors, 543–544
  clinical description, 538
  drug treatment research, 547
  DSM-IV-TR criteria, 538–539
  genetics, 544–545
  mood disorders and, 224–225
  Nun's study, 538–539
  overview, 556
  statistics, 538–539
  testing, 538
  vaccine for, 551
American Association of Mental
  Retardation (AAMR), 519–521
American Journal of Insanity, 13
American Journal of Psychiatry, 13
American Law Institute (ALI) rule,
  563–565
American Psychiatric Association
  (APA), 13
Amnesia, 191–192
Amnesic disorder, 549–550, 554
Amniocentesis, 523
Amphetamine, 298
Amphetamine use disorder, 401–402
Amygdala, 44
Amyloid beta peptides, 545
Amyloid plaques, 544–545
Anabolic-androgenic steroids, 410
Analog models, 101
Anandamide, 408
Anatomy of Melancholy (Burton), 12
Anger, 59
Angina pectoris, 323

Anhedonia, 473
Animal magnetism, 16
Animal models
  learned helplessness, 54–55
  substance abuse, 412
Animal phobia, 143
Anna O., 17–18, 181, 196
Anomic suicides, 250
Anorexia nervosa
  case study, 266
  characterization, 261
  clinical description, 266–267
  cross-cultural issues, 269–271
  developmental considerations,
    271–272
  DSM-IV-TR criteria, 267
  medical consequences, 267
  overview, 306
  psychological disorders with,
    267–268
  statistics, 269
  subtypes, 267
  treatment, 281–282
  weight loss and, 265
ANS (autonomic nervous system), 44
Antabuse. *See* Disulfiram
Antagonist substitution, 418
Antagonist treatments, 418
Antagonists, 47
Antecedent-behavior-consequence
  sequence, 76–77
Antidepressants, 239–241. *See also*
  specific antidepressants
Antigens, 316
Antipsychotic drugs
  characterization, 484
  commonly used, 489
  delirium treatment, 535
  development, 489–490
  effectiveness, 490
  noncompliance with, 490–491
Antisocial personality disorder
  (ASPD). *See also* Conduct disorder
  arousal theories, 446–550
  case study, 443–444
  characterization, 443
  clinical description, 444
  criminality and, 445–446
  defining criteria, 444–445
  developmental influences,
    448–449
  DSM-IV-TR criteria, 444
  gender differences, 177–179, 435
  genetic factors, 446
  integrative model, 449
  neurobiological factors, 446
  ODD and, 504
  prevention, 450
  psychological dimensions, 448
  psychopathy and, 445–446
  social dimensions, 448
  somatization disorder link,
    177–179
  substance abuse and, 416

treatment, 449–450
underarousal hypothesis, 446
Anxiety
  defined, 121
  GABA-sensitive neurons and, 412
  sexual dysfunction and, 365
  stress and, 313–315
Anxiety disorders
  brain wave activity and, 231
  bulimia and, 265
  causes, 123–125
  characterization, 121–122
  definitions, 121
  depression and, 92–93, 226–229
  generalized, 127–132
  integrated model, 125–126
  mood disorders and, 225
  OCD, 159–163
  overview, 168–169
  panic and, 60
  panic without agoraphobia,
    132–141
  PTSD, 152–159
  specific phobia, 141–148
  suicide and, 127
Anxiety Disorders Interview Schedule,
  74
*Anxiety Disorders Interview Schedule for
  DMS-IV (ADIS-IV),* 74, 93
Anxiolytic substance abuse, 399–401
APA. *See* American Psychiatric
  Association
Aphasia, 541
APO (apolipoprotein) E4 gene, 545
APP (amyloid precursor protein),
  545
Appearance, 72
ARC (AIDS-related complex),
  318–319
Aristotle, 14
Arousal, 357–358, 446–550
Asians
  alcohol use, 397–398
  dementia in, 546
  eating disorders in, 271
  homelessness in, 560
  hypochondriasis in, 173
  insomnia in, 291
  smoking in, 336–337
  substance-related abuse, 415
ASPD. *See* Antisocial personality
  disorder
Asperger's disorder, 515–516
Assertiveness training, 333
Assessment. *See also* Clinical assessment; Diagnosis
  behavioral, 74–77
  case study, 69–70
  defined, 69
  gender bias, 436
  interviews, 71–74
  key concepts, 71
  neuroimaging, 82–84
  neuropsychological testing, 82

Assessment (continued)
observations, 76–77
physical examination, 74
psychological testing, 77–82
psychophysiological, 84–85
schizophrenia, 495
sexual behavior, 361–363
text messaging in, 495
virtual reality in, 495
Association
free, 20
loose, 72
studies, 112, 482–483
Astrology, 11
Asylums, 15–16
Atherosclerosis, 323
Athletes, 413
Attention deficit/hyperactivity disorder (ADHD)
amphetamine treatment, 401
case study, 502–503
clinical description, 502–504
DSM-IV-TR criteria, 504
genetics, 505
misdiagnosis, 224
statistics, 503–504
treatment, 506–507
Atypical response, 3–4
Auditory hallucinations, 218, 472
Augmentative communication strategies, 525
Autism
biological factors, 514–515
case study, 511–512
causes, 514
characterization, 511
clinical description, 512–513
DSM-IV-TR criteria, 512–513
genetics, 514–515
myths, 514
neurobiological factors, 515
social dimensions, 514
Autohypnotic model, 199
Autoimmune disease, 317
Aversion
sexual, 356–357
therapy, 418–420
Avoidance, 134
Avoidant personality disorder, 457–458
Avolition, 472

B cells, 317
Bandura, Albert, 55–56
Barbiturates
clinical description, 399–401
history, 399
use statistics, 400
Bariatric surgery, 287
Basal ganglia, 43–44
Bazelon, David, 563
BDD. See Body dysmorphic disorder
Behavior
assessing, 74–77
cardiovascular disease and, 321
criminal, 445–446
cross cultural, 114–115
disorganized, 474
health-related, 311
heart disease and, 324
heterosexual, 346–347
homosexual, 346
mental status exam, 72
nongenomic inheritance, 39–40
self-injurious, 76–77
study of, 35–36
studying over time, 112–114
target, 74
Behavior modification
AIDS prevention, 335–336
benefits, 334–335

injury prevention, 335
smoking prevention, 336–337
Stanford Three Community Study, 337–338
Behavior of Organisms, The (Skinner), 24
Behavior rating scales, 76
Behavioral family therapy, 492–493
Behavioral medicine, 311
Behavioral therapy
beginnings of, 23–24
classical conditioning, 22–23
cognitive processes, 54
model development, 22–25
operant conditioning, 24–25
rise of, 23
Behaviorism, 16
Benzodiazepines. See also specific drugs
characterization, 399
discovery, 14
GABA molecules and, 47
for GAD, 131
treatment, 418
use, 400
Beta-adrenergic receptors, 48
Beyond Freedom and Dignity (Skinner), 24
Bianchi, Kenneth, 195
Bias, 436
Bill and Melinda Gates Foundation, 64
Binet, Alfred, 81
Binge drinking, 397–398
Binge-eating disorders
characterization, 261
dieting and, 274
overview, 306
treatment, 281
Binge-eating-purging, 267
Bini, Lucio, 13
Biofeedback, 84, 331–332
Biological factors. See also Genetic factors
anxiety disorders, 123–125
autism, 514–515
chronic pain, 328
dementia, 543–545
DID, 199
eating disorders, 276
mental retardation, 521–522
mood disorders, 228–231
psychological disorders and, 31–32
PTSD, 199
sexual dysfunction, 363–364
substance-related disorders, 411–412
suicide, 251
Biological model, 7–8
Biological tradition
consequences, 14
humoral theory, 11–12
nineteenth century, 12–13
treatment development, 13–14
Bipolar disorders
case studies, 215–216, 248
depression versus, 216–217
DSM-IV-TR criteria, 216
duration, 216–217
genetic influences, 229
identifying, 215
IPSRT for, 247
medication for, 241–242, 246–248
onset, 216–217
stressful life events and, 232
types, 215–216
BIS (behavioral inhibition system), 124, 446–447
Black box, 57
Bleeding, 12
Bleuler, Eugen, 467–468
Blind sight, 56

Blood pressure, 322
Blood-injury-injection phobia, 2, 142
BMI (body mass index)
hypertension and, 322
obesity, 283
table, 263
Body dysmorphic disorder (BDD)
case study, 185
causes, 188–189
clinical description, 186
statistics, 186–188
treatment, 186–188
Body image, 272–274, 277
Borderline personality disorder, 20
case study, 450
causes, 451–453
characterization, 434–435
clinical description, 451
DSM-IV-TR criteria, 451
integrative model, 453
suicide and, 251–252
treatment, 453–454
Brady, James, 564
Bradykinesia, 542
Brain. See also specific regions
alcohol effects, 396–397
anxiety-associated area, 124
blame, 572
dopamine pathways, 49
fear response and, 57–58
neuroimaging, 82–84
neurotransmitters, 46–50
nicotine receptors, 404–405
placebo effects, 339
psychosocial influences, 51–53
serotonin pathways, 48
stimulation, 243
structure of, 42–44, 485–486
Brain stem, 42, 44
Breathalyzer test, 395
Breathing-related sleep disorders, 295, 298
Breuer, Josef, 17, 18
Brief Psychiatric Rating Scale, 76
Brief psychotic disorder, 477
Bulimia nervosa
case studies, 262, 264, 275, 280
characterization, 261
clinical description, 264–265
cross-cultural issues, 269–271
developmental considerations, 271–272
DSM-IV-TR criteria, 264
medical consequences, 265
overview, 306
psychological disorders with, 265
psychological treatments, 279–280
statistics, 268–269
Bupropion imipramine, 506
Burke, Chris, 518

Cabin fever. See Seasonal affective disorder
Caffeine addiction, 394
Caffeine use disorders, 405–406
CAH (congenital adrenal hyperplasia), 351
Cancer
denial, 334
overview, 342
psychosocial effects, 319–321
Cannabinoids, 408
Cannabis sativa. See Marijuana
Cardiovascular disease
behavior and, 324–325
CHD, 323–325
hypertension, 321–323
negative emotions and, 325
overview, 342
Cardiovascular system, 321

Card-sort scores, 379
Caregivers, 546, 548
Case study method, 102–103
CAT (Children's Apperception Test), 78
CAT (computerized axial tomography) scans, 82–84
Catalepsy, 218
Cataplexy, 298
Catatonic immobility, 474
Catatonic type of schizophrenia, 475
Catcher in the Rye, 3
Catharsis, 157
Caudate, 44
Cell death, 312
Central nervous system. See CNS
Central sleep apnea, 295
Cerebellum, 44
Cerebral cortex, 44
Cerebral vascular accidents, 321
Cerletti, Ugo, 13
CFS. See Chronic fatigue syndrome
Charles VI of France, 9, 25
CHD. See Coronary heart disease
Chemical transporter, 37
Child abuse
borderline disorder and, 452–453
DID and, 197, 199
Munchausen syndrome by proxy, 181
pedophilia, 376–377
Childhood disintegrative disorder, 511–512
Children
ADHD, 502–507
aggression in, 448
antisocial personality disorder in, 450
autistic, 511–515
conduct disorder, 445–456
drug abstinence programs, 421
dysthymic disorder in, 213
eating disorders in, 271–272
false memories, 199–201
FAS, 397
of felons, 446
GAD treatment, 132
gender nonconformity, 382
learning disorders, 507–511
mania in, 233
mood disorders in, 222–224
normal/abnormal behavior in, 501–502
obesity in, 283–284
ODD in, 504
PTSD in, 153, 155
resilient, 65
separation anxiety disorder in, 143–144
sexual abuse of, 376–377
sleep disorder treatments, 299
sleep terrors, 136
Chinese culture
eating disorders in, 271
hypochondriasis in, 173
insomnia in, 291
smoking in, 336–337
Chocolate addiction, 393
Choking phobia, 143
Choleric personality, 12
Chromosomes, 34
Chronic fatigue syndrome (CFS), 328–330
Chronic pain
biological aspects, 328
characterization, 326
denial and, 334
gate control theory, 328
overview, 342
psychosocial aspects, 326–328
reduction therapies, 328–330

Chronic PTSD, 154
Cigarette smoking. *See* Nicotine use disorders
Cingulated gyrus, 44
Circadian rhythm sleep disorder, 295–296
Circadian rhythms, 230–231
Civil commitment
  case study, 561
  conflicting interests, 561
  criminalization and, 560
  criteria for, 558–560
  dangerousness defined, 559–560
  deinstitutionalization and, 560–561
  function, 557
  history, 557–558
  homelessness and, 560–561
  mental illness defined, 559
  overview, 562
  strict procedures and, 561–562
  Supreme Court rulings, 560, 562
Classical categorical approach, 86
Classical conditioning, 22–23
Classification
  approaches, 86–87
  defined, 85
  function, 86
  reliability, 87–88
  validity, 88
Clients. *See* Patients
Clinical assessments
  schizophrenia, 495
Clinical description, 6–7
Clinical efficacy axis, 570
Clinical interviews
  mental status exam, 71–73
  sample questions, 75–76
  semistructured, 73–74
Clinical practice guidelines, 570–572
Clinical psychologists, 5
Clinical significance, 101–102
Clinical utility axis, 571
Clomipramine, 162
Clonidine, 506
Cluster A personality disorders, 441–443
Cluster B personality disorders, 443–457
Cluster C personality disorders, 457–461
CNS (central nervous system), 40–42
Cocaine intoxication
  clinical description, 402–403
  DSM-IV-TR criteria, 402
  history, 402
  progression, 393–394
  statistics, 403
Coercive family practice, 448
Cognition
  borderline disorder and, 452
  emotions and, 57–60
  learned helplessness, 54–55
  mood disorders and, 234–235
  prepared learning, 56
  substance abuse, 413–414
  unconscious and, 56–57
Cognitive disorders
  amnesic, 549–550
  delirium, 533–535
  dementia, 535–549
  overview, 533, 554–555
Cognitive science, 54
Cognitive-behavioral group therapy, 151
Cognitive-behavioral self-management training, 336
Cognitive-behavioral treatment
  depression, 244
  eating disorders, 279, 281–282
  GAD, 131–132
  hypochondriasis, 175

mood disorders, 243–244, 246
panic disorders, 140–141
SAD, 221
somatization disorder, 179
suicide prevention, 253
Cohort effect, 113
Cohorts, 113
Collective unconscious, 20
Commitment. *See* Civil commitment; Criminal commitment
Comorbidity
  anxiety disorders, 126–127
  issue of, 91
  personality disorders, 436
  SAD, 221
Comparative treatment research, 106
Competence determination, 566
Comprehensive stress- and pain-reduction programs, 332–333
Comprehensive System, 78
Compulsions, 159–160
Conditioned stimulus, 22
Conduct disorder. *See also* Antisocial personality disorder
  arousal theories, 446–450
  characterization, 445–446
  DSM-IV-TR criteria, 447
  genetic influences, 446
  neurobiological influences, 446
Confound, 100
Conscientiousness, 432
Contingency management, 420
Control groups, 100, 105–106
Controlled drinking, 420
Conversion, 171
Conversion disorder
  case study, 179–180, 182
  causes, 183–184
  clinical description, 179–180
  DSM-IV-TR criteria, 180
  related disorders, 180–181
  statistics, 182–183
  treatment, 184
  unconscious mental processes and, 181–182
Coronary heart disease (CHD)
  characterization, 323
  denial and, 334
  psychosocial factors, 323–325
  Stanford Three Community Study, 337–338
Correlation
  benefits, 103–104
  coefficient, 103
  defined, 103–105
  epidemiology, 104–105
  types of, 103
Cortisol
  mood disorders and, 230
  psychopathy and, 448
  stress and, 312
Counseling psychologists, 5
Countertransference, 21
Course, defined, 6
Covert sensitization, 379, 420
CPAP (continuous positive air pressure), 298
Crack cocaine, 393–394
Creativity, mood disorders and, 225–226
Creutzfeldt-Jakob disease, 542
CRF (corticotropin-releasing factor), 312–313
Criminal commitment
  defined, 563
  insanity defense, 563–564
Criminalization, 560
Criminals. *See also* Psychopathy
  ethnicity and, 448
  genetic influences, 446
  treatment, 449–450

Criterion gender bias, 436
Cross-cultural factors
  anorexia nervosa, 269–271
  behavior, 114–115
  bulimia nervosa, 269–271
  research, 114–115
  schizophrenia, 494
Cross-generational effect, 113
Cross-sectional designs, 113
Cross-tolerance, 417
Cultural factors. *See also* Sociocultural factors
  behavior, 114–115
  borderline disorder, 453
  dementia, 546
  eating disorders and, 269–271
  gender identity disorder, 350–351
  insomnia, 292
  mood disorders, 225
  panic disorders, 135
  schizophrenia, 480
  sexual dysfunction, 366–367
  sexuality, 348
  specific phobia, 145
  suicide rate, 250
Cultural-familial retardation, 524
Culture of Narcissism, The (Lash), 456
Cyclothymic disorder, 216–217
Cyproterone acetate, 381

Dahmer, Jeffrey, 103, 375, 564
Dalmane. *See* Flurazepam
Dangerousness, 559–560
DARE (Drug Abuse Resistance Education), 421
Darwin, Charles, 57
DAT1 genotype, 505
DBT (dialectical behavior therapy), 453
DCS (D-cycloserine), 152, 164
Death instinct. *See* Thanatos
Deep brain stimulation, 243
Defense mechanisms
  define, 18
  examples of, 18
  fear and, 57
Defensive scale (K), 80
Deinstitutionalization, 560–561
Delayed sleep phase, 296
Delirium
  case study, 533–534
  characterization, 533
  clinical description, 534–535
  DSM-IV-TR criteria, 534
  overview, 554
  prevention, 535
  statistics, 534
  treatment, 535
Delta waves, 84
Delusional disorder, 476–477
Delusions
  defined, 72
  mood disorders and, 218
  schizophrenic, 470–471
  subtypes, 477
Delusions of grandeur, 218
Dementia
  alcohol-induced, 396
  Alzheimer's type, 538–540
  biological factors, 543–545
  caregivers, 546, 548
  case study, 536
  causes, 543–546
  characterization, 535
  classes, 537–538
  clinical description, 536–537
  costs of, 537
  due to other medical conditions, 541–543
  medical interventions, 547
  overview, 555

  prevention, 549
  psychosocial treatments, 547–549
  statistics, 537–538
  substance-induced, 543
  treatment, 546–548
  vascular, 540–541
Dementia Praecox, 468
Dementia pugilistica, 545
Demons, 8
Dendrite, 40
Denial
  cancer, 334
  CHD, 334
  chronic pain, 334
  defined, 19
  stress reduction, 334
Dependence
  abuse and, 391
  addiction and, 393
  alcohol statistics, 398
  definitions, 392
  disease model, 415
  drug-specific table, 393
  DSM-IV-TR criteria, 391
  environmental factors, 411
  moral weakness model, 414–415
  steroid, 410
Dependent personality disorder, 458–459
Dependent variables, 99
Depersonalization, 190–191
Depersonalization disorder, 190–191
Depo-Provera. *See* Medroxyprogesterone
Depressants. *See* specific drugs
Depression. *See also* Major depression
  anxiety and, 92–93, 226–229
  brain wave activity and, 231
  bulimia and, 265
  cognitive triad, 234
  cognitive vulnerability, 234
  genetic influences, 229
  humoral theory, 11
  learned helplessness and, 233
  stress and, 313–315
Derailment, 72
Derealization, 190
Desensitization, systematic, 23
Designer drugs, 401, 409–410
Development
  across life spans, 20
  antisocial personality disorders and, 448–449
  critical periods, 33
  psychoanalytic stages, 19–20
  schizophrenia, 479–480
  sexual orientation, 348–350
Developmental disorders
  ADHD, 501–507
  case studies, 501
  common, 501
  learning, 507–511
  mental retardation, 518–527
  overview, 530–531
  pervasive, 511–518
  prevention, 525–526
  psychopharmacogenetics, 526
Deviation IQ, 81
Diabetes, 285
Diagnosis. *See also* Clinical assessment
  ADHD, 224
  biological tradition, 14
  classification, 86–88
  creation, 92–94
  DSM-III, 88–89
  DSM-IV, 89–92
  labeling issues, 92
  mixed anxiety-depression, 92–94
  pre 1980, 88
  premenstrual dysphoric disorder, 93–94

Diagnosis (*continued*)
strategies, 85–86
supernatural model, 7–11
Diagnostic and Statistical Manual (DSM-III)
creation of, 88–89
description, 85
problems with, 88–89
Diagnostic and Statistical Manual (DSM-IV-TR)
ADHD criteria, 504
alcohol use disorder criteria, 395
Alzheimer's disease criteria, 539
amnesia criteria, 192
amnesic disorder criteria, 550
amphetamine intoxication criteria, 401
anorexia nervosa criteria, 267
antisocial personality disorder criteria, 444
anxiolytic intoxication criteria, 400
avoidant personality disorder criteria, 457
axis system, 89–90, 431
bipolar disorder criteria, 216
borderline personality disorder criteria, 451
breathing-related sleep disorder criteria, 295
bulimia nervosa criteria, 264
caffeine intoxication criteria, 406
cannabis intoxication criteria, 408
case study, 90
circadian rhythm sleep disorder criteria, 295–296
cocaine intoxication criteria, 401
conduct disorder criteria, 447
conversion disorder criteria, 180
creation of, 89
criticisms, 91–92
cultural considerations, 90–91
cyclothymic disorder criteria, 217
delirium criteria, 534
delusional disorder criteria, 477
dependent personality disorder, 459
depersonalization disorder criteria, 191
depression criteria, 208
dysthymic disorder criteria, 211
exhibitionism criteria, 373
factitious disorder criteria, 181
fetishism criteria, 372
format, 89–90
frotteurism criteria, 372
GAD criteria, 128
gender identity disorder criteria, 351
hallucinogen intoxication criteria, 409
histrionic personality disorder criteria, 455
hypnotic intoxication criteria, 400
hypoactive sexual desire disorder criteria, 356
hypochondriasis criteria, 173
insomnia criteria, 291
major depression criteria, 210
mania criteria, 208
mental retardation, 519
narcissistic personality disorder criteria, 456
narcolepsy criteria, 295
nicotine withdrawal criteria, 405
nightmare disorder criteria, 301
nonspecific paraphilia criteria, 376
OCD criteria, 160, 460
opioid intoxication criteria, 407
orgasmic disorder criteria, 359
pain disorder criteria, 185

panic disorder criteria, 133–134
paranoid personality disorder criteria, 438
parasomnia criteria, 300
pathological gambling criteria, 423
pedophilia criteria, 376
personality disorder classification, 432–433
premature ejaculation criteria, 360
primary hypersomnia criteria, 294
psychotic disorder criteria, 377–378
PTSD criteria, 154
schizoid personality disorder criteria, 440
schizophrenia, 470, 474–476
schizotypal personality disorder criteria, 442
sedative intoxication criteria, 400
sexual arousal disorder criteria, 358
sexual masochism criteria, 374
sexual sadism criteria, 374
sleep disorder criteria, 289
sleep terror criteria, 301
sleepwalking criteria, 301
social considerations, 90–91
social phobia criteria, 133–134
somatization disorder criteria, 176
specific phobia criteria, 141
substance abuse criteria, 391
substance dependence criteria, 391
substance intoxication criteria, 391
tasks force issues, 93
trance and position criteria, 194
transvestic fetishism criteria, 374
vascular dementia criteria, 540
voyeurism criteria, 373
Diagnostic and Statistical Manual (DSM-V)
neuroscience-based categories in, 95
personality disorder criteria in, 461
somatoform disorder criteria in, 202
Diana, Princess of Wales, 261–262
Diastolic blood pressure, 322
Diathesis-stress model, 36–38, 232–233
DID. *See* Dissociative identity disorder
Dieting, 274
Diffuse optical imaging, 84
Dimensional approach, 87
Diminished capacity, 563–564
Directionality, 103–104
Disintegrative disorder, 511
Disorder of written expression, 507
Disorders, defined, 4
Disorganized behavior, 474
Disorganized speech, 473–474
Disorganized type of schizophrenia, 474
Displacement, 18, 19
Dissociation, 56
Dissociative amnesia, 191–192
Dissociative anesthetics, 410
Dissociative disorders
amnesia, 191–192
case study, 191–192
characterization, 171
depersonalization, 190–191
fugue, 192–193
identity, 193–201
overview, 189–190, 205
trance, 193
Dissociative identity disorder (DID)
case study, 194–195
causes, 197–198
characteristics, 194–195

characterization, 194
clinical description, 194
faking, 195
memory and, 199–201
PTSD and, 198
statistics, 197
suggestibility and, 198–199
treatment, 201
Dissociative trance disorder, 193
Distant Mirror, A (Tuchman), 8
Distress. *See* Personal distress
Dix, Dorothea, 15–16
DMT (dimethyltryptamine), 409
DNA (Deoxyribonucleic acid), 34
Dominant gene, 34
Dopamine
ADHD and, 505
characterization, 48–50
cocaine and, 403
mood disorders and, 229–230
pleasure consequence, 423
schizoid personality and, 441
schizophrenia and, 483–485
substance abuse and, 412
Dorsal horns of spinal column, 328
Double depression, 210–211
Double helix, 34
Double-blind control, 106
Down syndrome, 522–523, 544, 545
Dream analysis, 20
Driving addiction, 393
Drug holidays, 108
DSM-III. *See Diagnostic and Statistical Manual* (DSM-III)
DSM-IV-TR. *See Diagnostic and Statistical Manual* (DSM-IV-TR)
DSM-V. *See Diagnostic and Statistical Manual* (DSM-V)
DST (dexamethasone suppression test), 230
DTs (delirium tremens), 396
Durham rule, 563
Durham v. United States, 563
Duty to warn, 567
Dysmorphophobia, 186
Dyspareunia, 360–361
Dysphoric disorder, 93–94
Dysphoric manic episode, 209
Dyssomnias, 289, 307
Dysthymic disorder
clinical description, 210
DSM-IV-TR criteria, 211
duration, 213
with major depression, 210
subtypes, 213

Eating disorders. *See also* Anorexia nervosa; Binge-eating disorders; Bulimia nervosa
anorexia nervosa, 261
bingeing, 268
biological dimensions, 276
developmental considerations, 271–272
dietary restraint, 275
drug treatments, 278–279
family influences, 275–276
increases in, 261–262
integrative model, 277–278
overview, 261–262, 306
prevention, 282–283
psychological dimensions, 276–277
psychological treatments, 279–282
social dimensions, 272–276
sociocultural factors, 262
statistics, 268–269
suicide and, 261
weight concerns, 282
weight gain strategies, 282

Echolalia, 514
ECT (electroconvulsive therapy)
history, 13–14
for mood disorders, 242–243
for schizophrenia, 489
EEG (electroencephalogram), 84, 231
Ego, 17–18
Ego and the Mechanisms of Defense (A. Freud), 19
Ego psychology, 19
Egoistic suicides, 250
Ejaculation, 360
Elderly
anxiety disorders in, 225
borderline disorder in, 434–435
dementia in, 537
GAD in, 129
mood disorders in, 224–225
panic disorders in, 134
paranoid personality disorder in, 439
social networks and, 63
suicide in, 249
Electra complex, 19
Electrodermal responding, 84
Electrolyte imbalance, 265
Emotional disorders. *See* Mood disorders
Emotions
components, 58–59
contagion, 10
evolution of, 57
expressed, 487–488
negative, 325
phenomena, 58
physiology and, 57–58
psychological disorders and, 32–33
psychopathology and, 60
role of, 57
Empathy, 22
Endocrine system, 45–46, 230
Endogenous opioids, 328
Endophenotypes, 446
ADHD, 483
borderline disorder, 451
defined, 110
schizophrenia, 483
Entwistle, John, 402
Environmental factors
antisocial personality disorder, 448
dependence, 411
genes interaction, 36–39
hostility, 487
immune system, 317
obesity, 286
sexual dysfunction and, 367
Ephedra sinica, 401
Epidemiology, 104–105
Epinephrine, 45, 46
Epstein-Barr virus, 328
Equifinality principle, 64–65
Erectile disorder, 357, 370
Ergotism, 408
Erikson, Eric, 20
Erotomanic delusion, 477
Erotophobia, 366
Essential hypertension, 322
Ethical Principles of Psychologists and Code of Conduct, 116
Etiology, 99
Event-related fMRI, 84
Event-related potential, 84
Evidence-base practice guidelines, 570–572
Evil eye, 60–61
Evoked potential, 84
Excitement, 313–315
Exhaustion, 312
Exhibitionism, 373
Exner, John, 78

Expert witnesses, 567–568
Explanatory therapy, 175
Explicit memory, 57
Exposure and ritual prevention, 162–163
Exposure-based treatments
    clinical guidelines, 570–572
    panic disorder, 138–139
    prevention, 51
    social phobia, 151
Express emotion, 487–488
Expressive language disorders, 509
External validity, 99–101
Extinction, 23
Extrapyramidal symptoms, 490
Extroversion, 432
Eye-tracking technologies, 512
Eysenck, Hans, 24

Facial agnosia, 536
Factitious disorders, 180–181
Faking, 195
False Memory Syndrome Foundation, 199
Familial influences
    antisocial personality disorders, 448
    eating disorders, 275–276
    mood disorders, 228–229
    psychopaths, 448
    schizophrenia, 487–488
    substance-related disorders, 411
    suicide, 228–229
Family studies, 110–111
FAS. See Fetal alcohol syndrome
Fatalistic suicides, 250
Fear. See also Panic disorders
    cultural factors, 60–61
    emotion of, 58
    gender factors, 61–62
    purpose, 57–58
Fearlessness hypothesis, 447
Fellatio, 373
Fetal alcohol syndrome (FAS), 397, 521
Fetishism
    characterization, 373
    DSM-IV-TR criteria, 372
    transvestic fetishism, 373–374
Fight or flight syndrome
    anxiety disorders and, 122, 124
    BIS and, 447
    characterization, 57
5HT (5-hydroxytryptamine), 47–48
Fluoxetine, 240, 364
Flurazepam, 298
fMRI (functional magnetic resonance imaging), 84
Folie à deux, 477–478
Forebrain, 42, 44
Formal observation, 76
Foster, Jodie, 564
Fox, Michael J., 542
Fragile X syndrome, 523–524
Franklin, Benjamin, 16
Free association, 20
Fright disorders, 60
Frigo phobia, 145
Frontal lobe, 44
Frotteurism, 372
Functional communication training, 108
Functional genomics, 411

GABA (gamma-aminobutyric acid)
    anxiety disorders and, 123–124
    barbiturates and, 400
    characterization, 42, 47
    opiates and, 412
    system, 395–396
GAD. See Generalized anxiety disorder

Galen, 11
Gambler's Anonymous, 424
Gambling. See Pathological gambling
Gambling addiction, 393
Gate control theory, 328
Genain quadruplets, 481
Gender
    bias, 436
    nonconformity, 352
    roles, 61–62, 236–237
Gender differences. See also Men; Women
    ADHD, 503
    ASPD, 177–179
    autism, 513
    BDD, 187
    causes, 504–506
    delusions, 477
    depression, 229
    GAD, 129
    HIV/AIDS incidents, 336
    mood disorders, 221–222, 225
    pain, 328
    panic disorders, 134–135
    personality disorders, 435–436
    schizophrenia, 479
    sexual dysfunction, 355
    sexuality, 346–348
    social phobia, 149
    somatization disorder, 177
    suicide rate, 249–250
    weight consciousness, 272–274
Gender identity disorders
    case studies, 350–352
    causes, 351–352
    characterization, 345
    defining, 350–351
    DSM-IV-TR criteria, 351
    overview, 386
    treatment, 352–354
General adaptation syndrome, 312
Generalizability, 101
Generalized amnesia, 191
Generalized anxiety disorder (GAD)
    case study, 128
    causes, 129–131
    clinical description, 127
    DSM-IV-TR criteria, 128
    onset, 129
    physical symptoms, 129
    statistics, 129
    treatment, 131–132
Genes
    ADHD, 505
    defined, 34
    environmental interaction, 36–39
    nature of, 34–35
    overemphasis on, 39–40
    study of, 35–36
Genetic factors
    ADHD, 505
    adoption studies, 111
    Alzheimer's disease, 544–545
    ASPD, 446
    autism, 514–515
    biological aspects, 110
    borderline disorder and, 452
    family studies, 110–111
    Huntington's disease, 542
    mental retardation, 521–522
    mood disorders, 228–231
    Parkinson's disease, 542
    schizophrenia, 480–483
    substance-related disorders, 411, 415
    twin studies, 111–112
Genetic linkage analysis, 112
Genetic markers, 112
Genital herpes, 309
Genotypes, 110
Germ theory, 12

GHB (gamma-hydroxybutyrate), 298, 410
Glial cell-derived neurotrophic factor, 546
Globus hystericus, 143
Glutamate system, 396
Grandeur, delusions of, 470
Grandiose delusion, 477
Grandiosity, 456, 477
Grave disability, 558
Grey, John P., 12–13
Grief, 213–215
Groups, 105–106
GSR (Galvanic skin response), 84
Guilhem, Arnaut, 8–9
Guilty but mentally ill, 565–566
Gun control, 564
Gynecomastia, 353

Halcion. See Triazolam
Hallucinations
    assessing, 72
    DSM-IV-TR criteria, 409
    hypnologic, 294
    mood disorders and, 218
    schizophrenic, 471–472
    use disorder, 407–409
Hallucinogens, 395. See also specific drugs
Halstead-Reitan Neuropsychological Battery, 82
Hara-kiri, 250
Harris, Robert Alton, 190
Haslam, John, 467–468
Hawking, Stephen, 92
Head trauma, 541, 545
Health. See also Physical disorders
    anger and, 59
    behavior and, 311
    behavior modification, 334–338
    psychology, 311
    social networks and, 62–63
Heart attack. See Myocardial infarction
Hebephrenic schizophrenia, 474
Helper T cells, 317
Hendrix, Jimmy, 389
Hermaphrodites. See Intersex individuals
Heroin, 393
Heroin addiction, 394
Heterosexuality
    behavior, 346–347
    development, 348–350
Hierarchy of needs, 21
High blood pressure. See Hypertension
Hinckley, John W., Jr., 564–565
Hippocampus, 44, 230
Hippocrates, 11–12
Histrionic personality disorder, 435, 454–455
HIV/AIDS, 9–10
    dementia-associated, 541
    immune system and, 317
    overview, 342
    prevention, 335–337, 342
    psychosocial effects, 318–319
Hoarding, 160
Homelessness, 560–561
Homosexuals
    amphetamine use, 402
    behavior, 346
    development, 348–350
    eating disorders in, 268
Hormones. See also specific hormones
    defined, 45
    sexual dysfunction and, 370
Horney, Karen, 20
HPA (hypothalamic-pituitary-adre-

nocortical) axis
    anxiety disorder and, 124
    characterization, 46
    mood disorders and, 230
    stress and, 312–313
Human Genome Project, 110
Human Sexual Inadequacy (Masters, Johnson), 368
Humanistic theory, 21–22
Humoral theory of disorders, 11–12
Huntington's disease
    brain deterioration and, 485
    characterization, 34
    motor movement and, 542
Hypersensitive gag reflex, 143
Hypersomnia. See Primary hypersomnia
Hypertension, 321–323
Hypertension medication, 364
Hypnagogic hallucinations, 294
Hypnosis, 16–17
Hypnotic use disorder, 399–401
Hypoactive sexual desire disorder, 355–356
Hypochondriasis
    case study, 171–172
    causes, 174–175
    clinical description, 172–173
    DSM-IV-TR criteria, 173
    historical concept, 171
    statistics, 173
    symptoms, 173–174
    treatment, 175
Hypofrontality, 485
Hypomanic episode, 209
Hypothalamus, 44, 46
Hypothesis, 99, 100
Hypothesis testing, 243
Hysteria
    ancient definition, 12
    category of, 94
    mass, 10
    stigma, 171

ICD. See International Classification of Diseases and Related Health Problems
Id, 17–18
Ideas of reference, 72, 441
Idiographic strategy, 85
Illness phobia, 143, 172
Immune system
    characterization, 315
    function, 316–317
    pathways, 317
    stress and, 315–316
Immunoglobulins, 317
Impacted grief reaction, 214
Impairment, 3
Implicit memory, 56–57
Impulse-control disorders
    defined, 389
    intermittent explosive disorder, 422
    kleptomania, 422–423
    pathological gambling, 423–424
    pyromania, 423
    trichotillomania, 424
Impulsivity, 451
Inappropriate affect, 474
Incest, 376–377
Independent genetic influence, 39
Independent Living Skills program, 492
Independent variables, 99
Inferiority complex, 20
Influenza, 442
Informed consent, 116, 569
Infrequency scale (F), 80
Inhibited orgasm, 358–359
Injury prevention, 335, 343

Insanity defense
    diminished capacity, 563–564
    history, 563–564
    public opinion, 564–565
    reactions to, 564–566
    reforms, 565–566
Insanity Defense Reform Act, 563, 565
Insel, Thomas, 52
Insomnia. See Primary insomnia
Insulin shock therapy, 13
Integrative approach model
    ASPD, 449
    borderline disorder, 453
    depression therapy, 245
    development, 24
    eating disorders, 277–278
    insomnia, 292–293
    models, 31–33
    mood disorder therapy, 237–239
    multidimensional, 31
    pervasive developmental disorders, 517
    schizophrenia, 493
    substance-related disorders, 415–417
Intellectual functioning, 72
Intermittent explosive disorder, 422
Internal validity, 99–101
International Classification of Diseases and Related Health Problems (ICD), 88, 93
Interoceptive avoidance, 134
Intersex individuals
    characterization, 350
    treatment, 353–354
Interventions. See also Treatments
    dementia, 547
    mood disorders, 245–246
    schizophrenia, 489–491, 491–493
Intrapsychic conflicts, 18
Introspection, 23
Intrusive thoughts, 162
Inverse agonists, 47
Involuntary commitment. See Civil commitment
IPSRT (interpersonal and social rhythm therapy), 247
IPT (interpersonal psychotherapy)
    bulimia nervosa, 279
    mood disorders, 244–245
IQ (intelligence quotient)
    autism, 513–514
    genetics, 35
    mental retardation, 519–520
    test development, 81–82
Ischemia, 323

Jackson v. Indiana, 566
Japanese culture, 149
Jealous delusion, 477
Jet lag, 295–296
Jones, Mary Cover, 23
Joplin, Janis, 389
Jung, Carl, 20

Kaczynski, Ted, 564
Kandel, Eric, 36
Kansas v. Hendricks, 562
Kernberg, Otto, 20
Ketamine, 485
Killer T cells, 317
Klein, Melanie, 20
Kleptomania, 422–423
Koch, Ed, 561
Korean culture, 415
Kraepelin, Emil, 14, 86, 467–468

La belle indifférence, 180, 183
Lanugo, 267

Latinos
    alcohol use, 397–398
    homelessness in, 560
    insomnia in, 291
    obesity in, 269
    panic disorder in, 135
    specific phobia in, 145
    suicide in, 249
Law. See Mental health law
L-dopa, 484
Learned alarms, 126
Learned helplessness
    characterization, 54
    mood disorders and, 233–234
    observation of, 55
Learning
    observational, 56
    prepared, 56
    social, 55–56
Learning disorders
    case study, 507
    causes, 509–510
    clinical description, 507–508
    related disorders, 509
    statistics, 508–509
    treatment, 510–511
Lesch-Nyhan syndrome, 522–524
Lesions, psychopathology of, 50–51
Leukocytes, 316
Libby, Lewis "Scooter," 567
Libido, 18
Lie scale (L), 80
Lifelong, 354
Life-span development
    equifinality principle, 64–65
    influences, 64
    theory of, 20
Limbic system
    function, 44
    structure of, 43
Linkage studies, 482–483
Lithium, 241–242, 247–248
Localized amnesia, 192
Loftus, Elizabeth, 567
Loiseua, Bernard, 250
Long alleles, 37
Longitudinal designs, 113–114
LSD (d-lysergic acid diethylamide)
    addition test, 393–394
    characterization, 408–409
Luria-Nebraska Neuropsychological Battery, 82

Ma-huang, 401
Macrophages, 316–317
Madden, John, 121–122
Magical thinking, 441, 479
Magnetic resonance imaging. See MRI
Maintenance treatment, 246
Major depression disorder. See also Depression
    bipolar disorder versus, 216–217
    case study, 211–212
    clinical description, 210–212
    cognitive-behavioral therapy for, 244
    DSM-IV-TR criteria, 209
    duration, 212–213
    with dysthymic disorder, 210
    ECT for, 242–243
    in elderly, 225
    grief and, 213–215
    late onset, 224
    MAO inhibitors for, 239–240
    onset, 212–213
    overview, 208–209
    postpartum, 219
    SSRIs for, 239–242
    suicide and, 251–252
    types, 210–212

Major depressive episode, 208
Malingerers, 567–568
Malingering, 180
Mania
    in children, 223, 233
    DSM-IV-TR criteria, 209
    dysphoric, 209
    overview, 208–209
Manson, Charles, 564
MAO (monoamine oxidase)
    mood disorders, 239–240
    social phobia, 151
Marijuana
    addiction test, 393
    history, 407
    medical use, 408
    tolerance, 407–408
Marker genes, 482–483
Marriage, 235
Maslow, Abraham, 21–22
Masochism. See Sexual masochism
Mass hysteria, 10
Mass suicides, 250–251
Masturbation, 347
Mathematics disorder, 507–508
MDMA (methylene-dioxymethamphetamine)
    addictiveness rating, 394
    characterization, 401
    effects, 410
Measurements, 107–108
Medications. See also specific drugs
    hypertension, 364
    neurotransmitters based, 484
    panic disorders, 138
    pervasive developmental disorders, 517
    PTSD, 158
    sexual disorder treatment, 370
    social phobia, 151
Medina v. California, 566
Meditation, 332, 343
Medroxyprogesterone, 298, 381
Medulla, 44
Melancholy, 8–9, 11
Melanin, 296–297
Melatonin, 296
Memory
    explicit, 57
    false, 199–201
    implicit, 56–57
    loss of, case study, 191
    real, 199–201
Memory wallets, 547
Men
    arousal disorders, 357–358
    ASPD in, 177–178
    orgasmic disorders, 359
    panic disorders in, 135
    sexuality myths, 368
    suicide in, 249–250
Mendel, Gregor, 34
Mental health law
    case studies, 561, 569
    civil commitment, 557–562
    competence issues, 566
    criminal commitment, 563–568
    duty to warn, 567
    expert witnesses, 567–568
    perspectives on, 557
    right to refuse treatment, 569
    right to treatment, 568
    therapeutic jurisprudence, 566
    trends in, 557
Mental hygiene movement, 16
Mental illness. See also Psychological disorders
    behavior types, 476–479
    criminalization of, 560
    legal definition, 559

Mental retardation
    biological factors, 521–522
    case study, 518–519
    causes, 521–524
    characterization, 518
    chromosomal influences, 522–524
    clinical description, 519–521
    DSM-IV-TR criteria, 519
    genetics, 521–522
    onset age, 520
    overview, 531
    psychological factors, 524
    social factors, 524
    statistics, 521
    treatment, 524–525
Mental status exam, 71–74
Mercury, 515
Mescaline, 394
Mesmer, Anton, 16
Mesmerism, 16
Methadone, 417–418
Methamphetamine addiction, 394, 425
Methylphenidate, 293, 505
Meyer, Adolf, 25
Midbrain, 44
Middle Eastern cultures
    OCD in, 161
    PTSD in, 155
Minnesota Multiphasic Personality Inventory (MMPI), 79–81, 567–568
Minnesota Multiphasic Personality Inventory (MMPI) for adolescents, 79
Mixed manic episode, 209
Mixed sleep apnea, 295
MMPI. See Minnesota Multiphasic Personality Inventory
M'Naghten, Daniel, 563, 565
M'Naghten rule, 563
Modafinil, 298
Modeling, 56
Modern mass hysteria, 10
Mood disorders. See also Major depression
    in adolescents, 222–224
    Alzheimer's disease and, 224–225
    anorexia nervosa and, 267
    anxiety disorders and, 225
    atypical features specifier, 217–218
    biological dimensions, 228–231
    bipolar disorders, 215–217
    brain wave activity and, 231
    bulimia and, 265
    case studies, 207, 243
    catatonic features specifier, 218
    in children, 222–224
    chronic features specifier, 218
    circadian rhythms and, 230–231
    cognitive vulnerability, 234–235
    combined treatments, 245–246
    creativity and, 225–226
    cultural differences, 225
    defined, 58
    ECT for, 242–243
    in elderly, 224–225
    integrative theory, 237–239
    interpersonal psychotherapy, 244–245
    learned helplessness and, 233–234
    life events and, 231–233
    longitudinal course specifiers, 219
    maintenance treatment, 246
    medication for, 239–242
    melancholic features specifier, 218
    neurotransmitters and, 229–230
    overview, 207–208, 258–259
    prevalence, 221–226
    prevention, 245–246

psychological dimensions, 231–235
psychotic features specifier, 218
rapid-cycling specifier, 219
seasonal pattern specifier, 219–220
structure, 209–210
TMS for, 242–243
treatment, 239–248
types of, 259–260
in women, 235–237
Mood incongruent hallucination. *See* Delusions
Moods
assessing, 72
defined, 58
Moon, moods and, 10–11
Moral principles, 18
Moral therapy, 14–16
Moral weakness model, 414–415
Morel, Benedict, 467–468
Mountain climbing addiction, 393
MRI (magnetic resonance imaging), 82–83
Multidimensional integrative approach, 31
Multimodal Treatment of Attention Deficit/Hyperactivity Disorder (MTA) study, 506–507
Multiple baselines, 108–110
Multivariate analysis, 35
Munchausen syndrome by proxy, 181
MUSE, 370
Mutilations, 187–188
Myocardial infarction, 323
Myocardial stunning and, 323–324
Myocardium, 323

Naltrexone, 418
Narcissistic personality disorder, 455–457
Narcolepsy, 294–295
National Alliance for the Mentally Ill, 562
Native Americans
alcohol use, 397–398
depression in, 222, 225
FAS in, 397
Natural environment phobia, 142–143
Nature *versus* nurture. *See also* Environmental factors; Genetic factors
defined, 34
diathesis-stress model, 36–38
reciprocal gene-environment model, 38–39
Nefazodone, 240
Negative affect, 93
Negative cognitive styles, 234
Negative correlation, 103
Negative reinforcement, 413
Negativistic personality disorder, 437
Nerve fibers, 328
Nervous breakdown, 155
Neurasthenia, 328
Neurobiological factors
ADHD, 506–507
antisocial personality disorder, 446
anxiety disorders, 123–124
autism, 515
learning disorders, 510
PTSD, 157
schizophrenia, 483–487
sexual dysfunction, 363
substance-related disorders, 411–412
suicide, 251
Neurofibrillary tangles, 544
Neurohormones, 230
Neuroleptics, 14, 489. *See also* Antipsychotic drugs

Neurons, 40, 412
Neuropsychological testing, 82
Neuroses, 19
Neurosis, 171
Neurosurgery, 163
Neurotransmitter pathways, 49
Neurotransmitters
defined, 46
discovery, 46–47
function of, 483
major, 47–49
medications based on, 484
mood disorders and, 229–230
release of, 42
NGRI (not guilty by reasons of insanity), 563–566
Nicotine use disorders
Alzheimer's disease and, 544
characterization, 403
Chinese example, 393–394
DSM-IV-TR, 404
effects of, 405–406
Night eating syndrome, 284
Nightmares, 300
NMDA (*N*-methyl-d-aspartate), 485
Nocturnal panic, 135–136
Nomenclature, 85
Nomothetic strategy, 85
Nondemand pleasuring, 369
Noradrenaline. *See* Norepinephrine
Norepinephrine, 48, 229–230
Norms, 4
Nosology, 85
NREM (nonrapid eye movement), 294, 300
Nucleus, 44
Nun's study, 538–539

Obesity. *See also* Eating disorders
bingeing association, 270–271
BMI, 263, 283
causes, 284–286
epidemic, government role, 303
immigrants and, 269–270
overview, 306
prevention, 287
social dimensions, 272–273
statistics, 283–284
treatment, 286–287
Object relations, 20
Observational learning, 56
Observations
ABCs, 76–77
formal, 76
Observations on Madness and Melancholy (Haslam), 467
Obsessions, 159–160
Obsessive-compulsive disorder (OCD)
assessing, 73
BDD and, 186, 188–189
biological causes, 50–51
case study, 159, 459
causes, 161–162
clinical description, 159, 459–460
DSM-IV-TR criteria, 160, 460
intrusive thoughts, 162
statistics, 161
treatment, 162–163
Occipital lobe, 44
OCD. *See* Obsessive-compulsive disorder
O'Connor v. Donaldson, 560–561
ODD. *See* Oppositional defiant disorder
Oedipus complex, 19
Oedipus Rex, 19
Olanzapine, 485
Openness to experience, 432
Operant conditioning, 24–25
Operational definition, 76

Opioids
releasing neurons, 412
use disorder, 406–407
Oppositional defiant disorder (ODD), 504
Orbital surface, 50
Orgasm disorders, 358–360, 369
Orgasmic reconditioning, 380
Oxytocin, 515

P300 amplitude, 412
Pain. *See also* Chronic pain
gender differences, 328
levels of, 326
sexual, 360–361
Pain disorder, 184–185
Pa-leng, 145
Panic, 60, 122
Panic attacks, 61, 122
Panic control treatments, 139
Panic disorders. *See also* Fear
case study, 132–133
causes, 136–138
clinical description, 133
cultural factors, 135
DSM-IV-TR criteria, 133–134
nocturnal, 135–136
onset, 134
statistics, 134–136
treatment, 138–141
types, 132
Papaverine, 370
Pappenheim, Bertha. *See* Anna O.
Paracelsus, 10
Paranoia, 402
Paranoid personality disorder, 438
Paranoid type of schizophrenia, 474
Paraphilia
case studies, 377–379
causes, 377–379
defined, 345
drug treatments, 381
DSM-IV-TR criteria, 376
exhibitionism, 373
female, 377
fetishism, 372–376
overview, 372
treatment, 379–381
treatment outcomes, 380
voyeurism, 373
Parasomnias
DSM-IV-TR criteria, 289
overview, 307
treatment, 300–302
Parkinson's disease
characterization, 542
drugs for, 484
motor difficulties, 490
Paroxetine, 140
Passive-aggressive personality disorder, 437
Pasteur, Louis, 12
Pathological gambling, 423–424
Pathological grief reaction, 214
Patient uniformity myth, 102
Patients
average, 102
practice guidelines and, 570–572
research rights, 569–570
right to refuse treatment, 569
right to treatment, 568
Pavlov, Ivan, 22–23, 54
PCP (phencyclidine), 393–394, 485
Pedophilia, 375, 376–377
Penile prostheses, 371
Penis envy, 19
Pepys, Samuel, 152–153
Performance anxiety, 149
Performance scales, 81
Periodic limb movement disorder, 291

Persecution, delusions of, 72, 471
Persecutory delusion, 477
Personal distress, 2–3
Personality disorders
antisocial, 443–450
aspects, 431
avoidant, 457–458
borderline, 450–454
categorical models, 432–433
characterization, 431
cluster A, 441–443
cluster B, 443–457
cluster C, 457–461
clusters, 432–433
comorbidity, 436
dependent, 458–459
development, 433–435
dimensional models, 432–433
gender differences, 435–436
histrionic, 454–455
narcissistic, 455–457
origins, 434
overview, 464–465
paranoid, 438–439
schizoid, 439–441
schizotypal, 441–443
statistics, 433–435
studies of, 436–437
Personality inventories, 79–81
Person-centered therapy, 22
Pervasive developmental disorders
Asperger's disorder, 515–516
autism, 511–515
characterization, 511
overview, 531
treatment, 516–518
PET (positron emission tomography) scans, 83–84
Phantom limb pain, 327
Phase delays, 298
Phenotypes, 110
Phlegmatic personality, 12
Phobias. *See also* specific fears
criteria, 2
illness, 172
social, 148–152
specific, 141–148
Phototherapy, 299
Physical disorders
AIDS, 318–319
behavior modification for, 343
cancer, 319–321
cardiovascular system, 321
chronic fatigue syndrome, 328–330
chronic pain, 325–328
genetics and, 340
health-related behavior, 311
hypertension, 321–323
injury control, 343
psychosocial factors, 310–311
psychosocial treatment, 328–330
relaxation techniques, 343
stress and, 311–318
stress factors (*See* Stress)
Physical examinations, 74
Pick's disease, 542
Pinel, Philippe, 15, 16–17
Pituitary gland, 46
PKU (phenylketonuria), 34, 522
Placebo control groups, 105
Placebo effects, 105, 339
Plastic surgery, 189
Plato, 15
Pleasure principle, 18
PMS (premenstrual syndrome), 94
PNI (psychoneuroimmunology), 317
PNS (peripheral nervous system)
characterization, 40
functions, 44, 45
structure, 45

Poddar, Prosenjit, 567
Police power, 558
Polysubstance abuse, 389
Positive correlation, 103
Positive psychology, 55
Positive reinforcement, 412–413
Possession, 9–10
Postpartum depression, 219
Posttraumatic stress disorder (PTSD)
  borderline disorder *versus*, 453
  case study, 153
  causes, 156–157, 199
  clinical description, 152–154
  complications, 158
  DID and, 198
  statistics, 154–156
  symptoms, 153
  treatment, 157–159
  types, 154
Practice guidelines, 570–572
Premarital sex, 347
Premature ejaculation, 360
Premenstrual dysphoric disorder,
  93–94
Prepared learning, 56
Presenilin 1, 545
Presenilin 2, 545
Presenting problems, 6–7
Prevalence, defined, 6–7
Prevention
  antisocial personality disorders,
    450
  delirium, 535
  dementia, 549
  developmental disorders, 525–526
  eating disorders, 282–283
  exposure and response, 51
  HIV/AIDS, 342
  injury, 335
  mood disorders, 245–246
  obesity, 287
  research, 112–113
  sleep disorders, 299–300
  substance-related disorders, 421–
    422, 425
  suicide, 253
Primary hypersomnia, 293–294, 298
Primary insomnia
  case study, 290
  causes, 291–292
  clinical description, 290–291
  DSM-IV-TR criteria, 291
  integrative model, 292–293
  medical treatment, 298
  statistics, 291
  treatments for, 299
Primary process, 18
Proband, 110
Problem-solving courts, 566
Prognosis, defined, 6
Progressive muscle relaxation, 332
Project MATCH, 421
Projection, 19
Projective tests, 77–78
Prostaglandin, 370
Protection and Advocacy for
  Mentally Ill Individuals Act, 568
Prototypes, 4
Prototypical approach, 87
Prozac. *See* Fluoxetine
PSG (polysomnographic evaluation),
  289
Psilocybin mushrooms, 394
Psychiatrists, 5
Psychoactive substances, 390
Psychoanalysis, 16
Psychoanalysts, 20
Psychoanalytic theory
  defense mechanisms, 18–19
  development of, 17
  development stages, 19–20

pioneers, 16–17
  structure of mind, 17–18
  techniques' functions, 20–21
Psychodynamic psychotherapy, 21
Psychodynamic treatment, 516–517
Psychological disorders. *See also*
  Mental illness; specific disorders
  behavioral influences, 31
  biological influences, 11–14,
    31–32
  biologically-based, 50–51
  bulimia and, 265
  causation, 7
  clinical description, 6–7
  criteria, 2–5
  defined, 2
  developmental influences, 33
  emotional influences, 32–33
  global influences, 64
  historical conceptions of, 7–8
  history timeline, 166–167
  integrative approach, 24
  multidimensional models, 31–34
  one-dimensional models, 31–34
  outcomes, 7
  psychological tradition, 14–25
  scientific method, 24
  social influences, 33
  stigma, 63
  suicide and, 251–252
  supernatural tradition, 8–11
  treatment, 7
Psychological dysfunction
  criteria defining, 2–5
  defined, 2
  prototypes, 4
Psychological model, 7–8
Psychological testing
  intelligence, 81–82
  personality inventories, 79–81
  projective, 77–78
Psychological tradition
  asylum reform, 15
  behavioral model, 22–25
  humanistic theory, 21–22
  mental hygiene movement, 16
  moral therapy, 14–16
  psychoanalytic theory, 16–21
Psychoncology, 319
Psychopathic deviation (Pd) scale, 80
Psychopathology. *See also*
  Psychological disorders
  behavioral theory, 54–57
  cognitive theory, 54–57
  emotions and, 60
  genetic contributions, 34–40
  health effects, 62–63
  neuroscience and, 40–54
  science of, 5–7
Psychopathy
  brain functions, 447–448
  characteristics, 445
  developmental influences,
    448–449
  fearlessness hypothesis, 447
  treatment, 449–450
Psychopharmacogenetics, 526
Psychophysiological assessment,
  84–85
Psychosexual stages of development,
  19
Psychosocial, 14
Psychosocial factors
  AIDS, 318–319
  antisocial personality disorder, 448
  autism, 514
  brain structure/function, 51–53
  cancer, 319–321
  CFS, 328–330
  CHD, 323–325
  chronic pain, 326–328

dementia, 545–546
  hypertension, 321–323
  mental retardation, 524
  physical disorders and, 310–311
  schizophrenia, 487–488
  sexual dysfunction, 364–367
Psychosocial treatment
  biofeedback, 331–332
  comprehensive programs,
    332–333
  delirium, 535
  meditation, 332
  relaxation, 332
Psychotherapy. *See* IPT (interpersonal psychotherapy)
Psychotherapy by Reciprocal Inhibition
  (Wolpe), 102
PTSD. *See* Posttraumatic stress disorder
Purging
  immigrant populations and,
    270–271
  techniques, 264–265
Pyromania, 423

Quantitative genetics, 35

Rachman, Stanley, 24
Randomization, 100–101
Rape, sadistic, 374–376
Rapid eye movement. *See* REM
Rationalization, 19
Rauwolfia serpentine. *See* Reserpine
Rayner, Rosalie, 23
Reaction formation, 19
Reactivity, 76
Reading disorders, 507–508, 509
Reagan, Ronald, 564, 569
Reality principle, 18
Reality testing, 163
Rebound insomnia, 293
Receptors, 40–41
Recessive gene, 34–35
Reciprocal gene-environment
  model, 38–39, 232
Reference, ideas of, 72
Reinforcement, 412–413. *See also*
  Positive reinforcement
Relaxation techniques, 332, 343
Reliability, 71, 87–88
REM (rapid eye movement)
  antidepressants effects on, 298
  defined, 289
  mood disorders and, 230–231
  narcolepsy and, 294
  nocturnal panic and, 135
Reno, Janet, 542
Repeated measurements, 107–108
Replication, 116
Repression, 19
Research
  adoption studies, 110–111
  Alzheimer's disease, 547
  analog models, 101
  average client, 102
  basic components, 99–101
  behavior over time, 112–114
  case study method, 102–103
  clinical significance, 101–102
  comparative treatment, 106
  concepts, 99
  control groups, 105–106
  by correlation, 103–105
  cross-cultural, 114–115
  defined, 105
  design, 99
  ethics, 116–117
  by experiment, 105–106
  family studies, 110–111
  genetic linkage analysis, 112
  genetics, 110–112

group designs, 105
  hypothesis, 100
  methods, 102–110
  patients' rights, 569–570
  prevention, 112–113
  programs, 115–117
  replication, 116
  single-case designs, 107–110
  statistical significance, 101–102
  twin studies, 111–112
  validity, 99–101
Reserpine, 14
Residual type of schizophrenia,
  475–476
Retail therapy, 161
Retarded ejaculation, 359
Reticular activating system, 44
Retrograde ejaculation, 359
Retrospective information, 113
Rett's disorder, 511–512
Reuptake, 46
Rheumatoid arthritis, 317
Riggins v. Nevada, 569
Right to refuse treatment, 569
Right to treatment, 568
Ritalin. *See* Methylphenidate
Rogers, Carl, 22
Roker, Al, 287
Roman Catholic Church, 8–9, 11
Rorschach inkblot test, 78
Rorschach, Hermann, 78
Running addiction, 393
Rush, Benjamin, 15

SAD. *See* Seasonal affective disorder
St. John's wort, 240
Sakel, Manfred, 13
Sakit gila, 114
Salinger, J. D., 3
Sanguine, 11–12
Schizoaffective disorder, 476
Schizoid personality disorder, 457
  case study, 440
  causes, 441
  characterization, 439
  clinical description, 440
  DSM-IV-TR criteria, 440
  treatment, 441
Schizophrenia
  adoption studies, 482
  antipsychotic medications,
    489–491
  assessment, 495
  association studies, 482–483
  biological interventions, 489–491
  brain structure and, 483–485
  case studies, 468–469, 471–472
  cross cultural treatment, 494
  cultural factors, 480
  defined, 467
  development, 479–480
  disorganized symptoms, 473–474
  dopamine and, 441, 483–485
  DSM-IV-TR criteria, 470,
    474–476
  effects of, 469–470
  endophenotypes, 483
  familial influences, 487–488
  history of, 467–468
  integrative treatment approach,
    493
  linkage studies, 482–483
  negative symptoms, 472–473
  neurobiological factors, 483–487
  positive symptoms, 470–472
  prenatal influences, 486–487
  prevention, 494
  psychosocial influences, 487–
    488
  psychosocial interventions,
    491–493

psychotic disorders related to, 476–479
relapse rate, 479
schizotypal personality and, 442
statistics, 479
stress and, 487
subtypes, 474–476
symptom identification, 468–469
symptoms, 469–474
treatment, 488–494
twin studies, 481–482
violence and, 469–470
Schizophrenia Genesis: The Origins of Madness (Gottesman), 480
Schizophreniform disorder, 476
Schizophrenogenic mother, 487
Schizotypal personality disorder
case study, 441
causes, 442
characterization, 441
clinical description, 441–442
DSM-IV-TR criteria, 442
treatment, 442–443
Scientific method, 24
Scientist-practitioners, 5–6
Script theory, 367
Seasonal affective disorder (SAD)
causes, 220
characterization, 219–220
circadian rhythms and, 230–231
comorbidity, 221
light treatment for, 220–221
prevalence, 220
Secondary process, 18
Sedative use disorder, 399–401
Selective amnesia, 192
Selective mutism, 509
Self-actualizing, 21
Self-injurious behavior, 76–77
Self-monitoring, 76
Senior Apperception Test, 78
Sensate focus, 369
Sensorium, 72
Separation anxiety disorder, 143–144
Septum, 44
Sequential design, 113
Serotonin
borderline disorder and, 451
characterization, 47–48
mood disorders and, 229
psychopathy and, 447–448
Sex addiction, 393
Sex reassignment surgery, 352–353
Sexual abuse
DID and, 199
OCD and, 459
repeat offenders, 562
Sexual arousal, 378
Sexual desire disorders, 355–357
Sexual dysfunction
alcohol and, 364
arousal disorders, 357–358
biological factors, 363–364
case study, 368
cultural factors, 366–367
desire disorders, 355–357
gender differences, 355
generalizations, 354–355
medical treatments, 370–371
orgasm disorders, 358–360
overview, 387
physical factors, 367–368
psychological factors, 364–366
psychosocial treatments, 368–370
sexual pain disorders, 360–361
social factors, 366–367
treatment, 368–371
Sexual masochism, 374–376
Sexual orientation, 348–350
Sexual pain disorders, 360–361
Sexual sadism, 374–376

Sexuality
assessing, 361–363
culture differences, 348
dysfunction (*See* Sexual dysfunction)
gender differences, 346–348
myths, 368
normal, 345–346
paraphilia, 371–379
Shaping, 24
Shared psychotic disorder, 477–478
Shift work, 295–296
Shinkeishitsu, 149
Shopping addiction, 393
Short alleles, 37
Short-term commitment, 559
Sildenafil, 370
Simon, Carly, 148
Simon, Théodore, 81
Single-case experimental designs
characterization, 107
multiple baseline, 108–110
repeated measurements in, 107–108
withdrawal, 108
Sinoaortic baroreflex arc, 31
Situational phobia, 142
Skinner, B. F., 24–25
Sleep apnea, 291
anxiety disorder and, 136
breathing problems and, 295
hypersomnia and, 293
medical treatment, 298
Sleep attacks, 295
Sleep disorders
breathing-related, 295
case study, 293
categories, 289
circadian rhythm and, 295–298
DSM-IV-TR criteria, 289
environmental treatments, 298–299
insomnia, 290–298
medical treatments, 298
mood disorders and, 230–231
narcolepsy, 294–295
overview, 288–290, 307
prevention, 299–300
primary hypersomnia, 293–204
psychological treatments, 299
Sleep efficiency, 289
Sleep paralysis, 294–295
Sleep stress, 292
Sleep terrors, 136, 300–301
Sleepwalking, 301
Smith, Anna Nicole, 411
Smith, Robert Holbrook, 419
Smoking. *See* Nicotine use disorders
Smooth-pursuit eye movement, 483
SNS (somatic nervous system)
functions, 44, 46
structure, 44
Social Cognition and Object Relations Scale, 78
Social learning, 55–56
Social learning model. *See* Behaviorism
Social networks
elderly and, 63
health and, 62–63
Social phobia
bulimia and, 265
case study, 148
causes, 149–151
clinical description, 148–149
incidences, 149
treatment, 151–152
Social stigma, 63
Social support
AIDS and, 336–337
caregivers, 546, 548

chronic pain, 327–328
mood disorders and, 237
networks, 62–63
Sociocultural factors
DSM-IV, 90–91
eating disorders, 262, 272–276
paranoid personality disorder, 439
psychological disorders, 33
PTSD and, 156–157
substance abuse, 414–415
suicide, 249
Somatic delusion, 477
Somatization disorders
ASPD link, 177–179
case study, 176
causes, 177–179
clinical description, 176–177
DSM-IV-TR criteria, 176
identification of, 175–176
overview, 204
statistics, 177
treatment, 179
Somatoform disorders
ancient definition, 12
body dysmorphic, 185–189
characterization, 171
conversion disorder, 179–184
DSM-V changes, 202
hypochondriasis, 171–175
pain disorder, 184
somatization disorder, 175–179
Somnambulism, 301
Specific phobias
causes, 145–147
clinical description, 141–144
defined, 131
DSM-IV-TR criteria, 141
onset, 144
statistics, 144–145
treatment, 147–148
types, 142–144
SPECT (single photon emission computed tomography), 84
Speech, disorganized, 473–474
Spinal column, 328
Spitzer, Robert, 88
SSRIs (serotonin-specific reuptake inhibitors)
bulimia nervosa, 280
characterization, 48
hypochondriasis, 175
mood disorders, 239–241
OCD, 162
panic disorder treatment, 138
PTSD, 158
sexual dysfunction side effect, 364
social phobia, 151–152
Standardization, 71
Stanford-Binet test, 81
STAR*D (Sequenced Treatment Alternatives to Relieve Depression), 240
State v. Campanaro, 564
Statistical significance, 101–102
Stem cells, 546
Steroids. *See* Anabolic-androgenic steroids
Stimulants. *See also* specific drugs
effects, 395
types, 401–406
Stimulus generalization, 22
Stress
anxiety and, 313–315
anxiety disorders and, 125–126
BDD and, 187
depression and, 313–315
excitement and, 313–315
gender differences, 62
HPA and, 312–313
immune response and, 315–318
life events and, 231–233, 252

mood disorders and, 231–233
myocardial stunning and, 323–324
nature of, 311–312
physiology of, 312–213
response, 313
schizophrenia and, 487
sleep, 292
supernatural model, 8–9
Stress hormone. *See* Cortisol
Stress reduction
denial and, 334
drug therapies, 333–334
muscle tensing exercise, 334
psychosocial therapies, 328–330
Strokes. *See* Cerebral vascular accidents
Stroop paradigm, 56
Structure of mind, 17–18
Stuttering, 509
Sublimation, 18
Substance dependence. *See* Dependence
Substance-induced dementia, 543
Substance-related disorders
agonist substitution, 417–419
alcohol, 393–398
amphetamines, 401–402
antagonist substitution, 418
aversion therapy, 420
aversive treatment, 418–419
barbiturates, 399–401
biological dimensions, 411–412
biological treatments, 417–419
bulimia and, 265
caffeine, 405–406
case study, 389–390
causes, 411–417
cocaine, 402–403
component treatment, 420–421
controlled use, 420
criminal aspects, 566
defined, 389
dementia and, 543
dependence level, 391–394
depressants, 395–401
diagnosing, 394–395
impatient facilities, 419
integrative model, 415–417
intoxication level, 390–391
involvement levels, 390–394
medication for, 419
moral weakness model, 414–415
nicotine, 403–405
opioids, 406–407
overview, 389–390
prevention, 421–422, 425
psychological dimensions, 412–413
psychosocial treatments, 419–421
relapse prevention, 421
social dimensions, 414–415
twelve programs, 419–420
use level, 390
Subthreshold, 90
Suggestibility, 198–199
Suicidal attempts, 250
Suicidal ideation, 250
Suicide, 251–252
anxiety disorder and, 127
borderline disorder and, 453
causes, 250–251
Durkheim's types, 250–251
eating disorders and, 261
incidents, 248
psychological disorders and, 251–252
publicity and, 252
risk factors, 251–252
SSRIs and, 240
statistics, 249–250
treatment, 252–254

Superego, 17–18
Supernatural model
  defined, 7
  demons, 8
  mass hysteria, 9–10
  melancholy, 8–9
  moon and stars effects, 10–11
  stress, 8–9
  treatments, 9–10
  witches, 8
Suppressor T Cells, 317
Supreme Court rulings, 560, 562
Susceptibility genes, 545
Susto, 60
Symptom substitution, 21
Synaptic cleft, 42
Syncope, 31
Syphilis, 12–13
Systematic desensitization, 23
Systolic blood pressure, 322

T cells, 317
T4 cells, 317
Taijin kyofusho, 188
*Tanasoff v. Regents of the University of
  California,* 567
Tarasoff, Tatiana, 567
Tardive dyskinesia, 490
Target behavior, 74
Taxonomy, 85
Television addiction, 393
Temple-Wisconsin study, 235
Temporal lobe, 44
Tend and befriend, 62
Testability, 100
Testing. *See* Neuropsychological test-
  ing; Psychological testing
Testosterone, 370
Text messaging, 495
Thalamus, 44
Thanatos, 18
THC (tetrahydrocannabinols), 408
Thematic Apperception Test, 78
Therapeutic communities, 449
Therapeutic jurisprudence, 566
Thompson v. County of Alameda,
  567
Thorndike, Edward L., 24
Thought process, 72
Thought-action fusion, 162
Threshold, 93

Thyroxine, 45
Tic disorders, 509
Time-management training, 333
Titchener, Edward, 23
TMS (transcranial magnetic stimula-
  tion), 242–243
Tobacco use. *See* Nicotine use dis-
  orders
Token economy, 491
Tolerance, 417
Transcendental mediation, 332
Transference, 20
Transinstitutionalization, 561
Transvestic fetishism, 373–374
Trauma, 197–198
Treatments. *See also* specific therapies
  ADHD, 506–507
  antisocial personality disorders,
    449–450
  avoidant personality disorder, 458
  biological tradition, 13–14
  borderline disorder, 453–454
  delirium, 535
  dementia, 546–548
  effectiveness, 570
  gender identity disorder, 352–354
  histrionic personality disorder, 455
  intersex individuals, 353–354
  learning disorders, 510–511
  maintenance, 246
  mental retardation, 524–525
  narcissistic personality disorder,
    456–457
  outcome research, 116
  paraphilia, 379–381
  pervasive developmental disorders,
    516–518
  psychopaths, 449–450
  right to, 568
  right to refuse, 569
  schizophrenia, 488–494
  sexual dysfunction, 368–371
Triazolam, 298
Tricyclic antidepressants, 239–241,
  298
Tuchman, Barbara, 8
Tuke, William, 15
Twelve-step programs, 419–420, 424
Twin
  antisocial behavior, 446
  Chang and Eng, 40

IQ, 35
  procedures, 111–112
  schizophrenia, 481–482
  sexual orientation, 349
  stressful life events, 232
  substance-related disorders, 411
Twinkie tax, 303
Type A behavior pattern, 324
Type B behavior pattern, 324

UFOs (unidentified flying objects),
  294–296
Unconditional positive regard, 22
Unconditioned response, 22
Unconditioned stimulus, 22
Unconscious
  cognitive science and, 56–57
  mind, 17
  vision, 56
Underarousal hypothesis, 446–
  447
Undifferentiated somatoform disor-
  der, 177
Undifferentiated type of schizophre-
  nia, 475
University of California at Los
  Angeles (UCLA), 569–570

Vacuum device therapy, 371
Vaginismus, 361, 367
Validity, 88
Variability, 107–108
Variables, 99–100
Vascular dementia, 540–541
Vasovagal syncope, 31
Venlafaxine, 240
Ventral tegmen-opioid releasing
  neurons, 412
Viagra. *See* Sildenafil
Violence
  in children, 448, 450
  schizophrenia and, 469–470
  substance abuse and, 399
Virtual reality, 495
Voluntary commitment. *See* Civil
  commitment
von Meduna, Joseph, 13
Voodoo, 60–61
Voyeurism, 373
Vulnerability, 37

Walden Two (Skinner), 24
Watson, John B., 23
Wechsler Adult Intelligence Scale, 81
Wechsler Preschool and Primary
  Scale of Intelligence, 81
Weight loss programs, 286–287
Wernicke-Korsakoff syndrome,
  396–397, 550
Western Collaborative Group Study,
  324
Williams, Ricky, 148
Wilson, Carnie, 287
Wilson, William, 419
Witches, 8
Withdrawal
  defined, 391
  delirium, 396
  designs, 108
  nicotine, 405
  opiate, 418
Wolpe, Joseph, 23–24
Women
  Alzheimer's prevalence in, 540
  arousal disorders, 358
  body image and, 272–274, 277
  borderline disorder in, 452
  conversion disorder in, 182–183
  dangerousness and, 559
  GAD in, 129
  insomnia in, 291
  mood disorders in, 235–237
  orgasm disorders, 359
  panic disorders in, 134–135
  paraphilia, 377
  sexuality myths, 368
  somatization disorder in, 177
  stereotypical traits, 435
Women's health Initiative Memory
  Study, 540
Work addiction, 393
World Health Organization, 64, 88
Wyatt v. Stickney, 568

X chromosomes, 34
X-linked genes, 522
X-rays, 82

Y chromosomes, 34
Yerkes-Dodson curve, 446
Youngberg v. Romeo, 568

TO THE OWNER OF THIS BOOK:

I hope that you have found *Abnormal Psychology: An Integrative Approach,* Fifth Edition, useful. So that this book can be improved in a future edition, would you take the time to complete this sheet and return it? Thank you.

School and address: _____

_____

Department: _____

Instructor's name: _____

1. What I like most about this book is:_____

_____

_____

2. What I like least about this book is: _____

_____

_____

3. My general reaction to this book is: _____

_____

_____

4. The name of the course in which I used this book is: _____

_____

5. Were all of the chapters of the book assigned for you to read? _____

   If not, which ones weren't? _____

6. Did you find the CD-ROM helpful in reviewing symptoms of particular disorders before you took

   tests? _____ If not, are there improvements that you might recommend? _____

_____

7. In the space below, or on a separate sheet of paper, please write specific suggestions for improving

   this book and anything else you'd care to share about your experience in using this book.

_____

_____

FOLD HERE

WADSWORTH
CENGAGE Learning

BUSINESS REPLY MAIL
FIRST-CLASS MAIL   PERMIT NO. 34   BELMONT CA

POSTAGE WILL BE PAID BY ADDRESSEE

Attn: Jaime Perkins, Psychology Editor

Wadsworth, Cengage Learning
10 Davis Dr
Belmont CA 94002-9801

FOLD HERE

OPTIONAL:

Your name: _____ Date: _____

May we quote you, either in promotion for *Abnormal Psychology: An Integrative Approach,* Fifth Edition, or in future publishing ventures?

Yes: _____   No: _____

Sincerely yours,

David H. Barlow, V. Mark Durand

AXIS I

Disorders Usually First Diagnosed in Infancy, Childhood, or Adolescence

Learning Disorders (Academic Skills Disorders)

Reading Disorder (Developmental Reading Disorder)/Mathematics Disorder (Developmental Arithmetic Disorder)/Disorder of Written Expression (Developmental Expressive Writing Disorder)

Motor Skills Disorder

Developmental Coordination Disorder

Pervasive Developmental Disorders

Autistic Disorder/Rett's Disorder/Childhood Disintegrative Disorder/Asperger's Disorder/PDD Not Otherwise Specified

Disruptive Behavior and Attention-Deficit Disorders

Attention-Deficit/Hyperactivity Disorder/Oppositional Defiant Disorder/Conduct Disorder

Feeding and Eating Disorders of Infancy or Early Childhood

Pica/Rumination Disorder/Feeding Disorder of Infancy or Early Childhood

Tic Disorders

Tourette's Disorder/Chronic Motor or Vocal Tic Disorder/Transient Tic Disorder

Communication Disorders

Expressive Language Disorder (Developmental Expressive Language Disorder)/Mixed Receptive/Expressive Language Disorder (Developmental Receptive Language Disorder)/Phonological Disorder (Developmental Articulation Disorder)/Stuttering

Elimination Disorders

Encopresis/Enuresis

Other Disorders of Infancy, Childhood, or Adolescence

Separation Anxiety Disorder/Selective Mutism (Elective Mutism)/Reactive Attachment Disorder of Infancy or Early Childhood/Stereotypic Movement Disorder (Stereotypy/Habit Disorder)

Delirium, Dementia, Amnestic, and Other Cognitive Disorders

Deliria

Delirium Due to a General Medical Condition/Substance-Induced Delirium/Delirium Due to Multiple Etiologies

Dementias

Dementia of the Alzheimer's Type; With Early Onset: if onset at age 65 or below; With Late Onset: if onset after age 65/Vascular Dementia/Dementias Due to Other General Medical Conditions/Substance-Induced Persisting Dementia/Dementia Due to Multiple Etiologies

Amnestic Disorders

Amnestic Disorder Due to a General Medical Condition/Substance-Induced Persisting Amnestic Disorder (refer to specific Substance for code)

Substance-Related Disorders

Alcohol Use Disorders

Amphetamine (or Related Substance) Use Disorders

Caffeine Use Disorders

Cannabis Use Disorders

Cocaine Use Disorders

Hallucinogen Use Disorders

Inhalant Use Disorders

Nicotine Use Disorders

Opioid Use Disorders

Phencyclidine (or Related Substance) Use Disorders

Sedative, Hypnotic, or Anxiolytic Substance Use Disorders

Polysubstance Use Disorder

Schizophrenia and Other Psychotic Disorders

Schizophrenia

Paranoid Type/Disorganized Type/Catatonic Type/Undifferentiated Type/Residual Type

Schizophreniform Disorder

Schizoaffective Disorder

Delusional Disorder

Brief Psychotic Disorder

Shared Psychotic Disorder (Folie à Deux)

Psychotic Disorder Due to a General Medical Condition

With Delusions/With Hallucinations/Substance-Induced Psychotic Disorder

Psychotic Disorder Not Otherwise Specified

Mood Disorders

Depressive Disorders

Major Depressive Disorder/Dysthymic Disorder/Depressive Disorder Not Otherwise Specified

Bipolar Disorders

Bipolar I Disorder/Bipolar II Disorder (Recurrent Major Depressive Episodes with Hypomania)/Bipolar Not Otherwise Specified/Cyclothymic Disorder

Mood Disorder Due to a General Medical Condition

Substance-Induced Mood Disorder

Mood Disorder Not Otherwise Specified

Anxiety Disorders

Panic Disorder

Without Agoraphobia/With Agoraphobia

Agoraphobia without History of Panic Disorder

Specific Phobia (Simple Phobia)

Social Phobia (Social Anxiety Disorder)

Obsessive-Compulsive Disorder

Posttraumatic Stress Disorder

Acute Stress Disorder

Generalized Anxiety Disorder (Includes Overanxious Disorder of Childhood)

Anxiety Disorder Due to a General Medical Condition

Substance-Induced Anxiety Disorder

Anxiety Disorder Not Otherwise Specified

(Continued on next page)

Somatoform Disorders

Somatization Disorder

Conversion Disorder

Hypochondriasis

Body Dysmorphic Disorder

Pain Disorder

Somatoform Disorder Not Otherwise Specified

Undifferentiated Somatoform Disorder

Factitious Disorders

Factitious Disorder

Factitious Disorder Not Otherwise Specified

Dissociative Disorders

Dissociative Amnesia

Dissociative Fugue

Dissociative Identity Disorder (Multiple Personality Disorder)

Depersonalization Disorder

Dissociative Disorder Not Otherwise Specified

Sexual and Gender Identity Disorders

Sexual Dysfunctions

Sexual Desire Disorders: Hypoactive Sexual Desire Disorder; Sexual Aversion Disorder/Sexual Arousal Disorders: Female Sexual Arousal Disorder; Male Erectile Disorder/Orgasm Disorders: Female Orgasmic Disorder (Inhibited Female Orgasm); Male Orgasmic Disorder (Inhibited Male Orgasm); Premature Ejaculation/Sexual Pain Disorders: Dyspareunia; Vaginismus/Sexual Dysfunctions Due to a General Medical Condition/Substance-Induced Sexual Dysfunction

Paraphilias

Exhibitionism/Fetishism/Frotteurism/Pedophilia/Sexual Masochism/Sexual Sadism/Voyeurism/Transvestic Fetishism

Gender Identity Disorders

Gender Identity Disorder: in Children/in Adolescents and Adults (Transsexualism)

Eating Disorders

Anorexia Nervosa

Bulimia Nervosa

Eating Disorder Not Otherwise Specified

Sleep Disorders

Primary Sleep Disorders

Dyssomnias: Primary Insomnia; Primary Hypersomnia; Narcolepsy; Breathing-Related Sleep Disorder; Circadian Rhythm Sleep Disorder (formerly Sleep-Wake Schedule Disorder)/Parasomnias; Nightmare Disorder (Dream Anxiety Disorder); Sleep Terror Disorder; Sleepwalking Disorder/Sleep Disorders Related to Another Mental Disorder

Sleep Disorder Due to a General Medical Condition

Substance-Induced Sleep Disorder

Dyssomnia Not Otherwise Specified

Parasomnia Not Otherwise Specified

Impulse Control Disorders Not Elsewhere Classified

Intermittent Explosive Disorder

Kleptomania

Pyromania

Pathological Gambling

Trichotillomania

Impulse-Control Disorder Not Otherwise Specified

Adjustment Disorder

Adjustment Disorder

With Anxiety

With Depressed Mood

With Disturbance of Conduct

With Mixed Disturbance of Emotions and Conduct

With Mixed Anxiety and Depressed Mood

Unspecified

Other Conditions That May Be a Focus of Clinical Attention

Pyschological Factors Affecting Medical Condition

Medication-Induced Movement Disorders

Relational Problems

Relational Problem Related to a Mental Disorder or General Medical Condition/Parent–Child Relational Problem/Partner Relational Problem/Sibling Relational Problem

Problems Related to Abuse or Neglect

Physical Abuse of Child/Sexual Abuse of Child/Neglect of Child/Physical Abuse of Adult/Sexual Abuse of Adult

Additional Conditions That May Be a Focus of Clinical Attention

Bereavement/Borderline Intellectual Functioning/Academic Problem/Occupational Problem/Childhood or Adolescent Antisocial Behavior/Adult Antisocial Behavior/Malingering Phase of Life

Problem/Noncompliance with Treatment for a Mental Disorder/Identity Problem/Religious or Spiritual Problem/Acculturation Problem/Age-Associated Memory Decline

AXIS II

Personality Disorders

Paranoid Personality Disorder

Schizoid Personality Disorder

Schizotypal Personality Disorder

Antisocial Personality Disorder

Borderline Personality Disorder

Histrionic Personality Disorder

Narcissistic Personality Disorder

Avoidant Personality Disorder

Dependent Personality Disorder

Obsessive-Compulsive Personality Disorder

Mental Retardation

Mild Mental Retardation/Moderate Mental Retardation/Severe Mental Retardation/Profound Mental Retardation